A GUIDE TO
THE BEST FICTION

A GUIDE TO
THE BEST FICTION

ENGLISH AND AMERICAN,
INCLUDING TRANSLATIONS FROM
FOREIGN LANGUAGES

By

ERNEST A. BAKER

AND

JAMES PACKMAN

NEW AND ENLARGED EDITION

NEW YORK
BARNES & NOBLE, INC.
Publishers & Booksellers since 1873

First published 1903 as a
Descriptive Guide to Best Fiction
by Swan Sonnenschein & Co. Ltd.

New edition, enlarged and thoroughly revised
published 1913 as
A Guide to Best Fiction
by George Routledge & Sons Limited

New and enlarged edition
with James Packman
published 1932

Reissued 1967
by Routledge & Kegan Paul Ltd.
Broadway House, 68-74 Carter Lane
London, E.C.4
Reprinted 1968

Printed in Great Britain

PREFACE

TECHNICALLY, this is the third edition of a work first published in 1903 ; but at every reappearance
the book has undergone such a complete transformation that it has been substantially a new one.
It is a book that has grown up, rather than been put together in the ordinary way, even of works
of reference. No man in his senses, without the accumulation of material supplied by years of
reading and annotating, would face such an undertaking as to survey the whole field of English
and American fiction and attempt to characterize every individual item of any importance. The
actual scheme of this work is even bigger, since it embraces also the fiction in foreign languages that
happens to have been translated into English. Begun, some thirty years ago, as a descriptive
catalogue of an actual library of fiction, it expanded, under the fostering encouragement and the
practical aid of the late William Swan Sonnenschein (afterwards Stallybrass), who with his own
hand inserted most of the bibliographical details, into a more comprehensive guide. Between 1903
and 1913 more material accumulated. The book was very greatly enlarged and almost entirely
rewritten in the edition of 1913. Certain portions had been similarly expanded in the two volumes
of *History in Fiction* (1908), and these were again further expanded and largely rewritten in the
more comprehensive *Guide to Historical Fiction* (1914).

Since the last day of December, 1911, the terminus reached in the 1913 edition of the Guide,
there has been an enormous output of new fiction, and the number of foreign novels turned into
English has been proportionately even greater. Hence the task of preparing a new edition was
one to shrink from, and would never have been undertaken without the prospect of collaboration,
even though Mr. Stallybrass generously offered to do the bibliographical work once more. This
he was preparing to perform when he died last year, after services to readers, bibliographers, and
librarians such as no member of his profession has surpassed. Fortunately, I was able to enlist a
colleague in one of the most esteemed of my former students at University College, Mr. James
Packman, a scholar and a trained librarian, who has manfully carried out the drudgery of inserting
the requisite bibliographical details, compiling the elaborate index, filling in many gaps among the
descriptive notes, and supplying or verifying the thousand and one items of information needed in
a work that is called upon to answer all sorts of questions besides those relating to the literary
quality of any given book.

The object has been to supply as complete a list as might be of the most notable prose fiction
in English, with as much characterization of the contents, nature, and style of each book as would
go into a few lines of print. Manifestly, such a list must include along with the very best many
novels that cannot be described as even among the second-best. It is a guide, not an autocratic
proclamation that such and such are the world's best novels, and that all the rest are inferior. A
proclamation of that sort would instantly meet with the same fate as sooner or later has befallen
certain too authoritative pronouncements, whose authors have singled out what they considered
the best books without reflecting that " best " is a relative term, relative, that is to say, not only
to the other things with which there is a comparison, but also to the purposes of the books and the
needs of readers. " Best " really means most suitable for some individual or for promoting some
particular purpose. It is hoped in the present case that those using the Guide will be enabled to see
for themselves what novels are recognized by most intelligent people as the best, and how and why
they are the best, and also what others come nearest to them in interest and artistic merit.

This does not claim to be a bibliography, in the strict professional sense of the word, although it supplies enough bibliographical particulars for general purposes. Long titles are frequently abbreviated; sub-titles, when they are really descriptive, often appear in the notes. The dates given are those of the first publication of each work in book form, the date of serial or other publication being added only when it is of special interest. More books that are now out of print have been included even than in the last edition of the Guide, the fact being indicated in the notes. Many interesting novels that had been long out of print at the time of the first and the second editions were afterwards reprinted, and the attention of publishers is again called to many that still remain unprocurable or have been sold out since.

The first great alteration that users of previous editions of the Guide will notice is that the contents have now been arranged under one alphabetical list of authors. Formerly, the division was first into national categories, and then into chronological groups. Although the authors were indexed alphabetically, so that the works of any given novelist could easily be found, this arrangement tended to be rather cumbrous, and it would have been still more cumbrous now that there are far larger numbers of foreign novels to be catalogued. The result would have been a long series of national guides, some of them very bulky. Both this and the chronological arrangement are much less useful at a time when there has ceased to be any lack of literary histories dealing with the fiction of the different countries. Many works that are now read only by students of the history of literature have been omitted for like reasons. Of a good many early novels or works that were almost novels, not excluding the long French prose romances of the seventeenth century, nearly all of which were turned into English almost as fast as they appeared, accounts are given in my *History of the English Novel* (Vols. I–IV, Witherby), a more suitable place to which the reader is directed. But those who wish to know what French, Russian, German, Italian, and other foreign novels have been translated, and those who want to see a list of the best American fiction, or the best novels by Scottish, Welsh, Irish, Canadian, Australian, and other British novelists, will find all these novelists grouped under proper heads in the index. That index also gives the titles of the works included in the general list, not omitting the chief items in collections of short stories, and is also a key to pseudonyms, hyphened names, and the like. Through an accidental disarrangement, these hyphened names do not appear always under the first or always under the second name. For this mishap only apologies can be offered, and readers are begged to refer to the index if some author with a double name appears at first sight to be missing.

Not quite so large and disproportionate an allowance of historical fiction has been included this time, although some critics may think that the authors have been generous enough. A new edition of the *Guide to Historical Fiction* has been asked for, and will now be prepared. This will be arranged on the same lines as the last, which have proved the handiest for general use, and it will of course include a group of sections dealing with the best of the war novels.

We intended at first to insert the prices of books; but after consideration decided to omit a piece of information that speedily grows out of date and misleading. Two or three have been carefully selected when a number of editions of any given work are available. Where American novels have been republished in England with an altered title, or English novels with a different title in America, the spurious designation is quoted in the note. The original titles of foreign novels are given in Roman type, along with the date of first publication, after the English title, in most cases when they are not practically identical, except in Russian and other languages of which the transliteration is not uniform, or when the information would be of trifling value to the ordinary reader. The authors do not profess to have read the English translations of the majority of the foreign novels listed. In the case of Russian or of Scandinavian languages, which they could not read in the original, it is much pleasanter to use a French or a German translation, and probably the French or German version will be more accurate as well as of superior literary merit. Translation seems to be a sweated industry, and publishers can hardly expect sound work for the miserable pittance offered. A friend recently took the trouble to collate with the original text a translation from the German, which was a recent " best seller ", and found upwards of forty complete misunderstandings of the author's meaning. Nor can the publishers be congratulated on the choice they make of works to be translated. Over and over again it has proved that a writer's master-pieces have been ignored and his poorest work Englished. But, evidently, it is not English publishers alone that are to blame. M. André Gide, in his recent book *Divers*, complains to André Thérive that " les traductions restent confiées le plus souvent à des êtres subalternes " ; and that the foreign publisher, evidently including the English publisher, demands so much for the rights of translation that there is no margin for properly remunerating the wretched translator. He rightly urges that it is not much of a translator who is content to give only the meaning of a text.

The authors have done their best to provide all the information necessary ; but in many cases the sources have been scarce and unreliable. They hope that a fair degree of accuracy has been attained, although the possibilities of error in such a work are innumerable, and faults of both omission and commission can hardly be avoided. Except a few translated works, only books published before the end of 1930 come within the purview. Their thanks are due to many kind helpers, almost too many to mention. Mr. W. C. Berwick Sayers, Chief Librarian of the Croydon Public Libraries, and Mr. W. E. Doubleday, late Chief Librarian of the Hampstead Public Libraries, lent them large quantities of books ; and along with their acknowledgments the authors would like to congratulate those libraries on possessing a large and well-selected stock of fiction in English and other languages. To Mr. Doubleday also thanks are due for reading the book in proof. Miss Elizabeth Stuyvesant, of the New York Public Library, and Professor H. D. Gray, of Stanford University, California, checked the lists of American novels and offered many valuable suggestions. Mr. L. C. Wharton, of the British Museum, put his linguistic knowledge at our disposal by correcting the transliteration of Slavonic names and some other details ; and Mr. I. C. Gröndahl, of University College, London, and Prince D. S. Mirski were good enough to glance through the Scandinavian and the Russian entries respectively. We are most grateful to them all. I should also like to express my indebtedness to the Editor of *The Nation*, now absorbed in *The New Statesman and Nation*, for allowing me to use a very large mass of notes on novels which I contributed to *The Athenæum*, during the years just anterior to its being absorbed in *The Nation and Athenæum*.

ERNEST A. BAKER.

" Although our productions have afforded more extensive and unaffected pleasure than those of any other literary corporation in the world, no species of composition has been so much decried. From pride, ignorance, or fashion, our foes are almost as many as our readers. And while the abilities of the nine-hundredth abridger of the History of England, or of the man who collects and publishes in a volume some dozen lines of Milton, Pope, and Prior, with a paper from the *Spectator*, and a chapter from Sterne, are eulogized by a thousand pens,—there seems almost a general wish of decrying the capacity and undervaluing the labour of the novelist, and of slighting the performances which have only genius, wit, and taste to recommend them. ' I am no novel-reader—I seldom look into novels—Do not imagine that *I* often read novels—It is really very well for a novel.'—Such is the common cant.—' And what are you reading, Miss——? ' ' Oh, it is only a novel ! ' replies the young lady ; while she lays down her book with affected indifference, or momentary shame. ' It is only *Cecilia*, or *Camilla*, or *Belinda* ; ' or, in short, only some work in which the greatest powers of the mind are displayed, in which the most thorough knowledge of human nature, the happiest delineation of its varieties, the liveliest effusions of wit and humour are conveyed to the world in the best-chosen language."

—(JANE AUSTEN.)

Guide to the Best Fiction

ABBOT, John Henry Macartney [Australian ; *b.* 1874.] *Castle Vane.* 1920
Bushrangers in New South Wales, in the time of Governor Bligh. [Angus and Robertson, Sydney.]

ABBOTT, Rev. Edwin Abbott [1838–1926]. *Philocristus : memoirs of a disciple of Christ.* 1878
Supposed to be written in Britain by a Galilean who witnessed the events. A narrative of Christ's ministry and death, based on the higher criticism. [Macmillan, 1916 : o.p.]

—— *Onesimus, Christ's Freedman : memoirs of a disciple of St. Paul.* 1882
A similar reconstruction of the progress of Christianity in Asia Minor, Greece, and Rome (A.D. 46–86). [Macmillan : o.p.]

—— *Silanus the Christian.* 1906
Autobiography of a Roman in the second century (A.D. 118–63) who attends the lectures of Epictetus at Nicopolis, and afterwards finds the teaching of Paul and the Gospels superior. [Cambridge Press ; Macmillan, New York : o.p.]

ABBOTT, Rev. Jacob [American ; 1803–79]. *The Franconia Stories.* [juvenile.] 1853
(v. 1) *Malleville ; Wallace.* (v. 2) *Mary Erskine ; Mary Sell.* (v. 3) *Beechnut ; Rodolphus.* (v. 4) *Ellen Linn ; Stuyvesant.* (v. 5) *Caroline ; Agnes.* The best of a great number of historical stories written expressly for children, whose minds the author addressed with rare tact and sympathy. His contributions to juvenile literature were enormous, and are of importance in literary history. [10 vols. in 5, Harper, New York : o.p. ; in 1 vol., Warne, 1872 : o.p.]

ABOUT, Edmond François Valentin [French ; 1828–85]. *Tolla* (Tolla, 1855). 1855
A summary of the problems of modern Italy, and a satire on the proud and poverty-stricken nobility living in their gloomy palaces ; depicting with more sympathy the picturesque life of the humbler classes, and the beautiful scenes of nature and art. About was accused of using an earlier novel, *Vittoria Savelli,* as material for *Tolla.* [Hamilton : o.p. ; Munro, New York : o.p.]

—— *The King of the Mountains* (Le roi des montagnes, 1856). 1897
An extravagant picture of Greek brigandage. Hadji Stavros holds the Government, the army, and the gendarmes in terror, and makes robbery a safe and dignified, as well as a lucrative profession. Gallic wit and irony season in the most piquant manner a story brimful of entertaining incident. [Transl. by Richard DAVIE, Heinemann : o.p. ; an earlier transl., by Sir C. F. L. WRAXALL, *sub tit. The Greek Brigand ; or, The King of the Mountains,* 1862 : o.p. ; *id., illus.* by G. Doré, Macmillan 1884 : o.p. ; transl. by Florence CREWE-JONES, *illus.,* Cupples, New York, 1924.]

—— *Madelon* (Madelon, 1863).
A courtesan ruins a pack of wealthy victims, marries an elderly millionaire, and puts in motion a series of big schemes for making money, which result in the bankruptcy of a town. In the last chapter she finds herself in a position to ruin a German principality. A satire on the corrupt institutions and unhealthy society of France under Louis Philippe. [o.p.]

—— *Trente et Quarante* (Trente et quarante, 1865). 1899
Farcical in plot, turning on an Italian exile's love for a girl, whose father, a captain in the Grand Army, frowns on the match. A critical incident is the captain's unintentional exploit of breaking the bank at Baden. [Transl. by Lord NEWTON, Arnold : o.p.]

—— *The Fellah* (Le Fellah : souvenirs d'Égypte, 1869). 1870
A tale of Egyptian life in About's own day. [Transl. by Sir Randall ROBERTS, Chatto ; Munro, New York : o.p.]

ACEBAL, Francisco [Spanish ; *b.* 1866]. *Face to Face ; and, Dolorosa : two novels of modern Spain.* 1906
In *Face to Face,* the downfall of the old aristocratic regime before the onslaught of capitalism and industrialism is represented in the encroachments of an English ironfounder on the estates of an impoverished marquess in northwest Spain. The Mater Dolorosa is the mother of an idolized son of successful tradespeople, whom she and his father educate to be an artist. He grows ashamed of his humdrum parents, and breaks his mother's heart by selfish extravagance. [With pref. by Martin HUME, Constable : o.p.]

ACHARD, Louis Amédée Eugène [French ; 1814–75]. *Blush-Rose* (Belle-Rose, 1847). 1913
A romance of cape and sword in the days of Louis XIV, Louvois, and Condé ; scenes Franche-Comté and Holland (1663–72). [An abridged translation by E. A. VIZETELLY, Holden : o.p.]

—— *The Golden Fleece* (La toison d'or, 1875). 1900
The Turkish wars in Austria, in the time of Louis XIV and Louise de la Vallière (1663–4). [Page, Boston : o.p. ; Macqueen : o.p.]. *La Chasse Royale* (1849–50) appears not to have been translated.

I

ACHILLES TATIUS [Greek, of Alexandria; *flor. c.* A.D. 540]. *The Most Delectable and Pleasant Historye of Clitophon and Leucippe:* written in Greeke by Achilles Stacius an Alexandrian, and now newlie translated into Englishe by W. B[URTON].   1577

Erotica, or *Leucippe and Clitophon*, is the most successful imitation of the style of romance exemplified by *Theagenes and Chariclea*, and the nearest to Heliodorus in point of date. Clitophon is supposed to tell the writer the whole story of his love for his cousin Leucippe, their disastrous voyage to Alexandria, escapes from shipwreck, from robbers, from amorous commanders, etc. Principal scenes, Tyre, Alexandria, and Ephesus. There is more bustle and incident than in the *Æthiopica*, and also more improbability. Incidents and descriptions were borrowed from late Greek poets, and in turn served as models to romantic poets and sentimental novelists after the Renaissance. [Transl. by W. B[URTON ?]; also *The Loves of Clitophon and Leucippe*, Englished by Anthony HODGES, 1638. Transl. by Rev. Rowland SMITH (with Heliodorus and Longus), *sub tit. The Loves of Clitopho and Leucippe*, in *Greek Romances of Heliodorus, Longus, and Achilles Tatius* (Bohn's Lib.), Bell (Harcourt, New York): o.p. Gk. text, ed. with transl. by Stephen GASELEE, (Loeb Classics) Putnam, New York (Heinemann) 1917; Burton's transl. reprinted from 1597 edition, ed. by Stephen Gaselee and H. F. M. Brett-Smith, Blackwell, Oxford, 1923.]

" ACKWORTH, John " [Rev. Frederick R. Smith; *b.* 1854]. *Clogshop Chronicles.*   1896
—— *The Scowcroft Critics; and other tales.*   1898

Two collections of brief stories and sketches, largely in the Lancashire dialect. The characters are factory-workers and others in a village, and most of them Methodists. Homely humour and homely pathos, racy genre-painting and character-drawing. [(1) C. H. Kelly: o.p.; Epworth Press; (2) Clarke; o.p.]

—— *Doxie Dent: a Clogshop chronicle.*   1899
Some of the people of *Clogshop Chronicles* reappear in this kindred story of a winsome girl. [C. H. Kelly: o.p.]
—— *The Minder: a story of the courtship, call, and conflicts of John Ledger, minder and minister.*

1900
The life of a Lancashire operative, his love affairs and his call to the ministry. Full of local colour, sketches of homely people and manners, rustic Methodism, etc.; the dialogue largely in north-country dialect. [Marshall: o.p.]

—— *The Coming of the Preachers: a tale of the rise of Methodism.*   1901
The coming of Methodism into the coarse, unspiritual life of a north-country village, the persecution it meets with, and the growth of religion among the better minds in response to John and Charles Wesley's preaching. [Hodder: o.p.]

ACLAND, Peregrine [Canadian]. *All Else is Folly: a tale of war and passion.*   1929
A war-novel that reflects the point of view of a section at least of the Canadian Expeditionary Force. [Constable; McClelland, Toronto; Coward McCann, New York.]

ADAMS, Andy [American; *b.* 1859]. *The Log of a Cowboy.*   1903
A very direct and realistic narrative of a great cattle-drive from Texas to the north. An excellent account of the cowboys of thirty years ago by a man who worked in that capacity for ten years. [Houghton, Boston; *illus.* by R. Farrington Elwell, 1927; Constable: o.p.]
—— *A Texas Matchmaker.*   1904
—— *The Outlet.*   1905
—— *Cattle Brands: a collection of western camp-fire stories.*   1906
—— *Reed Anthony, Cowman: an autobiography.*   1907

These convey with the same knowledge and fidelity the actualities of ranch life. The growth of a big cattle-ranch during the great cattle-boom, and all the various incidents of the life of a cowboy, are vividly described in the first three, and the last story is a similarly truthful account of an American who goes on the Texas Trail after the Civil War, and achieves fortune in the cattle-trade and the land-boom of the eighties. [All Houghton, Boston; Constable: o.p.]

ADAMS, Arthur Henry [New Zealander; *b.* 1872]. *Tussock Land: a romance of New Zealand and the Commonwealth.*   1904
Good descriptions of New Zealand life—Dunedin, a sheep run in the far south, Sydney, etc. The author is a New Zealander and a poet. [Unwin: o.p.]
—— *Galahad Jones.*   1910
The idyll of a middle-aged Australian bank-clerk. [Lane.]
—— *Grocer Greatheart.*   1915
An assorted set of characters, shipwrecked on a tropical island; they find their natural levels under primitive conditions. [Lane.]
—— *The Australians.*   1920
A study of Australian political and social life. [Nash: o.p.]

ADAMS, Henry [American; 1838–1918]. *Democracy: an American novel.*   1880
A political novel comprising a story of real interest and a delightful character in Mrs. Leigh. Depicts the political society of Washington, its corruptions, intrigues, and cabals, with realism and not a little pessimism. The various diplomats, senators, and members of Congress are very humanly portrayed; actual people have been pointed out as the originals; and scandals like the bribery case which hastens the *dénouement* have their counterparts in chapters of recent history. [Holt, New York; repr. 1925; Unwin, 1926.]

ADAMS, I. William [American]. *Shibusawa; or, The Passing of Old Japan.*   1906
A romance telling of the fall of the Shogun and the restoration of the Mikado, and giving a good account of the transformation of old manners and customs with the progress of Western culture. [Putnam, New York: o.p.]

ADAMS, Samuel Hopkins [American ; *b.* 1871]. *Revelry.* 1926
A melodramatic account, rather caricature than satire, of American politics and the White House, Markham representing Harding (President, 1920–3). The whole gang of politicians is shown as corrupt and debauched. [Boni, New York ; Brentano.]

ADCOCK, Arthur St. John [1864–1930]. *East End Idylls.* 1897
—— *In the Image of God : a story of Lower London.* 1898
Two series of stories carefully presenting the life of the very poor in London, with little heightening for literary effect, and not so monotonously gruesome as such realistic studies often are : the Cockney speech faithfully rendered. [(1) Bowden, o.p. ; Mansfield, New York ; o.p. (2) Skeffington : o.p.]

ADDERLEY, The Hon. and Rev. James Granville [*b.* 1861]. *Stephen Remarx : the story of a venture in ethics.* 1893
A miniature story of a clergyman who preaches socialism and humanitarianism and tries to establish a practical brotherhood ; with a longer story very similar in aim. [Arnold (Dutton, New York) ; Brown & Langham, 1904 ; o.p.]
—— *Paul Mercer : a story of repentance among millions.* 1897
Paul, the son of a millionaire, goes exploring among the poor and the ameliorating agencies of the East End, is converted to Christian socialism and founds a large manufacturing community. Full of criticism of the plutocratic regime and descriptive of the numerous humanitarian bodies. [Arnold : o.p.]

ADDISON, Joseph [1672–1719]. *The Spectator.* 1711–14
The *Spectator* contains many critical or satirical pictures of society, moral apologues, and character-sketches knit into a kind of memoir, such as that of Sir Roger de Coverley, all of which were important as aiding the development of the novel towards delineation of real life. The periodical essay went a stage further than the "character," whole volumes of which were published by Overbury, Butler, Earle, and numerous other writers of the preceding age. The essay not only analysed and criticized characters in a philosophical way, but showed them actually immersed in the practical affairs of life. [8 vols., Dent, 1897 ; o.p. ; ed. G. A. Aitken, 6 vols. (New Universal Lib.), Routledge (Dutton, New York) ; ed. H. Morley, with good index by Wheeler, Routledge (Dutton, New York) : o.p. ; (Bohn's Lib.), 3 vols., Bell (Harcourt, New York) ; 4 vols. (Everyman's Lib.) Dent (Dutton, New York) 1909.]

" ADELER, Max " [Charles Heber Clark ; American ; 1841–1915]. *Out of the Hurly-Burly ; or, Life in an Odd Corner.* 1874
A farrago of absurd and highly diverting incidents ; farce of an extravagant kind. [Coates, Philadelphia : o.p. ; Routledge (1921).]
—— *Transformations.* 1883
Short pieces of a like extravagance, e.g. *Mrs. Shelmire's Djinn*, the Aladdin fable transplanted to American soil. [Ward & Lock : o.p.]
—— *Captain Bluitt.* 1901
—— *In Happy Hollow.* 1903
—— *The Quakeress.* 1905
More in the form of regular novels, with some good character-drawing. [(1) Coates, Philadelphia ; Ward & Lock : o.p. ; (2) Coates ; o.p. ; (3) Winston, Philadelphia.]

AGATE, James Evershed [*b.* 1877]. *Responsibility.* 1919
A story of Manchester life, in the form of a soliloquy written in hospital. The narrator recalls his early life as a cotton trader in Manchester, and subsequent escape to London to become a novelist. [Richards.]
—— *Blessed are the Rich.* 1924
A somewhat flamboyant account of the son of a Manchester chemist, and his escape from the dullness of matrimony. [L. Parsons : o.p.]

" AGNUS, Orme " [Rev. John C. Higginbotham]. *Jan Oxber.* 1900
Dorset stories in broad dialect, comic or tragic, and all rich in rustic character. Jan is a stout-hearted peasant whose love is embittered by a wrong inflicted on his wife, and who develops into a village Hampden. " Orme Agnus " is obviously a disciple of Mr. Hardy, though pronouncedly an optimist. [Ward & Lock ; Page, Boston : o.p.]
—— *Love in Our Village.* 1900
The sentimental side of the Dorsetshire peasant, set forth with the same racy handling of character and humorous speech, and with touches of pathos ; e.g. *The Poet's Love*, tale of a consumptive lad who writes verses that he fondly imagines to be poetry, and *The Dethronement of the King*, how two lasses give their deceitful lover a thrashing and humble his pride. [Ward & Lock ; Page, Boston : o.p.]
—— *Zike Mouldom.* 1902
Zike, according to the author, represents the angel in the nature of a Lancashire navvy. He is a character prone to excess, a powerful will rioting in sheer devilry or rushing into extremes of self-sacrifice. Both this and the other sketches are decidedly sentimental versions of rustic life, and the good moral is an important part. *The Wooing of Kezia* is brisk comedy. [Ward & Lock ; Page, Boston : o.p.]
—— *Sarah Tuldon.* 1903
—— *Sarah Tuldon's Lovers.* 1909
Sarah is a shrewd and strong-willed village girl, who subjugates her lazy and slatternly parents, makes the whole family clean and industrious, and marrying a rich farmer, becomes queen of the village, and carries out a crusade against ignorance, filth, and neglect. Her story is full of broad comedy. [(1) and (2), Ward & Lock ; (1) Little & Brown, Boston : o.p.]
—— *Nance of Manchester.* 1912
A consumptive girl from the slums is sent to Dorset : she dies, but not before her personality and courage have impressed themselves on her companions. [Methuen : o.p.]

3

AGUILAR, Grace [1816–47]. *The Days of Bruce.* 1834
A tale of the Scottish war of independence against Edward II (1306–14), in the old-fashioned heroical style, offering in the three women feminine idealizations of lofty fortitude, over-confidence, and tender innocence, overwhelmed by the violence of a revolutionary era. [Routledge (Dutton, New York) : o.p. ; *illus.* by H. M. Brock, Pearson, 1905 : o.p. ; Seeley ; Burt, New York.]

—— *The Vale of Cedars ; or, The Martyr.* 1850
A notable Englishman's adventures in Spain under Ferdinand and Isabella ; Torquemada and the Holy Inquisition and the persecution of the Jews in Spain (1479–1501). [Routledge (Dutton, New York) ; intro. by W. Jerrold, *illus.* by T. H. Robinson, Dent, 1902 : o.p.]

AICARD, Jean [French ; 1848–1921]. *The Diverting Adventures of Maurin* (Maurin des Maures : comme on rit chez nous, 1908). 1910

—— *Maurin the Illustrious* (L'illustre Maurin : suite et fin des memorables aventures de Maurin des Maures, 1908) [sequel]. 1910
Maurin, a sort of pendant to Tartarin, is the Robin Hood and Don Juan of the Monts des Maures, a wild region of hill and forest overlooking the Var. These two volumes chronicle his exploits as hunter and as lover, and, above all, his galégeades, an elaborate Provençal jest at which he is a past master. [(1) & (2), transl. by Alfred ALLINSON, Lane.]

AINSWORTH, William Harrison [1805–82]. *Rookwood.* 1834
A Gothic romance, the career of Dick Turpin the highwayman (1705–39) ; the story of his famous ride to York probably applies more accurately to Swift Dick Nevinson (1676). [*Original Illustr. Ed.*—with the illustrations of both Cruikshank (1836) and John Gilbert (1851)—Routledge (Dutton, New York), 1875. (Chandos Cl.), Warne, London & New York, 1929.]

—— *The Admirable Crichton.* 1837
The career of James Crichton and adventures at the Court of Henri III : scene, Paris in 1579. [*Illus.* by Hablot K. Browne, Routledge, 1853 ; (Everyman's Lib.), Dent (Dutton, New York) ; Warne, New York.]

—— *Jack Sheppard.* 1839
A tale of criminal life more realistic, less romantic, than *Rookwood*. An idealization of roguery that, like Lytton's *Paul Clifford*, has been frequently condemned for immoral tendency (1702–24). [*Original Illustr. Ed.*, after Cruikshank, Routledge (Dutton, New York) ; Warne, New York.]

—— *The Tower of London.* 1840
Quite a product of Mrs. Radcliffe's art, with scenes of broad comedy added. The historical matter is the tragic story of Lady Jane Grey's hopeless conspiracy and execution (1553–4). Old London with its picturesque buildings furnishes the theatre of these events. [*Original Illustr. Ed.*, Routledge (Dutton, New York) ; (Everyman's Lib.), Dent, 1910 ; (World's Classics), Oxford Press, 1910 ; Harrap, 1926 ; Nelson, 1928 ; Collins (Canterbury Classics) 1930 ; 2 vols., Burt, New York ; Warne, New York.]

—— *Old St. Paul's.* 1841
History of a London grocer and his family during the years of the Plague and the Fire (1665–6) ; rich in local and historical colour and in portraits of celebrities. [*Original Illustr. Ed.*, Routledge (Dutton, New York) ; (Everyman's Lib.) Dent, 1911 ; Harrap 1926 ; Warne, New York.]

—— *Guy Fawkes ; or, The Gunpowder Treason.* 1841
A view of the plot favourable to the Catholics ; scenes, the midlands and London (1605–6). [*Original Illustr. Ed.*, Routledge (Dutton, New York) ; Warne, New York.]

—— *The Miser's Daughter.* 1842
A lurid, thoroughly Radcliffian story, written to show the evils of avarice. The life of the coffee-houses, of Ranelagh and Vauxhall, is depicted in the course of a young man's adventures about town (1744). [*Original Illustr. Ed.*, after Cruikshank, Routledge (Dutton, New York) ; Warne, New York.]

—— *Windsor Castle.* 1843
The Earl of Surrey and the mythical Fair Geraldine, Herne the Hunter, Cardinal Wolsey, Henry VIII, and two of his wives, Anne Boleyn and Jane Seymour, are the personages whose well-known stories are woven together in this romance. [*Original Illustr. Ed.*, Routledge (Dutton, New York) ; (Everyman's Lib.). Dent, 1915 ; Harrap, 1927 ; Warne, New York.]

—— *St. James's ; or, The Court of Queen Anne.* 1844
The Duke and Duchess of Marlborough and Abigail Hill, afterwards Mrs. Masham, play a conspicuous part in this story of court intrigues, the Sacheverell case, Guiscard's attempt upon Harley, etc. (1707–14). [Routledge (Dutton, New York).]

—— *James the Second.* 1848
London at the time of the Revolution of 1688, the trial of the Bishops, and the coming of the Prince of Orange. [3 vols. Colburn : o.p. There has been no modern re-issue.]

—— *The Lancashire Witches.* 1849
A romance of Pendle Forest and Whalley Abbey, dealing with trials for witchcraft at Lancaster in 1612, embodying the story of the Pilgrimage of Grace (1536) in the introduction. Contains plenty of topographical history dealing with Lancashire. [*Original Illustr. Ed.*, after John Gilbert, Routledge (Dutton, New York) ; Warne, New York.]

—— *The Star Chamber.* 1854
Trial of Sir James Mompesson (1621) ; an inferior work. [*Original Illustr. Ed.*, Routledge (Dutton, New York) ; Warne, New York.]

—— *Mervyn Clitheroe.* 1858
Manchester in 1820. [Routledge (Dutton, New York).]

—— *Ovingdean Grange.* 1860
A tale of the South Downs, old Brighthelmstone, etc., and the escape of Charles II : the historical basis very shaky. [*Original Illustr. Ed.*, Routledge (Dutton, New York).]

AINSWORTH, William Harrison (*continued*). *The Constable of the Tower.*   1861
Fall of the Protector Somerset (1549–52). [Routledge (Dutton, New York).]

—— *Cardinal Pole ; or, The Days of Philip and Mary*   1863
The marriage business (1554–8). [*Illus.* by F. Gilbert, Routledge, 1881 : o.p.]

—— *John Law, the Projector.*   1864
The Bank of Mississippi schemes ; shifts from London (1705) to Paris (1715–20). [*Illus.* by F. Gilbert, Routledge, 1881.]

—— *The South Sea Bubble.*   1868
An account of the South Sea Company, and a story of people ruined by the smash (1720). [Routledge : o.p.]

—— *Boscobel ; or, The Royal Oak.*   1872
Prince Charlie's escape after Worcester, and his preservation by the Penderels (1651). [*Original Illustr. Ed.* Routledge (Dutton, New York).]

—— *Preston Flight ; or, The Insurrection of 1715.*   1875
The Jacobite rebellion of 1715, described in a painstaking manner, along with a conventional love plot, of which Lord Derwentwater is the central figure. A characteristic example of Ainsworth's later works. [Routledge, 1879 (Dutton, New York).]

—— *The Leaguer of Lathom.*   1876
The war in Lancashire, siege of Manchester, and the Earl of Derby's exploits (1642–51). [Routledge, 1880 : o.p.]
[*Works*, 17 vols., Routledge ; 10 vols., Warne ; 8 vols., Burt, New York.]

AKSAKOV, Sergĕi [Russian ; 1791–1859]. *Years of Childhood.*   1916
—— *A Russian Schoolboy* [sequel].   1917
—— *A Russian Gentleman* [sequel].   1917
Aksakov published these chronicles of the Bagrov family in 1856, and his Russian gentleman, Stepan Mikhailovitch Bagrov, was generally recognized as a study of his own grandfather. So too the schoolboy is obviously Aksakov, the story ending with his arrival at the age of fifteen. The work thus consists in the main of authentic recollections of the life of landed gentry in Russia at the end of the eighteenth and the beginning of the nineteenth century. Aksakov was obviously a most impressionable youth ; his reminiscences come back to him with all the vividness and delight of an original experience. He is not satirical, or moralistic, or philosophical ; he simply puts down what he saw and experienced with quiet, artless literalness, and proceeds in a placid, epical manner suited to the simple, leisurely existence of those remote days. Stepan is a notable personage. He settles down like an ancient patriarch on a vast estate in the government of Orenburg, near the Urals, and there rules his family, his serfs, his flocks and herds. Beside this tyrannical and hot-tempered but honourable figure are grouped many others, some adorable, some repulsive or ridiculous. Then on his own childhood Aksakov writes of what he calls " the golden age," and re-lives the fevers and raptures of that ecstatic time with such zest as if he had never ceased to be a boy. [(1), (2), and (3), transl. by J. D. DUFF, Arnold : o.p. ; (World's Classics), Oxford Press, 1923–4 ; transl. by M. C. BEVERLEY, etc., *sub tit. Chronicles of a Russian Family,* (Broadway Transl.) Routledge (Dutton, New York), 1924.]

ALARCÓN, Pedro Antonio de [Spanish ; 1833–91]. *Brunhilde ; or, The Last Act of Norma* (El Final de Norma, 1855).   1891
This was a boyish performance which Alarcón later let slide into oblivion. [Transl. by Mrs. DARR, Lovell, New York : o.p.]

—— *The Strange Friend of Tito Gill* (El Amigo de la Muerte).   1890
A grotesque fantasy, of which the chief personage is Death. [Transl. by Mrs. F. J. A. DARR, Lovell, New York : o.p. ; *The Friend of Death,* adapted by H. J. SERRANO, 1891 : o.p.]

—— *The Three-cornered Hat* (El Sombrero de tres picos, 1874).   1905
Alarcón's masterpiece of vivacious and witty story-telling ; the amusing little love-tale of the still romantic days before modern Spain. Scene : a village in Andalusia (1804–12). [Transl. by Lady GOODENOUGH, Nutt : o.p. ; transl. by Jacob S. FASSETT, (Borzoi transl.) Knopf, 1918.]

ALBANESI, Effie Maria [*née* Anderson ; *b.* 1866]. *The Beloved Enemy.*   1913
A girl's unhappy marriage, subsequent struggle for independence, and eventual happiness. [Methuen : o.p.]

—— *Truant Happiness.*   1918
An unsophisticated tale of domestic life, typical of this prolific author's production at her best. [Ward & Lock : o.p.]

ALCOTT, Louisa May [American ; 1832–88]. *Hospital Sketches ; and, Camp and Fireside Stories.* 1863
Based on—almost a literal reproduction of—Miss Alcott's letters to her family, when acting as a hospital nurse at Washington during the war (1862–3). [Little & Brown, Boston (repr. 1872).]

—— *Little Women ; or, Meg, Jo, Beth and Amy.*   [juvenile] 1868
—— *Little Women Married ; or, Wedded ; also called " Good Wives "* [sequel].   1869
A bright and genial didactic story of childhood and home life, portraying four girls who are wholesome types, and following their growth to womanhood. One of the most truthful delineations ever penned of American village life. Moralistic, but not theological ; in fact, Miss Alcott rarely alludes to religious questions. [(1) Little & Brown, Boston ; Blackie ; Routledge ; Macmillan ; Oxford Press. *Illus.,* Little & Brown, Boston ; Low. (2) Blackie ; Low ; Hodder. *Little Women and Good Wives* (Everyman's Lib.) Dent (Dutton, New York) ; Seeley.]

—— *An Old-fashioned Girl.*   [juvenile] 1870
Commonplace people and commonplace events : the coming of a country girl to a fashionable Boston family, their failure, and her goodness and self-sacrifice rewarded by the love of a manly fellow. [Little & Brown, Boston ; Low. *Illustrated,* Little & Brown, Boston ; Winston, Philadelphia, 1928 ; Low.]

—— *Little Men : life at Plumfield with Jo's boys.*   [juvenile] 1871

ALCOTT, Louisa May (*continued*). *Jo's Boys, and How They Turned Out* [sequel]. [juvenile] 1886
Companion novels on parallel lines. [(1) Little & Brown, Boston ; Low, 1906 ; (Everyman's Lib.), Dent, 1911 ; *illus.*, Low ; Winston, Philadelphia, 1928 ; Saalfield, Akron ; (2), *illus.*, Little & Brown, Boston ; Low.]
—— *Work : a story of experience.* [juvenile] 1873
Life of a New England girl of superior birth, who goes out to earn her living, and, as housemaid, actress, governess, and, finally, as a wife, shows energy and adherence to the right. In the minor characters, and in the humorous dialogue, the influence of Dickens is patent. [Little & Brown, Boston ; Low.]
—— *Eight Cousins ; or, The Aunt Hill.* [juvenile] 1875
Story of a set of boys and girls, whose diverse characters and ways are drawn with a thorough enjoyment of and affection for children, and with plenty of fun. They have no precocious traits, but appeal to mature readers by their naturalness and the light they throw on questions of training and education. [Little & Brown, Boston ; Low. *Illus.*, Little & Brown, Boston ; Low.]
—— *Rose in Bloom* [sequel]. [juvenile] 1876
The cousins as they are a few years after their European holiday ; principally their love-stories. [Little & Brown, Boston ; Low. *Illus.*, Little & Brown, Boston ; Low.]
—— *Under the Lilacs.* [juvenile] 1877
The tale of a circus boy, his dog, and the friends they made. [Little & Brown, Boston ; Low, 1907. *Illus.* Little & Brown, Boston ; Low.]
—— *Jack and Jill : a village story.* [juvenile] 1880
Happy experiences of a boy and girl recovering from the effects of an accident. [Little & Brown, Boston ; Low, 1907. *Illus.*, Little & Brown, Boston ; Low.]
—— *Spinning-Wheel Stories.* [juvenile] 1884
Stories read to a party of children in the Christmas holidays. [Little & Brown, Boston ; Low : o.p.]
[*Works : Aunt Jo's Scrap Bag*, 6 vols. ; *Little Women Series*, 8 vols. ; *Spinning Wheel Series*, 4 vols. ; Little & Brown, Boston.]

ALDANOV, Mark Aleksandrovich [or Landau ; Russian ; *b.* 1888]. *The Ninth Thermidor.* 1921
—— *The Devil's Bridge* [sequel]. 1928
—— *Saint Helena, Little Island* [sequel]. 1923
An historical trilogy, inspired by the stone monster nicknamed Le Penseur, on Notre Dame, Paris. Robespierre is a prominent figure in the first, Napoleon in the last volume. Scenes range from London to Brussels, Paris, and St. Helena (1793–1821). [Transl. by A. E. CHAMOT, Cape ; Knopf, New York.]

ALDINGTON, Richard [*b.* 1892]. *Death of a Hero.* 1929
Purports to tell the " whole truth " about Victorian hypocrisy and the war. An exceedingly bitter, often hysterical indictment, which however throws a good deal of light upon the state of mind of some at least of those who had suffered. [Chatto ; Covici, New York.]
—— *Roads to Glory.* 1930
Includes the contents of *At all Costs* and *Two Stories*. Thirteen tales of the war and its aftermath, uniformly lugubrious. The one theme repudiated is the glory of war. Ugly incidents of trench-fighting, thoughts at the grave of a German soldier, the tragedy of a life ending in death for desertion, experiences after demobilization, post-war neurasthenia and suicide : these are the topics of stories that read like facts only in part subdued to the purposes of art. [Chatto.]

ALDRICH, Thomas Bailey [American ; 1836–1907]. *The Story of a Bad Boy.* 1869
Autobiography in the main. The bad boy is a New Orleans lad who comes to be educated at a New England seaport, of pronouncedly puritanical character. Makes one realize vividly the narrow range of boyish experience and imagination, the immense sorrows arising from petty troubles, and the exquisite fascination of the average boy's adventures and mischievous escapades. Comic as a whole, with bits of boyish pathos, home-sickness, love-sickness, etc. [Several eds., Houghton, Boston ; Macmillan, New York, 1930 ; *illus.* Houghton, Boston ; Winston, Philadelphia, 1928.]
—— *Marjorie Daw, and other People : short stories.* 1873
Artful little stories, wit characterizing not only the style but the manipulation of plot. *Marjorie Daw* leads up, by a climax, to an unforeseen conclusion, making a fool of the reader in a good-natured way. Hawthorne praised the delicate art and subdued pathos of *Père Antoine's Date Palm*. Every tale is logically worked out, rounded and complete in itself, and usually ends in a surprise. *Marjorie Daw* appeared first in the *Atlantic Monthly* (April, 1873). [Several eds., Houghton, Boston ; Douglas, Edinburgh : o.p. ; *illus.* by H. M. Brett, Houghton, Boston.]
—— *Prudence Palfrey.* 1874
A nearly impossible plot, developed with wit and plausibility—how a murderer and thief from the gold-diggings acts as minister in a New England village, wins the heart of his flock, and very nearly that of Prudence. [Houghton, Boston ; Routledge : o.p.]
—— *The Queen of Sheba.* 1877
A novelette connected with *Marjorie Daw* by the character of Flemming. Compact of humour and sensation, one of the most striking incidents being the escape of the lunatics from an asylum, after locking in their keepers. Scenes, a New Hampshire village and then Switzerland. [Houghton, Boston (repr. 1905) ; Douglas, Edinburgh, 1885 : o.p.]
—— *The Stillwater Tragedy.* 1880
His most elaborate novel. A murder and the detection of the murderer are the groundwork. The various aspects of life in a manufacturing village, the passions and calamities of a strike, are realistically depicted ; and a love-story introduces romance. [Houghton, Boston ; 2 vols., Douglas, Edinburgh, 1886 : o.p.]
—— *Two Bites at a Cherry ; with other tales.* 1893
The title-story is a good specimen of his ingenious and delicate workmanship. [Houghton, Boston ; Douglas, Edinburgh : o.p.]
[*Works* (Revised Ed.), 9 vols., Houghton, Boston.]

ALEMÁN, Mateo [Spanish ; *c.* 1550–1609]. *The Rogue ; or, The Life of Guzman de Alfarache* (Vida y hechos del pícaro Guzmán de Alfarache, 1599). 1622

One of the most famous rogue-stories, presenting a lively view of people and manners in Spain and Italy. Guzman, a low, canting scoundrel, whose rascally doings either get himself into trouble or injure his employers, appears as street beggar, man of fashion, sharper, pimp, religious student, and in other characters. But the story is portentously overloaded, to modern tastes, with moral disquisitions of an irrelevant and conceited kind. [Transl. by J. Mabbe in full-flavoured English, 1622 : reprint, with introd. by J. Fitzmaurice Kelly, (Tudor Translations), 4 vols., Constable (Knopf, New York), 1924 ; Navarre Soc., 1928.]

" ALERAMO, Sibilla " [Rina Faccio, *née* Cottino ; Italian ; *b.* 1878]. *A Woman at Bay* (Una Donna, 1906). 1908

An exceedingly frank and passionate statement of woman's right to freedom and sexual equality, in the autobiography of a refined girl driven by circumstances into a wrong sort of marriage, which becomes such a living hell that she seeks escape in suicide. [Transl. by Maria H. Lansdale, Putnam : o.p.]

ALEXANDER, Eleanor Jane [Irish]. *The Rambling Rector.* 1904

Character-drawing and pictures of life and manners among Church of England people in Ulster ; clerical life sympathetically drawn. [Arnold : o.p. ; Longman, New York : o.p.]

ALEXANDER, Miriam [Mrs. Stokes ; Irish]. *The House of Lisronan.* 1912

A dramatic story about the vengeance taken by an Irishman upon the Dutchman who has dispossessed him from his estates, and whose daughter he has married, in the times of the persecutions under William and Anne. Typical characters of the times, hedge-schoolmaster, priest, etc., are well drawn ; William III is introduced in an unfavourable light. [Melrose : o.p.]

—— *The Green Altar.* 1924

Depicts the fortunes of a Munster family, in modern times—the revolt of the younger generation who are carried away by the political upheavals. [Melrose : o.p.]

" ALEXIS, Willibald " [Georg Wilhelm Heinrich Häring ; German ; 1798–1871]. *The Burgomaster of Berlin* (Der Roland von Berlin, 1840). 1843

A story of German nobles and townsfolk under the Emperor Frederick III (1442–70). One of the best of a series of romances by a successful imitator of the Waverley novels—" Walter Scott of the Mark "—dealing with the history of Brandenburg. Häring first attained popularity by his *Walladmor* (1823), described as " freely translated from the English of Sir Walter Scott, with a preface by Willibald Alexis." This deceived even Scott's admirers. *Die Hosen des Herrn von Bredow* (1846–8), *Ruhe ist die erste Bürgerpflicht* (1852), *Isegrimm* (1854), *Der Wärwolf*, and *Dorothe* (1856) are notable among the untranslated novels by Häring. [3 vols., Saunders & Otley : o.p.]

ALLARDYCE, Alexander [Scottish ; 1846–96]. *The City of Sunshine.* 1877

Treats not only of Anglo-Indian people, but of the Hindu, in a way that appeals to the educated of that race. Much of the interest is religious ; caste, education, justice, the betrothal of infants, money-lending, and similar problems have light thrown on them ; and there are specimens of Hindu character from the Ganges basin. [3 vols., Blackwood : o.p.]

—— *Balmoral : a romance of the Queen's country.* 1893

A romance of the '15, with Balmoral, Deeside, Lochnagar, and Dunnottar Castle as scenes. In the picture of the mustering of the Jacobite clans before Sheriffmuir, the author shows a wide acquaintance with Highland genealogy and local history. The daughter of the Farquhars, the old lairds of Balmoral, is the heroine ; the hero represents the London Jacobites. [3 vols., Blackwood : o.p.]

" ALLEN, Grant " [Charles Grant Blairfindie Allen ; Canadian ; 1848–99]. *Philistia.* 1884

A farcical picture of Socialism. The important characters are all Socialists either actively or passively, and the hero endures afflicting trials for his convictions before he obtains a competence as editor of a Socialist journal. [Chatto.]

—— *Ivan Greet's Masterpiece ; etc.* 1893

Ivan Greet seeks among the negroes of Jamaica the leisure and tranquillity denied him by a London life, composes his masterpiece and dies. A faithful mulatto girl devotes her life to his baby and to the task of getting the manuscript printed, but this is accidentally burned, and in a scene of acute pathos she and the little one die exposed to a tropical tempest. A good index to the quality of the fifteen tales and sketches that follow. [Chatto.]

—— *The Woman Who Did.* 1895

She refuses to marry her lover, and enters into a free union with him, but dies a martyr to the author's gospel of free love. A bold and aggressive manifesto, quite inoffensive as a story. [De La More Press : o.p. ; G. Richards, 1919 : o.p. ; Little & Brown, Boston, 1926.]

—— *Twelve Tales, with a Headpiece, a Tailpiece, and an Intermezzo ; being select stories.* 1899

A Confidential Communication is the sardonic history of a murder by mistake ; *The Rev. John Creedy*, a tragic study of the racial question in a negro missionary who reverts ; *The Child of the Phalanstery*, public infanticide in advanced society centuries hence ; *The Curate of Churnside*, how an æsthetic, soft-hearted young curate puts his uncle out of the way to secure an income for his betrothed and himself—a grim *jeu d'esprit ;* and in *John Cann's Treasure* a man sacrifices honesty, position, and in the sequel his reason, for a treasure that turns out worthless. Fair specimens, not only of the tales in this volume, but of Grant Allen's fiction generally, which is nothing if not novel and startling. [Grant Richards : o.p.]

ALLEN, James Lane [American ; 1849–1925]. *Flute and Violin ; and other Kentucky tales.* 1891

Stories of the author's native country, the Blue-Grass region of Kentucky, and of its hardy agricultural folk, true Anglo-Saxons. Mostly pathetic in motive : *Two Gentlemen of Kentucky*, a touching, sadly humorous story of master and slave ; *The White Cowl* and *Sister Dolorosa*, two stories of monastic life ; *King Solomon*, a vagrant white who redeemed his character by acting as grave-digger in the dreadful cholera year, 1833.

ALLEN, James Lane (*continued*).

Flute and Violin, and others, have some of the delicate art and imagination of Hawthorne, and the natural description is akin to Thoreau's. [Macmillan, New York and London. *Two Gentlemen of Kentucky*, reprinted from this book, Macmillan, New York.]

—— *A Kentucky Cardinal.* 1895

The title refers to a cardinal bird, and indicates the subtle motive that underlies a story characterized by feminine sensibility. An act of unkindness to this shy child of nature brings misunderstanding into two young people's courtship. A refined study of personality and sentiment, penetrated with a tender love of nature. Perhaps of most interest for its descriptions of Kentucky. The time is half a century since. [Macmillan, New York and London.]

—— *Aftermath* [sequel]. 1896

A companion idyll consisting of meditations and fanciful disquisitions on life. A pure and beautiful portrayal of courtship and marriage is embodied in the little tale, tinged at the end with delicate pathos. The dominant motive is the conflict between the love of nature and the humaner love of wife and home. [Macmillan, New York and London. With *A Kentucky Cardinal*, *illus.* by Hugh Thomson, Macmillan, New York.]

—— *Summer in Arcady.* 1896

The common incidents of a girl's courtship by a young farmer. The idyll is imaginatively handled, and the sights and sounds of woods and fields in summer are harmonized into a poetic symphony. [Macmillan, New York and London, o.p.]

—— *The Choir Invisible.* 1897

A sentimental story of Kentucky in the years following the War of Independence, very delicate in analysis of feeling, and in the emotional use of landscape. The theme is that of an honest and pure affection between a man and a woman separated by marriage. Deals exclusively with the inner life, and is almost devoid of external incident, though the perilous conditions of existence in the colonizing days are brought out by glimpses of Indian warfare. [Macmillan, New York and London. *Illus.* by Orson Lowell, Macmillan, New York.]

—— *The Increasing Purpose.* 1900

A young Kentuckian, brought up to believe in the literal inspiration of the Bible, enters as a student for the ministry in the Lexington College. The story shows his awakening to a wider belief and his own loss of faith, until a woman, knowing little of theology, reconciles him to life and to the truest religion. [Macmillan, London and New York : o.p. ; *sub tit. The Reign of Law : a tale of the Kentucky hemp-fields*, Clark, Toronto : o.p.]

—— *The Mettle of the Pasture.* 1903

A spiritual tragedy worked out on the same delicate lines. A young man who had a liaison at college, confesses to the girl he loves, wrecking both their hearts. [Macmillan, New York and London : o.p.]

—— *The Bride of the Mistletoe.* 1909

First of a " trilogy " studying " the inner heart of thinking, feeling, suffering human beings." This story of the Kentucky forests is about a scholar immersed in his book and the torture of his wife who feels that she has little part in his real life. [Macmillan, New York and London : o.p.]

—— *A Heroine in Bronze ; or, A Portrait of a Girl : a pastoral of the city.* 1912

A pleasant idyll of a young writer in New York, and his courtship. [Macmillan, New York.]

—— *The Sword of Youth.* 1915

A Civil War episode (1863–5). The youth has joined up, but is summoned to his mother's death-bed. The moral question to be decided is whether he shall obey the call or stick to his post. [Macmillan, New York and London ; Century Co., New York.]

—— *A Cathedral Singer.* 1916

—— *The Kentucky Warbler.* 1918

Two more sentimental stories, largely concerned with children, in his popular manner. [(1) Macmillan, New York and London ; (2) Brown, New York ; Nash, 1920.]

ALMQVIST, Karl Jonas Ludwig [Swedish ; 1793–1866]. *Sara Videbeck* (Det går an, 1838) ; *and, The Chapel* (Kapellet, 1838). 1919

The former, a masterly piece of realism, was written to show what was the novelist's idea of a free marriage. The other is a simple and charming study of an ideal pastor and his affectionate congregation of poor fisherfolk. [Transl. by Adolph Burnett BENSON, American-Scandinavian Foundation, Oxford Press.]

ALTSHELER, Joseph Alexander [American ; 1862–1919]. *The Sun of Saratoga.* 1897

The War of Independence and the capitulation of General Burgoyne (1777). [Appleton, New York and London.]

—— *A Soldier of Manhattan.* 1898

Capture of Ticonderoga, battle of Quebec, etc. Montcalm and Wolfe appear (1758–60). An English officer's love for the daughter of a French seigneur. [Appleton, New York and London.]

—— *A Herald of the West.* 1898

Describes the attack on Washington and the battle of New Orleans, and depicts the deep animus against England fostered by the events preceding this war (1811–15). [Appleton, New York and London.]

—— *In Hostile Red.* 1900

The Revolutionary War in 1777–8 ; the British under Howe in Philadelphia, his march to New York, and the battle of Monmouth. [Doubleday, New York : o.p.]

—— *In Circling Camps : a story of the Civil War.* 1900

From the election of Lincoln to the surrender of Lee ; Gettysburg is a big battlepiece. [Appleton, New York and London.]

ALTSHELER, Joseph Alexander (*continued*). *The Wilderness Road.* 1901
The Indian wars in Kentucky, defeat of St. Clair and victory of Wayne (1791–4). [Appleton, New York and London.]
—— *My Captive.* 1902
The war in South Carolina (1781), the battle of the Cowpens between the English under Tarleton and the Americans under Morgan. [Appleton, New York and London.]
—— *Before the Dawn : a story of the fall of Richmond.* 1903
The final stages of the Civil War, the battle of the Wilderness, Grant's advance upon Richmond, and the surrender of Lee (1863–5). Scenes of action vigorously presented, with less interesting domestic scenes. [Doubleday, New York : o.p. ; Hutchinson : o.p.]
—— *The Forest Runners.* [juvenile] 1908
—— *The Free Rangers : a tale of early days along the Mississippi.* [juvenile] 1909
—— *The Riflemen of the Ohio.* [juvenile] 1910
Exciting and instructive tales for boys about the early settlers in Kentucky and the Indian wars (1775–81). [(1), (2), and (3), Appleton, New York and London.]
—— *The Last of the Chiefs.* [juvenile] 1909
The Sioux campaigns and the deeds of General Custer in Montana. [Appleton, New York and London ; Hodder ; Grossett, New York.]
—— *The Candidate.* 1924
A romance of the American journalistic and political world. [Appleton, New York and London.]

AMMERS-KÜLLER, Jo van [Dutch]. *The House of Joy : a story of stage life in Holland* (Het Huis der Vreugden : roman van tooneel-leven, 1922). 1924
The story of a daughter of impoverished Dutch gentlefolk who seeks success on the stage, related by a sympathetic schoolmistress. [Philpot : o.p. ; transl. by H. van WYKE, Dutton, New York, 1929.]
—— *The Rebel Generation* (De Opstandigen : een familie-roman, 1925). 1928
The history of a family in Leyden for three generations (1840–1927), especially of the reaction of the women against the social standards and restraints of their elders. [Transl. by M. W. HOPER, Dent ; Dutton, New York.]
—— *Tantalus* (1928). 1930
Also a family history and a study of revolt from tradition and conservatism, illustrated by the case of an unfaithful husband who at length drives his forbearing wife, whom he still loves, to divorce him. A plea for more enlightened ideas on marriage. [Transl. by G. T. RENIER and Irene CLEPHANE, Cape ; Dutton, New York.]

AMORY, Thomas [1691–1788]. *The Life and Opinions of John Buncle, Esq.* 1756–66
An extraordinary medley of oblique autobiography and disquisitions on religious controversy, philosophy, mathematics, and other recondite subjects. Buncle is, like the author, a bigoted Unitarian, a good liver, and in all respects a character, who marries and buries seven wives and then settles down to a meditative old age. Eating and drinking, the charms of his miscellaneous wives, the comfortable side of nature, and so on, are dilated upon with untiring gusto. The book is probably the finest example of unconscious humour in any literature. [Edited by E. A. Baker (Library of Early Novelists), Routledge (Dutton, New York), 1904.]

ANDERSEN, Hans Christian [Danish ; 1805–75]. *The Improvisatore ; or, Life in Italy* (Improvisatoren, 1834). 1845
This book was the result of his delight in Italy, which he visited about 1832–3. It is a fanciful story of Rome and theatrical life, with autobiographical chapters on his own childhood, and these the most charming part. The pictures of old Italy before the revolution are full of strong imaginative life and poetic colour. [Transl. by Mary HOWITT, Ward & Lock, 1863 : o.p. ; Houghton, Boston.]
—— *O. T. : a Danish romance* (O. T., 1836). 1870
A complicated story of treachery on the one hand, and on the other of a woman's great devotion and the sufferings of her unhappy son. With *A Danish Fiddler* (1837), which likewise contains vivid descriptions of scenery and manners. [Houghton, Boston.]
—— *Only a Fiddler* (Kun en spillemand, 1837). 1845
"The best of his romances" (E. Gosse). [Transl., with *O. T.*, 3 vols., Bentley : o.p. ; Houghton, Boston.]
—— *Danish Fairy Tales and Legends* (Eventyr og historier, 4 vols., 1862–71). 1846
His most characteristic work was the series of fairy-tales, wonder-stories, and humorous fables, in which he utilized and reshaped the old folk-lore of the north, the Æsopic fables, and other material, and created a new mythology of his own, which afterwards inspired storytellers of such diverse characters as Hawthorne and Lewis Carroll. Full of wisdom charmingly conveyed, and grounded on sound experience of life, Andersen's stories always have a definite and convincing touch of reality in spite of the adventurous fantasy. Their naïveté, their tenderness, and the evident love for children and the weak, are a most ingratiating trait. [Transl. by H. W. DULCKEN, Routledge ; transl. by Caroline PEACHEY and H. W. DULCKEN, Macmillan, London and New York, 1905 ; (complete) Oxford Press ; (60 stories ed. by J. K. Craigie, *id.* ; (Everyman's Lib.), 2 vols., Dent, 1906 ; transl. by Mrs. LUCAS, *illus.*, Dent ; 40 stories transl. by M. R. JAMES, Faber, 1930.]

ANDERSON, Mrs. Ada Woodruff [American]. *The Heart of the Ancient Firs : a story of the Pacific North-West.* 1908
Presents life as it was in the seventies in the Puget Sound region, Seattle, Olympia, etc., after the opening of the Northern Pacific Railway. Mrs. Anderson lives at Seattle. [Little & Brown, Boston : o.p.]

ANDERSON, Arthur James [*b.* 1863]. *The Romance of Fra Filippo Lippi : a new version of the story of the Friar-artist and the Nun Lucrezia.* 1909
The argument is that Fra Filippo was not a Don Juan but a faithful husband. Vasari's version and others

ANDERSON, Arthur James (*continued*).

    are given in the appendix (1456–69). [S. Paul (Dodd & Mead, New York) : o.p. ; *sub tit. The Joyous Friar*, *illus.* with reproductions of his paintings, Stokes, New York, 1927.]

—— *His Magnificence : a novel of Lorenzo de' Medici.*   1913

    A similar "new version" of the career of Lorenzo the Magnificent, from the conspiracy of the Pazzi to his death (1478–92). [S. Paul (Dodd & Mead, New York) : o.p.]

ANDERSON, Miss H. M. *Kelston of Kells.*   1927

    An historical novel covering some ten years (1669–79) and Scottish, English, and French scenes, and embracing a large number of historical as well as fictitious characters, from the Court of Charles II and that of Louis XIV, from those involved in the strife between Covenanters and Episcopalians in Scotland, in the intrigues between the two Courts, etc. [Blackwood ; Ryerson Press, Toronto.]

ANDERSON, Sherwood [American ; *b.* 1876]. *Windy McPherson's Son.*   1916

    An inchoate, immature attempt at a diagnosis of American life, less facetious and satirical than Sinclair Lewis's and more searching. Subject, the quest for an object in life. Sandy's life is followed from his feckless boyhood in an Iowa village : his start as a newsboy, his rise to millions in Chicago, his revolt from the creed of money-making, the marriage that proves a failure, and his final impulsive exodus with a batch of children whom he has picked up to make into men and women for the new age. All that emerges so far is the utter futility of the ideals that now rule America. [Cape, New York.]

—— *Marching Men.*   1917

    Like McPherson, Beaut McGregor is a man of superabundant energy who is perplexed by the general confusion and cannot discern his own goal. He throws up a promising career at the Bar, to form his army of " marching men " from the workers of Chicago, in readiness for any enterprise worthy of their manhood. [Cape, New York.]

—— *Winesburg, Ohio : an intimate history of everyday people.*   1919

    A newspaper reporter's stories of an Ohio township where life is pretty dreary, stamped down by the hypocrisies and inhibitions that Mr. Anderson hates. He looks behind the veil of outward behaviour, and finds very different impulses and passions smouldering in that region, where pharisaic codes and sexual repressions are responsible for much suffering, thwarted lives, and disastrous insurrections. [Cape, New York and London (1922).]

—— *Poor White.*   1920

    Another strong man is disenchanted by material success, and looks round hopelessly for some purpose, some worthy activity, for himself and the world. [Huebsch, New York ; Cape (1922).]

—— *The Triumph of The Egg ; and other stories.*   1921

    Short stories strikingly devoid of plot, *dénouement*, and the other usual tricks ; like Chekhov's or Katherine Mansfield's, not like those of W. W. Jacobs or Kipling. Largely explorations of the borderland of consciousness, obscure apprehensions, and involuntary impulses, too dark and undefinable for explicit statement. Like D. H. Lawrence, of whom he is the American counterpart, Sherwood Anderson often has " no words," as he says in the prologue ; hence the apparent inconsequence of some of the tales. The title-story just shows up the poor futility of life. In *Seeds*, we look under the shell, and are afraid. The man in *The Door of the Trap* remembers how " life had stepped out of his grasp." Deeper intuitions, the call of something greater, sound in *Out of Nowhere into Nothing* and *The Other Woman*. Every story is a protest against the mechanical, the sophisticated, the conventions that are framed to shut out reality. [Viking Press, New York ; Cape.]

—— *Many Marriages.*   1922

    Mr. Anderson's disquieted individual here is a man who has fallen in love with his secretary, and before going off with her expounds to his wife and daughter the reasons why his marriage had been a failure. [Viking Press, New York.]

—— *Horses and Men.*   1923

    Race-courses and saloons are the scenes, farmers and stable-boys the characters, and also the narrators of these stories, which, nevertheless, all have the imaginative Andersonian touch. *The Man who became a Woman*, *The Sad Horn Blowers*, and *The Man's Story*, may be taken as typical. [Viking Press, New York ; Cape.]

—— *Dark Laughter.*   1925

    Another example of " mental impressionism," which seizes and fixes the formless sensations, aches, cravings, which are usually kept down and even disavowed. A journalist and his wife have got on each other's nerves ; he simply disappears. " I'm setting out on a little voyage of discovery . . . I thought I'd take a little trip into Myself . . . God knows what I'll find." Like almost all American men, he felt he was out of touch with things—" stones lying in the fields, the fields themselves, houses, trees, rivers, factory walls, tools, women's bodies, sidewalks, people on sidewalks, men in overalls, men and women in automobiles." The affair with the other woman is as D. H. Lawrence might have imagined ; it is as if Nature had intervened to rectify human mistakes. And so is the " Dark Laughter " of the negro women—like that of knowing spirits watching the blind efforts of men to find themselves. [Boni, New York ; Cape.]

ANDREEV, Leonid Nikolaevich [Russian ; 1871–1919]. *Silence ; and other stories* (1889–1902).

     1910

    Andreev is not a true realist but a man goaded to madness and despair by the unanswerable riddles and incurable wretchedness of the world, who evolves types out of his inner consciousness, and exhibits them in a story that is really a solution, or at least the statement, of a moral problem. *Silence* is the study of a harsh, superior, dignified village priest who misunderstands his daughter's silence until she commits suicide in despair ; and then his lot is silence, gloom, and madness. *Snapper* analyses the feelings of an ill-used dog who has one glimpse of human kindness. *The Little Angel* and *Pyetka* are keenly sympathetic studies of the pathos of child life ; the former tells of a poor boy and his wax angel, which melts away on the stove whilst he sleeps ; the latter shows a town boy's glimpse of paradise in his brief stay in the country. *An Original* introduces us to a government clerk who gains applause by an avowed penchant for negresses, and has, much to his disgust, to live—and to die—up to his reputation. *The Tocsin* is a realization of the

ANDREEV, Leonid Nikolaevich (*continued*).

horrors of revolt and incendiarism. [Transl. by W. H. LOWE, Griffiths : o.p.; *Silence*, transl. by John COURNOS, Frank-Maurice, Philadelphia. A re-issue, *sub tit.. The Little Angel*; *and other stories*, 1915 (contents the same, save for the addition of *The Wall* (1901), an allegory of the state of Russia, hemmed in by bureaucratic control), Hodder : o.p.; Knopf, New York.]

—— *The Abyss* (1902). 1929

An early example of Andreev's analysis of the viler elements of character which lie dormant in the human soul —a story of brutish passion suddenly overwhelming a hitherto innocent man. [Transl. by John COURNOS, Golden Cockerel Press; an earlier transl. by Marya GALINSKA appeared in *Hours spent in Prison*, 1909.]

—— *Judas Iscariot* (Juda Iskariot i drugïe) : *forming, with Eleazar* (Lazarus), *and Ben Tobit, a biblical trilogy* (1903–7). 1910

Anatomizes the emotions rather than the motives of Judas, who betrays his Master out of insane jealousy— the development of madness through excessive egotism, intense love of Christ, and jealousy, is followed with pathological exactness. *Eleazar* (Lazarus) is the story of Lazarus' awful existence—a terror to men —after his resurrection. *Ben Tobit* is about a Jerusalem merchant who all the while the Crucifixion is going on suffers torture from an aching tooth and pays no attention to external events. [Transl. by W. H. LOWE, Griffiths : o.p.]

—— *The Red Laugh* (1904). 1905, new ed. 1914

Scenes in the Russo-Japanese war. [Transl. by Alexandra LINDEN, Unwin : o.p.]

—— *When the King Loses His Head* (1905) *; and other stories.* 1920

Includes *Judas Iscariot* and *Ben Tobit* (*vide supra*). *The Life of Father Vassily* (Fivensky, 1903) is one of Andreev's most powerful stories. It deals with the problem of evil; a priest all his life tormented by un- deserved misfortune wavers in his faith. Also included are *Dies Irae* (1910), and *Marseilles* (1903). [Transl. by A. J. WOLFE, International Pub. Co., New York.]

—— *The Dark* (T'ma, 1906). 1922

An intellectual puts to himself the question " Have I the right to be virtuous, so long as there is evil in the world ? " Accordingly he throws in his lot with the lowest prostitutes and outcasts. [Transl. by L. A. MAGNUS and K. WALTER, Hogarth Press : o.p.]

—— *The Seven Who were Hanged* (1908). 1909

The experiences of seven revolutionaries and other condemned persons waiting their execution are anatomized. [Transl. by H. BERNSTEIN, Ogilvie, New York; Fifield : o.p.; with *The Red Laugh*, Modern Lib., New York, 1918.]

—— *Sashka Jigouleff* (1911). 1925

A novel inspired by the deeds of the Maximalists. A young man of good family turns bandit in the Volga forest region. [Transl. by Luba HICKS, McBride, New York.]

—— *The Confessions of a Little Man during Great Days.* 1917

The diary of a middle-aged clerk in Petrograd during the war. The failure of the banks, and the fear that Russia has been betrayed, leads him from panic to despair; finally he gets what comfort he can from proceeding to the front to serve with an ambulance. [Transl. by R. S. TOWNSEND, Duckworth.]

—— *Satan's Diary* (Dnevik Satony, 1920). 1920

A posthumous novel left unrevised at the author's death. Satan has taken upon himself the body of an American millionaire by way of a joke, only to find himself hopelessly outmatched in villany and guile by the average human being. [Transl. by H. BERNSTEIN, Boni, New York.]

ANKER-LARSEN, Johannes [Danish ; *b.* 1874]. *The Philosopher's Stone* (De vises sten, 1923). 1924

A long philosophical novel, symbolizing man's search after God, in terms of the progress through life of a boy of sensitive character who falls into adversity. [Transl. by A. G. CHATER, Knopf, New York and London.]

—— *Martha and Mary* (Martha og Maria, 1925). 1926

A simple tale of two little country girls, who after separation are reunited, and form each the complement of the other. [Transl. by A. G. CHATER, Knopf, New York and London.]

—— *A Stranger in Paradise* (Sognet, som vokser ind i Himmelen, 1928). 1929

A sweetly sentimental tale of a saintly peasant lad, who discerns the heaven that lies about him on this earth and remains an inspiration to his fellows even after his untimely death. [Transl. by Ruth Gastberg JORDAN, Knopf, New York and London.]

" ANNUNZIO, Gabriele d' " [Gaetano Raspagnetto ; Italian ; *b.* 1863]. *The Child of Pleasure* (Il Piacere, 1889). 1898

D'Annunzio is the exponent of the pagan element in the Italian character, an element which came out strongly in the poetry of Carducci. This is his first presentation of a type which reappears constantly as the hero of his romances. Sperelli, a Roman poet, worshipper of beauty, devotee of art, completely absorbed in his own sensations, is avowedly a rendering of the author's own personality, and exponent of an æstheticism that takes the place of morality. His life is merely the commonplace existence of a young man about town with his innumerable amours, and the real interest lies in the analysis of his emotions and of the utter degradation of soul in which he ends. From the dissolute crowd stand out the figures of this egotist and two of his loves, one a second Lesbia, the other a pure and noble woman whom he corrupts. [Transl. by G. HARDING, Heinemann : o.p.; Page, Boston (repr. 1922); Modern Lib., New York.]

—— *Episcopo and Company* (Giovanni Episcopo, 1892). 1896

A brief dramatic tale of a man who allows himself to be dominated by those with whom he comes into contact, first by a brutal fellow-clerk, and subsequently by a loose woman. [Transl. by M. Leonora JONES, Stone, Chicago : o.p.]

—— *The Victim* (L'Innocente, 1892). 1898

The tragic story of moral retribution falling on a husband, Tullio Hermil, for his unbridled lust and egoism, and on his wife for an act of momentary weakness : the history of their inner lives, with an extreme paucity

" ANNUNZIO, Gabriele d' " (*continued*).

of external incident. The victim is the unwanted illegitimate child, brutally got rid of by Tullio. In this man's brother the author paints a man of high morality and affectionate disposition ; and this figure and that of the grand old peasant Giovanni di Scordio are admittedly the fruit of his reading of Tolstoy. [Transl. by Georgina HARDING, Heinemann : o.p. ; *sub tit. The Intruder*, transl. by Arthur HORNBLOW, Page, Boston.]

—— *The Triumph of Death* (Il Trionfo della Morte, 1894). 1895

His most elaborate analysis of erotic emotion, terrible as an exposure of human sensuality. The frenzied passion of the egoist Giorgio Aurispa for Ippolyta, which demands more than human nature can give, alters by a morbid process into homicidal mania. This story is peculiarly the vehicle for the author's mystical philosophy of individualism and æsthetic hedonism, and the influence of his reading in Tolstoy, Maeterlinck, Nietzsche, Zola, is obvious in numerous passages. The episode of a visit to the sanctuary of Casalbordino, where the diseased and the crippled are seeking miraculous relief, is more horrible in its description of repulsive sights than anything in *Lourdes*. These three novels, *The Romances of the Rose*, constitute a trilogy, linked together, not by identity of character or connexion of events, but by unity of feeling and thought. *The Triumph* and *The Flame of Life* are the most magnificent examples of d'Annunzio's art, an art which for the understanding reader makes up for the debased morality, the emptiness, and even the vulgarity of the life portrayed. In this art, a chief element is the prose style, superbly vivid, the incisive force of its metaphors incomparable. Even through a translation, some of this excellence can be perceived. [Transl. by Georgina HARDING, Heinemann : o.p. ; transl. by A. HORNBLOW, Page, Boston.]

—— *The Virgins of the Rocks* (Vergini delle Rocce, 1896). 1899

First of a new trilogy, *The Romances of the Lily*. A symbolical and poetic story, which has been compared to a gorgeous canvas by Burne-Jones or Rossetti. The sensuous and egoistic d'Annunzian hero, the degenerate Claudio Cantelmo, brooding over his dream of restoring his famous house, comes in quest of a wife to a castle where dwell three beautiful ladies, each the type of some spiritual excellence. The author exhausts his powers of voluptuous description in surrounding these fairy-like creatures with an atmosphere of poetry. The other two volumes are to be entitled *The Prodigy* and *The Annunciation*. [Transl. by A. HUGHES, Heinemann : o.p. ; transl. by Annetta Halliday and Guiseppe ANTONA, *sub tit. The Maidens of the Rocks*, Page, Boston ; Modern Lib., New York.]

—— *The Flame of Life* (Il Fuoco, 1899). 1900

First of *The Romances of the Pomegranate*. The psychological history of a liaison, in which the passion and self-submission of the woman (a famous tragic actress) are sacrificed to art, and still more to the capricious sensuality of Stelio Effrena, the artist panting for all variety of sensations, the d'Annunzian superman. Supposed to be an analysis of the author's own amour. Full of d'Annunzio's æsthetic ideas and the interpretations of artists, e.g. Michelangelo, Dürer, Wagner. To be followed by *The Dictator* and *The Triumph of Life*. [Transl. by Kassandra VIVARIA, Heinemann : o.p. ; Page, Boston ; Modern Lib., New York.]

—— *Tales of my Native Town* (Le Novelle della Pescara, 1902). 1920

The common scene of these stories is the Adriatic town of Pescara. They are vivid and only too realistic presentations of ugly, bestial, mean, and revolting things, their only apparent significance being that, as the introducer Mr. Hergesheimer puts it, they merge " into the general confusion of existence." In other words, they are alleged slices of life. [Transl. by G. MANTELLINI, with introd. by Joseph Hergesheimer, Doubleday, Garden City Press, New York ; Nash.]

" ANSTEY, F." [Thomas Anstey Guthrie ; *b.* 1856]. *Vice Versâ ; or, A Lesson to Fathers.* 1882

A ludicrous blend of the modern *conte* with fantasy like the *Arabian Nights*. The drollery of the situation is attained by a change of personality between a schoolboy and his staid old father ; after that the ordinary and probable events of school-life become exquisitely comic in their sober realism. [Murray ; Appleton, New York : o.p.]

—— *The Giant's Robe.* 1883

A weak young man pretends to be the author of a play sent him by a friend in India. The unfolding of his character in the stress of such a situation, and the remorse that drives him to confess, mingle more serious elements with the comic. [Murray ; Appleton, New York : o.p.]

—— *The Tinted Venus : a farcical romance.* 1885

The goddess Aphrodite reanimates an ancient statue and fastens herself on to a foolish hair-dresser in London—the grandeurs of classical paganism and the banalities of our common modern life in ludicrous apposition. [Arrowsmith ; Harper, New York : o.p.]

—— *A Fallen Idol.* 1886

An extravaganza, worked out with artful plausibility ; and a trenchant, though covert, satire on the esoteric Buddhism rampant at the time. [Murray ; Lippincott, Philadelphia : o.p.]

—— *The Pariah.* 1889

More of a novel, and a very good one ; strong in the handling of character and feeling. The neglected son of a parvenu father who wishes to enter society and marries a widow of good breeding but no money. The unhappy boy, ignorant and unpolished, finds himself in the bosom of a family who hate and despise him. [Murray.]

—— *Lyre and Lancet : a story in scenes.* 1895

A poet, author of *Andromeda*, and a " vet," owner of the prize bull-dog " Andromeda," are each mistaken for the other at a baronet's country seat, and the ensuing complications, ludicrous in the extreme, hit off satirically a number of contemporary types. [Murray : o.p. ; Macmillan, New York : o.p.]

—— *Baboo Jabberjee, B.A.* 1897

Parodies of stilted contributions to Indian newspapers " written by conceited baboos." [(Wayfarer's Lib.), Dent (Dutton, New York).]

—— *The Brass Bottle.* 1900

A burlesque fantasy with an unbottled genie for hero, who is liberated by a young architect, and repays his benefactor by an embarrassing series of miracles. Cf. *Mrs. Shelmire's Djinn*, by " Max Adeler," a story with the same motive. [Murray ; (as play), Heinemann ; Appleton, New York : o.p.]

"ANSTEY, F." (*continued*). *In Brief Authority.*　　　　　　　　　　1915

　　The family of Mr. Wibberley-Stimpson become for a time the Royal House of Märchenland, retaining their
　　suburban characters in spite of the gnomes, dragons, fairy godmothers, and such-like, that they meet
　　there. [Murray.]

—— *The Last Load.*　　　　　　　　　　1925

　　Stories, sketches, and essays contributed to magazines, and not previously published in book form. [Methuen.]

APOLLONIUS OF TYRE. *Kynge Appolyn of Thyre.*　　　　　　　1510

　　Oldest extant version in euphuistic Latin prose—a translation from the Greek. The well-known story of An-
　　tiochus, King of Syria, his unnatural love for his daughter, and the riddle he propounds ; and of Apollonius,
　　King of Tyre, whose queen, believed to be dead, is consigned to the waves ; Apollonius subsequently falling
　　in love with his own daughter, but at length discovering her true parentage and recovering his long-lost
　　queen—the story dramatized in Shakespeare's *Pericles.* There were numerous variants in the Middle
　　Ages (*Gesta Romanorum,* Gower's *Confessio Amantis,* etc.). Wynkyn de Worde's translation was from a
　　French prose romance. [The transl. quoted was by COPLAND, printed by Wynkyn de Worde ; a limited
　　edition in facsimile was reprinted from the unique copy in the library of the Duke of Devonshire in 1870.
　　A transl. by Laurence TWINE, *sub tit. The Patterne of painefull adventures : containing the most excellent,
　　pleasant, and variable Historie of the strange accidents that befell unto Prince Apollonius, the Lady Lucina,
　　his wife, and Tharsia, his daughter,* was printed in 1576 and again in 1594. Reprint of latter ed., Canwell,
　　New York, 1903 : o.p. There was an Anglo-Saxon rendering of this story from the Latin (but only a
　　fragment is extant), published with a modern English transl. by Benjamin Thorpe (1834).]

APULEIUS, Lucius [*b. c.* A.D. 125]. *The Metamorphoses ; or, Golden Ass.*　　　1566

　　Various theories have been read into this famous romance : certain of the Christian fathers perceived in it
　　a fantastic allegorical defence of Christian morality ; many have deemed it autobiographical, St. Augustine
　　even assenting cautiously to the probability that the transformation was a fact. There is no reason to
　　seek any other object but profane entertainment. Lucius of Madaura, the supposed narrator, on a visit
　　to Thessaly, the country of magic, is accidentally changed into an ass, and meets with the most extra-
　　ordinary train of adventures of a tragi-comic order, before he is released from his bestial situation. The
　　story deals largely with the black art, and with amorous adventures, in which the author gives free rein
　　to a " profligate imagination." By far the most beautiful part of the book is the tale of Cupid and Psyche,
　　related by one of the dramatis personæ. Here the sentiment is pure, and the writer's emotion lifts his
　　imagination on a nobler flight. That the Latin novel is a product of literary decadence, a bastard off-
　　shoot of poetry, is proved *inter alia* by the rhetorical and euphuistic style that Apuleius saw fit to adopt.
　　[*The xi Bookes of the Golden Asse, containing the Metamorphosie of Lucius Apuleius,* transl. by William
　　ADLINGTON, 1566, with introd. by C. WHIBLEY (Tudor Translations), Nutt, 1894 : o.p. *The most pleasant
　　and delectable Tale of the Marriage of Cupid and Psyche, done into English by William Adlington,* with a
　　Discourse on the Fable by Andrew LANG (*Bibliothèque de Carabas*), Nutt, 1887 : o.p. ; revised by
　　S. Gaselee, (Loeb Classics) Heinemann (Putnam, New York) 1915 ; (Abbey Classics) Simpkin (Small, Boston)
　　1922 ; Chapman, 1924 ; *illus.,* Lane, 1923. *The Marriage of Cupid and Psyche,* transl. by Charles STUTTA-
　　FORD, *illus.* by Jessie Mothersole, Nutt, 1903 : o.p. ; *Cupid and Psyche,* (Temple Cl.) Dent. *The Meta-
　　morphoses, or Golden Ass,* transl. by H. E. BUTLER, 2 vols., Oxford Press, 1910.]

ARABIAN NIGHTS' ENTERTAINMENTS : *consisting of One Thousand and One Stories told by the
Sultaness of the Indies to divert the Sultan from the execution of a bloody vow* (Hazár Afsána,
alluded to in tenth century).　　　　　　　　　　　　　1704–17

　　The one book in Arabian literature which has cosmopolitan interest. A huge collection of entertaining tales
　　of unknown origin. Scheherazade, wife of a tyrannical Sultan, is supposed to tell her lord a story each
　　night in order to avert the decree that each of his brides shall live but one day. The stories of Aladdin,
　　Sinbad the Sailor, of Haroun-al-Raschid, the jovial Caliph, Ali Baba and the Forty Thieves, and many
　　others, are as well known to English people of every age as any stories from their native literature. The
　　stories are fantastic, but the portraiture of Oriental life is the most graphic and authentic that we have.
　　They rank with those of the *Decameron* as supreme examples of the art of the short story. The title quoted
　　at head of note is that of the English rendering of GALLAND's transl. from Arabic into French. The
　　handiest English transl. is, however, LANE's, which was originally published 1838–40. The 1877 edition
　　of Lane gives text of 1859 edn., which was collated with Lane's own annotated copy of first edn. *Aladdin*
　　and *Ali Baba* are added from present editor's transl. from M. ZOTENBERG's Arabic text and the English
　　version of Galland. Lane's very copious notes on Mohammedan religion, superstitions, laws, customs,
　　dress, literature, etc., have been omitted or cut down. What notes there are appear at foot of page ; and
　　textual variations at end of each vol. The other two standard translations are PAYNE's and Sir Richard
　　BURTON's. Lane translated rather more than 100 tales, Payne 266, Burton 267 (171 primary and 96
　　secondary). Lane used a defective version, and omitted to an undue extent ; Payne and Burton translated
　　from a collation of the best versions. Payne " first taught the world what *The Nights* really is," says
　　Burton. His translation is scholarly, and in strong, masculine English, though larded with needlessly
　　coarse expressions. Burton's is said to be practically an adaptation of Payne's. Lady Burton's edn.
　　was modified for family reading by J. Huntly McCARTHY, and afterwards ed. by her, the omissions amount-
　　ing to 215 pp. out of 3156. It comprises only 10 out of the 16 vols. Burton's translation, whatever the
　　method of its making, is notable among all translations for its learned and painstaking accuracy, truth
　　to the letter and the spirit of the original, and for its racy and expressive but unchastened style. He was
　　unsurpassed as an orientalist, and his rendering shows a masterly command of both Arabic and English.
　　SMITHERS omits many gross passages in Burton's original edn., but restores four-fifths of those left out
　　of the first 10 vols. in Lady Burton's edn. [Transl. by E. W. LANE (1839–41) Chatto, 1930 ; with additions
　　from Galland's translation, *illus.* by Frank Brangwyn (1896), 6 vols., Palmer, 1922 (Lippincott, Phila-
　　delphia) ; *illus.* by Wood, 6 vols., Dent 1901. Ed. by E. W. L. Griffis from the text of Dr. Jonothan
　　SCOTT, 4 vols., *illus.,* Lothrop, Boston ; transl. by GALLAND, Routledge (Dutton, New York) ; by John
　　PAYNE, 9 vols., and 3 supplementary vols., Villon Soc., 1882–4 : o.p. ; by Sir Richard BURTON, with notes,
　　10 vols., and 6 supplementary vols., *priv. prin.,* " Benares " 1885–6 : o.p. ; the same edn., revised by

ARABIAN NIGHTS' ENTERTAINMENTS (*continued*).
> Lady BURTON (for household reading) 6 vols., Waterlow 1887–8 : o.p. ; the same repr. and ed. by Leonard C. SMITHERS, 16 vols., in 12 vols. (containing " Supplemental Nights," biography of the book, notes, and index), Nichols, 1894 : o.p. See also *New Arabian Nights*.]

ARDAGH, W. M. *The Magada*. 1910
> Tells of the Spanish capture of the Grand Canary (1482–92). [Lane.]

—— *The Knightly Years*. 1912
> After shifting to Spain under Ferdinand and Isabella, this romance comes back to the Canaries, at the time of their reduction by the Spaniards (1480–5). [Lane : o.p.]

ARISTOCRACY. 1888
> A satire, published anonymously, upon the too flattering pictures of society offered to the public by contemporary novelists. The characters are said to be well-known people. The book depicts barely one decent character, and the panorama of English life is wholly depressing. [Appleton, New York : o.p.]

ARLEN, Michael [formerly Dikran Kuyumjian ; Armenian, naturalized British ; *b*. 1895]. *Those Charming People*. 1923
> A long and dandified sub-title describes this as " a tapestry of the fortunes, follies, adventures, galanteries (*sic*) and general activities of Shelmerdene (that lovely lady)," and so on. The stories range in kind from the clever silliness and recherché bathos of Ronald Firbank to Kipling's " blugginess," e.g. *The Smell in the Library*. Not satirical, like Mr. Aldous Huxley ; but the author's complacency towards his stern, silent, expensive, stupid patricians—" shoes by Lobb "—and their womenkind, no better than they should be, has much the same effect. [Collins ; Doubleday, Doran, New York.]

—— *The Green Hat*. 1924
> A popular romance, written in that mincing, exaggerated style that Mr. Arlen has made his own, recounting the exploits and the fate of a heroine of uncertain morals and improbable charm. " It makes one feel as if one were drinking Benedictine and eating caramels on an empty stomach in a Turkish bath " [Gerald Gould]. [Collins ; Doubleday, Doran, New York.]

—— *May Fair*. 1925
> This has a sub-title of similar length and foppery, but the contents are evidently modelled on the *New Arabian Nights*. Several stories do not come badly out of the comparison, though the posturing of the style and some feeble climaxes and *dénouements* would have annoyed Stevenson. [Collins ; Doubleday, Doran, New York.]

—— *Lily Christine*. 1929
> Another sophisticated story of life in the upper classes—for those in the lower who admire them. Lily Christine's marriage to a charming, irresponsible, and utterly selfish husband comes to a tragic end. It is all very unimportant, but the glittering, frothy style washes it down. [Hutchinson ; Doubleday, Doran, New York.]

ARMSTRONG, Martin Donisthorpe [*b*. 1882]. *The Goat and Compasses*. 1925
> A quiet, detached story of village life, showing sympathy and humour in the characterization. [Cape.]

—— *The Stepson*. 1927
> The quiet of the countryside here gives place to tragedy—an old farmer marries a young wife, who against her will falls in love with his son. A powerful human drama convincingly handled. [Cape.]

—— *St. Christopher's Day*. 1928
> The break-up of married life between two people of forty, whose motives and reflections are given turn and turn about. [Gollancz ; *sub tit. All in a Day*, Harper, New York.]

—— *The Fiery Dive*. 1929
> Six stories varying in kind from *The Widow of Ephesus*, a simple retelling of that hoary legend, and the hagiographic *Saint Hercules*, to the typically modern title-story, of love turned to indifference. *Sombrero* is a sea-tale of 1810, after Conrad. *Portrait of the Misses Harlowe* and *In the Wilds*, both after Katherine Mansfield, hinge on their analysis of women. [Gollancz ; Harcourt, New York.]

—— *The Sleeping Fury*. 1929
> The self-sacrificing passion of love in a weak and not very intelligent woman, roused by a lover some years after marriage and subsequently by her daughter—a rather inconsequential story, told however in a graceful style and with sympathetic comprehension of character and of the little things of life. [Gollancz ; Harcourt, New York.]

—— *Adrian Glynde*. 1930
> The inner and outer life of a sensitive boy, his temperamental differences with a commonplace, selfish mother, his experiences at a public school, where he runs away, in France, at the Royal College of Music, etc. The charm of the book is in the picturing of quite ordinary life, and of several pleasing characters. [Gollancz.]

ARNIM, Mary Annette Gräfin von [*née* Beauchamp, now Countess Russell]. *Elizabeth and her German Garden*. 1898
> The chatty and reflective journal of an English lady married to a German nobleman, and employing her time in the congenial solitude of amateur gardening. Jottings on all kinds of topics, from flowers and wreaths to babies and ethics, and humorous sketches of the husband, " the Man of Wrath," and other people, including a biting one of her *bête noire*, a young woman with a note-book. [Macmillan, London and New York ; (Home Lib.), Burt, New York ; with *coloured illustrations* by S. H. Vedder, Macmillan.]

—— *The Solitary Summer*. 1899
> The same kind of meditations, observations, and sketches of nature and human life by this female hermit living in close communion with nature in her secluded garden. Preaches an eloquent sermon on the positive value of intercourse with nature and the blessedness of repose. [Macmillan ; also *illus., id.*]

—— *The Benefactress*. 1902
> Anna Estcourt, aged twenty-five, coming into a small property in North Germany, philanthropically offers a home to twelve distressed ladies. This somewhat farcical scheme is worked out with considerable serious-

ARNIM, Mary Annette Gräfin von (*continued*).

ness, and there are scenes that border on tragedy ; but as a whole the book is quietly comic, full of superficial but caustic sketches of character and manners. The writer is a close observer of German country-folk ; and the novel, though weak in structure, is unified by the personal charm and the feeling for nature already noted. [Macmillan.]

—— *The Adventures of Elizabeth in Rügen.* 1904
Tells how Elizabeth goes on a driving tour round the island of Rügen. The pictures of the Baltic, the coast dunes, the pine forests, the fields, and the sky effects are done with her most delicate art. Even more characteristic is the comic account of Elizabeth's journey, the farcical sketches of people she meets, and her caustic *obiter dicta.* [Macmillan.]

—— *The Princess Priscilla's Fortnight.* 1906
The idyllic life of a charming princess and an old courtier, who escape from the oppressive atmosphere of the grand ducal home and rusticate in a Somersetshire village. The tranquil course of their existence is marred, rather gratuitously, by a murder episode. [Macmillan ; Scribner, New York.]

—— *Fräulein Schmidt and Mr. Anstruther.* 1907
Letters of an independent young German lady to a weak Englishman, who is engaged to her and then falls in love with someone else. Interesting less for the sentimental drama involved than for the sharp observation and shrewd judgments of the writer, who is another Elizabeth in her piquant humour. Contains some well-drawn portraits, e.g. the professor and other inhabitants of Jena. [Macmillan ; Scribner, New York : o.p.]

—— *The Caravanners.* 1909
Chiefly a too cruel caricature of a fatuous German baron, who tells his story of a week's caravanning in Kent. [Macmillan ; (Caravan Lib.) *id.* ; Doubleday, New York : o.p.]

—— *The Pastor's Wife.* 1914
A rather tragic domestic tale of an English girl married to an East Prussian pastor. The description of the village, and of her relations with her country neighbours, are in the author's best manner. [Macmillan.]

—— *Christopher and Columbus.* 1919
Twin sisters of seventeen, half-German by birth, are packed off from England to America during war-time. Their difficulties, and progress under the care of a wealthy American bachelor, provide a graceful if superficial comedy, with a good deal of sentiment. [Macmillan ; Doubleday, New York.]

—— *Vera.* 1921
The man who drove Vera to suicide and then married the young and inexperienced Lucy is a monster of fatuous and self-centred uxoriousness and bullying egotism, compared with whom Sir Willoughby Patterne himself is modesty and unselfishness incarnate. Though the satire is overdone, Lucy and her plucky little aunt, in their relations with this gentleman, stir our interest. [Macmillan ; Doubleday, New York.]

—— *Love.* 1925
With sprightly humour and expert craftsmanship the author draws plentiful diversion from the marriage of a headstrong young fellow to a charming woman old enough to be his mother, whose daughter is wife to a clergyman old enough to be her father. The situation is too much, however, for the comedy not to turn sour at last. The author soothes her animosity against the other sex with the corrosive portrait of the uxorious clergyman preaching " love." [Macmillan ; Doubleday, New York.]

—— *Expiation.* 1929
Portrays a weak and foolish woman, disinherited by her husband on account of a flabby love-affair ; she has to depend on his relatives, who make life a misery for her. All the characters, save an old grandmother, are knaves or fools ; but the satire is so well distributed that it never becomes excessive. There is drama too in the meeting between Milly and her long-separated sister. [Macmillan ; Doubleday, Doran, New York.]

ARNOLD, Mrs. John Oliver [*née* England]. *Megan of the Dark Isle.* 1914
Life in Anglesea in the eighteen-fifties. Some old Welsh legends are incorporated. [Alston Rivers : o.p.]

ARNOLD, Matthew [1822–88]. *Friendship's Garland.* 1871
" Being the Conversations, Letters and Opinions of the late Arminius, Baron von Thunder-ten-Tronckh ; collected and edited, with a Dedicatory Letter to Adolescens Leo, Esq., of the *Daily Telegraph.*" This imaginary German is the author's stalking-horse for an attack on British Philistines and their ways of thinking and speaking. A book that did some useful destructive work in its time, along with Arnold's *Culture and Anarchy*, his theological criticisms, etc. Witty and consistently ironical : many of its phrases and paradoxes are now classical. [Murray.]

ARNOLD, William Delafield [1828–59 ; brother of preceding]. *Oakfield ; or, Fellowships in the East.* 1853
The hero, a young Oxford man, brought up in strict ideas of duty and conduct, goes to India and is revolted by the dissipation and indifference of the English, both military and civil, and their total neglect of the natives' well-being (*c.* 1849). His censures are sharpened by his ignorance of real life. Includes a narrative of the second Sikh war and the battle of Chillianwallah. [2 vols., Longman : o.p.]

ARRAS, Jean d' [French]. *Melusine* (1382–91). *English about* 1500
A popular romance, founded on a legend of great antiquity, similar in idea to the famous story of Cupid and Psyche. The supernatural being, Melusine, marries Raymondin on condition that he never sees her on a Saturday, a condition that he breaks after living with her many years and begetting ten sons. Much of the romance is taken up with the heroic gests of the sons, each of which has some preternatural feature. The end is pathetic, like that of Arnold's *Forsaken Merman.* Melusine changes into a serpent, and, with mutual lamentations, husband and wife are parted by their inevitable doom. [Part i., the text, ed. A. K. Donald (Early English Text Soc.), Oxford Press, 1895. This prose romance is much finer—and more poetical—than the metrical *Romans of Partenay*, translated from a poem composed about fourteen years later on the same legend : the latter also is published by the Early English Text Soc.]

ARTHUR OF LITTLE BRITAIN : *the History of the Valiant Knight, Arthur of Little Britain : a romance of chivalry, originally translated from the French by John Bourchier, Lord Berners.*
16th century.
First MS. fifteenth century ; first French edn. 1493. Probably composed in the reign of Charles VI. Said to have been a source of Spenser's Arthurian material, though not properly Arthurian but of the same species of irresponsible fiction as the *Amadis*. Arthur is son of the Duke of Brittany, and loves a maid of low degree, but his parents compel him to marry a lady of noble birth. The low-born damsel gets hold of the bride's dowry and a wondrous ring—whence interesting complications. Wild adventures, fights with dragons and giants, tourneys and battles with myriads of foes, recall *Amadis of Gaul*. There was an English edn. printed by Copland (1582), and another by Redborne (1609). [New edn. reprinted from that of Robert Redborne with preface by E. V. UTTERSON, 1814.]

ARTHUR, Frederick. *The Mysterious Monsieur Dumont.* 1912
Dumont is a woman in disguise, survivor of a family guillotined during the Terror. Though a Royalist, she is in touch with Danton, Robespierre, and the secret societies, and afterwards with Napoleon. History is imported wholesale : La Vendée, the Noyades, the fall of Danton and of Robespierre, etc. [Murray ; Devin-Adair, New York.]

—— *The Great Attempt.* 1914
A story of the Pretender, differing from hundreds of others in that it tries to show history from both sides. [Murray.]

—— *The Accuser.* 1927
A novel of the Popish plot, in which Titus Oates is a prominent figure (1678–9). [Nash.]

ARTSUIBASHEV, Mikhail Petrovich [Russian ; 1878–1927]. *Breaking Point.* 1915
Artsuibashev's is a coarse imitation of the Russian " realism of despair," harsh sensationalism and avoidance of decent reticence making up for real strength. The subject here is the moral depression which was the state of the majority in a backwater town of southern Russia at this era. The writer dwells on the blank purposelessness that leads to a philosophy of suicide. [Transl., Secker ; Viking Press, New York.]

—— *Tales of the Revolution* (1904–7). 1917
Five tales of horrors and depravities committed during the revolution of 1905–6. [Transl. by Percy PINKERTON, Secker : o.p. ; Viking Press, New York.]

—— *Sanine* (1907). 1916
A novel that won a passing vogue by the cleverness and the unabashed frankness with which it mirrored the life and the sentiments of young Russians in the period following the abortive revolution of 1905. There are long discussions, alternating with love episodes in which the writer gives his sensualism free rein. Sanine is a shoddy sort of superman, preaching enjoyment, indifference, sexual freedom. He was taken seriously for a time. [Transl. by Percy PINKERTON, preface by Gilbert Cannan, Secker ; new ed., preface by Ernest Boyd, Viking Press, New York, 1926.]

—— *The Millionaire.* 1915
The first of these three novelettes is about a wealthy man, sick and tired of his empty life, who commits even suicide ineffectively. *Ivan Lande*, which made a great hit in 1904, is a satirical sketch of a saint whose extravagant virtues bring him universal contempt—perhaps a gibe at Tolstoy. *Nina* is a story of bestiality and slaughter which shows the author at his worst. [Transl. by Percy PINKERTON, Secker : o.p.]

ASCHE, Shalom [Polish Jew ; b. 1880]. *The Mother.* 1930
Describes the life of a family of Polish-Jew emigrants ; their existence in Poland, dominated by the figure of the mother, and their arrival in New York ; there the younger generation break away from the matriarchal tradition. [Transl. by N. AUSÜBEL, Boni, New York.]

ASHFORD, Daisy. *The Young Visitors : or, Mr. Salteena's Plan.* 1919
Written at the age of nine, with obligations to " Ouida ", but without much punctuation. Mr. Salteena's plan, to become a real gentleman and marry haughty Miss Monticue, provides amusing high-falutin pictures of society. [With introd. by Sir J. M. Barrie, Chatto : Doubleday, Doran, New York.]

" ASHTON, Helen " [Mrs. Helen Rosaline Jordan ; b. 1891]. *A Background for Caroline.* 1929
The heroine is born in 1877, and the story follows her growth, spiritual and mental, leaving her a widow after the war. From the background of the social life of this period, she emerges as a clear and attractive character. [Benn ; Harcourt, New York.]

ASKEW, Mrs. Alice J. de C. [*née* Leake] and ASKEW, Claude Arthur Carey [*d.* 1917]. *The Shulamite.* 1904

—— *The Woman Deborah* [sequel]. 1910
In the first, we find Deborah Krillet, the " Shulamite," married to a brute of a Boer farmer, who loves her passionately, sjamboks her relentlessly, and drives her into a blameless love for her tyrant's overseer. On the tragic death of her husband the lovers are pathetically parted ; but in the sequel harrowing complications arise, for the sundered lovers engage themselves, by a most improbable coincidence, to a brother and sister, the end being death to the Shulamite's old adorer and madness to herself. [(1), Nash ; Unwin ; (2), Unwin.]

—— *The King's Signature.* 1912
A passable melodrama of the Ruritanian school. [Chapman : o.p.]

—— *The Golden Girl.* 1913
A story of a young man's disillusionment, mingled with fantastic improbabilities. [Ward & Lock : o.p.]

—— *Trespass.* 1915
Passion and expiation on a Boer farm. The characters are well-drawn. [Everett : o.p.]

ATHERTON, Mrs. Gertrude Franklin [*née* Horn ; American ; *b.* 1857]. *Los Cerritos : a romance of modern times.* 1890
Los Cerritos is an abandoned ranch in Southern California, on which poor whites and Mexican half-breeds have squatted. The wealthy owner attempts to eject them, with exciting consequences. [Lovell, New York : o.p. ; Heinemann : o.p.]

—— *The Doomswoman.* 1892
Spanish life in California in the eighteen-fifties. [Tait, New York : o.p. ; Lane.]

—— *Patience Sparhawk and Her Times.* 1897
A highly-coloured history of the New York career of an over-intelligent, undisciplined girl from a Californian ranch, her experiences among people of fashion, love affairs of an unchastened kind, life as a lady journalist, post-matrimonial flirtations, etc., with lively sketches of modern life and character. [Macmillan, New York : o.p.]

—— *American Wives and English Husbands.* 1898
A beautiful San Francisco girl, half Creole, marries the son of an English peer, and their life is not immediately successful. Criticizes Americans as severely as English aristocrats. [Dodd & Mead, New York : o.p. Murray ; revised edition, entitled *Transplanted*, Dodd & Mead, New York, 1919.]

—— *The Californians.* 1898
Tells with the same sort of exuberant and emotional realism the story of a woman's heart. Magdaléna, a daughter of the ancient Spanish owners of the soil, in her lack of natural endowments and in the frankness with which her emotions are analysed, is a Californian Jane Eyre. The cloistered luxury of the rich hidalgo's home, and the effete type of civilization for which it stands, are contrasted with the uncouth, strenuous life of the modern Yankee. [Macmillan, New York : o.p. ; Lane : o.p.]

—— *A Daughter of the Vine.* 1899
A frank and searching study of a woman who through the tragic effects of her parents' sins is a dipsomaniac. [Dodd & Mead, New York, 1923 ; Nisbet : o.p.]

—— *The Valiant Runaways.* 1899
A romance of California before the Union ; a picture of incessant feuds and adventure, showing the Spaniards in their decadence. [Dodd & Mead, New York : o.p. ; Nisbet : o.p.]

—— *Senator North.* 1900
The heroine, Betty Madison, is a Washington belle from the Southern States, who takes an interest in politics, and fascinates the elderly senator who gives his name to the novel. Opens up many political and social questions, amongst them the racial problem, which is illustrated by a pathetic episode. [Dodd & Mead, New York, 1914 ; Lane.]

—— *The Aristocrats.* 1901
A novel that came out anonymously and made a sensation. Written in the form of letters by the young Lady Helen Pole to an English friend, during a year spent in the Adirondacks among the most exclusive sets in American society. These people and their affectations are cuttingly, if superficially, satirized, especially the literary coteries, over-refined and " emasculated " according to this outspoken young lady, whose views on modern decadence and emancipation display no excess of prudery. [Lane, New York and London.]

—— *The Splendid Idle Forties.* 1902
An enlarged and revised edition of *Before the Gringo Came* (1892) : thirteen tales of old California and the romantic, passionate, half-Oriental life of the Spanish caballeros, under Mexican rule, before the advent of the improving Yankee. [Stokes, New York, 1914 ; Macmillan.]

—— *The Conqueror.* 1902
" The True and Romantic Story of the Birth, Life, and Death of Alexander Hamilton, Statesman, Orator, and Soldier " (1757-1804)—a novel of a eulogistic sort, based on the Hamilton family papers and public records of the West India Islands. Meant originally for a biography. Introduces Washington, Lafayette, Laurens, Adams, Madison, Burr, and Hamilton's other friends and enemies. [Revised ed., Stokes, New York, 1918 ; Macmillan.]

—— *Rulers of Kings.* 1904
The Rulers are a multimillionaire and his son, who have dealings with South American and European politics, hobnob with the Kaiser and the Emperor of Austria, etc., the son marrying the Princess of Hungary, and so on. [Harper, New York : o.p. ; Macmillan : o.p.]

—— *Rezánov.* 1906
The heroical career of a Russian empire-builder in California (1806), and his love-story ; a romance of high politics and love, of a conventional order. [Modern Lib., New York, 1919 ; Pearson : o.p.]

—— *Ancestors.* 1907
A long, unequal, exuberant novel of smart society and politics in England and life in California, Mrs. Atherton's wide knowledge and dramatic vigour making the latter far the strongest part of the book. Traces the development of a man with Celto-Saxon ancestors on one side and Spanish-American on the other, but the problem of heredity is complicated by many crossing interests. [Harper, New York : o.p. ; Murray : o.p.]

—— *The Gorgeous Isle.* 1908
A characteristic specimen of the romance of passion and the problem novel, one of the lovers being an inebriate and—a poet. Scene, the tropic island of Nevis in the West Indies, in 1842, when this was a fashionable winter resort with one of the most luxurious hotels in the world, and the haunt of wealthy English and Americans, who furnish Mrs. Atherton with a variety of characters. [Doubleday, New York : o.p. ; Murray.]

—— *Julia France and Her Times.* 1912
Gives an account of the American suffragist movement ; the heroine is forced into rebellion by her husband's ill-treatment, and becomes a leader in the cause of women's rights. [Macmillan, New York : o.p. ; Murray : o.p.]

ATHERTON, Mrs. Gertrude Franklin (*continued*). *Sisters-in-Law*. 1921
>The conflict between two women of opposite types of character, against a background of San Francisco society in the period 1906–18. [Stokes, New York; Murray.]

—— *Dormant Fires*. 1922
>Social life in San Francisco in the sixties and seventies. [*Sub tit. Sleeping Fires*, Stokes, New York; Murray.]

—— *Black Oxen*. 1923
>A psychological study of a woman of fifty-eight who after rejuvenation treatment becomes as one of twenty-eight. [Boni, New York; Murray.]

—— *The Immortal Marriage*. 1927
>The story of Pericles and Aspasia converted very cleverly into a modern novel. The latest authorities on the history of Athens and Miletus (445–429 B.C.) have been read up, and there results a very lively picture of the golden age with all its well-known figures, though it is clearly from the point of view of a modern and an ardent feminist. [Boni, New York; Murray.]

—— *Vengeful Gods : a processional novel of the fifth century* B.C. (*concerning one Alcibiades*). 1928
>The chequered career of Alcibiades (424–404 B.C.) similarly modernized, not however without allusion to the Greek idea of nemesis. The ambitious hero is puzzled and then passionately attracted by a masterful woman from Egypt, where the female sex rules : hence the materials for a romantic plot. (American title : *The Jealous Gods*). [Boni, New York; Murray.]

—— *Dido Queen of Hearts*. 1929
>The story of Dido's flight from Tyre, the founding of Carthage, and the visit of Æneas, following the Virgilian account. Dido appears as a strong-willed feminist, whilst Æneas is a superstitious bore. [Boni, New York; Chapman.]

ATTENBOROUGH, Gladys Mary [Mrs. Percy Linaker]. *The Rich Young Man : a comedy with digressions*. 1929
>The charming characters of Samela and her self-appointed guardian Mr. Twig, an eccentric dealer in antiques, and their discussions upon innumerable subjects, outweigh in interest the slender love-story. [Cassell; Stokes, New York.]

AUBRY, Octave [French; *b*. 1881]. *The Empress Might-have-Been* (Marie Walewska). 1925
>Napoleon and Mme Walewska, the divorce of Josephine, and the marriage with the Archduchess Marie Louise. [Transl. by H. E. DWIGHT, Cape; Harper, New York.]

—— *The Lost King* (Le roi perdu—Louis XVII retrouvé, 1924). 1926
>The affair of the Dauphin, Louis XVII (1793–1803) in an account of the investigations of a secret agent. [Hopkinson; Stokes, New York.]

—— *Gaspard Hauser : the orphan of Europe* (Gaspard Hauser, l'orphelin de l'Europe). 1930
>Based on the life of the mysterious youth, supposed heir to the throne of Bavaria, whose appearance caused so much stir throughout Europe (1812–33). [Transl. by Elizabeth NICHOLAS, Gollancz.]

AUCASSIN ET NICOLETTE. *Edited and rendered into modern English by F. W.* BOURDILLON. 1887
>A quaint little Provençal romance of the twelfth century, a prose-poem (*cante-fable*) of the sovereignty of true love, the hero a gentle knight of France, and the heroine a maiden of unknown birth, who proves to be daughter of the King of Carthage. Most striking perhaps in its grafting of vivid actuality upon pure romance—nothing more realistic than certain passages has come to us from mediæval literature. Composed in an alternation of prose and verse intended for recitation by the trouvère or jongleur. [(*a*) Transl. by Andrew LANG, Nutt (1887) 1904 : o.p. ; with 12 photogravures by Gilbert James (Photogravure Ser.), 1902 : o.p. ; (*b*) Rendered by F. W. BOURDILLON (Dryden Lib.), Kegan Paul (1887) 1903 ; (*c*) Transl. by M. S. HENRY, and versified by E. W. THOMSON, Schulze, Edinburgh, 1902 : o.p. ; (*d*) Transl. by Laurence HOUSMAN (with *Amabel and Amoris*, an original story in imitation of *Aucassin*), (1902), Chatto, 1925 ; (*e*) Transl. by Eugene MASON, Dent ; with other mediæval romances and legends, (Everyman's Lib.), Dent (Dutton, New York), 1900.]

AUDOUX, Marguerite [French]. *Marie-Claire* (1910). 1911
>In the introduction, Mr. Arnold Bennett describes the genesis of this little masterpiece, the work of a sempstress, and, indeed, the record of her own life. Whether " a divine accident," as he calls it, or a product of rare genius, the book, in style and composition and in economy of means, is an example of the finest impressionist art. Interprets the inner sense of childhood ; the characters and incidents of convent life, the indoor and outdoor life of a farm in the Sologne, being limned with delicate, indelible touches, as if she were transcribing the impressions of things on her inmost soul. [Transl. by J. N. RAPHAEL, Chapman : o.p. ; Doran, New York : o.p.]

—— *Valserine ; and other stories* (1910–12). 1912
>*Valserine*, a sketch for a longer work, is about a little diamond-cutter whose father is imprisoned for smuggling ; the rest are brief sketches of children, domestic incidents, the little things of life. [French text, with transl. by J. N. RAPHAEL, Chapman : o.p.]

—— *Marie-Clair's Workshop* (L'atelier de Marie-Claire, 1920). 1920
>Continues the life-story of Marie, now a sempstress in Paris—the joys and sorrows of working life, the humours and misfortunes of her associates, Gabrielle, who goes wrong, and the gruff, warm-hearted " Bouledogue " ; we leave her on the eve of marriage. [Transl. by F. S. FLINT, Chapman : o.p.]

AUERBACH, Berthold [German ; 1812–82]. *Spinoza : the life of a thinker* (Spinoza : ein Denkerleben, 1837). 1882
>Auerbach's studies of the Spinozan philosophy led to the abandonment of his intention to enter the Jewish priesthood, and the beginning of his literary career. This is an idealized biography of the man in the form of a novel, faithfully recording the cardinal events of Spinoza's life (1632–77)—the Spanish persecutions, his love for a Christian girl, excommunication from the Synagogue, etc., together with the essence of his philosophy, in conversations that reproduce verbally the *Ethics* and *Tractatus*. [Transl. by E. NICHOLSON, 2 vols., Tauchnitz, Leipzig, (Low) : o.p.]

AUERBACH, Berthold (*continued*). *Poet and Merchant* (Dichter und Kauffmann, 1840). 1877
"A picture of life from the times of Moses Mendelssohn" (*c.* 1729–86). [Holt, New York : o.p.]

—— *Village Tales from the Black Forest* (Schwarzwälder Dorfgeschichten, 1843). 1849
Village tales of southern Germany, sketching in a charming way the simple people of these secluded valleys ; though idealistic, preserving their peculiar traits, and throwing sidelights on German conditions early in the nineteenth century. They are saturated with Auerbach's philosophy, a legacy from Spinoza, and teach that we should try to comprehend motives and never despise or ridicule. Many of the peasants themselves are rustic philosophers. [Transl. by J. E. TAYLOR, Bogue : o.p. ; by C. GÖPP, Holt, New York, 1875 : o.p.]

—— *The Professor's Wife : a tale of Black Forest life* (Die Frau Professorin, 1847). 1851
In Lorle, the innkeeper's daughter, pure in heart, simple, devout, the author bids us see "a type of the original form of humanity, the primeval completeness, in its perfection, undisturbed by the twofold forces of history and culture." Married to an ambitious painter, she stifles amid the artifices and falsehoods of society in a German Court town, and their union ends in grief and disappointment. The author's hopeful and benign philosophy is an integral part of the tale ; but the narrative is quite simple and straightforward and there is no resemblance to a problem-novel. [Transl., London, 1851 : o.p. ; transl. by F. E. HYNAM, Drane, 1903 : o.p.]

—— *Little Barefoot ; or, Strive and Trust* (Barfüssele, 1856). 1872
A delicate, child-like fairy-tale of peasant life, with a barefoot maiden for heroine. Very characteristic of Auerbach in his simpler style ; rendering faithfully the dull, grinding life of the German village, but combining with these realistic elements the beauty of ideal humanity, and interpreting with tender fancy the poetry of life. Purity, faith, self-sacrifice are shown to be of God as much as are the birds and flowers. [Transl. by H. W. DULCKEN, Routledge : o.p. ; as *The Barefooted Maiden*, Low, 1857 : o.p. ; by E. B. LEE, Holt, New York, 1876 : o.p.]

—— *Christian Gellert ; and other sketches.* 1858
Idylls of German provincial life and rural character : the first a study of the poet Gellert, and the rude but sensitive countryman who repays him in his own way for the benefit of his verses (1715–69). *The Stepmother*, with its thoroughly German characters and environment, is a humorous tale. [Low : o.p., Sonnenschein, 1882 : o.p.]

—— *Joseph in the Snow* (Joseph im Schnee, 1860). 1861
A simple story of peasant life ; the theme, redemption through tribulation. [Transl. by Lady WALLACE, with *The Clockmaker* (*Edelweiss*), Saunders : o.p.]

—— *Edelweiss* (Edelweiss, 1861). 1869
A Black Forest idyll of greater length than the *Tales*, depicting the homely life of a clock-making community. The married life of a clockmaker and the innkeeper's daughter, who with her pride and unjust reproaches leads him a miserable life, till a terrible accident awakes her to her error. A pathetic tale, with a few glints of humour, teaching how daily intercourse becomes in time a mutual education. [Transl. by E. FROTHINGHAM, Holt, New York : o.p. ; transl. by C. T. BROOKS, Dulau (1877) : o.p.]

—— *On the Heights* (Auf der Höhe, 1865). 1867
The best of his definitely philosophical romances, an elaborate story of Court and village life, which are contrasted for didactic purposes. The king in a German state slights his pure and high-souled queen by loving a maid-of-honour. Discovering the intrigue, the queen separates herself from her husband, while Irma, though saved from suicide, lives a humble life of toil in the country, and alone with the contemplation of her sin, arrives at last at the serenity of repentance. The book is full of theoretical ideas on life and conduct, put in the mouth of the different personages. [Transl. by F. E. BUNNETT, 3 vols., Tauchnitz, Leipzig (Low) : o.p. ; same transl., Burt, New York ; transl. by S. A. STERN, Holt, New York, 1875–1912 : o.p.]

—— *The Country House on the Rhine* (Das Landhaus am Rhein, 1869). 1870
About a slave-trafficker who has made a fortune, and settles down in country society, until he is unmasked. There is much philosophizing, and discussion about the education of his son, whose tutor makes a fine character of him. [Transl., 3 vols., Bentley : o.p. ; *sub tit. The Villa on the Rhine*, 2 vols., Holt, New York : o.p.]

—— *The Good Hour ; or, Evening Holiday* (Zur guten Stunde, 1872). 1876
A collection of sketches of German life, with many humorous touches. [Transl. by H. W. DULCKEN : o.p.]

—— *Brigitta* (Brigitta, 1880). 1880
A peasant-story of a didactic kind. The daughter of a peasant, ruined and brought to his grave by a swindler, is a nurse in a hospital where her enemy comes as a patient ; and in a fit of indignation she maltreats him, but instantly repents and expiates her act by serving him till his death. [Transl. by Clara BELL, Tauchnitz, Leipzig (Low) : o.p.]

AUMONIER, Stacy [1887–1928]. *Olga Bardel.* 1916
Depicts the slum childhood of a little Jewish girl, a musical genius. [Methuen : o.p. ; Doubleday, Doran, New York.]

—— *Just Outside.* 1917
The story of a writer striving to find his true place in the world. [Methuen : o.p. ; Doubleday, Doran, New York.]

—— *The Querrils.* 1919
An ironical exposure of cant : the attempt of an upper-class family to ignore the suffering and ugliness in life brings its natural retribution, mainly upon the undeserving. [Methuen : o.p. ; Doubleday, Doran, New York.]

—— *One After Another.* 1920
Stories introducing queer types, and dealing in situations rather than persons. [Hutchinson : o.p. ; Macmillan, New York.]

AUMONIER, Stacy (*continued*). *The Love-a-Duck ; and other stories.* 1921
> Well-constructed stories of the magazine type, e.g. *The Great Unimpressionable*, about a young soldier who is left unmoved by all his wartime experiences, but is touched to the quick by the death of his dog. [Hutchinson ; *The Golden Windmill ; and other stories*, Macmillan, New York.]

—— *Overheard : fifteen tales.* 1924
> A varied collection, relying for interest upon the unexpected ending. *The Friends* is a good sketch of a pair of bibulous salesmen. [Heinemann ; Doubleday, Doran, New York.]

AUSTEN, Jane [1775–1817]. *Sense and Sensibility.* 1811
> A study of character and manners in a very delicate, precise, miniature style ; the characters just everyday people, drawn as they are without exaggeration ; the minute differences of human nature delicately pencilled ; the satire directed against mere commonplace foolishness, conceit, and vulgarity, rather than vice or eccentricity. In truth, the social failings and personal foibles are self-revealed rather than satirized, and make spontaneous comedy. In the comparison of the two sisters there may be implied an ironical criticism of the sentimentalists of the school of Richardson, etc. One is judgment, self-control, sanity ; the other imagination, feeling, sentimentality : the very different course of their respective love affairs points the moral. Based on an early novel in letters, *Elinor and Marianne*, recast in 1797–8, as *Sense and Sensibility*, and revised before publication in 1811. *Northanger Abbey* was finished 1798–9, before this.

—— *Pride and Prejudice.* 1813
> A priggish lover and a high-spirited girl are brought together at last, in spite of antipathy, by the natural growth of esteem. But the interest of passion and plot is a small thing with Miss Austen compared with the observation of character and humour, making foibles and vulgar selfishness a perfect delight to the reader —take, e.g., the selfish father, Mr. Bennet, the absurd clerical toady Mr. Collins, Mrs. Bennet the anxious mother, and even the failings of the too exalted heroine. This novel in its first form, entitled *First Impressions*, was written 1796–7, after *Elinor and Marianne*, the first draft of *Sense and Sensibility*. It was offered for publication, declined, and held up until the success of *Sense and Sensibility*.

—— *Mansfield Park.* 1814
> Her most considerable piece of work, not in mere dimensions, but in the mastery of a difficult problem—a houseful of young people in love with the right or the wrong person. Fanny Price, certainly one of Jane's most estimable young women, is quietly contrasted with Sir Thomas Bertram's flighty daughters, products of a careless education. Her unobtrusive love-affair eventually has its consummation in a wise and harmonious marriage. The most objectionable person, Mrs. Norris, is let down very lightly. In truth, nowhere is the difference between true comedy and satire better exemplified.

—— *Emma.* 1816
> Emma is a pretty girl of sterling character and more will than she can properly manage. She thinks she knows what is best for everybody, and is a prey to many deceptions. She is imposed upon, and imposes upon herself ; it is a long while before she sees things as they are, and recognizes where her own happiness lies. Her hero is one of Jane's sober, clear-eyed, and perfect men. The Fairfax and Churchill subplot furnishes a comedy of dissimulation contrasting didactically with Emma's honesty. A formidable snob and vulgarian, Mrs. Elton, and a good-natured bore, Miss Bates, who would be insufferable outside these pages, are among the more laughable characters.

—— *Persuasion.* 1818
> A tender, wistful tale, more of a love story than is Miss Austen's wont, with a vein of refined pathos, though the issue is happy. *Persuasion*, which was finished in 1817, has the exquisite charm of self-betrayal, the escape of a tender emotion long suppressed : here we can see her nearest approach to letting herself go. Anne Elliot parts from her lover, but after years of absence he returns, old love reasserts its sway, and they marry.

—— *Northanger Abbey.* 1818
> Though not published until 1818, this was written 1798–9 and entitled *Susan*, revised in 1803 and sold for publication ; it may perhaps have been rewritten or touched up later, before it appeared posthumously. Begun as a parody of sentimentalism and the romantics, it developed into the genre which was to be peculiarly Jane Austen's—the portrayal in sober and faithful tints of the quiet middle-class life she knew ; the satire restrained, the comedy all-pervasive. The heroine is a girl in the first innocent bloom of youth, a devotee of Mrs. Radcliffe, whose entry into life is attended by the collapse of many illusions.

—— *Lady Susan ; The Watsons.* 1871
> The former is a novelette in letters, supposed to have been written early ; never published by the authoress. The subject, an unpleasant sort of intrigue by an unpleasant woman, is uncharacteristic, and Prof. Goldwin Smith rightly calls the book a mere exercise. *The Watsons* (c. 1804) also is a mere fragment, the beginning of a thoroughly characteristic study of family life in a country town ; provincial vulgarity and the revulsion which a cultivated girl feels on coming back to a homely and ill-mannered family are the principal themes.

—— *Love and Freindship ; and other early works.* 1922
> *Love and Freindship* is a very piquant, out-and-out burlesque of the high-falutin romantic novel. The story is told in letters, the childish artlessness of which makes the satire more piquant. *Lesley Castle* is also in letters, with less story to tell, but not less quizzing of romantic sensibility. Exquisitely childish, but with the childishness of genius, are also *The History of England . . . by a partial, prejudiced, and ignorant historian*, and the collection of pattern letters and the *Scraps* with which the little book ends.
> [Novels in 5 vols. (*Northanger Abbey* and *Persuasion* in 1 vol.), each with introd. by Austin Dobson and *illus.* by Hugh Thomson or C. E. Brock, Macmillan, 1902 ; (Everyman's Lib.), Dent (Dutton, New York), 1906 ; ed. by R. W. Chapman, Oxford Press, 1923 (new ed., 1926). In 6 vols. (English Idylls), with coloured *illus.* by C. E. Brock, Dent (Dutton, New York), 1907–9. *Works*, 10 vols., Chatto, 1908 ; 5 vols., Macmillan, 1882 : 5 vols., (*Persuasion, Lady Susan*, and *The Watsons* in 1 vol.), (Georgian Series), Nash (Dodd and Mead, New York) ; in 7 vols., with introds. by Frank Swinnerton, Secker (Dodd and Mead, New York) ; in 6 vols., Bigelow Brown, New York ; in 5 vols., Little & Brown, Boston. *Lady Susan*, Oxford Press,

AUSTEN, Jane (*continued*).
　1925; *The Watsons, id.,* 1927; *The Watsons,* Appleton, New York, 1923. *Love and Friendship,* with
　introd. by G. K. Chesterton, Chatto, 1922 ; also Phœnix Lib., *id. Sanditon : fragment of a novel written
　in January–March* 1817, Oxford Press, 1925.]

AUSTIN, Alfred [Poet Laureate ; 1835–1913]. *The Garden that I Love ; 2 series.*　1894–1907
—— *In Veronica's Garden.*　1897
—— *Lamia's Winter Quarters.*　1899
—— *Haunts of Ancient Peace.*　1902
—— *A Poet's Diary.*　1904
　Scarcely novels, though the character-drawing perhaps authorizes us to call them fiction. A series of journals
　　of leisurely life in an old, secluded garden, where the poet converses with the admiring Lamia on the joys
　　of gardening, art and literature, politics, nature, and human nature. [(1), (2), (3), (5), Macmillan ;
　　(4), *id. :* o.p.]

AUSTIN, Jane [*née* Goodwin ; American ; 1831–94]. *A Nameless Nobleman.*　1881
　The scene is laid in Plymouth, a New England village making ready for the reception of a clergyman who
　　is bringing home his wife. Religious in tone. [Houghton, Boston.]
—— *Dr. Le Baron and his Daughters : a story of the old colony.*　1890
　The doctor is son of the Nameless Nobleman in the former romance. This tale deals more discursively with
　　later phases of social life, embodying many traditions and legends. [Houghton, Boston.]
—— *Standish of Standish.*　1890
—— *Betty Alden, the First-Born Daughter of the Pilgrims* [sequel].　1891
　Two tales of the pilgrims of Plymouth Colony, and of Miles Standish, one of the early heroes (*c.* 1620).
　　[(1) and (2), Houghton, Boston ; (1), Ward & Lock : o.p.]
—— *David Alden's Daughter ; and other stories of colonial times.*　1892
　Twelve stories, each representing some noteworthy character or epoch of colonial times. [Houghton, Boston.]

AUSTIN, Mary [American ; *née* Hunter ; *b.* 1868]. *The Basket Woman : fanciful tales for children.*　1904
—— *Lost Borders.*　1909
—— *The Trail Book.*　1918
　Stories of the Indians now dwelling in the Western deserts, by one who has lived like them, and spent years
　　between the Sierra Nevada and the Moldave desert studying their life and lore (see her chapter on " Aboriginal
　　Literature," in the *Cambridge History of American Literature*). [(1), (3), Houghton, Boston ; (2), *id.,* o.p.]
—— *Isidro.*　1905
　Adventures in Alta California in the early nineteenth century, the last days of the Catholic missions. Spanish
　　and Portuguese settlers and Indians, and the loves of Isidro and the Commandante's lost daughter.
　　[Houghton, Boston : o.p. ; Constable : o.p.]
—— *Outland.*　1910
　A dream-fantasy which might well have been inspired by Sir James Barrie : a pair of " House-Folk " are
　　captured by the " Outliers," a community which preserve the habits and simple virtues of primitive man,
　　and whose retreats are impenetrable by the ordinary mortal. [First published under pseudonym of
　　" Gordon Stairs," London ; new ed., Boni, New York, 1919.]

AVELING, Francis [*b.* 1875]. *Arnoul the Englishman.*　1908
　England under Henry III and France under St. Louis. Deals largely with the University of Paris, and the
　　differences of Regularists and Secularists in the time of Aquinas. A painstaking piece of work. [Methuen :
　　o.p. ; Herder, St. Louis.]

" AYSCOUGH, John " [Monsignor Count Francis Browning Drew Bickerstaffe-Drew, 1858–1928].
　Marotz.　1908
　The interest of this romance is emotional and spiritual, and differentiates it entirely from the ordinary run
　　of fiction. Marotz is a good woman drawn at full length, a postulant who leaves her convent to marry.
　　Her life and parting with a worthless husband, the sad career of their son, and her final happiness are
　　related in a manner that brings out the author's earnest philosophy of life. Peasants, nuns, and other S.
　　Italian and Sicilian figures are drawn with force and sincerity. [Chatto ; Putnam, New York : o.p.]
—— *Dromina.*　1909
　" Sad stories of the death of kings " is the writer's motto. He pictures a noble old Catholic house in Ireland
　　early in the nineteenth century, descended from Irish kings, titled by the Stuarts, and sending forth
　　claimants to thrones. A Louis XVII, an Emperor of Hispaniola, a king of the gipsies, are among the
　　tragic personages. Mr. Ayscough's romance is an affair rather of atmosphere than incident ; he has
　　the poetic gift of revealing the " something far more deeply interfused " in human life. [Arrowsmith :
　　o.p. ; Putnam, New York : o.p.]
—— *San Celestino.*　1909
　The story of Pietro di Morrone (1215–96), the Celestine V who resigned the papacy after five months. He
　　founded the Order of the Celestines (1260). [Murray ; Putnam, New York : o.p.]
—— *Hurdcott.*　1911
　A love-drama of the spirit, not the flesh, enacted in a fine old village amid the Wiltshire downs, at the time
　　of Hazlitt and Charles and Mary Lamb, who just set foot upon the stage. Hurdcott, the half-Sicilian
　　Consuelo, and the half-Hindu Basil are beautiful with the light of other worlds ; but there are more
　　mundane characters among their friends and relations, drawn with the right infusion of humour.
　　[Chatto ; Herder, St. Louis.]
—— *Faustula.*　1912
　Faustula is a little Vestal Virgin, and is put to death under the Emperor Julian when she confesses her love
　　for a Christian boy (340–363). [Chatto : o.p.]

"**AYSCOUGH, John**" (*continued*). *Monksbridge.* 1914

A little domestic chronicle of a girl with social ambitions in the sixties, with several attractive characters. [Chatto ; Longman's, New York.]

—— *Fernando.* 1918

The parentage, home and school life, and spiritual development, of a young convert to the Roman Church. [Long ; Kenedy, New York : o.p.]

—— *Jacqueline.* 1918

The heroine is the unsuspecting wife of a German spy moving in high society. The characterization is good. [Chatto ; Kenedy, New York.]

—— *A Prince in Petto.* 1919

The hero, a son of Charles Edward by Lady Margaret Stuart, remains ignorant of his birth, whilst serving the Young Pretender. There is a good picture of the fallen Stuarts and their circle in Rome. [Chatto.]

—— *Abbotscourt.* 1919

A characteristic delineation of provincial society, clerical circles especially. [Chatto.]

—— *Dobachi.* 1923

A romance of a small New England seaport ; the two principal characters are converted to Catholicism. [Macmillan, New York.]

AZEGLIO, Massimo Taparelli, Marchese d' [Italian ; 1798–1866]. *The Challenge of Barletta* (Ettore Fieramosca, 1833). 1880

An historical novel in Manzoni's style dealing with Gonsalvo di Cordova's defence of the town of Barletta, on the Adriatic (1503). Azeglio was Victor Emmanuel's prime minister, and was succeeded by Cavour. His two novels met with a *succès d'estime*, but are far less interesting than his autobiography. [2 vols., W. H. Allen : o.p.]

—— *The Maid of Florence* (Niccolò dei Lapi, 1841). 1853

The defence of Florence against the arms of Clement VII and Charles V, described from Varchi's account, and a vivid picture of the Florentines in the passions and anxieties of that strenuous time (1529–30). [Transl. by W. FELGATE, 3 vols., Bentley : o.p.]

"**AZORIN**" [José Martinez Ruiz ; Spanish ; b. 1876]. *Don Juan* (Don Juan, 1922). 1923

A quiet, meditative story : Don Juan in a reincarnation becomes the antithesis of his former self. [Transl. by Katherine Allison PHILLIPS, Knopf.]

AZUELA, Mariano [Mexican ; b. 1873]. *The Under Dogs* (Los de Abajo, 1919). 1929

The Mexican revolution of 1914–15, presented in the form of fiction, with typical characters drawn to the life, and the gloomy and confused atmosphere reproduced, but with no plot and no particular stress on the incidents. Don Azuela was a participant in the revolution. [Transl. by E. MUNGUÍA, junr., Brentano's, New York ; Cape.]

BABCOCK, Mrs. Bernie [*née* Smade ; American ; b. 1868]. *The Soul of Ann Rutledge.* 1919

The love-story of Abraham Lincoln, whose early career at New Salem and Springfield is described. [Lippincott, Philadelphia and London.]

—— *The Soul of Abe Lincoln.* 1923

Lincoln's life from his nomination for president to his assassination, interwoven with a love-story. [Lippincott, Philadelphia and London.]

BABCOCK, William Henry [American ; b. 1849]. *Cian of the Chariots : a romance of Arthur's Court.* 1898

A very serious attempt to reconstruct Arthurian Britain, by an author who in *The Two Lost Centuries of Britain* (1890) had written an imaginative monograph, based on historical indications, dealing with the period between the Roman evacuation and the establishment of Saxon rule. [Lothrop, Boston : o.p.]

—— *The Tower of Wye.* 1901

This likewise handles history in a very painstaking manner, exerting imagination only in filling up the gaps in existing records. The time is the Claiborne-Calvert contest of 1634–51, between Virginia and Maryland over their rival claims to Kent Island, and the chief characters and incidents, as well as the early conditions of the settlers, are well authenticated. [Coates, Philadelphia : o.p.]

—— *Kent Fort Manor.* 1902

Here there is less reliance on history ; the middle period of the American Civil War and the years following hardly provide any incidents or characters that can be recognized as historical, though the conditions existing in Chesapeake and Washington and the characters of those times and places are faithfully drawn. [Winston, New York : o.p.]

BABEL, Isaac [Russian ; b. 1894]. *Red Cavalry* (Konarmia, 1923). 1929

Scenes and stories of the Polish campaign of 1920–21, from the point of view of a soldier in the Red Army. Not a continuous or even an episodic story, but disconnected pictures and anecdotes, some in the very words of ignorant muzhiks or Cossacks and showing the obscure working of a primitive brain. The things related are ugly enough ; murdering, raping, sacrilege, filth, destruction, are the common features of daily life. The Red soldier asks fate for " the simplest of proficiencies—the ability to kill my fellow men." [Transl. by Nadya HELSTEIN, Knopf, New York and London.]

BACCHELLI, Riccardo [Italian ; b. 1891]. *The Devil at the Long Bridge* (Il Diavolo al Pontelungo, 1927). 1929

Founded on the later life of the Russian revolutionary Bakunin, dealing with his experimental Communist settlement at Locarno, and the abortive rising in Bologna (of which city the author is a native) in 1874. [Transl. by Orlo WILLIAMS, Longmans.]

BACHELLER, Irving Addison [American ; *b.* 1859]. *Eben Holden : a tale of the North Country.*
1900
A rambling, sentimental novel of life in the Adirondacks fifty years ago, introducing Horace Greeley and Abraham Lincoln. Interest centres in the faithful old servant, Eben Holden, who is lovingly drawn. Life in the woods and fields is depicted with no little charm. [Grosset, New York ; Unwin : o.p.]

—— *D'ri and I : memoirs of Col. Ramon Bell, U.S.A.* 1901
Vivid descriptions of forest, lake, and river, near the St. Lawrence (1812). The story and the characters are naught. [Harper, New York : o.p. ; Grosset, New York : o.p. ; Richards : o.p.]

—— *Darrel of the Blessed Isles.* 1903
The Blessed Isles are the land of poetry and imagination. Knowing Shakespeare, Milton, and the Bible by heart, Darrel (1835–55), the old clock-tinker and philosopher of the backwoods, teaches all men a more perfect wisdom, charity, contentment. The book is fragrant with these qualities, and with a deep and understanding love of nature. A book of pregnant sayings, a philosophy of life, rather than a story ; yet it portrays several examples of beautiful character, and has some moving scenes. [Harper, New York : o.p. ; Grosset, New York : o.p. ; Methuen : o.p.]

—— *Vergilius : a tale of the coming of Christ.* 1904
Vergilius is a Roman patrician and a favourite of the Emperor. Sent to Rome, he hears of the expected Advent. [Harper, New York, London : o.p.]

—— *Cricket Heron.* 1909
Autobiography of a wandering boyhood and business life during the railroad boom and the industrial development in New York City of the latter half of the 19th century ; telling of Abraham Lincoln's death and of Commodore Vanderbilt and Andrew Carnegie. [*Sub tit. The Hand-Made Gentleman : a tale of the battles of peace*, Harper, New York : o.p. ; title as above, Unwin : o.p.]

—— *The Light in the Clearing : a tale of the North Country in the time of Silas Wright.* 1917
Silas Wright (1795–1847), senator, and governor of New York, who declined nomination for the presidency, is a conspicuous figure in this leisurely story of country life in New York State and at Washington (1831–44) ; President Van Buren appears. Even the supposed autobiographer seems to be a real person. The rest of them are old-fashioned, homely, humorous figures, such as the author has already revived from a beautiful past in other novels. [Bobbs-Merrill, Indianapolis ; Collins : o.p.]

—— *A Man for the Ages : a story of the builders of Democracy.* 1919
A racy book that has a respectable place among the innumerable character-studies of Lincoln. [Bobbs-Merrill, Indianapolis.]

—— *Father Abraham* [sequel]. 1925
Continues the life-story of Lincoln from the beginning of the Civil War until his death. [Bobbs-Merrill, Indianapolis.]

—— *The House of the Three Ganders.* 1928
An exciting story about two boys and an old soldier. One of the boys is killed ; the other two unite to solve the mystery of his death. [Bobbs-Merrill, Indianapolis ; Hutchinson.]

—— *A Candle in the Wilderness : a tale of the beginning of New England.* 1930
The adventures of two young men who emigrate from England to Boston in 1634. References for many of the incidents are given in a note. [Bobbs-Merrill, Indianapolis ; McClelland, Toronto.]

BACON, Francis, Baron Verulam, Viscount St. Albans [1561–1626]. *The New Atlantis.* 1635
Certain voyagers discover an unknown land in the Pacific inhabited by a people of higher civilization than that of Europeans. In this unfinished tale Bacon embodies much of his philosophy, and makes suggestions, such as the utility of scientific academies, that have borne fruit since ; it is also a good example of his English prose. [Cambridge Press ; Macmillan ; Oxford Press ; ed. by G. C. Moore Smith, Macmillan, New York ; with More's *Utopia* (Broadway Translations), Routledge (Dutton, New York), 1925.]

BACON, Fryer. *The Famous Historie of Fryer Bacon.* 1627
" Containing the Wonderfull Things that he did in his life : also the manner of his death ; with the lives and deaths of the two Coniurers, Bungye and Vandermast." An Elizabethan version of an earlier story of the great Franciscan (1214–92) and his achievements, which are after the manner of the time ascribed to necromantic powers. Notable as the story on which Greene based his finest play. [Repr. in W. J. Thoms' *Early English Prose Romances*, Routledge (Dutton, New York) : see p. 465.]

BAERLEIN, Henry [*b.* 1875]. *On the Forgotten Road.* 1909
The story of the Children's Crusade (1212), told by a peasant. France under Philip Augustus and twenty-three years' captivity in Egypt (down to 1235). [Murray : o.p.]

—— *The House of the Fighting Cocks.* 1922
The story of a Spanish student in Mexico when Maximilian was trying to establish himself as Emperor (1866–7). [Parsons : o.p. ; Harcourt, Brace, New York : o.p.]

BAGE, Robert [1728–1801]. *Hermsprong ; or, Man as He is Not.* 1796
In some sort an imitation of Richardson ; good in its drawing of feminine character. Bage belonged to the revolutionary school of novelists headed by Godwin and Holcroft, whose teachings were in accord with those of Rousseau and Tom Paine—the rights of man, life according to Nature, social equality, etc. This is perhaps the most important of his novels, contrasting the deficiencies of things as they were with the beauties of an utopian colony planted among the redskins in North American forests, and extolling the virtues of man in a state of nature. [British Novelists, No. 48, 1810 ; o.p.]

BAGOT, Richard [1860–1921]. *A Roman Mystery.* 1899
The sensational part of the story turns on a case of " lupomanaro," the terrible hereditary madness that occurs not infrequently in Italy. Fashionable life, domestic affairs, politics, and religious intrigue at Rome are the other materials. [Methuen : o.p. ; Digby & Long : o.p. ; Lane, New York : o.p.]

BAGOT, Richard (*continued*). *Casting of Nets.* 1901

The author was a Roman Catholic, well known as a controversialist attacking priestly methods of securing converts. An agnostic peer, nominally a Protestant, marries a Catholic, whose relatives try to convert him ; a series of painful events enforce the author's arguments. [Everett : o.p. ; Lane, New York : o.p.]

BAILEY, Henry Christopher [*b.* 1878]. *My Lady of Orange.* 1901

A tale of the Dutch rising against Philip II—deeds of derring-do in Holland during 1573, ending with the relief of Alkmaar ; the narrator an English soldier of fortune. Alva, Vitelli, William the Silent, and Diedrich Sonoy are introduced. [Longmans : o.p. ; Ward & Lock ; Longmans, New York : o.p.]

—— *Karl of Erbach : a tale of Lichtenstein and Solgau.* 1903

Solgau seems to be a Swabian state (*c.* 1630, time of Thirty Years' War). Interest divided between exciting adventure and the sprightly dialogue of two romantic lovers. [Longmans : o.p. ; Ward & Lock ; Longmans, New York : o.p.]

—— *The Master of Gray.* 1903

The Master is Patrick Gray, 6th Lord Gray, a prominent intriguer in the days of Mary Queen of Scots, whose infamous desertion of his mistress's cause is excused on the plea of his love. But for this historical licence the story follows the records with exemplary faithfulness. Period of Mary's captivity (1580–7) ; Elizabeth, James VI, Sidney, Walsingham, Burleigh, etc., appear. [Longmans, London and New York : o.p.]

—— *Beaujeu.* 1905

Adventures, love-scenes, political intrigue, etc., in James II's reign and after the Revolution (1678–88). [Nelson : o.p.]

—— *Springtime.* 1907

An exciting romance of the early period of the Renaissance in Lombardy. The style is Mr. Hewlett's heavily dashed with Kipling. [Nelson ; *sub tit. Under Castle Walls*, Appleton, New York : o.p.]

—— *Raoul, Gentleman of Fortune.* 1907

Concerned with the revolt of the Netherlands (1574–84), siege and relief of Leyden, siege of Antwerp, the Prince of Parma, and the doings of a French adventurer. [Hutchinson : o.p. ; Appleton, New York : o.p.]

—— *The God of Clay.* 1908

A character-study of Napoleon from his days as an artillery lieutenant to the First Consulate (1788–99). [Hutchinson : o.p. ; Brentano, New York : o.p.]

—— *Colonel Stow.* 1908

Introduces Cromwell, Rupert, and other typical characters, historical and fictitious, Civil War period (1643–5) ; but more of a novel of manners than historical romance. [Hutchinson : o.p. ; *sub tit. Colonel Greatheart*, Bobbs-Merrill, Indianapolis : o.p.]

—— *Storm and Treasure.* 1910

A story of Sussex, Nantes, and the Vendean War (1793–4). [Methuen o.p. ; Brentano, New York : o.p.]

—— *The Lonely Queen.* 1911

Elizabeth as princess and then as queen (1540–66) ; Sir William Cecil the most conspicuous among her famous contemporaries. [Methuen : o.p. ; Doran, New York : o.p.]

—— *The Sea Captain.* 1914

Exciting adventures in the Mediterranean and the English Channel, at the time of the pirate Barbarossa and Spanish naval efforts against England ; time of Mary and Elizabeth. [Methuen ; Doran, New York : o.p.]

—— *The Gentleman Adventurer.* 1914

Miscellaneous adventures with Jacobites in England, time of William III, and then in the West Indies. [Methuen ; Doran, New York : o.p.]

—— *The Highwayman.* 1915

Not only a tale of the road, but of the Jacobites, and Queen Anne, Lady Masham, etc. (1714). [Methuen : o.p. ; Dutton, New York ; o.p.]

—— *The Gamesters.* 1916

The interest of a novel of manners is combined with the usual excitements, scenes chiefly Dresden and Frankfurt. Frederick the Great, still a young man, appears on friendly terms with an Englishman (1728–40). [Methuen ; Dutton, New York : o.p.]

—— *The Young Lovers.* 1917

A romance of the Peninsular War (1810–13). [Methuen ; Dutton, New York.]

—— *The Pillar of Fire.* 1918

A good historical picture of the times of the Risorgimento (1859–60) ; Palmerston and Mazzini appear in the London scenes, and Napoleon III, Victor Emmanuel, Cavour, and Garibaldi, in the Italian. [Methuen.]

—— *Barry Leroy.* 1919

The adventures of an English spy at home and on the Continent bring on the stage Bonaparte, Talleyrand, Nelson, Pitt, and other great people (1793–1800). [Methuen ; Dutton, New York : o.p.]

—— *His Serene Highness.* 1920

The romantic masquerade of an eighteenth-century gentleman from Sussex as prince of the little state of Salm, on the German border, lands him in unexpected responsibilities and a labyrinth of intrigue. [Methuen : o.p. ; Dutton, New York : o.p.]

—— *The Fool.* 1921

A tale of the times of Henry II in England and France (1153–89). The murder of Becket is an episode. [Methuen ; Dutton, New York.]

—— *Call Mr. Fortune.* 1921

—— *Mr. Fortune Speaking.* 1930

The first and last of half a dozen volumes of detective mysteries, which are amusing but have no pretence to intellectual subtlety, featuring an investigator who combines the methods of Sherlock Holmes with the

BAILEY, Henry Christopher (*continued*).
 manner of one of Mr. Wodehouse's heroes. [(1) Methuen ; Dutton, New York ; (2) Ward & Lock ; Dutton, New York.]

—— *The Plot.*   1922
 The Popish Plot furnishes the historical groundwork (1678). [Methuen.]

—— *The Rebel.*   1923
 The defeat of Garibaldi at Mentana and the Franco-German War mark out the historical framework of a story that has also English and Irish episodes (1866–71). [Methuen.]

—— *Knight-at-Arms.*   1924
 The Knight is a French seigneur who accompanies the Italian expedition of Charles VIII : a crowd of famous names appear (1483–94). [Methuen : Dutton, New York : o.p.]

—— *The Merchant Prince.*   1926
 The rise of a master-merchant under Edward IV and Richard III (1460–85) ; principal scenes, Southampton and the New Forest. [Methuen ; Dutton, New York.]

—— *Bonaventure.*   1927
 Spanish plots against Elizabeth furnish the poet-hero with adventure and serve to introduce a number of great figures (1586–7). [Methuen.]

—— *Judy Bovenden.*   1928
 The story of a Kentish squire and his daughter in the Waterloo period (1813–15). Good presentation of the social life of the day, with Beau Brummell and the Prince Regent in leading parts. Scenes, Weald of Kent and Brighton. [Methuen.]

BAILLIE-SAUNDERS. Margaret [*née* Crowther ; *b.* 1873]. *Black Sheep Chapel.* 1918
 A mystery novel, with a ritualistic church in the north of London for background. [Hurst & Blackett : o.p.]

BAIN, Francis William [*b.* 1863]. *A Digit of the Moon : a Hindoo love-story.* 1899
 Part of a cycle of sixteen stories, entitled *The Churning of the Ocean of Time*, each named after a digit ($\frac{1}{16}$ part) of the moon. A fairy-tale of a misogynist king who falls in love with a portrait, and after searching out the original, puts to her a series of riddles that baffles her reluctance. Full of Oriental humour and wisdom tricked out in a whimsical dress. [" Transl. by F. W. BAIN " ; really an original work by this fine Orientalist.]

—— *The Descent of the Sun : a cycle of birth.*   1903
—— *A Heifer of the Dawn.*   1904
—— *In the Great God's Hair.*   1904
 Further imitations of, or rather essays in, Oriental fiction.

—— *A Draught of the Blue.*   1905
 An Indian myth, stated to be " translated from the original MS.," and, like the others in this curious series of exotic masterpieces, acknowledged to be an authentic interpretation of the mythological fancy of Hindustan.

—— *An Essence of the Dusk.*   1906
 The tragic story of a king's son of surpassing strength and beauty, who finds a wondrous city in the desert inhabited by women and a sad old king, whose daughter is haunted by a curse. He becomes the haunted princess's lover, and essays to overcome the powers of evil ; but after strange ordeals of enchantment both prince and princess perish. The style of all these stories is as rich, sensuous, and fanciful, both in matter and diction, as that of the *Arabian Nights*. They may well be termed Indian rather than English fiction, because they seem to be derived from Oriental legend. They are far more truly the real thing than any of the eighteenth-century imitations of Eastern story. [" Transl. from original MS."]

—— *An Incarnation of the Snow.*   1908
—— *A Mine of Faults.*   1909
 Title derived from a Sanskrit *double entente* describing woman, " Lender of beauty to the dusk," or, " A mine of faults." Three Hindu love-tales. [" Transl. from original MS."]

—— *The Ashes of a God.*   1911
—— *Bubbles of the Foam.*   1912
—— *A Syrup of the Bees.*   1914
—— *The Livery of Eve.*   1917
—— *The Substance of a Dream.*   1919
 Further essays in the same exotic genre. [All Methuen ; Putnam, New York ; Riccardi Press (Medici Soc.), 1913–20.]

BAKER, Amy J. [Mrs. Maynard Crawford]. *The King's Passion.*   1920
 The King is Edmund of East Anglia, who loves the daughter of the King of Ireland, and the material is drawn from Roger of Wendover. [Long : o.p.]

BAKER, George Philip [*b.* 1879]. *The Magic Tale of Harvanger and Yolande.* 1914
 Adventures in greenwood, camp, and city, of a youth in search of " the best thing in the world." Recalls *The Glittering Plain*. [Mills & Boon : o.p. ; Doran, New York.]

—— *The Romance of Palombris and Pallogris.*   1915
 A pastiche of Arthurian romance. [Mills & Boon : o.p.]

BAKER, James [1847–1920]. *The Gleaming Dawn.*   1896
 A romance of England in the time of the Wyclifites and of the Hussite wars in Bohemia (1396–1420). [Chapman : o.p.]

—— *The Cardinal's Page : a story of adventure.*   1898
 Bohemia, Prague, Burgstein, and England (1427–32), the hero a page in the service of Cardinal Henry Beaufort, who was a figure also in the previous novel. The author had travelled largely in the countries that provide the scenes. [Chapman : o.p.]

BAKER, Mrs. L. A. ["Alien"; New Zealander]. *The Untold Half.* 1899
    A dramatic romance of passion enacted amid the wild and solitary mountain scenery of Lake Manapouri and the Cathedral Peaks in New Zealand. [Hutchinson: o.p.; Putnam, New York: o.p.]

—— *The Devil's Half-Acre.* 1900
    A romance of sin and expiation, with pictures of rough life in a mining district of New Zealand. The dominant figure is a religious fanatic known as "The Prophet," with an evil past. [Unwin: o.p.]

BALFOUR, Sir Andrew [Scottish; 1873–1931]. *By Stroke of Sword.* [juvenile] 1897
    Adventures in Drake's time, in Fife, Devon, and on the Spanish Main (*c.* 1585). [Nelson.]

—— *To Arms!* 1898
    A Stevensonian romance of the Jacobite rising, which in Scotland was defeated at Sheriffmuir (1715), with melodramatic adventures in Paris. [Methuen: o.p.; Page, Boston: o.p.]

—— *Vengeance is Mine.* 1899
    Adventure in Scotland and in France during the Hundred Days. [Methuen: o.p.; New Amsterdam Book Co., New York: o.p.]

—— *The Golden Kingdom.* [juvenile] 1903
    An imitation of Stevenson and Rider Haggard. Story of the quest for a kingdom of gold in Central Africa (*c.* 1700). [Nelson; Page, Boston: o.p.]

BALLANTYNE, Robert Michael [1825–94]. *Snowflakes and Sunbeams; or, The Young Fur Traders* 1856
    In later editions entitled *The Young Fur Traders.* Embodies, in the form of a story for boys, the author's experiences in Canada, of which he had published a rough diary in *Hudson's Bay; or, The Wilds of North America* (1848). [Nisbet; Oxford Press; Blackie; Nelson, New York.]

—— *Ungava: a tale of Esquimau Land.* 1857
    A similar yarn about North Labrador (1831). [Nisbet; (Everyman's Lib.), Dent (Dutton, New York); Blackie; Nelson, New York.]

—— *Coral Island.* 1857
—— *The Gorilla Hunters* [sequel]. 1861
    Here Ballantyne writes adventure stories about scenes that he was not personally acquainted with. [(1) Nisbet; Blackie; (Everyman's Lib.), Dent (Dutton, New York); Nelson, New York; (2) Nisbet; Blackie; Collins; Nelson, New York.]

—— *The Life Boat.* 1864
—— *The Lighthouse.* 1865
—— *Fighting the Flames.* 1867
—— *Deep Down.* 1868
    Stories of heroic work and adventure, on the Goodwin Sands, in northern lighthouses, with the fire brigade, and the Cornish miners, all carefully prepared for by information acquired on the spot. [(1) Blackie; Nelson, New York: o.p.; (2) Blackie; Oxford Press; Nelson, New York; (3) Nisbet; Blackie; (4) Nisbet; Blackie.]

—— *Erling the Bold.* 1869
    "A tale of the Norse Sea Kings." [Nisbet; Blackie; Nelson, New York.]

—— *The Norsemen in the West.* 1872
    The Pre-Columbian discovery of America. [Nisbet.]

—— *In the Track of the Troops.* 1878
    The Russo-Turkish War (1877–8). [Nisbet: o.p.]

—— *The Red Man's Revenge.* 1880
    The Red River Expedition (1869–71). [Nisbet.]

BALZAC, Honoré de [French; 1799–1850]. La comédie humaine:—
    Balzac has been described as a demographer rather than a novelist. His *Comédie humaine*, a stupendous fragment, was designed as a complete and systematic survey of the life of man in its various manifestations, a design carried out so far as to produce the fullest representation extant of modern civilization. He lacked humour, sympathy, refinement, and the passion for beauty. Balzac's dramatic energy and profound sense of the romance of life, however, make his novels as mere stories enthralling in incident and alive with actuality. He may be regarded as the founder of the school of Naturalism in fiction; he is a finer Naturalist than any Zola; and from that point of view his novels have been arranged according to his own classification, which emphasizes the systematic nature of his survey.

SCENES OF PRIVATE LIFE

—— *At the Sign of the Cat and Racket, etc.* (La maison du Chat-qui-Pelote, 1830). 1896
    The novelette thus entitled is the touching history of a draper's daughter who marries out of her sphere, and fails to win the affection that is a necessity of her nature. Depicts quiet bourgeois life with Dutch minuteness, and gives a detailed painting of a large business establishment. *The Sceaux Ball; or, The Peer of France* (1830), satirizes people who affect to despise business. Sir Walter Besant describes *The Purse* (1832) as "one of the most charming little bits of love, innocence, and nature in all Balzac." *La Vendetta* (1830) is the story of a rich and talented girl of Corsican parentage, who marries a man with whom her family is at feud, and reaps a harvest of calamities; *Madame Firmiani* (1832) is a bright, slight social comedy. [Also in Everyman's Lib.]

—— *A Woman of Thirty, etc.* (La femme de trente ans, 1831). 1897
    A group of stories in which the interest and pathos depend, more or less directly, on the attachment of married ladies to men who are not their husbands. *La Grenadière* (1832), written in one day, is full of tender

BALZAC, Honoré de (*continued*).

pictures of Balzac's native Touraine. *The Woman of Thirty*, like *Le lys dans la vallée*, develops a favourite motive of Balzac's, an attractive young woman sacrificed to a dull husband. *A Forsaken Lady* (*La femme abandonnée*, 1832), *The Message* (1832), and *Gobseck* (1830), are brief pieces of considerable interest.

—— *La Grande Bretêche, etc.* (1830–42).　　　　　　　　　　　　　　　　　　　　1896

La grande Bretêche is a ruined and deserted mansion on the Loire, the scene of a deceived husband's terrible vengeance. *Another Study of Woman* (1831) is a similar tale of intrigue and revenge near the Beresina during the Russian campaign. *A Study of Woman* (1831), *The Imaginary Mistress* (*La fausse maitresse*, 1842), and *Peace in the House* (*La paix du ménage*), are all very short stories. *Albert Savarus* (1842), a story of passion and intrigue, is more elaborate ; an unscrupulous girl in love with the hero persuading her rival that he is unfaithful, and, when she has driven him into a monastery, leaving no stone unturned to make life a misery for the deceived woman.

—— *A Marriage Settlement* (Le contrat de mariage, 1835), *etc.* (1830–44).　　　　　1898

A Marriage Settlement, recounting the negotiations about a marriage settlement, a spendthrift mother plotting to get the better of her son-in-law, shows the author's practical acquaintance with the details of finance and law. *A Start in Life* (*Un début dans la vie*, 1844) is a humorous history of a young man of inordinate vanity, whose infirmity gets him into great difficulties, but who is at length cured by drastic treatment. *A Second Home* (*Une double famille*, 1830) tells how an honourable and worthy man, estranged by the coldness and lack of sympathy of his bigoted wife, takes a mistress and has a second family. Retribution comes upon him through his children.

—— *The Atheist's Mass* (La messe de l'athée, 1836), *etc.* (1831–44).　　　　　　　1896

The first (*La messe de l'athée*, 1836), commemorating a brotherly friend of Balzac's, is the pathetic story of an infidel's tribute to the religion of a great and modest soul, who had been to him more than a father in his days of adversity. The longest story, *Honorine* (1844), is of a husband who watches over the unloving wife who deserted him. He employs a deputy to win her back, with disastrous consequences. *Colonel Chabert* (1832) is more deeply tragic : the colonel renounces wealth, fame, and even his own identity, rather than punish the wife who treated him infamously. In *The Commission in Lunacy* (*L'interdiction*, 1836), Judge Popinot is an ideal portrait of a just and charitable man : this and *Pierre Grassou* (1841) are short pieces. [Also in Everyman's Lib.]

—— *A Daughter of Eve* (Une fille d'Ève, 1838), *etc.* (1838–40).　　　　　　　　1897

In *A Daughter of Eve* (1839) a man of the world rescues his young wife from a false position, and saves his own honour, with a delicacy that does him infinite credit. *Letters of Two Brides* (*Mémoires de deux jeunes mariées*, 1842) contrasts the married life of two girls who have been brought up together, and contains a surpassing picture of true motherhood. The other wife is an exaggerated romantic, and her story verges on the incredible. [*The Two Young Brides* (transl.), with a critical introduction by Henry JAMES, Heinemann, 1902.]

—— *Beatrix* (1839–44).　　　　　　　　　　　　　　　　　　　　　　　　　　1896

A love-drama laid in an old-fashioned corner of Brittany, the quaint manners of which furnish an interesting picture of bygone phases of life. A fascinating and heartless coquette is passionately loved by a fine young Breton, who is the object in turn of several maidens' affection. Two admirable types of womanly character are drawn among the latter.

—— *Modeste Mignon* (1844).　　　　　　　　　　　　　　　　　　　　　　　1896

The ultra-romantic Modeste Mignon falls in love with the portrait of a famous poet, and enters into correspondence with him, like Mme Hanska with the author. This is the beginning of an amusing entanglement. She is rescued from the embarrassment by her father, who gives her the opportunity of choosing between the real and the sham poet, and the upshot of the comedy is surprising.

SCENES OF PROVINCIAL LIFE

—— *Pierrette ; and, The Abbé Birotteau* (1832–40).　　　　　　　　　　　　　1896

Two short novels—*Les célibataires I ; Pierrette* (1840)—the story of a saintly girl victimized and ultimately done to death by a pair of wretches; *Le curé de Tours* (1832)—a minor episode in the ecclesiastical life of Balzac's native Tours. The Abbé, an amiable, unambitious epicure, just as his modest ideals of a comfortable latter-life are about to be fulfilled and he beholds a happy vista to the grave, finds himself robbed of house and home by an ambitious priest. Shows up the intrigues and social factions that ferment in a provincial town.

—— *Eugenie Grandet* (1833).　　　　　　　　　　　　　　　　　　　　　　1896

The lifelong martyrdom of a character of exaggerated beauty ; innocent, gentle, faithful, and long-suffering ; sacrificed first to her father's inhuman avarice, and then to the brutal indifference of husband and lover. Yet wrongs and slights to her innocent love only reveal more grandly the fortitude and strength of her soul. Père Grandet is one of Balzac's monomaniacs, a portentous figure of concentrated avarice ; and the dull and colourless existence of the miser's household makes a gloomy and hideous picture. Perhaps this is Balzac's nearest approach to a perfect work of art, his novels being as a rule lacking in composition and unity. [Also in Everyman's Lib.]

—— *The Lily of the Valley* (Le lys dans la vallée, 1835).　　　　　　　　　　　1897

The pathos of innocent suffering and self-renunciation long drawn out, in the struggle between love and duty of a pure woman, married to a bad husband, and tempted by her love for a young and amiable man. The Lily dies a martyr to her fidelity—but in spite of her saintliness she remains a strong and interesting character, and no mere idealization.

—— *The Jealousies of a Country Town, etc.* (Les rivalités—La vieille fille, 1836).　1898

The Old Maid is a comedy with grotesque characters, especially the old maid, whose misfortunes are at once ludicrous and pathetic, and her suitor, the Chevalier de Valois—a strange pair of originals. In *The Collection of Antiquities* (*Le cabinet des antiques*, 1839) a young rake commits forgery, and is saved from disgracing his aristocratic family by the influence of a certain great lady and the skill of the family notary.

BALZAC, Honoré de (*continued*). *A Bachelor's Establishment* (Les célibataires II—Un ménage de garçon en province, 1842). 1896

The Bachelor is a rich old uncle of the Bridau family, the eldest son of which contrives to marry his uncle to a pretty housekeeper, then marries her himself and inherits the property, and after a disreputable career ends his life miserably.

—— *Parisians in the Country, etc.* (Les Parisiens en province—L'illustre Gaudissart, *and* La muse du département, 1833–43). 1898

Gaudissart the Great (1833), a favourite character of Balzac's, reappears in *César Birotteau, Cousin Pons,* and elsewhere ; the present story is slight and very comic, describing how the commercial traveller and insurance agent Gaudissart is induced by a wag to try his persuasive talents on a lunatic. *The Muse of the Department* (1843) is more elaborate ; the subject largely irregular love. Many important characters are included : Lousteau, an objectionable fellow, is said to be a sketch of the critic Jules Janin. Bianchon appears in a pleasant rôle, and the women are mostly prepossessing.

—— *Ursule Mirouët* (1841). 1896

A didactic novel written specially for the young person, dealing with Swedenborgianism and clairvoyance : the innocent and pious heroine converts her guardian, who is an atheist. But in spite of the supernatural element, the novel gives a realistic picture of the placid life and uncorrupted manners of a provincial town, Nemours, the characters of a little group of amiable old men, and the meanness and greed of rapacious relatives. [Also in Everyman's Lib.]

—— *Lost Illusions* (Illusions perdues, 1837–9). 1897
—— *A Distinguished Provincial at Paris* [sequel]. 1897

Connected stories which virtually form one long novel, the most comprehensive and the most representative of any in the series, in fact an epitome of the *Comédie humaine,* entitled respectively, *Illusions perdues I, Two Poets,* and *Eve and David ;* and *Illusions perdues II* and *Un grand homme de province à Paris.* Lucien de Rubempré, a weak and dandified young author, is the central figure throughout. After scandalizing the people of Angoulême by his platonic relations with a great lady, he goes to Paris as her protégé, full of confidence about the sensation he is to make. His disillusionment begins without delay. First taken up by the Cénacle, a coterie of literary men, he is soon dropped by them, and enters upon journalism. Parisian journalism is abominably corrupt, and Lucien, after a meteoric career, goes back to his native city, ruined in money, morals, and health. His calamities also involve his blameless relatives, the young married people, Eve and David, two quiet and industrious tradespeople, a model of conjugal fidelity. This group of novels is crowded with living characters of every shade of evil and goodness. Society in the provinces and the literary and artistic world of Paris are represented with remorseless realism, and the meanness, treachery, and depravity of mankind scathingly exposed. *A Harlot's Progress* (*Splendeurs et misères des courtisanes*) is the conclusion of this long history. [(1) also in Everyman's Lib.]

SCENES OF PARISIAN LIFE

—— *The Thirteen* (Histoire des treize, 1833–4). 1898

The Thirteen are a secret brotherhood of men belonging to the most widely separated ranks and professions, and bound to each other by indissoluble ties, who make themselves into a force superior to the law—a story full of melodramatic interest. *Ferragus* (1833) celebrates conjugal love ; and *The Duchess of Langeais* (1834) narrates a woman's self-abandonment to passion, the lover's contempt, and her suicide. She is probably drawn from Balzac's quondam friend, the Duchesse de Castries, who repulsed his advances, when they became embarrassing.

—— *Old Goriot* (Le père Goriot, 1835). 1896

A grandiose example of the tendency to simplify and hyperbolize character, to reduce a personality to one overmastering passion or instinct, noted already in the *Scenes of Provincial Life.* Goriot, another of Balzac's monomaniacs, symbolizes the extravagance of paternal sacrifice : " he is the modern King Lear," impoverishing himself to give his daughters dowries, and when they are reduced to straits by their depravity, stripping himself to save them. In this pathetic figure centres a lurid spectacle of social corruption ; the most infernal and the most despicable inhabitants of the criminal world are grouped around him, and over all the grim and sinister features of the Maison Vauquer flings its malevolent shadow. (Also in Everyman's Lib.]

—— *The Rise and Fall of César Birotteau* (Histoire de la grandeur et de la décadence de César Birotteau, 1837). 1896

The career of a perfumer, with social ambitions, who speculates heavily, is robbed by his associates, and becomes a bankrupt, but has the pluck and integrity to retrieve his honour. The characters are nearly all of a wholesome kind, and César himself is an ordinary man, whose virtues and foibles are so human that he wins the reader in spite of his absurdities. The bankruptcy proceedings have often been cited as a witness to Balzac's familiarity with the intricacies of French law. [Also in Everyman's Lib.]

—— *A Princess's Secrets* (Les secrets de la princesse de Cadignan, 1838–9). 1898

A drawing-room comedy containing some of Balzac's acutest observations on social life. A queen of fashion and a great writer are the principals. The profligate, brilliant, and worldly-wise princess courts the accomplished master of theoretical wisdom—a representation of Balzac himself—thus symbolizing " the seduction of genius by experience." The other piece, *Bureaucracy* (Les employés, 1838) gives the comedy of intrigue in a public office. M. Rabourdin, head of a bureau, has a scheme for reducing the staff, and the draft is stolen by an underling. The plots and counterplots are very amusing. The heroine is Madame Rabourdin, who makes adroit use of feminine arts to aid her spouse.

—— *A Harlot's Progress* (Splendeurs et misères des courtisanes, 1838–47). 1897

Four main episodes or connected stories concluding the history of Lucien, who at the close of the last episode had come into the power of the ruffian Vautrin : *Esther Happy : What Love Costs an Old Man* (Combien l'amour revient aux vieillards) ; *The End of Evil Ways* (Où mènent les mauvais chemins) ; *Vautrin's Last*

BALZAC, Honoré de (*continued*).

Avatar (*La dernière incarnation de Vautrin*). Lucien lives for a while in outward honour in the highest society of Paris, but at length the crimes of his accomplice involve him in ruin and ignominy, and the sole refuge is suicide. Vautrin's history is highly melodramatic : after a career of successful villainy he falls into the clutches of the law, and renouncing his associates becomes chief of police. A terrible panorama of the underworld of Paris, with its abandonment to dissipation, its crimes and miseries ; yet a picture never wholly lacking in the beauty of human kindness and purity unspotted in the midst of depravity. (See also p. 28, *Lost Illusions, etc.*). [2 vols.]

—— *The Unconscious Mummers, etc.* (Les comédiens sans le savoir, 1846). 1897
Short stories : *Les comédiens sans le savoir* (1846), *A Prince of Bohemia* (1845), *A Man of Business* (*Un homme d'affaires*), *Gaudissart II* (1844), *The Firm of Nucingen* (*La maison Nucingen*) containing a remarkable dialogue in which four accomplished scandalmongers tear Parisian society to tatters. *Facino Cane* is a notable Balzacian example of a whole romance compressed into one episode. The Venetian prince, introduced as a poor blind musician in Paris, is an incarnation of the lust for gold, one of those preternatural developments of a single passion in which Balzac delights.

—— *Cousin Betty* (Les parents pauvres I.—La cousine Bette, 1846). 1897
A repulsive picture of the corrupt life of Paris, harsh in its portrayal of infamous types, and the realistic exposure of lust and greed, passion, hatred, and jealousy, obscurely working together beneath the surface. The Baron Hulot is a tragic example of sensuality ruining character and breaking up the family. His mistress, Mme Marneffe, has become a synonym for the rapacious courtesan. Leslie Stephen said of Balzac, " Paris is a hell ; but hell is the only place worth living in." Adeline Hulot and her daughter Hortense are, nevertheless, delicate types of womanhood. In the peasant woman, Cousine Bette, the author shows us the poor relation overwhelmed with injuries and indignities and meanly avenging the offences to her vanity.

—— *Cousin Pons* (Les parents pauvres II.—Le cousin Pons, 1847). 1897
Exposes the selfishness, vanity, and corruption of Parisian life with the same relentless realism, in the lower social world of the minor theatres, lodging-house keepers, curiosity shops, poor artists, and bohemians. Over against this sordid section of society is set the beautiful friendship of two old musicians, the sentimental Schmucke and Cousin Pons. Much artistic interest : Pons is a virtuoso who, in spite of poverty, has collected a treasury of beautiful things, and these Balzac describes with the gusto of a connoisseur. [Also in Everyman's Lib.]

—— *The Middle Classes* (Les petits bourgeois, 1856–7). 1899
Said to have been finished by Charles Rabou, but probably not his work to any large extent. A study of the bourgeois classes of Paris, minute in its account of municipal affairs, and the colossal complications of a petty intrigue. One of the longest novels in the *Comédie humaine.*

SCENES OF POLITICAL LIFE

—— *A Gondreville Mystery* (Une ténébreuse affaire, 1841). 1898
A tragic story with an intricate mystery-plot, concerned with a Royalist conspiracy against Napoleon. With its collapse the police are hot on the scent of aristocrats. The plots and counterplots of the police and a devoted bailiff, allied with a kinswoman who reminds one of Scott's Di Vernon, are thrilling. Her interview with Napoleon on the field of Jena reaches the sublime. *An Episode of the Terror* (1831) is an affecting little anecdote of some Royalists in Paris and their strange encounter with an arch-enemy.

—— *The Seamy Side of History* (L'envers de l'histoire contemporaine, 1846–8). 1897
Contains two episodes in the history of a Brotherhood of Consolation, a secret society of men joined together for the purpose of remedying the evils which society neglects. In one, the father and son of an invalid lady endure the extremes of want in order to maintain her in the aristocratic luxury she was used to before the Revolution. Madame de la Chanterie, persecuted and outraged, yet never failing in faith and fortitude, is the most sublime figure in the *Comédie humaine. Z. Marcas* (1840)—strange anticipation of Gambetta, both in character and history, as Anatole de la Forge pointed out—is a brief psychological study of a politician, a man possessed of one idea and absolutely incorruptible and indefatigable in pursuit of it.

—— *The Member for Arcis* (Le député d'Arcis, 1847). 1898
A posthumous novel, completed by Charles Rabou. Minute and quietly faithful portraiture of provincial folk, belonging to the set of studies originating in Balzac's visits to Champagne and the neighbouring departments.

SCENES OF MILITARY LIFE

—— *The Chouans* (Les Chouans ; ou, la Bretagne en 1799, 1829). 1896
An essay in historical romance as written by Scott. Deals with the Royalist struggle in Brittany in 1799, the facts of which Balzac carefully investigated on the spot. Hence the local colour is first-rate. He did not take sides, and the thievish Chouans are not in any way idealized. Balzac made his story centre in an exciting love-drama, and so won a first success after those pseudonymous romances of his which are now forgotten. (Originally called *Le dernier Chouan ; ou, la Bretagne en* 1800.) [Also in Everyman's Lib.]

SCENES OF COUNTRY LIFE

—— *The Country Doctor* (Le médecin de campagne, 1833). 1896
A minute description of country life in the hilly region about Grenoble ; the agricultural doings, the wretchedness of the peasantry, and M. Benassis' persevering attempts to ameliorate their condition, furnish a good example of Balzac's indefatigable realism. In this practical philanthropist, the reformed sinner who becomes a public benefactor, an ideal figure is created, a great soul, unselfish, full of love for man, unconquerably patient. Balzac said of his patient labour that it was the Gospel in action. [Also in Everyman's Lib.]

—— *The Country Parson* (Le curé de village, 1839). 1896
In this novel the subject is very similar—country life and a man's efforts to improve the lot of the peasantry. A good deal of melodramatic interest is intermixed. [Also in Everyman's Lib.]

PHILOSOPHICAL STUDIES

BALZAC, Honoré de (*continued*). *The Wild Ass's Skin* (La peau de chagrin, 1831).   1896
One of Balzac's flights of pure imagination, yet one of his gravest commentaries on human life. The allegory of a miraculous piece of shagreen which gives the owner certain powers of self-gratification, but is also the measure of his life. Balzac is essentially a materialist and a determinist. In all his studies of social life, he represents man as governed and controlled by the circumstances of his world. At the same time, there is a mystical side to his philosophy, and he feels that the fundamental viciousness of man's nature needs to be restrained by the fear of retribution. [Also in Everyman's Lib.]

—— *Seraphita* (Séraphita, 1834–5) (1831–5).   1897
A mystical story inspired by Mme Guyon and Swedenborg—a study of the destiny of the soul, and of the power of unbounded faith. *Louis Lambert* (1832) is peculiarly interesting as being founded on facts in the writer's life ; Louis Lambert is Balzac, who actually wrote the essay. *On the Will*, a study of a great intellect in a feeble body, and of the ravages that result, is full of semi-scientific speculation. *The Exiles* (Les proscrits, 1831) introduces Dante.

—— *The Unknown Masterpiece, etc.* (Le chef-d'œuvre inconnu, 1831) (1831–5).   1896
All early works, full of power and freshness, philosophical only in that they go below the surface of things, and evoke deeper thoughts and feelings. *Christ in Flanders* (1831) is an apologue : a miracle appearing to a chance gathering of rich and poor sifts and separates the simple and full of faith from the sophisticated and spiritually blind. *Farewell* (*Adieu*, 1830) gives a vivid picture of war—the retreat from Moscow— and a portrayal of a woman crazed by suffering and horror, finding in animal insensibility repose from human agony. *El Verdugo* (1831) is a harrowing episode of the French occupation of Spain : a son compelled to be the executioner of his family ; and *The Conscript* (Le réquisitionnaire, 1831), a touching little drama in one act—a tragedy wrought by the Terror. In *A Seaside Tragedy* (*Un drame au bord de la mer*, 1834) a father justifiably kills his own son. *The Red House* (L'auberge rouge, 1831) is a Gothic romance, tempered with humour ; and *The Elixir of Life* (L'elixir de longue vie, 1831), a terrifying story of a voluptuary, Don Juan Belvidéro, who believes he is to have a second span of life given him for repentance, but is caught in his own trap ; grimly ironical in its satire of human avidity. *Les Marana* (1832) and *Melmoth Reconciled* (1835) are sombre little pieces. [*Christ in Flanders, and other stories* is in Everyman's Lib.]

—— *A Father's Curse, etc.* (L'enfant maudit, 1831) (1831–9).   1898
A grim story of a far-off age. In *Gambara* (compare with *Cousin Pons*), a wild and visionary musical genius is studied with equal sympathy and knowledge of the art. Music is again the theme in *Massimilla Doni* (1839), a rich fantasy, played out in modern Venice, its grandiose symbolism representing the gradual dehumanizing of man's nature by excessive indulgence in pleasure. Also *Maître Cornelius*, 1832.

—— *The Quest of the Absolute* (La recherche de l'absolu, 1834).   1896
A similar metaphysical study, but lacking the romantic interest. Subject, a modern alchemist, who sacrifices himself and his family to his belief in the philosopher's stone. The home and surroundings of the man, and the details of his scientific labours, are drawn with characteristic minuteness, and two admirable types of womanly virtue and affection are portrayed in his wife and daughter. [Also in Everyman's Lib.]

—— *About Catherine de' Medici* (Sur Catherine de Medici, 1843).   1897
A study of that powerful individuality, the unscrupulous queen of Henry II, contemporary with the Sieur de Balzac, Seigneur d'Entragues, from whom the author claimed descent. [Also in Everyman's Lib.]

—— *The Peasantry* (Les paysans, 1844).   1896
An account, veracious and sympathetic, of the life of the peasant (Balzac had lived in a country town most of his life), far from attractive in its presentation of the greed and land-hunger of the better class, and of the brutality, lawlessness, and immorality prevailing among the poorer. A wealthy count tries to establish himself on a fine estate, but arouses the hostility of the country-side, and is eventually driven by accumulated annoyances to leave the district. [Transl. by Ellen MARRIAGE, Clara BELL, and James WARING ; ed. by G. SAINTSBURY, 40 vols., ea. with 3 etchings ; Dent (Dutton, New York), 1895–9 ; new ed., 18 vols., Bigelow Brown, New York ; 15 vols. indicated above are reissued in Everyman's Lib., Dent (Dutton, New York) ; transl. by Katherine Prescott WORMELEY, 40 vols., Roberts, Boston : o.p. ; new ed., 35 vols., Little & Brown, Boston. Caxton Edn., 53 vols., Caxton Pub. Co., 1909 : o.p. The dates given above are those of the translations in Dent's edition ; most of the novels had been translated previously.]

BANDAMANNA SAGA: *the story of the banded men.*   1890
" The latest of the independent Icelandic sagas." " The Icelandic Sagas—the prose-histories of the fortunes of the great Icelandic houses—are the last, and also the finest, expression and record of the spirit and the ideas belonging properly to the Germanic race in its own right, and not derived from Rome or Christendom." This is a comedy, the only complete example among the sagas. The story of a great lawsuit, or, as the translators put it, " the greatest legal conspiracy known in the time of the Icelandic commonwealth " ; a singularly sarcastic narrative of greed and chicanery, with caustic personal sketches. Throws a searching light on the Icelandic legal system and the way the later nobles utilized its forms as instruments of private aggrandizement, whilst the spirit of the law was despised and flouted. Scene in N. Iceland (*c.* 1050–60). " An essentially plebeian story." There are two recensions of the text, (*a*) Northern, end of thirteenth to middle of fourteenth century, ed. by H. FRIDRIKSSON, Copenhagen (1852), and (*b*) Western, beginning of fifteenth century, ed. by G. J. C. CEDERSCHIOLD, Lund (1874). [Transl. by William MORRIS and Eiríkr MAGNÚSSON ; with *Howard the Halt* and *Hen Thorir*, (Saga Lib.), Quaritch.]

BANDELLO, Matteo [Italian ; 1480–1562]. *Le Novelle* (1554–73).   1890
Bandello, Bishop of Agen, was the most important of the Italian *novellieri*. His *novella* is a popular story, akin to the French *fabliau*, full of spirited action, and true to the life of his time, a dissolute period. The subjects and manner of treatment are extremely various, tragic and comic, romantic and amatory, with rather clumsy satire of the clergy, well exemplified by several in Pinkerton's selection. He constantly boasts that they are founded on fact, and the actual incidents introduced are said to have been very offensive to many families of high rank. His stories, of which there were something like two hundred, abound in

BANDELLO, Matteo (*continued*).

powerful dramatic situations, of which the Elizabethan playwrights made excellent use ; but as a rule they are singularly empty of personal character. The Venetian romance of *Gerardo and Elena*, Cornelio's comic adventures at Milan, Don Diego's constancy and his mistress Ginevra's stubbornness, and the grim tales of *Violante* and *Simone Turchi*, are representative stories. Noblest of all is the *Romeo and Juliet*, with the original climax, more sublimely pathetic than that adopted by Shakespeare from a French adaptation. Beaumont and Fletcher's *Triumph of Death* was founded on the tale of Violante. Many other Elizabethan plays took their plots from Bandello. [*Le Novelle*, 2 vols., E. Bari : Giuseppe Laterza, 1910. Transl. by John PAYNE, 6 vols., Villon Society ; *Twelve Stories*, selected and transl. by Percy E. PINKERTON, Nimmo, 1894 : o.p. ; *Tragical Tales*, ed. by H. HARRIS (Broadway Transl.) Routledge (Dutton, New York), 1924.]

BANG, Herman Joachim [Danish ; 1857–1912]. *Ida Brandt* (Ludvigsbakke, 1896). 1928

A story told almost entirely in dialogue. Out of the stream of small-talk emerge two figures, Ida, nurse in a mental hospital, and a young doctor, a feckless person to whom she is too generous, and who deserts her. [Transl. by A. G. CHATER, Knopf, New York and London.]

BANGS, John Kendrick [American ; 1862–1922]. *A House-boat on the Styx.* 1896

—— *The Pursuit of the House-boat : further account of the doings of the Associated Shades under the leadership of Sherlock Holmes, Esq.* [sequel]. 1897

Shakespeare, Mozart, Dr. Johnson, Delilah, Lucrezia Borgia, Barnum, Artemus Ward, and Pheidias are among the *dramatis personæ* of these absurdities. [(1) and (2), Harper, New York and London.]

BANIM, John [Irish ; 1798–1842]. *The Fetches.* 1825

Second of the *O'Hara Tales*, a series of novels planned with his brother Michael to do for Ireland what the Waverley novels had done for Scotland. They further proposed, " To insinuate, through fiction, the causes of Irish discontent, and to insinuate also that if crime were consequent on discontent it was no great wonder ; the conclusion to be arrived at by the reader, not by insisting on it on the part of the author, but from sympathy with the criminals." This is a characteristically sombre tale of superstition acting upon morbid imaginations. The Fetches are spirits that appear to the friends and kinsfolk of people about to die. [Duffy, Dublin : o.p.]

—— *The Boyne Water.* 1826

A very fine historical novel of the Jacobite and Williamite wars, the political and military history carefully elucidated—from the Catholic point of view—and the two kings, Sarsfield and other generals, and minor characters of the period (1685–91) vividly portrayed. Fine descriptions of the wild coasts of Antrim, and of the battle of the Boyne and siege of Limerick. [Duffy, Dublin : o.p. ; Kenedy, New York, 1865 : o.p.]

—— *The Nowlans.* 1826

A grim and painful story recounting the temptation and fall and the subsequent repentance of a young priest. Brings out strongly the mysticism and constitutional melancholy of the Celtic race. [Duffy, Dublin : o.p.]

—— *The Denounced ; or, The Last Baron of Crana.* 1826

The troubles of two Roman Catholic families after the treaty of Limerick (*c.* 1696), their persecutions by the Protestants, the doings of the Rapparees, etc. [Duffy, Dublin : o.p. ; Kenedy, New York, 1865 : o.p.]

—— *The Conformists.* 1829

Illustrates the effect of the Penal Laws under which education was denied to Roman Catholics (*c.* 1728). A disappointed lover by conforming brings disgrace on his family and ousts his father from his property. [Duffy, Dublin : o.p.]

BANIM, Michael [Irish ; 1796–1874]. *Crohoore of the Bill-hook.* 1825

One of the most popular of the *O'Hara Tales*. A tragical story of the Whiteboys, in the times (1815–25) when the unfortunate peasantry, wrung by the persecutions of tithe-proctors and penal laws, retaliated most savagely in the crimes of the secret societies. Kilkenny and neighbourhood are the scenes. [Duffy, Dublin : o.p.]

—— *The Ghost Hunter and his Family.* 1833

A complicated mystery novel of the usual melodramatic type, with good pictures of everyday life in Banim's native town, Kilkenny. [Simms and M'Intyre : o.p. ; (World-Wide Lib.), Aldine Co., 1913 : o.p., P. J. Kenedy, New York, 1865 : o.p.]

—— *The Bit o' Writing.* 1838

A collection of twenty stories, the title-piece showing the humorous side of Banim at his best and an admirable picture of peasant life. [Kenedy, New York, 1865 : o.p. Title-story, with *The Ace of Clubs*, Gill, 1886 : o.p. ; Simpkin, 1886–9 : o.p.]

—— *The Town of the Cascades.* 1864

Sets forth the dire consequences of intemperance among the peasantry in County Clare ; the town is Ennistymon, on its beautiful river-gorge near the Cliffs of Moher. [Chapman : o.p.]

BANIM, John and Michael. *John Doe ; or, The Peep o' Day.* 1825

The first of the *O'Hara Tales*, all but the first chapter written by John Banim. Story of a secret brotherhood, the Shanavests, which a young man gets mixed up with through motives of revenge (period 1808). [*Peep o' Day ; or, Savourneen Deelish*, Routledge : o.p. ; Kenedy, New York, 1865 : o.p.]

—— *The Croppy.* 1828

A careful version of the history of the 1798 rebellion, from the standpoint of a liberal Irishman, who views the horrible doings of his misguided countrymen with mingled pity and contempt. A lot of conventional novelistic business is thrown in. [Duffy, Dublin : o.p. ; Kenedy, New York, 1865 : o.p.]

—— *Father Connell.* 1840

A very winning and pathetic character-portrait of a country priest who lays down his life for the orphan boy he has befriended. Father Connell was drawn from a priest Banim knew well, and other characters from his native Kilkenny and the peasants of the neighbourhood are sketched with much kindliness and humour. [Kenedy, New York, 1865 : o.p.]

BANKES, George Nugent. *An Eton Boy's Letters.*   1901
Reproduces as nearly as is consistent with some literary form the ways of thinking, composition, and even spelling, of the average boy. The boy is shrewd and observant, and has a sense of humour; hence the journal of school life and the character-sketches are often very amusing. [o.p.]

BAṄKIMACHANDRA CHAṬṬOPĀDHYĀYA [Bengali; 1838–94]. *Kopal Kundala* (Kapala-Kundala, *c.* 1872).   1885
A romance of Bengali life some 300 years ago. [Kegan Paul: o.p.]

—— *The Poison Tree: a tale of Hindu life in Bengal* (Bisha Brikkha, 1872).   1884
Exhibits an intimate acquaintance with Hindu life and character of his own times. [Transl. by Miriam S. KNIGHT, Unwin: o.p.]

—— *Chandra Shekhar.*   1904
The adventures of a spirited girl married to a staid old Brahmin. She runs away with a rascally Englishman, but eventually returns in penitence. The Nawab and the Begum of Bengal appear (late eighteenth century). Wretchedly translated. [Luzac: o.p.]

—— *Bajani.*   1929
The romance of a blind flower-seller who turns out to be an heiress, and eventually, happily married, recovers her sight. Interesting for the account of domestic life and manners in the Bengal of last century, and the position of the woman in the household. [Transl. by P. MAJUMDAR, Book Co., Calcutta.]

BANKS, Mrs. George Linnæus [*née* Isabella Varley; 1821–97]. *God's Providence House.*   1865
A tale of 1791 and the emancipation of the slaves. Mrs. Banks lays the scenes of her novels chiefly in the neighbourhood of Chester and Manchester, the history of which she has studied with industrious research. There is a strong religious and moral bias in her domestic stories. [S. Paul: o.p.]

—— *The Manchester Man.*   1879
Based upon history " recorded and unrecorded " (1799–1831), and deals with " absolute people, events, and places "—the materials culled from various periods. The dress, the manners and speech, the details of business and manufacturing life, are studied and set down with the care of an archæologist. Contains an elaborate picture of bygone Manchester, and the Peterloo riots of 1819, with striking anecdotes and characters (e.g. the Rev. Joshua Brooks). [Abel Heywood, Mancs., 1895: o.p. *Illus.* by Green & Fitton, *id.*, 1896: o.p.]

—— *Forbidden to Wed.*   1883
The characters are chiefly Manchester tradespeople (*c.* 1778–1804), and doubtless real personages. The economic and social conditions of the town, the streets and buildings as they existed, and the domestic life are carefully portrayed. The love story of a tradesman's daughter and an officer's son forms the plot; circumstances and prejudices forbid them to wed. Chester and Buxton are the scenes partly. [Abel Heywood, Mancs.: o.p.]

—— *Bond Slaves: the story of a struggle.*   1893
A story of the Luddite agitation in the northern and midland counties, chiefly Yorkshire (1811–13), worked out with her usual elaborate care for written and oral evidence. [Griffith & Farran: o.p.]

BANKS, Mrs. Nancy Huston [American]. *Oldfield.*   1902
Life and manners in a country town in Kentucky, in the middle of last century. [Macmillan, New York and London: o.p.; Grosset, New York: o.p.]

—— *Round Anvil Rock.*   1903
Brings in several historical persons and incidents in the early days of Kentucky (time of Peter Cartwright, the Methodist preacher, the battle of Tippecanoe, etc.). Philip Alston, the noted desperado, is handled very sentimentally. [Macmillan, New York and London: o.p.]

BARBEY D'AUREVILLY, Jules Amédée [French; 1808–89]. *Bewitched* (L'ensorcelée, 1858)   1928
Barbey d'Aurevilly was an aristocrat, a conservative, and a romantic, well-read in English literature, and an admirer of Scott and Byron, as well as of his compatriot Chateaubriand. This gloomy tale, laid amidst the desolate *landes* of Cotentin, is full of echoes from *Guy Mannering*. It is theatrical, and the machinery creaks; but the scenes brought about are undoubtedly impressive. A conscience-stricken priest who has been a leader of the Chouans, and a woman cursed by a fatal passion for him, are the figures in whom tragedy centres. [Transl. by L. C. WILLCOX, Harper, London and New York.]

—— *The Diaboliques* (Les diaboliques, 1874).   1925
Tragic stories—as a character puts it, " the tragedy of hell "—by a romantic whose realistic power falls little short of Balzac's, the creator of Goriot and Vautrin. His salient characters yield themselves to furious passions that carry them headlong into crime and disaster: e.g. *A Woman's Vengeance.* The romantic fire and splendour are scarcely curbed by a grim humour and the heroic frankness of a realism undaunted by the horror of some ghastly situations. *Les dessous des cartes* and *À un dîner d'athées* are graphic pictures of Restoration manners as well as first-class examples of his dramatic story-telling. [Transl. by Ernest BOYD; introd. by Sir E. Gosse, Knopf, New York and London.]

—— *A Story without a Name* (Une histoire sans nom, 1882).   1919
Only a little longer than one of the *Diaboliques*, this recounts a mysterious domestic tragedy and its dreadful *dénouement*. Barbey d'Aurevilly, as usual, takes great pains with the setting, the cliff-girt township of Forez in the Cevennes, and a lonely château in Cotentin. The villain of the piece, a sacrilegious priest who turns bandit during the Revolution, is reminiscent of *L'ensorcelée.* [Transl. Brentano, New York.]

BARBUSSE, Henri [French; *b.* 1875]. *The Inferno* (L'enfer, 1906).   1918
Zolaesque studies of various people in the next room by a man who watches and listens through a chink in the wall. Loose-knit and unequal in quality, the prevailing tone sombre and despairing. Peasants, children, an estranged husband and wife, a dying man and a priest, an old doctor, are among the subjects inspected and anatomized. [An abridged transl. by Edward J. O'BRIEN, Boni, New York: o.p.]

BARBUSSE, Henri (*continued*). *We Others : stories of fate, love, and pity* (Nous autres, 1914). 1918

Favourable examples of the logical force combined with intensity of feeling, but no sentimentality, of these tales and sketches are *Immobility, The Green Spectre, The Funeral March, Saar, The Mother, The Most,* and *The Name.* [Transl. by W. Fitzwater WRAY, Dent.]

—— *Under Fire : the story of a squad* (Le feu : journal d'une escouade, 1916). 1917

A powerful and famous example of the excessively " realistic " school of war-novelists, insisting on the more repellent aspects of trench-warfare—the filth, the vermin, the stench, the charnel-house horrors. [Transl. by W. Fitzwater WRAY, Dent ; *id.,* Everyman's Lib. ; with *Light,* Dent, (Dutton, New York), 1929.]

—— *Light* (Clarté, 1919). 1919

A counterblast to d'Annunzio's imperialist and internationalist propaganda. In the mental awakening of a smug, dispirited clerk, a typical lower middle-class Frenchman, who becomes a *poilu,* the author symbolizes the new light—detection of the old shams and the old tyrannies, a simpler outlook on life, the hope of universal peace and brotherhood. [Transl. by W. Fitzwater WRAY, Dent ; *v.* also *Under Fire, supra.*]

BARCLAY, John [1582–1621]. *Argenis ; or, The Loves of Poliarchus and Argenis.* 1611

An allegory with political double-meanings grafted on to the romance of gallantry and heroism, such as was coming into vogue in France. Barclay reconstructs the map of Europe, and, bestowing classical names on the leading personages of the religious wars, weaves an elaborate and perplexing romance full of surprises and occult significations. Sicily represents France ; Poliarchus, Henry IV ; Usinulca, Calvin ; Hyanisbe, Queen Elizabeth ; the Hyperaphanii, the Huguenots ; etc. [Transl. by Kingsmill LONG, folio, Lond., 1625 ; transl. into English—the prose by Sir Robert Le GRYS, kt., and the verses by Thos. MAY, esquire, Lond., 1628 ; *The Phœnix, or the History of Polyarchus and Argenis ;* transl. from Latin (by Clara Reeve), 4 vols., London, 1771, all o.p. ; seventeenth-century Latin editions abound, many in the Elzevir format.]

BARING, Hon. Maurice [*b.* 1874]. *A Triangle : passages from three notebooks.* 1923

The domestic drama in which the five principal characters, a charming and high-spirited woman temperamentally unsuited to her scholarly husband, a painter, and a neighbour of crude, strong character separated from his wife, are involved, is revealed to us through the notebooks of three independent observers in turn. [Heinemann ; Doubleday, New York.]

—— *C.* 1924

The biography of a young man who promised literary genius : from nursery, preparatory school, introduction to the world of books, Oxford, to his attempts at diplomacy, the Bar, journalism, etc. The account of his literary enthusiasms is charming, and the austere taste of his critical friend Burstall bracing. C.'s last years are saddened by his vacillation between two women, one of them a modern Lesbia. [2 vols., Heinemann ; Doubleday, New York.]

—— *Cat's Cradle.* 1925

High society in Rome, London, and all over Europe through a long stretch of the last century, depicted with enormous prolixity in the story of an Englishwoman married to a very rich Italian prince. The jealous prince and his argus-eyed mother almost worry her into unfaithfulness, and the end is disaster. But there is still an immense amount of sentimental analysis, of many pairs of thwarted, or clandestine, and a few more fortunate lovers. [Heinemann ; *illus.* by Daphne Baring, Doubleday, New York.]

—— *Half-a-Minute's Silence ; and other stories.* 1925

The first part consists of ten stories of Russian life, written before the war ; the title-story records the thoughts of a house-party in the brief silence preceding departure ; *Dirge in Marriage* is about a tragic peasant marriage ; *The Governor's Niece* is a female anarchist of 1906. The rest are varied, ranging from *The Alternative,* in which we have glimpses of Napoleon, Wordsworth, Shelley, etc., as they might have been had circumstances been different, to *The Thief,* a little satire upon schoolmasters. [Heinemann ; Doubleday, New York.]

—— *Daphne Adeane.* 1926

Daphne is dead before the story begins, but her beauty, her intelligence, and something of her personality seem to be reincarnated in the heroine, who marries too hurriedly a man who is still in love with another woman, whence much misunderstanding and philanderings with others before they become true man and wife. Told in enormously diffuse conversations, and with some wholesome casuistry from a Roman Catholic priest. [Heinemann ; Harper, New York.]

—— *Tinker's Leave.* 1927

A young Englishman goes to Russia as a Press correspondent at the time of the Russo-Japanese war—witnesses a battle, falls in love with a nurse, talks interminably with the Russian officers. The story, however, is but a peg upon which to hang the author's own impressions of Russia and Manchuria, and many arguments carried on by a cosmopolitan set of characters ranging over poetry, music, and religion. [Heinemann ; Doubleday, Doran, New York.]

—— *Comfortless Memory.* 1928

A tender and moving story of a young painter's idyll in Rome with a woman who had formerly been the mistress of another. He is separated from her by the intervention of old friends, and she dies of grief. [Heinemann ; *sub tit. When They Love,* Doubleday, Doran, New York.]

—— *The Coat without Seam.* 1929

The coat bequeathed by Christ to the Roman soldiers is like Christopher's life—a life without seam. This difficult person is marked out for disillusionment ; he fails in love, in literature, in most things. Incidentally, we are taken to Constantinople, Petrograd, and Rome, and entertained to well-informed conversations on international politics, religion, and many other topics. [Heinemann ; Knopf, New York.]

BARING, Hon. Maurice (*continued*). *Robert Peckham.* 1930

Peckham is a loyal Englishman and also a devout Catholic who cannot accept the Reformation, is exercised in spirit by his father's adherence to the policy of the Crown, is tragically wedded, and in old age exiles himself to Rome. The story, which covers the latter years of Henry VIII and the earlier of Elizabeth, is too restrained and unimpassioned, and certainly too much of an apologia. [Heinemann ; Knopf, New York.]

BARLAAM AND JOSAPHAT. 1896

A book of enormous interest to students of folk-lore and of the successive transformations of apologues and other stories in their passage from language to language. Eastern in origin, its first appearance in literature being in Greek, among the writings of John of Damascus (a Syrian monk of the eighth century). Through the Latin, it was adapted in metrical or prose form into most European languages, appearing as *The Lyf of Saynt Balaam* in Caxton's edition of the *Golden Legend* (1483). A Middle English prose version was printed in a prospectus by Dr. C. HORSTMANN in 1877 (see Jacob's *Barlaam and Josaphat*). It is a Christianized version of the history of Gautama, the Buddha, with whom Josaphat, son of the persecuting King Abenner, has been identified. Josaphat, it has been predicted, will acquire glory in another kingdom and adopt the faith persecuted by his father. He is brought up in strictest seclusion, and only after a time learns of the ills to which humanity is liable : disease, poverty, and death. He hears of the Christian religion from the eremite Barlaam, who in the disguise of a merchant teaches him the true faith and the blessedness of celibacy. Associated in the Government with his father, he spreads Christianity, and after Abenner's death surrenders the crown, retiring to the desert to commune with Barlaam, whom he buries, and at length, after some years, himself passes away. An important feature of the work is the number of parables related by Barlaam. These are found in the *Kalilah ve Dimnah*, etc., and have been adapted by innumerable story-tellers. The most famous (through the *Speculum Hystoriale* of Vincent de Beauvais) is the casket story utilized in the *Merchant of Venice* ; but the provenance and subsequent history of the main and the subsidiary stories are questions that have yielded a literature of their own, the best compendium of which is J. Jacobs' *Barlaam and Josaphat, English Lives of Buddha* [Nutt, 1896], where Caxton's version is reprinted. The Ethiopic version of the legend has been edited, with an English transl., by Sir E. A. WALLIS BUDGE. [2 vols., Cambridge Press (Macmillan, New York), 1923.]

BARLOW, Jane [Irish ; 1860–1917]. *Irish Idylls.* 1892

Detached sketches of life among the poor cottars in a moorland hamlet in Connaught, rendering with sober fidelity the character, the manners, and emotions of these people of restricted life but large imagination, oppressed with poverty, but full of hope, deeply religious and trustful in Providence. Widow M'Gurk, Ody Rafferty, Mrs. Kilfoyle, and Father Rooney are drawn with subtle penetration and much quiet humour. The sadness of the picture is further lightened by the sensitive eye which sees the dignity of poverty and the goodness and charity that may dwell in lowly hearts. This and the later stories are remarkable for their pure, pellucid, and refined prose. [Hodder : o.p. ; Dodd & Mead, New York, 1917 : o.p.]

—— *Kerrigan's Quality.* 1893

Similar sketches, connected by a slight plot, the strange and dramatic chain of circumstances by which a girl learns the dreadful fate of her missing lover. There is much humour in the judgments passed by village gossips on their pet aversion, Kerrigan, an enriched peasant returned from Australia, who entertains a family of quality. [Hodder : o.p.]

—— *Strangers at Lisconnel.* 1895

Rather more genial stories about the Bogland, which Miss Barlow depicts with so much of the poetry of landscape, adding some fresh characters to those introduced in *Irish Idylls*, the most delightful of which is the poor old hedge-schoolmaster, Mr. Polymathers. The selection still remains very narrow, however, omitting such characteristic types as the Irish priest, the money-lender, and the agitator. [Hodder : o.p.]

—— *Maureen's Fairing ; and other stories.* 1895

Eight little stories, chiefly of life in Ballyhoy, a pleasanter place than Lisconnel. [Dent ; Macmillan, New York : o.p.]

—— *Mrs. Martin's Company ; and other stories.* 1896

Seven stories, chiefly of a light and humorous kind, very tender in their sketching of poor, refined, good-hearted people. Mrs. Martin is a devout old soul living in an out-of-the-way spot, to whom a sort of latter-day miracle happens, quite credibly, of course, with the result that she gets no lack of company to cheer her loneliness. *A Very Light Railway* is a touching sketch of child-life, and *A Case of Conscience* a police-court comedy. [Dent (Macmillan, New York) : o.p.]

—— *A Creel of Irish Stories.* 1897

The Keys of the Jest tells how a myth grows up in a child's mind, the sketch of the little girl and the household of broken-down gentry drawn with characteristic tenderness ; *The Snakes and Norah* is a little tragi-comedy of a peasant girl's temptation and the monster born of remorse ; *Three Pint Measures*, a comic sketch of low life ; and *A Proud Woman*, a humorous character-portrait of an old Irishwoman, a poor huckster with the pride of a duchess. Half a dozen sketches of the same West Irish peasantry. [Methuen : o.p. ; Dodd & Mead, New York : o.p.]

—— *From the East unto the West.* 1898

Nine stories about the Lisconnel folk, and six Oriental tales curiously resembling her Irish tales in many features. *The Puzzle of Jarbek* is an excellent sample of her story-telling, a fearsome but comic adventure with a lion in the desert. [Methuen : o.p.]

—— *From the Land of the Shamrock.* 1901

Delicate interpretations of Irish character in the form of brief anecdotes, evoking the fatalism and the poetry so deeply rooted in the Celtic peasant. [Methuen : o.p. ; Dodd & Mead, New York : o.p.]

—— *The Founding of Fortunes.* 1902

The story of a scapegrace boy in a bog-cabin who steals a purse, and by persistence and an eye to the main chance gets rich. Some of the folk reappear from *Kerrigan's Quality*. [Methuen : o.p. ; Dodd & Mead, New York : o.p.]

BARLOW, Jane (*continued*). *By Beach and Bogland: a book of Irish stories.* 1905
—— *Irish Neighbours.* 1907
Two collections of characteristic stories—seventeen apiece. [(1) Unwin: o.p.; (2), Hutchinson: o.p.]
—— *Irish Ways.* 1909
A story like *Ourselves and Our Island* gives a kind of conspectus of the Irish question, in so far as it is a problem of racial character. The other stories are much in the accustomed vein, portraying the finer qualities of the poorest peasants in the West, and bringing out with subtle and poetic insight the unobtrusive beauties of the desolate bogland. In all these tales the dialect is reproduced with the most scrupulous pains. [*Illus.*, Allen: o.p.]
—— *Mac's Adventures.* 1911
A pretty character-portrait of an idolized child—Irish, of course. She cuts a figure in eight stories. [Hutchinson: o.p.]
—— *Flaws.* 1911
A very elaborate but otherwise very characteristic novel, with characters from the genteel and the peasant classes. [Hutchinson: o.p.]
—— *Doings and Dealings.* 1913
Thirteen stories of the peasants; they show a relative falling off. [Hutchinson: o.p.]
—— *In Mio's Youth.* 1917
A novel published after the author's death. It has an intricate and not very well-knit plot, and is about a decaying landed family, with a medley of sons and daughters and a sensitive and imaginative adopted child. [Hutchinson: o.p.]

BARMBY, Beatrice Helen [*d.* 1904]. *Rosslyn's Raid; and other tales.* 1903
A fierce saga of Border fighting in Elizabethan times. Rosslyn—the reckless, chivalrous Border lord—though sketched in such brief compass, is a creation of extraordinary vigour. Also two shorter tales, of which *The Slave of Lagash* takes us back to ancient Chaldæa. [Duckworth: o.p.]

BARNES, James [American; *b.* 1866]. *For King or Country.* 1896
Twin brothers in a Tory family in New Jersey; one remains a Loyalist, the other joins the patriots. [*Illus.*, Harper, New York.]
—— *Yankee Ships and Yankee Sailors.* 1897
Thirteen romantic episodes occurring on the ships that fought in the war of 1812, by the author of *Naval Actions of War in* 1812. [Macmillan, New York; *illus.*, *id.*, 1928.]
—— *A Loyal Traitor.* 1897
An excellent boys' story of the war of 1812, the hero a waif from Connecticut, who sees fighting on a privateer, is captured and sent to Dartmoor, but escapes. [Harper, New York.]
—— *Drake and his Yeomen.* 1899
" A true account of the character and adventures of Sir Francis Drake as told by Sir Matthew Maunsell his friend and follower " (*c.* 1572–88). [Macmillan, New York and London.]
—— *Midshipman Farragut.* 1902
Two years of the future admiral's boy life with Commodore Porter (1812–14). [(Young Heroes of our Navy), Appleton, New York.]

" BARNETT, John " [John Reginald Stagg]. *The Rebel Lady.* 1915
The story of Grania, chieftainess of the O'Malleys, prominent in the Irish wars of Elizabeth. Introduces Raleigh and Essex (1589–1601). [Nisbet: o.p.]

BAROJA, Pío [Spanish (Basque); *b.* 1872]. *The Lord of Labraz* (El Mayorazgo de Labraz, 1902). 1926
Good in the picturing of a little town in the Cantabrian Alps, and of an impoverished but still ostentatious hildalgo. The second volume of a trilogy, *Tierra Vasca*, the remaining volumes of which, *La Casa de Aizgorri* (1900) and *Zalacaín el Aventurero* (1909), have not been translated. [Transl. by Aubrey F. G. BELL, Knopf, New York and London.]
—— *The City of the Discreet.* 1917
Depicts the social and political life of Cordova some fifty years ago. [Transl. by Jacob S. FASSETT, Knopf, New York.]
—— *The Quest* (La Busca, 1904). 1922
—— *Red Dawn* (Aurora Roja, 1904). 1924
—— *Weeds* (Mala Hierba, 1904). 1923
Together these form a trilogy, *The Struggle for Life* (*La Lucha por la Vida*), which is a dispassionate unveiling of the depravity and filth of the scum of Madrid. The story tells of the adventures of a young man from the country who is soon corrupted to the level of the dissolute life which surrounds him in the city; in many scenes and incidents, full of vigorous description, we meet all types of rogue, vagabond, and social outcast. [Transl. by Isaac GOLDBERG, Knopf, New York; *id.*, London, 1926.]
—— *Cæsar or Nothing* (César ó Nada, 1910). 1919
Cæsar Monçada sets out to reform and modernize Spain, meets with steady opposition from the Church, and at length subsides into an ordinary country gentleman. A dry and unemotional book, enlarging on the view that Spain requires iron discipline from a competent individual. [Transl. by Louis How, Knopf, New York and London (1922).]
—— *The Tree of Knowledge* (El Arbol de la Sienca Novela, 1911). 1928
Portrays the life of an unsuccessful medical student in Madrid, and the life of the poor of that city. [Transl. by Aubrey BELL, Knopf, London and New York.]

BARR, Amelia Edith [*née* Huddleston; Scottish born, American by adoption; 1831–1919]. *Jan Vedder's Wife.* 1885

A story of the Shetland Isles and the primitive inhabitants, descendants of the Norsemen, and of their homely and picturesque life. The motive is incompatibility of temperament between a correct wife and a good-tempered, unstable husband. [Dodd & Mead, New York; Warne: o.p.; J. Clarke: o.p.]

—— *Between Two Loves.* 1886

A touching story of rural life in the West Riding, permeated with a kindly sense of the inherent goodness of human nature. The cotton-spinner, loving his employees, loving his mills, widely sympathetic, is the most important character. [Dodd & Mead, New York: o.p.; Barse & Hopkins, New York: o.p.; Warne: o.p.; J. Clarke: o.p.]

—— *A Daughter of Fife.* 1886

Life and character in a Scotch fishing village; the hearty and deeply religious people are drawn with simplicity and without analysis. [Dodd & Mead, New York: o.p.; Warne: o.p.; J. Clarke: o.p.]

—— *Paul and Christina.* 1887

A picture of the rude weather-beaten fishermen of the Orkneys, and the wild surroundings of their life; and their fierce and often heroic struggles with circumstances and with temptation. [Dodd & Mead, New York: o.p.; J. Clarke: o.p.]

—— *Master of his Fate.* 1888

A small group of strongly accentuated, racy Yorkshire natives; a man fails to win happiness by marrying an heiress, but attains it and his own self-respect by a manly effort to make his fortune. [Dodd & Mead. New York: o.p.; Rand, New York: o.p.; *sub tit. In Spite of Himself: a tale of the West Riding*, J. Clarke: o.p.]

—— *The Bow of Orange Ribbon.* 1888

The old Dutch folk of New York, sturdy, quiet, and godly folk, and the rakish and dare-devil soldiery of King George just before the War of Independence (1756). A Dutch maiden's love for one of the most hare-brained of the young Englishmen is the motive. [Dodd & Mead, New York; J. Clarke: o.p.]

—— *The Maid of Maiden Lane* [sequel]. 1900

The year 1791 in New York City—a momentous year, in which the question whether New York or Philadelphia should be the seat of government led to many hot discussions. The death of Franklin, the large influx of French refugees, and the division of opinion regarding English rights in the lost colonies, enter into the story. [Dodd & Mead, New York; Unwin: o.p.]

—— *Remember the Alamo.* 1888

A tale of the revolt of the Americans in Texas against Mexican rule (1836). Davy Crockett, Sam Houston, and Santa Anna figure prominently; and the storming of the Alamo is the chief incident. [Dodd & Mead, New York.]

—— *Friend Olivia.* 1890

An historical study of Quaker life in the early days of Cromwell, favouring the Puritans and severe towards the Cavaliers. Cromwell and the men of his party, such as Baron Keldar, George Fox, and Olivia's father, the religious enthusiast Prideaux, are well portrayed, while the other side is represented by caricatures. [Dodd & Mead, New York; J. Clarke: o.p.]

—— *Bernicia.* 1894

A study of the hopes and disappointments, the social and political forces, of the period after the Jacobite outbreak of 1745. The great Methodist Revival takes a prominent place, and Whitefield is introduced (1748). [Dodd & Mead, New York: o.p.; Pearson: o.p.; Melrose: o.p.]

—— *A Knight of the Nets.* 1894

A sentimental, optimistic story of fisher-folk in a Fifeshire village, and of a neighbouring family of the land-owning class connected with them by the son's ill-fated marriage with a poor girl. [Dodd & Mead, New York: o.p.]

—— *Trinity Bells.* 1899

Tranquil, idyllic pictures of life in New York a century ago, connected into a narrative of family life. The heroine's father is captured by Algerian pirates, and this episode is the sole exception to the sobriety of the tale. [Dodd & Mead, New York; *illus.* by C. M. Relyea, Grossett, New York: o.p.; Unwin: o.p.]

—— *Was it Right to Forgive?* 1900

The unhappy domestic life of a pair of married couples, son and daughter of a Dutch Calvinist family on the one hand, daughter and son of grand New York people on the other. The two children of old Filmer are unfaithful and dissolute, while the Dutch wife and husband bear and forgive and win happiness for all in the end. [International Pub. Co., Chicago: o.p.; Unwin: o.p.]

—— *The Black Shilling.* 1904

Witchcraft trials at Salem and Boston, and the savage crusade of Cotton Mather and his father (1691–2). [Dodd & Mead, New York: o.p.; Unwin: o.p.]

—— *The Belle of Bowling Green.* 1906

A simple and quiet picture of life among the wealthy Dutch inhabitants of New York, who lived aloof from the war (1812–14), and yet were not unaffected by it. [Dodd & Mead, New York; Long: o.p.]

—— *The Strawberry Handkerchief: a romance of the Stamp Act.* 1908

The same people and scenes half a century before, at the time of the Stamp Act (1765). [Dodd & Mead, New York: o.p.; J. Clarke: o.p.]

—— *The House on Cherry Street.* 1909

The same in George II's time (1732–4) in the glory of its English colonial life, and the palmy days, also, of slavery and piracy. [Dodd & Mead, New York; Laurie: o.p.]

BARR, Robert [Scots-Canadian; 1850–1912]. *In the Midst of Alarms.* 1894

A journalist's love-story, illustrating Canadian country life at the time of a threatened Fenian invasion from the United States. [Methuen: o.p.; Stokes, New York.]

BARR, Robert (*continued*). *The Countess Tekla.*   1898
Adventures on the Rhine borders (*c.* 1273–91) ; the heroine a high-spirited countess who, after many perils, is wooed and won by an emperor in disguise. [Methuen : o.p. ; Stokes, New York : o.p.]

—— *The Strong Arm.*   1900
Brief tales of action, chiefly in mediæval Germany ; the Prince-Bishop of Trèves appears again, with other fighting prelates, and that sinister tribunal the *Vehmgericht* of Westphalia plays a dramatic part. *Converted* is grimly humorous ; the *Warrior Maid* is a story of Nelson. [Methuen : o.p. ; Stokes, New York : o.p.]

—— *A Prince of Good Fellows.*   1902
Eleven spirited stories about that versatile personality James V, the Scottish Haroun al Raschid, poet, etc. [Chatto.]

—— *Cardillac.*   1909
A romance of the early part of Louis XIII's reign (1617–18), introducing the Queen-Mother, Marie de Médicis, etc. [Mills & Boon : o.p. ; Stokes, New York : o.p. ; Grossett, New York : o.p.]

—— *The Swordmaker.*   1910
Frankfort and the predatory Rhine barons of the fourteenth century. [Mills & Boon : o.p. ; Grossett, New York : o.p.]

BARRÈS, Maurice [French ; 1862–1923]. *Colette Baudoche* (Les bastions de l'Est ; Colette Baudoche : histoire d'une jeune fille de Metz, 1909).   1919
A testament to Barrès' uncompromising nationalism. Colette, a fair young French girl in Metz, loves and is loved by a worthy German, but sacrifices him and herself on the altar of patriotism. [Transl. by F. W. HUARD ; Doran, New York : o.p.]

—— *The Sacred Hill* (La colline inspirée, 1913).   1929
The history of three enthusiastic priests, Léopold Baillard and his two brothers, inspired with mystical ideas, who in Lorraine during the eighteen-thirties set up a religious organization which ultimately came under the ban of the Church. [Transl. by Malcolm COWLEY ; Macauley, New York.]

BARRETT, Eaton Stannard [Irish ; 1786–1820]. *The Heroine ; or, The Adventures of Cherubina.*   1813
A burlesque attack on the blood-curdling romances fashionable at the time. Cherubina is crazed by reading these, disowns her yeoman father, adopts a high-flown name, and has many mirthful adventures in London and in a deserted castle, where she tries to establish herself with a retinue of attendants. Barrett was an Irish poet. [With introduction by Walter Raleigh (Oxford Lib. of Prose and Poetry), Clarendon Press, 1909 ; introd. by Michael Sadleir (Rescue Series), E. Mathews (Stokes, New York), 1928.]

BARRIE, Sir James Matthew [Scottish ; *b.* 1860]. *Better Dead.*   1887
An extravaganza : the "Society for Doing Without Some People," and its trade in slaughter of celebrities who have done their work, is a farcical variant on the theme of De Quincey's *Murder as a Fine Art,* or of Stevenson's *Suicide Club.* [Allen & Unwin ; Scribner, New York.]

—— *Auld Licht Idylls.*   1888
Disconnected character-sketches and anecdotes of the gossips, the village worthies, the weddings, christenings, funerals, and, in fact, the whole humble domestic life of the small Forfarshire market-town of "Thrums" or Kirriemuir early in the nineteenth century. Only the pleasanter aspects are given. With that exception, the sketches are realistic, and draw freely on autobiographical material. Full of humorous dialogue in broad Scots. Sir James Barrie is one of the sentimentalists, and akin to Sterne as well as to Galt, Christopher North, and George MacDonald. [Hodder ; Scribner, New York. *Illus.* by Wm. Hole, Hodder.]

—— *When a Man's Single.*   1888
The struggles of a dour, self-educated Scot, a Thrums saw-miller, who goes to London and wins fortune as a leader-writer, with the ups and downs of his courtship of a girl of higher social station. Comic sketches of life in a newspaper office, and of the author's place of nativity. [Hodder ; Scribner, New York.]

—— *A Window in Thrums.*   1889
A sequel to the *Idylls* ; stories and sketches, some humorous, some farcical, and some pathetic, knit together by the history of a family of cottars. Its distinguishing quality, next to the thumb-nail sketches of native humorists, is the author's reverence for simple piety and the domestic affections. [Hodder ; Scribner, New York ; Burt, New York. With *coloured illus.* by A. C. Michael, Hodder (Scribner, New York).]

—— *My Lady Nicotine.*   1890
A bundle of journalistic sketches (contributed to the *St. James's Gazette*) of a little coterie of devout smokers, their lifelike, if sometimes farcical, conversations, escapades, misadventures, and sentimental musings. [Hodder ; Scribner, New York.]

—— *The Little Minister.*   1891
A romantic fantasia on the Thrums motive : the love affairs of the Auld Licht minister and a beautiful and sprightly "Egyptian," who is a lady in disguise, give the book more of the structure of a novel than the foregoing. The sketches of character and of Scottish manners and religious sentiments are very humorous, and there are passages of concentrated pathos. [Cassell ; Scribner, New York.]

—— *Sentimental Tommy.*   1896
First volume of the life-history of a Thrums boy, whose unconquerable insincerity and habit of posing, even to himself, typify the artistic temperament. From the back-streets of London Tommy is suddenly transported to the real Thrums, which has hitherto been to him a kind of elysium, painted in golden tints by his mother. Then begins a delightful epic of boyhood and girlhood, in which the magic creator of fantasies and cloud-cuckoo-towns lets himself go. [Cassell ; Scribner, New York.]

—— *Tommy and Grizel* [sequel].   1900
Continues the biography of Tommy the writer to his unanticipated death. As he grows older his self-consciousness becomes more pronounced, and each act of his is penetrated with affectation as he views everything through a literary atmosphere as so much "copy" ; his flirtations are theatrical posturings,

BARRIE, Sir James Matthew (*continued*).

his whole life is make-believe, either for the benefit of his friends and admirers or in sheer self-deception. There has certainly been no such comedy of sentimentality since Sterne—Meredith's anatomy of the fine shades and the nice feelings in *Sandra Belloni* is meant to be satirical realism. The large-hearted Grizel is a noble creature, and would be comparable to the patient Griselda, if we could believe even in the poetic possibility of her existence ; and the minor figures, Aaron Latta, Corp, Mr. Cathro, Gavinia, the serial novelist Pym, and the degenerates from London society are drawn with strokes of the old Thrums humour. [Cassell ; *illus.* by Bernard Partridge, Scribner, New York.]

—— *The Little White Bird.* 1902

A wayward and eccentric fantasia in which Kensington Gardens are turned into a land of enchantments. The first half tells how an old fogey interests himself in a young couple and becomes a second father to their little boy. Then Peter Pan comes into the story—the little boy that never grew up—and we are launched upon a fairy epic that must captivate any child. [Hodder ; Scribner, New York.]

—— *Peter and Wendy.* 1911

This is the story of *Peter Pan*, the children's comedy, turned into a novel, with pictures recalling the stage scenes of that irresponsible fantasy. Peter is Sentimental Tommy, and Wendy is Grizel, reduced to infantile standards. [Hodder ; *illus.* by F. D. Bedford, *id.*, Scribner, New York.] [*Works : Novels, Stories, and Sketches,* Uniform Ed., 11 vols., Scribner, New York ; (Thistle Ed.), *id.* ; (Peter Pan Ed., etc.), *id.*]

BARRILI, Anton Giulio [Italian ; 1836–1908]. *The Eleventh Commandment* (L'undecimo Comandamento, 1881). 1882

The chief characters of this gay little comedy are a brotherhood of modern friars who have shut themselves away from society in order to pursue their archæological researches. But a pretty girl becomes a novice and teaches them an eleventh commandment. [Gottsberger, New York : o.p. ; 2 vols., Remington, 1883 : o.p.]

—— *A Noble Kinsman.* 1885

A plot-novel, dealing with the intrigues and embarrassing situations that arise through the loss of a will. The scene is Naples, and the history of a family for two generations is recounted with graphic sketches of character. [Transl. by H. A. MARTIN, 2 vols., Unwin : o.p.]

—— *The Devil's Portrait* (Il Ritratto del Diavolo, 1882). 1885

A novel of plot, that is chiefly melodramatic, but also contains faithful reproduction of the ideas and talk in Italian studios. Spinello Aretino, a talented artist of five centuries ago, loses his betrothed mysteriously, and after exposing and avenging the villainy committed on him and her, goes mad, and dies. [Transl. by Miss E. WODEHOUSE, 2 vols. ; Remington : o.p. ; Gottesburger, New York : o.p.]

—— *The Princess's Private Secretary* (Il Lettore della Principessa, 1885). 1893

A feeble plot, but good delineation of manners and political life ; the style refined and urbane. [Digby & Long : o.p.]

"BARRINGTON, E." [Mrs. Lily Adams Beck, *née* Moresby ; Canadian]. *"The Ladies!" A shining constellation of wit and beauty.* 1922

Sketches of eighteenth-century ladies : Lady Mary Wortley Montagu with her son, in *My Lady Mary* ; the famous beauties, the Gunning sisters, one of whom became Duchess of Hamilton, in *The Golden Vanity* ; how Fanny Burney left Queen Caroline's service and married General D'Arblay, in *A Bluestocking at Court.* [Unwin ; Little, Boston.]

—— *The Chaste Diana.* 1923

The story of the actress, Lavinia Fenton, the original Polly of Gay's *Beggar's Opera* (1727–32). [Lane ; Dodd & Mead, New York.]

—— *The Gallants, following according to their wont the Ladies.* 1924

Sentimental episodes from history : *The King and the Lady,* Queen Eleanor and Fair Rosamond ; *Her Majesty's Godson,* Sir John Harington (1561–1612) receives letters conveying a love-story ; *The Pious Coquette* is about the Thrales, Dr. Johnson, and Boswell ; *The Prince's Pawns* is about William of Orange before the English revolution ; *The Beau and the Lady* presents Brummell and Mrs. Fitzherbert. [Little & Brown, Boston ; Harrap.]

—— *The Divine Lady.* 1924

Lady Hamilton, from her girlhood as Emma Hart to the famous liaison with Nelson. [Dodd & Mead, New York ; Harrap.]

—— *Glorious Apollo.* 1925

A free treatment of Byron and his love affairs. [Dodd & Mead, New York ; Harrap.]

—— *The Exquisite Perdita.* 1926

The story of Mary Robinson, with sketches of the celebrities she came into contact with. [Dodd & Mead, New York ; Harrap.]

—— *The Thunderer.* 1927

A romantic history of Napoleon and Josephine, chiefly on the personal side, with portraiture of their entourage. [Dodd & Mead, New York ; Harrap.]

—— *The Empress of Hearts.* 1928

Marie Antoinette is the heroine ; tells the story of the famous necklace theft. [Dodd & Mead, New York ; Harrap.]

—— *The Laughing Queen.* 1929

Cleopatra's affairs with Julius Cæsar and with Mark Antony, treated in the way of a modern sex-novel. Mark Antony is depicted as a bloated sensualist, and Cleopatra is regarded as actuated by political motives. [Dodd & Mead, New York ; Harrap.]

BARRINGTON, Michael. *The King's Fool.* 1904
A romance of the Middle Ages and the land of the troubadours. Yvot, a noble lad, appears in the guise of a jester amid the pomps and revelries of a king's Court; his secret tragedy is full of pathos. [Blackwood: o.p.]

—— *The Reminiscences of Sir Barrington Beaumont, Bart.* 1902
Autobiography of a Georgian gentleman in London, Paris, and Sweden (1775–1812), portrait of Axel Fersen (who is the hero), and glimpses of Horace Walpole, Marie Antoinette, etc. [Blackwood: o.p.]

—— *The Knight of the Golden Sword.* 1909
Grahame of Claverhouse (whom the author tries to vindicate), and less prominently, Charles II and James II, Waller, Pepys, etc. (1672–89). The author has since published a life of his hero, Dundee (1911). [Chatto: o.p.]

—— *The Lady of Tripoli.* 1910
Another troubadour romance; scenes, Bordeaux and Tripoli (1146–7). Rudel appears. [Chatto: o.p.]

—— *David Arnot.* 1927
Adventures of a student of medicine in Italy and in Galloway, in the time of the persecution of witches, etc. (1571–2). [Lockwood.]

BARRY, Rev. William Francis [Irish; 1849–1930]. *The New Antigone.* 1887
A doctrinaire novel, propounding various political and sociological questions, and dealing with Anarchist and Nihilist agitators. The drama of passion and self-immolation, in which Hippolyta Valence is the protagonist, is full of ideality. Imbued by her Nihilist father with belief in the rightness of free love, she acts upon her principles—to the sorrow of herself and her lover. Long digressions and descriptive passages somewhat mar the artistic effect. [Macmillan: o.p.]

—— *The Two Standards.* 1899
The wealthy and idle classes of to-day judged from a high moral standpoint. Interest centres in the heroine, her struggle for a better standard of human conduct, the hopes and disillusions of her married life. She has intimate relations with a man of genius, evidently meant for Wagner. [Unwin: o.p. Century Co., New York: o.p.]

—— *Arden Massiter.* 1900
A young English socialist, in Italy as a newspaper correspondent, gets immersed in the strife of the Camorra and the various revolutionary forces devastating and transforming the country. A broad picture of the overburdened peasantry, the intriguing clergy, the corrupt politicians, and the general conditions of Italian life. [Unwin: o.p.]

—— *The Wizard's Knot.* 1901
A novel of Irish life, influenced by the new Irish movement in literature—the tragic loves of a gentleman and a peasant girl. The peasantry with their humours, superstitions, and poetry, are presented with insight, and there is a moving description of the famine in South West Cork. [Unwin: o.p.]

—— *The Dayspring.* 1903
The love romance of a talented young Irishman in Paris at the close of the Second Empire. The widowed countess he loves, his friend the Legitimist, and the necromantic villain, are the exotic souls in whom Dr. Barry delights. Incoherent, melodramatic, a fairy-tale in construction; but full of ideas—Celtic ideas, both Irish and French in origin—and remarkable for an almost lyrical enthusiasm. A lurid picture of the Commune, with sketches of Rochefort, Thiers, Gambetta, etc. [Unwin: o.p.; Dodd & Mead, New York: o.p.]

BARTLETT, Vernon [b. 1894]. *Calf Love.* 1928
The love-affairs of a young English student living with a middle-class German family; a good picture of post-war Germany. [Constable; Lippincott, Philadelphia.]

"BARTRAM, George" [Henry Atton; 1853–1915]. *The Thirteen Evenings.* 1901
Miscellaneous stories told in a club smoking-room, sensational, mystical, Rabelaisian, and bucolic. Three, of the West Indies, present extremely unfamiliar phases of life, and the sketches of rustic originals from the English Midlands are full-flavoured and humorous. Forcible and terse in style and treatment, sometimes coarse. Kipling's influence is apparent. [Methuen: o.p.]

—— *The Longshoremen.* 1903
Smuggling, from the preventive's standpoint. The real hero is a gigantic exciseman, a martyr to duty, a true man of action. The Sussex town of Hoigh, with its canting mayor and smuggling justices, and the open or surreptitious attempts to bring them to book, make brisk comedy; whilst the harsh, muscular characters come out in savage deeds of lust and revenge. The author was in the Custom House service. [Arnold: o.p.]

—— *Lads of the Fancy.* 1906
A "muscular" novel of 1811. Life in London and the Shires in the great days of the ring and fashionable gambling. [Duckworth: o.p.]

BASKETT, James Newton [American; b. 1849]. *As the Light Led.* 1900
A long and leisurely country love-story, located in Northern Missouri, when the political issues of that region were seriously affected by the disputes of the Immersionists and Pædobaptists. The characters are farmers and their people. [Macmillan, New York and London: o.p.]

BAUM, Vicki [German; b. 1888]. *Grand Hotel* (Menschen im Hotel, 1929). 1930
A romance of the picaresque order, with a whole group of adventurers of both sexes, who have the unmistakable stamp of flesh and blood. A needy, cancer-stricken clerk goes to the most expensive hotel in Berlin to have a last fling, and becomes speedily involved in the affairs and cross-purposes of a swindling baron, a famous Russian dancer, a beautiful typist, and the august head of his own firm. The characters have a fascinating quality, and the drama plays itself out with brilliance. [Admirably transl. by Basil CREIGHTON, Bles.]

BAYLOR, Frances Courtenay [Mrs. G. S. Barnum; American; 1848–1920]. *Juan and Juanita.* 1887
Mexico and Texas form the background of the story, which sketches the Indian graphically. [Houghton, Boston; *illus.* by Gustaf Tenggren, *id.*, 1926.]

BAZIN, René François Nicolas Marie [French; *b.* 1853]. *A Blot of Ink* (Une tache d'encre, 1888). 1892
A pretty sentimental comedy, effectively bringing out the antipathy between town and country people. A student upsets some ink over the manuscript of a professor who is reading in the Bibliothèque Nationale, and incurs his displeasure, the incident causing various complications when the student falls in love with the professor's daughter. [Transl. by " Q " (A. T. QUILLER-COUCH) and P. FRANCKE, Cassell: o.p.]

—— *This, my Son* (Les Noëllet, 1890). 1908
M. Bazin stands in literature for the old ways—the Church, the aristocracy, peasant proprietorship. Here he elaborates a tragedy to show how the son of a Vendéan farmer makes a fatal mistake in despising the life of his father, securing an education by pretending that he wants to be a priest, and trying to satisfy his ambitions by going to Paris. [Transl. by A. S. RAPPOPORT, Sisley: o.p.]

—— *Redemption* (De toute son âme, 1897). 1908
The daily life, the pleasures, the love affairs, and the dreams of the young girls in a millinery establishment at Nantes, form the milieu, in which Henriette, the head milliner, devotes her whole soul to a work of redemption in brightening the lives of those about her. [Transl. by A. S. RAPPOPORT, Hutchinson: o.p.; Scribner, New York: o.p.]

—— *Autumn Glory; or, The Toilers in the Field* (La terre qui meurt, 1899). 1899
The last pages in the history of a yeoman family in the marshes of La Vendée, who have been on the land longer even than the old nobility, and now are forced to leave it. Represents, in idyllic fashion and with tragic melancholy, the inroads of modernity, the fall of ancestral houses, and the collapse of estates. Old Lumineau is a peasant that Millet might have painted. [Transl. by Mrs. Ellen WAUGH, Jarrold, Norwich: o.p.]

—— *The Children of Alsace* (Les Oberlé, 1901). 1912
A novel inspired with passionate love for the soil of Alsace, and with equally passionate feeling for its people living under foreign rulers, laws, and culture. The Oberlé family is divided into those who accept and those who kick against the German regime. Dramatized and acted in 1902. [Transl. with pref. by A. S. RAPPOPORT, Collins; Brentano, New York.]

—— *The Nun* (L'isolée, 1905). 1908
An attempt to excite odium against the French Government for their expulsion of the religious orders. Describes the life of five nuns in Lyons and their ministrations among the poor. When they are ejected, the timid and sensitive Sister Pascale falls a prey to a handsome blackguard, and goes to the dogs. [Newnes: o.p.; Scribner, New York: o.p.]

—— *By Faith Alone* (Le blé qui lève, 1907). 1908
Returns to the idealized picturing of nature, landscape, and the simple beauty of country life, in which M. Bazin had already rivalled, in his own way, the rustic novels of George Sand. A story of peasant life in the Nivernais, extolling the virtues of fraternity—not of the pattern held out by trade unions and socialists, but on the model of a working community, which he describes, directed by Jesuits in Belgium. The labour troubles of the woodcutters in Nièvre, the patient efforts of a village priest, and the misfortunes of landed gentry who fail to do their duty, combine to point the moral. [Nash: o.p.; *sub tit. The Coming Harvest*, Scribner, New York: o.p.]

—— *The Redeemer* (Davidée Birot). 1913
The romance of a schoolmistress and a slate-quarryman is made the vehicle for a discussion of clerical versus anti-clerical influence on education. [S. Paul: o.p.; *sub tit. Davidée Birot*, transl. by Mary D. FROST, Scribner, New York.]

—— *Those of his own Household* (Madame Corentine). 1914
A homely story, with a Breton setting, about a separated husband and wife who are reconciled through the agency of their daughter. [Transl. by L. M. LEGGATT, Devin-Adair, New York.]

BEACH, Rex Ellingwood [American; *b.* 1877]. *The Spoilers of the North.* 1906
—— *The Barrier.* 1907
Two stories of the Alaska goldfields, sketching the rough, profane gold-seekers and their squaws and children of the mining camps with the picturesque pen of a Bret Harte, and not without the poetic touch that brings up the feel of the wilderness and the unknown immensity around the settlements. The French-Canadian 'Poleon Doret, in *The Barrier*, is a most human character; the rest are the ruck of miners and adventurers, brutal outside but sentimentalists within, and satanic ruffians who keep the melodrama exciting.

—— *The Silver Horde.* 1909
The duel of a young lover in search of fortune and the millionaire whom he hopes to make his father-in-law. The former is struggling to establish a canning site on a wonderful salmon-river in Alaska; the latter is the head of a rival trust. [(1), (2), and (3), Harper, New York and London; Burt, New York; Hodder.]

—— *The Ne'er Do Well.* 1911
—— *The Net.* 1912
—— *The Rainbow's End.* 1916
Romances that take us to Panama in the first, and to Cuba before the Spanish War in the last, whilst *The Net* is about the activities of the Mafia in Sicily and New Orleans. [(1), (2), and (3), Harper, New York; Burt, New York; (2) and (3), Hodder.]

—— *The Auction Block.* 1914
The heroine marries the son of a wealthy man, and her influence cures him of his craze for drink and pleasure, and stimulates him to work. More serious in tone than usual. [Harper, New York; Burt, New York; Hodder: o.p.]

BEARD, Wolcott le Cléar. [American; b. 1867]. *Sand and Cactus.*   1899
    Brief stories of life in the central Southern States; telling and humorous in style; shows influence both of Bret Harte and of Rudyard Kipling, e.g. *A Brother to St. James* and *Liver's Responsibility*. [Scribner, New York: o.p.; Unwin: o.p.]

BEARDSLEY, Aubrey Vincent [1872–98]. *Under the Hill: a romantic novel.*   1903
    A trifle hardly amounting to a story, describing, in recherché æsthetic phrases, how the Abbé Fanfreluche (Tannhaüser) assists at the toilet of the Lady Venus, sups and flirts with her, and watches her feed her pet unicorn. It is Beardsley's decorative letterpress to his characteristic drawings. In the current edition, *Under the Hill; and other essays in prose and verse*, a few odd letters, poems, and sayings make up the exiguous tale of his literary works. [Lane; Dodd & Mead, New York (1929).]

BEAUMONT, Mary. *A Ringby Lass: and other stories.*   1895
    A little love-tale of rustic Yorkshire folk in the early forties. The lass is a loyal, unsophisticated girl, who sacrifices herself heroically for her father's sake. With some shorter tales also largely in dialect, and a pathetic study of a Maori wife who reverts to savagery. [Dent: o.p.]

—— *Joan Seaton: a story of Parsifal.*   1896
    A touching story of the Yorkshire dales, strong in local colour and in rendering the dialect. [Dent; with intro. by Dr. R. F. Horton, (Everyman's Library) Dent (Dutton, New York), 1912.]

—— *The New Woman; and other stories.*   1899
    Title-story personifies the duty of work in two women who set passion aside. Also *The Avenger*, a pathetic tale; and *His Wife's Hand*, a village story of a ruffian's reformation. [J. Clarke: o.p.]

BEAUREPAIRE, Quesnay de ["Jules de Glouvet"; French; 1838– ?]. *The Woodman* (Le forestier, 1880).   1892
    This story of Jean Renaud the poacher is to be regarded as the protest of a member of the idealist school of French fiction against the prevailing naturalism. [Transl. by Mrs. John SIMPSON, Harper, New York, 1892: o.p.]

BECKE, George Louis [Australian; 1848–1913]. *By Reef and Palm; and other stories.*   1894
    Short tales of life among the natives and wild seamen in the South Sea Islands. [With *The Ebbing of the Tide*, Unwin (Lippincott, Philadelphia), (Collected ed., 1924).]

—— *His Native Wife.*   1896
    A little romance of the South Seas. The Polynesian heroine in the *dénouement* murders the woman whom she suspects of courting her European husband, illustrating the thesis of racial incompatibility. [Unwin: o.p.; Lippincott, Philadelphia: o.p.]

—— *The Ebbing of the Tide: South Sea stories.*   1896
    Twenty-one tales of Europeans and natives afloat and ashore in Polynesia. *Luliban of the Pool* and *Hickson* are bloodthirsty tales of the irregular amours of whites and coloured women. *A Boating Party of Two* is a dark story of brutality and revenge. Scenery, manners and customs, and racial peculiarities of the South Sea islanders vividly represented. [*Vide By Reef and Palm, supra.*]

—— *Rodman the Boatsteerer; and other stories.*   1898
    Fierce, melodramatic stories, representing a bygone state of things among the traders, whalers, slavers, and natives of Polynesia and Malaysia, some harking back to the times when Australia was a convict settlement. Rodman heads a mutiny on a Yankee slaver, and is the only survivor of the boat's crew who escape. The sketch includes a vivid account of whale-fishing. *The Trader* is a tale of fiendish revenge. *The Trader's Wife*, with its incident of a woman cut in two by a shark, is not more "bluggy" than divers others. The strange contrasts of character in Europeans and natives, the irregular morals, Yankee brutalities, crimes of lawless men, are depicted with vivid actuality, and so is the fairy atmosphere of the coral isles. [Unwin (Lippincott, Philadelphia)].

—— *Edward Barry, South Sea Pearler.*   1900
    A sensational story with sketches of nautical life and of the natives of the South Seas. Barry finds himself chief officer on a ship whose skipper was murdered by a rascal who has seized the vessel. [Unwin; Page, Boston.]

—— *Helen Adair.*   1903
    Helen is an Irish girl who gets herself convicted as a felon in order that she may follow her father, transported to Botany Bay. [Unwin (Lippincott, Philadelphia).]

BECKE, George Louis, and Jeffery, Walter [b. 1861]. *A First Fleet Family.*   1895
    Almost more fact than fiction, and wholly dressed in historical garb, with close reproduction of eighteenth-century expressions and ways of thinking—the story of the colonization of New South Wales, with sketches of the felon-colonists and their governors (1787–92). [Unwin: o.p.; Macmillan, New York: o.p.]

—— *The Mutineer: a romance of Pitcairn Island.*   1898
    Founded on the history of the famous mutiny on H.M.S. *Bounty* and the subsequent settlement of the mutineers on a desert isle (1787–90). [Unwin: o.p.; Lippincott, Philadelphia: o.p.]

BECKER, Wilhelm Adolf [German; 1796–1846]. *Gallus; or, Roman Scenes of the Times of Augustus* (Gallus, oder Römische Scenen, 1838).   1844
    Manners and customs (*c.* 31 B.C.–A.D. 14) learnedly and ponderously depicted in the form of a novel, with notes and excursuses. [Transl. by Rev. F. METCALFE, Longmans, London and New York.]

—— *Charicles; or, Illustrations of the Private Life of the Ancient Greeks* (Charikles, Bilder altgriechischen Sitte, 1840).   1845
    The story, such as it is, opens about the year 330 B.C. Both *Charicles* and *Gallus* are handbooks for students, and are now very much behind modern research; notes and excursuses. [Transl. by Rev. F. METCALFE, Longmans, London (o.p.), and New York.]

BECKFORD, William [1759–1844]. *The History of the Caliph Vathek: an Arabian tale from an unpublished MS.*   *French version finished* 1782

A brilliant medley of Oriental magic and Western comedy. The sultan Vathek, a despot of portentous attributes, whose Court and courtiers are depicted with a mingling of burlesque and Eastern magnificence, commits a series of detestable crimes at the instance of a diabolical Giaour, who leads him at length to the Hall of Eblis, an inferno whose torments are pictured with Dantesque imagination. Beckford hated women, and his female personages are etched in with vitriolic satire. Written in French, 1782. Published in English, 1784. [Ed. by R. Garnett, with etchings by Nye, Lawrence & Bullen, 1893: o.p.; with coloured plates by W. B. Handforth, Routledge, 1912; ed. by Guy Chapman, 2 vols., Constable (Houghton, Boston), 1929; *illus.*, ltd. ed., Nonesuch Press, 1929.]

BÉCQUER, Gustavo Adolfo Dominguez [Spanish; 1836–70]. *Romantic Legends of Spain* (Varias Poesías y Leyendas, 1885).   1909

Bécquer was the Spanish Hoffman or Poe. He wrote *Rimas*, and prose legends, full of fantastic dream, in a style of polished simplicity. [Transl. by Cornelia F. BATES and Katherine M. BATES, Crowell, New York: o.p.; see also p. 210, *sub nom.* Gabriela Cunninghame Graham.]

BEDDOE, David M. *The Honour of Henri de Valois.*   1905

Describes Mehemet Ali's conquest of Syria, capture of Acre, etc. (1828–32). A spirited story of love, heroism, and a soldier's honour, worked out with due regard to historical fact. [Dent: o.p.]

—— *The Lost Mameluke.*   1913

The life and death of an Englishman who becomes an Egyptian, and is killed fighting against his former compatriots at the battle of the Nile (1789–91). [(Wayfarer's Lib.), Dent (Dutton, New York).]

BEDEL, Maurice [French; b. 1884]. *Jerome; or, The Latitude of Love* (*Jerome: 60° latitude nord*, 1928).   1928

A rather fatuous comedy contrasting the Northern and Southern temperaments. A young Parisian falls in love with a Norwegian girl. [Transl. by Lawrence S. MORRIS, Duckworth; Viking Press, New York.]

—— *Molinoff; or, The Count in the Kitchen* (1929).   1929

The Count is an impoverished Russian, who has to take service as *chef* in the château in Touraine owned by a rich Bolivian planter. There is satire as well as light comedy in the contrasts of real aristocrats with cosmopolitan plutocracy, and in the social success of the charming Russian when he manages to conceal his occupation during his employer's absence. [Transl. by Lawrence Shackelford MORRIS, Duckworth; Viking Press, New York.]

BEECHER, Henry Ward [American; 1813–87]. *Norwood; or, Village Life in New England.*   1866

Life in a thriving village just before the Civil War (c. 1861); the principals, a parson of the old school, who holds philosophical duels with the physician, an eccentric sage, and other gossips, Rose, the doctor's daughter, and her suitors. One of the lovers is a young hero, though a dullard, and proves his worth on the field of Gettysburg, where Rose acts as nurse. [Fords, Howard & Hulbert, New York: o.p.]

BEER, Thomas [American; b. 1889]. *Sandoval: a romance of bad manners.*   1924

Reproduces with fidelity the social atmosphere of New York in the seventies. [Knopf, New York.]

—— *The Road to Heaven: a romance of morals.*   1928

The impressionist technique of this is interesting; it conveys the sense of the passing show impingeing on several minds. The strained cleverness of the slangy dialogue may be trying for English readers. But the episode—it is merely a quick sequence of love affairs in the life of a knock-about young man—is a sort of searchlight into the underworld, and more particularly the literary hinterland, of New York, where wild dissipation, nervous exhaustion, and suicide are rampant. [Knopf, New York and London.]

BEERBOHM, Max [b. 1872]. *Zuleika Dobson; or, An Oxford Love Story.*   1911

A comic fantasy of undergraduate life at Oxford, admirably true and admirably satirical: Zuleika a bewitching Artemis who drives everyone mad with hopeless passion. [Heinemann; Dodd & Mead, New York; Modern Lib., New York, 1926.]

—— *Seven Men.*   1919

Five characteristic pieces of playful humour, not without sting. *Enoch Soames* and *Savonarola Brown* are "dud" literary men of the eighteen-nineties. Soames makes Faust's bargain with the devil, to look into futurity and see what his fame will be a century hence. Brown writes a play which is composed of all the worst absurdities of bad melodrama. *Maltby and Braxton* makes extravaganza of the jealousy of two rival "best-sellers." *James Pethell* is a study of gambling monomania, and *A. V. Laidley* of a still commoner form of unbalanced mentality. [Heinemann; Knopf, New York.]

—— *A Christmas Garland.*   1922

A collection of amusing skits in the form of Christmas stories told in the manner of well-known writers; among the best are those after Henry James, Kipling, Arnold Bennett, and Hewlett. [Heinemann; Dutton, New York.]

—— *The Dreadful Dragon of Hay Hill.*   1928

Another delicately ironical fable, about a pair of lovers in the year 39,000 B.C., and their adventures with a dragon, in the district which is now Berkeley Square. [Heinemann.]

BEGBIE, Harold [1871–1929]. *An English Family: the memoirs of Hugh Frothingham of Longworthy.*   1919

An account of a family in transition from the Victorian to the Georgian age. A fair example of this writer's plodding realism. [Hutchinson: o.p.]

—— *Black Rent.*   1928

Another realistic tragedy—a surgeon, unhappily married, falls under suspicion of murdering his wife, and after the wreck of his life, finds hope in the service of the League of Nations. [Mills and Boon.]

BEHN, Mrs. Aphra [1640–89]. *Novels.* 1698
The Royal Slave (Oroonoko), The Fair Jilt, The Nun, Agnes de Castro, The Lover's Watch, The Case for the Watch, The Lady's Glass to Dress Herself by, The Lucky Mistake, The Court of the King of Bantam, The Adventure of the Black Lady. Mrs. Behn wrote a large number of licentious plays, one novel of singular merit, *Oroonoko*, and a number of short histories, on the model of the old Italian *novella*. They are inspired by the same romanticism as the contemporary heroic drama, and are all on variations of the one theme—the omnipotence of love. The realism is tentative and crude. *Oroonoko* has a truth and power unexampled in these. It is the story of an heroic negro who is kidnapped and sold into slavery in Surinam, where Aphra perhaps witnessed his sufferings and magnanimity. As a glorification of the natural man, this book anticipated Rousseau, and as an emancipation novel, Mrs. Stowe. Some other novels, and these not the least interesting, will be found in the edition of her *Works*, edited by the Rev. Montague Summers, ltd. ed., Heinemann, 1915. [With introd. by E. A. Baker (Library of Early Novelists), Routledge, 1905 (Dutton, New York.)].

BELDEN, Jessie [*née* Van Zile ; American ; *b.* 1857]. *Antonia.* 1901
A tale of colonial New York, and Dutch colonists in the Hudson River districts (1640–50). [Page, Boston : o.p. ; Murray : o.p.]

BELL, Florence Evelyn Eleanore, Lady [*née* Olliffe ; 1851–1930]. *Miss Tod and the Prophets.* 1898
An old maid with luxurious tastes and straitened means learns that the earth is to be destroyed by a comet, and resolves to obtain the maximum enjoyment out of her little capital in the brief period left. [Macmillan : o.p.]

BELL, John Joy [Scottish ; *b.* 1871]. *The Whalers.* 1914
Six sketches of whaling in Iceland waters, featuring genuine and attractive Norwegian fishermen. [Holden : o.p.]

BELL, Robert Stanley Warren [*b.* 1871]. *Tales of Greyhouse.* 1901
One of a series of wholesome and vivacious stories of school life, written for boys—and others. [Black ; Macmillan, New York.]

BELLAMY, Edward [American ; 1850–98]. *Looking Backward, 2000–1887.* 1888
The imaginary narrator awakes from a miraculous sleep and finds himself in Boston in A.D. 2000. A Socialist millennium reigns, all human ills being banished by the power of universal wealth. *My Afterdream*, by Julian West (Unwin, 1900 : o.p.), is a rejoinder and a criticism in the shape of another prophetic romance. [Houghton, Boston ; Routledge.]

BELLOC, Joseph Hilaire Pierre [*b.* 1870]. *Lambkin's Remains.* 1900
The venerable Oxford don has left a dull and ponderous commentary on success, sleep, and notable events in the learned and the ordinary world. Some ironical or merely jovial verses mingle with the prose. [Vincent, Oxford : o.p.]

—— *The Aftermath ; or, Gleanings from a Busy Life ; called upon the outer cover for purposes of sale, Caliban's Guide to Letters.* 1903
Light satire of a literary and academic kind on the literary and academic character. The best thing is the mock manual of instructions to the literary aspirant, sarcastically pigeon-holing the stunts and dodges of modern journalism. The humour overflows into the introduction and " opinions of the Press." [Duckworth ; Dutton, New York.]

—— *Emmanuel Burden, Merchant of Thames Street, London.* 1904
A similar satire on heavy, dull, conventional respectability. [Methuen ; Scribner, New York : o.p.]

—— *Mr. Clutterbuck's Election.* 1908
Light satire of foolish and mischievous tendencies in the political life of our day—bolstering of commercial interests by Government and the like. A stupid City man gains a fortune by lucky blundering, wins an election, is unseated, and gets knighted through the whim of a man with social influence. The author's anti-Semitism comes out violently. [Nash.]

—— *A Change in the Cabinet.* 1909
A further skit on bumptious commercialism, " high finance," and the impudent jobbery and corruption of professional politics. [Methuen.]

—— *Pongo and the Bull.* 1910
More of the same clever though sketchy satire of the pretentious vulgarity of industrial civilization, of professional politics, and sham " democracy " run as a job for the titled and moneyed classes. Mr. Belloc is French by birth and temperament, and an earnest Roman Catholic. [Long, 1929.]

—— *The Girondin.* 1911
The experiences of a young man in 1792 who is impressed into the army of the Republic and killed at Valmy. Extremely vivid in the picturing of actualities, as if by an eye-witness. [Nelson.]

—— *The Green Overcoat.* 1912
A comic variation of the ordinary detective tale—a professor of Subliminal Psychology is inveigled into forgery, and tries to cover his tracks by a pretended attack of amnesia. By the lure of modern publicity and high pay he is led into a series of articles and public lectures on his bogus experiences in the psychic world. [Arrowsmith ; McBride, New York.]

—— *Mr. Petre.* 1925
A very harmless person is mistaken for an American millionaire of irascible temperament, and notwithstanding his protests is forced to sustain the rôle. Some excellent satire on political and social institutions, and the medical profession. [*Illus.* by G. K. Chesterton, Arrowsmith ; McBride, New York.]

—— *Belinda : a tale of affection in youth and age.* 1928
An idyllic melodrama of Regency times, told with considerable elegance and not a little irony. [Constable ; Harper, New York.]

BELLOC, Joseph Hilaire Pierre (*continued*). *But Soft—We are Observed !* 1928

The year is 1979 ; Lady Caroline Balcombe, admirably portrayed, is Foreign Secretary of the Communist Government, which is by tradition attached to the Anarchist party. At her instigation, police, detectives, and magistrates harry an inoffensive youth who is mistaken for the envoy of a foreign power, in a fashion which is curiously similar to that of the present day. The 37 illustrations by G. K. Chesterton, equally with the text, are in the best vein of these authors' combined productions of light but forcible social satire. [*Illus.* by G. K. Chesterton, Arrowsmith ; *sub tit. Shadowed !* Harper, New York.]

—— *The Missing Masterpiece.* 1929

Elaborate but rather thin facetiousness on the theme of the modern picture-expert and the difference in real artistic value between originals and first-class copies, with Mr. Belloc's usual anti-Semite gibes. [*Illus.* by G. K. Chesterton, Arrowsmith ; Harper, New York.]

—— *The Man who made Gold.* 1930

An undergraduate and a don discover and exploit a magical process for manufacturing gold, and the latter subsequently becomes entangled in the world of high politics, finance, and corruption that Mr. Belloc is always denouncing. With incidental satire of an Anglican hostel for the poor and other objects. [*Illus.* by G. K. Chesterton, Arrowsmith.]

BELLOC-LOWNDES, Marie Adelaide [Mrs. Lowndes, *née* Belloc ; *b.* 1868]. *Barbara Rebell.* 1905

Barbara's life at St. Germain, and later in London after an unhappy marriage. The first part comprises a view of the French Court in its splendour just before 1870. [Heineman : o.p. ; Rickey, New York : o.p.]

—— *Mary Pechell.* 1912

A quiet romance with a pleasing heroine. [Methuen : o.p. ; Scribner, New York.]

—— *Studies in Love and Terror.* 1913

Five stories, one of which, *The Woman from Purgatory*, deals in the supernatural. [Methuen : o.p. ; Scribner, New York.]

—— *Good Old Anna.* 1915

A trusted German servant becomes half-unwittingly the tool of a spy, despite her love for England and her mistress. The end is tragic. [Hutchinson : o.p. ; Doran, New York : o.p.]

—— *Lilla : a part of her life.* 1916

The problem of a husband who returns after being reported missing in the war to find his wife married again, is solved by the timely death of the second husband. [Hutchinson : o.p. ; Doran, New York : o.p.]

—— *From the Vasty Deep.* 1920

The solution of a murder mystery by means of spiritism and a girl-medium. [Hutchinson ; Doran, New York : o.p.]

—— *Duchess Laura : certain days of her life.* 1929

Dramatic and melodramatic incidents centre in that admirable figure of a woman, the Duchess. [Ward, Lock.]

BENDA, Julien [French ; *b.* 1867]. *The Yoke of Pity* (L'ordination, 1912). 1913

A philosopher's solution of one of the most poignant questions : is a man of talent to sacrifice his life-work, if need be, to the claims of affection, or the converse ? The problem is worked out with a stern regard for truth yet a compassionate sense of the pangs inevitable to either *dénouement*. A thinker leaves his mistress, in spite of pity, rather than desert the path he has marked out for himself. But, when in later years his child becomes a cripple, he is confronted with a more terrible dilemma. [Transl. by Gilbert CANNAN, Unwin ; Holt, New York : o.p.]

BENECKE, Else Cecilia Mendelssohn [1873–1917]. [*transl.*] *Tales by Polish Authors.* 1915

Stories by Sienkiewicz, Stefan Żeromski, Adam Szymánski, and two by Wacław Sieroszewski ; well translated. [Blackwell, Oxford.]

BENECKE, Else C. M., and BUSCH, Marie [*translators*]. *More Tales by Polish Authors.* 1916

Six stories by Szymánski, Sieroszewski, Żeromski, Wladyslaw St. Reymont, and Boleslaw Prus (Alexandr Glowacki). *Two Prayers* and *Maciej the Mazur*, by the first-named, are tragic recitals of the sufferings of homesick Poles in Siberia ; Sieroszewski's *The Chukchee* introduces us to the primitive Yakuts of the far North. *The Returning Wave*, by Prus, is a grim picture of industrial exploitation by a brutal German ; *The Trial*, by Reymont, shows the peasant doing justice for himself in his misgoverned and neglectful country ; and *The Stronger Sex*, by Żeromski, contrasts ironically a well-meaning do-nothing doctor and an idealistic school-teacher who is faithful even unto death. [Blackwell, Oxford ; Longmans, New York : o.p.]

—— *Selected Polish Tales.* 1921

Prus, Szymánski, Żeromski, and Reymont are here represented, together with stories by J. Kaden-Bandrowski and Mme Rygier-Nalkowska. [(World's Classics) Oxford Press.]

BENÉT, Stephen Vincent [American ; *b.* 1898]. *Spanish Bayonet.* 1926

A striking picture of the South, especially the Floridas, in the years just preceding the American Revolution (1769–74). [Doubleday, Doran, New York ; Heinemann.]

BENNET, Robert Ames [American ; *b.* 1870]. *For the White Christ : a story of the days of Charlemagne.* 1905

Aims at a comprehensive view of mediæval history (778–85), and shows militant Christendom striving to conquer heathendom and Mohammedanism in the reign of Karl the Great. A young viking Olver is substituted for the legendary Oliver, and with Roland, Karl the Great, Willikind, Fastrada, and other historical personages acts a leading part in the wars in the Pyrenees and across the Rhine. [McClurg, Chicago : o.p. ; Putnam, London : o.p.]

—— *A Volunteer with Pike : the true narrative of one Dr. John Robinson and his love for the fair Señorita Vallois.* 1909

The Louisiana purchase, Aaron Burr's treasonable plot, and Zebulon M. Pike's expedition across the Rockies into Colorado. All the important incidents of the story are historical, and contemporary life in the United States, in the Indian country, and in Mexico is carefully depicted. [McClurg, Chicago : o.p.]

BENNET, Robert Ames (*continued*). *The Shogun's Daughter.* 1910

In an account of the American mission to Japan under Commodore M. C. Perry in 1853, the author gives a panorama of Japanese life during the Shogunate, and recounts the panic in Yedo, the assassination of the Shogun, and other events which led to the ultimate transformation of the country and people. [McClurg, Chicago : o.p.]

BENNETT, [Enoch] Arnold [1867–1931]. *A Man from the North.* 1898

A young man of middling abilities comes to London, full of ambitions, and eventually settles down to the average lot. A story told in a very simple and natural way, showing a gift for the presentation of things vividly and at the same time with a sense of their ulterior significance. [Methuen, Doubleday, Doran, New York.]

—— *Anna of the Five Towns.* 1902

The varieties of human nature observed in Mr. Arnold Bennett's own region, the Potteries, are faithfully portrayed ; but the stress here is on certain strong, quiet, unassuming types of womanhood, ignorant of worldly wisdom but capable of great heights of self-renunciation. Anna suddenly inherits £50,000, and remains as poor as ever. The rich miser, the financier of Methodism, to whom " the circuit was a going concern," is the focusing-point of some good-humoured satire of that body. [Methuen ; Doubleday, Doran, New York : o.p.]

—— *Leonora.* 1903

The history of an unhappy marriage in the same region and among similar people. [Chatto.]

—— *A Great Man.* 1904

A satire on the literary tastes of the great majority. The great man is a solicitor's clerk who takes to writing novels, and even becomes a playwright, and by catchy titles and other meretricious effects captures the British public and makes enormous gains. [Methuen ; Doubleday, Doran, New York : o.p.]

—— *Tales of the Five Towns.* 1905
—— *The Grim Smile of the Five Towns.* 1907

Slight stories of the Potteries district, several of them effectively contrasting London and provincial life, the impression made on the provincial by his first experience of the metropolis, and vice versa. [(1) Chatto ; (Phœnix Lib.), *id.* ; (2) Collins ; (Phœnix Lib.), Chatto.]

—— *Whom God hath Joined.* 1906

The history of two divorce cases in two closely related households, studied with most exact realism, the sole improbability being the coincidence of the two. The erring wife, and the injured wife and daughter, are excellent examples of the author's understanding of women. Scene, one of the towns in the Potteries. [Methuen ; Doran, New York : o.p.]

—— *The Old Wives' Tale.* 1908

The lives of two women from girlhood to death, two ordinary types whose experience of life illustrates the passage of an epoch, the engulfment of the mid-Victorian era by overwhelming modernity being typified in the disappearance of the Five Towns in an industrial metropolis with all the crudity and vulgarity of to-day. The staid and unromantic sister who lives out her life in Bursley is finely contrasted with the energy and self-reliance of her more fastidious sister, who makes her own fortune abroad and has interesting experiences during the siege of Paris. The first half of the book is rich in ironical satire of provincial respectability and pharisaical evangelicalism. On the whole, this is the masterpiece of his realism, to which nothing in human life came amiss. Nothing failed to evoke his passionate joy in life itself. [Hodder ; Benn ; Doubleday, Doran, New York ; Grosset, New York.]

—— *Buried Alive.* 1908

A farcical entertainment, with bits of satire in the vein of *A Great Man.* An eminent and eccentric painter changes identities with his dead valet, and extravagant complications ensue. [Methuen ; Doubleday, Doran, New York.]

—— *The Glimpse : an adventure of the soul.* 1909

A spiritual adventure related with circumstantial realism. A man falls into a trance and has a glimpse of the life outside and around that which we are conscious of ; and the experience changes his attitude towards his wife, his villainous friends, and his fellows in general. [Chapman ; Appleton, New York : o.p.]

—— *Helen with the High Hand : an idyllic diversion.* 1910

A preposterous comedy. The masterful Helen, a school-teacher in the Five Towns, turns a crabbed and miserly old relative into a fine gentleman, and makes him spend his money in a princely style that he would never have dreamed of. [Chapman ; Nelson ; Doran, New York.]

—— *Clayhanger.* 1910
—— *Hilda Lessways* [sequel]. 1911
—— *These Twain* [sequel]. 1916

Character and personal relations are the main theme of this trilogy, but it is also a compendium of social evolution. The brief story of Darius Clayhanger, child of poor work-people when youngsters of seven went out to earn their own living, is a pathetic, almost blood-curdling preliminary which strikes the historical note. Clayhanger is his son Edwin, the outer and inner history of whose boyhood, youth, and young manhood follows, with his passages of affection for Janet Orgreave, the most captivating figure in the book, his meeting with Hilda Lessways, and the matters that are related from her side in the second novel. That is concerned with Hilda's young womanhood in the Five Towns, her unlucky marriage with a bigamist, and the meeting with Clayhanger which results in their falling in love. The third novel takes up the story years later, when Hilda and Edwin are wedded, and is a searching study of married life, and of " the lofty and incomprehensible marvels of human nature." The pair suffer agonies from the friction and opposition of their two wills, till Edwin makes the grand discovery of life, the actuality of injustice, and they settle down to a safe, mediocre, disillusioned compromise. The three books are packed with lifelike individuals, among whom stand out the brilliant Orgreaves and the magnificent, vindictive, hypocritical Auntie Hamps. [(1), (2), and (3), Methuen ; Doubleday, Doran, New York ; complete in 1 vol., *sub tit. The Clayhanger Family*, 1925, Methuen.]

BENNETT, [Enoch] Arnold (*continued*). *The Card : a story of adventure in the Five Towns.* 1911
A light-hearted and light-headed history of a bland adventurer who makes his way rapidly from slum to affluence and the dignity of mayor by dint of good-humour, cheek, and bold reliance on his luck. [Methuen ; sub tit. *Denry the Audacious*, Doubleday, Doran, New York.]

—— *The Matador of the Five Towns ; and other stories.* 1912
Five are labelled " tragic " and seventeen " frolic." *The Matador* is a poignant little sketch of a great full-back, darling of the Five Towns. In *The Glimpse* may be seen the germ for the novel of that title. Mr. Bennett's technique is at its best in the eight pages of *The Letter and the Lie*. [Methuen ; Doubleday, Doran, New York.]

—— *The Regent : a Five Towns story of adventure in London.* 1913
" The Card," partly by accident but more by shrewdness and his remarkable inspiration of the moment, acquires a plot near Piccadilly Circus and puts up the Regent Theatre. The mountebank actor-manager, the boosting suffragette, the Azure Club and the young Yeatsian intellectuals are hit off with a pretty mixture of admiration and satire. [Methuen.]

—— *The Price of Love.* 1914
A slighter novel of the *Clayhanger* kind. The salient figures are a young man of weak moral fibre, a woman of sterling but by no means uncommon character, and a charwoman, counterpart in her patient and modest endurance to Flaubert's famous old servant, with an English vein of humour to distinguish her. [Methuen ; Harper, New York : o.p. ; Burt, New York : o.p.]

—— *The Lion's Share.* 1916
A feminine pendant to *The Card*. The young woman who would like the lion's share comes from Essex, but is spirited enough to be a heroine from the Five Towns. She flirts with the suffragist movement, and marries a French violinist, her experiences in London and Paris occasioning luxuriant descriptions of luxurious living. [Cassell ; Doubleday, Doran, New York.]

—— *The Pretty Lady.* 1918
The life of a courtesan, meant to be frank and uncompromising, but as Bennett recognized afterwards, vitiated by his sentimental treatment of this young woman. There is some satire—of the frivolity that went on during the calamities of the great war—the self-contradictions of a society that had gone insane. [Cassell ; Doubleday, Doran, New York.]

—— *The Roll Call.* 1919
An unsatisfactory addendum to the *Clayhanger* trilogy. Edwin's stepson wins recognition as an architect, has two love affairs, and joins up at the outbreak of war. [Hutchinson : o.p. ; Doran, New York : o.p.]

—— *Mr. Prohack.* 1922
Full of Mr. Bennett's undiscriminating joy in life. Mr. Prohack comes by chance into tons of money ; he and his son spend it ; and if there be any moral it is in the absurdity of this senseless expenditure and the fools it makes of its devotees. [Methuen ; Doubleday, Doran, New York.]

—— *Lilian.* 1922
A slight story of fast life in London and on the Riviera, with some serious touches in the treatment of Lilian's relations with other women. [Cassell ; Doubleday, Doran, New York ; Grosset, New York.]

—— *Riceyman Steps.* 1923
The all-seeing eye that made the world of the Five Towns living and substantial in *The Old Wives' Tale* and the *Clayhanger* series, and saw the essential beauty that exists in the commonest and drabbest human things, here transfers its vision to dismal back streets in Clerkenwell. Mr. Earlforward—business-name Riceyman—is a bookseller in this dull neighbourhood, whose miserliness brings himself and his wife to their deathbeds in a year of married life : they die of under-nourishment. The appealing figure in a sordid story is the devoted, childlike maidservant and charwoman Elsie. Her unconscious heroism and naïve struggles with a prickly conscience reveal the depth of Mr. Bennett's tenderness and the delicacy of his humour. [Cassell ; Doubleday, Doran, New York.]

—— *Elsie and the Child : a tale of Riceyman Steps.* 1924
This pathetic creature, so beautiful in her lowliness and unnoticed greatness, in her later life. [Cassell ; Doubleday, Doran, New York.]

—— *Lord Raingo.* 1926
A period novel, and one of those written by the author to amuse himself—and the reader. Raingo is another self-made millionaire, with a gift for organizing publicity, which brings him into the War Cabinet. Full of portraits which may be recognizable but are not to be taken too seriously, and amusing as a picture of intrigue and chaotic disorder at Whitehall. [Cassell ; Doubleday, Doran, New York.]

—— *The Strange Vanguard : a fantasia.* 1928
A self-made millionaire from the Five Towns provides the dash of character and humour required in this otherwise extravagant story of financial rivalry, abduction in a palatial yacht, and expensive revelling at Rome, Monte Carlo, and Marseilles. [Cassell ; Doubleday, Doran, New York.]

—— *Accident.* 1928
Expanded out of the matter of a short story by a talent for making unimportant detail interesting. A rich gentleman's journey to the Riviera, a railway accident, his chance meeting with his daughter-in-law, and reconciliation of this rebellious lady with her husband, who wants to be a Labour M.P. [Cassell ; Doubleday, Doran, New York.]

—— *Imperial Palace.* 1930
The whole intricate economy of a vast luxury hotel, from the financial deals for gaining control of it down to the working of the laundry and the engine-room and what goes on in the staff dining-room, laid bare with an eager delight in complex detail and in such a spectacle of opulence and splendour. The director's sentimental skirmishes with the brilliant daughter of the leading financier, and his discreet union with the young woman who has worked her way up through the business, merely share the interest with the Imperial Palace itself. [Cassell ; Doubleday, Doran, New York.]

BENNETT, John [American ; *b.* 1865]. *Master Skylark.* 1897
  About a Stratford boy in London (1596) who is befriended by Shakespeare. [Century Co., New York ; *illus.* by H. Pitz, *id.,* 1922 : Harrap.]
—— *The Story of Barnaby Lee.* [juvenile] 1900
  The founding of the colonies of New York and Maryland : Peter Stuyvesant and Governor Calvert appear (1664). A boy's adventures among pirates, etc. [Century Co., New York ; Warne : o.p.]

BENOIT, Pierre [French]. *Atlantida* (L'Atlantide, 1919). 1920
  A romance of adventure in North Africa : a French officer is captured in the desert by a people ruled by a mysterious woman. [Transl. by Mary C. Tongue and Mary Ross, Duffield, New York.]

BENSON, Arthur Christopher [1862–1925]. *The House of Quiet.* 1903
—— *The Upton Letters.* 1905
—— *The Gate of Death : a diary.* 1906
—— *Beside Still Waters.* 1907
—— *The Altar Fire.* 1907
—— *At Large.* 1908
  These are either mixed collections of essays or a kind of " imaginary portraits," as Pater would call them, a good deal more than essays but not quite novels. They contain a thread of biography—or auto-biography—and much introspective portraiture, or self-revelation thinly disguised. Both *The House of Quiet* (1903) and *The Upton Letters* (1905), the latter in epistolary form, give us the ruminations of a man of culture and leisure on all sorts of matters, the ethical equation being always at the back of his argu-ment. The titles indicate the slight degree of difference between the others. *Beside Still Waters* (1907) describes the moods and meditations of a contemplative man, averse from practical affairs, but anxious to find the work which he believes allotted him by God's scheme of providence. He settles down at last as a lonely scholar at Cambridge, and in *At Large* more of his impressions of English scenery, education, religion, conduct, literature, and what-not are presented in Mr. Benson's mellifluous prose, which is as emotional as Pater's but less subtle and less ornate. *The Altar Fire* adopts the same kind of machinery, and again the development of character is weak and vague, the real interest lying in the essays, sermons, or dissertations which are strung together on the biographical thread. [(1) Murray ; Dutton, New York : o.p. (2) Murray ; Putnam, New York. (3) Smith & Elder : o.p. ; Putnam, New York : o.p. (4) Smith & Elder : o.p. ; Putnam, New York : o.p. (5) Smith & Elder : o.p. ; Putnam, New York : o.p. (6) Smith & Elder : o.p. ; Putnam, New York.]
—— *The Orchard Pavilion.* 1914
  Three Oxford undergraduates of 1880, an agnostic materialist, a hedonist, and a clergyman, discuss their views on life. After thirty years they meet again and compare results, with an easy victory for Christianity. [Murray ; Putnam, New York.]
—— *Chris Gascoyne : an experiment in solitude ; from the diaries of John Trevor.* 1924
  A young man of charming presence, failing to save society by his admirable conversation, seeks refuge in the solitude of the country, where he meditates and falls in love. [Murray ; Dutton, New York.]
—— *Cressage.* 1927
  A quiet chronicle, with little or no plot, of the relationship between Walter, a detached and introspective young man, and Helen, of exactly opposite character, whom he admires but does not love. [Heinemann.]
—— *Basil Netherby : stories.* 1927
  With *The Uttermost Farthing,* a pair of capable ghost stories. [Hutchinson.]

BENSON, Blackwood Ketcham [American ; *b.* 1845]. *Who Goes There?* 1900
—— *A Friend with the Countersign* [sequel]. 1901
  A Union spy loses his memory, and serves, down to Gettysburg, with the Confederates (1861–3). In the sequel he pursues his calling, and sees most of the actions and manœuvres from both sides (1863–5). An accurate and almost too minute account of the whole course of the war, giving maps and references to the War Records ; with a great deal of exciting personal adventure. [(1) and (2), Macmillan, New York and London : o.p. ; Grossett, New York : o.p.]
—— *Bayard's Courier : a story of love and adventure in the cavalry campaigns.* 1902
  The early stages of the war (1862). General Stuart and Stonewall Jackson. Actions recounted in great detail and maps inserted. [Macmillan, New York and London : o.p.]
—— *Old Squire : the romance of a black Virginian.* 1903
  Plenty of history, little character ; the adventures of a negro in the Gettysburg campaign, which is described with great detail, two maps assisting the reader to follow the manœuvres (1863–4). Two brothers fight on opposite sides. Much dialect, negro and Irish. [Macmillan, New York and London : o.p. ; Grossett, New York : o.p.]

BENSON, Edward Frederick [*b.* 1867 ; brother of A. C. Benson]. *Dodo : a detail of to-day.* 1893
  A smart representation of smart society, which made a hit partly because the heroine was alleged to be a thinly disguised sketch of a well-known lady. A paradoxical jocularity, and satire tempered with com-placent appreciation, are the salient qualities. [Methuen ; Appleton, New York : o.p. ; Ogilvie, New York.]
—— *Limitations.* 1896
  Theme, the limitations of life and art : the two exponents, a woman who fails to win the man she loves, and a sculptor who aims at the great Hellenic ideals but gets his bread by producing trivial statuettes. [Ward & Lock ; Harper, New York : o.p.]
—— *The Babe B.A.* 1897
  A jovial comedy of University life at Cambridge, with some hilarious scenes. Mr. Stewart and Mr. Longridge are glorified likenesses of Oscar Browning and J. E. Nixon of King's, Mr. Benson's college. [Heine-mann : o.p. ; Putnam, New York : o.p.]
—— *The Vintage.* 1898

BENSON, Edward Frederick (*continued*).   *The Capsina* [sequel].   1899
Quiet, idyllic scenes of country life and manners, and episodes of violent adventure during the Greek War of
Independence (1820). Greeks and Turks, shepherds, village maidens, and truculent ruffians, make a
motley crowd. Historic personages figure ; even Apollo comes on the stage. The Capsina is a winsome
Amazon, who performs wonders of valour, but at last perishes tragically. The seas and mountains of
Greece are lavishly depicted as background. [(1) and (2), Methuen ; Harper, New York : o.p.]

—— *Mammon & Co.*   1899
A return to the smart, self-indulgent society of *Dodo*. Aristocratic company-promoters, baccarat-swindlers,
a woman who goes wrong and is perhaps meant as an awful warning of the results of mammon-worship,
a Mrs. Malaprop, and other serio-comic figures are presented half complacently and half satirically.
[Collins ; Appleton, New York : o.p.]

—— *The Princess Sophia.*   1900
A fantasia, mixing comedy and sensation, after the manner of *The Prisoner of Zenda*. The Princess Rhodope
is a born gamester ; she turns her domain into another Monte Carlo, but obtains as much congenial
excitement from the intrigues of her husband and her diplomats as from the roulette table. [Heinemann ;
Harper, New York : o.p.]

—— *The Luck of the Vails.*   1901
A tissue of unlikely events plausibly narrated : the villain, a great-uncle who plots to murder the young heir
of the family, is interesting as a study of the criminal temperament, and recalls Wilkie Collins's Count
Fosco. [Jenkins ; Appleton, New York : o.p.]

—— *The Challoners.*   1904
A more serious treatment than is usual with Mr. Benson of family estrangement through the vagaries of
character, illustrated in a brother and sister who make their own lives, one by a musical career, the other
by her marriage, in opposition to their father, an orthodox clergyman. Some of the by-characters are
interesting, particularly the paradoxical Lady Sunningwell, and the satire of hide-bound parochialism
is amusing. [Heinemann : o.p. ; Lippincott, Philadelphia : o.p.]

—— *An Act in a Backwater.*   1905
—— *The Image in the Sand.*   1905
—— *The Angel of Pain.*   1906
Various novels on the same general pattern, realism tempered with emotional and melodramatic excitement.
[(1) Heinemann ; (2) Nelson ; Lippincott, Philadelphia : o.p. ; (3) Heinemann : o.p. ; Lippincott,
Philadelphia.]

—— *Account Rendered.*   1911
Handles four characters more searchingly—Lord Tenby and his mother, an anxious, insincere woman, a young
girl he marries, and a young man that his bride really loved. The complications hinted at in this description of the cast are worked out on the basis of character. [Heinemann ; Doubleday, New York : o.p.]

—— *Mrs. Ames.*   1912
A slight but happy satire on the social affairs of a small country town. [Hodder : o.p.]

—— *Dodo the Second.*   1914
This is the daughter of the original Dodo by her second marriage. [Hodder : o.p.]

—— *Arundel.*   1914
Combines his usual witty execution with some seriousness of plot ; a marriage of convenience is disturbed by
a more romantic love, in a setting of smug suburbanism. [Unwin : o.p.]

—— *The Oakleyites.*   1915
A satire upon the "artistic" society of an old-world town (Rye), and the romance of a novelist who writes
pot-boilers against his better judgment. [Nelson : o.p.]

—— *David Blaize.*   1916
A pleasant and understanding story of schoolboy life at a private school. [Hodder ; Doubleday, Doran, New
York.]

—— *The Freaks of Mayfair.*   1916
Light social satire in Mr. Benson's most natural vein. [Foulis : o.p.]

—— *Mr. Teddy.*   1917
A quiet little comedy, a man in love at the age of forty. [Benn.]

—— *Up and Down.*   1918
A diary, month by month, of Europe from 1914 to 1917, told in the correspondence of two men-friends, the
one upon an Italian island, the other, middle-aged, at home. [Hutchinson : o.p.]

—— *David Blaize and the Blue Door.*   1918
An *Alice-in-Wonderland* adventure of a small boy with his nursery animals and toys. [Hodder ; Doubleday,
Doran, New York.]

—— *Robin Linnet.*   1919
The young hero proceeds from Cambridge to the front with the Grenadier Guards, and his death leads to the
reconciliation of his parents. [Hutchinson : o.p.]

—— *Dodo Wonders.*   1921
A resurrection of the popular heroine of earlier novels, now middle-aged and in reflective mood. [Hutchinson :
o.p.]

—— *Lovers and Friends.*   1921
A love story of social England in war-time, one of the best of this author's productions in this vein. [Unwin ;
Benn.]

—— *David of King's.*   1924
Continues the history of David Blaize, now at the University. [Hodder ; *sub tit. David Blaize of King's,*
Doubleday, Doran, New York.]

BENSON, Edward Frederick (*continued*). *Alan.* 1924
The life and doings of an egoist, amongst highly literary folk. [Unwin ; Doubleday, Doran, New York.]

—— *Mezzanine.* 1926
A woman, ten years her husband's senior, retains his love against the competition of a beautiful girl. [Cassell ; Doubleday, Doran, New York.]

—— *Paying Guests.* 1929
Exploits the humours of a superior boarding-house ; the dominating colonel, attractive young wife, and the rest of them. [Hutchinson ; Doubleday, Doran, New York.]

—— *The Inheritor.* 1930
" A story of youth " ; a handsome and brilliant young fellow in a modern environment turns out to be the inheritor of a primeval curse. [Hutchinson, Doubleday, Doran, New York.]

BENSON, Very Rev. Monsignor Robert Hugh [1871–1914 ; brother of preceding]. *By what Authority ?* 1904
A novel illustrating the troubles of Catholics in Elizabeth's time (1569–90) ; scenes, London and northern England. [Burns & Oates (Kenedy, New York).]

—— *The King's Achievement.* 1905
A Catholic's view of Henry VIII's conduct towards the monasteries illustrated by the destruction of Lewes Priory (*c.* 1534–40)—very controversial. More, Fisher, Thomas, Lord Cromwell, etc., appear. [Burns & Oates (Kenedy, New York).]

—— *The History of Richard Raynal, Solitary.* 1906
Supposed to be reprinted from a MS. found at Rome—the history of an English hermit in the fifteenth century. A study of Quietism, with portraits of Henry VI, Cardinal Beaufort, and others. [Burns & Oates ; Herder, St. Louis : o.p.]

—— *The Queen's Tragedy.* 1906
An erudite apologia for Queen Mary of England by this eminent Roman Catholic divine. The Princess Elizabeth, Philip of Spain, Cardinal Pole, and others are introduced (1553–8). [Burns & Oates ; Herder, St. Louis : o.p.]

—— *The Sentimentalists.* 1906
Begins a series of religious and spiritualistic studies of present-day life, chiefly of people in the class that goes to Eton and Oxford. They deal with religious experiences of the most esoteric kind, and are as much propagandist arguments for the supreme truth of Catholicism as novels in the ordinary sense. [Burns & Oates ; Benziger, New York : o.p.]

—— *A Mirror of Shalott.* 1907
Short stories revealing Father Benson's craftsmanship at its best, and suffused with spiritual imagination and poetry. [Pitman : o.p. ; Benziger, New York : o.p.]

—— *Lord of the World.* 1907
A romance of 2050 A.D., with sensational descriptions of the material aspects of life in the future, though primarily intended to set forth the conflict of principles between the two great camps of Humanitarianism and of believers in the Catholic God. [Pitman : o.p. ; Dodd & Mead, New York.]

—— *The Conventionalist.* 1908
More controversial than ever. A study of people in conventional county society, and the incursion of the supernatural into their lives. Some characters reappear from *The Sentimentalists*. [Burns & Oates ; Herder, St. Louis : o.p.]

—— *The Necromancers.* 1909
A young convert to Rome whose love has just died falls under the spell of an enthusiastic and successful medium, and is barely rescued from madness. Argues that spiritualism is a perilous commerce with diabolic powers which are lying in wait to enthral the soul. [Burns & Oates ; Herder, St. Louis.]

—— *A Winnowing.* 1910
A wealthy young Catholic, devoted to sport and mundane interests, is caught back from the brink of death, having " become aware of a real world of spirit, and all the rest." He builds a convent, and proposes that he and his wife shall become monk and nun. The sequel is a psychological surprise. The usual sensuous descriptions of Roman ceremonial, especially of the life of monastics. [Hutchinson : o.p. ; Herder, St. Louis.]

—— *None Other Gods.* 1910
Another spiritual biography inculcating that the two worlds are one. A peer's son enters the Roman Church, takes to poverty and the life of a gentleman tramp, and sacrifices himself to the bitter end in working out his scheme of purgation and devotion to the spirit. [Hutchinson : o.p. ; Herder, St. Louis.]

—— *The Dawn of All.* 1911
A vision of the world in 1973, when the Church has become omnipotent. A fulsome but very unalluring picture of sacerdotalism rampant. [Hutchinson : o.p. ; Herder, St. Louis.]

—— *The Coward.* 1912
An analysis of a young man, who possesses moral but no physical courage, in conflict with his setting, an old English family to whom such courage is precious. [Hutchinson : o.p. ; Herder, St. Louis.]

—— *Come Rack ! Come Rope !* 1912
The persecution of Roman Catholics under Elizabeth, the martyrdom of the Jesuit Campion, and the ill-treatment of Mary Queen of Scots, depicted in a manner that runs counter to the views of Protestant historians. [Burns & Oates (Kenedy, New York) ; Dodd & Mead, New York.]

—— *An Average Man.* 1913
A study in religious psychology, with some social satire. The hero, having entered the Catholic Church, on his sudden access to wealth abandons it, against the highest dictates of his nature. [Hutchinson : o.p. ; Dodd & Mead, New York.]

BENSON, Very Rev. Monsignor Robert Hugh (*continued*). *Initiation.*   1914
Beginning with a broken engagement to a ruthlessly selfish girl, the tragedy of the wealthy and vigorous hero gradually deepens, until in the pain of a fatal inherited disease he learns that suffering can only be turned to good by quiet acceptance as part of a Divine plan. In the handling of the story, no less than in his efficient characterization and unobtrusive moral purpose, this marks the highest level of Mgr. Benson's work. [Hutchinson : o.p. ; Dodd & Mead, New York ; Kenedy, New York.]

—— *Oddsfish.*   1914
A novel that brings in the leading personages and salient events of the close of the reign of Charles II (1678–85)—the Popish plot, the Rye-House plot, and Monmouth's rebellion. [Burns & Oates (Kenedy, New York) ; Dodd & Mead, New York.]

—— *Loneliness.*   1915
A *prima donna*, on the eve of fame, loses at once her voice, her best friend, and her lover. In this desolation she is forced to return to her faith, and realize her true happiness in religion. [Hutchinson ; Dodd & Mead, New York ; Kenedy, New York.]

BENSON, Stella [Mrs. O'Gorman Anderson ; *b.* 1892]. *I Pose.*   1915
A futurist or post-impressionist novel, with a self-devoted suffragette, a ship's gardener, a sanctimonious clergyman, and other figures posing as comedians, but symbolizing the tragedy of human ignorance, unsympathy, and helplessness. Flashes of realism and also of wit and poetry, diversify the topsy-turvy narrative. [Macmillan, London and New York.]

—— *This is the End.*   1917
Extravaganza of much the same stamp, the dream-world of beauty and goodness in mad juxtaposition with the humbug and banality of the actual world—before the war. A typical comic figure is the thick-skinned, self-satisfied female novelist, who is also active in organized philanthropy—one of Miss Benson's aversions. [Macmillan, London and New York.]

—— *Living Alone.*   1919
A fantasy almost as free as those of James Stephens ; the scene alternately the London streets and a magic boarding-house on a quiet island in the Thames. Satire of a civilization that engages illogically in war is mingled with uproarious farce, as when during an air-raid, the dead come out of their graves thinking it is the last day—the dialogue here is magnificent. [Macmillan, London and New York.]

—— *The Poor Man.*   1922
He is such a very poor specimen that interest is diverted to the magical descriptions of California and later of China, where the author now resides. The incidental satire of American taste in literature, of the boosting methods of publishers' travellers, and of the emancipated, dilettante, philandering set, is also diverting. [Macmillan, London and New York.]

—— *Tobit Transplanted.*   1931
The history of the exiled Tobit and his family, from the Apocrypha, is a parallel that throws into clear definition the personal, domestic, matrimonial, and financial predicaments of certain Russian refugees in Manchuria. Characters and situations correspond, perhaps too exactly ; the lambent humour playing about them is the author's own. [*Sub tit. The Far-away Bride*, 1930, Harper, New York ; Macmillan.]

BENSON, Wilfred. *The Foreigner in the Family.*   1929
The foreigner marries into a family of *nouveaux riches*, who have the usual snobbish tendencies ; but he proves himself a truer gentleman than the descendant of their predecessors at Sheppenhanger Court. A mixture of serious comedy and of farce and caricature. [Hogarth Press ; Harcourt, New York.]

—— *Dawn on Mont Blanc : being incidentally the tragedy of an aggravating young man.*   1930
An amusing comedy of life in Geneva, with some incidental satire upon bureaucrats of the League of Nations. [Hogarth Press.]

BENTLEY, Edmund Clerihew. *Trent's Last Case.*   1913
Although his only novel, this ranks with the best of English detective fiction. In combining character-drawing and love-interest with plot, it falls into line with the work of A. E. W. Mason. [Nelson.]

BENTLEY, Phyllis Eleanor [*b.* 1894]. *Carr.*   1929
" Being the biography of Philip Joseph Carr, manufacturer, of the village of Carr Foot, in the West Riding of Yorkshire, written by his grand-daughter, Mary Elizabeth Carr." An intimate and very detailed chronicle, supposed to have been reconstructed from diaries, letters, and the usual sources of biography, commencing in 1854 and coming down to Carr's death in 1927. [Benn.]

—— *Trio.*   1930
After five slighter novels, Miss Bentley here writes on a larger and more elaborate scale. Three young women, old schoolfellows, are very faithfully drawn, and their different destinies, shaped by their very different characters, are traced with dramatic truth. A West Riding town forms the background. [Gollancz.]

BÉRAUD, Henri [French ; *b.* 1885]. *Lazare* (Lazare, 1924).   1925
An exciting sensation novel constructed on the idea of double personality. A man develops this as the result of a terrible accident and the mental shock. May be compared, unfavourably, with Mr. de la Mare's more poetical story, *The Return*, or with Stevenson's famous morality, *Dr. Jekyll and Mr. Hyde*. [Transl. by Mrs. Harold Sandwith, Butterworth ; better translation by Eric Sutton, Macmillan, New York.]

BERESFORD, John Davys [*b.* 1873]. *The Hampdenshire Wonder.*   1911
Satirizes modern Positivism, whether academical or that of the man in the street. Also, a plea for mystery and romance. The prodigy is born with a finer intellect than Newton's, and rapidly acquires more learning than a dozen *Encyclopædia Britannicas*. His effect on all he comes in contact with is surprising and amusing. [Sidgwick & Jackson ; Secker.]

—— *The Early History of Jacob Stahl.*   1911

—— *A Candidate for Truth* [sequel].   1912

BERESFORD, John Davys (*continued*). *The Invisible Event* [sequel]. 1915

This trilogy deals with a pathological case. A Camberwell boy of Jewish, Irish, and German blood is crippled from infancy and never becomes quite normal. In the second part, though flabby and morbidly intro-spective, he is moulded by circumstance and trial into an individual ; and in the sequel the history of his hesitating and doubt-haunted alliance with Betty is a study appealing both to our human sympathies and to our psychological interests. The influence of Butler's *Way of all Flesh* is observable in the attention paid to heredity and other factors of development. [Sidgwick & Jackson ; Doubleday, Doran, New York.]

—— *Goslings*. 1913

Imagines the effect upon this civilized world of ours of a pestilence coming from Russia and killing off nearly all the male population. [Heinemann : o.p. ; *sub tit. The World of Women*, Macauley Co., New York : o.p.]

—— *The House in Demetrius Road*. 1914

Tries by the usual realistic procedure to show how the efforts of two lovers to save an older man who is a dipsomaniac react upon their relations to each other. [Heinemann : o.p. ; Doubleday, Doran, New York : o.p.]

—— *These Lynnekers*. 1916

Dickie Lynneker breaks away from the conservative traditions of his ancient family, to pursue success in a modern world that is strange to them. Though the characters scarcely come to life, the social contrasts are brought out vividly. [Cassell : o.p. ; Doubleday, Doran, New York : o.p.]

—— *God's Counterpoint*. 1918

An analytical study of the sexual inhibitions in a man brought up on narrow puritanical lines, and thus led to regard the sexual side of love as bestial and degrading. [Collins : o.p. ; Doran, New York : o.p.]

—— *The Jervaise Comedy*. 1919

Again the conflict of old and new. The Jervaises are prouder and more aristocratic even than the Lynnekers. Hence this highly " artificial English comedy," when the daughter is believed to have eloped with the chauffeur. [Collins.]

—— *An Imperfect Mother*. 1920

The mother is a genuine and attractive character up to the point where the novel becomes a piece of psycho-analysis. [Collins ; Macmillan, New York.]

—— *Revolution*. 1921

Scenes in a revolution brought about by a general strike staged in a village of the Midlands, where one of Mr. Beresford's neurotic heroes forms a local committee of public safety. More interest is sought in this humani-tarian enterprise and in this gentleman's sentimental affairs than in the larger issues. [Collins ; Putnam, New York.]

—— *Love's Pilgrim*. 1923

The love predicaments of another neurotic person, whose parent wet-blankets all his affairs, and wants to mother him indefinitely. [Collins ; Bobbs-Merrill, Indianapolis.]

—— *The Monkey Puzzle*. 1925

As much by long conversations as by the incidents, the novelist deals with the old question, whether we should ever interfere with others for their own good. The efforts of a husband and wife to save a bibulous artist end in discomfiture and a scandal in the village. [Collins ; Bobbs-Merrill, Indianapolis.]

—— *That Kind of Man*. 1926

A conscientious and rather dull literary man has an outbreak of romance, but returns to conjugal fidelity and subsides into his old rut. [Collins ; *sub tit. Almost Pagan*, Bobbs-Merrill, Indianapolis.]

—— *The Tapestry*. 1927

At turning-points, Fortescue acts with unwonted decisiveness, as at the dictate of some inscrutable volition. His ups and downs in life are distressing ; but at length he sees them as weaving the pattern of a tapestry— psycho-analysis slides into mysticism. [Collins ; Bobbs-Merrill, Indianapolis.]

—— *Real People*. 1929

A medical man discovers that he enjoys the gift of " intuitional diagnosis," and accepts it as proof of a super-natural world and his own immortality. The really real people, however, are some humorous young folk who satirize and scandalize society ; and there is further comedy in the fine shades of snobbishness contrasted. [Collins.]

—— *Love's Illusion*. 1930

A plain tale, not a psychological inquiry. A man thirty years later recalls how as an innocent, clean-minded young fellow he was drawn into an illicit affair with a girl whom he tardily found to be only " an erotic young animal." [Collins ; Viking Press, New York.]

—— *Seven, Bobsworth*. 1930

Amiable satire on a financial magnate and a newspaper lord and the menagerie of cranks who settle in a bungalow town which they establish. [Faber.]

BERG, Bengt Magnus Kristoffer [Swedish ; *b.* 1885]. *The Motherless*. 1924

A nature-story of the Northern forests, the Finns and the Lapps. The hero is a bear-cub. [Transl. by Charles Wharton STORK, Doubleday, New York.]

BERGMAN, Hjalmar [Swedish ; *b.* 1883]. *God's Orchid* (Markurells i Wadköping, 1913). 1924

Portrays old-fashioned aristocratic life of a Swedish cathedral-town, into which is projected a self-made financier, once an innkeeper. [Transl. by E. CLASSEN, Knopf, New York.]

BERGSÖE, Carl Vilhelm Otto [Danish ; 1835–1911]. *The Bride of Roervig* (Bruden fra Rörvig, 1872). 1877

A romantic story of the Roervig sands in Zealand, told by a Copenhagen professor ; with descriptive passages. The Danish novelist has also written *Fra Piazzo del Popolo* (1876) ; *Fra den gamle Fabrik*, etc. [Transl. by Nina FRANCIS, Tinsley : o.p.]

BERNARD, Charles de [Pierre Marie Charles de Bernard du Grail de la Villette ; French ; 1805–50]. *Gerfaut* (1838). 1893

A story of intrigue with a tragic—or melodramatic—ending, but different from the ordinary story of the kind. The author adopts an ironical attitude ; his hero, a fatigued literary man, is recommended by his physician to take this species of amusement as a restorative, and never shows a spark of passion in his amour. The book gives a vivacious picture of literary and artistic, on the one hand, and patrician society on the other ; but its strength is in the presentation of character. [Transl. by A. A. PAGE, Laird, Chicago : o.p. ; also in *French Romanticists*, 10 vols., Sawyer ; another tr., *sub tit. A Fatal Passion*, has been published : o.p.]

—— *The Lion's Skin* (La peau de lion ; et, la chasse aux amants, 1841). 1889

The pseudo-hero masquerades in a liaison as " the lion," and is cut out by the real " lion." [Transl. by E. VIZETELLY, Vizetelly : o.p. ; with *The Lover Hunt*, New York, 1853 : o.p.]

BERNHARD, Marie [German ; b. 1852]. *The Rector of St. Luke's.* 1891

A love story and study of character. The chief people are a girl, her lover (an artist whose past has an ugly blot which he dare not confess, and who yet will not marry her without confessing), and the rector, who knows the truth, but will not betray it even to win the girl's love. [Transl. by E. L. LATHROP, Worthington, New York : o.p.]

BERTRAM, Anthony [b. 1897]. *The Sword Falls.* 1930

An epic of the commonplace : a lawyer's clerk, despite blows dealt by the war to himself and his children, emerges with the unfailing philosophy of everyday life. [Allen and Unwin ; Harper, New York.]

BESANT, Sir Walter [1838–1901]. *The Revolt of Man.* 1882

A satirical extravaganza, picturing a future when women are in supreme command in State, army and navy, and private life. But man rebels, overthrows the feminine regime and the religion of the ideal woman, and—women are glad of it. [Chatto.]

—— *All Sorts and Conditions of Men.* 1882

An Utopian fancy, the Palace of Delight in Whitechapel has since, in some measure, been realized. But Besant lays most stress on human nature, and tells his readers to distrust politics and learn to help themselves. [Chatto ; Burt, New York.]

—— *Dorothy Forster.* 1884

The domestic history of the Forsters of Bamborough Castle during the unquiet years of Jacobite intrigue which culminated in the fatal rising of 1715, of which the autobiographer's brother was the General. Dorothy tells her own story in a garrulous fashion, giving intimate views of life among the gentry of Northumberland, portraying the characters of the chivalrous Earl of Derwentwater, whom she loved and refused on the score of religion, of her self-indulgent brother, and several fictitious characters, such as the humorous and pathetic Mr. Hilyard. The tragic narrative of the rebellion leads the reader at length to London, into Georgian society, and into Newgate and the Tower. [Chatto.]

—— *The Children of Gibeon.* 1886

Poverty, social reform, and the influence of caste, exhibited in a Hoxton romance. A baronet's and a washerwoman's daughters are brought up together in ignorance of their different origin, as an experiment to show the effects of hereditary character and of breeding. [Chatto : o.p. ; Harper, New York : o.p. ; Burt, New York, o.p.]

—— *The World went very well then.* 1887

Adventure, love, and war in the years 1744–62 ; the scene chiefly at Deptford, on the Thames, and on board ship. [Chatto ; Harper, New York : o.p.]

—— *For Faith and Freedom.* 1888

A story of the Puritans in James II's reign, Monmouth's rebellion, the expulsion of the recusants, and the life of the exiles in the Barbados plantations (1662–88). [Chatto ; Harper, New York : o.p. ; Burt, New York : o.p.]

—— *Beyond the Dreams of Avarice.* 1895

On the evils of colossal wealth. An immense fortune has grown up around a nucleus created by fraud ; and, the last owner dying intestate, a flock of claimants appear. Interest centres in the real heir, kept in ignorance of his wealth by his father, who believes the ill-gotten riches to be accursed. [Chatto ; Harper, New York : o.p.]

—— *A Fountain Sealed.* 1897

A pretty, but not a very plausible romance, based on the exploded story of Prince George's (afterwards George III) love affair with the Quakeress, Hannah Lightfoot (1760). [Chatto ; Stokes, New York.]

—— *The Orange Girl.* 1899

A picture of the streets, taverns, mansions, and theatres of London, and of Newgate and its strange inhabitants, 150 years ago, painted by an antiquary. The heroine, Nell Gwyn's double, poor girl, great actress, fine lady, and convict, magnanimously saves the hero, on trial on a false charge, and suffers for him. [Chatto ; Nash ; Dodd & Mead, New York : o.p.]

—— *The Lady of Lynn.* 1901

A bustling story of eighteenth-century Lynn, though the pictures of fashionable life are but superficial. A beautiful heroine, her bluff sailor lover, and a wicked peer who conspires to get hold of her money, are the boldly contrasted protagonists. [Chatto ; Dodd & Mead, New York : o.p.]

—— *No Other Way.* 1902

Eighteenth-century London, Newgate, debtors' prisons, taverns, cockpits, citizens, serving-folk, and ruffians described as if by an eye-witness. A fashionable lady, hopelessly in debt, takes advantage of the law that transfers a woman's liabilities to her husband by marrying a negro sentenced to death. [Chatto ; Dodd & Mead, New York : o.p.]

BESANT, Sir Walter, and RICE, James [1844–82]. *Ready-Money Mortiboy.* 1872

Old Mortiboy is a miser and the offspring of misers, who builds up a huge fortune by grinding the poor and ruining the well-to-do. His son, an unscrupulous but well-meaning young man, is at once nemesis to

BESANT, Sir Walter, and RICE, James (*continued*).

the old Shylock and dispenser of poetic justice to the various characters. Life in the country town where Mortiboy's bank is established, and many phases of shady life in London and elsewhere are exploited. [Chatto; Collins, London and New York.]

—— *The Golden Butterfly.* 1876

How an American oil-king dispenses his millions on an abortive humanitarian enterprise. This magnanimous, egotistical fellow, invincibly amiable in spite of discomfiture, is of course the centre of interest. The minor characters are the butt of keen satire, deriding dilettantism and the like; but incidents and characters border on extravaganza. [Collins, London and New York.]

—— *'Twas in Trafalgar's Bay; and other stories.* 1879

A pretty little love tale of Lyme Regis in 1803–5; the hero a fine old smuggler, and the lovers a country maid and the son of a City knight. Then, a story of a curious robbery, with sketches of Canadian life to-day; a City tale; and *Le Chien d'Or*, a tale of French Quebec in 1697. [Chatto.]

—— *The Chaplain of the Fleet.* 1881

A story of the famous gaol and of Epsom in George II's reign, well furnished with antiquarian lore about the streets, houses, theatres, and social life. [Chatto; (Wayfarer's Lib.), Dent.]

BEVAN, Tom. *Beggars of the Sea.* 1903

A fair specimen of a number of historical romances of adventure, especially for boys. The earlier stages of the protracted struggle with Spain; the Gueux, the terrible siege of Haarlem (1573), etc. [Nelson.]

—— *A Hero in Wolf-skin.* 1904

The struggle between the Romans and the Goths; scenes, the Danube and Rome under Gallus (250–1). [R.T.S.: o.p.; Jacobs, Philadelphia: o.p.]

—— *A Trooper of the Finns.* 1905

A fierce narrative of fighting between Finns and Croats. The hero is a young English soldier of fortune, in the Thirty Years' War (1630). [R.T.S.]

BEYLE, Marie-Henri ["De Stendhal"; French; 1783–1842]. *Red and Black: a chronicle of the nineteenth century* (Le rouge et le noir, 1830). 1898

The introspective autobiography of Julien Sorel, an egotistic and morbid young man, his struggles with adversity, his intrigues and crimes. In ground-plan resembles the old picaresque novel, a rogue's adventures in different social spheres; in method and spirit the book is new and all but unique. The coldness and irony are definitely anti-romantic. Having constructed a character of definite attributes, the author proceeds to experiment with him, observing, with the unimpassioned interest of a scientist, his conduct, thoughts, and emotions in given circumstances. Julien exposes his motives frankly, good and base, his high ideals or shabby self-seeking, the knavery of his early amours, and the mixture of real passion and theatrical propensities that characterizes his tragic intrigue with a high-born girl, and brings him to the guillotine. Beyle was an idolator of Bonaparte, whose inspiration is apparent in Sorel's exposition of the creed of individualism. [Transl. by E. P. Robins, 2 vols., Smithers: o.p.; by C. Tergie (a poor transl.), Brentano, New York (Downey): o.p.; by Horace B. Samuel, Routledge (Dutton, New York) 1916; by C. K. Scott-Moncrieff, 2 vols., Chatto (Boni, New York) 1926; *id.*, Modern Lib., New York, 1929.]

—— *The Chartreuse of Parma* (La chartreuse de Parme, 1839). 1901

Passion in all its purity and intensity, its fieriest results, and its most tragic consequences, is here portrayed with the same moral detachment, objectivity, and unfailing knowledge of human life. The scene is a little Italian Court, whither the young adventurer Fabrice has found his way, and in dramatic importance plays second fiddle to the fascinating Duchess Sanseverina and her jealous lover, the astute minister, Count Mosca. The book opens with a famous narrative of the battle of Waterloo. It is a novel that set a standard of flawless technique, of the lucid unfolding of character and motive, of accurate comprehension of the inherent disorder of life, that has rarely been approached in dramatic narration. [Transl. by Lady Mary Lloyd, with preface by Maurice Hewlett, Heinemann; new transl. by C. K. Scott-Moncrieff, 2 vols., Chatto (Boni, New York), 1926.]

—— *The Abbess of Castro* (L'abbesse de Castro, 1839); *and other stories.* 1925

This story of savage loves and hatreds in 16th century Italy was composed by Stendhal from the record of the actual case in a contemporary manuscript, i.e. from the same kind of materials as supplied some of the groundwork for the *Chartreuse de Parme*. It is the history of an amour between a girl of noble family and a young brigand, attached to the Colonna faction, then engaged in a sanguinary feud with the Orsini clan. The girl later becomes abbess and violates her vows; her trial took place in 1572. It is Stendhal's cool, sarcastic irony that differentiates this from innumerable stories which recall Bandello and Giraldi Cinthio. [Transl. by C. K. Scott-Moncrieff, Chatto; Boni, New York.]

BIDDER, Mary [Mrs. Horace Porter]. *Westminster Cloisters: the story of a life's ambition.* 1887

The story of a monkish artist in the days of Richard I, Queen Eleanor, and Prince John (1193). [Wells Gardner.]

—— *In the Shadow of the Crown.* 1899

This novel of the times of Edward II and Edward III (1323–33) brings these two figures on the stage in an arresting way, and still more strikingly John of Eltham, Duke of Cornwall, with the queen, Isabella, and Roger Mortimer. [Constable: o.p.]

BIERCE, Ambrose [American; 1842–1914?]. *In the Midst of Life.* 1891

Bierce was a skilful manipulator of sensational effects, and though he never wrote a novel he is responsible for a large number of grim and terrible stories, the realism of which accentuates and is accentuated by his sardonic attitude. These are chiefly episodes in the Civil War. The present collection was first entitled *Tales of Soldiers and Civilians.* [Boni, New York; Modern Lib., New York; Nash; (Phœnix Lib.), Chatto.]

BIERCE, Ambrose (*continued*). *The Monk and the Hangman's Daughter.*   1892

     A Gothic romance, suffused with poetic glamour, about a young monk who falls passionately in love with a girl whose father's trade makes her an outcast. Severe though the struggle is between inclination and his religious vows, earthly love triumphs ; the result is tragic. Bierce's story is adapted from Danziger's English version of a tale by Richard Voss. [Boni, New York, Cape.]

—— *Can Such Things Be ?*   1893

     Twenty-four sketches of the uncanny, ghosts, survivals of personality, and such-like terrors. *One Summer Night* and *John Mortonson's Funeral* are brief essays in pure horror ; *Moxon's Master* is a powerful story on the Frankenstein theme ; here the machine-man goes insane, through the maladjustment of a small part. [Boni, New York ; (Traveller's Lib.), Cape.]

—— *Ten Tales.*   1925

     Representative of the best of his stories, selected, with an introduction, by A. J. A. Symons. [First Edition Club ; Foyle.]

—— *The Eyes of the Panther ; and other stories.*   1928

     The Eyes of the Panther is an excellent example of Bierce's handling of the uncanny ; this and the other stories in the volume are arranged from *In the Midst of Life* and *Can Such Things Be ?* There are several good tales, e.g. *The Major's Story*, mingled with other work, to be found in *Collected Works*. [Cape ; Boni, New York.]

BIKÉLAS, Demetrios [Greek ; 1835–1908]. *Loukis Laras* (1879).   1881

     A story of the Greek revolution (1821–2) ; the reminiscences of a Chiote merchant. This author is the leading novelist of modern Greece. [Transl. from Greek by J. GENNADIUS, Macmillan.]

—— *Tales from the Ægean.*   1894

     Sketches of contemporary Greek life, simple and natural in style, refined in feeling and sentiment. [Transl. from the French by L. E. OPDYCKE, McClurg, Chicago.]

BINDLOSS, Harold [*b.* 1866]. *Ainslie's Ju-Ju.*   1900

     A trading venture into the hinterland of Lagos, Nigeria, leads a party of Europeans into terrible straits and perils, from which the hero owes his escape to the possession of a mystic ju-ju or talisman. [Chatto : o.p.]

—— *A Sower of Wheat.*   1901

—— *The Mistress of Bonaventure.*   1903

—— *A Damaged Reputation.*   1906

—— *By Right of Purchase.*   1908

—— *The Greater Power.*   1909

     Novels depicting the rough life of settlers in Canada, the result of first-hand observation. All Mr. Bindloss's stories are full of exciting adventure, on the Western prairies, in the wilds of Africa, and elsewhere, and of the hard experiences of sailors, ranchers, engineers, and explorers. [(1) and (2) Chatto ; (2) (Wayfarer's Lib.), Dent ; Stokes, New York : o.p. ; (3) Ward & Lock ; Fenno, New York : o.p. ; (4) and (5) Long : o.p. ; Stokes, New York : o.p.]

—— *Sadie's Conquest.*   1917

     A story of the Saskatchewan prairie, and of two friends of different stamp, the more stable of whom wins the hotel-keeper's level-headed daughter. [Ward & Lock.]

—— *A Moorside Feud.*   1930

     Life of a man from Alberta on a Cumberland sheep-farm : the dialect is rather laboriously reproduced, but the north-country hardness brought out well. [Ward & Lock ; *sub tit. Rancher Jim*, Stokes, New York.]

BINNS, Ottwell [*b.* 1872]. *A Hazard of the Snows.*   1921

     There is some character-drawing in this romance of adventure in Canada. [Ward & Lock.]

BIRABEAU, André [French]. *Revelation.*   1930

     A mother, after her son's death, discovers him to have been a sexual pervert. Her grief, and efforts to enlighten her husband, make a painful story. [Transl. by UNA, Lady TROUBRIDGE, Gollancz ; Viking Press, New York.]

BIRD, Robert Montgomery [American ; 1803–54]. *Nick o' the Woods ; or, The Jibbenainosay.*   1837

     Gives us the redskin, not idealized as by Cooper, but in all his natural ugliness. An episode of Indian warfare in Kentucky. Hero and heroine are carried off by savages, and, after strange alternations of escape and recapture, in which the whites always come off victorious from the brink of death, they are restored to safety and wealth, and the villain is killed. Nick is an unctuous Quaker, who privily carries on a sanguinary war with the Indians (who had massacred his wife and children), at the same time preaching love and peace. [Routledge : o.p. ; Burt, New York : o.p.]

BIRKENFELD, Günther [German ; *b.* 1901]. *A Room in Berlin* (Dritter Hof Links, 1929).   1930

     A ghastly picture of poverty and overcrowding and their results, starvation, prostitution, incestuous love, suicide. Apparently written for humanitarian purposes. [Transl. by Eric SUTTON, Constable ; Boni, New York.]

" BIRMINGHAM, George A."** [Canon James Owen Hannay, Irish ; *b.* 1865]. *The Seething Pot.*   1905

     The rector of Westport, Co. Mayo, and canon of St. Patrick's, Dublin, was a member of the Gaelic League, and in his earlier novels, which were a makeshift sort of fiction, tried to give a simple and sympathetic account of critical episodes of Irish history. His political attitude was nationalist in the most liberal sense, and he showed fellow-feeling even for opponents. The present romance deals with the violent political cross-currents of Parnell's time. [Arnold ; Doubleday, Doran, New York : o.p.]

" BIRMINGHAM, George A." (*continued*). *Hyacinth.* 1906

Deals with current politics, from a Protestant standpoint, and satirizes a Roman Catholic sisterhood. [Hodder : o.p. ; Doran, New York : o.p.]

—— *Benedict Kavanagh.* 1907

This has the same general subject, but shows less bias. The hero has to make up his mind whether he will be a quiet, prosperous citizen or a " patriot." [Hodder : o.p.]

—— *The Northern Iron.* 1907

Deals with the northern movement in the year of the rebellion of 1798, and of the defeat before Antrim. There are portraits of representative figures from both sides. [Talbot Press, Dublin ; Norman & Remington, Baltimore : o.p.]

—— *The Bad Times.* 1908

A good general view of all sorts and conditions at the period of Isaac Butt's Home Rule movement, in the seventies. Shows up the evils due to the operations of the Land League. [Methuen ; Doubleday, Doran, New York : o.p.]

—— *Spanish Gold.* 1908
—— *The Simpkins Plot.* 1911
—— *The Major's Niece.* 1911

In these three novels, bound together by the delightful personality of " J. J.," Mr. Birmingham leaves serious historical fiction for light comedy and farce. The Rev. J. J. Meldon is an extremely unorthodox clergyman from the west of Ireland, who in the first novel performs miracles of agility, valour, and address in a competitive search for hidden treasure ; in the second engineers a plot for getting rid of an objectionable agent ; and in the third triumphs absurdly over difficulties caused by a visit of the Lord-Lieutenant. He is an irresistible talker, a champion liar, a shrewd and satirical critic of things in general. His observations on Irish affairs are full of sound sense. The sceptical Major Kent, the impish Marjorie, and dozens of English and native characters are capitally drawn. [(1) Methuen ; Doubleday, Doran, New York ; (2) Nelson ; Doran, New York : o.p. ; (3) Hodder ; Doran, New York : o.p.]

—— *The Search Party.* 1909

Farcical incidents inaugurated by a crazy anarchist in a western village. [Methuen ; Doran, New York : o.p.]

—— *Lalage's Lovers.* 1911

In a kindred vein, with another humorous creation in the hoydenish Lalage Beresford. [Methuen ; Doran, New York : o.p.]

—— *The Inviolable Sanctuary.* 1912

A madcap heroine of fifteen, a dignified schoolboy, sailing-boats, laughter, and love on the west coast of Ireland. [Nelson ; *sub tit. Priscilla's Spies*, Doran, New York : o.p.]

—— *The Red Hand of Ulster.* 1912

Farce and wholesome satire. An American millionaire engineers an Irish revolution, enlisting hot-heads, waverers, shufflers, and simple fools. [Murray ; Doran, New York : o.p.]

—— *The Adventures of Dr. Whitty.* 1913

The comedy of local politics and personal eccentricities in a village of western Connaught. [Methuen ; Doubleday, Doran, New York : o.p.]

—— *General John Regan.* 1913

More light satire of Irish types, one at least revived from *Spanish Gold.* [Hodder : o.p. ; Doran, New York : o.p.]

—— *The Lost Tribes.* 1914

Makes comedy out of a high-handed American lady's schemes for boosting a village in Galway and running a miracle-play. [Murray ; Doran, New York : o.p.]

—— *Gossamer.* 1915

A more serious novel, dealing with international finance : a banker of German extraction whose interests are in England, finds himself, at the outbreak of the war, in the dilemma between loyalty to his country or to his business. The introduction of an Irish Nationalist character provides for an account of the situation in Ireland in 1914. [Methuen : o.p. ; Doubleday, Doran, New York : o.p.]

—— *Minnie's Bishop ; and other stories of Ireland.* 1915

Some serious stories and more of a comic sort. Those which deal with Ireland—not all do—depict sympathetically the miseries of the western peasants. [Hodder : o.p. ; Doubleday, Doran, New York : o.p.]

—— *The Island Mystery.* 1918

An extravagant story of an American millionaire who purchases an island in the Ægean, to satisfy his daughter's ambition to become a queen, finding on it secreted stores of petrol for submarines. [Methuen.]

—— *Our Casualty ; and other stories.* 1919

Short stories of the humours of characters of his usual type. The title-story, of hospital officialdom—a minor casualty is listed for immediate burial. [Skeffington : o.p.]

—— *Up, the Rebels !* 1919

The Sinn Feinn countermove of a young lady who seizes the post office, and shuts up the police in an Irish country town when conscription is threatened, gives rise to some excellent fun. [Methuen.]

—— *Inisheeny.* 1920
—— *The Lost Lawyer.* 1921
—— *The Major's Candlesticks.* 1929

Further comedies on Irish soil. [(1), (2), and (3), Methuen ; (3), Bobbs-Merrill, Indianapolis.]

—— *Good Conduct.* 1920

The heroine is an attractive tomboy refreshingly free from sentiment. [Murray.]

"BIRMINGHAM, George A." (continued). *The Grand Duchess.*   1924
The author breaks fresh ground here : a set of attractive and new characters go hunting for a wonderful diadem in Hungary. [Hodder.]

—— *Bindon Parva.*   1925
The scene of the comedy is a village on the Dorset coast. [Mills & Boon ; Bobbs-Merrill, Indianapolis.]

—— *Wild Justice.*   1930
An ingenious murder story, put in the mouth of a comical parson with a fierce grudge against the Royal Irish Constabulary. [Methuen ; Bobbs-Merrill, Indianapolis.]

—— *The Hymn Tune Mystery.*   1930
A well-known hymn-tune furnishes a cryptogram on which hangs the mystery of some stolen jewelry. Light farce dexterously handled. [Methuen.]

BIRRELL, Olive. *Love in a Mist.*   1900
A sympathetic study of a fanatical devotee of socialism, who wrecks his life and sacrifices the welfare of his family. His daughter's love for a humble but heroically unselfish character, and his tragic death, are the chief matters of the domestic drama, and his ill-assorted household furnish comic relief. [Smith & Elder : o.p.]

BJÖRKMAN, Edwin August [Swedish-American ; b. 1866]. *The Soul of a Child.*   1922
—— *Gates of Life* [sequel].   1923
An intimate and revealing psychological study of boyhood and adolescence, the first book distinguished also by its pictures of Swedish life and customs. [(1) and (2), Knopf, New York.]

BJÖRNSON, Björnstjerne [Norwegian ; 1832–1910]. *Synnöve Solbakken* (Synnöve Solbakken, 1857).   1881
Begins a series of short, simple stories of peasant life in Norway, in which Björnson won his first fame by portraying the honest farmers and labourers, among whom he had dwelt, with a truthfulness to the life as he saw it, warmed by sincere fellow-feeling, which was something new in Norse literature. This pastoral describes the refining of a rough and passionate youth, " Synnöve Sunnycheek," by the influence of a pure love. [Transl. by Julie SUTTER (1881), Heinemann (Macmillan, New York), 1894 : o.p.]

—— *Arne* (Arne, 1858).   1866
Gives us the same primitive, unsophisticated people, and simple ways of life and thought, in the same transparent style, conveying in an enchanting fashion the poetic atmosphere and glamour of the North. Arne is the son of a maiden, betrayed but afterwards married by a village coxcomb, who brutally maltreats her. The lad's story is carried down to his own love and marriage. [Transl. by Walter Low, Strahan : o.p. ; Heinemann (Macmillan, New York), 1889 : o.p.]

—— *A Happy Boy* (En glad gut, 1860).   1896
The simple record of the growth, love, ambition, and final success of a peasant, with faithful delineations of country life. The old pastor's care for the talented boy, who might have followed the devil as easily as he follows his good angel, is described with a simplicity that veils the subtlety. [Transl. by Mrs. W. ARCHER, Heinemann (Macmillan, New York) : o.p.]

—— *The Fisher Lass* (Fiskerjenten, 1868).   1896
A book typically Norse in characters, manners, and ideas, aiming to show the strength of native talent and to vindicate the theatre. The life of a wayward girl of humble origin, who is seized with an ambition to go on the stage. [Transl. by Mrs. W. ARCHER, Heinemann (Macmillan, New York) : o.p.]

—— *The Bridal March* (Brude-Slaatten) ; *and other stories* (1873).   1883
A Norse *Romeo and Juliet*—a tale of passion breaking down the fate that overshadowed a family for generations ; with eight idylls of peasant life, among them, *A Dangerous Wooing*, a comic story ; *Blakken*, " a vigorous bit of disguised autobiography, of which not the author but a horse is the ostensible hero " ; *The Father* (Faderen), a tragedy set forth in marvellously few words. These tales were the work of the years 1856–69. [*Bridal March* and *One Day* (Een daag), ed. by Sir E. Gosse, Heinemann, 1896 ; Macmillan, New York : o.p.]

—— *Magnhild* (Magnhild, 1877).   1897
A critical study of marriage, and altogether a more complex book ; peasants and landscapes depicted as before, together with a higher society, and more attention to the cares and problems of modern life. Magnhild is a woman of fine nature, married to a brute, whose talents and aspirations are driven back into herself. Her self-searchings, yearnings, and discouragements are forcibly rendered. [With *Dust*, Heinemann (Macmillan, New York).]

—— *Captain Mansana* (Kaptejn Mansana, 1878) ; *and other stories* (1880–2).   1883
Captain Mansana is a story of the Italian war of independence which the author states to be founded on fact, drawing a parallel between the title-character and the socialist Lassalle. *The Railroad and the Church-yard* (Jernbauen og kirkegaarden, 1867) and *Dust*, briefer pieces, are Norse stories, very modern in thought : the last, a suggestive study of the right way to instruct children in religious ideas. [*Captain Mansana* and *Mother's Hands* (Mors hænder), Heinemann ; Macmillan, New York : o.p.]

—— *The Heritage of the Kurts* (Det flager i byen og på havnen, 1884).   1892
A concise treatment of the Rougon-Macquart problem of heredity. The Kurts are a race of turbulent, sensual and eccentric gentlefolk, whose nature from generation to generation seems to be quite unamenable to the curbs of civilized society. The author traces the various branches of the family, bringing out with minuteness the effects of inherited aptitudes and of variation, the problem resolving itself into the question how Thomas Rendalen, half Kurt, half peasant, will conduct himself in life—whether the new blood will make him a useful member of society. The urgent social questions arising in the course of the story are stated with frankness, and with indignation against shams and hypocrisy. [Heinemann : o.p. ; 2 vols., Macmillan, New York : o.p.]

BJÖRNSON, Björnstjerne (*continued*). *In God's Way* (På Guds veje, 1889). 1890

An indictment of conventional morality, dealing, in the artistic form of a novel, with the case of an innocent woman married to a corrupt libertine, and her persecution by society when she takes the law into her own hands and frees herself. Denounces the unjust censoriousness of modern society, and exalts true purity of life ; but is no mere tract—the reserved strength and the thorough art of this group of novels being a striking quality throughout. [Transl. by E. CARMICHAEL, Heinemann : o.p.]

—— *Absalom's Hair* (Absalons haar) ; *and, A Painful Memory* (Et stygt barndomsminde, 1894) 1898

Allegorical in a very broad and very modern sense, the title glancing obliquely at the sensual failings of Rafael Kaas. A story of Norwegian life in town and country, which reads like a string of extraordinary anecdotes related by an eye-witness. Rafael and his mother are a pair of impulsive beings, frankly individual to the verge of eccentricity, and determined to live their own lives without submitting to interference or restraint. The other is a story of a murder and an execution. [Heinemann ; Macmillan, New York : o.p.]

—— *Mary* (Mary, 1906). 1909

Mary is a splendid Olympian creature worthy of a rôle in the Volsung myths. The very greatness of her nature causes her to make a terrible mistake ; dishonour is about to overwhelm her ; but a lover, whose generosity equals hers, saves her on the brink of self-immolation. Admirably translated. [Transl. by Mary MORISON, Heinemann : o.p. ; Macmillan, New York : o.p.]

BLACK, Ladbroke Lionel Day [*b.* 1877], and Robert LYND [*b.* 1879]. *The Mantle of the Emperor.* 1906

An Irishman's adventures mixed up with the career of Louis Napoleon, afterwards Napoleon III, down to his escape from Ham (1830–46). [Griffiths : o.p.]

BLACK, William [Scottish ; 1841–98]. *A Daughter of Heth.* 1871

His first and best novel, though *A Princess of Thule* is the most popular. Black was a romancer who got his picturesque and his atmosphere, not from the past, but from strange and beautiful scenery. He excels in verbal landscape-painting. This novel takes us to a Scottish village and on a trip along the Highland coast. The inhabitants are sketched in a lively fashion, bringing out their peculiarities of feeling, prejudice, and speech. The main characters are a mischievous and dare-devil but manly boy, son of a Presbyterian minister ; and his cousin, a half-French girl, whose sunny and refined disposition clashes with the rigid Puritanism of the northern village. Love and marriage give her opportunity to prove her capacity for self-sacrifice. [Collins, London and New York.]

—— *The Strange Adventures of a Phaeton.* 1872

History of a coaching tour from London to Edinburgh through the loveliest scenery of England. The travellers are four, a married pair who talk and bicker amicably, and an unmarried pair who make love. Parodied by Bret Harte in his *Condensed Novels.* [Low : o.p. ; Harper, New York : o.p.]

—— *A Princess of Thule.* 1874

A weak, pleasure-loving artist woos and wins a beautiful Highland girl, and brings her into the hothouse atmosphere of London, where she pines for the air and freedom of her Hebridean home. Ultimately her true and unaffected nature works on his character and makes a man of him. The wonderful colours and changes of sea and sky and mountain in the Hebrides inspire many a descriptive page, and the rich park-lands of southern England, so different in their beauty, are feelingly depicted. [Low : o.p. ; Harper, New York.]

—— *The Maid of Killeena ; and other stories.* 1874

The maid is a peasant sister to the " Princess," and heroine of a pretty idyll of the Hebrides, in which the simple, homely life of the dwellers in the isles and the romance of their habitat are lovingly depicted. [Low ; Harper, New York : o.p.]

—— *Macleod of Dare.* 1879

A tragic story, bringing shallow and garish fashionable life into contact with the noble simplicity of Highland society. Catastrophe results from the marriage of a brave and chivalrous young chief with a London lady. [Low : o.p. ; Harper, New York : o.p.]

—— *White Wings : a yachting romance.* 1880

A happy love tale, told with an accompaniment of beautiful views of sea and land, seen in a cruise along the coast of Scotland. [Low : o.p. ; Harper, New York : o.p.]

—— *In Far Lochaber.* 1888

Elaborates the contrast between the rough and genuine Highland gentry, with their humane and liberal religious feelings, and the straitness and intolerance of the " unco guid " in the Lowland manufacturing town. Rich in description of the wild mountainous region round Ben Nevis. [Low : o.p. ; Harper, New York : o.p.]

—— *Wild Eelin : her escapades, adventures, and bitter sorrows.* 1898

The tragical love tale of another Highland girl, own sister to the Princess of Thule. Black's favourite motive, the noble simplicity of Highland life in contact with modern decadence, reappears again, and there is a poetic rendering of the clan spirit as it survives at the present day. Scene, Inverness. [Low ; Harper, New York : o.p.] [*Works :* in 18 vols., Low ; in 5 vols., Burt, New York.]

BLACKBURN, Douglas. *A Burgher Quixote.* 1903

Ostensibly the memoirs written by himself of Sarel Erasmus, nominal author of the amusing satire on Boer officialdom, *Prinsloo of Prinsloosdorp* (MacLeay : o.p.). An ironical narrative, satirizing Boer character in the persons of those rogues and skulkers who fought for their country from various discreditable motives. Sarel the law-agent, his brother the horse-stealer, the traitor Andries Brink, and the humorous Paul du Plooy, are made to depict their own characters. Ben Viljoen and Joubert are drawn with generous appreciation. [Blackwood.]

—— *Richard Hartley, Prospector.* 1905

A South African novel ; society on the Rand. life on the veld, and the character of the Boer. [Blackwood.]

BLACKMORE, Richard Doddridge [1825–1900]. *Clara Vaughan.* 1864

Like the majority of Blackmore's novels, an attempt to naturalize romance in a modern environment. A melodramatic tale which was taken to be by Miss Braddon : a petulant and obstinate heroine's adventures, before she comes into her rightful heritage, mixed up with the history of a Corsican vendetta. Word-landscapes of Devon, Gloucestershire, and Corsica ; and many sketches of eccentric character, such as the Devonshire prodigy, Huxtable, with his wrestling feats, and the farcical Balak and Balam and other cockneys. [Low ; Scribner, New York : o.p.]

—— *Cradock Nowell : a tale of the New Forest.* 1866

Enshrines several rustic types and eccentrics, such as Parson Rosedew (a sketch of Blackmore's clerical uncle, Hey Knight) and Dr. Hutton ; the story is involved and abounds in sensation, the style charming for those who prize euphuism in a modern dress. [Revised ed., 1873 ; Low : o.p. ; Scribner, New York : o.p.]

—— *Lorna Doone.* 1869

A romance of Exmoor in Stuart times (*c.* 1673–88). John Ridd, one of Blackmore's stalwart yeomen, rescues Lorna from the robber Doones. This is their history from childhood to marriage, with episodes and pictures of life in the world outside as well as in the quiet homesteads of Exmoor. Humorous Tom Faggus, the terrible brigand Carver Doone, and Judge Jeffreys are among the characters—all drawn with a peculiar kindliness and gusto. The scenic descriptions of the lovely region about Lynmouth and the Badgeworthy Water are invested with a poetic glamour that befits the tale. Though *Lorna Doone* made little stir at the time of its appearance, it has had innumerable imitations since, and it signalized a return to the romanticism in historical fiction that Thackeray excluded in *Esmond, The Virginians, Barry Lyndon,* and *Denis Duval.* The Doones were a myth, if founded on certain insignificant facts. [Harper ; Low ; Putnam, New York. *Illus.* : Low ; Scribner, New York ; Harper, New York ; (Everyman's Lib.) Dent (Dutton, New York) ; (World's Classics) Oxford Press.]

—— *The Maid of Sker.* 1872

The romance of a foundling, the missing daughter of a Devon family, told by an old fisherman, Davy Llewellyn, who overflows with mother-wit. Opens with sketches of life in Glamorganshire ; passes then to Devon, where, in a wild and lawless state of society, the diabolical Parson Chowne is represented as the brutal despot of his parish (1782–98). Exciting episodes, such as a hurricane and a wreck, poetical descriptions, and many racy characters. [Low ; Scribner, New York : o.p.]

—— *Alice Lorraine : a tale of the South Downs.* 1875

A romance of Sussex and Kent during the Napoleonic wars (1811–14) ; full of startling incident and adventure, the ancient house of Lorraine being involved in disasters that have to be drastically remedied in the last chapter ; the heroine a modern Antigone. [Low ; Scribner, New York : o.p.]

—— *Cripps the Carrier : a woodland tale.* 1876

Luke Sharp, the lawyer, plots to abduct an heiress, and actually proves her dead and buried ; but his nefarious plans are overset, chiefly by the agency of Mr. Cripps, an original whose raciness and humour are characteristic of Blackmore's country-folk. Rural Oxfordshire is the scene, and most of the persons introduced are homely and rude. [Low ; Scribner, New York : o.p.]

—— *Erema.* 1877

Though the chief characters are English and Scottish, the scene is laid in California, New York, and Washington. Plot-interest is dominant and tragic, but the humour of the characterization and the beauty of the surroundings lighten the gloom. [Low : o.p. ; Scribner, New York : o.p.]

—— *Mary Anerley.* 1880

Story of an old Yorkshire family : smuggling adventures, service in the navy, and pictures of life on the coast about Flamborough (1777–1805). Brings out well the racy and jovial disposition of the Yorkshire people, and depicts several original characters, like the York agent, Mordacks, the family lawyer, and the hero himself, who is heir to an estate but elects to live humbly. [Low ; Harper, New York : o.p. ; Scribner, New York : o.p.]

—— *Christowell.* 1882

A beautiful village on the eastern edge of Dartmoor is the scene, and the tale covers a large extent of that wild region. Happy and affectionate family life and homely characters, with some episodes of terror as a contrast, make up the story. The gardener, Cap'n Larks, is a kind of self-portrait of Blackmore. [Low ; Scribner, New York : o.p.]

—— *Springhaven.* 1887

Nelson and Napoleon and the contemplated invasion of England are prominent in the complicated plot which provides the excitement, while a set of homelier and obscurer figures furnish interest of a quieter complexion. Sketches some fine types of heroism, of human kindness, gossips, and humorists, not the least attractive being Admiral Darling. [(Everyman's Lib.), Dent (Dutton, New York). *Illus.* by Alfred Parsons and F. Barnard, Low : o.p.]

—— *Kit and Kitty.* 1890

The hero is a poor market-gardener, and the life depicted is of the lowliest, but both hero and heroine are lifted high by the sweetness of their characters. A simple tale, with a dash of romance. Blackmore was a most unmercenary market-gardener himself. [Low : o.p. ; Harper, New York.]

—— *Perlycross : a tale of the western hills.* 1894

A leisurely romance with a mystery which turns out to be a hoax. Scenes of rural life in eastern Devon just before the 1832 Reform Bill, portraits of village worthies and much descriptive work. The river Perle is Culmstock River, and several village worthies were drawn from people Blackmore knew in his boyhood. Scoffs at modern cant about education. [Low : o.p. ; Harper, New York : o.p.]

—— *Tales from the Telling House.* 1896

Four tales of past and present. *Slain by the Doones* is a little study on the theme of *Lorna Doone ; Crocker's Hole,* a story of the catching of a mighty trout, is quite an epitome of Blackmore's humorous story-telling and loving description of nature, and also of his nervous, racy, meandering prose. [Low ; Scribner, New York : o.p.]

BLACKWOOD, Algernon [*b.* 1869]. *The Empty House ; and other ghost stories.* 1906
—— *The Listener ; and other stories.* 1907
—— *John Silence, Physician Extraordinary.* 1908
—— *The Lost Valley ; and other stories.* 1910
Three ghost-story books and a novel dealing cleverly with occult and ghastly themes, by methods at times simply blood-curdling, at others employing all the craft of a mental pathologist familiar with the theories of modern spiritualism. Dr. Silence is a mental Sherlock Holmes who unravels a lot of absurd mysteries by the aid of " psychometry." *A Suspicious Gift* in the first book, and *The Willows, Max Hensig,* and *May Day Eve* in the second collection are good examples of the genre. [(1), (2), (3), and (4), Nash ; (1), (2), and (4), Knopf, New York : o.p. ; (3), Dutton, New York.]
—— *Jimbo : a fantasy.* 1909
Experiences " beyond the veil " of a child delirious from brain fever—brilliant descriptions of a flight through infinite space. [Macmillan.]
—— *The Education of Uncle Paul.* 1909
Uncle Paul is a middle-aged business man from the wilds of Canada, who has preserved the illusions of childhood, and so wins the freedom of a little band of captivating children and their wonderful dreamland. [Macmillan, London and New York.]
—— *The Human Chord.* 1910
A fantastic house of cards built upon a little elementary acoustics : a crazy thaumaturge discovers how to bottle sounds and translate them into form and energy. As an extreme essay in investing absurdity with the atmosphere of reality it is interesting. [Macmillan, London and New York.]
—— *The Centaur.* 1911
Two mysterious Russian peasants turn out to be survivals from the ancient and venerable race of Centaurs, noble beings living on a higher plane than ours. [Macmillan, London and New York : o.p.]
—— *Pan's Garden.* 1912
" A volume of nature stories." [Macmillan ; *illus., id.*]
—— *A Prisoner in Fairyland : the book that " Uncle Paul " wrote.* 1913
A fantasy continuing *The Education of Uncle Paul.* [Macmillan, London and New York.]
—— *Incredible Adventures.* 1914
Five stories of psychic influences, dreams, and reincarnation, showing careful analysis and an imaginative sense of the past ; in *A Descent into Egypt,* an English scientist is absorbed into the " memory life " of ancient Egypt and loses his personality. [Macmillan, London and New York : o.p.]
—— *Ten-minute stories.* 1914
Stories of weird but futile wonders, at their best when concerned with real life. [Murray : o.p. ; Dutton, New York : o.p.]
—— *The Extra Day.* 1915
A romance of three children of seven, in " a kind of hazy, ecstatical, nursery, Watts-Dunton land. Only plump Maria knows anything definite about it, and she won't say " (*Times Literary Suppl.*). Nevertheless, it achieves a fantastic beauty and the illusion of wonder. [Macmillan, London and New York.]
—— *Julius le Vallon.* 1916
Reincarnated souls endeavour to expiate the sins of their pre-existence upon another planet. Discarded bodies, spirits of wind and fire, play their part, rising to a climax in the Jura mountains. [Cassell ; Dutton, New York.]
—— *The Wave : an Egyptian aftermath.* 1916
Reincarnation—ancient Egyptians, lovers and enemies, reappear, their fundamental natures—sensuality, greed, cruelty, cunning, or the opposites—still the same though toned down by the centuries. [Macmillan ; Dutton, New York : o.p.]
—— *Day and Night Stories.* 1917
Psychic thrillers, John Silence wrestling with the Fourth Dimension. [Cassell : o.p. ; Dutton, New York : o.p.]
—— *The Promise of Air.* 1918
Middle-aged Joseph Wimble and his daughter become absorbed by the rapture of bird-life and the joys of air, somewhat to the astonishment of everyday Mrs. Wimble. [Macmillan : o.p. ; Dutton, New York.]
—— *The Garden of Survival.* 1918
In this dreamy story a husband tells how his dead wife's spirit reacts on his from the other world, awakening his soul with the thrill of beauty—key to the goodness of the universe. [Macmillan ; Dutton, New York.]
—— *The Dance of Death : and other tales.* 1928
A selection of six of his best stories of the supernatural from books already published : *The Dance of Death, A Psychical Invasion, The Old Man of Visions, The South Wind, The Touch of Pan, The Valley of the Beasts.* [Jenkins ; Dial Press, New York.]
—— *Dudley and Gilderoy : a nonsense.* 1929
Dudley is a parrot, and Gilderoy a cat ; together they escape from a country house up to London ; understanding of animal nature and quaint absurdity are well blended. [Benn ; Dutton, New York.]
BLACKWOOD, Algernon, and WILSON, Wilfred. *The Wolves of God ; and other fey stories.* 1921
Fifteen stories of mystery and hauntings, among the best being *The Decoy* and *The Man who Found Out.* [Cassell ; Dutton, New York.]
BLAKE, M. M. *The Siege of Norwich Castle.* [juvenile] 1893
A story of the Norman Conquest and the rising of Waltheof and the Earls of Norfolk and Hereford (1073-96), strong in local colour. [Seeley.]

BLAKE, M. M. (*continued*). *The Glory and Sorrow of Norwich*. [juvenile] 1899
Edward III and the Black Prince at Norwich, the Hundred Years' War, and the plague at Norwich (1340–50). [Jarrold: o.p.; Page, Boston: o.p.]

—— *Grantley Fenton*. [juvenile] 1902
A boy's story of Napoleon at Elba (1814–15). [Jarrold: o.p.]

BLAKE-FORSTER, Charles Ffrench [Irish]. *The Irish Chieftains; or, A Struggle for the Crown*. 1872
A very learned account of the Williamite wars in Ireland, weaving the national events and the fortunes (1689–1770) of the O'Shaughnessy and Blake-Forster clans (Co. Galway) into a novel. Not only battles and sieges and the Continental deeds of the Irish Brigade, but home politics and the working of the penal laws are carefully studied (from an Irish-Jacobite standpoint), and well documented in the appendix. [Whittaker, 1874: o.p.]

BLANCHARDYN AND EGLANTINE. *Caxton's Blanchardyn and Eglantine*. *c.* 1489
Translated from a French prose version of a *roman d'aventure* in some 4,800 octasyllabic lines, *Blanchardin et Orgueillose d'Amors* (earliest version thirteenth century). Blanchandin or Blanchardin, son of a king of Frise (Phrygia), falls in love with the Princess of Tormadai and, after the usual series of adventures, disasters and escapes, weds her in peace. Caxton's pedestrian rendering is fairly close to the French prose, which expanded and altered the poem considerably both in style and matter. [From Lord Spencer's copy, completed from the original French and the second English version of 1595; ed. Dr. Leon KELLNER (Early English Text Soc.), Oxford Press (1890) 1906.]

BLAND, Mrs. Edith Hubert [*née* Nesbit; 1848–1924]. *In Homespun*. 1896
Ten stories told in homely English by rustic characters, mostly women, of south Kent and the Sussex downs. [Lane: o.p.]

—— *The Story of the Treasure Seekers; being the adventures of the Bastable children in search of a fortune*. [juvenile] 1899
A mock romance; the adventures of a family of six children in London, who fall into endless scrapes and whimsical exploits. Andrew Lang praised it highly, and said, " Give it to children." [Unwin: o.p.; Benn, 1930; Stokes, New York: o.p.; *vide The New Treasure Seekers, infra*.]

—— *The Wouldbegoods*. [juvenile] 1901
A similar story about children, for children and others. [Unwin: o.p.; Benn, 1930; Harper, New York; *vide The New Treasure Seekers, infra*.]

—— *The Red House*. 1902
The adventures and blunders and the joys of a young couple who enter upon their housekeeping career in a rambling old country house that has been left them. [Methuen: o.p.; Harper, New York: o.p.]

—— *The New Treasure Seekers*. [juvenile] 1904
—— *Oswald Bastable* [sequel]. [juvenile] 1905
Further episodes in the mischievously adventurous lives of the Bastable family. [(1) Unwin: o.p.; Stokes, New York: o.p.; (2) Wells, Gardner: o.p.; *The Bastable Children*, containing *The Treasure Seekers*, *The Wouldbegoods*, and *The New Treasure Seekers*, with introd. by Christopher Morley, Coward McCann, New York; Benn, 1928.]

—— *The Incomplete Amorist*. 1906
The doings of a flirtatious artist in an English rectory and Paris studios. [Constable: o.p.; Doubleday, New York: o.p.]

—— *Man and Maid*. 1906
Amusing magazine stories, some of them concerned with ghosts—not of a serious kind. [Unwin: o.p.]

—— *The Railway Children*. [juvenile] 1906
—— *These Little Ones*. [juvenile] 1909
Two further collections of amusing exploits and experiences of very original children. [(1) Wells Gardner: o.p.; Macmillan, New York; (2) Allen & Unwin: o.p.]

—— *Daphne in Fitzroy Square*. 1909
An independent young lady's independent career among art students and artists—amusing in the way of Mrs. Bland's children episodes, with love passages of a rather warmer complexion. [Allen & Unwin: o.p.; Doubleday, New York: o.p.]

BLASCO IBÁÑEZ, Vincente [Spanish; 1867–1928]. *The Mayflower: a tale of the Valencian seashore* (Flor de Mayo, 1895). 1921
A tragedy of the fisher folk of the Cabañal, the shore near Valencia. In the quality of its realism, no less than the beauty of the conclusion, this is spoken of as his finest work; the over-emphasis of his later style is absent. [Transl. by Arthur LIVINGSTONE, Dutton, New York; Unwin.]

—— *The Cabin* (La Barraca, 1898). 1917
What is best in this book is the graphic description of farming, and of the motley agricultural population and the whole Spanish countryside; the story is rather forced. It is about a family of nomads who establish themselves on a ruined farm in Valencia, cultivate the untilled fields, and prosper exceedingly, until after some years their envious neighbours turn them out. [Transl. by Francis Haffkine SNOW and Beatrice M. MEKOTA, Knopf, New York; Hurst & Blackett: o.p.]

—— *The Torrent* (Entre Naranjos, 1900). 1921
A story of passion, in modern Spain; a young deputy becomes infatuated with an opera singer, but is persuaded to desert her to make a marriage of convenience. [Transl. by Isaac GOLDBERG and Arthur LIVINGSTONE, Dutton, New York; Unwin.]

—— *Sonnica* (Sónnica la Cortesana, 1901). 1912
Tells the story of Hannibal in Spain, scenes Saguntum and Rome (*c.* 218 B.C.). The data supplied by Livy and by archæological research are worked up with romantic vigour. [Transl. by Frances DOUGLAS, Duffield, New York; Long, 1915: o.p.]

BLASCO IBÁÑEZ, Vinçente (*continued*). *The Shadow of the Cathedral* (La Cathedral, 1903). 1909
This characteristic novel centres in the splendid cathedral of Toledo, stronghold of the despotic ecclesiasticism to which Spain owes her present decadence. A young seminarist brought up amid these influences goes out into the world, and is disillusioned, his religious zeal turning to a hot enthusiasm for science. Imprisoned as an anarchist, he returns a physical wreck to the cathedral, where he is sheltered by his orthodox brother. The story ends in an ironical tragedy, the self-sacrifice and eloquent teaching of the enthusiast serving only to inflame his simple-minded hearers with the idea that revolution means destruction. [Transl. by Mrs. W. A. GILLESPIE, Unwin ; Dutton, New York, 1919.]

—— *The Intruder* (El Intruso, 1904). 1928
The Church and the College of Jesuits are the intruder : the scenes are laid among miners and iron-founders in Bilbao. [Transl. by Mrs. W. A. GILLESPIE, Dutton, New York.]

—— *The Mob* (La Horda, 1905). 1927
The English title is a mistranslation. What the author depicts, with his usual energy and no doubt some exaggeration, is the rabble of pariahs and outcasts who form the nether strata in a great city like Madrid. There are unsympathetic glimpses of the other world, of bourgeois and hidalgos ; but even the caricatures such as Mosco the poacher, Robin Hood of the Guadarama, the hoary old vagabond Zarathustra, with his wife, queen of the rag-pickers, and pious Brother Vincent, are done with a friendly humour. [Transl. by Mariano Joaquin LORENTE, Butterworth ; Dutton, New York.]

—— *The Fruit of the Vine* (La Bodega, 1905). 1919
A vigorous story of the wine-growing district round Xeres ; the bestiality of the labourers is shown to be the fruit of their drunken habits and of their brutal domination by the landowners. [Transl. by Isaac GOLDBERG, Dutton, New York.]

—— *Woman Triumphant* (La Maja Desnuda, 1906). 1920
The title in the original is borrowed from one of a famous pair of paintings by Goya in the Prado ; it is as if the author were haunted by the very spirit which inspired those portrayals of womanhood. This is the story for a young painter, inflamed with passion for his art, whose life is spent in quest of the ideal woman to transfer to his canvas as an apotheosis of sexual beauty ; forced by circumstances to pander to the commercial ends of art, and hampered by the scruples and jealousy of his wife, who fails him as a model, he meets only defeat. [Transl. by Margaret KENISTON, Dutton, New York.]

—— *Blood and Sand* (Sangre y Arena, 1908). 1913
A vigorous story of the bull-ring, with a bull-fighter hero. [Transl. by Mrs. W. A. GILLESPIE, Unwin ; Dutton, New York, 1922.]

—— *The Dead Command* (Los Muertos Mandan, 1909). 1919
A lover torn between tradition and his desire for love. Scene, the Balearic Isles. [Transl. by W. F. DOUGLAS, Duffield ; Unwin (1923).]

—— *The Four Horsemen of the Apocalypse* (Los cuatro Jinetes del Apocalipsis, 1917). 1918
Opens with a superb picture of a rich old gaucho on the Argentine pampas, who takes a young Frenchman into his employ and gives him his eldest daughter, the younger running off with a German. Long after comes the great war, and the last part of the family history shows us the retreat from the Marne, the foppish young grandson's death in action, and the Frenchman's luxurious château ravaged by the invaders. [Transl. (clumsily) by Charlotte Brewster JORDAN, Dutton, New York ; Constable.]

—— *Our Sea* (Mare Nostrum, 1918). 1919
"Our sea " is, of course, the Mediterranean, which, with the Spanish seaboard, is lovingly described. The story is about the owner of a small trading-vessel, whose affections are engaged by an attractive German spy. He runs petrol for submarines, is stricken with remorse when his son is torpedoed, and finally contrives to wreak vengeance. [Transl. by Charlotte Brewster JORDAN, Dutton, New York.]

—— *The Temptress* (La Tierra de Todos, 1922). 1923
A fascinating woman makes trouble on an Argentine ranch between an unsophisticated Spanish girl and her English lover. [Transl. by Leo ONGLEY, Dutton, New York ; Butterworth.]

—— *The Pope of the Sea : an historical medley* (El Papa del Mar, 1925). 1927
The story of the rival Popes, the Spanish Benedict XIII and the legitimate Boniface IX ; scenes, Avignon and Spain (*c.* 1389). [Transl. by Arthur LIVINGSTON, Dutton, New York.]

—— *Unknown Lands : the story of Columbus.* 1929
The great discoverer's character and story are well rendered, against a sound historical background, though for catch-penny reasons mixed up with the sugary idyll of two very young and innocent lovers. [Transl. by Arthur LIVINGSTON, Dutton, New York ; Butterworth.]

BLATCHFORD, Robert [*b.* 1851]. *A Son of the Forge.* 1894
The autobiography of a poor waif from the Black Country, who goes through the horrors of the Crimean War, is invalided, but fights a hard battle for existence in London, winning a comfortable position in the end, and the love of a true wife and of true friends. [Innes : o.p.]

—— *Tommy Atkins of the Ramchunders.* 1895
A realistic story of life in the ranks of the British army by an ex-sergeant. The author is a well-known socialist, whose stories are meant as object-lessons. [*Clarion* Press : o.p.]

BLEST-GANA, Alberto [Chilean ; 1831–1920]. *Martin Rivas* (Martin Rivas : novela de costumbres Chilenas). 1916
This account of a young fellow who goes to Santiago in 1850 to make his fortune, and who also wins a bride, is apparently written to illustrate economic, social, and political conditions, including the revolutionary troubles of 1851. The revelations of human nature in Chile, especially on the feminine and erotic side, are interesting. [Transl. by Mrs. Charles WHITHAM, Chapman : o.p.]

BLOCH, Jean Richard [French ; *b.* 1884]. —— *and Co.* (—— et Cie., 1918). 1929
A family of Alsatian Jews transfer their cloth-mill to a small French town after 1871, and prosper exceedingly, largely at the cost of the older inhabitants. The dramatic theme is the conflict between the individual

BLOCH, Jean Richard (*continued*).

and the family, identified with the business to the annihilation of their humanity. It is an example of thorough-going realism, reminiscent of Balzac, though dwelling more on externals. [Transl. by C. K. SCOTT-MONCRIEFF, with introd. by Romain Rolland, Simon & Schuster, New York ; Gollancz.]

—— *A Night in Kurdistan* (La nuit kurde, 1925). 1930
A singular attempt to capture the barbaric intensity and violence of Oriental passion. The raid of a Kurdish chieftain upon a town of Nestorian Christians plunges us into a staggering series of murders and ravishings, furious infatuations, and calm self-immolation for the sake of revenge. [Transl. by Stephen Haden GUEST, Gollancz ; Simon & Schuster, New York.]

BLOEM, Walter [German ; *b.* 1868]. *The Iron Year* (Das eiserne Jahr, 1911). 1914
A story, marked by passages of grim realism, of the Franco-Prussian War (1870). The daughter of a German general falls in love with a French staff-officer just before the outbreak of war, and later becomes a nurse at the front. [Transl. by Stella BLOCH, Lane : o.p.]

—— *A Son of his Country.* 1921
"An imaginative novel dealing with George Washington's youth." [Transl. by Frederick H. MARTENS, Harper, New York.]

BLOUNDELLE-BURTON, John Edward [1850–1917]. *The Hispaniola Plate* (1683–1893). 1894
Story of the loss of the Hispaniola plate off San Domingo at the end of the seventeenth century, and of the search for and recovery of it in the nineteenth century through the finding of a manuscript. [Cassell : o.p.]

—— *A Gentleman Adventurer : a story of Panama.* 1895
Founded on the history of the famous project for seizing Panama from the Spaniards in 1698 ; an exciting tale of buccaneering exploits. [Melrose : o.p.]

—— *In the Day of Adversity.* 1896
A romance of French history towards the end of the Louvois ministry (1690–2). [Methuen : o.p. ; Appleton, New York : o.p.]

—— *Across the Salt Seas.* 1898
Nautical adventure, partly founded on the history of the wars with the French and Spanish ; the siege of Vigo, the exploits of Marlborough, Rooke, etc. (1702–4). [Methuen : o.p. ; Stone, Chicago : o.p.]

—— *The Scourge of God.* 1898
Persecution of the Huguenots, and Jean Cavalier's rising in the Cevennes (1702–4) ; adventures of a young Englishman. [Clarke : o.p. ; Appleton, New York : o.p.]

—— *Fortune's my Foe.* 1899
Love, revenge, and adventure in the latter days of George II's reign. Much of the action takes place on shipboard, and Hawke's famous victory off Quiberon furnishes a concluding battle-piece (1741–59). [Methuen : o.p. ; Appleton, New York : o.p.]

—— *The Sword of Gideon.* 1905
The brave emprise of a cavalry officer, broken for duelling, connected up with the siege of Liége and other events when Marlborough was fighting in Flanders (1702). [Cassell : o.p.]

—— *The Land of Bondage.* 1905
Ireland and England in 1727, and James River, Virginia, in 1728 ; a young nobleman sent to the plantations, adventures with Indians, etc., down to 1747. [White : o.p.]

—— *Knighthood's Flower.* 1906
Reign of Louis XIII, the Huguenots, La Rochelle, etc., from 1628 to death of Richelieu (1642). [Hurst : o.p.]

—— *Traitor and True.* 1906
Plot of the " Prince de Beaurepaire " (Louis de Rohan) to depose Louis XIV (1669–74). [Long : o.p.]

—— *The King's Mignon.* 1909
France in 1588 during the wars of the League, in the period succeeding the murder of Guise. [Everett : o.p.]

—— *A Fair Martyr.* 1910
Marseilles during the 1720 Plague, and Paris about 1740 ; adventures of an Englishman and 'views of social life under Louis XV. [Everett : o.p.]

—— *The Sea Devils.* 1914
Adventures of an Englishman in Lisbon and elsewhere in Portugal, and his sufferings under the Inquisition. Time of the Armada (1588). [White : o.p.]

BLYTH, James [*b.* 1864]. *Juicy Joe : a romance of the Norfolk marshlands.* 1903
Paints the inhabitants of a Marshland village as a set of lazy, drunken, vicious sots, with nothing above the brutes but low cunning and hypocritical devotion to church or chapel—a picture as ugly as *La Terre*, though executed without unpleasant grossness. A London girl marries Juicy Joe, and comes to a tragic end, the drama being artistically staged amidst the impressive scenery of the marshes. An unselfish old woman redeems the story from utter squalor. [Richards : o.p.]

—— *The King's Guerdon.* 1906
The Norfolk marshes at the time of the Plague and the sea fights with the Dutch ; Charles II, Rochester, Pepys are introduced. [Digby & Long : o.p.]

—— *Napoleon Decrees.* 1914
Another romantic novel of Norfolk and Suffolk, with Continental episodes—the doings of a French spy, in Napoleon's time (1804). [White : o.p.]

BOCCACCIO, Giovanni [Italian ; 1313–75]. *Amorous Fiametta* (1341). 1587
" Wherein is sette downe a catalogue of all and singular passions of love and jealousie incident to an enamored yong gentlewoman, with a notable caveat for all women to eschew deceitfull and wicked love, by an apparent example of a Neapolitan lady, her approved and long miseries . . . done into English by B. Giovano del M. Temp." This sub title briefly describes Boccaccio's analytical **story** of Fiammetta's love

BOCCACCIO, Giovanni (*continued*).
for Panfilo (Boccaccio himself) and the stories she tells of other luckless passions. [Transl. by B. Giovano del M. Temp. (B. Yong, or Young, of the Middle Temple), 1587, with introd. by Edward Hutton, Navarre Soc. (Boni, New York).]

—— *The Decameron* (Il Decamerone, 1358). 1886
The stories in the *Decameron* are models for all time of one great class of fiction, the story that is objective and told for its own sake, having no purpose beyond entertainment, aiming at no interpretation of life, non-moral and matter-of-fact, and not in any way philosophical or poetical. A party of ten ladies and gentlemen, who have retreated to a charming asylum from plague-stricken Florence in the year 1348, are supposed to tell each other a hundred stories in ten consecutive days. Some of these are tragedies, some comic, some idylls : love is always the favourite motive. Boccaccio took most of his plots from the current fiction of his time, from the popular French *fabliaux*, from Oriental and classical sources, from actual history and tradition. Many of the subjects are sensual and very frankly dealt with ; but contemporary manners and morals, which are faithfully reflected in the stories, must fairly be held responsible. [Transl. by John Payne (1886), *illus.* by L. Chalon, 2 vols., Lawrence & Bullen, 1893 : o.p. (the most literal English translation) ; 2 vols., Boni, New York, 1924 ; with introd. by Thomas Wright (1873), Murray, Derby, 1878 : o.p. ; by Sharpe, 4 vols., Gibbings, 1896 : *illus.* by Clara Tice, introd. by R. Garrett, etc., 2 vols ; Boni, New York, 1925 ; *Forty Tales from the Decameron*, Routledge, 1884 ; by J. M. Rigg, with preface by J. A. Symonds (Library of Early Novelists), Routledge (1905), Dutton, New York ; (the best working edition).] The earliest [known] complete transl. into English (from the French of Antoine le Maçon, and consequently anything but exact), a fine example of post-Elizabethan prose, is *The Decameron Preserved to Posterity by Giovanni Boccaccio, and Translated into English Anno* 1620 ; ed., with introduction by Edward Hutton, 4 vols. (Tudor Translations.) [Nutt : o.p.]
Exceedingly full references to Boccaccio's sources, to analogous stories, and to rehandlings of his motives in later literature, are given in *The Decameron : its sources and analogues.* By A. C. Lee. [Nutt (1909) : o.p.]

BODKIN, Matthias M'Donnell [Irish ; *b.* 1850]. *Lord Edward Fitzgerald.* 1896
A Nationalist novel embodying the romantic incidents in the early life of the famous rebel, his relations with the Indians, and his life in Ireland. The facts are genuine, but liberties have been taken with the dates (1780–95). [Talbot Press, Dublin.]

—— *The Rebels* [sequel]. 1899
Lord Edward's later career (1796–8), Castlereagh's preparations for suppressing the rebellion, Humbert's invasion, etc. [Talbot Press, Dublin.]

—— *In the Days of Goldsmith.* 1903
Sketches Goldsmith, Burke, Garrick, Johnson, in a novel of manners and conversation. [Long : o.p.]

—— *Patsy the Omadhaun.* 1904
One of several volumes of short stories, largely in the brogue, recounting comic exploits and adventures and bringing out the humorous side of the peasants. [Chatto : o.p.]

—— *True Man and Traitor.* 1910
Robert Emmet's story from his Trinity days to its tragic close. Besides his love affair with Sarah Curran, many romantic incidents of a fictitious kind are combined with the facts (1803). [Talbot Press, Dublin.]

BOJER, Johan [Norwegian ; *b.* 1872]. *The Power of a Lie* (Troens magt, 1900). 1903
A weak and not strictly honest man, to exonerate himself from a false charge, actually forges a letter ; and the man who signed the bond so persuades himself that he is the injured party that he lets the falsehood stand though the other is ruined. A searching study of moral deterioration, and of the attitude of a not over-intelligent public towards a question of truth and falsehood. [Transl. by Jessie Muir, Hodder ; Century Co., New York, 1920.]

—— *A Pilgrimage* (Pilgrimsgang, 1902). 1924
The book opens with a masterly piece of realism—a description of a maternity home for the poor. Thereafter it is a study in hysteria—a woman who has surrendered her illegitimate baby to be adopted by an unknown family, makes havoc of her own life, and that of the man she marries, in the fruitless quest of her lost child. [Trans. by Jessie Muir, Century Co., New York ; Gyldendal : o.p.]

—— *Treacherous Ground* (Vort rige, 1908). 1912
A penetrating study of those processes of self-deception by which we try to disguise, even to ourselves, our meanness and love of ease under pretences of generosity and conscientiousness. Erik Evje proposes to make amends for the methods by which his father piled up wealth, by a scheme for the betterment of his workpeople ; but he shirks the greater sacrifice demanded when a big landslip threatens disaster to the whole project. [Transl. by Jessie Muir, Hodder : o.p. ; Century Co., New York ; *sub tit.* Our Kingdom, Hodder, 1920 : o.p.]

—— *Life* (Liv, 1911). 1920
Contrasts an egoist consumed with jealousy of a comrade's success, with others who enjoy life to the full and mould it to their own purpose. [Transl. by Jessie Muir, Century Co., New York ; Gyldendal : o.p.]

—— *The Prisoner who Sang* (Fangen som sang, 1913). 1924
Superficially, this is an account of a psychological case—a peasant youth whose zest for experimenting with life, and playing new rôles, leads him from lying and petty cheating as a child to serious crime and forgery, until in the end he is quite unable to distinguish between his real self and the personality he has assumed for the moment. But throughout, there is the implicit question, what is real personality and what false ? And in the career of Bruget, too, there is expressed in allegorical terms that zest and craving for the fullness of life which is the theme of *The Great Hunger*. [Century Co., New York ; Hodder : o.p.]

—— *The Great Hunger* (Den store hunger, 1916). 1918
The protagonist of the drama, in which moral ideas of profound import are at issue, is a man who has worked up from the bottom to eminence and riches as an engineer, and then is ruined. But in suffering and adversity he attains a victory that material success could never give. [Transl. by W. J. A. Worster and C. Archer, Hodder (1929) ; Century Co., New York ; Grosset, New York.]

BOJER, Johan (*continued*). *The Face of the World* (Verdens ansigt, 1917). 1919
Dr. Mark is morbidly obsessed by the wrongs of humanity, and presently devotes all his powers to the salvation of a wretched monomaniac, who in the end repays his work by a monstrous act of mischief. [Transl. by Jessie Muir, Hodder : o.p. ; Century Co., New York.]

—— *God and Woman* (Dyrendal, 1919). 1921
Here there is no glozing over of the hardness, selfishness, and mental torpor of the Norwegian peasant. Dyrendal is a fine old farm near Trondhjem, Johan Bojer's native district. It is acquired by a stroke of speculation on the part of Hans Lia, the gipsy-natured husband of the chief character. But the pair are never really happy. Martha wants to show that she is as good as the woman for whom she had been jilted. But, though rich, Hans remains a drunken churl, and she is childless. To carry on the house that they have founded, they adopt a nephew. The ultimate results are disappointing, and what embitters the situation, they are themselves chiefly to blame. [Transl. by A. R. Shelander, Moffat, New York ; Augsberg Co., Minneapolis.]

—— *The Last of the Vikings* (Den siste viking, 1921). 1923
An epical delineation of the Lofoten fisheries. The arduous struggle for life and the rude heroism of the men are finely presented, not without glimpses of their deeper spiritual qualities. [Transl. by Jessie Muir, Century Co., New York.]

—— *The Emigrants* (Vor egen stamme, 1924). 1925
A moving and glowing picture of the life of Norwegian pioneers in the Dakota wilderness. They come out, a motley group, each intent on making his fortune and returning home ; but the bonds of comradeship, cemented by dangers and difficulties nobly shared and overcome, prove stronger than the calls of the old life ; as memories of their native land recede and grow dim, a new home, America, appears. [Transl. by A. G. Jayne, Century Co., New York ; Grosset, New York ; Hodder.]

—— *The New Temple* (Det nye tempel, 1927). 1928
The two children of Peer Holm (of *The Great Hunger*) have been brought up by their aunt at Bruseth. Lorentz is deeply religious, and sets out upon a quest for the true God, to find at length that God is to be found only in love and the service of humanity. [Transl. by C. Archer, Hodder ; Century Co., New York.]

" BOLDREWOOD, Rolf " [Thomas Alexander Browne ; Australian ; 1826–1915]. *Robbery under Arms*. 1888
Rolf Boldrewood fixed the type of his novels in the first, also one of his best, in which a bushranger, in prison awaiting death, tells his story from the critical moment when the convict showed his children the hiding-place of the stolen cattle, through incident after incident to the final tragedy. Depicts bad and good characters as they are, with no sentimentalism and little extenuation. [Macmillan, London and New York.]

—— *A Colonial Reformer*. 1890
Tells about the introduction of fencing runs instead of shepherding. Totty Freeman, the selector's daughter, is a good specimen of his indigenous types of people. [Macmillan : o.p.]

—— *A Sydney-side Saxon*. 1891
A rough Australian squatter, starting as a pauper, by shrewdness and industry grows rich. He tells his own life-story artlessly and vividly, and offers a splendid advertisement to would-be emigrants. [Angus & Robertson, Sydney and London.]

—— *Nevermore*. 1892
Spirited stories of wild life on the goldfields. [Macmillan : o.p.]

—— *A Modern Buccaneer*. 1894
A graphic nautical tale, depicting the life of a Sydney sailor, adventures in the Pacific along with a filibustering skipper, fights with natives, and a good deal of shady life. [Macmillan : o.p.]

—— *The Squatter's Dream*. 1895
Contains characteristic pictures of exploring, trekking, and sheep-farming on the large scale in the old days before the gold rush. Adventures with bushrangers and natives, and experiences of drought and floods, evidently based on personal experience. [Angus & Robertson, Sydney and London.]

—— *War to the Knife ; or, Tangata Maori*. 1899
Adventures in New Zealand in the sixties, at the time of the Maori war. The hero is a lovelorn English gentleman, who emigrates, and takes part in the fighting. Bishop Selwyn appears. [Macmillan : o.p.]

—— *Babes in the Bush*. 1900
The successful career of a broken-down gentleman who in mid-century years emigrates to New South Wales with his family and takes to farming. A leisurely narrative, full of descriptions of outdoor life, racing, exploring, trekking, duelling, etc. [Macmillan : o.p.]

BONE, David William [Scottish, b. 1874]. *The Brassbounder*. 1910
Experiences of an articled apprentice round the Horn to San Francisco in a 3000-ton barque. The author is his own illustrator, and both in his prose, heavily salted with nautical vernacular, and in his hard-bitten lines, is vigorously picturesque. [Duckworth ; Dutton, New York.]

BONE, Florence. *The Morning of To-day*. 1907
A tale of the North Riding at the time of Jacobite intrigue and Methodist revivalism (early eighteenth century). John Wesley appears, and young university men, clergy, gentlefolk, and shepherds are among the varied characters. [Methodist Book Co., New York.]

BONE, Gertrude Helena [Mrs. Muirhead Bone, *née* Dodd]. *Children's Children*. 1908
An extremely simple tale of the poorest and humblest people in some remote country place by the sea. The old peasant farmer, bereaved of children and grandchildren, is invested with the simplicity and the dignity of tragic endurance. Drawings by Muirhead Bone. [Duckworth.]

—— *Women of the Country*. 1913
Portrays a number of types of peasant womenfolk, inarticulate but solid, against a dull and gloomy country background. The main figure is a woman of quiet charity who befriends a young girl whom a farmer has made his mistress. [Duckworth.]

BONE, Gertrude Helena (*continued*). *The Cope.* 1930
An artist's legendary story of a twelfth-century nun at Whitby, and the making of a wondrous cope. Appropriately " decorated by Stephen Bone." [Medici Soc.]

BOOTH, Edward Charles [*b.* 1870]. *The Cliff End.* 1908
Holderness villagers painted by one who loves simple, strong, racy character and has a fine sense of humour. An engaged man falls in love with another girl : this is almost all the plot there is. A village post-girl, whose chief distress in life is that everybody wants to marry her ; and a genial, bohemian High Church priest, are characteristic figures. [Unwin ; *sub tit. The Post-Girl*, Century Co., New York : o.p. ; Grosset, New York : o.p.]

—— *The Doctor's Lass.* 1910
The doctor takes charge of the sweetheart who jilted him, finds that he is in love with her, and learns at the same moment that she has become engaged. [Unwin ; Century Co., New York : o.p.]

—— *Bella.* 1912
A slighter affair, staged at Scarborough. A poet in love, more or less paternally, with a beautiful child, is tempted by the demirep mother. [Unwin ; Appleton, New York : o.p.]

—— *Fondie.* 1916
Fondie (Foolish) is the village nickname for a humble dreamer, a mute poet, whose worship and devotion are not for this world and lose him the too human heroine. This wild flirt and tomboy, epitome of the joy of life, is a most unconventional creation. The dialect of Holderness is reproduced almost too faithfully. [Duckworth ; Appleton, New York.]

—— *The Tree of the Garden.* 1922
This time, the primitive heroine is an ignorant, base-born, brow-beaten peasant girl, whose simple adoration is of tragic compass. But the humility and submissiveness which are her virtues make her an easy prey to the vulgar woman-hunter who steals a march upon her lover. [Duckworth ; Appleton, New York.]

—— *Miss Parkworth ; and three short stories.* 1924
In the long title-story, a cross, superannuated, straight-laced spinster, who worries the life out of her servant-maid, becomes a human creature again when the latter gets into trouble and makes a confidant of her mistress. *The Caretaker* is a miniature *Mr. Badman* : stupid egotism running its course and receiving its deserts. A more terrible little masterpiece is *The Will of God*, in which divine providence is confronted with the inexhaustible devotion of human love, in a mother with an idiot son. *The Slate* is the neat unmasking of an impostor. [Unwin ; Dodd & Mead, New York.]

—— *The Treble Clef.* 1924
Definitely a novel of character : it succeeds in the difficult task of making a good woman, a gentle, faultless, self-effacing creature, interesting and never insipid. This is Mrs. Holmroyd. Other figures are Dickensian, e.g. Elizabeth, amusing, and also, with her poor tormented soul, touching and impressive ; or Councillor Burford, who however is more than Dickensian because he has a mind. The sentimentalism suggests Sterne, but Sterne without the posturing and affectation. [Unwin ; Benn ; Dodd & Mead, New York.]

—— *Kith and Kin.* 1929
A village tragedy of Holderness—the life-long feud of two brothers. Careful and austere art, a style packed with aphorisms, and exact reproduction of dialect, are the foremost characteristics. [Duckworth.]

BOOTHBY, Guy Newell [1867-1905]. *Doctor Nikola.* 1896
—— *Farewell, Nikola.* 1901
These are average specimens of this prolific, crude, and once popular author's work. He aimed at sensation pure and simple, and gathered his materials from every source : gigantic adventurers, gory monsters, and supernatural beings are as common as ordinary men of the world and fascinating heroines. Mystery and horror, colossal wealth, blood-thirsty vendettas, are the favourite machinery. [(1) Ward & Lock ; Westbrook, New York ; (2) Ward & Lock : o.p. ; Lippincott, Philadelphia : o.p.]

BORDEAUX, Henri [French ; *b.* 1870]. *The Fear of Living* (La peur de vivre, 1903). 1913
In a preface written four years after the first publication of this novel, the author makes clear that his attack is upon that selfish evasion of human responsibilities and conflicts and sorrows which is such a common attitude in our day. He puts before us a woman sorely tried, whose children have not shrunk from the allotted task, and who in poverty and bereavement waits cheerfully for the end. [Transl. by Ruth Helen DAVIS, Dutton, New York ; Dent : o.p.]

—— *The Will to Live* (Les Roquevillard, 1906). 1915
The past, rooted in the family, gives the *force de vivre*, says the dedication. The honour of an ancient family of lawyers, with an estate close to Chambéry, is jeopardized by the son's elopement with a lady who helps herself to her husband's money. In the trial, Roquevillard senior saves him by invoking the well-known reputation of their house. [An American transl. by Pitts DUFFIELD, Duffield, New York ; Nash : o.p.]

—— *A Mind Awakened* (Les yeux qui s'ouvrent, 1908). 1915
A novel with a thesis—that the sacredness of the family demands the sacrifice of individual feelings, and at the same time condones individual frailties when its rights are vindicated. A husband, a learned historian, who has left his wife through incompatibility comes back to her when his eyes are opened, and his partner sacrifices her love to the interests of the family. Scenes, Grenoble and the Isère valley. [Transl. by Ruth Helen DAVIS, Dent : o.p. ; *sub tit. Awakening*, same transl., Dutton, New York, 1914.]

—— *The Parting of the Ways* (La croisée des chemins, 1909). 1911
A clever physician ambitious of a career in pure science, and a society girl who accepts when she thinks him conducive to social success but throws him over when at the call of duty he buries himself in his native Dauphiné—in these two and the homely, loyal wife who becomes the mother of the doctor's children is signified a double contrast, ambition and duty, the garish lure of Paris and the peace and beauty of sub-Alpine Dauphiné. [Transl. by Louise Seymour HOUGHTON, Chatto : o.p. ; Duffield, New York.]

BORDEAUX, Henri (*continued*). *The Woollen Dress* (La robe de laine, 1910).   1912
Sugary pathos decked out with pretty vignettes of the Savoy forests.   A very rich man woos and weds a country girl, whose purity is outraged by the free-and-easy Parisian society into which he forces her to enter. She dies of a broken heart, and he expiates his criminality by solitary flying until the machine crashes. [Transl. by Ruth Helen DAVIES, Duffield, New York.]

—— *Footprints beneath the Snow* (La neige sur les pas, 1912).   1913
A girl from Savoy marries an eminent French architect, deceives him, and when he repudiates her goes off with her lover to the Alps.   The man is killed in climbing the Velan, she escapes, and her husband forgives her.   But in the second part we are told that not until he realizes that it was his rival who loved her with full understanding, can they re-establish a perfect union.   [Transl. by Mary Seymour HOUGHTON, Duffield, New York ; Bell : o.p.]

—— *The House* (La maison, 1913).   1914
The life of a family in an old country house, recounted in leisurely, idyllic fashion and with an eye for character : note particularly, the pious, sweet-tempered mother, the father, a medical practitioner with Royalist leanings, the grandfather, disciple of Jean-Jacques, the daughter who takes the veil, and the benevolently despotic cook.   [Transl. by Louise Seymour HOUGHTON, Duffield, New York ; Dent : o.p.]

—— *Annette and Philibert : the new children's Crusade* (La nouvelle croisade des enfants, 1914).   1930
This is a propagandist novel for young people.   Two little Savoyards preach a new Crusade, and set out for Rome at the head of two-score boys and girls, of the whole band two arriving at the Vatican.   [Transl. by the Benedictines of Teignmouth, *illus.* Sands.]

—— *The House that Died* (La maison morte, 1922).   1922
A tragic tale of a family of mountaineers, one of whom murders his brother to obtain the latter's wife.   Each in their own way, the various members of the family, including even the dead man's son, labour to expiate the stain on their honour, rather than seek revenge, although the crime has wrecked all their lives.   Scene, the Haute-Maurienne.   [Transl. by Harold HARPER, Unwin ; Duffield, New York.]

BORDEN, Mary [Mrs. Edward Lewis Spears ; American ; *b.* 1886]. *Jane, our Stranger.*   1923
After James, of *The Golden Bowl* and *The Ambassadors*.   Main theme, an American marrying into a French house and failing to establish harmony with their very different ideals and social codes—except that the American is here a woman.   James gives the comedy of manners, with a tragic turn at the end ; this is the tragi-comedy of morals and sentiments, with some violent incidents lapsing almost into melodrama.   [Knopf, New York ; Heinemann.]

—— *Jehovah's Day.*   1929
Attempts a bird's-eye view of the progress of life from its first beginnings until the present day, locating a group of modern characters in the eternal procession of time, and linking them back with the primeval ancestors of mankind.   [Doubleday, Doran, New York ; Heinemann.]

—— *A Woman with White Eyes.*   1930
An elderly woman, who is erroneously described as blind to the emotional side of things, tells the story of her life and her dearest friend in retrospect.   It is a varied, lively, and often melodramatic tale, of New England and abroad : sentimental affairs, travel, married life with a bad husband, etc.   The American characters are admirably hit off.   Brooding mysteriously in the background is the strange Finnish giant, the " great sensual brute vowed to chastity," who exercises an inveterate fascination on the imaginary narrator's mind.   [Doubleday, Doran, New York ; Heinemann.]

BORROW, George Henry [1803–81]. *The Bible in Spain ; or, the Journeys, Adventures, and Imprisonments of an Englishman in an Attempt to Circulate the Scriptures in the Peninsula.*   1843
Recounts Borrow's adventures as an agent of the Bible Society in the Peninsula, 1835–9.   Perhaps the descriptive passages are finer even than those in *Lavengro* ; and the accidents of travel, the strange rencounters, the singular people met with, and the characteristic observations on national manners and idiosyncrasies, make a story no less fascinating ; though we do not get the inimitable self-revelation which is a unique ingredient in *Lavengro*.   " Vagrom " writers like Stevenson and Belloc draw their inspiration as much from Borrow as from Sterne.   [Murray (*illus.*) ; (World's Classics), Oxford Press ; (Everyman's Lib.), Dent (Dutton, New York) ; (Pocket ed.), Lane ; Putnam, New York.]

—— *Lavengro ; the Scholar, the Gipsy, the Priest.*   1851
—— *The Romany Rye* [sequel].   1857
Lavengro and its sequel, *The Romany Rye*, are the sacred books of those who confess the gospel of vagabondage. Borrow was a natural wanderer, a passionate lover of nature for her own sake, though in no sense a naturalist ; with a genius for graphic description of both scenery and human character.   They are really Borrow's autobiography down to 1825, with a veil of mystery purposely thrown over it.   They describe his wanderings over the three kingdoms, his strange adventures, literary struggles in London, vagrancy with gipsies, etc. The characters are of a piece, odd and striking, often disreputable people, removed as far as possible from the ordinary ; and the strange incidents and the glamour of his descriptions give us a most enchanting blend of romance and realism.   Dr. Jessopp calls it a story " which, in the exquisite beauty of its setting and the inimitable blending of the elements of gentle pathos and rugged tenderness—in the dialogue—it would be difficult to find a parallel for in modern English literature."   Borrow's pure, racy, and finely cadenced English is a delight to connoisseurs of prose.   [(1) and (2), Murray ; (World's Classics) Oxford Press ; also in 1 vol., *id.* ; (Everyman's Lib.) Dent (Dutton, New York) ; (Pocket Ed.) Lane ; Putnam, New York ; Knopf, New York ; *illustrated*, Murray ; P. Davies ; Macmillan.   *Works :* Definitive Ed., Murray ; Norwich Ed., ed. by C. K. Shorter, 16 vols., Constable (Wells Gardner, New York).]

BOSBOOM-TOUSSAINT, Anna Louisa Geertruida [1812–86 ; Dutch ; *née* Toussaint]. *Major Frank* (Majoor Frans, 1874).   1885
A study of the social position of women, delineating a number of agreeable persons, whose idiosyncrasies are set forth by means of conversation.   There is a collected edition of Mrs. Bosboom-Toussaint's novels in 25 vols. (Hague, 1885–8).   [Transl. by J. AKEROYD, Unwin : o.p.]

BOURGET, Paul Charles Joseph [French ; *b.* 1852]. *A Cruel Enigma* (Cruelle énigme, 1885). 1887
One of Bourget's earliest successes in the field of psychological analysis. A young man, the pampered idol of his mother and grandmother, has an affair with a married woman. His passion is proof even against the knowledge of her treachery to him ; his mother, who had been his informant, he comes to mistrust and even hate. Such is love, a cruel enigma. [Transl. by J. CRAIG, Vizetelly : o.p.]

—— *A Love Crime* (Un crime d'amour, 1886). 1887
Like its predecessor, *Cruelle énigme*, well illustrates the clear, unbiased, scientific method of M. Bourget in his earlier novels. A dissection of the minds of two persons involved in a guilty liaison : the man a careless libertine, who sees nothing in the intrigue but a pleasant adventure ; the woman, a passionate creature, who looks on it as the very object of her existence. Her punishment is to discover her lover's real character ; his comes from the poison of his own egotism. [Gibbings : o.p.]

—— *André Cornélis* (André Cornélis, 1887). 1889
Traces with the same remorseless psychology the history of a man who sets himself to discover the murderer of his father when the detectives have utterly failed, and who perseveres in spite of opposition from his relatives and the consciousness that success will bring misery on his dearest and best. [Brentano, New York ; with *Sins of Desire*, Collins, 1930.]

—— *A Living Lie* (Mensonges, 1887). 1896
A similar diagnosis of sexual passion divorced from love. Sad and repellent as a story, yet a superb example of M. Bourget's keen and searching analysis of the human soul. [Transl. by John DE VILLIERS, Chatto : o.p. ; *sub tit. Our Lady of Lies*, by G. F. MONKSHOOD and E. TRISTAN (Lotus Library), Brentano, New York (1910) 1921 ; Collins.]

—— *The Disciple* (Le disciple, 1889). 1898
Psychological analysis carried out with as much scientific accuracy as if an elaborate experiment were being reported. Thesis, the fatal effect of a great philosopher's abstract doctrines on the mind of an egoistic disciple. Intended as a warning of the evils to be feared from sceptical philosophies that perhaps dissolve the bases of morals, and as an antidote to some of his own works. Poorly translated. [Unwin : o.p. ; Scribner, New York : o.p.]

—— *A Woman's Heart* (Un cœur de femme, 1890). 1891
A study of conduct and manners in which keen analysis is tempered with too complacent picturing of the refinements of modern luxury. The duality of the feminine nature is the philosophical theme. Translation largely expurgated. [Transl. by Ernest TRISTAN, (Lotus Lib.) Brentano, New York, 1902 ; Collins.]

—— *Pastels of Men* (Nouveaux pastels, 1891). 1892
Studies of character and motive, of which the novelette entitled *A Saint* may be taken as a specimen. A mercenary and ambitious literary man outrages, by a mean theft, the hospitality of an Italian ecclesiastic. The saintly old man, guardian of a deserted monastery, heaps coals of fire on the head of the youth by presenting him with the coins he had taken, and, as it were, saves his soul. The manner and method of M. Bourget's model, Henry James, is constantly brought to mind by these sketches. [Transl. by Katherine P. WORMELEY, 2 parts in 1, Little & Brown, Boston : o.p.]

—— *A Saint ; and others* (Un saint, 1893). 1892
The *Saint* is already noted under *Pastels*. The other stories in this small sample collection of M. Bourget's short stories are typical of his more popular manner. [Transl. by J. GRAY, Osgood : o.p. ; Harper, 1894 : o.p.]

—— *A Tragic Idyll* (Une idylle tragique, 1896). 1896
Two friends in love with one woman in the *demi-monde* at Cannes ; the heroine " a neurasthenic lady in search of passion through divers essays of dreamy fancies." M. Bourget loves to paint the wealthy pleasure-seeking classes of French society, and dwells with delight on all the apparatus of luxury, furniture, works of art, etc. [Transl. by Wm. MARCHANT, Scribner, New York : o.p. ; Downey : o.p.]

—— *Some Portraits of Women* (Voyageuses, 1897). 1898
Six essays in psychological analysis done in various parts of the world ; the subjects drawn as usual from the section of society in which luxury and the race for pleasure are the paramount interests. [Transl. by Wm. MARCHANT, Scribner, New York : o.p. ; Downey : o.p.]

—— *The Blue Duchess* (La duchesse bleue, 1898). 1902
A rewriting of *Trois âmes d'artistes*, produced in his early psychological period. A painter, a dramatist, and an actress are the exponents of the thesis that art may be moral whilst the artist is ignoble and abject. [Transl. by E. TRISTAN, (Lotus Lib.) Brentano, New York, 1908 ; Collins.]

—— *Domestic Dramas* (Drames de famille, 1900). 1900
Three studies in the psychology of modern life : *Un homme d'affaires* deals with the vengeance of a deceived husband, who forces his reputed daughter to give up the man of her choice ; in *The Day of Reckoning* two parents appropriate trust-money in order to give their only son a suitable education. As always, the author shows the hidden working of emotion and motive. [Transl. by W. MARCHANT, Scribner, New York : o.p. ; Downey : o.p.]

—— *Divorce : a domestic tragedy of modern France* (Un divorce, 1904). 1904
A problem-novel attacking French marriage laws, and upholding the strict view of the Roman Catholic Church on the evil of divorce. The characters are anatomized in M. Bourget's best psychological style—the hard-hearted, free-thinking engineer married to the *divorcée*, and her son Lucien, another kind of free-thinker, whose love affairs go awry through the religious scruples of his mother and the complications of the laws. [Transl. by E. L. CHARLWOOD, Unwin : o.p.]

—— *The Weight of the Name* (L'émigré, 1907). 1908
A marshalling of the conflict between aristocracy and democracy, religious devotion and free-thought, in the person of an ambitious and energetic young man, son of a marquess, who sees every career closed to him by the inveterate feud between his caste and the republic. The personal tragedy of the situation, the conflict of ideas, desires, and, presently, of emotions—when the young man loves a bourgeois woman—are set forth with the usual psychological elaboration, and their social significance is clearly demonstrated. [Transl. by G. B. IVES, Gay & Hancock ; Little & Brown, Boston : o.p.]

BOURGET, Paul Charles Joseph (*continued*). *The Night Cometh* (Le sens de la mort, 1915). 1916
A famous surgeon, a convinced positivist, jealous of his beautiful wife and stricken by a fatal disease, persuades her into a covenant not to survive him. He is contrasted with the young man who loves her, simple, unscientific, unsceptical, in a crude and illegitimate attempt to prove pragmatism by showing the effects of their different attitudes to the unknown. Scene, a war-clinic in Paris. [Transl. by G. Frederic Lees, Chatto : o.p. ; Putnam, New York.]

—— *The Gaol* (La geôle, 1923). 1924
The gaol is the force of heredity, in this case a tendency towards suicide in a moment of emotional crisis : the son of a father who had shot himself after a political scandal is saved from such a fate, when he learns that his wife has betrayed him, by the intervention of his mother. The translation, at any rate, is uninspired. [Transl. by F. Mabel Robinson, Unwin ; Brentano, New York.]

"BOURNE, George" [George Bourne Sturt ; 1863–1927]. *The Bettesworth Book : talks with a Surrey peasant.* 1901

—— *Memoirs of a Surrey Labourer : a record of the last years of Frederick Bettesworth.* 1907

—— *Lucy Bettesworth.* 1913
Not novels, except that art has given to an actual document a truth superior to mere fact. "Bettesworth" was one of the poorest class of country labourers, a man quite uneducated, but of real personal worth, and, in spite of his ignorance of things outside his own small world, possessed of shrewdness, wisdom, and no little native wit. Mr. Bourne, his employer in the last years of his life, writes down his sayings and doings in a patient, Boswellian journal, adorning them in no way except by making the grammar and dialect a little more intelligible. What art he applies is in sketching the surroundings of the man and his petty traits of character in a feeling way. Hence the book has a truth different, if not superior, to the ordinary realistic work of fiction. Its evidences of the patient suffering, the stoical endurance, and the inextinguishable courage and charity of a fine relic of our ancient peasantry, touch one's heart and enlarge one's sense of kindred with a power of homely pathos few books achieve. [(1), (2), and (3), Duckworth.]

"BOWEN, Marjorie" ["George Preedy" ; Gabrielle Margaret Vere Campbell, afterwards Mrs. Costanzo, now Mrs. Arthur L. Long]. *The Viper of Milan.* 1906

—— *The Glen o' Weeping.* 1907

—— *The Sword Decides.* 1908
Exuberant historical stories, artless, lurid, emotional, and often quite subversive of historical truth, but certainly absorbing as romances, and settling down to a more serious interpretation of the past in the later books. *The Viper of Milan* is about Gian Galeazzo Visconti, the tyrant of Milan. *The Glen o' Weeping* tells of clan feuds and the Glencoe massacre ; *The Sword Decides* relates the crimes of Giovanna of Naples. [(1), Long : o.p. ; Doubleday, New York : o.p. ; Burt, New York : o.p. ; (2) Long : o.p. ; *sub tit. The Master of Stair*, Doubleday, New York : o.p. ; (3) Nelson ; Doubleday, New York : o.p.]

—— *I Will Maintain.* 1910
Begins a trilogy celebrating the greatness of William of Orange, his struggle for supremacy with the two De Witts, the events in London and at the Hague that led to the Revolution, and the domestic life of William and Mary at Kensington (1672–7). [Methuen ; Dutton, New York : o.p.]

—— *Defender of the Faith.* 1911
State affairs and romantic happenings in London and at the Hague (1672–9) ; chief personages, William of Orange, the Princess Mary, Charles II, and Danby. [Methuen ; Dutton, New York : o.p.]

—— *God and the King.* 1911
Ends the trilogy of William of Orange. A rather tearful account of William and Mary in England, their domestic life at Kensington, and confusing political troubles (1688–1702). [Methuen ; Dutton, New York : o.p.]

—— *Mr. Washington.* 1912
The more famous episodes of Washington's career (1753–81). [*Sub tit. The Soldier from Virginia*, Appleton ; Nelson ; title as above, Methuen (1915)].

—— *The Quest of Glory.* 1912
The adventures of Vauvenargues in the French army at the siege of Prague, and his life afterwards in Paris (1742–7). [Methuen ; Dutton, New York : o.p.]

—— *A Knight of Spain.* 1913
Don John of Austria at Lepanto and as viceroy of the Netherlands (1571–8) : more romance than history. [Nelson ; Dutton, New York : o.p.]

—— *The Governor of England.* 1913
More carefully historical : the life of Oliver Cromwell. [Methuen ; Dutton, New York : o.p.]

—— *Prince and Heretic.* 1914

—— "*William, by the Grace of God——*" [sequel]. 1916
The whole career of William the Silent ; the rising of the Netherlands against Philip II, the siege of Leyden, assassination of William of Nassau, the St. Bartholomew massacre, murder of Coligny, etc. (1555–84). [(1) Methuen : o.p. ; Dutton, New York : o.p. ; (2) Methuen ; Dutton, New York.]

—— *The Carnival of Florence.* 1915
Florence during the time of Savonarola's ascendancy ; he is the main figure in the book. Pico della Mirandola and Piero and Giovanni de' Medici are introduced. The novel ends with Savonarola's death (1498). [Methuen ; Nelson ; Dutton, New York : o.p.]

—— *Yesterdays : stories from an old catalogue.* 1916
Twelve costume-stories of passion and incident, supposed to be woven round the trinkets in an old museum. The Regency, the reign of Charles II, eighteenth-century Venice, Paris in 1747, the battle of Sedgemoor, Exeter in 1719, Spain early in the seventeenth century, Scotland and Florence at the same date, provide the settings ; and we come across Lady Castlemaine, Lord Muskerry, Lord Pawlett, Cardinal Duplessis, and others known to history. [Smith & Elder : o.p. ; Dutton, New York : o.p.]

"BOWEN, Marjorie" (*continued*). *The Third Estate.* 1917
> The story of the more democratic section of the States-General (1789–91). [Methuen: o.p.; Dutton, New York: o.p.]

—— *Kings-at-Arms.* 1918
> The wars of Charles XII of Sweden and Peter the Great of Russia (1700–18). [Methuen: o.p.; Dutton, New York: o.p.]

—— *The Burning-Glass.* 1918
> Reconstructs the love-story of Julie de Lespinasse, the Marquess de Mora, and the Comte de Guibert, author of the *Essai de tactique*, both of whom she loved in her own way, and of d'Alembert, whom she allowed to love her for sixteen years without response (1764–76). [Collins; Dutton, New York: o.p.]

—— *Mr. Misfortunate.* 1919
> A romanticized life of the Young Pretender, from his escape after Culloden to his union with Clementina Walkenshaw (1746–52). He is seen going from bad to worse in Paris, Avignon, and Venice, with Henry, Duke of York, Locheil, Keith, Wogan, and others about him. [Collins.]

—— *The Cheats.* 1920
> The tragic story of James de la Cloche or Jacques de Rohan, a natural child of Charles II, the mystery of which is examined by Andrew Lang in *The Valet's Tragedy* (1903). [Collins.]

—— *Dickon.* 1929
> The story seems to have been devised in order to do justice to the character of Richard III, whom Miss Bowen regards as having been deliberately maligned by the Tudors for dynastic reasons. She here makes him out a real hero. [Hodder.]

—— *The Rocklitz.* 1930
> The Countess Rocklitz, defeated in her attempt to become the wife of the last Protestant Elector of Saxony, becomes his mistress and the power behind the throne. The great people at the Court are well characterized, and the state of Saxony in the bad years after the Thirty Years' War is faithfully depicted. [Published under pseudonym of "George PREEDY," Lane; *sub tit. The Prince's Darling*, Dodd & Mead, New York.]

BOYCE, Rev. John ["John Peppergrass"; Irish-American, 1810–64]. *The Spae Wife; or, The Queen's Secret: a tale of the days of Elizabeth.* 1853
> Fine portraiture of the Scots Spae Wife gifted with second-sight, of Alice Wentworth, daughter of a persecuted Roman Catholic baronet, of an Irish gentleman in Mary Queen of Scots' retinue, and of Queen Elizabeth —anything but an attractive picture. [Noonan, Boston: o.p.]

BOYD, James [American; b. 1888]. *Drums.* 1926
> Lavish in description and picturesque dialogue, the writer striving to reproduce the colour of life. Time of the American Revolution (1771–80); scenes, North Carolina, London, etc. Paul Jones and his privateering exploits are a feature. [Scribner, New York; Unwin.]

—— *Marching On.* 1927
> In the experiences of one of the landless white men who loves the daughter of a rich and well-born owner of a large plantation, the condition of things in North Carolina is depicted just before and during the war (1859–65). The young man sees plenty of fighting, but it is the marching that wears him down. He spends his last three of the war-years a prisoner with the Yankees. [Scribner, New York; Heinemann.]

"BOYD, Martin A'Beckett" [Martin Mills; Australian; b. 1893]. *The Montforts.* 1928
> An account of the development of modern Australia, traced through the vicissitudes of three generations of a family. [Constable.]

"BOYLESVE, René" [René Tardiveau; French; 1867–1926]. *Daily Bread* (La becquée, 1901). 1929
> The domestic life of a large household of grandparents, uncles, aunts, and children, in Touraine, seen through the eyes of a little boy, who precociously observes their jealousies, suspicions, and quarrels, and their personal peculiarities, and at the same time is sensitive to the sights and sounds and tranquil rustic atmosphere. The dominant figure is the formidable old woman who manages the whole property, sharp-eyed, sharp-tongued, close-fisted, and obstinately intent on the affairs of this world and not of hereafter, but who at any rate is unquenchably loyal to the family and sees that each member gets his *becquée*, his daily mouthful. [v. infra.]

—— *The Child at the Balustrade* (L'enfant à la balustrade, 1903) [sequel]. 1929
> The little boy continues his observations. His father, a notary, has now married again, and much of the comedy, which has a pathetic side, arises from the jealousy of influential friends at his purchase of the reversion of a desirable property from the balustrade of which one commands the whole village and all that goes on there. They send him to Coventry, and he is heart-struck at the defection of ancient intimates, who contradict his faith in human nature. [Transl. by Jane HUTCHINSON, *sub tit. The House on the Hill*, 1904, Nutt: o.p.; (1) and (2), transl. (1 vol.) by H. V. MARROT, *sub tit. Young Vigilance*, Mathews, 1929.]

—— *A Gentlewoman of France* (Madeleine jeune femme, 1912). 1916
> Madeleine, whose exalted, enthusiastic temperament displayed itself in a previous novel, *La jeune fille bien élevée*, is here shown wedded without love in a marriage of convenience, and resisting the seductions of the gay set in Paris. Her inner life is finely portrayed, the book has been compared with *The Mill on the Floss*. The English rendering is dull. [Transl. by Aphra WILSON, Stanley Paul: o.p.]

BRADDON, Mary Elizabeth [Mrs. John Maxwell; 1837–1915]. *Lady Audley's Secret.* 1862
> A fair representative of her numerous novels, which aim, not to represent life, but to construct a series of incidents that shall keep the reader's curiosity incessantly on the stretch. The fictitious death and burial of a woman and the mysterious disappearance of a man are the mainspring of this.

—— *Aurora Floyd.* 1863
> A fascinating and wealthy girl, having married a worthy man, is flung into a dilemma by the reappearance of a low fellow whom she had eloped with and married in her teens. He is murdered and suspicion falls on her, but the real culprit is unmasked in the end.

BRADDON, Mary Elizabeth (*continued*). *John Marchmont's Legacy.* 1863
A dramatic story of a woman's revenge on her stepdaughter, after the latter has married the man they both love. Through an all but fatal accident to him, the girl is kidnapped, and he is led to believe her dead. At the moment he is about to marry again, she reappears; the plot is unmasked, and her guilty cousin who has been scheming to secure the inheritance, sets fire to the ancestral mansion and dies in the flames.

—— *Eleanor's Victory.* 1863
How Eleanor, starting from a vague clue, proceeds by gradual steps to identify her father's murderer and bring him to book.

—— *Henry Dunbar.* 1864
A mystery-plot, the solution of which breaks upon the reader's mind by slow degrees—a man's impersonation of a murdered millionaire.

—— *Joshua Haggard's Daughter.* 1876
Contains more characterization than was usual with Miss Braddon. The starting-point is a stern minister's marriage to a pretty child-like waif whom he has rescued from a vagabond life.

—— *Weavers and Weft ; and other stories.* 1877
Characteristic novelettes of incident. The title-story deals with a mercenary marriage, sensualism, and jealousy. *Christmas in Possession* and *Sir Luke's Return* are farces.

—— *An Open Verdict.* 1878
A rich heiress is believed by her neighbours, including her lover, to have caused her father's death, though the crime could not be brought home. Her complete innocence is established in the last chapters and poetic justice dispensed to friends and enemies.

—— *Ishmael.* 1884
Deals with Paris under the rule of the third Napoleon, from the *coup d'état* of 1851, which is vividly described, down to 1868. Many historical personages are introduced.

—— *Mohawks.* 1886
London in the days of Bolingbroke and Walpole (1726–7).

—— *London Pride.* 1896
The Plague, Lady Castlemaine, etc. (1649–78).

—— *In High Places.* 1898
Surrey, London, and Paris in the earlier years of Charles I (1628–45). Portraits of Buckingham, the Queen of France, Mazarin.

—— *The Infidel : a story of the great revival.* 1900
A heroine of obscure birth, a Voltairean by education, marries a peer on his death-bed, and keeps true to his memory in spite of affection for a young kinsman. She is strongly influenced by the preaching of Whitefield and Wesley, and devotes her latter life to good works. The general picture of the Methodist revival is drawn with sympathy and care.

—— *Miranda.* 1913
A spoilt girl makes an unhappy marriage with a degenerate poet. The characters have life, despite their old-fashioned traits.

—— *Mary.* 1916
One of her most mature works. Mary had been seduced when a mere girl, and is rescued by a charitable and public-spirited young man in the Government service.
[*Works :* (Author's Ed.), 62 vols., Simpkin.]

BRADLEY, Rev. Edward ["Cuthbert Bede"; 1827–89]. *The Adventures of Mr. Verdant Green, an Oxford Freshman.* 1853–57
The tomfoolery, high-jinks, and hoaxes of undergraduate life at Oxford. Though the author was not an Oxford man, he was correct enough in depicting the actual manners and customs of the University, exaggerating for the purposes of low comedy. [Jenkins. *Illus.* by the author, Routledge (Dutton, New York) : o.p. ; *The Adventures and Further Adventures of Mr. Verdant Green,* Young, Liverpool : o.p.]

—— *Little Mr. Bouncer and his Friend, Mr. Verdant Green* [sequel]. 1857
Chiefly a supplemental portrait of little Mr. Bouncer, the most comical of the author's Oxonians. [*Illus.* : J. Blackwood, 1890 : o.p. ; with *The Adventures, supra,* and *Tales of College Life,* 3 vols., Little & Brown, Boston : o.p.]

BRADY, Rev. Cyrus Townsend [American ; 1861–1920]. *For the Freedom of the Sea.* [juvenile] 1899
Duel between the *Constitution* and the *Guerrière* in the war of 1812. [Scribner, New York : o.p.]

—— *The Quiberon Touch.* 1901
An English-French story, the taking of Quebec and Hawkes' victory off Quiberon (1754–9). [Appleton, New York ; *sub tit. Little France,* Greening : o.p.]

—— *A Doctor of Philosophy.* 1903
A very pathetic story of the colour taint. The doctor of philosophy is an accomplished girl who is deeply in love with a young man of old and distinguished family in Philadelphia. Suspecting that there is a strain of negro blood in her veins, she marries the rector of a negro church, finds life with him impossible, and commits suicide. [Scribner, New York : o.p. ; Harper, London : o.p.]

—— *A Little Traitor to the South : a war-time comedy with a tragic interlude.* 1904
The attempt of one of the American "Davids" or submersibles to sink the *Wabash.* Scene, Charleston. [Grosset, New York : o.p. ; Macmillan : o.p.]

—— *The Two Captains.* 1905
Nelson and Napoleon (whose exaggerated figures overshadow everything else in the story) in the Mediterranean (1793–8). Ends with a spirited account of the battle of the Nile. [Macmillan, New York : o.p.]

BRADY, Rev. Cyrus Townsend (*continued*). *The Patriots.*   [juvenile] 1906
The Confederate General Lee is virtually the hero ; the other patriots are Grant and Lincoln. [Dodd & Mead,
New York : o.p. ; *sub tit. The Patriots of the South*, Cassell : o.p.]

—— *The Blue Ocean's Daughter.*   [juvenile] 1907
A romance of the British-American sea-fights from 1782, with a sailor heroine who marries an English lord.
[Moffat, New York : o.p. ; Greening : o.p.]

—— *The Adventures of Lady Susan* [sequel].   1908
A brisk romance of Portsmouth and the Atlantic in the days of George III (who appears in person). Lady
Susan (*sic*) meets with her adventures in running away from her husband, Lord Aldenford. [Moffat,
New York : o.p. ; *sub tit. The Adventures of Susan*, Greening : o.p.]

—— *On the Old " Kearsage."*   [juvenile] 1909
The naval side of the Civil War, the sinking of the *Cumberland* by the *Merrimac* (1862), and the duel between
the *Alabama* and the *Kearsage* (1864). [Scribner, New York.]

—— *The Sword Hand of Napoleon.*   [juvenile] 1914
A romance of the Russian campaign and the retreat from Moscow, with Napoleon as the dominant figure.
[Dodd & Mead, New York : o.p. ; Hodder : o.p.]

—— *The Eagle of the Empire.*   [juvenile] 1915
The Hundred Days and Waterloo, with Napoleon, Ney, and the other marshals well to the fore. [Doubleday,
Doran, New York : o.p. ; Burt, New York : o.p. ; Hodder : o.p.]

" BRAMAH, Ernest " [Ernest Bramah Smith]. *The Wallet of Kai Lung.*   1900
The adventures of an ingenious and ingenuous Chinaman among rogues and thieves and more roguish man-
darins, and the wonderful tales he tells to get himself out of difficulties when captured by brigands. The
stilted talk is an amusing travesty of Chinese ways of speaking and thinking, and the superstitious,
hypocritical courtesy and other celestial foibles are similarly burlesqued. Rich in sound aphorisms.
[Richards ; Methuen ; (Travellers' Lib.), Cape ; Doubleday, Doran, New York.]

—— *The Mirror of Kong-Ho.*   1905
A more laboured essay in the same genre. [Cayme Press, 1929 (Doubleday, Doran, New York).]

—— *Kai Lung's Golden Hours.*   1923

—— *Kai Lung Unrolls His Mat.*   1928
Further instalments of the preceding. [(1) and (2), Richards ; Doubleday, Doran, New York ; (1) Cape.]

—— *A Little Flutter.*   1930
The allusion in the title is to the last-surviving specimen of the Patagonian Groo-Groo, dispatched to the
aviary of a man who has been left a large legacy on condition that he devotes his life to ornithology.
The joke becomes intricate and hilarious with the disguising of an escaped convict in the skin of the
deceased bird. [Cassell.]

BRAY, Anna Eliza [*née* Kempe ; 1790–1883]. *The White Hoods.*   1828
A novel, readable to children, describing the revolt of the citizens of Ghent (1380–2), the deeds of Philip van
Artevelde, etc. The localities were carefully studied by the authoress. [Chapman, 1884 : o.p.]

—— *The Protestant.*   1828
Deals with the persecution of the Protestants under Mary (*c.* 1556–8). At the time of its appearance, in the
days of Catholic Emancipation, it made great stir. [Chapman, 1884 : o.p.]

—— *Romances of the West.*   1845–6
*Fitz of Fitz-Ford ; Warleigh ; Courtenay of Walreddon ; Henry de Pomeroy ; Hartland Forest ; Trelawny of
Trelawne.* Romances of the chief families of Devon and Cornwall, founded on the local antiquities,
legends, and domestic annals. Robert Southey suggested this method of composition to Mrs. Bray, who
had married the vicar of Tavistock. Longman published her romances in 10 vols., 1845–6. [All,
Chapman, 1884.]

BREBNER, Arthur [1870–1922]. *Patches and Pomander.*   1911
Complicated intrigue and love-doings at Whitehall in the days of Charles II and Lady Castlemaine, and
elsewhere in London, introducing some companionable characters. [Blackwood : o.p.]

BREBNER, Percy James [" Christian Lys " ; 1864–1922]. *A Royal Ward.*   1909
South Devon and London under the Regency, smuggling and other exciting doings. [Cassell : o.p. ;
Little & Brown, New York : o.p.]

—— *A Gentleman of Virginia.*   1910
Adventures in the Reign of Terror of a gallant Virginia boy, who was fired by a visit of Lafayette to his
father's home. [Macmillan, London and New York : o.p.]

—— *The Brown Mask.*   1910
The highwayman's mask conceals a lady's lover, in the days of Monmouth's rebellion ; scenes, Hants and
Somerset, London and Dorchester in 1685. [Cassell : o.p.]

—— *The Turbulent Duchess.*   1915
The romantic performances of a certain duchess in Germany at the time of Turenne's invasion of the Palatinate
(*c.* 1674). [Hodder : o.p. ; Little & Brown, Boston : o.p.]

BREMER, Fredrika [Swedish ; 1801–65]. *Novels.*   1843–50
I : *The Neighbours, Hopes, Twins, Solitary, Comforter, Suppers, Trälinnan* ; II : *The President's Daughter*,
2 parts ; III : *The Home, or Life in Sweden* ; *Strife and Peace* ; IV : *A Diary, the H—— Family, Axel
and Anna.* The Neighbours (1837, transl. 1844) is the best example of her quiet delineations of domestic
life in Sweden : much in the style of Jane Austen. *The H—— Family* (in the second series of her
Sketches of Everyday Life) (1831, transl. 1844) shows her quiet humour to best advantage. This book
made her reputation as a novelist. The interest in all her stories is strongly ethical, and is well sustained,
many fine scenes opening out as the drama of human life proceeds on its quiet way. Translated by Mary
Howitt. [(Bohn's Lib.) Bell (Harcourt, New York).]

BREMER, Fredrika (*continued*). *The Home.*   1843
A patient chronicle of family life in its homeliest details—the trials and troubles of the early period after
marriage, the fuller understanding and deeper happiness that ensue ; the joys and sorrows of the children,
their different characters, and how their destinies hinge thereupon. A whole moral philosophy illustrated
in the domestic microcosm. [Transl., 2 vols., Putnam, New York ; see also her *Novels, supra.*]

—— *A Poet's Bazaar : a romance* (En diktares bazar, 1842).   1846
" A charming miscellany " (E. Gosse). [Transl., 3 vols., Bentley : o.p.]

—— *Hertha* (1856).   1856

—— *Father and Daughter* (Far och dotter, 1858).   1859
Later novels expressing her ideas on the education and emancipation of women. [(1) Transl. by Mary HOWITT,
Hall : o.p. ; (2) transl. by the same, Hall : o.p.]

BRETON, Frederick [1864–1902]. *True Heart.*   1898
Reformation times in Switzerland (1514–25) ; Paracelsus, Œcolampadius, Erasmus. Largely philosophical in
motive. [Richards : o.p.]

—— *God Save England !*   1899
Adventure and passionate love in the times of Edward III and his successor. The history of the Cinque
Ports and the reprisals made on our coasts by the French, the doings of a doughty Scottish admiral, etc.,
furnish plenty of action (*c.* 1377). [Richards : o.p.]

BRINIG, Myron [American]. *Singermann.*   1929
The Singermanns are a Jewish family from Rumania settled in an American mining town. The interest of
the book is not in any story but in the close study of individuality and intense parental feeling in conflict.
[Farrar & Rineheart, New York ; Cobden-Sanderson.]

BRITON, E. Vincent. *Some Account of Amyot Brough.*   1884
Social and domestic life at Penrith, Westerham, etc. ; with Wolfe's campaign terminating an intimate study of
his life (1727–59). [Seeley.]

BROD, Max [German ; *b.* 1884]. *The Redemption of Tycho Brahe* (Tycho Brahes Weg zu Gott,
1916).   1928
Introduces the great Danish astronomer and Kepler in a castle of Bohemia, symbolizing the mystical as against
the scientific interpretation of the universe. [Transl. by Felix Warner CRESSE, Knopf, New York and
London.]

—— *Reubeni—Prince of the Jews* (Reubeni, 1925).   1928
A vivid and colourful romance of the Renaissance ; the hero spends his youth in the Jewish ghetto of Prague,
which he forsakes to fall in love with a Christian girl, only to reappear in 1524 in Venice as a great
Jewish nationalist leader. Machiavelli and Michelangelo appear in this latter half. [Transl. by Hannah
WALLER, Knopf, New York and London.]

—— *The Kingdom of Love* (Zauberreich der Liebe, 1928).   1930
A confused and confusing story. The hero's feud with a fellow-student at Prague and his experiences with
the Zionists in Palestine are tedious reading in comparison with the beauty of his love-story. [Transl.
by Eric SUTTON, Secker.]

BRODSKY, Anna [Russian]. *Natasha : the story of a Russian woman.*   1910
Written in English. A chronicle of happy domestic life at the country seat of a great Russian noble, with
scarcely a glimpse of the social troubles and the tyranny of the bureaucracy, though the book ends with
the mutiny at Odessa in 1905. Natasha and her sister Tanya are appealing figures, whose fortunes and
matrimonial crosses, happily ending, carry us through scenes at Vienna, Kiev, and in France. [Dent : o.p.]

BRÖGER, Karl. [German ; *b.* 1886]. *Pillbox 17 : the story of a comradeship-in-arms* (Bunker 17,
1928).   1930
By the German Labour poet. A tremendously realistic narrative of a few days' fighting in a German pillbox
by a machine-gun unit in the third battle of Ypres. [Transl. by Oakley WILLIAMS, Butterworth.]

BROMBY, Rev. Charles Hamilton [1814–1907]. *Alkibiades : a tale of the great Athenian war.*   1905
Attempts to justify the character of Alcibiades (420–404 B.C.), following history rather laboriously. Xenophon,
Plato, Thucydides, etc., are drawn upon, sometimes verbatim. [Simpkin : o.p.]

BROMFIELD, Louis [American ; *b.* 1895]. *The Green Bay Tree.*   1924
Centres in an independent woman, with personality enough to defy convention, and sometimes probability,
in the resolve to live her own life. Her intense individuality stands out in relief against the herd of
empty, timid, suspicious, or grasping and sordid people in a " progressive " steel city of the Western
Reserve, as her career is a dramatic contrast to the mechanical mass-movement of American " civilization."
Among other interesting figures are the imperious but philosophic mother and the sister whose craze for
self-immolation buries her at length among the Carmelites. A play, *The House of Women,* was based
on this. [Stokes, New York ; Grosset, New York ; Unwin.]

—— *Lilli Barr.*   1925
Continues the attack on outworn attitudes and prejudices. Lilli is the crude cousin who emancipates herself
at the instigation of the indomitable Lily Shane, and becomes a musician of world-wide celebrity.
[*Sub tit.* Possession, Stokes, New York ; Grosset, New York ; Unwin, 1926.]

—— *Early Autumn : a story of a lady.*   1926
Further transvaluation of social and ethical standards. Our sympathies are claimed for a woman of forty
who married into a famous New England family that for three centuries had " worshipped a harsh,
changeable, invisible goddess called Duty." She is offered the chance of escaping from this warped
existence, and at any rate secures for her child freedom to be " simple and friendly and human and
complete." The people who spend their arid lives " arranging the lives of others " and wallowing in the
luxury of martyrdom are caustically anatomized. In this and the next novel several characters from
the foregoing reappear. [Stokes, New York ; Grosset, New York ; Cape.]

BROMFIELD, Louis (*continued*). *A Good Woman.* 1927
Here also many cherished values tend to be reversed. The good woman is really a domineering person, with a streak of sexual weakness, who manages her son's spiritual as well as worldly affairs, with fatal results for him. He fails as a missionary and in matrimony, and dies on the eve of salvation through the woman whom he ought to have loved. The satire of emotional religiosity, of misguided missionary enterprise, and of obsolete conventions, is severe, and several of the women portrayed are repulsive. The polemical aim tends to distort the truth of character and motive. [Stokes, New York ; Grosset, New York ; Cape.]

—— *The Strange Case of Miss Annie Spragg.* 1928
The novelist jumps from Italy to the American prairies and back, and from now to the days of our grandfathers and back again ; hence a series of linked episodes and portraits of various characters, mostly bizarre. Raciest of these are the American missioner, Cyrus Spragg, a sort of Mormon Rasputin ; his offspring, the afflicted Miss Spragg, that faded voluptuary the Principessa d'Orobelli, and the irrepressible barmaid Bessie Cudlip, who so improbably fathers a Duke's cousin and marries a man of fortune. [Stokes, New York ; Grosset, New York ; Cape.]

—— *Twenty-four Hours.* 1930
One of those many recent novels that owe their scheme to the film. A swift succession of scenes and a bewildering crowd of New Yorkers pass rapidly across the screen, representing many social and moral —and unsocial and immoral—types, the old and the new rich, the night-club queens, and the inevitable " gunman." [Stokes, New York ; Cambridge Univ. Press.]

BRONNEN, Arnolt [German ; *b.* 1895]. *S.O.S.* (O.S., 1929). 1930
This account of the political intrigues and agitation fomented by the Poles in Upper Silesia after the war is manifestly an appeal for a revision of the problem of the German eastern coalfield and industrial towns. [Secker.]

BRONTË, Anne [" Acton Bell " ; 1820–49]. *The Tenant of Wildfell Hall.* 1848
Chiefly of biographical interest, giving the mournful story of Branwell Brontë's debased life, and meant as a warning example to young people. The homely realism and earnest moralizing are a contrast to the transforming imagination of her two sisters. [*v. infra.*]

BRONTË, Charlotte [" Currer Bell " ; 1816–55]. *Jane Eyre.* 1847
For Charlotte Brontë's first novel see below—*The Professor.* This is the autobiography of a woman of strong and original character, whose plain face was an innovation among heroines, as her love for an ugly and elderly hero indicated a recoil from stereotyped romance. Obviously written out of her own inner life ; autobiographical in the passionate expression of personal feeling, of a woman's yearning towards a fuller life, of revolt from social conventions, unnatural repression of feeling, and narrow religious dogmas. —in a word, it deals with the great modern theme of self-realization, to be treated more systematically by Meredith two or three decades later. In a sense, Charlotte and Emily Brontë were the first novelists of the nineteenth century, the first in whose work the romantic revival became apparent, the life of the spirit taking the place of intellect and reason. [Ed. by (Sir) W. Robertson Nicoll, with *The Moores* (a fragment), Hodder, 1902 : o.p. : *v.* also *infra.*]

—— *Shirley.* 1849
In *Shirley* Charlotte Brontë is again autobiographical to a large extent, the external incidents revolving round the home life of a Yorkshire millowner who suffers in the riots occasioned by the Orders in Council restricting trade during the great French war. Most of the characters are drawn from life, the men-folk being poorly caricatured and satirized for their impermeability to feminine ideas. The proud and passionate Shirley was drawn from her sister Emily ; the girl who is her bosom friend was also from life. Pastoral and moorland Yorkshire is depicted in the spirit of Wordsworth. The general theme is the same —" What was I created for, I wonder. Where is my place in the world ? " This is not only Shirley's problem, but that of all Charlotte Brontë's heroines.

—— *Villette.* 1853
Also composed largely of personal experiences and observations of life in the Brussels *pensionnat*, where Charlotte Brontë spent some years among many singular and not a few unpleasant people whose portraits she here puts on record. Lucy Snowe, another embodiment of her ideal of girlhood and nascent love, and the irascible preceptor, Paul Emanuel, are, like Jane and Shirley, " exceptional characters," in the Meredithian sense, beings living on a higher plane of thought and emotion than average humanity. A love-story of the same intensely spiritual nature as in all the Brontë novels, in which love is the means of realization of one's highest self in an ideal union.

—— *The Professor.* 1857
A first study for *Villette.* Scene, the same *pensionnat* at Brussels, where a pair of unworldly characters, the innocent heroine and the young professor, are attracted by natural kinship, and advance from sympathy to love. The publishers wanted more incident and excitement : so Charlotte Brontë kept this back and it was issued at last posthumously.

BRONTË, Emily Jane [" Ellis Bell " ; 1818–48]. *Wuthering Heights.* 1847
A weird drama of love, hate, and revenge, laid amid the sombre dales and fells of moorland Yorkshire ; the chief character, a fierce, elemental nature, in whom both affection and hatred grow into fixed ideas, pursuing their objects even beyond the grave. Around this terrible figure are a group of men and women, some akin to him in fiery will and uncurbed passion, some pitifully weak ; several are drawn with a firm hand and an uncanny insight into human nature and an intimate knowledge of local manners and speech. Like her sister Charlotte, Emily Brontë had a fund of creativeness in her intense and passionate nature : they looked within rather than at the world outside. Clumsy in workmanship, this strange masterpiece is like a Greek play fitted into the framework of a modern novel, with a current of deep poetry that overwhelms the barriers of realism and carried us into the limitless sea of elemental feeling and tragic strife. [*Works* of the Sisters Brontë, ed. Clement Shorter, 10 vols., (vol. 1 : *Poetry*, 2 : *Wuthering Heights*), Hodder (Doran, New York), 1910–11 : o.p. ; *Works*, 6 vols., with *Life* by Mrs. Gaskell (vol. vii.), Murray ; *Works* (Temple Edn.) 12 vols., Dent ; *Works*, with 60 *coloured illus.* by Edmund Dulac, Dent : o.p. ; *Works*, 6 vols., Bigelow Brown, New York. SEPARATELY : (Everyman's Lib.), Dent (Dutton, New York) ; (World's Classics), Oxford Press.]

BROOKE, Emma Frances [*d.* 1926]. *A Superfluous Woman.* 1894
A viewy novel on the woman question. The eccentric life of a society beauty, who at the beginning of the novel is tired of existence and thinks of dying, is recalled to life and its opportunities by a sentimental East End doctor, and has a variety of experiences as kitchen-help, lover of a Scottish peasant, and wife of a wicked peer. This gentleman makes her life a martyrdom ; but she works heroically till her death. [Heinemann : o.p. ; Cassell, New York : o.p.]

—— *The Engrafted Rose.* 1900
Rosamunda is a changeling, whose father had been forced by fear of disinheritance to marry his father's protégée a few hours before the death of his wife, Rosamunda's mother. This crime begets a series of tragic events in years to come. The story has character-drawing, earnest thought about the phases of life depicted, and some humorous dialogue, in the vernacular of Northern England, among servants and rustics. [Hutchinson : o.p. ; Duffield, New York : o.p.]

BROOKE, Mrs. Frances [*née* Moore ; 1724–89]. *The History of Lady Julia Mandeville* 1763
A novel in letters dealing with the tragic loves of an aristocratic pair who are as impeccably virtuous and high-minded as their faultless parents. Typical of the age of sensibility, and conventional in plot and *dénouement*; but interesting as a link between Richardson and Fanny Burney. Mrs. Brooke also wrote *Emily Montague* (1769) and *The Excursion* (1777), besides plays, etc. [Ed. by E. Phillips Poole, Scholartis Press, 1930.]

BROOKE, Henry [Irish ; 1703–83]. *The Fool of Quality ; or, The History of Henry, Earl of Moreland.* 1765–70
Brooke was a man of strong individuality who was looked upon in the days of George II as a literary luminary, and was famous later as an authority on agrarian and agricultural matters in Ireland. His friend Wesley adopted this book in an abridged form (*The History of Henry, Earl of Moreland*) as a handbook of the Christian virtues. It purports to describe the education of an ideal nobleman. The hero is brought up by an uncle, who gives him unlimited means for relieving poverty, etc. The pictures of boyhood were unmatched till Hughes wrote *Tom Brown's Schooldays*. Very inchoate ; the personal history of this quixotic young man is overshadowed by frequent homilies and dissertations on politics, morals, and social amelioration ; the theology is that of Brooke's future editor, Charles Kingsley—the identity of Goodness and God. [Ed. Kingsley, abridged and with biographical preface (highly eulogistic), Macmillan, 1873 : o.p. ; the same edn., with a new Life of the Author (based on unused family records) by E. A. Baker (Library of Early Novelists), Routledge (Dutton, New York), 1906. (New Pocket Lib.), 2 vols., Lane.]

BROOKFIELD, Mrs. Charles [Frances Mary, *née* Grogan]. *My Lord of Essex.* 1907
A painstaking account of the Earl of Essex's expedition to Cadiz in 1596, the craft of Sir Robert Cecil, and the character of Elizabeth. [Pitman : o.p.]

—— *A Friar Observant.* 1909
The Friar is one of the dispossessed in 1539, and wends on a pilgrimage from his Welsh convent through Germany, meeting with abundant adventures and with Luther, whose portrait is not attractive. [Pitman : o.p. ; Herder, St. Louis : o.p.]

BROOKS, Elbridge Streeter [American ; 1846–1902]. *In Leisler's Times.* [juvenile] 1880
Knickerbocker New York, Jacob Leisler, and the militia insurrection (1688–91). [Lothrop, Boston : o.p.]

—— *A Son of Issachar.* 1890
A melodramatic romance with Judas Iscariot and the young man of Nain whom Christ raised from the dead as chief figures. Attempts to justify Judas's motives, and for this purpose brings in a complicated series of plots and insurrections against Herod and the Romans (A.D. 33). [Putnam, New York : o.p.]

—— *A Boy of the First Empire.* [juvenile] 1895
A Paris waif becomes a page in the palace. Domestic life of Napoleon, etc. (1806–15). [Century Co., New York : o.p. ; Partridge : o.p.]

—— *A Son of the Revolution.* [juvenile] 1898
A boy's story in the West at the time of Aaron Burr's conspiracy (1805–7) and later. Burr, Clay, Jefferson, and Andrew Jackson are introduced. [Wilde, Boston, 1916 : o.p.]

—— *Master of the Strong Hearts.* [juvenile] 1899
The defeat and massacre of General Custer by the Sioux (1876). [Dutton, New York : o.p.]

BROSTER, Dorothy Kathleen. *The Yellow Poppy.* 1920
A tale of western France and Paris, in the time of the Chouans (1799–1800). [Duckworth ; McBride, New York.]

—— " *Mr. Rowl.*" 1924
The misfortunes and adventures of a French officer on parole in England, time of the Peninsular War (*c.* 1813). [Heinemann ; Doubleday, Doran, New York.]

—— *The Flight of the Heron.* 1925
—— *The Gleam in the North* [sequel]. 1927
—— *The Dark Mile* [sequel]. 1929
Jacobite romances, the first concerned with the Forty-five itself and the escape of Prince Charlie (1745–6), the second with the wanderings of Archibald Cameron, brother of Locheil (1752–3) ; the third with the betrayers of Dr. Cameron, and the subsequent lives of characters from the previous two books (1754). [(1), (2), and (3), Heinemann ; (1), Dodd & Mead, New York ; McClelland, Toronto ; *illus.*, Coward, McCann, New York, 1930.]

BROSTER, Dorothy Kathleen, and TAYLOR, Gertrude Winifred. *Chantemerle : a romance of the Vendean war.* 1911
A royalist romance of La Vendée (1792–4), politics and civil war sharing the interest with a problem of love and friendship that borders on tragedy. [Heinemann ; Brentano, New York : o.p.]

BROUGHTON, Rhoda [1840–1920]. *Cometh up as a Flower.* 1867

An innocent, impulsive girl loves a handsome soldier, but has to marry a rich husband to bolster up the family finances. A simple, melancholy story of disappointed passion, related by the heroine herself in a way that is really the perfection of art, in a minor sphere. The quiet touches of the character-drawing, the lively fancy and the humour are constant features of Miss Broughton's novels. [Macmillan : o.p. ; Appleton, New York : o.p.]

—— *Not Wisely, but too Well.* 1867

A girl of loving disposition throws away her heart upon an unworthy man—a muscular libertine of the Guy Livingstone type—and when life becomes intolerably dreary, she almost succumbs to a great temptation and never rises from the conflict. [Macmillan : o.p. ; Appleton, New York : o.p.]

—— *Red as a Rose is She.* 1870

The heroine is a very human mixture of truth and folly, self-respect and cowardice, qualities that give rise to the bitter and the sweet vicissitudes of her love-story. Her deceptions are paid for by suffering, and in the end she is restored to sincerity and happiness. [Macmillan : o.p. ; Appleton, New York : o.p.]

—— *Good-bye, Sweetheart !* 1872

The story of a headstrong, coquettish, and often very foolish heroine, her casual conquests and her love for a man who shares her passion, a love ruined by her own folly and ending in her death. [Macmillan : o.p. ; Appleton, New York : o.p.]

—— *Nancy.* 1873

Depicts the merry, undisciplined life of a neglected family of youngsters, with a selfish and indifferent father, among whom Nancy grows up an unkempt, but generous and faithful girl. Then we see her married, a fine example of womanhood, with a worthy husband. Her innocent imprudence is partly the cause of some episodes of scandal and jealousy. [Macmillan : o.p. ; Appleton, New York : o.p.]

—— *Joan.* 1876

Joan is a gracious and sweet-tempered girl, brought up in refinement and then sent to live with a family of good-natured but vulgar cousins. Her love-story runs far from smoothly, but reaches happiness in the end. [Macmillan : o.p. ; Appleton, New York : o.p.]

—— *Second Thoughts.* 1880

The taming of a shrew—light comedy, with a varied series of character-sketches and a spice of caricature in the poet Challoner. [Macmillan : o.p. ; Appleton, New York : o.p.]

—— *Belinda.* 1883

Belinda, outwardly cold and impassive, burning with concealed passion, is on the verge of stooping to folly, but is saved in time. A rather more complicated story than the foregoing ; a number of characters, who furnish comic effect, e.g. the vulgarly ironical Sarah, her grandmother, and her dogs. Scene, Dresden. [Macmillan : o.p. ; Appleton, New York : o.p.]

—— *Doctor Cupid.* 1886

Goes deeper than usual in the psychological treatment of character. A group of love affairs, prosperous or the reverse, principally those of two sisters, one of whom dies. [Macmillan : o.p. ; Lippincott, Philadelphia : o.p.]

—— *Alas !* 1890

An emotional story, dealing with a mother and her daughter, and the girl's unhappy love-affairs. Oxford, Florence, and Algiers are the scenes. [Macmillan : o.p. ; Appleton, New York : o.p.]

—— *Mrs. Bligh.* 1892

The romance of a clever widow and a distinguished sculptor, in Chelsea and Anglesea. [Macmillan : o.p. ; Appleton, New York : o.p.]

—— *A Beginner.* 1894

An unsophisticated young lady writes anonymously a novel which is branded as improper and causes a world of embarrassment among relatives, friends, and lovers. A comic episode, with light ridicule of the provincial reviewer and other varieties of the genus critic. [Macmillan : o.p. ; Appleton, New York : o.p.]

—— *The Game and the Candle.* 1899

A somewhat cynical story of a woman's passion and disillusionment ; the characters drawn with Miss Broughton's wonted candour and effervescent satire. [Macmillan : o.p. ; Appleton, New York : o.p.]

—— *Foes-in-Law.* 1900

The same congenial theme as in several of her earlier novels—the varied life of a large family of young people and the strained relations between various members. Two sisters-in-law head the hostile forces, a pair of well-contrasted characters, whose mutual influence and gradual progress to a better understanding are related with sprightly humour. [Macmillan : o.p.]

—— *Lavinia.* 1902

The central situation is rather painful—Lavinia out of gratitude to her guardian-uncle sacrifices her love. Comic relief is furnished by the satirical sketches of a parvenue and her sentimental daughter and of a bevy of too frank children. [Macmillan : o.p.]

—— *A Waif's Progress.* 1905

The waif is a charming young person, the daughter of a hard-drinking sportsman and a coquettish mother, and herself a baggage. Her relations with an ill-assorted married pair make an interesting story, not without comedy. [Macmillan : o.p.]

—— *Mamma.* 1909

A comedy in the ironical mood, a sort of feminine pendant to Meredith's *Egoist.* Mamma is a spoiled old lady, who with exquisite grace and amiability makes her children helots and their lives a burden. An admirable example in its details of Miss Broughton's polished technique and of her humorous insight. [Macmillan : o.p.]

BROUGHTON, Rhoda (*continued*). *A Fool in her Folly.* 1920
A lady of eighty tells how when she was a girl she wrote a daring novel, *Love*, to the horror of her parents, and afterwards met a daring lover with whom she lived it over again. Light, flippant, and amusing. [Odhams : o.p.]

BROWN, Alec. *Green Lane ; or, Murder at Moat Farm.* 1930
Malicious gossip hounds the unfortunate gentleman-farmer to suicide. A good sensation story, weak however in character-drawing. [Cape.]

BROWN, Mrs. Alice ["Martin Redfield"; American; *b.* 1857]. *Meadow-Grass : tales of New England life.* 1895
Short tales of New England village life, characterized by good-humour, optimism, and a keen delight in the open air. *Heartsease, Joint Owners in Spain, Farmer Eli's Vacation*, are good representatives. [Houghton, Boston ; Dent : o.p.]

—— *Tiverton Tales.* 1899
A further series having much the same qualities. [Houghton, Boston.]

—— *King's End.* 1901
A quiet story of life in a New England mountain village, in the style made familiar by Miss Wilkins ; full of insight into rustic character, such as that of the rough, manly young farmer and his deaf mother, of the spiritually minded elder, and of the young woman with the call to go preaching. [First entitled *April Showers*; Houghton, Boston : o.p. ; Constable : o.p.]

—— *The Mannerings.* 1903
A delicate, perhaps too tenuous, study of the deeper relations of true wedlock, as exemplified in three pairs of men and women. Very American in its puritanism, very feminine in its lack of realism and its etherealized portraits of men. A tender sense of the divinity of life and the supreme excellence of a love that renounces its own gratification, broods over the book, and is crystallized in the character of Elinor. [Houghton, Boston ; Nash : o.p.]

—— *Paradise.* 1905
A New England village tale with parallel interests. Simple as a story, the real significance being in the inner life, not in the outward incident. Not lacking in quiet humour, however, and rather too exact in the reproduction of a racy but uncouth vernacular. [Houghton, Boston ; Constable : o.p.]

—— *The County Road.* 1906
Thirteen stories embodying the same refined idealism and delicate fancy in the simple annals of New England folk, their love affairs, domestic incompatibilities, and the difficulties of married life. Little of the shadows of life, plenty of its comedy. [Houghton, Boston ; Constable : o.p.]

—— *The Story of Thyrza.* 1909
A very pathetic and emotional story of an imaginative girl who is betrayed, and has to earn her son's bread as a sempstress. Her trials are not finished here, for the son does not appreciate the simple honesty of her self-devotion. [Houghton, Boston ; Constable : o.p.]

—— *Country Neighbours.* 1910
A sheaf of similar stories, emphasizing the romance of humble lives and the fine qualities which sympathetic discernment knows not to be the monopoly of superior people. The beauty of Mrs. Brown's fancy comes out admirably in *Flowers of Paradise*, and her delicate humour in such idylls as *Gardener Jim* and *The Gay House*, though her artistic sphere is so limited and monotonous. [Houghton, Boston : o.p. ; Constable : o.p.]

—— *The Prisoner.* 1916
A country novel of New England that raises various moral problems, especially that of the effect of imprisonment upon the members of a man's family. Some conventional plot-stuff about his wife's theft of a necklace unfortunately confuses the issue. [Macmillan, New York : o.p.]

BROWN, Charles Brockden [American ; 1771–1811]. *Wieland ; or, The Transformation.* 1798
Brown was the first American novelist to count in literary history. He got rid of the more artificial elements in the contemporary styles of Mrs. Radcliffe, " Monk " Lewis, and other Gothic romancers, and laid his action in American scenes. A mysterious voice bids Wieland sacrifice his wife and children to show his obedience to Heaven ; but this oracle is only another fanatic who happens to be a ventriloquist. All Brown's romances are sensational in matter, grandiloquent in style, and animated with the social ideas of Godwin and Mary Wollstonecraft. [McKay, Philadelphia, 1887 ; together with *Memoirs of Carwin the Biloquist, a fragment*, ed. with introd. by Fred Louis Pattee, Harcourt, New York, 1926.]

—— *Ormond.* 1799
The least sensational of his novels ; portrays a woman of surpassing virtue, who rises superior to the ills of circumstance, little and great : a long and harrowing recital of moral and physical anguish and petty annoyances nobly endured. [*vide infra.*]

—— *Arthur Mervyn ; or, Memories of the Year 1793.* 1800
This account of the terrible visitation of yellow fever that devastated Philadelphia may be compared in its realism with Defoe's *Journal of the Plague Year*. Brown was absent from Philadelphia at the time, but went through a similar time of pestilence at New York in 1798 ; so that he draws on personal experience, though his characters are fictitious. [2 vols., McKay, Philadelphia, 1887.]

—— *Edgar Huntly ; or, Adventures of a Sleep-Walker.* 1801
A melodramatic novel, full of surprising incidents, and abounding in descriptions of the Alleghany region. There are scenes of Indian warfare, in which the redskin is less idealized than in Cooper's romances ; but Brown knew little about them or their country. A murder effected by a somnambulist supplies the mystery, the elucidation of which is the principal motive ; there are, in fact, two somnambulists. [Ed. with introd. by David Lee Clark, Macmillan, New York, 1928. *Novels*, ltd. ed., 6 vols., McKay, Philadelphia.]

BROWN, G. B. [" George Douglas " ; Scottish ; 1869–1902]. *The House with the Green Shutters.* 1901
A violent antidote to the sentimentality of the Kailyard novel, showing the grim and ugly side of life in a small Scottish township, the hatred and jealousy, the brutality, hypocrisy, and slander that are ineradicable traits of the supposed worthies. The gradual collapse and catastrophe of the bullying Gourlay and his family is dramatized on strict classical lines, and our sympathies are left with the victim of his own folly, the only figure having any strength or dignity. The others are a libel on human nature. [Introd. by J. B. Priestley, (Traveller's Lib.), Cape, 1929 ; with introd. by George Blake, Modern Lib., New York, 1927.]

BROWN, Katharine Holland [American]. *Diane.* 1905
Story of a communistic settlement of French people on the Mississippi, in the years before the war (1856) ; the traffic in runaway slaves, Captain John Brown, the Abolitionists, etc. [Doubleday, New York : o.p. ; Heinemann : o.p.]

—— *The Father.* 1929
The mixed fortunes of a household who settled on the unreclaimed Illinois prairie in 1850, when Abolitionist and Pro-Slavery agitation and the " Underground Railway " were in full swing. The father, a fervid Abolitionist editor, is the friend of Lincoln, Emerson, Horace Mann, Hawthorne, and the Alcotts ; Lincoln makes a very picturesque appearance. The authoress wields a lively descriptive pen. [Day, New York ; Grosset, New York ; Heinemann.]

BROWN, Vincent. *A Magdalen's Husband.* 1904
—— *The Dark Ship.* 1904
—— *The Disciple's Wife.* 1905
—— *The Sacred Cup.* 1905
—— *Mrs. Grundy's Crucifix.* 1906
Well-constructed novels of the kind that illustrate a point of view, satirizing the self-righteousness and half-unconscious hypocrisy that cloak the real heartlessness and the greedy appetite for scandal of upper middle-class society, the society which sits in the best pews, subscribes ostentatiously to missions, presides over charity bazaars. Intent on showing up one aspect of human nature, the writer falls at times into caricature ; yet many of his figures are drawn with memorable truth and fairness, a good few with the happiest humour, and his books leave the conviction that fine feeling and noble character are still to be found in the world. [(1), (2), (3), (4), Duckworth ; (5), Hutchinson ; (4), Putnam, New York : all o.p.]

—— *The Glory and the Abyss.* 1910
Draws and differentiates with great skill the members of a peasant family in Sussex, the brother, Peter Bonoor, of two sisters who have been seduced by the squire's villainous son being a memorable character. The author's portraiture of the gentlefolk is as biting as in *Mrs. Grundy's Crucifix*, but not quite so successful. [Chapman : o.p. ; Dutton, New York : o.p.]

—— *Mayfield.* 1911
A faithless husband, a good and patient wife, a deserving lover, and the difficulties of divorce as regards the poor. [Chapman : o.p. ; Brentano, New York : o.p.]

BROWN, William Garrott [American ; 1868–1913]. *A Gentleman of the South.* 1903
The father of this Gentleman of the South, owner of a great plantation in the Black Belt, slew his friend in a duel and wrecked the happiness of two generations. His son sacrifices his life to make atonement (1847–8). A study of chivalrous hearts, refined ideals, and self-sacrificing motives, leading up to one tremendous scene. The pathos is a powerful indictment of this false code of honour. [Macmillan, New York : o.p.]

BRUDNO, Ezra Selig [Jewish-American ; b. 1877]. *The Tether.* 1908
The life of a Jewish poet, a waif from the slums of Boston, who is sent to school and college by a benevolent lady, and earns his living with his pen. Illustrates the obstacles put in the way of a Jew by both Christians and his own people. [Lippincott, Philadelphia : o.p.]

BRUUN, Laurids [Danish ; b. 1864]. *Van Zanten's Happy Days.* 1920
The lives of Dutch settlers in New Zealand and the Polynesias (1846–1904). [Gyldendal : o.p.]

BRYDEN, Henry Anderson [b. 1854]. *Tales of South Africa.* 1896
Miscellaneous tales about Dutch, English, Bushmen, and others ; truthful in local colouring, and with a sporting flavour. [Constable : o.p.]

—— *An Exiled Scot : passages in the life of Ranald Cameron.* 1899
Adventures of a Jacobite refugee in the neighbourhood of Capetown (1746–56). Overflows with incident, perils among savages, etc. ; the picture of life among the Dutch colonists carefully drawn. [Chatto : o.p. ; New Amsterdam Book Co., New York : o.p.]

—— *From Veldt Camp-Fires : stories of South Africa.* 1900
The rough, adventurous life of the Boers on the veld, wild experiences among Kafirs and Bushmen, sketched by one who has lived in the country. [Hurst : o.p.]

BRYUSOV, Valery [Russian ; 1873–1924]. *The Fiery Angel* (1907). 1930
An historical romance of the time of Luther, supposed to be narrated by a German mercenary. [Transl. by Ivor MONTAGU and Sergei NALBANDOV, Toulmin.]

—— *The Republic of the Southern Cross ; and other stories.* 1918
Bryusov is a Russian Poe, with differences. The title-story depicts a million-peopled city on the Antarctic continent laid waste by a psychical epidemic. The mysteries of personal identity, the shadowy problems of dreams, half-existence, hysteria, and madness are the other themes. [Transl, with introd. essay by Stephen GRAHAM, Constable : o.p.]

BUCHAN, John [Scottish ; b. 1875]. *Sir Quixote of the Moors : being some account of an episode in the life of the Sieur de Rohaine.* 1895
Romantic adventures of a French gentleman who befriends a proscribed Scottish family after Culloden. [Unwin ; Holt, New York : o.p.]

BUCHAN, John (*continued*). *Scholar Gipsies.* 1896
Sketches of scenery and humanity on the upper Tweed ; full of Arcadian feeling. [Lane.]

—— *John Burnet of Barns.* 1898
Scenes, the Lowlands and the Netherlands (*c.* 1678–83). John Burnet is for Church and State, but changes his views when, a fugitive amongst the Covenanters, he becomes acquainted with their pious and lofty character. [Lane ; Dodd & Mead, New York.]

—— *A Lost Lady of Old Years.* 1899
A Stevensonian novel of Edinburgh and the Highlands. The two famous Jacobites of the '45, Lord Lovat and Murray of Broughton, are introduced. [Lane.]

—— *The Half-Hearted.* 1900
A study of a typically modern character : a dilettante, unready, and self-distrustful, with a reputation for cowardice, shows himself at a moment of failure and peril capable of supreme heroism—at that moment he dies gloriously. Scenes, Scotland and the mountainous frontier of India. [Hodder ; Houghton, Boston.]

—— *The Watcher by the Threshold.* 1902
—— *Grey Weather.* 1909
Short stories, remarkable for hard thinking and imaginative form, a number of them dealing with the supernatural. *The Watcher by the Threshold* describes the survival of a clan of prehistoric men in the wilds of the Highlands. [(1) Blackwood ; (2) Lane : o.p.]

—— *Prester John.* 1910
A South African romance with some blood-curdling adventures in the mountains. [Nelson ; *sub tit. The Great Diamond Pipe*, Dodd & Mead, New York, 1911 : o.p. ; title as above, Doubleday, Doran, New York.]

—— *The Moon Endureth : tales and fancies.* 1912
One of the best of the historical stories is *The Lemnian*, which tells how a man of Lemnos was accidentally an eye-witness of the stand of Leonidas at Thermopylae. *The Company of the Marjolaine* shows the Young Pretender in his inglorious later years. Another tale leaves a haunting physical sense of the metaphysical idea of space. [Blackwood.]

—— *Salute to Adventurers.* 1915
Adventures of a young Scot at home and in Virginia about 1685. [Nelson ; Houghton, Boston.]

—— *The Thirty-Nine Steps.* 1915
—— *Greenmantle* [sequel]. 1916
—— *Mr. Standfast* [sequel]. 1919
A trilogy of thrilling, though wildly impossible adventures, wherein Col. Hannay and his friends frustrate a German secret service organization of superhuman power and ingenuity. The fields of action are Scotland, Asia, and the western front respectively. [(1), Blackwood ; (1), (2), and (3), Hodder ; with *The Three Hostages, sub tit. Four Adventures of Richard Hannay*, 1 vol., *id.*, 1930 ; Doubleday, Doran, New York : (1) and (3) : o.p.]

—— *The Path of the King.* 1921
Fourteen stories of heroic adventure, from the times of the Vikings (*Hightown under Surfell*) to that of Abraham Lincoln (*The End of the Road*). [Hodder ; Doubleday, Doran : o.p.]

—— *Huntingtower.* 1922
A peaceful Glasgow grocer becomes involved with Bolshevists, who have kidnapped an heiress and hold her in a Scottish mansion ; with the aid of some stout-hearted local youngsters he enables her to regain her freedom. [Hodder ; Grosset, New York.]

—— *Midwinter.* 1923
Adventures of a Jacobite agent in the Oxford and Derby districts in 1745. Dr. Johnson as a young man is a prominent figure ; General Oglethorpe also appears. [Hodder ; Houghton, Boston ; Grosset, New York.]

—— *The Three Hostages.* 1924
A revolutionary conspiracy of post-war fanatics, led by a master-mind, is frustrated by Hannay, the hero of *The Thirty-Nine Steps.* [Hodder ; Houghton, Boston ; Grosset, New York.]

—— *John MacNab.* 1925
The familiar trio of sportsmen lay a wager that they will successfully poach from three Highland estates, due notice being given. Their methods, the excitement of the chase, and the ludicrous situations into which it leads them, provide sufficient interest, despite the peaceful nature of the adventure. [Hodder ; Houghton, Boston.]

—— *The Dancing Floor.* 1926
Old pagan rites are revived in modern Greece, and the heroine is rescued from an intended human sacrifice. [Hodder ; Houghton, Boston.]

—— *Witch Wood.* 1927
A careful historical picture of the times of Montrose and the Covenanters (by Montrose's biographer). The theatre of events is the Lowlands (1644–5), and interest centres in a minister who preaches a liberal doctrine in an age of bigotry and of such superstitions as witchcraft, and so incurs the charge of heresy and is excommunicated. [Hodder ; Houghton, Boston.]

—— *The Courts of the Morning.* 1929
High adventure and some capital fighting, in the frustration of a plot to gain world-power, engineered by an evil genius who discovered natural supplies of a peculiarly potent drug. [Hodder ; Houghton, Boston.]

—— *Castle Gay.* 1930
Several of the doughty heroes of *Huntingtower* here take a vigorous part in the adventures eventuating through the efforts of Evallonian revolutionaries to gain over a powerful newspaper magnate. [Hodder ; Houghton, Boston.]

BUCHANAN, Robert Williams [Scottish; 1841–1901]. *The Shadow of the Sword.*   1875
An epical, Hugoesque novel of the Napoleonic wars (1813–15). A Breton fisherman refuses to serve under Napoleon, holding war to be forbidden by Christianity; and is persecuted, outlawed, and driven insane. During the Hundred Days he tries to assassinate the Emperor. An earnest polemic against war and national ambition. [Chatto: o.p.]

—— *God and the Man.*   1880
A grandiose romance inspired by an ethical idea, the vanity and folly of individual hate. A man bitterly wronged pursues the villain relentlessly until both are face to face with death at the extremity of the habitable world; then, as it were in the presence of God, he pardons and rescues his foe. The loftiness of the argument, which precludes character-drawing, and of the ultimate scene amid the polar ice, again recalls Victor Hugo. [Chatto: o.p.]

BUCK, Mrs. Pearl S. [American]. *East Wind, West Wind.*   1930
A young Chinese girl brought up under Eastern conventions is married to a Westernized husband; the complications that ensue, more particularly when his brother returns home with an American wife, are worked out by one who has an intimate knowledge of the country. [Day, New York.]

BUCKLEY, William [Irish]. *Croppies Lie Down: a tale of Ireland in '98.*   1903
Aims at reproducing the horrors of the Wexford rising with complete realism. The characters are drawn in a most lifelike manner, but rather more than justice is done to the English statesmen and their agents. [Duckworth: o.p.]

—— *Cambia Carty; and other stories.*   1907
Realistic description—not very agreeable for the people of Cork and Youghal—of the lower and middle classes in Youghal. [Maunsell: o.p.]

"BUCKROSE, Miss J. E." [Mrs. Annie Edith Jameson, *née* Foster; b. 1868]. *A Little Green World.*   1909
"A Village Comedy without a Plot and without a Problem." [Hutchinson: o.p.; Putnam, New York: o.p.]

—— *A Golden Straw.*   1910

—— *The Pilgrimage of a Fool.*   1910

—— *Down our Street: a provincial comedy.*   1911
The lives and personal relations of average, domesticated people, their monetary difficulties, commercial successes and the opposite, homely fêtes, love troubles or happy courtings, etc.—described with quiet, unpretending realism. Little country places are the usual scene; that of *A Golden Straw*, for instance, is a lonely spot on the coast of Holderness. [(1), (2), and (3), Mills & Boon: o.p.; (3) Jenkins; (3) Putnam, New York.]

—— *The Grey Shepherd: the growth of a legend.*   1916
The shepherd is credited with supernatural powers, and when he dies becomes the subject of a myth. [Hodder: o.p.]

—— *The Matchmakers.*   1916
Village life, especially the struggles of the small farmer, treated with sympathetic insight. The efforts to marry the rector's daughter and the squire, and the embarrassments caused to the former whose heart is set elsewhere, make an amusing story. [Hodder: o.p.; Doubleday, Doran, New York: o.p.]

—— *Æsop Dancing; or, The Heart of Oliver Goldsmith.*   1930
The life of Goldsmith from childhood until his death (c. 1734–1774), told as a connected story. Johnson, Boswell, and several others of that circle are introduced; many of their better-known sayings are incorporated into the conversation. Very suitable for younger readers. [Nash.]

BULFIN, William [Irish]. *Tales of the Pampas.*   1900
Free-and-easy, broadly humorous stories of rough life in Argentina, where Irish settlers are numerous. The contrasts of Spanish and Hibernian character give point to several of the tales. [Unwin: o.p.]

BULLEN, Frank Thomas [1857–1915]. *The Log of a Sea Waif.*   1899
Largely autobiographical—portrays the hard life aboard the merchant service in the early seventies. [Murray.]

—— *A Sack of Shakings.*   1901

—— *Deep-sea Plunderings: a collection of stories of the sea.*   1901

—— *A Whaleman's Wife.*   1902

—— *Sea Wrack.*   1903

—— *Sea Puritans.*   1904

—— *A Son of the Sea.*   1905

—— *Sea Spray.*   1906

—— *Frank Brown, Sea Apprentice.*   1906

—— *The Call of the Deep: being some further adventures of Frank Brown.*   1907

—— *Confessions of a Tradesman.*   1908

—— *Cut off from the World.*   1909
Stories of the sea, into which Mr. Bullen works his vast experience of life on the ocean, his observation of everything alive, and his strong religious sense of character. *Sea Puritans* is the romance of the life of Admiral Blake, and comprises many moving scenes of action ashore and afloat in the stirring days of the Commonwealth (1643–57). Mr. Bullen's favourite theme is the simple one of a lad's rise to manhood in the mercantile marine. *Confessions of a Tradesman* is partly autobiography. [(1) Collins: o.p.; McClure, New York: o.p.; (2) Murray; (3) Hodder: o.p.; Appleton, New York: o.p.; (4) Murray; (5) Hodder: o.p.; (6) Nisbet: o.p.; Jacobs, Philadelphia: o.p.; (7) Hodder: o.p.; (8) Nisbet; Dutton, New York; (9) id.: o.p.; (10) Hodder: o.p.; (11) Unwin: o.p.]

BULLETT, Gerald William [*b.* 1894] *Mr. Godly Beside Himself : an adventure in two days.* 1924
A pleasant fantasy, pointing the contrast between the real and the desired. Mr. Godly is a respectable City man, until one day his typist leads him into Fairyland for an all-too-brief space. [Lane ; Benn ; Boni, New York.]

—— *The History of Egg Pandervil.* 1928
—— *Nicky, Son of Egg* [sequel]. 1929
A chronicle-novel of two lives ; in the first, we follow Egg from boyhood on his father's farm (about 1830) and leave him a grocer, comfortably married, with one son. Throughout he is an unfulfilled character, worthy of better things than fate has given him. Like another egg, the story is good in parts. [(1) and (2) Heinemann ; Knopf, New York ; together : 1 vol., *sub tit. The Pandervils,* 1930, Heinemann.]

BULLOCK, Shan F. [Irish ; *b.* 1865]. *Ring o' Rushes.* 1897
Sketches of real life among Irish peasants. In *His Magnificence* an enriched peasant returns to his native village and tries to show off his grandeur, but is deservedly humbled by a poor woman. *Her Soger Boy* recounts a mother's innocent fraud and her soldier lad's savage retaliation. *Rogue Bartley* masquerades as a man of property and "spoils the Egyptians." [Ward & Lock : o.p. ; Duffield, New York : o.p.]

—— *The Barrys.* 1899
Descriptions of life in the author's native Fermanagh, and faithful studies of contrasted character. Frank Barry, the most living, is one of those emotional people who seem able to love, sincerely and, in a way, faithfully, two women at once ; his character is thrown into relief against the sterling qualities of the peasantry. [Harper : o.p. ; Doubleday, New York : o.p.]

—— *Irish Pastorals.* 1901
Sympathetic and patriotic sketches of peasant life in Cavan, conveying a very strong impression of the sternness and harshness of the labourer's lot. They form a series of genre-pictures—Turf-cutters, Mowers, Reapers, Diggers, etc. [Richards : o.p. ; McClure, New York : o.p.]

—— *The Squireen.* 1903
The brief wedded life of a loving, sensitive, patient woman and a masterful, egotistic man, a gentleman-farmer in Donegal. An honest and sympathetic portrayal of the faults of character and the imperceptible steps that lead to happiness or unhappiness. The harsh Presbyterians of Gorteen remind one of the stiff-necked people in the New England novels of Miss Wilkins. [Methuen : o.p. ; McClure, New York : o.p.]

—— *Dan the Dollar.* 1906
Dan is a crude, sordid, self-made man from America, who comes back to Ireland with crude American notions of improving the "God-forsaken country." His brutal, materialistic nature is contrasted with a small group of native unregenerate and unspoiled Irish people. [Maunsell : o.p.]

—— *Master John.* 1909
An old retainer's yarn about a successful man who returns to Fermanagh and buys a place with a curse upon it. [Laurie : o.p.]

—— *Hetty : the story of an Ulster family.* 1911
The currents of sympathy and of estrangement in a family traced, with sincere feeling and understanding and careful drawing of character. [Laurie : o.p.]

—— *The Loughsiders.* 1924
A pleasant tale of small things, picturing the life of Ulster farming-folk. [Harrap ; Dial Press, New York.]

BUNGENER, Louis Félix [French ; 1814–74]. *The Preacher and the King ; or, Bourdaloue in the Court of Louis XIV* (Un sermon sous Louis XIV, 1845). 1853
One of the several religious stories of Louis XIV's reign (1642–1715), written by a Protestant historian of German origin to support his party. [Transl. with introd. by G. POTTS, Nelson, 1853 : o.p. ; Lothrop, Boston : o.p.

BUNIN, Ivan Alekseyevich [Russian ; *b.* 1870]. *The Village* (Derevnya, 1910). 1923
Presents a terrible and powerful picture of the poverty and barbarity of Russian village life in the period following the revolution of 1905. The main characters are a pair of brothers of opposite characters, one a successful man of business, the other a mystical idealist ; both come to a sorry end. [Transl. by Isabel HAPGOOD, Secker ; Knopf, New York.]

—— *The Dreams of Chang* (1916) ; *and other stories* (1911–16). 1923
The title-story is about a dog and his master, a dissolute seaman in Odessa. Included also are the *Gentleman from San Francisco* (see below), and the two long stories *Brethren* and *A Goodly Life* ; the former contrasts the attitude towards life of the native and the Englishman in Ceylon ; the latter is the autobiography of a servant-girl. [Transl. by Bernard Gilbert GUERNEY, Knopf, New York ; Secker.]

—— *The Gentleman from San Francisco* (Gospodin iz San Frantsisko, 1915) ; *and other stories* (1915–16). 1922
The title-story is one of the best known of Bunin's shorter works ; it paints in unlovely colours the closing days of an American millionaire's life on the Riviera. Of the remaining four, *The Son,* the story of a young man's attachment to a woman old enough to be his mother, is a little masterpiece of tragic irony. [Transl. by D. H. LAWRENCE, S. S. KOTELIANSKY, and Leonard WOOLF, Hogarth Press ; Boni, New York.]

—— *Mitya's Love* (1925). 1926
The passionate idealising love of a youth of seventeen for a girl unworthy of him is the theme of the poet in this imaginative tale. [Transl. from the French by Madeline BOYD, Holt, New York.]

BUNNER, Henry Cuyler [American ; 1855–96]. *The Midge.* 1886
A story of the French quarter of New York. [Scribner, New York : o.p.]

—— *The Story of a New York House.* 1887
A study of typical local and family history—quiet, uneventful American realism ; as a picture of life melancholy in tone. [Scribner, New York : o.p.]

BUNNER, Henry Cuyler (*continued*). *Zadoc Pine ; and other stories.* 1891
Chiefly incidents narrated in happy journalistic style, not without art ; comic and pathetic. [Scribner, New York : o.p.]
—— *The Runaway Browns.* 1892
The experiences of a couple who shut up house and wander forth among all sorts of people—tinkers, strolling players, and the like. A whimsical book, filled with curious observations on life and character. [With *More Short Sixes*, Scribner, New York, 1917.]
—— *Made in France.* 1893
" French tales retold with a U.S. Twist." [*Puck* Office, New York : o.p.]
—— *Love in Old Clothes ; and other stories.* 1896
The best of three volumes of short, humorous stories, " in which the artist keeps turning up the unexpected." [Scribner, New York.]

BUNYAN, John [1628–88]. *The Pilgrim's Progress from this World to That Which is to Come.* 1678–84
The first and best part, the story of Christian's pilgrimage, was written in prison in 1675. Describes the toils and trials of the Christian's mortal life under the guise of a journey from the City of Destruction to the New Jerusalem. One of the most absorbing allegories, because the least artificial, the characters interesting in themselves, intensely alive, and meeting with experiences fruitful in natural drama. Bunyan's prose is the simplest and purest English, homely, yet capable of sublime effects. Incidentally, he drew graphic pictures of his time in scenes from English provincial life, and types of human nature from his own keen-eyed observation. [Facsimile of 1st ed. (1678), Noel Douglas, 1928 ; Critical text, ed. J. Brown, Hodder, 1886 ; (Golden Treasury Series), Macmillan, 1862 ; ed. G. Offor, Bliss, 1897 ; (Temple Classics), Dent, (Dutton, New York), 1898 ; with introd. by C. Whibley, Constable, 1926 ; ed. by J. B. Wharey, Oxford Press, 1928.]
—— *The Life and Death of Mr. Badman.* 1680
A counterpart to the history of Christian. Relates the progress of a sinner to perdition, in a dialogue between Mr. Wiseman and Mr. Attentive, with many discussions by the way on points of doctrine. The rude country life of Charles the Second's time is painted with faithful realism, and the story is a natural and straightforward kind of narrative, illustrating the whole Christian theory of sin and retribution. [With *Grace Abounding* (Everyman's Lib.), Dent (Dutton, New York), 1928].
—— *The Holy War.* 1982
A more elaborate and complicated allegory : the strife between celestial and infernal hosts, led by Prince Emmanuel and Diabolus, for the city of Mansoul. The sects inside and outside the Anglican Church are all represented in the struggle, which unfortunately turns in the main on quibbling points of doctrine. But the old Parliamentarian soldier makes his battles and sieges impressive, and some of the minor characters are racy personages. [(Temple Classics) Dent (Dutton, New York) ; Bagster, 1928 ; R.T.S.]

BURCHELL, Sidney Herbert. *In the Days of King James ; or, Romances of London in the Olden Time.* 1898
Three stories : *The Goldsmith of Cheape, The King's Prerogative,* and *The Aldgate.* Carefully written with regard to historical and antiquarian accuracy, and equipped with notes (1603–15). [Gay & Bird : o.p.]
—— *The Duke's Servants.* 1899
A romantic story of the famous band of players, in London, in rural Derbyshire, and elsewhere. The Duke of Buckingham and his assassin Felton figure (1624–8). [Gay & Bird : o.p. ; Little & Brown, Boston : o.p.]
—— *Daniel Herrick : the romance of a news-writer.* 1900
The London of Charles II in the Plague year, 1665. Herrick's adventures in quest of his patron's daughter, whom the king had pursued with his attentions. [Gay & Bird : o.p.]
—— *My Lady of the Bass.* 1903
Recounts the historic seizure of the Bass Rock by four Jacobites, and its defence for three years against the authorities (1691–4). Below the author's usual level. [Gay & Bird : o.p.]
—— *The Prisoners of Carisbrooke.* 1904
Charles I and the governor of Carisbrooke ; scene, I. of Wight and London (1641–9). [Gay & Bird : o.p.]
—— *The Mistress of the Robes.* 1905
The Court of Queen Anne, her Grace of Marlborough, and Mrs. Masham. [Hurst : o.p.]
—— *The Shepherd of the People.* 1924
A story of life in Washington in the earlier half of the Civil War, when Lincoln was troubled with foes and traitors on his own side (1861–3). William Lloyd Garrison also appears. [Gay & Hancock.]

BURKE, Thomas [*b.* 1887]. *Limehouse Nights.* 1916
Sketches of London's East End and the Chinese quarter especially. The author holds something of a monopoly in that field ; but garishness and sentimentality tend to spoil his effects. [Cassell ; McBride, New York ; Grosset, New York ; *illus.* by Mahlon Blain, McBride.]
—— *Twinkletoes : a tale of Chinatown.* 1917
An attempt at unvarnished realism, ruined or redeemed by the poet's delight in the highways and tunnels of the East End and his joy in contrasting beauty and innocence with the ugly and squalid. [Cassell ; McBride, New York.]

BURNAND, Sir Francis Cowley [1836–1917]. *Happy Thoughts.* 1866
A farcical diary of social misadventures, funny predicaments on the railway, the high-road, and elsewhere, and other experiences of a clumsy and bashful gentleman, whose innocent exposure of his own foibles is a chief part of the fun. [With an introd. by Robert Lynd, Methuen, 1930.]
—— *Happy-Thought Hall.* 1872
—— *My Time and what I've Done with it.* 1874

BURNAND, Sir Francis Cowley (*continued*). *More Happy Thoughts.* 1879
Facetious anecdotes, scraps of conversation, social adventures, etc., marked by humorous exaggeration and genial satire of the minor failings of human nature. Appeared originally in *Punch.* [(1) and (3), Bradbury : o.p. ; (2), Macmillan : o.p. ; Burns & Oates : o.p.]

BURNETT, Frances Eliza [*née* Hodgson ; afterwards Mrs. Stephen Townsend ; American, but English by birth ; 1849–1924]. *That Lass o' Lowrie's.* 1877
A story of the author's native Lancashire. Loving portraiture of the humble life of the working classes. The romantic plot tells how a young engineer marries the brave daughter of a savage and drunken miner, after she had saved his life. [Grosset, New York, 1913 : o.p. ; Warne.]

—— *Vagabondia* [*previously called Dolly*]. 1877
Good-humoured pictures of life in a shiftless English household : portraits of girls and boys in their happy childhood and amid the troubles of dawning maturity ; sympathetic and often humorous. [Scribner, New York : o.p. ; *sub tit. Dolly,* Warne : o.p.]

—— *Haworths.* 1879
A tragic story of the same lowly domestic life of the Lancashire work-people. [Scribner, New York ; Warne : o.p.]

—— *Louisiana.* 1880
Portrait of a simple and beautiful type of Southern girlhood ; a pathetic story, embodying scenes of life in the mountain region of North Carolina. [Scribner, New York : o.p. ; Warne : o.p.]

—— *Through One Administration.* 1883
A poignant drama enacted amidst the brilliant social life and the political corruption of Washington. A woman married to a politician of the worst type loves and is loved again by an old wooer. Both are true and conscientious people, and the pathos of the situation is that the lover watches the husband using his wife for base political ends. [Scribner, New York : o.p. ; Warne : o.p.]

—— *Little Lord Fauntleroy.* [juvenile] 1886
A fairy-tale in real life. The seven-year-old hero, living among vulgar people in New York, suddenly becomes heir to a selfish and crusty old earl, goes to England and fascinates everybody, including his ogreish grandsire. The contrasts of character are trenchant, as befits a book for children, the good folk being very good and the bad intensely bad ; and there is plenty of sob-stuff. [Scribner, New York ; Warne ; McClelland, Toronto, 1930 ; *illus.* by Reginald Birch, Scribner, New York.]

—— *Sara Crewe ; Little Saint Elizabeth ; and other stories.* [juvenile] 1888
More fairy-tales of modern life ; fresh and naively humorous. Sara Crewe is a persecuted little drudge, to whom a good fairy comes in the person of a rich Indian gentleman, bringing her a fortune. (The story was re-issued in a new form—and spoiled—as *A Little Princess,* 1905.) Editha, an innocent maiden of seven in *Editha's Burglar,* gives the burglar her own toys and trinkets, and persuades him to leave her father's. [Scribner, New York ; *sub tit. Little Saint Elizabeth ; and other stories,* Warne. *A Little Princess,* *illus.,* Scribner, New York ; Warne.]

—— *The One I Knew the Best of All : a memory of the mind of a child.* [juvenile] 1893
The life of a little playwright and romancer of the nursery, confessedly autobiographical. [*Illus.,* Scribner, New York ; Warne : o.p.]

—— *The Captain's Youngest ; Piccino ; and other stories.* [juvenile] 1894
A touching tale of a little boy's devotion and death for his sister's sake. *Piccino* is another tale of childhood readable both by children and adults. [Scribner, New York : o.p. ; Warne : o.p. ; *Piccino ; and other child stories, illus.,* Scribner, New York.]

—— *A Lady of Quality : being a most curious hitherto unknown history related by Isaac Bickerstaffe.* 1896
Supposed to be written in the seventeenth century. As a child this singular lady is a little daredevil, as a girl a hoyden, indulging in clandestine love passages ; when marriageable she weds an aged earl, and on his death becomes a duchess. In a fit of fear and passion she murders an old lover, laying the ghost of her past for ever ; and in spite of remorse and the constant risk of discovery, she lives out her life pleasantly and in outward honour.

—— *His Grace of Osmonde* [sequel]. 1897
The Lady of Quality's husband ; scenery, costume, and manners *c.* 1690–1720. [(1) and (2), Scribner, New York ; Warne.]

—— *In Connection with the De Willoughby Claim.* 1899
Country life in Tennessee about the time of the Civil War (1861). A leisurely and rambling story, peopled by interesting and attractive characters, with sketches of homely life. [Grosset, New York, 1913 : o.p. ; Warne.]

—— *In the Closed Room.* 1904
A fanciful, spiritualistic story of a lonely child and her secret—imaginary—playmate. [McClure, New York : o.p. ; Hodder : o.p.]

—— *T. Tembarom.* 1913
An old-fashioned story of a poor American boy who turns out to be the heir to a Yorkshire mansion. [Century Co., New York ; Hodder.]

—— *The Head of the House of Coombe.* 1922

—— *Robin* [sequel]. 1922
The romance of an idealized boy and girl, childhood friends, who are separated and ultimately come together again. [(1) and (2), Stokes, New York ; McClelland, Toronto ; Heinemann.]

BURNETT, William Riley [American ; *b.* 1899]. *Little Cæsar.* 1929
Of historical importance as an intimate study of the mentality and domestic surroundings of a member of a gang of gunmen, during the recent activity of bootleggers in the United States. [Dial Press, New York ; Cape.]

BURNETT, William Riley (*continued*). *Iron Man*. 1930
> The story of a good-hearted, thick-headed prize-fighter, his trainer and stanch friend, and his wife, who is his evil genius. Realistic in the American style, with slangy Yankee dialogue. [Dial Press, New York; Heinemann.]

BURNEY, Fanny [Mme. D'Arblay; 1752–1840]. *Evelina; or, A Young Lady's Entrance into the World*. 1778
> Miss Burney was a sharp-eyed girl, daughter of a distinguished musician and historian of music—an indefatigable reader and a precocious writer of poems, plays, and stories for her own amusement—in a family well-off for friends, where she had plentiful opportunities of watching the kind of people to be seen in drawing-rooms, in the streets, and at smart places of entertainment. In *Evelina* she puts her observations together in a novel with a sketchy plot. Evelina's introduction to town, her visits to relatives and entrance into fashionable society, are the occasion for lively sketches of the surface things of London—its people and pleasures, life in theatre and ballroom, at Marylebone Gardens, the Pantheon, etc.; and of the people of fashion, the eccentrics, the conceited, and the vulgar; the last in particular being sharply satirized in the persons of Evelina's uppish relatives, the Branghtons, with their affected gentility and snobbishness. Miss Burney had doubtless read *Betsy Thoughtless*, by Mrs. Haywood. Dr. Johnson hit her off as a " character-monger." [Ed. by Annie Raine Ellis, (Bohn's Popular Lib.) Bell (Harcourt, New York) (1883) 1913; ed. by R. Brimley Johnson, 2 vols., (Everyman's Lib.) Dent (Dutton, New York) 1909; 2 vols., (Temple Classics) *id.*, 1903. *Illus.* by Hugh Thomson, Macmillan, 1903; ed. by Sir Frank D. Mackinnon, with *illustrations* from contemporary sources, Oxford Press, 1930.]

—— *Cecilia; or, The Memoirs of an Heiress*. 1782
> A more studied and elaborate work. A rich heiress is left to the tender mercies of three guardians, a characteristic trio, who, with the fortune-hunters and admirers besieging her, are sketched with a satirical pen. The comedy of manners is somewhat submerged by the multiplication of characters and the distracting interests of a melodramatic plot, and she was prone to exhaust the possibilities of her creations, and so exhaust the reader's enjoyment of them; but her great scenes are magnificent.
> In these two novels and in her *Diary* she gave her best, and there is a complete falling off in *Camilla* (1796) and *The Wanderer* (1814), which brought her £3,000 apiece, but little credit either then or since. [2 vols. (Bohn's Lib.), Bell (Macmillan, New York), 1883; 1 vol. (York Lib.), Bell (Macmillan, New York), 1904; edited by R. B. Johnson, 3 vols., Dent, 1893: all o.p.]

BURT, Katherine Newlin [Mrs. Maxwell Struthers Burt; American; b. 1882]. *The Grey Parrot*. 1926
> The development of three men, inhabitants of a small town on the Hudson river, contrasting the religious and the scientific outlook upon life. [Houghton, Boston; Hutchinson.]

—— *Cock's Feather*. 1928
> Apart from the subsidiary characters and their affairs which react upon it, this is simply a variant of the drama of two men and a woman, with the stress on the making and matching of personalities in a perfect union. The steadfast, philosophic husband is in conflict with the romantic, idealistic wife, and with the arrogant lover who tries to dominate her. It is an ethical case, expounded, as it were, by highly self-conscious characters. The reader should not be put off by the artificial style, bookish dialogue, and lack of humour. [Houghton, Boston; Heinemann.]

BUTCHER, Rev. Charles Henry [1833–1907]. *The Oriflamme in Egypt*. 1905
> The Crusade of St. Louis (IX) and Earl Longsword, the capture of Damietta and the defeat at Mansourah (1248–50). Also a glimpse at Henry III's England, and village life in the days of the miracle plays. Matthew Paris (the writer's authority) figures. Dr. Butcher was engaged at Cairo for a quarter of a century in historical research. An interesting account of the Coptic church. [Dent: o.p.]

BUTLER, Samuel [1835–1902]. *Erewhon; or, Over the Range*. 1872
—— *Erewhon Revisited Twenty Years Later, both by the Original Discoverer of the Country and his Son* [sequel]. 1901
> A satire on most of the institutions, ideas, customs, and the very bases of modern civilization, by a sturdy freethinker. Our modern Gulliver stumbles upon a great nation, hidden behind inaccessible mountains, which has reverted to an older stage of civilization and improved it by establishing, in some cases, the exact contrary of our institutions (e.g. they punish disease and deal with crime by medical treatment), and in other cases absurd exaggerations (e.g. musical banks corresponding to our churches where treasure is laid up for spiritual fruition, and colleges of unreason where hypothetics is taught instead of practical wisdom, cf. compulsory Greek). Much of the satire (take, for example, " The Book of the Machines ") is at least as telling now as when it was written. *Erewhon* (Nowhere), published in 1872, had a revival of interest later, when Butler wrote *Erewhon Revisited* (1901), in which the traveller, who escaped in a balloon, finds that the Erewhonians have grafted on to their religion a worship of the mysterious visitant who made such a miraculous ascension twenty years ago, with curious perversions of his *logia*. [(1) and (2), Cape; (Traveller's Lib.), *id.*; Dutton, New York; (1), Modern Lib., New York, 1927.]

—— *The Way of All Flesh*. 1903
> Butler wrote two satires but only one novel, which is in more than one sense the novel of his life. The tale is told by a family friend of the hero, who obviously corresponds in many traits and circumstances to Butler himself, and it has transpired that some of the letters were actually written by the father and the mother of Butler. His immediate ancestry, his infancy, home life, education, and the failure and disasters of young manhood, are related, with caustic criticism of the unsympathy and stupidity of conventional parents, and, in general, of sentimentalism, cant, priestcraft, and other social plagues. Butler was an independent critic of Darwinism with strong views on heredity and the race-memory which he regarded as a vital agency in life and in evolution. These views run through the book, which, though philosophical and even biological, is a work of art, not merely a concrete exposition of a theorem. Plenty of humour in the character-drawing: Butler is most serious when apparently most flippant. [Cape; (Traveller's Lib.), *id.*; Nash, 1928; Dutton, New York; Modern Lib., New York, 1917; Macmillan, New York, 1925.]

BYNNER, Edwin Lassetter [American ; 1842–93]. *Agnes Surriage.* 1886

A love-romance of colonial times, based on the story of Sir Charles Henry Frankland, who fell in love with a beautiful servant at an inn at Marblehead, and ultimately married her in gratitude for his escape from the earthquake at Lisbon (1755). [*Illus.*, Houghton, Boston, 1923.]

—— *Penelope's Suitors.* 1887

Penelope Pelham tells us in her diary how she came to throw over her lover Edward Buckley, and to become the wife of the governor of Massachusetts. A fresh, artless story of a young girl's heart. [Houghton, Boston.]

—— *The Begum's Daughter.* 1890

A tale of New Amsterdam in 1689–90 : the episode of the Leisler rebellion admirably told. [Houghton, Boston : o.p.]

—— *Zachary Phips.* 1892

A Boston boy who took part in the mysterious Western expedition of Aaron Burr (1804). [Houghton, Boston.]

BYRNE, Bryan Oswald Donn [Irish-American ; 1889–1928]. *The Foolish Matrons.* 1920

Dissolving views of the insane competition in display and extravagance and the defiant immorality of the most " advanced " set in New York, with a few married couples in the foreground. The selfish, conceited woman with literary ambitions and the wife who flirts with a millionaire to help her husband in his business career both come to grief. [Harper, New York ; Low.]

—— *Messer Marco Polo.* 1921

An old peasant tells his cronies the tale of the great adventurer and lover, in racy Irish-English, and in the romantic way of an old Gaelic saga, steeped in magic and poetry and beauty. [Century Co., New York ; Low.]

—— *The Wind Bloweth.* 1922

Out of his knockabout life, his strange love-ventures in different parts of the world, and incessant frustration, Shane Campbell hammers out a philosophy of life : " Success is in yourself, not outside yourself," and " There is a great Master and there is a Plan." It is all told in a rhapsodical way, with touches of oral legend and tags of English and Gaelic verse. [Century Co., New York ; Grosset, New York ; Low.]

—— *Blind Raftery and his wife Hilaria.* 1924

The great old poet in his wanderings about Ireland in the time of the South Sea Bubble (a century out of the right time), weds a beautiful lady from Spain, who had been the thrall and concubine of a rapacious Welsh money-lender. A poetical story told in the saga style. [Century Co., New York ; Low.]

—— *Hangman's House.* 1925

A romance of Irish country life, racing, hunting, and the like, in the Dublin country last century. [Century Co., New York ; Grosset, New York ; Low.]

—— *An Untitled Story.* 1925

A strangely beautiful, sad story of a nun who ran away with an Irishman, and had to obey the inner voice that commanded her to return. American title, *O'Malley of Shanganagh*, though it first appeared in the *Century Magazine* as above. [Century Co., New York ; Low.]

—— *The Power of the Dog.* 1926

The hero is a loyal Irishman attached to the staff of Lord Castlereagh, whereas his wife was the daughter of a rebel whom Castlereagh had executed. The story alternates between him in London, and his wife who loyally remains in Ireland, with the Napoleonic era as historical background. There are brief sketches of many figures of the time, Napoleon, Nelson, etc., but of these Castlereagh only, of whom an unflattering portrait is drawn, is an important character. [Low.]

—— *Brother Saul.* 1927

Retells, in the same semi-poetic way, the story of St. Paul, from his youth at Tarsus to his end in Rome. [Century Co., New York ; Grosset, New York ; Low.]

—— *Crusade.* 1928

An Irish knight in Palestine in the period following the Crusades. The Crusaders, and in particular the Knights Templars, are represented as sorry stuff, and eventually the hero turns Mohammedan to escape his enemies and marry the daughter of his previous captors. [Little & Brown, Boston ; Low.]

—— *Destiny Bay.* 1928

Nine stories of village life, love, gipsies, horses, prize-fighters, in a village on the north coast of Ireland. [Little & Brown, Boston ; Low.]

"CABALLERO, Fernán" [Cecilia Boehl von Faber ; Spanish ; 1796–1877]. *The Sea-Gull* (La Gaviota, 1848). 1867

A simple, unaffected narrative of ordinary life in an Andalusian village, thoroughly Spanish in tone, with some sentimental moralizing. The authoress was daughter of a German father and a Spanish mother. [Transl. by A. BETHELL, 2 vols., Bentley : o.p.]

CABELL, James Branch [American ; b. 1879]. *Gallantry.* 1907

Twelve stories of amorous adventure in the fashionable world of George the Second's time. They read like burlesques of the romance of " tushery," if we lose sight of the warning, " Half in masquerade, playing the drawing-room or garden comedy of life." Mr. Cabell's ironical attitude here is indeed very close to the spirit of Congreve, if a little too cynical, too delighted with his disillusionments. [Revised ed. 1922, McBride, New York ; Lane.]

—— *Chivalry.* 1909

Here the constraint of irony is less apparent, and Mr. Cabell lets himself go in high-flown heroics. The difference between the philosophy of chivalry, which is that of the troubadours and the mediæval courts of love, and the more cynical philosophy of gallantry, is now clearly defined. [Revised ed., 1921, McBride, New York ; Lane.]

CABELL, James Branch (*continued*). *The Cords of Vanity: a comedy of shirking.* 1909
The erotic adventures of Robert Townsend in a Virginia that seems to be still in the age of gallantry of France and England two or three centuries ago. [Revised ed., 1920, McBride, New York; Lane.]

—— *The Soul of Melicent: a comedy of woman-worship.* 1913
Entitled *Domnei* in the revised edition of 1920 (*Domnei* is Old French for Ladies). A story supposed to be adapted from *Le roman de Lusignan* by the apocryphal Norman poet Nicholas of Caen. In Perion and Melicent, who is a daughter of Manuel of Poictesme, we see the apotheosis of chivalric love, which neither exile to the ends of the earth nor possession of the beloved one's body by another can abate. It is an admirable specimen of Mr. Cabell's ironical extravaganza. [Revised ed., 1920, McBride, New York; Lane.]

—— *The Rivet in Grandfather's Neck: a comedy of limitations.* 1915
Returns to modern times and a romanticized Virginia. An American colonel, with a pedigree, and his pretty wife are given the rôle of Hans Andersen's chimney-sweep and the shepherdess. [Revised ed., 1922, McBride, New York; Lane.]

—— *The Certain Hour: dizain des poètes.* 1916
The introduction proclaims the writer's æsthetic creed, that style is the be-all and end-all of literature—and apparently of life. The ten stories of the dilemmas faced by his men of letters illustrate this. Let the artist stand aloof, and not dissipate by taking part in the drama the force which has been given him for the perfecting of his " lovelier version." [McBride, New York.]

—— *The Cream of the Jest: a comedy of evasions.* 1917
We may, presumably, recognize the writer himself in the dual personality of his romancer Felix Kennaston, who loves to wander forth from his home in Lichfield into the wondrous land of his imagining. [Revised ed., 1921, McBride, New York; Modern Lib., New York; Lane; *illus.* by Frank C. Papé, 1927, McBride, New York; Lane.]

—— *Beyond Life: dizain des demiurges.* 1919
This should be read as a proem to the series of romances forming the cycle of Dom Manuel and his followers and descendants—all his children of the spirit. Romance, the glory begotten of imagination, is our refuge and consolation in the despair of any clear answer to the riddle of the Sphinx. Three attitudes are open to choice: " the gallant, the chivalrous, and the poetic solutions of human existence." These three themes are illustrated, in isolation or interwoven, in the stories that follow. It has been pointed out, rightly, that the book is heavily indebted to Mr. Machen, especially to that writer's *Hieroglyphics*. [McBride, New York; Modern Lib., New York; Lane.]

—— *Jurgen: a comedy of justice.* 1919
A much-praised fantasy which may be taken as an allegory of the sceptical modern mind, its quest of pleasure and its disillusionment; or, in other words, of realism versus romance. Jurgen, the middle-aged pawn-broker, recovers his youth, and has for paramours Guenevere, the Lady of the Lake, and other half-divine ladies, makes his way into hell and into heaven, but returns to his homely old wife. It is the consecrated creed of Epicurus tempered with the Cabellian doctrine of compromise. Mr. Cabell's indebtedness to Anatole France and Mr. Arthur Machen is plainer to anyone in this book even than elsewhere. Readers who do not relish sniggering humour should, however, be warned that it is a sort of phallic romance. [Enlarged ed., 1921, McBride, New York; Lane; *illus.* by Ray F. Coyle, McBride, New York; *illus.* by Frank C. Papé, Lane: o.p.; Grosset, New York.]

—— *Figures of Earth: a comedy of appearances.* 1921
By holding his tongue and never thinking, the swineherd Manuel wins " a dreadful name for impenetrable wisdom and for boundless resource," and becomes Count of Poictesme and the beloved of queens who are mighty magicians. But like Jurgen, that other impersonation of realism, he cleaves stolidly to his fellow-drudge, the homely Niafer. In short, through all the pseudo-mediæval and mythological extravagance, the oceans of fee-faw-fummery, the smartness and self-conceit, this is a simple allegory of human life and the quest for beauty, success, happiness—futile, since man is the sport of the unknown, and to attain his will does not content his desires. [McBride, New York; Lane; *illus.* by Frank C. Papé, *id.*]

—— *The High Place: a comedy of disenchantment.* 1923
The adventures of Florian, son of the Duc de Puysanges. Period about 1732. [*Illus.* by Frank C. Papé, McBride, New York; Lane.]

—— *The Silver Stallion: a comedy of redemption.* 1926
After Manuel's translation, his widow institutes a cult of the Redeemer of Poictesme, and unbelievers are persecuted by St. Holmendis of Philistia. This is the book of the sagas of his comrades in arms, who penetrate to the uttermost regions of the universe, even to hell and heaven. Gonfal reaches the land of the Fundamentalists, who worship Pygé-Upsizugos and sing the hymn of the Star-Spangled Buttock. The votaries of Art for Art's sake are also satirized, in the interests of realism and utilitarian art. [McBride, New York; Lane; *illus.* by Frank C. Papé, McBride, New York.]

—— *The Music from behind the Moon.* 1926
—— *Something about Eve: a comedy of fig-leaves.* 1927
—— *The White Robe: a saint's summary.* 1928
Further stories and romances which, like the post-Homeric narratives, are a sequel to the cycles of Dom Manuel and Jurgen, the Achilles and the Ulysses of Poictesme. Mr. Cabell alternates between his mythical land of chivalry, Poictesme, and his own Virginia, which he transfigures into a sort of dreamland and a suitable scene for his episodes of gallantry. After skimming " the cream of the jest," only the most ardent devotees of ironical make-believe will go on to a deeper draught. [(1), Day, New York; (2), McBride, New York; Lane; *illus.* by Frank C. Papé, *id.*; (3), *illus.* by Robert E. Locker, McBride, New York; Lane.]

" **CABLE**, Boyd " [Ernest Andrew Ewart; Australian; *b.* 1878]. *By Blow and Kiss.* 1914
Life in the sheep country of New South Wales—of which the author had personal experience. [Hodder: o.p.]

"CABLE, Boyd" (*continued*). *Action Front.*   1916
—— *Front Lines.*   1918
   Stories or sketches of life in trench, dug-out, and the heat of conflict. [Murray.]

CABLE, George Washington [American ; 1844–1925]. *Old Creole Days.*   1879
   Seven stories of New Orleans, portraying the Creoles with tenderness, knowledge, and peculiar charm, artfully
      reproducing the quaint music of their broken English. Revealed a phase of American life never before
      described in literature. Cable's mastery of pathos is finely shown in *The Belles Demoiselles Plantation*,
      and his droll humour in *Posson Jone.* [Scribner, New York, 1907 ; Hodder : o.p. *Illus.* by Herter,
      Scribner, New York : o.p.]
—— *The Grandissimes : a story of Creole life.*   1880
   A long and rambling novel, with many loose-knit episodes, which is a full, rich picture of New Orleans and
      the neighbouring plantations, forests, and bayous as they were in the year of the Louisiana purchase.
      The exclusive old Creole families, the negro households, the Indians, Yankees, and swarming aliens, are
      all graphically presented. Realism is mingled with romance, and romance chequered with tragedy.
      [Scribner, New York, 1908 ; Hodder : o.p.]
—— *Madame Delphine ; Carancro ; and Grande Pointe.*   1881
   The first is a touching story of humble heroism in an old quadroon woman of New Orleans, throwing pathetic
      light on the racial prejudices that make life miserable for people of tainted blood. The other two appear
      later as episodes in *Bonaventure* (see below). [Scribner, New York : o.p. ; Douglas, Edinburgh : o.p.]
—— *Dr. Sevier.*   1884
   The long, despairing struggle of a young married pair in the prosperous world of New Orleans before the
      war. The Doctor is an elaborate study of an exceptional type of character. The old Creole town,
      streets, houses, and people are drawn in great detail, all sorts of brogues mingling in the dialogue.
      [Scribner, New York ; 2 vols., Douglas, Edinburgh : o.p.]
—— *Bonaventure : a prose pastoral of Acadian Louisiana.*   1888
   An idyllic love-story, with humour in the character-sketches of the innocent and homely Acadians exiled in
      Louisiana ; theme, the development of a saintly character from a nature originally selfish. [Scribner,
      New York ; Low : o.p.]
—— *John March, Southerner.*   1894
   A study of reconstruction in an old town battered by the recent Civil War, now the meeting-place of Northern
      promoters and irreconcilable Southerners. The meteoric career of financial companies, the intrigues,
      quarrels, and final collapse, supply plenty of incident. The characters are historical types ; Leggett,
      the half-breed, a servile, insolent scoundrel, who conspires with a white villain to ruin March, the amiable
      old judge, etc. [Scribner, New York ; Low : o.p.]
—— *The Cavalier.*   1901
   A complicated romance by a sympathizer with the Confederates. Several stirring chapters of fighting in
      Mississippi ; but the principal interest is in the character-drawing and the analysis of feeling and motive.
      [*Illus.*, Scribner, New York, 1903 ; Murray : o.p.]
—— *Kincaid's Battery.*   1908
   A romance of New Orleans at the opening of the Civil War (1861). Kincaid is a young artillery officer, a
      favourite with the girls. [Scribner, New York : o.p. ; Hodder : o.p.]
—— *The Flower of the Chapdelaines.*   1918
   A young American attorney obtains an introduction to a select coterie of Creole society in old New Orleans,
      and falls in love. The best part of the book is in two old manuscripts describing the escape of a family
      of negro slaves. [Scribner, New York ; Collins.]

CAFFYN, Kathleen Mannington [*née* Hunt ; "Iota" ; Irish ; *d.* 1926]. *A Yellow Aster.* 1894
   A study in eccentricities, of whom the principal is an abnormal girl, the offspring of two unparental scientists.
      The problem is to show how this "sexless" creature becomes "sexful" as the result of maternity.
      [Hutchinson : o.p. ; Appleton, New York : o.p.]
—— *Children of Circumstance.*   1894
—— *A Comedy in Spasms.*   1895
—— *A Quaker Grandmother.*   1896
—— *Anne Mauleverer.*   1899
   Novels with the same strong leaven of up-to-date feminism, but more mature in character-drawing and clear
      rendering of life. [(1), Hutchinson (Appleton, New York) : o.p. ; (2) and (3), Hutchinson : o.p. ; (4),
      Methuen (Lippincott, Philadelphia) : o.p.]
—— *Patricia : a Mother.*   1905
   Another problem-novel—the question of a woman's inability to understand her son's wife has to be resolved.
      [Hurst & Blackett : o.p.]
—— *The Fire-Seeker.*   1911
   A lively story in which the reaction of character upon character is well and truly handled. [Nash : o.p.]

CAHAN, Abraham [American ; Lithuanian-Jew by birth ; *b.* 1860]. *The White Terror and the
   Red.*   1905
   The Nihilist plots and the assassination of Alexander II, and the persecution of the Jews under Alexander III ;
      scenes, first Germany and then Russia. [Barnes, New York : o.p. ; Hodder : o.p.]
—— *The Rise of David Levinsky.*   1917
   This work of a Yiddish writer is possibly the best novel by any immigrant. In the career of a pious Jew
      who leaves his Russian village and builds up a great clothing business, it subsumes the enterprise,
      industry, and success of Russian Jews in America. Levinsky is a personality, and his trials of conscience
      are profoundly interesting. [Harper, New York.]

CAHUN, Léon [French; 1841–1900]. *The Adventures of Captain Mago* (Les aventures du capitaine Magon; ou, une exploration phénicienne mille ans avant l'ère chrétienne, 1875). 1876
Imaginary account of a Phœnician expedition, 1000 B.C. [Scribner, New York: o.p.]

—— *The Blue Banner* (La bannière bleue). 1877
Adventures of a Mussulman and a pagan in time of Crusades and Mongol conquest; scenes: Mongolia, Turkestan, Syria (1194–1254). [Low: o.p.; Lippincott, Philadelphia: o.p.]

CAINE, Oliver Vernon [b. 1862]. *Face to Face with Napoleon*. 1898
An English boy's adventures in the Great French War in Germany (1812–13). [Nisbet; *illus.*, Black, 1930.]

—— *In the Year of Waterloo* [sequel]. 1899
Continues the adventures of the English boy and his German cousin through the Hundred Days. [Nisbet; *illus.*, Black, 1930.]

—— *Wanderer and King: a story of the youth of Charles II.* [juvenile] 1903
A very free handling of the story of the king's flight after Worcester (1651); based on the *Boscobel Tracts* and Mr. Allan Fea's *Flight of the King.* [Nisbet.]

CAINE, Sir Thomas Hall Henry [1853–1931]. *The Shadow of a Crime*. 1885
A romance of Cumberland in the early days of the Quakers (*c.* 1650–60). Theme, renunciation on the grand scale. A false suspicion of murder threatens a dalesman's family with ruin, and to save his loved ones he avows the crime, though innocent. He is saved on the very scaffold by the confession of the real murderer. Similar coincidences give rise to many scenes of emotional stress. The first of a series of Hugoesque romances, which strive to catch the epical note by exhibiting passion and virtue on a titanic scale. [Chatto; Nash; Burt, New York.]

—— *A Son of Hagar.* 1886
A Cumberland romance with the same grandiose conception and treatment; theme, fraternal villainy. A talented and cultivated man, bitterly passionate and vindictive, schemes his brother's ruin. [Chatto; Nash; Burt, New York.]

—— *The Deemster.* 1888
A similar essay in the prose epic. Scene, the Isle of Man. A homicide is tried by his father, the Bishop, according to ancient usage, and is sentenced to live as an outcast in a desolate corner of Man. Here in misery and affliction he works out his own redemption, and in time of pestilence offers his life as atonement to the people. [Chatto; Nash; Burt, New York.]

—— *The Bondman.* 1890
A theatrical tale of uncurbed, lawless crimes and illimitable revenge. Scenes, Iceland and the Isle of Man during the Napoleonic wars. The dominant situation arises from a son's lifelong efforts to avenge his mother, the object of his fatal quest being his own brother. Scenes, events, and minor characters are strange and bizarre; even nature provides, as a fitting accompaniment, volcanic eruptions and earthquakes for the sensational events. [Cassell; Burt, New York; Appleton, New York, 1928.]

—— *The Scapegoat.* 1891
Here the favourite thesis of atonement is illustrated in a semi-poetic romance of Jewish life in Morocco. Israel Ben Oliel cleanses himself from the guilt of a tyrannical and extortionate life by abandoning his dignities amidst the jeers of the populace, and living the life of a John the Baptist in the wilderness. [Cassell; Appleton, New York: o.p.]

—— *The Manxman.* 1894
Theme, a good young man's surrender to passion, and the retribution falling on himself and others. Left in charge of his friend's sweetheart, he betrays the trusting and simple-minded Pete. Remorse drives him to confess, and the magnanimous victim actually smoothes the way for his betrayer to marry the divorced heroine. [Cassell; Appleton, New York: o.p.]

—— *The Christian.* 1897
Proposes to survey the religious life of London. Two passionate and sensuous beings are the protagonists; and as the emotional interest of the story of their loves and estrangements becomes keener, the philosophic purpose is wellnigh lost sight of. [Cassell; Appleton, New York; Grosset, New York.]

—— *The Eternal City.* 1901
A still more ambitious propagandist romance, the moral, religious, and political tendencies of the contemporary world being typified in the life of Rome and Italy. Personal interest centres in the loves of two characteristic figures, the Tolstoyan socialist Rossi, "a noble, natural man" endowed with irresistible energy, and the beautiful Roma, who atones for early frailty by heroic devotion. In plot resembles his previous melodramas, wildly improbable and visionary, the sequence of events being carried down to A.D. 1950, when a new Republic has been established with the Lord's Prayer as its charter. An immense prodigality of detail, vigorous theatrical scenes, an incessant flow of sentiment and emotion, pages of high-pitched oratory, and highly coloured descriptions, dazzle and confound the intelligent reader. [Cassell; Grosset, New York.]

—— *The Prodigal Son.* 1904
—— *The White Prophet.* 1909
—— *The Eternal Question.* 1910
Similar novels to the two foregoing. As time goes on Sir Hall Caine devotes himself more and more unreservedly to pulpit melodrama. The White Prophet is a Christ-like Mahdi. [(1) and (2) Cassell; (3) Heinemann: (1) Appleton, New York; (2) Grosset, New York: o.p.]

—— *The Woman Thou Gavest Me.* 1913
An unutterably tedious didactic novel on married life, a great favourite however with Sir Hall Caine's more devoted admirers. [Cassell; Lippincott, Philadelphia; Burt, New York.]

CAIRNES, Captain William Elliott. *The Coming Waterloo.* 1901
A military romance of the year 1903, when it is supposed England, Germany, and Austria will be arrayed against France and Russia, and a campaign in N. France will be decided by the defeat of the French in a great night attack. Very realistic and up-to-date in the details of tactics, artillery, and military apparatus generally ; artless as fiction. [Constable.]

CALVERTON, Victor Francis [formerly George Goetz ; American ; *b.* 1900]. *Three Strange Lovers.* 1930
A trio of stories the peculiarity of which is in the psychological technique, which searches the depths of consciousness whilst neglecting externals. All three deal with abnormal cases, a neurotic in an asylum relating his erotic experiences, and so on, the will-to-power in each story expressing itself in the impulse to sexual dominance. [Macaulay, New York.]

CAMBRIDGE, Ada [Mrs. George Frederick Cross ; Australian ; *b.* 1844]. *The Three Miss Kings.* 1891
—— *Not All in Vain.* 1892
Love-stories descriptive of social and domestic life in Australia or England, by an Australian novelist. [(1) and (2) Heinemann ; Appleton, New York ; both o.p.]
—— *Path and Goal.* 1900
The life of a doctor who comes from Australia and settles in a cathedral town (Ely), where he falls in love at various times with three girls, none of whom he is destined to marry. [Methuen : o.p. ; Appleton, New York : o.p.]

CAMPBELL, Frances. *For Three Moons.* 1900
Incidents of a voyage home from Queensland, love-making, troubles with a violent dipsomaniac, and small talk. The incidents reach a melodramatic force at times. [Digby & Long : o.p.]

CAMPBELL, Wilfred [Canadian ; 1861–1919]. *A Beautiful Rebel : a romance of Upper Canada in* 1812. 1909
The United States war, battle of Queenstown Heights, and death of Sir Isaac Brock. [Hodder : o.p. ; Doran, New York : o.p.]

CANAVAN, Michael Joseph [American]. *Ben Comee.* [juvenile] 1899
" A tale of Rogers's Rangers " ; life in and about Lexington at the time of the Fort William Henry massacre and the fall of Ticonderoga (1757–9). [*Illus.* by George Gibbs, Macmillan, New York.]

CANFIELD, Dorothy [Mrs. Dorothea Frances Fisher ; American ; *b.* 1879]. *Gunhild : a Norwegian-American episode.* 1907
The story of a party of American tourists in Norway, contrasting a native peasant lass, a magnificent primitive animal, with a highly cultivated girl, one of the party. There are some fine descriptions of mountain scenery. [Holt, New York : o.p. ; Constable : o.p.]
—— *The Squirrel-Cage.* 1912
An intimate and leisurely account of domestic life in a small New England village, methodically chronicling the little events and the dull routine, and discovering interest in characters that have not much to distinguish them from the average. [Holt, New York ; Grosset, New York.]
—— *The Bent Twig.* 1915
The daughter of an intellectual pair, who are all for the simple life, has cravings for art, and luxury, and beauty ; but is presently pulled up by the warning against the " beauty that can't endure disharmony in conduct, the fine true ear for the deeper values, the foundations——" The story is told with immense earnestness, immense minuteness, and immense dullness. Many pages are devoted to the social life of a co-educational university, with the absurd snobbishness that prevails ; but the tone is too serious for any attention to the comic side. [Holt, New York ; Grosset, New York ; Constable.]
—— *Hillsboro People.* 1915
Sympathetic stories and character-studies of village life. Some poems by Sarah M. Cleghorn are included. [Holt, New York ; Cape.]
—— *The Real Motive.* 1916
More of the same sort, and further poems by Sarah Cleghorn. *From a Life of Two Months* is about a mother's relations to her first baby. Some peculiar views of heredity are the basis of *A Good Fight.* The artist who found inspiration in his own wretchedness and was sterilized by contentment is the theme of *The City of Refuge.* According to *An Academic Question,* poverty is considered a misdemeanour in the American university world. [Holt, New York ; Long.]
—— *Home Fires from France.* 1918
Powerful scenes of French village life during the war, showing the courage and pertinacity of those left derelict by the tide of battle, and the sufferings they had to endure. The authoress worked in France at that time, and these were written to help interpret the French spirit to her countrymen. [Holt, New York ; Constable : o.p.]
—— *The Brimming Cup.* 1921
Dorothy Canfield's representative novel. Pictures, with fond regard for the tiniest detail, home life in a quiet village, the growing up of the children, the parties and merry-makings, the arrival of interesting visitors, and so on. Amid all this, a self-questioning young woman, still cherishing the memory of brilliant days in Rome, feels baffled by the riddle of existence, especially her own dreary lot. Beauty, youth, romance, poetry are gone : what is left ? The situation threatens tragedy. She all but succumbs to the temptation to leave her husband and the children, now living their own lives. In the analysis of her mental conflict there is perhaps more ethical and psychological hair-splitting and moral eloquence than the personality of the potential lover quite justifies. [Grosset, New York ; Cape.]

CANFIELD, Dorothy (*continued*). *Rough-Hewn.* 1922
This novel reaches its goal, a marriage of true minds, by a circuitous route. In seven alternate books it follows the two lives, from childhood, school-days, college, and an opening career in business or music. The man is an Emersonian thinker, with no interest in women; the woman hates love because of a tragedy in her mother's life; both are worried about their place and duties in the world: hence much self-examination and moral debate. Bayonne and Rome, as well as America, yield a collection of remarkable characters. [Harcourt, New York; Grosset, New York; Cape.]

—— *Raw Material.* 1923
Brief character-studies and sketches from life, the " raw material " out of which fiction is constructed. [Harcourt, New York; Grosset, New York; Cape.]

—— *The Home-Maker.* 1924
An extremely able and conscientious woman feels that there is no real sympathy or understanding between her and her husband. He becomes an invalid, and she has to carry on the business, whilst his lot is to stand as a sort of buffer between her well-meant despotism and the children. Characteristically full of little domestic incidents, endless talk, and the like, all of which tend to mask the psychological difficulties of the case. [Harcourt, New York; Grosset, New York; Cape.]

—— *The Deepening Stream.* 1930
Some twenty years in the life of an American woman are treated here with Miss Canfield's habitual seriousness. In the earlier part, the trials and emotional reactions of a sensitive brother and sister amid the discords of life in the uncultured West; and in the more interesting later part, the experiences of Matey and her husband on war-work in France, and the contrasts between French and American points of view, are related with sure and quiet insight and no little piquancy. [Harcourt, New York; Cape.]

CANKAR, Ivan [Slovene; 1876–1918]. *The Bailiff Yerney and his Rights.* 1930
The masterpiece of a Slovene novelist. A fine old peasant who has worked a farm with admirable success for forty years is turned out by his master's son and heir, and his appeals for equity are unavailing. [Transl. by Sidonie Yeras and H. C. Sewell Grant, with introd. by Janko Lavrin, Rodker.]

CANNAN, Gilbert [*b.* 1884]. *Round the Corner : being the life and death of Arthur Christopher Folyat.*
1913
A study of the way character develops in a very ordinary sort of family, a clergyman's family in a Lancashire town, the members of which somehow never come up against realities—" life is always round the corner." The book may well be compared with Butler's *Way of All Flesh*, at any rate in its seriousness. (Mr. Cannan published a study, *Samuel Butler*, in 1915.) [Nash; Boni, New York.]

—— *Old Mole ; being the surprising adventures in England of Herbert Jocelyn Benham, M.A. sometime sixth-form master.* 1914
An erratic schoolmaster gets the sack, and marrying the girl who had compromised him joins a troupe of strolling players. But this highly improbable story is of minor account relatively to the analysis of Old Mole's mental experiences of love, jealousy, and subsequent most magnanimous forgiveness. See also *Old Mole's Novel* (Secker). [Secker: o.p.; Appleton, New York.]

—— *Young Earnest : the romance of a bad start in life.* 1915
The bad start is a marriage that does not content the very serious René, who satisfies his craving for completeness and his philosophy of life by regaining his first love, after throwing up a solid academic career and driving a taxi-cab. A candid and thoughtful study of personal and social problems, especially of life in such great centres as Manchester and London. [Unwin; Appleton, New York.]

—— *Windmills : a book of fables.* 1915
Three satires in the form of Gulliverian stories and otherwise, of militarist nationalism, female despotism, and modern pauperism. [Secker: o.p.; Viking Press, New York.]

—— *Mendel : a story of youth.* 1916
A discussion-novel which is also dramatic; theme, Art, or rather, Art and Life. Mendel is a Jew, and the Jews of the East End, immigrant or indigenous, are intimately portrayed. He is recognizably a man of genius, making his way by trial and error towards an artistic method. Many characters have their say, and the sexual business is not irrelevant. But the debates of Mendel and the blatant yet not insincere Logan are more interesting, and open up far-reaching views of the past and future of painting. [Unwin: o.p.; Doran, New York: o.p.]

—— *Three Pretty Men.* 1916
They are three penniless young Scots, two of whom make good, in the material sense, and the third, Jamie, serves to bring out the worldly unsuccess but the spiritual superiority of other ideals. It is a very searching study of the blighting effects of commercialism in modern life. (American title, *Three Sons and a Mother*.)

—— *The Stucco House* [sequel]. 1918
James and his brother in the south Lancashire industrial town reappear, and the philosophic vivisection of our chosen way of living continues. The wife, small-minded, narrowly conventional, miserly, joyless, is a grimly representative figure. An admirable contrast to her ugliness is the Scots servant Tibby, who also reappears from the earlier novel, and brings a breath of poetry and human simplicity into the drab household. [(1) Methuen: o.p.; Doran, New York: o.p.; (2) Unwin.]

—— *Mummery : a tale of three idealists.* 1918
Satire of the commercial theatre. An actor-manager who is a business man and nothing else, contrasts with a futurist painter, an actress who at any rate is an enchanting woman, and a playwright who is said to write masterpieces. These three are out for reform. The tangle .of motives is skilfully disentwined. [Collins: o.p.]

—— *Anatomy of Society.* 1919
A more ambitious analysis than Mr. Swinnerton's and the more patient, over-conscientious craftsmen's, of the demoralization that prevailed just after the war. [Chapman: o.p.]

CANNAN, Gilbert (*continued*). *Pink Roses.* 1919

The mental and moral revolution, the gulf between pre-war and post-war minds, standards of conduct, scales of value, attitudes ; elucidated in the story of a wealthy C3 young man who stays at home, whilst his friends disappear or are physically wrecked. The man of intellect learns instinctive perceptions from a " pretty lady " with whom he has a liaison, and comes to despise the old shams and bogus ideals. [Unwin.]

—— *Pugs and Peacocks.* 1921

Also a study of intellectual chaos produced by the war. The hero, a professor of mathematics, in reaction against the wave of emotional patriotism, becomes associated with a pacifist organization. Later, again led by his emotions, he veers to the orthodox position. Throughout, he remains that type of inconclusive, uncertain character frequent in this author's work. [Hutchinson : o.p.]

CANNON, Cornelia James [Mrs. Walter Bradford Cannon ; American ; *b.* 1876]. *Red Rust.* 1928

A boy who comes with his parents to settle in New Sweden, Minnesota, devotes his life to finding a strain of wheat that will be proof against red rust. Despite poverty, lack of education, ridicule, locusts and other scourges, he succeeds, but dies before he can reap the benefit. [Little & Brown, Boston ; Hodder.]

—— *Heirs.* 1930

An old cloth-mill in New Hampshire is a focusing-point in this emotional story of the Polish immigrants who are steadily supplanting the descendants of the original New Englanders. It is the profound social changes going on around that give significance to the personal happenings, touching as these are in themselves. [Little & Brown, Boston ; McClelland, Toronto ; Hodder.]

ČAPEK, Karel [Czech ; *b.* 1890]. *The Absolute at Large* (1923). 1927

Wellsian scientific fantasy, with some satire upon politics and clericalism. An engineer perfects a machine which destroys matter, thereby liberating the absolute or spiritual essence—and consequently uprooting society. [Macmillan.]

—— *Krakatit.* 1925

A symbolical tale, told with quaint imagination, about a scientist whose life is devoted to the discovery of explosives. He creates Krakatit, a terrific agency of wholesale annihilation ; his life thenceforth is a nightmare ; financiers, ministers, a princess even, combine to wrest the secret from him. Only when he has realized the futility of destructive force, and forgotten the secret of Krakatit, does he begin to find peace. [Transl. by Lawrence HYDE, Bles ; Macmillan, New York.]

CAPES, Bernard Edward Joseph [*d.* 1914]. *The Lake of Wine.* 1898

About an immensely valuable ruby, and the plots and counterplots of which it is the occasion (*c.* 1800). Gallants and ruffians are the actors ; the passions revealed are mostly evil. Style tends to preciosity. Has been described as blending Stevenson's skill with Le Fanu's creepiness. [Heinemann : o.p. ; Appleton, New York : o.p.]

—— *Adventures of the Comte de la Muette.* 1898

Action and love-making during the Reign of Terror ; gruesome incidents brilliantly related ; the style, as usual, full of Meredithian mannerisms. [Blackwood : o.p. ; Dodd & Mead, New York : o.p.]

—— *Our Lady of Darkness.* 1899

A story of intrigue and adventure, fantastic in style and matter, with a courtesan and priestess of anarchy as dominant figure, and some historic names among the subordinate personages, historical events being used as the imaginative setting (1780–93). [Blackwood ; Dodd & Mead, New York : o.p.]

—— *At a Winter's Fire.* 1899

A collection of stories mostly of the grim sort that we associate with Poe. *An Eddy on the Floor* is a peculiar ghost story that has quite his mixture of horror and fascination. *Jack and Jill* is rather of the kind invented by Munchausen. The others are somewhere between these. [Methuen : o.p. ; Doubleday, New York : o.p.]

—— *From Door to Door.* 1900

Short stories of an uncommon, fastidious type, in an elaborate, highly Latinized style. *A Coward* describes a man's feelings when threatened with death by fire. *A True Princess* records the aristocratic sufferings of a patrician lady who has caught a cold from a servant-maid. [Blackwood : o.p. ; Stokes, New York : o.p.]

—— *Joan Brotherhood.* 1900

The history of a foundling girl, who marries a parson secretly, and is led by ambition to be an actress, to her own undoing. Contains much painful incident, and deals boldly with shady phases of life. [Pearson : o.p.]

—— *Love Like a Gipsy.* 1901

A love-romance opening in Canada at the time of the American Revolution (1778). Somewhat bizarre in plot and often grotesque in characterization. Overshadowed almost to the end with threatening tragedy. Gives a glimpse of Brighton and its frivolities in the Prince Regent's time, and a sketch of Mrs. Fitzherbert. [Constable : o.p.]

—— *A Castle in Spain.* 1903

A self-conscious adventurer, given to analysing his emotions, goes from the Netherlands, via England, to the Peninsula, to rescue the Dauphin, Louis XVII, from a Talavera convent. Strange scenes and characters, mysterious spies, ingratiating traitors, carnage-piled battlefields and haunted forests—depicted in a curiously inlaid style, full of ghoulish suggestiveness (1785–1810). [Smith & Elder : o.p.]

—— *The Secret in the Hill.* 1903

Treasure-hunting, smuggling, etc., in early Victorian days ; scenes, near Ipswich. Adventures of two admirable boys. [Smith & Elder : o.p.]

—— *The Extraordinary Confessions of Diana Please.* 1904

Diana is a female picaroon, daughter of a rake and a nun. She passes through many grotesque and horrible adventures, is at Paris during the Reign of Terror, and at Naples in the revolution of 1798, where she sees Nelson and Lady Hamilton (1771–99). [Methuen.]

CAPES, Bernard Edward Joseph (*continued*). *A Jay of Italy.* 1905
A highly coloured, fantastic story of mediæval Italy, the hero a saint-like youth who endeavours to reform the corrupt court ; scene, Milan under Galeazzo Maria Sforza (1476). [(Wayfarers' Lib.), Dent.]

—— *A Rogue's Tragedy.* 1906
Doings of a libertine hero in Savoy and Piedmont just before the French Revolution, against the dawning influences of which he pits his strength, but dies a sacrifice to unrequited love (1783). [Methuen : o.p.]

—— *The Love Story of St. Bel.* 1909
A vigorous, fantastic, theatrical romance of Italy in 1374—Siena and Maremma—full of fighting, intriguing, murdering, love-making, with the impressive figure of St. Catherine brooding over the scene. More restrained in style than the foregoing. [Methuen : o.p.]

—— *Jemmy Abercraw.* 1910
An unreal story of a gentleman-highwayman in 1758-60, who impersonates the Young Pretender. [Nelson ; Brentano, New York : o.p.]

—— *Historical Vignettes.* 1910
Short stories and sketches that may serve for imaginative portraits of such celebrities as *Fair Rosamund, Margaret of Anjou, Queen Elizabeth, Louis XIV, George I,* etc. [Unwin : o.p. ; revised ed., with 12 new sketches, 1912 ; Sidgwick : o.p. ; Stokes, New York : o.p.]

—— *The Pot of Basil.* 1913
The marriage of Isabella, daughter of the Duke of Parma, to the Archduke Joseph (II) of Austria (1759), is the historical datum of this striking novel. [Constable : o.p.]

—— *The Story of Fifine.* 1914
A romance of travel in Paris and Provence. [Constable : o.p.]

—— *If Age Could.* 1916
Contrasts the characters of a middle-aged man and his young ward—the one amiable and weak, the other utterly selfish. [Duckworth : o.p.]

—— *Where England Sets her Feet.* 1918
A romantic novel of Elizabethan London, the borders of Dartmoor, and the sea (1560-85) ; Raleigh, Robert Dudley, Earl of Leicester, and Sir Richard Grenville are more or less prominent. [Collins.]

—— *The Skeleton Key.* 1919
A workmanlike detective story, embroidering on the Sherlock Holmes theme, with a well-kept if rather incredible surprise for the finish. [Collins : o.p.]

"CARBERY, Ethna" [Mrs. Seumas McManus, *née* Anna Johnston ; Irish ; 1866–1902]. *The Passionate Hearts.* 1903
Tender and melancholy, poetic and beautiful studies of love in an Irish girl, a Donegal peasant, with idyllic pictures of the coast and mountain scenery. [Gill, Dublin : o.p. ; Irish Pub. Co., New York.]

—— *In the Celtic Past.* 1904
Stories from the Ossianic cycle, retold in a beautiful prose. [Gill, Dublin : o.p. ; Funk & Wagnalls, New York.]

CARBERY, Mary [Irish]. *Children of the Dawn.* 1923
Pictures Ireland in the times of the Druids, utilizing legendary material on immigrants from Greece, Egypt, Palestine, etc., who taught the worship of the Unknown God and the arts of civilization. [Heinemann : o.p.]

CAREY, Rosa Nouchette [1840–1909]. *Wee Wifey.* 1869
—— *Wooed and Married.* 1875
—— *Uncle Max.* 1887
—— *Only the Governess.* 1888
—— *The Sunny Side of the Hill.* 1908
Sunny, wholesome domestic fiction of no high literary merit but enjoyable to a large class of readers. [All Macmillan ; Lippincott, Philadelphia.]

—— *Not like other Girls.* 1884
A mother and three daughters, suddenly reduced from affluence to poverty, earn their living by dressmaking. Cleverness and good sense win them success, and they are rewarded by offers of marriage and by a restoration of fortune. [Macmillan ; Lippincott, Philadelphia.]

—— *Barbara Heathcote's Trials.* 1885
Home life of a family of girls, all differing in character, all wilful. Barbara is a blunt, outspoken girl, whose very candour leads her into misunderstandings and troubles. [Macmillan ; Lippincott, Philadelphia.]

—— *Life's Trivial Round.* 1900
Like the foregoing, a simple, unaffected account of the ordinary events of domestic life, a quiet picture of little things, with nothing more exciting than the wedding festivities that crown the story. [Hutchinson : o.p. ; Lippincott, Philadelphia.]

—— *Rue with a Difference.* 1900
Quiet domestic life in a cathedral town, the love affairs of a stepmother and a stepdaughter, and a set of pleasant, well-conducted characters sketched in a lifelike manner. [Macmillan ; Lippincott, Philadelphia.]

CAREY, Wymond. *Monsieur Martin : a romance of the Great Swedish War.* 1902
Scenes : Sweden, England, France (1699-1719). [Blackwood : o.p. ; Putnam, New York : o.p.]

—— *For the White Rose* [sequel]. 1903
The English and Continental Jacobites ; their intrigues with Alberoni and other statesmen all over Europe, and their attempts in Scotland, with their defeat in Glenshiel (1716-19). Monsieur Martin comes on the scene again, when it has been shifted to the camp of Charles XII of Sweden. [Blackwood : o.p.]

CAREY, Wymond (*continued*). "*No. 101.*"   1906
Exciting adventures of a secret agent in the time of Louis XV, whose brilliant, dissolute court is alternately the scene with the camps and battlefields of the Low Countries (1740–50) during the War of the Austrian Succession. [Blackwood ; Putnam, New York : o.p.]

CARLETON, William [Irish ; 1794–1869]. *Traits and Stories of the Irish Peasantry.* (Two Series.)
    1830–3
Carleton called this, and rightly, his greatest work. The plan on which it begins, subsequently abandoned, is that the cronies sitting round the fire in Ned McKeown's cabin should tell a story apiece. In these short stories and descriptions of the manners and ways and emotions of the Irish peasants, he serves up the best of his autobiographical material, in the form that suited him best and drew out his innate artistic gifts. And so we get a matchless presentation of the real life of the peasants, their quick temper and variable nature, now moody, now gay, capable of the deepest feeling, of fiercely vindictive passions, and of crime. He reproduces the brogue and turns of speech with truth and humour. The *Party Fight and Funeral* is a boisterous and spirited narrative of a faction fight ; *Phil Purcel the Pig Driver*, a caricature of a Connaught peasant that has been adopted as typical of Irishmen ; *The Lianhan Shee* and *The Midnight Mass* show his deep feeling for nature. *The Poor Scholar*, a portrait from life, and *Tubber Derg, or the Holy Well*, with its "hero beggar," are two touching stories. *Wildgoose Lodge* is a tale of lawless revenge. Others, e.g. *Dennis O'Shaughnessy going to Maynooth*, a comic story of a novice who falls in love, are of a humorous kind. Carleton's realism is almost over-faithful in detail, yet by no means free from caricature and exaggeration. He said of his *Lough Derg Pilgrim*, "It resembles a coloured photograph more than anything else." Carleton had none of the popular and brilliant comedy of Lever, or his fertility in farcical character ; but his insight into the Irish mind and temperament, his knowledge of Irish traditions, thoughts, manners, idiosyncrasies, was enormously deeper. From Lever we get the amusing Irishman, the stage buffoon ; from Carleton a numerous gallery of authentic types, peasants drawn by one who was himself a peasant, and gifted with what he called an extraordinary power of unconscious observation and a tenacious memory. [Complete, Routledge (Dutton, New York) : o.p. ; 4 vols., *illus.*, Dent : o.p. ; *Stories of Irish Life*, with introd. by Darrel Figgis, Talbot Press, Dublin ; *Wildgoose Lodge, and other Irish tales*, Putnam, New York.]

—— *Fardarougha the Miser ; or, The Convicts of Lisnamona.*   1839
A well-constructed story dealing tragically with the passion of avarice. Fardarougha has been compared with Balzac's *Père Goriot*, and several of the other characters are admirable, and avowedly drawn from living originals. The emotional struggle between avarice and parental love brings in scenes of intense sorrow and gloom. Honour, the wife, is a beautiful portrait of an Irishwoman, and is said to be drawn from Carleton's own loved mother. [Ed. by D. J. O'Donoghue, Downey, o.p. ; Kenedy, New York : o.p.]

—— *Valentine McClutchy, the Irish Land Agent.*   1845
A passionate indictment of the tyranny and rapacity of land agents, the evils of non-residence, the hypocrisy of canting attorneys who hang on to the landlord class, the violence of the Orange faction, and the partisanship of juries. Paints terrible scenes of eviction and the like—unquestionably charged with memories of a cruel outrage perpetrated on Carleton's father—with many droll situations. [Duffy, Dublin : o.p. ; Kenedy, New York : o.p.]

—— *Paddy-go-Easy and his wife Nancy.*   1845
Sketches an easy-going, reckless, good-for-nothing peasant—not a fair example of the species—with much raciness and humour. [Duffy, Dublin : o.p.]

—— *Rody the Rover.*   1845
Rody is an agent of the Ribbonites, who are painted as a set of rascals and spies (*c.* 1820–40). [Duffy, Dublin : o.p.]

—— *Art Maguire ; or, The Broken Pledge.*   1847
A temperance story—the downward career of a man utterly ruined by drink. [Sadlier, New York : o.p.]

—— *The Black Prophet : a tale of the Irish famine.*   1847
One of his most powerful novels, rich in both pathos and humour and in studies of female character. Written amid the trials and sufferings of a terrible famine (1846–7), the record of an earlier visitation Carleton had himself passed through, and of the typhus epidemic of 1817—a tragic testimony to the endurance and devotion of the Irish people. [Lawrence and Bullen, 1899, o.p. ; Kenedy, New York : o.p.]

—— *The Emigrants of Ahadarra.*   1847
Contains some beautiful scenes of rural life and also some of his bitterest scenes of sorrow and anguish, with pen portraits from the life, e.g. the old patriarch, Dora McMahon, the Burkes, and the Hogans. [Routledge : o.p. ; Kennedy, New York : o.p. ; in *Works*, 10 vols., Sadlier, New York : o.p.]

—— *The Tithe-Proctor.*   1849
A rancorous and perverted study of the anti-tithe campaign, giving a biased version of a notorious agrarian crime, the murder of the Bolands. [Duffy, Dublin : o.p. ; Kenedy, New York : o.p.]

—— *The Squanders of Castle Squander.*   1852
"An attempt to portray the life of the gentry, a task for which Carleton was imperfectly qualified." An acrid and unpleasing story, feebly mimicking Lever's jovial style. [o.p.]

—— *The Poor Scholar* (1830) ; *and other tales.*   1853–5
A selection of nine of Carleton's last stories, the title-story one of his most touching. Carleton himself learnt at a hedge-school. [Duffy, Dublin : o.p.]

—— *Willie Reilly and his Dear Colleen Bawn.*   1855
A story based on a popular legend of Ulster, which had been told in countless ballads and in artless prose. A poor example of Carleton's work. Tells with more romance than realism of the days (1745–52) when the priests were persecuted and hunted, and a Catholic lover had small chance of wedding a Protestant heiress. [With introd. by E. A. Baker (Half-forgotten books), 1904, Routledge : o.p. ; Burt, New York : o.p.]

CARLING, John R. *By Neva's Waters : being an episode in the secret history of Alexander I.* 1907
A complicated plot-novel of international politics and love at the Russian Court at the time of the murder of the Emperor Paul (1801). Elizabeth of Baden, wife of the Tsar Alexander I, is the more august of the heroines. [Ward & Lock : o.p. ; Little & Brown, Boston : o.p.]

CARLYLE, Thomas [tr.]. *Translations from the German : Musaeus, Tieck, Richter.* 1827
MUSAEUS : *Dumb Love, Libussa, Melechsala ;* TIECK : *The Fair-haired Eckbert, The Trusty Eckart, The Runenberg, The Elves, The Goblet ;* RICHTER : *Schmelzle's Journey to Flaetz, Life of Quintus Fixlein. Dumb Love* is a charming idyll of two lovers who could not speak to each other ; with some supernatural and comic effects. *Libussa* is a pretty myth about the origin of Bohemia, told in a homely style, which also gives charm to *Melechsala*, the tale of a captive crusader rescued by the daughter of the Egyptian sultan (cf. *Huon of Bordeaux*). In *Eckbert*, TIECK mingles the wonderful and mysterious with commonplace reality, in a gloomy tale of fatalism. *Eckart* is a fine old knightly legend of Burgundy, and *The Runenberg* a version of the Tannhäuser myth. In *The Elves*, we have the fairy world depicted as kind and lovely to those who are innocent and good. *The Goblet* is a symbolist story of a magic vessel, and teaches a subtle moral. For *Quintus Fixlein* see under Richter. *Schmelzle* is an exaggerated portrait of a coward ; an inimitable caricature of a single foible, rather overburdened with Jean Paul's incurable drollery. [(Library edn.), 3 vols., Chapman (includes his transl. of Goethe's *Wilhelm Meister*) ; (Century edn.), 2 vols., Chapman (Scribner, New York) ; Page, Boston.]

CAROSSA, Hans [German ; b. 1878]. *A Childhood* (Eine Kindheit, 1922). 1930
This is probably in substance autobiography rather than fiction. It is the exquisitely sensitive and evocative art with which the author, a distinguished poet and physician, brings before us the sensations and emotions of a child, that entitles it to a high place among the imaginative re-creations of childhood. [Transl. by Agnes Neill SCOTT, Secker.]

CARPENTER, Edward Childs [American ; b. 1872]. *Captain Courtesy.* 1906
Covers much of the history of Old California during the " Bear Flag " war, the attempt of the Mexican Government to expel American settlers, General Castro's murderous raids, the American revolution aided and abetted by General Kearny and Colonel Frémont, Admiral Stockton's capture of San Pedro and Los Angeles, the battle of San Gabriel, and the admission of California to the Union (1840–2). The scene is centred in the mission of San Gabriel, near Los Angeles. [Jacobs, Philadelphia : o.p.]

—— *The Code of Victor Jallot : a romance of New Orleans.* 1907
Deals with one of the plots that were rife among the French and Spanish of Louisiana at the time of the purchase (1803). The hero is a gentleman-barber and poet, dancing-master and fencing-master, who checks one of these intrigues against the American authorities. Governor Claiborne, the Spanish Marquess Casa Calvo, and the French colonial prefect Lausset are among the characters. [Jacobs, Philadelphia : o.p.]

CARR, Mrs. Alice Comyns [née Strettell]. *The Arm of the Lord.* 1899
A tragedy of humble life, involving a stubborn, unforgiving Methodist yeoman and the wayward grandchild whom he would fain save from damnation. [Duckworth : o.p.]

CARR, M. E. *Love and Honour.* 1901
A novel with a certain infusion of history, concerned with Westphalia in the time of Jerome Bonaparte (1807–13). [Smith & Elder : o.p. ; Putnam, New York : o.p.]

CARREL, Frederic [b. 1869]. *The Realization of Justus Moran.* 1900
A study of pessimism. The two characters represent intelligence and instinct respectively ; they love each other, separated though they are by conventional morality, and the struggle of the man's reason against his passion is the motive of a tragic drama. [Long : o.p.]

" CARROLL, Lewis " [Rev. Charles Lutwidge Dodgson ; 1832–98]. *Alice's Adventures in Wonderland.* 1865
—— *Through the Looking-Glass ; and What Alice Found There.* 1871
Lewis Carroll invented a new kind of fairy tale, several degrees more fantastic than Andersen's, drawing on modern science and all sorts of modern ideas for materials, and finding its most characteristic expression in droll irrelevance and the ludicrous distortion of familiar things. Though written for children and inspired by the prattle and innocent charm of children, the wit, the fanciful humour, and the subtlety of many of its under-meanings can be fully appreciated only by educated people. Lewis Carroll, further, was a genuine poet, and his songs and snatches of verse are very beautiful, even when most absurd, in their sensuousness and haunting cadences. [(1) and (2) *illus.* by J. Tenniel, Macmillan (1911) ; in 1 vol. (Everyman's Lib.) Dent (Dutton, New York), 1929 ; Collins 1928 ; (1) *illus.* by Thomas Maybank, Routledge ; by Arthur Rackham, Heinemann ; by Charles Robinson, Cassell ; by W. H. Walker, Lane ; with orig. *illus.* by Tenniel, Riccardi Press, 1914.]

—— *Sylvie and Bruno.* 1889
—— *Sylvie and Bruno Concluded* [sequel]. 1893
In these later tales his comic imagination applies itself to the regular duties of the fabulist, to enforce what he held right in conduct and religion. The ideas are more recondite ; and, though the first object is entertainment, the didactic purpose is strongly pronounced. [(1) and (2), Macmillan.]

CASTLE, Agnes [née Sweetman ; d. 1922], and CASTLE, Egerton [1858–1920]. *The Pride of Jennico.* 1898
A romance of adventure (1771–3), with a surprise plot and some comedy—passages in the life of Capt. Basil Jennico, scion of an ancient English family, who inherits princely estates in Moravia, and meets with strange adventures through his courtship of a fascinating princess, only child of a reigning house. Agnes Castle was the sister of M. E. Francis. [(Wayfarer's Lib.), Dent ; Nash.]

—— *The Bath Comedy.* 1900
A jealous husband, a doting wife, and a dashing widow who intervenes disastrously to reconcile the two, start a complicated train of misadventures, which in a day or two end farcically and happily. Scene, fashionable Bath during the Beau Nash regime, middle of the eighteenth century. [Macmillan : o.p. ; Stokes, New York : o.p.]

CASTLE, Agnes, and CASTLE, Egerton (*continued*). *Incomparable Bellairs* [sequel]. 1904
 Seven further episodes in the history of that impersonation of the gay, elegant, artificial eighteenth century, Mistress Kitty Bellairs. Romantic comedy, reproducing the atmosphere of the time by the conventional stage-methods. [Constable : o.p. ; Stokes, New York : o.p.]

—— *French Nan* [sequel]. 1905
 A comedy of character and manners, in the genre of *Incomparable Bellairs*, etc., with a *Taming of the Shrew* motive ; scene, Georgian London. [Smith & Elder : o.p.]

—— *The Secret Orchard.* 1901
 Probably designed for a play ; full of stage talk and theatrical situations. The hero, a handsome duke descended from the Stuart kings, is wedded to a beautiful and spotless lady, from whom he conceals his profligate indulgences in the "Secret Orchard." Bright comedy nearly to the end, which is tragic. [Macmillan : o.p. ; Stokes, New York : o.p. ; Grosset, New York : o.p.]

—— *The Star Dreamer.* 1903
 The Star Dreamer is a young baronet whose heart has been turned to gall by a love crime. He shuts himself up in his tower and studies the stars. Into this lonely life comes the daughter of his kinsman, an old alchemist and collector of simples. They love, but almost insuperable obstacles confront them. The characters are quaint, their surroundings full of glamour, and the style well attuned. Scene, a weird old manor-house in Wilts (*c.* 1810–20). [Long, 1929 ; Stokes, New York : o.p.]

—— *If Youth but Knew.* 1906
 A love-romance of Westphalia when Jerome Bonaparte was king, with a characteristic figure of a tragic old musician, who sings to the hero about the joys of youth and lends picturesqueness to the tale (1812–14). [Nelson ; Macmillan, New York : o.p.]

—— *My Merry Rockhurst : some episodes in the life of Viscount Rockhurst, a friend of the King, at one time Constable of His Majesty's Tower.* 1907
 Eight stage-like episodes in the career of a rakish comrade of the second Charles. [Murray ; Macmillan, New York : o.p. ; Grosset, New York : o.p.]

—— *Flower o' the Orange ; and other stories.* 1908
 Similar romances of the early eighteenth century, of the '45, 1749, and earlier periods, and ranging from Italy to England and Galloway. [Methuen : o.p. ; Macmillan, New York : o.p.]

—— *Wroth.* 1908
 The same kind of material more long drawn out, ranging from Tunbridge Wells to Compiègne and Florence (1816–17). [Murray ; Macmillan, New York : o.p.]

—— *Love Gilds the Scene and Women Guide the Plot.* 1912
 Tales of London, Bath, and the road, in which Lady Kilcroney, formerly Kitty Bellairs, re-enters. [Murray.]

—— *The Ways of Miss Barbara.* 1914
 Typical of the numerous bright romances of the eighteenth century which these authors have provided. [Murray.]

—— *The Black Office ; and other chapters of romance.* 1917
 Stories of the war with France after the peace of Amiens. One deals with the "Black Office," set up for secret Government purposes : two with the prohibition of gold export and the guinea-running carried on from our shores ; and two others portray Edinburgh characters and the gloom and mystery of the old town. [Murray.]

—— *Pamela Pounce : a tale of tempestuous petticoats.* 1921
 Fashionable circles at Cheltenham, Canterbury, London, Weymouth (1788), with Lady Kilcroney, Queen Charlotte, and the Prince of Wales upon the boards. [Hodder : o.p. ; Appleton, New York.]

CASTLE, Egerton [1858–1920]. *The Light of Scarthey.* 1895
 A pretty, unreal romance of a romantic time, Napoleon's Hundred Days. Characters, the recluse of Scarthey Lighthouse, who lost his love twenty years ago and sees her daughter come back like a spirit from the grave, the dare-devil privateer, the villainous brother, smugglers and preventives. [Macmillan : o.p. ; Stokes, New York : o.p.]

—— *Young April.* 1899
 A sprightly story of a young man's thirty days of crowded life, love and adventure. Suddenly learning he has inherited the vast wealth and honours of a duke, he devotes a month of freedom to the pursuit of unfettered happiness. [Macmillan, London and New York : o.p.]

—— *Marshfield the Observer ; and, The Death Dance : studies of character and action.* 1900
 Five stories, mostly related by an eccentric observer of the minds and emotions of men and women, with his interesting comments. Chiefly fantastic or ultra-romantic stories of unruly passion, remorse, etc. *The Death Dance* is a spirited tale of the war in Hungary in 1849, and *Endymion in Barracks* a psychological sketch of a dreamer who takes to the soldier's life. [Macmillan : o.p. ; Duffield, New York : o.p.]

CATHER, Willa (Sibert) [American ; *b.* 1876]. *O Pioneers !* 1913
 The making of Nebraska, as it were epitomized, in thirty years of the history of a Swedish family of settlers. Foremost in worth and energy stands the beautiful Alexandra Bergson, the true pioneer. But the lesser characters, children or their elders, are also drawn with the peculiar intimacy and the sense of amplitude and abounding life which is Miss Cather's distinctive mark. [Houghton, Boston ; (Riverside ed.), *id.*, 1929 ; Heinemann.]

—— *The Song of the Lark.* 1915
 The heroic female character here is Thea Kronborg, who breaks away from the cramping environment of her Colorado village and becomes a great singer. [Houghton, Boston ; Murray.]

—— *My Ántonia.* 1918
 Early days in Kansas and Nebraska, in the recollections of a lawyer and railroad-builder who was born on the prairie and knew the strangely diversified characters portrayed—a vision of history transforming a primitive

CATHER, Willa (Sibert) (*continued*).

into a modern complex world in less than an average lifetime. It is the fascination of the past that inspires the portrait of Ántonia, a girl of intense vitality and prickly temperament, who after an age of privation conquers by dint of a true heart and indomitable courage—not a romantic figure, but one well worth putting beside Marie Chapdelaine. [Houghton, Boston ; *illus.*, *id.*, 1926 ; Heinemann ; (Windmill Lib.), *id.*, 1930.]

—— *Youth and the Bright Medusa.* 1920

The first and best four of these eight stories give an aching perception of the stuffiness and squalor of average life in the towns of the Middle West. In *Paul's Case* the nausea of it all drives a young fellow to steal a thousand dollars, enjoy a glorious week of dissipation, and jump under a train. [Knopf, New York ; Heinemann.]

—— *A Lost Lady.* 1923

Hardly more than the portrayal of a bewitching woman, whose beauty and charm is for years an inspiration to the man who tells her story—in the Henry James manner. Her husband, a gallant old pioneer who has survived from the days of great-hearted adventurers into the new epoch of " shrewd young men, trained to petty economies," is as fine a figure as she. But the beauty of the old neglected landscape perishes, and the lady herself becomes a symbol of disenchantment. [Knopf, New York ; Heinemann.]

—— *The Professor's House.* 1925

An odd book : a study of atmosphere rather than of actualities. The middle-aged professor, still working and popular, happy in his home life, with his children settled, yields to a sense of defeat, feels he has made a mistake somewhere, that he is really alone in the world, and being useless might as well go out of it. The interpolated story of a boy's adventures in New Mexico seems to have its point in the professor's theory of a revival of youth in some men. [Knopf, New York ; Grosset, New York ; Heinemann.]

—— *My Mortal Enemy.* 1926

A character-sketch, in the form of a younger friend's reminiscences, of a wilful, high-strung, jealous woman— a symbol of human disenchantment—who at the end of married life laments that " People can be lovers and enemies at the same time." [Knopf, New York ; Heinemann.]

—— *Death Comes for the Archbishop.* 1927

The life and missionary work of two high-souled priests who after 1851 establish the Roman Church in New Mexico, enduring untold hardships, perils, and heart-breaking reverses. From the opening tableau of the cardinals dining on the lofty terrace in sight of Rome to the death-scene of the saintly apostle of the Indians, the book is richly pictorial. Both racial and individual traits come out strongly in the character-drawing. [Knopf, New York ; Heinemann ; *illus.* by Harold von Schmidt, 1929, Knopf, New York ; Heinemann.]

CATHERWOOD, Mrs. Mary Hartwell [American ; 1847–1902]. *The Romance of Dollard : an historical romance of Canada.* 1889

Woven round an historical episode of 1660, when Dollard, with a devoted band of Hurons, repulsed a horde of Iroquois invading New France. The high-souled heroine, the valiant Dollard, and the courageous Huron, Annahotaha, are fine characters if a little unsubstantial. [Century Co., New York ; Unwin : o.p.]

—— *The Lady of Fort St. John.* [juvenile] 1892

A picturesque story of Acadia (French Nova Scotia) in 1645, based on historical records. Two French nobles, holding seigniories from the King of France, are at feud, and one of them, a profligate and unscrupulous protégé of Louis XIII, besieges the fort, which is heroically defended by the wife of his enemy. [Houghton, Boston ; Low : o.p.]

—— *Old Kaskaskia.* [juvenile] 1893

Life in the North-west ; French and English character well contrasted. [Houghton, Boston : o.p.]

—— *The White Islander.* 1893

A romance of the old Indian wars, getting much of its effect from the pictorial treatment of river and forest scenery ; characters, a chief and an Indian girl, a white fugitive and a French girl, captive among the redskins. [Century Co., New York : o.p. ; Unwin : o.p.]

—— *The Chase of Saint Castin ; and other stories.* 1894

Seven strenuous tales of French, Indian, and English, in the romantic period two centuries ago, before the French were expelled from Canada and the Lakes. [Houghton, Boston : o.p.]

—— *The Days of Jeanne d'Arc.* [juvenile] 1897

A careful study of the period *c.* 1412–31, emphasizing the moral beauty and valour of the inspired peasant maid. [Century Co., New York : o.p. ; Gay & Hancock : o.p.]

—— *Spanish Peggy.* [juvenile] 1899

A short story of early Illinois, with an attractive picture of Lincoln as a young man. [Stone, Chicago : o.p.]

—— *Lazarre.* 1902

Lazarre is the Dauphin (Louis XVII, who died in the Temple) and is imagined to have been smuggled across to America as an idiot. He regains his reason, and has to decide whether he shall reassert his claims to the throne or sacrifice all to love. [Bobbs-Merrill, Indianapolis : o.p.]

—— *The Story of Tonty.* 1904

Adventures of the Sieur de la Salle and his friend the one-armed lieutenant Tonti in Canada and Texas (1678–1687). Plenty of history, excellent descriptions of scenery and of the Indians ; character-drawing a failure. [McClurg, Chicago.]

CENA, Giovanni [Italian ; 1870–1917]. *The Forewarners* (Gli Ammonitori, 1903). 1908

A formless, abrupt, intensely sincere novel, that reads like chapters torn out of actual life. The autobiography of a proof-reader in Turin, a poor man, finely cultivated, a thinker and a dreamer, whose record throws a flood of light on the miserable, wasted lives of poor people dwelling in the great blocks of flats in Turin, and on the agonizing social problems which await solution. [Transl. by Olivia Agresti ROSSETTI ; with Preface by Mrs. Humphry WARD ; Murray ; Doubleday, New York : o.p.]

CERVANTES SAAVEDRA, Miguel de [Spanish ; 1547–1616]. *Galatea : a pastoral romance* (1585). 1867

An unfinished pastoral on the conventional pattern of Sannazaro and Montemayor, afterwards laughed at in *Don Quixote*, where, however, the author pays a sly compliment to his own production. Said to have been his own favourite among his works, and meant to be completed by a second part. The characters are the usual nymphs and shepherds engaged in amorous converse on the banks of the Tagus, singing love-songs, etc. Full of digressions and episodes, of rhetorical flights and philosophical disquisitions, with profuse imitations of classical mythology. A better model of Spanish prose than *Don Quixote*, though the prose has the rather tedious graces of imitative romance. [Transl. by G. W. J. GYLL (Bohn's Lib.), Bell (Harcourt, New York) : o.p. ; by J. FITZMAURICE-KELLY, Gowans & Gray, Glasgow : o.p.]

—— *Don Quixote de la Mancha* (1605–15). 1612–20

One of the greatest books in the world—a satire on romances of chivalry, and an interpretation of human life by a profound comic philosopher. Incidentally, as it were, the story depicts with perfect realism the Spanish world of the time in all its principal phases. The minor characters are the everyday people whom the author and his readers were best acquainted with, and are strongly national and even local in their traits. No better representation exists of Spanish life at that period. The immortal pair, Don Quixote, the mad idealist, and Sancho Panza, the quintessence of vulgar commonsense, have been copied in numerous literary forms. [Transl. by H. E. WATTS, 5 vols., Quaritch, 1888–9 (the best transl. for the scholar and bibliophile : has lavish notes and excursuses) ; by J. ORMSBY, 4 vols., Smith & Elder (Cheap edn., ed. J. F. KELLY, 4 vols., Gowans & Gray, Glasgow, 1901) ; by T. SHELTON (1612–20), 4 vols. (Tudor Translations), Nutt, 1896 : o.p. ; by SHELTON, 3 vols. (Lib. of English Classics), Macmillan, 1900 ; by SHELTON, *illus.* by Daniel Vierge, 4 vols., Unwin, 1907 ; by P. MOTTEUX (1822), 2 vols. (Bohn's Popular Lib.), Bell ; 2 vols., (Everyman's Lib.) Dent (Dutton, New York) ; by C. JARVIS (1801), 2 vols in 1, Routledge, 1889 ; Harper, London and New York, 1923 ; Warne, 1926 ; *illus.* by Heath Robinson, Dent, 1927 ; by Robinson SMITH, Routledge, (Dutton, New York) (1910), 1924.]

—— *Exemplary Novels* (Novelas exemplares, 1613). 1640

Written 1588–1603 ; picaresque stories, miniature romances, and mere anecdotes ; all designed, though light in tone, to enforce a moral. To Spaniards, it has been pointed out, they are what Boccaccio's tales are to Italians. Some are remarkably modern in style. One of the best is *Rinconete and Cortadillo*, a comic story of two knaves, that gives a humorous account of the vagabond characters for which Seville was famous. Pointed and witty, full of brisk action and of humorous portraits from all grades of society, but most strikingly of the picaresque class—gipsies, thieves, bonarobas, and the like—in whose adventures Cervantes relates his own experiences in Italy, Spain, and Africa. [Transl. by J. MABBE (1640), 2 vols., Lippincott, London and Philadelphia, 1900 ; *The Spanish Ladie* (with two other tales), Oxford Press, 1928 ; by W. K. KELLY, (1846) (Bohn's Lib.), Bell (Harcourt, New York) ; by N. MACCOLL, 3 vols., R. B. Johnson : o.p.]

—— *The Travels of Persiles and Sigismunda* (Los Trabajos de Persiles y Sigismunda, 1617). 1619

" A Northern history, wherein amongst the variable fortunes of the Prince of Thule and the Princesse of Friesland, are interlaced many Witty Discourses, Morall, Politicall, and Delightful." An imitation of the *Theagenes and Chariclea* of Heliodorus, and, like that intricate romance, a series of tribulations, misadventures, perils, and fortunate escapes sustained by a pair of lovers, the daughter of a queen of Friesland and the son of a queen of Thule. [Translator unknown ; reprinted 1639 and 1741 : o.p. ; transl. by L. Dorothea STANLEY, 1854 : o.p.]

CHAMBERS, Robert William [American ; *b.* 1865]. *The Red Republic : a romance of the Commune.* 1895

The romantic adventures of a chivalrous American student and a noble young lady, enemies of the Communist chief of the police department in Paris (1871). Based to large extent on facts, the author having studied public and private sources of information. [Putnam, New York : o.p.]

—— *The Haunts of Men.* 1898

Multifarious stories of American or Canadian life. *Pickets*, a story of fraternizing outposts during the Civil War ; *Smith's Battery*, an exciting incident of the same period ; *Enter, the Queen*, a farcical piece ; *Another Good Man*, an extravagance, etc. [Stokes, New York : o.p.]

—— *Lorraine.* 1898

A romance of the Franco-German War, especially the battles of Saarbrück and Sedan. [Harper, New York ; Putnam, London : o.p.]

—— *Ashes of Empire.* 1899

The siege of Paris ; the escape of the Empress. [Stokes, New York.]

—— *The Cambric Mask.* 1900

An exciting romance of commercial rascality culminating in a violent attempt to expel the hero from his farm in Mohawk County. He is rescued from almost certain death by a girl, who marries him. [Stokes, New York ; Unwin.]

—— *Cardigan.* 1901

A spirited romance of the troublous times preceding the Revolution (1774–5). Unhistorical interests predominant—Cardigan's love, and extraordinary adventures among Indians. Scenes : Mohawk Valley, Pittsburg, and Lexington. Hero is nephew of Sir William Johnson, who like Walter Butler, Molly Brandt, and some others, is a well-known character from history. [Harper, New York ; Constable : o.p.]

—— *The Maid-at-Arms* [sequel]. 1902

A very romantic romance ; scene, Tryon County and Fort Stanwix, where the Loyalists enlisted the services of the Indians. A number of historical persons from both camps are introduced, among them the Butlers, Johnsons, Molly and Joseph Brandt. [Harper, New York ; Long.]

CHAMBERS, Robert William (*continued*). *The Maids of Paradise.* 1903

Opens with a fiery description of the battle of Wörth and the famous charge of the cuirassiers. In the second part we are shown the closing incidents of the war from the point of view of a Breton seaport (1870–1). An unscrupulous American steals the Crown jewels of France, and in the guise of a Communist leader plans a yet bigger haul. The imaginary narrator is a police-officer on his trial. [Harper, New York : o.p. ; Burt, New York : o.p. ; Constable : o.p.]

—— *The Reckoning.* 1905

Fourth in the series that began with *Cardigan* and *The Maid-at-Arms* (the third part not yet published). The closing incidents of the War of Independence, its effect upon the great landed families in the northern part of New York State (1781), the doings of the Oneidas, etc. Washington figures, and most of the characters are real people. [Appleton, New York : o.p. ; Grosset, New York : o.p. ; Constable : o.p.]

—— *The Fighting Chance.* 1906

The love-story of a man touched with hereditary dipsomania and a society girl—two of the few tolerable people in a crowd of fashionable New Yorkers. Describes with evident complacency the snobbishness and luxury, the vulgar, glittering smartness, and the pinchbeck sentimentality of these empty-headed time-killers. [Appleton, New York : o.p. ; Unwin.]

—— *The Younger Set.* 1907

Another fulsome panorama of life among " the rich and the great, the steel kings, and copper kings, and oil kings, and their heirs and dauphins," the smart set being contrasted with a healthier generation that seems to be growing up. A chivalrous young soldier, who divorced his wife out of sheer unselfishness, comes back to New York and has passages of reviving affection, but marries a finer type of girl. [Appleton, New York : o.p. ; Constable : o.p.]

—— *Ailsa Paige.* 1910

A rather slight and melodramatic Civil War story, with some excellent fighting scenes, especially of McClellan's unsuccessful campaign in the peninsula. [Appleton, New York ; Newnes.]

—— *The Common Law.* 1911

A typical specimen of the fashionable American novel of fashionable life—sentimental, unreal, and luscious in its description of the fainéant rich. The fashionable hero, who is an artist, wants to marry his model—hence the imbroglio. [Grosset, New York ; Newnes.]

—— *The Crimson Tide.* 1919

The murder of the Russian imperial family and the atrocities of the Battalion of Death provide suitable interest in the earlier part, but the novel goes to pieces in the later scenes in New York. [Appleton, New York and London.]

—— *The Little Red Foot.* 1921

A Red Indian romance of 1774–7, dealing with the Iroquois and Burgoyne's expedition. [Doubleday, Doran, New York ; Hodder.]

—— *The Man they Hanged.* 1926

The hero is the famous Captain Kidd in the eventful ten years before his hanging in 1701 ; scene, chiefly New York. [Appleton, New York and London.]

—— *Marie Halkett ; a true story.* 1926

Rum-running and murder off the American coast. [Unwin.]

—— *The Drums of Aulone.* 1927

Adventures of a French girl in Paris, London, and Canada, at the time of Mme de Maintenon and the Huguenot persecution, events leading to the expulsion of James II, and the repulse of the English fleet from Quebec. [Appleton, New York and London.]

—— *The Painted Minx.* 1930

A romance of the occupation of New York by British troops (1777–81). Major André plays a large part. [Appleton, New York and London.]

CHAMIER, Capt. Frederick [1796–1870]. *Ben Brace of Nelson's " Agamemnon."* 1835

Ben Brace's autobiography is really a study of Allen, Nelson's faithful servant. Forms a naval history of the wars from 1797–1816. An imitation of Captain Marryat. [Ed. by E. A. Baker (Half-forgotten Books) 1905, Routledge : o.p.]

—— *The Life of a Sailor.* 1834
—— *The Saucy Arethusa.* 1836
—— *Jack Adams.* 1838

Similar nautical stories of the great wars. Chamier saw service in the American War of 1812 and later, but his knowledge of the earlier period was based on investigations for his continuation of James's *Naval History*. [All o.p.]

—— *Tom Bowling : a tale of the sea.* 1839

A composite portrait, based on the histories of a famous captain of a frigate, Richard Bowen, and of Nelson's flag-captain, Hardy, with others : the name Tom Bowling was lifted from Smollett's *Roderick Random*. Capture of Martinique, seizure of the Cape, the action off Algeciras in 1801, and other events, slavishly plagiarized from history (1780–1815, especially 1794–5). [Ed. by E. A. Baker (Half-forgotten Books), Routledge, 1905 : o.p.]

CHAMIER, George [Australian]. *Philosopher Dick : Adventures and Contemplations of a New Zealand Shepherd.* 1890

The shepherd, a cultured, meditative man, spends years of his life in the solitude of a mountain sheep-farm. This is not merely description of the wild existence of settlers and the details of sheep-farming thirty years ago, but also an analytical study of solitude and its effect on a thoughtful mind. [Unwin : o.p.]

CHAMISSO DE BONCOURT, Ludwig Carl Adelbert von [German ; 1781–1838]. *The Shadow-less Man : Peter Schlemihl* (Peter Schlemihl's wundersame Geschichte, 1814).   [juvenile] 1824
The story of the man who sold his own shadow was written partly as a diversion from his scientific studies and partly to entertain the children of a friend. [Transl. by Sir J. BOWRING, Whittaker : o.p. ; *illus.* by Gordon Browne, Chatto, 1910.]

CHAMSON, André [French ; *b.* 1900]. *Roux the Bandit* (Roux le bandit, 1925)   1929
Roux is a Cévennois peasant who refuses to fight in the great war, and is hunted by the gendarmes, revered and fed by the villagers. [Transl. by Van Wyck BROOKS, Scribner, New York ; Gollancz.]

CHAPMAN, Mrs. Maristan [American ; *b.* 1895]. *The Happy Mountain.*   1928
The hackneyed tale of the raw youth who goes off to see the world, his sweetheart left at home, and the rascally would-be seducer, seems to have been written to show off the uncouth dialect and manners of the Kentucky mountaineers. [Viking Press, New York ; Grosset, New York ; Philip Allan.]

CHARDONNE, Jacques [French ; *b.* 1884]. *Eva* (Eva ; ou le journal interrompu).   1930
The story is a trite and slender affair, how a husband is cured of his infatuation for a dull and egotistic wife ; it is handled, however, in a very unconventional and arresting way. [Transl. by Viola Gerard GARVIN, Gollancz.]

CHARLES THE GRETE. *The Lyf of the Noble and Crysten Prynce ; translated from the French by William Caxton and printed by him.*   1485
Translated from the prose romance *Fierabras*, which was a compilation partly from Vincent de Beauvais' *Speculum Historiale* and partly from the late twelfth century *chanson de geste, Fierabras.* The English metrical romance *Sir Ferumbras* is from this *chanson*, which was probably the central portion of a longer poem known as *Balan. The Sowdone of Babyloyne* is probably taken from the same lost poem. Caxton follows the original so slavishly that at times, the editor points out, difficulties have to be explained by reference to the French. The book purports to be a life of Charlemagne, and begins with a genealogical history of the early kings of France ; but it contains far more fable than fact. After briefly relating how Charles was elected Emperor of Rome and delivered the Holy Land from the miscreants, it launches out into more marvellous incidents, for which the wars with the Saracens supplied material. Outstanding episodes are : Oliver's fight with the giant Fierabras ; the capture of the Twelve Peers by Balan, the Saracen " Admiral," and their succour by the hand of Balan's daughter Floripas, who afterwards marries Guy of Burgoyne ; the forcing of the marvellous Bridge of Mantrible, and the death of Balan ; Charlemagne's conquest of Spain, the duel of Roland and the giant Ferragus, the treason of Ganelon, the French defeat and the death of Roland at Roncesvalles. The book covers the same ground as that of the metrical romances *Sir Ferumbras, The Sowdone of Babyloyne, Roland and Vernagu,* and the *Song of Roland.* [Edited, with introd., notes, and glossary, by Sidney J. H. HERRTAGE, 2 vols. (Early English Text Soc.), Oxford Press, 1881. Retold by Robert STEELE, G. Allen, 1895 : o.p.]

CHARLES, Elizabeth [*née* Rundle ; 1828–96]. *Chronicles of the Schönberg-Cotta Family.*   [juvenile] 1863
The domestic and civic side of Luther and Melanchthon's lives (1503–47) ; a book founded on painstaking research, and animated largely by a didactic purpose. [Nelson : o.p. ; Partridge : o.p. ; Dodd & Mead, New York : o.p. ; Burt, New York ; Augustana Co., Minneapolis.]

—— *Diary of Mrs. Kitty Trevelyan.*   [juvenile] 1864
" A story of the times of Whitefield and the Wesleys " (1745–50). [Nelson : o.p.]

—— *The Draytons and the Davenants.*   [juvenile] 1867
—— *On Both Sides of the Sea* [sequel].   [juvenile] 1868
The Civil War, the Commonwealth, and the Restoration. Strong domestic and religious. interest. Baxter, Foxe, Bunyan, etc., come in. First story covers 1637–49, and the sequel 1649–66. [(1) and (2), Nelson : o.p.]

—— *Conquering and to Conquer.*   [juvenile] 1876
Told by a centenarian abbess—the days of her youth, the persecutions, the Christian life of her mother and herself, the slow conversion of her philosophic father, the careers of Jerome and St. Augustine. The year 404 was signalized by the sacrifice of the monk Telemachus as a protest against the gladiatorial shows. [S.P.C.K. : o.p. ; Dodd & Mead, New York : o.p.]

CHARLTON, Randal. *Mave.*   1906
A tragedy of insensate primordial passion, enacted in some country place, forest-girt, in some past time, apparently the eighteenth century. Mave is an innocent and ignorant child, who loves divinely because her lover is her God. But misfortunes separate them ; and meanwhile Mave's beauty rouses in a grave ascetic, a thinker absorbed in books and theory, such passions as hurl him into folly, insanity, murder. [Methuen : o.p.]

—— *The Virgin Widow.*   1908
A sombre tale from beginning to end, apparently of the time of William IV. A man's passionate, undivulged love, a mysterious murder, a woman's perjury for a man who she thinks is in love with her, and her tragic death. [Methuen : o.p. ; Dillingham, New York : o.p.]

CHASE, Beatrice [Olive Catharine Parr ; *b.* 1874]. *The Heart of the Moor.*   1914
Rather than tell a story, this and other works of this author attempt to capture the spirit and atmosphere of Dartmoor. [Jenkins ; Benziger, New York : o.p.]

CHATEAUBRIAND, François René, Vicomte de [French ; 1768–1848]. *Atala* (Atala ; ou, les amours de deux sauvages dans le désert, 1801).   1884
Originally an episode in *Les Natchez,* and later incorporated in *Le Génie du Christianisme.* A famous prose idyll of resurgent romanticism—" a sort of poem," says the author, " half descriptive, half dramatic . . . to which I have tried to give the most ancient forms ; it is divided into prologue, narrative, and epilogue." Recounts in an elevated strain the passionate love of two beings, who are not really savages, but have

CHATEAUBRIAND, François René (*continued*).

the freedom of the savage with the knowledge and susceptibility given by European training. The fervid descriptions of woods and prairies and mighty rivers often reach the sublime, in spite of rhetoric and sentimentality ; but the extent to which Chateaubriand freed himself from convention can be realized only by comparison with the Radcliffian romances. He had himself wandered in the solitudes of the North American backwoods, where the scenes take place. [Transl. by J. S. HARVEY, *illus.* by Gustave Doré, Cassell, 1884 : o.p. Transl. by Caleb BINGHAM, *sub tit. Atala ; or, The Love and Constancy of Two Savages in the Desert,* in 1802, ed. W. L. Schwartz, Stanford University Press (Milford) 1931.]

—— *René : a tale from the French* (René, 1802). 1813

A long reverie, in which an unhappy man (a shadow of Chateaubriand himself) reviews his life and cries out for the happiness that earth cannot give ; in short, an expression, like Goethe's *Werther*, of the *mal du siècle*, the disillusionment and *tædium vitæ* from which there is no escape but suicide. Lyrical in the diction, which shows strongly the influence of Macpherson's *Ossian*. More even than in *Atala*, with which it is linked by the introduction of Charles as René's confidant, the scenery is but a vehicle to express the surging emotions. First included with and then detached from the *Génie du Christianisme*. [o.p.]

—— *The Two Martyrs : a moral tale* (Les martyrs ; ou, le triomphe de la religion chrétienne, 1809). 1819

A prose epic, utilizing the miracles and the heroes of Christianity in lieu of the demigods and marvels of classical poetry, to present an ornate and comprehensive picture of Christianity rising superior to paganism. Borrows deliberately the methods of Homer, Virgil, Milton, and Tasso. Invocations in right epic style, strange voyages, supernatural wonders in camp and city, scenes above and below the earth, angels, demons, and mythical men—all are freely introduced, sometimes with magnificent impressiveness. [Transl. by W. J. WALTER.]

CHÂTEAUBRIANT, Alphonse de [French ; *b.* 1877]. *The Keynote* (Monsieur de Lourdines : histoire d'un gentilhomme campagnard, 1911). 1912

A pensive, elegiac, not to say sentimental, idyll of Poitou, the forest scenery and bucolic life prettily rendered. Like Wordsworth's *Michael*, the châtelain is ruined by his prodigal son ; but the latter comes home, and is moved to remorse on listening to his lonely father's violin. The date is 1840, and the decay of the landowning class is typified. [Transl. by Lady Theodora DAVIDSON, Hodder : o.p. ; Doran, New York : o.p.]

CHÂTELAINE OF VERGI, THE (1282–8). 1903

Paraphrase of a mediæval poem (1282–8), which showed a distinct approximation to the modern novel in its treatment of real life. M. Raynaud conjectures that it was based on an actual scandal at the Court of Burgundy (1267–72) ; but Prof. Brandin contests this. The story is very tragic. A knight secretly loves the châtelaine, and the jealous Duchess of Burgundy wrings from him the secret ; the lady dies of a broken heart and the knight kills himself. Bandello and Marguerite of Navarre both had versions of such a story. [Done into English by Alice KEMP-WELCH. Ed. with introd., by L. BRANDIN, PH.D. ; with contemporary *illus.*, Chatto ; Oxford Press, New York.]

CHEKHOV, Anton Pavlovich [Russian ; 1860–1904]. *The Black Monk ; and other stories.* 1903

Chekhov is often compared with Maupassant ; but his art is finer and subtler, and the matter and spirit of his stories entirely different. He evokes an irresistible sense of actuality by plunging us into the troubled, restless stream of everyday life. We feel the confusion, the incoherence, and yet the hidden connexions, the " altogetherness " of the human world. There is none of the simplification, none of the emphasis, the insulation of the significant, which are characteristic of Western art : nothing could differ more from ordinary " intellectual realism." His characters are infinitely various ; but those that stand out are morbid, neurotic, over-sensitive Russians, oppressed by the banality of life or its tragedy. Of these twelve tales, *The Black Monk* is about the phantom conjured up by the unhealthy imagination of a hard-worked and disappointed professor ; *In Exile, Rothschild's Fiddle,* and *Two Tragedies* are studies of mental and moral wretchedness. [Transl. by R. E. C. LONG, Duckworth.]

—— *The Kiss ; and other stories.* 1908

The kiss is given in mistake to a poor, shy, clumsy young officer—this is a touching analysis of a momentary impulse of strong emotion, of an insignificant thing which is deeply significant to the individual concerned. *The Muzhiks* is a terrible and pitiful sketch of the peasantry, steeped in ignorance and misery. In *The Princess*, a plain-spoken doctor shows a fine lady how completely heartless she is. In *The Runaway*, a little boy in a hospital is terror-stricken by the sight of suffering and death. There are no crises here, no climaxes. As in his plays, Chekhov somehow dramatizes the undramatic, and arouses a keen sense of absorption and suspense even when nothing much happens. The exquisite delicacy with which we are made to see what is continually overlooked or denied or dissembled, is the very antithesis, for example, of the coarse and savage realism of Gorky. [Transl. by R. E. C. LONG, Duckworth.]

—— *Stories of Russian Life.* 1914

Most of these stories can be read elsewhere, several in preceding volumes by the same publisher. This is a laboured and ineffective translation. The last and longest, *The Ravine*, is one of Chekhov's best, and thoroughly typical. It is a moving picture of life in a small industrial village. There are dishonest tradesmen, credulous muzhiks, flaunting women, no better than they should be, a simple peasant girl, brutally maltreated but accepting her fate with the patience of utter simplicity, a young fellow who has been coining roubles, living in dread of the inevitable detection, and so on. From the confusion, the incoherence, the chiaroscuro of ugly and beautiful, foul and innocent, cruel and soft-hearted, there emerges, as always in Chekhov's stories, a poetic beauty, a harmony, as from a great, complex picture—even a moral beauty, that redeems this heterogeneous world from all its deformities. [Transl. by Marion FELL, Duckworth ; Scribner, New York.]

—— *The Bet ; and other stories.* 1915

All but one are short stories, showing, with Chekhov's clairvoyance, how things happen and how things are felt. *The Bet* shows a man coming to despise what he has sacrificed his all for. *The Fit* is a saddening

CHEKHOV, Anton Pavlovich (*continued*).

glimpse of prostitution ; *Misfortune*, a subtle analysis of the power of the senses. *A Tedious Story* appears elsewhere under a slightly different title. [Transl. by S. KOTELIANSKY and J. Middleton MURRY, Allen & Unwin.]

—— *The Steppe ; and other stories.* 1915

Stories of rural Russia, most of which also appear in other collections, e.g. *The Hollow*, elsewhere called *The Ravine*. *The Steppe* is the narrative of a schoolboy's journey, in motley company, across the great flats of middle Russia. In its perfect naturalness, the accidental way it begins and ends, the passing incidents, the various glimpses of character, it is an epitome of Russian life and of the art of Chekhov. *Of Love* may well be compared—and contrasted—with *The Statue and the Bust*. [Transl., awkward and unidiomatic, by Adeline Lister KAYE, Heinemann : o.p.]

—— *Russian Silhouettes : more stories of Russian life.* 1915

A Journey by Cart relates the similar experience of an elderly schoolmistress to that recounted in *The Steppe*. *The Bishop* portrays a fine old churchman, growing weary of life and its trivial duties but ever stronger and stronger in faith. *At Christmas-time* is the tale of the letter sent by two old people to their married daughter, and of the reception it gets. [Transl. by Marian FELL, Scribner, New York ; Duckworth.]

—— *The Darling ; and other stories.* 1916

Good examples of Chekhov's penetrating vision and a sensitiveness too tender for irony. *Neighbours* brings out finely the Russian failing : loftiness of attitude and intent, stupidity and ineffectiveness in action. [Transl. by Constance GARNETT ; introd. by Edward Garnett, Chatto (Macmillan, New York).]

—— *The Duel ; and other stories.* 1916

Here appear *The Princess* (see above) and *At Home*, two notable pieces. The latter relates with all Chekhov's tenderness, how a father rouses his little boy's imagination with a story, when he had utterly failed to move him with precepts and warning. [Transl. by Constance GARNETT ; introd. by Edward Garnett, Chatto (Macmillan, New York).]

—— *The Lady with the Dog ; and other stories.* 1917

Early and late work. One of the earlier, *The Black Monk*, appears above. Most are gloomy and pessimistic in feeling, but admirable examples of Chekhov's technique. There is humour, however, in the darkest, and notably in the long piece, *An Anonymous Story*. [Transl. by C. GARNETT, Chatto (Macmillan, New York).]

—— *The Wife ; and other stories.* 1918

A husband, in the title-story, tells his tale of unhappy married life. In *A Dreary Story*, a study of old age, the numbing sense of failure and disillusionment overwhelms. In *Difficult People*, personal rancours end in tragedy. There is a contrasting beauty in *The Student* and in *Happiness* ; and *Gusev* is one of those stories that bring out, as only Chekhov can, the harmony and beauty immanent in a world that seems so squalid and hopeless. [Transl. by Mrs. C. GARNETT, Chatto ; Macmillan, New York.]

—— *The Bishop ; and other stories.* 1919

Stories chiefly of priests and peasants. The longest, *The Steppe* (see also above), is a supreme example of the unity his æsthetic method impresses upon the heterogeneity of things. [Transl. by Mrs. C. GARNETT, Chatto (Macmillan, New York).]

—— *The Schoolmistress ; and other stories.* 1920

First-class examples of Chekhov's delicate and beautiful art : e.g. *Exile*, *Misery*, and *The Cattle-dealers*. [Transl. by Constance GARNETT, Chatto (Macmillan, New York).]

—— *The Chorus-Girl ; and other stories.* 1920

The long story, *My Life : the story of a provincial*, portrays a young man who obeys his impulse to work for the cause of the poor, sacrifices his position, and becomes a common workman. His father's harshness alienates him, and leads to his sister's downfall. But he finds no real solution to the difficulties of life. *A Father* sketches the reverse, successful son and miserable father. Includes also *At a Country House, On the Road, Zinotchka, Ivan Matveyitch, Bad Weather, A Gentleman Friend, Verotchka, A Trivial Incident*, and *Rothschild's Fiddle*. [Transl. by Constance GARNETT, (*Works, v.* 8) Chatto (Macmillan, New York).]

—— *The Horse-Stealers ; and other stories.* 1921

The Horse-Stealers ; Ward No. 6 ; *An Avenger ;* and nineteen shorter sketches. [Transl. by Constance GARNETT, (*Works, v.* 10) Chatto (Macmillan, New York).]

—— *The Schoolmaster ; and other stories.* 1921

The Schoolmaster ; Betrothed ; Enemies ; The Examining Magistrate ; and twenty-five shorter tales. [Transl. by Constance GARNETT, (*Works, v.* 11), Chatto (Macmillan, New York).]

—— *The Cook's Wedding ; and other stories.* 1922

Many of these twenty-five stories deal in very kindly fashion with children or animals ; *Home* propounds an interesting problem of moral education ; *Sleepy* portrays a miserable ill-used servant-girl ; *Kashtanka* is the story of a dog. [Transl. by Constance GARNETT, (*Works, v.* 12) Chatto (Macmillan, New York).]

—— *Love ; and other stories.* 1922

Includes *The Death of a Government Clerk*. Eleven of these twenty-four sketches are early work published posthumously. Completes Mrs. Garnett's transl. of Chekhov's work. [Transl. by Constance GARNETT, (*Works, v.* 13) Chatto (Macmillan, New York) ; *Selected Tales*, (25 from the whole body), *id.*]

—— *The Grasshopper ; and other stories.* 1926

Some of Chekhov's very best are included here, though the titles may be different : e.g. *The Black Monk, The Wager, In the Ravine*. The title-piece is an excellent illustration of his restrained power : a social butterfly is married to a medical man whose genius she utterly fails to comprehend. He lets himself become fatally infected with diphtheria. *The Wager* might be read as an apologue, and a great one. A man accepts

CHEKHOV, Anton Pavlovich (*continued*).
a two million wager from a wealthy banker to stay fifteen years in solitary confinement. The end is strange and impressive. The English of the translation is uneven and at times illiterate. [Transl. by A. E. Chamot, Stanley Paul, McKay, Philadephia.]

CHERBULIEZ, Charles Victor [French ; 1829–99]. *Count Kostia* (Le comte Kostia, 1863). 1873
Cherbuliez may be ranked, in a rough-and-ready way, with our Henry Seton Merriman. This striking melodrama, in which the heroine masquerades as a boy and fraternizes with the young man who is to be her lover, is a fair example of his brilliant and inventive fiction, with its lively dialogue, punctuated with epigram. The lady's father, the Count Kostia, is a moody and tyrannical Russian living in a castle on the Rhine. How his doubts as to his daughter's legitimacy are set at rest, and how the love affair is to end happily, are the business of the plot. [Transl. by Ashley, Holt, New York : o.p.]

—— *The Romance of an Honest Woman* (Le roman d'une honnête femme, 1867). 1874
A high-spirited woman, married to a coxcomb, rebels against his assumed superiority of sex. While he coquets with another woman, she plays the same game with such adroitness that at length he is brought to reason. The character of the heroine, brought up in seclusion, her honesty and dignity, and intellectual keenness tempered by extreme ignorance of the world, make an interesting study. The charms of country life in Dauphiné are the burden of many descriptive passages. [Transl., Gill, Boston : o.p.]

—— *Prosper Randoce* (1868). 1874
Prosper Randoce is a typical product of his day, a literary man of cold disposition, who is for ever simulating deep emotion and enthusiasm. His weaknesses are aptly accentuated by his juxtaposition with a man of exactly opposite disposition, a confirmed sceptic, thoroughly amiable and kind-hearted. [Transl. by C. Benson, Holt, New York : o.p.]

—— *Joseph Noirel's Revenge* (La revanche de Joseph Noirel, 1870). 1874
The scene is Geneva, where the heroine appears as the joy of her parents' household, and in the troubles of her married life and the tragic closing scene bears herself courageously and with abnegation of self. In the catastrophe, Marguerite, wronged by her husband, calls on her socialist lover to stab her and afterwards himself. [Transl. by West, Holt, New York : o.p.]

—— *The Blue-Eyed Meta Holdenis* (Méta Holdenis, 1873). 1881
Meta is a fascinating adventuress, but so impetuous that through sheer imprudence she fails to secure either of her lovers. Next to Meta, Tony the painter stands out conspicuous, a mixture of impulsiveness and worldly wisdom ; and the tale of his two love affairs with the German siren illustrates capitally Cherbuliez's art in developing a plot out of the natural play of character. [Vizetelly : o.p. ; Maclaren, Edinburgh, 1904 : o.p. ; Appleton, New York : o.p.]

—— *Miss Rovel* (1875). 1875
An international novel roughly handling eccentricities, scene Geneva again. An untamed English girl becomes intimately acquainted with a retiring scholar, who, having been disappointed in love, is a confirmed misogynist. The novelist brings about some piquant situations in arranging a match between the pair. [Transl. by Shaw, Estes, Boston : o.p.]

—— *Samuel Brohl and Partner* (Samuel Brohl et Cie., 1877). 1880
A bizarre and complicated plot-novel, full of unexpected situations. Brohl the German Jew, a clever and unscrupulous rascal, personates a deceased Polish count with amazing success, and nearly manages to carry off an heiress. [Vizetelly : o.p. ; Dodd & Mead, New York : o.p. ; Burt, New York, 1906 : o.p.]

—— *Jean Têterol's Idea* (L'idée de Jean Têterol, 1878). 1878
A peasant, affronted by a haughty aristocrat, goes away and makes a colossal fortune, and, on returning to his native village, finding his enemy dead, manages by financial strategy to get the son into his power. The price of redemption is that the baron's daughter shall marry the parvenu's son ; but the latter revolts from such a bargain, and, renouncing the authority of his father, goes off to earn his own living. The result of this magnanimous course of action is a love-match. [Burt, New York, 1906 : o.p.]

—— *The Tutor's Secret* (Le secret du précepteur, 1893). 1893
The scholarly young tutor of two attractive girls, handicapped as a lover by his position, tells his own tale, of which the termination is not a prosperous one for him. [Transl. by R. Derecheff, Arnold : o.p.]
The following have not been translated : *L'aventure de Ladislas Bolski*, a character-study on Cherbuliez's favourite lines—determinist if not avowedly fatalistic. Ladislas is a Pole, the son of a traitor, chivalrous, ardent, unstable, who puts himself to the test by a year of probation, serving the revolutionary committee at Paris, and succumbs to his own fundamental weakness. *La ferme du Choquard*, agricultural people delineated in a way radically the same, that is to say, woven into a story, in which character is the motive force.

CHESNEY, Sir George Tomkyns [1830–95]. *A True Reformer.* 1873
Opens with chapters of Anglo-Indian life at Simla under Lord Mayo (1869–72), and continues the hero's autobiography in England, where he tries as M.P. to pass a measure for reforming the army. Contains a large amount of special technical knowledge, which is carefully explained. [3 vols., Blackwood : o.p.]

—— *The Dilemma : a tale of the Mutiny.* 1876
How the English in an up-country station are surprised by the Mutiny and forced to defend their home desperately against odds. A dramatic story, founded on first-hand information, and full of the interest of individual character. [Blackwood : o.p.]

—— *The Private Secretary.* 1881
A young philanthropist falls in love with his private secretary ; but as his income depends on his offering marriage to a cousin, he is for a time hindered from marrying her, and induces her to become his mistress. Interest is concentrated on the heroine, on her gradual falling in love, and the mental struggle between self-respect and the dread of poverty for herself and her orphan brother. [3 vols., Blackwood : o.p.]

CHESNUTT, Charles Waddell [American ; b. 1858]. *The Conjure Woman.* 1899
Sketches of negro life in the Southern States told in dialect by an old coloured servant. The natural environment is depicted poetically as a sylvan background to the play of character and racial idiosyncrasy. [Houghton, Boston ; Gay & Bird : o.p.]

CHESNUTT, Charles Waddell (*continued*). *The Wife of his Youth ; and other stories of the colour line.* 1899

A calm, sympathetic, impartial survey of the negro race in the United States, and all the problems connected with their economic position in the South or the social stigma attached to those in the North. The author's knowledge is wide and profound. [Houghton, Boston : o.p.]

—— *A Matter of Principle.* 1900

A comedy making admirable fun of the snobbery prevailing in the Blue Vein circles, i.e. the Mulattoes who will have nothing to do with their black cousins. A young lady who is nearly white rejects a most eligible suitor under the impression that he is a pure negro. [o.p.]

CHESSON, Nora [Mrs. Winifred Hugh, *née* Hopper ; Irish ; 1871–1906]. *The Bell and the Arrow.* 1905

A love-story with interesting character-drawing of Devonshire gentlefolk, e.g. the exquisite love-stricken old spinster. Not a very remarkable novel, yet one worth reading with Mrs. Chesson's poetical work, which so often has the same subdued sense of the tragic. [Laurie : o.p.]

—— *Father Felix's Chronicle.* 1907

A priest gives his memories of the troublous times of Henry IV (1367–1413), times which the author has studied with care and industry. [Ed. by W. H. Chesson, Unwin : o.p. ; Wessels, New York : o.p.]

CHESTERTON, Gilbert Keith [*b.* 1874]. *The Napoleon of Notting Hill.* 1904

Brilliant nonsense, not the serious tomfoolery of some later stories, although the last paragraph indicates that even a joke may suggest things that are " real and passionate." A London suburb half-a-century from now becomes an independent city, with walls, provost, and pageantry, and sanguinary war arises when its rights and autonomy are threatened by modernizing neighbours. The author's delight in mediævalism, colour, heroism, and bloodshed—on paper—have full fling. [Hodder ; Musson Co., Toronto.]

—— *The Man who was Thursday.* 1908

Here the Rabelaisian fun is fast and furious. The oracles are masquerading as clowns and harlequins : wisdom flashes out in star-showers. The story seems as empty and preposterous as a nightmare ; then, suddenly, it has a meaning. A club of seven anarchists are in a plot to destroy the world ; six of them, after terrific efforts to run each other to earth and foil the deadly scheme, turn out to be police officers in disguise. But narrative and talk are a form of dialectic. The chief detective sitting in the darkness had given each man his commission. It is all an allegory of human life, the everlasting struggle in which man finds it so hard to distinguish friend from foe, right from wrong ; where the whole basis and ultimate sanction of his faith must be an enigma. [Arrowsmith ; Dodd & Mead, New York ; Modern Lib., New York.]

—— *The Ball and the Cross.* 1910

The starting-point is the arrival of Lucifer in an airship, from which a holy man from Bulgaria alights on the ball of St. Paul's. But, again, under a veil of irresponsible extravaganza shines steadily—or unsteadily—a truth of great moment. All the world is mad, and madness is the only sanity : down with eugenics, bureaucracy, and all the other tyrannies ! [Wells, Gardner ; Lane, New York.]

—— *The Innocence of Father Brown.* 1911
—— *The Wisdom of Father Brown.* 1914
—— *The Incredulity of Father Brown.* 1926
—— *The Secret of Father Brown.* 1927

Paradoxical yet for the most part philosophically convincing variants of the ordinary detective story ; Father Brown is the Chestertonian Sherlock Holmes, whose detective faculty is simply the philosopher's penetration into the working of the normal mind. [(1), (2), (3), and (4), Cassell ; (1), (2), and (3) Dodd & Mead, New York ; (4), Harper, New York. *The Father Brown Stories* (the four complete in 1 vol.) Cassell, 1929.]

—— *Manalive.* 1912

Another philosophic extravaganza, cryptically expounding the author's views on society, religion, the Church of England, etc. The attitude of romantic bewilderment at things as they are is the only sane one. [Arrowsmith ; Dodd & Mead, New York.]

—— *The Flying Inn.* 1914

An extravaganza of the maddest kind, waging a crusade against those who would refuse us any more cakes and ale. When the modern puritans have made drinking and the sale of liquor an indictable offence, two champions of freedom and joviality set up a peripatetic tavern to outwit Malvolio. A satire very good in parts, and to be taken seriously—in parts. [Methuen ; Dodd & Mead, New York ; Doubleday (Garden City Co.), New York.]

—— *The Man who knew too much ; and other stories.* 1922

Twelve stories each unravelling some fantastic mystery. In their own queer fashion, their hyperbole of situation and character, at once unreal and convincing, the mysteries are parables of certain social evils, and the solutions demonstrate the folly of slipshod thinking and of deduction from hypotheses instead of facts. [Cassell ; Harper, New York ; Burt, New York.]

—— *The Poet and the Lunatics : episodes in the life of Gabriel Gale.* 1929

The chief agent in the fantastic adventures, mystifications, and surprising solutions is here a freakish poet and painter. Good examples are *The Yellow Bird, The Shadow of the Shark, The House of the Peacock,* and *The Purple Jewel.* [Cassell ; Dodd & Mead, New York.]

—— *Four Faultless Felons.* 1930

The Chestertonian hyperbole and paradox find their mark here in mock " detective stories " rehabilitating the characters of four members of the Club of Men Misunderstood. Chestertonian anti-Semitism and Catholic propaganda come off second-best in the entertainment. [Cassell ; Dodd & Mead, New York.]

CHILDERS, Robert Erskine [Irish ; 1870–1922]. *The Riddle of the Sands.* 1903

An excellent story of espionage : the adventures of a pair of Englishmen cruising off Friesland, who discover a secret German naval base ; intended to demonstrate the possibility of a German invasion of England. [Sidgwick ; Lauriat, Boston.]

CHIRIKOV, Evgeny Nikolaevitch [Russian]. *Marka of the Pits* (1911).   1930
    A pretty crude example of the fiction written a quarter of a century ago to show up the poverty and degradation of Russian life. Marka is a spirited girl living in hideous surroundings in a town on the Volga. [Transl. by L. ZARINE, Alston Rivers.]

CHOLMONDELEY, Mary [*d.* 1925]. *Sir Charles Danvers.*   1889
    A plot-novel, reviving as hero a character from an earlier novel, *The Danvers Jewels.* Satire against stupid conventions and stupid people, who figure in plenty, often dropping into caricature. The writer's strength is not in portraying individuals, but in the dramatic presentation of universal emotions. [Macmillan : o.p.; Harper, New York : o.p.]

—— *Diana Tempest.*   1893
    In an unwary moment a ruined uncle is tempted into a bet that launches a series of murderous plots against his rich nephew. His helpless and remorseful suspense, the peril of his victim, and the melodramatic justice that falls on his own son, are the sensational elements of the story. Then we get the hero's chequered love affairs, social scenes more or less satirical, and varied phases of character. Diana is a high-spirited girl, superior to the petty ambitions of fashionable life, who rejects wealth rather than honour. [Macmillan ; Appleton, New York : o.p.]

—— *Red Pottage.*   1899
    Strong in the psychology of motive and conduct in arbitrary and exacting circumstances. The initial situation of a very dramatic plot results from a duel by casting lots and the guilty man's failure to carry out the sentence on himself. Censures religious savagery and other kinds of humbug, and caricatures a narrow-minded parson and some pseudo-literary people. [Nash : Harper, New York : o.p.]

—— *Prisoners—Fast Bound in Misery and Iron.*   1906
    Like all Miss Cholmondeley's novels, this is a romantic situation grounded and worked out on a sound basis of natural motive. An innocent man suffers imprisonment (in Italy) for murder, in order to shield the charming but selfish woman whom he loves ; and she keeps silence. [Hutchinson : o.p. ; Copp, Clark, Toronto : o.p.]

—— *Notwithstanding.*   1913
    A quiet novel of country life, about a girl who is saved only by accident from an indiscretion, and later falls in love with the cousin of the man who had compromised her. [Nash ; *sub tit. After All*, Appleton, New York.]

CHOPIN, Kate [American ; *d.* 1904]. *Bayou Folk.*   1894
    Stories and characterizations of the descendants of Acadian exiles in Louisiana, among whom the original traits seem to have been preserved in exceptional purity—an indolent, irresponsible race, keenly alive to personal honour and sensitive to passion—by a Southern lady who knows and loves them. [Houghton, Boston : o.p.]

CHOTZINOFF, Samuel [American]. *Eroica : a novel based on the life of Ludwig van Beethoven.*   1930
    Deals with the great composer's life at Bonn and Vienna. [Simon & Schuster, New York.]

CHRISTIE, Agatha [*née* Miller ; now Mrs. Max Mallowan]. *The Mysterious Affair at Styles.*   1921
—— *The Murder on the Links.*   1923
—— *Poirot Investigates.*   1925
    Good examples of that ingenious confection described by the late Lord Birkenhead—" the detective novel is a gigantic imposture practised on a credulous public." [(1), (2), (3) ; together, *An Agatha Christie Omnibus*, Lane, 1931 ; (1), (2), and (3), Dodd & Mead, New York.]

CHURCH, Rev. Alfred John [1829–1912]. *Two Thousand Years Ago.*   [juvenile] 1885
    Spartacus and Mithridates (72–63 B.C.) : scene Sicily and Asia Minor and the Mediterranean. [Seeley : o.p. ; *sub tit. Lucius ; the adventures of a Roman boy*, Dodd & Mead, New York, 1924.]

—— *To the Lions.*   [juvenile] 1889
    The Christians in the persecution under Trajan, and the younger Pliny as governor of Bythinia (110). [Seeley ; Putnam, New York : o.p.]

—— *The Burning of Rome.*   [juvenile] 1892
    A story of Nero's days (64–70). [Seeley ; Macmillan, New York : o.p.]

—— *Lords of the World.*   [juvenile] 1898
    The fall of Carthage and Corinth (146 B.C.). [Seeley : o.p. ; Scribner, New York : o.p.]

—— *The Crown of Pine.*   [juvenile] 1905
    Rome and Corinth in the reign of Claudius (*c.* 41–8). The banishment of the Jews, St. Paul's preaching, the Isthmian games and the exploits of a Greek athlete. [Seeley ; Scribner, New York : o.p.]

CHURCH, Rev. Alfred John, and SEELEY, Richmond. *Patriot and Hero.*   [juvenile] 1889
    A story of Maccabæan times (174–161 B.C.). Originally entitled *The Hammer.* [Seeley.]

CHURCH, Samuel Harden [American ; *b.* 1858]. *John Marmaduke : a romance of the English invasion of Ireland in* 1649.   1889
    A thoroughly historical novel, studiously retailing the events of the Cromwellian reduction of Ireland to soon after the massacre of Drogheda (1649). Marmaduke is an officer under General Ireton and an idolizer of Cromwell. [Putnam, New York and London : o.p.]

—— *Penruddock of the White Lambs.*   [juvenile] 1903
    Cromwell's times in Holland, England, and America (1655). [Stokes, New York : o.p.]

CHURCHILL, Winston [American ; *b.* 1871]. *The Celebrity : an episode.*   1898
    Satirizes an author, whose books had become fashionable, but who is shown as a vain and shallow woman-hunter. He is made the victim of an elaborate practical joke. [Macmillan, New York and London.]

CHURCHILL, Winston (*continued*). *Richard Carvel.*   1899

An autobiography dealing with the period of the Revolution, and, like *Esmond*, written in contemporary language. Maryland and its fine old landed gentry, life on the high seas, Georgian London, with portraits of Garrick, Fox, Walpole, and Paul Jones, provide excellent material for the patriotic romancer. [Macmillan, New York and London; Grosset, New York.]

—— *The Crisis.*   1901

A painstaking study of the Civil War and its causes (1860–5); scene, chiefly St. Louis. The fierce political movements of the time personified in representative characters. Lincoln, Grant, and Sherman appear; while the lovers are a Yankee and a Southern lady. The story deals with the descendants of the Carvel family who have migrated to Missouri. [Macmillan, New York and London; Grosset, New York.]

—— *The Crossing.*   1904

A boy's life and adventures during the great Western movement (1780–1804) after the American Revolution. Andrew Jackson, George Rogers Clark, Daniel Boone, Sevier, and other famous names appear. Clark is the real hero, his march to N. Ohio and treaty with the Indians being a cardinal episode. The multitude of characters, the many and various but converging interests, and stirring scenes of action in the heroic days, form a big panorama of the changes that passed over the lands bordering the Mississippi during this period. [Macmillan, New York and London; Grosset, New York.]

—— *Coniston.*   1906

An exposure of the Boss system, as it worked in a young district during Grant's presidency, probably instigated by Roosevelt's crusade against civic corruption. Mr. Churchill's villainous politician capitulates to sentiment when the conflict is between ambition and love. [Macmillan, New York and London.]

—— *Mr. Crewe's Career.*   1908

An indictment of American " business politics." The two lovers are children of the chief counsel to a railroad corporation and the president of the line, two men who have successfully controlled the politics of an Eastern State in order to keep up dividends. Dedicated to those engaged in the struggle for purer politics. *The Crisis, The Crossing, Coniston,* and *Mr. Crewe's Career* are a quaternion of novels connected in idea, as exhibiting successive epochs of progress in politics and civilization. [Macmillan, New York and London.]

—— *A Modern Chronicle.*   1910

Married life in aristocratic New York, where divorce is easy but not respectable. The history of a beautiful, sensitive, and brilliant girl, who marries the wrong man. Timid and over-reticent, though it touches on fast life where the ice is very thin. Professes to analyse, but the analysis is only skin deep. Obviously written with a pious regard for the literary censorship, and consequently lacking reality. [Macmillan, New York and London.]

—— *The Inside of the Cup.*   1912

An Americanized *Robert Elsmere*, turning less on the conflict of faith and doubt than on that between conservative dogma and practical application of the spirit of Christ in personal and social relations. An earnest but half-educated minister, product of the theological seminaries, suddenly becomes alive to the fact that his fashionable church and the fashionable religion are simply a screen of respectability behind which the chief of his flock carry on their fraudulent company-promoting, sweating, brothel-keeping, and slum-landlordism. A readable book, not very searching or convincing, but likely to do some good by opening blind eyes. A fair specimen of this author's latest style. [Macmillan, New York and London; Grosset, New York.]

—— *A Far Country.*   1915

A corporation lawyer who has carried through divers shady transactions, having loved and lost, is forthwith converted to the higher life. [Macmillan, New York; Grosset, New York.]

—— *The Dwelling-Place of Light.*   1917

American industrialism, the harsh lot of the women caught in its toils, and the alleged misdoings of the Industrial Workers of the World: these and allied problems are woven into a sentimental story with an edifying conclusion. [Macmillan, New York.]

CID. *The Chronicle of the Cid* (Spanish; 16th century).   1808

Transl. from three books, (1) *Cronica del Cid* (printed 1552), a secondary history based on Alfonso's *Estoria de Espanna*, (2) *Cronica General de España* (printed 1541), which may possibly have been the source of the former chronicle (both are of high antiquity as MSS.), (3) *Poema de mio Cid* (composed, *c.* 1135–75), the oldest poem in Spanish. Southey also made some use of the *Romancero del Cid*, ancient ballads of little historical authority. The life of the Cid, Ruy Diaz de Bivar (*b.* 1030–40, *d.* 1099) has been related by Ramón Menéndez Pidal, in *La España del Cid* (Madrid, 1930). The *Poema de mio Cid* is a sound historical document, so far as an epic can be such. In the *Historia Roderici* (*c.* 1140) there is an accretion of legend. In effect, Southey's compilation ranks as a historical fiction; but it has the strength and the dramatic energy of reality, and differs from the Spanish romances of chivalry as a hero-saga differs from Italian opera. The career of the Cid, as here related, gives a unity and an order like that of epic narrative to the incidents of the wars between the kings of Castille, Aragon, and Navarre, and the struggles with the Moors. The outstanding episodes are the repeated banishment of the Cid, his wars with the Moors, the capture of Valencia (which he erects into a kingdom for himself), the outrage of the Cid's sons-in-law, the Infantes of Carrion (who, by the way, are mythical) upon his daughters, and the avenging thereof, with the death of the Cid and the last battle, where his dead body puts the Moors to flight. [Transl. by Robert SOUTHEY, Warne; (Universal Lib.), Routledge.]

" CLARE, Austin " [Miss W. M. James]. *By the Rise of the River.*   1899

Studies and sketches in South Tynedale: parochial literature, pure and simple; local character and customs and local dialect faithfully reproduced. [Chatto: o.p.]

—— *Court Cards: chiefly the Knave of Hearts: a romance of the little game played between England and Scotland at the close of the sixteenth century.*   1904

The famous moss-trooper, Kinmont Willie, and King James of Scotland's jester, Archie Armstrong, are the foremost figures in this story of sheep-stealers and Court intrigues (1596–1600). [Unwin: o.p.]

CLARETIE, Jules Arsène Arnaud [French ; 1840–1913]. *Agnès : a romance of the siege of Paris.* 1909
M. Claretie, who wrote several other novels which have not been translated, was a newspaper correspondent during the war, and staff-officer in the National Guard during the Commune. [Transl. by Ada SOLLY-FLOOD, Stock : o.p.]

CLARK, Barrett Harper [American ; *b.* 1890], and LIEBER, Maxim [*ed.*]. *Great Short Stories of the World.* 1925
Some two hundred examples from all over the world and from ancient and modern literature, with an introduction to each racial group. [McBride, New York ; Heinemann.]

CLARKE, Donald Henderson [American ; *b.* 1887]. *Louis Beretti.* 1929
Portrays the New York " gunman " as, after all, a human being, who has become a gangster, not from original wickedness, but through the natural effect of circumstance upon character, and who cherishes the virtues of the gangster, above all, loyalty, which makes his like so formidable. [Vanguard Press, New York ; Knopf.]

CLARKE, Mrs. Henry. *A Trusty Rebel ; or, A Follower of Warbeck.* [juvenile] 1905
The rising of Perkin Warbeck (1492–9). [Nelson : o.p.]

CLARKE, Isabel Constance. *By the Blue River.* 1913
The wife of a financier convicted of fraud begins life afresh with her little son in the French colony of Algiers. [Hutchinson : o.p. ; Benziger, New York : o.p.]

—— *The Potter's House.* 1916
The theme is divorce and the right to re-marry, treated from the Roman Catholic point of view. [Hutchinson : o.p.]

CLARKE, Marcus Andrew Hislop [Australian ; 1846–81]. *For the Term of his Natural Life.* 1874
Convict life in Tasmania in the thirties and forties, pictured realistically with all its hideous accompaniments of brutality and innocent suffering, and no concession to poetic justice ; a careful study of the facts. Graphic sketches of Australasian scenery are interspersed. [Macmillan ; Ward & Lock ; Laird, Chicago : o.p.]

CLARKE, Mrs. Sarah M. S. [*née* Pereira]. *The Duke's Page.* 1901
The short, brilliant, and somewhat incomprehensible career of Maurice, Duke (and afterwards Elector) of Saxony, from his accession to the dukedom to his death (1531–53). Other characters introduced are Charles V and his ministers Alva and Granvella, Luther and Carlowitz, Mary and Elizabeth Tudor. [Nisbet : o.p.]

" CLEEVE, Lucas " [Mrs. Kingscote, *née* Wolff ; *d.* 1908]. *As the Twig is Bent.* 1901
A good example of this author's fiction, which portrays some of the least admirable phases of modern society. Here we are introduced to the company of shady financiers, whose ways are exposed with intimate knowledge of technical detail. How a young man of good impulses grew up through the influence of surroundings and associates to be an accomplished swindler, and how after all he was reformed through love. [Digby & Long : o.p.]

CLELAND, Robert [Scottish]. *Inchbracken.* 1883
A simple story presenting intimate views of life and manners in a parish near the Highland border at the time of the Disruption and the formation of the New Kirk. A young minister is the central person ; round him are grouped his relatives, the members of his congregation, etc. [Wilson & M'Cormack, Glasgow : o.p.]

CLEMENCEAU, Georges [French ; 1841–1929]. *The Surprises of Life* (Les embuscades de la vie, 1903). 1920
Pungent sketches and stories of French country folk, by a sceptical, ironic, and sometimes cynical philosopher. Two of the finest are *Flower o' the Wheat* and *Six Cents*. [Transl. by Grace HALL, Nash.]

CLIFFORD, Sir Hugh [*b.* 1866]. *In a Corner of Asia.* 1899
Eight sympathetic stories of native life in the Malay Peninsula, by one who knows it intimately. A fierce and lawless state of things is portrayed, elemental tragedies, village idylls, stories of dacoity and superstition. A favourite specimen is *Kûlop Sûmbing*. [Unwin ; McBride, New York.]

—— *Bush Whacking ; and other sketches.* 1901
Brief, realistic sketches of hard life in distant places. They bring one into touch with heroic and elemental things—the struggles of civil servants and other Britishers, of French missionaries, and the like, with untoward circumstances ; native life in Malaysia, etc. *Sally, a Study* (1904) and *Saleh, a Sequel* (1908) are about a young Malay prince, educated in England, who realizes the futility of his attempted Europeanization and goes back to his native land. [All Blackwood : o.p. ; (1), *illus.* by Mahlon Blaine, Heinemann (Harper, New York), 1929.]

—— *The Downfall of the Gods.* 1903
A romanticized version of the overthrow of the Khmer empire of Cambodia (thirteenth century), the violation of the temples, the expulsion and massacre of the Brahmins, and the subsequent anarchy. Sir Hugh tries to concentrate the glamour and insensate passion of the East in the unbridled desire of the insurgent Chun for a beautiful slave of the temple, and the violent tragedy which is the consummation. [Murray : o.p. ; Dutton, New York : o.p.]

—— *A Free-Lance of To-day.* 1911
The Free-Lance is a young Englishman who goes on a gun-running expedition into Acheh, meets with adventures, and is strongly tempted to denationalize himself and settle down among the Malays. On its more serious side the book is a study of the Malayan character as compared with the European, the terrible example of a renegade Englishman, a witch-doctor, pointing the moral. [Methuen : o.p.]

—— *Malayan Monochromes.* 1913
Grim stories of Malay life, bringing out the cruelty and superstition of the natives. [Murray ; Dutton, New York : o.p.]

CLIFFORD, Mrs. William Kingdon [*née* Lucy Lane ; *d.* 1929]. *Mrs. Keith's Crime.* 1885
A novel developing a morbid state of mind, a certain individual's view of human life and of right and wrong, without plot or much incident. A loving mother, dying of a disease that has also attacked her child, fearful of leaving her little one to the harsh mercies of the world, ends its life by giving it an overdose. [Nash ; Harper, New York : o.p.]

—— *Love-Letters of a Worldly Woman.* 1891
Three suites of letters—*A Modern Correspondence, Letters of a Worldly Woman, On the Wane*—each setting forth the history of an affair of the heart from the woman's point of view, very frank in their avowal of feminine passion, strength and weakness. One-sided, of course ; the women, whether weak or strong, appearing as in all respects superior to their lovers, who are either Philistines, incapable of the finer feelings, or Turks, who exploit them in the most cold-blooded selfishness. [(Wayfarer's Lib.), Dent (Dutton, New York), 1915 : o.p. ; Harper, New York : o.p. ; Caldwell, Boston : o.p.]

—— *Aunt Anne.* 1892
A domestic novel, centred in one character, the pathetic Aunt Anne, an old and wrinkled woman, sentimental and foolish as a young girl ; poor, yet extravagant, and lavish with her gifts ; a curious blending of diverse human features. [Hodder ; Harper, New York : o.p.]

—— *A Woman Alone : three stories.* 1901
The first and most important is the curious and sombre history of an ill-assorted marriage between a reserved and selfish English gentleman and an enthusiastic and ambitious Hungarian. There follows a comic sketch. [Duckworth ; Appleton, New York : o.p.]

—— *Sir George's Objection.* 1910
A pretty love-tale, with Maggiore and the mountains for its setting. Sir George's objection is to his son's marrying a girl whose father had died in prison. The end contrived is a happy one, however. [Nelson : o.p.]

—— *The House in Marylebone.* 1917
The working girls who inhabit this house provide a set of fugitive characters whose lives are touched upon in every aspect. [Duckworth.]

CLIVE, Mrs. Archer [Caroline, *née* Meysey-Wigley ; 1801–73]. *Paul Ferroll.* 1855
Paul murders his wife in order to marry a girl he loves, and manages to avert suspicion and live a happy life with his new wife and his daughter. At length, however, the guilt is brought home and his condemnation kills his wife, while he escapes with his daughter and settles down to a repentant life abroad. Mrs. Clive was a minor poet, whose *IX Poems by V——* appeared in 1840. [Chatto : o.p. ; Scholartis Press (McKee, New York), 1929.]

—— *Why Paul Ferroll killed his Wife* [sequel]. 1860
The names are changed in the sequel, but the characters represent the same *dramatis personæ*. An equally gloomy narrative, every character and every particle of the environment taking the hue of the dominant situation. The hero is a man whose intellectual powers have raised him so high that he thinks himself superior to moral laws : absolutely selfish, fearless, and remorseless, he commits his crime and lives securely till events betray his guilt. [Chatto : o.p.]

CLOUSTON, Joseph Storer [*b.* 1870]. *The Duke.* 1900
A modern high-society farce. A young duke, instead of entering on his inheritance, allows an eccentric Irishman to assume the ducal rôle for a month. [Arnold : o.p. ; Longmans, New York : o.p.]

—— *The Lunatic at Large.* 1900
—— *Count Bunker* [sequel]. 1906
Another absurdity in a conventional modern environment. [(1), Blackwood ; Brentano, New York ; (2), Blackwood : o.p. ; Brentano, New York.]

COBB, James F. *The Watchers on the Longships.* [juvenile] 1878
Life on the Cornish coast and in the lighthouse at the end of the eighteenth century. [Wells Gardner.]

—— *In Time of War : a tale of Paris during the siege and the Commune.* [juvenile] 1880
Brittany, the siege of Paris and the Commune (1870–1). Originally published *sub tit. Workman and Soldier.* [Frowde : o.p.]

COBB, Thomas [1854–1932]. *The Judgment of Helen.* 1899
A social comedy in one act, a matchmaker outwitted by her two protégées : plot and motives developed by means of dialogue, which, like the story, is light and frothy. [Lane : o.p.]

—— *Scruples.* 1900
A drawing-room comedy of manners, with a group of hesitating characters entangled in a mesh of love at cross-purposes. The story of the heroine's scruples and the final *dénouement* is told by means of coruscating dialogue. [Richards : o.p. ; Lane, New York : o.p.]

—— *The Dissemblers.* 1900
A trite dilemma of courtship—two lovers being hurried by a compromising incident into a premature engagement —worked out with the stage play of a regular comedy. [Lane.]

—— *Severance.* 1901
A similar drawing-room comedy, a little broader in effects than the foregoing ; misunderstandings in courtship and married life are the motives. As usual, there is hardly any character-drawing. [Lane : o.p.]

—— *The Bishop's Gambit.* 1901
Various complications threaten disaster to the love affairs of the bishop's two daughters, but are cleared up in course of the plot. [Richards : o.p.]

—— *A Change of Face.* 1904
—— *Mrs. Erricker's Reputation.* 1906
—— *The Anger of Olivia.* 1910

COBB, Thomas (*continued*). *Andrew and His Wife.* 1914
—— *Mrs. Latham's Extravagance.* 1915
    Similar comedies unfolded by means of light and nimble dialogue, free from sentimentality and with the barest suggestion of character-drawing. [(1), Methuen: o.p.; (2), Rivers: o.p.; (3) and (4), Mills & Boon: o.p.; (5), Chapman: o.p.]

COBBOLD, Richard [1797–1877]. *The History of Margaret Catchpole.* 1845
    The story of an actual Suffolk woman (1773–1841), who was imprisoned for horse-stealing (1797), broke gaol, and was transported, afterwards marrying and living at Sydney till her death. [With introd. by Clement Shorter (World's Classics), Oxford Press, 1907.]

COCKTON, Henry [1807–53]. *Valentine Vox, the Ventriloquist.* 1840
    By means of his ventriloquial gifts, the hero perpetrates enormous practical jests that beget scenes of screaming farce. These, with his love affairs, satirical sketches of London life, and some sensational episodes, such as that of a man immured in a lunatic asylum and deliberately driven mad by torture, make up a lengthy novel of the Pierce Egan and *Pickwick* variety. To a certain extent it is a novel of purpose, and is said to have brought about a revision of the lunacy laws. [Jenkins; Burt, New York; McKay, Philadelphia.]
—— *Sylvester Sound, the Somnambulist.* 1844
    A weak attempt to follow up the success of the former book. [Jenkins; Dutton, New York: o.p.]

COFFIN, Charles Carleton [American; 1823–1896]. *Daughters of the Revolution and their Times.* 1895
    Outbreak of the Revolution, the state of public feeling, Boston massacre, Tea-Party, battle of Lexington, etc. (1767–76). The author has written a number of books on this period. [Houghton, Boston: o.p.]

COKE, Desmond [1879–1931]. *Sandford of Merton.* 1903
    A parody of the conventional Oxford novel. Published under the pseudonym "Belinda Blinders, edited by Desmond F. T. Coke." [Simpkin: o.p.]
—— *The Bending of a Twig.* 1906
    An admirable novel of public schoolboy life at Shrewsbury. [Re-written 1908, Oxford Press.]
—— *The Comedy of Age.* 1906
    A view of undergraduate life at Oxford, through the eyes of a 'Varsity man who has become a society entertainer. [Chapman: o.p.]
—— *The Golden Key: a comedy of temperaments.* 1909
    Deals with character as it is moulded by the entry upon work and business. [Chapman: o.p.]
—— *The School Across the Road.* 1909
—— *Beauty for Ashes.* 1910
    Further stories chiefly of school and university life. All these novels convey an intimate reading of character in boys and men in the prime of life, and realistic pictures of the many aspects of school and college, the clubs, debates, friendships, entertainments, and the intellectual and emotional currents of life, with plenty of comedy and now and then a touch of pathos. [(1), Oxford Press; (2), Chapman: o.p.]
—— *Youth, Youth!* 1919
    "A book of schoolboy rags"; the moral, character tells. [*Illus.* by H. M. Brock, Chapman.]

COLE, Sophie [*b.* 1862]. *A London Posy.* 1917
    An idyll of Gough's Court and Dr. Johnson's house, with the Dictionary as a compendium of *Sortes Johnsonianæ.* The hero is an unselfish and long-suffering boy who watches over a pair of twins, and there are two courting couples and other pretty characters to match. [Mills & Boon: o.p.]

COLERIDGE, Christabel Rose [1843–1921]. *Minstrel Dick.* [juvenile] 1896
    The last days of the Black Prince; scenes, Berkhampstead and Chelsea (1376). [Wells Gardner: o.p.]
    See also YONGE (Charlotte M.).

COLERIDGE, Hon. Gilbert James Duke [*b.* 1859], and COLERIDGE, Marion [*née* Darroch; *d.* 1917]. *Jan van Elselo.* 1902
    England, France, Spain, Holland, *temp.* Philip II (1559–73), hero a page to William of Orange. Closes with the Spanish reign of terror in the Low Countries. Not accurate in minor historical details. [Macmillan: o.p.]

COLERIDGE, Mary Elizabeth [1861–1907]. *The King with Two Faces.* 1897
    A romance dealing with the events that led to the assassination of Gustavus III of Sweden in 1792, the cabals of the nobility, the siege of Gothenburg, the king's revocation of the constitution, etc. (1789–92). The Parisian episodes introduce Marie Antoinette, Count Fersen, Mme de Staël, and others. Suffused with her curious mysticism. [Arnold: o.p.]
—— *The Fiery Dawn.* 1901
    Same theme as in Dumas' *She-Wolves,* the Duchesse de Berri's attempt to place her son on the French throne (1831–2). Historical and other characters drawn with fullness and care, plenty of strenuous action and strong touches of tragedy; yet on the whole a vague and dreamy romance, like the others by Miss Coleridge. [Arnold: o.p.; Longman, New York: o.p.]

"COLETTE" [Sidonie Gabrielle Gauthier-Villars, *née* Colette, afterwards Mme de Jouvenal; French; *b.* 1873.] *The Vagrant* (La vagabonde, 1910). 1912
    The vagabond is a music-hall star who is courted by a worthy and substantial bourgeois, but mindful of her former bondage refuses at the last moment to marry again. In a sequel, *L'entrave,* she has some heart-burnings when she accidentally sees her lover happily married and a father. [Transl. by Charlotte Remfrey KIDD, Nash. This translation was republished, with some slight alterations, as a new novel, under a new title, *Renée Néré,* in 1931; and was accepted by reviewers, if not by readers of Mme Colette, as a fresh work of that author. This is by no means the only instance of old translated work being palmed off on the public as new.]

"COLETTE " (*continued*). *Mitsou ; or, How Girls grow Wise* (Mitsou ; ou, Comment l'esprit vient aux filles, 1917). 1930

The affair of a music-hall star and a young airman who is repelled by her vulgarity, but whose disenchantment, it is hinted, will not be final. Mme Colette at one time was famous on the variety stage. [Transl. by Jane TERRY, Boni, New York ; Gollancz.]

—— *Chéri* (Chéri, 1920). 1929

Candid and unsentimental analysis of the characters and motives of a middle-aged courtesan and a young man with whom she is in love, and whom she feels she must lose as the years ruin her charms. [Transl. by Janet FLANNER, Boni, New York ; Gollancz.]

—— *The Gentle Libertine* (L'ingénue libertine, 1928). 1930

In understanding of the heart and imagination of a young girl, this is Colette's ripest work. Her innocent libertine (the English title is a mistranslation) nurses a passionate interest in the deeds of the Paris apaches, and would love to run away with the leader of a gang. Then, disappointed with marriage to her cousin and confidant, she experiments with clandestine love, till her husband's magnanimity teaches her that there is something better. [Transl. by R. C. BENÉT, Gollancz ; Farrar & Rinehart, New York.]

—— *Fanny and Jane* (La seconde, 1929). 1931

Farou, a big, blonde, bullying composer of vaudeville, is the centrepiece, with his womenfolk, his wife, and her bosom-friend, to whom the incontinent fellow makes love indiscriminately. Sympathy is centred, however, in the wife, and in the process of intuition by which she becomes aware of the situation. A novel almost wholly in dialogue ; statement by the method of allusion and suggestion. [Transl. by Mrs. Viola GARVIN, Gollancz.]

"COLETTE " and "WILLY " [Henri Gauthier-Villars ; French ; b. 1859]. *Claudine at School* (Claudine à l'école, 1900). 1930

This first of a series, continued in *Claudine à Paris* (1901), *Claudine en ménage* (1902), and *Claudine s'en va* (1903), with a belated sequel *La maison de Claudine* (1922), tells how an intelligent girl of fifteen goes to a school in the provinces, watches with an amused eye the goings on of the red-headed mistress and her pretty assistant and the erotic school-doctor, and by the time she has finished knows everything that she shouldn't. The wit and the easy art of the telling are admirable. [Transl. by Janet FLANNER, Gollancz ; Boni, New York.]

COLLINGWOOD, William Gershom [b. 1854]. *Thorstein of the Mere : a saga of the Northmen in Lakeland.* 1895

In style an imitation of the sagas ; in matter, a restoration of the history of Cumberland and Westmorland in the tenth century, when the Northmen had settled there, and, allied with the decadent Welsh, a few Gaelic stragglers, and the Scottish kings, were resisting the encroaching Saxon. The battle of Brunanburh (A.D. 937) is a dramatic incident. Old place-names, archæological remains, local traditions, and a certain amount of ascertained history, with a plentiful leavening of fancy, are wrought into a romance of the eponymous hero of Coniston Water or Thurston's Mere. [With introd. by E. Thomson, Heinemann, 1929.]

—— *The Likeness of King Elfwald.* 1917

A similar attempt at an imaginative re-creation of the Viking age in Northumbria and Western Scotland and the isles (787–808). The king is Elfwald II of Northumbria. [Titus Wilson : o.p.]

COLLINS, William Edmund Wood. *A Scholar of his College.* 1900

A leisurely novel of conventional design, giving life-like pictures of country-house society and people at Oxford. [Blackwood : o.p.]

COLLINS, William Wilkie [1824–89]. *Antonina.* 1850

Alaric in Italy—a really fine historical novel (408–10). [Chatto : o.p. ; Harper, New York.]

—— *Hide and Seek.* 1854

A novel depending on a long-kept secret. Plot : how a brother, having hunted out the destroyer of his sister, relinquishes his vengeance for the sake of his friend, the villain's son. Moral purpose : to show how by kindness and patience the life of a deaf and dumb girl may be made happy. [Chatto ; Harper, New York : o.p.]

—— *After Dark.* 1856

A series of stories told by a painter whose sight is failing. *The Yellow Mask*, a story of Pisa, has much of the grisly effect of Poe's tales. A jealous woman masks herself with a waxen cast of a man's dead wife and nearly kills him with horror. [Chatto ; Dodd & Mead, New York.]

—— *The Dead Secret.* 1857

Here plot-interest completely overrides the human interest, sustaining the reader's curiosity up to the moment when the secret is revealed. There are, however, some scenes and characters (e.g. Uncle Joseph) that stir our emotions or entertain with Dickensian humours. The old Cornish house with its mysterious associations recalls Mrs. Radcliffe. [Chatto ; Harper, New York : o.p.]

—— *The Woman in White.* 1860

Develops the mechanics of plot to a stage that confounds the simple-minded reader though not the critical. Collins adopts the attitude of inviting the reader's ingenuity in discovering the identity of a puppet-heroine and detecting the real object of a villainous conspiracy. The arch-villain, Count Fosco, has a certain amiability and some human idiosyncrasies which save him from forfeiting all sympathy by his crimes, and he, Mrs. Catterick, and Fairlie are the three best-drawn of Wilkie Collins's characters. Collins was the most expert novelist in what Stevenson called the carpentry of plot. This is an excellent example of his complicated mystifications, every part of which is accurately dovetailed and subordinated to the *dénouement*. [Chatto ; Collins ; (Everyman's Lib.), Dent (Dutton, New York) ; (World's Classics) Oxford Press ; Harper, New York ; Putnam, New York, 1917.]

—— *No Name.* 1862

Less of a puzzle-plot than the last, preferring to foreshadow events. The disadvantage of illegitimate birth is the leading motive—a girl deprived of her father's money by this misfortune tries under a false name to marry the heir ; another unscrupulous woman protects the invalid hero. Capt. Wragge, the swindler, and his wife are comic figures. [Chatto ; Collins, London and New York.]

COLLINS, William Wilkie (*continued*). *Armadale.*   1866

The mainspring of this story, which abounds in coincidence, is a crime the effects of which come to a head in the second generation. An attempt to deal imaginatively with the physical and moral results of heredity. A feminine counterpart to the villain Fosco plays a signal part, giving her life to save her lover from the fatal consequences of her own crime. The amorous gardener, Abraham Sage, and Miss Gwilt are capitally done. [Chatto; Harper, New York: o.p.]

—— *The Frozen Deep ; and other tales.*   1866

The Frozen Deep is a romantic drama : the heroine, who is gifted with second sight, has a vision of her lover stranded upon an iceberg with a rival suitor ; eventually the latter sacrifices his life for the sake of his enemy. The remaining two, *The Dream Woman* and *John Jago's Ghost*, are stories of crime. [Chatto.]

—— *The Moonstone.*   1868

The theft of a celebrated jewel, and its quest and restitution by devoted Hindu priests, after an Iliad of adventures, to the idol from whose forehead it had long ago been wrenched, make an intricate story. An excellent mystery-plot, borrowing strong romantic effect from the dark and mysterious Brahmins. The old servant, Gabriel Betteridge, the police-inspector Cuff, and Miss Clack are good comic characters, studied from Dickens. [Chatto; Collins; Harper, New York; Dial Press, New York, 1925; Dodd & Mead, New York; with introd. by T. S. Eliot, Oxford Press, 1928.]

—— *Man and Wife.*   1870

A fierce onslaught upon athleticism, the villain being a champion boxer, runner, and a savage in manners and morals. The defects of the Irish and Scottish marriage laws, the tyrannical power of husband over wife in England, are the causes of the chief disasters involved in an exciting plot. [Chatto; Harper, New York.]

—— *Poor Miss Finch.*   1872

A sensation novel, with a blind girl as heroine, a hero suffering from epileptic fits, and a great amount of surgical and medical details in the plot business. As usual, full of complicated intrigue involving good people and bad. Poor Miss Finch, a lovable girl, though little more than a child in character, is at length married to a good, silly young fellow, Oscar, who, with his twin-brother Nugent, is the focus of some puzzling situations. [Chatto; Harper, New York: o.p.]

—— *The New Magdalen.*   1873

The tragic redemption of a camp-follower, time of the Crimean War. [Chatto; Harper, New York: o.p.]

—— *Heart and Science.*   1883

An assault on vivisection, the most prominent character being engaged in practical biological research. Enlivened by humorous descriptions of Scottish life and character by a vivacious child. [Chatto: o.p.; Harper, New York: o.p.]

—— *Little Novels.*   1887

These show in little the characteristics of his full-length novels, ingeniously complicated plot, ravelled and then unravelled, and a weakness for supernatural incident. [Chatto; Harper, New York: o.p.]

COLONNA, Francesco [Italian; *c.* 1435 (or 49)–1527]. *Hypnerotomachia : The Strife of Loue in a Dreame* (Polyphili Hypnerotomachia, 1467).   1592

" Supposed to be the allegorical record of the priest Colonna's passion for a nun." Told in the form of a marvellous dream, in which the lover is conducted through the temples and tombs of Greece and Egypt, and to the isle of Cythera, where he beholds the festivals of Venus and Adonis. The style of the Elizabethan rendering is adorned with the most sumptuous rhetoric of the time. [Original transl. by Sir Robert DALLINGTON(?), with a selection of strangely decorative cuts from the Italian original of 1498, ed. by Andrew LANG, (Tudor Lib.), Nutt, 1890: o.p.]

COLUM, Padraic [Irish; *b.* 1881]. *A Boy in Eirinn.*   1913

A pretty story of an Irish peasant-boy and his outlook on the world, how he learns the old legends, etc. [Dent (1915): o.p.; Dutton, New York.]

" COMBE, T." [Mlle Adèle Huguenin; French]. *Jonquille ; or, The Swiss Smuggler.*   1891

Jonquille, an Amazonian maiden in a village of the Jura, is the queen of a band of smugglers. A young watchmaker, longing for freedom and release from sedentary toil, marries her and joins the band ; but the new activities do not satisfy him ; he would fain go to the colonies, while his marriage restrains him. [Transl. by Beatrix L. TOLLEMACHE, Percival: o.p.]

COMPTON, Herbert E. *The Inimitable Mrs. Massingham.*   1900

A romance of Gretna Green, with a beautiful country girl as heroine, who later becomes a favourite actress. The streets and inhabitants of bygone London, and life on a convict ship and at Botany Bay are vigorously depicted from authentic records (1799). [Chatto: o.p.]

—— *The Queen can do no Wrong.*   1904

Full of excitement. A story of Queen Caroline, for whom the author holds a brief (1796–1821). [Chatto: o.p.]

COMSTOCK, Harriet Theresa [*née* Nichols; American; *b.* 1860]. *The Queen's Hostage.*   1906

Pictures life in London and at Court about 1590, portraying Elizabeth, Ben Jonson, and Shakespeare, and describing a performance of *Love's Labour's Lost* at the Globe. [Little & Brown, Boston: o.p.]

CONDER, Arthur R. *The Seal of Silence.*   1901

A comedy by a young Oxford man, who died just before the issue of this, his first and only novel. Undergraduate manners are illustrated in the account of a reading-party in Devonshire. [Smith & Elder: o.p.]

CONGREVE, William [1670–1729]. *Incognita ; or, Love and Duty Reconciled.*   1692

Among the latest progeny of sentimental romanticism, but in some points an anticipation of the comic fiction about to be inaugurated by Fielding. Very brief, as novels went in those days, fruit of the idle hours of a fortnight's time ; and very dramatic, the plot comprehending exactly three days. Scene, Florence, " two couples so oddly engaged in an intricate amour," ending their affairs in satisfactory weddings, after a rapid series of intrigues and imbroglios which are related with a mixture of fashionable sentiment and

CONGREVE, William (*continued*).

mock-heroic raillery. The first published work of the author. [Ed. by H. F. Brett-Smith (Percy Reprints) Blackwell, Oxford (Houghton, Boston), 1922 ; ed. by F. W. Bateson, in *Works*, 1 vol., Davies (Minton & Balch, New York), 1930.]

"CONNELL, John" [John Henry Robertson ; Scottish ; *b.* 1909]. *Lyndesay.*　　1930

A try at a Scottish *Tom Brown's Schooldays*, by a writer whose recollections of Loretto are still fresh. [With introd. by Compton Mackenzie, Cape.]

CONNOLLY, James Brendan [American ; *b.* 1868]. *Out of Gloucester.*　　1902

Vivid stories of seafaring life on the Newfoundland banks, etc., obviously from personal experience. [Scribner, New York ; Hodder : o.p.]

—— *The Crested Seas.*　　1907

Thirteen stories of Newfoundland and Nova Scotia mariners and their strenuous conflict with the waves. [Scribner, New York ; Duckworth : o.p.]

"CONNOR, Ralph" [Rev. Charles William Gordon ; Canadian ; *b.* 1860]. *Black Rock : a tale of the Selkirks.*　　1898

—— *The Sky Pilot : a tale of the foot-hills.*　　1899

Stories of rough life in the far West. Sketches of cowboy life and character, and of the mountains and the prairies, with a pervasive tinge of religious sentiment. The Sky Pilot is a saintly young evangelist, who converts the turbulent ranchers in a little frontier village of the Rockies, and then dies. [(1) and (2) Revell, New York ; Hodder ; Grosset, New York ; McClelland, Toronto.].

—— *Patrol of the Sun-Dance Trail.*　　1914

A characteristic novel of vigorous open-air life in Western Canada—the North-West Mounted Police and roving Indians. [Burt, New York ; Hodder.]

CONRAD, Joseph [Feodor Józef Konrad Korzeniowski ; Pole, writing in English ; 1857–1924].

Almayer's Folly : a story of an Eastern river.　　1895

—— *An Outcast of the Islands* [sequel].　　1896

The history of a European married to a Malayan wife, who reverts to her ancestral savagery. He lives a miserable life among the fierce Malays and Dyaks of Borneo, and the tragedy culminates when his beloved daughter forsakes him to marry a savage. The awful effect on the mental and moral nature of the solitude and the contact with savagery is brought out with intense imaginative skill. Conrad carried *Almayer's Folly* about with him on his voyages, before finishing it during a stay ashore.

—— *The Nigger of "The Narcissus" : a tale of the forecastle.*　　1897

An account of a voyage home from India in an old-fashioned sailing ship. A wonderfully realistic description of rough seafaring life, by one who has been a seaman, and has moreover a poetic imagination. The description of a storm rivals the finest performances of Loti. The unfortunate negro and the rest of the ship's crew are striking characters portrayed with a deep sense of humanity and not without strokes of saturnine comedy. [Original American title, *The Children of the Sea*.]

—— *Tales of Unrest.*　　1898

The two little dramas, *Karain : a memory* and *The Lagoon*, and the grisly tale, *An Outpost of Progress*, illustrate the fierce tropical character of the Malay. *The Return* is a conjugal tragedy of civilized English life, a psychological study of the disastrous collision between two incompatible temperaments ; much below Conrad's usual standard.

—— *Lord Jim : a tale.*　　1900

Conrad's *Hamlet*. A brave young officer in the mercantile navy loses his head in a moment of dire emergency and is cashiered. His weak point is a too vivid imagination. In a career of self-devotion and heroic adventure among the savages of Malaysia he strives to rebuild his shattered self, the higher self that was his ideal and his criterion. Descriptions of the sea finer even than Loti's, but totally different in method. Conrad was an out-and-out impressionist, like Sterne in some ways, giving sensations and impressions as they would occur to the spectator. Like Henry James, he left it to the reader to correlate the memories and reports from different friends of the unfortunate hero.

—— *Youth : a narrative ; and two other stories.*　　1902

Youth is from his own life, his voyage to the East in a coffin ship, a sustained struggle with the sea, with accidents in port and with a burning cargo, and the indelible picture of that new world left on his mind, steeped in the glamour of youth and the glamour of the sea. *Heart of Darkness* interprets, in the same imaginative and autobiographical way, the gloom and strangeness and demoralizing isolation of a European's life among West African savages. *The End of the Tether* is a longer story, about a captain who dissembles the terrible fact that he is going blind.

—— *Typhoon ; and other stories.*　　1903

Four stories of intermediate length—" long-short "—all more or less nautical. *Typhoon* is one of the greatest descriptions of a ship in a storm in any literature, equal at least in its tremendous actuality to the famous narrative in Loti's *Mon Frère Yves*, and superior in its characteristic subjectivity. Capt. McWhirr is a good type of Conrad's imperturbable, unimaginative, supremely competent master-mariners. *Amy Foster* is a grim analysis of fundamental incompatibility between a commonplace girl and a strange, imaginative waif who becomes her husband. *Falk* and *To-morrow* are shorter stories illustrating Conrad's humour as well as his tragic power.

—— *Nostromo : a tale of the seaboard.*　　1904

Episodes of adventure and daring exploit in the revolutionary broils of the American republic of Costaguana, loosely connected into a long story, in which the man of action, Nostromo, a rich Englishman and his admirable wife, an old Garibaldian, brigands, politicians, adventurers, and others make a motley crowd of personages. The narrative is straightforward, for Conrad, and not made up of impressions gathered from different quarters ; but here as elsewhere, not merely the singularity of the characters, but also the inescapable loneliness of the individual, come out profoundly and poignantly.

CONRAD, Joseph (*continued*). *The Secret Agent : a simple tale.* 1907

A new kind of detective novel. The story of a notorious attempt to blow up Greenwich Observatory, told in Conrad's peculiar way, the personality and mental atmosphere of the secret agent and the concatenation of motives that bring about the attempt being anatomized with his usual clairvoyance. (The Assistant Commissioner was drawn from Sir Robert Anderson). A glimpse into a hidden phase of London life, illustrating his masterly handling of the base, sinister, and squalid elements of humanity.

—— *A Set of Six.* 1908

Characterized by the author as "romantic, ironic, indignant, desperate, military, and pathetic." *Gaspar Ruiz* is a piece in the *Nostromo* vein, and *The Informer* in that of *The Secret Agent*. *The Brute* is a character study of a ship, with a dreadful climax ; *The Duel* a magnificent piece of story-telling about two officers of Napoleon ; *The Anarchist* is admirably ironical ; and *Il Conde*, about an invalid who flies from a Neapolitan assassin only to die in an inhospitable climate, is hardly less so.

—— *Under Western Eyes.* 1911

Undertakes for the benefit of the Western reader to interpret Russian feelings and ways of thought from the inside. The people anatomized are a circle of political refugees and plotters in Genoa, and the pathology of crime, fear, distrust, and treachery is worked out with something of Dostoevsky's gloomy strength and insight into the secrets of the human soul. One rare figure, that of Natalia Haldin, is a welcome relief to the more sombre and repulsive elements of character so remorsely presented.

—— *'Twixt Land and Sea : tales.* 1912

Three stories. *A Smile of Fortune* is told by a ship's captain who somehow manages to convey the queer charm of a sulky young lady. *The Secret Sharer* is wonderful in the power of suggestion and atmosphere : it is the story of a skipper who keeps a fugitive from justice in his cabin and gives him an opportunity to escape. *Freya of the Seven Isles* is all Conrad in a nutshell, a tragic story of overweening confidence and the revenge of Fate. A chivalrous young sailor, owner of a brig in the Dutch East Indies, is outwitted and brought to ruin by a disappointed rival, the stolid captain of a Dutch gunboat. Even in the longer stories, Conrad never conveyed the poetry of the Eastern seas more beautifully.

—— *Chance : a tale in two parts.* 1913

One of his more popular books, probably because it is one of his rare love-stories. The real theme is the anguish of two kindred souls who long fail to recognize each other's love across the gulf of misunderstanding. The story is made more intricate by the method of its telling, the narratives of several witnesses being ultimately pieced together in a manner parallel to that of Henry James, whom Conrad admired as a fellow-craftsman.

—— *Within the Tides : tales.* 1915

Four tales : *The Planter of Malata, Because of the Dollars,* and the two following which are superior work. *The Partner* is the story of a plot to defraud a marine insurance company, told with grim humour. *The Inn of the Two Witches* is about a gruesome adventure in Spain, excellently told, but in itself at least as old as the *Decameron*.

—— *Victory : an island tale.* 1915

The situation in *Chance* is transposed : here another persecuted girl is saved from infamy by a chivalrous hero, who is almost as rare a personality as Capt. Anthony the poet. He is a Swede, who preaches quietism, abstinence from action, for the world is evil. Conrad dwells heavily on that evil in the hideous comedy of the three ruffians who assail the lovers in their lonely outpost amid the ocean archipelago.

—— *The Shadow Line : a confession.* 1917

Here as elsewhere chance is the agency of good or of evil. Chance makes the young man who tells the story captain of a vessel ; but all "the immense forces of the world" are against him in the task of bringing her home. Something occult, perchance the evil spirit of the old skipper, seems to have drawn a line at 8° 20′, past which she may not go. By heroic endurance the captain and a dying seaman get her into port.

—— *The Arrow of Gold : a story between two notes.* 1919

Two lovers in a "world eaten up with charlatanism of all sorts so that even we, the simple, don't know any longer how to trust each other." The world depicted is the Carlist society of the mid-seventies, when the Pretender was in Spain, and his supporters in France and elsewhere were plotting, intriguing, and gun-running to keep him afoot. Doña Rita, who thrills and fascinates the hero, one of the gun-runners, has at any rate the charm of mystery. Chief scene, Marseilles.

—— *The Rescue.* 1920

Conrad's favourite contrast : civilization, safety, ease, versus freedom and heroic action, is here set out very elaborately in the arbitrary doings of Capt. Lingard, a stalwart seaman who co-operates in the enterprise of restoring a dispossessed rajah and in the sufferings and the interesting behaviour of the various members of a yachting party accidentally involved in the ensuing outbreak of elemental forces.

—— *The Rover.* 1923

The Rover is an old sea-captain with a shady past, infinitely resourceful, calmly fatalistic, who with a characteristic gesture of magnanimity throws his life away in a scheme for outwitting Nelson, then blockading Toulon. Most of the incidents take place on a lonely farm in the Giens peninsula, where an old woman and her niece, brooding over the revolutionary massacres, dwell with a bloodthirsty sans-culotte, a Robespierre in miniature. These and the naval officer who loves the niece form one of those groups of strange individualities prized by Conrad, who with stroke after stroke of action and circumstance weaves round them a sombre atmosphere of suspense and terror.

—— *Tales of Hearsay.* 1924

The Warrior's Soul has for its last terrible *mise en scène* the retreat from Moscow : it is a terse example of Conrad's scorching irony. *Prince Roman*, a tale of Poland and the revolution of 1831, is interesting in reminiscences of the author's native country. Of the other two, *The Black Mate* was probably the first story he ever wrote, *The Tale* is a war-story of a fog-bound vessel off a perilous shore.

CONRAD, Joseph (*continued*). *Suspense: a Napoleonic novel.* 1925
An unfinished romance in the genre of *Nostromo*. The beginnings of some large complication of incident that defies conjecture are picturesquely set forth in the position of a young English squire at Genoa, at the moment when the general hopes and fears are centred on the captive Napoleon at Elba.
[*Works* : 22 vols., Dent ; 21 vols., Gresham Co. (in sets) ; 18 vols., Harrap (except 8, 20, and 21) ; 24 vols. Doubleday, Doran, New York. Also, (1) and (2), (17), and (19), Nash ; Unwin ; Benn (Essex Lib.) ; (3) and (7), Heinemann ; (4), Nash ; Unwin ; (5) and (6), Blackwood ; (9), Laurie ; Methuen ; (10), (11), (13), (15), Methuen ; (20), Nash ; Unwin. *The First and Last of Conrad*, Benn, 1929, contains (1), (2), (17), and (19) in 1 vol.]

CONRAD, Joseph, and FORD, Ford Madox. *Romance.* 1903
Adventures of a young Englishman of family who finds himself in the notorious Cuban stronghold of Rio Medio, and becomes involved in a series of romantic and terrifying experiences ; with splendid passages and brilliant scenes—the work of two not quite harmonious collaborators. [Dent ; Doubleday, New York.]

CONSCIENCE, Hendrik [Fleming ; 1812–83]. *The Year of Miracles* (Het Wonderjaar, 1837). 1837
Scenes in the Flemish rebellion against Spain (1566). The author was by origin French, born in Antwerp ; an enthusiastic student of Flemish history, and a close observer of the manners and character of the Flemings, he began a revival of the national literature by his writings in the despised Flemish language. [o.p.]

—— *The Lion of Flanders* (De Leeuw van Vlaanderen, 1837). 1855
A tale dealing with the struggle of the Flemish people to defend their liberties and independence against the aggressions of Philip le Bel, King of France ; the battle of Courtrai. The scene is laid mostly in or around Bruges, and the palmy days of the old city are depicted (1298–1302). [Murphy, Baltimore ; Burns & Oates ; Collins.]

—— *Tales of Flemish Life* (1850–1). 1854
The Recruit ; Mine Host Gansendonck ; Blind Rosa ; The Poor Nobleman. [(1) and (3), with *The Miser*, (4) with *The Amulet*, Burns & Oates ; Murphy, Baltimore ; *The Village Inn-Keeper, v. infra*.]

—— *Veva ; or, The War of the Peasants* (De Boerenkryg, 1853). 1855
Invasion and occupation of the Austrian Netherlands (Belgium) by the French (1793–8). [Burns & Oates : o.p. ; Murphy, Baltimore.]

—— *Ludovic and Gertrude* (1854). [juvenile] 1895
A romance dealing with the domination of Spain in the Netherlands (1567–73), the rule of Alva, and the revolt of the Gueux. Scene : Antwerp. [With *The Young Doctor*, Murphy, Baltimore ; with *Wooden Clara*, Burns & Oates : o.p.]

—— *The Lost Glove.* 1885
—— *The Pale Young Maiden* (sequel, 1872). 1894
Another pair of novels from a series depicting Flemish life in the past and to-day. Portraiture of ordinary people and normal incidents. [English translations of the following tales are also available : *The Miser ; The Miser and Other Stories ; The Demon of Gold ; Tales of Flanders ; The Curse of the Village ; Geraldine ;* all Burns & Oates.]

—— *The Fisherman's Daughter.* [juvenile] 1893
A tale of Flanders in the time of the French Revolution (1794). [Brentano, New York : o.p. ; with *The Village Innkeeper*, Burns & Oates, 1906 : o.p. ; Murphy, Baltimore.]

—— *The Young Doctor* (1860). 1906
Continues the admirable series of stories portraying Flemish home life in the most intimate and sympathetic style. Conscience wrote several series of novels, and many were translated into English, French, German, and Italian during the fifties and sixties. [Burns & Oates.]

CONSTANT DE REBECQUE, Henri Benjamin [French ; 1767–1830]. *Adolphe : an anecdote found among the papers of an unknown person* (1816). 1816
Constant is alleged by his editor, M. de Lescure, to have referred to his connexion with Mme de Staël in his *Adolphe*, although Ellénore, the unfortunate mistress of Adolphe, does not correspond in any way with the illustrious *savante*. Rather, she is a synthesis of all the writer's ephemeral loves. Adolphe enters into relations with Ellénore as a sentimental episode ; but the woman regards the bond more seriously, and dies, in the sequel, broken-hearted. It is a frank confession of egoism, satiety, and disenchantment, ruthless in the psychological dissection of the too sophisticated romanticist, incapable of a pure emotion. [Transl. by A. WALKER : o.p. ; transl. by Paul HOOKHAM, Knopf, New York. 1925 ; by J. Lewis MAY, McKay, Philadelphia.]

CONVERSE, Florence [American ; b. 1871]. *Long Will : a romance.* 1903
The story of William Langland, author of *Piers Plowman*, on the Malvern Hills and in London at the Court of Richard II. Wat Tyler, John Ball, Jack Straw, Chaucer, and Gower come into the story, which conveys the atmosphere of the age with ability (1381). [(Everyman's Lib.), Dent (Dutton, New York).]

" CONWAY, Hugh " [Frederick John Fargus ; 1840–85]. *Called Back.* 1884
A bold, terse, and thrilling melodrama, based on the idea of a man's temporary loss of memory. The first of the modern " shilling shockers," it met with immense success and was dramatized. [Nash ; Ogilvie, New York.]

—— *A Family Affair.* 1885
A plot-novel of the Wilkie Collins type, with some character and delineation of domestic life, conversation and social incident, and touches of comedy in the idiosyncrasies of a pair of brothers. [Macmillan : o.p.]

—— *A Cardinal Sin.* 1886
A complicated plot-novel, with a murder and a young man's adroit intrusion of himself into another's place and fortunes. [Eden : o.p. ; Holt, New York : o.p.]

CONWAY, Moncure Daniel [American ; 1832–1907]. *Pine and Palm.*   1887
    A detailed survey of the state of things existing in the North and in the South just before the Civil War. A
        pair of friends, Northerner and Southerner, at Harvard, quarrel on the slavery question, and each agrees
        to reside a year in the other's country. [Holt, New York : o.p.]

CONYERS, Dorothea [Mrs. J. White Nantenan, *née* Smythe ; Irish ; b. 1873]. *Peter's Pedigree.*
                                                                                          1904

—— *Aunt Jane and Uncle James* [sequel].   1908
    A couple of good Irish stories of hunting, horse-dealing, and sentimental affairs. [(1), Arnold ; (2) : o.p.]

—— *The Strayings of Sandy.*   1906
    One of a number of vivacious Irish stories, drawing chiefly on the society of hunting people, horse-dealers,
        officers in garrison towns, spendthrift gentry, and happy-go-lucky peasants. This is about what a London
        business man sees on a holiday on the West Coast. [Hutchinson : o.p.]

—— *The Conversion of Con Cregan.*   1909
—— *Two Impostors and a Tinker.*   1910
—— *The Arrival of Antony.*   1912
—— *Sandy Married.*   1913
    Similar stories of the turf, and the dealers, sharpers, and sporting gentry connected with it, the scenes and the
        characters chiefly Irish and drawn with knowledge and some exaggerations. ([1] and (2), Hutchinson :
        o.p. ; (3) Arnold : o.p. ; Dutton, New York : o.p. ; (4) Methuen.]

—— *For Henri and Navarre.*   1911
    The usual recital of derring-do, opening with the massacre of St. Bartholomew, and giving a strong portrait of
        Henri IV. [Hutchinson : o.p.]

—— *Old Andy.*   1914
    Irish life, humour, and pathos, with some appealing characters. [Methuen.]

—— *The Financing of Fiona.*   1916
    Country life in Ireland : Fiona inherits a big house but no money, and learns wisdom from an unfortunate
        experience with paying guests. [Allen & Unwin.]

—— *B.E.N.*   1919
    Episodes of the hunting-field, linked together by Ben, an orphan girl making her own way as a whip. [Methuen :
        o.p.]

—— *Follow Elizabeth.*   1929
    Good fun is provided by a wealthy Englishman hunting in Ireland. [Hutchinson.]

COOKE, Grace [American ; *née* MacGowan ; b. 1863], and Alice MACGOWAN [b. 1858]. *Return.*
                                                                                          1905
    Georgia and the savannahs (1739), depicted, with a sense of historical atmosphere, by two descendants of the
        patriots who fought for the land. A passionate Charleston girl is the herione of the romance, which has
        considerable character interest. [Page, Boston : o.p. ; Hodder : o.p.]

COOKE, John Esten [American ; 1830–86]. *The Virginia Comedians : from the MSS. of C.
Effingham, Esq.*   1854
—— *Henry St. John, Gentleman* [sequel].   1858
    The masterpiece of many novels in which this " Virginian of the Virginians " attempted to restore the picturesque
        bygone times of his country. Scenes of life in Williamsburg, once the Southern Boston (1763–5) ; the streets
        and mansions, taverns and theatre, the old courtly society, chivalrous and gentle characters belonging to
        the territorial families, are all portrayed with an idealizing pen. The sequel deals with events in the
        Shenandoah Valley (1774–5). [(1) Appleton, New York : o.p. ; (2) Harper, New York : o.p.]

—— *Surry of Eagle's Nest.*   1866
    Stonewall Jackson, Lee, J. E. B. Stuart, Pelham, and Ashby are drawn as they appeared to a companion in
        arms during the early stages of the war on the Southern side (1861–3). Cooke was on Stuart's
        staff. [Donohue, New York.]

—— *Hilt to Hilt : days and nights on the banks of the Shenandoah* [sequel].   1869
    This and *Mohun* continue the eye-witness's story of the Southern army's campaigns (in 1864). [Dillingham,
        New York : o.p.]

—— *Mohun ; or, The Last Days of Lee and his Paladins* [sequel].   1869
    The Civil War and the last days of Lee. [Dillingham, New York : o.p.]

—— *Colonel Fairfax ; or, The Master of Greenway Court.*   1868
    Deals with the valley of the Shenandoah again, in 1748–81. [Dillingham, New York : o.p.]

—— *Doctor Van Dyke.*   1872
    " A story of Virginia in the last century." [Appleton, New York : o.p.]

—— *My Lady Pokahontas : a true relation of Virginia, writ by Anas Todhill, Puritan and pilgrim.*   1879
    The famous story of the chieftain Powhatan's daughter who saved the life of John Smith by throwing herself
        between him and his executioners. She afterwards came to England, where we are introduced to Shake-
        speare at the Mermaid who is supposed to draw his Miranda from the fair Indian. [Houghton, Boston.]

COOKE, Marjorie Benton [1876–1920]. *Cinderella Jane.*   1918
    Portrays a bright and arresting character, and gives a woman's view of certain much-debated social questions.
        [Jarrold : o.p. ; Doubleday, New York : o.p.]

—— *The Threshold.*   1918
    Joan Babcock is another attractive creation whose activities transform the lives of a rich, easy-going uncle and
        nephew and rouse them to a sense of their responsibilities. [Jarrold : o.p.]

COOKE, Marjorie Benton (*continued*). *The Cricket.* 1919
Excellent in portraying a delightfully precocious, spirited, and impulsive child, who wears out a succession of governesses and fails on the stage, before meeting her destined lover in Bermuda. [Jarrolds : o.p. ; Burt, New York.]

COOKE, Rose [*née* Terry ; American ; 1827–92]. *The Deacon's Week.* 1884
The Deacon, with considerable fortitude, relates his experiences of a protracted meeting, and the story is told by Mrs. Cooke with keen appreciation of the humours of New England character. [Pilgrim Press, Boston : o.p.]

—— *The Sphinx's Children, and other People's.* 1886
Two collections of miscellaneous short stories from the same source. [Houghton, Boston : o.p.]

—— *Steadfast : the story of a saint and a sinner.* 1889
Life and trials of a young minister in Connecticut Valley in the early eighteenth century. A presentation of New England character, founded on the history of the times. [Houghton, Boston.]

—— *Huckleberries Gathered from New England Hills.* 1891
Vernacular tales, like the huckleberry, typical of plain, hardy New York characters, e.g. *A Town Mouse and a Country Mouse*, a story truly Yankee in motive and idiom. [Houghton, Boston : o.p.]

COOPER, Edward Herbert [1867–1910]. *The Monk Wins.* 1900
A novel of the turf, with a rich young sportswoman for heroine, who keeps a stud and has intimate dealings with trainers and bookmakers ; the dialogue appropriately enlivened with slang and technical jargon. " The Monk " is a racehorse. [Duckworth : o.p. ; Stone, Chicago : o.p.]

COOPER, James Fenimore [American ; 1789–1851]. *The Spy : a tale of the Neutral ground.* 1821
An exciting romance of the War of Independence (1780), localized in the region where the loyalists took refuge, introducing Washington (under an *alias*), and other heroes, but paying small regard to historical fact. The hero, Harvey Birch, is a thorough American, well individualized, and Cooper lays his scenes in a country he knew by heart. [Collins, London and New York ; Ginn, New York and London ; Putnam, New York and London ; Page, Boston ; Macmillan, New York ; *illus.*, Houghton, New York ; Minton & Balch, New York ; with introd. by Henry Seidel Canby, 3 vols., Rudge, New York, 1928.]

—— *The Pilot.* 1824
A nautical romance packed with scenes of storm and fight, and descriptions of the many aspects of the sea by one who had been a sailor. Celebrates the exploits of the famous American rover Paul Jones (1747–92) in English waters ; period 1778–9. Rich also in humorous character ; Long Tom Coffin, whose native soil was the sea, is a famous creation. [Putnam, New York and London ; Page, Boston ; *illus.*, Minton & Balch, New York.]

THE LEATHER-STOCKING TALES :

—— *The Deerslayer ; or, The First War-Path.* 1841
—— *The Last of the Mohicans.* 1826
—— *The Pathfinder ; or, The Inland Sea.* 1840
—— *The Pioneers ; or, The Sources of the Susquehanna.* 1823
—— *The Prairie.* 1826
A famous quintet of romances (ranged above in chronological order of incident, not as they were written) which gave the red man a place in literature such as Scott had recently given to the Highlander. They are linked together by the career of Natty Bumppo, or Hawkeye, Cooper's inimitable backwoodsman, a romantic embodiment of the virtues of both races, and of Chingachgook, his Indian counterpart, equally idealized. In *The Deerslayer* his youth and early adventures are recounted ; next, we find him in the prime of manhood, and are plunged into the romantic incidents of the Old French War (1756–7) ; then we have his love for Mabel Dunham ; in *The Pioneers* he is a man of seventy near Lake Otsego, where he had passed his boyhood ; and lastly, in *The Prairie*, an old trapper of eighty years, on the Upper Missouri, driven west by the inroads of civilization. There is little historical background ; but the vivid descriptions of wood, lake, and prairie, and of the daily life of Indian and huntsman, gives the finest imaginable picture extant of natural scenes and human conditions that have long passed away. [*The Leatherstocking Tales*, 5 vols., Houghton, Boston, 1898–9 ; Page, Boston ; Winston, New York ; Putnam, New York ; (Everyman Lib.), Dent (Dutton, New York) ; (1) and (2), *illus.*, Scribner, New York, 1929 ; (1), (2), and (4), *illus.* by H. M. Brock, (3), by C. E. Brock, Macmillan ; (5), *id.* : o.p.]

—— *Lionel Lincoln ; or, The Leaguer of Boston.* 1825
Boston at the opening of the war ; the skirmish at Lexington and the battle of Bunker Hill are well done, but the rest is inferior, and the series of patriotic novels which this was to inaugurate, was never continued (1775). [Putnam, New York and London ; Page, Boston ; Routledge.]

—— *The Wept of the Wish-ton-Wish.* 1827
An episode in the war of King Philip of Pokanoket (1675–6). [Putnam, New York and London ; Page, Boston ; Routledge.]

—— *The Red Rover.* 1828
A tale of adventure on the deep, with racy characterization and lively episodes, the hero a former pirate who fights for his country in the War of Independence. [Putnam, New York and London ; Page, Boston.]

—— *Mercedes of Castile ; or, The Voyage to Cathay.* 1841
Columbus and the discovery of America (1469–93). [Putnam, New York and London ; Page, Boston ; Routledge.]

—— *Wing-and-Wing ; or, Le Feu-follet.* 1842
Adventures of a French privateer in the Mediterranean (1798–9) ; Nelson appears. [Putnam, New York and London ; Page, Boston ; Routledge.]

—— *Wyandotté.* 1843
Adventures on the Upper Susquehanna ; the siege of a block-house.

COOPER, James Fenimore (*continued*). *Afloat and Ashore.* 1844

The autobiography of Miles Wallingford : deals with the iniquities of impressment, and contains some of Cooper's best accounts of sea-fighting. [(1) and (2), Putnam, New York and London ; Page, Boston.]

—— *Satanstoe.* 1845

—— *The Chainbearer.* 1845

—— *The Redskins.* 1845–6

Three inferior stories, forming a sequence, on the early history of colonial New York, through three generations (1750–1829) ; frontier life, etc. ; a mine of information on manners, social and political matters, etc. ; controversial, attacking Puritanism and the agrarianism of the Anti-Rent party. [(1), (2), and (3), Putnam, New York and London ; Page, Boston ; (1), Routledge.]

—— *Oak Openings.* 1848

A story of bee-hunting and fights with redskins on Lake Michigan ; the result of the writer's own travel in the unsettled West the year before. [Putnam, New York and London ; Page, Boston ; Routledge.] [*Works :* 33 vols., Putnam, New York and London ; 32 vols., Page, Boston ; 29 vols., Houghton, Boston.]

COPPARD, Alfred Edgar [*b.* 1878]. *The Black Dog ; and other stories.* 1923

The title-story, like Mr. Coppard's other work, recalls Chekhov : it is essentially undramatic. Neither the expected nor the unexpected comes to pass. The magnificent girl at the public-house offers herself to the fastidious young aristocrat, and he does not even notice that she is offering. *Alas, poor Bollington !* likewise has no *dénouement* : things drift, and are as they were. There are more inhibitions than decisions or actions in all these stories. Such is life. [Cape ; (Traveller's Lib.), *id.* ; Knopf, New York.]

—— *Fishmonger's Fiddle : tales.* 1925

These show the same conception of life and the same technique ; but are superior, perhaps, in seizing the real, the concrete. Mr. Coppard loves rare, odd, bizarre characters and behaviour. He is astonishingly unsentimental, detached, cold-blooded. . Take, for instance, *The Jewel of Jeopardy, The Watercress Girl,* or *A Three-handed Reel* ; or, for his disdain for the expected, take the title-story. [Cape ; (Traveller's Lib.), *id.* ; Knopf, New York.]

—— *Pink Furniture : a tale for lovely children with noble natures.* 1930

An extravagant tale, but by no means conventionally extravagant, of two children's adventures in fantastic places. Not without satire, particularly of the traditional wonder-story, yet well-adapted for young readers. [*Illus.* by Nancy Bankart Gurney, Cape, London and New York.]

COPPÉE, François Édouard Joachim [French ; 1842–1908]. *Henriette ; or, A Corsican Mother* (Henriette, 1889). 1889

A story of young love, which teaches that a true and unselfish passion, though humble, is stronger than a mother's devotion. [Transl. by E. WAKEFIELD, Worthington, New York : o.p.]

—— *Blessed are the Poor* (Les vrais riches, 1892). 1894

A vivacious story founded on the commonplace that true riches consist in virtue and resignation. [Transl. by W. HEATON, with introd. by T. P. O'CONNOR, Heinemann : o.p.]

—— *The Rivals* (Rivales, 1893). 1893

A sentimental tale of a young poet who is tempted to desert his humble fiancée for the wealthy and popular actress who had paved the way for his success. He dies, and the two who had loved him, both now reduced to poverty, make common cause in misfortune. [Harper, New York : o.p.]

—— *The Guilty Man* (Le coupable, 1896). 1912

A story of moral retribution, intended to demonstrate how neglect and an ill-applied penal system create the criminal. A young law-student deserts his mistress when she is about to have a child. This boy, though the object of her unselfish devotion, is left destitute at her death ; he is sent to a reformatory, and involved with a set of bad characters ; eventually, under a momentary impulse, he commits murder. The judge who is to try him is no other than his father. Two others of Coppée's best novels, *Une idylle pendant le siège* (1875) and *Toute une jeunesse* (1890) have not been translated. [Transl. by R. H. DAVIS, Greening : o.p.]

CORELLI, Marie [Minnie Mackay ; of Scottish-Italian parentage ; 1864–1924]. *A Romance of Two Worlds.* 1886

Tacks on to an ordinary novel of everyday life the gospel of electricity, which the writer professes to be the outcome of her psychical experiences. This novel, with its spiritualizing methods, or rather its materializing of spiritual things so as to bring them closer to commonplace experience, may be regarded as the type of a long series of fictions, of which the more important are quoted below. [Methuen ; Burt, New York.]

—— *Vendetta : the story of one forgotten.* 1886

Propagates the same theosophic creed of the ever-living spirit within each one of us, identified later on with radio-activity. [Methuen ; Burt, New York.]

—— *Thelma.* 1887

Intended as " a love-story pure and simple," and a digression from her spiritualistic propaganda. A romance of Norway and of English society, full of elaborate description. Thelma is supposed to be a daughter of Norse sea-kings, and to show her regal nature by ruling as a queen in society. [Methuen ; Burt, New York.]

—— *Ardath : the story of a dead self.* 1889

A sequel to the *Romance of Two Worlds* ; in fact, these, with *Vendetta, Lilith, Barabbas,* and *The Master Christian,* are " all linked together by the one theory," and " are the result of a deliberately conceived plan and intention." [Methuen ; Burt, New York.]

—— *Wormwood.* 1890

The horrors of absinthe-drinking in Paris are dealt with in the same transcendental manner. [Methuen ; Burt, New York.]

CORELLI, Marie (*continued*). *Barabbas: a dream of the world's tragedy.* 1893

A melodrama founded on the Gospel story of the betrayal and crucifixion of Christ. The motives of Judas and Barabbas are attributed to sexual passion or patriotic zeal. Splendiferous scenic accompaniments. [Methuen; Lippincott, Philadelphia; Burt, New York.]

—— *The Sorrows of Satan.* 1895

Another transcendental melodrama of modern life. The devil is hero, and it is sought to show that he has a pathetic side. [Methuen; Lippincott, Philadelphia.]

—— *The Mighty Atom.* 1896

Protests against over-education and the folly of bringing up children without a religious belief. The rich, vulgar, and tyrannical father, whose wife has left him, dismisses the first tutor because he teaches the boy about God and immortality. The next tutor believes in the atom as the beginning of creation. But the boy's natural questioning about the why and the wherefore of things is unsatisfied by such philosophy. He hangs himself in order that he may see for himself whether a little friend has really gone to heaven. [Methuen; Lippincott, Philadelphia.]

—— *The Master Christian.* 1900

The dedication, " To those Churches who quarrel in the name of Christ," speaks for the book, which is a clamorous invective against the Churches, especially the Roman and High Anglican, arraigning the clergy, though the chief character is a cardinal. The finding of the Christ-child by this unworldly priest outside Rouen cathedral is a touching incident; henceforth " Manuel " attends the cardinal regularly, and is at length brought into the presence of the Pope. The plea is that the Church should reform her creed on scientific lines and her ethics on socialistic. Multifarious incident and interspersed homilies. [Methuen; Dodd & Mead, New York; Burt, New York.]

—— *Temporal Power: a study in supremacy.* 1902
—— *God's Good Man: a simple love-story.* 1904
—— *The Treasure of Heaven: a romance of riches.* 1906
—— *Holy Orders: the tragedy of a quiet life.* 1908
—— *The Life Everlasting: a romance of reality.* 1911

Perhaps these are described sufficiently by their titles, in the light of the foregoing notes. The writer was an emotional lady who believed that she was sent into the world with a mission—to inculcate her rather crude brand of theosophy, to fight against Romanizing tendencies in the English Church, and show up moral abuses in general. [(1) Methuen; Dodd & Mead, New York; (2) Methuen; Dodd & Mead, New York; Burt, New York; (3) Constable; Burt, New York; (4) Methuen; Stokes, New York: o.p.; (5) Methuen; Grosset, New York.]

CORKERY, Daniel [Irish; *b.* 1878]. *A Munster Twilight.* 1916

Sixteen diversified tales of Co. Cork and Kerry, ranging from the poetical *Ploughing of Leacana-Naomh* to the idyllic *Child Saint.* [Talbot Press, Dublin; Stokes, New York: o.p.]

—— *The Threshold of Quiet.* 1917

The inner life of several people, who really have an inner life, but externally are very ordinary and meet with no unusual experiences, is traced with peculiar intimacy and tenderness, and their depth of feeling and essential fineness brought to light. [Talbot Press, Dublin.]

CORNFORD, Leslie Cope [1867–1927]. *The Master Beggars of Belgium.* 1897

Period of the Inquisition and the revolt of the Dutch (1568–70). [Wayfarer's Lib.), Dent, 1915 (Dutton, New York: o.p.).]

—— *Northborough Cross.* 1901

Delineations of the manners and peculiarities of ecclesiastical society in a cathedral town, animated apparently by a virulent dislike for the clergy, who, compared with the laity, are represented as rotten and corrupt; several of the characters are repulsive degenerates. [Allen & Unwin: o.p.]

COTES, Mrs. Everard [Sarah Jeanette, *née* Duncan; Canadian; 1861–1922]. *A Social Departure: how Orthodocia and I went round the world by ourselves.* 1890

A kind of *Innocents Abroad*: first of a series of travel books and social sketches in which the Old World is shown as it appears to Transatlantic eyes. Recounts, with much facetiousness, the journey of two unprotected girls from America through Japan, India, Egypt, etc. [Chatto: o.p.; Appleton, New York: o.p.]

—— *An American Girl in London.* 1891

Compares British conventionality with American freedom. The piquancy of the young lady's comments on British manners and customs owes as much to her naïve misunderstandings as to the revelation of trans-atlantic ways of thinking. [Chatto: o.p.; Appleton, New York: o.p.]

—— *His Honour and a Lady.* 1896

The comedy of Anglo-Indian social and official life. One lieutenant-governor falls a martyr to his stubborn honesty, the next wins signal success because he is a consummate hypocrite. The chatter of officials' wives, the humours of class distinctions, the queer character of the baboo and his wonderful English are amusingly caught. [Macmillan: o.p.; Appleton, New York: o.p.]

—— *A Voyage of Consolation.* 1898

A sequel to *An American Girl in London.* Another *jeu d'esprit* of transatlantic travel, an American senator, his wife and daughter touring in Europe. [Methuen: o.p.; Appleton, New York: o.p.]

—— *The Path of a Star.* 1899

Somewhat graver, though the main thing is still comedy and light satire. A group of contrasted characters in Calcutta; a beautiful young Salvationist, a brilliant actress, a society lady, and two Oxford friends; all of whom fall in love with the wrong persons. [Methuen: o.p.]

COTES, Mrs. Everard (*continued*). *The Imperialist.*　　　　1904
　　Life in a Canadian township ; trade, religion, local politics, and the evolution of a young statesman ; with some sentimental matters. [Constable : o.p.]

—— *Cousin Cinderella.*　　　　1908
　　Told by Mary Trent herself, the Canadian cousin on a visit to England, where she wins a young lord in competition with an American heiress. The usual lively pictures of English society, with an implied criticism from the American and Canadian standpoint. [Methuen : o.p. ; Grosset, New York : o.p.]

COTTON, Albert Louis. *The Company of Death.*　　　　1905
　　The ten days' revolt in Naples against the Spanish domination (1647) ; the fisherman-dictator Masaniello, the painter Salvator Rosa. [Blackwood : o.p.]

COUPERUS, Louis Marie Anne [Dutch ; 1863–1923]. *Footsteps of Fate* (Noodlot).　　　　1890
　　An imaginative study of fatalism : characters, two Dutchmen and an English girl, whom one of them loves. The poor man, an emasculate creature, sponges on his wealthy friend, and when he fears he will lose by his friend's marriage, yields to the impulse to estrange the lovers. The state of mind of a man who would fain impute his crimes to Fate or the innate defects of character is forcibly exhibited as a case of moral pathology. As omens and presages have hinted from the beginning, the end is tragedy for all. [Transl. by Clara BELL, Heinemann : o.p.]

—— *Majesty* (Majesteit).　　　　1893
　　A study of the life of royalty ; scene, the empire of Lipara, an autocratic state in southern Europe ; personages, the reigning Emperor, the Crown Prince, the royal family, friends, courtiers, and nobility. Interest centres in the growth and trials of a young prince, whose sensitive nature is morbidly oppressed by the terrible responsibilities of his position and the lack of real compensations. [Transl. by A. Texeira DE MATTOS and E. Dowson, Unwin : o.p. ; new transl. by the former, Dodd & Mead, New York, 1921.]

—— *Ecstasy : a study of happiness* (Extaze).　　　　1892
　　A widow with two children and a middle-aged bachelor fall in love, and work themselves into such a state of unhealthy ecstasy that they dare not put their love to the test of everyday life. They decide to separate rather than spoil the illusion which they have built up. [New transl. by A. Texeira DE MATTOS, Dodd & Mead, New York, 1919.]

—— *Eline Vere.*　　　　1889
　　Life of a neurotic, introspective woman, bored with society at the Hague, bored with life on a country estate, and just as bored with the quasi-bohemian existence she leads with some relatives in Brussels. Her engagement to an eligible young Dutchman fails to make her any happier ; she breaks it off, and after much unhappiness of her own making commits suicide. [Transl. by J. T. GREIN, Chapman : o.p.]

—— *Psyche.*　　　　1898
　　A fairy-tale or moral allegory. [Transl. by B. S. BERRINGTON, Rivers : o.p.]

—— *Small Souls* (De Kleine Zielen, 1902).　　　　1914

—— *The Later Life* (Het Late Leven) [sequel].　　　　1915

—— *The Twilight of the Souls* (Zielenschemering) [sequel].　　　　1917

—— *Dr. Adriaan* (Het Heilige Weten) [sequel].　　　　1918
　　A study of the human soul in transition from empty worldliness to a desire for understanding and wisdom ; at the same time a cruel picture of the utter boredom, pettiness, and spite underlying Dutch family life in all its phases. In these four volumes Couperus has rendered the spirit of Holland better than in any other of his works. [Transl. by A. Texeira de MATTOS, Heinemann ; Dodd & Mead, New York.]

—— *Old People and the Things that Pass* (Van Oude Menschen: die Dingen die voorbijgaan, 1906).
　　　　1918
　　Three old people, a great-grandmother who had betrayed her husband, the lover who killed him, and the doctor who knew of the deed, are seen waiting and brooding on their secret knowledge ; and around them the children and grandchildren, some of whom know or suspect. This is a novel that contemplates life from a comprehensive view-point, and presents characters that are profoundly alive and conscious of realities. [Transl. by Alexander Texeira DE MATTOS, Dodd & Mead, New York ; Butterworth.]

—— *The Tour : a story of ancient Egypt* (Antiek-Toerisme, 1911).　　　　1920
　　A learned descriptive account of Alexandria, Memphis, etc., at the time of Tiberius (A.D. 20), in the shape of a rich young patrician's tour. [Transl. by A. T. DE MATTOS, Dodd & Mead, New York ; Butterworth.]

—— *The Comedians : a story of ancient Rome* (De Komedianten, 1917).　　　　1917
　　A well-informed but not very lively picture of Rome, the imperial Court, the men of letters, the Apostle John, etc. (A.D. 76). [Transl. by J. Menzies WILSON, Cape ; Doubleday, Doran, New York.]

—— *Eighteen Tales.*　　　　1924
　　Little stories woven, for the most part, out of every-day incidents of life ; selected from contributions to *Het Vaderland.* *Uniform and No Uniform* and *The Imagined Life* deal with the world of might-have-been ; *Two Pairs of Twins* is a comedy. [Transl. by J. KOOISTRA, White : o.p.]

COURNOS, John [born in Russia ; b. 1881] [ed.]. *Short Stories out of Soviet Russia.*　　　　1930
　　Horror and pity characterize the best of these stories of the revolution and the civil war : e.g. *The Child* by Vsevolod Vanov or *The Man You Couldn't Kill* by Sergeyev-Tzensky. Efim Zozulya's *Tale about Ak and Humanity* is a satire giving comic relief, and there are stories from Pilniak, Babel, Aleksei Tolstoy, Vladimir Lidin, etc. [Dent ; Dutton, New York.]

"COURTELINE, Georges" [French; 1861–1929]. *The Bureaucrats* (Messieurs les ronds-de-cuir).　　　　1928
　　Light and amusing satire upon the Civil Service, appropriately illustrated by D. Nachsen. [Transl. by Eric SUTTON, Constable.]

COWAN, James [New Zealander ; b. 1870]. *The Adventures of Kimble Bent : a story of wild life in the New Zealand bush.*　1911
　The hero deserted, and lived with the Maori for thirteen years about the middle of the nineteenth century, witnessing horrible scenes of cannibalism and massacre in the ruthless war of British conquest. [Whitcombe & Tombs : o.p.]

COYLE, Kathleen [Irish]. *A Flock of Birds.*　1930
　The mental experiences of a condemned man and his nearest relations, in the Black-and-Tan period in Dublin, between sentence and execution, related from the mother's point of view—pathos subdued to beauty. [Cape ; Dutton, New York.]

CRACKANTHORPE, Hubert M. [1865–96]. *Wreckage ; and other stories.*　1893
　Little masterpieces of stern, tragic realism, of a kind more common in French literature than in English : a relentless exposure of the seamy side of modern life, terrible in their cold, unimpassioned statement of the saddest things. Read, for instance, *A Conflict of Egoisms* or *A Dead Woman.* [Heinemann : o.p.]

—— *Sentimental Studies.*　1895
　Not quite up to the same level, though *Battledore and Shuttlecock* is in the same genre. Crackanthorpe's fine, thrifty art and also his gentle disposition are well exemplified in *A Set of Village Tales.* [Heinemann : o.p.]

—— *Vignettes.*　1896
　A little collection of scraps and impressionist sketches from his note-books ; the most characteristic perhaps is *Anthony Garstin's Courtship.* [Lane : o.p.]

—— *Last Studies.*　1897
　A sheaf gleaned after Crackanthorpe's death, with an unappreciative introduction by Henry James. [Heinemann : o.p.]

"CRADDOCK, Charles Egbert" [Mary Noailles Murfree ; American ; 1850–1922]. *In the Tennessee Mountains.*　1884
　Eight stories, strong in the dramatization of fierce, primitive natures, of the rugged and uncouth dwellers in the Great Smoky Mountains ; reproducing the rude dialect, and describing the magnificent scenery of the forest ranges and gloomy valleys with extraordinary pictorial vigour. [Houghton, Boston.]

—— *Where the Battle was Fought.*　1884
　Characters of a more elevated class : an old Southern general and his daughter, victims of the war, a young officer her lover, lawyers, financiers, and the society of a country town in Tennessee. The story turns on powerful motives and feelings that hardly come to the surface, the two lines of interest being the growth and ultimate ripening of love between the officer and Marcia, and a deep-laid plot to rob another young lady of her fortune. What gives the book a peculiar imaginative colouring is the proximity of the old battlefield, haunting the lives of men and unconsciously swaying their souls. [Houghton, Boston.]

—— *The Prophet of the Great Smoky Mountains.*　1885
　The classic portrayal of the Tennessee mountaineer, the sublimity of his domicile, the squalor and lawlessness that condition his life, and the finer aspirations struggling in his soul. Singles out two characters from the crowd of brutal and lawless hillmen and primitive villagers, Hiram and Dorinda ; the one a moody, introspective preacher, a Bunyan worsted by his doubts ; the other a girl of beautiful nature, born in a family of rascals and idlers. [Houghton, Boston ; Chatto : o.p.]

—— *In the Clouds.*　1887
　Here again the interests are largely spiritual and ideal ; and in the exuberant descriptions of nature, the influence of physical surroundings on the mind is traced. A tragic story, the faithful heroine, bewildered by her troubles, going mad. [Houghton, Boston.]

—— *The Despot of Broomsedge Cove.*　1889
　A longer novel picturing very fully the magnificent phenomena of the mountain regions, and the varied life in homestead, tavern, and store, of this strange, motley people. Three figures are very characteristic : the domineering and fiery young hero, the proud and fascinating heroine, and her sarcastic grandmother. The plot hinges on a mysterious murder. [Houghton, Boston : o.p.]

—— *In the Stranger People's Country.*　1891
　The story of an American Don Quixote ; a rugged, courageous, and lofty figure. A dramatic story, well grounded in realism which accentuates the ideality of its main theme. [Harper, New York : o.p.]

—— *His Vanished Star.*　1894
　Mountaineers and townspeople delineated in the same objective manner, one young native being singled out for deeper portraiture : the omen of a "temporary star" which he takes to himself supplies the title. The doings of "moonshiners," with their illicit still, the pursuit of a man on a murder charge, the ill-starred scheme of a capitalist for building a huge sanatorium, and certain love affairs furnish abundance of plot interest. [Houghton, Boston : o.p. ; Chatto : o.p.]

—— *The Young Mountaineers.*　1897
　Short stories, chiefly about young men and their exploits and adventures ; see, e.g., *A Mountain Storm.* The grand aspects of nature are made great use of. [*Illus.* by Malcolm Fraser, Houghton, Boston.]

—— *The Story of Old Fort Loudon.*　1899
　A story of the Seven Years' War in North America (1758), and the massacre at Fort Loudon by the Cherokees. [Macmillan, New York : o.p.]

—— *A Spectre of Power.*　1903
　The struggles of the French and English in the Mississippi Valley (1762). [Houghton, Boston : o.p.]

—— *The Storm Centre.*　1905
　The growth of understanding and affection in difficult circumstances—a widow of Confederate sympathies growing to love a Federal officer, invalided at her house. [Macmillan, New York and London : o.p.]

"CRADDOCK, Charles Egbert" (*continued*). *The Amulet.* 1906

English frontier fighting with the Cherokee Indians in Tennessee (1763), the jealousies and quarrels of the young officers, a love affair, and Indian superstitions, worked into a romance. [Macmillan, New York and London : o.p.]

—— *The Windfall.* 1907

Scene, Colbury, a dead old town in Tennessee, where a travelling fair is stranded, one of the showmen, Lloyd, serving to link together and contrast the opposite spheres of society. He is the submerged gentleman who comes in for the windfall. The love-story centres in a country girl of fine primitive nature, and is broken by savage outbursts of passion and by exciting incidents between revenue officers and the moonshiners. [Duffield, New York : o.p. ; Chatto : o.p.]

—— *The Fair Mississippian.* 1908

A romantic story of an old house on a lonely cotton plantation on the Mississippi, with supernatural and semi-supernatural effects and love adventures. [Houghton, Boston.]

CRAIGIE, Pearl Mary Teresa [*née* Richards ; " John Oliver Hobbes " ; 1867–1906 ; American by birth]. *Tales.* 1894

Four very actual and searching stories of modern society, rather fantastic in idea, pessimistic and cynical in criticism of life, clever and epigrammatic in style. *The Sinner's Comedy* (1892) is typical. The sinner's wife is an admirable woman, despised and slighted by her husband, whereas she might have been the good genius of a finer man, whose life is a blank without her. The irony of fate—or rather of human society—is set forth with bitter pathos. *Some Emotions and a Moral* (1891), a tragical love-tale, is a good introduction to Mrs. Craigie's curious blend of the real and the imaginary world. The other stories are *A Study in Temptations* (1893) and *A Bundle of Life* (1894), both rather strange and morbid in their main theme, and embracing some charmingly eccentric by-characters. [Unwin ; Stokes, New York : o.p.]

—— *The Gods, Some Mortals, and Lord Wickenham.* 1895

A good man's marriage to a woman with a past, treated from a lofty standpoint. The husband's is a pathetic story of forsaken ideals. Lord Wickenham, confidant of the husband and official commentator, expounds the moral that a man should marry the goddess that he loves and not from mere weakness stoop to earth. [Unwin ; Appleton, New York : o.p.]

—— *The Herb Moon : a fantasia.* 1896

A little drama of the bizarre kind dear to Mrs. Craigie—the prolonged and interrupted courtship of a supposed widow, who has a living husband in an asylum. She is a pathetic type of suffering womankind ; the man is a strong, pure-natured, taciturn character. [Unwin : o.p.]

—— *The School for Saints.* 1897

—— *Robert Orange* [sequel]. 1900

Two parts of a rambling life-history that opens up some moral problems. The more significant characters are uncommon in type, highly intellectual, lofty in their ideals, touched with decadence, thoroughly modern. The hero and his friends discuss religion, the greater issues of life, and other matters of deep emotional interest in a very solemn and self-conscious way. Robert Orange, a paragon among feminine heroes, loves a woman whose husband proves to be living, and they part ; yet when the husband dies leaving them free, the idealist and visionary renounces love and seeks peace in the cloister ; he has already abandoned a brilliant political career. Orange is an idealized study of Disraeli, who further is introduced in person. [(1) and (2), Unwin ; Stokes, New York : o.p.]

—— *The Serious Wooing : a heart's history.* 1901

A story of high society, castigating its pettiness and insincerity with pointed wit. The headstrong heroine, sacrificing all to her forbidden passion, appears respectable compared with the empty and cynical worldlings who constitute this spurious aristocracy. [Unwin ; (Wayfarer's Lib.), Dent.]

—— *Love and the Soul Hunters.* 1902

Introduces us to the world of throneless princes, morganatic marriages, subterranean diplomacy, and high finance, the most compelling figure being a *demi-mondaine* of consummate cleverness hailing from America. Her daughter, a wholesome English girl, is loved by a libertine prince—" a sentimental soul-hunter, a specialist in souls "—and a sour German doctor : which of them will win ? As usual, all the characters, always and everywhere, talk glibly like critics of life, not actors in it. [Unwin ; Funk & Wagnalls, New York : o.p.]

—— *The Vineyard.* 1904

A sarcastic, paradoxical, and not over-convincing picture of middle-class mediocrity, modern affectation of culture, and undiluted philistinism, in a provincial town, with the usual impersonations of decadence that Mrs. Craigie affects. [Unwin : o.p.]

—— *The Dream and the Business.* 1906

A family of Nonconformists in Bayswater, some middle-class Hampstead people, a lord and his lady unsatisfactorily mated, and other modern personalities, some commonplace and some complex and bizarre—drawn with little sympathy, though less satire than pervades the last book (Mrs. Craigie was a Roman Catholic). Vague and inconclusive as a story—in Mrs. Craigie's way—but abounding in keen flashes of insight into life and the objects of life, religion, society, culture and barbarism, and in her old brilliant epigram. Gladstone makes an appearance. [Unwin ; Appleton, New York ; (Wayfarer's Lib.), Dent.]

CRAIK, Dinah Maria [*née* Mulock ; 1826–87]. *The Ogilvies.* 1849

Mrs. Craik wrote a long series of mediocre domestic novels with a strong didactic tendency, of which the better are given here. This is a story of first love, told with plenty of sentiment and some scenes of pathos, as, for example, that of Leigh's death. [Macmillan : o.p. ; Harper, New York : o.p.]

—— *Olive.* 1850

The main story—there are divers underplots—is an attempt to make an attractive heroine of a cripple who is without beauty ; the latter half deals with the cripple's successful attempt to convert her agnostic husband. [Macmillan, 1890 ; Harper, New York : o.p.]

CRAIK, Dinah Maria (*continued*). *John Halifax, Gentleman.* 1856

This is Mrs. Craik's finest story—her full-length portrait of an ideal man. By faithfulness and courage he rises from extreme poverty to wealth, and marries a girl of gentle family. The period covered is 1780–1834, and we get peeps at Lady Hamilton and other celebrities, glimpses of the riots caused by the introduction of steam machinery, and a pleasing chronicle of old-fashioned life in a provincial town (Tewkesbury). It is supposed that Halifax was studied from Handel Cossham, son of a Gloucestershire carpenter, and later a wealthy colliery proprietor. [Everyman's Lib.), Dent (Dutton, New York), 1907; Warne; Harrap; Macmillan, London and New York; Harper, New York; Dodd & Mead, New York; Crowell, New York; *illus.* by C. M. Brock, Seeley; by Warwick Goble, Oxford Press, 1914.]

—— *A Life for a Life.* 1859

A problem-novel, dealing with the nemesis of a repented crime and assailing capital punishment. A man attacks another under extreme provocation and accidentally kills him. He keeps the act secret until, later on, he loves a woman, who turns out to be his victim's half-sister. [Hurst & Blackett: o.p.; Harper, New York: o.p.]

—— *Mistress and Maid.* 1862

A sober tale of humble life, didactic like the rest. Both mistress and maid are womanly and exemplary people, the one gaining the reader's sympathy by her determined struggle with adversity, the other by her simplicity and loyalty and the pathos of her love romance. [Hurst & Blackett: o.p.; Harper, New York: o.p.]

—— *The Woman's Kingdom.* 1868

Less ambitious, but shows some mastery of feminine character. The love stories of two sisters are contrasted. The plain sister is loved for her good disposition and happy home life; the beauty is incapable of deep affection, and her lover's life and her own are marred by her selfishness and inconstancy. [Hurst & Blackett: o.p.; Harper, New York: o.p.]

CRAKE, Rev. Augustus David [1836–1890]. *Æmilius.* [juvenile] 1871

A tale of the Decian and Valerian persecutions, and the Persian defeat of Valerian; scenes, Rome, Antioch, Nisibis, etc. (250–269). [Mowbray (Morehouse, Milwaukee), 1921.]

—— *Edwy the Fair; or, The First Chronicle of Æscendune: a tale of the days of St. Dunstan.*

[juvenile] 1874

Edwy as prince and then as king, his invasion of Mercia and his defeat, with Dunstan, Queen Elgiva, and Edwy's brother Edgar among the prominent characters. [Longmans, London and New York, 1928.]

—— *Alfgar the Dane; or, The Second Chronicle of Æscendune.* [juvenile] 1875

Tells in the form of a fictitious diary the tale of the struggle with the Danes—Ethelred the Unready and Edmund Ironside versus Sweyn and Canute. [Longmans, London and New York, 1925.]

—— *The Rival Heirs: being the third and last chronicle of Æscendune.* [juvenile] 1882

The battle of Hastings, and subsequent struggles between Englishmen and Norman. Harold, William the Conquerer, and Hereward make their appearance. Ends with the First Crusade and the capture of Jerusalem. [Longmans (1926).]

—— *The Last Abbot of Glastonbury: a tale of the dissolution of the monasteries.* [juvenile] 1884

Scenes, Glastonbury, Dartmoor, Exeter (1524–47). [Mowbray; (Morehouse, Milwaukee).]

—— *The House of Walderne: a tale of the cloister and the forest in the days of the Barons' Wars.*

[juvenile] 1886

Sussex, Kenilworth, and Oxford during the Barons' Wars (1253–64). [Longmans, London and New York, 1926.]

CRAMB, J. A. *Schönbrunn: a romance of Napoleon.* 1918

A thin veneer of fiction covers an attempt to give an analysis of the mind of Napoleon during three days at the time of the signing of the treaty of Schönbrunn (October, 1809). [Putnam.]

CRANE, Stephen [American; 1871–1900]. *The Red Badge of Courage.* 1895

An extraordinary example of psychological portraiture—subject, the state of mind of the soldier in action; the brilliant work of an inexperienced youth who studied the phenomena at second-hand. Consists virtually of one episode, the protracted battle of Chancellorsville (1863). [Appleton, New York (1925); Heinemann.]

—— *The Little Regiment.* 1896

Similar stories and studies, the title-story an episode in a big engagement; the effect of actuality obtained by an introspective mode of relation, strange and striking epithets being added and added until a detailed picture is before the eye. [Appleton, New York: o.p.; Heinemann: o.p.]

—— *The Third Violet.* 1897

Developed entirely in dialogue, spiced with Yankee slang. A poor, proud artist loves a wealthy girl, and subdues his pride to propose only in the last chapter. Bohemian scenes of struggling artist life in New York. Extremely realistic in reproduction of slovenly, illiterate talk and slangy manners. [Appleton, New York: o.p.; Heinemann: o.p.]

—— *The Open Boat.* 1898

Stories as vivid as his earliest masterpiece, with the addition that Crane had now seen action for himself. Title-story based on his escape from the *Commodore* during the Cuban War; tales of sea and land, filibustering expeditions, narrow escapes, humorous incidents, etc. [Doubleday, New York: o.p.; Heinemann: o.p.]

—— *Active Service.* 1899

A war correspondent's adventures in love and war during the Græco-Turkish campaign (1897) where Crane served in this capacity. Very rough and slangy in style. [Stokes, New York: o.p.; Heinemann: o.p.]

—— *The Monster; and other stories.* 1896

The longest story, *The Monster*, condensed into a series of pithy scenes and dialogues, is the realistic development of a ghastly idea. A negro servant, with unexpected heroism, rescues his master's son from a

CRANE, Stephen (*continued*).

burning house and is hideously disfigured. The master, a village doctor, concentrates his science on the task of saving the life of this horrible wreck of humanity, and his stubborn devotion involves him in ruin. *His New Mittens* is a story of boy life. [Harper, New York : o.p.]

—— *Wounds in the Rain : a collection of stories relating to the Spanish-American war of 1898.* 1900
Similar impressionist pictures of warfare by a correspondent who was in the thick of it, e.g. *The Price of Harness*, a tale in the same genre as *The Red Badge*. [Stokes, New York : o.p. ; Methuen : o.p.]

—— *Bowery Tales.* 1900
George's Mother (Arnold, New York : o.p., 1896) and *Maggie : a girl of the streets* (Appleton, New York : o.p. ; Heinemann, 1896)—two studies of slum life in New York, by a disciple of Tolstoy, who professed unshrinking fidelity, and evolved a hideous picture of squalor, brutality, and crime. [Heinemann : o.p. ; *Maggie*, illus. by Bernard Sanders, ltd. ed., Newland Press, New York, 1930.]

—— *Whilomville Stories.* 1900
Tales and studies of American child-life ; the misadventures, practical jokes, amusing foibles and antics of precocious youths of eight and nine, humorously related. *Shame*, *The Carriage Lamps*, and *Making an Orator* are amusing sketches of boy-nature. [Harper, New York : o.p.]

CRANE, Stephen, and BARR, Robert (" Luke Sharp "). *The O'Ruddy.* 1903
An amusing, rollicking, unreal story written round a capital Irishman—" a fairy story for grown-ups." [Stokes, New York : o.p. ; Methuen : o.p. *Works :* 12 vols. (in sets), ed. by Wilson Follett, ltd. ed. Knopf, New York and London, 1925–6.]

CRAVEN, Mrs. Augustus [Pauline Marie Armande Aglaé, *née* de la Ferronays ; French ; 1808–91]. *Fleurange* (1871). 1872
A cosmopolitan novel, showing wide knowledge of the world, and comprising scenes of domestic life in Germany, of conventual and aristocratic life in Italy, and of the Court of Petersburg, where the writer's father was ambassador. Amongst the characters the strong and womanly heroine stands out as a conception worthy of the best traditions of the old French nobility. Mrs. Craven is best known as the author of the *Récit d'une sœur*, an intimate record of her family life. [Transl. by E. Bowles, 2 vols., Smith & Elder : o.p.]

CRAWFORD, Francis Marion [American ; 1854–1909]. *Mr. Isaacs.* 1882
A thrilling mystery novel of Indian life that has something of the fascination of the *Arabian Nights*. The esoteric Buddhist who captivates the English girl, is said to be drawn from a notorious Persian merchant who had a dispute with the Nizam about a famous diamond. [Together with *With the Immortals*, Macmillan, New York ; alone, Macmillan.]

—— *Doctor Claudius.* 1883
A romance almost as improbable, though the mystery is not connected with the supernatural. In the main, a love-story of the good old sort, with an Admirable Crichton hero and sparkling dialogue. Time, that of Lytton's viceroyalty and the second Afghan war. [Together with *Zoroaster*, Macmillan, New York and London ; alone, Nelson.]

—— *To Leeward.* 1883
An Englishwoman married to an Italian is unfaithful, and is murdered in revenge. [Macmillan, New York ; Ward & Lock : o.p.]

—— *A Roman Singer.* 1884
A garrulous old man recounts the career of a fortunate Italian peasant boy, who became a great tenor and won the hand of a beautiful lady. [Macmillan, New York and London ; Nelson.]

—— *Zoroaster.* 1885
A Persian romance of the times of Darius and the prophet Daniel, brilliant in *mise-en-scène* ; the ideas modern. Opens with a tableau of Belshazzar's feast. [*Vide Dr. Claudius, supra.*]

—— *An American Politician.* 1885
A story of politics in Boston, by one not particularly familiar with the subject. [With *Marion Darche*, Macmillan, New York ; Ward & Lock : o.p.]

—— *A Tale of a Lonely Parish.* 1886
A quiet study of commonplace life and of the characteristics of a small group of average people in the country. [*Vide A Cigarette-Maker's Romance, infra.*]

—— *Saracinesca.* 1887
—— *Sant' Ilario* [sequel]. 1889
—— *Don Orsino* [sequel]. 1892
—— *Corleone : a Sicilian story* [sequel]. 1898
A panorama of Roman society from 1865 to the present day, set forth in the annals of a princely house. The first two are a romance of passion and jealousy, in which the loves of the chaste and beautiful Corona and Sant' Ilario are the central interest : family feuds and reconciliations, duels, battles, suicide, furnish violent incidents, while Roman life is presented in a host of public and private characters, priests of all grades, gallant nobles like Prince Saracinesca and Sant' Ilario, Don Orsino (son of the latter, grandson of the former), Count Spicca and other prominent members of Roman society, and many side-studies of inconspicuous people. The corruption of public life is exposed, and the obscure forces agitating the financial world are the special subject in *Don Orsino*, where the young hero occupies himself with the building speculations that were such a striking phenomenon in the recent history of Roman business. *Corleone* is a Sicilian episode in the history of the Saracinesca, bringing them into contact with the Corleone, " the worst blood in Italy," and the Mafia. Marion Crawford, as an American residing in Rome, had an intimate knowledge of Italian life and character. [(1) Macmillan, New York ; Blackwood ; (2), (3), and (4), Macmillan, New York and London.]

CRAWFORD, Francis Marion (*continued*). *Marzio's Crucifix*. 1887

Strong in realistic portraiture of lower and middle class Italians. Pre-eminently a study of a single personality, that of a born artist, true descendant of Cellini and the Renaissance. This man is an unbeliever and a fanatical anarchist, hating his brother, a priest and his own patron. The crucial incident brings out his moral cowardice by the touchstone of a projected murder which is never perpetrated. [With *A Lady of Rome*, Macmillan, New York ; alone, Macmillan.]

—— *Paul Patoff*. 1887

The many-coloured life of modern Constantinople is painted in a series of vivacious scenes at the beginning of the story. Two brothers are the chief characters, one of whom disappears mysteriously, and a tangle of sensational events is the result. [Macmillan, New York and London.]

—— *With the Immortals*. 1888

A conference near Sorrento, where Crawford was living, in which the geniuses of all time—Cæsar, Francis I, Bayard, Leonardo da Vinci, Pascal, Dr. Johnson, Chopin, Heine—talk about all sorts of subjects and utter grave reflections on life. [*Vide Mr. Isaacs, supra.*]

—— *Greifenstein*. 1889

A story of German militarism ; scene, the Black Forest. [With *Khaled, infra*, Macmillan, New York.]

—— *A Cigarette-Maker's Romance*. 1890

Marion Crawford was always an admirable craftsman, ingenious as a constructor of plots, deft in execution. This novel and, perhaps, *Marzio's Crucifix* are works of more genuine artistic merit. This is a pathetic little romance, worked out on almost regular dramatic lines, and comprehending just two days. Scene, Munich, with a small group of foreign characters, the most engaging of whom are a quixotic Count, and a poor Polish girl, beautified by self-denying love. [With *A Tale of a Lonely Parish*, Macmillan, New York ; alone, Macmillan ; Nash.]

—— *Khaled : a tale of Arabia*. 1891

An Oriental fantasia with a genie for hero, who craves from Allah the gift of a human soul and life hereafter, and is bidden to earn the boon by winning a woman's love. [*Vide Greifenstein, supra* ; alone, Macmillan.]

—— *The Witch of Prague*. 1891

A novel of hypnotism based on a Bohemian legend. [Macmillan, New York.]

—— *The Three Fates*. 1892

An analytical novel after Howells and Henry James, dealing with society life in New York ; the character of a hesitating, untrustworthy man, is subtly evolved, and there is a good deal of emotional interest. [Macmillan, New York.]

—— *The Children of the King*. 1893

This is the surname of a race of Calabrian peasants ; the last representative, an heroic, primitive character, is contrasted with a cultured but worthless aristocrat. The peasant's devotion to a hopeless love is the soul of tragedy, but the *dénouement* is violent and melodramatic. [With *The White Sister*, Macmillan, New York ; alone, Macmillan.]

—— *Pietro Ghisleri*. 1893

Ghisleri is something like the traditional Byronic hero, a self-contained, somewhat taciturn man, with a dark reputation, but in reality a generous, even heroic, character. How he and a good English girl, two apparently antipathetic characters, come in the end to love each other is one thread of the plot, another is about a criminal conspiracy directed against these two by a jealous, neurotic woman. The pleasures, jealousies, and quarrels of the gay set in Roman high society are portrayed with evident familiarity, and we are introduced again to several of those gentlemen of noble lineage and chivalrous manners who are such good company in previous stories. [Macmillan, New York.]

—— *Katherine Lauderdale*. 1894

—— *The Ralstons* [sequel]. 1894

The beginning of another great family chronicle like the Saracinesca series. The Lauderdales are a wealthy family in New York, who with their social intimates are set before us in a gallery of analytical portraits almost in the style of Henry James. The leading motives are clandestine marriage and its consequences, and the efforts to reform an inebriate, John Ralston. [(1) and (2), Macmillan, New York.]

—— *Love in Idleness : a Bar Harbour tale*. 1894

A charming little tale that was the author's own favourite. [Macmillan, New York and London : o.p.]

—— *Casa Braccio*. 1895

A violent tale of passion, with some melodrama arising from a peasant's long-cherished vengeance. The under-characters are chiefly peasants. Scene, Subiaco in the Sabine hills. The Americans and the genteel characters are of the average kind. [Macmillan, New York.]

—— *Taquisara*. 1896

Plot contains much melodrama, and some revolting features ; a conventional love-story is combined with it. Veronica, the heroine, by far the finest character, is a young girl, last of a wealthy and princely house, a strong, unconventional nature, with high ideals of duty and a will to realize them. [Macmillan, New York and London.]

—— *A Rose of Yesterday*. 1897

The heroine is a singularly noble woman, intelligibly and convincingly portrayed ; the book is an emphatic protest against the laxity of marriage laws in America. [With *The Heart of Rome*, Macmillan, New York ; alone, Macmillan.]

—— *Via Crucis: a romance of the Second Crusade*. 1899

A melodramatic romance of the days of Stephen and the Second Crusade (c. 1146–9), dealing chiefly with the adventures of a brave English knight. Eleanor of Aquitaine, wife successively of Louis VII and of Henry II of England, and Bernard of Clairvaux are prominent. The feuds of Stephen and Matilda are among the motives. [Macmillan, New York and London.]

CRAWFORD, Francis Marion (*continued*). *In the Palace of the King : a love story of Old Madrid.*
1900
A story of passion, in the court of Philip II at Madrid (1574), brief and compact as a play. The king's brother, the chivalrous Don John of Austria, loves a lady of the Court, and by his determination to marry her, brings himself into collision with his hard and cruel brother, and with the more powerful of his counsellors. [Macmillan, New York and London.]

—— *Marietta : a maid of Venice.*
1901
Marietta, daughter of a wonderful old glassblower of enormous wealth, loves, and is loved, by her father's workman, a foreigner, who is assailed by the jealous plots of the citizens. Based on actual incidents (*c.* 1470). [Macmillan, New York and London.]

—— *Cecilia : a story of modern Rome.*
1902
The two lovers have met in a former state of existence, but the lady has unfortunately become engaged to her dream-lover's dearest friend—a situation that has to be arbitrarily resolved. The psychical interest is deepened by the author's realistic treatment of Italian life. [Macmillan.]

—— *Soprano : a portrait.*
1905
—— *The Primadonna* [sequel].
1908
—— *The Diva's Ruby* [sequel].
1908
A trio of stories giving the complicated love affairs, the operatic career, and many romantic experiences of an English girl in London and New York. Clever melodrama ballasted with some good character-drawing. [Under the collective title *The Singer's Trilogy*, (1) *sub tit. Fair Margaret*, (2), (3) as above, Macmillan, New York and London.]

—— *Arethusa.*
1907
A dashing romance of love and intrigue in Constantinople (1376), the hero a Venetian merchant who figures in history, and Arethusa a beautiful slave who turns out to be the adopted daughter of a Greek noble. A plot for ousting the usurper Andronicus and reinstalling the deposed Johannes provides incident ; but the book is chiefly imaginary adventure, and hardly attempts to be historical in manners, character, or atmosphere. [Macmillan.]

—— *Stradella : an old Italian love-tale.*
1909
A posthumous love-comedy with grim features, about a seventeenth-century Sicilian, who is a composer and a musician and wins the betrothed of a Venetian senator. The plot brings in the assassins of Monadelschi, who met his death by command of Christina of Sweden. [Macmillan, New York and London. *Works* (Sorrento ed.) : 30 vols., Macmillan, New York.]

CREANGĂ, Ion [Roumanian ; *b.* 1837]. *Recollections ; and other tales.*
1930
Four stories selected from *Scrierile Lui Ion Creangă* (1890–2). The longest, *Recollections from Childhood*, is a set of reminiscences of the author's early years among the peasants of Moldavia. [Transl., Dent.]

CREED, Sibyl. *The Vicar of St. Luke's.*
1901
A High-Church clergyman's attempts to introduce ritualism, the open and the underhand opposition of his parishioners, and his secession to Rome. Criticizes the Anglo-Catholics. The character-drawing has power, e.g. the honest and unfortunate vicar, his two curates, and the hysterical girl who loves him and nearly works his ruin. [Longmans : o.p.]

CRESSWELL, Clarice M. *The Making and Breaking of Almansur.*
1915
The story of Mansur, who rose from humble scribe to be regent for the Caliph in Cordova (tenth century). [Chatto : o.p.]

CRIPPS, Arthur Shearly [*b.* 1869]. *A Martyr's Servant : the tale of John Kent,* A.D. 1553–1563. 1915
—— *A Martyr's Heir : the tale of John Kent,* A.D. 1563–1594 [sequel].
1916
A narrative of the early Jesuit missions (1553–94) in south-east Africa (Makaronga and Monomotapa) ; the martyr is Gonçalo de Silveira. [Duckworth.]

CROCKETT, Samuel Rutherford [Scottish ; 1860–1914]. *The Stickit Minister ; and some common men.*
1893
A typical story-book of the Kailyard school. Stories, somewhat after the manner of Galt, of Galloway villagers, largely in dialect. The work of the minister, and the doctrinal discussions and criticisms of his flock are the theme of some. The Stickit Minister is an example of patience and altruism, who gives up all his substance to his brother, and makes no complaint when repaid with ingratitude. More sentiment and sentimental description than either plot or character, with humour that lies, as the author puts it " near the Fountain of Tears." Cleg Kelly makes his début in two stories. [(Essex Lib.), Benn, 1929 ; Macmillan, New York : o.p. ; Caldwell, Boston : o.p.]

—— *The Raiders.*
1894
—— *The Dark o' the Moon : being certain further histories of the folk called " Raiders "* [sequel].
1902
Melodramatic tales of fighting and smuggling on Solway Moss and the Border (*c.* 1720–30). Moss-troopers, smugglers, and gipsies furnish plenty of adventure and gruesome incident ; and there is harrowing pathos in the episode of Willie, the child-martyr, and his mother. [(1) Unwin ; Nash ; (Essex Lib.), Benn, 1929 ; Macmillan, New York : o.p. ; (2) Macmillan ; Harper, New York : o.p.]

—— *The Lilac Sunbonnet.*
1894
A characteristic specimen of the author's sentimental love-making. The rendering of Galloway scenery and domestic life and character among humble people gives the story local interest. [Unwin ; Appleton, New York.]

—— *Bog-Myrtle and Peat.*
1895
Chiefly stories of Galloway, with a few going farther afield. In *The Minister of Dour*, an old-fashioned minister acts an heroic part, both in subjugating his lawless parishioners and in fighting the plague. *A Cry Across the Dark Water* is a weird little romance of the Galloway Highlands—retribution falling at last on

CROCKETT, Samuel Rutherford (*continued*).

a false lover. Then come tales of contemporary life in the villages and homesteads, with sentimental or sarcastic sketches of homely character, among which Kit Kennedy, ne'er-do-weel, makes his début, and a series of *Tales of the Kirk* in the rustic theological genre now so familiar. [Sands : o.p. ; Appleton, New York : o.p.]

—— *The Men of the Moss-Hags.* 1895
Episodes of the persecution of the Covenanters under Claverhouse (1679–80), the obverse of the picture painted by Scott in *Old Mortality*. [Pitman : o.p. ; Macmillan, New York : o.p.]

—— *Cleg Kelly, the Arab of the Streets.* 1896
Cleg is an Edinburgh street arab of Irish parentage, a boy of sharp and tenacious character, stanch to his friends, a terror to his foes and theirs. His father is a criminal, and his upbringing fits him for a life of roguery ; but the boy's escapades are the mere effervescence of youthful energy, and he keeps straight in the main. When Edinburgh gets too hot to hold him, the scene shifts to a farm-house in Galloway. [Smith & Elder : o.p. ; Appleton, New York : o.p.]

—— *The Grey Man.* 1896
An exaggerated and melodramatic account of the deadly feuds of Galloway about 1601–11. The murder of Sir Thomas Kennedy of Culzean and the events leading up to it are historical, as well as the figures of the murderous villain, John Mure of Auchendrane, and his son. [Unwin ; Harper, New York : o.p.]

—— *Lochinvar.* 1897
Adventures of the famous ballad-hero in the service of William of Orange, and in Scotland after the English Revolution. Battles, plots, escapes, adventures among the Western Isles, and plenty of love-making. [Methuen : o.p. ; Harper, New York : o.p.]

—— *The Standard Bearer.* 1898
The scene is laid in the wilds of Galloway and in Edinburgh (*c.* 1685–90). The struggles and persecutions of the Covenanters furnish the historical basis for a robustious story. [Methuen : o.p. ; Appleton, New York : o.p.]

—— *The Red Axe.* 1898
A sensational story of the wild and lawless Dukes of the Wolfmark in the Germany of the Thirty Years' War. [(Wayfarer's Lib.), Dent ; Harper, New York : o.p.]

—— *The Black Douglas.* 1899
A sensational romance of mediæval Scotland (1439–40) ; doughty knights, herculean yeomen, abnormal villains, wizards and werwolves. [(Wayfarer's Lib.), Dent ; Doubleday, New York : o.p.]

—— *Kit Kennedy.* 1899
A pendant to *Cleg Kelly* ; a further sketch of boy nature and rustic character in Galloway, avowedly picturing the circumstances and influences amid which the author grew up. Kit is a brave lad whose efforts to be good and to earn an honest living are handicapped by a disreputable father. [J. Clarke : o.p.]

—— *The Silver Skull.* 1901
A rousing story of Apulia during the struggle between France and Austria, with an Amazonian heroine, and a bountiful supply of plots, escapes, gory deeds, and thrilling adventures (1815–20). The author has utilized the papers left by Sir Richard Church, who pacified the province. [Smith & Elder : o.p. ; Stokes, New York : o.p.]

—— *Strong Mac.* 1904
Another tale of wild life in Galloway, with a scene or two from the Peninsular War. [Ward & Lock.]

—— *Maid Margaret of Galloway.* 1905
The successive love-affairs of the Fair Maid of Galloway, who appears as a child in *The Black Douglas*. She was wife to two Earls of Douglas. Admirable passages of thrilling narrative are interlarded with mawkish sentiment and crude word-painting in the author's less chastened style. [Hodder : o.p. ; Dodd & Mead, New York : o.p.]

—— *The Cherry Riband.* 1905
Loves of a Covenanter's son and a girl in the camp of the persecutors. A characteristic story of Dumfries and the Bass Rock in the days of Claverhouse. [Hodder : o.p. ; Barnes, New York : o.p.]

—— *The White Plumes of Navarre : a romance of the Wars of Religion.* 1906
Opens with St. Bartholomew, shifts to southern France and Spain, brings in the plots of Catherine de Médicis and the Guises, the horrors of the Inquisition, and the sinister figure of Philip II. [R.T.S. ; Dodd & Mead, New York : o.p.]

—— *The Moss-Troopers.* 1912
A semi-historical romance of love and adventure among smugglers on Solwayside and in London in Queen Charlotte's time. [Hodder : o.p.]

CROFTS, Freeman Wills. *The Cask.* 1920
A detective-novel that has received the highest praise for the mechanical construction of the plot, and anything but praise for the psychology or human probability of the *dénouement*. [Collins ; Boni, New York ; Burt, New York.]

—— *Inspector French's Greatest Case.* 1925
—— *Inspector French and the Starvel Hollow Tragedy.* 1927
Further workmanlike specimens of detective fiction. [(1) and (2), Collins ; (1) Boni, New York ; (2) Harper, New York.]

CROKER, Mrs. Bithia Mary [*née* Sheppard ; Irish]. *Proper Pride.* 1882
An Anglo-Indian story, written to amuse, with some delineation both of European manners and character and of the natives. [Chatto.]

CROKER, Mrs. Bithia Mary (*continued*). *A Bird of Passage.* 1886
> The same kind of circulating-library fiction; love-making in the Andamans, garrison life, amusing sketches of the typical Irish carman, Irish servants, and broken-down gentry. [Chatto.]

—— *Diana Barrington.* 1888
> Anglo-Indian life in a military station; the story draws on the authoress's intimacy with Irish character as well as her sympathetic knowledge of the Indian native. [Chatto.]

—— *Interference.* 1891
> Opens in Ireland and closes in an Indian hill-station. Largely a story of calamities falling on the good characters through the agency of the evil-doers. [Chatto.]

—— *Mr. Jervis: a romance of the Indian Hills.* 1894
> The comedy of Anglo-Indian social life, with a pathetic portrait of a renegade Englishwoman who succumbed to the trials of the Mutiny. [Chatto; Nelson; Lippincott, Philadelphia: o.p.]

—— *Village Tales and Jungle Tragedies.* 1894
> Stories of native life in India, kindly in spirit and intimate in their realism. *A Free-will Offering* is a tiger story elevated to tragedy by the self-devotion of a native whose kin have been devoured, and who lures the man-eater to the rifles. In *The Betrayal of Shere Bahadur* a villainous rajah outwits an Englishman by sacrificing a centenarian elephant. [Chatto.]

—— *In the Kingdom of Kerry.* 1896
> Seven sketchy little stories of poor folk, written in a light and merry style. [Chatto.]

—— *Beyond the Pale.* 1897
> A light and amusing novel of country life in Ireland, sketching the peasants and broken-down gentry, without going very deeply into the Irish temperament or throwing much light on Irish troubles. A millionaire's son loves a poor girl whom misfortunes have put beyond the pale of society, but she is in reality the sole representative of the noble family whose house and lands now belong to the millionaire. [Chatto; Fenno, New York: o.p.]

—— *Terence.* 1899
> Very similar, though the plot is inverted, a rich Australian girl loving the ruined heir of the once princely house of Desmond. Contains exciting episodes, piquant sketches of life in Kerry and of society at an anglers' inn, with comedy of a broad and sometimes vulgar kind, turning on jealousy and scandal. [Chatto; Buckles, New York: o.p.]

—— *Angel.* 1901
> An Anglo-Indian love-tale, with an engaging heroine, a wayward and passionate girl, to whom rather masculine traits combined with real womanliness give a piquant charm. [Methuen; Dodd & Mead, New York: o.p.]

—— *Johanna.* 1903
> She is a beautiful but foolish Kerry girl who runs away to Dublin, and falling into a lodging-housekeeper's clutches, becomes a household drudge. [Methuen.]

—— *A Nine Days' Wonder.* 1905
> Utilizes a well-worn idea—a girl from an Irish cabin is acknowledged as the daughter of a peer, and astonishes society and the reader by her countrified candour. [Methuen: o.p.]

—— *Lismoyle: an experiment in Ireland.* 1914
> A young English heiress spends six months in a decayed Tipperary mansion, and is involved in a love-affair and other amusing situations. [Hutchinson: o.p.; Brentano, New York: o.p.]

—— *Bridget.* 1918
> Social life in Ireland presented with her wonted ability for drawing character, in a story hingeing on the efforts of interested relations to prevent the heroine from following the course that would obviously bring her the greatest happiness. [Hutchinson: o.p.]

—— *Blue China.* 1919
> The character of the crafty and intriguing niece of the enthusiast in old china is interesting. [Hutchinson: o.p.]

—— *Odds and Ends.* 1919
> Mostly Irish stories, the subjects varying from ghosts to racing. [Hutchinson: o.p.]

CROLY, George [Irish; 1780–1860]. *Salathiel, the Immortal: a history.* 1827
> An impressive example of Gothic romance, on the old theme of the Wandering Jew, embellished with Oriental scenery and Oriental grandiloquence. [Republished under title *Tarry Thou Till I Come*, Funk & Wagnalls, New York.]

CROSBIE, Mary [Irish, born in England]. *Kinsmen's Clay.* 1910
> Refined ideals—this is the keynote of the character-drawing, the doings, and the sentiments in this Irish novel, with its crowd of individualized persons grouped around a humorous old lady and her intimates. [Methuen: o.p.]

—— *Bridget Considine.* 1914
> Another thoughtful book. Bridget is of Irish parentage though born in London, and when she goes to the west of Ireland she marries a landowner, who, however, bitterly disappoints her. [Bell: o.p.]

CROTTIE, Julia M. [Irish; b. 1853]. *Neighbours.* 1900
> Twenty sketches of unpleasant aspects of human nature in a stagnant town in Munster. Very truthful, the gossip skilfully reported, the humours and the ingrained melancholy and superstition brought out with fidelity. [Unwin: o.p.; *sub tit. Innisdoyle Neighbours*, Magnificat, Manchester N.H.]

—— *The Lost Land: a tale of a Cromwellian-Irish town, being the autobiography of Miss Annita Lombard.* 1901
> A sort of impassioned summary of Irish history (1780–97) and an indictment of Anglo-Saxon ascendancy, throwing strong light on feelings and political conditions. The loss of a much-loved mother, the fruitless patriotism of a brother, the heroine's own disappointed hopes of her country's resurrection are the tragic elements of a sombre story. [Unwin: o.p.]

CROWE, Catherine [*née* Stevens ; 1800–76]. *Susan Hopley ; or, The Adventures of a Maid-Servant.*
1841
The maid-servant eventually turns out to be a colonel's daughter, though she lives many years as a household drudge. To the domestic story is added plot-interest in the murder of Susan's brother and the events that enable her to convict the murderer. [Routledge, 1883 : o.p.]

—— *Lilly Dawson.* 1847
Brought up in a family of smugglers, the heroine runs away, and after a hard life comes across her relations, gentlefolk. She will not be a fine lady, however, and marries the lover of her humbler days. The author protests against the inferior education given to women, and points out the qualities in which women surpass men. [Routledge, 1878 : o.p.]

—— *The Night Side of Nature.* 1848
A collection of stories and anecdotes of ghosts, apparitions, warnings, trances, haunted houses, etc., asserted to be facts, but derived from all kinds of veracious or doubtful sources. [Edited by E. A. Baker (Half-forgotten Books), Routledge : o.p.]

—— *Linny Lockwood.* 1854
Like *Lilly Dawson*, a fair example of domestic fiction, with a plot like that of *East Lynne*. Betrayed by her husband, Linny finds herself the servant of his deserted mistress, whom she nurses on her death-bed. [o.p.]

CROWLEY, Mary Catherine [American]. *A Daughter of New France ; with some account of the gallant Sieur Cadillac and his colony on the Detroit.* 1901
A brilliant picture of Canada, or New France, under Louis XIV, the Regency of Orleans, and the early years of Louis XV, when the province was governed by Count Frontenac—nearly all the prominent statesmen, explorers, missionaries, soldiers, and Indian chiefs of the period 1687–1735 are introduced, and not only the chief historical events but the buildings, the manners and customs, and trading and military usages are delineated. [Little & Brown, Boston : o.p.]

—— *The Heroine of the Strait : a romance of Detroit in the time of Pontiac.* 1902
Does the same service for the period 1760–70, the story centring in the detection and collapse of the famous conspiracy of Pontiac and the early history of Detroit. [Little & Brown, Boston : o.p.]

—— *Love Thrives in War : a romance of the Frontier in 1812.* 1903
Here again the historical and the romantic events centre in Detroit (1805–32). The destruction of the settlement by fire in 1805, the surrender to the British in 1812, and the American victory on Lake Erie in 1813 are the cardinal incidents. [Little & Brown, Boston : o.p.]

—— *In Treaty with Honour : a romance of Old Quebec.* 1906
Describes the struggle of French Canada for independence, its defeat, and the reforms that ensued (1837–9). Dr. Theller, L. J. Papineau, Lord Gosford, governor of Lower Canada, and President Van Buren are prominent in a host of characters from the annals of the time. [Little & Brown, Boston : o.p.]

CROWTHER, Dr. Philpot [" Gak Tsok-sin "]. *The Travail of his Soul.* 1899
A story of Chinese life, showing great familiarity with Chinese ways and character, and containing suggestions as to the right means for amelioration. [Jarrold : o.p.]

CULLEY, Christopher. *Lily of the Alley.* 1918
A stirring tale of ranch life in Mexico, cowboys, outlawry, love, and fighting. [Cassell : o.p.]

—— *Billy McCoy.* 1919
A Stevensonian or Conradian romance, with plenty of thrills in Billy's experiences among the murderous White-caps. Mexico is depicted with the magical touches of one who has lived in and loved it. [Cassell.]

CULLUM, Ridgwell [*b*. 1867]. *The Story of the Foss River Ranch.* 1903

—— *The Hound from the North : the story of a Canadian farm.* 1904
The best thing in these stories is the faithful presentment of the scenery and atmosphere of the great North-West. [(1) and (2) Page, Boston ; (1) sub tit. The Devil's Keg, Chapman ; (2) Chapman.]

—— *In the Brooding Wild : a mountain tragedy.* 1905
The tragedy of two brothers, who fall in love with the same woman, amid the titanic scenery of the Rockies. [Page, Boston ; Burt, New York ; Chapman : o.p.]

—— *The Watchers of the Plains.* 1909
The story is crude and incredible melodrama, but the free air of the prairies, and the picturesque life of the Indians in the Bad Lands of Dakota and south Nebraska, are brought before the mind with intense vividness. [Burt, New York ; Chapman.]

—— *The Compact : the story of an unrecorded conspiracy in South Africa.* 1909
—— *The Sheriff of Dyke Hole : a story of a Montana mining camp.* 1910
Similar novels of fierce, strenuous life on the frontiers of civilization, sketching character with rough and effective realism, and racy vernacular dialogue, and conveying the spell of nature's vast and solitary aspects with imagination. [(1) Doran, New York : o.p. ; Chapman ; (2) Burt, New York ; Chapman.]

—— *The Trail of the Axe : a story of the Red Sand Valley.* 1911
Pictures with the same vigour and acknowledged fidelity the rugged life of a lumber camp in W. Canada. A strike and desperate rioting give lurid scenes toward the finish. [Burt, New York : o.p. ; Chapman ; Nelson.]

—— *The One-Way Trail.* 1911
A similar story of ranch life in Montana. [Burt, New York ; Chapman.]

—— *The Golden Woman.* 1913
The romance of an innocent girl in a gold-mining camp in Montana. [Chapman ; Macrae Smith, New York.]

—— *The Law of the Gun.* 1918
Another romantic story of elemental things—crime, revenge, love, and the terror of sudden death—on Canadian prairies and in the Rockies among the gold-diggers. [Macrae Smith, New York ; Burt, New York ; Chapman.]

CULLUM, Ridgwell (*continued*). *The Tiger of Cloud River.*   1929

A lumberman is shanghaied on board an Arctic whaler on the eve of his marriage, returns after two years' hardship to execute vengeance and make a fortune, and finally discovers the son whom he has never seen. [Cassell; Lippincott, Philadelphia.]

CUMBERLAND, Gerald [1879–1926]. *The Poisoner.*   1921

The poisoner is the force of heredity from parents, one a murderer, the other a drunkard, acting upon the life of a musical genius. After repeated lapses, he ends in suicide upon learning his father's crime. [Richards: o.p.]

—— *Striving Fire.*   1924

A loosely-hung story of family conflict, the children against the parents and against each other. [Richards; Brentano, New York.]

CUMMINS, Maria Susannah [American; 1827–66]. *The Lamplighter.*   [juvenile] 1854

A moral book for the young; diffuse, sentimental, and exclamatory: very widely read a generation ago. [Houghton, Boston, 1882; Burt, New York; Donohue, Chicago; Collins; Epworth Press; Ward & Lock.]

—— *Mabel Vaughan.*   [juvenile] 1857

Entirely didactic; a model heroine does her duty as sister and daughter, and is rewarded with the hand of a model senator. Laboured and artificial, though not without an occasional touch of nature. [Houghton, Boston: o.p.; Routledge: o.p.]

CUNNINGHAM, Sir Henry Stewart [1832–1920]. *Wheat and Tares.*   1860

A short love-story, with a brilliant and clever young man for principal, whose egoism and adroit mastery of people and events remind one of George Eliot's Tito Melema. Background, society in a seaside town; the conversation characterized by wit and repartee and free handling of sentimental, moral, and religious topics. [Macmillan: o.p.]

—— *Late Laurels.*   1864

Main idea: the contrast between a nature of genuine simplicity and nobleness and a brilliant but artificial character, a product of modern social influences. Sketches of society; smart and lightly sarcastic dialogue. [2 vols., Longmans: o.p.]

—— *The Chronicles of Dustypore.*   1875

Anglo-Indian official and social life in a station of the Sandy Tracts and in a pleasure resort among the hills. A gay little comedy, largely satirical, involving a variety of motives, love in particular; with plenty of lively dialogue. [Murray.]

—— *The Heriots.*   1889

The heroine becomes engaged to a wealthy M.P., who introduces her to the cream of English society, an episode that enables a number of characters to be amusingly sketched. Then she finds she is really in love with another man, poor like herself, to whom the novelist marries her in the last chapter. Sparkling dialogue. [Macmillan: o.p.]

—— *Sibylla.*   1894

The story of the young spendthrift, who breaks his father's heart, disappears after ruining the family property, and comes to light again only to cause embarrassment, is of minor interest compared with the sketches of character and society. Politics and the lighter themes of a pleasure-loving world fill many pages with animated talk. [2 vols., Macmillan: o.p.]

CUNNINGHAME, Alice. *The Love Story of Giraldus: a romance of the twelfth century.*   1907

Gerald of Wales, the narrator, enters the Church when he believes his love is lost for ever. Eleanor of Poitou, wife of Henry II, is a central figure, and life at the French Court, the University of Paris, and on the Welsh Borders is rendered with studious care. [Griffiths: o.p.]

CURTIS, George William [American; 1824–92]. *Prue and I.*   1856

A story or an essay according to the classifier's point of view. Rather, a train of inconsequent musings on life, which the narrator shares with his wife and comrade, Prue—the story and musings give an ideal picture of serene and sympathetic wedlock. Often the reveries take fantastic shapes, as in the story of Titbottom's spectacles, the property of which is to show the real character beneath each man's exterior. A quiet humour and a reverent faith in goodness and charity give these fables and reminiscences a grace like that of Lamb's more personal essays. [Burt, New York; with *Lotus Eating* (Everyman's Lib.), Dent (Dutton, New York), 1910; with *The Public Duty of Educated Men*, Macmillan, New York and London, 1919.]

CURWOOD, John Oliver [Canadian]. *Swift Lightning.*   1920

Story of a Canadian wolf-dog. [Hodder; Cosmopolitan Book Co., New York.]

"CUSHING, Paul" [Roland Alexander Wood-Seys; b. 1854]. *The Blacksmith of Voe.*   1887

A village story of the Peak of Derbyshire, with some description of local customs and scenery—a quarrel and a supposed murder, the return of the imaginary victim twenty years later, and a love affair as means of poetic justice. [Blackwood: o.p.]

CYRANO DE BERGERAC, Savinien [French; 1620–55]. *The Comical History of the States and Empires of the Worlds of the Moon and the Sun* (1662).   1687

A translation of two posthumous romances, *L'histoire comique des états de la lune* (*c.* 1656), and *L'histoire comique des états du soleil* (1662). These were humorous satires of the pedantic science of the day, especially of fantastic theories about the moon. Bishop Godwin's *Man in the Moon* probably gave the suggestion, and Cyrano de Bergerac in turn influenced Swift, and later writers of imaginary voyages. [Transl. by A. LOVELL, Upham: o.p.; *Voyages to the Moon and the Sun*, transl. by Richard ALDINGTON (Broadway Transl.), Routledge (Dutton, New York), 1923.]

CZAYKOWSKI, Michael [afterwards Sadyk Pasha; Polish; 1804–86]. *The Black Pilgrim.*   1900

A story of the struggle for faith and freedom in the Balkan peninsula, written by a Pole who was naturalized in Turkey and became a pasha. A very Oriental story in the violence of its passion and the rapidity of its adventures. A Bulgarian brought up as a Turk is the hero, the heroine is the Christian daughter of a pasha, and the multifarious characters typify the wild and romantic life of the Balkans (*c.* 1806). [Transl. by Count C. S. DE SOISSONS, Digby & Long: o.p.]

DAHN, Julius Sophus Felix [German ; 1834–1912]. *A Struggle for Rome* (Ein Kampf um Rom, 1876). 1878

A great historical novel dealing with the struggles of the Ostrogoths, after the death of Theodoric (526), against the Eastern Emperor Justinian, the campaigns of Belisarius (527–49), the defeat of Totila (522) and of the last king of the Ostrogoths (553). [Transl., 3 vols., Bentley : o.p.]

—— *Felicitas*. 1883

Illustrates the story of the German migrations into the regions about Salzburg (476). Dr. Dahn was a great scholar and historian, like Ebers, rather than a novelist. [Transl., McClurg, Chicago : o.p.]

—— *A Captive of the Roman Eagles* (Bissula, 1894). 1902

The Romans and the Alemanni (Germans) near Lake Constance (378) ; the poet Ausonius figures. [Transl. by Mary J. SAFFORD, McClurg, Chicago : o.p.]

—— *The Scarlet Banner* (Gelimer, 1894). 1903

Overthrow of the Vandal king Gelimer in Africa, by Belisarius (533–4). [Transl. by M. J. SAFFORD, McClurg, Chicago : o.p.]

DALE, Harrison Clifford [b. 1885] [ed.]. *Great Ghost Stories, collected and edited ; with an introduction on the ghost story.* 1930

Fifteen English, Scottish, Irish, American, Continental, and Eastern stories, most of them celebrated examples of the kind, which is carefully analysed and subdivided in the introduction. [Jenkins.]

DALIN, Talmage. *European Relations : a Tyrolese sketch.* 1892

An international sketch of America and of Tyrol, of the mountain scenery of which the book is full. A girl has two love affairs—one abortive, indeed hardly begun, the other quickly consummated with a cousin. The older lover is a study of hesitancy and want of courage. [Unwin : o.p. ; Cassell, New York : o.p.]

DALTON, Moray. *The Sword of Love.* 1920

Story of the plot against Lorenzo and Giuliano de' Medici, and the assassination of the latter, related by a soldier of fortune. Scene, Florence (1477–8). [Collins.]

DAMPIER, E. M. Smith. *Oil of Spikenard.* 1911

A novel of 1752–6, with a Jacobite plot and a glimpse of the Pretender ; but the real story is how the too-perfect daughter of an Oxford scholar yields her heart to a loyal lover and learns not to be a prig. [Melrose : o.p.]

DANA, Richard Henry [American ; 1815–82]. *Two Years before the Mast.* 1840

The classical account of seafaring in a merchant sailing-ship of the old days. Dana, after leaving college, served his two years in a Boston vessel, for the sake of his health, and this is a faithful record of his experiences—a realistic, unexaggerated picture of life on shipboard in all its details. There is no lack of human interest, and the descriptions of the sea itself and of the glorious run home before the wind are full of spirit and vivid truth. [Houghton, Boston ; Crowell, New York, 1917 ; Macmillan, New York and London ; (Everyman's Lib.), Dent (Dutton, New York) 1911 ; *illus.* by Mahlon Blain, Sears, New York, 1927 ; by Edward A. Wilson, Donnelley, Chicago, 1930.]

DANE, Clemence [Winifred Ashton]. *Regiment of Women.* 1917

Woman's rule in a girls' school, of the old-fashioned fashionable kind ; contrasted with an ultra-modern example of co-education, and held up to execration for its inquisitorial and repressive methods. A brilliant mistress stands for the old ideal of absolutism. But her individual interest overwhelms the scholastic thesis. She is a human vampire, fascinating, ruthless, feeding her cold heart on the devotion of pet after pet. One little thing, in a fit of captiousness, she drives to suicide. To this heart-rending tragedy there is an anti-climax in the prosperous love-story of a victim saved from the siren. Psycho-analysis is employed by the rescuer to cure this other girl's obsessions. [Heinemann ; Macmillan, New York.]

—— *First the Blade : a comedy of growth.* 1918

A much more ordinary affair than the previous novel. The commonplace man and the charming girl, and the setting in a Kentish village, are scarcely adequate subjects for the subtle analysis and confidential discussion that the novelist expends upon them. [Heinemann ; Macmillan, New York.]

—— *Legend.* 1919

Sketches with a mordant pen a little coterie of literary and artistic people, pure intellectuals, who are swept with consternation when at the dramatic moment they learn that their great idol, an accomplished novelist, has fallen a victim to that romantic myth, an earthly passion. [Heinemann.]

—— *The Babyons : a family chronicle.* 1928

Four little tragic romances, dated 1750, 1775, 1820–73, and 1902–6, in the history of an old family of baronets in Devonshire, to whose successive generations there clings a fatal curse. [Heinemann ; Doubleday, Doran, New York.]

DANE, Clemence, and **SIMPSON**, Helen de Guerry [b. 1897]. *Enter Sir John.* 1928

An entirely new departure—this is an ingenious detective story, in which Sir John Saumarez, actor-manager and man-about-town, clears a young actress accused of murder. [Hodder ; Cosmopolitan Book Co., New York.]

—— *Printer's Devil.* 1930

An amusing detective-story, the liveliest figures in which are a literary lady running a publishing business and the irrepressible publicity agent. [Hodder.]

DANE, Joan. *Prince Madog, Discoverer of America : a legendary story.* 1909

Expanded from the tradition of Madog's western voyage in 1170 as preserved in the abbey MSS. of Conway and Strata Florida. [Stock : o.p.]

DANIEL-ROPS, Henry [French ; b. 1901]. *The Misted Mirror* (L'âme obscure). 1930

A very serious, uncompromising, and unsentimental study of the problem of post-war youth, who gives back such a misty reflection of ourselves. The dark soul is that of a rebellious, sceptical young fellow, who comes back from the war, and tries to make life bow to his will rather than to fit himself into life. His sexual

DANIEL-ROPS, Henry (*continued*).
> affairs bring him no satisfaction, his friendships have tragic endings, his father in Savoy is dying of remorse. The close of the book shows him older and wiser, but hardly nearer tranquillity. [Transl. by R. H. MOTTRAM, Secker.]

DANILEVSKY, Grigori Petrovich [Russian ; 1829–90]. *The Princess Tarakanova : a dark chapter of Russian history* (1884). 1891
> Deals with a mysterious pretender, who seems to have been the tool of Prince Radziwill, the leader of the conspiracy of Radomsky ; she was treacherously enticed on board the admiral's ship by Count Orlov, at the orders of the Empress, imprisoned in Petersburg, and tradition says was drowned by the rising waters of the Neva (1775–6). [Transl. by I. DE MOUCHANOFF, Sonnenschein : o.p.]

—— *Moscow in Flames* (1886). 1917
> The French invasion of Russia, from the Russian point of view, and the later life of a young nobleman and his betrothed. [Transl. by A. S. RAPPOPORT, S. Paul : o.p.]

DARROW, Clarence [American ; b. 1857]. *Farmington.* 1904
> Recollections of the author's childhood, the village school, parents, and neighbours, inspired this autobiography of a boy's early years and approach to manhood ; quiet, but refreshingly true to life. [Viking Press, New York ; Boni, New York, 1925 ; Cazenove : o.p.]

"**DART**, Edith." *Rebecca Drew.* 1910

—— *Likeness.* 1911
> The first is set in a rustic environment with village characters and simple human motives, Rebecca being the daughter of an ancient line of yeomen, incompatibly mated to a bohemian. The second is a rather daring comedy of the City and Park Lane, turning on a resemblance between two girls. This, however, brings us back eventually to rustic scenes in Devon. [(1), (2), Mills & Boon : o.p.]

DASENT, Sir George Webbe [1817–96]. *Popular Tales from the Norse.* 1859
> A fine English rendering of the fascinating collection of fairy-tales and beast-fables from primitive Norse folk-lore made by Asbjörnsen and Moe, which possibly supplied suggestions to Hans Andersen for some of his stories. Their spontaneity is the most striking characteristic ; they are nature-myths, childish fancies emanating from unsophisticated observation of the ways of animals, dreams of the wonder-world, and romantic fantasies, some with morals, all enjoyable for their own sake. Prefixed is a valuable introduction (87 pp.) on the *Origin and Diffusion of Popular Tales.* [Transl. by DASENT, *illus.*, Routledge, 1907 ; Lippincott, Philadelphia, 1910.]

—— *Annals of an Eventful Life.* 1870
> Containing in the form of a novel a good deal of the author's autobiography. He was a great Scandinavian scholar, and had travelled in Iceland. [Hurst & Blackett : o.p.]

—— *Tales from the Fjeld : a series of popular tales from the Norse of P. Ch. Asbjörnsen.* 1874
> A further collection of the same kind. [Transl. by DASENT, with 140 illustrs. by Moyr Smith, Gibbings, 1896 : o.p. ; Putnam, New York.]

—— *The Vikings of the Baltic.* 1875
> A story of the Vikings, Sweyn, Hakon, and Olaf Trygvason, in the last quarter of the tenth century. Dasent translated the great saga of Burnt Njal (*q.v.*) into fine English. [3 vols., Chapman : o.p.]

DAUDET, Alphonse [French ; 1840–97]. *Little Good-for-Nothing* (Le petit chose, 1868). 1885
> A simple, pathetic story, in the restrained style which preceded the Tartarin extravaganzas. The diminutive hero, a compound of weaknesses and strength of will, meets with slights and persecution as usher in a huge college, and again in his life in Paris ; the struggle with poverty, the yielding to temptation, and the rescue by a devoted brother, embody reminiscences of the author's early life. Some of the humorous episodes and characters, and the sentimentality, show very distinctly Daudet's partiality for Dickens. [Transl., *sub tit. Little What's His Name* (and other stories), Little & Brown, Boston.]

—— *Letters from My Mill* (Lettres de mon moulin, 1869). 1880
> Seventeen tales and descriptive sketches written in a ruined mill on the Camargue ; delicate renderings of Provençal things, interpreting the brightness and gaiety of the native temperament and satirizing its foibles with humorous affection. Extremely various, ranging from old legends to pictures of modern life, from *The Pope's Mule*, a sketch of the Middle Ages, to *The Stars*, a meditative pastoral. The outdoor aspects, the hills, rocks, and woods, are sketched in exquisite vignettes. [Transl. (with *Monday Tales*, etc.), Little & Brown, Boston.]

—— *Tartarin of Tarascon, Traveller, " Turk," and Lion-Hunter* (Aventures prodigieuses de Tartarin de Tarascon, 1872). 1896
> A new and inimitable kind of extravaganza, satirizing Daudet's Provençal compatriots with a geniality and an irresistible gusto that remove any offence. Tartarin, like Pickwick, is a new figure in literature, a caricature of the imaginative and unveracious Meridional, with his incorrigible propensity for exaggeration and bragging. He sets out on an expedition to Algeria to prove his reputation for valour and resource, and meets with adventures as monstrous as those of Don Quixote. [With *Tartarin on the Alps* (Everyman's Lib.), Dent (Dutton, New York) ; Little & Brown, Boston.]

—— *Artists' Wives* (Les femmes d'artistes, 1874). 1896
> Brief sketches of character, many of them lightly satirical, and all giving the impression of being drawn from personal observation, of the wives of literary men, actors, painters, and sculptors. The moral seems to be that it is very hard to find a suitable mate for the artistic temperament. [Transl. by L. ENSOR, Dent : o.p. With *Tartarin*, above, Little & Brown, Boston.]

—— *Fromont Junior and Risler Senior* (Fromont jeune et Risler aîné, 1874). 1894
> A sentimental story of middle-class Paris, and the mean, drab world of the Marais shopkeepers. A partnership between two incompatibles, their wives' jealousies, and an unpleasant intrigue are the chief interests. Sidonie Chèbe is a peculiarly French example of a vain and heartless woman, whose mischief-making works havoc among her friends. On the other hand, the novel contains plenty of Daudet's Southern

DAUDET, Alphonse (*continued*).

humour, especially in the delectable figure of the superannuated actor Delobelle, who has not acted for ten years, but is determined not to give up the stage. [Transl. by E. VIZETELLY, Hutchinson (Lippincott, Philadelphia): o.p.; see also *Robert Helmont*.]

—— *Robert Helmont: the diary of a recluse* (Robert Helmont, 1874). 1896

The journal kept by a non-combatant during the siege of Paris and the German occupation, vividly depicting the sufferings of the besieged, and the emotions awakened in a sensitive mind by the actualities of war. [Transl. by L. ENSOR, Dent: o.p.; transl. (with *Fromont jeune et Risler aîné*), Little & Brown, Boston.]

—— *Jack* (Jack, 1876). 1897

Emotional pictures rather than a regular novel—pictures connected by the history of an illegitimate boy, whose life is a career of misery relieved only by death. The young martyr and his worthless mother were drawn from life, and certain denizens of the bohemian world in Paris are caricatured. The imitation of Dickens is palpable; the harrowing pictures of the Moronval Academy have an obvious likeness to Dotheboys Hall. [Transl. by L. ENSOR, 2 vols., Dent: o.p.; transl., 2 vols., Little & Brown, Boston: o.p.]

—— *The Nabob* (Le nabab, 1877). 1878

A satirical picture of life under the Second Empire, emphasizing the different phases of vulgar brilliance, hollowness, baseness, and rapacity. Recognizable scandals are introduced, and many figures are obvious caricatures of well-known people: e.g. the Duke de Mora (Morny) and the Irish Doctor Jenkins. The Nabob is a man from the south of France, who rises from poverty to immense wealth by operations in Tunis. His début in society is very comic; but, in spite of his ignorance, he impresses himself on the reader as better than the great people with whom he is associated. [Transl., 2 vols., Little & Brown, Boston; with introd. by Prof. TRENT, Heinemann, 1902. (Lotus Lib.) Brentano, New York (Collins).]

—— *Kings in Exile* (Les rois en exil, 1879). 1896

Another alleged portrayal of actual persons, the chief figure an exiled King of Illyria holding his Court in Paris. He is a weak and dissolute man, caring for nothing but his pleasures; but the queen is a real queen, living for her ambition, ready to sacrifice everything to see her husband on the throne again. The most appealing character is the little prince, last of the royal house, the hope of his mother, shattered by a cruel accident. [Transl. by L. ENSOR and E. BARLOW, Dent; transl., Little & Brown, Boston.]

—— *Numa Roumestan; or, Joy Abroad and Grief at Home* (Numa Roumestan, 1880). 1884

Daudet's fullest and most serious concentration of Provençal characteristics in an individual. Numa's genius for lying, his sham enthusiasms and irrepressible impudence, achieve a dazzling success; he wins a rich and beautiful wife, and at thirty is Minister of Fine Arts. This career seems to be suggested by the life of Gambetta, but Numa is not an actual portrait. This *grand méridional* is in conduct a very reprehensible person, his follies, deceptions, absurdities, are detailed with keen satire; yet the gaiety and audacity of the Southern temperament subjugate the reader, while the nobler nature of his Parisian wife seems cold. In this pair it is sometimes contended that Daudet sketched the characters and bohemian existence of himself and his wife. Henry James says that here " he has achieved the feat of becoming objective to his own vision." [Transl. (with *Rose et Ninette*), Little & Brown, Boston.]

—— *The Evangelist* (L'évangéliste, 1883). 1883

A rather forced satire on fanatical Protestantism and intolerance. The dominating figure is a woman, bigoted, overbearing, implacable, whose religious zeal is a curse to her neighbours; and the principal episode is her evil influence on a young girl whose affectionate disposition is frozen hard by this sombre Calvinism. [Transl. by C. H. MELTZER: o.p.; transl. (with *The Little Parish Church*), Little & Brown, Boston.]

—— *Sappho* (Sapho, 1884). 1886

The history of a young man's utter moral ruin through his infatuation for a Manon Lescaut of our days—a veritable artist in debauchery. A characteristic study of Parisian manners and morals. [Transl. by MAXWELL: o.p.; transl. (with *Between the Flies and the Footlights*, etc.), Little & Brown, Boston. (Lotus Lib.), Brentano, New York.]

—— *Tartarin on the Alps* (Tartarin sur les Alpes, 1885). 1896

To establish his glory more firmly, Daudet's mock-hero now undertakes the conquest of the Alps, encouraged thereto by his belief that the notorious dangers were invented by successful climbers to enhance their credit. Great is the harvest of ludicrous incident, especially when the lion-hunter and his comrade are, as they think, brought face to face with death. There is also a mock-romance, out of which Tartarin emerges very absurdly. [Transl. by H. FIRTH, Dent: o.p.; see also *Tartarin of Tarascon*, p. 129.]

—— *La Belle Nivernaise* (La belle Nivernaise, 1886). 1892

An idyll of life on the Seine, portraying sympathetically a little group of humble characters. [Transl. by R. ROUTLEDGE, Unwin (Cassell, New York): o.p.; with *The Support of the Family*, Little & Brown, Boston.]

—— *One of the Forty* (L'immortel, 1888). 1888

A savage pasquinade on the Academy, by one of the unelect. Mercilessly personal in its satire, and intensely bitter in the final scene, where the inept Astier-Réhu is driven to suicide by the wife whose intrigues had ensured his election. [Transl. by A. W. and M. de G. VERRAL, Sonnenschein: o.p.; transl. (with *The Struggle for Life*), Little & Brown, Boston.]

—— *Port Tarascon* (Port-Tarascon, 1890). 1890

Tartarin's last great enterprise is to lead a company of his fellow-citizens to found a utopian colony in the South Seas. [Transl. by Hy. JAMES, Low (Harper, New York): o.p.; transl. (with *La Fédor*), Little & Brown, Boston.]

—— *Rose and Ninette* (1892). 1892

A frankly realistic study of irregular unions and the vices of fast society. Endeavours to show that marriage can never be completely dissolved, and insists pathetically on the miserable consequences of divorce, especially to the children. [Unwin: o.p.; see also *Numa Roumestan*, *supra*.]

[*Novels*, transl. by Katharine Prescott WORMELEY and others, 14 vols., Little & Brown, Boston.]

DAVIDSON, John [Scottish ; 1857–1909]. *Perfervid : the career of Ninian Jamieson.* 1890
The first part, *The Campaign of Ninian Jamieson*, is a farce about a Scottish provost, whose fortune was derived from whisky, and who imagines himself a descendant of the Stuarts and rightful King of Scotland ; he takes an absurd little fellow called Cosmo Mortimer to be his fool, and finds a young lady willing to humour him. The second part, *The Pilgrimage of Strongsoul and Saunders Elshander*, has no particular connexion with the first, save that it is a story told by Cosmo about Ninian's son—the boy takes himself to be Strongsoul, and sets out on a new Pilgrim's Progress, fighting errand boys and giants, and rescuing an heiress. [Ward & Downey : o.p.]

—— *Baptist Lake.* 1894
Plotless and rather scattered in its interest ; but contains some suggestive sketches of character and striking thoughts about life. The anti-hero Baptist is a self-indulgent charlatan who exalts sensuality into a shoddy æstheticism. [Ward & Downey : o.p.]

—— *A Full and Free Account of the Wonderful Mission of Earl Lavender, which leaked out one night and one day : with a history of the pursuit of Lord Lavender and Lord Brumm by Mrs. Scamler and Maud Emblem.* 1895
A novel harking back somewhat to the romantic motives of *Perfervid*. [Ward & Downey : o.p.]

DAVIGNON, Henri [French]. *The Two Crossings of Madge Swalue* (Jean Swalue, 1919). 1919
Madge is an Englishwoman married to a great-hearted young bourgeois of Bruges. She cannot adapt herself to Flemish social life, and they come to England to live. But Swalue is killed in the war, and the widow returns to Bruges, so that his son may be born on Flemish soil. [Eng. version by Tita Brand CAMMAERTS, Lane.]

DAVIS, Elmer Holmes [American ; b. 1890]. *Giant-Killer.* 1928
Retells the story of David from a rationalistic standpoint : David is a weak youth, who can always find someone to kill his giants for him, whilst he takes the credit ; thus, Goliath is killed by a drunken soldier ; later, when David is king, it is Joab who does all the work. [Day, New York ; Harrap.]

DAVIS, John ["Owen Hall" ; d. 1907]. *In the Track of a Storm.* 1896
The troubled career of a supposed highwayman and convict, the victim of a miscarriage of justice ; scenes of convict life in New South Wales. [Chatto (Lippincott, Philadelphia) : o.p.]

DAVIS, Richard Harding [American ; 1864–1916]. *Gallegher ; and other stories.* 1891
Gallegher is an impish office-boy on a newspaper, who in a most exciting episode runs a criminal to earth. The others are miscellaneous stories of smart life in New York, the last three introducing the genial Van Bibber. [Scribner, New York, 1915.]

—— *Van Bibber, and Others.* 1892
Rollicking anecdotes of reprobate and dissipated life in New York, the doings of shady characters, etc. Van Bibber is a rich young clubman. a quaint mixture of happy-go-lucky temperament and acuteness, of innocence and knowingness : an unconscious humorist. [Harper, New York ; Garden City Co., New York.]

—— *The Exiles ; and other stories.* 1894
A sketch of a colony of American outcasts in Tangier, with a humane moral. *The Right of Way*, apparently a narrative of actual experience, heightened a little by the verve and humour of the writer, a journalist and an indefatigable traveller. [Harper, New York : o.p.]

—— *The Princess Aline.* 1895
A comedietta of modern knight-errantry : an American painter chases across Europe a German princess, with whose portrait he has fallen in love. [Harper, New York : o.p.]

—— *Soldiers of Fortune.* 1897
Scenes of action and adventure all over the globe. The hero, an Admirable Crichton, is successively a sailor, an English officer in the Soudan, a chasseur d'Afrique fighting the Arabs, a German baron, a cowboy, and a great promoter of railways. A South American revolution is a central episode. [Scribner, New York, 1920 ; Heinemann : o.p.]

DAVIS, William Stearns [American ; 1877–1930]. *A Friend of Cæsar : a tale of the fall of the Roman republic.* 1900
Adventures of a friend of Julius Cæsar in the period 51–40 B.C. Cæsar and Antony and Cleopatra are introduced, together with the crossing of the Rubicon and the battle of Pharsalia. [Macmillan, New York, 1925.]

—— *"God Wills It" : a tale of the First Crusade.* 1901
Adventures of Richard Longsword, a redoubtable young Norman cavalier, settled in Sicily. He wins the hand of the Byzantine princess, takes the vows of a Crusader in expiation of a crime, is robbed of his bride by the Egyptian Emir, but regains her under romantic circumstances at the storming of Jerusalem by the French. Godfrey of Bouillon, Tancred, Peter the Hermit, and Urban II figure (1094–9). [*Illus.*, Macmillan, New York, 1924.]

—— *Falaise of the Blessed Voice : a tale of the youth of St. Louis, King of France.* 1904
A graceful story of the young St. Louis, and of a plot to separate him from his queen (c. 1237). The finest character is a blind peasant girl, whose "blessed voice" is the means of checkmating the conspirators. [*Sub tit. The White Queen*, Macmillan, New York, 1925.]

—— *A Victor of Salamis : a tale of the days of Xerxes, Leonidas, and Themistocles.* 1907
Describes the Isthmian games, the Panathenaic festival, and the battles of Thermopylæ, Salamis, and Platæa (481–479 B.C.). [Macmillan, New York.]

—— *The Friar of Wittenberg : a tale of the times of Martin Luther.* 1912
The story is related by an intimate companion of Luther, and gives the chief incidents of his career from the Nailing of the Theses to his abduction to the Wartburg (1517–21). Scenes, Germany and Papal Rome ; chief characters, Luther, Melanchthon, Pope Leo de' Medici, and the Emperor Charles V. [Macmillan, New York.]

DAVIS, William Stearns (*continued*). *The Beauty of the Purple: a romance of imperial Constantinople twelve centuries ago.* 1924

The victorious campaign of Leo the Isaurian against the Saracens is the main episode (712–18). [Macmillan, New York.]

—— *Gilman of Redford: a story of Boston and Harvard College on the outbreak of the Revolutionary War.* 1927

A young fellow from Harvard is the hero of this story of the outbreak and subsequent incidents of the American Revolution (1770–75). [Macmillan, New York.]

—— *The Whirlwind: an historical romance.* 1929

" Being the story of the French Revolution as it was seen by René de Massac, deputy to the National Assembly and general of the Republic." [Macmillan, New York.]

DAWSON, A. J. [*b.* 1871]. *Daniel Whyte: an unfinished biography.* 1899

A man's life from boyhood to maturity ; from the moral and didactic standpoint. Daniel serves a hard apprenticeship at sea in the merchant service, a phase of his life that introduces several uncommon people ; later he is a journalist in Australia and in London. [Methuen : o.p.]

—— *African Nights' Entertainments.* 1900

White and native life in Morocco and on the West Coast of Africa, dealt with realistically and sometimes photographically, after Kipling. Many of the subjects are horrible and repulsive, but ventilate serious problems, such as that of intermarriage between different races. *Ben Hamed el Askar, Prince Djalinak, A Moorish Hero,* and *Juanita* set the modern Moor in an attractive light. *The Purser's Own Romance* is a striking fragment of West African life. [Heinemann : o.p. ; Dodd & Mead, New York : o.p.]

—— *The Story of Ronald Kestrel.* 1900

The struggles, the punishment at the hands of critics, and the ultimate success of a young literary man ; with sketches of life in Morocco and in New South Wales. [Heinemann : o.p. ; Appleton, New York : o.p.]

—— *Joseph Khassan, Half-Caste.* 1901

The central character is a study of temperament and heredity in a half-caste, son of a Turk and his Spanish wife. He is a man of gifts and subtle charm, who fails through lack of the northern fibre and the northern sense of honour. The scene is chiefly Morocco, which the author is intimately acquainted with. [Heinemann : o.p.]

DAWSON, Coningsby William [*b.* 1863]. *The Road to Avalon.* 1911

A strange visionary romance of the Arthurian world, a charcoal-burner's son going in quest of the dead king, and meeting Sir Heureux and Sir Douloureux, Sir Specious, Sir Torment, and other allegorical beings. [Hodder : o.p. ; Doran, New York : o.p.]

DAY, Frank Parker [Canadian ; *b.* 1881]. *Rockbound.* 1928

A story of a primitive community upon an island off Nova Scotia, which displays close acquaintance with the life of the fishermen of the Great Banks, and their unusual dialect. [Doubleday, Doran, New York.]

DAY, Susanne R. *The Amazing Philanthropists: being extracts from the letters of Lester Martin, P.L.G.* 1916

A very human, entertaining, and cheering medley of episodes observed by a lady P.L.G. in southern Ireland, a lady who herself was an excellent woman and a bit of a character. [Sidgwick.]

DAY, Thomas [1748–89]. *Sandford and Merton.* 1783–89

A pedagogic novel, advocating the adoption of more enlightened methods of education, and appealing to the young with stories and improving talks which set forth the truths and charms of science and virtue. [*Illus.*, Routledge (Dutton, New York : o.p.) n.d.]

DEARMER, Mabel [Mrs. Percy Dearmer ; *née* White ; 1872–1915]. *The Orangery: a comedy of tears.* 1904

An extremely sentimental love-comedy—sentimental in the finer sense—with successful pictures of society life in George III's days (1796). [Murray.]

—— *The Alien Sisters.* 1908

This likewise deals with experiences of life that are strongly emotional. The two sisters are the heiress of a rich baronet and his illegitimate daughter, with both of whom the heir to the baronetcy has love passages. [Murray.]

DE BLÁCAM, Aodh [Irish]. *The Ship that Sailed too Soon ; and other stories.* 1919

Directly or indirectly about Ireland past or present, and full of a passion for all things Irish. *Tales of my own People* and *Pages from Portabeg* seem to be about actual experiences. The favourite key is melancholy and pathetic, and a fondness for the ghostly touch is evident in the title-story. [Talbot Press, Dublin.]

—— *The Lady of the Cromlech.* 1929

About a romantic chase through Ireland after a girl whom the hero met in Paris—and whom he finds at last in his own village. Those who like Borrow will recognize a minor effort in his genre. [Murray ; *sub tit. The Flying Cromlech,* Century Co., New York.]

DE CRESPIGNY, Mrs. Philip Champion. *Tangled Evidence.* 1924

A detective story with an ingenious plot. [Cassell.]

DEEPING, George Warwick [*b.* 1877]. *Uther and Igraine.* 1903

A prose *Idyll of the King*—the loves of King Arthur's father and mother. The author has a genius for description, a sensuous, rhythmical, pictorial style. The characters are poetically imagined, the passions hot and intense ; yet they are neither ancient Britons nor Arthurian knights and damsels after Malory, but modern young ladies and gentlemen who have read their Tennyson. [Cassell ; Knopf, New York, 1928 ; Grosset, New York.]

DEEPING, George Warwick (*continued*). *Love Among the Ruins.*　　1904
　　Has the Arthurian atmosphere and centres in Avalon, but time and place are really quite undefined. Flamboyant word-painting of a great uprising of the poor against their knightly oppressors—pageants, battles, and carnage in a riot of pictorial adjectives. [Cassell.]

—— *The Seven Streams.*　　1905
　　A romance of corresponding vagueness. A knight goes out to avenge his sister and to overthrow the Papal despotism. [Cassell.]

—— *Bess of the Woods.*　　1906
　　Here Mr. Deeping renounces his fantastic mannerisms and tells a straightforward, if conventional, story of smuggling, hid treasure, hard-drinking sportsmen, and a wild young lady delivered from a shameful marriage, a century and a half since. [Cassell; Harper, New York: o.p.]

—— *Bertrand of Brittany.*　　1908
　　The early life of the renowned Bertrand du Guesclin and his no less renowned wife Tiphaine. A stormy romance of trials and troubles, shames and triumphs, culminating in the great combat between English and Breton champions at Rennes (1356). [Cassell.]

—— *Mad Barbara.*　　1908
　　Barbara meets with wild adventures in running to earth the murderer of her father, Sir Lionel Purcell. It is Charles the Second's reign, and we hear about the Plague and the Popish Plot, and see Samuel Pepys. [Cassell.]

—— *The Red Saint.*　　1909
　　A romance of the Kent and Sussex woodlands in Simon de Montfort's days, the foes of the beautiful Red Saint being undone at the battle of Lewes. [Cassell.]

—— *The Lame Englishman.*　　1910
　　The siege of Rome; Mazzini and Garibaldi in 1849. [Cassell.]

—— *Joan of the Tower.*　　1911
　　The exploits of the doughty Pelleas, monastery-bred, who goes forth to succour the oppressed in the reign of the tyrant John. [Cassell.]

—— *Fox Farm.*　　1911
　　A pathetic idyll of country life to-day—the vagabondage and tribulations of mind of a farmer stricken blind and of a faithful woman, with some additional studies of character. [Cassell.]

—— *Sincerity.*　　1912
　　A young doctor, full of the latest ideas in medical science, finds that he can make little headway against the prejudices and narrowness of a small country town, though he eventually wins success in London. [Cassell.]

—— *The House of Spies.*　　1913
　　The house is on the Sussex seaboard near Battle, in the time of the Napoleonic scare (1803). A French spy plays a foremost part. [Cassell.]

—— *The King behind the King.*　　1914
　　Another novel of that trite subject the Peasants' Revolt of 1381; scenes chiefly the forest-region of Kent and Sussex, and the usual historical figures. [Cassell; McBride, New York: o.p.]

—— *Martin Valliant.*　　1917
　　The story of a monk who finds his true self in the defence of a woman; time of Richard III and Henry VII. [Cassell; McBride, New York: o.p.]

—— *The Prophetic Marriage.*　　1920
　　The downfall of a youthful idealist whose marriage is unhappy. Finally, when he is a war-time colonel, his troubles come right. [Cassell.]

—— *Lantern Lane.*　　1921
　　A novel of incident, with Charles II prominent; scenes London and Surrey. [Cassell.]

—— *The House of Adventure.*　　1921
　　A romance centring in the restoration of a devastated French village. Clemenceau is introduced. [Cassell; Macmillan, New York; Burt, New York.]

—— *Orchards.*　　1922
　　The author makes the most of his skill at evoking the historical "climate." The scenes are in the Cotswolds and at Oxford in Prince Rupert's time (1642–3). [Cassell.]

—— *Apples of Gold.*　　1923
　　A novel of manners with some character interest, and local and historical colour—Covent Garden and thereabouts in 1715–25. [Cassell.]

—— *Sorrell and Son.*　　1925
　　A sententious account of the struggles of an ex-officer to provide for himself and for his son; to give the boy an education, Sorrell works as an hotel boots, rising to managership, whilst the son enters the medical profession. [Cassell; Knopf, New York.]

—— *Old Pybus.*　　1928
　　A variation on the theme of *Sorrell and Son*; a boy finds that though his parents are wealthy, his grandfather is a boots: none the less, he makes him his closest companion. [Cassell; Knopf, New York.]

—— *Exiles.*　　1930
　　A story of English folk in Italy; how a girl is disillusioned by a vicious novelist, but finds her place in life in assisting those of weaker calibre than herself. [Cassell; *sub tit. Exile*, Knopf, New York.]

DEFOE, Daniel [1663–1731]. *Robinson Crusoe.*　　1719
　　Founded on the actual experiences of Alexander Selkirk, cast away on an uninhabited island, and on many other accounts of solitaries; and, as to the geographical detail, on Defoe's wide reading in Dampier and other travellers. A minutely circumstantial account of Crusoe's shipwreck and escape, and the methodical

DEFOE, Daniel (*continued*).

industry whereby he makes himself a comfortable home. A masterpiece of spurious history intended to be accepted as truth, and a book that has been a model for realistic romances ever since. Though it is only by stretching a point that any of his books can be defined as novels, Defoe was of epoch-making importance in the history of fiction. He wrote to satisfy a popular demand for facts, and so established realism as the new basis for romance. [Ed. H. Kingsley (Globe edn.), Macmillan, 1879 ; ed. J. W. Clark (Golden Treasury Series), Macmillan, 1868 ; Dent (Macmillan, New York), 1895–6 ; vol. vii, Defoe's *Novels*, etc., 7 vols. (Bohn's Stand. Lib.), Bell ; ed. C. Whibley, 3 vols., Constable ; (World's Classics) Oxford Press.]

—— *Memoirs of a Cavalier.* 1720

"A military journal" of the wars in Germany under Gustavus Adolphus and in England under Charles I, (1632–48) ; rather history than romance, though made up from contemporary newspapers and other authorities. The battles and other military events are magnificently described, and so accurately and circumstantially that the book has deceived the ablest critics. [Constable ; vol. ii, Defoe's *Novels*, (Bohn's Stand. Lib.), Bell.]

—— *Life, Adventures, and Piracies of Capt. Singleton.* 1720

This and the next are excellent examples of Defoe's pseudo-history and pseudo-biography, which pretended to be authentic, and were perfectly faithful accounts of contemporary life. The boy Singleton was kidnapped and sold to gipsies, headed a band of mutineers, crossed Africa from Madagascar, and became a successful pirate. This part is made up from authentic tales of travellers, and the detailed account of Central Africa has often been taken as far in advance of the best geographical knowledge of that day. Defoe's nearest approach to a humorous character, William the Quaker, comes into this tale. [(Everyman's Lib.), Dent (Dutton, New York) ; Bell : o.p. ; (World's Classics) Oxford Press.]

—— *The Fortunes and Misfortunes of Moll Flanders.* 1722

A masterpiece of naturalistic fiction, which in recent years was translated into French as a classic of that genre. Moll went to the bad in early life, was five times married (bigamously or legitimately she little cared), a thief and a harlot, and eventually a penitent. She tells her story with a plain sincerity that both captivates and appals, so dreadful are the facts set down, without comment save the occasional apostrophes for mercy which Defoe, as moralist, felt it incumbent upon him to interject. [(Abbey Classics) Simpkin ; with *Roxana*, ed. E. A. Baker (Early Novelists), Routledge (Dutton, New York), 1906.]

—— *A Journal of the Plague Year.* 1722

A plain, matter-of-fact narrative, fortified by documentary proofs that give it the semblance of history. It is indeed a masterpiece of tragic history, fairly comparable to the descriptions of great cities in the throes of pestilence by Thucydides and Milton. [With Cruikshank's illustrations, Routledge : o.p. ; ed. H. Morley, Routledge (Dutton, New York) : o.p. ; Bell : o.p. ; (Everyman's Lib.) Dent (Dutton, New York) ; Constable.]

—— *Life and Adventures of Colonel Jacque.* 1722

A pendant to *Moll Flanders* as a view of shady life—this biography of a convict has frequently been reprinted among accounts of genuine highwaymen. By birth a gentleman, the hero fell among depraved people, was brought up to be a thief, and after a life of rascality was sent to the plantations. Like *Moll Flanders*, gives a vivid and touching picture of the submerged in London, the ways of the criminal classes, etc. [Dent (Macmillan, New York), 1895 : o.p. ; Bell : o.p. ; Constable.]

—— *The Fortunate Mistress, Lady Roxana.* 1724

Another narrative of moral corruption—the life of a courtesan among the upper classes. The beautiful daughter of a French refugee, she marries a fool who levants, and then goes to the bad. She gains wealth by wily scheming, but in the end is disgraced, and dies in gaol. There is a Quaker landlady in the story who is interesting as a character. But the finest part of *Roxana* is towards the end, where a climax of terror and suspense is engineered. The story was finished by another hand, who blundered with dates, etc. [2 vols., Dent (Macmillan, New York), 1895 : o.p. ; Knopf ; (Abbey Cl.), Simpkin (Small, Boston) ; with *Moll Flanders* ; see above.]

—— *The Memoirs of an English Officer.* 1728

Long accepted as authentic memoirs, but now recognized as one of Defoe's fictions. A realistic narrative of the wars, particularly of the Earl of Peterborough's daring but unfortunate campaign in the Peninsula, in the form of a biography. There was a Capt. George Carleton actually serving in the operations ; hence long uncertainty as to the real authorship. [o.p.]

DE FOREST, John William [American ; 1826–1906]. *Seacliff ; or, The Mystery of the Westervelts.* 1859

The mystery overshadowing this New York family concerns a forgery into which a villainous lawyer entrapped Mrs. Westervelt as a girl. Here we have the love-story of her daughter, and of a young man who cannot make up his mind as to which of the pair he loves. Some tragedy is involved, but comic scenes and dialogues diversify the tale. [o.p.]

—— *Miss Ravenell's Conversion from Secession to Loyalty.* 1867

A rather famous novel, giving a contemporary diagnosis of American feeling at the time of the Civil War, particularly of the prejudices, animosities, and domestic troubles of the rebels. We have the Southern father of Yankee proclivities, the Virginian colonel who fights for the Federalists, and the Knickerbocker lieutenant with his amusing wit and wickedness. The heroine, a pure-minded girl, loves a libertine colonel : the real hero is the honest soldier who wins her later. Gives a full account of the campaign in the southwest. [Harper, New York : o.p.]

—— *Kate Beaumont.* 1871

A South Carolina vendetta, an obstacle to true love, is the mainspring of the plot. Portrays the home life and social life of typical people, the relations of master and slave, etc., with satire of certain phases of Southern sentiment and prejudices. [Estes, Boston : o.p.]

DE FOREST, John William (*continued*). *Overland*. 1871

Rich in travel pictures, containing also several originals among its minor characters, and a variety of American types, Mexicans, Irish, Germans, Indians, and others. A poetical narrative of a voyage through the terrible Great Cañon is one of the purple patches. [Sheldon, New York : o.p.]

—— *Justine's Lovers*. 1878

An attempt to imitate the ordinary " woman's novel," which imposed on all the critics as to the writer's sex. The sympathetic account of a young woman's experiences, particularly of the feelings and motives determining her attitude towards marriage, is remarkable for frank analysis of the female mind. Political affairs at Washington are the subject of one episode, which is said to show personal animus. [o.p.]

" DEHAN, Richard " [Clotilde Inez Mary Graves ; *b.* 1863]. *The Dop Doctor*. 1910

A lurid romance, in a fulsome, Ouidaesque style, giving vivid pictures of the S. African War and the siege of Gueldersdorp (Mafeking, 1900). The Dop Doctor is a fashionable physician under a cloud, who rehabilitates his character by devotion and courage, and wins a bride. Some of the incidents are hideous. [Heinemann ; Doubleday, New York.]

—— *Between Two Thieves*. 1912

As highly coloured and not more coherent : scenes in the revolution of 1848 and the *coup d'état* of Louis Napoleon —who cuts an ugly figure—are followed by scenes in Turkey and the Crimea, all serving to introduce the celebrities of the time, under their own names or transparent disguises. [Heinemann ; Stokes, New York : o.p.]

—— *The Man of Iron*. 1915

Bismarck is, of course, the man of iron, and the chief incidents and leading personages of the Franco-German War are brought into play with this writer's usual freedom. [Heinemann ; Stokes, New York.]

DEKOBRA, Maurice [French ; *b.* 1885]. *The Madonna of the Sleeping-Cars* (La madone des sleepings, 1925). 1927

We have not seen the English translation of this work, the only importance of which is that it had an enormous sale in France and has been done into English. The original is crude pornography combined with a preposterous tale of adventure among the " Bolsheviks." Readers claim to identify the nymphomaniac heroine with a society lady. [Transl. by Neil WAINWRIGHT, Laurie ; Payson & Clarke, New York.]

" DELAFIELD, E. M. " [Edmée Elizabeth Monica Dashwood, *née* De La Pasture ; *b.* 1890]. *Zella Sees Herself*. 1917

Zella is a self-centred person who is always trying to be what she thinks the world will admire ; she is continually posing, without however being actually insincere or making us dislike her. This not uncommon type is drawn with a penetrating eye for the complexities of life and alertness for its humours. [Macmillan ; Knopf, New York : o.p.]

—— *The Pelicans*. 1918

Two sisters who love each other so tenderly that their divergences of character and different ways of settling the most momentous problems affect them to the quick, are the central subject of this very affecting study, which takes in, further, a considerable group of minor personages. [Heinemann : o.p. ; Knopf, New York : o.p.]

—— *The War-Workers*. 1918

Severe satire upon the " efficient " type of woman, who during the war gained an adventitious importance as director of a supply depot. [Heinemann : o.p. ; Knopf, New York : o.p.]

—— *Consequences*. 1919

Here again attention is centred on an unbalanced, unstable person, like yet unlike Zella, whose inability to see things as they are and whose inconsistencies and changes of front involve her in failure and misery. [Hodder : o.p. ; Knopf, New York.]

—— *Tension*. 1920

Beneath the comedy of eccentric characters, there is the serious problem of an energetic girl engaged to a paralysed and disabled man. [Hutchinson : o.p. ; Macmillan, New York.]

—— *The Heel of Achilles*. 1921

The heroine is another Zella in her egoism, though here this vice assumes a more subtle form—the inability to care for anyone to the extent of sacrificing her feelings for their sake. Only after her daughter marries against her wishes is this lesson of love brought home to her. [Hutchinson : o.p. ; Macmillan, New York.]

—— *Humbug : a story in education*. 1921

A satire directed against stupid parents, schoolmistresses, and husbands. But the characters are types rather than individuals, and poor types at that. [Hutchinson ; Macmillan, New York.]

—— *The Optimist*. 1922

The Victorian parent is satirized in the character of Canon Morehard, who, though apparently fervent, honest, and good, stands revealed in his true colours when his children grow up and one by one founder. [Macmillan, London and New York.]

—— *Turn Back the Leaves*. 1930

A study of " psychological and religious environment " in an old Roman Catholic family, and of the moral strains and the suffering which result from a marital lapse and the husband's forgiveness. He, the erring wife, her admirable successor, and the children, are drawn with great care and with striking impartiality ; the tragic gloom is unrelieved. [Macmillan ; Harper, New York.]

—— *Diary of a Provincial Lady*. 1930

The incidents of an average lady's existence in the country and on visits to town, jottings for character-sketches, good-humoured but penetrating comments, such as might well be put down for her own amusement. [Macmillan.]

DE LA MARE, Walter John [*b.* 1873]. *Henry Brocken : his travels and adventures in the rich, strange, and scarce-imaginable regions of romance.*   1904
A susceptible young man's " adventures among masterpieces " rhapsodized into a romantic narrative, in which figure Lucy Gray, Jane Eyre and Rochester, Gulliver, la Belle Dame sans Merci, Annabel Lee, and Criseyde, with other immortal personages from poetic brains. [Collins ; Knopf, New York, 1924.]

—— *The Return.*   1910
Dissociation of personality treated as a supernatural theme. A man is seized and occupied by the ghost of a dead Frenchman. His wife and friends question his identity. But the comic possibilities of the situation are not exploited : it is the mental torments of the victim, threatened with loss of wife, daughter, friends, even his own personality, that rivet attention. [Revised ed. 1922 ; Collins ; Knopf, New York.]

—— *Memoirs of a Midget.*   1921
The autobiography of a diminutive woman shut by her strange physical lot into a world of her own, whence she looks on humanity as if through a spy-hole. There is a second midget, and some other people who are drawn with an effort to blend Dickens's humour with a more penetrating psychical vision. [Collins ; Knopf, New York ; Grosset, New York, 1930.]

—— *The Riddle ; and other stories.*   1923
The Riddle is an apologue not easy of interpretation. The other fourteen pieces are all of the borderland— of life and death, the seen and the unseen, sanity and insanity. Old houses haunted by whispers of past inmates, persons more at home in the other world than in this, magic and mystery, are the dominant themes. *Out of the Deep* and *The Creatures* are atmospheric studies hinting at things beyond this world ; also *The Vats*, which are the reservoirs of time. *Seaton's Aunt* is seasoned with a grotesque, macabre humour. [Faber & Gwyer ; Knopf, New York.]

—— *The Connoisseur ; and other stories.*   1926
More stories with the same general characteristics ; *Mr. Kempe* or *All Hallows* may be cited as among the most compelling and beautiful of this collection. [Collins ; Knopf, New York.]

—— *On the Edge : short stories.*   1930
More from the haunted borderlands of waking and dreaming, the natural and the supernatural ; some grue- some, some grotesquely humorous, some terrifying, others tender or beautiful, in Mr. de la Mare's poetic way. *At First Sight* and *Willows* are two of his best. [Faber.]

DELAND, Margaretta Wade [*née* Campbell ; American ; *b.* 1857]. *John Ward, Preacher.* 1888
The typical novel of a New England lady who, like, and yet unlike, Mrs. Humphry Ward, carries the philosophical realism of George Eliot a further stage (cf. *Robert Elsmere*, published almost simultaneously). John Ward is a rigid Calvinist, his religion " grounded on damnation," whose austere conscience brings him into conflict with his agnostic wife. The happy, untroubled life of a sequestered village, inhabited by old-fashioned gentlefolk of lovable traits, gives a pleasant background to the tragedy, which is relieved further by a happy love affair. Over the personalities of the Anglican rector, whose kindness and common sense are so superior to his theology, and of the two innocent maids, the author's humour plays tenderly. [Houghton, Boston ; Warne.]

—— *Sidney.*   1890
Is it worth while to love in this mortal life of ours ? This is the psychological problem. A father, heart-broken at the loss of his wife, brings up his daughter Sidney in a philosophy of life from which the element of sexual love has been carefully excluded ; but it is love that awakens her spiritual consciousness and leads her to a deeper life of feeling. [Houghton, Boston.]

—— *The Story of a Child in Old Chester.*   1892
Another psychological problem : the history of a child of uncontrolled imagination, whose little heart was hungry. [Houghton, Boston.]

—— *Mr. Tommy Dove ; and other stories.*   1893
Character-portraits and episodes in the loves of several among the sweet-tempered and unspoiled inhabitants of Mrs. Deland's ideal world. *Mr. Tommy Dove* is a characteristic story of middle-aged courtship. In *A Fourth-Class Appointment*, the pathetic history of two women who keep a country post-office, Mrs. Deland laughs tenderly at the unsophistication of these true-hearted people. [Houghton, Boston : o.p.]

—— *Philip and his Wife.*   1894
States, without trying to resolve, some of the problems raised by ill-assorted marriages, and suggests ideas on the lawfulness of divorce and other questions. Philip's wife is a clever and fascinating woman who is almost completely non-moral, though endowed with the good impulses actuating nicer people. The husband's interests are concentrated on the welfare of his own soul. [Houghton, Boston.]

—— *The Wisdom of Fools.*   1898
Short stories propounding various difficult problems, moral and social, by similar means. [Houghton, Boston : o.p.]

—— *Old Chester Tales.*   1899
George Eliot crossed with Mrs. Gaskell seems the artistic genealogy of the author in these chronicles of a New England Cranford, peopled by quaint old characters full of humour and gentle goodness, where nothing happens more exciting than a tea-party and the small vicissitudes of domestic life, e.g. *Good for the Soul* and *Where the Labourers are Few.* [Harper, New York and London ; *illus.*, id.]

—— *Dr. Lavendar's People.*   1903
Six more Old Chester tales, characterized by the same unpretentious but refined art. They reveal the rarer graces of personality in what seem quite ordinary people, emphasizing them with perhaps a little excess of sentimentality. *The Grasshopper and the Ant, Amelia,* and the *Stuffed Animal House* are good examples of both her humour and her pathos. [Harper, New York and London.]

—— *An Encore.*   1907
—— *R. J.'s Mother ; and some other people.*   1908

DELAND, Margaretta Wade (*continued*). *The Way to Peace.* 1910
—— *The Voice.* 1912
—— *Partners.* 1913
—— *The Hands of Esau.* 1914
—— *Around Old Chester.* 1915
—— *The Promises of Alice.* 1919
—— *An Old Chester Secret.* 1920
—— *New Friends in Old Chester.* 1924
Collections of magazine stories and character-sketches, all on the old lines. [(1)–(6), (8), and (9), Harper, New York : o.p. ; (7) and (10), Harper, New York.]
—— *The Rising Tide.* 1916
The heroine is in the rising tide, that is, she is a crude and impulsive member of the rising generation, who is chastened and made more lovable by bitter experience. [Harper, New York ; Murray.]

DE LA PASTURE, Mrs. Henry [afterwards Lady Clifford ; Elizabeth, *née* Bonham ; b. 1866.]
Catherine of Calais. 1901
A romantic and sentimental girl, who falls in love with an elderly baronet, high-minded, but priggish. She is not an uncommon type, but is drawn with sympathy and insight. The story is rather diffuse and wordy ; its strength is in the drawing of certain female characters, amiable or unpleasant. [Murray ; Dutton, New York : o.p.]
—— *Catherine's Child* [sequel]. 1908
Old friends from the first book mingle with new faces in this life of Catherine's daughter, down to her marriage. The women, as before, are excellently drawn, from the aged dowager, Catherine's mother-in-law, to those precocious girls Lily and Philippa. [Smith & Elder : o.p. ; Dutton, New York : o.p.]
—— *Peter's Mother.* 1905
—— *The Grey Knight.* 1907
—— *Master Christopher.* 1911
Domestic life, family troubles, love's cross-currents, social solecisms, and the like, described with plain, plodding realism, the story in all three works meandering on in a leisurely, gossipy way. Character is the foundation of each novel, and the lights and shades of female character in especial are brought out strongly. [(1) and (3), Murray ; (2), Smith & Elder : o.p. ; (2) and (3), Dutton, New York : o.p.]

DE LA ROCHE, Miss Mazo [Canadian ; b. 1885]. *Jalna.* 1927
—— *Whiteoaks* [sequel]. 1930
A chronicle made up of the petty loves, interactions, and contrasted characters of the sundry members of a farming clan in the vicinity of Winnipeg—a matriarchal establishment dominated by a virile grandmother. [(1) and (2), Macmillan, Toronto and London ; Little & Brown, Boston.]

" DELEDDA, Grazia " [Madame Madesani-Deledda ; Sardinian ; b. 1876]. *After the Divorce* (Dopo il divorzio, 1902). 1905
The wife of a man sentenced to a long term of imprisonment obtains a divorce, and marries again. Only misery ensues, which develops into tragedy when her former lover returns. [Transl. by M. H. LANSDALE, Holt, New York : o.p.]
—— *Ashes : a Sardinian story* (Cénere, 1904). 1908
Madame Deledda is a Sardinian, and in this novel she depicts with realistic thoroughness, though without pretence to psychological analysis, the primitive, impulsive, hot-blooded nature of the Sardinian peasantry, so little affected by the current of modern civilization. The story is sad and ugly. A girl is led away by a married man, cast out by her father, leaves her illegitimate son to the care of others, and goes utterly to the bad. The climax is when her son, a young law student, searches for and eventually discovers his mother in the most terrible degradation. [Transl. by Helen Hester COLVILL, Lane : o.p.]
—— *Nostalgia* (Nostalgie, 1905). 1905
A study of weak, pitiful natures—a neurotic, discontented wife and her husband who becomes a rich woman's kept lover to provide her with the luxuries she craves. The life of the real Romans of Rome. of whom the tourist and archæologist and the fashionable world know nothing, is depicted with knowledge and realism. [Transl. by Helen Hester COLVILL, Chapman : o.p.]
—— *The Woman and the Priest* (La madre, 1920). 1922
How a young parish priest falls in love with an attractive girl, and the efforts of his mother to hold him to his vows—a story whose swift, direct narration emphasizes the quick passions of the Sardinian peasantry. [Transl. by Mary G. STEEGMAN ; new ed., *sub tit.* The Mother, with preface by D. H. Lawrence, Cape, 1927 ; Macmillan, New York (1923).]

DELL, Floyd [American ; b. 1887]. *Moon-Calf.* 1920
—— *The Briary-Bush* [sequel]. 1921
A semi-autobiographical pair of novels which are " an exploration of the dark continent of the mind." Moon-Calf, the poet Felix Fay, grows up among the towns and villages of Illinois, learns from his own blunders and rebellions and from those who are friendly and sympathetic or merely commonplace, and so arrives at a wider vision. But the sequel finds him still the prey of loneliness and conflict. This is the story of him and Rose-Ann. He is a journalist in Chicago, capable of sound creative work but distrustful of his own ability ; she a woman with a passion for spiritual freedom, who fears to be absorbed in a profound personal union. Their free marriage ends in a rupture. But after long estrangement they learn that marriage is not freedom, it is surrender and the birth of a new personality. Freedom is playing at life ; marriage is taking life seriously. [Doran, New York ; Macauley Co., New York ; Heinemann : o.p.]

DELL, Floyd (*continued*). *Souvenir.*　　1929

Felix Fay, of *The Briary-Bush*, long ago divorced from Connie, is here found living happily if prosaically with a second wife, and troubled by his relations to his and Connie's son. There is much sound criticism of American family life and recent social phenomena. [Doubleday, Doran, New York; Jarrolds.]

DELONEY, Thomas [? 1543–1600]. *Jack of Newbery.*　　1597

Full title, *The Pleasant History of John Winchcomb, in his younger years called Jack of Newbery, the famous and worthy clothier of England.* Deloney, the silk-weaver of Norwich, a noted ballad-singer, was probably commissioned by the cloth-merchants to compose this life of one of their order. Jack was a real person, who lived at Newbury under Henry VII; but his history is merely traditional. Deloney, however, knew the town, and in this account of the rise of a successful tradesman, whilst borrowing freely from the jest-books and popular tales, he produced the earliest example of homely realism and racy character-drawing in English fiction. See the admirable study, *Thomas Deloney : le roman des métiers au temps de Shakespeare* (1926) by Abel Chevalley, who has also translated Deloney's novels into French. [In *Works, vide infra.*]

—— *The Gentle Craft.*　　1597–8

Deloney wrote this to please the cordwainers. It consists partly of the stories of St. Hugh, Crispin, Crispian, and Ursula, and other legends of the craft, and then of the lives of many London worthies, genuine or traditional. This desultory scheme gave Deloney a free hand to portray racy characters and paint many admirable scenes of low comedy. [In *Works, vide infra.*]

—— *Thomas of Reading ; or, The Sixe Worthie Yeomen of the West.*　　*Earliest extant edition,* 1612

This too was written to please the clothiers, and is a better-constructed story of the same kind as *Jack of Newbery*. Thomas Cole was probably a legendary person, and much interesting lore is introduced on the wealth and character of his order, and curious local customs and privileges, such as the gibbet law of Halifax. Henry I's reign is the imaginary period, but the golden age of the industry in Henry VIII's time is that actually depicted. The more romantic chapters are concerned with the king's brother, Robert of Normandy, and the Lady Margaret, whom he loves; and there is a powerful melodramatic episode, the murder of Cole, which fascinated Swinburne. [6th ed. (1632), repr. in W. J. Thoms' *Early English Prose Romances*, see p. 465. Included in *The Works of Thomas Deloney*, edited from the earliest extant editions and broadsides by F. O. Mann, with an introduction and notes, Clarendon Press, 1912.]

DEMING, Philander [American; 1829–1915]. *Adirondack Stories.*　　1880

Quiet, realistic stories, together giving a pretty full picture of life in the wild Adirondack region of northern New York. Typical is *Lisa Ann*, the tender little story of a commonplace girl who elopes from her husband, a frothy, emotional revivalist. By hard work and self-sacrifice he redeems his character, and the girl comes home. [Houghton, Boston : o.p.]

—— *Tompkins ; and other folks.*　　1885

Simple stories and sketches of humble country folk, in the same vein. *Tompkins* is about a girl who supports her lover in his college days, and dies before he learns of the debt. [Houghton, Boston.]

DE MORGAN, William (Frend) [1839–1917]. *Joseph Vance : an ill-written autobiography.*　　1906

A long novel of many characters drawn from a lifelong acquaintance with the streets of London in the transitional period from Dickens's age. It is rather loosely put together, the life of Joseph from boyhood onwards being the one thread of union; but the excellence of the book is entirely in the characters, or in the episodes that reveal the peculiarities of character, the ambition of the author being to rival Dickens on Dickens's best side. The gallery of portraits is rich and varied—and there is reason to believe that many are real portraits. First comes Joseph's father, one of the finest originals in the preposterousness of his humour. Then we have Joe's mother, and her successor, the little maid-of-all-work "Miss Dowdeswell"; Dr. Thorpe and his delectable family, with those fascinating embodiments of womanhood, Lossie and Jane. These stand out among the crowd, every one of which is a distinct creation, whether drawn from the slums of Joe's boyhood or the middle-class society of later years. [Heinemann; Holt, New York.]

—— *Alice-for-Short : a dichronism.*　　1907

Alice is a dear little girl rescued by a good-hearted but ineffectual young artist from a dreadful home. She grows up with his own family, and the story covers her life and that of a crowd of friends, relations, haphazard connexions, for something like a quarter of a century. The characters are not merely interesting and lifelike, but Mr. De Morgan—much like Henry Kingsley—makes the reader in love with them, so that when one of them drops out of the story it is as if we had buried a friend. Alice both as babe and woman, Peggy the sister of the artist Charley Heath—in whose story the author has used up a good deal of personal material—the whole family, indeed, of the Heaths; Pope and Chappell, the Protestant and Catholic firm of church-window manufacturers; old Verrinder with his unutterably pathetic story; the bevy of youngsters, etc., are drawn with a charming naturalness, and the humour is all-persuasive. There is tragedy in the story also, deepened and spiritualized by the psychical interests of the author. [Heinemann; Holt, New York; Grosset, New York.]

—— *Somehow Good.*　　1908

A story in which the psychical preoccupations of Mr. De Morgan's mind furnish the very basis of the plot, which turns on a man's total loss of memory through an accident, and his recovery after a series of amazing complications have resulted. The strength of the book, however, is rather in the truth and fertility of the character-drawing. There is deep tragedy in the preliminaries of the story, but "somehow, good" becomes "the final goal of ill." [Heinemann; Holt, New York; Grosset, New York.]

—— *It Never Can Happen Again.*　　1909

A long, two-plot novel—(*a*) the growth of jealousy in a dull, affectionate wife, and of passion in the husband for a splendid society beauty, at the time when the Deceased Wife's Sister Bill puts the wife's title in jeopardy; (*b*) a "Little Nell" story of a blind sailor and his daughter. The former is a masterpiece in the analysis of imponderable motive, the latter a tragic idyll of exquisite beauty and pathos. There is such a leisurely insistence on every detail in the story that the reader feels himself a part of it, and the

DE MORGAN, William (Frend) *(continued).*
characters—the muscular Rev. Athelstan and his womenfolk, the magnificent Judith and her people, Challis and Marianne and the prurient Miss Eldridge ; nay, the very domestic servants—all seem to be familiar acquaintances. [Heinemann : o.p. ; Holt, New York.]

—— *An Affair of Dishonour.* 1910
A study of character, conduct, and conscience, laid in the seventeenth century, but hardly historical, save that the battle of Solebay, or Southwold (1672), is a spectacular episode. There is an apparition to remind us of Mr. De Morgan's psychical interests, but of his characteristic humour and geniality not a trace. [Heinemann ; Holt, New York.]

—— *A Likely Story.* 1911
Returns to the genre of *Somehow Good* ; a very unlikely story. A lower middle-class and an upper middle-class family circle come into relations in their affairs of love or uncongenial wedlock, the *deus ex machina* being an old Italian picture that talks. [Heinemann ; Holt, New York.]

—— *When Ghost meets Ghost.* 1914
An enormous complication of circumstances brings about the rediscovery of each other, in old age, of two affectionate and devoted twin-sisters who had believed one another dead. Poring fondly over the past, De Morgan tells the story with his customary garrulity (in 892 pages), and resuscitates the usual large crowd of grown-up people and children with their various love-affairs and other matters. [Heinemann ; Holt, New York.]

—— *The Old Madhouse.* 1919
Left unfinished ; the last chapter is by Mrs. De Morgan. The regular brand of realistic reminiscence ; a throng of characters, and a story with a stronger dash of romance than usual, and more of the supernatural. Interest centres in an unstable young fellow unfortunately in love with the wife of his best friend. [Heinemann ; Holt, New York.]

—— *The Old Man's Youth.* 1921
Also left unfinished, the " Narrative of Eustace John " standing as De Morgan wrote it, " The Story " being put together and inserted in the gaps and at the end by his widow. Eustace John composes his reminiscences in Chelsea Infirmary, and leaves the makings of a story and a characteristic picture of a family living in Mecklenburgh Square about the time of the Indian Mutiny. [Heinemann ; Holt, New York.]

DEMPSTER, Charlotte Louisa Hawkins [1835–?]. *The Hôtel du Petit-St.-Jean : a Gascon story.* 1869
The simple life and manners of a southern French town pictured with delicate touches and an affectionate sympathy with Provençal ways and ideas. The little idiosyncrasies of a crowd of characters, from the Préfet and Préfette downwards, are humorously sketched. The main thread of the triple story is concerned with the growth of Marie's character—a sunny and impulsive girl to whom pathetic experiences bring gravity and wisdom. Much is made of the lovely scenery of the Garonne. [Smith & Elder : o.p.]

—— *Véra.* 1871
Véra is a high-born Russian, who loses her boy-lover at Inkermann, and in the course of years gives her hand to the English officer who accidentally slew him. The scenes that set forth this operation of Destiny, as the author regards it, occur in Moscow, the Crimea, Italy, Nice, London, etc. Véra's bright and careless disposition is deepened by troubles and experience of the world, till at last love gives her a new view of life. [Smith & Elder : o.p.]

—— *Iseulte.* 1875
Memoir of a Frenchwoman, noble by birth and by character, who meets with some of the most tragic calamities of life, but by fortitude and unselfishness rises superior to fate, and is rewarded with a middle-age of happiness. Her sister, who is entrapped into a convent and sacrifices her love, is a pathetic counterpart to the lovely character of Iseulte. Life in the provinces and at the front during the convulsions of 1870 is described, and the virtues of the old nobility are contrasted with plebeian vulgarity and self-seeking. [Smith & Elder : o.p.]

—— *Blue Roses ; or, Helen Malinofska's Marriage.* 1877
A story of hopes and ideals unfulfilled. The Polish heroine fails to attain, in her marriage with a Devonshire squire, the happy love that she had dreamed of in her joyous girlhood, and she dies in estrangement. Polish life and characters favourably depicted and contrasted with an unpleasant set of English people. [Paul : o.p.]

DENNIS, Geoffrey Pomeroy [b. 1892]. *Mary Lee.* 1922
The autobiography of a child brought up with barbaric severity by Plymouth Brethren. In Aunt Jael and her circle we have a grim but comprehending study of fanaticism bordering on insanity ; Mary herself is so sure and sympathetic a revelation of repressed but vigorous feminine character that critics assumed the author to be a woman. [Heinemann ; Knopf, New York.]

—— *Declaration of Love : undiplomatic correspondance between Paris and Berlin.* 1927
An analysis, in four letters, of a modern love match. The emphasis is rather heavily on the intellectual side, but there is the same charming introspective observation and sensibility as in *Mary Lee.* [Heinemann ; Knopf, New York.]

DE QUINCEY, Thomas [1785–1859]. *Klosterheim ; or, The Masque.* 1832
A Radcliffian story of the turbulent period in the Thirty Years' War preceding the Imperialist victory of Nordlingen (1633–4). A tyrannical landgrave, allied with the Swedes ; the Catholic Klosterheimers, gallantly aiding the other side ; and a mysterious apparition who discomfits the Landgrave in his own palace, and afterwards turns out to be the rightful ruler, are the *dramatis personæ.* [In his *Collected Writings* (14 vols.), vol. xii., Black, 1896.]

—— *The Incognito ; or, Count Fitzhum* (1824). *The King of Hayti* (1823). *The Dice* (1823). *The Fatal Marksman* (1823). *The Avenger* (1838).
The first two are humorous tales, the third a tale of necromancy and devilry, all from the German. *The Fatal Marksman* is a version of the German story made familiar by Weber's opera *Der Freischütz* ; *The Avenger,*

DE QUINCEY, Thomas (*continued*).

a sensational story of a series of murders, ultimately proved to have been the deliberate work of a wealthy young gentleman of Jewish extraction. It is much in the style of the author's *Murder considered as one of the Fine Arts*, with its sensational appendix. [In his *Collected Writings* (14 vols.), vols. xii., xiii., Black, 1896–7.]

DE SELINCOURT, Hugh [*b.* 1878]. *A Soldier of Life.* 1916
Explores the consciousness of a maimed and shattered ex-soldier, who has come to realize the urgency with which his true self demands beauty and reality, and is led to understand the essential balance of life. [Constable ; Macmillan, New York : o.p.]

—— *Nine Tales ; with an introduction by Harold Child.* 1917
Promising stories of a philosophic cast, e.g. *The Last Quality.* *Men and Brothers* satirizes our present social attitudes. The others range from the almost Tolstoyan pathos of *The Sacrifice* to the beauty of *Arethusa*. [Nisbet : o.p.]

—— *The Cricket Match.* 1924
The comedy of a village cricket match provides the setting for a shrewd and humorous delineation of a group of country characters, comprising every type, from workman to parson and dandy. Nor are the players' wives forgotten. [Cape.]

—— *Never in Vain.* 1929
Portrays a man haunted by the fear that his wife is loved by his best friend, and seeking by means of a vague, indeterminate philosophy and much quoting of Blake, to find a solution to the dilemma. [Gollancz.]

DEVEREUX, Blanche. *Star of Mercia : historical tales of Wales and the Marches.* 1922
From the times of St. David and Gildas to the eve of the Conquest (fifth to eleventh century). No little imagination is used in the portrayal of historic characters and the depicting of bygone scenes. [Cape : o.p.]

DIAZ FERNANDEZ, José [Spanish ; *b.* 1899]. *The Blockhouse* (El Blocao). 1930
Seven stories of the war in Morocco. They depict, with a concentrated and almost savage realism, the brutal and ugly side, especially the sexual aspects of Spanish military service. [Transl. by Helen B. Newsome, Hopkinson.]

DICKENS, Charles [1812–70]. *Sketches by Boz.* 1836–7
Random sketches and episodes drawn from life in London among the poor and the lower middle classes. Manners are portrayed with vivid truth or recognizable caricature, but the great things are such humorous extravaganzas as the "Election for Beadle." Dickens is the novelist of the lower classes as Thackeray is of the upper ten, but there is a profound distinction between these two great comic artists. Though Dickens gives a faithful picture of the surroundings and the conditions of life in the middle period of last century, he is anything but a realist in the more important sphere of human character. Thackeray was a satirical realist : Dickens's genius was essentially humorous and fantastic. He used human nature as material for creative work ; and a poetic imagination found full scope, not only in fantasies like *The Chimes* and *A Christmas Carol*, but in grotesque beings like Quilp, Mrs. Gamp, the Wellers, and Mr. Micawber. He has few affinities in English literature, unless it be Sterne and Smollett, both in different ways. This creative and transforming impulse of his is shown from the beginning.

—— *The Posthumous Papers of the Pickwick Club.* 1837
Here we have exuberant fancy, and an imagination richly stored with human material collected in his early experiences in the streets of London, at work on the random scheme of adventure with which Pierce Egan and Theodore Hook had amused people a decade before. It was begun as a sporting chronicle to illustrate a set of comic plates by R. Seymour ; hence the prowess of Mr. Winkle, who soon however is reduced to a minor rôle. An absurd club sends four members on a journey of research through England ; the four meet with an immense profusion of comic adventures and curious people, many of whom add to the entertainment by telling their stories. Among the host of characters drawn from every nook and corner of London and provincial life stand out conspicuously Mr. Pickwick, Sam Weller and his sire, the fat boy, Mrs. Bardell, Messrs. Tupman and Snodgrass, Mr. Jingle, Mr. Nupkins, Bob Sawyer, Job Trotter, and many others whose idiosyncrasies are as indelibly fixed in our minds as are the chief creations of Shakespeare.

—— *The Adventures of Oliver Twist.* 1838
A dramatic plot combining the fortunes of a poor boy, brought up in a workhouse, with the misdeeds and the punishment of a gang of thieves. As a picture of the criminal classes showing the burglar, the pickpocket, and the coiner in their dens and the poor in their slums, the book is worthy of Defoe. Bill Sikes is a hideous portrait of a complete scoundrel, a product of our penal system ; and the Jew, Fagin, is a companion picture. The comic passages give us such humorous creations as Mr. Bumble, the Artful Dodger, and Charlie Bates. Rose Maylie and Mr. Brownlow are characters of a more engaging kind.

—— *Nicholas Nickleby.* 1839
This too has a melodramatic plot, of which the mainspring is the antagonism of the good Nicholas and his bad uncle, the usurious Ralph Nickleby. And again the strength of the book is in the numerous comic characters, incidents, and situations—the Mantalinis, the Squeers family and their detestable school, Dotheboys Hall, the Cheerybles, Mr. Vincent Crummles, and Mrs. Nickleby and such bizarre objects as Sir Mulberry Hawk Lord Verisopht, and Madeline Bray. The tale somewhat resembles Smollett's picaresque narratives.

—— *Barnaby Rudge.* 1840–1
An historical novel giving a lurid tableau of the orgies and incendiarism of the "No Popery" riots in 1780. Lord George Gordon is an actor, and the principal events are founded on fact. Intertwined is a private story with some characteristic traits, e.g. in the Vardens, the Willets, Miss Miggs, and Simon Tappertit.

—— *The Old Curiosity Shop.* 1840–1
Combines diverse elements—the sentimental idyll in which the etherealized and pathetic Little Nell and her grandfather are protagonists ; the light comedy in which figure those sportive creations Dick Swiveller and the Marchioness, Kit Nubbles, Sophy, Miss Wackles, Cheggs, and Chuckster ; and the gloomy grotesque of Quilp and his doings. People in those days enjoyed the mawkish sentiment and the semi-poetic rhapsody of the idyllic part.

DICKENS, Charles (*continued*). *Christmas Books.* 1843–8
Little tales written for Christmas, in which realism and fantasy are mingled, kindliness and love for the poor being the dominant theme. *A Christmas Carol* makes its ghostly appeal to the hard old miser, and *The Chimes* is a variation of the same motive. *The Cricket on the Hearth* is an idyll of home life; *The Battle of Life*, an imaginative deliverance on resignation; and *The Haunted Man*, a fairy tale having the beauty of kindness for its moral.

—— *Martin Chuzzlewit.* 1844
A novel of multifarious scope, containing comedy, caricature, farce, melodrama, and tragedy; shifting from England to America and back again. The selfish family of the Chuzzlewits are technically the central interest in what plot there is, and the regeneration of young Martin may be regarded as the moral motive. But the characters are as richly varied as the incidents, and comprise such epitomes of human nature's tricks and foibles as Mr. Pecksniff and his daughters, Charity and Mercy, and Mark Tapley, Tom Pinch, Mrs. Todgers, Chollops, Poll Sweedlepipes, the Hon. Elijah Pogram, Jefferson Bricks, Betsey Prig and the immortal Sairey Gamp, whose wonderful patter, gliding naturally into blank verse, shows the grotesque imagination of Dickens at the height of its power. The American interludes betray animus, and were so taken across the Atlantic.

—— *Dombey & Son.* 1848
The moral purpose is to anatomize pride and illustrate its strength and weakness. Slenderly attached to the main story developing this idea is the pathetic episode of little Paul Dombey's invalid life and death. Then the history of Mr. Dombey moves on to his business failure and the chastening of his pride; Edith Dombey and Mr. Carker belong to the melodrama. Farcical affairs such as the Pipchin establishment and the Blimber academy are not even travesties of anything actual; whilst such diverting freaks and gargoyles as Capt. Cuttle, Capt. Bunsby, and Mrs. MacStinger, afterwards Mrs. Bunsby, are more or less consciously creations after Smollett. Among the characters which are pure Dickens may be named Mr. Toots, the admirable Toodles family, Mrs. Chick and Miss Tox, Susan Nipper, Cousin Feenix, and perhaps those caricatures, Major Bagstock and the Rev. Melchisedek Howler.

—— *David Copperfield.* 1850
Of considerable interest as autobiography and self-revelation, telling something of the pathetic story of his own early struggles, and setting down other cherished memories. David's hard youth, the sentimental idyll of his first marriage and the firmer happiness of his union with Agnes, are the connecting thread among the varied episodes and eccentric, humorous, and lovable characters. An episode of seduction brings in the melodramatic. Miss Betsey Trotwood, Barkis, Micawber, the Peggottys, Mr. Dick, Mrs. Gummidge, Miss Mowcher, and Tommy Traddles are among the pleasing grotesques; the sanctimonious villain, Uriah Heep, is one of the repulsive. Little Emily, Steerforth, Rosa Dartle, Murdstone, and Mr. Littimer are among the memorable characters introduced here.

—— *Bleak House.* 1853
A plot-novel with two chief threads, a proud lady's expiation of a sin done in youth and the humorous chronicle of a huge and interminable lawsuit. Connected with these are a crowd of personages—the hero Carstone, Poor Jo, Mrs. Jellyby the philanthropist, Mr. Chadband, Snagsby, Mr. Tulkinghorne, Sir Leicester Dedlock, Mr. Bucket, the police-officer, Esther Summers, Mr. Turveydrop, the Bagnets, Guppy, and two sketches from life, Boythorn and Harold Skimpole (Savage Landor and Leigh Hunt).

—— *Hard Times.* 1854
A tract-novel inspired by Carlyle's Philosophical Radicalism—a protest against tyrannous utilitarianism and political economy divorced from human feeling. The stage is a hideous manufacturing town created by the two apostles of fact, Gradgrind and Bounderby, and the drama is chiefly enacted by Gradgrind's children brought up on facts, and ruined spiritually by the complete neglect of sympathy and sentiment.

—— *Little Dorrit.* 1857
Satirizes the Civil Service under the style of the Circumlocution Office. Also pictures prison life, Little Dorrit's father being Father of the Marshalsea. The melodramatic element appears in the history of the House of Clennam; with the usual complement of originals: Mr. F.'s Aunt, the Meagles, Pancks, Mr. Nanby, Mr. Casby, Flora Finching, Miss Wade, Tallycoram.

—— *A Tale of Two Cities.* 1859
An historical novel inspired by Carlyle's *French Revolution*, the style of which it constantly echoes. A powerful, melodramatic story of the Reign of Terror (1789–94), leading up to the famous scene of Sydney Carton's self-immolation at the guillotine, now well-known on the boards.

—— *Great Expectations.* 1861
An excellent tale for children; the story of poor Pip has touching chapters, and there are several characters akin to those of Dickens's best period, e.g. Joe Gargery and Miss Havisham, Uncle Pumblechook, Mr. Wosple, Magwitch, Orlick. The Thames marshes furnish a sombre background.

—— *Our Mutual Friend.* 1865
A complicated story, with a few minor figures, like Boffin, Wegg, Eugene Wrayburn and Lizzie Hexam having the characteristic stamp.

—— *Christmas Stories.* 1854–67
Chiefly minor miscellaneous stories and sketches contributed to the Christmas numbers of *Household Words*. *The Seven Poor Travellers*, *The Holly Tree*, and *Mugby Junction* are sketches of travelling, inns, old-fashioned hostelries, etc. *Somebody's Luggage* is a discourse on waiters, and *Mrs. Lirriper's Lodgings*, a characteristic picture of London lodging-house life.

—— *The Mystery of Edwin Drood.* 1870
An unfinished melodrama centring in a mysterious murder and enacted amid the picturesque closes and cathedral-buildings of old Rochester (Cloisterham), with scenes in an opium den in Shadwell. The scenic elements create a deep impression of gloom and tragedy, and the plot is an excellent piece of construction. Contains some characteristic types of villainy and passion, and some grotesquely humorous figures, who at least reflect the creations of his best period, e.g., Canon Crisparkle, John Jasper, Mr. Sapsea.

DICKENS, Charles (*continued*).

[Editions of Dickens's Works, published by Chapman & Hall :—

(*a*) Library Editions : 8vo, with the original *illustrations* (National Edn.), 40 vols., 8vo (1906–7) (sold in sets only) : o.p. *Illustrated* Lib. Edn., 30 vols., 1873–6 : o.p. ; (Centenary Edn.) 36 vols.

Chapman & Hall are also the English agents for the Autograph Edn. of Dickens's complete writings, ed. F. G. Kitton, in 56 vols., pub. by Sprout, of New York (only 250 sets printed). An edn., edited by A. J. Hammerton and illustrated by Harry Furniss, is published by the Educational Book Co. (1910).

(*b*) Smaller Editions : (Universal Ed.), 22 vols. ; (Original Illustrated Ed.), 20 vols. ; (Fireside Ed.), 22 vols. ; (Oxford India Paper Ed.), 17 vols. ; Popular Ed., 22 vols.

(*c*) By other Publishers : *illus.*, in 20 vols. ; (*Great Expectations* and *Hard Times* in 1 vol.), Macmillan ; 29 vols., (Everyman's Lib.), Dent (Dutton, New York) 1906–25. 29 vols., Nelson, 1908–25. *Dickens Dictionary*, ed. by G. A. Pierce and W. A. Wheeler, gives a key to the characters and principal incidents in the novels, Chapman & Hall, 1878. The *Dickens Dictionary*, by A. J. Philip, is a similar work, dealing with the characters, localities, etc., of the novels and miscellaneous works, alphabetically arranged, Routledge (Dutton, New York), 1909 ; the *Dickens Concordance* : a compendium of names and characters and principal places mentioned in all the works of Dickens, ed. by Mary Williams, Griffiths, 1907 ; the *Dickens Encyclopædia*, ed. by A. L. Hayward, " an alphabetical dictionary of every character and place mentioned, with notes," Routledge, 1924.]

DICKENS, Mary Angela [granddaughter of Charles Dickens]. *A Mere Cypher.*   1893

A shrinking, unesteemed woman becomes the good angel of an unhappy young man, saves him from ruin and helps him to win his love. Her character is one of extreme pathos, overwhelmed as she is by the slights and tyranny of a wretched marriage. [Macmillan : o.p.]

—— *A Valiant Ignorance.*   1894

Julian Romayne's history is a study of hereditary tendency and the successive steps from unresisted temptation to ultimate crime. Rendered all the more tragic by the mother's vain attempt to keep him ignorant of his father's sins. Inspired by Ibsen. [Macmillan : o.p.]

—— *Against the Tide.*   1898

A man affected by homicidal mania corrupts and ruins his rich brother-in-law, and ultimately commits murder and suicide. Pathos and tragic suspense arise from the pardonable complicity of a young girl, who has kept the secret and sees her lover separated from her as a consequence. [Hutchinson : o.p.]

—— *The Debtor.*   1912

The story of a woman's miraculous cure through prayer, and her conversion to Catholicism.

DICKESON, Alfred. *Tychiades : a tale of the Ptolemies.*   1903

A too erudite story of Ptolemy II's times, supposed to be written in Greek and saved from the Alexandrian library. Adventures of a young Greek. Contains some anachronisms, but is an interesting picture of life in the still youthful city (280 B.C.). [Unwin : o.p.]

DICKINSON, Goldsworthy Lowes [*b.* 1862]. *The Magic Flute : a fantasia.*   1921

A fantasy amplifying the story of Mozart's opera. [Allen & Unwin ; Macmillan, New York.]

DICKINSON, H. N. *Keddy : a story of Oxford.*   1907

College life at Oxford from the inside, the escapades of fast young men, raggings, and a breach of promise case as a finish. Lifelike character-drawing with abundance of satire ; the best, Keddy and his larkish friend Bobby, sanctimonious tutors, and a muscular parson. [Heinemann : o.p.]

DICKSON, Harris [American ; *b.* 1868]. *The Black Wolf's Breed.*   1900

The warrior-hero is a French captain who served under Bienville, governor of Louisiana, during the latter days of Louis XIV, shortly after La Salle had made his memorable voyage down the Mississippi and thus sowed the seeds of the mighty quarrel which culminated in the Seven Years' War (*c.* 1700). The story is mainly laid at Biloxi, in Louisiana, but sometimes moves to Versailles and Paris ; it gives a good idea of frontier life in a new European settlement among the Indians. [Bobbs-Merrill, Indianapolis : o.p. ; Methuen : o.p.]

—— *The Siege of Lady Resolute.*   1902

The story is founded on the legend of the wealthy merchant Anthony Crozat and his project for making himself Prince of Louisiana. Protestants in the Cevennes at the time of Jean Cavalier and the Camisards (1702–15), and Louisiana under Iberville, Crozat, and Cadillac. Mme de Maintenon is the heroine's bitter foe. [Harper, New York and London : o.p.]

—— *She that Hesitates.*   1904

A story of the Princess Charlotte of Brunswick that married Alexis, the son of Peter the Great. It is supposed that she was not liked by her husband, but escaped to Louisiana, where she marries her French lover (1715–18). [Bobbs-Merrill, Indianapolis : o.p. ; Ward & Lock : o.p.]

DIDEROT, Denis [French ; 1713–84]. *The Nun* (La religieuse, 1796).   1797

This remarkable work was written in 1760, and seems to have been the outcome of a hoax, the appended letters of Suzanne Simonin being really concocted by Diderot and Grimm and sent to the Marquis de Croismare, who thought them genuine. The story is based, at any rate, on the facts of Suzanne's enforced entrance into the cloister, her fruitless appeal to the law, and her eventful escape. But the work is of most importance as a novel. Suzanne portrays herself and her mental sufferings, in the account of her persecution by the bigoted in one convent and her narrow escape from corruption by the perverted superior of the other, in a manner displaying a command of character-drawing and analysis of motive and conduct, which makes this Diderot's finest essay in fiction. Long before the book was published, the reforms virtually demanded by this attack on the monastic system were matters of history. [Transl. by Francis BIRRELL (Broadway Transl.), Routledge (Dutton, New York).]

—— *Rameau's Nephew* (Le neveu de Rameau, 1805).   1897

A satire on Parisian society as it was just before the Revolution ; in the form of a dialogue which gives a view of the world as seen through the eyes of a parasite. Rameau's disreputable nephew is a philosophic scamp, full of wise and wicked saws, as well as lively modern instances. 1805 was the date of Goethe's

DIDEROT, Denis (*continued*).
    translation ; this singular and rather perplexing book was not published in French till 1823. [Transl.
    by S. M. HILL, Longman : o.p. ; transl. by Mrs. Wilfred JACKSON, Chapman & Hall (McBride, New
    York) 1926.]

DILL, Liesbet [Frau von Drigalski ; German ; *b.* 1877]. *The Boundary Post* (Der Grenzpfahl,   1925).   1930
    A domestic story that brings to a head the personal and racial problems created by the transference of Lorraine
    to France. The heroine is a German, whose father and husband have both died in the war. [Transl.
    by Eleanor d'Esterre STAHL, Benn.]

DILLON, Mary G. [*née* Johnson ; American]. *The Leader.*   1906
    To-day's or yesterday's politics. An idealized portrayal of William Jennings Bryan. [Doubleday, New
    York : o.p.]

—— *The Patience of John Morland.*   1909
    A political novel of Washington (1820–30), rather on Mrs. Humphry Ward's plan. Kitty McCabe is really
    Margaret O'Neill, who married John Henry Eaton of Tennessee, Secretary of War in Jackson's Cabinet
    and afterwards Minister to Spain. Andrew Jackson, Clay, Calhoun, Monroe, Daniel Webster, and Martin
    van Buren appear. [Doubleday, New York : o.p. ; Nash : o.p.]

" DINARTE, Sylvio " [Viscount Alfredo d'Escragnolle-Taunay ; Portuguese]. *Innocentia.*   1889
    A story of the prairie regions of Brazil. [Transl. and *illus.* by J. W. WELLS, Chapman : o.p.]

DISRAELI, Benjamin, Earl of Beaconsfield [1804–81]. *Vivian Grey.*   1826
    A fantastic sketch, much like Lytton's *Pelham*, prefiguring with its burlesque and persiflage the lighter elements
    of Disraeli's mature novels of political life. It recounts the youth of a dandy and adventurer, who makes
    himself the favourite of a marquess and engineers a new party, but is caught intriguing and ends his career.
    Said to owe its idea to the attempted cabal of the Duke of York and the Marquess of Hertford against
    Canning on the Catholic question. Horace Grey is a faithful portrait of the novelist's father, Isaac
    D'Israeli. The latter part of the book degenerates into a false, semi-poetic romanticism. Disraeli's
    novels show kindred qualities in literature to the forces that took him to the top in his political career—
    brilliance of intellect, far-sighted views, and a love of theatrical effect. [Edited with biographical introd.
    (a very luminous one) by Lucien Wolf, 2 vols., De La More Press, 1904 : o.p.]

—— *Alroy* (1833). *Ixion in Heaven* (1833). *The Infernal Marriage* (1833). *Popanilla* (1828).
    Alroy is a wild Oriental romance of the days of the Jewish captivity ; *Ixion* recounts in burlesque fashion the
    old legends of Juno and Jove's eternal vengeance, with droll admixture of mundane foibles and elaborate
    etiquette, and with a side reference to Disraeli's own ambitions. *The Infernal Marriage* (of Proserpine
    with the king of Hades) satirizes the modern " marriage for an establishment." Elysium is a caricature
    of high society, its luxuries, idleness, and scandals. *Popanilla* is a good-humoured Gulliverian satire on
    Benthamite schemes for reforming the social and political system. The Captain, born and bred on a primi-
    tive island, comes to England, and is introduced to artificial society. [In 1 vol., Longman ; (1), (2), (4),
    and *Count Alarcos*, Lane ; (1) alone, (2), (3), and (4) in 1 vol., Davies.]

—— *The Young Duke.*   1831
    There are shrewd political hits in this story of the detrimental young aristocrat and his reformation ; otherwise
    it is not much more than a garish picture of the world of fashion and frivolity. [With *Count Alarcos*, in
    Longman's ed. ; with *The Rise of Iskander* and *The Infernal Marriage*, in Lane's ed.]

—— *Contarini Fleming.*   1832
    Disraeli regarded this as forming with *Alroy* and *Vivian Grey* a sort of trilogy, those giving his real and his
    ideal ambitions, this his poetic character. Contarini would fain be a poet, but is dissuaded by his statesman
    father and by his own failure. He wanders off and has many adventures, psychical and other, visits the
    Contarini palace in Venice, loves against human and divine ordinances, and loses his love—in short, the
    story is a sort of amalgam of *Alastor* and *Childe Harold*, and the hero a thin blend of Shelley and Byron,
    with an undue admixture of extravagance and sheer silliness with much that is wiser and more sincere.
    [With *The Rise of Iskander*, in Longmans' ed.]

—— *Henrietta Temple.*   1837
    A passionate love tale ; the hero is engaged to an heiress who is to save his estates from ruin, but falls in love
    with the beautiful Henrietta. Contains a little of Disraeli's peculiar comedy.

—— *Venetia.*   1837
    A love-story founded on the history of Byron and Shelley ; the women are drawn with unusual truth and
    restraint.

—— *Coningsby ; or, The New Generation.*   1844
    Disraeli had now entered Parliament and this novel and the two that follow are much more than novels.
    Coningsby is a political manifesto with a practical aim, to furnish a programme for the Young England
    party. Coningsby is the grandson of a profligate marquess who is a standing monument to the great
    families who calmly asserted their immutable right to rule England. His friendships, his social experiences,
    and entry into political life entail a review of the political condition of England (1832–4), and criticism of
    the misgovernment and undefined principles of the Tories under Peel and their anti-reform manœuvres.
    Tory underlings, toadies, and political humbugs are caricatured. Sidonia, the great Jew financier, represents
    Disraeli's Hebrew enthusiasms ; Rigby is the Right Hon. J. W. Croker ; the Marquess of Monmouth is
    probably Lord Hertford (Thackeray's Steyne), Lord Henry Sidney is Lord George Manners, afterwards
    Duke of Rutland ; and Coningsby's original was George Smythe, afterwards Lord Strangford. [(Every-
    man's Lib.), Dent (Dutton, New York, 1911).]

—— *Sybil ; or, The Two Nations.*   1845
    One of our earliest serious social studies of the two great classes, the rich and the poor, from the practical
    standpoint of a politician. Compares the miserable conditions of the people, reduced by the tyranny of
    wealth to slavery, starvation, vice, and infanticide, with the kindlier life of the Middle Ages. This is the

DISRAELI, Benjamin, Earl of Beaconsfield (continued).

real problem for any political party that is to endure, and the Conservatives must make it a chief plank in their platform : the policy of laissez faire will no longer work. Pungent satire of aristocratic and political tinkers. Romantic interest is supplied by the love of a nobleman for a Chartist's daughter. Barrow Bridge, near Bolton, Lancs., is the model village described. [(World's Classics), Oxford Press, 1925 ; (Caravan Lib.), Macmillan.]

—— Tancred ; or, The New Crusade. 1847

Last part of what Disraeli called " a real Trilogy," setting forth the new Conservative doctrine. A fantastic story in Disraeli's most theatrical style, relating how the heir to a dukedom, after sundry adventures in patrician society, related with plenty of satire, goes in quest of light to the Holy Land, where in a trance it is revealed to him that the regeneration of Christendom must come from a new Anglican Christianity refined by Judaism. The pages of Eastern life are admirably graphic, and show his native affinity ; the Emir Fakredeen is a great creation. The end fantastic and abrupt, and the meaning left in the air.

—— Lothair. 1870

A Corinthian but far from superficial picture of the highest society of England, by one who had lived in its midst, and of the ruling classes after the two Reform Bills. Gay and operatic in style—flattering in tone, the satire of vanity and selfishness of a bantering and hardly serious kind. Lothair, who is to inherit immense possessions, is the object of a conspiracy to make him a Roman convert, and on the other hand, of Protestant intrigues. He wavers, impelled to and fro by doubts and the fascinations of two romantic ladies, champions of Catholicism and of freedom respectively. The late Marquess of Bute was pointed out as the original of Lothair ; Mazzini (Mirafiori) and Garibaldi appear in the Italian episodes. Monsignor Capel, who figures as Mgr. Catesby, died recently in North California, of which he was prelate-in-charge. Gaston Phœbus is said to be a sketch of Matthew Arnold.

—— Endymion. 1880

The romantic history of Endymion and his sister Myra (1830–40) is an allegory with an autobiographic meaning ; and the other characters are either important social types or representatives of great people of a later day. A book full of double meanings and of aphorisms enunciating the writer's political philosophy, and his mature views upon the Reform Act and its consequences, the conflicts and cabals of Whigs and Tories, Chartism, the potato famine, the Papal Bull, and many other vexed topics. One character, the snobbish St. Barbe, is a crude skit on Thackeray. [With Falcone (a posthumous fragment), in P. Davies's ed.]

Works : (Hughenden ed.) 11 vols., Longmans, 1919. With introds. by the Earl of Iddesleigh, 11 vols., Lane ; also, (Pocket ed.), id., 9 vols. With introds. by Philip Guedalla, 12 vols., Davies (Knopf, New York) 1927–8. Other eds. are noted under titles.]

DIVER, Maud Katherine Helen [née Marshall ; Anglo-Indian]. Captain Desmond, V.C. 1907

Mrs. Diver obviously has an intimate knowledge of military life in a cantonment on the north-west frontier of India a generation ago. Her captain is the regulation hero of the lady novelist—tall, intrepid, iron-willed, soft-hearted. Married to a silly wife, he falls mutually in love with her bosom friend. The issue must needs be tragic for someone, and Mrs. Diver sacrifices the poor little wife. Incident plentiful and exciting.

—— The Great Amulet. 1908

The same milieu and a number of the same characters. The hero is another captain who marries in haste, and leaves his wife in a fit of jealousy, almost at the church door. When they meet again in India and his passion revives, tragedy seems imminent, but a pleasing conclusion is arranged.

—— Candles in the Wind. 1909

Completes the " trilogy." A study of the same scenes of life and many of the same characters ; the general thesis, apart from the romantic sentiment, being the fine ideals of duty and strenuous self-devotion and loyalty, developed under the stress of military service in the midst of ignorant Orientals and constant danger from hostile tribesmen and disease. [(1), 2), and (3), Blackwood ; Dodd & Mead, New York ; together in 1 vol., sub tit. Men of the Frontier Force, Newnes, 1930.]

—— The Hero of Herat. 1912

—— The Judgment of the Sword [sequel]. 1913

Similar fictions, centring in a hero who penetrates into Afghanistan and afterwards is present at the defence of Herat in the first Afghan war (1837–41). In the sequel, he takes his part in the subsequent events, the terrible retreat, the reinvasion, the capture of Cabul, etc. Many of those historically associated with these events come on the stage. [(1) and (2), Murray ; (1), Putnam, New York ; (2), id., o.p.]

—— Desmond's Daughter. 1916

She is daughter to Captain Desmond, V.C., and her story brings in the usual Anglo-Indian scenes and historical incidents of the Tirah campaign of 1897. [Blackwood ; Houghton, Boston.]

DIX, Beulah Marie [Mrs. George H. Flebbe ; American ; b. 1876]. Hugh Gwyeth : a Roundhead cavalier. [juvenile] 1899

Battle of Edgehill and affairs in Oxford, the Royalist capital (1642–3). The hero is brought up by his grand-father, a Roundhead, and fighting with the Cavaliers, finds his own father. [Illus., Macmillan, New York.]

—— Soldier Rigdale : how he sailed in the " Mayflower," and how he served Miles Standish. 1899

Story of a boy among the colonists and the Indians (1620–1). [Illus., Macmillan, New York, 1926.]

—— Mistress Content Cradock. 1899

A love-story of the old colonizing days, kindly in its portraiture of the religious exiles, though overweighted with local and historical erudition. [Barnes, New York : o.p. ; Allenson : o.p.]

—— The Making of Christopher Ferringham. 1900

A love-story of Massachusetts (1652–4), with some careful pictures of the times, e.g. of the Quaker persecutions. [Macmillan, New York.]

DIX, Beulah Marie [American], and **HARPER**, Carrie A. [American]. *The Beau's Comedy.* 1902
A young pet of English fashionable life is taken for a French spy by the Massachusetts colonists (1745). Scenes, London and Sunderland in the Connecticut Valley. [Harper, New York and London : o.p.]

DIX, Edwin Asa [American ; b. 1860]. *Deacon Bradbury.* 1900
A study of upright and self-reliant character in the stress of moral conflict. The Deacon's son, for honest reasons, confesses to a theft of which he is innocent, and his father suffers so much in the pious community to which they belong that he loses his faith in goodness and Providence, and leaves the church. [Century Co., New York : o.p. ; Macmillan : o.p.]

DIXELIUS, Hildur Emma Eufrosyne [Swedish ; b. 1879]. *The Minister's Daughter* (Prästdottern, 1920). 1927
—— *The Son* (Prästdottern's son, 1921) [sequel]. 1928
—— *The Grandson* (Sonsonen, 1922) [sequel]. 1928
A trilogy unfolding a drama of village life in Sweden, in the early years of the nineteenth century ; excellent in local colour. [(1), (2), and (3), transl. by Anna C. SETTERGREN, Dutton, New York ; Dent.]

DIXON, Ella Nora Hepworth [daughter of W. H. Dixon]. *The Story of a Modern Woman.* 1894
The orphaned daughter of a renowned professor tries to live a useful and independent life. Failing to become an artist, she earns a precarious livelihood in byways of literature ; she loses her lover, but fights on doggedly. The future of the lonely woman, as foreshadowed on the last page, is a melancholy one. In her satire on the shams and corruptions of society life the authoress is very much in earnest. [Heinemann : o.p.]

DIXON, Thomas [American ; b. 1864]. *The Leopard's Spots.* 1902
—— *The Clansman* [sequel]. 1905
—— *The Traitor* [sequel]. 1907
Cover the history of the Reconstruction period, the murder of Lincoln (1865), the doings of the Ku Klux Klan, who banded themselves together, after the war, to protect white interests in the South, and the dissolution of this society in 1872. [(1), (2), and (3), Doubleday, New York : o.p. ; (2), Grosset, New York ; (1), De La More Press : o.p. ; (2) Heinemann : o.p.]
—— *The Southerner.* 1913
A portrayal of Lincoln, chiefly during the war (1861–3), by a sympathizer with the South, who tries to make out that by nature and temper the President was really a Southerner. [Appleton, New York and London.]
—— *The Victim.* 1914
A companion study of Jefferson Davis, aiming to present his " real character unobscured by passion or prejudice." Summarizing the Southern leader's early career, it concentrates on the crucial period 1860–7. [Appleton, New York and London : o.p.]

DODD, Catherine Isabel. *Lords of Red Lattice : being some chronicles of the Crathornes of Crathorne.* 1930
A pleasant story of English country life in the late eighteenth century, revolving around the effect of an ancestral curse. [Jarrolds.]

"**DOFF**, Neel" [C. Lerigiers]. *Keetje.* 1930
A piteous story of the underworld of Amsterdam—the life of a girl who has to become a prostitute to support her parents and brothers and sisters, and whose fine nature eventually frees her from this horror to become the partner of an heroic young philanthropist. [Transl. from the French by Frederic WHITE, Hutchinson.]

DOLE, Nathan Haskell [American ; b. 1852]. *Omar the Tentmaker.* 1899
Omar Khayyám, author of the Rubaiyat, imagined as hero of an old Persian love-story. Introduces such celebrities as Malik Shah Seljuki, the minister Nizāmu 'l Mulk, etc. [*Illus.*, Page, Boston ; Duckworth : o.p.]

DORGELÈS, Roland [French ; b. 1886]. *Wooden Crosses* (Les croix de bois, 1919). 1921
The actualities of trench warfare on an unspecified sector of the French front, and the experiences of a little group of *poilus* who are in the thick of it ; all presented with terrible realism. [Transl., Putnam, New York.]
—— *Saint Magloire.* 1923
An ironical story suggested perhaps by the newspaper head-line " If Christ came to Chicago." Magloire is a true saint, whose courage, eloquence, and selfless energy have performed miracles among the heathen. Returning to France, he is fêted and interviewed and creates such a sensation that his bourgeois relatives are embarrassed and the mayor finds it difficult to keep order. But the wonder is forgotten in nine days, and Magloire's own confidence that he will save the civilized world too ends in tragic failure. [Transl. by Pauline DE CHARY, Collins.]
—— *The Cabaret up the Line* (Le cabaret de la Belle Femme, 1922). 1930
Fourteen stories (including five from *Les croix de bois*) of trench life, attacks and raids, and other war-time experiences of a *poilu*. The translation, by Brian Lunn and Alan Duncan, is not first-class. [Lane.]
—— *Departure* (Partir, 1927). 1928
A set of characters outward bound from Marseilles to the East are dissected with ready wit and no little satire, and their commonplaces make a contrast to the exotic background against which they play their parts. [Transl. by Pauline E. RUSH, Simon & Schuster, New York ; Gollancz.]

DORR, Julia Caroline [*née* Ripley ; American ; 1825–1913]. *In Kings' Houses : a romance of the days of Queen Anne.* 1898
A charming picture of life at Windsor early in the eighteenth century, drawing Queen Anne and her intimates with a sympathetic touch, and rendering the manners and atmosphere of the time with much art. [Page, Boston ; Duckworth : o.p.]

DOS PASSOS, John Roderigo [American ; *b.* 1896]. *Three Soldiers.* 1921
One of the grimmest among war-books. The experiences of three men in the American army in France are made to bring out powerfully the demoralizing effects upon the educated mind of the horrors of modern warfare. [Doubleday, New York.]

—— *Manhattan Transfer.* 1925
Attempts for New York what Joyce did for Dublin. The plan is not the same as in *Ulysses*, but the method is similar, and hence came the staccato, elliptical style, violent and slangy, stringing words together to evoke flashlight pictures. What story there is comes in short snatches, rather as in Huxley's *Point Counter Point*. But, anyhow, the effect of life as it goes rushing on, noisy, confused, terrifying, is caught, from moment to moment, the ruthless, stunning, stupefying life of a monstrous city in the " jazz age." A whole crowd of people from every class, tramp and criminal, millionaire and politician, are shown feverishly striving for pleasure or passion, for wealth or for mere existence. Most come to an evil end, and such philosophy as emerges is pessimistic rather than tragic. [Harper, New York ; Constable.]

—— *The 42nd Parallel.* 1930
This extraordinary production has a wider range, raking in its subjects from all over North America. It comprises, a series of ironical biographies, of Burbank, Bill Heywood, Debs, Carnegie, Edison, and Steinmetz ; a " news-reel " professedly gathered from the popular journals of 1900–1917 ; the " camera-eye " filming " the stream of consciousness " in the *Ulysses* way ; and five terse expressionist stories of the underworld,—the whole lot as unbeautiful in manner as in subject. This is to be the first part of a trilogy. [Harper, New York ; Constable.]

DOSTOEVSKAYA, Lyubov Thedorovna [Russian ; *b.* 1869]. *The Emigrant* (1913). 1916
An interesting study, by Dostoevsky's daughter, of a Russian type, the idealist who cannot square herself with actualities. The subject is a woman, out of sympathy with the new ideas of social reconstruction after the Russo-Japanese war, who seeks change and rest in Italy, experiments with Roman society and the Church, becomes a nun, but deserts the cloister for a husband. Still unable to escape her temperament, she commits suicide. [Transl. by Vera MARGOLIES, with introd. by Stephen Graham, Constable : o.p. ; Brentano, New York : o.p.]

DOSTOEVSKY, Thedor Mikhailovich [Russian ; 1821–81]. *Poor Folk* (1846). 1887
Dostoevsky's stories, long or short, are the most searching studies of abnormal, distressed, tormented, and criminal minds in any literature ; written with a sympathy and an intensity of insight that indicate something abnormal in the brain of the writer. This was written before his death-sentence and reprieve and the subsequent exile to Siberia (1849–59) ; hence it is not typical of his mature genius. Yet it is a powerful, compassionate, deeply pathetic story of the submerged, telling of the happy and innocent comradeship of two young people : a poor clerk, whose life is a perpetual struggle for bread, embittered by continual slights to his self-love ; and a girl, equally poor, isolated and despised, whose friendship is the one solace of his existence. [Transl. by H. S. EDWARDS, 1887 ; Harper, New York : o.p. ; by Lena MILMAN, 1894, Mathews : o.p. ; *v.* also *The Gambler.*]

—— *White Nights ; and other stories* (1848). 1918
White Nights ; Notes from Underground ; A Faint Heart ; A Christmas Tree and a Wedding ; Polzunkov ; A Little Hero ; Mr. Prohartchin. [Transl. by Constance·GARNETT, (*Works, v.* 10), Heinemann (Macmillan, New York).]

—— *An Honest Thief* (1848) ; *and other stories* (1848–76). 1919
The title-story and two others, *The Peasant Marly* and *The Dream of a Queer Fellow*, are perhaps those in which the beauty and the tragedy of life, in the piercing vision of Dostoevsky, reach the greatest heights. *An Unpleasant Predicament* is an almost cruelly lifelike and biting chronicle of a *faux pas* and its consequences to the doer. *Another Man's Wife* is a broad comedy to appreciate which we must change our accepted values. *The Heavenly Christmas Tree*, in the Hans Andersen vein, though tragic, is hardly worthy of Dostoevsky ; but his peculiar humour comes out well in some of the rest. [Transl. by Constance GARNETT, (*Works, v.* 11), Heinemann (Macmillan, New York).]

—— *The Friend of the Family ; or, Stepantchikovo and its inhabitants* (1859). 1884
Dostoevsky's first novel after his Siberian exile. The chief figure is a repulsive companion who worms his way into the confidence of his employer, and succeeds in dominating him and his womenfolk—a picture of petty egoism carried almost to the point of insanity. [With *The Gambler*, Vizetelly : o.p. ; with *Nyetochka Nyezvanov*, transl. by Constance GARNETT, (*Works, v.* 12), Heinemann (Macmillan, New York) 1920.]

—— *The Insulted and Injured* (1861). 1915
In point of construction and also as a piece of story-telling this stands perhaps foremost among Dostoevsky's works. It is first-class melodrama, like the best of Dickens, and combines therewith the profound psychological interest that is peculiarly Dostoevsky's. It is one of those books which have given rise to the idea that he preaches " a religion of suffering." The little group of principal characters includes two women who endure the extremes of wrong and ignominy. Over them towers one of those monstrous egoists, cold-hearted, clear-headed, ruthless in procuring his vicious pleasures, whom he can draw with such a terrifying power. The underworld of Petersburg diffuses a sombre, sinister light over the whole exciting drama. [Transl. by Constance GARNETT, (*Works, v.* 6), Heinemann (Macmillan, New York).]

—— *The House of the Dead* (1861–2). 1881
In this autobiography of a Russian landowner condemned to penal servitude in Siberia, Dostoevsky hardly troubles to disguise his own experiences. He traces the different effects of imprisonment on the moral nature, in the life-stories of a group of criminals. It is a terrible record of the anguish of the prisoner's lot—hunger, cold, torture, and the squalor of debased companionship, and a burning appeal for justice to the oppressed. [Transl. by Marie von PHILO, *sub tit. Buried Alive*, 1881 ; title as above (Everyman's Lib.), Dent (Dutton, New York), 1911 ; by Constance GARNETT, (*Works, v.* 5), Heinemann (Macmillan, New York), 1915.]

DOSTOEVSKY, Thedor Mikhailovich (*continued*). *Crime and Punishment* (1866). 1886

First of the great quaternion in which Dostoevsky sounded the deepest abysses of the soul, and explored the most agonizing problems that beset the human spirit—problems which are subsumed in the momentous question, Does God exist ? Such questions had hitherto been debated in dramatic terms only by the greatest playwrights, in the *Prometheus*, the *Oresteia*, *Hamlet*, *Lear*, *Faust*. These four novels, if novels they are to be called, are gigantic imaginative experiments, in which the mental conflicts, doubts, and speculations Dostoevsky had lived through are objectified. The protagonists are colossal figures representing facets of man's intellect and will ; they are human, yet superhuman ; in short, they are at once individuals and symbols, and have no counterparts except in the heroes of these mighty plays. Dostoevsky does not recoil from the most appalling facts, and is not afraid to contemplate the most shameless and revolting acts and motives or to ponder the most rebellious and blasphemous protests. His Raskolnikov, convinced by his theories that he has the right, deliberately murders an old pawnbroker and her sister. But he is not a complete immoralist ; he justifies his act by the argument of the greater good ; " he does not free himself an instant from conscience and his own mediocrity " (André Gide). He proceeds even to repentance and expiation. Not so the frigid Svidrigailov, who does not pay even a lingering obeisance to moral codes ; he is one of those awful creations of Dostoevsky who have gone beyond good and evil and are a law to themselves. [Transl. by F. WHISHAW, (Everyman's Lib.) Dent (Dutton, New York) 1911 ; by Constance GARNETT (*Works*, v. 4), Heinemann (Macmillan, New York) 1914.]

—— *The Gambler* (1867) ; *and other stories*. 1915

The Gambler is comparatively a slight piece, but a capital instance of Dostoevsky's strength and swiftness in unthreading a tangle of confused and conflicting motives and interests. The gambler, in love with a girl above him in rank, stakes all on the Roulettenburg tables, loses, and is lost. His, however, is but one affair among a whirl of hazards and passions and breathless crises, which are bewildering to the reader and overdo perhaps Dostoevsky's avowed policy of using swift and exciting narrative to carry off the philosophic implications. [With *Poor Folk*, transl. by C. J. HOGARTH, (Everyman's Lib.) Dent (Dutton, New York). With *Poor People* and *The Landlady*, transl. by Constance GARNETT (*Works*, v. 9) Heinemann (Macmillan, New York) 1917.]

—— *The Idiot* (1868). 1887

This attacks the problem of evil and its correlative, the question of the existence of God, from the other side. Dostoevsky puts into a world of foolishness, vice, pretence, and sordid ambitions, a being who in childhood had suffered from mental disease, and who with an intellect of more than ordinary power retains the simplicity and clear insight of a child. In the *Idiot*, he tried to realize his idea of " a truly perfect and noble man " ; this Prince Myshkin of his, an epileptic like himself, is the champion of humanity. The deeply absorbing drama in which he is a protagonist turns on the salvation of a woman, Nastasya Filipovna, who had been corrupted in young girlhood. She is a wonderful creation, and her career one long tragedy. The passion that ruins is chiefly represented by her insensate lover Rogozhin, another of those dark figures invested with symbolic import. The closing scene is heart-rending. The issue goes beyond tragedy. Personality does not triumph even in defeat. Man, even the good man, is overwhelmed. Evil remains omnipotent. Yet there are passages of high comedy. In many scenes, the well-worn motive of the *ingénu* and the *enfant terrible* elicit humorous effects, and such admirable characters as Mme Epanchin and the buoyant and optimistic General Ivolgin show to what profit Dostoevsky had sat at the feet of Dickens. [Transl. by F. WHISHAW, Vizetelly, 1887 : o.p. ; transl. by Constance GARNETT, (*Works*, v. 2), Heinemann (Macmillan, New York) 1913 ; by Eva M. MARTIN, (Everyman's Lib.) Dent [Dutton, New York).]

—— *The Eternal Husband* (1870) ; *and other stories*. 1917

Marcel Schwob considered *The Eternal Husband* Dostoevsky's masterpiece, not quite unreasonably. It lays bare the complex mental states of a man who years ago seduced a wife, and is brought into the closest contact with the dead woman's husband and the daughter, now grown up, whom he recognizes as his own. Does the husband know ? Is he jealous ? The guilty man cannot decide the tormenting question. Dostoevsky's favourite thesis, that love and hate are profoundly akin and change into each other imperceptibly, is here developed in the intense light of his insight into the obscure regions of the soul. Another masterly tale is *The Gentle Spirit* (1876). But this cannot be said of *The Double* (1848), in spite of its amazing ingenuity. [Transl. by Constance GARNETT, (*Works*, v. 8), Heinemann (Macmillan, New York).]

—— *The Possessed* (1871). 1914

Dostoevsky prefaced this novel with a summary of the parable of the swine. He shows a group of Nihilists propagating ideas and fomenting revolution in a provincial town, in an atmosphere of rabid enthusiasm, mental uncertainty, and mutual suspicion, which has comic as well as tragic aspects. The sentimental romancer Karmazinov is a caricature of Turgenev. The great character of the book, Stavrogin, was an after-thought ; Dostoevsky recast the story to make this the terrible central personage. Stavrogin is all intellect and energy : he coldly sacrifices love, self, even pride, to the realization of his will. He is the man-god, dominating the mind of Shatov and Kirillov, the simple, honest peasant and the idealist, who kills himself because he knows God does not exist. His dominating personality prompts to heroic devotion and to ruthless crimes. He is prophetic of the subversive Bolshevism of half-a-century later. In this crowded drama, in which Dostoevsky deliberately speeds up the action to carry off the meaning, he objectifies, as was his wont, his most searching and most desolating thought on the ultimate problems, on the value or the worthlessness of life. His stern mental debates and the doctrines he had derived or developed from Hegel, Schopenhauer, and Nietzsche, and tested in his own moral conflicts, are the express or the underlying dramatic motives. Stavrogin's and the speeches of Ivan Karamazov, in the subsequent book, are the most fearless statements of the tragic alternatives of human existence ever put into fiction. [Transl. by Constance GARNETT (*Works*, v. 3), Heinemann (Macmillan, New York) ; *Stavrogin's Confession ; three hitherto unpublished chapters of The Possessed*, transl. by S. S. KOTELIANSKY and V. WOOLF, Hogarth Press, 1922.]

DOSTOEVSKY, Thèdor Mikhailovich (*continued*). *A Raw Youth : a novel in three parts* (1875).
1919

In his imaginary autobiographer Dostoevsky has here drawn a character who is a frank exponent of the Nietzschean " will to power " ; perhaps he has portrayed a phase of his own immaturity, and shown the foolishness of it without unsympathy or satire. The raw youth, poor and illegitimate though he is, determines to be a Rothschild ; and to that end starves himself, shuns and decries women, and so on : he is a romantic, with the romantic deficiency of balance, but, at any rate, without any sentimental self-pity. [Transl. by Constance GARNETT (*Works*, v. 7), Heinemann (Macmillan New York).]

—— *The Brothers Karamazov* (1879–80).
1912

His last and perhaps his greatest work ; unfinished, although the main action is ended before the abrupt close. Enormously long, notwithstanding, and crowded with characters, even though the essential personages are few. These are profoundly human, yet characteristically superhuman figures ; incarnations of the most violent and unbridled passions and aberrations ; symbols, yet not merely symbols ; individuals with a tremendous life and energy. Old Karamazov is the embodiment of bestial sensuality, unrestrained by moral or sentimental feeling. Of his three sons, Ivan is pride of intellect, in revolt against the apparent disorder of the world, revolt against the idea of God, ruler of such a senseless universe ; Dmitri, easy-going, sensual, impulsive, good-natured, romantic, is his inevitable antagonist ; Aloysha is a Christ-like being surpassing even Myshkin ; he represents human nature in its fulness, rich in tenderness and fellow-feeling for all things, he has in him the makings of a saint. There are two notable women-characters, who are subsidiary to these chief actors ; and one of Dostoevsky's most beautiful and sublime creations, Father Zossima, a serene, unworldly being, who has gone through the fire and issued cleansed, pure, sanctified. Old Karamazov is killed by the ugly and sinister Smerdyakov ; but who, morally, is his murderer ? In the tria of Dmitri for the murder of his father, and the ensuing miscarriage of justice, there is a certain parallel to *The Ring and the Book*—human evidence is studied and judged from a different angle. [Transl. by Constance GARNETT (*Works*, v. 1), Heinemann (Macmillan, New York) ; same, 2 vols. (Everyman's Lib.), Dent (Dutton, New York, 1927).]

DOUGALL, Lily [Canadian ; 1858–1923]. *Beggars All.*
1891

Inculcates love for one's neighbour as the sole philosophy of human life. A little family of American ladies, in utter distress through illness and poverty, are the central characters ; one, a modest and sensitive girl, answers a matrimonial advertisement and marries a man for the sake of her suffering relatives—and finds that the man is a thief. [Longmans : o.p.]

—— *The Mormon Prophet.*
1899

An apologetic study of the career of the famous Joseph Smith, and of the Mormons at the height of their struggle (1823–44). [Black : o.p. ; Appleton, New York : o.p.]

DOUGLAS, George Norman [Scottish ; b. 1868]. *South Wind.*
1917

Belongs to the cynical, half-complacent, half-ironical picturing of frivolous, sophisticated, demoralized or unmoral life, done by Oscar Wilde, Firbank, Michael Arlen, etc., with Anatole France further in the distance. The volcanic Mediterranean isle of Nepenthe is Capri, where the author lived—he was born in Austria. Apart from natives, who hardly count, it is inhabited by persons under various sorts of cloud, a rich epicurean Scotsman, an artistic Italian count who forges an antique statuette, etc., whose number is increased by the arrival of a South African bishop and sundry other unusual persons. Not much story ; but the incidents are funny in the manner of musical comedy, and the conversations are very witty indeed, with hints of something else that the author refrains from putting into plain English. [Secker ; Dodd & Mead, New York ; Macmillan, New York, 1929 ; *illus.* by Valenti Angelo, Dodd & Mead, New York ; by John Austen, 2 vols., Argus Press, Chicago, 1929.]

—— *They Went.*
1920

An essay in myth-making, written in Brittany and inspired by Breton folk-lore as an irreverent variation of the legend of the Roi d'Ys. It is about a city and its king and queen and cruel princess, and how it was overwhelmed by the sea. The characters, one and all, from the boorish monarch to the druidess, patron of all feminists, are highly modern and diverting types. [Chapman ; Dodd & Mead, New York.]

—— *In the Beginning.*
1928

A facetious attempt to depict the infancy of mankind soon after their creation by the Father of the Gods, when the gods themselves, various demigods, satyrs, and other beings who have now disappeared, inhabited the earth or heaven, and sported or otherwise interfered with people's business. [Chatto ; (Phœnix Lib.), *id.* ; Day, New York.]

" DOUGLAS, Theo " [Mrs. H. D. Everett]. *Nemo.*
1900

Hypnotism and spiritualism, and more human elements than are usual in this class of story. A conjurer transfers the soul, or the psychical activities, of his daughter to an automaton. The daughter's struggle between love and revolt from her father's remorseless pursuit of the occult gives rise to some touching passages. [Smith & Elder : o.p.]

—— *Cousin Hugh.*
1910

The traffic in escaped prisoners ; scene, the south coast about 1809. [Methuen : o.p.]

DOWIE, Ménie Muriel [Mrs. E. A. Fitzgerald, formerly Mrs. Henry Norman ; b. 1867]. *Gallia.*
1895

A society novel of the " fast " type touching rather freely on bohemian life in artistic Paris and on sex problems. [Methuen : o.p.]

—— *The Crook of the Bough.*
1898

The hero is a modernized Turk, a patriot and a soldier, who cherishes advanced ideas about woman and her influence on social and moral progress. But the woman he loves disappoints him, deteriorating intellectually and morally to the status of an Oriental. [Methuen : o.p. ; Scribner, New York : o.p.]

DOWIE, Ménie Muriel (*continued*). *Love and His Mask.* 1901
The thesis which the novelist seeks to prove is that, in questions of marriage, passion is everything and mere respect and admiration nothing. Bold in design, with a set of well-drawn characters from high society. [Heinemann : o.p.]

DOWLING, Richard [Irish ; 1846–98]. *The Mystery of Killard.* 1879
The mystery is connected with an inaccessible rock on the forbidding coast of Clare. and a certain treasure. But the central and most original idea is that of " a deaf mute who, by brooding on his own misfortune, grows to envy and then to hate his own child, because the child can hear and speak." [3 vols., Tinsley : o.p.]

—— *Old Corcoran's Money.* 1884
The first of various sensational plot-novels to which the author now turned his attention. A miser, his stolen money, and the detection of the thief, with sketches of life in southern Ireland, and some character-drawing. [Chatto : o.p.]

DOWNEY, Edmund [" F. M. Allen " ; Irish ; b. 1856]. *Anchor-Watch Yarns.* 1884
Humorous stories told by old salts in a seaport public-house.

—— *Through Green Glasses.* 1887

—— *From the Green Bag.* 1889
Comic episodes of pseudo-history by a humorist of County Waterford, Dan Banim—e.g. the burlesque account of King James's escape after the battle of the Boyne, the loves of Dermot MacMurrough and Devorgilla, and the true story of Lambert Simnel the impostor ; in the second collection, St. Patrick, Horatius, and Julius Cæsar come on the stage.

—— *The Merchant of Killogue : a Munster tale.* 1894
A picture of life and politics in an Irish provincial town, highly praised by Reade. Amusing election scenes. [3 vols., Heinemann : o.p.]

—— *Dorothy Tuke.* 1905
A story of the sea. [Hurst & Blackett : o.p.]

—— *Dunleary : humours of a Munster town.* 1912
Comedy of a genial, old-fashioned sort, with none of the brogue, and indeed little that is distinctively Irish. Fourteen diverting anecdotes of the R.M., the mayor and councillors, the leading tradespeople, skippers, etc., of a decayed seaport of about 1,300 inhabitants. *The Rivals*, about the feud between two editors, is a delectable anthology of invective. [Low : o.p.]

DOYLE, Sir Arthur Conan [Irish ; 1859–1930]. *A Study in Scarlet.* 1887
A sensational story in two parts : the first deals with adventures in Utah and the wrong committed by two brutal Mormons on a girl and her lover ; the second is the history of a mysterious double murder committed in London and, by the agency of Sherlock Holmes, shown to be the work of the wronged lover, who thus, after many years, attains his revenge. [Ward & Lock ; Burt, New York ; with *The Sign of Four*, Harper, New York, 1904.]

—— *Micah Clarke.* 1888
Told by a humble adherent of the Duke of Monmouth—the whole story of the rising in Somerset, the triumphant advance towards Bristol and Bath, and the tragic rout at Sedgemoor (1685). A rattling narrative of fights and adventures. Robert Ferguson, Monmouth, and Jeffreys appear. [Longmans, London and New York ; Murray ; Harper, New York ; Burt, New York.]

—— *The Sign of Four.* 1889
The story of a vendetta in which Sherlock Holmes figures again. [Murray ; Lippincott, Philadelphia ; Burt, New York ; with *A Study in Scarlet, vide supra*.]

—— *The Firm of Girdlestone.* 1890
A plot-novel of commercial roguery. Two London merchants, a sanctimonious scamp and his ruffianly son, plot to murder a ward and use her money to bolster up the business ; after complicated intrigues and many scenes of violence, the girl is saved by her lover, and the villains come to a bad end. [Chatto ; Murray ; Burt, New York.]

—— *The White Company.* 1891
Exploits of a company of English bowmen in France and Castile under the Duke of Lancaster. Du Guesclin, Chandos, and other paladins come on the stage. A stirring narrative of hard blows and feats of arms, inspired by Scott and Froissart (*c*. 1366–7). [*Illus.* Murray ; Harper, New York ; Burt, New York ; Dodd & Mead, New York.]

—— *The Refugees : a tale of two continents.* 1891
A Huguenot romance of Louis XIV's reign, the French episodes dealing with intrigue and adventure in the style of Dumas (there is a favourable portrait of Madame de Maintenon) and the American half, an essay in the style of Fenimore Cooper (*c*. 1684–90). [Longmans ; Murray ; Harper, New York.]

—— *The Adventures of Sherlock Holmes.* 1892
—— *The Memoirs of Sherlock Holmes.* 1893
—— *The Return of Sherlock Holmes.* 1905
Detective stories forming the life-history of the amateur thief-taker who first appeared in *A Study in Scarlet*. He is a man of superhuman powers of observation, inductive sagacity, and combination, whose exploits are usually accompanied by gruesome and thrilling incidents. *Facile princeps* amongst detective stories, at any rate after Poe, whom the author confessedly takes as his pattern. [(1), (2), and (3), Murray ; (1) and (2), Harper, New York ; Burt, New York ; (3), Doubleday, New York.]

—— *The Great Shadow.* 1892
A little drama of the Napoleonic terror, with a fine tableau of Waterloo. The heroine jilts the hero and elopes with an officer of the Imperial Guard. [Arrowsmith ; Harper, New York.]

DOYLE, Sir Arthur Conan (*continued*). *Round the Red Lamp : being facts and fancies of medical life.* 1894

Realistic stories of operations and other episodes of medical life, sketches of old-fashioned doctors, medical students and their pranks, a Waterloo veteran, and other picturesque figures, with miscellaneous stories of an exciting trend. [Murray ; Appleton, New York.]

—— *The Exploits of Brigadier Gerard.* 1896

Self-related exploits of an officer of the *Grande Armée*, a fire-eater, a braggart, and in many ways a type of French virtues and foibles. The eight stories are roughly connected into a memoir, each centring in some sensational deed, the perils and prowess of which are by no means belittled in the mouth of the genial narrator. Napoleon, Wellington, and many another celebrity pass through these scenes of action and adventure all over Europe (1807–14). [Murray ; Appleton, New York : o.p.]

—— *Adventures of Gerard* [sequel]. 1903

Further exploits of this obtuse, fire-eating, gasconading hussar, in the Peninsular War, in England as a prisoner-of-war, in the retreat from Moscow, and at Waterloo (1808–15) ; characterization of the same slap-dash kind, the incidents sensational and exciting. [Murray ; Elder ; McClure, New York : o.p.]

—— *Rodney Stone.* 1896

A sporting novel of the " Corinthian " days of Brummell, Charlie Fox, Sheridan, and the Prince Regent (George IV), (1796–1803), with a great deal of lore about the ring : there are two memorable descriptions of " a fight to a finish." One of the most interesting figures is the superfine buck, Tregellis. Nelson, Lady Hamilton, Sir Philip Francis, and many other notable people are sketched in a rough-and-ready way. [Murray ; Appleton, New York.]

—— *Uncle Bernac.* 1897

A story of the camp at Boulogne and the projected invasion of England (1805). Napoleon is vividly sketched. The hero and narrator is an *émigré* noble who serves under the emperor ; Bernac is the villain, a treacherous uncle who has usurped the family estates. [Murray ; Appleton, New York : o.p.]

—— *The Tragedy of the Korosko.* 1898

The disasters and hairbreadth escapes of a pleasure-party of Europeans in a trip up the Nubian Nile, where they fell into the hands of the Baggaras. [Murray ; Lippincott, Philadelphia.]

—— *The Green Flag ; and other stories of war and sport.* 1900

A miscellaneous collection of stories of action and of humorous incident. The title-story, like some others, is martial, and deals with an Egyptian campaign ; Capt. Sharkey is a bloodthirsty pirate ; *The Slapping Sal* also tells about a valorous pirate ; and some of the others are reminiscent of Sherlock Holmes, the Brigadier Gerard, and others of the author's creations. [Murray ; McClure, New York : o.p.]

—— *The Hound of the Baskervilles.* 1902

One of the most complicated problems solved by Sherlock Holmes. The criminal whom he eventually runs to earth has employed a savage hound—believed to be the ancestral curse of the Baskervilles—to frighten to death a rich old baronet, to whom he supposes himself next of kin. [Murray ; Garden City Co., New York.]

—— *Sir Nigel.* 1906

A stirring romance of the period just antecedent to that of *The White Company*, which should be read as the sequel. Gives a vigorous description of the battle of Poitiers (1348–56). [Murray ; McClure, New York : o.p.]

—— *The Last Galley : impressions and tales.* 1911

Sensational stories of Brigadier Gerard, of adventures on the Spanish Main, prize-fighters, lepers, pirates, etc., some of them pretty creepy ; and exciting episodes from history, ancient, mediæval, and later. [Murray ; Doubleday, New York.]

—— *The Lost World.* 1912

Two professors and two other Englishmen come across a region in the Amazon valley where the Jurassic period still persists, with its flora and fauna, pterodactyls, dinosaurs, iguanodons, and other beasts that we know only in fossil form, still flourishing. The scientific squabbles of Challenger and the other professor provide incidental comedy. [Murray ; *illus.*, Oxford Press ; Doran, New York.]

—— *The Poison Belt.* 1913

Further adventures of Challenger and his friends, who take precautions to remain alive, whilst all other life on the earth ceases for a time. [Hodder ; Doran, New York : o.p.]

—— *The Valley of Fear.* 1915

The story falls into two parts ; in the first, Sherlock Holmes solves a murder mystery, engineered by a secret society ; the second describes that society and their capture, in a wild American valley. [Murray ; Doran, New York : o.p. ; Burt, New York.]

—— *His Last Bow : some reminiscences of Sherlock Holmes.* 1917

War-time stories of the great amateur detective, now living on a small farm near Eastbourne and prepared to put his genius at the service of the Government. [Murray ; Doran, New York : o.p.]

—— *Danger ! and other stories.* 1918

The title-story was a warning against invasion, written eighteen months before the war. The amusing *Fall of Lord Barrymore* is of Regency days. [Murray ; New York : o.p. ; Burt, New York.]

—— *The Case-Book of Sherlock Holmes.* 1927

Brings together the final stories of the great detective. [Murray ; Doubleday, Doran, New York. *The Complete Sherlock Holmes*, containing *The Adventures, Memoirs, Return, His Last Bow*, and *The Case Book*, Murray (Doubleday, Doran, New York), 1929. *Sherlock Holmes Long Stories*, containing *A Study in Scarlet, Sign of Four, Hound of the Baskervilles*, and *Valley of Fear*, Murray, 1929.]

—— *The Maracot Deep ; and other stories.* 1929

The title-story is a rather lame effort in the style of H. G. Wells's scientific romances. Of the other three, the best is *When the World Screamed*. [Murray ; Doubleday, Doran, New York.]

[*Tales*, 6 vols. in 1, Murray, 1929.]

DOYLE, C. W. [American ; *d.* 1903]. *The Shadow of Quong Lung.* 1900
  Realistic stories of the Chinatown quarter of San Francisco ; connected together by the mysterious and threatening shadow of a diabolical monster who lives by kidnapping Chinese women, and employs the resources of modern science to carry out his crimes. [Lippincott, Philadelphia : o.p. ; Constable : o.p.]

"DOYLE, Lynn" [Leslie Arthur Montgomery ; Irish ; *b.* 1873]. *Mr. Wildridge of the Bank.* 1916
  A comedy of northern Irish life—the hero attempts to establish a factory which will bring prosperity to the town. There is some lively character-drawing. [Duckworth ; Stokes, New York.]

DRACHMANN, Holger Henrich Herholdt [Danish ; 1846–1908]. *The Cruise of " The Wild Duck " ; and other tales (chiefly from* Smaa Fortællinger, 1884). 1893
  The title-story and *Round Cape Horn* are sea-tales, adventurous in spirit and full of a passion for the sea. *She Died and was Buried* is a touching story, with an uncommon vein of satire. Herr Drachmann was a great Danish poet and novelist. [Unwin : o.p.]

DRAKE, Henry Burgess [*b.* 1894]. *The Schooner " California ".* 1926
  Nautical adventures about 1849, manifestly inspired by Conrad and Herman Melville. [Lane ; Harper, New York.]

—— *Cursed be the Treasure.* 1926
  Romantic adventure—smugglers, hidden treasure, murder—more in the Stevensonian vein. [Lane ; Vanguard Press, New York.]

—— *The Children Reap.* 1929
  The most interesting pages are those depicting the sub-tropical scenery and savage life of the mountain region of Formosa, where the author has travelled. [Lane ; Vanguard Press, New York.]

—— *Shinju.* 1929
  A young Englishman in love with an enchanting Japanese girl comes up against the inexorable dilemma of racial incompatibility. The writer is thoroughly conversant with the minutiæ of Japanese manners and ancestral taboos. [Lane.]

DREISER, Theodore [American ; *b.* 1871]. *Sister Carrie.* 1901
  A very plain, unassuming, and unconventional history of a young woman led into vice by her love of pleasure, and the parallel history of the moral deterioration of a man. The life of the lower middle classes in New York and Chicago is depicted with the industrious realism of a Zola, and something of the vision and power, if not of Tolstoy, at least of a Gorky. Mr. Dreiser came to the front at the time when the short-lived Frank Norris was the leader of a naturalistic movement in American fiction. [Boni, New York, 1921 ; Constable.]

—— *Jennie Gerhart.* 1911
  A similar piece of work, undramatic, inartistic, but thoroughly honest and not without serious thought, although Mr. Dreiser admits that he is unable to make up his mind about anything. Contrasts the fortunes of two families, German and Irish immigrants. Jennie, child of an unsuccessful German, falls a prey to the pleasure-loving son of the enterprising Irishman. Whether of deep-laid purpose or not, the book illustrates the rottenness of a complex social fabric resting on materialism. [Boni, New York, 1923 ; Constable.]

—— *The Financier.* 1912
—— *The Titan* [sequel]. 1914
  Though lacking the charm that won popularity for his first two novels, these are very fair specimens of his patient and voluminous method, and of the sincerity and confused strength that impresses the American public. The ruthless, successful, cynical, and dissolute Frank Catherwood is drawn, at any rate as regards the main points of his career, after the great financier Charles T. Yerkes. There was to have been a third novel to complete this " Trilogy of Desire," bringing the predatory millionaire to London, but it has not appeared. [(1), revised ed., Boni, New York, 1927 ; (2), Boni, New York, 1923 ; (1) and (2), Constable.]

—— *The Genius.* 1915
  Another enormous hunch of life, after consuming which we know a great deal more about farming, railroading, the work and struggles of artists in New York, Paris, and elsewhere, magazine-editing, publicity business, and finance, than most of us want. A great deal of it is realism for the sake of realism. Willa is a painter who shows phases of life which are for the most part " but casually glanced at, things which because they were commonplace and customary were supposedly beyond the pale of artistic significance." Here can be read Mr. Dreiser's own artistic creed, although Willa could hardly have been so exhaustive. Willa is a genius of ebullient but fitful energy, made and marred by his weakness for women, and a victim of drift. The philosophy of the book is that of a Hall Caine or Corelli. [Boni, New York, 1923 ; Constable.]

—— *Free ; and other stories.* 1918
  Eleven slighter stories of the dull, soul-crushing life of those gripped by the vast American machine. *Free* is about a man released at sixty from a marriage that has blighted his personality. *The Second Choice* shows a young girl thrown into just such a union through the baseness of a lover. *Nigger Jeff* is a tale of lynching. There are also stories of rival journalists, a terrific battle of ants, etc. [Boni, New York ; Modern Lib., New York, 1914.]

—— *Twelve Men.* 1919
  In the main, studies of character, faithfully delineating people he has actually known. [Boni, New York ; Modern Lib., New York, 1928.]

—— *An American Tragedy.* 1925
  An enormously long diagnosis of the life of a crude young man, from boyhood to the electric chair. Every circumstance, relevant or irrelevant, bearing upon the murder of his unwanted mistress, is conscientiously recorded. His apprehension, trial, and execution are reported in detail, occupying most of the second part. Before he dies, the condemned man writes an address to the world, affirming his redemption : " My task is done, the victory won." [2 vols., Boni, New York ; in 1 vol., *id.*, 1929 ; 1 vol., Constable.]

—— *A Gallery of Women.* 1928
  A companion volume to *Twelve Men.* [2 vols., Boni, New York ; Constable.]

DRIBERG, Jack Herbert. *People of the Small Arrow.* 1930
An imaginative picture of tribal life in N.E. Uganda, a region where the author worked as administrator. [*Illus.* by Pearl Binder, Routledge ; Brewer, New York.]

DRISCOLL, Clara [American]. *In the Shadow of the Alamo.* 1906
Stories of the San Antonio Valley, illustrating Texas history from the Spanish conquest till to-day. [Putnam, New York : o.p.]

DRUMMOND, Hamilton [*b.* 1857]. *For the Religion : the records of Blaise de Bernauld.* 1898
—— *A Man of His Age* [sequel]. 1900
Historical romances of the religious wars in France (1562–8). Scenery, costumes, and historical personages carefully studied. [(1) Smith & Elder : o.p. ; (2) Ward & Lock : o.p. ; Harper, New York : o.p.]
—— *A King's Pawn.* 1900
A story of Henry of Navarre and of Blaise de Bernauld, hero of the two foregoing (1583–4). [Blackwood : o.p. ; Doubleday, New York : o.p.]
—— *The Beaufoy Romances.* 1902
Episodes in the life of the Sieur de Beaufoy during the reigns of Charles VII and Louis XI. *The Madness of Mesnil* and *The King comes to Beaufoy* are the most readable. [Ward & Lock : o.p. ; *sub tit. The Seigneur de Beaufoy*, Page, New York : o.p.]
—— *The Cuckoo.* 1906
Illustrates the relations of the peasantry and the feudal lords in France at the time of the religious wars. [White : o.p.]
—— *Shoes of Gold.* 1909
The gallant hero is sent by Louis XV and Choiseul to the Court of Peter III of Russia to win over the Empress Catherine : hence an account of the Orloff plot, and the deposition and murder of the Tsar (1761–2). [Stanley Paul : o.p.]
—— *The Justice of the King.* 1911
Louis XI and the Dauphin in 1482–3, with sketches of Villon, Commines, etc. [Stanley Paul : o.p. ; Macmillan, New York.]
—— *Greater than the Greatest.* 1915
Deals with the conflict of the Emperor Frederick II, " Stupor Mundi," and Gregory IX (1227). [S. Paul : o.p. ; Dutton, New York : o.p.]
—— *The Great Game.* 1918
A romantic novel of ambition, Court intrigue, and faithful love, in the days of the Grand Monarque and his minister Louvois (1670). [S. Paul : o.p.]
—— *The Betrayers.* 1919
Hinges on the feud between the Emperor Frederick II and Innocent II (1245–8). [S. Paul : o.p. ; Dutton, New York : o.p.]
—— *A Maker of Saints.* 1919
The hero and lover is a sculptor, Marco Fieravanti of Forli, known as the Maker of Saints. Dante appears in this romance of Italy in the times of the Guelfs and Ghibellines. [S. Paul : o.p. ; Dutton, New York : o.p.]
—— *Chattels.* 1922
Like *The Cuckoo*, pictures the miserable lot of the peasantry, this time under Charles VII and Louis XI. [S. Paul : o.p.]

DRURY, Major William Price [*b.* 1861]. *Bearers of the Burden.* 1899
Random stories of the British Empire ; several of them lively, facetious, or touching, e.g. *Terence of Trinity, Lachrymæ Christi, Shinnybeggar, The Cocoa Valve.* The influence of Rudyard Kipling is obvious. [Lawrence & Bullen, o.p. ; Putnam, New York : o.p.]
—— *The Passing of the Flagship ; and other stories.* 1902
Patriotic stories of a like stamp, by an officer who has seen much active service. [Chapman : o.p.]

DU BOIS, William Edward Burghardt [American ; *b.* 1868]. *The Souls of Black Folk.* 1903
—— *The Quest of the Golden Fleece.* 1911
—— *Dark Princess.* 1928
Stories and novels by a University professor who is of part negro descent and has written several important works on the racial question in the United States. He is a vehemently enthusiastic advocate of the rights of the negro. [(1) and (2) McClurg, Chicago ; (2) o.p. ; (3) Harcourt, New York.]

DU CHAILLU, Paul Belloni [French ; 1837–1903]. *Ivar the Viking : a romantic history based upon authentic facts of the third and fourth centuries.* 1893
Based on the invalid results of his investigations in writing *The Viking Age.* The life of a Norse boy of the third and early fourth centuries. Du Chaillu maintains that the English are more Norse than Saxon. [Murray : o.p. ; Scribner, New York : o.p.]

DUDENEY, Mrs. Henry Ernest [*née* Alice Whittier ; 1866–1930]. *Folly Corner.* 1900
An energetic kind of realism applied to rather disagreeable yet characteristic phases of modern life—the hypnotism of a mind by passion. Bigamy and its consequences are the motives ; and the chief subject is a girl whose character is a strange mixture, a very modern type of adventuress. [Heinemann : o.p. ; Holt, New York : o.p.]
—— *Men of Marlowe's.* 1900
" Marlowe's " is Gray's Inn, and there are eleven tales, mostly about the young inhabitants and their free-and-easy existence ; humorous and pathetic by turns, revelling in the unorthodoxy of uncurbed youth. [Long : o.p. ; Holt, New York : o.p.]

DUDENEY, Mrs. Henry Ernest (*continued*). *The Third Floor.*   1901

An amusing and somewhat sensational story of a strong-minded young woman of a modern stamp, who lives alone and unprotected in a London flat. Many queer characters come on the stage. The most moving episode is that of the lecturer on social purity, tardily reconciled to the husband whom she had divorced. [Methuen : o.p.]

—— *The Story of Susan.*   1903

Old-fashioned people and manners, quiet home scenes, parties, balls, scandals of high and low life, in a small country town near Brighton, in 1839–46—in the *Cranford* style. A predominant feature of Liddeshorn is the harsh and intolerant Methodism, which is described with kindly satire. Susan, whose lightness and coquetry are all on the surface, is deeply in love with a Methodist, a paragon of piety. A mistake of hers and his quixotism cause years of separation and misery to both. [Heinemann : o.p.]

—— *The Maternity of Harriott Wicken.*   1899

—— *The Wise Woods.*   1905

—— *Rachel Lorian.*   1909

—— *A Large Room.*   1910

Similar novels of old-fashioned life pervaded by a quiet but freakish spirit of comedy—the comedy that strikes fire from the rough edge of character. The first, however, is serious, tragic ; the second comes nearest to the present day ; all have that criticism of our common human nature which is always pertinent and engrossing. Mrs. Dudeney presents finely, especially in *Rachel Lorian*, the nobler side of love. [(1), Heinemann ; (2), (3), and (4), Heinemann : o.p. ; (1) Brentano, New York : o.p. ; (3) Duffield, New York : o.p. ; (4) Macmillan, New York : o.p.]

—— *Gossips Green.*   1906

Gossips Green is a quiet village on the south coast (1790–1815), where a lad saved from shipwreck is adopted by two peasants. He grows into a brilliant, intelligent man, and the love-tale of his maturity is moving. [Cassell : o.p. ; *sub tit. The Battle of the Weak*, Dillingham, New York : o.p.]

—— *Maids' Money.*   1910

How two old maids, whose womanhood has been repressed, come into money, and try, though faded and forty, to enjoy what life has for women, not excepting love. The pair are a humorous contrast, their would-be suitors are another. Mrs. Dudeney makes much of the fine shades of character in people by no means remarkable, and of the elusive comedy in quite ordinary events. [Heinemann : o.p. ; Duffield, New York : o.p.]

—— *What a Woman Wants.*   1914

The heroine, after unrewarded devotion to her brother and sister, and to a lover who deceives her, finds happiness at last as the wife of a sailor whom she had met years before. There is a good description of the hardships and monotony of life on a Sussex farm in the earlier part of the book. [Heinemann : o.p.]

—— *The Secret Son.*   1915

A country tragedy of seduction and retribution, dominated by the character of the woman, now grown old, who has to tell the story of her life to an illegitimate son, when fate has made him an actor in a similar drama. [Methuen : o.p.]

—— *Manhood End.*   1920

A domestic chronicle of a clergyman and his wife, who live in the flat country near Chichester, the influence of which appears in their characters. [Hurst : o.p.]

—— *The Next Move.*   1925

A romance in a quiet Sussex setting, emphasizing the sanctity of marriage. [Collins.]

DUHAMEL, Georges [French ; *b.* 1884]. *New Book of Martyrs* (Vie des martyrs, 1917).   1918

M. Duhamel went to the front as a doctor, and these are scenes in a hospital, and most inspiring character-sketches of the maimed and tortured heroes. [Transl. by Florence SIMONDS, Heinemann.]

—— *Civilization, 1914–1918* (1918).   1920

Sixteen scenes in a hospital near the front on the Vesle. The ghastly wounds, the torments, the evil smells, the flies and other abominations are served up raw, to point the irony indicated in the title. Lighter pieces hit off the foibles of society ladies on the nursing staff ; and among those satirizing French obsequiousness to authority in a field-officer's uniform, *Discipline* is first-class comedy. [Transl. by T. P. COMVIL-EVANS, Allen & Unwin.]

"DUIMOV, Osip" [O. I. Perelman ; Russian ; *b.* 1878]. *The Flight from the Cross.*   1916

Very Russian in spirit. Each character feels the call of the spirit, and loathes himself for his weakness in not responding. [Transl. by G. M. Foakes, LAURIE : o.p.]

DUKE, Winifred [Scottish]. *Scotland's Heir.*   1925

Edinburgh, Derby, and the Highlands (1745–46). Prince Charles Edward is the principal character ; Lord Lovat and Clementina Walkinshaw appear. [Chambers, Edinburgh ; *sub tit. Heir to Kings*, Stokes, New York.]

—— *King of the Highland Hearts* [sequel].   1929

Continues the story of Prince Charlie after Culloden ; his wanderings in Scotland, and his sojourn in France and Rome until his death. [Chambers, Edinburgh ; Stokes, New York.]

—— *The Drove Road.*   1930

A romance with an historical background of the '45 rebellion. [Jarrolds.]

DUMAS, Alexandre Davy de la Pailleterie [French ; 1802–70]. *The Chevalier d'Harmental* (1843).   1894

Dumas' most characteristic work was the long series of novels dealing with French history, in which he employed his fertile imagination and theatrical genius in revivifying episodes and personages from the time of the Renaissance to near his own day. It is history brilliantly romanticized rather than historical romance in the style of Scott, who preferred to keep eminent historical characters in the backgrounds. At the

DUMAS, Alexandre Davy de la Pailleterie (*continued*).

same time, Dumas' finest characters are either pure creations or obscure adventurers, like d'Artagnan, endowed with new life by the great romancer. His vigour of improvization ran at such a pace that he had to use the services of various hacks to embody his ideas and inventions, and of all but a few, and these the finest of the romances, it is difficult to say which has a complete right to bear his name. This gives the inner history of the conspiracy of Cellamare (1718), in which many great nobles entered into negotiations with the King of Spain to carry out the schemes of Cardinal Alberoni for changing the French succession during the early years of Louis XV and the regency of Orleans. Well aware of what is going on, the regent's unscrupulous minister, the Abbé Dubois, bides his time, and at a chosen moment explodes the plot, turning the conspiracy into a farce. With the exception of the hero and his love, practically all the characters are well-known people. The adventurer Roquefinette is often compared with Scott's Captain Dalgetty, who may have suggested the character. [Also entitled *The Conspirators.*]

—— *The Regent's Daughter* (Une fille du régent, 1845) [sequel].   1894
The final stages of this theatrical conspiracy (1719), its development in Brittany, where an active revolt took place, and the proceedings at the Court of the regent. Some of the most amusing scenes are those in which the life of the prisoners in the Bastille is sketched.

—— *Ascanio* (1843).   1895
Romance and history inextricably interwoven, the historic incident on which the story is founded being Benvenuto Cellini's visit to Paris and the Court of Francis I (1540). The titular hero is an apprentice of the Florentine artist. Many famous names appear, such as the king, the Duchesse d'Étampes, the Dauphine Catherine de Médicis, Diane de Poictiers, Rabelais, and Clement Marot. Scandalous chronicles and true and untrue anecdotes of Parisian and Court life are worked into the fabric (also entitled *Francis the First ; or, The sculptor's apprentice and the provost's daughter*).

—— *Sylvandire* (1844).   1897
An early romance that helps to fill the gap between the *Vicomte de Bragelonne* and the *Chevalier d' Harmental*, the period represented being the close of Louis XIV's reign, during the gloomy and sanctimonious years of Madame de Maintenon's ascendancy, soon to be followed by the licentious gaieties of the Duke of Orleans' regency (1708–16). One of the episodes of the love-story that forms the main action is the unjust imprisonment of the hero in the Bastille.

—— *The Count of Monte Cristo* (Le comte de Monte-Cristo, 1844–5).   1894
The impressive story of a long captivity in the Château d'If. The escape of Edmond Dantès in the guise of a corpse is one of the most thrilling of romantic inventions. The rest is clever melodrama—the gigantic scheme of revenge by which the Marseilles sailor, now the lord of untold wealth, makes life a hell for those who had wronged him. Maquet and Fiorentino were his collaborators in this romance. [Also in Everyman's Lib.]

—— *The Three Musketeers* (Les trois mousquetaires, 1844).   1846
This and the two following make a cycle of romances, retailing the exploits of four heroes from youth to age, and presenting a magnificent panorama of contemporary history (1626–71). The feud between Richelieu and Anne of Austria bulks large, and the adventures of the three guardsmen with their redoubtable and versatile Gascon comrade, d'Artagnan, are intimately connected with affairs of state (1626–28). Political intrigue, Court life, duelling and fighting provide a ceaseless flow of absorbing incident. It was this book, in which Dumas enjoyed the co-operation of Auguste Maquet in suggesting and planning the story, that marks the real beginning of Dumas' great work as an historical romancer. The two had been working together since 1839.

—— *Twenty Years After* (Vingt ans après, 1845) [sequel].   1846
Anne of Austria's regency, the insurrection of the Fronde, and the execution of Charles I of England mark out the period (1648–9).

—— *The Vicomte de Bragelonne ; or, Ten Years Later* (Dix ans plus tard ou le Vicomte de Bragelonne, 1848–50) [sequel].   1858
Praised by Stevenson as the greatest of all romances : the great closing scenes in the lives of the four musketeers (period, 1660–71 ; Mazarin's ministry and the early days of the Grand Monarque). Court life, the great personages of this epoch, and state affairs are described with fair accuracy, although facts and fiction are mingled. Mazarin and the king are prominent, and romantic interest attaches to Mlle de la Vallière, the tender-hearted mistress of Louis XIV ; Madame de Montespan, Fouquet and Colbert, the great rival ministers of finance, the Man in the Iron Mask, and other famous persons figure among the characters. Much material for this great trilogy was drawn by Dumas from an earlier memoir now translated into English : *Memoirs of Monsieur D'Artagnan, Captain-Lieutenant of the 1st Company of the King's Musketeers* (French edn. Cologne, 1701–2). By Gatien de Courtilz de Sandras, a purveyor of fictitious memoirs and pseudo-history who gave Defoe the idea of his *Memoirs of a Cavalier* and other fictions. Transl. by R. NEVILLE, 3 parts, Nichols, 1898–9 : o.p. [(1), (2), and (3) also in Everyman's Lib.]

—— *Marguerite de Valois* (La reine Margot, 1845).   1894
Begins a new historical cycle, the *Valois Romances* (1572–85), the period when Charles IX and Henry III were kings and Catherine de Médicis was reigning. Her antagonism to Henry of Navarre is a recurring motive. The chief historical event here is the massacre of St. Bartholomew, which, with the murder of Coligny, is fully described. Coconat, one of the two heroes, took an active part in the persecution of the Huguenots. Both he and the other hero, La Mole, the lover of Marguerite, Queen of Navarre, are historical, though their characters and positions are suitably romanticized. The queen is painted in very favourable colours, though Henry of Navarre is the noblest character in the book, and the true hero of the Valois cycle.

—— *La Dame de Monsoreau* (1846) [sequel].   1894
The troubles of Henry III (1578), the contending factions represented by a host of historical personages, including the king, the Guises, and the Huguenots, with Henry of Navarre at their head. Contains one of Dumas' finest creations, the jester Chicot. The romantic incidents revolve round Bussy d'Amboise

DUMAS, Alexandre Davy de la Pailleterie (*continued*).

and Diane de Meridor, wife of De Monsoreau. Bussy's heroic defence against overwhelming numbers when set upon at the instigation of the Duke of Anjou, is one of the famous fights in literature. Sometimes published in English as *Chicot the Jester*.

—— *The Forty-Five Guardsmen* (Les quarante-cinq, 1848) [sequel].　　　1894

A medley of romance and tragedy; the "Forty-Five," Henry III's famous bodyguard, playing a subordinate part to Chicot. The chief dramatic event is the vengeance of the Dame de Monsoreau on the Duke of Anjou for the murder of her lover. Period, 1585. [(1), (2), and (3), also in Everyman's Lib.]

—— *The War of Women* (La guerre des femmes, 1845–6).　　　1895

Deals with the later phases of the war of the Fronde; the imprisonment of the Prince de Condé and his relatives by Mazarin, the revolt incited at Bordeaux by his wife, and the various cabals and dissensions consequent on these acts, form the historical part; while a romance of love and adventure is interwoven, and several fictitious or semi-fictitious characters are introduced. Period of the regency of Anne of Austria (1650).

—— *The Chevalier de Maison-Rouge* (1846).　　　1895

Fifth and last of the Marie-Antoinette romances, though written earlier; deals with the last act of the tragedy, the doing to death of the Dauphin and the execution of the queen (1793). Many fictitious characters, including the titular hero. Artistically an inferior work. [Also in Everyman's Lib.]

—— *Agenor de Mauléon* (Le bâtard de Mauléon, 1846).　　　1897

A narrative of the great wars in the fourteenth century, introducing such paladins of romance as Du Guesclin, Chandos, the Black Prince, and such a monster as Pedro the Cruel of Spain; founded on a story told to Froissart by the redoubtable Bastard de Mauléon; the mediæval chronicler appears in person. Scene, chiefly Spain in 1361.

—— *The Two Dianas* (Les deux Dianes, 1846–7).　　　1894

Said to be entirely the work of Paul Meurice. Goes back to the time of Francis I and his short-lived successor Henry II (1521–74). Catherine de Médicis, Mary of Scotland, and the heads of the Catholic and Huguenot factions are among the historical personages. The pathetic encounter of the Huguenot Renaudie with his old bosom friend Pardaillan, and the story of the defence of St. Quentin and the tumult of Amboise, are splendid pieces of romance.

—— *Memoirs of a Physician* (Mémoires d'un médecin, 1846–8).　　　1894

First of five Marie-Antoinette romances, covering 1770–93, the period of the decadence of the monarchy, and the reigns of De Pompadour and Du Barry. This story (1770–4) of the quack Balsamo, identified with the mysterious Count Cagliostro, is supposed to be based on a memoir of worse than dubious authenticity.

—— *The Queen's Necklace* (Le collier de la reine, 1849–50) [sequel].　　　1894

An account of the scandalous affair of the Diamond Necklace in accordance with the known facts, though Balsamo's connection with the intrigue is taken for granted. The period (1784–5) is the beginning of the ill-fated reign of Louis XVI, and Marie Antoinette makes her first appearance. Only in part by Dumas.

—— *The Black Tulip* (La tulipe noire, 1850).　　　1895

A love-romance associated with the Haarlem tulip craze and intertwined with scenes from Dutch history (1672–5), when William of Orange lent himself to the agitation against the brothers De Witt, the patriotic defenders of Dutch liberty. [Transl. by CONNOR, with introd. by R. GARNETT, Heinemann, 1901; also in Everyman's Lib.]

—— *Olympe de Clèves* (1852).　　　1894

A very romantic story of the early years of Louis XV (1727–9): one of the few authentic episodes is Cardinal Fleury's conspiracy to corrupt the morals of the king. The interest centres in the actress Olympe de Clèves and her lover, a young novice in the Jesuit seminary, the life and organization of which are very fully described.

—— *Ange Pitou; or, The Taking of the Bastille* (Ange Pitou, 1852).　　　1894

A full and striking picture of Paris and Versailles in 1789; the taking of the Bastille one of the most dramatic episodes. The characters include the royal family, the courtiers and ministers, the revolutionary leaders, members of the National Assembly, and a host of obscure agitators and loyalists, and the multitudinous forces which were agitating the French world are well illustrated. Breaks off with the invasion of Versailles.

—— *La Comtesse de Charny* (1853–5).　　　1894

Avowedly history, not romance. The flight of the king and queen to Varennes, the proceedings of the various Assemblies, the march of the Marseillais to Paris, the massacres of the Terror, the Prussian war, and the battle of Valmy, and finally the execution of Louis XVI, are the principal events (1792). The characters embrace a legion of historic names. The Count and Countess de Charny, faithful adherents of the royal family, assist at the Varennes incident, and throughout the story display heroic devotion. For the end of the series see above, *The Chevalier de Maison-Rouge*.

—— *The Page of the Duke of Savoy* (Le page du duc de Savoie, 1855).　　　1894

The period is almost identical with *Les deux Dianes* (1528–80), and many characters reappear, among them the adventurers who stormed the old fort of Calais; but the troupe of soldiers of fortune, among them the diverting Procope, are new. Philibert, Duke of Savoy, is the central personage. It was a period that witnessed the abdication of the Emperor Charles V, the accession of Philip II, the struggle for supremacy between the queen-mother Catherine de Médicis and the Guises, and the growth of the Reformation.

—— *The Companions of Jehu* (Les compagnons de Jéhu, 1857).　　　1895

A romance with innumerable historic incidents interwoven which serves as a sequel to *The Whites and the Blues*. Chiefly concerned with the Royalist insurrections in La Vendée and Brittany, and the exploits of Georges Cadoudal. The heroine's lover, leader of the Royalist Companions of Jehu, is guillotined, partly through the agency of her brother, one of Napoleon's aides-de-camp. Period 1799–1800. Also entitled *Roland Montrevel* (1860).

DUMAS, Alexandre Davy de la Pailleterie (*continued*). *Black : the story of a dog* (Black, 1858).
1895

A touching story of a spaniel, which illustrates Dumas' great affection for animals. Period, 1793–1842.

—— *The She-Wolves of Machecoul* (Les louves de Machecoul, 1859) ; *and, The Corsican Brothers* (Les frères corses, 1845).
1895

The first, otherwise entitled *La Vendée*, deals with the Duchesse de Berri's attempt to stir up an insurrection in that province in 1832. The two girls nicknamed the " She-Wolves " are among Dumas' most attractive creations, and the story of their love is touching. It is in this book that Dumas lifted an entire episode from Scott's *Rob Roy*. *The Corsican Brothers* is a melodramatic tale of occult sympathy between twin brothers.

—— *Monsieur de Chauvelin's Will* (Le testament de M. Chauvelin, 1861) ; *and, The Woman with the Velvet Necklace* (La femme au collier de velours, 1859).
1897

The first of these short romances depicts the close of Louis XV's reign, and is a terrible but accurate picture of royal debauchery and debased Court life. Closes with the dreadful scene of the king's death by small-pox. The Marquis de Chauvelin was one of the companions of Louis' debaucheries (1774). The second story is an episode of the Reign of Terror (1793), and the famous story-teller Hoffmann is the hero. The scene of Madame du Barry's death by the guillotine is historical.

—— *The Neapolitan Lovers* (1916) ; *Love and Liberty ; or, Nelson at Naples* (1918) (La San-Felice, 1865).
1916–18

Two romances based on the true and very moving story of Luise Sanfelice, heroine of the Parthenopean revolution of 1798–9, and utilizing material obtained by Dumas from the secret archives of Naples. Nelson, Sir William and Lady Hamilton, the king and queen, and Admiral Caraccioli who was hanged, appear on the scene. It is a laboured work, remarkable for the generous portrait of the heroic Nelson. [(1) and (2), transl. with introd. by R. S. GARNETT, S. Paul.]

—— *The Whites and the Blues* (Les blancs et les bleus, 1867–8).
1895

Carries on the annals of the Revolution to the Directory and the rise of Bonaparte (1793–9). The early portion, *The Prussians on the Rhine*, is based on the personal experiences of Dumas' friend, Charles Nodier. Then come the great episode of the rising of Thirteenth Vendémiaire, the street fighting that brought Bonaparte to the front, the Directory, and finally the *coup d'état* of Eighteenth Fructidor. Appended is a narrative of the luckless expedition to Egypt, *The Eighth Crusade*. [" Aramis Edn.," 25 vols., ea. with col. front and 5 plates, Routledge, 1911 ; " Fleur de Lis Edn.," 18 vols., Routledge (Dutton, New York) ; mainly o.p. ; " Dent's Edn." (the most complete), 48 vols., ea. with etched and photogravure illustrations, Dent ; " Everyman's Lib.," 9 vols., Dent (Dutton, New York) ; (cheap ed.) 23 vols., Methuen ; " Handy Lib. Edn.," 48 vols., Little & Brown, Boston ; 40 vols., Page, Boston.]

DUMAS, Alexandre Davy de la Pailleterie, *fils* [French ; 1824–95]. *The Lady with the Camelias* (La dame aux camélias, 1848).
·1902

The pathetic story of a courtesan, who conceives a pure passion ; founded on a true story and obviously patterned after *Manon Lescaut*. The subject is treated with all the delicacy possible, where the vices and follies of a great city are to be described realistically. [Transl. with critical introduction by Edmund GOSSE, Heinemann, 1902 (Modern Lib., New York).]

DU MAURIER, George [1834–97]. *Peter Ibbetson.*
1894

Du Maurier, the black-and-white artist, wrote three novels out of the materials furnished by his personal memories of life in Paris and other places in France and Belgium, the best of them, though not the most popular, being the first. It is a melancholy, dreamy book on the idea of a supernatural gift enabling the hero to meet his lost love in the dreamland of the past. Reminiscences of a happy childhood at Passy are the real basis. *Illus.* by the author. [Harper, London and New York, 1917.]

—— *Trilby.*
1895

Made up partly of Du Maurier's reminiscences of bohemian life in Paris, and partly of a story of hypnotic influence over a beautiful girl. It was this inferior sensational element which brought the story fame, especially in the dramatized form. In spite of the poignant sadness, the book is mainly a comedy, full of spontaneous mirth and bonhomie. [Harper, London and New York ; Collins.]

—— *The Martian.*
1898

Returns to the theme of *Peter Ibbetson*—France in the forties, Parisian and provincial happy domestic life, Belgian scenes, Malines and its dignified clerical society. The romantic side is concerned with a dream influence from Mars that supplies the hero with literary inspiration, whilst utopian adumbrations of a nobler race of men inspire Du Maurier the draughtsman. [Harper, London and New York.]

DUNBAR, Paul Laurence [American ; 1872–1906]. *Folks from Dixie.*
1898

" Twelve stories which portray with insight the spiritual, moral, social, and domestic life of the Southern negro." Mr. Dunbar was a coloured author with fervid sympathy for his race and the power to interpret its characteristics dramatically. [Dodd & Mead, New York.]

—— *Strength of Gideon ; and other stories.*
1900

Two stories of life in the South : " have not been outdone in truth, delicacy, and the art of happy omission." [Dodd & Mead, New York : o.p.]

DUNCAN, Professor Norman [Canadian by birth ; 1871–1916]. *The Way of the Sea.*　1903

Vivid but very unequal stories of the Newfoundland fishermen and their perils and hardships in the icy seas of the North. Closely akin in style and dialect to Mr. Kipling's *Captains Courageous*. *The Strength of Men, The Breath of the North, In the Fear of the Lord*, and *A Beat t' Harbour* are good specimens of his character-drawing and dramatic strength. [McClure, New York.]

—— *Doctor Luke of " The Labrador."*
1904

—— *The Mother.*
1905

DUNCAN, Professor Norman (*continued*). *Dr. Grenfell's Parish, the Deep-sea Fisherman.*   1905
Further sea-stories in the same vigorous and incisive style. [(1), Revell, New York; (2) and (3), *id.*, o.p.]

DUNHAM, B. Mabel [Canadian]. *The Trail of the Conestoga.*   1924
The " conestoga " (the Canadian " covered wagon ") carries a party of German Mennonites from Pennsylvania to Ontario, in the days following the American Revolution. Based on old family documents and letters. [Macmillan, New York.]

DUNNE, Finley Peter [Irish-American; *b.* 1867]. *Mr. Dooley in Peace and in War.*   1898
—— *Mr. Dooley in the Hearts of his Countrymen.*   1899
Humorous colloquies, on topics of the day, of the Irish-American Dooley and his friend Hennessey, in a New York bar-room—discussing in an exaggerated brogue the Dreyfus case, Kipling's writings, American habits and institutions, the Standard Oil Company, Trusts, the Tariff, Ocean Travel, and politics from a point of view very different from that of the English press. The satire is thoroughly Irish, fanciful, exaggerated, farcical, fertile in bulls. [(1) and (2), Small, Cambridge, Mass.; (1), De La More Press: o.p.; Routledge: o.p.; (2), De La More Press: o.p.]

—— *Mr. Dooley's Philosophy.*   1900
—— *Mr. Dooley's Opinions.*   1901
—— *Observations by Mr. Dooley.*   1902
—— *Dissertations by Mr. Dooley.*   1906
—— *Mr. Dooley Says.*   1910
—— *Mr. Dooley on Making a Will and Other Necessary Evils.*   1919
Similar olios of talk and satire. [(1), Harper, New York; Heinemann; (2) Russell, New York: o.p.; Heinemann; (3), Russell, New York: o.p.; (4), Harper, New York: o.p.; (5) and (6), Scribner, New York; Heinemann.]

" DUNOIS, Dominique " [French]. *The Natural Mother.*   1929
A novel that won the Femina prize. A grim illustration of two human traits—attachment to the land, specially strong in the French peasant, and woman's yearning for love and motherhood. [Transl. by Angelo S. RAPPOPORT, Macaulay, New York; Jarrolds.]

DUNSANY, Edward John Moreton Drax Plunkett [18th Baron; *b.* 1878]. *The Gods of Pegana.*   1905
—— *Time and the Gods.*   1906
—— *The Sword of Welleran; and other stories.*   1908
Lord Dunsany has invented a new mythology, and may be almost said to have devised a new language to describe it. He skims the cream of old and new romance, giving a concentration of all that is most strange, poetical, grotesque, and glamorous, in his tales of unknown gods, untravelled deserts, ghostly peoples, cities, and temples, and cataclysms of which no echo has heretofore been heard. Mr. Sime's ghoulish and grotesque illustrations are, as a rule, finely in harmony with the sense. [(1), Mathews; Luce, Boston; (2), Putnam; Luce, Boston; (3), Allen & Unwin; Luce, Boston.]

—— *A Dreamer's Tales.*   1910
Similar experiments in artificial glamour, chiefly of the sad, forlorn, and macabre type. Visions of unheard-of lands and rivers, dead cities, and monstrous deserts and haunted forests, peopled by mysterious habitants of human or unknown kind. [G. Allen: o.p.; Luce, Boston; with introd. by Padraic Colum, Modern Lib., New York, 1919.]

—— *Fifty-one Tales.*   1915
All short tales of the fantastic, allegorical, suggestive, or satirical kind. The range of titles, from *The Death of Pan* to *Taking Up Piccadilly*, indicate the diversity of the contents. [Mathews; Little, Boston.]

—— *Tales of Wonder.*   1916
A mixture of up-to-date smartness and the grim or grotesque: e.g. the sardonic *Bureau d'Echange de Maux*, the ghastly *Loot of Loma*, and *Thirteen at Table*, in which the stricken Don Juan speaks in a manner worthy of his fame to the ladies who haunt him. *A Story of Land and Sea* is a rousing farcical story of a pirate who puts wheels to his ship and sails the Sahara. [Mathews.]

—— *Tales of War.*   1918
Thirty-two pen-pictures: e.g. the exquisite little sketch *England, The Last Mirage, Punishment, A Walk in Picardy, The Movement.* [Putnam.]

—— *Tales of Three Hemispheres.*   1920
The author goes to his lands of dream by usually unnoticed turnings out of our own familiar streets, and the otherworldly atmosphere is conjured up—though it would have been more compelling had the art not been so over-literary. [Unwin; Luce, Boston.]

—— *The King of Elfland's Daughter.*   1924
Elfland is given the circumstances of reality in this quest of Alveric for the princess's hand. [Putnam, London and New York.]

—— *The Charwoman's Shadow.*   1926
Spain provides a happy setting for this tale of fantastic magic—a penniless hidalgo sends his son to a wizard to learn the art of alchemy. [Putnam, London and New York.]

DURAND, Rt. Hon. Sir Henry Mortimer [*b.* 1850]. *Helen Treveryan.*   1892
Adventures and love affairs of a young English officer, killed by Afghans. The second Afghan War (1878–9) is described in circumstantial style (the author was present), with criticisms of the position of the British in India. [Macmillan: o.p.]

DURAND, Rt. Hon. Sir Henry Mortimer (*continued*). *Nadir Shah*. 1908
> The author proposed to write a history of Nadir Shah, but found that the materials were more fitted for a romance. In describing the career of the great conqueror he has throughout treated known facts with proper respect. Sir Mortimer's knowledge of Persian life and history is hardly surpassed. [Constable: o.p.; Dutton, New York: o.p.]

DURRANT, William Scott [*b*. 1860]. *Cross and Dagger: the Crusade of the Children*, 1212.
[juvenile] 1910
> The youth who joins the juvenile crusaders falls into the hands of the Chief of the Assassins, witnesses the Christian defeat at Damietta, and later joins the order of St. Francis of Assisi (1212–22). [(Wayfarer's Lib.), Dent; Lane, New York: o.p.]

DUSSERRE, Antonin [French]. *Jean and Louise* (Jean et Louise, 1912). 1913
> Like M. Guillaumin, M. Dusserre is a farmer, and here gives us a faithful picture of the yeomen and peasants of the Cantal, the glens and fells of which are charmingly described. [Transl. by John N. RAPHAEL, Chapman: o.p.; Doran, New York: o.p.]

DUTT, Romesh Chunder [Bengali; 1848–1909]. *The Slave Girl of Agra*. 1909
> An enlarged rendering of a story describing life under the Moguls which the author wrote in Bengali some thirty years earlier. [Unwin: o.p.]

DUUN, Olav [Norwegian; *b*. 1876]. *Good Conscience* (Det gode samvite, 1916). 1928
> The history of three generations of yeomen dwelling on a western fjord, in the Namdalen region, north of Trondhjem. They are guilty of shady transactions, even of crimes, and are worried by conscience. But this is not a didactic story; it is an artistic handling of moral situations, and satirizes pietism, the doctrine of sacrifice, and the morbid sense of sin. Among several arresting characters, the most striking is the innocent girl who feels that to grasp life firmly she must know evil as well as good. [Transl. by Edwin Björkman, Harper, New York.]

—— *The Trough of the Wave* (Juvikingar I, 1929). 1930
> First of a six-volume work *The People of Juvik*, the original of which is written in the Landsmaal or popular language, not the literary language of Norway. The saga-like style goes well with this, and with the history of the family of primitive, almost barbarous farmers living a century ago on a Norwegian fjord. The outstanding embodiment of the family virtues and vices is here the masterful old Pier Anders; but the hereditary strain is also an interesting factor in the two sons. This chapter in the family annals deals with a period of decline, to be followed by revival. [Transl. by A. G. CHATER, Knopf.]

EBERS, Georg Moritz [German; 1837–98]. *An Egyptian Princess* (Eine ägyptische Königstochter, 1864). 1870–1
> Ebers was a learned Egyptologist, docent at Jena, and professor at Leipzig. He travelled in Egypt, and in 1867–8 published his monumental work— *Egypt and the Books of Moses*. The object of his romances was definitely educational, to convey a knowledge of Egyptian history and antiquities in a popular way. They are not, however, a slavish reconstruction of bygone ages; the writer deals with his materials imaginatively, and makes his characters think and feel as modern Europeans. He takes some historic personages, such as Cambyses, Amasis, or Sappho, and weaves fact and fiction together, not refraining from an occasional anachronism. Here the action opens in Hellas, passes into Persia, and finally makes Egypt the theatre of events (528–522 B.C.). [Transl. by E. GROVE, 2 vols., Tauchnitz, Leipzig (Low): o.p.; transl. by Emma S. BUCHHEIM (Bohn's Lib.), Bell (Harcourt, New York, 1887); Burt, New York.]

—— *Joshua: a tale of Biblical times* (Josua: eine Erzählung aus biblischer Zeit, 1867). 1890
> The Jews and the Holy Land (*c*. 1250 B.C.). [Transl. by Clara and M. BELL, 2 vols., Tauchnitz, Leipzig (Low): o.p.]

—— *Uarda: a romance of ancient Egypt* (Uarda, 1877). 1877
> The inner history of the Regent's conspiracy to usurp the throne while Ramessu II was warring against the Aramæans, whom he defeated at Kadesh; principal scene, Thebes, in 1352 B.C. The conspirators are among the chief characters; the more agreeable ones including the daughter of Ramessu, the half-Greek Uarda, and the poet Pentaur, hero of the national epos. Contains a really valuable mass of learning about manners and habits of life, religious rites and superstitions, and the various currents of thought, rationalistic and reactionary. The plot is a modern one of infants changed at birth, and a happy resolution of difficulties crowned by marriage; motives and passions those of our own time. [Transl., 2 vols., Tauchnitz, Leipzig (Low): o.p.; Burt, New York.]

—— *Homo Sum* (Homo sum, 1878). 1878
> "I am a man and a sinner." A tale of the Anchorites (330), who sought escape from the world and from themselves at the foot of Sinai. [Transl. by Clara BELL; 2 vols., Tauchnitz, Leipzig (Low): o.p.; Burt, New York.]

—— *The Sisters* (Die Schwestern, 1880). 1880
> An Egyptian romance of 164 B.C., time of Ptolemy Philometer and Euergetes II. [Transl. by Clara BELL, 2 vols., Tauchnitz, Leipzig (Low): o.p.]

—— *The Burgomaster's Wife: a tale of the siege of Leyden* (Die Frau Bürgermeisterin, 1881). 1882
> Chronicles that decisive event in the foundation of Holland's independence, the siege of Leyden by Valdez (1574), when the starving and plague-stricken Dutch cut the dykes and let the sea flood their rich lands that the Gueux might sail up to the walls and relieve them. [Transl. by Clara BELL, Macmillan: o.p.]

—— *The Emperor* (Der Kaiser, 1881). 1881
> Richly and intimately pictorial, describing the Roman dominion and the early growth of Christianity in Egypt. Hadrian and the Empress Sabina figure. [Transl. by Clara BELL, Low: o.p.]

EBERS, Georg Moritz (*continued*). *Serapis* (1885).　　　　　　1885
    Deals with the struggle of Christians and Pagans at Alexandria in the time of Theodosius I, and the destruction of the temple of Serapis (391). [Paul : o.p.]

—— *The Bride of the Nile* (Die Nilbraut, 1887).　　　　　　1887
    The Moslem invasion of Egypt, and an outburst of native patriotism ; the strife of Christian sects, pagans, and Moslems (643). [2 vols., Gottsberger, New York : o.p.]

—— *Per Aspera* (Per Aspera, 1892).　　　　　　1892
    A picture of Alexandria in the later Roman period, when Bassianus (Caracalla) was Emperor (A.D. 211–17). [Transl., 2 vols., Tauchnitz, Leipzig (Low) ; *sub tit. A Thorny Path*, Appleton, New York.]

—— *Cleopatra* (Kleopatra, 1894).　　　　　　1894
    A romance of Cleopatra's later days ; scene, Alexandria (30 B.C.). [Transl. by Mary J. SAFFORD, Appleton, New York : o.p.]

—— *In the Blue Pike : a romance of German civilization at the commencement of the sixteenth century* (Im blauen Hecht, 1896).　　　　　　1896
    One of his non-Egyptian novels, a sort of Dutch painting of life in a provincial town (Nuremberg in 1517) just before the Reformation. The *Blue Pike* is an inn frequented by all classes. Tetzel, the seller of indulgences, who provoked Luther, is a prominent figure. [Transl. by Mary J. SAFFORD, Appleton, New York : o.p.]

—— *Barbara Blomberg : an historical romance* (1897).　　　　　　1897
    Deals with German Court life at Ratisbon and Brussels, under Charles V (1546–76). Barbara is a beautiful singer, the mother of Don John of Austria, who captivates the moody emperor ; and the plot deals with her efforts to recover her son from his imperial father. Grandees and courtiers, dignitaries of the Church, and the statesmen of this great epoch appear on the stage. [Transl. by Mary J. SAFFORD, 2 vols., Appleton, New York : o.p.]

—— *Arachne : an historical romance* (Arachne, 1898).　　　　　　1898
    A novel of manners in ancient Alexandria (274 B.C.) during the reign of the second king of the house of Ptolemy. Portrays the life of Greek sculptors and their models, and the licentious Court ruled by Queen Arsinoë and her boon companions. Arachne is a statue : much studio talk about æsthetics, realism in art, and the like, which sounds very like the nineteenth century. [Transl. by Mary J. SAFFORD, 2 vols., Appleton, New York : o.p.]
    [*Works* (transl.), 15 vols. (sold in sets only), Appleton, New York : o.p. ; 10 vols., Bigelow Brown, New York.]

EÇA DE QUEIROZ, José Maria [Portuguese ; 1843–1900]. *Our Lady of the Pillar* (O Defunto, 1879).　　　　　　1906
    Eça de Queiroz is acclaimed as the founder of the realist school in Portugal, but his really typical works have not been translated. This is a story of fifteenth-century Spain, a story of passionate love and jealousy, mystery and horror, told with intense imagination and vivid realism, and also with artistic economy of means and effect. [Transl. by E. PRESTAGE, Constable : o.p.]

—— *The Sweet Miracle* (Suave Milagre, 1879).　　　　　　1905
    This also is a work of finished art—a fanciful story of the Holy Land and the days of Christ, with the poignancy of meaning of a fine apologue. [Transl. by E. PRESTAGE, Nutt : o.p. ; Mosher, Portland, Maine.]

—— *Perfection.*　　　　　　1923
    Retells with piquant irony the story of Ulysses and Calypso—a Ulysses sated by his charmer's unchanging perfection, and longing for his wife. [Transl. by Charles MARRIOTT, Selwyn & Blount ; Knopf, New York.]

ECCLES, Charlotte O'Conor [Irish ; d. 1911]. *Aliens of the West.*　　　　　　1904
    Half a dozen tales of Toomevara, an imaginary little township on the Shannon, telling of lives and events by no means out of the common, and showing what existence was like in a place rent by class feeling and religious antipathies. The story of the disillusioned girl who ultimately becomes a nun is very pathetic. She has also written *The Rejuvenation of Miss Semaphore* and *A Matrimonial Lottery*, slighter and less serious affairs. [Cassell : o.p.]

ECCOTT, W. J. *Fortune's Castaway.*　　　　　　1904
    The Duke of Monmouth, Henrietta, Lady Wentworth—in a more innocent rôle than that recorded in history—Judge Jeffreys, William of Orange, etc. [Blackwood : o.p.]

—— *His Indolence of Arras.*　　　　　　1905
    Court intrigues in the days of Louis XIV (1665–7). The scene moves from the provinces to Paris, and includes elopements, duels, ambushes, and the usual paraphernalia of the modern historical novel. [Blackwood : o.p.]

—— *The Hearth of Hutton.*　　　　　　1906
    Experiences of a Cumberland squire in the '45, down to Falkirk (1746). [Blackwood : o.p.]

—— *The Red Neighbour.*　　　　　　1908
    Adventure and intrigue in Paris and at the camp of Turenne (1675) ; Louvois and La Fontaine are among the characters. [Blackwood : o.p.]

—— *A Demoiselle of France.*　　　　　　1910
    Adventures of an Abbé in 1662, in which appear Louis XIV, Colbert, La Fontaine, Molière, etc. [Blackwood : o.p.]

—— *The Mercenary.*　　　　　　1913
    A Scot's adventures in the Thirty Years' War, at the sack of Magdeburg and the first battle of Breitenfeld (1631). [Blackwood : o.p.]

ECKSTEIN, Ernst [German ; 1845–1900]. *Quintus Claudius : a romance of imperial Rome* (Die Claudier, 1882).　　　　　　1882
    A good picture of social life in Rome and Baiæ, under Domitian (A.D. 95–6). [Transl., Gottsberger, New York : o.p.]

ECKSTEIN, Ernst (*continued*). *Prusias: a romance of ancient Rome under the Republic.* 1882
The slave revolt under Spartacus (73–71 B.C.). [Transl., 2 vols., Gottsberger, New York: o.p.; revised ed. 1884: o.p.]
—— *Aphrodite: a romance of ancient Hellas* (1886). 1886
Greece about 551 B.C. [Transl., Gottsberger, New York: o.p.]
—— *The Chaldean Magician.* 1886
" An adventure in Rome in the reign of the Emperor Diocletian " (c. 284–305). [Transl., Gottsberger, New York: o.p.]
—— *Nero: a romance.* 1889
Nero, Agrippina, Octavia, the freedwoman Acte loved by Nero, Tigellinus, Poppæa, Pætus Thrasea, Annæus Seneca, and the other well-known figures in the drama of Nero's profligate career and shameful death (c. 54–68). [Transl. by Clara BELL and Mary J. SAFFORD, 2 vols., Gottsberger, New York: o.p.]
EDEN, Hon. Emily [1797–1869]. *The Semi-attached Couple.* 1860
An entertaining novel of manners, notable for its picture of high life in the days of the great Whig families. [(Rescue Ser.), with introd. by John Gore, Mathews, (Stokes, New York), 1927.]
EDGAR, John George [1834–64]. *Cressy and Poictiers.* 1865
Story of the Black Prince's page, in the wars with the Scots and the Hundred Years War (1344–76). [Routledge; (Everyman's Lib.), Dent (Dutton, New York), 1906.]
—— *Runnymede and Lincoln Fair.* 1866
A story of King John's vicissitudes, the Great Charter, the defeat of Louis, son of Philip Augustus, at Lincoln, and other historical matters (1214–17). [(Everyman's Lib.), Dent (Dutton, New York), 1908.]
EDGEWORTH, Maria [Irish; 1767–1849]. *The Parent's Assistant.* 1796–1800
Simple tales, with very obvious morals, adapting her father's maxims to the understanding of children. A famous book in its way, containing among the rest *Simple Susan*, *The Purple Jar*, and *Lazy Laurence*. The original *Parent's Assistant* was a joint work with her father Richard Lovell Edgeworth, educational reformer and friend of Thomas Day (see p. 132). [Routledge; *illus.* by Chris Hammond, Macmillan, 1903.]
—— *Castle Rackrent.* 1800
A novel in which Miss Edgeworth was free from the interference of her father, and obeyed the dictates of imagination, enriched with early recollections of life in Ireland (the annals of an Irish house, an immortal picture of the broken-down gentry. The character-portraits of Sir Patrick, Sir Murtagh, Sir Kit, Sir Condy, and the other squireens and their retainers, and the anecdotes of boisterous, irresponsible life, put into the mouth of an old servitor who is himself a character, are manifestly the work of a great novelist, and the moral—the nemesis of self-indulgence—is too sure and universal to be a hampering element here. [Putnam, 1906. With *The Absentee*, *illus.* by Chris Hammond, Macmillan, 1898; with *The Absentee* (Everyman's Lib.), Dent (Dutton, New York), 1909.]
—— *Belinda.* 1801
This was heavily handled by her father, and is essentially didactic, embodying their ideas on woman's sphere and duties and on moral philosophy in general. More of a novel than the foregoing, yet manifestly constructed to show off certain contrasts of character—Belinda, the ideal of maidenhood and womanly good sense, the fast society woman who chaperons her, the profligates and fatuous beaux, the admirable wife and mother, the burlesque asserter of woman's rights, and the girl, brought up like a hothouse flower, who goes to the bad. [*Illus.* by Chris Hammond, Macmillan, London and New York, 1897.]
—— *Early Lessons; and, Moral Tales.* 1801–15
Harry and Lucy (begun early but not completed till 1826) is a moral tale urging children to be their own teachers. *Frank and Rosamund* contains a certain allowance of entertainment with a full measure of edification. *Early Lessons* appeared 1801–15, and *Moral Tales* (1801): the former were republished 1822–6 in a revised form. [Routledge (Dutton, New York): o.p.]
—— *Popular Tales.* 1803
Depicts the rustic world, farm life, fields, cottage children, and quiet unstirred by great events. Simple themes and simple language, child-like characters and the patent moral, make these tales eminently suitable for the young (e.g. *Lame Jervas*, *The Limerick Gloves*, *The Lottery*, *To-morrow*, *Out of Debt out of Danger*). [*Illus.* by Chris Hammond, Macmillan, London and New York, 1903.]
—— *Leonora.* 1806
This is believed to have been written to confute Madame de Staël's *Delphine* and its advanced views on women. Lady Leonora is an exemplary English wife, whose husband is seduced by a woman imbued with French views of gallantry. This siren writes pages of " sentimental metaphysics " to her confidant in France; on the other hand, Leonora and her friends and her erring husband moralize the situation in the best English style. The whole is in letters, which show how competently Miss Edgeworth could handle violent emotions. [Dent, 1893: o.p.]
—— *Vivian.* 1809
The sad career of a vain, weak man, who with the best intentions in the world manages to ruin himself, lose the girl he loves, run away with a fashionable woman, and marry a lady he does not care for. One of the novels that Sir Walter Scott praised in a memorable saying. [Dent, 1893: o.p.]
—— *Tales from Fashionable Life.* 1809–12
Vol. 1.—*Ennui*—Lord Glenthorn is bored to death by wealth, society, luxury, and the lack of anything to do or any incentive to exert himself. On going to his estates in Ireland he meets with troubles that bring out his manhood, and the final test of character is the dilemma when he finds that his foster-mother is actually his mother and that the legitimate Lord Glenthorn is the village farrier.
Vol. 2.—*Almeria, Madame de Fleury,* and *The Dun*—Almeria, a girl of no family with £200,000 of her own, is taken up by a fashionable lady and dazzled with the lure of marriage to a title, but the result is disappointment, and she finds herself left on the shelf, a snubbed and embittered old maid. Mme de Fleury is a charitable aristocrat who befriends and educates some children of the people, and through their gratitude

EDGEWORTH, Maria (*continued*).

escapes harm under the Terror. *The Dun* is an undisguised sermon on the wickedness of extravagance and the cruelty of not paying one's tailor's bills.

Vol. 3.—*Manœuvring*—The " heroine " is an " intriguess " who cannot be sincere and open ; her attempts to secure a vast fortune and titles for her children at the cost of their happiness only bring confusion and ridicule on herself.

Vol. 4.—*Vivian*—this is a study of a man of weak will, who is led astray by his snobbish and ambitious mother and by other unhappy influences. Most of the characters are synthetic compounds of moral qualities rather than live human beings.

Vol. 5.—*Emilie de Coulanges*, is a short story of altogether finer quality than these examples of ethical theorems embodied in stories. *The Absentee.*

Vol. 6.—*The Absentee* concluded (see below).

[4 vols., Routledge : o.p. ; *Ennui*, Dent, 1893 : o.p.]

—— *The Absentee.* 1812

Exposes in all its ill-consequences one of the rankest abuses of Irish landlordism. Lord Clombrony, though fond of Ireland, is an absentee, because his vulgar wife hankers after fashionable life in " London " ; the tenants meanwhile are left to the rapacity of dishonest agents, and the estate goes to ruin. Shows up the hollowness of society life, and, in the Fanny Burney manner, satirizes the contemporary fop, the empty-headed soldier, fortune-hunters male and female, and slaves of fashion living beyond their means. A kindlier humour is lavished on Larry, the postilion, Sir Terence O'Fay, the good-natured and witty hanger-on, and that fine Irish gentleman, Count O'Halloran. Written originally as a play, and then put in a second series of *Fashionable Tales.* [Dent, 1893 : o.p. ; (*vide* also *Castle Rackrent*).]

—— *Patronage.* 1814

Her longest novel, written 1811–13. Based on a story told her by her father. The characters are numerous, and unfortunately hardly any are Irish ; the most prominent are types of good and bad principles, and in the complications of the political and social intrigue moral issues are always to the fore. Lord Oldborough, the haughty, ambitious minister, is a strong figure in the Sir Ulick O'Shane manner ; Buckhurst Falconer is a warm-hearted but unstable man, whose moral decadence moves compassion. [2 vols., Routledge, 1893 : o.p. ; 2 vols., Dent, 1893 : o.p.]

—— *Harrington.* 1817

Said to have been written to make amends to the Jews, at the instance of a Jewish lady who reproached her with having made so many of her brethren ridiculous, e.g. Mordecai, in *The Absentee.* Harrington in childhood was frightened into antipathy to Jews, and trying to cure his weakness went to the opposite extreme. Then he falls in love with the beautiful and cultured daughter of a Jew, and after the machinations of a villainous rival are foiled, marries her. But the authoress gives her case away by showing that the lady is not a Jewess after all. The No-Popery riots of 1780 make an exciting episode. [Dent, 1893 : o.p.]

—— *Ormond.* 1817

Ormond aspires to be an Irish Tom Jones, but under correction from an estimable lady, mother of a charming girl, he decides to emulate Sir Charles Grandison. But the beauty of this novel is elsewhere, for it contains King Corny (another Sir Condy) and Sir Ulick O'Shane, among her oddest and most humorous creations, and some of her gayest and brightest scenes, and the dialogue is full of humour and drollery. [Dent, 1893 : o.p. ; *illus.* by Carl Schloesser, Macmillan, London and New York, 1903.]

—— *Helen.* 1834

A poor story with good character-studies, written after her father's death, and so without his wonted counsel and encouragement. The moral aim is to show what social troubles arise from addiction to fibs and " white lies." [Routledge, 1893 : o.p. ; *illus.* by Chris Hammond, Macmillan, London and New York, 1903.]

EDSCHMID, Kasimir [German ; *b.* 1890]. *Lord Byron : the story of a passion* (Lord Byron, 1929). 1930

Makes careful use of the best authorities, but treats Byron with extreme good-nature. Quite candid about the liaison with his half-sister, without being severe. Byron's character emerges in a not-unamiable light, and the portraits of Hobhouse, Lady Caroline Lamb, Lady Oxford, Lady Melbourne, the Countess Guiccioli, and the rest, are pleasing and vivid. [Transl. by Eveline BENNETT, Toulmin (Cayme Press).]

EDWARDES, Amelia Ann Blandford [1831–92]. *Barbara's History.* 1864

The character and inner life of a girl, the romance of her courtship, her experiences in a German college (a part related with intimate sketching of national and local traits), and her romantic marriage, with a number of minor characters, such as Mr. Sandyshaft, stern and irascible externally, but inwardly full of kindness, drawn with quiet humour. [Hurst & Blackett : o.p.]

—— *Debenham's Vow.* 1870

Gives an excellent description of blockade-running into Charleston harbour during the American Civil War. [Hurst & Blackett : o.p.]

—— *Lord Brackenbury.* 1880

Like *Barbara*, comprises much portraiture of foreign people and society, and careful descriptions of foreign towns and scenery ; the old manor-house and other local details from Cheshire are also accurately studied. [Hurst & Blackett : o.p.]

EDWARDES, Rev. Ticknor [*b.* 1865]. *The Honey-Star.* 1913

—— *Tansy.* 1914

Pleasant novels of Sussex country life, by a naturalist and authority on bee-keeping. [(1) and (2), Hutchinson : o.p.]

EDWARDS, Matilda Barbara BETHAM [1836–1919]. *Dr. Jacob.* 1868

Life in Frankfurt and certain little German towns ; English and German characters, the chief of whom, the sexagenarian Dr. Jacob, a " noble but oblique " nature, appears first as a man of brilliant intellect, fascinating manners, and lofty aims, but shows his lack of principle in love-passages with some young women, and subsides into the unhonoured old age of a selfish epicurean. [Blackett : o.p.]

EDWARDS, Matilda Barbara BETHAM (*continued*). *Bridget*. 1877
> The development of Bridget's character from impulsive and thoughtless girlhood to a mature and affectionate woman is the central motive of this story, which comprises a variety of character-studies with their several love-tales. [3 vols., Hurst : o.p.]

—— *Brother Gabriel*. 1878
> Gabriel, a young Irish monk, is expelled from his monastery in southern France, and, forced by circumstances to live with an English girl as her brother and protector, falls deeply in love. A study of religious devotion battling with desire for freedom, and of passion yielding to saintly unselfishness. [Hurst : o.p.]

—— *A Romance of Dijon*. 1894
> France before 1789 ; a simple love-story quite subservient to the careful study of the feelings and attitude of the peasantry towards the *ancien régime* and the earlier movements of the Revolution. [Black : o.p. ; Macmillan, New York : o.p.]

—— *The Dream Charlotte : a story of echoes*. 1896
> A village story of Normandy during the Revolution, of which but the faintest echoes are audible, while Charlotte Corday hardly appears in person in these memoirs of her kin and of the Huguenots, whose sufferings were ending with the dawn of a new order. [Black : o.p. ; Macmillan, New York : o.p.]

—— *A Storm-Rent Sky*. 1898
> This depicts the tranquil life that went on in the forest regions of eastern France, where Danton was born ; and then gives his career and death (1789–94). [Hurst : o.p.]

—— *The Lord of the Harvest*. 1899
> Quiet rural life in Suffolk before the repeal of the Corn Laws ; largely taken up with description of local customs and modes of life. [(World's Classics), Oxford Press, 1913.]

—— *A Suffolk Courtship*. 1900
> A pleasant picture of Suffolk fifty years ago, in the happy days of agriculture. Quiet town life in Ipswich and farming in the shire are well depicted in the course of a narrative of several love affairs. [Hurst : o.p.]

—— *Mock Beggars' Hall*. 1902
—— *A Humble Lover*. 1903
> Homely and unpretentious stories of rustic life in Suffolk fifty years or more ago, yeomen, gentry, clergymen, and farm-hands, simply and faithfully drawn. [(1) and (2), Hurst : o.p.]

EEDEN, Frederik Willem van [Dutch ; *b.* 1860]. *The Deeps of Deliverance* (Van de Koele Meren des Doods, 1900). 1900
> A very solemn and serious psychological study of a young Dutch girl and the development of her character—almost pathological in the close study of temperament in its more recondite phases ; but the general drift is " the joy of spiritual growth in intensest suffering, and the purification of natural desires." [Transl. by Margaret ROBINSON, Unwin : o.p.]

—— *The Quest* (De Kleine Johannes, 1892). 1905
> " A mingling of novel, epic, fairy-tale, and ethical and philosophic treatise." The author is a recognized leader in the modern school of Dutch thought. [Transl. by L. C. W., Luce, Boston : o.p. ; *Little Johannes* ; transl. by Clara BELL, with introd. by A. LANG, Heinemann, 1895 : o.p.]

EGAN, Pierce [Irish ; 1772–1849]. *Life in London ; or, The Day and Night Scenes of Jerry Hawthorn, Esq., and his Elegant Friend, Corinthian Tom, accompanied by Bob Logic, the Oxonian, in their Rambles and Sprees through the Metropolis.* 1821–8

—— *Finish to the Adventures of Tom, Jerry, and Logic in their Pursuits through Life in and out of London* [sequel]. 1828
> A series of sketches of Cockney life that appeared in monthly parts illustrated by Cruikshank ; remarkable as one of the earliest of picture-novels. They deal with the favourite haunts of pleasure-seekers, and copiously reproduce the slang and cockneyisms of Londoners, spiced with puns and word-play. The rollicking adventurers are in the sequel either reformed or disposed of by unseasonable death. Dickens adopted this form of random adventures and burlesque in the *Pickwick Papers*. [*Life in London*, col. ill., Chatto, 1869 : o.p. ; *Finish*, Reeves & Turner, 1889 : o.p. ; (Plain and Coloured Series), Methuen, 1890 : o.p.]

" **EGERTON**, George " [Mrs. Golding Bright, Mary Chavelita, *née* Dunne]. *Keynotes*. 1893
> Sketches and slight stories of the *femme incomprise*, etc. ; introspective studies of woman's impulses, which are acknowledged without false shame—the dialogue very plain-spoken, and the influence of Ibsen very apparent in the ideas, though the methods are rather those of the French school. [Lane ; Little & Brown, Boston : o.p.]

—— *Discords*. 1894
> George Egerton was a contributor to the *Yellow Book*, and has been described as a feminine Crackanthorpe. This early work, with its approximation to the attitude and methods of the French naturalists, might substantiate the claim. The grimmest and strongest tale is *Wedlock* ; the most penetrating psychologically, though not the most concise, is *Gone Under*. [Lane.]

—— *Symphonies*. 1897
> Similar studies of the feminine temperament and aspirations ; outspoken and sometimes slangy in style. Angling reminiscences gave the outdoor atmosphere in *Keynotes* ; here the feeling for nature is appealed to by word-painting of Continental scenery, particularly of the Basque country. Two of the best stories are *The Captain's Book* and *Oony*. [Lane.]

—— *Fantasias*. 1898
> Half a dozen short sketches, in a dainty, yet vigorous, manner. *The Mandrake Venus* is a scathing denunciation of irregular relations between men and women. [Lane.]

—— *Rosa Amorosa*. 1901
> Very literary love-letters. The authoress seems to have embodied her ideal self in the woman who writes, and in her emotional confidences we have an apotheosis of sexual feeling. Descriptions and reveries of

"EGERTON, George" (*continued*).
> all kinds diversify the diary of sentiments, in sensuous and fanciful prose. [Richards, o.p. ; Brentano, New York : o.p.]

EGGE, Peter [Norwegian ; *b.* 1869]. *Hansine Solstad : the history of an honest woman* (1925). 1929
> Peter Egge is a native of Trondhjem, whose plays and novels show a close study of the minds of peasants and ordinary townspeople, and an interest in social ethics. Here his heroine is a peasant girl unjustly accused of theft ; the effects of the slander remain with her through life. [Transl. by Jess H. JACKSON, Doubleday, Doran, New York.]

EGGEBRECHT, Axel [German ; *b.* 1899]. *Pilgrim to the Abyss.* 1930
> The life-story of a god-daughter of the Tsar Alexander II, from 1866 to 1924. A strong, embittered personality, she suffers wrongs and humiliations, and schemes for the wealth and power that will enable her to avenge herself. A dark and painful story, redeemed by the author's psychological force and insight. [Transl. from the German by Mildred M. BOZMAN, A. H. King, New York ; Methuen.]

EGGLESTON, Edward [American ; 1837–1902]. *The Hoosier Schoolmaster.* 1871
> The lawless and homely pioneer life of Indiana (*c.* 1830–5), described by a man who was an itinerant preacher in the West, and knew that life intimately. The schoolmaster boards round among the farmers, and the story is about his love for a servant-girl whose mistress wants him for her daughter. He is brutally persecuted by the settlers, but all is righted eventually. [Judd, New York ; Macmillan, New York, 1928 ; Routledge : o.p.]

—— *The End of the World.* 1872
> A novel dealing with the life of the poor whites of Indiana [o.p.].

—— *The Circuit Rider : a tale of the heroic age.* 1874
> The author was himself at one time a circuit rider among the Methodists in southern Ohio (1809–12). Full of incident, the hero meeting with persecution, but getting ample reward in the end for his loyalty and courage. [Scribner, New York ; Epworth Press.]

—— *Roxy.* 1878
> Scenes of life in a town of southern Indiana at the time of the Tippecanoe campaign (1811). A story full of vigorous and picturesque incident, and at the same time a study of character development in the heroine, Roxy. [Scribner, New York.]

—— *The Hoosier Schoolboy.* 1882
> "A sentimental sermon against the harshness of rural schools." [Scribner, New York : o.p.]

—— *The Graysons : a story of Illinois.* 1888
> Another detailed picture of the turbulent life of the pioneers ; scene, Illinois (about 1850). Abraham Lincoln is introduced as counsel in a murder trial. He convicts the leading witness of perjury and brings home the guilt. [Century Co., New York ; Paterson, Edinburgh : o.p.]

—— *The Mystery of Metropolisville.* 1891
> A minor novel, the scene Minnesota. [Thompson, New York : o.p.]

—— *The Faith Doctor.* 1891
> Realistic delineation of life in New York, showing much the same characteristics, modified by the influence of Howells. Throws strong light on Christian Science, faith-healing, and other ideas that had recently gained a hold on the popular mind. [Appleton, New York : o.p.]

EGIL SKALLAGRIMSSON, *the Story of : being an Icelandic family history of the ninth and tenth centuries.* 1893
> History of a tragic feud between three generations of a great baronial house and King Harold Fairhair and his successors. Scenes changing from Norway and Iceland to Sweden, the Far North, Russia, Holland, and the British Isles. There is special interest for Englishmen in Egil's dealings with Athelstan. Gives a lively account of the first settlers in Iceland. The saga is no doubt accurate in substance, though epic in style ; and the pictures of home and Court life, the adventures of Vikings and the wars in England and Norway have the stamp of reality. Egil, who at first strikes one as an overbearing savage, towers over the rest as one of the invincible champions of old, a nobler Grettir ; his generosity, dauntless bravery, and keen sense of honour winning full sympathy. Kveldulf, Skallagrim, and Thorolf, his elders, and the noble Arinbjorn, his friend, are strong types of the free-spirited barons ; and the tyrant king with his family is likewise powerfully drawn. Ranks high among the sagas of action and adventure. Egil (*c.* 898–988) was a great poet ; his verses are well translated, and the famous lament for his sons is rendered in an adequate manner. [Transl. by Rev. W. C. GREEN, Stock : o.p. ; transl. by E. R. EDDISON, Cambridge University Press, 1930 ; Macmillan, New York.]

EJE, Andreas [Swedish]. *A Horrible Suspicion.* 1920
> A murder-mystery in a Swedish country town. [Transl. by Elaine A. WOOD, Bale.]

"ELDERSHAW, M. Barnard" [Marjorie Faith Barnard and Flora Sydney Patricia Eldershaw ; Australians]. *A House is Built.* 1928
> The story of a family of British traders in the early days of Australia—the social and commercial life of Sydney in the period 1837–1884 is depicted in considerable detail. [Harrap ; Harcourt, New York.]

"ELIOT, George" [Mary Anne Cross, *née* Evans ; 1819–80]. *Scenes of Clerical Life.* 1858
> George Eliot was the most philosophical of the great novelists. She carried ethical interests and analysis of motive much farther than Mrs. Gaskell, as was natural to one who had been immersed in religious and philosophic criticism from youth to middle-age, when she began to write her novels, and she was always oppressed by a sense of her responsibility as a guide and teacher. *Scenes of Clerical Life*, described by her as "Sketches illustrative of the actual life," contains *Amos Barton*, a story full of humanism, portraying the home life of a poor curate, commonplace in character and appearance, and his wife, a being of adorable kindness and devoted love ; *Mr. Gilfil's Love Story*, the bygone romance of an elderly gin-drinking man, a

" ELIOT, George " (continued).

tragic little drama of passion and jealousy ; and *Janet's Repentance*, the awakening and moral rebirth of a beautiful woman, driven by harsh treatment to drink. Ordinary life is interpreted in the light of spiritual ideals, and the humour and pathos of common things are revealed with delicate art.

—— *Adam Bede.* 1859

Adam Bede goes deeper into the dark places of human nature, and sets forth a coherent philosophy of conduct and inexorable retribution. An innocent country lass is seduced by the young squire ; and crime, remorse, suffering for the innocent as well as the evil-doers, are the tragic consequence. The rustic aphorist, Mrs. Poyser, is the most humorous creation, and the inspired preacher, Dinah Morris, the most exalted. Both are idealizations of people George Eliot knew. Village life, the farmyard, and all the ordinary aspects of country life a hundred years ago, are presented with the minute strokes of a Dutch painter. Loamshire is North Staffordshire, and Stonyshire, Derbyshire. Dinah Morris's original, Elizabeth Evans, aunt by marriage of George Eliot, actually preached at Wirksworth. In fact, many characters in this novel and later are studied from people the author knew and loved.

—— *The Mill on the Floss.* 1860

Another deeply significant tragedy of the inner life, enacted amidst the quaint folk and old-fashioned surroundings of a country town (St. Ogg's is Gainsborough). The conflict of affection and antipathy between a brother and sister, and again in the family relations of their father, is a dominant motive ; but the emotional tension rises to a climax in Maggie's unpremeditated yielding to an unworthy lover and betrayal of her finer nature. Brother and sister (they stand psychologically for George Eliot herself and her brother Isaac) are purified and reconciled only in death. Among the characters whose humours provide many comic pages the three aunts are famous ; there is the wonted prodigality of aphorisms.

—— *Silas Marner, the Weaver of Raveloe.* 1860

A country idyll of a century ago : contains in small compass the finest elements of the longer novels. The wronged and despised weaver shuts himself up with his gold in misanthropic solitude ; but his gold is stolen, and a ministering angel comes in the shape of a little child to win him back to hope and love. Sin and its tragedy, innocence with its powers for good, are the themes worked out with the usual strict causation ; while village humorists sustain passages of genial comedy.

—— *Romola.* 1863

This novel marks the transition to a more systematic kind of philosophical realism and the gradual exhaustion of her humour. It is based on a special study of Florentine history in the epoch 1492–1509, the days of Lorenzo de' Medici, and the saintliness and all-conquering energy of Savonarola are finely portrayed. *Romola* is a sternly tragic novel of temptation, crime, and retribution. The weak butterfly Tito mortally wrongs his benefactor and believes himself safe from the consequences ; but the net of destiny closes round and he meets with his proper doom. The spiritual growth of Romola, tried by many ordeals and many undeserved wrongs, is the artistic contrast to the base career of Tito.

—— *Felix Holt, the Radical.* 1866

This is a feebler work altogether. Holt is a champion of the working-men at the period just after the Reform Act, and is in love with a girl of the better classes. The doctrine evolved from the study of industrial and social conditions is that true progress must come from internal reform rather than from legislation. Gerald Massey, the poet, is believed to be the original of Felix Holt.

—— *Middlemarch : a study of provincial life.* 1871–2

Pictures with intense realism and a wealth of detail the divers characters, social cliques, and complex life of a provincial town. A novel almost destitute of plot, yet unified by the dominant idea of moral causation into a tragic drama of deserted ideals and failure. Dorothea's unfulfilled aspirations, Casaubon's barren pedantry, Bulstrode's hypocrisy, Lydgate's ambition quenched by an unsuitable marriage, all illustrate the fundamental theorem ; the happier lives of Caleb (said to be a study of George Eliot's father) and Mary Garth enforce the moral. Dorothea is the final incarnation of the ideal imaged in Maggie and Romola, and was drawn from Mrs. Mark Pattison ; but Casaubon is not Pattison.

—— *Daniel Deronda.* 1876

Sets forth a grave, spiritual conflict. The chief actors are a gay and accomplished girl, and her husband, a selfish tyrant who exemplifies the blighting influences of purely material civilization in the modern world. Closely connected is the story of the unselfish Deronda and Mordecai, Jewish leaders in a Zionist scheme. The longest and heaviest of her novels. A sombre book, with little humour.

[Edns. of " George Eliot's " works : (Library Edn.), 10 vols., Blackwood, o.p. (Lippincott, Philadelphia) ; (Standard Edn.), 21 vols., Blackwood (Scribner, New York) ; (New Cabinet Edn.), 17 vols., Blackwood ; (Warwick Edn.), 14 vols., Blackwood ; (Popular Edn.), each book in 1 vol., 8 vols., Blackwood. 7 vols. (excluding *Middlemarch*), (Everyman's Lib.) Dent (Dutton, New York). *American Edns.* : 21 vols., Page, Boston ; 22 vols., Houghton, Boston ; 17 vols., Scribner, New York ; 8 vols., Little & Brown, Boston ; 10 vols., Bigelow Brown, New York.]

ELLIOT, Robert. " *Act of God.*" 1907

Life on an emigrant ship a quarter of a century ago, in all its picturesque and all its disgusting features, ending with the horrors of a fire ; the whole done with a vivid and a merciless pen. [Duckworth : o.p.]

ELLIOTT, Sarah [née Barnwell ; American ; 1848–1928]. *The Felmeres.* 1886

Depicts the conflict between rationalism and Christianity. The heroine is a young woman of great purity of character, carefully brought up without creed of any kind. [Holt, New York : o.p.]

—— *A Simple Art.* 1887

An imaginative study of average life, that goes beneath the surface aspects of character : the story of a man who failed. He was a carpenter in a pioneer town of Texas and became a preacher. [Ireland, New York : o.p.]

—— *Jerry.* 1890

Scenes in south-western and far western States. From the pilgrimage of the forlorn little boy towards the setting sun, through all his vicissitudes of poverty and wealth, the reader is conscious of impending tragic fate. [Holt, New York : o.p.]

ELLIOTT, Sarah (*continued*). *John Paget.*   1893

An arraignment of fashionable religion. As the daughter of Stephen Elliott, first Protestant Episcopal Bishop of Georgia, this writer, in her candid treatment of religious and social questions, has won much attention. [Holt, New York: o.p.]

—— *The Durket Sperret.*   1898

A story of the Tennessee mountains, pitched near the University of Sewanie. [Holt, New York: o.p.]

ELLIS, Beth. *Barbara Winslow, Rebel.*   1903

A tale of the Bloody Assizes (1685). Barbara, a perfect spitfire, helps two rebels to escape, and is herself arraigned before Judge Jeffreys, whom she browbeats as ably as he could do it himself. After a wildly improbable series of adventures, she and her lover get off scot free. [Blackwood: o.p.]

—— *The Moon of Bath.*   1907

Bath in 1745 (Beau Nash's reign) ; a lover mistaken by the Jacobite fashionables for a Whig spy. [Blackwood: o.p. ; *sub tit. The Fair Moon of Bath*, Dodd & Mead, New York: o.p.]

—— *The King's Spy.*   1910

A similar novel of intrigue, in the Dumasian style, time of the espousals of William and Mary and John Churchill's courtship of Sarah Jennings. [Blackwood: o.p.]

—— *A King of Vagabonds.*   1911

The story of Perkin Warbeck (1489–97). [Blackwood: o.p.]

ELLIS, Edward Sylvester ["H. R. Gordon"; American; 1840–1916]. *Seth Jones of New Hampshire.*   [juvenile] 1860

A romance of Western frontier life and adventure ; reprinted with preface and notes by the aged author— good example of the "dime" novel. [Dillingham, New York, 1907: o.p.]

—— *Uncrowning a King.*   [juvenile] 1896

Follows carefully the history of the attempt of the famous Indian chieftain, King Philip of Mount Hope, to destroy the settlements in New England (1675–6). [Penn. Pub. Co., Philadelphia ; Cassell: o.p.]

—— *The Cromwell of Virginia.*   [juvenile] 1904

Deals with Bacon's rebellion (1676) : a sequel to *Uncrowning a King.* [Coates, Philadelphia: o.p.]

—— *Patriot and Tory.*   [juvenile] 1904

Much authentic history is woven into this story of the American Revolution, of which the great episode is the battle of Monmouth, New Jersey, when the Americans under Charles Lee were repulsed, but Washington eventually defeated the British. [Winston, Philadelphia: o.p.]

—— *The Last Emperor of the Old Dominion.*   [juvenile] 1904

A further sequel dealing with the Indian wars and the burning of Jamestown. E. S. Ellis has written a large number of adventure stories for boys, dealing with perils among Indians, etc., several of them instructive historically. [Coates, Philadelphia: o.p.]

ELLIS, Henry Havelock [b. 1859]. *Kanga Creek: an Australian idyll.*   1922

The experiences of a young English school-teacher in the backwoods of Australia ; the author himself taught in New South Wales for four years (1875–9). [Golden Cockerell Press ; Chaucer Head, New York.]

ELLIS, John Breckenridge [American ; b. 1870]. *Fated to Win.*   1910

Depicts the Angles and Saxons in their original homes on the Baltic, and their coming to Britain (*c.* 616). Æthelfrith of Northumbria, Penda of Mercia, and Edwin, future King of Northumbria, and the struggle for supremacy in the midlands and north of England.   [*Sub tit. The Soul of a Serf*, Laird & Lee, Chicago.]

ELRINGTON, Miss H. *Ralph Wynward.*   [juvenile] 1903

Desmond's rebellion and the sack of Youghal (1578–9). One of a number of similar historical tales for children. [Nelson: o.p.]

EMERSON, Dr. Peter Henry. *Caoba, the Guerilla Chief: a real romance of the Cuban rebellion.* 1897

Caoba is a negro chief who joins the rebels against the Spaniards (*c.* 1870). Negro savagery and Spanish misgovernment lead the author to hope for American intervention. [Nutt: o.p. ; Scribner, New York: o.p.]

EPHTALIOTIS, Argyris [Greek ; b. 1849]. *Tales from the Isles of Greece: being sketches of Greek peasant life* (1894).   1897

Miscellaneous tales, romantic, idyllic, and genre pictures of peasant life in the Greek islands of that day ; with three stories of the war of independence. [Transl. by W. H. D. Rouse, Dent: o.p.]

ERCKMANN, Émile [French ; 1822–99], and **CHATRIAN, Alexandre** [French ; 1826–90]. *Madame Thérèse ; or, The Volunteers of '92* (1863).   1864

These two Lorrainers wrote a long series of Alsatian peasant stories, truthful and charming in local colour, and saturated with the historical spirit. Their earliest successes were concerned with the Napoleonic wars. Madame Thérèse is a *vivandière* whom a country doctor rescues from among the wounded in a skirmish, and nursing her falls in love (1792–3). Scene, a quiet hamlet near Strasbourg ; the Republic before the advent of Bonaparte, in its fresh fervour of liberty, is regarded through the simple understandings of the peasants, their talks and domestic anxieties, while the great military movements sweep irresistibly over their village. [Transl., Scribner, New York: o.p.]

—— *Friend Fritz* (L'ami Fritz, 1864).   1877

The story of an old bachelor who marries a little country maiden in an Alsatian village ; little incident, much portraiture of rustic life and character in his friends, dependents, and boon companions. [Ward & Lock: o.p. ; Scribner, New York.]

—— *The Conscript* (Histoire d'un conscrit de 1813, 1864).   1865

Annals of the French campaigns of 1812–13—quaintly and charmingly put in the simple language of a peasant —designed to expose the wickedness of war. The Conscript is an unfortunate peasant, half a cripple,

ERCKMANN, Émile, and CHATRIAN, Alexandre (*continued*).
whose love affairs and prospects in life are ruined by the call to arms. At Phalsbourg he witnesses the passage of the *Grande Armée*, and then is involved in the disasters culminating at Leipzig. [Transl., *The Conscript* and *Waterloo* (Everyman's Lib.), Dent (Dutton, New York), 1909 ; Scribner, New York.]

—— *Waterloo* (Waterloo : suite du conscrit de 1813, 1865) [sequel]. 1865
Sequel to *The Conscript*, though in historical sequence *The Blockade* intervenes. All three are peasant stories which read like narratives of individual experience. [Scribner, New York ; see also *The Conscript, supra.*]

—— *A Man of the People* (Histoire d'un homme du peuple, 1865). 1871
His own story told by a peasant who took part in the Revolution of 1848, with comments on men and politics. His early days as a journeyman in Saverne, and his coming up to the capital, bring in descriptions of country life in Paris. [2 vols., Bentley : o.p.]

—— *The Blockade of Phalsbourg* (Le blocus : épisode de la fin de l'empire, 1867). 1869
The invasion of France by the Allies in 1814, and the siege of Phalsbourg, in the Vosges. An old Jew lays in a supply of wine with a view to profiting by the scarcity : the fate of this wine occasions great suspense. During the siege, which ends with Napoleon's abdication, the old huckster and his family drive a roaring trade. Much play of comic eccentricity among the trade-bands (e.g. such incidents as employer being disciplined by employee), while the Jew's moralizings on war are full of humour. [Ward & Lock : o.p. ; Scribner, New York.]

—— *The Story of a Peasant* (Histoire d'un paysan, 1868–74). 1871–4
4 vols. : *The States-General*, 1789 ; *The Country in Danger*, 1792 ; *Year One of the Republic*, 1793 ; and *Citizen Bonaparte*, 1794–1815. A continuous story of the Revolutionary period, from a peasant's point of view. First a picture of pre-revolutionary days, showing the hardships of the peasants under the monarchy ; then come the awakening to their rights as citizens, and the great episodes of the Revolution and the wars. A domestic story is interwoven with the historical events. [Transl. by C. J. HOGARTH, (Everyman's Lib.) 2 vols., Dent (Dutton, New York) ; Scribner, New York.]

—— *The Story of the Plébiscite* (Histoire du plébiscite ; racontée par un des 7,500,000 oui, 1872). 1872
An intelligent tradesman describes the political condition of France just before the *débâcle* of 1870–1, the unreadiness of the military authorities, and the rottenness of the imperial regime ; with a vivid picture of life in a Vosges village, the local incidents of the war, and the troubles of the country people. [Smith & Elder : o.p. ; Scribner, New York : o.p.]

—— *The Brothers Rantzau* (Les deux frères, 1873). 1874
A story told by a schoolmaster, a self-taught naturalist, who has a knack for describing landscapes as well as human nature, about two brothers, in a little village of the Vosges, who quarrel over an inheritance, and carry the feud to bitter extremes. In the course of years their two children fall in love with each other and marry, yet their hatred never relaxes. A plea for national education. [Low : o.p.]

—— *A Campaign in Kabylia* (Une campagne en Kabylie, 1874). 1876
Fighting in Algeria against the Kabyles (1871), a good story for boys, like most of the foregoing. [Ward & Lock : o.p.]

"ERNST, Otto" [Otto Ernst Schmidt ; German ; b. 1862]. *Roswitha : being leaves from the life of my little daughter.* 1913
An intimate and delicate, and entirely delightful little picture of childhood. [Transl. by A. C. CATON, A. C. Caton : o.p.]

ERSKINE, John [American ; b. 1879]. *The Private Life of Helen of Troy.* 1925
This diversion by a learned professor at Columbia University is a modern reinterpretation of the Homeric story : what was said and done after the return from Troy. Helen is a frank, emancipated woman, who repudiates the idea of dirty linen, and anyhow would wash it in public. Related in an enormously protracted dialogue, very colloquial and very American : readers who cannot stomach Landor on the same subject will probably like it. [Bobbs-Merrill, Indianapolis ; Nash.]

—— *Galahad : enough of his life to explain his reputation.* 1926
Retells from Malory and Gaston Paris the tale of Galahad, with his mother Elaine as the really important character. [Bobbs-Merrill, Indianapolis ; Nash.]

—— *Adam and Eve ; though he knew better.* 1927
Borrows Rossetti's enigmatic Lilith, to make her the disturbing influence between the ancient pair. [Bobbs-Merrill, Indianapolis ; Nash.]

—— *An Experiment in Sincerity : a story of our time.* 1930
A wife who makes a cult of sincerity, finding her husband not quite straight with her about another woman, leaves the two together and goes off. But the runaway returns and the locum tenens has to quit. Mr. Erskine's irony plays with the difference between what people would like to do and to be, and the face they feel they have to present to the world. (*Sub tit. Sincerity*, Bobbs-Merrill, Indianapolis ; Putnam.]

—— *Uncle Sam in the Eyes of his Family.* 1930
Tries to hit off the Yankee temperament and the movements and infatuations of to-day, in the doings of Uncle Sam, his brothers and sisters, nephews and nieces, and their fellow townsfolk. [Bobbs-Merrill, Indianapolis ; Putnam.]

ERVINE, St. John Greer [Irish ; b. 1883]. *Mrs. Martin's Man.* 1915
Her husband betrays and leaves her, then, after sixteen years, comes back to her a drink-sodden idler. Sound character-drawing, against a dreary background of town life in Ulster. [Allen & Unwin ; Macmillan, New York.]

—— *Changing Winds.* 1917
A discussion-novel : interlocutors, an unheroic hero, his more virile, disappointed father, and some other well-defined characters who are personally less attractive. They talk at large on Labour problems, the war, Irish affairs ; and their mixture of callowness and common sense is lifelike. [Allen & Unwin ; Macmillan, New York.]

ERVINE, St. John Greer (*continued*). *The Foolish Lovers.* 1920
A romantic Ulsterman, the son of a grocer, meets failure and disillusion in London, and returns to his native land for choice. [Collins ; Macmillan, New York.]

ESCHOLIER, Raymond [French ; *b.* 1882]. *The Illusion* (Dansons la trompeuse, 1922). 1923
Life in a quiet corner of France under the Pyrenees, shown as in a talking film—the landowners and *métayers*, faithful old servants, a Voltairian survival of the *ancien régime*, grumbling and malicious peasants, and a curé trying vainly to save their souls. But the centre of the picture is occupied by the little old lady, very tenderly portrayed, trying desperately amid her dusty furniture and bibelots and her big house and park to keep the illusion of youth. [Putnam, London and New York.]

—— *Comes the Blind Fury* (La nuit, 1923). 1925
The interesting part of this book is the earlier chapters, dealing with the inevitable clash between a spirited girl, illegitimate child of a scapegrace son, and her bourgeois grandparents in an old-fashioned provincial town. The old man does not believe in education, and keeps the poor thing locked up. Later, Henriette goes blind, and ultimately goes to the bad altogether, the author apparently trying to lay the blame on heredity rather than on her extraordinary upbringing. [Transl. by J. Lewis MAY, Dodd & Mead, New York ; Lane.]

ESLER, Erminda [*née* Rentoul ; Irish]. *The Way of Transgressors.* 1890
A long novel of family life. Class prejudice in country society, and the effect of culture above her station on a girl's character, are the earlier motives ; then more people and wider interests come in. [Low : o.p.]

—— *The Way They Loved at Grimpat.* 1894
Little comedies and tragedies in the lives of village girls in an unknown English hamlet, told in a simple manner, with refined realism and no dialect. [Low : o.p.]

—— *'Mid Green Pastures.* 1895
More about the Grimpat people ; slight stories and character-sketches of humble folk, containing several types of what is best in human nature, e.g. *Jamie Myles* and *Miss Chrissie's Protégé*. *The Idealist* is about a village authoress. [Low : o.p.]

—— *A Maid of the Manse.* 1895
Idyllic sketches of country life and manners among Presbyterians in county Donegal, half a century ago. Miss Esler is the daughter of a Presbyterian minister in that county. [Low : o.p.]

—— *The Wardlaws.* 1896
A grave domestic story, worked out on the basis of character, laid in an Irish rural district. [Smith & Elder : o.p.]

ESPINA, Concha [Spanish ; *b.* 1877]. *Mariflor* (La Esfinge Maragata, 1911). 1924
Combines a romantic idyll with a realistic account of the lives of the peasants of northern Spain. [Transl. by Frances DOUGLAS, Macmillan, New York.]

ESPINEL, Vincente [Spanish ; 1551–1634]. *The History of the Squire Marcos de Obregon* (Relaciones de la Vida del Escudero Marcos de Obregón, 1618). 1816
Written towards the end of the sixteenth century. Lesage modelled the character of Gil Blas on Obregón, and borrowed many incidents from this story, which was written by an aged priest with a view to moral edification, and speedily translated into French. [Transl. by Major A. LANGTON : o.p.]

"EUSTACE, Robert" [E. Rawlins]. *The Hidden Treasures of Egypt.* 1925
" Compiled and adapted from the records of Ptahmes, Third Prophet of Ammon Piromis of Thebes and Prince of the North and South. (Epoch about 1300 B.C.)." A story of the Exodus, Moses, etc., and Egypt under the nineteenth dynasty. [Simpkin Marshall.]

EVANS, Caradoc [Welsh]. *My People.* 1915
—— *Capel Sion.* 1916
Uncompromisingly " realistic " delineations of the uglier side of the Welsh peasantry. [(1) and (2), Hutchinson ; Duffield, New York : o.p.]

—— *Nothing to Pay.* 1930
This time, Mr. Evans's hatred of his Welsh compatriots and satire of their baseness, greed, depravity, and sanctimoniousness finds a target in a village-boy from Cardiganshire, who by practising every meanness becomes a flourishing draper. [Faber ; Norton, New York.]

EVANS, Charles Seddon [*b.* 1883]. *Nash and Some Others.* 1912
The distinction of these tales of schoolboys is that they portray types from the elementary schools of London—full of the characteristic Cockney spirit and humour. [Arnold ; Heinemann (1928).]

EVANS, Howel. *A Girl Alone.* 1917
Realism that does not shrink from vulgar, harrowing, or repulsive subjects, and brings out the common humanity that survives in the depths. [Richards : o.p. ; Putnam, New York.]

EWALD, Carl [Danish ; 1856–1908]. *My Little Boy.* 1906
The history of a father and his first-born, from just before the boy's birth up to the day when he " hands him over to society "—sends him to school. Exquisitely fanciful, delicately ironical ; but the fancy and the irony pierce unerringly to the deeper truths of life. [Transl. by Alexander Texeira DE MATTOS, Methuen ; Scribner, New York.]

—— *Two Legs ; and other stories.* 1907
—— *The Queen Bee ; and other nature stories.* 1907
—— *The Spider ; and other tales.* 1907
—— *The Old Room.* 1908
—— *The Pond ; and other stories.* 1909
Fanciful little romances and allegories of birds, animals, crabs, insects, and plants, all talking in character ; some rather grim, but the majority humorous and pleasingly didactic, pervaded with a coherent philosophy

EWALD, Carl (*continued*).

of Ewald's own. [(1), Transl. by DE MATTOS, Methuen : o.p. ; Scribner, New York ; (2), by G. C. M. SMITH, Nelson : o.p. ; (3), Transl. by DE MATTOS, Scribner, New York : o.p. ; (4), transl. by DE MATTOS, Scribner, New York ; (5), Butterworth.]

EWART, Wilfred Herbert Gore [1892–1922]. *Way of Revelation : a novel of five years.*   1921

A sober and just account of war from several aspects. To a careless group of boys and girls, the crisis brings fulfilment, for good or evil, of the fundamental potentialities in the character of each. The horror of the trenches is brought home without recourse to grossness or brutality, and the social disintegration in England is seen as a tragedy hardly less acute though of a different order. Whilst the craftmanship shows faults and some crudity, the power and sincerity of the book make amends. [Putnam ; Appleton, New York.]

EWING, Juliana Horatia Orr [*née* Gatty ; 1841–85]. *Jackanapes.*   [juvenile] 1883

Written for children ; the story of a gallant boy's self-devotion, in the time of Waterloo. The best-known of her many stories and a favourable specimen of her sympathetic drawing of child-character and the joys and sorrows and the humours of childhood. [*Illus.* by Gordon Brown and Randolph Caldecott, S.P.C.K. With *Daddy Darling's Dovecot*, and *The Story of a Short Life*, (Everyman's Lib.) Dent (Dutton, New York), 1916. *Illus.* by H. M. Brock, Bell (Harcourt, New York). Putnam, New York. *Illus.*, McKay, New York.]

—— *Mrs. Overtheway's Remembrances.*   [juvenile] 1868
—— *The Brownies ; and other tales.*   [juvenile] 1870
—— *A Flat Iron for a Farthing.*   [juvenile] 1873
—— *We and the World : a book for boys* (2 parts).   [juvenile] 1873
—— *Jan of the Windmill : a story of the plains.*   [juvenile] 1876

Mrs. Ewing was the daughter of Mrs. Gatty, the author and editor of children's books hardly less delightful. She wrote an admirably pure and pellucid style, and her truth to nature and whimsical humour are charming to both old and young readers. These books—and she wrote many others scarcely at all inferior—are classics amongst literature for children. [(1), *Illus.* by Gordon Browne, S.P.C.K. ; *illus.* by M. V. Wheelhouse, Bell (Harcourt, New York) ; with *Other Tales*, (Everyman's Lib.), Dent (Dutton, New York), 1916 ; (2), *illus.* by Alice B. Woodward, 1910 ; (3), *illus.* by M. V. Wheelhouse, 1908 ; (4), *id.*, 1910 ; (5), *id.*, 1919, Bell (Harcourt, New York.]

EYRBYGGJA SAGA : *the story of the Ere-Dwellers.*   1891

With *The Story of the Heath Slayings.* Translated by William MORRIS and Eiríkr MAGNÚSSON, who describe it as " a mixture of a saga, or dramatically told tale, and a chronicle record of events outside its aim and purpose." It is in fact one of the most miscellaneous of the sagas, comprising the stories and traditions belonging to a whole district ; and full of information about the manners and institutions of the heathen ages. The salient personages are Snorri the Priest, a wily schemer, no great fighter, but vengeful and pitiless when opportunity serves ; the brave and generous Arnkel ; Steinthor of Ere ; and the romantic champion Biorn, lover of Thurid. Vendettas, piracies, hauntings, and pitched combats form the various threads of interest. Period 884–1031 ; principal events between 986 and 998. Written between 1230 and 1260 according to Vigfússon. [Transl., see *Heiðarviga Saga, infra.*]

FABRICIUS, Johann [Dutch]. *Vain Love.*   1931

A romantic tale of passion, revenge, and disillusionment vividly presented against the colourful backgrounds of Capri and South America. [Transl., Gollancz.]

FADYEEV, Aleksandr Aleksandrovich [Russian ; *b.* 1901]. *The Nineteen.*   1929

Adventures and personal experiences of a band of miners, peasants, and other Soviet irregulars in Siberia during the Russian civil war. [Transl. by R. D. CHARQUES, Martin Lawrence ; International Pub. Co., New York.]

" FAIRLESS, Michael " [Margaret Fairless Barber, daughter of Archdeacon Barber, 1869–1901] *The Gathering of Brother Hilarius.*   1901

A cloister story of Edward III's time (1348–50). The spiritual life of a novice whom his superior sends into the world to learn experience. Scenes, Westminster, English villages at the time of the Black Death, and Florence, where he is trained as a limner. Full of wisdom and love for mankind, he comes back to be prior of his monastery. [Duckworth ; Dutton, New York : o.p.]

—— *The Roadmender.*   1902

Less a story than musings on life and death, pervaded with a sense of gentle melancholy, which the sad circumstances of their writing explain. The author suffered from a painful and incurable malady, of which she subsequently died, and this little book was dictated to the sister at a nursing home. [Duckworth ; Dutton, New York ; *illus.* with 20 photographs by W. F. Taylor, *id.* Medici Soc.]

FALKBERGET, Johan [Norwegian ; *b.* 1879]. *Lisbeth of Jarnfjeld.*   1930

A tragic account of a girl who marries, though her love is fixed upon another, and the miseries she and her husband endure. The atmosphere of the Norwegian mountain country is well rendered. [Transl. by R. GJELSNESS, Allen & Unwin ; Norton, New York.]

FALKNER, John Meade [*b.* 1858]. *The Lost Stradivarius.*   1895

A psychical romance of some fifty years ago. An old Italian melody and a Stradivarius, unearthed in an Oxford college, cast a mysterious spell over a young man, and bring him under the fatal influence of a spirit, who in his days of life and lust had been the owner. [Blackwood : o.p. ; Appleton, New York : o.p.]

—— *Moonfleet.*   1898

A romance of Hampshire and Dorset about 1757–8. The quest for a lost diamond and smuggling furnish the chief episodes, centring in a deep and secret cavern and an ancient family vault. Finely worked out, and not lacking in character-drawing. [Arnold.]

FALKNER, John Meade (*continued*). *The Nebuly Coat.* 1903
An imaginative romance of like quality laid in an old-world minster town. The title refers to the coat of arms of Lord Blandamer, and the plot is concerned with this nobleman's efforts to get rid of the proofs that his grandfather was a bigamist and his own claim to the estates invalid. [Murray.]

FARADAY, L. Winifred [tr.]. *The Cattle Raid of Cualgne* (Tain bó Cuailgne): *an ancient Irish prose epic.* 1904
A close student's translation from two of the oldest and rudest MSS., the *Leabhar na h-Uidhri* (*Book of the Dun Cow*) and the *Yellow Book of Lecan* (late seventh or early eighth century) of a central episode of the Cuchullin cycle. Like Miss Hull's *Cuchullin Saga* in its literal exactness rather than Lady Gregory's more popular recension. No notes. [(Grimm Library), Nutt: o.p.; Scribner, New York: o.p.]

FARINA, Salvatore [Sardinian; 1846–1918]. *Love Blinded* (Amore bendato, 1874). 1879
A little drama of conjugal life among the upper middle-classes in Milan. A young husband and wife, thinking they do not love each other, agree to part; but the husband is stricken with temporary blindness, and, while the wife nurses him, they fall in love with each other. [Transl. by " Marcellina," Charing Cross Pub. Co.: o.p.]

—— *Signor I* (Il Signor Io, 1880). 1888
Story of a girl's marriage against her father's wishes, and their ultimate reconciliation; told with sympathy and pathos. [Transl. by the Baroness Langenau, Gardner, Paisley: o.p.]

FARJEON, Benjamin Leopold [1838–1903]. *Grif: a story of Australian life.* 1866
Poverty, villainy, and innocence in the end triumphant; an *Oliver Twist* of Melbourne and the diggings at the time of the Gold Rush. Grif is a street-arab and a thief, but brave and capable of all the virtues. On the one hand we have Grif, a virtuous and unfortunate wife, and the misguided husband; on the other, a gang of desperadoes and bushrangers. [Hutchinson: o.p.]

—— *The Mystery of M. Felix.* 1890
Sensational stories of murder and mystery, and its ultimate explanation, on the same general lines as Gaboriau's detective stories. [(1), Hutchinson: o.p.; (2), Ward & Downey: o.p.; (3), White: o.p.]

—— *Blade-o'-Grass.* 1874
A humanitarian novel picturing the different fates of twin sisters, one happily adopted by respectable people, the other left to the hard mercies of slum life. [Hutchinson: o.p.]

—— *Samuel Boyd of Catchpole Square.* 1899
A thrilling detective story, less inartistic than the average. [Hutchinson: o.p.; New Amsterdam Book Co., New York: o.p.]

FARJEON, Eleanor. *Gypsy and Ginger.* 1920
A playful story of married housekeeping on a novel plan that is fitted to amuse both children and grown-ups. [Dent: o.p.]

FARMER, James Eugene [American; b. 1867]. *Brinton Eliot: from Yale to Yorktown.* 1902
Undergraduate life at Yale before the War of Independence, and adventures with the American army. Fiercely anti-British in sentiment. Benjamin Franklin, Beaumarchais, Louis XVI, and Benedict Arnold are introduced. [Macmillan, New York: o.p.]

" FARNINGHAM, Marianne " [Mary Anne Hearne; 1834–1909]. *A Window in Paris.* [juvenile] 1898
Paris during the siege and the Commune (1870–1). [Clark: o.p.]

FARNOL, (John) Jeffery [b. 1878]. *The Broad Highway: a romance of Kent.* 1910
A spirited chronicle of Regency days, built on picturesque lines, with a love-plot as an extra; scene, the forest country near Sevenoaks. Corinthians, fine ladies, tramps, highwaymen, and villagers jostle each other in pages redolent of Borrow. [Low; Little & Brown, Boston; Burt, New York.]

—— *The Amateur Gentleman.* 1913
The same sort of story, with scenes in Kent and London, the hero coming in for money and being introduced to fashionable society. [Low; Little & Brown, Boston; Burt, New York.]

—— *The Chronicles of the Imp.* 1915
The pranks and adventures of a small boy, mingled with some rather sugary romance. [Low.]

—— *Beltane the Smith.* 1915
Adventures of an outlaw in mediæval England. [Low; Little & Brown, Boston; Burt, New York.]

—— *The Definite Object.* 1917
The jaded millionaire finds an object at length in a charming heroine, and has the further satisfaction of helping divers friends and paying off old scores on an odious foe. New York slum life and several amusing oddities are depicted, with a full measure of American slang and the popular mixture of sentiment and sensation. [Low; Little & Brown, Boston.]

—— *Our Admirable Betty.* 1918
A costume novel of George the First's time. [Low; Little & Brown, Boston.]

—— *The Geste of Duke Jocelyn: a romance in prose and verse.* 1919
A romance of chivalry in Mr. Farnol's swaggering prose and swinging verse. [Low; Little & Brown, Boston.]

—— *Black Bartlemy's Treasure.* 1920

—— *Martin Conisby's Vengeance* [sequel]. 1921
Adventures on land and the high seas, with the Spanish Inquisition, pirates, etc. [(1) and (2), Low; Little & Brown, Boston; Burt, New York.]

—— *The Loring Mystery.* 1925
The business pivots on a murder, scene, Sussex. [Low; Little & Brown, Boston; Burt, New York.]

—— *The High Adventure.* 1926
The same ingredients as in most of the foregoing, scenes in the south-eastern counties. [Low; Little & Brown, Boston.]

FARNOL, (John) Jeffery (*continued*). *Over the Hills: a romance of the Fifteen.* 1930
" Being the narrative of Adam (called Thursday), with particulars of his adventures, his joys, and sorrows, his friends and right-beloved enemy." Excitement is provided by a trick marriage, a shipwreck on the coast of Scotland, and an attempted assassination. [Low; Little & Brown, Boston.]

FARRAR, Frederick William, Archdeacon [1831–1903]. *Julian Home: a tale of college life.* 1859
A specimen of several didactic stories of school and college life by this author. Julian is a good young man who meets with impediments and sorrows in his college and university career, but emerges all the stronger and fitter for his future life as a clergyman. The characters who meet with the author's reprobation are the fast young men who do not read, and indulge in expensive dissipation. [Black; Ward & Lock; Macmillan, New York.]

—— *Gathering Clouds.* 1896
A similar didactic romance, giving a view of the Byzantine Empire under Arcadius and Honorius, at the time of the pagan reaction against Christianity (A.D. 387–438), the world overmastering the Church. It is also a popular history of S. Chrysostom and of his stand against the growing dissoluteness and corruption. [Longmans: London and New York.]

" FARRÈRE, Claude " [Charles Bargone; French; b. 1876]. *The House of the Secret* (La maison des hommes vivants). 1923
An exciting mystery story. [Transl. by Arthur LIVINGSTON, Dutton, New York.]

—— *Thomas the Lambkin, Gentleman of Fortune* (Thomas l'agnelet). 1924
Adventures of St. Malo pirates, mainly in the Caribbean and South America. [Transl. by Leo ONGLEY, Dutton, New York; Butterworth.]

FARRINGTON, Margaret Vere [*née* Livingstone; b. 1863]. *Fra Lippo Lippi.* 1890
A touching little love-romance, into which are woven the facts of the painter's history, with abundant local colour (1412–69). [Putnam: o.p.; *id.*, New York.]

FAULKNER, William [American]. *Soldier's Pay.* 1926
By a Georgian writer. Theme, the American soldier's return to his people, who have no further use for him and no sympathy or understanding of his outlook. The ex-service men are strangers, almost outcasts, uncomprehended and uncomprehending. Even their old sweethearts recoil from their maimed and scarred lovers. [Boni, New York; Chatto.]

—— *The Sound and the Fury.* 1929
The tragedy of madness in a decayed Georgian family, treated with powerful imagination. One of the uncles is a mental defective, and an idiot son brings catastrophe on the old house. [Cape, New York; Chatto.]

FAUSET, Jessie Redmon [American]. *There is Confusion.* 1924
A study of the social injustice of America towards the negro, developed through an account of two families; the two principal actors, the artistic Joanna and Peter Bye, an ambitious medical student, are excellent pieces of character-drawing. [Boni, New York: Chapman.]

FAUSTUS: *the History of the Damnable Life and Deserved Death of Dr. John Faustus* (Faustbuch, 1587). 1592
—— *The Second Report of Dr. John Faustus; containing his appearances and the deeds of Wagner* (Wagnerbuch, 1593). 1594
The former book is of high interest as being the direct source of Marlowe's greatest play. It is a translation from the German *Faustbuch*, published at Frankfort, 1587, or from the reprint that probably appeared in 1588; the chapters were reduced from 68 to 62. The German author was evidently a man of powerful imagination, even though he borrowed from traditionary sources. The real Faustus was, in all probability, " a miserable charlatan," and by no means the large, heroic spirit imagined by the poets; and the *Faustbuch* represents an intermediate stage between the actual man and the later idealizations. In the darker passages an extremity of physical horror is reached that Poe or Meinhold could not surpass. The translator deserves credit for his strong, natural, and straightforward English. The Second Report [a translation of the *Wagnerbuch* (1593)] is supposed to be written by an English gentleman, student in Wittenberg, where Faustus lived and sold himself to the devil. It adduces evidence as to the authenticity of the story, and then goes on to recount the doings of Wagner, the servant of Faustus, especially how he aided the Christians in a great war with the Turks in Austria. It is inferior in every way to the former work. [Both in Thoms's *Early English Prose Romances*, see p. 465.]

FAWCETT, Edgar [American; 1847–1904]. *A Hopeless Case.* 1880
Portrays a very conventional and aimless section of New York society, and emphasizes its shortcomings by introducing a high-spirited girl with right ideals. [Houghton, Boston: o.p.]

—— *A Gentleman of Leisure.* 1881
The comedy of caste in American society. An anglicized American comes to New York, expecting to find a free and unconventional life prevailing there; anticipating barbarism and vulgarity, he discovers the existence of an American aristocracy, more exclusive even than the European. Among the types satirized are the anglomaniacs, well versed in the English peerage. [Houghton, Boston: o.p.]

—— *An Ambitious Woman.* 1883
An ambitious girl of humble station strives, with ups and downs of success, to secure a place in the most select society of New York. [Houghton, Boston: o.p.]

—— *The House at High Bridge.* 1886
Plot based on a similar idea to that of Mr. Anstey's *Giant's Robe*, i.e. the theft of another man's literary work. Draws realistically the sordid life of would-be genteel people, with their petty economies, doubtful tastes, and cheap ambitions. [Houghton, Boston: o.p.]

FEA, Allan [b. 1860]. *My Lady Wentworth.* 1909
The loves of Monmouth and Henrietta, Lady Wentworth, and Monmouth's rebellion. The author has written a history of the family, *The Loyal Wentworths*. [Mills & Boon: o.p.]

FELD, Rose Caroline [American ; *b.* 1895]. *Heritage.*   1928
Chronicles with ruthless, well-nigh intolerable realism, the monotonous struggles of a small family on a stony farm in New Hampshire. The woman who as wife, mother, and grandmother exerts the driving force is as grim as one of the Fates. No humour and but faint gleams of tenderness relieve the austerity. [Knopf, New York and London.]

FÉNELON, François de Salignac de la Mothe [French ; 1651–1715]. *The Adventures of Telemachus* (Les aventures de Télémaque, 1699).   1699
An operatic blend of Homeric epic and Italian pastoral, written in a consciously poetic prose ; based on those books of the *Odyssey* which relate the adventures of the son of Ulysses in his quest for his father. The ancient world is depicted as a golden age. Composed as a lesson in virtue, piety, and political wisdom for Fénelon's pupil, the young Duke of Burgundy, but taken as a satire on the Court of Louis XIV. The sensuousness and the doubtful morality of the Archbishop's paganism were severely chastized in P. V. Faydit's *Télécomanie* (1700). [Transl. by Dr. HAWKESWORTH, Houghton, Boston.]

FENN, George Manville [1831–1909]. *A Little World.*   1877
Chiefly a story of humble life and a worthy organist's struggle with adverse circumstances, plot-business being introduced by the mysterious disappearance of a baronet's son. Some amusing people from the neighbourhood of Seven Dials contribute many lighter pages. Fenn was better-known as a prolific writer of fiction for boys ; *e.g. Nat the Naturalist* (1882), *Middy and Ensign* (1883), *The Silver Cañon, Menhardoc, Bunyip Land* (1884), *The Devon Boys, Dick o' the Fens* (1887), *Quicksilver* (1888), *Real Gold* (1893), *Steve Young* (1893), *The Black Bar* (1893), *Blue Jackets* (1893), and *Nic Revel* (1898). [(1), 3 vols., H. S. King : o.p. ; (2), (5 : o.p.), (6), (7), (8), and (9), Blackie ; (3) and (13), Oxford Press ; (4) and (12), Low ; (10) and (14), Chambers ; (11), S.P.C.K. : o.p.]

FERBER, Edna [American ; *b.* 1887]. *Cimarron.*   1930
A novel that subsumes the history of Oklahoma ; hero, a masterly young lawyer, editor, idealist, pioneer. He gradually deteriorates into a mere soldier of fortune, whilst his wife develops from an inexperienced girl into a practical and tenacious business woman. The ill-treatment of the Indian tribes, the growth of the primitive town of Osage, and the discovery of fabulous wealth in oil, give materials for some big scenes. [Doubleday, New York ; Heinemann.]

FERGUSSON, Robert Menzies [Scottish]. *The Silver Shoe-Buckle : a tale of the '15.*   1909
A short story based on historical and topographical knowledge, especially about the Ochils, and provided with notes. [Digby & Long : o.p.]

FERNALD, Chester Bailey [American ; *b.* 1869]. *The Cat and the Cherub ; and other stories.*
                                                                                                1896
The Chinese of San Francisco are the amusing subject of these tales, which differ widely from those of C. W. Doyle. The author enters with interest and real sympathy into the curious workings of the Celestial mind. [Century Co., New York : o.p. ; *sub tit. Chinatown Stories,* Heinemann : o.p.]

—— *Under the Jackstaff.*   1903
Eleven stories of the sea told by an Irish man-o'-war's man ; some mysterious, all of them powerful. [Century Co., New York : o.p.]

FERRIER, Susan Edmondstone [Scottish ; 1782–1854]. *Marriage.*   1818
Galt pictured the inhabitants of a Lowland village ; Miss Ferrier dealt with better-class people and the would-be genteel. This is a rambling, ill-constructed novel, which, however, attains its main object, to bring out contrasts of manners and character, the sharpest opposition being between the young lady, a spoilt child of English fashionable life, who elopes with the son of a Highland laird and is brought to live in his uncouth home, and the set of originals she finds there, rough, honest, overflowing with fussy kindness, and with humours that delight the reader but disgust the heroine.

—— *The Inheritance.*   1824
Here Miss Ferrier manages her highly romantic plot better, but the comedy of manners is of the same complexion : her models here are Fanny Burney and Jane Austen rather than Galt. An heiress is all but ousted from her inheritance, is deserted by her mercenary lover, but marries the right one. The real entertainment, however, is not in the story but in the highly original examples of Scottish character, eccentrics, vulgarians, sentimental misses, a pompous and loquacious lord, specimens of county society, a nabob and his family, and the writer's masterpiece, the indefatigable gossip and busybody, Miss Pratt.

—— *Destiny ; or, The Chief's Daughter.*   1831
Rather a falling off from the other two. The plot turns on the title to certain estates, and the fortunes of a young lady who eventually marries the rediscovered heir. Sketches of clan and village life, the chief's household and retainers in their faded magnificence, divers satirical portraits, and a fierce caricature of a Presbyterian minister, are in her old style.
[Each in 1 vol., Routledge (Dutton, New York) : o.p. ; edited by R. B. Johnson and *illus.* by Nelly Erichsen, each work in 2 vols., Dent, 1894 : o.p. ; with introds. by Lady Margaret Sackville, 4 vols., Nash, 1929 ; *Marriage,* (Everyman's Lib.), Dent (Dutton, New York), 1928.]

FETHERSTONHAUGH, V. [Canadian]. *Mrs. Jim Barker ; and, Frosts of June.*   1899
Two fresh and vivacious novelettes, depicting English country society and Anglo-Canadian life, the latter element giving a picturesque variety to both tales. [Chapman : o.p.]

FEUCHTWANGER, Lion [German ; *b.* 1884]. *The Ugly Duchess* (Die hässliche Herzogin, 1923).
                                                                                                1926
The life and times of Margareta, Duchess of Tyrol, are made to live again by methods as forcible as in *Jew Süss.* Here the principal scenes are in Tyrol and Bavaria, in the period 1330–60. The ugly duchess herself is drawn with great vigour, and besides this dominating protagonist a considerable number of historical personages come more or less prominently into the picture, among them the blind king of Bohemia, Pope Clement VI, and William of Occam. [Transl. by Willa and Edwin MUIR, Secker ; Viking Press, New York.]

FEUCHTWANGER, Lion (*continued*). *Jew Süss* (Jud Süss, 1925). 1925

A broad and lurid picture, employing realism for romantic ends, of Wurtemberg in the period 1730–40. Above the bull-like duke, Karl Alexander, and his sycophantic Court, his Jewish counsellor Josef Süss Oppenheim stands dominant, broken only when his daughter falls a victim to the monarch's lust. Then he plans revenge, enjoys it, and is put to death content. The political affairs of the duchy, intrigues and scandals at the Court, the open and latent feuds of Catholic, Protestant, and Jew, and the general life and manners of the people, are vigorously and frankly depicted ; actual historical events hardly come in at all, except for passing allusions. For a biography of the hero see *Jew Süss Oppenheimer*, by Dr. Curt Elwenspoek, transl. by E. CASTLE, 1931. [Transl. by W. and E. MUIR, Secker ; *subtit. Power*, Viking Press, New York.]

—— *Success : three years in the life of a province* (Erfolg : drei Jahre beschichte einer Provinz, 1930). 1930

A strong, over-voluminous, over-crowded, and over-weighted study of social conditions and political corruption and intrigue in Bavaria in the years 1920–23, with sidelights on human injustice throughout the planet. The complicated story hinges on a miscarriage of justice involving the director of an art gallery in Munich and several other public men, and brings in a political movement which can be identified with the Ludendorff-Hitler affair of 1923. [Transl. by Willa and Edwin MUIR, Secker.]

FEUILLET, Octave [French ; 1821–90]. *The Little Countess* (La petite comtesse, 1857). 1881

Feuillet was the novelist of aristocratic society in France ; his snobbishness and his jejune idealism will not endear him to present-day readers. A pathetic tale with a bitter *dénouement* ; how a dry, staid man of letters and a gay young countess are drawn towards each other by genuine love, in spite of first impressions ; but the prejudices of the fast society which is her sphere cause misunderstanding with tragic results. [Vizetelly : o.p.]

—— *The Romance of a Poor Young Man* (Le roman d'un jeune homme pauvre, 1858). 1908

An idealized portrait of the old nobility ; one of those gay, idyllic romances in which everything comes right— Henry Harland justly called it a fairy-tale. The poor young man is a marquess who has been left penniless by a spendthrift father, and has to become a land steward in order to earn his living, or else adopt methods that he does not approve. His decision to accept honest work as his duty leads to a romance which has many ups and downs, but leaves him married to the girl he loves. [With critical introd. by H. HARLAND, Heinemann.] Between this novel and *Un mariage dans le monde* appeared the following : *Sibylle* (1862), *Monsieur de Camors* (1867), and *Julia de Trécœur* (1872), the pathetic story of a woman's disastrous love for her stepfather, and the conflict between passion and duty. *Le journal d'une femme* followed in 1878. Translations do not appear to be available. Of *Julia de Trécœur* it has been said, " Ce roman contient tout Feuillet."

—— *A Marriage in High Life* (Un mariage dans le monde, 1875). 1886

A characteristic study of woman and marriage, the author having little faith in the strength of woman under temptation. The parties to this marriage fail to agree ; the wife is drawn into the fast life of Parisian society, and the husband lets her go her own way ; but a friend intervenes and saves her. [Maxwell : o.p. ; transl. by C. LOGAN, Porter & Coates, Philadelphia : o.p.]

—— *Aliette* (La morte, 1886). 1886

Told in letters of a bereaved husband. A man of culture, an unbeliever, after considerable opposition marries the daughter of a pious family. The girl has one ambition—to convert her husband. Another woman, who is an agnostic, falls in love with him. The wife dies, the husband marries this woman, and then learns that she poisoned his wife. The inner life of the man, and his terrible awakening, make a study of absorbing interest. [Transl. by SIMPSON, Warne : o.p. ; by J. H. HAGER, Appleton, New York, 1886 : o.p.]

—— *An Artist's Honour* (Honneur d'artiste, 1890). 1891

Subject, a mistaken marriage between a bourgeois painter and a girl of aristocratic birth, who loves his friend, a man of her own class. On the one hand, we have a tragic situation led up to by the author's reading of character ; on the other hand, he charms by his witty analysis of class prejudice and the distinctions of manners. [Cassel, New York : o.p.]

FEYDEAU, Ernest-Aimé [French ; 1821–73]. *Fanny ; or, The Revelations of a Woman's Heart* (Fanny, 1858). 1860

An analytical novel that was a popular but not quite an artistic success. The lover tortures himself with jealousy of his mistress's husband, and stoops to the most contemptible shifts to spy upon her conduct. [Vickers : o.p.]

—— *The Secret of Happiness* (Le secret de bonheur, 1864). 1867

The secret is that to do good is the destiny of man. A moralizing French count, with his wife and family, disgusted by European society, go to Algeria, and lead a useful and natural life among the Arabs, whose primitive virtues point the satire against civilization. [Edmondston & Douglas, Edinburgh : o.p.]

FIELD, Eugene [American ; 1850–95]. *A Little Book of Profitable Tales*. [juvenile] 1895

Some twenty simple stories, sketches, fables, and fairy-tales, inspired by the author's tender appreciation of children ; largely in dialect. [Scribner, New York.]

—— *The Love Affairs of a Bibliomaniac*. 1896

A whimsical little book that has a peculiar charm for the book-hunter, and something of the poetic beauty that characterizes the author's verse. [Scribner, New York.]

FIELDING, Henry [1707–54]. *The Adventures of Joseph Andrews*. —— 1742

Begins and ends as a burlesque of Richardson's *Pamela*, but, taken as a whole, is a magnificent " comic epic " of the road, patterned on Cervantes, and to a smaller extent on Le Sage, Scarron, and Marivaux. The worldly-wise vestal Pamela reappears as Mrs. Booby, and her brother Joseph, the footman, is represented as repelling the overtures of a woman of quality. The servants and connexions of a squire's family in the country include those famous originals : Parson Adams, designed as a character of perfect simplicity and goodness, Mrs. Slipslop, Peter Pounce, and Parson Trulliber. In a long disquisition Fielding analyses the novel as a comic epic in prose. Fielding was probably the author of *Shamela* (1740), a rather scurrilous parody of Richardson's novel, and here made use of some of the comic materials again. [Ed. Saintsbury,

FIELDING, Henry (*continued*).

2 vols., Dent (Macmillan, New York), 1893 ; (Bohn's Lib.), Bell (Harcourt, New York) ; (World's Classics) Oxford Press, 1929 ; Scholartis Press, 1929 ; Dodd & Mead, New York ; Scribner, New York.]

—— *A Journey from this World to the Next.*   1743

A Lucianic fable. The journey gives occasion for much quizzing of human nature, the satire growing more unequivocal when Minos decides, in grim sardonic style, on the various claims to enter Elysium. Humorous descriptions of literary immortals follow, and then a lengthy account of Julian the Apostate and his transmigrations. Probably written earlier than *Joseph Andrews*. [In his *Miscellanies*, ed. G. Saintsbury, 2 vols., Dent (Macmillan, New York), 1893 ; see also next book.]

—— *The History of Mr. Jonathan Wild the Great.*   1743

A masterpiece of sustained irony, an ostensible biography of the noted thief-taker hanged at Tyburn in 1725, being at once a satire on the human folly of worshipping greatness even when divorced from goodness, and a lampoon on Walpole and the jobbers and place-hunters ruling—and robbing—the country. [This and the *Journey* appeared in the *Miscellanies*, 3 vols. (1743). In 1 vol., Routledge (Dutton, New York) ; *Miscellanies*, ed. G. Saintsbury, 2 vols., Dent (Macmillan, New York), 1893. With Defoe's *Life of Jonathan Wild*, Knopf.]

—— *Tom Jones : the history of a foundling.*   1749

His most elaborate and comprehensive work. The complete and unexpurgated history of a young man of strong natural impulses, a good disposition, and no overpowering sense of morality. Fielding planned it as a " Comic Epic," and built the plot with care, a plot turning on the recognition of Jones's birth and on the fortunes of his love for an adorable girl. Life in country and town in the year 1745 ; with a great crowd of characters of all sorts and conditions, from the squirearchy and the rakes and fashionable women of London down to the domestic servants and even gipsies and tinkers. Squire Western and Partridge are comic gems of the finest quality ; Allworthy is an idealized portrait of Ralph Allen, and Sophia (like Amelia) a picture drawn with reverent passion from Fielding's dead wife. Fielding aims at a philosophical representation of life, and in the essays prefixed to his chapters gives many dissertations on literature and art, and on the actions and characters of the story. *Tom Jones* is of the highest importance in the history of literature, as indicating the lines on which the modern novel of manners was to be written ; Thackeray, the most distinguished of Fielding's followers, avowedly took it for his model in *Pendennis*, and it justifies the digressions and asides of George Eliot and other novelists. [Ed. Saintsbury, 4 vols., Dent (Macmillan, New York), 1893 ; 2 vols., (Bohn's Lib.), Bell (Harcourt, New York) ; Routledge (Dutton, New York) ; Macmillan, 1900 ; Methuen ; Lane (Dodd & Mead, New York) ; 2 vols., Knopf, 1924.]

—— *Amelia.*   1751

This comes closest of all Fielding's novels to actuality, for he was drawing upon his personal experiences as a London magistrate, and was anxious to show up the disorders of society in his pictures of licentious pleasures, depravity and crime, and the horrors of Newgate. Amelia, "the perfect model of an English wife," he drew from his own first wife. It is the touching story of a married couple in an uphill struggle with adversity, the hero as weakly good-natured as Tom Jones—or more so. Dr. Harrison and Col. Bath are the most original creations. [Ed. Saintsbury, 3 vols., Dent (Macmillan, New York), 1893 ; (Bohn's Lib.), Bell (Harcourt, New York) ; Routledge (Dutton, New York.)]

[*Novels*, ed. by G. Saintsbury, 12 vols., Blackwell, Oxford ; Boni, New York ; 6 vols., Bigelow Brown, New York.]

FIELDING, Sarah [sister of Henry Fielding ; 1714–68]. *Adventures of David Simple in Search of a Faithful Friend.*   1744

A moralizing novel, inspired by Richardson's *Pamela*. The misadventures and perplexities of a serious young man in quest of an ideal friend, whom he finds at last in the beautiful and amiable Camilla. One volume was mainly devoted to exposition of character in a number of individuals, the other to episodes of life in London. [Ed. E. A. Baker, Routledge (Dutton, New York) : o.p.]

FIGGIS, Darrell [Irish ; 1882–1925]. *Jacob Elthorne.*   1914

The life story of a strong, hard man, lacking humour and charity ; after a hard and impoverished youth he achieves some fame as a writer ; but both in his work and in his relations with his wife, a popular novelist of the cheaper sort who grows apart from him, he is a disappointed man. [Dent : o.p.]

—— *Children of Earth.*   1918

The author lives in Achill Island (the Maolan of the novel) and has studied the inhabitants closely. He depicts them as a very primitive race, given to elemental passions and haunted by pagan ideas of the occult influences of the earth. All this is the sombre groundwork in the story of a girl compelled to marry one man whilst loving another. [Talbot Press.]

FINDLATER, Jane Helen [Scottish ; b. 1866]. *The Green Graves of Balgowrie.*   1897

A touching story of eighteenth-century gentlefolk in Fife. Two unhappy sisters are brought up by an unkind mother, whose vagaries develop into insanity, whereupon they are befriended and educated by a good-hearted minister. [Methuen : o.p.]

—— *A Daughter of Strife.*   1897

A touching domestic story of gentlefolk in Fife (*c.* 1710–40), with firmer handling of character and motive. [Methuen : o.p.]

—— *The Story of a Mother.*   1903

Life in a Highland manse a hundred years ago. The story somewhat tame, interest lying in the small family circle of characters and their relations toward each other—the rigid, unsympathetic minister, his young and finely endowed wife, and her beloved son. [Nisbet : o.p.]

—— *The Ladder to the Stars.*   1906

An optimistic book, with a fine character of a girl, that takes its inspiration from a little picture of Blake's figuring the struggle to realize our ideals. [Methuen : o.p. ; Appleton, New York : o.p.]

—— *Seven Scots Stories.*   1912

Magazine stories, some humorous, some pathetic, e.g. *The Bairn-Keeper*, about a little girl who has to take charge of both baby and grandmother of a slatternly farmer's wife. [Murray ; Dutton, New York.]

FINDLATER, Jane Helen (*continued*). *A Green-Grass Widow; and other stories.* 1921
Four stories: *The Green-Grass Widow* gives a lively picture of Scottish gipsies. [Murray.]

FINDLATER, Mary [Scottish; b. 1865; sister of preceding]. *Over the Hills.* 1897
A quiet story of Scottish villagers and others, homely characters, chiefly feminine. One that stands out is a study of a non-moral woman, and the wiles wherewith she hoodwinks her lovers, while a simpler and nobler girl is placed in strong contrast. [Methuen: o.p.]

—— *Betty Musgrave.* 1899
A domestic story, portraying a noble-hearted girl in squalid surroundings. A delicate character study of better-class folk. [Methuen: o.p.]

—— *A Narrow Way.* 1901
An uneventful, sometimes dull, story of domestic life in Edinburgh, portraying chiefly, in a very delicate yet penetrating manner, two characters, an old-fashioned Presbyterian spinster aunt, and an innocent, sane, and sweet-natured girl, in whom freedom is an inborn passion. [Methuen: o.p.]

—— *The Rose of Joy.* 1903
The same modest and unpretentious realism, presenting a family of not uncommon people, so as to show the very elements of character, the delicate shades of temperament, and the deeper beauty of spiritual traits. In Susan, the daughter of a feckless middle-class home, Miss Findlater's subdued art finds apt expression. [Methuen: o.p.; McClure, New York: o.p.]

—— *A Blind Bird's Nest.* 1907
Deals with a sadder theme, the life of a motherless girl whose father was sentenced to penal servitude. [Methuen: o.p.]

—— *Tents of a Night.* 1914
The heroine, after a broken romance, is restored to spirit in a period of travel in Brittany. Both she and a schoolgirl friend are attractive creations, and the Breton setting is well done. [Murray.]

FINDLATER, Mary and Jane Helen. *Tales that are Told.* 1901
Short stories written separately by the two sisters. The strongest and most characteristic are the domestic stories of the Scotch middle-class, several of which have a dash of romance; e.g. *My Little Hester*, delicate analysis of a girl's dread of the supernatural; *In Hopefield Square*, containing a fine old lady; *Void of Understanding*, the tale of an idiot's self-devotion. [Methuen: o.p.]

—— *Crossriggs.* 1908
Domestic and social life in a quiet village near Edinburgh, in the times before the Disruption. Poor in incident, but fertile in pleasant if not striking character, the unobtrusive differences in which are skilfully brought to light. [Nelson; Nash.]

—— *Penny Monypenny.* 1911
A long family history of Scottish gentlefolk in whom clan feeling strongly persists. [Murray.]

—— *Seen and Heard Before and After* 1914. 1916
Six sketches, of which five are by Jane Findlater. *The Little Tinker*, which points the contrast between gipsy and civilized life, may be singled out. Others are war-stories. [Murray.]

FINLAY, Rev. Thomas A., S.J. ["A. Whitelock"; Irish; b. 1848]. *The Chances of War.* 1877
An historical study of the failure of the Confederation of Kilkenny, and the wars in Ireland during 1646–9. Good account of the battle of Benburb and Ireton's advance against Limerick; Owen Roe O'Neill, Rinuccini, Sir Charles Coote, etc., thoroughly portrayed. Catholic and nationalist, but fair. [Gill, Dublin: o.p.]

FIRBANK, Arthur Annesley Ronald [1886–1926]. *Odette: a fairy tale for weary people.* 1905
Probably this is Firbank's most touching and poetical story, and distinctly better than Oscar Wilde's artificial efforts in the style of Andersen and Malory. It sounds like a legend: a little French girl wanders out from the château on the Loire to find the Virgin, and rescues a desperate woman from her evil life. [With 4 *illus.* by Albert Buhrer, Grant Richards, 1916.]

—— *Vainglory.* 1915
A slight bit of half-cynical impressionism: Mayfair and a vague old cathedral town, with some inconsequential business about a lady and a stained-glass window in which she hopes to perpetuate herself. Small talk, hovering between wit and nonsense. [Duckworth; Brentano, New York.]

—— *Inclinations.* 1916
The same sort of gossamer stuff, with little story, the characters so vaguely outlined they might be interchangeable. They talk in an absentminded way, uttering witticisms that usually fail to come off—in short, just agreeable nonsense. [Duckworth.]

—— *Caprice.* 1917
A little fantasy of theatrical affairs, sketching the go-as-you-please life of the eighteen-nineties in rapid touches of colour and dialogue. A callow enthusiast runs away from her home in the cathedral close, and in no time finds herself running a playhouse.

—— *Valmouth: a romantic novel.* 1919
Exhibits a set of perverted individuals, mostly women, regaling each other with inadequately oxygenated nastiness. Firbank's cunning use of dialogue and his delicately indelicate humour is worthy of a better subject. [Duckworth.]

—— *The Princess Zoubaroff.* 1920
Similar sketching of sylphs and satyrs from Mayfair society, witty or would-be witty patter, closely skirting the suggestive and even the obscene. [Duckworth.]

—— *Santal.* 1921
A brilliant pastiche, depicting in hot Oriental colours a day in the life of a young Arab—the mosque, the bazaars, the desert. There is a fatalistic moral drawn from the Koran—resignation and trust in the All-Wise.

FIRBANK, Arthur Annesley Ronald (*continued*). *Prancing Nigger.* 1925

Firbank's object was apparently to evade formal narrative : in truth, he rarely had any story to tell. This enacts itself. Prancing Nigger, who has got religion, comes with his family from the village where they have run naked, to the pleasure city of Cuna-Cuna, and they admire, from the back-seats, the splendours and gilded depravities of its millionaires and duchesses, and utter ingenuous, if not innocent remarks. [Duckworth ; Brentano, New York.]

—— *The Works of Ronald Firbank.* 1929

Introduction by Arthur Waley ; biographical memoir by Osbert Sitwell. Vol. 1—Vainglory (1915) ; Vol. 2— Odette (1905), Inclinations (1916), Caprice (1917) ; Vol. 3—Valmouth (1919), The Princess Zoubaroff (1920) ; Vol. 4—Santal (1921), The Flower beneath the Foot (1923) ; Vol. 5—Prancing Nigger (1925), Concerning the Eccentricities of Cardinal Pirelli (1926). [5 vols., Duckworth ; Brentano, New York.] Ronald Firbank, who died at the age of 39, is described as a " primitive."

FISHER, Vardis [American]. *Toilers of the Hills.* 1928

Presents in fresh but unromantic terms the hard life of early settlers in Idaho—a man winning through by the strength and obstinacy of his temper, his wife crushed by the toil and loneliness. [Houghton, Boston ; Gollancz.]

FITZPATRICK, Kathleen [Irish]. *The Weans at Rowallan.* 1905

Amusing pictures of children, remarkably lifelike, not untinged with pathos or with the native melancholy of the peasant. [Methuen : o.p.]

FITZPATRICK, Sir James Percy [1862–1931]. *Jock of the Bushveld.* 1907

A vivid story for boys of a boy's life in S. Africa, by a charming story-teller who knew the country intimately, and never wrote better on the subject. [Longmans.]

FLANDRAU, Charles Macomb [American ; *b.* 1871]. *The Diary of a Freshman.* 1901

History of a first year at Cambridge (Mass.), forming a detailed picture of manners and customs in an American university. [Doubleday, New York : o.p. ; Heinemann : o.p.]

FLAUBERT, Gustave [French ; 1821–80]. *Madame Bovary* (1857). 1893

Perhaps the most perfect, certainly the most artistic work of realistic art in any language ; a faithful interpretation of actual life, infinitely painstaking in its rendering of all the significant facts by means of the exact phrase and the one word that corresponds to truth. It is a plain history of the slow but inevitable moral degeneration of a weak woman. Filled with sentimental ideas about life, she marries a stupid but indulgent doctor, and soon finds herself bored by the dullness of their rustic existence. She takes a lover, and after him a second, ruins her husband by her extravagance, and then poisons herself, the husband discovering her infidelity and dying broken-hearted. The passionless candour of the narrative, the patient rendering of the squalor and narrowness of provincial life and of its effect on the woman's mind, make this a landmark in the history of naturalism. In spite of the author's cold neutrality—he hated the life and the characters that he drew, and worked against the grain—the moral is obvious. [Original transl. by Eleanor Marx AVELING, Knopf, London and New York, 1919 ; (Everyman's Lib.), Dent (Dutton, New York), 1928 ; Cape, 1930. Transl. with introd. by Henry JAMES, Heinemann, 1902. Transl. by J. Lewis MAY, Lane (Dodd & Mead, New York), 1928.]

—— *Salammbô* (1862). 1886

Salammbô is a Carthaginian princess, sister of Hannibal ; and the history of the imperial city of Africa in its death-struggle with the revolted mercenaries (241–36 B.C.) fills a succession of gorgeous and appalling scenes. Episodes of riot and torture, the hideous ceremonial of Moloch worship, the barbarous personality of the various leaders, are brought before the eye with tremendous vividness. A wealth of archæological learning is applied by the author of *Madame Bovary* to the composition of this huge realistic canvas, which with George Eliot's *Romola* of the year after (1863) began a new tradition in historical fiction. [Transl. by J. S. CHARTRES, Gibbings : o.p. ; by J. W. MATTHEWS, De La More Press, 1901 : o.p. ; same transl., *illus.* by H. Mackey, Mandrake Press, 1930 ; transl. by Ben Ray REDMAN, *illus.* by Mahlon Blaine, Day, New York, 1927 ; another transl., Brentano, New York, 1919 ; with engravings by Robert Gibbings, ltd. ed., Random House, New York, 1929.]

—— *The Sentimental Education* (L'éducation sentimentale, 1869). 1898

A long and laborious novel, almost entirely lacking in plot or story, but forming a veritable encyclopædia of manners and morals in mid-nineteenth century Paris ; the hero a good-natured, aimless young man whose life is a failure, and most of the other characters examples of the failure to achieve happiness. With stern fidelity to the most humdrum facts of life, and practised observation of the springs of action, Flaubert reviews this world of foolish mortals, and shows the nothingness in which such a life must end. Some of the characters are masterpieces of individual portraiture, e.g. the wonderful courtesan La Maréchale and the adorable Mme Arnoux. [Transl. by D. F. HANNIGAN, 2 vols., Nichols : o.p. ; another transl., Knopf, 1928 ; Brentano New York, 1922.]

—— *The Temptation of St. Anthony* (La tentation de Saint Antoine, 1874). 1896

A play for reading, rather than a novel. The famous temptation appears as a wonderful vision passing before the eyes of the anchorite in his desert hut. Wealth and luxury are offered him in the most alluring manner ; he is transported to the imperial Court, takes on the personality of famous kings, the pagan gods pass in procession before him, while the tempter mocks at Christianity ; philosophers, heretics, magicians appear and argue to corrupt his faith, and the devil reveals to him all the mysteries of the world. [Transl. by D. F. HANNIGAN, Nichols : o.p. ; by René FRANCIS, Duckworth, 1910 : o.p. ; same, *illus.*, Lane : o.p. ; by Lafcadio HEARN, Richards (Harriman, New York), 1911 : o.p. ; another transl., Brentano, New York, 1923 ; *illus.*, ltd. ed., Washburne, New York, 1930.]

—— *Bouvard and Pécuchet* (1881). 1896

Posthumous and unfinished. A full-length portrait of two members of the Parisian bourgeois, a pair of " narrow-minded, credulous, conventionally vicious Frenchmen," done with a satirical intent and an unfalteringly realistic method. [Transl. by D. F. HANNIGAN, Nichols : o.p.]

FLECKER, James Elroy [1884–1915]. *The King of Alsander.* 1914
A kind of short " New Arabian Night " about a studious young grocer who becomes king of a belated mediæval State somewhere in the latitude of Italy. The author is better known as a poet. [Allen & Unwin ; Knopf, New York.]

" FLEMING, George " [Miss Julia Constance Fletcher ; *b.* 1858]. *Kismet* (later called *A Nile Novel*). 1877
The talk, flirtations, and love-making of a party of English and American tourists in a voyage up the Nile ; the book is something between a love-story and a travel-novel. [Macmillan : o.p. ; Little & Brown, Boston.]
—— *Vestigia.* 1884
A familiar picture of Italian life at Leghorn, especially of the fisher-folk and other humble people. The heroine, daughter of a fine old sailor, is an innocent maidenly girl, gentle, but capable of heroic self-sacrifice. The interest centres in her lover, who has been entangled with a revolutionary society and is deputed to assassinate King Humbert. [Macmillan : o.p.]
—— *Andromeda.* 1885
A love-novel, with English and Italian characters and Tyrolese scenery. The principal situation is that of a betrothed girl in love with her lover's friend, and the pure ideals of the book and the consistency of the character-drawing render it a moving story of self-sacrifice. [2 vols., Bentley : o.p.]

FLETCHER, Joseph Smith [*b.* 1863]. *When Charles I was King.* 1892
A Yorkshire story of the Civil War, the battle of Marston Moor, and the siege of Pontefract. [Gay & Hancock ; Black.]
—— *The Wonderful Wapentake.* 1894
Journalistic sketches of man and nature as observed in the Yorkshire district of Osgoldcross. Some are essays in the style of Richard Jefferies ; others tend towards the short story. [Lane : o.p.]
—— *Where Highways Cross.* 1895
A country story, of the Arcadian order, of the charming agricultural region round about Pontefract, of which the author is a native. [Dent : o.p. ; Macmillan, New York : o.p.]
—— *Life in Arcadia.* 1896
Sketches of nature and of human nature in Yorkshire ; humorous and pathetic by turns. [*Sub tit. The Arcadians*, Long, 1930.]
—— *In the Days of Drake.* [juvenile] 1896
Adventures of a Yorkshire boy in Mexico and as a prisoner of the Inquisition (1578–80). [Blackie : o.p. ; Rand & McNally, Chicago : o.p.]
—— *At the Gate of the Fold.* 1896
A simple country story, simply told ; the observations of outdoor phenomena and of the details of country life much in the manner of Jefferies. [Ward & Downey : o.p. ; Macmillan, New York : o.p.]
—— *Mistress Spitfire : edited from the original MSS.* [juvenile] 1896
The Civil War period again (1642–4), and the siege of Pontefract. [Collins, 1930 ; McClurg, Chicago : o.p.]
—— *The Builders.* 1897
The growth and entry into life of a young man, his matrimonial mistakes and the consequences. Reflects incidentally on the conventional training of youth in pious families. Scene, Yorkshire. [Methuen : o.p.]
—— *The Paths of the Prudent.* 1899
The career of a bewitching and too clever heroine, who plays with her lovers and outwits her master, a genial and humorous Yorkshire landlord. [Jarrolds, 1929 ; Page, Boston : o.p.]
—— *From the Broad Acres.* 1899
More chronicles of loves and marriages, trials and joys, of the Yorkshire countryman, racy with the bucolic spirit ; sadder than most of the preceding. [Richards : o.p.]
—— *Morrison's Machine.* 1900
The inventor of a valuable machine loses his memory, and his employer yields to the temptation to steal the invention : this is the basis of a melodramatic plot. [Hutchinson : o.p.]
—— *The Harvesters.* 1900
A simple story of modern farming life, with the love affairs of two idealized rustics, to which a poaching incident contributes a bit of melodrama. [Long : o.p.]
—— *David March.* 1904
A romance of Charles II and Judge Jeffreys' times (1683) ; scenes, the Wakefield neighbourhood and London, where Wren comes in. [Jarrolds, 1929.]
—— *The Town of Crooked Ways.* 1912
The characters are drawn from business men, bank officials, and the like, in a small country town, and the story illustrates the unscrupulous dealings and municipal corruption that can go on underground in such a society. [Newnes ; Dana Estes, Boston : o.p.]
—— *Perris of the Cherry-Trees.* 1913
A tragedy in which the coarser aspects of Yorkshire village life are well brought out. [Jenkins ; Doubleday, New York.]
—— *I'd Venture all for Thee! a romance of the Yorkshire coast.* 1913
A Jacobite story of Boroughbridge, York, and the North Riding, after the Forty-five (1746). [Jarrolds, 1930 ; Doubleday, New York.]
—— *Malvery Hold.* 1917
Mystery and sensation, staged round an old cathedral town that looks like Chichester. [Ward & Lock : o.p.]
—— *Heronshawe Main : the story of a Yorkshire colliery.* 1918
An account of an autocratic colliery-owner, and the bitter struggle between him and his workmen, settled only by the outbreak of the war. [Ward & Lock : o.p.]

FLETCHER, Joseph Smith (*continued*). *The Middle Temple Murder.* 1919
—— *Wrychester Paradise.* 1921
Two good examples of this author's many mystery stories. [(1) and (2), Ward & Lock ; (1) and (2), *sub tit.*
The Paradise Mystery, Knopf, New York.]

FLEURON, Svend [Danish ; *b.* 1874]. *Grim : the story of a pike* (Grum, 1919). 1921
A nature-story, with good descriptive passages, in particular those dealing with the struggle for existence beneath
the water. [Transl. by Jessie MUIR and W. EMMÉ, Knopf.]
—— *Kittens : a family chronicle.* 1920
The author is a well-known Danish writer of nature-stories. [Holden.]

FOGAZZARO, Antonio [Italian ; 1842–1911]. *The Woman* (Malombra, 1881). 1896
A youthful blending of Byronic sentimentalism and romance with modern realism. The chief figures are a
passionate, impulsive, neurotic woman, who loves music, Baudelaire, and lonely reveries amid the Alpe dei
Fiori, and a struggling author whose love she repulses. But the lady is fascinated by a dream that he
and she are reincarnations of two old, unhappy lovers—a morbid obsession that is subtly worked out to its
conclusion in a tragic scene of madness. The novelist's earlier work was a tale in verse, *Miranda* (1874).
[Transl. by Thorold DICKSON, Unwin (1907) : o.p. ; Lippincott, Philadelphia.]
—— *Daniele Cortis* (Daniele Cortis, 1885). 1887
Dramatizes very movingly a conflict between passion and the ordinances of society and the Church. Cortis
is a democratic politician, who loves his married cousin, their long vacillation between love and duty
terminating in the victory of the latter. Besides the interesting study of character and conduct in these
two, their circle of friends are well portrayed, while the politics and finance of the capital help to explain
the character of Cortis. Fogazzaro is an expert in the art of evolving a story by means of natural
dialogue. [Transl. by Mrs. I. R. TILTON, Holt, New York : o.p. ; transl. by S. L. SIMEON, Remington,
1890 : o.p.]
—— *The Patriot* (Il piccolo Mondo antico, 1896). 1906
—— *The Man of the World* (Il piccolo Mondo moderno, 1901) [sequel]. 1907
—— *The Saint* (Il Santo, 1906) [sequel]. 1906
" The little old world " of the first novel is the Valsolda and the Alpine environs of Lugano, and the period
the middle of last century, just before the expulsion of the Austrians : the original is largely written in
the local dialect. The quiet, unchequered, unsophisticated life of this old-world society is rendered with
the charm of boyish memories. Franco and Luisa Maironi are the parents of the Piero Maironi who is
the central figure of the other two novels, and who represents the diverse instincts and propensities inherited
from them. Franco, a noble Brescian, marries and has differences with an intellectual, free-thinking
girl of humbler rank. The tragic sufferings of this pair are brought to an end by a scene of reconciliation,
just before Franco is killed in the war of 1859. The next two books deal with the two great phases in
the life of Piero, the son, who in the second novel is in love with Jeanne Dessalle, a woman unhappily
married, and, like Luisa, an agnostic. Passion is about to overcast all barriers, when Piero's spiritual
transformation changes everything. In the third novel, Piero reappears as the monk Benedetto, a man
inspired like Francis of Assisi with a mission for reforming the Church. He is, in fact, the artistic embodiment of the Modernist creed ; and his story corresponds to some extent with *John Inglesant* and *Robert
Elsmere*, and also with Zola's *Rome*. Needless to say, it has been placed on the Index. [Transl. by M.
PRICHARD-AGNETTI, (1), (2), and (3), Hodder : o.p. ; Putnam, New York ; (1) and (2) : o.p. ; (3), (Wayfarer's Lib.), Dent, 1917.]
—— *Leila* (Leila, 1910). 1911
A companion novel to *The Saint*. The Saint's influence works powerfully on Massimo Alberti, who is intended
as a husband for Leila, a difficult girl who for a long while repels him. There are two main currents of
interest in the book, this study of passion and repugnance, and the analysis of Italian religion during the
later courses of the Modernist movement and of the different types of clerical character in the Church.
[Transl. by Mary PRITCHARD-AGNETTI, Hodder : o.p. ; Doran, New York : o.p.]

FOOTE, Mary [*née* Hallock ; American ; *b.* 1847]. *The Led-Horse Claim : a romance of a mining
camp.* 1883
Romance in a realistic setting—a Californian *Romeo and Juliet*, ending happily. The feud is between two
mining superintendents, and the wild and perilous life of the region gives a specific character to the story.
[Houghton, Boston ; Warne : o.p.]
—— *John Bodewin's Testimony.* 1886
Mining and civil engineering in western Arkansas. [Houghton, Boston : o.p.]
—— *The Chosen Valley.* 1892
An episode in the reclaiming of the great waste lands in the West. Two men are engaged in a vast irrigation
enterprise, one an energetic and unscrupulous promoter, the other a dour Scot, a conscientious engineer,
who puts his very soul into the work, and dies a martyr to his design. The clash of character between
these men and between their children, who become lovers, makes interesting drama. [Houghton,
Boston : o.p.]
—— *Cœur d'Alène.* 1894
The same combination of careful realism and romantic plot. Hero and heroine are brought together by the
perils and terrors of a sanguinary labour war between a mining syndicate and a union in the wild West.
[Houghton, Boston.]
—— *The Royal Americans.* 1910
An eighteenth-century story dealing with the Schuyler family and Quaker life, and extending from Montcalm's
capture of Oswego (1756) to the Revolutionary War (1757). [Houghton, Boston : o.p. ; Constable : o.p.]

FORBES, Esther [Mrs. A. C. Hoskins ; American]. *O Genteel Lady !* 1926
Literary society in Boston and Concord—Emerson, Whittier, Thoreau, Holmes, Longfellow, the Alcotts—
and in England—Tennyson and George Eliot. [Houghton, Boston ; Grosset, New York ; Heinemann.]

FORBES, Esther (*continued*). *A Mirror for Witches ; in which is reflected the Life, Machinations, and Death of Famous Doll Bilby, who with a more than feminine perversity preferred a Demon to a Mortal lover : Here is also told How and Why a Righteous and Most Awful Judgment befel her, destroying both Corporeal Body and immortal Soul.* 1928

This mimics the awe-stricken, matter-of-fact old-time relation of cases of witchcraft, the one modern touch being the occasional humour. Charmingly " embellished with 12 wood-engravings by Robert Gibbings." [Houghton, Boston ; Heinemann.]

FORBES, Lady Helen Emily [*b.* 1874]. *His Eminence : a story of the last century.* 1904

Character and intrigue in an ancient town of northern Italy, which Bonaparte was on the point of invading— an ambitious cardinal, the widowed duchess, and the Court circle (1794 *c.*–1800). [Nash : o.p.]

FORBES, Hon. Mrs. Walter R. D. [Eveline Louisa, *née* Michell ; *b.* 1866]. *Leroux.* 1908

Leroux, the Republican soldier, saves a noble's daughter from the guillotine by marrying her, and subsequently rises to the dignity of general (1783–94). Bonaparte, Barras, Masséna, etc., come on the stage, which is shifted from France to Italy, Switzerland, etc. [Greening : o.p.]

FORBES-MOSSE, Irene [German ; *b.* 1864]. *The Little Death* (Der kleine Tod). 1921

Autobiographical notes, sketches, reminiscences by a grand-daughter of Bettina von Arnim. [Transl. by Mrs. Henry HEAD, Allen.]

—— *Don Juan's Daughters* (Don Juan's Töchter, 1928) ; *together with Dream Children, and The Burden.* 1930

Three playful, poetical stories, ranging from pathos to comedy. [Transl. by Miss Oakley WILLIAMS, with introd. by Vernon Lee, Lane.]

—— *Katinka* (Kathinka Plüsch, 1929). 1930

The world of a little German town in the latter years of the great war, and after. [Transl. by Miss Oakley WILLIAMS, Lane.]

FORD, Corey [" John Riddell," ; American ; *b.* 1902]. *The John Riddell Murder Case : a Philo Vance parody.* 1930

A reviewer, tortured to death by the professional reading of best-sellers, lures the authors into his study and puts them to death : he is " brought to trial and acquitted by every jury in the country." A crude burlesque of the mannerisms of Dreiser, Sherwood Anderson, Calvin Coolidge, Richard Halliburton, Will Durrant, Beverley Nichols, etc. [*Illus.*, Scribner, New York and London.]

FORD, Ford Madox [formerly Hueffer ; *b.* 1873]. *The Fifth Queen ; and How She Came to Court.* 1906

—— *Privy Seal ; his last venture* [sequel]. 1907
—— *The Fifth Queen Crowned* [sequel]. 1908

A trilogy depicting the history of Katharine Howard and the Court of Henry VIII from 1540 to her execution. Mr. Hueffer's forte is vigorous scene-painting like Hewlett's, bustling activity rather than action in the true dramatic sense. His curt dialogue conduces to a strenuous kind of realism, resulting in a general appearance of lustful, treacherous, half-savage life—a Court with the manners of a slum. He achieves speaking likenesses—without going much into the psychology of motive—of Henry and his consort, Lord Cromwell, Cranmer, the Lady Mary, Throckmorton, Bishop Gardiner, and many other courtiers, statesmen, and nobles (1539–42). [(1) and (2), Rivers : o.p. ; (3), Nash : o.p.]

—— *An English Girl.* 1907

The impressions of a well-bred English girl on a visit to New York, her bewilderment at the spectacle of millionaire society, the plague of journalists, the blatant advertising, the vulgar standards of conduct, and the unfathomable contrast between these and European ideas. A kind of static comedy with no particular story to tell, but a number of piquant characters from both sides of the Atlantic. [Methuen : o.p.]

—— *The Half Moon : a romance of the Old World and the New.* 1909

Opens with a graphic picture of Rye in Jacobean times, and closes with the narrative of Henry Hudson's famous voyage to the West. But the real interest belongs to the story of Edward Coleman, the sailor, savagely persecuted by the machinations of a woman he had slighted. [Nash : o.p. ; Doubleday, New York : o.p.]

—— *The Portrait.* 1910

Portrays actual people, e.g. Sir Francis Dashwood and the Hell Fire Club, and other kindred characters of mid-eighteenth century. (See Johnstone's *Chrysal.*) Glimpses of prison life, Methodism, etc. [Methuen : o.p.]

—— *Ladies whose Bright Eyes.* 1911

A clever confusion of present and past—a publisher of the baser sort, a sordid exploiter of the craze for printed matter, is transformed into the personality of a Greek slave, journeying from Palestine in 1326, and witnessing vivid scenes of life in the days of chivalry. [Constable.]

—— *Mr. Fleight.* 1913

Satizes corruption in politics, and modern journalism. A Jewish millionaire endeavours to realize his ambition of succeeding in political life. Aided by a friend who contributes cynical but practical advice, he buys a magazine, sits for Parliament, and contracts a profitable marriage. [Latimer : o.p.]

—— *The Young Lovell.* 1913

A Border romance of the period 1485–6, introducing Bishop Sherwood of Durham and others. [Chatto : o.p.]

—— *Some Do Not* ——. 1924
—— *No More Parades* [sequel]. 1925
—— *A Man Could Stand Up* [sequel]. 1926
—— *Last Post* [sequel]. 1928

A tetralogy intended to give, in a number of impressionist scenes, a panorama of England in the years preceding

FORD, Ford Madox (*continued*).

and during the war. The central figure is Tietjens, Yorkshireman, idealist, blessed with a singularly unfaithful and revolting wife. In the second volume he is in command of a camp at the base, until her intrigues make trouble. The third deals with the armistice and the emotions of men suddenly released from the nightmare of perpetual danger, whilst the concluding volume brings us to the joys of peace, when the characters sort themselves out into civil life as best they can. [All, Boni, New York; Duckworth; (1), (2), and (3), Grosset, New York.]

—— *A Little Less than Gods.* 1928

The stirring times of the Hundred Days, the downfall of Napoleon, and the plot which secured the escape of Marshal Ney, are the historical thread with which is interwoven the tragic romance of a pair of less-exalted characters. Scenes, Corsica and Paris (1815). [Viking Press, New York; Duckworth.]

See also *sub nom.*, CONRAD, Joseph.

FORD, George. *The Larramys.* 1897

A tale of unruly passion and of a Devonshire farmer's life. [Hutchinson: o.p.]

—— *'Postle Farm.* 1899

Study of rustic Devonshire character and dialect, with some more sophisticated people thrown among the primitive folk. [Blackwood: o.p.; Dodd & Mead, New York: o.p.]

FORD, Paul Leicester [American; 1865–1902]. *The Hon. Peter Stirling, and What People Thought of Him.* 1894

The rise and progress of an ideal statesman, who in the midst of the corruption and intrigues of American politics maintains the virtues of disinterested honour, humane sympathy with all classes, and constancy to the "American idea"—Stirling's college life, professional struggles, and success as a lawyer; his first love affair, and his maturer affection for the old love's daughter. [Holt, New York (54th ed., 1929); Grosset, New York, 1930.]

—— *Janice Meredith.* 1899

A long, sentimental romance of New Jersey and New York, centring in a wonderful heroine who captivates friends and foes. The battles and other incidents of the American Revolution (*c.* 1780), and many celebrities—Washington, Major André, and English generals—are conscientiously drawn. [Dodd & Mead, New York, 1919; Constable: o.p.]

FORESTER, Cecil Scott [b. 1899]. *Payment Deferred.* 1921

A study of the demoralization of a secret murderer, haunted by the fear of discovery, and finally hanged for a crime of which he was innocent. [Lane.]

FORMONT, Maxime [French; b. 1864]. *The Child of Chance* (Le semeur, 1907). 1908

A strong, suggestive study of an abnormal case, that of a woman forbidden to marry, who deliberately and without passion realizes the mission of woman—maternity. [Lane: o.p.]

FORREST, Charles E. *All Fools Together: a bucolic history.* 1925

Family feuds and intrigues between a skinflint miller and his son, in the rural Essex of the early nineteenth century. [Collins: o.p.]

FORREST, R. E. *Eight Days.* 1891

The Eight Days of the escape from Delhi; historically correct. Contains a portrait of General Nicholson. [Smith & Elder: o.p.]

—— *The Bond of Blood.* 1896

Founded entirely on the writer's acquaintance with the customs and feelings of the Rajputs. Embodies a motive quite foreign to European ideas: a man's life is pledged for his master's debt, and he brings down a curse on the defaulter's head by slaying his own mother as an expiatory victim. [Unwin: o.p.]

—— *The Sword of Azrael: a chronicle of the Great Mutiny, by John Hayman, Major-General.* 1903

Adventures of an English officer escaping from among the revolted Sepoys. [Methuen: o.p.]

FORSTER, Edward Morgan [b. 1879]. *Where Angels fear to Tread.* 1905

A young widow, from the irreproachable Sawston, falls in love with an ineligible Italian at Monteriano, and marries him; whence there is trouble for her respectable mother-in-law and family over the custody of the posthumous child. The people who spend their lives in making little sacrifices for objects they don't care for, to please people they don't love, who never learn to be sincere or to enjoy themselves, are pungently contrasted with the happy-go-lucky Italian's *joie-de-vivre*. [Arnold; Knopf, New York; Garden City Co., New York.]

—— *The Longest Journey.* 1907

A typical intellectualist novel, consisting rather of criticism of life than of anything resembling life; the characters, "clever people," are points of doctrine, not human beings. The title is from the famous lines on dull monogamy in *Epipsychidion*; and the subject, personal relations in general, is in its particularity the marriage of a young intellectual and a philistine. Trouble arises from the existence of an illegitimate brother, whom they try to ignore, one from "sexual snobbery," the other from more sordid motives. Good satire of a big grammar school trying to be an Eton or Harrow. [Arnold; Knopf, New York.]

—— *A Room with a View.* 1908

The conflict between grundyism and timidity, in alliance with masculine egotism and arrogance, and the instinct for freedom, is fought out in a Florence *pensione* and on the neighbouring hills. A lover whom all would approve carries off his Andromeda from the claws of the dragon, who is simply Meredith's Egoist writ small. But it is noticeable that the girl's revolt is unconscious—Samuel Butler and the psycho-analysts have contributed to the new treatment of the motives that work in the dark. [Arnold; Knopf, New York.]

—— *Howard's End.* 1910

The permanent contrast between the two worlds, that in which personality grows and the other where it is suppressed, is exposed in the contacts of two sensitive modern girls and the successful Wilcoxes—the life of the mind and soul, and the practical, money-making life, "that which has made Britain what it

FORSTER, Edward Morgan (*continued*).

is." The Schlegels come into closer relations with the Wilcoxes through a most unlikely series of events ; but at least they learn, " How dare Schlegels despise Wilcoxes, when it takes all sorts to make a world ? " [Arnold ; Knopf, New York ; Garden City Co., New York.]

—— *The Celestial Omnibus ; and other stories.* 1911

Pretty fancies, with just a pinch of realism, the injunction " Cherish your dreams " giving them a common purport. Hence the humour as well as the deeper symbolism of Pan frightening a picnic-party on an Italian hillside, of the bus running daily to Elysium, the faun making friends with a bored curate, and the " other kingdom " discovered in the park of a highly decorous gentleman in Herts. [Sidgwick ; Knopf, New York.]

—— *A Passage to India.* 1924

Various persons essay to make the passage from West to East, but the twain cannot be made to meet. " The world . . . is a globe of men who are trying to reach one another and can best do so by the help of good will plus culture and intelligence " ; but the English official classes in India are shown resisting real intercourse through ineradicable prejudice and snobbishness, or making farcical and futile pretences at bridging the gulf. The mother and the betrothed of a hidebound chief magistrate, and a cultivated intelligent Asiatic, become involved in a great trial in court, which would have been magnificent comedy had it been made clear what did in fact take place in the Marabar caves. [Arnold ; Harcourt, New York ; Grosset, New York.]

—— *The Eternal Moment ; and other stories.* 1928

Eight tales, among them the exquisite *Story of a Siren.* [Sidgwick ; Harcourt, New York.]

FORSTER, Robert Henry [1867–1923]. *In Steel and Leather.* 1904

Northumberland and Yorkshire during the Wars of the Roses, the siege of Dunstanborough and the battle of Sedgeley Moor (1461–5). [Long : o.p.]

—— *Strained Allegiance.* 1905

Adventures among the Jacobites in Northumberland ; local colour very good. The hero is a Whig and loves a fair Jacobite (1715). [Long : o.p.]

—— *The Arrow of the North.* 1906

Northumberland and the Border in the reigns of Henry VII–VIII. The adventurous career of an Englishman from his youth up. Siege of Norham Castle (1497), battle of Flodden (1513). Praised for excellence of the historical geography. [Long : o.p.]

—— *A Jacobite Admiral.* 1908

Northumberland and the Jacobites in 1714. [Long : o.p.]

—— *Harry of Athol.* 1909

Warkworth Castle and Hotspur, the Scots at Hamildon Hill, Mortimer and Glendower at Bramham Moor (1402–8). [Long : o.p.]

—— *Midsummer Morn.* 1911

A Tynedale romance of Border raids in the closing sixteenth century. [Long : o.p.]

—— *The Little Maister.* 1913

Jacobites on the coast of Northumberland and Prince Charley at Carlisle (1745). [Long : o.p.]

FORTESCUE, Sir John William [b. 1859]. *The Drummer's Coat.* 1899

Exmoor, the Peninsular War and Corunna in 1808–9. A story that seems to have been written for children, but is worth anybody's reading as a study of child-life, soldiers, and animals. [Macmillan.]

FOSTER, Catherine and Florence. *A Reel of No. 8 ; and, Suddaby Fewster. By " Flit and Ko."* 1897

Two Holderness stories, very largely in dialect. [Brown, Hull : o.p.]

—— *The Goblin.* 1900

A somewhat formless story, a medley of dialogue, episodes of child-life and character-sketches. The " Goblin " and his friends are diverting children, while the grown-up people look like caricatures from life. The domestic manners and the scenery of Holderness are sketched with intimate local knowledge. [Wells Gardner : o.p.]

FOTHERGILL, Jessie [1851–91]. *Aldyth.* 1876

A girl refuses, from a sense of duty to her younger sisters, to emigrate with her lover, and ten years later is treacherously supplanted by one of them. A very old-fashioned domestic story of the trials that purify character. [Macmillan : o.p.]

—— *The First Violin.* 1877

A sympathetic picture of German musical life, the hero being leader of an orchestra in Düsseldorf. [Macmillan ; Brentano, New York ; Burt, New York ; McKay, New York.]

—— *Probation.* 1880

A story of the Lancashire cotton famine of 1863, setting forth on the one side the distress of the poor operatives, and on the other the loves of a wealthy girl, a hot champion of women's rights, and a clever man who engages her energies and enthusiasms in really useful work. [Macmillan : o.p. ; Fenno, New York : o.p.]

—— *Kith and Kin.* 1881

Like the foregoing, a good example of the novel suited for family reading. The hero is the grandson of a wealthy squire, disinherited and earning his living as a clerk. His grandsire learns accidentally the true position of the young man, whom he had supposed to be in comfortable circumstances. This is the starting-point of the plot. [Macmillan : o.p. ; Burt, New York : o.p.]

—— *From Moor Isles.* 1888

A small group of characters, male and female ; Brian, a study of the artistic temperament, in which the author always shows especial interest, the impulsive Inez, and the fine-natured daughter of the people, Alice Ormerod, with her devotion and unreciprocated love. [Macmillan : o.p. ; Holt, New York : o.p.]

FOULKE, William Dudley [American ; *b.* 1848]. *Maya : a story of Yucatan.*   1900
A romance of sixteenth-century adventure, based on explorations among the ruined cities of Yucatan, and utilizing legendary history, including an account of an early Spanish adventurer who saw the old Maya civilization of Yucatan. [Putnam, New York and London : o.p. With *Songs of Eventide*, and *Heloise*, Bobbs-Merrill, Indianapolis, 1928.]

FOUQUÉ, Friedrich Heinrich Karl, Baron de la Motte [German ; 1777–1843]. *Undine* (1811).   1818
One of the most beautiful of modern imitations of the primitive folk-tale. Based on a legend from Paracelsus. A water-nymph by marrying a mortal gains a soul, but with it all the pains and penalties that are the lot of mortality. Fouqué manages to invoke the haunting sense of mysterious beauty and dread that overwhelms one in listening to Schubert's folk-songs. [Transl. with illustrations by J. Tenniel, 1845 : o.p. ; transl. by E. Gosse, Lawrence & Bullen, 1896 : o.p. ; adapted by W. L. Courtney, *illus.* by A. Rackham, Heinemann (Doubleday, New York), 1909 ; other transl., Simpkin ; Putnam, New York ; Houghton, Boston. With *Sintram*, Tauchnitz, Leipzig (Low) : o.p.]

—— *Aslauga's Knight* (Aslauga's Ritter).   1827
Aslauga, the daughter of Sigurd and Brynhild, is mentioned in the *Volsunga Saga*. The good knight Froda, inspired by the accounts of her beauty and nobility which he has read in ancient books, devotes himself to her service, and she endues him with irresistible prowess. The earthly love-story of Froda, Edwald, and Hildegardis, and the supernatural matters, are combined with the same delicate and unconscious art. [Transl. by Carlyle (German Romance, q.v.) ; (with *Undine*) *illus.* by Gordon Browne, with introd. by Charlotte M. Yonge, Gardner, 1896 : o.p. ; see also *Sintram, infra*.]

—— *Sintram and his Companions* (Sintram und seine Gefahrten, 1820)   1820
A poetical apologue of human life suggested by Dürer's famous picture of Death and the Devil, and invested with Fouqué's characteristic atmosphere of weird fantasy. Several other minor tales have also been translated in the last century. [Transl. by Julius Hare, 1820 : o.p. ; by A. C. Farquharson, Methuen : o.p. Other transl., Constable : o.p. ; Putnam, New York ; (with *Aslauga's Knight*, Temple Classics for Young People), Dent (Dutton, New York) : o.p. ; with *Undine, illus.* by Gordon Browne, Stokes, New York, 1909).]

FOURE SONNES OF AYMON, *The Right Pleasaunt and Goodly Historie of the ; Englisht from the French by William Caxton, and printed by him about* 1489.
From a prose romance entitled *Les Quatre Filz Aymon*, or *Renaud de Montauban*, one of the most widely translated of the Charlemagne romances. This was a free rendering of an ancient *chanson de geste*, of which the earliest extant text belongs to the twelfth century. Local memories of the redoubtable Renaud (he was sixteen feet high), and of his horse Bayard, are current still in the Ardennes. Aymon was one of Charlemagne's dukes. His sons revolt from the emperor and set all the French chivalry at defiance, repelling the greatest paladins from their strongholds, and defeating them in the field. Renaud ventures to Paris and wins a horse-race on Bayard against Roland himself. Their cousin Maugis carries off Charlemagne by enchantment. At last Renaud goes to the Holy Land, performs miracles of valour against the Saracens, and returns to work as a common labourer at Cologne, where he dies, and is reverenced as a martyr. Aymon is a fine example of feudal loyalty ; Charlemagne appears as a cruel tyrant, openly flouted by the powerful barons—a symptom of the decadence of monarchical power at the time of the composition of the poem. Roland, Oliver, Turpin, Ogier the Dane, and Naymes play their part in this long romance (600 pages), which in Caxton's version was one of the English " popular novels " of Tudor days. [Edited, with introd., by Octavia Richardson (Early English Text Soc.), 2 vols., Oxford Press, 1884–5 ; *Renaud de Montauban :* first done into English by William Caxton and now abridged and retransl. by Robert Steele, G. Allen, 1897 : o.p. This is a popular adaptation.]

FOURNIER, Alain [French ; 1886–1914]. *The Wanderer* (Le grand Meaulnes, 1913).   1928
A strangely fascinating story told in an artless way by a crony of the boy-hero. The crony is a schoolmaster's son, and the inside and outside of a French school in the Sologne are depicted from a lad's point of view. Through the same wondering eyes, also, we see the Wanderer, and are thrilled by the epic of his four days' escape from school, the romantic awakening in the old château, and the haunting quest for his love. Though related in matter-of-fact terms, it reads like a poetic allegory of unattainable ideals. It is said to be a transposition of Fournier's own pathetic love-story. [Transl. by François Delisle, Constable ; Houghton, Boston ; Macmillan, Toronto.]

FOWLER, Ellen Thorneycroft [Hon. Mrs. Alfred Laurence Felkin ; *b.* 1860]. *Concerning Isabel Carnaby.*   1898
The good things in Miss Fowler's books are the table-talk of humble people, who have nothing to do with the smart society furnishing the chief stage figures. The humours of a Methodist household contrasted with the showy frivolity of London society. Isabel, the society girl, loves a Methodist tutor, but her arrogance leads to a rupture, which is made up, however, when he fathers a scandalous novel written by her. [Hodder : o.p. ; Appleton, New York.]

—— *A Double Thread.*   1899
A story of flashy worldlings and dull provincials, very like the last in its bright dialogue and too abundant repartee and epigram : everybody without exception is given to the manufacture of sayings. A soldier has love affairs with two girls, one poor, the other rich, who in the *dénouement* prove to be the same person ! [Hutchinson : o.p. ; Appleton, New York.]

—— *The Farringdons.*   1900
The humours of Methodist society again brought into piquant juxtaposition with the fashionable world ; the story comparatively unimportant, except as a framework for the sketches and caricatures of people and manners. The Methodist heroine is the centre of interest, but such figures as Mrs. Hankey and Mrs. Bateson are more characteristic. Their small-talk on religion and providence, and on more frivolous subjects, bubbles over with smartness and epigram. Locality, the Black Country (Silverhampton is the writer's own Wolverhampton). [Hutchinson : o.p. ; Appleton, New York : o.p.]

FOWLER, Ellen Thorneycroft (*continued*). *In Subjection.* 1906

Isabel Carnaby's married life in happy subjection to Paul Seaton, her distinguished husband, and the love affairs of an Anglo-Indian girl who retains instincts inherited from Hindu forefathers ; with some plot business. [Hutchinson : o.p. ; Dodd & Mead, New York : o.p.]

FOX, John William, Junior [American ; 1862–1919]. *A Cumberland Vendetta ; and other stories.* 1896

Stories of the savage mountaineers of Kentucky. *A Mountain Europa* is a good example of the way rather violent romance is invested with local colour. A lovely but quite uneducated maid of the hill-country is beloved and won by a man from New York, and shot by her drunken father on her wedding-day. [Scribner, New York : o.p.]

—— *The Kentuckians.* 1898

An episode in the political annals of Kentucky. Two orators are rivals ; one champions the turbulent, homicidal mountaineers of the Cumberland range, the other represents the " Blue Grass " landowners. Their political feud merges into rivalry in love, and ends in a contest of magnanimity. [*Illus.* Scribner, New York, 1909.]

—— *The Little Shepherd of Kingdom Come.* 1903

The early part—life in the Kentucky mountains, among settlers and hunters—is wholly delightful, if a little too sentimental. The psychological interest begins with the Civil War, when the young hero, like his native State, is torn asunder by his sympathies with either side. The Confederate cavalry general, Morgan, is a prominent figure. [Scribner, New York ; Constable : o.p.]

—— *Crittenden : a Kentucky story of love and war.* 1905

The Cuban war—good scenes of fighting. A Kentuckian finds his patriotism towards the Union flag aroused by a foreign war. [Scribner, New York, 1920 ; Constable : o.p.]

—— *The Trail of the Lonesome Pine.* 1908

A tale of the lawless early days of Kentucky and the Virginia border, family feuds, illicit distilling, land booming, prospecting for minerals, love, hate, and revenge. [Scribner, New York ; Constable : o.p.]

—— *The Heart of the Hills.* 1913

A lusty tale of blood-feuds, murder, politics, and romance, in the hill country of Kentucky. [*Illus.*, Scribner, New York.]

—— *Erskine Dale, Pioneer.* 1920

The War of Independence in Virginia and Kentucky (1774–84). Mainly a story of adventures with the redskins. [Scribner, New York ; Hodder : o.p.]

FOX, Marion. *The Seven Nights.* 1910

Scenes, Brittany and Kent in the days of Wat Tyler's rising (1381). The stage is set with more regard for the realities of life, and the story of the knight-errant's quest, the wrath of the peasantry, and the final tragedy is told with more insight into character and the motives that agitated men in those times, than in the average historical romance. [Stock : o.p.]

—— *The Hand of the North.* 1910

London in 1601, Hexham, and the Border are the successive scenes. Brings in the Earl of Essex's plot and the Earl of Southampton. [Lane : o.p.]

—— *The Bountiful Hour.* 1912

Cowper and John Newton at Olney, and Chelsea in the times of the Methodists and of the Prince Regent. [Lane.]

" FRANCE, Anatole " [Jacques Anatole Thibaut ; French ; 1844–1924]. *Jocaste ; and, The Famished Cat* (Jocaste, 1879 ; and, Le chat maigre, 1879). 1912

In his first work of fiction published, the novelette *Jocaste*, Anatole France told a somewhat fantastic story that skirts melodrama. A wife who suspected that her husband was being poisoned but was too timid to interfere, persuades herself that she is answerable for his death, and commits suicide. The hard-headed doctor who loves her, but whose rôle it is to look on, evidently stands for Anatole himself. The Chat Maigre is an eating-house in the Latin quarter, frequented by coloured people and disreputable writers and artists. The rather sketchy story is about a young mulatto from Haiti, who wastes his time painting and falling in love, when his father has sent him to Europe to pass his baccalaureate. A general trait of these amusing characters is that they act first and think afterwards, if they ever think at all. [Transl. by Mrs. Agnes FARLEY.]

—— *The Crime of Sylvestre Bonnard* (Le crime de Sylvestre Bonnard, 1881). 1891

Bonnard is a genial old savant, gourmand, and sentimentalist, who lives by himself among his books, sees a few visitors, and indulges his philosophic humours. Affection for the daughter of his old love induces him to become her guardian ; and the crime consists in his capturing her by a ruse. (In the revised version of 1903, Jeanne becomes the granddaughter instead of the daughter of Clémentine.) The tender cynicism of the old epicurean is mild and inoffensive, when compared with the wicked mockery of things spiritual in later works. It is Anatole France in his most amiable mood ; full of curious learning, worldly wise but not too hard-headed, writing prose the wit and grace of which are sheer seduction. [Transl. by Lafcadio HEARN.]

—— *The Aspirations of Jean Servien* (Les désirs de Jean Servien, 1882). 1912

Written 1872 and considerably revised before publication in 1882 ; his first analytical work (see preface to the first ed.). A young Parisian of the artisan class, whose intellectual ambitions are thwarted by circumstances, and whose dreams and idealisms end in disillusionment and his sentimental aspirations in disappointment, joins up in 1870–71, and is shot during the Commune. His story embodies reminiscences of the author's early life and mental development, and well illustrates the sceptical philosophy which he had at that epoch imbibed from Renan. [Transl. by Alfred R. ALLINSON.]

—— *My Friend's Book* (Le livre de mon ami, 1885). 1913

There is little of Anatole's cynicism or delight in naughtiness in these episodes, dialogues, and dreams in the

" FRANCE, Anatole " (*continued*).

lives of two children ; rather he dwells with fond delight on the surviving memories of his own infancy. The book falls into two halves : the history of the delightful Pierre up to sixteen, and the childhood of Pierre's fascinating little daughter Suzanne. [Transl. by J. Lewis MAY.]

—— *Balthasar* (1889). **1909**

A medley of early Christian and hagiographical and modern themes. *Balthasar* is an unfamiliar version of the Bible tale of the Magi. This and *l'étui de nacre* and *le puits de Sainte-Claire* are collections of stories written for the most part as vehicles of ideas ; they convey by suggestion or inversion or irony Anatole's sceptical attitude to accepted doctrines and his own easy-going epicurean philosophy of life. [Transl. by Mrs. John Lane.] *Honey-Bee*, a long story for " old-fashioned children," has been issued separately also. [Lane, 1911.]

—— *Thaïs* (Thaïs, 1890). **1909**

A story of ancient Alexandria and the Thebaid that challenges comparison with Flaubert's *Tentation de St. Antoine*, but falls short in certainty of aim and consistency. Philosophers and courtesans, voluptuaries and anchorites, are contemplated in the light of a sceptical Parisian's philosophy, and depicted with irony and a curious double-edged banter—what has been called his " satanism " is perhaps excessive. A debauchee turned eremite essays the perilous errand of converting the courtesan Thaïs, the light o' love of his unregenerate days. He succeeds ; but the image of carnal beauty haunts him in his cell and drives him from salvation. [Transl. by R. B. DOUGLAS.]

—— *Mother of Pearl* (L'étui de nacre, 1892). **1908**

Sixteen short stories and sketches of an equally miscellaneous kind, religious, hagiographical—in the ironical way of Anatole France—and frankly modern. The famous *Procurator of Judæa* is among them, and also the not less characteristic—though its tender humanism is such a contrast to the sardonic story of Pilate— *Our Lady's Juggler*. Poorly translated. [Transl. by A. ALLINSON, ed. by Frederic CHAPMAN.]

—— *At the Sign of the Queen Pédauque* (La rôtisserie de la reine Pédauque, 1893). **1910**

The conversations and adventures—amorous, bacchanalian, and other—of the motley frequenters of an eating-house in early eighteenth-century Paris. Foremost in interest among these strange creatures is the Abbé Coignard, a monk of abandoned habits, childlike disposition, and powerful intellect : this Rabelaisian figure is a humorous representation of the author himself and of his libertarian creed. Anatole France dug his style out of the old monkish books, and his inimitable irony thereby acquired a richer savour. [Transl. by Mrs. Wilfred JACKSON ; also by J. A. V. STRITZKO, Gibbings, 1910 : o.p. ; re-issued, with introd. by J. B. Cabell, Modern Lib., New York, 1923.]

—— *The Opinions of Jérôme Coignard* (Les opinions de Jérôme Coignard, 1893). **1913**

In the discourses and ruminations of the genial and humorous Abbé Coignard, so charming a figure in *La rôtisserie de la reine Pédauque*, the author pretty frankly expounds a philosophy that is simply negative, and makes merry at the expense of revolutionaries and conservatives, rationalists and Catholics, philosophers and scientists alike, concluding, " I have no illusions about men, and rather than hate them I despise them." Jules Lemaître called this " the most thoroughgoing breviary of scepticism that has appeared since Montaigne." [Transl. by Mrs. Wilfred JACKSON.]

—— *The Red Lily* (Le lys rouge, 1894). **1908**

Physical enjoyment is the mainspring of life in this story of an emotional, self-indulgent Frenchwoman's liaisons with two men, the second of whom she loves with passion. Apart from the felicity of its style, the book is peculiarly interesting for its portraits : the bohemian poet Choulette is a composite, chiefly of Verlaine ; the sculptor Dechartre is France himself (Paul Vence, the essayist, is put there as a blind) ; Miss Bell is Mary Robinson. [Transl. by Winifred STEPHENS.]

—— *The Garden of Epicurus* (Le jardin d'Épicure, 1894). **1908**

Little essays, sketches, anecdotes, aphorisms as luminous as Joubert's, and other miscellaneous items from magazines and journals—various facets of the author's urbane personality and wiser and sadder thought. The crowning treasure of the book is *How I Discoursed one night with an Apparition on the first Origin of the Alphabet*, an imaginative survey of history, in which dry old facts and legends are endowed with a new life by the sheer irradiation of common sense. The translations are correct enough in this series, but rarely give any sense of the exquisite felicity and delicacy of the original. [Transl. by Alfred ALLINSON.]

—— *The Well of Saint-Clare ; and other stories* (Le puits de Sainte-Claire, 1895). **1908**

A kind of ecclesiastical and hagiographical *Decameron* ; supposedly stories in the Tuscan dialect told by an old priest, who believed in God on the evidence of Holy Scripture and in accordance with the teachings of the Church, and laughed at those simple philosophers who believed in Him on their own account without being under any obligation to do so. The original is notable for the perfection of its prose style. [Transl. by A. ALLINSON.]

—— *The Wickerwork Woman* (Le mannequin d'osier, 1897). **1910**

Here too the satire is covert and restrained, but none the less murderous in effect. M. Bergeret—a projection of himself less fanciful and less sentimentalized than his Sylvestre Bonnard—and others are found discoursing on current politics, literature, philosophy, life. [Transl. by M. P. WILLCOCKS.]

—— *The Elm-Tree on the Mall : a chronicle of our own times* (L'orme du mail, 1897). **1910**

First of the series *L'histoire contemporaine*, comprising also *Le mannequin d'osier*, *L'anneau d'amethyste*, and *M. Bergeret à Paris*, in which France, who had sided with Zola in the *Affaire*, lets fly at the anti-Dreyfusards in general, and their allies, clericals, anti-Semites, and the " Black Party " of reactionaries, monarchists, and bellicose nationalists. In this apparently harmless piece, a set of old cronies in a provincial town chat together about all manner of things—people, society, and politics. [Transl. by M. P. WILLCOCKS.]

—— *The Amethyst Ring* (L'anneau d'amethyste, 1899). **1919**

Proceeds with the general vivisection of French society and politics during the *Affaire*. The placid pagan philosopher M. Bergeret is the one figure of real dignity beside the shallow bigots, raving anti-Dreyfusards, and the sordid intriguers and adulterers, whose whole scheming has for its final achievement the elevation

" FRANCE, Anatole " (*continued*).

of a nincompoop to an episcopal see. Considerable allowance must be made for the author's polemical bias : his cardinal-archbishops, heads of seminaries, professors of theology, are systematically overdrawn. On the other hand, in the amiable M. Bergeret, it is to himself and his party that he is too kind. [Transl. by B. DRILLIEN.]

—— *Pierre Nozière* (1899).   1916

The life of Pierre and his impressions of the universe form a characteristic medley of fiction and discursive musings on all sorts of topics, from " the Scriptures and the Zoological Gardens " to " The Origin of Creeds," " The Function of Intellect," and " The Birth of Superstition." Pierre Nozière's travels in France yield yet more of the author's profane learning on the history and legends of the Church. Five tales told by Mme Nozière to Pierre are omitted here, appearing in *The Merrie Tales of Jacques Tournebroche.* [Transl. by J. Lewis MAY.]

—— *A Mummer's Tale* (Histoire comique, 1903).   1921

A beautiful actress loves a young diplomat ; but, whenever she is about to give herself to him, the spirit of a former lover, who had blown his own brains out, rises threateningly. The main story is ostensibly that of her triumphs at the Odéon and the Théâtre Français, the real interest being artfully put in the side-show. The genial cynic Dr. Trublet is a fellow to the Abbé Coignard. [Transl. by C. G. ROCHE.]

—— *Crainquebille, Putois, Riquette, and other profitable tales* (Crainquebille, Putois, Riquet, et autres récits, 1904).   1915

Sixteen of his deservedly best-known stories, very well translated from the point of view of style. " *Crainquebille* is the *Candide* of Anatole France," says Victor Giraud. The eponymous here is the Paris coster who falls a victim to the blind operation of the constabulary and judicial machine. *Putois* is an extravagant extension of the Mrs. Harris motive—the Bergerets create him so circumstantially that no one doubts his existence. [Transl. by Winifred STEPHENS.]

—— *The White Stone* (Sur la pierre blanche, 1905).   1909

A Socratic discussion on the present and the future of mankind, by a party of intellectuals met in the Forum of Rome. The author's critical and sceptical mind traverses the course of history, reviews the Yellow Peril and the White Peril—to the Yellow races—and perceiving a fatalistic movement in the tendency of things prophesies a new order in which capitalism and national government will have yielded to the advance of Socialism. [Transl. by C. E. ROCHE.]

—— *The Merrie Tales of Jacques Tournebroche ; and, Child Life in Town and Country* (Les contes de Jacques Tournebroche ; Filles et garçons—Nos enfants, 1908).   1909

Jérôme Coignard, Jacques's revered master, reappears in one of these stories in an adventure as fine as any in *La reine Pédauque.* Charlemagne and his paladins, the Dominican friars, and other primitive figures from the dark ages and the Renaissance, perform in characteristic rôles, to which the modern chronicler gives an ironical import. [Transl. by A. ALLINSON.]

—— *Penguin Island* (L'île des pingouins, 1908).   1909

An ironical history of the human race—past, present, and future—in the annals of the Penguins, a nation of birds which were accidentally baptized in mistake for men. More cynical, though less morose, than Swift's *Gulliver,* and not less wholesale in its mockery. In a style parodied from some hagiographical legend, it describes the unfortunate blunder of the aged saint who evangelized the Penguins ; and wild burlesque is carried down through the ages, until, in still distant cataclysms, over-civilization comes to wreck. Pessimism was never expressed in more daring persiflage. The satire of French history is of more limited interest, and the elaborate ridicule of the Dreyfus case rather a bore. [Transl. by A. W. EVANS.]

—— *The Gods are Athirst* (Les dieux ont soif, 1912).   1913

This essays to reinterpret the history of the Terror, from the fall of the Girondists to the overthrow of Robespierre, through a story of the Commune in which the actors are not mere historical figures, nor mere representatives of party or of political ideals, but human beings with an urgent private life of their own. Among them, Brotteaux des Ilettes and the painter Gamelin and his mistress stand out memorably. [Transl. by Alfred ALLINSON.]

—— *The Revolt of the Angels* (La révolte des anges, 1914).   1914

The guardian angels in Paris throw up their job, and joining hands with the seraphim, cherubim, and lower orders of the fallen host prepare a modern scientific campaign against Jahveh. The love affairs and general goings on, troubles with the police, and disturbances of various households, are all very funny. A magnificent caricature of an old-fashioned librarian is the subject of some uproarious episodes. In the original this displays Anatole's ironic style at its wittiest, and the maxims and the survey of human history are memorable. [Transl. by Mrs. Wilfrid JACKSON.]

[*Works,* 45 vols., complete, ed. by Frederic Chapman and James Lewis May (translators as shown above), Lane ; also *illus.* and cheap eds. of several, *id.* Uniform ed., 31 vols., Dodd & Mead, New York ; also other eds., *id.*]

" FRANCIS, M. E." [Mrs. Francis Blundell, *née* Sweetman ; Irish ; *d.* 1930]. *In a North Country Village.*   1893

Sketches and actual episodes of agricultural life in Lancashire, reported by a lady of the parish, who has a keen eye for unvarnished human nature. [Harper : o.p. ; Little & Brown, Boston : o.p.]

—— *The Story of Dan.*   1894

An Irish tale, brief and tragic, of a magnanimous peasant, infatuated with a worthless girl, for whom he sacrifices himself blindly and uselessly. [Harper : o.p. ; Houghton, Boston : o.p.]

—— *Maime o' the Corner.*   1897

A touching tale of Lancashire and Liverpool ; theme, self-renunciation among the poor and lowly. [Harper : o.p.]

—— *Yeoman Fleetwood.*   1900

Country life in southern Lancashire (1815–20). A yeoman of faultless character loves a girl who is above him

"FRANCIS, M. E." (*continued*).

in social rank, and who has captivated George, Prince of Wales, at Brighton. Glimpses of Mrs. Fitzherbert, Beau Brummell, and the dissolute prince. [Longmans : o.p.]

—— *Pastorals of Dorset.*　　1901

Characteristic stories of Dorset folk, with an eye chiefly for the pleasant side of local peculiarities, and more affinity to the poet Barnes than to the pessimist Hardy. Brings out finely the feelings of the people at home during the South African War. [Longmans : o.p.]

—— *Fiander's Widow.*　　1901

Fiander was an elderly farmer, whose charming young widow woos his old friend when she finds she cannot manage the farm. Makes humorous capital of the self-interest, the conservatism, and the cunning of the Dorset rustic. [Longmans : o.p.]

—— *North, South, and Over the Sea.*　　1902

Fifteen short stories of humble life in Lancashire, Dorset, and Ireland, e.g. *The Girl he left behind him* and *Blackbird's Inspiration.* [*Illus.*, Newnes : o.p.]

—— *The Manor Farm.*　　1902

A farm-house comedy in Dorset—the humours and contrariness of two farmers and their womenfolk, with a love affair that puts things straight. [Longmans : o.p.]

—— *Lychgate Hall.*　　1904

Lychgate Hall is a haunted old mansion at Great Crosby, near Liverpool. The author is at her best in describing homely old country people. [Longmans : o.p. ; *id.*, New York.]

—— *Dorset Dear : idylls of country life.*　　1905

Unaffected simplicity and sincerity are the characteristics of these stories. *Postman Chris*, a pretty tale of a rustic wooing, and perhaps the best, *Keeper Guppy*, with some telling character-sketches, are worth sampling. [Longmans : o.p. ; *id.*, New York.]

—— *Wild Wheat : a Dorset romance.*　　1905

Another country tale, with an attractive heroine ; the poorer country-folk especially are well delineated. [Longmans : o.p. ; *id.*, New York.]

—— *Simple Annals.*　　1906

Stories portraying the simple joys and sorrows of working-women. [Longmans.]

—— *Stepping Westward.*　　1907

Miscellaneous tales of the same humble folk ; e.g. *Lwonesome Lizzie* and *Our Brother's Burdens.* *Lady Lucy* is historical. [Methuen : o.p.]

—— *Galatea of the Wheatfield.*　　1909

A Dorset story of a gentleman lover and a peasant maid. [Methuen : o.p.]

—— *Noblesse Oblige.*　　1909

French refugees in a Berkeley Square mansion, time of French Revolution (1794). [Long : o.p.]

—— *The Wild Heart.*　　1910

A tragic tale of a poacher with a passionate instinct for nature ; his unpremeditated crime and disastrous love. [Smith & Elder : o.p.]

—— *Gentleman Roger.*　　1911

Roger turns labouring man and weds a farmer's daughter. [Sands : o.p.]

—— *The Story of Mary Dunne.*　　1913

The poignant story of a charming Irish girl who becomes the prey of the traffickers in "White Slaves." [Murray ; Longmans, New York.]

"FRANCIS, M. E." and **BLUNDELL, Margaret.** *Wood Sanctuary.*　　1930

A simple, old-fashioned story of two or three people in a Welsh village and their sentimental affairs. [Allen & Unwin.]

FRANK, Leonhard [German ; b. 1882]. *The Robber Band* (Die Räuberbande, 1920).　　1928

An account, sympathetic and often amusing, of a band of schoolboys in Munich who organize a secret society ; the main object however is to explore the adolescent mind, and offer a psychological diagnosis of the cause of their anti-social behaviour. [Transl. by Cyrus T. BROOKS, Cape, New York ; Davies.]

—— *The Cause of the Crime* (Die Ursache, 1920).　　1928

Freudian psychology applied as special pleading against judicial punishment. A young fellow has murdered his former schoolmaster in a sudden fit of rage, provoked by the recollection of punishments inflicted in the past ; the defence, which he elaborates in the Court, is that not he, but the victim himself, is really the guilty party, for the true cause is a psychological complex established in him by the master in his schooldays, and this is the normal and inevitable consequence. [Davies.]

—— *A Middle-Class Man* (Der Bürger, 1924).　　1930

Herr Frank here incarnates his impassioned sympathy for the poor and oppressed in a young man who sacrifices a promising career to face the hardships and obloquy of a socialist agitator. But the devoted hero harks back to respectability, and, much to the reader's surprise, achieves remarkable success as a banker. Then a sense of dereliction maddens him, and after a breakdown he goes off on a wild journey through Europe—a fantastic episode symbolical of the quest for the ego. [Transl. by Cyrus BROOKS, Davies.]

—— *Carl and Anna* (Karl und Anna, 1927).　　1929

A tale of two German prisoners on the Russian steppe, idealizing a common war incident. Richard talks so much about his wife that Carl falls in love, contrives to escape, and poses as Anna's husband. Puzzled but not deceived, she accepts the man who knows her better than ever Richard did. Their profound, well-nigh mystical community of feeling gives a singular beauty to this episode. Then Richard comes back. [Transl. by Cyrus BROOKS, Peter Davies ; Putnam, New York.]

FRANK, Leonhard (*continued*). *Brother and Sister* (Bruder und Schwester, 1930).   1930

Two children separated by their parents' divorce, meet and fall in love and marry. The splendour of their passion and the upheaval of their souls when they discover their blood relationship are analysed with power if not with the finality demanded by such a problem. [Transl. by Cyrus BROOKS, Cape, New York; Davies.]

FRANKAU, Gilbert [*b.* 1884]. *Peter Jackson, Cigar Merchant : a romance of married life.*   1920

The story of a merchant, engrossed in his business, who is broken in the war, and, emerging from his ordeal with a spirit refined and softened by suffering, finds peace and sanity in winning the affection of his wife. [Hutchinson ; Knopf, New York.]

FRANZOS, Karl Emil [German ; 1848–1904]. *The Jews of Barnow* (Die Juden von Barnow, 1877).   1882

Pathetic stories of Jews in a Polish ghetto, with little narrative interest, capturing the reader's sympathies by the humanity, the suffering, and fortitude of these uncouth characters set amid such grim surroundings. [Munro, New York : o.p. ; transl. by M. W. MACDOWALL, Blackwood (1883) : o.p.]

—— *For the Right* (Ein Kampf ums Recht, 1882).   1887

The hero, an unlettered peasant, as village judge is inspired with an indefatigable zeal for justice, and through good and evil report strives for the right. Laid in the region of the Carpathians, giving us a view of the Slavonian country people, and of the institutions of old Austria (1835–49). [J. Clarke : o.p. ; Harper, New York : o.p.]

FRASER, Mrs. Hugh [*née* Crawford]. *The Custom of the Country ; or, Tales of New Japan.*   1899

Stories and pictures of new Japan, chiefly of an emotional character ; e.g. the title-story and the pathetic story of a foreigner's liaison with a Jap. An enthusiastic love for things Japanese pervades the book. [Hutchinson : o.p. ; Macmillan, New York : o.p.]

—— *The Stolen Emperor : a tale of Old Japan.*   1903

Of the time when the actual power was in the hands of the great feudatories. The authoress is familiar with Japan and its history. [Long : o.p.]

FRASER, Ronald. *Rose Anstey.*   1930

Three bachelor brothers in a roomy mansion in Belsize Park, a fine old housekeeper, and a captivating girl who marries the youngest, only to come to a tragic end, are the principals in this story, which is rather in the De Morgan vein. [Cape.]

FRAZER, Robert Watson [1854–1921]. *Silent Gods and Sun-steeped Lands.*   1895

Seven brief stories and sketches—an intimate and realistic presentation of native life and ideas in modern India. [Unwin : o.p. ; Stokes, New York : o.p.]

FREDERIC, Harold [American ; 1856–98]. *Seth's Brother's Wife.*   1887

Minute delineation of country life in an out-of-the-way district in New York State ; the dull routine and coarseness of farming set forth without palliation, with realistic accounts of local journalism, from editor down to compositor, and of the machinery of elections. [Scribner, New York : o.p. ; Chatto : o.p.]

—— *The Lawton Girl.*   1890

Life in a small manufacturing town, with its political, industrial, and social turmoil. [Scribner, New York ; Chatto : o.p.]

—— *In the Valley.*   1890

Episodes preceding or occurring early in the War of Independence among the Dutch of the Mohawk valley, the battle of Oriskany (1757–80), etc., supposed to be related by a Dutchman deeply prejudiced against the British cause, the whole narrative burning with racial hatred. [Scribner, New York ; Heinemann : o.p.]

—— *The Copperhead : and other stories of the North during the Civil War.*   1893

Stories bringing out the animosities and violent revenges characterizing the life of stay-at-home people during the Civil War. (In the Mohawk valley and elsewhere, a sympathizer with the South was called a " Copperhead.") [Scribner, New York : o.p. ; Heinemann : o.p.]

—— *Marséna ; and other stories.*   1894

Further stories of New York State in the wartime. Marséna, a village coquette who has the war fever, contrives to send two of her lovers to the front, where, dying on the field, they wake to the irony of their position, for she cares for neither. [Scribner, New York : o.p. ; Unwin : o.p.]

—— *Illumination.*   1896

A subjective study of character, which in America bears the significant title, *The Damnation of Theron Ware.* Theron is an earnest, zealous, and narrow young Methodist minister in a town where there are many Irish and the Roman Catholics are very active. His " illumination " is the work of a priest who teaches him that religion is an appeal to the emotions, a learned agnostic who instructs him in the Higher Criticism, and more powerfully still, of a captivating and unscrupulous girl who plays on his sensuous instincts. From narrow orthodoxy the transition is quick to doubt and unbelief. [*Sub tit. The Damnation of Theron Ware,* Duffield, New York, 1915 ; Boni, New York, 1924 ; Heinemann : o.p.]

—— *The Deserter ; and other stories.*   1898

The Adirondacks in the Civil War time ; *A Day in the Wilderness* is worth reading. [Lothrop, Boston : o.p.]

—— *Gloria Mundi.*   1898

A posthumous novel, unfinished. The character of the young Christian Tower who unexpectedly finds himself the heir of a duke is the completest thing in the book, which deals critically with English society, the feminist movement, Jewish character, etc. [Duffield, New York ; Heinemann : o.p.]

—— *The Market-Place.*   1899

A study of the methods and morals of the London stock exchange in the career of a daring and unscrupulous financier, who by a deal wins a colossal fortune, chiefly at the expense of the rogues. [Stokes, New York : o.p. ; Heinemann : o.p.]

FREEMAN, Harold Webber [*b.* 1899]. *Joseph and His Brethren.*   1928

FREEMAN, Harold Webber (*continued*). *Down in the Valley*. 1930
Quiet, slow-moving novels of country life, which render to the fertile lowlands of Suffolk a service similar to that of Miss Kaye-Smith to Sussex. [(1) and (2), Chatto ; Holt, New York ; (1), Grosset, New York.]

FREEMAN, Richard Austin [*b.* 1862]. *The Mystery of 31, New Inn*. 1912
—— *The Puzzle Lock*. 1925
Representative of a number of highly ingenious and compact detective mysteries, unravelled by a medico-legal expert who relies on scientific analysis to effect a solution. [Hodder ; Dodd & Mead, New York.]

FREMDLING, A. [Irish]. *Father Clancy*. 1904
Loosely connected pictures of the heterogeneous people and the various incidents of life in a small town in Kerry ; extraordinarily vivid and picturesque, though not always perhaps free from erroneous impressions. Father Clancy, the dominating figure, is an unselfish, unworldly parish priest, beloved of his flock, and set off by the unpleasant character of his vicious curate. Abounds in flashes of keen insight into the humours and the pathos of Irish character. [Duckworth : o.p.]

FRENCH, Allen [American ; *b.* 1870]. *The Colonials*. 1902
Adventures of a hero and heroine in the backwoods near Detroit—a study of winter life among the Indians —the " Tea-Party," the retreat from Concord, the battle of Bunker Hill, and the siege of Boston by Washington (1772–6). Anti-British. [Doubleday, New York : o.p. ; De La More Press : o.p.]

FRENSSEN, Gustav [Schleswig-Holsteiner ; *b.* 1863]. *The Three Comrades* (Die drei Getreuen, 1898). 1907
A story of life at home on the coast of Schleswig-Holstein whilst the Franco-German war was going on. [Transl. by L. Winstanley, Constable : o.p. ; Dana Estes, Boston : o.p.]

—— *Jörn Uhl* (1901). 1905
Frenssen is the novelist of Schleswig-Holstein, the country and inhabitants, the colour and atmosphere of which he portrays, not only with convincing fidelity, but with clear, calm, philosophic vision on the one hand, and on the other with a poetic imagination that makes these hard-worked toilers on the barren soil as impressive as the figures in Millet's pictures. This is his simplest and finest story, and Jörn Uhl's ill-fated efforts to save the family acres admirably enunciate his sage and wholesome philosophy of life. It may be compared with Bazin's *La terre qui meurt*, as a picture of the break-up of the old farming aristocracy ; but the moral idea is deeper, and the pathos of human life in general expressed in a more impressive and far-reaching way. The battle of Gravelotte is an episode, and the Franco-Prussian war weighs heavy in the background. [Transl. by F. S. Delmer, Constable : o.p. ; Page, Boston ; Modern Lib., New York.]

—— *Holyland* (Hilligenlei, 1906). 1906
A confused and confusing novel, describing the humble seafaring folk on the borders of the German Ocean, with the same realism, but losing the design in the details. Kai Jans in his purity and self-abnegation symbolizes Christ, a Christ blindly striving to find his heavenly Father, and to bring heaven down upon earth, but eternally baffled by the incurable defects of human nature. [Transl. by Mary Agnes Hamilton, Constable : o.p. ; Page, Boston.]

—— *Peter Moor's Journey to South-West Africa : a narrative of the German campaign* (Peter Moor's Fahrt nach Südwest, 1906). 1908
The German war of extermination against the Herreros (1904), related from the point of view of a peasant volunteer. The unspeakable horrors of warfare in the bush, the ravages of thirst, hunger, and disease among the soldiers as well as the hunted natives, and the whole monstrous absurdity of the death-struggle, in which Peter and his comrades are the blind instruments of a ruthless policy of expansion, are brought crushingly before us with all Frenssen's imaginative realism. [Transl. by Margaret May Ward, Constable : o.p. ; Houghton, Boston : o.p.]

—— *Klaus Heinrich Baas : the story of a self-made man* (1909). 1911
Tells how the son of a farm-labourer in Holstein, by dint of imagination, business energy, and endurance, wins commercial success and also the self-knowledge which Frenssen prizes so much higher. Peasant life in a village and market-town of Ditmarch, and the crowded metropolitan life of Hamburg, are presented with clear understanding of the sad realities as well as the false glamours of modern existence. [Transl. by E. E. Lape and E. F. Read, Macmillan : o.p.]

—— *The Paster of Poggsee* (Der Pastor von Poggsee, 1921). 1931
The life of a simple, honest pastor among the peasants and fisher folk of Holstein ; submerged by misfortune during the unhappy period of the war, but rising from it with renewed fervour to preach a doctrine of spiritual rejuvenation. In part no doubt autobiographical, for Frenssen, like his hero, was a minister, and the son of a carpenter. [Transl. by Katharine G. Potts, Harrap.]

—— *Otto Babendiek* (1926). 1930
A long and leisurely autobiographical story, beginning in a village on the west coast of Schleswig, then dealing with a period in Munich and Otto's first marriage, with the war on the eastern front and Otto's life as a prisoner near Petrograd, and lastly with his return to Germany and union with the old comrade of his childhood. [Transl. by Huntley Paterson, Harrap ; *sub tit. The Anvil*, Houghton, Boston.]

FREYTAG, Gustav [German ; 1816–95]. *Debit and Credit* (Soll und Haben, 1855). 1856
A realistic study of German society about 1848, illustrating the effects of the industrial revolution in making the middle class the backbone of the country. The struggle for existence is represented by a proud baron, member of an effete aristocracy, endeavouring to stave off ruin by entering into commerce, and a wholesale grocer whose mercantile enterprises are successful. There is considerable humour in the characterization. Freytag's prejudices as a native of Silesia come out strongly in the way Teutonic virtues are contrasted with the racial foibles of Jew and Slav, and Prussian claims are advanced to the hegemony of Germany. Freytag's most popular book ; it reached its hundredth edition in five years, and long came next to the Bible as a best-seller. [Ward & Lock : o.p. ; transl. by Mrs. G. Malcolm, Bentley, 1858 : o.p.]

FREYTAG, Gustav (*continued*). *The Lost Manuscript* (Die verlorene Handschrift, 1864). 1865
A study of the scholarly side of German life, the experiences of a professor at Leipzig University in his search for the lost books of Tacitus, and the inner life of the University, set forth with plenty of incident and varied character-drawing. The professor does not find the MS., but he wins an adorable maiden. Later on, however, he becomes so absorbed in his labours that he neglects his wife, who is embarrassed by the attentions of a libertine prince. [Kegan Paul: o.p.; Open Court Pub. Co., Chicago.]

—— *Our Forefathers: Ingo and Ingraben* (Die Ahnen; Ingo und Ingraben, 1872). 1873
The first of a series of romances which proposed to trace the history of a German family from the fifth-century immigration to the founding of the new German Empire, and so exhibit the permanence of the heritage from the past and its value as a factor in social evolution. Thuringia, in A.D. 357, is the scene. Ingo is a fugitive Vandal prince at the period of the great migration, who fights with the Alemanni against the Romans, and after his escape takes refuge at the Thuringian Court. Ingraban is his descendant in the time of Charlemagne (724), and comes into contact with the Christian missionaries labouring among the barbarous Slavs. [Transl. by Mrs. MALCOLM, 2 vols., Asher: o.p.; *Ingo, Ingraben*, Holt, New York: o.p. The other six stories have not been translated; they comprise: *Das Nest der Zaunkönige* (1873), *Die Brüder vom deutschen Hause* (1874), *Markus König* (1876), *Die Geschwister* (1875), and *Aus einer kleinen Stadt* (1880).]

FRITH, Henry. *Under Bayard's Banner*. [juvenile] 1893
The Chevalier de Bayard, battle of Ravenna, etc. (1512). [Cassell: o.p.]

FROUDE, James Anthony [1818–94]. *The Two Chiefs of Dunboy*. 1889
An historian's essay in fiction—an Irish tale composed of some materials used in writing his *English in Ireland*. The theatre of events is the O'Sullivan country in S.W. Cork (1750–98), and the political movements are depicted from an unsympathetic English point of view. [Longman: o.p.]

FULK FITZ WARINE. *The History of Fulk Fitz Warine, an outlawed baron in the reign of King John* (Fouke Fitz Warin, c. 1322). 1855
The French paraphrase of an Anglo-Norman *chanson de geste* composed late in the thirteenth century, traces of poetic diction being legible in the prose. Fitz Warine was a powerful baron who took arms against John, leagued himself with the Welsh, and held out successfully for many years, until he was pardoned. Based on family traditions, and true in the main, though it contains some curious inaccuracies (e.g. at least two Fitz Warines have been used up in the composition of the hero; cf. Barbour's *Bruce*), and a few of the conventional extravagances foisted in by the trouvère. Scene, principally Ludlow Castle and the Welsh border; most of the places can be identified still. As interesting, and almost as natural, as a modern novel; the historical characters forcibly sketched in, and the life and conditions of the time so well rendered that the book is of high historical value. [Ed. with transl. and notes by Thos. Wright, Warton Club, 1855: o.p.; transl. Alice Kemp-Welch, with intro. by L. Brandin (The King's Classics), Chatto, 1904: o.p. There is an excellent critical edition of the French text, ed. by L. Brandin (*Les Classiques français du moyen age*), Champion, Paris, 1930.]

FULLER, Anna [American; 1853–1916]. *Pratt Portraits: sketched in a New England suburb*. 1892
—— *Later Pratt Portraits: sketched in a New England suburb*. 1911
Brief character-sketches, with little in the way of incident. The members of the Pratt family are racy individuals, especially Aunt Betsy and Old Lady Pratt. [(1), Putnam, New York; (2), Putnam, New York and London: o.p.]

FULLER, Henry Blake ["Stanton Page"; American; 1857–1929]. *The Chevalier of Pensieri-Vani; together with frequent references to the prorege of Procopia*. 1891
The Chevalier is a poor but discerning art enthusiast; and other connoisseurs, Italian, German, French, and American, make up the tale of characters. Pisa, Orvieto, Rome, Ravenna, Venice, and Florence are described, with their buildings, pictures, statues, antiquities, and, above all, their *cognoscenti*, in a singularly humorous, fanciful, and vivacious narrative. [Century Co., New York: o.p.]

—— *The Châtelaine of La Trinité*. 1892
Another æsthetic pilgrimage to Europe, in much the same strain.

—— *The Cliff-Dwellers*. 1893
Portrays the dwellers in a huge, many-storied building called the "Clifton" as typical representatives of the rapid and multitudinous life of modern Chicago. The merest thread of connected narrative. Social ambitions are satirized. [Harper, New York: o.p.]

—— *With the Procession*. 1895
Another Chicago novel, the ordinary incidents of business and social life serving to illustrate the differences of character in a small group of people, the different ways in which they work out their destinies, and the varying results of wealth and social success on character. [Harper, New York: o.p.]

—— *From the Other Side*. 1898
—— *Under the Skylights*. 1901
—— *Waldo Trench, and Others*. 1908
Short stories of Chicago or of American tourists in Europe, mostly expressive of the author's personal artistic and archæological interests. [(1), Houghton, Boston: o.p.; (2), Appleton, New York: o.p.; (3), Scribner, New York: o.p.]

—— *On the Stairs*. 1918
Something of a self-portrait. Memoirs of a Chicago gentleman, an amateur, but no more, of art, who is unable to reconcile himself to the fierce life of the place. [Houghton, Boston.]

—— *Not on the Screen*. 1930
How a provincial young fellow gets his social education in New York from a girl of old family, and eventually, in spite of the treacherous manœuvres of an enemy, happily marries her. The real interest of the book is in the quiet satire of the writer's fellow-countrymen. [Knopf, New York and London.]

FULTON, David Kerr. *The Witch's Sword.* 1908
>A stirring tale of the times after Flodden (1513), full of moving incident hingeing on a double resemblance, the hero's father being supposed to have died on the battlefield instead of King James, of whom he was the very counterpart. [Arnold : o.p.]

"FUTABATEI" [Taksunosuke Hasegawa ; Japanese ; *d.* 1909]. *An Adopted Husband* (Sono Omokage). 1919
>Russian realism was evidently the inspirer of this novel of Tokio and of a professor's affair with the natural sister of his formidable wife ; but the prettiness and charm of things Japanese redeem it from any ugliness. [Transl. by Buhachiro MITSIU and Gregg M. SINCLAIR, Knopf, New York ; Hutchinson.]

GALE, Zona [Mrs. W. L. Breeze ; American ; *b.* 1874]. *Friendship Village.* 1908
>Stories giving a picture of village life in the Middle West that has been compared with *Cranford.* An earlier novel, *The Loves of Pelleas and Etarre* (1907), was a similar mixture of sentiment and humour. [Macmillan, New York and London : o.p.]

—— *Friendship Village Love Stories.* 1909
—— *Neighbourhood Stories.* 1914
—— *Peace in Friendship Village.* 1919
>More of the same sort about the same delectable retreat. [(1), (2), and (3), Macmillan, New York.]

—— *Miss Lulu Bett.* 1920
>The idyllic atmosphere of the village (the site is shifted and it is now called Warbleton, but it remains outwardly the same) is here shattered. Miss Gale has grown out of her sentimentalism and learned the uses of irony, which gives a new significance to the drudging and down-trodden Lulu, with her clearing vision of the inane, affected, pompous, overbearing creatures that these people really are. [Appleton, New York and London.]

GALLET, Louis [French]. *Captain Satan* (Le capitaine Satan, 1899). 1900
>Adventures of Cyrano de Bergerac in the early part of Louis XIV's reign. [Jarrold : o.p. ; *sub tit. Adventures de Cyrano de Bergerac*, Fenno, New York : o.p.]

GALLI DE BIBIÉNA, Jean [French ; 1709 ?–79 ?]. *The Fairy Doll* (La poupée, 1744). 1925
>Something of a prose counterpart to Pope's *Rape of the Lock* ; depicts the same manners and society, though here Paris replaces London, and lascivious abbés the gallants of the Court. The doll is a sylph, whose earthly mission is to cure abbés of their foppery ; she enters the household of one destined for her work of redemption, and relates the history of a lover's humiliation at the hands of his mistress, contrived by her ; not forgetting to add a lesson on the methods of address whereby the female heart may be softened. Her wit, elegance, and beauty, coupled with her mastery of polite usages, turn her victim from a fop to a slave. [Transl. by H. B. V., with introd. by Shane Leslie, Chapman ; McBride, New York.]

GALLON, Tom [1866–1914]. *The Rogue in Love.* 1900
>A good example of this author's imitations of the sentimental melodrama and humorous drawing of character from low life, of which Dickens is the great exponent. The rogue is an inmate of Wormwood Scrubs gaol, who acts the good fairy to a queer old waiter's innocent daughter, falls in love, and is changed into an honest man. [Hutchinson : o.p.]

—— *The Golden Thread.* 1904
>Deals in the same way with low life and people of the vulgar stockbroker class. [Nash : o.p.]

—— *Peplow's Paper-Chase.* 1904
>A dying father tells his son to study the daily papers, which are more conducive to happiness than is generally believed. The resulting adventures are amusingly fantastic. [Hutchinson : o.p.]

—— *Memory Corner.* 1912
—— *Levity Hicks.* 1913
—— *Young Eve and Old Adam.* 1913
>Further novels of a light and pleasant kind. [(1), (2), and (3), Long : o.p.]

—— *It Will Be All Right.* 1914
>An art-dealer arranges a pretended suicide ; his subsequent efforts to regain his identity and estate provide a lively story. [Hutchinson : o.p.]

GALSWORTHY, John [" John Sinjohn " ; *b.* 1867]. *From the Four Winds.* 1897
—— *A Man of Devon.* 1901
>Sets of stories, afterwards rearranged in *Caravan* (1925).

—— *Villa Rubein ; and other stories.* 1900
>The first (1900) deals with the emotional life of two wedded lovers, who are artists to the core, a Tyrolese painter, born a peasant, and his English wife ; and portrays the people and the scenery of Tyrol. Republished with stories more characteristic of his later development—*A Man of Devon* (1901), *A Knight, The Salvation of a Forsyte*, and *The Silence*—in 1909 ; afterwards rearranged in *Caravan* (1925).

—— *The Island Pharisees.* 1904
>A biased and not very effective criticism of English society, institutions, and the prevailing national character, intended to reveal the mental forces that make for acceptance of things as they are by the ninety and nine, and revolt by the hundredth man, the strong in himself, the true idealist. Shelton " is surely not the hundredth Pharisee," and his journey " is but a ragged effort to present the working of the truth, ' All things that are, are wrong,' upon the truth, ' All things that are, are right,' " so says the preface. [Putnam, New York.]

—— *The Man of Property.* 1906
>An exposure of the emptiness and blind egotism of a certain stratum of society, the comfortable moneyed class, demoralized by idleness and lack of imagination—a duller and, if possible, a more useless section

GALSWORTHY, John (*continued*).

than the butterflies of smart society. Several generations of the Forsytes are taken as the epitome of this class; their solid and highly respectable but humdrum existence passes before the eyes, and the aimlessness of it is brought into sharp relief by the development of a love drama between two very different people who have been drawn into relations with the Forsytes by circumstances. Later embodied in *The Forsyte Saga*.

—— *The Country House.* 1907
The Pendyce family represents the squirearchy as the Forsytes represented the propertied classes in town. The landed proprietor, and the whole system of which he is the keystone, are anatomized here with the same thoroughness; and the inmost springs of character are disclosed in a drama of passion at strife with the institution of marriage. One character, Mrs. Pendyce, is drawn with rare subtlety—a tender and beautiful portrait of an English lady.

—— *A Commentary.* 1908
Twenty sketches of English characters, typical of every grade from the street hawker to the man of fashion, and all pointed to bring out the indifference of the upper classes to the wrongs of the poor; afterwards rearranged in *Caravan* (1925).

—— *Fraternity.* 1909
Brings into juxtaposition the highly cultivated, fastidious, hothouse existence of a set of upper-middle-class people in Kensington, and the distressing facts of life in the neighbouring slums. The emotional situation, how a weak literary man becomes involved with a girl who has been a model, is analysed so as to display the significance of social relations, prejudices, and feelings, and show how a slight alteration of attitude in one person may react through complex ways and set up unheard-of vibrations in our sensitive society. Artistically, Mr. Galsworthy succeeds better here probably than in any other of his longer works.

—— *A Motley.* 1910
Twenty-eight stories showing almost as many different aspects of human circumstance and social condition at the present day. Criticism is implied in each—indignant criticism in most—but the author leaves the moral to his reader. *The Prisoner* is a poignant exposure of the inhumanity of imprisonment; *Apotheosis* and *The Japanese Prince* are amusing satires of the man of routine; *Courage* and *Compensation* represent foreigners—not with the knowledge and cogency with which low life at home is sketched in *Once More* and *For Ever*. There is real poetry in *A Parting* and *The Meeting*. These stories were rearranged in *Caravan* (1925).

—— *The Patrician.* 1911
Caste feeling is here seen at odds with individuality and passion. The Patrician is an idealist whose admirable schemes for the government of his country all but come to grief through his love for a woman separated from her husband. His sister, too, saves herself just in time from social catastrophe by not accepting the quixotic adventurer whom she loves. The drama is worked out with much analysis of the inner struggle of principle—or sense of social responsibility—and feeling. A novel showing Mr. Galsworthy's wonted sympathy, knowledge, and insight, and his judicial detachment.

—— *The Dark Flower.* 1913
The dark flower is passion—a madness that impels to breaches of the marriage contract, of friendship, and even of reputation. A man with a charm for women that is hardly made intelligible has successive affairs which are figuratively described as Spring, Summer, and Autumn, and settles down after middle-age to what is presumably Winter, bidding farewell to the dark-red flower and remaining soberly true to the wife of his bosom.

—— *The Freelands.* 1915
A novel of the same class as *The Man of Property* and *The Country House*, in which a landed family provide the characters, and the landless toilers the problem—that of our present inequalities and injustices. Three stable brothers and one of revolutionary tendencies are drawn as much for polemical reasons as for artistic, and their womenfolk, much more pleasingly, for their own sake.

—— *Beyond.* 1917
Mainly the life of a highly temperamental woman, love-child of an army officer, and her curiously impulsive affairs. In the things that matter, she always goes "beyond" other people. Depicts, apparently without any satirical motive, characters and manners curiously devoid of any fundamental seriousness or fineness of morals.

—— *Saint's Progress.* 1919
The recalcitrant daughter of a clergyman who cannot see the world as it is, has a war-baby.

—— *Tatterdemalion.* 1920
An unequal collection of tales and sketches written in war-time, most if not all included in *Caravan*.

—— *The Forsyte Saga.* 1922
The Man of Property is here combined with its sequels, *In Chancery* (1920) and *To Let* (1921), the chronicle being formally equipped with a family tree, the whole book to be further supplied with sequels continuing the record into the fourth generation. In these memoirs of one large ramifying family, the history of the upper middle-classes since the accession of Victoria is written down, as it appears to Mr. Galsworthy's social vision, and brought into its proper perspective as one principal phase of social development or social decadence. It is his largest and most representative book. The various sequels to *The Forsyte Saga* are assembled in *A Modern Comedy: the second part of the Forsyte Chronicles, including The White Monkey, The Silver Spoon, and Swan Song, and two interludes*, 1929.

—— *The White Monkey.* 1924
The title refers to a painting, said to convey the warning, "Eat the fruits of life, scatter the seeds, and get copped doing it." This is the story of a very risky marriage between love and disappointment, the ardent Michael Mont and Fleur, one of the Forsytes.

—— *Caravan: the assembled tales of John Galsworthy.* 1925
Fifty-six pieces, written 1900–23, from previous collections. The author's object having always been to

GALSWORTHY, John (*continued*).

exhibit a society and the types of people who compose it, many of these belong to the established English genus entitled " charactery " by the seventeenth-century followers of Theophrastus. Forsytes or their like make divers appearances. Thus the first, *Salvation of a Forsyte*, records the one flash of romance in the safe and humdrum career of one of that breed.

—— *Two Forsyte Interludes.* 1927

Jon Forsyte, in the Southern States, meets and woos an American girl : this is the idyllic first interlude. The other is staged at Washington, where Soames Forsyte and Jon's mother, ancient foes, are brought again into contact.

—— *Swan Song.* 1928

A further addendum to the *Saga*, dealing with Fleur's insatiate passion for Jon and its tragic consequences, and with the death of Soames. The general strike of 1926 comes into the story. In these sequels, Mr. Galsworthy seems less pleased with the post-Victorian generation and its manners than he was even with their fathers and grandparents.

—— *On Forsyte 'Change.* 1930

Some twenty stories of the Forsytes at various dates from 1821 to 1918. Good examples are *Hester's Little Tour*, *Aunt Juley's Courtship, Midsummer Madness*, and *Cry of Peacock*.

[*Works*: Grove Ed., 21 vols.; Popular Ed., 18 vols., Uniform Ed., 17 vols., Heinemann; Scribner, New York. *The Forsyte Saga, A Modern Comedy*, and *Caravan*, 3 vols. each, also 1 vol. each, *id.* ; an edition of the Novels in 21 vols. is also published by Harrap.]

GALT, John [Scottish ; 1779–1839]. *The Ayrshire Legatees.* 1821

Galt may be described as the earliest Kailyard novelist, if the honour is not more justly Scott's, on the strength of his faithful and humorous pictures of lowland character and racy representation of dialect. This novel, modelled on the great classic of epistolary humour, *Humphry Clinker*, tells how the Pringle family went to London, saw the " lions," and what they thought about the proceedings on George III's death, and the divorce of Queen Caroline. Displays the same keen relish of mother-wit and goodness, and the same detailed painting of personality as *The Annals* (written earlier, published later). [*Vide* also *Annals of the Parish, infra.*]

—— *The Annals of the Parish.* 1821

An attempt to rival *The Vicar of Wakefield* : pictures the characters of an Ayrshire village (1760–1810), from the minister downwards, with raciness, humour, and pathos ; in the form of a journal by the village minister, a kindly old man, whose three wives are drawn at full length. Contains a touching story of an old widow, whose husband is drowned, and who by heroic efforts brings up her family well. Smollett's influence is visible in such vitriolic portraiture as the death-scene of the blaspheming Cayenne. The American War and its effects, smuggling, the invasion of utilitarianism and philosophic radicalism, come in for discussion and anecdote. [(Everyman's Lib.), Dent (Dutton, New York), 1910 ; with *The Ayrshire Legatees*, with introduction by G. S. Gordon, Oxford Press, 1908. *Illus.* by C. E. Brock, Macmillan ; *v.* also *infra*.]

—— *The Provost.* 1822

The Annals, so to speak, in another edition, by a magistrate who chronicles half a century of life in a Galloway township. He is a shrewd and observant Scot, but less reflective and narrower in outlook than the minister. The cases that come before him, the careers of local unfortunates, village politics, and the jobbery which affords him his little pickings, are his favourite texts. Coleridge praised the book, pointing out how admirably " Selfness is united with a *Slyness* and a plausibility eminently successful in cheating the man himself into a happy state of constant self-applause." (*Times Literary Supplement*, Sept. 30, 1930.) [*v. infra.*]

—— *Sir Andrew Wylie of that Ilk.* 1822

A novel of broader humour, not free from coarseness, with a witty character in Sir Andrew. (Lord Sandford is a sketch of Lord Blessington.) [*v. infra.*]

—— *The Entail : or, The Lairds of Grippy.* 1823

Contains one of the author's most humorous characters, Leddy Grippy, an inimitable Scotswoman. Coleridge regarded this and *The Provost* as Galt's finest work. [World's Classics, Oxford Press, 1913 ; *v.* also *infra*.]

—— *Ringan Gilhaize.* 1823

An attempt to emulate Scott's *Old Mortality* : a story of the Covenanters and the battle of Killiecrankie. [*v. infra.*]

—— *The Last of the Lairds.* 1826

Here Galt paints in his humorous way an old-fashioned set of people, grouped round a decayed, ignorant, and empty-headed old laird. Many of them are well endowed with racy individuality ; but a certain talkative and meddlesome Scotswoman is the masterpiece. [Each work, ed. by S. R. Crockett, D. S. Meldrum, and W. Roughead, Grant, Edinburgh, 1928.]

GARBORG, Arne [Norwegian ; 1851–1924]. *Peace* (Fred, 1892). 1929

Garborg's first book, *Trætte mænd* (1891) was a severe indictment of the shallow agnosticism in favour at that time, repugnant to a genuine freethinker like himself. This is an exposure of " narrow pietistic Christianity." It is an exceedingly gloomy study of a man, a peasant, formerly a schoolmaster, in Garborg's native Jæren, who makes terms with God, and then fears that this self-regarding religion is really a pact with the Devil. Fear develops into mania, bringing disaster on the individual and his family. The book is largely autobiographical. [Transl. by William D. CARLETON, American-Scandinavian Foundation, Norton, New York ; Allen & Unwin.]

—— *The Lost Father* (Den burtkomne faderen, 1899). 1920

Contains much of Garborg's ripest wisdom. Gunnar, the emigrant brother of Paul Hove in *Peace*, comes back disillusioned, and Paul teaches him how to find happiness in old age. The book is full of fine sayings. The right question we should ask ourselves is, How shall I get a meaning into *my* life ? Values, in Garborg's philosophy, evidently derive from the principle of developing personality to the utmost. [Transl. by Mabel Johnson LELAND, Stratford, Boston.]

GARDNER, Edmund Garratt [*b.* 1869]. *Desiderio.* 1902
A story of love and hate in the warlike times of that redoubtable Pope, Julius II ; the opulent and luxurious life of the cities, intrigues in Court and Church. Desiderio is of the Arvirardi, Dukes of Cittanova. Professor Gardner is a recognized Italian scholar. [Dent : o.p.]

GARLAND, Hamlin [American ; *b.* 1860]. *Main-Travelled Roads : six stories of the Mississippi valley.* 1891
—— *Prairie Folks.* 1892
Two sets of stories picturing, with sober realism and compelling sincerity, the dull, hopeless, overburdened life of the Western farmer and his hands, the homespun style, aiming at no literary graces, strengthening the picture. Born on a Wisconsin farm, Mr. Garland went with his father to Iowa and then to Dakota, missed ordinary schooling, and as a boy had to work like a man, as he relates in his autobiographical volumes, *Boy Life on the Prairie* (1899), *A Son of the Middle Border* (1917), and *A Daughter of the Middle Border* (1921), and the semi-historical studies, *Trail-Makers of the Middle Border* (1926) and *Back Trailers from the Middle Border* (1928). [(1), Harper, New York ; (2), *id.* : o.p.]

—— *A Little Norsk ; or, Ol' Pap's Flaxen.* 1892
Depicts the same hard life in frankly realistic fashion, animated by fierce indignation against the hard lot of the Western farmer. [Appleton, New York : o.p.]

—— *Jason Edwards : an average man.* 1892
The squalid side of Boston. Edwards is an unfortunate artisan with a cultivated daughter, whose journalist sweetheart comes to the rescue when they meet with more troubles as settlers in Dakota. [Thacker & Co. : o.p.]

—— *A Member of the Third House.* 1892
Another essay in political fiction. [o.p.]

—— *A Spoil of Office : a story of the modern West.* 1892
The history of a Western farm hand who rises to be a member of the national legislature at Washington. The early part is a realistic account of his struggle to educate himself, and of local politics. The latter part is controversial, denouncing the corruption of existing parties, and advocating the Populist programme. [Rev. ed., 1897, Appleton, New York : o.p.]

—— *Rose of Dutcher's Coolly.* 1896
Chicago life, painted with the same quiet, stern, forcible realism, " sombre veracity," as it has been pithily called : a presentment that is also an arraignment. Mr. Garland is, or was, a disciple of Henry George. Transparently honest, he is out to denounce oppression and enlist support for a programme of economic and social reform. These earlier stories, however, stand much higher artistically than those in which he has not been content to work upon his recollections of the grim struggle for life on the prairie farms but sought to show up corrupt politics or to exploit his material for the purposes of ordinary sentimental and romantic fiction. [Harper, New York.]

—— *The Eagle's Heart.* 1900
Life on the prairie among cowboys and blacklegs : the career of a gallant, impetuous boy, whose loyalty steers him through many obstacles. [Harper, New York ; Heinemann : o.p.]

—— *Her Mountain Lover.* 1901
Deserts realism for more conventional, commercial fiction. A picturesque and shrewd, but rough and ignorant cowboy from Colorado comes to London to sell a gold mine, and there has sentimental experiences with a woman novelist. His naïve criticisms of English things are amusing, the Yankeeisms repellent. [Century Co., New York ; Heinemann : o.p.]

—— *The Captain of the Gray-Horse Troop.* 1902
—— *The Light of the Star.* 1904
—— *The Tyranny of the Dark.* 1905
—— *The Long Trail.* 1907
—— *Money Magic.* 1907
—— *The Shadow World.* 1907
—— *Cavanagh, Forest-Ranger.* 1910
—— *Victor Ollnee's Discipline.* 1911
—— *The Forester's Daughter.* 1914
These are novels of the ordinary stamp having less of the force and authenticity that marked the semi-autobiographical stories enumerated above. They mingle incidents of travel, adventure, and pioneering in the Western States, the Klondike, etc., from the eighteen-sixties to the present day, with the regular stuff of fiction. [(1), (3), (4), (6), (7), (9), Harper, New York ; (2), (5), and (8) : o.p.]

—— *Hesper.* 1903
A romantic story in which the refinements of civilization and the semi-barbarous world of cowboys and gunmen are brought into vivid contrast—a pampered girl from New York is plunged into the life of the ranges and mining camps. [Harper, New York.]

—— *The Moccasin Ranch : a story of Dakota.* 1909
A story, with considerable dramatic force in it, of a settler, his wife, and one or two others, on the Dakota prairie in 1883, when the virgin soil was being taken up by the immigrants. The struggles and trials of the squatters, the wild, hard life of the plains, and the physical and moral effect on the men and women plunged into it, are depicted. [Harper, New York : o.p.]

—— *Other Main-Travelled Roads.* 1910
A later instalment of the stories reminiscent of Mr. Garland's early experiences of prairie life. [Harper, New York.]

—— *They of the High Trails.* 1915
Sketches of vanishing Western types ; the chapter headings, *The Grub-Staker, The Trail Tramp, The Outlaw,* etc., indicating their nature. [Harper, New York.]

GARNETT, David [*b.* 1892]. *Lady into Fox.* 1922
Recounts with quiet, Defoe-like realism, how a woman was transformed into a fox, and the embarrassing results. [Chatto; Knopf, New York; *v.* also *infra.*]

—— *A Man in the Zoo.* 1924
Another experiment in fantasy: the account of a man who voluntarily becomes an exhibit in the Zoo. [Chatto; Knopf, New York; with *Lady into Fox*, Doubleday, New York.]

—— *The Sailor's Return.* 1925
A sailor comes back to England in 1858, and settles in a Dorsetshire inn appropriately named "The Sailor's Return"; bringing with him his wife Tulip, a negress who in her own land was a king's daughter. The efforts of Tulip, a gentle and child-like creature, to please her husband, the tragedy of their child's death, and the bitter hostility of the neighbours, which results, after the sailor's death, in her becoming the drudge of the inn of which she had been mistress, make a pathetic story whose power is enhanced by the quiet matter-of-fact manner of its telling. [Chatto; (Phœnix Lib.), *id.*; Knopf, New York; Garden City Co., New York.]

—— *Go She Must!* 1927
A rehandling of the not uncommon theme of a clergyman's daughter who breaks away from dull surroundings and finds a husband in the bohemian artistic world of Paris. [Chatto; Knopf, New York; Garden City Co., New York.]

—— *No Love.* 1929
After the two freak books, returns to the usual type of novel. This belongs to the Butler group of scientific studies, and also has something of the Zolaesque *roman expérimental*, a touch of the laboratory case. A wife whose husband has gone to the war is thrown with his old friend, and they become lovers. But she returns to her husband, only to run away again. What is wrong with a man who cannot get on with wife or friend? Want of love is the fault in his disposition—so it is concluded. [Chatto; Knopf, New York.]

GARNETT, Olive. *Petersburg Tales.* 1900
Four analytical studies of Russian social conditions and the emotional undercurrents of life in that country: essays in the manner of Henry James and Turgenev. *Ronkoff* illustrates the evils of bureaucratic institutions; *Vetrova* is a record of a terrible political punishment and the impression it made on various individuals and the public. [Heinemann: o.p.; Houghton, Boston: o.p.]

—— *In Russia's Night.* 1918
Gives a good picture of Russian life, in a country mansion and in Petersburg, in the period 1904 to 1905, ending with the revolution of that year. [Collins: o.p.]

GARNETT, Richard [1835–1906]. *The Twilight of the Gods; and other tales.* 1888
The title story is a witty travesty of the Prometheus legend, the titan being released from durance when the Christian mob ejects the pagan gods. Some two dozen shorter stories are of the same sardonic trend; the close-knit construction, the parsimony of effect, and the strong, masculine style, being quite after the classic model. [New and augmented edn., Lane, 1906; Dodd & Mead, New York; with *Other Tales*, introd. by T. E. Lawrence, Knopf, New York, 1926.]

GARNETT, Mrs. Robert Singleton [*née* Roscoe; *b.* 1869]. *The Infamous John Friend.* 1909
A very realistic character-study of a man in the days of the Regency, who is a spy in the French pay when Bonaparte's invasion is expected, but in private life a good and affectionate husband. [(Traveller's Lib.), Cape; Holt, New York: o.p.]

GARSHIN, Vsévolod Mikhailovich [Russian; 1855–88]. *Stories* (1878–87). 1893
Sketches and stories by a young writer of abnormal sensitiveness and unbalanced genius, who saw intensely and analysed deeply, and in his pity for suffering humanity and his longing for beauty was sometimes carried away by a lyrical emotionalism beyond the limits of prose fiction. The pictures of the Russo-Turkish war of 1877, in which Garshin served till he was wounded, are vivid and poignant. *Four Days* (see below) is a fearful indictment of war. Most terrible of all, and perhaps unique as a record of mental disease by one who has suffered, is the story of his own insanity. [Transl. by E. L. Voynich, Unwin; Knopf, New York.]

—— *The Signal; and other stories.* 1915
Grim studies of sensitive minds trying to adjust themselves to the terrible realities of existence. Grimmest, perhaps, is *Four Days*, the experiences of a soldier lying disabled on the battlefield. *Nadjeja Nicolaievna* is the life of a prostitute recounted in her own words. [Transl. by Rowland Smith, Duckworth: o.p.; Knopf, New York.]

GARSTIN, Crosbie Alfred Norman [1887–1930]. *The Owl's House.* 1923
—— *High Noon* [sequel]. 1925
—— *The West Wind* [sequel]. 1926
A romance of adventure among gipsies, smugglers, slavers, privateers, and other lawless characters, at the end of the eighteenth and the beginning of the next century, ranging from Cornwall to Morocco and the West Indies. [All Heinemann; Stokes, New York; Burt, New York.]

—— *China Seas.* 1930
An eventful voyage from Singapore to Hong-Kong, with a typhoon on the way that serves to show what the officers and passengers are made of, episodes of piracy, and love business between an English captain and a Chinese girl. Such figures as Gaskell, Mackail, and Olga Vollberg are hastily but appetizingly sketched. [Chatto.]

GĄSIOROWSKI, Waclaw [Polish]. *Napoleon's Love Story* (1903). 1905
A somewhat heavy historical study of Warsaw life and European politics rather than a novel (1806–12). Madame Walewska's self-abandonment to Napoleon for her country's sake. A novel, says the *Speaker*, "that cannot be neglected by students of Napoleonic literature." [Transl. by Count S. C. de Soissons. Duckworth: o.p.]

GASKELL, Lady Catherine Milnes. *Old Shropshire Life.* 1904
> Tales and legends of Much Wenlock and neighbouring halls and villages, from the beginning to the end of the eighteenth century, told in a homely style well suited to young people. Illustrated with beautiful photographs of the actual places. [Lane : o.p.]

GASKELL, Elizabeth Cleghorn [*née* Stephenson ; 1810–65]. *Mary Barton ; and other stories.* 1848
> An early attempt to depict the very poor sympathetically, and to study their social problems from a human standpoint. A tragic story of factory-hands in Manchester, the cardinal incident a murder with which Mary's lover is wrongly charged. Reveals the workings of motive and conscience, and draws some beautiful types of intrinsic nobility and fortitude. *Cousin Phyllis* is an affecting love story, set in pastoral surroundings. *My French Master* is a touching portrayal of an *émigré*, whose politeness and refined nobility realize the old ideals of his order. Written during 1845–7. [(Everyman's Lib.), Dent (Dutton, New York), 1912 ; v. also *infra*.]

—— *Ruth ; and other tales.* 1853
> A seduced girl by a pious fraud brings up her child honourably, but afterwards suffers for the deceit and brings retribution on the minister who assisted her. A controversial book, one of the first to claim the same standard of purity for men and women. *Mr. Harrison's Confessions* is a humorous sketch of a spinster-ridden township, in the style of *Cranford* ; the scene, Duncombe, is the same Knutsford. In this set of stories, industrial conditions in Lancashire are treated with far more truth and sympathy than by Dickens in *Hard Times* (1854). [v. *infra*.]

—— *Cranford ; and other tales.* 1853
> By far the finest of her novels, and worthy to stand with the *Vicar of Wakefield* and the works of Jane Austen. Dainty miniature-painting, of a little old-fashioned, peaceful country town (Knutsford, in Cheshire, where the author spent her early days), inhabited by widows and elderly spinsters living in genteel poverty. A finely graduated series of characters, rich in feminine whimsies and foibles ; with humorous descriptions of bygone etiquette, tea-drinkings, and gossip, and several episodes that appeal to the heart. Captain Brown and Miss Matty are two of her sweetest characters. *The Moorland Cottage* is a touching story, in which Edward and Maggie Brown play the part to be enacted by Tom and Maggie Tulliver (in *The Mill on the Floss*) and in which also there are a pair of weak and fretful mothers ; and *The Crooked Branch*, a dark and almost incredible tragedy : how a beloved son goes astray, and at length becomes so abandoned that he robs his aged parents. [(Everyman's Lib.), Dent (Dutton, New York), 1908 ; *illus.* by C. E. Brock, *id.*, 1926 ; Methuen ; Routledge ; Bell (Harcourt, New York) ; Houghton, Boston.]

—— *Lizzie Leigh ; and other tales.* 1854
> The title-piece is a short novel condensed into a short story : the idyll of Will and Susan in sharp contrast with Lizzie's disasters. *Lady Ludlow*, a more leisurely character-portrait, has something of Jane Austen's synthesis of humour and beauty. This feudal lady, compact of prejudice and wisdom, shrewdness and obstinacy, kindliness and affection and aristocratic hauteur, is one of Mrs. Gaskell's finest creations. In *A Dark Night's Work*, she appears clearly as a precursor of George Eliot : this is a condensed novel dealing with an unpremeditated and hushed-up crime, and the long-delayed nemesis. As usual with Mrs. Gaskell, humorous stories alternate with sad ones. [v. *infra*.]

—— *North and South.* 1855
> Another study of the labour question, on a broader scale than *Mary Barton*, from the standpoint of a just and philanthropic manufacturer, who marries the heroine. Pleads for more human relations between employers and employed, just as Charles Reade does in *Put Yourself in his Place* (1870), and aptly contrasts the temperament and spirit of the north and the south, the country of the great manufacturers and that of the landed proprietors. [(Everyman's Lib.), Dent (Dutton, New York), 1912 ; v. also *infra*.]

—— *Sylvia's Lovers.* 1863
> Written after the Cotton Famine of 1862–3, of which the final chapters are particularly reminiscent. Theme, the mistakes and disappointments of love and wedlock. The sufferings of whale-fishers and other humble folk of old Whitby (Monkshaven) during the French wars (1797–1800), and their indignation at the cruelties of impressment, deepen the pathetic feeling. St. Sepulchre is the Hospital of Holy Cross, near Winchester. [(Everyman's Lib.), Dent (Dutton, New York), 1911 ; Routledge ; v. also *infra*.]

—— *Wives and Daughters.* 1866
> Left unfinished, and completed by the writer's daughter. Goes deeply into motive and the growth of character ; the issues just the natural issues of ordinary life, and the characters shown in all the complexity and diversity that the ordinary characters of real life exhibit ; e.g. Molly, a loyal and sunny-natured girl, and the second Mrs. Gibson, a subtly insincere and egotistic woman. Like *Cranford*, has Knutsford for scene.
[Editions of Mrs. Gaskell's *Works* : Knutsford ed., 7 vols., Murray ; Putnam, New York. In 10 vols. (including *Essays*, etc.), with introd. by Clement Shorter, Oxford Press (World's Classics), 1906–15.]

GAULOT, Paul [French ; *b.* 1852]. *The Red Shirts : a tale of the Terror* (Les chemises rouges, 1893). 1894
> Deals with the Terror and the famous Batz Conspiracy (1793–4). [Transl. by J. A. J. DE VILLIERS, Brentano, New York (Collins).]

GAUNT, Mary (Elizabeth Bakewell) [Mrs. Hubert Lindsey Miller ; Australian ; *b.* 1872]. *Dave's Sweetheart.* 1894
> Story of life in an Australian police camp. [2 vols., Arnold ; o.p.]

—— *Deadman's : an Australian story.* 1898
> A tale of modern bush life, and an analysis of the mental effects of the vast solitudes on the mind of an educated man. [Methuen : o.p. ; New Amsterdam Book Co., New York ; o.p.]

—— *A Wind from the Wilderness.* 1919
> Adventures in China and Tibet ; the hero a self-possessed young doctor who attaches herself to an American mission in Yang Cheng, whence the party have to make their escape from rioters. [Laurie : o.p.]

GAUNT, Mary (Elizabeth Bakewell) *(continued).* *The Surrender; and other happenings.* 1920

Eleven short stories of the war and other subjects, e.g. *The Surrender* and *Captain Pettifer and the U Boats.* *The Temple of the Great Beneficence* and *White Wolf* are about risings in China. [Laurie: o.p.]

—— *Joan of the Pilchard.* 1930

Opens in this country, in the days of the press-gangs, takes us on the voyage that ended in the mutiny of the *Bounty*, and then to Australia. Bligh is well drawn. [Benn.]

GAUTIER, Judith [French; daughter of Théophile Gautier; 1846–1917]. *The Imperial Dragon.* 1928

A romance of Old China : the story of a young peasant-boy who heads a revolt, and his companions, a poet and a girl. [Transl. by M. H. BOURCHIER, Brentano, New York and London.]

GAUTIER, Théophile [French; 1811–72]. *Mademoiselle de Maupin* (1835). 1893

A free glorification of the sensuous side of love, unrestrained and even monotonous in its repetition of erotic scenes, redeemed only by the writer's devotion to the cult of beauty and by his magnificent prose, though he was not uninfluenced by the joy of flouting bourgeois philistinism. [Transl. by Burton RASCOE, Knopf, London and New York, 1925 ; by G. F. MONKSHOOD, Brentano, New York (Collins) ; transl. by VIZETELLY, *illus.*, Washburne, New York, 1929.]

—— *The Romance of a Mummy* (Le roman de la momie, 1858). 1886

An Egyptian story of the time of the plagues and of the flight of the Israelites through the Red Sea, with brilliant descriptions of arts, manners, customs, and buildings, embodying recent archæological discoveries. [Transl. by M. YOUNG, 1886 : o.p. ; with *The Quartette*, Harrap, 1901 : o.p. ; by Augusta McC. WRIGHT, Lippincott, Philadelphia.]

—— *Captain Fracasse* (Le capitaine Fracasse, 1863). 1897

Reconstitutes the life and manners of the time of Louis XIII (1610–43), the costumes, customs, and castles of the nobility, the streets of Poitiers, Paris, and other cities, with vivid realistic detail. Adventures of a ruined baron, who joins a troupe of strolling players and takes the title-part in a comedy, *The Rodomontades of Captain Fracasse.* The soubrette of the band is a girl of mysterious origin, whom he loves and has to fight for with a powerful and unscrupulous young duke. The opening chapters depicting the baron's Château of Misery are a celebrated example of descriptive art ; and the fights with bravos, the abductions, the storming of a castle, and other scenes, are wonderfully picturesque and exciting. [Transl. by Ellen M. BEAN, Duckworth : o.p. ; Page, Boston ; transl. by the same, with *etchings* by Delort, 2 vols., Macqueen, 1901 : o.p. ; transl. by F. C. de SUMICHRAST, Appleton, New York, 1926 ; another transl., Brentano, New York (Collins).]

Much of Gautier's finest work seems never to have been translated. His artistic gifts shine most clearly in his stories of smaller compass, collected in *Fortunio* (1838), *Jettatura*, *La morte amoureuse*, a wonderful ghost-story, *Militona* (1847), etc. [*La morte amoureuse* was translated by Lafcadio HEARN, *sub tit. Clarimonde* (with *The Mummy's Foot* and *King Candaules*), Jack, 1908 : o.p. ; by Paul HOOKHAM, *sub tit. The Beautiful Vampire*, McBride, New York, 1927.]

GAY, Marie Françoise Sophie [*née* de la Valette ; French ; 1776–1852]. *Marie de Mancini* (1840). 1898

A novel of the time of Mazarin, Anne of Austria, Condé, etc. (1655–9). Madame Gay's best novels were *Léonie de Montbreuse* (1813) and *Anatole* (1815). [Lawrence & Bullen : o.p.]

GAYE, Phœbe Fenwick. *Vivandière.* 1929

The love-story of a camp-follower, a pathetic figure, and of a French lieutenant of noble birth, during Napoleon's campaign in Russia (1812). [Secker ; Boni, New York.]

—— *Good Sir John.* 1930

Sir John Falstaff, in a somewhat emasculated edition, is the principal character. [Secker ; Boni, New York.]

GEORGE À GREEN, *The History of George à Green, Pindar of the town of Wakefield : his Birth, Calling, Valour, and Reputation in the Country, with divers pleasant, as well as serious passages in the course of his life and fortune* (1155–94). 1706

Makes a crude sort of novel out of the traditional exploits of the doughty Pindar, or Pound-keeper, by connecting them with the Earl of Kendall's rebellion, during Richard's absence in the Holy Land. Robin Hood is introduced, and fights George à Green, to prove that Maid Marian is more beautiful than the Pindar's Beatrice. A grand fight with quarter-staves, in the town of Merry Bradfield, is described in the last chapter. [repr. in W. J. Thoms' *Early English Prose Romances*, see p. 465].

GEORGE, Walter Lionel [1882–1926]. *The City of Light.* 1912

The scene, bourgeois life in Paris ; the theme, an indictment of the supremacy of the family and the *mariage de convenance.* The French setting is genuinely achieved. [Constable : o.p. ; Brentano, New York : o.p.]

—— *The Second Blooming.* 1914

Three methods of avoiding boredom are followed by the wives of representatives of commerce, politics, and the law : to wit, domesticity, political advancement, and adultery. [Unwin ; Little & Brown, Boston.]

—— *The Making of an Englishman.* 1914

Autobiography of a Frenchman who makes up his mind to be an Englishman, and in time becomes more English than the English. He has trouble when he wants to marry an English girl. The scheme enables the novelist to criticize and compare English and French life in almost every aspect, and to be caustic on English peculiarities. [Long ; *sub tit. Little Beloved*, Little & Brown, Boston : o.p.]

—— *Olga Nazimov ; and other stories.* 1915

Contains twenty-nine sketches, mainly satirical little dramas ; some, Cockney sketches, are humorous. [Mills & Boon : o.p.]

—— *Blind Alley.* 1919

A study of England in war-time and of many of the questions raised by the war, especially those that react upon conduct. [Unwin.]

GEORGE, Walter Lionel (*continued*). *Caliban.*   1920
> The career of a newspaper magnate, from the days when he founded a school magazine, until he becomes a power in politics ; as the title implies, he and his world are vulgar and sordid materialists, in whom the sense of beauty or of things spiritual has no place. [Methuen.]

GERARD, Dorothea [Madame Longard de Longgarde ; 1855–1915]. *Orthodox.*   1888
> The chief interest of E. and D. Gerard's novels is the local colour, the peculiarities of society, manners, religion, and custom being described from observation on the spot. In this love-story of a Polish Jewess and an Austrian lieutenant—scene, a town in Austrian Poland—the manners, customs, and the religious feelings of the two nations are thrown into instructive contrast. [Routledge : o.p. ; Appleton, New York : o.p.]

—— *Recha.*   1890
> Shows the ugly side of Jewish life in a miserable Galician town, where Recha's father, a sternly orthodox Jew, employs his daughter as an instrument for fleecing the foolish young Austrians. [Blackwood : o.p.]

—— *One Year.*   1899
> Deals with Polish characters and manners in eastern Galicia ; motive, a man's love for a girl whose father ruined his own father by cheating at cards. [Blackwood : o.p. ; Dodd & Mead, New York : o.p.]

—— *Sawdust.*   1901
> A Ruthenian *Romeo and Juliet* ; modern industrialism at odds with decadent aristocracy, a pushing German, who opens a sawmill in a Carpathian village, representing one, and an impoverished Polish count, whose daughter is loved by the miller's son, the other. [Heinemann : o.p. ; Winston, Philadelphia : o.p.]

—— *The Supreme Crime.*   1901
> Depicts in considerable detail Ruthenian life in Austria, especially the priests of the Greek Church and their households. The story is tragic : a husband is brought to believe his innocent wife guilty of poisoning her sister, whom he had loved. [Methuen : o.p. ; Crowell, New York : o.p.]

—— *The Million.*   1901
> Describes racial characteristics and manners in Galicia. The impulsive heroine sacrifices her love to her father's social ambition ; nothing but crime and misery results. [Methuen : o.p. ; Dodd & Mead, New York : o.p.]

—— *A Glorious Lie.*   1912
> The hero of this tragic romance commits bigamy, and is spared the immediate consequences by the glorious lie of his first wife, who avows that she is only his mistress. In an early episode he fights in the Austrian army at Königgratz. [Long : o.p.]

" GERARD, E. D." [Emily Gerard and Dorothea Gerard]. *Reata ; or, What's in a Name?*   1880
> Reata is half Mexican half German, whose wild freak, begun in frolic but continued in earnest, leads to serious embarrassments. The Mexican scenes are studied from life. [Blackwood : o.p.]

—— *Beggar my Neighbour.*   1882
> Sketches life in Poland half a century back; has some character interest. [Blackwood : o.p.]

—— *The Waters of Hercules.*   1885
> Staged amid the wild scenery of the borders of Hungary and Rumania ; local characters, manners, and superstitions are utilized. The plot turns on the search for a certain mysterious abyss with a legendary history, and involves such picturesque scenes as an encounter with brigands and a great forest fire. [Blackwood : o.p.]

—— *A Sensitive Plant.*   1891
> Life of a girl affected from childhood with morbid timidity and shyness. She is made an attractive figure by the unselfishness that at length overcomes her nervousness and sends her forth to do a generous act. Both England and Venice are depicted. [Blackwood : o.p. ; Appleton, New York : o.p.]

" GERARD, Morice " [Rev. John Jessop Teague ; 1856–1929]. *The Red Seal.*   1907
> Somerset during the Monmouth rebellion ; Judge Jeffreys the chief historical actor, and James II an important figure. [Cassell : o.p.]

—— *The Adventures of an Equerry.*   1907
> Concerned with the early life of John Churchill (Marlborough) and his marriage with Sarah Jennings, the war in the Low Countries, siege of Maestricht, etc. [Cassell : o.p.]

—— *A Rose of Blenheim.*   1907
> The days of Marlborough again, ending with Blenheim (1704). The hero is sent to Paris to find out Louis XIV's plans, and gets involved in a tangle of adventures. [Hodder : o.p.]

—— *The Broken Sword.*   1910
> A romance of 1688, when James II was trying to subvert the laws of England and William of Orange saved the country. A love drama is enfolded in the historical movement. [Hodder : o.p.]

—— *The Last Link.*   1911
> A Roman Catholic house in Suffolk, and Jacobite plotting in the time of William III (1690). [Hodder : o.p.]

—— *The Heart of a Hero.*   1913
> The loves of General Wolfe and Miss Lowther. In the earlier scenes, at Bath, Taunton, and London, the aged Beau Nash, Pitt, and other celebrities figure ; the later chapters deal with the war in Canada and the battle of Quebec (1757–59). [Hodder : o.p.]

—— *The Countess of Zelle.*   1919
> The romantic career of a valiant Yorkshireman who served in France under Churchill and Turenne and is graciously permitted by the Grand Monarch to marry a great lady of the Rhineland. [Odhams : o.p.]

GERHARDI, William Alexander [Scottish ; *b.* 1895]. *Futility : a novel on Russian themes.*   1922
> Chekhov shows the weakness and futility of the Russian character, Gerhardi the futility of any action in a world so complicated and unintelligible as this which has got out of control since the war. Here the situation is farcical—a middle-aged man carrying his triple household of relatives and hangers-on in a wild-goose chase across Siberia to Vladivostok, and back again to Omsk, in a hopeless attempt to save

GERHARDI, William Alexander (*continued*).
the insolvent gold-mines, sole support of the whole nondescript crowd. Presumably, the central figure is an image of Mr. Gerhardi's father, who was a wealthy manufacturer in Petersburg before the war, which ruined him; and much of the rest is no doubt founded on what the writer saw during his experiences in Russia, Siberia, and the Far East. [Duckworth; Duffield, New York.]

—— *The Polyglots.* 1925
A go-as-you-please narrative of adventures in Mukden and the neighbouring parts at the time of British intervention in Russian affairs. The world is upside-down, and the chaos is reflected in the confusing nature of the story. Things happen anyhow, and the characters are likewise—rich families hunted by Bolshevists, mushroom generals, muddle-headed administrators, wretches driven insane with their troubles, swindlers, women of easy virtue doing a thriving trade, etc. The "hero" is in love with an empty-headed girl, and half the story is about his vacillations and self-questionings. [Duckworth; Duffield, New York.]

—— *Pending Heaven.* 1930
Extravaganza that is palpably too clever: the novelist Max Fisher's literary and erotic adventures have no perceptible connexion or meaning, except the disenchantment and nihilism of post-war attitudes to life. [Duckworth; Harper, New York.]

GERSTÄCKER, Friedrich Wilhelm Christian [German; 1816–72]. *Germelshausen.* 1888
A little German classic—the quaint story of a sunken village which comes to life one day in every hundred years. [Sever, Cambridge (Mass.); transl. by Clara M. LATHROP, Crowell, New York (1906): o.p.; Harrap.]

GESTA ROMANORUM. *c.* 1440
A collection of Latin stories compiled late in the thirteenth or early in the fourteenth centuries; author unknown and country unascertained; intended as edifying examples for the use of preachers. English translation printed by Wynkyn de Worde, 1510–5. A parallel compilation to that of the Chevalier de la Tour-Landry, all the tales, whatsoever their nature and origin, being burdened with a Christian moral. Sources various—Oriental, classical, and mediæval. A Latin translation of the fables of Bidpai, the Arabian fables of the Spanish Jew, Petrus Alphonsus, ancient chronicles now lost, and the decadent classical authors, were all drawn upon largely; but the various MSS. differ considerably in their contents. The history is false, the characters are fictitious, and the title—the *Acts of the Romans*—purely gratuitous; it is a miscellany of Oriental romance and apologue, beast fables, classical tales, miracle stories, and legends of the Virgin, costumed in the external features of mediæval life. All the stories are allegorized or otherwise interpreted in a moralizing way, often with the most absurd results. It is important in literary history as a storehouse whence Italian, French, and English writers, poets, novelists, and playwrights, obtained many of their plots. [*Latin text*, rec. H. Oesterley, Berlin, 1872; rec. A. Keller (Bibl. d. deutsch. National-Liter.), Quedlinburg, 1841; rec. W. Dick, Leipzig, 1890. *English transl.* by Rev. C. Swan (1824), (Bohn's Lib.), 1877: o.p.; re-ed. Thos. Wright, Chatto: o.p.; with introduction by E. A. Baker (Broadway Transl.), Routledge (Dutton, New York), 1912; *Selections*, ed. by M. Komroff, Dial Press, New York.]

GIBBON, Perceval [South African, of Welsh parentage; 1879–1926]. *Souls in Bondage.* 1904
A powerful story of Dutch half-breeds, blacks, and Europeans in a small town apparently in Orange River Colony; a revelation of ugly facts, with a harrowing tragedy at the end. [Blackwood: o.p.]

—— *Vrouw Grobelaar's Leading Cases.* 1905
Mostly gruesome stories of Boers and South African natives, in the mouth of a shrewd and not unkindly Dutchwoman. A strong interpretation of Boer character, and of their treatment of the Kafirs, with glimpses of superstition and folk-lore. *Vasco's Sweetheart*, *The Avenger of Blood*, and *Tegalash* are among the best. [Blackwood: o.p.; McClure, New York: o.p.]

—— *Margaret Harding.* 1911
Margaret is a patient in a sanatorium for consumptives on the Karoo, whose indiscretions in making friends with a Kafir involve her in serious trouble with the prejudiced whites. The gulf between the European and the natives is brought out, and various broken-down whites in the colonial police, an alcoholic doctor, an old buck from Pall Mall, a Boer farmer, and others, are drawn with humour. [Methuen: o.p.]

—— *The Second Class Passenger; and other stories.* 1913
Stories of action and adventure, the settings Paris, Russia, East Africa, etc., with incidents as diverse as their scenes—hypnotism, second-sight, fighting with ruffians, and so on—adventures told with something of the romantic glamour of Conrad. [Methuen: o.p.]

GIBBS, (Arthur) Hamilton [b. 1888]. *Cheadle and Son.* 1912
A story of Oxford life—a slacker makes good. [Chatto: o.p.; *sub tit. Rowlandson's Oxford*, Dutton, New York: o.p.]

—— *The Hour of Conflict.* 1914
An Oxford man falls in love with the daughter of a French restaurant-keeper. [S. Paul: o.p.; Doran, New York: o.p.]

GIBBS, Sir Philip [b. 1877]. *The Street of Adventure.* 1909
A romance of Fleet Street, with the world of authors, journalists, illustrators, and the like, depicted with inside knowledge and affection. [Heinemann; Dutton, New York, 1920.]

—— *Oliver's Kind Women.* 1912
An odious, coxcombical young man and other unpleasant things put before us with this author's wontedly deft treatment of bohemian life. [Heinemann; Dana Estes, Boston: o.p.]

—— *Helen of Lancaster Gate.* 1912
This rather commonplace story of a girl freed by her father's ruin from the social obstacles between her and her lover includes a charming character-study of Helen and her vivid, if less pleasing husband. [Herbert & Daniels: o.p.]

—— *A Master of Life.* 1913
The idealistic nature of Titus Harsnett, a millionaire employer, who faces seriously the problems of his position, is responsible for that apparent failure which is so often the concomitant of moral success. [Cassell.]

GIBBS, Sir Philip (*continued*). *The Custody of the Child.* 1914

Discusses the evils of divorce, from the standpoint of the child of the marriage. [Hutchinson : o.p.]

—— *Venetian Lovers.* 1921

Eight stories of the aftermath of war, set in various countries of Europe. [Hutchinson : o.p.]

—— *The Reckless Lady.* 1924

The lady in question is an inveterate gambler, and the plot turns on her efforts to support her children, whilst hiding from them the means she adopts. [Hutchinson ; Doubleday, Doran, New York.]

—— *The Age of Reason.* 1928

A superficial analysis of modern tendencies in life—the problems entailed by the marriage of a woman of orthodox views to a non-religious scientist, whose two children have been brought up on modern lines. [Hutchinson ; Doubleday, Doran, New York.]

—— *Darkened Rooms.* 1929

The theme is spiritualism, which is represented as often fraudulent and always dangerous. The heroine, an attractive actress, is duped, after the death of her lover, by a vulgar trickster who represents himself as directed and controlled by the dead man's spirit. [Hutchinson ; Doubleday, Doran, New York.]

—— *The Hidden City.* 1929

The hidden city is the inner consciousness of man, which is explored by the doctor hero, whose work brings him into contact with specimens of many types and classes, in especial a young neurotic whom he rescues. [Hutchinson ; Doubleday, Doran, New York.]

GIDE, André [French ; *b.* 1869]. *The Immoralist* (L'immoraliste, 1903). 1930

This has been taken as an apologia or as a manifesto of M. Gide's philosophy ; but in the preface he repudiates any such interpretation, and as usual declines to speak out. It is the autobiography of a detrimental, who appears to be a sort of experimental illustration of hedonism and moral irresponsibility pushed to the logical extreme. A savant, and in some sort even an ascetic, he throws over all that he has hitherto cherished, and lives a life of pure individualism, encouraged by his oracular friend Menalcas (the Ménalque of *Les nourritures terrestres*). Preferring evil to good, he pursues it even at his own expense ; he poaches his own preserves, teaches a native boy to lie and steal, lets his devoted wife die of sheer neglect. It is a triumph of psychological science and art, and the translation gives an adequate idea of the limpid style. [Transl. by Dorothy BUSSY, Knopf, New York and London.]

—— *Strait is the Gate* (La porte étroite, 1909). 1924

A unilinear story, like that kindred masterpiece *La symphonie pastorale*, and one that may perhaps be read as a valediction to M. Gide's ancestral Huguenotism. A young man relates the ups and downs of his love for a girl whose heart is to him a *terra incognita*. He is mystified and maddened by her apparent capriciousness, the result of a premature glimpse of evil and her craving for a purity and holiness not of this world. Not till she dies, worn out with the struggle for perfection, does her journal reveal the secret of her attitude. [Transl. by Dorothy BUSSY, Knopf, New York and London.]

—— *Two Symphonies* (La symphonie pastorale, 1919 ; Isabelle, 1911). 1931

A Swiss pastor rescues a blind waif, teaches her after the Laura Bridgman method, and falls in love, persuading himself by unconscious sophistry that their love is blessed by Christ. By a medical operation she is cured, and recognizes at once that it is the old man's son she loves. There is no escape from the tragic dilemma but by her suicide. The tale is told with reticence and beauty, and the clash of two philosophies of conduct, the primitive, non-coercive ethics of the gospel and the sterner Pauline code, is subtly combined with the drama of motive. [Transl. by Dorothy BUSSY, Knopf, New York.]

—— *Lafcadio's Adventure* (Les caves du Vatican, 1922). 1928

Breaks all the rules of probability and structural form, but remains undeniably amusing, and the satire though aimed rather at random registers many hits. There are five sections, loosely connected by the absurd canard that the Freemasons have kidnapped Leo XIII and that an impostor occupies the throne of St. Peter. The devout subscribe to a fraudulent crusade, the more foolish go to Rome and meet with queer misadventures. Less farcical are the histories of the atheist converted by a supposed miracle who relapses into modern science, and the Tartuffian novelist who has a fit of freethinking. But the idea canvassed is whether an unmotived crime is conceivable, and the born picaro, Lafcadio, Gide's immoralist hero, supplies the instance. [Transl. by Dorothy BUSSY, *sub tit. The Vatican Swindle*, Knopf, New York, 1925 ; Knopf, London, with title and date as above.]

—— *The Counterfeiters* (Les faux monnayeurs, 1925). 1927

Termed his first novel by the author. Very unlike the ordinary novel, in its lack of plot, sequence, or clearly defined theme. Many subjects are canvassed in the dialogues and the issue of certain episodes, and perhaps the conflict between reality and the ideal reality of the novelist, or between the real world and the order we would impose upon it, is behind the extracts from a journal kept by the novelist Edward and his sketches for a novel, *The Counterfeiters*, for which some of the characters and incidents are seen providing materials. Edward is half an immoralist ; some of the others are entirely that. Several of these boys and older men are unsavoury people ; but are, fortunately, not too real, merely impersonations of moral and intellectual attitudes. It is a novel of ideas, like *Wilhelm Meister* or *l'education sentimentale*, and full of psychological and literary brilliances. " Paul Ambroise " is Paul Valéry ; Alfred Jarry comes on the scene in person. [Transl. by Dorothy BUSSY, Knopf, New York and London.]

—— *The School for Wives* (L'école des femmes, 1929). 1929

A young woman's journal before and after marriage, which must be read in an ironical light. Her lover, subsequently her husband, is a person like Meredith's Sir Willoughby Patterne with a stronger dash of Tartuffe. [Transl. by Dorothy BUSSY. Knopf, New York and London.]

GIELGUD, L. E. *Red Soil.* 1926

An account of the early days of the Russian Revolution of 1917 ; the experiences of a group of officers and refugees in a village. [Heinemann ; Doubleday, Doran, New York.]

GIELGUD, Val. *Gathering of Eagles.* 1929

A melodramatic romance of Napoleon's campaign in Russia—a young Pole fighting with the French endures the hardships of the retreat with the girl he loves. [Constable ; *sub tit. White Eagles : a story of* 1812, Houghton, Boston.]

GIFFORD, Evelyn. *Provenzano the Proud.* 1904

Siena in the wars of Guelfs and Ghibellines. Defeat of Conradin of Hohenstaufen by Charles of Anjou at Tagliacozzo, and of the Sienese by the Florentines (1268–9). [Smith & Elder : o.p.]

" GILBERT, George David " [Miss Mary Lucy Arthur ; Irish ; 1882–1919]. *The Island of Sorrow : an historical novel* 1797–1808. 1903

Less a novel than a biographical study of Robert Emmet's career (1796–1803). The author tries to be impartial, but cannot divest herself of the English lack of sympathy with Ireland. Lord Edward Fitzgerald is fairly drawn, but Curran is libelled as a domestic monster. [Long : o.p.]

—— *The Bâton Sinister.* 1903

Henrietta, Lady Wentworth is supposed to tell the story of Monmouth, whom she loved (1674–85). [Long : o.p.]

—— *To My King Ever Faithful : the love story of Mrs. Fitzherbert,* 1782–1837. 1909

The author dealt with this subject in a romance, *In the Shadow of the Purple* (1902), and, having pursued her researches, writes the story over again here. She was preparing an historical study on Mrs. Fitzherbert and her family. [Nash : o.p.]

GILBERT, Rodney Yonkers [b. 1889]. *The Indiscretions of Lin Mang.* 1929

By the Peking correspondent of the *North China Daily News,* whose acknowledged familiarity with Chinese life vouches for accurate drawing of character, manners, and scenery. The seamy side of the Chinese world during recent years is pungently exposed in the picaresque experiences of a native adventurer. [Murray.]

GILCHRIST, Robert Murray [1868–1917]. *A Peakland Faggot.* 1897

Very brief tales and scenes of life in the Peak of Derbyshire, with an accentuated version of the dialect, pictures of cottage interiors, and realistic studies of rustic character. [Faber & Gwyer.]

—— *The Courtesy Dame.* 1900

One of the author's full-length novels, also laid in the Peak, and utilizing local scenery, characters and manners, with much dialect. Main situation, a young girl in love with an aged peer. [Heinemann : o.p. ; Dodd & Mead, New York : o.p.]

—— *Road Knight.* 1913

Village social life, the narrowness and snobbery of the upper set and the humours of the rustics, are well rendered in this uneventful story of Peak district folk. [Holden : o.p.]

GILKES, Arthur Herman. *Kallistratus : an autobiography.* 1897

The Second Punic War ; battles of Lake Trasimene and Cannæ, and the death of Hannibal (218–216 B.C.). [Oxford Press, 1911 : o.p.]

—— *Four Sons.* 1909

The Samnite War (338 B.C.) and Alexandria (307 B.C.). [Oxford Press, 1912 : o.p.]

GILLIAT, Rev. Edward [1841–1915]. *God Save King Alfred.* [juvenile] 1901

A good example of a number of sound and stirring historical stories for boys : Alfred the Great, Edward Atheling, the siege of Rochester, etc. (885–6). [Macmillan : o.p.]

GILLMAN, Henry [b. 1833 ; American ; Irish by birth]. *Hassan, a Fellah.* 1898

A story of modern Palestine, making picturesque use of the people and the scenery. [Little & Brown, Boston : o.p.]

GILSON, Captain Charles James Louis [b. 1878]. *The Spy : a tale of the Peninsular War.* [juvenile] 1910

This too is one of many capital historical romances. It describes the battles and sieges from Roleia and Talavera to Badajoz (1808–12). [Oxford Press.]

GIOVANNI FIORENTINO, Ser [Italian]. *The Pecorone* (Il Pecorone, 1378 ; *first printed* 1558). 1897

The title means the Big Sheep, the Simpleton. In inception, this book, the author and true date of which are to some extent conjectural, was an imitation of the *Decameron,* especially in the framework, a priest and a nun, in love with each other, telling stories alternately and ending each with a canzonet. First come a number of amusing stories chiefly of erotic adventure, which are not dissimilar to Boccaccio's, but not so licentious, though free enough, and with a moral as a rule by no means on the side of the angels. There follow a series of historical anecdotes recounting the feuds of Guelf and Ghibelline (Ser Giovanni was himself a Guelf, but is fair to both sides), and of the Neri and Bianchi, with other episodes in Florentine history of the fourteenth century ; and, finally, adaptations or excerpts from the Italian chronicles of Giovanni Villani (with whom our author is sometimes identified), and even historical and legendary stories out of Livy. Like the other *novellieri,* Giovanni borrowed from the *Gesta Romanorum,* the *fabliaux,* collections of Eastern stories, and other available sources ; he shows more skill as a story-teller than as an inventor. Variants of many of the tales will be found in Boccaccio, Straparola, Massuccio, Bandello, Sacchetti, etc. ; Shakespeare used the story of Giannotto in the *Merchant of Venice.* There is more of the bloom of Troubadour romance than we get in Boccaccio or Sacchetti. [Dated 1378, first printed Milan, 1558 ; now first transl. into English by W. G. WATERS, *illus.* by E. R. Hughes, Lawrence & Bullen, 1897 : o.p.]

GIRAUDOUX, Jean [French ; b. 1882]. *My Friend from Limousin* (Siegfried et le Limousin, 1922). 1923

A French prisoner-of-war loses his sense of nationality, and imagines himself a German. He is restored to his senses by the influence of a comrade. [Transl. by Louise Collier WILLCOX, Harper, New York.]

GISLI THE OUTLAW, *the Story of.* 1866

Finest of the lesser sagas; scene, north-west of Iceland (930–78). A tragic story of extreme pathos, the cruel system of blood-feuds carrying havoc into the bosom of an affectionate family, and an unmerited curse pursuing Gisli to his death. Brave, generous, and faithful, he is one of the most engaging of the heathen champions. His verses, charmingly translated by Dasent, are by a thirteenth-century writer. The entire story is poetical, the beautiful idea of the Dream Ladies lifting these grim episodes into the higher realm of imagination. Nevertheless, the everyday scenes, the family relations, the ancient observances and superstitions, manners and morals, and the scenes of swift action, are described in such a minute and familiar manner as to carry instant conviction to the reader's mind. [Transl. by Sir G. W. DASENT, Edmonston & Douglas, Edinburgh: o.p.; in *Tales of the Norsemen* (juvenile), Collins, 1928.]

GISSING, Algernon [Brother of following; b. 1860]. *A Secret of the North Sea.* 1899

A melodramatic story of farmers and fisher-folk on the Northumberland coast, whose rude speech is reproduced. Turns on the lifelong enmity of two neighbours, and shows nothing but the dark side of these people. The scenery of sea, sky, and moorland gives breadth and atmosphere. [Chatto: o.p.]

—— *Knitters in the Sun.* 1903
—— *Baliol Garth.* 1905
—— *The Dreams of Simon Usher.* 1907
—— *The Unlit Lamp.* 1909
—— *The Herdsman.* 1910
—— *One Ash.* 1911

Studies of rustic life in a northern county, with plenty of realism in the details, the characters boldly outlined, Mr. Gissing's object being to show vice, stupidity, and passion as the critical factors in life which bring ruin and misery on more than the wrongdoers. The follower of Mr. Hardy can be recognized in the imaginative treatment of landscape, the psychology, and the rather arbitrary mechanics of the plots—everything conspires to express the fatalism of his view of life. [(1) and (2), Chatto: o.p.; (3), Chatto; (4), (5), (6), White: o.p.]

GISSING, George Robert [1857–1903]. *The Unclassed.* 1884

Gissing was one of the most serious and conscientious students of modern conditions, particularly in the lower middle classes, and wrote with a faithfulness and sincerity that but for his lack of humour would have made him one of our great novelists. Like Balzac, he was a demographer. He worked in crowds, or rather social groups, and it is these that impress themselves on the memory rather than any individual creations. He discloses in a powerful and luminous way the realities of life to-day, especially in great towns like London, and not only shows up social maladies, but illustrates the working of ameliorative agencies, particularly socialism. In *The Unclassed* he attacks a most dispiriting problem in an idealistic fashion. The " Unclassed " are the " daughters of joy," and the author would show that even these are not utterly lost. Two girls are rescued, or rescue themselves, and live an honest and womanly life; one of them devoting herself nobly to the work of helping the poor and fallen. Waymark is obviously Gissing himself. [(Essex Lib.), Benn, 1930; Fenno, New York: o.p.]

—— *Demos: a story of English socialism.* 1886

A very earnest examination of socialism in its effect on various minds; the principal character is a demagogic workman who comes into money and gradually lapses from integrity and his high ideals. The finer natures of the woman who loves him and of the woman of gentle nurture whom he marries bring in the pathos of human tragedy, while his old companions and his relatives afford studies of idiosyncrasy and human kindness amongst the working classes. Much more honest as a study of life as it is than the earlier novel. [With introd. by Morley Roberts, Nash, 1928; Dutton, New York.]

—— *Thyrza.* 1887

Tells the story of a London factory girl whose imaginative and spiritual disposition stands out in relief against squalid surroundings. Full of tragic human interest, to which the many by-characters contribute, e.g. the artisan-student, the young Ruskinian teaching among the workmen of Lambeth, and a working-man who is an agnostic and socialist. [Nash, 1928; Dutton, New York.]

—— *A Life's Morning.* 1888

A tragedy that was transmogrified and given a happy and incongruous ending, because James Payn thought the reader's nerves would not stand it as it was originally designed. Emily Hood renounces the man she loves, because her father has committed suicide in circumstances that might bring disgrace upon her future husband. [Murray; with introd. by Morley Roberts, Nash, 1928; Dutton, New York.]

—— *The Nether World.* 1889

Pictures in a stern and impressive way the obscure, poverty-stricken multitudes of Clerkenwell, brutalized by the inhuman struggle for bread, half of them criminals or in close touch with criminals, a nether world of squalor and misery. Among the drab crowds that move before us stand out the family of a worthy man ruined by misfortune, with a son and a daughter driven to felony and immorality; and, on the other hand, a little group of ideal characters engaged in a lofty struggle with evil, in which they are worsted by circumstances. Here Gissing appears as a sad-eyed Dickens. [With introd. by Morley Roberts, Nash, 1928; Dutton, New York.]

—— *The Emancipated.* 1890

Presents a series of characters who have liberated themselves from the restraints of creed and moral law. The emancipated women are morbid, self-questioning types, whose histories are records of failure and unhappiness, relieved by the episode of Miriam's wooing and marriage to a rough and honest man and their happy after-life. [Lawrence & Bullen: o.p.]

—— *New Grub Street.* 1891

A pessimistic study of the literary life under modern conditions, much of the poignancy due to an autobiographical element. The writer, who is a business man, succeeds, while those of superior talent and finer artistic

GISSING, George Robert (*continued*).
conscience fall into distress and ruin. [With introd. by Morley Roberts, Nash, 1928 ; Dutton, New York ; Modern Lib., New York, 1926.]

—— *Born in Exile.*   1892
The hero, a compound of base and honourable qualities, is ambitious of rising in the world and of mixing with cultivated society, but is handicapped by the disadvantages of his early life and by personal qualities attributed to heredity. [Black : o.p.]

—— *The Odd Women.*   1893
A curious phase of modern life, the forlorn lot of the superfluous women. The ineffectual struggles of a group of gently nurtured women who have no hope of wedlock, and a girl's unhappy marriage for the sake of a home, related with his usual realism. [Sidgwick ; Macmillan, New York : o.p.]

—— *In the Year of Jubilee.*   1894
Satirizes the vulgarity and barbarism of the lower middle-class, presenting a humorous commentator in a man with a mania for statistics, and a number of typical characters drawn and analysed with candour and realism. [Lawrence & Bullen : o.p. ; Appleton, New York : o.p.]

—— *Eve's Ransom.*   1895
Dwells on the sordid aspects of lower middle-class life, and describes how Eve's artistic and social aspirations are awakened by a visit to Paris. [(Essex Lib.), Benn, 1929 ; Appleton, New York : o.p.]

—— *The Whirlpool.*   1897
Theme : the irresistible attraction which London, with its pleasures, excitements, and extravagance, has for a numerous class of people, who may depart for a season, but are drawn again into the fatal vortex. The cultured life has no time for children, and sterility is the common result. Is there not better hope even in Rudyard Kipling's ideal of man as the active animal and fighter ? This and like questions arise in the course of the novel. There is a melodramatic central episode—the heroine's husband in a fit of jealousy kills a man in mistake, the tragic sequel depending on very shaky psychology. [Lawrence & Bullen : o.p. ; Stokes, New York : o.p.]

—— *Human Odds and Ends.*   1897
Sketches and jottings of many phases of life, rarely amounting to a story, yet significant and full of penetration ; e.g. *Comrades in Arms*, the abortive love affair of a literary man and a literary woman ; *Lord Dunfield*, a severe picture of aristocratic barbarism ; *Raw Material* and *The Beggar's Nurse*, glimpses of the sadness and infamy of life under modern conditions. [Sidgwick.]

—— *The Town Traveller.*   1898
An unwontedly bright story, bringing out the humours of a group of London people of a commonplace, typical kind ; a good-natured " commercial," a Cockney girl, a lodging-house keeper, and so on, in Kennington. [Methuen ; Stokes, New York : o.p.]

—— *The Crown of Life.*   1899
The first part autobiographical. One of Gissing's restrained tragedies of modern existence—how a man misses love, the crown of life. [Methuen.]

—— *Our Friend the Charlatan.*   1901
Comedy of the kind that makes you think how unpleasant everybody is. Deals with higher strata of society and satirizes shallow " culture." The Charlatan is a product of modern education, who puts himself forward as a politician with a theory. (This bio-sociological theory is really borrowed from Prof. Jean Izoulet's *La cité moderne*). The unpleasant characters are true to modern conditions, and the analysis is fair though severe. [Chapman : o.p. ; Holt, New York : o.p.]

—— *The Private Papers of Henry Ryecroft.*   1903
The mellowest, kindest, and most human fruit of Gissing's pen. Pathetic in its autobiographic interest, as Ryecroft only too plainly reflected the struggles and disillusionments of Gissing's own career as an author, which ended untimely the year this was published. A defeated literary man comes into an annuity, gives up book-making, and settles down to quiet happiness and contemplation in the country. This is his diary in spring, summer, autumn, winter ; with his observations of nature, people, books, and himself—a captivating revelation of Gissing's own mind and heart. [Constable ; Dutton, New York ; (Everyman's Lib.), 1927, Dutton, New York ; with introd. by Paul Elmer More, 1918, Modern Lib., New York ; by Thomas Seccombe, 1920, Mosher, Portland, Me.]

—— *Veranilda : an unfinished romance.*   1904
A scholarly and workmanlike, but colourless, historical romance, depicting the dying struggles of Rome and Italy during the Gothic invasion under Totila, just after the brilliant exploits of Belisarius (544–6). Veranilda is a Gothic princess, loved by a Roman noble. [(World's Classics), Oxford Press, 1929.]

—— *Will Warburton.*   1905
Brighter and less bitter in tone than earlier work, and filled with a spirit closely akin to optimism. Four main characters ; Warburton is a merchant ruined by the speculations of his partner, who to retrieve his fortunes and maintain mother and sister, sacrifices the respectability in which he has been reared, and which is so dear to him, and becomes a grocer. His friend, a painter whom in better days he had assisted, wins cheap success at the expense of his art, and with it the girl Warburton loved. But the grocer's shop turns out a success, and another lady appears not too proud to wed the owner. [(World's Classics), Oxford Press, 1929.]

—— *The House of Cobwebs ; and other stories.*   1906
A collection of very significant and representative fragments, which, like *Human Odds and Ends*, shows how admirably Gissing could work on a small scale. Introductory survey by Thomas Seccombe. [Constable ; Dutton, New York : o.p.]

GIUSTI, Arndt. *An Artist Passes.*   1929
A frankly unmoral specimen of picaresque fiction. The pseudo-hero is a thoroughpaced but seducing rogue, a Mexican peon who runs after a woman to the United States and then to Paris, murders the lady, and after a chequered attempt to win success as a painter, comes back to Mexico. [Chatto.]

GJELLERUP, Karl Adolf [Danish; 1857–1919]. *The Pilgrim Kamanita: a legendary romance*
(Der Pilgrimen Kamanita, 1906). 1911
A romance of the latter days of the Buddha and his death, a well-informed and admirable interpretation of
Buddhism. [Transl. by J. E. LOGIE, Heinemann: o.p.]

—— *Minna* (Minna, 1889). 1913
Minna is first loved, lightly, by a Danish painter, and then, very seriously, by a student at a Dresden polytechnic.
She is torn between her feelings towards both, and even when she marries her first love the mental agony
continues, till she dies in an asylum. It is in this inner tragedy that interest centres. [Transl. by C. L.
NIELSEN, Heinemann: o.p.]

GLADKOV, Feodor Vasilievich [Russian; b. 1883]. *Cement.* 1929
A nightmarish picture of one corner of the Russian inferno. A soldier back from the front manages to get
the colossal cement-works restarted and economic life restored. He and one or two other powerful figures
stand out from a crowd representing all the elements of greed, idealism, hatred, cowardice, and primitive
force, seething in the cauldron from which a new world may emerge. [Transl. (far from lucidly) by A. S.
ARTHUR and C. ASHLEIGH; Lawrence; International Publishing Co., New York.]

GLASGOW, Ellen Anderson Gholson [American; b. 1874]. *Phases of an Inferior Planet.* 1898
Morbid phases of bohemian life; realistic and analytical. An ill-matched pair live out the first miserable
epoch of married life in cheap apartments in New York, and part after the death of their child. Later
they are reconciled, but die before they are re-united. [Harper, New York: o.p.; Heinemann: o.p.]

—— *The Voice of the People.* 1900
A poor boy's political ambitions, and rise to a high position in his native State. Life in Virginia during the
Reconstruction period, the quality, the poor whites, and the negroes, many of them quaint and humorous,
and the natural scenery and luxuriant gardens, are freely sketched; the story diffuse and desultory.
[Doubleday, New York; Heinemann: o.p.]

—— *The Battle Ground.* 1902
First part a sympathetic portrayal of the wealthy Virginians before secession, second half a vivid picture of the
war, stressing rather the mournful underside of war than the heroic—halts and bivouacs, hospitals, the
miseries of non-combatants, and the like. Fair to both sides, though as a whole it gives the Southern tragedy.
[Doubleday, New York; Constable: o.p.]

—— *The Deliverance.* 1904
Romance of a large tobacco plantation in Virginia twenty years ago. [Doubleday, New York; Constable: o.p.]

—— *The Romance of a Plain Man.* 1909
This is a " self-made " man of the people whom the Virginians try to ostracize and deprive of an aristocratic
wife: time, the years after the Civil War. A typical American story of matrimonial trials and their effect
in developing the sterling qualities of character. [Doubleday, New York; with introd. by Hugh Walpole,
Garden City Co., New York, 1926.]

—— *The Miller of Old Church.* 1911
An alluring picture of rural Virginia, its pleasant scenery and pastoral atmosphere. More thought, more
criticism of life, appears in this and the subsequent novels, compared with the foregoing, especially in
the treatment of character. [Hurst, New York: o.p.; Murray.]

—— *Virginia.* 1913
Compared with the earlier novels, this is a much more searching study of modern tendencies; and the irony
and pungency of the style make the critical attitude clearer. Virginia learns that life is not such plain
sailing as she had imagined it. She does not succeed in keeping her egoistic husband, and her intense
affection for her children has to be its own reward. Hence her life is sufficiently tragic. [Doubleday,
New York.]

—— *Life and Gabriella: the story of a woman's courage.* 1916
Having witnessed her sister's unhappy marriage, Gabriella is spirited enough to defy genteel Southern traditions
and goes to New York to earn her living as a milliner. But she too suffers much the same fate. [Doubleday,
New York; Murray.]

—— *The Builders.* 1919
Takes sides with the misunderstood man. His wife under the outward show of beauty and sensibility is a thoroughpaced egotist, and makes her husband out to be a bully and a failure. [Doubleday, New York; Murray.]

—— *One Man in his Time.* 1922
The conflict between the spirit of progress and conservatism, illustrated in the persons of Gideon Vetch, a
governor of Virginia, and the aristocratic suitor of his daughter. [Doubleday, New York; Murray.]

—— *The Shadowy Third.* 1923
Seven ghost-stories. [Doubleday, New York: o.p.]

—— *Barren Ground.* 1925
Rural life in Virginia during the last century: a girl's efforts to win forgetfulness of an unhappy romance by doing a
man's work, restoring a neglected farm to fertility. [Doubleday, New York; Grosset, New York; Murray.]

—— *The Romantic Comedians.* 1926
An elderly Virginian judge fancies he has regained his youth on becoming a widower, and marries a pretty
young thing, with the natural results. Caustic humour and piquant characterization of several ages of
women, together with the comic opposition of modern freedom and time-worn restrictions, furnish both
criticism and amusement. [Doubleday, New York; Burt, New York; Murray.]

—— *They Stooped to Folly: a comedy of morals.* 1929
The subject is the alteration of ordinary attitudes and values, not only in the post-war generation, but also
in their elders. Lots of discursive talk and canvassing of rather incoherent ideas that lead nowhere in
particular. These are interesting, however, and the author's humour is a saving grace. [Doubleday,
New York; Heinemann.]

GLASPELL, Susan [formerly Mrs. G. C. Cook, now Mrs. Norman Matson ; American ; *b.* 1882].

Fidelity.   1915

A pendant to *Babbitt* : that gave the materialism and stupidity of the middle classes in the Middle West, this gives their moral philistinism. It shows up, not the men, but the women, and humour is lacking. It is the harrowing study of a woman's persecution by pharisees and cowardly slaves of convention ; it is another version of "The woman who did." Ruth Holland goes off with a married man, the man having been goaded into it by a cold-blooded, rancorous wife, who refuses to divorce him, whilst Ruth is ostracized. The doctor who defends her receives the treatment meted out to his counterpart in *An Enemy of the People*. [Small, Boston ; Jarrolds : o.p.]

GLEIG, Rev. George Robert [1796–1888]. *The Subaltern*.   1825

Less a novel than actual reminiscences of the last stages of the Peninsular War, in which the author (afterwards Chaplain-General of the Forces) served as ensign—the siege of San Sebastian, Pampeluna, St. Jean de Luz (1812–5). [Blackwood, 1907 ; (Everyman's Lib.), Dent (Dutton, New York), 1915.]

GLENN, Isa [Mrs. S. J. Bayard Schindel ; American]. *Transport*.   1929

Almost entirely in dialogue and the most unmitigated American slang. A ship's load of officers and their womenfolk are making the trip across the blazing Pacific from San Francisco to Manila, and spend the whole three weeks in outdressing, snubbing, backbiting, flirting with, and talking scandal about each other, whilst two old campaigners pursue a finer though still unlawful love affair, and incidentally save one or two from the consequences of their own or others' folly. The satire is extraordinarily pungent and searching, with more than a touch of the psychoanalyst in its unmasking of hidden motives. [Knopf, New York and London.]

—— *A Short History of Julia*.   1930

Miss Glenn has already written several novels on the South, including the hostile *Southern Charm*. This is a riper and more catholic survey of the two races living side by side in Georgia, typified in two women, whose lives are made to touch our sympathies profoundly. [Knopf, New York and London.]

GLOWACKY, Aleksandr ["Boleslaw Prus" ; Polish, 1847–1912]. *The Pharaoh and the Priest* (1897).   1902

Reign of Rameses XIII (eleventh century B.C.). The struggle between the secular and the ecclesiastical forces. [Transl. by Jeremiah CURTIN, Little & Brown, Boston : o.p. ; Low : o.p.]

GLYN, Elinor Clayton [*née* Sutherland]. *The Visits of Elizabeth*.   1901

A young lady's letters to her mother, recording her observations on manners and customs, characters and conversations, during visits to country houses in England and France. The cynical reflections on smart society and its free-and-easy morals, of which this was the foretaste, are continued in the following, and one or two other novels which deal frankly with irregular liaisons.

—— *The Reflections of Ambrosine*.   1902
—— *The Damsel and the Sage : a warrior's whimsies*.   1903
—— *The Vicissitudes of Evangeline*.   1905
—— *The Sayings of Grandmama*.   1908
—— *Elizabeth Visits America*.   1909

[All Duckworth ; *Works*, 10 vols., Author's Press, Auburn, 1926.]

GOBINEAU, Comte Joseph Arthur de [French ; 1816–82]. *The Lucky Prisoner* (Le prisonnier chanceux, 1846).   1926

A romance of the French religious wars prior to the massacre of St. Bartholomew, with a youthful Don Juan for hero, and Diane de Poitiers a prominent figure. Brantôme and De Méré also appear. [Transl. by F. M. ATKINSON, Heinemann ; Doubleday, New York.]

—— *The Pleiads* (Les pléiades, 1874).   1928

This long and discursive novel is of interest now chiefly as pleasantly illustrating Gobineau's social philosophy ; his idea, for example, that a few fine personalities outweigh in value whole multitudes of the mediocre and sordid, is crystallized in his Pleiads, especially in the three young men, an Englishman born in Bagdad, a Frenchman, and a Teuton, whose ordeals, as much intellectual as sentimental, before they are duly mated, give serious import to the medley of love-stories. The characters are hardly substantial enough to arouse more than a tepid sympathy ; but the coquettish great lady who at long last finds out what it is to be in love, and her counterpart, the hereditary grand duke, with his many failures crowned at last by a successful marriage, are amusing if somewhat "intriguing". Gobineau's urbane style and discursive wit would redeem an inferior story. [Transl. by F. SCANLAN, Knopf.]

GODWIN, William [1756–1836]. *Caleb Williams ; or, Things as They are*.   1795

Not primarily, as Leslie Stephen described it, an imaginative version of *The Political Justice* (1793), though sociological ideas are at the back of the writer's mind in working out his ghastly climax of oppression and fear. A youth finds his beloved master to be guilty of murder, and is persecuted by the alarmed murderer, until he is compelled reluctantly to denounce him. Then each is overwhelmed by the consciousness of the other's "greatness of mind." Denounces the inelastic rule of human justice as represented by the law. [Edited by E. A. Baker, Routledge, 1904 : o.p. With introd. by Van Wyck Brooks, Greenburg, New York, 1926.]

—— *St. Leon : a tale of the sixteenth century*.   1799

A respectable gentleman, a model husband and estimable father, becomes possessed of the elixir of life and the philosopher's stone. But immortality and inexhaustible riches fail to ensure happiness to a human creature. St. Leon is dogged by misfortune, distrusted by friends and foes, imprisoned by the Inquisition, and his sufferings in Switzerland and Hungary give rise to some powerful scenes in the Gothic style. [o.p.]

—— *Fleetwood ; or, The New Man of Feeling*.   1805

A Gothic novel revolving round the motive of jealousy—an earlier *Griffith Gaunt*. A lurid succession of brain-storms culminate in violent madness—the result of groundless suspicion on the part of a worn-out and misanthropic roué, married to a young wife. [o.p.]

GOETEL, Ferdynand [Polish]. *From Day to Day.* 1930

An Austrian-Pole who was a prisoner-of-war in Turkestan, where he had a liaison, appears here in the act of writing a novel about these experiences and at the same time keeping a journal of his life at home, his unromantic relations with his wife, the temptation of another light o' love, etc. The one thing is a commentary on the other, and provides the other with an artistic *dénouement.* [Transl. by Winifred COOPER, Mathews.]

GOETHE, Johann Wolfgang von [German ; 1749–1832]. *The Sorrows of Werther* (Die Leiden des jungen Werther, 1774). 1779

A story that seemed to voice the romanticism and regrets of an age saturated with sceptical philosophy and with the sentimentalism of Rousseau. Certain passages between Goethe himself and some friends and the suicide of a disappointed young man gave him the outline of a story that reflected a phase of his own emotional history. An ardent idealist falls hopelessly in love, and dies rather than face the anguish of renunciation. Written in the form of a journal (1771–2), it is an intimate and poignant study of a mind diseased, and therewithal a dramatic picture of the people and the society among whom his lot was cast. [First transl. by Richard GRAVES ; transl. by W. RENDER : o.p. ; transl. by R. D. BOYLAN (with *Elective Affinities*), Bell ; newly transl. by Dr. William ROSE, Scholartis Press (McKee, New York), 1929.]

—— *Wilhelm Meister's Apprenticeship* (Wilhelm Meister's Lehrjahre, 1778–96). 1839

A study of culture in the widest sense of the word, tracing the life of a man from boyhood to maturity, recounting his youthful dreams and aspirations, his love, his first contact with the world and the loss of his illusions ; in short, the whole process by which he finds his true place and duties as a citizen of the human world, and abandoning merely individual aims accepts his position and so ends his apprenticeship. The various phases are handled with extreme elaboration ; the story of Wilhelm's life as an actor is so carefully told, with such profound disquisitions on the education and growth of an actor and on the dramatic art, that this has been often asserted to be the aim of the book. It is full of various and beautiful characters, of imaginative and poetical passages, of a broad, humane philosophy ; it is indeed " an incalculable work." Sir John Seeley reads its intention as follows : " That we should give unity to our lives by devoting them with hearty enthusiasm to some pursuit, and that the pursuit is assigned to us by nature through the capacities she has given us." Goethe said, " In the novel it is chiefly *sentiments* and *events* that are exhibited ; in the drama, it is *characters* and *deeds*." " The novel-hero must be suffering, at least he must not in a high degree be active." Wilhelm does nothing, intends nothing, is the sport of circumstances and emotions ; and many other characters seem to exist simply to luxuriate in the varieties of sentimental experience. [Transl. by Thomas CARLYLE (Library edn., see Carlyle, p. 93) ; (Centenary edn.) 2 vols., Chapman (Scribner, New York) : o.p. ; (People's edn.) 2 vols., Chapman (Scribner, New York) : o.p. ; transl. by R. D. BOYLAN, Bell.]

GOGOL, Nikolai Vasilievich [Russian ; 1809–52]. *St. John's Eve, etc.* (1829–36). 1886

Gogol was a Little Russian or Ukrainian, and a large proportion of his stories deal with peasant life in Little Russia, which is, or was, more primitive, more free-and-easy, more picturesque, than elsewhere. *St. John's Eve* is a powerful story showing Gogol's lifelike drawing of his countrymen at its best ; *Old-Fashioned Farmers* sketches an elderly couple living in a sequestered country house in idyllic happiness ; *How the Two Ivans Quarrelled* is a magnificently humorous tale of town life ; *The Cloak*, an intensely moving story of a poor official in Petersburg, who is the butt of his fellow-clerks. [Transl. by Isabel F. HAPGOOD, Maxwell : o.p. ; Crowell, New York : o.p.]

—— *Evenings on a Farm near Dikanka* (1831). 1926

Eight stories, Gogol's earliest productions, concerned with the life of the peasants of his own district and village of the Ukraine, their folklore and legends of the past, and the natural beauty of the countryside. [Transl. by Constance GARNETT, Chatto (Knopf, New York).]

—— *Taras Bulba : a story of the Dnieper Cossacks* (1834). 1886

A fierce epical narrative of the bloody wars of the Zaporogian Cossacks against the Poles. Taras with his own hand shoots one of his sons who has turned traitor ; the other is captured and put to torture before his father's eyes. Taras exacts a terrible revenge by devastating the country, and dies in the midst of his foes. The scenes of tumult and battle ring with the names of heroes, and the blows and wounds of personal encounters ; the rhythm is that of some fierce old *chanson de geste.* Gogol was himself a Cossack, and incorporated legends handed down among his people. [Transl. by Isabel F. HAPGOOD, Knopf, New York ; (Everyman's Lib.) Dent (Dutton, New York), 1917 ; transl. by Mrs. Constance GARNETT, *sub tit. Mirgorod* (with *Old-World Landowners, Viy*, and *Ivan Ivanovich and Ivan Nikiforovich*, Chatto (Knopf, New York) 1929).]

—— *The Diary of a Madman.* 1930

An attempt to give a realistic history of the mind of a lunatic. His delusions are presented for the most part with strict regard to psychological truth, though never without that compassionate feeling for everything human congenital to the great Russian novelists. The pathos at length enforces a close more dramatic than mere psycho-analysis would warrant. [Transl. by Prince MIRSKY, Cresset Press ; McKee, New York.]

—— *Tchitchikoff's Journeys ; or, Dead Souls,* (Mertruya Dushi, 1842). 1886

Gogol founded the realistic school of Russian fiction. His novels and stories are almost to be described as improvizations, in their lack of order and precision ; but they relate truthfully and vividly exactly what he saw. His human portraiture of all orders of Russian people—reminding one in its freshness and humour of the *Pickwick Papers*—has suggested a superficial comparison with Dickens. He has been likened, quite as justly, to Cervantes and Lesage, and again to Swift. This, his greatest novel, albeit unfinished, leaving an important earlier episode not cleared up, is a tale of the old days of serfdom, when the peasants were registered and counted as " souls," and those who died between the registrations were denominated " dead souls." An adventurer buys up a large number of these at nominal prices, and then raises money on the certificates. This farcical proceeding gives opportunity for humorous and often bitterly satirical pictures of the Russian landowning class, who are represented as utterly effete and ridiculous, while such men as Manyelov, who talk about schemes for ameliorating the lot of the serfs, are in reality the worst of masters. There are besides a crowd of ne'er-do-wells, spendthrifts, ineffectuals, mad dreamers and schemers, corrupt,

GOGOL, Nikolai Vasilievich (*continued*).

easy-going, or martinet officials, with a model landowner to point the moral.   The second part, posthumous and partially destroyed, is in all respects inferior to the first, but of interest to students of Russian life.   [A rough transl., with interpolations, was published by Hurst & Blackett, *sub tit. Home Life in Russia*, 1854 : o.p.   Transl. by Isabel F. HAPGOOD, 2 vols., Crowell, New York : o.p. ; another transl., Vizetelly, 1887 : o.p. ; the same, with connecting passages from Charrière's French version (1885), and Dr. Zahartchenko's sequel, notes, etc., a defective transl. (see *Athenæum*, April 10, 1915), *sub tit. Dead Souls*, with introd. by Stephen Graham, Unwin, 1915 ; transl. by D. J. HOGARTH (Everyman's Lib.) Dent (Dutton, New York), 1915 ; transl. by Constance GARNETT, 2 vols., Chatto (Knopf, New York), 1923 ; Benn, 1929.]

GOLDING, Louis [*b.* 1895]. *Forward from Babylon.*   1920

A profound and sensitive study of Jewish life and of the religious problem facing the emancipated Jew.   The son of a stern and deeply religious member of the Synagogue, after a protracted struggle with his father, wins his freedom, and takes up his work in life unfettered by obsolete restrictions.   [Christophers.]

—— *Day of Atonement.*   1925

Jewish communities in Russia, superstitious hatred by the muzhiks, a pogrom, and refugee life in Manchester slums—all focused in the pathetic history of a young couple.   Rabbinic profundities, rites and observances, and the intensity of religious devotion, are described with evident familiarity.   Between the bigotry and intolerance of Jews and Gentiles there seems little to choose.   [Knopf, New York ; Chatto.]

—— *Give up your Lovers.*   1930

Continues the story, the crucial situation arising from the mutual love of a young Jew and an English girl, and the consequent conflict etween the younger generation and their elders, who cling firmly to ancient customs and pride of race.   [Heinemann ; Cosmopolitan Book Co., New York.]

GOLDSMITH, Henry [Australian]. *Euancondit.*   1895

A story of Australia in the sixties.   [Sonnenschein : o.p.]

GOLDSMITH, Oliver [Irish ; 1728–74]. *The Citizen of the World.*   1762

An essay in the supposed Oriental manner then in vogue, consisting of letters from a Chinese philosopher studying Western society in London to his friend at home (cf. Montesquieu's *Lettres persanes*).   Sketches of the various aspects of London life, in coffee tavern, drawing-room, streets, and places of public entertainment (cf. *Spectator* and *Tatler*), with a mere suggestion of a continuous story.   Manners, literature, art, politics, religion are handled in the style of a social critic, with interludes of dialogue and the humours of some originals drawn from life, e.g. Beau Tibbs and the Man in Black, the latter perhaps a fancy portrait of Goldsmith himself.   [Edited by J. W. M. Gibbs (with *Polite Learning*), (Bohn's Lib.), Bell (Macmillan, New York), 1885 : o.p. ; edited by Austin Dobson and *illus.* by H. Railton, 2 vols. (Temple Library), Dent, 1891 : o.p. ; 2 vols. (Temple Classics), Dent (Dutton, New York), 1893.]

—— *The Vicar of Wakefield.*   1766

The Vicar is a lovable mixture of virtue and foible, shrewdness and simplicity, unselfishness and vanity ; a blameless and pathetic figure, who is tried like Job by undeserved misfortune.   He and his family, a group of simple, rustic characters, drawn with delicate touches of eccentricity, make an Arcadian picture of affectionate family concord—a picture tinged with a regretful longing that often breaks out into poetry.   The idyll is rudely disturbed by the villainy of a seducer ; troubles come thick and fast, but after sounding the depths of affliction all are restored to happiness and prosperity.   The Vicar was drawn from Goldsmith's father, and doubtless some of the other characters were sketched from old acquaintances.   Goldsmith's style is the perfection of classical English.   [Edited by Austin Dobson (Parchment Lib.), Paul ; with memoir by D. Masson, Macmillan, 1883 ; (Pocket Lib.), Routledge (Dutton, New York) ; edited by M. Macmillan, Macmillan ; (World's Classics), Oxford Press, 1901 ; (Everyman's Lib.), Dent (Dutton, New York), 1908.   *Illus. Edns. : illus.* by Hugh Thomson, Macmillan, 1890 ; the same, Pocket Edn., *id.*, 1902 ; with 13 facs. coloured *illus.* by J. M. Wright, Black, 1903 ; with 25 coloured *illus.* by C. E. Brock, Dent (Dutton, New York), 1904.   *Facsimile Repr.* of 1st edn., 2 vols., Stock, 1885 : o.p.]

GONCHAROV, Ivan Aleksandrovich [Russian ; 1812–91]. *A Common Story* (1847).   1894

A classical study of the inveterate conflict of ideas in Russia, between the reformers and the old regime, as exhibited in the career of a member of the landowning classes, who has vague ideas of political and social reform.   The hero goes to Petersburg and begins his official life full of enthusiasm and belief in his future ; but the deadening influences of political life soon affect him, and he is glad to return to his estates.   The story reflects the struggle between the new ideas and those of the old regime.   [Transl. by Constance GARNETT, Heinemann : o.p.]

—— *Oblomov* (1858).   1929

Goncharov's best and most famous novel, well translated.   Oblomov typifies the Russian temperament—sensitive, imaginative, full of good intentions, but stricken with lassitude and indecision, and doomed to be for ever ineffectual.   The companion portrait of Olga, whom he loves but surrenders out of sheer apathy and self-contempt to the pushful Stoltz, is a foil and a contrast.   Goncharov's affinity to Turgenev is obvious, even from this brief analysis.   [Transl. by Natalie A. DUDDINGTON, Allen & Unwin ; Macmillan, New York.]

—— *The Precipice* (1870).   1915

In this translation Goncharov's novel is curtailed to about one-third of the original.   It is a plot-novel, with hero, villain, two sisters of opposite dispositions, and a fine, patriarchal grandmother.   The plot turns on character, temperament, and personal relations, and both the hero, the potential artist, and the two young women are well-drawn and their motives truly analysed.   [Hodder : o.p. ; Knopf, New York : o.p.]

GONCOURT, Jules [French ; 1830–70] and **Edmond de** [French ; 1822–96]. *Renée Mauperin* (1864).   1903

A typical example of the Goncourts' pictures of contemporary life : a study of bourgeois society.   Its strength is in its workmanship, and the keen-eyed observation and accurate reproduction of even the trivialities in everyday existence.   A morbid story ; its long-drawn agony painful.   [Transl., with critical introd. by J. FITZMAURICE-KELLY, Heinemann, 1902 ; another transl., Modern Lib., New York.]

GONCOURT, Jules and Edmond de (*continued*). *Germinie Lacerteux* (1865).   1887
Here their naturalism is still more thoroughgoing. Germinie is a poor girl of the lowest classes, having no physical or mental attractiveness, born a drudge, and destined to be maltreated and enslaved by the brutishness of man. Into her depressing history the Goncourts poured out the mass of particulars which they had accumulated by patient and accurate observation of her class, and so produced an authoritative picture of manners and a cogent demonstration of the influence of environment upon the individual. [Transl. by Ernest BOYD, Knopf, New York and London, 1922.]

GOODWIN, Maud [*née* Wilder ; American ; b. 1856]. *The Head of a Hundred in the Colony of Virginia.*   1895
Tells of the settlement of Jamestown (1619–22). Much the same in historical groundwork as Mary Johnston's *By Order of the Company.* [Little & Brown, Boston : o.p. ; Dent : o.p.]

—— *White Aprons* : *a romance of Bacon's rebellion in Virginia in 1676.*   1896
The title alludes to the ruse employed by the rebels in placing the wives of Governor Berkeley's officers in front of their works until the fortifications were completed. Bacon is the champion of popular liberty (1676). The heroine comes to England and meets Dryden and Pepys. [Little & Brown, Boston : o.p. ; Dent : o.p.]

—— *Sir Christopher* : *a romance of a Maryland manor in 1644.*   1901
Adventures of a Somersetshire knight, a Cavalier, in the pioneering days in Maryland. [Little & Brown, Boston : o.p. ; Ward & Lock : o.p.]

—— *Veronica Playfair.*   1910
Life in George I's reign in London, at Pope's villa at Twickenham, and at Bath. Pope, Bolingbroke, Swift, Lady Mary Wortley Montagu, and Benjamin Franklin figure. [Little & Brown, Boston : o.p. ; Warne : o.p.]

GORDON, Samuel [1871–1927]. *Sons of the Covenant.*   1900
A study of the Jews in East and West London, telling of the useful life of two youths, who do excellent work for the less fortunate of their people. An optimistic book, which does not shirk realities. [Sands : o.p. ; Jewish Pub. Soc., Philadelphia : o.p.]

—— *The Ferry of Fate* : *a tale of Russian Jewry.*   1906
A story of Russian persecution, opening with the expulsion of Jews from the University of Odessa. Baruch makes his way into the higher bureaucracy at the expense of denying his religion. Mr. Gordon has been called the Jewish Kipling. [Chatto : o.p. ; Duffield, New York : o.p.]

—— *The Lost Kingdom* : *the passing of the Khazars.*   1926
An historical novel, dealing with the kingdom of Khazaria, in the Crimea (968). [Shapiro, Vallentine.]

" GORKY, Maksim " [Aleksyei Maksimovich Pyeshkov ; Russian ; b. 1869]. *Tales from Gorky* (1894–9).   1902
Nine altogether, with a biographical sketch. *Chelkash* (1895), one of the best-known masterpieces, and *Twenty-Six of Us*, appear below. *A Rolling Stone*, the life of a born vagabond, a sworn enemy of morality and conventional respectability, is a perfect summary of Gorky's philosophy, and wholesomely satirical in its scornful branding of " shoddy honesty." *In Steppe* and *One Autumn Night*, if not others, commemorate actual incidents in Gorky's life among the vagrants, the outcasts, the lovers of freedom, winds and deserts, the foes of society, whose manner of life and revolutionary morals he consistently extols, whilst obviously depicting them as better-educated and wiser-minded than they ever were. Also *The Green Kitten, Comrades, Her Lover, Chums*. [Transl. by R. Nisbet BAIN, Jarrold : o.p. ; Brentano, New York.]

—— *Comrades* (Mat', 1897).   1907
A melancholy and indignant description of the brutalized life of men, women, and children in a Russian factory, and of the revolutionary activities of the Labour leaders before 1905. The book was written for propagandist purposes, and this purpose is incarnated in the patient, ignorant woman turned into a revolutionary when she realizes the meaning of socialism. [Hodder (new ed.), 1915 : o.p. ; *sub tit. Mother*, Appleton, New York and London (new ed., 1921).]

—— *Creatures that Once were Men* (Byoshii Lyudi, 1897).   1905
Melancholy pictures of the destitute and the fallen, who resort to a doss-house belonging to a rich and cynical merchant. [Transl. by J. K. M. SHIRAZI, Rivers : o.p. ; Modern Lib., New York, 1918.]

—— *The Orloff Couple ; and, Malva* (1897).   1901
The first is perhaps Gorky's finest story. Orloff, the cobbler, has some likeness to Fomá Gordyéeff, the millionaire ; he, too, is disgusted with the flatness of life, and yearns for opportunities of heroism. Orloff and his wife in their hovel, the monotony of their existence, and the sudden spell of strenuous work for humanity during the epidemic, are depicted with fidelity and abundance of detail. In *Malva* the descriptions of the sea show Gorky's poetic feeling for nature, and the heroine is a notable creation (Gorky is always at his best in portraying women). [Transl. by Emily JAKOWLEFF and Dora B. MONTEFIORE, Heinemann : o.p. ; transl., *sub tit. Orloff and His Wife*, Scribner, New York : o.p.]

—— *Fomá Gordyéeff* (1899).   1901
A great piece of realism and spiritual insight, though formless, and overburdened with Nietzschean philosophizing. Fomá Gordyéeff (Thomas the Proud) is the son and heir of a rich merchant, but is oppressed by the falsehood and viciousness of conventional life, and wears himself out in blind efforts to find an outlet for his natural energies. The merchant classes at Nijni Novgorod, the teeming life of the Volga, are portrayed with intense realism, unreticent and unselective. Fomá's father, the domineering, unscrupulous trader, has been identified with a famous millionaire who died in a monastery. [Transl. by Isabel F. HAPGOOD, Unwin ; Scribner, New York ; *sub tit. The Man who was Afraid*, transl. by H. BERNSTEIN, Benn (1929).]

—— *Twenty-six Men and a Girl* (1899).   1902
The twenty-six men labour in a dark underground bakery (as Gorky himself had done), and the only gleam of joy in their dismal life is a young girl whom they idolize. But she falls a prey to a dissolute soldier,

"GORKY, Maksim" (*continued*)**.**
and the extinction of their one glimpse of fairness and purity is the last pang of tragedy. *Chelkash* relates how a defiant, unscrupulous, successful ruffian seduces a stupid country lad ; the workings of the two minds are revealed with astonishing force. [Transl. by Emily JAKOWLEFF and Dora B. MONTEFIORE, Duckworth ; *Chelkash and other stories*, Knopf, New York.]

—— *The Outcasts ; and other stories* (1900).   1902
Includes *Waiting for the Ferry* and *The Affair of the Clasps*. [Transl. by D. B. MONTEFIORE, Emily JAKOWLEFF, and Vera VALKHOVSKY, Unwin : o.p.]

—— *Three Men* (Troye, 1900–1).   1902
A long novel like *Fomá Gordyéeff*. The life of Ilya Lunev, son of a convict, from boyhood onwards. Ilya starts work with a rag-and-bone man, and lives with the dregs of society. His hardships, shames, and disillusionments, and the crime that leads to his death, are chiefly of interest for the terrible pictures of the vagabonds, thieves, courtesans, and the poorest classes of workers in Russia. The women, as usual, are vividly done. [Transl. by Charles HORNE, Pitman : o.p. ; by A. LINDEN, *sub tit. Three of Them*, Unwin ; Knopf, New York.]

—— *The Spy : the story of a superfluous man* (1908).   1908
This, like *Comrades*, is a propagandist novel, but reverts to the tone of pessimism. The spy is a poor, timid peasant who becomes a tool of the police. The reactionary movement, due to the rally of the Black Hundreds, and the despair of the people at the collapse of constitutionalism, are set forth with horrifying realism. [Transl. by T. SELTZER, Duckworth : o.p. ; Viking Press, New York.]

—— *A Confession* (1908).   1910
A Russian's Pilgrim's Progress. From the abysmal despair which seems the inexorable conclusion, from the universal debauchery of the monks and the ruthlessness of officialism, the Pilgrim struggles on to a faith in the people as a united force. " Thou art my God, O Sovereign people, and creator of all gods which thou hast formed from the beauties of thy spirit in the travail and torture of thy quest." [Transl. by F. HARVEY, Everett : o.p.]

—— *Tales of Two Countries.*   1914
The two countries are Italy and America, in both of which Gorky had resided. [Viking Press, New York : o.p. ; Laurie : o.p.]

—— *Through Russia : a book of stories.*   1922
Ten tales of Russian life ; *Gubin, A Woman*, and *Kalinin*, are some of the best. [Transl. by C. J. HOGARTH, (Everyman's Lib.) Dent (Dutton, New York).]

—— *The Story of a Novel ; and other stories.*   1925
The Story of a Novel ; The Sky-Blue Life ; An Incident ; The Rehearsal ; The Hermit. [Transl. by Marie ZAHREVSKY, Dial Press, New York ; Jarrolds.]

—— *Decadence.*   1927
Depicts the changing conditions of Russian life during the latter half of last century, ending with the revolution of 1905, as they affect the lives of a family of merchants in a provincial town. [Transl. by Veronica SCOTT-GATTY, Cassell ; McBride, New York.]

—— *Bystander.*   1930
First part of a trilogy, yet itself very long, covering the period 1881–94, from the assassination of Alexander II to the coronation of Nicholas II. This prolixity is due to the combination of realistic portraiture of life and society with incessant philosophical discussion of Russian affairs. Gorky has here tried to portray the intelligentsia, instead of the lower classes. This records the childhood and adolescence of one of them, and his troubles under the old regime. [Transl. by Bernard Guilbert GUERNEY, Cape.]
The second instalment, *The Magnet* (transl. by Alexander BAKSHY) has just appeared (1931). It is a critical survey of the revolutionary movement during the last two decades of the nineteenth century, and the first two of the twentieth ; in short, a study of the evolution of Bolshevism out of the vague and conflicting ideas of the earlier age, as illustrated by Samghin's gradual transformation into a representative Bolshevist, largely through the moral impact upon his selfish and conceited nature of a love-affair with a devoted woman. [Cape.]

GOSSE, Sir Edmund [1849–1928]. *The Secret of Narcisse.*   1892
Scene, Bar-le-Duc in the sixteenth century ; life at the ducal Court, mediæval manners, dresses, superstitions, feasts, and jollity are presented, but the story is of a melancholy cast and tragic in its termination. [Heinemann ; Tait, New York : o.p.]

GOUGH, George Wodey. *The Yeoman Adventurer.*   1916
—— *The Terror by Night.*   1922
—— *A Daughter of Kings.*   1930
Historical romances which emphasize the coarseness and brutality of the eighteenth century, and present the reverse side of the pictures drawn by A. and C. Castle. Walpole appears in *A Daughter of Kings ; The Yeoman Adventurer* is concerned with the Jacobite rebellion and its suppression by " Butcher " Cumberland. *The Terror by Night* is a series of romantic episodes in which a gentleman adventurer plays the chief part. [(1), Methuen ; (2), Blackwood ; (3), Skeffington.]

GOULD, Nat [1857–1919]. *A Northern Crack.*   1917
The career of a race-horse and very full measure of the seamy side of the turf. [Long : o.p.]

—— *The Smasher.*   1917
The hero and his mare have a hard time in the northern Australian deserts ; later on, the foal, which is a " smasher," makes a sensation at Kalgoorlie with its performances on the race-course. [Long : o.p.]

—— *The Rider in Khaki.*   1918
About a wounded officer who returns home, only half-recovered, to ride his own horse in a great steeplechase. [Long : o.p. ; Whitman, New York.]

GOULD, Nat (*continued*). *Fast as the Wind.* 1918
Horse-racing and crime, an escape from Dartmoor, etc. [Long : o.p. ; Whitham, New York.]

—— *Won on the Post.* 1919
Vivid descriptions of races at Epsom, York, and elsewhere, and, of course, love-making everywhere. [Long : o.p.]

—— *The Steeplechaser.* 1919
The career of a wonderful horse who twice wins the Grand National, and is the centre of a pleasant bevy of sportsmen and their womenfolk. [Long : o.p.]

—— *A Chestnut Champion.* 1920
The hero, an emigrant to Sydney, shares the triumphs of a well-known trainer and generally has a successful run in life. [Long : o.p.]

—— *Racing Rivals.* 1920
A breezy tale of two half-brothers, who have inherited their father's love of racing. [Long : o.p.]

—— *The Sweep Winner.* 1920
A story of New South Wales and Queensland and the rescue of a woman from a Chinese scoundrel and his white accomplice. [Long : o.p.]

GOULD, Rev. Sabine BARING [1834–1924]. *Mehalah : a story of the Salt Marshes.* 1880
A powerful and imaginative story of peasant folk on the east coast, in which character and melodrama are mixed in fairly equal parts. Mehalah is a country girl of strong and passionate nature, the heroine of some painful episodes ; there is racy humour in the talk and doings of several rustic people. [Murray.]

—— *John Herring.* 1884
A sombre story of village life and half-savage, primitive characters on the borders of Devon and Cornwall. Imaginative description of places and of old families and their histories, the legends connected with the Dartmoor antiquities, etc. Strong in dialect. [Smith & Elder : o.p.]

—— *Court Royal : a story of cross-currents.* 1886
The last act in the reign of a ducal family, brought low by chronic extravagance. Attention is concentrated on the career of a poor girl, pawned to the Jew who holds the chief mortgages and uses them as instruments of revenge for a personal outrage ; she inherits the Jew's wealth, marries a rich parvenu, and ends as mistress of the duke's late mansion. The eclipse of the aristocratic house is treated as a serious problem of modern social tendencies, though Joanna's career is all melodrama. [Murray.]

—— *Red Spider.* 1887
Aims at picturing realistically and preserving the features of village life on the borders of Devon and Cornwall as it was fifty years or more ago. The yeoman farmer class is depicted with many individual touches. [Chatto ; Appleton, New York : o.p.]

—— *The Gaverocks.* 1888
The sensational plot turns on wife-murder. The characters are accentuated types of Cornish villagers in bygone times : the peasants, callous, unlovable people ; the gentry represented by a brutal old squire of an obsolete stamp and his family—a rudely picturesque group. Local customs, superstitions, and other folk-lore copiously exploited [Murray ; Lippincott, Philadelphia : o.p.]

—— *Richard Cable, the Lightshipman.* 1888
An Essex peasant marries an heiress—the pathos of humble life, relieved with farce. The story at length transports us to Cornish scenes, and there is a fine description of a great wreck. [Murray ; Lippincott, Philadelphia : o.p.]

—— *Eve.* 1888
Scene : Morwell Hall, a romantic and historic spot on the Tamar, at the edge of Dartmoor (*c.* 1820). Legends of the moor, pixies, a convict's escape, etc. [Chatto : o.p. ; Appleton, New York : o.p.]

—— *Grettir the Outlaw.* [juvenile] 1889
An exciting story of desperate feats, combats with berserks and with the spirit of Glam, etc., and an instructive account of the old Icelandic mode of life (*c.* 997–1031). Based on a famous saga. [Blackie ; Scribner, New York : o.p.]

—— *Urith : a tale of Dartmoor.* 1891
Turns partly on Monmouth's rebellion (1685) ; full of stormy incident and acts of passion and malice ; the scenery and antiquities of the moor, and the manners and customs of the rugged inhabitants, are presented with abundant knowledge. [Methuen : o.p.]

—— *Margery of Quether ; and other stories.* 1891
Margery is an uncanny story ending in preparations for a witch-burning ; scene, Lamerton, near Tavistock. *At the Y* is another tale of bygone Dartmoor. [Methuen : o.p.]

—— *In the Roar of the Sea.* 1892
Strong in description of the rugged coast of north Cornwall ; the characters as usual not prepossessing, but drawn with a powerful hand. [Methuen ; Street, New York : o.p.]

—— *Cheap-Jack Zita.* 1893
A very sensational story of the Ely fens in 1815. [Methuen : o.p. ; Tait, New York : o.p.]

—— *Noémi : a story of rock-dwellers.* 1895
France under Charles VII, at the time of the long struggle with England (*c.* 1450) ; the heroine, an Amazonian Jewess. Local features, such as the wondrous rock-fortress on the Dordogne, play a considerable part in the tale. [Methuen : o.p. ; Appleton, New York : o.p.]

—— *Kitty Alone : a story of three fires.* 1895
Teignmouth and the fringes of Dartmoor in the rick-burning days (*c.* 1820). Kitty is one of the writer's best women-characters ; and her uncle, Pasco Peperill, who commits arson to get the insurance, is a rascal strongly portrayed. Describes " Brunel's Folly "—the Atmospheric Railway. [Methuen : o.p.]

GOULD, Rev. Sabine BARING (*continued*). *The Broom-Squire.* 1896

Deals with the historic murder of a sailor near the Devil's Punchbowl, Hindhead, in 1786, by three men who were hanged at this spot ; and with life in the neighbourhood. Mehetabel is a striking character. [Methuen ; Stokes, New York : o.p.]

—— *Dartmoor Idylls.* 1896

Magazine stories of the primitive moorland folk, descriptive of the wild and barren but ever-varying scenery, and full of local and archæological lore. [Methuen : o.p.]

—— *Guavas, the Tinner.* 1897

A melodrama of passion, villainy, and triumphant virtue, enacted in the wildest part of Dartmoor ; embodying much antiquarian lore, about the Stannary Laws, the manners and customs of the tin-miners, and the superstitions that prevailed down to the Elizabethan age and even after. [Methuen : o.p.]

—— *Bladys of the Stewponey.* 1897

A Shropshire romance (1790) turning on the marriage of a hangman, who manages to conceal his identity, with the pretty daughter of an innkeeper. Contains some ghastly scenes, like the execution of a woman by burning. [Methuen : o.p.]

—— *Perpetua.* 1897

The persecutions of Christians at Nîmes (A.D. 213) ; a learned archæological work. [Pitman : o.p. ; Dutton, New York : o.p.]

—— *Domitia.* 1898

An antiquary's picture of Court life in Rome during the reign of terror under Domitian (76–96) ; takes liberties with history. The heroine is the tyrant's unhappy wife. [Heinemann : o.p. ; Stokes, New York : o.p.]

—— *Pabo the Priest.* 1899

A story of Wales in the time of Henry I (1115–20), who was trying to force Roman discipline on the independent Welsh Church, with a view to subjugating the people. Strong in local colour. [Methuen : o.p. ; Stokes, New York : o.p.]

GOURMONT, Remy de [French ; 1858–1915]. *The Dream of a Woman* (Le songe d'une femme : roman familier, 1899). 1927

An erotic novel in letters, by various young woman-hunters and their female counterparts, all of whom plume themselves on their moral and intellectual emancipation. They are, of course, not live characters, only attitudes, illustrations of the author's *Physique de l'amour*. One of the men-philosophers contends, " My sensualism is stoical," " Love is always a matter of gastronomy." The most illuminated of the women avows her scheme of life to be to enslave men through their lusts. [Transl., Boni, New York.]

—— *A Night in the Luxembourg* (Une nuit au Luxembourg, 1906). 1912

In his jaded literary man's dream of a night of Oriental bliss in the transfigured gardens of the Luxembourg, Remy de Gourmont gave a loose to his sensuous imagination, and cleverly at the end leaves us wondering whether the lovely paramour is not a real woman after all. [Transl. Luce, Boston.]

—— *A Virgin Heart* (Un cœur virginal, 1907). 1921

The author suggests alternative subtitles : " a novel without hypocrisy," " a physiological novel " ; the second will do. He takes a special case of the physiology of love—an innocent girl's induction, premising that " a young girl is not merely an unawakened heart, but a young human body in all its completeness." The elderly roué who awakens her senses but shilly-shallies at the question of marriage, is cut out by a younger man who plays a dirty trick on his rival. [Transl. by Aldous HUXLEY, Allen & Unwin ; Brown, New York.]

—— *Mr. Antiphilos, Satyr* (Lettres d'un satyre, 1913). 1922

The satyr is a chance survival from the golden age, when he and his like were forces akin to Nature herself. He is a most convenient exponent of Remy de Gourmont's philosophy of instinct versus reason, nature versus society. It is a pagan *éloge* of sensualism and promiscuity, rather than the satire of social restrictions and social sophistries announced in the preface. [Trans. by JOHN HOWARD, Lieber & Lewis, New York.]

GOZLAN, Léon [French ; 1803–66]. *The Emotions of Polydore Marasquin* (Les emotions de Polydore Marasquin, 1857). 1888

An extravaganza in Jules Verne's manner. Marasquin is cast away on an island in the Malay archipelago, and is enslaved by the inhabitants, who are monkeys : full of wild incident and of descriptions of tropical scenery. For some reason the better-known *Aristide Froissart* (1843) and the characteristic blood-curdler, *Histoire de cent trente femmes* (1852) have not been translated. [Vizetelly : o.p.]

GRAÇA ARANHA, José Pereira da [Brazilian ; b. 1868]. *Canaan.* 1920

A novel of contemporary South America : an idealistic German emigrates to Brazil, hoping to find there a purer moral atmosphere than at home, and is disillusioned. [Transl. from the Portuguese by Mariano Joaquin LORENTE, Four Seas Co., Boston ; Allen & Unwin.]

GRACE, Alfred A. [New Zealander]. *Tales of a Dying Race.* 1901

Stories republished from the Sydney *Bulletin*, depicting the Maoris of New Zealand after the manner of Bret Harte and Rudyard Kipling. [Chatto : o.p.]

GRAHAM, John William [b. 1859]. *Neæra : a tale of ancient Rome.* 1886

The Rome of Tiberius (A.D. 26) ; portraits of the tyrant, Sejanus, Apicius, and others. The famous banquet of Apicius elaborated into a dramatic episode. By the machinations of a profligate woman Neæra is abducted to Capreæ, and the episode serves to introduce descriptions of the splendour, the sensuality, and the crimes of this imperial hermitage. [Macmillan : o.p.]

—— *Harlaw of Sendle.* 1901

Motive of the love-story, the scruples of a high-minded young man who loves an heiress. But the main interest lies in the portraiture of certain Cumberland originals. [Blackwood : o.p.]

GRAHAM, Gabriela Cunninghame [*née* De la Balmondière; *d.* 1906]. *The Christ of Toro; and other stories.* 1908
Stories and vignettes of clerical life in Spain and Mexico, written in early life by the late Mrs. Cunninghame Graham, with two translations from Gustavo Becquer, *Tres Fechas* and *La Mujer de Piedra*. [Nash: o.p.]

GRAHAM, Robert Bontine Cunninghame [Scottish; *b.* 1852]. *The Ipané.* 1899
Sketches of travel and pithy stories, portraits of exotic types and individuals, and bits of elemental drama, collected by a globe-trotter, an inveterate Ishmaelite, who lays stress on the contrast between civilized dullness and real life. The subjects are chiefly South American; but there are striking glimpses of Scotch character in *A Survival, Heather Jock,* and *Salvagia;* while *S.S. Atlas,* the narrative of a tramp's voyage across the Atlantic, is one of the finest sketches. [Unwin; Boni, New York.]

—— *Thirteen Stories.* 1900
A traveller's yarns from all over the globe, describing foreign and irregular ways of life with the mordant vigour of an etching, and with amazingly few strokes of lifelike dialogue, sketching such strong, simple types as the "Forty-niner" of Rio Grande, the skipper of the German tramp, the desperate band of hounded Apaches, the Arab blindly dying to do his chieftain's bidding. A love of free self-assertion and a hatred of the shams of civilization barb innumerable epigrams. [Duckworth.]

—— *Success.* 1902
"How few successful men are interesting!" The vulgarity and inconsequence of success, the relative grandeur of lost causes, the meanness of our convention-ridden, machine-made civilization, such is the burden of these essays, short tales, and sketches of life in all parts of the world. The biting, acrimonious style is very characteristic. [Duckworth; Stokes, New York, 1917: o.p.]

—— *Progress; and other sketches.* 1905
Progress is a sardonic account of the wiping out of a Mexican community by the forces of law and order. The other essays, impressions, or bits of stories, wander back to Morocco, Yorkshire, Scotland; and vary in subject, but all harp on the rights of the unconventional freeman against the Philistine. [Duckworth: o.p.; Stokes, New York, 1917: o.p.]

—— *His People.* 1906
Similar sketches from all the world over, the most sympathetic being those concerned with the failures, the desolate and oppressed. Almost every story has a dig at our boasted civilization. *Fate,* a pessimistic tale, *Le Chef, Signalled, Dagos, A Wire-walker,* and two Scottish stories, *Miss Christine Jean* and *Ha Til Mi Tuliadh,* are admirable specimens. *A Memory of Parnell* is a passionate apologia. [Duckworth.]

—— *Faith.* 1909
Brilliant but depressing episodes of all manner of life, similar in general complexion to the foregoing. *At the Ward Toll* is a picturesque study in melancholy on a lovely Highland road. *At the River* is an Oriental fantasia put realistically, and evidently true. In *Maktub* an old beggar is the impersonation of the Oriental doctrine of Kismet. [Duckworth; Stokes, New York: o.p.]

—— *Hope.* 1910
More railing against the shams and hypocrisies of the world, rather memories than stories, and every one an intimate revelation of the man himself. They range over Spain, Morocco, South America, Scotland, etc. *The Fourth Magus* tells of the king from the East who arrived only in time for Calvary. *My Uncle* and *Un Monsieur* are kindlier portraits, the latter well worthy of Flaubert. [Duckworth; Stokes, New York: o.p.]

—— *Charity.* 1912
Mordant irony finds expression in the sketch *Charity,* and in the preface, which is really a story; whilst *Aunt Eleanor* is a wonderful creation, a typical Scottish character, and, like *A Meeting,* offers a contrast to the meanness and sordidness out of which the others have their birth. [Duckworth.]

—— *A Hatchment.* 1913
A collection of sketches, mainly descriptive; *Los Indios* and *El Rodeo* are fine accounts of two aspects of South American life; *Bismillah* is a delicate Theocritean idyll, a contrast to the heady matter of the rest. [Duckworth.]

—— *Scottish Stories.* 1914
Collects together the Scottish stories of previous volumes—stories which recapture the atmosphere of the author's native land, and present vivid pictures of characteristic and notable types. [Duckworth: o.p.]

—— *Thirty Tales and Sketches.* 1929
These are selected from previous books, one or two being taken from each. The selection is made by Edward Garnett. [Duckworth; Viking Press, New York.]

GRAHAM, Stephen [*b.* 1884]. *The Lay Confessor.* 1928
A picture of Russia in the period of revolution, in particular, how the upheaval affects the lives of two men and a girl. [Benn; Knopf, New York.]

—— *St. Vitus Day.* 1930
An imaginative reading of recent history—the conspiracy that brought about the assassination of the Archduke Franz Ferdinand at Serajevo in 1914. The quiet, matter-of-fact account of the diabolical treatment meted out to the alleged assassin, Gavro Princip, is appalling. [Benn.]

GRAHAME, Kenneth [*b.* 1859]. *The Golden Age.* 1895
Sketches of childhood by a man who still loves the fanciful pleasures and has not forgotten the feelings of children. The characters are a little family of five children left to themselves and creating a little world of their own.

—— *Dream Days.* 1898
Takes up the story, if story it can be called, when the children are entering upon the threshold of adult life. The same imaginative impressionism, half-forgotten things seen through a mist of dreamy longing. [(1) and (2), Lane; Nelson; Dodd & Mead, New York; Garden City Co., New York. *Illus.* by M. Parrish, Lane; Dodd & Mead, New York; by Lois Lenski, Lane.]

GRAHAME, Kenneth (*continued*). *The Wind in the Willows.* 1908
> A charming make-believe in which animals, with man-like foibles, figure as men—Mole, Rat, the Badger, and a romantic stranger—and have adventures in which the animals' point of view and the human interchange with humorous inconsistency. [Methuen ; Harrap ; Scribner, New York. *Illus.* by Wyndham Payne, Methuen ; by Nancy Barnhart, Scribner, New York.]

"GRAND, Sarah" [Mrs. Frances Elizabeth Haldane McFall, *née* Clarke ; Irish ; *b.* 1862]. *Ideala.* 1888
> A portrait of a woman of original and wayward nature, a character "by suffering made strong"; one of the earliest sketches of the New Woman. [Heinemann : o.p.]

—— *The Heavenly Twins.* 1893
> Less a coherent story than a string of multifarious incidents and moralizing passages intended to advocate greater freedom for women : a wife discovers her husband's past, and declines to live with him. Some of the characters are eccentrically humorous, others idealizations of the writer's views on life. The episode in Book IV, *The Tenor and the Boy* (which has been published separately) is about a young wife, disguised as a boy, and a sensitive young man, who discovers her sex when rescuing her from drowning. [Heinemann.]

—— *The Beth Book.* 1897
> The biography of a girl who believes she has genius, and who is a type of the New Woman. This also is full of moralizing tirades about modern society, the masculine regime, etc., but is not quite so chaotic. [Heinemann : o.p.]

—— *Babs the Impossible.* 1901
> The history of Babs begins with her precocious girlhood, and is carried on to the age of love-making. First we have the family squabbles of this *enfant terrible*, and then her flirtations with a romantic peer and his friend. The other characters are chiefly women, more or less neurotic and eccentric, in a remote country place, where bachelors are hard to come by. [Hutchinson : o.p.]

—— *Adnam's Orchard.* 1912
> A better-constructed novel of country life, from the landed gentry down to the labouring-man, many of them finely characterized. Adnam with his schemes for educating the rustics finds he has a hard furrow to turn. Sarah Grand is not less in earnest here, but she manages to state her views on social regeneration in a more artistic and objective way. [Heinemann : o.p. ; Appleton, New York.]

GRANT, Charles [American ; 1841–88]. *Stories of Naples and the Camorra.* 1897
> Grant lived among the Neapolitans from 1872 to 1878. His affable and sympathetic disposition ingratiated him, not only with the tradespeople or *galant'uomini*, but with the much more exclusive *lazzaroni*, peasants, and fisher-folk. A methodical observer, he sets down honestly just what he sees, without any romantic bias. *Peppiniello* is a street boy living from hand to mouth : no novelist has explored a lower stratum of humanity. *Gabriele*, the longest story, describes the tragedies that follow on any violation of the barrier between the *lazzaroni* and the better classes. *Don Antonio* recounts the rise to authority of a Camorrist, and *Domenico* is a darker story of a ruffianly agent of the same formidable society, into whose secret organization Grant seems to have won a completer insight than any other foreigner. [With introductory memoir by J. B. Capper, Macmillan, New York and London : o.p.]

GRANT, James [Scottish ; 1822–87]. *The Romance of War ; or, The Highlanders in Spain.* 1846
> Grant's typical romance—love-making in Perthshire, Highlanders in the Peninsular War, and the Waterloo campaign (1812–15) ; battle scenes, duels, flirtations, and sketches of Spanish character and manners ; the narrative ending with the hero's return to Scotland and union with his love. All Grant's novels are suitable for boys. [Warne, London and New York.]

—— *The Adventures of Rob Roy.* 1848
> A collection of anecdotes and traditions about the career of the doughty cateran (*c.* 1715), with very little if any fiction. [o.p.]

—— *The Adventures of an Aide-de-Camp.* 1848
> Campaigning and miscellaneous adventure in Italy (1806–8), battle of Maida, and siege of Scylla. Zingari, brigands, patriots, French and British soldiers, all play their part. [Warne, London and New York.]

—— *Bothwell ; or, The Days of Queen Mary.* 1851
> The career of Mary's evil spirit, Bothwell (1566–77). Opens in Norway, where he is an ambassador to the Danish king, with scenes of shipwreck and peril. Lady Bothwell's piteous tragedy, the murder of Darnley, Bothwell's amour and marriage with Mary, his miserable end as a captive in Malmö. [o.p.]

—— *The Scottish Cavalier ; or, The Revolution of 1688.* 1851
> Dundee and the battle of Killiecrankie ; with scenes in the Low Countries, the battle of Steinkirke, etc. [o.p.]

—— *Philip Rollo ; or, The Scotch Musketeers.* 1854
> Scottish soldiers of fortune in the Thirty Years' War, chiefly in Denmark ; Tilly, Wallenstein, and Gustavus Adolphus, etc. (1626–9). [o.p.]

—— *The Yellow Frigate ; or, The Three Sisters.* 1855
> The romantic and tragic incidents that marked the close of James III's reign, the insurrection of the nobles, the battle of Sauchieburn, and the murder of James (1488), followed by the sea-fights with the English in the Firth of Forth. The fiction has a more prosperous ending. [Nelson.]

—— *Harry Ogilvie ; or, The Black Dragoons.* 1856
> A Royalist story of the Great Civil War (1638–51). Scotch politics and religious feuds, the Solemn League and Covenant, invasion of England, coronation of Charles II at Scone, the battle of Inverkeithing and the sack of Dundee, with, of course, a love-story running through the narrative. [o.p.]

—— *Frank Hilton ; or, The Queen's Own.* 1857
> Scenes of regimental life, a troopship voyage to Aden, the hero's adventurous mission as envoy to an Arab sultan, winding up with a big battle in which the Arabs are severely beaten. Sketches of Oriental life, scenery, religious and superstitious observances, and Oriental tales. [Routledge.]

GRANT, James (*continued*). *Lucy Arden.* 1859

A narrative of the Jacobite rebellion in 1715, with racy character-sketches of the leaders and the more prominent rank and file. The hero gets mixed up with the rising, but escapes punishment and wins the heroine of the love-story. Grant shows much irresponsible originality in making out " General " Forster to be a good-natured debauchee, whose fondness for women nearly led to his capture by the enemy. [o.p.]

—— *Mary of Lorraine.* 1860

Battle of Pinkie (1547) and the question of the marriage of Mary, Queen of Scots (1548). [o.p.]

—— *The Captain of the Guard.* 1862

James II of Scotland and the House of Douglas, from the execution of the sixth Earl to the stabbing of the eighth Earl by the king at Stirling. Scenes : Edinburgh, Galloway, and Flanders (1440–52). [o.p.]

—— *Second to None.* 1864

Adventures of a penniless gentleman, who serves in the Scots Greys under the Duke of Cumberland in Hanover (1759) ; camp life, an exciting night-action, swift and strange turns of fortune, escapes, disguises, rescues, amours ; a rapid succession of melodramatic events, with plenty of horror to flavour. [o.p.]

GRANT, Judge Robert [American ; 1852–1914]. *The Confessions of a Frivolous Girl.* 1880

The ante-matrimonial experiences of a fashionable girl in New York, particularly her behaviour towards a trio of suitors, one of whom she marries after enjoying her fill of balls, flirtations, and liberty. The frivolity of the fashionable American girl, her vulgarity and boisterous manners, along with the foibles of divers masculine types, are the object of satire. [Houghton, Boston : o.p.]

—— *The Reflections of a Married Man.* 1892

The various experiences of conjugal life, with the self-revealing reflections of the author ; lightly humorous.

—— *The Opinions of a Philosopher.* 1893

Philosophy drawn from a happy married life in Boston, pervaded with a quiet humour and a high appreciation of the possibilities of wedded companionship. [(1) and (2), Scribner, New York ; (1) : o.p. ; Warne : o.p. ; together, *sub tit.* A Married Man, Scribner, 1925.]

—— *The Bachelor's Christmas : and other stories.* 1895

Half a dozen stories of fashionable society in Boston. [Scribner, New York : o.p.]

—— *Unleavened Bread.* 1900

Study of a woman's character as illustrated by her career and the people with whom she comes in contact—a woman whose ambition and energy are out of all proportion to her ability. The three matrimonial chapters of her biography form, as it were, three separate tales, three contrasted phases of American life. [Scribner, New York ; Hutchinson : o.p.]

—— *The Undercurrent.* 1904

A characteristic story of Judge Grant's—serious, methodical, patiently observant, full of criticism from the point of view of an experienced man of the world, illustrating the modern problems of love, marriage, business, religion. The theatre of events is Benham, a thriving lumber city. [Scribner, New York : o.p. ; Hutchinson : o.p.]

—— *The Chippendales.* 1909

The Chippendales are an old Boston family, rooted in tradition and the New England conscience, whose family mansion is bought and whose exclusive social sphere is invaded by a scion of modern commercialism, the bustling Blaisdell. [Scribner, New York ; Stanley Paul : o.p.]

GRAS, Félix [Provençal ; 1845–1901]. *The Reds of the Midi* (Li rouge dóu miejour, 1896). 1896

—— *The Terror* [sequel]. 1898

—— *The White Terror : a romance of the French Revolution and after* [sequel]. 1900

A living picture of the whole of the revolutionary era by a Southern novelist, who puts it in the homely words of a rustic, and so attains an air of verisimilitude in a very artistic and charming way. The supposed narrator is a peasant from Provence, who marches to Paris with the Marseilles battalion, and is an eye-witness of all that he describes. The first book depicts the unsettled state of Paris after the fall of the Bastille, and then tells how the insurrection broke out anew, and how the mob sacked Versailles. In the sequel the Reign of Terror is in full blast, Marat figures prominently, and the king is executed. The scene in the last volume changes back to the South and faction-torn Avignon ; Valmy and other battlefields are described, and then, more briefly, the rise and career of Napoleon. Everything falls into right perspective from the consistency with which the point of view of a man of the people is maintained, even in the running commentary of the unlettered hearers. [Transl. by Mrs. JANVIER, (1), (2), and (3), Heinemann : o.p. ; Appleton, New York (new ed. 1928–30).]

GRAVES or GREAVES, Richard [1715–1804]. *The Spiritual Quixote : or, The Summer's Ramble of Mr. Geoffry Wildgoose : a comic romance.* 1772

Like Smollett's *Launcelot Greaves*, a clumsy satire on the *Don Quixote* plan, the young Oxonian Wildgoose adopting Methodism and perambulating Gloucestershire and Somerset with his trusty Sancho, Jeremiah Tugwell, the cobbler. Episodes in the conventional novelistic style are tacked on, and there are interesting denunciations of contemporary follies in manners and dress. Graves was rector of Claverton, near Bath. [With introd. by Charles Whibley, 2 vols., Davies, 1926.]

GRAVES, Robert [b. 1895]. *My Head ! My Head !* 1925

" Being the history of Elisha and the Shunamite woman : with the history of Moses as Elisha related it, and her questions put to him." An imaginative and more personal re-telling of the Book of Kings. [Secker ; Knopf, New York.]

" GRAY, Maxwell " [Miss Mary Gleed Tuttiett ; 1847–1923]. *The Silence of Dean Maitland.* 1886

As a young curate, a future dignitary of the Church seduces a girl, commits manslaughter, and allows his dearest friend to suffer penal servitude for the crime. Afterwards he lives a good and useful life, with occasional twinges of conscience, till the friend is released from prison and forgives him, whereupon the Dean makes public confession and dies. [Routledge ; Burt, New York.]

"GRAY, Maxwell" (*continued*). *The Last Sentence.* 1893

A barrister, having married a girl of low station, learns that she has perished in a fire ; in point of fact, she is alive, and accidentally sees him courting another woman, the shock causing her death. By a strange series of events, he condemns as judge his own daughter for child-murder, and her innocence is proved barely in time to save her from death. [Heinemann : o.p. ; Appleton, New York : o.p.]

—— *The House of Hidden Treasure.* 1898

An old-fashioned plot-novel, with a villain of the old school, who intercepts letters and in general maintains the traditions of his office. The lively heroine belongs to the type of girl who is at once fascinating and exasperating. [Heinemann : o.p. ; Appleton, New York : o.p.]

GREEN, Anna Katherine [Mrs. Rohlfs ; American ; b. 1846]. *The Leavenworth Case.* 1878

A good example of this writer's many detective novels. She is a successful follower of Wilkie Collins. [Putnam, New York (new ed., 1913) ; Routledge : o.p.]

—— *The House of the Whispering Pines.* 1910

A similar story of criminal investigation culminating in a trial scene in New York State. [Putnam, New York (new ed., 1917) ; Nash.

GREEN, Evelyn EVERETT [1856–1931]. *Six Stories, narrated by Max von Pochammer.*

1900

The first story may be taken as type of this prolific writer's many domestic stories for young girls : the love-tale of a German pastor, a learned man, but simple-hearted, a believer in Providence, who chooses his wife by a sign from above, and wins her love after years of waiting. [Leadenhall Press : o.p.]

—— *Evil May-Day.* [juvenile] 1893

An historical story of London in 1517 ; the prentices' riot against foreign craftsmen, attack on Newgate, etc. [Nelson.]

—— *Shut In : a tale of the wonderful siege of Antwerp.* [juvenile] 1894

The siege and capture of Antwerp by the Duke of Parma (1585). [Nelson : o.p.]

—— *A Clerk of Oxford.* [juvenile] 1897

Oxford, Kenilworth, the battle of Lewes, etc. (1264). [Nelson : o.p.]

—— *Tom Tufton's Travels.* [juvenile] 1897
—— *Tom Tufton's Toll* [sequel]. [juvenile] 1898

Adventures of highwaymen, etc. (1704). [(1), Nelson ; (2), *id.* : o.p.]

GREEN, Julien [American, of French birth ; b. 1900]. *Avarice House* (Mont-Cinère, 1926). 1927

A sort of Virginian *Wuthering Heights*, without the poetry. A skinflint mother and her ignorant, victimized daughter, who is strong-minded enough to retaliate but only brings down general disaster, are the protagonists of a squalid, uncouth story, the gloom of which is obstinately unrelieved by even a glint of humour. In the method of his story-telling M. Green seems to be intent on illustrating the theories of the behaviourists. [Transl. by Marshal A. BEST, Harper, New York ; Benn.]

—— *The Closed Garden* (Adrienne Mesurat, 1927). 1928

The same relentless analysis of a mental case, the same piling up of the agony, the same behaviourist procedure appear in this story of a lonely young girl in a small French town who works herself into a state of desperation through the belief that she is guilty of her father's death. The power of it grips and absorbs ; one can't put the book down, yet one groans for the end. [Transl. by Henry Longan STUART, Harper, New York ; Heinemann.]

—— *The Dark Journey* (Léviathan, 1929). 1929

Lays bare the smouldering passions and sudden, obscure impulses that end in crime. A man goaded to murder by the discovery that the girl he loves is a *cocotte* ; the girl herself, more sinned against than sinning ; the stupid, selfish woman who corrupted her ; and another woman who is a concise study of sadism, are the cardinal figures in a drama conducted entirely by means of psychological analysis. [Transl. by Vyvyan HOLLAND, Harper, New York ; Heinemann.]

—— *Christine ; and other stories* (Le voyageur sur la terre, 1930). 1930

Essays in morbid or at any rate abnormal psychology, rather than lucid stories. The longest probes curiously a case of dissociation of personality ending in suicide. *The Keys of Death* deals gloomily and obscurely with a situation that might have been given a comic turn. The two others are of the slightest, including *Leviathan*, which is a footnote to *The Dark Journey*, the murderer dying of remorse when he is safe from justice. [Transl. by Courtney BRUERTON, Harper, New York ; Heinemann ; *The Pilgrim on the Earth, illus.*, ltd. ed., Harper, New York (Blackamore Press), 1929.]

GREENE, Graham. *The Man Within.* 1929

Combines a story of adventure, the shifts and straits of a young man fleeing from the band of Sussex smugglers whom he has betrayed to the revenue officers, with a very modern psychological analysis of the cause of his cowardice. The trial of the smugglers at Lewes assizes is a powerful scene. [Heinemann ; Doubleday, Doran, New York.]

GREENE, Robert [c. 1560–92]. *Pandosto, the Triumph of Time ; or, The Pleasant History of Dorastus and Fawnia.* 1588

A pastoral, written in the euphuistic style, based on a Polish tale, and used by Shakespeare as material for *A Winter's Tale.* Plot, scenery, and characters, with the chronological and topographical mistakes, are all reproduced there. Pandosto is Leontes, Dorastus, Florizel, and Fawnia, Perdita. Greene was a fertile romancer, and his other stories are of great interest to the student of literature. [Ed. P. G. Thomas (Shakespeare Classics) with Second Day of Puget de la Serre's *Pandoste* (1631) in French (1907), Oxford Press.]

GREENE, Sarah Pratt [*née* McLean ; American ; b. 1855]. *Cape Cod Folks.* 1881

A series of personal sketches. The fictitious characters were so easily identified with their caricatured models that the publishers were mulcted in damages in a libel suit, and the author gained lucrative notoriety. [Grosset, New York.]

GREGOR, Joseph [German ; *b.* 1888]. *The Sisters of Prague* (Die Schwestern von Prag, 1929).
1930
The three sisters, in their tumbledown castle, masquerading in scenes from Goethe, Schiller, and Donizetti, seem to be all in love with the runaway husband of one of them. *Adephi, or the happiness of man, War with God,* and some of the shorter tales, are equally enigmatic. [Transl. by Albert BEAUMONT and Eric SUTTON, Secker.]

GREGORY, Augusta, Lady [*née* Persse ; Irish] [tr.]. *Cuchulain of Muirthemne : the story of the men of the Red Branch of Ulster ; arranged and put into English by Lady Gregory.*   1902
Not a tale nor a series of tales, but the redaction of a whole primitive literature, the legends of Cuchulain, "the Irish Achilles," or " the Irish Herakles," as he is variously described.   The extant MS. literature amounts to some 2,000 octavo pages, the MSS. being principally pre-twelfth century ; the tales assumed their present form between the seventh and the ninth centuries.   Not a Gaelic scholar herself, Lady Gregory has translated them from various sources, English and foreign, collating different authorities.   But like Malory, she has not aimed at literal accuracy, but has selected and suppressed what she thought desirable, and, where necessary, introduced links to strengthen the whole.   For this reason, Irish scholars compare this unfavourably with the more literal collection made by Miss Hull, criticizing Lady Gregory for creating an artificial unity, and for leavening these primitive sagas with the modern ideas of Connaught and Munster. The stories that form landmarks are the *Birth of Cuchulain, Bricriu's Feast, The Fate of the Children of Usnach, The War for the Bull of Cuailgne, The Battle of Rosnaree, The Only Son of Aoife, The Great Gathering at Muirthemne,* and *The Death of Cuchulain.*   The war for the bull (*Tain bó Cuailgne*) is the central saga. The language of this translation is somewhat too artificially archaic ; Mr. Yeats calls it, " the beautiful speech of those who think in Irish."   Though written in prose, the book is poetry in essence and style— romance saturated with mythology, and breaking momently into lyricism (the irregular metres are rendered into prose).   Characters of epic grandeur, the exterminating feuds of savage tribes, battles and single combats, feats of strength and endurance, scenes of feast and ceremony, wonderful enchantments, with wild passions and splendid lyrical laments, are knit together in a fairly unbroken narrative.   A meritorious endeavour to popularize the primitive legends of Celtic Ireland.   [With preface by W. B. Yeats, Murray ; Scribner, New York ; *Cuchulain the Hound of Ulster,* by Eleanor HULL, is a recension of the legends for children ; Harrap, 1909 : o.p. ; *illus.,* Crowell, New York.]

—— *Gods and Fighting Men : the story of the Tuatha de Danaan and of the Fianna of Ireland.*   1906
Cuchulain of Muirthemne is a popular redaction of the heroic legends, this of the divine and the Fenian legends of Ireland, in other words of the Ossianic legends, current orally or in MSS. in both Ireland and Scotland. Mr. Nutt considered that whilst the Cuchulain cycle belonged to the aristocratic class and died out in Scotland, the survival of the legends of Finn and the Fianna in that country proves them to be "non-Aryan folk-literature partially subjected to Aryan treatment."   These stories are independent of the Cuchulain cycle, and in like manner have been furnished with legendary connexions linking them with the Christian age.   They are myth, not history.   Even the period of their composition is uncertain ; the oldest MSS. belong to the eleventh and twelfth centuries, but their stories are 100 to 250 years more ancient ; a large number are in fourteenth-century MSS., and were redacted in the thirteenth or fourteenth centuries. The bulk consists of narrative poems, the Scottish written in the fifteenth to seventeenth centuries, the Irish in the sixteenth to nineteenth.   Lady Gregory has followed the same method of borrowing from the best authorities, though she has not scrupled to modify the text, and has adopted the same colloquial peasant prose as in her former recension.   From the following list of sixteen books it will be noticed that many of the sagas cited here appear also under other translators.   Part I, *The Gods :—The Coming of the Tuatha de Danaan ; Lugh of the Long Hand ; The Coming of the Gael ; The Ever-Living Living Ones ; The Fate of the Children of Lir.*   Part II, *The Fianna :—Finn, Son of Cumhal ; Finn's Helpers ; The Battle of the White Strand ; Huntings and Enchantments ; Oisin's Children ; Dearmuid ; Dearmuid and Grania ; Cnoc-an-air ; The Wearing Away of the Fianna ; The End of the Fianna ; Oisin and Patrick.*   For those who will not read all of them, the following stand out as pre-eminent examples of the literature : the epic *Battle of the White Strand* fought by the Fianna to keep the foreigners out of Ireland ; the flight of Dearmuid and Grania, with its correspondences to the Arthurian story ; the tragic story *The End of the Fianna,* Oisin's lament for the days that have passed away, and the famous colloquy of Oisin and St. Patrick.   [With preface by W. B. YEATS, Murray ; Scribner, New York.]

—— *Poets and Dreamers.*   1906
An ingathering of legends, and even translated talks with peasants, from modern Irish, ballads and other poems (best of all, those of the blind Raftery, a wandering minstrel of sixty years ago), two little folk-plays from the Irish of Dr. Douglas Hyde, *The Twisting of the Rope* and *The Marriage,* and miscellaneous sketches giving Lady Gregory's personal impressions of Irish people of to-day.   *A Book of Saints and Wonders* [Murray] is a similar gleaning from modern sources.   [Murray : o.p. ; Scribner, New York : o.p.]

GREGORY, Jackson [American ; *b.* 1882].   *Wolf Breed.*   1917
Gold-finding, jewel-hunting, and love in the North-West Territory.   [Dodd & Mead, New York : o.p. ; Grosset, New York ; Hurst.]

GRENFELL, Sir Wilfrid Thomason [*b.* 1865].   *Tales of the Labrador.*   1916
The only blemish on these stories of the back of beyond is their excessive sentimentality.   [Houghton, Boston ; Nisbet.]

—— *Labrador Days : tales of the sea toilers.*   1919
Stories of the struggle against sea and snow of the fishermen, trappers, and Eskimos, told by the great authority on Labrador.   [Houghton, Boston ; Hodder.]

GRETTIS SAGA : *the story of Grettir the Strong.*   1869
A sombre story, simpler in plan than most of the sagas, and less encumbered with genealogical and other extraneous matter ; has much the same plan as a modern biographical novel.   Grettir is a man of prodigious strength and indomitable courage, whose irascible temper gets him into a succession of scrapes for men illegally slain, and involves him at last in outlawry.   He holds his own in defiance of innumerable foes for nearly twenty years, and then is killed lying on his sick-bed (*c.* 997–1031).   As a prose epic of

GRETTIS SAGA (*continued*).

simple, heroic character, of strenuous deeds, and unflinching bravery, it is one of the finest things in northern story ; the supernatural episodes are peculiarly Icelandic in character. Vigfússon sees in the saga three separate parts : the first, Historical, based on an original *Grettis saga* ; the second, Mythical, comprising an Icelandic version of the Beowulf legend ; and a third, Fabulous and Romantic, derived from indigenous folk-tales and from foreign romance. He thinks the saga was edited into this final shape about 1300–10. [Transl. by Eiríkr MAGNÚSSON and William MORRIS (*Works*, vol. 7), Longmans ; transl. by George Ainslie HIGHT (Everyman's Lib.), Dent (Dutton, New York).]

" GRÉVILLE, Henri " [Alice Marie Céleste Durand, *née* Fleury ; French ; 1842–1902]. *Sylvie's Betrothed* (Le fiancé de Sylvie, 1882).　　1882

The central situation is a delicate one, but the author's refinement makes the story wholesome. Sylvie, an impulsive girl, almost unconsciously falls in love with her guardian, and he as innocently returns her regard, but, striving to do his duty by her, induces her to engage herself to a young lover. When Sylvie dismisses her fiancé, the situation becomes acute ; but the *dénouement* exhibits the triumph of goodness, and teaches that " we must not live for ourselves alone." [Transl. by M. N. SHERWOOD, Peterson, Philadelphia : o.p.]

—— *Nikanor* (1887).　　1889

A Russian story, illustrating elevated ideals of conduct and character. The history of a grand seigneur, an egoist, who causes a love-child to be brought up secretly. Impelled by a sense of duty, he gradually experiences such feelings of paternity as melt the ice enveloping his heart. [Transl. by Éliza E. CHASE, Chatto.]

Mme Durand has also written *L'héritière*, *Péril* (1891), *Jolie propriété à vendre*, *Un vieux ménage* (1893), *Fidèlka*, *L'aveu* (1894), *Ariadne* (1878), (transl., Burt, New York, 1906 : o.p.), *The Beauraud Mystery* (transl., Mershon, New York, 1900 : o.p.), etc.

GREY, Zane [American ; *b.* 1875]. *The Last Trail*.　　1916

Pioneer life a hundred years ago in the Ohio valley—after Fenimore Cooper. [Burt, New York ; Hodder.]

—— *The Spirit of the Border*.　　1916

This impressive story of pioneers in the Ohio Valley a century since, of the white renegade, and the burning of the Moravian village, is partly founded on documents left by the writer's ancestor Colonel Zane. [Burt, New York ; Hodder.]

GRIEG, Nordahl [Norwegian ; *b.* 1902]. *The Ship Sails On* (Skibet gaar videre, 1924).　　1927

A realistic account of tramp steamer life—both afloat and ashore. [Transl. by A. G. CHATER, Knopf, London and New York.]

" GRIER, Sydney Carlyon " [Hilda Gregg ; *b.* 1868]. *In Furthest Ind. : the narrative of Mr. Edward Carlyon of the H.E.I.C.'s service.*　　1894

Imaginary autobiography of an East India Company's servant, who is persecuted by the Inquisition, and visits the Court of the Great Mogul (*c.* 1660–85) ; founded on historical research. [Blackwood : o.p.]

—— *An Uncrowned King : a romance of high politics.*　　1896
—— *A Crowned Queen : the romance of a Minister of State* [sequel].　　1898

Imaginary politics, diplomacy, and palace intrigue in a fictitious kingdom of Thracia, supposed to resemble in its conditions those unsettled Balkan States that were under the thumb of Russia. Love plays an active part in the drama. A diplomatist of vast pretensions, Count Cyril Mortimer, comes to the front as the tales proceed. [(1) and (2), Blackwood.]

—— *The Kings of the East* [sequel].　　1900

Mortimer reappears as premier of Thracia. The schemes of a Jewish " United Nation Syndicate " for repossessing the Holy Land provide the cardinal motive. Mixed up with the affairs of princes and diplomatists, which are conceived on a scale befitting the chancelleries of western Europe, are a variety of love-romances, happy or tragic. [Blackwood.]

—— *Like another Helen*.　　1899

India in the eighteenth century, and the series of historical events connected with the Black Hole incident (1755–7). Told in letters between two girls, one of whom resembles strongly Richardson's Clarissa ; the language and sentiment of the period laboriously reproduced. [Blackwood.]

—— *The Warden of the Marches*.　　1901

Scene, a fort on the Khemistan frontier, which the Warden, one of the forward school, has made strong against the turbulent tribesmen ; until a new commissioner, a theorist and bureaucrat, comes and upsets his policy, and a brisk war results. A love-story is mixed up with these matters. Forms a sequel to *The Advanced Guard*, which appeared later. [Blackwood : o.p.]

—— *The Advanced Guard*.　　1903

A frontier novel, with a fine British soldier (perhaps a study of Lord Roberts) as most conspicuous personage. The love affairs go tragically. Contains a terrible picture of a native dungeon, and of an officer who succumbs to its tortures and embraces Mohammedanism. Period, just before the Mutiny. [Blackwood.]

—— *The Great Proconsul : the memoirs of Mrs. Hester Ward, formerly in the family of the Honble. Warren Hastings, Esq., late Governor-General of India.*　　1904

A favourable account of Warren Hastings in the latter half of his official career (1777–1818). Sir Eyre Coote, Philip Francis, Sir Elijah Impey, etc., are brought in. [Blackwood.]

—— *The Heir*.　　1906
—— *The Heritage* [sequel].　　1908
—— *The Prize* [sequel].　　1910

Another ingenious set of political romances, giving the career of a young man who turns out to be head of the Theophanis, and leading us through a complication of personal and international imbroglios. [(1), (2), and (3), Blackwood.]

"GRIER, Sydney Carlyon" (*continued*). *The Path to Honour.*　1909
—— *The Keepers of the Gate* [sequel].　1911
　　Political and patriotic novels of India and a frontier state, seventy years ago, the sequel dealing with the
　　　Mutiny. [(1) and (2), Blackwood.]
—— *A Young Man Married.*　1909
　　A romance of the Peninsular War (1812–13); not equal to the Indian novels. [Blackwood.]
—— *One Crowded Hour.*　1912
　　A good account of the expedition of the Thousand against the Bourbons in Sicily and Naples, centring in
　　　the adventures of two Englishmen who join the patriot army. [Blackwood.]
—— *Writ in Water.*　1913
　　Imaginary politics in a West Indian island *c.* 1870, continuing the career of Sir Robert Charteris, of *The
　　　Path to Honour.* A negro rising is put down sternly, and the governor later has to bear the stigma of
　　　brutality. [Blackwood.]
—— *England Hath Need of Thee.*　1916
　　Imaginary Indian politics: troubles in a buffer state and on the north-eastern frontier, a disastrous punitive
　　　expedition, Anglo-Indian society a generation ago. [Blackwood.]
—— *The Strong Hand.*　1920
—— *Out of Prison* [sequel].　1922
　　Historical pictures rather than fictitious history, dealing with Germany and France and their political relations
　　　from Jena to the entry of the allies into Paris (1806–14). Napoleon (an unfriendly portrait), Josephine,
　　　the Electress Louisa Frederika, Queen Hortense, Jerome Bonaparte, and many other historical personages
　　　are leading *dramatis personæ.* [(1) and (2), Blackwood.]
—— *A Brother of Girls.*　1925
　　Political life, high diplomacy, and war, through the experiences of a young Englishman on a foreign mission,
　　　in the period from the treaty of Amiens to the retreat from Moscow (1802–12). Napoleon, the Tsar
　　　Alexander I, and Frederick William of Prussia, and their chief ministers come into the picture.
　　　[Blackwood.]

GRIESE, Frederic [German; *b.* 1890]. *Winter* (Winter, 1927).　1929
　　Depicts peasant life in northern Germany, as bleak and harsh as the life of nature itself, where winter is
　　　bitter and summer brings only drought. [Transl. by D. L. Adler HOBMAN, Longmans, London and New
　　　York.]

GRIFFIN, Edith Aceituna [*b.* 1876]. *A Servant of the King.*　1906
　　The story of the Earl of Strafford down to his execution (1640–2). [Blackwood: o.p.]

GRIFFIN, Gerald [Irish; 1803–40]. *Tales of the Munster Festivals.*　1827–32
　　Faithful and racy sketches of the Kerry and W. Clare peasantry and the small gentry; home life, the hedge-
　　　schools, smuggling, love and seduction, troubles with Government officials, etc. [Routledge: o.p.;
　　　Sadlier, New York: o.p.]
—— *The Collegians; or, The Colleen Bawn: a tale of Garryowen.*　1828
　　A rather formless novel which was dramatized in a well-known play by Dion Boucicault. Here Griffin appears
　　　as the novelist of the better class of Irish yeomen, a very true and faithful interpreter of native character.
　　　The story is founded on fact—a poor girl is seduced and forsaken for a wife of higher station. Scenes:
　　　Limerick and Killarney. [Talbot Press, Dublin; Warne, New York: o.p.]
—— *The Invasion.*　1832
　　A painstaking study of western Ireland in the eighth century, the fortunes of the O'Haedha sept, on Bantry
　　　Bay, giving a little narrative interest. Archæological notes are supplied by Eugene O'Curry. [Duffy,
　　　Dublin: o.p.]

GRIFFITHS, Major Arthur George Frederick [1839–1908]. *In Tight Places: some experiences
of an amateur detective.*　1900
　　A collection of short detective stories that deal little with the repellent aspects of crime, though concerned
　　　with shady life and the hunting down of felons. Very matter-of-fact and unsentimental in manner.
　　　The author was an authority on police and crime, and had been a governor and a Government inspector
　　　of prisons. [Jarrold: o.p.]

GRIGORÓVICH, Dmitry Vasilievich [Russian; 1822–1899]. *The Cruel City.*　1891
　　A picture of life in Petersburg. The motive is comic: a young man comes up from the country to seek his
　　　fortune among his city relatives; but they turn out to be by no means wealthy, and they fleece the
　　　unhappy youth. Grigoróvich's pictures of country life, factory life, etc., are remarkably truthful and
　　　of real ethnographical value. [Transl. by E. de L. PIERSON, Cassell, New York: o.p.]
—— *The Fisherman* (1853).　1916
　　Rather heavy as a story, but the intimate character-drawing of various types of Russian workers is valuable.
　　　The advent of the factory is shown making havoc of the old village life. [Transl., with preface, by A. S.
　　　RAPPOPORT, McKay, Philadelphia (S. Paul).]

GRIMMELSHAUSEN, Hans Jacob Christoph [German; *c.* 1625–76]. *The Adventurous Simplicissimus; being the description of the life of a strange vagabond named Melchior Sternfels von Fuchs-
shaim* (Der abentheurliche Simplicissimus, 1669).　1912
　　This famous German offshoot of picaresque fiction recounts the diversified experiences of a young fellow, half
　　　rogue, half simpleton, during the Thirty Years War. Simplicissimus is born in 1622, just after the battle
　　　of Höchst, is captured by troopers ten years later, "springs" into the world after Nördlingen, 1634, and
　　　down to the battle of Jankow in 1645 suffers all manner of vicissitudes in the war. His subsequent
　　　history is not less extraordinary, and ceases to be entertaining only in the later continuations to the
　　　original novel. Grimmelshausen borrows freely from Spanish picaresque fiction, from Boccaccio, Ban-
　　　dello, and other *novellieri*, and from Sidney's *Arcadia* and other romances. Though a work of fiction,

GRIMMELSHAUSEN, Hans Jacob Christoph (*continued*).

it is the most authentic picture left by that age of the state of society and of the horrors of this most terrible of wars. In matters of fact its accuracy has been verified ; and it is obvious that in the main episodes the author put down what came before his eyes ; even his accounts of such incidents as the witches' sabbath are according to what he believed. The coarseness and brutality of manners in numerous scenes and the atrocity and bestiality of the soldiers are done with a frankness and down-rightness that are often revolting. [Transl. for the first time into English, by A. T. S. GOODRICH, Heinemann : o.p. ; same, with introd. by William Rose (Broadway Transl.), Routledge (Dutton, New York), 1924.]

GRIMSHAW, Beatrice Ethel [Irish]. *The Sorcerer's Stone.* 1914

The adventures of a party seeking an immense diamond in Papua. [Hurst ; Winston, New York : o.p.]

—— *Red Bob of the Bismarcks.* 1915

Adventures of treasure-hunters in New Guinea. [Hurst : o.p. ; *sub tit. My Lady of the Island : a tale of the South Seas*, McClurg, Chicago : o.p.]

—— *Nobody's Island.* 1917

A lady suspected of having poisoned her husband betakes herself to a Pacific isle and marries an old flame—a story giving the novelist an opportunity to display her knowledge of Polynesia. [Hurst : o.p. ; Doubleday, New York.]

—— *The Terrible Island.* 1920

A very effective sensation story of an island of evil repute in the neighbourhood of New Guinea, effective also in local colour. [Hurst : o.p. ; Macmillan, New York.]

GROGAN, Walter E. *The King's Cause.* 1909

Deals with Rupert's capture of Bristol and surrender to Fairfax ; the hero handicapped as a hero by his rôle as Royalist spy. [Milne : o.p.]

GROOME, Francis Hindes [1851–1902]. *Kriegspiel : the war game.* 1896

Gipsy life delineated by an eminent authority, the author of *Gypsy Folk-Tales* (1898). An English baronet, son of a Romany mother, is kidnapped, and travels over England and the Scottish border in a gipsy caravan, Suffolk, Berwick, and Edinburgh being the chief scenes. Romany manners and customs, life under canvas, language and folk-lore, are presented in a striking way. [Ward & Lock : o.p.]

GUBSKY, Nikolai [Russian writing in English]. *The Gladiator.* 1930

In the gladiator, an elderly disillusioned clerk to the Supreme Court, in Petersburg before the revolution, is concentrated the tragedy, and, in a manner peculiarly Russian, the grotesque humour of the book. He is robbed for fifteen years of his wife, inmate of an asylum. Parallel and contrasted, runs the strange love-story of the younger Kanshin. [Mathews.]

GUERRAZZI, Francesco Domenico [Italian ; 1804–73]. *Beatrice Cenci* (Beatrice Cénci : storia del Secolo XVI, 1854). 1858

A novel of the sixteenth century dealing with the subject of Shelley's famous tragedy. Guerrazzi wrote a poetical romance, *La Battaglia di Benevento* (1827), and a very fine historical novel, *L'Assedio di Firenze* (1836), on the fall of the Florentine republic. [Transl. by C. A. SCOTT, Ward & Lock : o.p.]

GUEST, Lady Charlotte Elizabeth [*née* Schreiber ; 1812–95] [tr.]. *The Mabinogion : from the Welsh of the Llyfr Coch o Hergest (the Red Book of Hergest).* 1849

The nucleus of this book and the portion that gave it the title is the series of primitive mythological tales known as *The Four Branches of the Mabinogi*, which are connected together by the person of Pryderi. They have been equated (see a primer entitled *The Mabinogion*, by Ivor B. John, David Nutt) to Snorri's compilation of Icelandic mythology in the Prose Edda, and were perhaps intended for the instruction of bardic students. *Pwyll, Prince of Dyfed* recounts the marriage of Pwyll and Rhiannon, and leads up to the birth of Pryderi. *Branwen, Daughter of Llyr*, is the story of an unfortunate marriage between a Welsh princess and an Irish king, and of the exterminating war that arose thereupon, with the exploits of the gigantic Bran. *Manawyddan, Son of Llyr*, tells how Pryderi is carried off by enchantment, and a whole country laid desolate by a spell. *Math, Son of Mathonwy*, whose kernel is a legend about the introduction of swine into Wales, is likewise full of marvellous incident, and contains the two greatest of Welsh enchanters, Math and Gwydion. These legends probably got their present form about the tenth or eleventh century, but are much older in origin. Closely affiliated to them in manner and inspiration are five other British stories. *Kilhwch and Olwen ; or, The Twrch Trwyth* tells how King Arthur and his hosts chased a monstrous boar, and performed other feats required by the father of Olwen before she was given in marriage to Kilhwch : a " wild and whirling " story overburdened with allusions to other British legends. *The Dream of Rhonabwy* also brings in Arthur, but in a dream, in which the Ravens of Owain appear destroying the sons of the nobles of Britain. *The Dream of Maxen Wledig* relates to the Roman Emperor Maximus ; *Lludd and Llevelyn* to the famous King Lud, brother of Cassivelaunus. *Taliesin*, in prose and verse, narrates the wonderful birth and sayings of the greatest Welsh bard. The other three stories are less distinctively Welsh, and nearer akin to the Continental romances of Arthur. *The Lady of the Fountain* corresponds to Chrétien de Troyes' *Yvain*, and an English adaptation thereof, *Yvain and Gawin*, in Ritson's *Metrical Romances*, vol. I (Gwalchmai is better known as Gawain). The hero is Owain, a knight beloved by Arthur, who slays the warder of a magic fountain, and becomes the consort and protector of a widowed countess. *Peredur, the Son of Evrawc*, is the most archaic of the Grail legends, of which Perceval or Peredur was the original hero. (See list of versions *sub tit. High History of the Holy Graal*, and Mr. Alfred Nutt's primer, *The Legends of the Holy Grail*, Nutt). *Geraint, the Son of Erbin*, is the well-known story retold in Tennyson's *Enid*, and corresponds to Chrétien's *Erec et Enide*. Lady Charlotte Guest edited the *Mabinogion* with this beautiful translation in 1849 (3 vols., Llandovery : o.p.), and published the translation and notes without the text in 1877 (Quaritch : o.p.). Her book was taken from a fourteenth-century MS., all except *Taliesin*, of which the oldest extant MS. belongs to the seventeenth century. Should be read in close connexion with the sagas of Celtic Ireland, as well as with the Arthurian romances. [With note on the literary history of the tales, by Alfred NUTT ; (Everyman's Lib.), Dent (Dutton, New York), 1906 ; and in the Welsh Library, vols. i.–iii., Unwin.]

GUEULETTE, Thomas Simon [French ; 1683–1768]. *The Thousand and One Quarters of an Hour*
(Contes tartares, 1723). 1893
One of the most readable of the imitations of the Arabian Nights produced at this date, in rivalry with the more brilliant tales of Count Hamilton. Gueulette used his imagination, but borrowed ideas and incidents from Oriental fiction and even from contemporary novelists. [Edited by Leonard C. SMITHERS, H. S. Nichols & Co. : o.p.]

GUICCIARDI-FIASTRI, Virginia [Italian]. *From Opposite Shores* (Da opposte rive). 1914
A tale full of pathos, redeemed from mere emotionalism by the beauty of acceptance in the sorely-tried widow whose story it chiefly is, and the general sense of beauty. This north Italian peasant heroine gives up her socialist lover for the sake of the Church, and then has to make the sacrifice of her daughter. [Transl. by Hélène ANTONELLI, Göschen : o.p.]

GUILLAUMIN, Émile [French ; b. 1873]. *The Life of a Simple Man* (La vie d'un simple). 1919
The daily life of a husbandman from cradle to grave, admirable in conveying the mental attitude and the humble philosophy of a French peasant. The author is himself a farmer. [Transl. by Margaret HOLDEN, Selwyn & Blount.]

GULL, Cyril Ranger ["Guy Thorne" ; 1875–1923]. *The Serf.* 1902
Shows the dark side of social conditions in Stephen's reign (1136). The hero Hyla avenges an outrage committed by his lord, but is caught at last, and suffers a horrible death. Scene, the Fen country. [Greening : o.p.]

—— *The House of Torment.* 1910
Also a rather gruesome story of Suffolk, and of Spain in the time of Philip and Mary (1555), dealing with an English martyrdom and the Inquisition. [Greening : o.p.]

GUNNARSSON, Gunnar [Icelander, writing in Danish ; b. 1889]. *Guest the One-eyed* (Gjest den enöjede, 1913). 1920
A sensational romance of Copenhagen and Iceland ; hero, a violinist-financier ; villain, his clerical brother, who seduces a girl and denounces his own father for the deed. [Transl., Gyldendal : o.p.]

—— *The Sworn Brothers : a tale of the early days of Iceland* (Fóstbrædur, 1919). 1920
Not merely doughty Vikings warring and colonizing in Iceland, but also the domestic life, the heathen rites, and the natural surroundings of the early Icelanders, are vividly presented here. [Gyldendal : o.p.]

—— *Seven Days' Darkness.* 1930
The scene is Reykjavik, and the darkness is due to a volcano, simultaneously with whose eruption an epidemic of influenza is ravaging the city. Such is the setting of a gloomier drama, of temperamental antipathy and smouldering passion between two men, one of whom loves the other's wife. The character-drawing is notable for the strong individuality of the traits. [Transl. by Roberts TAPLEY, Macmillan Co., New York.]

GWYNN, Stephen Lucius [Irish ; b. 1864]. *The Old Knowledge.* 1901
A well-written book, though not quite a successful novel. Attempts to combine two elements, a modern love-story in a Donegal setting (the author has written an excellent topographical work on Donegal), and the character and visionary ideas of a Celtic seer. The study of folklore and mysticism is interesting. [Macmillan : o.p.]

—— *John Maxwell's Marriage.* 1903
The tyrannous conduct of Protestant landowners in the north of Ireland, and the bitter feelings of the dispossessed Catholics (1761–79). A strong story, telling of a forced marriage, an autocratic father, and the quixotry of a spirited young man who joins the insurgent colonists in America and dabbles in nationalist schemes. Manners and characters admirably delineated. [Macmillan : o.p.]

—— *The Glade in the Forest.* 1907
Seven short stories chiefly of peasant life in Donegal, e.g. *The Grip of the Land*, a moving story of a small farmer's passionate struggles and his eldest son's emigration. [Maunsel : o.p.]

—— *Robert Emmet : an historical romance.* 1909
Treats on the lines of a novel the closing episode in Emmet's career, the attempted insurrection in Dublin (1803), and uses his love for Sarah Curran, daughter of the great orator, as a cardinal motive. Gives a map of Dublin in 1803, and is carefully exact. [Macmillan : o.p.]

"GYP" [Gabrielle Sibylle Marie Antoinette de Riquetti de Mirabeau, Comtesse de Martel de Janville ; French ; b. 1850]. *Little Bob* (Petit Bob, 1882). 1900
Dialogues with an acute and witty boy of eight, the proverbial *enfant terrible*, whose sayings are unconsciously satirical of older people and of their conventional, insincere ways. [Transl. by Alys HOLLARD, Heinemann : o.p.]

—— *Chiffon's Marriage* (Le mariage de Chiffon, 1894). 1895
The history of a husband more absorbed in politics than in his wife, who allows men to pay her attentions, but learns this is not the way to happiness. With plenty of good humour, raillery, and wit, Gyp amuses herself with lively sketches of the caprices, the pleasures, and the frivolous fashions of fast society. [Transl. by Mrs. Patchett MARTIN, Hutchinson : o.p. ; by Mrs. E. L. COFFEY, Hurst, New York : o.p.]

—— *Those Good Normans* (Ces bons Normands ! 1895). 1896
Light banter and satire of the people of Normandy in a series of sketches. These Normans of Gyp's are narrow and mean, selfish and vulgar characters ; but the portraiture is not meant altogether seriously. [Transl. by Marie JUSSEN, Rand & McNally, Chicago : o.p.]

HABBERTON, John [American ; 1842–1921]. *Helen's Babies : by their latest victim.* 1876
An amusing story of young children, which captured the public. [Dodd & Mead, New York ; Appleton, New York and London ; Routledge ; *illus.* by Mary La Fetra Russell, Stokes, New York ; by Eva Roos, Chatto.]

HABBERTON, John (*continued*). *Budge and Toddie*. 1877
Further adventures of Helen's Babies, illustrating the difficulty of taking care of other people's children. [Grosset, New York ; *sub tit. Other People's Children*, Routledge : o.p.]

—— *Brueton's Bayou*. 1882
A Western story full of bright conversation. [Lippincott, Philadelphia : o p ; Chatto : o.p.]

HACKLÄNDER, Friedrich Wilhelm von [German ; 1816–77]. *The Countess of St. Alban ; or, Lost and Found* (Namenlose Geschichten, 1851). 1854
A picture of the superficial aspects of actual life, the author's strength being description ; busy streets, still life, etc., vividly depicted. He has been called, very erroneously, "The German Dickens." Other novels by the same author are *Behind the Counter* (*Handel und Wandel*, 1850), 1867, and *Clara ; or, Slave Life in Europe* (*Europäischer Sklavenleben*, 1856), 1880. His best untranslated novels include *Eugen Stielfriend* (1852) and *Krieg und Frieden* (1859). [Hodgson : o.p.]

HAGGARD, Sir Henry Rider [1856–1925]. *Dawn*. 1884
—— *The Witch's Head*. 1884
Exciting novels of adventure in Africa, then still to a large extent a dark continent. [(1) and (2), Longmans, London and New York ; (1), Harrap ; (2), Hodder.]

—— *King Solomon's Mines*. 1886
A highly coloured romance of adventure in the wilds of Central Africa in quest of King Solomon's Ophir ; full of sensational fights, blood-curdling perils, and extraordinary escapes. [Cassell ; Longmans, New York.]

—— *Allan Quatermain* [sequel]. 1888
A similar compound of realism and fantasy. A subterranean river in Africa leads the adventurers to a city in the interior of the earth, where the hero courts the queen and involves all in civil war. Quatermain was drawn from the famous hunter F. C. Selous. [Longmans, London and New York ; Hodder ; Harrap.]

—— *Jess*. 1887
Gives a good picture of the home life of the Boers. [Murray ; Longmans, New York.]

—— *She*. 1887
Another wonder-story, with realistic and gruesome details worked in. "She" is a mighty queen and enchantress in an imaginary African region ; she has lived many centuries and had amorous passages with the hero when, in an early stage of existence, he was a Greek. [Longmans, London and New York ; Hodder.]

—— *Maiwa's Revenge ; or, The War of the Little Hand*. 1888
—— *Mr. Meeson's Will*. 1888
All similar in general characteristics, fantastic marvels and realistic travel-pictures of Africa and elsewhere, with no end of thrilling adventure, gory scenes of slaughter, and unexpected escapes. [(1) and (2), Longmans, London and New York ; (1), Hodder.]

—— *Colonel Quaritch, V.C.* 1888
A country story of a lost family treasure and its recovery. [Longmans, London and New York ; Hodder.]

—— *Allan's Wife ; and other stories*. 1889
More about Allan Quatermain. [Longmans, London and New York ; Hodder.]

—— *Cleopatra*. 1889
"Being an account of the fall and vengeance of Harmachis, the royal Egyptian, as set forth by his own hand." Not an historical novel so much as one of the usual Haggard type in which Cleopatra and the rest play the chief rôles. [Longmans, London and New York ; Hodder ; Harrap.]

—— *Eric Brighteyes*. 1891
The same kind of thing with imaginary history added. The first takes us back to ancient Egypt and draws a lurid picture of the times ; the third is a romance of the Scandinavian Vikings in Iceland, before 999 A.D. [Longmans, London and New York ; Hodder ; Harrap.]

—— *Nada, the Lily*. 1892
Continues the adventures of Umslopogas, the Zulu hero of *Allan Quatermain*. [Longmans, London and New York ; Hodder ; Harrap.]

—— *The People of the Mist*. 1894
A "record of barefaced and flagrant adventure," the author calls it. The hero goes to Africa, rescues a beautiful girl from a detestable slave-trader, destroying the rascal's lair ; and after various thrilling experiences goes in quest of the wondrous gems in the City of the People of the Mist. [Longmans, London and New York ; Hodder.]

—— *Montezuma's Daughter*. 1894
A sensational romance of the Spanish Inquisition and of Cortez in Mexico (1515–25). [Longmans, London and New York ; Hodder ; Harrap.]

—— *Heart of the World*. 1896
A pilgrimage of daring adventurers to the wild interior of Mexico, where they reach a pre-Aztec City of the Heart, inhabited by a degenerate race. [Longmans, London and New York ; Harrap.]

—— *Swallow*. 1899
A story of the Great Trek (1836). [Longmans, London and New York.]

—— *Black Heart and White Heart : and other stories*. 1900
The title-story deals with the loves of two Zulus, in which an English trader plays a sinister part. Cetewayo is a prominent figure. *Elissa* is a tale of the Phœnician Zimbabwe in Rhodesia. *The Wizard* is a vigorous tale of missionary effort in Central Africa. [Longmans, London and New York.]

—— *Lysbeth : a tale of the Dutch*. 1901
A story of the Netherlands revolt against Philip II, beginning at Leyden when Lutheranism was just beginning

HAGGARD, Sir Henry Rider (*continued*).

to lay hold of the northern Netherlands, and ending with the siege of that city, and with a picture of the principal characters living peacefully in the author's loved city of Norwich (1571–74). [Longmans, London and New York.]

—— *Pearl Maiden.* 1902

A tale of the fall of Jerusalem (A.D. 70). Spectacular and crudely exciting, quite untouched by the historical spirit. Finely illustrated by Mr. Byam Shaw. [Longmans, London and New York.]

—— *The Brethren.* 1904

Pays more attention than usual with this writer to character and motive. Two brethren are in love with one woman, niece of Saladin, who kidnaps her from England, and the romantic events then work themselves out in Palestine. Ends with the capture of Jerusalem (*c.* 1185–88). [Cassell.]

—— *Ayesha : the return of She.* 1905

Continues the miraculous career of " She " after reincarnation. [Ward & Lock ; Garden City Co., New York.]

—— *Fair Margaret.* 1907

Margaret is the daughter of a converted Jew in Henry VII's reign, and with her lover meets with terrifying adventures in Ferdinand and Isabella's Spain, when the Inquisition was persecuting the Jews (1491–1501). [Hutchinson : o.p. ; Longmans, New York.]

—— *The Yellow God : an idol of Africa.* 1908

About a Chinese idol that exercises a tragic power upon those who come into contact with it. [Cassell ; Cupples, New York : o.p.]

—— *The Lady of Blossholme.* 1909

Another exciting romance of the eastern counties and London in Henry VIII's reign, time of the Pilgrimage of Grace and Thomas, Lord Cromwell (1535–6). [Hodder.]

—— *Red Eve.* 1911

A romance of the eastern counties, Venice, Avignon, and the battle of Creçy ; the frightful shadow of the Black Death brooding over all. [Hodder : o.p. ; Doubleday, New York : o.p.]

—— *The Mahatma and the Hare : a dream story.* 1911

A subtle and imaginative handling of mystical and supernatural effects, and at the same time an appealing argument in defence of the lower animals against sport. [Longmans ; Holt, New York : o.p.]

—— *Marie.* 1912

The story of Allan Quatermain in young manhood, at the time of the Great Trek (1836). [Cassell ; Longmans, New York.]

—— *Child of Storm.* 1913

Continues the story of Allan Quatermain ; he is in Zululand, and his adventures end for the time being with the battle of the Tugela (1856). [Cassell ; Longmans, New York.]

—— *The Wanderer's Necklace.* 1914

A flat, pinchbeck story of a young Dane of the Viking age in Byzantium, inadequately enlivened with some good fighting incidents. [Cassell ; Longmans, New York.]

—— *The Holy Flower.* 1915

Allan Quatermain describes an early adventure—a journey into Africa in search of a fabulous orchid. [Ward & Lock.]

—— *The Ivory Child.* 1916

Quatermain conducts an expedition into Central Africa in search of a lady who has been spirited away by magic. [Cassell ; Longmans, New York.]

—— *Finished.* 1917

Quatermain in the Transvaal and Zululand (1877–84) ; the Zulu wars, Cetewayo, and the battle of Isandhl-wana. This completes the trilogy, of which *Marie* and *Child of Storm* were the previous instalments. [Ward & Lock ; Longmans, New York.]

—— *Moon of Israel : a tale of the Exodus.* 1918

Pharaoh is supposed to be the usurping Amenmeses. [Murray ; Longmans, New York.]

—— *The Ancient Allan.* 1920

Lady Ragnall (of *The Ivory Child*) has brought back from Africa a drug which throws herself and Allan back to their previous existence as lovers in Egypt about 400 B.C. [Cassell ; Longmans, New York.]

—— *She and Allan.* 1921

All the familiar characters from the former romances reappear, though they are rather past their best form. [Longmans, London (o.p.), and New York.]

—— *The Virgin of the Sun.* 1922

Adventures of an Englishman in Peru in the latter half of the fourteenth century. [Cassell ; Doubleday, New York.]

—— *Wisdom's Daughter : the life and love story of She-Who-Must-Be-Obeyed.* 1923

The marvellous Ayesha here appears as the daughter of an Arab chief in the fourth century B.C. [Hutchinson ; Doubleday, New York.]

—— *Queen of the Dawn.* 1925

A romance of Egypt under the shepherd-king Apepi, in the eighteenth century B.C. [Hutchinson ; Longmans, New York.]

—— *Belshazzar.* 1930

Haggard's vigorous sensationalism tends to become emasculated by a misplaced zeal for historical and archæological accuracy, in this love-romance of a brave young Egyptian and a granddaughter of Zedekiah, who is coveted by the royal prince of Babylon. [S. Paul ; Doubleday, New York.]

HAGGARD, Sir H. Rider, and LANG, Andrew. *The World's Desire.* 1891
A sensational romance of ancient Egypt that brings in both the Exodus of the Israelites and the death of Ulysses. [Longmans.]

HALE, Edward Everett [American; 1822–1909]. *The Man Without a Country.* 1861
A homily on the obligation of patriotism, embodied in the fictitious memoirs of an American officer who said he wished never to hear of the United States again, and for punishment had his wish fulfilled. The story has been accepted before now as authentic. [Little & Brown, Boston; Putnam, New York; Altemus, Philadelphia; Ginn, New York and London.]

—— *If, Yes, and Perhaps: four impossibilities and six exaggerations, with some bits of fact.* 1868
Eleven stories and sketches, some humorous, some serious and to a certain extent didactic, others mere flights of fancy; all characterized by a realism that makes them seem to be leaves out of the author's personal experience. [Houghton, Boston: o.p.]

—— *Ten Times One is Ten: the possible reformation.* 1870
A little story, full of vivacious humour, but with a serious meaning, viz. to sketch a practical scheme for the world's regeneration. Crammed with fertile ideas on life, and resolutely optimistic. [Little & Brown, Boston.]

—— *In His Name.* 1873
A romance of the Waldenses (c. 1179), inspired by the Christian life of those martyrs. The heroine is daughter of a weaver of Lyons of the kin of the saintly Peter Waldo, founder of the society called the Poor Men of Lyon. [Little & Brown, Boston; Seeley: o.p.]

—— *Ups and Downs: an every-day novel.* 1873
The ups and downs of business life, illustrated by the hard struggle and ultimate prosperity of several young people, with their courtship and happy marriages. [Little & Brown, Boston: o.p.]

—— *Philip Nolan's Friends: a story of the change of Western Empire.* 1876
Time of the Louisiana purchase (1803). [Little & Brown, Boston.]

—— *The Skeleton in the Closet.*

—— *My Double.* 1895
Droll extravaganzas worked out with all the minuteness and matter-of-fact style appropriate to an account of real but astonishing occurrences. [(1), o.p.; (2), Lawson, St. Paul, Min.: o.p.]

—— *Mr. Tangier's Vacations.* 1888
A series of diverting situations, glimpses of life in country and town, and the novel and fertile ideas prompted by a lawyer's flight into the country from overwork. [Little & Brown, Boston: o.p.]

—— *New Ohio: a story of East and West.* 1892
A tale of the settling of Ohio by New Englanders at the close of the eighteenth century. [Cassell, New York: o.p.; *sub tit. East and West: a story of New Ohio*, Cassell, London: o.p.]

HALÉVY, Ludovic [French; 1834–1908]. *Marriage of Love* (Un mariage d'amour, 1881). 1886
The heroine is an attractive Parisian girl, whose ambition is to marry out of the respectable bourgeois sphere to which her people belong, but who finds that she must take whom Providence offers. Contains sympathetic pictures of tranquil home life among the middle classes. [Transl. by BOGAERDE and NEWILL, Simpkin: o.p.; by F. H. POTTER, Dodd & Mead, New York: o.p.]

—— *The Abbé Constantin* (1882). 1897
One of the best examples of the " healthy novel "—*roman honnête*—an innocent and sentimental form of literature portraying the middle classes, and read by them, and containing none but worthy characters. An idyllic story, with a charming and most meritorious priest as the leading figure, and two American ladies, Mrs. Scott and her sister, who are attractive renderings of transatlantic character. [Transl. by Thérèse BATBEDAT, Macqueen: o.p.; Burt, New York; Dodge, New York.]

—— *Criquette* (1883). 1891
Criquette also is a pure and estimable character, who begins life as a flower-girl, and after some juvenile successes on the stage becomes an actress. Her first lover is unworthy, and deserts her, but she remains loyal; and when at length she allies herself with another, it is only to give up her life for him. [Transl. by A. D. HALL, Rand & McNally, Chicago, 1891: o.p.]

—— *Parisian Points of View: tales.* 1894
Nine stories and sketches selected from Halévy's numerous tales, very characteristic of their bright and effervescent qualities and of the author's peculiarly dramatic methods. [Transl. by E. V. B. MATTHEWS, Harper, New York: o.p.]

HALIBURTON, Thomas Chandler [Canadian; 1797–1865]. *The Clockmaker: the sayings and doings of Sam Slick of Slickville.* 1838–41
Sam has some traits of an American Sam Weller—he is a witty rogue, fond of abusing people, especially his own countrymen—the Blue-noses—slangy, conceited, knowing how to do everything better than anybody else, always ready for a " trade " or a piece of practical roguery, fervently believes in the union of English and Americans, and expounds the author's high Tory opinions. This and the following novels contain little plot, but no end of yarns, ludicrous fancies, and shrewd saws. Haliburton, who was Chief Justice in Nova Scotia, knew how to draw a sharp, life-like and terribly offensive caricature of Nova Scotians and Yankees, and no doubt many of his portraits were easily recognized at the time. The book founded the school that has produced " Artemus Ward " and " Mark Twain," not to mention Mr. Dooley and David Harum. [Edited by E. A. Baker (Half-forgotten Books), Routledge; Houghton, Boston; Dutton, New York; ed. by Ray Palmer Baker, with bibliography, Doran, New York, 1923. *Illus.*, Musson Co., New York, 1929.]

—— *The Letter Bag of the " Great Western."* 1839
Humorous sketches of Yankee manners and customs, in the form of letters supposed to be taken from the mail-bag of a steamship. [In his *Works*, 3 vols., Routledge: o.p.]

HALIBURTON, Thomas Chandler (*continued*).   *The Attaché; or, Sam Slick in England.*
1843–4
A satire on British manners and customs.   [Routledge : o.p. ; Dick, New York : o.p.]

—— *The Old Judge ; or, Life in a Colony.* 1849
Sketches from life of people in Nova Scotia, in the shape of a tourist's narrative.   The time referred to is that of the Canadian rebellion of 1837–8.   The facetious effects are emphasized by innumerable puns, jests, *double-ententes*, and distorted spelling.   [Munro, New York : o.p.]

—— *Wise Saws and Modern Instances.* 1853
A further collection of the doings and sayings of Sam Slick ; a mingling of worldly wisdom, commercial smartness, and pungent satire.   [Dick, New York : o.p.]

—— *Nature and Human Nature.* 1855
Professes to deal with the same subject as Juvenal, the whole life of man.   Full of characteristic aphorisms. [Dick, New York : o.p.]

HALL, Anna Maria [Mrs. S. C. Hall, *née* Fielding ; Irish ; 1801–81].   *Sketches of Irish Character.*
1829
Tries to portray the characters, ways, and surroundings of the villagers of Bannow, Co. Wexford—where she had lived as a girl—in the manner of Miss Mitford.   [*Illustrated* by Cruikshank, Maclise, and others, Chatto, 1892 : o.p.]

—— *Lights and Shadows of Irish Life.* 1838
The same sort of material is happily strung together to make a three-volume novel of peasant life.   [3 vols., Colburn : o.p.]

—— *The Whiteboy.* 1845
A too optimistic story of a young Englishman who tries to improve the lot and engage the sympathies of the peasants during the Whiteboy troubles.   [Routledge : o.p.]

—— *Stories of the Irish Peasantry.* 1851
Twenty tales which endeavour to show that the enmity of landlord and peasant is due to misunderstanding, or the influence of bad habits such as intemperance, superstition, and general lack of discipline—which the author thinks might easily be remedied.   [Chambers : o.p. ; *Tales of Irish Life and Character*, McClurg, Chicago, 1910.]

HALL, Miss Evelyn Beatrice [" S. G. Tallentyre "].   *Early Victorian : a village chronicle.* 1910
A quiet, keen, and humorous description of village society eighty years ago—apparently Eltham, the author's place of residence.   [Murray ; *sub tit. Basset : a village chronicle*, Moffat, New York : o.p.]

HALL, Henry Fielding [" Henry Fielding "].   *Thibaw's Queen.* 1899
A story of life in Upper Burma at the present day, fairly realistic in its portrayal of manners and customs and native character, though much embroidered with romance.   [Harper, London and New York : o.p.]

—— *Palace Tales.* 1900
Light and airy stories of Court life in Burma, supposed to be transcriptions from stories that were current among the courtiers before the country became British, but obviously Anglicized in more than the language. Mysteries, drolleries, and love scenes of a fairyland order, bedecked with the flowers and odours and brilliance of a tropical land.   [Harper, London and New York : o.p.]

—— *One Immortality.* 1909
A rather vague, meditative, and occasionally mystical book, thrown into the form of a novel, but not concerned with incident or motive or character so much as general truths.   The characters are fellow-travellers from Venice to India, and are brought together to discuss many things, largely from the contrasted standpoints of West and East.   [Macmillan, London and New York : o.p.]

HALL, Marie [*née* Sibree, 1839–85].   *Andrew Marvel and his Friends.* [juvenile] 1873–4
A careful historical study of Kingston-upon-Hull and its worthies, with its relations to the history of England during the Protectorate and the reign of Charles II.   The two sieges of Hull by the Royalists in 1642–3, and the life of the poet Marvel, are the most important historical matters.   [A. Brown & Sons, Hull : o.p.]

HALL, Radclyffe.   *The Well of Loneliness.* 1928
This protracted and over-charged history of the unmerited sufferings of a woman who is born a sexual invert, is a protest against social injustice as much as a novel.   It was banned in this country, but had a thriving sale on the Continent, especially among the prurient-minded, to whom it was no doubt a severe disappointment.   It has pathos, it has beauty in places, but is not a good novel.

" HALSHAM, John " [G. Forrester Scott].   *Idlehurst : a journal kept in the country.* 1898
—— *Lonewood Corner : a countryman's horizons.* 1907
Something between a novel and a string of musings and *obiter dicta*, written by a literary man who has sought nature and the simple life in the country and gardening.   Friends and neighbours and village worthies are sketched, and their views on life set forth, and the author gives us his own ideas (as they occur) on most things under the sun.   [(1) and (2), Smith & Elder (Dutton, New York) : o.p.]

HAMBLEN, Herbert Elliott [American ; *b.* 1849].   *The General Manager's Story.* 1897
Old-time reminiscences of railroading ; an exciting record of sensational adventure, picturing, technically and realistically, the everyday life on an American railway.   [Macmillan, New York : o.p.]

HAMILTON, Bernard [*b.* 1863].   *Coronation.* 1902
The days of Prince Hal (Henry V) and Sir John Fastolf (*c.* 1413–5) ; ends with an account of the battle of Agincourt.   [Ward & Lock : o.p.]

—— *The Giant.* 1926
A romantic treatment of Danton's career and of the Revolution, with his figure standing gigantically out in the well-known crowd (1774–84).   [Hutchinson.]

HAMILTON, Elizabeth [Scottish ; 1758–1816].   *The Cottagers of Glenburnie.* 1808
A homely tale, didactic in aim, portraying lowly life and character in rural Scotland.   [Simpkin, 1888 : o.p.]

HAMILTON, Lord Ernest William [Scottish ; *b.* 1858]. *The Outlaws of the Marches.* 1897
A romance of 1587 in Liddesdale and the Border country. [Unwin : o.p. ; Dodd & Mead, New York : o.p.]

—— *Mary Hamilton : her life and history.* 1901
Mary Hamilton is one of Mary Queen of Scotland's Marys, and the plot runs that she is Darnley's wife, rendering his marriage with the Queen bigamous. While it takes liberties with history, shows careful study of the period (cf. *The Queen's Quair*, p. 239). [Methuen : o.p.]

HAMILTON, Rev. John Arthur [*b.* 1845]. *The MS. in the Red Box.* 1903
Isle of Axholme in the Fens, when the Dutch, under Vermuyden, were engaged in draining the country, and had collisions with the inhabitants. Romance of the Weyman brand with plenty of local colour. Hero loves a Dutch girl, and his rival is president of the Council of the North. The curious title states that the MS. of the book was received by the publisher in a mysterious manner ; the book was published anonymously, although by that time the author's name had been disclosed. [Lane : o.p.]

—— *Captain John Lister.* 1906
The story of a Parliamentarian during the Civil War, centring in the same district. [Hutchinson : o.p.]

HAMILTON, Lillias [*d.* 1925]. *A Vizier's Daughter : a tale of the Hazara War.* 1900
A novel of Afghan life, as tragic and sombre as actual life under the Ameer is said to have been. It narrates the brief and unhappy career of an heroic daughter of the Hazaras, a rude but worthy race of highlanders. She has to flee the pursuit of a savage general, seeks refuge in the household of a royal minister at Cabul, and lays down her life for her protector. The delineation of manners and ways of life in Afghanistan make the book much more than a novel : the author was Court physician to the late Ameer, whose idiosyncrasies are the subject of a careful portrait. [Murray : o.p.]

HAMILTON, Margaret. *Poor Elizabeth.* 1901
A tragedy of character, utterly unrelieved in its gloom and anguish ; the history of a marriage between a beautiful Eurasian and a highly correct Englishman. His hardness of heart and cold superiority are exposed remorselessly ; her passionate and impulsive nature, driving her at last to crime, is handled with sympathy and evident knowledge of the racial problems involved. [Hurst : o.p.]

HAMILTON, Patrick [*b.* 1904]. *The Midnight Bell : a love story.* 1929
The hero is a bar-tender, whose romantic attachment to a prostitute leaves him a poorer but a wiser man. Humour and sentiment recall De Morgan. [Constable ; Little & Brown, Boston.]

HAMLET IN ICELAND : *the Ambales Saga.* 1898
" Being the Icelandic romantic Ambales Saga, edited and translated, with extracts from five Ambales Rimur and other illustrative texts, for the most part now first printed, and an introductory essay, by Israel GOLLANCZ." Of importance chiefly on account of the use Shakespeare made of another version of the same story. The present version belongs to the sixteenth or the early seventeenth century, the major part of it having been derived from Saxo Grammaticus, the Danish historiographer (late twelfth century) and remodelled under the influence of popular folk-tales, Carlovingian and Arthurian romances, and the stories of Tamburlane. But there are probably elements of the pre-Saxo legend surviving in the Icelandic text. In his learned prolegomena, Gollancz analyses the contents of this barbarous and sanguinary story, showing among other interesting derivations how the Roman legend of Junius Brutus and the Tarquinii was incorporated. [Nutt : o.p.]

HAMLEY, Major-General William G. *Traseaden Hall.* 1882
A long, meandering story, extending from the beginning of the Peninsular War to the peace that followed Waterloo, and shifting from an English country town to Portugal and Spain. Provincial life and regimental life are both depicted with fullness and intimacy. [3 vols., Blackwood : o.p.]

HAMSUN, Knut [Norwegian ; *b.* 1859]. *Hunger* (Sult, 1890). 1899
A morbidly sensitive young writer in Christiania records his experiences of poverty, semi-starvation, and the thousand and one afflictions that try his nerves. [Transl. by George EGERTON, Duckworth ; with intro. by Edwin Bjorkman, Knopf, New York, 1920 ; Grosset, New York.]

—— *Mysteries* (Mysterier, 1892). 1927
As in *Hunger*, the hero Nagel represents the author, in some aspects at least, whilst it has been suggested that the idiot Minutten equally portrays a different side of that same character. Nagel falls from the clouds into a little seaside town, strikes up an intimacy with the local idiot, falls in love with two ladies, one young and proud, the other a humble old maid, and eventually commits suicide. Like Pan, Nagel is a creature of unregulated impulse, with a sensitive, even mystical approach to the phenomena of life. [Transl. by A. G. CHATER, Knopf, London and New York.]

—— *Shallow Soil* (Ny jord, 1893). 1914
A rather exaggerated satire of dandified literary people in Christiania, who are made to appear both foolish and depraved. [Transl., with introd., by Carl Christian HYLLESTED, Duckworth : o.p. ; Knopf, New York, 1921.]

—— *Pan* (Pan : af løjtnant Thomas Glahns papirer, 1894). 1920
The beauty of this novel is in the pantheistic vision of nature which impassions the hero and makes the whole book lyrical. The scene is the Nordland forest region, where this man conceives a love—for a capricious woman—that is strong enough to embrace death when he loses her. [Transl. by W. WORSTER, Holden ; Knopf, New York.]

—— *Victoria* (Victoria, 1898). 1923
A very poetical, impassioned, and impassioning story of a young man's love, glorious though ill-fated. [Transl. by Arthur G. CHATER, Holden ; Knopf, New York.]

—— *Mothwise* (Sværmere, 1904). 1921
A light and pleasant story, with which it is not amiss to begin one's reading of Hamsun. [Transl. with introd., by W. W. WORSTER, Holden ; *sub tit. Dreamers*, Knopf, New York.]

—— *Wanderers—Autumn ; and, With Muted Strings* (Under höststjernen, 1906 ; and En vandrer spiller med sordin, 1909). 1922
The much-travelled and long-experienced Knut Pedersen is undisguisedly an impersonation of the novelist

HAMSUN, Knut (*continued*).

himself, and in the incidents and conversations and descriptive pages of the two books here rendered into one the author gives an unusually direct expression of his sentiments on life and nature, not omitting, of course, vexed questions like the problems of marriage. [Transl. by W. WORSTER, Holden; Knopf, New York.]

—— *Benoni* (Benoni, 1908).   1925

—— *Rosa* (Rosa, 1908) [sequel].   1926

Norwegian peasant types fill this wide canvas, and are portrayed with serene humour :—Benoni, a clever fellow who gets on in the world through his industry ; Rosa, whom he woos, and after sundry misadventures makes his wife ; Edvarda, who reappears from *Pan*, older and a prey to religious mania ; but, above all, Mack of Sirilund, wealthy merchant, born leader, who holds in his hands the destinies of them all. [(1) and (2), transl. by A. G. CHATER, Knopf, London and New York.]

—— *Children of the Age* (Börn av tiden, 1909).   1921

Offers a strong and graphic picture of the almost feudal conditions still persisting in rural Norway in the latter half of the last century, in the portrait of a despotic aristocrat and his relations with the people of his estate.

—— *Segelfoss Town* (Segelfoss by, 1915) [sequel].   1925

Here the Segelfoss estate, on the death of its former despotic owner, falls into hands which lack his personality and cannot maintain his prestige. It passes through the usual phases of industrial development. The people fall an easy prey to the perils of popular education, cheap politics, and democracy. Meanwhile the cobbler starves, for people no longer want his old-fashioned work. [(1) and (2), Transl. by J. S. SCOTT, Knopf, New York and London.]

—— *Growth of the Soil* (Markens gröde, 1917).   1920

This won the Nobel prize in 1920, and is probably his best-known novel. It is a great epic of labour and of the natural life. The peasant Isak carves his farm out of the primeval forest, establishes a home for his family, and so founds a human community. [Transl. by W. W. WORSTER, Holden ; Knopf, New York ; Grosset, New York.]

—— *The Women at the Pump* (Konerne ved vandposten, 1920).   1928

A lengthy novel of Norwegian womenfolk and their village gossip, in which there is told a story of moral degradation, not without pathos. [Transl. by A. G. CHATER, Knopf, New York and London.]

—— *Chapter the Last* (Sidste kapitel, 1923).   1929

A sardonic picture of a sanatorium and its ugly collection of inmates, who are seen clinging with bloodthirsty tenacity to a life that they should rather hasten to be quit of. [Transl. by A. G. CHATER, Knopf, New York and London.]

—— *Vagabonds* (Landstrykere, 1927).   1930

—— *August* (August) [sequel].   1930

Nowhere is Hamsun more intensely Norwegian than in this pair of connected stories ; he is so intent on showing the physiognomy, the manner and tone, the ways of thinking of the Norwegians in the 1870's, that the foreign reader will often find himself at a loss to comprehend. The first is the delightfully humorous story of two vagabonds, Edevart and August, one happy-go-lucky, open-handed, and a lover, the other a wild grotesque who challenges comparison perhaps with Falstaff, at any rate with Tartarin. August returns to his native village, in the sequel, and introduces new ideas, with uproarious results. [Transl. by Eugene GAY-TIFFT, Coward McCann, New York.]

HANCOCK, Albert Elmer [American ; 1870–1915]. *Henry Bourland : the passing of a cavalier.*
    1901

The author, a Northerner, endeavours to enter into the feelings of the South during the disasters of the Civil War and the still more intolerable wrongs of the Reconstruction period (1861–6). Urgent problems such as that of the negro are handled suggestively. The hero is a Virginia gentleman, invested with the tragic charm of his order. [Macmillan, New York : o.p.]

HANSSON, Ola [Norwegian]. *Young Ofeg's Ditties.*   1895

Psychological analysis of the most microscopical kind, applied chiefly to sad themes. [Transl. by George EGERTON, Lane : o.p.]

HAO CH'IU CHUAN : *The Breeze in the Moonlight : the second book of genius.*   1926

The best Chinese romance, written in the fourteenth century, relating the adventures of an exceedingly perfect pair of lovers beset by innumerable villainies ; renowned in China for its style. A translation, entitled *Hau Kiou Chooan, or, The Pleasing History*, edited by Bp. Percy, was published by Dodsley in 1761. A much-condensed version (based on the translation by Sir J. F. Davis, *sub tit. The Fortunate Union*, 1829), entitled *Shueypingsin*, appeared in 1899 [Kegan Paul: o.p.]. The present translation is made from the French version of George Soulié de Morant (1925). [Transl. from the French by H. BEDFORD-JONES, Putnam, New York.]

HARBEN, William Nathaniel [American ; 1858–1919]. *Abner Daniel.*   1902

—— *The Substitute.*   1903

—— *The Georgians.*   1904

—— *Mam' Linda.*   1907

—— *Gilbert Neal.*   1908

—— *The Redemption of Kenneth Galt.*   1909

The most striking of more than a dozen novels by a Georgian writer, picturing life mostly in Georgian villages or country towns, the talk largely in the local patois. The plots are based on moral problems. In *The Substitute*, a young man's life and love affairs are marred for a season by his father's conviction for theft. Dwight, the candidate for the legislature, has to choose between humane instincts and the fury of the lynching populace who flog Mam' Linda's son. Both Gilbert Neal and Abner Daniel, who reappears in

HARBEN, William Nathaniel (*continued*).

The Georgians, are great talkers, and their unworldly wisdom and practical sagacity express Mr. Harben's feelings about life. He has the true American optimism and idealistic sentiment ; and this inspires his genial character-drawing, which is apt to escape appreciation in the rush of exciting incident. Kenneth Galt is an ambitious railroad man whose crime was the betrayal of a girl ; and we have not only his redemption but that of a youth as much sinned against as sinning, who was his scapegoat. [(1), Burt, New York ; (2), Harper, New York ; (3) and (4), *id.* ; o.p. ; (5), Harper, New York ; (6), *id.* : o.p.]

HARCOURT, Colonel Alfred Frederick Pollock. *Jenetha's Venture.*   1899

A story of the siege of Delhi. [Cassell : o.p.]

—— *The Peril of the Sword.*   1903

The march to Cawnpore and the relief of Lucknow. The author's chief anxiety is to be accurate historically, and he succeeds. [Skeffington : o.p.]

HARDY, Arthur Sherburne [American ; *b.* 1847]. *But Yet a Woman.*   1883

A study of the inner springs of human conduct in the light of high ideals ; scene, an old French town, and the principal character a French maiden destined to the convent, who is awakened to love. The people and the ways of thinking thoroughly French. [Houghton, Boston.]

—— *The Wind of Destiny.*   1886

Another psychological and ethical study, with French and American characters and scenery. [Houghton, Boston.]

—— *Passe Rose.*   1889

A semi-poetical romance of Franks and Saxons in the Ardennes region in the ninth century. Passe Rose is a lovely Provençal waif. Guy of Tours, Charles the Great, monks and Court ladies are among the actors in a drama actuated by the simple, unmixed passions of half-civilized people. [Houghton, Boston.]

—— *His Daughter First.*   1903

In the latest manner of Mr. Howells. The rather complicated and delicate relations—sentimental or financial—of four women and three men in New York and a country house in New England—one pair being a high-strung girl and her father who wants to marry again—all set forth with the most sensitive manipulation of the fine shades of character and motive. [Houghton, Boston.]

HARDY, Thomas [1840–1928]. *Desperate Remedies.*   1871

A plot-novel of the Wilkie Collins brand, with some touches of Hardy's powerful sketching of village life, rustic gossips, and nature.

—— *Under the Greenwood Tree.*   1872

The first of the Wessex novels proper, the common groundwork of which is a very vivid delineation of the people of Dorset and the neighbouring counties, and of the natural life and scenery. The local dialect is used with great literary skill and raciness. These novels are essentially dramatic ; a series of personal histories in which the end is inexorably determined by the conflict of insensate passion and circumstance, as in a Greek play. The protagonists are chiefly yeomen, tradesmen, or others somewhat above the rank of peasants ; these last play their part almost entirely in the comic scenes. The composition is on the grand scale, an architecture making visible the fabric of causation. Hardy's frankness indicates to some critics a leaning to naturalism, but his realism is only the medium for a high poetic imagination, which instinctively personifies Nature herself as having a chief hand in the play. This first characteristic novel is an idyll of village life, in which the members of a carrier's family and the village choir, a gathering of rustic oddities, furnish a sort of comic chorus to the love-affairs of a rustic boy and girl. Here one can hear but a few faint accents of the irony which was to be the main burden of his later fiction. [Harrap ; Chatto ; Boni, New York ; Garden City Co., New York ; *v.* also *Works, infra.*]

—— *A Pair of Blue Eyes.*   1872–3

This, on the contrary, is elaborately ironical. Two friends are in love with the same Cornish girl, who loves both and marries neither, the end poignant tragedy. The story turns on the mutual misunderstandings of the friends and similar sins of innocence on the maiden's part. The author's gloomy determinism begins to show itself here in the abundant coincidences that seem like fatality. A little village on the Cornish coast is the principal scene. [Harrap ; *v.* also *Works, infra.*]

—— *Far from the Madding Crowd.*   1874

Breathes irony in its very title : the tragi-comedy of rural life ; the stormy passions, thwarted purposes, and shattering griefs which are the reality behind the idyllic externals. A harrowing episode of seduction, desertion, and death, and a melodramatic episode of disappointed love and homicidal jealousy, are attached to the main story, how Gabriel Oak wins at last his Rachel, Bathsheba. The routine of agricultural work, outdoor life on the farm, the natural surroundings, the weather, the nightly heavens, make a setting that brings out poetically man's cosmic insignificance. [Harrap ; *v.* also *Works, infra.*]

—— *The Hand of Ethelberta : a comedy in chapters.*   1876

Deals with both Wessex and society in London. Ethelberta is the author's Becky Sharp. A girl of lowly birth, she is clever enough to flourish for a time as a fine lady, a successful crusader against caste prejudice, but she ends as wife of an aristocratic debauchee. Unconquerable loyalty to her needy brothers and sisters is her redeeming virtue.

—— *The Return of the Native.*   1878

A drama of passion and nemesis, enacted amidst the wild and solemn scenery of an imaginary heath, and animated profoundly by the author's philosophy of revolt. The landscape overture is famous—Egdon Heath is as it were a protagonist in the drama, the environment that influences decisively the lives of those who dwell there. The Heath is a symbol also of something more vast, the entire order of Nature, in which man is but an insignificant particle. Behold the quandary in which the working of natural laws has placed mankind ! Fatal misunderstandings between dear relatives, and the subtle and imperceptible yielding to temptation which leads to crime and death, are the determining motives. Clym Yeobright and his mother and the exotic Eustacia Vye are among his finest impersonations of human longing and disillusionment, anguish, and endurance. [Harrap ; Modern Lib., New York ; *v.* also *Works, infra.*]

HARDY, Thomas (*continued*). *The Trumpet Major.*   1879

A genial and happy love-story, more soberly realistic than the foregoing in its picture of family life and of a fickle sailor lover. The anxiety and suspense prevailing in the southern counties during the Napoleonic terror is a leading motive, and we get a glimpse of George III and his family at their favourite watering-place of Weymouth. *The Trumpet Major* has been successful on the boards of a rustic theatre.

—— *A Laodicean ; or, The Castle of the De Stancys : a story of to-day.*   1881

Another minor novel of Wessex and society. The heroine a weaker Ethelberta and the motive somewhat similar : feudal prestige superseded by brains and money.

—— *Two on a Tower : a romance.*   1882

A fanciful and unreal story with a strong dash of poetry ; the hero an amateur astronomer burning to devote his life to science. An older lady of higher social status loves him, and thus creates one of the ironical situations in which Hardy delighted.

—— *The Mayor of Casterbridge.*   1886

In the foregoing, at any rate before *Two on a Tower*, Hardy was prone to invoke external agencies as the powers thwarting human designs and controlling destinies. From this point onwards he shows his characters bearing their fates within them, in the master-tendencies of their appetites and wills. Here we have Henchard, an impetuous, domineering tradesman, who for a long while commands success, but whose egotism and obstinacy, without any strange conjunction of accident, eventually work his ruin. The scene is Dorchester and its immediate surroundings, and the local scenery is employed with wonderful suggestiveness. [Harrap ; Modern Lib., New York ; *v. also Works, infra.*]

—— *The Woodlanders.*   1887

Here too all the chief personages come to grief through yielding the reins of life to their passions, whether noble or the reverse. It is a sylvan pastoral of central Dorset, imbued with a pagan delight in the beauty and the bounteousness of nature, the human figures appearing, as it were, part and parcel of the landscape. A love-tale of the conventional kind holds the foremost place ; but the underplot is lofty and austere tragedy, an idyll of unrequited love, of which the two protagonists are, in all their homeliness and simplicity, as majestic as the figures of Æschylus, while the nature-worship and the pagan sentiment recall Theocritus. [Harrap ; *v. also Works, infra.*]

—— *Wessex Tales.*   1888

Six stories of medium length, some comic but the majority austere. *The Three Strangers*, which won exceedingly high praise from Stevenson, is a one-act drama, the surprising *dénouement* of which is a piece of sardonic humour ; *The Withered Arm*, a gruesome tale of the supernatural ; *Interlopers at the Knap* and *Fellow-Townsmen*, fatalistic stories of mistaken marriages, good specimens of those tales in which everything goes awry ; *The Distracted Preacher*, a love-story of a smuggling parish seventy years ago.

—— *A Group of Noble Dames.*   1891

Ostensibly legends of Dorsetshire historic families, collected and related by the members of a field club. Chiefly tragi-comedies of wedlock, and as grim and sardonic as anything he has written.

—— *Tess of the D'Urbervilles : a pure woman faithfully presented.*   1891

The tragic history of a woman betrayed. Tess is the completer portrait of the ideal woman sketched in the previous novels, a daughter of the primeval soil of Wessex, and at the same time a tragic symbol of the author's fatalism. The title is a challenge : Tess, the author contends, is sinned against, but not a sinner ; her tragedy is the work of tyrannical circumstances and of the evil deeds of others in the past and the present, and more particularly of two men's baseness, the seducer, and the well-meaning intellectual who married her but is not emancipated enough to reject old prejudices or recognize the pearl that the swine have rejected. The pastoral surroundings, the varying aspects of field, river, sky, serve to deepen the pathos of each stage in the heroine's calamities, or to add beauty and dignity to her tragic personality. [Harrap ; *v. also Works, infra.*]

—— *Life's Little Ironies.*   1894

Brief stories containing the quintessence of the author's fatalism, with a series of broadly comic stories, *A Few Crusted Characters*, appended as a sort of antidote. [Harrap ; *v. also Works, infra.*]

—— *Jude the Obscure.*   1895

This is a novel in which art is hampered by intellectualism ; it is as polemical as *Tess*, and not redeemed by the pity or the beauty of that lofty and austere tragedy. It is the story of a peasant scholar's foiled ambition, and from beginning to end is sombre and in many of the incidents extremely painful. The influence of character upon character, here an influence entirely for evil, is the argument implied in Jude's conjugal history, with its repeated alternations of divorce and reconciliation. Jude himself, the sensual Arabella, the neurotic Sue, and the feeble Tillotson form a quadrilateral of contending forces which must produce the resultant which the novelist has calculated. The end is the extinction of pure and lofty ideals by the hideous brutality of existence, an end in which Jude's suicide is not the most tragic incident. [Harrap ; Modern Lib., New York ; *v. also Works, infra.*]

—— *The Well-Beloved : a sketch of a temperament.*   1897

A fantastic *jeu d'esprit* about an artist in pursuit of his ideal woman. He sees his vision embodied successively in three generations, and last of all woos the granddaughter of his first love. Portland is the principal scene, but there is less local colour than usual.

—— *A Changed Man, The Waiting Supper, and other tales ; concluding with the Romantic Adventures of a Milkmaid.*   1913

A sheaf of twelve items from the magazines (1881–1900) : Hardy called them " minor novels." The last and longest is a pretty fantasy, and one of the only two with a happy ending. Otherwise the dominant temper is gloomy and ironical, and the motive of nearly all, matrimonial tragedy. *A Tryst at an Ancient Earthwork* may be singled out as a notable specimen of Hardy's quiet and impressive art.

[*Works* (Uniform Ed.) ; (Pocket ed.) ; (Wessex ed.) Macmillan ; (novels), 18 vols. Macmillan ; Harper, New York. *Short Stories* (collected in 1 vol.), Macmillan, 1928.]

HARKER, Mrs. Lizzie Allen [*née* Watson ; *b.* 1863]. *A Romance of the Nursery.*   1902

HARKER, Mrs. Lizzie Allen (*continued*). *Concerning Paul and Fiammetta.*　1906
　　Two story-books about children which people of any age can enjoy. The children are delightful little originals, with a fantastic imagination to which the author's whimsical yet natural and unpretending style is charmingly attuned. [(1) (Enlarged ed.) and (2), Murray ; Scribner, New York.]

—— *The Little People.*　1903
—— *His First Leave.*　1907
　　Further stories of young people—boys, girls, and grown-ups—Wycherleys and others. [(1), Murray : o.p. ; (2), Lane : o.p. ; (2), revised ed., *sub tit. Montagu Wycherly*, Murray ; Scribner, New York, 1921.]

—— *Miss Esperance and Mr. Wycherley.*　1908
　　About an old maid and an Oxford don living in a village on the Firth of Forth, and the coming of two boys into their quiet domestic existence. Tender character-drawing in an atmosphere reminiscent of *Cranford* ; readable by young as well as grown-up people. [Murray ; Scribner, New York. *Illus.* by Sybil Tawse, Murray.]

—— *Master and Maid.*　1910
　　The innocent flirtations and other captivating goings-on of an impulsive Irish girl, domiciled with a staid and dignified house-master at a public school. The perfect ease with which the characters are hit off by means of lifelike and vivacious dialogue is a characteristic of all Mrs. Harker's stories. [Murray ; Scribner, New York : o.p.]

—— *Mr. Wycherley's Wards.*　1912
　　Continues *Miss Esperance and Mr. Wycherley* after the death of Miss Esperance ; the wards are the two boys, and Allegra, a gifted Greek girl whom Mr. Wycherley adopts. The latter is an interesting sketch of the artistic temperament in a child. [Murray ; Scribner, New York : o.p.]

—— *The ffolliots of Redmarley.*　1913
　　A happy domestic romance of the tomboy children of a Cotswold family. [Murray ; Scribner, New York.]

—— *Jan and her Job.*　1917
　　A fresh and humorous story of a young woman who has to take charge of a batch of children through the death of her sister and her brother-in-law's defection. Opens in India, a little before the great war. [Murray ; Scribner, New York.]

—— *Allegra.*　1919
　　Allegra throws over the playwright who dramatized a trashy novel and made it worth her taking the principal part, then falls in love with the original author ; but her revulsion is complete when he sends her the rest of his works. Allegra wisely sticks to the stage. [Murray ; Scribner, New York.]

—— *Black Jack House.*　1930
　　The trials of a husband of the tradesman class married to a wife with an illegitimate war-baby. This precocious infant, a credit to her patrician father and to the creator of Paul and Fiammetta, excites his jealousy—hence the mother's tears. [Murray.]

HARLAND, Henry [American ; *b.* in Petersburg ; 1861–1905]. *The Yoke of the Thorah.*　1887
　　Probably the best of Harland's early stories, which were crude and violent sensation novels, issued under the pseudonym of Sidney Luska. A study of Jewish life in New York, particularly of German Jews. The young hero loves a Yankee girl, but his religious and racial feelings are so worked upon by his uncle, a Rabbi, that he jilts her. His marriage to a commonplace Jewess is followed by his intensely pathetic death. [Cassell : o.p.]

—— *Mea Culpa : a woman's last word.*　1891
　　An amusing book, though the end is tragic ; several of the characters are humorous, especially the musician, Armadis. [Street, New York : o.p.]

—— *Mademoiselle Miss ; and other stories.*　1893
　　Five stories that mark a change of temper and style : Harland had now come under French influences, and in 1894 became editor of the *Yellow Book*, the organ of the Æsthetes. The most remarkable are the title-sketch, of an English governess who finds herself in a very Parisian hotel, and the touching *Funeral March of a Marionette*. Maupassant had obviously taught Harland how to make the most of his rather fine little talent. [Lane.]

—— *Grey Roses.*　1895
　　Continues in a like strain. Harland's stories are rather the light confectionery of the art than serious novels, but within their own limits they are delicately and seductively compounded. [Lane.]

—— *Comedies and Errors.*　1898
　　Miscellaneous stories, gay or sad, delineating ordinary people of the world. *The Queen's Pleasure* and *The Invisible Prince* deal with the possible humours and consolations of the life of royalty. [Lane.]

—— *The Cardinal's Snuff-box.*　1900
　　This and the next are excellent illustrations of the note on *Grey Roses* : it is a novelist's love-romance. He has made a heroine of a lovely girl whom he meets again as an Italian duchess, widowed. He has thus unconsciously prepared the way for his courtship. [Lane ; Dodd & Mead, New York.]

—— *The Lady Paramount.*　1902
　　Another popular novel without the genuine basis of reality that gave strength to *Mademoiselle Miss*, etc. [Lane ; Dodd & Mead, New York.]

—— *My Friend Prospero.*　1904
　　The fairy-tale of two lovers made happy by a beneficent godmother, translated into terms of modern society life, a penniless English aristocrat meeting an Austrian princess in a wonderful castle embosomed amongst remote Italian mountains. Sensuous description and felicitous chatter are the chief material of the novel, in which manner far outweighs matter. [Lane ; Nelson.]

HARRADEN, Miss Beatrice [*b.* 1864]. *Ships that Pass in the Night.*　1893
　　The ships are human souls that speak each other in this earthly night of sorrow and uncertainty, each with

HARRADEN, Miss Beatrice (*continued*).
its message of comfort and hope. The scene is an Alpine health resort, where many people, sorely tried in the voyage of life, come within hail and exert their various influences on one another's lives. A well-meaning, sentimental story that made many a reader's heart throb. [Blackwood ; Dodd & Mead, New York.]

—— *Hilda Strafford.* 1897
A rather didactic story of a selfish wife who needs awakening to all that affection and devotion might do for her husband. [Blackwood : o.p. ; Dodd & Mead, New York : o.p.]

—— *Katharine Frensham.* 1903
Has a similar moral, but the parts are reversed, the woman is the fine character, and the man weak and hysterical. [Blackwood.]

HARRINGTON, James [1611–1677]. *Oceana.* 1656
Half a romance of the conventional quasi-historical type, half a serious treatise on government. The account of his fictitious commonwealth, particularly the debates and the sketches of statesmen—which clearly refer to contemporary politics—have some humorous touches ; but the main part is grave theory enforcing such principles as a maximum allowance of landed property, election by ballot, etc., derived from Venice and Sparta. [Ed. H. Morley, Routledge, 1887 (Dutton, New York).: o.p. ; ed. by S. L. Liljegren, Nutt, 1924.]

HARRIS, Corra May White [Mrs. L. H. Harris ; American ; *b.* 1869]. *A Circuit-Rider's Wife.* 1910
The work of an American Methodist minister on circuit duty ; a very human story of his various experiences as seen through the eyes of his wife. [Altemus, Philadelphia ; Constable : o.p.]

—— *A Circuit-Rider's Widow.* 1916
—— *My Son.* 1920
Further sketches of Methodism and Methodists in Georgia. [(1) and (2), Doubleday, Doran, New York : o.p.]

HARRIS, Frank [1856–1931]. *Elder Conklin ; and other stories.* 1895
Sketches of rough life in Kansas, done with extraordinary actuality. The Elder, a conscientious Puritan, deliberately does wrong for his daughter's sake, who, as it ironically happens, is quite unworthy of his devotion. A searching study of motive and of manners, intertwined with a narrative of courtship. *Gulmore the Boss* is another transcript from life, showing how elections are worked. *Eatin' Crow* and *The Best Man in Garotte* depict life in a mining district, a state of things made familiar by Bret Harte. [Lane ; Brentano, New York.]

—— *Montes the Matador ; and other stories.* 1900
Montes is a bit of Spain, a story of love and hate, hot passion and abounding life ; bull-fighting is described with the enthusiasm of one who enters into the spirit of the game. *First Love* is a girl's affection for a shabby-natured young man, to whom she attributes all sorts of high qualities. *Sonia* is the history of an Englishman's liaison with a Nihilist. [Lane ; Brentano, New York.]

—— *The Bomb.* 1908
The history of an anarchist outrage in Chicago, 1886 ; told in the first person by the perpetrator, with the startling realism of the tales mentioned above. In diagnosing the motives that led up to the event, Mr. Harris not only gives an interesting psychological study, but writes a kind of pamphlet on the cruel conditions of American industrialism, the brutality of the police, and other social grievances. [Long : o.p. ; Brentano, New York.]

HARRIS, J. Henry. *Faith : a story of Saint Porth.* 1899
An attractive picture of pious and sound-hearted seafaring folk in Cornwall, contrasted with the egoism and faithlessness of their son, who is spoiled by London and the ways of Mammon, and becomes an agnostic. [Nisbet : o.p.]

—— *Our Cove.* 1900
Intimate little pictures of a Cornish village and its people, old and young ; anecdotes in the vernacular, of local peculiarities, observances, and superstitions. [Pollard, Truro : o.p.]

—— *The Luck of Wheal Veor ; and other stories of the mine, moor, and sea.* 1901
Impressions of the old-fashioned Cornish peasant, his superstitions, his pietism, and his humours. Almost wholly in dialect. The eponymous tale deals with the " nuggies " or spirits of the mine, still implicitly believed in. [Gay & Bird : o.p.]

HARRIS, Joel Chandler [American ; 1848–1908]. *Uncle Remus.* 1881
A collection of folk-stories from Georgia in negro dialect, only a little touched up by the novelist. Uncle Remus, a shrewd and humorous old negro, is a product of the plantation system, his mind a rich store of beast-fables, the moral of which is always cunningly adapted to the foibles of his hearers. The hero of most of the tales is Brer Rabbit, and Brer Fox usually comes off worst in the encounter of wits ; in fact, the victory of craft over strength is the favourite motive, as in the mediæval beast-epic of *Reynard the Fox.* [Appleton, New York and London ; Routledge ; Chatto ; see also *seq.*]

—— *Nights with Uncle Remus.* 1883
A further collection, in which the author begins to embroider more upon the primitive folk-story. Three new-comers help Uncle Remus with his tales, each maintaining his own peculiarity of dialect and distinctive personality. [Houghton, Boston ; Routledge ; Chatto ; with *Uncle Remus*, Routledge.]

—— *Mingo ; and other sketches in black and white.* 1884
Four bizarre tales in the same humorous lingo, giving a comic picture of the negroes in Georgia before or just after emancipation. [Houghton, Boston ; Douglas, Edinburgh : o.p.]

—— *Free Joe ; and other Georgian sketches.* 1887
Familiar pictures of Georgian life before and after the Civil War. They portray the slave and his master, and the various members of the slave-owning community, in a pleasant light, dwelling by preference on the kindlier aspects of their relations. The title-story is deeply pathetic. [Scribner, New York : o.p. ; Routledge : o.p.]

HARRIS, Joel Chandler (*continued*). *Balaam and His Master ; and other sketches and stories.* 1891

Besides the title-story, contains *Ananias, Mom Bi, The Old Bascom Place,* and two others. The melancholy and pathetic side of the negro character predominates in these stories, which, however, present a great variety of types, e.g. the faithful and heroic Balaam and Ananias, and the grotesque Mom Bi. [Houghton, Boston ; Harper, London : o.p.]

—— *Uncle Remus and His Friends.* 1892

A further series of fables by this rude and uncouth Georgian Æsop. Brer Fox, Brer Rabbit, the wolf, the bear, and other characters reappear, each a racy personality of well-marked traits. The character of the wily and good-natured old humourist is considerably developed. [Houghton, Boston.]

—— *Aaron in the Wildwoods.* [juvenile] 1897

The adventures of a runaway slave, Aaron, and of Little Crotchet the cripple—a fantastic, broadly humorous story. [Houghton, Boston ; Harper, London : o.p.]

—— *Tales of the Home Folk in Peace and War.* 1898

Stories on all kinds of subjects from dogs to negroes and babies, with many sketches of the people at home in Georgia during the Civil War. [Houghton, Boston.]

—— *The Chronicles of Aunt Minervy Ann.* 1899

A shrewd and garrulous old negress, own sister to Uncle Remus, tells similar stories in the drollest way and the same broad patois, commenting on passing events with sagacity and humour. [Scribner, New York : o.p.]

—— *On the Wing of Occasions.* 1900

Five stories of the times of the Civil War, including the exciting escape of a Southern spy from New York, a plot to kidnap President Lincoln, and divers very attractive portraits of Southern humorists, daring scouts, and an inimitable Anglo-Irishman. [Doubleday, New York : o.p.]

—— *A Little Union Scout.* 1901

Campaign of General Nathan Bedford Forrest (1864). Adventures of a soldier in chase of a Federal scout, who turns out to be a bewitching damsel. Good characters. [Doubleday, New York : o.p. ; Duckworth : o.p.]

HARRISON, Frederic [1831–1923]. *Theophano : the Crusade of the Tenth Century : a romantic monograph.* 1904

As romance of small account, but interesting as a reconstruction of a period of history (956–9). Constantinople and the decadent empires of East and West in the midst of the great struggle by which the Saracens were held in check. The reconquest of Crete is a magnificent episode, and the chapters describing the life of the great mediæval cities, Byzantium in the reign of Nicephorus Phocas, Rome under Otto, Cordova under the Abassids, etc., are not only picturesque and full of life, but show the grip and insight of the experienced historian. [Chapman : o.p.]

HARRISON, Henry Sydnor [American ; 1880–1930]. *Queed.* 1911

A very popular novel which gives a complacently realistic view of the crude social atmosphere and the pushful ideals of American city life. Queed, the young " revolutionary sociologist," an over-educated young man with " high-falutin " but useless ideas of his mission in life, is seriously disenchanted by contact with actualities and the demands of a yellow newspaper on which he is employed. [Houghton, Boston ; Constable.]

" HARRY, Myrian " [Mme Perrault-Harry ; French ; b. 1875]. *The Little Daughter of Jerusalem* (La petite fille de Jérusalem). 1918

By a native of Jerusalem, of mixed Russian and German parentage, who depicts the strange intermingling of races and creeds. [Transl. by Phœbe ALLEN ; introd. by Jules Lemaître, Dent : o.p.]

HARTE, Francis Bret [American ; 1839–1902]. *The Luck of Roaring Camp ; and other sketches.* 1870

Bret Harte's early stories are a unique record at first-hand of the strenuous, lawless times of the gold rush in the 1850's to the Pacific slope. He was a writer strongly akin to Dickens, though not lacking in originality ; prone to melodrama, sentimental in his trick of seeing the angel under the skin of wastrel and cut-throat ; admirably realistic in his power of giving actuality to the most daring conceptions of character and romantic incident. The " Luck " is a babe whose coming among the brutal and uncivilized miners in the Californian settlement makes their lives better and more humane. *The Outcasts of Poker Flat, Miggles, Tennessee's Partner, Mliss,* and many others are vivid limelight pictures of the gold-digging communities. Appended is a boisterous set of parodies, *Sensation Novels Condensed,* ridiculing with clear, critical insight and cruel satire the masterpieces of many of the famous novelists of the middle of the nineteenth century. [Houghton, Boston ; Chatto ; (Everyman's Lib.), Dent ; Macmillan, London and New York, 1928.]

—— *Condensed Novels (sometimes entitled Sensation Novels).* 1870

—— *Condensed Novels : new burlesques.* 1902

The former is an excellent series of parodies on Fenimore Cooper, Miss Braddon, Dumas, Charlotte Brontë, Marryat, Hugo, Michelet, Lytton, Reade, Disraeli, Dickens, and others ; the latter a less successful collection on Anthony Hope, Doyle, Caine, Kipling, Corelli, and others. [(1) and (2), Houghton, Boston ; in 1 vol., Chatto.]

—— *Flip ; and, Found at Blazing Star.* 1872

A picturesque little romance, with a highly melodramatic conclusion. Flip is a half-wild, half-clad virgin, living with her mad old father in the midst of mountains and forests, and courted by a mysterious stranger. The ring " found at Blazing Star " is the beginning of a mysterious series of incidents and of a love affair between an ingenuous young digger and a very smart girl ; this also closes in melodrama. [Houghton, Boston ; Chatto.]

—— *Gabriel Conroy.* 1876

His one serious attempt to write a full-length novel. The sensations begin with the straits of a party of settlers driven to cannibalism by famine, and culminate in an earthquake which performs the functions of *deus ex machina.* Humorous scenes are interlaced with the murders, lynching, miraculous escapes ; and a

HARTE, Francis Bret (*continued*).

perplexing tangle of villainy, love and jealousy, intrigue and counter-intrigue, is unravelled in an astonishing trial scene. Among the characters that bear the stamp of Dickens may be singled out the fascinating desperado, Jack Hamlin, and Colonel Starbottle, a swashbuckler advocate (both well known from other novels) ; but the most original is Gabriel himself, stupid but self-forgetful. [Houghton, Boston ; Chatto.]

—— *In the Carquinez Woods.* 1883

A story of the old melodramatic kind, but also a powerful rendering of the wonder and mystery of the forest (the culminating scene a forest conflagration and stampede of beasts). The heroine, a coarse, rowdy girl from the dancing-saloons, becomes, under the influence of love, a refined and gentle woman, capable of patient suffering. Other characteristic figures are the half-breed lover and the hypocritical Baptist minister. [Houghton, Boston ; Longmans : o.p.]

—— *On the Frontier.* 1884

Three tales. *Left Out on Lone Star Mountain* is a characteristic idyll, bringing out the lawlessness of the miners, and also the innate sense of justice which gave them a code of their own administered by Judge Lynch. Four disheartened diggers are plotting to desert their comrade when he discovers gold and brings them the joyful intelligence, his unselfishness overwhelming them with penitence. [Houghton, Boston.]

—— *Maruja.* 1885

A more sustained story, full of the usual violent contrasts and melodramatic surprises. The heroine is half-Puritan, half-Spanish, a wild and wilful beauty, with a motley circle of lovers, strongly coloured representatives of Californian life. [Houghton, Boston ; Chatto.]

—— *The Crusade of the " Excelsior."* 1887

A mixture of fantasy and realism, the plot arising from the arrival, by accident, of the American ship *Excelsior* at a secluded port in Lower California. Here the crew meet with droll adventures, and with some exceedingly funny people. [Houghton, Boston ; Chatto.]

—— *A Phyllis of the Sierras ; and, A Drift from Redwood Camp.* 1888

The first story, which brings the old order and the new into strange juxtaposition, is about an abortive love affair between an English baronet's son and a Western girl, the Englishman's financial ruin, and his marriage to a blacksmith's daughter, now a millionaire. The " Drift " is a weak and cowardly miner, who is carried on a river-flood among the Indians and adopted by them as heaven-sent chief. [Houghton, Boston ; Chatto : o.p.]

—— *Cressy.* 1889

The love-story of the master and a pupil in a South Californian school. Less desultory than most of this author's tales, animated by the same fun and humour. [Houghton, Boston ; Chatto.]

—— *A Waif of the Plains.* 1890

Story of a boy's adventures in California. [Houghton, Boston ; Chatto.]

—— *Colonel Starbottle's Client ; and some other people.* 1892

Eight stories of the South and the West and one of England. [Houghton, Boston ; Chatto : o.p.]

—— *Sally Dows ; and other stories.* 1893

Four tales. Title-story, an incident of Reconstruction times. [Houghton, Boston : Chatto.]

—— *Clarence.* 1895

Time of the Civil War and of Reconstruction. [Houghton, Boston ; Chatto : o.p.]

—— *From Sand Hill to Pine.* 1900

Seven stories in the old manner, and of the old gold-mining days of California, e.g. *A Jack and Jill of the Sierras, A Belle of Canada City.* [Houghton, Boston ; Chatto : o.p.]

—— *Under the Redwoods.* 1901

Stories well representative of Bret Harte's various styles, and including some of his best. *Three Vagabonds of Trinidad* is a powerful and touching little story of an Indian, a China boy, and a faithful dog ; and *Bohemian Days* brings before us vividly the half-veiled struggle between respectability and lawlessness that marked the early days of San Francisco. [Houghton, Boston ; Chatto.]

—— *Openings in the Old Trail.* 1902

His usual sentimental melodrama—desperadoes and virtuous villains. Life in Sierra Nevada, however, is presented with excellent realism. [Houghton, Boston ; Chatto.]

[Complete works, Riverside Edition, 20 vols. ; California Ed. (1929), 10 vols., Houghton, Boston.]

HARTLEY, M. *Beyond Man's Strength.* 1909

Tries to make interesting a period " not well known to the general reader " (1814–49). Tells of the Piedmontese rising of 1821 and its collapse, and the 1848 rising which ended at Novara (1849). Shelley, Byron, and Cavour appear, but the most arresting figure is that of Charles Albert of Savoy. [Heinemann : o.p.]

—— *A Sereshan.* 1911

Another industrious compilation, describing frontier fighting with brigands in the Croatian regiment under Radetzky, the revolution in Vienna, and the Hungarian insurrection ; Kossuth, General Guyon, and Jellachich the Ban looming large. [Mills & Boon : o.p.]

HARTLEY, Mrs. May [*née* Laffan ; Irish]. *Hogan, M.P.* 1876

A discursive and garrulous novel of Catholic society in Dublin and the country, revealing the social currents that underlie political movements. Hogan is a struggling barrister, ambitious and energetic, but not particularly scrupulous. He gets into Parliament in an underhand way, runs a brief course of prosperity, then fails ignominiously. Characters numerous and representative, but few appeal to the sympathies ; yet their social manœuvres, petty intrigues, ambitions, gossip and scandal are often diverting. The writer's object is to show up the permanent effects of the wrong methods of education pursued by the Roman Catholics. [Macmillan : o.p.]

—— *Christy Carew.* 1880

Irish people and Irish society, the secular rivalry of the churches, the problem of mixed marriages and the social disabilities of Roman Catholics, studied and criticized with some anti-Catholic bias. [Macmillan : o.p.]

HARTLEY, Mrs. May (*continued*). *Ismay's Children.*   1887
    A conscientious study of many classes of Irish people from the point of view of the "quality"; the scene laid
        amid the squalid and mournful wilds of County Cork, in the times of Fenian activities and midnight drillings.
        [Macmillan : o.p.]

HAŠEK, Jaroslav [Czech ; *d.* 1923]. *The Good Soldier Schweik.*   1930
    An hilarious though overlong satire of the Austrian Empire and the Austrian army, which was secretly circulated
        among the Czech troops and caused wholesale disaffection. Schweik is an accomplished malingerer, who
        discomfits every attempt to reduce him to obedience and makes his superior officers and everything Austrian
        a laughing-stock. [With grotesque *illus.* by Joseph Lada, transl. by Paul SELVER, Heinemann ;
        Doubleday, Doran, New York.]

HATTON, Joseph [1840–1907]. *By Order of the Czar : the tragic story of Anna Klopstock, Queen
    of the Ghetto.*   1890
    A sensational novel ; prohibited in Russia for its bold handling of the persecution of the Jews. [Hutchinson : o.p.]

HAUFF, Wilhelm [German ; 1802–27]. *Josephine ; or, The Beggar-girl of the Pont-des-Arts* (Die
    Bettlerin vom Pont-des-Arts).   1844
    The lover finds the original of a portrait that he has fallen in love with to be the ill-used wife of a brutal baron,
        whom he ultimately induces her to forsake, and then marries her. Highly romantic and improbable.
        [Transl. by John NISBET, *sub tit. A Constant Lover,* 1893, Unwin : o.p.]

—— *Lichtenstein ; or, the Swabian league* (Lichtenstein, 1826).   1846
    Deals with Swabia under Duke Ulrich of Würtemberg, who was driven out by the Swabian league in 1519 ;
        a novel very popular in Germany, on account of its good local colour and successful imitation of Scott's
        narrative style. [Transl. by F. WOODLEY and W. LANDER, Bruce & Wyld : o.p. ; transl. by R. F. CRAIG,
        Digby & Long, 1897, *sub tit. Marie of Lichtenstein* ; Nister : o.p. ; Dutton, New York, 1901.]

HAUPTMANN, Gerhart Johann Robert [German ; *b.* 1862]. *The Fool in Christ, Emanuel Quint*
    (Der Narr in Christo, Emanuel Quint, 1910).   1911
    A long and rambling account of a half-witted peasant, the victim of religious hysteria, who re-enacts in modern
        times the principal events in the life of Christ, and is misunderstood, and persecuted. [Transl. by Thomas
        SELTZER, Viking Press, New York ; Methuen : o.p.]

—— *Atlantis* (Atlantis, 1912).   1912
    The German doctor and the Swedish dancer with their love story, formally the connecting-link, fade into
        insignificance in comparison with the broad imaginative view of our complex modern life, as beheld on the
        vast liner crossing the Atlantic, or in the furious stress of business and pleasure in the United States, a
        view that is essentially critical and philosophical. [Transl. by Adèle and Thomas SELTZER, Viking Press,
        New York ; Laurie : o.p.]

—— *The Heretic of Soana* (Der Ketzer von Soana, 1918).   1923
    Story of a priest betrayed by sensual love. The scenery of Monte Generoso and its neighbourhood is well
        described. [Transl. by Bayard Quincey MORGAN, Viking Press, New York ; Secker.]

—— *Phantom* (1923).   1923
    The confession of a criminal, written down after repentance. A young fellow falls a victim to megalomania ;
        the fantasy transforms his life, and leads him into debt and crime. Unlike Stavrogin, his aberration is
        something alien to his nature ; imprisonment restores his balance, and he resumes his original self. [Transl.
        by Bayard Quincey MORGAN, Viking Press, New York.]

—— *The Island of the Great Mother* (Die Insel der grossen Mutter : oder das Wunder von Ile des
    Dames, 1924).   1925
    A rather heavy *jeu d'esprit*, or perhaps a philosophical fantasy. A big pleasure ship comes to grief in the Pacific,
        and her freight of over-civilized women, habituated to ease and luxury, are sent ashore in the boats. They
        found a monosexual community, which thrives in this hospitable climate, and dissembling the fact that
        a growing boy is among them, attribute the steady yield of births to supernatural agency. [Transl. by
        Willa and Edwin MUIR, Secker ; Viking Press, New York.]

HAUSRATH, Adolf D. ["George Taylor" ; German ; 1837–1909]. *Antinous : a romance of
    ancient Rome* (1880).   1882
    Hadrian's famous minion (117–30) is the chief figure in this romance, with his dreams and despairing act of
        suicide. The character of Hadrian, the tricks and the virtues of contemporary paganism, the contentions
        of the Christian Church, are all set forth with a careful attention to history and archæology. [Transl.
        M. J. SAFFORD, Gottesburger, New York : o.p. ; transl. by J. D. MORELL, Longmans, 1884 : o.p.]

—— *Klytia : a story of Heidelberg Castle* (1883).   1883
    Germany torn by contending sects, Lutherans, Calvinists, and Catholics (1570) ; Erastus appears. Amid
        such scenes a pathetic story is worked out, with a moral that duty is more important than dogma. [Transl.
        by S. F. CORKRAN, 2 vols., Tauchnitz, Leipzig (Low) : o.p. ; transl. by M. J. SAFFORD, Gottesberger, New
        York, 1884 : o.p.]

—— *Jetta ; or, Heidelberg under the Romans* (1884).   1886
    A tragic chronicle of the great struggle on the debatable land of the Neckar and Rhine, between the Alamanni
        and the decadent Romans under Valentinian (fourth century). [Transl. by Sutton CORKRAN, Kegan Paul :
        o.p.]

—— *Father Maternus : a romance of the sixteenth century* (Pater Maternus, 1898).   1911
    A learned picture of religious life about 1511, centring in two German Augustinians who pay a visit to Rome,
        and dwelling on the corruptions and the anti-Semitic violence of the time. Not much of "romance"
        about it. [Dent : o.p.]

HAWKER, Marie Elizabeth ["Lanoe Falconer" ; 1848–1908]. *Mademoiselle Ixe.*   1890
    A quiet domestic story of country life, with a singularly vivid portrait of a Russian governess who is a Nihilist—
        the tragedy intensely affecting. "One of the finest short stories in English" (*Saturday Review*). [Unwin : o.p.]

HAWKER, Marie Elizabeth (*continued*). *Cecilia de Noël.*   1891

An unique sort of ghost story. The ghost appears in a country house to seven different people, giving them the impression that it is a lost soul. Miss Hawker's fine touch appears in the effect produced on each of these people's minds. [Macmillan : o.p.]

—— *Hôtel d'Angleterre ; and other stories.*   1891

Short stories revealing the same delicacy of touch in handling the finer shades of sentiment, the elusive subtleties of quite ordinary life and everyday character. *Violin Obbligato* is perhaps her finest achievement. [Unwin : o.p.]

—— *Old Hampshire Vignettes.*   1907

A little collection of stories depicting old-fashioned life in the neighbourhood where she lived, viz. near Hurstbourne Priors. [Macmillan : o.p.]

HAWORTH, Paul Leland [American ; *b.* 1876]. *The Path of Glory.*   1911

A workmanlike historical novel of the conquest of Canada (1754–59), culminating in Wolfe's glorious exploit at Quebec. [Little & Brown, Boston : o.p. ; Ham-Smith : o.p.]

HAWTHORNE, Julian [American ; 1846–1913 ; son of Nathaniel Hawthorne]. *Garth.*   1877

A much-elaborated story of country life in New Hampshire, going into the details of family connexions, and so assembling a large variety of characters. A painter's love-story is the chief subject ; there are long talks on Swedenborgianism, etc. [Appleton, New York : o.p. ; Chatto.]

—— *Sebastian Strome.*   1879

Strives " to tell of the birth and first infancy of a man's heart, and of sundry vicissitudes befalling other hearts in consequence thereof." A serious study of a strong but selfish character, chastened to unselfishness by the consequences of his folly and crimes. The simultaneous deaths of his father and a girl he had betrayed are two among many tragic episodes. [Appleton, New York : o.p. ; Chatto : o.p.]

—— *Dust.*   1883

An intricate plot based on the far-fetched idea of a man's act of self-sacrifice, whereby he shields a gambling scamp at the expense of his own good name and fortune. [Houghton, Boston : o.p. ; Chatto : o.p.]

—— *Archibald Malmaison.*   1884

A creepy tale with a good idea boldly worked out. [Funk, New York.]

—— *Beatrix Randolph.*   1884

The plot hinges on the successful attempt of a New York impresario to pass off an amateur with a magnificent voice in place of a prima donna who failed to appear. [Houghton, Boston : o.p. ; Chatto : o.p.]

HAWTHORNE, Nathaniel [American ; 1804–64]. *Fanshawe.*   1828

A minor work, reprinted 1876, before then practically unknown. An old-fashioned romance, embodying reminiscences of the author's college days—a much-idealized picture of Bowdoin, where he was educated. Already exhibits the grace and clearness of the prose style that is one of the distinctions of all the following books. [Houghton, Boston ; *v. Dolliver Romance, infra.*]

—— *Twice-Told Tales.*   1837–42

Hawthorne's novels and stories always present small groups of figures in ideal-relations. They hinge upon some critical event rich in spiritual suggestiveness. Hutton calls them " ideal situations, expanded by minute study and trains of clear, pale thought into the dimensions of novels." The gloomy Calvinistic theology of his forefathers, that haunted the writer's imagination whilst his intellect revolted from it, gives a sombre colour to the more serious tales. This series contains the *Legends of the Province House* and other imaginative readings of pre-Revolutionary traditions, several of which involve supernatural incident, e.g. *The Gray Champion, Endicott and the Red Cross*, and, most characteristic, *Lady Eleanore's Mantle*, a perfect example of his method of putting a moral idea into an artistic concrete, the mantle being at once a symbol of the lady's heartless egoism and the physical cause of calamity to her fellow-creatures. Akin to these, in visionary qualities and profound knowledge of the heart, are such apologues as *The Threefold Destiny*, an allegory of human endeavour, *The Wedding Knell, The Minister's Black Veil, The Great Carbuncle*, and *Dr. Heidegger's Experiment*. The ethical conflicts are handled exclusively as intellectual and artistic material, not in order to edify. Then there are compact pictures of New England life, and contemplative sketches pervaded by a serene philosophy, like *Toll-Gatherer's Day, A Rill from the Town Pump, Chippings with a Chisel* ; some of these have the light vivacity of a fairy-tale. [2 vols., 1 vol., Houghton, Boston ; 2 vols. (Chandos Classics), Warne ; (Everyman's Lib.), Dent (Dutton, New York), 1911 ; Macmillan.]

—— *Mosses from an Old Manse.*   1846

A second batch of " twice-told tales." Of the gloomier imaginative projections of moral ideas two of the best examples are *Rappaccini's Daughter* and *Young Goodman Brown* ; the latter a story of diabolical influence, with impressive forest scenery. *Roger Malvin's Burial* is a tragic tale of remorse and long-delayed expiation in the romantic days of Indian warfare (1725). Among the lighter pieces one of the best is *The Celestial Railroad*, a comic parody of the *Pilgrim's Progress* and a satire on modern insincerity. [2 vols., 1 vol., Houghton, Boston ; Macmillan, New York ; (Bohn's Lib.), Bell (no Amer. ed.).]

—— *The Scarlet Letter.*   1850

A masterpiece in the style of art described above by R. H. Hutton—a philosophical handling of the problem of sin and remorse. A Calvinist minister in the early Puritan days of Massachusetts commits adultery with a married woman, and with his accomplice makes terrible expiation. An austere study of the workings of a guilty mind, and a deeply pathetic book, though pity is not allowed to intrude : the protest against the inhuman mercilessness of the old Puritan morality is strictly tacit. Hawthorne's fantastic symbolism brings the crime and its searing effects on the heart visually before us. [Houghton, Boston ; Scribner, New York ; Routledge ; (Everyman's Lib.), Dent (Dutton, New York) ; (World's Classics), Oxford Press ; Macmillan, London and New York ; with *The Blithedale Romance*, Houghton, Boston.]

—— *The House of Seven Gables.*   1851

A brighter and more humorous story, which he carefully described as a romance, not a novel, though the analysis of character is stern and uncompromising, and the writer dwells, as is his wont, upon the endless and incalculable consequences of past mistakes and misdeeds. In the last generations of a decaying family he

HAWTHORNE, Nathaniel (*continued*).

presents a series of quaint, fanciful, and grotesque figures, rich in eccentricity and the subtler essences of character ; and conjures up a picture unsurpassed as a symphony in which background and atmosphere play a dominant part. [Houghton, Boston ; Routledge ; (Everyman's Lib.), Dent (Dutton, New York), 1907 ; Macmillan, London and New York ; (World's Classics), Oxford Press ; with *The Snow Image*, Houghton.]

—— *A Wonder Book for Boys and Girls.* 1851

—— *Tanglewood Tales ; being a Second Wonder Book.* 1853

Two series of tales adapted from the old Greek myths, rendered more vivid to the childish imagination by the intimate touches which stress the moral import and make the wonders plausible. As conscientious in their art as the stories already enumerated. [(1), Houghton, Boston ; Macmillan, London and New York ; Oxford Press ; *illus.* by Walter Crane, Houghton, Boston ; by Arthur Rackham, Doran, New York, 1922 ; (2), Houghton, Boston ; Macmillan, London and New York ; Oxford Press ; *illus.*, Houghton, Boston ; Batsford, London ; (1) and (2) in 1 vol., Houghton, Boston ; (Everyman's Lib.), Dent (Dutton, New York) ; *illus.* by Gustaf Tenggren, Houghton, Boston ; by Maxfield Parrish, Duffield, New York ; by H. Granville Fell, Dent (Dutton, New York).]

—— *The Snow Image ; and other Twice-Told Tales.* 1851

The title-story described as " A childish miracle " is a fantastic apologue, contrasting a matter-of-fact man who believes only what he sees with a woman who through life " had kept her heart full of childish simplicity and faith," and so perceived " truths so profound that other people laughed at them as nonsense and absurdity." *The Great Stone Face* is a parable not unlike in motive to the *Threefold Destiny*, describing a very noble, modest, and spiritual type of character, and abounding in poetical imagery. *Main Street* is a characteristic meditation on human life, its aspects and vicissitudes ; in form a review of the changes which have come over a New England town in the long years since the colonizing days. *Old News* and *Old Ticonderoga* are of a similar cast. *The Devil in Manuscript* is a comic piece ; while the tragic imagination that invests the problems of sin and its demoralizing power with such tremendous symbolism in *The Scarlet Letter*, finds a congenial theme in the story of *Ethan Brand* and his search for the unpardonable crime, setting forth the injury to the soul which comes from purely intellectual ambitions. [Houghton, Boston ; W. Scott : o.p. ; *v. also House of Seven Gables, supra.*]

—— *The Blithedale Romance.* 1852

A dreamy, idealized account of the famous " Transcendental Picnic," the communistic settlement at Brook Farm. The brilliant and passionate Zenobia is drawn imaginatively from Margaret Fuller, and the contemplative Miles Coverdale stands in the same way for Hawthorne himself. A light and joyous tale for the most part, in spite of Zenobia's tragic suicide, after which the book goes off on visionary excursions into clairvoyance, mysticism, and esoteric speculation. [Houghton, Boston ; (Everyman's Lib.), Dent (Dutton, New York).]

—— *The Marble Faun ; or, The Romance of Monte Beni.* 1860

A philosophical novel with a melodramatic plot ; theme—" is sin . . . merely an element of human education ? " The faun-like Donatello, an anomalous creature " mystified " between the Real and the Fantastic, is suddenly awakened to moral consciousness and remorse by an unpremeditated murder. The New England maiden, Hilda, is said to be a portrait of Hawthorne's own daughter. Art and nature in Italy, the architecture, paintings, and sculpture (especially American scupture) of Rome, and Catholic ceremonial, are the subjects of long passages of description. [Houghton, Boston ; (Everyman's Lib.), Dent (Dutton, New York) ; *sub tit. Transformation,* (Bohn's Popular Lib.), Bell.]

—— *The Dolliver Romance ; and other pieces.* 1864

—— *Septimius Felton ; or, The Elixir of Life.* 1872

—— *Doctor Grimshawe's Secret : a romance.* 1883

—— *The Ancestral Footstep.* 1884

Posthumous and unfinished romances, mostly dealing with psychological and ethical themes. All of these were, as Julian Hawthorne tells us, connected with a project for composing a novel with English scenes. [(1), (2), (4), with *Fanshawe*, in 1 vol., Houghton, Boston ; (3), Houghton, Boston.]

[*Works :* Riverside Ed., 13 vols. ; *illus.*, Graylock Ed., 22 vols., Houghton, Boston.]

HAWTREY, Valentina. *Perronelle.* 1904

Contains number of entertaining and natural characters ; the atmosphere of fifteenth-century Paris caught felicitously and with little apparent effort. [Lane : o.p.]

—— *Suzanna.* 1906

This has like merits. The scene is France under Charles V, and then Flanders, at the time of Philip van Artevelde's revolt (1362–82). [Murray : o.p. ; Holt, New York : o.p.]

—— *In a Desert Land.* 1915

An English family history, from the time of the Peasants' Revolt of 1381 and Wyclif's preaching to the eve of the modern era ; scenes, Gloucestershire and the west Midlands. [Cassell : o.p. ; Duffield, New York : o.p.]

" HAY, Ian " [John Hay Beith ; Scottish ; *b.* 1876]. *Pip : a romance of youth.* 1907

Pip is a delightful boy ; not clever, but modest, loyal, and the " right stuff." We watch his career from kindergarten to public school, and from school to his wooing of an admirable girl. [Blackwood ; Houghton, Boston.]

—— *The Right Stuff : episodes in the career of a North Briton.* 1908

Robin Fordyce, a huge, muscular, raw Scot, is shown in various stages of his progress from bursar at Edinburgh University, and callow stupefaction at the wonders of Auld Reekie, to the dignity of Privy Councillor and Secretary of State. [Blackwood ; Houghton, Boston.]

—— *A Man's Man.* 1909

More heroes and heroines of the same pleasing brand, showing what they are made of in the bigger affairs

"HAY, Ian" (*continued*).

of life as well as in the society of their families and their friends. There are episodes of undergraduate life at Cambridge, and more strenuous scenes at sea, showing the same healthy sentiment and reliance on the best in human nature. [Blackwood ; Houghton, Boston.]

—— *A Safety Match.* 1911

The married life of a mine-owner and the eldest of a brood of children—happily drawn. The writer's invincible optimism is evident in the pleasing, if superficial, characterization, and his avoidance of the deeper aspects of things, in such an episode, for example, as the labour struggle. [Blackwood ; Houghton, Boston.]

—— *Happy-Go-Lucky.* 1913

An exuberant and sentimental comedy—a young Cambridge man falls in love with a girl of sterling character whose mother keeps a Bloomsbury lodging-house. There is plenty of farce in the opposition of his mother, Lady Adela, to Tilly and her Cockney brother. [Blackwood ; Houghton, Boston.]

—— *A Knight on Wheels.* 1914

A jolly comedy, portraying a number of odd or ordinary people, including some boys and girls of a healthy type. The story of the swindling of charitable dupes for benevolent and useful purposes is full of light entertainment. [Hodder ; Houghton, Boston.]

—— *The First Hundred Thousand : being the unofficial chronicle of a unit of K*1. 1915

Probably the best of that ephemeral literature of army life produced during the years of war. This is a record of the training of a Highland battalion, from depôt to front line ; with plenty of comedy, and glorification of the soldier's calling. [Blackwood.]

HAY, John [American ; 1838–1905]. *The Breadwinners.* 1884

A conservative study of social questions, especially the increasing contests between labour and capital, in a town of Ohio. Realistic, not only in representing characters and actions, but in conveying the tone and atmosphere of this provincial town. Published anonymously, but believed to be the work of Lincoln's erstwhile private secretary, the author of *Pike County Ballads* (1871). [Harper, New York : o.p. ; Warne : o.p.]

HAY, Marie [Baroness Herbert von Hindenburg ; b. 1873]. *The Winter Queen : a romance.* 1910

A biography of Elizabeth of Bohemia, daughter of our James I, in a romantic form. Her palmy days at Heidelberg, the battle of the White Mountain, and her sorrowful retirement at the Hague. [Constable : o.p. ; Houghton, Boston.]

—— *Mas'aniello : a Neapolitan tragedy.* 1913

A carefully documented account of the Neapolitan revolution of 1647, led by the fisherman Tommaso Aniello. [Constable : o.p.]

HAY, William Gosse [Australian ; b. 1875]. *Herridge of Reality Swamp.* 1907

A grim story of the cruel sufferings of convicts in New South Wales in the thirties, perils from savages, Herridge's superb heroism, and melodrama to wind up with. [Unwin.]

—— *The Escape of the Notorious Sir William Heans, and the Mystery of Mr. Daunt : a romance of Tasmania.* 1918

This history of an English gentleman imprisoned in the convict settlement at Hobart, Tasmania (*c.* 1830–40), conveys with extraordinary power the grinding anguish of captivity. [Allen & Unwin.]

—— *Strabane of the Mulberry Hills.* 1929

Tasmania in 1841. [Allen & Unwin.]

HAYASHI, Viscount Tadasu [Japanese ; b. 1850] (ed.). *For his People : being the true story of Sogoro's sacrifice.* 1903

The original Japanese version is called *The Cherry Blossom of a Spring Moor.* A story grounded on one of the old heroic plays ; the stilted diction preserving the right native flavour. The village headman appeals to the Shogun (early seventeenth century) on behalf of his fellows, knowing well that death is the inevitable penalty. A life-like picture of the manners and oppressive conditions of the feudal age. *Tales of Old Japan*, by Lord REDESDALE, also gives the story. [Harper : o.p.]

HAYDEN, Eleanor G. *From a Thatched Cottage.* 1902

—— *Turnpike Travellers.* 1903

—— *Rose of Lone Farm.* 1905

—— *Travels round our Village.* 1905

—— *Islands of the Vale.* 1908

Miss Hayden's books, whether descriptive essays and sketches, fictitious tales, or novels on the usual pattern, are based on genuine observation of country people and their ways (apparently in Berkshire). She sketches their characters with conscientious truth, reproducing the rustic dialogue, racy sayings, and unconscious humour with obvious fidelity. *Turnpike Travellers* is about tramps ; *From a Thatched Cottage* presents the grimmer sides of rural life ; the rest are very pleasing, though devoid of any pastoral make-believe. [(1), (2), (4), Constable : o.p. ; (3), Smith & Elder : o.p. ; (5), Murray.]

HAYES, Frederick William. *A Kent Squire.* 1900

—— *Gwynett of Thornhaugh* [sequel]. 1900

Contain much history, public and private, some of it founded on a rare pamphlet, *Life and strange adventures of Ambrose Gwinett* (1770), relating to France, England, and Holland about 1712–5. The Court of Versailles, the intrigues connected with the peace of Utrecht, the squire's dealings with the Jacobites, etc., are the principal motives of a wild and breathless series of adventures. Louis XV, the Regent, and Marlborough are prominent figures. Written as one book, but split for convenience of publication. [(1) and (2), Hutchinson : o.p.]

—— *The Shadow of a Throne.* 1904

The story of the Dauphin (1793–1808) ; connected with the foregoing into a sort of trilogy. The history very carefully studied. Barras, Fouché, Josephine de Beauharnais, etc., well portrayed. [Hutchinson : o.p.]

HEAD, Richard [1637 ?–1686 ?]. *The English Rogue described in the Life of Meriton Latroon, a witty extravagant, being a compleat History of the most Eminent Cheats of both Sexes (by Richard Head and Francis Kirkman).* 1665–71

A crude, coarse, indecent, but racy story, in the form of the autobiography of a professional thief. Francis Kirkman, a bookseller, wrote a second part, licensed 1668, and in 1671 a 3rd and 4th parts were published. Head's life was a loose and adventurous one, and supplied him with material for a small library of works on canting, trepanning, and the villainous practices of the day. [Reprinted in 4 vols., Chatto, 1874 : o.p. ; Routledge (Dodd & Mead, New York), 1928.]

HEARD, Adrian. *Rose in the Mouth.* 1927

A novel of the French Revolution, bringing in the Dauphin—and his supposed rescue—Danton, Marat, Robespierre, etc. [Ward & Lock.]

HEARN, Lafcadio [American ; 1850–1904]. *Youma.* 1890

The only regular novel written by this singularly sensitive interpreter of exotic moods and characters. A picture of Martinique at the time of the negro insurrection in 1848 ; an idyll closing in blood and horror. Youma is a devoted slave, who clings to her white charge rather than to her negro lover. [Harper, New York : o.p. ; Low : o.p.]

—— *Kwaidan : stories and studies of strange things.* 1904

For the most part, a re-telling of Japanese folk-tales from the *Hyaku-Monogatari* and other sources ; magic plays a great part in these. One or two are original tales. [Houghton, Boston ; Cape.]

HEDDLE, Ethel Forster [Mrs. W. Marshall]. *Marget at the Manse.* 1899

A simple tale, sketching various dwellers in a fishing-village of Fife. [Wells Gardner : o.p.]

HEIDENSTAM, Carl Gustaf Verner von [Swedish ; b. 1859]. *A King and his Campaigners* (Karolinerna, 1897). 1902

Vague, impressionistic sketches of Charles XII and Sweden, and the battle of Pultava (1697–1718). *The Keeper of the Castle Stores,* the tale of an old woman's heroism, is perhaps the best. [Duckworth : o.p.]

—— *The Charles Men* (1897–8). 1920

An historical novel giving a faithful account of Charles XII of Sweden (1697–1718), his wars, the defeat at Pultava, and his death before Fredrikshald, and also of the miseries of the Swedish people. [Transl. by Charles Wharton Stork, American-Scandinavian Foundation (Oxford Press), 1920.]

—— *The Tree of the Folkungs* (Folke filbyter, 1905, *and* Bjälboarvet, 1907). 1920

Part 1—*Folke filbyter,* deals with the end of the Viking age in Sweden and the stormy events attending the establishment of Christianity and the suppression of heathenism ; Part 2—*The Bellbo Heritage,* with the era of the wars with the Danish king, Waldemar III. [Transl. by A. G. Chater, Knopf, New York and London.]

—— *The Swedes and their Chieftains.* 1925

Main episodes in the history of Sweden, from the Stone Age to the nineteenth century. [Transl. by Charles Wharton Stork, American-Scandinavian Foundation (Oxford Press).]

" HEIMBURG, W." [Bertha Behrens ; German ; b. 1850]. *Her Only Brother* (Ihr einziger Bruder, 1882). 1888

A domestic novel ; scene, an old home on the Baltic shore, interest centring in the lives of three women of different character. Depicts the petty details of quiet, homely life, old-fashioned manners, and restrained emotions. Typical of many novels by this authoress. [Transl. by J. W. Wylie, Crowell, New York : o.p.]

—— *Incurable* (Meraner Novellen, 1864). 1890

Diary of an invalid girl, at Meran, supposed to be dying. There she meets a young man of congenial character, also supposed to be on the brink of the grave, and their talk about the serious problems of death and life occupies the major part of the diary. [Transl. by Mrs. W. H. Eve, Nutt : o.p.]

HEIÐARVIGA SAGA : *the story of the Heath-Slayings.* 1891

" Unquestionably the oldest of all the sagas of Iceland " ; originally rough and incoherent in style, and has come down to us in a sadly mutilated state. Dramatic account of how Bardi exacts signal vengeance on the Gislungs for the murder of his brother Hall, the climax being a battle on the great heath connecting the N. and W. of Iceland, between Northlanders and Southlanders. Snorri the priest, with his wonted cunning, acts the part of conciliator. Date not certain, somewhere between 1013 and 1021. [Transl. by W. Morris and E. Magnússon (with *Eyrbyggja Saga*), (Saga Lib.), Quaritch.]

HELIODORUS. *An Æthiopian History written in Greeke : very wittie and pleasaunt* (4th century.) 1569

Theagenes and Chariclea, often entitled *Æthiopica* ; written by Heliodorus, who was probably Bishop of Tricca in Thessaly, born in Syria, lived at end of fourth century. The story opens with a scene in the delta of the Nile, during the period before the Alexandrian wars when Egypt was ruled by a satrap of the Persian monarch. Chariclea, who eventually proves to be daughter of the king of Ethiopia, a lady of ravishing charms and Greek complexion though of African lineage, has just been captured by pirates. She and her Thessalian lover Theagenes, who passes as her brother, escape during the confusion occasioned by an attack on the outlaws. This is the prelude to a long series of adventures, in which the lovers repeatedly fall into the hands of robbers, amorous satraps, and other formidable personages, and invariably escape by means of stratagem, disguise, or unexpected accident, the improbable history being concluded by the recognition of Chariclea's royal birth, and union with Theagenes. The descriptions of costumes, manners, and ceremonies are picturesque, and of some interest to archæologists. Chariclea is tolerably well drawn, and the " sugared " sentiment made this a favourite pattern to story-writers from the time of its first appearance down to the Elizabethan age, and even that of the seventeenth-century romances of sentiment in France. Heliodorus imitated Homer, Euripides, and to a less extent Æschylus, in incidents, construction, style, and also in his employment of supernatural machinery. [Englished by Thomas Underdowne, other editions 1577, 1587, and 1605 (reprinted with introd. by C. Whibley (Tudor

HELIODORUS (*continued*).

Translations, (Nutt, 1895: o.p.); the ed. of 1587, edited by G. Saintsbury (Abbey Classics), Simpkin (Small, Boston), 1924; revised, and partly re-written by F. A. WRIGHT (Broadway Transl.), Routledge (Dutton, New York), 1923. Other transls., *The History of Chariclea and Theagenes: gathered for the most part out of Heliodorus, a Greeke authour* (in *The Amorus and Tragical Tales of Plutarch*, transl. by James SANDFORD, 1567); also transl. by W. LISTE (1623); by Nahum TATE and another, *sub tit. The Triumphs of Love and Constancy*, 1686, and one published in 1791 on which is based the revised transl. by Rev. Rowland SMITH (*see* Achilles Tatius, *supra*).]

HELLSTRÖM, Erik Gustaf [Swedish; *b.* 1882]. *Lacemaker Lekholm has an Idea* (Snörmakar Lekholm får en idé, 1927).   1930

A grandson's return from the United States to the grandfather's centenary evokes this survey of the Lekholm family, mainly during two generations. Many varieties and shades of good and bad appear among the characters, and their conduct of life and fortunes are equally diverse. But the author is a believer in heredity, and demonstrates how the dramatic contrasts are the results of intermixture of strains. [Transl. by F. H. LYON, Allen & Unwin.]

HELYAS, *Knight of the Swan, the History of.*   1512

Printed by Wynkyn de Worde, 1512; extant edition printed by Copland, and dedicated to Edward, Duke of Buckingham, who claimed descent from the fabulous hero, said to be grandfather of Godfrey of Bouillon. Translated from a French prose romance printed in 1504. The legend is of great antiquity, and is referred to in Flanders early in the fourteenth century. There was a French romance in 30,000 verses, which was probably the original of a little poem in English alliterative verse, the *Chevelere Assigne*. The knight's brothers were changed to swans to escape the vengeance of their wicked grandmother, who had persuaded their father, King Orient, that his wife had committed an abominable crime. When this falsehood is miraculously cleared up, the romance goes on to tell how the brethren are restored to human shape, how valiant deeds are done, and the house of " Boulyon " founded by the seed of Helyas. [W. J. Thoms, *Early English Prose Romances*, p. 465.]

HEMINGWAY, Ernest [American; *b.* 1896]. *In Our Time.*   1925

This collection of sketches forms a curious experiment in technique—each is labelled by consecutive chapters, though each is about a new set of characters and a fresh theme; whilst interspersed are a further set of brief episodes, which appear to have no connexion whatever with the rest. Considered individually, several of the stories, e.g. *My Old Man, Indian Camp, Soldier's Home*, have power, which is enhanced by the laconic style in which incidents and facts are reported rather than described. [Boni, New York; Cape.]

—— *Fiesta.*   1926

A ghastly and depressing picture of a group of Americans resident in Paris—sub-human creatures to whom drink and sexual promiscuity afford the only interests in a life which the aftermath of war has deprived of all meaning or direction. As one character says: " You're an expatriate . . . fake European standards have ruined you. You drink yourself to death. You become obsessed with sex. You spend all your time talking, not working." There are some fine pages, where the scene shifts to Spain, in particular a description of bull-fighting; but the amount of liquor consumed in the course of the story (probably a record in literature) distracts the reader's attention from the issues in which the characters, a nymphomaniac and her lover, who is incapacitated as the result of a wound, are involved. American title, *The Sun Also Rises*. [Scribner, New York; Cape.]

—— *A Farewell to Arms.*   1929

At once among the most revealing of all the recent war-novels, and one that on the personal side reaches the greatest heights of beauty and tragedy—in the love-story of the supposed narrator and the V.A.D. Mr. Hemingway served and was wounded on the Italian front, and his account of the advance and the subsequent disorderly retreat is that of an eye-witness. His narrative method is peculiar: the apparent artlessness is due to his setting down acts and impulses but not motives or reflections; a psychological critic defines this as behaviourist fiction. Prudish readers should be warned that, like Homer, he is very plain-spoken. [Scribner, New York; Cape.]

HÉMON, Louis [French; 1880–1913]. *Maria Chapdelaine.*   1921

The simple, heroic life of settlers in the province of Quebec, presented by one who believes that the most human heart of all human hearts is that of the French-Canadians. Maria is the child of two simple primitive, god-fearing people, and inherits their fine qualities. She is loved by a splendid young backwoodsman, who perishes in the winter-bound forest. But happiness of a sobered kind remains for her. [Transl. by W. H. BLAKE, Macmillan, New York and London; *illustrated, id.*, New York.]

HENDERSON, George [ed.]. *The Feast of Bricriu* (Fled' Bricrend): *an early Gaelic saga.* 1899

A saga transcribed from older MSS. into the *Book of the Dun Cow*, and probably an amalgam of two at least, and more likely four, separate and very different versions. Not a primitive saga, but romanticized. Belongs to the Cuchullin cycle, the same tale being an episode in Lady Gregory's *Cuchulain of Muirthemne*. That hero contends in a series of competitive feats with Conall and Loigaire, for the championship of Ulster and the privileges appertaining thereto; the origin of the contest being the desire of Bricriu, giver of the feast, to raise up strife and enmity among his powerful guests. " Bricriu of the Evil Tongue," says the editor, " is the counterpart of Conan of the Ossianic cycle, of Sir Kaye of the Arthurian romances "; his love of taunts and satire leads eventually to his death by violence. [Edited with introduction and notes (Irish Texts Soc.), Nutt: o.p.]

HENDERSON, Rev. Wright. *John Goodchild.*   1909

Deals with the railway mania of 1845. [Murray: o.p.]

HENRY, Arthur [American; *b.* 1867]. *A Princess of Arcady.*   1900

A dreamy, idyllic story portraying a number of unworldly characters who are very much out of their element in the midst of modern civilization. The Paul and Virginia of the tale play out their idyll on the utopian stage of an islet within sight of New York. A book full of sympathy with the best things in human nature, of love for children, for animals and plant life. [Doubleday, New York: o.p.; Murray: o.p.]

HENSA-THORIS SAGA : *the story of Hen Thorir.* 1890
" An old saga, belonging to the earliest group of the domestic tales of ancient Iceland." The artless style and construction are thoroughly in keeping with the primitive manners and passions it delineates. Hen Thorir is an avaricious and evil-minded pedlar, an Icelandic Shylock, to whose greed and resentment, through the curious legal customs, the public-spirited chief, Blund-Ketil, is tragically sacrificed. Date of Blund-Ketil's burning, A.D. 964 or 965. The consequent lawsuit led to Thord Gelli's constitutional reforms, *c.* 964. Scene, South-west Iceland. [Transl. by W. MORRIS and E. MAGNÚSSON (Saga Lib.), Quaritch.]

HENTY, George Alfred [1832–1902]. *The Young Franc-Tireurs, and their Adventures in the Franco-German War.* 1871
Henty had served as war correspondent, and went through the siege of Paris. He wrote an enormous number of serial stories for boys, healthily exciting, patriotic, and instructive ; very popular, and very much of a muchness in character and quality. Most of them will be found in the *Guide to Historical Fiction.* [Oxford Press ; Donohue, New York.]

HERBERT, Alan Patrick [b. 1890]. *The Secret Battle.* 1919
A disenchanting picture of war, in the history of a romantic youth who is in the Gallipoli campaign, and, his spirit broken by the incessant horrors, is shot for cowardice. [Methuen ; Knopf, New York.]

—— *The House by the River.* 1920
It is a charming young poet who lives with his charming wife in the house by the river, and it is a happy home happily depicted. But one day all is changed, by the curious misadventure which makes him unexpectedly a murderer. [Methuen ; Grosset, New York.]

—— *The Trials of Topsy.* 1928
Comic adventures of a modern young lady, which cover most fields of feminine activity, from hunting the curate to sitting in Parliament ; poured out in breathless style in a welter of letters. Reprinted from *Punch.* [Unwin.]

—— *The Water Gipsies.* 1930
In the Dickens tradition without being too imitative. Among Thames barge-dwellers and others of the same class, Mr. Herbert has hunted out a miscellany of amusing and engaging natural oddities and more ordinary people, and shown them amid their pleasures and follies and minor tragedies, with the geniality and bon-homie that is his great characteristic. [Methuen ; Doubleday, New York.]

HERGESHEIMER, Joseph [American ; b. 1880]. *The Lay Anthony.* 1914
A rambling story, out of which emerges the sheepish character of the hero, who remains " pure," rejects the advances of a mad scientist's daughter, and returns home to find that the girl he loves is dead. [Revised ed., 1919, Knopf, New York ; Doubleday, Doran, New York ; Heinemann.]

—— *Mountain Blood.* 1915
A tragedy of the elemental passions, stage a village in the Appalachian mountains, the scenery accentuating the brooding sense of fatality. Gordon inherits tainted Highland blood, and comes to grief through his wilfulness and lack of business capacity, which make him an easy prey to the wealthy traders who are foreclosing on the heavily mortgaged farmers. Mr. Hergesheimer's method is highly pictorial, and the descriptions of mountain, forest, skies, and storms are perhaps overdone. [Knopf, New York ; Garden City Co., New York ; Heinemann.]

—— *The Three Black Pennys.* 1917
This is a costume novel, or a period novel, or a bunch of such—a genre much affected by this novelist. Scene, what is now the iron region of Pennsylvania. The successive histories of three men, sprung from a family in which there is a hereditary Welsh taint ; moody, unsocial, lonely beings who cannot fit into the frame of society. They appear in (1) Colonial days, the courtly Ludowica Winscombe furnishing the contrast of exotic elegance with ruggedness ; (2) the age of steam and railways ; and (3) the grime and din of to-day. [Knopf, New York ; Grosset, New York ; Heinemann.]

—— *Gold and Iron.* 1918
Three stories, of Georgia not long ago and of the New England seaboard a century since. *Tubal Cain* aptly exemplifies the author's descriptive power, with its turn for symbolism. In the psychology of the man and woman in *Wild Oranges* there is a hint of drama unusual in Mr. Hergesheimer. [Heinemann ; *Tubal Cain,* Knopf, New York, 1922 ; *Wild Oranges, id.,* 1922.]

—— *Java Head.* 1919
Another gorgeously coloured costume piece : theme, the eternal opposition of West and East. A sea-captain brings home to the little old-world town of Salem a Chinese wife. The rococo bizarrerie of this wonderful Oriental figure, swathed in rich vestments like an idol, and compassed about by ceremonial of remote antiquity and inexorable strictness, with the puritan town as a background, is curiously charming. Emulating Conrad, the novelist also strives to evoke the magic of the sea. This is perhaps the best example of his descriptive prose. [Knopf, New York ; Grosset, New York ; Heinemann.]

—— *The Happy End.* 1919
Short stories of an admittedly artificial kind, and certainly below Mr. Hergesheimer's recognized level. His grocer, he said, was as responsible for them as anyone. [Knopf, New York ; Heinemann.]

—— *Linda Condon.* 1919
The strange and subtle ways in which personality grows and becomes set are studied here, in the case of the neglected daughter of a fashionable courtesan. Linda grows up a detached, self-contained, critical being, a strange mixture of innocence and an angel's experience of good and evil. The man she marries and the great sculptor whom she inspires are but subsidiary to the growth and illumination of this one soul. Yet all three are chosen spirits, and each has individual interest. [Knopf, New York ; Heinemann.]

—— *Cytherea.* 1922
Portrays a group of American men and women of the prosperous middle-class, whose lives are reined in by convention, and are barren of intellectual or spiritual values, tormented by vague discontents which they mistake for passion, and a sexual urge of which they are unable to attain fulfilment or mastery. [Knopf, New York ; Heinemann.]

HERGESHEIMER, Joseph (*continued*). *The Bright Shawl.*   1922
Watching the disillusionment of his nephew after the war, a man looks back at his own youth, when he served
in the cause of Cuban freedom, and his feeling for a dancer, whose bright shawl was a symbol of romance.
[Knopf, New York ; Garden City Co., New York ; Heinemann.]

—— *Balisand.*   1924
A modern introspective novel in a historical setting—Virginia in 1784–1801, in times when Jefferson and the
Democrats were agitating the nation against the conservative policy of Washington.   Bale of Balisand is
one of the backwoodsmen.   But this is historical fiction of an unusual kind, seeking less to rehearse events
or reanimate actual persons than to recapture the lineaments and atmosphere of the past.   Hence across
the tragic story, we see the drinking, dicing, racing, and fox-hunting gentry of old Virginia, living a stately
life amid their households of slaves.   [Knopf, New York ; Grosset, New York ; Heinemann.]

—— *Tampico.*   1926
A vigorous melodrama of the Mexican oilfields.   Bradier, the manager, is by disposition a bandit, and sticks at
nothing to achieve his ends.   [Knopf, New York ; Heinemann.]

—— *The Party Dress.*   1930
A woman of forty reawakes to the possibilities of love—a tragic story that excites little sympathy, embellished
with the author's usual glowing descriptions of houses, dresses, perfumes, dinner-parties, dinner-tables,
and the like.   [Knopf, New York and London.]

—— *The Limestone Tree.*   1930
A Kentucky pendant to *The Three Black Pennys*.   The chequered and often violent and tragic annals of the
Sash and Abel families, from the heroic days of the settlers, through the fierce feuds of Federalists and
Constitutionalists, and through the Civil War, which saw the kinsmen enlisted on opposite sides, down to
modern times.   Not only the strong personal interest, but the wide historical outlook and the implied
contrast with the more orderly North, give this distinction among the author's books.   [Knopf, New York.]

HERRICK, Robert [American ; *b.* 1868].   *The Gospel of Freedom.*   1898
Mr. Herrick was at this time Professor of Rhetoric at the University of Chicago, and a student of philosophy
and social science.   This is the first of a long series of novels having a definitely practical aim : to show
up the evils of the present social scheme, especially those that have grown to alarming dimensions in America
through the vast increase and ill-distribution of wealth and the craze for luxury.   [Macmillan, New York.]

—— *The Web of Life.*   1900
A realistic, and to a great extent, a philosophic study of modern American life : the scene is Chicago, and the
writer's views of society there are penetrating.   The hero is a doctor, and the organization of medical
practitioners is well brought out.   Having saved the life of a drunkard by an operation that injures the
brain, he falls in love with the man's wife, and the situation thus produced is a specimen of the problems
raised.   The story of the woman's futile effort to realize her character in this chaos of repressing forces,
and her suicide, is tragic, but it is not unwholesome.   [Macmillan, New York.]

—— *Jock o' Dreams ; or, The Real World.*   1901
Another critical study of modern American society.   The hero tests by experience various kinds of life, and is
repelled by the heartlessness and self-indulgence that he sees.   There is a pleasant glimpse of Harvard.
[Macmillan, New York.]

—— *The Common Lot.*   1904
Here the master-evil of contemporary life, extravagance and the unscrupulous pursuit of wealth, is illustrated
by the case of an architect who connives in the frauds of dishonest builders.   [Macmillan, New York.]

—— *The Memoirs of an American Citizen.*   1905
The dazzling career of a country lad who eventually rises to the Senate is shown to be due to trickery, graft,
and legal chicanery, and to be paid for by his steady demoralization.   [Macmillan, New York.]

—— *Together.*   1908
A long, serious, and rather ponderous study, in the differing cases of some half-dozen married couples in moneyed
New York, of the factors that make for or against a perfect marriage union.   The method is severely realistic,
and the moral is brought home to us by the natural development of circumstances.   The blame for most
failures is with the women, whose selfish pursuit of ideals, not wrong in themselves, is too often at the
expense of their husbands, who become mere wealth-producing helots.   [Macmillan, New York.]

—— *A Life for a Life.*   1910
An excursion into fantasy and mystery ; an unfortunate departure from his true path, the critical study of
actualities.   [Macmillan, New York : o.p.]

—— *The Healer.*   1911
Another very serious study of life's problems.   The Wild Man is a medical idealist, sickened by the commercialism
of his profession, who goes into the wilds of Canada to lead a life like Thoreau, practising as a healer in the
settlements and among the Indians.   He saves the life of a girl from the fashionable world, and marries her,
and she with her social ambitions and extravagance all but brings him to ruin.   [Macmillan, New York : o.p.]

—— *One Woman's Life.*   1913
Further criticism, especially of the American woman, the idle, decorative social type evolved by wealth and
luxury and glorified by foolish novelists.   This specimen is an ambitious spendthrift who ruins the man she
loved and married, and does her worst for her best friend of the same sex, then marries again.   [Macmillan,
New York.]

—— *His Great Adventure.*   1913
Here again the critic of society quits his true field and attempts to produce amusing melodrama of the
conventional kind.   [Macmillan, New York : o.p.]

—— *Clark's Field.*   1914
A sociological and ethical study which is as much a sermon aiming at enlightenment and reform as a novel,
though some of the characters have life and charm.   A poor child inherits property that rapidly develops
and makes her a millionaire, and what she and her husband make of it is a lesson on " the absurdity of

HERRICK, Robert (*continued*).
the family inheritance scheme by which property is preserved for the use of blood descendants of its owner, irrespective of their fitness to use it." With criticism of the education that makes the inheritors of wealth " likely to become selfish, egotistical, and purse-proud in a few years." [Houghton, Boston : o.p. ; Mills & Boon : o.p.]

HERSCH, Virginia [*née* Davis ; American]. *Bird of God.*   1929
A painstaking effort to reconstruct the life of El Greco from the scanty facts available ; with a bibliography of sources. [Harper, New York and London.]

HEWLETT, Maurice Henry [1861–1923]. *The Forest Lovers.*   1898
Pure romance in the style of Malory and of the mediæval stories of Arthur and the recent work of William Morris—the wanderings and adventures of a knight and a peasant girl whom he has rescued. The spirit and atmosphere of the age of knight-errantry are recaptured in all their glamour, the scenery of a poetized New Forest, and the picturesque castles, halls, towns, dress, and pageantry giving the impression of a splendid piece of embroidered tapestry. [Macmillan ; Nelson ; Scribner, New York.]

—— *Little Novels of Italy.*   1899
Five stories of Renaissance times ; admirable pieces of historical actuality based on close study of the period. In *The Duchess of Nona* an Italian adventurer brings home his beautiful and stupid English bride, and tries to make her a tool in his ambitious schemes, but is.checkmated by her simple fidelity. *Madonna of the Peach-Tree* is a more poetical fantasy of a peasant girl. All give a realistic impression of life as it went on day by day in mediæval cities, and at the same time reflect the swift changes from comedy to tragedy, the dramatic contrasts of exquisite culture and diabolical crime that characterized the epoch. [Macmillan : o.p. ; Scribner, New York.]

—— *The Life and Death of Richard Yea-and-Nay.*   1900
An imaginative and dramatic reading of the character and life-history of Richard Cœur-de-Lion, poetical rather than actual in style and method. Richard's passionate, reckless, and domineering personality is painted in hot colours ; and the lady of his knightly passion is a perfect creature of romance, beside whom Berengaria seems quite a secondary figure. Departing from strict accuracy in the record of events, it is a brilliant, perhaps too brilliant, reconstruction of the manners and emotions, the poetry and pageantry of the age of tournaments and crusades. Bertran de Born the troubadour, Henry II, Sancho the Wise, the Abbot Milo, are at once historical figures and Meredithian creations, in the sense of being exceptional, not normal beings. [Macmillan, London and New York : o.p.]

—— *New Canterbury Tales.*   1901
Stories supposed to be told in 1450, suffused with the best Renaissance spirit, the spirit of chivalry, the worship of love, the devotion to women, combined with a vigorous sense of love and delight in action. They tell of Edward III and the Countess of Salisbury, of the Ghetto, of the border wars with the Welsh, etc. A collection to be put side by side with *Little Novels of Italy.* [Macmillan ; Scribner, New York.]

—— *The Queen's Quair ; or, The Six Years' Tragedy.*   1904
A very elaborate study of Mary Stuart and of all the baffling problems of her career (1561–7), in the manner of *Richard Yea-and-Nay*, but more modern and realistic. Analyses her very soul ; discovers the woman beneath the queen ; reveals depths of passion and of feminine weakness with remorseless scrutiny. All the great historic figures appear at full length beside her, Murray, Morton, Chastelard, Rizzio, Darnley, Ruthven, Bothwell—the last as the evil genius of the tragedy. A stern, magnificent picture of a most dramatic period—a reading of history by the light of human passion. [Macmillan ; Nelson ; Scribner, New York.]

—— *Fond Adventures : tales of the youth of the world.*   1905
Four stories that seem to be equally inspired by Meredith (in psychology and also in style) and by Kipling (in the strength and harshness of their actuality) ; scenes, France, England, and Italy in the Middle Ages. *The Heart's Key* is a grim tale of love and vengeance in lawless feudal days ; scene, a hill-fortress near Toulouse. *Brazenhead the Great* is a brilliant miniature of town life at the time of Jack Cade's rebellion (1450). *Buondelmonte's Saga* describes a famous Florentine vendetta in the manner of the *Laxdaela Saga* : it is based on Ser Giovanni's eighth day, " How the parties of the Guelfs and Ghibellines arose." *The Love Chase* presents the hot, passionate life of Milan in the Sforza period with sardonic realism. [Macmillan ; Harper, New York : o.p.]

—— *The Fool Errant : being the Memoirs of Francis Strelley, Esq., Citizen of Lucca.*   1905
A true spiritual Quixote—an English gentleman, committing what the world considered a venial sin, flings away rank and wealth, and sets out on a fantastic pilgrimage to earn forgiveness. His adventures in Italy (1721–41) among all classes of the people are as good in their motley entertainment as any picaresque romance ; but the main interest is in the strong, visionary character of Strelley, and the diversity of figures he meets with in that unconventional and profoundly unmoral society. His lack of humour is a fertile occasion of comedy. [Heinemann : o.p. ; (Wayfarer's Lib.), Dent ; Scribner, New York.]

—— *The Stooping Lady.*   1907
Meredithian in the general situation, the psychology, and the style. A young lady of aristocratic lineage stoops to love a chivalrous butcher. It is the year 1809 and the Radical days of Cobbett and Sir Francis Burdett ; and, not only are we treated to a lively imbroglio of warring motives and social dissensions, but also to episodes of the stormy politics of the early reform movement. There is plenty of piquant character-drawing and plenty of Mr. Hewlett's wit and humour. [Macmillan ; Dodd & Mead, New York : o.p.]

—— *The Spanish Jade.*   1908
An Englishman in Spain, half a century ago, falls in with a sort of Carmen, and becomes involved in a vendetta that brings out the elemental violence of Spanish character. A brief story, like *Carmen*, but characteristically unlike Merimée in the hot splendour of its descriptive method, which is, nevertheless, wonderfully effective. [Cassell : o.p. ; Garden City Co, New York.]

—— *Halfway House : a comedy of degrees.*   1908

HEWLETT, Maurice Henry (*continued*). *Open Country : a comedy with a sting.* 1909
—— *Rest Harrow : a comedy of resolution.* 1910
These form a trilogy connected by the author's unorthodox philosophy of life, and by the character of Mr. Senhouse, a Borrovian gentleman, who wanders about Europe in a tent, teaches ladies the wrongness of marriage, devotes his days to wild gardening in desolate places, and his nights to preaching or thinking philosophic anarchism.   In the first novel he provides a solution to the love problems of Mary Middleham, wedded to an aged husband, who took her from a humble sphere, but attracted by a sensual amorist. She finds happiness, however, in a free union with the philosophic vagabond, who nevertheless, in the second novel, is stated to have already conceived a finer and deeper passion for the real heroine in the trilogy, Sanchia, a perfect Artemis with a perfectly human soul.   But Sanchia, led away by her worshipper's own teaching, yields herself to a swinish country squire.   The last novel of the three witnesses her deliverance, with spirit, at any rate, still unsmirched, from this unworthy thraldom, and the story closes in an apotheosis of nature worship, free love, and mystical paganism.   As might be expected in fiction intended as a solvent of the prevailing social prejudices, many of the characters stand chiefly for intellectual points of view, and many long dialogues—and longer letters—[Separately repr. *sub tit. Letters* (from Senhouse) *to Sanchia upon things as they are*, Macmillan ; Scribner, New York]—are of the nature of Socratic discussions, distinguished by Mr. Hewlett's ironical humour and biting epigram.   But many other characters appear who have a life of their own, if not much like the normal citizen ; and among these may be instanced the Percival family, headed by the City merchant and his snobbish wife, their bevy of singular daughters, their aristocratic friend Lady Maria—a sort of female Major Pendennis—and the slangy, rattling, stanch friend, the good-hearted Chevenix. [(1), Chapman : o.p. ; Scribner, New York : o.p. ; (2), Macmillan : o.p. ; Nelson ; Scribner, New York : o.p. ; (3), Macmillan : o.p. ; Scribner, New York.]
—— *Brazenhead the Great.* 1911
Four episodes in the exciting career of the robustious soldier of fortune who made such a figure in *Fond Adventures* (p. 239).   Scenes : Italy, France, and England. [Murray ; Scribner, New York.]
—— *The Song of Renny.* 1911
Tries to renew the success of his first novel, *The Forest Lovers*.   A prose *roman d'aventure*, as the mediæval jongleur would have called it, having, like the romances of Mr. Warwick Deeping, Mr. Hewlett's imitator, no definite time or place, but revolving round the city of Maintsonge, capital of the realm Jadis.   Savage fighting, incessant love-making, glamour *ad libitum* ; the style a rich tapestry of chivalric splendour. [Macmillan : o.p. ; Scribner, New York.]
—— *Mrs. Lancelot : a comedy of assumptions.* 1912
Poetic comedy after Meredith : Mrs. Lancelot is a figure to compare with Nesta or Aminta (in *One of our Conquerors*).   Four striking main characters : the self-suppressed, routine-ridden husband ; the Duke, a combination of Disraeli's Monmouth, Wellington of the *Dispatches*, and a kindly Voltaire or Anatole France ; the nymph-like Georgiana Lancelot ; and the poet, one who lives poetry as well as writes it. [Macmillan : o.p. ; Century Co., New York : o.p.]
—— *Lore of Proserpine.* 1913
Fantastic tales, on the lines of Greek mythology, introducing the reader to the world of fauns and dryads— *The Gods in the Schoolhouse, Oreads*, and *A Boy in the Wood* indicate the contents. [Macmillan : o.p. ; Scribner, New York.]
—— *Bendish : a study in prodigality.* 1913
A continuation in which Mrs. Lancelot reappears, together with the Duke and the Shelleyan poet.   Interest now focuses on Bendish, an incarnation of Byron.   Moore, Sydney Smith, Rogers, and Leigh Hunt also come in. [Macmillan : o.p. ; Scribner, New York.]
—— *A Lover's Tale.* 1914
A tale of Iceland in the tenth century, based on the Cormac saga. [Ward & Lock ; Scribner, New York.]
—— *Frey and his Wife.* 1916
Early Scandinavia in a modernized and somewhat flat version of a matrimonial saga. [Ward & Lock : o.p. ; McBride, New York : o.p.]
—— *Love and Lucy.* 1916
A marriage made rather than marred by the intrusion of the inevitable third party.   A romantic Meredithian novel ; the characterization good. [Macmillan : o.p. ; Dodd & Mead, New York : o.p.]
—— *Thorgils of Treadholt.* 1917
The saga of a man's courageous battle with sorrow and hardship. [Ward & Lock : o.p. ; Dodd & Mead, New York.]
—— *Gudrid the Fair.* 1918
The story of Gudrid and Freydis and of the discovery of Vinland, from the Eirikr saga and other sources. Excellent for young readers. [Constable : o.p. ; Long ; Dodd & Mead, New York.]
—— *The Outlaw.* 1919
Fifth in the series of *Sagas Retold*.   A very simple and bald modernization of the saga of Gisli the outlaw and the famous feuds. [Constable : o.p. ; Long ; Dodd & Mead, New York : o.p.]
—— *The Light Heart.* 1920
Another saga retold : the avenging of Thorgar by Thormod. [Chapman : o.p. ; Holt, New York : o.p.]
—— *Mainwaring.* 1920
The rise of a Labour leader to Cabinet rank, in the political world of the seventies.   Disraeli and Gladstone figure, under the names of Bentivoglio and Hardman.   The hero is a character-study recognizably after Meredith, although Hewlett deprecated the assertion (see *Times Literary Supplement*, February 24 and March 3, 1921). [Collins ; Dodd & Mead, New York.]
HEWLETT, William. *The Child at the Window.* 1915
Miscellaneous observations of the crowded and diversified life of our day gravitate together in this story of a restless and not very attractive young woman. [Secker : o.p. ; Duffield, New York : o.p.]

HEWLETT, William (*continued*). *Telling the Truth : a novel of analysis.* 1913
Runaway schoolboy, journalist, novelist, and lover made happy after all, the hero is his own biographer and the critic of much that is generally accepted in our modern world. [Secker : o.p. ; Duffield, New York : o.p.]

—— *Introducing William Allison.* 1916
Allison meets with many sorts of people and experiences, in town and in a Brixton boarding-house, which show off the writer's keen observation ; but the whole is unco-ordinated and inconclusive. [Secker : o.p. ; Duffield, New York : o.p.]

HEYSE, Paul Johann Ludwig [German ; 1830–1914]. *The Dead Lake ; and other tales* (1867). 1870
Among the most beautiful of these *Novellen* are the title-story, and *Doomed, Beatrice, The Beginning and End.* All characteristic of his method of interpreting human and social life ; shadowy and idealistic, concentrating chiefly on mental and emotional elements. [Transl. by M. WILSON, Tauchnitz, Leipzig ; (Low) : o.p.]

—— *The Children of the World* (Kinder der Welt, 1873). 1882
His finest novel ; a typically German story, keenly interesting as a faithful reflection of the pessimism and scepticism then dominant in German thought, and further as expressing the hopes and jubilation which followed the victory over France. Very imaginative in form and treatment, rising into poetry now and then, and full of thought and criticism of life. [3 vols., Chapman : o.p. ; revised ed. (1894), Holt, New York.]

—— *In Paradise* (Im Paradiese, 1875). 1878
The Paradise Club is composed of artists in Munich, gathered together by a set of congenial spirits who would fain make head against the conventions of a Philistine society, and live a life of their own in which they may find scope for individuality. [2 vols., Appleton, New York : o.p.]

—— *La Marchesa : a story of the Riviera ; and other tales.* 1887
Three uncommon stories (including *Her Excellency's Daughter* and *A Divided Heart*), all sad ; the inner life of passion and feeling, the deeper springs of character revealed with a minimum of external description, with an absence of fact that demands close attention. Novelettes that aim at finish and artistic perfection of form. [Transl. by John PHILIPS, Stock : o.p.]

HEYWARD, Du Bose [American ; *b.* 1885]. *Porgy.* 1925
About a crippled beggar and his friends, describing with sympathy and insight negro life in Charleston. The book of a successful play. [" Decorated by Theodore Nadejen," Doubleday, New York ; Grosset, New York ; *illus.* by Elizabeth O'Neill Verner, Doubleday, New York, 1928 ; *unillustrated* (Traveller's Lib.), Cape.]

—— *Mamba's Daughters.* 1929
The social evolution of a negro family in Charleston. Mamba succeeds in raising her station and becoming servant to a white family ; her grandchild wins fame as a singer. [Doubleday, Doran, New York ; Grosset, New York ; Heinemann.]

HICHENS, Robert Smythe [*b.* 1864]. *The Green Carnation.* 1894
An audacious comic fantasy, satirizing the ways of society and parodying the mannerisms of Oscar Wilde and the æsthetes. [Heinemann : o.p. ; Argus Co., Chicago, 1929.]

—— *An Imaginative Man.* 1895
A man of cynical and misanthropic temperament gives way to his morbid impulses, with the result that he becomes a maniac. Scene, Cairo, with pictorial descriptions of the desert and the city, particularly of the seamy side of native life. The writer adopts an unusual moral standpoint, and his satire of the dullness, the petty hypocrisies and cant of modern people is very scathing. [Heinemann ; Appleton, New York : o.p.]

—— *Flames : a London fantasy.* 1897
The spiritualistic plot, how a sort of human Mephistopheles seizes one man's personality and seduces another, has a serious bearing on the problem of moral influence. It is a weird story, akin on one side to *Dr. Jekyll and Mr. Hyde*, and on the other to the realistic studies of low and evil life by Zola and his imitators ; very long. Cuckoo Bright, though belonging to the lowest class of women, is represented as capable of returning to purity through love for a good man. [Heinemann ; Grossett, New York : o.p.]

—— *The Londoners : an absurdity.* 1897
An enormous farce, fairly successful as an attempt to be consistently funny for several hundred pages. [Heinemann ; Stone, Chicago : o.p.]

—— *The Slave.* 1899
Another fantasy, interwoven with realism : the heroine is a creature with a passion for jewels whose loss by theft of a wondrous emerald is a cardinal incident. [Heinemann : o.p. ; Stone, Chicago : o,.p,.]

—— *Tongues of Conscience.* 1900
Five stories of remorse carried to morbid extremes ; such as a man haunted by the cry of his dead child whom he had neglected, and a wife who poisons her husband because he writes immoral fiction. [Methuen ; Stokes, New York : o.p.]

—— *The Prophet of Berkeley Square.* 1901
Pure farce in the same genre as *The Londoners.* [Methuen : o.p. ; Dodd & Mead, New York, 1918.]

—— *Felix : three years of a life.* 1902
An introspective study, reminding the reader strongly of Bourget ; the interest centres in the character of a woman who is a victim of the morphia habit. An unpleasant story, but one of the strongest examples of Mr. Hichens's analytical work. [Methuen ; Stokes, New York.]

—— *The Woman with the Fan.* 1904
The luxuries and frivolities, the men and women of pleasure, and the morbid and decadent features of smart society in London, drawn with almost photographic realism, and with complacency rather than satire. [Methuen ; Nash ; Grosset, New York : o.p.]

HICHENS, Robert Smythe (*continued*). *The Garden of Allah.* 1904

A too heady and unbalanced novel, inspired by the spell of the vast deserts of northern Africa and also by the appeal of the Roman Church. A Russian monk yields to the call of passion. [Methuen ; Stokes, New York.]

—— *The Call of the Blood.* 1906

In a like strain. An Anglo-Sicilian is here the victim of his Southern temperament and pays tragically for disloyalty to the marriage bond. [Methuen ; Harper, New York : o.p.]

—— *A Spirit in Prison* [sequel]. 1908

It is the tortured spirit of a woman who for sixteen years broods over the memory of her husband and then discovers that he had been unfaithful, a secret piously kept from her by two devoted men, one of whom loves her. Naples and the scenery of the bay and islands provide a chromatic accompaniment of storm and sunshine to the changing moods. [Hutchinson : o.p. ; Stokes, New York : o.p.]

—— *Barbary Sheep.* 1909

—— *Bella Donna.* 1909

Novels inspired by the scenery and the elemental human nature of Africa and the East ; Morocco, Atlas, and the Sahara, or Egypt, with their strange conglomeration of modern and ancient, primeval desert and the luxury and squalor of civilization, furnishing the stage. The descriptive passages are numerous and exuberant, recalling the magical pens of Loti and Fromentin. Ishmaelitish Europeans, disappointed women of fashion, renegade monks, and other morbid and exotic types, are brought into contact with the more primitive native elements, and there is always a hot, tempestuous drama of passion that tempts the author's powers of emotional, semi-lyrical rhapsody. [(1) Methuen ; Harper, New York : o.p. ; (2) Heinemann ; Lippincott, Philadelphia.]

—— *The Fruitful Vine.* 1911

Gives a vivacious picture of society in Rome, and one of his fullest portraits of a woman of fine character. The principal parties are a retired diplomat and his wife, and the story hinges on her childlessness. [Unwin ; Stokes, New York : o.p.]

—— *The Way of Ambition.* 1913

A composer of sacred music is persuaded by his worldly wife, after an agonizing struggle with his conscience, to devote his genius to opera. In the end, however, disaster tries the mettle of both, and the man's strength finds itself matched by the woman's love. The story is told with the author's usual command of feeling and atmosphere. [Methuen ; Stokes, New York : o.p.]

—— *In the Wilderness.* 1917

An emotional story with emotive character-drawing, of a man and a woman whose sympathies are broadened by a great sorrow. [Methuen ; Stokes, New York.]

—— *Mrs. Marden.* 1919

The heroine is an egoistical society woman, indifferent to all except her son. His death in the war opens her eyes to the necessity of something in life beyond pleasure ; she fails to find comfort either in orthodox religion or in spiritualism, and only illness and suffering bring her at last a sense of spiritual values. [Cassell].

—— *Snake-Bite ; and other stories.* 1919

Six stories : three of the East, in his familiar vein ; *The Lighted Candles*—a mystery in Rome ; *The Lost Faith*—a woman faith-healer loses her gift when attempting to cure her lover. [Cassell.]

—— *The Gates of Paradise.* 1930

Mostly tragic and terrifying stories, e.g. *The Inn* and *The Grip*, the scenes of both which are the deserts of northern Africa. In every one some gust of passion is the agency that brings prosperity and happiness to ruin, though, characteristically, local colour is by no means a subordinate factor. [Cassell.]

—— *The Bracelet.* 1930

A neat and competent society novel, the big scene being a trial for slander. [Cassell ; Cosmopolitan Book Co., New York.]

HIGGINSON, Mrs. Sarah Jane [*née* Hatfield ; American ; *b.* 1840]. *A Princess of Java : a tale of the Far East.* 1887

A novel containing many elements of an amusing kind, e.g. the character-sketches of Dutch people and natives of Java, even to some extent reproducing the speech. [Houghton, Boston : o.p.]

HIGGINSON, Thomas Wentworth [American ; 1823–1911]. *Malbone : an Oldport romance.* 1869

An old-fashioned, leisurely novel ; scene, a venerable seaside town of New England, where modern fashionable life comes into contact with the indigenous characters. Malbone himself is an interesting study of temperament, and there is beauty in the characters of " Hope " and Emilia. [Lee & Shepherd, Boston : o.p.]

HIGH HISTORY OF THE HOLY GRAAL, The ; *translated from the French by Sebastian Evans.* 1898

From the first volume of *Perceval li Gallois ou le conte du Graal* (edited by Ch. Potvin, 1866), which, Dr. Evans contends, is " the first and most authentic " version of the Grail legend. He tries to prove by an ingenious argument that it was written about 1220. The general opinion of scholars is, however, that this French prose romance is a very late version. An early Welsh translation exists and has been published with an English translation by the Rev. R. Williams in his *Selections from the Hengwrt MSS.* (2 vols., Richards, 1876–92). The " most archaic form " of the story extant has been translated in Lady C. Guest's *Mabinogion* under the title *Peredur*. This and the metrical *Syr Percyvelle of Galles* (*Thornton Romances*, 1844) show strong traces of the original non-Christian elements of the legend. A list of the other versions of the legend, with a brief history of its growth and transformations, will be found in Mr. Alfred Nutt's primer, *The Legends of the Holy Grail* (David Nutt). Only Chrétien de Troyes' *Conte del Graal* and Wolfram von Eschenbach's *Parzival*, the most important mediæval forms from the literary point of view, chapters 13–18 of Malory's *Morte Darthur*, Tennyson's *Holy Grail*, and Wagner's opera *Parsifal* need be

HIGH HISTORY OF THE HOLY GRAAL, The (*continued*).

mentioned here. Perceval, " the best knight in the world," was the original hero of the Grail quest, although his place was ultimately taken by Lancelot's son Galahad. In the present singularly confused version, the adventures of Gawain and Lancelot take up inordinate space. We have Gawain's wanderings in quest of the Grail, his winning of the sword whereof John was beheaded, and his journey to the castle of King Fisherman ; then Perceval's boyhood in the forest, his first acquaintance with chivalry and journey to Arthur's Court, with a long story of his achievements repeating much of the Gawain story. Perceval eventually rescues his mother who is oppressed by the Lord of the Moors, and then sets sail on his last voyage. A wild and mystical tale of knight-errantry, full of enchanted forests, marvellous castles, monsters, giants, and knights of superhuman strength, tournaments, single combats, strange ordeals ; the whole interpenetrated with a deeply religious spirit. Transl. into a poetic prose that adopts the graces and quaintnesses of Tudor English without being slavishly archaic. [2 vols. (Temple Classics), Dent, (Dutton, New York). *Illus.* by Jessie King, Dent, 1903 : o.p. ; also in Everyman's Library, Dent (Dutton, New York).]

HIGH TREASON : *a romance of the days of George II.* 1902
Love affairs of a Jacobite and a Hanoverian, the Young Pretender's visit to London ; painstaking sketches of George Selwyn and the prime minister Pelham (1744–50). [Murray.]

" HILL, Headon " [Francis Edward Grainger ; 1857–1927]. *The Cottage in the Chine.* 1913
—— *The Crimson Honeymoon.* 1914
Average specimens of this author's competent sensationalism. The first is about a nobleman who is a secret smuggler, the second is a murder mystery which lives up to its title. [(1) and (2), Ward & Lock.]

—— *The Man from Egypt.* 1917
An exciting detective novel, about a poisoning case. [Ward & Lock : o.p.]

—— *The Skeleton Finger.* 1924
—— *The Great Bluff.* 1925
Further examples of this author's mystery stories. [(1), Ward & Lock : o.p. ; (2), Ward & Lock.]

" HILLIERS, Ashton " [Henry M. Wallis]. *Memoirs of a Person of Quality.* 1907
Adventures of a younger son who leaves the army and lives among Yorkshire Quakers. The incidents are exciting, the characters miscellaneous, and his experiences give views of every kind of life in different parts of England a century since. [Heinemann : o.p. ; Fitzgerald, New York : o.p. ; *sub tit. Fanshawe of the Fifth*, McClure, New York : o.p.]

—— *As it Happened.* 1909
The quest of an Anglo-Indian major for the children of an old comrade brings about a similar series of multifarious experiences, illustrating the author's vast knowledge of the period (1778–9). Madras, Chester, London, and Gibraltar (during the siege) are the successive scenes, and we get another glimpse of Quaker life. [Hutchinson : o.p. ; Putnam, New York : o.p.]

—— *The Master Girl.* 1910
A remarkably imaginative reconstruction of life in the Stone Age. [Methuen : o.p. ; Putnam, New York : o.p.]

—— *Demi-Royal.* 1915
A crowded picture and eventful story of the period from Trafalgar and Austerlitz to the birth of Victoria (1805–19), in the form of an autobiography. Public and private life are both represented, together with the military events ; the Ellwoods and other Quakers appear, and the story is linked with the Prince Regent and Mrs. Fitzherbert. Many other notable people figure less conspicuously. [Methuen ; o.p.]

HINKSON, Henry Albert [Irish ; *b.* 1865]. *Father Alphonsus.* 1898
A Catholic priest falls in love and marries. He ends as a Carthusian monk. [Unwin : o.p.]

—— *Up for the Green.* 1898
One of the numerous romances that commemorated the centenary of the Irish rebellion ; a vigorous narrative which reviews the camp life of both sides. [Lawrence & Bullen : o.p.]

—— *The King's Deputy.* 1899
Adventures of a young man from Galway in Dublin ; duels, love-making, and serio-comic scenes at the Court of the Viceroy, who cuts out the hero and gives his title to the book. Grattan, Curran, Napper Tandy, Sir John Parnell, etc., appear. [Lawrence & Bullen : o.p. ; McClurg, Chicago : o.p.]

—— *The Splendid Knight.* [juvenile] 1905
The Spanish Main and Eldorado, the Incas, and Sir Walter Raleigh, whose adventurous friend, a wild Irishman, is the hero. [White : o.p.]

HOARE, Rev. Edward Newneham. *The Brave Men of Eyam.* [juvenile] 1881
The story of " the Desolation of Eyam," a Derbyshire village near Chatsworth, by the Plague. [S.P.C.K. (1929).]

HOBHOUSE, Violet [Irish ; *née* McNeill ; 1864–1902]. *Warp and Weft.* 1899
A conscientious rendering of homely aspects of life in Antrim. [Skeffington : o.p.]

HOCKING, Rev. Joseph [*b.* 1860]. *A Flame of Fire.* 1903
Three Cornishmen in Spain in the days of the Inquisition (1587–8). [Cassell ; Revell, New York.]

—— *Follow the Gleam.* 1903
A story of Marston Moor (1640–6). Cromwell, Charles I, and Strafford appear. [Hodder : o.p.]

—— *The Chariots of the Lord.* 1905
Monmouth's rebellion, Sedgemoor, the trial of the Seven Bishops, the coming of William of Orange (1685–8). [R.T.S. ; Eaton & Mains, Chicago.]

—— *The Sword of the Lord.* 1909
A romance of Henry VIII's reign and the Reformation in Germany ; the hero goes on a secret mission to Luther in Wittenberg (1517). [Cassell ; Dutton, New York : o.p.]

HOCKLEY, William Browne. *Pandurang Hari.* 1826

The adventurous career of a Hindu in the Deccan early in the nineteenth century, purporting to be a rough-and-ready translation from a native MS.; full of knowledge of the Mahrattas during the anarchy that preceded the British occupation of their country. [With preface by Sir Bartle Frere (1875), Chatto, 1891: o.p.]

—— *Tales of the Zenana; or, A Nawab's leisure hours.* 1874

A kind of Indian Arabian Nights; excellent stories, largely comic. [2 vols.: o.p.]

HODSON, James Lansdale. *Tall Chimneys.* 1929

About a group of owners and operatives in the cotton-mills of Oldham; a notable delineation of modern Lancashire life and character. [Hodder.]

—— *Grey Dawn—Red Night.* 1929

A restrained, yet intensely tragic story of the war. As in *Her Privates We*, the hero is an educated man serving in the ranks, who is killed on the eve of gaining his commission. The first half of the book is devoted to "Grey Dawn," his early years in Manchester, where from office boy he rose to newspaper reporter. There is quick, clear portraiture, truth, and some touches of beauty. [Gollancz; Doubleday, Doran, New York.]

"HOELLRIEGEL, Arnold" [Richard Arnold von Bermann; Austrian; b. 1883]. *The Forest Ship: a book of the Amazon* (Das Urwaldschiff). 1930

The romantic account of a journey up the Amazon and over the Andes, manifestly inspired by Conrad, which has more of the interest of descriptive travel than of fiction. [Transl. by Ethel Colburne Mayne, Putnam.]

HOFFMANN, Ernst Theodor (Wilhelm) Amadeus [German; 1776–1822]. *Weird Tales* (1814–22). 1885

Vol. i: *Biographical Notice, The Cremona Violin, The Fermata, Signor Formica, The Sand-Man, The Entail.* Vol. ii: *Arthur's Hall, The Doge and Dogess, Master Martin the Cooper, Mlle de Scudéri; Gambler's Luck, Master Johannes Wacht.* Hoffmann was a versatile but ineffectual sort of man, who painted, composed operas, conducted orchestras, and as a last resource wrote a series of fantastic romances, beginning with the *Vision auf der Schlachtfelde von Dresden* in 1814. *Die Serapionsbrüder* appeared in 1819–21. In 1816 he was made a councillor in the supreme court, and won considerable reputation as a jurist. Hoffmann's imagination was as morbid and macabre as Poe's, though he had not the same power of psychological suggestion. He borrowed ideas from the established school of fantastic story-tellers—Richter, Tieck, von Arnim, Chamisso—and from folk-lore, embellishing what he took with his own grotesque and often diabolical fancy. He revelled in horrors, and not only made his readers' flesh creep, but was too fond of outraging their most sacred feelings. There was, says Carlyle (*Miscellaneous Essays*, vol. i), "in Hoffmann's character something playerlike, something false, brawling and tawdry, which we trace both in his writings and his conduct . . . the light of his fine mind is not sunshine, but the glitter of an artificial firework." "He loved Art with a deep, but scarcely with a pure love, not as the fountain of Beauty, but as the fountain of refined Enjoyment; he demanded from it not heavenly peace, but earthly excitement." *The Sand-Man* and *Master Martin the Cooper* may be read as examples of Hoffmann at his very best. [A new transl. by J. T. Bealby, 2 vols., Nimmo: o.p.; Scribner, New York: o.p.]

—— *The Serapion Brothers* (Die Serapionsbrüder, 1819–21). 1886–92

Vol. i: *The Story of Serapion, The Story of Krespel, An Interrupted Cadence, The Poet and the Composer, A Fragment of the Lives of Three Friends, The Artus Hof, The Mines of Falun, Nutcracker and the King of Mice, The Singers' Contest, Automatons, The Doge and the Dogaressa, Master Martin, The Stranger Child.* Vol. ii: *The Life of a Well-known Character, Albertine's Wooers, The Uncanny Guest, Mademoiselle Scudéri, Gamblers' Fortune, Signor Formica, Phenomena, The Mutual Interdependence of Things, The King's Betrothed.* [Transl. by A. Ewing, 2 vols. (Bohn's Lib.), Bell: o.p.; Macmillan, New York: o.p.]

HOGG, James [Scottish; c. 1770–1835]. *The Private Memoirs and Confessions of a Fanatic* (originally, *The Confessions of a Justified Sinner*). 1824

A strange and ghastly novel depicting a man afflicted with religious mania, who believes himself attended and urged into crime by a familiar spirit. He murders various people, among them his brother, and then, accused and about to be convicted of still more heinous offences, commits suicide. Prof. Saintsbury suggests that Lockhart had a principal hand in the book. Hogg figures constantly as one of the principal spokesmen in the *Noctes Ambrosianæ*. [New edn. *sub tit. The Suicide's Grave*, J. Shiels (Lippincott, Philadelphia), 1895: o.p.]

HOLCROFT, Thomas [1745–1809]. *Anna St. Ives.* 1792
—— *Hugh Trevor.* 1794–7

Holcroft was the most intransigent of the philosophic radicals. These were among the earliest of many propagandist novels animated by the creed of Rousseauism, expounding revolutionary principles of government and social organization, attacking law, property, and the class system. The first paints an ecstatic picture of mankind living in utopian bliss, sans government, sans laws, and, above all, sans property. Frank Henley is the representative of philosophic virtue, like Bage's Hermsprong. The second story is about another idealist, harshly treated by the world, who learns that a human revolution cannot be achieved in a day. Cf. Godwin's novels (above). [o.p.]

HOLDSWORTH, Ethel. *The Taming of Nan.* 1919

Nan is the wife of a North-Country pastor, and she is not tamed until she finds religion and then nearly loses her daughter. The queerly-matched pair and their friends and relations are cleverly drawn. [Jenkins.]

HOLLAND, Rev. Josiah Gilbert [American; 1819–81]. *The Bay Path: a tale of New England colonial life.* 1857

A story of the early settlers in the Connecticut valley (1638), aiming at quiet portraiture of life and character rather than romance. A shrewd but obstinate man set down in a community of decorous and conventional people, and a foolish, excessively scrupulous minister, are points of interest. [Scribner, New York: o.p.]

HOLLAND, Rev. Josiah Gilbert (*continued*). *Miss Gilbert's Career: an American story.* 1860
   A study of contemporary life in a factory village, exhibiting with keen perception and humour the virtues and foibles of Yankee character. [Scribner, New York: o.p.; Ward & Lock: o.p.]

HOLME, Constance. *Beautiful End.* 1918
   This is the name of a farm, the tenant of which is an unbusiness-like, visionary person, who fails to make good and in old age becomes dependent on one of his sons. The son's wife does her utmost to make the old man miserable, but he lives in a land of dreams and finds consolation in his fiddle. [Mills & Boon.]

—— *The Splendid Fairing.* 1919
   A tragic story of a struggling farmer and his wife, the latter driven insane by her brother-in-law's gibes, the sombre marshland scenery giving the right tragic atmosphere. [Mills & Boon.]

HOLMES, Oliver Wendell [American; 1809–94]. *The Autocrat of the Breakfast Table.* 1858
   Only in a limited sense a novel. The sayings, thoughts, and set discourses of a philosopher, who holds forth on every chance topic to his fellow-lodgers in a boarding-house. Full of alert wisdom, droll humour, and shrewd observation of life. The scraps of poetry are among his finest verse. The character-sketches and the little love plot give the book a right to be classed as fiction. [Houghton, Boston; (New Universal Lib.), Routledge; (Everyman's Lib.), Dent (Dutton, New York); (World's Classics), Oxford Press; Macmillan, London and New York.]

—— *The Professor at the Breakfast Table.* 1859
—— *The Poet at the Breakfast Table.* 1872
   The author characterized these as the wine squeezed out in the press after the first juice that runs of itself from the fruit. They resemble the *Autocrat* in plan, the table-talk of an omniscient pundit holding forth on general subjects, while a thread of story is woven into the fabric, that of the *Professor* recalling episodes in *Tristram Shandy*, while in the *Poet* there is less humour and more gravity. The whole series is steeped in the very winning personality of Dr. Holmes—a personality akin to that of Charles Lamb—a characteristic that makes them a thing unique. [(1) and (2), Houghton, Boston; (New Univ. Lib.), Routledge; (Everyman's Lib.), Dent (Dutton, New York); (World's Classics), Oxford Press; Collins.]

—— *Elsie Venner.* 1861
   A compound of faithful realism and of psychical fancy. A mother dies in childbirth through a rattlesnake's bite, and the virus gives her child a serpentine character. This weird idea is worked out amid the surroundings and characters of a commonplace village, sketched with fidelity and humour. Elsie's love for a young schoolmaster, and a wild young fellow's love for her, are the chief matters of the little drama that precedes her untimely death. [Houghton, Boston; Burt, New York; Routledge.]

—— *The Guardian Angel.* 1867
   A psychological study of heredity and moral responsibility. In Myrtle Reed contradictory instincts and aptitudes from diverse types of progenitors meet, her lower nature is at war with her higher and the conflict throws her into a form of religious hysteria. The wise student, Myrtle's guardian angel, Byles Gridle, the hypocritical minister Joseph Bellamy Stokes, the humorous, gifted Hopkins, and other types are portrayed in the same analytical fashion. [Houghton, Boston; Low: o.p.]

—— *A Mortal Antipathy.* 1885
   A third novel of this experimental kind, another product of Dr. Holmes's medical speculations on character and heredity. [Houghton, Boston; Douglas, Edinburgh: o.p.]
   [*Prose Works*, 11 vols., Riverside Ed., Houghton, Boston.]

HOOD, Hon. Alexander Nelson [Duke of Bronte; b. 1854]. *Adria: a tale of Venice.* 1902
   First and last a novel of locality. The author shows a fine appreciation of Venice, its people, its art, and the subtle spirit of the place. Time of the revolt headed by Manin, and the bombardment and capture by the Austrians (1848–9). [Murray.]

HOOK, Theodore Edward [1788–1841]. *Sayings and Doings.* 3 Series. 1824–8
   Novelettes of a farcical or serious kind; many of the characters caricatures, or at least portraits of his friends and familiars, and of people well known in society; largely dealing with pleasantries and hoaxes; e.g. *The Sutherlands*—a somewhat farcical story of two brothers, one headstrong, the other over-cautious, whose widely different matrimonial schemes land them both in disagreeable consequences. In *Doubts and Fears*—a thorough-going farce—a lady-killer intrigues simultaneously with his wife, separated from him, and her daughter, with lamentable results. *Gervase Skinner*—a stingy country bumpkin, lady-killer in an artless way—is made the victim of sharps and adventurers: this is a farcical sketch with a number of caricatures of pleasant and unpleasant people, among them Kekewich, who may have suggested Mr. Jingle. *Cousin William* is a sentimental society tale of passion and its consequences. Frivolous stuff for the most part, yet not devoid of value for the delineations of contemporary life. [Bentley, 1872: o.p.; *Choice Humorous Works*, Chatto.]

—— *Maxwell.* 1830
   A plot-novel, hingeing on a mystery disclosed in the last chapters. The characters, as usual with Hook, much addicted to puns. Godfrey Moss, a queer mixture of generosity and egotism, vulgarity and refined habits, is said to be drawn from George IV's led-parson, Cannon. [Routledge, 1873: o.p.]

—— *Gilbert Gurney.* 1836
   A boisterous comedy, made up chiefly of Hook's own escapades and the characters of his intimates, young men about town, with their practical jokes and smart talk. Satirical sketches of cockneys, dinners, and other jovial scenes, city society; also anecdotes of real people, gibbeting their petty foibles. [Routledge, 1871: o.p.]

—— *The Ramsbottom Letters.* 1872
   An old lady's diary during a tour on the Continent, enlivened profusely by her malapropisms and strokes of unconscious humour. [o.p.]

"**HOPE**, Anthony" [Anthony Hope Hawkins; b. 1863]. *A Man of Mark.* 1890
   The farcical inner history of a revolution in the imaginary South American republic of Aureataland. [Nelson: o.p.; Rand, New York: o.p.]

"HOPE, Anthony" (*continued*). *Father Stafford*. 1891

A country-house comedy, with a party of four in love with each other, but the wrong couple betrothed. To set this state of things right with proper regard for the convenances and for the feelings of the young ladies demands a great deal of diplomacy and finesse. The comedy works itself out with chat and repartee, and with satire that glances over the surface of things, while deeper emotions are stirred in the case of the sworn celibate, whose life is wellnigh wrecked by love for the witty heroine. [Cassell: o.p.; Nelson; Holt, New York.]

—— *A Change of Air*. 1893

A revolutionary poet, being received in county society and falling in love with the daughter of a country squire, modifies his old opinions and exasperates the cranky village doctor, who has taken the poems for his gospel: much epigrammatic dialogue. [Methuen; Holt, New York: o.p.]

—— *The Prisoner of Zenda*. 1894
—— *Rupert of Hentzau* [sequel]. 1898

The extraordinary adventures of Rudolf Rassendyll in an imaginary kingdom in Austrian Tyrol. Duels and hairbreadth escapes, palace intrigues and conspiracies, and two episodes in which the hero takes advantage of his likeness to impersonate the king, fill the two volumes with romantic incident. The characterization also is romantic—the chivalry of the hero, the princely nature of the heroine, and the cool energy of the villain. Rapid and witty conversation is a feature in common with Mr. Hope's quieter novels. But the distinctive effect is got by placing a thoroughgoing romance of cape and sword in a nineteenth-century environment, and this, with the device of the imaginary State, has been the keynote of numerous imitations. [(1) and (2), Arrowsmith; Harrap; Holt, New York.]

—— *The Indiscretion of the Duchess*. 1894

A novelette combining tragedy and comedy in small compass—the adventures of a diamond necklace and the love affairs of two couples; the characters French. [Arrowsmith: o.p.; Holt, New York: o.p.]

—— *The God in the Car*. 1894

The love affair and the experiences in society and in his own more strenuous sphere of a modern " Juggernaut," a man of strong, aggressive personality who promotes a company to develop vast concessions in South Africa. [Methuen: o.p.; Appleton, New York: o.p.]

—— *The Dolly Dialogues*. 1894

One of the best things Mr. Hope has given us as a masterly example of literary technique. Smart and witty chat between a society lady and her admirer, whom she is alleged to have jilted; the characters lightly sketched and connected into a slight tale. [Methuen; Harrap; Holt, New York: o.p.; New York Book Co.: o.p.]

—— *Comedies of Courtship*. 1896

Six stories of the humours of courtship as observed by the non-interested person. Characteristic examples of the author's pointed and vivacious dialogue, and of his easy sketching of drawing-room society. [Innes: o.p.; Scribner, New York: o.p.]

—— *Phroso*. 1897

Adventures of an English nobleman on a Greek island—sensational fighting, murdering, and love-making in rapid succession. [Methuen; Harrap; Stokes, New York.]

—— *Simon Dale*. 1898

An amusing fantasia, sketching Restoration manners. The hero, a country squire, is the king's rival for the favours of Nell Gwyn. Brilliant dialogue and exciting intrigue. [Methuen; Nash; Stokes, New York: o.p.]

—— *The King's Mirror*. 1899

A romance concerning itself in a thoughtful way with character, yet still imaginary character in a purely imaginary world. The autobiography of a young German potentate—how he frees himself from tutelage, and how his pleasure-loving nature is subdued to the duties of his position, to which even passion must give way. The courtiers and politicians, princesses and women of the world, who are the minor characters, are all conceived in the half-serious, half-comic spirit of the earlier novels. [Methuen; Harrap; Appleton, New York: o.p.]

—— *Quisanté*. 1900

Quisanté is the political adventurer; a knave in his dealings, yet at times rising to the plane of the born statesman; intellectually strong, weak in body, with an indomitable will. A beautiful aristocrat, fascinated by his brilliant personality, throws in her lot with his, rejecting the gentlemanly and honest Marchmont. The book is mainly an elaborate development of this situation and its consequences to each. The hero dies in harness, and the lady remains loyal in life and in death. The society scenes are characterized by the usual comedy and persiflage. [Harrap; Stokes, New York: o.p.]

—— *Tristram of Blent: an episode in the history of an ancient house*. 1901

History of a curious *cause célèbre*: the two claimants to the peerage and estates of Blent, the accredited heir and his beautiful cousin, are tacitly in love with each other; a situation fertile in comedy and in the lights and shades of character—the eccentric Tristrams and several others being finely delineated. [Murray; Harrap; Nash; McClure, New York: o.p.]

—— *The Intrusions of Peggy*. 1902

Peggy is an impulsive, self-reliant young lady who intrudes into divers sections of London life, and plays a part in some complicated episodes with a medley of different characters. The differences of manners and personal idiosyncrasy are touched in with the usual art, and a certain air of romance is thrown over the whole story. [Murray; Harper, New York: o.p.]

—— *Double Harness*. 1904

The serio-comedy of married life, half a dozen wedded couples coming out more or less unhappily. Though the person who gets the best of it is a self-indulgent bachelor, the upshot of Mr. Hope's worldly wisdom is not entirely cynical, but just this—that at the worst a little mutual forbearance and sympathy will help even the badly mated to rub along together. [Hutchinson: o.p.]

"HOPE, Anthony" (*continued*). *A Servant of the Public.* 1905

An essay in the more complex style of Henry James. Ashley, the centre of interest among a number of characters, has to choose between the world of business and success embodied in a millionaire's daughter, and the attractions of art, love, and all that, associated with a pretty actress, who, however, has a husband to divorce. Motives are analysed, but the general motive is rather tenuous and inconclusive. [Methuen : o.p. ; Stokes, New York : o.p.]

—— *Tales of Two People.* 1907

Sixteen stories which are thoroughly representative of Mr. Hope's compromise between the claims of fine art and the attractions of popularity ; the characters mostly agreeable, well-bred people, with a few whose snobbishness or vulgarity is lightly chastised ; and the plots of a slight, fanciful, or comic strain. [Methuen : o.p.]

—— *The Great Miss Driver.* 1908

Presents an average section of society and a set of average characters, but further introduces some touches of the fantastic comedy typified in the Zenda romances. Miss Driver is a young woman of great wealth and spirit, surrounded by admirers and aspirants, who unfortunately injures her character both in the social and the artistic sense by running off with a lover—not her betrothed. [Methuen : o.p. ; McClure, New York : o.p.]

—— *Mrs. Maxon Protests.* 1911

Mrs. Maxon, a self-assertive woman, leaves the unappreciative Maxon, and after one or two unsuccessful attempts at unorthodox marriage settles down with an Irishman. Not at all improper in tone despite the theme. A "half-hearted onslaught on the established social code" (*Spectator*). [Methuen ; Harper, New York : o.p.]

—— *A Young Man's Year.* 1915

After two unsuccessful love-affairs, a young lawyer finds his true mate, and is set on the road to success, in the course of a year. [Nelson : o.p. ; Appleton, New York : o.p.]

—— *Captain Dieppe.* 1918

A further excursion in the Zenda manner—a mysterious castle, a soldier of fortune, and a charming heroine. [Skeffington : o.p. ; *sub tit. The Secret of the Tower*, Appleton, New York.]

—— *Beaumaroy Home from the Wars.* 1919

A mystery story with a pleasant original in Beaumaroy. [Methuen.]

—— *Lucinda.* 1920

Lucinda elopes with an undesirable on the wedding-day fixed for a thoroughly eligible person, and suffers the natural results. Fortunately, she becomes a widow and has another chance. [Hutchinson : o.p.]

HOPE, Miss Jessie Graham. *A Cardinal and his Conscience.* 1901

Catherine de Médicis, the Cardinal of Lorraine, etc. (1563–72). [Smith & Elder : o.p.]

—— *My Lord Winchenden.* 1902

Love affairs of Lord Winchenden and the wife he abducted. Scenes : London, Battersea, Chelsea, and Clapham, in Charles II's time (1672–3), with glimpses of political agitation at the time of the Test Act. Jeffreys, Ken, etc., appear. [Smith & Elder : o.p.]

—— *The Triumph of Count Ostermann.* 1903

A graceful love-romance, overweighted somewhat with the personality of Peter the Great in his declining years. Despising her low-born husband, Princess Maria learns at length that she has been married to a man of real greatness. In the scenes of Court life, its actual brutality is by no means realistically treated. [Smith & Elder : o.p. ; Holt, New York : o.p.]

—— *The Gage of Red and White.* 1904

The heroine is Jeanne d'Albret, daughter of Marguerite d'Angoulême, sister of Francis I. At the age of twelve she is married, unwillingly, to the Duke of Cleves. A piece of history, hardly a novel or even a story. [Smith & Elder : o.p.]

—— *The Lady of Lyte.* 1905

Alludes to, but hardly describes in a way intelligible to the ordinary novel-reader, the Popish Plot and the contention between the Court party and the opposition ; and brings in most of the famous names of the time (1678). [Methuen : o.p.]

HOPE, Matilda [Scottish]. *Because of the Angels.* 1883

Based on the early history of the Irvingite Church and the passing of the Reform Bill. Character-sketches of Scottish people in Scotland and in London, and descriptions of Scottish scenery. [2 vols., Longmans : o.p.]

HOPE, Thomas [1770–1831]. *Anastasius ; or, Memoirs of a Modern Greek.* 1819

A faithful picture of Greek and Turkish life in the Levant. Anastasius is a type of the modern Greek as Byron drew him, a thorough rascal, cunning and treacherous. The long and elaborate story of his adventures is full of digressions describing manners and ways of life with a Dutch love of detail. Hope was Dutch in origin and a great Eastern traveller. [o.p.]

HOPKINS, Tighe [*b.* 1856]. *For Freedom.* 1899

A story of the war of Italian liberation, bringing Garibaldi on the stage (1859). [Chatto : o.p.]

—— *The Silent Gate : a voyage into prison.* 1900

Stories and vivid sketches of modern prison life, largely humorous and friendly in their realistic portraiture of criminals. [Hurst : o.p.]

HORNUNG, Ernest William [Australian ; 1866–1921]. *A Bride from the Bush.* 1890

The governing situation of this social comedy is the awkward position of an uncultured bride from Australia on her introduction to her husband family's circle and to society in England. [Murray ; Scribner, New York : o.p.]

—— *The Boss of Taroomba.* 1894

The "Boss" is a dashing young woman, owner of Taroomba, who rules the men on her Australian sheep-farm

HORNUNG, Ernest William (*continued*).
    with spirit. The story is short—the arrival of a German piano-tuner, a young man with ambitions, his chats with the sympathizing " Boss," and a scene of violence and bravery when the pair defend a storehouse against a gang of bushrangers. [Sands : o.p. ; Scribner, New York : o.p.]
—— *The Rogue's March.* 1896
    The theme is unpleasant, but the story is a vigorous narrative of convict life in early New South Wales. [Cassell : o.p. ; Scribner, New York : o.p.]
—— *Young Blood.* 1898
    The struggle and ultimate success of a young man whose father has been disgraced by bankruptcy. The boy tries to get work in the City, has a rough experience as teacher in a private school, and succeeds as a magazine contributor. A mystery plot with a farcical company-promoter and a melodramatic villain. [Cassell : o.p. ; Scribner, New York : o.p.]
—— *The Amateur Cracksman.* 1899
    The exploits of Raffles, a gentleman-burglar, related with almost unpardonable gusto. [Nash ; Scribner, New York.]
—— *The Belle of Toorak.* 1900
    A little tragi-comedy of bush life : a young " boss " shelters an escaped convict, believing him to be his own father, the situation being complicated by the presence of his rich and fashionable *fiancée.* Exciting incidents ensue, with descriptions of wild life on the sheep-farm. [De la More Press : o.p.]
—— *Fathers of Men.* 1912
    A thoughtful story of boyhood and public school life. [Murray ; Scribner, New York.]

HORSLEY, Reginald [American]. *Stonewall's Scout : a story of the American Civil War.* 1896
    Contains an admirable narrative of Gettysburg (1861–3). [Harper, New York : o.p. ; Low : o.p.]

HOUGH, Emerson [American ; 1857–1923]. *Fifty-Four Forty, or Fight.* 1900
    The dispute about Oregon (1844–6) : the American cry was for the whole—up to the 54.40 parallel. The story is laid chiefly in Washington and Montreal, and brings Calhoun, Clay, Tyler, Everett, and Sam Houston on the scene. [Bobbs-Merrill, Indianapolis : o.p. ; Grosset, New York ; Hodder.]
—— *The Girl at the Half-way House : a story of the Plains.* 1900
    A broad picture of life in the West at the time of the general movement to undeveloped lands after the Civil War. Hero, a young captain in the Federal army, whose fortunes as a pioneer, typical of a chapter in American national history, are more interesting than his love-story. [Appleton, New York and London.]
—— *The Mississippi Bubble.* 1900
    John Law's love-story, escape from Newgate, adventures among Iroquois in New France, and the success and failure of his gigantic bank (1696–1730). One of the ordinary run of romances. [Bobbs-Merrill, Indianapolis : o.p. ; Grosset, New York ; Appleton.]
—— *The Purchase Price.* 1910
    A story bringing in the slave question and other political matters of the period, 1850–51 ; scene, chiefly Washington. [Bobbs-Merrill, Indianapolis : o.p. ; Grosset, New York ; Hodder : o.p.]
—— *The Magnificent Adventure.* 1916
    A Virginian romance of 1803–9, having Aaron Burr's daughter as a central figure, and bringing in Burr himself and President Jefferson, and also the explorers Lewis and Clark with their adventures in the Far West. [Appleton, New York and London ; Hodder.]
—— *The Covered Wagon.* 1922
    A romance of adventure in the Western movement of 1848. [Appleton, New York and London ; Hodder.]
—— *North of 36.* 1923
    Adventures in Texas in 1867, trail-making, cattle-driving, and troubles with the Comanches. [Appleton, New York and London ; Hodder.]

HOULT, Norah. *Poor Women.* 1928
    Five studies of women for whom life has little more to offer ; an ageing prostitute, a bullied servant-girl, an elderly spinster living on the charity of relatives, and the like. [Scholartis Press ; Harper, New York.]
—— *Time, Gentlemen ! Time !* 1930
    The mind of a confirmed drunkard faithfully anatomized, with equally lifelike characterizations of the wife and children. [Heinemann ; *sub tit. Closing Hour,* Harper, New York.]

HOUSMAN, Clemence. *The Unknown Sea.* 1898
    An allegorical rhapsody of the sea and its deep, inscrutable influence over the soul of man. The hero Christian woos and wins a soulless mermaid, who stands for the cruel and inhuman life of the waters ; and in the sequel he dies for her redemption. [Duckworth : o.p.] ·

HOUSMAN, Laurence [*b.* 1867]. *An Englishwoman's Love-Letters.* 1900
    Published anonymously. The tragic love-story of a young lady and an Oxford undergraduate, told in her letters, which are remarkable for a free display of emotion unusual in prose. By various devices, beyond the ordinary methods of realism, the book aims at the effect of a true narrative, and this, with the enigma of its authorship and its considerable literary merits, fascinated the public at the time of its appearance. [Murray ; Doubleday, New York : o.p. ; Altemus Co., Philadelphia.]
—— *A Modern Antæus.* 1901
    Suggested by the myth of Antæus, who remained unconquerable as long as he drew strength from Mother Earth, a theme on which Mr. Housman has also written a poem. It is a long realistic novel of English country life.
—— *John of Jingalo.* 1912
—— *The Royal Runaway* [sequel]. 1914
    Amusing satires of monarchical institutions, the dramatic censorship, and other outstanding features of English life to-day. [Chapman : o.p.]

HOUSMAN, Laurence (*continued*).   *The Sheepfold : the story of a shepherdess and her sheep and how she lost them.*   1918
The moving life-story of a simple soul who fashioned for herself a very unconventional idea of God—a God who sent adversity in order to strengthen and so expected thankful joy in all circumstances.   [Duckworth.]

HOWARD THE HALT, *The Story of.*   1890
With *The Banded Men* and *Hen Thorir* ; translated by William MORRIS and Eiríkr MAGNÚSSON.   A brief and very dramatic saga, the human nature in which comes home to one powerfully.   The main story is how the aged and worn-out Howard is worried and excited by his wife to such a pitch that he avenges his murdered son with unexpected prowess.   This characteristic—the valour of a doddering old man—is reiterated in Atli the Little's surprising energy, and, with a difference, in the slaying of a champion by two lads.   Has a solid historical basis, with local and genealogical inaccuracies due to the reciter's ignorance (*prob.* 1001–3).   [Transl. (Saga Lib.), Quaritch.]

HOWARD, Blanche Willis [Mme von Teuffel ; American ; 1847–98].   *One Summer.*   1875
A very ordinary love-story, brightly told.   The lovers who are made happy in the end are a young man and a young lady from the city, spending a holiday in a New England village.   [Houghton, Boston ; o.p. ; Douglas, Edinburgh : o.p.]

—— *Guenn : a wave of the Breton coast.*   1883
A tragedy of love.   A painter, passionately devoted to his art, takes for his model a beautiful Breton maiden, and unwittingly wins her love, then goes away unconscious of the blow he has dealt her.   [Houghton, Boston ; Warne : o.p.]

HOWARD, Blanche Willis, and SHARPE, William.   *A Fellowe and His Wife.*   1892
Correspondence of a husband living in Germany and a wife studying art in Italy ; an absolutely sincere and confidential correspondence, the subject of which is the wife's danger from a web of intrigue surrounding her in her artist world.   [Houghton, Boston ; Harper, London : o.p.]

HOWARD, Edward [*d.* 1841].   *Rattlin the Reefer.*   [juvenile] 1836
—— *Jack Ashore.*   [juvenile] 1840
Nautical romances in a similar style to Marryat's, and often attributed to him, as they appeared anonymously under his editorship.   The author also wrote *The Old Commodore* (1837), *Outward Bound* (1838), and *Sir Henry Morgan the Buccaneer* (1842).   [Routledge : o.p.]

HOWARTH, Anna [South African].   *Katrina : a tale of the Karoo.*   1898
Domestic life at the time of the great epidemic of smallpox (1859) ; Katrina is a Dutch girl.   This and the following are of no particular consequence as literature, but of value as simple, vivid, and sincere pictures of a life with which the writer is perfectly familiar.   [Smith & Elder : o.p.]

—— *Sword and Assegai.*   1899
Adventures during the Kafir wars of the years 1846 and 1851, based on history and local knowledge.   [Smith & Elder : o.p.]

—— *Norah Lester.*   1902
Lift of Dutch and English in the Transvaal in the eighteen-nineties, and the sufferings of English refugees ; worked into a complicated love-story.   [Smith & Elder : o.p.]

HOWE, Edgar Watson [American ; *b.* 1854].   *The Story of a Country Town : an ante-mortem statement.*   1883
One of the first examples of grim realism applied to life in the Middle West.   A story of dark passion and terrible retribution, amid the joylessness of a small town in the eighteen-seventies.   [Harper, New York, 1917 ; with introd. by Carl Van Doren, Boni, New York, 1926 ; *illus.*, Dodd & Mead, New York, 1922.]

HOWELL, Edward Butts [*b.* 1879] [*tr.*].   *The Restitution of the Bride ; and other stories from the Chinese.*   1926
Six stories from the *Chin Ku Ch'i Kuan* (*Marvellous Tales*), a collection of tales said to have been written in the early half of the seventeenth century by various hands.   [Laurie ; Brentano, New York.]

HOWELLS, William Dean [American ; 1837–1920].   *Their Wedding Journey.*   1871
Things seen and heard by a pair of Bostonians on their honeymoon to Canada and back—the places and the people, copious talk, a few incidents, and continuous interchange of light moralizing on the passing show and its possible inwardness.

—— *Their Silver Wedding Journey* [sequel].   1899
The Marches are now middle-aged, and keep up the same rippling current of observation and reflective chat throughout the voyage and the tour through Germany.   Among their fellow-travellers are a young couple over whose incipient love-affair Mrs. March maternally and unobtrusively presides.   [(1), With additional chapter on *Niagara Revisited*, Houghton, Boston, 1899 ; (2) Harper, New York.]

—— *A Chance Acquaintance.*   1873
A more serious story.   A highly cultivated gentleman from Boston, a courtly prig, attaches himself to a party of tourists from the West, and wins the heart of a romantic and unsophisticated girl.   The mutual attraction and utter incompatibility of the pair are delicately indicated.   The Bostonian's exclusiveness and over-refinement keep him hesitating, and a happy accident reveals to the girl the inferiority of his character.   [Houghton, Boston ; Douglas, Edinburgh : o.p.]

—— *A Foregone Conclusion.*   1875
An "international novel," the canals and palaces of Venice (where Mr. Howells was consul) being the scene of the love drama.   An agnostic priest loves an American girl, but religious prejudices and natural misunderstandings lead at length to an unhappy ending.   [Houghton, Boston ; Douglas, Edinburgh : o.p.]

—— *The Lady of the " The Aroostook."*   1878
A love-story in which provincial manners in New England are contrasted with those of the town ; the heroine an attractive girl, countrified without being vulgar.   [Houghton, Boston ; 2 vols., Douglas, Edinburgh : o.p.]

HOWELLS, William Dean (*continued*). *The Undiscovered Country*. 1880

A study of New England spiritualism, the Shakers, the spiritualistic aberrations of a mesmerist, etc. [Houghton, Boston ; 2 vols., Douglas, Edinburgh : o.p.]

—— *A Fearful Responsibility*. 1881

The responsibility rests on an American professor in Venice with a young girl under his charge, who is wooed by an Austrian officer. The love-affair has an abortive conclusion, leaving only a burden of regret to all concerned. [Houghton, Boston ; (with *Tonelli's Marriage*), Douglas, Edinburgh : o.p.]

—— *A Modern Instance*. 1881

Some approach is visible here to the method of Henry James, in his earlier phase. But the realism, though extremely minute and overburdened with the meaningless trivialities of everyday existence, is mainly superficial ; it does not take us very far into the consciousness of the selfish and dissipated Bartley Hubbard or the wife whom he deserts. It is an animated story of life in a Maine village, in which Howells has dealt as faithfully as he could with some ugly tendencies of modern decadence, without however leaving us with a deeper understanding. [Houghton, Boston.]

—— *Doctor Breen's Practice*. 1881

Dr. Breen is a young lady who adopts the medical profession after an unfortunate love affair, and practises in a small seaside town in Maine. She is an example of New England Puritanism, strongly developed on the moral rather than the religious side, and her struggle for success in the face of stupid prejudice is interesting. [Houghton, Boston.]

—— *Out of the Question ; and, At the Sign of the Savage*. 1883

The first a little satire on the subject of caste and its despotic rule in American society, almost feminine in its insight into woman's character ; the other a light and humorous tale. [Houghton, Boston ; Douglas, Edinburgh : o.p.]

—— *A Woman's Reason*. 1883

Has the characteristic elements, fine dissection, etc., along with some unusual romantic features and fine descriptions of life on the Pacific atolls. [Houghton, Boston.]

—— *The Rise of Silas Lapham*. 1885

Silas is a crude, uneducated man, who makes his fortune by methods not above criticism, but manly and capable of better things when his conscience is awakened—a compendium of human virtues and vices, drawn with insight, tenderness, and humour. The efforts of the prosperous Laphams to get into Boston society, with their mistakes and disillusionments, the sentimental tragi-comedy of the two daughters, in love with the same young man ; and Lapham's business troubles, are more or less neatly woven in to make the plot. [Houghton, Boston ; 2 vols., Douglas, Edinburgh : o.p.]

—— *Indian Summer*. 1886

An amiable little story of love at middle-age ; scene, Florence. An emotional girl throws herself at the head of an elderly American, and he, good-hearted gentleman, fails to realize that he is in love with the widowed lady who is chaperoning her. The hardly noticeable shocks and subtle changes of mood and feeling are brought out with a delicacy almost like that of James. Colvile's wit and unaffected charm casts a spell even on the little daughter of the elder lady, and the child is not a negligible factor in the sentimental drama. [Houghton, Boston ; 2 vols., Douglas, Edinburgh : o.p.]

—— *The Minister's Charge ; or, The Apprenticeship of Lemuel Barker*. 1887

An upright and sincere but awkward and countrified boy is induced to go to Boston by the city clergyman's praise of his verses. His homely nature is repelled by the conventions and flippancy of society ; and, discouraged in his literary ambition, he goes through various humble employments, settling down as a country teacher. The clergyman, with his efforts to do right with his flock, and his amiable fibs, is a very different character. [Houghton, Boston.]

—— *April Hopes*. 1887

The April time of courtship : the quarrels, reconciliations, and all the vicissitudes of comedy and tragedy that chequer the loves of two young people. [Harper, New York : o.p.]

—— *Annie Kilburn*. 1888

Town and country life depicted in low tones ; the heroine, the ardent evangelist, the brilliant bohemian, and other New Englanders are done in a life-like way. As a realistic treatment of dipsomania the book is more serviceable than a tract. Several of the characters reappear in *The Quality of Mercy*. [Harper, New York.]

—— *A Hazard of New Fortunes*. 1890

New York life and the strife of classes painted on a wider canvas, again through the eyes of Mr. and Mrs. March. He has come there to conduct a magazine, and their adventures in search of apartments are amusing. The doings of a German family enriched by a boom and trying to push their way into society, illustrate vulgarity at odds with intelligence and breeding. More serious are the fierce labour struggles, into which one of the sons throws himself. Then there is the contrast between the audacious and versatile Fulkerston and the mean and aimless man of talent Beeton. All is viewed against an impressive metropolitan background. [Harper, New York.]

—— *An Imperative Duty*. 1891

The casuistical question involved in this elaborate examination of motive is whether it was an imperative duty to reveal the fact that the heroine is tainted with negro blood. [Harper, New York : o.p. ; Douglas, Edinburgh : o.p.]

—— *The World of Chance*. 1891

A shadowy story about the regeneration of society upon the principles inculcated by Tolstoy. Peace Hughes, a strong, self-reliant girl, daughter of a cranky socialist, is an unusual type among the author's heroines. [Harper, New York : o.p.]

—— *The Quality of Mercy*. 1892

Has a crowd of diverse characters, the defalcating treasurer of a company, whose flight and return are the gist

HOWELLS, William Dean (*continued*).

of the story, his two daughters, the chairman of the company, and a brace of young pressmen. [Harper, New York : o.p.]

—— *The Coast of Bohemia.* 1893

A love-novel—and Mr. Howells excels in the handling of courtship—with a trio of characters, the lovers and a romantic friend. [Harper, New York.]

—— *A Traveller from Altruria.* 1894

A Utopian novel, expounding the author's altruistic faith, formulated less distinctly in several other novels. The Altrurian, in the course of a dialogue, passes in review the most striking phenomena and tendencies of social life in America ; the snobbish exclusiveness and the lack of sympathy, the tyranny of individualism incarnated in the millionaire. Over against this arraignment is placed the great Altrurian ideal of equality and Christian brotherhood. [Harper, New York.]

—— *An Open-Eyed Conspiracy : an idyll of Saratoga.* 1897

Gives a vivid idea of the typically American life at this watering-place. Merely relates how Mr. and Mrs. March had a beautiful country girl left in their charge, and half-intentionally brought about an engagement between her and a young author. A most ordinary adventure, told with minutest description of every step in its progress, and with a sub-current of humour. [Harper, New York : o.p. ; Douglas, Edinburgh : o.p.]

—— *The Story of a Play.* 1898

Mrs. Maxwell allows her own love-story to be utilized in the composition of the play, and her feelings are wrung as a result of the indiscretion. Miniature-painting of the finest shades of motive and feeling in a small group. [Harper, New York and London : o.p.]

—— *Ragged Lady.* 1899

The life of a New England girl from childhood to her second marrriage. Round her are grouped a variety of Americans, who are nearer to a comic type. Scenes, America and Italy. [Harper, New York and London : o.p.]

—— *A Pair of Patient Lovers.* 1901

Five stories representative of the author's latest manner. Three are little comedies of courtship, with Mr. and Mrs. March posing once again as sympathetic and abetting spectators. Slight, and as uneventful and unemotional as ever, but interesting and ingratiating in their portraits of ordinary American men and women. [Harper, New York and London : o.p.]

—— *The Kentons.* 1902

The European tour of a retired judge and his family, and the embarrassments caused by the attentions of an ineligible suitor to one of the daughters—a story told with kindly humour and engaging portraiture of the ordinary people we meet in the world. [Harper, New York.]

—— *Questionable Shapes.* 1903

Three psychical stories. *His Apparition* is chiefly farce, but the two others are finer studies of the mental effect of occult phenomena. In *The Angel of the Lord*, a man haunted by the idea of death loses his fear just before the end. *Though One Rose from the Dead* deals in a very subtle way with the development of telepathy between a lonely wife and her husband. [Harper, New York.]

—— *Letters Home.* 1903

An intricate comedy of character and manners developed with masterly ease in letters written by a set of nicely differentiated people. A strong feature of the book is the freshness and charm with which it brings out the peculiar fascination New York has for the stranger. [Harper, New York and London : o.p.]

—— *The Son of Royal Langbrith.* 1904

A group of attractive people and a pleasing love affair. The title refers ironically to a son's idealization of the memory of a worthless father. [Harper, New York and London : o.p.]

—— *Miss Bellard's Inspiration.* 1905

The comedy of an engagement and the misunderstandings of a married pair, which suggest such ideas of the risks of marriage to Miss Bellard that she breaks off with her lover. The end, however, is not unhappy. [Harper, New York and London : o.p.]

—— *Between the Dark and the Daylight.* 1907

A Sleep and a Forgetting, and six other stories of abnormal states of consciousness. [Harper, New York.]

—— *Through the Eye of the Needle : a romance with an introduction.* 1907

A satirical picture of American society in New York by a visitor from Altruria, followed by a description of the simplified and happy life of the Altrurians themselves, by the lady who returns as his wife. [Harper, New York : o.p.]

—— *Fennel and Rue.* 1908

A superfine example of Mr. Howell's artistic skill in the delicate analysis of shades of temperament in over-sensitive people. A young novelist, a lion-hunting hostess, and a nervous young lady who gets into a humiliating position are the characters. In ground plan, little more than an episode, a situation composed of quite trivial elements, but the trivialities are made to disclose factors of human individuality and human relation that are full of subtle significance. [Harper, New York : o.p.]

—— *New Leaf Mills.* 1913

A charming picture of farming life in the Middle West, in the middle of last century. [Harper, New York.]

—— *The Leatherwood God.* 1916

Suggested by the doings of an impostor in the early days of Ohio who gave himself out to be God. The story of idolatry in the old-fashioned settlement is thin enough ; but a real reverence for the God ideal lies behind the old magistrate's rather cynical philosophy. [Century Co., New York : o.p. ; Jenkins.]

—— *The Vacation of the Kelwyns.* 1920

" An idyll of the middle eighteen-seventies." [Harper, New York.]

HOWELLS, William Dean (*continued*). *Mrs. Farrell.* 1921
The heroine is a young widow in a New England boarding-house. Appeared in the *Atlantic Monthly* under the title of *Private Theatricals* in 1875. [Harper, New York.]

HUCH, Ricarda Octavia [German; b. 1864]. *Defeat.* 1928
—— *Victory* [sequel]. 1929
A sequence, *Garibaldi and the New Italy* (*Die Verteidigung Roms*, 1906–7), dealing with Garibaldi and Mazzini (1848–9). [Transl. by Catherine Alison PHILLIPS, Knopf.]

HUCKEL, Oliver [American; b. 1864]. *A Dreamer of Dreams: being a new and intimate telling of the love-story and life-work of "Will Penn, the Quaker."* 1916
Supposed to be an authentic narrative rearranged from a diary found in an old chest: some historical sources are cited. The scenes change from London and Oxford to Paris and the New World, and Milton and Cromwell appear among the historic personages. [Crowell, New York: o.p.]

HUDSON, Charles Bradford [American]. *The Crimson Conquest: a romance of Pizarro and Peru.* 1907
Fighting, love, and adventure in sixteenth-century Peru; a Spanish captain and a princess of the Incas. [McClurg, Chicago: o.p.; De La More Press: o.p.]

"HUDSON, Stephen" [Sidney Schiff]. *Richard Kurt.* 1919
First of a series tracing the growth of an artist who becomes a novelist after reaching the age of forty. Here we are shown him as an idle, rich young man, married to an ambitious, unfaithful woman, in a world of pleasure and frivolity—London, Brussels, Nice, Biarritz, Sicily. [Secker; *v.* also *infra.*]

—— *Elinor Colthouse.* 1921
This goes back chronologically to explain how Richard came to marry his elegant, heartless American wife, with whom there could never be any intellectual or spiritual union. [Secker; *v.* also *infra.*]

—— *Prince Hempseed.* 1923
Goes back still further, to Richard's childhood and youth, and shows the gradual awakening of his soul amidst people and distractions that leave him indifferent. It is academic fiction, trying to investigate life scientifically, without however any Freudian appeals to the subconscious: this is fiction more akin to Henry James or Stendhal than to Joyce or D. H. Lawrence. [Secker; *v.* also *infra.*]

—— *Tony.* 1924
Tony, an obtuse, self-indulgent, entirely conscienceless person, on his deathbed tells his brother Richard the story of his life, especially how Richard Kurt's inscrutable behaviour appears to him—James's method of revealing characters and events through the medium of a well-defined personality. [Constable; Knopf, New York.]

—— *Myrtle.* 1924
Nine stories, of or by nine different people, through whom we see Myrtle, who does not come in directly. [Constable; Knopf, New York.]

—— *Richard, Myrtle, and I.* 1926
Three characters discuss "The problem of creative activity," in reference to Richard, viz. Richard himself, the mere man with his human avocations and his love for Myrtle; Myrtle his wife, who may throw in her lot either with husband, or with the artist in him; and, thirdly, Richard's æsthetic super-self. Note the influence of Proust. [Constable; Knopf, New York.]

—— *Celeste.* 1930
A collection of brief stories that proceed by the indirect method, someone talking about someone else or comparing notes about the person who is the actual subject. [*Illus.* by John Nash, Blackamore Press.]

—— *A True Story.* 1930
Richard Kurt and its three sequels are here combined; and in this uninterrupted form the Proust influence is much more clearly apparent. [Constable; Knopf, New York.]

HUDSON, William Henry [1841–1922]. *The Purple Land that England Lost: being the narrative of one Richard Lamb's adventures in the Banda Oriental, in South America, as told by himself.* 1885
The romantic adventures of a young Englishman in the Banda Oriental (Uruguay) half a century ago. His love of nature and gipsy temperament make his experiences in wonderful surroundings very delightful, and the Spanish-American character is vividly portrayed. [Duckworth; Dutton, New York; *v.* also *Green Mansions, infra.*]

—— *A Crystal Age.* 1887
A very imaginative kind of Utopia, in which, among other things, sexual love is eliminated, the community being organized, like the bees, with a Queen Mother, etc. A life free from passion, strife, and vulgarity and carnal appetites is presented with a rare sense of beauty, and then contrasted with actuality in the person of a man of commonplace habits and motives. [Duckworth; Dutton, New York.]

—— *El Ombú.* 1902
El Ombú is a deserted farm-house with which a terrible history of crime and calamity is associated. Powerful tales of the South American pampas early in last century, at a time when might was right, and horrible deeds were perpetrated in the strife between white men and the aboriginal savages. Hudson tells his story and draws his stern, vengeful men—men with devil in them—in the clean, objective way of Merimée. The gloomy story of *Marta Riquelme*, driven mad by the Indians and a heartless husband, persuades the Jesuit priest who relates it that malignant spirits exist, warring against God and righteousness. [Duckworth; (reissued as *South American Sketches*, Duckworth, 1909: o.p.); *sub tit. Tales of the Pampas*, Knopf, New York, 1926; *v.* also *Green Mansions, infra.*]

—— *Green Mansions: a romance of the tropical forest.* 1904
A more modern *Atala* (see Chateaubriand)—the loves of a European and a beautiful maiden of mysterious origin and a diviner nature, who, like Kipling's Mowgli, knows the language of the beasts and is their

HUDSON, William Henry (*continued*).
> friend. Paints with the imagination of a poet and the knowledge of a great naturalist the wild, multitudinous life of the vast forests of Venezuela. [Duckworth ; Knopf, New York ; *illus.*, Duckworth, 1929. *South American Romances*, containing *The Purple Land*, *El Ombú*, and *Green Mansions* in 1 vol., Duckworth, 1930.]

—— *Dead Man's Plack ; and, An Old Thorn.* 1920
> For Hudson, this is a somewhat commonplace handling of the legend rather than the history of Elfrida, who is supposed to have been responsible for the death of her first husband in order to marry King Edgar. That she killed her stepson Edward is more probable. The other and briefer story is more worthy of Hudson's imagination, telling of the sheep-stealer, torn from wife and children to be hanged—a history blended in some magical way with the eternal beauty of an old tree. [Dent ; Dutton, New York.]

HUEFFER, Oliver Madox [brother of Ford Madox Ford ; 1877–1931]. *Hunt the Slipper.* 1913
> A mystery-story in light vein, about a sporting Englishman searching New York for an unknown granddaughter. [S. Paul : o.p.]

—— *Cousins German.* 1930
> An exciting plot-novel, starting in Mexico at the outbreak of the great war, and transporting us in due course into the trenches, a leading motive of the writer being to show what good chaps his comrades were, and how war brought out their sterling qualities. The spy business has a tragic side. [Benn.]

HUGH OF RUTLAND. *The Life of Ipomydon* (*14th century*). 16th century.
> A prose romance adapted from an English rhyming poem which was translated in the fourteenth century from the Anglo-Norman Hugh of Rutland's French poem, written about 1185. [The MS. belongs to Marquess of Bute. The French *Hippomédon* was ed. by Kölbing and Koschwitz, 1890. An English *Life of Ipomydon* was printed by Wynkyn de Worde, only one copy known.]

HUGHES, Richard [*b.* 1900]. *A Moment of Time.* 1926
> Short stories, e.g. *Lochinvárovič*—the hero plays Lochinvar to a Balkan maiden, with the aid of a Ford car ; *Martha*—the child of a waitress in London's Chinatown is taught by a derelict artist, and soon outstrips him in his art by dint of her native genius. [Chatto ; (Phœnix Lib.), *id.*]

—— *A High Wind in Jamaica.* 1929
> A pack of children have adventures with real pirates, in the early days of steam navigation. The matter-of-fact ways in which they take the experience make an interesting study of child mentality. The descriptions of a tornado and an earthquake in Jamaica are remarkable. [Chatto ; *sub tit. The Innocent Voyage*, Harper, New York ; reissued with English title as above, Harper, New York, 1930.]

HUGHES, Rupert. *The Golden Ladder.* 1924
> A romance woven round the life of Elizabeth Bowen, who married the American politician Aaron Burr at the age of sixty. Introduces Alexander Hamilton ; the duel between him and Burr is an incident. Scenes, New York and Paris (1794–1865). [Hurst ; Burt, New York.]

HUGHES, Thomas [1823–97]. *Tom Brown's Schooldays.* 1856
> Judge Hughes may be grouped with the exponents of muscular Christianity, and is certainly one of the most healthy and unaffected. This is a spirited account of Tom's early days in the country and his life at Rugby under Dr. Arnold, telling of his fights and friendships, bird-nesting and poaching, school sports and escapes, with a most infectious sympathy for boyhood. The love of truth and manliness, Tom's honesty, loyalty, and reverence for what is better than himself, make, and were intended to make, a strong appeal to young readers. [Macmillan, London and New York ; Routledge ; (Everyman's Lib.), Dent (Dutton, New York) ; Oxford Press ; Sidgwick and Jackson (Stokes, New York) ; Houghton, Boston. *Illus.* by Edmund J. Sullivan, Macmillan, London and New York ; by Louis Rhead, Harper, London and New York.]

—— *Tom Brown at Oxford.* 1861
> Tom Brown's collegiate life—an ideal picture of a young Englishman, the athlete, scholar, gentleman. Most of the characters are new. Too obtrusively didactic, although the book is silent on the inner life of the university, the prevailing thought, religious tendencies, and educational activities. Ends with Tom's marriage and a matrimonial homily. [Macmillan, London and New York ; Burt, New York.]

HUGO, Victor [French ; 1802–85]. *Han of Iceland* (Han d'Islande, 1823). 1825
> A sensational and revolting tale of Iceland, having an allegorical bearing on the circumstances of Hugo's life at the time. The love-story is inspired by his passion for his future wife ; the monster Han symbolizes the obstacle to his marriage. A " wild and whirling romance of an impossible Iceland." [Transl. 1825 : o.p. ; 2 vols., Dent : o.p. ; Little & Brown, Boston ; *sub tit. The Outlaw of Iceland*, Brentano, New York (Collins) ; with *The Last Day of a Condemned Criminal*, Page, Boston.]

—— *Under Sentence of Death ; or, Last Day of a Condemned Criminal* (Le dernier jour d'un condamné, 1829). 1900
> The powerful title-story is a realistic account of the thoughts and sensations of a condemned man about to die : a plea for the abolition of capital punishment. *Told Under Canvas* (Bug-Jargal, 1826) is an episode of the horrible negro rebellion against the whites in Haiti early in the nineteenth century. *Claude Gueux* (1834) is a story founded on fact, though Claude is altered from a scoundrel into a hero. More special pleading against capital punishment (a prisoner in a fit of pardonable passion has killed his gaoler). [Transl. by Eugenia de B., Dent : o.p. ; (New Universal Lib.), Routledge (Dutton, New York) : o.p. ; *v. also supra.*]

—— *Notre-Dame de Paris* (1830). 1899
> Hugo afterwards incorporated this into a trilogy with *Les misérables* and *Toilers of the Sea*, as one of the great manifestations of the Fate or Ananke with which man is at odds. This hidden force is symbolized by the superhuman grandeur and multitudinous imageries of the cathedral. The first part of the book is a panorama of mediæval life—religious, civic, popular, and criminal—drawn with immense learning and an amazing command of spectacular effect. These elements are then set in motion in a fantastic and grandiose drama, of which the personages are romantic sublimations of human virtues and passions—Quasimodo, the hunchback, faithful unto death ; Esmeralda, incarnation of innocence and steadfastness ; Claude Frollo, Faust-like type of the antagonism between religion and appetite. Splendours and absurdities,

HUGO, Victor (*continued*).

the sublime and the grotesque are inextricably mingled in this strange romance. The date is fixed at the year 1482. [Transl. with critical introd. by Andrew Lang, Heinemann, 1902 : o.p. ; '' Notre Dame Edn.,'' 2 vols., Routledge : o.p. ; (Everyman's Lib.), Dent (Dutton, New York) ; 2 vols., Little & Brown, Boston ; 2 vols., Page, Boston.]

—— *Les misérables* (1862).   1900

A still vaster panorama of French life in the first half of the century, aiming to exhibit the fabric of civilization in all its details, and to reveal the cruelty of its pressure on the poor, the outcast, and the criminal. Jean Valjean, a man intrinsically noble, through the tyranny of society becomes a criminal. His conscience is reawakened by the ministrations of the saintly Bishop Myriel (said to be portrayed from Bishop Miollis of Digne) ; and Valjean, reformed and prosperous, follows in the good bishop's footsteps as an apostle of benevolence, only to be doomed again by the law to slavery and shame. The *demi-mondaine* Fantine, another victim of society ; her daughter Cosette, one of those whom suffering makes sublime ; Marius, an ideal of youth and love ; Myriel, the incarnation of Christian charity, are the leading characters of this huge morality, which is thronged with representatives of the good in man and the cruelty of society. Magnificent descriptions that leave a lifelong impression on the reader, scenes invested with terror, awe, repulsion, alternate with tedious rhapsodies. Realism mingles with the incredible. It is '' rather the chaos of a prose epic than a novel.'' [Transl. by J. C. Beckwith and others, 10 vols., Dent : o.p. ; by Charles E. Wilbur, (Everyman's Lib.) Dent (Dutton, New York) ; Routledge ; 4 vols., Little & Brown, Boston ; transl. by Isabel F. Hapgood, Crowell, New York, 1906 ; *illus.*, Dodd & Mead, New York ; abridged, Macmillan.]

—— *Toilers of the Sea* (Travailleurs de la mer, 1866).   1866

A prose-poem of the sea, representing the eternal conflict of the elemental powers of nature against the will of man. Jersey and the neighbouring seas are the theatre of the struggle, and the life of the mariner, the flora and fauna of the ocean and its isles, the infinite aspects of the sea in storm and calm, are depicted with a characteristic mixture of minute realism and rhapsodical eloquence. The interest is focussed on Gilliatt's superhuman combat with the waves, out of which he issues triumphant, only to be worsted in the hour of victory by a woman's caprice. Nature is personified as a living antagonist, the forces of nature are arrayed as a mighty army, and the battle of the man and the tempest is one of the most enthralling scenes in literature. [Transl. by W. Moy Thomas, 1866 : o.p. ; by M. W. Artois, 4 vols., Dent : o.p. ; Routledge ; (Everyman's Lib.) 2 vols., Dent (Dutton, New York) ; 2 vols., Little & Brown, Boston ; Page, Boston.]

—— *By Order of the King ; or, The Man Who Laughs* (L'homme qui rit, 1869).   1901

An extraordinary fantasy giving a burlesque picture of English life and institutions at the time of the Stuarts, and satirizing princes, lords, bishops, and popular servility. The love of the mutilated heir of Clancharlie for the blind Dea, the only one who recognizes his beautiful nature, is a tender idyll. Sheer sensation and sublimity, grotesque comedy and utter tragedy alternate in this strange work. [4 vols., Dent : o.p. ; '' Notre Dame Edn.,'' 2 vols., Routledge : o.p. ; 2 vols., Little & Brown, Boston ; 2 vols., Page, Boston. *Sub tit. The Laughing Man*, Collins.]

—— *Ninety-Three* (Quatre-vingt-treize, 1873).   1900

A grandiose, rhetorical romance of the Revolution, which hurtles across the stage like an earth-shaking act in the drama of destiny, the incidents centring in a Breton district, where the Royalists attempt an insurrection, and culminating in the siege and destruction in blood and fire of a Chouan stronghold. As in the foregoing, everything is placed in its elemental relations. The powerful, titanic figures are abstractions, representatives of humanity in the mass, or rather of a particular epoch in human progress—history itself, or the destiny of nations, is, as it were, one of the personages of the drama. The scenes of strife and carnage, the episodes of panic and suspense, are done with a terrific strength and actuality, even though errors of observation are frequent. [Transl. by Jules Gray, 2 vols., Dent : o.p. ; '' Florin Edn.,'' Routledge : o.p. ; Collins ; Little & Brown, Boston ; with *Bug-Jargal*, etc., 2 vols., Page, Boston.]

HULL, Eleanor [Irish] [ed.].   *The Cuchullin Saga in Irish Literature : being a collection of stories relating to the hero Cuchullin, translated from the Irish by various scholars.*   1898

Compare this with Lady Gregory's *Cuchulain of Muirthemne*, a more literary recension that takes considerable liberties with the text and arrangement of the stories. This is intended for students, and contains a long introduction on the literary qualities and historical aspects of the saga, and on the mythology. It makes no attempt to harmonize different versions ; omissions are carefully indicated ; and, whilst it leaves out much that Lady Gregory incorporates, it includes several other stories relating to Cuchulain, viz. *The Birth of Conachar, How Conachar gained the Kingship over Ulster, The Siege of Howth, The Tragical Death of Conachar, The Phantom Chariot of Cuchullin.* [(Grimm Library), Nutt : o.p.]

HUME, Fergus W. [New Zealander ; *b.* 1859]. *The Mystery of a Hansom Cab.*   1887

The plot is based on murder in a cab, and mystery is piled upon mystery. Exciting melodrama. Scene : Melbourne. [Jarrold : o.p. ; Hurst, New York : o.p. ; Ogilvie, New York.]

HUMPHREY, Frank Pope [American]. *A New England Cactus ; and other tales.*   1892

Village life in Massachusetts and Rhode Island in the Puritan times (1640–50) ; simple little episodes of love-making, etc. ; e.g. the title-story and *A Belated Lover.* [Cassell, New York : o.p. ; Unwin : o.p.]

HUNGERFORD, Margaret [*née* Hamilton ; 1855–97]. *Molly Bawn.*   1878

A love-tale of a tender, frivolous, and petulant Irish girl, who flirts and arouses her lover's jealousy, and offends against the conventions in all innocence. A gay and witty story, spiced with slang and touched with pathos. [Jenkins ; Burt, New York.]

—— *Airy Fairy Lilian.*   1879

A light novel of country society in England ; frivolous, slangy, and smart ; with pleasant characters, an engaging heroine, happy love affairs, and sparkling dialogue. These are the best of a number of love-tales having little if any literary pretensions. [Smith & Elder : o.p. ; Lippincott, Philadelphia : o.p. ; Burt, New York.]

HUNGERFORD, Margaret (*continued*). *The O'Connors of Ballynahinch.* 1896
A light domestic story of people of the landlord class in Cork ; but the local colour is practically non-existent. [o.p.]

HUNT, James Henry Leigh [1784–1859]. *Sir Ralph Esher.* 1832
" Memoirs of a Gentleman of the Court of Charles II, including those of his friend, Sir Philip Herne " (in the time of the Plague and the war with the Dutch, 1662–70). [Colburn : o.p.]

HUNT, Miss Violet. *The Maiden's Progress : a novel in dialogue.* 1894
The social career of Moderna, a *blasée* drawing-room beauty, her flirtations and disappointments, and how she found herself. Tart satire on social frailties. [Chapman : o.p. ; Harper, New York : o.p.]

—— *A Hard Woman : a story in scenes.* 1895
A series of lively dialogues, developing the story of a clever, but shallow and selfish woman and her gradual moral declension. [Chapman : o.p. ; Appleton, New York : o.p.]

—— *The Way of Marriage.* 1896
A dozen frothy tales about getting married, the happy couples usually having at least one " past " in the background ; the last story, *Mrs. Arne*, is a try at the horrible. [Chapman : o.p.]

—— *The Human Interest : a study in incompatibilities.* 1899
Farcical in plot, and in the drawing of the characters a satire on some modern types—the literary woman innocent of worldly knowledge, the egotistic painter, etc. Dialogue lively and pointed. [Methuen : o.p. ; Stone, Chicago : o.p.]

—— *Affairs of the Heart.* 1900
Love episodes, comic or sad, of which the salient characteristic is the smartness and cynicism of the style. The male creatures are all contemptible ; the women mostly silly, or else clever flirts. [Freemantle : o.p.]

—— *The Celebrity at Home.* 1904
The celebrity is a novelist who is taken up by society ; we see him through the eyes of his entirely disillusioned, but very perspicacious daughter of fourteen, in the cold and dispassionate light of his family, to whom he is no hero. [Chapman : o.p.]

—— *The Workaday Woman.* 1906
Sketches the fortunes of a group of women earning their own living. The heroine, who tells the story, is a paid companion, whose fate is to be snubbed and bullied. There are rather cruel portraits of less pleasing types, sentimentalists, sycophants, and adventurers. [Laurie : o.p.]

—— *The Doll.* 1911
Matrimonial troubles and misunderstandings, innocent, though involving at any rate one divorce case—a good number of characters, feminine chiefly, clearly individualized. [Stanley Paul.]

—— *Their Lives.* 1916
Analysis of a Victorian family—emphasizing their hypocrisy and selfishness, with the moral that these things were responsible for the war. [S. Paul : o.p.]

HUNTER, Sir William Wilson [1840–1900]. *The Old Missionary.* 1895
An idyllic picture of India in the early days of the nineteenth century, with a dignified and touching central figure. [Frowde : o.p.]

" HUNTINGTON, H. S." [Herbert Huntington Smith ; American ; 1851–1919]. *His Majesty's Sloop Diamond Rock.* 1904
The " Sloop " is a rocky islet near Martinique fortified by the British in the time of the great French wars (1802–3). [Houghton, Boston.]

HUON OF BURDEUX. *The Boke of Duke Huon of Burdeux : done into English by Sir John Bourchier, Lord Berners, and printed by Wynkyn de Worde about* 1534.
One of the three most popular Charlemagne romances. The original *Huon of Bordeaux* was a *chanson de geste*, probably of the middle part of the thirteenth century, of which no less than seven continuations are extant, four of them incorporated in this translation. To the simple story of courtly broils and deeds of arms was added the more diversified interests of Arthurian romance and the Oriental magic that had come into vogue. The dwarf Oberon was of Teutonic origin, though placed here in Oriental surroundings. The *chanson* was reduced to prose in 1454, and printed in 1513 at Paris ; Lord Berners translated it probably between 1525 and 1533. The first part corresponds to the original *chanson*, and its main lines are as follows : Huon and Gerard, sons of one of Charlemagne's Peers, are treacherously waylaid by the king's dissipated son Charlot, whom Huon, not knowing him, slays. So far the story is true to mediæval conditions. For the offence, Huon is sent on an absurdly perilous quest to Babylon, where he is befriended by Oberon, king of the Fairies, and by this aid performs many wonderful feats. Howbeit, for his sins, he falls into grievous trouble on the way home, but at the end is miraculously delivered. The second part embraces (*a*) *La Chanson d'Esclaramonde*, wherein the Emperor Raoul besieges Bordeaux and tries to seize Huon's duchess ; Huon goes to the East for succour, has many preposterous adventures, meeting with Cain and Judas Iscariot, and at length saves Bordeaux ; (*b*) *La Chanson de Clarisse et Florent*, which relates the wooing of their daughter Clariet along with many absurd extravagances ; (*c*) *La Chanson d'Ide et Olive*, an unpleasant story of Ide, daughter of Clariet and Florence, who disguises herself as a man, and is actually wedded to the daughter of the Emperor of Rome ; (*d*) *La Roman de Croissant*, the great-grandson of Huon. As in the *Four Sons of Aymon*, Charlemagne is portrayed as a vengeful tyrant, the increasing power of the nobles being reflected in the more dignified rôle accorded to the Peers. [Berners' translation, edited by S. L. LEE (Sir Sidney Lee) (Early English Text Soc.), 4 vols., Kegan Paul, 1882–4 : o.p. The same retold by Robert STEELE (i.e. the first part only, modernized and abridged) : o.p. ; G. Allen, 1895 : o.p.]

HUS, John. *The Last Days of John Hus : an historical romance* (1902). 1909
A brief " anonymous account of the trial and martyrdom of John Hus," not " strictly speaking an historical document," but " a tale based upon original sources." [Transl. from the original Czech, with an introduction, by W. R. MORFILL, R.T.S. : o.p.]

HUSSEY, Eyre. *Miss Badsworth, M.F.H.* 1905

Portrays a strong-minded woman who, under the provisions of an eccentric will, has to perform the duties of M.F.H. [Longmanns : o.p.]

HUTCHINSON, Arthur Stuart-Menteth [*b.* 1880]. *The Happy Warrior.* 1912

A buoyant, vehement, emotional story of the " tricks and chances " of life, exemplified in the disputed succession to a peerage. The hero lives up to Wordworth's ideal of " The Happy Warrior." [Hodder ; Little, Boston.]

—— *The Uncertain Trumpet.* 1929

A harmless, dull, mechanical story, with no literary qualities whatever, but no worse or better than others of this writer which have secured him a public. [Hodder ; Little & Brown, Boston ; McClelland, Toronto.]

HUTCHINSON, Horatio Gordon [*b.* 1859]. *Little Lady Mary ; and, Her Best Friend.* 1900

Two tales of self-sacrifice. Lady Mary is an audacious and dashing woman of fashion and the heroine of a pathetic story ; a group of lovable characters. [Smith & Elder : o.p.]

—— *A Friend of Nelson.* 1902

A loose account of Nelson and the Baltic campaign, based on a diary kept by the author's ancestor ; it has been criticized for historical inaccuracies. Brings in an imaginary plot of Bonaparte's to assassinate Nelson. Scene, largely, Ashdown Forest (1803–5). [Longmans : o.p.]

—— *Crowborough Beacon.* 1903

Country life at Tunbridge Wells and on the borders of Kent and Sussex, early last century—a rather languid, conventional story—local history, folk-lore, smuggling, sectarian jealousy, the intrigues of a Roman Catholic priest, and wrongful suspicions of murder are the ingredients. [Smith & Elder : o.p.]

HUTTEN ZUM STOLZENBERG, Freiherr von [Bettina von Hutten, *née* Riddle ; American ; *b.* 1874]. *Pam.* 1905

—— *Pam Decides.* 1906

Pam, the irregular relative of highly aristocratic people, is a girl of strong character, who leads her own life in bohemian style in spite of her friends' affectionate remonstrances. The story is thoroughly alive and natural, without either the merits or the defects of mere literature. *Pam* tells of this young girl's struggle against her passion for a " magerfu' man," as Barrie would put it : the sequel, of her happier after-life and union with a reliable lover. [(1), Dodd & Mead, New York : o.p. ; Heinemann ; (2), Dodd & Mead, New York : o.p. ; *sub tit.* What Became of Pam, Heinemann.]

—— *Beechy ; or, The Lordship of Love.* 1909

The magnetic figure here is the beautiful daughter of a Roman noble and an English governess, drawn with the same clever impressionism as Pam ; and her bohemian musical life (in the days of popular opera in the early eighties), her stay with the dead governess's suburban relatives, and then her début in society as a musical star, are in the old vein. An episode with an aristocratic Lothario gives the book its title. [Stokes, New York : o.p. ; *sub tit.* The Lordship of Love, Hutchinson : o.p.]

—— *The Green Patch.* 1910

Three stories, each almost a novel. Similar studies of temperament, chiefly attractive but in some cases the reverse, in the stress of married life. The wayward Daffy is of the same order as Pam. [Stokes, New York : o.p. ; Hutchinson : o.p.]

—— *The Bag of Saffron.* 1917

The biography of a minx, with incidental portraits of other people in a distinctively feminine style ; the best chapters are about her early life in a Yorkshire village. The title refers to a bit of rank romanticism. [Appleton, New York ; Hutchinson : o.p.]

—— *Eddy and Édouard.* 1929

A light affair about a youth of mingled French and American parentage, torn between the two divergent trends of his dual nature. [Hutchinson ; Doubleday, Doran, New York.]

HUTTON, Edward [*b.* 1875]. *Frederic Uvedale.* 1901

A sketch of a beautiful unworldly character, a modern knight of the Grail. He is a young Roman Catholic, in whose soul two alien impulses are at war—a pagan love of nature and life, and a mysticism that urges him towards the monastic ideal. His education in England and experiences among the Italian clergy and in the riots at Milan are the outer incidents ; but the main interest is spiritual. [Blackwood : o.p.]

—— *The Mastiff of Rimini : chronicles of the House of Malatesta.* 1906

The life of the despot of Rimini, Sigismondo Pandolfo Malatesta (*d.* 1328), thrown into the form of a novel (*illus.*). [Methuen ; Dutton, New York : o.p.]

HUXLEY, Aldous Leonard [*b.* 1894]. *Limbo.* 1920

Two longish stories and five trifles. *Richard Greenhow* is a farcical case of dual personality ; as " Dr. Jekyll " Greenhow is a serious thinker and writer, as " Mr. Hyde " he is a female purveyor of sloppy fiction. *Happily Ever After* is a sentimental affair hingeing on the war, ending ironically. A machine-gun fire of universal mockery is kept up all through. [Chatto ; Doubleday, Doran, New York.]

—— *Crome Yellow.* 1921

In this brief novel, Mr. Huxley already introduces his house-party, talking, philandering, and busied in the pretentious avocations of the moneyed intellectual—afterwards a favourite device. All is observed from the point of view of a raw youth in love with a more experienced girl. There is a painter among the crowd who has done with cubism, an amateur archæologist, a writer of books with " uplift," a clergyman ingeminating Armageddon. The satire of these current types looks more flippant than it really is. [Chatto ; Doubleday, Doran, New York.]

—— *Mortal Coils.* 1922

Five tales ; best, *The Gioconda Smile* and *Permutations among the Nightingales*. In the former, a wealthy hedonist who has failed to marry " his betrothed of the spirit " is charged with the murder of his wife, and it turns out that she did it. The other is a picture of sordid sensual intrigue, poetized and idealized by the actors, in an idyllic Italian setting—in dramatic form. [Chatto ; Doubleday, Doran, New York.]

HUXLEY, Aldous Leonard (*continued*). *Antic Hay.*　1923

The demoralized, disillusioned, despairing post-war world, with no purposes, no aim even distantly imagined, no originality or strength of personality ; portrayed in what has the semblance of a story but is really satire in the classic form, episodic, a succession of incisive sketches of character : Lypiatt, the bad artist, truculent and abusive, whose heart is in the right place only the brain isn't there ; the pathetic demirep, Mrs. Viveash ; the assimilators, picking up and distorting the latest catchwords, etc. The satire is pessimistic and all-embracing. [Chatto ; Doubleday, Doran, New York.]

—— *The Little Mexican.*　1924

Six characteristic stories ; the long story *Uncle Spencer* embodies a boy's recollections of his eccentric uncle, and his war-experiences in Belgium. *Young Archimedes* is about children in Italy—less mordant in tone than the rest. [Chatto ; *sub tit. Young Archimedes ; and other stories*, Doubleday, Doran, New York.]

—— *Those Barren Leaves.*　1925

The same mixture of inconsequent story, cynical character-drawing, and Socratic dialogue. A little crowd of disenchanted hedonists are engaged in psycho-analysing themselves in public at the Italian castle belonging to a wealthy Englishwoman. Wisdom drops continuously from the lips of these experienced but dissatisfied people : some of Calamy's sayings are actually very wholesome. Note the diabolical cleverness of the scenic descriptions. [Chatto ; Doubleday, Doran, New York.]

—— *Two or Three Graces ; and other stories.*　1926

Charactery almost in the old style of Butler and Addison, with development of two or three crucial episodes that exhibit and define what the characters essentially are ; and, as a background, a portrayal of the sophisticated, amoral, riotous life of the gay set to-day, glorying in their blasphemies and their superiority to old-fashioned restraints. Grace, the woman with no personality of her own, is " just what circumstances or her imagination and other people happen to make her." [Chatto ; Doubleday, Doran, New York.]

—— *Point Counter Point.*　1928

An embittered vivisection of the vices and depravities of the idle section of society , with no religion, no philosophy, no codes or ideals remaining : nothing to distinguish between good and bad or provide a purpose even in their amusements. No plot, no story, no art except swift characterization and pungent dialogue— even the incidents are merely points counter points. The thought and learning, scientific, philosophical, æsthetic, are overwhelming. But even the most enlightened character, Rampion, has little to say for our encouragement ; and the author's own attitude seems to be nearer to Spandrell's, the hater of life. [Chatto ; Doubleday, Doran, New York ; Grosset, New York.]

—— *Brief Candles : stories.*　1930

Another saturnine anatomy of contemporary manners and morals, e.g. *The Claxtons*, a caricature of religious affectation. [Chatto ; Doubleday, Doran, New York.]

HUYSMANS, Joris-Karel [French ; 1848–1907]. *En Route* (1895).　1896
—— *The Cathedral* (La cathédrale ; 1898) [sequel].　1898
—— *The Oblate* (L'oblate, 1903) [sequel].　1924

In method, Huysmans was a disciple of Zola, and almost outvied his master in the frankness and the grossness of his naturalism. The sphere of his subject-matter is narrower, but he goes far deeper than Zola into the abysses of human nature, especially the abnormal and diseased. These three novels, and some that preceded but were never translated, are introspective chapters in the life of a literary man, Durtal, who obviously corresponds more or less directly to Huysmans himself. Jules Lemaître calls him the modern René of fiction (see Chateaubriand). In a previous novel, *Là-Bas*, we see Durtal overwhelmed with pessimism, dallying on the one hand with religious mysticism, and on the other hand dipping into mediæval and modern diabolism and stirring up the dregs of exhausted sensuality. *En route* shows him still struggling desperately in the sensual bog, but gradually surrendering to religious influences, especially the æsthetic charms of Catholic worship. The elaborate descriptions of religious art, vestments and ritual, music and architecture, and of their potent influence on Durtal's mind, are extreme examples of the naturalistic method. The grossness of the original has been largely eliminated in this translation. *En route* is a perfect guide-book to the churches of Paris, not merely describing their exteriors and interiors with the utmost fullness and the critical attitude of an ecclesiologist, but also dealing with the performances of clergy and choirs, and with the daily life of each church. A similarly close account of the manner of life in a retreat follows, and this contains some of the best portraits of character. In *The Cathedral*, Chartres is depicted with exceeding fullness—the building, the stained glass, sculpture, and ceremonial, are the subject of a series of subtle descriptive essays. *L'oblat* records the last stage of Durtal's penitence and conversion, which he consummates by becoming a monk. [(1) and (2), transl. by Clara BELL, (3), by E. PERCIVAL, Routledge (Dutton, New York).]

HYDE, Douglas [Irish] [ed.]. *The Adventures of the Lad of the Ferule ; The Adventures of the Children of the King of Norway : two Irish romantic tales of the sixteenth and seventeenth centuries.*　1899

The first is an example of the popular tales that were handed down from age to age. The traditional matter comes from the Middle Ages, though perhaps never committed to paper until a century or two ago. The Lad of the Ferule is a mysterious being who appears to Murough, son of Brian Boru, and, carrying home for him the spoils of a miraculous hunting, demands as guerdon a certain ferúle that lies at the bottom of a lake. Ultimately, Murough slays a serpent and delivers the Land of the Ever Young, which lies below the lake. Being made for linguistic purposes, the translation is not very readable in any of these publications of the Irish Texts Society. The editor thinks the *Adventures of the Children of the King of Norway* was a written story even so early as the fourteenth century. It has always been a great favourite with Irish scribes, and was probably not handed down as a folk-tale for many generations before being committed to writing. It is a long story of enchantment and miraculous adventures, " in which much of the stock-in-trade of the Celtic story-teller is employed." The outset of the adventures is how the three princes are put under *geasa*, or enchantment, by a lady, which obliges them to search for her throughout the world, she meanwhile changing herself into a cat and then a swan. [Edited and translated for the first time with introduction, notes, and glossary (Irish Texts Society), Nutt : o.p.]

HYNE, Charles John Cutcliffe Wright [*b.* 1866]. *The Adventures of Captain Kettle.* 1898
—— *Further Adventures of Captain Kettle.* 1899
Medleys of nautical adventure, piratical feats, and humorous incidents, of which the hero is a truculent but diverting old skipper. In the sequel he is settled down comfortably on a Welsh farm. [(1), Pearson; Dillingham, New York: o.p.; (2), Pearson; Federal Bk. Co., Boston: o.p.]
—— *Prince Rupert the Buccaneer.* 1901
The story—put into the mouth of a girl who followed Rupert in the guise of his secretary, who was never found out and who never told her love—of Blake's pursuit of Rupert and the Royalist fleet out of Europe into the West Indies, after the execution of Charles I (1651–2). [Methuen; Stokes, New York: o.p.]
—— *Thompson's Progress.* 1902
A poor nameless boy by indomitable energy and self-confidence becomes a peer and a millionaire. Manufacturing life in Bradford (1840–50 and onward), the Ku Klux Klan in the Southern States. Good poaching scenes. [Harrap; Macmillan, New York: o.p.]
—— *Captain Kettle, K.C.B.* 1903
Another sequel to the previous adventure-books. [Pearson; Federal Bk. Co., Boston: o.p.; *Captain Kettle,* Omnibus Ed., Newnes, 1929.]

ILF, Ilya [*Russian*], and **PETROV**, Evgeny [*Russian*]. *Diamonds to Sit On: a Russian comedy of errors.* 1930
A Russian farce in the Gogol genre. A mother-in-law secretes the family jewels in one of the drawing-room chairs, and the inheritor, unluckily with the aid of a rascally adventurer, tracks down the furniture, scattered during the revolution, only to find the treasure rifled. [Transl. by Elizabeth HILL and Doris MUDIE, Methuen; Harper, New York.]

INCHBALD, Elizabeth [*née* Simpson; 1753–1821]. *A Simple Story.* 1791
A novel of sensibility, written in 1777. A coquettish girl, whose foolishness is charged against the old boarding-schools and their obsolete methods of education, marries her guardian, a Catholic priest, after tormenting him with her caprices. She is unfaithful and dies in misery, leaving a legacy of misfortune to her daughter. Mrs. Inchbald wrote bad plays for the stage, and there is a stilted, theatrical manner about this one successful novel of hers that is curious but not unpleasing. [Routledge, 1884, o.p.; with *Nature and Art,* De la Rue, 1880: o.p.; with introd. by G. L. Strachey (Oxford Library of Prose and Poetry), Oxford Press, 1908.]
—— *Nature and Art.* 1796
A formal exhibition of the defects of our accepted system of social morality, contrasting the characters of two cousins, one educated in a deanery, the other imbibing the truths of nature (according to Rousseau's creed) on an island inhabited by savages. The latter's criticisms of the sophistications and artificialities of the world are good satire. Contains one scene of extreme pathos, where a girl is condemned to death by the man who seduced her. [Cassell's National Library, 1886: o.p.]

INGEMANN, Bernhard Severin [*Danish*; 1789–1862]. *Waldemar* (Valdemar Seier, 1826). 1841
Ingemann was a Danish poet and novelist who wrote a number of realistic tales and a series of historical romances in Scott's style, of which this, *Valdemar Seier* (1826), and *Prinds Otto af Danmark* (1835) are the best. This deals with the time 1204. [3 vols., Saunders & Otley: o.p.] His village tales, *The Doomed House, The Secret Witness, All Souls' Day,* and *The Aged Rabbi,* have been translated in Mrs. Anne S. BUSHBY's *The Danes, Sketched by Themselves: stories by Danish authors.* [3 vols., Bentley, 1864: o.p.]

IRVINE, Alexander [*Irish*; *b.* 1863]. *My Lady of the Chimney Corner: a story of love and poverty in Irish peasant life.* 1914
The chief character is an impoverished woman drawn from the author's mother, living in Antrim, where he was born. [Unwin; Collins; Century Co., New York: o.p.]
—— *The Souls of Poor Folk.* 1921
A further novel of Ulster peasant life. [Collins.]

IRVING, Washington [*American*; 1783–1859]. *Salmagundi; or, The Whim-Whams and Opinions of Lancelot Langstaff, Esq., and others.* 1807–8
A serial miscellany of essays and sketches, comprising *inter alia* Addisonian memoirs of the Cockloft family, and satirical letters from a Turkish exile in New York, after the model of Goldsmith and Montesquieu. [2 vols., Putnam, New York; Bell.]
—— *A History of New York, by Deidrich Knickerbocker.* 1809
Begun as a parody of a pretentious history, carried on as a burlesque in which fact and droll fiction are inextricably mingled in a peculiarly American manner; introduces a good deal of kindly satire of the old Dutch inhabitants of Manhattan Island, which actually offended their living descendants. Diedrich is a representative of these decaying families of New York, an eccentric old bachelor, whose idiosyncrasies are very diverting. The style is that of the classic English writers of the eighteenth century. [2 vols., Putnam, New York; ed. by S. Williams and T. Macdowell, Harcourt, New York; Bks. III–VII, Macmillan, London and New York; *illus.,* 1 vol. and 2 vol. eds., Putnam, New York; by James Daugherty, Doubleday, New York, 1928.]
—— *Rip Van Winkle; and, The Legend of Sleepy Hollow.* 1819
Humorous fantasies, in which the primitive Dutch folk living in the wooded and hilly country bordering on the Hudson are delineated in a racy style, as they were long ago. In the first, a man's supernatural sleep through years that transform his native village from ancient to modern, is the motive, which may have been borrowed from some European legend; in the second, a headless horseman plays a mock-tragic part. The prose of these idylls is that of Addison and Goldsmith, and a quieter humour than the drollery of the Knickerbocker history pervades them. [*Illus.* by G. H. Broughton, Macmillan, London and New York; by Eric Pape, *id.* Lippincott, Philadelphia and London. Separately, *illus.,* Putnam, New York; *Rip Van Winkle, illus.* by N. C. Wyeth, McKay, Philadelphia; by Arthur Rackham, Heinemann.]

IRVING, Washington (*continued*). *Bracebridge Hall; or, The Humourists.* 1822
Like so many of the essays in the *Sketch Book*, this is a sympathetic picture of pleasant phases of English country life, and recalls the very similar sketches by Addison in the Sir Roger de Coverley papers. [Putnam, New York (1 vol. and 2 vol. eds.) ; *illus.*, 2 vols., Putnam, New York ; by R. Caldecott, Macmillan, London and New York.]

IRWIN, Margaret [Mrs. J. R. Monsell]. *None so Pretty.* 1930
This is historical fiction in which the historical colour is entirely subordinated to the interest in character and the interplay of motives. Prince Rupert, Sir Thomas Browne, and Cardinal Mazarin come on the scene, but quite as naturally as any others implicated in the story of Nan and her untoward love-affairs. [Chatto ; Harcourt, New York.]

IRWIN, Will [American ; *b.* 1873]. *Youth Rides West: a story of the seventies.* 1925
Adventures in the Rockies of Colorado and among miners. [Knopf, New York ; Cape.]

ISAACS, Jorge [Spanish-Argentine ; 1857–95]. *Maria* (Maria : novela Americana, 1870). 1890
A simple but poetic story of romantic love, set amid the author's native scenery. The beauty of its description, and the insight shown into South American character won it great popularity. [Transl. by Rollo OGDEN, Harper, New York (1925.).]

ISTRATI, Panaït [Greek-Rumanian, writing in French ; *b.* 1884]. *Kyra, my Sister* (Kyra Kyralina). 1930
Depicts with merciless realism the hideousness of the Oriental underworld. Kyra and her mother are brutally maltreated by her father and his abandoned comrades, and Kyra is carried off by a Turk and put in his harem. But the chief character is her brother, who also is corrupted by the Turk. His childhood and his wanderings as a pedlar in the towns along the Danube are an engrossing story. [Transl. from the French by Anthony THORNE, Toulmin ; also Cayme Press ; American transl. by James WHITALL, Knopf, New York, 1926.]

—— *The Bandits* (Les Haïdoucs). 1930
A romantic and very picturesque novel of the internecine war in Roumania, in mid nineteenth century, between the bands of haïdoucs, champions of the peasantry, and the oppressive feudal landowners. Some of the scenes are horrifying. (Written in French, originally in two parts published separately.) [Transl. by W. A. DRAKE, Knopf.] The above, with *Uncle Anghel* [Knopf, New York, 1927 ; *sub 'tit.* *Balkan Tavern*, Toulmin, 1931], are the four parts of a sequence, *Les récits d'Adrien Zograffi* (1924–6).

JACKS, Lawrence Pearsall [*b.* 1860]. *Mad Shepherds; and other human studies.* 1910
By the well-known professor of philosophy. To all appearance, sketches from life and records of actual conversations among a set of hard-headed, clear-thinking, village characters. Shoemaker Hankin is a jewel, but of far rarer quality is the shepherd Snarley Bob—a type perhaps unexampled in fiction—uncultivated, even brutish in externals, but having the clear brain and embracing vision of a Spinoza. By native insight he perfects a system of breeding as fruitful as Mendel's theories. By untaught reasoning and meditation he gets to an intellectual standpoint that puts him on a level with the clearest European philosophers and the profoundest of Hindu mystics. The book is a pertinent criticism of talking people who never get near " the bigness o' things." [*Writings, vol.* 1, Williams & Norgate ; Holt, New York : o.p. ; *illus.*, Williams & Norgate.]

—— *Philosophers in Trouble: a volume of stories.* 1916
Six further stories framed on the Comtist plan of " constructing types on the basis furnished by science." *Bracketed First* shows pithily how difficult it is to pass from abstract ethics to the trying sphere of actuality. *The Poor Man's Pig* satirizes the sweeping generalizations of socialist demagogues. *The Chest of Cedar* contrasts the empty religiosity of a fashionable preacher with the austere religion that will never be popular in a world like the present. *Not Convincing* sets forth the idea of the whole universe as " a work of Literary Art," but is too aptly described by its title. [*Writings, vol.* 3, Williams & Norgate ; Holt, New York : o.p.]

—— *Among the Idol-Makers.* 1917
Appeared originally in 1911. *Made out of Nothing* is the satire on modern-antique making which confers a title on the volume. It describes a one-man firm supplying prehistoric implements, mummies, idols, and any curious object wanted by any collector, however mad. The longest story is *The Tragedy of Professor Denison* and the most poignant *Helen Ramsden*. [*Writings, vol.* 6, Williams & Norgate ; Holt, New York : o.p.]

—— *All Men are Ghosts.* 1917
First appeared in 1913. " Illusion is an integral part of Reality " is the theme developed in the title-story ; and the kindred fantasia, *Panhandle and the Ghosts*, inverts the ordinary ghost-story by representing the " living "—if so they may be termed—haunting the disembodied. [*Writings, vol.* 5, Williams & Norgate : Holt, New York.]

—— *The Country Air.* 1917
" A wise stupidity was the keynote of Mr. Jeremy's life," and of several of these stories, character-sketches, and dialogues with rustics, all of them forming a philosopher's criticism of life, and some directed at specific problems, e.g. *Mary* at feminine emancipation, and *That Sort of Thing* at the Public School system. [*Writings, vol.* 4, Williams & Norgate ; Holt, New York.]

—— *Legends of Smokeover.* 1921
Five eccentric, almost insane figures contribute a satire upon Manchester and its industrial conditions, too indefinite however to be vital. [Hodder ; Doubleday, Doran, New York.]

—— *Heroes of Smokeover.* 1926
Stories in rather lighter vein which introduce as characters those members of the social life of Smokeover of whom the city may be justly proud, and regard as the best types of its production : men such as self-made scientists and doctors risen from the ranks stand high. [Hodder ; Doran, New York.]

JACKSON, Helen Maria [*née* Fiske, afterwards Mrs. Hunt; American; 1831–85]. *Saxe Holm's Stories* (*two series*). [juvenile] *c.* 1870
Stories of American life, thoughtful and interesting. [*First Series*, Scribner, New York; *Second Series, id.*: o.p.]

—— *Ramona.* 1884
Written to expose the injustice of the United States Government's policy towards the Indians. Scene, southern California; the authoress takes one of the mission Indians for her hero, while picturing old-fashioned life on the Spanish rancho, the household, the pastoral occupations, and the religious observances, and telling a tragic love-story. [Little & Brown, Boston; *illus., id.,* 1928; Low: o.p.]

JACOB, Violet [Mrs. Arthur Jacob, *née* Kennedy-Erskine; Scottish]. *The Sheep Stealers.* 1902
A romance of Herefordshire and Brecknock, time of the Rebecca riots (1843–4), which arose through the increase of highway tolls. A young farmer gets mixed up with a murder case and then embarks in the sheep-stealing traffic. His love affairs go wrong, and the sequel is tragic. Strong, uncouth, simple characters and elemental emotions are portrayed against a background in perfect keeping. [Heinemann: o.p.; Putnam, New York: o.p.]

—— *The Interloper.* 1904
Country life and manners on the east coast of Scotland. A romance of family history—a young laird loves and is beloved, but learns that he is illegitimate and nameless. Some interesting and thoroughly natural portraiture of men and women. Realizes the past (1801–2) without straining after effect. [Heinemann: o.p.; Nelson.]

—— *The History of Aythan Waring.* 1908
Much on the lines of *The Sheep Stealers.* Scene, the Wye Valley, Crickowell, and the Brecon hills in the times of contraband trade and fights with excisemen; the hero is found guilty of attempted murder. [Heinemann: o.p.; Dutton, New York: o.p.]

—— *Irresolute Catherine.* 1909
A maid on a farm and her lovers—one a shepherd, the other a rich gentleman; with sketches of Welsh Baptists. [Murray: o.p.; Doubleday, New York: o.p.]

—— *Flemington.* 1911
A novel of 1745 laid in the neighbourhood of Brechin and Montrose, and mingling the interests of character and incident in the manner of the Waverley novels. [Murray: o.p.]

—— *Tales of my own Country.* 1922
Short homely stories of Scottish countryfolk. [Murray.]

JACOBS, William Wymark [*b.* 1863]. *Many Cargoes.* 1896
Miscellaneous yarns in sailor's lingo: love scenes on shipboard (*A Love Passage*), a female tartar (*The Cook of the "Gannet"*), practical jokes (*A Change of Treatment*), and funny misadventures (*In Mid Atlantic*); portraits of old salts, Thames bargees, bigamous captains (*Mated*), love-lorn mates, and the like. The comedy in this and the subsequent tales is as delightfully unreal as Sheridan's. The characters produce it at high pressure, and enjoy it as much as we do. They are average people with single traits absurdly exaggerated, and everybody is either a butt or endowed with extraordinary powers of wit and sarcasm. [Methuen; Stokes, New York.]

—— *The Skipper's Wooing.* 1897
The skipper and his crew go from port to port in search of a missing man, his sweetheart's father, and meet with absurd adventures. Another short tale is appended, *The Brown Man's Secret.* [Pearson; Methuen; Stokes, New York.]

—— *Sea Urchins.* 1898
Deals chiefly with life in the mercantile marine. The boy who fondly believed he was aboard a pirate is a diverting specimen of the urchins. [Methuen.]

—— *A Master of Craft.* 1900
Presents a ludicrous situation aboard a coasting schooner; the skipper gets engaged to three young women at once, and extricates himself by a sham suicide. [Methuen; Stokes, New York.]

—— *Light Freights.* 1901
Sixteen more far-fetched yarns—incredible hoaxes, retaliations, and broad repartees. *The Resurrection of Mr. Wiggett* is about a bullying and boastful landlord who produces the alleged eye-witness of his exploits, only to be let down worse than ever. Ginger and Peter Russett, in *A Marked Man,* persuade their mate to be tattooed and pass himself off as a long-lost son. In *A Question of Habit,* a ship's boy pretends to be a runaway girl, and is petted by all on board. [Methuen; Dodd & Mead, New York.]

—— *At Sunwich Port.* 1902
The kidnapping of a bad-tempered captain and the wooing of his daughter by his enemy's son provide most of the fun. [Methuen; Scribner, New York.]

—— *The Lady of the Barge.* 1902
Principally jests of the usual sort; absurd predicaments, funny mistakes, tables turned, biters bit, and so on. *The Monkey's Paw* is of the contrary stamp, though the surprise is characteristic. The paw is a talisman with the power to grant wishes. A father wishes, and the wish is literally—but tragically—fulfilled. [Methuen; Stokes, New York.]

—— *Odd Craft.* 1903
—— *Short Cruises.* 1907
Similar collections of pleasantries, varied with an occasional excursion into the realm of the uncanny. Police-men, landsmen, mariners, Thames-side people, womenfolk, make admirable fooling. [(1) and (2), Methuen; Scribner, New York.]

—— *Dialstone Lane.* 1904
Three extremely commonplace individuals—arrant landlubbers—make an expedition to the South Seas in search of a treasure which turns out a hoax. Their preposterous adventures, the conversations of a shrewd

JACOBS, William Wymark (*continued*).
sea-captain, and the love affairs of his termagant niece are knit rather perfunctorily into a long story. [Methuen ; Scribner, New York.]

—— *Captains All.* 1905
Farces and drolleries of mariners and others on land, with one grisly tale of the sea—*Over the Side*. *The Temptation of Burge*, a converted burglar, is one of the most comic. The farcical characters, and the admirable way they express themselves, make the somewhat clumsy plots pass muster. In *Four Pigeons*, the ingenious Bob Pretty, the poacher, makes one of his appearances. [Hodder : o.p. ; Scribner, New York.]

—— *Salthaven.* 1908
A much less farcical comedy than the preceding, but the humour is well sustained in the characters and the household affairs of a sea-captain and an attractive widow. [Methuen ; Scribner, New York.]

—— *Ship's Company.* 1911
Another draught from the same fount—ludicrous farce enacted by the stock seamen, small shopkeepers, spinsters, wives, and widows. [Nelson, Hodder.; Scribner, New York.]

—— *Night Watches.* 1914
More in the same genre, mostly comic, but one, *The Three Sisters*, a minor effort in the same vein as *The Monkey's Paw*. [Chapman ; Scribner, New York.]

—— *The Castaways.* 1916
A bank-clerk comes into a fortune, and the subsequent absurdities culminate in a mock mutiny on a yacht, with a sequel not foreseen by the ringleader. [Nelson ; Scribner, New York.]

—— *Deep Waters.* 1919
Further experiences and amusing predicaments of Peter Russet, Ginger Dick, Sam Small, and others, e.g. *Dirty Work* and *Shareholders*. [Nash ; Scribner, New York.]

—— *Sea Whispers.* 1926
More stories of the night-watchman, with one or two excursions into the uncanny and horrible. [Hodder ; Scribner, New York. Cheap eds. of most of the above are also published by Nelson.]

JACOBSEN, Jans Peter [Danish ; 1847–1885]. *Marie Grubb: a lady of the seventeenth century* (1876). 1917
A large-scale reconstruction of bygone life (*c.* 1655–95), bringing in divers historical events, such as the defence of Copenhagen against the Swedes (1658), and a number of kings and prominent statesmen. But the essence of the book is in the tragic life of Marie Grubbe, thrice married and twice divorced. [Transl. by Hanna Astrup LARSEN; American Scandinavian Foundation (Oxford Press) ; Knopf, New York, 1925.]

—— *Niels Lyhne* (Niels Lyhne, 1891). 1919
In many respects this is autobiographical ; Niels is a native of Jutland, an artist, and a freethinker. Here we follow the workings of his inner life, culminating in the final scene where on his death-bed he steels himself to hold fast to the convictions of his lifetime, in face of the terrors of death. [Transl. by Hanna Astrup LARSEN, American Scandinavian Foundation (Oxford Press).]

JAMES, George Payne Rainsford [1801–60]. *Richelieu ; or, A Tale of France.* 1829
James's first novel, a good example of his accuracy and power of visualizing the past, and of his defects— lack of humour and general dulness. Praised by Scott. The inner history of the ill-fated conspiracy of Cinq-Mars (1642), and of the events leading to the fall of Richelieu, incorporated with a story of Court intrigue. Louis XIII, Anne of Austria, and the cardinal are drawn with care and learning. Chavigni, the bold, unscrupulous, good-hearted plotter, is a type that often reappears in James. St. Germain, Paris, the Bastille are the principal scenes. [Routledge (Dutton, New York) : o.p. ; (Everyman's Lib.), Dent (Dutton, New York), 1906.]

—— *De l'Orme ; or, Le Comte de Soissons.* 1830
Adventures among Pyrenean smugglers, the crimes of a diabolical noble, hairbreadth escapes, and grandiose scenery, in the style of Mrs. Radcliffe. The revolt of the Catalans from Philip of Spain and the conspiracy of the Comte de Soissons are the historical matters introduced (1619). [Routledge (Dutton, New York) : o.p.]

—— *Darnley ; or, The Field of the Cloth of Gold.* 1830
Old English life in Tudor times : domestic scenes, pageants and revelry, Court life, and the famous meeting of Henry and Francis (1520) ; with the wonted love romance and melodrama worked in. [Routledge (Dutton, New York) : o.p.]

—— *Philip Augustus ; or, The Brothers in Arms.* 1831
Baronial France (1199–1214) overrun by the rebellious banditti and free companies. The adventures of the Sire de Coucy, John of England's persecution and murder of Prince Arthur, and the battle of Bouvines (1214). History worked in with more than his usual care. [Routledge (Dutton, New York) : o.p.]

—— *Henry Masterton ; or, The Adventures of a Young Cavalier.* 1832
Autobiography of a Cavalier—a picture of the Royalist downfall that should be read with Scott's *Woodstock*. Shows the Roundheads in the same offensive light, confiscating the goods of malignants for their own benefit ; and represents the Puritans as snuffling hypocrites. That fine king's officer Goring, and the Parliamentarian Ireton, are vigorously portrayed (1645–51). [Routledge (Dutton, New York) : o.p.]

—— *Mary of Burgundy ; or, The Revolt of Ghent.* 1833
Similar in theme to Scott's *Quentin Durward*, but treated differently ; the turbulent history of the burghers of Flanders and their incessant revolts from their several lords. Heroine, Mary, daughter of Charles the Bold ; hero, the patriotic young President, Albert Maurice, citizen of Ghent (1456–77). [Routledge (Dutton, New York) : o.p.]

—— *John Marston Hall ; or, The Little Ball of Fire.* 1834
A sequel to *Henry Masterton*. The dazzling career of a conceited young Scot, during the plots and battles of the New Fronde (*c.* 1642–8) ; related by himself. Condé, Turenne, Mazarin, and Anne of Austria are among the historical portraits. [Routledge (Dutton, New York) : o.p.]

JAMES, George Payne Rainsford (*continued*). *One in a Thousand ; or, The Days of Henry Quatre.*
1835

A novel of the League (1589–90), taking up the story of the religious wars just before the murder of Henry III and the battle of Ivry. With the romanticism of the complex plot are combined careful studies of the history, portraits of Henry IV, of the Duke of Mayenne, head of the Guises, and a vivacious picture of the Leaguers in Paris. [Routledge (Dutton, New York) : o.p.]

—— *Attila ; or, The Huns.*
1837

A young Roman exile seeks an asylum in Attila's camp, and so becomes spectator of his devastating march across Europe against the Rome of Valentinian, and of the tremendous encounter between the Huns and the Visigoths (452–3). [Routledge (Dutton, New York) : o.p.]

—— *The Huguenot ; or, The French Protestants.*
1838

Love and persecution in Poitou at time of Dragonnades and revocation of the Edict of Nantes (1685). Intrigues of ministers and favourites at the Court of the Grand Monarque ; the crafty Louvois, bigoted Madame de Maintenon, Bossuet, and Marshal Schomberg. The horrors of the Bastille. [Routledge (Dutton, New York) : o.p.]

—— *Henry of Guise ; or, The States of Blois.*
1839

A novel of the League (1588), the Huguenot Henry of Navarre appearing in an unfavourable light. A brave young adherent of the great Duke is nominally hero as well as lover, but the true hero is Henry of Guise. Both he and the incompetent Henry III make sound historical portraits. The king's debaucheries at Vincennes and the factious state of Paris are impressively described. The finale is the Duke's assassination at Blois. [Routledge (Dutton, New York) : o.p.]

—— *The King's Highway ; or, In the Age of William III.*
1840

The conspiracy of Fenwick, Barclay, and Charnock (1696–7). The king and the Duke of Berwick well portrayed. Jacobite plots, attempts to abduct, and highway robberies. [Routledge (Dutton, New York) : o.p.]

—— *The Man-at-Arms.*
1840

A Huguenot story of the third religious war, that of Jarnac and Moncontour (1569–72)—a time marked by great disasters, the murder of Condé and the massacre of St. Bartholomew. The Catholic League and the Guises are in disfavour throughout, and their commander-in-chief, the Duke of Anjou, Queen Elizabeth's suitor, is the villain of the piece. [Routledge (Dutton, New York) : o.p.]

—— *Castelnau : or the Ancient Regime.*
1841

A sound and well-made novel of the Midi and Paris and Versailles under Louis XV, who, with Louvois, Mme du Barry, and the Duke and Duchess de Choiseul, is a prominent figure (1756–74). The corruption at Court and the systematic espionage of the police are matters heavily insisted upon. [Longmans : o.p.]

—— *The Jacquerie.*
1841

Time of the Hundred Years' War and the Jacquerie (1357–8). [Routledge (Dutton, New York) : o.p.]

—— *The Brigand ; or, Corse de Leon.*
1841

Opens amidst the Alpine scenery of Savoy, moves to Paris and the Court, the Louvre and Fontainebleau, all elaborately depicted ; among the prominent figures are Diane de Poitiers and Henry II of France, with whose fatal wound in a tournament the narrative closes (1558–9). [Routledge (Dutton, New York) : o.p.]

—— *The Woodman ; or, Bosworth Field.*
1842

Richard III and the Earl of Richmond (Henry VII). [Routledge : Dutton, New York : o.p.]

—— *Forest Days ; or, Robin Hood.*
1843

One of his best novels ; the Barons' Wars, Simon de Montfort, Prince Edward (I), and the battle of Evesham. Scenes : Derbyshire, Notts, Sherwood Forest, and Worcestershire in 1265. [Routledge (Dutton, New York) : o.p.]

—— *Agincourt ; or, The Times of Henry V.*
1844

Rich in lore from historians, poets, and romancers—the chivalric story of Henry of Monmouth, as Shakespeare portrays him before his accession, and as victor at Agincourt ; with scenes of old English life in London and the country, pictures of the Burgundian court and of Flanders, and portraits of celebrities like Philip the Good, Count of Charolois, afterwards Duke of Burgundy (1413–5). [Routledge (Dutton, New York) : o.p.]

—— *Arabella Stuart ; or, The Days of James I.*
1844

Love story of Arabella and William Seymour, and plot to make her Queen ; a sentimental tragedy. Takes liberties with history. Harsh portraits of James I, his favourite Rochester, and the latter's paramour the Countess of Essex ; Raleigh, Cobham, Markham, etc., are introduced, with the Main Plot, Bye Plot, and the murder of Overbury (1603–15). [Routledge (Dutton, New York) : o.p.]

—— *Rose d'Albret ; or, The Leaguers.*
1844

A Radcliffian romance of intrigue, with incidental pictures of France in the year of Ivry (1590), under the rule of Henry of Navarre, but torn asunder by the machinations of the League, headed by the Duke of Mayenne. [Routledge (Dutton, New York) : o.p.]

—— *The Smuggler.*
1845

A picture of smuggling and smugglers in Kent at middle of eighteenth century, with an account of how the trade received a crushing blow from the Customs and the military. General ruffianism relieved by a few strong characters and by love-making under difficulties. The good-natured but gruff Mr. Zachary Croyland and his well-intentioned, meddling sister supply low comedy. [Routledge (Dutton, New York) : o.p.]

—— *Arrah Neil ; or, Times of Old.*
1845

The historical part of this sentimental romance is one of the earliest episodes of the war, the attempt of the king's party to obtain possession of Hull, the magazine of the north (1642). Capt. Barecolt, one of James's few low-comedy characters, is a tolerable reflection of Capt. Dalgetty. [Routledge (Dutton, New York) : o.p.]

—— *Heidelberg ; or, The Winter King.*
1846

The first part a glowing picture of Heidelberg, the Rhine and the Neckar, and the gorgeous court of Frederick V, Elector Palatine, the " Winter King." The last is a narrative of his disasters as King of Bohemia, the battle

JAMES, George Payne Rainsford (*continued*).

of the Weissenberg, the fall of Prague, and the sack of Heidelberg (1619–20). His wife Elizabeth, daughter of our James I and ancestress of the Hanoverian line, is a tragic figure. [Routledge (Dutton, New York) : o.p.]

—— *The Castle of Ehrenstein ; or, A Romance of Princes.* 1847

A romance of mediæval Germany, of historical atmosphere rather than facts (*c.* 1208–12). The struggles and intrigues of princes and barons, fitfully controlled by the authority of Emperor and Pope. [Routledge (Dutton, New York) : o.p.]

—— *The Forgery.* 1849

Probably the best of his novels of contemporary life. [Routledge (Dutton, New York) : o.p.]

—— *The Fate.* 1851

Social life with some appearances of historical figures—Monmouth, Churchill, Jeffreys, Monk, etc. Monmouth's rebellion is the big historical episode towards the end. The scenes shift from Lincolnshire and Nottinghamshire to Dorset and Somerset. [Routledge (Dutton, New York) : o.p.]

—— *Gowrie ; or, The King's Plot.* 1851

The Gowrie conspiracy (1599–1600). The author assumes that James VI (I of England), his special *bête noire*, fabricated the plot in order to do a blameless young noble to death. Scenes : Padua, France, Scotland. [Routledge (Dutton, New York) : o.p.]

—— *The Old Dominion.* 1856

A romance of Virginia and the Southampton massacre (1831). [Routledge (Dutton, New York) : o.p.]

—— *Leonora d'Orco ; or, The Times of Caesar Borgia.* 1857

The "veracious history" of Leonora and Lorenzo Visconti (1494–5). The troublous times of the French Charles VIII's invasion of Italy, of Cesare Borgia and Leonardo da Vinci. [Routledge (Dutton, New York) : o.p.]

JAMES, Henry [American ; 1843–1916]. *A Passionate Pilgrim ; and other tales.* 1875

The Passionate Pilgrim, American heir to an English estate, is a much-idealized hero, in whom Anglomania becomes a dreamy poetic passion. In *Madame de Mauves*, an American girl married to a French nobleman believes that ancient lineage means everything noble and refined, but is cruelly undeceived : yet her inherited inhibitions render her proof against the New Englander who would fain be Perseus to her Ariadne. [Houghton, Boston ; with *The Reverberator, etc., Works, vol.* 18, Macmillan.]

—— *Roderick Hudson.* 1875

Roderick, an epitome of the strength and the weakness of genius, is a young American sculptor taken to Italy by one of Mr. James's rich virtuosi. There, after spasmodic production of a few masterpieces, the flame of his genius expires. He outrages the love of his betrothed, and flouts his benefactor ; but we are led to regard him as a beautiful, irresponsible animal, and to pity rather than blame him, useless though he be. [Revised edn. (1911), Houghton, Boston ; Macmillan, *Works, vol.* 7.]

—— *The Madonna of the Future ; and other tales.* 1875

International stories, chiefly about Americans on the Continent. The first is a delicate and affecting little story of an artist in Florence, with limitless ambitions but no power to carry them out, and of the masterpiece that was never painted. For *Madame de Mauves* see above. [*v. A Passionate Pilgrim, supra.*]

—— *The American.* 1877

A good example of the *émigré* novel, scientifically expounding the differences of national manners and breeding, traditional standards and ideals, and the impossibility of reconciling such opposites. A self-made American goes to Europe to enjoy his " pile," and becomes engaged to a French widow of noble family. The match is a good one for both parties, but at length the powers that rule this exclusive social world deliver their verdict : the engagement must be annulled. The American's pluck and good nature are happily contrasted with the colossal pride and essential meanness of the old noblesse. [Houghton, Boston ; *Works, vol.* 2, Macmillan.]

—— *The Europeans.* 1878

A brother and sister from Europe, American by extraction, come to seek their fortune among relatives near Boston. Great part of the interest is in the impression made on outsiders by the serious and colourless life of these modern descendants of the Puritans. [New ed. (1906), Houghton, Boston ; *Works, vol.* 3, Macmillan.]

—— *Daisy Miller : a comedy.* 1878

The tragi-comedy of a sprightly American girl holidaying on the Continent, and getting into scrapes and compromising situations through her natural innocence and delightful ignorance and her superiority to the conventions. " Daisy Millerism " was for some time a byword with the American globe-trotter. [Houghton, Boston ; with *An International Episode*, Harper, New York ; Macmillan, New York. With *Other Stories, Works, vol.* 23, Macmillan.]

—— *An International Episode.* 1879

A social comedy turning on the problem whether an English nobleman will marry a beautiful American girl. The lady is a dignified specimen of her countrywomen, proud, well-bred, and too disinterested to give her hand where she does not give her heart. [*v. supra.* In *Lady Barbarina, etc., Works, vol.* 19, Macmillan.]

—— *Washington Square.* 1881

One of the stories not afterwards revised. Considered by Americans his best delineation of life in the United States. Scene, the oldest and stateliest quarter of New York. Idea, the disillusionment of a girl who finds that her suitor is only in love with her fortune. The irony is kindly, and the characters are very sympathetically analysed. [Harper, New York ; Boni, New York ; *Works, vol.* 5, Macmillan.]

—— *The Portrait of a Lady.* 1881

Isabel Asher is one of James's most complete studies of either sex ; she sets out consciously to explore life, to " make her life fine," and the development of her personality is followed from girlhood to her complex maturity. There are other characters drawn on a large scale in the foreground. Scenes, America, London,

JAMES, Henry (*continued*).

Paris, Italy. Here we see James introducing the tragic element of conflict and suspense which later makes *The Golden Bowl* so essentially dramatic. [Houghton, Boston ; 2 vols., *Works*, vols. 6–7, Macmillan.]

—— *The Siege of London ; The Point of View.* 1883

In *The Siege of London*, a little comedy of manners, an adventuress of strong American proclivities lays siege to an English baronet and wins him by sheer adroitness. In *The Point of View* we have impressionist sketches, "instantaneous mental photographs," of American life, in the form of letters by Europeanized Americans ; and in *The Pension Beaurepas*, studies of foreign Americans and native Americans as they appear to European eyes ; with side-lights on the influence of foreign culture and other nice problems of nationality. [(1), and *Pension Beaurepas*, Houghton, Boston ; (1), (2), and (3), in *Lady Barbarina, Works,* *vol.* 19, Macmillan ; (1), with *Madame de Mauves*, (2) and (3) and *An International Episode*, 2 vols. Macmillan.]

—— *Stories Revived.* (*Two series*). 1885

The Author of "Beltraffio" gives the tragedy of the literary artist, on the personal and domestic side of life. His wife represents the antagonistic, the philistine, spirit. She sacrifices her son rather than allow him to fall a prey to the malign influence of his father's heterodox writings. *Pandora* sketches a new type, the self-made American girl, a product of recent tendencies in American society. Five other stories in the first series and seven in the other, of which several, e.g. *The Last of the Valerii* and *The Romance of Certain Old Clothes*, trench on the supernatural. [*The Author of "Beltraffio," Works, vol.* 21, Macmillan ; *Pandora*, in *Daisy Miller, etc., Works, vol.* 23, *id.* ; *The Last of the Valerii, etc., Works, vol.* 26, *id.*]

—— *The Bostonians.* 1886

One of his few American novels, which might have been more adequate "had he not forgotten so much about American life." The Bostonians are gently satirized, especially the apostles of feminism and other faddists. The affairs of various people in love, an elopement, and the question whether the runaway couple will be happy or starve, are the chief points of interest. [2 vols., *Works*, vols. 8–9, Macmillan.]

—— *The Princess Casamassima.* 1886

The later doings of an American adventuress whose ambitious guardian secured a prince for her husband, as related in *Roderick Hudson*, the hero of which she captivated. Scene transferred to London, where the Princess, hating her husband, amuses herself by sympathizing and making love with the socialists. She is an excellent specimen of the "dangerous" woman ; a vagabond by birth, an empress in her superb egoism and reckless generosity, potentially an angel or a fiend. The vast revolutionary plot of the socialists brings in a romantic element unusual in James's novels. [2 vols., *Works*, vols. 10–11, Macmillan.]

—— *The Aspern Papers ; and other stories.* 1888

A writer is anxious to secure, as material for his life of the poet Aspern, certain papers which are supposed to be in the custody of an old lady-love of the poet's in Florence. With infinite trouble and address he contrives to overcome the privacy of the lady, his tactful diplomacy is about to be rewarded, when the whole thing turns out to be a misunderstanding. [Boni, New York ; *Works*, vol. 17 (with *The Turn of the Screw*), Macmillan ; Secker.]

—— *The Reverberator.* 1888

A comedy of manners with two lines of interest ; incompatibility between a cultivated family of South Carolinians settled in France and the vulgar relatives of a pretty American girl loved by the son ; and the scandalous violation of private life by modern journalism. [With *Other Stories, Works, vol.* 18, Macmillan.]

—— *The Tragic Muse.* 1891

A long novel, with a double plot and a very large allowance of characters ; much concerned with art and stage affairs, the result of James's experiments with theatrical work. Aims at "an immense and exquisite correspondence with life," but marks no real advance towards his more elaborate technique. The theme of the more important of the stories intertwined is "the quick development of an uncouth girl into a famous actress." [2 vols., Houghton, Boston ; 2 vols., *Works*, vols. 12–13, Macmillan.]

—— *The Lesson of the Master ; and other stories.* 1892

First a piece of ironical comedy—a man takes the advice of one whom he idolizes, and finds that while he has made the mistake of his life the other has, all unconsciously, reaped the benefit. In *Brooksmith* the rare personality of a butler is subtly drawn, a trophy of the author's untiring quest for preciosities of character. *Sir Edmund Orme* is a new kind of ghost-story exampled later in the full-length novelette *A Turn of the Screw* (1898). [(1) *Works, vol.* 20, Macmillan ; *v.* also *The Turn of the Screw* ; *Brooksmith*, in *Daisy Miller, etc., Works, vol.* 23, Macmillan ; *Sir Edmund Orme*, in *The Altar of the Dead, etc., Works, vol.* 22, *id.*]

—— *The Real Thing ; and other tales.* 1893

The Real Thing illustrates the author's theories of art, and throws much light on the impressionism, as opposed to actuality, of his later work. A broken-down lady and gentleman offer themselves to an illustrator as models, supposing themselves, as being the "real thing," infinitely superior to the professional, who merely poses ; but the artist in the end thinks differently. Literary and artistic life comes in a good deal in these five stories ; e.g. in *Greville Fane*, a humorous story of a successful "lady novelist." [Macmillan, New York ; (1), in *Daisy Miller, etc., Works, vol.* 23, Macmillan ; *Greville Fane*, in *The Author of Beltraffio, etc., Works, vol.* 21, *id.*]

—— *The Wheel of Time ; and other stories.* 1894

Two other stories, *Owen Wingrave* and *Collaboration*. The latter resembles *The Lesson of the Master* in motive ; a young French writer wishing to collaborate with a German musician, gives up his sweetheart on account of her anti-Teutonic animus ; and in the sequel the German wins her. [Harper, New York : o.p. ; (1), and *Collaboration*, in *Lord Beaupré, etc., Works, vol.* 27, Macmillan ; *Owen Wingrave*, in *The Altar of the Dead, etc., Works, vol.* 22, *id.*]

—— *Terminations.* 1895

The Death of the Lion makes game of a clique of admirers gathered round a decadent novelist, who dies of a cold while they are waiting to hear him read his MS. *The Middle Years* portrays a young novelist of

JAMES, Henry (*continued*).

promise who is dying, and, in spite of a friend's devotion, expires with a prayer on his lips for another chance to carry out his life's work. *The Altar of the Dead* illustrates the writer's growing fondness for mystical themes. A man founds an altar for those he loved who have passed away, and institutes a kind of sacramental service. The *dénouement* has a surprising turn. [Harper, New York : o.p. ; Heinemann ; the three stories cited occur in *Works*, vols. 20, 21, and 22, Macmillan, respectively.]

—— *The Figure in the Carpet.* 1896

A bantering *jeu-d'esprit* on the pretensions of critics to find an esoteric significance in their pet authors. One expert after another is hot on the scent of " the buried treasure, the general intention " in the novels of their idol ; but each one dies before the imaginary writer of the tale can secure the precious secret. [In *The Lesson of the Master, etc., Works, vol.* 20, Macmillan.]

—— *The Other House.* 1896

Contains a fine tragic character in Rose Armiger, a nature of repressed but passionate energy. Culminates in an unwonted outbreak of emotion. [Macmillan, New York : o.p. ; Heinemann.]

—— *The Spoils of Poynton.* 1897

A domestic comedy hingeing on the destinies of a fine old country house, full of articles of virtu, which an elderly lady who is passionately fond of the place schemes to retain when her son, the actual owner, gets married. The heart-burnings and squabbles are terminated by a very ironical catastrophe. [Houghton, Boston ; Heinemann ; with two other stories, *Works, vol.* 15, Macmillan.]

—— *What Maisie Knew.* 1897

The method of gradual revelation through the brain of an actor in the drama who is also an observer, the method of his final masterpieces, is well displayed in this " attempt to print the figure of life as it falls upon the very acute vision of a little girl." Maisie is the child of divorced parents who have married other people, and she is the innocent and uncomprehending witness of an intrigue between the step-parents. [Scribner, New York ; with *In the Cage*, and *The Pupil, Works, vol.* 16, Macmillan.]

—— *In the Cage.* 1898

A telegraph girl's glimpses of high society. She takes a keen interest in a love affair, and out of the telegrams passing through her hands, pieces together a romance. [Stone, Chicago : o.p. ; *v. supra.*]

—— *The Two Magics.* 1898

The Turn of the Screw employs the same device of impressions conveyed through a mind into which we are directly gazing. Hence it is one of the most dreadful of ghost-stories, the ghosts making their presence felt without any romantic nonsense. They are two evil beings, straight from hell, who have secured a grip on the souls of two children, and made them partners in the abominations of their own secret life. *Covering End* is a little comedy concerned with the doings of a captivating American, who makes a raid on an old country house after the manner of her compatriots. [Macmillan, New York, 1924 ; *The Turn of the Screw*, Boni, New York, 1924 ; Secker ; in *The Aspern Papers, etc., Works, vol.* 17, Macmillan ; with *The Lesson of the Master*, Modern Lib., New York, 1930.]

—— *The Awkward Age.* 1899

In such a novel as this James can be seen turning his psychological apparatus in a speculative direction, tracing out a tendency, a phase of social behaviour, to a stage hardly discernible in the world of reality. His " collection of natural affinities " outrun all their predecessors in the decadent arts of free living and experimenting with good and evil, especially evil. The incidents slight, the action purely intellectual and emotional, the dialogue so nebulous and allusive that a sustained effort is required to follow it. [Harper ; Heinemann ; *Works, vol.* 14, Macmillan.]

—— *The Soft Side.* 1900

More studies of psychical phenomena and of the abnormal. *John Delaroy* contrasts the vulgar attitude of an editor anxious to exploit a dead writer's life with the reverent affection of his sister. *Europe* anatomizes the feelings of three ladies, obliged to postpone their tour on the Continent because their aged mother will not die. *The Great Good Place* is a study of an intangible phase of consciousness, dreamland and its connexions with waking thoughts. *Paste* describes the suspicions aroused through the discovery of a valuable necklace among the effects of a deceased lady of moderate means. Some of these psychical and fantastic stories are of a still more esoteric kind. [Macmillan, New York : o.p. ; Methuen : o.p. ; *John Delaroy*, in *Lord Beaupré, etc., Works, vol.* 27, Macmillan ; the remaining three cited, in *The Author of " Beltraffio," etc., Works, vol.* 21, *id.*]

—— *The Sacred Fount.* 1901

A further example of his taste for occult ideas in their psychological aspects. A society sketch in which is elaborated the fanciful idea that youth may be a fount to rejuvenate age. Of interest chiefly as a " technical exercise." [Scribner, New York ; *Works, vol.* 29, Macmillan.]

—— *The Wings of the Dove.* 1902

Three minds become each in turn the stage on which we are shown what is going on : Kate Croy's, Densher's, and Milly Theale's. Kate and Densher are pledged to each other, and Kate persuades her lover to pay attentions to Milly, so that the pair may subsequently enjoy the fortune which would almost certainly be left to Densher when the dying girl is gone. James has not escaped some obscurity in the process of disentangling the complication of motives, which are ever subtly changing. Milly, " the Dove," is one of his most delicate creations—shadowed by Fate, marked down for extinction before her splendid chances of joy can be realized, pathetically sure that the will to live might be re-created if she loved and were loved in return. [2 vols., Scribner, New York ; *Works, vols.* 30–1, Macmillan.]

—— *The Ambassadors.* 1903

Regarded by James as his best-constructed novel : a finished example of his latest artistic method. Strether, the chief ambassador, is sent to England by the wealthy queen of a philistine town in New England to rescue her son. But the rescuer's eyes are gradually opened to the beauty of a world that has made the fugitive into one of James's perfect men, and he himself is the one to entreat Chad to stay. " Live all you can ; it's a mistake not to," is the philosophy ultimately announced. The whole history of the case,

JAMES, Henry (*continued*).

subtle and complicated, though the incidents are all on the same plane, is set forth in the mirror of Strether's consciousness. [Harper, New York ; 2 vols., *Works, vols.* 32–33, Macmillan.]

—— *The Better Sort.* 1903

Eleven stories of which *The Beast in the Jungle* and *The Birthplace* may be considered typical. Both are curious psychological studies. In the former, a man's life is embittered by his conviction that he is marked out for a terrible calamity, inconceivable and unexampled ; and he realizes, just too late, that he has missed a great blessing which lay ready to his hand—that is the calamity, the unknown " beast in the jungle." The point of the other is the effect upon a cultivated and critical being, caretaker and showman of a literary shrine—it might be at Stratford-on-Avon—with a legend attached to it having very little basis in ascertained fact. [Scribner, New York ; Methuen : o.p. ; *The Beast in the Jungle*, in *The Altar of the Dead, etc., Works, vol.* 22, Macmillan.]

—— *The Golden Bowl.* 1905

Here the opposition and interlacing of motive and the impossibility that any of the four chief characters should speak out, result in an even greater complexity ; but the situation is inch by inch laid bare, and the drama of changing attitudes and feelings runs its course with triumphant clarity. This is a work that falls short of none in the power of showing all that may be going on beneath the polished screen of apparently frank and affectionate intercourse ; more, of conveying " the horror of the thing hideously *behind*, behind so much trusted, so much pretended, nobleness, cleverness, tenderness." [2 vols., Scribner, New York ; *Works, vols.* 34–5, Macmillan.]

—— *The Finer Grain.* 1910

Five stories which are polished examples of delicate art—close-patterned mosaics of his meticulous psychology— and at the same time tolerably free from the later mannerisms of Mr. James. *The Velvet Glove* records an incident in the life of an eminent author, who is entreated by a lady to write a log-rolling preface to her trashy novel. *The Bench of Desolation* is unusually full of tender emotion ; it tells how a man and a woman who parted under threats of a breach-of-promise action come together again after many years. [Scribner, New York ; *The Velvet Glove*, and *The Bench*, both in *Maud Evelyn, etc., Works, vol.* 28, Macmillan.]

—— *The Outcry.* 1911

A comedy of to-day rich in implications of characteristic subtlety, about a great picture, the authorship of which provides the experts with a nice controversy, and its threatened sale to America. A peer in need of ready money, his daughter's matrimonial schemes complicated by various side-issues, her caddish aristocratic suitor, the pushing American millionaire who bids extravagant thousands for the picture, the young art critic of the scientific school, are combined into a straightforward story, the psychology of which is made much clearer than was Mr. James's wont in the later novels. [Scribner, New York ; Methuen : o.p.]

[*Works*, 35 vols., Macmillan ; also Pocket ed., *id.*]

—— *The Sense of the Past.* 1917

A young American, heir to an old London house, finds himself, not merely studying the past as an enthusiastic antiquary, but enveloped in it. He takes on the personality of his kinsman and namesake of 1820, and meets the friends and relations of Jane Austen's time. But he fails to be a full member of this vanished world : he cannot talk its language, seize its point of view ; they are puzzled, suspicious ; and at last he takes flight. [Scribner, New York ; Collins.]

—— *The Ivory Tower.* 1917

Left unfinished through loss of interest during the war years. James's latest technique, the application of " my dramatic principle, my law of successive Aspects, each treated from its own centre," is well exemplified in the story how a cultivated man with no money-sense comes unexpectedly into the inheritance of a millionaire. His mental reactions to the overwhelming change of circumstances and to the utterly anti-pathetic characters and motives of the people among whom he is plunged—possessors, or would-be possessors, of vast predatory fortunes rusticating in their luxurious cottages at Newport, Rhode Island are the theme. [Scribner, New York ; Collins.]

JAMES, Montagu Rhodes [*b.* 1862]. *Ghost Stories of an Antiquary.* 1904

—— *More Ghost Stories of an Antiquary.* 1911

These stories are the work of a well-known scholar, and they exploit the element of supernatural mystery and horror, in especial hauntings by elementals, in a finished and compelling manner. *Whistle and I'll Come to Thee* may be singled out as one of the most gruesome and effective of the collection. [(1) and (2), Arnold ; Longmans, New York.]

—— *A Thin Ghost ; and others.* 1919

Five polished examples of Dr. James's cunning preparation of the atmosphere and felicitous handling of the sensational climax. [Arnold ; Longmans, New York.]

—— *A Warning to the Curious ; and other ghost stories.* 1925

More on the same lines, hardly up to the level of previous books. *The Haunted Doll's House* however is a good tale. [Arnold ; Longmans, New York.]

JANSON, Gustaf [Swedish]. *Abraham's Sacrifice* (Abrahams Offor, 1902). 1903

A sermon against war, with the struggle in South Africa (1900–2) for text. Anti-British, and emphatic on the alleged " methods of barbarism." A Boer general finds that his son has indiscreetly betrayed a secret— hence the sacrifice. [Transl., Methuen : o.p.]

—— *Pride of War* (Lögnerna). 1912

Seven stories of the Italian campaign in Tripoli during the war with Turkey (1911), which constitute one of the most unmitigated denunciations of militarism ever written. On the face of it, they are exaggerated : no army was ever so permeated with brutality and lust of murder ; no war so lacking in any vestige of justification. As propaganda, anyhow, this is strong stuff. [Sidgwick : o.p.]

JANVIER, Thomas Allibone [American ; 1849–1913]. *Colour Studies.* 1885

Four stories, reprinted from *The Century Magazine* ; each complete in itself, yet connected into a greater whole,

JANVIER, Thomas Allibone (*continued*).
> illustrating the early struggles of the painter's career in New York ; the bohemianism, the easy-going life of the studios, the genial, unconventional characters. [Scribner, New York : o.p. ; Bickers : o.p.]

—— *The Aztec Treasure-House : a romance of contemporaneous antiquity.* 1890
> Romance as adventurous as Rider Haggard's *She*. A professor of archæology, a priest, a young Mexican, and two Yankee railroad men discover an Aztec city, which has been miraculously shut away in a mountain valley for a thousand years. A good deal of interesting antiquarian lore is worked in. [Harper, New York, 1918.]

—— *At the Casa Napoléon.* 1912
> Four stories about cosmopolitan bohemian life in a New York café. [Harper, New York : o.p.]

JEANS, Alice. *The Stronger Wings.* 1909
> Gives an analysis of the main currents and undercurrents of the revolutionary period in Austria and Hungary (1848-9), with portraits of Metternich and Field-Marshal Windischgrätz. [Stock : o.p.]

JEFFERIES, John Richard [1848–87]. *Greene Ferne Farm.* 1880
> A short and simple bucolic story, with good descriptive passages of outdoor life and some authentic touches of country character. [Smith & Elder : o.p.]

—— *Wood Magic : a fable.* 1881
> The first account of Bevis, the small boy who was to figure, a little older, as the hero of a great juvenile epic. Bevis is, of course, Jefferies himself, and in this " jungle book " of English fields and woods he records his early revellings in the natural things around him. [Longmans, London and New York ; Collins.]

—— *Bevis : the story of a boy.* 1882
> One of the greatest of boy's books, being written, with very few lapses, in the very spirit of a boy. In the doings of Mark and Bevis, Jefferies relived more gloriously the adventures of his brother and himself in their Wiltshire homeland. In the big reservoir near Coate, the pair behold a real ocean. They explore forests and jungles, build a canoe and a raft and ascend the Nile and Mississippi and more fabulous rivers. They discover wild beasts and savages, and their deeds make a veritable epic, all of it the more fascinating for the author's passionate enjoyment of nature and the infectious delight with which he recalls how they used to make their own weapons and tools and do everything for themselves. In this respect, the comparison is with Defoe. [Duckworth ; (Everyman's Lib.), Dent (Dutton, New York), 1930.]

—— *The Dewy Morn.* 1884
> A singularly unconventional novel. A half-poetical expression of the great naturalist's pantheism, if the term can be used, at all events of his nature-worship, his belief in the purity of nature, in the unity of mind and body, and in the truth and excellence of passion as an expression of natural life. The love-tale and its curious psychological drama is sometimes intermitted, and the novelist breaks forth into lyrical descriptions of natural phenomena and man's healthy delight in nature. The book is also a pamphlet, but that part is irrelevant. [2 vols., Bentley : o.p. ; Macmillan, 1900 : o.p.]

—— *After London ; or, Wild England.* 1886
> Civilized England is overwhelmed by a cataclysm, and the country slowly reverts to a state of nature, while the few surviving inhabitants adopt the barbarous life of early ages. Little story, but the progress of nature's invasion is related with lavish and minute description of animal and plant life. [Duckworth.]

—— *Amaryllis at the Fair.* 1887
> A poor novel, but a masterly picture of country life. Proceeding by his usual method of word-painting, Jefferies gives us a real sense of character in the Iden family, whose daily life is in the closest touch with nature. Out of his minute observation of the things that most of us pay little heed to, Jefferies builds up a general impression of nature's life that is singularly full and ample. Dictated to his wife whilst he was dying. [Duckworth.]

JEFFERY, Walter [b. 1861]. *The King's Yard : a story of Old Portsmouth.* 1903
> A novelist's version of a notorious case—the half-successful plot of an American, John Hill or John the Painter, during the War of Independence, to fire Portsmouth Dockyard. Full of minute particulars about the old town, the " mateys " of the yard, and other features of the time (1776–7). [Everett : o.p.]
> See also *sub nom.* BECKE.

JENKINS, Herbert George [1876–1923]. *Bindle : some chapters in the life of Joseph Bindle.* 1916
> A vivacious divertisement : Mr. Bindle is an oddity whose verbal and practical jokes show understanding of human nature and some bent for extravagance. [Jenkins ; Stokes, New York : o.p.]

—— *The Night Club.* 1917
> Bindle again, as the foremost figure among the heterogeneous members. [Jenkins.]

—— *The Adventures of Bindle.* 1918
> Amusing episodes that often degenerate into horseplay. [Jenkins.

—— *Mrs. Bindle.* 1921

—— *The Bindles on the Rocks.* 1924
> Further instalments of the above. [Jenkins.]

JENKINS, John Edward [1838–1910]. *Ginx's Baby : his birth and other misfortunes.* 1870
> A satire on English benevolent institutions, illustrating, by the absurd efforts of a poor man to get rid of his baby, the dangers to be feared from a vast pauper proletariat. The author sums up as follows : " Philosophers, Philanthropists, Politicians, Papists and Protestants, Poor Law Ministers and Parish Officers—while you have been theorizing, debating, wrangling, legislating, and administering —Good God ! between you all, where has Ginx's baby gone to ? " [Mullan, Belfast : o.p.]

JENSEN, Wilhelm [German ; 1837–1911]. *Karine* (Karin af Sverig, 1872). 1896
> Reign of Gustavus Vasa (1523–60). [Transl. by Emma A. EUDLICH, McClurg, Chicago : o.p.]

JENSEN, Johannes Vilhelm [Danish ; b. 1873]. *The Long Journey* (Den lange Rejse, 1919–22). 1922
> A book in three parts : *Fire and Ice* (*Det Table Land* and *Bræen*), *The Cimbrians* (*Cimbrernes Tog* and *Norne*),

JENSEN, Johannes Vilhelm (*continued*).

and *Christopher Columbus* (*Christoffer Columbus*), reconstructing from the evidence of science, legend, and history the life of man in northern Europe from the Stone Age to the eve of the modern era. [Transl. by A. G. CHATER, Knopf, New York.]

JEPSON, Edgar [*b.* 1864]. *The Professional Prince.* 1917

The jaded prince engages a double to perform his duties whilst he enjoys himself as an ordinary mortal. [Hutchinson : o.p.]

JEROME, Jerome Klapka [1859–1927]. *Three Men in a Boat.* 1889

A comic history of a picnic up the Thames, a medley of buffoonery and droll musings on familiar things. [Arrowsmith ; Holt, New York.]

—— *Sketches in Lavender, Blue, and Green.* 1897

Social sketches, little stories, thumb-nail portraits and skits, inspired by the same comic-paper style of humour. [Longmans : o.p. ; Holt, New York : o.p.]

—— *Three Men on the Bummel.* 1900

A humorous narrative of a journey on the Continent, mainly in Germany. [Arrowsmith.]

—— *Paul Kelver.* 1902

Shows the influence of Dickens in the portrayal of childhood, and in the pathos and touches of broad comedy which is not the light drollery of the earlier books. [Hutchinson : o.p. ; Dodd & Mead, New York : o.p.]

—— *Tommy & Co.* 1904

Farcical sketches exploiting the bohemianism of the journalistic world. [Hutchinson : o.p.]

—— *The Passing of the Third Floor Back.* 1907

The vulgarities and humours of a boarding-house. [Hurst ; Dodd & Mead, New York.]

—— *Malvina of Brittany.* 1916

Six stories, some e.g. *The Lesson*, in fantastic vein ; but those of real life, e.g. *The Fawn Gloves*, a tale of a fastidious man, are more successful. [Cassell : o.p.]

JERROLD, Douglas William [1803–57]. *Mrs. Caudle's Curtain Lectures.* 1846

The comic irony of wedlock ; a shrewish wife's nocturnal harangues at her husband : originally appeared in *Punch*. [(World's Classics), Oxford Press, 1907 ; Foulsham, 1925 ; with *original illustrations*, R. Brimley Johnson, 1902 : o.p.]

JERVEY, Theodore Dehon [American ; *b.* 1859]. *The Elder Brother.* 1907

Owen Wister refers to this book in the preface to *Lady Baltimore* (q.v.). Its importance lies in the thoughtful consideration given to the political, social, and racial problems that have arisen in the South as the legacy from the Reconstruction period. [Neale Pub. Co., Washington : o.p.]

JESSE, Fryniwyd Tennyson [Mrs. Harold Marsh Harwood]. *The Milky Way.* 1913

A light-hearted picaresque medley, concerned with a pair of bohemian artists in Provence. [Heinemann ; Doran, New York : o.p.]

—— *Beggars on Horseback, and other stories.* 1915

Eight stories ; *The Ladder* is a story of a girl hanged for the murder of her father, based on the case of Mary Blandy (1751). *Why Senath Married*, an ironical account of rustic marriage. [Heinemann ; Doran, New York : o.p.]

—— *Secret Bread.* 1917

How a bastard was elevated above his legitimate brethren, and surmounted his difficulties by the aid of a fine-minded pastor—a long and far from superficial novel giving intimate studies of Devonshire farming and a progressive landowner's improvements (1857–1900). [Heinemann ; Doran, New York : o.p.]

—— *The White Riband : or, a young female's folly.* 1921

An amusing pastiche of Victorian romance. [Heinemann.]

—— *Moonraker ; or, The Female Pirate and her Friends.* 1921

An exciting sea-story of Cornwall and Haiti and the deeds of Toussaint l'Ouverture (1801–3). [Heinemann ; Knopf, New York.]

—— *Tom Fool.* 1926

The sea in its beauty and terror, holding despotic rule over its lover and victim, is here the dominant theme ; through many pages of striking description and poetic beauty in the account of Tom Fould's career, from the day when as a lad he and his parents sailed for Australia, until, still in the prime of youth, he meets his doom, we follow his ambition to make the sea his career, his craving for moments of danger when man is pitted against the elements, his friendship for the owner's son, by nature a landsman, and his brief idyll of married life, from which the sea soon claims him. [Heinemann ; Knopf, New York.]

—— *Many Latitudes.* 1928

The qualities of clear and vigorous narration which distinguish her longer novels are not lacking in these stories : *The Two Helens* is a tale of the sea, a sketch on the lines of *Tom Fool* ; *Greater Love*, perhaps the best of them, shows the poignant irony of mother-love unrewarded ; the Irish rebellion of 1916 is the background of the little tragedy, *Virtue*. *Featherbeds* takes us to Cornwall, where the dilemma of a farmer's wife about to make off with a commercial traveller is resolved in an original and dramatic fashion. [Heinemann ; Knopf, New York.]

—— *The Lacquer Lady.* 1930

Mandalay and Upper Burma at the time of the British conquest of 1885. The interest centres in a girl of mixed English, Italian, and Burmese origin, whose resentment at the loss of a lover impels her to betray the French intrigues with King Thebaw to the British. [Heinemann ; Macmillan, New York.]

JESSEN, Franz de [Danish]. *Katya : a romance of Russia.* 1914

The author is a Danish journalist with an intimate knowledge of eastern Europe. [Heinemann : o.p.]

JEWETT, Sarah Orne [American ; 1849–1909]. *Deephaven.* 1877

Quiet, undramatic character-drawing, in the manner of *Cranford*, of the old-world inhabitants of a decayed

JEWETT, Sarah Orne (*continued*).
seaport in New England, viewed by a pair of girls making holiday, who laugh, not without kindly appreciation, at the quaint old people. Miss Jewett's humour and the spirituality of her perceptions bring her very near to Hawthorne. [Houghton, Boston; Constable: o.p.; illus., Houghton, Boston.]

—— *Country By-Ways.* 1881
Fragmentary reminiscences, glimpses of New England life and human nature, pervaded by the same restful atmosphere and the placid charms of home and of homely affection. [Houghton, Boston.]

—— *The Mate of the " Daylight " ; and, Friends Ashore.* 1884
Sketches and studies, some budding into little incidents, others mere bits of still life. A lowly New England King Lear is the subject of *A Landless Farmer*; *An Only Son* is a piece of restrained emotion; and *The New Parishioner* is typical in its quiet interest. [Houghton, Boston.]

—— *A Country Doctor.* 1884

—— *A Marsh Island.* 1885

—— *A White Heron ; and other stories.* 1886
Simple, uneventful, and perhaps rather monotonous stories of quiet, beautiful life in rural New England, portraits of old acquaintances, and loving pictures of common people, interpreting their more elusive graces and bringing out the kindly side of the Puritan character. [(1), (2), and (3), Houghton, Boston.]

—— *The King of Folly Island ; and other people.* 1888
A typical collection of Miss Jewett's best. The King is a misanthropic hermit, self-exiled with his daughter on a barren islet; and his story shows the spiritual bent of Miss Jewett's imagination, but hardly her humour. [Houghton, Boston; Duckworth: o.p.]

—— *Strangers and Wayfarers.* 1890
Similar portraiture of New England folk, native types and also new-comers like the Irish; all pervaded with a gentle and charitable humour, e.g. *The Town Poor, The Luck of the Bogans, A Winter Courtship, By the Morning Boat.* [Houghton, Boston; Harper, London: o.p.]

—— *A Native of Winby ; and other tales.* 1893
Less stories than sketches of pregnant situations, bringing out traits of temperament. *The Native* describes the visit of a successful man, half shamefaced, half in self-display, to his native village; *Decoration Day* is a study of patriotic emotion; *The Passing of Sister Barsett*, a typical piece of New England life; and there are two sketches of Irish New Englanders, in which the broad speech accentuates the humour. [Houghton, Boston: o.p.]

—— *The Country of the Pointed Firs.* 1896
Further portraits and scenes of quiet life, rich in spiritual beauty and in humour—the treasure-trove of a summer holiday at a seaside village in Maine. The homely and old-fashioned characters are among her finest drawings from the life—venerable old people who have kept the freshness and innocence of youth; shy, unsophisticated men; women immersed in household cares; quaint originals, full of old-world graces, like the weather-beaten captain with his tale of a spirit-city within the Arctic Circle, the herb-gatherer, and other childlike Wordsworthian figures. [Houghton, Boston; (Traveller's Lib.), Cape.]

—— *The Queen's Twin ; and other stories.* 1899
The Queen's Twin is an old woman in Maine, whose life has points of coincidence with Queen Victoria's. All the tales show the same affectionate delight in quaint and gentle types of humanity. The humorous sayings of the Irish women are in the raciest dialect. [Houghton, Boston; Smith & Elder: o.p.]

—— *The Tory Lover.* 1901
A love-tale—not in Miss Jewett's characteristic way—introducing the vigorous personality of the redoubtable Paul Jones. [Houghton, Boston: o.p.; Smith & Elder: o.p.]
[*Best Stories*, selected, with preface, by Willa Cather, 2 vols., Houghton, Boston, 1925.]

JOHNSON, Owen McMahon [American; b. 1878]. *Arrows of the Almighty.* 1901
A study of American life in the period immediately following the Civil War, the interest centring in the development of character in a man who feels the natures inherited from father and mother struggling in himself, as it were, for mastery. Covers nearly forty years. [Macmillan, New York and London: o.p.]

—— *In the Name of Liberty.* 1905
A ghastly picture of the crimes and atrocities of the maddened populace—the minor and unknown characters in the frightful tragedy of the Terror (1792-3)—set in a grimmer light by contrast with Nicole's love-idyll. [Century Co., New York: o.p.; *sub tit. Nicole, or, In the Name of Liberty*, Macmillan, London: o.p.]

JOHNSON, Richard [1573 ?-1659]. *The History of Tom a Lincoln, the Red Rose Knight.* 1607
The hero is the son of King Arthur and a nun of Lincoln. He goes to " Fayerie Land," and has an amour with the Amazonian queen, whom he deserts. After ridding the land of Prester John of a dragon, he marries the daughter of that monarch. The ensuing adventures are just as preposterous. The book is a vulgarization of the style of romance exemplified by the *Morte d'Arthur*, the *Amadis*, and the *Faerie Queene*, and is written in a debased kind of euphuism. It is interesting as showing what delighted the " general reader " of those days. The author also wrote *The History of the Seven Champions of Christendom* [illus., Blackie; Stokes, New York, 1913] and *The History of Tom Thumb*, for the same illiterate public. [7th ed. (earliest extant), 1635: o.p.; reprinted in W. J. Thoms', *Early English Prose Romances*, see p. 465.]

JOHNSON, Dr. Samuel [1709-84]. *Rasselas, Prince of Abyssinia.* 1759
A lay sermon on " the Vanity of Human Wishes," written when Johnson was in profound sorrow for the death of his mother; the most majestic example of his prose. Belongs to the philosophic meditations on human destiny, in the form of allegory, dialogue, or fable, in which the periodical writers loved to indulge. The prince escapes from his happy valley in quest of a satisfactory object in life, but returns to his paradise again with a sager acceptance of man's limitations. The book was contemporary with Voltaire's *Candide*, and the conclusion is not very different from the famous *Il faut cultiver notre jardin*. [Edited by G. Birkbeck Hill, with introduction and notes, Clarendon Press, 1887; (Ariel Booklets), Putnam, New York; (New

JOHNSON, Dr. Samuel (*continued*).

Universal Lib.), Routledge (Dutton, New York), 1905 ; ed. by R. W. Chapman, Oxford Press, 1927. With introd. by G. K. Chesterton, *illus.* by D. Percy Bliss, Dent (Dutton, New York). *Facsimile Reprint of 1st edn.*, 2 vols., Stock, 1884 : o.p.]

JOHNSTON, Sir Harry (Hamilton) [1858–1927]. *The Gay-Dombeys.*　　1919

Traces, on a somewhat overcrowded stage, the fortunes of the descendants of Dickens' characters (in *Dombey and Son*) until the modern period (1914). [With preface by H. G. Wells, Chatto ; Macmillan, New York.]

—— *Mrs. Warren's Daughter : a story of the women's movement.*　　1920

Continues the life-story of Vivie (from *Mrs. Warren's Profession*) who becomes a militant suffragette and eventually marries a scientist. [Chatto ; Macmillan, New York.]

—— *The Man Who Did the Right Thing.*　　1921

The best thing in this book is the picture of life in East Africa in the last decade of the nineteenth century. [Chatto ; Macmillan, New York.]

—— *The Veneerings.*　　1922

Follows the lives of the principal characters in *Our Mutual Friend* from 1864 until 1907, through England, France, America, and South Africa. [Chatto ; Macmillan, New York.]

JOHNSTON, Henry [Scottish]. *Chronicles of Glenbuckie.*　　1889

A gallery of character-portraits and stories illustrating Scottish character : subjects, the elders of the kirk, the doctor, the minister, and the weavers and soutars of an Ayrshire village at the time of the Disruption ; village politics, Church doctrine, and courting. [Douglas, Edinburgh : o.p.]

—— *Kilmallie.*　　1891

Similar sketches of nature and humanity in a village in the west of Scotland. [Ward & Downey : o.p.]

—— *Dr. Congleton's Legacy : chronicles of North Country byways.*　　1896

The story unimportant, interest centring in the humours of the Scottish village, e.g. the schoolmaster, Saunders M'Phee. [Methuen : o.p. ; Scribner, New York : o.p.]

JOHNSTON, Mary [American ; b. 1876]. *Prisoners of Hope.*　　1898

A hot-coloured romance of Virginia (c. 1649–51), when the colony was seething with disaffection caused by the sending of rebels to the plantations. The hero, one of the convicts sold into this slavery, joins in a rising against the Government. His love for his master's daughter leads to a series of sensational events. Much description of the landscapes and the stately homes of Virginia, in the times of Sir William Berkeley. [Houghton, Boston ; *sub tit. The Old Dominion*, Butterworth.]

—— *To Have and to Hold.*　　1900

A beautiful maid-of-honour, ward of the king, escapes a libertine nobleman, the king's favourite, by fleeing to Virginia with the cargo of brides sent out by the Company (1621). She marries a rough, stanch settler, a famous swordsman, who defends his wife against the favourite, and they meet with strange adventures. Daringly and dazzlingly unreal, full of vigorous movement, characters boldly outlined, and polychromatic scenery. [Houghton, Boston ; *sub tit. By Order of the Company*, Butterworth.]

—— *Audrey.*　　1902

A very romantic story of Virginia (1727), the hero a rich proprietor and man of fashion ; the heroine, daughter of a backwoodsman, robbed of home and relatives by the Indians. [Houghton, Boston ; Butterworth.]

—— *Sir Mortimer.*　　1904

A romance of the Spanish Main, introducing Queen Elizabeth, Drake, Thomas Doughty, Sidney, the Countess of Pembroke, etc., and successfully attempting the euphuistic speech of the period just before the Armada. [Houghton, Boston : o.p. ; Butterworth.]

—— *Lewis Rand.*　　1908

Rand is the son of a tobacco-planter, in the days of Hamilton, Jefferson, and Aaron Burr, when animosities were keen between Republicans and Federalists (c. 1805), who by ability and egotism rises to distinction in the State, but becomes implicated in Burr's conspiracy, and in a fit of passion commits a murder. Strong in the intense style of character-drawing. [Houghton, Boston ; Butterworth.]

—— *The Long Roll.*　　1911

Like the last, this contains at least as much history as romance, and the account of the Valley Campaign and the opening chapters of the Civil War (1861–3) are extremely full and minute. Stonewall Jackson is drawn on a large scale as the hero, and there are many smaller portraits of his subordinates, the life of a particular regiment being vividly presented. [Houghton, Boston ; Butterworth.]

—— *Cease Firing.*　　1912

The American Civil War again (1862–5) : this and the preceding novel afford a wide general view and bring many famous personages to the front or back of the stage. The point of view is that of the South. [Houghton, Boston ; Butterworth.]

—— *Hagar.*　　1913

Deals with social questions and the position of women ; Hagar is the daughter of Virginian aristocrats, who emancipates herself and works for the enfranchisement of women. [Houghton, Boston ; Butterworth.]

—— *The Witch.*　　1914

A romantic novel of the last days of Elizabeth and the reign of James I ; a graphic picture of England at the time of the trials for witchcraft. [Houghton, Boston ; Butterworth.]

—— *The Fortunes of Garin.*　　1915

A romance of the Crusades and the land of the troubadours ; Richard Cœur de Lion and Saladin appear. [Houghton, Boston ; Butterworth].

—— *The Wanderers.*　　1917

A presentation, in nineteen episodes, of the gradual spread of culture and the emancipation of women, from primeval times until the French Revolution. [*Illus.* by Willy Pogány, Houghton, Boston ; Butterworth.]

JOHNSTON, Mary (*continued*). *The Laird of Glenfernie.* 1919
Adventures in Scotland, Paris, Rome, and Egypt, with a Jacobite hero who escapes after Culloden. [Butter-worth ; *sub tit. Foes*, Harper, New York : o.p.]

—— *Michael Forth.* 1919
Here the interest is chiefly religious questions and the social and commercial conditions prevailing in Virginia after the Civil War. [Little, Boston (1926) ; Butterworth.]

—— *Admiral of the Ocean Sea.* 1922
Columbus and his voyages, Ferdinand and Isabella of Spain (1490–1503). [Butterworth ; *sub tit.* " 1492," Little, Boston.]

—— *Croatan.* 1923
The voyage from Plymouth and the settlement in Croatan Island, off the coast of North Carolina, in Raleigh's time (1587). [Little, Boston ; Butterworth.]

—— *The Slave Ship.* 1924
More Jacobite adventures after Culloden, in Virginia, the west coast of Africa, and Jamaica, with a great deal about the slave trade and the Virginia plantations. [Little, Boston ; Butterworth.]

—— *The Great Valley.* 1926
The valley is that of the Shenandoah in Virginia, where a Scottish minister settles with his family (1735–60). Washington and Governor Dinwiddie make their appearance. [Little, Boston ; Butterworth.]

JOHNSTON, Richard Malcolm [" Philemon Perch " ; American ; 1822–98]. *Dukesborough Tales.* 1871

—— *Old Times in Middle Georgia.* 1897
Fifteen stories by an able Southern novelist, describing with considerable monotony of character and motive, but not without humour, the petty social bickerings and more virulent religious differences that coloured life in Georgia in the first half of the nineteenth century. Largely in a very grotesque and uncouth dialect. [(1), Appleton, New York : o.p. ; (2), Macmillan, New York : o.p.]

JOHNSTONE, Charles [c. 1719–c. 1800]. *Chrysal ; or, The Adventures of a Guinea.* 1760–5
Not a novel in the proper sense, but a disguised chronicle of contemporary events loosely strung together on the autobiography of a guinea as it passes from hand to hand. Johnstone's plan had been adopted already in the adventures of the halfpenny and the shilling in Richard Bathurst and Addison's stories in *The Adventurer* and *The Tatler.* The present edition gives a key to most of the characters, which include General Wolfe and Miss Lowther (afterwards Duchess of Bolton), the Countess of Yarmouth (mistress of George II), Frederick the Great, Ferdinand of Brunswick, Byng, Chatham, Whitefield, Sandwich, Henry Fox, Lord George Sackville, Charles Churchill, Bute, Sir Francis Dashwood, Wilkes, Bubb Dodington and the other members of the Hell-fire Club (for which this is the principal document), Dr. John Hill, the famous quack, Foote, and many other leading people. The most notorious episodes of contemporary history are dished up by Johnstone in a very prejudiced and scurrilous way ; but the book has many good points, such as its incisive portraiture, and throws light on public opinion at the time of its writing. An earlier novel of the same kind was *The History of Pompey the Little, or the Life and Adventures of a Lap-dog* (1751), and later there were *The Adventures of a Black Coat* (1760), *The Adventures of a Bank-note* (1770), *The Life and Adventures of a Cat* (1781), *The Adventures of A Rupee* (1782), *Memoirs of a Flea* (1785), etc. [*Chrysal*, edited with introduction by E. A. Baker (Library of Early Novelists), Routledge (Dutton, New York), 1907.]

JÓKAI, Mor [Maurus ; Hungarian ; 1825–1904]. *The Day of Wrath* (Szomorú Napok, c. 1850). 1900
A powerful, melodramatic picture of Hungarian life in the early half of the nineteenth century, crowded with lurid figures, some of them typical of a people of strong passions, some purely mythical creations. Scenes of startling force, such as the one where a man decapitates his wife, are characteristic of Jókai, whose romances are a blend of Scott and Dumas, with a Magyar infusion of violence and fantasy. [Transl. by R. Nisbet BAIN, Jarrold : o.p. ; McClure, New York : o.p.]

—— *The Lion of Janina ; or, The Last Days of the Janissaries* (1852). 1897
The Lion is the redoubtable Ali Pasha (d. 1822), and the book gives a spirited and gorgeous description of Turkish life, and of his stubborn and sanguinary resistance to the Turkish forces (1819). [Transl. by R. Nisbet BAIN, Jarrold : o.p. ; Harper, New York : o.p.]

—— *Timar's Two Worlds* (Az arany ember, " A Man of Gold "). 1888
A kind of Magyar *Monte Cristo*, though a thoroughly characteristic work ; wildly imaginative and almost impossible in characters and incidents, faithful in treatment of scenery and surroundings : the people delineated differ widely from Western types, their traits are Oriental and fantastic. The action takes place in Lower Hungary, on or near the Danube, and the passage of the Iron Gates is a memorable episode. [Transl. by Mrs. H. KENNARD, Blackwood : o.p.]

—— *'Midst the Wild Carpathians* (1852). 1894
A romance of the Golden Age of Transylvania and the struggle with the Turks (1662–6) ; very picturesque in its spectacle of semi-barbaric life and the scenery of mountain and forest. Deals with the elevation of Apafi, a country gentleman, to the throne, by a whim of the Sultan. [Transl. by R. Nisbet BAIN, Jarrold, 1897 : o.p. ; Page, Boston : o.p.]

—— *The Slaves of the Padishah : the Turks in Hungary* (1853). 1902
Sequel to *'Midst the Wild Carpathians*. Like the latter, centres in Michael Apafi, last independent prince of Transylvania ; and his Machiavellian minister, Michael Teleki, Csaky, Kucsuk, Feriz, Azrael, etc., reappear. A most exciting tale of a tumultuous period (1764–90), and, it is affirmed, not a bit exaggerated. [Transl. by R. Nisbet BAIN, Jarrold : o.p.]

—— *An Hungarian Nabob* (Egy magyar nábob, 1856). 1898
A richly coloured picture of aristocratic life (1822), just before the times of Széchenyi, full of vivid, bustling scenes, various native characters, and humorous and dramatic incidents. The central figure is a Hungarian

JÓKAI, Mor (*continued*).

potenate of vast estates, living amidst a crowd of retainers, wassailing companies, women, gamblers, fools, gipsies. The plot relates to the intrigues of his dissolute heir, and his marriage with a young girl which serves to baffle them. [Transl. by R. Nisbet BAIN, Jarrold : o.p. ; Doubleday, New York : o.p.]

—— *Halil the Pedlar : a tale of old Stamboul* (1854).   1901
The romanticized history of Halil Patrona, a poor huckster, who headed a rebellion, dethroned a Sultan, and became prime minister to his own nominee (1730). Halil, much idealized, yet a fine incarnation of Turkish character, is the central figure of a story full of colour and romance. [Transl. by R. Nisbet BAIN, Jarrold : o.p.]

—— *Debts of Honour.*   1900
Full of vigorous incident and abrupt changes from grave to gay, in spite of the gloomy theme—the annals of a family burdened with a curse that leads at last to a grim catastrophe. The national insurrection in Hungary (1848) comes in. [Transl. by A. B. YOLLAND, Jarrold : o.p. ; Doubleday, New York : o.p.]

—— *The Poor Plutocrats* (1860).   1899
A sensational story of the adventures and daring deeds of a brigand, " Fatia Negra," or the Black Mask, who plays two rôles, the other being that of a respectable baron. [Transl. by R. Nisbet BAIN, Jarrold : o.p. ; Doubleday, New York : o.p.]

—— *The New Landlord* (Az úi földesúr, 1862).   1868
The passive resistance of the Hungarians to the Austrian domination during the " Bach Era " (1849–59), when the Austrian premier Alexander von Bach was trying to Germanize Hungary, exhibited in the persons of a stubborn old gentleman whose estates are ruined, his imprisoned nephew, and the titular hero, who becomes at length a hot antagonist of the Government. [Transl. by Arthur J. PATTERSON, 2 vols., Macmillan : o.p.]

—— *The Baron's Sons* (A kösziü ember fiai, 1869).   1900
Condensed from *The Sins of the Stony-hearted Man*, a romance of the Hungarian revolution (1848) : romanticized history, full of thrilling deeds and perils that are semi-historical. The baron's widow, instead of carrying out his death-bed wishes, abets her sons in their revolt from Austria. [Transl. by P. F. BICKNELL, Macqueen : o.p. ; Page, Boston : o.p.]

—— *Black Diamonds* (Fekete gyémánlok, 1870).   1896
Another high-pitched story of love and picturesque incident ; life among the wild miners of Bondavar, and social and commercial life in Budapest. Ivan is a faultless hero, of surpassing virtues and accomplishments. The translation is largely abridged. [Transl. by Francis A. GERARD, Jarrold : o.p. ; Harper, New York.]

—— *Pretty Michal* (1876).   1892
A grim and sinister narrative of extraordinary incidents said to be founded on fact ; both exciting and pathetic. Scene, Kassa, in northern Hungary, when the Turks were barbarously oppressing the Magyars (*c.* 1650). [Transl. by R. Nisbet BAIN, Jarrold : o.p. ; Doubleday, New York : o.p.]

—— *The Nameless Castle* (1877).   1898
A romance of French and Magyar : how a daughter of Marie Antionette sought an asylum in a Hungarian stronghold, and how Napoleon's emissaries gave chase (*c.* 1804–9). [Transl. by S. E. BOGGS, Doubleday, New York (Jarrold, 1899) : o.p.]

—— *Manasseh : a story of the stirring days of '48* (1878).   1901
Life among a primitive people hidden away in far Transylvania (1848–59). The opening scenes are laid in Rome, and the view of the corrupt society there forms a striking contrast to the pastoral simplicity and savage warfare that succeed. Somewhat abridged. [Transl. by P. F. BICKNELL, Macqueen : o.p. ; Scott, 1908 : o.p. ; Page, Boston : o.p.]

—— *The Green Book ; freedom under the snow* (1879).   1897
The story of a Nihilist conspiracy against Alexander I of Russia (1825). Depicts realistically and with strong individual characterization the various classes of the Russian people, the stormy politics and seething discontent. Court intrigue affords some scenes of comedy. [Transl. by Mrs. WAUGH, Jarrold : o.p. ; Harper, New York.]

—— *The Strange Story of Rab Ráby* (1879).   1909
A sound historical study of Hungarian life and politics under Joseph II (1780–90). Ráby, with the emperor's countenance, tries to introduce a reform scheme which would liberate the people from the tyranny and corruption of the ruling classes, who invoke the Hungarian constitution, and by fair means and foul strive to checkmate and even assassinate him. [Jarrold : o.p.]

—— *The Tower of Dago* (extracted from *Targallyak*, 1882).   1899
A gory yet impressive melodrama of fraternal hatred and revenge. [Sands : o.p.]

—— *Told by the Death's Head : a romantic tale.*   1903
A ghoulish fantasy. The skull of a malefactor relates all his crimes and experiences. An excellent picture of the times (1688) by virtue of the wealth of minute learning poured out. [Transl. by S. E. BOGGS, De La More Press (Saalfield, Akron, O.) : o.p.]

—— *Eyes Like the Sea* (A tengerszemü hölgy, 1890).   1893
The author's own romantic history : he tells the story of his life as a boy and his later experiences. Gives broad views of the political movements in Hungary during the last two generations. The heroine is a fascinating figure. [Transl. by R. Nisbet BAIN, Lawrence & Bullen : o.p.]

—— *Dr. Dumány's Wife* (1891).   1891
History of the strange marriage of Dr. Dumány, the Silver King : deals with political life. Opens with a powerful description of a railway accident on the St. Gothard. [Transl. by F. STEINITZ, repr. of 1st ed. (Cassell, New York, 1891), *sub tit. There is no Devil*, Jarrold : o.p. ; Doubleday, New York : o.p.]

—— *A Christian but a Roman.*   1900
A romance of the early Christians in the time of the Emperor Carinus, with whose murder and the accession of Diocletian the story ends. Scene, Rome and its vicinity, 283–5. [Doubleday, New York : o.p.]

JÓKAI, Mor (*continued*). *Tales from Jókai.*   1904
Characteristically trenchant, fantastic, and grim. *The Bad Old Times* gives a terrible idea of the times of the Tartar invasion. *The Red Starosta* is a grisly story of an inherited curse. [Transl. by R. Nisbet BAIN, Jarrold : o.p.]

JONES, Mrs. E. Brandram. *In Burleigh's Days.*   1916
History and character-drawing of historical personages, such as Shakespeare, Bacon, Burleigh, James I, and Sir Thomas Overbury (1588–1612). Sequel, *The Second Cecil,* (1917). [(1) and (2), Lang : o.p.]

—— *The Friar's Niece.*   1930
A romance of the Barons' wars, woven round the figure of Roger Bacon. [Heath.]

JONES, Emily Beatrix Coursolles [Mrs. F. L. Lucas ; *b.* 1893]. *Quiet Interior.*   1920
A quiet story that is truly concerned with the inner world of thought and feeling. Its heroine learns by the renunciation of one with whom she might have been happy—but only at her sister's cost—that she has really found happiness, since she has put herself in harmony with reality. The other characters are adequate and lifelike. [Cobden-Sanderson : o.p.]

JONES, Margam [Welsh]. *The Stars of the Revival.*   1910
A sympathetic and revealing study of the religious spirit in Wales early last century. [Long : o.p.]

JÓSIKA, Baron Miklós [Hungarian ; 1796–1865]. *'Neath the Hoof of the Tartar* (Abafi, 1836). 1905
By Jókai's precursor in Magyar romance, who wrote some sixty novels. Commemorates, in Scott's style, the stirring period when Hungary was overrun by hordes of Mongols under Batu Khan (*c.* 1340). [Transl. by R. Nisbet BAIN, Jarrold : o.p.]

JOYCE, James [Irish ; *b.* 1882]. *Dubliners.*   1914
Here we see the realist trying his hand in a series of sketches—studies for a picture, but not the picture itself. There is nothing exciting in these stories ; there are a few dramatic moments, with the drama undeveloped. Half-tones of shade and colour make all the contrasts. Close observation, especially of faces and peculiarities of manner, and a penchant for the ugly and repulsive, are obvious traits. The characters are, at first, children, especially of the poorer classes in Dublin, then loafers, bar-crawlers, servant-girls, small clerks, etc. Neither sympathy nor satire appears ; the writer is impassive. [Cape ; Viking Press, New York ; Modern Lib., New York.]

—— *A Portrait of the Artist as a Young Man.*   1916
Apparently written (1904–1914) as a prelude to *Ulysses,* and as evidently autobiographical ; the childhood, boyhood, and young manhood of the writer seen by fitful but intense flashes. A succession of moods, conflicts with himself or with others, and, above all, conversations. There is here much in common with the " Expressionism " of Miss Richardson and D. H. Lawrence. Stephen Daedalus is shown at home, then at Clongowes, the Jesuit college, afterwards at Belvedere, and lastly at the University in Dublin. The story is formless ; the dialogue, ragged scraps of sentences spat out by incoherent boys and youths, with an unholy gusto for blasphemy and stinks ; many things are disgusting. But there is a strange power in certain scenes. The account of Stephen's spiritual conflicts and of the spell cast upon him by the Jesuits may well be compared with the story of a seminarist, *L'empreinte,* by Edouard Estaunié. [Cape ; Viking Press, New York ; Modern Lib., New York.]

—— *Ulysses.*   1926
An attempt to revolutionize the art of fiction, as evolved by Fielding and his predecessors and developed since. Towards this the two preceding books were experimental studies. The novel has become sophisticated, and offers a distorted and inadequate image of life, chiefly through its omissions. Joyce therefore undertakes to put everything in, and to cram the whole heterogeneous life of a big city, Dublin, into the record of one day. An immense crowd, almost all the individuals in which can be identified by Dubliners, come into one scene or another ; but the eye is focused upon two men, and now and then one woman, who are subjected to the " Expressionist " process : Stephen Daedalus, now emancipated from Clongowes and Belvedere, Mr. Bloom the advertising-agent, and his wife. Mr. Joyce is determined to unveil the background of consciousness, the irrational forces that determine behaviour, the double life that we all lead. This conflict between inner and outer is symbolized in Bloom and Stephen, the astute, easy-going, sensual nature and the self-conscious, educated, imaginative product of age-old culture. There is also an allegory. Erudite admirers delight in tracing the buried but exact correspondence to the successive episodes of the *Odyssey.* Bloom is Ulysses, Stephen Telemachus, Mrs. Bloom Penelope. No realism of the dirty corner and no wildest imaginative flights daunt Mr. Joyce, who soars from unmentionable places and scenes of the foulest debauchery on such apocalyptic fantasies as the Walpurgis Night in the brothel, and whose uproarious humour and gigantic grotesquerie need fear no competition except from Rabelais, who, by the way, indulged in similar flights of " Dadaism." His book is difficult, through sheer learning and allusiveness, and requires a commentary (e.g. *James Joyce's Ulysses : a study,* by Stuart Gilbert, 1930, Faber). He not only has a marvellous style of his own, but is a master of all styles, and gives a burlesque example of every one from the Bible to the *Daily Mail.* Critics and every serious student of the history of art will always have to read *Ulysses* ; but it is very properly banned to those who would extract and wallow in the filth ; and, though an experiment worth making, it must be described as a colossal mistake, a magnificent and perhaps epoch-making failure.

JOYCE, Patrick Weston [Irish ; 1827–1914] [ed.]. *Old Celtic Romances ; translated from the Gaelic.*
                                                                    (2nd and enlarged edition) 1894
A dozen carefully selected tales, chiefly from the ancient prose literature. *The Fate of the Children of Lir* and *The Fate of the Children of Turenn* are from *The Three Tragic Stories of Erin.* Lir's children were changed into four white swans by a step-mother's enchantments. The sons of Turenn involve themselves in an Odyssey of woes for the murder of a kinsman under the shape of a pig. *The Voyage of Maildun* is well-known in Tennyson's version, which, however, is not much like the original. It is the oldest of the mythical voyages (cf. Brendan), written down in the ninth century, some of the incidents from the Æneid. The wonders met with in this voyage on the ocean of romance exceed those described by Homer—the Isle of Red-hot Animals, the Miller of Hell, a lonely country beneath the waves, an island standing on one pillar, etc.

JOYCE, Patrick Weston (*continued*).

The next three, *The Fairy Palace of the Quicken Trees*, a story of the enchantment of Finn and his deliverance by the hero Dermat O'Dyna, the humorous wonder-story of *The Pursuit of the Gilla Dacker*, and the romantic story of Finn's tyranny and Dermat's chivalry in *The Pursuit of Dermat and Grania*, supplemented by some shorter pieces, belong to the great Fenian cycle, concerning Finn, Oscar, Oisin, Dermat, etc,., The stories are not given in their entirety, nor with the literalness required by philologists ; but are suitable for popular reading. Notes and list of proper names. [Longmans, London and New York ; Talbot Press, Dublin.]

JUAN MANUEL, Infante Don [Spanish ; 1282–1347]. *Count Lucanor* (El Conde Lucanor, 1575). 1868

Otherwise called *The Book of Patronio* (El Libro de Patronio) and *The Book of Examples* ; the Spanish *Decameron* or *Arabian Nights*, written 1328–35. Fifty-one stories of various origins—Æsopian, Oriental, and mediæval —related by Patronio the councillor to his patron Count Lucanor. They are mostly adapted to the manners and superstitions of Spain, and to the national taste for moralizing. Juan Manuel was the second great prose writer of Spain, and in his Castilian prose he forged a weapon of admirable force and temper. " The honour of being the forerunner of the real modern short story must be awarded to the Spanish prince " (Martin Hume). [Transl. by J. YORK, *illus.* by L. S. Wood (Broadway Transl.), Routledge (Dutton, New York), 1924.]

JUDD, Sylvester [American ; 1813–53]. *Margaret : a tale of the real and the ideal, of blight and bloom.* 1845

An inchoate, improbable book, that is of some importance in the history of American fiction, and possesses individuality. The life of a Massachusetts village early in the century, the religious worship, rustic festivals, the prevailing intemperance, and the manners of the time, are depicted with great realism. The religious and social movements which were in the air are interpreted with the bias of a Unitarian, who was also an advocate of peace and of temperance, and strongly opposed to slavery and capital punishment. Mixed up with the sad story are rhapsodical descriptions of nature in the fields and the woodlands, full of thought and deep feeling. [Roberts, Boston : o.p. ; Ward & Lock : o.p.]

KAFKA, Franz [German-Czech ; 1883–1925]. *The Castle* (Das Schloss, 1930). 1930

One of the three unfinished novels which the author left behind him. An allegory broadly resembling *The Pilgrim's Progress*, but much more philosophical in the character of the pilgrim's arduous progress towards salvation. The reader who masters the intellectual enigmas will have some reward in the comic scenes. [Transl. by Willa and Edwin MUIR, Secker ; Knopf, New York.]

KAGAWA, Rev. Tokohiko [Japanese ; b. 1888]. *Before the Dawn* (Shisen Wo Koete). 1924

An account of life in the slums of Tokyo, written by the secretary of the Japanese Labour Federation. [Transl. by I. FUKANOTO and T. SATCHELL, Chatto ; Doubleday, Doran, New York.]

KALLAS, Madame Aino [*née* Krohn ; Finnish]. *The White Ship : Esthonian tales* (1923). 1924

Simple, powerful stories, often suffused with the beauty and pathos of suffering, depicting Esthonian peasant characters of the middle of the last century, mainly downtrodden, and under the yoke of slavery. The authoress (whose husband is an Esthonian) says : " The majority are the outcome of the spirit of opposition awakened in one coming from the comparative freedom of Finland by the feudal atmosphere that until recently prevailed in Esthonia. Few only of the stories are entirely imaginative." Two deal with punitive measures taken against the peasants after the revolt of 1905. [Transl. by Alex MATSON, Cape, London and New York.]

—— *Eros the Slayer : two Esthonian tales.* 1927

Barbara von Tisenhusen is a story of Esthonia in the sixteenth century ; the second, *The Rector of Reigi*, tells of a man's fortitude under tragic misfortune. [Transl. by Alex MATSON, Cape, London and New York.]

—— *The Wolf's Bride : a tale from Esthonia.* 1930

The wife of a forester in Esthonia is changed into a werwolf, hunts cattle and sheep at night and keeps house by day, till her husband discovers her secret and she is burned to death by the villagers. The story, which is told with a rare simplicity and beauty, won the Finnish State Prize for Literature (1928). [Transl. by Alex MATSON and Bryan RHYS, Cape.]

KALLINIKOV, Josif [Russian ; b. 1890]. *Women and Monks.* 1930

A rambling novel of portentous length, and devoid of every artistic merit save vivid description, which seems to have been written to expose the profligacy of Russian monks. From 1905 to the revolution of 1917, the monastery to which the two principal scoundrels, or anti-heroes, belong shelters the morals of a brothel : then the Bolshevists arrive. [Transl. by Patrick KIRWAN, Secker ; Harcourt, New York.]

KARAMZIN, Nikolai Mikhailovich [Russian ; 1766–1826]. *Russian Tales by Karamsin.* 1803

—— *Tales from the Russian of Karamsin.* 1804

Karamzin's sentimental stories are chiefly memorable for the wild popularity excited by one of them, *Poor Liza* (1792), a harrowing story of seduction. The pond where she drowned herself in the Simony Monastery, was once a favourite pilgrimage. Karamzin wrote a well-known *History of Russia*. [(1) Transl. by J. B. ELRINGTON : o.p. ; (2) transl. by A. A. FELDBORG : o.p.]

KATAEV, Valentin [Russian ; b. 1897]. *The Embezzlers.* 1929

Drunkenness and peculation, and the silliness of the herd, furnish sustained comedy, with only one or two strokes of sadness, in this mocking picture of the underworld of pleasure-seekers in Russia. [Transl. by L. ZARINE ; with introd. by Stephen Graham, Benn ; Dial Press, New York.]

KAUFFMAN, Reginald Wright [American ; b. 1877]. *Daughters of Ishmael.* 1911

A novel written to expose the horrible realities of prostitution and the white slave traffic in New York, and incidentally showing up the wholesale corruption of the police and the Government officials who profit by the ghastly business. Rigorously based on facts, and related with as little offensiveness as the nature of the subject permits. [With pref. by John Masefield, Laurie.]

KAUFFMAN, Reginald Wright (*continued*). *Broken Pitchers.*   1912
Sixteen short sketches on the same subject, and in the same manner, as *Daughters of Ishmael*. [Laurie:
o.p.]

KAVANAGH, Julia [Irish ; 1824–77]. *Madeleine : a tale of Auvergne.*   1848
A love-story, rich in pictures of places and manners in Auvergne (1804), unfortunate and pathetic in its issue :
the disappointed Madeleine devotes her life to founding and fostering an orphanage. [Ward & Lock,
o.p. ; Kilner, Philadelphia.]

—— *Nathalie.*   1850
Scene, Normandy ; the country life and characters sketched from memories of a youth spent there. Nathalie
is a sprightly and impulsive Provençal, whose errors of tact and judgment bring on herself many troubles ;
the old Canoness is a fine old native type. A tender, sentimental story, thoroughly naturalized as a
delineation of French character. [Hurst & Blackett : o.p. ; Appleton, New York : o.p.]

—— *Adèle.*   1857
An idyllic picture of happy life in an old château, with affectionate and truthful drawing of French life and
manners ; the sunny-natured and high-born heroine in the sequel marries an Englishman. [Hurst &
Blackett, o.p. ; Appleton, New York : o.p.]

—— *Silvia.*   1870
To set before us the character and fortunes of this pretty Italian is the main object of the novel, which contains
pictures of scenery and country life in Italy and France, and character-sketching of French people and
English living abroad. Silvia is a wilful girl, loyal and true, ignorant but gifted, and a winning character.
Her love affairs with an English engineer, and his melodramatic vendetta with a rascally innkeeper, are
the chief materials of the romance. [Appleton, New York : o.p.]

—— *Two Lilies.*   1877
A pair of beautiful girls, intrinsically unlike in character, one of whom, after the proverbial troubles, is married
to the hero, who has had love passages with both. Character-sketches of English people in Normandy,
and some farcical pages, with descriptions of a picturesque Norman town. [Blackett, o.p. ; Appleton,
New York : o.p.]

—— *Forget-me-nots.*   1878
Compact little tales of quiet French life, sketches of girls, etc., mostly happy and peaceful in motive, but touched
now and again with pathos, e.g. the peasant idyll, *By the Well*, a complete romance in miniature, the
thoroughly native *Story of Monique, Mimi's Sin*, and other Norman stories. [3 vols., Bentley : o.p.]

KAYE, Michael W. *The Duke's Vengeance.*   1910
—— *The Cardinal's Past.*   1910
—— *For Braganza.*   1911
Romances of foreign history, first dealing with Louis XI and Charles the Bold (1471), the second with a plot
against Richelieu (1626), and the third with Portugal under Spanish domination in the seventeenth century.
[(1), (2), and (3), Greening : o.p.]

—— *The King's Indiscretion.*   1920
An exciting historical novel about the Broglie affair under Louis XV (1764), when a mad scheme was hatched
for invading England under a flag of truce. Choiseul and the Chevalier d'Eon are among the personages.
[S. Paul : o.p.]

KAYE-SMITH, Sheila [Mrs. Theodore Penrose Fry]. *The Tramping Methodist.*   1908
—— *Starbrace.*   1909
Historical novels of Kent and Sussex, the first giving an inspiring idea of a vagabond preacher about 1799,
and the other concerned with Rye and the neighbourhood at a period fifty years earlier. [(1) and (2),
Cassell ; Dutton, New York ; McClelland, Toronto.]

—— *Isle of Thorns.*   1913
The heroine is an unconventional girl who goes vagabonding through Sussex, to learn that " the road of excess
leads to the palace of Wisdom." [Cassell ; Dutton, New York ; McClelland, Toronto.]

—— *Three against the World.*   1914
The general theme is the break-up of a Sussex family, by death, imprisonment, and unhappy love. The story
of the two brothers and a sister is amusing and affecting ; but as usual the rural background is the thing
in this novel. [Chapman ; *sub tit. Three Furlongers*, Lippincott, Philadelphia : o.p.]

—— *Sussex Gorse : the story of a fight.*   1916
A Sussex *Mayor of Casterbridge*, without the catastrophe that engulfs Henchard or his tragic grandeur. The
son of a farmer, in the days of the enclosures, vows that he will buy and reclaim the furze-covered moor
of Boarzell, and bit by bit succeeds, but at the expense of his own soul and of the degradation of his children
and his two wives. It is the history of a monomaniac, and has a sound realistic background. [Nisbet ;
Cassell ; Knopf, New York ; McClelland, Toronto.]

—— *The Challenge to Sirius.*   1917
A long novel handling character and love-motives in the author's usual way, with the Isle of Oxney as back-
ground, and a man's experiences with the Confederates in the American Civil War as an excursion.
[Nisbet ; Cassell ; Dutton, New York ; McClelland, Toronto.]

—— *Little England.*   1918
A Sussex village disturbed and lacerated by the war, yet still going on steadily, as it has done for countless
generations. [Nisbet ; Cassell ; McClelland, Toronto ; *sub tit. The Four Roads*, Doubleday, Doran,
New York.]

—— *Tamarisk Town.*   1919
The man who " made " Marlingate will not give up Marlingate for the woman he loves. But she kills herself,
and after that he revenges himself on the rival to Brighton which he created, and the place degenerates
into a vulgar tripper-resort. [Cassell ; Dutton, New York ; McClelland, Toronto.]

KAYE-SMITH, Sheila (*continued*). *Green Apple Harvest.* 1920

Undertakes, but hardly succeeds, to show how a hot-blooded young rustic was converted from his drinking and wenching by the Calvinist Pope of Goudhurst. The landscape-painting is, however, well done, and the realism is thorough in the detail—one learns quite a lot about mixed farming in this and *Sussex Gorse.* [Cassell ; Dutton, New York ; McClelland, Toronto.]

—— *Joanna Godden.* 1921

Joanna inherits the paternal farm, and being independent and self-willed runs it herself. This is the story of her business success and her less prosperous love-affairs, the marsh country round Romney and Rye providing the background. [Cassell ; Dutton, New York ; McClelland, Toronto.]

—— *The End of the House of Alard.* 1923

The Alards are a county family who have held their land since the early sixteenth century, and now in the war period are plunged into the struggle to keep it. Now is the heyday of the small farmer. Sir John's children come to see the folly of trying to keep up appearances ; the elder sons die, and the youngest prefers to enter a monastery to striving to maintain the family tradition. [Cassell ; Dutton, New York ; Grosset, New York ; McClelland, Toronto.]

—— *Iron and Smoke.* 1928

The story of Isabel, a wealthy ironmaster's daughter, and her marriage to an impoverished squire who weds her for her dowry, is dominated by the conflict between the tradition of agriculture and the desire to make money by industry. [Cassell ; Dutton, New York.]

—— *Shepherds in Sackcloth.* 1930

The old Kentish parson and his wife, and the Methodist preacher with his unhappy love affairs, are humanly drawn ; but there is more about Anglo-Catholic Church disputes than is wanted in a novel. [Cassell ; Harper, New York.]

KEARY, Annie Maria [Irish ; 1825–79]. *Janet's Home.* 1863

An uneventful story of home life, its joys and sorrows, daily hopes and cares ; with delicate drawing of average characters in the family of a poor tutor who married a well-born girl. [Macmillan : o.p.]

—— *Oldbury.* 1869

Resembles *Cranford* in its delineation of character and manners in a small country town. An Evangelical clergyman, amiable, but narrow-minded and lacking in moral fibre, is domineered over by the female leader of the serious party in Oldbury, is tried by the loss of his wife, and finds his religion not adequate as a source of comfort ; Mrs. Cutwidge, an egotistic woman who believes herself an agent of Providence, and the quaint, tender-hearted old lady Mrs. Berry, are the other chief persons. The plot deals with the troubles of an innocent family, one of whose members is a convict, and the pathos of a girl's love when she fears the shame that will take her lover from her. [Macmillan : o.p.]

—— *Castle Daly.* 1875

Irish life at the time of the famine and the Smith O'Brien insurrection. The plot deals with many romantic and tragic vicissitudes, and furnishes views of the starving peasantry and their squalid but contented existence, and of the landowning classes. The Dalys are half English. Mr. Daly, who is shot in mistake for an agent, is beloved of his tenantry ; one son joins in the rising, another, educated at Eton and prejudiced in favour of England, is ultimately converted to Home Rule. The author is studiously impartial. There are other English and Irish types (the nationalist O'Donnell being probably a portrait), also descriptions of scenery in Galway and Connemara. [Macmillan : o.p. ; Winston, New York : o.p.]

—— *A York and Lancaster Rose.* 1876

Contrasting characters of two girls. [Macmillan : o.p.]

—— *A Doubting Heart.* 1879

A fine novel left unfinished, and completed by Mrs. MacQuoid. [Macmillan : o.p.]

KEARY, Charles Francis [1848–1917]. *A Mariage de Convenance.* 1890

Two characters, an abnormally selfish man and a devoted woman, and their melancholy story developed in letters. [Unwin : o.p.]

—— *The Journalist.* 1898

Realism of a very thoroughgoing and laborious sort, the life and ideas of a young journalist who comes under the influence of Ibsenism. [Methuen : o.p.]

—— *High Policy.* 1902

The same method—realistic reporting—applied to political society in England thirty or more years back. A clever young M.P., with fine ideas but very little backbone, makes a beautiful Irish girl his Egeria, and all but succeeds in corrupting her to the standards of the degenerate, self-indulgent world he is mixed up with. [Unwin : o.p.]

—— *Bloomsbury.* 1905

A study of culture and socialism in Bloomsbury ; crowded with characters, several of them strikingly drawn. [Nutt : o.p.]

KEATING, Joseph [Irish by birth ; *b.* 1871]. *Son of Judith : a tale of the Welsh mining valleys.* 1901

A melodramatic tale of hatred and long-cherished revenge. A betrayed mother devotes her life to the training of her boy, whom she destines to be his father's murderer. Culminates in a ghastly scene. [G. Allen : o.p.]

KEATS, Miss Gwendoline [" Zack " ; *d.* 1910]. *Life is Life ; and other tales and episodes.* 1898

Life is Life is a longish story of Australian life, rising by a climax of calamity to heights of pathos. A lawless and passionate scoundrel, who wrecks the lives of wife and son and dies impenitent, is the most powerful figure, while a humble old woman, by her kindness and endurance and her pithy sayings, expounds the thought that " life is life." The other stories deal with Australian, German, Italian, and Devon folk, the last speaking in broad dialect. [Blackwood : o.p. ; Scribner, New York : o.p.]

—— *On Trial.* 1899

A study in primitive ethics. A country girl commits a felony for the sake of a weak lover, who makes her life

KEATS, Miss Gwendoline (*continued*).

a wreck and is too cowardly to stand by her, though miserably conscious of his degradation. The Devonshire dialect gives point to the humorous sayings of the country folk. [Blackwood : o.p. ; Scribner, New York : o.p.]

—— *The White Cottage.* 1901

The man who engages the reader's sympathies, though by no means a hero, is robbed of the woman he loves by a village libertine, whom he subsequently convicts of bigamy. Most of the characters are fisher-folk, who are subjected to drastic analysis. [Constable : o.p. ; Scribner, New York : o.p.]

—— *Tales of Dunstable Weir.* 1901

Seven tales told in dialect by a Devonshire labourer. Not unrelieved by humour, they are chiefly melancholy. Primitive character and primitive passions are delineated, with no intrusion of plot or of irrelevant problems, e.g. *Benjamin Parrot's Fancy* and *Mary Amelia Spot.* [Methuen : o.p. ; Scribner, New York : o.p.]

—— *The Roman Road.* 1903

Roland, inheriting " Groot "—the wherewithal to pay his debts—learns he is illegitimate ; shall he keep silence, or deliver the property to the rightful heir ? The foolish, guilty soul of the mother is, however, the chief object of the reader's interest. *The Balance* is a drama of three souls—a debauched novelist, a moral wreck ; his loyal friend ; and a girl both love. *The Thoughty Ones* is a story of children. There is in all three tales a parsimony of phrase, of description, of narrative, that demands hard thinking. They have the abstract, riddling manner of the apologue. [Constable : o.p. ; Scribner, New York : o.p.]

KEIGHTLEY, Sir Samuel Robert [Irish ; *b.* 1859]. *The Crimson Sign.* [juvenile] 1894

Adventures before and after the siege of Derry (1689–90). [Hutchinson : o.p. ; Harper, New York : o.p.]

—— *The Cavaliers.* [juvenile] 1895

Cromwell and Charles ; the latter's captivity at Carisbrooke (1644–8). [Hutchinson : o.p. ; Harper, New York : o.p.]

—— *The Silver Cross.* [juvenile] 1898

Mazarin, Mme de Chevreuse, and others, figure in a romance in the manner of Dumas. [Hutchinson : o.p.]

—— *The Pikemen : a romance of the Ards of Down.* [juvenile] 1903

The Presbyterian " United Men," and the events that led up to their abortive rising (1798). Good character of a spy. Scoto-Irish dialect ; Nationalist bias. [Hutchinson : o.p.]

KEITH, Edward. *The Keeper of the Rede.* 1929

A deserving attempt to preserve the Redesdale dialect, in a spirited novel of Border life in Northumberland in the fifteenth century. [Reid & Co., Newcastle-upon-Tyne.]

KELLERMANN, Bernard [German ; *b.* 1879]. *The Sea* (Das Meer, 1911). 1925

A grim and realistic portrayal of the lives of Breton fisher folk. [Transl. by Sasha Best, Cape.]

—— *The Tunnel* (Der Tunnel, 1913). 1915

A scientific romance rather reminiscent of Jules Verne—the projection and construction of a great Transatlantic tunnel. [Macauley Co., New York.]

—— *The Ninth of November* (Der 9te November, 1920). 1925

An indictment of war ; the moral and material upheaval in Berlin society is graphically portrayed. [Transl. by Caroline V. Kerr, Cape ; McBride, New York.]

KENNEDY, Bart [1861–1930]. *A Man Adrift : being leaves from a nomad's portfolio.* 1899

The autobiography of a poor man, who goes across the Atlantic, through the States to Klondike and back ; working his way as seaman, oyster-fisher, navvy, gold-digger ; often in peril, sometimes in prison, always at odds with organized society, and fighting hard and incessantly for subsistence. [Greening : o.p. ; Stone, Chicago : o.p.]

—— *A Sailor Tramp.* 1902

Vivid sketches of vagabond life at sea, in Texas, etc. [Richards : o.p.]

—— *Slavery : pictures from the depths.* 1905

A vivid description, largely autobiographical, of the life of the poor in Manchester—as seen through the eyes of a boy as he grows to manhood, by way of the workhouse, cotton-mills, and similar employments. [Treherne : o.p.]

—— *In a Tramp Camp.* 1906
—— *The Vicissitudes of Flynn.* 1909

Similar chronicles of the struggle for life among the disinherited of the earth, drawn from a chequered personal experience, and rich in the sayings and thinkings and doings of the elemental man. Mr. Kennedy was a more " literary " Supertramp. [(1) Cassell : o.p. ; (2), Nash : o.p.]

KENNEDY, John Pendleton [" Sol. Second Thoughts " ; American ; 1795–1870]. *Swallow Barn : or, A sojourn in the Old Dominion.* 1832

Attractive pictures of rural Virginia in the early years of the century—quiet description of old-fashioned, genial society, of hearty and hospitable people, and a phase of happy life that was soon to pass away. [Harcourt, New York, 1929.]

—— *Horseshoe Robinson : a tale of Tory ascendency in 1780.* 1835

A strongly local story of South Carolina during the War of Independence (1757–80), founded on personal memories of actual events, and portraying historical people. [Putnam, New York : o.p. ; Burt, New York, 1928.]

KENNEDY, Margaret [Mrs. B. Davis ; *b.* 1896]. *The Constant Nymph.* 1924

The eternal feud between order, civilization, tameness, and the freedom of the artistic temperament, is typified in the unstable marriage of a pattern young lady, daughter of an Oxford don, and the composer Lewis Dodd, who is as brutal and titanic as Emily Brontë's Heathcliff. An unforgettable family group is Sanger's Circus, the women and children, legitimate and illegitimate, of a disorderly musical genius, one of whose daughters plays the part of Cathie to Dodd's Heathcliff. [Heinemann ; Doubleday, New York.]

KENNEDY, Margaret (*continued*). *Red Sky at Morning.* 1927
The fortunes of twin children of an eccentric poet, who is accused of murder. Their gaiety and brilliance in London society is overshadowed by the prospects of such a heritage. [Heinemann ; Doubleday, New York.]

—— *The Fool of the Family.* 1930
The fool of the Sanger family is the ineffectual Caryl, whose unhappy rivalry in love with his brother, the musical genius Sebastian, is the main concern of a story as swift and as crowded with incident and change of scenery as *The Constant Nymph.* [Heinemann ; Doubleday, New York.]

KENNEDY, Patrick [" Harry Whitney " ; Irish ; 1801–73]. *The Banks of the Boro : a chronicle of the County of Wexford.* 1867
A country tale by the well-known student of Irish mythology and antiquities, embodying a mass of local tales, ballads, and legends, illustrating in picturesque variety the home life, the customs and traditions, and the mercurial temperament of the peasant. [M'Glashan & Gill, Dublin, 1875 : o.p.]

KENNEDY, Sara Beaumont [*née* Cannon ; American]. *Joscelyn Cheshire.* 1901
Adventures in North Carolina during the War of Independence ; gallant deeds of high-spirited dames as well as of brave men. Principal scene, Hillsboro, where the Americans under Greene and the British under Cornwallis were successively quartered. [Doubleday, New York : o.p.]

—— *The Wooing of Judith.* 1902
A love-tale of Virginia, at the time when it was the refuge of the Cavaliers, after the king's execution (1649–51). Historical in setting, not in plot. [Doubleday, New York : o.p. ; Hodder : o.p.]

—— *Cicily : a tale of the Georgia March.* 1911
A love-story with the Civil War as background—a living picture of Atlanta and the South during the last phases of the struggle, November, 1864, to April, 1865. [Doubleday, New York : o.p. ; Hodder : o.p.]

KESTER, Vaughan [American ; 1869–1911]. *John o' Jamestown.* 1907
Supposed to be related by the hero of the story, a friend of Capt. John Smith. A romance of the founding of Jamestown and the first settlements in Virginia. [Bobbs-Merrill, Indianapolis.]

—— *The Prodigal Judge.* 1911
The South in the early part of the nineteenth century, the plots for a slave insurrection, and a fine study in Judge Slocum Price. [Bobbs-Merrill, Indianapolis ; Methuen : o.p.]

KETTLE, Rosa Mackenzie. *The Mistress of Langdale Hall.* 1872
A domestic story of life in the West Riding on the fringe of the manufacturing district. Several characters hold managers' and other positions in mills. A daughter's estrangement from her parents by cleaving to an eccentric and imperious relative, with whom they are at feud, is the motive, which leads to some emotional scenes. [Unwin : o.p.]

KICKHAM, Charles Joseph [Irish ; 1826–82]. *Sally Cavanagh ; or, The Untenanted Graves.* 1869
Kickham was a Fenian journalist, who in 1865 was sentenced to fourteen years' penal servitude for treason-felony. His novels are strongly Nationalist, " the work of a man of warm, tender, homely heart—a man born and bred one of the people about whom he writes " (Rev. S. J. Brown, s.j.). A simple love-tale of people belonging to the class of small farmers ; the tragedy a consequence of landlordism and emigration. Written in prison. [Duffy, Dublin : o.p.]

—— *Knockagow ; or, The Homes of Tipperary.* 1879
A novel unreservedly praised by Irish critics. A series of living pictures of the different inhabitants and the changing phases of existence in a Tipperary village, rich in first-hand observation of the most sympathetic and keen-eyed sort. [Duffy, Dublin : o.p.]

—— *For the Old Land : a tale of twenty years ago.* 1886
Another love-story of the same good brand, pathetic in its sympathy with the peasant's love of home and the pangs of emigration, with a lighter side in the comic pictures of bailiffs and police and the fine old humorist Rody Flynn. [Gill, Dublin : o.p.]

KIELLAND, Alexander Lange [Norwegian ; 1849–1906]. *Garman and Worse* (Garman og Worse, 1880). 1884
Life and character in a little western seaport town in Norway (no doubt, his native Stavanger) graphically depicted by one who had himself sprung from the well-to-do shipowning families, into whose home circle we are introduced. All the people of the township are portrayed with obvious familiarity, good humour, and kindly touches of satire. Two of the most attractive are the old brothers, the Consul and the Attaché ; the two clergymen, again, are interesting figures, and the whole of this provincial bureaucracy is set before the reader with convincing reality ; the everyday talk, the weather, the physical aspects of the country filling in the picture with faithful detail. [Transl. by W. W. Kettlewell, Kegan Paul : o.p.]

—— *Skipper Worse* (Skipper Worse, 1882). 1885
Continues the history of Worse, and tells of his joining the Garman firm and of his married life. This profane and delightfully humorous old mariner is the object of a determined attempt by his mother-in-law to convert him. This comedy, however, does not detract from the author's seriousness in dealing with the Haugian religious movement among the people. The character of Hans Nilsen, the lay-preacher, is a worthy pendant to that of the skipper. [Transl. by the Earl of Ducie, Low : o.p.]

—— *Tales of Two Countries* (Nye novelletter, 1880). 1891
Characteristically Norse stories, slight sketches of life, with now and then intensely realistic glimpses into the inner things of life. [Transl. by William Archer, Harper : o.p.]
Nye novelletter is partly transl. also by R. L. Cassie in *Norse Tales and Sketches*, 1896. [Stock : o.p.]

KIMMINS, Miss Grace T. [" Sister Grace," of the Bermondsey Settlement]. *Polly of Parker's Rents.* 1899
A humanitarian study of slum life, by a worker among the poor and the lost. Polly is the child of a thievish family, an undisciplined but generous girl, who is reformed and after many harsh experiences, happily married. [Bowden : o.p.]

KING, Grace Elizabeth [American ; *b.* 1852]. *Balcony Stories.* 1893
A collection of stories, some slight and sketchy, some complete little dramas, dealing with life in the Southern States, e.g. *Grandmother's Grandmother, A Crippled Hope, The Old Lady's Restoration.* [Macmillan, New York, 1925 ; Warne : o.p.]

—— *The Pleasant Ways of St. Médard.* 1916
The life of a family uprooted from their plantation in the South by the Civil War. [Macmillan, New York and London, 1927.]

KING, Maude Egerton. *Studies in Love.* 1900
Quiet, ultra-sentimental idylls of love and the country ; plotless and uneventful, but elevated occasionally by poetic feeling : e.g. *Love in the Woods.* [Dent : o.p. ; Dutton, New York : o.p.]

KING, Richard Ashe [" Desmond B. O'Brien " ; Irish]. *The Wearing of the Green.* 1886
A love-story from Ireland, particularly good in the minor characters ; hard on English people, and kindly disposed to the Irish and their grievances. [Chatto : o.p.]

—— *Bell Barry.* 1891
An exciting story, laid in Ireland, then in Liverpool, and in part aboard a liner. The Irish servants and other minor characters, and a stolid, good-natured Yorkshireman provide a good deal of humorous talk. [Chatto : o.p.]

KING, William Benjamin Basil [American ; 1859–1928]. *Let Not Man Put Asunder.* 1901
Almost a tractate against divorce—as it flourishes in the United States. Husband and wife are both strong personalities, the woman by no means a pleasant one. The author enforces his moral by a curiously symmetrical arrangement of four married pairs, who are divorced, and in two cases re-married. [Harper, New York : o.p. ; Grosset, New York, 1914 : o.p.]

KINGSLEY, Rev. Charles [1819–75]. *Alton Locke, Tailor and Poet : an autobiography.* 1850
A tract as well as a novel ; an embodiment of the doctrines of Christian socialism, inspired by Carlyle and by Kingsley's master, F. D. Maurice. It exposes the evils of " sweating " in realistic pictures of the London poor, and enters indignantly into the broader question of the condition of England at the time of the Chartist agitation (1838–42). The history of a life made abortive by the tyranny of circumstances. Alton Locke is a strenuous fighter for the rights of his fellows, who goes to prison for the cause and dies tragically. Among the characters is prominent the generous and fierce old Scot, Sandy Mackaye. [Macmillan ; (Everyman's Lib.), Dent (Dutton, New York).]

—— *Yeast.* 1851
A fierce social pamphlet rather than a novel, giving expression to the discontent seething in rural districts—the thread of romance, a young fox-hunter's love for an idealist and ascetic girl, merely stringing together denunciatory pictures of the condition of the country labourer, his poverty, immorality, insanitary surroundings, the tyrannous game laws, poaching, and so on. It also opens up problems of faith and scepticism. Appeared in *Fraser's Magazine* in 1848, and is therefore his first novel. [(Everyman's Lib.), Dent (Dutton, New York) ; Collins.]

—— *Hypatia ; or, New Foes with an Old Face.* 1853
Hellenic Egypt (*c.* 413–5), when Christianity and paganism were at war, depicted with scholarship and no little dramatic power ; Goths, Romans, Greeks, and a crowd of minor races come on the stage ; and there is great variety of situation and incident, of dramatic and emotional passages. The heroine is the famous votress and martyr of Neo-Platonism, and the " squire-bishop " Synesius of Cyrene, is also a brilliant historical reconstruction. The polemics of old heresies and old religions have a significant bearing on recent controversies, and enable Kingsley to exalt " Muscular Christianity " at the expense of what he held to be modern errors. [Macmillan ; (Everyman's Lib.), Dent (Dutton, New York) ; *illus.,* Oxford Press.]

—— *Westward Ho !* 1855
A kind of national saga bodying forth the spirit of adventure that sent Drake, Raleigh, Hawkins, Grenville, and their compeers to wreck the world-empire of Spain in the East and West hemispheres. An impassioned narrative of high achievement, culminating in the overthrow of the Armada. A band of young adventurers from Devon sail on a fanciful quest to the Spanish Main. Though Kingsley had not yet been there, he paints the American scenery magnificently. He idealizes his heroes, who are faultless young men from Cambridge, rather than the fierce and lawless natures depicted by Elizabethan playwrights. The prose-epic of Muscular Christianity. [Macmillan ; Dent (Dutton, New York) ; Oxford Press ; Dodd & Mead, New York ; Scribner, New York ; many other eds.]

—— *The Heroes ; or, Greek Fairy Tales for my Children.* [juvenile] 1856
The stories of Perseus and Andromeda, the Argonauts, and Theseus, retold in a simple, straightforward style, like a modern tale of adventure, so as to be intelligible and delightful to children. The moral tone of all Kingsley's work is here, but it does not overweight the stories, as happened to some of Hawthorne's *Tanglewood Tales.* [Macmillan ; (Everyman's Lib.), Dent (Dutton, New York) ; Oxford Press ; *illus.* by G. Soper, Doubleday, Doran, New York.]

—— *Two Years Ago.* 1857
The story revolves round the life of a rationalist, and, besides the personal interests, opens up many problems of conduct and religion. Contains perhaps his best characterization of lifelike individuals, and in general is more of a novel and less of a pamphlet or romance than any of his other books. There are many descriptive passages dealing with the scenery of Devon and North Wales. Muscular Christianity is definitely embodied in the athletic parson. [Macmillan ; Collins.]

—— *The Water-Babies : a fairy tale for a Land-Baby.* 1863
A poor little chimney-sweep is carried off by a good fairy, and being equipped with gills is introduced to the marvels of the world of waters. The aim is didactic. The pretty little fables which alternate with the gay burlesque inculcate the love of nature, the beauty of purity, cleanliness, simplicity, reverence. [Macmillan ; Oxford Press ; *illus.* by Jessie W. Smith, Dodd & Mead, New York ; by W. Heath Robinson, Houghton, Boston ; by E. A. Cox, Dent. With *Glaucus,* (Everyman's Lib.), *id.* Many other eds.]

KINGSLEY, Rev. Charles (*continued*). *Hereward the Wake ; last of the English.* 1866

A direct and not unsuccessful imitation of the sagas—the whole spirit of the book Scandinavian. Hereward is half a Dane, and refuses to fight under the West Saxon Harold. His career is like that of the usual saga hero—a wild, unruly youth, outlawry, brilliant exploits abroad, and a return home at last to fight for his patrimony in the Fens. A singular contrast to Macfarlane's Hereward—he is no true patriot, but a fierce, passionate, unmanageable hero, a true Viking, with fits of Berserk madness. A very free rendering of history (1070–1), but full of live touches and a genuine sense of tragedy. Kingsley's most " muscular " novel. [Macmillan ; (Everyman's Lib.), Dent (Dutton, New York) ; Oxford Press.]

[*Works*, 18 vols., Macmillan.]

—— *The Tutor's Story : an unpublished novel . . . revised and completed by his daughter Lucas Malet.* 1916

Largely a very early work, with some features in common with *The Water-Babies* ; otherwise very like Kingsley's other fiction. [Murray ; Dodd & Mead, New York.]

KINGSLEY, Henry [1830–76]. *The Recollections of Geoffrey Hamlyn.* 1859

Henry Kingsley was more of a novelist than his brother ; he excelled where Charles was weak, in the delineation of character. His first two novels were his best, freshly made from an abundant store of personal recollections, Kingsley having lived a nomadic, knockabout life as a boy in Devon, and then on the cattle-stations and goldfields of New South Wales. *Geoffrey Hamlyn* is the history of a family and their friends, who leave Devon and settle on farms in New South Wales, where the villain of the piece, transported as a convict, turns up as head of a fiendish gang of bushrangers. The incidents are thrilling, the scenes of happy family life and the portraits of healthy sterling character are fascinating, and the glorious scenery of Gippsland is depicted with a vivid pen very different from his brother's elaborate word-painting. [(Everyman's Lib.), Dent (Dutton, New York), 1900 ; (World's Classics), Oxford Press, 1925.]

—— *Ravenshoe.* 1862

This too is a family romance, but far richer in character, and altogether more masterly than the experimental *Geoffrey Hamlyn*. One of the raciest figures observes, " I have seldom or never met with a great house with so many queer elements about it " as Ravenshoe. The squire, his scapegrace brother, the old priest, the children, servants, fishermen, and the rest of the West Country folk, are drawn with Kingsley's wonderful appeal to our affections ; even the villains and the blackguards have a certain bonhomie. Still more indelible is the impress on our memories of such characters as the grand seigneur Lord Saltire, the old dowager Lady Ascot, and the fine rustic squire old Humby. [(Everyman's Lib.), Dent (Dutton, New York), 1906 ; (World's Classics), Oxford Press, 1925.]

—— *Austin Elliot (with, The Harveys).* 1863

A slight story with beautiful characters, a charming friendship, and a love affair that is like an idealized friendship. Eton, Wales, and Scotland are the principal scenes, and the beauty of nature is conveyed with his wonted charm. [Ward & Lock : o.p. ; *ed.* by C. K. Shorter, Longmans, New York.]

—— *The Hillyars and the Burtons : a story of two families.* 1865

As inchoate as anything he wrote, but also as charming, particularly in the reminiscences of the family life of the Kingsleys in the old Chelsea rectory where he spent his boyhood. A baronet's family and the family of a blacksmith are brought into contact by events. Kingsley pursues the fortunes of the several members in Chelsea and in Australia, and portrays a notable set of honest, manly, and affectionate people. Sketches of Australian life and scenery show his high spirits and his enthusiasm for that country. [Ward & Lock : o.p. ; Longmans, New York : o.p.]

—— *Silcote of Silcotes.* 1867

A family chronicle, showing a number of strong, masterful, clashing personalities in the act of development ; chief among them Silcote, the " Dark Squire," a powerful, bullying, yet engaging old " Berserk." Terse, critical, sarcastic dialogue ; situations rather too monotonously charged with dramatic irony. Scenes : a fine old English country house, a great school, and Italy during the war of liberation (1859), with the battlefields of Montebello and Palestro. Touches on Puseyism. [Ward & Lock : o.p. ; Longmans, New York : o.p.]

—— *Mademoiselle Mathilde.* 1868

A romance of England and France during the French Revolution. Marat is a prominent figure, and Robespierre and Camille Desmoulins come on the stage. The first half light comedy, the second melodrama, with the massacres of the Abbaye for the catastrophe. [Ward & Lock : o.p. ; Longmans, New York : o.p.]

—— *Stretton.* 1869

Like most of his novels, a group of characters rather than a series of events ; no construction ; works round somehow to a trice of marriages, and ends anyhow. Recounts the childhood, life at school and at Oxford, and the early manhood of children of several county families in Shropshire. Sets forth the same great ideal of honest, noble, and affectionate manliness. Aunt Eleanor, the frank, sarcastic, warm-hearted farmer, is the figure we remember the book by, rather than the paragon Roland Evans, who flings up a brilliant career to throw himself into the turmoil of the Indian Mutiny. [Ward & Lock : o.p. ; Longmans, New York.]

—— *Old Margaret (with other stories).* 1871

A story of the people of Ghent in the time of Philip the Good of Burgundy (*c.* 1400). Plenty of action, description and character, and of his peculiar touches of human nature. The Van Eycks are brought in. [Ward & Lock : o.p. ; Longmans, New York : o.p.]

—— *The Harveys (with, Austin Elliot).* 1872

The history of a very bohemian family ; pictures of life as varied as the characters. Old Mr. Harvey, shiftless and irresponsible, simple-minded, but shrewd in the pursuit of theological difficulties ; his favourite son, the artist, whose school life and early career are alive with adventure : these and the rest of the family, with their pecuniary troubles and cheery disposition, are portraits conceived in Kingsley's usual buoyant and humorous spirit. Has a good deal to say about spiritualism. [*v. Austin Elliot, supra.*]

KINGSLEY, Henry (*continued*).   *Valentin : a French boy's story of Sedan* (*with, Number Seventeen*).   [juvenile] 1872
Kingsley was a war correspondent with the German army, and the first Englishman to enter Metz, and was an eye-witness of the *débâcle* of Sedan.   [Ward & Lock : o.p. ;   Longmans, New York.]

KINGSTON, William Henry Giles [1814–80].   *Peter the Whaler.*   [juvenile] 1851
—— *Digby Heathcote.*   [juvenile] 1860
Rousing stories of adventure by sea and land, wholesome and inspiring for boys.   [(1), (Everyman's Lib.), Dent (Dutton, New York), 1906 ;   Oxford Press ;   (2), Routledge : o.p. ;   Dutton, New York : o.p.]
—— *Hurricane Hurry.*   [juvenile] 1873
Adventures of a naval officer, chiefly with the British fleet (1764–81).   [Oxford Press ;   Pott, New York : o.p.]
—— *The Three Midshipmen.*   [juvenile] 1873
—— *The Three Lieutenants.*   [juvenile] 1875
—— *The Three Commanders.*   [juvenile] 1876
—— *The Three Admirals.*   [juvenile] 1878
Adventure stories, putting an exhilarating ideal of devotion to duty before the minds of boys.   [(1), (2), (3), and (4), Oxford Press ;   Blackie ;   (1), (Everyman's Lib.), Dent (Dutton, New York) ;   (2), and (3), Dutton, New York : o.p.]
—— *From Powder-Monkey to Admiral.*   [juvenile] 1883
Naval adventures during the great struggle with the French and their allies in the revolutionary era.   [Oxford Press ;   Armstrong, New York : o.p.]

KIOKUTEI, Bakin [Japanese ;   1767–1848].   *A Captive of Love* (Kumono Tayema Amayo Notsuki).   1886
Kiokutei Bakin is reckoned among the greatest of Japanese novelists ;   of his enormous output this and the following alone have appeared in English.   [Transl. by Edward GREY, Lee & Shepherd, Boston (Gowans & Gray, Glasgow) : o.p.]
—— *Glimpses of Dreamlands* (Musōbiōye Koshō Monogatari).   1881–2
A moral allegory, recounting the hero's progress through various resting-places on the soul's journey ;   such as the Land of Childhood, the Village of Lust, and the City of Pleasure.   [Transl. by L. MORDWIN, 2 vols., Yokohama.]

KIPLING, Rudyard [*b.* 1865].   *Plain Tales from the Hills.*   1887
Candid and sometimes scathing pictures of Anglo-Indian life and manners, at Simla and elsewhere, and superficial sketches of the natives ;   written for the *Civil and Military Gazette*.   The peculiar catchy realism has been compared to a searchlight shining intensely on successive portions of the subject and constantly uncovering the dirty aspects of life.   The following are representative of this initial stage of the author's development :   *A Germ-destroyer, His Wedded Wife, Tod's Amendment, In the House of Suddhoo, Beyond the Pale, The Gate of the Hundred Sorrows,* and an uproarious farce, *The Taking of Lungtungpen.*
—— *Soldiers Three ; The Story of the Gadsbys ; and, In Black and White.*   1888–9
The first set consists of episodes in the Indian life of three British privates, a swaggering Irishman of drunken propensities and humorous tongue, who is also a man if ever there was one, a phlegmatic Yorkshireman, and a peppery little Cockney, a trio of fast friends, who stand shoulder to shoulder in many perils and escapades, and in the not less trying ordeals of peace.   A wonderfully actual presentation of the surface aspects of life in the ranks.   Each man keeps to his native vernacular, and the barrack-room talk is freely reproduced, with its garniture of oaths and slang.   A delight in strenuous muscular life animates the stories, the battle-pieces are filled with true martial spirit and unrestrained joy in bloodshed.   *The Gadsbys* is a morbid episode of married life in the officers' quarters, cast into the dramatic form of colloquial, slipshod talk.   *In Black and White* purports to be translations of native stories, and to show, from the inside, the native character and way of looking at things; these are thoroughly Oriental in style and imagery; a good example is *In Flood-Time*, an idyllic story which a native tells to an Englishman.
—— *Wee Willie Winkie ; Under the Deodars ; The Phantom 'Rickshaw ; etc.*   1888–9
Wee Willie Winkie shows more love of children than insight into their minds.   The prevailing theme of *Under the Deodars* is an ugly one, " men and women playing at tennis with the seventh commandment " ;   the unspeakable Mrs. Hauksbee (from *Plain Tales*) is a prominent figure.   The *'Rickshaw* is a psychical story of a kind to try the nerves ;   an Englishwoman, cruelly misused by her lover, returns to haunt him in the very streets of Simla.   All are first-rate examples of the art of story-telling, even when the treatment of character is at fault.
—— *The Light that Failed.*   1891
An ill-knit but intensely realistic narrative of bohemian life, the uncouthness of which is, however, overcharged.   The ambitious and swaggering hero is a war-artist, who goes blind, loses his love and his ambition, and is robbed of his one masterpiece.   Full of the lust of life and the joy of action.
—— *Life's Handicap : being stories of mine own people.*   1891
Further doings of the famous three, e.g. *The Incarnation of Krishna Mulvaney*, a fine piece of boisterous comedy, and the touching revelation of Mulvaney's character in *The Courting of Dinah Shadd*.   Stories at large of Anglo-Indians, e.g. *The Man Who Was*, an uncanny yarn about a man's return from worse than death ;   *Without Benefit of Clergy*, the pathetic narrative of an Englishman's liaison with a Mohammedan ;   *The Mark of the Beast, Bertram and Bimbi, At the End of the Passage*, and *The Return of Imray*, ghastly tales of lycanthropy, murder, haunting, and the like.   Also some tales of native life, e.g. *The City of Dreadful Night, The Finances of the Gods*, and *Nangay Doola.*
—— *Many Inventions.*   1893
My Lord the Elephant and *In the Rukh* foreshadow the ampler studies of animal-character in the *Jungle Books*. *The Finest Story in the World* is a tale of metempsychosis, staggering in its imaginative actuality.   *Brugglesmith* is a character-farce.   In *His Private Honour* and *Love o' Women* the three privates reappear, but the

KIPLING, Rudyard (*continued*).

themes are more serious—conscience, remorse, and retribution—though the manner is as boisterous as ever. *Badalia Herodsfoot* is a realistic picture of the ugliest kind of Whitechapel life. An allegory, *The Children of the Zodiac*, and various other evocations of life in the East, add to the diversity.

—— *The Jungle Book.* 1894
—— *The Second Jungle Book.* 1895

Fables of man and beast in India, poetical rather than allegorical, aiming to interpret the actual character and mode of reasoning of the animals, so far as human insight and sympathy can go. The laws of the jungle, the distinct habits of the different nations, the natural phenomena of the desert, and the effect of drought and of human hostility are depicted with essentially the same realism as the author applies to human subjects. Mowgli, the wolves' foster-child, the friend and free companion of the jungle-folk, is one of the most fascinating creations in modern literature.

—— *Captains Courageous.* 1897

Hardly more than a short story depicting the life of New England fishermen on the high seas, the harsh lingo and the uncouth technicalities being reproduced. Tells how an invertebrate and pampered young millionaire is accidentally torn from his mother, and made a man by drastic treatment at the hands of a rough but kindly skipper.

—— *The Day's Work.* 1898

More cosmopolitan in subject and various in style. India is the scene in *The Bridge Builders*, an imaginative story of a great engineering feat, which combines in one purview the modern Englishman, the native as he thinks and acts, and the still living mythology of Hindustan ; *The Tomb of his Ancestors* and *William the Conqueror* are a twofold story of English fortitude and self-devotion in the presence of famine. American locomotives are the *dramatis personæ* of ·007 ; *The Ship that Found Herself* likewise gives a tongue to brute mechanism ; in *A Walking Delegate* the characters are horses ; *The Maltese Cat* is a vivacious story in the *Jungle Book* genre ; and the poetical story of dream-life, called *The Brushwood Boy*, is of the same sentimental and semi-lyrical class as *The Finest Story in the World*.

—— *Stalky & Co.* 1899

A counterblast to *St. Winifred's, Eric,* and all kinds of goody-goody literature and sentimentality. Goes deeper into the queer psychology of the boy, though it must be admitted these are not quite like other boys, if on the whole they are better. Episodes in the lives of three boys at an army college (Westward Ho ! in Devon). The three are weird individuals in their exclusiveness and knowingness, but Stalky is of the stuff of which heroes are made ; their exploits make them a terror to the masters and their unappreciative schoolfellows. Stalky's original is Major-General L. C. Dunsterville, author of *The Adventures of Dunsterville* (1920), and *Stalky's Reminiscences* (1928). Beetle, one of his two henchmen, is said to be a portrait of the author himself, who was educated at this college.

—— *Kim.* 1901

Mr. Kipling's solitary triumph on the scale of the full-length novel, and his fullest portrayal of what he can present better than any man—the life of modern India, native and European. Kim is a street-arab from Lahore, derelict child of an Irish soldier ; an alert, precocious little vagabond, whose apprenticeship to the secret service gives him a unique education in the shady walks of Anglo-Indian life. His journeys through India as the disciple of an old Lama bring before the reader a rich panorama of the multifarious life of the country.

—— *Just-So Stories for Little Children.* 1902

More fantastic beast-fables than the *Jungle Book* stories, cleverer and more laboured ; describing in burlesque style *How the Whale got his Throat, How the Leopard got his Spots, How the Rhinoceros got his Skin, How the Alphabet was Made,* and so on. Perhaps the very best is *The Elephant's Child*, which tells how the elephant got his trunk. [*Illus.* by the Author.]

—— *Traffics and Discoveries.* 1904

Stories more discursive in subject and uneven in quality. *They* ranks with *The Brushwood Boy* and *The Finest Story in the World* as pure imagination, a subtle fantasy in which even a motor-car becomes a thing of romance. It describes a blind lady with powers of supernal vision denied to those who have eyes, and in its exquisite tenderness for little ones recalls Lamb's pathetic *Dream Children*. The other stories are brilliant snapshots of many subjects, from the humorous doings on a British cruiser in *The Bonds of Discipline* and the naval manœuvres in *Their Lawful Occasions* to the crude imperialism of the Boer war stories, *The Captive* and *A Sahib's War*.

—— *Puck of Pook's Hill.* 1906

Two children encounter Puck the immortal fairy on the top of the South Downs, and he tells them a wonderful story of the Stone Men and the fatal discovery of weapons made of metals. A childlike attempt to re-create the past, enlisting history—and pre-history—and folk-lore for the purpose.

—— *Actions and Reactions.* 1909

More miscellaneous than the previous collections. *A Habitation Enforced* tells how an American millionaire and his wife acclimatize themselves in an old-world Sussex village. *A Deal in Cotton* is an African tale, and a matchless example of Mr. Kipling's clairvoyance in its portrait of the mighty slave-dealer. In *The House Surgeon* his ghostly imagination has its fling. In *Garm—a Hostage* we are reintroduced to Privates Ortheris and Learoyd in an excellent story of a bull-terrier. *With the Night Mail* is a fantasy of the year A.D. 2000. Americans, Anglo-Indians, Jews, Arabs, Hindus, and animals are presented with unerring truth, each speaking after his kind.

—— *Rewards and Fairies.* 1910

A continuation of the *Puck of Pook's Hill* theme. Later episodes of English history, in the same magic dress, bringing home to us the identity of the past and the present. The poems interspersed are triumphs of metrical skill.

—— *A Diversity of Creatures.* 1917

No falling off in craftsmanship is evinced in these products of Mr. Kipling's maturity, nor in command of the inexhaustible variety of life. The occult enters in one way or another into *The Dog Hervey, In the same Boat,*

KIPLING, Rudyard (*continued*).

and *Swept and Garnished*. There are three farces, *The Vortex*, *The Horse Marines*, and *The Village that Voted the Earth was Flat*, the last a crescendo of uproarious fun outdoing all his earlier examples in that vein. *Regulus* is a Platonic dialogue. Stalkey and Beetle reappear, and Sikhs, Goorkhas, and other natives recall *Kim*. *The Land* celebrates the eternal, autochthonous British peasant.

—— *Debits and Credits.* 1926

Contains some astonishing examples of realistic technique, and of a style that Mr. Kipling has made for himself— in some, the technique is everything and the subject of small importance. The prevailing theme is the war. *A Madonna of the Trenches* is told, almost in the Henry James manner, in spasmodic confessions by an hysterical boy ; it is about a psychical incident, and is inspired with a flaming conception of romantic love. *The Wish House* mingles magic and realism, and *The Janeites* is good criticism of Jane Austen. [*Works :* Macmillan ; Doubleday, New York ; 23 vols., in sets, Scribner, New York ; 10 vols., in sets, Bigelow Brown, New York.]

—— *Thy Servant a Dog. Told by Boots ; edited by Rudyard Kipling.* 1930

The story of a miscellaneous group of English dogs, related by one of them. The doggie viewpoint is admirably maintained, and the whole is capital fun. [*Illus.* by G. L. Stampa, Macmillan ; *illus.* by Margaret Kirmse, Doubleday, Doran, New York.]

KIPLING, Rudyard, and Wolcott BALESTIER [American]. *The Naulahka.* 1892

Western civilization and commercialism in grotesque contact with Oriental manners—a Californian speculator follows his love, a medical missionary, to India, amuses the Rajah, fights and conquers his favourite queen, and has many adventures. [Macmillan ; Doubleday, New York.]

KIRBY, William [Canadian ; 1817–1906]. *The Golden Dog : a romance of the days of Louis Quatorze in Quebec.* 1877

The work of a poet and folk-lorist ; a long historical romance, rich in local colour, and based on a legendary story of the early days of fur-trading. Scene, the French province of Quebec, time of Louis XIV (1748–9). [Page, Boston.]

KIRK, Ellen [*née* Olney ; American ; *b.* 1842]. *A Lesson in Love.* 1881

A lawyer engaged to a client falls in love with a pretty little girl who is opposed to her as plaintiff in a will suit. The situations lasts long enough to bring out the character of this able but selfish and feebly con- scientious man, and is closed by his *fiancée's* discovery of the fact. [Houghton, Boston.]

—— *A Midsummer Madness.* 1885

A picture of country-house life on the banks of the Delaware, an agreeable medley of love-making, happy and careless existence, and sketches of nature. [Houghton, Boston.]

—— *The Story of Margaret Kent.* 1886

A story of violent social contrasts, brisk in movement. [Houghton, Boston : o.p.]

—— *Queen Money.* 1888

Phases of American life, showing the effects of the race for wealth upon a young man of simple, refined tastes and worthy ideals, who had hitherto lived in the country. The moral aim is not obtrusive ; and the world of brokers, financiers, plutocrats, and the quieter one of intellectual people unaffected by the covetous passion, afford scope for character-drawing and sober incident. [Houghton, Boston : o.p.]

—— *The Story of Lawrence Garthe.* 1894

Story of a man who makes a mistake in an early marriage, divorces his wife, and is rewarded with happiness in his next venture. In the sub-plot the affairs of two other lovers are related ; but the chief interest is in the character of the divorced wife, an intrepid and brilliant adventuress, whose sins against the social code appear to no one more scandalous than to her duenna, an advanced woman whose theories would sanction them all. There is satire also in the chapter on the " Fin-de-Siècle Club." Scene laid in New York. [Houghton, Boston.]

KIRKLAND, Joseph [American ; 1830–94]. *Zury, the Meanest Man in Spring County.* 1887

Illinois life in the pioneer days, superficially represented, but with accuracy of detail. The memoirs of an exceedingly quaint personage, who reappears in the next story, form the plot. [Houghton, Boston : o.p.]

—— *The McVeys : an episode.* 1888

Sketches of Illinois life a little later, connected into a slender story by the reappearance of the same characters, illustrating the homely, colourless nature of the prairie life, and the moral forces shaping it which were destined to act powerfully in the great national movement of the next generation. Abraham Lincoln, the young advocate, plays an important part, as in Eggleston's *Graysons*. The leading incidents refer to a young engine-driver, who is aroused out of an immoral intrigue by a genuine passion for a womanly girl. [Houghton, Boston : o.p.]

KITCHIN, Clifford Henry Benn. *Death of My Aunt.* 1929

A detective novel in which interest is directed rather to the psychology of the victim's relatives than to the solution of the crime. [Hogarth Press ; Harcourt, New York.]

KIVI, Alexis [or Stenvall ; Finn ; 1834–72]. *Seven Brothers* (1870). 1929

An epical family history of northern Finland—seven brothers of vast strength and thick heads, are bent on overcoming everything by brute force ; they flee their homestead and take to the wilds, but intelligence soon conquers, and they return to their village, to the difficulties of life, and the joys of civilization. Kivi was a Finnish poet, and this is his greatest achievement in prose. There is a saga-like lustiness and humour in both the adventures and the characters of the seven heroes ; and interspersed are passages, Aapo's tale of the Pale Maiden in particular, of great lyrical beauty. Above all, the mystery and fascination of the vast forest is rendered in terms which remain in the reader's imagination. [Transl. from the Swedish by Alex. MATSON, Faber ; Coward McCann, New York.]

KLOERSS, Sophie [German]. —— *and Sons.* 1930

The history of three generations of a shipowning family at Hamburg, a lighter novel in the manner of Thomas Mann's *Buddenbrooks*. [Transl. by Edward CATTLE, Hurst.]

KNIPE, Emily [*née* Benson; *b.* 1870], and KNIPE, Alden Arthur [*b.* 1870]. *A Maid of '76.*
1915

A story of the American Revolution—the efforts of a loyalist to reconcile king and colonies. Scenes, Boston and London; Washington and George III are introduced. [Macmillan: o.p.; *id.*, New York.]

—— *The Shadow Captain.* 1925

The hero is Captain Kidd, shown as an honest seaman unjustly condemned, who escapes hanging to clear his name and avenge himself on his enemies. Scenes, London and New York (1701–3). [Lane; Dodd & Mead, New York.]

KOERNER, Hermann T. [German]. *Beleaguered: a story of the uplands of Baden.* 1889

Villingen (1633–4). [Putnam, New York: o.p.]

KOHN, Salomon [German]. *Gabriel: a story of the Jews in Prague (Gawriel).* 1882

Period, early in the seventeenth century. [Transl., Tauchnitz, Leipzig (Low): o.p.]

KOMROFF, Manuel [American, born in Russia; *b.* 1890]. *Coronet.* 1929

A sixfold panorama of the misdeeds of aristocracy from Florence in 1600 to Chicago in 1919—rather in the Merezhovski style, with elaborate symbolism extra. Napoleon, Chopin, Murat, Balzac, and other notabilities are superficially sketched, and there are such historical episodes as the retreat from Moscow. [Coward McCann, New York; McClelland, Toronto (both in 2 vol. and 1 vol. editions). 1 vol., Harrap.]

—— *The Grace of Lambs.* 1925

Stories about Russia and the Russians; *Thumbs* depicts a characteristic peasant, good-humoured and stupid, who is roused to murderous rage by an officer's cruelty to a pet bird. [Boni, New York; Cape.]

—— *Two Thieves.* 1931

An imaginative version of the Crucifixion story, in which the figure of Christ is pointedly disregarded and those who were crucified with Him are the heroes. An Arab, brutally wronged under Herod, and a Jewish slave, are the prime movers in a plot against the Roman power. They are seized and put to death by the authorities, who are little aware of the tremendously greater importance of their fellow-victim. [Coward McCann, New York.]

KORMAKS SAGA: *the life and death of Cormac the Skald.* 1902

Prose and verse, the latter rendered with great spirit. The love-tale of a poet—poor, proud, wayward but true—and a frivolous woman who jilts him (not howbeit without excuse), and despises the greatness of his passion. His genius and daring contrast dramatically with her fickleness and selfishness. Cormac, Irish in name and nature, turns Viking, and performs many deeds of valour (*c.* 930–60). Much like a modern romance in feeling, yet substantially true. Put into literary form probably between 1250 and 1300, and a faithful transcript of the oral version two centuries older. Contains the best account of holmgang, the Icelandic duello. [Transl. by W. G. COLLINGWOOD and Jon STÉFANNSON, *illus.* by Collingwood, Holmes, Ulverston: o.p.]

KOROLENKO, Vladimir [Russian; 1853–1921]. *The Vagrant; and other tales.* 1887

Admirably finished stories, hardly inferior in force and beauty of execution to Turgenev's. Korolenko spent many years in exile at a remote settlement in Siberia, and he pictures the life there with deep impressiveness. *The Vagrant* relates the escape of a band of exiles; *Sketches of a Siberian Tourist* are full of the observations of an imaginative mind, and are chiefly autobiographical; all are pervaded with the spirit of the scenery and the characteristic melancholy of the Slav, yet with no bitterness. The translations from Korolenko are defective. [Transl. by Mrs. A. DELANO, Crowell, New York: o.p.]

—— *The Blind Musician.* 1890

A beautiful story of the development of a musical genius, who is born blind; over-subtle perhaps in its psychological analysis of an emotional temperament strongly influenced by nature—nature in the Ukraine. [Transl. by " STEPNIAK " and WESTALL, Ward & Downey: o.p.; by Mrs. A. DELANO, Little & Brown, Boston: o.p.]

—— *The Saghalien Convict; Easter Eve.* 1892

Inspired by his own exile (1881–4) in the dreary, sub-Arctic province of Yakutsk, where he was sent for refusing to take the oath to Alexander III. [(Pseudonym Lib.), Unwin: o.p.]

—— *In Two Moods.* 1892

A rather reticent study of the Nihilist movement of 1873–5, sketching the young Russian enthusiast in warm and sympathetic colours; along with a very characteristic psychological portrait. [Transl. by " STEPNIAK," Ward & Downey: o.p.]

—— *Makar's Dream* (1885). 1892

Makar, a drunken old Yakut muzhik, dreams he is brought to the house of the great Taïon or judge to be tried for his sin this beautiful fable the problem of redemption is worked out with the familiar characters and scenes life as factors. *Bad Company* is a pathetic tale reminiscent of Korolenko's half-Polish, half-Cossack parentage, and of his early life in Volhynia. [(Pseudonym Lib.), Unwin: o.p.]

—— *The Murmuring Forest; and other stories.* 1916

The title-story (1886) is concerned with Little Russia in the feudal period, the oppression of the serfs, and the nemesis that overtakes one of the oppressors. It is a little drama of love and jealousy. For *Makar's Dream* and *In Bad Company*, see above. The other, *The Day of Atonement*, is a bright and humorous story of a southern town within the Jewish pale. [Transl. with an introd. by Marian FELL, Duckworth: o.p.; Duffield, New York.]

KOSTROMITIN, G. J. [Russian]. *The Last Day of the Carnival.* 1893

A lurid picture of a public holiday in a provincial town, a day of brutal indulgence passed in continual dread of the knout and of Siberia; claims to be accurate. [(Pseudonym Lib.), Unwin: o.p.]

KRASNOV, Petr Nikolaevich [Russian; *b.* 1869]. *Kostia the Cossack.* 1930

General Krasnov is a Cossack, and this patriotic historical novel celebrates the struggle between the Don Cossacks and the Turks, in the time of the early Romanov tsars, for the possession of Azov. It is an epical story of fiery deeds and terrible carnage, recalling Gogol's *Taras Bulba*; yet there is also a Tolstoyan

KRASNOV, Petr Nikolaevich (*continued*).

 vision of the disenchanting realities behind the exploits and the pageantry, a sense of frustration paralysing the most heroic souls. A bad translation. [Transl. by Olga VITALI and Natalie TSYTOVITCH, Duffield, New York; Allen & Unwin.]

KRASZEWSKI, Józef Ignacy [Polish; 1812–87]. *The Jew* (1865).   1890

 The scene is the insurrection of 1860, the later developments of which drove the author into exile. [Transl. by Linda da KOWALEWSKA, Heinemann.]

—— *The Countess Cosel: a romance of history of the times of Augustus the Strong* (Hrabina Kosel, 3 vols., 1881).   1901

 The Countess is the reigning favourite at the Court of Augustus the Strong, Elector of Saxony, sometime King of Poland (1706–27); and her story is one of intrigue, interesting but unedifying. History predominates over romance. [Transl. by Count S. C. DE SOISSONS, Downey: o.p.]

KREUTZ, Rudolph Jeremias [Norwegian]. *Captain Zillner* (Den store frase).   1919

 An impassioned diatribe against war: records the experiences in the rank and file of the Austrian Army; enthusiastic mobilization, incompetent, cowardly, and selfish officers; terrors and gallantry of the fighting line. [Transl. by W. J. A. WORSTER, Hodder.]

KRONENBERGER, Louis [American]. *The Grand Manner*.   1929

 Historical fiction made to look as much as possible like authentic biography. It is the story of the last king of Hedenstrom, a minor German state; after troubles with the democratic elements and with his son, he abdicates, and the latter scenes are of his exile and poverty in Paris. [Boni, New York; Gollancz.]

KRUIZHANOVSKAYA, V. I. *The Torch-Bearers of Bohemia* (c. 1900).   1916

 A crude and one-sided historical romance of the Bohemian nationalist struggle under John Hus in the fifteenth century (1401–14): written apparently for propagandist purposes; the anti-German bias is obvious. [Transl. by Juliet M. SOSKICE, Chatto: o.p.; McBride, New York: o.p.]

KUPRIN, Aleksandr Ivanovich [Russian; b. 1870]. *The Duel* (1905).   1916

 Probably Kuprin's most famous story. It is about a sensitive young intellectual who has tragic misunderstandings with his brutal fellow-officers, and shows up the stupid and ugly side of army life in a way that before this date would never have been tolerated. The translation of this Russian novel is typically slipshod. [Allen & Unwin; previously translated by M. F. HARVEY, *sub tit. In Honour's Name*, 1907; Everett: o.p.]

—— *Sulamith* (1908).   1926

 Retells the Biblical story of Solomon and the Shulamite woman of the *Song of Songs*, with a wealth of exotic Eastern colour. [Transl. by B. G. GUERNEY, Adelphi Co., New York.]

—— *Yama—the Pit* (1909–13).   1930

 The Pit is a brothel in southern Russia; both the women and the men who haunt the place are drawn with psychological penetration, and without evasion or sentimentalism. The paralysing boredom which is the prostitute's lot, the contemptible rascality of the trade in women—these are the strongest impressions left. [Hamilton; Argus Press, New York; also transl. by Bernard Guilbert GUERNEY, privately printed, N. L. Brown, 1922.]

—— *The River of Life; and other stories*.   1916

 Four excellent examples of Kuprin's handling of the Russian *conte*, all excellently translated. Kuprin was curious of every side of life, and every type of character in the heterogeneous population of southern Russia. With a keen eye for local colour and the contrasts of the visible scene, he is not afraid to go below the surface in his character-drawing, although he does it with the tenderness as well as the skill of the artist who loves humanity. [Transl. by S. KOTELIANSKY and J. Middleton MURRY, Maunsel: o.p.]

—— *A Slav Soul; and other stories*.   1916

 A selection carefully omitting Kuprin's stories referring to women, a subject on which the editors regard him as " self-conscious and awkward." Most of the fifteen included are concerned with the peasantry, " the most enigmatical, the greatest, and the most abased people in the world." Mr. Graham compares these with Kipling's: they are dramatic, humorous, and told with the art of a first-class raconteur. Some are stories suitable for children, and hardly inferior to Hans Andersen's. [With an introd. by Stephen Graham, with *Captain Ribnikov*, Constable: o.p.]

—— *Sasha*

 Kuprin, interpreter of moods, disconsolate and despairing moods in especial, is not here at his best the pangs of hopeless love, hints of a pogrom, the squalor of back-streets in a great seaport, Odessa developed in vivid scenes against a sky uniformly overcast. [Transl. by Douglas ASHBY; pref. J. A. T. LLOYD, S. Paul: o.p.; McKay, Philadelphia, 1928.]

—— *The Bracelet of Garnets; and other stories*.

 A translation by a Russian American of a number of stories selected by Kuprin himself, including *The Thieves*, *The Jewess*, *Anathema*, and *The Læstrygonians*. The last-named is a sketch of fisher of the Black Sea and their natural surroundings. *The Bracelet* is a little love romance. [Transl. PAVLOVSKY, Scribner, New York.]

—— *Gambrinus; and other stories*.

 Gambrinus is the story of a sensitive fellow unconsciously adapting himself to misfortune: a fiddler in a beer house, he serves in the Russo-Japanese War, then comes back after two years to delight his old audience; after the revolution of 1905, he reappears again, now maimed and crippled. Also included are *Monte Carlo* and *Roach Hole*. [Transl. by B. G. GUERNEY, Adelphi Co., New York.]

KURZ, Isolde [German; b. 1853]. *Tales of Florence* (Florentiner Novellen, 1890).   1919

 Two romances; the better one, *The Marriage of the Dead*, is of the time of the pestilence described by Boccaccio; *Saint Sebastian*, of that of Lorenzo de' Medici and Savonarola. [Transl. by Lilian DUNDAS, Hutchinson.]

LACLOS, Pierre Ambroise François Choderlos de [French ; 1741–1803]. *Dangerous Acquaintances* (Les liaisons dangereuses, 1782). 1924

A long and elaborate chronicle of corrupt morals and systematic seduction, which is a masterpiece of psychological drama in the minute epistolary form exemplified by Richardson's *Clarissa*. Written as a satire on the cold-blooded depravity of the old noblesse. The intellectual interest is profound, though the matters are so intolerably repellent. [Transl. by Richard ALDINGTON (Broadway Transl.), Routledge (Dutton, New York.]

LA FARGE, Oliver [American ; b. 1901]. *Laughing Boy.* 1929

A sympathetic interpretation of Indian life—the story of a pair of Navajo lovers. [Houghton, Boston ; Constable.]

LA FAYETTE, Marie Madeleine Pioche, Comtesse de [*née* de la Vergne ; French ; 1634–93]. *Zayde : a Spanish history, or romance* (Zayde, histoire espagnole, 1670) 1690

In plot, akin to the old style of romance. Two Spanish grandees retire from the Court, and meditate on the wrongs they have suffered from others and those which were due to their own conduct. A Moorish princess is cast ashore in their neighbourhood, and one of these nobles falls passionately in love ; the truthful painting of sentiment and emotion shows the same psychological power as her other novel. [" By Monsieur Segray " (i.e. Jean Regnauld de Segrais, and the Countess de la Fayette). Done into English by D. PORTER : o.p.]

—— *The Princess of Cleves* (La princesse de Clèves, 1678). 1892

A story that marks an epoch in literary history as a long stride from the love romances of Scudéry and Calprenède (whose style she had imitated in *Zayde*), towards the realistic methods and the spirit of modern fiction. The characters are still royal and aristocratic personages, but the evolution of the love-story is by the natural unfolding of motive and character, and the emotions and incidents are those of real life. The story opens in 1558, in the reign of Henry II, with the marriage of Mary of Scotland to the Dauphin. Numerous celebrities of that time appear, at least in name ; but the characters are to a large extent drawn from well-known people of Louis XIV's reign, and the story may in a certain sense be a reflection of Mme de la Fayette's sentiments towards La Rochefoucauld, who is sometimes credited with having had a hand in it. [Transl. by T. S. PERRY, 2 vols., Osgood : o.p. ; transl. by H. ASHTON (Broadway Transl.), Routledge (Dutton, New York), 1927. See Taine's *Essais de critique*, and D'Haussonville's *Mme de la Fayette*, Hachette, 1891 ; Harper, 1912 : o.p.]

LAFFAN, Mrs. Robert Stuart de Courcy [Bertha Jane, *née* Grundy, *formerly* Mrs. Leith Adams]. *Madelon Lemoine.* 1879

A novel of conventional design and peopled by conventional characters, but in many respects lifelike and truthful. Madelon is a beautiful woman of unknown antecedents who makes her home in a seaside place in the West, and becomes by turns a source of blessing, a mark for gossip, an object of love, and a victim of trial. Mrs. Laffan has written about a dozen other novels of the same calibre. [Sonnenschein : o.p.]

LAFON, André [French ; 1885–1915]. *Jean Gilles, schoolboy* (L'élève Gilles, 1912). 1914

This was awarded the Academy prize. It is the poignant story of a little boy who slowly finds out, from the way he is treated by the other boys, that there is something peculiar about him—he is the son of a lunatic. [Transl. by Lady Theodora DAVIDSON, Bell : o.p. ; Putnam, New York : o.p.]

LAGERLÖF, Selma Ottiliana Lovisa [Swedish ; b. 1858]. *The Story of Gösta Berling* (Gösta Berlings saga, 1891). 1898

A most singular and unconventional story, or chain of stories, woven into a prose epic or saga, in which the mercurial and daring Gösta, unfrocked priest, drunkard, lover, and poet, is the chief hero, and a whole Round Table of reckless gallants share his exploits, ordeals, and troubles. It all takes place in a romantic region of Sweden, bordering on Norway, forest-clad, infested with beasts, watered by torrents and lakes ; and the time lies somewhere back in the half-civilized past. [Transl. by Pauline Bancroft FLACH, Doubleday, New York ; (Marbacka ed.), *id.*, 1928 ; transl. by Lillie TUDEER, Chapman & Hall, 1899, revised by Velma Swanston HOWARD, American Scandinavian Foundation, 2 vols., (Oxford Press), 1918.]

—— *The Miracles of Antichrist* (Antikrists mirakler, 1897). 1898

A poetical and partly allegorical story of Sicily, setting forth, side by side with a touching love-tale, the conflict between Christianity and the materialistic cult of socialism. Portrays the childish and superstitious, impulsive and revengeful people, with some comic characters ; many word-pictures of the superb scenery of Etna and the subjacent region, and of the cities and the natives. [Transl. by Pauline Bancroft FLACH, A. F. Bird : o.p. ; Doubleday, New York.]

—— *From a Swedish Homestead* (En herrgårdssägen, 1899). 1901

Another series of fanciful tales, quieter and more pensive in character than *Gösta Berling*, and lacking the artistic unity of that wild masterpiece ; but like it in the serious purpose half hidden in the imaginative form. The first and longest is about an insane man won back to mental health by love ; the second is a life of St. Olaf, curiously mingling Christian and mythological features. The others are shorter, miscellaneous pieces, anecdotes, and fables, often pathetic, full of insight into the life of humanity, and warmed by a kindly humour. [Transl. by Jessie BRÖCHNER, Heinemann (Doubleday, New York).]

—— *The Queens of Kungahälla ; and other sketches* (Drottningar i Kungahälla, jämte andra berättelser, 1899). 1904

Imaginative sketches of historical and other characters : e.g. *Sigrid Storråde*, concerning the Queen of Sweden and Olaf Trygvason of Norway, and *Astrid*, about a daughter of the King of Sweden by a serf. [Transl. by C. FIELD, Laurie.]

—— *Jerusalem* (Jerusalem, I–II, 1901–2). 1903

In this epical narrative of a mystical evangelizing movement which culminates in an abortive Zionist mission to the Holy Land, Miss Lagerlöf leaves her native Värmland for the neighbouring province of Dalarna, equally primitive and remote from civilization. She chronicles the family history of the Ingmarssons, a race of peasant-farmers, through two generations. She shows how even the peasant's age-long devotion

LAGERLÖF, Selma Ottiliana Lovisa (*continued*).
to the land yields at the call of religion, although her own sympathies are not with the fanatic. It is a story that at many points touches sublimity. [Transl. by Jessie BRÖCHNER, Heinemann : o.p. ; the very American translation by Velma Swanston HOWARD (Doubleday, New York ; Laurie) is incomplete, in spite of the words " the end."]

—— *The Girl from the Marsh Croft* (En saga om en saga, 1904). 1910
Nine short stories, with a literary autobiography entitled *The Story of a Story*. [Transl. by Velma Swanston HOWARD, Laurie ; Doubleday, Doran, New York.]

—— *Herr Arne's Hoard* (Herr Arnes penningar, 1904). 1923
An excellent example of Miss Lagerlöf's power of blending the real with the supernatural into a finished whole. It is the story of how a rich man was plundered, and his family murdered, by three Scottish soldiers of fortune in sixteenth-century Sweden, and of the divine vengeance which overtook them ; the telling suggests the simplicity and finality of an old ballad. [Transl. by A. G. CHATER, *illus.* by Wendal : o.p. ; *sub tit. Treasure*, Doubleday, Doran, New York ; with *Other Sketches*, transl. by C. FIELD, Laurie.]

—— *The Wonderful Adventures of Nils* (Nils Holgerssons underbara resa genom Sverige, 2 vols., 1906–7). 1907

—— *The Further Adventures of Nils*. 1911
Fanciful stories written to supply a child's reading book for schools, about a boy's dream of animals and birds. [Transl. by Velma Swanston HOWARD, Doubleday, New York ; (Marbacka ed.), *id.*, 1928.]

—— *Liliecrona's Home* (Liljecronas hem, 1911). 1914
A pleasant tale for children, of a jolly old pastor in Värmland, who is visited by a watersprite long ago evicted from the lake that once flowed where now is his glebe, and, unhappily for him, married by this mischievous elf. [Transl. by Anna BARWELL, Dent (Dutton, New York).]

—— *The Emperor of Portugallia* (Kejsaren av Portugallien: en Värmlandshistoria, 1914). 1916
In this novel of domestic life among simple villagers, the moral and dramatic interest lies in the tragic requital of a father's selfless love by a selfish daughter. Miss Lagerlöf's insistence upon spiritual instead of material values, and her delicate perception of beauty and significance in trivial things, come out strongly in the character of Jan Rüffleck. In the extremity of grief, Jan's wits wander, and he styles himself " Emperor," yet he retains the nobility and charity of his normal self. [Transl. by Velma Swanston HOWARD ; Hodder : o.p. ; Doubleday, New York.]

—— *The Outcast* (Bannlyst, 1918). 1920
Although the period here is that of the great war, and the battle of Jutland provides matter for a pacifist postscriptum, this is a story that reads like a mediæval saga. It is stranger than romance, though the dramatic truth is undeniable. Scene, the western seaboard of Sweden. Out of the humility and unselfishness which his ostracism has nourished, the pariah becomes a teacher of men and a champion of the Life that overcomes Death. [Transl. by W. WORSTER, Holden ; Doubleday, New York.]

—— *Mårbacka*. 1924
Reminiscences, portraits, and legends of the authoress's ancestral home. [Transl. by V. S. HOWARD, Doubleday, Doran, New York ; Laurie ; also *illus.*, *id.*]

—— *The General's Ring* (Löwensköldska ringen, 1925). 1928
The ring is stolen from the grave of a fierce old officer of Charles XII, and his ghost avenges itself on innocent and guilty for three generations, till a devoted young girl restores it. For the sequels see below. [Transl. by Francesca MARTIN, Doubleday, New York ; Laurie.]

—— *The Ring of the Löwenskölds ; including The General's Ring, Charlotte Löwensköld* (1925), *and Anna Svärd* (1928). 1930
The theme of the turbulent nature of the Löwenskölds is richly developed in the further course of the trilogy. A century after the affair of the ring, Charlotte Löwensköld is thrown over by her betrothed, whom she has led to believe her tinged with the family greed. But this man also comes of the same unstable blood. He weds an illiterate peasant, and rushes from one excess to another, ere, after years of missionary service in Africa, he learns wisdom and settles down peaceably with his wife. But that is only part of the complicated drama. [Transl. by Velma Swanston HOWARD, Doubleday, New York ; Laurie.]
[*Works*, 11 vols., Doubleday, New York.]

LAMPEL, Peter Martin [German ; *b.* 1894]. *Youth Betrayed* (Berratene Jungen, 1929). 1930
Herr Lampel, the playwright, here deals appealingly with the case of those misguided youths who for various motives were enlisted into the Black Army and involved in the abortive Kapp-Putsch. [Transl. by Agnes PLATT, Shaylor.]

" LANCASTER, G. B." [Edith Lyttleton ; New Zealander]. *Sons o' Men*. 1904
Short stories of sheep-run life in New Zealand ; strong local colour—very local—relating to the South Island. [Melrose : o.p.]

—— *A Spur to Smite*. 1905
Life in town and bush amid the beauties of New Zealand and on the shores of Samoa. [Melrose : o.p.]

LANDON, Letitia Elizabeth [Mrs. Maclean ; 1802–38]. *Ethel Churchill ; or, The Two Brides*. 1837
The days of the first Georges ; a touching story, with some wit and tender sentiment in the dialogue. Historic characters come on the stage, e.g. Sir Robert Walpole. L.E.L. was a popular poet in the time of Mrs. Hemans. [o.p.]

LANDOR, Walter Savage [1775–1864]. *Pericles and Aspasia*. 1836
The most famous example of Landor's stately dialogues, and the one that in form is the nearest approach to a novel. Fills in the story of Pericles and the brilliant hetaira, told in outline by historians ; and gives a vivid idea of the intellectual and social life of Athens in the Golden Age, Alcibiades, Socrates, Aristophanes, Anaxagoras, Sophocles, etc., figuring in this series of familiar letters. Landor's majestic periods, sculptured epigrams, and polished verse are admirably suited to the nobility of the theme. [In *Works*, Dent (Scribner, New York) ; Scott : o.p.]

LANE, Elinor Macartney [Mrs. Francis Rantour Lane; American; 1864–1909]. *Nancy Stair.* 1905
Edinburgh (1768–88). Robert Burns and William Pitt are introduced, the former not too favourably. Nancy Stair, poetess and student of law, is a very charming and life-like figure, as portrayed by her father (*c.* 1801). The tale ends in melodrama. [Appleton, New York; Heinemann.]

LANE, Mrs. John [*née* Anna Eichberg, formerly Mrs. King; American by birth]. *Kitwyk.* 1902
Cranford-like sketches of the society and individuals of a little old-fashioned town in Holland a hundred years ago; playful, sentimental, and full of affectionate observation. Little episodes, complete in themselves, knit together into a longer narrative. [Lane.]

LANG, Andrew [Scottish; 1844–1912]. *A Monk of Fife.* 1895
The youthful adventures of a monk of Dunfermline, who has been a Scottish archer in the French service and had much intercourse with Joan of Arc. Besides her glorious and tragic story, the romance deals in love, villainy, fighting, and hairbreadth escapes. The monk writes the tale in the language and manner of the age (1429–31). [Longmans, London and New York: o.p.]
See also Haggard, Sir H. Rider, and A. Lang (p. 221), and Mason, A. E. W., and A. Lang (p. 332).

LANG, John. *The Wetherbys; or, A few Chapters of Indian Experience.* 1850
A journalist's picture of Anglo-Indian life and manners before the Mutiny (*c.* 1845); caustic in its satire and caricatures of bygone types of English and half-castes. Ferozeshah supplies a battle-piece. [Chapman: o.p.]

LARNED, Augusta [American; 1835–*c.* 1920]. *Village Photographs.* 1887
Sketches of a representative village of New England; realistic though not too frank. Altogether they form an almost exhaustive account of a rustic community, the life-histories of a large number of people being related as they appear to the neighbours, illustrating how little real privacy there is in such a little world. Feminine characters predominate. [Holt, New York: o.p.]

LARRETA, Enrique [Spanish (Argentine); *b.* 1875]. *The Glory of Don Ramiro* (La Gloria de Don Ramiro, 1908). 1924
A vivid picture of Spanish life in the days of Philip II (1570–1605). [Transl. by L. B. WALTON, Dent; Dutton, New York.]

LARSEN, Hanna Astrup [ed.]. *Norway's Best Stories.* 1928
Twenty-one stories representing Björnson, Lie, Kielland, Garborg, Skram, Bull, Hamsun, Krag, Kinck, Aanrud, Hilditch, Egge, Bojer, Scott, Duun, Falkberget, Fönhus, and Undset. There are brief biographical notes. The translations are made by Anders Olbeck. [American-Scandinavian Foundation, Norton, New York; Allen & Unwin.]

—— *Sweden's Best Stories.* 1928
Representing Ahlgren, Bo Bergman, Engstrom, Geijerstam, Heidenstam, Levertin, Lagerlöf, Hallström, Molin, Nordström, Martha áf Sillén, Siwertz, Söderberg, Strindberg, and Topelius; with brief biographical notes. [Transl. by Charles Wharton STORK, American-Scandinavian Foundation, Norton, New York (Allen & Unwin).]

—— *Denmark's Best Stories.* 1928
Stories by Andersen, Bang, Blicker Goldschmidt, Drachmann, Gunnarsson, Jacobsen, Jensen, Larsen, Nexö, Pontoppidan, Schandorph, Skjoldberg, Söiberg, and Wied. There are brief biographical notes. [American-Scandinavian Foundation, Norton, New York (Allen & Unwin).]

LARSEN, Nella [American]. *Passing.* 1929
A study of a woman of part negro descent, who passes for a white, and has a white husband, though there is an inbred craving to revert to her own race. The authoress is herself of negro ancestry. [Knopf, New York and London.]

LA SALE, Antoine de [French; *c.* 1388–1462 (?)]. *The Fifteen Comforts of Rash and Inconsiderate Marriage; or, Select Animadversions upon the Miscarriages of a Wedded State; done out of French. The fourth edition, with the addition of three Comforts.* 4th edn., 1694
A translation of *Les Quinze Joies de Mariage* (1462) accredited to La Sale on the strength of an acrostic in one MS.; another rendering or adaptation is the famous *Batchelor's Banquet* of Thomas Dekker. The *Quinze Joies* is an astonishing example of malicious realism and cynical moralizing ages before Balzac and Anatole France, but not so many ages after the fabliaux. La Sale is also credited with the authorship of the famous farce, *Pathelin*, and the compilation and part-authorship of the *Cent nouvelles nouvelles*, a work imitated from the *Decameron* and inspired to some extent by the *Facetiae* of Poggio. [This translation is a very rare chap-book which differs in many details from *The Fifteen Comforts of Matrimony, with an addition of Three Comforts more, wherein the various Miscarriages of the Wedded State, and the miserable Consequences of Rash and Inconsiderate Marriages are laid open and detected.* London, 1760: o.p. There was also a translation, *The Fyftene Joyes of Maryage*, by Henry FIELDING, printed by Wynkyn de Worde, 1509; new transl. by Richard ALDINGTON, (Broadway Transl.) Routledge (Dutton, New York), 1926.]

—— *The History and Pleasant Chronicle of Little Jehan de Saintré, and of the Lady of the Fair Cousins* [1459], *together with the Book of the Knight of the Tower Landry. An English translation by Alexander Vance.* 1862
L'histoire et plaisante cronique du Petit Jehan de Saintré et de la jeune Dame des Belles Cousines sans autre nom nommer. Little Jehan is a page of honour, whose bringing up and adventures at Court are an amusing and naively realistic account of the manners, morals, and ceremonial of the ages of chivalry, especially as regards the intercourse of the sexes. La Dame des Belles Cousines instructs the unsophisticated youth in the arts of love, and the sequel, where she succumbs to a low intrigue related in fabliau style, is supposed to be a fling at the theory of *l'amour courtois. La Tour-Landry* is so much abbreviated here as to be of little value. [Chapman & Hall: o.p. *Little John of Saintré*, transl. by Irvine GRAY, Routledge, 1931.]

LATHROP, George Parsons [American; 1851–98]. *In the Distance.* 1882
A recondite, imaginative conception is the basis of this story, the great hill of Monadnoc " in the distance " deeply influencing the lives of Edith and her lovers in their holiday-resort among the mountains. [Scribner, New York: o.p.]

LATHROP, George Parsons (*continued*). *An Echo of Passion.* 1884

A painful episode in the life of a young married couple, the motives carefully worked out to give a truthful rendering of spiritual conflict. [Scribner, New York : o.p. ; Douglas, Edinburgh : o.p.]

—— *Would You Kill Him ?* 1890

Holsclaw, the subject of what seems to be a plea against capital punishment, is a well-intentioned, but somewhat weak man, who with very little blame attaching to himself, sees his married life about to be wrecked by the sudden disclosure of an old engagement he had concealed. In a violent dispute he accidentally kills the person threatening him ; hence the title. [Harper, New York : o.p.]

LA TOUR-LANDRY, Geoffroy de [French ; 14th century]. *The Book of the Knight of La Tour-Landry, Compiled for the Instruction of his Daughters.* Middle 15th century.

Written 1371-2 ; first printed in French 1514 ; translated into English by Caxton [see below], 1483, and printed by him 1484. The present is a much older translation, however, which existed only in MS. until now ; it is not so bald and literal as Caxton's, and renders the spirit of the original more faithfully. A multifarious collection of didactic stories, pious examples, parables, miracle-tales, and the like ; from Holy Scripture, classical sources, and the legends of chivalry. They inculcate the virtues of piety, chastity, modesty of dress and demeanour, spiritual and worldly wisdom. La Tour-Landry is a castle in Anjou ; its ruins are still visible. [Translated from the original French in the reign of Henry VI, and edited, with introduction and notes, by Thomas WRIGHT (Early English Text Soc.) (1868), revised ed., 1906, Oxford Press. Ed. by G. S. TAYLOR, Hamilton, 1930. See also *The Booke of Thenseygnementes and Techynge that the Knyght of the Towre made to his Doughters.* By the Chevalier Geoffroy De La TOUR-LANDRY. Edited, with notes and a glossary, by Gertrude Burford RAWLINGS, Newnes, 1903 : o.p. This is a selection from Caxton's translation. Of less value to students than the preceding, it has been adapted for general reading by the omission of those coarse and plain-spoken anecdotes and expressions that were characteristic of the age. The language has not been modernized. A selection of the original translated by Alexander VANCE appeared in 1862, see above, La Sale, *Little Jehan de Saintré.*]

LAUDER, Sir Thomas Dick [Scottish ; 1784-1848]. *The Wolfe of Badenoch.* 1827

Career of Alexander Stewart, Earl of Buchan (*d.* 1394), son of Robert II (1371-90). Strong in local and antiquarian colour relating to the Speyside region and Morayshire (1388-94). [With pref. by R. B. Cunninghame Graham, Mackay, Stirling (Simpkin), 1930.]

LAUT, Agnes Christina [Canadian ; *b.* 1871]. *Lords of the North.* 1901

The far north of Canada a hundred years ago, when fierce rivalry was raging between the great fur-trading companies. A man's quest for his wife, kidnapped by Iroquois, and his comrade's love-affair, form the two streams of incident. Pioneer life among the savages and adventure in the trackless wilderness. [Heinemann : o.p. ; Doran, New York : o.p.]

—— *Heralds of Empire : being the story of one Ramsay Stanhope, lieutenant to Pierre Radisson in the northern fur trade.* 1902

Adventures in the wilderness, and the exploits of the famous pioneer Radisson in the Hudson Bay region fighting the French (1671-83). [Appleton, New York : o.p.]

LA VERGNE, Mme Cécile Josephine Julie [French]. *The Spire of Caudebec.* 1909

A slight story of the fifteenth century. [Transl. by Constance, Countess DE LA WARR, Sands : o.p.]

LAWLESS, Hon. Emily [Irish ; 1845-1913]. *Hurrish ; a study.* 1886

An impressive picture of the half-barbarous peasantry on the Atlantic shore, deeply sympathetic in its rendering of their sombre and imaginative temperament. Hurrish is a generous, lofty, and appealing type of primitive manhood. The writer gives a very unfriendly account of the doings of the Land League. [Methuen : o.p.]

—— *Major Lawrence, F.L.S.* 1887

Chiefly a character-portrait of a simple-minded and great-hearted gentleman. [Murray : o.p.]

—— *With Essex in Ireland.* 1890

Supposed to be the secretary's journal of the expedition of Lord Essex to suppress the rebellion in Tyrone, reproducing the contemporary language and modes of thought. Based on historical documents, the narrative pictures in a graphic way the miserable state of Ireland day by day, recounting the ambushes, battles, and skirmishes that in 1599 beset the progress of the expedition. A mournful and terrible narrative. [Methuen : o.p.]

—— *Grania : the story of an island.* 1892

On the barren, melancholy Aran Isles, off the Galway coast, inhabited by a primitive race of fishermen, whose dreamy and humorous temperament, with its strain of gloom, is interpreted with sympathetic tenderness, is played out a tragedy, the actors a pure and lofty fisher-girl, a true child of nature, her saintly sister, and the lover, typically Irish in his goodness and in his vices. [Smith & Elder : o.p.]

—— *Maelcho : a sixteenth-century narrative.* 1894

A gloomy account of the natives beyond the **Pale,** and their struggles with the English in the time of the Desmonds (1577-82) ; a story well authenticated, bringing out all the horrors of the English conquest. [Methuen : o.p. ; Appleton, New York : o.p.]

—— *Traits and Confidences.* 1898

Detached tales and sketches of character, plans, and scenery, with some historical matter towards the end. [Methuen : o.p.]

—— *The Book of Gilly ; edited by Emily Lawless.* 1906

A vivid picturing of life on Inishkey, an islet in Kenmare Bay, as beheld through the eyes of a little boy. [Murray.]

LAWLESS, Hon. Emily, and BULLOCK, Shan F. [Irish ; *b.* 1865]. *The Race of Castlebar.* 1913

An Englishman tells, without prejudice, the story of Humbert's invasion of Ireland (1798). The narrative is based on the account written by Joseph Stock, Bishop of Killala, who was captured by Humbert. [Murray : o.p.]

LAWRENCE, Charles Edward [1870–1928]. *Pilgrimage.*   1907
    A tale of the middle ages, with plenty of satire on the religious and social institutions of the time. [(Wayfarer's Lib.), Dent (Dutton, New York) : o.p.]

—— *The Arnold Lip.*   1913
    The comedy of a young man who scandalizes his conventional family by adopting an illegitimate baby. [Murray : o.p.]

—— *Mrs. Bente.*   1918
    A woman of the streets succeeds in marrying a visionary curate who has vowed to save her soul. But the woman is irreclaimable and drags him to the verge of ruin, not, however, without serving as an instrument for satirizing the smug and snobbish inhabitants of their country parish. [Collins : o.p.]

—— *Youth Went Riding : a romance.*   1918
    A harebrained young champion goes out to defeat wicked barons and rescue ladies—and to furnish ironical entertainment. [Collins.]

—— *Such Stuff as Dreams.*   1919
    A clerk is enabled, as the result of a cerebral lesion, to see London peopled by those men and women of the past whose personality is strong enough to survive ; lesson—" we must bring in the Past to mend our ideals in the Present." [Murray.]

—— *The God in the Thicket.*   1920
    A fantasy set in the Forest of Argorie. Into the world of Harlequin and Columbine, a poor musician of genius enters. He compounds with Pan, who lurks behind all, to exchange his gift for the love of Punchinello's daughter, but loses gift and love alike. [Dent.]

—— *The Iron Bell.*   1921
    Grim realism—the life of despair of a woman of the lower classes overshadowed by insanity. [O'Connor : o.p.]

—— *The Old Man's Wife.*   1926
    A young woman unhappily married leaves her husband, who is subsequently murdered. Only after her trial and condemnation does the real murderess confess. [Murray.]

—— *Underneath.*   1928
    Similar in plan to *No. 5, John Street*—the hero abandons his wealth to live for a year amongst the homeless and workless. His experiences whilst tramping in search of work, and when employed as a greengrocer's assistant in Islington, are strongly described ; but realism degenerates into sentimentality in certain of his encounters with women of the streets. [Murray.]

LAWRENCE, David Herbert [1885–1930]. *The White Peacock.*   1911
    This long and rather crude novel covers a long span in the lives of various young people growing up together on the fringes of Derbyshire and Nottinghamshire. The picturing of nature and of farm life is beautifully done. The deeper interest lies in the incessant conflict between deep and half-recognized instincts and affinities and the social influences that try to thwart them, especially in the case of a man who fails to marry the girl who was his natural mate, and eventually declines into sloth and drunkenness. [Secker.]

—— *The Trespasser.*   1912
    The Trespasser wins another woman's husband away, and the result is uttermost tragedy for him, whilst she survives to love again. The idyll of their stolen honeymoon on the Isle of Wight is beautiful with the impassioned imagination that transmutes visible things into poetic symbols. The tragedy which turns beauty to poison is the dreadful sense that nothing can bridge the gulf between the two minds. But for a few lapses, Lawrence's style is here at its best. [Duckworth ; Secker ; Kennerley, New York : o.p.]

—— *Sons and Lovers.*   1913
    Largely autobiographical, like his play, *The Widowing of Mrs. Holroyd* (1914), and like that containing a fine portrait of a mother, wife of a drunken collier, who despite piteous circumstances brings up her family decently. The early part presents life through the eyes of Mrs. Morel ; in the later, centring in her son Paul, we are led among baffling complexes and subtleties. This is concerned with his incipient love-affairs ; and in Miriam, the woman who " over-refined " the sex-instinct in Paul, we have one of Lawrence's inscrutable beings, whose emotions and curious antagonisms seem to be inadequately analysed, except perhaps to a Freudian expert. In the end, after passages with another girl, Paul recognizes that it is his mother that he really loves—in short, the Œdipus complex has him in its grip. [Duckworth ; Secker ; Boni, New York ; Argus Co., Chicago.]

—— *The Prussian Officer ; and other stories.*   1914
    In the first two, both of German soldiers, a sudden uprush of elemental, i.e. unconscious impulse, physical rather than mental, launches a man into crime. The longest story, *Daughters of the Vicar*, shows the clash between intellect and instinct in two sisters ; one, fighting down physical repulsion, marries a poor reed of a man who saves her from her father's poverty, the other sets class-prejudice at defiance and chooses a sturdy collier. Some of the rest are about miners or country people in the Nottingham district, and the verbal evocations of nature in field and woodland are exquisitely done. For tense, bloodless tragedy, *Shadow in the Rose Garden* is a little masterpiece. [Duckworth ; Secker ; Huebsch, New York : o.p.]

—— *The Rainbow.*   1915 (*rev. ed.*) 1926
    The original edition was withdrawn for censorship reasons. In this novel, Lawrence dealt with the conflicts and soul-storms of sex on an almost epical scale. The characters mostly belong again to the rural neighbourhood of Ilkeston and Nottingham, and embrace three generations of English middle-class people and some Poles connected with them by marriages. The more prominent are what is vulgarly called " over-sexed " ; and the men are not, to use his own phrase, " manly men." Of the two principal women, the Pole finds equilibrium in the routine of child-bearing, the half-English girl, imaginative and passionate but unable to discover her perfect mate, comes to grief. She insists " on creating life to fit herself " ; and on her tragic story Lawrence lavished some of his most beautiful writing. [Secker ; Boni, New York (1924) ; Viking Press, New York.]

LAWRENCE, David Herbert (*continued*). *The Lost Girl.* 1920

The girl belongs to the same mining folk as Paul Morel, in *Sons and Lovers*, and breaks away from her dull environment to marry an Italian. The magnetic effect of his " psyche " upon hers is described in the technical terms of Freudian analysis ; but there is little of the powerful handling of impulse and passion that distinguished the former novel. [Secker ; Boni, New York.]

—— *Women in Love.* 1921

This, in some sort a sequel to *The Rainbow*, sums up the author's mystical theories of sex, still tentative and inchoate, still obscure also, and by no means stated in a way to conciliate criticism. There are three women, of different temperament, among them Ursula Brangwen in her after-life, and two men of opposite natures, one of whom, almost the author's direct mouthpiece, craves something " beyond love, beyond any emotional relationship." This man, an intellectual if ever there was one, ascribes our demoralization to our self-consciousness—" Better be animals, mere animals with no mind at all, than this, this *nothingness*." [Secker ; Boni, New York.]

—— *Aaron's Rod.* 1922

More inchoate than most of Lawrence's novels, it is on the standing subject, the chaos of impulses and incoherent aspirations in the break-up of established moral standards—life in a state of revolution with no terminus in sight. The miner, Aaron Sisson, with his passion for music, who after various adventures wanders off to Italy, is evidently Lawrence himself. There is some vivid character-drawing, and life in Florence is charmingly pictured. " You are your own Tree of Life, roots and limbs and trunk. Somewhere within the wholeness of the tree lies the very self, the quick ; its own innate Holy Ghost. And the Holy Ghost puts forth new buds, and pushes past old limits, and shakes off a whole body of dying leaves." Such is the doctrine propounded in this and developed in later novels. [Secker ; Boni, New York.]

—— *Kangaroo.* 1923

We are told here that a novel should be a " thought-adventure," and this, with its long discussions and meditations on life and civilization, is verily such. In the adventures of an Englishman who goes to Australia and is all but captured by the new revolutionary Australianism of the self-appointed liberator Kangaroo, a kind of mystic Shavianism is preached, in which we see Lawrence groping for a creed. We hear still more about " the God-wife, the life-prompting, the Holy Ghost." " A dark, mysterious God hovers behind the human conflict, and the victory is with those who can seize and identify themselves with this dark master of human destiny." The Australian scene has never been painted more magically, or the Australian mentality more truthfully summed up. [Secker ; Boni, New York.]

—— *The Ladybird.* 1923

In the first of these three stories, the Bohemian count and the thrilled society woman who feels the mystic call, the infernal witchery, of a deeper world than that of her old conventional self and of her solid British husband, are striking illustrations of the new psychology. We peer again into the dark tracts of the subconscious in the other tales. The soldier-boy in *The Fox* kills a woman by a calculated accident, through some unconscious hate or homicidal impulse ; and the older woman responds to some occult charm in the boy, otherwise her antipathy. In *The Captain's Doll*, where post-war life in a Tyrolese pleasure-haunt is vividly evoked, the German women have little other distinction than these dim, unanalysable traits. [Secker ; *sub tit. The Captain's Doll : three novelettes*, Boni, New York.]

—— *England, my England.* 1924

Ten stories, each a glimpse into the deep, inscrutable life of the natural man, the " sheer immediacy of blood-contact with the substantial world " that, according to Lawrence, makes for happiness—the lonely soul, " brooding on the face of the uncreated flux, as a bird on a dark sea." *Tickets, please* and *Samson and Delilah* both turn on the humours of the sexual appeal. *Monkey Nuts, You touched Me*, and *The Horse-dealer's Daughter* deal with it in different ways. *The Blind Man* shows the other side, instinctive antipathy. [Secker ; Boni, New York.]

—— *St. Mawr ; together with The Princess.* 1925

St. Mawr is a horse, and also a symbol—of that untamed life of natural things which is in entire opposition to the domesticated existence of men to-day, men who are not really alive. " I don't know one single man who is a proud living animal. I know they've left off really thinking." Men have eliminated this, " in the process called civilization, and hence they have eliminated life." In the passages between the two women who sense all this and in certain persons of the contrary stamp, Lawrence gives a loose to his scorching humour. The other story is thoroughly characteristic and expresses the same ideas ; it also depicts the mountain scenery of New Mexico superbly, as *St. Mawr* does that of Arizona. [Secker ; Knopf, New York.]

—— *The Plumed Serpent (Quetzalcoatl).* 1926

A woman goes to Mexico, and finding two men trying to revive the old native religion, after long hesitation throws in her lot with them, and marries one, an Indian general. Merely as a travel-book, this at least equals *Eothen* and *The Bible in Spain*, as a revelation of the inmost character of a country and a race. In Mexico, naturally, Lawrence finds in full activity the spiritual forces whose extinction he deplores elsewhere. Readers may perhaps think the myth-making chapters too diffuse, and the hymns and ceremonies overdone. [Secker ; Knopf, New York.]

—— *The Woman who Rode Away ; and other stories.* 1928

Ten altogether. The title-story is a compact variant of *The Plumed Serpent*—a mine-owner's wife in Mexico is lured by the call of the wild and rides away to the Indians. *Glad Ghosts* and *Jimmy and the Desperate Woman* both strain probability in the effort to show up the inferiority and baseness of " this half-death which we call life." *The Last Laugh*—of Pan at Hampstead—is frankly an imaginative flight. On the other hand, *Two Blue Birds, Smile*, and *In Love* are delicate little studies of the interplay of temperament that seem at first sight to be entirely outside Lawrence's ambit. But as in *Sun*, a simple tale of sun-bathing, his mystical vision is always there, fastened upon the essentials. [Secker ; Knopf, New York.]

—— *Lady Chatterley's Lover.* 1929

A book rightly suppressed in Great Britain. Lawrence, with his strong views on the " spiritual body " and

LAWRENCE, David Herbert (*continued*).
the importance of the sexual life, evolved a vague and heterodox morality of his own, and in the exasperation of persecution and controversy wrote this very indecent book as a sort of challenge. [Including *My Skirmish with Jolly Roger*, privately printed; expurgated ed., 1932, Secker.]

—— *The Virgin and the Gipsy*. 1930
Posthumous, and left with some improbabilities, even in the culminating scene, which would perhaps have been smoothed away. One of his most successful figures of a young girl, cast in his favourite mould, daughter of a poor-spirited rector in a Derbyshire village, is drawn to a gipsy, as Lady Chatterley is to her gamekeeper. The clergyman's old mother is wonderful in her repulsiveness. [Secker; Knopf, New York.]

LAWRENCE, D. H., and SKINNER, Miss M. L. *The Boy in the Bush*. 1924
Apparently Miss Skinner contributed the rich and intimate knowledge of unkempt life in Western Australia, and perhaps helped in giving accuracy to the unmitigated patois of the dialogue. *Kangaroo* was a discussion novel, this is a good story, the history of the boy's self-development—on Laurentian lines. Much of it hinges on his struggle with the brutal Easu, who personifies the evil forces which he must instinctively combat. He finds himself when he enters the grey-blue paradise of the bush, "where man has to begin all over again." There, in passages of magnificent prose that is half-poetry, it is told how, nearing the primal source of life, he realizes his "spiritual body," which Easu and his like would degrade and subjugate to the sensual body. [Secker; Boni, New York.]

LAWRENCE, George Alfred [1827–76]. *Guy Livingstone; or, Thorough*. 1857
Lawrence wrote a number of crude, defiant, and theatrical romances of contemporary life, proclaiming his gospel of victorious manhood. His "physical force doctrine" was called by detractors the creed of "Muscular Blackguardism." Guy is his representative hero, a Byronic, arrogant, aristocratic young man, of prodigious bodily strength and implacable temper—a Berserk out of his element in an age of peace and civilization, who discharges his pent-up energies in libertine amours and physical sports, in the lack of more serious fields for his prowess. His fellows, including the old crony who writes the memoir, love him in spite of his cruelty and egoism. The supposed biographer introduces congenial anecdotes, such as the defence of a house against Irish moonlighters by a handful of gentlemen, with tremendous carnage. Brilliantly satirized in Bret Harte's *Condensed Novels*. [With introd. by E. A. Baker (Half-forgotten Books), Routledge (Dutton, New York), 1903 : o.p.]

—— *Sword and Gown*. 1859
Here another champion of muscularity, "the Cool Captain," wins the heart of a society beauty and then divulges that he has a wife living. He is eventually killed in the Crimea, whither the girl has followed him as a hospital nurse. The novelist hopes that heaven may have mercy on this bold rider's soul. [Routledge : o.p.]

—— *Brakespeare; or, The Fortunes of a Free-Lance*. 1868
An historical and romantic version of the muscular novel. Brakespeare is a free companion, like the famous mercenary Sir John Hawkwood. An almost epical panorama of the great days of Cressy and Poitiers, the days of Manny and Chandos (1346–56). After bearing the brunt of a hundred combats, Lawrence's champion falls at the hands of Du Guesclin. The fighting scenes reveal the inspiration of the Norse sagas, which were at the height of a fresh popularity in Lawrence and Kingsley's time. [Routledge.]

—— *Breaking a Butterfly: Blanche Ellerslie's ending*. 1869
Another embodiment of Lawrence's doctrine of the overman. His style is often vivid and imaginative, but at its worst as florid and pretentious as Ouida's, and by no means "a well of English undefiled." [Tinsley : o.p.]

—— *Hagarene*. 1874
Lawrence's idea of an adventuress. [Chapman : o.p.]

LAWSON, Henry Hertzberg [Australian; 1867–1922]. *While the Billy Boils*. 1897
Lawson's stories are chiefly of note for their intimate picturing of actual life in the bush. These are a characteristic set of painfully realistic sketches of the hardships in the life of a settler. The best are *The Drover's Wife* and *His Father's Mate*. [Angus & Robertson, Sydney; Cape.]

—— *On the Track; and, Over the Sliprails*. 1901
Similar stories and pictures of human nature in the bush, presenting a rough and lawless manner of life, and characters of a rude and disreputable class—tramps, sharpers, gold-diggers, wastrels, as well as squatters, cattle-drivers, sheep-shearers, etc.—accentuating the more sombre aspects of Australian life. [Angus & Robertson, Sydney (Australian Book Co., London).]

—— *The Country I come from*. 1901
Short sketches and concise character-portraits of bush life—in their masculine vigour and terse expressiveness, as in their sharp contrasts and grim touches of reality, not unlike Bret Harte. [Blackwood : o.p.]

—— *Joe Wilson and his Mates*. 1901
—— *Children of the Bush*. 1902
Similar pictures of the Australian world by the well-known Australian poet. [(1) and (2), Angus & Robertson, Sydney (Australian Bk. Co., London).]

LAXDAELA SAGA. 1899
This famous saga contains some of the greatest characters and grandest scenes in northern literature. After the customary historical and genealogical recital, full of interesting minor episodes, come the stories of Hoskuld and his son Olaf the Peacock, two of the noblest Icelanders (before 890–1031); then the careers of the brave and chivalrous Kjärtan Olafson (978–1003) and his foster-brother Bolli; and side by side with these the dramatic story of Gudrun and her four marriages. The great tragic event of the story is the slaying of Kjärtan by Bolli, which is followed by the usual series of blood-feuds. Snorri the priest makes his appearance towards the end of the saga. "It is a modern prose version of the Niblung tragedy. . . . Kjärtan stands for Sigurd, Gudrun . . . in the place of Brynhild, wife of Gunnar" (W. P. Ker). (Probably first put together in thirteenth century.) [Transl. by Muriel A. C. PRESS, (Temple Classics) Dent; transl. by Thorstein VEBLEN, Viking Press, New York, 1925.]

LEACOCK, Stephen Butler [Canadian; *b.* 1869]. *Literary Lapses : a book of sketches.*   1910
By the Professor of Political Science at McGill University. Jocular tales and sketches by a new humorist, sometimes in the vein of Artemus Ward or Mark Twain, and sometimes in quite his own. *Boarding House Geometry* is a good sample of the best. [Dodd & Mead, New York ; Lane.]

—— *Nonsense Novels.*   1911
Not parodies of particular books, but absurd burlesques of the types of fiction now or recently in vogue, e.g. the detective novel, the Kailyard school, psychical romance, anticipations. [Lane ; Dodd & Mead, New York ; Garden City Co., New York.]

—— *Sunshine Sketches of a Little Town.*   1912
A masterpiece of humour and sympathetic observation of life as it was in the small towns of Ontario before the war—a life that has now passed away. Orillia, Ont., is said to have been the original " little town." [Dodd & Mead, New York ; Lane.]

—— *Arcadian Adventures with the Idle Rich.*   1914
Pokes fun at certain types of wealthy Americans of both sexes. [Lane ; Dodd & Mead, New York.]

—— *Further Foolishness : sketches and satires on the follies of to-day.*   1917
This instalment is on the whole forced and unduly boisterous. [Lane ; Dodd & Mead, New York.]

—— *Winsome Winnie ; and other new Nonsense Novels.*   1920
Five parodies of established types of fiction—the detective story, the marooned lovers, and so on—and three other sketches. [Dodd & Mead, New York ; Lane.]

LEADBITTER, Eric. *Rain before Seven.*   1915
A consistently low-pitched history of the first twenty-five years in the life of a thoroughly dull, unexciting fellow, who finds more satisfaction in a clerkship than in developing his musical talent. [Allen & Unwin.]

—— *Perpetual Fires.*   1918
A quiet, uneventful history of a Northumberland family through three generations, focusing interest upon the subtler influences of environment and tradition in the characters and their relations to each other. [Allen & Unwin.]

—— *Shepherd's Warning.*   1920
The comedy, pathos, and good cheer of rural life (1890–1910). The central figure, an old ploughman, resisting time and change, expresses well the spirit of the soil. [Allen & Unwin.]

LEAHY, A. H. [Irish ; *b.* 1857] (ed.). *The Courtship of Ferb : a romance of the Cuchulain cycle.*   1902
Appears in Lady Gregory's version of the Cuchulain legends as *The Wedding of Maine Morgor.* Maine, son of Maeve and Ailell of Connaught, goes to Rath Ini in Ulster to marry Ferb, daughter of Gerg. Conchubar, King of Ulster, aided by the Fomor, attacks them in the house. Maine and Gerg fall, and both hosts are all but exterminated. A sort of Irish *cante-fable,* translated into prose and verse from the German of Prof. Windisch. [(Irish Saga Lib.), Nutt.: o.p.]

—— *Ancient Heroic Romances of Ireland.*   1905
Vol. i contains five stories : *The Courtship of Etain* (two versions from Egerton MS. 1782 and the *Leabhar na h'Uidhri* ; *Mac Datho's Boar* (*Book of Leinster*) ; *The Sick-bed of Cuchulain* (*Leabhar na h'Uidhri*) ; *The Exile of the Sons of Usnach* (*Book of Leinster*) ; and *The Combat at the Ford* (*Book of Leinster* version). Vol. ii. contains five of the lesser tains : *The Tain bó Fraich, Dartada, Regamon, Flidais,* and *Regamna* (Mr. Leahy has altered the accepted names). The verses interspersed in the prose, and the last four lesser tains or preludes, have been translated, not satisfactorily, into English verse ; the prose rendering is scholarly, exact, and admirably conveys the spirit of the original. [Transl. into prose and verse (Irish Saga Lib.), 2 vols., Nutt : o.p.]

LEBLANC, Maurice [French ; *b.* 1864]. *The Exploits of Arsène Lupin* (Arsène Lupin, gentleman cambrioleur, 1907).   1912
Arsène is a super-criminal, with all the resources of modern civilization at his disposal, who plays the part of a Robin Hood, preying on plutocratic society. Eventually he turns over a new leaf and becomes head of the detective service. [Transl. by A. T. de Mattos, Mills & Boon ; Ogilvie, New York.]

—— *The Bomb-Shell* (L'éclat d'obus, 1914).   1914
The impersonations of a woman spy, the kidnapping of a son of the Kaiser, various murders, etc.—an exciting story of the frontier region during the early part of the great war. [Transl. by A. Texeira de Mattos, Hurst & Blackett : o.p.]

—— *The Crystal Stopper* (Le bouchon de cristal).   1913
An exciting impossible story of a crime by motor-bandits, and Lupin's daring exploit in rescuing an innocent comrade from the guillotine. [Transl. by Alexander Texeira de Mattos, Hurst & Blackett : o.p. ; Doubleday, New York : o.p.]

—— *The Golden Triangle* (Le triangle d'or, 1915).   1917
An exciting story turning on the efforts of a Turkish banker in France to export gold for the benefit of the friends of the Central Powers. Arsène Lupin helps to checkmate him. [Transl. by A. Texeira de Mattos, Hurst & Blackett : o.p. ; Macauley, New York.]

—— *Coffin Island.*   1920
A skilful excursion into the realms of sheer horror. [Hurst : o.p.]

—— *The Teeth of the Tiger.*   1915.
More adventures of Lupin. [Transl. by A. T. de Mattos, Hurst : o.p.]

" **LE BRETON**, John " [Thomas Murray Ford]. *Mis'ess Joy.*   1900
A novel of character, picturing rustic society in Kent during the Regency. Mis'ess Joy is an illegitimate girl, who, through mistaken motives, encourages the man who should have married her to marry her half-sister, and thus prepares misery for herself and others. [Macqueen : o.p. ; Routledge : o.p.]

LEE, Charles James [*b.* 1870]. *Cynthia in the West.* 1900
The social intercourse, the sensitive artistic life, and the love-making of a colony of painters in a Cornish village, where a Diana-like beauty is the cynosure of masculine eyes. There are bits of rustic humour, and the charms of the Cornish shore inspire several descriptive passages. [De La More Press : o.p.]

—— *Our Little Town ; and other Cornish tales and fancies.* 1909
Similar sketches of village life, some like *The Defeat of the Amazons* evoking considerable mirth. [Dent ; Dutton, New York : o.p.]

LEE-HAMILTON, Eugene [1845–1907]. *The Romance of the Fountain.* 1905
Ponce de Leon's quest for the legendary Fountain of Youth, and the discovery of Florida (1512–21). [Unwin : o.p.]

LE FANU, Joseph Sheridan [Irish ; 1814–73]. *The Fortunes of Col. Torlogh O'Brien.* 1847
Le Fanu had already written *Cock and Anchor : a tale of Old Dublin* (1845), a gloomy novel of no importance. This is a good historical novel of 1689–91, when the Jacobites and Williamites were fighting and plotting to ruin each other. The battle of Aughrim is well described. [Duffy, Dublin : o.p.]

—— *The House by the Churchyard.* 1863
Le Fanu's element was the gruesome and the uncanny, and he produced some remarkable tales in the manner of Poe. This is a murder mystery in which a sinister and ingenious ruffian, Black Dillon, cuts a grim figure. The setting gives scenes of social life in a colony of officers and their families at Chapelizod, the suburb of Dublin. [Duffy, Dublin : o.p.]

—— *Uncle Silas : a tale of Bartram Haugh.* 1864
The ward of Uncle Silas is the heroine. He is a mysterious and malevolent old man who schemes to marry her to her profligate cousin and to get hold of her money. Fair means failing, a fiendish plot is contrived, into which, however, one of the accomplices, a wicked French governess, falls a victim. [With introd. by M. R. James, (World's Classics), Oxford Press, 1926.]

—— *In a Glass Darkly.* 1872
Five stories from the diary of a German neuropath—a banquet of horrors. In one a clergyman is haunted by a loathsome familiar in the shape of a black monkey, and is driven to suicide. Swedenborgianism, crime, obsessions, vampires, trances, and other stimulants of creepy sensations are freely utilized. *Green Tea* is Le Fanu's masterpiece of terror, unless this be *Carmilla*, a more poetical story of vampirism. [Nash ; *illus.*, Davies, 1929.]

—— *The Purcell Papers.* 1880
Stories comic or mysteriously sensational, collected after Le Fanu's death by A. P. Graves, who prefixes a memoir. *Passages in the Secret History of an Irish Countess* and *A Chapter in the History of a Tyrone Family* are in his more characteristic vein. [Bentley : o.p.]

LE FEVRE, Raoul [French ; 15th cent.]. *Caxton's Recuyell of the Historyes of Troye.* 1475
Translated from a prose compilation (1464) by Raoul le Fevre, from the Latin prose chronicle of Guido delle Colonne (1287). Guido's pretended history ousted from popular favour the huge poem of Benoît de Sainte-More, the *Roman de Troie* (1165), hitherto the standard account of the pseudo-Homeric transactions. These classical romances contained many picturesque scenes, chivalric and fantastic adventures, and were, unintentionally, a faithful mirror of the times when they were composed. Both Benoît's and Guido's attained immense popularity, were often redacted, and translated into several languages. Caxton's rendering also went into numerous editions. Printed at Bruges—the first book printed in English. [Faithfully reprinted from the unique perfect copy of the original, and edited, with critical and bibliographical introduction, glossary, and detailed index of persons and places, by H. Oskar SOMMER. 2 vols., Nutt, 1894.]

LE FRANC, Marie [French]. *The Whisper of a Name* (Grand-Louis l'innocent, 1928). 1928
A woman deserted by her lover finds rest in an old house in Brittany. There she encounters Louis, whom the war has robbed of all recollection of the past. Her pity, as she endeavours to heal his shattered intellect, soon turns to love. [Transl. by George and Hilda SHIVELEY, Nash & Grayson ; Bobbs-Merrill, Indianapolis.]

LE GALLIENNE, Richard [*b.* 1866]. *The Quest of the Golden Girl.* 1896
A whimsical tale of the walking tour of a latter-day troubadour in search of his ideal bride. The fanciful irresponsibility of the style, the sensuousness, and the imitation of Sterne's mannerisms and sentimentality are characteristic of the author. [Lane ; Dodd & Mead, New York ; Garden City Co., New York.]

—— *The Romance of Zion Chapel.* 1898
The story of a bereaved lover, introspective and morbidly sentimental, inspired with much of the passion and abandon of Rossetti's love-sonnets. Incidentally tells how the æsthetic renaissance was brought to Coalchester. [Lane ; *id.*, New York : o.p.]

—— *Young Lives.* 1899
The early struggles and self-education of a poet amid uncongenial surroundings ; autobiographical to some extent, and personal in some of its sketches. [Arrowsmith, Bristol : o.p.]

LEHMANN, Rosamund. *A Note in Music.* 1930
A sensitive but rather uneven study of two mismarried women in a northern industrial town, whose apathetic, resigned existence is disturbed by a pair of visitants from a more brilliant world. [Chatto.]

LEIGHTON, Robert [Scottish ; *b.* 1859]. *The Thirsty Sword.* [juvenile] 1892
The Norse invasion of Scotland and the battle of Largs (1262–3). [Blackie : o.p. ; Scribner, New York : o.p.]

—— *Olaf the Glorious.* [juvenile] 1894
Career of Olaf Trygvason, boyhood as a slave in Esthonia, life at Court of Valdemar of Russia, his unsuccessful invasion of England (battle of Maldon), and his glorious death (963–1000). Gives a map. [Blackie ; *illus.*, Macmillan, New York, 1929.]

—— *The Golden Galleon.* [juvenile] 1897
Sir Richard Grenvil's famous sea-fight in the *Revenge* off the Azores (1591). [Blackie ; Scribner, New York : o.p. ; Burt, New York : o.p.]

LEIGHTON, Robert (*continued*). *Cap'n Nat's Treasure.*   [juvenile] 1902
Liverpool in 1776. [Partridge : o.p.]

LEMAÎTRE, Jules [French ; 1853–1914]. *Serenus ; and other stories of the past and present* (Sérénus, 1886).   1920
The eponymous story, gently ironical, is about a sceptical Roman who by a chapter of accidents is condemned to death as a Christian, and so becomes enrolled in the catalogue of martyrs. In *Myrrha* (1894) a Christian maiden is, rather too effusively, depicted as in love with Nero, and fancying herself actuated by the motive of service to God. [Transl. by A. W. EVANS, Mathews.]

LENNOX, Charlotte [*née* Ramsay, daughter of Lieut.-Governor of New York ; 1720-1804]. *The Female Quixote ; or, The Adventures of Arabella.*   1752
An imitation of Cervantes. Arabella's mental nutriment has been romances of the Scudéry type, and thence she has got all her ideas of life. In every stranger she sees a knight-errant, and romantic adventures in the most trivial events, herself committing extravagant follies until restored to reason by the sermons of her friends, when she marries a worthy man. [o.p.]

" LE NOTRE, G." [Louis Léon Théodore Gosselin ; French ; *b.* 1857]. *The House of the Combrays.* 1903
The Chouans, Georges Cadoudal, etc. (1804–14). More of an historical study than a novel, the author adhering scrupulously to fact ascertained by research, even in matters of detail. [Transl. by J. B. GILDER, with introd. by Victorien SARDOU, Dodd & Mead, New York : o.p. ; Harper, London : o.p.]

LEONOV, Leonid [Russian ; *b.* 1899]. *The Thief.*   1931
A writer seeks copy in the lowest quarter of Moscow, living with a gang of dissolute and rascally characters. Interest is directed principally towards their leader, a misdirected genius, who had been a hero in the Red Army, and now, disillusioned, has turned his exceptional talents to theft. The novel is published ; the thief makes an exemplary reformation. [Transl. by Hubert BUTLER, Secker.]

LE POER, John Patrick. *A Modern Legionary.*   1904
Adventures of a young Irishman in the Foreign Legion of the French Army. Service in Algeria and Tonquin, described with such fidelity that it reads like a journal of actual experiences. [Methuen : o.p.]

LEPPER, John Heron [Irish ; *b.* 1878]. *A Tory in Arms.*   1916
A vigorous story of the Belfast and Carrickfergus district (1715–19). [G. Richards.]

—— *A North-East Corner.*   1917
A quieter story of the same people, with political matters in the forefront, although the essential interests lie in personal relations and feelings. [G. Richards.]

LERMONTOV, Mikhail Yurievich [Russian ; 1814–41]. *A Hero of our Time* (1839).   1854
A poet's novel, semi-autobiographical, strongly imaginative, and full of description of Circassian scenery, and of the condition of the country at the time of the war with Russia. The hero is a true Russian, a man with vague hopes and aims who accomplishes nothing and is disillusioned by life. [Transl. by T. PULSZKY, 1854 ; transl. by LIPMANN, Vizetelly, 1886 : o.p. ; text and transl. by J. N. SCHNURMANN, *sub tit.* *A Modern Hero,* Cambridge Press (Macmillan, New York), 1899 ; transl. *sub tit.* *The Heart of a Russian,* by J. H. WISDOM and Marr MURRAY, Herbert & Daniel, 1912 : o.p. ; same, *sub tit.* *A Hero of Our Time,* Knopf, New York, 1924.]

LEROUX, Gaston [French ; 1868–1927]. *Balaoo.*   1913
Balaoo is an ape from Java, in short, a brother german of Pithecanthropus, who, like Peacock's Sir Oran Haut-Ton, figures in human guise. Let loose on a French town, he is responsible for a reign of terror, but indirectly also for much merriment at the expense of the townsfolk. [Transl. by Alexander Texeira de MATTOS, Hurst & Blackett : o.p.]

—— *The Bride of the Sun.*   1916
A picturesque and exciting romance of Peru and the Incas, in the Rider Haggard style. [Transl., Hodder : o.p. ; McBride & Nast, New York : o.p.]

LESAGE, Alain René [French ; 1668-1747]. *Asmodeus ; or, The Devil on Two Sticks* (Le diable boiteux, 1707).   1896
Lesage is the finest product of the picaresque school, for earlier examples of which see especially Aleman, Mendoza, Quevedo. This was begun as an imitation of a novel by Guevara, but the idea developed on independent lines. A profligate young student secures the henchmanship of a demon, and journeys through Spain in miraculous fashion, meeting with a host of adventures. The book is a string of realistic episodes, full of wit, malice, and acute observation of life akin to that of the fashionable collections of *caractères* ; many of the personages were drawn from the writer's contemporaries. [Sisley : o.p. ; Nimmo, 1881 ; o.p. ; new ed. Navarre Soc., 1928 (Boni, New York) ; transl. by Joseph THOMAS, *illus.,* Doubleday, Doran, New York, 1925.]

—— *Gil Blas* (Histoire de Gil Blas de Santillane, 1715–35).   1761
Both the form of this masterpiece of picaresque romance and the characters and incidents were borrowed from Spain. It portrays all sides of life and all classes of people, in a series of changing scenes, incident to the hero's adventurous career as he rises stage by stage from the condition of valet to that of confidant of the prime minister of Spain. A " comedy in a hundred acts," it has been justly called, the humour being too good-natured and tolerant to be described as satire. [Transl. by H. van LAUN, 3 vols., Simpkins, 1885–6 : o.p. ; by Tobias SMOLLETT (1761), ed. G. SAINTSBURY, 3 vols., Nimmo, 1881 : o.p. ; same, (World's Classics), 2 vols., Oxford Press ; same tr., with introd. by W. Morton FULLERTON ; (Early Novelists), Routledge, 1913 (Dutton, New York).]

—— *Vanillo Gonzales* (Estevanille Gonzalès, 1734) ; *and, The Bachelor of Salamanca* (Le bachelier de Salamanque, 1736).   1881
Two more Spanish stories, the first romantic, the second realistic or picaresque. The memoirs of the Bachelor of Salamanca, Don Cherubin, have much the same essential design as the foregoing, satirizing in the same tolerant way many kinds of people and society. *Vanillo Gonzales* was apparently based on a Spanish novel with a similar title (1640) ; it was translated into English by Smollett, who confessedly owed a great deal to Lesage [(1) Transl., Nimmo : o.p. ; (2) Transl. by J. TOWNSEND, Nimmo : o.p.]

LEVER, Charles James [Irish ; 1806–72]. *The Confessions of Harry Lorrequer.* 1839–40

Loosely connected stories and sketches of garrison life in Cork, full of high spirits and jocularity, very Irish in the stagey sense, very unreal. " All the pleasures of life are set before us ; wit, wine, and women, fighting and loving, daring leaps, absurd hoaxes, mad Irishmen." Thackeray parodied it as a prominent example of that once flourishing book the rollicking novel in his *Novels by Eminent Hands,* christening the boisterous hero Harry Rollicker. [(Everyman's Lib.), Dent (Dutton, New York), 1907 ; Nelson ; Little & Brown, Boston. *Illus.* by " Phiz," Macmillan.]

—— *Charles O'Malley, the Irish Dragoon.* 1841

A random and reckless chronicle (1808–14) of boisterous fun, personal humours, love-making, and martial adventures, many good stories being redressed. After Galway and Dublin, the Peninsular War, and the romantic countries and inhabitants of Portugal, Spain, and France, furnish the *mise en scène* and never-ending chances of adventure, and of comic and tragic incident. The humorous figure Major Monsoon is a real personage, who assigned to Lever, for a consideration, the right to use him and his adventures. Baby Blake, the romping Irish girl, is another sketch from life ; and Mickey Free, with his farcical eccentricities and droll repartee, a diverting specimen of the Irish lower classes. [Routledge : o.p. ; Burt, New York ; McKay, New York ; *illus.* by Rackham, Nisbet (Putnam, New York) : o.p. *illus.,* Collins.]

—— *Jack Hinton.* 1841

Another diverting farrago of love-making, high life in Dublin, adventure, and rollicking humour. Full of portraits, e.g. Curran, and others nearly as well known in their day ; Father Tom Loftus (sketched from Rev. Michael Comyns), a not overdrawn portrait of the jolly Irish priest ; Tipperary Joe, a good low-comedy character ; Corny Delaney, Mrs. P. Rooney, etc., all taken from life. The dialogue is piquant and racy, and makes effective use of the brogue. [Nelson, London and New York ; *illus.* by " Phiz," Macmillan ; 2 vols., Little & Brown, Boston : o.p.]

—— *Tom Burke of Ours.* 1844

A lively yarn about Irish soldiers on service abroad, in the wars of the Consulate and Empire ; the Peninsular chapters founded largely on Napier's history of that war. The usual infusion of Irish anecdote ; the sketches from French life based on Lever's own experiences. Napoleon appears, and the Austerlitz and Jena campaigns are described with considerable fullness. [*Illus.* by " Phiz," Macmillan. 2 vols., Little & Brown, Boston : o.p.]

—— *Arthur O'Leary.* 1844

A miscellany of adventures based on Lever's own experiences—in Canada, student life at Göttingen, the Napoleonic wars, etc. [*Illus.* by Cruikshank, Macmillan. Little & Brown, Boston.]

—— *The O'Donoghue.* 1845

Lever is now trying to be more serious, and his criticism of economic and social conditions and of native character is at any rate more thoughtful. Portrays the decaying gentry at the time preceding the outbreak of 1798, when French emissaries were stirring up discontent, and the armament led by Hoche was in preparation. The selfish old chief of the O'Donoghues, brooding in his ruined tower over the lost glories of his house, the moody son, tempted and betrayed by detestable miscreants who made a traffic in conspiracy, are melancholy creatures. The fruitless efforts of a rich Englishman to ameliorate the lot of his tenants produce a sad comedy, young ladies provide love-making of a genteel romantic kind, and there is a plenteous flow of Irish humour. [Downey : o.p. ; Routledge, New York : o.p.]

—— *The Martins of Cro' Martin.* 1847

Shows the practical working of the Emancipation Act ; scene, Connemara, where the selfish landlord Martin is defeated at an election and leaves his estates in disgust to the tender mercies of an agent. [2 vols., Routledge : o.p.]

—— *The Knight of Gwynne.* 1847

A thoughtful study of Irish life and character (1808–24), at the time of the legislative union, founded on Lever's own experiences in Antrim and Derry. The Knight is an ideal picture of an Irish gentleman, courageous, loyal, high-minded, and chivalrous ; supposed to be a portrait of the Knight of Kerry. [2 vols., Routledge : o.p.]

—— *Roland Cashel.* 1850

A characteristic story of adventure, love, and legal intrigue, Roland being nearly kept out of his estates by a villain, and from his true love by an old flame from the republic of Columbia. The Dean of Drumcondra is drawn from Archbishop Whately. [2 vols., Routledge : o.p.]

—— *The Daltons.* 1852

His longest novel. The selfishness of an absentee landlord, incidents of the Austro-Italian war of 1848, and the Italian revolution, military life in Austria and Italy, Anglo-Italian life at Florence, the doings of priests, etc. [2 vols., Routledge : o.p.]

—— *Maurice Tiernay, the Soldier of Fortune.* 1852

A story of the Napoleonic wars, Humbert's attempt on Ireland, the death of Wolfe Tone, the Austrian siege of Genoa, etc. (1793–1809). [Routledge : o.p. ; Harper, New York : o.p.]

—— *The Dodd Family Abroad.* 1853–4

The Continental adventures of a family whose heads are full of absurd notions on the manners and customs of foreigners ; related in letters by the actors themselves on the plan of Smollett's *Humphry Clinker,* bringing out the foibles of each writer. The Dodds are not altogether caricatures, but typify the prejudices, self-assertiveness, and ignorance of the British traveller. Written in Italy. [2 vols., Routledge : o.p. ; Harper, New York : o.p.]

—— *The Confessions of Con Cregan.* 1854

An Irish *Gil Blas,* in the style of his early tales. Con has exciting adventures in Quebec, Texas, and Mexico, before coming back to Ireland. Published anonymously, it was attributed to a new and formidable rival of Lever's, whose contemporaneous book, *The Daltons,* was compared with it unfavourably. [Routledge : o.p.]

LEVER, Charles James (*continued*). *Sir Jasper Carew.* 1855
Jasper's autobiography is prolific in adventure. He is mixed up with the wild social life and turbulent politics of Dublin in the early days of the Irish Parliament, is implicated in revolutionary schemes in France, a secret agent in London, where he meets Fox and Pitt, etc. Covers the period *c.* 1782–1805. [o.p.]

—— *The Fortunes of Glencore.* 1857
A plot-novel written to show that Lever's talent was the unravelling of human motive. Lord Glencore misjudges his wife and disowns his son, all being made right after a variety of adventures in W. Ireland and in Italy. Billy Fraynor is the fun-maker of the story. [Routledge : o.p.]

—— *Davenport Dunn.* 1859
Another picaresque novel—the astonishing histories of two adventurers. Dunn is a financial swindler, whose operations involve the fortunes of princes, and whose daily life is an incessant alternation of luxurious indulgence and rapid achievement ; the other scoundrel is a '' leg,'' whose sporting cheats are on a like scale, and who eventually knocks his rival on the head. [2 vols., Routledge : o.p.]

—— *One of Them.* 1861
A minor story utilizing Lever's own experiences as a consul abroad. From N. Ireland the story shifts to Florence, with scenes of diplomatic life, and a plenty of sensational incident. Quackinboss, a droll Yankee, and a nondescript Irish M.P. are the principal figures. [Routledge : o.p. ; Harper, New York : o.p.]

—— *Barrington.* 1862
Social and domestic life among middle-class people in Co. Kilkenny. A fire-eating major and a country doctor are capital figures. Young George Barrington's character and story are those of Lever's own son. [Routledge : o.p.]

—— *A Day's Ride.* 1864
A Quixotic extravaganza—the Irish and Continental adventures of a Dublin apothecary's son, Mr. Algernon Sydney Potts. [Routledge : o.p.]

—— *Luttrell of Arran.* 1865
A romantic story of the Aran Isles and Galway. Young Luttrell's bride, a peasant girl brought up to be a lady, is one of Lever's best women characters. [Routledge : o.p.]

—— *Tony Butler.* 1865
Diplomatic life, the Garibaldian war, etc. Major M'Caskey, soldier of fortune, is the purveyor of comedy. [o.p.]

—— *Sir Brooke Fossbrooke.* 1866
Reproduces much of the humour and frolic of his earlier tales, the mess-room scene in the officers' quarters at Dublin, with which it opens, recalling the sprightly comedy of *Harry Lorrequer*. The vigorous story that fol ows, however, is more serious, though hardly better, in its characterization and portraiture of real life. [Routledge : o.p. ; Harper, New York : o.p.]

—— *The Bramleighs of Bishop's Folly.* 1868
The Bramleighs are a family of rich parvenus, divided into three camps, one headed by an exclusive lady, an earl's daughter, who has married for money ; another composed of Col. Bramleigh and his set, who fight by fair means and foul against a French pretender to the estates ; and a third composed of three honourable and straightforward younger people, who are the peace party. The attack and repulse of the claimant cause much tragi-comedy, and bring out forcibly the heterogeneous characters of the family. Scenes : Co. Londonderry about Coleraine, and Italy. [Routledge : o.p. ; Harper, New York : o.p.]

—— *That Boy o' Norcott's.* 1869
A lively and romantic story, full of striking characters of a very various and very theatrical type. The hero enters the business house of a Jew, and loves his master's daughter ; is sent by her on a mission to Hungary, and falls in with the inamorata of his father, just as she is widowed. [Routledge : o.p. ; Harper, New York : o.p.]

—— *Lord Kilgobbin.* 1872
Pictures of a bohemian and thoroughly Irish section of society in the 1860's. Kilgobbin is a wellnigh ruined squireen, one of James II's unrecognized peers, a reckless, cheerful Hibernian ; Atlee is a characteristic hero of Lever's, a Trinity student of boundless ability, versatile, ambitious, and a bit of a charlatan, who makes himself a career in spite of obstacles ; the heroine, half-Irish daughter of a Greek prince and adventurer, is another of those all-conquering beauties, around whom Fenians, soldiers, politicians, and vice-regal officials gather as lovers. [Routledge : o.p. ; Harper, New York : o.p. ; *illus.* by Luke Fildes, Macmillan.]

—— *Gerald Fitzgerald the Chevalier.* 1899
Adventures of a legitimate son of the Young Pretender, by an Irishwoman. He is recognized as a claimant to the English Crown, and comes in contact with Mirabeau, Alfieri, Madame Roland, the Pretender and his Court at Rome, etc. Appeared as a serial in the *Dublin University Magazine* ; republished twenty-seven years after Lever's death. [Downey : o.p. ; New Amsterdam Book Co., New York : o.p. ; Harper, New York : o.p.]

LEVY, Amy [1862–89]. *Miss Meredith.* 1889
Miss Meredith is an English governess, living with an Italian family at Pisa, who has a love affair with a younger son. A story worked out with a simple but admirable realism, which gives us great and trivial things, events, circumstances, and traits of personality, just as they affect the mind. The view of life is passionate and despairing. [Hodder : o.p.]

—— *Reuben Sachs.* 1889
A sad and not very sympathetic portrayal of Jewish people in London, their character, domestic life, religious feelings, and peculiarities of thought. An ambitious young politician loves and is loved by the heroine, but puts worldly advancement before passion. He succeeds : she marries a rich but commonplace husband, and learns one day that Reuben is dead. [Macmillan : o.p.]

LEWIS, Arthur. *The Pilgrim.* 1910
A leisurely story of Gregory VII.'s time, and the glories of the Papal Court at the time of the struggle with the Emperor Henry IV (1075–84). The Welsh pilgrim is loved of two noble ladies. [Blackwood : o.p.]

LEWIS, D. B. Wyndham. *At the Sign of the Blue Moon.* 1924

Brief journalistic skits, caricatures, and parodies, from the *Daily Mail*, on modernist poetry, Freudism, bolshevism, the arrogance of the expert, the literary foibles of Yeats, Belloc, Kipling, Housman, and others, and a great many other topical subjects. [Hutchinson.]

—— *At the Blue Moon Again.* 1925

More of the same kind, not quite so bright and witty. [Methuen.]

LEWIS, Matthew Gregory [1775–1818]. *Ambrosio ; or, The Monk.* 1795

A Gothic tale of terror that differs from the Radcliffian type in being unsentimental and not attempting to explain away the supernatural horrors. A coarse melodrama—Ambrosio is an abandoned monk whose licentious crimes meet their due in his being carried off by the devil. Lewis also translated from the German *The Bravo of Venice*, 1804. [Ed. E. A. Baker (Lib. of Early Novelists), Routledge (Dutton, New York), 1907 ; Brentano, New York, 1924.]

LEWIS, Percy Wyndham [American ; *b.* 1886]. *Tarr.* 1918

A most unconventional novel. Against a bohemian background in Paris are set some unattractive individuals— most prominent, a contemptible German and a female compatriot, with the vaguely outlined Tarr, an English student. [Knopf, New York ; (Phœnix Lib.), Chatto.]

—— *The Wild Body : A Soldier of Humour ; and other stories.* 1927

A dozen sketches, more like those from a traveller's note-book than the work of a novelist, chiefly from Brittany since the war. The writer's eye is avowedly for people's " nastiest propriums and kinks "—" When we say ' types of humanity,' we mean violent individualities, and nothing stereotyped." He has his own standard of what is comic ; and his harsh, brutal, and aggressively vulgar style may be piquant to some yet affront a good many readers. [Chatto ; Harcourt, New York.]

LEWIS, Sinclair [American ; *b.* 1885]. *Our Mr. Wrenn : the romantic adventures of a gentle man.* 1914

An early novel alleged to be largely autobiographical. Mr. Lewis was born in Minnesota, son of a medical man —whence his well-informed interest in that profession. He was a journalist and an editor before *Main Street* gave him celebrity, and has led an extremely mobile life. [Harcourt ; Cape.]

—— *The Trail of the Hawk : a comedy of the seriousness of life.* 1915

—— *The Job.* 1916

An account of a commonplace girl winning success in the world of business in New York. Una Golden is an honest if prosaic type, who begins as a stenographer and works her way up. [Harcourt, New York ; Cape.]

—— *The Innocents : a story for lovers.* 1917

A slight affair about the mishaps of an elderly married couple who open a tea-room at Cape Cod. [Harper, New York.]

—— *Free Air.* 1919

An early novel, not before published. It is about an impecunious young motor-engineer who falls in love with a wealthy girl, and wins her in a romantic chase over half America : preaches the favourite gospel of anti-snobbery. [Harcourt, New York : o.p. ; Grosset, New York ; Cape.]

—— *Main Street : the story of Carol Kennicott.* 1920

Employs the time-honoured motive of the *femme incomprise* to satirize the barbarism and boredom of life in a small Minnesota " city." A college girl from Minneapolis, burning with pure aspirations, marries the local doctor. Full of expectations, she finds that Gopher Prairie is a street of shacks, inhabited by sordid, money-grubbing, gossiping oafs, who resent her schemes for making it civilized and comely. [Harcourt, New York ; Cape.]

—— *Babbitt.* 1922

Life of a typical American business man of facile morals, a real estate agent in the flourishing town of Zenith. Babbitt's confused thinking, on trade-unions, labour agitation, strictly limited business integrity, chambers of commerce, citizens' leagues, population and prosperity, and most of the other questions canvassed at the present day, is scathingly satirical, but the American public have taken it good-naturedly. [Harcourt, New York ; Cape.]

—— *Martin Arrowsmith.* 1925

A candid treatment of the medical profession in America. Arrowsmith is a Lydgate who refuses to be led astray either by a frivolous wife or by the boosting self-advertisement of his rivals. Here and elsewhere, Mr. Lewis may be called the American H. G. Wells. There is copious discussion, in the Wells manner. But, whereas Mr. Wells preaches scientific progress, Mr. Lewis is ridiculing commercialized medicine, commercialized education, and the general vulgarity and stupidity of much American life. [Harcourt, New York ; Cape.]

—— *Mantrap.* 1926

A comedy in this author's early manner, of the adventures of a lawyer on a camping holiday in the Canadian North-West. [Harcourt, New York ; Cape.]

—— *Elmer Gantry.* 1927

A vigorous indictment of hot-gospellers and those who run after them. Elmer is a perfervid hypocrite, and his life provides many sensations. He is, however, well-matched by a lady evangelist with whom he lives, who is exposed without mercy. [Harcourt, New York ; Grossett, New York ; Cape.]

—— *The Man who Knew Coolidge : being the soul of Lowell Schmaltz.* 1928

Hurls devastating satire upon the self-complacent American citizen, and upon his cherished idols—democracy, " manly sports," family life, efficiency, culture, and religious uplift. It is a masterly piece of work, for the " constructive and Nordic citizen " here dissected under Mr. Lewis's scientific scalpel reveals himself as at once a worm and a living portrait of our next-door neighbour. [Harcourt, New York ; Cape.]

—— *Dodsworth.* 1929

A satire upon that process of American self-education which consists of a tour in Europe. Sam Dodsworth and his wife are contrasted types ; the woman wishes to acquire the veneer of civilization which she finds in the East, the man prefers the rough but honest traditions which, with all their limitations,

LEWIS, Sinclair (*continued*).
constitute the true American spirit. On the whole, he comes off best. Interesting, too, is the impression gained of Europe by these typical tourists—confused, superficial, but intelligent. [Harcourt, New York ; Cape.]

LEWISOHN, Ludwig [American ; *b.* in Germany, 1882]. *Stephen Escott.* 1930
Escott is a divorce lawyer, who in half a dozen stories illustrates what he considers the different kinds of love, and propounds his heterodox views of sex and marriage. [Harper, New York ; *sub ttt. The Memoirs of Stephen Escott*, Butterworth.]

LIDIN, Vladimir [Russian ; *b.* 1894]. *The Apostate.* 1931
A graphic view of conditions in Moscow and of the working of Soviet schemes is afforded by this story of the moral downfall of an engineering student and his subsequent self-rehabilitation. [A clumsy transl. by Helen CHROMSCHOFF, Cape.]

LIE, Jonas Lauritz Idemil [Norwegian ; 1833–1908]. *The Visionary ; or, Pictures from Nordland* (Den Fremsynte ; eller Billeder fra Nordland, 1870). 1893
Inspired by memories of his boyhood in the wild Arctic region of Nordland ; scenes and characters novel, but all animated with warm and vigorous life by the author's sympathy and imagination. The love-tale, with its tragic ending, is peculiarly tender, the young heroine a beautiful embodiment of affectionate womanhood. [Transl. by Jessie MUIR, Hodder : o.p.]

—— *Little Grey (from* Fortaellinger og skildringer fra Norge, 1872). 1873
A very moving story of a shrewd, hardy, ill-used horse.

—— *The Barque Future : life in the Far North* (Tremasteren Fremtiden ; eller liv nordpaa, 1872). 1879
A novel rich in social significance, illustrating the onset of industrialism and the decline of old-established orders in the community. A great commercial house, the head of which is ruined by a scoundrel, focuses interest : the rescuer and inheritor of its fortunes is a capable and energetic man of the people. Björnson's example obviously has much to do with the inception of this and the next book. [Scott, Chicago : o.p.]

—— *The Pilot and his Wife* (Lodsen og hans hustru, 1874). 1876
A study of married life, the history of the pilot and his wife from childhood upwards. The wife, a true and loving woman, sacrifices herself wholly to her husband ; but in him jealousy growing into mania subjects her to a continual ordeal, till at length she is forced to assert herself and place herself on a footing of equality ; the result is reconciliation and happy union. The character and career of the mariner, with his life of adventure all over the world, particularly in South America, are made v ery interesting. [Transl. by G. W. TOTTENHAM, Blackwood, 1877 : o.p. ; by Sara C. (Mrs. Ole) BULL, Griggs, Chicago : o.p.]

—— *One, of Life's Slaves* (Livsslaven, 1883). 1895
The realistic story of a young smith's apprentice in the Norwegian capital, a child of shame, and his tragic struggle with poverty and the hopelessness of things as they are. He owes his final failure to his yielding to physical appetite. [Transl. by Jessie MUIR, Hodder : o.p.]

—— *The Family at Gilje* (Familien paa Gilje, 1883). 1920
Presents an excellent picture of domestic life in the forties, in the household of a provincial dignitary. But the main concern is with the parents' efforts to marry off their daughters advantageously, and with the frustration of the daughters' efforts to marry for love. [Transl. by Emil OLSON, American-Scandinavian Foundation (Oxford Press) ; by S. C. EASTMAN, Doubleday, New York, 1923.]

—— *The Commodore's Daughters* (Kommandörens döttre, 1886). 1892
A candid and realistic study of the question of women's rights to choose their own mates. The love affairs of the Commodore's daughters, one obedient to convention, the other a rebel, both turn out unhappily. [Transl. by H. L. BRAEKSTAD and Gertrude HUGHES, Heinemann.]

—— *Weird Tales from Northern Seas* (Trold, I–II, 1891–2). 1893
Poetical stories of the semi-conscious region of man's soul, where Lie perceived impulses surviving from our life at an earlier stage of evolution. This mysterious region of demons, nixies, and trolls has its counterpart in the strange and barren Arctic world, with its intense contrasts of bright ephemeral summer and long winter night, and the magnificent scenery of mountain and sea-shore. [Transl. by R. Nisbet BAIN, Kegan Paul : o.p.]

—— *Niobe* (Niobe, 1894). 1897
Niobe is the loving wife of a village doctor, whose children are infected with modern ideas of emancipation. The elder son talks the modern cant about art, and fails successively as musician, journalist, and actor ; the second speculates, and involves his family in disgrace and ruin ; a daughter gives herself over as a medium to a spirit-conjurer. Nemesis descends at last with terrible completeness, but all through it is the noble and long-suffering mother who appeals to our compassion. [Transl. by H. L. BRAEKSTAD, Heinemann : o.p.]

LILJENCRANTZ, Ottilie Adaline [Norwegian-American ; 1876–1910]. *The Ward of King Canute.* [juvenile] 1903
The story of Edmund Ironside and his defeat by Canute. [McClurg, Chicago : o.p.]

—— *The Thrall of Leif the Lucky : a story of Viking days.* [juvenile] 1904
An essay in the saga style, telling about a young English noble, captured by the Danes, and sold into slavery in Norway in the days of Olaf Trygvason (*c.* 995–1000). Miss Liljencrantz, born in Chicago, wrote her stories in English. [Ward & Lock : o.p. ; McClurg, Chicago : o.p.]

—— *The Vinland Champions.* [juvenile] 1905
Romance of the Viking settlers on the coast of North America. [Ward & Lock : o.p.]

—— *Randvar the Songsmith : a romance of Norumbega.* 1906
A legendary romance of the Norsemen in America and the fabled city of Norumbega ; fighting, love-making, werwolves, etc. [Harper, New York : o.p.]

LILLY, William Samuel [1840–1919]. *A Year of Life.*   ·   1900
A philosopher's essay in novel-writing. A society story of the conventional kind, but full of original and serious thinking on political, social, moral, and religious matters. [Lane : o.p.]

LINDE, Marie [Afrikander]. *Among Privileged People* (Onder bevoorregte Mense, 1925).   1927
A vivid picture of Dutch life on farms in Cape Colony and in Cape Town. Said to be the first novel translated from Afrikaans. [Transl. E. M. ARDERNE and G. A. TOMLINSON, S. Paul.]

" LINDSAY, Harry " [H. Lindsay Hudson]. *Methodist Idylls.*   1897
—— *More Methodist Idylls.*   1899
Portraits and biographical sketches from a Puritan connexion in Wales, containing several characters of much individuality and pathos, outlined with affectionate care. Piety, renunciation, fortitude, are taught in the way of parables by these " annals of the poor." [(1) and (2), Bowden : o.p.]

" LINNAKOSKI, Johannes ." [Victori Peltonen ; Finnish]. *The Song of the Blood-Red Flower.*
         1920
A romance of city and forest life in Finland. [Transl. by W. WORSTER, Holden ; Dodd & Mead, New York].

LINSKILL, Mary [1840–91]. *Tales of the North Riding.*   1871
Portray lovingly the rough and simple, strong and good-hearted Yorkshire folk, whose dialect is faithfully reproduced. *The Vicar's Daughter* tells of the conversion of a cold, self-sustained girl to tenderness and love, through a great peril. *Theo's Escape* is a domestic story of a girl, the mainstay of a home, who nearly loses her chance of happiness for the sake of her shiftless family. [Macmillan : o.p.]

—— *Between the Heather and the Northern Sea.*   1884
A sentimental love-story, full of descriptive passages of the moors and coasts of Yorkshire, by a close observer of nature [Macmillan : o.p.]

—— *Hagar.*   1887
A simple little love-story, tinged with melancholy, but not tragic ; with portraiture of the country-folk and scenery of the Yorkshire coast. [J. Clarke : o.p.]

LINTON, Eliza [*née* Lynn ; 1822–98]. *Grasp your Nettle.*   1865
Sober delineation of ordinary life in a small circle of country society, living in their own little world, immersed in their own petty projects and interests, local gossip and family squabbles. The rector's wife and daughter, the Calvinistic curate awkwardly in love with a bewitching foreigner, the Dorcas Society, old maids and old bachelors, such are the characters. The nettle to be grasped by the heroine's husband is the threat of troubles and disgrace that may arise from the reappearance of his first wife, believed to be dead. [Murray.]

—— *Lizzie Lorton of Greyrigg.*   1866
A Cumberland parish in early nineteenth-century years, in a state of semi-barbarism and irreligion, with a devout young ritualist newly appointed as rector. Lizzie Lorton, a half-savage young beauty, brought up in a narrow home and panting for a fuller life, is loved by the young Oxonian, but prefers a muscular but worthless fellow, who flirts with and jilts her. Here are the elements of a drama having some sensational features. The minor characters bring in comic views of life among the dalesmen : the dialect faithfully reproduced. [Ward & Lock : o.p.]

—— *Sowing the Wind.*   1867
A rather didactic novel of character, with a disastrous married life as main theme. Sympathy is concentrated on a woman of energetic and loyal character, whom her husband loves for her physical beauty. The course of events exposes the weakness of this sensual and selfish man, who dies tragically before the end, leaving his wife to marry a brave and worthy lover. [Chatto : o.p.]

—— *The True History of Joshua Davidson, Christian Communist.*   1872
A didactic novel, the memoirs of a young working-man, who, in his mistakes and readjustments to the ideal, typifies the follower of Christ. [Methuen : o.p.]

—— *Under Which Lord.*   1879
The rival lords for a woman's devotion are her husband and the priest. A tract disguised as a novel, very one-sided in its illustration of the moral. The hero is a saintly agnostic, much idealized, the object being to show the evils of priestly interference ; the orthodox Christian is depicted as a tyrant and a bully. [Chatto.]

—— *The Autobiography of Christopher Kirkland.*   1885
Mrs. Lynn Linton may be identified with Christopher, and she gives her own account of the incompatibilities that led to her separation from Linton, with portraits of Panizzi, Douglas Cook, and others. [3 vols., Bentley : o.p.]

LIPSETT, Caldwell [Irish]. *Where the Atlantic Meets the Land.*   1896
Sixteen short sketches, several dealing—not too sympathetically—with Donegal peasantry, passionate and childish beings, in whose undisciplined natures tragic and humorous elements are close neighbours. [Lane : o.p.]

LIZARS, Robina, and LIZARS, Kathleen Macfarlane [Canadians]. *Committed to His Charge.*   1900
A sketchy delineation of social life in an old-fashioned village in Canada. The aim of the authors is chiefly to satirize the ladies of the parish. [Greening.]

LLOYD, Ellis [Welsh]. *Scarlet Nest.*   1919
A good portrayal of Nonconformist peasantry in a Welsh mining village. [Hodder : o.p.]

LLOYD, John Arthur Thomas [*b.* 1870]. *The Three Destinies.*   1912
Analysis of the character of a young man incapable of choosing between three girls—finding his true mate only after unsuccessful experiences with the other two. [S. Paul : o.p.]

—— *Prestige.*   1920
Like Gissing's *New Grub Street*, an attack upon sordid commercialized journalism, with lively pictures of editors and their underlings. [S. Paul : o.p.]

LLOYD, John Uri [American ; *b.* 1849]. *Stringtown on the Pike.*   1900
A long, digressive novel of Kentucky in the early sixties, full of negro dialect not easily intelligible. An old nigger, who mixes up Christian ideas and African superstitions, is the most humorous and racy character. [Dodd & Mead, New York ; Hodder : o.p.]

LLOYD, Nelson McAllister [American ; *b.* 1873]. *The Chronic Loafer.*   1901
Tales told in dialect by the Loafer, the Patriarch, the Miller, the Tinsmith, and other members of a set of originals outside a store in a primitive village of Pennsylvania. [Taylor, New York : o.p. ; Heinemann : o.p.]

—— *A Drone and a Dreamer.*   1901
How a middle-aged dilettante is aroused from the indolent, self-indulgent existence to which he has consecrated the remainder of his life by a frank, outspoken girl. [Taylor, New York : o.p. ; Heinemann : o.p.]

LOBEIRA, Vasco de [Portuguese ; *d.* 1403 ?]. *Amadis of Gaul* (Amadis de Gaula, 1508).   1619
Supposed author, Vasco de LOBEIRA the Portuguese (*d.* 1403), the first known edn. (1508) gives the author as Garcirodriguez de MONTALVO ; Kelly says Joham de LOBEIRA (1261–1325). But a French origin has been claimed by Scott and others, and there are weighty arguments for a Castilian original (fourteenth century). Cervantes called it the earliest and best of the Spanish romances of chivalry. (It is mentioned in the Spanish translation of Egidio Colonna's *De Regimine Principum, c.* 1350.) First printed at Salamanca, 1508. Thomas PAYNEL translated a selection, *The Treasurie of Amadis of Fraunce* (1567), and Anthony MUNDAY, " a dismal draper of misplaced literary ambitions " (Kelly), translated the *Amadis* and several continuations (1589–1619), both from the French. The period of the story is antecedent to that of Arthur, but geography and chronology are as imaginary as in the *Fairy Queen.* Like the Arthurian and Carlovingian romances, *Amadis* reflects the manners, religion, and the ideas of love, honour, and morality that prevailed when it was written. Obviously inspired by Arthurian romance and the *romans d'aventure,* the action exhibits the same variety of incident ; there are monsters, giants, and enchantments without end ; but the author's inventions have nothing of the Celtic glamour and mysticism. Gaula is Wales. Beginning with the romantic birth and casting away of Amadis, the story recites his adventures as Child of the Sea, and proceeds to interweave two threads, his career as a knight-errant of invincible prowess and the vicissitudes of his love for Oriana. The adventures of his brother Galaor are another thread. Oriana's jealousy and its consequences, the wars with the race of Giants, the deeds of Amadis in the disguise of Beltenebros and, later, as the Knight of the Green Sword, and the great war for the hand of Oriana, are brought to a natural end by the ordeal of the Forbidden Chamber and the marriage of hero and heroine. But a large number of continuations, in Spanish, French, and Italian, carry the history much further, dealing in a markedly inferior manner with the exploits of descendants and kinsmen. Amadis is a mirror of courtesy and knightly valour, of chastity and fealty to his love ; in him every virtue is carried to excess. Noble sentiment shines through every episode, and inspires many admirable sayings. Merely by curtailing the prolixity of his original Southey reduced the story to half its length. He used the Spanish version of Garcia Ordoñez de Montalvo (1508), who added the fourth book ; but he kept before him Munday's version, for the sake of its antique language. [Transl. by A. MUNDAY, 1589–1619 ; 5th Part, transl. ANON., 1664 ; 6th, by F. KIRKMAN, 1652 ; 7th, 1693 ; note also Paynel's *Treasurie of Amadis* (1567) ; but the most serviceable rendering is SOUTHEY's translation of the first four books, 1803. New edn., 3 vols., 1872 ; see also *Amadis de Gaula :* a poem in three books. Freely transl. from the French of Nicolas de Herberay des Essarts by William Stewart ROSE, *c.* 1803.]

LOCKE, William John [West Indian born ; 1863–1930]. *Derelicts.*   1897
The principal character suffered imprisonment for fraud, but patiently endeavours to live a new life in spite of the ostracism of society. His hopeless love for a lady, who through exceptional events is flung derelict upon the world, and his rivalry with his strait-laced cousin, an upright but pharisaical clergyman, are the main lines of a piteous story that nevertheless ends in happiness. [Lane ; Dodd & Mead, New York.]

—— *The White Dove.*   1899
A father pays blackmail in order to shield his son from the knowledge of his illegitimate birth, and retain his whole-hearted confidence. [Lane.]

—— *The Usurper.*   1901
A philanthropic millionaire faced by the question, shall he make restitution of the wealth that came to him through a fraud, and therewithal abandon his schemes for the welfare of mankind. [Lane.]

—— *The Morals of Marcus Ordeyne.*   1905
Diary of a baronet, recluse, and student, and of his ward, an innocent and helpless girl rescued from a harem. Locke displays here the rather fine mixture of whimsical irony and gay insouciance which continued now to redeem even his melodrama. [Lane ; Dodd & Mead, New York.]

—— *The Beloved Vagabond.*   1906
Career of a picturesque, fascinating, unreal ne'er-do-well ; like all Locke's novels, an unconventional manipulation of conventional material. [Lane ; Dodd & Mead, New York ; Burt, New York.]

—— *Septimus.*   1909
A childlike inventor unexpectedly involved in the drama of real life. [Lane ; Dodd & Mead, New York.]

—— *Simon the Jester.*   1910
An improbable story of the sudden conversion of an invertebrate dilettante into a man with a faith in life, purpose, and a will. [Lane ; Dodd & Mead, New York.]

—— *The Glory of Clementina Wing.*   1911
Another clever comedy of this very unreal world. Clementina is an unprepossessing female of thirty-five with a " heart of gold " ; the other chief character is a grotesque idealist who plays at being Timon. [Lane ; Dodd & Mead, New York.]

—— *The Joyous Adventures of Aristide Pujol.*   1912
Aristide is a happy irresponsible Provençal, whose adventures, mainly amatorial, include teaching English and selling quack medicines. Locke knew and loved the middle and poorer classes in the South of France, and ultimately made his home among them. [Lane.]

LOCKE, William John (*continued*). *Jaffery.* 1915

The hero is a strong, lusty fellow, able to achieve all sorts of feats, but powerless to decide which of two girls is his proper mate. The sub-plot, about an author who filches the manuscript of a successful novel, and how the secret is kept, knits the whole into a more compact story than others of this author's similar romances, and the character of Liosha, an untamed child of nature whom Jaffery eventually marries, is diverting. [Lane.]

—— *The Wonderful Year.* 1916

A schoolmaster at a crammer's who tries to teach French and is sacked because examinations are the single objective, a girl art-student in Paris, a philosophic oddity, the Marchand de Bonheur, and a charming American ; their affairs of the heart, and still more their progress towards living the perfect life. [Lane ; Dodd & Mead, New York.]

—— *The Red Planet.* 1917

The story is told and the hero portrayed by a survivor of the South African War. The faulty hero makes good in the recent great war. [Lane.]

—— *The Rough Road.* 1918

Education is the problem. The war gives his real schooling to a young fellow brought up in cotton-wool, and turns him from a lap-dog into a man. [Lane ; Dodd & Mead, New York.]

—— *The Coming of Amos.* 1924

An unreal story of a fashionable portrait-painter on the Riviera, his young nephew fresh from a wild Australian sheep farm, and a lovely Russian princess ; the whole thickly sugar-coated with Locke's usual urbanity. [Lane ; Dodd & Mead, New York.]

—— *The Great Pandolfo.* 1925

Pandolfo is a wealthy and domineering egoist who has to come to grief before he wins the love of an impoverished widow. [Lane ; Dodd & Mead, New York.]

—— *The Old Bridge.* 1926

A romance of misunderstandings in Florence, turning upon the mating of youth with age. This experiment is made by two couples, and turns out successful only when the lesson of honesty and mutual adaptation is learnt. [Lane ; *sub tit. Perella*, Dodd & Mead, New York ; Grossett, New York.]

—— *The Town of Tombarel.* 1930

Nine little dramas of Provence, with themes suited to that amorous and quick-passioned countryside ; the narrator is the mayor of a small town, and his petty foibles add to the fun. [Lane ; Dodd & Mead, New York.]

—— *The Shorn Lamb.* 1930

The plot turns upon the impersonation of a dead man by his twin brother. [Lane ; Dodd & Mead, New York.]

LOCKHART, John Gibson [Scottish ; 1794–1854]. *Valerius.* 1821

A classical novel recounting the story of a Romano-Briton's visit to Rome, and the persecutions under Trajan (A.D. 110). [Blackwood : o.p.]

—— *Adam Blair.* 1822

A gloomy story of insensate passion and remorse ; the protagonists, a Presbyterian minister and Charlotte Campbell, wife of another man. The harvest of retribution is terrible. Blair confesses publicly, and tries to expiate his crime by resigning the pastorate and becoming a farmer. Characters and natural scenery contribute powerfully to the sombre effect. [Blackwood : o.p.]

—— *Reginald Dalton.* 1823

Oxford undergraduate life ; a tale that has some pathetic touches, but, as a whole, has much of the rollicking and fanciful spirit of the *Noctes Ambrosianæ* : town and gown riots, a duel, and the like, are characteristic incidents. [Blackwood : o.p.]

LODGE, Thomas [1558–1625]. *Rosalynde : Euphues Golden Legacie, found after his death in his cell at Silexedra.* 1590

A pastoral idyll which is the most famous of the imitations of Lyly and Sidney, and noteworthy as the source of Shakespeare's *As You Like It*, which borrowed plot, scenery, and characters (Shakespeare added Jaques, Touchstone, and Audrey). It is a version of the old tale of *Gamelyn*, sometimes included in the *Canterbury Tales*. [*Illus.*, Routledge ; ed. by W. W. Greg (Shakespeare Classics), Oxford Press, 1907.]

LONDON, Jack [American ; 1876–1916]. *Son of the Wolf : tales of the far North.* 1900

—— *The God of his Fathers : tales of the Klondyke.* 1901

—— *The Children of the Frost ; and other stories.* 1902

Jack London was a Californian who worked for many years as unskilled labourer, longshoreman, etc., and was a tramp, then a university student, before joining in the gold rush to the Klondike. These stories of life in that region are intensely graphic, and full of his violent energy and a genuine though unchastened poetry. [(1), Garden City Co., New York ; Mills & Boon ; (2), Macmillan, New York : o.p. ; Donohue, New York : o.p. ; Heinemann : o.p. ; Mills & Boon.]

—— *The Call of the Wild.* 1903

A wonderful autobiography of a dog, who loses his friend and master and relapses into wolfdom. The scene is still the Klondike, and there is a vivid account of a journey over the Chilcoot Pass. Like Landseer, Jack London could not refrain from sentimentalism and made his dog a human being ; in short, he put something of his own fiery and rebellious psychology into him. [Macmillan, New York ; McKay, New York ; Heinemann.]

—— *The Sea-Wolf.* 1904

A grim picture of a Norwegian sealer who is a combination of superman and savage. [Macmillan, New York ; Grosset, New York ; Heinemann.]

—— *The Game.* 1905

A vivid story of prize-fighting. [With *Before Adam*, Macmillan, New York ; alone, Heinemann.]

LONDON, Jack (*continued*). *White Fang.*   1907
 The obverse of *The Call of the Wild.* In this case, a wolf is civilized into the likeness of a dog. [Macmillan, New York ; Methuen.]

—— *Before Adam.*   1907
 Out of dreams which are supposed to be racial reminiscences of primordial times, Mr. London reconstructs a picture of life in the Pleistocene age. [With *The Game, supra,* Macmillan, New York ; alone, Laurie.]

—— *The Iron Heel.*   1908
 Supposed to be written about 2630 from a MS. describing the great and bloody revolt against the trust system between 1912 and 1932. [Macmillan, New York ; Everett : o.p. ; Mills & Boon.]

—— *Martin Eden.*   1909
 Eden has had a knockabout life as a sailor, and falling in love with a girl used to middle-class refinement and luxuries, tries to write. He is rejected by editors, and the girl jilts him. The abysmal contrast between the genius of this man, his vital ideals and the big realities of life, and, on the other hand, the narrow, unintelligent mediocrity of the " cultured " classes is brought out with characteristic force. [Macmillan, New York ; Grosset, New York ; Heinemann.]

—— *Burning Daylight.*   1910
 One of his more sentimental versions of life. Daylight is a young man of stupendous energy, who makes millions at Klondike and, in a fit of idealism, renounces his wealth. [Macmillan, New York ; Grosset, New York ; Heinemann.]

—— *The Cruise of the " Snark."*   1911
 A characteristic story of a voyage in the Pacific, based on his own travels. [Macmillan, New York ; Mills & Boon.]

—— *John Barleycorn ; or, Alcoholic Memoirs.*   1913
 Semi-autobiographical, drawing on his recollections of alcoholism. [Century Co., New York.]

—— *The Mutiny of the Elsinore.*   1915
 The hero begins his voyage in the Pacific as a helpless landlubber, but before the end he is capable of quelling a mutiny and sailing the ship. [Macmillan, New York ; Mills & Boon.]

—— *Jerry of the Islands.*   1917
 Another long story of a dog, said to be of " real adventures " in the Solomon Isles. [Macmillan, New York ; Mills & Boon.]

—— *Hearts of Three.*   1918
 " The raw red drama and tragedy of the primitive mediæval melodrama of sentiment and passion of the New World Latin," is the author's description of this novelized film of Americans, Spaniards, and peons in quest of the treasures of Sir Henry Morgan and the Mayas. [Macmillan, New York ; Mills & Boon.]
 [*Works,* 21 vols., Macmillan, New York.]

LONGFELLOW, Henry Wadsworth [American ; 1807–82]. *Hyperion.*   1839
 The musings, love-making, and dreams of a young poet, a pilgrim in Germany and Switzerland ; no doubt representing a phase in Longfellow's youth. Beginning with a poet's grief, it preaches an optimistic lesson of courage and confidence in the future. [Houghton, Boston, 1882 ; with *Kavanagh* and *Evangeline,* McKay, Philadelphia ; W. Scott : o.p.]

LONGUS. *Daphnis and Chloe : Excellently describing the Weight of Affection etc., finished in a Pastorall . . . and therefore termed by the name of The Shepheards Holidaie.* By ANGEL DAY. 1587
 Nothing is known about Longus, who is vaguely ascribed to the end of second or beginning of third century. This idyll is a late expression in prose of the pagan spirit of Theocritus, Bion, and Moschus ; and, whether it did actually furnish a model to Tasso, Sanazzaro, and Montemayor through Amyot's translation into French (1559) or otherwise, was undoubtedly imitated by many writers in the pastoral style, down to the author of *Paul et Virginie.* Daphnis and Chloe are the adopted children of a goatherd and a shepherd on the isle of Lesbos, and this in the main is the simple story of their learning to love and their happy marriage. They are represented as living in a state of nature and innocence ; they love without restraint— and there is a lack of restraint in the recital of certain incidents ; but this remains one of the purest expressions of simple passion and pagan revelling in natural beauty ; and the harmonious composition and elaborate, sensuous style have been happily reproduced by the translators into modern languages. [Transl. by Angel Day, ed. by Joseph JACOBS (Tudor Lib.), Nutt, 1890 : o.p. ; edited, with Greek text and notes, by W. D. LOWE, Bell (Macmillan, New York), 1908. Another transl. by George THORNLEY (1657), ed. by G. Saintsbury, (Abbey Classics) Simpkin (Small, Boston), 1920 ; same transl., *illus.,* Bles ; Golden Cockerel Press (Chaucer Head, New York), 1923. Another transl. by James CRAGGS, 1720 : o.p. Another transl. by Rev. Rowland SMITH (see Achilles Tatius, *supra*). This translator based his rendering on a " select " translation (by C. V. LE GRICE) published at Truro in 1803, restoring omitted passages and incorporating the fragment discovered in 1810 by P. L. COURIER. Transl. (a beautiful version) by George MOORE, Heinemann, (1924), 1927.]

LOOS, Cécile Ines [German-Swiss]. *Matka Boska—Mother of God.*   1930
 The distinction of this tragic history of an unintelligent and illiterate Polish serf-girl is the art with which the poor creature is made symbolical of the author's doctrine of good and evil and the wrongs and sufferings of mankind. [Transl. by Margaret GOLDSMITH, Cape.]

LÔPEZ DE UBEDA, Francisco [Spanish]. *La Picara ; or, The Triumphs of Female Subtility : enriched with three pleasant novels* (La Picara Justina, 1605).   1665
 Sometimes ascribed to Fra Andrés Pérez. An imitation of *Guzman de Alfarache.* Justina is the daughter of an innkeeper, who had trained her to dupe the customers, a practice which she pursues, on an extended scale, after his death, among the inhabitants of Leon and Castile. [Rendered into English by John DAVIES of Kidwelly, 1665 : o.p. ; *La Picara Justina ; the Spanish Jilt,* made English by Captain John STEVENS (1707), repr. 1889, without name of publisher : o.p. Also transl. as *The Life of Donna Rosina, The Spanish Pole-cat,* and under other titles.]

LORIMER, George Horace [American; *b.* 1868]. *Letters from a Self-made Merchant to his Son.* 1902
Sets forth in a knowing style a philosophy of life and business not unlike that of *David Harum.* [Dodd & Mead, New York; Methuen.]

—— *Jack Spurlock, Prodigal.* 1908
This also is less story than commentary, philosophizing destructively on the selfish and ignoble ideals of New York society; the language so unsparingly slangy and American that English readers will be continually nonplussed for a meaning. [Doubleday, New York: o.p.; Murray: o.p.]

LORIMER, Norma Octavia [*b.* 1864]. *Mirry-Ann.* • 1900
Village life among the fishing population of the Isle of Man, the local characters, the manners and customs, drawn with knowledge. [Methuen: o.p.; Appleton, New York: o.p.]

—— *On Etna: a romance of brigand life.* 1918
Exciting, and good in its local colour. [S. Paul: o.p.]

—— *Catherine Sterling.* 1918
Love affairs meandering from Japan to Italy and England. [S. Paul: o.p.]

LORRAINE, Rupert. *The Woman and the Sword.* 1908
The times of Laud and the Star Chamber, and also of the Thirty Years' War (*c.* 1634). Scenes: Somerset, London, and Germany. A good depiction of rough military life, with an English soldier of fortune for hero. [Unwin: o.p.; McClurg, Chicago: o.p.]

" LOTI, Pierre " [Louis Marie Julien Viaud; French; 1850–1923]. *Rarahu* (Le mariage de Loti, 1882). 1890
Like many, perhaps the majority, of Loti's stories, this is a fragment of half-disguised autobiography. Its theme is that of *Atala,* the loves of a civilized man and a savage. *Atala* was deliberately designed as a poem in prose; this, more spontaneous, is quite as much a poem, the lyrical emotion of the writer breaking into passionate laments for the sadness of satiety and the brevity of joy. Rarahu is a girl of Tahiti who is loved and then abandoned by a sailor. The child-like soul of the savage, the sensuous charm of the tropic isles, the ephemeral ecstasy of passion—all this is invested with a glamour that haunts; but the poignancy is in the refrain—the littleness of human life measured against nature and eternity. Originally entitled *Rarahu: idylle polynésienne* (1880). [Transl. by Clara BELL, Paul: o.p.; same transl., *sub tit. The Marriage of Loti,* Laurie, 1930; same, *sub tit. Tahiti,* Stokes, New York.]

—— *Constantinople* (Aziyadé, 1879). 1928
—— *A Phantom from the East* (Fantôme d'orient, 1892) [sequel]. 1892
The tragic history of a European's love for a Circassian slave in a harem. Both books are intensely lyrical; the sequel is a passionate lament for happiness that has flown. Loti returns to the scene of his amour after seven years of absence, and is awakened at last to the greatness of Aziyadé's love and sacrifice. The beautiful scenery of Constantinople and its romantic environs is the theme of long descriptive passages. As usual in Loti's romances, the autobiographic substratum is very apparent. [(1), Transl. by Marjorie LAURIE; (2), transl. by J. E. GORDON, Unwin: o.p.; (1) and (2) together, *sub tit. Constantinople,* Laurie, 1928.]

—— *The Romance of a Spahi* (Le roman d'un spahi, 1881). 1890
A French soldier's life in Africa, and his affairs with a negress. Jean is another of Loti's creatures made all of impulse, and the book is a revelation of the enervating and debauching effect of the African climate and free intercourse with natives upon a European nature of weak stamina. [Transl. by M. L. WATKINS, Brentano, New York (Collins).]

—— *My Brother Yves* (Mon frère Yves, 1883). 1887
A long and rambling novel, containing the most vivid and imaginative word-pictures of the sea in its innumerable aspects, and not less beautiful and sensuous descriptions of the landscapes, flowers, and summers of Brittany; through all of which runs the characteristic undertone of melancholy. The story is a most affecting idyll of friendship between the midshipman Loti and a humble friend and shipmate, a drunken but stanch and delightful Breton sailor. [Transl. by Mary P. FLETCHER, Vizetelly: o.p.; transl. by W. P. BAINES, *sub tit. A Tale of Brittany,* Laurie, 1924 (Stokes, New York).]

—— *An Iceland Fisherman* (Pêcheur d'Islande, 1886). 1887
Equal to the last as a poetic rendering of the life and wonder of the sea, and his masterpiece of artistic construction and of pathos. A story of the utmost simplicity, the loves of a Breton girl and a Breton sailor, a fisherman in the stormy seas of Iceland, their two years of hesitation, the brief and merry wedding festival, the sailor's departure never to return. The one theme beats through it as in a fugue—the fleetingness of joy, the sadness of inexorable fate. [Maxwell: o.p.; transl. by Anna Farwell de Koven, McClurg; Chicago, 1899; transl. by W. P. BAINES, Laurie (Stokes, New York), 1924.]

—— *Madame Chrysanthème* (Madame Chrysanthème, 1887). 1897
The amusing interlude of Loti's temporary liaison with a dainty Japanese in Nagasaki, who seems to have bored him. The character of the Japanese is presented ironically and unfairly, but the scenery is exquisitely done. [Transl. by Laura ENSOR, Routledge (Dutton, New York): o.p.; same transl., *sub tit. Japan,* illus., Laurie (Stokes, New York), 1925.]

—— *A Child's Romance* (Le roman d'un enfant, 1890). 1891
Dreamy, half-poetical reminiscences of his own childhood spent in a beautiful countryside (Oléron), which is lovingly depicted as a harmonious background, unspoiled by the inroads of modernity, and peopled by primitive, old-world folk. A recurring motive is the pathos of the difference between the child world as it lingers in memory and the real scenes when the man revisits them. [Transl. by Clara BELL, Gottsberger, New York: o.p.]

—— *The Book of Pity and Death* (Le livre de la pitié et de la mort, 1891). 1892
Detached studies, in which recurs over and over again as a *leitmotif* the sentiment of human annihilation and the pity we owe to the lower creatures. *The Sorrow of an Old Convict* is a pathetic little tale of a prisoner and his pet, and *The Life of Two Cats* charmingly inculcates tenderness for dumb animals. [Transl. by T. P. O'CONNOR, Cassell: o.p.]

"LOTI, Pierre" (*continued*). *Ramuntcho* (Ramuntcho, 1897). 1897

An idyll of the Basque country, the tale of two childish lovers whose parents are bitter enemies. As is his wont, Loti discourses most exquisite music on the pathetic fallacy. The sadness of the tale seems to be the inmost expression of the forlorn and beautiful landscapes of this Pyrenean borderland. Loti failed to understand the Basque temperament, but his pen-pictures of the country are in his finest style. [Transl., Brentano, New York ; transl. by W. P. BAINES, *sub tit. A Tale of the Pyrenees*, Laurie (Stokes, New York), 1922.] An intervening story, *Mâtelot* (1893), the most lachrymose and ultra-sentimental of all his books—the life and death of a French marine—has not yet been turned into English.

—— *Disenchanted* (Les désenchantées, 1906). 1906

Expresses the new pangs, the crushed hopes and stultified longings of the modern Turkish lady, who has received a Western education, but cannot free herself from the revolting slavery of the harem. Constantinople and the shores of the Bosphorus are described in a long succession of enchanting pictures. [Transl. by Clara BELL, Macmillan : o.p. ; Macmillan, New York, new ed., 1924.]

LOUD, Emily S. [Australian]. *Taurua ; or, Written in the Book of Fate.* 1899

The scenery, people, superstitions, and legendary lore of the South Seas treated in a romantic and idealistic manner from the native point of view. [Low : o.p.]

LOVER, Samuel [Irish : 1797–1868]. *Rory O'More.* 1837

Rory is an idealization of Irish good-nature, suggested by Lover's popular song, " Rory O'More." Essays to prove that a few desperadoes were responsible for the more heinous atrocities of the '98, and that the Irish peasantry are naturally too kind-hearted to commit such excesses. Tries to be serious, but cannot help falling into melodrama and the broadest comedy. [Edited with introd. by D. J. O'Donoghue, Constable : o.p. ; Burt, New York ; McKay, Philadelphia.]

—— *Handy Andy.* 1842–3

The blunders and misadventures of a happy-go-lucky servant, an exaggeration of the stage Irishman, with other laughable episodes introducing more stage characters, gentry, peasants, and vagabonds. [Edited with crit. introd. by D. J. O'Donoghue, Constable : o.p. ; (Everyman's Lib.), Dent (Dutton, New York), 1907 ; Jenkins ; Burt, New York ; McKay, Philadelphia ; *illus.*, Little & Brown, Boston, 1927.]

—— *Legends and Stories of Ireland.* 1844

Localized romances and racy scraps of folk-lore worked up into stories with a plot, mostly comic and farcical. Among the most laughable are *The Gridiron, Paddy the Sport*, and the mock-epic *Barny O'Reirdon the Navigator*, the buoyant, muddle-headed hero of which follows into the Atlantic a ship bound for Bengal, in the belief that he will reach the fabulous paradise of Fingal. [With introd. by D. J. O'Donoghue, Constable : o.p. ; Ward & Lock : o.p. ; Sadlier, New York : o.p.]

LOWELL, Robert Traill Spence [American ; 1816–91] *The New Priest in Conception Bay.* 1858

A poet and evangelist's story of Newfoundland people and their deeply religious character. The discussions of church government and theology are prolix, but involve some humorous presentation of character. The sea, the skies, and the lonely shores of the island, the scene of the author's pastoral labours, are lovingly depicted. [Dutton, New York (1889) : o.p.]

LOWRY, Henry Dawson [1869–1906]. *Wreckers and Methodists.* 1893

—— *Women's Tragedies.* 1895

Two series of chiefly pathetic little stories interpreting the grave, masculine character of the moorland folk of Cornwall, though they aim rather at artistic and spiritual effect than at realism ; e.g. *The Man in the Room*. [(1) and (2), Lane : o.p.]

—— *A Man of Moods.* 1896

A more commonplace novel inspired by the flower-fields of Scilly. A literary man marries a native ; they disagree, and he returns to London, but the charm of the place and the folk draw him back. [Sands : o.p.]

LUBBOCK, (Alfred) Basil [b. 1876]. *Round the Horn Before the Mast.* 1902

—— *Jack Derringer : a tale of deep water.* 1906

—— *Deep Sea Warriors.* 1909

—— *The China Clippers.* 1914

Realistic records of the daily routine and the multifarious experiences of life in the old-fashioned sailing-ship. The author knows it at first hand, and has the knack of reproducing his impressions with extraordinary vigour. [(1), Murray ; Dutton, New York, 1928 ; (2), Murray : o.p. ; (3), Methuen : o.p. ; Dodd & Mead, New York : o.p. ; (4), Brown : o.p.]

LUCAS, Edward Verrall [b. 1868]. *Listener's Lure : an oblique narration.* 1906

Letters and replies written by a number of imaginary correspondents, people in all sorts of stations and of various characters, who touch on the most miscellaneous topics and incidents of life, the humorous aspects of which are happily brought out. A little story runs through the farrago, and a handful of characters are sketched with Mr. Lucas's artful touches of tender appreciation and delicate satire. [Methuen ; Macmillan, New York : o.p.]

—— *Character and Comedy.* 1907

A miscellany of Elia-like essays, reflections of a book-lover, sketches of character, meditative anecdotes, and finally a witty series of short stories told in letters, *Life's Little Difficulties* (from *Punch*), choice examples of epistolary conversation and oblique narrative. Humorous side-lights on Lamb, Dr. Johnson, John Mytton, the Irish " king " Bagenal, and other worthies, exhumed from forgotten books and periodicals of the last two centuries. [Methuen ; Macmillan, New York : o.p.]

—— *Over Bemerton's : an easy-going chronicle.* 1908

A nondescript commentary on many phases of life in London in the year 1908, not disdaining actual people and well-known incidents, by a kindly old bachelor who comes home to settle down after thirty years in South America. Quite in the genial, urbane style of the *Spectator*. [Methuen ; Macmillan, New York : o.p. ; Grosset, New York : o.p.]

LUCAS, Edward Verrall (*continued*). *The Slowcoach.*   [juvenile] 1910
> A very readable account of the experiences of some delightful children on a gipsy-van holiday.   [Wells Gardner : o.p. ; Macmillan, New York.]

—— *Mr. Ingleside.*   1910
> A middle-aged, disappointed man, who has accepted the gifts and the refusals of life, and found a genial philosophy.   To his home on the Embankment many friends come in, and the discussions on passing events, modern movements, books and the like, remind one of *Over Bemerton's*.   [Methuen ; Macmillan, New York.]

—— *London Lavender.*   1912
> Further chronicles in the style of *Over Bemerton's*, recording droll incidents and traits of character, not excepting bits of news that roused gossip in their time ; all very charming, desultory, and pleasant to dip into at odd moments.   [Methuen ; Macmillan, New York.]

—— *Landmarks.*   1914
> The life of a young man, from childhood up to the commencement of his career as a writer, viewed as a series of significant episodes.   [Methuen : o.p. ; Macmillan, New York.]

—— *The Vermilion Box.*   1916
> Letters of various people of various ages forming a commentary on the war news, the scares, and most of the other favourite topics in the period 1914–15.   [Methuen : o.p. ; Doran, New York : o.p.]

—— *Genevra's Money.*   1922
> A contrast between older and younger generations, cast in a loose mould that allows the author to range lightly over many subjects, from musical comedy to the Church.   [Methuen ; Doubleday, Doran, New York.

—— *Windfall's Eve : an entertainment.*   1929
—— *Down the Sky.*   1930
> Entertainments that conduct the reader through the English counties and afterwards to Ceylon, with the desultory love-story of a gentleman from the British Museum, and talks and interludes that smack of the essayist rather than the delineator of character.   [(1) and (2), Methuen ; Lippincott, Philadelphia.]

LUCAS, Frank Laurence [*b.* 1895]. *Cécile.*   1930
> The disillusionments of wedded life and a woman's ill-starred craving for love and happiness are the motives of this novel, which has an historical setting, opening in 1776, just before the fall of Turgot.   Scenes, Paris and the country.   The strong character is not the erring Cécile, but her elder sister Andrée, a woman of clear vision, one of those who refuse to make terms with life and suffer inevitably but magnanimously. [Chatto ; Holt, New York.]

LUCAS, Reginald Jaffray [1865–1914]. *When all the World is Young.*   1908
> A young man's life from Eton to Parliament and the eve of marriage, chronicled and annotated in the letters of a shrewd and scholarly father.   [Humphreys : o.p.]

LUCIAN [*c.* A.D. 120–*c.* A.D. 200]. *The True History.*   1634
> A broad satire on the poets and historians who purveyed extravagant tales, e.g. Homer and Ctesias, who are cited by name, and many other dignified writers.   Lucian relates how with fifty companions he set sail through the Pillars of Hercules, and was carried up to the moon, where they were enlisted by the monarch Endymion to fight against the armies of Phaeton, king of the Sun.   After numerous adventures of the most monstrous kind the ship is swallowed up by a sea-serpent a hundred miles long, in whose interior they visit wondrous regions, but eventually sail out and reach the Happy Isles.   Rabelais' voyage of Pantagruel, Cyrano de Bergerac's wonderful travels, and the exploits of Swift's Gulliver are among the populous lineage of this incredible history.   [Transl. by Francis HICKES (1634), *illus.* by William Strang, J. B. Clark, and Aubrey Beardsley, with introd. by Charles Whibley, A. H. Bullen, 1902 : o.p. (orig. pub. with Greek text in 1894) ; *illus.*, Golden Cockerel Press (Chaucer Head, New York), 1927 ; transl. by H. W. and F. G. FOWLER, in vol. ii. of *Works of Lucian*, transl., 4 vols., Oxford Press, 1905.   Transl. by A. M. HARMON, (Loeb Lib.) Heinemann (Putnam, New York), 1913–25 ; by W. L. COLLINS, Blackwood (Lippincott, Philadelphia).]

LUDLOW, James Meeker [American ; *b.* 1841]. *The Captain of the Janizaries.*   [juvenile] 1886
> Scanderbeg (Iskander Bey) and the fall of Constantinople.   Good descriptions of Turkish life and religion, and of the life and folk-lore of Albania and the Balkans.   [Harper, New York.]

—— *Deborah : a tale of the times of Judas Maccabaeus.*   [juvenile] 1901
> Portrays contemporary Judaism in its conflict with Syria under Antiochus Epiphanes (217–5 B.C.)   [Revell, New York ; Nisbet : o.p.]

—— *Sir Raoul : a tale of the theft of an Empire.*   1905
> A romance of the Black Forest, Venice, and the Bosphorus (1202–4), concerned with the diversion of the Fourth Crusade from the conquest of the Holy Land to the capture of Constantinople.   [Revell, New York ; Oliphant, Edinburgh : o.p.]

—— *Avanti ! A tale of the resurrection of Sicily,* 1860.   [juvenile] 1912
> A story of the liberation of Sicily, the landing of the Ten Thousand, and the battle of Palermo.   [Revell, New York.]

LUDWIG, Otto [German ; 1813–65]. *Between Heaven and Earth* (Zwischen Himmel und Erde, 1856).   1911
> A village tragedy, involving a family of slaters in Thuringia ; it reveals the jealousy and hatred that may underlie apparently peaceful country life.   This is accounted Ludwig's finest novel.   [Transl. by W. METCALFE, Gowans & Gray : o.p.]

LUKASH, Ivan [Russian]. *The Flames of Moscow.*   1930
> A crowded, spectacular, and somewhat confused historical novel, opening, in the prologue, with the assassination of the Tsar Paul I in 1799, and culminating in the firing of Moscow and the retreat of the Grand Army, which the young hero witnesses as a prisoner of the French.   The Decembrist conspiracy of 1825 comes into the epilogue.   [Trans. (well) by Natalie DUDDINGTON, Peter Davies ; Macmillan, New York.]

LUNDEGÅRD, Axel Wilhelm [Swedish; *b.* 1861]. *The Storm Bird: a historical silhouette with background and frame* (Stormfågeln, 1893). 1895
A picture of Vienna in 1848, with discussions on the difficulty of realizing ideals in human society. [Transl. by Agnes KILGOUR, Hodder: o.p.]

LUNN, Arnold Henry Moore [*b.* 1888]. *The Harrovians.* 1913
The most pertinent opinion on this Harrow novel is that of Alec Waugh: " This book, as no other book has done, photographs the life of a Public School boy stripped of all sentiment, crude and raw, and is of its kind, the finest school story written. . . . Of course, a storm of adverse criticism broke out at once. . . . What fools all these people were ! " (*The Loom of Youth*). [Methuen: o.p.]

" LYALL, Edna " [Ada Ellen Bayly; 1857–1903]. *Donovan: a modern Englishman.* 1882
—— *We Two* [sequel]. 1884
A study of a supposed agnostic, who is estranged from religion by adversity rather than disbelief. Without touching on the real problems of agnosticism, the writer, in the course of a long domestic narrative of this young man's misfortunes and love affairs, shows how his innate goodness keeps him straight and leads him eventually by the help of his wife to the Christian fold. Luke Raeburn is to some extent a reflection of Bradlaugh. [(1) and (2), Hurst ((1): o.p.); Appleton, New York: o.p.; Burt, New York.]

—— *The Golden Days.* 1885
Chiefly concerned with the home life of Algernon Sydney at Knole Park in " good King Charles's golden days," his arrest, and execution (1682–4). [Hurst: o.p.; Harper, New York: o.p.; Burt, New York.]

—— *To Right the Wrong.* 1893
Labours to achieve a sympathetic but temperate portrayal of John Hampden and his career (1642–3). [Hurst & Blackett; Harper, New York: o.p.]

—— *In Spite of All.* 1901
A didactic novel of the same sentimental stamp, bringing in the Civil War, Falkland, Laud, etc. (1640–5). [Hurst & Blackett: o.p.; Longmans, New York: o.p.]

LYELL, William Darling [Scottish; 1860–1925]. *The House in Queen Anne Square.* 1920
Sensation, crime, and intricate plot combined with some literary merit, reminiscent of Wilkie Collins. The scene is Edinburgh. [Blackwood; Putnam, New York.]

—— *The Justice Clerk.* 1923
A melodrama of Edinburgh in 1794. [Hodge, Edinburgh: o.p.]

LYESKOV, Nikolai [Russian; 1831–95]. *The Sentry; and other stories.* 1922
The title-story is about a humane officer and a sentry who quits his post to save a man from drowning, in the despotic times of Nicholas I. Lyeskov wrote a large number of novels and tales most of which have apparently missed the attention of English translators. This selection hardly does justice to the lively humour which pervades much of his work. He excited enmity by his hostile portraya of Nihilists. [Transl. by A. E. CHAMOT, Lane; Knopf, New York.]

—— *Cathedral Folk* (Soboryane, 1872). 1924
The second volume of a trilogy, relating the chronicles of an imaginary provincial town, Stavgorod, devoted to portraits of clerical life. This was Lyeskov's most successful and popular work ; in Father Tuberozov and his deacon Akhila he created an outstanding pair of characters, the latter providing an example of his genius for comedy. It is by virtue of this trilogy that he has been compared to Trollope. [Transl. by Isabel HAPGOOD, Knopf, New York; Lane.]

—— *The Enchanted Wanderer.* 1926
An excellent portrayal of a typically Russian character, poetic, imaginative, and a wanderer by nature. [Transl. by A. G. PASCHKOFF, Jarrolds.]

LYLY, John [155¾–1606]. *Euphues, the Anatomy of Wit.* 1579
—— *Euphues and his England* [sequel]. 1580
Lyly is famous, in the first place, for his *Euphues*, a work that combined the courtly treatise on manners and morals with characters and a story, and so initiated, and to some extent determined, the nature of the modern novel as an interpretation of life ; and in the second place for his work as a dramatist. *Euphues* and its sequel form a didactic story, the object of which is to present the ideal gentleman. It is a story of pure abstractions, having less realism than the romances it superseded, and the human interest is thin and languid. But its style caught the popular taste and provoked endless imitations. Euphuism, this elaborate tissue of antithesis, simile, and allusion, pointed with alliteration and balanced cadences, was not Lyly's invention. It began in England with Lord Berners's *Froissart*, and was all the mode with Gosson, Pettie, and others. Lyly perfected and popularized it, and gave all such fashions a label for future use. [*Euphues*, ed. E. Arber (English reprints), 1904, Constable ; contains Chronicle of life, works, and times ; introd. and bibliog. The best ed. of all his works is *The Complete Works of John Lyly*, ed. by R. W. Bond, 3 vols., Clar. Press, 1902. Mr. Bond's invaluable researches are epitomized by J. D. Wilson, with an acute exegesis, in *John Lyly*, Bowes & Bowes, Cambridge, 1905 ; (1) and (2), also, ed. by M. W. Croll and H. Clemons, Dutton, New York, 1916.]

LYNCH, (John Gilbert) Bohun [1884–1929]. *Glamour.* 1912
A story of adventure in modern Greece. For a romance of action, it is too true to life, in that two-thirds of the action is wholly irrelevant to the matter on hand. [Murray: o.p.]

LYND, Sylvia [Mrs. Robert Lynd; *née* Dryhurst]. *The Chorus: a tale of love and folly.* 1915
Less a story than a succession of smart and epigrammatic conversations, providing a running commentary on the affair between a successful artist-craftsman and a young girl who works with him. [Constable: o.p. ; Dutton, New York: o.p.]

—— *The Mulberry Bush ; and other stories.* 1925
Short sketches, several of which, e.g. *The Mulberry Bush, Eat, Drink, and Be Merry, The Sybarite*, deal in an understanding manner with children and their outlook upon life. [Macmillan ; Minton, New York.]

LYNDE, Francis [American; 1865–1930]. *The Helpers.* 1899
—— *The Grafters.* 1904
—— *The Quickening.* 1906
—— *Empire Builders.* 1907
The first two deal with business and politics in Denver and the mining regions, etc. The third—scene, the Tennessee coal and iron fields—touches on problems of faith and doubt as well as the conflicts of commercialism. The fourth deals with railway building in the West, plotting contractors in Denver, the New York Stock Exchange, etc. [(1), Houghton, Boston; (2), (3), (4), Bobbs-Merrill, Indianapolis: o.p.]
—— *Mr. Arnold.* 1923
Virginia in 1780; the hero plots to kidnap Benedict Arnold. [Bobbs-Merrill, Indianapolis; Methuen: o.p.]
LYONS, Albert Neil [b. 1880]. *Clara: some scattered chapters in the life of a hussy.* 1912
This account of a dishonest servant-girl who becomes a flower-seller provides a capable delineation of cockney characters of the lowest classes. [Lane.]
—— *Simple Simon: his adventures in the thistle patch.* 1913
A satire, with good characterization, upon boards of guardians, charity societies, and the like. [Lane; Dodd & Mead, New York.]
—— *Moby Lane and Thereabouts.* 1916
Short sketches, some humorous, some satirical, of life in a Sussex village, e.g. *Befriending her Ladyship*, a comedy about district visitors. [Lane; Dodd & Mead, New York.]
—— *A London Lot.* 1919
Based on the play *London Pride.* The people are cockneys and the copious dialogue is of Mr. Lyons's best. [Lane.]
LYSAGHT, Edward E. [Irish]. *The Gael.* 1919
A political tract rather than a novel, dealing with rural Ireland and the Sinn Fein movement. The rebellion of Easter, 1916, and English prison life are described. [Maunsel, Dublin: o.p.]
LYSAGHT, Sidney Royse [Irish]. *The Marplot.* 1893
A young enthusiast marries a music-hall actress, and her past comes to light on the wedding-day. He lives as a cowboy in America for some years, comes back to Ireland, and falls in love with a fair patriot, reaping nothing but tragedy. [Macmillan.]
—— *One of the Grenvilles.* 1899
A long and desultory novel, the main business arising out of a love complication: it is essentially a novel of character, however, and follows the fortunes of an old family over a considerable period. Several personalities of a fine old type are delineated on an ample scale. [Macmillan.]
—— *Her Majesty's Rebels.* 1907
The central figure in this study of Irish politics (1875–91) corresponds very closely in the details of his private career, which involves him in flagitious relations with several women, to Parnell; but the writer deprecates any imputation of having drawn on the personal character of the great leader. [Macmillan: o.p.]
—— *My Tower in Desmond.* 1925
An autobiographical description of Irish life, in the country near Mallow. [Macmillan, London and New York.]
LYTTON, Edward George Earle Lytton Bulwer, Baron [1803–73]. *Falkland.* 1827
A Byronic crime-novel, which Lytton withdrew from circulation in his collected works on account of its doubtful morality. [Published in his works (*infra*) in the vol. containing *Zicci*, which is a short sketch of *Zanoni* and first appeared in *The Monthly Chronicle* of 1841.]
—— *Pelham; or, The Adventures of a Gentleman.* 1828
A precocious delineation of a man of the world, aiming to show that worldly experience need not corrupt a man's heart or debase his ideals. Superficially, Pelham is frivolous, foppish, effeminate; underneath he is a man of principle and high ambition. Many sketches of people then living. [o.p.]
—— *Devereux.* 1829
An historical novel in which Lord Bolingbroke figures. Steele, Addison, and Swift, Pope, Col. Cleland (supposed original of Will Honeycomb), Beau Fielding ("Orlando" of *The Spectator*), Kneller, Colley Cibber, Richard Cromwell, Lady M. Wortley Montagu, the Duke of Wharton, etc., take minor parts. [o.p.]
—— *The Disowned.* 1829
A "metaphysical" novel, the characters representing certain moral qualities. Attempts to relieve the abstract nature of the plot by episodes of passion and the adventures of two heroes and a gigantic scoundrel sketched from a notorious swindler. [o.p.]
—— *Paul Clifford.* 1830
Denounces "a vicious Prison Discipline and a sanguinary Pénal Code," and advocates a reformatory method. A very tragic story with a "gentleman highwayman" for hero, and a dramatic climax confronting father and son as judge and criminal. Thackeray in *The Yellowplush Memoirs* and elsewhere treated Lytton and his glorified scoundrels and innocent criminals to much wholesome satire. [o.p.]
—— *Eugene Aram.* 1832
Another of Lytton's sympathetic studies of criminals—the story of the famous murderer, executed 1759. As a critic sarcastically put it, "How Eugene Aram, though a thief, a liar, and a murderer, yet being intellectual, was amongst the noblest of mankind." [o.p.; Collins.]
—— *Godolphin.* 1833
"A singular mixture of love, politics, gossip, gambling, satire, prophecy, and astrology." Hero and heroine are both scions of the nobility; but the latter is devoted by her father's dying wish to the destruction of the aristocracy. In pursuit of this aim, though loved by Godophin, she marries another. Then, on her husband's death, she joins her lover in Italy, to find him entangled with another woman, and all are involved in tragedy. Much criticism of the aristocracy, and many predictions of their downfall. Appeared anonymously, rousing speculations as to the real authorship. [*v. infra.*]

LYTTON, Edward George Earle Lytton Bulwer (*continued*).   *The Pilgrims of the Rhine.*   1834
>   An extravaganza mingling elves and fairies with more mundane creatures, and propounding his ideas of human life. The English fairies visit their kindred of the Rhineland. [*v. infra.*; also (Everyman's Lib.), Dent (Dutton, New York), 1909.]

—— *The Last Days of Pompeii.*   1834
>   A learned and fairly successful picture of the splendid and luxurious Roman society of the reign of Titus (A.D. 79), based for its local colour on Lytton's study of the Pompeian antiquities and Pliny's famous account of the eruption. Spoiled by too much eloquence. [*v. infra.* Also (Everyman's Lib.), Dent (Dutton, New York), 1908; *illus.*, Scribner, London and New York.]

—— *Rienzi, the Last of the Tribunes.*   1835
>   Another romance in which Lytton tried to rival Scott. It gives a careful historical picture of the stormy politics of Rome and Italy in the period 1313–54, and Rienzi's fight for Italian freedom and unity. [Routledge; (Everyman's Lib.), Dent (Dutton, New York), 1911.]

—— *Ernest Maltravers ; and, Alice, or The Mysteries.*   1837–8
>   A complicated love-romance, the sequel giving the solution of an extremely hazardous plot. Maltravers, a rich and aristocratic young man (whose literary brilliance seems a reflection of Lytton's), loves and loses a beautiful girl of the lowest class, seeks consolation in distant travel and adventure, and parades like Byron " the pageant of a bleeding heart." Politics, social intrigue, legal plots, and a murder or so, lead on to a conclusion satisfying to the most ardent sentimentalist. Published in 1838 as parts 1 and 2 of *The Eleusinia*. [o.p.; *Ernest Maltravers*, Warne.]

—— *Leila.*   1838
>   A romance of Spain and the Moors, making a picturesque use of the stormy incidents of the conquest of Granada. [*v. infra.*]

—— *Night and Morning.*   1841
>   A romantic and highly improbable story of great length, profuse in coincidence as any of Lytton's, reciting the fortunes of two sons of a wealthy man who had concealed his marriage and left no proofs of their right to the estates. Exciting adventures and hair-breadth escapes in England and abroad, villainous doings among sharpers and coiners in Paris, love complications, etc., come to an end with the recovery of the missing documents. [o.p.; Routledge; Nelson.]

—— *Zanoni.*   1842
>   A story of a secret brotherhood of remote origin, who possess the secret of eternal youth, a subject that obsessed Lytton. The hero, having lived many centuries, marries a lovely opera singer, resigning his gifts of supernatural vision and immortality, and perishes in the Reign of Terror. A gloomy and, at times, a ghastly story, but Lytton's favourite. *Zicci* was a first sketch of this novel. [o.p.; Little & Brown, Boston.]

—— *The Last of the Barons.*   1843
>   The tragic story of Warwick the King-Maker and his strife with Edward IV. The battle of Barnet (1471) is described at length ; and besides giving the facts of history, the novel attempts to analyse in a philosophical way the social tendencies of this changeful epoch. But, after all, it is Lytton's first-rate story-telling that has preserved this and his other historical novels from oblivion. [*v. infra.* Also (Everyman's Lib.), Dent (Dutton, New York), 1907; Oxford Press.]

—— *Lucretia ; or, Children of the Night.*   1847
>   An adaptation of the story of Thomas Griffiths Wainewright, the virtuoso and poisoner. Lucretia, the arch-criminal, is a character with redeeming traits ; but the rest of the villains and their nefarious deeds are so revolting that the book aroused a good deal of protest at the time of its appearance. [*v. infra.*]

—— *Harold ; or, The Last of the Saxon Kings.*   1848
>   The tragic history of Harold's fall ; elaborate descriptions of the battles of Stamford Bridge and Hastings and of English life in the eleventh century ; as accurate historically as Lytton could make it. [Routledge; (Everyman's Lib.), Dent (Dutton, New York) ; (World's Classics), Oxford Press, 1908.]

—— *The Caxtons.*   1849
>   The first of a group of novels of manners professing a criticism of life grounded on Lytton's principle of the Real and the Ideal. Takes the form of family memoirs by Pisistratus Caxton, a modern Tristram Shandy. The blend of realism and didactics is Lytton's, but the manner is that of Sterne. Mr. and Mrs. Caxton are a toned-down, Victorian Mr. and Mrs. Shandy ; the soldier-uncle, with his Wellington-worship and genealogical crotchets, is a sort of Uncle Toby ; idealism triumphs in the high-minded and high-bred Sedley Beaudesert. This group of novels, in spite of the attitudinizing, offers a graphic picture of society in that day, and also of political life. Lytton's faith in a natural aristocracy of well-born, well-bred, and patriotic Englishmen, which gave strength and consistency to the statesman, gives the novelist a similar unity and significance in his character-drawing and general picture of life. It is the same inspiration that comes out more epically in his historical novels. [*v. infra* ; also Nelson.]

—— *My Novel ; or, Varieties of English Life.*   1853
>   Continues the theme of *The Caxtons*—" the amusements, the pleasures, and the passions of the idle members of English society," i.e. the squirearchy and country-houses. A multitude of characters are introduced, centring in a wealthy country squire and his family, their connexions, and the magnates and ordinary inhabitants of the parish. [*v. infra.*]

—— *What Will he do with it ?*   1858
>   Another novel by " Pisistratus Caxton " in the style of *The Caxtons* and *My Novel*. [*v. infra.*]

—— *The Haunted and the Haunters.*   1859
>   A short story that came out in *Blackwood*—a masterpiece of terrifying supernaturalism more uniformly successful than the following, which is usually bound up with it. [*v. infra*, with *The Pilgrims of the Rhine* ; *v.* also *The Coming Race*, *infra*.]

LYTTON, Edward George Earle Lytton Bulwer (*continued*). *A Strange Story.* 1862

A grisly story of supernatural influence, on a much more elaborate scale, with a regular plot and a number of characters, believers or sceptics. Has a good deal of the stage trickery common in ghost literature, but attains some thrilling psychological effects. [o.p.]

—— *The Coming Race.* 1871

A Utopian romance of the philosophic kind. The scene is below the surface of the earth, where a branch of the human race, lost ages ago, has developed a higher order of civilization and of mechanical art. [*v. infra*; with *The Haunted and the Haunters*, (World's Classics), Oxford Press, 1928.]

—— *Kenelm Chillingly.* 1873

Another didactic novel developing his philosophy of the Real and the Ideal, and criticizing everyday life. The muscular hero acquires a more wholesome view of life, after being the heir to a baronet and therefore predestined to wickedness, by living in the slums and working as a labourer. [*v. infra.*]

—— *The Parisians.* 1873

A view of Parisian society in all its ranks and phases—the old noblesse, financial and industrial magnates, bohemians, workmen, and socialists, with their various interests and activities, at the period ending in the siege of Paris. Philosophical and didactic like the foregoing—the characters often mere mouthpieces for the author's own doctrines. [2 vols., with *The Coming Race*, *v. infra*.]

—— *Pausanias the Spartan.* 1876

A posthumous historical romance (relating to 470 B.C.), unfinished, ed. by Lytton's son.

[Editions of Lytton's *Works*, published by Routledge: (New Knebworth Edn.), 29 vols. (Dutton, New York); (Stevenage Edn.), 29 vols. (Dutton, New York); those so marked are o.p. in these editions. Also, 32 vols., Nickerson, Boston; Warwick ed., ltd., Page, Boston; 25 vols., *illus., id.*]

"**MAARTENS, MAARTEN**" [Joost Marius Willem van der Poorten-Schwartz; Dutch, writing in English; 1858–1915]. *The Sin of Joost Avelingh.* 1890

This and the following are written in correct and forcible English by a Dutch novelist. Truthful genre-painting of homely Dutch life, with lifelike characters, and an interesting psychological study of the quixotic Joost. The plot pivots on a murder. [Constable; Appleton, New York: o.p.]

—— *An Old Maid's Love: a Dutch story told in English.* 1891

An unsophisticated Dutch student is in love with a Dutch girl, while a bewitching French vicomtesse loves him and carries him off to a little Eden on Lake Maggiore. [Constable.]

—— *God's Fool: a Koopstad story.* 1892

A psychological and ethical study of a strong young man whose intellect is that of a child, and who had lost three senses by an accident in childhood, analysing the mental states and difficulties of this sensitive and emotional being, shut off from his fellow-creatures, whom he ardently desires to benefit with his wealth. [Macmillan: o.p.; Appleton, New York.]

—— *A Question of Taste.* 1892

The quiet, humdrum life of a group of Dutch people of the middle class; thoroughly true to the commonplace interests of average family life. Scanty in incident, but motives are exposed with humour, insight, and satire. [Constable.]

—— *The Greater Glory.* 1894

An indictment of "infamy in high places, contrasting worldly power with the greater glory of great thoughts and unselfishness." One compares it instinctively with Thackeray's *Newcomes* for its general theme, the peculiar tone of its satire, and the accomplished realism of its representation of average life and character. [Constable; Appleton, New York: o.p.]

—— *My Lady Nobody.* 1895

A delineation of Dutch society that comes still nearer to Thackeray's manner—realism portraying human beings neither better nor worse than they are, a running commentary by the author, cynicism and sarcasm, much like Thackeray's, though differentiated by the writer's peculiar humour. The crowd of characters gathered round a decayed baronial family represent the old aristocracy, the moneyed bourgeois, the lower middle-class, and, with harsh satire, the lower classes in the country. The gist of the story is the life of a parson's daughter who marries the Baron and, after his death, by great self-sacrifice keeps the estate together in the teeth of obloquy. [Constable.]

—— *Her Memory.* 1898

A society story, with a good deal of ironical comedy and analysis of sentiment. Subject, a bereaved husband's sorrow, ending only with his next wedding; and the cynical moral, that the world is too much in the end for merely private griefs and aspirations. [Constable; Appleton, New York: o.p.]

—— *Some Women I have Known.* 1901

A dozen women of various countries portrayed in a form that hovers between the character-sketch and the short story. They are well diversified, but most are either unhappily married or ill appreciated. The prevailing tone is comedy with, now and then, shrewd touches of satire. The reader will perhaps be struck most by the author's cosmopolitanism. [Constable, Appleton, New York: o.p.]

—— *My Poor Relations.* 1903

Short stories, some dramatic, some mere character-studies, chiefly of Dutch peasants, all alike admirable in their sober and homely Dutch painting. The realism of Mr. Maartens shows well in *The Banquet*. More tragic is *The Mother*, and *Jan Hunkum's Money* is a grim bit of comedy. [Constable: o.p.]

—— *Dorothea: a story of the pure in heart.* 1904

An enormously long and amorphous novel, brimful of human experience and wisdom, and crowded with characters, who represent on the one side the garish world of pleasure and excitement, Paris, the Riviera, and Montreux, and on the other the better part expressed in the sub-title and the character of Dorothea. One of the best observed of the host of characters is the husband, Col. Sandring. [Constable.]

"MAARTENS, MAARTEN" (*continued*). *The Healers.* 1906

The characters of the Dutch professor of medicine and his poetess-wife provide a solid and humorous background to the main story, that of their son, who achieves a wonderful cure by psycho-therapy, and so wins fame. A good deal of fun is poked at those scientists who admit nothing but physical forces in their interpretation of nature. [Constable : o.p. ; Appleton, New York : o.p.]

—— *The Woman's Victory ; and other stories.* 1906

A collection of emotional stories—about artists, politicians, and more especially women. [Constable : o.p.]

—— *The New Religion.* 1907

Deals in rather broad satire at the expense of medical men, specialists, and fashionable cures : a criticism of those who give excessive care to the body, at the expense of the spirit. [Methuen : o.p. ; Appleton, New York : o.p.]

—— *Brothers All : more stories of Dutch peasant life.* 1909

Another collection of stories, of which *The Library*, *Tuberculin*, and *Teetotal* may be taken as specimens of his lighter vein, and *The Death Way* and *The Contract* of his pathos. [Methuen : o.p. ; Appleton, New York : o.p.]

—— *Harmen Pols—Peasant.* 1910

Rough-sketches the characters and elaborates the domestic relations and the moral and monetary complications of three Dutch families, struggling peasant farmers. Impressionist drawing of real life, seasoned with plot-effects. [Methuen : o.p. ; Lane, New York : o.p.]

—— *Eve : an incident of Paradise Regained.* 1912

The problem of a girl used to a care-free, happy family life, married to a stolid burgomaster engrossed in his local affairs. After the loss of her child, and a passionate episode with an airman, she regains happiness through the consolations of religion. [Constable ; Dutton, New York : o.p.]

"M'AULAY, Allan" [Miss Charlotte Stewart of Ardvoirlich ; Scottish ; *b.* 1863]. *The Rhymer.* 1900

An episode in Burns's life connected with his platonic amour with Clarinda (Mrs. Maclehose) is made the peg on which to hang the story of an ingenuous girl's love and estrangement (1787). [Unwin : o.p. ; Scribner, New York : o.p.]

—— *Black Mary.* 1901

Kindly portraiture of Perthshire folk a hundred years ago, bringing out strongly their hardness and their integrity. In the half-caste daughter of a ne'er-do-well emigrant to the West Indies, a much-idealized picture is presented of invincible goodness and generosity. Black Mary's life of hardship, peril, and disappointment nobly borne is pathetic. [Unwin : o.p.]

—— *Poor Sons of a Day.* 1902

The most melancholy side of the '45, the sufferings of relatives, sweethearts, and also of those brave men who threw themselves into the movement though they despaired of its success. Æneas MacGregor is one of the last, his heroic little sweetheart Mally is a winsome representative of the Whigs. As might be expected from the subject, the story is extremely sentimental. [Nisbet : o.p.]

—— *The Eagle's Nest.* 1909

An attempt to "puzzle out the secret" of Napoleon by a character-study of his early years in Corsica, when he was alternately supporting and intriguing against Paoli (1779–92). [Lane : o.p.]

MACAULAY, Rose. *The Lee Shore.* 1912

The man in whom sympathy centres is an ineffectual person who ends on the lee shore of poverty and vagabondage. His endearing qualities are good-nature, invincible cheerfulness, and a sense of honour, which are thrown into relief by comparison with one of fortune's favourites and with his own disreputable half-brother. [Hodder ; Doran, New York : o.p.]

—— *Views and Vagabonds.* 1912

A humorous survey of contemporary life and social ideas and prejudices, rather than a novel. A Cambridge man of good family marries a girl of the working-classes, to show he is no empty idealist. The woman is a genuine human creature, and in herself confutes the fallacy of regarding the poor as by nature different from their betters. [Murray : o.p. ; Holt, New York : o.p.]

—— *The Making of a Bigot.* 1914

Here the protagonist is a young man so incredibly broad-minded and catholic that he not merely sympathizes with but even joins all the sects, parties, and movements, however mutually exclusive. But to make life livable and marry a Tory he has to choose some form of bigotry. This sprightly idea at any rate gives scope for versatile character-drawing and plenty of humorous but not ill-natured criticism of life in all its modern diversity. [Hodder : o.p.]

—— *Non-Combatants and Others.* 1916

The different views of the war held by different people, and its different effects upon themselves and especially upon a woman who, in the course of it, finds herself thrown in with, now her own people, genteel and earnest, then certain dull and unresponsive but very human middle-class folk, and finally a callous and flippant artistic set who are out for pleasure as usual. [Hodder : o.p.]

—— *What Not : a prophetic comedy.* 1919

A jesting satire upon the future menace of official control, centring in the Ministry of Brains, whose function is the compulsory mental education of the citizen, by the elimination of the unintelligent. The Minister himself, falling a victim to a charming girl, shipwrecks his own theories, and the Ministry falls before a popular outburst. Miss Macaulay's wit has more laughter than bitterness. [Long.]

—— *Potterism : a tragi-farcical tract.* 1920

Potterism is the slogan of Mr. Potter's newspapers ; it is " the usual British mixture of humbug, sentimentality, commercialism, and genuine feeling." The anti-Potterites, some of whom are of his own family, say that it is based "on fear, ignorance, vulgarity, mental laziness, sentimentality, and greed." This is a shrewd satire of the public opinion dispensed by the gutter-press during the war years. [Collins ; Boni, New York.]

MACAULAY, Rose (*continued*). *Dangerous Ages.*   1921
The women of three generations in a family find that there are at least three dangerous ages. The early thirties are perilous, and so are the forties. But sixty-three is still more dangerous—for the young and active grandmother, who thinks she has brains, and falls an easy prey to the psycho-analysts. The wisest and happiest person is the great-grandmother, who is not an intellectual, but enjoys the serenity of age like a true philosopher. [Collins ; Boni, New York.]

—— *Mystery at Geneva : an improbable tale of singular happenings.*   1922
A satirical comedy about a reporter at the League of Nations Assembly in Geneva, who turns out to be a girl in disguise. [Collins ; Boni, New York.]

—— *Told by an Idiot.*   1923
The intellectual and moral history of a clergyman's family (1879–1923)—Victorian, *fin-de-siècle*, Edwardian, and Georgian periods, pungently characterized. The clergyman keeps losing his faith, is an Anglican, a Unitarian, a Roman Catholic, a proselyte of the Ethical Church, etc., according as conscience, and too much study, compel. History makes the plot, the great war furnishes the *dénouement*. [Collins ; Boni, New York ; Grosset, New York.]

—— *Orphan Island.*   1924
A satire upon conventions, shams, and artificial class-distinctions. An island in the South Seas inhabited by the descendants of a shipload of orphan castaways ruled by the Smith clan is rediscovered by an English family. Clever characterization, plenty of sheer fun, and many home-thrusts at convention, prudery, and class-prejudice. [Collins ; Boni, New York.]

—— *Crewe Train.*   1926
The title suggests a wrong direction in life. The heroine suffers from a vague distaste for every form of activity other than physical, but is finally enmeshed in the normal routine of civilized life. However, she is by nature too awkward and tiresome to be the instrument of more than very mild satire of middle-class convention. [Collins ; Boni, New York ; also with the two preceding, in 1 vol., Collins, 1928.]

—— *Keeping up Appearances.*   1928
A study of dual personality in the daughter of parents of widely different social standing and ideals, and how this young woman endeavours to meet the demands of her complex nature, her actual achievements falling far short of her aspirations. [Collins ; *sub tit. Daisy and Daphne*, Boni, New York.]

—— *Staying with Relations.*   1930
The usual witty conversations, on any mortal subject, and some novelties in the way of character, with much about a visit to Guatemala, which brings in several vivid and exciting chapters and one strong emotional passage. Miss Macaulay is anxious to show up the fallacy of calling people types, and accordingly exhibits each individual behaving quite differently from what that assumption would imply ; hence a certain lack of her usual spontaneity. [Collins ; Boni, New York.]

" McCALL, Sidney " [Mary Fenollosa, *née* McNeill ; American]. *The Breath of the Gods.* 1905
Japan at the outbreak of the Russian War, by one who knows and loves the country. The centre of attraction is a Japanese girl educated in America. [Little & Brown, Boston : o.p. ; Hutchinson : o.p.]

—— *The Dragon Painter.*   1906
A Japanese artist whose feeling towards the invaders is finely expressed. [Little & Brown, Boston : o.p. ; Stanley Paul : o.p.]

McCALLIN, William [Irish]. *Ulster Fireside Tales.*   1921
Nine stories of homely farm-life, turning mainly upon leases, lawsuits, and such-like, with a good rendering of the dialect of Northern Ireland. [Heath Cranston : o.p.]

McCARTHY, Justin [Irish ; 1830–1911]. *The Waterdale Neighbours.*   1867
A novel of character—the contrasted life-story of two men, one a manly and upright worker, the other a political tu ncoat, a Chartist who joins the Tories for the sake of personal success and, when ruin stares him in the face, commits an act of treachery that is quickly followed by retribution. [Chatto.]

—— *A Fair Saxon.*   1873
The fair Saxon's lover is an Irish M.P., whose chivalry leads him into embarrassing entanglements with the Fenians, and brings his political career to an abrupt close. Dashing and incisive sketches of men and women, often satirical. [Chatto : o.p.]

—— *Dear Lady Disdain.*   1875
" A free, friendly, half-boyish sort of nature, which seemed to turn with impatience and even contempt from sentimentalisms and love-making "—such is the heroine, and there are other fresh and attractive characters, as well as sundry eccentrics. The plot moves on with little complication to the happy conclusion. [Chatto.]

—— *Mononia.*   1901
The attempted rising of 1848 in a town in Munster (? Cork) worked into a happy love-story. A Nationalist version of the events, but fair. [Chatto.]

McCARTHY, Justin Huntly [Irish, son of above ; b. 1860]. *If I were King.*   1902
A successful melodrama turned into a brilliant fairy-tale, in which history is altered **freely**. Hero, the reprobate poet, François Villon (1462–3), who is made Constable of France for **one week**, to satisfy a caprice. Dramatized as *The Vagabond King.* [Heinemann ; Harper, New York.]

—— *Needles and Pins* [sequel].   1907
Villon is now husband of Katherine de Vaucelles and Lord of Moncorbier. [Hurst : o.p. ; Harper, New York : o.p.]

—— *The Flower of France.*   1906
A careful and sympathetic life of Joan of Arc, eked out with touches of imagination. Afterwards dramatized. [Hurst : o.p. ; Harper, New York : o.p.]

—— *The Illustrious O'Hagan.*   1906
A light melodrama of court intrigue in a German principality early in the eighteenth century, with twin brothers, the O'Hagans, as joint-heroes. Copyrighted for the stage. [Hurst : o.p. ; Harper, New York : o.p.]

McCARTHY, Justin Huntly (*continued*). *Seraphica: a romance.* 1907
    Seraphica is a daring and wilful little duchess—scenes, eighteenth-century Paris and Artois—who wins the obstinate prince she loves by masking herself as a gallant and delivering him from various awkward situations. [Hurst: o.p.; Harper, New York: o.p.]

—— *The Gorgeous Borgia.* 1908

—— *The God of Love.* 1909
    Two melodramatic novels of Renaissance Italy, the first of Rome in the days of the Borgias, the other the story of Dante and Beatrice (1290). [(1) and (2), Hurst: o.p.; Harper, New York: o.p.]

—— *The King Over the Water.* 1911
    Tells the story of Wogan's rescue of Clementina Sobieska. (See also Mason's *Clementina* and Miss Poynter's *Madamscourt*.) [Hurst: o.p.; Harper, New York: o.p.]

—— *The Fair Irish Maid.* 1911
    A romance of Ireland in the days of the Dandies. [Hurst: o.p.; Harper, New York: o.p.]

—— *In Spacious Times.* 1916
    The love-story of an Englishman of the school of Drake—a strange wooing that began in comedy and nearly ended in tragedy. [Hurst: o.p.; Lane, New York: o.p.]

—— *Henry Elizabeth.* 1920
    Love and adventure in Devon, on Lundy Island, at the Court of Elizabeth, and in shady haunts in London (1568). [Hurst: o.p.; Lane, New York: o.p.]

McCHESNEY, Dora Greenwell [1871–1912]. *Kathleen Clare.* 1895
    The story of Strafford's viceroyalty of Ireland (1637–41) told in pseudo-Elizabethan English in the diary of an imaginary kinswoman. [Blackwood: o.p.]

—— *Miriam Cromwell, Royalist.* 1897
    The story of Cromwell's niece; from Edgehill to Naseby and the king's execution (1641–9). [Blackwood: o.p.; Way, New York: o.p.]

—— *Rupert, by the Grace of God.* 1899
    Intrigue, war, and adventure, hingeing on a plot for placing Prince Rupert on the English throne (1645–6). [Macmillan: o.p.]

—— *Cornet Strong of Ireton's Horse: an episode of the Ironsides.* 1903
    A Roundhead story, from Marston Moor to the fall of Bristol (1644–5). [Lane: o.p.]

—— *Yesterday's To-morrow.* 1905
    Charles II, Prince Rupert, and Restoration history generally as a mere background to a story with some slight character-drawing, pivoting on the identity of James de la Cloche (Henri de Rohan), Charles II's oldest natural son (1668). [Dent: o.p.]

—— *The Wounds of a Friend.* 1908
    A romance of Elizabethan Virginia, adventures among Indians and on the high seas, and a rather vague and sketchy drama of mistaken revenge transporting us to the English Court (1585–90). [Murray.]

—— *The Confessions of Richard Plantagenet.* 1913
    Posthumous and left unfinished, but presenting a new view of Richard's character, as less black than usually painted (1471–85). [Murray.]

MacDONALD, George [Scottish; 1824–1905]. *Phantastes: a faerie romance.* 1858
    A fairy-tale for grown-up people which, like Meredith's almost contemporary *Shagpat*, teaches a lesson of valour and self-control. Full of poetry both in verse and prose, it uses many of the old properties of fairyland, and shows a fecund and novel imagination. [(Everyman's Lib.), Dent (Dutton, New York), 1916; with *The Portent*, McKay, Philadelphia.]

—— *David Elginbrod.* 1863
    Began a series of Aberdeenshire stories, largely in broad Saxon dialect, which later on begat the Kailyard novelists, Barrie, Crockett, "Ian Maclaren," etc. It is a story of humble life, centring in two saintly personalities, a dignified and pious Scottish peasant and his daughter. A characteristic vein of mysticism runs through the story. [Cassell; McKay, Philadelphia.]

—— *The Portent: a story of second sight.* 1864
    Excels even *Phantastes* in a truly Celtic power of evoking illusion. It is the love-tale of two beings whose spiritual natures are connected by a mystical affinity. The tale closes amid tragic hints and forebodings, but the poetical treatment gives it all a strange, unearthly beauty. [Chatto; *The Portent; and other stories*, Unwin, 1909; v. also *Phantastes, supra*.]

—— *Alec Forbes of Howglen.* 1865
    Portrays the inhabitants of an Aberdeenshire village, and contains MacDonald's most charming pictures of boys. Alec's boyhood, his university life in Glasgow, his temptation and fall, and his final restoration, are a kind of modern *Pilgrim's Progress*. [Cassell; McKay, Philadelphia.]

—— *Annals of a Quiet Neighbourhood.* 1866
    Character-portraits and studies of conduct chiefly in a Scottish parish, e.g. an amiable parson, epitome of all the virtues, a number of oddities whose talk is very humorous, the various inmates of an ancient hall— the imperious mistress, the dilettante and egotistic musician, the edifying heroine, and the wanton little sprite Gladys. Ethical and religious interest is paramount, and a spirit of good-will towards men pervades the book, which was the first to bring its author into wide repute. [Routledge; McKay, Philadelphia.]

—— *The Light Princess.* [juvenile] 1867

—— *At the Back of the North Wind.* [juvenile] 1870

—— *The Princess and the Goblin.* [juvenile] 1871
    Delicate and fanciful stories for children—lighter essays in the style of *Phantastes*, full of the same glamour and the same ethical teaching. [(1), *illus.*, Blackie; Putnam, New York; (2), *illus.* by Arthur Hughes,

MacDONALD, George (*continued*).
Blackie; Burt, New York; (3), *illus.* by Helen Stratton, Blackie; by Arthur Hughes, Lippincott, Philadelphia. Other eds., (1), (2), and (3), *illus.*, Lippincott, Philadelphia; McKay, Philadelphia; Macmillan, New York, 1926.]

—— *The Seaboard Parish.* 1868
History of a long holiday spent by a clergyman and his family on the Cornish coast (Bude). Many incidents; but the interest centres in the clergyman's talks, which voice the author's beliefs concerning things in heaven and things on earth. An ideal picture of family happiness and concord. [S. Paul: o.p.; McKay, Philadelphia.]

—— *Robert Falconer.* 1868
An interesting study of Calvinism and of the growth and manhood of a philanthropist, who puts in action the author's ideas of what should be done. The joys and woes of boyhood are finely sketched; and the musical soutar, Dooble Sammie, with his love for his old fiddle, and the Calvinistic grandmother, brimming over with affection which she thinks it her duty to repress, are touching figures—the latter a portrait of MacDonald's own grandmother. [Hurst & Blackett: o.p.; McKay, Philadelphia.]

—— *Malcolm.* 1875
—— *The Marquis of Lossie* [sequel]. 1877
The life-history of a boy, the heir to an earldom, who, stolen in infancy, was adopted by a Highland piper and brought up to be a fisherman. [(1) and (2), Cassell; McKay, Philadelphia; (2), Burt, New York.]

—— *St. George and St. Michael.* 1876
A love-tale of Puritan and Royalist (1641-6). Hero the Earl of Glamorgan, who is represented as the king's scapegoat in the affair of the intrigues for bringing over an Irish army. The second Marquess of Worcester is prominent among the men and women from both sides. [S. Paul: o.p.; McKay, Philadelphia.]

—— *Thomas Wingfold, Curate.* 1876
Traces the conversion of a clergyman from mere professional lip-service to a hearty and genuine faith in God. Interwoven is the story of a youth who accidentally kills a heartless girl to whom he is strongly attached. He is led to repentance and peace by the curate's influence. [S. Paul: o.p.; McKay, Philadelphia.]

—— *Paul Faber, Surgeon.* 1879
In some sort a sequel to *Thomas Wingfold.* How a doctor, devoted to his profession and eager in the service of humanity, is led by painful experience, sorrow, and love for his neighbour to a belief in God. English Nonconformity is depicted in far from attractive colours. [S. Paul: o.p.; McKay, Philadelphia.]

—— *Sir Gibbie.* 1879
Spiritual history of a Christ-like character, and sketches of more than one person to whom the unseen is more real than the seen. [Cassell; (Everyman's Lib.), Dent (Dutton, New York), 1914; Burt, New York; McKay, Philadelphia.]

—— *Castle Warlock: a homely romance.* 1882
Annals of a God-fearing family, whose piety and otherworldliness bring them near to ruin, from which they are saved by the discovery of an ancestral hoard. [Paul: o.p.; *sub tit. Warloch o' Glenwarloch,* McKay, Philadelphia.]

—— *Donal Grant.* 1884
Portrays another of these men of lowly life who influence their neighbours for good, a noble, unselfish being, who wears religion as a familiar everyday garment. There is a little too much of the conventional plot-novel in the mysterious and sensational elements of the story. [Paul: o.p.; McKay, Philadelphia.]

—— *What's Mine's Mine.* 1886
The story of an exiled chief and his brother, forced to sell their lands and emigrate with the remnant of the clan. Their influence for good on two English girls, daughters of their supplanter, and the contrast of their broad views of God's fatherhood with the stern Calvinism of their mother are leading motives. [Routledge; McKay, Philadelphia.]

—— *Heather and Snow.* 1893
Another romance of Aberdeenshire, with dialogue in the usual "broad Saxon." An athletic and religious peasant girl, her brother, half-witted but spiritually strong, the hero and his unpleasant mother are the more prominent characters. [Chatto; Harper, New York: o.p.]
[*Works,* 24 vols., McKay, Philadelphia.]

MacDONALD, Ronald [Scottish; *b.* 1864]. *The Sword of the King.* 1900
Love and adventure in the England of James II, and in Holland under William of Orange. Deals incidentally with some of the events that preceded and contributed to the English Revolution (1678-88). [Murray: o.p.; Century Co., New York: o.p.]

McFADYEN, Ferdinand [Scottish]. *All Smoke.* 1930
A number of characters, mostly unbeautiful, mean, hard-fisted, malicious, sly, gross, vulgar, and unctuously respectable, are drawn in all their harsh lineaments from the people in a Scottish industrial town. But the picture is saved from complete ugliness by the finer traits of some, and the author's sure handling of motive and causation. [Constable; R. R. Smith, New York.]

MACFARLANE, Charles [1799-1858]. *The Camp of Refuge.* 1844
An extremely vivid story of Hereward's famous stand against the Conqueror in the Fens of Ely. Aims at historical accuracy rather than romance, and achieves a most convincing picture of everyday life in town and cloister. [Edited by (Sir) G. L. Gomme, maps, etc., Constable (Longmans, New York), 1897: o.p.; ed. by E. A. Baker (Half-forgotten Books), Routledge, 1904.]

—— *A Legend of Reading Abbey.* 1845
A similar account of the turbulent state of England in the reign of Stephen (1135-54), centring in the vicissitudes that befell the monks of Reading. [Edited by (Sir) G. L. Gomme, maps, etc., Constable (Longmans, New York), 1898: o.p.; ed. by E. A. Baker (Half-forgotten Books), Routledge, 1904: o.p.]

MACFARLANE, Charles (*continued*). *The Dutch in the Medway.*   1845

Deals with a disgraceful episode of English history, the blockading of the Thames by a Dutch fleet under De Ruyter (1667), which was followed by the ignominious peace of Breda.   Founded on Pepys, who is one of the characters of the domestic story.   [With Foreword by S. R. Crockett, J. Clarke, 1897 : o.p.]

McFEE, William [Scottish ; *b.* 1881]. *Casuals of the Sea : the voyage of a soul.*   1916

Very casual in construction : it is not obvious whether the soul in question is that of the determined young woman who enters the *demi-monde* and afterwards marries respectably, or her brother the street-arab, who goes to sea and then marries the buxom proprietrix of a pub.   Those who want to know all about the inside of the engine-room on a tramp-steamer will find enough to satisfy them here. [Secker ; Doubleday, New York.]

—— *Captain Macedoine's Daughter.*   1920

A voyage and the ship's company of queerly assorted people, and more particularly the emotional affairs in which the beautiful Artemisia Macedoine has the rôle of fatal enchantress—all watched and commented by the chief engineer Spenlove, a cynical philosopher who denounces the mirage of romantic love.   [Secker ; Doubleday, New York.]

—— *Pilgrims of Adversity.*   1928

A romantic novel with many external resemblances to *Nostromo*, though the technique is not Conrad's.   The captain, chief officers, and engineers of a cargo-steamer get mixed up with an incipient revolution in the Central American state of Costaragua.   The characters are stated to be drawn from life, and include Britishers, Americans, Spaniards, half-breeds, and others. [Heinemann ; Doubleday, New York.]

—— *North of Suez.*   1930

A war-story centring in Port Said, which is made out to be a cess-pool of vice and iniquity, villainous intrigue and general corruption.   The writer shows himself intimately acquainted with the place and the numerous races congregated there.   [Heinemann ; Doubleday, New York.]

—— *Sailors of Fortune.*   1930

Fourteen stories of the Afro-Iberian line or of the Greek archipelago and the Levant, the interest at least as much in character as in the adventures.   Captain Muster of the *Biskra* is the most striking figure, and like Jimmy Russell the press photographer keeps reappearing.   *A Son of the Commodore* is an imaginative solution of the mystery of the *Vestris*.   Another good yarn is *The Vanished Passenger*.   [Heinemann ; Doubleday, New York.]

MacGILL, Patrick [Irish ; *b.* 1891]. *Children of the Dead End : the autobiography of a navvy.*
                                             1914

The writer declares that this is mostly autobiographical, and paints a sombre, realistic picture of life in Glenties, Co. Donegal, where the " Navvy Poet " was born.   No less piteous and disturbing are his revelations of life among the labouring-classes in Scotland.   There he goes on tramp and finds a job at Kinlochleven, where, close to nature at its wildest, the navvies are herded in foul slums.

—— *The Rat-Pit* [sequel].   1915

In this sequel, the realism is probably overcharged, although, no doubt, the horrors of slum-life and of the houses of ill-fame in Glasgow are from direct observation.   The girl from Donegal whom the hero loves in *Children of the Dead End* here dies a woman of the streets.   [(1) and (2), Jenkins ; (1), Dutton, New York : o.p. ; (2), Doran, New York : o.p.]

—— *Glenmornan : a story of Donegal.*   1918

A " Return of the Native " to a Donegal glen, which is also perhaps autobiographical, at least in part : some of the strange peasant-girls seem to be drawn from life.   The descriptions of priest-ridden people, hard-working, but afflicted with prejudices and class-jealousies, are instructive if not pleasing.   [Jenkins ; Doran, New York : o.p.]

—— *Maureen.*   1919

The tragic story of a love-child in Donegal, opening up vistas of peasant character, mysticism, and super-stition. [Jenkins ; McBride, New York : o.p.]

MACHEN, Arthur [*b.* 1863]. *The Chronicle of Clemendy.*   1888

Seventeen stories, apparently intended as part-burlesque, part-imitation of mediæval romance, with plenty of talk about monks and beer, and not much else.   One of the more successful, *How the Folk of Abergavenny were pestered by an Accursed Knight*, tells how a craftsman made a knight in armour to ring the clock-bell, and how the knight came to life and did untold mischief. [Revised ed. 1925, Secker ; Knopf, New York.]

—— *The Hill of Dreams.*   1907

A youth of morbidly sensitive temperament falls so completely under the spell of dream-reconstructions of the past, that they usurp the functions of normal life, and lead him to misery and suicide. [Secker ; Knopf, New York.]

MACHRAY, Rev. Robert [Scottish ; *b.* 1857]. *Grace O'Malley, Princess and Pirate.*   1898

The protracted struggle between English and Irish that ended in Carew's barbarous pacification of Ulster (*c.* 1579).   Scenes on the west coast, and plenty of exciting incident. [Cassell : o.p.]

M'ILROY, Archibald [Irish ; 1860–1915]. *When Lint was in the Bell.*   1897

—— *By Lone Craig-Linnie Burn.*   1900

Two series of local stories of the Scoto-Irish folk of Ulster, the chat of village gossips, character-sketches of doctor, minister, agent, and innkeeper, quaint blends of Scotch and Irish traits.   Most of the tales are of an idyllic kind.   [(1), M'Caw, Belfast : o.p. ; (2), Unwin : o.p.]

—— *The Auld Meetin' Hoose Green.*   1898

Similar stories of the Antrim peasants, and a rendering of the thoughts and feelings of rustic Presbyterians —much in the style of the Kailyard novelists. [M'Caw, Belfast : o.p.]

—— *A Banker's Love Story.*   1901

Begins in town (Belfast) among bank-clerks and their superiors, and goes on at Craig-Linnie and Ballinasloe, where the writer is thoroughly at home. [Unwin : o.p.]

M'ILROY, Archibald (*continued*). *The Humour of Druid's Island.* 1902

Further tales from N.E. Antrim. " A series of very short anecdotes told to one another by the Presbyterian country people, in their peculiar Scoto-Irish dialect, and full of the dry, ' pawky ' humour of the North. Gives glimpses of the manners and life of the place " (Rev. S. J. Brown, s.J.). [Hodges & Figgis, Dublin : o.p.]

MacILWAINE, Herbert C. [Australian]. *Dinkinbar.* 1898

A vivacious story of life on a Queensland cattle-station, strong in local colouring. [Constable : o.p.]

—— *Fate the Fiddler.* 1900

A rambling tale of cattle-farming in Western Australia or Queensland, of love-making, and of treachery between partners, two men of strongly marked characters. Depicts life on a cattle-run, the loneliness of the desert, the ways of animals, and, above all, the types of humanity produced by these conditions. [Constable : o.p. ; Lippincott, Philadelphia : o.p.]

—— *The White Stone : the story of a boy from the Bush.* 1900

A boy's physical and moral growth to young manhood ; his schooldays, schoolfellows, friends and enemies, and the masters, vigorously portrayed ; with the troubles arising from the ignorant Australian lad's introduction to English school life. Boy-life in the bush, cattle-farming, gold-mining, and nature in Australia are described with much enthusiasm. [Wells Gardner.]

—— *The Undersong.* 1903

Eight stories of bush life and town life, gold-digging, and more fantastic subjects. *Billy Durbey* brings into tragic contact the civilization, and heedless strength of the modern Australian and the weakness and ignorance of the poor savage. *A Microcosm of Empire* is the tale of a conflict for municipal rights between Celt and Saxon in a mining township. *Jasper Townshend's Piccaninny* gives a powerful rendering of the loneliness of a woman's life in the bush. [Constable : o.p.]

MACKAIL, Denis. *The Square Circle.* 1930

A London square housing forty and odd families supplies the people, chiefly of that class in which convention has full sway, and a single year the petty emotions, mild tragedies, and light comedies here put on record. A lot of padding makes the book too long. [Hodder.]

McKAY, Claude [American ; *b.* 1890]. *Banjo.* 1929

A collection of dramatic sketches of negro life in Marseilles. The central character, Banjo, is a primitive, good-natured idler, full of animal vitality. In the mouth of Ray, a negro intellectual, are presented some views on the colour problem. [Harper, New York and London.]

—— *Home to Harlem.* 1928

Portrays vividly the seething coloured life of the negro town, a whirl of prostitutes, returned soldiers with money to burn, and jazz. [Harper, New York and London.]

MACKENNA, Robert William [Scottish ; *b.* 1874]. *Flower of the Heather.* 1922

—— *Through Flood and Fire.* 1925

Stories of love and adventure in the days of Claverhouse and the Covenanters (1680–5) ; with local colour from Dumfries and Galloway. [Murray.]

McKENNA, Stephen [*b.* 1888]. *Sonia : between two worlds.* 1917

A flashy and melodramatic chronicle of fashionable life in England, decadents, intellectuals, politicians, and so on, from 1898 to 1915, with a heroine who may be compared to Dodo. [Methuen ; Doubleday, Doran, New York.]

—— *Sonia Married.* 1919

Continues the history of Sonia, who marries a man blinded in the war and subsequently elopes with an M.P. [Hutchinson : o.p. ; Doubleday, Doran, New York.]

—— *Midas and Son.* 1919

The hero is a young man of highly-strung temperament, who goes to pieces through the enormous fortune inherited from his father. [Methuen : o.p. ; Doubleday, Doran, New York.]

—— *The Oldest God.* 1926

In the guise of a handsome man-about-town, Pan appears amid a house-party of the shady *nouveaux-riches*. There is, however, more argument than action. [Butterworth ; Little & Brown, Boston.]

—— *Happy Ending.* 1929

A wife shilly-shallying with a lover, and a sensible husband, a hard-working judge, who sees what is going on and brings the affair to an end without anybody being much the worse. [Cassell.]

—— *The Redemption of Morley Darville.* 1930

A highbrow novelist who has abused a popular rival is introduced by the latter to the gilded society which he had despised. Falling in love with a titled lady, he changes his style and writes society novels, but the result is to disillusion the lady, and his rival has an ironical revenge. [Cassell ; Dodd & Mead, New York.]

—— *The Cast-iron Duke.* 1930

Social intrigue, among a crowd of miscellaneous people of clashing interests, with an imperious old duke as arbiter of their differences. [Cassell.]

MACKENZIE, Agnes Mure [Scottish ; *b.* 1891]. *Without Conditions.* 1923

A romance of Aberdeenshire with an attractive heroine, amid an atmosphere of crinoline and convention in the 1840's. [Heinemann.]

—— *The Quiet Lady.* 1926

The difficulty of a man loved by two equally charming, though very different Scottish ladies. Scene, mainly the Outer Hebrides (1816–17). [Heinemann ; Doubleday, New York.]

—— *Keith of Kinnellan.* 1930

A previous novel, *Lost Kinnellan*, is here combined with its sequel, *The Falling Wind*, the whole giving, somewhat in the poetic manner of a ballad, the history of Keith, married to a warm-hearted, but homely

MACKENZIE, Agnes Mure (*continued*).

and unimaginative woman, and in love with a girl who is her opposite. The first half is strong and moving, though the tragic part is handled lightly ; the second part fine-spun and protracted. [Constable ; R. R. Smith, New York.]

MACKENZIE, (Edward Montagu) Compton [Scottish ; *b.* 1883]. *The Passionate Elopement.* 1911

A brilliant costume-piece, depicting the fashionable frivolities of an eighteenth-century spa—the card-parties, routs, drinking the waters, cock-fighting, flirting both innocent and the reverse, and the exaggerated etiquette—in a sort of mock-heroic style. It is the romanticism of Stevenson, Anthony Hope, and Hewlett—a glittering exterior with something real behind, for under the fantastic mannerisms and the veneer of affectation we gradually become aware that these puppets are men and women : the comedy changes its note, and the strutting M.C. reveals himself a very hero. [Secker ; Putnam, New York.]

—— *Carnival.* 1912

Theatrical in manner and matter, although where the author stands on the sure ground of personal familiarity he is realistic enough. Thus his ballet-girl is a plausible invention, and the stage with its disreputable hangers-on is painted with a sure brush, whilst the Cornish farmer whom she marries is a figment of melodrama. [Secker ; Appleton, New York.]

—— *Sinister Street.* 1913–14

A book so long that it had to be cut in halves which were published separately, each of them longer than most novels. Michael Fane, destined to be conspicuous in the series of novels that follow, is launched upon the world. His boyhood in West Kensington and his schooldays at St. Paul's School are depicted with an almost photographic realism and a lyrical enjoyment of life that do not always blend without discord. Then, as the hero gets beyond adolescence, he is found rubbing shoulders with curious examples of moral ugliness and mental obliquity, in short, has the adventures in the general world and the under-world appropriate to picaresque fiction. The sister who has musical genius, the young ritualists, the bibulous cook, the decadent æsthete, and various others are lively studies in which an interest in the morbid aspects is prominent. [2 vols., Secker ; vol. I, *sub tit. Youth's Encounter* (1913), and vol. II, *Sinister Street* (1914), Appleton, New York.]

—— *Guy and Pauline.* 1915

From among the multitude of characters in *Sinister Street* these two emerge, become engaged, and presently the engagement is broken off. The course of the love-story, among the Cotswold streams and meadows, is beautiful and idyllic. In the accompaniments, there is abundance of Mr. Mackenzie's minute and candid treatment of actuality. [Secker ; *sub tit. Plasher's Mead*, Harper, New York.]

—— *The Early Life and Adventures of Sylvia Scarlett.* 1918

The tradition of Scarron, Le Sage, and Petronius of the *Satyricon* is here represented as true, not only to " Southern Italy in the time of Nero," but also to " Southern England in the time of Victoria." Sylvia is a regular picara, of doubtful parentage and unhealthy upbringing, who plumbs the depths of vice and comes up a mixture of cynicism and hardheadedness and tenderness and charity. Her life drags us all over the world, and takes us into all sorts of disreputable company and through many farcical as well as some pathetic adventures. [Secker ; Harper, New York.]

—— *Sylvia and Michael : the later adventures of Sylvia Scarlett.* 1919

Another picaresque book, sequel to both the last-named and *Sinister Street* ; the pace even quicker, as we are whirled about from Petrograd to Bucharest and the Greek island where it ends, amidst the noise of the war. Michael Fane and Sylvia, tried, scarred, and disillusioned, yet not denuded of ideals, gravitate together, and the story ends on a chord of rapturous hope. [Secker ; Harper, New York.]

—— *Poor Relations.* 1919

Chiefly farce, the characters brand-new. The romantic playwright John Touchwood comes back wealthy from America, and finds himself the protector of a herd of sponging relatives, all of them drawn with incisive strokes, no lack of comic incident, and Mr. Mackenzie's unfailing gift of vitality. [Secker ; Harper, New York.]

—— *The Vanity Girl.* 1920

A new sort of *Vanity Fair*, with Dorothy Lonsdale, the girl at the " Vanity " for Becky, the monkey-faced Houston for Lord Steyne, and the Earl of Clarehaven for Rawdon Crawley. Dorothy, however, changes her character after marriage, and discovers a self-sacrificing mission—to provide the Clares with a son to continue the old house. A clever but mechanical novel. [Cassell ; Harper, New York.]

—— *The Altar Steps.* 1922
—— *The Parson's Progress* [sequel]. 1923
—— *The Heavenly Ladder* [sequel]. 1924

The life-story of Mark Lidderdale, a young Anglo-Catholic clergyman who, after many difficulties and much discussion, enters the Roman Catholic Church. There is much about parish work, and the conflict between High and Low Church ; but the third book, concerning Mark's ministry in a Cornish village, is more dramatic and is said to be based on fact. [(1), (2), and (3), Cassell ; Doubleday, Doran, New York.]

—— *The Old Men of the Sea.* 1924

An extravagant story of a mixed bag of adventurers who found a South Sea island settlement. [Cassell ; Stokes, New York.]

—— *Fairy Gold.* 1926

A romantic idyll, slight but pleasant—the setting, a pair of tiny islands off the west of England. [Cassell ; Doubleday, Doran, New York.]

—— *Vestal Fire.* 1927

The humours and vagaries of a group of sophisticated and eccentric folk, residents on a Mediterranean island. The theme recalls *South Wind* ; the treatment is unreservedly comic. [Cassell ; Doubleday, Doran, New York.]

—— *Extremes Meet.* 1928

MACKENZIE, (Edward Montagu) Compton (*continued*). *The Three Couriers.* 1929
Experiences of a secret-service agent in Constantinople ; intrigues, counter-intrigues, lavish excitement, and a good deal of comedy. The author was engaged in Intelligence work in that field during the war. [(1) and (2), Cassell ; Doubleday, Doran, New York.]

—— *Extraordinary Women.* 1928
Pokes fun at the homosexual women who are so earnest and solemn about their perversion. [Secker ; Vanguard Press, New York.]

—— *April Fools : a comedy of bad manners.* 1930
More about the poor relations. The quarrelsome Touchwood family are presented by John with his house in Hampshire, on condition that they live there together. The upshot which he wickedly foresees is an uproarious series of malicious or harmless practical jokes. The children are delightful creatures. [Cassell ; Doubleday, Doran, New York.]

MACKENZIE, Henry [Scottish ; 1745–1831]. *The Man of Feeling.* 1771
An attempt to rival the fashionable sentimentality of Sterne. A disjointed story ; the hero a shy, sentimental youth, absolutely faultless ; the heroine correspondingly superfine. He dies of joy when she admits she loves him. His various experiences of life are set forth in scenes of voluptuous pathos, the characters idealized so far that the reader's sympathy is sought even for thieves and courtesans. [Ed. by Hamish Miles, Scholartis Press (McKee, New York), 1928 ; with *The Man of the World* (New Universal Lib.), Routledge.]

—— *The Man of the World.* 1773
Less irregular in structure as a novel, having a complicated plot. Intrigue, gambling, seduction, robbery, Newgate, an infamous baronet, etc. ; the ordinary novelistic stock-in-trade, dealt with, however, from the pathetic standpoint and with careful avoidance of impropriety. [*v. supra.*]

—— *Julia de Roubigné.* 1777
A novel in letters which Talfourd, Christopher North, and Allan Cunningham thought highly of for its pathos ; comparatively brief. The French heroine marries an elderly suitor to help her distressed father, and then her first love reappears. The husband out of jealousy poisons her, and afterwards learning her innocence puts an end to himself. All these novels were published anonymously. [2 vols., Chaucer Head Press, New York.]

MACKENZIE, William Cook [Scottish ; b. 1862]. *The Lady of Hirta.* 1905
The abduction of Lady Grange, kinswoman of the Earl of Mar, and the search for her among the Hebrides (1739). Lord Lovat, Duncan Forbes of Culloden, etc., appear. [Gardner, Paisley.]

—— *The Shirra : a tale of the Isles.* 1910
The Shirra, or Sheriff, a big shipowner, and his son are the chief figures in a love-romance of the days of smugglers and privateering a century ago. [Gardner, Paisley : o.p.]

MACKIE, John [Canadian ; b. 1862]. *The Devil's Playground.* 1894
A romance of love and adventure culminating in the wildernesses of W. Canada : theme, two lovers parted and thrown together by fortune, who hold out to the end against the devil's temptations. Largely descriptive of scenery and the wild life of settlers. [Unwin : o.p. ; Stokes, New York : o.p.]

—— *The Prodigal's Brother.* 1899
A romance of the North-West Provinces at the time of Riel's rebellion (1885). The writer was an officer in the Canadian Mounted Police. [Jarrold : o.p.]

—— *The Man Who Forgot : a strange experience.* 1901
This strange plot of a man's loss of memory is said to be founded on fact. His accident involves him in embarrassing situations, such as being taken by detectives for a notorious dynamitard. Describes an ocean voyage and the eruption of Krakatoa. [Jarrold : o.p.]

MACKIE, Pauline Bradford [Mrs. Herbert Müller Hopkins ; American ; b. 1874]. *The Washingtonians.* 1903
The politics and political wire-pulling at Washington, when the city was full of barracks and military hospitals, with the war dragging on (1864). The principal figure is a candidate for the presidency, an American Aristides ; his secretary, and his intriguing daughter, Lincoln and his wife, are the next in importance in a crowd of characters. Implacably Federal in spirit. [Page, Boston : o.p. ; Bell : o.p.]

" MACLAREN, Ian " [Rev. John Watson ; Scottish ; 1850–1907]. *Beside the Bonnie Brier Bush.* 1894
A typical production of the Kailyard school of novelists (see Galt, Barrie, MacDonald, etc.). Sketches and stories of a Scottish village (Drumtochty), realistic in the minute delineation of manners and idiosyncrasies. *Domsie* is an old-fashioned dominie, a scholar, and a pattern of self-sacrifice ; *A Doctor of the Old School*, a still more exalted example of patient altruism. Theology is a favourite motive, village connoisseurs of doctrinal points contributing largely to the comedy ; and the pathos of family relations is, of course, a very pervasive feature. [Hodder ; Dodd & Mead, New York.]

—— *The Days of Auld Langsyne.* 1895
More idylls of Drumtochty, not quite so spontaneous. *A Triumph in Diplomacy* illustrates Scottish canniness, and the indigenous qualities of piety, family affection, and external impassivity. Pathos is much sought after, and death-bed scenes are frequent, though it is the faith and hope and the fortitude and love rather than the suffering that are dwelt on. Burnbrae, Drumsheugh, Jamie Soutar, and others are on their way to becoming household names in Scottish fiction. [Hodder ; Dodd & Mead, New York.]

—— *Kate Carnegie and those Ministers.* 1896
Character sketches and anecdotes loosely connected. The most original yet a thoroughly representative figure is Rabbi Saunderson, a man of colossal learning, but childlike in his simple faith and unselfishness. The chapter which tells how the gentle old man was urged by conscience to prosecute his beloved friend, Kate's lover, for heterodox preaching, is typical of this sentimental school. [Hodder : o.p. ; Dodd & Mead, New York : o.p.]

"MACLAREN, Ian" (*continued*). *Afterwards; and other stories.* 1898
Fourteen stories, chiefly sentimental and pathetic, a few humorous. *Afterwards* relates how an easy-going, selfish husband realizes with tragic suddenness on the death of his neglected wife " that Christ had lived with him for more than ten years, and his eyes had been holden." One or two deal with Drumtochty folk again, as in the death of the old schoolmaster Domsie ; but the author has gone farther afield than usual. His habit of embodying sermons in stories has grown upon him. [Hodder : o.p. ; Dodd & Mead, New York : o.p.]

—— *Young Barbarians.* 1901
A school-story located in a Tayside village, probably made up of recollections of the author's own boyhood. Rough and hearty good-humour and plenty of farcical fun are the leaven of these scenes of mischief and practical jocularity, stand-up fights and life in school. The two principal characters are an impish lad, " Speug," and a not unkindly schoolmaster, " Bulldog," who believes in the stick. [Hodder : o.p. ; Dodd & Mead, New York : o.p.]

—— *Graham of Claverhouse.* 1908
A life of Dundee thrown into the shape of a novel, with character-drawing of those around him. Very fair to both parties, in spite of the author's instinctive leaning towards the Covenanters. [Murray : o.p. ; Cupples & Leon, New York : o.p.]

McLELLAN, William [Irish]. *Spanish John.* 1898
Adventures of Colonel John McDonell, when a lieutenant in the Regiment Irlandia, in the service of the King of Spain, operating in Italy (1744–6). Spanish John goes on a mission to the Pretender, but reaches Scotland after Culloden. [Harper : o.p.]

McLELLAN, William, and M'ILWRAITH, Jean Newton. *The Span o' Life.* 1899
The 1745 rebellion, Louisbourg and Quebec. The hero, Maxwell, is a real personage, and his adventures in the Jacobite rising in Scotland and afterwards in the great struggle with the French in Canada are, very loosely, founded on fact (1745–59). [Harper : o.p.]

MacMAHON, Ella [Irish]. *Fancy O'Brien.* 1909
A tragic story of the undoing of a Dublin girl ; realistic without any grossness ; scenes, Dublin and Bray. [Chapman : o.p.]

MacMANUS, Miss L. [Irish]. *Lally of the Brigade.* 1899
Italy in the War of the Spanish Succession. Hero an Irish Jacobite in the French army, fighting against Austrians under Prince Eugène (1702). The surprise of Cremona, etc. Miss MacManus is a Catholic writer, whose novels are based on careful historical research. She has published several other novels well suited for children ; e.g. *The Silk of the Kine* (1896). [Unwin : o.p. ; Page, Boston : o.p.]

—— *Nessa.* 1904
The Cromwellian settlement in Co. Mayo (1654). [Sealy, Dublin : o.p.]

—— *In Sarsfield's Days : a tale of the siege of Limerick.* 1906
Dramatized as *O'Donnell's Cross*. A powerful story of a wayward Irishwoman during the siege of Limerick in the Williamite wars (1690). [Gill, Dublin ; *sub tit. The Wager,* Buckles, New York : o.p.]

—— *Nuala : the story of a perilous quest.* [juvenile] 1909
Nuala, after many adventures, saves the historic *Cathach,* or ancient battle-book of the O'Donnells, in the times of Napoleon in Austria. [Browne & Nolan, Dublin.]

MacMANUS, Seumas [Irish ; *b.* 1869]. *In Chimney Corners.* 1899
Irish folk-tales, artistically rendered, strong in native qualities and humour ; not much less fanciful than the same writer's *Donegal Fairy Stories* (1904). [Harper : o.p. ; Doubleday, New York ; Irish Pub. Co., New York.]

—— *Through the Turf Smoke : the love, lore, and laughter of old Ireland.* 1899
Short stories, both comic and pathetic, of Donegal peasants, by the son of a peasant farmer. [Unwin : o.p. ; Doubleday, New York : o.p.]

—— *A Lad of the O'Friels'.* 1903
Annals of a poor Donegal hamlet in the times of the liberator O'Connell—politics and debate at the cobbler's, the schoolmaster's courtship, the harvest fair, and other episodes in the life of a peasant lad. Avowedly, the author dwells, in preference, on the pleasant and cheerful things in the Irishman's lot. [Digby & Long : o.p. ; Irish Pub. Co., New York.]

—— *The Bend of the Road* [sequel]. 1912
Short stories and sketches, showing the same sensitive appreciation of peasant humours and sympathy with peasant feelings. [Gill, Dublin : o.p. ; MacManus, New York : o.p.]

—— *Yourself and the Neighbours.* 1914
A further collection of Donegal peasants, showing no falling off in intimacy, humour, or pathos. [Devin-Adair, New York ; Irish Pub. Co., New York.]

—— *Tales that were Told.* 1919
Folk-tales from Donegal—romance, adventures, enchantments, and so on. [Talbot Press, Dublin : o.p.]

MACMILLAN, Malcolm Kingsley. *Dagonet the Jester.* 1886
A pathetic village story of the Great Civil War time, having little to do with those great events. The central figure is a gay and whimsical jester, whose pleasantries are quenched by the cold atmosphere of Puritanism. [New ed., Macmillan.]

MacMUNN, Sir George Fletcher [Anglo-Indian ; *b.* 1869]. *A Freelance in Kashmir : a tale of the great anarchy.* 1915
Adventures in Kashmir about 1804, excellent in local colour and in the knowledge shown of the period when Lake and the future Duke of Wellington were smashing up the power of the Mahrattas. [Murray ; Dutton, New York : o.p.]

"**MACNAMARA**, Brinsley" [A. E. Weldon; Irish]. *The Valley of the Squinting Windows.* 1918
  A bitter account of Irish life in Meath; hatred, vendettas, murder are the order of the day, each man taking the greatest pleasure in his neighbour's misfortune. Such miserable death-in-life is ascribed to the want and land-hunger of the people, and their misgovernment. [Low.]
—— *The Clanking of Chains.* 1920
  This account of life in an Irish provincial town, a hotbed of meanness, jealousy, and self-seeking, is an indictment of those qualities which make Ireland, in the author's opinion, her own worst foe. [Talbot Press.]

MACNAMARA, Lewis [Irish]. *Blind Larry: Irish idylls.* 1897
  Artless records of life among the very poor in the west of Ireland, the fruit of kindly observation and, obviously, essays in the *Thrums* style. Larry is a poor blind fiddler, whose one joy in life is his son, and he turns out a reproach to his father. *Katty's Wedding* is a very Irish bit of farce, and *Mulligan's Revenge* expresses the vindictive passions of the Celt, an episode of jealousy and crime, alleviated at the close by penitence and reconciliation. [Jarrold: o.p.]

MACNAUGHTAN, Miss Sarah [Scottish; *d.* 1916]. *Selah Harrison.* 1898
  A sombre story of a penitent prodigal, who becomes a missionary, and after devoted work is killed by natives; a study of religious enthusiasm. [Macmillan: o.p.]
—— *The Fortunes of Christina M'Nab.* 1901
  A spirited character-story of Scots people, full of shrewd humour bordering on farce. [Methuen: o.p.; Appleton, New York: o.p.]
—— *A Lame Dog's Diary.* 1905
  The Lame Dog—an Englishman crippled in the South African war—and a charming widow amusing themselves with a diary in which the peculiarities of their neighbours are gently satirized. [Murray; Dodd & Mead, New York.]
—— *The Three Miss Graemes.* 1908
—— *Us Four.* 1909
  Both stories are made up of recollections of Miss Macnaughtan's childhood in the western Highlands. The Miss Graemes are transplanted thence to civilized England. [(1) and (2), Murray: o.p.; (2), Dutton, New York: o.p.]
—— *The Andersons.* 1910
  History of a Scots family on their way up in the social scale, and their intimate friends; genial and humorous character-drawing, tea-parties and other domestic scenes fruitful in sly comedy; matrimonial schemes and the like being the chief attraction, especially in the earlier part, which is laid in a west coast village. [Murray: o.p.; Dutton, New York: o.p.]
—— *Four Chimneys.* 1912
  A touching yet cheerful little story of the house "Four Chimneys," and a lovable woman who behaves with the quiet greatness of sterling worth in the hour of the family's disaster. [Nelson: o.p.]
—— *Snow Upon the Desert.* 1913
  A somewhat disjointed novel of Anglo-Indian life, with a strong character in Miss Antrobus, a lady with a doubtful past who does not fail, however, in self-possession or in making her personality score. [Hodder: o.p.; Dutton, New York: o.p.]
—— *Some Elderly People and their Young Friends.* 1915
  Contrasts the Victorian with the younger generation, and combines pleasant portraits of both with quiet satire. [Murray; Dutton, New York: o.p.]

McNEILE, Cyril ["Sapper"; Scottish; *b.* 1888]. *Bull-Dog Drummond.* 1920
  This big, powerful, and daredevil ex-officer, with more intelligence than he has credit for, finding peace dull, gets blissfully involved in fighting an absurd world-plot engineered by foreign financiers and "Bolsheviks" for the ruin of Great Britain. Through hair-raising perils and hairbreadth escapes, in which probabilities are set at naught, he comes out winner with a bride. [Hodder; Grosset, New York.]

MacNICHOLL, Shaw. *Between the Days: being the writing of Jean Bruyard. A story of Franche Comté.* 1925
  A chronicle of French peasant life from 1870 until 1914, as recorded by an old vine-dresser, whose life is intimately bound up with that of his god-daughter. [Blackwood.]

M'NULTY, Edward [Irish; *b.* 1856]. *Misther O'Ryan: an incident in the history of a nation.* 1894
  A short story, a picture of real life in a small country town. O'Ryan, speaking an exaggerated brogue, is a blethering political humbug, who starts a branch of the League and gets returned for the borough. The scenes of agitation, boycott, and crime are very ugly, and have been stigmatized as a monstrous caricature. [Arnold.]
—— *The Son of a Peasant.* 1897
  A tragi-comedy of life among lower middle-class people in a small provincial town. Humorous but insistent on the meaner aspects of human character. A far-fetched plot closing in hideous tragedy. [Arnold: o.p.]

MAGINN, William [Irish; 1794–1842]. *Miscellaneous Works—Prose and Verse; ed. R. W. Montagu.* 1885
  Chiefly facetious miscellanies composed on the same plan as the *Noctes Ambrosianæ*, as, e.g. the *Memoirs* and the *Maxims of Morgan O'Doherty*. There are short stories also, e.g. *The Man in the Bell*, *Bob Burke's Duel with Ensign Brady*, and—the most famous—*A Story without a Tail*. [2 vols., Low (Scribner, New York): o.p.; *A Story without a Tail*, with introd. by George Saintsbury (Rescue Series), Mathews, 1927.]

MAISTRE, Count Xavier de [Savoyard; 1764–1852]. *A Journey Round My Room* (Voyage autour de ma chambre, 1794); *and, A Nocturnal Expedition Round My Room* (Expédition nocturne autour de ma chambre, 1825). 1843
  Two little masterpieces of prose style and quaint meditative fancy. The first is a whimsical account of the

MAISTRE, Count Xavier de (*continued*).
author's experiences and reflections during confinement to his quarters in Turin. He surveys the various objects in his room, weaves little romances about them and about his mistress, and moralizes on his servant; all in the manner of Sterne's sentimental lucubrations, with even more of the sentimental posing. The other is similar in motive and design. [(1), Transl. by H. ATWELL, Chatto (1871), 1883: o.p.; Putnam, New York; (1) and (2), transl. by J. ANDREWS, Simpkin, 1900: o.p.]

MAITLAND, Mrs. Ella Fuller. *The Saltonstall Gazette.* 1896
A series of essays or letters written in the polished and urbane manner of the eighteenth century, and held together by a slight thread of personal reminiscences. [Chapman: o.p.]

MAITLAND, Mrs. Ella Fuller, and POLLOCK, the Rt. Hon. Sir Frederick. *The Etchingham Letters.* 1899
Correspondence of a baronet and his sister, setting forth a story of the conventional kind, along with their views on modern life and character, on art, and on literature, expressed in the Addisonian manner, and reflecting two attractive personalities. [Murray; Dodd & Mead, New York: o.p.]

MAITLAND, Mrs. Ella Fuller, and BERNARD, R. Spence. *The Clere Family*, 1927 to 1928. 1929
Amusing family correspondence, in modern style, recording the history of sundry matrimonial affairs. [Chapman.]

MAJOR, Charles ["Edwin Caskoden"; American; 1856–1913]. *When Knighthood was in Flower.* 1898
The love-story of Charles Brandon, Duke of Suffolk, and Henry VIII's sister, Mary Tudor (1513). [Grosset, New York; Nash.]

—— *Dorothy Vernon of Haddon Hall.* 1902
Another *réchauffé* of the legend about Dorothy Vernon and Sir John Manners, which has been proved to have not the slightest historical foundation. The ostensible raconteur brings in a love affair of his own with the Dauphine, Mary, Queen of Scots. [Macmillan, New York and London; Grosset, New York.]

—— *Yolanda, Maid of Burgundy.* 1905
Yolanda is Mary of Burgundy, the daughter of Charles the Bold, and the incidents are to some extent the same as those of Scott's *Quentin Durward* and *Anne of Geierstein*, supplemented by her marriage to Maximilian (I) of Austria. [Macmillan, New York.]

—— *A Gentle Knight of Old Brandenburg.* 1909
A tragi-comedy of the Prussian Court in the time of Frederick William I and the youth of Frederick the Great. The Princess Wilhelmina and her lover (afterwards her husband), Henry, Prince of Bayreuth, are the principals; and most of the many characters are from history. The whole novel has a strangely "up-to-date" flavour. [Macmillan, New York.]

—— *The Little King.* 1910
"A story of the childhood of Louis XIV, King of France." [Macmillan, New York.]

"MALET, Lucas" [Mary St. Leger Harrison, *née* Kingsley; 1852–1931]. *Colonel Enderby's Wife.* 1885
A pessimistic study of the disenchantments of real life, in the tragedy of an ill-assorted marriage between a trusting middle-aged man and a heartless woman. [Methuen; Appleton, New York: o.p.]

—— *Little Peter: a Christmas morality for children of any age.* 1887
An idyll of country life with a little group of diverse characters: an old bookworm and his patient wife, a charcoal-burner and a cowherd, and a flirting servant-maid. [Oxford Press (new ed., 1929); Doran, New York: o.p.]

—— *A Council of Perfection.* 1888
Character and motive illustrated in a love episode of unusual shape. A woman, verging on middle age, has devoted her life to her father, a selfish and unsympathetic bookworm. Suddenly her heart is awakened by a man who is not worthy of her: hopes of a new life inspire her with feelings like those of youth; but when her lover is at her feet she renounces the temptation. Embellished with descriptive passages of English country life and Swiss travel-sketches. [Methuen: o.p. Appleton, New York.]

—— *The Wages of Sin.* 1890
A young painter gets entangled with a Cornish girl, whose coarse beauty makes her a desirable model; and when he tries to live down his sin, and, more tragically, when he loves a pure and worthy girl, his old paramour and their child reappear to wreck all his future, and at last drive him to his death. [Methuen; Fenno, New York: o.p.]

—— *The Carissima: a modern grotesque.* 1896
A domestic drama enacted in a Genevese hotel, wherein some consciences are brought to the test. The Carissima is engaged to a man haunted by a loathsome hallucination, and plots with another suitor to get rid of him. Some unmitigated bores are brought in for comic purposes. [Methuen: o.p.; Stone, Chicago: o.p.]

—— *The Gateless Barrier.* 1900
A spiritualistic romance founded on the idea of bringing back the dead by will-power in conjunction with intense love. [Nash; Dodd & Mead, New York.]

—— *The History of Sir Richard Calmady: a romance.* 1901
Sir Richard, a baronet of enormous wealth, was maimed from birth, and goes through life a misshapen dwarf. In the central portion of this long and elaborate history, we see him falling a victim to the lusts of the flesh and the natural instincts of revolt against his horrible fate. Passion wrecks but love redeems him—this is the moral of the author's sentimental philosophy. [Methuen; Dodd & Mead, New York: o.p.]

—— *The Score.* 1910
Two stories—*Out in the Open*, an actress gives up her lover, a M.P., not to spoil his career, characters from *Sir Richard Calmady*; the other, *Miserere Nobis*, an Italian story of murder, confession, and attempted suicide. [Murray: o.p.; Dutton, New York: o.p.]

"MALET, Lucas" (*continued*). *Adrian Savage.*   1911
> A prolix story the general trend and leading characters of which are unpleasant and even repulsive—scenes, Paris and Stourmouth (Bournemouth), and the English characters conceited, pushing, vulgar people, strikingly unlovable. Adrian loves the disillusioned widow of a great artist of ill repute, and is loved—tragically—by the unattractive Joanna, whose morbid, suffering character is the strength of the book. [Hutchinson : o.p. ; Harper, New York : o.p.]
>
> See also Kingsley, Charles.

MALLOCK, William Hurrell [1849–1923]. *The New Republic : culture, faith, and philosophy in an English country house.*   1877
> The first of a series of satires on contemporary philosophers, religious thinkers, politicians, etc. The real *dramatis personæ* are : " Storks " (Huxley), " Stockton " (Tyndall), " Herbert " (Ruskin), " Donald Gordon " (Carlyle), " Jenkinson " (Jowett), " Mr. Luke " (Matthew Arnold), " Saunders " (Prof. Clifford), " Rose " (Walter Pater), " Leslie " (Mr. Hardinge), " Seyden " (Dr. Pusey), " Lady Grace " (Lady Dilke), " Mrs. Sinclair " (Mrs. Singleton, afterwards Lady Currie [" Violet Fane "]). Mallock himself said, " In each case I have tried to make the character representative of the views held by the originals, [rather] than of the originals themselves." [Chatto ; Scribner, New York : o.p.]

—— *The New Paul and Virginia : positivism on an island.*   1878
> A similar burlesque of the religious ideas of Huxley, Tyndall, Clifford, and Frederic Harrison. [Chatto : o.p. ; Scribner, New York : o.p.]

—— *A Romance of the Nineteenth Century.*   1881
> Almost a novel, handling in a semi-abstract way a psychological problem of love, the personages being English idlers on the Riviera. As an exposition of certain tendencies of contemporary life it has resemblances to *Without Dogma* by Sienkiewicz. The hero, agnostic, pietist, and sentimental philanthropist, fails through the lack of a steadfast dominating principle ; the heroine succumbs to her woman's craving for love. [Chatto : o.p. ; Fenno, New York : o.p.]

—— *The Individualist.*   1899
> Makes game of the belief that the poorer classes are amenable to culture, by means of burlesque of social reforms, half-disguised caricatures of actual people, and exaggerations of the failings and vulgarities of the ill-bred. [Chapman.]

MALO, Henri [French ; b. 1868]. *The Romantic Passion of Don Luis.*   1925
> Don Luis sets sail with the Armada, and is wrecked upon the Flanders coast, where he is drawn into the political life of the Low Countries. [Transl. by Helen PRESTON, Harrap ; Dial Press, New York.]

MALORY, Sir Thomas. *Le Morte Darthur : Sir Thomas Malory's Book of King Arthur and of his Noble Knights of the Round Table.*   1485
> Printed by Caxton in 1485. A redaction of the Arthurian legends from various English and French versions. These sources, and the extent of Malory's indebtedness to each, are exhaustively treated by Dr. H. O. Sommer in his monumental reprint of Caxton's text, with excursus on Malory's English, a valuable introduction on Malory, and copious variant readings, notes, etc. Malory did not always utilize the finest version of an episode ; and modern poets, e.g. Tennyson, would have done better had they gone nearer the fountain-head for their readings of the legends (e.g. to the *Mabinogion* or Chrétien de Troyes) ; nevertheless his book is a great storehouse of knightly tales of adventure, feats of arms, strange enchantments, mystical enterprises like the Grail quest, and of immortal love-tales like those of Lancelot and Guenevere, Tristan and Iseult, Geraint and Enid. Caxton published it as a handbook to the manly virtues of chivalry ; and in spite of the " vain amoratorious " element denounced by the Puritans, it remains one of the most nobly inspiring books in our English tongue. Malory's unique place in our literature is due, at least as much as to the tact of his selection, to the strong, simple English in which he writes, with its command of vivid suggestion and its noble cadences. [Ed. Israel Gollancz, 4 vols. (Temple Classics), Dent, 1897 ; *illus.* by Beardsley, Dent (new ed. 1927) ; ed. A. W. Pollard, 2 vols., Macmillan, 1900 ; abgd., 1917 ; ed. with an introd. by Sir E. Strachey (Globe Edn.), Macmillan ; *The Boy's King Arthur*, ed. Sidney Lanier, Low. *The Morte Darthur*, verbatim repr. of Caxton's original ed., with Introduction, Variants, Notes, Glossarial Index, and Study of the sources of Malory, by H. O. SOMMER, and a Study of Malory by A. LANG ; 3 vols., 4to, Nutt 1889–91 : o.p. ; also 2 vols., Roxburghe, or in 3 vols., Roxburghe : o.p.]

MALOT, Hector Henri [French ; 1830–1907]. *No Relations* (Sans famille, 1878).   1880
> A picaresque novel recounting the adventures of a lovable boy, an English foundling, in France and elsewhere. Varied pictures of life, in town and country, among thieves, vagabonds, and simple rustics with sad and mirthful episodes, and touching sketches of character. The romance of vagabondage is brought before us further in scenes from the life of a wandering musician with his wonderfully attractive animals. [Transl. by M. LAFFAN, Macmillan : o.p. ; transl. by Florence CREWE-JONES, *sub tit. Nobody's Boy*, Cupples, New York, 1916, new ed. 1930.]

—— *Doctor Claude* (Le docteur Claude, 1879).   1882
> A curious portrayal of a man who is outwardly honest and respectable, but at bottom a monstrous criminal. [2 vols., Vizetelly : o.p.]

—— *Conscience* (1888)   1891
> In a reunion of ambitious young men, advocates, writers, etc., one of them, a physician of great talent, argues from scientific premises that there is no such thing as conscience. [Transl. by Julia S. RAE, 2 vols., Bentley : o.p. ; by L. A. RICE, Worthington, New York : o.p.]

—— *A Mother* (La mère, 1890).   1890
> Portrays the seamy side of outwardly reputable life in Paris with realism and satire. The class depicted is that of well-to-do manufacturers, financiers, etc., and wealthy young men of pleasure. Shows how a man, healthy in mind and body, might be taken for a madman and deprived of his liberty : an attack on science and justice in France. [Transl. by J. SCHÖNBERG, Belford Co., Chicago : o.p.]

MANING, Judge Frederick Edward [New Zealander ; 1812–83]. *Old New Zealand.*   1863
> " A tale of the good old times, and a history of the war in the north against the Chief Heke, in the year 1845,

MANING, Judge Frederick Edward (*continued*).
told by an old chief of the Ngapuhi tribe, also Maori traditions. By a Pakeha Maori." Regarded as a classic portrayal of Maori life whilst yet free from foreign influence. [Whitcombe & Tombs ; ed. by Dr. Hocken, Oxford Press, 1922.]

MANN, Francis Oscar. *The Golden Quill.* 1924
" A romance of the fourteenth century." A pleasant story of a scribe and illuminator working in London, which introduces Chaucer. The author edited the work of his predecessor, Thomas Deloney (*q.v.*). [Blackwood, Oxford.]

MANN, Heinrich [German ; brother of Thomas Mann ; b. 1871]. *Berlin, the land of Cockaigne* (Im Schlaraffenland : ein Roman unten feinen Leuten, 1900). 1929
A bitter satire on wealthy and fashionable society in Berlin before the war, painted in many scenes of gross and nauseating debauchery. A simple youngster from the country is taken under the patronage of a newspaper magnate of colossal wealth and power. There is a banquet scene which recalls that of Trimalchio. Through an error of tact, the poor hero falls from grace, and suffers shameful punishment and abandonment. [Transl. by Axton D. B. CLARK, Gollancz ; *sub tit. In the Land of Cockaigne*, Macauley, New York.]

—— *The Patrioteer* (Der Untertan, 1911). 1921
The first of a trilogy (*Die Armen, Der Kopf*, 1925, not translated), which review and pass judgment upon the social and political life of Germany under the old regime. This pillories a domineering manufacturer, and the blind patriotism of the middle classes. [Transl. by Ernest BOYD, Harcourt, New York.]

—— *The Little Town* (Die kleine Stadt). 1930
The rejuvenescence of a little Italian town, roused to a fresh joy in life and to a fuller intensity of all the passions, good or bad, as by a breath of ozone, at the visit of an opera company, is the theme of this slight but very humorous novel, which is notable also for its crisp and diversified character-drawing and its broad and tolerant philosophy. [Transl. by Winifred RAY, Secker.]

—— *The Royal Woman* (Eugénie, 1928). 1930
The story of Napoleon III and the Empress Eugénie is curiously interwoven in this complicated novel with the story of a German consul in one of the Hanseatic towns in 1873, and his flirting French wife. [Transl. by Arthur J. ASHTON, Mathews ; Macauley, New York.]

MANN, Mary E. [Mrs. Fairman Mann, *née* Rackham]. *Susannah.* 1895
A young lady in reduced circumstances goes out as general servant, so that she may be able to nurse her dying brother. She meets with some comic experiences of life and some severe trials, and the upshot is that she loses a doubtful lover and gains a true one. A household tyrant, slave to her paragon of a son, and several young bohemians, furnish comedy, but the great merit of the story is its impartial truth to the realities of life. [Unwin : o.p. ; Harper, New York : o.p.]

—— *The Patten Experiment.* 1899
A comedy of character, with a fanciful plot. A wealthy family try to live for a week on a labourer's wages, and meet with unexpected difficulties. [Unwin : o.p.]

—— *Out in Life's Rain.* 1899
The history of two children who, like John Halifax, are loyal and true in the face of bitter trials : a simple story of real life. [Hutchinson : o.p.]

—— *Among the Syringas.* 1901
Portraiture of average humanity and of the joys and troubles of the average life ; commonplace characters, good and evil mixed, with their vulgarity and weakness and moments of inspiration and courage, from among whom the heroine stands out, but is no ideal creature. There is humour in the scenes of child-life. [Unwin : o.p.]

—— *The Fields of Dulditch.* 1901
Chapters of the humblest country life as it really is, without any of the forced pathos, exaggeration, or disturbing optimism usual in fancy pictures of the rustic. Mostly they give us the grim side, with the workhouse in the middle distance, e.g. *Ben Pitcher's Little Elly, Gran'mawther, The Lost Housen.* But *Our Mary* is a humorous sketch of a " general," and in others, the different aspects are interpreted with penetration. [Digby & Long : o.p.]

—— *Olivia's Summer.* 1902
A tragic story—an old maid, the daughter of a rector, marries a successful but uncultivated man of the village ten years her junior. [Methuen : o.p.]

—— *The Mating of a Dove.* 1902
A story of country gentry in straitened circumstances that brings real pathos out of the pressure of class distinctions and the struggle to keep up appearances. Amy Dove, a creature of fine spiritual beauty, in her simplicity loves the village carpenter, but has to marry the doctor. [Unwin : o.p.]

—— *Mrs. Peter Howard.* 1903
A moving story of temptation and resistance thereto, with a group of characters, well varied in small compass, in a country town. [Methuen : o.p.]

—— *Gran'ma's Jane.* 1903
The story of a little girl from childhood onwards, in a dismal early-Victorian home at Norwich. Realistic in its drawing of both pleasant and unpleasant characters, the childhood of Jane sketched with much idyllic charm, while the story has tragic sides presented in all their grimness and truth. [Methuen : o.p.]

—— *The Parish Nurse.* 1905
Sketches village life and society with the usual realism. A lady undertakes the duties of parish nurse. [Methuen : o.p.]

—— *The Eglamore Portraits.* 1906
The domestic embarrassments and unpleasantness endured by a young couple domineered over by a disagreeable mother-in-law. A hackneyed situation handled in a straightforward manner. [Methuen : o.p.]

MANN, Mary E. (*continued*). *The Memories of Ronald Love.* 1907
—— *Avenging Children* [sequel]. 1909
Domestic stories of Norwich and East Anglia in mid-Victorian days. The first has a pathetic study of a child; the interests of the second are more conventional—clandestine love, an elopement, the caddishness of a legitimate son and the chivalry of his bastard brother. [(1) and (2), Methuen: o.p.]
—— *The Sheep and the Goats.* 1907
Draws faithfully and humorously the coteries and characters of a little town where the son of a local draper has been made rector. He and the woman he loves, and a spoilt doll of a girl whom he quixotically champions, are the best among many interesting likenesses of human nature. [Methuen: o.p.]
—— *A Sheaf of Corn.* 1908
Nineteen stories in Mrs. Mann's realistic style, dealing with rustics in E. Anglia; several are gloomy and repellent. [Methuen: o.p.]
—— *Bound Together.* 1910
Short stories chiefly of the hard and squalid side of peasant life, with more of the sensational, sentimental, and farcical than in *The Fields of Dulditch*. [Mills & Boon: o.p.]
—— *When a Man Marries.* 1916
A homely tale, narrated by a girl whose life is wholly bound up in a few strong affections; it presents a clear picture of her own small world. [Hodder: o.p.]

MANN, Thomas [German; *b.* 1875]. *Buddenbrooks* (Die Buddenbrooker: Verfall einer Familie, 1901). 1924
The history of four generations of a family in Lubeck, the author's native city, from the eighteen-thirties to the seventies, analogous to the *Forsyte Saga*, but richer in personal character. The interplay of motive and changing social conditions, the conflict of commercialism and finer ideals, the clash of family tradition and the demands of individuality: all these are thoughtfully elucidated; but it is with such a mixed but life-like figure as Antonie that the book tends to become identified. [Transl. by H. T. Lowe-Porter, 2 vols., Secker, Knopf, New York.]
—— *Royal Highness* (Königliche Hoheit, 1909). 1916
Princely life in a small German State, and the elaborate ceremonial of the archducal Court. The central figure of the story is not the archduke, but his brother, an ineffectual person. But all the characters are interesting, not excepting the peasants. [Transl. by A. Cecil Curtis, Sidgwick; Knopf, New York.]
—— *Death in Venice* (Der Tod in Venedig, 1912). 1925
Three stories are included in this volume, each a psychological study of a genius. *Death in Venice* has been acclaimed as " the finest novelette produced in our generation." The other two are *Tristan* and *Tonio Kröger* (1903), his own favourite work. [Transl. by H. T. Lowe-Porter, Secker; with introd. by Ludwig Lewisohn, Knopf, New York, 1930; transl. by Kenneth Burke, Knopf, New York, 1925.]
—— *A Man and his Dog* (Herr und Hund, 1919). 1930
Bashan and his master and their adventures are but a peg for the novelist's view of life in growing suburbs. [Transl. by Herman George Scheffauer; Knopf. Previously issued *sub tit. Bashan and I*, 1923, Collins.]
—— *The Magic Mountain* (Der Zauberberg, 1924). 1927
A grim, absorbing psychological study of the inmates of a Swiss sanatorium for consumptives—a prose-epic woven of different psychological themes, realized on a larger scale than in *Tonio Kröger*. [Transl. by H. T. Lowe-Porter, 2 vols., Secker; Knopf, New York.]
—— *Early Sorrow* (Unordnung und frües Lied, 1926). 1929
A little story about a professor's family and his small daughter, which displays an exquisitely tender and sympathetic insight into childish nature and parental love. [Transl. by H. T. Lowe-Porter, Secker; Knopf, New York.]
—— *Mario and the Magician* (Mario und der Zauberer, 1930). 1930
A little story that transmits an uncanny spell—of a German family's experiences whilst holidaying at a seaside town in Italy. On a basis of strict actuality, the novelist raises an atmospheric superstructure that holds us fast. The culmination is in a sinister scene in which a mountebank conjurer exerts hypnotic powers, as if he were evil itself incarnate. [Transl. by H. T. Lowe-Porter, Secker; Knopf, New York.]

MANNING, Anne [1807–79]. *The Maiden and Married Life of Mary Powell.* [juvenile] 1850
The family life of the poet Milton, set forth in the autobiography of his wife (1643–6). Their meeting and courtship, their London life, the famous estrangement that led to the tracts on divorce, and their ultimate reconciliation, related with fullness of detail and deep feminine sympathy. Written in a close imitation of the old prose. [With *Deborah's Diary*, *illus.* by John Jellicoe and Herbert Railton, Routledge; (Everyman's Lib.) Dent (Dutton, New York), 1908.]
—— *Deborah's Diary* [sequel]. [juvenile] 1858
The life of Milton's daughter by his second wife; scenes, London and Chalfont (1665–6) [with *Mary Powell*, *v. supra*.]
—— *The Colloquies of Edward Osborne, Citizen and Clothworker of London.* 1851
The founder of the ducal house of Leeds tells his own story, in charmingly old-fashioned language, from the day when he was entered apprentice on London Bridge (1547–59). A pretty story that is substantially true. [*Illus.* by Jellicoe and Railton, Routledge; Dutton, New York: o.p.]
—— *The Household of Sir Thomas More.* 1851
A restoration of the man and his times, in the imaginative form of a journal by his daughter Margaret; founded on Erasmus and other authorities and imitating the contemporary style (1522–35). [Routledge; Chatto; *illus.* by C. E. Brock, Dent: o.p.; with Roper's *Life of More*, (Everyman's Lib.), Dent (Dutton, New York).]
—— *The Commentaries of Ser Pantaleone.* 1856
The story of Tasso and Leonora d'Este, sister of the Duke of Ferrara, told by the lady's gentleman-usher

MANNING, Anne (*continued*).
(1565–71). The poet's supposed attachment to this princess is said, with more or less foundation, to have been one of the causes that led to his confinement in 1579. [o.p.]

—— *Cherry and Violet: a story of the Plague.* [juvenile] 1864
London during the Fire and the Plague (1665–6). [*Illus.* by Jellicoe and Railton, Nimmo: o.p.; Dodd & Mead, New York: o.p.]

—— *The Old Chelsea Bun-house.* [juvenile] 1866
A quiet little tale, with pictures of bygone society (eighteenth century) woven round scenes which Miss Manning knew and loved. [*Illus.* by Jellicoe and Railton, Routledge: o.p.; Dutton, New York: o.p.]

—— *Passages in the Life of the Faire Gospeller, Anne Askew.* [juvenile] 1866
The story of the famous martyr (1546). [Bentley, o.p.; Dodd & Mead, New York: o.p.]

MANNING, Frederick. *Her Privates We, by Private 19022.* 1930
The strength of this book on the great war is in the portrayal of the mind of the rank and file, on the Ancre and Somme in 1916, through the experiences of an educated man who fell before he won his commission. It is an abridgment from a work in two volumes, *The Middle Parts of Fortune*, privately printed; the author is known as a poet. [Davies; Putnam, New York.]

"MANSFIELD, Katherine" [Kathleen Beauchamp, afterwards Mrs. Middleton Murry; New Zealander; 1889–1923]. *In a German Pension.* 1911
A dozen sketches of greedy, bloated, enamoured, or snobbish Germans, of one sex or the other, tending towards caricature. Immature: Katherine Mansfield was dissatisfied with them and refused to republish them after the war. She felt that they had not the veracity, the tolerance, the perfect understanding, at which she aimed. *The Swing of the Pendulum* is more characteristic. A girl in a discontented and rebellious mood nearly falls a prey to an enterprising man. Her victory restores her spirit. [Constable; Knopf, New York.]

—— *Bliss; and other stories.* 1920
The themes here for the most part are the unconsidered trifles of life; little happens beyond the ordinary routine; but shown as events in the minds of the people concerned, with all their reactions and faintest vibrations, they appear in their true import. *Prelude* is simply the account of a family move to a new home in the country—apparently in New Zealand. It is enough to acquaint us intimately with a whole group of characters and their various outlook on life. The bliss of the title-story is poisoned by the *dénouement*. *Psychology*, *Pictures*, and *The Man without a Temperament* are typical of her indefatigable "searching after truth." She is as skilled and keen-sighted as Chekhov, if without his wide and varied experience and his tragic power. [Constable; Knopf, New York.]

—— *The Garden Party; and other stories.* 1922
The title-story alone would suffice to show that Katherine Mansfield has now perfected her technique, her wonderful ability to convey even the "overtones, half tones, quarter tones." Her imaginative self-identification with the object, animate or inanimate, is so complete that her characters seem to reveal their whole mentality without the least departure from ordinary natural life. She was so absorbed in reality, that she at length ceased to shrink from the vile or the ugly, having glimpses of something beyond that redeems even the worst. "Beauty triumphs over everything in Life." [Constable; Knopf, New York; Garden City Co., New York.]

—— *The Dove's Nest; and other stories.* 1923
The first pictures a group of timid ladies at a Mediterranean *plage* entertaining a glossy American; every line is a delicate touch of life, etched in with a tenderness and humour not otherwise expressed. So, too, the poignancy and the satire of *The Doll's House* are conveyed with no syllable of comment. Compare this with that sardonic masterpiece *The Fly*. [Constable; Knopf, New York.]

—— *Something Childish; and other stories.* 1924
Mostly if not entirely earlier work than *Bliss*. Nearly thirty sketches and impressions, all of the briefest in the point of duration of time, instantaneous photos, so to speak: the thoughts of a tired girl in a big millinery establishment; the impressions of a tiny child who was kidnapped; glimpses of fellow-travellers; the domestic manœuvres and heart-burnings incidental to the purchase of new dresses for the kids; the mentality of a madman; nude snobbishness in a Turkish bath; young, innocent love—and disillusionment. *Sixpence* gives the anguish of self-reproach felt by a man who whipped his little son; *Poison* is an ultra-modern *novella*, *The Woman at the Store* a tale of the Australian bush that comes near Kipling. [Constable; *sub tit. The Little Girl; and other stories*, Knopf, New York.]

MANZONI, Alessandro [Italian; 1785–1873]. *The Betrothed* (I Promessi Sposi, 1825). 1875
The best known of Italian prose romances. Scene, Milan, Lecco, and the shores of Lake Como, at the time of the Spanish domination (1628–30); the author carefully cites his authorities for the historical details. The saintly Cardinal Federigo Borromeo is nobly portrayed. The agonies of famine and pestilence in Milan make an impressive episode, though Goethe objected to the elaboration of its historical treatment. From the revolt that followed it start the series of dramatic adventures, invented by the author, which made the book's fame. It is, further, a faithful picture of life in Italy at that epoch, full of insight into human nature, and of sympathy with the poor and lowly; the descriptive passages show the poet's love of beauty.
One hundred and sixteen Italian editions have been issued (37 printed at Milan, 18 at Florence, 11 at Naples, 7 at Lugano, 6 at Turin, 3 at Parma, 3 at Mendrisio, 2 at Leipzig, 2 at Malta, 1 each at Leghorn, Placentia, Pesaro, Vienna, Rome, Brussels, and London, 20 in Paris). Of translations, 17 in German, 19 French, 10 English, 3 Spanish, 1 Greek, Swedish, Dutch, Russian, Hungarian, and Armenian (*Athenæum*, August 18th, 1877). [2 vols. (Bohn's Lib.), Bell (Harcourt, New York); with introd. by R. SABATINI, (International Lib.) McKay, Philadelphia; transl. by Daniel T. CONNOR, Macmillan, New York (1924).]

MARAN, René [French]. *Batouala* (1921). 1922
The scene is the French Congo, and the author himself is a negro. In incidents from the life of a native chief are set forth, with intimate knowledge of native psychology, the deplorable results of exploitation by the whites. [Transl. by Adèle S. SELTZER, Boni, New York.]

MARGUERITE D'ANGOULEMÊ [Queen of Navarre; French; 1492–1549]. *The Heptameron.* 1558
A framework series of stories and novelettes in imitation of Boccaccio's *Decameron*. A party of ladies and gentlemen are imprisoned by floods in the Pyrenean village of Cauterets, and pass the time by telling tales. Many of these are drawn from the fabliaux, the licentious *Cent nouvelles nouvelles*, and the Italian novellieri, and all are more or less erotic, scandalous, and salacious. Amorous stratagems and intrigues, incidents at Court, histories in which the monks cut a discreditable figure, are the chief material. Though the comedy is so easy-going and licentious, the writer claims that her aim is serious, and even conducive to sound morality. [The *Heptameron* has been translated for the " Society of English Bibliophilists " from the authentic text of Le Roux de Lincy, including the notes, etc. (5 vols., 1894), by W. K. KELLY (Bohn's Lib., 1855 : o.p.) ; 5 vols., Gibbings (Lippincott, Philadelphia), 1898 : o.p. ; by A. MACHEN (privately printed in 1886) ; (Lib. of Early Novelists), Routledge (Dutton, New York), 1905 ; Knopf, New York, 1924 ; another transl., with preface by G. Saintsbury, and original *illustrations*, 5 vols., Navarre Soc. (Boni, New York), 1928. *The Fortunate Lovers*, 27 of the less offensive stories, transl. by A. Mary F. ROBINSON, with notes and introduction, Redway : o.p.]

MARGUERITTE, Paul [French ; 1860–1918] **and Victor** [French ; *b.* 1866]. *The Disaster* (Le désastre, 1898). 1898
First number of a series—*Une époque*—half history, half fiction, dealing with the terrible events of 1870–1. Zola's *Downfall* was written from the point of view of the common soldier ; these represent the views of the officers, being written by the sons of the brave General Marguéritte. This novel describes the disastrous campaign on the N.E. frontier, particularly the operations round Metz ; it is minutely and exactly true in detail, and the prolonged agony of the beleagured army is vividly depicted. [Transl. by F. LEES, Chatto : o.p. ; transl., Brentano, New York.] Two sequels, *Les tronçons du glaive* (1901), and *Les braves gens* (1901), dealing with *La defense nationale* (1870–1) and *Épisodes* (1870–1), continue the narrative with the siege of Paris, and the movements of the armies of the North and the East, and of the two armies of the Loire, the French soldier and the peasant being carefully studied. The only English translation is *Strasbourg*, from *Les braves gens*, which contains a graphic account of the siege and bombardment of that town. [Transl. by " S. G. TALLENTYRE," Smith & Elder, 1915 : o.p.]

—— *The Commune* (La Commune, 1904). 1904
Concludes the series with an impartial account of the Commune, based, like the three foregoing, on a painstaking study of the events and a sympathetic consideration of the causes. Full of deep pity for the unhappy workmen of Paris who hoped to regenerate society by establishing the Commune. Compared with the knowledge, insight, and seriousness shown in these four, most of the other novels dealing with the time are mere adventure stories. Not, however, very artistic—the imaginary episodes are sandwiched in with the actual history, the design being to present the tempestuous scenes of insurrection, riot, and massacre as they appeared to the eyes of typical characters. Not a meritorious translation. [Transl. by F. LEES and R. B. DOUGLAS, Chatto : o.p.]

—— *Vanity* (Vanité, 1907). 1907
More a piece of sociological analysis with a definite thesis than a novel. Theme, the vanity of money-making, expounded in the members of a wealthy bourgeois family whose outward careers and inner life are laid bare in the style of Balzac and Maupassant. [Transl. by K. S. WEST, Chatto : o.p.]

MARGUERITTE, Victor [French ; *b.* 1866]. *The Frontiers of the Heart* (Les frontiers du cœur, 1911). 1913
A study of marriage between aliens, a Frenchwoman and a cultivated, scientific Prussian, and of the unendurable conflict between national sentiment and personal affection, whilst a war, that of 1870–1, is going on. Scenes, Paris, Marburg, Amiens, etc. [Transl. by Frederic LEES, Heinemann : o.p. ; Stokes, New York : o.p.]

—— *The Bachelor Girl* (La garçonne, 1922). 1923
A young woman engaged to a man in a good position sees her fiancé in a compromising situation with another woman, and determines to have her revenge. The chronicle of the " good time " in which she rivals the worst profligacy of the opposite sex defies literary conventions of decency. [Transl. by Hugh BURNABY, Philpott.]

MARIVAUX, Pierre Carlet de Chamblain de [French ; 1688–1763]. *The Life of Marianne ; or, The Adventures of the Countess of* —— (La vie de Marianne, 1731–36). 1736–42
Never completed. Marivaux is a curious study in the history of fiction, and the question of the relation between his novels and those of Richardson is a perplexing subject. Marivaudage has been defined as " the metaphysic of love-making." His novels are studies of sentimentality, the actors analysing their feelings for the benefit not only of themselves but of each other. The language in which this sensibility is expressed must be studied in the original ; it is a singular, and for its purposes, a masterly style. This novel " is a picture of social life, and a study, sometimes infinitely subtle, of the emotions of his heroine ; her genius for coquetry is finely allied to her maiden pride ; the hypocrite, M. de Climal—old angel fallen— is a new variety of the family of Tartufe " (Edward Dowden). " The real importance of *Marianne* in the history of fiction is that it is the first example of a novel of analysis rather than of incident (though incident is still prominent), and the first in which an elaborate style, strongly imbued with mannerism, is applied to this purpose " (Saintsbury). [3 vols., 1736–42 : o.p. ; transl. by Mrs. Mary COLLIER, *sub tit.* The Virtuous Orphan ; or, The Life of Marianne, Countess of ——, 1747: o.p. ; same, 4 vols., Lond., 1784 : o.p. ; another transl. is *The Hand of Destiny ; or, The Life of Marianne*, by Sir G. CAMPBELL, Ward & Lock, 1889 : o.p.]

" MARLITT, Eugenie " [Eugenie John ; German ; 1825–87]. *At the Councillor's : or, A Nameless History* (Im Hause des Kommerzienrats, 1877). 1877
A fair specimen of this prolific writer's sentimental fiction. Illustrates the unsettled state of the country after the Franco-German war, the troubles caused by sudden alterations of fortune, etc. [3 vols., Bentley : o.p. ; Lippincott, Philadelphia.]
Other novels are : *Gold Else* (1868), 1868 ; *The Old Mam'selle's Secret* (1868), 1869 ; *The Princess of the Moor* (1872), 1872 ; *The Second Wife* (1874), 1874. [All, Ward & Lock : o.p. ; Lippincott, Philadelphia.]

MARMONTEL, Jean François [French ; 1723–99]. *Moral Tales* (Contes moraux, 1761).   1895
Oriental and classical tales, stories of eighteenth-century France, and romantic scenes after the manner of Fénelon and Florian. [*Selections* by G. SAINTSBURY, G. Allen : o.p.]

MARNAN, Basil [South African]. *A Daughter of the Veldt.*   1901
A biographical novel covering twenty-five years of a young woman's life, and presenting a realistic picture of semi-civilized life in South Africa. Boers and Britons, black sheep and white, the former predominating, are portrayed impartially. [Heinemann : o.p. ; Holt, New York : o.p.]

MARRIAGE, Caroline. *The Luck of Barerakes.*   1903
Barerakes, the lonely farm on the Yorkshire moors, with its atmosphere of gloom and terror, is another Wuthering Heights, and the " Black Dog," its owner, a more repulsive Heathcliff. Begins with a murder done on the moors a century ago, and works out, with a deep sense of tragedy, the lifelong fear and remorse it leaves to those implicated, the deadly influence it exerts on the characters of themselves and their kindred and the heritage of shame to succeeding generations. A very careful transcript of the local speech. [Heinemann : o.p.]

MARRIOTT, Charles [*b.* 1869]. *The Column.*   1901
A high-flown and bizarre story, with a mystical heroine and other characters who are not very like average human beings, but have, for the reader who cares to understand them, much interest of a purely intellectual kind. The scene is Cornwall, where the heroine's father, pagan, scholar, and hermit, has set up a Doric column, which becomes the symbol of his daughter's cult of nature and the elements. The narrative style and the dialogue are euphuistic, epigrammatic, obviously Meredithian. [Lane : o.p.]

—— *Love with Honour.*   1902
Not so far-fetched in subject or style—a curious problem in the moral casuistry of love. The hero, a young man who has read *Lavengro*, Carlyle, and Whitman, and wants to put their gospel into action ; the heroine, a girl of lofty and delicate principles of conduct ; a fine old martinet ; an æsthetic villager, etc. Scene, a beautiful village in Gloucestershire. [Lane : o.p.]

—— *Ginevra.*   1904
Another Cornish vestal with a pagan soul, a poetess worshipping nature, satirically contrasted with a mere literary woman. The girl rises to the heights when she and a painter fall in love ; but he asks her to wait, her pride is insulted, and she steels herself to seek content in work and her lonely fame. [Methuen : o.p.]

—— *Mrs. Alemere's Elopement.*   1905
Opens with a comic situation—Alemere visits Dick's mother to commiserate with her on his wife's elopement with Dick—after which the sequence of events is ordinary and unstrained. Mrs. Alemere, remorselessly analysed, is a frivolous woman of a low but common type, whose beauty injures the lives of three men. [Nash : o.p.]

—— *The Wondrous Wife.*   1907
A novel of passion that shows independent and sensible thought on the mutual influence of people's acts and the restraining claims of marriage. The central incident is again an elopement, this time of an unfaithful husband, whose wife is perhaps the strongest woman yet painted by Mr. Marriott. [Nash : o.p. ; Bobbs-Merrill, Indianapolis, 1913.]

—— *The Kiss of Helen.*   1908
Another suggestive study of the fine shades of passion—and perhaps of a love more etherealized than passion ; the conclusion is enigmatic. [Nash : o.p. ; Lane, New York : o.p.]

—— *The Intruding Angel.*   1909
The intruding angel is compassion, which leads a man to pardon his unfaithful wife, at the expense of a woman who loves him, and to accept the fatherhood of an illegitimate child. [Hurst : o.p. ; Lane, New York : o.p.]

—— *Now !*   1910
" Now ! " is the motto of a brotherhood pledged to live their own lives—to do really what we mildly approve as the beautiful dreams of poets and idealists. The two lovers, a Lavengro, with less propensity for the dull and conventional than George Borrow himself, and a young Diana born of highly respectable parents, cast prejudice and prudence to the winds for the comradeship of nature. [Hurst : o.p. ; Lane, New York : o.p.]

—— *The Dewpond.*   1912
The main theme is the liaison between a young novelist and the wife of a politician, related by a woman observer. The " Dewpond " is youth, with its free attitude towards sex and convention. [Hurst : o.p. ; Lane, New York : o.p.]

—— *Subsoil.*   1913
There is more discussion of painting and various social and artistic problems in this novel, than character-drawing or narrative. [Hurst : o.p.]

—— *The Catfish.*   1913
The hero is an imaginative, dreamy fellow, only spurred on to find his real vocation by the " catfish," an idealistic girl who thoroughly understands his temperament. Eventually he finds satisfaction in establishing a novel type of shop, where he sells the best quality goods at the lowest possible rates. [Hurst : o.p. ; Bobbs-Merrill, Indianapolis : o.p.]

—— *The Unpetitioned Heavens.*   1914
The hero is a young novelist of sensitive and fastidious character, who forgoes marriage with a wealthy woman, rather than sacrifice his pride or his ideals. [Hutchinson : o.p.]

MARRIOTT-WATSON, Henry Brereton [New Zealander ; 1863–1921]. *Galloping Dick.*   1895
Adventures of a gentleman of the road who flourished in the reigns of Charles II and James II. [Lane.]

—— *The Princess Xenia.*   1899
A romance of intrigue on *Zenda* and *Prince Otto* lines. A millionaire plays with the destinies of an imaginary German State. [Harper : o.p.]

MARRIOTT-WATSON, Henry Brereton (*continued*). *The Rebel.*   1900
Amazing adventures and exploits of the Earl of Cherwell, who defends a lady's honour against the Duke of
    York's designs, and is engaged in " the Rising at Taunton in 1684." The diction modelled on the con-
    temporary style. Depicts the corrupt and brilliant life of the Court. [Heinemann: o.p.; Harper, New
    York: o.p.]
—— *Chloris of the Island.*   1900
A sensational romance of the period 1800–10. The indomitable hero fights single-handed against a lawless Irish
    family, who live in an island stronghold off the Cornish coast, and have dealings with Napoleon. The
    plot is complicated by his love affair with the daughter. [Harper: o.p.]
—— *The Skirts of Happy Chance.*   1901
Nine very slight, but clever and fantastic stories of the adventures of a rich young nobleman—a philanderer
    and a scamp, with a gift for impersonation. [Methuen: o.p.]
—— *The House Divided.*   1901
An entertaining story of social life in 1732. [Harper: o.p.]
—— *Captain Fortune.*   1904
Adventures in Cornwall, and on the way to the king at Oxford (1643). Machine-made romanticism. [Methuen:
    o.p.]
—— *Twisted Eglantine.*   1905
Perhaps his best story; certainly contains his best character—the gorgeous and invincible beau, with his
    alternate selfishness and generosity. Restores felicitously the Regency days (*c.* 1809–20). [Methuen:
    o.p.; Appleton, New York: o.p.]
—— *The High Toby.*   1906
" Further chapters in the Life and Fortune of Dick Ryder, otherwise Galloping Dick, sometime Gentleman
    of the Road." [Methuen: o.p.]
—— *The King's Highway.*   1910
" Further episodes in the life of Richard Ryder, otherwise Galloping Dick, sometime gentleman of the road."
    [Mills & Boon: o.p.]
—— *Alise of Astra.*   1910
Another romance of the *Zenda* type, the frustration by an Englishman of a plot to substitute a baby heir to a
    mid-European Grand Duchy. [Methuen: o.p.; Little & Brown, Boston: o.p.]
—— *The House in the Downs.*   1914
Adventures with smugglers and other gentry on the Sussex coast, at the time of Napoleon's threatened landing
    and of the naval manœuvres of Villeneuve and Nelson (1805). [Nelson.]
MARRYAT, Capt. Frederick [1792–1848]. *Frank Mildmay; or, The Naval Officer.*   1829
Marryat had served as midshipman under Lord Cochrane on board the *Impérieuse*, and wrote this sea-novel
    on board the *Ariadne*. In two and a half years' service he is said to have seen fifty engagements, many
    very brilliant; and he had authentic material for the life of perpetual adventure and activity that is
    here described. Certain notabilities of his day are supposed to be sketched among the very multi-
    farious characters, and the book is made up of reminiscences, except that it has a fictitious plot and
    hero.
—— *The King's Own.*   1830
His first book, *Frank Mildmay*, was made up of reminiscences in the form of fiction; this, constructed of like
    materials, is more of a novel, following Scott the historical novelist and Smollett the delineator of nautical
    humours. The opening chapters give a full account of the mutiny at the Nore (1797), followed by the
    adventures of a daring smuggler, who impresses the young hero into his crew. It is in this novel that
    appears the famous story of an English captain who deliberately loses his frigate on a lee shore in order to
    wreck a French line-of-battle ship.
—— *Newton Förster.*   1832
Has a romantic plot, opening with a terrible shipwreck and the rescue of an infant, who in the end proves to
    be the heiress of a French marquess that Newton becomes acquainted with in the West Indies. Farcical
    scenes of connubial strife, society on shipboard, wrecks, escapes, and the usual frolics and escapades.
—— *Peter Simple.*   1834
Much more natural and racy; the journal of a sailor, from the day he is entered as midshipman to his marriage
    and retirement as Lord Privilege. Peter, the supposed dunce, with his real sagacity, his misadventures
    and lucky escapes from every peril and quandary; the pungent character-sketches, like Mr. Chucks and
    romancing Capt. Kearney, escapes from shipwreck, cutting-out expeditions, and adventures of the fugitive
    prisoners, make up a lively and humorous picture of naval life.
—— *Jacob Faithful.*   1834
The hero tells his own story from infancy upwards. His life at a charity school, apprenticeship to a Thames
    waterman and life on the river till he and young Tom get impressed and see service on board a frigate,
    are episodes crammed with ludicrous incident The vulgar Turnbulls and their attempts to be fashionable,
    the theatrical picnic party, the " Domine," and the incurable punster, Old Tom, provide continual
    mirth.
—— *Mr. Midshipman Easy.*   1836
Founded, like his first novel, on Marryat's personal experiences of active service round the coasts of France
    and Spain during the great war; full of horseplay, absurd incident, and miscellaneous jocosity, as well as
    thrilling nautical adventure; rich in salt-water and other characters, such as the philosophic father and
    the silly mother; full also of yarns which Munchausen might have fathered.
—— *Japhet in Search of a Father.*   1836
Not a sea-novel; a picaresque story pure and simple, closely modelled on Smollett. Japhet and Timothy are
    another Roderick and Strap; Aristodemus the soothsayer is a second Cadwallader, Mr. Cophagus and
    Mr. Pleggett, the rival apothecaries, recall Potion and Crab.

MARRYAT, Capt. Frederick (*continued*). *Snarleyyow ; or, The Dog Fiend.* 1837

A story of William III's reign. The dog which plays such a prominent rôle belongs to a rascally lieutenant commanding a small vessel hunting for smugglers. The lieutenant's avarice gets him mixed up with the Jacobites, and when he has quite filled up the cup of his cruelties and treachery, it is at their hands he meets with his doom. Lieut. Vanslyperken and his dog are grotesques, verging on the horrible ; but the story has many episodes of characteristic fun and comedy, Short and the widow furnishing the broadest mirth.

—— *The Phantom Ship.* 1839

A seventeenth-century narrative ; the story of Philip Vanderdecken's arduous search for and successful but calamitous discovery of his father, the " Flying Dutchman."

—— *Masterman Ready ; or, The Wreck of the " Pacific."* 1841

A well-meaning story that children like—a wreck, Crusoe life on an island, a fight with savages, and the heroic death of the fine old sailor, Masterman Ready, through the carelessness of a naughty boy.

—— *The Children of the New Forest.* [juvenile] 1847

A Royalist family, especially the young people, near Lymington (1647).

[Editions of Marryat's *Novels*, published by Routledge : (King's Own Edn.), ed. by W. L. Courtney, 24 vols., ea. with 6 photogravures (Dutton, New York) ; (Frank Mildmay Edn.), 20 vols., *id.*, both mainly o.p. *Illus.* by Sullivan, Brock, Pegram, and others, 6 of the novels, Macmillan ; ed. by R. Brimley Johnson, 22 vols., ea. with 3 etchings, Dent (new ed., 1929) ; 24 vols. *illus.*, Page, Boston.]

MARSHALL, Archibald [b. 1866]. *Peter Binney, Undergraduate.* 1905

—— *Richard Baldock : an account of some episodes in his childhood, youth, and early manhood, and of the advice that was freely offered to him.* 1906

—— *Exton Manor.* 1907

—— *Many Junes.* 1908

—— *The Eldest Son.* 1911

Novels of family life in the country ; a hunting family—the Clintons in South Meadshire—bulking prominently ; the leading interest character, or the kind of incident that reveals character. Most of the characters are quite ordinary people, like peppery but good-natured old Squire Clinton—but interesting on that very account, so truly are they rendered. A few more unusual figures give touches of comedy now and then, and there are some roguish children done to the life. [(1) and (2), Rivers : o.p. ; (3) and (4), Methuen : o.p. ; (5), Collins ; (1)–(5), Dodd & Mead, New York.]

—— *Watermeads.* 1916

The easy-going squire and his wife illustrate the difference between people with light natures and those with heavy natures. Monetary difficulties and the struggles of a family clinging to the ancestral home bring out the contrast : the man is contented, in spite of his troubles ; the woman unhappy, even when circumstances improve. [S. Paul : o.p. : Dodd & Mead, New York.]

—— *Abington Abbey.* 1918

A worldly-minded and snobbish clergyman, his submissive wife, and the daughters of a wealthy banker are among the prominent characters of this readable story. [S. Paul : o.p. ; Dodd & Mead, New York.]

—— *The Graftons* [sequel]. 1922

In this sequel we meet the same set of characters, and follow the love-affairs and marriages of the two daughters. [Collins ; Dodd & Mead, New York.]

—— *The Hall and the Grange.* 1921

The contrast and misunderstandings between the sons of an old county family, the eldest, an old-fashioned squire, the younger in business. [Collins ; Dodd & Mead, New York.]

MARSHALL, Emma [*née* Martin ; 1830–99]. *In Colston's Days : a story of Old Bristol.* 1883

The story of Edward Colston, the philanthropist (1636–1721), and descriptions of old Bristol in the time of the Great Rebellion ; like the rest of the writer's novels, a quiet story conveying moral and religious truths in a form acceptable to young people. [Seeley.]

—— *In the East Country with Sir Thomas Browne.* 1884

The home life of the author of *Religio Medici* ; scenes, chiefly the neighbourhood of Norwich. [Seeley ; Dutton, New York : o.p.]

—— *Under the Mendips.* 1885

Life in Somerset, the Bristol riots, etc. (1831). [Seeley.]

—— *On the Banks of the Ouse.* 1887

Life at Olney (*c.* 1767–87) ; the poet Cowper and his friend John Newton, Vicar of Olney. [Seeley.]

—— *Bristol Diamonds.* 1888

Bristol at the end of the eighteenth century ; the quaint manners, the minuets, pump-rooms, etc. Hannah More is introduced. [Seeley : o.p.]

—— *Under Salisbury Spire.* 1889

A tender and conscientious study of the life and times of the saintly divine and poet George Herbert (1613–33), the subject of one of Isaac Walton's *Lives*. [Seeley : o.p.]

—— *Winchester Meads.* 1890

A study of the stanch and saintly Bishop Ken (1672–88) ; full of local charm, particularly for old Wykehamists. [Seeley.]

—— *Winifrede's Journal.* 1892

Times of Charles I (1637–56) ; the heroine shares the fortunes and trials of Bishop Hall of Exeter and Norwich. [Seeley ; Macmillan, New York : o.p.]

—— *In the Service of Rachel, Lady Russell.* 1892

The unfortunate William, Lord Russell's home life, his plots and execution (1682–94). [Seeley : o.p.]

MARSHALL, Emma (*continued*). *Penshurst Castle.* 1893
The domestic life of Sir Philip Sidney (1581–6). [Seeley.]

—— *The White King's Daughter.* 1895
Civil War times, the Princess Elizabeth, Carisbrooke. [Seeley : o.p.]

—— *The Master of the Musicians.* 1895
Life and times of Handel (1742–59). [Seeley : o.p.]

—— *Kensington Palace in the Days of Queen Mary II.* 1895
A study of Queen Mary's character, based on recent researches and memoirs ; largely an apology for her alleged indifference to the cause of her father, the dethroned king, James II. Includes the pathetic story of her little son, the Duke of Gloucester. [Seeley : o.p.]

—— *By the North Sea.* 1896
Cromwell's granddaughter Bridget Bendysh (1694–5). [Jarrold : o.p. ; Whittaker, New York : o.p.]

—— *A Haunt of Ancient Peace : memories of Mr. Nicholas Ferrar's house at Little Gidding, and of his friends, Dr. Donne and Mr. George Herbert.* 1897
A visit to this pious hermitage in the time of the Great Civil War is recorded in J. H. Shorthouse's *John Inglesant.* [Seeley : o.p.]

—— *In the Choir of Westminster Abbey.* 1897
The famous composer Henry Purcell (1658–95) and the beautiful actress Mrs. Bracegirdle are the central figures. [Seeley.]

—— *Castle Meadow : a story of Norwich a hundred years ago.* 1897
The two characters round whom the story is written are the musical prodigy William Crotch (1775–1847) and the painter Old Crome (1768–1821). [Seeley.]

—— *The Young Queen of Hearts.* 1898
The Princess Elizabeth and her brother, Henry, Prince of Wales, the ill-fated prince who died before he came to the throne in succession to his father, James I ; scenes, largely, Coombe Abbey, in Warwickshire, and Coventry (1602–13). [Seeley.]

—— *Under the Dome of St. Paul's.* 1898
The later years of Sir Christopher Wren (1709–23). [Seeley : o.p.]

—— *The Parson's Daughter : her early recollections and how Romney painted her.* 1899
Illustrated by portraits after Gainsborough and George Romney, the originals of which are the subjects of a quiet domestic tale (1790–1811). [Seeley.]

MARSHALL, Leslie A. [Translator]. *Builders of New Rome ; and other Lettish tales.* 1924
The title-story, by Jans Poruks, illustrates the desire for knowledge amongst schoolboys ; *The Cat's Mill*, by Karlis Skalbe, is a fairy-tale ; also included are *Memories of Summer*, by Janis Akuraters, and three tales by Rudolfs Blaumanis. [Dent.]

MARTIN, A. D. *Una Breakspear.* 1926
A novel of the Commonwealth and Restoration times, illustrating the political and religious fanaticism disturbing the nation and oppressing the clergy. [James Clarke.]

MARTIN, Mrs. George [*née* Madden ; American ; *b.* 1866]. *Emmy Lou : her book and heart.* 1902
" School days of a very bewildered and very real little girl. Incidentally satirizes some school methods and manners." [Doubleday, New York.]

MARTIN, Mrs. Herbert. *Jock's Ward.* 1899
A touching story of a stanch boy, a street-arab, and of a broken man whom he rescues from misery and remorse. [Pearson : o.p. ; Fenno, New York : o.p.]

MARTINEAU, Harriet [1802–76]. *Deerbrook.* 1839
A village story of the good old-fashioned sort, describing two rival families, their narrowness and jealousy, and the evils of gossip. Miss Martineau had already made money and reputation by her stories illustrating the science of political economy, taxation, the poor law, etc.—*Illustrations of Political Economy*, 9 vols., 1832–4—a striking outcome of the rage for the diffusion of useful knowledge. She considered *Deerbrook* her best work. [Murray.]

—— *The Hour and the Man.* 1840
An early *Uncle Tom's Cabin.* The man is Toussaint l'Ouverture, and the hour that of the black revolution in Haiti (1791–1803). Toussaint is an almost incredible paragon, and the savagery and guilt of the native chiefs are not recognized by the author, who makes an idyll out of a series of frightful convulsions. She keeps fairly close to the historical records, but her knowledge of local conditions was ridiculed by Judge Haliburton in *Sam Slick*, and it is obvious that she was unduly fascinated by the idea of a negro acting successfully in the sphere of political and social government upon the principles she most cherished. [Edited by E. A. Baker (Half-forgotten Books), Routledge, 1904 (Dutton, New York) : o.p.]

—— *The Playfellow.* 1841
A series of children's stories—still readable—comprising *Settlers at Home*, *The Peasant and the Prince*, *Feats on the Fiord*, and *Crofton Boys*. [(1), o.p. ; (2), Ginn, Boston ; (3), *illus.* by Rackham, Dutton, New York ; by Artzibashev, Macmillan, New York ; with *Merdhin* (Everyman's Lib.) Dent (Dutton, New York) ; (4), Heath, New York.]

MASEFIELD, John [Poet Laureate ; *b.* 1878]. *Captain Margaret.* 1908
A novel of adventure in Devon and Cornwall and the Spanish Main (dating 1685–8), written on modern psychological lines, the leading figure a very unattractive woman-hunter. [Richards ; Cape ; Macmillan, New York.]

—— *Multitude and Solitude.* 1909
A literary man loses the woman he loves, and roused to a new vision of the seriousness of life and the futility of a literature and an art which the multitude disdains, resolves to build up a character, and do a work that shall be worthy of her, and, as it were, complete the noble life which has been cut off. Seeking a

MASEFIELD, John (*continued*).
cure for sleeping-sickness in the depths of West Africa, amid hardships, disease, and the horrors of solitude, he gets at the real stuff of life. [Richards ; Cape ; Macmillan, New York ; Garden City Co., New York.]

—— *Martin Hyde, the Duke's Messenger.*　　　　　　　　　　　　　　[juvenile] 1910
A boy's adventures in the service of the Duke of Monmouth, time of the rebellion (1684–5). [Wells Gardner ; Little & Brown, Boston.]

—— *Lost Endeavour.*　　　　　　　　　　　　　　　　　　　　　　1910
Strange adventures of an English lad and a Spaniard in the buccaneering days on the Spanish Main and in Virginia, from 1692 onwards. The peculiar charm of the book is the glamorous atmosphere Mr. Masefield's poetic vision casts over all. [Nelson ; Macmillan, New York.]

—— *The Street of To-day.*　　　　　　　　　　　　　　　　　　　1911
Attempts a critical diagnosis of modern social conditions, from the point of view of eugenics, but rather with the imaginative fervour of a poet than the detachment of a scientist or philosopher. A man of science proposing to amend society by a revolutionary hygiene, a shallow, neurotic woman of the parasitic type, and a " genuine " woman, who is his good genius, illustrate Mr. Masefield's arguments. [Dent : o.p. ; Dutton, New York.]

—— *Jim Davis.*　　　　　　　　　　　　　　　　　　　　　　　1911
An adventure story of smugglers, spies, etc., in Napoleon's time, in Devon and then on the high seas. [Wells Gardner ; *illus.*, Stokes, New York ; McKay, New York ; *sub tit. The Captive of the Smugglers*, Page, Boston.]

—— *Sard Harker.*　　　　　　　　　　　　　　　　　　　　　　1924
A breathlessly exciting adventure story of an American republic, prone to revolution ; time, some twenty years ago. Rum-running, silver-mining, simmering sedition, devil-worship, grafted by a repulsive Jew on indigenous savagery. Harker's love is abducted, and he is left ashore and has marvellous escapes. But there is too much talkee-talkee, which takes the edge off the suspense and ruins probability. [Heinemann ; Harrap ; Macmillan, New York.]

—— *Odtaa.*　　　　　　　　　　　　　　　　　　　　　　　　1926
Another novel on the same lines, a succession of amazing adventures, with several poetical descriptions of wild nature. [Heinemann ; Macmillan, New York.]

—— *The Midnight Folk.*　　　　　　　　　　　　　　　　　　　1927
A dream-fantasy for children, about a little boy whose governess is a witch, and who meets such delightful folk as Nibbins the Cat and Bitem the Fox. [Heinemann ; Macmillan, New York.]

—— *The Hawbucks.*　　　　　　　　　　　　　　　　　　　　　1929
A rustic comedy, the characters of which have been met before in his poem *Reynard the Fox* ; the " Hawbucks " are the suitors of the lovely Carrie Harriedew—there is plenty about horses and hunting, but the men and women are queer stuffed lay-figures. [Heinemann ; Macmillan, New York.]

MASON, Arthur Edward Woodley [*b.* 1865]. *The Courtship of Morrice Buckler.*　1896
A semi-historical romance after the style of Dumas. Opens tragically with a story of Monmouth's rebellion (1685), and passes, with episodes of exciting and unexpected incident, from England to Tyrol. The heroine is Tyrolese. [Hodder ; Nash ; Macmillan, New York : o.p.]

—— *Lawrence Clavering.*　　　　　　　　　　　　　　　　　　1897
Love and intrigue, Lake District and Carlisle (1715). [Ward & Lock ; Hodder ; Dodd & Mead, New York.]

—— *Miranda of the Balcony.*　　　　　　　　　　　　　　　　　1899
A romantic and intricate story of rascality, love, and adventure. Sketches of life in Scilly, Tangier, Spain, and Devon give the action a changing environment. [Hodder ; Nash ; Macmillan, New York : o.p.]

—— *Clementina.*　　　　　　　　　　　　　　　　　　　　　　1901
A particularly close imitation of Dumas. Princess Clementina Sobieska is the bride-elect of the Old Pretender ; and the chivalrous Irishman Wogan, who with his three comrades revives immortal memories, loving her himself has to further the marriage in spite of perilous obstacles. On this situation is based a thrilling romance, full of theatrical vigour, the end very painful. Without much regard for historical accuracy, the author draws a disenchanting portrait of the ruined Stuart (temp. 1720). [Methuen ; Hodder ; Stokes, New York : o.p.]

—— *The Four Feathers.*　　　　　　　　　　　　　　　　　　　1902
A serious kind of novel bringing into play the moral ideas by which high character is forged and tempered. The son of a line of soldiers, though brave in the highest sense, mistrusts his nerve, and is branded a coward. As a captive at Omdurman, he expiates his error in the noblest way. [Murray ; Hodder ; Nash ; Macmillan, New York.]

—— *The Broken Road.*　　　　　　　　　　　　　　　　　　　1907
A good story of intrigue and fighting on the North-West frontier, after a loyal ruler has been rendered hostile by his treatment at the hands of an Englishwoman. Condemns the practice of educating native princes at English universities, where their minds are confused by unassimilated Western ideas. [Murray ; Hodder ; Nash ; Scribner, New York.]

—— *At the Villa Rose.*　　　　　　　　　　　　　　　　　　　1910
A very capable detective story, the action of which takes place near Dijon. The author's stock detective, Hanaud, with his English foil, Ricardo, here make their début ; they are a whimsical and well characterized pair. [Hodder ; Scribner, New York.]

—— *The Turnstile.*　　　　　　　　　　　　　　　　　　　　　1912
The hero is an Antarctic explorer who is frankly out for political honours, and loses the respect of his wife, a youthful idealist, in that atmosphere of self-seeking and intrigue ; to regain it, however, when he forsakes politics for his former vocation. [Hodder ; Scribner, New York.]

MASON, Arthur Edward Woodley (*continued*). *The Four Corners of the World.* 1917

A miscellaneous collection of stories; in *One of Them*, a man prevented by ill-health from going to the front captures a German spy in England; *Green Paint* describes a novel and amusing way to make a fortune out of South American revolutions. [Hodder; Scribner, New York.]

—— *The Summons.* 1920

How a physically disabled man does good service in the war by hunting enemy submarines off Spain. [Hodder.]

—— *The Winding Stair.* 1923

A capital story of romance and adventure in France and North Africa—a young French officer is betrayed by love into deserting his military duty, but at the instance of his wife, makes good and redeems his honour. [Hodder; Doubleday, Doran, New York.]

—— *No Other Tiger.* 1927

A hard-bitten and courageous hero, a charming lady to be protected, a mystery to be solved—these, salted with some grim horrors and sweetened with a little love, are the ingredients from which this author can without fail concoct a thrilling yarn. [Hodder; Doubleday, Doran, New York.]

—— *The Prisoner in the Opal.* 1928

The ingredients are much as before, but the horror, in this case a secret magical society and the Black Mass, and the characters, who form a house-party near Bordeaux, are well done. [Hodder; Doubleday, Doran, New York.]

—— *The Dean's Elbow.* 1930

An ambitious chemist engaged in industrial research is the dashing central figure. He eventually attains a peerage; but his success is blighted by the long-delayed consequences of a wrong committed in the first episode—the really interesting part of the story—when he takes a girl on a yachting cruise and afterwards deserts her. [Hodder.]

MASON, Arthur Edward Woodley, and LANG, Andrew. *Parson Kelly.* 1900

A comedy of manners, with a fine lady and her lovers, as well as Jacobite intriguers involved in the Jacobite conspiracies after the rebellion of 1715. Some are historical characters; but the chief personage, the witty and coquettish Lady Oxford, is purely fictitious. [Longmans: o.p.; *id.*, New York.]

MASON, Caroline [*née* Atwater; American; *b.* 1853]. *A Woman of Yesterday.* 1900

A thoroughly American study of religious life, sombre and deeply Puritan. Largely taken up with the history of a Utopian settlement founded by a Christian socialist. The stern Calvinism of the heroine and her husband is modified, as they grow older, into a milder and broader religion. [Doubleday, New York: o.p.]

—— *A Lily of France: a romance of the sixteenth century.* 1901

The struggles of Protestants in France and Holland (1558–81) and the love-story and married life of William the Silent and Charlotte, Princess of Bourbon-Montpensier. [American Baptist Pub. Soc., Philadelphia; Hodder: o.p.]

—— *The Binding of the Strong.* 1908

The story of Milton's relations with his wife, Mary Powell, and the conquest of his passion for Delmé Davies. [Revell, New York; Hodder: o.p.]

MASSUCCIO OF SALERNO [Italian; mid. 15th century]. *Novellino* (1476). 1895

A collection of fifty disconnected stories, bluntly realistic, after the manner of Boccaccio, and reputed to be the most licentious of the Italian novels. A few are in the vein of genuine *buffo*, a few are tragedies pure and simple, but the majority of the others either satirize or castigate the clergy and unchaste women. Massuccio himself states that his tales are founded on actual incidents; and he was certainly less indebted than most of his colleagues to the time-honoured *fabliaux* and folk-tales. [Transl. by W. G. WATERS, *illus.* by E. R. Hughes, 2 vols., Lawrence & Bullen: o.p.]

MASTERS, Edgar Lee [American; *b.* 1869]. *Mitch Miller.* 1920

The author of that terrible outcry of disillusionment, *Spoon River Anthology* (1915), which checked any idealizing tendencies on the part of recent novelists, here enters into rivalry with Mark Twain. Mitch and Skeet Kirby (who tells the story in his boyish lingo) believe that Tom Sawyer and Huck Finn are real, and try to emulate their great adventures, in their own Illinois village. It is a jolly account of a charming friendship, ending in the death of the young hero Mitch. But the ugly side of American life is not omitted: there is a trial for murder, and sermonizing on " hired orators, hired newspapers, hired clergymen, hired lawyers, and hired officials." [Macmillan, New York; Grosset, New York.]

—— *Children of the Market Place.* 1922

A young Englishman arrives in Illinois to take possession of an estate, and becomes the friend of Stephen Arnold Douglas, the Democratic politician (1813–61), whose life and career are the main theme, affording a broad view of the stormy period leading to the war. [Macmillan, New York.]

—— *Skeeters Kirby.* 1923

The story of Mitch's pal and biographer, and more or less the author's own story. [Macmillan, New York.]

MATHER, James Marshall [*b.* 1851]. *Lancashire Idylls.* 1895

Eight stories of the country folk, in the manner of Sir James Barrie's stories of Thrums: the speech strongly vernacular. [Warne: o.p.]

—— *The Sign of the Wooden Shoon.* 1896

A longer story, pathetic in motive, portraying the same people, with some touches of humour. [Warne.]

—— *By Roaring Loom.* 1898

More idylls of the Lancashire operatives. [Bowden: o.p.]

MATHERS, Helen [Mrs. Henry Reeves; 1853–1920]. *Comin' thro' the Rye.* 1875

Abounds in romping comedy, not only in the account of the heroine's tomboy girlhood. Her love-story, with its crosses and perils, is tragic. A fair specimen of a numerous issue of sentimental novels by this writer. It first appeared anonymously, and was taken by many readers to be the work of Rhoda Broughton. [Jenkins; Appleton, New York: o.p.]

MATHEW, Frank [Irish ; *b.* 1865]. *The Spanish Wine.* 1898
A brief tale of passion and jealousy in troubled Elizabethan Ireland. Chief figure a beautiful lady whose haughty and capricious temper involves in tragedy all who come under its spell. Has a touch of Celtic mysticism. Scene, Dunluce Castle, Co. Antrim. [Lane : o.p.]

—— *Defender of the Faith.* 1899
A story of Henry VIII's loves and intrigues, as witnessed by Henry Percy, sixth Earl of Northumberland. A subtle blend of history and romance, with the figures of Anne Boleyn, Lord Cromwell, and others, thrown out in relief (1530–40). [Lane : o.p.]

—— *One Queen Triumphant.* 1899
The historical motive is how Mary of Scotland was brought to the scaffold. She and her rival Elizabeth are the foremost in a crowd of celebrated personages. The hero and his brother are implicated in the Babington plot. [Lane : o.p.]

—— *Love of Comrades.* 1900
A romantic tale of the days of Strafford (1640), with a sprightly and adventurous Irish heroine who masquerades as a boy and performs dashing exploits. [Lane : o p.]

—— *The Royal Sisters.* 1901
The intrigues, family jealousies, and conspiracies that were going on while Edward VI lay dying, forming the prelude to Mary's reign and persecution (1553). Mary herself and Princess Elizabeth, Lady Jane Grey, and Northumberland and his sons Guildford and Robert, Renard, Wyatt, Pembroke, and Arundel, are the chief personages of the drama, and their characters are carefully drawn. Largely in dialogue. [Long : o.p.]

MATTHEWS, James Brander [American ; *b.* 1852]. *The Story of a Story ; and other stories.* 1893
Stories that aim at both realism and artistic effect ; the picture of magazine-editing seems to contain some actual portraiture. [Harper, New York : o.p.]

—— *Vignettes of Manhattan.* 1894
—— *Outlines in Local Colour.* 1897
—— *Vistas of New York.* 1911
Each volume contains a dozen stories and sketches of life in New York. [(1), (2), and (3), Harper, New York : o.p.]

MATURIN, Charles Robert [Irish ; 1782–1824]. *Melmoth, the Wanderer.* 1820
The most powerful of the Gothic romances of mystery and terror which Mrs. Radcliffe, Monk Lewis, and others made fashionable at the time of the " Revival of Wonder." The motive of Faust and Mephistopheles is combined with that of the Wandering Jew or the Flying Dutchman, and with the favourite business of the elixir of life. The writer's imagination revels in the mysterious and the horrible, and, unlike Mrs. Radcliffe, leaves his nightmares to work their full effect. [3 vols., Macmillan, 1892 : o.p.]

MAUGHAM, Henry Neville. *Richard Hawkwood.* 1906
The hero is a great-grandson of the famous condottiere, Sir John Hawkwood (see Lawrence's *Brakespeare,* p. 292), and is in the service of Lorenzo de' Medici, who is a preponderant figure. Leonardo, Botticelli, and Pico della Mirandola also come on the stage and talk, and both Florentine politics and Renaissance culture are freely illustrated (1477). [Blackwood : o.p.]

MAUGHAM, William Somerset [*b.* 1874]. *Liza of Lambeth.* 1897
Twelve months in the life of a factory girl, described with hideous realism, the depravity and vile language of the lowest classes being set down without modification. [Cape ; Doubleday, Doran, New York.]

—— *Orientations ; and other stories.* 1899
Six short stories, ranging from *The Choice of Amyntas,* an allegorical fairy-tale, to the realism of *Daisy,* a study of sordid characters and motives among the lower middle-class. [Unwin : o.p.]

—— *The Hero.* 1901
A bitter story, reproducing with scrupulous realism all the grimness of life, but nothing of its gaiety or humour— the narrow interests and petty society of a village, the unsympathetic and stupid characters, the prejudices that embitter existence. The hero's tragedy results from an engagement, entered into as an inexperienced youth, which he is unable to repudiate when, as a grown man, he becomes aware that he does not love. [Hutchinson : o.p.]

—— *Mrs. Craddock.* 1902
—— *The Merry-go-round.* 1904
Further examples of " relentless realism," depicting factory-hands, villagers of a debased breed, etc. Histories of depravity and crime, related with the foul language and grimy details that stamp this genre. [(1) and (2), Heinemann : o.p.]

—— *The Explorer.* 1907
—— *The Magician.* 1908
Stories displaying the same realistic technique. The last is a powerful handling of the uncanny, conscientiously free from melodrama—the monstrous individual who rejoices in the title of the Magician produces ghastly scenes by the creation of living homunculi. [(1) and (2), Heinemann ; Doubleday, Doran, New York.]

—— *Of Human Bondage.* 1915
A long biographical novel that owes something to both Zola and Samuel Butler. The sorry career of a man with a club-foot, a nervous temperament and a morbid lack of self-confidence. From schooldays onwards, his life is a succession of defeats and fresh starts, all embittered by a sense of his deformity. It is embittered worst of all by his infatuation for a stupid, conceited woman who becomes a prostitute—a forcible, but, like much of the rest, an overcharged creation. This is probably the author's best book : though unbalanced, it has sincerity and power. [Heinemann ; Doubleday, Doran, New York ; Grosset, New York.]

MAUGHAM, William Somerset (*continued*). *The Moon and Sixpence.* 1919

The case of Gauguin transposed. Strickland is a middle-aged stockbroker, who takes up painting, throws over his family, and like the Frenchman goes to Tahiti and dies a leper. His brutal concentration on his art, his violent sexuality, his callous indifference to love, friendship, kindness, are forcibly presented ; but there is no revelation of the inner man or demonstration of his genius. He remains a picturesque enigma. [Heinemann ; Doubleday, Doran, New York.]

—— *The Trembling of a Leaf : little stories of the South Sea Islands.* 1921

Six dramatic sketches of Europeans and natives in the islands of the Pacific. [Heinemann ; Doubleday, Doran, New York.]

—— *The Painted Veil.* 1925

A perfunctory tale of marital infidelity in a Chinese city (Hong-Kong). The sketch of a town at the height of a cholera epidemic is the one thing of value. [Heinemann ; Doubleday, Doran, New York.]

—— *Cakes and Ale : or, The Skeleton in the Cupboard.* 1930

A sarcastic portrait of an author, a genial old bohemian, very different from the reverential idea provided for his admirers by his second wife, now widowed, who commissions another novelist to do the official biography. Good characterization of the two wives, especially of the first, who bolted. [Heinemann ; Doubleday, Doran, New York.]

MAUPASSANT, Henri René Albert Guy de [French ; 1850–93]. *Boule de Suif* (1880). 1899

Technically, this is one of the finest short stories ever written, and furthermore a brilliant example of Maupassant's sardonic humour. Boule de Suif (" Bladder of Lard "), a *fille de joie*, in an episode of the German occupation, proves herself morally the superior to a party of highly reputable people who despise her, and yet are anxious to profit by the conveniences of her trade. First appeared in *Les Soirées de Médan* (see p. 516). [Also transl. with introd. by A. SYMONS, *illus.*, Thevenot, Heinemann : o.p.]

—— *A Woman's Life* (Une vie : l'humble verité, 1883). 1888

An anatomy of married life and all its disillusionments, carried out with a ruthless and almost brutal frankness. [Also transl. (Boulevard Novels) by Henry BLANCHAMP (Lotus Library), Brentano, New York, 1902.]

—— *Yvette ; and other stories* (1884). 1904

Ten in all—*Miss Harriet, The Umbrella, The Piece of String, On Sale*, etc. *Yvette* is a triumph in the fine art of narration, and splendidly exhibits Maupassant's dexterity in revealing the elusive heart of a woman. It is a peculiarly French love-tale of the *demi-monde*—Yvette being the daughter of the " Marquise " Obardi, a woman in the same situation as that described in *Mrs. Warren's Profession*. Instead of the usual irony verging on cynicism, the author here expresses—or at least impresses the reader with—a sense of agonizing pathos. [Also transl. by Mrs. John GALSWORTHY, with pref. by Jos. CONRAD, Duckworth, (Knopf, New York).]

—— *Pierre and Jean* (Pierre et Jean, 1888). 1890

The preface is a memorable manifesto of the school of " Art for Art's sake," a laudation of objective realism as opposed to mere subjective analysis. A sombre and tragic study of bourgeois life, the tale of two brothers, one of whom is suddenly led to suspect that the other is the child of his mother's adultery. With infinite reluctance he compels himself to follow up the inquiry, while the mother, impassive and remorseful, awaits the discovery of her guilt. A superb example of Maupassant's faculty for observing the infinite details of life and reproducing them with unerring artistic fidelity. [Transl. by Clara BELL, Heinemann, 1902 ; this transl in *Collected Novels*, Knopf ; by Hugh CRAIG, Brentano, New York, 1899.]

—— *The Odd Number : thirteen tales.* 1889

The title-story is a faithful transcript of life and manners in a Norman village, accurate and convincing in the revelation of thought and emotion, and showing with characteristic irony how big issues hang on trifling events. Maupassant surpassed himself in portraying his countryman, the Norman peasant. [Also transl. by Jonathan STURGES, with introd. by Henry JAMES, Harper, New York.]

—— *A Coquette's Love* (Notre cœur, 1890). 1890

An unemotional, unsentimental, and unsarcastic study of the heart. Mariolle's mistress is a woman incapable of passion, who simply permits him to love her—a response to his ecstasies of desire that drives him to jealousy and eventual disillusionment. He finds consolation in the child-like affection of a girl of the people, whom he saved from brutality. The idle, luxurious, most recherchée of Parisian sociaty is depicted with magnificent realism. [Belford, New York : o.p. ; *sub tit. Notre cœur* in Laurie's edn.]

—— *Stories from Maupassant.* 1903

A selection evidently governed by reluctance to provoke the philistine ; representative, nevertheless, of Maupassant's exquisite technique, his unsurpassed faculty of observation, and his sense of the irony of things. The two best are *The Return* and *Night* ; the former an Enoch Arden story with a commonplace ending that is convincingly true to life. [Transl. by Elizabeth MARTINDALE, with preface by Ford Madox HUEFFER, Cape, 1928.]

[*Works :* transl by Marjorie LAURIE, 10 vols., Laurie (Brentano, New York) ; *Collected Novels and Stories*, transl. by Ernest BOYD, Storm JAMESON, Mrs. John GALSWORTHY, and others, 14 vols., Knopf, London and New York ; another transl., complete, with introds. by Edmund GOSSE and Arthur SYMONS, 10 vols., Bigelow Brown, New York, 1909. There are also *Complete Novels*, 1 vol., and *Complete Short Stories*, 1 vol., Black, New York ; *Eighty-eight Short Stories*, Knopf, 1930.]

MAURIAC, François [French ; *b.* 1885]. *Destinies* (Destins, 1926). 1929

Mauriac is the novelist of Bordeaux and the wine-growing regions of the Landes. Here his theme appears to be the incalculable effect of character in thwarting human effort to control our destinies. A dour old wine-grower has pinched and slaved and added acre to acre ; and now at death's door he sees the last of his family, his two grandsons, one, a charming ne'er-do-well, killed in a motor-escapade, the other entering the priesthood and renouncing his rights of inheritance. So the one object for which he had toiled vanishes in smoke. [Transl. by Eric SUTTON, Secker ; Covici, New York.]

MAUROIS, André [French; *b.* 1885]. *The Silence of Colonel Bramble* (Les silences du colonel Bramble, 1918). 1919

Depicts the mess-room life of the officers in a Highland regiment at Poperinghe and elsewhere on the western front. The doctor, the sportsmanlike *padre*, the French interpreter who drops into poetry, and, above all, the good old colonel, are pleasantly drawn. [Transl. by Jules CASTIER and Ronald BOSWELL, Lane; transl. by Thurfrida WAKE, Appleton, New York, 1930.]

—— *Ariel: a Shelley romance* (1923). 1924

An imaginative study of the poet's life and career, to his death in 1822, which deals pretty arbitrarily with some of the problems still outstanding, in relation to Harriet and Mary. [Transl. by Ella D'ARCY, Lane; Appleton, New York.]

—— *Bernard Quesnay* (1926). 1927

A thoughtful study of post-war attitudes to life. A young lieutenant returns in 1919 to take his place in the paternal cloth-mill, in Eure-et-Loir, and after withdrawing from a liaison and making other renunciations, settles down to the humdrum but worthy lot of a captain of industry. The technical and commercial aspects of the story are capitally done. [Transl. by Brian W. DOWNS, Cape; Appleton, New York.]

—— *Mape: the world of illusions* (Meïpe: ou la délivrance, 1926). 1926

The title is that of a dream-country where a girl finds deliverance from the day's ennuis: only there, it is hinted, are any of us really happy. This is the text for three stories. Two are pretty little novels made out of well-known incidents: how Goethe created Werther, and so healed the wounds of his first love-affairs; how the Siddons sisters loved the painter Lawrence, and how their deaths inspired their mother's greatest moment in tragedy. The other is an ironic study of a man shaping his conduct on patterns from Balzac and Stendhal. [Transl. by Eric SUTTON, Lane; Appleton, New York.]

—— *Whatever Gods may be* (Climats, 1928). 1929

The first part, a man's confession to his second wife, is a poignant study of jealousy. He had married a frail, but exquisite and enchanting girl, whose portrait is the most beautiful thing in the book. In the second part, her successor tells the story of her own marriage, in which the jealousy is now on the woman's side. [Transl. by Joseph COLLINS, Cassell.]

—— *Voyage to the Land of the Articoles* (Voyage aux pays des Articoles, 1928). 1929

In this satirical frolic, two voyagers in the Pacific make a landfall on an island, private property colonized by Articoles, mad literati who have no use for real life except as "copy," and who spend their lives analysing and recording their inner experiences, while the mob of Beos, or Beotians, attend to their material wants. [Transl. by David GARNETT, Cape; Appleton, New York.]

MAXWELL, Sir Herbert Eustace [Scottish; *b.* 1845]. *A Duke of Britain.* 1895

A romance of Novantia, or ancient Galloway, in the fourth century, a learned work by an antiquarian and historian. [Blackwood: o.p.]

—— *The Chevalier of the Splendid Crest.* 1900

England and Scotland at the time of the Scottish war of independence (1314). Full of archæological learning; for example, there are plans of the battle-ground of Bannockburn and of the city of Winchester, and much detail about domestic and outdoor life, while the earlier portion is written in a kind of Middle English. [Blackwood: o.p.]

MAXWELL, William Babington [son of Mrs. John Maxwell (Miss Braddon); *b.* 1876]. *The Ragged Messenger.* 1904

—— *Vivien.* 1905
—— *The Guarded Flame.* 1906
—— *Hill Rise.* 1908
—— *Seymour Charlton.* 1909
—— *The Rest Cure.* 1910

On the whole, these may be summed up as realistic studies of modern life in familiar phases, with threads of romance woven in. The writer's favourite problem is the aftermath of marriage. In *The Guarded Flame*, a great philosopher neglects his young wife, who falls in love with his secretary. In *The Rest Cure*—these are perhaps the two best of the lot—the situation is parallel, a man whose mind has been concentrated on his business affairs learns, when he has broken down, of his wife's unfaithfulness. In both novels the awakening comes about in the most tragic circumstances, and the writer spares no jot of bodily or mental anguish to intensify the horror. (1), Butterworth; (2) and (3), Methuen; Butterworth; (1), (2), and (3), Dodd & Mead, New York; (4), Methuen: o.p.; Cupples, New York: o.p.; (5), Hutchinson: o.p.; (6), Methuen: o.p.; (5) and (6), Appleton, New York: o.p.]

—— *Mrs. Thompson.* 1911

Two unhappy marriages—Mrs. Thompson's, a woman of exceptional organizing power, who has built up a successful business, and falls weakly in love at forty-five, and that of her daughter. [Butterworth; Nash; Dodd & Mead, New York.]

—— *The Devil's Garden.* 1913

The finest part of this otherwise melodramatic novel is the last third, in which the conscience of a man who has committed an undetected murder—an execution, as he regards it—is aroused, and he presently finds moral and religious salvation in sacrificing his own life. [Butterworth; Dodd & Mead, New York.]

—— *The Mirror and the Lamp.* 1918

A thoughtful piece of work built round a rather trite spiritual theme. The best are the minor characters, the Rev. Mr. Walsden and his wife, the sergeant, and Mrs. Churchill; those in the forefront are vague and less alive, in comparison. [Cassell; Butterworth; Dodd & Mead, New York.]

—— *The Great Interruption.* 1919

Twelve popular stories of the war period, of which the most cheerful and entertaining is *Christmas is Christmas*, and the most magic *A German in the Village*. [Hutchinson: o.p.]

MAXWELL, William Babington (*continued*). *A Remedy against Sin.* 1920
Definitely a plea for more liberal divorce laws. [Hutchinson : o.p.]

—— *Children of the Night.* 1925
Nine stories of crime and criminals in London. [Butterworth.]

—— *We Forget Because We Must : a story of decades and lustres.* 1928
Thirty years in the lives of a well-to-do middle-class couple living in a London suburb. Inevitably, as the years progress, the incidents of joy or sorrow in their lives pass away into insensibility. [Hutchinson ; Doubleday, New York.]

—— *Himself and Mr. Raikes.* 1929
A not altogether effective history of an ineffective young man, who is not sure of his own sincerity, or of his physical courage. [Hutchinson.]

—— *To What Green Altar ?* 1930
A young woman falls in love with a dipsomaniac, effects his cure, and attains an idyllic existence in Provence. [Hutchinson ; Doubleday, Doran, New York.]

MAXWELL, William Hamilton [Irish ; 1792–1850]. *Stories of Waterloo.* 1829
A farrago of Irish stories, sensational, with a dash of Hibernian character and local colouring. Not only Quatre Bras, Ligny, and Waterloo, but also battles in the Peninsula War, are among the incidents. [Ed. by E. A. Baker (Half-forgotten Books), Routledge (Dutton, New York) : o.p.]

MAYNE, Ethel Colburne [born in Ireland]. *Gold Lace : a story of girlhood.* 1913
Attacks the unchivalrous and overbearing behaviour of the English garrison of a town in southern Ireland ; the heroine revolts against the tradition of subservience to their unwanted attentions. [Chapman : o.p.]

—— *One of our Grandmothers.* 1916
A very sympathetic study of the dawning womanhood and the passionate struggle against undue dependance on father or husband, amid the drawbacks of her provincial surroundings, of an Irish girl in the 1860's, who has an imaginative temperament and musical genius. Killarney is attractively pictured. [Chapman : o.p.]

—— *Come In.* 1917
The faculty manifested in these fourteen short stories is a peculiar insight into the almost imperceptible jars and incongruities and subconscious antipathies of temperament. In *The Separate Room* a case of the Freudian wish is worked out to a painful climax. *Four Ballrooms* gives a series of lighter and even comic examples of natures meeting and leaving a more or less enduring impress on each other. *Lovells Meeting* sketches a fickle lover's mind awakened from its egotism by death. [Chapman : o.p.]

—— *Blindman.* 1919
The same quality of sensitive, subtle insight into the workings of human nature characterizes this set of stories. *The Letter on the Floor* and *The Man of the House* are studies of morbid perversions ; *The Hair of the Dog* pokes fun at the obtuse, hearty type of Englishman. [Chapman : o.p.]

—— *Inner Circle.* 1925
Campaign, The Picnic, and *The Shirt of Nessus* are among the best of this collection of stories. [Constable ; Harcourt, New York.]

MAYO, William Starbuck [1812–95]. *Kaloolah ; or, Journeyings to the Djébelkumri.* 1849
A wild romance of adventure on the deep and in Africa, wherein the author embodied much autobiography, mainly of his boyhood and schooldays in New York State. The adventures culminate in the marriage of the young American hero, Jonathan Romer, to a princess in Central Africa, exciting scenes of life in forest and desert, hairbreadth escapes, fights with slave-traders and natives, being the chief incidents. The contrast between the primitive society where he is expatriated and his native land affords the adventurer opportunity for some Gulliverian satire. [*Illus.* by Fredericks, Putnam, New York.]

MEAKIN, Nevill G. Myers [*b.* 1876]. *The Assassins : a romance of the Crusades.* 1902
A glittering, hot-blooded romance of the Third Crusade. Philip of France, Cœur de Lion, and Saladin appear in familiar rôles, but interest is focused on their enemies, and the hero is an Arab owning allegiance to the Sheik of the Mountain, head of the Assassins. [Heinemann : o.p. ; Holt, New York : o.p.]

MEINHOLD, Johann Wilhelm [German ; 1797–1851]. *Mary Schweidler, the Amber Witch* (Maria Schweidler die Bernsteinhexe, 1843). 1844
Meinhold was an opponent of the Tübingen school of Biblical criticism, and wrote this account of what he describes as " The most interesting trial for witchcraft ever known," as an authentic historical document, in order to show how easily such critics could be taken in. The plain realism, purporting to be the unvarnished statement of an eye-witness, and the frightful intensity of horror it conveys, rival Defoe's *Journal of the Plague* ; and it is not to be wondered at that Meinhold deceived his readers completely, and succeeded to some extent in discrediting the methods of the Tübingen critics. Pomerania (1628–9), in the torments of the Thirty Years' War, is the grim theatre in which Pastor Schweidler and his daughter go through their terrible ordeal. A gruesome atmosphere of superstition and diabolism pervades the book, and with this the characters, all firmly etched in, the spiteful old witch, the libidinous sheriff, the timid judge, and the pious but mercenary pastor, are well in keeping. But for the poetic justice of the end, one would take it for truth. [Transl. by Lady Duff GORDON, Nutt : o.p. ; Scribner, New York : o.p. ; (World's Classics) Oxford Press, 1929.]

—— *Sidonia the Sorceress ; the supposed Destroyer of the whole Reigning Ducal House of Pomerania* (1861). 1893
Sidonia (executed 1620) having failed in her scheme to marry the young Duke Ernest Louis von Wolgast, entered a convent, and subsequently by magic arts rendered the whole princely race childless, for which she was beheaded and afterwards burned. Meinhold says, " I do not here distinctly declare whether Sidonia be history or fiction." He introduces his supernatural views of Christianity, in the belief that the rationalists will be more likely to peruse them if presented in a work not avowedly philosophical. [Transl. by Lady WILDE (with *Mary Schweidler, the Amber Witch*), 2 vols., Reeves & Turner, 1894 : o.p.]

MELDRUM, David Storrar [Scottish ; *b.* 1865]. *The Story of Margrédel.* 1894

Realistic pictures of domestic life in the author's native place, the old Fifeshire seaport, Kirkcaldie, in the early nineteenth century. A Kailyard novel with a melodramatic plot about the fate of the Oliphants. [Blackwood ; Putnam, New York : o.p.]

MELVILLE, George James WHYTE [1821–78]. *Captain Digby Grand : an autobiography.* 1853

A novel after Lytton's style (cf. *The Caxtons*, etc.), with sporting scenes and characters grafted on. Whyte-Melville's speciality was the sporting novel, people with daring hunters of both sexes, social scenes and country-house life—everything, in short, connected with the hunting-field. [Ward & Lock : o.p. ; Longmans, New York.]

—— *Tilbury Nogo, an Unsuccessful Man.* 1854

Mr. Nogo, a wealthy sportsman, writes his own reminiscences in a chatty and desultory way, with many a regretful reflection thrown in. Runs with the hounds, after-dinner talks about dogs and horses, scenes of high play and cheating, desperate flirtations, are loosely combined into a story. Mr. Nogo would be a great hunter, but his prowess hardly equals his desires. [Ward & Lock : o.p. ; Longmans, New York : o.p.]

—— *The Interpreter.* 1858

A serial novel, changing its scenes from England to Turkey, Vienna, Hungary, and the Crimea. Naughty characters, e.g. an Hungarian princess employed by the Austrian Government to seduce her lover, a wicked guardsman, etc. ; but they are regarded through a rosy atmosphere that veils the unpleasantness. As to the events connected with the Crimean War, it may be mentioned that Melville served in the Turkish contingent. [Ward & Lock : o.p. ; Longmans, New York.]

—— *Holmby House.* 1860

A romance of 1644–9—Newbury, Naseby, the captivity and death of the king. Mary Cave, the high-souled heroine, is perhaps the author's best female character ; and Cromwell is introduced in an unprejudiced portrait. [Ward & Lock : o.p. ; Longmans, New York.]

—— *Market Harborough ; or, How Mr. Sawyer went to the Shires.* 1861

A sporting novel of Leicestershire ; published with a rollicking tale, *Inside the Bar ; or, Sketches at Soakington.* [Ward & Lock : o.p. ; Longmans, New York.]

—— *The Gladiators : a tale of Rome and Judaea.* 1863

An energetic story of Rome and the Holy Land (A.D. 69–70). The hero, a noble British slave, is loved by a beautiful patrician, who in turn is loved by the Tribune Placidus, a subtle compound of sensuality and ambition. Britons and Roman nobles fight in the arena ; then the scene is transferred to Jerusalem, the siege of which takes up the later chapters. The defeat and death of Vitellius afford lurid scenes of tumult and carnage, and the finale is dramatic. [(New Universal Lib.), Routledge ; (Everyman's Lib.), Dent (Dutton, New York) ; Longmans, New York.]

—— *The Queen's Maries.* 1864

The story of Mary Queen of Scots and her marriage with Darnley ; Holyrood, Stirling, etc. (1561–5) [Collins, London and New York ; Longmans, New York.]

—— *Cerise.* 1866

A melodramatic tale of Louis XIV's last days and the regency of Orleans (1715–20) ; love entanglements, Court intrigues, privateering, adventures in the West Indies, and dealings with the Jacobites. [Ward & Lock : o.p. ; Collins, New York.]

—— *Sarchedon : a tale of the Great Queen.* 1871

Egypt and Assyria in the times of Semiramis (2000 B.C.). The priests of Baal play a conspicuous part, and by a bold anachronism the author introduces events in Egypt just before the Exodus. [Ward & Lock : o.p. ; Longmans, New York.]

—— *Satanella : a story of Punchestown.* 1872

A racy racing story, showing the best side of military and sporting life—hearty good fellows are the typical characters. The fate of the heroine and her favourite mare (both called Satanella) is tragic. [Ward & Lock : o.p. ; Longmans, New York.]

—— *Katerfelto : a story of Exmoor.* 1875

A semi-historical novel of 1763, crowded with incident and picturesque character, gipsies, deer-hunters, and other inhabitants of the moor. Stag-hunting is described with the zest and knowledge of a keen sportsman. [Ward & Lock ; Longmans, New York : o.p.]

[*Works*, 24 vols., Thacker, (Lane, New York), 1898–1902 : o.p.]

MELVILLE, Herman [American ; 1819–91]. *Typee : a romance of the South Seas.* 1846

Not much adulterated with fiction. Melville depicts the natives of the Marquesas islands, an amiable race of cannibals, with truth and accuracy, and does not embroider much upon his own adventures when he was left there with Toby, his friend Greene (1842–3). His exposure of the evils caused by missionary interference with the primitive ways of the natives, and of the demoralization due to European vices imported by traders, raised such an outcry that these important passages were deleted from all editions until the modern collected edition of his works (1922).

—— *Omoo* [sequel]. 1847

Melville thought that Toby (Richard Tobias Greene) had deserted him ; but on the publication of *Typee* he heard all about his adventures after leaving the Marquesas, and used this material for *Omoo*. [(1) and (2), Cape ; (New Universal Lib.), Routledge ; (Everyman's Lib.), Dent (Dutton, New York) ; (World's Classics) Oxford Press (unexpurgated version) ; Dodd & Mead, New York ; Page, Boston.]

—— *Mardi and a Voyage Thither.* 1849

A "Romance of Polynesian adventure" containing some of Melville's best chapters of the natural history of the sea, including the mariner and the multitudinous fauna of the Pacific. After weeks in the solitudes of the ocean, the wanderers, one of whom, the Skyeman Jarl, is a character, reach Mardi, the wondrous archipelago, a Gulliverian nowhere half evolved from Maori folk-lore and half a caricature of Europe. [Cape ; Boni, New York ; Page, Boston.]

MELVILLE, Herman (*continued*). *Redburn: his first voyage.* 1849

In the form of autobiographical fiction, Melville here relates how he entered the merchant service (1837) and sailed as a ship's boy to England and home again. It is a grim, disillusioned, and even a disgruntled picture of life on shipboard and in the horrible streets of Liverpool. Mr. Masefield had eulogised this pioneer novel of the life of a sailorman, and paid it the compliment of borrowing from it in *Dauber*. [Cape; Constable (R. R. Smith, New York); Boni, New York.]

—— *White Jacket; or, The World in a Man-of-War.* 1850

An unvarnished picture of life on a United States frigate, based on Melville's own experiences when he served as a common sailor. The kindly and humorous Englishman Jack Chase indemnifies the reader for the oppressive series of hardships and tyrannical discipline. [Cape; (World's Classics) Oxford Press, 1924; Page, Boston.]

—— *Moby-Dick; or, The Whale.* 1851

A unique book, fused and shot incandescent from the furnace of a fierce and gloomy imagination, brooding on the persecuted lot of humanity, and feeding itself on the transcendental dreams and the cosmic imagery of Sir Thomas Browne and De Quincey and the fulminations of Carlyle. Incorporates episodes of Melville's whaling voyages on the *Acushnet,* the scientific accuracy of which has been praised by the experts. In structure, ill-proportioned and clumsy, the greatness being in the climaxes; it is, perhaps, the most powerful rendering in prose literature of the eternal conflict of man and fate. Captain Ahab, leader of this strange whale-hunt from ocean to ocean, is a Satanic hero (in the sense of Blake's interpretation of Milton) and at the same time a symbol of mankind confronting and defying the evil energies of the universe. A book that seemed insane to the world of 1851, was rediscovered twenty years ago, and has influenced Conrad and many other moderns. [Cape; (Everyman's Lib.) Dent (Dutton, New York); (World's Classics), Oxford Press; Dodd & Mead, New York; Page, Boston; Boni, New York; Doubleday, New York (Kennerley, London).]

—— *Pierre; or, The Ambiguities.* 1852

This has very reasonably been regarded as Melville's *Hamlet,* and was indeed written at a time when he was absorbed in Shakespeare. It is a strange, incoherent novel, the work of a great imagination in a state of disillusionment and furious revolt. A young man of lofty and passionate ideals, to right the wrong done by his own father in leaving an illegitimate child to neglect and want, strives and fails in a course of superhuman action, strives in short to act " angelically," and the end is tragedy. The enigma of the book has been interpreted very satisfactorily by Mr. Grant Watson (*New England Quarterly*, April 1930). [Constable, 1923: o.p.; Dutton, New York, 1929; Knopf, New York and London, 1930.]

—— *Israel Potter: his fifty years of exile.* 1855

From the Life of Potter published in 1824, Melville refashioned this congenial record of human effort and endurance ending in hopeless misery. Potter fought at Bunker Hill (1775), served as messenger from Horne Tooke and other sympathizers to Dr. Franklin at Paris, fought under Paul Jones—the duel of the *Bon Homme Richard* and the *Serapis* is a tremendous battlepiece—but fell again into English hands and lived in toil and penury in London for forty-five years—" a long life still rolling in early mishap." [Cape; Boni, New York, 1924; Page, Boston.]

—— *Piazza Tales.* 1856

Six magazine stories, the best of which are *Benito Cereno* and *The Encantadas.* The former, a gruesome story of piracy on the high seas, is a curious anticipation of the impressionist method developed later on by Conrad—the incidents being set down as they crowd upon the attention of the surprised observer and their significance gradually revealing itself, as happens in actuality. The other, the scene of which is the Galapagos, not less poetically evokes the loneliness and the savage beauty of Oceania and the intrinsic majesty of human suffering. [Constable (R. R. Smith, New York), 1929; the two stories named, with *Billy Budd* and *Bartleby the Scrivener*, in *Shorter Novels*, Boni, New York, 1928; *Benito Cereno, illus.,* ltd. ed., Nonesuch Press (Random House, New York), 1927.]

—— *The Confidence-Man: His Masquerade.* 1857

A long and laboured novel that deservedly fell flat, satirizing the objectionable people collected on a passenger boat from St. Louis to New Orleans. [o.p.]

—— *Billy Budd.* 1928

His last book, published forty years after his death. A tragic story, remarkable for the sober exaltation of the ultimate scene, in which Billy, who has without premeditation slain a villainous petty-officer, accepts the execution of his captain's sentence with the cheerful stoicism of innocence and with a blessing on his judge. [*v. Piazza Tales, supra.*]

[*Novels*, 7 vols., Cape; Nickerson, Boston; *Works* (sets only), 16 vols., Constable, 1922–4, (vols. 1–12 o.p.).]

MENDÈS, Catulle (Abraham) [French; 1841–1924]. *Number* 56 (Rue des Filles-Dieu, 56; ou l'héautonparatéroumène, **1895**). 1929

The title-piece is a very acute study of amnesia. A respected citizen commits a crime when mad with drink and a violent quarrel, and knows nothing about it. The story, told with admirable Gallic humour, is how he unconsciously runs the criminal, himself, to earth. The others, shorter pieces, are essays in the art of making the flesh creep. [Transl. by Phyllis MÉGROZ, Laurie.]

MENDOZA, Diego Hurtado de [Spanish; 1503–75]. [?] *Lazarillo de Tormes: the pleasant history of Lazarillo de Tormes* (La Vida de Lazarillo de Tormes, y de sus fortunas y adversidades, 1554). 1576

Attributed to the poet Diego Hurtado de Mendoza, though without sufficient proof. Original model of that thoroughly Spanish production, the *novela picaresca*, or rogue-story. Lazaro, autobiographer and hero, son of a miller and a trull, enters the service of all kinds of people, and gets on by flattery and cunning, until he ends as town crier of Toledo. This plan enables the author to describe many aspects of Spanish life—low life especially—with accuracy and pointed wit; and a motley assortment of characters, the rogue's successive masters, the blind beggar, the skinflint priest, the alguazil, the starving hidalgo, etc. The character-portrait of the vendor of indulgences led to the banning of the book by the Inquisition;

MENDOZA, Diego Hurtado de *(continued).*

in spite of which it was speedily translated into French, German, Italian, and English. There was an English transl. by David ROWLAND in 1576, and Martin Hume mentions a 1568 version, *The Marvelus Dedes and Lyf of Lazaro de Tormes.* A sharp, cynical wit accentuates the satire. [Transl. (with Alemán's *Guzman*) by BRADY, 2 vols., Nimmo, 1882 : o.p. ; *The Life of Lazarillo de Tormes*, transl. by Sir Clements MARKHAM, Black, 1908 : o.p., is inaccurate as a translation and inadequate on the editorial side ; transl. by Louis How, Kennerley, New York, 1917 : o.p. ; transl. by Mariano Joaquin LORENTE, Luce, Boston, 1924 ; together with the continuation by Juan de LUNA, (Rogues Bookshelf), Greenburg, New York, 1926.]

MENZIES, John [Scottish]. *Our Town, and Some of its People.* 1894

Sketches of Fife folk ; on the face of it, a bundle of reminiscences, with real incidents and real people disguised in a thin dress of fiction. The old industry of the place was weaving, and the survivors of the craft tell a brave tale about the happy times before railways took away the population to larger towns. Glimpses of home life, humorous squabbles, sketches of old cranks and gossips. [Unwin : o.p.]

MEREDITH, George [1828–1909]. *The Shaving of Shagpat : an Arabian entertainment.* 1855

A burlesque of the Oriental story mingling humorous extravaganza with sheer poetry, and conveying a Meredithian lesson in practical ethics. Imagination often takes wing in flights of irregular verse, and the wisdom expresses itself in rhymed aphorisms with an Oriental ring, though it may be doubted whether there is not at least as much Celtic fantasy, of the *Mabinogion* type, learned from Meredith's father-in-law, the author of *The Misfortunes of Elphin.* George Eliot reviewed the book, and compared its exuberant imagery to that of the *Arabian Nights.*

—— *The Ordeal of Richard Feverel.* 1859

Meredith's novels combine the scientific analysis and philosophical criticism which were carried to such a pitch by George Eliot with the free imagination and passionate intensity brought into English fiction by the Brontës. They show in action the philosophy of human life, the development of personality with a view to the continuous evolution of the race, that is formulated in his poems. His novels must, further, be studied in the light of his great *Essay on Comedy*, for the Comic Spirit hovers over even the most poetic and the most profoundly tragic situations. *Richard Feverel* and its immediate successor are the best introduction to Meredith, being easy to read, alive with human interest, and rich in his finest qualities, with few of the mannerisms and obscurities that baffle readers of his later works. An egoistic father brings up his son on an abstract system of education, which breaks down when Richard arrives at the threshold of manhood and falls in love. Here is the ordeal. The comedy of life ends in tragedy the most heart-rending. The characters are many and various : the Meredithian hero Richard, the innocent and noble Lucy, the cynic Adrian whose witticisms express one phase of the satire, the philosophic father and the aphorisms of the *Pilgrim's Scrip* which express another side, chivalrous Austin Wentworth, the bewitching *demi-mondaine* Mrs. Mount, and Meredith's finest low-comedy figure, the lodging-house keeper, Mrs. Berry. Adrian Harley was suggested by the character of Maurice FitzGerald, Edward's nephew. The lyricism of the love chapters reaches levels hardly attained since *Romeo and Juliet.*

—— *Evan Harrington.* 1861

The son of a fashionable tailor, brought up in aristocratic tastes and associations, suddenly finds himself saddled with the responsibility of his father's debts. On one side is duty, on the other his love for a well-born maiden. How Evan comes through the ordeal, happily, yet without abjuring his manhood, is the main business of a sustained comedy in which the subtle conflict of class prejudice is developed with infinite humour. Evan and Rose Jocelyn, his father the Great Mel and his austere mother, the two Cogglesbys, and the fascinating and unscrupulous Countess de Saldar, are each in their way thoroughly Meredithian creations. But the book is largely autobiographical, and Meredith's grandparents and aunts can be recognized in Mr. and Mrs. Mel and the countess.

—— *Sandra Belloni.* 1864
—— *Vittoria* [sequel]. 1866

Two novels comprising the life-story of a noble Italian, a woman of genius. The former deals with the comedy of English society, the domestic life of a parvenu family, and Sandra's unprosperous love for a young man who is Mr. Meredith's type of the sentimentalist, a favourite object of his satire. The book is indeed largely a diagnosis of sentimentalism, which, beside the pseudo-hero, is represented by a set of finely graduated persons, such as the Miss Poles, who typify the Fine Shades and the Nice Feelings, Sir Purcell Barrett, who dies for an impossible ideal, and the nobler sentimentalists, Merthyr Powys and Georgiana Ford. Over against these are the real people : Sandra, who is simplicity, passion, and genius incarnate, the irascible impresario, Pericles, vulgar Mr. Pole, and the still more vulgar and impossible Mrs. Chump who remind one of Dickens. The public career of Sandra, now the great singer Vittoria, transports us to Italy ; and soon we are immersed in the riots and battles of the abortive insurrection of 1848. The whole history of the rising, from the preliminary conspiracies to the final collapse, is told with an epical enthusiasm for liberty, but with impartial consideration for the views and motives of both sides. Some thirty important characters appear, types of the Italian leaders and agitators, Austrian officers and English sympathizers, and the tragedy of sentimentalism is carried to its bitter close in the after life of Wilfrid Pole.

—— *Rhoda Fleming.* 1865

A simple, intensely dramatic story of middle-class people : the heroine is the daughter of a yeoman, the hero a farmer. In the rustic scenes, farmers and their women-folk, pot-house company and overfed labourers, furnish plenty of low comedy. But the main action is serious, culminating in scenes of heartfelt tragedy, even though the dramatic stress is alleviated at the end. Rhoda, a simple, heroic nature, devotes her all to saving her sister, betrayed and deserted by a false lover, who repents, but too late. The characters are multifarious, ranging from Father Gammon, the stolid, stupid hind, and old Anthony Hackbut, haunted by the money-demon, to the vivacious Anglo-Indian widow Mrs. Lovel, a too enigmatic mixture of evil and good.

—— *The Adventures of Harry Richmond.* 1871

A typical example of Meredith's poetic comedy : incidents and characters, though in nature and grouping often wildly romantic, are justified by the psychology. A kaleidoscopic story—changing from country

MEREDITH, George (*continued*).

to town, from England to Germany—the personages equally multifarious—obstinate Squire Beltham, the fascinating and erratic pretender Richmond Roy, Harry's princess love Ottilia, a goddess of earth, sober and womanly English Janet, Kiomi the gipsy maiden, an English Carmen, and many another character quickened with intense individuality. Peculiarly rich in imaginative descriptions of country and town, of sea and forest, both in England and on the Continent. All is seen through the eyes and imagination of Harry, the hero whose personality is being developed through trial and defeat. But as in *Richard Feverel*, the figure of the father is by no means of minor dramatic importance.

—— *Beauchamp's Career.* 1876

Beauchamp, the Radical, studied from Captain (afterwards Admiral) Maxse, a dear friend of Meredith, is a chivalrous and impetuous champion of the oppressed ; and his history gives a broad view of the politics of mid-century England in the light of Carlyle's teaching. Entwined with the comedy of politics is the comedy of love set forth in the emotional history of Beauchamp, who is successively enamoured of three women, French Renée, the English gentlewoman Cecilia, and the sage and loyal Jenny. Beside these three studies of feminine character, the still more subtle one of Rosamund Culling holds a prominent place among the numerous figures. Some of these were drawn from his friends, and the election was an historical event. The hero's fate, emblematic of his " rocket-mind," is untimely and tragic. The descriptive passages are magnificent, moments of exalted feeling fused indissolubly with some vision of beauty.

—— *The Egoist : a comedy in narrative.* 1879

Contains little of the romance or the poetry of *Richard Feverel*, *Harry Richmond*, and *Beauchamp's Career* ; it is the finest example of Meredith's realism and analytical power. A psychological comedy, mercilessly laying bare the soul of a spoiled child of fortune, outwardly a pattern of conventional virtue, inwardly a thrall to selfishness ; tragical in its exposure of the secret egoism that is in all men. In many ways this novel typifies the author's idiosyncrasies, the dramatic structure of his plots, his satire—of John Bull, of the masculine regime and the sultanic treatment of women—the wit and subtlety of his dialogue, and the profoundly philosophical purpose of his art. Clara Middleton, whose engagement to the hero and its rupture are the pith of the story, is a charming personification of his refined ideas of women ; and the genial epicure, her father, the boy Crossjay, and Vernon Whitford (said to be a sketch of Leslie Stephen) are all intensely Meredithian creations. The novel is very long, the time of the action very brief, each act in the drama being developed with huge elaboration.

—— *The Tragic Comedians : a study in a well-known story.* 1880

An episode of actual history, interpreted imaginatively and cast into a form like Greek tragedy with dialogue and chorus, but not departing in any vital point from fact—the fatal love story of Ferdinand Lassalle (1825–64). Alvan and Clotilde are a pair of characteristic figures, the former a powerful and predominant nature, whose egoistic conception of love and woman betrays him to his death.

—— *Diana of the Crossways.* 1885

The story of a woman of genius, suggested in its main lines by the career of the Hon. Caroline Norton, though the famous episode of the selling of the Cabinet secret is not authentic. The dialogue, more particularly Diana's talk, is witty and coruscating even for Meredith, and the prologue is a choice specimen of the hard reading he offers. The heroine's love troubles from the disaster of her first marriage to her congenial and happy union with the strong and sensitive Redworth, her literary career, and the vicissitudes of her legal troubles, make a chequered story. The novel was written as a bid for popularity ; but the aphoristic, allusive, and cryptic first chapter is a strange obstacle.

—— *One of our Conquerors.* 1891

Meredith's more oracular and elusive style of thought and writing here takes its full fling. The story of a millionaire of vast ideas and unconquerable energy, who began his career by marrying a rich old widow. From her he ran away with her young companion. Everything prospers with him, though he can never get into society. Their daughter, kept in ignorance, he seeks to marry to an embryo earl. His schemes end in catastrophe, but the daughter, a picture of what woman will be, marries where she has given her heart. Full of thought, humour, and criticism of our present conditions of life.

—— *Lord Ormont and his Aminta.* 1894

Even more drastic in its handling of the marriage question, and, unlike the last novel, revolutionary. The old lord, a man who has not " rounded Seraglio Point," drives his wife into the arms of her lover, the loyal and practical Weyburn. Hero and heroine strive against a passion that infringes human, but not, the author pleads, divine law. The old story of Lord Peterborough and Anastasia Robinson is said to have suggested the plot.

—— *The Tale of Chloe ; and other stories.* 1895

Chloe is a brief, tense drama ending in a great act of self-immolation ; scene, Bath in the eighteenth century, in the brilliant world of beaux and fine ladies caustically depicted in Smollett's *Humphry Clinker*. *Farina*, written about the same period as *Shagpat*, is a burlesque romance in the German fashion, embodying a legend of Cologne in the twelfth century. Knights and robber-barons, burghers and maidens, saints, fairies, and devils make a strange medley of characters. *General Ogle and Lady Camper* is a little social comedy, quite in his own vein ; and *The House on the Beach*, a humorous tale of more homely people, was written under the influence of Dickens.

—— *The Amazing Marriage.* 1895

Like *One of our Conquerors*, an unorthodox treatment of a marriage problem, and quite as difficult to read. Carinthia, " the Whitechapel Countess," one of the noblest of his tragic figures, is married precipitately and then neglected by a cynical young earl, whose remorse and unavailing efforts to win her back make a sardonic comedy. Woodseer is said to be a sketch of R. L. Stevenson ; he is the customary sayer of epigrams. The book is rich in word-landscapes of Alpine scenery, etc.

—— *Celt and Saxon.* 1910

Meredith's posthumous novel, unfinished, though it runs to three hundred pages. Contrasts John Bull and the Celtic temperament. His Irish mouthpieces give scope for Meredith's characteristic poetry. In

MEREDITH, George (*continued.*)
fact, the novel is thoroughly characteristic of his manner, though the later course of the story is unfortunately an insoluble problem.
[*Novels*, 16 vols., Constable; Scribner, New York.]

MEREZHKOVSKY, Dmitry [Russian; *b.* 1866]. *The Death of the Gods* (1896).   1901
First part of a huge trilogy, *Christ and Anti-Christ*, designed to interpret " the everlasting contest between the idea of a God-Man and the idea of a Man-God," in other words, Christian and pagan ideals. With an imagination steeped in ancient history and archæology, the novelist depicts the struggle between light and darkness in the soul of the Emperor Julian, and throughout all the peoples of his dominions (337–63). The result is a succession of gorgeous tableaux representing dissolute city life, wars in Germany and Persia, controversies and squabbling among pagan philosophers and Christian prelates. [Transl. by Herbert TRENCH, Constable; Putnam, New York.]

—— *The Forerunner* (1901).   1902
Called in Russian *The Resurrection of the Gods*, because Merezhkovsky sees in the Renaissance a new fusion of pagan and Christian ideals. A eulogy of individualism in the character and career of that many-sided genius, Leonardo da Vinci, and an elaborate study of the artistic temperament. Raphael, Michelangelo, Savonarola are disparaged, and other foils to the grandeur of Leonardo are such historical characters as Pope Alexander VI, Cesare Borgia, Charles VIII, Machiavelli. Period 1494–1519. [Transl. by H. TRENCH, Constable; *sub tit. The Romance of Leonardo da Vinci*, 2 vols., Putnam, New York; transl. by B. G. GUERNEY, Modern Lib., New York, 1928.]

—— *Peter and Alexis* (1905).   1905
Conclusion of the trilogy. Peter the Great and his imbecile son Alexis are but the protagonists in a vast and crowded drama representing the whole life of Russia at that epoch (1715–18). [Constable: o.p.; Putnam, New York.]

—— *December the Fourteenth* (1922).   1925
The story of the revolutionary outbreak against Nicholas I, and the relentless treatment meted out by the Tsar to those implicated. [Transl. by Natalie DUDDINGTON, Cape; International Pub. Co., New York.]

—— *The Birth of the Gods* (Rozhdenie Bogov, 1924).   1926
—— *Akhnaton, King of Egypt* (1924) [sequel].   1927
Two connected sets of stories, first of Crete, then of Egypt. In the first group, the life of Minoan Crete is reconstructed. Tutankhamon, son-in-law and envoy of the Egyptian king, appears, and Dio, the Cretan virgin, priestess of the sacred bull, is introduced. She comes to recognize that such religion is evil, and kills the bull. In the following book, Dio is associated with King Akhnaton and his mystical ideas of reforming the world and establishing universal peace. [(1) and (2), transl. by Natalie DUDDINGTON, Dent; Dutton, New York.]

MERIMÉE, Prosper [French; 1803–70]. *Chronicle of the Reign of Charles IX* (Cronique du règne de Charles IX, 1829).   1889
Fictitious memoirs of the conflict between Catholics and Huguenots under Charles IX and of the eve of St. Bartholomew (1550–74), in which Merimée draws on his historical and antiquarian knowledge, presenting an animated picture of the epoch. The Huguenot hero is an engaging figure, typical of his age; the characters, nearly all fictitious, are drawn with force and accuracy. This is Merimée's one long novel. [Transl. by Geo. SAINTSBURY, 2 vols., Nimmo: o.p.; transl. by Theodore BOLTON, *sub tit. Diane de Turgis : a chronicle, etc.*, Arnold Co., Arnold, U.S.A.]

—— *The Abbé Aubain; and, Mosaics* (Mosaïques, contes et nouvelles, 1833).   1903
A selection comprising some of Merimée's choicest work in his own peculiar field, the short story, e.g. *The Etruscan Vase, Lokis, Venus of Ille, The Blue Chamber, Djoumane, Mateo Falcone, Tamango*, and *How we Stormed the Fort*, polished gems of objective imagination, psychical fancy, sardonic comedy, and a realism that is sufficient unto itself. No writer has surpassed Merimée in this particular kind of art. [Transl. by Emily Mary WALTER, with introd. by Arthur SYMONS, De La More Press; also *Golden Tales*, Dodd & Mead, New York, 1929.]

—— *Colomba : a Corsican story* (1830).   1853
A little drama of Corsican life, into which is precipitated the sense of beauty and strangeness that seems to belong to this land, where assassination is still a recognized means of settling differences. Colomba is a young Corsican in whom the vendetta spirit is incarnate, while her brother, who ought to avenge his father's death, is Parisianized and emancipated from ancestral barbarism. The touches of local colour, the outlined under-characters, and the romantic scenery combine into a perfect artistic whole. [Transl. by A. R. SCOBLE, Bentley: o.p.; by Lady M. LLOYD, see *Carmen, infra*; by SHERMAN, Crowell, New York: o.p.]

—— *Carmen* (1847).   1887
The tale so well known from Bizet's opera, which is founded on it. Very brief; the story of a Spanish gipsy, in whose nature are concentrated the primitive instincts of the savage, chief among them a passion for freedom. The tale is pure romance, the method calmly realistic, and it is a masterpiece of pure objective art. The scenery and costumes of Spain add to its picturesque qualities. [Transl. by E. H. GARRETT, Dent, 1896: o.p.; Little & Brown, Boston: o.p.; *Colomba* and *Carmen*, transl. by Lady M. LLOYD (Masterpieces of French romance), Heinemann; another transl., Putnam, New York; Altemus, Philadelphia.]

MERRICK, Leonard [*b.* 1864]. *The Man Who Was Good.*   1892
—— *Cynthia.*   1896
—— *The Worldlings.*   1900
—— *When Love Flies out o' the Window.*   1902
—— *Conrad in Quest of his Youth.*   1903
—— *Whispers about Women.*   1906

MERRICK, Leonard (*continued*). *The House of Lynch.*   1907
Well-constructed novels describing the surface of modern life with considerable realism, but no pretence at deep analysis. The plots may be built upon a rather fantastic basis, as, for example, that of the last story, where the daughter of one of the world's richest men proposes to and marries a struggling artist, and in the upshot gives her dead father's hundred million dollars to retrieve the wrongs which he committed in gaining the pile. But if the idea is ultra-romantic, Mr. Merrick's narrative method is sober, circumstantial, and plausible, and his character-drawing equally so. [(1), (2), (3), (4), (6), (7), Hodder ; Dutton, New York ; (5), Nash : o.p.]

—— *The Man Who Understood Women ; and other stories.*   1908

—— *All the World Wondered.*   1911
Collections of workmanlike stories of bohemian life in Paris and of English life, the French ones sparkling and vivid in catching the air of Montmartre. *At the Sign of the Bleeding Heart*, in the second book, is a good example of the humorous sort. [(1), Hodder ; Dutton, New York ; (2) Methuen : o.p.]

—— *The Position of Peggy Harper.*   1911
An ironical novel, put together with Mr. Merrick's expert craftsmanship, neatly satirizing a world that gives success to the third-rate and despises real talent, a vulgar actress and a playwright too good for his public being the cases in point. [Hodder ; Dutton, New York.]

—— *While Paris Laughed.*   1918

—— *A Chair on the Boulevard.*   1920
More stories of Tricotrin and bohemian life in Paris. [(1) and (2), Hodder ; Dutton, New York.]

—— *To Tell You the Truth.*   1922
Stories of the magazine type about Paris, with pathos and sentiment in *Picq Plays the Hero*, and comedy in *Aribaud's Two Wives* and *That Villain Her Father*. [Hodder ; Dutton, New York.]

—— *The Little Dog Laughed.*   1930
Satires, extravaganzas, and miscellaneous sketches. The Parisian trio, Tricotrin, Pitou, and Lajeunie reappear amusingly, with others hardly less diverting. Other stories ring the changes on mirth and gravity, love and tears. [Hodder ; Dutton, New York ; Musson, Toronto.]

" MERRIMAN, Henry Seton " [Hugh Stowell Scott ; 1862–1903]. *With Edged Tools.*   1894
The pair of heroes, both in love with the same girl, go to Africa, the west coast and the interior, meet with extraordinary adventures and win huge fortunes. Epigrams and smart sayings enliven the narrative. [Murray ; Harper, New York : o.p.]

—— *The Sowers.*   1896
A workmanlike novel, utilizing Russian conditions—the gulf between the aristocracy and the people, the exactions of foreign agents, and the plots of reformers—for sensational effect. [Murray ; Harper, New York.]

—— *In Kedar's Tents.*   1897
Adventures of an Irishman in the Spanish service fighting the Carlists, and the inner history of a desperate plot to kill the Queen-Regent (1838–9). Sketches of typical Spaniards, of manners and customs, and of scenery. [Murray ; Nash ; Dodd & Mead, New York : o.p.]

—— *Roden's Corner.*   1898
The history of a huge commercial plot, with descriptions of industrial life ; coloured by indignation against trusts and monopolies and modern forms of organized charity. [Murray ; Harper, New York : o.p.]

—— *The Isle of Unrest.*   1899
A complicated romance of Corsica in 1868–70. An old-established family feud, an heiress's love for a young officer called out by the German war, and the intrigues of a French commandant to possess himself of gold existing on the family estates, furnish excitement. [Murray ; Dodd & Mead, New York : o.p.]

—— *The Velvet Glove.*   1901
Spain under Marshal Prim, in the turmoil of Carlist agitation (1870–1). Opens at Saragossa with the assassination of a wealthy nobleman. The plots and counterplots to get his fortune into Jesuit hands for the service of Don Carlos, and on the other side to secure it for his daughter, make exciting reading. [Murray ; Dodd & Mead, New York : o.p.]

—— *The Vultures.*   1902
History of a plot of Russian Nihilists and insurgent Poles at Warsaw. The Vultures are secret agents of foreign governments, of whom three, the strong Englishman Cartoner, the witty and volatile Frenchman Deulin, and the humorous American Mangles, with his sister Joolz, the platform woman, are striking and amusing characters. Opens with an account of Alexander II's assassination in 1881. [Murray ; Harper, New York.]

—— *Barlasch of the Guard.*   1903
Side-scenes of Napoleon's Russian campaign (1812)—the spy system that made Europe a network of intrigue ; the plots of *émigrés* and Prussian nationalists ; adventures of private soldiers, like Barlasch, the devoted, war-worn soldier of the Guard. Describes the gallant defence of Dantzig by Rapp. [Murray ; McClure, New York : o.p.]

—— *The Last Hope.*   1904
Story of a mythical son of the murdered Dauphin (Louis XVII) who is supposed to have escaped from the Temple. The young man, mate of a small vessel, is sought out in his humble home in a Suffolk fishing village, and made the pivot of a Royalist plot. The one striking character is a certain Anglo-Parisian banker. Scenes, England and France in 1849–51. [Murray.]

—— *Tomaso's Fortune ; and other stories.*   1904
Nineteen magazine stories. *Tomaso's Fortune* is a Balearic idyll ; *The Mule* takes us under Spanish sierras ; *Stranded* presents a manly figure of an Atlantic captain who makes the one mistake of his life and wrecks his boat ; *The Wandering Jew* is a terror-striking glimpse of cholera in a remote station in India. [Murray.]

"MERRY, Andrew" [Mrs. Mildred H. G. Darby, *née* Gordon-Dill; Irish; *b.* 1869]. *The Green Country.* 1902
—— *Paddy Risky; or, Irish Realities of To-day.* 1903
Two collections of short stories about Ireland and Irish peasantry, from the point of view of the landlord, but fair and sympathetic. [(1) and (2), De La More Press: o.p.]
—— *The Hunger: being realities of the famine years in Ireland,* 1845–8. 1910
Only the form is fiction; the facts, indeed, were so horrible they had to be toned down in the telling. The author got her evidence from oral statements and private documents, as well as the sources open to all. [Melrose: o.p.]

MERWIN, Samuel [American; *b.* 1874]. *The Road to Frontenac.* 1901
The French occupation of Canada (1687). [Doubleday, New York: o.p.; Murray: o.p.]
—— *The Whip Hand: a tale of the Pine Country.* 1903
Recounts a stiff fight against a lumber trust; scene, Michigan. [Doubleday New York: o.p.]
—— *The "Merry Anne."* 1904
Describes with skilful actuality lumber carrying and smuggling on Lakes Huron and Michigan. [Macmillan, New York and London: o.p.]
—— *Anthony the Absolute.* 1914
A travel-diary of the East—how an American scientist falls in love with the runaway wife of a repulsive drunkard. [Century Co., New York: o.p.; Richards: o.p.]
—— *The Honey Bee.* 1915
The title suggests the unmarried woman who devotes herself to business, and the theme is the gradual atrophy of feminine and sexual instincts in one whose life is spent in commercial dealings. [Bobbs-Merrill, Indianapolis: Nash: o.p.]
—— *Silk: a legend.* 1923
A fanciful romance of a mandarin in China engaged in the silk trade in the first century of our era. [Houghton, Boston; Constable.]

MERWIN, Samuel, and WEBSTER, Henry Kitchell [American; *b.* 1875]. *The Short-Line War.* 1901
Opened up a new field for fiction—the romance of trade and finance. Story of the fight for the possession of a line connecting two great railways A rapid, vigorous narrative of commercial rivalry and intrigue, culminating in a display of force that has to be put down by the military. A love-tale is bound up with these events. [Macmillan, New York and London: o.p.]
—— *Calumet "K."* 1901
Calumet "K" is a two-million grain elevator, which Charlie Bannon has to build against time. How he succeeds in doing so in the teeth of persons who are interested in delaying the work, and of the "walking delegates," is the story. Its heroine is Bannon's typist. [Macmillan, New York.]

MEYER, Annie [*née* Nathan; American; *b.* 1867]. *Robert Annys, Poor Priest.* 1901
A romance of the Peasants' Revolt, 1381, in Richard II's reign, distinguished by powerful treatment of emotional scenes. Based on a study of authorities, and avowedly owing much to William Morris's *Dream of John Ball*, the book reflects sympathetically the feelings and aspirations of men like Wyclif and Ball. The author of *Piers Plowman* is introduced in a new and unromantic light. [Macmillan, New York: o.p.]

MEYER, Conrad Ferdinand [German; 1825–98]. *The Saint* (Der Heilige, 1880). 1930
A romance of Henry II and Thomas Becket, distinguished by the great German romancer's genius for dramatizing fine souls in whom the inexplicable latent in human greatness remains a very real element. [Poorly transl. by Edwin Franklin HAUCH, Simon & Schuster, New York.]

MEYER, Kuno [1858–1919] [ed.]. *The Vision of MacConglinne* (Aislinge Meic Conglinne): *a twelfth-century Irish wonder-tale.* 1892
A primitive tale (in prose intermixed with verse) combining two elements rather perplexingly—satire of the abbot and monks of Cork, and the vision of the Lake of Milk, which reveals to the gleeman MacConglinne how King Cathal may be delivered from the demon of gluttony that has been the bane of his land. Full of extravagance and comic fancy. Probably originated in a folk-tale about a marvellous land of plenty; opens up a number of difficult problems to the student of early literature and folk-lore. [Edited with transl. by Kuno MEYER, with literary introduction by W. WOOLNER, Nutt: o.p.]
—— *The Voyage of Bran, Son of Febal, to the Land of the Living.* 1895–7
An old Irish saga, now first edited, with translation, notes, and glossary by Kuno Meyer. With an essay upon the Irish vision of the Happy Otherworld, and the Celtic doctrine of rebirth, by Alfred NUTT. Vol. i., *The Happy Otherworld*; vol. ii., *The Celtic Doctrine of Rebirth*. [(Grimm Lib.), Nutt: o.p.]

MEYNELL, Viola [Mrs. John Dallyn]. *Lot Barrow.* 1913
The heroine is a farm servant, whose character is portrayed with a graceful insight. She has the slow brains and simplicity of the country combined with a capacity for delicate and genuine emotion. [Secker: o.p.; Badger, Boston: o.p.]
—— *Modern Lovers.* 1914
The central character is a girl so accustomed to trivial deceit that she is false even to herself; her two lovers, rival professional divers, are absorbed in their art. Intimacy of detail lends itself to the drawing of fine shades of character, but the total effect is wanting in life. [Secker; Badger, Boston: o.p.]
—— *Columbine.* 1915
A study of a man lacking in self-discipline and humour, wavering between two loves. All the characters, in especial the vacuous dancer of whom he is enamoured, are drawn with skill and wit. It is this skill, together with her pleasant style, that constitute the value of this author's work. [Secker: o.p.; Putnam, New York: o.p.]

MEYNELL, Viola (*continued*). *Narcissus.* 1916
Two brothers contrasted, the one ordinary, the other consumed by a wasting egoism; a study in failure. [Secker : o.p.; Putnam, New York : o.p.]

—— *Second Marriage.* 1918
The fortunes of three daughters of a Fen-country farmer. The setting is well-realized, but the beauty is of still-life rather than of the living. [Secker; Doubleday, Doran, New York.]

—— *Antonia.* 1921
The expression of a mood—a tantalized, vague longing—more than a story. The characters have interest, but the whole effect is thin and unreal. [Secker.]

" MICHAËLIS, Karin " [Katharina Marie Bech, *née* Brøndum; Danish; b. 1872]. *The Child :*
Andrea. 1905
Not so much a story as the simple unfolding of a tragic situation in all its emotional significance. The little girl Andrea dies, loved by her parents who are estranged from each other, and they in their loneliness are reconciled over her grave. [Transl. by John Nilsen LAURVIK, Duckworth : o.p.; Elder, San Francisco.]

—— *The Dangerous Age : letters and fragments from a woman's diary* (Den farlige Alder, 1910).
1911
This is the diagnosis of a morbid psychological case—the autobiography of a woman of forty who revolts from matrimony and eventually loses both husband and lover. Exceedingly frank in analysing the secret instincts of a sensuous woman. [Transl. with introd. by Marcel PRÉVOST, Lane; Macauley Co., New York; o.p.]

—— *The Governor.* 1913
A gloomy melodrama of sexual aberration and distorted passions, staged on a grim island the scenery of which is meant to intensify the horrible fascination. [Transl. by Amy SKOVGAARD-PEDERSEN, Lane : o.p.]

MIKKELSEN, Ejnar [Danish; b. 1880]. *Frozen Justice.* 1922
A grim story of Alaska, showing the debasing influence of civilization upon the Eskimo. The background is well done. [Transl. by A. G. JAYNE, Holden; Knopf, New York.]

MIKSZÁTH, Kálmán [Hungarian; b. 1849]. *The Good People of Pawlocz* (1892). 1893
Mikszáth is called the " Hungarian Bret Harte." Fifteen of his stories, picturing the vices, crimes, and superstitions of the peasant classes among his countrymen; almost unrelievedly wretched. [Transl. by C. BINGHAM, *illus.* (folio), Dean : o.p.]

—— *St. Peter's Umbrella* (1896). 1900
Racy sketches of Slovak and Magyar peasantry and townsfolk in an out-of-the-way corner of Hungary, connected by a whimsical story about an umbrella, which impressed the simple villagers as a portion of the ceremonial of a burying, and also played a part in bringing two lovers together. [Transl. by B. W. WORSWICK, Jarrold : o.p.]

MILLE, Pierre [French; b. 1865]. *Two Little Parisians* (Caillou et Tili). 1913
A tenderly amusing tale of two small children at Paris, really interpreting the child's mind and point of view, so difficult for the adult to seize. [Transl. by Bérengère DRILLIEN, Lane.]

—— *Barnavaux* (Sur la vaste terre, 1905). 1915
Introduces the author's hero, the shrewd, phlegmatic, humorous, case-hardened French soldier of marines, who might well be a messmate of Kipling's famous soldiers three. (M. Mille was the first French translator of Kipling.) Here a principal scene is Madagascar, and the natives are drawn to the life, with their strange ways of thinking, their superstitions, etc. No doubt, the author has utilized the local folk-lore. Transl. by Bérengère DRILLIEN, Lane.]

—— *Under the Tricolour* (Barnavaux et quelques femmes, 1908). 1915
Thirteen tales in the same thoroughly French variation of the Kipling style, of soldiers and marines in the French colonies, from Equatorial Africa to Cochin China. Active service in the desert, hardships and perils on the rivers and in the tropical forests, and the uglier side of life at military posts and in trading-stations, are made interesting by the personal touch. [Transl. by Bérengère DRILLIEN, Lane.]

—— *Louise and Barnavaux* (Louise et Barnavaux, 1912). 1916
In the longer second part of this series of tales, chiefly episodes in Barnavaux' career, he has left the service and is back in Paris, and, his polygamous habits a thing of the past, is living with his " wife " Louise —quite a respectable citizen. Some of the other sketches are pretty grim, of *actes passionelles*, in spots like Port Said. [Transl. by Bérengère DRILLIEN, Lane.]

MILLER, Thomas [1807–74]. *Royston Gower ; or, The Days of King John.* 1838
An historical romance of Nottingham Castle and Sherwood Forest (1207–13). [Ward & Lock : o.p.]

—— *Gideon Giles the Roper.* 1840
Miller, the " Basket-maker " of Nottingham, was a humble poet and nature-lover who in this novel, much of which is conventional rubbish, managed to picture the rustic Midlander of his time (the Chartist period) with remarkable truth and lifelikeness. Ben Brust, the indefatigable trencherman, with his primitive philosophy of life, is a character drawn with real humour. [Edited by E. A. Baker (Half-forgotten Books), Routledge (Dutton, New York) : o.p.]

MILLIN, Sarah Gertrude [*née* Liebson; American; b. 1889]. *God's Step-Children.* 1924
Discusses the problem of the negro : a missionary in Africa, holding that there should be no distinction of race, puts his theory into practice by marrying a native woman. The results are traced through four generations. [Boni, New York; Constable.]

—— *The Coming of the Lord.* 1928
A tragic story set in South Africa—the passion of a Jewish doctor for the wife of an Englishman, complicated by the clash of the mingled nationalities, English, German, Jew, Hindu, and native, which are involved. [Boni, New York; Constable.]

344

MILLS, Weymer JAY [American; b. 1880]. *The Ghosts of their Ancestors.* 1906
A comedy written in mockery of American ancestor-worship. Jonathan Knickerbocker, a New Yorker in the eighteen-thirties, absorbed in piling up wealth and reverencing his family, is confronted by the disreputable ghosts of his forefathers and consents to his daughter's marriage to a grandfatherless man. [Fox & Duffield, New York: o.p.]

—— *The Van Rensselaers of Old Manhattan.* 1907
A love-tale of New York in the Revolutionary period, and the coming of President Washington. [Stokes, New York: o.p.]

MIRÔ, Gabriel [Spanish; b. 1879]. *Our Father San Daniel* (Nuestro Padre San Daniel, 1921). 1930
Intensely and uncompromisingly Spanish, both the picture of the small cathedral town, teeming with priests and soaked in ecclesiasticism, and the manner in which the characters and the tragic happenings are, as it were, taken for granted rather than described. The coloured, opulent prose of the original marks the author as of the symbolist school. [Transl. Charlotte Remfrey KIDD, Benn.]

MIRRLEES, Hope. *Madeline, one of Love's Jansenists.* 1919
A charming reconstruction of French family life in the mid-seventeenth century—the epoch of Mlle de Scudéry, whom Madeline apes with the devoted folly of youth, until she is completely divorced from reality. [Collins.]

MITCHELL, Silas Weir [American; 1829–1914]. *Hephzibah Guinness.* 1880
Three little stories of Quakers in Philadelphia, incidentally presenting a picture of the manners and observances of the straitest members of the sect. Two are quiet love-stories, though one has a tragic motive. [Century Co., New York: o.p.]

—— *Roland Blake.* 1886
The earlier part is a story of action, camps and battles in the Civil War; the latter a love idyll. [Century Co., New York: o.p.]

—— *Far in the Forest.* 1889
A tale of the great Pennsylvanian forest before the war, when life in that wild region was of an heroic kind. Not so much a romance as a story of character and the interaction of character. Two personages stand out: the heroine, introduced at the bedside of her dying husband, and the German scientist whom fate brings into her life at this crisis. [Century Co., New York: o.p.; Unwin: o.p.]

—— *Characteristics.* 1892

—— *Dr. North and His Friends* [sequel]. 1900
"Selections from the table-talk of an intimate coterie of highly cultivated men and women, who meet constantly at each other's houses and discuss books, art, religion, ethics, and themselves." [(1) and (2), Century Co., New York: o.p.]

—— *Hugh Wynne, Free Quaker.* 1897
An aged Quaker's story of the men and the events of the War of Independence. Washington and Lafayette, Major André, Howe, and Dr. Rush are drawn at length. Makes a good deal of the contrast between the old Quaker society, with its ideals of brotherly love, and the battles, duels, plots, and bitterness prevailing around. [Century Co., New York (new ed. 1922); Unwin: o.p.]

—— *The Red City: a novel of the second administration of President Washington* [sequel]. 1908
The events take place in the Quaker city, Philadelphia, when it was the seat of government during Washington's second administration, and arise from a young French vicomte's scheme of vengeance on the man who had brought about his father's death (1792–5). Jefferson and Hamilton are among the historical people brought in. [Century Co., New York; Macmillan: o.p.]

—— *The Adventures of François: Foundling, Thief, Juggler, and Fencing-Master.* 1898
The Dumasian adventures of a little Ishmaelite adrift in the Paris streets during the Terror, a light-hearted, irresponsible rascal, who tells his own astonishing history (1777–93). The dog Toto, and the Marquess de Ste. Luce, a fascinating old reprobate, are salient characters. [Century Co., New York; Macmillan.]

—— *The Autobiography of a Quack; and, The Case of George Dedlow.* 1900
The death-bed narrative of a rascally doctor. A curious study of the mind of a professional cheat, the medical details handled realistically, the author being himself an accomplished physician. His professional knowledge stands him in good stead also in *The Case of George Dedlow*, the story of a soldier who had all his limbs amputated and nearly lost his sense of identity. The case was widely accepted as genuine when the tale appeared (1880), and subscriptions are said to have been sent in. [Century Co., New York: o.p.]

—— *Constance Trescott.* 1905
A story of the South after the Civil War. [Century Co., New York: o.p.]

—— *A Diplomatic Adventure.* 1906
Supposed to be told by a secretary to the American legation in Paris, in 1862, about a stolen dispatch and Napoleon III's efforts to persuade England to acknowledge the Confederate States as a nation. [Century Co., New York: o.p.]

—— *A Venture in 1777.* [juvenile] 1908
A boy's story of boys' adventures in Philadelphia, at Valley Forge, etc. [Jacobs, Philadelphia: o.p.]

—— *Westways.* 1913
Before and after the Civil War in Pennsylvania (1855–65), violent political conflicts, the siege of Vicksburg, etc. [Century Co., New York; Unwin: o.p.]

MITCHISON, Naomi Margaret [*née* Haldane; b. 1897]. *The Conquered.* 1923
A fine romance about a chieftain of the Veneti during Cæsar's campaign in Gaul (58–46 B.C.). Vercingetorix is introduced, and the book ends with his death as a captive in Rome. The sympathies of the author are, as in all her stories about Gaul, with the conquered rather than the conquerors. [Cape; Harcourt, New York.]

MITCHISON, Naomi Margaret (*continued*). *When the Bough Breaks.* 1924
Three of these stories are about Cæsar's Gallic wars and Vercingetorix ; *The Triumph of Faith* deals with Colossæ in the time of St. Paul ; the title-story is about Italy and the Danube at the beginning of the fifth century. [Cape ; Harcourt, New York.]

—— *Cloud Cuckoo Land.* 1925
Greece and the west coast of Asia Minor during the latter part of the Peloponnesian War, and the supremacy of Sparta (late fifth century B.C.) ; the story is based on Xenophon. [Cape ; Harcourt, New York.]

—— *Black Sparta.* 1928
Tales of Grecian life—particularly of domestic scenes. [Cape ; Harcourt, New York.]

—— *Barbarian Stories.* 1929
Miniatures of life in far-off times, from the early Bronze Age to the eleventh century, with a tale of 1935 to end up. Scenes—Dorset, Ireland, Italy, Gaul, Rome, Ravenna, Russia, Constantinople. The tales have a modern flavour, told as they are from the point of view of the men chiefly concerned. [Cape ; Harcourt, New York.]

—— *The Hostages ; and other stories for boys and girls.* 1930
Half new, half earlier tales adapted for young readers. All are historical, and furnish vivid pictures of life or lively versions of famous episodes, from 396 B.C. to A.D. 1110. So lively that modern slang is not proscribed. [Cape.]

MITFORD, Bertram [South African]. *A Romance of the Cape Frontier.* 1891
The first of a long series of narratives of adventure among the savages and wild beasts of South Africa, usually concerned with such eventful periods as those of the Zulu, Matabele, and Boer wars ; and with English colonists and soldiers, Dutch, Kafirs, Zulus, etc., for dramatis personæ. A romantic love-tale always runs through these pictures of wild life, warfare, and scenery (1877-8). [Heinemann : o.p.]

—— *The Gun Runner : a romance of Zululand.* 1893
(1878-9.) [Chatto : o.p. ; Fenno, New York : o.p.]

—— *The Luck of Gerald Ridgeley : a tale of the Zulu border.* 1893
[Chatto : o.p.]

—— *The King's Assegai : a Matabele story.* 1894
(1893.) [Chatto : o.p. ; Fenno, New York : o.p.]

—— *The Sign of the Spider : an episode.* 1896
Fighting with Matabele, etc., and love-making among Europeans (c. 1890-3). [Methuen : o.p. ; Dodd & Mead, New York : o.p.]

—— *The Induna's Wife.* 1898
The wars of the great heroes of Zululand, Dingaan and Umzilikazi, with the Boers (1836-40). [White : o.p.]

—— *Aletta.* 1900
South Africa on the eve of the Boer War and during its first stages, depicted with knowledge and no unfriendliness to the Boers and Oom Paul Kruger. [White : o.p.]

—— *The Word of the Sorceress.* 1902
Laid at the time of the Zulu war (1878-9) ; brings in Cetewayo, and describes the catastrophe of Isandhlwana. [Hutchinson : o.p.]

MITFORD, Mary Russell [1787-1855]. *Our Village : sketches of rural character and scenery.* 1824-32
A series of essays giving the finest descriptions extant of the natural surroundings, the people, high and low, the manners and customs, festivals—in short, the whole life of a Berkshire village in the first quarter of the nineteenth century. Realistic and pictorial in manner, full of keen and loving observation ; the style polished and repolished with exquisite art ; yet purely external and devoid of dramatic interest, but for which deficiency they would challenge comparison with Mrs. Gaskell's *Cranford*. [(Temple Classics), Dent (Dutton, New York) ; Dodge, New York. *Illus.* by Hugh Thomson, Macmillan, 1898 ; with 25 coloured plates by C. E. Brock, Dent (Dutton, New York), 1904 ; by Hugh Thomson and A. Rawlings, Macmillan, 1910 : o.p.]

MOIR, David Macbeth [Scottish ; 1798-1851]. *Life of Mansie Wauch, Tailor in Dalkeith.* 1828
Dr. Moir, the " Delta " of *Maga* and a minor poet, in this history of the childhood, schooling, and later life of a hard-working man, and of the prentices, councillors, and provost, with some pathetic episodes, many mirthful ones, and a racy account of the resurrectionists, wrote a novel worthy to stand on the shelf near John Galt : many of the scenes are strongly akin to the boisterous conviviality of the *Noctes Ambrosianæ*. [Blackwood, 1895 ; *illus.* P. Davies (1911).]

MOLANDER, Harold [Swedish]. *The Fortune-Hunter* (1897). 1905
A gayer *Three Musketeers*, of the days of Gustavus Adolphus and Wallenstein (1629), with a picaroon hero. [Transl. by Karin H. CAGNEY. Heinemann : o.p.]

MOLESWORTH, Mary Louisa [*née* Stewart ; Scottish ; 1839-1921]. *" Carrots " : Just a Little Boy.* 1876
—— *The Cuckoo Clock.* 1877
—— *Grandmother Dear.* 1878
—— *Adventures of Herr Baby.* 1881
—— *Peterkin.* 1902
All simple, unaffected tales of child life, told for children, without obtrusive didacticism. Of like quality are *Us* (1885), *Four Winds Farm* (1886), *The Rectory Children* (1889), *The Girls and I* (1892), *The Carved Lions* (1895), *This and That* (1899), *The Wood Pigeons and Mary* (1901). [All Macmillan, London and New York (9 and 10 : o.p.)]

MONELLI, Paolo [Italian ; *b.* 1891]. *Toes Up* (Le Scarpe al Sole : storie di Alpini, di muli, et di vino, 1921). 1930
> Stories, which appear to be rather reminiscences than fiction, of the war on a sector of the Italian front, showing the growth of the spirit of revolt and indignation out of which Fascism had its birth. [Transl. by Orlo WILLIAMS, Duckworth ; Harcourt, New York.]

MONKHOUSE, Allan Noble [*b.* 1858]. *Men and Ghosts.* 1918
> Two friends of very different moral character, fall in love with a girl of bright, attractive personality, who seems strongly influenced by some force entirely beyond their comprehension. [Collins : o.p.]

—— *True Love.* 1919
> A romance of the journalistic and theatrical worlds of Manchester, on the eve of the great war. [Collins.]

—— *Suburb.* 1925
> Short sketches, for the most part quiet and amusing, of surburban life in Manchester. [Philpot.]

MONTAGU, Lily H. *Naomi's Exodus.* 1901
> The story of a clever young Jewess, out of sympathy with her narrow surroundings, who suffers chastening troubles in endeavouring to find a more congenial sphere. [Unwin : o.p.]

MONTAGUE, Charles Edward [1867–1928]. *A Hind Let Loose.* 1910
> Mordant, but on the whole good-humoured satire upon the journalistic world of Manchester, though the satire often gives place to sheer comedy. The chief character is an irrepressible Irishman who writes leaders for two papers on opposite political platforms, one vituperating the other. The portraits of the rival editors are pieces of very telling irony. Montague was sub-editor of the *Manchester Guardian.* [Methuen ; Doubleday, New York.]

—— *Fiery Particles.* 1923
> Stories mostly about war-time incidents, e.g. *In Hanging Garden Gully.* Rivalry between a couple of *embusqués* for unmerited decorations provides comedy and satire in *Honours Easy.* [Chatto ; Doubleday, New York.]

—— *Right Off the Map.* 1927
> Combines an exciting story—the conflict between an imaginary State and its neighbour—with brilliant satire upon war and war-makers ; financial magnates, press, and demagogues who brought the war about, and rascally contractors, inefficient leaders, and rash optimists who were responsible for defeat. Contrasted, however, with these are the actual fighters, in their heroism and devotion to duty. [Chatto ; Doubleday, New York.]

—— *Action ; and other stories.* 1928
> Thirteen varied stories, the best of which is *Action,* a fine account of a perilous Alpine climb ; also *A Cock and Bull Story,* a little epic of the front line ; others, e.g. *The Great Sculling Race,* are sporting stories in lighter vein. [Chatto ; Doubleday, New York.]

MONTEMÔR, or MONTEMAYOR, Jorge de [Portuguese ; *d.* 1561]. *Diana* (Diana Enamorada, 1558-9). 1598
> One of the most celebrated of the pastorals that succeeded the romances of chivalry. It was modelled on the *Arcadia* (1502) of the Neapolitan Sannazaro who, like Baptista Mantuanus and Boccaccio in his *Ameto,* sought refreshment in the charms of the woods and fields from the jaded life of cities. Sannazaro pictured his simple life in placid scenes that form a setting to eclogues imitated from Virgil. Montemayor's is a complete romance with human interest and pathos. The plot is how three swains, who have loved and lost, or loved and forsaken, meet by the river Esla, and tell the story of their griefs. They are joined by nymphs and shepherdesses, who likewise have their tales to tell of unrequited affection. All journey to the temple of Diana, whose priestess gives each a potion inducing oblivion of the old love and growth of a new, for which the priestess furnishes partners. Contains much lyrical verse. Influenced Sidney, whose *Arcadia* is likewise a mingling of chivalric and pastoral elements. Montemayor's prose is not so euphuistic and overstrained as Sidney's. [Transl. by Bartholomew YONG (1598), together with supplements by Alonzo PEREZ (1564) and Gaspar Gil POLO (1564). *The Story of the Shepherdess Felismena* (from Book II of YONG's transl.) was included in Collier's *Shakespeare's Library* (q.v.). YONG's transl. was finished 1583 : o.p.]

MONTESQUIEU, Charles Louis de Secondat, Baron de la Brède et de [French ; 1689–1755]. *Persian Letters* (Lettres Persanes, 1721). 1892
> A book copied sixty years later by Goldsmith in his *Citizen of the World.* A criticism of the social and religious conditions of contemporary France, in the form of letters written by two Asiatics in exile at Paris to their friends in Persia. The one personage, an arrogant but philosophical Oriental, is a serious portrayal of the Asiatic character ; while the other, in lighter vein, gives amusing impressions of European manners and usages, vices and follies. An expression of freethought, and of the reaction against monarchical and ecclesiastical despotism expounded later in a more systematic way in the *Esprit des lois.* [Transl. by John DAVIDSON, 2 vols., *priv. prin.* London : o.p. ; new ed., (Broadway Transl.) Routledge (Dutton, New York) ; Dial Press, New York, 1929.]

—— *The Temple of Gnidus* (Le temple de Gnide, 1725). 1888
> A rhetorical and exotic pastoral—reading like a translation from verse into prose, a thing French will not stand—aiming to put life into Greek antiquities in the same way as Barthélemy's *Jeune Anacharsis.* Describes in seven chants the loveliest of the abodes of Venus. [Transl., with preface, by O. UZANNE, Vizetelly : o.p.]

MONTGOMERY, Florence [1843–1923]. *Misunderstood.* 1870
> Probably the best of Miss Montgomery's long series of child-novels (written rather for older people but mostly readable by children too) is this touching story, in which she studies and criticizes the education of children in the case of two motherless boys neglected by their father. One of the brothers, misunderstood by father and governess, grows lawless in pure innocence, his innate nobleness leading him astray. [Macmillan (last ed., 1930).]

MONTGOMERY, Florence (*continued*). *Thrown Together.* 1872

A sensitive girl, unappreciated by her parents, and a petted boy are thrown together ; and their mutual influence is not only good for them, but brings their respective parents to a better understanding of their children's dispositions and their own responsibilities. [Macmillan : o.p.]

—— *Prejudged.* 1900

A love-idyll in a French *pension*, an English girl falling in love with a mysterious young man, towards whom at first she had conceived an instinctive antipathy. [Macmillan.]

"MONTGOMERY, K. L." [Kathleen and Letitia Montgomery ; Irish]. *Major Weir.* 1904

The story of the famous warlock burnt in Leith Walk, Edinburgh, in 1670. [Unwin : o.p.]

—— *The Cardinal's Pawn.* 1904

The story of Bianca Capello (see Symonds's *Story of the Renaissance*) and of Fiamma Bonaventuri, twin sister of her boy-husband, who marries a young Englishman. A rapid, improbable, thrilling succession of dramatic adventures. A little artificial and obscure in style. Presents the gorgeous life of mediæval Venice in a fascinating manner (1587–9). [Unwin ; McClurg, Chicago : o.p.]

—— *The Ark of the Curse.* 1906

Describes the hideous persecution of the Cagots, "the accursed race," in Henry III's France. [Hurst : o.p.]

—— *Colonel Kate.* 1908

An energetic romance of the '45, with a vehement lady as foremost figure, and next to her the ill-fated Simon Fraser, Lord Lovat, and his more honourable son. [Methuen : o.p.]

—— *The Gate-Openers.* 1912

A tale of the Rebecca riots in Carmarthenshire in 1843–4 (see Violet Jacob's *Sheep Stealers*). [Long : o.p.]

—— *Maids of Salem.* 1915

The witch craze in Cotton Mather's time, in Salem and Boston (1691–5). [Long : o.p.]

MONTRESOR, Miss F. F. *Into the Highways and Hedges.* 1895

The impressionable, cultivated Margaret weds the street preacher Thorpe, and learns afterwards to love him for his fortitude in unmerited sufferings. He is an unlearned, illogical, quixotic being, full of faith and energy in the pursuit of his ideal ; his rival for Margaret's affection is a hard-headed Jew. [Hutchinson : o.p. ; Appleton, New York : o.p.]

—— *The One Who Looked On.* 1895

A chapter of family history told by a motherly Irish aunt. Among the character-sketches is that of an English Q.C., a hard, unemotional man externally, whose heart is found to be truly benevolent. [Hutchinson : o.p. ; Appleton, New York : o.p.]

—— *False Coin or True.* 1896

A nameless orphan, rescued from domestic drudgery by a French mesmerist, acts for him as medium, and wins him fame and profit. She falls in love with an honest, thick-headed Scot ; and when love beckons one way and duty to her invalided guardian another, shows herself capable of true gratitude. [Hutchinson : o.p. ; Appleton, New York : o.p.]

—— *At the Cross Roads.* 1897

Like the foregoing, interesting for the moral issues involved, and strongly didactic. The heroine a very modern figure, hard-grained but capable of intense passion, showing her strength by waiting seven years for her convict lover and exerting herself to prove his innocence. [Hutchinson : o.p. ; Appleton, New York : o.p.]

—— *The Alien.* 1901

A mother's conspiracy to give her illegitimate son the inheritance of another. [Methuen : o.p. ; Appleton, New York : o.p.]

—— *Through the Chrysalis.* 1910

A clear-headed study of a girl of mixed character, whose sins do not deprive her of the reader's sympathy and regard, and of her succumbing to the temptation to a course of deceit. [Murray.]

MOORE, Frank Frankfort [Irish ; b. 1855]. *The Jessamy Bride.* 1897

A novel founded on an actual story of the eighteenth century, introducing Goldsmith and Mary Horneck (the Jessamy Bride), Dr. Johnson, Burke, and Garrick (1774). [Hutchinson : o.p. ; with introd. by C. Morley, Duffield, New York, 1926 ; Garden City Co., New York, 1928.]

—— *The Fatal Gift.* 1898

A novel of manners of the eighteenth century. The famous Irish beauties the Misses Gunning are the leading characters. [Hutchinson : o.p. ; Dodd & Mead, New York : o.p.]

—— *Nell Gwyn, Comedian.* 1900

Court life in Restoration times, the chief parts being sustained by Nell Gwyn, Lady Castlemaine, the Duchess of Portsmouth, Sir Charles Sedley, and Jack Churchill, afterwards Duke of Marlborough. [Pearson ; Brentano, New York : o.p.]

—— *A Nest of Linnets.* 1901

Sheridan, and the Linleys at Bath (1771–3). [Hutchinson : o.p. ; Appleton, New York : o.p.]

—— *Castle Omeragh.* 1903

—— *Captain Latymer* [sequel]. 1907

Exciting adventures and trustworthy pictures of the West of Ireland during the Cromwellian wars (1649–50). The Fawcetts are a Protestant family who have gone Irish, and in the sequel the eldest is sent to the West Indies by Cromwell. [(1), Constable : o.p. ; Appleton, New York : o.p. ; (2), Cassell : o.p.]

—— *The Messenger.* 1907

John Wesley's love-story ; scene, Cornwall in 1740. [Hodder : o.p. ; *sub tit. The Love that Prevailed*, Cupples, New York : o.p.]

—— *Fanny's First Novel.* 1913

Fanny Burney, the author of *Evelina*, and her circle—Garrick, Dr. Johnson, etc. [Hutchinson : o.p. ; Doran, New York : o.p.]

MOORE, Frank Frankfort (*continued*). *The Rescue of Martha.*   1913
 A novel of eighteenth-century life, utilizing the case of Francis Hackman and Martha Ray, mistress of Lord Sandwich, murdered by the former (1779). See Boswell's *Life*, April 16, 1779. [Hutchinson: o.p.]

—— *The Ulsterman : a story of to-day.*   1914
 The chief character is a tyrannical millowner—a picture of the drab materialism and bigotry of the Ulster character, as well as of its rugged determination. [Hutchinson: o.p.]

MOORE, George [Irish ; *b.* 1857]. *A Modern Lover.*   1883
 Called by Arnold Bennett, " The first realistic novel in England," i.e. the first attempt to follow Flaubert, Maupassant, the Goncourts, and Zola. Mr. Moore says, " The novel, if it be anything, is contemporary history, an exact and complete reproduction of [the] social surroundings of the age we live in." This gives the career of a bad artist, who deserts the " moderns " because their path is too difficult, and succeeds only through the influence of women—he is actually elected A.R.A. as the result of an intrigue. Full of the art talk of the period. Mr. Moore rewrote it as *Lewis Seymour and some Women* (1917). [Heinemann ; Brentano, New York.]

—— *A Mummer's Wife.*   1884
 The wife of a small shopkeeper in the Potteries runs away with the manager of a travelling company of actors, and goes on tour with him. But jealousy makes her impossible, she is dropped out of the programme, and takes to solitary drinking. Her degradation is traced with a stern yet merciful pen—Flaubert's without the irony. [Heinemann ; Brentano, New York, 1917.]

—— *A Drama in Muslin : a realistic novel.*   1886
 Irish society in the days of the Land League and the Phœnix Park murders (1879–82). A rather savage description of gentry and nobility expecting ruin at any moment, mothers fishing for coronets, daughters ready to accept anything in the shape of a husband, bachelors and widowers preying on the ignorant and innocent. A period novel, much overcharged, and unconvincing on artistic grounds as well as through lack of probability ; republished, with very slight revision, as *Muslin*, 1915. [Heinemann ; Brentano, New York.]

—— *Confessions of a Young Man.*   1888
 An early book of self-revelations, now reissued with a new preface. The young man goes to Paris as an art student and mixes with the *demi-monde* of artists, actors, literary men, and bohemians. Interesting for its original and piquant criticisms on life, art, and literature, its impressions of life " seen through a temperament," and its ideas of the novel as a truthful study of social history. [Heinemann ; Brentano, New York.]

—— *Spring Days : a realistic novel.*   1888
 A good example of quiet, literal, unrefracting realism applied to a commonplace subject ; with no satire, no irony, no intrusion of the author whatever. Yet he enables us to form a just estimate of the shoddy, second-rate people inhabiting a residential place near Brighton, and to perceive the barbarism and vulgarity of these prosperous, middle-class individuals, with their flabby young men and frivolous, flirting girls. [Laurie : o.p. ; Brentano, New York.]

—— *Esther Waters.*   1894
 A study of low life in England, especially of people connected with the turf. The household of a racing squire, described as it appears to Esther the scullery-maid, is broken up on the squire's bankruptcy, and the crowd of servants, trainers, jockeys, and stablemen disperse, most of them to get a living on the racecourse or in shady business in London. Esther, the scullery-maid, being ruined, suffers the miseries of a lying-in hospital. After many troubles, she marries her old lover, who now keeps a low public-house and is a bookmaker. [Revised ed., 1920, Heinemann ; Laurie ; Brentano, New York.]

—— *Evelyn Innes.*   1898
—— *Sister Teresa* [sequel].   1901
 One book, divided for convenience of publishing—a woman's life during the perilous age ; perhaps the fullest full-length of a woman in English fiction. Evelyn is a musical genius, who elopes to the Continent with a rich amateur, then falls in love with an Irish poet and mystic, comes under the influence of a priest, and finds peace with a sisterhood at Wimbledon, becoming a postulant. The story is told in enormous detail, the author following Balzac's method of exhaustive analysis and explanation of the characters and their mental states. He also follows the note-book realists in pouring into it masses of erudition. As an æsthete, he fills pages with descriptions of pictures, rooms, and furniture ; as a Wagnerian, he makes his heroine's conduct turn largely on musical experiences ; and his interest in religion is accountable for more about Roman Catholic doctrine and observances than is actually relevant. [(1) and (2), Benn ; (2), Unwin ; (1), Appleton, New York ; (2), Brentano, New York.]

—— *The Untilled Field.*   1903
 Written in 1900, when Moore, Yeats, and Edward Martyn were trying to found an Irish theatre. The stories were translated into Irish as fast as written, to further the literature and language movement. These stories are avowedly suggested by places and atmospheres—Duncannon and the villages round Dublin, the bogs of the West. They are among Moore's best. Interest in the good and the bad of humanity, humorous appreciation, love, tenderness, and now and then poetry, are integral qualities. Ireland, depopulated by emigration, is now an untilled field ; the remnant are priest-ridden, yet it is often the parish-priest who alone stands between his people and desperation. That is the dominant theme. [Heinemann.]

—— *The Lake.*   1905
 Too long to be included in the *Untilled Field*, but very like the foregoing. A conscientious and introspective priest drives a young woman from the parish, and then comes to realize that it was jealousy and not impersonal morality that actuated him. His meditations and heart-burnings are poetically blended with the scenery of Killarney, the wild life, and the legends. [Heinemann ; Appleton, New York.]

—— *The Brook Kerith : a Syrian story.*   1916
 Joseph of Arimathea is the witness through whom the story is told, but the subject is Jesus, a Palestine shepherd and member of the brotherhood of the Essenes, with a mystic understanding of nature in which he perceives God. Listening to the Baptist, he is carried away by enthusiasm, and believes himself to be the promised

MOORE, George (*continued*).
Messiah, but afterwards grows bitterly remorseful for such presumption. Jesus suffers crucifixion, and is laid in the sepulchre. But he is not dead, and Joseph secretly nurses him and shelters him from the priests till he can return to the Essenes. It is rationalist interpretation of the confused evidence, done with artistic simplicity and tenderness. Only rarely is there a touch of irony in the spirit of Anatole France. A profound and beautiful theism pervades the whole. [Laurie ; Macmillan, New York.]

—— *Héloïse and Abélard.* 1921
An introduction to the famous letters. After careful study of the documents, the whole story of the famous liaison and its sequel is related in enormous detail and in the leisurely manner of the old romances or those of William Morris. Full of mediæval colour and large romantic episodes. Even the controversies between Realists and Nominalists and the course of reading in the Latin poets with which Héloïse beguiled her leisure are described with scholarship and a scarcely pardonable excess. It is a work of the Art for Art's sake school, an elaborate piece of make-believe, Moore's sensualist philosophy finding its counterpart in Abélard's " Love is enough." [Heinemann ; Laurie ; 2 vols., Boni, New York.]

MOORE, Dr. John [Scottish ; 1730–1803]. *Zeluco : various views of human nature.* 1786
A didactic novel reflecting on the education of youth. Zeluco, the lurid villain, and his persecuted and engaging wife Laura are a pair of stock characters of conventional fiction, like the two Scots, Whig and Jacobite, who fight a duel over the reputation of Mary Queen of Scots. [Last ed. 1822 : o.p.]

MOORE, Thomas [Irish ; 1779–1852]. *The Fudge Family in Paris.* 1818
A series of journalistic skits written under the name of Thomas Brown the Younger, inspired by a sojourn of Moore and Rogers in Paris in 1817. [o.p.]

—— *The Epicurean.* 1827
An essay in the manner of *Vathek*, supposed to be translated from a Greek manuscript found in Egypt. Supernatural and other adventures of an Epicurean philosopher who embraces Christianity and is persecuted by the Memphian hierarchy. Time, third century, reign of Diocletian. It is really a prose amplification of his poem *Alciphron*, afterwards published along with it. [Longman, 1864 : o.p.]

MOORMAN, Frederic William [1872–1919]. *Tales of the Ridings.* 1920
—— *More Tales of the Ridings.* 1920
Country tales in the dialect of Yorkshire, by a professor of English at Leeds University, author of *Songs of the Ridings*, etc. [(1) and (2), Mathews.]

MORAES, Francisco de [Portuguese]. *Palmerin of England* (1547–8). 1581
Palmerin is hero of the most important family of chivalric romances after the Amadis cycle. The original *Palmerin de Oliva* is said to have been written by a carpenter's daughter, but Francisco Vázquez of Ciudad Rodrigo may have been the author. First printed at Salamanca, 1511 ; translated into English by Anthony MUNDAY, through the French and Italian (1588) ; he translated the history of Palmerin's son, *Primaleon* (1512) in 1597. Like Amadis, the hero is of romantic birth and extraordinary prowess. He goes forth as a knight-errant in search of adventures, slays numerous monsters, fights the Grand Turk, marries Polinarda, daughter of the emperor of Germany, and becomes emperor of Byzantium. The book contains many warm love scenes. There were many continuations in Spanish, French, and Italian, the most famous of the whole series being the sixth book, *Palmerin de Inglaterra*, by Francisco de Moraes, which Munday translated partly through the French, and partly from a Portuguese version through the Italian (SOUTHEY edited and abridged this translation, 4 vols., 1807). This relates the early adventures of Palmerin and Florian, twin children of Palmerin's daughter Flerida and King Duardos of England, adventures resembling those of Valentine and Orson. The chief scenes of their exploits are England and Constantinople. In emulation of Amadis and Galaor, they fight with each other, and with giants, knights, pagans, and other foes innumerable. Of the monotonous and perplexing chronicle of knight-errantry the most interesting episode is that concerning the Perilous Isle. The knights and giants are fairly well drawn ; the female characters are nullities. Cervantes eulogized the book with enthusiasm. Ford's romance, *Parismus, Prince of Bohemia* (1598), is founded on *Palmerin*. [Transl. by Anthony MUNDAY, 1588 : o.p. ; by Thomas CREED, 1586 : o.p. ; *Palmerin of England*, transl. from the Portuguese of Francisco de Moraes by Robert SOUTHEY, 4 vols., London, 1807 : o.p. ; *Palmerin of England*, by W. E. PURSER, Browne & Nolan, Dublin, 1904, discusses problems of authorship, etc.]

MORAN, James J. [Irish]. *The Dunferry Risin'.* 1894
A good tale of the Fenian movement, by one who belonged to the Irish Republican Brotherhood ; it is an account of an attempted insurrection (1867–8), and the actors are faithfully drawn and not without humour. [Digby & Long : o.p.]

MORAND, Paul [French ; b. 1888]. *Open All Night* (Ouvert la nuit, 1922). 1923
Half a dozen *épatant* sketches of emancipated, topsy-turvy life in different parts of post-war Europe, with startling female types as centre-pieces—the fair agent of the International at Barcelona, the Russian princesses earning their bread as waitresses in a Pera café, the hunted Jewess at Buda-Pesth, the lady-secretary of the society for *Nacktkultur*, the Roman demi-mondaines, etc. [Transl. by N.B.V., Knopf ; Boni, New York.]

—— *Closed All Night* (Fermé la nuit, 1923). 1924
Companion pictures to the preceding, of types of men of the aftermath of war. [Chapman.]

—— *Black Magic* (Magie noire, 1928). 1929
Eight sardonic tales of negroes and mulattoes of various tints, in Haiti, the United States, and Africa, bringing out the basic and ineradicable savagery of the race and its liability to revert to ancient superstitious practices. Under the influence of the Russian terror, one negro starts a Bolshevist revolution in Haiti and takes to Voodoo. A wealthy and highly educated octoroon lady on a pleasure trip to Liberia, stops behind in the bush. [Transl. by Hamish MILES, Heinemann ; Viking Press, New York.]

MORDAUNT, Elinor (Evelyn May) [*née* Clowes]. *Lou of the Ranges.* 1913
The story of a girl in Australia in revolt against masculine domination. [Heinemann : o.p. ; Sturgis, New York : o.p.]

MORDAUNT, Elinor (*continued*). *Bellamy.* 1914
The value of this novel lies in its pictures of the life of mill-hands in the silk factories of North Staffordshire. [Methuen : o.p. ; Lane, New York : o.p.]

—— *The Family.* 1915
In this story of a large yeoman family, the eldest, a boy of sensitive temperament, and the one sister who can sympathize with him, are the outstanding characters. [Methuen : o.p. ; Lane, New York : o.p.]

—— *The Processionals.* 1918
About a father and his young daughter who escape from the domination of their relatives and begin a new existence together in the East End. [Cassell : o.p.]

—— *The Dark Fire.* 1927
A romance of Australia and the South Seas, dealing in black magic and sorcery. [Hutchinson ; Century Co., New York.]

MORE, Hannah [1745–1833]. *Cœlebs in Search of a Wife.* 1808
The only readable survivor of a series of didactic stories by this celebrated bluestocking. Cœlebs visits a number of families and inspects the young ladies, the character-sketches and evaluations of personal qualities, humorous exposure of faults and affectations, being the results of his survey. [James Blackwood, 1879 : o.p.]

MORE, Sir Thomas [1478–1535]. *Utopia ; translated by Raphe Robynson.* 1516
Published in Latin at Louvain, the satire making it risky to publish in England. The author meets a comrade of Amerigo Vespucci, and hears about the isle of Utopia—Nowhere—the perfect government of which is contrasted with the lamentable state of England. Draws a condemnatory picture of English society, finance, laws, the luxury of the rich and misery of the labouring class, a picture touched in with humorous satire. Then the Utopian system is expounded—national education, sanitary laws, limited hours of labour, ethical philosophy—a socialist system, prophetically modern. [*Utopia*, transl. Ralphe ROBINSON, ed., with introd. and notes, by J. Churton Collins, Oxford Press, 1908 ; with Latin text of 1518 edition, ed. by J. H. Lupton, *id.*, 1895 ; with Roper's *Life*, ed. by J. R. Lumby, Camb. Univ. Press ; (Bohn's Popular Lib.) Bell (Harcourt, New York) ; with Bacon's *New Atlantis* (Broadway Transl.) Routledge (Dutton, New York), 1925 ; with *A Dialogue of Comfort against Tribulation*, (Everyman's Lib.) Dent (Dutton, New York). *More's Millennium*, ed. by Valerian Paget, gives the *Utopia* in modern English ; Rivers, 1909 : o.p. Also included in *Ideal Commonwealths*, ed. by Prof. H. Morley, Routledge (Dutton, New York).]

MORGAN, Charles [*b.* 1894]. *Portrait in a Mirror.* 1929
A curiously interesting study, in autobiographical form, of the mind of the artist, with many illuminating glimpses into the working of the imagination in its effort to penetrate to realities. The portrait of the girl who was about to marry someone else is never painted. But the imaginary writer strives to pierce to her spirit ; and the interest lies in the struggle between sacred and profane love. [Macmillan ; Knopf, New York.]

MORGAN, Lady [Sydney, *née* Owenson ; 1783 ?–1859]. *The Wild Irish Girl.* 1806
A sentimental love-tale by a perfervid girl with a mania for reviving all the ancient tokens of nationality. Glorvina, in whom Lady Morgan's contemporaries discerned much self-portraiture, is the last descendant of a line of Connaught princes, for centuries at feud with the earls who dispossessed them. The heir to the earldom woos her in disguise, and after romantic vicissitudes they are publicly united. [Routledge : o.p. ; Haverty, New York : o.p.]

—— *O'Donnel.* 1814
The impoverished scion of a princely house, intended to typify the heroic virtues of the native aristocracy. A plea for Catholic emancipation ; represents the young Irishmen oppressed by penal laws and driven into foreign service. The hero's career is consummated by a fortunate marriage with a dowager-duchess. Much idealized, yet truly Irish, sketches of all ranks ; the society chapters vulgar in tone and full of broad comedy. The governess transformed by marriage into a duchess is the author's own portrait. [Downey : o.p.]

—— *Florence M'Carthy.* 1816
A kidnapped heir asserts his claim to a peerage and estates, and unwittingly woos the romantic Florence, to whom he was betrothed in his youth. Among the comic people, Crawley is memorable as Lady Morgan's caricature of her enemy J. W. Croker. [o.p. ; Sadlier, New York : o.p.]

—— *The O'Briens and the O'Flahertys.* 1827
An attempt to imitate Scott's historical romances. The biography of a patriot who after the 1798 tragedy escapes to the Continent, where his career is brilliant, and where he marries the heroine. Scenes of old Irish society, wild landscapes, exciting adventures. Like the others, highly sentimental, and hot for nationalism and Catholic emancipation. [o.p. ; Haverty, New York : o.p.]

MORGAN-DE-GROOT, Dr. J. [*b.* 1868]. *The Affair on the Bridge.* 1909
Dutch village life given in the style of an old Dutch painting. [Blackwood : o.p.]

MORIER, James Justinian [1780–1849]. *The Adventures of Hajji Baba of Ispahan.* 1824
—— *Hajji Baba in England* [sequel]. 1828
The most brilliant picture we have in English literature of society and manners in Persia, done on the convenient plan of a Spanish rogue-story, by a great traveller and diplomat with an unrivalled knowledge of the people. The sequel relates the comic adventures of a Persian ambassador and his suite in London, and makes capital of the amusing contrasts between Persian and English customs. The book is a masterpiece of comic literature, Morier having a wonderful knack for developing choice idiosyncrasies of character. [(1), (Everyman's Lib.), Dent (Dutton, New York), 1914 ; (World's Classics), Oxford Press, 1923 ; Dulau ; *illus.*, Macmillan (1895) ; Knopf, New York, 1926 ; (2), (World's Classics), Oxford Press, 1925.]

MORLEY, Christopher Darlington [American ; *b.* 1890]. *Parnassus on Wheels.* 1917
—— *The Haunted Bookshop.* 1919
Light fantastic romances, with an agreeable literary flavouring. The first is about a young man who goes

351

MORLEY, Christopher Darlington (*continued*).
round the countryside with a travelling library ; the second has a good deal to say about books and authors. [(1) and (2), Doubleday, Doran, New York.]

—— *Thunder on the Left.* 1925
A fantasy of adult life as seen through the eyes of a child. On his tenth birthday, Martin is transported into the future ; the other children of the party are grown up, his little girl friend is married, and he, still a child in spirit, appears as her artist-lover—with incongruous results. [Doubleday, New York ; Heinemann.]

MORRIS, Gouverneur [American ; *b.* 1876]. *Aladdin O'Brien.* 1902
A Northern story of the whole course of the Civil War, but fairly impartial. Opens in New England, and follows the struggle in the South. [Century Co., New York : o.p. ; Cassell : o.p.]

MORRIS, William [1834–96]. *The Dream of John Ball.* 1888
An idyll made out of historical materials, i.e. the facts of the Kentish Rising in the reign of Richard II (1381), expressing Morris's ideals of social regeneration in the life and deeds of men of that age who were striving to enlighten and amend the lot of their fellows. [With *A King's Lesson*, Longmans, London and New York.]

—— *A Tale of the House of the Wolfings and all Kindreds of the Mark ; written in prose and in verse.* 1889

—— *The Roots of the Mountains.* 1890
Prose counterparts to the poet's metrical romances. First a story of the Goths in their tribal period (fourth century A.D.), when they were fighting the Romans. Scene, the Mark, a clearing in the great forests somewhere in the Danube region. There is a mythic breadth about the conception of the story, and the prose style is modelled on the severe, simple, and antique style of the sagas. It is the same with the other story of the Goths. *The Roots of the Mountains* is laid in a subsequent age, the epoch of village communities ; this has less of the primeval grandeur and more of the softer side of romanticism. [(1) and (2), Longmans, London and New York.]

—— *The Story of the Glittering Plain.* 1890
Time and place quite indefinite. A fanciful story, like most of those that follow, pouring out the riches of Morris's exuberant fancy, his delight in the beauty of mediæval art, and longings for that " shadowy isle of bliss," that golden era which he was striving toward more practically in his socialist preaching and artistic reforms. [Longmans, London and New York.]

—— *News from Nowhere ; or, An Epoch of Rest : being some chapters from a Utopian romance.* 1891
Formulates the same gospel in clearer terms. A socialist-artist's dream of a future London, when the socialist revolution has taken place, painting in rich hues the dress, furniture, and all the accompaniments of everyday life as they might be were commercialism destroyed and the love of art universal. [Longmans, London and New York ; Kerr, Chicago, 1917.]

—— *The Wood Beyond the World.* 1895
Pure romance as it might have been written by Malory, whose style Morris constantly echoes, as he does the rambling scheme and glamorous incidents of the chivalric lays. The wanderings and encounters of a young hero with beings of supernatural strength in a wondrous unknown land. [Longmans, London and New York.]

—— *The Well at the World's End.* 1896
The longest and most elaborate of these imaginative stories or prose poems, brimful of marvellous incident, enchanted landscapes, and the atmosphere of fairyland. [2 vols., Longmans, London and New York.]

—— *The Water of the Wondrous Isles.* 1897
—— *The Sundering Flood.* 1898
Similar romances, both posthumous. A delight in strangeness, in sensuous beauty, and a luxuriant imagination, combined with a curious realism, are the salient traits of these essays in mediæval romance. [(1) and (2), Longmans, London and New York.]
[*Works*, ed. by May Morris (his daughter), 24 vols., Longmans.]

MORRIS, William [tr.]. *Old French Romances done into English.* 1896
The Tale of King Coustans the Emperor, The Friendship of Amis and Amile, The Tale of King Florus and the Fair Jehane, The History of Over Sea. A translation of four romances belonging to the thirteenth century, almost contemporary with *Aucassin and Nicolette*, which, whatever their origin, are a faithful expression of the thought and feeling of mediæval France. The first is mythical history, the miraculous career of Constantius Chlorus, father of Constantine the Great, and the strange fulfilment of prophecies made before his birth ; scene, Byzantium. The next is a legend of true friendship between two heroes of the Carlovingian wars, the Damon and Pythias of mediæval romance ; their devotion culminates in Amile's sacrifice of his children to save his friend. The story of Jehane, a very pretty, improbable romance of a wife disguised and serving as her husband's esquire unbeknown to him, contains the root incident of *Cymbeline*—the wager about a wife's virtue. The most powerful of the four is the last, the tragic story of the Countess of Ponthieu, which was dramatized in the eighteenth century. Morris's archaic and sensuous prose is an admirable medium for the reproduction of these romances. [G. Allen : o.p. ; Scribner, New York : o.p. ; in vol. XVII of *Collected Works*, Longmans ; each tale separately (except *King Florus*), Mosher, Portland, Me.]

MORRIS, William, and **MAGNÚSSON,** Eiríkr [trs.]. *Three Northern Love-stories ; and other tales.* 1875
The first three have many marked features in common ; all turn on the enforced marriage of a daughter in love with another man, each contains charming snatches of impromptu verse. *The Story of Gunnlaug the Worm-tongue and Raven the Skald* is supposed to be the work of Ari. Scenes : W. Iceland, England, and Norway, A.D. 985–1008. Two rival poets, the masterful, hot-blooded Gunnlaug, and the dark, vengeful Raven, love a maiden. The cunning Raven supplants his gallant rival, whom she loves, and betrays him in the holmgang. Historical in substance ; gives interesting glimpses of the northern Courts. *Frithiof the Bold*

MORRIS, William, and MAGNÚSSON, Eiríkr (*continued*).

is a fourteenth-century romance, based perhaps on an early historical poem or saga. The son of a bersir loves a sister of the kings of Sogn, who despise and hate him, but after many wild adventures he brings their schemes to naught. In his reckless bravery, his song-craft, and chivalrous sense of honour, Frithiof is a regular troubadour. The Swedish poet Tegnér (1782–1846) composed a *Frithjofs Saga*. *Viglund the Fair*, a fifteenth-century story, is pure romance, and strangely modern in sentiment. The episode of Viglund's parents is like the story of young Lochinvar. He loves the sister of his foemen, and a witch-wife is suborned to destroy him. The *dénouement* is remarkable for a display of the nice sense of honour that is so foreign to the earlier savagery. *Hogni and Hedinn*, amplified from a tale in the Skáldskaparmál, is an absurd blend of mythology and hero tale. *Roi the Fool* is a Norse adaptation of an Oriental story. *Thorstein Staff-Smitten* is a genuine little saga, telling of a youth's unexpected derring-do ; the principle of revenge is tempered by a more chivalrous personal feeling. [Longmans.]

MORRIS, Judge William O'Connor [Irish ; 1824–1904]. *Memoirs of Gerald O'Connor.*   1903

Based on family documents and traditions. The autobiography of an ancestor of the author, who served in the Williamite wars (1689–91), went to France with Sarsfield and was on the staff of Marshal Villars. Describes the conquest and the confiscations in Ireland, and the battles of the War of the Spanish Succession. [Digby & Long : o.p.]

MORRISON, Arthur [*b.* 1863]. *Tales of Mean Streets.*   1894

Fifteen naturalistic stories of the London poor : hawkers and their women-folk, their fights and brutal love-making, poverty, filth, thieving, all presented with the most graphic realism, and without anything whatever to relieve the squalor and the gloom. *Lizerunt* is typical, a horrible narrative of courtship and conjugal brutality. [Methuen ; Modern Lib., New York.]

—— *A Child of the Jago.*   1896

The misery, foulness, and brutality of the poorest, drawn with the same unshrinking realism, and scarcely any comic or emotional relief. The life of a little boy, who leaves his thieving for a time to work in a shop. The district pictured is the scene of continual fights and bloodshed, brightened only by a muscular priest's courageous work. [Methuen : o.p. ; Stone, Chicago : o.p.]

—— *To London Town.*   1899

A much less depressing study of East Enders, delineating manners and characters full of individuality, in a grade of humble society not so squalid and criminal. Centres in the fortunes of a poor family near the Docks ; there are scenes of low comedy and vignettes of Epping Forest. [Methuen : o.p. ; Stone, Chicago : o.p.]

—— *Cunning Murrell.*   1900

Murrell is a witch-finder in an Essex village fifty years ago, a curious personality, half superstition, half charlatanry. He was suggested partly by an original who left actual documents. [Methuen : o.p. ; Doubleday, New York : o.p.]

—— *The Hole in the Wall.*   1902

Scene, the Ratcliff Highway, in its worst days, some thirty years ago ; characters, an observant boy, a picturesque pair of murderers, an innkeeper who received stolen goods, and other shady people ; the events well in keeping, and related with the usual realistic skill and a great deal less of the unrelieved gloom notable in *Mean Streets*. [Methuen : o.p. ; McClure, New York : o.p.]

—— *Divers Vanities.*   1905

Short stories chiefly of the same class of subject, but also some humorous ones, e.g. *Lost Tommy Jepps*—a little masterpiece—and *A Tale of Tricks*. [Methuen : o.p.]

—— *Green Ginger.*   1909

Sixteen short tales, largely of the rustic worthies from Essex whom we sampled in *Cunning Murrell*. [Hutchinson : o.p. ; Stokes, New York : o.p.]

MORROW, Honoré Willsie [*née* McCue ; American]. *Forever Free : a novel of Abraham Lincoln.*   1927

A most conscientious work, even the dialogue being founded on facts taken from the best authorities—of which a long list is given. It deals with Lincoln's first two years at the White House, the final incidents that made war inevitable, the battles from Bull Run to Antietam, and the political and personal manœuvres going on behind the scenes. At the same time it has all the features of a rich domestic novel, with Lincoln and his wife as hero and heroine, and their children making delightful byplay. Much of the dramatic tension arises from Lincoln's efforts to stir up McClellan. The war-correspondent William Russell is an engaging figure, but all the prominent men of the day make their entry as the tale goes on. A woman spy is responsible for a streak of melodrama. [Morrow, New York ; McClelland, Toronto ; Cape.]

—— *With Malice toward None* [sequel].   1928

This carries on the story to the end of the war. The disturbing factor in the life of the Lincolns is now the political dissensions and intrigues, even in the Cabinet, which hamper the President's efforts to evolve a scheme of reconstruction that would satisfy all parties. Most of the previous characters reappear, with the negro politician Douglass and Lincoln's son Robert as newcomers. A further list of authorities : but the many quotations from the poets are remarkably incorrect. [Morrow, New York ; McClelland, Toronto ; Cape.]

—— *The Last Full Measure* [sequel].   1930

Completes the trilogy ; this covers the Booth conspiracy and the last six months of Lincoln's life (1865). [Morrow, New York.]

—— *Splendour of God.*   1930

The story of Adoniram Judson and the first Baptist mission in Burma (1814–50). [McClelland, Toronto ; Hodder.]

MORROW, William Chambers [American ; 1853–1923]. *A Man, his Mark.*   1899

A tragic drama laid amid the Alpine scenery of California. There are two actors, a man who has lost his beloved, and the woman who has caused his loss, and whom he repays by an act of heroic sacrifice. [Lippincott, Philadelphia : o.p. ; De La More Press : o.p.]

MOSS, Geoffrey. *Defeat.* 1924

Six tales of post-war Germany; on the whole, a heartrending picture of individuals suffering for the sins of others. The title-story shows the French engineering a Secessionist plot in the occupied territory, and brutally doing to death a chivalrous German officer. The destitution of the educated classes, the debauching of innocent girls, and the brutalization of the workers in the Ruhr, are the other subjects. [Constable.]

MOSZKOWSKI, Alexander [German]. *The Isles of Wisdom.* 1925

A Gulliverian satire: the narrator visits a group of islands, each of which is populated by the devotees of some new philosophy or modern craze. [Transl. by H. J. STENNING, Routledge.]

MOTT, Jordan Lawrence [American; b. 1881]. *Jules of the Great Heart.* 1905

Life of a free trapper in the early days of the Hudson Bay Company. A series of episodes, each a short story, detailing the various aspects of his existence and his incessant fight with nature. Gives the French-Canadian patois well. [Century Co., New York: o.p.; Heinemann: o.p.]

—— *To the Credit of the Sea.* 1907

The Labrador fisher-folk. [Harper, New York and London: o.p.]

—— *The White Darkness; and other stories of the great North-West.* 1907

The gloom, mystery, and terror of the wilderness finely expressed. [Outing Pub. Co., New York: o.p.; Heinemann: o.p.]

MOTTA, Luigi [Italian]. *Flames on the Bosphorus* (Fiamme sul Bosforo). 1920

A vivid account of the capture of Constantinople by the Turks (1453). [Transl. by Helen ZIMMERN, Odhams: o.p.]

MOTTRAM, Ralph Hale [b. 1883]. *The Spanish Farm.* 1924

What happens to the Ferme l'Espagnole, near Hazebrouck, is subordinate to the character of Madeleine, the strong, competent Flemish daughter of the farmer. She is a wonderful manager, who impresses herself on the miscellaneous sorts of soldiers and civilians during the war, and also on her peasant neighbours. And the history of her love affairs is a profoundly interesting study of human personality. [Chatto; Dial Press, New York.]

—— *Sixty-Four, Ninety-Four!* 1925

—— *The Crime at Vanderlynden's.* 1926

Captain Dormer, a sober and competent temporary officer, attempts to straighten out the business at the Farm: an ironical account of wasted time and strength, contrasting, by implication, the momentous events that are passing with the futilities of the daily round of those engaged in the war. [Chatto; Dial Press, New York.]

—— *The Spanish Farm Trilogy, 1914–18.* 1927

Collects the three previous novels into one, with connecting links and epilogues. [Chatto; Dial Press, New York.]

—— *Our Mr. Dormer.* 1927

Deals with three generations of a solid business family connected with a bank in the eastern counties, and offers a brief conspectus of the social history of the last century. The author has written a history of Banking. [Chatto: Dial Press, New York.]

—— *The English Miss.* 1928

This is a study in character—the development of a girl, athletic, healthy, and without any great depth of sensibility, from childhood to maturity, during the war. [Chatto; Dial Press, New York.]

—— *The Boroughmonger.* 1929

Scenes of provincial society in Norwich in the Reform period, with some account of the political jobbery of the landed nobility, woven into rather a confused story. [Chatto; Little & Brown, Boston.]

—— *Europa's Beast.* 1930

Skene, of *The Spanish Farm*, is now in love with a woman whose husband's mind has been affected by a wound. When the husband is killed in a flying accident, they marry. A story of quite ordinary people made interesting by admirable workmanship. [Chatto; *sub tit. A Rich Man's Daughter*, Harper, New York.]

MOUAT, James [Australian]. *The Rise of the Australian Wool Kings.* 1892

A somewhat thin romance of Port Philip, interspersed with much valuable information respecting the rise of the wool kings. Author is a descendant of James Mouat, of Yarraberb, one of the original pioneers of the Bendigo goldfields. [Sonnenschein: o.p.]

MOULT, Thomas. *Snow over Elden.* 1920

A quiet love-story, little more than a series of pictures, set in the Peak district, the author's native region. [Heinemann.]

" MOWBRAY, J. P." [Jeanie Pearl Wheeler, *née* Mowbray; American], and her late Husband, Andrew Carpenter **WHEELER** [American; d. 1903]. *A Journey to Nature.* 1901

A New York stockbroker, threatened with heart disease, is sent by his doctor into the country to lead a natural existence, in other words, " to cease to live," for a year. This is the record of the semi-animal life of himself and his son, his talks with a rough and hearty old doctor, and his love passages with a country girl. He is a sort of sophisticated Thoreau, a lover and an observer of nature, and prone to meditate on what he sees. But in his reveries he always has an eye for effect, and his style scintillates with smart sayings and allusions. [Garden City Co., New York; Constable: o.p.]

MRAZOVIĆ, Milena [Bosnian]. *Selam: sketches and tales of Bosnian life* (1893). 1899

Eight slight but sympathetic sketches of the little known and harshly treated inhabitants of the hills of Bosnia and Herzegovina, by one who knows and loves them. Many of the subjects are really Turkish. [Transl. by Mrs. WAUGH, Jarrold: o.p.]

" MÜHLBACH, Luise " [Klara Mundt, *née* Müller; German; 1814–73]. *Old Fritz and the New Era.* 1872

—— *Frederick the Great and his Court* (1853). 1867

"MÜHLBACH, Luise" (*continued*). *Berlin and Sans Souci ; or, Frederick the Great and his Friends* [sequel]. 1867

—— *Frederick the Great and his Family* [sequel]. 1867

—— *The Merchant of Berlin* (Johann Gotzkowsky). 1867

—— *Louisa of Prussia and her Times.* 1872

—— *Napoleon and the Queen of Prussia* [sequel]. 1867

—— *Napoleon in Germany.* 1867

—— *Napoleon and Blücher.* 1868

—— *Andreas Hofer.* 1868

—— *Prince Eugene and his Times.* 1872

Luise Mühlbach's novels are a patient and methodical amplification of the bare historical record, designed to illustrate any given period according to the letter and spirit of historical fact. The characters are all prominent people and nearly all historical, and the result is a continuous narrative of high politics, Court life, diplomacy, and war, in which personal motive and intrigue play a considerable part. It is, in short, history written in the form of a novel. Arranged above in chronological order of events. [Appleton, New York : all o.p. except (1), (2), (9), and (11).]

MUIR, Robert James [Scottish]. *The Mystery of Muncraig.* 1900

Delineations of character in the style of Galt form the best part of this story of the Stewartry of Kirkcudbright ; the mystery attaches to a squire and a farmer who have been implicated in piratical enterprises. [Unwin : o.p.]

MUJAMORI, Asartaro [Japanese]. *Tales of the Samurai.* 1921

Tales of the days of feudalism, introducing historical characters, e.g. Masamune, persecutor of the Christians, and Iyemitsu. The author is professor of English in Tokyo. [Tokyo.]

MULHOLLAND, Rosa [Lady Gilbert ; Irish ; 1841–1921]. *Nanno.* 1899

A deeply sympathetic and in its own way realistic novel of very humble life, Nanno being a workhouse child who rises to heights of self-sacrifice through the sound influence of homely people. Scenes : Dublin, Youghal, and Ardmore. [De La More Press : o.p.]

—— *Onora.* 1900

Onora is a daughter of poor parents, who goes into service at a farm in County Waterford, and is loved by one of the sons of her mistress. A careful study of humble life, the pathos of which, and the sterling goodness of obscure people, are rendered with womanly sympathy. [De La More Press : o.p.]

—— *The Tragedy of Chris : the story of a Dublin flower-girl.* 1903

A similar theme to that of her masterpiece, *Nanno.* Chris is a workhouse girl who falls into the clutches of the white slave traffic. [Sands : o.p. ; Herder, St. Louis.]

—— *The Return of Mary O'Murrough.* 1908

A pathetic story, Mary returns from the States to her home near Killarney to find her lover in gaol, a victim of police injustice. An impeachment of the laws under which the peasantry were suffering. [Sands : o.p. ; Herder, St. Louis.]

—— *O'Loghlin of Clare.* 1916

Brings out the hardships suffered by Roman Catholics under the penal laws. A story of a Catholic landowner and his family in Co. Clare (1746). Mrs. Delany is a figure. [Sands : o.p. ; Kennedy, New York : o.p.]

MÜLLER, Professor Friedrich Max [German ; 1823–1900]. *German Love : fragments from the papers of an alien* (Deutsche Liebe). 1858

A thoroughly poetic story in idea and execution, reciting with refined tenderness the history of a pure affection, platonic first by choice and then by necessity. [Transl. by S. WINKWORTH, Chapman : o.p. ; Longmans, 1877 : o.p. ; transl. by G. P. UPTON, *sub tit. Memories : a story of German love,* M'Clurg, Chicago.]

MUNRO, Hector Hugh [" Saki " ; 1870–1916]. *The Chronicles of Clovis.* 1911

Sporting tales and sketches, flippant and farcical, extremely clever at absurd epigram and occasional parody ; with two stories of the horrible, *Sredni Vashtar* and *The Hounds of Fate.* [Lane ; Viking Press, New York.]

—— *The Unbearable Bassington.* 1912

An all too indiscriminately brilliant novel of character and social affairs, where all but the people mocked at are accomplished wits. [Lane ; Viking Press, New York.]

—— *Beasts and Super-Beasts.* 1914

Thirty-six amusing trifles, concerned with witty individuals who without fail score hits over a duller adversary. [Lane ; Viking Press, New York.]

—— *When William Came.* 1916

England as it might have been under German domination—a land of enervated shopkeepers, intent only on sport and safe living—comedy that develops into more than ephemeral sarcasm. [Lane ; Viking Press, New York.]

—— *The Toys of Peace ; and other Papers.* 1916

The Wolves of Cernogratz and *The Interlopers* may be singled out, with diffidence, as the best ; but *Shock Tactics, Louis, Excepting Mrs. Pentharby,* and the title-piece bring out, scarce less aptly, the subtle, elusive humour and quaintness of thought characteristic of Saki. [Lane ; Viking Press, New York.]

MUNRO, Neil [Scottish ; 1864–1930]. *The Lost Pibroch ; and other shieling stories.* 1896

A Highlander's tales of the Western Highlands ; the modern crofter classes, inspired pipers, antique legends and superstitions, raids and murders in the old turbulent days, inspired by the recent Celtic movement— " Fiona MacLeod " and also Stevenson. Gives a glossary of Gaelic terms. [Blackwood.]

—— *John Splendid : the tale of a poor gentleman and the little wars of Lorn.* 1898

Like *Esmond,* this aims at historical realism and dwells on the horrors and barbarities instead of the romance of war. It is an instructive contrast to Scott's *Legend of Montrose,* the material being almost identical,

MUNRO, Neil (*continued*).

viz. the war in Argyllshire with the Royalists under Montrose (1642–5). John Splendid himself is one of the most victorious attempts to capture that elusive thing the Highland character ; he is a typical Gael, akin to Stevenson's Alan Breck. The only defect is that he is as modern in his point of view as his interpreter. [Blackwood ; Dodd & Mead, New York : o.p.]

—— *Gilian the Dreamer : his fancy, his love, and adventure.*　　　　1898

An interpretation of the visionary and poetic side of the Gaelic character. Gilian is a born poet, unfitted to grapple with the practical necessities of existence, and he endures ills and humiliations at the hands of inferior men. But his nature asserts itself strongly, and at length he finds the poetical expression for which he has been half-unconsciously striving. The minor characters are very various, and form a picture of Highland village life (Inverary) just after Waterloo. [Blackwood ; Dodd & Mead, New York : o.p.]

—— *Doom Castle.*　　　　1901

Intrigue, love, and adventure in the Western Highlands after the '45. The hero a gallant French nobleman, who comes north to seek out a traitor ; the other characters, Highlanders, who display the author's familiar understanding of the Celtic nature, and some Lowlanders with humorous traits. [Blackwood ; Doubleday, New York : o.p.]

—— *The Shoes of Fortune.*　　　　1901

A showy kind of Stevensonian romance, bringing in the Young Pretender and Miss Walkenshaw. Scotland and France (1755). [Blackwood ; Dodd & Mead, New York : o.p.]

—— *Children of Tempest.*　　　　1903

Inspired by the grand elemental aspects of nature in the Outer Hebrides—Uist and Benbecula—rather than by interest in the human figures. What plot interest there is hangs upon a certain treasure, concealed by the Jacobites and destined to be the dowry of a young girl. Her brother is a priest, and most of the characters are Catholic peasants. Dialect, customs, etc. (*c.* 1800). [Blackwood.]

—— *Fancy Farm.*　　　　1910

A romantic love-comedy enacted on the west coast of Scotland, the lovers a rather eccentric baronet—" a splairger," as he calls himself—and a long-headed cousin who plays a waiting game. [Blackwood.]

—— *Ayrshire Idylls.*　　　　1912

Ten stories of Scottish life, some about historical personages (Johnson and Burns appear) ; others, such as *The Three Brothers*, are tales of peasant life. [Blackwood ; *illus.*, Macmillan, New York.]

—— *The New Road.*　　　　1914

The making of General Wade's road into the Highlands after the Forty-five is alluded to in the title. Accurate local and historical colour, with a severe characterization of the turncoat, Simon Fraser, Lord Lovat. [Blackwood.]

—— *Jaunty Jock ; and other stories.*　　　　1918

Eleven tales, mainly historical, from which *Young Pennymore*, the tragedy of a Jacobite suspect in 1752, and *A Return to Nature*, in which a country law agent returns to the manner of his marauder ancestors, may be singled out. [Blackwood.]

MURASAKI SHIBUKU, Lady [Japanese ; 978 (?)–1031 (?)]. *The Tale of Genji* [*The Tale of Genji—The Sacred Tree—A Wreath of Cloud—Blue Trousers*] (Genji Monogatari, printed 1650).　　　　1925–8

" The most celebrated of the classical Japanese romances." Written, between 1001 and 1015, by a lady of the Court, some of whose other literary work is extant. Genji is the son of the Mikado by his favourite concubine. Court life, political intrigues, and the love-affairs of the hero are the theme. Murasaki displays sentiment, wit, and a keen, often critical observation of men and manners in her thoroughly realistic presentation of the life of Japanese high society of the epoch. [Transl. by Arthur WALEY, with introds. and appendices, 4 vols., Allen ; Houghton, Boston. A translation of 17 out of the 54 chapters was made by Baron KENCHIO SUYEMATSU in 1882 (Trübner : o.p.).]

MURGER, Henri [French ; 1822–61]. *Bohemians of the Latin Quarter* (Scènes de la vie de Bohême, 1851).　　　　1895

A rambling novel composed chiefly of detached scenes of life among the struggling authors, students, and grisettes who were the associates of Murger's early days, all of them depicted with a most infectious humour and delight in good fellowship. Most of the anecdotes and of the happy band of comrades are, doubtless, historical ; we know, at any rate, that the hospital scene is true. The two grisettes, Mimi and Musette, in the love episodes, are both touching figures of a time that has completely vanished. [Transl., *sub tit.* *The Latin Quarter*, by Ellen MARRIAGE and John SELWYN, De La More Press, 1901 : o.p. ; Brentano, New York (Collins) ; in *French Romancists*, 10 vols., Sawyer.]

" MURON, Johannes " [Gustav Keckeis ; German ; *b.* 1884]. *The Spanish Island* (Die spanische Insel, 1926).　　　　1930

A well-informed but rather heavy historical novel on the theme of Columbus's discovery of Hispaniola (Haiti) in 1492 and the rivalries, dissensions, and intrigues that followed, down to 1500. Christopher's brother, Bartholomew, governor of the island, is a prominent character, and various Spaniards, Italians, and natives are carefully drawn. [Transl. by Florence Low, Secker.]

MURRAY, David Christie [1847–1907]. *A Life's Atonement.*　　　　1880

A gloomy story, told partly as autobiography. The hero, on the point of seeing his ambition fulfilled, being in difficulties with a money-lender and urged by necessity and luck, robs a stranger, and by misadventure kills him. Thereupon begins his life's atonement : he works as a dock labourer in London, and is not recognized as author of the crime till on his death-bed. [Chatto.]

—— *Joseph's Coat.*　　　　1881

A young fellow is compelled by circumstances to leave his wife, whom he married secretly, and to pass off their child as some one else's. On this foundation a complicated plot is based, exemplifying the law of nemesis and bringing happiness to innocent sufferers. [Chatto.]

MURRAY, David Christie (*continued*). *Old Blazer's Hero.* 1887
> The characters and doings of a mine surveyor and his rival : Old Blazer is a mine. The hero is one of those seemingly commonplace characters who on occasion rise to heights of heroism ; the rival is a selfish, handsome, engaging scamp. [Chatto.]

—— *A Dangerous Catspaw.* 1889
> The dire temptation that leads an impecunious young barrister into crime, a clever rascal's nearly successful plot to secure him and his booty, and the counterplottings of a detective, share the interest with a quiet love-story. [Longmans: o.p.]

MURRAY, Rosalind [Mrs. A. J. Toynbee ; Scottish]. *The Leading Note.* 1910
—— *Moonseed.* 1911
> Domestic life at home and abroad, the strengths and weaknesses, affinities or angularities of character that lead to mutual understanding and lasting affection or the reverse—described with a simplicity and directness and a cold detachment that give it all a singularly unemotional effect. [(1) and (2), Sidgwick : o.p.]

—— *Hard Liberty.* 1929
> Though not devoid of incident, this is in the main the character-study of a talented, but selfish, unamiable, and self-tormenting man, whose sole refuge from the miseries of his loneliness is in science. [Chatto ; Harcourt, New York.]

MURRY, John Middleton [*b.* 1889]. *Still Life.* 1916
> A set of highly self-conscious, dissatisfied people are shown exploring themselves and each other and striving to find some mode or plan of existence that is worth while. Anne leaves her stodgy husband and elopes with Maurice, the latter thinking he has eloped with her. Then he returns to Madeleine, who no longer wants him. But it is less the events than the talk and self-vivisection of these subtle and abnormal characters that is the point. [Constable.]

—— *The Voyage.* 1924
> There is no voyage, only talk about this and the emotional relationships in another little coterie of intellectuals and discontented seekers for a way to live. [Constable.]

MUSAEUS, Johann Karl August [German ; 1735–1787]. *Legends of Rubezahl ; and other tales* (1803). 1845
> Musaeus put into a literary dress a number of legends, etc., in his *Volksmärchen der Deutschen* (1782–6). His *Legends of the Enchanted Knights* was transl. by KENNEDY (Longman : o.p. 1857). See also Carlyle, *Translations from the German.* He also wrote a kind of parody of Richardson in *Grandison the Second ; or, The German Grandison* (*Grandison der Zweite*, 1760). [Cundall : o.p.]

MUSSET, Alfred de [French ; 1810–57]. *Confessions of a Child of the Century* (Confessions d'un enfant du siècle, 1836). 1892
> A semi-autobiographical expression of Musset's sense of disgust and disillusionment after the Byronic eruptions of his early career. The hero has been aroused from a course of debauchery by his father's death, and he falls in love. Libertinism has made him a cynic and a sceptic, incapable of a pure attachment ; his love degenerates into fits of passion and jealousy, which beckon him on to murder and suicide. Finding happiness out of reach, he bids his mistress farewell. Musset's experiences with George Sand on the famous sojourn in Italy inspire his disgusted portraiture of woman. (Among untranslated pieces may be mentioned *Contes et nouvelles*, superior in art and interest to his longer essay in fiction, e.g. *Le fils de Titien*, *Pierre et Camille*, *Frédéric et Bernerette*, and *Mimi Pinson*, tender, natural, and fanciful creations of a poetic mind. [Transl. by K. WARREN, Sergel, Chicago : o.p. : *sub tit. A Modern Man's Confession*, Brentano, New York.]

MYERS, Leopold Hamilton [*b.* 1882]. *The Orissers.* 1922
> The suspicions, jealousies, plots, and intrigues over the will of a millionaire ; exhaustive analysis of the various consciences, and discussions of the abstract principles in the light of recent American psychology. [Putnam.]

—— *The Clio.* 1925
> In the story of the revolution in Amazonia, which is secretly being run by a Byronic peer who has come up the Amazon with a crowd of pleasure-loving, erotic guests, the author has achieved a blend of Conradian romance and sentimental intrigue, with a superabundance of incidents in the nude that are usually left to the imagination. [Putnam ; Scribner, New York.]

—— *The Near and the Far.* 1929
> A vivid imaginative picture of Indian life in the time of Akbar. [Cape ; Harcourt, New York.]

" NADEL, Henri " [Henri Josepf Vendel ; French ; *b.* 1892]. *Down the Red Lane.* 1930
> A diary of the war, emphasizing the fear and horror that threatened the very foundations of sanity. The author joined the French army at the age of twenty. [Transl. by Blair TAYLOR ; preface by Romain Rolland, Bobbs-Merrill, Indianapolis.]

NASHE, Thomas [1567–1601]. *The Unfortunate Traveller ; or, the Life of Jack Wilton.* 1594
> The nearest approach to realism in English fiction before Deloney. Nashe's object was to write a sensation story, showing that real life was as exciting as anything imagined by the romancers ; and he produces several lurid and ghastly episodes, in which the life of that " hell of iniquity," Italy, where he had probably not travelled, furnish circumstance and verisimilitude. Historical persons—e.g. Surrey, More, Erasmus, Luther, and Cornelius Agrippa, not to mention the mythical Geraldine—actual events, and accounts of famous cities in Germany, France, and Italy, are introduced into a mixed recital which seems to have been written as a counterblast to other story-tellers. [Ed. with *Essay on Life and Writings of Nash*, by Edmund Gosse, Chiswick Press, 1892 ; o.p. ; ed. by H. F. B. Brett-Smith, Blackwell, Oxford, 1927.]

NAZHIVIN, Ivan Fedorovich [Russian ; *b.* 1874]. *Rasputin.* 1930
> Interesting only in so far as it deals with that period of history (1905–22) which has seen Russia's transformation. [Transl. by C. J. HOGARTH, Knopf, London and New York.]

NEALE, Rev. John Mason [1818–66]. *Duchenier; or, The Revolt of La Vendée.*　　1848
A Royalist story of 1793–4; scenes, La Vendée, Paris, and London. [S.P.C.K.]
—— *Theodora Phranza.*　　1857
A story closing with the fall of Constantinople (1453). Neale was an Anglican divine who wrote a long series of historical tales for children, most of them illustrating Church history. This and the preceding are among the best of these. [S.P.C.K.]

NEEDELL, Mrs. John Hodder [Mary Anna, *née* Lupton; 1830–?]. *The Story of Philip Methuen.*
1886
Character and the influences that mould character. Philip is an ascetic, trained for the priesthood, inured to self-control, and tenacious of his ideal. Anna is an egoist, passionate, revengeful—the result of early neglect. The other characters also show the effects of training and environment. The novel exhibits Philip sacrificing his own happiness in life and that of his love to save the reckless Anna from a slur on her good name; his quixotism brings tragic consequences. [Warne: o.p.; Appleton, New York: o.p.]
—— *Stephen Ellicott's Daughter.*　　1891
A pathetic story, the characters endowed with an exalted virtue and an active altruism transcending ordinary human nature. [Warne: o.p.; Appleton, New York: o.p.]

NĚMCOVÁ, Božena [Czech; 1820–62]. *The Grandmother: a story of country life in Bohemia* (Babička).　　1891
A tale of Bohemian peasants, resembling Auerbach's; contains much folk-lore, and sketches of manners and customs. [Transl. by Frances GREGOR, McClurg, Chicago: o.p.]

NEMIRÒVITCH-DANTCHENKO, Vasili [Russian; b. 1848]. *With a Diploma; and, The Whirlwind* (1894).　　1915
The work of a very fertile and very popular novelist who applies himself mainly to the short story. The first is about the self-regeneration of a peasant girl, the other contrasts the inner life and the social conduct of a girl belonging to a much higher class. Both stories are significant of the moral changes going on in Russia before the revolution. [Transl. by W. J. Stanton PYPER, Maunsel: o.p.; Luce, Boston.]
—— *Princes of the Stock Exchange.*　　1914
A satirical picture of society and business life in Petersburg. [Transl. by A. S. RAPPOPORT, S. Paul: o.p.]

NEMIROVSKY, Irene [Russian, writing in French]. *David Golder* (1929).　　1930
Golder is of course a Jew, of unbounded rapacity and unscrupulousness. The history of his international financial schemes is told in swiftly-changing scenes, down to his evil end. [Transl. by Sylvia STUART, Constable; Boni, New York.]

NEUMAN, Berman Paul [b. 1853]. *The Uttermost Farthing.*　　1900
A study of rancour and revenge in a girl who believes a certain man to be the cause of her father's ruin. In the sequel, destiny and love turn the tables, and she gives her heart where she hated. [Blackwood: o.p.]
—— *The Rise and Glory of the Westell-Browns.*　　1914
A family chronicle of a little London draper of sterling character, who makes a fortune, loses it through his children's mismanagement, and has to make a fresh start to provide for the family. [Hodder: o.p.]

NEUMANN, Alfred [German; b. 1895]. *The Deuce* (Der Teufel, 1926).　　1928
An attempt in the *Quentin Durward* genre, presenting Louis XI and his barber-favourite, Oliver Necker (1468–88). [Transl. by Huntley PATERSON, Heinemann; *sub tit. The Devil*, Knopf, New York.]
—— *The Rebels* (Rebellen, 1927).　　1929
—— *Guerra* (Guerra, 1928) [sequel].　　1930
The revolutionary movements of 1848, particularly in the duchy of Tuscany. [Transl. by Huntley PATERSON, (1), Heinemann; Knopf, New York; (2), Knopf, London and New York.]

NEUMANN, Robert [Austrian; b. 1897]. *Flood* (Sintflut, 1929).　　1930
The narrator tells the uneventful story of his life until he comes to the terrible period following the war, as a prelude to a gruesome but absorbing picture of Vienna in the grip of starvation, brutal profiteering, and frenzied luxury. [Transl. by William A. DRAKE, Putnam; Covici, New York.]

NEVINSON, Henry Woodd [b. 1856]. *The Valley of Tophet.*　　1896
Depicts the people of one of the lowest mining districts in England, in twelve stories, almost entirely pathetic in motive. [Dent: o.p.; Holt, New York: o.p.]

NEVYEROV, Aleksandr [Russian; 18?–1923]. *Tashkent, the City of Bread.*　　1930
The ghastly sufferings and patient endurance of the Russian peasantry in the famine of 1921 are soberly but poignantly brought out in the narrative of a boy's plucky tramp for 1,300 miles to Tashkent, which he imagines to be a city of plenty. [Transl. by Reginald MERTON and W. G. WALTON, Gollancz.]

NEW ARABIAN NIGHTS, The.　　1882
Select tales not included in the translations of Galland or of Lane. Not to be confused with the so-called *New Arabian Nights—Arabian Tales, or a Continuation of the Arabian Nights Entertainments*, stated to be newly transl. from original Arabic into French by Dom CHAVIS and M. CAZOTTE, and thence into English by Robert HERON, 4 vols. (Edin. and Lond., 1792), 3 vols. (Lond., 1794). This was based on Arabic MSS., but the translation was so free that it is usually regarded as a poor imitation of *The Arabian Nights*. Two new tales, *Mengraby the Magician* (which suggested to Southey the idea of *Thalaba*) and the farcical *Robber Caliph*, were memorable additions, however. [Transl. by W. F. KIRBY, Sonnenschein: o.p. See also *Arabian Nights Entertainments*.]

NEWBOLT, Sir Henry John [b. 1862]. *Taken from the Enemy.*　　1892
Story of a plot to rescue Napoleon (1821). [Chatto.]
—— *The Old Country: a romance.*　　1906
Life in England in the twentieth and in the fourteenth centuries so portrayed as to reveal the intrinsic oneness—
" In Eternity there is no distinction of Tenses " (Browne). The more significant characters live in both

NEWBOLT, Sir Henry John (*continued*).

ages ; they step back from to-day into the year 1356, the time of the Black Prince and of the battle of Poitiers, which is magnificently described. [Smith & Elder : o.p. ; Murray, 1929 ; Dutton, New York : o.p.]

—— *The New June.*   1909

Court life, monastic life, and the fortunes of certain young nobles and squires in the days of Richard II, who is a prominent figure—all described in the same spacious style and with an almost aggressive modernity of manners and speech (1396–1403). [Blackwood : o.p. ; Dutton, New York : o.p.]

—— *The Twymans.*   1911

A rather miscellaneous novel, with faithful—and inspiring—episodes of school life—a midland grammar school and Clifton College—and an idealistic story of a fine-souled youth's great renunciation of the things of this life. [Blackwood ; Lippincott, Philadelphia : o.p.]

—— *Aladore.*   1914

An allegorical romance in the archaic style of Malory, about a prince who becomes a pilgrim in order to reach the dream-city of Aladore and win his heart's desire. [*Illus.* by Lady Hylton, Blackwood.]

NEWMAN, John Henry, Cardinal [1801–90]. *Loss and Gain.*   1848

More of a Platonic dialogue than a novel ; subject, the Roman supremacy and the defects of Anglicanism ; the hero, a projection of Newman's own personality, at once shy and bold, simple and profound, occasionally satirical. The story of his conversion brings in some delicate and intimate sketches of Oxford life. [Longmans, London and New York ; Burns and Oates.]

—— *Callista : a sketch of the 3rd century.*   1856

The story of an African martyr at Sicca, under the emperor Decius (*c.* 250), with interesting studies of demoniacal possession, religious emotion, and the fear of eternal punishment. Divagations on theological and devotional questions. [Longmans, London and New York ; Burns & Oates (Kenedy, New York) ; Browne & Nolan, Dublin.]

NEWTE, Horace Wykeham Can [*b.* 1898]. *Ruth, the Woman Who Loved.*   1916

—— *He Whom I Follow* [sequel].   1917

Ruth is a tragic figure, successively betrayed by a rake, abandoned by her lover, and married to a blackguard ; in the sequel, which is a less convincing story, she achieves happiness in company with a mystic who leads a wandering existence. Several of the minor characters are good sketches of vicious and unpleasant types. [(1) and (2), Mills & Boon : o.p.]

—— *The House that Fell, and the Decline and Fall of a Suburb.*   1917

A pedestrian story enlivened by satirical laughter, presenting some fifty denizens of villadom—for the most part snobs, fools, gossips, flirts, harridans, or at any rate commonplace people, with a few worth more friendly appreciation. [Mills & Boon : o.p.]

NEXØ, Martin Andersen [Danish ; *b.* 1869]. *Pelle the Conqueror* (Pelle Erobreren, 1906–10).   1913–17

The life of a Labour leader, in four parts : *Boyhood* (1906), *Apprenticeship* (1914), *The Great Struggle* (1916), *Daybreak* (1917). The author was a shoemaker ; and Pelle, first a herdboy on the land, reluctantly takes to that trade in Copenhagen. The early two volumes picture feelingly and with a wealth of intimate touches the life of the poor in the Danish capital, without narrowing the focus too much from life in general. Then comes the growth of class-consciousness and Pelle's devotion to the great idea of the solidarity of Labour. The account of the employers' lock-out and the general strike that paralyses the capitalist forces is probably the most brilliant ever written. The trade unions have won, but sweating and poverty still go on. Pelle comes out of prison, after serving an iniquitous sentence, to resume the fight, but on other ground. With the aid of a wealthy friend, he sets up a co-operative colony—which at least provides the author with a good propagandist ending. [(1), (2), and (3), transl. by Jessie MUIR, (4), by Bernard MIALL, Sidgwick ; Holt, New York ; (1) is o.p. In 1 vol., P. Smith, New York, 1930.]

—— *Ditte, Girl Alive !*   1920
—— *Ditte, Daughter of Man* [sequel].   1921
—— *Ditte, Beyond the Stars* [sequel].   1922

This trilogy (*Ditte Menneskebarn*, 1917–19), is again a tragic and realistic picture of life in the slums of Copenhagen. Ditte is an illegitimate child, enters domestic service, is seduced, and meets an untimely death. It is a portrayal of a noble character amidst sordid surroundings. [(1) and (2), transl. by A. G. CHATER and Richard THIRSK, (3) by Asta and Rowland KENNEY ; Holt, New York ; Heinemann : (1) and (2) o.p.]

NICHOLS, Beverley [*b.* 1899]. *Prelude.*   1920

A public school novel that is far from unfavourable to that institution. The over-sensitive boy whose trials and miseries are followed is very sympathetically analysed. [Chatto.]

NICHOLSON, Meredith [American ; *b.* 1866]. *The House of a Thousand Candles.*   1905
—— *The Little Brown Jug at Kildare.*   1908
—— *The Lords of High Decision.*   1909

Popular novels introducing the romantic elements of mystery, adventure, and sensation into prosaic life. *The Little Brown Jug* is a pretty little farce of life in the South ; the *Lords of High Decision* is a more serious and strenuous novel. [(1), Bobbs-Merrill, Indianapolis : o.p. ; Grosset, New York ; Gay & Hancock ; Nelson ; Black, 1929 ; (2), Bobbs-Merrill : o.p. ; *sub tit.* The War of the Carolinas, Nelson ; (3), Doubleday, New York : o.p. ; Gay & Hancock : o.p.]

—— *Otherwise Phyllis.*   1913

A sentimental comedy of a Hoosier township, with a vivacious heroine. [Burt, New York : o.p.]

—— *Broken Barriers.*   1922

A girl sets out to earn her own living in a Middle Western city, and falls in love with an engineer—hence conflict between career and home-making. [Scribner, New York ; Burt, New York, 1924.]

NICHOLSON, Meredith (*continued*). *Best Laid Schemes.* 1922
Six stories of business and political life. [Scribner, New York.]
—— *The Cavalier of Tennessee.* 1928
The love-story of Andrew Jackson. [Bobbs-Merrill, Indianapolis.]
NIETSCHMANN, Hermann Otto [" Armin Stein "; German; *b.* 1840]. *Prince Albrecht of Branden-
burg: a story of the Reformation* (Kardinal Albrecht, 1882). 1907
The titular hero was Archbishop and Elector of Mainz, and a cardinal at the time of the Reformation, and
Tetzel was his commissioner for the sale of indulgences. [Transl. by Mrs. M. E. H. IRELAND, German
Literary Board, Burlington, Ia.]
NISBET, Hume [Australian; *b.* 1849]. *Bail Up!* 1893
A romance of bushrangers and bushmen in early Queensland; pure melodrama. This and the next two are
good specimens of this writer's many novels. [Chatto: o.p.]
—— *A Bush Girl's Romance.* 1894
A tale of adventure, in which Captain Wildrake, an epicurean bushranger, performs prodigies of prowess and
cruelty. Apart from these sensations, there is vivid drawing of life in Western Australia. [White: o.p.]
NIVEN, Frederick John [Scottish; *b.* 1878]. *Justice of the Peace.* 1914
A realistic study of a Glasgow family—a suspicious and selfish woman wrecks the lives of her husband and
of her artistic son. [Nash: o.p.; Boni, New York, 1923.]
—— *The S.S. "Glory".* 1915
Rough and brutal life on an Atlantic cattle-boat is effectively presented. [Collins; Doran, New York: o.p.]
—— *The Lady of the Crossings.* 1919
An attractive blend of romance and adventure in a small township of western America. [Hodder: o.p.]
—— *The Three Marys.* 1930
A workmanlike novel, recounting the life of a Scotsman and his relations with three women, a peasant girl,
a Glasgow woman with whom he has his first affair, and a beautiful Londoner whom, to his cost, he
ambitiously marries. [Collins.]
NJALS SAGA. 1861
The greatest of the sagas, whether in the national scope of its action, the beauty and distinction of the
characters, or in the pathos and epical grandeur of the narrative (*c.* 1230–80). Njal is one of the old
statesmen and lawgivers, a reverend figure; his friend Gunnar, among the noblest of the great chiefs;
Hallgerda, an evil woman drawn on an heroic scale; and the minor characters are boldly delineated.
Falls naturally into three parts: the first, representing probably a lost " Gunnar's Saga," is the touching
story of Njal and Gunnar's friendship, and the fatal enmity of their wives, with the woes it brings on
the two households; in the second part is worked out the tragedy that culminates in the magnificent
scene of Njal's burning; and the third, where the champions Flosi and Kari are protagonists, relates the
events, down to the battle of Clontarf, whereby retribution is wrought on the burners. The saga has
furthermore high importance as history, giving a detailed picture of the social and political life centring
in the Althing, with portraits of the foremost Icelanders of the time. Vigfússon calls it " the Saga of
the Law." He points out also (Prolegomena to *Sturlunga Saga*) that the author, or editor, was unquestionably a lawyer, and an Eastlander, who makes blunders as to the Westland topography, and handles
the facts with considerable freedom. Period, 850–1017, especially the years 959–1011. [*The Story of
Burnt Njal*; transl. by Sir G. W. DASENT, 2 vols., Edmonston & Douglas, 1861: o.p.; with an abridg-
ment of Dasent's learned introduction on history, religion, and social life, De La More Press, 1900: o.p.;
Doubleday, New York, 1912: o.p.; (Everyman's Lib.), Dent; also an abridgment for children with
introd., etc., by Allen FRENCH, *sub tit. Heroes of Iceland, illus.*, Nutt, 1905: o.p.]
NOBLE, Edward [*b.* 1857]. *The Edge of Circumstance.* 1904
—— *The Waves of Fate.* 1905
—— *Fisherman's Gat; a story of the Thames estuary.* 1906
—— *The Grain Carriers.* 1908
—— *Lords of the Sea.* 1909
—— *Chains.* 1910
Novels of the sea and the mercantile marine, that owe something to both Kipling and Conrad. The story
in the first book of the salving of a coffin ship by a Scots skipper and his engineer, who board a derelict
and tow their own ship home, is not unworthy of the former. The second recalls *Lord Jim*, describing
the sudden collapse of a man's will, a skipper who leaps for safety in a collision and leaves his crew and
passengers to their fate. His shame and contrition are acutely analysed. Mr. Noble draws ordinary
men and women in a lifelike way, but his gift is for episodes that try the nerves and illustrate the
psychology of bravery and cowardice. He assumes a mission for exposing the nefarious ways of shipowners who send crews to sea in unsound vessels, and is full of sarcasm against the tyranny of wealth.
[(1), (2), (3), (4), Blackwood; (5), Methuen; (6), Constable: all o.p. except (2); (1), Dodd & Mead, New
York: o.p.]
—— *Dust from the Loom: a romance of two Atacamas.* 1914
The romantic idyll of an English naval captain and a Chilean girl. [Constable: o.p.]
—— *The Bottle-Fillers.* 1915
A tragedy of seafaring life, again directed against the abuses caused through unscrupulous shipowners.
There are good descriptions of life on a tramp steamer. [Heinemann: o.p.]
—— *The Pulse of Darkness: a tale of Eastern seas.* 1928
A drama of vengeance played out on the Hong-Kong–London passage, in the days of sail. There is a good
description of a volcanic eruption. [Jarrolds; Houghton, Boston, 1929.]
NOELDECHEN, Wilhelm [German]. *Baron and Squire.* 1892
The Thirty Years' War (1619–48); Tilly, Richelieu, etc. [Transl. by Sarah M. S. CLARKE, Nisbet: o.p.]

NORDLING, Johan [German]. *The Moonlight Sonata* (Quasi una Fantasia). 1911
A romantic study of Beethoven in Vienna when he was becoming totally deaf. [Melrose : o.p. ; Sturgis, New York : o.p.]

NORRIS, Charles Gilman [American ; brother of following ; b. 1881]. *Salt : the education of Griffith Adams.* 1918
—— *The Amateur.* 1919
Thoughtful, serious studies of American life. The second resolves the problem of an artist who hopes to win success by exploiting a passing fashion. [(1) and (2), Dutton, New York ; Constable.]
—— *Brass.* 1921
The varied marriage experiences of the hero illustrate the dangers, due to selfishness, divorce, lovelessness, etc., which beset the married man. Setting, San Francisco. [Dutton, New York ; Heinemann.]
—— *Bread.* 1923
The disillusionment of a young girl wishing for independent life—the conflict between marriage and a career. [Dutton, New York ; Unwin.]
—— *Pig Iron.* 1925
The life-story of the son of a poor Massachusetts family, winning money and position, but no satisfaction, in New York. [Dutton, New York ; Murray.]

NORRIS, Frank [American ; 1870–1902]. *McTeague.: a story of San Francisco.* 1899
Norris was the most promising of the American naturalists, and still probably the best. He clearly perceived that Zola was " the very head of the romanticists," yet Zola was at least his precursor in this unmitigatedly realistic picture of Californian life. It gives the stupidity, the animalism, and the grinding poverty of the labouring classes. McTeague is as strong and almost as much a brute as if he were a cart-horse ; the other characters are on a par. It is a story of steady degeneracy through poverty, loveless wedlock, and, in two cases, the insensate lust for money. [Doubleday, New York; De la More Press: o.p.; Heinemann.]
—— *Blix : a love idyll.* 1899
A young journalist and a girl of strong, wholesome character enter into a partnership which develops by insensible degrees into a closer affection. The same Zolaesque reproduction of life with photographic detail. Scenes, California and New York. [Doubleday, New York ; De La More Press : o.p.]
—— *A Man's Woman.* 1900
Studies of character, chiefly in a virile heroine and a pair of Arctic explorers : a glorification of strength and fortitude and modern enterprise. [Doubleday, New York ; De La More Press : o.p.]
—— *The Octopus : a story of California.* 1901
First part of an unfinished trilogy, which was to show up the iniquities of the selfish and brutal warfare of the capitalists against the community. In this the scene is California, where over vast spaces the grain to feed the world is seen germinating and ripening like a great natural force, though tended by a host of toilers. Far away are the consumers, and, in between, the wheat is the plaything of merchants and speculators playing ducks and drakes with prices and ruining each other by bearing or bulling. The octopus is the railway system which holds the farmers in the hollow of its hand, and can squeeze them of their hard-won earnings. [Doubleday, New York (repr. 1930) ; Nelson.]
—— *The Pit.* 1903
Here the speculators are seen manipulating prices, and the whole game of controlling the distribution of the food-supply is exhibited in full swing. Gives the inner and outer history of a deal in the Chicago wheat-pit, of a colossal corner in which the welfare of millions is staked on a gamble for private profit. *The Wolf*, which was to describe a famine, was never written. [Doubleday, New York (repr. 1930) ; De La More Press : o.p. ; Nelson.]
—— *A Deal in Wheat ; and other stories of the New and Old West.* 1903
—— *The Third Circle.* 1909
Two collections of somewhat inferior stories, the second lot—all early—edited by W. Irwin. [(1), Doubleday, New York ; De La More Press : o.p. ; (2) Dodd & Mead, New York ; Lane.
—— *Shanghaied : a story of adventure off California coast.* 1904
A romance based on the same realism of experience. [De La More Press : o.p. ; Nelson.]
—— *Vandover and the Brute.* 1914
Written in 1895, though not published till 1914. The tragedy of a young man's struggle against the baser instincts of his nature, and his defeat—a defeat that involves his artistic career, and leaves him a drink-sodden outcast in San Francisco. Far from flawless, it is an interesting early example of his detailed realism. [Doubleday, New York ; Heinemann : o.p.]
[*Works*, 10 vols., Doubleday, New York ; also *illus., id.*]

NORRIS, Kathleen [Mrs. Charles Gilman Norris, *née* Thompson ; American ; b. 1880]. *Saturday's Child.* 1914
A sentimental story inculcating a homely moral about a girl clerk who dreams of the good things of life, but finds her truest happiness in marriage with one of like humble station. [Macmillan, New York : o.p. ; Grosset, New York.]
—— *The Story of Julia Page.* 1915
Depicts a girl whose early years have been spent among sordid surroundings in San Francisco, now redeemed and reconstructing her life under the influence of love. [Doubleday, Doran, New York ; Murray.]
—— *The Lucky Lawrences.* 1930
About the grandchildren of a family of original settlers in San Francisco, who have retained only the family pride out of their fortune. [Doubleday, Doran, New York ; Murray.]

NORRIS, William Edward [1847–1925]. *Mademoiselle de Mersac.* 1880
A quiet story, carefully portraying not unusual types of French and English character, with pictures of leisurely life and social doings in Algiers and England. The heroine and her true lover are embodiments of the ideal

NORRIS, William Edward (*continued*).

virtues of the *ancienne noblesse*, while the English lover is a mixture of bad and good. [Smith & Elder : o.p.]

—— *Matrimony.* 1881

Like many others by this writer, a slight tale, with good natural dialogue and character-drawing of the external kind. Mr. Norris abounds in types of people we often meet, such as the hero's father, a fine old gentleman with an unkind tongue and a generous heart, always performing kind actions. [Murray ; Fenno, New York : o.p.]

—— *No New Thing.* 1883

The history of an Anglo-Indian lad, of sharp, unscrupulous, superficial nature, who is a contrast to the stronger and simpler English people with whom he is brought into contact, especially the kind-hearted woman who befriends him. [Murray.]

—— *Adrian Vidal.* 1885

The conjugal infelicities experienced by a young novelist of somewhat shallow, pleasure-loving disposition, and his eventual reconciliation with his wife. [Murray.]

—— *Chris.* 1888

The love affairs of a young heiress and her trio of suitors, ending pleasantly after a series of doubts and perplexities. Scene, Cannes and London. [Macmillan : o.p. ; Hurst, New York : o.p.]

—— *Major and Minor.* 1888

The old story of a man's sterling affection for a girl above him in wealth and station, and the discomfiture of a less worthy rival. [Bentley : o.p.]

—— *The Rogue.* 1889

The same realistic delineation of character and manners, with a strong dash of comedy and good-natured satire. The Rogue is an easy-going fellow, who has been a scamp, and tries to pass himself off as a decent and respectable member of society. [Macmillan : o.p. ; Street, New York : o.p.]

—— *Miss Shafto.* 1889

Made up of character-sketches, talks, love-making, and the like, altogether forming a humorous picture of the ordinary intercourse of people in good society. [Macmillan : o.p. ; Hurst, New York : o.p.]

—— *Marcia.* 1891

The married life of two people who are not sympathetic, the man honest but hard, the woman selfish and frivolous ; the everyday existence of people moved by petty and unworthy motives is depicted with almost painful realism. The son's happy love-making brightens the later chapters. [Murray ; Harper, New York : o.p.]

—— *Billy Bellew.* 1895

The hero is a simple, almost silly, young man, but unselfish and amiable, who eventually meets with a fate too heavy for his deserts. [Chatto : o.p. ; Harper, New York : o.p.]

—— *The Fight for the Crown.* 1898

The humours of political differences between a Conservative husband and a Liberal wife. Makes use of the Home Rule controversy. [Seeley ; Harper, New York : o.p.]

—— *Giles Ingilby.* 1899

A colourless, unemotional story depending for interest on the minute drawing of characters who represent just the average mediocrities of everyday life. A love-story, a disappointed lover going to South Africa, complications happily disentangled, are the main features of the plot. [Methuen : o.p. ; Biddle, Philadelphia : o.p.]

—— *The Flower of the Flock.* 1900

A rich and luxurious young man, amiably selfish, reckless, and incompetent, but idolized by his mother and bowed down to by his kin, is played with and landed by a knowing American widow, and thus saved from the consequences of an act that in a more responsible person would be severely reprobated. [Nisbet : o.p. ; Appleton, New York : o.p.]

—— *His Own Father.* 1901

A story of the ups and downs of courtship, with touches of melodrama, as in the account of a missing father who reappears to untie the tangled skein of difficulties. [Hurst : o.p.]

—— *Pauline.* 1908

Pauline Daguerre, an actress who has divorced her husband, meets with crushing generosity the efforts of an aristocratic mother to save her son, in love with Pauline, from an ineligible marriage. She is the strength of the novel, the other characters being quite ordinary ; but the story grips one rather more than the average of Mr. Norris. [Constable : o.p.]

—— *Vittoria Victrix.* 1911

The story of Vittoria's suitors—a young peer, an American millionaire, and the famous sculptor who tells it. [Constable : o.p. ; Brentano, New York : o.p.]

—— *The Triumphs of Sara.* 1920

A typically workmanlike novel. The hard-headed, philistine Sara triumphs over the æsthetic modernist, Estelle. [Hutchinson : o.p.]

NORTON, Hon. Caroline Elizabeth Sarah [*née* Sheridan ; Irish ; 1808–77]. *Stuart of Dunleath : a story of modern times.* 1851

A leisurely and highly elaborated novel of the old-fashioned type, going into minutest particulars about home and family surroundings, family history, etc. There are nearly a score of separate characters, chiefly Scotch—the heroine is an immaculate creature, the hero, a weak man, who risks his ward's fortune, loses it and disappears, returning to find her wedded to a brute. She dies of a broken heart. Said to embody a good deal of veiled autobiography. Mrs. Norton was the original of Meredith's *Diana of the Crossways*. [Ward & Lock : o.p.]

NORTON, Hon. Caroline Elizabeth Sarah (*continued*). *Lost and Saved.* 1863
A special pleading for women wronged, maintaining that the men suffer too lightly and the women out of all proportion to their faults. The girl who is shamed is innocent, while a society woman, whose offences are many, presents a fair face to the world. Among the crowd of minor characters the vulgar and magnificent Marchioness of Updown is conspicuous. [Hurst & Blackett : o.p.]

—— *Old Sir Douglas.* 1868
The hero is an elderly Scot, a high-bred Christian gentleman, weak-natured, but in his generosity and chivalrous loyalty a Bayard. These traits he exhibits disastrously in his indulgent policy towards a profligate nephew, and again when entrapped into a belief in his wife's unfaithfulness. The domestic plot has side-scenes of society life, in which there is satire of social types, such as the pharisaical old dowager, a grim and bigoted Presbyterian, the selfish fast man, and the stiff-necked Scot. [Macmillan : o.p.]

NORWAY, Arthur Hamilton [b. 1859]. *Parson Peter.* 1900
A romance of Devon. Parson Peter is a representative of the old order, a keen sportsman and a lover of the sea, consort of smugglers, and contemner of the law, a generous and amiable personality. The operations of smugglers and preventives, a little love-romance, and an undercurrent of tragedy furnish the action. [Murray : o.p.]

NORWAY, George. *Willoughby Manor.* [juvenile] 1902
A story of old Liverpool, and the siege of Havre, held by the Huguenots aided by the English (1562). [Nimmo & Hay, Edinburgh : o.p.]

NOYES, Alfred [b. 1880]. *Walking Shadows : sea-tales and others.* 1918
Straightforward magazine stories, mainly sea-yarns of war-time. [Hodder ; Stokes, New York.]

—— *The Hidden Player.* 1924
Eleven stories, each turning upon some drama of spiritual experience—emotion strained beyond the bounds of reality. In *The Troglodyte*, a man spends his life in a cave awaiting the return of the fiancée of his youth, a victim of the white slave traffic. *The Wine Beyond the World* is the best, an ironical little comedy. [Hodder : o.p. ; Stokes, New York.]

NYBURG, Sidney Lauer [American ; b. 1880]. *The Chosen People.* 1917
Jewish life in Baltimore and the differences between orthodox and reformed Jews, Zionists and anti-Zionists : hero, an idealistic young rabbi who shows great self-sacrifice for the sake of the poor of his own race. [Lippincott, Philadelphia.]

O'BRIEN, William [Irish ; 1852–1928]. *When We Were Boys.* 1890
Written in gaol by an Irreconcilable : a lively political story of Fenians and Nationalist agitation ; scene, Glengarriff (1866–7). [Longman : o.p. ; Talbot P., Dublin.]

—— *A Queen of Men : a romance of Ireland.* 1898
A highly coloured romance of the famous Grania, sea-queen of the O'Malleys (see also R. Machray's *Grace O'Malley*, p. 315) in the stormy years contemporary with Elizabeth (1588–92) ; scenes, Galway and Clare Island ; written in a lingo full of Spanish, Irish, and slang. [Unwin : o.p.]

"O'BYRNE, Dermot" [Arnold Bax ; Irish]. *Children of the Hills : tales and sketches of western Ireland in the old time and the present day.* 1915
Seven stories, fanciful and often weird : *Ancient Dominions*, a description of pagan worship in the sea-caves of Donegal ; *Hunger*, the devastation of Ireland under Carew ; *The Call of the Road*, a humorous account of vagabondage. [Maunsel, Dublin : o.p.]

—— *Wrack ; and other stories.* 1918
Wrack caricatures the supposed mutual suspicion and antipathy between English tourists and Irish peasants. *Before Dawn* is truer to life ; and *From the Fury of the O'Flaherties* is a dreadful picture of the Irish clan-feuds in the Middle Ages. The other tales are founded on ancient myths. [Talbot Press, Dublin.]

O'BYRNE, W. Lorcan [Irish ; 1845–1913]. *The Knight of the Cave ; or, The Quest of the Pallium.* 1906
Well grounded in historical and antiquarian learning, and an informative picture of England under Stephen, of social and religious conditions in Ireland, and of Rome, Tivoli, etc. There is a visit to St. Bernard at Clairvaux. [Blackie : o.p.]

—— *The Falcon King.* 1907
Scenes and episodes of Welsh, English, Irish, Icelandic, and other history (1146–70), all very carefully studied. [Blackie : o.p. ; Talbot Press, Dublin.]

ODOEVTSEVA, Irma [Russian]. *Out of Childhood.* 1930
In a singularly reticent, delicately suggestive way, making more of atmosphere than of concrete fact, tells the story of three Russian refugees living almost destitute in a French *pension*, after the father had been shot by the Bolshevists : the mother, still young in spirit, and her daughters, the impetuous Vera and the vivid and passionate Louka, hardly more than a child. Vera marries ; but the villainous, seducing Arsenin still hangs round her ; and tragedy comes in with the insane passion he inspires in the young girl. [Transl. and *illus.* by Donia NACHSHEN, Constable ; R. R. Smith, New York.]

O'DONNELL, Peadar [Irish]. *Islanders.* 1928
Pictures the hard life of fishermen upon an island off the Irish coast, in particular Mrs. Doogan and her family, their troubles and their courage in adversity. [Cape ; *sub tit. The Way it was with Them*, Putnam, New York.]

—— *Adrigoole.* 1929
A romance of the poorest type of Donegal peasant, told with humour and local idiom, which brings out their courage and cheerfulness amid great hardships and grinding poverty. [Cape ; Putnam, New York.]

O'DONOVAN, Gerald [Irish]. *Father Ralph.* 1913

This is frankly a bitter attack on the Catholic Church and the ecclesiastical system in Ireland, but it gives also a valuable picture of Irish life. [Macmillan : o.p.]

—— *Waiting.* 1914

A further attack on the Catholic priesthood : a young man of anti-clerical views loses his post as a schoolmaster, and is unfairly hampered in his attempts to secure political office. [Secker.]

O'DUFFY, Eimar Ultan [Irish ; b. 1893]. *King Goshawk and the Birds.* 1926

Begins as a promising satirical extravaganza on the imbecilities, injustices, and social outrages of " civilization," when somewhere in the near future the earth is entirely enslaved by colossal millionaires. A reforming philosopher brings back Cuchulain from the other world, and he begets a hero fit to right matters. But the mixture of Aristophanic exaggeration and Celtic rodomontade over-reaches itself and falls flat. [Macmillan, London and New York.]

OEHLENSCHLÄGER, Adam Gottlob [Danish ; 1779–1850]. *Wayland Smith* (Velent Smed). 1847

A prose trifle from the pen of the great poet and dramatist, who wrote several novels and idylls not translated. A modern romanticized rendering of an ancient legend, Germanic in origin, but blended with Latin myths about Vulcan, Dædalus, etc. The Lay of Volund in the Poetic Edda was probably composed about A.D. 900 by a Norwegian, who got the tale from England, where it was well known at an earlier period (see *Saga-Book of the Viking Club*, vol. ii). The legend is traced in Scandinavian, German, and French literatures under the names Völund, Wieland, Galans, etc. In the *Thidreks Saga* it is connected with the Völsung legend. Vaulundur and his brothers, sons of the King of the Finns, migrate to a summer land, and marry three Swan-maids (Valkyries), who leave them after nine years. He distinguishes himself as a marvellous smith, but is enslaved and maltreated by the Swedish king Nidudr (Nithud), on whom he wreaks a terrible vengeance, and takes flight. Oehlenschläger, who wrote the story in Danish, *c.* 1800 (afterwards in German, whence it was translated), has embellished it with the usual features of the sentimental fairy-tale most pleasingly exemplified by Fouqué. [Transl. from the German of Oehlenschläger, by Elizabeth KINNEAR, with a dissertation on the legend, by Depping and Pickering, 1847 ; Michel : o.p.]

O'FLAHERTY, Liam [Irish ; b. 1896]. *Spring Sowing.* 1924

—— *The Tent ; and other stories.* 1926

—— *The Mountain Tavern ; and other stories.* 1929

Three collections of short stories displaying the same unbridled vehemence and force of imagination as the longer works. They are mostly sketches of peasant life, fierce and primitive passions vividly presented. [(1)–(3), Cape ; (1), Knopf, New York ; (2), Boni, New York ; (3), Harcourt, New York.]

—— *The Informer.* 1925

The story of Gypo Nolan, who betrays a wanted murderer to the police, and is tried and executed by the Irish Communist leaders. The Dublin underworld is drawn in lurid colours, but over all towers the figure of Gypo, a primitive half-animal creature of immense strength. We follow him in his savage attempts to ease his sense of guilt, during his one night of freedom with the blood-money in his pocket ; we are introduced to every secret of his savage mentality. He is a titanic creation—a human brute, with a brute's cunning, defeated by superior intelligence. [Cape (also in Traveller's Lib., 1929) ; Knopf, New York.]

—— *Mr. Gilhooley.* 1926

This elderly retired Dubliner, an introvert, afraid of death, disappointed with life, the " voluptuary " as his friends call him, falls helpless to the physical seductions of a loose woman, and in a fit of jealousy strangles her. The strife of tenderness and hatred, half-stifled idealism and mere sensuality, in this man's soul, makes a tragic monodrama. The realism, though it shirks no grossness, rises naturally into poetry, in its outlook on the immensities beyond the individual. [Cape ; Harcourt, New York.]

—— *The Assassin.* 1928

Analyses the mentality of a murderer, whose mind shifts rapidly from extremes of joy to blank despair, before and after the deed, which he had plotted for three years. [Cape ; Harcourt, New York.]

—— *The House of Gold.* 1929

The central figure is a peasant who has amassed wealth as a shopkeeper and usurer, and is the supreme power in his village ; the story, which is confined within twenty-four hours, shows him terrorizing over the villagers, until he meets his deserts. [Cape ; Harcourt, New York.]

OGLE, Anne Charlotte [" Ashford Owen " ; 1832–1918]. *A Lost Love.* 1855

A slight story, with delicate pathos and sentiment, which won the approval of Swinburne and Tennyson. The heroine is a girl of sweet and devoted nature, who is deserted by her lover for a more profitable match. For modern readers, there is a charming old-world flavour in this account of the conventions and the daily round of a society that is so remote. [American title, *Georgie* ; republished by Murray, 1920.]

O'GRADY, Standish Hayes [Irish ; 1832–1915] [ed.]. *Silva Gadelica*, 1–31 : *a collection of tales in Irish, extracts illustrating persons and places.* 1892–3

[Edited from the MSS., with translations and notes. Vol. i, Irish text ; vol. ii, Translation and Notes ; Williams and Norgate : o.p.]

O'GRADY, Standish James [Irish ; 1846–1928]. *The Bog of Stars.* 1893

Nine stories of Elizabethan times in Ireland, " not so much founded on fact as in fact true." Told with the epical energy that marks all Mr. O'Grady's narratives, bringing out clearly the savagery and internecine feuds of the Irish chieftains and the selfishness and cruelty of the English. [Unwin : o.p.]

—— *The Coming of Cuculain : a romance of Ireland.* 1894

An imaginative romance of the heroic age of Ireland—a little history and a great deal of myth and legend. [With introd. by A. E., Talbot Press, Dublin.]

O'GRADY, Standish James (*continued*). *In the Gates of the North* [sequel].
Continues the epic story of Cuculain, telling how he held the Ulster fords against the armies of Maeve. [Talbot Press, Dublin.]

—— *Ulrick the Ready ; or, The Chieftain's Last Rally.*   1896
A story of 1600–2, of Philip III's Armada, and the battle of Kinsale, picturing vividly the clan feuds and the unsettled state of the country. [Sealy & Bryers, Dublin : o.p. ; Talbot Press, Dublin.]

—— *In the Wake of King James ; or, Dun Randal on the Sea.*   1896
The Jacobites and the rapparees of Connaught in the years following James II's expulsion from Ireland (1691–1700). Not reliable historically. [(Wayfarer's Lib.), Dent.]

—— *The Flight of the Eagle ; or, Red Hugh's Captivity.*   1897
Tells the story of Hugh Roe O'Donnell's kidnapping and his escape from Dublin Castle in 1591, in the same spirited fashion, basing the details on contemporary documents. [Sealy & Bryers, Dublin : o.p. ; Talbot Press, Dublin.]

—— *The Triumph and Passing of Cuculain.*   1919
A modern simplification of the Cuculain cycle is completed in this third volume of the series beginning with *The Coming of Cuculain* and *In the Gates of the North*. [Talbot Press, Dublin.]

O'HANRAHAN, Michael [Irish]. *When the Norman Came.*   1920
A story of warfare in Ireland during the twelfth century when Diarmid MacMurrough, King of Leinster, applied for help to the English king. [Talbot Press, Dublin.]

OHNET, Georges [French ; 1848–1918]. *Serge Panine ; or, Can you Blame Her ?* (Serge Panine, 1881).   1883
A drama of passion, resolving itself into a duel between a resolute bourgeois of noble character and an aristocratic wastrel. Worked out with a playwright's knowledge of *mise-en-scène*. One of the few works of Ohnet's that have found favour with critics. Under the general title of *Les batailles de la vie* he wrote a series of novels dealing with social life, in a more or less popular, melodramatic vein : these have been severely handled by the leading critics. [Transl. by Jessie HAMILTON, Tubbs, Manchester : o.p. ; Vizetelly : o.p.]

—— *The Ironmaster ; or, Love and Pride* (Le maître de forges, 1882).   1884
Like the following, portrays the wealthy bourgeois classes and the fringes of the aristocratic society with which they are in more or less intimate contact, and lays emphasis on the solid virtues of the former. Here we have the daughter of a baroness wedded to an honourable and magnanimous plebeian, whom she wrongs, but she is won from indifference to passionate love by his admirable conduct. [Warne : o.p. ; Rand & McNally, Chicago : o.p.]

—— *Doctor Rameau* (Le docteur Rameau, 1888).   1888
A very dramatic novel, in which a man eventually discovers that the girl he had believed to be his daughter is not so, but continues to regard her as his child because of his affection for her. [Transl. by Mrs. Cashel HOEY, Chatto : o.p. ; Lippincott, Philadelphia : o.p.]

—— *Will* (Volonté, 1888).   1896
A melodrama, with strongly accentuated types of character, and a pathetic *dénouement*. [Transl., Gibbings : o.p. ; Brentano, New York : o.p.]

—— *A Last Love* (Dernier amour, 1889).   1890
A good average specimen of his working out of a melodramatic plot. Here it is a contest between two women for the affection of the husband of one of them. [Transl. by A. D. VANDAM, Chatto : o.p. ; Lippincott, Philadelphia : o.p.]

—— *Love's Depths* (Le lendemain des amours, 1893).   1899
Another melodrama of irregular passion, diabolical revenge, and spotless virtue. [Transl. by Fred ROTHWELL, Chatto : o.p.]

—— *The Lady in Grey* (La dame en gris, 1895).   1895
A gruesome murder by a ruffian of the type dear to Eugène Sue, and a liaison of the kind common in the *demi-monde*, form the gist of the story. [Tower Pub. Co. : o.p.]

—— *The Eagle's Talon* (La serre de l'aigle, 1912).   1913
An historical novel of the Chouans, the Pichegru conspiracy, and the executions of the Duc d' Enghien and of Georges Cadoudal (1804). [Transl. by Helen MEYER ; Putnam, New York : o.p.]

OHTA, Takashi [Japanese], and **SPERRY**, Margaret [American]. *The Golden Wind.*   1930
Perhaps this may be at bottom autobiography. It records the experiences of a political exile from Japan, who serves with the revolutionary forces in China till he is disillusioned, carries out an arduous mission for love, and is all the while in quest of wisdom. Descriptions, dialogues, and reflections, with the sententious style, aptly convey the deeper spirit of the East. [Boni, New York ; Cape.]

O'KELLY, Seumas [Irish ; 1881 ?–1918]. *The Lady of the Deerpark.*   1917
A quiet romance of western Ireland. [Methuen : o.p.]

—— *Waysiders : stories of Connacht.*   1917
Mainly the tragedies of the humble dwellers in the wilds of Connaught, related with the imagination of a poet and with touches of Celtic mystery. Talbot Press, Dublin.]

—— *The Golden Barque ; and, The Weaver's Grave.*   1919
The first title belongs to a little cycle depicting life on a canal barge, the best stories being *Billy the Clown* and *The Derelict*. The other is a picturesque and macabre story in the manner of Synge. [Talbot Press, Dublin ; Putnam, New York.]

—— *Hillsiders.*   1921
Six sketches, simple and genial, of life in western Ireland. [Talbot Press, Dublin.]

OLAF TRYGVASON. *The Saga of Olaf Trygvasson, who reigned over Norway* A.D. 995 *to* A.D. 1000.　　　　　　　　　　　　　　　　　　　　　　　　　　　　　　　　　　1895

Neither history nor fiction, but, like Southey's *Cid*, a compilation of general sagas containing both ; it is told in the simple epic manner, and contains scenes and passages of like order to the best in the sagas proper. This life of Olaf Trygvason, the favourite hero of Norse history, and as Carlyle says, " the wildly beautifullest man in body and in soul that one has ever heard of in the north," is a redaction of the following part of Snorri's *Heimskringla*, the legendary life of Olaf by Odd Monk (late twelfth century), extracts from *Landnamabok* and *Kristni Saga*, the greater part of *Hallfred's Saga*, a summary of *Laxdaela*, Sigmund Prestisson's life in the *Faereyinga* (see *Thrond of Gate*), various poetical extracts, and a number of miscellaneous stories and minor sagas otherwise unknown. To distinguish it from the *Heimskringla* narrative, which is a great epical history of the kings of Norway, this is often known as the *Great O. T. Saga.* The text is taken from Fornmanna Sögur (printed 1825). The story goes back as far as the times of Harold Fairhair ; the birth, life, and reign of King Hakon (*b.* 918, *d.* 960) are related. Then there is an account of the unsettled times before Earl Hacon (*d.* 995) and Hacon's reign, probably all from the *Heimskringla*. The early adventures of Olaf as a refugee in Garda (Muscovy) and as a Viking, launch us at once on the main current of heroic story. Olaf's wars and warlike attempts to spread the Christian faith, and the subsidiary episodes, lead in a great climax to the tremendous battle of Swold. But the chronicler disbelieves in Olaf's death by drowning, and supplies an apocryphal history of his deeds after his miraculous disappearance. The supernatural plays a conspicuous part ; the Devil appears as Odin, the enemies of the faith as Trolls ; there are innumerable prophetic dreams, portents, and premonitory warnings. The translator would place the date of the compilation about the middle of the thirteenth century. [Transl. by J. SEPHTON, Nutt : o.p.]

OLDHAM, Henry [American]. *The Man from Texas : a Western romance.*　　　　　1884

Career of a brilliant guerrilla general on the Southern side in the Civil War, told by a sympathizer. [Peterson, Philadelphia : o.p.]

OLDMEADOW, Ernest James [*b.* 1867]. *Susan.*　　　　　　　　　　　　　　　　1907
—— *The Scoundrel.*　　　　　　　　　　　　　　　　　　　　　　　　　　　　1907
—— *Aunt Maud.*　　　　　　　　　　　　　　　　　　　　　　　　　　　　　1908
—— *Antonio.*　　　　　　　　　　　　　　　　　　　　　　　　　　　　　　1909

Leisurely novels, well written and good in rendering character, the last chronicling the suppression of the monasteries in Portugal (1834) and the efforts of a young monk to make money in the wine trade with England in order to restore a suppressed house. [(1), (2), (3), (4), Richards : all o.p. except (4) ; (3), McClure, New York : o.p. ; (4), Century Co., New York : o.p.]

—— *Coggin.*　　　　　　　　　　　　　　　　　　　　　　　　　　　　　　1920

Coggin is a queer, solitary child, the son of a marine-store keeper, about the middle of the last century. [Richards : o.p.]

OLIPHANT, Laurence [1829–88]. *Piccadilly.*　　　　　　　　　　　　　　　　　1870

First published in *Blackwood's Magazine*, soon after the brilliant traveller and war correspondent had come under the influence of the mystical evangelist Harris. It is a satire on contemporary society, describing ironically how a mercenary aristocrat introduces a family of moneyed nobodies to fashionable circles in London. Tilts at a variety of objects which the bohemian author detested, and covertly expounds his peculiar theosophy, grounded on Swedenborgianism and the gospel of the inner life. [Blackwood : o.p. ; R. Smith, New York, 1930.]

—— *Altiora Peto.*　　　　　　　　　　　　　　　　　　　　　　　　　　　　1883

A similar mixture of satirical comedy and mysticism in the loose form of a society novel ; Altiora is victimized by her guardians. An unconventional pair of American girls and their caricature of a Yankee chaperon are genially sketched, but the love scenes are abstract dialogues on such subjects as matter and spirit, humanitarian ideals, etc. [Blackwood ; *illus.*, Blackwood : o.p.]

OLIPHANT, Margaret Oliphant [*née* Wilson ; Scottish ; 1828–97]. *Passages in the Life of Mistress Margaret Maitland.*　　　　　　　　　　　　　　　　　　　　　　　　　　　　　1849
—— *Lilliesleaf* [sequel].　　　　　　　　　　　　　　　　　　　　　　　　　1856

An old-world picture of Scottish character and manners, much in the style of Galt, but more refined and tender. The mystery and suspense attaching to Anne Ross's endeavours to clear her brother's good name form a strong interest. Warmly praised by such a severe critic as Jeffery. [(1) and (2), Ward & Lock : o.p.]

—— *Katie Stewart : a true story.*　　　　　　　　　　　　　　　　　　　　　1856

A romantic story of Fifeshire (*c.* 1735–60), connected with events of the '45, but not historical, though the Young Chevalier is introduced. [Blackwood : o.p.]

—— *Salem Chapel.*　　　　　　　　　　　　　　　　　　　　　　　　　　　1863

Mrs. Oliphant's Carlingford novels stand out, like Trollope's Barchester series, high above the very numerous and unequal tale of her books. This is the first of the set. Depicts a Nonconformist " connexion " in the little English town of Carlingford, where the hero, a clever and ambitious student, has just arrived from college as minister. His advanced views almost end in a schism, and the history of his struggle with the congregation is fertile in comedy. Mixed up with this portion of the plot is a melodramatic story. Rich in character-drawing—Tozer, the deacon, with his vulgarity and ignorance conjoined with thorough manliness and liberality of mind ; the pettifogging trustees and their vulgar, match-making womankind, intent on their social squabbles and jealousies ; and the hero's mother, a character of a higher type. [With *The Doctor's Family*, Blackwood : o.p. ; (Everyman's Lib.), Dent (Dutton, New York).]

—— *The Rector ; and the Doctor's Family.*　　　　　　　　　　　　　　　　1863

The Rector, a learned Oxford don, finds his new parish of Carlingford a sphere of life and duty for which he is totally unfit ; and after various experiences, which to the reader are very humorous, he gives up the

OLIPHANT, Margaret Oliphant (*continued*).

living and returns to his college. The Doctor is a struggling practitioner, on whose hands is unexpectedly thrown the care of his shiftless brother's wife and family from Australia. He is filled with consternation ; but the wife's sister, a stout-hearted girl, heroically bears the burden of their improvidence and selfishness. The Doctor falls tumultuously in love with her, but she declines to abandon her self-imposed duty. [Blackwood.]

—— *The Perpetual Curate.*   1864

More of the Carlingford people, characterization being always the main interest—the curate himself with his long and stubborn fight against circumstances, and the long-awaited marriage which is, after all, but the commencement of new cares ; his brother, who resigns a fat living to join the Roman Church ; their women-folk, especially the two maiden aunts, the convert's silly little wife, and Mrs. Morgan, who suddenly realizes that she has been dwelling in an ideal world, with an imaginary self and a too-perfect husband, whereas the facts are humdrum and conventional. [With *The Rector, supra*, Blackwood : o.p.]

—— *Miss Marjoribanks.*   1866

Miss Marjoribanks is the daughter of the hard-headed doctor of Carlingford, whom, on his being left a widower, she thinks it is her duty to console. The doctor does not want to be consoled, and her sentimental attempts are laughably frustrated. Still more fruitful in comedy are her efforts to take the lead in Carlingford society, and to raise the tone of thought. This young lady ranks with the immortal Tozer as a living figure, to whose creating sympathy and satire have gone in about equal proportions. The whole book is alive with humour. [Blackwood : o.p. ; Collins, London and New York ; Munró, New York : o.p.]

—— *Phœbe, Junior : the last chronicle of Carlingford.*   1876

A domestic story ; the fortunes of the younger Phœbe, a granddaughter of the inimitable Deacon Tozer, and daughter of a dissenting minister whom circumstances have raised in the social scale. A pleasant character, frank and honest, bearing her superiority of education and position with dignity and kindness, and a variety of minor characters, the moneyed contractor and his loutish son, whom Phœbe tames and civilizes, Nonconformists and Church-people, tradesmen and gentry, all depicted with kindly humour. [Hurst & Blackett : o.p.]

—— *Madonna Mary.*   1866

A numerous gallery of womankind of all ages, married and single, lovable and the reverse, seen in a domestic environment into which only one or two not very masculine men are allowed to penetrate. Madonna Mary, quiet and dignified, and her tearful and lackadaisical sister, are among the many contrasts. Deep affection between women, petulant jealousy developing with age into crabbed ill-humour, a woman's unspoken love, the widow's schemes for her boys' futures, such are the motives of the story. [Ward & Lock : o.p.]

—— *The Minister's Wife.*   1869

Landscapes and seascapes from the west of Scotland give colour to this story, and so do the fervid, poetical nature of the dwellers in Lochshire, with the descriptions of the revival and of the simple religious emotions of the cottars. The focus of interest is Ailie, the beautiful young religious enthusiast ; next come her lover, a rake turned preacher, and Isabel, the minister's wife. Their troubles and sorrows give pathos. [Hurst & Blackett : o.p.]

—— *Ombra.*   1872

Ombra is a shadowy creature of contradictions, bewitching, but jealous and ill-tempered, now passionately sincere, now stooping to untruth ; her mother, however, is the striking personality of the book, a subtle mixture of worldliness and goodness, affectionate yet shrewdly reserved ; and Kate Courtenay, the one who attracts our sympathies, is a beautiful, transparent soul, her very faults amiable. [Ward & Lock : o.p.

—— *Whiteladies.*   1875

Has a good deal of Mrs. Oliphant's fine humour. The staid and elderly ruler of Whiteladies, Miss Susan, whose prudence is above suspicion, is almost involuntarily tempted to instigate and abet a fraud in the interests of the family property, and her mingled feelings of remorse and triumph produce a situation at once pathetic and humorous. [Chatto : o.p.]

—— *The Story of Valentine and his Brother.*   1875

A romantic story, compounded of the elements of character, with one profoundly moving scene that brings into juxtaposition the extremes of human fate. The grandson of a Scottish peer marries a gipsy vagrant, who vanishes with her twin sons, but after seven years brings Valentine to the home of his kindred, and again disappears. Circumstances and the mystic affinity of blood lead the two together, though unaware of their relationship. [Blackwood : o.p.]

—— *The Curate-in-Charge.*   1876

An idyll of English village life, with some engaging characters. The elderly curate-in-charge is passed over in favour of a younger clergyman ; and his indignant daughter learns to love the usurper. [Macmillan : o.p.]

—— *A Beleaguered City : a story of the seen and the unseen.*   1878

One of her poetic romances of the spirit world. How the souls of the just came back to the French town of Semur, and put the quick to flight. Brings the unseen world into contact with the living and commonplace by Defoe-like strokes of realism and character-drawing. There is much humour in the portrait of the mayor, but as a whole the book is solemn, deeply pathetic, and inspired with devout faith. [Macmillan : o.p.]

—— *He that Will Not when he May.*   1880

As claimant to an estate, the hero's good humour and honesty deserve success, while he executes poetic justice on the perverse and capricious gentleman who is disinherited. Some complications and mystery simply and easily unfolded. [Macmillan : o.p.]

—— *A Little Pilgrim in the Unseen.*   1882

A tale of the same imaginative origin as *A Beleaguered City* : how a simple-minded woman awakes to the life beyond death. Sequel, *The Land of Darkness*. [Macmillan.]

OLIPHANT, Margaret Oliphant (*continued*). *The Ladies Lindores.* 1883

A needy gentleman, succeeding to a Scottish peerage, would make his daughters' marriages subserve his social ambitions. He gives the refined Lady Car to the wealthy boor Pat Torrance ; but the younger daughter disappoints his scheme for winning a marquess, and marries her lover. Rich in character (e.g. Old Rolls) ; pathos mingled with the brighter qualities. [3 vols., Blackwood : o.p.]

—— *Lady Car* [sequel]. 1889

The tragedy of Lady Car's wretched marriage is hardly alleviated, though her brutal husband dies, and she weds her old lover ; for the hero she had idealized has grown indolent in middle age, and his lofty enthusiasms have flown, while she has the still bitterer sorrow of watching the son of Pat Torrance grow up as brutal as his father. [Longman : o.p.]

—— *The Wizard's Son.* 1884

Second sight and a haunted castle share interest with the character-drawing. A commonplace young man succeeds to an old estate in Scotland, and thus ordinary modern life is brought into touch with the uncanny. The mystery is explained after the manner of Mrs. Radcliffe. The touching sketch of a mother striving with adversity and disappointment is not without a personal reference to the authoress. The Crofter question comes in. [Macmillan : o.p.]

—— *Joyce.* 1888

A romance like *Valentine* ; the heroine, brought up by peasants, turns out to be the child of rich parents. Her hesitation between a high-born and a low-born lover, and her peasant's scorn for the elaborate formality of genteel life, make a humorous story. The most satirical among the character-sketches is that of an Anglican clergyman and his " female accomplice." [Macmillan : o.p.]

—— *The Land of Darkness.* 1888

A pendant to her *Little Pilgrim*. Her conception of Hell—a place of horror and torment, but not utterly hopeless, since faith and resolution can find a way of escape. Contains also *On the Dark Mountains* and a sequel to the *Little Pilgrim*. [Macmillan : o.p.]

—— *Neighbours on the Green.* 1889

Dinglefield Green is an aristocratic Cranford, inhabited by a little colony whose several stories are told here. *Lady Denzil* is the pathetic story of the most amiable and dignified of these characters. *My Neighbour Nelly* is lighter in theme, and *The Stockbroker at Dinglewood*, though sad in its ending, is mainly a comedy. [Macmillan : o.p.]

—— *The Railway Man and his Children.* 1891

A millionaire, risen from the ranks, generous, open-handed, loyal ; his youthful wife, a cultured woman whom he wins late in life ; his bourgeois children, offspring of an earlier marriage ; and other persons rich in idiosyncrasy, are the principals in the story. [Macmillan : o.p.]

—— *The Cuckoo in the Nest.* 1892

A baronet's half-imbecile son marries an inn-keeper's daughter ; he soon dies, but the young woman ingratiates herself with the baronet, and at his death finds herself in possession of the whole estate, to the horror of the local gentry and the dismay of the family. She puts herself right, in the end, by an act of magnanimity. The writer's sympathies are with the heroine, who is no Becky Sharp, but a shrewd, self-reliant, and not ungenerous girl ; and her invasion of genteel society evokes extremely comic scenes. [Hutchinson : .o.p.]

—— *Old Mr. Tredgold : a story of two sisters.* 1896

A selfish, vulgar, and sordid old man is Mr. Tredgold, and these unpleasant attributes are inherited by one daughter, while the other, a better woman, suffers the reverses of fortune. Characters drawn just as they are, without alleviation or satire, and with no undue regard for poetic justice. [Longman : o.p.]

OLLIVANT, Alfred [1874–1927]. *Owd Bob, the Grey Dog of Kenmuir.* 1898

Sketches of the Cumberland dalesmen and their doughty tykes, a book full of love and knowledge of animals and of the life of the shepherds on the fells. The fights are incessant between Bob, Son of Battle, and the hideous Red Wull ; but the sagacity and loyalty of the dogs are made as much of as their feuds, and the author gives them characters full of individual traits and capacities. [Heinemann ; *sub tit. Bob, Son of Battle*, Doubleday, New York ; *illus.* by Margaret Kirmse, Heinemann ; Doubleday, New York.]

—— *Danny : story of a Dandy Dinmont.* 1903

A story of the same kind, but not so good, though the 1902 edition was withdrawn and revised. [Murray : o.p. ; Macmillan, New York : o.p.]

—— *Redcoat Captain : a story of that country.* 1907

Tells allegorically " the one story, and it is the best story in the world," the story of life's meaning, that " in the end love must win." [Murray : o.p. ; Macmillan, New York : o.p.]

—— *The Gentleman : a romance of the sea.* 1908

A fast and furious story of a Nelsonian midshipmite in 1805, when Napoleon was daily expected in Sussex, and of an attempt to kidnap the English admiral. This and the one preceding are written in a strangely simple, almost child-like style that has a force and charm of its own. [Allen & Unwin ; Nelson.]

—— *The Royal Road.* 1912

The misery and squalor of London life is well conveyed in this story of the progress of a Cockney boy down the " royal road " by way of failure, consumption, and despair, to death. [Allen & Unwin.]

—— *Boy Woodburn : a story of the Sussex Downs.* 1918

An open-air story about a girl who trains a Grand National winner. [Jenkins ; Doubleday, Doran, New York.]

—— *Two Men : being the first part of a romance of two worlds.* 1919

The theme is the strength of heredity and the moulding power of circumstance on character, in three generations of a family in the Sussex Downs. [Allen & Unwin ; Doubleday, New York.]

—— *Old For-ever.* 1923

A tale of the North-West Frontier at the time of the last Afghan war (1879), but not particularly historical. The chief characters are a major and his wife. [Nelson ; Doubleday, New York.]

OMAN, Carola [Mrs. Carola Mary Anima Lenanton ; daughter of Sir Charles Oman ; *b.* 1897].
Crouchback.   1929
The heroine is Anne, wife of Richard III. Life in the fifteenth century and episodes in the Wars of the Roses, are brought vividly before us ; Richard himself appears much less black than he is generally painted. Hodder ; Holt, New York.]

—— *Miss Barrett's Elopement.*   1930
The story of Robert Browning & Elizabeth Barrett. [Hodder ; Holt, New York.]

ONIONS, Oliver. *The Odd-job Man.*   1903
The redemption of a man of flawed character—a theme worked out unconventionally and with an eye for the intricacies of motive. London life, respectable and the reverse, sketched with actuality, not untempered by touches of Dickens, e.g. the brotherly model, and the vengeful lover who with an innocent girl and a woman of rare nobility are reshaping influences on the hero. Amusing satire of cheap journalism, second-rate art, etc. [Murray.]

—— *Widdershins.*   1911
Nine magazine stories of the supernatural or abnormal. *The Beckoning Fair One* and *Hic Jacet*, in the Henry James manner, deal, the one with the obsessions of an author in an ancient house, the other with the vain efforts of a writer of detective fiction to write for art's sake. *Benham* is a sketch of a mad sculptor, *Phantas* an Elizabethan tale in the genre of *The Finest Story in the World.* [Secker.]

—— *In Accordance with the Evidence.*   1912
—— *The Debit Account* [sequel].   1913
—— *The Story of Louie* [sequel].   1913
This trilogy gives the story from three points of view. First comes a quiet, prosaic account of the feelings and reflections that led to a very business-like murder—Jim Jeffries "executes" the abject little rat who is about to marry the commonplace girl Jim loves. In the second, Jeffries watches his wife growing more and more suspicious and enlightened. His death is followed by her suicide. The third tells the story as a third person, a strong, independent, clear-sighted woman, sees it : she is the great character of the whole story, which incidentally gives " close-up " pictures of a business college in Bloomsbury, office life, journalism, etc. Reissued complete in one volume, entitled *Whom God hath Sundered* (1925). [Secker ; Doubleday, Doran, New York.]

—— *The Two Kisses.*   1913
The main characters are a group of art-students, of whom two girls, with the men they marry, are of strongly contrasted types—the one a shallow intellectual, the other solid, shrewd, and having a sense of humour. [Methuen : o.p.]

—— *A Crooked Mile.*   1914
Continues the later lives of the characters from *The Two Kisses.* The intelligentsia, crammed with half-digested ideas and windy talk, come in for severe satire. [Methuen : o.p.]

—— *Ghosts in Daylight.*   1924
Five stories of the unseen and the uncanny, e.g. *The Woman in the Way*, a tale of exorcism in the seventeenth century ; *The Real People*, an author creates so strong a character that it becomes a real person to him, and influences his life. [Chapman.]

—— *The Painted Face.*   1929
In *The Painted Face*, a modern Italian girl returns to the ritual of the Greek gods, and comes to her death. In *The Rosewood Door*, an old door exercises a tragic influence over those who pass it. *The Master of the House* is a tale of Indian magic. [Heinemann.]

—— *The Open Secret.*   1930
As serious an exploration of character and of human relations as the earlier trilogy, though it falls short in lifelikeness. Begun seven years before the date of publication, when there was more to be said for the view that Europe was dominated by the conflict between Bolshevism and Fascism. [Heinemann.]

OPIE, Amelia [*née* Alderson ; 1769–1853]. *The Father and the Daughter.*   1801
A conventional novel characterized by harrowing pathos. A young lady betrayed by a libertine, leaves home and falls into terrible troubles, the culmination of which is that her father goes mad and dies of grief. [o.p.]

—— *Adeline Mowbray ; or, Mother and Daughter.*   1804
A satire on the new woman : the heroine is a ridiculous travesty of Mary Wollstonecraft, the main incidents of her life and her connexion with Godwin. Adeline refuses to marry, and lives with her lover until his death, whereupon she meets with persecution and contumely till she dies in great misery. [3 vols., Longman, 1805 : o.p.]

OPPENHEIM, Edward Phillips [*b.* 1866]. *The Man and his Kingdom.*   1899
A romance of the Zenda type, concerned with an imaginary socialist colony in South America. [Ward & Lock ; Little & Brown, Boston : o.p.]

—— *The World's Great Snare.*   1900
A romance of adventure and love in an American mining camp and in England. The hero comes in for a fortune by the help of a daring and unselfish girl, who has been his mistress ; and he has to choose between her and an aristocratic bride. [Ward & Lock ; Lippincott, Philadelphia : o.p.]

—— *A Millionaire of Yesterday.*   1900
An intricate plot, dealing with the financial schemes of a man who won a rich concession in West Africa, but who deserted his partner, and has to face damaging allegations in consequence. These financial difficulties and the complications arising when he falls in love with the partner's daughter make a lively story. [Ward & Lock (repr. 1929) ; Little & Brown, Boston : o.p.]

—— *The Survivor.*   1901
The " Survivor " is an ambitious poet, and the character next in importance is a beautiful siren, who would fain pose as his patroness. The plot is fertile in sensations, but there are natural and lifelike character-

OPPENHEIM, Edward Phillips (*continued*).
drawing and sympathetic pictures of nature amid the woods and the fells. [Ward & Lock ; Little & Brown, Boston.]

—— *Master of Men.* 1901
—— *The Great Awakening.* 1902
Plot-novels on much the same kind of plan, dealing with financial and other villains, selfish society ladies, intricate imbroglios of all kinds, always ending satisfactorily for those who deserve it. [(1) Methuen ; (2) Ward & Lock ; (1) and (2) Little & Brown, Boston : o.p.]

OPPENHEIM, James [American ; *b.* 1882]. *The Olympian.* 1912
A study of New York high finance, and the effect of dollars on both high and low in business life. [Harper : o.p.]

—— *Idle Wives.* 1914
A teaching of theory by example : an American wife leaves husband and children to work out her own idea of a woman's duty to society. Gives an unalluring picture of both upper and lower strata in New York social life. [Century Co., New York : o.p. ; Nash : o.p.]

ORCUTT, William Dana [American ; *b.* 1870]. *Robert Cavelier.* 1904
Adventures of an ex-Jesuit in New France, in La Salle's time ; he is one of the first in the Mississippi valley. Keeps close to history (1662–82). [McClurg, Chicago : o.p. ; Heinemann : o.p.]

—— *The Flower of Destiny.* 1905
A romance written round Louis Napoleon's escape from Spain, the *coup d'état*, and Eugénie, afterwards empress (1846–52). [McClurg, Chicago : o.p.]

ORCZY, Baroness Emmuska [Mrs. Montague Barstow ; *b.* 1865]. *The Scarlet Pimpernel.* 1905
—— *I Will Repay* [sequel]. 1906
—— *The Elusive Pimpernel* [sequel]. 1908
—— *The League of the Scarlet Pimpernel* [sequel]. 1919
—— *Lord Tony's Wife* [sequel]. 1917
—— *The Triumph of the Scarlet Pimpernel* [sequel]. 1922
—— *Eldorado* [sequel]. 1913
—— *Sir Percy Hits Back* [sequel]. 1927
A long series of connected stories (arranged above in order of incident) detailing the feats and adventures of Sir Percy Blakeney, who rescues victims from the guillotine in France during the Revolution. Light, full of exciting incident, and enormously popular. [(1) and (2), (5)–(8), Hodder ; (3), Hutchinson : o.p. ; (4), Cassell ; (1), Putnam, New York ; (2), Lippincott, Philadelphia ; (3), Dodd & Mead, New York ; (4), (5), and (7), Doran, New York : o.p. ; (6), Burt, New York ; (8), Doran, New York.]

—— *A Son of the People.* 1906
—— *The Tangled Skein.* 1907
—— *Beau Brocade.* 1908
—— *Petticoat Government.* 1910
—— *The Nest of the Sparrowhawk.* 1911
Further exciting melodramas with historical backgrounds ; *A Son of the People* is a faithful account of peasant life in Hungary in the stormy days of the introduction of machinery, and describes the authoress's own estates. *The Tangled Skein* is a sentimental story of Mary's reign ; *Beau Brocade* portrays a chivalrous highwayman in Jacobite days ; *Petticoat Government* is a popular romance of the Pompadour, the Pretender, and the French Court in 1745 ; *The Nest of the Sparrowhawk* is a love-romance of the Protectorate. [All Hodder, except (4), Hutchinson : o.p. ; (3), Lippincott, Philadelphia ; (4), Doran, New York : o.p.]

—— *The Bronze Eagle.* 1915
A story of the Hundred Days, and the treasure seized by Talleyrand at the flight of Marie Louise. [Hodder.]

—— *A Sheaf of Bluebells.* 1917
An ingenious and exciting story of Royalist plotting after the coronation of Napoleon I. [Hutchinson : o.p.]

—— *The Honourable Jim.* 1924
The experiences of a Roundhead husband and his Cavalier wife. [Hodder ; Burt, New York.]

ORENBURGSKY, Sergei Gussiev [Russian ; *b.* 1867]. *The Land of the Fathers.* 1925
—— *The Land of the Children.* 1928
A tremendous panorama of Russian life before and during the Bolshevist revolution and civil war. [Transl. by Nina Nikolaevna SELIVANOVA, Longmans, New York.]

O'RIORDAN, Conal O'Connell [F. Norreys Connell ; Irish ; *b.* 1874]. *The Young Days of Admiral Quilliam.* 1906
A sea-story of 1805 with an autobiographic hero who makes himself out a fool. [Blackwood : o.p.]

—— *Adam of Dublin : a romance of to-day.* 1920
Begins a life-history, with the potential hero's infancy. Illegitimate and born in a slum, Adam has sparks of genius. Here and in the subsequent volumes everything is seen from his single point of view, and his imagination and sensitiveness give depth and ulterior significance to the figures that emerge from the crowd. His mother and his putative father are of the hideous world explored by the naturalists ; but their ugliness is veiled—why " paint the merely sordid " ? Of a very different stamp are the kindly, childlike priest, the philosophic Mr. Macarthy, and certain figures portrayed from political society in Dublin. [Collins.]

—— *Adam and Caroline* [sequel]. 1921
Still a boy, Adam is in love, or thinks he is, with one girl and then another, which sentimental experiences are to persist as a background in his consciousness even when he grows up and has other affairs. The lively style, not devoid of bulls and other Irishisms, is a striking feature of both novels. [Collins.]

O'RIORDAN, Conal O'Connell (*continued*). *In London* [sequel]. 1922

He arrives in the English metropolis at the beginning of the great war, by accident, and as casually drifts on to the stage, where he is surprisingly successful and has further emotional experiences. Some autobiography may be detected here. There is a farcical account of the long run of a worthless play, and the actor-manager and his wife are gently caricatured. [Collins ; Harcourt, New York.]

—— *Married Life* [sequel]. 1924

Hardly yet a man, and innocently inclined towards a more sympathetic person, he finds himself mated with a conceited, heartless beauty, who makes life intolerable. The theatrical business goes on ; actors and actresses have humorous or sentimental rôles ; and Irish characters reappear, with indirect glimpses of the Black-and-Tan atrocities in Dublin. Also the talk about things on heaven and earth goes on interminably, with notable aphorisms from Mr. Macarthy. [Collins.]

—— *Soldier Born : a story of youth.* 1927

—— *Soldier of Waterloo : a story of manhood* [sequel]. 1928

The hero is a young Irishman ; the first part describes his boyhood and early life in Dublin ; in the second he comes to England, meets the Princess Charlotte (who falls in love with him) and takes part in the battle of Waterloo. [Collins ; together, *sub tit. Yet Do Not Grieve*, Scribner, New York, 1928.]

ORLOVSKY, R. [Russian]. *Nadia ; or, Out of the Beaten Track.* 1888

Life of an enthusiastic woman who from childhood has been affiliated with secret revolutionary societies : at Zürich she mixes with a crowd of Russians all discussing Nihilist problems. She aspires towards a higher and better life, but it is only with the utmost difficulty that she rends the bonds that have been woven round her by her fellow-conspirators. [Transl. by Baroness LANGENAU, 3 vols., Sonnenschein : o.p.]

ORZESZKO, Madame Eliza [Polish ; *née* Pawlowska ; 1842–1910]. *An Obscure Apostle* (Meir Ezofowicz, 1885). 1899

A study of Jewish life in Poland, embracing sketches of all classes, the fiercely orthodox heads of the synagogue, the town Jews, and the patriarchal landowners, drawn without prejudice, and with sympathetic insight into the social and religious troubles of this portion of the race. The personal interest attaches to a young Jew who has broken with his people's traditions. The feud between the two parties in the Jewish village seems to symbolize the universal strife between darkness and light. [Transl. by Count S. C. DE SOISSONS, Greening : o.p. ; by Iza YOUNG, *sub tit. Meir Ezofovitch*, Allison, New York, 1898 : o.p.]

—— *The Interrupted Melody* (Pieśń Przerwana, 1896). 1912

A short tale of a ducal romance. [Transl. by M. OCHENKOWSKA, Melrose : o.p.]

—— *The Modern Argonauts* (Argonauci, 1900). 1901

A powerful treatment of a familiar subject, life and happiness wrecked through the engrossing pursuit of riches. The Jason of the story is a multimillionaire, who forgets the home affections, neglects his wife, and leaves his children to their own devices, while he is absorbed in financial enterprises. The story ends in overwhelming tragedy. [Transl. by Count S. C. DE SOISSONS, Greening : o.p. ; by Jeremiah CURTIN, *sub tit. The Argonauts*, Scribner, New York : o.p.]

OSBOURNE, Lloyd [American ; *b.* 1868]. *The Queen versus Billy.* 1900

Stories of blacks and whites in the Solomon Isles, by the Vice-Consul in Samoa. The title-story is about a negro who, though probably innocent, is condemned for the murder of a white man. He becomes a favourite on shipboard, and every chance is given him to escape, but the pathetic humour of the story is that Billy insists on being shot. [Scribner, New York ; Heinemann : o.p.]

—— *The Infatuation.* 1909

The sentimental history of a railway president's daughter, who refuses a number of suitors, and then falls desperately in love with an actor and makes a runaway marriage. Their married life is at first a failure, and the lady has to undertake the redemption of the man. [Bobbs-Merrill, Indianapolis : o.p. ; *sub tit. Harm's Way*, Mills & Boon : o.p. ; see also p. 450, *sub nom.* Stevenson, R. L.]

" OSGOOD, Irene " [Mrs. R. Harborough Sherard, *née* De Belot ; American ; *b.* 1875]. *To a Nun Confess'd : Letters from Yolande to Sister Mary.* 1909

Sentimental analysis of a woman hopelessly in love, the neglected wife of a self-centred Englishman. The letters are supposed to have been written to a nun and discovered in one of the French convents disestablished by the Government. [Dana Estes, Boston : o.p. ; Sisley : o.p.]

OSSORGIN, Mikhail [Russian ; *b.* 1878]. *A Quiet Street* (Sivtzev vrazhek). 1930

A poignant story of Russian life during the revolution, bringing out the tragic sufferings of the intellectuals under the new order. Ossorgin was exiled by the Bolshevists in 1922. [Transl. by Nadia HELSTEIN, Secker ; Dial Press, New York.]

" OUIDA " [Mdlle Marie Louise de la Ramée ; 1839–1908]. *Strathmore.* 1865

Ouida's novels, it has been well said, " suggest a schoolgirl's dream of the *grande passion*." They portray not real life, but an inexperienced, imaginative, and emotional young lady's idea of what life ought to be. Ouida's feeling for beauty, her tenderness and sympathy for the poor and distressed, are so engaging, and her revelation of the feminine heart is so interesting, that a few of her novels can be read in spite of their glaring faults. In *Strathmore* the cold-hearted, gifted, and immensely strong hero falls a victim at last to the charms of an unscrupulous beauty, to whom he sacrifices everything, and in a fit of misguided jealousy kills his bosom friend in a duel. The rest of the novel is taken up with his immeasurable revenge on the woman, who in the end unexpectedly changes her evil nature and forgives Strathmore. In the descriptions and amorous scenes the writer gives full rein to her sensuous imagination.

—— *Chandos.* 1866

A garish and gushing romance, with a glorified libertine as hero, who is likened to Goethe " because the list of his loves is long." This dazzling creation keeps a harem in Park Lane, and is constantly in pursuit of his ideal, embodied in miscellaneous women, other men's wives as a rule. The story is decorated throughout with luxurious upholstery, gorgeous millinery, magnificent language and cookery.

" OUIDA " (*continued*). *Under Two Flags.* 1867

The author's best novel, good in spite of the florid extravagance of her descriptions and the unreality of the world depicted. The numerous episodes of exciting action, fox-hunts in the shires, battles of French and Kabyles in Algeria, are well described, and the book is full of imagination of an Oriental kind. The characters are all idealizations of good or bad, and stand out well. The hero is a handsome, aristocratic guardsman of superhuman virtues and vices (it is hard to say which are regarded with more complacency by his creator). His lodgings in Piccadilly surpass Oriental Courts in luxury and magnificence. Men adore him, women pet him, his riotous living never impairs his daredevil courage or his superb physique, etc. The next best character is an " unsexed " but heroic little French *vivandière*.

—— *Tricotrin.* 1868

Tricotrin is an agnostic and a bohemian ; but his virtues are near perfection : he is handsome, an accomplished artist, learned, wise. The heroine is a castaway, whom he rescues from poverty. A main motive of a sentimental story is Tricotrin's self-abnegation in keeping his love unspoken.

—— *Puck.* 1870

The autobiography of a lapdog born in low society, and passing through various stations of life, which he describes in Ouidaesque language.

—— *A Dog of Flanders ; and other stories.* 1872

Also tells the story of a dog, whose fortitude and affection are scathingly contrasted with the cruelty and meanness of the human beings who maltreat him as a poor beast of burden. Belgium and France are the scenes of these tales. *The Branch of Lilac* culminates in the fighting of the Communists and Versaillists in Paris.

—— *Pascarel.* 1873

Highly coloured descriptions of Florence and other Italian cities and lovely landscapes. Pascarel is a born actor, and a son of the people, who plays to simple villagers and shuns the applause of cities. His love is an innocent waif, and a cardinal incident turns on the jealousy of her and her mistress. As usual, many " improper " people figure among the characters.

—— *Two Little Wooden Shoes.* 1874

An innocent little Brabant girl is petted by a rich painter, who leaves her to her peasant lover ; but, hearing he is sick, she walks to Paris to offer succour and love, and finding him sunk in debauchery, flies home and dies.

—— *Signa.* 1875

Signa is a foster-child of nature, a lad with a genius for art and music, in whose mind bold and striking thoughts on life and God are instinctive. Luxuriantly descriptive of the beautiful mountains and forests of the sub-Alpine region, and of the ancient monasteries and strongholds of Italy.

—— *Ariadne.* 1877

Another child of nature, innocent, impulsive, passionate, is depicted as a born sculptor. Her perilous camaraderie with artists and connoisseurs introduces voluminous talk about art and the ancients (full of characteristic inaccuracies).

—— *Moths.* 1880

As typical as any of Ouida's gushing ignorance of life and rhapsodical passion for romance. The love of an ignorant young lady for a great singer, told entirely from the girl's point of view.

—— *A Village Commune.* 1881

Describes a modern Italian village under the so-called regime of Liberty. In reality, a political adventurer rules the community as an irresponsible autocrat, grinding the poor with impositions, rooting out every cherished custom or survival, and utilizing public pretexts to serve his own ends.

—— *In Maremma.* 1882

Musa, the daughter of a ferocious brigand, is another of these children of nature, who makes a solitary home in an Etruscan tomb, amid the wilds of Maremma. Her intercourse with other human beings only leads to treachery, robbery, and martyrdom.

—— *The Waters of Edera.* 1900

Pictures the squalid inhabitants of an Italian district, and denounces the corruption and tyranny of the Government. Tells how a primitive and pagan lord of the soil fights a hopeless battle against a foreign company representing civilization and industrialism.

[All, Chatto ; Lippincott, Philadelphia ; (10) and (12), o.p. ; (3) also Burt, New York ; (6) also Putnam, New York ; *illus.*, Macmillan, New York.]

OUTHWAITE, R. L. [South African], and **CHOMLEY, C. H.** [South African]. *The Wisdom of Esau.* 1901

A plain story, with little pretensions to literary qualities, but stamped with sincerity ; dealing with colonial life in Victoria half a century ago. The authors expose the ill-working of the Gavan Duffy Land Act and the infamous proceedings of the land-grabbers. The pioneer farmer who is the hero suffers a terrible series of wrongs. [Unwin : o.p.]

OVERTON, Gwendolen [*b.* 1876]. *The Heritage of Unrest.* 1901

A study of the relations between the Apaches in New Mexico and Arizona and the U.S. Government during the latter part of the nineteenth century, and to some extent an impeachment of American policy ; historical characters like General Crook are portrayed, and the local conditions, the ways of the Indians and whites set forth. The plot centres in the fortunes and the moral history of a female half-breed. [Macmillan : o.p.]

OWEN, John [*b.* 1878]. *Many Captives.* 1930

There is little story but admirably perceptive character-drawing in this quiet and finely written portrait of a Suffolk village. [Gollancz.]

" OXENHAM, John " [William Arthur Dunkerley]. *John of Gerisau.* 1902

—— *Under the Iron Flail.* 1902

—— *Barbe of Grand Bayou.* 1903

"OXENHAM, John" (*continued*). *Lauristons.*   1910
—— *The Coil of Carne.*   1911
—— *Broken Shackles.*   1914

Absorbing love-business and exciting adventure are the main ingredients of all these popular romances, which deal with war, e.g. the 1866 campaign in Austria in *John of Gerisau*, the Crimea in *The Coil of Carne*, the Franco-German campaigns in *Under the Iron Flail*, and the Southern States in *Barbe*. [(1) Hodder ; (2) and (3), Unwin ; (4), o.p. ; (5) and (6), Methuen : o.p.]

—— *My Lady of the Moor.*   1916

A Dartmoor tale, the heroine said to be drawn from a Devonshire authoress. [Longmans, London and New York.]

OZAKI, Yei Theodora [Madame Yukio ; Japanese]. *Warriors of Old Japan ; and other stories.*
                                                                                                    1909

A rendering of ten old native stories by a lady whose father and husband are Japanese—folk-tales of a mythological or allegorical nature, in which giants and supernatural beasts play a considerable part. [*Illus.* by Japanese artists, Constable : o.p. ; Houghton, Boston.]

—— *Romances of Old Japan.*   1919

Eleven stories admirably translated from the Gidayu or musical drama and other native sources ; chiefly of bygone times, e.g. *The Tragedy of Kesa Gozen*, *Loyal even unto Death*, and *Ursato, or the Crow of Dawn*. [Brentano, New York.]

PAGE, Thomas Nelson [American ; 1853–1922]. *In Ole Virginia.*   1887

Stories of the Southern States, plantation life and family life, mostly in negro dialect. *Polly* is an exception, where the spokesman is a profane, hard-drinking, devil-may-care old planter. [Scribner, New York ; Heinemann : o.p. ; *illus.* by A. B. Frost, Scribner, New York.]

—— *Two Little Confederates.*   [juvenile] 1888
—— *Among the Camps.*   [juvenile] 1891

(1) Home life in Virginia during the war; the two boys are left on a plantation while the men are at the front. [Scribner, New York.] (2) Four short stories about children in the South. [Scribner, New York.]

—— *Elsket ; and other stories.*   1891

A little Norwegian tragedy : Elsket, descendant of the Vikings, is wooed and deserted by an English lover, and dies in her grief ; whilst he suffers a terrible revenge. The other stories are chiefly of the South and comprise some comic narratives, like *George Washington's Last Duel* and *Plaski's Tunament*, overflowing with negro humour. [Scribner, New York.]

—— *The Burial of the Guns ; and other stories.*   1894

Six tales of the days before and after the Civil War, depicting the South, with deep affection for the old patriarchal society but without blindness to its darker side. *The Burial of the Guns* is a gallant, pathetic episode of the last phases of the war. This and the others contain some very tender and affecting sketches of character. [Scribner, New York : o.p. ; Ward & Lock : o.p.]

—— *Red Rock : a chronicle of Reconstruction.*   1898

A crowded story of the Reconstruction period, centring in the Red Rock plantation and its strange vicissitudes of ownership. The unhappy Southern landowners and their faithful negroes are drawn sympathetically ; and, on the other hand, the detested " carpet-baggers," the persecuting instruments of the Federal Government, appear in an odious light. [Scribner, New York ; Heinemann : o.p.]

—— *Gordon Keith.*   1903

Long and prolix—the biography of a Southern gentleman, put forward as an exemplar of Southern virtues. Son of a ruined planter, he gets his living in many walks of life, giving opportunity for descriptions of cities and villages in the South, and of plutocratic society in New York, with too ample records of many love affairs. [Scribner, New York ; Heinemann : o.p.]

—— *John Marvel, Assistant.*   1909

A novel on the same ample scale, dealing with the friendship and deep affection of three men who meet in a Southern college, their work as pastor, as socialist teacher, etc., and the different issues of their love for the same girl. A good study of the development of character and of social unrest in the West and the South. [Scribner, New York ; Laurie : o.p.]

PAGET, Miss Violet [" Vernon Lee " ; b. 1856]. *Penelope Brandling.*   1903

Story of an old house on the Welsh coast (1772–3), the head-quarters of a gang of smugglers and wreckers, who terrorize a young baronet and his wife on their entering upon the property. [Unwin : o.p.]

PAIN, Barry Eric Odell [1864–1928]. *In a Canadian Canoe.*   1891

A medley of absurdities, humorous fables, and droll wit, with a sediment of serious thought. One of the best is *The Celestial Grocery*, in which the fantastic humour slips almost imperceptibly into genuine pathos. [Harper : o.p.]

—— *Stories and Interludes.*   1892

Similar compositions, brief and sketchy, some in verse. Even the superficially trifling hint at deeper meanings, e.g. the little parable of Bertillon and Bruno. [Harper, London and New York : o.p.]

—— *Playthings and Parodies.*   1893

Parodies, imitations, and humorous lucubrations, full of whimsical but quiet fun, and generally burdened with a suggestion of grave meanings. [Cassell : o.p.]

—— *The Octave of Claudius.*   1897
—— *An Exchange of Souls.*   1911

Two psychical stories, the former intensely realistic and horrible. [(1), Harper : o.p. ; (2), Nash : o.p.]

PAIN, Barry Eric Odell (*continued*). *Eliza.*   1900

—— *Eliza's Husband* [sequel].   1903

—— *Eliza Getting On* [sequel].   1911

—— *Exit Eliza* [sequel].   1912

    Amusing matrimonial and housekeeping experiences, the husband a serious, methodical young man who gets on in business, the wife a woman with a sense of humour ; much in the style of Grossmith's *Diary of a Nobody.* [(1), Cassell : o.p. ; (2), Chatto ; (3), Cassell : o.p. ; (4), Cassell : o.p.]

—— *The One Before.*   1902

    Pure extravaganza in Mr. Anstey's vein. [Nelson : o.p. ; Scribner, New York : o.p.]

—— *The Exiles of Faloo.*   1910

    A comic picture of a South Sea island where a body of genteel swindlers and other fugitives from London society have settled and established a club ; the satire particularly neat and unobtrusive, the characters adroitly combined so as to bring out each other's foibles. [Methuen : o.p.]

—— *Stories in Grey.*   1912

    Miscellaneous short stories, ranging from anecdotes of diablerie and studies in the uncanny to the condensations of humorous story-telling called " Miniatures." [Laurie : o.p.]

—— *Mrs. Murphy.*   1913

    Anecdotes of a London charwoman. [Laurie : o.p. ; repr. in *Humorous Stories*, 1930.]

—— *One Kind and Another.*   1914

    Several of these are serious stories, but those in lighter vein, e.g. *Detection without Crime*, four skits about an amateur detective whose clues lead only to absurdity, are more effective. [Methuen : o.p.]

—— *The Problem Club.*   1919

    Good comic stuff reprinted from magazines ; the twelve members of the club each set out to solve some ridiculous problem of real life. [Collins.]

—— *The Death of Maurice.*   1920

    A well-constructed mystery story. [Skeffington : o.p.]

—— *Humorous Stories.*   1930

—— *More Stories.*   1930

    Two posthumous collections of Barry Pain's best, mostly items that have appeared already in the volumes preceding. The gem of the whole lot is certainly that ingenious and exciting tale *The Exiles of Faloo.* [Laurie.]

PAINE, Albert Bigelow [American ; *b.* 1861]. *The Bread Line : a story of a paper.*   1901

    The story of four sanguine young men who started a paper in New York and in a year were reduced to the " Bread Line," i.e. the receipt of charity. The humorous treatment is entertaining, and compensates for the technicalities of the subject. [Century Co., New York : o.p.]

PAINTER, William [1540–94]. *The Palace of Pleasure.*   1566–7

    A famous treasury of stories from Boccaccio, Bandello, Cinthio, Ser Giovanni, Straparola, Guevara, Marguerite of Navarre, etc., in most cases the first translations into English. The Elizabethan dramatists quarried many of their plots here ; e.g. *Romeo and Juliet*, *All's Well that Ends Well*, and *Measure for Measure*. [Ed. Joseph Jacobs, 3 vols. (a *verbatim* repr. of Haslewood's Ed. of 1813), Nutt, 1890 : o.p. ; 4 vols., *illus.*, Cresset Press (McKee, New York), 1930.]

PALACIO VALDÉS, Armando [Spanish ; *b.* 1853]. *The Marquis of Penalta* (Marta y María, 1883).   1886

    Maria is affianced to the Marquis, a man of the world, who takes his religious duties easily ; but she is afflicted by religious scruples, and fears that their union will be a surrender to carnal desires. She is a most interesting case of exaggerated mysticism, and, as in the *Doña Perfecta* of Galdós, the novelist utilizes her pious extravagance to satirize the morbid influence of the clergy, and, further, their interference in political affairs, a Carlist agitation springing out of the personal complication. Life in an old town (Avilès) in the author's native Asturias is depicted in a very picturesque and animated way ; but the glory of the novel, as of *Sister Saint Sulpice*, and of *José* and *La Aldea Perdida* (1903), which seems to have escaped translation, is the felicitous delineation of character. [Transl. by N. H. Dole, Crowell, New York.]

—— *Riverita* (1886).   1886

    In this and the next novel the heroine is the author's wife (now dead) : she appears here as a captivating child. Valdés is compared, by the late Fitzmaurice-Kelly, with those thorough going, notebook realists, the Goncourts ; but in these early novels Spanish ideas are predominant.

—— *Maximina* (Maximina, 1887) [sequel].   1888

    A simple plot, with more interesting characters, including dignified Spanish dons and fascinating ladies. Maximina is a shy and modest maiden, with a reserve of strong character ; her husband, a more ordinary person, is chastened by misfortune into a worthier mate. Sister Saint Sulpice is a friend of Maximina in Madrid. [Transl. by N. H. Dole, Crowell, New York.]

—— *The Fourth Estate* (El Cuarto Poder, 1888).   1901

    A tragic story of wedded life ; prime actors a husband, a heartless and guilty wife, and her noble sister, who loves the man, but sacrifices herself to make them happy. Many of the episodes are entertaining, sketching the humours of provincial society (in Asturias) and satirizing corrupt journalism. [Transl. by Rachel Challice, De La More Press : o.p.]

—— *Sister Saint Sulpice* (La Hermana San Sulpicio, 1889).   1890

    A thoroughly Spanish story, in spite of obvious French influences ; scene, Seville, the warm, many-coloured, passionate life of which makes a lively picture. The Andalusian Sister Saint Sulpice, who leaves her convent after taking the vows for four years, is loved by a Galician, but the match is opposed by her mother. The interest, however, is chiefly in the drawing of characters and manners. [Transl. by N. H. Dole, Crowell, New York.]

PALACIO VALDÉS, Armando (*continued*). *Froth* (La Espuma, 1890). 1891
A work of rather heavy realism emulating the contemporary French naturalists. The fashionable life of Madrid, shady financial doings, the tyranny of capital, the corrupt pleasures and adulteries of the fast set, and the coarseness of manners that makes them peculiarly repulsive ; with no plot beyond the story of a liaison and its wretched termination. A gallery of representative characters is presented in the harshest colours. [Transl. by Clara BELL, Heinemann.]

—— *Faith* (La Fé, 1892). 1892
Notable for the characterization of its heroine Obdulia. [Transl. by Isabel HAPGOOD : o.p.]

—— *The Grandee* (El Maestrante, 1893). 1894
Provincial society and the secluded life of the rural gentry. Lancia represents Oviedo half a century ago. Earlier half full of quaintness and humour ; second half tragic, dealing with a revengeful mother's crimes. Brings out in a striking fashion the pride and narrowness of the Spanish upper classes, and their antique picturesqueness. [Transl. by Rachel CHALLICE, Heinemann.]

—— *The Joy of Captain Ribot* (La Alegría del Capitán Ribot, 1899). 1900
As a picture of nobility of character, the triumph of honesty and manly feeling over libertinism, this book, written in denunciation of " the eternal adultery of the French novel," is one of his finest. In the lady of the piece we have a model of a true wife. Captain Ribot begins to court her, but is shamed by her purity and dignity. Has a good deal of distinctively Spanish humour, but the characterization often falls into caricature. Contains a good picture of bourgeois life and manners in Valencia. [Transl. by Minna C. SMITH, Downey : o.p. ; World Fiction Lib., 1923.]

PALGRAVE, William Gifford [1826–88]. *Hermann Agha : an Eastern narrative.* 2nd ed. 1872
One of our great Oriental romances. The author, who lived as a Jesuit missionary among the scenes he describes so brilliantly, claims that his story is truer than even the *Arabian Nights* to the true Orient. It is really the story (1762–8) of Hermann Wolff, the favourite officer of Ali Bey, who revolted from the Porte in 1768 and ruled Egypt till 1771, when he overran Syria, but was at last defeated. A thrilling narrative of Hermann's adventures at Bagdad, Diar-Bekr, and in the desert, and of his perilous amour with a beautiful Arab. Transfused with a passionate love of the desert and the free life of the Bedouin, as *Lavengro* is with the outdoor spirit of the gipsy. [H. S. King & Co. : o.p.]

PALTOCK, Robert [1697–1767]. *The Life and Adventures of Peter Wilkins, a Cornishman.* 1751
An imitation of *Robinson Crusoe* and *Gulliver's Travels*. Wilkins is carried in a boat to a strange land, " back of beyond," where he lives in solitude till he finds there are human inhabitants who can fly. One of them, a winged woman, falls into his hands, and lives with him as his wife. [*Facsimile Repr.*, ed. A. H. Bullen, 2 vols., Reeves and Turner, 1884, o.p. ; with original *illus.*, Dulau ; (Everyman's Lib.), Dent (Dutton, New York) ; *illus.* by Edward Bawden, Dent (Dutton, New York), 1928.]

PANZINI, Alfredo [Italian ; *b.* 1863]. *Wanted—a Wife* (Io cerco Moglie, 1920). 1929
An inferior and artificial story about a man in search of a wife, and the various girls whom he meets. Better works of this author, *Il Libro dei Morti* (1893), and *Le Fiabe della virtù* (1905) have not been translated. [Transl., N. L. Brown, New York.]

PARDO BAZÁN, Emilia [Signora Quiroga ; Spanish ; 1851–1921]. *The Son of the Bondwoman* (Los Pazos de Ulloa, 1886). 1907
The Condesa Pardo Bazán was an enthusiastic follower of Zola, whose principles she extolled in her *Cuestión Palpitante*, a study of modern realism. In later days, she frittered away her undeniable talents in various and often frivolous directions. This is a naturalistic picture of life in an old-fashioned village in Galicia. The chief figure is an indolent and self-indulgent hidalgo, the Marquess of Ulloa, who for years has been under the thumb of his steward, a plundering, masterful rogue. The marquess wants to marry, but unfortunately the steward's daughter has long been his mistress. Complications begin with the advent of the bride, and events soon turn to tragedy—a tragedy evolving naturally out of the conflicting forces of character. The sequel, *La Madre Naturaleza* (1887), has not been translated into English. [Transl. by Ethel H. HEARN, Lane.]

PARIS AND VIENNE : Hystorye of the noble ryght valyaunt and worthy knyght Parys, and of the fayr Vyenne the Daulphyns doughter of Vyennoys. 1484
A tale of knight-errantry, Catalonian in origin, translated into Provençal about 1430, and into French in 1459 by Pierre de la Sippade. Probably translated into English from the French version. One of the least affected and least incredible of the mediæval stories. Paris is of much lower degree than his lady-love, and when at length he ventures to ask her hand he is repulsed with threats and ignominy. They are married secretly ; then Paris goes to the East and lives at Babylon disguised as a " Moure," winning the favour of the Soldan, whereby he is enabled to rescue Vienne's father from captivity in Alexandria, and to win his bride. [Edited by W. C. HAZLITT, from the copy printed by Caxton ; with preface, glossary, and notes, and printed for the Roxburghe Lib., 1868 : o.p.]

PARKER, Eric [*b.* 1870]. *The Sinner and the Problem.* 1901
The life of a small group of people closely observed and playfully rendered, with a good deal of what may be called literary self-consciousness and no little sentiment. The characters seem to be genuine portraits, and the best of them are the two schoolboys nicknamed the Sinner and the Problem, whose ways are very true to boy-nature. [Macmillan, London and New York : o.p.]

—— *Promise of Arden.* 1912
About a family of children, the eldest of whom, Peggy, who mothers the rest, is portrayed with considerable charm. [Murray.]

PARKER, Sir Gilbert [Canadian ; *b.* 1862]. *Pierre and his People.* 1892
Stories of love and adventure, chiefly in the Hudson Bay Territory ; a presentment of native character and life by one who knows it intimately. Pierre, the half-breed, is an unpleasant character finely drawn. [Methuen ; Harrap ; Harper, New York : o.p.]

PARKER, Sir Gilbert (*continued*).   *The Translation of a Savage.*   1894
Describes the complications that ensue on an Englishman's marrying an Indian girl in Canada and sending her to his parents at home. [Methuen ; Harrap.]

—— *An Adventurer of the North.*   1895
" Being a continuation of the personal histories of *Pierre and his People*, and the last existing records of Pretty Pierre." [Methuen ; Harrap ; Harper, New York.]

—— *When Valmond came to Pontiac.*   1895
A picturesque romance about a traditional son of Napoleon, with some good character-drawing and intimate studies of manners among the French inhabitants of a Canadian town. [Methuen ; Harrap ; Harper, New York.]

—— *The Trail of the Sword.*   1895
A romance of Canada and New York, full of valorous feats and thrilling adventures.   One episode is the attempt of Admiral Phips to capture Quebec (1691) (cf. Miss Crowley's more accurate reading of history in *A Daughter of New France*, p. 126). [Methuen ; Harrap ; Appleton, New York : o.p.]

—— *The Seats of the Mighty.*   1896
Several chapters of the great struggle, culminating in the battle of Quebec, which dispossessed France and enthroned England in North America.   Wolfe and other famous characters appear. [Methuen ; Harrap ; Appleton, New York.]

—— *The Pomp of the Lavilettes.*   1897
A Canadian village story of the time of Papineau's abortive insurrection (1837).   Best character an Irish ne'er-do-well, whose humour atones for his misdeeds, of which, furthermore, he repents. [Methuen ; Harrap ; Appleton, New York : o.p.]

—— *The Battle of the Strong : a romance of two kingdoms.*   1898
Opens with the battle of Jersey, and is continued into the great war between England and France (1781–93), with episodic glimpses of the Revolution and the Vendéan tragedy.   Scene, chiefly Jersey, sometimes Brittany ; the local colour carefully studied. [Methuen ; Harper, New York : o.p.]

—— *The Lane that had no Turning ; and associated tales.*   1900
Twenty-six stories and sketches of the French-Canadians, the author's compatriots ; comic and tragic, melodramatic and grotesque.   The longest is the story of a seigneur who is all but driven mad by an hereditary malady, and at length commits a murder.   The principal figure, however, is his noble wife who shields and fosters him to the last. [Heinemann : o.p. ; Harper, New York : o.p.]

—— *The Right of Way : being the story of Charley Steele and another.*   1901
The most striking of many romantic episodes is the absolutely new life led by a man who for a time lost his memory through an accident. " Beauty Steele," the Montreal barrister, talented and eloquent, but a dipsomaniac, belongs to a favourite type of the author's.   The simple life and unsophisticated characters of a French-Canadian village are well portrayed. [Harrap ; Grosset, New York.]

—— *The Weavers.*   1907
A complicated story of political intrigue and adventures among the Arabs in Egypt fifty years ago, the hero a Quaker of mysterious birth. [Heinemann : o.p. ; Harper, New York.]

—— *The Judgment House.*   1913
A novel of English and South African life in the time of the Boer War (1896–1902). [Methuen ; Harper, New York.]

—— *The World for Sale.*   1916
A novel of Romany life in the great North-West. [Heinemann ; o.p. ; Nelson.]

—— *Wild Youth and Another.*   1919
Wild Youth is an effective story of a dour, elderly rancher in Askatoon married to a young wife, who falls in love with a young farmer near by.   The other, *Jordan is a Hard Road*, is a sentimental affair concerned with a bandit who reforms, and then is killed whilst holding up one last train in order to provide a dowry for his daughter. [Hutchinson : o.p. ; Lippincott, Philadelphia.]

—— *No Defence.*   1920
A romance of Ireland, London, and Jamaica, at the close of the eighteenth century.   The mutiny at the Nore (1797) is an episode. [Hodder : o.p. ; Lippincott, Philadelphia.]

—— *The Power and the Glory.*   1925
Canada and Quebec again, in the time of Frontenac, La Salle, and Henri de Tonti ; adventures on the Mississippi, and scenes at Versailles (1672–87). [Hodder ; Harper, New York ; Burt, New York.]

PARRISH, George Randall [American ; 1858–1923].   *When Wilderness was King ; a tale of the Illinois country.*   1904
A romance of the second war with England and the massacre of Fort Dearborn (1812). [McClurg, Chicago : o.p.]

—— *My Lady of the North : the love story of a Gray.*   1905
Virginia and Shenandoah during the Civil War ; Fisher Hill and other actions described : hero a Federal, heroine on the Confederate side (1864–5).   General Lee and General Grant appear. [McClurg, Chicago ; Burt, New York ; Putnam, London : o.p.]

—— *A Sword of the Old Frontier : a tale of Fort Chartres and Detroit.*   1905
A conventional story of a French officer's mission to Pontiac, adventures in the wilds, and love affairs (1763). [McClurg, Chicago : o.p. ; Putnam, London : o.p.]

—— *Bob Hampton of Placer : a tale of two soldiers of the Seventh.*   1906
The Indian campaign of 1875 and the battle of Little Big Horn.   General Custer and the officers of the 7th Cavalry are drawn from history. [McClurg, Chicago : o.p. ; Putnam, London : o.p.]

—— *My Lady of the South.*   1909
Exciting romance centring in an old Kentucky house, where the heroine, about to be forced into an unwelcome

PARRISH, George Randall (*continued*).
marriage, is wedded by an imposter bridegroom who subsequently wins her affection. [*Illus.*, McClurg, Chicago.]

—— *Beyond the Frontier.* 1915
Love and adventure in the Canadian backwoods at the time of the rivalry between La Salle and La Barre, and the exploits of La Salle's comrade Henri de Tonti (1682–5). [McClurg, Chicago : o.p. ; Burt, New York ; Jarrolds : o.p.]

—— *Molly Macdonald.* 1924
Similar ingredients, period two centuries later (1868) when Custer was campaigning against the Indians ; scenes, Kansas and Arkansas. [McClurg, Chicago : o.p. ; Jarrolds : o.p.]

PARRY, Major Gambier. *The Story of Dick.* 1892
A study of normal and healthy growth of character in a boy, the son of a soldier in India, who wins the love of everybody with whom he comes in contact. [Macmillan : o.p.]

" PASTON, George " [Miss Emily Morse Symonds]. *A Fair Deceiver.* 1897
The "fair deceiver" is engaged to the man who ought to marry her sister : this is the crucial situation. Interesting appreciation of artistic subjects. [Harper : o.p.]

—— *The Career of Candida.* 1898
Candida is a sympathetic portrait of the New Woman, and her story a thoughtful statement of the disadvantages of being born a woman. Contains some mild satire on contemporary ways. [Chapman : o.p. ; Appleton, New York : o.p.]

PATER, Walter [1839–94]. *Marius the Epicurean, his Sensations and Ideas.* 1885
History of the mental and moral growth of a Roman thinker, friend of Galen and Marcus Aurelius. The books consists chiefly of meditations, philosophical disquisitions, and reviews of the great schools of thinkers, criticisms of personalities, such as that of the imperial philosopher, and of the social and moral phenomena of the times ; all set forth in a refined, meditative prose. From Cyrenaicism the philosopher gradually works his way to a more spiritual attitude, coming under the influence of the Christian Church, of which an impassioned picture is given ; and he dies a kind of martyr, though not formally received within the Christian communion. There are many pages delineating the outward life and manners of Rome in the second century. [2 vols., Macmillan, London and New York ; (Caravan Lib.), *id.* ; (Traveller's Lib.), Cape ; 2 vols., lt. ed., Medici Soc.]

—— *Imaginary Portraits.* 1887
A Prince of Court Painters ; *Sebastian von Storck* ; *Denys l'Auxerrois* ; and *Duke Carl of Rosenmold*— essays in fictitious biography, with no dramatic play, but a most delicate interpretation of character and environment. Watteau is the central figure in the first ; the others are fanciful creations in which philosophical influences, like that of Spinoza, and artistic feelings and ideas are portrayed against a vague historical background. [Macmillan, London and New York.]

—— *Miscellaneous Studies.* 1895
A posthumous collection of essays containing two similar pieces of biographical fantasy, *Apollo in Picardy* and *Emerald Uthwart*, the latter embodying reminiscences of his own boyhood and education at Canterbury. [Macmillan, London and New York.]

—— *Gaston de Latour : an unfinished romance.* 1896
Philosophical, tracing the development of a refined and cultivated mind which finds ultimate satisfaction in the things of the spirit. Period of the French wars of religion in the sixteenth century ; the massacre of St. Bartholomew (1572) is an incident, and Ronsard and Montaigne make their appearance. Placid and idyllic pictures of country life in La Beauce, and elaborate descriptions of Chartres cathedral are in the same delicate, meandering style. [Macmillan, London and New York ; Mosher, Portland.]

PATERSON, Arthur Henry [b. 1862]. *A Son of the Plains.* 1895
An exciting story of the Santa Fé Trail in the early seventies, before the railways, when the overland journey was one of incessant peril from Indians and lawless whites. [Macmillan, London and New York : o.p.]

—— *The King's Agent.* 1902
A conventional story of Marlborough and the forger Young's plot against William III (1692). Portraits of Sarah, Duchess of Marlborough, William III, the Princess Anne, and her husband. [Heinemann.]

PATTERSON, John Edward [1866–1919]. *Fishers of the Sea.* 1908
—— *Watchers by the Shore.* 1909
—— *Love like the Sea.* 1911
Stories of seafaring life, fishermen, longshoremen, sailors, etc., in which Mr. Patterson, who has also written poetry, draws upon his own long experience of life on shipboard and vagabondage in many parts of the world. His first story pictures the fisher-folk of Grimsby, the next deals with the Sussex coast, and the third is a novel on the regular lines. [(1), Murray, (2), Methuen : o.p., (3), Heinemann.]

—— *The Story of Stephen Compton.* 1913
Gives a good account of the life of workers in the cotton-spinning industry, in which Stephen spends his earlier years. Subsequently he enters politics, and preaches the doctrine of solidarity between capital and labour. [Heinemann : o.p.]

—— *The Passage of the Barque " Sappho ".* 1919
A nautical novel thronged with salt-water types, among whom stands out a half-mad old captain whose dream of the Sargasso Sea comes true. [Dent : o.p.]

PATTON, James Blythe. *Bijli, the Dancer.* 1898
An episode of native Indian life, revealing the inner and emotional side of Mohammedan character and domestic manners. Bijli belongs to the most dishonoured class of women, but her capacity for true affection invests her with dignity. [Methuen : o.p. ; Page, Boston : o.p.]

PAULDING, James Kirke [American; 1779–1860]. *The Dutchman's Fireside.* 1831
Sole survivor of a number of satires, sketches, and novels, written by a collaborator of Washington Irving in *Salmagundi*. A thoroughly native and local novel, and patriotic, too, in its eulogy of Yankee character. Sensational and sentimental features alternate with quaint facetiousness; and the portraiture of Dutch settlers and Indian braves is incisive and racy. [Scribner, New York: o.p.]

PAYN, James [1830–98]. *Lost Sir Massingberd.* 1864
An ingenious plot-novel, revolving round the mysterious disappearance of a "colossally nefarious" baronet. Payn was a follower of Trollope, whose better qualities he now and then reproduced, e.g. in his best story *By Proxy*. [Collins, London and New York.]

—— *Married Beneath Him.* 1865
Contains some humorous scenes and a good many jokes, with a pair of diverting journalists. [Chatto; Munro, New York: o.p.]

—— *Blondel Parva.* 1868
A concise example of the novel of plot. A ruined man insures his life for the benefit of his wife and daughter; then disappears. When, later on, his daughter is entangled with two suitors, one of these, the villain, threatens to expose the fraud; but after divers complications a happy conclusion is reached. [2 vols., Bradbury: o.p.]

—— *Bentinck's Tutor.* 1868
A plot-novel, hingeing on the reappearance of a young heir supposed to be drowned, and the discomfiture of the villains. Local colouring from the Lake District (which Payn knew well enough to write a guide-book). [Chatto.]

—— *Not Wooed, but Won.* 1871
Full of incident; how an attractive heroine with a large circle of admirers is lucky enough to secure a fortune by one marriage and an estimable lover by the next. [Chatto.]

—— *Fallen Fortunes.* 1876
The plot excites the reader's suspense as to whether the virtuous people will or will not be rewarded with a fortune. Quiet portraiture of character, e.g. the jocular Mr. Dalton and the selfish and offensive Mrs. Campden. [Chatto: o.p.; Appleton, New York: o.p.]

—— *By Proxy.* 1878
A strong plot-novel dealing with English people in China and at home, and containing many passages descriptive of northern Chinese landscapes and ways of life. [Chatto: o.p.]

—— *Less Black than We're Painted.* 1878
Very favourable to the theatrical profession; the heroine an actress, who reforms her spendthrift husband and steers a happy and prosperous course through severe trials. [Chatto.]

—— *A Grape from a Thorn.* 1881
Life at a watering-place, follies and vanities of fashionable people, the Jacobite craze of a country gentleman, and similar stuff, treated in a light satirical vein. The love-story concerns a high-born girl, the "Grape," and a pair of bohemian friends. [Chatto.]

—— *The Canon's Ward.* 1884
Depicts a placid, kindly group of people, at their head the scholarly and amiable old Canon, into whose blameless life sorrow comes ungently. The Ward makes a secret marriage; but, her husband being drowned, a man uses his knowledge of the case to make her marry him. A happy conclusion is skilfully arranged. [Chatto; Dodd & Mead, New York: o.p.]

—— *The Heir of the Ages.* 1886
The title refers to a wonderful discovery of a lost Saxon treasure. The main interest is in a governess who takes to writing and suddenly becomes famous, and the doings of a villain who makes love to her in his wife's lifetime. [Murray.]

PAYNE, Will [American; b. 1865]. *The Money Captain.* 1898
A bold journalist in Chicago exposes the clandestine relations existing between a corrupt municipal body and a "gas duke." With this plot dealing with modern actualities a love-story is interwoven. [Stone, Chicago: o.p.]

—— *The Story of Eva.* 1901
Has been described as "a sort of idealized *Esther Waters*." Eva's married life is a failure, and she enters into an irregular union with a weak man. The story of their life together and of the interaction of their characters is worked out, though rather inconclusively. The scene is laid in Chicago. [Houghton, Boston: o.p.; Constable: o.p.]

—— *Mr. Salt.* 1903
Business life in Chicago and the 1893 panic. [Houghton, Boston: o.p.]

PEACOCK, Thomas Love [1785–1866]. *Headlong Hall.* 1816
Peacock was a satirist of striking individuality, who parodied the views of contemporary romanticism, Liberal politicians, and progressive thinkers, in absurd dialogues interspersed with exquisite snatches of poetry. He may be compared with Aristophanes, Lucian, Cyrano de Bergerac, and Voltaire, and also with Fielding the satirist and the later Samuel Butler. His first novel was a Rabelaisian satire on contemporary men of letters and philosophers, who are pilloried as faddists and their views criticized by the method of *reductio ad absurdum*. [(Everyman's Lib.), Dent (Dutton, New York); Routledge, 1906. With *Nightmare Abbey*, illus.* by Millar, Macmillan, London and New York; (World's Classics), Oxford Press, 1929.

—— *Melincourt.* 1817
A longer satire with more plot, and some likeness to Swift's *Gulliver*. The mock-hero, a priggish disciple of Rousseau, an anti-slavery enthusiast, etc., prepares a tame monkey, Sir Oran Haut-ton, to enter Parliament. The election for One Vote is a farcical episode, satirizing the effete pocket-borough system, and there is plenty of high jinks and high spirits. Southey, Coleridge, Wordsworth, Canning, etc., are caricatured. [*Illus.* by Townsend, Macmillan, London and New York, (1896, 1927.)]

PEACOCK, Thomas Love (*continued*). *Nightmare Abbey*. 1818

An amusing farce of great literary interest, caricaturing Byron as Mr. Cypress, Coleridge as Mr. Flosky, and Shelley, in a friendly way, as the misanthropic Scythrop, with his ludicrous entanglement with two girls—the plot is that of *The Rivals*. Extravagant sketches of contemporary cranks, poets, and mystics, many of them still easy to identify, fill up the canvas. [Routledge, 1906, Oxford Press, 1924 ; see also *Headlong Hall*.]

—— *Maid Marian*. 1822

A rollicking version of the Robin Hood legend, with oblique satire on English politics and reformers from the Conservative point of view—though Peacock is no party man. Melodious songs abound. Planché dramatized the tale. [Routledge, 1906 ; with *Crotchet Castle, illus.*, Macmillan, London and New York (1895, 1927).]

—— *The Misfortunes of Elphin*. 1829

His most eccentric novel, a semi-poetical burlesque of ancient Welsh history and legend, and at the same time a covert satire on the rival arguments of British politicians during the Reform Bill agitation, symbolized by the sapping and overthrow of the great sea wall. The sayings and doings of that immortal inebriate Seithenyn are exquisitely humorous, and the war songs, lyrics of love and drinking gave many gems to the anthologies. [Routledge, 1906 ; with *Crotchet Castle*, (World's Classics), Oxford Press, 1924 ; with *Rhododaphne*, a poem, *illus.* by Townsend, Macmillan, London and New York (1897), 1927.]

—— *Crotchet Castle*. 1831

Probably his most famous story, if not his best. Consists of Aristophanic mockery of what he regarded as fads and extravagances. A house-party of crotcheteers and other comic creatures meet and talk. Dr. Folliott, the jovial athletic parson, the exposer of shams, is, like Seithenyn, Dr. Opimian, and others, a piece of genuine humanism and no mere intellectual butt. [Routledge, 1906 ; *v. Maid Marian : v. Misfortunes of Elphin*.]

—— *Gryll Grange*. 1860

More of a regular novel than the rest, but the main element is still Aristophanic satire and shrewd criticism of social tendencies. Dr. Opimian, like Dr. Folliott, makes liberal amends for Peacock's early assaults on the clerical order. [Routledge, 1906 ; *illus.* by Townsend, Macmillan, London and New York, 1896, 1927].

[*Works* (complete, 10 vols.), ed. with introd. by H. F. B. Brett-Smith and C. E. Jones, ltd. ed. (in sets), *Halliford* ed., Constable (Wells, New York), 1924–5.]

PEAKE, Charlotte M. A. *Eli of the Downs*. 1920

The biography of a shepherd on the Wiltshire border in the 1870's. After the tragedy of his wife's death has broken his uneventful life, he travels in Colombo and the Klondike, and then returns to England, where the story was recounted to the author between 1908 and 1914. One may compare it with the work of George Bourne. [Heinemann : o.p.]

PEAKE, Elmore Elliot [American ; b. 1871]. *The Shape of Fear ; and other ghostly tales*. 1898

Concise stories of the supernatural, largely of evil spirits who help their familiars to gratify their desires. *A Grammatical Ghost* is a humorous tale ; while *Their Dear Little Ghost* and *From the Loom of the Dead* are pathetic. [Macmillan, New York : o.p.]

—— *The Darlingtons*. 1901

Typical of American realism, honest and scrupulously faithful to everyday life, minutely biographical, often tedious, and not much concerned with literary form. A railroad centre in the West is the scene, and the principal characters are the family of a railroad president, immersed in railway business. In one son an interesting case of dipsomania is studied, but the most attractive personalities are the spirited, self-reliant daughter and her lover, a Methodist minister, a " character " in every sense of the word. [McClure, New York : o.p. ; Fenno, New York : o.p. ; Heinemann : o.p.]

PEARCE, Joseph Henry [b. 1856]. *Esther Pentreath*. 1891

Among the miners of the Land's End peninsula sixty years ago. A story of primitive people, tragic in its intricate web of accident and human error, though lightened by the idyll of Esther's love and wedlock. A terrible shock injures the other lover mentally, and the resulting estrangement leads on to catastrophe. [Unwin : o.p.]

—— *Inconsequent Lives*. 1891

An intensely realistic study of the home and village life of the Cornish fisher-folk, bringing out the callous natures and selfishness that render them, not the people of primitive virtues that the romancers portray, but a people of mixed qualities, who make each other suffer, and yet live a hard life of toil and privation with endurance. Resembles Thomas Hardy's novels in both its realism and its melancholy. [Heinemann : o.p.]

—— *Eli's Daughter*. 1896

A pessimistic tale of fisher and mining folk in Cornwall, enlivened by the light-hearted love-making of two rustics, Eli's daughter and a young fisherman. The gaiety does not last long, for a stalwart farmer also comes a-courting, and misfortunes fall thick. [Heinemann : o.p.]

—— *Ezekiel's Sin : a Cornish romance*. 1898

A pathetic story of fisher-folk. The old fisherman Ezekiel one day pulls up a drowned man with a large sum of money tied round him, and yields to the temptation to keep it, for his favourite daughter's sake. But the gold is the beginning of troubles to him and his loved ones, and he finds no peace till on his death-bed. [Heinemann : o.p. ; J. F. Taylor, New York : o.p.]

—— *Youth goes a-Marketing*. 1901

A similar drama of humble life, the love-story of a young Cornishman and two girls of wholly opposite natures ; like the foregoing, worked out strictly on the lines of character-development, incident being of comparatively trifling interest. A village of tin-miners is the scene. [G. Allen : o.p.]

PEARD, Miss Frances Mary [1835–1923]. *The Rose Garden.* 1872
Scene, Bayonne and district, pictured by one who knows and loves the country, delights in the gardens and the sunlight, and sees the beauty and interest of everyday life. The love-story of two French maidens, quiet and delicately sentimental. A poodle furnishes the comedy. [Murray.]

—— *The White Month.* 1880
A story of Brittany and the Franco-German War ; the heroine a pretty Breton maiden. Scenery, a desolate part of Brittany ; the village and interiors depicted. [Smith & Elder : o.p.]

—— *His Cousin Betty.* 1888
Two cousins with little in common are persuaded by a stratagem that they love each other. When betrothed and really in love, they discover that their coming together has not been spontaneous, and the resulting situation is in many ways pathetic. [3 vols., Bentley : o.p.]

—— *Catherine.* 1893
A love-tale of the times of the Napoleonic wars : peaceful English life in contrast with the haunting fears that prevailed. The characters of two lovers are tested by the heroine's loss of beauty. [Innes : o.p. ; Harper, New York : o.p.]

—— *The Interloper.* 1894
Provincial and domestic life in France. A weak but attractive baron is saved from calamity by a rich bourgeois wife, not merely through her wealth, but by her good sense and devotion. [2 vols., Bentley ; Harper, New York : o.p.]

—— *Donna Teresa.* 1899
A love-tale of English people in Rome and Sicily. A man asks a girl to marry him, and falls in love with the deeper and truer character of her sister : the solution is melodramatic. [Macmillan : o.p.]

—— *Number One and Number Two.* 1900
A quiet, slight, readable love-story of a similar kind, with some very ordinary but very real characters, who play their part amid scenes of travel, Cairo, the Nile, and Gibraltar. [Macmillan : o.p.]

PEARSE, Patrick Henry [Irish ; 1880–1916]. *The Mother ; and other stories.* 1916
Stories strongly tinged with the mysterious charm of Celtic folk-lore, e.g. *The Mother*, or *The Road*. *The Keening Woman* is a pathetic tale of the mother of a murderer. [*Collected works*, vol. 2, Talbot Press, Dublin, 1917.]

PEASE, Howard. *The Mark o' the Deil ; and other tales.* 1894
Racy stories of Northumberland peasants and their ways, written chiefly in unadulterated dialect (with a glossary). [Unwin : o.p.]

—— *The White-Faced Priest ; and other Northumbrian episodes.* 1896
Similar, though less gloomy, portraits of pitmen and other indigenous characters. [Swan & Morgan, Newcastle-on-Tyne : o.p.]

—— *Tales of Northumbria.* 1899
Similarly realistic studies and stories of pitmen and other natives of miscellaneous grades and characters, very masculine and humorous in tone. [Methuen : o.p.]

—— *Magnus Sinclair.* 1904
A Northumberland and Scots Border story of Cavaliers, Cromwellians, and Covenanters, rather ponderously equipped with historical and topographical erudition (1649–51). The author is an amateur of fencing, and makes the most of encounters with the sword, e.g. the hero fights a duel with Cromwell. [Constable : o.p.]

—— *Of Mistress Eve : a tale of the Southern Border* [sequel]. 1906
Carries on the story from the battle of Worcester to the Restoration (1652–60). [Constable : o.p.]

—— *The Burning Cresset : a story of the last rising of the North.* 1908
The story of the 1715 and the Northumberland rebel, the young Earl of Derwentwater. Brings in " General " Forster and his sister, whom Derwentwater loved. [Constable : o.p.]

—— *With the Warden of the Marches ; or, The Vow by the " Nine Stane Rig."* 1909
Chiefly grim and bloody tales of Liddesdale and the Marches, in the time of Mary Queen of Scots and other historical periods. Heavily equipped with antiquarian learning and unmitigated dialect. [Constable : o.p.]

—— *Border Ghost Stories.* 1919
Melodramatic tales of witches, warlocks, hauntings, and spectres ; strongest in their local colour. [E. Macdonald : o.p.]

PEMBERTON, Sir Max [b. 1863]. *The Iron Pirate.* 1893
An exciting story of wholesale plundering by a formidable vessel, driven by electricity and manned by a rough and motley crew. A sensation story in Jules Verne's style, without his scientific imagination. [Cassell ; Street & Smith, New York.]

—— *The Impregnable City.* 1895
A series of thrilling adventures, in a style midway between Dumas and Jules Verne, centring in the fortunes of an impregnable city built on a Pacific island. After repulsing the French and Russian fleets, the city is captured by the escaped prisoners, and the hero rewarded with his bride. [Cassell.]

—— *A Gentleman's Gentleman.* 1896
A picaresque romance : the adventures and shady exploits of a seventeenth-century baronet, who lives by his wits, related by his valet, another clever rogue. [Innes : o.p. ; Harper, New York : o.p.]

—— *The Phantom Army.* 1898
A sensation story of the doings of an imaginary army of outlaws on the European continent. [Pearson : o.p. ; Appleton, New York : o.p.]

—— *The Garden of Swords.* 1899
Adventures in the Franco-German War, particularly during the siege of Strasburg and at the battle of Wörth. The personal thread is the tragic experiences of a French officer and his wife. [Cassell : o.p.]

PEMBERTON, Sir Max (*continued*). *Signors of the Night.* 1899
Stories of adventure in Venice (1701–6). [Pearson: o.p.; Dodd & Mead, New York: o.p.]
—— *Feo.* 1900
Adventures in England and on the Continent of a beautiful singer at the Vienna opera, and an Austrian prince, whose marriage the Austrian authorities try by force and fraud to prevent. [Hodder: o.p.]
—— *The Footsteps of a Throne.* 1900
A sensation-novel of high life, the thrilling love-story of an English peer and a gambling Russian princess. London, Moscow, and the Caucasus furnish the scenes. [Methuen: o.p.; Appleton, New York: o.p.]
—— *I Crown Thee King.* 1902
A romance of Mary Tudor and Wyatt's attack on London; scene, largely, Sherwood Forest (1554). [Methuen: o.p.]
—— *Beatrice of Venice.* 1904
Love adventures of a French officer in Venice and Verona, while Napoleon was fighting his campaigns in Italy, in 1797. [Hodder: o.p.; Dodd & Mead, New York: o.p.]
—— *The Hundred Days.* 1905
An exciting love-tale, with glimpses of Napoleon and the political and military movements (1815). [Cassell; Appleton, New York: o.p.]
—— *My Sword for Lafayette.* 1906
Lafayette's story told by a faithful comrade, in France and America (1777–8), in England, and back on the Continent during the French Revolution. [Hodder: o.p.; Dodd & Mead, New York: o.p.]
—— *Sir Richard Enscombe.* 1908
Tells of the mad orgies of the Hell Fire Club, at Medmenham Abbey (see C. Johnstone's *Chrysal*, p. 271.) [Cassell: o.p.; Harper, New York: o.p.]
—— *The Virgin Fortress.* 1912
Adventures of an Englishman fighting with the Germans before Metz (1870). [Cassell: o.p.]
—— *Leila and her Lover.* 1913
A romance of high society. [Ward & Lock: o.p.]
—— *Millionaire's Island: a veracious story of a man, two women, and an idea.* 1913
An amusing farce about a millionaire who elopes with a princess, and hopes, though in vain, to escape from the problems of the outside world by retirement upon an island. [Ward & Lock: o.p.]
—— *The Great White Army.* 1915
A surgeon-major's recital of the sufferings of the *Grand Armée* after Borodino, at Moscow, and during the retreat (1812). [Nelson.]
—— *Paulina.* 1922
Love and other adventures in Venice, at the time of the French invasion and the fall of the Venetian republic (1797–8), in Paris, and in London, many well-known personages making their appearance. [Cassell: o.p.]

PENDLETON, Louis Beauregard [American; b. 1861]. *In the Wire Grass.* 1889
A story of South-Western life, with an interesting romance and descriptions of local scenes and manners. [Appleton, New York: o.p.]
—— *The Sons of Ham.* 1895
Written to show that the "colour line" in society must remain. [Little & Brown, Boston: o.p.]

PENNELL, Elizabeth [*née* Robins; American; b. 1855]. *Our House and the People in It.* 1910
Hardly fiction at all perhaps. The misadventures of a lady with a queer assortment of servants in a flat on the Embankment. Reads like notes of actual happenings and actual characters, and real friends of Mr. and Mrs. Pennell, like Whistler, Phil May, Beardsley, come into the story. [Houghton, Boston: o.p.; Unwin: o.p.]

PENNY, Fanny Emily [*née* Farr; Anglo-Indian]. *The Outcast.* 1912
The outcast is an Indian who returns from England a Christian; his miseries and persecution are forcibly portrayed. [Chatto.]
—— *Love in the Hills.* 1913
The scene is the Nilgiri Hills, and there are good accounts of the everyday life of a hill station. [Chatto.]
—— *Love in a Palace.* 1915
Exhibits the different outlooks on marriage of the East and the West, in the romance of an Indian prince and an English girl. [Chatto.]
—— *A Love Tangle.* 1916
The contrasts of Eastern and Western ideals, and a winning portrait of an Indian assistant-superintendent of police who was educated in England but remains an Asiatic of the highest type. [Chatto.]
—— *Love by an Indian River.* 1916
Shows the writer's familiarity with both the Indian and the Government point of view in regard to big engineering undertakings. The lady from California and other characters are naturally drawn. [Chatto.]
—— *Missing!* 1917
Affords instructive glimpses of zenana life. The ranee and her Rajput husband are drawn with insight and charm; the intriguing dowager ranee is comic. [Chatto.]
—— *A Love Offensive.* 1918
This time the scene is Ceylon, and native customs and folk-lore, especially concerning snakes, add interest. It is a war-story, about an Englishman escaped from the Germans. [Chatto.]
—— *The Two Brides.* 1929
Deals with the problem of child-wives in India. [Hodder.]

PENTREATH, Dolly. *In a Cornish Township.* 1893

Recollections of a parish clerk (supposed to have been written in 1818), in modern dialect. Sketches of old-world characters, tales of smuggling, and humorous adventures. [Unwin : o.p.]

PEREDA, José María de [Spanish ; 1833–1906]. *The Last of the Breed ; and other stories.* 1916

Five tales, selected from *Escenas Montañesas* (1864) and *Tipos y Paisajes* (1871), two famous sets of stories, drawing with convincing truth of feature and of atmosphere both the country folk of his native Montaña and the sophisticated and dandified people of Madrid. Pereda was the founder of the modern realistic novel in Spain, in which he revived the tradition of Cervantes and the picaresque novelists. [Transl. by D. FREEMAN, Nutt : o.p.]

PEREZ, Isaac Loeb [Russian Jew ; b. 1851]. *Stories and Pictures.* 1906

Perez, a native of Samosez in the government of Lublin, Russia, is considered the leading writer in Yiddish, the language spoken by the Jews in Russia, Poland, Austria, Roumania, and America. [Transl. from the Yiddish by Helena FRANK, Jewish Pub. Co., Philadelphia : o.p.]

PÉREZ GALDOS, Benito [Spanish (Canaries) ; 1845–1920]. *Lady Perfecta* (Doña Perfecta, 1876) 1894

The social problem which engrosses so much of the author's interest, the struggle between scientific and social enlightenment and the tyrannous obscurantism of the Church, is here set forth in the domestic conflict of a group of characters and the political strife agitating a provincial town. Doña Perfecta is a devout lady whose daughter is sought by a promising young man, a representative of modernism. A wily priest is her chief ally, and eventually the rival intrigues drag in a host of forces on either side, the anarchic elements that exist beneath the surface in modern Spain being strikingly revealed. [Transl. by Mary WHARTON, Unwin : o.p. ; by M. J. SERRANO, *sub tit. Doña Perfecta*, Harper, New York, 1895 : o.p.]

—— *Leon Roch* (La Familia de León Roch, 1878). 1888

A novel of life and passion, dealing with the tendencies and problems of the new era, the main action being the conjugal troubles of a sceptical husband and a deeply religious wife, who fail in their efforts to persuade each other : the issue is misery and separation. The various social classes, decadent aristocrats, pseudo-religious enthusiasts, unbelievers, etc., are well portrayed. [Transl. by Mrs. Clara BELL, 2 vols., Paul : o.p.]

—— *Marianela* (1878). 1893

A blind young man of wealth is the hero ; he idealizes the poor stunted peasant girl who acts as his guide into an image of beauty. Their talks on the things around them and on themselves are characterized by a quaint and artless simplicity that is very touching. The young man recovers his sight and Marianela's dream ends abruptly. [Transl. by Mary WHARTON, Digby & Long : o.p. ; by Helen W. LESTER, McClurg, Chicago, 1892 : o.p.]

—— *Saragossa* (Zaragoza). 1899

The siege of Saragossa (1808–9) ; one of many brilliant retellings of episodes in the long war of Spanish independence. [Transl. by Minna C. SMITH, Little & Brown, Boston : o.p.]

—— *Trafalgar* (1879). 1884

These last are two of a series of 46 vols. (*Episodios nacionales*, 1873–1912) dealing with the Spanish war of independence. Here a young Spaniard's adventures in Cadiz and the neighbourhood are followed by an extremely good historical account of Trafalgar. [Transl. by C. BELL, Trübner : o.p.]

PERRIN, Alice [*née* Robinson ; Anglo-Indian ; b. 1867]. *East of Suez.* 1901
—— *The Spell of the Jungle.* 1902
—— *The Stronger Claim.* 1903
—— *Idolatry.* 1909
—— *The Charm.* 1910

Novels showing intimate knowledge, not only of the external aspects of native and European life in India—missionaries, military and other officers—but of the superstitions of the Hindu, his magic and spiritualism, and of the inner life of the Eurasian half-caste and his kind. [(1), Treherne : o.p. ; (2), S. Paul ; (3), Chatto ; Harrap ; (4), Chatto ; (5), Methuen : o.p. ; Fitzgerald, New York : o.p.]

—— *The Happy Hunting Ground.* 1914

India is the happy hunting-ground for husbands ; the story describes the trials and difficulties of an Anglo-Indian wife. [Methuen.]

—— *Separation.* 1917

A husband busy in irrigation work in India and a wife enjoying herself in London society. The daughter insists on visiting India, and eventually marries a Hindu. [Cassell : o.p.]

PERRY, Bliss [American ; b. 1860]. *The Broughton House.* 1890
—— *Salem Kittridge ; and other stories.* 1894
—— *The Plated City.* 1895

Life in a Connecticut industrial city. The dominant motive is class prejudice, illustrated chiefly in the troubles of Tom and his half-sister, who are threatened with ostracism because their mother is suspected of being a quadroon. [(1), (2), (3), Scribner, New York : o.p.]

—— *The Powers at Play.* 1899

Short stories of American life of the day. [Scribner, New York : o.p.]

PERRY, Walter Copland [1814–1911]. *Sancta Paula : a romance of the fourth century*, A.D. 1902

Prepared for by study of Jerome, Gibbon, Milman, Dill, Thierry, etc. ; heavily encumbered with history. But the figures of Saints Jerome and Paula stand out well. Detailed pictures of Rome under Valentinian, Byzantium under Valens, and the hermits in the Egyptian deserts (362–403). [Sonnenschein : o.p.]

PERSIAN TALES : *The Thousand and One Days.* 1714–15

Rivalled the *Arabian Nights* in European popularity early in the eighteenth century. Englished from *Les Mille et Un Jour* [*sic*] *Contes Persanes traduits en François, par M. Pétis de la Croix* (1710–2). Their

PERSIAN TALES (*continued*).

provenance is doubtful. Le Sage is said to have "assisted" the translation. Anyhow, the stories are based on Oriental stories, and render the magic and mystery of the East, as well as actual manners and customs and beliefs, with the same brilliance as the rival collection. There is more of the element of fantasy and enchantment, and much more sentimentality, the old nurse who tells the tales to soothe a beautiful princess who has lost her faith in man keeping mainly to the one theme of true love. [Transl. from the French by M. Ambrose PHILIPS, Lond., 1714–15, many later editions : o.p. ; see also *Turkish Tales* (p. 475).]

PERUTZ, Leo [German ; *b.* 1884]. *Where will you Fall?* (Wohin rollst Du, Üpfelchen ? 1928). 1930

After hunting down the brutal Russian commandant who had ill-treated him and his mates in a prison camp, the would-be revenger finds him selling toys in the gutter, and his hatred melts away. Incidentally pictures Moscow in a state of revolution (1919). [Transl. by Hedwig SINGER, Methuen.]

PETERKIN, Mrs. Julia [*née* Mood ; American ; *b.* 1880]. *Scarlet Sister Mary.* 1928

Among the black people on this old Southern plantation Si'Mary and the stanch cripple Budda Ben are regarded as "the two toughest sinners in the whole county." Mary may be "de wickedest sinner Gawd ever made " ; but this crude and ignorant expositor of an indulgent philosophy is a brilliant creation, standing out against a background of selfish, pharisaic, and otherwise uncharitable fellow-creatures. [Bobbs-Merrill, Indianapolis ; Gollancz.]

PETRONIUS ARBITER [probably Gaius, *d. c.* 66 A.D.]. *The Satyricon.* 1694

Only a fragment remains of a voluminous series of picaresque adventures, comic pictures of life, and good stories (e.g. "The Widow of Ephesus"), which is the Roman equivalent of the famous Milesian tales— the *fabliaux* of antiquity. The author is probably to be identified with Nero's courtier and companion in debauchery, the Petronius mentioned by Tacitus ; but the legend that he wrote the work in his last moments and sent it as a testamentary gift to Nero is absurd. The general plan of the recital is lost with the missing portions, and consequently the attitude of the writer may be misunderstood ; but apparently he stands alone among the great satirists of the world in picturing the most abominable excesses of luxury and vice with the frank sympathy of a sensualist. The most brilliant episode is the Banquet of Trimalchio, a freedman of enormous wealth, who entertains a crowd of parasites in extravagant and ostentatious style, the vulgarity, ignorance, and pretentiousness of these social sycophants being painted with inimitable force. Other episodes ridicule the literary fashions of the age. There are parodies of contemporary poets, and verse passages and epigrams that seem to be essays in rivalry of Lucan, etc. The style, where it is not a burlesque of vulgar and illiterate speech, is a model of the finest prose of the Silver Age ; and the art with which the typical characters of this abandoned period are made to move and speak redeems what Dunlop calls "the most remarkable fiction which has dishonoured the literary history of any nation." [*The Satyr of Titus Petronius Arbiter,* "made English by Mr. BURNABY and another," with introd. by C. K. Scott-Moncrieff, (Abbey Cl.) Simpkin (Small, Boston), 1923. Made English by Mr. WILSON and several others, 1708, *privately repr.* (400 copies) 1899 ; transl. by John ADDISON, 1736. Transl. by Michael HESELTINE (Loeb Cl.) Heinemann (Putnam, New York), 1913 (with Seneca's *Apocolocyntosis,* a satire upon Claudius Cæsar). Transl., unexpurgated, by W. C. FIREBAUGH, 2 vols., Boni, New York, 1922 ; revised, with pref. by C. WHIBLEY, Longmans, 1927. Transl. by J. M. MITCHELL, (Broadway Transl.) Routledge (Dutton, New York), 1923. *Cena Trimalchionis,* ed. with transl. and notes by W. D. LOWE, Bell, 1905.]

PETTIE, George [1548–89]. *A petite Pallace of Pettie his pleasure : contaynyng many pretie Hystories by him set foorth in comely colours and most delightfully discoursed.* 1576

Pettie got the idea of his collection from Painter's *Palace of Pleasure,* and his style from the same sources as gave Lyly his euphuism. Only a dozen tales—Sinorix and Camma, Tereus and Progne, Germanicus and Agrippina, Amphiaraus and Eriphile, Icilius and Virginia, Admetus and Alcest, Scilla and Minos, Curiatius and Horatia, Cephalus and Procris, Minos and Pasiphae, Pigmaleons freinde and his Image, Alexius. [Ed. I. Gollancz, 2 vols. (King's Classics), Chatto.]

PHELPS, Elizabeth Stuart [Mrs. Herbert Dickinson Ward ; American ; 1844–1911]. *The Gates Ajar.* 1868

A religious story, relating in a diary the meditations and aspirations of a girl who has lost a beloved brother. Immortality and the nature of the future life are the principal themes, and the writer ventures on imaginative glimpses into the celestial paradise, where the interests and occupations of terrestrial existence are still carried on. Appearing soon after the Civil War, when many were mourning relatives, the book leapt into popularity. [Houghton, Boston ; Low.]

—— *Men, Women, and Ghosts.* 1869

Miscellaneous tales of which the predominant qualities are simplicity and sympathy. *Kentucky's Ghost* is a thrilling ghost-story ; and *In the Gray Goth,* an affecting incident of life among the lumbermen of the Maine forests. [Houghton, Boston : o.p.]

—— *The Silent Partner.* 1871

A philanthropical novel, dealing with the wrongs of labour in New England. The heroine, a child of wealth and luxury, is aroused to her responsibilities as sleeping partner in an industrial firm, and devotes her life henceforward to the betterment of the workpeople. [Houghton, Boston.]

—— *The Story of Avis.* 1877

Memoirs of a married pair in a university town. The wife sacrifices a brilliant future as a painter to a husband of good intentions but feeble will, who is incapable of appreciating her character. [Houghton, Boston : o.p. ; Routledge : o.p.]

—— *An Old Maid's Paradise.* 1879

A simple tale of everyday summer life in a seaside cottage. The troubles of furnishing, the perplexities of housekeeping, the antics of a terrier, the idiosyncrasies of three or four homely people : there is nothing else in the book. [With *Burglars in Paradise,* Houghton, Boston : o.p.]

PHELPS, Elizabeth Stuart (*continued*). *Burglars in Paradise* [sequel]. 1886
A comic sequel to the preceding, the same realistic sketching and portraiture, with a series of burlesque incidents. [See *An Old Maid's Paradise*.]

—— *Doctor Zay.* 1882
A plea for women's right to the higher education and an independent career. Doctor Zay is a high-minded girl who earns her own living as a physician. The main interest is in the influence of her steadfast character on a weak and aimless young man, whom she gradually lifts to her own level, and, after many repulses, grows to love. [Houghton, Boston.]

—— *Beyond the Gates.* 1883
—— *The Gates Between.* 1887
These elaborate the rather crude idea of her first book, *The Gates Ajar*. A woman falls into a trance after a fever, and dreams she is in heaven. She thinks she passes several years in the Celestial City, which is a sort of Utopia described in a minute and familiar manner, and that she meets with people famous in history. [(1), Houghton, Boston; (2), *id.*: o.p.]

—— *Though Life us do Part.* 1908
A doctor at a New England seaside place, his wife who is his social superior, his patients with whom he flirts, etc. When matters reach a critical point the doctor enlists for the Spanish War, and is reported killed, but this is only the beginning of the plot-business. [Houghton, Boston: o.p.; Constable: o.p.]

PHILLIPPS-WOLLEY, Clive [Canadian; *b.* 1854]. *The Chicamon Stone.* 1900
Adventures in the mountains and among savages in Alaska and the Yukon region, in search of a gold reef; comprising travel pictures of these wild, desolate, and perilous lands. [Smith & Elder: o.p.]

PHILLIPS, David Graham [American; 1867–1911]. *The Great God Success.* 1901
—— *Her Serene Highness.* 1902
—— *A Woman Ventures.* 1902
Novels displaying more honest—if prejudiced—realism than literary grace. Mr. Phillips stood for the middle-class view of the luxuries, follies, and sins of the uppermost class in America, which he depicts in a rough and merciless style, not without indicating an obvious moral. He is particularly hard on the gilded, selfish, and imperious women of the upper ten, and he was shot in 1911, it is said by a self-appointed avenger of the sex. [All Stokes, New York: o.p.]

—— *The Master Rogue: the confessions of a Crœsus.* 1903
A clerk in a dry-goods store makes up his mind to be a millionaire and does it. A brutal, sordid story from the objective point of view. The Rogue dies, worth a hundred millions, more wretched than a beggar, the abhorred of all mankind, including his own family. [McClure, New York: o.p.; De La More Press: o.p.]

—— *Golden Fleece.* 1903
The American adventures of a fortune-hunting earl. [McClure, New York: o.p.; De La More Press: o.p.]

—— *The Social Secretary.* 1905
Social comedy: a millionaire engages an expert to coach him in the mysteries of social behaviour. [Bobbs-Merrill, Indianapolis: o.p.; Gay & Hancock: o.p.]

—— *The Second Generation.* 1907
Love-stories of a young man and his sister, brought up by a self-made man who leaves his wealth away from them in order that they may be hardened by the same struggle as he had gone through. [Appleton, New York.]

—— *Light-Fingered Gentry.* 1907
Explores the inner working of the great insurance companies and the luxurious lives of the plutocrats of Fifth Avenue. [Appleton, New York.]

—— *Old Wives for New.* 1908
A very drastic handling of the situation, common where divorce is easy, in which a man who married in a fit of youthful passion finds at forty that his wife is intolerably unsympathetic, and hankers after his fair allowance of romance. Hardly literature; but almost all the characters except the hero—a Byronic millionaire—are drawn naturally and convincingly, and not without streaks of humour, especially the commonplace wife and her pathetic struggles with obesity. A railway accident, a murder, and other exciting incidents add to the interest of candid realism some of the attractions of the ordinary plot-novel. [Appleton, New York: o.p.]

—— *The Fashionable Adventures of Joshua Craig.* 1909
A low-bred, blatant, self-made politician (said to be drawn from life) by sheer force of cheek and bluff compels a refined lady of the highest Washington society to think herself in love and to marry him. Remarkable for a brutal but masterly handling of difficult psychological crises, and a savage kind of realism in the character-drawing. [Appleton, New York: o.p.]

—— *The Hungry Heart.* 1909
The organ alluded to belongs to a well-educated, intellectual, and energetic young lady, married to a rich Southerner, whose life is monopolized by chemical experiments in quest of a new fuel. She feels herself neglected, sees no object in life, and takes up with another man. [Appleton, New York: o.p.; Heinemann: o.p.]

—— *The Husband's Story.* 1910
A savage impeachment of the snobbishness of the American rich and the European aristocrat, especially the female snob as exemplified in a wife of the commonest origin who is society-mad. The author's sympathies are with the husband, who by tireless energy piles up millions for his wife to spend. Though his style is often uncouth, his downright, brutal sincerity, strong "horse sense," and determination to tell the nastiest truths about the vile basis of millionairedom and the foolishness of the lazy classes, makes this not only a biting satire, but a handbook for social reformers. He says, "Caste is made by those who look up, not by those who look down." [Appleton, London and New York: o.p.]

PHILLIPS, David Graham (*continued*). *Susan Lenox : her fall and rise.* 1917

Realism as detailed and uncompromising as Dreiser's : the anatomy of an American prostitute. We follow Susan throughout her career ; an innocent girl driven to flight by the harshness of her relatives, she attempts to earn an honest living in spite of obstacles that crowd her path. In desperation she is driven to the streets ; but her innate character and self-respect enable her to rise from the sordid progress through New York's underworld, and achieve fame as an actress. The author's object is to expose the social and economic causes which are responsible for such cases, and the drab infamy of their lives ; sentimentalism and lurid colours are equally eschewed. [2 vols., Appleton, New York and London. Together, 1 vol., *id.*]

PHILLPOTTS, Eden [*b.* 1862]. *Down Dartmoor Way.* 1895

Ten tales of Dartmoor and the neighbourhood, dealing with simple folk and describing beautiful landscapes, e.g. *A Curse Half Spoke*, two scenes in a mariner's life, at home in Devon, and cast away on the ocean— an idyll poetizing a bit of superstition ; *Brake-Fern Weir*, a tragic story told by a water-bailiff to an angler on the Dart ; *Children of the Mist*, the brief career and self-immolation of a lion-hearted boy. [Harper : o.p.]

—— *Lying Prophets.* 1897

A Cornish novel of seduction and retribution that has been described by some as a weaker *Return of the Native*, and by others as equal to *Esther Waters*. [Butterworth.]

—— *Children of the Mist.* 1898

A long and crowded novel of a Dartmoor village and its beautiful surroundings, in the style of Hardy's Wessex novels. Embraces a number of varied personalities—the mercurial hero, his vengeful rival, some finely drawn women, a village poet, farmers, gipsies, parish humorists, etc. Many of the dialogues and witticisms are very comic and racy in their broad Devon. [(Widdecombe ed.) Macmillan.]

—— *The Human Boy.* 1899
—— *The Human Boy Again* [sequel]. 1908

Facetious tales and sketches of school life from the boy's point of view—practical jokes, mock-heroic escapades, queer idiosyncrasies, the humours of class routine and of schoolmasters. [(1), Methuen ; Harper, New York ; (2), Chapman : o.p.]

—— *Sons of the Morning.* 1900

Country people of a village on the edge of Dartmoor depicted in the manner of Hardy. Shows the same fatalistic feeling, and the same treatment of rustic humours and scenery. There are three principal actors, a yeoman's daughter, who manages her own farm, and a pair of contrasted lovers. [(Widdecombe ed.), Macmillan.]

—— *The Good Red Earth.* 1901

A short novel in which the idea of Nature, as embodied in the fields, trees, and lanes of the apple country between Dartmoor and the sea, predominates in the writer's imagination over the merely human part. Thus the book is largely descriptive of outdoor life, the rustic characters acting in a plot of a conventional order. [Arrowsmith : o.p.]

—— *The Striking Hours.* 1901

Fourteen stories of a village (Gidleigh) near " Dartymoor," told by old Devon worthies in a literary solution of the vernacular. Of the tragic, *Sam of Sorrow Corner* is the most powerful ; *Right of Way*, a funeral story, is racy and humorous ; *The Red Rose* is a tender idyll of courtship ; and the longest, *The Devil's Tight Rope*, admirably epitomizes the author's finer characteristics. [Methuen : o.p. ; Stokes, New York : o.p.]

—— *The River.* 1902

Ranks with *Children of the Mist* as by far the best work of Mr. Phillpotts. The life of a simple, pious countryman, a moorland gamekeeper, whose religion and heroic patience are sorely tried by the falsehood of the woman he was about to marry. [Methuen ; (Widdecombe ed.), Macmillan ; Nash.]

—— *The American Prisoner.* 1904

A story of when thousands of French and American prisoners were herded in the war prison at Princetown, and goaded by their miseries into several desperate outbreaks (1814). The characters are stamped with melodramatic traits—the gentleman farmer with his lost amphora, his daughter with her three lovers, and the fierce, avaricious, unsexed beldame, Lovey Lee, who plots to set the prisoners free, and then betrays them. [Methuen : o.p.]

—— *The Farm of the Dagger.* 1904

A story of the same period and the same occurrences, complicated with a vendetta between two yeomen farmers. [Newnes : o.p.]

—— *The Secret Woman.* 1905

An ugly story of clandestine indulgence, and the jealousy of a good and religious woman who kills her husband in a fit of passion. Here the real tragedy begins, involving the sons, who witnessed the act, and the secret woman, the cause of it. [Methuen ; (Widdecombe ed.), Macmillan ; Nash ; (as play), Duckworth.]

—— *The Portreeve.* 1906

A Dartmoor *Mayor of Casterbridge*—the ill-starred career of a stiff-necked countryman, who falls a victim to the rancour of a slighted woman. Mr. Phillpotts is now entering on his titanic phase, and the novels of this period depict fierce, turbulent characters, savage passions and crime ; with less of the careful drawing of temperament and the rustic humours which redeemed his earlier stories. [(Widdecombe ed.), Macmillan.]

—— *The Whirlwind.* 1907

Scene, near Lydford and Great Links Tor. The usual tragic factors slightly rearranged and forcibly handled— a simple, gigantic, God-fearing labourer, his wife who goes wrong, and a vengeful rival. [(Widdecombe ed.), Macmillan.]

—— *The Mother.* 1908

Another vehement melodrama of ungovernable passion, revenge, and superhuman forbearance, with a fine figure of a mother tenderly drawn. [(Widdecombe ed.), Macmillan ; *sub tit. Mother of the Man*, Dodd & Mead, New York : o.p.]

PHILLPOTTS, Eden (*continued*). *The Three Brothers.* 1909
Returns to character-drawing with a crowd of rustic people, focusing attention on three sexagenarians, one of whom, a crusty misanthrope, is supposed to turn sentimentalist in his dotage. Enormously long-drawn-out discussions and far-fetched scenic displays. [(Widdecombe ed.), Macmillan.]

—— *The Haven.* 1909
Scene, a fishing village in Devon ; the shopkeepers and farming population being described as well as the mariners and their family life. [Murray : o.p. ; Lane, New York : o.p.]

—— *The Thief of Virtue.* 1910
An open-hearted, breezy old farmer brings up a son who is the fruit of his wife's intimacy with an old sweetheart, and has his latter days embittered by the young man's incompatibility of character. [Murray ; (Widdecombe ed.), Macmillan.]

—— *Demeter's Daughter.* 1911
A problem in which a Dartmoor thatcher and his wife and family provide the factors for the reader to work out, with the usual elaborate scene-painting and patient character-drawing of the country folk. [(Widdecombe ed.), Macmillan.]

—— *The Beacon.* 1911
Another three-cornered love-story, the girl a philosophically loquacious barmaid. Contains one character from real life, not mere literary gestation, the hard old miser Mortimore. Scene, N.E. Dartmoor—under Cosdon. [(Widdecombe ed.), Macmillan.]

—— *The Forest on the Hill.* 1912
A family feud, culminating in murder, between Dartmoor villagers. [(Widdecombe ed.), Macmillan.]

—— *The Lovers.* 1912
The romance of an American prisoner escaped from Princetown and a farmer's daughter who befriends him. [Ward & Lock : o.p. ; Rand, New York : o.p.]

—— *The Joy of Youth.* 1913
The story of an unconventional artist who stirs up Devon county society, and makes off with the fiancée of a stolid Conservative squire, is made the peg on which to hang much discussion of art and literature, particularly when the scene shifts to Florence. [Chapman : o.p.]

—— *Widecombe Fair.* 1913
No plot and hardly any story ; just a Teniers-like painting of the whole life of a Dartmoor village. [Murray ; (Widdecombe ed.), Macmillan ; Little & Brown, Boston.]

—— *The Master of Merripit.* 1914
Highwaymen and romance on Dartmoor a century ago. [Ward & Lock : o.p.]

—— *The Judge's Chair.* 1914
Seventeen stories of Dartmoor, of which *The Two Farmers*, a tragic story of the rivalry of two brothers, *The Apostates*, about children who set up a pagan idol on the moor, and *The Point of View*, a comedy concerned with the ill-starred efforts of a third party to reconcile husband and wife, may be singled out. [Murray : o.p.]

—— *Brunel's Tower.* 1915
Describes life in a pottery works near Dartmouth. The workers provide a crowd of amusing characters, and the potter's art is amply described. This begins a projected series of novels, each to be written round some localized industry. [(Widdecombe ed.), Macmillan.]

—— *Faith Tresilion.* 1916
A Cornish romance of smuggling, love, etc., in the 1820's. [Ward & Lock : o.p. ; Macmillan, New York : o.p.]

—— *Chronicles of St. Tid.* 1917
Simple anecdotes, mainly of the humours of courtship, told by an old rustic of his friends and neighbours in a Cornish village inhabited by slate-quarriers. [Skeffington : o.p. ; Macmillan, New York.]

—— *The Spinners.* 1919
Industrial life in a Dorset spinning-mill near Bridport. [Heinemann.]

—— *Storm in a Teacup.* 1919
A comedy of rustic characters. [Heinemann ; Macmillan, New York.]

—— *Evander.* 1919
The idyllic story of an Italian peasant and her husband, and of the god Apollo, with whose intellectual votary she runs away ; also of Bacchus, who reconciles her and her husband. [G. Richards.]

—— *Miser's Money.* 1920
A quiet story of two generations of Dartmoor folk. [(Widdecombe ed.), Macmillan.]

—— *Eudocia : a comedy royal.* 1921
A romance of Constantinople in 1076, under the Empress Eudocia, widow of Constantine XI. [Heinemann ; Macmillan, New York.]

—— *Orphan Dinah : a new Dartmoor story.* 1921
A good example of the maturer Phillpotts, with well-developed characters and more command of the descriptive writing. [Macmillan.]

—— *Black, White, and Brindled.* 1923
Short stories of average merit, concerned with islands of the South Seas. [G. Richards ; Macmillan, New York.]

—— *The Treasures of Typhon.* 1924
Epicurus and Menander appear in this love-tale of ancient Athens. [G. Richards ; Macmillan, New York.]

—— *The Jury.* 1927
A murder case, staged entirely in the court-room where the jury are deliberating on the evidence, and viewed through their eyes. [Hutchinson ; Macmillan, New York.]

PHILLPOTTS, Eden (*continued*). *The Torch ; and other tales.* 1929
Fifteen magazine stories, the first and one or two others about criminals, the rest deal with plain and harmless Dartmoor rustics, who are often the story-teller's mouthpiece. [Hutchinson ; Macmillan, New York.]

—— *Tryphena.* 1929
The heroine, the illegitimate daughter of a Devon squire, is brought up by a peasant family as their own child, and subsequently resists her father's claims on her, in favour of the local blacksmith. [Hutchinson ; Macmillan, New York.]

—— *The Three Maidens.* 1930
The love-affairs of three Devonshire village-girls divide the interest with the talkative folk at the village inn. [Hutchinson ; R. R. Smith, New York.]

—— *Alcyone : a fairy story.* 1930
Tells in a lively, if sometimes slangy and sometimes stilted way, how a priggish young intellectual from Athens and an oread in Arcadia fell in love with each other, until he bored her with his epigrams and heavy seriousness. The woodland setting is well done. [Benn ; R. R. Smith, New York.]

—— *Cherry Gambol ; and other stories.* 1930
Sound character-drawing is employed for comic purposes, and is spiced with excellent rustic dialogue, in the title-story and indeed in most of this collection, which is all in the Widecombe vein. [Hutchinson.]

PHILLPOTTS, Eden, and BENNETT, Arnold. *The Statue : a story of international intrigue and mystery.* 1908
A clever, extravagant melodrama of high finance, murder, and the marvels of scientific invention. [Cassell : o.p. ; Moffat, New York : o.p.]

PICKTHALL. Marmaduke William [*b.* 1875]. *Saïd the Fisherman.* 1903
The career of an adventurer (1860–82), who begins life as a poor fisherman on the Syrian coast, takes part in the Druses' massacre of Christians, becomes a rich merchant in Damascus, is ruined, and after grievous vicissitudes perishes at Alexandria in Arabi's revolt. One of our finest Oriental novels, worth comparing with *Hajji Baba* and *Hermann Agha*, in its faithful interpretation of Eastern humanity, with its humours, selfishness, fatalism, and the modes of thought usually so inscrutable to Europeans ; and hardly less remarkable for its complete objectivity of manner and self-effacement of the author. [Methuen ; Knopf, New York, 1925.]

—— *The House of Islam.* 1906
—— *Children of the Nile.* 1908
Mr. Pickthall wrote some novels of the ordinary modern type, and then returned to the Oriental scenes of his first, the Mohammedan world, the desert and the mosque, and the intricacies of Oriental character. He has recently embraced the Mohammedan religion. [(1), Methuen : o.p. ; Appleton, New York : o.p. ; (2), Murray : o.p.]

—— *Veiled Women.* 1913
In addition to picturing life in an Egyptian harem about 1870, the author enters into the spirit and philosophy of the Eastern womenfolk. [Nash : o.p. ; Duffield, New York : o.p.]

—— *Tales from Five Chimneys.* 1915
Five stories of the East : *Father Saba* is the tragedy of an Orthodox monk ; *Count Abdullah* is a picture of a Turkish scoundrel ; in *His Honour's Pleasure : a study in pure nerves*, the author's dislike for the Egyptians has free rein. [Mills & Boon : o.p.]

—— *The House of War.* 1916
Shows up the uselessness and absurdity of much of the missionary work carried on in the Near East. [Nash : o.p. ; Duffield, New York : o.p.]

—— *Knights of Araby.* 1917
A story of Arab lands (1066–1120), valuable for the accurate detail of its setting. [Collins.]

—— *Oriental Encounters : Palestine and Syria* (1894–5–6). 1918
This has the appearance of observations set down on the spot by a young adventurer among the Arabs, who learns their language and does his best to be on the most intimate terms with them. So, indeed, it claims to be in the preface. But it is of the family of *Lavengro* ; and, whether the incidents are recounted exactly as they occurred or not, these and the racy characters and the vivid dialogues portray Oriental life in the manner of the artist and the humorist rather than of the globe-trotter. [(Traveller's Lib.), Cape ; Knopf, New York.]

—— *The Early Hours.* 1921
Turkish peasant politics after the restoration of the Ottoman constitution, 1908. [Collins.]

PIDGIN, Charles Felton [American ; 1844–1923]. *Quincy Adams Sawyer and Mason's Corner Folks.* 1901
Thoroughly American, faithful to its particular phase of life, and unobtrusively humorous. Mr. Sawyer is the son of a rich Bostonian, and his kindly doings among the humble people of Mason's Corner are entertaining and touching. [Clark Pub. Co., Boston : o.p. ; Unwin : o.p.]

—— *Blennerhassett.* 1901
Develops the history of Aaron Burr and Harman Blennerhassett's treasonable scheme for conquering Texas and setting up a Southern republic (1805–7). [Clark Pub. Co., Boston : o.p. ; Grosset, New York.]

—— *The Further Adventures of Quincy Adams Sawyer and Mason's Corner Folks.* 1909
The same characters of the first book after eight years, with some others. [Page, Boston : o.p.]

PIER, Arthur Stanwood [American ; *b.* 1874]. *The Sentimentalists.* 1901
History of a family which tries to gain a footing in Boston society, and of their financial troubles ; rather difficult to the English reader unacquainted with the niceties of American social distinctions and the tortuous ways of stockbrokers. [Harper, New York : o.p.]

PILLING, William. *Ponce de Leon: the rise of the Argentine republic, by an Estanciero.* 1878
A novel which is said to be the most graphic history extant of the British invasion and the rise of Argentina (1806–19) ; anti-Spanish in bias, though the facts are said to be right ; based, no doubt, on the history of the Argentine rebellion by Bartolomé Mitre, the first President, which Pilling translated. [First published in 1878 by Chapman. Laurie, 1910 : o.p.]

PINKERTON, Thomas A. *John Newbold's Ordeal.* 1889
A novel of character, with vivacious portraiture of Biscoe, a vulgar, unscrupulous brewer ; Mrs. Newbold, " whose severity was so diluted with copious speech and qualified by religious sentiment " ; Archdeacon Newbold, " one of the most fortunate of holy clerks " ; Miss Leigh, the heiress ; and that remarkable personality Limb, the fox-terrier. [Sonnenschein : o.p.]

—— *The Spanish Poniard : being the story of the remorse of Ambrose Drybridge.* 1890
Scene, rural Warwickshire at the close of the Elizabethan age. The adventurers who followed Drake to the Spanish Main, and the fanatics who nourished their violent instincts on dreams of divine wrath and their own providential election, well represented (1620–42). [Sonnenschein : o.p.]

—— *The Last Master of Carnandro : the story of the revenge of Ronald Sinclair.* 1890
A successful, proud, and egotistical man is suddenly insulted and beaten so ignominiously that he becomes almost insane, and, with his whole being warped by hatred, devotes his life to revenge. [Sonnenschein : o.p.]

—— *A New Saint's Tragedy.* 1891
A story of middle-class life, strong in characterization, and with a good deal of humour. [Sonnenschein : o.p. ; Harper, New York : o.p.]

—— *The French Prisoner : a romance of Dartmoor and the western seas.* 1894
Adventures in the time of the Bonaparte scare, smuggling, duelling, etc., worked up with plenty of local colour. [Sonnenschein : o.p.]

—— *Dead Oppressors.* 1899
A ghastly story—a young man falls in love with his father's illegitimate daughter, and dies of the shock of discovery. [Sonnenschein : o.p.]

PIRANDELLO, Luigi [Italian ; *b.* 1867]. *The Outcast* (L'Esclusa, 1901). 1925
A man conceives the idea that his wife is unfaithful and turns her out. In desperation she goes to a former lover ; but her husband, unable to endure her absence, must perforce make peace. His preconceived idea has brought him the very misfortune he sought to avoid. [Transl. by Leo ONGLEY, Dutton, New York.]

—— *Late Mattia Pascal* (Il fu Mattia Pascal, 1904). 1923
A comedy which points the moral, that it is vain for a man to seek reality outside the circle wherein his own character and mode of life have circumscribed him. A librarian, weary of his monotonous existence and of harassing relatives, takes advantage of an accident to assume a new personality and a more colourful life in Rome. All goes well until he falls in love ; he realizes then that he is a living lie with no place in the scheme of things. But when he decides to fake another accident, throw off his assumed character and return home, he finds that his wife is re-married and his old existence too is closed to him. [Transl. by Arthur LIVINGSTONE, Dutton, New York.]

—— *The Old and the Young* (I Vecci e i Giovani, 1913). 1928
Gives a bitter and disillusioned picture of Italian social and political life in the nineties ; the old have forgotten the ideals for which they fought under Garibaldi ; the young have inherited only selfishness. All are immersed in the slough of political intrigue and corruption. A banking scandal in Rome and a labour revolt in Sicily provide the setting, wherein repulsive figures of financiers, politicians, and landed gentry struggle to amass money or to save their skins. Only, by contrast, the quaint figure of a Sicilian patriot stalks through the book. " He didn't think ; he merely felt " ; thereby retaining the essential purity and idealism that the others had lost. [Transl. by C. K. SCOTT-MONCRIEFF, 2 vols., Chatto ; Dutton, New York.]

—— *Shoot!* (Si Gira! Quaderni di Serafino Gubbio, operatore, 1916). 1926
Here the author identifies himself with a cinematograph camera-man—" the hand that turns the handle "—a passive observer. Dispassionately he analyses men and women playing at life—unreal shadowy things, by contrast to the band of outcasts he meets in a visit to a night-shelter. But he sees at last that man is inseparable from his illusions—life itself is a cinema show. [Transl. by C. K. SCOTT-MONCRIEFF, Chatto ; Dutton, New York.]

POE, Edgar Allan [American ; 1809–49]. *Tales of Mystery, Imagination, and Humour.* 1840–5
Extreme developments of the Gothic romance of Mrs. Radcliffe, Walpole, Maturin, and Brockden Brown, with a more calculated study of psychological effect. Impossible and improbable fictions, hallucinations, mysteries, phantoms, and other conceptions of overpowering horror, made credible for the moment by Defoe-like realism and closeness of reasoning ; e.g. *M. Valdemar,* the ghastly tale of a man mesmerized in the act of dying and kept in a state of semi-consciousness ; *A Descent into the Maelstrom,* a thrilling wonder-story attaining verisimilitude by matter-of-fact narration ; *Ligeia,* a psychical story of how a woman of powerful will returns from the dead and usurps the living body of her husband's second wife ; *The Fall of the House of Usher,* a dramatic piece that appeals poetically to our sense of the weird and mysterious ; *The Gold Bug,* a story of Captain Kidd's treasure ; *The Mystery of Marie Roget, The Purloined Letter, The Murders in the Rue Morgue,* the model for Conan Doyle and his school ; *Hans Pfaal,* the prototype of Jules Verne and H. G. Wells's impossible voyages ; with numerous other essays in pure sensation and the marvellous, detective riddles and grotesque humour, all constructed with consummate skill and power of suggestion. *The Narrative of A. Gordon Pym, of Nantucket* (1838), which is usually included in Poe's *Tales,* pretends in the same manner to be an authentic travel-book. [(Everyman's Lib.), Dent (Dutton, New York) ; (World's Classics) Oxford Press ; Harrap ; Brentano, New York. *Tales,* 5 vols., Putnam. *Illus.* with etchings, 3 vols., Routledge : o.p.]

PONTOPPIDAN, Henrik [Danish; *b*. 1857]. *Emmanuel ; or, Children of the Soil* (Muld, 1891). 1892

—— *The Promised Land* (Det forjaettede land, 1892) [sequel]. 1896
Two parts of a trilogy (*Muld, Det forjaettede land*, and *Dommens dag*, 1895 ; the third not yet translated) describing the career of a Danish pastor, who enters with enthusiasm into the cause of the peasants, at the time of their struggle in the seventies against reaction, marries a peasant girl, and adopts their manner of life. In the sequel it is shown that the idealist cannot utterly throw off the instincts of his order ; he loses the sympathy of his parishioners, and when he returns to city life his wife nobly accepts the inevitable parting from husband and children. [(1) and (2), transl. by Mrs. Edgar Lucas, Dent : o.p.]

POOL, Maria Louise [American ; *d*. 1898]. *Dally*. 1891
Tells the story of a poor girl of North Carolina, rescued from poverty and squalor, and brought up by a Yankee widow of sterling benevolence and probity. The talk is in dialect, and there are amusing incidents. [Harper, New York : o.p.]

—— *Roweny in Boston*. 1892

—— *Mrs. Keats Bradford* [sequel]. 1892
Practically the continuous biography of a New England girl, who goes to Boston to learn painting, and proceeds to a wider sphere in Paris, where she marries a Bostonian, then leaves him because marriage interferes with her art, but is ultimately reconciled. [(1) and (2), Harper, New York : o.p.]

—— *The Two Salomes*. 1893

—— *Out of Step* [sequel]. 1894
A bizarre psychological idea is the motive—a conscientious girl losing, or believing she has lost, her sense of right and wrong. A good deal of local colour from New England and Florida ; and some droll and pathetic passages. [(1) and (2), Harper, New York : o.p.]

—— *In a Dyke Shanty*. 1896
Story of an outing ; a series of strongly accented individuals, with their several love-stories. [Stone, Chicago : o.p. ; Page, Boston : o.p.]

—— *A Golden Sorrow*. 1898
Tragic history of a marriage for money. A pleasure-loving girl, who is made by her mother to desert her lover and marry a Spanish grandee, finds that she has wedded sorrow. The novelist contrives, however, to manage a happy ending. [Stone, Chicago : o.p.]

POOLE, Ernest [American ; *b*. 1880]. *The Harbor*. 1915
The theme is that of labour unrest in the evil conditions prevalent at the beginning of the century. The setting, New York harbour, plays an effective part in the story. Mr. Poole is a fellow-worker of Mr. Upton Sinclair's, whom he helped in collecting material for *The Jungle*. [Macmillan, New York and London ; Grosset, New York.]

—— *His Family*. 1917
A novel that won the Pulitzer Prize (1918). It is an equally serious and a deeper and riper study of a father whose mind is grievously exercised by his daughters, carried away by the mutinous ideas and passions of the new age. [Macmillan, New York and London.]

—— *His Second Wife*. 1919
A contrast of mind and temperament is drawn between two sisters, one fascinated by the giddy social life of New York, the other, of a deeper nature, who as his second wife undertakes to win her husband back to his earlier and nobler ideals. [Macmillan, New York and London.]

—— *The Avalanche*. 1924
A more commonplace romance—a newspaper magnate and a neurologist are rivals in love. [Macmillan, New York ; Nash.]

PORTER, Anna Maria [1780–1832]. *The Hungarian Brothers*. 1807
An early and very old-fashioned historical romance of Vienna in 1790–1800. [Warne : o.p. ; Lippincott, Philadelphia : o.p.]

PORTER, Jane [1776–1850]. *Thaddeus of Warsaw*. 1803
A sentimental idyll suggested by the exploits and tragic after-life of Kosciusko. Count Thaddeus Sobieski is a faultless hero of romance, disinterested, valiant, performing mighty deeds in his country's last struggle ; then, as a refugee in London, where he lives as a teacher of languages, the unparalleled nature of his misfortunes gives him a mysterious dignity. [Ed. by E. A. Baker (Half-forgotten Books), Routledge, 1905 (Dutton, New York) : o.p. ; (Home Lib.) Burt, New York, 1917. *Illus.*, Nisbet, 1892 : o.p.]

—— *The Scottish Chiefs*. 1810
A better story though not so famous, founded on Barbour's poem, *The Brus*, with its heroic story of Wallace and Bruce and the long war of Scottish Independence (*c*. 1296–1314). The writer's personal knowledge of the localities strengthens the work. [Routledge : o.p. ; *illus.* by T. H. Robinson, Dent : o.p. ; (Home Lib.), Burt, New York, 1921 ; Dutton, New York ; *illus.*, Scribner, New York, 1921.]

PORTER, William Sydney [" O. Henry "; American ; 1867–1910]. *Cabbages and Kings*. 1905

—— *The Four Million*. 1906

—— *The Trimmed Lamp*. 1907

—— *The Heart of the West*. 1907

—— *The Gentle Grafter*. 1908

—— *The Voice of the City : further stories of the four million*. 1908

—— *Roads of Destiny*. 1909

—— *Options*. 1909

—— *Strictly Business : more stories of the four million*. 1910

PORTER, William Sydney (*continued*). *Whirligigs.* 1910
—— *Sixes and Sevens.* 1911
Collections of short, smart, slangy, and up-to-date stories of to-day, many of them first published in the more popular magazines and in daily papers. The best rank with the cleverest kind of stories we get in the English *Strand Magazine* and its like. *Options* (sixteen stories of the cheap, smart kind) may be taken as an average specimen. Intellectually, they are on a par with the cinematograph practical joke. They are written in a conceited, slangy, knowing style : e.g. drinking champagne is described as "ingurgitating another modicum of the royal boose."
[*Works*, in 18 vols., Doubleday, New York. Also in 1 vol., *id.* ; Hodder ; *Best of O. Henry* (100 stories selected by " Sapper "), *id.*]

PORTMAN Lionel. *Hugh Rendal : a Public School story.* 1905
—— *The Progress of Hugh Rendal.* 1907
Hugh Rendal was acclaimed as " the most truthful story of school life that we know." Its characteristic was truthful description without any lapses into mere " effects " ; and the sequel, telling of Hugh's Oxford days, is equally veracious down to the moment when the distinguished blue falls in love, and the story ends in the approved sentimental fashion. [(1) Rivers : o.p. ; (2) Heinemann : o.p.]

POST, Waldron Kintzing [American ; *b.* 1868]. *Harvard Stories.* 1893
Stories of a group of undergraduates, depicting the manners and customs and the amusing incidents of college life, with representative character-sketches. [Putnam, New York and London : o.p.]
—— *Smith Brunt : a story of the Old Navy.* 1899
Sketches of a sailor's life in the times of the naval war between England and the youthful United States ; the fight between the *Shannon* and the *Chesapeake*, the defence of the frigate *Essex* at Valparaiso, etc. (1811–5). [Putnam, New York and London : o.p.]

POTTER, Margaret Horton [Mrs. John Donald Black ; American ; *b.* 1881]. *The House of De Mailly.* 1901
A long romance, laid partly in Maryland, where the French hero weds the New England heroine, and partly at Versailles, in the reign of Louis XV, who pursues the young wife unsuccessfully. Crowded with characters, the book draws a striking contrast between the free New England life and the profligate Court of France (*c.* 1741–8). [Harper, New York and London : o.p.]
—— *The Genius.* 1906
An extremely fine study of Tchaikowsky and the Russian musical world. [Harper, New York and London : o.p.]

" POUSSE-CAILLOUX." *His Majesty's Shirt Sleeves.* 1930
Stories that read like transcriptions of fact, of the perils, hardships, and fortitude of British officers on the frontiers of India and of Assam. Sepoys, Pathans, and Tibetans come into the picture. [Blackwood.]

POWYS, Theodore Francis [*b.* 1875]. *Black Bryony.* 1923
—— *Mr. Tasker's Gods.* 1925
—— *Mockery Gap.* 1925
In revolt at the sentimental presentation of country life, this author portrays the truth as he prefers to see it—rustics whose main occupation is animal-maiming and the begetting of illegitimate children. He would appear to have a mission to present, with wonderful art, life as a succession of sniggering indecencies alternating with episodes of bestial cruelty. [All Chatto ; Knopf, New York.]
—— *Mr. Weston's Good Wine.* 1927
The village and villagers of the story are no exception to Mr. Powys's skilful handling of the unclean and grotesque ; but amongst the medley of seducers and all too willingly seduced wanders the enigmatic figure of Mr. Weston, offering to all a draught of his good wine, which brings oblivion. [Chatto ; Knopf, New York.]
—— *Kindness in a Corner.* 1930
There is indeed rather more kindness in the rural corner here portrayed than one might have anticipated. [Chatto ; Viking Press, New York.]
—— *The White Paternoster.* 1930
The inhabitants of Mr. Powys's rustic world are queerer and uglier than the villagers and farmers most of us are acquainted with ; those of his twenty-six stories that incline to tragedy are grim and horrible, his comedy tends to the grotesque. Of the former kind *A Box of Sweets* and *What I lack yet* may be singled out, with *Christ in the Cupboard* and *The Baked Mole* as the most sardonic and appalling. Among the lighter, *Archdeacon Truggin*, *Another Godiva*, *Parson Sparrow*, and *Found Wanting* are notable. [Chatto ; Musson, Toronto.]

POYNTER, Eleanor Frances. *My Little Lady.* 1870
Madelon is the daughter of a professional gambler, an innocent girl surrounded by corruption. Her character and inner life and the character of the gambler are described, and the story tells of her helplessness and troubles after her father's death, the pathos of her convent life, and her yearnings for freedom. Spa, Liége, and Cornwall are the scenes. [Hurst & Blackett : o.p.]

PRAED, Rosa Caroline Campbell Mackworth [*née* Prior ; Australian ; *b.* 1852]. *An Australian Heroine.* 1880
In the early part there are sketches of bush life ; but the book deals principally with the life of the Australian in England. The authoress is a native of Queensland. [Ward & Lock : o.p.]
—— *Outlaw and Lawmaker.* 1893
Life and politics in Australia, bushranging, etc. [Chatto : o.p. ; Appleton, New York : o.p.]
—— *Mrs. Tregaskiss.* 1896
Vivid description of the rough life, the scenery of the bush, and the arid plains of Australia. A story of unlawful and unhappy love, the central figure being an imaginative woman of nervous temperament,

PRAED, Rosa Caroline Campbell Mackworth (*continued*).
who revolts from a dull and commonplace husband, a bushman. Brings out forcibly the influence on such a mind of the dreary environment and the rude, uncivilized life. [Chatto ; Appleton, New York : o.p.]

—— *Nùlma.* 1897
Nùlma, an innocent and beautiful Australian in the first bloom of womanhood, is brought into contact with a group of decadent people from English society, and, unfortunately, learns to love an unworthy man. The English circle gathered round the old governor, with their discreditable intrigues, are not attractively portrayed. [Chatto : o.p. ; Appleton, New York : o.p.]

PRAVIEL, Armand [French ; *b.* 1875]. *The Murder of Monsieur Fualdès* (L'assassinat de M. Fualdès, 1922). 1922
A novel woven out of a case that actually occurred at Rodez (1817–8). [Transl. by Doris ASHLEY, Collins ; Boni, New York.]

PRENTISS, Elizabeth [*née* Payson ; American ; 1818–78]. *Stepping Heavenward.*
[juvenile] 1869
The best of a series of once very popular stories, having a distinctly religious purpose (sequel to *Pressing Forward* : o.p.). [Altemus, Philadelphia ; Augustana, Minneapolis ; Donohue, Chicago ; Sears, New York, 1926 ; Routledge ; Collins ; Oxford Press.]

PRESCOTT, H. F. M. [*b.* 1896]. *The Unhurrying Chase.* 1925
A picturesque story of the twelfth century, the hero a squire to the Count of Angoulême, and Richard of Poitou (later Richard I), occupying a prominent place. Into this setting is woven a romance whose dominant motive is the conflict of ambition and earthly love with the love of God. We take leave of the hero about to set out with Richard on the Third Crusade (1188). [Constable ; Dodd & Mead, New York.]

PRÉVOST, Marcel [French ; *b.* 1862]. *A Woman's Tragedy* (L'automne d'une femme, 1892). 1913
A soft-hearted woman, married commercially to a rich banker, nurses, and, with qualms of conscience, becomes the mistress of the weak young hero, half her age. When he after long shilly-shallying decides to marry a girl of his own age, she nerves herself to the great sacrifice. A fair type of the fiction in which our accepted values are discounted ; sentimentality, regret, and remorse become the cardinal virtues. [Transl. by Helen K. HAYES, Bohemian Pub. Co. : o.p.]

—— *Guardian Angels* (Les anges gardiens, 1913). 1913
A clever, if not very sensible piece of fiction at the expense of the foreign governess in French homes. One of them, a German, seduces the master of the house ; the Englishwoman is a vampire, the Italian a fortune-hunter, and the one from Luxemburg succeeds in running off with the head of the family. A wretched translation. [Nash : o.p. ; Macauley Co., New York : o.p.]

—— *Benoit Castain* (L'adjudant Benoît, 1916). 1916
A young French soldier loves and loses, by death, the daughter of the man whom he killed for a spy. [Transl. Arthur C. RICHMOND, Macmillan, London and New York : o.p.]

—— *The Don Juanes* (Les Don Juanes, 1922). 1924
An analysis of love in the hands of four typical women of the post-war period. One is a young wife faithful to her older and less intelligent husband ; another, a business woman who is infatuated, and betrayed ; a third is loved by a mere youth, but finds herself psychologically unfit for marriage, and retires to a convent ; the fourth (and this is the dominant theme) adores a young man, whom she later discovers to be her own son ; but they find peace and happiness in the new relationship, since their love had been based on spiritual and intellectual affinity rather than passion. [Transl. by Jennie COVAN, Brentano, New York.]

—— *His Mistress and I* (Sa maîtresse et moi, 1923). 1927
The writer of this long-drawn confession is one of those Frenchmen who " fiddle harmonics on the strings of sensualism." He and his friend's mistress, a Russian Jewess, fall in love, and on the death of his beloved friend marry. Then he suffers agonies through suspecting that she had given the invalid an overdose to secure their freedom. There are further intricacies of sentiment : he is jealous of her adoration for the deceased, she feels that his suspicion has cheapened their bond. [Transl. by N. FLEMING, Hamilton ; Doubleday, Doran, New York].

—— *The Virgin Man* (L'homme vierge, 1929). 1930
A threefold story, in that it is presented from three points of view—the confession of a dead man who seduced a young girl, the girl's own case, and the judgment of the man she loves. [Transl. by Jack KAHANE, Shaylor.]

PRÉVOST D'EXILES, Abbé Antoine François [French ; 1697–1763]. *Adventures of a Man of Quality* (Mémoires d'un homme de qualité, 1728–33). 1930
Manon Lescaut is a part of the *Mémoires*, and the only portion very much read, although Sainte-Beuve thought highly of the entire book. The portion of the *Mémoires* here translated is that dealing with the Man of Quality's experiences in England. The Abbé Prévost had sojourned in this country, and was anxious to promote a kindlier view of English manners and a friendly understanding on the part of his countrymen. [Transl., with introd., by Maysie E. I. ROBERTSON (Broadway Translations), Routledge ; Dial Press, New York.]

—— *Manon Lescaut* (1731). 1770
The subject is the infatuation of an estimable but weak young man for a pleasure-loving woman, to whom he attaches himself in spite of the active opposition of his friends. They gain their living in the most shameful ways, and are at last driven into the wilds of America, where she dies in his arms. Handicapped as it might seem by these unromantic features, the story is an incomparable pæan of true love, the feeling genuine and pure. There is not a touch of sensuality or indelicacy. This famous book was originally an episode appended to *Mémoires et aventures d'un homme de qualité qui s'est retiré du monde* (1728–33),

PRÉVOST D'EXILES, Abbé Antoine François (*continued*).
a rambling work embodying incidents from his own life (see above). It was revised and reissued alone in 1753 ; this is the text on which all the translations, save Miss Waddell's, are based. [First English transl. of *Manon Lescaut*, 1770 ; transl., by George Dunning GRIBBLE, (Broadway Transl.), Routledge (Dutton, New York) 1925 ; by Burton RASCOE, Knopf, New York and London, 1919 ; with Merimée's *Carmen*, transl. by Edmund H. GARRETT, (Everyman's Lib.) Dent (Dutton, New York), 1929 ; another transl., Brentano, New York. *Illus.* with etchings by Leloir, Gebbie, Philadelphia (Sonnenschein) : o.p. ; *illus.*, ltd. ed., Dodd & Mead, New York (Lane), 1929. The text of 1731, translated for the first time, by Helen WADDELL, with introd. by George Saintsbury, Constable, 1931.]

PRICE, Miss Eleanor Catherine. *The Foreigners.*   1883
Intimate delineations of rural France, its people and manners, particularly of the provincial noblesse. The plot turns on the difference between French and English ways of arranging marriages and winds up sadly. [Chatto : o.p.]

—— *Alexia.*   1887
A simple story of the happy love affairs of two young people, whose passion is shown to be the natural outcome of their characters, sympathetic and estimable, though far from faultless. [Macmillan : o.p.]

—— *The Heiress of the Forest : a romance of Old Anjou.*   [juvenile] 1900
A quiet, old-fashioned story of an unhappy young heiress, destined to a hateful marriage, and the adventures that result in her deliverance. [Pitman : o.p. ; Crowell, New York : o.p.]

—— *Angelot : a tale of the First Empire.*   1902
A love-story of Anjou with a few incursions into contemporary politics (1811–2). [Newnes : o.p. ; Crowell, New York : o.p.]

PRICHARD, Katharine Susannah [Mrs. Hugo Throssel ; Australian ; *b.* 1844]. *Working Bullocks.*
                                                                                  1927

—— *Coonardoo : the well in the shadow.*   1929
This and the former are intimate presentments of Australian life, both of the whites and of the aborigines. Coonardoo is a native woman, deeply but impassively devoted to her white master : her portrait is a revelation of strange modes of being. [(1), Cape ; Viking Press, New York ; (2), Cape ; Norton, New York.]

—— *Haxby's Circus.*   1930
The gallantry and romance, and also the hardships and cruelty of circus life. [Cape.]

PRIESTLEY, John Boynton [*b.* 1894]. *Adam in Moonshine.*   1927
Adam becomes involved in a fantastic conspiracy, to further his pursuit of three girls, without however eventually winning any one of them. [Heinemann ; Harper, New York.]

—— *Benighted.*   1927
A party of travellers have to spend the night in an uncanny Welsh mansion. The husband and wife who have grown apart, the self-made millionaire, the girl with him, the world-weary young man, and the macabre inhabitants of the house, in turn reveal themselves in their true lights, wherein the good outweighs the evil, before the unexpected and tragic *dénouement* compels a readjustment of their lives. [Heinemann ; *sub tit. The Old Dark House*, Harper, New York.]

—— *The Good Companions.*   1929
A book as jolly as the title. Pickwickian in spirit and to a large extent in method. A number of people, otherwise most unlikely ever to be found in the same room, are started by circumstances and inclination on the picaresque track, and by a chapter of accidents come together. Hence we have a very odd set of musical entertainers touring from town to town, meeting with strange adventures, and showing off their picturesque foibles of character. It is a long story, on the grand simple lines as old as *Joseph Andrews*, but remarkably full of zest and youthfulness. [Heinemann ; Harper, New York (also in 2 vols.).]

—— *Angel Pavement.*   1930
Portraiture rather than plot is the chief distinction of this novel, in which a number of people, the sort we meet with in ordinary life and most of them weak, vicious, and even odious in themselves, play their part and are made intensely interesting. Angel Pavement, E.C., is the address of a City firm whose dealings with a commercial adventurer start the whole business. [Heinemann ; Harper, New York.] See also *sub nom.* WALPOLE, Hugh.

" PRIOR, James " [James Prior Kirk ; 1850–1922]. *Forest Folk.*   1901
Farm life in a Nottinghamshire village on the edge of Sherwood Forest, at the time of the Luddite riots and machine-wrecking. Character, or the growth and decay of character, is the main interest, the latter finely traced in the downfall of a talented young villager who ends his life as an outcast. [Palmer, 1929 ; Dodd & Mead, New York : o.p.]

—— *A Walking Gentleman.*   1907
A fine-flavoured Borrovian story of low life and the open road, thoroughly real and alive in its portraiture of the essential man, labourer, harvester, stonebreaker, factory hand, or tramp, and its psychology of the peer who takes to the wandering life out of disgust and boredom. [Constable : o.p. ; Dutton, New York : o.p.]

—— *Fortuna Chance.*   1910
The same command of local character and atmosphere here creates a lifelike picture of the villagers, shepherds, beggars, and gipsies, and also the gentlefolk of the Sherwood region and the Yorkshire and Derbyshire moorlands, at the time of the '45. Roland Chance gets mixed up with the Highlanders and is suspected of murder, and the romantic events of the latter part end in a dramatic trial scene (1725–46). [Constable : o.p.]

PRITCHETT, Victor Sawdon [*b.* 1900]. *The Spanish Virgin ; and other stories.*   1930
Ten mainly fanciful stories, *The Spanish Virgin* by far the longest, all of them real enough in their comprehension of humanity and the human problems. [Benn.]

PROUST, Marcel [French ; 1871–1922]. *Remembrance of Things Past* (A la recherche du temps perdu, 1913–1927).   1922–31

At the age of thirty-five, Proust withdrew from the world, shut himself in his room, and applied his remaining sixteen years to exploring the deeps of consciousness and reconstructing from the submerged but still existing debris the life of himself and of the brilliant society to which he belonged. The result was a work unique in the annals of fiction ; the comparison with the memoirs of Saint-Simon is more to the point. It is real, for as he said, nothing is more real than that which the self contains ; but it is not realism. *A la recherche du temps perdu* is a great concrete illustration of Bergson's philosophy of time and memory—Bergson was his kinsman by marriage. By the concentrated activity of intuition, it makes the past live again in the eternity of art. The Marcel of the story is Proust's own counterpart, and many if not most of the other persons, without being direct portraits, have their verifiable references in the personages of that era. It is a comprehensive view of an epoch of social history, as seen by one hypersensitive and critical eye, penetrating by a strange clairvoyance into the obscurities of personal character, examining and comparing feelings, tastes, motives, and attitudes, judging, expounding, and making generalizations, with a patience and a minuteness which can hardly be paralleled. Some will dispute the generalizations, as based too much on his own case. Marcel, like his creator, is of a morbid, apprehensive, passive, irresolute temperament, prone to disillusionment. But the subtlety and acuteness of his perceptions are unquestionable. The successive parts of this multiple work appear below. The last two volumes came out after the author's death.

—— *Swann's Way* (Du côté de chez Swann, 1913).   1922

The reader confronted and possibly confounded by the involved, parenthetic, incessantly qualifying style of Proust, will do well to realize at the outset that it was the natural expression of his mind and the fit instrument of his peculiar art. His style is rather of the seventeenth and eighteenth centuries than of to-day. Scott-Moncrieff produced its equivalent in English, without attempting to make it more lucid or easier to read. In this first part, Proust brings up from inner consciousness his reminiscences of childhood, and of parents, grand-parents, grand-aunts, and early friends. The little town of Combray is Illiers, not far from Chartres, where the family spent their summers with an uncle who had a large property there. If they went out, there were two directions open, one leading to the château of the Guermantes, the other past M. Swann's house. Incident after incident is called up, childish thoughts and ideas, naïve misconceptions, the most fugitive experiences with the associations that cling to them, sensorial images above all, scents, things tasted or things seen, which continue to evoke all the circumstances of the vanished past. Much related here, however, pertains to a remoter time, e.g. the love-story of M. Swann. This friend of the family, drawn probably from Charles Haas, is a rich Jew, son of a Government official on the Bourse, who is long regarded as nobody in particular but turns out to be a habitué of the highest society and a friend of the Prince of Wales. His passion for a woman whose reputation he learns too late in the day, who repeatedly betrays him, but whom he eventually marries, brings in tragic episodes of jealousy and suspicion. Marcel towards the end is in love with Swann's daughter Gilberte. [Transl. by C. K. SCOTT-MONCRIEFF, 2 vols., Chatto ; Holt, New York ; Boni, New York.]

—— *Within a Budding Grove* (A l'ombre des jeunes filles en fleurs, 1918).   1924

Awarded the Prix Goncourt (1919). Marcel's boyish affair with Gilberte comes to a disenchanting end, and presently he goes to the seaside for his health, under the watchful eyes of his grandmother, whom he tenderly loves, and the family servant Françoise, one of the most racy, touching, and beautiful creations Proust ever did. Admirable also are his portraits of the old diplomat, M. de Norpois, Bergotte the novelist, the gossipy old Marquise de Villeparisis, and younger friends, the fierily progressive intellectual, Saint-Loup, and the other aristocrat, the arrogant Charlus, drawn in the main from Count Robert de Montesquiou. The descriptive pages are exquisite—the church at Balbec, sea and sunsets from the hotel windows, etc. Marcel broods over his disappointment, and is thrown into reveries by any beautiful face he sees ; he is continually analysing the intense desire to go out of himself and mingle his life with that of another. His encounter with a joyous band of young girls on the shore is prophetic. [Transl. by C. K. SCOTT-MONCRIEFF, 2 vols, Chatto ; Boni, New York.]

—— *The Guermantes Way* (Le côté de Guermantes, 1920–21).   1925

Marcel is here a young man of fashion, admitted to the circle of the Duchess de Guermantes and the most exclusive society of the Faubourg Saint-Germain, which is pictured through such a microscopic lens that the account of a dinner-party at the duchess's takes up 120 pages. Here, but not here only, are many admirable discourses on snobbishness and class-feeling. Obtuse critics have called Proust himself a snob, on the score of his reverence for ancient and historic names, and his interest in these foibles. But his delineation of aristocratic *morgue* is sarcastic enough ; he broods characteristically over the diversified manifestations of this and its converse, with the fondness of a connoisseur delighting in the intrinsic beauty of human traits. Saint-Loup's liaison with an actress who plays fast and loose with him furnishes tragi-comedy. There are echoes of the Dreyfus affair, and the Baron de Charlus comes more and more to the front. [Transl. by C. K. SCOTT-MONCRIEFF, 2 vols., Chatto ; Boni, New York.]

—— *Cities of the Plain* (Sodome et Gomorrhe, 1922).   1927

Charlus is the prominent figure in this study of sexual inversion, a subject which has rarely if ever been treated with a more scrupulous regard for the truth. Homosexuality, says Proust, is an incurable disease, and the life of its victims a prolonged tragedy. The secrecy to which the invert is condemned, his corroding passions, the ceaseless fear of detection and ostracism, his terrible solitude—all this is brought out with a power and a knowledge unexampled, certainly in fiction. (Some detractors have charged Proust with " eavesdropping ! ") This is, of course, only a part of the book, which continues Marcel's mental evolution, life in the salons and in bourgeois coteries far outside the Guermantes circle. Social intrigues and social follies alternate with other themes, music, literature, painting, acting, and our reactions to these arts, always favourite subjects with Proust, who not only talks about Rembrandt and Boecklin, but invents artists, like the painter Elstir, the actress Berma, Vinteuil the musician, and the novelist Bergotte. [Transl. by C. K. SCOTT-MONCRIEFF, 2 vols., ltd. ed., Knopf ; Boni, New York.]

PROUST, Marcel (*continued*). *The Captive* (La prisonnière, 1923). 1929
Now it is the autobiographer who suffers the pangs of thwarted desire, suspicion, and jealousy. Marcel discovers that Albertine, one of the flowery band at Balbec, has a past, that she too is a sexual pervert, and he is tortured by the unconscious revelations in her efforts to dissemble the truth. He keeps her in durance, hesitating to marry her, afraid even to let her know the depth of his passion, lest what inclination she has towards him should vanish entirely. To love, he says, is to torment each other. They are continually feigning. Romantic love, the whole book seems to demonstrate, is a delusion. Love is always one-sided, a going-out of the individual, a craving to share another's life and individuality that can never be realized, for the self is private and inviolable. It is in his disquisitions on love that Proust sounds his saddest note—always the note of disillusionment. On this subject, as usual, he generalized too much from his own exceptional case, read the mental history of others too completely in the light of his own. [Transl. by C. K. Scott-Moncrieff, Knopf ; Boni, New York.]

—— *The Sweet Cheat Gone* (Albertine disparue, 1925). 1930
The grief-stricken introvert is brooding over his past with Albertine (whom Proust has allowed to die), and the tormenting problem of her frailties and deceptions. Other matters in this rather dull section are the degenerate Saint-Loup's marriage to Gilberte, who as Mlle de Forcheville forces her way into the Guermantes set, and that of the Marquess de Cambremer to the tailor Jupien's niece, soi-disant daughter of the Baron de Charlus. There is also a visit to Venice, and a charming glimpse of the aged M. de Norpois. But none of the other books is more typical of the method and intention of Proust. Here we see his intelligence at work upon the materials seized by intuition : the moral philosopher dwelling on each incident, however banal, to savour its essence, discover its sources in the least-explored regions of our mental being, its furthest reactions on conduct and personal relations. " Each reader is in reality the reader of himself." [Transl. by the late C. K. Scott-Moncrieff, Knopf ; Boni, New York.]

—— *Time Regained* (Le temps retrouvé, 1927). 1931
Nearing the end of life, the autobiographer shows us Paris during the German air-raids, and the last phases of Saint-Loup and Charlus, the latter in the final pit of abandonment. Then in a chapter of enormous length, he records a meditation on the crucial problem of his art, the development of that which is in time and perishes into that which is in our mental duration and remains. He makes his last entry into the Guermantes salon, where all the more familiar characters are present, changed with the lapse of years as society also has changed to its very foundations. And in a sort of epilogue he bids life farewell, confident that men will occupy " a place in Time infinitely more important than the restricted one reserved for them in space . . . like giants immersed in Time." [Transl. by Stephen Hudson, Knopf ; Boni, New York.]

PROWSE, Richard Orton [b. 1862]. *The Poison of Asps.* 1892
Tragic without the least sensational incident, the three persons to whom the reader's sympathy is engaged being the victims of the pettiness, the love of scandal and hatred of the unconventional, that characterize the society of a little country town. [Methuen : o.p.]

—— *Voysey.* 1901
The subject is sordid and at times revolting—the history of a liaison between Voysey and a sentimental, discontented wife. The author's method is exhaustive analysis after the manner of Henry James, while the frankness of his realism in certain scenes suggests Zola. The characters are dull, poor-spirited people, who in themselves have little interest. [Heinemann : o.p. ; Macmillan, New York : o.p.]

—— *A Gift of the Dusk.* 1920
A consumptive sentenced to death meditates in an Alpine sanatorium on the future that is imminent, and how to deal with the short span of life remaining ; and in a fellow-patient he finds love and a sharer in his new vision. [Collins : o.p.]

PRYCE, Miss Daisy Hugh [Welsh]. *Valda Hânem : the romance of a Turkish harem.* 1899
A British officer's intrigue with a Turkish pasha's beloved wife, who has been imbued with English ideals of romantic love. Intimate descriptions of the interior of a harem and of life in modern Cairo. [Macmillan, London and New York : o.p.]

—— *The Pasha.* 1901
The writer uses her extensive knowledge of life in Constantinople to draw an attractive portrait of a Turkish gentleman. This excellent man falls in love with an English governess and marries her ; their family life is pleasantly depicted. The Armenian question of 1896 has sidelights thrown on it favourable to the Turk. [G. Allen : o.p.]

PRYCE, Gwendolen [Welsh]. *John Jones, Curate.* 1901
The simple, uneventful life of country people in Anglesey, their ambitions, joys, and sorrows, woven into a pretty idyll. The authoress has been called " the Welsh Crockett " ; she has his truth to and love of the soil, without his sensationalism. [Unwin : o.p.]

PRYDZ, Alvide [Norwegian ; 1848–1922]. *The Heart of the Northern Sea* (Gunvor Thorsdotter til härö, 1896). 1907
A story of a little Norwegian haven, conveying the atmosphere and fascination of the sea in a beautiful way, and finer still as a luminous rendering of the national ideals of character. Gunvor is a dignified impersonation of the " rigid, northerly, cold conscience ", and her strength and purity are thrown into high relief by the weakness and hedonism of her lover, whom she resigns to a sensuous charmer. [Transl. by Tyra Engdahl and Jessie Rew, Allen & Unwin : o.p.]

—— *Sanpriel : the promised land* (Det lovede land, 1903). 1914
The promised land is resignation, the time when we enter into the life of the soul. This theme is worked out, with a lyricism that draws magic from the spacious heaths and fells, in the belated love of a weary woman for a being she had fled from in years gone by. [Transl. by Hester Coddington, Badger, Boston : o.p. ; Augsberg, Minneapolis ; Allen & Unwin : o.p.]

PSICHARI, Ernest [French ; 1883–1914]. *A Soldier's Pilgrimage* (Le voyage du centurion, 1914).
1916
Fictional in form, but in substance the history of his own conversion ; eloquent in the expression of mystical and religious feeling. The author was a grandson on his mother's side of Ernest Renan, and fell in action. [Transl. by E. M. WALKER and Harriet M. CAPES ; with introd. by Paul Bourget, Melrose.]

PUGH, Edwin William [b. 1874]. *A Street in Suburbia.* 1895
Impressionist sketches of people and manners in a Cockney neighbourhood ; the patois faithfully reproduced. [Heinemann : o.p. ; Appleton, New York : o.p.]

—— *Tony Drum, Cockney Boy.* 1898
A slight story of London characters founded on close observation. Tony and other denizens of the slums are drawn realistically in their squalid surroundings, but the sympathy and humour of the author show also what is pleasant and estimable in their life. [Heinemann : o.p. ; Holt, New York : o.p.]

—— *Mother-Sister.* 1900
The heroine of this story of low life is a stanch and self-reliant girl, daughter of an old prize-fighter and gaol-bird, who is more than a mother to her brothers and sisters ; one of these is a ne'er-do-well, another a factory-girl who runs away with a rascally bookmaker, and so on. Realistic, showing the pleasures and excitements, as well as the miseries, of the slums. [Hurst : o.p.]

—— *The Stumbling Block.* 1903
—— *The Fruit of the Vine.* 1904
—— *The Purple Head.* 1905
—— *The Spoilers.* 1906
—— *The Shuttlecock.* 1907
—— *The Enchantress.* 1908
—— *The Broken Honeymoon.* 1908
Novels that give a rather rose-coloured and optimistic picture of the poor and the lower middle-classes in the East and the South-East of London. The uglier sides—" the habitual squalor and the atmosphere of mean, pretentious poverty," and the sordid spirit of the average denizen of Suburbia—break through at times, as in the last novel, which tells about a seaside honeymoon. [(1), Long ; (2), Hurst ; (3), Newnes ; (4) and (5), Hurst ; (6), Heinemann ; Barnes, New York ; (7) and (8), Milne : all o.p.]

—— *Harry the Cockney.* 1913
Harry is the son of a London barber, who rises in life and becomes a lawyer—a good account of Cockney life and character. [Laurie : o.p.]

—— *The Quick and the Dead : a tragedy of temperaments.* 1914
An involved story contrasting the practical and the artistic temperaments—the admiration of the wife of a young engineer for the work of a decadent poet, whose literary executor the husband is, brings down disaster all round. [Chapman : o.p.]

PUGH, Edwin William, and BURCHETT, Godfrey. *The Heritage.* 1901
A gloomy study of the effects of hereditary alcoholism on the several members of a family. Though its influence acts in diverse ways, the taint in the blood proves to be the overmastering agent of their destinies, and the philosophy of the book is very pessimistic. [Sands : o.p.]

PURDON, Katherine Frances [Irish]. *The Folk at Furry Farm.* 1914
The little farmstead is somewhere in the middle of Ireland, and the inmates, men and women, and the tramps and others who call, are brought before us in the most intimate, racy, and entertaining way, as by one of their own class and education. [Talbot Press, Dublin.]

—— *Dinny of the Doorstep.* 1918
The history of two Dublin street-urchins, orphaned and left to a drunken stepmother, and of the mistakes of a charitable young lady to whom the feelings of the poor are a sealed book. The childish talk in Irish-English is charming. [Talbot Press, Dublin.]

PUSHKIN, Alexandr Sergyeevich [Russian ; 1799–1837]. *Prose Tales.* 1894
Pushkin's stories are chiefly native in subject, and his influence has been more profound, perhaps, than that of any other man of letters on succeeding Russian novelists. For *The Captain's Daughter*, see below. *An Amateur Peasant Girl* is the story of a flirtation ; *The Snowstorm*, an extraordinary episode, how a man marries a lady who believes him to be some one else ; *The Postmaster*, a pathetic tale of a pretty peasant girl's elopement with a passing hussar ; *The Queen of Spades* is a tragedy. [Transl. by T. KEANE (Bohn's Lib.), Bell (Macmillan, New York) : o.p. ; *The Queen of Spades*, with pref. by Prince D. S. Mirsky, Blackamore Press, 1929.]

—— *The Captain's Daughter* (Kapitanskaya Dotchka, 1836). 1859
Adventures of two lovers during the Pougachev rebellion in the time of Catherine II (1773). By means of brisk incident, forcible outlines of character, and sharp strokes of description and dialogue, Pushkin sets before us the various types of a savage period so incisively that the story makes the same impression as a drama. [Transl. by J. F. HANSTEIN (1859), and in *Prose Tales*, transl. by T. KEANE (Bohn's Lib.), Bell (Macmillan, New York) : o.p. ; transl. by Natalie DUDDINGTON, with introd. by E. Garnett, Dent, 1928 ; Viking Press, New York.]

P'U SUNG-LING [Chinese ; b. 1622]. *Strange stories from the Lodge of Leisures (from Liao-Chai-Chih-I, 1679, printed 1740).* 1913
A collection of 25 stories from a work renowned in China for the beauty and terseness of its style, and the wealth of metaphor and learned allusion. Magic and the supernatural are used extensively to provide a *dénouement*. [Transl. by Georges SOULIÉ, Constable ; another translation, *sub tit. Strange Stories from a Chinese Studio*, 2 vols., by H. A. GILES, appeared in 1880.]

PYLE, Howard [American ; 1853–1911]. *The Merry Adventures of Robin Hood, of great renown in Nottinghamshire.* [juvenile] 1883

This and the next three are the best of a dozen or so clever mosaics of traditional and historical material, which the author illustrates in a most appropriately picturesque style for young people. [Scribner, New York and London ; Newnes : o.p.]

—— *Within the Capes : a sea story.* [juvenile] 1885

A story of incident and adventure, dealing with the war-period of 1812–4. The sailor-lover goes abroad to seek his fortune and win a Quaker maiden, is cast away, endures many perils, returns, and nearly kills his sweetheart's new lover. [Scribner, New York : o.p.]

—— *Otto of the Silver Hand.* [juvenile] 1888

About a little German boy late in the thirteenth century. [Scribner, New York.]

—— *Men of Iron.* [juvenile] 1892

Pictures English life in the reigns of Henry IV and V (1400–18). [Harper, New York and London.]

"QUEEN, Ellery" [American]. *The Roman Hat Mystery.* 1929

—— *The French Powder Mystery.* 1930

Excellent specimens of the detective novel that consists of an honest intellectual problem honestly worked out. Before the end, every clue is in the reader's hands, and the solution should be inevitable. [Gollancz ; Stokes, New York.]

QUERIDO, Isaak [Dutch]. *Toil of Men* (Menschenwee, 1904). 1909

A Dutch *La Terre* ; a gloomy epic of agricultural life, more depressing in its catalogue of hopeless labour, brutal avarice, and brutish vice than even Zola's terrible masterpiece. The art is superb, and the brutalized rustics are etched in with almost intolerable force, now and then a figure conveying a tenderer pathos. [Transl. by Dr. F. S. Arnold, Putnam, New York ; Methuen.]

QUEVEDO Y VILLEGAS, Francisco Gomez de [Spanish ; 1580–1645]. *Pablo de Segovia* (Historia de la Vida del Buscón, llamado Don Pablos : Exemplo de Vagamundas y espejo de Tacaños, 1626). 1657

A rogue-novel on the established plan, with coarsely sketched scenes of bohemian student life, drawn from the writer's personal experience. (There are curious anticipations of Dotheboys Hall and similar Dickensian caricatures, and also of the wildest exaggerations of American humour.) The hero, son of a barber and a loose woman, engages in all sorts of rascally and licentious escapades, is imprisoned, and ends a disreputable career by emigrating to America. Chief scenes, Madrid and Seville. [*The Life and Adventures of Buscon the witty Spaniard* (1657) ; *The Comical Works of Don Francisco de Quevedo*, transl. by John Stevens (1707) ; *The Life of Paul, the Spanish Sharper*, contained in *The Works of Quevedo*, transl. by M. Pinneda (1745) : all o.p. *Illus.* by Daniel Vierge, Unwin : o.p. ; *Quevedo's Humorous and Satirical Works*, transl. by Sir Roger l'Estrange, John Stevens, etc., ed. by Charles Duff, (Broadway Translations) Routledge (Dutton, New York).]

—— *The Visions of Dom Francisco de Quevedo y Villegas* (Sueños, 1635). 1667

A satire of an apocalyptic design, *Visions and Discourses, concerning abuses, vices, and deceits in all offices and estates of the world*, afterwards parodied in verse and again in *The New Quevedo ; or, Visions of Charon's Passengers*, both 1702. [Made English by Roger l'Estrange, 10th ed., 1715 : o.p. ; repr. from 3rd ed. (1668), Methuen, 1904 : o.p.]

QUILLER-COUCH, Sir Arthur Thomas [" Q " ; b. 1863]. *Dead Man's Rock.* 1887

A sanguinary and outlandish romance of sixty years ago, put in the mouth of a Cornishman—the quest for the Great Ruby of Ceylon.

—— *The Astonishing History of Troy Town.* 1888

A burlesque account of certain doings in a quaint little seaport of Cornwall (Polperro, the author's native place). The characters are half-serious, half-farcical creations, not without friendly digs of satire at some of the little cliques with their affectations and absurdities. Ending with a country courtship. [(Wayfarer's Lib.), Dent ; Scribner, New York.]

—— *The Splendid Spur. Being memoirs of the adventures of Mr. John Marvel, a servant of His late Majesty King Charles I in the year 1642–3. Written by Himself and Edit. in Modern English by " Q."* 1889

A Royalist romance, particularly strong on the history of the campaign in Cornwall and the west of England generally (1642–3). [School edn., Cassell ; Nelson ; *illus.*, Doubleday, Doran, New York, 1927.]

—— *The Blue Pavilions.* 1891

Harwich and Holland, chiefly in the year 1691—a crowded episode in a young man's life. Two dauntless and eccentric old sea-captains, who quarrel over the guardianship of the hero, son of the woman they had loved and lost, are the most striking figures ; the villain is an adventurer who has dealings with all parties, including King James at St. Germain ; and King William and the future Duke of Marlborough appear in some humorous scenes. [(Wayfarer's Lib.), Dent ; Scribner, New York : o.p.]

—— *I Saw Three Ships.* 1892

A picturesque tale of the old times of wreckers and preventives on the Cornish coast, full of local colour ; with some ghost stories and other sensations, the rustic humours obviously inspired by Thomas Hardy.

—— *Noughts and Crosses : stories, studies, sketches.* 1893

Very diverse in scenes and characters, but nearly all far-fetched, bizarre, and even gruesome : admirable in execution. *Gabriel Foot*, the self-related experience of a fantastic and uncanny criminal ; *The Omnibus* and *Fortunio*, incisive little etchings of character ; *The Return of Joanna, From a Cottage in Troy, The Mayor of Gantick*, etc., specimens of Cornish life, humorous, grotesque, and oddly pathetic. *Bleakirk-on-*

QUILLER-COUCH, Sir Arthur Thomas (*continued*).

Sands, a Yorkshire story of a madman, is horribly thrilling, and the *Countess of Bellarmine* makes a good companion piece. *The Magic Shadow* is a weird little allegory. [Scribner, New York.]

—— *The Delectable Duchy: stories, studies, and sketches.*   1894
Scraps of legend, humour, romance, and tragedy of Cornish villages, country-folk and fishermen ; slightly connected, and told in such a manner as to seem as if the author merely reported them. [Scribner, New York : o.p.]

—— *Wandering Heath.*   1895
More short stories and sketches, racy of Cornish humanity and redolent of the past. *The Roll-Call of the Reef* is a ghostly fantasy, based on one of those terrible legends of foundered warships which haunt the fatal coasts of the Lizard. Humorous sketches of village politics and characteristic *Letters from Troy* (Polperro) are among the contents. [Scribner, New York : o.p.]

—— *Ia.*   1896
Ia is a strong-natured and pretty Cornish girl who courts a young preacher : sketches of manners and character among " the Elect," religious fisher-folk. [Scribner, New York : o.p.]

—— *The Ship of Stars.*   1899
A desultory story with interesting episodes : the life of a Devon village lad, a dreamer who develops into a strong and practical man. Scenes, Cornwall and Oxford. [Nelson.]

—— *Old Fires and Profitable Ghosts.*   1900
Imaginative and artistic experiments in the ghost-story, chiefly of spirits returning to the scenes of their human experience. The localities and the persons are mostly Cornish. *Once Aboard the Lugger* is a kind of abridged *Ia*. Another impressive little drama is staged among the Polar ice-floes, where some shipwrecked mariners, at the point of death, are cheered by a comforting presence. [Scribner, New York : o.p.]

—— *The Laird's Luck ; and other fireside tales.*   1901
Five in number. The title story belongs to the same supernatural kind as those of the preceding volume. The most considerable and the most striking, *The Two Scouts*, recounts the adventures of two scouts in the Peninsular War, one a Presbyterian, the other a Catholic, the radical differences of whose moral character are disclosed very dramatically. The others are various in subject and period, and unequal in power, though all show masterly handling of the short story. *Phœbus of Halzaphron*, a legend of Apollo in Cornwall, suggested by the discovery of relics of a temple, brings together in an artistic way Christian and pagan ideas. [Scribner, New York : o.p.]

—— *The Westcotes.*   1902
Dorothea Westcote, aged thirty-seven, falls in love with a handsome French prisoner, fifteen years her junior, and is cruelly awakened from her belated romance. A pathetic story, told with a fine courtesy and delicacy that save it from touching the ridiculous. An old Somersetshire country town in 1810 is the scene, and some good old-fashioned characters, French and English, are among the personages. [Coates, New York : o.p.]

—— *The White Wolf ; and other fireside tales.*   1902
Miscellaneous, the nautical stories either humorous or fanciful, the others sketches of temperament ; a ghost-story or two and more tales of Troy Town. [Scribner, New York : o.p.]

—— *The Adventures of Harry Revel.*   1903
The random adventures of a delightful foundling at Plymouth, at sea, and in Spain, with a charming Welsh-woman, and other originals. Covers a number of years down to the Peninsular War and the siege of Ciudad Rodrigo. [Scribner, New York : o.p.]

—— *Hetty Wesley.*   1903
Combines fiction and biography. Mehetabel (1723-1803), the most gifted sister of the Wesleys, was betrayed by a lover, and expiated her fall by marrying a clown—at least that is Q.'s interpretation. He argues that the harsh Puritanism of her father, whose unbending character is finely dramatized, contributed to her disaster. [Macmillan, New York : o.p.]

—— *Fort Amity.*   1904
From the British reverse at Ticonderoga to the repulse of the Americans before Quebec (1758-75). Adventures of an English officer in a French station and among the Ojibways—a quixotic young man who suffers worldly disgrace rather than sully his immaculate ideal of honour. Makes romantic profit of the picturesque scenery and the warlike circumstance. [Scribner, New York.]

—— *The Mayor of Troy.*   1905
A farcical chapter in the annals of Troy Town—the deeds of the Troy Volunteer Artillery during the Napoleonic scare of 1804. [Scribner, New York : o.p.]

—— *Shakespeare's Christmas ; and other stories.*   1905
In this miscellany, *Captain Wyvern's Adventures*, *Frenchmen's Creek*, and *Ye Sexes give Ear*, are scenes from Cornwall a century or two ago ; *Rain of Dollars* and *The Lamp and the Guitar* are incidents of the Peninsular War. [Dent ; Longmans, New York.]

—— *Shining Ferry.*   1905
A Cornish novel, with some striking people in it, e.g. the dissenter Samuel Rosewarne, the old clerk, etc.

—— *Sir John Constantine. Memoirs of his adventures at home and abroad, and particularly in the island of Corsica. Beginning with the year 1756. Written by his son, Prosper Paleologus, otherwise Constantine.*   1906
A romance of adventure, with some comedy of character at the beginning reminiscent of Sterne. The heroic deeds of a quixotic gentleman in the expulsion of the Genoese and the recovery of the crown of Corsica for Queen Emma (1756-60). [Scribner, New York : o.p.]

—— *Poison Island.*   1907
A romantic novel with a *Treasure Island* plot crossed with the fantastic of *The Ebb-Tide*, and in addition some

QUILLER-COUCH, Sir Arthur Thomas (*continued*).

Dickensian caricatures or humours, such as Miss Plinlimmon (from *Harry Revel*) and the Stimcoes, a more amiable Dotheboys gang (1813–4). [School ed., Dent ; Scribner, New York : o.p.]

—— *Merry Garden ; and other stories.* 1907

Seven romantic tales of Cornwall and the West ; *Merry Garden*, a pretty and spirited story of a pleasure garden near Plymouth and the people who frequented it ; *Hi-Spy-Hi*, a glimpse of the Napoleonic scare and the local fencibles ; and *Where the Treasure Is*, a finely conceived tale of a pair of fishermen.

—— *Major Vigoureux.* 1907

A slight but amusing story of the Scilly Isles, with a fairy-tale motive, and an ingratiating central character in the simple, chivalrous old soldier representing the obsolescent past. [Scribner, New York : o.p.]

—— *True Tilda.* 1909

The amazing adventures—told in a fairly plausible way—of a little circus-girl on tour ; not at all unlike parts of *The Old Curiosity Shop*, with a lot of picturesque and unexpected people among the strolling players and those they meet. [Scribner, New York : o.p.]

—— *Corporal Sam ; and other stories.* 1910

The title-story is about the siege of San Sebastian (1813) ; *The Copernican Convoy* and *Red Velvet* are of the Great Civil War.

—— *Lady Good-for-Nothing : a man's portrait of a woman.* 1910

An imaginative version of the story of Sir Harry Frankland and Agnes Surriage ; scenes, Boston and Lisbon, at the time of the earthquake (1755). [Nelson ; Scribner, New York.]

—— *Brother Copas.* 1911

Episodes in a College of Noble Poverty, the most distinguished among the inhabitants of which is the wise and scholarly bedesman, Brother Copas. Into his mouth Q puts a rich miscellany of reminiscences, conversations, and versatile comments on politics, literature, and the worldly or unworldly interests that disturb the little coterie. [Scribner, New York : o.p.]

—— *Hocken and Hunken.* 1912

One of his richest stories of Troy Town and its people. The two old skippers and their courtship of the well-provided and buxom widow are very entertaining. [Appleton, New York.]

—— *Nicky-Nan, Reservist.* 1915

How Alcibiades Penhaligon, a Cornish child of four, tracked a German spy and captured his gold. [Blackwood ; Appleton, New York.]

—— *Mortallone ; and Aunt Trinidad : tales of the Spanish Main.* 1917

The first is about a treasure-hunt ; Aunt Trinidad is a Bristol woman who marries a buccaneer.

—— *Foe Farrell.* 1918

A terrible story of vengeance and hate. A biologist's life-work is destroyed in a few minutes owing to a well-meaning but ignorant allegation that he experiments on living animals. [Collins ; Macmillan, New York.]

[*Works*, 32 vols., Duchy Ed., Dent, 1928, in progress.]

RABELAIS, François [French ; 1483 (or 90 or 95)–1552 (or 3)]. *Works* (1533–62). 1653–64

A wonderful combination of jovial buffoonery with satire grounded in an acute philosophy. The author proposed to write a burlesque of the current romances of chivalry : as he saw the possibilities of his theme, he brought his work nearer to human realities. Hence, while the characters are monstrous and grotesque caricatures, and the incidents extravagant, the book has a definite relation to life, and abounds in penetrating criticism, serious allegory, and profound humour. First the giant Gargantua comes on the scene : his exploits are full of absurdities and of satire on monks, priestcraft, the bigotry and pedantry of the age. Next Pantagruel, the real protagonist, is introduced ; his education, marvellous feats, adventures and experiences in real and fictitious places being related at great length. Then Panurge, the man of intellect without conscience, becomes for a time the centre of interest. Urquhart and those following him give a fair reproduction of Rabelais' extraordinary style, a style of which the motley colouring has, by Lanson, been compared to Rubens. Wit, tomfoolery, and rodomontade, puns and word-jingles, daring combinations of learned, popular, and obscene dialects, grotesque coinages, oratorical rotundities, —this style is the "orchestration of ideas." [Transl. by Sir Thomas URQUHART (Tudor Translns.), 3 vols., Nutt : o.p. ; by URQUHART and P. A. MOTTEAUX (1653–64), 5 vols., Gibbings, 1897 : o.p. ; same transl., 2 vols. (Bohn's Lib.) : o.p., 1849 ; same transl., *illus.* by G. Doré, Chatto, 1872 ; same transl., *illus.* by W. Heath Robinson, 2 vols., Navarre Soc. (Boni, New York) 1921 ; 5 vols., Lippincott, Philadelphia ; 1 vol., *id.* ; 1 vol., Chatto ; Simon & Schuster, New York, 1928 ; complete, ed. by I. Lewis May, 2 vols., Lane. *Gargantua and Pantagruel*, 3 vols., Chatto (Boni, New York), 1925. *Heroic Deeds of Gargantua and Pantagruel*, with introd. by D. B. Wyndham Lewis, 2 vols., (Everyman's Lib.) Dent (Dutton, New York), 1929. Transl. by J. PAYNE, *illus.* by G. L. Chalon, 2 vols., Lawrence & Butler : o.p. ; by W. F. Smith, 2 vols. Rabelais Club (A. P. Watt), 1893 : o.p. ; by J. M. Rigg, (Early Novelists Lib.), Routledge, 1905 : o.p. ; by S. Putnam, 3 vols., Covici, New York, 1929. *Readings in Rabelais*, ed. by Walter BESANT, 1884 Blackwood : o.p. ; Macmillan, New York.]

RABUSSON, Henri [French ; *b.* 1850]. *Madame d'Orgevaut's Husband* (Le mari de Mme d'Orgevaut, 1888). 1891

One of several studies of problems of wedlock. Madame d'Orgevaut learns from her husband that he has been dishonest, but has made restitution, and would fain live a straight life. Will she be able to love him still, having ceased to respect him ? The searchings of heart and bitter emotional experiences of the wife are pathetically related. At last the struggle is too great to be borne, and she leaves him to work out his salvation in solitude. [Transl., Jamieson, Chicago : o.p.]

RADCLIFFE, Anne [*née* Ward ; 1764–1823]. *The Castles of Athlin and Dunbayne : a Highland story.* 1789

A sham historical novel mixing up baronial and highland life on the north-east coast of Scotland with the courtly and chivalrous society of Gothic romance. Clan revenge provides the plot interest. Mrs. Radcliffe is of great importance in the history of romantic literature. She laid her plots in remote periods, and in countries she had never seen, thus avoiding any responsibility to fact. Picturesque ruins, distant mountains, forest-shrouded landscapes are described with rich but monotonous colour, in a semi-lyrical style. The scenic glamour prepares the reader for sensational occurrences that conjure up feelings of awe and terror ; but in the sequel she invariably dispels our apprehensions by some commonplace explanation of her ghosts and other mysteries. [o.p.]

—— *A Sicilian Romance.* 1790

A wicked marquess locks his wife up in his castle on the north coast of Sicily and marries again. Groans are heard from mysterious doors and ghostly figures appear. Ultimately his children liberate their mother, and retribution falls on the criminals. Date about 1580. Ideal descriptions of scenery give space and amplitude to the incidents. [o.p.]

—— *The Romance of the Forest.* 1791

A sequestered ruin of an abbey, a nefarious marquess and a poetical heroine, a murder, a mysterious skeleton, and eloquent word-pictures of the Alps of Savoy. About the same date. [Ed. D. Murray Rose (Half-forgotten Books), Routledge, 1904 : o.p. ; *id.*, Dutton, New York.]

—— *The Mysteries of Udolpho.* 1794

Centres in a gloomy castle in the Apennines, the haunt of brigands, where the heroine is immured by a sinister Italian. Haunted chambers and a mystic veil play blood-curdling parts among the horrors. The idyllic scenes interspersed might have been imagined by Rousseau. The Pyrenees, the Alps, Venice, and the Apennines supply an harmonious background. Date about 1580–90. [Ed. D. Murray Rose (Half-forgotten Books), Routledge, 1903 ; Dutton, New York, 1921.]

—— *The Italian ; or, The Confessional of the Black Penitent.* 1797

The plot is a young noble's love for a penniless orphan, and the unscrupulous efforts of his mother and of a demoniac villain, Schedoni, to thwart it. Attempted assassinations, the abduction and imprisonment of the heroine in a ghastly dungeon, the terrors of the Inquisition and perilous escapes provide the requisite sensations. Naples and the coast are the theme of the scenic rhapsodies. Date about 1764. [Routledge (1877), 1884 : o.p.]

" RAINE, Allen " [Mrs. Beynon Puddicombe, *née* Evans ; Welsh ; 1836–1908]. *A Welsh Singer.* 1897

Idyllic phases of Welsh life in a seaside village, combined with melodramatic episodes in London. A shepherd-girl develops into a popular contralto. [Hutchinson : o.p.]

—— *Torn Sails.* 1898

A sentimental idyll, the central incident tragic, but the end happy. The actors are Welsh peasants, working in a little sail-factory in a seaside hamlet of Cardiganshire. Native superstitions, pretty customs and ways of speech, and the storms and sunshine of the coast, give the atmosphere. [Hutchinson : o.p.]

—— *By Berwen Banks.* 1899

Gives idyllic pictures of the same people, with some little humour, and melodramatic business involving persons of a higher class. [Hutchinson : o.p.]

—— *Garthowen.* 1900

The heroine is a waif saved from a shipwreck through the warning of a wraith. Her life with a farmer's family amid the moors and mountains is narrated with abundance of natural description ; and there are sketches of her foster-brothers, a pair of contrasts, and of Nonconformist Welsh folk in general. [Hutchinson : o.p.]

RANSOME, Arthur [*b.* 1884]. *Swallows and Amazons.* 1930

A seducing Crusoe story of a family of children on an island on the English coast. [Cape ; Lippincott, Philadelphia.]

RASPE, Rudolph Eric [German ; 1737–94 ; attrib. to]. *Travels and Surprising Adventures of Baron Münchausen* (1800). 1785

A mock-serious recital of absurdly impossible feats and adventures—now a byword for extravagant braggadocio —originally intended as a satire on the *Memoirs* of Baron de Trenck. The authorship is attributed to Raspe, a German emigrant to London, and editor of Leibnitz and other works in English. A sequel (1792) was " humbly addressed to Mr. Bruce, the Abyssinian traveller," then seriously regarded as a De Rougemont or Dr. Cook. Original edn. in English (1785), transl. into German by BURGER (1800). [Putnam, New York ; Brentano, New York ; *Travels*, with the sequel, *Adventures of the Baron Münchausen in Russia*, ed. by William Rose, (Broadway Transl.) Routledge (Dutton, New York) 1923.]

RATHBONE, Hannah Mary [*née* Reynolds ; 1798–1878]. *So much of the Diary of Lady Willoughby as relates to her Domestic History, and to the eventful Period of the Reign of Charles I, the Protectorate, and the Restoration.* 1844–7

Both in style and format this was a charmingly successful attempt to reproduce a book of the period. Miss Manning (q.v.) modelled her *Mary Powell* (1850) and other domestic novels of past days on Mrs. Rathbone's little masterpiece, without, however, equalling her model. A sequel came out in 1847 and was embodied in the 1848 edn. [o.p.]

RAVĪNDRANĀTHA THĀKURA [Rabindranath Tagore ; Bengali ; *b.* 1861]. *Hungry Stones ; and other stories.* 1916

The kind of parables and allegories that are very well in such poetical work as *Fruit-Gathering*, put into the prose terms of real life. *The Victory* of the poet is the victory of those " who suffer and bear the burden

RAVĪNDRANĀTHA THĀKURA (*continued*).

of power." *Vision* teaches that physical blindness may confer "the power of seeing a world which is beyond all change." *Living or Dead* and other tales carry us into eternity : the woman who thought she had died cannot share duty and affection with the people of this world. [Transl., Macmillan, London and New York.]

—— *Mashi ; and other stories.* 1918

Brief sketches of native Bengali life, more superficial in treatment than *Hungry Stones.* [Transl. by various writers, Macmillan.]

—— *The Home and the World.* 1919

Relations of an Indian maharajah's wife with her husband and the outside world of politics, treated with the large and rather misty eloquence that we now expect from the poet-novelist. [Macmillan.]

RAWSON, Maud Stepney [*née* Fife]. *A Lady of the Regency.* 1900

The heroine of the love-romance is an affectionate servant of Queen Caroline ; hence a very full recital of the unhappy queen's life and misfortunes down to her death, with pictures of her Court, of such people as Brougham, Castlereagh, Grattan, the Regent, Queen Charlotte, etc., and of London at the time of the *cause célèbre* (1818–21). [Hutchinson : o.p. ; Harper, New York : o.p.]

—— *Journeyman Love.* 1902

The love-story of a young Bristolian in Paris is of less interest than the author's drawing of numerous celebrities of the eventful period, 1840–8. George Sand, Chopin, Heine, Lamartine, Berlioz, Countess Potocka, Madame de Girardin, Guizot, Louis Napoleon, etc., appear and talk, and the presentment, though ambitious, is not unsuccessful. [Hutchinson : o.p.]

—— *The Apprentice.* 1904

A story of Rye and its neighbourhood in 1820 ; the local and historical colour well done. [Hutchinson : o.p.]

—— *Tales of Rye Town.* 1905

A delicate embodiment of the sentiment of place. Stories from the time of Elizabeth onwards clustering about the old seaport of Rye, the Huguenot and Flemish refugees, etc. [Constable : o.p.]

—— *Morlac of Gascony.* 1915

Rye and Winchelsea in the time of Edward I (1287–93) when the French had designs on the Cinque Ports. [Hutchinson : o.p.]

RAYMOND, Ernest [*b.* 1888]. *Daphne Bruno.* 1926

—— *The Fulfilment of Daphne Bruno* [sequel]. 1926

Pleasantly patient, quiet, sympathetic portraiture of upper middle-class life ; a story of father and daughter, with too much sentimentality for some tastes. [Cassell ; Doubleday, Doran, New York.]

—— *The Old Tree Blossomed.* 1928

Another family piece—the son of a dull suburban household achieves honour in the war. [Cassell.]

—— *A Family That Was.* 1929

Opens in 1893, and gives a good account of the life of a clergyman's family at that period, and after. [Cassell ; Appleton, New York.]

RAYMOND, Walter [1853–1930]. *Misterton's Mistake.* 1888

A rural idyll of Somersetshire, with excellent delineation of gnarled rustic character. [Sonnenschein : o.p.]

—— *Love and a Quiet Life.* 1894

Sunny idylls of bucolic life in mid-Somerset half a century ago. The dialect is woven artistically into not only the talk but even the narrative, in all these stories and the longer novels that follow. [Hodder : o.p. ; Dodd & Mead, New York : o.p.]

—— *In the Smoke of War.* 1895

A plaintive little story of the suffering and anxiety inflicted on the ignorant country people by the Civil War. A friendless girl, her captured father, the absent lover, and a cowardly rustic wooer are the characters, and the scene is a village near Langport in Somerset, where the battle was fought (1645). [Arrowsmith, Bristol : o.p. ; Macmillan, Mew York : o.p.]

—— *Tryphena in Love.* 1895

A fanciful idyll of agricultural life in an old-world village. Mrs. Pettigrew is a milder Mrs. Poyser ; and the tomboyish, tender-hearted Tryphena, with her alleged lack of "feelings," is prettily contrasted with the rich young lady who captivates her lover without meaning it. [Dent ; Macmillan, New York : o.p.]

—— *Charity Chance.* 1897

A love-comedy in a little Somersetshire watering-place on the Bristol Channel. [Sands : o.p. ; Dodd, New York : o.p.]

—— *Two Men o' Mendip.* 1899

A tragic story of the Mendip Hills in the time of Hannah More, and her attempts to civilize the lawless and brutal lead-miners of Cheddar and the neighbouring villages. [Longmans : o.p. ; Doubleday, New York : o.p. Play, based on novel, same title, Folk Press.]

—— *No Soul Above Money.* 1899

Village life and character in Somersetshire, in the reign of Queen Anne. The catastrophe is the murder of a brother, followed by a terrible expiation and unutterable sorrow for the bereaved mother. [Longmans : o.p.]

—— *Good Souls of Cider Land.* 1901

Rambling tales, plotless, but full of human nature, of Somersetshire in the days before railways. The two longest, *Gentleman Upcott's Daughter* and *Young Sam and Sabina*, are fragrant idylls of love and courtship. Both were originally published several years earlier. [De La More Press : o.p.]

—— *Jacob and John.* 1905

A tender love-tale, and a youth's adventures as a captive of Sallee rovers. With humorous sketches of village life in Somerset at the time of the South Sea Bubble (1720). [Hodder : o.p.]

RAYMOND, Walter (*continued*). *A Book of Crafts and Characters.*   1907

A gathering of many stories and sketches of farmers, peasants, pedlars, public-house gossips, and other racy Somersetshire characters ; the dialogue well flavoured with humour and the ruminating philosophy of the countryman. [Hodder : o.p.]

—— *The Revenues of the Wicked.*   1911

A characteristic love-story of the western moors a hundred years ago ; a lawyer's clerk and a farmer's daughter are the chief people. [Dent : o.p. ; Dutton, New York : o.p.]

RAYNER, Miss Emma [American]. *Free to Serve : a tale of Colonial New York.*   1897

The heroine, a well-born English girl, finds herself in the startling position of a bond-servant in the colony. It is during the administration of the eccentric Lord Cornbury, and the manners and ways of the people, chiefly Dutch, are admirably portrayed. [Small & Maynard, Boston : o.p.]

—— *In Castle and Colony.*   1899

The Swedish and Dutch colonies on the Delaware, and the rivalry of Governor Printz and Peter Stuyvesant (1628–55). [Stone, Chicago : o.p.]

—— *Doris Kingsley, Child and Colonist.*   1901

A chapter in the history of the English colony of Georgia founded by James Oglethorpe, who tries to make it a barrier against Spanish encroachment from Florida. [Dillingham, New York : o.p.]

—— *Visiting the Sin.*   1901

A rather high-pitched romance of mountain life in Kentucky and Tennessee after the wartime—a daughter tries to avenge the supposed murder of her father. [Small & Maynard, Boston : o.p. ; Putnam : o.p.]

REA, Lorna. *Six Mrs. Greenes.*   1919

Analyses and contrasts, with irony and pleasant humour, six women, all wives or widows, and members of one family :—from old Mrs. Greene, all but bedridden, though still active in mind, to the latest married of her grandchildren. [Heinemann ; Harper, New York.]

READ, Opie Percival [American ; b. 1852]. *A Kentucky Colonel.*   1896

Portrays a very engaging exemplar of the old Southern aristocrat ; a keen sportsman, full of amiable foibles, kind and good, constantly being " taken in " with his own connivance : a man beloved by all. [Schulter, Chicago : o.p.]

—— *The Waters of Caney Fork : a romance of Tennessee.*   1898

A doctor's son comes back to his birthplace in a remote corner of the Tennessee woodlands, where life moves slowly ; there he makes friends with the homely folk, and loves a beautiful little girl whose mind has been unhinged from infancy. The story meanders on in a dreamy fashion, till at length an accident restores the maiden's reason, when the autobiographer wins the quiet happiness for which he longs. [Rand McNally, Chicago : o.p.]

—— *By the Eternal.*   1906

An adventure-story of New Orleans at the beginning of last century, with General Andrew Jackson as central figure. Based to some extent on unpublished documents. [Laird, Chicago.]

READE, Charles [1814–84]. *Peg Woffington.*   1853

A free portrait of the famous Irish actress (1720–60) in the imaginary emotional episode dramatized in *Masks and Faces* (1852) by Reade and Taylor. The culminating scene in both is a contest of magnanimity between the injured women. [Dent (Dutton, New York) ; with *Christie Johnstone*, Chatto ; Scribner, New York.]

—— *Christie Johnstone.*   1853

Based on Reade's knowledge and liking of Scotch fishing folk. A *blasé* nobleman goes among the fishing population of a town on the east coast of Scotland, and learns charity from their rough but sincere and hearty character, getting a taste of real life in an adventure that calls out his manhood. Christie and Peg Woffington are Reade's best women characters. [*v. supra.*]

—— *It is Never Too Late to Mend.*   1856

Attacks two social evils—the prison system, which is indicted for its culture of vice ; and greed for gold, exemplified in the Australian adventures of two gold-diggers. Founded on industrious research on a gigantic scale ; the prison chapters based on disclosures as to the cruelties practised at Winson Green gaol, Birmingham, 1851–3. Brown was sketched from Warder Evans (d. 1903). Many of the episodes are of an exciting melodramatic kind, but the most horrible rest on documentary proofs. Among the characters may be mentioned the saintly and chivalrous chaplain, Mr. Eden, who interferes in the odious tyranny of the prison. [Chatto ; Scribner, New York.]

—— *The Cloister and the Hearth.*   1861

As a piece of historical narrative, crowded with characters, brilliantly pictorial, and based on indefatigable study, this is one of our finest novels of the Middle Ages, taking the hero from the Netherlands through Germany and France to Italy and Rome, and depicting the state of all these countries (1465–85). Attempts with amazing success to reconstruct the whole life of the time. The hero is said to be the father of Erasmus, and his story to be true in the main. Filled from beginning to end with rapid adventure, with glowing and diversified scenes of life, and inspired with a brotherly feeling for human nature in all its phases. It is one of the finest products of the note-book method of writing fiction. [Chatto ; Dent (Dutton, New York) ; Oxford Press ; Collins ; Scribner, New York ; *illus.* by M. B. Hewerdine, Chatto, 1901 ; by Gordon Browne, Lippincott, Philadelphia.]

—— *Love Me Little, Love Me Long.*   1859

—— *Hard Cash* [sequel].   1863

Romances carefully built up on solid matters of fact, with an idealized pair of lovers in the simple chivalrous sailor, David Dodd, and the Diana-like Lucy Fountain. The hard cash is David's hard-earned fortune, fallen into the clutches of a swindler. David goes mad with the shock ; hence realistic descriptions of an asylum, founded on a mass of documents about lunacy and its treatment in private asylums, which evoked rabid criticism. Many subjects have obviously been got up, like a barrister's brief, and vast quantities of technical information are poured forth—University life at Oxford, the boat-race, a tea-

READE, Charles (*continued*).
clipper taking in cargo, a bank smash, speculation in Old Turks, the delinquencies of the medical profession, etc. [(1) and (2), Chatto; Scribner, New York; (2), Routledge; Collins.]

—— *Griffith Gaunt ; or, Jealousy.* 1866
A tragic romance of jealousy and the ruin it brings on innocent people. The pure and magnanimous heroine is wrongfully suspected by her husband, a despicable fellow, who eventually goes to the dogs; and he leaves her and marries again. Later on she is accused of murdering him, and a grim catastrophe is hardly averted by the generous activity of the other woman. A happy sequel is appended to these dark scenes. The realism offended prejudiced critics, and the novel was severely handled, among others by Swinburne. [Chatto; Scribner, New York; *illus.*, Harper, New York.]

—— *Foul Play.* 1869
Title refers to a young merchant's conspiracy to wreck one of his own ships and pocket the insurance money. The interest is divided between the steps by which this is brought to light and the adventures of two lovers on a desert islet in the Pacific; this Crusoe episode has several fresh and entertaining features, but the author's attempts to portray character and emotion are singularly unsuccessful. [Chatto; Collins; Scribner, New York; Putnam, New York, 1917.]

—— *Put Yourself in His Place.* 1870
Condemns rattening and the underhand methods of the trade unions, pleading for sympathy, in the place of hostility, between capital and labour. [Chatto; Scribner, New York.]

—— *A Terrible Temptation : a story of the day.* 1871
The man of letters, Rolfe, is Reade's own portrait. This was the novel which the American reviewers stigmatized as " carrion literature." [Chatto; Scribner, New York; Burt, New York.]

—— *A Simpleton.* 1873
—— *The Wandering Heir.* 1873
Two of his inferior later novels, the second suggested by the Tichborne case. [(1), Chatto; Scribner, New York; (2), with *Autobiography of a Thief, etc., id.*]

—— *A Woman Hater.* 1877
Depicts the insanitary conditions of village life. Hill Stoke is Stoke Row, a hamlet on the estate of Reade's brother at Ipsden. [Chatto; Scribner, New York.]

—— *The Perilous Secret.* 1884
A posthumous novel based on his Adelphi drama *Love and Money* (1882). [Chatto; Scribner, New York.]

—— *Single Heart and Double Face.* 1884
A novelistic version of his sensational play of the same name (1883). [With *The Course of True Love*, Chatto.]

—— *The Jilt ; and other tales.* 1884
—— *Good Stories of Man and Other Animals.* 1884
Two posthumous collections of his short stories. [Together, 1 vol., Chatto; Scribner, New York.]
[*Works :* 16 vols., Chatto; 17 vols., Scribner, New York; 18 vols., Page, Boston.]

REBREANU, Liviu [Roumanian]. *The Forest of the Hanged.* 1930
The story of a Transylvanian soldier conscripted into the Austro-Hungarian army in the great war, and finally hanged for desertion. Based no doubt on the experiences of the author's brother, who suffered a like fate. [Transl. by A. V. WISE, Allen & Unwin; Duffield, New York.]

REDESDALE OF REDESDALE, 1st Baron [Algernon Bertram Freeman-Mitford; 1837–1916].
Tales of Old Japan. 1871
Drawn from the folklore and popular literature of the Yedo period (1603–1867). *The Forty-Seven Ronins, The Loves of Gompachi and Komurasaki, Kazuma's Revenge, A Story of the Otokodaté of Yedo, Wonderful Adventures of Fimakoshi Jiuyémon, The Eta Maiden and the Hatamoto*, Fairy Tales, *The Ghost of Sakura, How Tajima Shumé was Tormented.* Concerning certain superstitions, Japanese sermons. Appendices. [Macmillan (1871), 1903.]

REED, Myrtle [Mrs. J. S. McCullough; American; 1874–1911]. *The Shadow of Victory : a romance of Fort Dearborn.* 1903
Story of a frontier fort in the days of Indian wars (massacre of Fort Dearborn, 1812); strongly anti-English, and inspired with the Monroe doctrine. [Putnam, New York; Methuen.]

REED, Talbot Baines [1852–93]. *The Adventures of a Three-guinea Watch.* 1881
—— *The Fifth Form at St. Dominic's.* 1882
—— *Reginald Cruden.* 1894
Baines Reed was a famous contributor to the *Boy's Own Paper*, for which he wrote this admirable series of stories for boys, dealing chiefly with school life and depicting memorable types of wholesome and manly boyhood. Among the rest may be mentioned *Follow My Leader* (1885), *A Dog with a Bad Name* (1886), *The Master of the Shell* (1887), *The Cock-House at Fellgarth* (1891), *Tom, Dick, and Harry* (1892), and the two following. [All R.T.S.]

—— *Sir Ludar : a story of the days of the great Queen Bess.* [juvenile] 1889
Scene laid in Antrim and elsewhere—time of the Armada (1585–90); the retaking of Dunluce Castle is a fine episode. [R.T.S.]

—— *Kilgorman.* [juvenile] 1894
Adventures in Donegal, in Paris during the Terror, at the battle of Camperdown, and in Dublin with the United Irishmen and Lord Edward Fitzgerald (1792–8). [With a memoir of the author by his friend J. Sime, Nelson : o.p.]

REEVE, Clara [1738–1803]. *The Old English Baron.* 1777
First entitled *The Champion of Virtue*; a very early and crude attempt to give a real historical setting to

REEVE, Clara (*continued*).

the Gothic romance by embodying the events of the Wars of the Roses (1455–85). There is some supernatural incident, by which a murder is discovered and an heir restored to his estates. [With Walpole's *Castle of Otranto*, Warne, 1872 ; with the same, *illus.* with etchings, Nimmo, 1883 ; o.p.]

REEVES, Amber [Mrs. Blanco White ; New Zealander]. *The Reward of Virtue.*   1911

Keen, accurate, satirical vivisection of commonplace femininity. A highly respectable mother bringing her daughter up with careful avoidance of every undesirable influence, idea, or emotion, and the daughter herself who becomes an exact fit to the environment so assiduously prepared, are both drawn with clear understanding of the world that is "mostly fools." [Heinemann : o.p.]

REID, Forrest [Irish ; *b.* 1876]. *The Bracknels : a family chronicle.*   1912

An honest picture of the unpleasing personalities, the discords, misunderstandings, and embarrassments of the Bracknel family, as observed by a tutor. A hard father, a passionate daughter, one vicious son, and another whose fine nature is wedded to a frail constitution—tragedy is inherent in the characters, and its oncoming is traced with unflinching regard for actuality. [Arnold : o.p.]

—— *Following Darkness.*   1912

Autobiography of an introvert, son of a repressive father and brought up among uncongenial people, in the Mourne Mountains and then in Belfast. In revolt from the religious teaching that is thrust upon him, he finds a refuge in occultism. [Arnold : o.p.]

—— *At the Door of the Gate.*   1915

An even gloomier psychological study, of narrow, stunted people in Belfast, and more especially of a young man's mental development, morbid through the odiousness of his surroundings. Much subdued, ironical satire. [Arnold : o.p. ; Houghton, Boston : o.p.]

—— *A Garden by the Sea : stories and sketches.*   1918

An Ulster Farm is a piece of grim realism, and has more local colour than the other stories. *Courage* is a ghost-story remarkable for its fineness. Several pieces depend for their beauty largely on the drawing of children. [Talbot Press.]

REMARQUE, Erich Maria [German ; *b.* 1898]. *All Quiet on the Western Front* (Im Westen nichts Neues, 1929).   1929

Illustrates in the history of one unit every phase of the common soldier's experience during the war—life in trenches, shelters, and shell-holes, raids and counter-raids, intensive bombardments, hospitals, doctors, nurses, etc. Comic relief is afforded by the incessant struggle to get food and an occasional bean-feast. The basis of the anti-militarist philosophy is that it is authority and the lust for power that corrupts man and is ultimately responsible for wars—schoolmaster, corporal, lieutenant, and so on to the Kaiser and the war party, each lusts to impose his will. [Transl. (inaccurately) by A. W. WHEEN, Putnam ; Little & Brown, Boston.]

REMINGTON, Frederic [American ; 1861–1909]. *Crooked Trails.*   1898

—— *Men with the Bark on.*   1900

Lifelike and forcible sketches of wild, rough life in Cuba and on the western frontier, both collections illustrated by the author, who was a famous artist. [(1), Harper, New York and London, 1923 ; (2), *id.* : o.p.]

RENDALL, Vernon Horace [*b.* 1869]. *The London Nights of Belsize.*   1917

Emphatically, the novel of an intellectual. It presents us with a rich man of wonderful spirit and versatility, an amateur detective, a raconteur, a *bon viveur*, a writer, who entertains if he does not edify profoundly. [Lane ; *id.*, New York : o.p.]

RENN, Ludwig [German ; *b.* 1899]. *War* (Krieg, 1928).   1929

A record of personal experience in the ranks of the German army, on the western front during the whole period of the war ; free from sensational or sentimental effect, but with no shirking of facts. Of particular interest is the brief account of the final collapse. [Transl. by Willa and Edwin MUIR, Secker ; Dodd & Mead, New York.]

REUTER, Fritz [German ; 1810–74]. *In the Year '13 : a tale of Mecklenburg life* (Ut de Franzosentid, 1860).   1867

A story of country life in Mecklenburg during the French occupation, revealing the depths of national feeling stirred by these events, the characters being mixed up with the public misfortunes and the proceedings of the invaders. [Transl. from the Platt-Deutsch by C. L. LEWIS, Tauchnitz, Leipzig : o.p.]

—— *An Old Story of my Farming Days* (Ut mine Stromtid, 1864).   1878

Reuter was the greatest writer in the popular and racy Platt-Deutsch dialect. He produced a good deal of admirable verse, depicting the village life of his native Mecklenburg with forcible realism and plenty of humour ; and then began a great series of prose tales which in bold realism, spontaneous gaiety, and tenderness easily surpassed all that he had done before. This is Reuter's masterpiece. It deals with common, everyday life, and aims at no exaggeration or effect ; but with the deep, imaginative insight into human nature, and the vitality belonging to great art, it gives us a picture of real life in rural Mecklenburg unsurpassed for truth and engrossing charm. The queer old bachelor Uncle Bräsig is one of the most delightful originals in German fiction. Touches significantly on the revolutionary currents stirring the deepest feelings of men about 1848. [Transl. by M. W. MACDOWALL, 3 vols., Tauchnitz, Leipzig (Low) : o.p. *Sub tit. Seed-time and Harvest* (1871), Lippincott, Philadelphia : o.p.]

REYMONT, Wladislaw Stanislaw [Polish ; 1868–1925]. *The Comedienne* (Komedjantka, 1896).   1921

Reymont's first novel : a picture of worthless and degenerate characters in the theatrical world of a Polish provincial town. [Transl. by Edmund OBEENY, Putnam.]

—— *The Promised Land* (Ziema Obiecana, 1899).   1927

Lodz in the eighties, with its newly founded industrial prosperity ; in particular, a young nobleman and factory owner, who is hardened and consumed by a lust for wealth. A piece of documented realism, with

REYMONT, Wladislaw Stanislaw (*continued*).
scenes taken from every type of city life, but inferior in characterization to *The Peasants*. [Transl. by Michel H. DZIEWICKI, 2 vols., Knopf, New York and London.]

—— *The Peasants (Autumn, Winter, Spring, Summer)* (Chlopi, 1902–9).   1925–6
A vast and detailed picture of peasant life in Poland, which won for its author the Nobel prize for 1924. It records intimately and faithfully nine years in the lives of a group of villagers, peasants engaged in ceaseless warfare with the soil and the elements to gain a bare living, whose psychology is clearly revealed in their actions. The tale rises to an epical grandeur as the unlawful love between Antek and his stepmother Yagna unfolds, and marches forward to the inevitable catastrophe. [Transl. by Michel M. DZIEWICKI, 4 vols., Jarrolds; Knopf, New York.]

REYNARD THE FOX, *The History of*, tr. William Caxton (*c.* 1422–91).   1481
A fable or beast-epic which had European currency in the Middle Ages, and attained its finest literary embodiment in the Low German and Flemish versions of the thirteenth, fourteenth, and fifteenth centuries. These were derived from the French, though the oldest versions known are in Latin. Complaints are made in the Lion's court against Reynard's roguery and insolence, but by craft and eloquence he evades them, and afterwards wins in the trial by combat. A comic mirror of the age, full of satire on roguish and sensual priests, and other delinquents; not pure allegory, but deeply humorous and ironical. [Ed. Joseph Jacobs, with historical excursus, *subscr.*, Nutt, 1893: o.p.; ed. Wm. Morris, o.p., Kelmscott Press, 1893. Free rendering of Caxton's Transl., ed. F. S. Ellis, Nutt, 1894: o.p. Ed. by W. S. Stallybrass, with *Physiologus*, (Broadway Transl.), Routledge (Dutton, New York), 1924. Also several juvenile editions. For texts, see *Le Roman de Renart*, ed. Ernest Martin, 3 vols., Strassburg, Trübner, 1882–7; and for history, etc., Martin's *Observations sur le Roman de Renart*, Trübner, Strassburg, 1887.]

REYNOLDS, Mrs. Baillie [*née* Gertrude Robins]. *A Castle to Let*.   1917
The experiences of an Oxford lady in a Hungarian castle, said to be haunted by a dragon. [Cassell; Doran, New York: o.p.]

REYNOLDS, Stephen [*b.* 1881]. *A Poor Man's House*.   1908
Mr. Reynolds is a student of the social problem who has understood the poor by living among them and testing sociology by experience. This is a book with an optimistic thesis, viz. that the poor have their own talent for happiness, only wanting to be left to themselves; and with their insight into life's fundamental realities have much to teach their educated superiors in the social scale. He prefers the bracing atmosphere of the Devon fishing-port to the smug utilitarian virtues of our artificial middle class. The book is virtually a direct record of his experiences among the fisher-folk, on the beach, in their homes, and in their daily labours on the sea, all which, with their personal traits, their manners, and their racy conversation, are hit off with an accuracy at times almost too conscientious. [Cape, 1928; Lane, New York: o.p.]

—— *Alongshore*.   1910
Twenty-six sketches of much the same subject under different aspects. Impressionist drawings of the actual nautical life of these mariners, their feats of craft and courage, their spicy talk and shrewd science of life, and, further, of the dramatic moods of the sea. [Macmillan: o.p.]

" RHOSCOMYL, Owen " [Capt. Owen Vaughan; Welsh]. *The Jewel of Ynys Galon*.   1895
A romance of Welsh piracy in the times of Sir Henry Morgan, the buccaneer (1635 ?–88); a mixture of adventure and legendary lore concerning a famous gem. [Longmans: o.p.]

—— *Battlement and Tower*.   1896
Adventure and history; the Civil War in North Wales (1644–5), the siege of Conway Castle, battle of Naseby, etc. [Longmans: o.p.]

—— *For the White Rose of Arno*.   1897
The story of the Welsh share in the Jacobite conspiracies that took effect in the 1745 rising and the march to Derby; claims to throw fresh light on those events. [Longmans: o.p.]

—— *The Shrouded Face*.   1898
A Carnarvonshire romance of war and love, claiming to be an historically accurate view of the turbulent Wales of the Elizabethan epoch. [Pearson: o.p.]

RHYS, Ernest [Welsh; *b.* 1859]. *The Whistling Maid*.   1900
An imaginative romance, in William Morris's style, of Edward II's time (*c.* 1325). The adventures of a high-born damsel, abducted by a half-crazed uncle, who tries to marry her to his adopted son. [Hutchinson: o.p.]

—— *The Man at Odds*.   1904
Smugglers, pirates, and detectives of Lundy and the Severn (1745). Disconnected, but has the right romantic atmosphere. Touches on the Methodist revival in Wales. [Hurst: o.p.]

RHYS, Grace [Mrs. Ernest Rhys, *née* Little; Irish; 1865–1929]. *Mary Dominie*.   1898
A tragic story of a peasant's seduction by the landowner's son and the long-delayed retribution that falls upon him, in the time of the land war. [Dent: o.p.]

—— *The Wooing of Sheila*.   1901
A fresh and simple idyll, with some touches of tragedy; a gentleman bringing up his son as a common labourer, and the latter marrying a peasant girl, after killing a young squire who tries to seduce her. The characters are farming people, small squires, servants, and labourers, and in their portrayal the authoress has seized much of the peculiar charm of the Irish temperament. [Methuen: o.p.; Holt, New York: o.p.]

—— *The Prince of Lisnover*.   1904
A boy and girl love-tale of Ireland in the sixties, by one who was born among the Irish peasantry and is always on their side. The story brings out strongly the devotion of the peasants to their old dispossessed lords. [Methuen: o.p.]

—— *The Charming of Estercel*.   1913
A poetical romance of Ulster at the time (1598–9) of the rebellion of Hugh O'Neill, Earl of Tyrone, and the

RHYS, Grace (*continued*).
expedition of Essex. History, however, is a minor element, compared with the passion for wild nature. The great horse Tamburlaine is as important a character as the famous destrier Bayard in *Renaud de Montauban*. [Dent.]

RHŶS, Sir John [Welsh], and J. Gwenogvryn EVANS [Welsh]. [eds.]. *Old Welsh Texts.* 1887
Vol. i., *Y Llyvyr Coch o Hergest (Red Book of Hergest I), Mabinogion*; vol. ii., *Black Book of Carmarthen*; vol. iii., *Red Book of Hergest II, Gyfrol, y Brutien*; vol. iv., *Book of Llan Dav (Liber Landaviensis)*; vol. v., *Book of Aneirin.* Reproductions of the great Welsh texts, some in facsimile, the others in different type exhibiting the differences of characters in the original MSS. The *Mabinogion*, the *Brut y Tywysogion, Brut y Saeson*, and other *Bruts* (of high historical and topographical importance as well as literary), the romance of Dares Phrygius, the Welsh version of Geoffrey of Monmouth's *History*, and a number of documents the main value of which is historical. The whole equipped with palæographical notes and other editorial illustrations, indexes giving modern place-names, autotype facsimiles, etc. [Privately printed, Oxford.]

RICE, Alice Caldwell [*née* Hegan ; American ; *b.* 1870]. *Mrs. Wiggs of the Cabbage Patch.* 1901
—— *Lovey Mary* [sequel]. 1903
—— *Sandy.* 1905
—— *Captain June.* 1907
—— *Mr. Opp.* 1909
Half-comic, half-pathetic stories, with a strong dash of not unwholesome sentiment, that might have been fathered by the Dickens of *A Christmas Carol*, though the humour has the right American flavour. The favourite scene is on the outskirts of a town, where the brave widow, Mrs. Wiggs, the orphan, Lovey Mary, and other children, old and young, talk delightfully and distinguish themselves in domestic emergencies. Sandy is an Irish stowaway. Mr. Opp is the great-hearted proprietor of the *Opp Eagle*, and, like all Mrs. Rice's best characters, a charming blend of the sublime and the ridiculous.
[All Century Co., New York ; (1) and (2), Hodder ; (3), (4) and (5), *id.*, o.p.]
—— *Quin.* 1921
An amusing trifle : the courtship of an aristocratic girl by an impecunious but enterprising young fellow. [Century Co., New York.]
—— *The Buffer.* 1929
A well-constructed didactic novel, on the old lines, with a number of familiar types, and among them an arrant example of a self-complacent clergyman. [Century Co., New York ; Hodder.]

RICHARDSON, Dorothy [Mrs. Alan Odle]. *Pointed Roofs.* 1915
The first of a series, *Pilgrimage*, forming the mental history of Miriam Henderson, through whose impressions from moment to moment the novelist gives the very sense of life, " the stream of consciousness " flowing incessantly on ; in short, it is a thorough-going example of " expressionism." This is the beginning, so far as there can be a beginning to such an amorphous thing. Miriam has entered upon life by breaking away from her home in England and teaching in a school in Hanover. Her casual relations with her colleagues and the girls, and her feelings about it all, are the staple of the record. [Duckworth ; Knopf, New York : o.p.]
—— *Backwater.* 1916
Aged eighteen, Miriam is back in London, to work as a governess in a school for the daughters of gentlemen. She continues the steady chronicle of her reactions to the world about her ; the trivial and the significant are all mixed up in the struggle to penetrate to inmost reality. [Duckworth ; Knopf, New York : o.p.]
—— *Honeycomb.* 1917
Here she is oppressed by the urgency of finding out whether Eve, her bosom friend, shares her feeling that she must go on registering her experiences " or lose hold of some essential thing." " The Kingdom of God is *within* you " : that is the inspiration of many passages of lyrical impressionism, alternating with acute and humorous bits of character-sketching, all, of course, discerned through Miriam's moods. [Duckworth ; Knopf, New York : o.p.]
—— *The Tunnel.* 1919
Clerk and lady-in-waiting to a flourishing firm of dentists in Wimpole Street, Miriam finds herself one of a circle of cultivated people. Casual talk and less pointless discussions go on, of all sorts of things—music, composers, freethinkers, shorthand-typists, and people, people ; with Miriam's critical reflections. We know more than we want about dentistry before we have finished. [Duckworth ; Knopf, New York : o.p.]
—— *Interim.* 1919
Life in a Bloomsbury boarding-house, work in Wimpole Street, talks with lodging-house keepers and the like, reveries in the street or in bed—so it goes on, with the continuity of a kinematograph. [Duckworth ; Knopf, New York : o.p.]
—— *Deadlock.* 1921
Miriam in love, which turns to disenchantment and deadlock. But for the time being she is more than ever alive to the beauty of outer things and of other people's experiences. In long walks about streets and parks, she explains England to her Russian fellow-boarder and exchanges ideas on most things under the sun. [Duckworth ; Knopf, New York.]
—— *Revolving Lights.* 1923
—— *The Trap.* 1925
—— *Oberland.* 1928
Further instalments of Miriam's life ; we take leave of her at the close of a holiday in Switzerland. No more have appeared ; but *Oberland* is in no sense a conclusion. [(1), (2) and (3), Duckworth ; Knopf, New York.]

RICHARDSON (Henrietta) [Mrs. J. G. Robertson, " Henry Handel Richardson "; Australian].
Maurice Guest. 1909
A satirical affairs in a university town on the Continent furnish the background to this novel of character. Miss Richardson came to the Conservatorium of Leipzig from her native Melbourne to study the piano, and here drew freely on her observations of life. [Heinemann ; Duffield, New York.]
—— *The Getting of Wisdom.* 1910
A satirical picture of a girls' school (the Presbyterian Ladies College in Melbourne was the original) and of the mistakes, scrapes, and quandaries of a girl from the country. [Heinemann : o.p. ; Duffield, New York.]
—— *Chronicles of the Fortunes of Richard Mahony—Australia Felix.* 1917
—— —— *The Way Home.* 1925
—— —— *Ultima Thule.* 1929
Based on early recollections, talks with former colonists, and research amongst Government files in Victoria, this trilogy surveys Australian history from the fifties onwards. It centres in the career of a medical man, who does brilliantly in Ballarat but comes to grief financially. He is a wrong-headed, irritable person, and leads his admirable wife a terrible dance without forfeiting her devotion. In the harrowing third volume, he goes from bad to worse, antagonising everyone in a village in the Back Blocks, and ending insane. The bulletin of his illness, the brutalities of the asylum, the details of the funeral, and the bewildered chatter of his innocent boy and girl, intensify the agony. The strength of the work is in the solidity and depth and vitality of the character-building. [(1), (2) and (3), Heinemann ; Norton, New York ; in 1 vol., *sub tit. The Fortunes of Richard Mahony,* Heinemann, 1930.]

RICHARDSON, Major John [Scots-Canadian ; 1796–1852]. *Wacousta ; or, The Prophecy ; a tale of the Canadas.* 1832
The importance of this novel, which is crammed with exciting incident and avowedly modelled upon the work of Fenimore Cooper, lies in its description at first hand of the early days of Canadian history, and of Indian warfare, in particular the rising under Pontiac, chief of the Ottawas, and his attack on Fort Detroit (1763). The author's grandfather was British commandant at Fort Amhurstburg. [Doubleday, Doran, New York ; *illus.,* Sully, New York, 1925.]
—— *The Canadian Brothers : or, The Prophecy Fulfilled. A tale of the late American War* [sequel].
1840
A graphic account, based on the author's own experiences, of the war of 1812, in which Richardson fought. Scenes, Amhurstburg, Kentucky (where he was imprisoned), and Queenstown. The story was re-written and toned down for publication in New York, *sub tit. Matilda Montgomerie* (1851). [o.p.]

RICHARDSON, Norval [American ; b. 1877]. *The Heart of Hope.* 1905
A Civil War novel, dealing with the siege of Vicksburg (1863–4). [Dodd & Mead, New York : o.p.]
—— *The Lead of Honour.* 1910
An adventure-story of 1830, dealing with Mississippi and Natchez (Adam's County). [Burt, New York : o.p. ; Pitman : o.p.]

RICHARDSON, Samuel [1689–1761]. *Pamela, or, Virtue Rewarded.* 1740–2
A didactic novel written in letters of great prolixity and minuteness, the outcome of a project for utilizing Richardson's epistolary gift to furnish people of all classes with examples of polite letter-writing and of just and prudent behaviour. The story of a maidservant of good and prudent upbringing whose virtue is pertinaciously assailed by her master. Epoch-making in literature as a study of the female heart. The point of view and the natural feelings of an ignorant, shrewd, pious, and practical girl of humble station are faithfully interpreted. Richardson's prudential scheme of morality provoked Fielding to write *Joseph Andrews* (1742). The second part of *Pamela* (1742) is dull and almost unreadable. [(Everyman's Lib.) Dent (Dutton, New York) ; Richardson's *Works,* ed. by Leslie Stephen, 12 vols., 1883 : o.p. ; 20 vols., Chapman : o.p. ; 19 vols., Pickering Club Classics, 1905 : o.p. ; 19 vols., Shakespeare Head Ed., Blackwell, Oxford, 1930.]
—— *Clarissa Harlowe ; or, The History of a Young Lady.* 1748
Richardson's masterpiece—the history of a beautiful woman sacrificed to a heartless libertine—written in letters, with a stronger leavening of dialogue, but the same minute, methodical realism in the anatomizing of mental states. Richardson describes the play of impulse and feeling with the same superabundance of relevant and irrelevant detail as Defoe used in describing physical occurrences. Dr. Johnson said that a single letter in one of his novels contained more knowledge of the human heart than the whole of *Tom Jones.* The book had enormous influence on European literature, inspiring Rousseau and arousing the enthusiasm of Diderot. [Abridged edition, Routledge, (Dutton, New York) : o.p. ; Holt, New York, 1922.]
—— *The History of Sir Charles Grandison, Bart.* 1753
Undertaken as a retort to those critics who thought Lovelace, the undoer of Clarissa, too attractive : Richardson's idea of a complete gentleman. Sir Charles is a wealthy and accomplished man of fashion, endowed with every possible virtue, adored by women, etc. The exemplary young English girl who eventually wins his hand is much the inferior of the tragic Clementina who loses him. Like *Clarissa,* it was originally published in seven vols, and contains about fifty characters portrayed with enormous detail in interminable letters. [Abridged ed., Routledge (Dutton, New York). *Letters from Sir Charles Grandison,* selected by George Saintsbury, 1904.]

RICHINGS, Emily A. *Broken at the Fountain.* 1916
A retelling of the well-known story of the pathetic Inez de Castro and her secret marriage to the Crown Prince of Portugal (1340–55). [Heath : o.p.]

RICHMOND, Grace (Louise) [*née* Smith ; b. 1866]. *At the South Gate.* 1928
A pleasant romance, about an unsuccessful author and his wife, who repay the hospitality of wealthy friends by reforming them from fast living. [Methuen ; Doubleday, Doran, New York.]

RICHTER, Jean Paul Friedrich [German; 1763–1825]. *The Invisible Lodge* (Die unsichtbare Loge, 1793). 1883
A romance containing a good deal of allegory and poetical criticism on man and his position in the world, the dualism of his spiritual and carnal nature, and the mockery of human society. A young author is educated by a genie in an underground dwelling, that he may behold nature with soul unspoiled—an imaginary version of Richter's own emotional life. [Transl. by C. T. BROOKS, Holt, New York: o.p.]

—— *Hesperus; or, Forty-five Dog-Post Days* (1794). 1865
Another poetical romance, very much involved, and embracing a great number of personages. The mystical hero loves a semi-divine being, an idealization of woman. Told in letters brought to the author by a dog. [2 vols., Trübner: o.p.; 2 vols., Holt, New York: o.p.]

—— *Flower, Fruit, and Thorn Pieces; or, The Married Life, Death, and Wedding of Firmian Stanislaus Siebenkaes, Parish Advocate in the Parish of Kuhschnappel* (Blumen-, Frucht-, und Dornenstücke, 1796). 1845
A strange combination of real life, dream, and philosophic reverie; the plot, thin and vague as always in Jean Paul—incidents in the history of an ill-assorted marriage between a poet and a good, dull woman. The upshot is fantastic and equally vague. The poet is made happy by the beautiful Natalie, a personification of feeling, imagination, poetry. De Quincey borrowed several of his grandiose dream-pieces from this book, which contains *The Dead Christ*, and other prose-poems. [Transl. by E. H. NOEL (with memoir by Carlyle), Smith: o.p.; 2 vols., Tickner & Fields, Boston, 1863: o.p.; transl. by A. EWING (Bohn's Lib.), Bell, (Macmillan, New York), 1877: o.p.]

—— *Quintus Fixlein* (Leben des Quintus Fixlein, 1796). 1827
Much in the same vein of domestic fiction, perhaps a little nearer to actuality; the style just as whimsical and digressive, pirouetting like a tumbler, incapable of plainness or simplicity, except in passages of deep feeling, where Richter becomes simple, straightforward, powerful, e.g. Fixlein and Thiennette's awakening to love. Passion in its divinest and chastest is expressed here in characters the most moving and spontaneous. Some of the grandest examples of Jean Paul's cosmic eloquence are in this book. [Transl. by T. CARLYLE, in *The Campagner Thal; and other writings*, Ticknor, Boston, 1864: o.p.]

—— *Titan: a romance* (1799–1803). 1862
Like the foregoing, the history of certain problematic characters, and of the reaction of the real world upon a priori theories and ideals. Chief personage, a German prince, who is brought up in ignorance of his rank, and ascends the throne as an enlightened monarch, destined to be a blessing to his people. Among other figures whose natures are of an exaggerated, "titanic" order, is the heroine, studied from Mme von Kalb, "the Aspasia of Weimar"; she is a woman of great talents and self-reliance, who has no religion or law but the dictates of her own being; and this, the tragedy teaches, is her ruin. In *Flegeljähre* (1804–5) Richter makes another attempt to realize his ideal of human personality, but as usual digresses widely from his philosophic object. See also Carlyle's *Translations from the German* (p. 93). [Transl. by C. T. BROOKS, 2 vols., Trübner: o.p.]

RICKERT, Martha Edith [American; b. 1871]. *Out of the Cypress Swamp.* 1902
A romance of Louisiana (1808–15); a strong, impassioned situation rising out of the question of colour, the hero, an octoroon, marrying a white woman. Adventures among the pirates of the Gulf of Mexico, the defence of New Orleans against the English, etc., with glowing descriptions of the country. [Methuen: o.p.]

—— *Golden Hawk.* 1907
A romance of Provence in the fourteenth century, and Avignon, then the residence of the Pope. [Baker & Taylor, New York: o.p.; Arnold: o.p.]

RIDDING, Lady Laura. *By Weeping Cross.* 1899
A simple and pathetic story, bringing before us in pictorial description the life of southern France in the period 1424–83—idyllic country life, beauty and romance, with horrors hard by. [Hodder: o.p.]

RIDGE, William Pett [1860?–1930]. *Mord Em'ly.* 1898
Life in south London slums, sketched by a keen-eyed, facetious observer, who is inclined to see things through a rose-coloured atmosphere. Mord Em'ly is the daughter of a charwoman and a convict, a mixture of generosity and self-reliance, with a taste for excitement that gets her into trouble. Domestic service, a "home," and life as waitress in a cheap eating-house, are her main experiences before she escapes to a comfortable marriage. [Pearson.]

—— *Outside the Radius: stories of a London suburb.* 1899
Fifteen tales portraying the manners, behaviour, humours and character of lower middle-class people, domestic servants, etc.; the themes mostly light and facetious or sentimental. [Hodder: o.p.; Dodd & Mead, New York: o.p.]

—— *A Son of the State.* 1899
The life of a young street-arab from Hoxton, who goes through a reformatory and a training-ship, developing in due course into a gallant sailor. Realism of the pleasant kind; the personal traits, the slang and repartee of the young people, and their precocious notions of life, detailed with much facetiousness. [Methuen: o.p.; Dodd & Mead, New York: o.p.]

—— *A Breaker of Laws.* 1900
Another sentimental study of Cockney character; the hero a rascal of an engaging kind, good-humoured, and full of mother-wit, a burglar who tries to reform, out of love for his wife, a simple Devonshire lass, but goes astray again to his own undoing. [Methuen: o.p.; Macmillan, New York: o.p.]

—— *London Only: a set of common occurrences.* 1901
Sympathetic sketches of the most commonplace varieties of life in London; the life of the streets, the shops, the middle-class and lower-class homes. [Hodder: o.p.]

—— *Lost Property.* 1902
The fortunes of a foundling, with sketches of the people she is thrown amongst on the fringe of the lower middle class and the poor. [Methuen: o.p.]

RIDGE, William Pett (*continued*). *Erb.*   1903
> Another good-humoured sketch of the same social grade, that of the small shopkeeper, the clerk, and the factory girl. Erb is a carman with a misguided zeal for Spencer, a socialist agitator with the " gift of the gab." [Methuen : o.p. ; Appleton, New York : o.p.]

—— *Mrs. Galer's Business.*   1905
> The story of a Clerkenwell laundress and her son. [Methuen : o.p.]

—— *On Company's Service.*   1905
> Life in the service of a great railway company. [Hodder : o.p.]

—— *Name of Garland.*   1907
> Rather better connected than most of these stories, and adorned with a very attractive character, the servant-girl Winnie Garland. Particularly good also in sketching the fine shades of class feeling and manners among the petty suburban people Mr. Ridge knew so intimately. [Methuen : o.p.]

—— *Splendid Brother.*   1909
> The pseudo-hero, clever, ingratiating, unscrupulous, imposes to the end on the admiring love of his mother and a stupid, but good and successful brother, the supposed biographer. Lifelike minor characters from the mean streets of New Cross and elsewhere. [Methuen : o.p.]

—— *Thanks to Sanderson.*   1911
> The homely affairs of a ticket-collector on the railway, his wife, and their son and daughter—a story with some sadness in it, which the author attenuates with his habitual facetiousness. [Long.]

—— *Madame Prince.*   1916
> The cheering history of the efforts of a mother, head of a dress-making establishment at Highgate, to bring up a family of four children. [Methuen : o.p. ; Doran, New York : o.p.]

—— *Top Speed.*   1918
> The principal character is " Pa," a dairyman of sterling qualities—a typical example of this author's London types. [Methuen.]

—— *The Bustling Hours.*   1919
> The heroine binds up an airman's leg in Regent's Park in the first chapter, and marries him in the last. [Methuen : o.p.]

—— *Well-to-do Arthur.*   1920
> An amusing story of reckless young people in Wood Green at the close of the war. [Methuen : o.p.]

—— *Bannerton's Agency.*   1921
> Another typical story of London life ; the heroine, an efficient and affectionate girl, redeems the errors of her rather foolish husband. [Methuen.]

—— *Miss Mannering.*   1923
—— *Rare Luck.*   1924
—— *Just like Aunt Bertha.*   1925
> Further similar stories of London types. [All Methuen.]

RIDLEY [Alice, Lady, *née* Davenport]. *Anne Mainwaring.*   1901
> A society woman's daughter marries without love in order to escape the uncongenial ties of social life and to practise her art, then falls in love with another man. [Longman : o.p.]

RIIS, Jacob August [American ; 1849–1914]. *How the Other Half Lives.*   1895
—— *Children of the Tenements.*   1903
> The writer was a well-known sociologist and agitator in the cause of social reform. He was a police reporter in New York, and took an active part in the small-parks movement and in tenement-house reform. These books are really sociological studies. [(1), Scribner, New York ; (2), Macmillan, New York.]

RILEY, William [*b.* 1866]. *Windyridge.*   1912
—— *Thro' a Yorkshire Window.*   1919
—— *Windyridge Revisited.*   1928
> Pen-portraits of dalesmen and daleswomen, farmers, the postmaster, the village constable, various idlers, and the delightful old vicar. [(1), (2) and (3), Jenkins ; (1), Appleton, New York.]

—— *Jerry and Ben.*   1919
> A couple of spinsters in a West Riding cottage and their dalesfolk neighbours are carefully drawn. [Jenkins.]

—— *Witch Hazel.*   1929
> A Yorkshire story, with an unconventional heroine who is gifted with second-sight. [Jenkins.]

RILKE, Rainer Maria [German ; 1875–1926]. *The Notebook of Malte Laurids Brigge* (Aufzeichnungen des Malte Laurids Brigge, 1908).   1930
> In the form of a fictitious life of a Danish poet in Paris, Rilke in this book wrote the inner history of his own childhood, and produced one of the most profound and beautiful works of self-revelation extant. Rilke was a poet, and this is the imaginative realism of a poet ; full of pain and sorrow, intensely affecting, but never in the least distorted by personal feeling or sentimentalism. [Transl. by John LINTON, Hogarth Press ; *sub tit. The Journal of My Other Self*, Norton, New York.]

RINDER, Edith Wingate [tr.]. *The Massacre of the Innocents ; and other tales by Belgian writers.*   1895
> *Massacre of the Innocents*, by M. Maeterlinck ; *Kors Davie, Ex Voto, Hiep-Hioup*, by G. Eekhoud ; *Fleur-de-Blé, St. Nicholas' Eve*, by C. Lemonnier ; *Trompe-la-Mort*, by A. Jenart ; *Pierre de la Baraque*, by L. Delattre ; *Shadowy Bourne*, by S. Richelle ; *Jacclard*, by G. Ganir ; *The Nile of St. Peter*, by E. Demolder ; *Mountebanks*, by H. Urdins. [Stone, Chicago : o.p.]

RING, Barbra [Norwegian ; *b.* 1870]. *Into the Dark* (Før kulden kommer, 1915).   1921
> Barbra Ring's other works are for young people. This is a tragic novel which will not be least memorable

RING, Barbra (*continued*).
 for its incidental wisdom and flashes of insight. It is the " confession " of a young woman who marries a man with whom she finds she has nothing in common—the end, her suicide. [Transl. by W. Emmé, Gyldendal : o.p. ; Knopf, New York.]

RIORDAN, Roger, and TAKAYANAGI Tozo [Japanese] [eds.]. *Sunrise Stories.* 1896
 Twenty examples of mediæval and modern Japanese legend and fiction. [Kegan Paul : o.p.]

RISING, Lawrence [American]. *Proud Flesh.* 1924
 An intimate picture of San Francisco and its society, a generation ago. [Boni, New York ; Unwin.]

RITCHIE, Mrs. David George. *The Human Cry.* 1911
 A slight tale, unfolding the tragedy of inherited madness, and analysing the mental crudities of a clever, unstable woman who thinks she has a mission, which she attempts to realize in turn in the Church, in politics, and in a vague theosophy. [Methuen : o.p.]

—— *The New Warden.* 1918
 The Warden of King's becomes infatuated with the empty-headed daughter of a scheming mother. There are other entertaining characters. [Murray.]

RIVES, Amélie [Mrs. J. A. Chanler, now Princess Troubetzkoy ; American ; b. 1863]. *Virginia of Virginia.* 1888
 An emotional story of passion, the chief figure being a half-savage girl, who atones for a sin by a deed of splendid generosity. [Harper, New York : o.p. ; Routledge : o.p.]

—— *The Quick or the Dead.* 1889
 A frank exposure of the doubts, hesitations, and repulsions of a young widow, who has loved her husband deeply, and now finds herself falling hopelessly in love with his younger cousin, who is his very image. [Lippincott, Philadelphia ; Routledge : o.p.]

—— *Barbara Dering* [sequel]. 1893
 A study of problems rather than of people, similarly frank in portrayal of passion, and of interest as a woman's view of the other sex. [Lippincott, Philadelphia : o.p. ; Chatto : o.p.]

—— *Tanis, the Sang-Digger.* 1894
 A wild, passionate girl of the Southern mountains, and her awakening to more spiritual ideas of love—a savage nature fighting against its lower impulses. The barbarous dialect is reproduced. [*Town Topics* Pub. Co., New York : o.p.]

RIVES, Hallie Erminie [Mrs. Post Wheeler ; American ; b. 1878]. *A Furnace of Earth.* 1900
 A study of morbid self-consciousness. A sensitive, introspective girl gets it into her head that she does not love her fiancé in the right way, and they part, becoming reconciled only after much needless suffering. [Camelot Co., New York : o.p. ; De La More Press : o.p.]

—— *Hearts Courageous.* 1902
 Scene laid in the colony of Virginia during the momentous days of determination for independence and the formation of the new republic, with character-sketch of Patrick Henry (1774–81). [Bobbs-Merrill, Indianapolis.]

—— *The Long Lane's Turning.* 1917
 Illustrates the evils of drink in the United States. [Dodd & Mead, New York : o.p. ; Hurst : o.p.]

ROBERTS, Baron Alexander von [German]. *Lou* (Lou, 1894). 1894
 A pathetic story of a young Nubian slave ; scene, Paris. [Transl. by Jessie Haynes, Heinemann : o.p.]

ROBERTS, Charles George Douglas [native of New Brunswick ; b. 1860]. *Earth's Enigmas.* 1896
 Forest stories ; the life of a logging camp ; the storms, incessant warfare of the beasts, etc. [Lamson : o.p. ; Page, Boston.]

—— *The Forge in the Forest.* 1897
 A romance of Acadia in the times of the French and English wars (1746–7), making good use of the natural surroundings and the primitive life of the colonists. The picturesque Black Abbé figures again in the next story. [Dent ; Page, Boston.]

—— *A Sister to Evangeline : the story of Yvonne de Lamourie.* 1900
 A story of the expulsion of the Acadians (1755), which aims at being fair to both sides. Life in the old days, the lovely aspects of nature in the Annapolis valley, the mysteries of woodcraft, and some unexciting incidents of the war. Longfellow's inspiration is manifest throughout. [Lane : o.p. ; Page, Boston.]

—— *The Heart of the Ancient Wood.* 1901
 Full of intimate and affectionate description of life in the vast forests of the northern parts of the United States : beasts and birds, woodcraft and human life, share the interest. A sort of North American *Jungle Book*, with animals as characters. The human actors are a mother and her little daughter who flee from the settlement into the wilderness. [Methuen ; Dent ; Page, Boston.]

—— *Barbara Ladd.* 1902
 A nature book with clever portraiture of animals. The story, what there is of it, relates to the love of a young loyalist for the rebel Barbara. Scenes : Maryland and Connecticut (1769–78). [Constable : o.p. ; Page Boston.]

—— *The Prisoner of Mademoiselle.* 1905
 A romantic story of a Boston captain and a charming Frenchwoman, in the times of the wars with the French. The finest part of the book is the description of nature in the vast Acadian forests. [Constable : o.p. ; Page, Boston.]

—— *The Backswoodsmen.* 1909
 Miscellaneous stories and sketches of the human and the wild life of the forest. [Ward & Lock ; Macmillan, New York.]

ROBERTS, Charles George Douglas (*continued*). *The Ledge on Bald Face.* 1918
The characters are eagles, bears, bull-moose, cocks, hawks, dogs, and some "humans," chiefly Americans. A most poetical war-tale is *The Eagle*. [Ward & Lock.]

—— *In the Morning of Time.* 1919
The prelude shows "the World without Man." The story is of primeval man and woman. [Dent; Stokes, New York.]

ROBERTS, Charles Humphrey [American; *b.* 1847]. *Down the O-hi-o.* 1891
Presents a series of vivid scenes of rural life among the Quakers on the north bank of the Ohio in the period just before the Civil War. [McClurg, Chicago : o.p.]

ROBERTS, Elizabeth Madox [American; *b.* 1885]. *The Time of Man.* 1926
The first novel of a Kentucky poetess. A very earnest, patient chronicle of a woman's life, through childhood, adolescence, marriage, and motherhood : a homely record, in which the petty domestic things bulk large, as we perceive them through this sensitive mind. Though it is all so solemn and so devoid of humour, there is some compensation in the poetry that somehow exhales from the backgrounds and the pastoral atmosphere. [Viking Press, New York ; Çape.]

—— *My Heart and my Flesh.* 1927
Adopts the expressionist technique of Dorothy Richardson and Virginia Woolf to exhibit the "stream of consciousness" in a girl from childhood to womanhood. She has musical talent ; but as the daughter of the Don Juan of a Kentucky village who has made her the half-sister of mulattoes and degenerates, she is dogged by poverty and defeat. A hideous picture is left on the reader's mind of these country-people's ignorance and squalor, and a brutishness worse than that of the animals they slaughter—with complete inhumanity. [Viking Press, New York ; Cape.]

—— *Jingling in the Wind.* 1928
A strange and not very comprehensible fantasy, the story of a miraculous rain-maker ; with some excursions into satire, on fundamentalism, advertising, medical rejuvenation, and other recent crazes. [Viking Press, New York ; Cape.]

—— *The Great Meadow.* 1930
A saga-like narrative of the long trek of the Virginians who followed Daniel Boone in 1777 to Caintuck and Harrod's Fort, combined with a rather stilted Enoch Arden story of a woman whose husband disappeared, to return when she had married again. Dwells on the spiritual dilemma when she has to choose between the two fathers of her children. [Introd. by Edward Garnett, Viking Press, New York ; Cape.]

ROBERTS, Margaret [*b.* 1833]. *Mademoiselle Mori : a tale of modern Rome.* 1860
Life in Rome during the insurrectionary period (1846–9). Domestic life of the orphan children of an English artist, their struggle with adversity and twofold love-story. Then private matters merge in public events, historic names and incidents come in, and there is a full account of the French siege of Rome. [Longmans : o.p.]

—— *The Atelier du Lys.* 1876
Life of an art student during the Reign of Terror (1793–5), mainly a story of private interest, with plenty of local colouring. The young heroine is the object of villainous machinations, which are happily frustrated. [Longmans : o.p. ; *id.,* New York.]

—— *In the Olden Time.* 1883
A tale of the Peasants' War in Germany (1524–5) ; scenes, the Thuringian forest and Tyrol. [Longmans : o.p.]

—— *The Fiddler of Lugau.* 1888
Home and civic life in a town of Saxony during the Napoleonic wars, with the petty animosities and public fears, and a pathetic story of love and loyalty. [Hatchard : o.p. ; Whittaker, New York : o.p.]

ROBERTS, Morley [*b.* 1857]. *In Low Relief.* 1890
A realistic story of bohemian life ; the hero an art critic, the heroine a model. But the realism is not merely superficial—it interprets the thoughts and ideals of men who inhabit a different world from the conventional. [Chapman : o.p. ; Appleton, New York : o.p.]

—— *The Earth-Mother.* 1896
A sculptor wreaks vengeance on a treacherous friend, and hides the body in a colossal statue of the "Earth-Mother." Dread of discovery and the irony of events drive him to suicide. [Downey : o.p.]

—— *The Great Jester : some jests of Fate.* 1896
Eighteen short stories of all kinds of life and from all over the globe ; scenes of wild colonial life in British Columbia and Australia, scenes afloat, and domestic scenes usually turning on unlawful passion. All express a fatalistic and sombre idea of life, many deal with the hallucinations of distempered minds. [Mentz : o.p.]

—— *Maurice Quain.* 1897
A study of London life below the surface, which strongly resembles some of Zola's novels in piling up details into one vast overpowering image endowed with a life of its own and having a shaping influence over the lives of men. The hero is a man whose will-power has been sapped by the deadly allurements of the city. The plot brings together people who are outside the pale of respectability, and the morality is the glorification of strength made popular by Rudyard Kipling. [Hutchinson : o.p.]

—— *A Sea Comedy.* 1899
A yarn, Rabelaisian in its broad humour, about a ship and a crew of ruined and lawless miners homeward bound from Australia, and the queer adventures that befell them. [Milne : o.p.]

—— *A Son of Empire.* 1899
Portrait of a strenuous soldier and explorer, with the complicated history of his persecution by his superiors and salvation by a clever girl—perhaps inspired by the story of Sir Richard and Lady Burton. [Hutchinson : o.p. ; Lippincott, Philadelphia : o.p.]

ROBERTS, Morley (*continued*). *The Colossus.* 1899

A mixture of fact and fiction about a man (for whom Cecil Rhodes is obviously the model), with grandiose schemes for the exploitation of Africa, and how these were affected by a woman's falling in love with him (1853–1902). [Arnold : o.p. ; Harper, New York : o.p.]

—— *The Descent of the Duchess.* 1900

An amusing trifle about a duchess who falls out of a train in embarrassing circumstances. [o.p.]

—— *The Plunderers.* 1900

A third of these combinations of romance and realism aiming to glorify physical force and jingoism. The history of a sort of " Jameson Raid," conceived by a Foreign Office clerk and put into effect by two daring Englishmen and an Albanian, to carry off the jewels of the Shah from Teheran. [Methuen : o.p.]

—— *Taken by Assault.* 1901

Love and adventure in the last Boer War and on the veld (1900–1). The indomitable hero gets into Pretoria to rescue a man, as the price of his betrothal to the heroine. [Sands : o.p.]

—— *Immortal Youth.* 1902

Irregular life and irregular love among artists' models and unsuccessful literary men in bohemian Chelsea. Parker Fullerton, hard-headed, cynical, but generous and passionately in love, and the Pandemian Sara, are striking characters. An emancipated and daringly tolerant philosophy of life is set forth in rather high-flown style. [Hutchinson : o.p.]

—— *Rachael Marr.* 1903

A powerful drama set in a Cornish village—the conflict between Rachael, a free child of Nature typical of the spirit of vital womanhood, and Anthony Perran her lover, a Puritan to whom all beauty seems evil. [Nash (1925) ; Knopf, New York.]

—— *The Blue Peter : sea comedies.* 1906

Five broad farces, largely at the expense of objectionable skippers, crimps, and conscienceless shipowners. The coarse humour and profanity of the modern sailorman reproduced without stint. [Nash : o.p. ; Page, Boston : o.p.]

—— *The Private Life of Henry Maitland : a record dictated by J. H.* 1912

This is the life of Gissing, with the names of persons and places changed : Harold Edgewood is Frederic Harrison ; John Harley, John Morley (the *Piccadilly Gazette* is the *Pall Mall Gazette*) ; John Glass, James Payn ; G. H. Rivers, H. G. Wells ; Edward Latter, Clement K. Shorter ; Edmund Roden, Edward Clodd. [Nash ; Doran, New York : o.p.]

—— *Time and Thomas Waring.* 1914

A middle-aged journalist, as a result of an operation, is led to review and make drastic alterations in his attitude to life, particularly towards his wife, daughter, and mistress. [Nash : o.p. ; Putnam, New York : o.p.]

—— *Ancient Mariners.* 1919

Racy and humorous nautical yarns, using—perhaps too freely—the sailor's vernacular. [Mills & Boon : o.p.]

—— *Hearts of Women.* 1919

Definitely a piece of special pleading for alteration in the marriage and divorce laws. [Nash : o.p.]

—— *The Mirthful Nine.* 1921

Nine farcical tales, based upon various eccentricities of character. [Nash.]

ROBERTS, Morley, and MONTESOLE, Max. *The Shadow of Allah.* 1900

Adventures of a Circassian in Constantinople, related by himself ; sensational intrigues and multifarious incident, side by side with views of life and politics and social movements, of the Western ideals of the Young Turkish party, and the stern piety of older patriots. [Long : o.p.]

ROBERTSON, Miss Frances Forbes [" Frances Harrod "]. *The Taming of the Brute.* 1905

A quixotic young lady undertakes to civilize an uncouth and degraded cousin, living among peasants in a remote corner of Wales. Fancy-dress scenes in the Pump-Room at Bath in the eighteenth century. [Methuen : o.p.]

ROBERTSON, William [Scottish]. *The Kings of Carrick : a historical romance of the Kennedys of Ayrshire.* [second edn.] 1890

First edn. entitled *The Kennedys.* Describes the terrible feud between the Cassillis Kennedys and the Kennedys of Bargany. John Mure of Auchendrane is the protagonist, and his death is the catastrophe of the tale. (See also Crockett's *Grey Man*, p. 124.) [o.p.]

—— *The Stone of Dunalter.* 1901

Scottish scenes, Culloden, etc. (1745–6). Local history carefully utilized. [Gardner, Paisley.]

—— *The Dule Tree of Cassillis.* 1904

An episode in the history of the Kennedys, Earls of Cassillis—the unscrupulous attempt of Earl Gilbert to seize the properties of Crossraguel Abbey, the crimes, slaughterings, and revenges that were the consequence (1564–71). See Scott's account in the notes to *Ivanhoe*. [Menzies, Edinburgh : o.p.]

ROBIN HOOD. *The Noble Birth and Gallant Achievements of that Remarkable Outlaw Robin Hood ; together with a true account of the many merry and extravagant exploits he play'd in twelve several stories. Newly collected into one volume by an Ingenious Antiquary.* 1678

A redaction into prose of ballads from the common garlands, most of which appear in Ritson's collection. The editor added a MS. life of the great outlaw, preserved in the Sloane Library ; this is a prose paraphrase of the ancient legend, *A Lytle Geste of Robyn Hode.* The twelve stories recount some of his most famous feats and adventures, such as the fights with the Tanner of Nottingham, with the Beggar, and with the Curtal Fryar (*alias* Friar Tuck, *alias* The Monk of Copmanhurst), his feats of archery, etc. Full of anachronisms. The period is supposed to be that of Henry VIII, instead of the early Angevin period (c. 1160–99). [o.p., but included in W. J. Thoms' *Early English Prose Romances*, see p. 465.]

ROBINS, Elizabeth [Mrs. George Richmond Parks, " C. E. Raimond "; American; *b.* 1862].
George Mandeville's Husband. 1894
Pure comedy ending unexpectedly in doleful tragedy. Some satire on recent features of society : the egotistic and empty authoress who terrorizes her spouse with her conceited faith in her mission may very well have been drawn from life. [Appleton, New York : o.p. ; Heinemann : o.p.]

—— *The New Moon.* 1895
A pathetic version of the not unhackneyed case of a clever man, married prematurely to a silly wife, finding too late a woman he can love. The lovers are strong-minded and self-restrained, but the struggle to be true to their principles is almost too much for human nature. A tragic accident cuts the Gordian knot. [Appleton, New York : o.p. ; Heinemann : o.p.]

—— *The Open Question : a tale of two temperaments.* 1899
A problem of character and heredity, the love of two cousins marked down as victims to consumption. Life and society in the defeated Southern States are both well delineated, and Mrs. Gano, though a subordinate character, is among those racy creations with whom one's memories of a book often become identified. [Harper, New York : o.p. ; Heinemann.]

—— *The Magnetic North.* 1904
A vivid account of the hardships and disappointments suffered by the emigrants on the long Yukon trail, of Eskimo life, and the building and management of a camp by the gold-diggers, is the finest part of this Klondyke novel. The characters are well drawn, but the novel is too full of dialogue and of digressions on the feminist question, etc. [Stokes, New York : o.p. ; Heinemann.]

—— *A Dark Lantern : a story with a prologue.* 1905
An ethical and psychological problem : the heroine, who has the author's sympathies, enters into an illicit union with a doctor. [Macmillan, New York : o.p. ; Heinemann : o.p.]

—— *Come and Find Me !* 1908
Another story of the frozen north and California, equally remarkable as a piece of enthralling narrative : the personal drama rather laboured in the psychology and far less interesting than *The Magnetic North.* [Century Co., New York ; Heinemann : o.p.]

—— *The Florentine Frame.* 1909
A story of fashionable American life, turning on a conflict in love between mother and daughter. The scene of the drama, " Hudson College," is Columbia University. [Moffat, New York : o.p. ; Murray ; Nash.]

—— *Where Are You Going To . . .?* 1913
A powerful and moving story of two sisters, brought up in innocence, who fall victims of the white slave traffic. The elder, who is the narrator, escapes, but her efforts to rescue her sister prove unavailing. [Heinemann ; *sub tit. My Little Sister,* Macauley Co., New York : o.p.]

—— *Camilla.* 1918
The spiritual dilemma of a woman who, though divorced from an unworthy husband, yet feels bound to him, and rejects an attractive and devoted suitor. [Hodder : o.p. ; Dodd & Mead, New York.]

ROBINSON, Agnes Mary Frances [Mme Duclaux, formerly Mme Darmesteter ; *b.* 1857]. *A Mediæval Garland.* 1897
Obscure episodes connected with history, showing chiefly the tragic side of the Middle Ages, and related with tender pathos. Italy and France are the scenes. *The Story of Antonio*—scene, Assisi, the death of St. Francis (1290). *Philip the Leal*—a few scenes in Cherbourg, where Humphrey, Duke of Gloucester, is governor, at the time of Joan of Arc's rising (1429). *The Ballads of the Dauphine*—scene, Chalons, where the Dauphine Margaret, daughter of James I of Scotland, neglected by her husband and persecuted by jealous and suspicious nobles, dies of a broken heart (1446). *Countess of Dammartin*—the great gulf fixed between the vassal and his lord by feudalism. Her husband being driven from his castle, the Countess seeks refuge among his dependants, who repulse her, all save one honest man, who guards and maintains her till the Count returns, and then is repaid by a contemptuous gift (1464). *The True Story of White-Rose and the Fair Sibyl*—the beautiful wife of a jeweller at Metz, is seduced by an English prince, renounced by her husband, and flung into prison by the citizens. She hangs herself at last— another example of the saying that the woman suffers. A story rich with mediæval colour, not without a subtle irony in the telling (1518). [Lawrence & Bullen : o.p.]

ROBINSON, Emma. *Whitefriars ; or, The Court of Charles II.* 1844
A descriptive romance of the Popish Plot, Rye House Plot, Restoration London—Alsatia, the thieves' paradise ; Titus Oates, Col. Blood, Shaftesbury, Buckingham, Charles II, and Claude Duval (1666–83). A glowing tableau of the Great Fire. [Edited by E. A. Baker (Half-forgotten Books), Routledge (Dutton, New York) : o.p. ; (cheap ed.), Funk, New York.]

—— *Whitehall ; or, The Days of Charles I.* 1845
A similar romance of the Civil War, centring in Oxford (1643–9), and crowded with notabilities. [Routledge : o.p.]

—— *Cæsar Borgia.* 1853
Rome and Florence at the time when Charles VIII of France was invading Italy ; Machiavelli and other famous personages figure. [o.p.]

ROBINSON, Frederick William [1830–1901]. *Grandmother's Money.* 1806
Robinson was one of the most industrious producers of novels in the three-volume period, since when he has been almost completely forgotten. His master was Dickens, but he went beyond his master in faithful realism, e.g. *Owen—a Waif* and *Jane Cameron.* He wrote 55 novels. This is a wholesome novel of character presenting average people with their faults and weaknesses as well as their homely virtues. The grandmother with her " unrelenting soul " and deep affections is a lovable being, and the hero, if not of the stuff of which heroes are usually made, is human, and his wife loves him. The plot with the misdoings of the false lover is rather involved. [Hurst & Blackett : o.p.]

—— *Owen—a Waif.* 1862

ROBINSON, Frederick William (*continued*). *Jane Cameron : Memoirs of a Female Convict.* 1863
In these two novels, the first picturing low life in London and the other low life in Glasgow, Robinson's photographic realism, says Theodore Watts-Dunton, reminds one of Defoe. Robinson anticipated the poor-life story of later times, and has had few superiors in humorous and sympathetic delineation of the London arab. [(1), Hutchinson : o.p. ; (2), 2 vols., Hurst & Blackett : o.p.]

—— *Female Life in Prison ; by a Prison Matron.* 1863
Began a series of novels dealing with prison life. This is based on the personal experiences of an actual prison matron. " For perfect realism it was worthy of Defoe " (Watts-Dunton). It was accepted by *The Times*, etc., as an authentic record. [Low : o.p.]

—— *Mattie—a Stray.* 1864
Mattie is a very humble heroine who has to work hard for her living, first as street hawker, then as grocer's book-keeper : but while she is outwardly far removed from the conventional heroines of fiction, her sterling honesty and upright character make her a more admirable type of human nature. The subordinate characters are petty shopkeepers, clerks, and mechanics, the various inhabitants, in short, of a mean quarter in London. [Ward & Lock : o.p.]

—— *Christie's Faith.* 1867
A very popular love-tale. The faith is Christie's faith in her lover. [Chapman : o.p.]

—— *The Courting of Mary Smith.* 1886
The story of a high-minded girl, who inspires a prosaic and illiterate cotton millionaire with a pure, self-abnegating love that seems at first sight incompatible with his character. [Maxwell : o.p.]

ROBINSON, Lennox [Irish ; *b.* 1886]. *A Young Man from the South.* 1917
A novel by a well-known Irish playwright, a former manager of the Abbey Theatre, Dublin. It is the story of a young man brought up as a Unionist and Protestant, who comes to Dublin and is there converted to whole-hearted Nationalism. Though written before the rebellion of 1916, it is a true interpretation of the spirit of the men and women of that time. [Maunsel, Dublin.]

ROBINSON, Maude. *The Time of her Life ; and other stories.* 1919
Studies of Quaker life and character, largely based on facts and introducing historical personages (1682–1875), e.g. Elizabeth Fry in 1817 (*Transported*). [Swarthmore Press : o.p.]

ROBINSON, Rowland Evans [American ; 1833–1900]. *Sam Lovel's Camps ; Uncle 'Lisha's Friends under Bark and Canvas.* 1889
Yarns and pictures of outdoor life and character portraits. The dialect is so closely and phonetically reproduced that Vermonters alone can fully appreciate its curious expressiveness. [Houghton, Boston : o.p.]

—— *Danvis Folks.* 1894
The same villagers of the beautiful region bordering on Lake Champlain, which is described with all the passion and observation of a nature-lover. Rural gossips, true Yankees (of the Vermont blend), honest, virile, and humorous characters ; written in dialect. [Houghton, Boston.]

—— *Uncle 'Lisha's Shop.* 1897
Slightly connected sketches and dialogues portraying a set of originals who meet in a shoemaker's shop in a Vermont village. The talk is unadulterated Yankee, and the book racy of the soil. [Houghton, Boston.]

ROD, Édouard [French-Swiss ; 1857–1910]. *White Rocks* (Les roches blanches, 1895). 1916
Two persons of full integrity, the pastor in a small Vaudois town (" Bielle " is the writer's native Nyon, on the Lake of Geneva) and the wife of a rich parishioner, fall in love, and after an agonizing struggle subdue their passion and resign themselves to the call of duty. The onlookers of the drama, which malicious gossip speedily detects, are drawn, with quiet humour, in all their individual traits. M. Rod's finer novels appear not to have been translated ; e.g. *La vie privée de Michel Teissier* and *L'ombre s'étend sur la montagne.* [Transl. by F. ROTHWELL, Palmer : o.p.]

RODENBERG, Julius [German ; 1831– ?]. *King by the Grace of God* (Von Gottes Gnaden). 1871
A careful study of the men and the politics of the days of Cromwell (*c.* 1646–7), containing life-like portrayals of the Protector, Charles I, Fairfax, and others, and good sketches in Cornet Joyce, the daring captor of the King, and in the hero, a colonel in Cromwell's own regiment. [3 vols., Bentley : o.p.]

RODOCANACHI, Emmanuel Pierre [French ; *b.* 1859]. *Tolla the Courtesan* (Tolla la courtisane ; esquisse de la vie privée à Rome en l'an du Jubilé 1700, 1897). 1905
Private life and manners at Rome. The loves of Tolla Boccadileone with Prince Constantine Sobieski and Don Gaetano Cesarini ; told in letters. Almost severely historical, notes being appended and authorities quoted. [Transl. from French by Frederick LAWTON, Heinemann : o.p.]

RODWAY, James. *In Guiana Wilds.* 1899
Life in an English settlement in Demerara (British Guiana) and among the Indians. An Englishman marries a half-breed, gets into monetary difficulties, and levants. Living among the savages, he marries a chief's daughter according to native rites. [Unwin : o.p.]

RODWELL, George Herbert Buonaparte (1800–52). *Old London Bridge : a romance of the 16th century.* 1849
Rodwell was proprietor of the Adelphi and a musician. This is a sensational version of the story told in more restrained style by Anne Manning in *The Colloquies of Edward Osborne*, the London apprentice who founded the ducal house of Leeds (1536–59). [Edited by E. A. Baker (Half-forgotten Books), Routledge (Dutton, New York) : o.p.]

RODZIEWICZÓWNA, Marya [Polish]. *Devaytis* (Dewajtis, 1889). 1901
A novel of peasant life in Lithuania, portraying its primitive folk with lively realism and no little humour. A lofty idealism shows itself in some of the characters, such as the hero, whose worship of the oak gives the book its title. [Transl., Jarrold : o.p.]

RODZIEWICZÓWNA, Marya (*continued*). *Anima Vilis: a tale of the great Siberian steppe*
(Anima Vilis, 1893). 1900
A rather melancholy story of country life in Siberia, as viewed under the best conditions, with a few hints of
the convict settlements; the romantic interest concerned with a gloomy hero, his misfortunes and his
troubled love affairs. [Transl. by Count S. C. DE SOISSONS, Jarrold: o.p.]

—— *Distaff* (Kądziel, 1899). 1901
A study of domestic intercourse and of feminine emancipation as it works in real life. An old-fashioned
woman who manages her farm with energy is the central figure, and the next in interest is a young woman
of advanced ideas that urge her to discontent and insubordination. [Transl., Jarrold: o.p.]

" ROHMER, Sax " [Arthur Sarsfield Ward; *b.* 1883]. *Dope: a story of Chinatown and the drug
traffic.* 1919
A case illustrating the tragic results of the drug traffic, and professedly founded on facts " personally observed."
[Cassell; McBride, New York.]

—— *The Dream-Detective: some account of the methods of Morris Klaw.* 1920
The device of this particular sleuth-hound is to dream a dream on the spot where the crime took place, and so
arrive at a clue. *The Tragedies in the Greek Room* may be read as a sample. [Jarrolds: o.p.; Doubleday,
Doran, New York.]

ROJÀS, Fernando de [attributed to] [Spanish]. *The Spanish Bawd, represented in Celestina; or,
The Tragicke-Comedy of Calisto and Melibea* (La Comedia de Calisto y Melibea) [first edn. known
1499]. 1631
A play or dialogue in 16 acts, extended later to 21. A tragedy of illicit passion; " a completely original
masterpiece," says Kelly, " unique in its kind." " His realism and his pessimistic fulness are above all
praise. . . . His purpose is to give a transcript of life, objective and impersonal, and he fulfils it, adding
thereunto a mysterious touch of sombre imagination." " His book took the world by storm . . . and
was passed from the Spanish stage to be glorified as *Romeo and Juliet*. Celestina acts as go-between to
the lovers, who in the end commit suicide. Not a picaresque novel, not a novel at all in form and method."
The genial old hypocrite, Celestina, with her inexhaustible worldly wisdom, is one of the great characters
of fiction. Translations of *The Tragicke Comedye of Celestina* appeared in 1530 (Martin HUME), 1591 (?),
and 1598 (?). MABBE's fine translation of 1631 was reprinted in W. E. Henley's *Tudor Translations*,
2 vols., 1894. Mr. Warner ALLEN contributes a long and learned introduction dealing with the rise of
realism, the question of the authorship of the *Celestina*, and the extraordinary history of the book, which
offended the Inquisition in Spain, and fell into obscurity in England, though one of the masterpieces of
literature. [Transl. by James MABBE, 1631. With *An Interlude of Calisto and Melebea*, ed. with introd.
on the Picaresque Novel and appendices, by H. Warner ALLEN, Routledge (Dutton, New York), 1908.]

ROKUJIU YEN [Ishikawa Toyonobu; Japanese]. *The Story of a Hida Craftsman* (Hida no
Takumi Monogatari, *c.* 1808). 1912
The author was an artist and the son of an innkeeper, himself carrying on his father's business. His romance
is full of wonderful adventures and mechanical achievements; it also comprises a touching love-story;
but its main charm is the rich infusion of proverbial philosophy, rendered with perfect understanding of
the Japanese genius by Mr. Dickins. [Transl. with annotations by F. V. DICKINS, with *illus.* by Hokusai,
Gowans & Gray, Glasgow: o.p.]

ROLFE, Frederick W. S. A. L. M. [" Frederick Baron Corvo "; 1860–1913]. *Stories Toto Told
Me.* 1898
—— *In His Own Image.* 1901
Books of Italian folk-lore in the form of tales, with which the loquacious young Toto regales his master, an
artist, the supposed recorder. The names and titles of his mythology, angels and virgins, saints and martyrs,
are Christian; the whole spirit is pagan, abounding in joviality and humour, and related with the familiar
irreverence begotten of primitive faith. [(1), Lane: o.p.; (2), Lane; Knopf, New York, 1925.]

—— *Don Tarquinio: a kataleptic phantasmatic romance.* 1905
Half extravaganza; a day of crowded life in the Rome of the Borgias (1495). Shows an intimate knowledge
of mediæval history and archæology, literature and philosophy; and conveys the effect of life and action
in spite of an affected style. [Chatto.]

ROLLAND, Romain [French; *b.* 1868]. *John Christopher* (Jean Christophe, 1904–12). 1910–13
A biographical novel, in ten volumes; subject, a musical genius born in a small German ducal town, beginning
with his actual babyhood, and so copious and discursive that it almost reaches the scale of a social treatise.
Among the most luminous and enchanting books of the long recital are those relating to his infancy and
comradeship with the fine old grandsire, formerly chief musician at the ducal Court. There is great pathos
in the history of the family poverty, the father's drunkenness (cf. Beethoven's father), the mother's heroism;
but the true interest is in the effect of these things on Jean Christophe's mind. Trained observation,
searching insight, and a philosophic criticism of life and society are brought to bear on every phase of his
development. We see the young musician composing—almost unconsciously—his first piece, the stage-
fright of his first appearance in public, his hesitations and misgivings when he takes the headship of the
family; the dawn of love—an episode treated with rare penetration; and so on to the artistic triumphs
and vicissitudes of maturity; all these episodes being handled with the same admirable balancing of
attention upon the inner and the outer aspects of life. M. Rolland is an idealist with a strong didactic
bent; and his belief in a regenerated Europe, with the best forces of French nationality heading the
triumphant attack on materialism, plutocratic corruption, and luxury, gives breadth of view to his survey
of Continental affairs. [Transl. by G. CANNAN, 4 vols., Heinemann; Holt, New York; in 1 vol., Holt,
New York, 1927.]

—— *Pierre and Luce* (Pierre et Luce, 1920). 1922
A quiet but earnest diatribe against militarism, in the shape of a tender idyll: two youthful lovers make the

414

ROLLAND, Romain (*continued*).

most of the time left before the boy is called up, and both perish in the catastrophe when the shell from Big Bertha falls on St. Gervais. [Transl. by Charles DE KAY, Holt, New York.]

—— *Clérambault* (Clérambault : histoire d'une conscience libre pendant la guerre, 1920). 1921

In the tragic experiences of a French professor whose mind is awakened to the folly of the war and who is hounded to death as a defeatist, the author enunciates in eloquent and cogent terms the enlightened individualistic philosophy which determined his own attitude during the world struggle. Though in form a novel, this is a work that may well be read and compared with Alain's *Mars ; ou la guerre jugée*. [Transl. by Katherine MILLER, Holt, New York.]

—— *Annette and Sylvie.* 1925

—— *Summer* [sequel]. 1925

—— *Mother and Son* [sequel]. 1927

A sequence, *The Soul Enchanted*, which analyses the soul of a girl, affording a companion picture to *Jean Christophe*. The first volume shows her, a sensitive creature hungry for affection and human relationship, after her father's death, seeking out his illegitimate daughter, a working girl with totally different standards of life, and succumbing to her fascination. The necessity of marriage turns her affections elsewhere. She has an illegitimate son, to whom she is devoted. The final volume brings us to·the war, where the expression of M. Rolland's pacifist philosophy occupies more place than the relationship ·between mother and son, which is however seriously affected by her activities on behalf of a prisoner of war. A final volume is still to appear. [(1), (2), and (3), Butterworth ; Holt, New York.]

ROLLESTON, Thomas William [Irish ; 1857–1920]. *The High Deeds of Finn ; and other bardic romances of ancient Ireland.* 1910

An attempt to present the old stories in an artistic form satisfactory to modern tastes. [With introd. by Stopford A. BROOKE, Harrap ; Crowell, New York.]

RÖLVAAG, Ole Edvart [Norwegian-American ; 1876–1931]. *Giants in the Earth : a saga of the prairie.* 1927

—— *Peder Victorious.* 1929

Novels dealing with the problems besetting the Norwegian immigrant in South Dakota. In the first, Per Hansa and his wife represent opposing forces, hunger for the new life and constancy to tradition. The sequel is concerned with the mother, who still clings to the old ways, and Peder, the youngest son, whom education soon transforms into the complete American. The author was professor of Norwegian in St. Olaf's College in Minnesota. [Transl. by Norah O. SOLUM and the author, Harper, New York.]

—— *Pure Gold.* 1930

A tale of the blighting effect of avarice on the lives of a Norwegian farmer and his wife in Minnesota. [Transl. by Sivert S. ERDAHL and author, Harper, New York.]

" ROMAINS, Jules " [Louis Farigoule ; French ; b. 1885]. *The Death of a Nobody* (Mort de quelqu'un, 1911). 1914

The death and funeral of a common labouring-man, and the reverberations set up by this event in the minds of those around him, friends and relatives or mere neighbours—a sensitive little study of the individual and the collective consciousness. [Transl. by Desmond MACCARTHY and Sydney WATERLOW, Allen & Unwin ; Viking Press, New York.]

—— *Lucienne* (1922). 1925

Reflective, analytical impressionism, again recording the sensations, intuitions, misgivings, elusive fancies that make up the mental life—in this case of a young girl, a music-mistress, who, incidentally, is very interesting on the effect of great music upon the performer. The tale is simple ; merely the domestic comedy in a little household where, unintentionally, she wins a husband. Everything is in the mode of the telling. Jules Romains has now published sequels, *Le don des corps* (1928) and *Quand le navire . . .* (1929), forming with this a trilogy, and giving the married life of the two young people in the most intimate detail. The whole is a plea for what the author calls *la religion sexuelle*, corporeal love developed into mysticism. One might perhaps describe it as the Song of Songs reduced to extremely vulgar prose. [Transl. by Waldo FRANK, Boni, New York.]

ROOK, Clarence. *The Hooligan Nights.* 1899

Reported conversations with a young criminal in London, who relates his escapades in cheating, burglary, and the various occupations of a professional law-breaker. The cant lingo is not easy. [De La More Press : o.p. ; Holt, New York : o.p.]

ROPES, Arthur Reed [b. 1859] and Mary E. ROPES. *On Peter's Island.* 1901

Petersburg in the reign of Alexander III is the scene, and the underground world of Nihilists, secret societies, spies, and secret police is represented in a story full of varied and exciting situations. Interest centres in a business plot, engineered by an " Oil King." [Murray : o.p.]

ROSCOE, Thomas [tr.]. *The Italian Novelists : trans. from the original.* 1825

Selections from the *Novelle antiche*, Boccaccio, Sacchetti, Ser Giovanni Fiorentino, Massuccio, Sabadino degli Arienti, Alessandro Sozzini, Agnolo Firenzuola, Gentile Sermini, Giovanni Brevio, Girolamo Parabosco, Giovambattista Giraldi Cinthio, Anton-Francesco Grazzini, Ortensio Lando, Straparola, Bandello, Sansovino, Luigi da Porto, Marco Cademosto da Lodi, Macchiavelli, Bernardo Illicini, Pietro Fortini, Niccolo Granucci, Salvuccio Salvucci, Anton-Francesco Doni, Erizzo, Ascanio Mori da Ceno, Malespini, Maiolino, Bisaccioni, Colombo, Bargagli, Bottari, Capacelli, Soave, Altanesi, Magalotti, Lodoli, Maria Manni, Girolamo Padovani, Luigi Sanvitale, Carlo Gozzi, Luigi Bramieri, Robustiano Gironi. [Warne, 1880 : o.p.]

—— *The Spanish Novelists : trans. from originals.* 1832

Selections from Manuel, *Lazarillo de Tormes*, Alemán, Cervantes, Quevedo, Juan Pérez de Montalbán, Antonio de Eslava, Donna María de Zayas i Soto Mayor, Matías de los Reyes, Christoval Lozano, Luis Vélez de Guevara, Isidro de Robles, Alonzo de Castillo Solórzano. [Warne, 1880 : o.p.]

ROSEGGER, Peter Ketteenfeier [Austrian ; 1843–1918]. *The Forest Schoolmaster* (Waldheimat, 1894).
1901
" A strange, sweet tale of an isolated forest community civilized and regenerated by the life of one man." [Transl. by Frances E. SKINNER, Putnam : o.p.]

—— *The God-seeker : a tale of Old Styria* (Der Gottsucher, 1894).
1901
The religious crime, of which this is virtually a true history, was committed in a remote part of the Styrian Alps, and relics are still preserved at Tragös (1493). The old pagan rites handed down to the villagers, who danced round the Need-fire on the Johannisburg, are described with powerful imagination. [Transl. by F. E. SKINNER, Putnam : o.p.]

—— *The Earth and the Fulness Thereof* (Erdsegen ; vertrauliche Sonntagsbriefe eines Bauern-knechtes, 1900).
1902
A newspaper magnate pledges himself, as a result of a wager, to live for a year as a farm-labourer ; but then, finding happiness in a life spent in communion with nature, he marries a peasant girl and settles down on a farm. [Transl. by F. E. SKINNER, Putnam, New York : o.p.]

—— *I.N.R.I. : a prisoner's story of the Cross* (I.N.R.I. Frohe Botschaft eines armen Sünders, 1905).
1905
A prisoner condemned to die retells the story of the Gospels, as the incidents and the character of Jesus appeared to him—a very simple, direct, and touching re-narration. [Transl. by Elizabeth LEE, Hodder : o.p. ; McClure, New York : o.p.]

ROSENKRANTZ, Baron Palle Adam Vilhelm von [Danish ; b. 1867]. *The Magistrate's Own Case.*
1908
A plot-novel skilfully handling a difficult piece of criminal investigation, which culminates in the trial of a Frankfort merchant for the murder of his friend, an English lord. The young magistrate who conducts the case is in love with the defendant's wife, whence further complications arise. [Methuen : o.p. ; McClure, New York : o.p.]

ROSS, Clinton [American ; b. 1861]. *The Scarlet Coat.*
[juvenile] 1896
A romance dealing with Lafayette's campaign and the surrender of Cornwallis. Description of siege of York-town. Historical studies of such significant types as the wealthy Virginian trimmer (1776–81). [Stone, Chicago : o.p.]

ROSS, Sir Ronald [b. 1857]. *The Revels of Orsera.*
1920
A legendary fantasy that reads like a variant of the story of Faust and Mephistopheles ; scene, the Urserental, at the foot of the Furka Pass, in 1495. A diabolic spirit from the glaciers of the Galenstock abets the knightly hero in his suit for the daughter of Count Reichenfels of Orsera. An appendix refers to a MS. authority for the story in the University of Basel. [Murray.]

ROSTAND, Maurice [French]. *The Crystal Coffin* (Le cercueil de cristal, 1920).
1921
The theme is the clash of ideas between a patriotic father and his son, who is a pacifist. The author is the son of the well-known dramatist. [Philpot.]

ROTH, Joseph [German ; b. 1894]. *Flight without End : a report* (Flucht ohne Ende, 1927).
1930
Presented as a direct and authentic record. An Austrian lieutenant, captured by the Russians in 1916, escapes to Siberia, but in 1919 falls into the hands of the Bolsheviks and serves with the revolutionaries for four years. He has had various liaisons and now finds his fiancée married to someone else. The end of all is disillusionment and despair. [Transl. by Ida ZEITLIN, Doubleday, Doran, New York ; Hutchinson.]

ROUSSEAU, Jean-Jacques [French ; 1712–78]. *Julia ; or, The New Heloïse* (La nouvelle Heloïse ; ou, Lettres de deux amans habitans d'une petite ville au pied des Alpes, 1761).
1820
A voluminous romance, told in letters, in which Rousseau seems to be feeding his imagination with the pleasures of satisfied love and the sentimental ecstasies of which destiny had deprived his heart. The egotistic hero loves his well-born pupil and is loved by her, but they are parted, and she marries another. Later, the lover is invited to return, and lives with the married pair. An Arcadian picture is drawn of pure and felicitous wedded life, and the true way of educating children as expounded in *Émile*. Criticizes, from a lofty standpoint, the sophisticated life of cities as compared with that of nature, and includes formal dissertations on suicide, duelling, charity, religion, etc. A landmark in the history of literature, in its praise of rural joys and plainness of living. [3 vols., Edinburgh : o.p.]

RUFFINI, Giovanni Domenico [Italian ; 1807–81]. *Lorenzo Benoni : or, Passages in the Life of an Italian.*
1853
The life of an Italian patriot and revolutionary, written in English by a refugee. Embodies the stories of Ruffini himself and his brother (Mazzini is introduced as Fantasio). Begins with his schoolboy republicanism ; then we have the story of 1831, its conspiracies and revolution, and a host of romantic personal episodes down to 1837. [Constable, Edinburgh : o.p.]

—— *Dr. Antonio.*
1855
Naples (1848–58). Love-tale of a patriot and the daughter of an exclusive English baronet. [Constable, Edinburgh, 1855 : o.p. ; Stott, 1890 : o.p. ; Dillingham, New York : o.p.]

—— *Lavinia.*
1860
A novel of plot, varied in scene, characters, and incidents, and in manner of narration. An Italian artist of republican tendencies, a French realist, a dog-fancying Spanish countess, two Roman swindlers, an Italian bishop, some English, and the heroine with her mercurial nature, are the chief characters. [3 vols., Rudd, New York : o.p.]

—— *Carlino.*
1870
A good example of the Continental short story. Extremely simple ; the story of an aristocrat who is subdued and humanized by the tender devotion of an affectionate young man ; with incidental sketches of characters and manners, both Italian and French. [Lippincott, Philadelphia : o.p.]

RUNKLE, Bertha [Mrs. Louis H. Bash ; American]. *The Helmet of Navarre.* 1901
A bustling romance of cape and sword, with a young adherent of Henry of Navarre for hero, and for scene Paris (1593-4), at the moment when the Huguenot king entered the city at the cost of a mass. [Century Co., New York.]

RUSSELL, George William [" A. E." ; Irish ; *b.* 1867]. *The Interpreters.* 1922
A philosophic story. In the middle of what is a sort of transcendental version of the Irish revolution, a world-rising against the nationalist and plutocratic dynasts of three centuries hence, a little knot of captured rebels discuss the basic principles of socialism and the cult of personality leading to the realization of a new world. [Macmillan.]

RUSSELL, John [*b.* 1885]. *Where the Pavement Ends.* 1921
Stories in the Kipling vein, each turning upon the unravelling of some bizarre situation. In *The Lost God*, a diver is washed ashore, and hailed by the natives as a god ; but he is unable to release himself from his diving-suit. [Butterworth ; Knopf, New York.]

—— *Far Wandering Men.* 1929
Ten stories of the South Seas—sailors afloat and ashore, revenge, and sorcery. [Butterworth ; Norton, New York.]

RUSSELL, William Clark [1844-1911]. *John Holdsworth, Chief Mate.* 1875
This and the two following are perhaps the three best of a long succession of nautical novels, in which extraordinary adventures and plot interest take the place of the rich character-drawing and humours of Smollett, Marryat, and Michael Scott. Here we have a variation of the *Enoch Arden* story, the husband losing his memory through shipwreck and exposure in an open boat. The interloper dies, and the couple are reunited, but the story remains sufficiently harrowing. [Low.]

—— *The Wreck of the " Grosvenor."* 1876
May be taken as the type of Clark Russell's narratives, which mingle realistic pictures of life on board and of the storms and beauty of the ocean, with ultra-romantic adventures. This is an exciting story of a mutiny and its consequences, with the usual love-plot. [Low ; Dodd & Mead, New York, 1923 ; Brentano, New York.]

—— *The Frozen Pirate.* 1877
A sailor in the Arctic comes upon an old wrecked ship, and finds an eighteenth-century pirate in a state of suspended animation. He is restored to life, and the story revolves round his doings in these strange circumstances. [Low ; Street, New York : o.p.]

RUTTER, Owen [*b.* 1889]. *Cain's Birthday.* 1930
The recorded facts of the mutiny of the *Bounty* are here connected up into a dramatic novel of character and motive. [Hutchinson.]

" RYCE, Mark." *Mrs. Drummond's Vocation.* 1911
Mrs. Drummond, a French-English girl of Boulogne, becomes the wife of a missionary in China, and on her widowhood has a liaison with a Russian prince, before settling down to a decorous life in Clapham. The point is the admirable facility and success with which women adapt themselves to life ; an idea brought out with truth of drawing and complete honesty, in spite of the satirical implication—the missionary, the fellow-minister, the fellow-labourers in China, the converted natives, the humdrum Clapham set, all being pictured with striking fidelity. [Heinemann : o.p. ; Macauley Co., New York : o.p.]

RYDBERG, Prof. Abraham Viktor [Swedish ; 1828-95]. *Singoalla : a mediæval legend* (1858). 1904
A fantastic saga-like romance of Sweden at the time of the Black Death (*c.* 1340). A knight weds a mysterious gipsy, loses his recollection, and after marrying a woman of his own race, is visited by the son of his early marriage, a youth with hypnotic powers. Describes a remote, wild life on the borders of Christendom and heathenism. By the learned author of *Teutonic Mythology.* The introduction on Swedish literature is misleading. [Transl. by J. FREDBÄRJ, W. Scott : o.p.]

—— *The Last Athenian* (Den Siste Athenaren, 1859). 1883
An interesting picture of the last days of antiquity (A.D. 361) and the struggling Christian sects, by a great historical scholar. [Petersen, Philadelphia : o.p.]

RYGIER-NALKOWSKA, Mme Sofja [Polish]. *Women : a novel of Polish life* (Kobiety). 1920
The histories of three unhappy women, told by an ardent feminist. [Transl. by Michael Henry DZIEWICKI, Putnam, New York.]

RYND, Evelyne Elsye. *Mrs. Green.* 1901
Mrs. Green is an entertaining old charwoman, quite a character, who propounds her views of things in general, and sketches in forcible colours the characters of friends and acquaintances. She is obviously a relative of Mrs. Gamp, and a similar Cockney dialect seasons her gossip. [Murray ; Putnam, New York : o.p.]

SABATINI, Rafael [Italian by birth ; *b.* 1875]. *The Lovers of Yvonne (being a portion of the memoirs of the Sieur Gaston de Luynes).* 1902
A sensational romance in the style of Dumas, Weyman, etc. ; scenes, Paris and Blois in the time of Mazarin. [Pearson ; *sub tit. The Suitors of Yvonne*, Putnam, New York : o.p.]

—— *The Tavern Knight.* 1904
Hero, a riotous Cavalier, time of Worcester (1651). [De La More Press : o.p. ; Newnes ; Houghton, Boston.]

—— *Bardelys the Magnificent.* 1906
Adventures in Louis XIII's reign, time of Orleanist rising and Montmorency's downfall (1632). [Nash : o.p. ; Newnes ; Houghton, Boston.]

—— *The Trampling of the Lilies.* 1906
The eve of the French Revolution and the Revolution itself (1789-93). Scenes : Picardy, Belgium, and Paris. [Hutchinson : o.p. ; Houghton, Boston.]

SABATINI, Rafael (*continued*). *Love at Arms.*   1907
—— *The Shame of Motley.*   1908
—— *The Justice of the Duke.*   1912
—— *The Banner of the Bull.*   1915
    Four romances that give an exciting picture of the turbulent era of the Renaissance in Italy, the first dealing with the Sforzas (*c.* 1500), the second with Cesare Borgia and his contemporaries (1498–1503) ; the other two books are collections of shorter stories. [(1) and (2), Hutchinson : o.p. ; (3), S. Paul : o.p. ; (4), Hutchinson ; (2) and (4), Houghton, Boston ; McClelland, Toronto.]
—— *St. Martin's Summer.*   1909
    The tragi-comedy of a château in Dauphiné (1615) ; an emissary of Marie de' Medici, Queen Regent, saves the heroine from a forced marriage. [Hutchinson : o.p. ; Newnes ; Houghton, Boston.]
—— *Anthony Wilding.*   1910
    A love-romance of Monmouth's rebellion, the duke, Lord Grey, and other followers appearing. [Hutchinson : o.p. ; *sub tit. Arms and the Maid, or, Anthony Wilding*, Putnam, New York : o.p.]
—— *The Lion's Skin.*   1911
    Hinges on the struggle between vengeance and filial instinct in a son brought up to avenge his mother. This motive, the South Sea Bubble, and Jacobite intrigues, provide abundant incident. Scenes : Paris and London (1721). [Stanley Paul : o.p. ; Houghton, Boston ; McClelland, Toronto.]
—— *The Strolling Saint.*   1913
    A vigorous romance of the Italian renaissance, culminating in the assassination of Pier Luigi Farnese, son of Paul III (1547). [S. Paul ; Houghton, Boston.]
—— *The Gates of Doom.*   1914
    The Atterbury plot and the doings of a Jacobite agent. Scenes, Chelsea, etc. (1721). [S. Paul ; McClelland, Toronto.]
—— *The Sea-Hawk.*   1915
    Exploits of a Barbary corsair in the Elizabethan time ; scenes, Cornwall and the Mediterranean. [Nelson ; Houghton, Boston ; McClelland, Toronto.]
—— *The Snare.*   1917
    An episode of the Peninsular War, when Wellington stood at bay behind the lines of Torres Vedras (1810). [Hutchinson ; Houghton, Boston ; McClelland, Toronto.]
—— *The Historical Nights Entertainment.*   1917–19
    Two sets of romantic versions of exciting historical episodes, English, Italian, etc. [2 vols., Hutchinson : o.p. ; 2 vols., Houghton, Boston.]
—— *Scaramouche.*   1921
    A romantic version of French history in the time of Necker and the first years of the Revolution ; scenes, Brittany and Paris (1788–92). [Hutchinson : o.p. ; Houghton, Boston ; McClelland, Toronto.]
—— *Captain Blood.*   1922
    An innocent British fugitive after Sedgemoor is transported to Barbados, and has sensational adventures in the West Indies. [Hutchinson : o.p. ; Houghton, Boston.]
—— *The Carolinian.*   1925
    A romance of South Carolina before the War of Independence and during its early stages (1775–9). [Hutchinson ; Houghton, Boston ; McClelland, Toronto.]
—— *Bellarion.*   1926
    Exciting adventures at Milan and elsewhere in the days of Gian Maria Visconti and the strife of Guelf and Ghibelline (1407–9). [Hutchinson : o.p. ; Houghton, Boston ; McClelland, Toronto.]
—— *The Nuptials of Corbal.*   1927
    The time is that of the Reign of Terror (1793), and Paris and the provinces furnish the background. [Houghton, Boston.]
—— *The Hounds of God.*   1928
    A romance of the Armada period ; the scene, England, and subsequently the Court of Philip of Spain and the Inquisition. [Houghton, Boston ; Hutchinson.]

SABIN, Edwin Legrand [American ; *b.* 1870]. *With Sam Houston in Texas : a boy volunteer in the Texas struggles for independence.*   1916
    A stirring novel, largely based on fact, suitable for young readers. There are several others of similar type, e.g. *With George Washington into the Wilderness, Into Mexico with General Scott*, etc. (*Trail Blazers Series*). [Lippincott, Philadelphia.]

SACCHETTI, Franco di Benci [Italian ; *c.* 1335–1410]. *Eighty-three Tales from Sacchetti.* 1907
    A follower of Boccaccio, who did not, however, adopt the connected plan of the *Decameron* or trouble much about artistic effect. A born raconteur, with a fund of experience accumulated as a man of affairs, telling pithy stories of the life of his day, most of them anecdotes of real occurrences chiefly of a humorous cast, others drawn from the *fabliaux* and the *Gesta Romanorum*. [Transl. by Mary G. STEEGMANN, with Preface by Dr. Guido BIAGI, Dent : o.p.]

SACHER-MASOCH, Leopold von [German ; 1836–95]. *Jewish Tales.*   1894
    A selection of twenty-six tales or character-studies, by a Galician, dealing with the Jews in those eastern European countries where their peculiar habits, prejudices, and superstitions are maintained with the least modification. [Transl. by H. L. COHEN, McClurg, Chicago : o.p.]

SACKVILLE-WEST, Victoria [Hon. Mrs. Harold Nicholson ; *b.* 1892]. *Heritage.*   1919
    A vigorous story, turning upon the effect of Spanish blood in a girl of the Weald of Kent, her unhappy marriage, and long-deferred union with her lover. The form in which it is told, first by the lover, then by his friend in England, finally in his journal, entails some lack of focus and unity. [Collins.]

SACKVILLE-WEST, Victoria (*continued*). *The Dragon in Shallow Waters.*   1921
> Two brothers, afflicted with an hereditary taint, gain domination over a village by their strength of body and character and their blind hatred of humanity. [Collins ; Putnam, New York.]

—— *The Heir : a love story.*   1922
> A story in the Henry James manner, about an insurance clerk who inherits a country house, and develops a new and greater personality under its influence. With four slighter stories. [Heinemann ; Doubleday, Doran, New York.]

—— *The Edwardians.*   1930
> A half-satirical view of high society in the early nineteen-hundreds—a scene of luxury and splendour, loose morals and outward decorum, centring in a vast mansion, not hard to identify, and an amorous young duke. Reciprocally dedicated to the author of *Orlando*, and not uninfluenced by the literary methods of Mrs. Woolf. [Hogarth Press ; Doubleday, Doran, New York.]

SADLEIR, Michael [*b.* 1888]. *Privilege.*   1921
> One of the sons of an old peer, notorious a century ago for his follies and extravagances, tells how the family goes to pieces in this modern age. The present generation, with their diversified temperaments and utter inability to adapt themselves to " an existence of a complexity undreamed of " by a more stable world, are well anatomized. [Constable ; Putnam, New York.]

—— *The Noblest Frailty.*   1925
> An English county family in the eighteen-sixties and onwards—the breakdown of family authority and traditions at the hands of a wilful girl. [Constable ; *sub tit. Obedience,* Houghton, Boston.]

" ST. AUBYN, Allan " [Frances Marshall, *née* Bridges]. *Mary Unwin.*   1899
> A domestic story of a country parson's family, where love and poverty run a hard race. A fair specimen of the author's work. [Chatto.]

" ST. CLAIR, William " [William Ford]. *Prince Baber and his Wives ; and, The Slave-Girl Narcissus and the Nawab of Lalput.*   1901
> Tales of native Indian life, by one who is intimately acquainted with the inner side of the native Courts. The extraordinary adventures of a princess, remarkable interviews with gorgeous courtesans, slave-dealings and the like, are woven into exciting narratives. [Sonnenschein : o.p.]

SAINT MARY MAGDALENE. *The Life of Saint Mary Magdalen* [Italian ; *c.* 14th cent.].   1903
> A story that shows the same simple and childlike imagination as that of the mediæval artists who painted the storied windows in the churches. The author, probably a little Italian burgher turned Franciscan, transfers to Palestine the scenery and manners of his own land. He tells of the feast of Bethany, the death and restoration of Lazarus, and the tragedy of Passion Week. Its pure and fervent piety and its quaintness have the charm of the Pre-Raphaelite painters. [Transl. by Valentina HAWTREY, Lane : o.p.]

SAINT-PIERRE, Bernardin de [French ; 1737-1814]. *Paul and Virginia* (Paul et Virginie, 1786-8).   1890
> An idyll of primitive natures, the classic expression of a favourite eighteenth-century idea, civilization coming into contact with and blighting unsophisticated man. Utopian sentimentalism, akin to that of the old Italian pastorals, is the inspiration, and the inhabitants of the Happy Valley are models of human perfection. The style of the original shows the first development of modern word-painting—language expressing sensation. [Routledge : o.p. ; Houghton, Boston ; McKay, Philadelphia. *Illus.* by Leloir, Routledge : o.p. ; by same, Altemus Co., Philadelphia ; by Laguillermie, Estes, Boston : o.p.]

SAINTINE, Xavier-Boniface [French ; 1797-1865]. *Picciola ; or, The Prisoner of Fenestrella* (Picciola, 1836).   1875
> The famous sentimental story of the Comte de Charny, a political prisoner, who solaced his captivity and saved himself from despair and madness by the cult of a tiny plant that sprang up between the paving-stones of the prison ; time, the earlier Napoleonic era. [Low : o.p. ; Caldwell, Boston : o.p.]

SALTUIKOV, Mikhail Evgrafovich [" Shchedrin " ; Russian ; 1826-89]. *The Gollovlev Family* (1880).   1916
> Saltuikov was a bitter satirist of Russian provincial society and administration ; here is depicted with mordant realism the decadence of a noble family. Gollovlev, nicknamed Judas, is an outstanding type of avarice and double-dealing. [Transl. by A. RIDGWAY, Jarrolds : o.p. ; by Natalie A. DUDDINGTON, Allen & Unwin, 1931.]

SALTUS, Edgar [American ; 1858-1921]. *Mr. Incoul's Misadventure.*   1886
> Like *Purple and Fine Linen* or *Daughters of the Rich,* the product of an exotic imagination turned loose among the details of fast and fashionable life in Paris and elsewhere. The atmosphere of his stories is redolent of wealth and luxury ; there is wit, often cynical, in the telling. [Brentano, New York, 1925.]

SALVERSON, Laura Goodman [Canadian]. *The Viking Heart.*   1923
> About a group of Icelandic settlers in the neighbourhood of Winnipeg, about 1870 ; following the course of their hardships and progress up to the present day, and showing how, out of their old loyalties to clan and country, there develops a new spirit of citizenship in the land of their adoption. [Brentano ; McClelland, Toronto.]

" SAMAROW, Gregor " [Oscar Meding ; German ; 1828-1903]. *For Sceptre and Crown* (Um Szepter und Kronen, 1873-4).   1875
> The best of Samarow's novels ; deals with the Austrian war (1866). He also wrote a novel entitled *Transvaal* (1897). [2 vols., H. S. King : o.p.]

SANBORN, Alvan Francis [American ; *b.* 1866]. *Moody's Lodging House ; and other tenement sketches.*   1895
—— *Meg McIntyre's Raffle ; and other stories.*   1896
> Two volumes of studies of the poorest classes in a great city, the pathos often ghastly. The title-story is an

SANBORN, Alvan Francis (*continued*).
    Irish idyll ; *Episodes in the Career of Shuffles* and *A Lodging House Bum* are studies of people depraved by
    untoward circumstances. [(1) and (2), Small & Maynard, Boston : o.p.]

"SAND, George" [Armandine Aurore Lucile Dupin, "Baronne" Dudevant ; French ; 1804–
    76]. *Indiana* (1832).   1850
    Inspired by *Paul and Virginia* ; another manifesto of the gospel of Nature, and the rebellion against a false
    and impure social scheme. Indiana is a Creole brought up in the wilds of the Ile de France, with an
    unlimited capacity for exalted love. Escaping from a vulgar Lothario, who is most convincingly drawn,
    she finds her destiny in a rather mysterious cousin, who has loved her dumbly and hopelessly from her
    childhood. [Peterson, Philadelphia : o.p.]

—— *Valentine* (1832).
    Like *Indiana*, a transcript of her own sentimental experiences, her rupture with M. Dudevant (portrayed as
    the husband in the novel), and her relations with Jules Sandeau. Poor and inchoate as a story, but rich
    in descriptive passages and the fervid expression of feeling.

—— *Lélia* (1833).
    Half a story of real life, half allegory, in which the characters represent certain moral and social tendencies
    and are chiefly interesting as the expression of the author's moods at a period of doubt and despondency.
    The style is semi-lyrical, rising at times into flights of poetry. An appreciative critic calls it, "This poem,
    so strange, incoherent, magnificent, and absurd." As the aggressive expression of the authoress's early
    doubts it aroused keen hostility.

—— *Jacques* (1834).   1847
    An impassioned eulogy of individualism and a hot renunciation of the trammels and falsehoods of philistine
    society. The Byronic Jacques, acting on the romantic principle of absolute freedom, lets his wife go off
    with her lover. The style is semi-lyrical, admirably fitted for the expression of reverie and emotion.
    George Sand had come back from her Cytherean journey to Italy with De Musset, and this is the first
    proclamation of her gospel of free love. [Harper, New York : o.p.]

—— *Mauprat* (1837).   1847
    A story of aristocrats in the provinces in the latter half of the eighteenth century. A refined girl married to
    a boorish cousin applies herself to the task of civilizing him, and succeeds in making him an estimable man
    by drawing out his better feelings. The situation is handled in a forcible way, and the book is full of ideas
    on life. [Transl. by Miss HAYES, 1847 : o.p. With introd. by Mrs. CRAIGIE, Heinemann, 1902 ; transl.
    by VAUGHAN, Little & Brown, Boston : o.p.]

—— *The Last Aldini* (La dernière Aldini, 1838).   1847
    The hero, Nello, a gondolier, wins the love of a countess, but sacrifices his affection to her worldly welfare ;
    and when he has achieved success as an opera-singer, he fascinates her daughter, once more magnanimously
    retiring. [Transl., *sub tit. The Last of the Aldinis*, by Miss HAYES, 1847 : o.p. ; transl., Peterson,
    Philadelphia : o.p.]

—— *The Master Mosaic Workers* (Les maîtres mosaïstes, 1838).   1847
    Her first socialist novel. A picture of Venetian life in the palmy days of the republic (time of Tintoretto),
    the interest centring in two master mosaists and their work. [Transl. by Miss HAYES, 1847 : o.p. ; transl.
    by C. C. JOHNSTON, Dent : o.p. ; with *The Devil's Pool*, Little & Brown, Boston : o.p.]

—— *The Journeyman Joiner ; or, The Companion of the Tour of France* (Le compagnon du tour de
    France, 1840).   1847
    Another humanitarian novel, preaching universal fraternity and the fusion of classes. The hero is an artisan,
    an ideal man of the people, devoting himself to the amelioration of his fellows ; the title refers to his
    membership of a trade union. This superhuman hero's pure love is contrasted with the sensual passion
    of a lower nature. [Transl. by Miss HAYES, Churton, 1847 : o.p. ; another transl., M'Glashan, Dublin :
    o.p.]

—— *Little Fadette* (La petite Fadette, 1840).   1849
    An idealistic pastoral of country life in Berri, portraying with fond delight the homely, sterling nature of the
    peasant children's friendships, the growth of love in a young girl's heart, and the transforming effect upon
    her character. The local colour is done to perfection. [Transl., 1849 : o.p. ; *sub tit. Fanchon*, 1874 : o.p. ;
    transl. by Jane M. SEDGWICK, Dent : o.p. ; Little & Brown, Boston : o.p. ; transl. by Hamish MILES,
    Scholartis Press (McKee, New York), 1929.]

—— *Consuelo* (1842–3).   1847
—— *The Countess of Rudolstadt* (La comtesse de Rudolstadt, 1843–5) [sequel].   1851
    Consuelo is George Sand's *Wilhelm Meister*, and with the sequel gives the life-story of a great singer who was
    also a woman of the noblest character. The tone of the entire history is romantic, the second part,
    especially, closing with an allegorical vision of humanitarian theosophy. Consuelo is introduced as a child
    of the streets in Venice, where her artistic gifts bring her to the notice of a fine old maestro. Her career
    takes her to Bohemia, Vienna, Berlin ; and among the personages she meets are the Empress Maria Theresa,
    Haydn, Metastasio, Frederick the Great. The life of the time (1740–86) is portrayed on a broad canvas,
    and in addition to innumerable incidents which are both dramatic and credible, the author gives enough
    adventure, mystery, fantastic journeying, imprisonments, abductions, escapes, to furnish out half a dozen
    sensation-novels. [Transl. (1), Weldon, 1876 : o.p., W. Scott, 1894 : o.p. ; (2), Weldon, 1877 : o.p.,
    W. Scott, 1894 : o.p.]

—— *The Miller of Angibault* (Le meunier d'Angibault, 1845–6).   1847
    The best of several novels preaching a kind of sentimental socialism. A democratic artisan and a baroness
    are in love, but the advocate of social equality will not marry the lady because she is rich. Later on
    misfortune overtakes the baroness, and she welcomes what will remove the obstacle to their union.
    [Transl. by Miss HAYES, 1847 : o.p. ; Weldon, 1878 : o.p. ; transl. by DEWEY, Little & Brown, Boston :
    o.p.]

"SAND, George" (*continued*). *The Devil's Pool* (La mare au diable, 1846).   1895

Perhaps the simplest and freshest of the Berrichon idylls, quiet, harmonious, and, above all, truthful and sensitive pictures of nature and country life, which mark intervals of repose between her tales of passion and the political and psychological novels. Merely the narrative of a rustic courtship, with four characters—a young farmer, an innocent little shepherdess, a child, and a mare. She had already written *Petite Fadette*, a pastoral in the same genre, *Jeanne* (1844), and there is a later one, *Les maîtres sonneurs* (1853), of which no translation seems to be available. All are charming in their tender picturing of placid, homely life and of the quiet beauties of nature in the country, if the human features are over-idealized. [Transl. by Jane M. SEDGWICK, with *François the Waif* (Everyman's Lib.), Dent (Dutton, New York), 1911 ; transl. by Hamish MILES, Scholartis Press (McKee, New York), 1929.]

—— *The Sin of M. Antoine* (Le peché de M. Antoine, 1847).   *c.* 1870

A doctrinaire novel ; theme, marriage and divorce. A magnanimous husband sets free his wife, who loves another man. The novel takes up the situation years after, and by the mediation of an innocent girl, the other man's daughter brings about a reconciliation and friendship between the first husband and the second. [Peterson, Philadelphia : o.p.]

—— *The Country Waif* (François le champi, 1849) ; *and, The Castle of Pictordu* (Le Château de Pictordu).   1930

François le champi is another of the Berrichon idylls, and was staged as a pastoral comedy in 1849. Simple as ever, the story tells with an art that seems artless how the friendship of Francis and the good Madelon grew into a sweeter affection. The other is a charming didactic tale of a little girl and her dream, mixing up the real and the supernatural in a fascinating way. [Transl. by E. COLLIS and P. H. WATSON, Scholartis Press (McKee, New York) ; (1), v. also *The Devil's Pool.*]

—— *The Snow Man* (L'homme de neige, 1859).   1871

A picturesque and very romantic tale of Swedish life in the eighteenth century, with striking descriptions of sport, hunting, and winter scenery. In the dramatic opening a great entertainment is being held in the castle of a powerful baron, and a player of marionettes makes his appearance, who is really the rightful heir. This is the key to the plot. [Transl. by V. VAUGHAN, Little & Brown, Boston : o.p.]

SANDEAU, Léonard Sylvain Jules ["Julien Sandeau" ; French ; 1811–83]. *Catherine : a village tale* (Catherine, 1845).   1860

An idyllic picture of life in a sequestered village, atmosphere and characters recalling the *Vicar of Wakefield*. Catherine, "the little virgin," daughter of a poor curé, is loved by a homely farmer and by a young viscount. The latter is weak and vacillating, and his friends oppose the match, so Catherine renounces him and marries the countryman. But her husband's magnanimity is still greater, for, believing his wife to be heart-sick, he goes away, leaving her in affluence, and comes back only when he has won her affection. [Transl. by W. ROBSON, Routledge, 1860 : o.p. ; by J. H. IRVING, Cupples, Boston : o.p.]

—— *Mademoiselle de la Seiglière* (1848).

Contrasts the old-fashioned noblesse (the Marquess de la Seiglière) and the nineteenth-century bourgeois (Bernard Stamply), who loves Hélène de la Seiglière. Dramatized afterwards by himself with a totally different *dénouement*. [o.p.]

—— *Madeleine* (1848).   1850

Another idealized picture of life. Madeleine's cousin is a young roué, whom despair and remorse are driving to suicide when Madeleine undertakes his reform. Dramatized by Couaillhac and Bourdain (1850), and successfully acted in Paris. [Transl. with an analytical review of the author by G. PLANCHÉ, Slater : o.p. ; transl. McClurg, Chicago : o.p.]

—— *The House of Penarvan* (La maison de Penarvan, 1858).   1878

A quiet delineation of the life of the old noblesse : the heroine, a beautiful patrician, excessively proud of her ancient house, of which she writes a history. Urged by pride of race rather than love, she marries the only other representative of the family, sacrifices him to the reactionary attempts of the Chouans, casts off her daughter for marrying a bourgeois, and is at length won back to human kindness by her grandchild. [Transl. by Lady G. FULLERTON : o.p.]

SANDY, Isabelle [French ; b. 1886]. *Andorra* (Andorra, ou les hommes d'airain, 1923).   1924

The value of this novel is entirely in the graphic account of life in Andorra and the patriarchal system of government which forms the whole framework of society. [Transl. by Mathilde MONNIER and Florence Donnell WHITE, Houghton, Boston.]

SARATKUMĀRA GHOSHA, A. [Bengali]. *The Prince of Destiny : the new Krishna.*   1909

Career of a young Indian prince educated in England—a panorama of Indian life and ideas with sidelights on Indian unrest. [Rebman : o.p.]

SARTORIS, Mrs. Adelaide [*née* Kemble ; American ; 1814–79]. *A Week in a French Country House.*   1867

The writer—Adelaide Kemble, the singer—says, "The papers are descriptions of places and things which I have seen and people whom I know." She sketches every person met with at Marny in a humorous, delicate, yet incisive manner that makes them wonderfully alive and individual. Her work has been justly compared with that of her editor, the authoress of *The House on the Cliff.* [American edn. : o.p. *Illus.* by Lord Leighton with Mrs. Richmond Ritchie, Smith & Elder : o.p.]

SATCHELL, William [New Zealander]. *The Toll of the Bush.*   1905

Life in the New Zealand Bush. [Macmillan : o.p.]

—— *The Greenstone Door.*   1914

A good story illustrating the troubles with the Maoris, in the time of Sir George Grey (1861–7). The Rev. J. R. Selwyn, afterwards Bishop of Melanesia, is among the historical personages. [Sidgwick : o.p. ; Macmillan, New York : o.p.]

SATTHIANADHAN, Mrs. S. [Hindu ; 1862–94]. *Kamala : a story of Hindu life.*   1894

SATTHIANADHAN, Mrs. S. (*continued*). *Saguna : a story of native Christian life.* 1895
Tales imbued with the Christian sentiments of the author. [o.p.]

SAUNDERS, John [1810–95]. *Abel Drake's Wife.* 1883
Realistic portraiture of poor people, mill hands, and domestic servants. Abel, a strike leader, leaves his wife, who, believing him dead, gets engaged ; her husband then reappears, to the dismay of wife and lover. [W. H. Allen : o.p.]

—— *A Noble Wife.* 1895
A pathetic memoir of Archbishop Cranmer's wife and the great episodes of the English Reformation of which they were central figures. [Jarrold : o.p.]

SAVI, Ethel Winifred. *Banked Fires.* 1919
A number of women and a doctor who finds himself in a compromising situation are well studied in this Anglo-Indian novel. [Putnam.]

SAVINKOV, Boris ["V. Ropshin"; Russian; 1879–1925]. *What Never Happened* (1912). 1917
An absorbing and substantially accurate picture of the terrorist outbreak of 1905, from the point of view of the revolutionaries themselves. Savinkov was an active member of the party ; hence his revelations have almost documentary value, and the portraits of terrorists are convincingly true to life. [Transl. by Thomas SELTZER, Allen & Unwin.]

—— *The Pale Horse* (1909). 1917
Anatomizes one type of revolutionary—the cold-blooded anarchist to whom death has become a commonplace, and life of no value—a contrast to Bolotov, the hero of *What Never Happened*. [Transl., Maunsel, Dublin : o.p. ; Allen & Unwin.]

SCARRON, Paul [French; 1611–60]. *The Comical Romance* (Le roman comique, 1651–7) ; *and other tales.* 1676
The adventures of a troupe of strolling players, who come to Le Mans, and play *Herod and Mariamne* in burlesque fashion, the tragedy being turned to farce by the mean habiliments of the actors, and ending in a fight with the owners of the clothes they have stolen. Of high importance as the earliest faithful picture of French provincial life, and, in its individual portraiture, a forerunner of the modern novel. Satirizes the affected diction, the unreal sentimentality, and the foppish heroics of Calprenède and Scudéry, of whose style Scarron's is the very antipodes—plain, coarse, maliciously plebeian. The narrative is interspersed with short, fanciful tales, borrowed from Spain, a contrast to the realism of Scarron's original work. He did not finish it, but sequels were supplied by the Abbé Preschac and the publisher, Offray (the latter is incorporated in Tom Browne's translation). The other tales are five erotic novelettes, with comic or tragic *dénouements*—*Avarice Chastised, or, The Miser Punished ; The Useless Precaution ; The Hypocrites ; The Innocent Adultery ; The Generous Lover, or, The Man of Deeds and not of Words.* [*Scarron's Comical Romance ; or, A Facetious History of a Company of Strolling Players*, transl. by P. PORTER, 1676 : o.p. ; transl. by Tom BROWNE, 2 vols., Lawrence & Bullen, 1892 : o.p.]

SCHAEFFER, Evelyn [American; *née* Schuyler]. *Isabel Stirling.* 1920
A biographical novel of New England and Arizona from the eighteen-fifties to the seventies, in which the broadening of religious attitudes is a main thread of interest. [Scribner, New York ; Nash : o.p.]

SCHAÜWECKER, Franz [German; *b.* 1890]. *The Furnace : an epic of the war.* 1930
The story of the war from the private soldier's point of view ; very long, laboriously realistic, graphic and very impressive in places, but on the whole one of those honest chronicles which have no artistic *raison-d'être*. [Transl. by R. T. CLARK, Methuen.]

SCHEFFEL, Johann Victor von [German; 1826–86]. *Ekkehard : a tale of the tenth century* (1857). 1872
An historical romance of the Huns in the tenth century—the life of a poet and a vivid picture of a Court and a convent. Disappointed in his ambitions and disgraced, the poet retires to a hermitage in the Alps, and there recovers the health of his soul. [Transl., 2 vols., Tauchnitz, Leipzig (Low) : o.p. ; (Everyman's Lib.), Dent (Dutton, New York).]

SCHICKELÉ, René [German; *b.* 1883]. *Maria Capponi* (1926). 1928
—— *The Heart of Alsace* (Blick auf die Vogesen, 1927) [sequel]. 1929
A sequence, *The Rhineland Heritage (Das Erbe am Rhein)* : a study of the present situation in Alsace, rent from the Germans and incorporated in France, with broad views of the state of things in Europe generally. [(1) and (2), transl. by Hannah WALLER, Knopf, New York and London.]

SCHILLER, Johann Friedrich von [German; 1759–1805]. *The Ghost-Seer, or Apparitionist* (Der Geisterseier, 1785–9). 1795
A long and complicated story of mystery and horror, the pseudo-supernatural groundwork being fully explained to the reader ; intended apparently as an antidote to the extravagance of Gothic romances, but in effect an incentive to their popularity. Left uncompleted. [Also *The Armenian, or Ghost-Seer*, transl. by Dr. RENDER, 4 vols. (first only is from Schiller, with continuation by Emanuel F. W. E. Follenius (1773–1809)), 1800 : o.p.]

SCHIMMEL, Hendrik Jan [Dutch; 1823–1906]. *The Lifeguardsman : a tale of the English revolution* (De Kaptein van de Lijfgarde). 1888
The experiences of a Dutch officer in the service of William of Orange during 1688–90, the Revolution, the settlement of the new reign, the Jacobite conspiracies, and the campaign of the Boyne, though these transactions are of less interest than the trials of a husband and wife whose fidelity is tested by long separation. The author was also known as a poet. [Black, 1888 : o.p.]

SCHLUMP : *the story of an unknown soldier* (Schlump : Geschichten und Abenteurer aus dem Leben des unbekannten Musketiers Emil Schulz, genannt " Schlump," von ihm selbst erzählt, 1928). 1929
Like *All Quiet on the Western Front*, the record of a young German infantryman throughout the course of the

SCHLUMP (*continued*).

war. There is a good deal about Schlump's love-affairs, and some broad humour; in the main it reads like a record of actual experience. [Transl. by Maurice SAMUEL, Secker; Harcourt, New York.]

SCHNITZLER, Arthur [Austrian; 1862–1931]. *Bertha Garlan* (Bertha Garlan, 1901). 1913

Sets the characters and works out the mental and emotional situation between a lover who has just lost his unfaithful wife and the mistress whom he had left. [Transl. by J. H. WISDOM and Marr MURRAY, Göschen: o.p.; Modern Lib., New York.]

—— *Little Novels* (Novellen). 1929

Ten sardonic tales of Viennese life, *The Stranger*, or *The Death of a Bachelor*, being excellent examples of Schnitzler's craftsmanship. [Transl. by Eric SUTTON, Constable; Simon & Schuster, New York.]

—— *The Road to the Open* (Der Weg ins Freie, 1908). 1913

Up to this date only Schnitzler's second novel. An epitome of Viennese life and of his versatile and penetrating art. Austrians and Jews are represented in the social picture, with their inevitable antagonisms. But the interest centres in the egotistical hero who would fain turn his face to the open, but yields to circumstance and disillusionment. [Transl. by Horace SAMUEL, Allen & Unwin; Knopf, New York.]

—— *Fräulein Else* (Fräulein Else, 1924). 1925

A short pathological study of a girl broken in spirit and health by the shame of an earlier incident. The story describes her mind, passing from morbid recollection to delirium, in the last few hours of her life. [Transl. by F. H. LYON, Philpot: o.p.; by Robert H. SIMON, Simon & Schuster, New York; transl. by F. H. LYON and Eric SUTTON, Constable, 1930.]

—— *Therese: the chronicle of a woman's life* (Therese: Chronik eines Frauenlebens, 1930). 1930

A long and uniformly grey study of the life of a governess, daughter of an ex-officer who ends in a madhouse, and of a literary mother who exploits her love-affairs for the sake of copy; inevitably she sinks by slow degrees from depth to depth, and is finally murdered by her illegitimate son.

SCHREINER, Olive [Mrs. Cronwright; " Ralph Iron "; South African; 1855–1920]. *The Story of an African Farm.* 1883

A novel as unusual in scheme and almost as poetical as *Wuthering Heights*, to which it has near resemblances —e.g. the solitary, self-reliant souls, Waldo and Lyndall, to Heathcliff and Catherine. These two, on an ostrich farm in the S. African veld, work out for themselves the universal problem of human life and destiny, the vast loneliness of the scenery symbolizing artistically the solitude and helplessness of man and the inscrutable might of nature. The earlier chapters, describing the childhood of Waldo and his friends, with the idyllic old Otto, Tante Sannie, the Boer housekeeper, and the humorous Bonaparte Blenkins, are by far the best of the book as a novel. Afterwards it becomes a philosophical pamphlet, full of powerful sayings and with one splendidly imaginative passage, the allegory of Truth, though this is put undramatically in the mouth of a chance stranger. [Unwin; Benn; Little & Brown, Boston; Burt, New York.]

—— *Dreams.* 1891

—— *Dream Life and Real Life.* 1892

Stories and fables of a gnomic and aphoristic kind, teaching Olive Schreiner's spiritual view of life; with other stories. [(1), Unwin; Benn; Little & Brown, Boston; Mosher, New York; (2), Unwin; (1) and (2) in 1 vol., Unwin.]

—— *Trooper Peter Halket of Mashonaland.* 1897

A tract for the times on the black and white problem of South Africa, in which Jesus Christ, coming in the flesh to Mashonaland, is the principal spokesman. A powerful attack on Rhodesianism. [Unwin; Little & Brown, Boston: o.p.]

—— *Undine: a queer little child.* 1928

This posthumous work is older than the *Story of an African Farm*, having been written between the ages of sixteen and twenty-one and finished about 1876. It is a human document rather than literature, the immediate expression of the ardent spiritual instincts of a young girl, who cannot help portraying herself in Undine Bock. The scenes of childhood and some of the characters have intense biographical interest, and the little girl's outbursts against Bible theology show how inevitable was her passage from Calvinism to atheism. [With introd. by S. C. Cronwright-Schreiner, Harper, New York; Benn.]

" SCHUBIN, Ossip " [Aloisia Kirschner; Russian; b. 1854]. *Erlach Court* (Erlachhof, 1887). 1889

A sentimental love-story, with a German hero, and scenes shifting from Germany to Paris. A subordinate episode is concerned with a married pair who fall in love with each other after nine years of indifference. [Transl. from the German by Mrs. A. L. WISTER, Lippincott, Philadelphia: o.p.]

—— *The Closing Door.* 1896

A study of the characters of two girls, full of insight into girl nature; contains much local colour. [Transl. from the German by Marie D. GURNEY, Dent: o.p.]

SCHÜLTZ, Heinrich [German]. *When Mammoths roamed the Frozen Earth.* 1930

A reconstruction of the life of the cave-man in Europe in the diluvial period when the mammoth was about to disappear. [Transl. by Frank BARNES, Cape.]

SCHURÉ, Édouard [French; b. 1842]. *The Priestess of Isis* (1907). 1910

A picture drawn by a well-known scholar and dramatist of Egypt and Pompeii just before the catastrophe. [Transl. by F. ROTHWELL, Rider: o.p.]

SCOLLARD, Clinton [American; b. 1860]. *A Man-at-Arms.* 1898

Milan; adventures of a soldier of fortune under Gian Galeazzo Visconti, Lord of Pavia (c. 1390–1402). [Page, Boston: o.p.; Nash: o.p.]

—— *The Son of a Tory.* 1901

A story of the siege of Fort Stanwix (1777), Col. Barry St. Leger, Walter Butler, and General Benedict Arnold. [Badger, Boston: o.p.]

SCOLLARD, Clinton (*continued*). *The Vicar of the Marches.* 1910
 Padua in the thirteenth century, Ezzelino da Romano, and Tiso di Campo Sanpiero. [Sherman & French, Boston : o.p.]

SCOTT, Mrs. Catherine Amy Dawson. *The Story of Anna Beames.* 1907
—— *The Burden.* 1908
—— *Treasure Trove.* 1909
 These novels form a threefold series of heavily realistic studies of " Some Women," their environment and its effect on their character. [(1) and (2), Heinemann : o.p. ; (3), Heinemann.]
—— *The Agony Column.* 1909
 A sober and serious study of a woman with sentimental cravings married to a man who does not fulfil her ideals, and dissatisfied with the common routine of life. She finds a responsive heart in a young Jew, and the results are tragic for herself and her middle-aged husband. [Chapman : o.p.]
—— *Madcap Jane ; or, Youth.* 1910
 With the last and next makes a new series " Some Wives." [Chapman : o.p.]
—— *Mrs. Noakes : an Ordinary Woman.* 1911
 Mrs. Noakes is disappointed in her husband, who abuses her trust in him, and in her son, who turns out a poor sort of creature. A sombre and pathetic, but thoroughly sincere study of actuality. [Chapman : o.p.]

SCOTT, Evelyn [Mrs. John Metcalfe ; American ; b. 1893]. *The Narrow House.* 1921
 An account, mainly in dialogue, of unhappy family life : a girl marries against the wishes of her parents, and lives with her husband's folk. [Boni, New York : o.p. ; Duckworth.]
—— *Escapade.* 1923
 This " creative autobiography " purports to be the true history of a very young woman and a married man who ran off together from the United States to Brazil and suffered the extremes of failure, discomfort, and even destitution and squalor. The authoress is a resident in Brazil. [Boni, New York ; Cape.]
—— *Ideals.* 1927
 Five character-sketches, aiming at photographic realism, devoted to the demolition of ideals. [Boni, New York.]

SCOTT, John Reed [American ; b. 1869]. *Beatrix of Clare.* 1909
 A romance of 1482–3, giving a favourable picture of Richard III, as a strong, resourceful, able man, without the physical deformity, faults, and crimes usually attributed. A careful historical narrative, bringing in the more prominent personages of that era. [Lippincott, Philadelphia : o.p. ; De La More Press : o.p.]

SCOTT, Michael [Scottish ; 1789–1835]. *Tom Cringle's Log.* 1833
 Scott was a Glasgow merchant who travelled widely and lived in the West Indies, collecting from all over the world the miscellaneous characters who people his two novels of adventure by sea and land, two novels as full as any books in our maritime literature of the veritable ocean magic. This is a wonderful farrago of thrilling adventure and brilliant pictures of the sea, ostensibly the diary of a midshipman during the great world-struggle of 1813–14. The scene shifts to the West Indies, Jamaica, Bermuda, Cuba, and other places, giving extensive descriptions of the scenery, towns, and inhabitants. Encounters with American frigates, with smugglers and privateers, droll anecdotes, Tom's kidnapping and life aboard the *Torch* and the *Wave*, make a picturesque and animated narrative which never slackens ; and the characters, e.g. Obediah, the Yankee pirate, Aaron Bang, the punster and buffoon (copied from life as they probably were), provide any amount of rough humour and horseplay, in the Smollett vein. First appeared (1829) in *Blackwood's Magazine.* [Low ; (Everyman's Lib.), Dent (Dutton, New York) ; Brentano, New York ; *illus.*, Low ; Dodd & Mead, New York.]
—— *The Cruise of the " Midge ".* 1834
 The second novel is exactly similar in scheme, or lack of scheme, the eventful life of a sailor—slaver-catching on the African coast ; visits to the Cape ; cruising in the West Indies ; pleasures and dangers, flirtations and duels, scenes of joviality and humour, with death always in the background. Tropical scenery is presented with the same vivid realism, and the salt-water characters are drawn with the same coarse vigour, strongly reminding one of Smollett's comic beasts in human form. First appeared in *Blackwood's Magazine.* [Edited by E. A. Baker (Half-forgotten Books), Routledge (Dutton, New York) : o.p. ; Collins.

SCOTT, Sir Walter [Scottish ; 1771–1832]. *Waverley ; or, 'Tis Sixty Years Since.* 1814
 A romance of the Jacobite Rebellion of 1745, begun by Scott in 1805, then laid aside, and in 1814 taken up and finished in three weeks. This, like many of the following tales, was first published anonymously. Opens in Scotland just before the outbreak, with scenes of Lowland life at the home of the jocular old baron of Bradwardine ; then the hero makes an excursion into the disaffected Highlands, and is soon plunged into the Jacobite movement. A memorable scene is the famous Holyrood ball. Waverley fights with credit at Prestonpans, accompanies the Highland army in their march to Derby, and returns to Scotland after Culloden. A tragic and moving episode is the trial and death of the gallant Highland chief, beside whom Waverley has fought throughout the campaign. His own lot is happier, for he marries the baron's daughter, and restores the glory of the Bradwardines. In germ the Waverley novels were the same kind of thing as Scott's metrical romances, but to the romantic and mediæval elements they add something of infinitely higher value. Here Scott's knowledge of human nature, his power of creating humorous characters most convincingly true to life, and his command of natural drama, find their sphere. His faithful drawing of indigenous Scottish types had a mighty influence upon the progress of realism, and compared with this the stimulus he gave to Dumas and the romancers is a minor matter.
—— *Guy Mannering ; or, The Astrologer.* 1815
 The plot very romantic, though the story is said to be founded on facts : the fortunes and misfortunes of an abducted heir. The wild coasts of Galloway are the chief scenes, with trips to Edinburgh and the Border ; and Scott brings in numberless types of native characters such as he had grown familiar with in his youthful peregrinations in search of old ballads and legends. The chivalrous yeoman Dandie

SCOTT, Sir Walter (*continued*).

Dinmont, the wild, romantic gipsy Meg Merrilies, Dirk Hatteraick, the villainous freetrader, Dominie Sampson, a simple, faithful old tutor who reminds one of Goldsmith, and the witty advocate Counsellor Pleydell are among Scott's most memorable creations. He was at his best the nearer he came to his own time, and this is laid in 1750–70.

—— *The Antiquary.* 1816

Comes nearer still and deals with life and manners in Forfarshire about 1795. As usual the official personages of the plot are gentry ; but it is in the humble fisherfolk, the picturesque old bedesman Edie Ochiltree, the antiquarian Oldbuck of Monkbarns, for whose hobbies and eccentricities Scott had a fellow-feeling, and in the humorous scenes where these figure, that the strength of this great novel is to be looked for. The broader comedy in which the swindling charlatan Dousterswivel is so roughly handled is also very characteristic (cf. *Woodstock*). The clumsy plot-work is straightened out in a conclusion which is arrant melodrama.

—— *The Black Dwarf.* 1816

A minor romance grounded on fact, bringing in a hideous and misanthropic recluse, suggested by a native of Tweeddale, who was only three and a half feet high, the depredations of freebooters on the Border, and the abortive proceedings of the Jacobites about the year 1706 when the Rebellion of 1715 was preparing.

—— *Old Mortality.* 1816

Perhaps the finest of Scott's properly historical novels, dealing with the rebellion and defeat of the Covenanters in 1685, the battles of Loudon Hill or Drumclog and of Bothwell Brig. Scott's Tory sympathies were with the other side, and he presents Grahame of Claverhouse, the scourge of the Covenanters, in a very favourable manner—while he lampoons the Presbyterian preachers, e.g. Poundtext. Mucklewraith and the fanatical old woman Mause Headrigg are impressive figures with a strain of madness in them, and the historic Balfour of Burley is depicted as a victim of religious frenzy. Scott's intimate knowledge of village life in Scotland, and his powers of delineating the characters of humble folk, are freely displayed in this novel. Old Mortality was a venerable enthusiast known to Scott, who got from him much of his material. On the other hand, his two cultivated gentlemen, Morton and Lord Evandale, are persons a century in advance of their time.

—— *Rob Roy.* 1817

Ultra-romantic, with its captivating heroine Di Vernon, the strange Northumberland house with its mysteries, and the complicated plot, which involves a young Englishman in the troubles of 1715, takes him on an adventurous excursion into Rob Roy's territory, and brings on the scene Rob Roy himself and the theatrical figure of his wife Helen Macgregor. The descriptions of Highland scenery about Loch Lomond helped to make Scotland a tourist district. On the other hand, the Baillie Nicol Jarvie and the canny gardener Andrew Fairservice rank high among the exponents of Scott's rich humour.

—— *The Heart of Midlothian.* 1818

Opens with an impressive account of the Porteous Riots in Edinburgh (1736) ; but the dramatic interest centres in the misfortunes of a peasant girl, Effie Deans, indicted for the murder of her illegitimate child, and the great heroism of her sister Jeanie, the noblest of Scott's heroines, whose prototype was a certain Helen Walker, who actually walked from Edinburgh to London, as Jeanie does, to obtain her sister's pardon from Queen Caroline. The faithful and kindly pictures of humble life again bear witness to Scott's keen observation of the small farmers, drovers, and other rustic inhabitants of the Lowlands. The crazy Madge Wildfire is another of those wild, grotesque women of whom Meg Merrilies is the type. Among the historical characters introduced are George II's wife Queen Caroline, the Duke of Argyle, and Captain Porteous. The romantic plot is a tissue of theatrical effects and strained coincidences.

—— *The Bride of Lammermoor.* 1819

The most tragic of Scott's romances, on which Donizetti's opera *Lucia di Lammermoor* is based. The last scion of a ruined family and the daughter of his ancestral enemy in possession of the estates fall in love. For a while there is a glimpse of hope and happiness ; but the ambitious mother opposes the match, prophecies and apparitions prognosticate tragedy, and the romance closes in death and sorrow. The scene is laid in East Lothian, near the sea, about 1695. Caleb Balderstone, the faithful retainer, is one of Scott's humorous creations, whose obstinate care for his unhappy master relieves the overpowering tragedy.

—— *A Legend of Montrose.* 1819

A brief but thrilling romance, concerned with the Royalists under Montrose in the Highlands in 1645–6, and based on the singular history of the young Earl of Menteith ; the facts much modified for romantic purposes. A wild tribe of Highlanders, the Children of the Mist, enact a sanguinary part in the drama, which embraces among its personages the famous Montrose, the puritan Marquess of Argyle, and other adherents of the King or the Parliament, and most memorable of all, Captain Dalgetty, a humorous portrayal of a soldier of fortune, which ranks with Scott's finest creations. Compare Scott's idealized version of this episode with Neil Munro's realistic study, *John Splendid*—the other side of the shield.

—— *Ivanhoe.* 1819

The author's first departure from Scottish themes, and his most popular book. Dictated while he was suffering from illness. A many-coloured picture of mediæval England at the period when Norman and Saxon had hardly begun to fuse, when the castles were the strongholds of baronial oppressors, and the woods full of outlaws. Brings together some of the most romantic names of the Middle Ages, Cœur de Lion, Robin Hood, Friar Tuck, Allan-a-Dale, Isaac of York, and Prince John ; the tale of Richard's clandestine home-coming being interwoven with the loves and adventures of a young Saxon knight. The tournament of Ashby-de-la-Zouch, the siege of Front-de-Bœuf's castle, the encounter of Brian de Bois-Gilbert with Ivanhoe, are now classic episodes to be found in many story-books. The period is about 1194, and Yorkshire and Leicestershire supply the principal scenes. Historical and chronological matters are handled with much licence.

—— *The Monastery.* 1820

SCOTT, Sir Walter (*continued*). *The Abbot* [sequel].   1820

Romances of Edinburgh and the Border country in the unsettled period that followed the Scottish defeat at Pinkie. The Monastery of Kennaquhair is Melrose, and most of the earlier events occur on Tweedside. A ghost, the White Lady of Avenel, plays a considerable part, and there is a caricature of an English courtier talking Euphuism. The whole story covers the period 1550–68, to the fall of Mary Queen of Scots, whose personality is sympathetically and inimitably drawn in the later scenes. The regent Murray her bastard brother, George Douglas her would-be rescuer, the Earl of Morton, and other famous people take part in the action. The obscure young man who is the hero attends the Queen in Lochleven Castle and is present at the battle of Dumbarton.

—— *Kenilworth.*   1821

Founded on Mickle's romantic ballad of *Cumnor Hall*; the tragic story of Amy Robsart, the martyred wife of Queen Elizabeth's favourite the Earl of Leicester (1575) : takes great liberties with history and chronology, and scarcely embodies the spirit of the times—the Renaissance, the Elizabethan unrest and enthusiasm. The Queen, Raleigh, Shakespeare, Burleigh, and other historic persons are introduced, and there are elaborate descriptions of the magnificent palace of Kenilworth and of the revels that celebrated the Queen's visit. Oxfordshire and Warwickshire are the principal scenes.

—— *The Pirate.*   1821

A romantic version of the career of a pirate executed in 1725. The scene lies in the Orkney and Shetland Isles, the primitive inhabitants of which are picturesquely described, with their quaint laws and customs two centuries ago. Norna of the Fitful-head is one of those semi-supernatural figures, like Meg Merrilies, and Blind Alice in *The Bride of Lammermoor*, which show Scott's ingrained romanticism.

—— *The Fortunes of Nigel.*   1822

Life in London and at the Court in the early days of James I (1604) ; with full portraits of the King, Prince Charles, Buckingham, Jingling Geordie, founder of Heriot's Hospital, and other historic personages. " No historical portrait that we possess," says R. H. Hutton, " will take precedence, as a mere portrait, of Scott's brilliant study of James I." The fortune-hunting Scots who followed James to England come in for humorous portraiture, and the courtiers, fops, servants, park-rangers, and the lawless population of Alsatia or old Whitefriars, the thieves' sanctuary, make up a motley crowd. Nigel is a young Scots nobleman, who, after an adventurous career, marries the daughter of a London watchmaker.

—— *Peveril of the Peak.*   1823

Has an ultra-romantic plot, in which a supposed deaf mute and a dwarf help defeat the machinations to separate hero and heroine. The historical datum is the bogus conspiracy revealed by Titus Oates : the hero's father is threatened with denunciation. The Peak of Derbyshire, the Isle of Man, and London are the scenes ; and among the personages are Charles II, his favourite the Duke of Buckingham, the Countess of Derby and Queen of Man (whose participation brings in a great deal of Manx lore), Col. Blood, and some of the obscurer ministers of the King's debaucheries.

—— *Quentin Durward.*   1823

Scott's first romance of Continental history. A rich and varied picture of the age when feudalism and chivalry were about to pass away. The chief scenes are in the frontier districts of France and Flanders ; and the Machiavellian Louis XI, headstrong Charles the Bold, and the rebellious Flemings, with the savage William de la Marck, the Wild Boar of Ardennes, Commines the historian, Oliver the barber, Louis' confidant, Galeotti the astrologer, Cardinal Balue, and Lord Crawford, chief of the Scottish Archers, are strongly portrayed. Among the historical incidents are several of the most impressive *mise en scène*, and the pure romance is absorbing. *Quentin Durward* made the same sensation abroad as *Waverley* had made in England.

—— *St. Ronan's Well.*   1823

Scott's attempt to rival Miss Austen in a comedy of character, manners, and small talk in a rural watering-place, Inverleithen on the Tweed. The plot has a tragic ending, but the strength of the novel is in the humours of such people as the landlady, Meg Dods, who has been described as " one of the very best low-comedy characters in the whole range of fiction."

—— *Redgauntlet : a tale of the eighteenth century.*   1824

Incorporates many reminiscences of Scott's youth. The scene is Cumberland and the Scottish district bordering on the Solway. The romantic affairs of the laird of Redgauntlet, his niece and her lover, are interwoven with an abortive Jacobite plot, the most memorable scene of which is the Young Pretender's (apocryphal) farewell to Britain. *Wandering Willie's Tale*, told by one of the characters, has been pronounced the finest short story in the language. The litigious, hard-hearted drunkard, Peter Peebles, is one of Scott's raciest characters.

—— *The Betrothed.*   1825

This and *The Talisman* compose the series of *Tales of the Crusaders*. The scene is Garde Douloureuse, a Norman castle on the Welsh border ; and the motive is first a feud with a Welsh prince, a suitor of the Norman heroine, and then the usurpation of her rights by her lover's kinsman. The *Tales* were to illustrate the disorders caused by the absence of the Crusaders. Time : reign of Henry II (1187).

—— *The Talisman.*   1825

A minor work with a feeble romantic plot. Presents, however, an animated picture of the Crusaders in Palestine (1189–92), with vivid portraits of Cœur de Lion and Saladin, who have several picturesque encounters both peaceful and armed, Berengaria, the Archduke of Austria, Philip Augustus of France, and the Prince Royal of Scotland, who, disguised as an obscure knight, is the nominal hero. The jealousies and squabbles of the generals of Christendom are comic ; but the most humorous scenes are those between Richard and his faithful old counsellor, the Lord of Gilsland.

—— *Woodstock ; or, The Cavalier.*   1826

A Royalist picture of the domination of the Parliament. The scene is the royal demesne of Woodstock, to sequestrate which commissioners have arrived, and are made the butt of a series of hoaxes, the royal lodge where they have their quarters being haunted by ghostly visitants. The romantic plot has for theme

SCOTT, Sir Walter (*continued*).

the love of a brave and generous Roundhead for the daughter of the keeper of Woodstock Park ; and his considerate behaviour when Charles comes as a fugitive after Worcester secures him the bride. Desborough, Harrison, Bletson, and Cromwell himself are introduced. Time, 1652 ; but the history quite untrustworthy.

—— *Chronicles of the Canongate. First Series : The Two Drovers ; The Highland Widow.* 1827

The Two Drovers is founded on the actual history of two cattle-dealers, an Englishman and a Scot, bosom friends, who quarrel over a petty difference, and the insulted Highlander stabs his comrade (1795). *The Highland Widow* is the story of a mother who causes her son to exceed his furlough, with the result that he is shot. Scott was a first-rate hand at the short story, but the best is the one he incorporated in *Redgauntlet*.

—— *The Surgeon's Daughter.* 1827

A melodramatic story said to be founded on fact. Scenes : Fifeshire and India (1780).

—— *The Fair Maid of Perth ; or, St. Valentine's Day.* 1828

Scotland in 1402, the time of Robert III ; a picture full of action and strife, the fierce dissensions of nobles, and the feuds of unruly clans. Perth and the vicinity are the scene, and one of the most memorable episodes is the Homeric battle on the South Inch between the Clans Chattan and Quhele.

—— *My Aunt Margaret's Mirror ; The Tapestried Chamber, or The Lady in the Sacque ; and the Death of The Laird's Jock.* 1828

The *Mirror* discloses a husband's infidelity (1702). *The Tapestried Chamber* is a ghost-story ; scene, a castle in the west of England (1782). *The Laird's Jock* is an episode of border strife—an old warrior dies of shame at witnessing the defeat of his son and the loss of an ancient sword, inherited from his ancestors (period, 1600).

—— *Anne of Geierstein ; or, The Maiden of the Mist.* 1829

Embodies the story of Charles the Bold, Duke of Burgundy, and the heroic Switzers who routed him at Nancy, and thus constitutes a sequel to *Quentin Durward*. The feudal magnificence of the Burgundian Court is thrown into picturesque contrast with the simple and hardy life of the mountaineers. Many romantic personages who lived about 1474–7 are introduced : Queen Margaret of Anjou, the troubadour King René of Provence, Charles the Bold, the merchant-earl of Oxford, and the secret tribunal the *Vehmgericht*. Oxford's son, the hero, weds a Swiss maiden.

—— *Count Robert of Paris.* 1831

A product of Scott's decadence ; subject : the brawls which ensued when the paladins of the First Crusade sojourned in Constantinople (1098). Alexander Comnenus the Emperor, Godfrey de Bouillon, and Count Robert, of the blood of Charlemagne, are among the leading characters, and the hero is an Englishman in the Emperor's bodyguard.

—— *Castle Dangerous.* 1831

Founded on Barbour's *Brus* and Hume's *History of the House of Douglas and Angus*. The story of the Ayrshire castle of the Black Douglas (1306–7), which was taken and re-taken many times during the war of Scottish independence.

[(*a*) Macmillan & Co. : (Border Edn., ed. by A. Lang), 24 vols., with 250 etchings, 1901, a reprint of the edn. pub. by Nimmo (1892–4) ; same, Large Type Edn., 25 vols. ; (Pocket Edn.), 25 vols. ; these follow the arrangement of the Border Edn. except that *Betrothed* and *Talisman* are in separate volumes. (*b*) A. & C. Black : (Dryburgh Edn.), 25 vols., with 250 photogravure plates, 1899 ; (Macmillan, New York), 1892–3 ; (Roxburghe Edn.), 48 vols., with 96 steel plates and 1,600 cuts, 1885 : o.p. ; (Standard Edn.), 25 vols., with frontispiece to each vol. ; (Centenary Edn.), 25 vols., with 158 steel plates (Baker & Taylor, New York), 1889–90 : o.p. ; (Victoria Edn.), 25 vols., with frontispiece to each vol. (25 vols., Lippincott, Philadelphia), 1897. (*c*) Dent : (Temple Edn.), 48 vols., (Dutton, New York) : o.p. ; (Everyman's Lib.), 24 vols., (Dutton, New York), 1908. (*d*) Nelson : (New Century Lib.), 25 vols., 1900–1. (*e*) Oxford Press, 25 vols. (*f*) Houghton, Boston (new edn.), 26 vols. (*g*) Page, Boston, ed. by A. Lang, 26 vols.]

SCUDDER, Vida Dutton [American ; *b.* 1861]. *The Disciple of a Saint : being the imaginary biography of Raniero de Landoccio dei Paglairesi.* 1907

A very delicate and a fairly complete character-portrait of St. Catherine of Siena (see also B. Capes's *Love Story of St. Bel*), through the imaginary memoirs of her secretary, a young Tuscan poet. The chief historical figures form a background to portraits of less-known or fictitious people, on whose lives the influence of the saint is finely brought out. [Dutton, New York (1927) ; Dent.]

SEAMAN, Owen [*b.* 1861]. *Borrowed Plumes.* 1902

Parodies of novelists, poets, and other writers of the day—Mrs. Craigie, Miss Fowler, Hall Caine, Marie Corelli, Mr. Dooley, Hewlett, Meredith, Lord Avebury, Mrs. H. Ward, W. E. Henley, Henry James, Maeterlinck, etc. The imitations are closer and more elaborate, much less summary and trenchant, than those of Bret Harte ; the humour of a subtler nature. [Constable ; Holt, New York.]

SEAWELL, Molly Elliot [American ; 1860–1916]. *Throckmorton.* 1890

Scene, a lowland Virginia neighbourhood ; time, immediately after the Civil War. [Appleton, New York : o.p.]

—— *Little Jarvis.* [juvenile] 1890

The American quarrel with France ; cruise of the frigate *Constellation*. The pathetic and heroic story of a boy midshipman (1798–1800). [Appleton, New York.]

—— *Midshipman Paulding.* [juvenile] 1891

A true story. Midshipman (later Commodore) Hiram Paulding distinguishes himself at the battle of Lake Champlain (1814). [Appleton, New York : o.p.]

—— *Decatur and Somers.* [juvenile] 1894

Adventures of these two American commanders in the war with Tripoli, the daring capture and burning of the *Philadelphia*, and blowing up of the *Intrepid* (1798–1804). [Appleton, New York.]

SEAWELL, Molly Elliot (*continued*). *The Sprightly Romance of Marsac*.   1896
> A lively little story that is almost a farce; impossibilities made plausible, incessant action and animated dialogue; *dramatis personæ*, a small group of Parisians. [Scribner, New York.]

—— *Francezka*.   1902
> A tragic romance, with a spirited and well-informed portrayal of Marshal Saxe, Adrienne Lecouvreur, Voltaire, and their times. [Bobbs-Merrill, Indianapolis; o.p.; De La More Press: o.p.]

—— *The Fortunes of Fifi*.   1903
> Napoleon and a Parisian actress. [Bobbs-Merrill, Indianapolis: o.p.]

—— *The Last Duchess of Belgarde*.   1908
> The intriguing Court of Louis XVI and after that the Terror. The estranged duke and duchess are drawn together again as prisoners in the Temple. [Appleton, New York: o.p.]

SEDGWICK, Anne Douglas [Mrs. Basil de Selincourt; American by birth; *b.* 1873]. *The Confounding of Camelia*.   1899
> A love-comedy, of which the principal motive is evolution of a girl's character from flagrant egoism to sincerity and humility: very frank in its treatment. [Heinemann: o.p.; Century Co., New York: o.p.]

—— *Valerie Upton*.   1907
> A psychological comedy of a very serious cast. Valerie, a figure of intense humanity, is contrasted with her priggish daughter, the "frosty, white-souled, high-principled Imogen," a shallow product of New England Puritanism. [Constable: o.p.; Nelson; *sub tit. A Fountain Sealed*, Houghton, Boston.]

—— *Amabel Channice*.   1908
> The story of a marriage failure. [Arnold; Century Co., New York: o.p.]

—— *Franklin Kane*.   1910
> A solid, cultivated, exalted American; a romantic girl who does not appreciate his sterling worth; divers other sentimental complications, and the misunderstandings and gradual enlightenment by which the right two are eventually brought together. [Arnold: o.p.; Houghton, Boston.]

—— *Tante*.   1911
> A similar study, as usual very diffuse, of the misunderstandings and contradictions of temperament. Tante, a great European pianist, subjugates the soul of a simple and clear-natured girl, who does not see the egoism and cruelty of this dangerous woman till her own life has been almost spoiled. [Arnold: o.p.; Century Co., New York: o.p.; Grosset, New York.]

—— *The Third Window*.   1920
> Malcolm was killed in the war, and his friend Bevis falls in love with the widow, who however receives a message, underlined by Malcolm's psychical sister, that marriages are continued in heaven and he awaits her there. It is the widow who kills herself. [Secker; Houghton, Boston.]

—— *Adrienne Toner*.   1921
> A serious analysis of a typical American girl, soulful, self-assured, and ignorant. In her relations with an English family, she exhibits at once the virtues and the defects of that type; a superficial efficiency, counterbalanced by a readiness to go to pieces owing to lack of foundation and tradition. [Arnold; Houghton, Boston.]

—— *Dark Hester*.   1929
> The author knows how to show the friction of discordant temperaments. Here it is the clash between old and new; an intelligent woman is repelled by the free and defiant intellectualism of her post-war daughter-in-law. What promises merely emotional cataclysms in a teacup develops into stormier drama. [Constable; Houghton, Boston.]

—— *Philippa*.   1930
> A father, essentially hard and selfish, and a daughter, with a cruel insight into the weaknesses and emotions of other people, sympathize with and love each other at the expense of both the former's wives. And yet this selfish affection founders when the daughter falls in love. It is an acute study of jealousy ravaging old affections and wrecking married happiness. [Constable; Houghton, Boston.]

SEDGWICK, Catharine Maria [American; 1789–1867]. *Hope Leslie*.   1827
> The best of a number of domestic novels depicting primitive life in a New England homestead, extolling the modest virtues of kindness and courtesy, honesty and self-improvement, and praising a single life for women. Apart from these moral purposes, her novels picture the bygone life of the village and farm in an attractive light. [2 vols., Harper, New York: o.p.]

SEELEY, Edith. *Under Cheddar Cliffs, a Hundred Years Ago*.   [juvenile] 1903
> Life among the ignorant and brutal lead-miners, farmers, and village folk, of the Mendip Hills in Somerset. Hannah More (1745–1833) is introduced, with her efforts to reform them; and William Wilberforce (1759–1833) just appears. [Seeley: o.p.]

SEGHERS, Anna [German; *b.* 1900]. *The Revolt of the Fishermen* (Aufstand der Fischer von St. Barbara, 1928).   1930
> Portrays the hard and bitter struggle against hunger and despair of the fishermen of a bleak Northern village; their strike for higher wages, and their defeat. Awarded the Kleist prize in Germany. [Transl. by Margaret GOLDSMITH, Mathews; Longmans, New York.]

SEI SHŌNAGON [Japanese; *c.* 1000]. *Pillow Sketches* (Makura Zōshi).   1929
> A kind of commonplace book, random reminiscences, stories, amorous adventures, and the odds-and-ends jotted down of a cultivated and intelligent woman attached to the Court (she is mentioned, and criticized, by Murasaki). Its main interest, perhaps, is that it is suffused with the spirit of its creator, but it makes an interesting pendant, though of a totally different nature, to Murasaki's *Tale of Genji*. [Transl. by Arthur WALEY; Allen; Houghton, Boston.]

SÉNANCOUR, Étienne Pivert de [French; 1770–1846]. *Obermann* (1804). 1903
A kind of meditative romance or protracted soliloquy, in letters, by a disciple of Rousseau, which made a deep impression on his contemporaries and on Matthew Arnold, but is almost unreadable now. Sénancour had already poured out the melancholy of a disillusioned soul, and preached atheism and stoical endurance, in his *Rêveries sur la nature primitive de l'homme* (1799). In *Obermann*, like Chateaubriand in *René*, but with a more agonized pessimism, he projects himself, bemoaning the futility of life and vainly essaying to soothe his sorrow and despair with the beauty and grandeur of Alpine scenery. [With biographical and critical introd. by A. H. WAITE, Welby, 1903: o.p.; transl by J. Anthony BARNES, 2 vols. 1910–14, W. Scott (Simmons, New York): o.p.]

SENIOR, Dorothy. *The Clutch of Circumstance.* 1908
An Arthurian romance inspired by Malory, bringing in the Knights of the Round Table, Cormac, King of Leinster, and other heroes. [Black: o.p.; Macmillan, New York: o.p.]

SERAO, Matilde [Madame Eduardo Scarfoglio; Italian; 1856–1927]. *Fantasy* (Fantasia, 1883). 1890
The contrasted lives of two women from girlhood upwards; one a simple, wholesome nature, the other neurotic and a prey to eccentric ideals. Into the quiet home life of the former with her young husband the other enters as a spirit of mischief. Henry James saw in some of the pictures of outdoor life the direct influence of Zola and Flaubert. The translators compare Madame Serao's realism with the work of Daudet in his more emotional moods. [Transl. by Henry HARLAND and "Paul SYLVESTER," Heinemann; U.S. Book Co., New York: o.p.]

—— *The Conquest of Rome* (La Conquista di Roma, 1885). 1902
A realistic picture of political life in Rome, especially the sides less known to foreigners. The portraits of deputies and others strike one as done from life, and the topographical minuteness is remarkable. The story tells how a provincial deputy failed in his ambition through an entanglement with a married woman. [Heinemann; Harper, New York.]

—— *The Ballet-Dancer* (La Ballerina, 1899); *and, On Guard* (All' erta Sentinella, 1889). 1901
The story of an unfortunate ballet-dancer, a woman "more sinned against than sinning." The other, simple in plan, gives the inside of prison life and noteworthy sketches of character in a Piedmontese governor of a prison and his little boy. The translation defective. [Heinemann: o.p.; Harper, New York: o.p.]

—— *Farewell Love* (Addio, Amore! 1890). 1894
A very luscious and effusive study of uncontrollable passion; the history of a girl who is a slave to love and dies a victim to her infatuation for a man who despises her. The life of the fashionable idle rich in Naples is painted in fulsome colours. [Transl. by Mrs. HARLAND, Heinemann: o.p.]

—— *The Land of Cockayne* (Il Paese di Cuccagna, 1891). 1901
A broad general view of Neapolitan life, and, more narrowly, an exposure of the gambling mania in that city, where lottery competitions flourished to an alarming extent. Depicts the tragedies caused by this fever, the most harrowing incident being the breakdown and death of a nobleman's daughter, who has been repeatedly hypnotized to make her foretell the winning numbers. [Heinemann: o.p.]

—— *After the Pardon* (Dopo il Perdono, 1904). 1909
An honest treatment of the psychology of passion—peculiarly Southern passion—in two lovers who retreat and go back, one to the husband, the other to the betrothed, whom they had betrayed. But pardon cannot restore the love that had already failed, nor penitence renew a life of virtue and happiness. The punishment of the lovers is that they go back to their sin, even when the sin has lost the old fascination. [Nash: o.p.]

—— *The Desire of Life* (Evviva la Vita). 1911
The principal scenes are in the Engadine. [Transl. by William COLLINGE, Collins (Brentano, New York).]

—— *Souls Divided* (Ella non rispose, 1914). 1919
A typical example of this writer's luscious and emotional work. Told in letters, it is the story of two lovers who are never united. The lady marries a wealthy English diplomatist, and when he dies is unable to trace her inamorato. So she pines away and dies. [Transl. by William COLLINGE, Collins (1930).]

SERVICE, Robert William [Canadian; b. 1876]. *The Trail of '98.* 1911
A love-melodrama, with strong pictures of the fierce life of the gold-hunters of Klondyke. [Unwin; Dodd & Mead, New York.]

SETON, Ernest Thompson [Canadian; b. 1860]. *Wild Animals I Have Known.* 1898
The author describes these tales as true. They are about real, individual animals—wolves, dogs, rabbits, crows, foxes, horses, etc.—whom he actually knew in various parts of N. America. He gets inside his animals and makes their characters clear by dint of knowledge, affection, and admiring sympathy. It is something quite different from Mr. Kipling's half-miraculous clairvoyance. His intense enjoyment and emotion carries him away at times into semi-poetical passages. [With 200 *drawings* by the author, Scribner, New York; Hodder.]

—— *Rolf in the Woods: the adventures of a Boy Scout with Indian Quonab and Little Dog Skookum.* 1911
A boy's book of life among the animals of an American forest. Rolf is on the American side in the war of 1812. [*Illus.* by author, Constable; Doubleday, New York.] Mr. Seton has written a large number of animal biographies and nature stories, which may be described as zoological novels, e.g. *Wild Animals I have known* (see above), *Biography of a Grizzly*, and *Two Little Savages.*

"SETON, Graham" [Lieut.-Col. Graham Seton Hutchison; b. 1890]. *The W Plan.* 1929
—— *The Governor of Kattowitz.* 1930
This is fictive history, rather than historical fiction. The first book shows Germany during the war arraying all her strength and exacting every sacrifice for the one purpose, defeating the allies. In the second, where the scene is Silesia and the Polish frontier after the war, the demobilized army is seen disintegrating into lawless bands, hostile to each other and hated by the peasantry. Germans, Poles, Bolshevists, and

"SETON, Graham" (*continued*).

    Jews are taken into account, especially in the qualities that make for survival, individual character being neglected or considered only in its representative aspects. [(1) and (2), Butterworth ; (1), Cosmopolitan Book Co., New York.]

"SETOUN, Gabriel" [Thomas Nicoll Hepburn ; Scottish ; *b.* 1861]. *Robert Urquhart.*   1896

    The love-romance of a schoolmaster in a Fifeshire village, with sketches of local characters, young and old maids, farmers, decayed weavers, and the gossips at the inn. A typical product of the Kailyard school ; Scottish in language and humour ; sentimental, but sane and healthy ; deeply, yet not obtrusively pious. Satirizes the old educational code in the person of a meddling schoolmistress. [Bliss : o.p. ; Fenno, New York : o.p.]

—— *The Skipper of Barncraig.*   1901

    The tragic story of a life turned from its natural bent : the hero is brought up to be a sailor, though he wants to be a musician. The success of the book is in the drawing of the characters, of the minor characters not least : the gossips and wiseacres of the Fifeshire sea-town, pit-folk, fishermen, country people, and seafaring men are quaint and life-like ; their talk is natural and humorous. [Constable : o.p.]

SEVEN WISE MASTERS : *the History of the Seven Wise Masters of Rome.*   *c.* 1505

    A cycle of stories originating in the East, known as the book of Sindbad or Sendabar, an Indian philosopher, *c.* 100 B.C. This original is unknown, though there is an analogous collection in Sanskrit. The book was rendered into Arabic, Persian, Syriac, Greek (*Syntipas*), Latin (*Dolopathos*) by Jean de HAUTESEILLE, monk of Haute-Seille ; French (*Li Romans di Dolopathos*), by the trouvère HERBERS, whence were derived German, Spanish, and English versions. *Li Romans des sept Sages* came from a different Latin original, and so again did the *Historia Septem Sapientium* (Cologne, soon after invention of printing), whence the work cited at head of this note was translated. The device adopted to link the stories is the familiar one of delaying a certain punishment by a series of entertaining recitals ; in this case a young prince falsely accused by his stepmother telling the tales to his father, the Roman emperor. The collection represents the remotest sources traceable of many stories used by the early Italian novelists. [Black-letter edns., printed by Wynkyn de Worde (*c.* 1505), Copland (1550), J. C. for E. Blackmore, etc. (1653), etc. ; repr. from ed. of 1520 by C. L. Gomme, Villon Soc. 1885 : o.p.]

SEYMOUR, Beatrice Kean [*née* Stapleton]. *Invisible Tides.*   1919

    The main situation is one afterwards handled by the authoress much more capably—the emotional triangle of wife, husband, and lover. When the lover is killed in the war, the wife returns. It is a careful—and rather too sombre—study of temperament, even of nerves : it is not so much what the characters are, as what takes place within them that is chronicled. [Chapman : o.p. ; Boni, New York.]

—— *The Romantic Tradition.*   1925

    More or less confessedly inspired by Meredith. Two thoroughly exceptional characters, the woman especially is such, are trying to achieve " a marriage of true minds " and to make it permanent. They all but succeed, in spite of the dramatic interferences of " the romantic tradition . . . of eternal love-making and chocolates," and—it must be added—of an incredible bit of melodrama at the end. [Chapman ; *sub tit. Unveiled*, Boni, New York.]

—— *The Last Day.*   1926

    A woman, of the same superfine strain as Enid in the previous novel, is seen trying to make up her mind between the husband who is her spiritual complement and the lover who appeals to her senses. [Chapman ; Boni, New York.]

—— *But not for Love.*   1930

    Here again is posited a high and refined standard of love, to make the perfect marriage ; and it is her sense of this that distinguishes the heroine from the rest of the ultra-modern young women. Falling short of her ideal, she ends the marriage tragically for both her husband and herself. [Chapman.]

SHAKESPEARE'S LIBRARY ; *the romances, novels, poems, and histories used by Shakespeare as the foundation of his dramas ; ed. by J. Payne Collier.* 2 vols.   1843

    Greene's *Pandosto* (*The Winter's Tale*) ; Lodge's *Rosalynd* (*As You Like It*) ; *The Histoire of Hamblet* (*Hamlet*) ; *Apollonius, Prince of Tyre* (*Pericles*) ; *Romeus and Juliet*, by Arthur Brooke ; *Rhomeo and Julietta*, from Paynter's *Palace of Pleasure* ; *Giletta of Narbona* (*All's Well that Ends Well*), ibid. ; *The Two Lovers of Pisa* (*Merry Wives of Windsor*) ; *The Historie of Apollonius and Silla* (containing part of plot of *Twelfth Night*), Rich's *Farewell to Military Profession*, 1606 ; *The Historie of Promos and Cassandra* (*Measure for Measure*), from Whetstone's *Heptameron of Civil Discourses*, 1582 ; *The Adventures of Giannetto*, from the *Pecorone* of Ser Giovanni Fiorentino, *Of a Jew Who Would for his Debt have the Flesh of a Christian*, from the *Orator* of Alex. Silvayn, transl. by A. MUNDAY, 1598, *The Choice of Three Caskets*, from the *Gesta Romanorum*, transl. by ROBINSON (*Merchant of Venice*) ; *The Story of a Moorish Captain*, from the *Heccatomithi* of Cinthio (*Othello*) ; *Queen Cordila*, a poem by John Higgins, from the *Mirror for Magistrates*, 1587 ; *The Paphlagonian Unkind King*, from Sir Philip Sidney's *Arcadia*, 1590 (Gloster and his sons in *King Lear*) ; *The History of Makbeth*, from Holinshed's *Chronicle* ; *The Shepherdess Felismena*, from the *Diana* of Montemayor, transl. by B. YOUNG, 1598 (*Two Gentleman of Verona*) ; *The Story told by the Fishwife of Stand on the Green*, from *Westward for Smelts*, 1620 (*Cymbeline*). [Thomas Rodd, 1843, o.p. Most of these works are reprinted in the new *Shakespeare Library*, with revised and annotated texts, and a most elaborate *apparatus criticus*, embracing introductions, notes, illustrative passages from originals of translations, etc., 11 vols., Oxford Press.]

"SHALOM 'ALEKHEM" [Solomon Rabinovitz ; Russian Jew ; 1859–1916]. *Stempenyu.*   1913

    The hero so named is a natural genius who goes wandering about the world fiddling and making love, till he is caught by a strong-minded woman and reduced to bondage. It is a fanciful, humorous, gnomic story, and the style of the Yiddish original is cunningly reflected in the quaint irregularity and deliberate clumsiness of the translation. [Transl. by Hannah BERMAN, Methuen.]

"SHALOM 'ALEKHEM" (*continued*). *Jewish Children.* 1920

Nineteen tales of Jewish children in Russian Poland, all told from a child's point of view, and veritable little masterpieces of poetic art. [Transl. by Hannah BERMAN, Heinemann; with introd. by Dorothy Canfield, Knopf, New York, 1926.]

SHARP, William [" Fiona Macleod "; Scottish; 1856–1905]. *Pharais: a romance of the Isles.* 1894

" Fiona Macleod " was a clear case of dual personality. Sharp's work under this name—so much more than a name to him that he said, Fiona dies if the secret is found out—differs entirely from the work he acknowledged. These are romances and visionary stories of the Western Isles, where he spent his boyhood, saturated with mysticism and Celtic faerydom, the style a sort of rhapsody that oft-times attains rare beauty, the beauty of " natural magic," though its monotony must be admitted, like the absence of humour and of any lightness of touch. This is a wistful little domestic drama, composed of the simplest and homeliest elements, spiritualized by the author's poetic vision, and by the grandeur of the stage amidst the storms and sunsets of the Hebrides.

—— *The Mountain Lovers.* 1895

A tragic pastoral of the Highlands that might belong to present or past, but is imbued with the mysticism of long ago. The actors are akin to the shadowy creations of ancient legend ; the significance of the action is spiritual and symbolical.

—— *The Sin-Eater ; The Washer of the Ford ; and other legendary moralities.* 1895–6

Collections of Hebridean lore and old Celtic legends. The latter belong to the time when Christianity was struggling with Druidism. The characters shadowy and lacking in human interest. *Muime Chriosd* is an Irish legend of St. Bridget, the foster-mother of Christ, and the Celtic elements mingle quaintly with the Gospel story.

—— *Green Fire.* 1896

A vague and tenuous story, a sort of Tristan legend of a Breton lady and the son of a Scottish chief. Dreamy descriptions of Brittany, the sea, and the Hebrides ; mystic visions, fears, and monitions creating an atmosphere of witching melancholy.

—— *The Laughter of Peterkin : a retelling of old tales from the Wonder World.* 1897

Peterkin is a somewhat superfluous " wonder-child," whose laughter is interjected into tragic episodes from old Celtic legend, *The Four Swans, The Fate of the Three Sons of Turenn*, etc.

—— *Silence Farm.* 1899

A gloomy, realistic story of life on a farm, ending in tragedy. Published under his own name.

—— *The Dominion of Dreams ; Under the Dark Star.* 1899

Some thirty chapters or " dreams " mingling Celtic fantasy and real life. *The White Heron* relates the earlier story of a character in *Pharais.*

—— *The Divine Adventure ; Iona : studies in spiritual history.* 1900

The first is a fable or allegory in the traditional Celtic manner. The Soul, the Will, and the Body go on pilgrimage towards the Hills of Dream, symbolizing man's quest for a solution of the mysteries of life and death, dissolution and eternity. *Iona* is an essay on the place of Iona in Celtic tradition.

[*Collected Works*, 7 vols., Heinemann (Duffield, New York), 1911. Vol. i. : *Pharais, The Mountain Lovers ;* ii. : *The Sin-Eater, The Washer of the Ford, and other Legendary Moralities ;* iii. : *The Dominion of Dreams, Under the Dark Star ;* iv. : *The Divine Adventure, Iona, Studies in Spiritual History ;* v. : *The Winged Destiny, Studies in the Spiritual History of the Gael ;* vi. : *The Silence of Amor, Where the Forest Murmurs ;* vii. : *Poems and Dramas.* Also Pocket Ed., same, with vol. 8, *The Laughter of Peterkin*.]

SHAW, Adèle Marie [American]. *The Coast of Freedom.* 1903

" A romance of the adventurous times of the first self-made American "—the career of Sir William Phips (1651–94), Governor of Massachusetts. Boston, time of Cotton Mather and the persecution for witchcraft (1681). [Doubleday, New York : o.p. ; Hodder : o.p.]

SHAW, George Bernard [Irish ; b. 1856]. *The Irrational Knot.* 1905

" The second novel of his Nonage " . . . " an early attempt . . . to write *A Doll's House* in English " ; written 1880, pub. 1905. Studies the sex question in the cases of a legal marriage and an irregular union, both between members of opposite social spheres, and concludes in favour of freedom. The hero is an electrical engineer and a *very* Admirable Crichton. [Constable ; Brentano, New York.]

—— *An Unsocial Socialist.* 1887
—— *Love Among the Artists.* 1889

The first and third " novels of his Nonage." The titles characterize them sufficiently : in artistic value they are entirely below comparison with the writer's plays. [(1) and (2), Constable ; Brentano, New York.]

—— *Cashel Byron's Profession ; also The Admirable Bashville, and an Essay on Modern Prize-fighting.* 1886

" No. 4 of the novels of his Nonage." Byron, the gentleman who becomes champion of the ring, and not only makes a good income by his profession but marries a lady, seems to be an adumbration, at least, of the superman. In one of the most significant passages in the book, he proves the supreme value of executive power : " A man that understands one art—even the pugilistic—understands every art." The novel is dramatized, or parodied, in a blank-verse play, which is an absurd travesty of Shakespearian and other kinds of romanticism. [Constable ; Brentano, New York.]

SHEEHAN, Rev. Patrick Augustine [Irish ; 1852–1913]. *My New Curate : a story gathered from the stray leaves of an old diary.* 1900

The diarist and commenator, the humorous Daddy Dan, priest of a sequestered, sleepy parish in Ireland, is an admirable contrast to the energetic young curate, used to the systematic work of an English city, who wants to perform the sweeping office of the new broom. His efforts fill the place with consternation. [Longmans, London and New York (1928) ; Burns & Oates.]

SHEEHAN, Rev. Patrick Augustine (*continued*). *Luke Delmege.*   1901
    The life of an Irish priest. " The main theme of this great novel is the setting forth of the spiritual ideals of the race and of the heights of moral beauty and heroism to which these can lead " (Rev. Stephen J. Brown, s.j.). Contrasts English and Irish views of life, and depicts in a masterly way the public and private events of the priest's daily routine and the typical incidents of life in Ireland. Canon Sheehan was parish priest of Doneraile. [Longmans, London and New York.]

—— *Glenanaar : a story of Irish life.*   1905
    A study of tainted heredity in a family of informers, opening with the trial of the Doneraile conspirators at Cork in 1829, when O'Connell saved the defendants (here described as innocent), and coming down to the great famine of 1848. [Longmans, London and New York.]

—— *Lisheen ; or, The Test of the Spirits.*   1907
    An idealistic member of the landlord class in Kerry puts his ideals of social regeneration into practice by living the life of a common labourer : cf. Tolstoy's *Resurrection* (see p. 469). [Longmans, London and New York.]

—— *The Blindness of Dr. Gray ; or, The Final Law.*   1909
    Strong in the portrayal of Roman Catholic clerical life in Ireland. Dr. Gray is a moral martinet who believes in strict justice, but finds as time goes on " that it is love, not law, that rules the world." A story with love interest of refreshing charm, considerable pathos, and criticism of politics, religion, and " the change in the mentality of the people," giving food for thought. [Longmans, London and New York.]

—— *The Queen's Fillet.*   1911
    A long and crowded romance of the whole revolutionary period in France, but concerned especially with the years 1798–94, from the beginnings of the Revolution to the fall of Robespierre. Tallyrand and the poet André Chénier are prominent among the historic figures. [Longmans, London and New York.]

—— *Miriam Lucas.*   1912
    The life-story of an attractive Irish girl provides scenes of life in Dublin and the slums of New York, in the late nineteenth century. [Longmans, London and New York.]

SHELDON, Rev. Charles Monroe [American ; *b.* 1857]. *John King's Question Class.*   1899
    A didactic novel expounding the author's ideas on living for the glory of God, on political and social abuses, on private vices (smoking, etc.), in a parson's replies to questions put by his pupils. The career of a girl who has a genius for music runs through these scenes. Specimen of a large series of once strangely popular didactic novels. [Grosset, New York : o.p. ; Heinemann : o.p.]

SHELLEY, Mrs. Mary Wollstonecraft [*née* Godwin ; 1797–1851]. *Frankenstein ; or, The Modern Prometheus.*   1818
    The best of the tales of mystery and horror written in friendly competition by Shelley, Byron, Polidori, and Mrs. Shelley at Geneva in 1816. It is a ghastly extravaganza, built up on the idea of a monster created on pseudo-scientific principles, and endowed with life, by a young German, whom the monster forthwith turns upon and keeps in anxiety and torment. [(Everyman's Lib.) Dent (Dutton, New York), 1913 ; Brentano, New York.]

SHEPPARD, Alfred Tresidder [*b.* 1871]. *The Red Cravat.*   1905
    An historical comedy. Crazy old Friedrich Wilhelm of Prussia, his grotesque chamberlain, a pair of court jesters, and other eccentrics, join in a most original and diverting fantasia (1730–1). A kidnapped Englishman, enlisted in the giant grenadiers, is the hero. [Hodder.]

—— *Running Horse Inn.*   1906
    A tragic novel of hatred and revenge, opening with the return of a Peninsular soldier to the inn near Herne Bay on the day his brother marries his old love. The character-drawing is strong, and rural life in the times just after Waterloo is rendered with truth and good humour. More than a glimpse is had of the unrest with which England was seething, and the Spa Fields riot of 1816 comes into the story. [Hodder ; Lippincott, Philadelphia : o.p.]

—— *The Autobiography of Judas Iscariot.*   1920
    Power sometimes degenerating into violence is the obvious quality of this interpretation of Judas, as a sort of Ishmael, who feels himself mocked and maddened into crime. [Allen & Unwin.]

—— *Brave Earth.*   1925
    A graphic story of the Reformation and the Western Rising (1549). The scene shifts from the west of England to France, Rabelais putting in an appearance at Lyons. [Cape ; Doubleday, Doran, New York.]

—— *Here Comes an old Sailor.*   1927
    A fairly successful attempt to give the social and moral colour of the Middle Ages. The time is the reign of John, who stands mainly in the background, the foreground being occupied by the domestic life of a religious house and of a Kentish family, and such a picturesque event as the sea-fight with the French off Sandwich (1217). [Hodder ; Doubleday, Doran, New York.]

—— *Tuck-of-Drum.*   1930
    Short stories aiming in like manner to evoke the past. *The End of the Sermon* is a vivid picture of Spaniards during the Peninsular war ; *The Cross at the Door*, a sombre one of mediæval Paris ; in the title-piece, three of Napoleon's veterans take part in the resistance to the Prussians in 1870. [Hodder.]

SHEPPARD, Elizabeth Sara [1830–62]. *Charles Auchester : a memorial.*   1853
    A sentimental rhapsody devoted to music and musicians ; Seraphael is an idealized portrait of Mendelssohn ; other characters are claimed to represent minor celebrities of the time. [McKay, Philadelphia, 1928].

SHERIDAN, Mrs. Frances [*née* Chamberlaine, 1724–66]. *Memoirs of Mrs. Sydney Biddulph.*   1761
    Written in opposition to the theory of poetic justice. " Every affliction is accumulated on the innocent heroine, in order to show that neither prudence nor foresight, nor the best dispositions of the human heart, are sufficient to defend from the evils of life " (Dunlop). The Abbé Prevost adapted the story sub tit. *Mémoires pour servir à l'histoire de la vertu : extraits du journal d'une dame* (1762). [o.p.]

SHERRIFF, Robert Cedric [b. 1896], and BARTLETT, Vernon. *Journey's End.* 1930
The well-known play transposed into a novel, without any detriment to the spirit of the original. [Gollancz ; Stokes, New York.]

SHIEL, Matthew Phipps [b. 1865]. *The Yellow Danger.* 1898
A sensation romance of the near future, and a glorification of jingoism on the largest scale. The Japanese and Chinese set the nations of Europe by the ears with the object of aggrandizing themselves when their enemies are exhausted. Battle and sea-fights of a monstrous and sanguinary kind succeed each other with bewildering rapidity. [De La More Press : o.p. ; Fenno, New York : o.p.]

—— *Contraband of War.* 1899
An exciting tale of high finance and politics during the Spanish-American war (1897–9). [De La More Press : o.p.]

—— *Cold Steel.* 1899
A rapid, melodramatic story of violent action, fighting, love-making, and intrigue, in the England of Henry VIII. That jovial monarch and Anne Boleyn appear, but the interest is not particularly historical. [Gollancz (1929) ; Vanguard Press, New York.]

—— *The Man-Stealers : an incident in the life of the Iron Duke.* 1900
A frankly sensational narrative of a French plot to kidnap the Duke of Wellington and avenge the exile of Napoleon ; impossible events simulating truth by sheer rapidity of narrative. [Hutchinson : o.p. ; Lippincott, Philadelphia : o.p.]

—— *The Lord of the Sea.* 1901
Another impossible romance in which modern inventions and scientific marvels are dexterously used for sensational effect. The hero is a Jewish Napoleon, who undertakes to subjugate the sea, as the land is subjugated under the present regime. The events by which he makes himself a mighty ruler in the earth are related with vigorous, if often crude, realism. [Gollancz (1929) ; Knopf, New York (1924).]

—— *The Purple Cloud.* 1901
A highly coloured story of an explorer who reaches the North Pole, and thereby releases an unknown force which blots out all human life, save himself and one woman. His experiences as a solitary wanderer in devastated Europe are the product of a vivid, unbridled imagination. [Gollancz (1929) ; Vanguard Press, New York.]

—— *The Weird O't.* 1902
An intriguing detective story intermingled with a good deal of philosophic doctrine. [Gollancz (1929).]

SHORTHOUSE, Joseph Henry [1834–1903]. *John Inglesant.* 1881
The spiritual biography of a very rare spirit who was a servant of Charles I, and afterwards acts as go-between to the Anglican and Romanist ecclesiastical parties. Historical events are subordinate, however, to the subjective narrative. In Mr. Ferrar's house at Little Gidding, among the Quietists, Inglesant becomes acquainted with the mysticism that was a common philosophy to certain Romanists and Anglicans ; and on the exposition of this doctrine, which reproduced itself in the Tractarian movement of our own times, the author concentrates his eloquence. Many great men appear, and the manners, the thought, and the religious feeling of the period in England and Italy are rendered with studious accuracy and deep sympathy. Such episodes as the election of a Pope and the plague at Naples are, as it were, careful historical monographs vivified by imagination. [Macmillan, London and New York ; (Caravan Lib.), *id.*]

—— *The Little Schoolmaster Mark : a spiritual romance.* 1883
A mystical story which borrows material from H. Jung-Stilling's autobiography (1750). [Macmillan : o.p.]

—— *Sir Percival.* 1886
Ostensibly told by a woman, about a nineteenth-century seeker after the Grail, an idealized young Englishman, in an idealized and beautiful society. [Macmillan : o.p.]

—— *The Countess Eve.* 1888
A spiritual romance, in which the Evil One, who comes on the scene, is foiled in his attempt to seduce two human beings : a study of human infirmity and proneness to temptation. Many pages of descriptive rhapsody of the beautiful mountains, forests, and lakes of Burgundy and the Jura. [Macmillan : o.p.]

—— *A Teacher of the Violin ; and other tales.* 1888
Short stories treating similar themes of spiritual aspiration, refined ideals of conduct, and the ennobling influences of the chivalrous past. The title-story is about a music-loving boy in Germany (1787) and his communings with Nature. Of the four others, the *Marquis de St. Pelaye* is most characteristic. [Macmillan : o.p.]

—— *Blanche, Lady Falaise.* 1891
A mystical, dreamy novel, largely a vehicle for the discussion of religious and moral ideas. Lady Falaise is a socialistic dreamer, whose very love rests on her ideals of social amelioration, and whose practical conduct is, in consequence, often wrong-headed and mischievous. [Macmillan : o.p.]

SIDGWICK, Cecily [Mrs. Alfred Sidgwick, *née* Ullmann ; " Mrs. Andrew Dean "]. *Isaac Eller's Money.* 1889
Intimate portraiture of a community of Frankfurt Jews settled in London, a squalid race of money-grubbers, contemptuous of anything better in life, with their less repellent women-folk. A love-story runs through. [Unwin : o.p.]

—— *The Inner Shrine.* 1900
Portraiture of some various characters, an innocent and high-minded girl, a very vulgar and pretentious married couple, a bright little boy, and others. Placed in a difficult situation, this engaging type of loyal girlhood, loved by a married man, and compromised by the two scandal-mongers, suffers no loss of dignity or of truth to the inner shrine. [Harper : o.p.]

—— *The Severins.* 1909
Extremely realistic and elaborate character-drawing of a number of major figures and not a few minor is the outstanding quality of all these novels. In the last, we have a sound, solid, conventional young English-

SIDGWICK, Cecily (*continued*).

man ; an idealistic social reformer, who is ruthlessly anatomized, together with his shiftless family and their German and Russian friends ; and a heroine of fine personality. [Methuen : o.p.]

—— *The Lantern Bearers.*   1910

The true romance in a familiar suburban setting. About the clandestine marriage of a very attractive pair who have to keep their union secret, with amusing results, the wife going out as a lady-help to one of her husband's friends. Much pointed characterization, e.g. the young German learning English methods of business, and his cousins with their desperate attempts to disguise their German origin. [Methuen : o.p.]

—— *Anthea's Guest.*   1911

Piquant character-drawing of both English people and Germans, nice people and vulgar, the guest of the good-natured Anthea being a delightful hussy of an adventuress who runs a successful career in both countries and elopes with Anthea's rich uncle. [Methuen : o.p.]

—— *Below Stairs.*   1913

A quiet story, with romance at the end, bringing home to one the dull and drab existence of servants in a large house. [Methuen : o.p.]

—— *Karen.*   1918

A vivid and amusing picture of German social life as it appears to an English girl invited to a friend's wedding in Germany, hitting off admirably such things as the arrogance and narrow conventionality of the Graf, the tutor's bad manners, and the detestation of England shown by the heroine's acquaintances. [Collins.]

—— *Masquerade.*   1930

An entertaining novel on well-known lines, with a number of clean-cut and amusing characters, and no lack of incidents. [Collins.]

SIDGWICK, Ethel [*b.* 1877]. *Promise.*   1910

—— *Succession : a comedy of the generations* [sequel].   1913

This is a long study of a youthful musical genius, the son of an English father and a French wife. It demonstrates the impossibility of control of the artistic impulse, and the torture which such a temperament provides for its possessor. Particularly in the sequel, there are many scenes of French life, with which the authoress is familiar. [(1) and (2), Sidgwick & Jackson ; Small, Boston.]

—— *Le Gentleman ; an idyll of the Quarter.*   1911

A love-story of bohemian life in Paris. [Sidgwick & Jackson ; Small, Boston.]

—— *Herself.*   1912

About an attractive Irish girl, who is a teacher in Paris, and later a governess in London. [Sidgwick & Jackson ; Small, Boston.]

SIDNEY, Sir Philip [1554–86]. *The Countess of Pembroke's Arcadia.*   1590

The first edition, containing the first three books, was not published till 1590, though written a decade earlier and widely circulated in MS. It was shown in 1907 by Mr. Bertram Dobell that these three books were a recast by Sidney of the original work (now distinguished as the " old *Arcadia* "). In 1593 a new edition was published in five books, the fourth and fifth being added to the three of 1590 from the old *Arcadia*. In the *Arcadia*, Sidney combined the pastoral romance of Sanazzaro and Montemayor with the romance of chivalry. It is a rambling story of the adventures of two shipwrecked princes, who in disguise woo the daughters of the king of Arcadia, and set in motion a train of events which are to fulfil a certain oracle. The book in both matter and expression is nearer poetry than prose fiction proper, mingling verse with a flowery and emotional prose elaborately cadenced, and imaging a more beautiful world than the real, in the manner expounded by Sidney in his *Apologie*. The action and the characters body forth his ideals of chivalrous virtue, heroic energy, and passionate love, and express his longing for a simpler and purer life than was his own lot amid the pomps and frivolities of Elizabeth's Court. Alexander supplemented " a defect in the third part," and Beling added a sixth book. Dr. H. O. Sommer's (only edn. since eighteenth century except Hans Friswell's abridgement, London, 1893 : o.p.) is a photographic reproduction of 1st ed., which contained only first three books (1891, Paul : o.p. Scribner, New York : o.p.). [Ed. E. A. Baker, with the additions of Sir Wm. Alexander and Richard Beling, a life, and intro. (Early Novelists), Routledge, 1907 (Dutton, New York) ; *Works*, 4 vols., ed. by Albert Feuillerat, Camb. Univ. Press (1912), 1926 ; Vols. I and II, *Arcadia*, *Poems* ; Vol. III, *Defence of Poesie*, etc. (Vol. IV, The *Older Arcadia*). The story of Argalus and Parthenia was often published separately in the seventeenth and eighteenth centuries, e.g. *The Unfortunate Lovers : the history of Argalus and Parthenia*. Black Letter, 1672.]

SIENKIEWICZ, Henryk [Polish ; 1846–1916]. *In Vain* (1863).   1899

A story of University life in Poland, chiefly remarkable for the penetration into various people's motives shown by the author, then under eighteen. The hero, a young lad, afflicted with a promiscuous love of women, is analytically portrayed, with his state of mind in his love affairs with two women. [Transl. by Jeremiah CURTIN, Dent : o.p. ; Little & Brown, Boston : o.p.]

—— *With Fire and Sword : an historical romance of Poland and Russia* (Ogniem i mieczem, 1886).

1890

—— *The Deluge : an historical romance of Poland, Sweden, and Russia* (Potop, 1888) [sequel].

1891

—— *Pan Michael : an historical romance of Poland, Russia, and the Ukraine* (Pan wołodyjowski, 1893) [sequel].   1898

The romance of Polish history from 1647 to 1674, composed on a scheme more vast and multitudinous even than Tolstoy's *War and Peace*. Sienkiewicz was the Scott and the Dumas of Poland, a magnificent improviser, who had delved in the ancestral records of many Polish houses, had a genius for character-drawing and narrative, and an expert's knowledge of strategy and tactics which stood him in good stead in his great romances of war and battle. The first part describes the terrible war that arose when the Ukraine Cossacks, reinforced by Tartars and Ottomans, revolted from Poland, triumphing at Korsún and suffering defeat at Sbarasz ; the next, still more voluminous, deals with the overwhelming invasion

SIENKIEWICZ, Henryk (*continued*).

of Poland and Lithuania by the Swedes, under Charles Gustavus (1654–5), and the splendid rally of the Poles ; and the third continues the story of the war with the Tartars. An accumulation of episodes, connected by various characters and their histories ; the personal interest very considerable, a number of figures, principally nobles, standing out from the crowd, many of them striking, savage, heroic, or saintly, some humorous or grotesque, others bold historical studies of personages like Sobieski, the Russian Hemnitski, the treacherous Radziwill, and King Kazimir. The general impression left is of a succession of scenes of battle, carnage, devastation, lust, and fiery heroism, now and then relieved by quieter episodes of village life and domestic peace. [Transl. by Jeremiah CURTIN, (1), (2), 2 vols., and (3), Little & Brown, Boston ; Dent : o.p.]

—— *Without Dogma : a novel of modern Poland* (Bez Dogmatu, 1891).   1893

Sets forth the conflict of modern paganism and Christianity, in the persons of a sceptical Polish dilettante and a girl of pure and earnest character. The man is a type of Slavonic incapacity for action, and in his conduct modern decadence is satirized. The long spiritual combat of the two lovers, separated by a woman's simple determination to do right, is narrated in a journal, in which their hearts and minds are explored with an insight which has suggested to many readers that Sienkiewicz was analysing the opposing elements in his own mind. A sad tale, unrelieved by a touch of happiness—the kind old Polish aunt almost the only pleasant character. [Transl. by Iza YOUNG, Dent : o.p. ; Little & Brown, Boston : o.p.]

—— *Lillian Morris ; and other stories.*   1894

Chiefly the fruit of his own experiences in Spain and the United States. *Lillian Morris* is the tragic account of an overland journey to California, and *Yannyol* the touching story of a forlorn child. [Little & Brown, Boston : o.p.]

—— *Children of the Soil : a novel of modern Polish life* (Rodzina Połanieckich).   1895

An elaborate novel of contemporary life in Poland, clearly interpreting the temperament of the Slav, and opening up the agricultural and other problems. The personal interest is chiefly in the story of the ups and downs of married life ; the women and still more particularly the children are admirably drawn. [Transl. by J. CURTIN, Dent : o.p. ; Little & Brown, Boston : o.p.]

—— *Quo Vadis ? a narrative of the time of Nero* (Quo Vadis ? 1895).   1896

The book that brought Sienkiewicz recognition throughout the European world. A broad, theatrical picture of Roman life in all its light and shade, splendours and horrors, bringing into salient contrast the licentiousness of paganism and the spiritual beauty of Christianity. Scenes of Court life and of Christian worship, the burning of Rome, and the massacres in the amphitheatre, are woven into a rapid narrative, which brings in a motley host of characters, all speaking in their proper roles, slaves, preachers, and imperial Romans. The Apostles Peter and Paul come on the stage, but the pagans are the most interesting characters ; Nero, for instance, an impressive figure in his strange and repulsive individuality—and Petronius Arbiter, the artist in refined sensuality, the worshipper of beauty, is the dominating personality of the book. [Transl. by J. CURTIN, Dent ; Little & Brown, Boston ; transl. by S. A. BINION and S. MALEVSKY, Routledge ; Crowell, New York.]

—— *Sielanka, a Forest Picture ; and other stories* (1893).   1898

Sielanka, the idyll of two young lovers in a forest, is a poetic rendering of the life of nature. The pathetic *Lighthouse Keeper of Aspinwall*, *Sachem*, and *Across the Plains* embody the author's American experiences, the last being the tragic story of an overland journey to California, chequered by the perils and privations of fifty years ago. Sachem, the last of the Black Snake Indians, appears as a circus performer in Texas. In *Yanko the Musician*, a story that brought every Polish reader to tears, a poor half-witted village lad falls a victim to his passion for music. *Yamyol* is a kindred sketch of a forlorn village boy. *The Bull-fight* is Spanish. In *The Diary of a Tutor in Poznan* and in *Bartek the Victor* the tyranny of the Germans in Poland is depicted. The Tutor is a poor little martyr to scholastic regulations. Bartek, a stupid, gigantic hero, performs miracles of prowess at Gravelotte and Sedan, but coming home is persecuted and sent to gaol because he is a Pole. The episode of the ignorant peasants coming out to fight they know not whom is a curious study of the psychology of war. [Transl. by J. CURTIN, Dent : o.p. ; Little & Brown, Boston : o.p.]

—— *In Monte Carlo.*   1899

A Polish artist, entangled with a *demi-mondaine*, falls in love purely and sincerely with a good woman. Depicts many shades of character, vile and noble. [Transl. by Count S. C. DE SOISSONS, Greening : o.p.]

—— *Tales* (Nowele, 1896).   1899

Minor stories, and fragmentary episodes, all thoroughly Slavonic in character. *A Country Artist* is a sentimental tale containing an imaginative description of organ-playing ; *In Bohemia*, a tale of irregular artist life ; *Anthea*, like *Quo Vadis ?* deals with classical times ; *The Duel* is a realistic story of life in the Ukraine. [Transl. by Count S. C. DE SOISSONS, G. Allen : o.p.]

—— *In the New Promised Land.*   1900

The tragic fortunes of a peasant and his daughter, decoyed to America by an emigration agent. They go out full of hope, and on landing are plunged into the deepest poverty. Their sufferings are heart-rending, and, though they endure with Slavonic patience, the father dies and the girl loses her reason. [Transl. by Count S. C. DE SOISSONS, Jarrold : o.p.]

—— *The Knights of the Cross : an historical romance of Poland and Germany* (Krzyżacy, 1900).
                    1900

Poland and Lithuania at the end of the fourteenth century, an heroic epoch of Polish history, when strife was hot with the Germans, headed by the savage Knights of the Cross. The exploits and love romance of a Polish knight are bound up with the historical events ; the characters are drawn to an heroic scale, and many of the incidents are stupendous. The author's love of horrors is as evident here as in his great trilogy. [Transl. by Jeremiah CURTIN, 2 vols., Dent : o.p. ; Little & Brown, Boston : o.p. ; transl., Sands, 1900 : o.p.]

—— *On the Field of Glory* (c. 1900).   1906

A strenuous national romance (unfinished) opening in the winter of 1682–3 (the times of John Sobieski), with

SIENKIEWICZ, Henryk (*continued*).
  five spectacular scenes of adventure in the forests and fierce warfare against the Turks. [Transl. by Henry BRITTON, Lane : o.p. ; transl. by J. CURTIN, Little & Brown, Boston : o.p.]

—— *Hania ; and other stories.*   1897
  Ten tales, mainly of Polish life. [Transl. by J. CURTIN, Dent : o.p. ; Little & Brown, Boston : o.p.]

—— *Whirlpools : a novel of modern Poland.*   1911
  [Apparently appeared first in English, and no Polish edn. yet ; Laurie : o.p. ; Little & Brown, Boston : o.p.]

SILBERRAD, Una Lucy [*b.* 1872]. *The Lady of Dreams.*   1900
  A gloomy story, with some melodramatic scenes. A mad uncle, his niece, whom he tries to shoot and who accidentally shoots him, and a doctor are the personages. The doctor persuades the much-tried girl to marry him, but her feeling for him is only friendship, and when she wakes out of the morbid, dreamy state of mind caused by her troubles, she loves another man. The scene is laid in the poor quarters of East London. [Heinemann : o.p. ; Doubleday, New York : o.p.]

—— *Desire.*   1908
  Desire, daughter of a wealthy man who dies intestate, has lived a self-indulgent life, but love and work make her a totally different woman. [Long ; Doubleday, New York : o.p.]

—— *Ordinary People.*   1909
  Faithful chronicling of the uneventful lives of quite ordinary people, done in such a way as to make them keenly interesting. Plot-building, however, introduces some improbable situations that are certainly not ordinary. [Nelson.]

—— *Sampson Rideout, Quaker.*   1911
  Rural life in the neighbourhood of Salisbury and Shaftesbury about the year 1700, a Quaker manufacturer in love with a lady of superior station. [Nelson.]

SIME, Miss J. G. *Our Little Life.*   1921
  Study of a working-girl's life in Montreal. [Richards.]

SIMMS, William Gilmore [American ; 1806–1870]. *Guy Rivers.*   1834
  The evil-doings of a border bandit and the fierce campaign against him give a picturesque historical element to this otherwise conventional novel. [o.p.]

—— *The Partisan.*   1835
—— *Mellichampe : a legend of the Santee.*   1836
—— *The Scout* (1st edn. entitled " *The Kinsmen* ").   1841
—— *Katherine Walton.*   1851
  A closely connected sequence of romances dealing with the War of Independence in the South, the scenes being mainly on the Carolina coast, about Charleston and old Dorchester. The actualities of the long domestic war, suspicions and fears among friends and kinsfolk, double dealings of traitors and patriots alike, together with scenes from the brilliant social life of Charleston and episodes in field and forest, are worked into an old-fashioned novel of plot and adventure. Historic notabilities appear (e.g. Marion, Sumter, Gates, Cornwallis, Tarleton) ; but native types of backwoodsmen, scouts, soldiers, etc., are the most original part of the work, as, e.g. Lieutenant Porgy, the Falstaffian *gourmet*, supple Jack Bannister, the boatman of Congaree, and the magnanimous Jack Witherspoon, who dies for his friend. [All o.p.]

—— *Woodcraft* (1st edn. entitled " *The Sword and the Distaff* ").   1854
—— *The Forayers.*   1855
—— *Eutaw* [sequel].   1856
  The same subject, and often the same characters, transferred to scenes in the interior, chiefly on the Santee and Congaree rivers. *Woodcraft* " furnishes a kind of comic after-piece to the Partizan series " (Van Doren). It has in Captain Porgy " the most truly comic character ever produced by this school of American romance." [All o.p.]

—— *The Kassique of Kiawah.*   1859
  A picturesque romance of Carolina in the seventeenth century. [o.p.]

SIMS, George Robert [1847–1922]. *Mary Jane's Memoirs.*   1887
—— *Mary Jane Married : tales of a village inn.*   1888
  Amusing autobiography of a servant-girl who marries a village innkeeper. [Chatto.]

—— *Memoirs of a Landlady.*   1894
  A garrulous old woman tells her experiences as proprietress of furnished apartments, hitting off with dry comment the humours of her husband, and the foibles of her queer assortment of lodgers. [Chatto : o.p.]

—— *The Small-part Lady ; and other stories.*   1900
  A miscellaneous dozen of stories that summarize this author's characteristics. Title-story is a bit of natural realism about a young chorus-lady, who gets advanced to a small part, much to the gratification of herself and her friends. *Miriam, The Third Floor,* and *Margaret Lorimer* are compact melodramas with touches of a humour like that of Dickens. [Chatto.]

SINCLAIR, May [*b.* 1879]. *Two Sides to a Question.*   1901
  Two analytical studies of woman's vocation. *The Cosmopolitan* presents a lady kept in durance by the purblind selfishness of a widowed father, who suddenly gets her freedom, and develops the great and complex soul that is in her by travel over the globe, dying in a fit of self-sacrifice. *Superseded* tells how a middle-aged arithmetic mistress in a high school finds herself in love. Her mental bewilderment is the last straw, and she is superseded. Humour in the character-drawing of elderly people relieves the critical moral psychology. [Constable : o.p. ; Taylor, New York : o.p.]

—— *The Divine Fire.*   1904
  A study, too heavily weighted with learned theory, of a poet who, like Francis Thompson, is out of his element in the mercenary trafficking and immoral compromises of the world—especially of the literary world—and

SINCLAIR, May (*continued*).

visits the depths of misery ; but, unlike Thompson, he at length wins recognition and the love he had worshipped from afar. Incidentally sketches an unscrupulous bookseller—the poet's father—successful editors, an æsthetic Oxford don, and other luminaries of the literary firmament. [Nash : o.p. ; Holt, New York.]

—— *Kitty Tailleur.* 1908

The tragedy of a woman's renunciation, with much on the psychology of sexual relationships. [Constable : o.p. ; *sub tit. The Immortal Moment*, Doubleday, New York : o.p.]

—— *The Creators ; a comedy.* 1910

Studies a group of geniuses, male and female, their attraction for each other, and the thwarting influence of their devotion to the divine fire. Shall Jane Holland, one of the gifted beings, marry Tanqueray, another of them whom she loves, or subside upon the commonplace Brodrick ? Genius demands virginity for its fulfilment. This and kindred problems are discussed with a plethora of talk. [Constable : o.p. ; Century Co., New York : o.p.]

—— *The Combined Maze.* 1913

Less overweighted with intellectualism than most of her novels, hence better story-telling. The subject is a London clerk and his admirable behaviour under the burden of an unfortunate marriage. [Constable : o.p. ; Macmillan, New York.]

—— *The Three Sisters.* 1914

The sisters are packed into a moorland vicarage, like the Brontës, and eat their hearts out in dullness and gloom, under the despotism of a sensual father who wants to marry again. One is a high-spirited, imaginative girl, a sort of Emily Brontë : her romance comes to nothing. The other two find their dull destinies in soulless marriages. An emotional and rhetorical study of the Brontë theme, in the new analytical manner. [Hutchinson : o.p. ; Macmillan, New York ; Doubleday, Doran, New York.]

—— *Tasker Jevons : the real story.* 1916

Jevons makes his way out of provincial journalism to celebrity as novelist and playwright, and shows just as much grit and push in overcoming his ingrained shyness and social disqualifications, particularly in his contacts with his wife's genteel relations. Tasker Jevons has been identified with Arnold Bennett. [Hutchinson : o.p. ; *sub tit. The Belfry*, Modern Lib., New York.]

—— *The Tree of Heaven.* 1917

Treats of the war-time and its tragedies, losses of relations and lovers, the moral anguish of a conscientious objector, etc. But by dwelling on the compensations—the heroic endurance of those that are left, the reconciliations and the friendships, the book leaves us with a deeper sense of human faith and courage. [Cassell : o.p. ; Macmillan, New York.]

—— *Mary Olivier : a life.* 1919

Here the repressive father of *The Three Sisters* is exchanged for a selfish and jealous mother, who makes Mary's life a failure, spoiling her chances in love and blighting her individuality, until the girl nerves herself to a combat with this repressive influence and emerges victorious. It is a study of the baneful effects of family life that Butler might have commended, with, however, more cases of sexual aberration and even incipient madness than he allowed himself in *The Way of All Flesh*. [Cassell ; Macmillan, New York.]

—— *The Life and Death of Harriet Frean.* 1920

This also is a concrete illustration of Freudian theories. Harriet suffers from a parental complex, and makes a general mess of her life. She falls in love with a friend's sweetheart, resigns him in deference to old-established prejudices—to the ultimate detriment of both herself and him. [Collins ; Macmillan, N.Y.]

—— *The Romantic.* 1920

A great display of psycho-analysis applied to a woman's husband, who is a coward. He is afraid of marriage, and on examination by a Freudian expert turns out to be sexually impotent. [Collins : o.p. ; Macmillan, New York.]

—— *Anne Severn and the Fieldings.* 1922

All the phenomena revealed by Freudian analysis, repression, buried complexes, sublimation, are exemplified in the sons of the over-motherly Mrs. Fielding, two of whom love Anne. The eldest, for reasons that are nothing else than morbid, sacrifices her and marries the wrong woman ; the youngest, less reprehensibly, sacrifices himself and remains celibate. Anne herself does not remain immune from the neurotic reactions naturally consequent on such a situation. [Hutchinson : o.p. ; Macmillan, New York.]

—— *The Rector of Wyck.* 1925

The Rector believes that God is love, and acts upon that simple creed. He and his wife cheerfully forgo all the pleasures of life, and are disappointed in their children, yet meet the end unembittered. A sermon on the text, " Christianity isn't so much a creed to be stated as a life to be lived." [Hutchinson ; Macmillan, New York ; Grosset, New York.]

—— *The History of Anthony Waring.* 1927

Quite short, though it extends from childhood to death. Waring is one of the undistinguished crowd, not clever or wise, who is unfortunate in his first affairs and marries a coarse-minded, jealous woman. And that is all. [Hutchinson ; Macmillan, New York.]

—— *Tales told by Simpson.* 1930

Tales of temperament and idiosyncrasy told by a genial young painter, showing off well Miss Sinclair's psychological methods. *Miss Tarrant's Temperament* appears to be meant as an ironical study of a nonentity. More unmistakably sardonic is the study of a father and daughter and her lover in *The Wrackham Memoirs*, and the simpler *Between the Lines* is effective. [Hutchinson ; Macmillan, New York.]

SINCLAIR, Upton (Beall) [American ; *b.* 1878]. *The Jungle.* 1906

Not his first novel—if novels they can be called rather than denunciations of glaring evils and appeals for instant reform—but the first signal success. This sensational exposure of the scandalously corrupt and insanitary methods of the Chicago meat-packers and their brutal treatment of their employees, led

SINCLAIR, Upton (*continued*).
to fierce agitation at home and in Europe and to drastic improvements. [Pub. by the Author; also Regan Co., Chicago; Laurie.]

—— *A Captain of Industry.* 1906
A similar indictment of the capitalist system, likewise well-documented with authentic incidents.

—— *The Metropolis.* 1908

—— *The Money-Changers* [sequel]. 1908
Two more of his propagandist novels, dealing with modern phases of commercialism and especially the Trusts, which are exhibited in league with New York financial magnates who aim at stultifying the Anti-Trust campaign. *The Money-Changers* appeared in a revised edition in 1923. [(1) and (2), Regan Co., Chicago; (1), Laurie.]

—— *Samuel the Seeker.* 1910
This might be described as an autobiographical allegory. [Regan Co., Chicago.]

—— *Love's Pilgrimage.* 1911
This too is autobiographical, plaintively describing the vain efforts of a poet to gain the ear of the world, and relating the story of his first marriage and of the disaster in which it ended. [Pub. by the author; Laurie.]

—— *Damaged Goods.* 1913
Based on Brieux' notorious play, *Les avariés*: a warning against the social dangers of sexual disease. [The author.]

—— *Sylvia.* 1913

—— *Sylvia's Marriage* [sequel]. 1914
The subject is still the horrors of venereal disease. The stupidity of parents who fail to instruct their children is fiercely criticized. [The author; (2), Laurie.]

—— *King Coal.* 1917
Exposes the iniquitous state of things alleged to be maintained by greedy capitalists in a mining area—apparently in Colorado. [Regan Co., Chicago; Hutchinson: o.p.]

—— *Jimmy Higgins.* 1919
American domestic troubles during the war, from the point of view of the worker, the internationalist, the rebel against tyranny—whether of kaisers or millionaires. Ends in horrible scenes of torture by the American police at Archangel. [Regan Co., Chicago; Hutchinson: o.p.]

—— *The Spy* (Am. title, 100%: *the story of a patriot*). 1920
This shows up the spying and persecution that went on among those who stayed at home. Peter Gudge is a loathsome example of a spy. [Regan Co., Chicago; Laurie: o.p.]

—— *Oil!* 1927
Makes characteristic use of the Teapot Dome scandal and the Sacco and Vanzetti affair. [Boni, New York; Laurie.]

—— *Boston.* 1928
A "contemporary historical novel"; "an effort at history" in its very full and impartial statement of the Sacco and Vanzetti case, which is based on all the evidence available at the time of writing. Parallel with this is a story of business and high finance referring to a famous law case, but introducing only fictitious characters. [2 vols., Boni, New York; Laurie.]

—— *Mountain City.* 1930
An ugly picture of Denver, the attack on American business methods and political corruption this time being directed at the exploitation of the oil-fields, and taking the form of the history of a ruthless young man's rise to wealth. [Boni, New York; Laurie.]

SITWELL, Osbert [*b.* 1892]. *Before the Bombardment.* 1926
A lampoon on Victorian tastes, conventions, and affectations, still rampant before the war in a watering-place easily identifiable as Scarborough. It is made into a sort of novel by an elaborate piece of ironical comedy in which a mysterious rich old lady is the quarry of a whole pack of gossips, scandal-mongers, and fortune-hunters. The bombardment shakes up this effete social world, but the satire widens to a Swiftian scope as it envisages the future. [Duckworth; Doubleday, Doran, New York.]

—— *Dumb-Animal; and other stories.* 1930
Seven fiercely satirical stories, directed mainly at "the stupid in England" who bear such a rancorous hatred "towards all manifestations of beauty." The one that will cause most heart-burnings is perhaps *Happy Endings*, which considers life at an army crammer's at Camberley, and the stupidity and futility of it all. *Charles and Charlemagne* is a good specimen of the macabre. Sir Robert Mainwroth, in *The Lovebird*, is brilliantly done. But for comic originality *That Flesh is Heir to* may well be preferred. [Duckworth.]

SIWERTZ, Per Sigfrid [Swedish; *b.* 1882]. *Downstream.* 1923
A powerful story of Swedish life, illustrating the corroding effects of selfishness and the pursuit of wealth for its own ends. [Transl., Gyldendal: o.p.; by E. CLASSEN, Knopf, New York.]

—— *Goldman's.* 1929
Character-studies from the inside life of a Stockholm business establishment, grouped round the figure of the Jewish owner. [Transl. by E. G. NASH, Allen & Unwin; Cosmopolitan Book Co., New York.]

SKELTON, Sir John [Scottish; 1831–97]. *Queen Mary's Holdfast.* 1896
In *Summers and Winters at Balmawhapple*, vol. i. A study of Patrick, Master of Gray, a traitor to Queen Mary of Scotland; highly praised by Froude. Explores a little by-path of history with learning and imagination. The same volume contains some other essays in Scottish fiction. [*Table Talk of Shirley*, 2 vols., Blackwood: o.p.]

SKRAM, Berthe Amalie [*née* Alver; Norwegian; 1846–1905]. *Professor Hieronimus* (1895). 1899
An exposure of the horrors of lunatic asylums, based on a personal experiment and written with the convincing

SKRAM, Berthe Amalie (*continued*).

realism of an avowed naturalist. Professor Hieronimus, the despot in charge of the institution described, is an astonishing personality. [Transl. by Alice STRONACH and G. B. JACOBI, Lane : o.p.]

SKRINE, Mrs. Mary Jessie Hammond [*née* Tooke ; *b.* 1856]. *The World's Delight.*   1901

Children's stories told from the child's point of view, in an unusually fresh and sympathetic way ; best of them, perhaps, *A Pedagogue, A Friend of Master Francis, The Godfather at Play,* and *Madame Prue.* [Lane : o.p.]

—— *The House of the Luck.*   1906

A novel showing the same skill and tenderness in interpreting the nature of the child. [Smith & Elder : o.p.]

—— *A Stepson of the Soil.*   1910

Simple country life and common characters, drawn with remarkable understanding, not only of their obvious traits, but also of the more intimate and secret thoughts and feelings which are usually hidden from the quality under the veil of reserve. An old man and his wife, their stepson, a wise woman, and others are drawn with delicate insight. [Arnold.]

—— *A Romance of the Simple.*   1911

A simple story of life in a sequestered village, depending for its interest and pathos on the truth and tenderness with which the soul of the rustic is revealed. The mind of the idiot son, and the sorrowful yearnings of his mother Patience are finely interpreted. [Arnold.]

SLADEN, Douglas Brooke Wheelton [*b.* 1856]. *My Son Richard.*   1901

The doings and the sayings of a "great company" of young men and young ladies at a summer resort on the Thames. The girls particularly are very ready at repartee and smart sayings about things in general. Copious descriptions of the river and its daily life. [Hutchinson : o.p.]

—— *The Curse of the Nile.*   1913

Egypt and the Sudan (1884–98)—the siege and fall of Khartum, and the rule of the Mahdi until Kitchener's final victory at Omdurman. Gordon, the Mahdi, etc., appear ; the story is rather lost in the history. [Nash.]

SLOSSON, Annie [*née* Trumbull ; American ; 1838–1926]. *Seven Dreamers.*   1891

An account in rich dialect of various eccentrics, people with a touch of mania. Aims to show the psychical value of such phases of mental history. [Harper, New York : o.p.]

—— *The Heresy of Mehetabel Clark.*   1892

The backslidings of this young woman from strict Calvinist doctrines are described in rich New England dialect by an old farmer who does not agree with her. [Harper, New York.]

—— *Dumb Foxglove ; and other stories.*   1898

Fantastic stories of New England, e.g. an old woman appears by mistake as chief mourner at a stranger's funeral, and is changed in consequence for life. [Harper, New York and London : o.p.]

SMALL, Sidney Herschel [American ; *b.* 1893]. *Fourscore.*   1924

The Americanization of German immigrant stock ; from the first arrival of a German youth in 1843, the fortunes of his descendants are traced through three generations. [Bobbs-Merrill, Indianapolis ; Unwin.]

SMEDLEY, Francis Edward [1818–64]. *Frank Fairleigh.*   1850

An old-fashioned kind of novel containing scenes of university life at Cambridge of a rather trite, facetious character, much in the rollicking style of Theodore Hook.

—— *Lewis Arundel ; or, The Railroad of Life.*   1852

Aims a little higher. A novel of upper-class society, with a moral. Lewis is a fine fellow, whose besetting sins, pride and passion, he overcomes through suffering and by the help of his friend, the bookworm Frere, a scorner of social conventions. The joker Bracy and the ass De Grandeville supply the comedy ; the tragedy hinges on the villainy of Lord Bellefield, a worldling and a gambler, the hero's evil genius. [(1), Routledge ; (2), *id.*, o.p. ; (1) and (2), Jenkins ; Dutton, New York.]

—— *Harry Coverdale's Courtship, and What Came of It.*   1855

A similar effusion to *Frank Fairleigh*, animated by high spirits and fun and by a wholesome enjoyment of the good things of life. Harry is a sporting squire, comfortably off, a lover of horses and a terror to poachers. He cuts out a wealthy rival, but is too fond of himself to value his wife aright until schooled by the troubles and jealousies of wedlock. [Routledge : o.p. ; Dutton, New York.]

SMILOVSKÝ, Alois Vojtěch [Czech ; 1837– ?]. *Heavens !*   1894

A good example of the work of this Bohemian novelist. A story of real life, with a simple plot, and a number of well-portrayed characters, e.g. Father Ovok, the man of practical sense, Father Ledecky, the rather selfish woman, and the serving men and women. [Transl., Sands : o.p.]

SMITH, Albert [1816–60]. *The Adventures of Mr. Ledbury.*   1844

—— *The Pottleton Legacy.*   1849

By the famous showman who introduced Mont Blanc to Britishers. Facetious novels sketching incidents of the life of the time in a clever journalistic way—the opening of a railway in a country district, going to the Derby, shady life in town—and hitting off notable types—company-promoters, impresarios, aeronauts, fast young men, and the like—in a style midway between Dickens and the comic papers. [(1), o.p. ; (2), Edited by E. A. Baker (Half-forgotten Books), Routledge (Dutton, New York) : o.p.]

SMITH, Mrs. Alice Prescott [American]. *Montlivet.*   1906

Montlivet, a chivalrous Frenchman, rescues the English heroine from the Indians, in the days of the early French settlements in Canada, the struggles with Huron and Iroquois and rivalries with the English (1695). [Houghton, Boston ; Constable : o.p.]

—— *Kindred.*   1925

The adventures of an English spy among the French and their Indian allies, at the time of the Seven Years' War (1758). [Houghton, Boston ; Heinemann.]

SMITH, Bertram. *Running Wild.*   1920

An extraordinarily tender and acute understanding of a little boy's mind and vision of life is evinced by this

SMITH, Bertram (*continued*).

book, by a man of charming personality who died at forty-one. [With a preface by Ward Muir, Simpkin.]

SMITH, Charlotte [*née* Turner ; 1749–1806]. *Ethelinde ; or, The Recluse of the Lake.*　　　1789

Mrs. Smith was a very capable woman who, like Mrs Oliphant in the following century, took charge of a large family when her husband came to grief, and to support them wrote some fifty novels. Here, the heroine's troubles in losing her lover, and being persecuted by the attentions of a married man, all finally removed by the lover's unexpected reappearance, are the pith of a sentimental story. Grasmere and the Lake mountains furnish the setting. [5 vols. : o.p.]

—— *The Old Manor House.*　　　1793

This is a competent domestic novel, with satirical passages on caste pride. The most prominent figure is a proud and autocratic old lady owning vast estates in the south of England—a very complete portrait drawn without satire. The destination of the property and the loves and adventures of the hero, who ultimately inherits, are the principal matters. He is engaged in the American War of Independence, and Mrs. Smith has much to say on the Government's blunders. [4 vols. : o.p.] Other novels by her are : *Emmeline, or the Orphan of the Castle* [4 vols., 1788] ; *Celestina* [4 vols., 1791] ; *Desmond* (favouring the spirit of the French Revolution), [3 vols., 1792] ; *The Banished Man* [4 vols., 1795] ; *Montalbert* [3 vols., 1795] ; *The Young Philosopher* [4 vols., 1798]. [All o.p.]

SMITH, Miss Constance. *Corban.*　　　1901

The principal figure is a French curé, whose humility and quixotic self-sacrifice exalt him above average humanity, without being untrue to life. His love-story is affecting, and tragedy is touched when the good priest is confronted with the dilemma of revealing a secret of the confessional or beholding his loved one unjustly condemned. [Hurst : o.p.]

SMITH, Lady Eleanor [b. 1902]. *Red Wagon : a story of the tober.*　　　1930

The life of a showman and the life of circus people, presented from the inside, in a way that suggests inside experience. [Gollancz ; Bobbs-Merril, Indianapolis.]

SMITH, Francis Hopkinson [American ; 1838–1915]. *Colonel Carter of Cartersville.*　　　1891

Character-portraits of people in the South : an extravagant but noble-hearted old Yankee ; his devoted henchman, Chad, an ex-slave ; and other old-fashioned folks. Draws an Arcadian picture of the relations between master and slave, now master and man, with a regretful feeling for the splendours of the old regime. Largely in dialect, the negro patois making the anecdotes funnier. [Houghton, Boston ; Harper, London : o.p.]

—— *A Day at Laguerres ; and other days.*　　　1892

Nine admirable short impressions of scenes and men in Mexico and other places. [Houghton, Boston ; Harper, London : o.p.]

—— *A Gentleman Vagabond ; and some others.*　　　1895

Stories illustrative of character. *John Saunders, Labourer*, a simple-minded, tender-hearted hero, sacrifices his life to save a cur. *A Knight of the Legion of Honour* is the tale of a true gentleman and of his romantic ride with a beautiful Polish countess in distress. [Houghton, Boston.]

—— *Tom Grogan.*　　　1896

" Tom " is a woman of extraordinary will-power and physique, who prosecutes her husband's trade, that of stevedore in New York harbour, after his death, in spite of hostility on the part of the union. This is the narrative of a grim episode in her life, her brave and stubborn fight with the unscrupulous Knights of Labour. [Houghton, Boston ; Macmillan, London : o.p.]

—— *Caleb West, Master Diver.*　　　1898

A record of warfare with the brute forces of nature—the obscure toil and heroism of New England mariners engaged in erecting a lighthouse. [Houghton, Boston ; Constable : o.p.]

—— *The Fortunes of Oliver Horn.*　　　1902

Society at Washington and New York, and in the South before and during the Civil War. [Scribner, New York : o.p. ; Newnes : o.p.]

—— *Colonel Carter's Christmas.*　　　1903

Reintroduces us to the genial hero of his first novel. [Scribner, New York : o.p.]

—— *The Under-Dog : stories.*　　　1903

Of the poor, the neglected, the submerged. [Scribner, New York.]

—— *The Tides of Barnegat.*　　　1906

Lives of fisher-folk on the coast of New Jersey, about the time of the Civil War. [Scribner, New York ; Hodder : o.p.]

—— *Peter : a novel of which he is not the hero.*　　　1909

Character-portrait of a charming old bachelor of the old-fashioned sort. [Scribner, New York ; Hodder : o.p.]

—— *Kennedy Square.*　　　1911

Aristocratic life in Maryland at the same epoch, with a fine portrait of a young buck of fifty and a glimpse of Edgar Allan Poe. Several characters from *Oliver Horn* re-enter. [Scribner, New York ; Laurie : o.p.]

SMITH, Horace [1779–1849]. *Brambletye House ; or, Cavaliers and Roundheads.*　　　1826

An antiquarian romance of the times of the Great Civil War, in imitation of Scott. Introduces historical personages and events profusely, even inserting passages from Defoe's *History of the Plague*. Brambletye House still stands, a conspicuous ruin, beside the railway between East Grinstead and Forest Row, on the edge of Ashdown Forest. [Weldon : o.p.]

SMITH, Miss Isabel. *The Minister's Guest.*　　　1900

The story revolves round a winsome girl, the guest of a minister in a small northern town where Nonconformity is strong. He loves her, and has to watch in silence the growth of her love for another. Nonconformist circles, the household of a sporting parson, and village life supply character-sketches. [Unwin : o.p. ; Appleton, New York : o.p.]

SMITH, Minna Caroline [American ; *b.* 1860]. *Mary Paget.* 1900
A romance of Tavistock and old Bermuda, *temp.* James I, the historic framework being the wreck of the *Sea Venture* which Shakespeare used in *The Tempest.* Mary's love-story in " the still vexed Bermoothes " is complicated by the struggle between the Established Church and Puritanism. [Macmillan : o.p.]

SMITH, Naomi Royde. *Summer Holiday or Gibraltar.* 1929
The story itself is slight—a crude young girl on holiday seduced by a hotel musician. Its merit lies in the skill with which commonplace and vulgar types are made real and interesting. [Constable.]

—— *The Island.* 1930
A morbid, not to say repellent theme—the mental and physical decay of a homosexual woman. The portrait of the poor creature, from sentimental girlhood to feeble-minded age, continually charmed, victimized, and deserted by the sensual egoist who is her bane, has the clarity of truth and the pitifulness of inevitability. [Constable ; Harper, New York.]

SMITH, Pauline [South African]. *The Little Karoo.* 1925
Ten sketches, written in simple yet poignant style, of life among the Dutch farmers and peasants of the Cape Colony veld, by the daughter of an English doctor there. [Cape ; Doubleday, Doran, New York.]

SMITH, William Henry [1808–72]. *Thorndale ; or, The Conflict of Opinions.* 1857
Meditations and discussions, thrown into a personal form as the autobiography of a man, tracing the growth of his mind through self-analysis and conversation with his friends. The autobiography is not without affecting passages, and there are impressions of nature at home and abroad ; but the main interest is philosophical ; questions of good and evil, immortality, realism and idealism, even such topics as the power of money, are dealt with in a desultory but earnest fashion. [Blackwood : o.p.]

SMOLLETT, Tobias George [1721–71]. *The Adventures of Roderick Random.* 1748
A string of picaresque adventures in the comic style of Cervantes and Le Sage, but more realistic, composed largely of personal reminiscences, particularly of the disastrous expedition to Cartagena (1741). Smollett has never been surpassed in a certain kind of coarse, graphic realism, seasoned with an hilarious spirit of low comedy, and caricature of people he knew in the flesh. His savage satire and inexhaustible invective produced many figures that have a certain artificial semblance of life, Roderick's henchman Strap and the Commodore Trunnion group. Tom Bowling and Jack Rattlin are the pleasantest of his saltwater company here ; Morgan the Welshman, Capt. Oakum, and Dr. Mackshane are the chief caricatures. [Ed. G. Saintsbury, (Bohn's Lib.), Bell (Harcourt, New York), 1895 ; 2 vols., Routledge (Dutton, New York) : o.p. ; (Everyman's Lib.) Dent (Dutton, New York), 1927 ; (World's Classics) Oxford Press, 1930.]

—— *The Adventures of Peregrine Pickle ; in which are included the Memoirs of a Lady of Quality.* 1751
Into this second novel he worked the same kind of material, adding a larger proportion of romantic and farcical business. Peregrine's schooling, his courtships (with most unsavoury interludes), his travels and amorous exploits on the Continent and in London, make a humorous but unedifying story. The realism is Hogarthian ; the caricature, it has been said—but this is only a superficial impression—gives us comic beasts rather than men. Smollett never did anything better than the Garrison chapters with those grotesque beings Commodore Trunnion, Lieut. Hatchway, the boatswain Tom Pipes, and Perry's aunt, Mrs. Grizzle. [2 vols. (Bohn's Lib.), Bell (Macmillan, New York), 1895 ; ed. G. Saintsbury, 4 vols., Gibbings, 1895 ; o.p. ; 2 vols., Routledge (Dutton, New York) : o.p. ; (Everyman's Lib.), 2 vols., Dent (Dutton, New York), 1930.]

—— *The Adventures of Ferdinand, Count Fathom.* 1753
Less consistently ironical than the *Jonathan Wild* of Fielding : the history of an unmitigated scoundrel, offspring of a repulsive old camp-follower. In his adventures and misdeeds, the broad comedy is superseded by a romantic handling of mysterious and blood-curdling incident. This is in fact the earliest of the Gothic romances. [Ed. G. Saintsbury, 2 vols., Gibbings, 1895 : o.p. ; Routledge (Dutton, New York).]

—— *Adventures of Launcelot Greaves.* 1762
A clumsy imitation of *Don Quixote.* Sir Launcelot, a rustic squire, rambles about the country as a redresser of grievances, and has an absurd rival in the novice Captain Crowe. Like Smollett's other novels, full of scurrilous satire of everything and everybody. Interesting as the first English novel to appear serially, and also for technical reasons as anticipating Dickens, etc. [With *Adventures of an Atom,* Routledge (Dutton, New York).]

—— *The Expedition of Humphry Clinker.* 1771
Written while he was dying—a riper book, more restrained, yet still pungent enough in its satire. The travels and observations of a Welsh family, a group of delightful oddities, through England, Scotland, and Wales : Matt. Bramble is a reflection of Smollett himself, his sister Tabitha is a second Aunt Grizzle, Lismahago is another wonderful grotesque. The sarcastic descriptions of towns and peoples are doubly comic from being in letters written by the different characters, with absurdly incompatible points of view. Parodies the language and manners of the Methodists. The Scottish portion is particularly familiar and racy, dealing with the scenes of Smollett's younger days. [Ed. G. Saintsbury, 2 vols., Gibbings, 1896 : o.p. ; (Bohn's Lib.), Bell (Macmillan, New York), 1895 : o.p. ; Routledge (Dutton, New York) ; ed. by L. Rice-Oxley, (World's Classics) Oxford Press, 1925 ; Modern Lib., New York, 1929.]
[*Works,* ed. by George Saintsbury, 12 vols., Navarre Soc. (Boni, New York), 1925 ; 12 vols., Jarrolds, 1916 : o.p. ; 6 vols., Bigelow Brown, New York.]

SMYTHE, Patrick G. [Irish ; *b.* 1856]. *The Wild Rose of Lough Gill.* 1883
An Irish novel of 1641–52 and the wars of the Confederation down to the fall of Galway, Owen Roe O'Neill and Myles Slasher figuring most conspicuously. [Gill, Dublin : o.p.]

SNAITH, John Collis [*b.* 1876]. *Mistress Dorothy Marvin.* 1895
A tale of action and adventure concerned with the intrigues that led to the dethronement of James II and the triumph of William of Orange (1685–8). Marlborough is introduced. [Ward & Lock ; Appleton, New York : o.p.]

SNAITH, John Collis (*continued*). *Willow the King: the story of a cricket match.* 1899
A *jeu d'esprit*, written largely in slang. The heroine, an audacious tomboy, plays a match at single-wicket, literally, for love. [Ward & Lock: o.p.]

—— *Broke of Covenden.* 1904
A novel obviously inspired by other novelists, more particularly Meredith. Broke is an egoist, in whom pride of race is developed to the verge of insanity, and who remains impassible, unflinching, under blows to his filial love almost as terrible as Lear's. Most of the characters are mere theorems, but slangy old Lord Bosket is a real humorist. [Long; Dodd & Mead, New York.]

—— *Patricia at the Inn.* 1906
An exciting romance of Cavalier and Roundhead after the battle of Worcester, adventures of Patricia and her husband, and of the fugitive Charles II, at a lonely seaside inn, the rascally landlord of which takes toll of both parties. [*Arrowsmith's Christmas Annual*, Arrowsmith, Bristol: o.p.; Dodge, New York: o.p.]

—— *William Jordan, Junior.* 1908
A fantastic book with many good things in it, but very uneven in merit. The experiences of a bewildered poetic soul in the different phases of modern life. A fine, grotesque being is the poet's friend William Dodson, with his humorous common sense and daring mendacities. [Long; Moffat, New York: o.p.]

—— *Araminta.* 1909
A beautiful, brainless heroine, backed by her managing aunt, a tyrannical old countess, takes fashionable London by storm. [Murray; Appleton, New York.]

—— *Fortune.* 1910
Adventures of an English soldier of fortune, Sir Richard Pendragon, in Spain and France in the time of the Emperor Maximilian and Louis XI. [Nelson: o.p.; Moffat, New York: o.p.]

—— *Mrs. Fitz.* 1910
A wildly romantic story of the *Zenda* kind attired in the habiliments of ordinary English life. The supposed circus-rider turns out to be the runaway daughter of the King of Illyria. [Smith & Elder: o.p.; Moffat, New York: o.p.]

—— *The Great Age.* 1915
An Elizabethan love-story with Shakespeare as chief personage and Burbage and Queen Elizabeth as occasional figures. [Hutchinson: o.p.]

—— *Mary Plantagenet: an improbable story.* 1918
No longer a mere understudy of Meredith, the author shows originality in plot, in dialogue garnished with spicy story, in piquant character-drawing, and the comedy of class-distinctions and the like. [Cassell: o.p.]

—— *Love Lane.* 1919
One of a little group of very ordinary, vulgar, and not very intelligent people, who are all hit off to the life, goes to the war, and through his talks with a comrade in the trenches somehow wakes up, sees things in a new light, and becomes a full-size human being. [Collins.]

—— *The Unforeseen.* 1930
A very perplexing murder case, the hero serving a life-sentence for seventeen years before being cleared: worked out perhaps too circumstantially for the reader to be taken in. [Hodder; Appleton, New York.]

SNOWDEN, James Keighley [*b.* 1860]. *The Plunder Pit.* 1898
A Stevensonian romance, reproducing the manners and language of Yorkshire in the early nineteenth century (1857). Gordale Scar is the scene of a sensational incident. [Methuen: o.p.]

—— *Barbara West.* 1901
The sad love-story of an innocent, babyish girl who is wronged by a vulgar rake. Aims to deal in a clean and sympathetic manner with a serious social problem. Graphic sketches of journalistic life and local idiosyncrasies in a small town of Yorkshire. [Long: o.p.]

—— *The Life Class.* 1908
Deals with allied problems of morals and good taste, in the differences of an art class in a Yorkshire town with the puritanical element on the local authority. The heroine of the controversy and of the love-story is a clean-minded art student and artist's model. [Laurie: o.p.]

—— *Jack the Outlaw.* 1926
Jack is a poacher, and the iniquity of the Game Laws is exposed. Good Yorkshire colour from Nidderdale; the period is 1841. [Simpkin.]

SÖDERBERG, Hjalmar Emil Fredrik [Swedish; *b.* 1869]. *Martin Birck's Youth* (Martin Bircks ungd-dom, 1901). 1907
Autobiographical in the main. The childhood, youth, and young manhood of a poet; his painful differences with a pious and conservative mother, and the monetary difficulties of himself and his mistress, raise many problems, which the author handles with the irony of a sceptic. [Transl. from the Swedish by Charles Wharton STORK, Harper, New York: o.p.]

SÖIBERG, Harry [Danish; *b.* 1880]. *The Sea King* (Søkongen, 1926). 1928
The life of fisher-folk in a West Jutland village, dominated by a hard-headed peasant. [Trans. Edwin BJÖRKMAN; Morrow, New York.]

SOKOLOV, Boris [Russian]. *The Crime of Doctor Garine.* 1928
A volume of short stories by a Russian emigré scientist. In *Strategy*, a female Bolshevik falls passionately in love with the White officer she is tracking. *In Stanitza* recounts the brutal horrors of village occupation by Red soldiers. [Transl., Covici, New York.]

" SOLOGUB, Fedor " [Feodor Kuzmich Teternikov; Russian; *b.* 1863]. *The Sweet-scented Name; and other fairy-tales, fables, and stories.* 1915
Sologub's works comprise some 20 volumes of novels, plays, poems, and short stories. In the last, which are often fables of a mere paragraph or two, he excels; the fable has a satirical, an ironical reflection;

" SOLOGUB, Fedor " (*continued*).

the fantasy, however bizarre, keeps tense hold of real life. Many, such as the first story *Wings*, the title-story, *Turandina*, and *Lohengrin* belong to the Hans Andersen genre; but Sologub is intensely Russian and more of a dreamer than the Dane. [Ed. by Stephen Graham. A more literal but not more faithful version of many stories is *The Old House ; and other tales*, transl. by John COURNOS. Secker : o.p.]

—— *The Old House.*   1915

The title-story, longest of the set, is a fanciful, elegiac tale of the last abortive rising against the Tsars. *The Uniter of Souls* and *The Invoker of the Beast* are still more fantastic. In *The White Dog*, a woman turns werwolf, and in *The Glimmer of Hunger*, a student runs amok and then commits suicide. [Transl. by John COURNOS, Secker : o.p.]

—— *The Little Demon* (Melki Bes, 1907).   1916

In his minute chronicle, powerful and accomplished as it is, of the gradual decline into insanity of a most unpleasant schoolmaster, selfish, stupid, malignant, lewd, Sologub sought by the example of perversity to rouse his countryman from their sensual slough. " In the literature of the world there is hardly a creature more absurd, more monstrous and appalling, more unreal in spite of his commonness, than this gymnasium teacher of an ordinary provincial town." [Transl. by John COURNOS and Richard ALDINGTON, Secker.]

—— *The Created Legend* (1908–12).   1916

A symbolical and fantastical story, a " created legend," with the Russian revolution of 1905 as background. The hero, like his author, is a poet, dreaming of a less chaotic and more beautiful world, and the heroine has visions of a day of freedom. The first part only of the original is translated ; in the two remaining ones, the scene is a group of imaginary islands in the Mediterranean. [Transl. by John COURNOS, Secker : o.p.]

SOMERVILLE, Miss Edith Œnone [Irish ; *b.* 1861], and " ROSS, Martin " [Miss Violet Martin, of Ross, Co. Galway ; Irish ; 1865–1915]. *Some Experiences of an Irish R.M.*   1899

—— *All on the Irish Shore : Irish sketches.*   1903

—— *Some Irish Yesterdays.*   1906

—— *Further Experiences of an Irish R.M.*   1908

Successive volumes of random sketches and anecdotes of squireens and sportsmen, servants, agents, peasants, and many other Irish types, of a generation that has now passed away, the incidents illustrating the adventures and misadventures of country-house life, the hunting-field, village quarrels, and so on. The realism is of the natural, unstudied type, and we have no more accurate reproduction of the brogue. The resourceful Flurry Knox has become a household name in his own country. The humour always seems spontaneous and unforced, though the authors stick to the Anglo-Irish tradition by insisting on the farcical side of everything. Scene, South-West Cork. *Some Irish Yesterdays* takes us to Connemara and the Aran Isles. [(1)–(4), Longmans, London and New York ; Nelson ; (1), (2), and (4), Harrap.]

—— *The Real Charlotte.*   1900

Perhaps the best of these collaborators' novels. " An unscrupulous woman works the ruin of a sweet-natured, ill-trained girl. . . . Land-agents, farmers, great ladies, drawn with impartial and relentless truth " (Rev. S. J. Brown, S.J.). [Longmans, London and New York ; Nelson.]

—— *The Silver Fox.*   1900

Sporting scenes in the West ; the peasants are caricatured. [Longmans, London and New York ; Nelson.]

—— *An Irish Cousin.*   1903

First edition 1889, rewritten 1903. A sporting young man's awakening to the realities of life, and his tragic love for a Canadian cousin. [Longmans, New York.]

—— *Dan Russel the Fox.*   1911

A sporting novel combining the same ingredients in a sustained story packed with entertaining characters. [Methuen.]

—— *In Mr. Knox's Country.*   1915

Flurry Knox and his formidable mother reappear, and are matched by the amazing and amusing Miss Larkie McRory and her tribe, in this further collection of fox-hunting, horse-racing, and queer-company stories of Munster. [Longmans, London and New York ; Nelson.]

—— *Mount Music.*   1919

A novel finished by Miss Somerville after her partner's death. It has less of the geniality and fewer of the sparkling dialogues to which they had used us, and there is sharp satire of that bane of Irish life, religious intolerance. The general theme is tragic, the passing of the Protestant landlord, as represented by the heroine's improvident father. This charming girl is loved by her Catholic cousin. A grim but powerful creation is " the big Doctor." [Longmans, London and New York ; Nelson.]

—— *Stray-Aways.*   1920

Put together after the death of Martin Ross ; more miscellaneous than the preceding, one item being an account of a holiday in Denmark. [Longmans, London (: o.p.) and New York.]

—— *The Big House of Inver.*   1925

The story of a great Irish family brought to ruin by its own vices, and the heroic but fruitless efforts of an illegitimate daughter of the house to restore its fortunes. Though enlivened by some wit and comedy, the story is tragic, and offers a picture of Irish life that contrasts with the preceding works. [Heinemann ; Doubleday, Doran, New York.]

—— *The Irish R.M. and his Experiences.*   1928

Collects together all the stories told by the R.M. [Faber.]

SOUVESTRE, Émile [French ; 1806–54]. *The Attic Philosopher* (Un philosophe sous les toits, 1850).   1883

The reminiscences and meditations of a humble Parisian philosopher, who prefers poverty and contentment

SOUVESTRE, Émile (*continued*).

to money and anxiety, lowly friends to wealthy kinsfolk, and finds his happiness in doing little acts of kindness. [Transl., Longman: o.p.; Burt, New York.]

SOUVESTRE, Pierre [French; 1874–1914], and **ALLAIN, Marcel** [French; *b.* 1885]. *A Nest of Spies: being the continued pursuit of Fantômas the elusive.* 1917

Juve, the French Sherlock Holmes, suspects Fantômas, the man of many disguises, to be responsible for a series of mysterious crimes, and eventually runs him to earth; but Fantômas is plainly not at the end of his resources. [Stanley Paul: o.p.]

SPENCER, Claire [Mrs. Harrison Smith]. *Gallow's Orchard.* 1930

Clandestine love, murder, and scandal-mongering in a puritanical Scots village; the story related by the schoolmaster, who was ruined through his passion for a kind of Beautiful White Devil. [Cape.]

SPIELHAGEN, Friedrich [German; 1829–1911]. *Problematic Characters* (Problematische Naturen, 1860). 1869

—— *Through Night to Light* (Durch Nacht zum Licht, 1861) [sequel]. 1870

Novels of purpose, and sternly logical studies of the more momentous problems and emotions of the period immediately preceding the 1848 revolution, comprising various individualist, Faust-like characters typical of the Prussian life of that time (*c.* 1840–8) in the aristocratic and bourgeois classes. [Transl. by Schele DE VERE, Holt, New York: o.p.]

—— *The Hohensteins* (Die von Hohenstein, 1863). 1870

Spielhagen's novels are long and elaborate studies in social evolution, dealing with vexed questions of their day. In these annals of three generations of the Hohenstein family a chapter of contemporary history, from 1848 onwards, is unrolled. The revolutionary Munzer is the principal exponent of the theme; around him are the numerous members of the family, whose various relations and interests illustrate the forces at work beneath the social movement. [Transl. by Schele DE VERE, Holt, New York: o.p.]

—— *Hammer and Anvil* (Hammer und Amboss). 1870

Spielhagen puts his reading of the social problem in the mouth of the governor of a prison. In the war of classes, some men are the hammers, the rest are anvils. But in a healthy society, each would realize that he is at once hammer and anvil, must accept his duties with his privileges. [o.p.]

—— *The Block House on the Prairie: German pioneers* (Deutsche Pioniere, 1871). 1882

The life of the German pioneers in America in the middle of the seventeenth century, and the difficulties and hardships of their existence on the outskirts of civilization. Episodes of Indian warfare, and of the conflicts between French and English. [Transl., City of London Pub. Co.: o.p.]

—— *The Breaking of the Storm* (Sturmflut, 1877). 1877

Draws a parallel between a devastating cyclone which wrought havoc in N. Germany, and the upheaval of social life in Berlin, during the recent financial crisis, caused by the irruption of the French milliards into the monetary world. The effects upon the State and upon society are laid bare, the rage for speculation, the decay of old-fashioned integrity, the extravagance of the upper classes, and the discontent of the poor. [Transl. by STEPHENSON, 3 vols., Bentley: o.p.]

—— *The Skeleton in the House* (Das Skelett im Hause, 1878). 1881

A humorous sketch of conjugal life; moral, that a man really loved by his wife may confess anything so long as it reaches her from his own lips. [Transl. by J. MARSDEN, Kolckmann: o.p.]

—— *Quisisana; or, Rest at Last* (Quisisana, 1880). 1881

A tender and touching idyll: a man of fine nature feels young at heart whilst he is growing old. [Nimmo: o.p.]

SPINNER, Alice [American]. *A Study in Colour.* 1894

Stories, or reminiscences, of the writer's residence on a West Indian island, chiefly concerned with the great gulf fixed between white and coloured peoples, and the overpowering desire of the negroes to have a half-breed child. [Unwin: o.p.]

SPITTELER, Carl [German-Swiss; 1845–1924]. *Prometheus and Epimetheus* (Prometheus und Epimetheus, 1880–1). 1931

A "prose-epic," dealing with the classical myth, and giving it a symbolical and didactic turn. The two brothers stand for opposed types, the one refusing to surrender his soul, or personal inspiration, the other allowing himself to be led by the voice of authority and convention. [Transl. by James F. MUIRHEAD, Jarrolds.]

—— *Two Little Misogynists* (Mädchenfeinde). 1922

An early tale by the author of the epic poem *Olympischen Frühling*. It records, with wit and psychological insight, the conversation of two boys of nine and ten, at a military school. [Transl. by Mme la vicomtesse DE ROQUETTE-BUISSON, Holt, New York.]

SQUIRE, John Collings [*b.* 1884]. *The Grub Street Nights Entertainment.* 1924

Nine clever and ironical stories, of authors and literary affairs; *The Man Who Kept a Diary* is about a fraud who got into society on the pretence that he was recording the scandals of the day for future publication; *The Lecture* concerns a popular writer who is moved to tell his audience, for the first time, his real opinion of them. [Heinemann; (Traveller's Lib.), Cape; Doubleday, Doran, New York.]

STACPOOLE, Henry de Vere Stacpoole [Irish; *b.* 1865]. *The Blue Lagoon.* 1908

An Adam and Eve story of a boy and girl left on a desert isle and loving each other in a state of nature. [Unwin; Benn; Lippincott, Philadelphia.]

—— *Patsy.* 1908

The story of a house-party in a big house in mid-Meath; both the English and Irish characters, the naughty children especially, amusingly drawn. [Unwin.]

—— *Garryowen: the romance of a racehorse.* 1910

An Irish story, evincing a close acquaintance with the peasants. The great character is the wily Moriarty, the trainer. [Unwin: o.p.]

STACPOOLE, Henry de Vere Stacpoole (*continued*). *The Ship of Coral : a tropical romance.*
1911
Treasure-seeking, piracy, smuggling, and marooning in the Caribbean, and idyllic love-romancing, with picturesque description of tropical scenery. [Newnes ; Duffield, New York : o.p.]

—— *The Street of the Flute-player.*
1912
Romance of the same sentimental brand, but the scene is Athens in the golden age. [Nash ; Duffield, New York : o.p.]

—— *The Order of Release.*
1912
Here the scene is Paris and Versailles in the time of Choiseul and Du Barry. [Hutchinson : o.p.]

—— *Monsieur de Rochefort.*
1914
A variation on the motives and scenes of the preceding. [Hutchinson : o.p.]

—— *The Reef of Stars : a romance of the tropics.*
1916
A treasure-hunt in New Guinea, with some thrilling episodes of murder and vengeance, a fight between the great scorpion and a giant centipede, and the indispensable love-affairs. [Hutchinson : o.p.]

—— *The Blue Horizon.*
1917
—— *In Blue Waters.*
1917
Stories of old sea-dogs, of all complexions, with the usual attractive ocean setting. [(1) and (2), Hutchinson : o.p.]

—— *Under Blue Skies.*
1919
A dozen tales of coral isles, beachcombers, hobos, kanakas, and the like—e.g. *A Problem of the Sea.* [Hutchinson : o.p.]

—— *The Beach of Dreams : a story of the true world.*
1919
Adventures in the usual vein ; the rich and lovely Cléo de Bronsart is cast away on Desolation Island, or Kerguelen's Land, and makes friends with the seals when she is left alone by the death of two unpleasant men who were the other two survivors. [Hutchinson : o.p.]

STAËL, Madame de [Anne-Louise-Germaine, *née* Necker, Baroness de Staël-Holstein ; French ; 1766–1817]. *Corinne ; or, Italy* (1807).
1894
A kind of idealized autobiography and picturesque tour couched in the form of a novel. " The first æsthetic romance not written in German " (G. Saintsbury). The story is defective ; the permanent interest is in the emotional history of two sympathetic and sensitive minds, as they contemplate Italian scenery, monuments, pictures, sculpture, literature, and manners. But this second novel has little of the unruly strength and pass on of the earlier *Delphine.* [Transl., with introd., by G. SAINTSBURY, 2 vols., Dent : o.p. ; by BALDWIN & DRIVER (Bohn's Lib.), Bell (Macmillan, New York), 1888 : o.p. ; another transl., Burt, New York ; McKay, Philadelphia.]

STEEL, Flora Annie [*née* Webster ; Scottish ; 1847–1929]. *Miss Stuart's Legacy.*
1893
Rich in kindly observations of Anglo-Indian life. Belle Stuart's love affairs and her mistaken marriage give the dramatic interest, but the best of the book is in the studies of native life and character, the Mohammedan soldier, the Hindu usurer, the barbarous Pathan, etc. [Heinemann.]

—— *From the Five Rivers.*
1893
Eight short stories of Hindu and Mohammedan life in the Punjab ; rural conditions, customs, habits, ideas, and prejudices, looked at as far as possible through Eastern eyes. [Heinemann ; Appleton, New York : o.p.]

—— *The Potter's Thumb.*
1894
The plot hinges on the efforts of an Indian magnate to get possession of the keys of the canal sluice-gates by the agency of an unprincipled Englishwoman ; the brave young custodian of the keys is brought to despair and death. The native characters are drawn with intimate knowledge. [Heinemann : o.p. ; Harper, New York : o.p.]

—— *Tales of the Punjab ; told by the People.*
1894
A collection of folk-tales in prose and verse. [Macmillan, London and New York.]

—— *The Flower of Forgiveness.*
1894
Sixteen short stories and sketches of the life, habits, and theosophic lore of the natives, written with touches of sympathetic mysticism, and with pathos. [Heinemann.]

—— *Red Rowans.*
1895
A Scottish novel, comprising good specimens of the writer's character-drawing, and descriptions of West Highland scenery, with a tragic catastrophe. [Heinemann : o.p.]

—— *On the Face of the Waters.*
1896
A study of the Mutiny ; punctiliously accurate, fiction never interfering with fact. Full of terrible scenes, like the massacre at Meerut, and the storming of the Delhi gate ; with careful portraits of native types, and of English officers and civilians. Pays considerable attention to sex problems, Ibsenism, and other modern fashions. [Heinemann : o.p. ; Nash ; Macmillan, New York.]

—— *In the Tideway.*
1897
A long short-story of Scots people. [Constable : o.p. ; Macmillan, New York : o.p.]

—— *In the Permanent Way ; and other stories.*
1897
The Second Story, At the Grand Durbar, The Blue-throated God, and *Glory of Woman* may be singled out as striking stories. Less individual characterization than in Kipling, but a more intimate knowledge of the inner life and thought of the native races. [Heinemann : o.p. ; Macmillan, New York : o.p.]

—— *Voices in the Night.*
1900
The plot matters are the good and evil fortunes of a young Englishman in the Indian Civil Service, and his love for a very modern governess. Striking studies of native life, descriptions of the plague, thoughts on miscegenation, caste, sanitation, intercourse of soldiers and natives, and other political and social problems. [Heinemann ; Macmillan, New York : o.p.]

STEEL, Flora Annie (*continued*). *The Hosts of the Lord.*   1900
A romance centring in an old dynastic city, and dealing with the problem of " the mutual assimilation of East and West without injury to either." The interests and characters are multitudinous ; Indians, Anglo-Indians, and people of mixed blood, soldiers, civil officials, missionaries (both Protestant and Roman Catholic), and natives of all grades and conditions are involved, the central theme being the ill-starred love of an Englishman for a half-Italian begum, which brings him into collision with a turbulent young Mohammedan. [Heinemann : o.p. ; Macmillan, New York : o.p.]
—— *In the Guardianship of God.*   1903
Seventeen short stories analysing Hindu character under various aspects, especially in its contact with Europeans. Four are noteworthy : *Little Henry and his Bearer*, the tale of a Thug's affection for an English child ; *Surâbhi*, the love of a Brahmin for his favourite cow ; *The Perfume of the Rose*, an ill-favoured native's devotion in the Mutiny ; and *The Reformer's Wife*, sketching an aristocratic Hindu with Western ideals. [Heinemann : o.p. ; Macmillan, New York : o.p.]
—— *A Prince of Dreamers.*   1908
A very thoroughgoing study of Akbar, the Great Mogul, and his ideals for the regeneration of the world. Mrs. Steel's intimate acquaintance with all the native types, and their creeds and religious feelings, enables her to enter fully into the mystical side of Akbar's work and aspirations, and to portray the multitudinous life of the period (contemporary with Elizabeth) with the realism exemplified in her modern stories of India. [Lane ; Doubleday, New York : o.p.]
—— *The Gift of the Gods.*   1911
A love-tale of an Hebridean island, incidentally throwing light on the crofter problem. [Heinemann : o.p.]
—— *King Errant.*   1912
A novel dealing with the reign and character of Baber (1493–1530), founder of the Mogul empire. [Heinemann : o.p. ; Stokes, New York : o.p.]
—— *The Adventures of Akbar.*   1913
Returns to the theme of her *Prince of Dreamers*, but takes his childhood in the mountains of Kandahar and Kabul. Readable by children. [Heinemann : o.p. ; Stokes, New York.]

STEPHENS, James [Irish ; *b.* 1882]. *The Crock of Gold.*   1912
An allegorical fantasy mingling old Irish myth with real peasant life, and propounding a revolutionary philosophy very similar to Blake's. " The greatest thing in the world is the Divine Imagination," says the Celtic god, Angus Og, when he wins the peasant girl Caitilin from her ravisher Pan. The boldness of the poetical vision is matched by the humour of the Philosopher, who puts the same doctrines more pithily. His Socratic conversations with gods and men are wonderful descants, as witty as they are profound. [Macmillan, London and New York ; *illus.* by Thomas Mackenzie, *id.*]
—— *The Charwoman's Daughter.*   1912
A story of the simplest : the tenderness, humour, and poetic imagination are what lift it above a hundred like it—of Dublin or elsewhere. The ignorant, dreamy child of the down-trodden but indomitable old charwoman is fascinated and terror-struck by a huge policeman who wants to prey upon her. Rescue comes unexpectedly. " Next to good the most valuable factor in life is evil," runs one of the admirable gnomic sayings. [Macmillan, London and New York (originally published in America, *sub tit. Mary, Mary*, Small, Boston : o.p.).]
—— *Here are Ladies.*   1913
Oracular tales in which a modicum of realism—but that is lively enough—serves to illustrate and vitalize a philosophic truth, which may be recondite but is always valuable. They range from broad humour to tragedy, and all have some touch of poetic imagination. The doctrine of life for the sake of life might have been drawn from Blake. [Macmillan, London and New York.]
—— *The Demi-Gods.*   1914
Approximates rather to the fantastic *Crock of Gold* than to the novel of real life. Angels and elves rub shoulders with tinkers and gombeen men, and the doings and conversation are a marvellous gallimaufry of poetic imagination and admirable common sense. [Macmillan, London and New York.]
—— *Deirdre.*   1923
The tragic story of Deidre and Naoise and Conachúr (Conchobor), the subject of poems and plays by Yeats, Synge, and others, is retold in a mixture of ancient and modern, Irish and English, prose and poetry. The fight of the Sons of Uisneac is a piece of truly Homeric narrative, and the end of the story simple and austere. [Macmillan, London and New York.]
—— *In the Land of Youth.*   1924
A more comic and fantastic set of mythic tales—of Tara and Etain, of Hy Brasil and the Lands of Faery, and of the Introduction to the Great Táin. Etain's elopements from husbands in one world to husbands in another, and other transits to the realm of the Shi, are typical legends of Samhain—May Eve. More akin to the humorous extravagances of the *Mabinogion* are the tales of the rival swineherds and of the man hanged who was too thirsty to die. [Macmillan, London and New York.]

STEPHENS, Robert Neilson [American ; 1876–1906]. *An Enemy to the King. From the recently discovered Memoirs of the Sieur de la Tournoire.*   1898
A story of Henry III and Henry of Navarre, Catherine de Médicis and the Guises, before and during the seventh Civil War (1578–9). [Page, Boston ; Methuen : o.p.]
—— *A Gentleman Player : his adventures on a secret mission for Queen Elizabeth.*   1899
Adventure and love in Elizabeth's reign (1601) ; the hero a comedian in the Lord Chamberlain's company along with William Burbage and Shakespeare. [Page, Boston ; Methuen : o.p.]
—— *Philip Winwood.*   1900
Home life in New York and English episodes (1763–86). Chiefly concerned with the hero's fears for the loyalty of his feather-brained wife, who has espoused the Loyalist side and is courted by a king's officer, while he fights for the Colonists. [Page, Boston ; Chatto : o.p.]

STEPHENS, Robert Neilson (*continued*). *Captain Ravenshaw ; or, The Maid of Cheapside.* 1901
An excellent picture of Elizabethan London. [Page, Boston ; Ward & Lock : o.p.]

—— *The Road to Paris : a story of adventure.* 1902
Prodigal of adventures, in the Pennsylvania woods, at Bunker Hill, in Canada, England, France, and Germany (*c.* 1760–80). [Page, Boston ; Ward & Lock : o.p.]

STEPHENSON, Nathaniel [American ; *b.* 1867]. *They that Took the Sword.* 1901
Life in Cincinnati before and during the Civil War (1861–2) ; a pleasing, perhaps a too pleasing, picture. A girl's lover is with the Northern army, and her relatives are with the Confederates. [Lane : o.p.]

—— *Eleanor Dayton.* 1903
Story of a Cincinnati family in the old days of Calvinism. The author is fond of dealing with the problems of character and the mysteries of life by means of symbolism. Stirring episodes of the Civil War enliven a very leisurely narrative. [Lane : o.p.]

STERN, Gladys Bronwyn. *Tents of Israel.* 1924
Introduces us to the whole tribe of Rakonitz, whose fortunes are followed in the two sequels. An enormous crowd of characters (a genealogical table is appended), overshadowed by the grandmother of the clan, are brought into play. It is upon Toni, the eldest grandchild of the senior line, and her cousin Danny, in their years of childhood, that interest is principally directed. [Chapman ; *sub tit.* The Matriarch, Knopf, New York.]

—— *A Deputy Was King.* 1926
Toni, now engaged in the millinery trade, her husband, and Val, a half-cousin, here hold the stage. [Chapman ; Knopf, New York.]

—— *Petruchio.* 1928
A light affair about an idealistic Englishman married to an Italian peasant girl, and how the shrew is effectively tamed. [Chapman.]

—— *Mosaic.* 1930
This latest volume of the history of the Rakonitz family is indeed a mosaic of characters and centripetal or centrifugal interests. The centre is that wonderful matriarchal woman Berthe Czelovar, *née* Rakonitz, whose life is followed for some sixty years. Hardly less admirable, however, is the very different figure of her sister Lettie, who shares her life in Paris. [Chapman ; Knopf, New York.]

STERNE, Laurence [1713–68]. *The Life and Opinions of Tristram Shandy, Gent.* 1759–67
A long and eccentric novel in which the author plays incessant jokes with the order and method of his narrative —the whimsical masterpiece of an inveterate jester. Tristram's father and Uncle Toby are the figures on which the eye is chiefly focused ; and with Dr. Slop, Corporal Trim, Mrs. Shandy, and Yorick, make an extraordinary and inimitable group of characters, humorous idealisms of a rare kind infinitely surpassing any caricature or burlesque. A medley of random drollery, satirical sporting with human virtues and foibles, philosophical digressions, with little unity or plot : it was intended to—and actually did—go on till the writer was dead. Sterne's peculiar sentimentality is unique, though many writers have tried to copy it, e.g. Carlyle, Jean Paul Richter, and Xavier de Maistre. [Edited by G. Saintsbury, 3 vols., Dent, 1894 ; (Everyman's Lib.), *id.*, with *Sentimental Journey*, 2 vols. (Temple Classics), Dent (Dutton, New York), 1899 ; Macmillan ; 3 vols., Shakespeare Head Ed., Blackwell ; (World's Classics), Oxford Press ; ed. by Wilbur Cross, Boni, New York, 1925. *Illus. Editions : illus.* by T. H. Robinson, Chatto (1902), 1907 : o.p. ; by John Austen, Lane (Dodd & Mead, New York) ; by Rowland Wheelwright, Brentano, New York, 1926].

—— *A Sentimental Journey through France and Italy.* 1768
Sterne himself is the traveller, and the journey with its incidents (many of which are not very chaste) is a vehicle for his sentimental moralizing on the absurdities, the elusive humour, and the pathos of human life. An admirable specimen of his style, and on the whole more pleasing to the uninitiated than the more freakish and grotesque *Tristram Shandy*. [Ed. by George Saintsbury, Dent, 1894. With *Tristram Shandy*, 2 vols. (Temple Classics), *id.* ; 2 vols., Macmillan. With *Journal to Eliza* (Everyman's Lib.), Dent (Dutton, New York), 1927. Ed. by Henry Morley, Routledge ; Methuen ; ed. by Wilbur Cross, Boni, New York, 1926. With introd. by Virginia Woolf (World's Classics), Oxford Press, 1928 ; ed. by Herbert Read, Scholartis Press (McKee, New York), 1928. *Illus.* by Norah McGuiness, Macmillan ; by Vera Willoughby, P. Davies (Stokes, New York).]

STEUART, Catherine [Scottish]. *By Allan Water : story of an old house.* 1901
In the guise of a novel, Miss Steuart relates the history of a family living in a change-house near Stirling, where Jacobites and adherents of King George meet and talk politics. The affairs of both the '15 and the '45 are dealt with from this point of view, and the real condition of the people has a good deal of light thrown on it. [Elliot, Edinburgh : o.p.]

STEUART, John Alexander [Scottish ; *b.* 1861]. *In the Day of Battle.* 1894
Thrilling adventures, partly in Scotland, partly in Mecca and the desert—an Eastern battle and a Bedouin raid, scenes of pilgrim life in Mecca and Mohammedan ceremonial, pictures of the wildly beautiful desert. [Low : o.p.]

—— *The Minister of State.* 1898
The career of a Highland herd, who becomes a Minister of State by the force of genius. Life in the Perthshire highlands, in London, etc. Didactic. [Dent ; Dodd & Mead, New York : o.p.]

—— *Wine on the Lees.* 1899
A strong Temperance novel, and a study of life among the London poor. Account of a family who made their money by the sale of drink, and of one of its members whose conscience is aroused, and who plunges into slum life to see how far drink is responsible for social evils. He is mortally wounded in a street fray. [Hutchinson : o.p. ; Dodd & Mead, New York : o.p.]

—— *The Eternal Quest.* 1901
A manly and hearty kind of story, portraying brave soldiers, ardent lovers, and other worthy people, nearly

STEUART, John Alexander (*continued*).

all Scottish. Deals with Magersfontein and the prowess of the Highland Brigade. [Hutchinson : o.p. ; Dodd & Mead, New York : o.p.]

—— *The Red Reaper.*   1905

A Royalist romance of Montrose's campaigns from Tippermuir to Philiphaugh, with the marquess himself as central figure and Argyle as his foil (1644–50). The obverse of the picture in *John Splendid* (see p. 355). [Hodder : o.p.]

—— *The Immortal Lover.*   1930

A novel made up out of the life of Burns. The author tries to bring out the beautiful element in the story of Mary Campbell ; but it is Jean Armour who really dominates Burns's life, here as in actual fact. [Harrap ; Lippincott, Philadelphia.]

STEVENS, A. de Grasse [American]. *Old Boston.*   1884

A kindly, appealing story of the days of the siege of Boston and the outbreak of the War of Independence (1773–6), thoroughly feminine in its sentiment and leisurely garrulity. George Washington, Warren, and others are introduced. [Scribner, New York : o.p. ; G. Allen : o.p.]

STEVENS, Ethel Stefana [Mrs. E. M. Drower]. *The Veil ; a romance of Tunisia.*   1909

A romantic novel about Sicilian, Arab, and French people in Tunis and the sacred city of Kairouan, pivoting on a threatened Arab insurrection ; but of most importance as an attempt to penetrate the mysterious character of the Arab and the profundity of his racial and religious antipathy to the European. The fascination of the things behind the Veil is finely realized ; and Si Ismael, the revolutionary dreamer, and the dancer Mabrouka are picturesque exponents of the strange reactions set up by the clash of East and West. [Mills & Boon : o.p. ; Stokes, New York : o.p.]

—— *The Earthen Drum.*   1911

A collection of stories on the same theme, the mystery of the Orient and its compelling fascination for Western peoples brought in contact with Eastern races. [Mills & Boon : o.p.]

—— *Sarah Eden.*   1914

Portrays a woman of unconventional though deeply spiritual character, who after a youth of self-sacrifice and work amongst the poor, founds a religious community in Jerusalem. There is a vivid though harsh description of life in that city. [Mills & Boon : o.p. ; Dodd & Mead, New York : o.p.]

—— *Magdalene : a study in methods.*   1919

It is the old-fashioned penitential methods of conducting rescue-homes for fallen women that are in question. The rigid patroness who is at loggerheads with another trustee of ultra-modern views has a past—hence the piquancy of the situation when her stepson falls in love with her long-lost daughter. [Cassell.]

STEVENS, Sheppard [American]. *The Sword of Justice.*   1899

The struggle between the French and the Spanish in Florida (*c.* 1565), a series of striking incidents which the author alleges to be substantially true. [Little & Brown, Boston : o.p. ; Gay & Hancock : o.p.]

—— *In the Eagle's Talon.*   1902

America and Paris prior to the Louisiana purchase (1803). [Little & Brown, Boston : o.p.]

—— *The Sign of Triumph.*   [juvenile] 1904

The story of the Children's Crusade (1212). [Page, Boston : o.p. ; Chapman : o.p.]

STEVENSON, Burton Egbert [American ; *b.* 1872]. *A Soldier of Virginia : a story of Colonel Washington and Braddock's defeat.*   1901

Fighting with French and Indians, the establishment of Fort Duquesne by the French, and the defeat of Braddock (1754–73). [Houghton, Boston ; Duckworth : o.p.]

—— *The Heritage.*   1902

The settlement of Ohio, St. Clair's defeat and Wayne's victory (1790–4). [Houghton, Boston : o.p.]

STEVENSON, Philip L. *A Gendarme of the King.*   1905

Rather military history than a novel—Frederick the Great and the battles of the Seven Years' War (1756–63). Hero a Jacobite Scot. [Hurst : o.p.]

—— *The Black Cuirassier.*   1906

A sombre narrative of the period covering the battle of Lützen and the assassination of Wallenstein (1632–4) ; more history than fiction, with an Irish hero. [Hurst : o.p.]

—— *A Gallant of Gascony : a romance of Marguerite de Valois.*   1907

A novel of intrigue at the French Court at the time of Marguerite's rupture with Henry (1585–6). [Hurst : o.p.]

—— *The Rose of Dauphiny.*   1909

Adventures of the Sieur de Roquelaure, a Huguenot, who sees much of both sides in the French wars of religion (1574–6). [Stanley Paul : o.p.]

—— *Love in Armour : or, The Experiences of Guy de Château-Bondeau in the French Wars of Religion.*

1912

Romance in the style of Dumas, " featuring " Charles IX, Marguerite de Valois, Henry of Navarre, etc. (1574). [S. Paul : o.p.]

STEVENSON, Robert Louis Balfour [Scottish ; 1850–94]. *The New Arabian Nights.*   1882

The fantastic adventures of a modern Haroun-al-Raschid in London, handled realistically and placed in a modern and familiar environment. *The Suicide Club* is a fantasy on somewhat similar lines to De Quincey's *Murder as one of the Fine Arts*, sporting with terror in an impish way. Romantic events are carried off by lively narrative, even when there is a deliberate excess of fantasy, as in *The Cream Tarts*. *The Rajah's Diamond* has a daring plot stringing together most heterogeneous scenes and characters, the coveted gem being a potent incentive to elaborate villainy and crime. In Stevenson's novels and stories, pure romance is made more effective by his dexterous technique, his command of verisimilitude, and insight into the psychology of the reader. In *The Pavilion on the Links*, the atmosphere of loneliness

STEVENSON, Robert Louis Balfour (*continued*).
and inscrutable terror conjured up by the deserted house on the shore is, characteristically, an element to which the story, perfectly in key with it, must be considered subordinate. [Also Chatto.]

—— *Treasure Island.* 1883
A masterpiece among romances for boys ; a story of piracy and concealed treasure in the middle of the eighteenth century ; the characters nearly all of a sinister kind : Pew, Black Dog, and Long John Silver are a villainous trio, strongly individualized, shedding an atmosphere of malignancy and terror. The scenery of isle and ocean contrasts vividly with the savagery of the action. [Also (Everyman's Lib.) Dent (Dutton, New York) ; *illus.* by Edmund Dulac, Doubleday, Doran, New York ; *etc.*]

—— *The Silverado Squatters.* 1883
Substantially the story of Stevenson's honeymoon, at Juan Silverado, amid the mountains and forests of California ; buoyant and humorous in tone, and abounding in impressionist descriptions of nature. [Also Chatto ; with others, *sub tit.* *The Amateur Emigrant*, Scribner, New York ; alone, ltd. ed., *illus.*, 1923.]

—— *Prince Otto.* 1885
Stevensonian in its fine, clear style ; Meredithian in its paradoxical psychology. A love-comedy, adapted from a tragedy, *Semiramis.* Scene, an imaginary German principality ; motive, the growth, under the stress of untoward events, of a true and intelligent affection between husband and wife. The atmosphere of Court intrigue and the subtle play of character among courtiers are well portrayed. [Also Chatto.]

—— *The Strange Case of Dr. Jekyll and Mr. Hyde.* 1886
A grim apologue of a supernatural change of personality, symbolizing the conflict between the good and the evil selves in man. [Also, with *Other Fables*, Longmans ; with *The Merry Men*, Scribner, New York ; (Everyman's Lib.), Dent (Dutton, New York).]

—— *David Balfour : vol. i. Kidnapped ; vol. ii. Catriona.* 1886 ; 1892
Kidnapped is a match for *Treasure Island* as pure romance, strenuous deeds, thrilling encounters, hairbreadth escapes occurring on almost every page ; yet the romantic scenery of the West Highlands is almost as important as the characters and the action. Alan Breck, the supposed Appin murderer (1751), is perhaps the finest of Stevenson's creations. But there is more characterization in *Catriona*, which is his chief success in drawing a woman, and love interest is an important element. The social and political condition of Scotland in the period succeeding the '45, and the persecution, military and legal, of the beaten side, are well depicted in the two stories, which cover the years 1746–51. In *Stevenson and the Scottish Highlanders* (1929), Mr. D. B. Morris shows how very carefully Stevenson had worked local records and clan history into the two books.

—— *The Merry Men ; and other tales and fables.* 1887
A galaxy of masterpieces in the art of short-story writing : the first is a weird tale of the Western Isles, a treasure from the Armada, an awful wreck, and a man's remorse driving him to his death ; the whole invested with a magical atmosphere of hoary legend and the scenery of ocean, mountain, and storm. *Will o' the Mill* is an exquisite fable of human life, with Alpine valley scenery ; *Thrawn Janet*, a blood-curdling ghost story in a Scottish village ; *Markheim*, a sombre murder-story, and *The Treasure of Franchard* are two masterly embodiments of Stevenson's philosophy of life ; *Olalla*, a tragic love-story of Spain. [Also Chatto ; with *Dr. Jekyll and Mr. Hyde*, Scribner, New York.]

—— *The Black Arrow.* 1888
In quality, an indifferent story for young readers. A Yorkist story of the Wars of the Roses. The characters are outlaws, barons, men-at-arms, and priests ; Richard III is prominent. The language is to some extent based on that of the *Paston Letters*. [*v.* also *infra.*]

—— *The Master of Ballantrae.* 1889
The downfall of a noble Scottish family involved in the Jacobite troubles (1745–64), recounted by a faithful steward. Two brothers are the protagonists : the elder, a romantic construction, a fascinating exterior but cruel heart, the younger, a plain, long-suffering man. These, with the old lord, their young kinswoman, and a showy French adventurer, make a group of the exceptional personalities that Stevenson loved to sketch. Full, perhaps too full, of surprises and strange situations ; but they are all prepared with convincing ingenuity. In one scene, the midnight duel, he achieved his masterpiece of dramatic effect. Mackellar the steward is a thoroughly Stevensonian blend of moral courage with physical cowardice. [With *The Black Arrow* (Everyman's Lib.), Dent (Dutton, New York).]

—— *Island Nights' Entertainments.* 1893
The Beach of Falesá, *The Bottle Imp*, and *The Isle of Voices* are stories of the South Seas into which Stevenson infused much of the eeriness and mystery that characterizes such Scotch tales as *The Merry Men* and *Thrawn Janet*, according to his well-known formula, that romance is " the poetry of circumstance." In the first a rough and unlearned trader is the story-teller, whose nautical slang and colloquialisms are woven into a forcible and expressive prose. On the lonely beach of a forest-clad isle, he is the mark of a rival trader's diabolical plot, the superstitions of the natives being excited so that he is tabooed and nearly frightened to death. The charm of the tale is the enthralling atmosphere of glamour and dread. Life and nature in the Pacific are described with the familiar realism of one who has lived there. *The Bottle Imp* is a fairy-story, an adaptation of a German folk-tale to the people and surroundings of the South Seas.

—— *Weir of Hermiston.* 1896
An impressive torso of a tragedy, on the motive of deep antipathy between father and son. The father is a study of the hanging judge Lord Braxfield, the son represents the dawning age of reason and mercy. The son's pathetic love-story was only begun when the pen fell from Stevenson's hand. Outlines a remarkable group of tragic personalities, hard, strong-natured Scotch folk. Old Edinburgh and the dun moorlands haunted by memories of martyred Cameronians form the austere background. Period 1813–14. [Also Chatto.]

—— *St. Ives.* 1897
A posthumous romance, finished by " Q." Stevenson called it " a mere tissue of adventures." An essay

STEVENSON, Robert Louis Balfour (*continued*).
in picaresque fiction, reciting the experiences of a French prisoner of war in Edinburgh Castle, and his adventures after escaping. St. Ives is the only gentleman among the prisoners, and suffers much in his dignity.

STEVENSON, Robert Louis Balfour, and STEVENSON, Fanny van der Grift. *The Dynamiter.*
1885
In the style of the *New Arabian Nights.* Mrs. Stevenson claims to have written all the stories except the *Explosive Bomb*; but unmistakable traces of Stevenson's handiwork and of his characteristic philosophy abound.

STEVENSON, Robert Louis Balfour, and OSBOURNE, Lloyd [*b.* 1868]. *The Wrong Box.*
1889
An absurd yet engrossing extravagance; the rival plotting of the heirs to two old men, survivors of a tontine scheme. The frantic endeavours of various people to get rid of a corpse, supposed to be one of these valuable old men, lead to surprising results. These farcical complications were the work chiefly of Mr. Osbourne, who is responsible also for the more sordid and horrible features of the next two stories.

—— *The Wrecker.* 1892
Parisian student life, shady financial doings in California, piracy on the high seas, and more gruesome incidents, brought into juxtaposition by an elaborate mystery plot. A skilful combination of romance and prosaic realism.

—— *The Ebb Tide : a trio and quartette.* 1894
Pirates and treasure again, woven into a tense psychological drama. The uncanny atmosphere of the lone isle in the Pacific with its solitary occupier is a large element in the total impression. The cynical Attwater, dead-shot and Christian revivalist, the desperate skipper, the villainous little Cockney, and the man of education gone to the dogs but clinging to his sense of honour, form the quartette.
[*Works* (including collaborations): Tusitala Ed., 35 vols., Heinemann (Ryerson Press, Toronto); Biographical Ed., with introd. by Mrs. Stevenson, 31 vols., Scribner, New York; South Seas Ed., 17 vols., *id.* (1925); *Novels, illus.,* 10 vols., Macmillan.]

STIMSON, Frederic Jesup [American ; *b.* 1855]. *King Noanett : a story of Devon settlers in old Virginia and Massachusetts Bay.* 1897
Pioneering and adventure (seventeenth century). [Scribner, New York ; Lane : o.p.]

STINDE, Ernst Wilhelm Julius [German ; 1841–1905]. *The Buchholz Family : sketches of Berlin life* (Die Familie Buchholz, 1886). 1886–7
Family annals giving a singularly full delineation of the manners, character, and domestic life of middle-class people in Berlin—their petty personal interests, gross tastes, and unrefined conversation. No satire, although there is some comedy of human character ; the kind and motherly Frau Buchholz is an unconscious humorist, and Frau Berzfeldt is responsible for many a shaft of mother-wit in the snubs she inflicts on her dear friends. [4 vols., Bell : o.p. ; (condensed), *sub tit. Masterful Wilhelmine,* by E. V. Lucas, Methuen, 1916 ; *sub tit. The Hausfrau Rampant,* Doran, New York : o.p.]

STIRLING, M. C. [Scottish]. *The Minister's Son ; or, Home with Honours.* 1882
The son of a Presbyterian father and a Highland mother, being disappointed in love, enlists and goes through the Afghan campaign and the march to Kandahar. Coming home, he finds his old love a widow, and having learned wisdom, is rewarded with her hand. Various sketches of Scotch character, including a drunken and humorous " soutar." [3 vols., Blackwood : o.p.]

STOCKLEY, Cynthia. *The Dream Ship.* 1913
A somewhat far-fetched story, vivaciously told, with an attractive heroine who writes and lives up to her pseudonym of Wanderfoot. Scenes, America, Jersey, and France. [Constable : o.p. ; Nash ; *sub tit. Wanderfoot,* Putnam, New York.]

—— *Wild Honey.* 1914
Seven short stories of a highly coloured, sensational kind, picturing English, Dutch, and natives in South Africa with evident knowledge—the title alludes to the wild charm of the veld. *Progress* is perhaps the best, unless that be the title-story. *Watchers by the Road* and *The Mollmeit of the Mountain* are very gruesome. [Constable : o.p. ; Long ; Putnam, New York : o.p.]

—— *Blue Aloes.* 1918
Four further South African stories that vividly depict persons and places. [Hutchinson : o.p. ; Putnam, New York.]

STOCKTON, Francis Richard [American ; 1834–1902]. *Rudder Grange.* 1879
The humorous experiences of a young couple who begin housekeeping in a derelict barge, and retain the name of " Rudder Grange " when they move to a more stable dwelling. This pair, their servant Pomona (drawn from Stockton's own maid), and the lodger are average characters drawn to the life, but the fun is that of comic opera. (Sequel, *The Rudder Grangers Abroad,* Scribner, New York.) [Scribner, New York ; (Wayfarer's Lib.), Dent. *Illus.* by A. B. Frost, Scribner, New York.]

—— *The Lady or the Tiger ; and other stories.* 1884
Ingenious stories, sparking with wit and covert satire, with comic surprises and irrelevant fun. The title-story, with its unexpected conclusion, is a masterpiece of elaborate wit, and *The Remarkable Wreck of Thomas Hyke* is a good example of Stockton's cool, realistic handling of the marvellous. [Scribner, New York ; Douglas, Edinburgh : o.p.]

—— *The Casting Away of Mrs. Lecks and Mrs. Aleshine.* 1886
The absurd Crusoe adventures of two prosaic matrons ; their methodical life on a desert isle, where they keep house as calmly and composedly as if they were at home in New England, set forth in a matter-of-fact manner that reads like a parody of Defoe. [With *The Dusantes,* Century Co., New York ; Low : o.p.]

STOCKTON, Francis Richard (*continued*). *The Dusantes* [sequel]. 1888
The Dusantes are the owners of this new Juan Fernandez, and they follow the Crusoe-ladies on the way home, to return the money paid for use of the property. The adventures are various, ingenious, and hilarious. [See *The Casting Away of Mrs. Lecks*.]

—— *The Late Mrs. Null.* 1886
Another absurd story, told with a matter-of-fact gravity that makes more than ever absurd the preposterous nature of the characters and their relations to each other. The negro parts have the most spontaneous humour; Aunt Patsy and the Jerusalem Jump are inimitable. [Scribner, New York: o.p.; Low: o.p.]

—— *The Hundredth Man.* 1887
Two stories intertwined—the one farcical, about a waiters' strike in a New York restaurant, the other, in places very pathetic, dealing with the deliberate and effectual attempt of a social theorist to break off an engagement between a pretty girl and a man he thinks unworthy of her. [Century Co., New York: o.p.; Low: o.p.]

—— *The Squirrel Inn.* 1891
An eccentric landlord of independent means, a scholar engaged in translating Dickens into ancient Greek, a teacher of moral philosophy working as a nurse, with other queer samples of humanity, meet together in this eccentric hostelry, and an orgy of funny incidents ends in three weddings. [Century Co., New York; Low: o.p.]

—— *Pomona's Travels.* 1894
The staid and competent but incalculable handmaid of the Rudder Grangers marries, and goes on a wedding trip through England and Scotland. Her journal hits off the characters of places and peoples with shrewdness and dry humour, her imperturbable common sense being a perennial source of amusement. [Scribner, New York: o.p.; Cassell: o.p.]

—— *The Adventures of Captain Horn.* 1895
A characteristic story of a quest for a treasure of the Incas, the interest dependent chiefly on Stockton's farcical handling of character. [Scribner, New York; Cassell: o.p.]

—— *Mrs. Cliff's Yacht* [sequel]. 1896
What is Mrs. Cliff to do with her millions? The question is worked out with the usual droll and paradoxical situations, which culminate in this plain and matter-of-fact old lady's going off in command of a steam yacht, manned by a synod of clergymen, fully armed, in pursuit of a treasure-ship captured by pirates. [Scribner, New York: o.p.; Cassell: o.p.]

—— *The Girl at Cobhurst.* 1898
Cobhurst, a ramshackle farm, becomes the property of a marriageable young man, whose matrimonial destinies are the object of intrigue and counter-intrigue between an eccentric old spinster and an autocratic cook; whence a series of topsy-turvy situations. Mild farce, with some felicitous sketches of character. [Scribner, New York: o.p.]

—— *The Associate Hermits.* 1898
The droll adventures of an elderly couple and a pretty girl who spend a holiday camping out. [Harper, New York: o.p.]

—— *A Bicycle of Cathay.* 1900
A village schoolmaster goes on a cycling tour and falls in love with every girl he meets, with other amusing adventures. Superficially like Mr. Wells's *Wheels of Chance*. [Harper: o.p.]

—— *Afield and Afloat.* 1901
Eleven short stories mixing fantasy and realism. Three are ghost stories. They sketch American characters and manners in a life-like way. *The Buller-Peddington Compact* puts before us a pair of crochety friends, and the mule story gives a graphic picture of old New Orleans. [Scribner, New York; Cassell: o.p.]

STODDARD, William Osborn [American; 1835–1925]. *Guert Ten Eyck.* [juvenile] 1893
A boy's adventures, chiefly about New York; Washington, Hamilton, Paul Revere, Nathan Hall, etc. This and the next two are good samples of a number of this writer's many and excellent stories for boys. [Lothrop, Boston.]

—— *With the Black Prince.* [juvenile] 1898
Invasion of France and battle of Creçy (1346). [Appleton, New York: o.p.]

—— *The Errand Boy of Andrew Jackson.* [juvenile] 1902
General Jackson; Mobile and New Orleans (1814). [Lothrop, Boston.]

STOKER, Bram [Irish; 1847–1912]. *The Snake's Pass.* 1891
A story of Mayo, sketching Irish types in a rough-and-ready way, and making sensational effect out of prophetic dreams, attempted murder, and " the strange phenomenon of a moving bog." [Collier: o.p.; Harper, New York: o.p.]

—— *Dracula.* 1897
A very successful handling of horrible sensations in a realistic way—a Gothic romance adapted to the more exacting requirements of *fin-de-siècle* readers. A terrible baron in a Transylvanian castle is the chief of an army of human vampires that prey on mankind and pursue their ravages as far as London, demanding all the determination and resource of the hero and his friends to exterminate them. [Rider (1921): o.p.; Doubleday, New York.]

STOKES, Whitley [1830–1909] [ed.]. *The Destruction of Dá Derga's Hostel* (Togail Bruidne Dá Derga). 1902
Apears in Lady Gregory's recension in a mutilated form as *The High King of Ireland*. Conary becomes king on condition that he abide by certain bonds imposed on him by his fairy kinsfolk. Having transgressed these conditions, he comes to his death in a great affray with outlaws, who attack Dá Derga's inn. Portents and marvels are characteristic of the story from beginning to end. [Bouillon, Paris: o.p.]

STONE, Christopher. *The Valley of Indecision.* 1920
A young man comes back from the war determined to renounce all worldly interests and preach the gospel of Christ. His people are unsympathetic, and oppose his decision. His and their attitudes are intelligently examined. [Collins : o.p.]

STONE, Grace Zaring [American]. *Bitter Tea.* 1930
What is most remarkable in this book is, not the story of the raw American lady's adventures amid the revolutionary troubles at Shanghai, nor the characters, although these are incisively drawn, but the contrast between American and Chinese mentality and between Western positivism and the ancient negative philosophy of China, the young lady and her captor, a Chinese general, being the interlocutors. [Bobbs-Merrill, Indianapolis, *sub tit. The Bitter Tea of General Yen* ; Cobden-Sanderson.]

STORM, Hans Theodore Waldsen [German ; 1817–88]. *Immensee ; or, The Old Man's Reverie* (Immensee, 1852). 1863
One of the simplest and most pathetic of North German stories ; almost devoid of incident, the charm of the book being in its exquisite feeling. Reinhardt and Elizabeth grow up as child-lovers, but are parted by inexorable circumstance, and he is left to a life of solitude. [Transl. by H. CLARK, Munster, 1863 : o.p. ; transl. by Irma Ann HEATH, Mosher, Portland, Me., 1902 ; Putnam, New York.]

STOWE, Harriet Elizabeth [*née* Beecher ; American ; 1812–96]. *Uncle Tom's Cabin ; or, Life among the Lowly.* 1852
An historic exposure of the barbarities of slavery, which did incalculable service for emancipation : a highly emotional book, as befitted its purpose. The characters are strongly accentuated types of virtue and villainy, e.g. Uncle Tom, Topsy, Eva, Harris, and the brutal Legree ; scenes, like the flogging to death, which were intended to appeal to public compassion, are relieved by passages of a tenderer pathos and a lively humour. [Houghton, Boston ; *illus.* by James Daugherty, Coward McCann, New York (McClelland, Toronto) ; Routledge ; Macmillan ; (Everyman's Lib.) Dent (Dutton, New York).]

—— *Dred : a tale of the Great Dismal Swamp.* 1856
Another anti-slavery manifesto, in the form of a novel of North Carolina, with another strong creation in Old Tiff. Dred, the runaway slave, is a wearisome ranter. The book preaches indirectly true ideals of humanity and religion, while satirizing bigotry and fanaticism. A new edition was published in 1866, called *Nina Gordon.* [Houghton, Boston.]

—— *The Minister's Wooing.* 1859
A semi-historical picture of Newport people in the time of the slave-trade, especially of their Puritanical life and sombre religious creed. Dr. Hopkins and Captain Aaron Burr are drawn, melodramatically, from life. The Doctor is about to marry his pupil, when her sailor lover appears, and he magnanimously releases her. [Augustana Co., Minneapolis.]

—— *The Pearl of Orr's Island : a story of the coast of Maine.* 1861
Chiefly quiet portraiture of a set of Puritan folk, pious, solemn, and honest, and somewhat dull ; their dullness the target for mild satire. There are thrilling episodes, but most of the story is very sober, ordinary love matters and wedded life, unconsciously humorous talk, and the diverting eccentricities of an attractive person, Miss Roxy, and of an unconverted original, Captain Kettridge. [Houghton, Boston ; Low : o.p.]

—— *Agnes of Sorrento.* 1862
A nobleman's love for a girl of the people, whose piety is offended by his infidelity to the Church. Savonarola's crusade and death are an important episode (c. 1492–8). [Houghton Boston ; Murray.]

—— *Oldtown Folks.* 1869
—— *Sam Lawson's Oldtown Fireside Stories.* 1872
Portraiture of bygone society, characters, and manners in a Massachusetts village (in Norfolk County about 1800)—Indians, Hibernians, English, Puritan home life, and ghosts. [(1) and (2), Houghton, Boston ; (1), Low : o.p.]

STRACHEY, Marjorie. *The Nightingale.* 1925
The story of Chopin and his relations with George Sand. [Longmans.]

STRACHEY, Ray [Mrs. Oliver Strachey, *née* Costelloe ; American ; b. 1887]. *Marching On.* 1923
A novel dealing graphically with the antecedents of the American Civil War : the anti-slavery movement, the Kansas-Nebraska Bill of 1854 and the disturbances that followed, the doings of John Brown and his seizure of Harper's Ferry, etc. (1845–61). [Harcourt, New York ; Cape.]

STRACHEY, St. Loe. *The Madonna of the Barricades : being the memoirs of George Lord Chertsey, 1847–48–49.* 1925
An historical novel in the form of memoirs, beginning in England and closing in the revolutionary Paris of 1848. Louis Napoleon and Karl Marx are brought in. [Cape ; Harcourt, New York.]

STRAIN, Mrs. Euphans H. [*née* M'Naughton ; Irish]. *A Man's Foes.* 1895
A tale of the conflicts between Protestants and Catholics in Ulster, and the siege of Londonderry (1689–90) ; anti-Catholic in feeling. [Ward & Lock : o.p. ; New Amsterdam Book Co., New York : o.p.]

—— *Elmslie's Drag-Net.* 1900
Five stories of a Scotch fishing-village in the north, etchings of elemental phases of character. *Bell Dundas*, a dour old woman who makes a hard fight for existence, handicapped by a shiftless husband ; a blind shepherd who forgoes revenge and saves his enemy's life on the storm-swept mountain-side ; these are good types of a virile, undemonstrative, yet deeply emotional people. [Methuen : o.p.]

—— *A Prophet's Reward.* 1908
A rather slow novel of Scottish politics in the days of the " Friends of the People " and the French Revolution (1778–93). [Blackwood : o.p.]

STRAPAROLA, Giovan Francesco [Italian ; *d. c.* 1557]. *The Nights* (Notte Piacevoli, 1554). 1894
Seventy-four stories, related during thirteen nights by a company of ladies and gentlemen, to amuse the Duke of Milan's daughter. They are derived from various sources—Italian tale-tellers, including Boccaccio,

STRAPAROLA, Giovan Francesco (*continued*).

the *fabliaux*, the Arthurian legends, Arabian literature, and folk-lore. Fantasy and fairy romance predominate, and many of the mythological stories have attained wide popularity since in adaptations by Hans Andersen, Grimm, and Perrault : *Puss in Boots* is perhaps the best known. There are also stories of knights and of the bourgeois classes, and characteristic drolleries ; while the rich, voluptuous life of the Italian nobility is depicted in warm colours as a background. [Transl. by W. G. WATERS, *illus.* by E. R. Hughes, 2 vols., Lawrence & Bullen : o.p.]

" STRATHESK, John " [John Tod ; Scottish]. *Bits from Blinkbonny : or, Bell of the Manse.* 1884
—— *More Bits from Blinkbonny.* 1884
Sympathetic sketches of Scottish village life between 1841 and 1851, very simple and realistic in manner, and largely concerned with the religious emotions of the peasant characters. [(1) and (2), Oliphant, Edinburgh : o.p.]

STRATZ, Rudolph [German ; *b.* 1864]. *His English Wife* (Seine englische Frau, 1913). 1915
She is not really very English, and the author in spite of his desire to do us justice falls into several absurd blunders about England and English ways. The events take place half in England and half in Germany, and it is doubtful whether Herr Stratz has ever visited the former. [Transl. by A. C. CURTIS, Arnold.]

STREET, George Slythe [*b.* 1867]. *The Autobiography of a Boy : being passages selected by his friend.* 1894
A clever piece of ironical story-telling. A mock-heroic portrait of the *fin-de-siècle* young man, non-moral, devoted to the gospel of self-indulgence. In the various episodes of college life and social intercourse he writes himself down a fool. [Lane.]
—— *The Wise and the Wayward.* 1897
A full-length novel satirizing in like fashion the dilettanti of society and similar moral delinquents. [Lane : o.p.]
—— *The Trials of the Bantocks.* 1900
An ironical biography by an admiring sycophant, castigating the snobs and vulgarians in moneyed society. Bantock is a banker, who, with his correct and highly respectable family, is plagued with parasitical friends and other social afflictions. [Lane : o.p.]

" STRETTON, Hesba " [Hannah Smith ; 1832–1911]. *Through a Needle's Eye.* 1878
A fair example of this writer's unpretentious but carefully wrought didactic fiction. A man does wrong in order to become owner and master of the family estate. He repents and makes due reparation, but his much-loved daughter suffers for his misdeeds. The various characters of a village, the Methodist preacher, the curate and his worldly wife, and some humbler people, are clearly drawn. [Paul, o.p. ; Dodd & Mead, New York : o.p.]

" STREUVELS, Stijn " [Frank Lateur ; Flemish]. *The Path of Life.* 1915
Stories of Flemish village life, displaying imaginative powers and an intense realization of the significant value of detail. [Transl. from the West Flemish by A. T. DE MATTOS, Allen & Unwin ; Dodd & Mead, New York : o.p.]

STRIBLING, Thomas Sigismund [American ; *b.* 1881]. *Birthright.* 1922
A negro educated at Harvard desires to raise the condition of his fellow-negroes. He returns to his native town, where both black and white reject his views, and leave him disillusioned and robbed of his self-confidence. [Century Co., New York ; Collins : o.p.]
—— *Fombombo.* 1923
Depicts the encounter of the hundred-per-cent. American with the Latin Americans of the South. Strawbridge, a small-arms drummer, imbued with the ideals of business and the philosophy of Babbitism, comes to Venezuela to do business with the tyrannical dictator who is creating a new State. How he fares there, and enlarges his mental horizon, and how he eventually elopes with the dictator's wife, and pulls off his business deal into the bargain, make up a romance containing plenty of sheer farce, and much satire of the foibles and weaknesses of both races. [Century Co., New York ; Nisbet.]
—— *Red Sand.* 1924
A Venezuelan bull-fighter falls in love with an American lady ; the contrast is presented with some irony, and the background is vivid. [Harcourt, New York ; Nisbet.]
—— *Teeftallow.* 1926
Another realistic story of the life of negroes in Tennessee, bringing out their humour and superstition, and the contrast between them and the " poor white." [Doubleday, New York ; Grosset, New York ; Nisbet.]
—— *Bright Metal.* 1928
A view of life in a small town in Tennessee—bigoted, ignorant, honeycombed with graft. The theme is rather similar to *Main Street* ; the heroine, an educated and somewhat foolish girl, attempts to engineer reforms by organizing the women of the district. She fails, partly from their traditional apathy, partly from the difficulties of her position, at once dependent on and disloyal to her husband. In the end she abandons the attempt and becomes a devoted wife. The tone of the book is not optimistic, and seems to suggest that any real reform must be a slow affair. [Doubleday, Doran, New York ; Nisbet.]
—— *Strange Moon.* 1929
Hardly a serious portrayal of life in Venezuela, but amusing and exciting. An American business man, who is after an oil-lease, is fooled by a commercial rival, and both get involved with shady people of both sexes. [Doubleday, New York ; Heinemann.]
—— *Backwater.* 1930
The population of a small town in Arkansas are pungently sketched, with their petty class-hatreds and their righteous anger at lawlessness. A detested bootlegger saves the town when the Mississippi breaks the levee, and gives the story a climax. [Doubleday, New York ; Heinemann.]

STRINDBERG, John August [Swedish ; 1849–1912]. *The Red Room* (Röda rummet, 1879). 1913
In these sketches of character and the interplay of character among the journalists and artists, all more or

STRINDBERG, John August (*continued*).

less down and out, who meet in a Stockholm café, Strindberg displayed a kindliness, even a touch of catholicity, and a humour rare in his later work. One or two of the men are fine incarnations of courage and endurance. But the object is evidently to satirize the comfortable, prosperous, bureaucratic bourgeois; and already Strindberg's obsession with the depravity of women is manifest: it is largely to them that the blame attaches for the failures of the other sex. [Transl. by Ellie SCHLEUSSNER, Latimer: o.p.; Putnam, New York: o.p.]

—— *Married* (Giftas, 1884; new ed. 1886).   1913
Twenty stories of married life, dealing almost exclusively with the disasters, the disillusionments, the degradations, and the diseases of matrimony. [Transl. by Ellie SCHLEUSSNER, Palmer: o.p.; Modern Lib., New York.]

—— *The Son of a Servant: a soul's development* (Tjensteqvinnans son, 1886-7).   1913
This is a novel composed largely of autobiographical material. Strindberg's father was of good family, but his mother was a waitress, hence the title. It deals with the hardships, hatreds, and discontents of his early life, and the record is continued in the *Confessions of a Fool* (see below). [Transl. by Ellie SCHLEUSSNER, Hutchinson; transl. by Claud FIELD, Putnam, New York: o.p.]

—— *By the Open Sea* (I hafsbandet, 1890).   1913
A Nietzschean superman and a supersexed woman and their emotional relations, ending in the hero's insanity. [Transl. by Ellie SCHLEUSSNER, Palmer: o.p.; Viking Press, New York.]

—— *Confessions of a Fool* (Die Beichte eines Thoren, 1893).   1912
Strindberg's own account of his married life, that is, with the vain and incompetent Siri, the actress, who was his first wife—he divorced her and was afterwards separated from two others, yet seems to have loved her in a way until the end. His play *The Father* is another version; neither of course must be taken too literally. This is a terrible vivisection of two mentalities, morbid and one of them disordered; for Strindberg regarded the inmates of mental asylums as the only sane people. The book is really the fourth part of his autobiographical novel *The Son of a Servant*; being forbidden in Sweden, it was published in Germany, hence the German title. [Transl. by Ellie SCHLEUSSNER, Viking Press, New York.]

—— *Fair Haven and Foul Strand* (1902).   1914
A further record of Strindberg's matrimonial disasters. [Transl., McBride, New York: o.p.; Laurie: o.p.]

—— *Tales*.   1903
Characteristically morbid yet idealistic stories, chiefly of the moulding of character by evil and suffering. Actuality, fairyland, and Sweden's historical past supply the circumstance. [Transl. by J. POTTS, Chatto; (Phoenix Lib.), *id.*, 1930.]

—— *In Midsummer Days*.   1913
These tales are mostly of pleasant themes and wholesome tendencies, and no better than thousands by inferior men. When, however, Strindberg reverts to his old antipathy, woman, as in *The Mystery of the Tobacco Shed*, he is strong and interesting. [Transl. by Ellie SCHLEUSSNER, Latimer: o.p.; McBride, New York: o.p.]

—— *The German Lieutenant; and other stories*.   1915
The title-story recounts a war-incident of 1870-1 and its effects on the life of a German officer—a powerful analysis of the attitudes war engenders in different minds. [Transl., Laurie: o.p.; McClurg, Chicago: o.p.]

STRONG, Leonard Alfred George [*b.* 1896]. *Doyle's Rock; and other stories*.   1925
Short tales and sketches, of simple and delicate emotion rather than incident. *The Farm, Tea at Maggie Reynold's, The Cottage* are characteristic and most successful. [Blackwell; Oxford.]

—— *Dewer Rides*.   1929
The tragedy of a young Dartmoor farmer whose character, more and more dominated by traits of coarseness and sensuality, is broken by unsuccessful love, and brings him to degradation. There is some beauty though much brutality in the telling. [Gollancz; Boni, New York.]

—— *The English Captain; and other stories*.   1930
Sketches and vivid emotional impressions; the title-story illuminates the contrast between English and Irish mentality. [Gollancz.]

STRUTT, Joseph [1749–1802]. *Queen-hoo Hall*.   1808
Strutt was a learned antiquarian who, disgusted by the anachronisms of the Radcliffian romancers, undertook to show how an historical story should be written. The work is full of archæological lore, and the speech and manners of the fifteenth century are reproduced accurately, without much life. Scott completed the book and prepared it for publication. [o.p.]

"STUART, Esmé" [Miss Leroy]. *Christalla, an Unknown Quantity*.   1900
The demure little bluestocking who is the heroine forms the link in a group of characters whose oddities and comicalities are prettily delineated. An excellent book for girls, like most of this writer's stories. [Methuen: o.p.]

STUART, Henry Longan [American; 1875–1928]. *Fenella*.   1911
Fenella is the daughter of a patrician clergyman and a Cornish farmer's daughter. Her life from girlhood up, her career as a dancer, and her love experiences make a long story with a touching close. [Doubleday, New York: o.p.; Chatto: o.p.]

STUART, Ruth [*née* McEnery; American; 1856–1917]. *The Golden Wedding; and other tales*.   1893
The pathetic and humorous aspects of negro life in the Southern States presented with sympathy. The title-story is a good example of the pathos, and *The Wilder Johnsing* of the fun. [Harper, New York: o.p.]

—— *Mr. Simpkinsville: character tales*.   1897
—— *Moriah's Mourning; and other half-hour sketches*.   1898
Seven and thirteen short stories respectively, chiefly about the South and the negro. [(1) and (2), Harper, New York.]

STURGIS, Howard Overing. *Tim.* 1891
A delicate portrayal of a sensitive boy's devoted affection for an older boy—a very touching story of a tender and self-forgetful character. [Macmillan : o.p.]

SUCKOW, Ruth [American ; *b.* 1892]. *Country People.* 1924
—— *The Odyssey of a Nice Girl.* 1925
—— *Iowa Interiors.* 1926
—— *The Bonney Family.* 1928
—— *The Kramer Girls.* 1930
—— *Cora.* 1930
Miss Suckow, who is a native of Iowa and runs the Orchard Apiary at Earlville, has a gift for portraying the uneventful everyday life of very homely people. She goes well below the surface, and makes us sympathize with their hopes and ambitions and disappointments, petty as these may seem to the casual observer. *Iowa Interiors* consists of a number of such domestic episodes. *The Kramer Girls*, history of three devoted sisters, is a fair example of her quiet—perhaps too quiet—manner. [All, Knopf, New York ; Cape.]

SUDERMANN, Hermann [German ; 1857–1928]. *Dame Care* (Frau Sorge, 1889). 1891
A symbolical tale of a boy born in a time of misfortune, and attended throughout life by Dame Care, the Spirit of Sorrow, but a boy who always bears himself manfully and with generous feeling for others. Realistic portraiture of the commonplace features of daily life, imaginative rendering of the nobler possibilities of character. [Transl. by Bertha OVERBECK, Harper ; Modern Lib., New York.]
—— *Regina ; or, The Sins of the Fathers* (Der Katzensteg, 1889). 1898
A tragic story of hate and love, plunging deeply into the hidden places of the mind ; scene, a Prussian village in 1814–15. The legacy of guilt and retribution is bequeathed to his son by a nobleman who turned traitor after Jena. Between this son, overwhelmed with the burden of shame, and Regina, a peasant girl, the victim of his father's profligacy, springs up a love, forbidden by human and divine laws, though essentially pure and heroic. [Transl. by Beatrice MARSHALL, Lane ; Dodd & Mead, New York.]
—— *The Wish* (Der Wunsch, 1891). 1894
A brief, intense, ruthless psychological study of a hidden sin. A wish, involuntarily uttered in a moment of strong excitement, repented of bitterly, and expiated by death. [Transl. by Lily HENKEL, Unwin : o.p. ; Appleton, New York : o.p.]
—— *The Undying Past* (Es war, 1894). 1906
A bloodless but powerful and impressive tragedy. A man who has killed the husband of his mistress in a duel comes home after four years to find her married to his best friend. The mental conflict aroused by her blandishments is developed with the same grim psychological force, and the complex character of the woman is set forth with admirable completeness. [Transl. by Beatrice MARSHALL, Lane : o.p.]
—— *The Song of Songs* (Das hohe Lied, 1908). 1909
Paints, with merciless realism and an infallible eye for the depravity of a luxurious, idle society, three sections of Berlin life, the plutocrats and the literary and artistic coteries on the fringe of plutocratic society, military life, represented by officers holding high commands and by the lower grades, and finally the courtesans who connect these corrupt worlds together. The heroine is the victim of a bloated sensualist, and falls from degradation to degradation ; the moral being the inevitable rottenness of a society that does not work. [Transl. by Thomas SELTZER, Viking Press, New York ; transl. by Beatrice MARSHALL, Lane, 1915.]
—— *The Indian Lily ; and other stories* (Die indische Lilie, 1911). 1911
Seven short stories, skilfully composed, dealing for the most part with irregular passion. *Thea, a Phantasy over the Samovar*, and *Merry Folk*, a story of Christmas, are on healthier themes. [Transl. by Ludwig LEWISOHN, Viking Press, New York ; Lane (1912).]
—— *The Mad Professor* (Der tolle Professor : ein Roman aus der Bismarckzeit, 1926). 1928
Offers a general picture of a German university town in the throes of conflict between the old Bismarckian national spirit and the newer liberalism. [Transl. by Isobel LEIGHTON and O. P. SCHINNERER, 2 vols., Boni, New York ; Lane.]
—— *The Journey to Tilsit* (Excursion). 1930
Four stories of the Lithuanian peasantry ; *Miks Bumbullis* is the strongest in local and racial features. The others deal, as was Sudermann's wont, with the universal facts of human life and with elemental passions. The title-story is a fair example of his dramatic power : a man who tries to get rid of his wife loses his own life instead. Tragedy also ends the idyll of the bond-servants Jons and Erdma, after years of toil and struggle. [Transl. by Lewis GALANTIÈRE, Liveright, New York.]

SUE, Marie Joseph Eugène [French ; 1804–59]. *The Mysteries of Paris* (Les mystères de Paris, 1842–3). 1845
A startling and incredible melodrama, professing to be a realistic picture of the Parisian underworld, the slaves of poverty and vice, swindlers, robbers, murderers. The central figure is a wealthy German prince who has ordained himself as a grand justiciar of society, to succour the unfortunate, remedy iniquities, and avenge guilt. His courage and physique bring him safely through scores of perilous encounters in his investigations amongst the haunts of crime, where he meets with a crowd of ruffians and outlaws, some, such as " The Schoolmaster " and his partner " La Chouette," among the most hideous creations of fiction. From this tragic company he rescues a poor, abandoned girl, whom he discovers to be his kidnapped child. This and *Le juif errant* appeared as a serial, and the humanitarian romanticism of the author, combined with his genuine knowledge of the lower classes, secured him countless readers. [Routledge : o.p. ; Burt, New York ; 3 vols., Bigelow Brown, New York, 1928 ; *illus.*, Page, Boston.]
—— *The Wandering Jew* (Le juif errant, 1844–5). 1845
A romance on the semi-supernatural theme of tradition, compounded of the same realistic and sensational ingredients, powerful in its command of terror ; no doubt, inspired by Maturin—whence, probably, the animus against Jesuits. [Routledge : o.p. ; 2 vols., Burt, New York ; 3 vols., Bigelow Brown, New York, 1928.]
[*Romances*, 20 vols., Nickerson, Boston.]

SULLIVAN, James Frank. *Queer-Side Stories.*   1900
> Fables, extravagances, and other satirical studies of modern life, chiefly on the non-political and social side.
> [Downey : o.p.]

SULLIVAN, James William [American ; *b.* 1848]. *Tenement Tales of New York.*   1894
> A series of miniatures painted in abodes of poverty by a devoted social reformer, who is a strong advocate of Swiss political methods. Touches of fun and mischief light up the prevailing sadness. [Holt, New York : o.p.]

SURTEES, Robert Smith [1779–1834]. *Handley Cross ; or, The Spa Hunt.*   1843
> A famous classic of the hunting-field, the work of an experienced and enthusiastic fox-hunter, cousin of the antiquary Surtees, who in his insatiable love of farce, broad caricature, and the high-flavoured vocabulary of stable and turf, was a minor Dickens, or at least the genuine offspring of the sporting miscellanists whose work was crowned and transcended by the *Pickwick Papers.* Furthermore, he was the historian of a world that railways and other innovations, and extravagances such as racing and betting, were shortly to displace. This is an almost interminable chronicle, describing how a village grew into a fashionable spa, and the pack of hounds kept by the farmers became the nucleus of the Spa Hunt. The one immortal among the farcical characters is Mr. Jorrocks, the cockney grocer and M.F.H., who reorganizes the hunt and has various squabbles with the magnates of the spa, winding up with a couple of lawsuits. [With the original coloured plates, and 100 other *illus.* by John Leech, Methuen ; ltd. ed., Harrap (Viking Press, New York), 1930.]

—— *Hillingdon Hall ; or, The Cockney Squire.*   1845
—— *Mr. Sponge's Sporting Tour.*   1853
—— *Ask Mamma ; or, The Richest Commoner in London.*   1858
—— *Plain or Ringlets ?*   1860
> Sporting novels of a similar stamp, depicting the manners and customs of the hunting fraternity and the technique of hunting, in the utmost detail—Surtees was the author of *The Horseman's Manual* (1831). Inns and watering-places, hunt-dances, hunt-breakfasts, horses and hounds, the idiosyncrasies of the expert and the fool, and a thousand similar matters come in for pungent description. All this is seasoned with uproarious and very unkind satire, and the women characters altogether are badly treated. [(1), (2), (3), and (4), with original illustrations, Methuen ; (2), Bles.]

—— *Hawbuck Grange ; or, The Sporting Adventures of Thomas Scott, Esq.*   1847
> Contains one of his finest accounts of a hare-hunt. [With eight original *illus.* by " Phiz," Methuen.]

—— *Mr. Facey Romford's Hounds.*   1865
> Mr. Romford describes himself as A.D.C., though he is only the assistant drains commissioner. But his zeal and prowess in the field redeems him. [With original *illus.*, Methuen.]
> [*Novels*, with original *illus.* by John Leech and Hablot K. Browne, 10 vols., ltd. ed., Eyre & Spottiswoode (Scribner, New York), 1930.]

SUTCLIFFE, Halliwell [1870–1932]. *A Man of the Moors.*   1897
> A tale of love and tragedy, with a good deal of sensation and some gruesome scenes. The author is a lover of the lonely moorlands of Yorkshire, and their wild, beautiful, and solemn aspects are reflected in every chapter. The Brontë neighbourhood of forty years ago is largely the scene, and the dialect is utilized. [Unwin.]

—— *Through Sorrow's Gates : a tale of the lonely heath* [sequel].   1904
> The best part of this is the close and enthusiastic description of the moors in the West Riding ; in the love-story and the tragic business the writer simply wallows in sentiment. Griff, the conqueror of the heath, and his intake are a fine impersonation of mankind's long struggle with the sterile forces of nature ; but the pathetic fallacy is ridden very hard throughout. [Unwin.]

—— *Ricroft of Withens.*   1898
> The rude old life of the moorland folk of the West Riding. A story abounding in violence and sensation. Adds historical interest by bringing the Jacobite chiefs of the '45 rebellion on the stage. [Unwin ; Appleton, New York : o.p.]

—— *Shameless Wayne.*   1900
> Chiefly concerned with a gory feud between two landed families ; descriptive passages of the moors and fells, of local superstitions, and bygone manners. [Unwin ; Dodd & Mead, New York : o.p.]

—— *Willowdene Will.*   1901
> Jacobites and highwaymen ; Yorkshire, Cumberland, and London. [Unwin.]

—— *Mistress Barbara Cunliffe.*   1902
> Yorkshire woolcombers and the cotton industry in the days before machinery (1830). Strongly marked provincial types drawn by one who lives among their very conservative children. [Unwin ; Crowell, New York : o.p.]

—— *Under the White Cockade.*   [juvenile] 1902
> A Jacobite's adventures in 1745-6. [Cassell ; Long.]

—— *A Benedick in Arcady.*   1906
> Honeymoon love in a cottage, with a well-experienced old Yorkshire couple as gardener and cook. [Unwin ; Dutton, New York : o.p.]

—— *Pam the Fiddler : a tale of the rising brooks.*   1910
> The story of the Nortons (i.e. of *The White Doe of Rylstone*) and their rising on behalf of Mary Queen of Scots in 1569. [Laurie : o.p.]

—— *The Lone Adventure.*   1911
> Adventures of the son of a Lancashire squire with Prince Charles Edward, from the march to Derby to the flight to Skye. [Unwin : o.p. ; Doran, New York : o.p.]

SUTCLIFFE, Halliwell (*continued*). *The Open Road.* 1913
Jacobite adventure in Yorkshire and Cumberland, the hero is taken for Prince Charlie (1745–6). [Ward & Lock.]

—— *The White Horses.* 1915
A Civil War tale of Yorkshire—the siege of Skipton Castle and that of York, and the battle of Marston Moor (1644). [Ward & Lock : o.p.]

—— *The Crimson Field : a Flodden tale.* 1916
The concluding battle-piece that provides the title is Flodden (1513). Local colour from Wharfedale, Durham, and Northumberland. [Ward : o.p.]

SUTHERLAND, Joan [Mrs. Richard Kelly ; *b.* 1890]. *Cavanagh of Kultann.* 1911
A tale of the North-West frontier of India, characters and environment much the same as those of Mr. Kipling's incisive stories, but the treatment fundamentally different, the strong, devoted district officer Cavanagh fighting an uphill battle with a jealous M.P. sworn to discredit his work. [Harper : o.p.]

—— *The Edge of Empire.* 1916
This also is semi-historical, introducing the Chitral expedition of 1895 ; but the main interest is manners and sentiment, and London and Paris come into the picture as well as N.W. India. [Mills & Boon.]

SUTTNER, Bertha, Baroness von [*née* Kinsky ; German ; *b.* 1843]. *Lay Down Your Arms : the Autobiography of Martha von Tilling* (Die Waffen nieder ! 1889). 1892
A woman's sufferings at home during the Italian war (1859) and the Schleswig-Holstein war, and at the front during the Austro-Prussian and Franco-German wars, in the course of which her two successive husbands meet their deaths. Realistic and pathetic ; written as a plea for the abolition of war, and translated under the auspices of the Peace Association. [Transl. by T. HOLMES, Longman : o.p.]

SVARNAKUMĀRĪ Devī [Mrs. Ghosal ; sister of Ravīndranātha Thākura ; Bengali ; *b.* 1857]. *An Unfinished Song.* 1914
A love-romance showing keen insight into the heart of a Hindu girl. [Laurie : o.p.]

—— *The Fatal Garland.* 1915
A tale of romantic love in fifteenth century Bengal. The heroine considers herself married to a young prince, who flings a garland of flowers about her neck, symbolic of matrimony. He does not fulfil his obligations, and she, though she marries the son of the Sultan, finds only misery. [Laurie : o.p.]

—— *Short Stories.* 1919
Fourteen tales of Bengali life, mostly from magazines, in India. [Ganesh, Madras.]

" SVEVO, Italo " [Ettore Schmitz ; Italian ; 1864–1928]. *The Confessions of Zeno* (La coscienza di Zeno, 1921). 1930
A young man undergoing treatment at the hands of a psycho-analyst writes down his reminiscences—adventures mainly amorous, which lay bare the fundamental weakness of his character. [Transl. by Beryl DE ZOETE, Putnam, New York.]

—— *The Nice Old Man and the Pretty Girl ; and other stories* (1927–9). 1930
Three short stories and a fragment published posthumously : the little bucolic fable, *The Mother*, dates from 1910. All are good examples of Svevo's passion for unveiling the secret motives and sordid feelings which he contends really actuate us, in spite of pretences and idealistic self-deception. The title-story is about an old man who has his last affair, is tortured with jealousy, and preaches morality to the girl he has seduced. *Generous Wine* (*Vino generoso*, 1927) is also about an old man's lapses and the nightmare which is the penalty. [Transl. by L. COLLISON-MORLEY, Hogarth Press.]

" SWAN, Annie S." [Mrs. Burnett Smith ; Scottish ; *b.* 1859]. *Aldersyde.* 1880
Country life on the Scotch border in the early nineteenth century ; a pathetic tale. Most of this fertile novelist's work is written expressly for girls, and is pronouncedly didactic in tone. [Oliphant, Edinburgh ; Methodist Book Concern, New York : o.p.]

—— *Adam Hepburn's Vow : a tale of Kirk and Covenant.* [juvenile] 1885
Dealing with the Cameronian rebellion of 1679 (the same as that treated by Scott in *Old Mortality*) ; suitable for girls. [Cassell : o.p.]

—— *Maitland of Laurieston : a family history.* 1891
About a lowland farmer, his household and their friends. The farmer is a type of honest, uncultured manliness, a devout Presbyterian, one of whose trials is to see his son first of all forsake the ancestral farm to become a professor, and then embrace agnosticism. The son is a fine character, who is gradually won back to Christianity by the sorrow of losing his child and by the pious fortitude of his wife. A large number of characters and various interests are dealt with in a manner that is more or less didactic ; the people, the manners, and the speech are pronouncedly Scotch. [Oliphant, Edinburgh ; Methodist Book Concern, New York : o.p.]

SWIFT, Jonathan [1667–1745]. *A Tale of a Tub.* 1704
Probably written about 1695. One of the most original and powerful satires ever penned. Swift's exclamation is famous : " Good God, what a genius I had when I wrote that book ! " The most specific object of the satire is formalism and pedantry in religion, the author taking the attitude of a loyal Church of England clergyman and belabouring the Roman Catholics and the Puritans. But the weak points of Anglican Christianity by no means escape censure, and the digressive style admits of the ridicule of all kinds of cant and prejudice. Swift's satire is profoundly philosophical in scope ; it goes to the roots of human nature and is applicable to all ages of history. The misanthropic prejudice of the book and its irreverence have been severely criticized, even by admirers. A consummate example of the author's clear, precise, virile prose and deadly logic. [With *The Battle of the Books*, etc., (Everyman's Lib.) Dent (Dutton, New York), 1909 ; ed. by C. A. Guthkelch and D. Nichol Smith, Oxford Press, 1920 ; alone, ed. by William Hodnett, *illus.*, Columbia Univ. Press, 1929.]

SWIFT, Jonathan (*continued*). *Travels into several remote Nations of the World, by Lemuel Gulliver.* 1726

In the account of his four wonder-countries Swift satirizes contemporary manners and morals, art and politics—in fact the whole social scheme—from four different points of view. The huge Brobdingnagians reduce man to his natural insignificance, the little people of Lilliput parody Europe and its petty broils, in Laputa philosophers are ridiculed, and finally all Swift's hatred and contempt find their satisfaction in degrading humanity to a bestial condition. The mordant satire and wayward humour are for men, but children can appreciate the simple and direct narrative that makes marvels appear quite everyday affairs. Swift's realistic method is an adaptation of Defoe's. See also p. 127, *Cyrano de Bergerac.* [(Temple Classics), Dent (Dutton, New York), 1896 ; illus. by Arthur Rackham (juvenile), *id.* Illus. by C. E. Brock, Macmillan ; by Cole, Lane, 1899. Facsimile Reprint, with introduction by Austin Dobson, Stock (1872), 1877 : o.p. *Gulliver's Travels and other Works,* exactly reprinted from 1st edn., and ed., with some account of Cyrano de Bergerac and his voyages to the sun and moon, by H. Morley, with note on the name " Gulliver " by J. P. Gilson (Library of Early Novelists), Routledge (Dutton, New York), 1906. Ed. by A. B. Gough, Oxford Press, 1915 ; Knopf, New York ; Putnam, London and New York ; 2 vols., Chaucer Head, New York. Reprint from 1st edn., ed. by Harold Williams, First Edition Club (McKee, New York), 1929. Swift's *Prose Works,* ed. Temple Scott, 12 vols., Bell, 1897–1908 ; vol. i., *Tale of a Tub,* etc. ; vol. viii, *Gulliver's Travels.*]

SWINBURNE, Algernon Charles [1837–1909]. *Love's Cross-currents : a year's letters.* 1905

The reprint of a novel which originally appeared serially as *A Year's Letters* in the *Tatler.* A characteristic revelation of the poet's mind, in characteristic prose. Displays his remarkable powers of sarcasm, and is a finished example of the finest epistolary style, the story interest altogether secondary. [Heinemann ; Harper, New York.]

SWINNERTON, Frank Arthur [b. 1884]. *On the Staircase.* 1914

The author's interest is in the fine distinctions of character in his three family groups in their Holborn flats ; he makes them talk—rather bookishly—and he analyses their complexities of attitude and motive down to the last detail. The twin love-stories of the ineffectual romantic and of the strong, efficient young man are subsidiary. [Methuen : o.p. ; Doran, New York.]

—— *The Chaste Wife.* 1916

This and the previous novel read as if partly composed of the writer's early experiences. The young man is a reviewer, who comes from a seedy family in Islington ; his father-in-law a literary dilettante, comfortably off. The contrast recalls Gissing, of whom the author had recently published a critical study. So does the concentrated observation of the straitened, humdrum lives of working-people. The title alludes to the drama of suspicion and incipient jealousy between the young man and his wife, two very clean-minded persons who had yearned for spiritual unity and self-surrender. [Secker : o.p. ; Doubleday, Doran, New York.]

—— *Nocturne.* 1917

" Life as it is, seen only more intensely " (H. G. Wells's preface). The evening escapade of an impulsive romantic girl, who is contrasted with her matter-of-fact but not less dynamic sister. Only the episode of one evening, but fraught with consequences that are with artistic economy only suggested. [Secker, Doubleday, Doran, New York.]

—— *Shops and Houses.* 1918

The same painstaking, argus-eyed drawing of the two social strata in a suburban place, where the well-to-do residents and the handful of gentry are not on speaking terms with the ever-increasing crowd of City clerks and butchers and grocers. There is a love affair ; but the emphasis is on the futility of such an existence and the petty snobberies, coming to a head when one irreproachable family discover that some vulgar people who have opened a shop hard by are their own relations. [Methuen : o.p. ; Doubleday, Doran, New York.]

—— *September.* 1919

A wife entering on middle-age, and an unfaithful husband, her hard and defiant rival, and the man who stirs an autumnal passion in herself, form the parallelogram of emotional forces which the novelist works out with his usual thoroughness. [Methuen : o.p. ; Doubleday, Doran, New York ; Grosset, New York.]

—— *Coquette.* 1921

A mental or moral study of the career of an adventuress, an Islington flapper, who pushes her way to the top in spite of an unfriendly world. Ends, rather unexpectedly, in an ugly murder-scene. [Methuen : o.p. ; Doubleday, Doran, New York.]

—— *Young Felix.* 1923

A family struggling with misfortune in a poverty-stricken suburb are depicted with the usual overwhelming realism ; but cheerfulness outweighs pathos, especially in the figures of Felix and his mother, who never complain though as poor as Lazarus. The " natural droll " and other oddities are experiments in humorous character-drawing. [Hutchinson : o.p. ; Doubleday, Doran, New York.]

—— *The Elder Sister.* 1925

A modern and more tragical version of the *Sense and Sensibility* theme, in the relations of two sisters to a caddish and rather shoddy young fellow who marries one and runs off with the other. Humdrum middle-class households drawn with careful touches and humour held in restraint. [Hutchinson : o.p. ; Doubleday, Doran, New York ; Grosset, New York.]

—— *A Brood of Ducklings.* 1928

Another careful exploration of a family group ; this time, a father, an affable dilettante, and his two daughters. Despite his anxious care for those he loves, he is unable to realize that they have grown to womanhood and desire marriage ; but there is no tragedy. They sail, more by luck than judgment, through the difficulties of the situation, and all turns out well. [Hutchinson ; Doubleday, Doran, New York.]

—— *Sketch of a Sinner.* 1929

The reader's interest is engaged rather with the gradual development of the heroine's character, and the

SWINNERTON, Frank Arthur (*continued*).

crystallization of her vague feelings of unrest, than with the trite theme—two love-affairs of a dissatisfied young wife. The family life of her and her husband, an elderly and unsuccessful antique-dealer, is well rendered; but the conclusion is mechanical and unsatisfying. [Hutchinson; Doubleday, Doran, New York.]

SWYNNERTON, Rev. Charles [ed.]. *Romantic Tales of the Punjab: with, Indian Nights' Entertainment.*   1908

A collection of primitive Aryan, or at any rate pre-Mohammedan legends from the Punjab; mostly myths, hero-tales, and beast-stories, of intense interest to children and of importance as folk-lore. Translated in a flowing idiomatic style that well conveys the native spirit, dialogue and other impassioned passages being given in verse. Two works are now combined in one volume with a short new preface. *The Romantic Tales* appeared in 1903, the *Indian Nights' Entertainment* in 1892. [Constable.]

SYMONS, Arthur [b. 1865]. *Spiritual Adventures: studies in temperament.*   1905

Studies of æsthetic perversion. *Christian Trevalga* analyses the mind of a pianist driven mad by a musical obsession. *Seaward Lackland* deals with a religious decadent who delights in outraging his own conscience. In *The Death of Peter Waydelin* we have an artist whose obsession is lubricity. *Esther Kahn* is a vigorous study of a Jewish actress whose histrionic genius suddenly matures through a spasm of baffled passion. [*Collected Works*, 9 vols., Secker, 1924; vol. 5 of *Collected Works*, 16 vols., Wells, New York, 1924; R. R. Smith, New York, 1930.]

SYRETT, Miss Netta. *The Child of Promise.*   1907

Her finest novel, bringing out her intellectual force and her humour. [Chapman: o.p.]

—— *Anne Page.*   1908

A sympathetic and appealing picture of "a woman who did." [Chatto: o.p.; Lane, New York: o.p.]

—— *A Castle of Dreams.*   1909

A clever blend of fancy and commonplace modernity, the dreamy Lady Bridgit coming from her Irish dream-castle into the common world of fashionable Londoners, and growing wiser through friendship and love. [Chatto; McClurg, Chicago: o.p.]

—— *Drender's Daughter.*   1911

A satire on eugenics. A wealthy crank brings up a peasant's daughter to be his wife and the mother of his children, but omits to take account of the human element in his protégée. [Chatto: o.p.; Lane, New York: o.p.]

—— *Barbara of the Thorn.*   1913

The heroine is a hyper-sensitive girl possessing psychic powers, who comes under the influence of two doctors, one hard-headed and practical, the other with an unhealthy passion for experiment. [Chatto.]

—— *Lady Jem.*   1923

Pepys is a leading figure in this romantic novel of London in the Plague year (1665). [Hutchinson: o.p.; *sub tit. Cupid and Mr. Pepys; a romance of the days of the great diarist*, Stokes, New York.]

—— *Strange Marriage.*   1930

The marriage is between a man on the eve of middle age and a girl of eighteen, who gets into a very modern set and has a lover. This, in the long run, becomes the means of bringing husband and wife truly together, and the latter history of their union is serene and happy. [Bles.]

SZÁSZ, Elsa [Hungarian]. *The Temple on the Hill.*   1912

The Hungarian authoress wrote this in English. The inhabitants of her Rumanian village are strange to us, but they are made very real, even the mad priest who sells absolution for payments on account of his Italianate temple, the peasant who mothers him, and the shepherd girl and her lover. There is moving tragedy in the story, but its artistic beauty is its most obvious merit. [Sidgwick.]

TABER, Ralph Graham [Canadian]. *Northern Lights and Shadows.*   1900

Tales and sketches of the primitive and little-known people, European and Eskimo, inhabiting sub-Arctic Labrador. *God's People* is about the Moravians. [Greening: o.p.]

"TAFFRAIL" [Commander Henry Taprell Dorling; b. 1883]. *Minor Operations.*   1917

Naval exploits, realistically described by one with professional knowledge—the deeds rather excessive. [Pearson: o.p.]

TANSLEY, F. C. *For Kett and Countryside: a tale of the Norfolk rebellion.*   1910

Robert Kett's rebellion in Norfolk (1549), during Edward VI's reign, related by another peasant, a friend of Kett. [Jarrold, Norwich: o.p.]

TARKINGTON, (Newton) Booth [American; b. 1869]. *The Gentleman from Indiana.*   1899

Strikes the keynote of all his fiction, which is in the Stevenson line, crossed with that of Anthony Hope; in short, Mr. Tarkington's literary pedigree is much the same as W. J. Locke's. All his love for Indiana went to the making of his petted hero, and he describes its skies and landscapes with as much delight as he does the townsfold of Plattville. This brilliant young man wages war against a gang of political rascals, and receives the popularity which is his due, especially from the young people of either sex. [Doubleday, Doran, New York; Nelson.]

—— *Monsieur Beaucaire.*   1900

A little drama of intrigue, laid in Bath during the Beau Nash regime. Complications arise when a French nobleman masquerades as a barber and falls in love with the reigning belle. [Doubleday, Doran, New York: Nelson: o.p.]

—— *The Two Vanrevels.*   1902

The hero of the love-story, a fiery abolitionist, is in Polk's war with Mexico. [Doubleday, Doran, New York; De la More Press: o.p.]

TARKINGTON, (Newton) Booth (*continued*). *The Conquest of Canaan.* 1905
An idealized young lawyer is popular with the rabble, and nevertheless is chosen mayor of his Indiana town. [Harper, New York and London.]

—— *In the Arena : stories of political life.* 1905
The result of Mr. Tarkington's years in the Indiana legislature (1902–3). [Doubleday, Doran, New York.]

—— *The Guest of Quesnay.* 1908
An American millionaire with a notorious past loses his memory through a motor accident, and arriving at the Norman village of Quesnay as an unrecognized person shines forth as an embodiment of all the virtues. [Doubleday, Doran, New York.]

—— *Penrod.* 1914

—— *Penrod and Sam.* 1916

—— *Seventeen.* 1916
Three stories of childhood and youth, amusing efforts in the Tom Sawyer vein, but not to be seriously compared with their model as authentic pictures of child life. [(1) and (2), Doubleday, New York ; Grosset, New York ; (3), Harper, New York ; (1), Hodder.]

—— *The Turmoil.* 1915
Another incredible reversal of fortune, Bibbs Sheridan suddenly becoming rich after years of futility. [Harper, New York.]

—— *The Magnificent Ambersons.* 1918
This also has an ultra-romantic plot, but the satire is good. [Doubleday, Doran, New York.]

—— *Alice Adams.* 1921
His most restrained book and by many thought to be his best. Brings out, mischievously but not unkindly, the little vanities and pretences of a young woman with good stuff in her, who has to make some sort of show among friends and acquaintances who are much better off and think everything of dress and amusement. The story is almost drowned in the too fluent dialogue, and ends, like so many of the foregoing novels, just when it begins to be interesting. [Doubleday, Doran, New York.]

—— *The Plutocrat.* 1927
Another comedy about philistines and highbrows ; the scene this time is Algiers and Tunis. [Doubleday, Doran, New York ; Heinemann.]

—— *Growth.* 1927
The Magnificent Ambersons, The Turmoil, and *The Midlander* are here rewritten and combined between one pair of covers. [Doubleday, Doran, New York.]

—— *Mirthful Haven.* 1930
About the daughter of a dissolute fisherman in a Maine village, who is educated by a wealthy relative. [Doubleday, Doran, New York.]

TARPEY, J. T. Kingsley. *Idylls of the Fells.* 1901
Stories of Yorkshire and Worcestershire, dwelling on the hardships of life, and the cruelty and injustice of convention. The first, *The Girl at the Gate,* is a fair sample, with the humanity and pathos of its portraiture of the little orphan and the rudely chivalrous " China-man," and its vivid rendering of the silence and sombre beauty of the fells. [Brimley Johnson : o.p.]

" TASMA " [Mme Jessie Fraser Couvreur ; Australian ; *d.* 1897]. *Uncle Piper of Piper's Hill.* 1889
Gives a vivid general idea of life in Victoria, some sixty years ago. [S. Paul : o.p. ; Harper, New York : o.p.]

—— *A Sydney Sovereign : and other tales.* 1890
Tales of Australian life, pathetic and decidedly morbid, but enlivened by a facile kind of facetiousness, e.g. *How a Claim was Jumped.* [S. Paul : o.p.]

—— *In Her Earliest Youth.* 1890
A conjugal drama ; a young and inexperienced wife, neglected by her hare-brained husband, nearly runs off with another man, but is saved on the eve of elopement. [S. Paul : o.p. ; Harper, New York : o.p.]

TAUTPHOEUS, Baroness Jemima von [*née* Montgomery ; 1807–93]. *The Initials.* 1850
A novel depicting everyday life in Bavaria, the personal interest centred in a young Englishman travelling for education and experience, and his love for a beautiful German girl, to marry whom he sacrifices his prospects. The novelist is at her best in drawing the natural contrast between the two German sisters. [Macmillan : o.p. ; Lippincott, Philadelphia.]

—— *Cyrilla.* 1853
A deeply tragic novel, accurately reproducing the details of the criminal trial of Assessor Lahn. [Bentley, 1872 : o.p.]

—— *Quits.* 1857
Long, with a straggling plot which marries the heroine at the end to the snob who slighted her at the beginning. Family life in London, followed by travel scenes in Bavaria and Tyrol, with a village drama of love and jealousy. The authoress satirizes vulgarity, but her own theory of life is not elevated. This novel introduced the Oberammergau passion play to the English. [Macmillan : o.p. ; Lippincott, Philadelphia.]

—— *At Odds.* 1863
Bavaria in Napoleon's time (1800–9), the family history interwoven with the disasters of S. Germany, from Hohenlinden to Hofer's insurrection in Tyrol. Plot : how a young man is obliged to marry a girl whom he has compromised by pure accident, while he loves her sister. Their quarrels, especially their political differences, last a long time and coincide with many signal historical events, from the father's death at Hohenlinden and the arrival of a French detachment at the countess's castle, right to the conclusion. [Macmillan : o.p. ; Lippincott, Philadelphia.]

TAYLER, Jenner [American]. *Mary Bray X Her Mark.* 1901
A picture of life in the Oregon woods. Mary is a trapper's daughter, illiterate, but shrewd and charming, with whom a young English gentleman falls in love. [Long : o.p.]

TAYLOR, Bayard [American ; 1825–78]. *Hannah Thurston.* 1864
Hannah is an advocate of woman's rights, who devotes her life to her mission as lecturer on the woman question, but unfortunately meets a man who awakens love. The story teems with fruitful ideas. [Putnam, New York : o.p.]

—— *Joseph and his Friend.* 1870
A quiet story of homely life in rural Pennsylvania, the author's own country ; like the former, abounding in fine ideas and rich in local colour. [Putnam, New York : o.p.]

TAYLOR, Mary Imlay [American]. *On the Red Staircase : a Russian story.* 1896
Court intrigues in Russia after the death of the Tsar Feodor, the riot of the Streltzi, and the regency of the Tsarevna Sophia (1682). [McClurg, Chicago : o.p.]

—— *An Imperial Lover.* 1897
A similar story of the Russian Court just after the Tsar Peter the Great had divorced his first wife Eudoxia, and before Catherine Shravonsky rose to power (1703–4). [McClurg, Chicago : o.p.]

—— *The House of the Wizard.* 1899
The reign of Henry VIII, death of Katharine of Aragon, and execution of Anne Boleyn. Numerous historical characters (1535–6). [McClurg, Chicago : o.p.]

—— *Anne Scarlet : a romance of Colonial times.* 1901
A story of Salem village and the witchcraft scare in Cotton Mather's times (1688). [McClurg, Chicago : o.p.]

TAYLOR, Col. Philip Meadows [1808–76]. *Confessions of a Thug.* 1839
An Indian romance of adventure and local colour by an Indian officer who possessed an intimate and extensive knowledge of native life and character. The incidents are very sensational. [(World's Classics), Oxford Press, 1916.]

—— *Tippoo Sultaun.* 1840
A story of the Mysore War (1788–9) in Sir Walter Scott's style ; a very full and elaborate picture of the times.

—— *Tara.* 1863
—— *Ralph Darnell.* 1865
—— *Seeta.* 1873
A series of three powerful tales illustrating three epochs in the history of India. " The historical events which form the foundation of each of these works are not only of the highest importance and interest, but, occurring strangely at almost exact intervals of a hundred years, are not exceeded in dramatic power by any actions in the history of India. " In that year a new political power arose in the English, and Clive won the battle of Plassey. *Tara* deals with the 1657 epoch ; the personages are all native, and the manners, costumes, and turbulent conditions of the land are carefully reproduced. *Ralph Darnell* deals with the events of 1757 and the Black Hole tragedy ; and in *Seeta* the literal fulfilment of a prediction that the rule of the English Company should come to an end in a hundred years is a motive in a narrative of the Mutiny (1857). " In each tale the great opposing interests are personified by great men, the characteristics of the rival races are brought out in examples which command admiration, and the romantic interest is secured by female characters of entirely novel types. " In the last, e.g., is portrayed a beautiful and noble Hindu woman, by marrying whom an Englishman scandalizes the European ladies, but who proves her worth by dying for him. The violent aspects of the Mutiny are hardly touched upon.

—— *A Noble Queen.* 1878
A romance illustrating one of the most important periods in the history of the Deccan. " The character of the noble Queen, Chand Beebee (contemporary with Elizabeth), is still popular in the country, and her memory is reverenced not only as the preserver of Beejapoor, but for the heroic resistance she made to the Mogul armies in their first invasion of the Deccan and siege of Ahmednugger. " [All, Kegan Paul, 1878–80 : o.p.]

TENREIRO, Ramón María [Spanish]. *The Handmaid of the Lord* (La Esclava del Señor). 1930
Autobiography of a much-tried woman from childhood to old age—an emotional picture of the vicissitudes that temper character. Life's purpose is self-devotion—to one's family and to God. The scenes change from near Corunna to Madrid, and his native Galicia is lovingly depicted by the novelist. [Secker.]

THACKERAY, Anne Isabella [Lady Ritchie ; 1838–1919]. *The Story of Elizabeth.* 1863
Thackeray's daughter excelled in delicate and thoughtful portraiture of character, sober in tint, restrained in feeling. The main situation is that of a man in love with the daughter of the woman who for twenty years has loved him. His is an unheroic, over-prudent nature, cursed with indecision. " Ely " is a childlike, wayward girl of varying moods, whose character is sobered and deepened by a near vision of death. One or two worldly-wise people are mouthpieces for caustic comments on life and conduct.

—— *The Village on the Cliff.* 1867
Expresses feelingly the sadness of sensitive natures condemned by fate to a cheerless and purposeless existence. A poor little governess loves a man who cares nothing for her, and marries from mistaken motives one who is not her true mate. Her girlish hopes and fears, her awakening to consciousness of her error, and her womanly conquest of passion are related with delicate sympathy. Impressionist sketches of Normandy give the keynote of feeling.

—— *Old Kensington.* 1873
A long novel full of musings on life that arise out of the incidents like the thoughts of an observer of actual events. Robert Henley is a scathing study of the genus prig ; the heroine a gentle poetical nature, whose growth is traced from youth up. Descriptions of scenery, the Thames, London, Cambridge, expressing its emotional effect on different temperaments.

THACKERAY, Anne Isabella (*continued*). *Bluebeard's Keys.*   1874
Little novels or long stories of which the essence is character—new illustrations of old fables and fairy tales.
An English family in Rome and an Italian marquess who loves the younger daughter are the personages
of the title story, which is a variation of the Bluebeard theme.

—— *Miss Angel.*   1875
A novel of manners (period 1765–8); Angelica Kauffmann and Sir Joshua Reynolds, with other celebrities.

—— *Mrs. Dymond.*   1886
A sweet-natured woman, whose life has little of the eventful, but appeals by its quiet goodness and unselfishness:
scene, France during the adverse months of the Franco-German war, which is set before us as it affected
the women and children. [All, Smith & Elder: o.p.]

THACKERAY, William Makepeace [1811–63]. *The Yellowplush Memoirs.*   1841
Contributed under various titles to *Fraser's Magazine* (1838–40), and supposed to be reminiscences of a self-
educated footman. A medley of extremely personal satire (Dionysius Lardner and Bulwer Lytton are
unmistakably travestied), facetious sketches of society above and below stairs, and the doings of an
aristocratic card-sharper, Mr. Deuceace. The farce is purposely vulgar in tone, and the scenes of brutality
are intentionally made odious by ironical sympathy with the rogues.

—— *The Christmas Books of M. A. Titmarsh.*   1847–55
Comprises *Mrs. Perkins's Ball* (1847), a farcical account of the guests and their behaviour, particularly of the
escapades of an Irish gentleman, The Mulligan; *Our Street* (1848), thumb-nail pictures of its inhabitants,
their families, servants, and followers—broad caricature; *Dr. Birch and his Young Friends* (1849), similar
sketches of school life; *The Kickleburys on the Rhine* (1851), ludicrous sketches of natives and Englishmen
abroad; *The Rose and the Ring* (1855), a mock-heroic tale of the Kings of Paflagonia and of Crim Tartary,
slily satirizing modern manners, etc. These farces and extravaganzas were lavishly illustrated by the author,
as they came out at successive Christmastides. Readable by children, amusing to readers of every age.

—— *The Book of Snobs.*   1848
Satirical monographs on the multifarious species of this national genus, which he hunts out from every rank
of society. Affectation, vulgarity, meanness, are illustrated with copious example and anecdote.
(Appeared in *Punch*, 1846–7).

—— *Vanity Fair; or, A Novel without a Hero.*   1848
His most representative novel—a picture of society on a broad canvas, embracing a great variety of characters
and interests, the object being to depict mankind with all its faults and meannesses, without idealization
or romance. Little set design, although the careers of Becky Sharp, the adventuress, and her husband,
Rawdon Crawley, make an apt contrast to the humdrum loves of the good hero and heroine, Dobbin and
Amelia. The nobility, fashionable people about town, the mercantile aristocracy and the needy classes
below them, are all portrayed in the most lifelike way. Episodes strong in tragedy, dramatic displays
of passion, are mingled with pure comedy. Thackeray combines comment with narrative even more
intimately than Fielding; to many readers, indeed, his sarcastic dissertations are the chief intellectual
delight. Lord Steyne is drawn from the Marquess of Hertford (cf. Disraeli's Monmouth), Mr. Wagg from
Theodore Hook, and Wenham from J. W. Croker.

—— *The History of Samuel Titmarsh and the Great Hoggarty Diamond.*   1849
A sort of miniature *Vanity Fair*, briefly recounting the history of a young man's life in London, his early
struggles, courtship, marriage, and family troubles; happy in its humour, now and then fiercely satirical,
e.g. in exposing the villainy of bubble companies, with some pages of affecting pathos. (Appeared in
Fraser's Magazine, 1841.)

—— *The History of Pendennis: his Fortunes and Misfortunes, his Friends and his Greatest Enemy.*
                                                                                               1849–50
Claims to have presented the contemporary young man without flattery or extenuation, as Fielding had
presented Tom Jones. Pendennis is in some way a reflex of Thackeray himself, at any rate, much
personal history is made use of; he is by no means an ideal hero, and in his egotism, vanity, and weakness he is only a trifle better than George Osborne, Amelia's showy lover in *Vanity Fair*. Introduces
a numerous gallery of characters, e.g. the womanly Laura, the gushing Miss Amory, the Irishman Capt.
Costigan, the old buck Major Pendennis, and the manly George Warrington. Thackeray avowed himself
a disciple of Fielding, whose method of faithful representation without any romantic or sentimental idealism
he tried to follow, not succeeding always, however, in eschewing sentimentality. He allowed himself the
same liberty of criticizing manners and morals in a running commentary, and he adopted the same ironical
tone, without, however, being able to maintain it consistently.

—— *The History of Henry Esmond, Esq., a Colonel in the Service of Her Majesty Queen Anne; written
by himself.*   1852
A chronicle of public and domestic events towards the end of the seventeenth century; ostensibly an autobiography written in George III's reign, and a successful reproduction of the modes of writing and
speaking then in vogue. Twice members of the Esmond family become involved in Jacobite plots; and
they are engaged in the Blenheim campaign and other historic affairs, which serve to introduce Marlborough,
Gen. Webb, Steele, Lord Mohun and his victim Hamilton, the Old Pretender, and other celebrities.
Actual events are inwoven with the family narrative, and the manners, dress, and habits of the time are
portrayed with scholarly exactness. The personal interest centres in Henry Esmond and the two women
whom he loves, Lady Castlewood and her daughter Beatrix: it culminates in episodes of moving tragedy.
Beatrix is taken up again in *The Virginians*; she is often characterized as the only woman completely
portrayed in English fiction. *Esmond* marked a renascence of English historical fiction and established
a new model, rejecting the standards of romanticism, and aiming at describing life as realistically as
contemporary writers might have represented it.

—— *The Newcomes: Memoirs of a Most Respectable Family; edited by Arthur Pendennis, Esq.*
                                                                                               1854–5
Thackeray's great " middle-class epic," the tragedy of worldliness. Contains hardly any distinct thread of

THACKERAY, William Makepeace (*continued*).

story, except Clive Newcome and Ethel's love affairs, which end in blank tragedy. Clive, like Pendennis, is a weak hero and does not escape satire. Depicts a society thronged with worldlings, false, self-seeking, whited sepulchres (Barnes Newcome is the most odious character Thackeray ever drew, and is remarkably akin to Fielding's Blifil) ; over against whom is set his ideal English gentleman, Col. Newcome. Realism triumphs alike in the beautiful Ethel Newcome, and in that terrible creation, the Old Campaigner, who makes Clive's and the Colonel's life a burden.

—— *Miscellanies* (4 vols.). 1855-7

Chiefly multifarious contributions (from 1837 onwards), to *Fraser's Magazine* and *Punch*, Vol. i : *Ballads ; Snob Papers ; The Tremendous Adventures of Major Gahagan* (1838-9), the latter, tall stories of an Anglo-Indian Munchausen, another of Thackeray's delightful Irishmen. *The Fatal Boots* (1839), a masterly anatomy of selfishness, and *Cox's Diary* (1840) are minor facetiæ. Vol. ii : *The Yellowplush Memoirs : Jeames's Diary* (1845-46) ; *Sketches and Travels in London : Novels by Eminent Hands* (1847) (these last are burlesque imitations, at the same time profoundly true criticisms, of Lytton, Lever, Disraeli, G. P. R. James, Cooper, etc.) ; *Codlingsby*, a most diverting travesty of *Coningsby* ; *Character Sketches*. Vol. iii : In *The Memoirs of Barry Lyndon, Esq., written by himself* (*Fraser*, 1844), the autobiographer is an Irish adventurer, card-sharper, and bully. The narrative is ironical (not so consistently as in the model, Fielding's *Jonathan Wild the Great*), the hero recounting his iniquities with pride and expectation of approval. Pictures European society before the French Revolution, principally in pleasure haunts or amid the camps and battles of the Seven Years' War (1756-63). *A Legend of the Rhine* (1845) is a burlesque of the mediæval story of barons and knight-errantry. *Rebecca and Rowena, a Romance upon Romance* (1850), is a mock-heroic sequel to Scott's *Ivanhoe*, making capital of the romantic glamour investing the Jewess to the disparagement of the Saxon heroine. *A Little Dinner at Timmins's* (1848) ; *The Bedford Row Conspiracy* (1840). Vol. iv : *The Fitz-Boodle Papers* (1842-3) are " reminiscences of a younger son, who moans over his poverty, complains of womankind generally, laughs at the world all round, and intersperses his pages with one or two excellent ballads "—the latter unveiling the humbug of things in general and of poetry in particular. *Men's Wives* (1843) ; *A Shabby-Genteel Story* (1840) ; *The History of Samuel Titmarsh and the Great Hoggarty Diamond* (1849)—see p. 462 for this last.

—— *The Virginians : a tale of the last century* [sequel to *Esmond*]. 1858-9

The memoirs of Esmond's two grandsons in America and England (1755-77), with the end of Beatrix as the deplorable Baroness Bernstein. George Washington, Dr. Johnson, Fielding, and Richardson are among the historical notabilities introduced, and the study of manners is excellent. The two heroes take opposite sides in the American War of Independence.

—— *Lovel the Widower*. 1861

A minor work based on a rejected play, *The Wolves and the Lamb*—the vulgar love affairs of a much-engaged young woman, who extricates herself from her other lovers and eventually marries Lovel.

—— *The Adventures of Philip on his Way through the World ; showing who robbed him, who helped him, and who passed him by*. 1862

A rambling story, containing several fine scenes and a beautiful character in the " Little Sister," the womanly friend of Philip. He, the son of a polished villain, determines to show his rectitude by his independence and disdain of social polish, and thus make his way. He tries to live by his pen, an episode which brings in the journalist world and bohemian Paris. A more elaborate continuation of *The Shabby-Genteel Story* (1840), and a minor counterpart of *Vanity Fair* and *The Newcomes*, out of which novels several characters step without further introduction.

—— *Catherine*. 1867-9

Described by its author as a narrative of " unmixed rascality, performed by persons who never deviate into good feeling," aiming to show how disgusting would be the records of thieves, cheats, and murderers, were their doings and language described according to their nature rather than handled in such a way as to create sympathy. A counterblast to Lytton's *Eugene Aram*, Ainsworth's *Jack Sheppard*, and Dickens's *Oliver Twist*. (Appeared in *Fraser's Magazine*, 1839-40.)

—— *Denis Duval*. 1867

A splendid fragment containing scenes worthy of Thackeray's best days. The old town of Rye in 1763-79, with its motley population of smugglers and refugees, old sea captains and Catholic gentry, is a very picturesque setting. Breaks off at the beginning of a thrilling episode, the capture of the *Serapis* by Paul Jones.

[*Illus. editions :* pub. by Smith & Elder : (Ed. de Luxe), 24 vols., 1878-9 : o.p. ; (Standard Ed.), 26 vols., (Lippincott, Philadelphia) : o.p. ; (Biographical Ed.) with biographical introductions by his daughter, Anne Ritchie, 12 vols., Murray (Harper, New York) ; Library Ed., 24 vols., Pocket Ed., 27 vols. Pub. by Dent : ed. by W. Jerrold, 30 vols., 1886 : o.p. Pub. by Macmillan : Ed. by Lewis Melville, 20 volumes ; Pocket ed., 8 vols. Pub. by Oxford Press, with 930 *illus.*, 24 vols. ; also India Paper Ed. *Without Illus. :* (Pocket Ed.), 27 vols., Murray (Houghton, Boston) ; eight titles in Everyman's Lib., Dent (Dutton, New York).]

" **THANET, Octave** " [Alice French ; American ; *b.* 1850]. *Knitters in the Sun*. 1887

Realistic stories with a strong ethical trend, exhibiting people of marked character in the stress of moral conflict. [Houghton, Boston.]

—— *Expiation*. 1890

" Deals with social conditions in Arkansas at the close of the Civil War." [Scribner, New York : o.p. ; Warne : o.p.]

—— *Otto the Knight ; and other trans-Mississippi stories*. 1891

Otto is a " knight of labour." Intimate and artistic studies of Arkansas life ; same class of subjects as the foregoing and the following. [Houghton, Boston : o.p.]

—— *Stories of a Western Town*. 1893

Workaday life in Iowa, from the standpoint of the people themselves ; the business trials, the injustices caused

"THANET, Octave" (*continued*).

by competition, strongly emphasized. *The Face of Failure* sketches an honest man who fails because he thinks other men as honest as himself; *Tommy and Thomas* is the story of an ambitious boy who becomes an eloquent—and honest—politician. [Scribner, New York; Low: o.p.]

—— *The Missionary Sheriff: incidents in the life of a plain man who tried to do his duty.* 1897

Six anecdotes of the Sheriff, or head of the police, in a country-town of Iowa, a man of sterling worth, sagacity, and Christian zeal. In the first story he saves the soul of a young felon, and keeps the knowledge of her son's disgrace from the poor old mother. In another, he arrests a scamp on the point of marrying a hypnotized girl; in *His Duty* he kills a band of Indians, and saves a family from massacre. In the last story the Sheriff is outwitted, but marries the girl of his heart. [Harper, New York and London: o.p.]

—— *The Heart of Toil.* 1898

Realistic stories of labour struggles in Illinois and Iowa, illustrating the hard lot of the striker and his half-starved family. In *The Non-Combatant* an inoffensive man is brought to the verge of ruin between the warring forces, though he has sympathies with both sides. *The Way of an Election* is a sketch of political characters, the venal stump-orator, the wire-puller, and the conscientious labour leader. *The Conscience of a Business Man* is a pathetic tale of a strike. [Scribner, New York: o.p.]

THARAUD, Jérome [French; *b.* 1874], and Jean **THARAUD** [French; *b.* 1877]. *The Shadow of the Cross* (L'ombre de la croix, 1918). 1919

Life in a village of Upper Hungary, especially the social life and religious ceremonial of Jews, and the experiences of a child of Jewish birth who is persecuted by the Christian children. [Transl. by Frances Delanoy LITTLE, Melrose: o.p.; Knopf, New York, 1924.]

THEISS, Frank [German]. *Farewell to Paradise* (Abschied vom Paradies, 1920). 1923

A delicate study of adolescent love, which captures some of the romance of extreme youth, and interprets the spirit of modern German children. [Transl. by H. T. LOWE-PORTER, Knopf.]

THEURIET, Claude Adhémar André [French; 1833–1907]. *The Marriage of Gerard* (Le mariage de Gérard, 1875). 1891

One of the best of several idyllic novels, the main charm of which is their delectable rural setting. The scenery is in perfect keeping with the simple beauty of the love-story, which tells how the son of an old chevalier resists his father's plans for an eligible marriage, and chooses his own bride. [Transl., *sub tit. Gerard's Marriage*, Burt, New York, 1906: o.p.]

—— *Angèle's Fortune* (La fortune d'Angèle, 1876). 1879

A story with a definite moral. The daughter of a lawyer's clerk in the provinces idealizes a young poet, while a worthy young fellow in her own walk of life loves her faithfully. Betrayed by the selfish poet, who fails in his ambition and absconds during the war, she is magnanimously taken to wife by the countryman, who adopts her child. [Transl. by M. N. SHERWOOD, Peterson, Philadelphia: o.p.]

—— *The House of the Two Barbels* (La maison des deux-Barbeaux, 1878). 1878

A little domestic comedy of southern France, and a tender picture of the charms of home life, so dear to the French author. An old-fashioned household of simple-minded and eccentric people is thrown into consternation by the arrival of two relatives from Paris, a fashionable lady and her brilliant daughter. [Appleton, New York: o.p.]

—— *The Godson of a Marquis* (Le filleul d'un marquis, 1879). 1881

The love of an illegitimate son is blighted by his ignoble birth, and in his despair he is on the verge of an intrigue with a married woman; but his troubles are brought to an end by the repentance and marriage of his father and mother. [Vizetelly: o.p.; Burt, New York, 1906: o.p.]

—— *Maugars Junior* (Le fils Maugars, 1879). 1880

An edifying love-story, with scenes of happy and virtuous country life and of vicious bourgeois life in a small town, bringing out the beauty of unselfishness, peaceful domesticity, and simplicity of life. [Vizetelly: o.p.; *sub tit. Young Maugars*, Appleton, New York: o.p.]

—— *Queen of the Woods* (Reine des bois, 1890). 1891

The heroine devotes herself to the care of a paralytic old man, her love-romance shattered by the discovery that she and her lover are children of one father. Theuriet's word-painting of the woods of Lorraine and the plains of the Loire is as exuberant as the work of Richard Jefferies. [Transl. by H. E. MILLER, Laird, Chicago.]

THOMAS, Edward [1878–1917]. *The Happy-go-lucky Morgans.* 1913

Less a story than a literary man's revocation of the scenes, the friends, the moods, and the dreams of his boyhood, in a now vanished house at Balham which was named after and preserved the memories of a place in Carmarthenshire. [Duckworth.]

THOMAS, Henry Elwyn [Welsh]. *The Forerunner.* 1910

Won the first prize at a national Eisteddfod. Story of a young evangelist in South Wales about 1635, his love romance and the persecution she endured. Throws light on manners, religious feelings, and the history of the Welsh after the decline of papal influences. [Lynwood: o.p.]

THOMAS, R. M. [Welsh]. *Trewern: a tale of the 'thirties.* 1901

A study of life in Carmarthenshire, the local manners and customs, the turbulent politics of the Reform Bill era, etc. (*c.* 1832). Two or three strong characters, members of the land-owning class, are carefully drawn. [Unwin: o.p.]

THOMPSON, Daniel Pierce [American; 1795–1868]. *The Green Mountain Boys.*

[juvenile] 1840

A romance of the settlement of Vermont (1775–7), embodying hero tales of Ethan Allen, incidents of the quarrels between Vermont and New York, and stirring episodes like the capture of Ticonderoga and Burgoyne's invasion, steeped in local colour. [Lothrop, Boston; Burt, New York.]

THREE

THOMPSON, Edward John [*b.* 1886]. *An Indian Day.* 1927
A vivid and thoughtful portrayal of Indian life and character, by a writer with an extensive knowledge of the land and the people. [Knopf, London and New York.]

—— *These Men, Thy Friends.* 1927
One of the few novels dealing with the Eastern theatres of war ; this covers the Mesopotamian campaign (1916–17), ending with the occupation of Bagdad. The principal characters are a Nonconformist padre and a doctor. The writing is restrained, often beautiful, when fighting is not the theme, vivid, and free from grossness. [Knopf ; Benn ; Harcourt, New York.]

—— *Night Falls on Siva's Hill.* 1929
A somewhat commonplace romance is the peg upon which is hung many fine descriptions of life in the Indian hill and jungle country ; there is more than a hint that the dominant European existence here portrayed may not endure for ever. [Heinemann ; Dial Press, New York.]

THOMPSON, Maurice [American ; 1844–1901]. *Alice of Old Vincennes.* 1901
Vincennes is an old town of French Indiana, and much local and family history is worked into this story of a high-spirited woman who does great deeds for her country's flag (1780). [Bobbs-Merrill, Indianapolis.]

—— *Sweetheart Manette.* 1901
A love-romance, centring in a charming girl who has at her feet a miscellaneous group of admirers—a Boston millionaire, a novelist, a speculator from Colerado, and a Southerner of old family. The surroundings of the old Creole town on the Gulf coast are pleasantly sketched. [Lippincott, Philadelphia : o.p.]

THOMPSON, N. P. [American]. *The Rangers.* 1851
Western campaigns of George Rogers Clarke (1779), by which the Lake regions were cut away from Canada. [Nichols & Hall, Boston : o.p.]

THOMPSON, Sylvia [Mrs. Theodore Dunham Lulling ; *b.* 1902]. *Chariot Wheels.* 1929
A careful study of the reactions between a devoted but disillusioned wife and her husband, a novelist to whom life is but so much material for his literary work—especially interesting in the third book, in which their daughter tells her own story. [Heinemann ; McClelland, Toronto.]

THOMS, William John [1803–1885] [ed.]. *Early English Prose Romances.* 1828, new ed. 1907
Combines the contents of Henry Morley's *Early Prose Romances* (Carisbrooke Library) with those in the former edn. by Thoms. Traditional stories of popular heroes or creatures of romantic fantasy, current in the Tudor period in the form of chap-books and the like. Many of them were dramatized by Elizabethan playwrights. In modern times Goethe and Wagner have utilized the Faustus legend and that of the Swan Knight. For *Reynard* see p. 404 ; *Thomas of Reading*, p. 138 ; *Robin Hood*, p. 411 ; *George a Green*, p. 195 ; *Tom a Lincoln*, p. 269 ; *Knight of the Swanne*, p. 236 ; *Faustus*, p. 170. *Robert the Deuyll*, an early French serio-comic tale of diabolical wickedness and plenary repentance ; afterwards located in Normandy. The earliest known version is in Latin prose (thirteenth century). *Virgilius*, from the Dutch translation of the French story ; an Italian folk-tale in origin, being the life and miracles of Virgil, the fabled enchanter, based on legends of the poet. *The History of Hamlet*, from Richard Bradnocke's version (1608). Hamlet's story was told originally by Saxo Grammaticus, the Danish historiographer (twelfth century) ; see *Ambales Saga*, p. 223. *Fryer Bacon*, an Elizabethan version of the earlier story of the great Franciscan (1214–92) and his achievements, with those of Bungay and Vandermast. *Guy of Warwick* is a twelfth or thirteenth century story of Athelstan's reign, embodying some episodes from the metrical *King Horn*, and connected in subject with the *Havelok* poem. The present highly grandiloquent and semi-metrical version was published at the end of the sixteenth century. *Friar Rush*, as savage a lampoon on the clergy as *Reynard*, is an old Danish tale, found in High German verse of the late fifteenth or early sixteenth century. The friar is a devil who enters a monastery, and commits all sorts of ludicrous physical and moral outrages on the monks. [New edn., rev. and enlarged (Library of Early Novelists), Routledge, 1924 (Dutton, New York).]

THORBURN, Septimus Smet [1844–1924]. *His Majesty's Greatest Subject.* 1897
The inner side of the political career of a Governor-General of India, written by a retired member of the Bengal Civil Service. [Constable : o.p. ; Appleton, New York : o.p.]

—— *Transgression.* 1899
Contains a detailed picture of Indian frontier work, a sensational love-story forming the thread of personal interest. [Pearson : o.p. ; Fenno, New York : o.p.]

THORESEN, Anna Magdalene [*née* Kragh ; Norwegian ; 1819–1903]. *Signe's History : a Norwegian tale* (Signes historie, 1864). 1865
Tragic history of a pretty peasant girl, daughter of a rich yeoman on the western seaboard of Norway, who is betrayed by the rector's son, and compelled by the stern puritanism of her father to bear her shame publicly. Character-drawing of rugged and primitive people, and sketches of their quaint customs and sombre life. [Transl. by Rev. M. R. BARNARD, Chapman : o.p.]

THÓRODDSEN, Jón Thorðarson [Icelandic ; 1819–68]. *Lad and Lass : a story of life in Iceland* (Piltur og Stúlka, 1850). 1890
A simple pastoral story of the loves of two young people in a remote dale, and of the various obstacles that keep them apart for several years. Told in the simple style appropriate to Icelandic fiction. [Transl. by Arthur M. REEVES, Low : o.p.]

THREE KINGS' SONS, *The ; Englisht from the French.* *c.* 1500
A fifteenth-century romance ; MS. transcribed in 1463, in Flanders, by David Aubert, who may have been the author ; Englished about 1500. Romance of a hackneyed note. Alfour, King of Sicily, nearly overwhelmed by the Turks, is succoured by three princes from England, France, and Scotland, who meet with the usual adventures and misfortunes, but at length drive out the invaders. Alfour is elected Emperor of Germany. The three princes being in love with his daughter, come back as kings to fight for her in a great tournament. The marriage festivities conclude the piece. [Ed. from the unique MS. by F. J. FURNIVALL, part I, Text (Early English Text Soc.), Oxford Press, 1895.]

THROND OF GATE, *The Tale of: commonly called Faereyinga Saga.* 1896
From the fourteenth-century Icelandic MS. called Flateybook, where the story is distributed into chronological segments, here put together again. History of two lifelong rivals. Thrond is a hard, crafty, selfish nature, sure to succeed by hook or by crook, a heathen who resists the introduction of Christianity into the Färoes by Olaf Trygvason (*c.* 976–1036). He is the centre of the picture; but the reader's sympathies are with his gallant adversary Sigmund, and still more with Sigmund's wife, "the Mighty Widow." A number of characters firmly drawn, dramatic incidents, and something of the artistic unity of a plot: such are this saga's characteristics. Sigmund's last fight is one of the finest scenes of action in the literature (written probably *c.* 1230). [Transl. by F. York POWELL, Nutt: o.p.]

THURSTON, Ernest Temple [*b.* 1879]. *The Five-barred Gate.* 1916
The fifth year of married life is the trying one. A young couple think they have said good-bye to romance, but after a time of doubt and questioning they recover hope. [Hodder: o.p.; Appleton, New York.]

—— *Portrait of a Spy.* 1928
A competent handling of exciting and sentimental business, concerning a girl spy in war-time France. [Putnam; Doubleday, Doran, New York.]

—— *The Rosicrucian.* 1930
The title-story in this collection employs the supernatural, and so does the better one, *Back to Burmah.* Expert plotting gives effectiveness to several others. [Putnam.]

THURSTON, Mrs. Katherine Cecil [*née* Madden; wife of preceding; *d.* 1911]. *John Chilcote, M.P.* 1904
An ingenious plot-novel on the old device of two persons so like each other than even nearest relations are taken in when a change of personality is contrived. Dramatized by Mr. E. Temple Thurston and produced in 1905. [Blackwood.]

THYNNE, Arthur Christopher. *Sir Bevil.* 1904
A Cavalier romance (1596–1643); Sir Bevil Grenvil (grandson of Sir Richard of the *Revenge*), the Parliamentarian Sir John Eliot, etc.; ends with the battle of Lansdown, where Waller was defeated near Bath. [Lane: o.p.]

TIERNAN, Mary Spear [*née* Nicholas; American]. *Homoselle.* 1881
Life on the James River in the *ante-bellum* period, an unprejudiced picture of people and manners by a Southerner. Rich in local colouring. [Fenno, New York: o.p.]

—— *Suzette.* 1885
A placid picture of happy family life in Richmond many years before the war, and of an old-established and genial society, which looked on slavery very much as a sacred institution. [Holt, New York: o.p.]

—— *Jack Horner.* 1890
Pictures of life in Richmond, the Confederate capital, during the last year of the Civil War (1865), describing the loves of a Southern girl and a Federal soldier, which are brought to a satisfactory conclusion in spite of adverse circumstances. [Fenno, New York: o.p.]

TIMMERMANS, Felix [Dutch]. *Droll Peter.* 1930
An idealized portrait of Pieter Brueghel the elder (*d.* 1569); a good account of Flemish life in the sixteenth century. [Transl. by Maida C. DARNTON and Wilhelmina J. PAUL, Coward McCann, New York; McClelland, Toronto.]

TINAYRE, Marguerite Suzanne Marcelle [French; *b.* 1877]. *The House of Sin* (La maison du péché, 1902). 1903
The struggle in France between the two ideals of life, the moral and religious and the sceptical and pagan, is poignantly figured in the tragic love-story of a young *gentilhomme de province*, descended from Jansenists and brought up by a saintly mother in the most rigorous asceticism, and a woman from the gay Parisian world. Mme Tinayre traces the effect of the clash of characters and hostile ideals in the most natural and convincing way; and in the bower of bliss attached to the old manor-house and in the beautiful country-sides provides a most artistic and harmonious setting. [Transl. by A. SMITH, Maclaren, Edinburgh: o.p.]

—— *The Shadow of Love* (L'ombre de l'amour, 1910). 1911
Here again is set forth with exquisite art the intellectual and emotional conflict between old faiths and new, science and positivism on the one hand, represented by the eugenist Dr. Cayrol, and on the other the Church, represented by his friend and opponent, the abbé. Scene, a country place in the department of the Lot. In the doctor's noble child, Denise, and her tragic love-story the tender humanism of Mme Tinayre is finely displayed; the close of the book is sad and pessimistic. [Transl. by A. ALLINSON, Lane: o.p.] Mme Tinayre has also written *L'amour qui pleure* (four stories of a melancholy strain), *Avant l'amour* (1897); *La rançon* (1898); *Hellé* (1899); *La vie amoureuse de François Barbazanges* (1904), "That tender and touching idyll"; *La rebelle* (1906). [All Calmann-Lévy, Paris.]

—— *Madeleine at her Mirror* (Madeleine au miroir, 1912). 1913
Essays and sketches, which are really the memories and meditations of a widow of thirty-five, who, we are told at the end, will marry again. The subjects are various; the feeling is often melancholy, but always full of charm, and not untouched with humour. [Transl. by Winifred STEPHENS, Lane.]

—— *Sacrifice* (La veillée des armes, 1914). 1916
Pictures what went on in the minds of the people in a Paris street during the forty-eight hours from July 31 to August 2, 1914—the reports of the Caillaux trial, the telegrams on the international crisis, the plans for summer holidays, and then the order for mobilization. [Transl. by M. Harriet M. CAPES, Melrose: o.p.]

TIREBUCK, William Edwards [Welsh; 1854–1900]. *Dorrie.* 1891
A lifelike and touching story of poor people in Liverpool, where Tirebuck was born and worked as a clerk. [Longmans: o.p.]

TIREBUCK, William Edwards *(continued).* *Sweetheart Gwen : a Welsh idyll.* 1893
Welsh country life as seen by boyish eyes, and a boy's love for a pretty, grown-up girl, his cousin. [Longman : o.p.]

—— *Miss Grace of All Souls'.* 1895
Life in a small coal-mining town, apparently in Lancashire ; the soul-crushing toil, the horrors of want, the strong affections and pathos of family life. The daughter of the worldly and compromising vicar is the heroine of a strike ; and the struggle between her ideals and love for her weak-kneed father are pathetically described. [Heinemann : o.p.]

—— *Tales from the Welsh Hills.* 1896

—— *Meg of the Scarlet Foot.* 1898
The best of several books written by one who aspired to be the novelist of Wales. [(1), Simpkin : o.p. ; (2), Harper : o.p.]

TOKUTOMI, Kenjiro [Japanese ; *b.* 1863]. *The Heart of Nami-San : a story of war, intrigue, and love* (Hototogisu). 1918
A long-winded, clumsy novel of the time of the Chino-Japanese war of 1894, valuable for the graphic picture of Japanese life and the way in which the individual's subordination to the family is made a vital element in the story. [English version with introd. by Isaac Goldberg, Stratford Co., Boston.]

TOLLEMACHE, Mrs. Beatrix L. [*tr.*]. *The Village Priest ; and other stories from the Russian of Militsina and Saltikov.* 1918
Elena Dmitrievna Militsina is the author of two, and Mikhail Evgrafovich Saltuikov (1826–89) of the other four stories. All bring us face to face with the childlike, patient, tragic character of the peasant. [Introd. by C. Hagberg Wright, Unwin : o.p.]

TOLSTOY, Count Aleksei Konstantinovich [Russian ; 1818–75]. *A Prince of Outlaws* (Knyaz Serébryany, 1863). (1892) 1927
A very fine and accurate study of the times of Ivan (IV) the Terrible. Amid the savagery of the Court, the figures of Boris Godunóv, General Morózov, and the hero stand out in contrast. Admirable in its artistic setting. [Previously transl. by Capt. H. C. FILMORE, sub tit. *The Terrible Czar*, 1892 ; by Jeremiah CURTIN, sub tit. *Prince Serbryani : an historical novel of the times of Ivan the Terrible and the conquest of Siberia*, Low, 1892 : o.p. ; the transl. cited, by Clarence Augustus MANNING, Knopf, 1927.]

TOLSTOY, Aleksei Nikolaievich [Russian ; *b.* 1882]. *The Road to Calvary* (Khozhdenie po Mukam, 1920–1). 1923
A realistic picture of life amid the intellectual circles of Russian society, from 1914 to 1917. The main characters are two sisters of good family, strongly affected by the new trend of ideas. [Transl. by R. S. TOWNSEND, Boni, New York.]

TOLSTOY, Count Leo Nikolaievich [Russian ; 1828–1910]. *Childhood ; Boyhood ; Youth* (1852–5). 1888
Three stories describing the infancy and upbringing of a child of good family ; autobiography mingled with fiction. Forms the first instalment of his mental and moral history, of which the great novels and the ethical treatises are, in one of their aspects, the continuation. Exposes the absurdities of the educational system then in vogue, and the hollowness of most of the current ideals of fashionable society, and is further a painful narrative of the workings of the soul in a sensitive and morbidly introspective child placed under such influences. *Childhood* was his first work, and like *Boyhood* stands high among the literature dealing with the life of children. In youth, the young man makes friends with Prince Nekludov (to reappear in *Lucerne*). In spite of fine resolutions, their life is a compromise with the world, and Tolstoy insists upon their failures. [Transl. by Isabel F. HAPGOOD, with *And What to do*, W. Scott : o.p. ; Crowell, New York ; by Leo WIENER, (Everyman's Lib.), Dent (Dutton, New York).]

—— *A Russian Proprietor ; and other stories* (1852–9). 1887
The first describes the well-meant but futile efforts of a young landowner to raise the status of his peasantry, efforts half benevolent, half selfish, encountered by stolid ignorance and invincible fatalism. No doubt, the story grew out of Tolstoy's own experiences after settling at Yasnaya Polyana in 1847. The subject of *Lucerne* is the disillusionment of a philanthropist, Nekludov, who champions a strolling muscian, and is rewarded only by the ridicule of society and the ingratitude of his protégé. *Two Hussars* contrasts the characters of a father and son, the one reckless, dare-devil, but generous and faithful to his friends ; the latter correct and well-instructed, but a heartless profligate. *Three Deaths* (1858–9), a fragment, subsumes the author's Nihilistic philosophy ; the three deaths are those of a lady living in the lap of luxury, of a poor muzhik, and of an ash-tree in the forest—an anticipation of *Ivan Ilyitch*. Several, including *Recollections of a Marker*, are unvarnished transcripts from his personal experiences ; the last relates to his own gambling days. *A Prisoner of the Caucasus*, the life of a captive officer in a Tartar village, pictures in a vivid way the whole surroundings of the half-savage mountaineers. [Transl. by N. H. DOLE, W. Scott : o.p. ; Crowell, New York.]

—— *The Invaders ; and other stories* (1852–61). 1887
In the first (1852), an incident of frontier fighting in the Caucasus, the imaginary romance of warfare is contrasted with the reality. Magnificent descriptions of the mountain scenery. We have reminiscences of the author's military life in *An Old Acquaintance* (1854–5) and *The Wood-cutting Expedition*, the latter a very realistic character-sketch of soldier life in the Caucasus, officers, men, and atmosphere portrayed as if in notes taken on the spot. *Lost on the Steppe* describes a sleigh ride over the steppe during a heavy snowstorm. The feverish hallucinations of the half-frozen traveller are well set off by the unemotional coolness of the driver. *Polikushka* (1860) is a gruesome tale of blind Fate hideously sacrificing innocent victims, and rewarding with joyous laughter those who profit by their disasters. *Kholstomir* also expresses the irony of fate, in the story of a horse from the racing stud to the knacker's yard. [Transl. by N. H. DOLE, W. Scott (Crowell, New York) : o.p. ; transl. by Leo WIENER, see *The Cossacks, infra.*]

TOLSTOY, Count Leo Nikolaievich (*continued*). *Sevastopol* (1855–6).   1889
  Three intensely realistic sketches of the Crimean war (1854–5), through which Tolstoy served as an officer
    inside Sevastopol ; they give three views of the great siege, in December, May, and August ; but the
    views are introspective and meditative, especially in the second part, which sets before us the inner life
    of the men engaged in the daily combat with death.   For the first time since Gogol, said his contemporaries,
    we have a Russian who tells us the truth.   [Transl. by Isabel F. HAPGOOD, W. Scott (Crowell, New York) :
    o.p. ; other transl., Methuen ; Collins (Brentano, New York) ; *Sevastopol, Two Hussars, and other Military
    Tales*, transl. by L. and A. MAUDE, Constable (1901), 1905 ; Funk, New York ; by Leo WIENER, see
    The Cossacks, infra.]

—— *The Cossacks : a tale of the Caucasus in* 1852 (1862).   1878
  Written, at least in part, while he was serving in the army of the Caucasus, and rich in descriptions of that
    superb region.   A story of the love of an educated Russian gentleman (in whom he probably sketches
    himself) for a beautiful savage.   Repudiates the false romanticism in the attitude of Byron and other
    fashionable writers towards primitive people.   The girl is a creature of instinct, and an insuperable barrier
    exists between her simple nature and the complex character of the man.   So their lives go on as if they
    had never met.   Tolstoy's crystal-clear style is not always reproduced in translations.   [Transl. by E.
    SCHUYLER, W. Scott (Gottsberger, New York) : o.p. ; by N. H. DOLE (with *Sevastopol, The Invaders*,
    and other stories), Crowell, New York, 1899 ; by Leo WIENER, Dent (Dana Estes, Boston), 1907 : o.p.
    The Cossacks ; and other tales of the Caucasus ; transl. by Louise and Aylmer MAUDE (World Classics),
    Oxford University Press, is a collection of stories that show perhaps better than any other Tolstoy's
    intense delight in the physical, outdoor life, and his marvellously observant eye.]

—— *War and Peace* (1864–9).   1886–9
  A panorama of Russian affairs, public and private, at the time of the Napoleonic wars—in four parts : *Before
    Tilsit* (1805–7) ; *The Invasion* (1807–12) ; *The French at Moscow*, and *Epilogue* (1812–20).   " A summary
    of the author's observations on human life in general " (De Vogüé).   A multitude of characters are
    presented, officers and men, both French and Russian, the hostile emperors and their suites, gentry living
    quietly in Moscow or on their estates, great people of fashion, serfs, and all intermediate classes.   The
    more important are portrayed from the inside, and the reader sees through their eyes, and coloured by
    their emotions, the entire life of the nation throughout this tremendous epoch, which the *Epilogue* carries
    down to the time of the Decembrists.   Real personages occupy almost as much space as the fictitious,
    and are drawn with the same unerring insight ; while in Prince André Bolkonski and Pierre Bezushov,
    whose life histories run through the book, are embodied two significant types of the Russian nobleman.
    Bezushov shows the ideas and sentiments most powerfully at work on the nation, which bore fruit in the
    Liberal movement—the Nihilism and Theosophy of a later date.   Like Levin in *Anna Karénin*, and like
    Count Tolstoy himself, Bezushov is initiated by a peasant into the gospel of resignation to God's will.
    Natasha and Princess Marie come second to Anna Karénin alone among Tolstoy's women.   The battle-
    pieces, Austerlitz, Friedland, Borodino, are not merely accurate historical studies, but wonderful analyses
    of the sensations and emotions of a combatant.   Whether as a dramatic portrayal of many individuals,
    with all their multifarious interests and ideals, in all their social relations near and remote ; or as a vast
    segment of human history, in which we are ever conscious of the steady onward march of time and of
    the ceaseless changes it brings about, this is probably the greatest of all novels.   [Transl. by N. H. DOLE,
    4 vols. in 2, W. Scott : o.p. ; 3 vols., also 1 vol., Crowell, New York ; by C. GARNETT, 1 vol., Heinemann,
    Dodd, New York, 3 vols., 1904–11 ; by Leo WIENER, 4 vols., Dent : o.p. ; Dana Estes, Boston, 1905 :
    o.p. ; repr. in 3 vols. (Everyman's Lib.), Dent (Dutton, New York), 1911 ; transl. by L. and A. MAUDE,
    (World's Classics), Oxford Press, 3 vols., 1922–3.]

—— *Anna Karénin* (1873–6).   1901
  This and *War and Peace* are the two greatest examples of Count Tolstoy's peculiar method of fiction, in which
    he does away with the accepted conventions, and gives a direct, truthful, unsentimentalized and
    unheightened transcript of life in all its multitudinous and complex phases as noted by his unrivalled
    observation and understanding.   His knowledge of life seems inexhaustible.   Matthew Arnold called this
    " Less a work of art, than a piece of life."   The main action is profoundly tragic—a woman of fine
    nature forsakes husband for lover, and after a bitter experience finds rest in suicide.   The connected
    story of Levin and his honest and happy love expresses the author's own disgust with the world, and
    his initiation into the peasant's simple obedience to the rule of God which gave him peace.   [Transl. by
    Constance GARNETT, 1 vol., Heinemann (Macrae Smith, New York) ; 1 vol., Lane, New York, 1901 ;
    by Leo WIENER, 3 vols., Dent (Dana Estes, Boston), 1905 ; transl. by R. S. TOWNSEND, 2 vols. : o.p. ;
    (Everyman's Lib.) Dent (Dutton, New York) ; by N. Haskell DOLE, W. Scott : o.p. ; Crowell, New
    York, 1886 ; Dodd & Mead, New York ; transl. by L. and A. MAUDE, 2 vols., (World's Classics) Oxford
    Press, 1919.]

—— *Ivan Ilyitch ; and other stories* (1884–6).   1887
  Tales and sketches, containing some of his most characteristic moral and social teaching.   The death of Ivan
    Ilyitch is a naturalistic study of the slow, insidious, inexorable progress of a fatal disease.   The anguish
    of the sufferer at his approaching end, and his inability to realize the meaning, are strikingly brought
    out in this remorseless vivisection of a common, dull, unreflecting soul.   *If you Neglect the Fire you don't
    put it out* is a parable on the evil consequences of anger and the duty of forgiveness ; *Where Love is, there
    God is also* and *A Candle* are similar fables of the peasants ; *The Two Pilgrims* is a parable of the con-
    straining power of a good life ; *Texts for Woodcuts, The Three Mendicants*, and *Popular Legends* are
    various ethical and religious apologues with Russian provincial life for their figures and setting.   *The
    Godson*, a consummate example of Tolstoy's genius for apologue, preaches the uselessness of trying to
    correct evil, and the power of unselfish goodness.   *Ivan the Fool* is an epitome of his most radical social
    teaching, thinly veiled in a homely story.   Non-resistance, the absurdity of militarism and commercialism,
    the all-sufficiency of labour are enunciated with great vigour.   [Transl. by N. H. DOLE, W. Scott (Crowell,
    New York) : o.p. ; *Death of Ivan Ilyitch, and other stories*, transl. by Constance GARNETT, Heinemann
    (Dodd & Mead, New York), 1902 ; transl. by Leo WIENER, see *Kreutzer Sonata, infra*.]

TOLSTOY, Count Leo Nikolaievich (*continued*). *The Long Exile ; and other stories for children.*
1888
Miscellaneous moral fables and simple delineations of peasant life, e.g. *What Others Live By, The Repentant Sinner, Bear-Hunting worse than Slavery, Scenes from Common Life, School Life, School Scenes.* [Transl. by Constance GARNETT, Heinemann : o.p. ; by N. H. DOLE, W. Scott (Crowell, New York) : o.p. *The Long Exile, and, Walk in the Light,* Crowell, New York.]

—— *The Kreutzer Sonata* (1890) ; *and, Family Happiness* (1859). 1890
Like *Ivan Ilyitch,* the *Kreutzer Sonata* is a very painful diagnosis of mental suffering and the horrors which are the result of our false views of life. Summarizes his ideas upon marriage, and denounces sexual immorality. A man who had led a licentious life before marriage discovers that romantic love is a delusion, comes quickly to hate his wife, and in a fit of jealousy murders her. He recounts his experiences as a warning to others. *Family Happiness* (1855) traces the emotional subsidence of two people from a state of romantic passion to one of commonplace affection. [W. Scott : o.p. ; *Kreutzer Sonata* (alone), W. Scott : o.p. ; transl. by Leo WIENER (with *Ivan Ilyitch* and *Dramatic Works*), Dent (Dana Estes, Boston), 1905 : o.p. *The Kreutzer Sonata ; and other stories,* transl. by A. MAUDE, (World's Classics), Oxford Press, 1924.]

—— *Master and Servant* (1895). 1895
One of Tolstoy's later stories expressing his gospel of the divine charity latent in human hearts. Describes with his inimitable realism the sudden transformation of a callous and selfish master who in a momentary impulse sacrifices himself for a devoted servant perishing in a terrible blizzard on the steppe. [Transl. by S. RAPPOPORT and J. C. KENWORTHY, W. Scott : o.p. ; *sub tit. Master and Man,* Crowell, New York ; with *Kreutzer Sonata* and *Dramas, id.* ; *Master and Man, and other Parables and Tales,* transl. by C. D. S. HOGARTH and Constance GARNETT (Everyman's Lib.), Dent (Dutton, New York), 1910.]

—— *Resurrection* (1899). 1900
First half of a novel designed to rival *War and Peace* in length, and in the fullness of its representation of life. Partly composed in his early period, the book is nevertheless in purpose a moral and social tract, enunciating Tolstoy's gospel of brotherhood, and exposing the evils of modern civilization most flagrant in Russia. The idealism is undiluted ; on the other hand, all officials, aristocrats, rich people, are fools, hypocrites, or brazen scoundrels. There is no sense of comedy here, or even the irony that pervades *War and Peace.* It is a furious indictment not only of the Russian criminal system, but of accepted morality. An aristocratic worldling, Prince Nekludov, brought face to face as juryman with the girl whom he ruined, repents, with Russian impulsiveness, and devotes his whole soul to the task of saving her. He offers to marry the abandoned prostitute ; he follows her to Siberia. His self-sacrifice is the moral regeneration of both. [Transl. by Louise MAUDE, *illus.* by Pasternák, Constable (1900), 1905 (Dodd & Mead, New York) ; (World's Classics) Oxford Press ; by Leo WIENER, 2 vols., Dent (Dana Estes, Boston), 1905 : o.p. ; by Aline P. DELANO, Crowell, New York, 1911.]

—— *Twenty-three Tales.* 1909
A selection of typical short stories, that may serve as an introduction to Tolstoy. [Transl. (World's Classics) Oxford Press.]

—— *In the Days of Serfdom ; and other stories.* 1911
Both early and late works. *Polikoúshka,* previously translated in *The Invaders* (see p. 467), describes the evils and the folly of serfdom, and the kindred imbecilities of conscription ; the characters are the retainers and serfs on a great estate. *God's Way and Man's* shows up more recent absurdities, the cruelty of the governmental system and the sufferings of different types of revolutionaries. [Transl. by L. and A. MAUDE, Constable : o.p.]

—— *The Forged Coupon ; and other stories and dramas.* 1911
The Forged Coupon (unfinished) is a powerful study of the infinite complexity of redoubtable consequences that may be produced by one thoughtless act. In working out this process, Tolstoy exhibits almost every class and type of Russian society. [Ed. by C. Hagberg Wright, Nelson : o.p.]

—— *Father Sergius ; and other stories and plays.* 1912
Father Sergius tells, characteristically, how a monk with a great reputation for holiness and self-renunciation learns from a simple girl that, after all, he is only a great egoist. [Ed. by C. T. Hagberg Wright, Nelson : o.p.]

—— *Hadji Murád ; and other stories.* 1912
Three collections of writings which Tolstoy deliberately withheld from publication, not because of any literary inferiority, but apparently through his gradual revulsion from art and absorption in ethical teaching. *The Forged Coupon* (see above) appears here again. (The French edn., *Le faux coupon,* also contains a wonderful story *The Devil* (1889), a drama of sensual obsession, a companion piece to the *Kreutzer Sonata*). *My Dream* is one of Tolstoy's most pathetic stories of the divine power of love and its infinite capacity for forgiveness. *Hadji Murád,* the longest of these stories, is an early production, giving a fine picture of the Caucasian struggle for independence (cf. *The Cossacks* and *The Invaders*). Tolstoy met Hadji Murád in 1851. [Ed. by C. T. Hagberg WRIGHT, Nelson : o.p. ; *id.* New York.]
[*Works,* 28 vols., 14 vols., transl. by Leo WIENER, Page, Boston ; *Novels and other works,* 24 vols., Scribner, New York, 1899–1902.]

TOMLINSON, Everett Titsworth [American ; *b.* 1859]. *For the Stars and Stripes.* 1909
A boy's story, founded on facts—the escape of a Federal soldier from a Southern prison. [Lothrop, Boston.]

TOMLINSON, Henry Major [*b.* 1873]. *Old Junk.* 1918
Newspaper " middles," conveying the spirit of place, sketches of human types, and bits of stories, all resembling the notes of a sharp-eyed and reflective traveller rather than fiction. A loving eye for ships and seas and coasts is much in evidence. Some of the later items are reminiscent of the great war. [Melrose (Hutchinson) ; Cape ; Knopf, New York.]

—— *Gallions Reach : a romance.* 1927
The author of *Youth* and *Typhoon* and *Heart of Darkness* might have fathered this story of a great adventure,

TOMLINSON, Henry Major (*continued*).

the shipwreck in eastern seas and the terrible journey into unexplored forests. The characters, also, Captain Hale, another M'Whirr, the scientist dissembling sentiment with cynicism, the half-mad ethnologist, the native Malays. Jimmy Colet in whom it all centres, acts on behaviourist formulas; hence, motives are lacking, and the whole business runs on accidental lines. Yet he, or his creator, does a lot of thinking, as if in every act or event it were necessary to get at the primary significance, unveil the mystery that underlies everything in this world. [Heinemann; Harper, New York; Grosset, New York.]

—— *All our Yesterdays.* 1930

Meditative chapters on the state of the world since 1900, and descriptive chapters on life in the trenches during the war, in Mr. Tomlinson's poetically expressive prose. Evidently semi-autobiographical, but also a philosophy of history in the best sense of the phrase. [Heinemann; Harper, New York.]

TOOMER, Jean [American]. *Cane.* 1923

Stories of the American negro, admirable in art and in their knowledge and truth; two of the most poetical are *Fern* and *Kabuis.* [Boni, New York.]

TOPELIUS, Zachris [Swedish; 1818–98]. *The King's Ring : being a romance of the times of Gustavus Adolphus and the Thirty Years' War.* 1901

This and the following belong to a series of novels depicting life in Sweden and Finland during the seventeenth and eighteenth centuries, entitled *Fältskärns berättelser*—" The Barber-Surgeon's Stories "—(1872–4). Topelius was a Swedish poet and novelist born in Finland. The period covered is 1631–5, that of the battles of Breitenfeld, Lützen, and Nördlingen. The great historical events are bound into a story full of romance and genial humanity, with description not only of military incidents but also of many sides of life in Germany and Sweden. [Transl., Jarrold : o.p.; Page, Boston : o.p.]

—— *Times of Battle and of Rest.* 1883

Second cycle of the " Surgeon's Stories." Times of Charles X and Charles XI (1654–97), the former's conquests in Poland and Denmark and the peaceful reign of the latter. All these stories are connected by the history of an aristocratic and a burgher family, the Bertelskölds and the Larssons. [Transl., McClurg, Chicago : o.p.]

—— *The Times of Charles XII.* 1884

Third cycle—Swedish and Finnish history identified with the fortunes of these two families, which depend upon the vicissitudes of the conquering but reckless king, whose victories, disasters, and romantic return from exile are related from the standpoint of stay-at-home countrymen. [Transl., McClurg, Chicago : o.p.]

—— *The Times of Frederick I.* 1883

The period succeeding the eventful reign of Charles XII, whose sister, Ulrica Eleonora, put the government into the hands of her consort, Frederick of Hesse-Cassel (1718–40). [Transl., McClurg, Chicago : o.p.]

—— *The Times of Linnæus.* 1884

The scientific labours of Linnæus and his disciples. Court affairs and national politics, and the domestic annals of the Larssons and Bertelskölds (1750–71). [Transl., McClurg, Chicago : o.p.]

—— *The Times of Alchemy.* 1883

Another generation of the same families; scenes, East Gothland and the Court at Stockholm (1771–2). [Transl., McClurg, Chicago : o.p.]

TOURGÉE, Albion Winegar [American; 1838–1905]. *Figs and Thistles.* 1879

Realistic stories of rough, rollicking life in the early days in Ohio. [Fords, New York : o.p.]

—— *A Fool's Errand.* 1879

—— *The Invisible Empire* [sequel]. 1883

Experiences of a Federal officer who went south after the war and lived there fifteen years (1865–80). A picture of the " carpet-bagger " period vividly painted; the Ku Klux Klan described incidentally. [In 1 vol., Fords, New York : o.p.]

—— *Bricks Without Straw.* 1880

A political novel of the South, treating various social conditions resulting from slavery. [Fords, New York : o.p.]

—— *Pactolus Prime.* 1890

The hero is a bootblack in a Washington hotel. Senators, doctors, lawyers, and judges are his customers, and he discusses aspects of the negro question with them. [Cassell, New York : o.p.]

TOZZI, Federigo [Italian; 1883–1919]. *Three Crosses* (Tre Croci, 1920). 1921

Detailed and vigorous realism, depicting the lives of three brothers in Siena, over whom hangs the fear that their crime of forgery will be detected. Exposure comes, they are ruined, speedily die, and are forgotten. The author was a self-taught peasant, whose autobiographical studies of peasant life roused interest. [Secker].

TRAUTWEIN, Susanne [German; b. 1886]. *The Lady of Laws* (Die schöne Richterin, 1925). 1929

The heroine, Ravegnana, is a lecturer in the University of Bologna in the turbulent setting of fifteenth-century Italy. Amid social disruption and personal temptations she retains dignity and integrity. [Transl. by H. E. PALMER and L. W. CHARLEY, Secker; Coward McCann, New York.]

" TRAVERS, Graham " [Margaret G. Todd, M.D.; Scottish; 1859–1918]. *Mona Maclean.* 1892

—— *Fellow Travellers.* 1896

—— *Windyhaugh.* 1898

—— *The Way of Escape.* 1902

—— *Growth.* 1909

Domestic fiction with good character-drawing, particularly of divinity students in Edinburgh half a century ago, illustrating educational and intellectual conditions. [(1)–(4), Blackwood [(1) : o.p.]; Appleton, New York : o.p.; (5), Constable : o.p.; Holt, New York.]

TRENCH, William Stewart [Irish; 1808–72]. *Ierne : a tale.* 1871
A study of agrarian crime in Ireland (by the land agent to Lord Lansdowne and other great owners), in which the author uses much of the knowledge he had obtained in researches for a history of the nation, which he refrained from publishing owing to the feeling occasioned by the controversy over the Irish Land Bill. He endeavours, by a careful consideration of the temperament of the people, to show the causes of the obstinate resistance by the Irish to measures undertaken for their benefit, and the method of cure. [2 vols., Longman : o.p.]

TRENT, Paul. *When Greek meets Greek.* 1916
The heroine conducts a fierce and complicated industrial war with an American manufacturer, and at the end marries him. [Ward & Lock : o.p.]

TROLLOPE, Anthony [1815–82]. *The Macdermots of Ballycloran.* 1847
A dark and pathetic story, about a ruined Irish family, an abduction, and a murder. It demonstrates how thoroughly the author had made himself acquainted with Irish character and Irish ways during his service with the Post Office in that country. He never again tried his public with anything so uniformly tragic. [Lane.]

—— *The Kellys and the O'Kellys.* 1848
A more cheerful book, equally good as a portrayal of characters and manners—in certain spheres. [Lane ; (World's Classics) Oxford Press, 1929.]

—— *The Warden.* 1855
The Warden, Mr. Harding, a gentle and innocent old cleric, living a quiet and contented life, is suddenly assailed by the newspapers for receiving the profits of a rich sinecure, and, half in fear of the odium thus created, half from conscientious scruples, resigns his income and accepts penury. The cathedral city with its ecclesiastical dignitaries was suggested by Salisbury. Trollope was an enormously prolific writer who turned out stories of sound workmanship with industrious punctuality. His realism and patient verisimilitude—aiming at no high imaginative creation—produced few characters of the first order : Mr. Harding, Mrs. Proudie and the Archdeacon, Lady Glencora, the Duke of Omnium, and Dr. Thorne, fall very little short of this, however ; they are concentrations of humanism and sober truth to life. He was incomparable in presenting clerical society with its peculiar humours and foibles. [Lane ; (Everyman's Lib.) Dent (Dutton, New York) ; (World's Classics.) Oxford Press ; Dodd & Mead, New York ; with introd. by Frederic Harrison, (Bohn's Lib.) Bell (Harcourt, New York) ; *illus.* by Ethel Galbain, Mathews ; *v.* also *infra.*]

—— *Barchester Towers.* 1857
Resumes the history of this episcopal society, the chief incidents being connected with the appointment of a new bishop, the troubles and disappointments this involves, and the intrigues and jealousies of the clergy. The characters comprise the henpecked bishop and his amazonian lady, the immortal Mrs. Proudie ; Archdeacon Grantly, son of the late bishop, who had hoped to succeed ; Mr. Harding ; the eccentric Stanhope family ; and the dean, canons, and other clergy of the cathedral, with their wives. [Lane ; (Everyman's Lib.) Dent (Dutton, New York) ; (Bohn's Lib.) Bell (Harcourt, New York) ; (World's Classics) Oxford Press ; 2 vols., Dodd & Mead, New York ; *v.* also *infra.*]

—— *The Three Clerks.* 1857
Three men in the Civil Service fall in love with three girls, whose differences of character are finely worked out. To the romantic interest is to be added that of deliberately ironical portraiture, two at least of the clerks being sketched from well-known people. [Lane ; (World's Classics), Oxford Press.]

—— *Doctor Thorne.* 1858
Concerned mainly with the fortunes and misfortunes of Mary Thorne, whose troubles commence with her birth. Beatrice Gresham and Mary, two attractive girls ; divers pairs of lovers, actual or potential, whose proceedings lead to some comic situations ; genial Dr. Thorne, a country practitioner of strong idiosyncrasies ; and the numerous figures of the aristocratic De Courcys, are admirable additions to the Barsetshire people. [Lane ; (Bohn's Lib.), Bell (Harcourt, New York) ; (Everyman's Lib.), Dent (Dutton, New York) ; 2 vols., Dodd & Mead, New York ; (World's Classics), Oxford Press, 1926 ; *v.* also *infra.*]

—— *Framley Parsonage.* 1861
Another section of Barsetshire society. The vicar of Framley, a weak but honest young man, is led astray and into debt by a spendthrift M.P., and finds himself in a false position. The other branch of the story deals with his sister's chequered love affair and marriage with young Lord Lufton. A great crowd of characters are engaged in the social functions, the intrigues and the match-making, the general effect of which is comic, though graver interest is never far off, and there are situations of deepest pathos. [Lane ; Murray ; (Bohn's Lib.), Bell (Harcourt, New York) ; (Everyman's Lib.) Dent (Dutton, New York) ; (World's Classics), Oxford Press, 1926 ; 2 vols., Dodd & Mead, New York ; *v.* also *infra.*]

—— *Orley Farm.* 1861–2
A lengthy chronicle of family life (two country houses supply most of the chief personages), events revolving round one figure, Lady Mason, a mixed character of guilt and innocence, weakness and strength, who forges a codicil in favour of her son and keeps the secret for twenty years. A chivalrous old baronet, his high-minded daughter-in-law, and a dry old lawyer, are all under the spell of Lady Mason's personality, and the drama of guilt and shame has a pathetic bearing on many lives. The legal case is complex and difficult, and the proceedings subserve the author's purpose of exposing the immorality of wrongful advocacy. A pair of bagmen and other minor characters relieve the graver matters with chapters of natural comedy. [Lane ; 3 vols., Dodd & Mead, New York.]

—— *The Small House at Allington.* 1864
Country life, its quiet, its pleasures and troubles, monotony and dullness, with digressions into boarding-house life in London and into high society. Many old friends appear in the usual concourse of characters, among whom stand out Mr. Crosbie, a snobbish and cowardly trifler, whose virtues are of the plausible sort, but whose temptation and repentance demand the reader's pity ; Lily Dale, the jilted maiden, amiable and weak Johnny Eames, and the aristocratic doll, Lady Dumbello ; all closely copied from life. Fifth

TROLLOPE, Anthony (*continued*).

of the Barsetshire series. [Lane ; 2 vols., Bell (Harcourt, New York) ; (Everyman's Lib.), Dent (Dutton, New York) ; 3 vols., Dodd & Mead, New York ; *v.* also *infra*.]

—— *Can You Forgive Her ?*   1864–5

A study of the half-realized motives and minor causes that determine conduct. She breaks off an engagement because she is infected with modern ideas on the duties and importance of women, and craves excitement. Plantagenet Palliser, who figures repeatedly in the Phineas novels, is a character here, a strong, haughty, and frigid English gentleman, a politician devoted to his country's service and a man of indestructible principle, yet entirely lacking in personal charm—a very representative national type. [Lane ; 3 vols., Dodd & Mead, New York.]

—— *Phineas Finn, the Irish Member.*   1866
—— *Phineas Redux.*   1874

In this pair of novels Trollope proposed to trace " the changes in men and women which would naturally be produced by the lapse of years." These he exemplifies not only in the hero, whose vanity brings him bitter disappointment, while his consistent honesty leads on to ultimate success, but in Lady Laura's tragic repentance for a mercenary marriage and the chequered lives of other characters. Trollope is as successful here in drawing political magnates as he had been with his clerical dignitaries, though, of course, the interest is not politics but personality. The sequel presents a great trial at the Old Bailey, one in which society is implicated. More characteristic are the domestic chapters, realistic hunting scenes, and the ordinary intercourse of country life. A noble M.F.H. and his very matter-of-fact courtship, his quarrels with his father, etc., furnish important interests. Mr. Turnbull is a satirical portrait of John Bright. [(1), 2 vols., (Everyman's Lib.), Dent (Dutton, New York), 1929 ; (1) and (2), 2 vols. each, with introds. by Frederic Harrison, Bell [(1) : o.p.]. (1) and (2), 3 vols. each, Dodd & Mead, New York.]

—— *The Belton Estate.*   1866

A quiet enough story, specially interesting for the leading character Will Belton, who is the author's very attractive presentment of himself. The women are good too, particularly the heroine in her quandary between two eligible suitors. [(World's Classics), Oxford Press, 1924 ; 2 vols., Dodd & Mead, New York.]

—— *The Last Chronicle of Barset.*   1867

The ecclesiastical society of *The Warden*, Mr. Harding, Mrs. Proudie, and the rest, make their last appearance. The dominant situation is one of intense anguish. A poor country clergyman, proud, learned, sternly conscientious, is accused of a felony, and the pressure of family want makes his guilt seem only too probable. His own agony, his wife's terror, and the distress of his daughter, affianced to the son of a neighbouring landowner, are ultimately relieved. [2 vols., Bell (Harcourt, New York) ; (Everyman's Lib.), Dent (Dutton, New York) ; 3 vols., Dodd & Mead, New York.]

The Barsetshire Novels, with introds. by Frederic Harrison, 8 vols. (the above and *The Small House at Allington*. 2 vols. each), Bell. Also, 6 vols., Lauriat Co., Boston, 1926. 14 vols. (vol. i, *Autobiography* ; vol. ii *The Warden*, the rest 2 vols. each), Shakespeare Head Ed., ed. by Michael Sadleir, Blackwell, Oxford (Houghton, Boston) 1929.]

—— *The Claverings.*   1867

Harry Clavering has to choose between the girl to whom he is engaged and his old love, who had jilted him, but now turns to him again, rich and a widow. In the minor characters, a county family and their friends, the parson and his family, etc., is exhibited the typical life of the landed gentry, their dinners, hunting, flirtations, and match-making, their egotistic social intercourse, family squabbles, and thoroughly matter-of-fact and unintellectual existence. [(World's Classics) Oxford Press, 1924.]

—— *He Knew He was Right.*   1869

A tragedy composed of the homeliest materials. The gradual estrangement of husband and wife, beginning with an insignificant difference and ending in strife and agony : the husband a portentous image of stupid and obstinate suspicion and proneness to take offence. [Ward & Lock : o.p.]

—— *The Vicar of Bullhampton.*   1869

Photographic portraiture of thoroughly English characters : a genial and manly country vicar, who champions the cause of a fallen girl and of a country fellow wrongly suspected of murder, and suffers obloquy therefor ; an unfortunate squire in love with the heroine, who loves somebody else ; a crusty old farmer, and so on. Episodes of homely life, with its everyday interests, humours, and sorrows, form a complexity like the complexity of actual life. [(World's Classics) Oxford Press, 1924 ; 2 vols., Dodd & Mead, New York.]

—— *Ralph the Heir.*   1871

Another political novel, the best chapters of which are the election scenes, founded on Trollope's own unsuccessful candidature for Beverley (1868). [o.p.]

—— *The Eustace Diamonds.*   1872

Trollope calls his Lady Eustace "an opulent and aristocratic Becky Sharp." Her unscrupulous lying darkens the mystery of the diamonds and brings about many unexpected and amusing turns in the story. There are several characters of a more agreeable type, and in the background people already familiar in *Phineas Finn*, etc. [Ward & Lock : o.p. ; 2 vols., Dodd & Mead, New York.]

—— *The Way We Live Now.*   1875

Portrays many phases of English life, high society, country life, the genteel and the humble, journalists, commercial men and the world in general, with a keen eye for weak and flagitious motive. An exposure of the marriage market and the brutal indelicacy of the haggling between such people as the ruined family of patricians and the rascally millionaire, who is prepared to subsidize them with his daughter and his thousands. Even the honest young man is not altogether attractive. [Chatto.]

—— *The Prime Minister.*   1876

Lady Glencora and Palliser, now Duke of Omnium, are the big characters of this book, which should be read after the Phineas novels and before *The Duke's Children* : they are developed here on a roomy canvas. The story itself is not first-rate, the political chapters are tiresome, and Lopez, who brings about the

TROLLOPE, Anthony (*continued*).

public attacks and misunderstandings with his wife that make the Duke's life miserable, is a poor creature. But in part at any rate this is excellent Trollope. [3 vols., Dodd & Mead, New York.]

—— *The Duke's Children.* 1880

The Duke after the death of his admirable wife is left alone to deal with the troubles of his three children, scapegraces or at least intolerably selfish, and his efforts to understand and sympathize with them are pathetic. Some good comedy enlivens an inferior story. [3 vols., Dodd & Mead, New York.]

—— *Is He Popenjoy?* 1878

One of his cleverest plots, with a Barsetshire touch in the amiable dean. [2 vols., Dodd & Mead, New York.]

—— *Ayala's Angel.* 1881

A light and pleasing, though long and ill-knit story, with a brace of heroines and a sort of double plot. Ayala is one of his most seducing young women and the best of a large crowd of living creations. [(World's Classics) Oxford Press, 1929.]

—— *Dr. Wortle's School.* 1881

The subject of scandal and blackmail and the question of throwing up an appointment gives this some superficial resemblance to *The Warden*. Dr. Wortle himself is at least a half-portrait of the author, a good characterization of one side of him. [(World's Classics) Oxford Press, 1928.]

—— *Mr. Scarborough's Family.* 1883

More sardonic perhaps than anything else of Trollope's. Mr. Scarborough keeps his two troublesome sons in order by having two different marriage certificates " up his sleeve," and declaring the elder illegitimate, then restoring him to the rights of primogeniture. [Chatto.]

TROLLOPE, Frances [*née* Milton ; 1780–1863]. *The Domestic Manners of the Americans.* 1831

A novel by the mother of Anthony Trollope, made up of her experiences during a three years' sojourn in America for business purposes. The caustic sketches of life and society aroused the same resentment in the United States as Dickens provoked later by his *American Notes*. Mr. Weller sarcastically advised Mr. Pickwick to go to America and write a book " about the Merrikins as'll pay all his expenses and more if he blows 'em up enough." [With introd. by Michael Sadleir, Routledge (Dodd & Mead, New York), 1927.]

—— *The Vicar of Wrexhill.* 1837

The title originally proposed—*The Unco Guid*— indicates the spirit of the book. The Vicar is a clergyman of an unpleasant type, sketched to a large extent from actual facts, and so realistically drawn that a storm of criticism and abuse was raised by the Low Church party. [o.p.]

—— *The Widow Barnaby.* 1839

—— *The Widow Married* [sequel]. 1840

—— *The Barnabys in America ; or, Adventures of the Widow Wedded* [sequel]. 1843

A ripost for her American remonstrants. This coarse Cockney emigrates to New Orleans after London has become too hot to hold her gambling husband, and, like her creator, writes a book on the Americans, but unlike her creator, takes them at their face value, and they accept her glorification with enthusiasm. [All o.p.]

TROLLOPE, Thomas Adolphus [1810–92 ; brother of Anthony Trollope]. *La Beata : a Tuscan Romeo and Juliet.* 1861

The sufferings of a poor flower-girl of Florence, forsaken by an artist. An idealized figure, exponent of the author's views on marriage, maintaining her inborn purity in spite of surrounding corruptions. Fierce Protestant bias, in the way the evil actions of this or that man are ascribed to priestly influence. [Ward & Lock : o.p]

—— *Marietta.* 1862

The scene is Florence, and the book is crammed with details about the city and its surroundings and the everyday life of middle-class people there. The central personage, Marietta, is impressive with her indomitable resolution and family pride. [Ward & Lock, o.p. ; Petersen, Philadelphia : o.p.]

—— *Beppo the Conscript.* 1864

A faithful study of the agricultural, domestic, and religious life of the peasants of Romagna, and their political and economic conditions, centring in the daily history of a prosperous family ; shows up the secret power of the priests. [Ward & Lock : o.p. ; Petersen, Philadelphia : o.p.]

—— *Dream Numbers.* 1868

Sympathetic drawing of the Italians in old-fashioned villages and country towns away from well-known tracks —happy domestic life, simple pleasures, harmless gossip, humble and ignorant country folk, with an episode of priestcraft, a tale of true love, and a destructive flood to lend dramatic interest. [3 vols., Chapman : o.p. ; Petersen, Philadelphia : o.p.]

—— *The Siren.* 1870

A murder novel ; scene, Ravenna and neighbourhood, with characteristic sketches of people and manners. A beautiful opera-singer, engaged to a marchese and courted by his heir, is strangely and very ingeniously killed : who is the criminal ? [3 vols., Smith & Elder : o.p.]

—— *Diamond Cut Diamond.* 1875

Also *The Golden Book of Torcello, Vittoria Accoromboni, The Duchess Veronica*, and other stories of Tuscan life, by an Englishman who lived among the people for many years. [Chatto : o.p.]

TROWBRIDGE, John Townsend [" Paul Creyton " ; American ; 1827–1916]. *The Three Scouts.* 1865

Tennessee in the war-time. [Lothrop, Boston, 1894.]

TROWBRIDGE, William Rutherford Hayes [*b.* 1866]. *A Girl of the Multitude.* 1902

An expansion of the true story of Eglée, a *fille de joie* of the Faubourg St Antoine, who devoted herself madly to the cause of Marie Antoinette, and tried to rescue the Duc d'Amboise, as related in the memoirs of

TROWBRIDGE, William Rutherford Hayes *(continued)*.
the Comte de Beugnot (1792–3). By the author of *The Letters of her Mother to Elizabeth*. [Unwin : o.p. ; Wessels, New York : o.p.]

—— *The Little Marquis of Brandenburg.* 1904
A really imaginative and interesting novel dealing with the early life of Frederick the Great, down to the execution of Katte (1712–30). [Hurst : o.p.]

TRUMBULL, Annie Elliot [American ; *b.* 1857]. *A Cape Cod Week.* 1898
Account of a seaside holiday undertaken by a party of American girls, who have many amusing adventures in their amateur housekeeping, and discourse funnily about Boston, culture, and other topics. [Barnes, New York : o.p. ; Allenson : o.p.]

TS‘AO CHAN [Chinese ; *c.* 1719–64]. *The Dream of the Red Chamber* (Hung Lou Meng, 1792). 1929
One of the finest Chinese romances, said to be the first realistic novel in that literature : recent investigators believe it to be largely autobiographical. Enormously long, and prolix (there are 421 characters), full of incidents of everyday life ; the plot hinges upon a youth, handsome and highly gifted, in love with two girls, both miracles of wit and charm. The characters are drawn in lively fashion, often with considerable wit ; interspersed are several short poems. Eighty chapters only of the whole were completed on the author's death ; the remaining forty were edited by Kao Ngoh. [Transl. by CHI CHEN WANG (of the New York Metropolitan Museum) with pref. by Arthur Waley, Doubleday, Doran, New York ; Routledge. A transl. of Book I by H. R. JOLY appeared in 1892 : o.p.]

"TUR, Eugenia" [Countess Elizaveta Vasil'evna Salias de Tournemir ; Russian]. *The Shalonski Family : a tale of the invasion of Russia.* 1882
The quiet country life of a pious Russian and his family, and the troubles created by the irruption of the French (1812) ; a simple story, related by a young girl. [Transl. by C. J. COOKE, Remington : o.p.]

TURGENEV, Ivan Sergyeevich [Russian ; 1818–83]. *A Sportsman's Sketches* (1852). 1896
Stories and studies loosely strung together on the thread of random adventures. The sketches of serfs and serfdom bring out touchingly the simple loyalty, affection, and immeasurable endurance of the Russian poor, and the book was instrumental in determining Alexander II to abolish serfdom. The scenery of central Russia is finely pictured. Turgenev's great characteristic is the pure objectivity of his method. He seems absolutely unbiased, so much so that one reader detects satire where another sees perfect sympathy. The characters appear to live and move independently of their creator, whose art is so complete that its subtlety and perfection are invisible except to the critical analyst. Exquisite examples of this art are *The Tryst, The Agent, The Singers* ; and of his drawing of peasants, *Yermolai and the Miller's Wife, Biryuk, Lebedyan*. [2 vols.]

—— *The Jew ; and other stories* (1846–68). 1900
The Jew is a psychological study of a man about to be hanged. The other four, written at various dates, are all melancholy. The epilogue *Enough* expresses the saddest of judgments on life, its brevity and worthlessness, while art is said to be only a fleeting image of beauty. *An Unhappy Girl*, the longest story, is the miserable history of a Russian gentleman's illegitimate daughter. From the ignoble humanity surrounding her she accepts persecution and ignominy ; but it is reserved for a young man whose nature is "too awfully symmetrical" to bring this proud, chaste girl to despair and suicide.

—— *The Diary of a Superfluous Man ; and other stories* (1850–64). 1899
This autobiography of an unfortunate man of limited mental powers finely exhibits Turgenev's abstruse explorations of the human heart, and also his Nihilism. *A Tour in the Forest* and *Yakov and Pasinkov* are tales that might have been included in *A Sportsman's Sketches*. *Andrei Kolosov* is a good specimen of his compact and pointed story-telling, reading like a piece of actual observation ; it is a curious study of love-making, or rather of the working of a young man's mind at the season of love-making, and the humour is as keen as the mental analysis.

—— *Rudin* (1855). 1894
Almost a satire, so ruthless is the showing up of the doctrinaire enthusiasm, the ineffectual idealism, and the weakness of principle in the unpractical Rudin, an embodiment of one of the most enervating traits in the national character, and of the ardent but barren Liberalism of the time ; yet removed from satire by the sympathy which even such weakness inspires in a critic of Turgenev's catholic insight. Rudin excites love in a girl far too good for him, and is brought into damaging contrast, in a most natural way, with a number of admirable but less showy types of the Russian gentry. "Of Turgenev's six novels," says Edward Garnett, "*Rudin* is the most perfect in form, by the harmony of its parts and absolute grace of modelling." Pokorsky is a sketch of Byelinsky.

—— *A Lear of the Steppes ; and other stories* (1855–70). 1898
The tragic tale of Harlov of the Steppes is a supreme example of Turgenev's imaginative interpretation of life, and of his habit of embodying the universal in an episode. It is the tragedy of a powerful nature ; and the novelist shows with exquisite art how the tragic event affects the household and relatives of the sufferer, and how the whole life of the community in which he lived is more or less influenced by his death. Among the other stories, *Faust* is a psychological study of a singular problem, the awakening of the imagination in a woman from whom imaginative literature has been carefully kept ; *Acia* is an imaginative souvenir of Turgenev's student-life in Germany.

—— *A House of Gentlefolk* (1859). 1894
A touching, refined, and beautiful story of two lovers separated by Fate. Lavretsky tells his love to Liza in the belief that his false wife is dead ; but the latter returns, and these two pure natures, in their different ways, suffer the bitterness of separation with noble patience. Liza is Turgenev's most beautiful woman character. [Also entitled *A Nest of Noblemen* ; sub tit. *Liza*, transl. by W. R. S. RALSTON, (Everyman's Lib.) Dent (Dutton, New York) 1914.]

—— *On the Eve* (1859). 1895
Another love-tale ending unhappily : in Elena the whole nature of a pure girl is revealed, and the minor characters are portrayed with similar intimacy. The foregoing novels belong to Turgenev's period of

TURGENEV, Ivan Sergyeevich (*continued*).

youthful dreams and enthusiasms; this marks the close of the Nicholas regime, and forecasts the new epoch. Elena symbolizes young Russia; Uvar Ivanovich represents the Slav, and points to the future unification of the Slav peoples.

—— *Fathers and Children* (1862). 1895

A novel that mirrored and revealed to Russian readers the real nature and significance of the momentous changes in the outlook upon life, the attitude to science, and the political and social ideas which were taking place in the minds of the younger generation at that epoch. The age that was passing and that about to dawn are represented each by a considerable variety of characters, both, after Turgenev's wont, being treated with the same artistic detachment. The character that in sheer intellectual interest and the complex elements of a strong personality stands out pre-eminent, both here and in Turgenev's novels as a whole, is Bazarov, the archetype of Nihilism, " the bare mind of Science applied to Politics." Beside him, the other people, with all their humours and foibles and conflicting personal interests, are quite secondary. The pathos of the close is overwhelming. [Also, *sub tit. Fathers and Sons*, transl. by C. J. HOGARTH, (Everyman's Lib.) Dent (Dutton, New York) 1922.]

—— *Smoke* (1867). 1896

Litvinov, a young Russian, betrothed to an innocent girl, is seized with a passion for a brilliant woman in society, who returns his love but shrinks from elopement. She, the matchless coquette, the woman of impulse and caprice, but devoid of any strength of character, is the heroine of the drama, though a maleficent one. Their phases of passion and hesitation are rendered in a few short scenes, with complete naturalness and absence of conventional artistry. In the onward march of humanity, says the author, the deeds and the sufferings of the individual are as smoke, full of spasms, convulsions, cataclysms, but annihilated in a moment. The empty, conventional, animal life of the aristocrat, the vain talk of frothy enthusiasts, are touched in with refined art.

—— *Virgin Soil* (1876). 1896

A reply to *The Possesssed* of Dostoevsky, which was itself called out by the Nihilist doctrines in *Fathers and Children*. Both Turgenev and Dostoevsky deal with the same theme: the subterranean world of political agitation and conspiracy then threatening the peace of Russia. Like *Smoke* (which also was written in exile from Russia), this is bitter in feeling and deeply pessimistic. The faint-hearted Neshdanov, despairing of the cause of socialism, in which he and the girl he loves are workers, takes his own life. The official classes are painted in dark colours. [2 vols.] [Also transl. by R. S. TOWNSEND, (Everyman's Lib.) Dent (Dutton, New York) 1911.]

—— *The Torrents of Spring* (1871); *and other stories* (1877). 1897

Like *Smoke* in plot. Sanin loves a pastrycook's daughter, but is carried off by a woman of his own set: the spring waters are muddied and choked. In after-life he reviews his treason and his wasted existence. Apart from this caustic diagnosis of Russian defaults, there is lively portraiture of various types at Baden, and several brilliant caricatures: *The Gentleman of the Steppe* is in a very different vein. This mixture of barbarousness and true gentility is inimitable; so is the bitter comedy of the *dénouement*.

—— *Dream Tales; and Prose Poems* (1882). 1897

Clara Militch is a tragic story of hallucination; *Phantoms*, a poetical rhapsody of a man's dealings with a sylphid, in a style akin to both Poe and De Quincey. Some nature symphonies and imaginative tales of wizardry and the supernatural follow, which have something of Coleridge's glamour.

—— *A Desperate Character; and other tales* (1847, etc.). 1901

Six tender studies, written at various periods of Turgenev's life, chiefly of characters that have failed, all dominated by the same motive of self-effacement and Nihilism. *The Brigadier* and *Pyetushkov* are similar in theme to the *Diary of a Superfluous Man*.

[The above works: transl. by Constance GARNETT, Heinemann; Macmillan, New York. 14 vols. transl. by Isabel F. HAPGOOD, Scribner, New York.]

TURKISH TALES: *consisting of several extraordinary adventures; with the History of the Sultaness of Persia and the Viziers.* 1708

This is a version of the Sindbad or Sendabar story (see *The Seven Wise Masters*), Indian in origin, and adapted into many Oriental and European languages. The connecting plot is how a queen, whose criminal advances to her stepson have been rejected, tries to destroy him; and his defenders, the forty viziers, tell the irate father stories of wicked women and loyal sons, the queen in opposition telling stories of wicked viziers and nefarious princes. One famous story, the *Santon Barsisa* (akin to *Faust*), was the origin of Lewis's *Monk*. Others were quoted in *The Spectator*. [Written originally in the Turkish Language by Chec ZADE for the use of Amurath II, and now done into English: o.p. Also included in *The Persian and the Turkish Tales Compleat*, 1714: o.p.]

TURLEY, Charles. *Godfrey Martin, Schoolboy.* 1902

—— *Godfrey Martin, Undergraduate* [sequel]. 1904

—— *The New Broom.* 1911

Healthy school-stories, with good character-drawing of boys and masters. [(1) Heinemann; Dutton, New York; (2), Heinemann: o.p.; (3), Nelson.]

TURNBULL, Francesse Hubbard [*née* Litchfield; Mrs. Lawrence Turnbull; American]. *The Golden Book of Venice.* 1900

Based on the career of the friar Paolo Sarpi (1552–1629), champion of the republic against the Church. The historical materials are carefully studied (1565–1607); the politics, the dialectics, and the artistic atmosphere are rendered with sympathy; and the heroine, an artist's daughter in her home beautiful with treasures of art, is tenderly portrayed. [Putnam, New York.]

—— *The Royal Pawn of Venice.* 1911

Deals similarly with Venice and Cyprus in an earlier day (1468–88). Catarina Cornaro, who married the King of Cyprus, is the heroine. [Putnam, New York.]

475

" TWAIN, Mark " [Samuel Langhorne Clemens ; American ; 1835–1910]. *The Celebrated Jumping Frog of Calaveras County ; and other sketches.* 1867

The Jumping Frog is a comic tale that tickled Artemus Ward ; it came out first in a newspaper (1865).

—— *The Innocents Abroad ; or, The New Pilgrim's Progress : being some account of the steamship " Quaker City's " pleasure excursion to Europe and the Holy Land.* 1869

His first success, though he had published his *Celebrated Jumping Frog, and other sketches* in 1867. A comic travel-book of the Mediterranean and the adjacent countries. A party of Yankee innocents adopt the rôle of cold-blooded philistines with no reverence for the works of art and antiquity, or the historical and sacred memorials about which the sentimental tourist raves, guide-book in hand. A satire on the " high-falutin " American globe-trotter, from the point of view of a practical, ignorant, sceptical Westerner. [Also Macmillan ; Dent ; Nash.]

—— *Roughing It at Home and Abroad.* 1872

Genial sketches of rough-hewn character and lawless life in the mining camps of Nevada, where the author was seeking his fortune in the early sixties, thrown into the form of fiction, and showing the New World as a contrast to the Old, which had been inventoried and assessed in the previous book. [With *Innocents at Home*, Chatto.]

—— *The Adventures of Tom Sawyer.* 1876

—— *Tom Sawyer Abroad* [sequel]. 1894

—— *Tom Sawyer, Detective* [sequel]. 1897

Tom is the perfect example of the bad boy who is essentially a good boy. This is, in fact, the *Tom Jones* of boyhood, and the distinction is set off by the pattern good boy Sid—albeit overdone and impossible—who is a sneak. In the adventures of Tom and Huck on the Mississippi, a regular boy's saga, we have what may be called real romance ; what reads like burlesque is, indeed, far more romantic than the Indian Joe melodrama and the real treasure. The fun admirable, the satire of that extravagant kind in which Twain revelled.

—— *A Tramp Abroad.* 1880

—— *More Tramps Abroad.* 1897

Two facetious narratives of the author's travels over the globe ; not precisely fiction, yet characterized by the same exaggeration of the characters of people and places as the foregoing—humorous impressionism they might be called. They are full of broad jokes, hilarious incidents, and mock-serious criticism, affecting the same impervious philistinism as the *Innocents* ; yet a piercing common sense that looks below the surface and detects real absurdities, pretences, and hypocrisies is quite as patent a quality as the humour. [The American title of (2) is *Following the Equator*.]

—— *The Prince and the Pauper.* 1881

A fantasia meant for children : how Prince Edward (VI), in Henry VIII's reign, changed positions with a beggar, and what came of it. Realistic in presenting mediæval life, showing up its selfishness, cruelty, and barbarism, as an antidote to the high romantic style. [Also *illus.* Dent.]

—— *The Stolen White Elephant.* 1882

New and old stories ; among the new *The Invalid's Story* is a very characteristic chapter. The titular piece is a huge burlesque. [Harper, New York ; Chatto.]

—— *Life on the Mississippi.* 1883

The most veracious of his autobiographical stories, and his own favourite. A record of bygone phases of life, observed by the young Mark Twain when he served as pilot on a Mississippi steamer ; the second part not much more, however, than an account of a visit in 1882 to the old scenes. This group of his books stands apart as his most serious studies of a life he was intimately acquainted with ; the effects of slavery, the fierce family feuds, the general lawlessness, lynching, etc., are described in the indignant spirit of the reformer.

—— *The Adventures of Huckleberry Finn.* 1885

Autobiographical in form, and hence more artistic than *Tom Sawyer*—a boy's epic of the Mississippi, the call of nature to the lad's imagination rendered with true poetry, in the boy's own rich rustic lingo. Tom and Huck are seen playing at brigands and parodying the Arabian Nights, and it is done with true insight and sympathy, and the same honest mockery of religiosity and humbug of any kind. Apparently the excrescent episode of the feud—too like the melodramatic stuff in *Tom Sawyer*—is meant as satire of idiotic lawlessness. [Also Harrap ; Nash.]

—— *A Yankee at the Court of King Arthur.* 1889

Burlesque of the historical romance. A Yankee of the most arrant modern type is plumped down in the middle of King Arthur's England, and a series of farcical incidents ensues. The serious purpose, which is not obtruded, is to strip off the glamour and tinsel of chivalry, as it appeared to the romancers, and show the evils and miseries that actually underlay it. [The American edition has the title, *A Connecticut Yankee in King Arthur's Court*.]

—— *Pudd'nhead Wilson.* 1894

A story of a sober kind, picturing life in a little town of Missouri, half a century ago, and vanished types, like the fine old gentleman, without fear and without reproach, who came of the first families of Virginia, and like Wilson himself, the lawyer, despised by the townsfolk, who have no sense of humour, until he proves himself a genius. The principal incidents relate to a slave of mixed blood and her almost pure white son, whom she substitutes for her master's baby. The slave by birth grows up in wealth and luxury, but turns out a peculiarly mean scoundrel, and, perpetrating a crime, meets with due justice. The science of finger-prints is practically illustrated in detecting the fraud.

—— *Personal Recollections of Joan of Arc : by the Sieur Louis de Conte (her Page and Secretary) ; freely translated out of the Ancient French.* 1896

Mark Twain's own favourite among his books. He worshipped the Maid, and only in the powerful narrative of the trial does his anti-romantic humour prevail. "A prose epic which seizes the undying charm of Joan's character."—*Nation.*

"TWAIN, Mark" (*continued*). *The Man that Corrupted Hadleyburg ; and other stories and sketches.* 1900

Exaggerated reminiscences, anecdotes of strange experiences, and fictitious episodes of a humorous kind. The Hadleyburg man inveigles the stainless citizens of an American town into a snare for their covetousness and vanity, and explodes their reputation for incorruptible probity. *The Esquimaux Maiden's Romance* is a characteristic farce related with mock gravity ; and *My First Lie*, a humorous parable, illustrates Mark Twain's ingrained didacticism.

—— *Captain Stormfield's Visit to Heaven.* 1908

Extravaganza of the usual irreverent kind written forty years earlier. The Skipper diverges from the recognized route and reaches Heaven by the wrong gate, his place of origin being in consequence a difficult problem for the janitor. A farcical description follows of his equipment with halo, harp, and wings, and his introduction to the inhabitants, the manners, and sights of the place.

—— *The Mysterious Stranger.* 1916

Written in dejection in 1898 and published after his death. Mark Twain in an apocalyptic dream, outlines a view of man and the universe which is little else than sheer negation, except that it tacitly affirms the intrinsic worth of morality. [*The Mysterious Stranger ; and other stories*, Harper, New York and London.]

"TWAIN, Mark," and WARNER, Charles Dudley [American ; 1829–1900]. *The Gilded Age.* 1873

Mark Twain and Dudley Warner were neighbours at Hartford, Conn., when they collaborated in this portrayal of their times ; the bitter account of the Easterners is Warner's, the humorist drew the Westerners, scoffed at Washington and Congress, and created the mighty optimist Colonel Sellars.

—— *The American Claimant.* 1892

Further doings of Colonel Sellars, of *The Gilded Age*. [Also with *Tom Sawyer Abroad*, Chatto.]
[*Works* ; various eds., some illustrated, Harper, New York ; Chatto. Other editions are noted.]

TYLEE, Edward Sydney. *The Red Cap.* [juvenile] 1907

The story of a boy's adventures during the French Revolution. [Nelson : o.p.]

—— *The Witch Ladder : a story of Somerset in the later days of Victoria.* 1911

The strength of this rather rambling story, some of which is rather weakly conventional, is in the dialect and the racy humour of the rustic sayings, and also in the truth with which the Somerset farmers and villagers are drawn, bringing out their native shrewdness and ineradicable superstitions. The suspicions of witchcraft alluded to in the title lead to amusing complications. [Duckworth : o.p.]

TYNAN, Katharine [Mrs. Henry Albert Hinkson ; Irish ; 1861–1931]. *The Handsome Brandons.* 1898

An old feud is healed by a marriage between two ancient houses. [Blackie : o.p.]

—— *The Dear Irish Girl.* 1899

A portrait-study of a captivating girl, and a sentimental love-story of middle-class society in Dublin and amid the wild scenery of Connaught. [Smith & Elder : o.p. ; McClurg, Chicago : o.p.]

—— *She Walks in Beauty.* 1899

The love-romance, chequered but happily ended, of three charming Irish daughters of impoverished gentlefolk, with humorous sketches of servants, villagers, and others. [Smith & Elder : o.p. ; McClurg, Chicago : o.p.]

—— *A Daughter of the Fields.* 1900

Another gracious Irish girl. Well educated and brought up to a refined and easy life, she applies herself to the drudgery of farm work rather than desert her toiling mother ; but the novelist finds her a husband and a more fortunate lot. [Smith & Elder : o.p. ; McClurg, Chicago : o.p.]

—— *Three Fair Maids ; or, The Burkes of Derrymore.* 1900

They are the daughters of an impecunious Irish gentleman, and their love-matches result from a scheme for paying-guests. [Blackie : o.p. ; Scribner, New York : o.p.]

—— *A Union of Hearts.* 1901

Another of these engaging love-stories ; the hero a faultless Englishman whose efforts for the good of his tenants gain him their dislike, the young lady an Irish heiress. Both the gentry and the peasants are efficiently drawn. [Nisbet : o.p.]

—— *A Girl of Galway.* 1901

Another winsome girl, living with her misanthropic grandfather in Connemara, and, of course, her love-affairs. [Blackie : o.p.]

—— *That Sweet Enemy.* 1901

A sentimental story of two Irish girls, children of a decayed house ; their love affairs, the hindrances to their happiness, and the matrimonial *dénouement*. [Constable : o.p. ; Lippincott, Philadelphia : o.p.]

—— *The Handsome Quaker.* 1902

Eighteen short stories of the peasantry—Katharine Tynan at her best. [Bullen : o.p.]

—— *A King's Woman.* 1902

Describes, from the point of view of a Quaker lady, a Loyalist in a Leinster country-house, the dark doings and evil passions of 1798. [Hurst : o.p.]

—— *Love of Sisters.* 1902

A love-story in which one sister unselfishly gives way, with plentiful character-drawing of some delightful elderly folk in the west of Ireland and at Dublin. [Smith & Elder : o.p.]

—— *A Daughter of Kings.* 1903

She is the daughter of a county family, and of course the descendant of chieftains, and has to make a living by taking the post of chaperon. The English house and her ruinous old home in Donegal are contrasted. [Nash : o.p. ; Benziger, New York : o.p.]

TYNAN, Katharine (*continued*). *The Story of Bawn.* 1906
A love-tale of Mrs. Hinkson's graceful kind, with characters Irish and aristocratic ; the misfortunes of a family in the claws of the money-lenders. Scene, Kerry in the sixties. [Murray ; McClurg, Chicago : o.p.]
—— *For Maisie.* 1907
English people of the most irreproachable circles furnish the characters here ; the two most engaging are a very successful builder who wins his way among the best people, and his adopted daughter Maisie. [Hodder : o.p. ; McClurg, Chicago : o.p.]
—— *Her Ladyship.* 1907
Her Ladyship, who comes into a great estate in Kerry, plays providence to her tenants and others. Besides the indispensable love-story, there is pathetic interest in the reduced lady starving in Dublin, and the girl dying of consumption. [Murray ; McClurg, Chicago : o.p.]
—— *Mary Gray.* 1908
A double love-story, that of Mary, the watchmaker's daughter, companion to a lady of title, and that of a fine soldier. [Cassell : o.p.]
—— *Cousins and others.* 1909
Eleven stories, chiefly of Irish people. The title-piece is about the salvation of an old family through a marriage and the discovery of some old papers. [Laurie : o.p.]
—— *John-a-Dreams.* 1916
The shy and diffident John-a-Dreams develops eventually into the quiet, self-reliant John-a-Deeds. [Murray.]
—— *The Man from Australia.* 1919
Here too the village setting in the west of Ireland is the thing. The sentimental story and plot business are a little trite. [Collins.]
—— *Denys the Dreamer.* 1920
A public-spirited landowner meets with opposition from the country people whom he would benefit by a scheme for reclaiming the foreshore. Among the engaging characters are a Jew moneylender and his wife. [Collins ; Benziger, New York.]

" TYTLER, Sarah " [Henrietta Keddie ; Scottish ; 1827–1914]. *Citoyenne Jacqueline.* 1865
A woman's lot in the Revolution ; a touching domestic story. Paris, the Luxembourg ; Charlotte Corday, etc. (1792–3). [Chatto.]
—— *What She Came Through.* 1877
Lover and heroine, servants on a farm, really belong to a superior rank in life, and the ignorance of each as to the other's antecedents gives peculiar opportunities for the play of character. Describes farming and country life in considerable detail. [Chatto : o.p.]
—— *St. Mungo's City.* 1885
Appreciative portraiture of Glasgow people, very racy and rich in local colour. A variety of characters, comic and pathetic—the poor, proud Mackinnon sisters, old-fashioned gentlewomen ; sweet-natured Eppie Drysdale ; the self-made business man, Auld Tam, etc. [Chatto : o.p.]
—— *Logie Town.* 1887
An old-fashioned Scottish township, full of characters humorously depicted. Brings out the mingled simplicity and self-importance of the Scot, the intimate association of classes, the powerful ties of kindred. [Ward & Downey : o.p.]
—— *The Macdonald Lass : a study from last century.* 1895
A careful and affectionate retelling of Flora Macdonald's heroic rescue of Prince Charlie after Culloden (1746). [Chatto : o.p.]
—— *The Witch Wife.* 1897
A gloomy story of the grim old days of witch-burning late in the seventeenth century ; only too faithful to what we know of the times. [Chatto : o.p.]
—— *Miss Nanse.* 1899
A quiet domestic story of an old Scottish seaport town of fifty years ago, full of pleasant characters. [Long : o.p.]
—— *A Young Dragon.* 1900
Country life on the moorlands, near the English Border, delineated with little incident and quiet, truthful characterization. A masterful old bachelor is dared into a wager that he will win a wife. He marries a simple-hearted, unselfish woman, who is shocked to discover the motive of his wooing. [Chatto : o.p.]
—— *A Daughter of the Manse.* 1905
Describes with moving pathos the long and heroic struggle for existence of the pastors who resigned their ministries at the great Disruption (1843). [Long : o.p.]
—— *Favours from France.* 1905
Story of a Scots laird and his family after the '45, in Edinburgh, where he has unfortunate lawsuits, and in Paris among Jacobite exiles. [Long : o.p.]
—— *Innocent Masqueraders.* 1907
The contrasted life of two girls abandoned on Blackheath (*c.* 1800), and brought up, the well-born infant by a farmer's wife, the other by a lady. [Long : o.p.]

UCHARD, Mario [French ; 1824–93]. *My Uncle Barbassou* (Mon oncle Barbassou, 1876). 1888
A fantastic and humorous account of an Oriental experiment in Paris. The uncle of the young Parisian hero was a sort of pasha, and, among other things, left to his nephew a harem of captivating young ladies, with one of whom the hero falls in love. [With 40 *etchings* after P. AVRIL, Vizetelly : o.p. ; Rand & McNally, Chicago, 1889 : o.p.]
ULFERS, S. [Dutch]. *Idylls of a Dutch Village* (Eastloorn). 1914
Ten sketches of the farmers and labourers and the parish minister in a village of Overijsel. The framing of

ULFERS, S. (*continued*).

meadows and cornfields and open skies gives something of the idyll to the general picture. But the uglier aspects of country life are not lost sight of. A simple, strong, unemotional people—that is the main impression conveyed. [Transl. by P. WILLIAMSON-NAPIER, Unwin ; Dutton, New York : o.p.]

UNAMUNO, Miguel de [Spanish (Basque) ; *b.* 1864]. *Mist* (*Niebla*, 1914).   1929

A philosophical discussion-novel of a pleasantly whimsical kind, the characters as it were having their own way independently of any original plan, and the hero consulting the author at his house in Salamanca on the question why he can't make up his mind to commit suicide. The deepest metaphysical issues are implied or suggested, with characteristically sceptical conclusions. [Transl. by Warner FITE, Knopf.]

UNDERDOWN, Emily. *Cristina : a romance of Italy in the olden days.*   1903

A sentimental novel based on incidents related by Dante, occuring at Siena and other places in his infancy. Conradin of Swabia and the battle of Tagliacozzo (1267–8). [Sonnenschein : o.p.]

UNDSET, Sigrid [Norwegian ; *b.* 1882]. *Jenny* (1911).   1920

An artless, ill-constructed, beginner's novel, that has many fine things in it. The characters are Norwegian art-students living at Rome, talking at the café table, love-making, and also finding their own selves. We are asked to believe that Jenny yields to a too-generous impulse and comes to a tragic end, whilst her worldly-wise friend, who never does anything unconventional, basks in fortune's sunshine. [Transl. by W. EMMÉ, Knopf ; transl. by A. GRIPPENWALD and J. ALEXANDER, Knopf.]

—— *Kristin Lavransdatter* (*Kransen*, 1920 ; *Husfrue*, 1922 ; *Korset*, 1922).   1929

This voluminous historical romance appeared first in English in three parts, as in the original language. Somewhat confused, or at least confusing, in the multitude of characters and of loosely connected episodes, it offers a vivid and highly detailed panorama of Norwegian life in the first half of the fourteenth century. The woman Kristin's life is followed from childhood to death ; and, though of course there are numerous figures of the other sex, it is Sigrid Undset's women who are really alive. The interest is largely psychological and moral. Historical personages like Erling Vidkunsson and King Magnus Eriksson appear only in the background ; yet the era is evoked with striking success. [Transl. by Charles ARCHER and J. S. SCOTT, (1), *The Garland* (American title, *The Bridal Wreath*), 1922 ; (2), *The Mistress of Husaby*, 1923 ; (3), *The Cross*, 1927 ; Knopf, London and New York. Complete in 1 vol., *id.*, 1929.]

—— *The Master of Hestviken.*   1928–30

A tetralogy resuscitating the outward lineaments and the very spirit of fourteenth-century Norway, although the author's attitude is entirely modern and the interest predominantly moral and religious. The authoress is a convinced Roman Catholic. Strong and exciting dramatic events and the clash of character and motive in a large group of personages overshadow the merely historical interest. But the epic of Olav Audunsson somehow manages to epitomize an epoch. [Transl. by A. G. CHATER, (1), *The Axe*, 1928 ; (2), *The Snake Pit*, 1929 ; (3), *In the Wilderness*, 1929 ; (4), *The Son Avenger*, 1930 ; Knopf, London and New York ; complete in 1 vol., *id.*, 1930.]

UPWARD, Allen [1863–1926]. *The Prince of Balkistan.*   1895

A romance of Court life and political intrigue in an imaginary Balkan State, somewhat of the *Zenda* type ; a remarkable anticipation of the state of things leading to Stambuloff's murder (1895). [Chatto : o.p. ; Lippincott, Philadelphia : o.p.]

—— *The Accused Princess.*   1900

A complicated story, of the comic-opera type, about a priceless ruby, owned by a Maharajah, a vassal of the English Government, and its extraordinary adventures. [Pearson : o.p.]

VACHELL, Horace Annesley [*b.* 1861]. *The Romance of Judge Ketchum.*   1896

About one-third is the fashionable English society novel of love and intrigue, the rest a melodramatic story of rough life in a Californian settlement. Here Judge Ketchum comes on the scene—a hard-headed Yankee with shrewd knowledge of human nature, whose ignorance and simplicity are as diverting as his broad humour. He turns out to be the heir to an English peerage. [Macmillan : o.p.]

—— *A Drama in Sunshine.*   1898

A romance of the land boom in California. A strenuous Yankee lawyer successfully booms an estate, and is on his way to fortune. But he has married a half-Spanish girl, and conflict arises between his ambition and her jealousy. Violent scenes of murder and vengeance result from the inflamed passions of dispossessed Irish squatters ; indeed the whole story is tragic, though an unexpected stroke in the last sentence averts a sad ending. [Nash : o.p. ; Fenno, New York : o.p.]

—— *The Procession of Life.*   1899

Ranching in California during the land boom (1890–4), with incidental sketches of society in a small township. [Nash ; Appleton, New York : o.p.]

—— *John Charity.*   1900

Adventures in Alta California (*c.* 1830–40) ; the hero fights under Alvarado against Mexico for independence, and meets with accidents in the field and with love complications among the pretty women. [Murray ; Dodd & Mead, New York : o.p.]

—— *Brothers : the true history of a fight against odds.*   1904

Begins with an extremely vivid and affectionate account of boy life at Harrow, and the doings of the two brothers, their particular chum, and an enchanting little girl. The seriousness comes on, however, in the sequel as the two brothers grow into men, the one empty, showy, and successful ; the other a most loving and lovable nature, sacrificing all to his idolized brother. Certain of the portraits are declared to be true to fact. [Murray ; Dodd & Mead, New York : o.p.]

—— *The Hill : a romance of friendship.*   1905

A Harrow story, suggested by Mr. G. W. E. Russell after reading *Brothers*, and one of the most natural in its presentment of the ways, and talk, and the very thoughts of healthy boyhood. The theme of a boy's

VACHELL, Horace, Annesley (*continued*).

worship for another who seems to have little response is worked out with fine insight and pathos. [Murray ; Dodd & Mead, New York.]

—— *John Verney* [sequel]. 1911

Deals with politics and business life, and shows the more prominent characters from *The Hill* immersed in serious affairs. Verney comes to grips again, both in politics and in love, with his old enemy, Demon, now a newspaper millionaire. [Murray ; Doran, New York : o.p.]

—— *The Paladin, as Beheld by a Woman of Temperament*. 1909

The young man who thinks himself a paladin is engaged to a girl, supposed to be rich, whose father leaves her nothing but liabilities. [Murray ; Dodd & Mead, New York : o.p.]

—— *Bunch Grass*. 1912

Good stories of life on a Californian cattle-ranch. [Murray ; Doran, New York : o.p.]

—— *Quinneys'*. 1914

Quinney is a dealer in antiques, who is saved from falling to the temptation of faking by his wife and daughter ; the latter's romance with his foreman provides the climax of an amusing tale. [Murray ; Doran, New York : o.p.]

—— *The Triumph of Tim : the life history of a chameleon*. 1916

Tim's triumph is in the attainment of self-knowledge. This is the mental and moral history of a very ordinary person, ably recorded. [Murray ; Doran, New York : o.p.]

—— *The Soul of Susan Yellam*. 1918

English village life, especially how characters were affected by the war. Notable are the old peasant woman who loses her faith and flies to the fortune-teller's cards, the jovial squire, the vicar, and the bibulous braggart " Uncle." [Cassell.]

—— *Whitewash*. 1920

A public-spirited doctor's campaign against a dishonest bailiff, who neglects the cottages owned by the lady of the manor, points a forcible indictment of obsolete methods of estate-management. [Cassell.]

—— *The Enchanted Garden ; and other stories*. 1929

The title-story is a delightful fantasy about two children who return after death to enjoy the garden in which they used to play. [Cassell.]

VALENTYNE AND ORSON. *The Hystorie of the Two Valyaunte Brethren, Valentyne and Orson, Sonnes unto the Emperor of Greece* (Valentin et Orson, 1489). *c.* 1560

A composition of the fifteenth century, closely connected in matter with the later Carlovingian romances ; first printed at Lyons, 1489. The Emperor drove out his wife, who was falsely accused (a version of the popular Griseldis legend), and she gave birth to twin sons in a forest ; Orson was suckled by a bear, and Valentine was brought up by his uncle Pepin, father of Charlemagne. Their true relationship is revealed by a Brazen Head. They fight the Green Knight and the giant Ferragus, King of Portugal. The latter part of the book recounts their wars with the Saracens in the East, the capture of the twelve Peers of France (an anachronism), with Pepin and the Emperor, and their safe deliverance. Marvels of a hackneyed kind, the feats of Pacolet and Adriman, rival enchanters, and combats with giants, dragons, etc., furnish the usual fare. [An English translation was printed by Wynkyn de Worde, another by Copland, and early in the seventeenth century it was retranslated by Henry WATSON : o.p.]

VALERA Y ALCALÁ GALIANO, Juan [Spanish ; 1824–1905]. *Pepita Jiménez* (1874). 1891

The theme is natural feeling and passion overcoming the restraints of sacerdotal training. The beautiful, passionate heroine is the wooer, the hero being a seminarist ; the love-tale is the self-revelation of these two in their letters. Light and sceptical in treatment, in construction rather loose and discursive, altogether a contrast to the realistic fiction then in its heyday abroad and shortly to be the mode in Spain. A thoroughly native production in feeling, method, and character, it marks the renaissance of Spanish fiction. [Transl. by Mary J. SERRANO, Heinemann : o.p. ; Appleton, New York : o.p.]

—— *Comendador Mendoza* (El Comendador Mendoza, 1877). 1893

The problem to be solved is how the Comendador Mendoza and Doña Blanca, who has deceived her husband, shall prevent their illegitimate daughter from inheriting the husband's wealth. The solution is the resultant of the different forces of human nature brought into play ; in other words, the characterization gives much the same sort of interest as that of a plot-novel, with deeper interests superadded. Mr. Fitzmaurice-Kelly describes it as " a transfigured piece of autobiography " ; certainly Valera put an undue proportion of himself into his characters in general. [Transl. by Mary J. SERRANO, Appleton, New York ; o.p.]

—— *Doña Luz* (1879). 1891

A many-sided picture of life in an Andalusian town, with much the same central situation as that in *Pepita Jiménez*. The theological discussions a little tiresome, and the missionary priest and Doña Luz—in whom Valera's pet theme of sensuous mysticism is embodied—are somewhat forced ; otherwise free from Spanish extravagance, and the social and political pictures true to life. [Transl. by Mary J. SERRANO, Appleton, New York : o.p.] Other novels are *Las Ilusiones del Doctor Faustino* (1875), *Juanita la Larga* (1895), and *De varios Colores* (1898).

VALLINGS, Harold. *By Dulvercombe Water : a love-story of 1685–9*. 1902

A side-scene of Monmouth's rebellion and its sequel. One brother personates another, and is tried by Judge Jeffreys. [Macmillan : o.p.]

—— *The Lady Mary of Tavistock*. 1908

The troubles of Sir Richard Grenvil's ill-used wife ; his villainous attempts to get hold of her property. A Devon story, bringing in the pastoral poet William Browne : time a little before the Civil War (*c.* 1630). [Milne : o.p.]

VALLOTTON, Benjamin [French-Swiss ; *b.* 1877]. *The Profit Family : a story of Lausanne* (La famille Profit, 1912). 1915

A chronicle of the small events of life, in the family of a professor of arithmetic in Lausanne. Interest focuses

VALLOTTON, Benjamin (*continued*).
upon César, the only son, a cripple from birth, and the marriage of one of the daughters. [Transl. by Louise CHATAWAY, Richards.]

—— *Potterat and the War* (De la paix à la guerre ; ce qu'en pense Potterat, 1915). 1917
Potterat is a retired police-superintendent at Lausanne, large-hearted, irascible, naif and idealistic but clear-headed, a born humorist—in short, he is a flattering epitome of Vaudois characteristics. He bows to Progress, when it ejects him from his house and garden on Lake Léman ; he provisions his flat and is prepared to fortify it if the Boches arrive. He spends far more than he can afford on Belgian refugees and other unfortunates. The one thing he cannot understand is the pusillanimous attitude of his own Government when other neutral nations are being maltreated. [Heinemann ; Dodd & Mead, New York.]

—— *The Heart of Alsace* (On changerait plûtot l'esprit de place, 1917). 1918
Presents a sympathetic and moving picture of Alsace prior to the war. The chief character is a Swiss tutor who comes to teach the sons of a wealthy manufacturer. The hard-headed business circles in which he moves are stirred to the depths by their patriotism, though they judge it better to remain passive and keep their French sympathies hidden, whilst waiting for the day of deliverance. [Heinemann ; Dodd & Mead, New York.]

VAN VECHTEN, Carl [American ; *b.* 1880]. *Peter Whiffle : his life and works.* 1922
Bohemian existence in Paris, queer, futile decadents running hither and thither and chattering, all to no apparent purpose, engaging in endless literary arguments about things and people of no importance—only mildly amusing, though the piece of necromancy at the close adds a touch of colour. [Knopf, New York and London.]

—— *Firecrackers : a realistic novel.* 1925
Presumably the " realistic " part is that wherein a group of half-wits of the New York moneyed class, with an impossible and insufferable child, are displayed ; the firecrackers are supplied by a mysterious personage, one Gunnar O'Grady, who appears and disappears for no apparent reason and in no human manner, performs acrobatics, and quotes Persian philosophy. [Knopf, New York and London.]

—— *Nigger Heaven.* 1926
Semi-detached studies of negro society in Harlem, where the wealthiest and the destitute are congregated. Sets forth vividly and feelingly the complex problems due as much to their own rigid class-distinctions and snobbery and to their hatred of any of their number who attempt to rise and emancipate themselves, as to their ostracism by the whites. The most interesting figure is that of a young negro educated at Harvard, whose fate is heart-rending. But we are given unimaginable glimpses into the African temperament, its propensity to violence, to lust and debauchery, to reckless display, in short to the vices of all the world intensified by a fundamental savagery. [Knopf, New York and London ; Grosset, New York.]

—— *Spider Boy : a scenario for a moving picture.* 1928
A light-hearted, rollicking extravaganza, making fun of the great film-making establishments at Hollywood, the grandiose pretensions of the producers, the conceit and jealousies of the stars, the gigantic prodigality of the whole business. The persecuted hero is a playwright who falls into the clutches of the film-lords, who want to exploit his notoriety, and to " put him through it " before he makes his escape. [Knopf, New York and London.]

—— *Parties : scenes from contemporary New York life.* 1930
Apparently a satire, at any rate a candid exposure, of the utter demoralization and futility of the boozing and sex-ridden crowd in the expensive night-clubs and private bars of Harlem—the state of things brought about by prohibition. [Knopf, New York and London.]

VAUCAIRE, Michel B. [French]. *Bolivar* (Bolivar el Liberta, 1928). 1929
The life-story of Bolivar, both in Europe and subsequently as leader of the revolt in Venezuela, in the first quarter of last century. [Transl. by Margaret Baines REED, Constable ; Houghton, Boston.]

VAZOV, Ivan [Bulgarian ; *b.* 1850]. *Under the Yoke.* 1893
A narrative of the unsuccessful revolt of the Bulgarians from Turkey (1875–6) ; realistic in an imaginative, pamphleteering way. Brings out vividly the differences of national character, and the deeper causes of defeat. [Heinemann, 1915.]

" VERESAYEV, V." [Vikenti Vikentievich Semedawiiz ; Russian ; *b.* 1867]. *The Confessions of a Physician* (1901). 1904
Autobiographical experiences, hardly flattering to the medical profession, of a young doctor. The novel caused some sensation on its appearance with the frankness of its disclosures. [Transl. by S. LINDEN, Richards : o.p.]

VERESHCHAGIN, Vasili Vasilievich [Russian ; 1842–1904]. *The War Correspondent.* 1894
Incidents in the Russo-Turkish war (1877). Vereshchagin was a famous battle-painter who was present at the crossing of the Shipka Pass and the storming of Plevna, and was dangerously wounded at the passage of the Danube. He went down with the *Petropavlovsky* during the Russo-Japanese war. [Osgood, London : o.p.]

VERGA, Giovanni [Sicilian ; 1840–1922]. *Cavalleria Rusticana ; and other stories* (*from* Vita dei Campi, 1880). 1928
Nine stories of Sicilian life ; the title-story is that from which the libretto of the opera was composed. [Transl. by D. H. LAWRENCE, Cape ; Harcourt, New York. *Cavalleria Rusticana*, transl. by A. STRETTELL, 1893 : o.p.]

—— *Little Novels of Sicily* (Novelle rusticane, 1883). 1925
Sicily of the eighteen-sixties—landowners, gentry, priests, and, above all, the peasants. These, in their poverty, oppression, and patience, arouse the author's deepest sympathies, and at the same time are drawn with a profound belief in the beauty of truth ; e.g. *Black Bread* (*Pane nero*), a moving tale of a young peasant and his wife, ruined by the father's death, descending into the depths of abject toil and poverty. [Transl. by D. H. Lawrence, Blackwell, Oxford ; Boni, New York.]

VERGA, Giovanni (*continued*). *The House by the Medlar Tree* (I Malevoglia, 1888).   1890
A realistic picture of peasant life in an Italian fishing hamlet by the author of *Cavalleria Rusticana*. The Sicilian novelist studied Maupassant and his master Flaubert; but his artistic method is in no sense imitative, rather it aims at the same ideals of uncompromising fidelity and personal detachment. The tale tells itself, with no obtrusive comment or explanation. It is the story of a grand old fisherman, whose god is financial integrity, and who exhausts his life and the life of his family in making reparation for debts incurred through misfortune. [Transl. by Mary A. CRAIG, Harper: o.p.]

—— *Maestro Don Gesualdo.*   1923
Second of the projected series, *I Vinti*, describing scenes of Sicilian life. Gesualdo is a wealthy peasant whose overbearing egoism and inability to adapt himself to the society he wishes to enter bring him to grief. [Transl. by D. H. LAWRENCE, Boni, New York; Cape.]

VERNE, Jules [French; 1828–1905]. *Five Weeks in a Balloon* (Cinq semaines en ballon, 1863).   1870
The precursor of a long series of scientific romances, especially accounts of extraordinary travels and discoveries. Jules Verne contrived some more or less plausible scientific marvel—a balloon, a monster gun, a submarine, or a strange geographical discovery—and on this datum built up a series of startling adventures. Here a party of balloonists go on an exploring journey across Central Africa. [Low; Ward & Lock; with *Around the World in Eighty Days*, (Everyman's Lib.) Dent (Dutton, New York), 1926.]

—— *A Journey into the Interior of the Earth* (Voyage au centre de la terre, 1864).   1872
A band of explorers go down the funnel of a volcano in Iceland, and are ejected near Stromboli in the Mediterranean, after journeying through the subterranean regions, where they find animal and vegetable productions akin to those of past geological periods. [Routledge; Oxford Press; Scribner, New York.]

—— *From the Earth to the Moon direct in 97 hours, 20 minutes* (De la terre à la lune; trajet direct en 97 heures, 1865).   1873

—— *Around the Moon* (Autour de la lune, 1869) [sequel].   1875
An adventurous party in America have a monster gun cast, and are shot to the moon. They are a comic set of people, and many of their experiences are very funny. Ardan is drawn from Verne's old friend Nadar, photographer and aeronaut. [In 1 vol., Low; Scribner, New York; Burt, New York.]

—— *The English at the North Pole* (Les Anglais au Pole Nord: aventures du capitaine Hatteras, 1866).   1875

—— *The Desert of Ice* (Le désert de glace, 1866) [sequel].   1876
Thrilling adventures during a voyage to the Pole; contains a number of odd people, plenty of pseudo-scientific marvels, and characteristic comedy. Captain Hatteras ranks with Phileas Fogg as one of Verne's best seriocomic figures. [In 1 vol., *sub tit. The Adventures of Captain Hatteras*, Routledge, 1876: o.p.; Collins.]

—— *Twenty Thousand Leagues Under the Sea* (Vingt mille lieues sous les mers, 1869–70).   1872
The wondrous voyages, piracies, and disasters of a submarine ship. The Byronic Captain Nemo is not a bad specimen of Verne's intrepid leaders. [Low; 2 vols. in 1, Routledge; (Everyman's Lib.) Dent (Dutton, New York); Scribner, New York; Burt, New York; Putnam, New York; *illus.*, Low.]

—— *Around the World in Eighty Days* (Le tour du monde en quatre-vingt jours, 1873).   1873
An English gentleman undertakes this project for a wager, but, in addition to the physical difficulties, his enemy puts every sort of impediment and danger in his way, so that from beginning to end he runs the gauntlet of incessant peril, though he is successful at the finish. Phileas Fogg is one of Verne's most striking creations. [Low; Routledge; *sub tit. Tour of the World in Eighty Days*, Scribner, New York; Burt, New York; see also *Five Weeks in a Balloon, supra.*]

—— *The Fur Country; or, Seventy Degrees North Latitude* (Le pays de fourrures, 1873).   1874
An astronomical expedition is astounded to find that the chosen station is outside the track of the eclipse; the explanation is that Cape Bathurst is a vast ice-floe covered with blown sand, and has been cut adrift by an earthquake. [Transl. by N. D'ANVERS, Low; Routledge.]

—— *The Mysterious Island* (L'île mystérieuse, 1874).   1875
Dropped from the Clouds, Abandoned, The Secret of the Island: stories of adventure, perils by sea, pirates, and wild beasts. [3 vols., Low; 3 vols. (Everyman's Lib.) Dent (Dutton, New York); 1 vol., *illus.*, Scribner, New York; *illus.* by Lloyd Osbourne, Sears, New York.]

—— *Dr. Ox's Experiment; and other stories* (Le docteur Ox, 1874).   1874
Life in a comatose village in Flanders is stimulated to effervescence by a dose of oxygen. The rascally German Jew Hakkabut is a caricature meant perhaps to confute those who said that Verne was a Polish Jew. [Low: o.p.]

—— *A Winter amid the Ice* (Un hivernage dans les glaces, 1874).   1876
The ascent of Mont Blanc. [Low: o.p.]

—— *Michael Strogoff, the Courier of the Czar* (Michel Strogoff, 1876).   1877
The herculean Strogoff is sent by the Czar with a letter to a commandant in Irkutsk, beleaguered by hordes of Tartars. Traversing the vast extent of Siberia, accompanied by a beautiful girl, he encounters every conceivable kind of peril, but escapes, and executes his mission. [Low; Scribner, New York; *illus., id.*]

—— *Hector Servadac* (Hector Servadac: voyages et aventures à travers le monde solaire, 1877).   1878
A voyage too extraordinary even for Jules Verne. A slice of Algeria is transferred to a comet, and the people on it are brought back two years later. [Transl. by E. E. FREWER, Low; Scribner, New York.]

—— *Dick Sands, the Boy Captain* (Un capitaine de quinze ans, 1878).   1879
Another thrilling yarn about a boy who is left in command of a ship, and wrecked in West Africa, about the time of Livingstone's expedition. There is a good deal of moralizing about slavery, adapted for the then juvenile market. [Transl. by E. E. FREWER: o.p.]

VERNE, Jules (*continued*). *Mathias Sandorf* (Mathias Sandorf, 1885).   1886
 Thrilling adventures in Hungary, about the frustration of a plot against the Austrian Government. The hero
 is betrayed and imprisoned ; he escapes, and after amassing great wealth, returns to execute a long-planned
 vengeance on a vast and picturesque scale. [Low : o.p.]
—— *The Castle of the Carpathians* (Le château des Carpathes, 1892).   1893
 A weird tale with necromantic effects, which the author calls romantic, but it is chiefly pure fantasy. [Low : o.p.]
 [*Novels*, containing *Twenty Thousand Leagues under the Sea, Around the World in Eighty Days, Hector Servadac,
 The Floating Island*, and *The Blockade Runners*, 1 vol., Gollancz, 1929.]

VESELITSKAYA, Lidia Ivanovna [" V. Mikulich " ; Russian]. *Mimi's Marriage* (Mimotchka,
 1891).   1893
 Scenes and characters drawn from life with a bantering and sometimes cynical pen—the bringing-up, marriage,
 and family life of a Russian girl. Well translated. [Introd. by C. Hagberg WRIGHT, Unwin : o.p.]

VIEBIG, Clara [Clara Cohn-Viebig ; German ; *b.* 1860]. *Our Daily Bread* (Das tägliche Brot,
 1903).   1909
 In the lives of two servant-girls, peasants from Schwerin, of the family of a greengrocer, and other Berlin people
 of the working class, Clara Viebig paints with photographic realism, and with intense nervous sympathy,
 the essential features of lower middle-class life in any great city. The squalor, drudgery, stupidity, meanness, and brutishness are heavily stressed, but the better qualities of such sturdy characters as the household
 drudge Mina redeem the picture from utter repulsiveness. No humour, and on the other hand, no
 didactic or sentimental bias : the truth of the picture speaks for itself. [Transl. by Margaret L. CLARKE,
 Lane : o.p.]
—— *The Sleeping Army* (Das schlafende Heer, 1904).   1929
 Depicts the conflict between Pole and Prussian in the eastern provinces of Germany in the closing years of
 last century. [Transl. by Gilbert WATERHOUSE, Benn.]
—— *Absolution* (Absolvo te ! 1906).   1908
 A powerful study of a gloomy and repellent theme—a woman's loathing for a husband to whom she has been
 wedded through poverty, and hatred driving her to crime. A story of the Russian-Polish border peasantry.
 [Transl. by H. RAAHANGE, Lane : o.p.]
—— *The Son of his Mother* (Einer Mütter Sohn, 1906).   1913
 A lady in Berlin who believes education stronger than heredity adopts the child of a peasant mother and brings
 him up in affluence. His innate savagery proves incurable, at any rate, before the novelist gives up the
 case and lets him die of heart disease. The story is told without humour, but the end is really moving.
 [Transl. by H. RASHAUGE, Lane : o.p.]

VIELÉ, Herman Knickerbocker [American ; 1856–1908]. *The Inn of the Silver Moon.*   1902
 A light comedy in a French setting. [Murray : o.p. ; Duffield, New York.]
—— *Myra of the Pines.*   1904
 A love-romance very pleasantly told, amid the Arcadian surroundings of the American backwoods. [Unwin :
 o.p. ; Duffield, New York.]

VIGA GLUM'S SAGA.   1866
 One of the earliest sagas. " Murdering Glum " is a grim, unscrupulous, implacable character, who has fits
 of laughter when the appetite for killing comes upon him. A sombre picture of the savage heathen days,
 and the events true : time, middle and end of tenth century. The verses interspersed are genuine. [*The
 Story of Viga Glum ;* transl. with notes and introductions by Rt. Hon. Sir Edmund HEAD, Williams &
 Norgate : o.p.]

VIGFÚSSON, Gudbrand [1827–89], and POWELL, F. York [1850–1904] (eds.). *Origines Islandicae :
 the more important sagas and other native writings relating to the settlement and early history of
 Iceland.*   1905
 This is the standard source-book for the Icelandic Sagas. [2 vols., Oxford Press.]

VIGNY, Alfred Victor, Comte de [French ; 1797–1863]. *Cinq-Mars ; or, The Conspiracy* (Cinq
 Mars ; ou, une conjuration sous Louis XIII, 1826).   1847
 A romance in Scott's style, giving a free account (though the accuracy is attested by footnotes) of the famous
 conspiracy against Cardinal Richelieu in the reign of Louis XIII. Cinq-Mars was the leader in it, holding
 treasonable relations with Spain. He and his youthful accomplice De Thou were beheaded at Lyons
 (1642). " According to Vigny, the novelist is a poet, a moralist, a philosopher, and history only lends him
 material. Beyond the positive reality, there is an ideal fact " (G. Pellissier). He was a poor story-teller,
 but the Cardinal is finely portrayed, by reason perhaps of the author's dislike. [Routledge : o.p. ; transl.
 by Wm. HAZLITT, *illus.* with etchings (1847), 2 vols., Low 1890 : o.p. ; transl. by Madge PEMBERTON,
 sub tit. The Spider and the Fly, S. Paul ; McKay, Philadelphia, 1926.]

VILLARI, Linda [Italian ; *née* Mazini]. *In Change Unchanged.*   1877
 A story of Florence and Bellosguardo, with a series of character-sketches and a more finished portrait of a
 brilliant talker, Miss Whitman, said to be a study of Mrs. Browning's dearest friend. Mme Villari has
 also written *In the Golden Shell : a story of Palermo* (1872) ; *When I was a Child ; or, Left Behind* (1885),
 all in English. [2 vols., Macmillan : o.p.]

VILLIERS DE L'ISLE-ADAM, Count Philippe Auguste Mathias de [French ; 1838–89]. *Sardonic Tales* (Contes cruels, 1883).   1927
 Cameos of delicate art picturing strange lives with a most sardonic malice. *Les demoiselles de Bienfilâtre*
 recounts the virtuous lapse of a daughter of joy, her death-bed confession and absolution. In *Véra*, a
 widowed husband, by force of imagination, reincarnates for himself the spirit of his wife. *Virginie et Paul*
 is a cynical inversion of the conventional idyll. *Le convive des dernières fêtes* turns out to be the public
 executioner. *Impatience de la foule* and *Les brigands* are satires on popular imbecility. The saturnine,
 nay satanic, humour of *La reine Ysabeau*, an anecdote of a royal courtesan, the queen of Charles VI, is

VILLIERS DE L'ISLE-ADAM, Count Philippe Auguste Mathias de (*continued*).

so tragic one dare not smile. [Transl. by Hamish MILES, Knopf.] A further series, *Nouveaux contes cruels*, 1889, appear not to have been translated.

VISRAMIANI : *the Story of the Loves of Vis and Ramin : a romance of ancient Persia.*   1914

One of the oldest novels in the world, originally written in Pahlavi long before the Moslem conquest of Old Persia in the seventh century. It was preserved in a poetical version (published under the title of *Wis o Rámín, an ancient Persion poem*, Calcutta, 1864–5), and also in a Georgian rendering from which this present work is translated. The story has many points of resemblance to *Tristan and Iseult*. Vis is the wife of Ramin, the brother of the great Shah Moabad. This aged monarch plays a part like that of Marc, alternately persecuting and pardoning the lovers, and, like Tristan, Ramin is seduced from his fealty to Vis at one period by a foreign charmer Gul. The story is full of varied incident, the characters are drawn in a simple epical way, and the love passages have all the luxuriant imagery and daring splendour of Oriental rhetoric. Like the *Arabian Nights*, this is a text-book of Oriental manners and customs, religion, and mythology, and its use in this respect is made fully available by the comprehensive classified index. The translation is done in a style admirably conveying the epic spirit of the original. [Transl. from the Georgian version by Oliver WARDROP (Oriental Translation Fund, New Series, v. 23, Asiatic Soc.]

VÖLSUNGA SAGA. *The story of the Volsungs and Niblungs, with certain songs from the Elder Edda.*

1870

A recension of the heroic myths about the Volsungs, Brynhild, and the Giukings, which appeared in fragmentary forms in the *Poetic Edda*. Inchoate, but studiously faithful to the original legends, of which it gives the fullest summary extant in Icelandic literature. By using material contained in different versions of the lays in the *Edda*, the translators have given their recension more of the character of a work of art. Put together in the decadent fourteenth century, long after the great saga time, this is still the most famous story in Northern literature, and the one that by its grand simplicity, noble conceptions of life and death, and sublime characters, appeals most forcibly to modern readers, although its ideas belong to a barbarous antiquity. Comprises the story of Sigmund, son of Volsung, and the magical sword called Gram ; the genealogy of Sigurd ; Sigurd's career ; the slaying of the Worm Fafnir, and Sigurd's love for Brynhild ; their fateful separation and death ; the marriage of Gudrun and Atli, and the tragic end of the Giukings or Niblungs. In the German epic, the *Nibelungenlied*, Siegfried takes the place of the incomparable hero Sigurd, as again in Wagner's *Ring of the Nibelungs*. William Morris's masterpiece, the epical *Sigurd the Volsung*, is on the same theme. [Transl. by Eiríkr MAGNÚSSON and William MORRIS, ed. by H. H. SPARLING (Scott Lib.), W. Scott : o.p. ; transl. by Margaret SCHLAUCH, Norton, New York, 1930.]

VOLTAIRE, François Arouet de [French ; 1694–1778]. *Tales* (1746–67).   1891

Babouc, Zadig, Plato's Dream, Candide, L'Ingénu, etc. A famous collection of dialogues, apologues, *contes*, expounding with inimitable art and wit a definite series of philosophic views on the conduct of life and society. *Babouc* is a satire on the evils of war, public and private immorality, and misgovernment. Its conclusion is that the good in human affairs compensates for the evil, and, that if things are not all good, they are, at all events, passable. *L'Ingénu* is a Huron transferred to Europe, whose naïve perplexities and searching questions expose the incompatibilities of Roman Catholic customs and formulas with the teaching of the Bible, and of social conventions with reason and true morality. Many of the tales are very short ; all are witty, thoughtful, and sincere applications of philosophic truths to the facts of life. [*Zadig and other Tales*, transl. by B. B. BOSWORTH (Bohn's Lib.), Bell (Harcourt, New York) ; *Zadig and other Romances*, transl. by H. I. WOOLF (Broadway Transl.), Routledge (Dutton, New York), 1923 ; by H. I. WOOLF and Wilfred S. JACKSON, Lane (Dodd & Mead, New York), 1926.]

—— *Candide ; or, All for the Best* (1759).   1759

A farrago of diverting incidents, the object of which is to burlesque the teleological philosophy of Leibnitz by a *reductio ad absurdum*, and controvert freewill by showing the inexorable power of circumstances. This it does with brilliant irony and implacable force. Both the old and the new worlds are shown to be full of crime and misery ; there is no true happiness or virtue on earth. Optimism is proved absurd. Therefore, let us give up theorizing and do our best—let us cultivate our garden. [With introd. by W. JERROLD, Redway, 1898 : o.p. ; transl. by Henry MORLEY, *illus.*, Dutton, New York, 1922 ; *Candide and Other Romances*, transl. by Richard ALDINGTON, (Broadway Transl.) Routledge, (Dutton, New York), 1927. Cheap ed. (Abbey Classics), Simpkin : o.p.]

—— *Zadig ; and other tales.*   1891

Further satire of effete dogmas, and comparisons of theory with realities. Zadig is a young Babylonian whose comic mishaps are pegs for the author's philosophic commentary ; main theme, the difficulty of securing happiness by reason of the malice of one's neighbours. Zadig tries to reform society, but finds human conventions and formulas invincible. In *Micromégas, a Philosophic Story*, the same doctrine is embodied, and the absurdities of humanity displayed, as it were, in cosmic perspective. [*v. supra.*]

VOYNICH, Mrs. Ethel Lillian [*née* Boole ; *b.* 1864]. *The Gadfly.*   1898

The writer's object seems to be to show a strong, passionate, magnanimous character driven by wrong and contumely into atheism. The scene is young Italy before the revolution (1833–46) : and the characters include patriots, conspirators, assassins, in their struggle with Austrian authorities, spies and ecclesiastics. The Gadfly, unacknowledged son of a priest, in his onslaught on religion and authority, ultimately comes into collision with his own father, now a famous cardinal. The tragic story ends in agony unlit by any gleam of hope or reconciliation. [Heinemann ; Holt, New York ; Grosset, New York.]

—— *An Interrupted Friendship* [sequel].   1910

Clears up a hiatus in the history of the Gadfly by relating his adventures in Ecuador (1838–41). It is a tragic story, the tragedy accentuated by the sombre humour ; the character-drawing incisive as ever. [Hutchinson : o.p. ; Macmillan, New York : o.p.]

—— *Jack Raymond.*   1901

The strongest section of this thoughtful novel deals with the boyhood of the orphan Jack Raymond, passed under the guardianship of a Cornish vicar, in whom cruelty has become a sort of mania. [Heinemann : o.p. ; Lippincott, Philadelphia : o.p.]

"WAKEMAN, Annie." *The Autobiography of a Charwoman.* 1900
Purports to be the actual life of a poor woman, merely translated into a literary form. The characteristic note is cheery acceptance of the world's hardships, of which she endures a woeful share in her lover's desertion and the brutality of her legal husband. [Macqueen : o.p. ; Routledge : o.p. ; Page, Boston : o.p.]

WALEY, Arthur (*tr.*). *The Lady who loved Insects.* 1930
Only some twenty pages from a lost romance written about eight hundred years ago, but enough to evoke a stage of civilization and modes of thought and feeling strangely remote yet full of charm. In the Lady who loved Insects and the Lady who loved Butterflies is suggested the eternal contrast between naturalness and servitude to convention. [Transl. from the Japanese, *illus.*, Blackmore Press.]

WALFORD, Lucy Bethia [*née* Colquhoun ; Scottish ; 1845–1915]. *Mr. Smith.* 1874
The comedy of social intercourse in a village and its neighbourhood, bestirred by the advent of a wealthy stranger whom the vulgar genteel are in doubt whether or not to receive. This simple-minded and modest gentleman is also the principal figure in the love-drama. Contains a variety of studies of human nature, and teaches an edifying lesson. [Longmans, New York.]

—— *Pauline.* 1877
Also didactic, showing how a man's love for a good woman is not sufficient to keep his undisciplined nature in the path of rectitude. Pauline is a refined, saintly, and religious character, whose love for the sinner gives deep pathos to some of the scenes. Minor characters like Pauline's aunts with their petty vanities furnish amusement. [Longmans, New York.]

—— *The Baby's Grandmother.* 1884
A touching domestic story, with a happy ending ; lengthy, chiefly taken up with very familiar portraiture of a dozen characters, grouped round one beautiful woman. [Longmans, New York.]

—— *A Stiff-Necked Generation.* 1885
A tragi-comedy of match-making and courtship ; the primary situation arising from a girl's refusal to accept her mother's protégé, a young lord, while she engages herself to a dashing, vulgar-minded soldier, whom she has idealized into a hero. [Longmans, New York : o.p.]

—— *A Mere Child.* 1888
Truthful, unambitious character-drawing of people in London and Scotland ; the female characters, as usual with Mrs. Walford, pleasant and winning, particularly the arch and captivating heroine ; the men less sympathetically drawn. [Blackett : o.p.]

—— *The Matchmaker.* 1894
A story of an aristocratic household and the little world they rule : a peer and his lady, with their peculiarities and weaknesses. [Longmans, New York.]

—— *Leddy Marget.* 1898
Sketches a good-hearted, evergreen old lady, whose lavish alms-giving provokes the ire of her last surviving son and his vulgar wife. [Longmans, New York.]

—— *Sir Patrick, the Puddock.* 1899
Peopled chiefly by vulgar parvenus, match-makers, and husband-hunters, and a plain-faced but sterling-hearted Scotch baronet as hero. [Pearson : o.p. ; Longmans, New York.]

—— *One of Ourselves.* 1900
A domestic comedy, embracing a number of vivacious characters. The self-complacent and consequential Mrs. Tom Farrell is the chief, head of a family outside of which she thinks there can be nothing admirable or respectable, an illusion sadly upset by the black sheep " Billy." The natural and unconventional Miss Colvins are good examples of the writer's warm-hearted English girls. [Longmans, New York.]

—— *The Enlightenment of Olivia.* 1907
Simple, straightforward stories of average people leading average lives, with no complex psychology, though plenty of good, sound, human nature. Olivia and her husband make a very prepossessing pair. [Longmans, New York.]

WALKER, William Sylvester [" Coo-ee " ; Australian ; b. 1846]. *When the Mopoke Calls.* 1898
A native Australian's descriptions of pioneering, gold-digging, cattle-farming, bushranging, and other phases of Australian life a quarter of a century ago, cast into the form of reminiscences, anecdotes founded on fact, and sketches of people he has known. [Long : o.p.]

—— *From the Land of the Wombat.* 1899
A collection of sketches similar to the foregoing. [Long : o.p.]

—— *Native Born.* 1900
A penniless man lands in Melbourne, meets with adventures and experiences of various kinds of life, including service in the Victoria Mounted Police, and comes off prosperously. Full of melodramatic incident, of realistic pictures of the bush and its natural glories, and the ways of English people and natives. [Long : o.p.]

—— *The Silver Queen : a tale of the Northern Territory.* 1908
—— *What Lay Beneath : a story of the Queensland bush.* 1909
—— *Blair's Ken.* 1910
More stories descriptive of bush life, pioneering and squatting, the natives, etc., by a man who knows most aspects of Australian and New Zealand life by practical experience. [All Ouseley : o.p.]

WALLACE, Edgar [1875–1932]. *The Ringer.* 1926
One of the best of an enormous number of mystery, adventure, and detective stories which compensate in excitement for what they may lack in subtlety. [Hodder ; Doubleday, Doran, New York.]

WALLACE, Helen. *Lotus or Laurel ?* 1900
Mother and daughter are great players on the violin, and the mother cannot bear to see her own fame eclipsed. A duel between two strong personalities and much musical gossip. [Arnold : o.p.]

WALLACE, Gen. Lewis [American ; 1827–1905]. *The Fair God ; or, The Last of the Tzins.* 1873
An archæological reconstruction of Mexican life at the time of the conquest (1519–20) ; exceedingly elaborate, brilliant in effects. [Houghton, Boston ; Warne. *Illus.* with 40 photogravures by Eric Papé, 2 vols., Houghton, Boston.]

—— *Ben Hur ; or, The Days of the Messiah.* [juvenile] 1880
A long and gorgeously coloured romance of Judæa and Antioch in the first century, abounding in florid scenes of pageantry. The plot is intricate, and the grammar not always faultless. It was the outcome of researches undertaken to verify the Christian gospel. [Harper, New York and London ; Warne ; Ward & Lock. *Illus.*, Harper, New York.]

—— *The Prince of India ; or, Why Constantinople Fell.* [juvenile] 1893
The hero takes the character of the Wandering Jew. Gives a florid picture of the Byzantine empire in the fifteenth century. [2 vols., Harper, New York.]

WALLER, Mary Ella [American ; b. 1885]. *Out of the Silences.* 1918
Indian life in the country of the Dakotas. [Little & Brown, Boston ; Melrose : o.p.]

"WALLIS, A. S. C." [Miss Adèle Opzoomer ; Dutch]. *In Troubled Times* (In Dagen van Strijd, 1878). 1883
The leading actors of the period (1563–72) in which Holland laid the foundations of her greatness (Margaret of Parma, Alva, Van Brederode, the Prince of Orange, etc.) are firmly drawn and with scrupulous regard for ascertained facts ; and the national movement is finely described. [Transl. by E. J. IRVING, Sonnenschein : o.p.]

—— *Royal Favour* (Vorstengunst, 1883). 1884
The hero is Person, son of a relapsed priest ; Melanchthon trains him to be a learned and high spirited man. He enters public life at the Court of Gustavus Vasa *c.* 1560 ; becomes chancellor to Eric XIV, and finds himself insensibly degraded until he is looked upon, and virtually is, the minister of the weak king's tyranny and cruelty. [Transl. by E. J. IRVING, Sonnenschein : o.p.]

WALLOTH, Wilhelm [German ; b. 1856]. *The King's Treasure House : a romance of Ancient Egypt* (Das Schatzhaus des Königs, 1883). 1886
Egypt before the Exodus. [Transl. by M. J. SAFFORD, Gottsberger, New York : o.p.]

—— *Empress Octavia* (Oktavia, 1885). 1900
Rome in the time of Nero. [Transl. by M. J. SAFFORD, Little & Brown, Boston : o.p.]

WALPOLE, Horace, Earl of Orford [1717–97]. *The Castle of Otranto.* 1764
A famous example of the Gothic romance of mystery and terror. Its extravagant events are supposed to occur in Italy in the twelfth and thirteenth centuries, but the historical setting is quite imaginary. Manfred, a tyrannical baron, his ill-used wife and beautiful daughter, with a gigantic apparition that haunts the castle, are the puppets in the tragedy. An historical curiosity that effectively was not more important in the history of the romantic revival than the Rev. Thos. Leland's *Longsword, an Historical Romance,* of two years earlier, which, however, is hardly readable now. [Chatto ; Stokes, New York ; ed. by Rev. Montague Summers, with *illus.* from the edition of 1796, Constable (Houghton, Boston) ; ed. by Oswald Doughty, Scholartis Press (McKee, New York), 1929.]

WALPOLE, Hugh Seymour [New Zealander ; b. 1884]. *Maradick at Forty : a transition.* 1910
Maradick is a stodgy business-man, stodgily married, who comes to life—the real life he has hitherto fought shy of—through aiding a young fellow in a genuine love-affair. A Cornish gentleman supposed to enjoy Satanic gifts furnishes horrors of an inoffensive kind. [Macmillan ; Doubleday, Doran, New York.]

—— *Mr. Perrin and Mr. Traill : a tragi-comedy.* 1911
The adventures of two ushers consumed with mutual jealousy and hatred, and other eccentricities in a private school in the west of England. [Macmillan ; *sub tit. The Gods and Mr. Perrin,* Doubleday, Doran, New York.]

—— *Fortitude : being the true and faithful account of the education of an explorer.* 1913
This long account of the boyhood and schooldays in Cornwall, and the struggles and astonishing success of a novelist, becomes really absorbing with the failure of his marriage to a society woman. [Macmillan ; Doubleday, Doran, New York.]

—— *The Duchess of Wrexe, her Decline and Death : a romantic commentary.* 1914
The octagenarian duchess lords it over her family, and represses the rising generation, especially the grand-daughter, who is in love with the wrong man. [Macmillan ; Nelson ; Doubleday, Doran, New York.]

—— *The Dark Forest.* 1916
Obviously the result of Mr. Walpole's experiences with the Red Cross in Galicia : war from the point of view of an Englishman, who is watching the moral predicaments of an Englishman unhappily in love with a Russian fellow-worker. Attempts to reach beyond the grim actualities to a more mystical view, symbolized in the title. [Macmillan ; Nelson ; Doubleday, Doran, New York.]

—— *The Green Mirror : a quiet story.* 1918
A slice out of the history of two families, the kind who " have made England what it is." The Trenchards are upset, and the mirror, symbol of their placidity, is shattered, when the daughter loves an emancipated and Russianized young fellow with a past and runs away to marry him. [Macmillan ; Doubleday, Doran, New York.]

—— *The Secret City : a novel in three parts.* 1919
A sequel to *The Dark Forest,* continuing the story amidst the revolution in Petrograd. But the secret city is also that in man's heart ; and the emotional drama in the minds of the Russian characters has tragic power. [Macmillan ; Doubleday, Doran, New York.]

—— *Jeremy.* 1919
The episodes of a by no means abnormal childhood, in a provincial cathedral city, presented, with very few lapses from consistency, through the impressions of the boy himself. [Cassell ; Doubleday, Doran, New York.]

WALPOLE, Hugh Seymour (*continued*). *The Captives : a novel in four parts.* 1920
> The most successful creation in this long book is the mystical parson, James Warlock. The errors and misfortunes of the two lovers and their eventual reunion, though they take up more space and prominence are less interesting or convincing. [Macmillan ; Doubleday, Doran, New York.]

—— *The Thirteen Travellers.* 1921
> Thirteen stories of representative types, the impoverished aristocracy, women workers in men's jobs, disabled soldiers, and so on, whose lives call for readjustment after the upheaval of war-time. [Hutchinson : o.p. ; Doubleday, Doran, New York.]

—— *The Young Enchanted.* 1921
> Some of the characters from *The Green Mirror* and *Fortitude* reappear. [Macmillan ; Doubleday, Doran, New York.]

—— *The Cathedral.* 1922
> A painstaking and ambitious work that challenges comparison with Trollope's Barchester series. Archdeacon Brandon is another Archdeacon Grantly, though his trial is less of a comedy and more of a tragedy. His sufferings are those of a Job. But the deathblow comes from a newcomer, the duel with whom reminds one of that decided by the appointment of Mr. Arabin. The conflict between the religion of authority and the religion of the spirit, personal religion and ecclesiasticism, Renan and the cathedral, is a new element showing the advent of modern ideas. [Macmillan ; Doubleday, Doran, New York.]

—— *Jeremy and Hamlet.* 1923
—— *Jeremy at Crale : his friends, his ambitions, and his one great enemy.* 1927
> Sequels giving the later history of Jeremy. [(1) and (2), Cassell ; Doubleday, Doran, New York.]

—— *Harmer John : an unworldly story.* 1926
> Johanson, of Swedish-English parentage, returns to Polchester to preach his gospel of physical perfection, and expounds far-reaching schemes whereby the city, sunk in squalor and inertia, may be made entirely perfect. He meets the usual fate of a prophet, and is done to death by the slum-dwellers whom he had tried to benefit. [Macmillan ; Doubleday, Doran, New York.]

—— *Wintersmoon.* 1928
> Depicts social life in the upper classes, in London and the country, whilst working out a quiet love-story. [Macmillan ; Doubleday, New York.]

—— *Hans Frost.* 1929
> The novelist's hero—unless the irony is intentional—is another novelist, on whom he thrusts greatness. Frost is the accomplished writer of facile, conventional, futile best-sellers, who suddenly realizes what it is he has been doing. He and his wife and niece are the principal among a number of characters whose little peculiarities are made much of. But the most successful part of the book is that dealing with the uncle and the young girl. [Macmillan ; Doubleday, Doran, New York ; Grosset, New York.]

—— *Rogue Herries.* 1930
> A romance of Carlisle and Borrowdale in the period 1730–70, with the Forty-Five as the main historical episode. [Macmillan ; Doubleday, Doran, New York.]

WALPOLE, Hugh, and PRIESTLEY, John Boynton. *Farthing Hall.* 1929
> A novel told in a series of letters between a pair of friends : recounting the domestic troubles of the one, and the exciting romance of the other. Some entertaining characters, a mysterious family in the Lake District, a night-club, a fight, are some of the ingredients of this exuberant and amusing collaboration. [Macmillan ; Doubleday, Doran, New York.]

WALTON, Mrs. Octavius Frank. *A Peep Behind the Scenes.* [juvenile] 1877
—— *Christie's Old Organ ; or, Home, Sweet Home.* [juvenile] 1882
> Didactic, tearfully pathetic, and very popular tales for children. The first tells about the hard life of a small girl in a travelling fair ; an old organ-grinder and a boy are the heroes in the next. [(1) and (2), R.T.S. ; (2), Altemus Co., Philadelphia.]

" WARD, Artemus " [Charles Farrar Browne ; American ; 1834–67]. *Artemus Ward ; his book.* 1862
—— *Artemus Ward ; his travels.* 1865
—— *Artemus Ward in London ; and other papers.* 1867
—— *Complete Works.* 1869
> Artemus Ward was a humorist whose distinguishing quality was the ludicrous confusion of sense and non-sense. His sketches of Mormon life and manners, his various travel-sketches, the lectures in which he affected the character of a travelling showman, relating absurd interviews with various notabilities, are all marked by this grotesque incongruity. While his lectures are but the shadows of what they were as delivered by his inimitable self, they are good examples of drollery and humour uncloaking the shams of modern life ; and in print their extravagances are made more ludicrous by the vagaries of spelling and typography. [With Memoir by E. P. Hingston, Dillingham, New York : o.p. ; Chatto ; *His Book*, Hutchinson ; *Selected Works*, Boni, New York, 1924.]

WARD, Mrs. Humphry [Mary Augusta, *née* Arnold ; 1851–1920]. *Robert Elsmere.* 1888
> The most painful side of the spiritual conflict between faith and agnosticism set forth in the life and love of a clergyman, who ultimately leaves the Church. Describes his home education and Oxford career, where he is influenced by various philosophical tutors (Mr. Grey is Prof. T. H. Green), and the sharper struggle when he becomes rector of a parish, and tragedy is added by growing estrangement from his evangelical wife. The psychological analysis is very minute ; the criticism inspired by older German theorists. Preaches a Christianity purified of supernatural accretions. The novel originated in a pamphlet provoked by the Bampton Lecture of the Rev. John Wordsworth, who ascribed " the present unsettlement in religion " to sin (1881). (Mrs. Ward had already published a novel with an educational thesis, *Miss Bretherton* (1885). Miss Bretherton was drawn from the contemporary actress, Mary Anderson.) [Murray ; Macmillan, New York.]

WARD, Mrs. Humphry (*continued*). *The History of David Grieve.* 1892

A study of religious and sociological problems rather than a true novel. David's relations to two women illustrate the pros and cons of lawful marriage and free union; his mental history—revivalism, secularism, socialism, and communism—opens up the broadest questions of the relation between man and man, and between man and God; he ends as an ardent theist or Unitarian. The wild surroundings of a moorland farm in northern Derbyshire and the savage recesses of Kinderscout are brilliantly depicted. David Grieve was drawn from J. R. Lancashire (see Frank Hall's *A Northern Pioneer : the story of J. R. Lancashire*, 1927). [Murray ; Macmillan, New York : o.p.]

—— *Marcella.* 1894

At once a kind of inductive study of modern political and social ideas in their reactions upon character, and a love-novel. Marcella is an able and accomplished woman who desires above all things to be of use, and at first believes the regeneration of the world is to be effected by means of socialism and the sweeping away of plutocratic institutions. In this first act of her history she comes under the influence of a political charlatan advocating socialism, and of a solid young nobleman of Liberal principles. Ultimately she learns by experience that doctrines are of less importance than character and personal action, and doubts whether the social order can be overset for the good of humanity. Dramatic scenes illustrate the game laws, agrarian distress, the struggles of slum-workers in London, after the manner of Kingsley's *Yeast*. [Murray ; Macmillan, New York : o.p.]

—— *The Story of Bessie Costrell.* 1895

A cottage tragedy in five brief acts, in which the author makes effective use of the close knowledge of humble country people of which she had shown glimpses in *Marcella* and elsewhere. A flighty woman is tempted to take from the hoard of a thrifty old labourer, and borrows beyond possibility of repayment. In the crucial scene she is confronted by her puritan husband, the labourer who had trusted her and now sees himself left to chance mercies, and the neighbours who make themselves her judges ; and she commits suicide. [Smith & Elder : o.p.]

—— *Sir George Tressady* [sequel to *Marcella*]. 1896

Continues the development of Marcella, and deals with a young politician, Tressady, in the same minute way. Tressady belongs to the opposition, and the cardinal incident is Marcella's successful attempt, at a critical moment, to win his vote for her husband's party. Too late she finds he is in love with her, and remorse urges her to atone, by her self-devotion, for the involuntary wrong to her husband and to Tressady's selfish and empty wife. The pseudo-hero's death is tragic. [Murray ; Macmillan, New York : o.p. ; Grosset, New York : o.p.]

—— *Helbeck of Bannisdale.* 1898

The tragic loves of a devout Roman Catholic and an agnostic girl. Like the foregoing, a tale of character and of passion, complicated by problems of thought. Both sides of the controversy are treated with sympathy ; Helbeck is a man of the noblest nature, and Roman dogmas, rites, and social agencies are carefully described. A feeling for nature is a vital trait in the heroine's character, and the scenery of the dales and fells between the Lake mountains and the sea plays a strong emotional part. The iron foundries at Barrow figure in one episode of overwhelming pathos. The book was written at Levens Hall, near Kendal, which was, with Sisergh Castle hard by, the original of the scene. [Murray ; Macmillan, New York : o.p.]

—— *Eleanor.* 1900

A more emotional story than the earlier : though the political and social life of modern Italy is studied minutely, the main interest lies in the drama of passion, two women of one character loving the hero, a literary man of high intellectual gifts. An affecting story, culminating in a scene of tragic renunciation. The minor personages comprise many representatives of the ideas, forces, and tendencies working for change in Italy, especially of the antagonism between the Papacy and the Italy of Garibaldi and Cavour. The ambassador was drawn from Lord Dufferin, and the case of Dr. Schell suggested Father Benecke. [Murray ; (Wayfarer's Lib.), Dent ; Harper, New York : o.p.]

—— *Lady Rose's Daughter.* 1903

Less a tendency novel, like the foregoing, than a novel of manners. The story of Lady H. Delafield and Julie Le Breton corresponds (save in the *dénouement*) with the famous episode of Mme du Deffand and Mlle de Lespinasse (see Ste.-Beuve's *Causeries du Lundi*). Several soldiers, statesmen, and other celebrities appear to be sketched in the characters. [Murray ; Harper, New York : o.p.]

—— *The Marriage of William Ashe.* 1905

An adaptation of the story of William Lamb (afterwards Lord Melbourne), Lady Caroline Lamb, and Lord Byron, to the circumstances of a time two generations later. [Murray ; Harper, New York.]

—— *Fenwick's Career.* 1906

A similar handling of the lives of George Romney and Benjamin Haydon, the painters, with one of Mrs. Humphry Ward's finest characters in the beautiful Eugénie de Pastourelles, on whom the love-tragedy hinges. [Murray ; Harper, New York : o.p.]

—— *Diana Mallory.* 1908

A love-drama played out in the sphere of high society and politics which Mrs. Humphry Ward habitually selects, the heroine a blameless and beautiful girl whose mother died under the stigma of murder. The story is, as usual, rather too heavily loaded with ethical problems and edifying solutions to be a perfect work of art. [Murray ; *sub tit. The Testing of Diana Mallory*, Harper, New York.]

—— *Daphne ; or, Marriage à la Mode.* 1909

An arraignment of the American attitude to marriage and divorce, and a picture of smart society in the States that is anything but agreeable. [Cassell : o.p. ; *sub tit. Marriage à la Mode*, Doubleday, New York : o.p. ; Burt, New York : o.p.]

—— *The Case of Richard Meynell.* 1911

A sequel to *Robert Elsmere*, Meynell, the Modernist rector of a country parish, marrying Elsmere's daughter. The history of Meynell's efforts to reform the Church from within, on the lines of a new Protestant

WARD, Mrs. Humphry (*continued*).

reformation, and of the opposition he meets with from an orthodox squire, is mixed up with a scandal connected with his ward, this unfair attempt to discredit him being utilized to enlist the reader's sympathies with his intellectual conflict. [Murray ; Doubleday, New York : o.p.]

—— *The Mating of Lydia.*   1913

Social ideas and social criticism—the evils of irresponsible landlordism, the manias of art-collectors, and the responsibilities of rank and wealth and of character—give extraneous interest to the course of a somewhat mechanical love-story. [Murray ; Doubleday, New York : o.p.]

—— *The Coryston Family.*   1913

An insidious attack on the woman in politics. Lady Coryston brings trouble on herself and her family through her mania for pulling the political wires. [Murray ; Harper, New York.]

—— *Eltham House.*   1915

Brings forward a hundred years and retells under other names the story of Holland House and the marriage troubles of Henry Fox, the first Lord Holland. [Cassell : o.p. ; Hearst, New York : o.p.]

—— *A Great Success.*   1916

A minor story, efficiently told. The success is that of the neglected wife of a literary lion, who snatches him from the toils of a formidable mistress of a salon. [Murray ; Hearst, New York : o.p.]

—— *Lady Connie.*   1916

The scene is the Oxford familiar to the authoress in the early eighties, where the wealthy and accomplished Lady Constance attracts a throng of admirers, to the dismay of her less gifted cousins, and fights her love-duel with a too arrogant suitor, a brilliant young intellectual and doughty athlete, who seems to belong to a more recent generation. [Smith & Elder : o.p. ; Hearst, New York : o.p.]

WARD, Lynd. *God's Man : a novel in woodcuts.*   1930

An interesting experiment : a story told without letterpress by means of more than a hundred pictures. [Cape.]

—— *Madman's Drum.*   1930

A further experiment in the same technique. [Cape.]

WARD, Robert Plumer [1765–1846]. *Tremaine ; or, The Man of Refinement.*   1825

Ward was a legal writer, politician, and society man, of whom Canning said that his law books were as pleasant as novels and his novels as dull as law books. This is a dull novel so far as story goes, though clever in style. It had more than a season's success owing to Ward's familiarity with the political and social circles delineated. [Tegg : o.p.]

—— *De Vere ; or, The Man of Independence.*   1827

A similar novel presenting the character of an ambitious statesman, believed on its appearance to be Canning, but, as the author stated, a composite study of Pitt, Canning, and Bolingbroke. Other characters were more exact portraits, e.g. Lord Mowbray and the Duke of Newcastle. It was a link between the doctrinaire fiction of the late eighteenth century and the political novels of Disraeli. [3 vols., Colburn : o.p. ; Harper, New York : o.p.]

WARD, Mrs. Wilfrid Philip [Josephine Mary, *née* Hope-Scott ; *b.* 1864]. *One Poor Scruple.* 1899

A study on the question of marriage with a *divorcé*, including an intimate delineation of Roman Catholic life and id as, with portraiture of women characters. [Longmans : o.p.]

—— *The Light Behind.*   1903
—— *Out of Due Time.*   1906
—— *Great Possessions.*   1909

Further studies of the problems of life confronting the modern Catholic. Mrs. Wilfrid Ward's handling of intellectual positions and analysis of character put her in the same class of novelist as her namesake, Mrs. Humphry Ward. [(1), Lane ; (2), Longmans ; (3), Longmans ; *sub tit.* House of Mirth, Putnam, New York : all o.p.]

—— *The Job Secretary : an impression.*   1911

The Job Secretary—a lady typist—comes to help a novelist, and the result is a strange incursion of real life into art, and, reciprocally, of artistic insight into a problem of real life. [Longmans, London (o.p.) and New York.]

—— *Not Known Here.*   1921

Remarkable for the character-drawing of an Englishman whose reputed German parentage brings him to grief, whilst he is constrained by regard for others from revealing the truth. [Hutchinson : o.p.]

WARDE, Evelyn B. *Elena.*   1910

Leading characters are Cesare and Lucrezia Borgia, both well studied (1492–1507). [Simpkin : o.p.]

WARE, William [American ; 1797–1852]. *Zenobia ; or, The Fall of Palmyra.*   1836

Letters written from Palmyra by a Roman, depicting the splendours of the desert city and its overthrow by Aurelian. A good historical picture of the life and manners of the early third century (*c.* 225–70) when Paganism and Christianity were at war. The author was a traveller and a scholar, and a Unitarian minister, whose religious views colour his presentation of historical periods. [Burt, New York : o.p. ; Caldwell, Boston : o.p. ; Warne : o.p.]

—— *Aurelian ; or, Rome in the Third Century* [sequel].   1838

First published under the title *Probus*. The persecution of Christians by the Emperor Aurelian (270). [Burt, New York : o.p. ; Estes, Boston : o.p. ; Warne : o.p.]

—— *Julian ; or, Scenes in Judæa.*   1841

The story of Christ and life in the Holy Land ; Herod, Pilate, etc. [Estes, Boston : o.p. ; Warne : o.p.]

WARNER, Charles Dudley [American ; 1829–1900]. *Their Pilgrimage.*   1887

The love-plot a mere thread ; minute and sometimes satirical descriptions of Southern watering-places ; almost a guide-book. [Harper, New York : o.p. ; Low : o.p.]

WARNER, Charles Dudley (*continued*). *A Little Journey in ihe World.* 1889

—— *The Golden House* [sequel]. 1895

The gradual deterioration of a woman who leaves her home in the country to become the wife of a notorious financier in New York. Wealth and the social life that wealth entails in America enervate her spiritual nature. In the Golden House where this pair dwell the reader's attention is concentrated on another couple. Jack Delaney is ruined by this self-indulgent society; but his ruin saves his character. [(1), Harper, New York: o.p.; Low: o.p.; (2), Harper.]

—— *That Fortune.* 1899

New York life, particularly in the financial world, the ins and outs of which are described with minute knowledge. The story is almost buried in detail. [Harper, New York: o.p. All in *Works*, 15 vols. (set), 1904, Sawyer.]

WARNER, Susan ["Elizabeth E. Wetherell"; American; 1819–85]. *The Wide, Wide World.* [juvenile] 1850

Pictures of past life and manners in New England, charged with pious evangelical teaching and with a very lachrymose pathos; the characters and incidents are of a thoroughly homely kind, and depicted with fidelity to the little things of life. [Lippincott, Philadelphia; Burt, New York; Epworth Press; Seeley.]

—— *Queechy.* [juvenile] 1852

A book of similar piety and sentiment. [Lippincott, Philadelphia; Routledge: o.p.]

WARREN, Samuel [1807–77]. *Passages from the Diary of a late Physician.* 1832–8

Twenty-eight of these papers came out in *Blackwood* from 1830 to 1837. Warren had been a medical student at Edinburgh, and was now engaged at the Bar. The work, which has plenty of melodramatic interest and parades its moral purpose, aroused criticism from the *Lancet* for divulging professional secrets. [Routledge (Dutton, New York).]

—— *Ten Thousand a Year.* 1841

A highly coloured sensation novel which once had immense vogue. The object is serious and edifying, but the book is full of extravagant comedy, not much above Theodore Hook's boisterous jesting satire on English legal forms and personages, and of farcical characters like Oily Gammon and Tittlebat Titmouse, the caricature of Lord Brougham as Mr. Quicksilver, and the draper's assistant who gets the £10,000 a year. [Routledge (Dutton, New York): o.p.; Burt, New York; 2 vols., McKay, Philadelphia.]

WARUNG, Price [Australian]. *Tales of Australian Early Days.* 1894

Powerful, grim tales of early convict days, graphically portraying the horrors of the old penal system in Norfolk Island, which made bad men fiends and converted even good men into tyrants. [Sonnenschein: o.p.]

—— *Tales of the Isle of Death.* 1897

A continuation of the author's revelation of the iniquities, brutalities, and grim humours of the transport settlement on Norfolk Island. [Sonnenschein: o.p.]

—— *Half-Crown Bob; and, Tales of the Riverine.* 1898

Stories, mostly of boat-life on the Upper Murray and contiguous rivers, full of raciness, local allusions, and colloquial colonialisms. [Sonnenschein: o.p.]

WASSERMAN, Jacob [German; *b.* 1873]. *Caspar Hauser* (Caspar Hauser: oder die Trägheit des Herzens, 1908). 1928

The fruit of the author's researches into the history of the mysterious "orphan of Europe." Here, not so much the historical aspect of the case is insisted upon, as the symbolical: an innocent being oppressed and crushed by the insensate evil of the world. Like Emanual Quint, Caspar is a simple soul, who seems, as if by some strange power, to evoke all that is best or worst in those with whom he comes into contact. [Transl. by Caroline NEWTON, Liveright, New York.]

—— *The World's Illusion* (Christian Wahnschaffe, 1919). 1921

A grandiose and complicated symbolic novel, ranging from city to city all over Europe and even to Argentina, and from the highest and most exclusive society to the lowest depths, and embracing many groups of characters, whose dramas alternate as in a cinema show. Christian Wahnschaffe, eldest son of a multi-millionaire industrialist, performs a Tolstoyan act of self-abnegation, renouncing name and wealth and submerging himself among the fallen and hopeless. He realizes that the justice of the universe is an illusion, and that the source of evil is in man himself. Only by living with and loving individual fellow-creatures can he even begin to do good. [Transl. by Ludwig LEWISOHN, 2 vols., Harcourt, New York; 1 vol., *id.*, Allen & Unwin.]

—— *Wedlock* (Laudin und die Seinen, 1925). 1926

Discusses the problems of marriage. A lawyer engaged in the divorce-courts becomes entangled with an actress, who draws him away from his normal social circles, until the claims of his conventional life reassert themselves. [Transl. by Ludwig LEWISOHN, Boni, New York; American Book Co.]

—— *World's Ends* (Der Wendekreis I, 1922). 1927

Five strong, deeply ironical, and generally quite characteristic stories, in a clumsy American rendering: e.g. *Golovin* and *Lukardis*. [Transl. by Lewis GALANTIÈRE, Allen & Unwin; Boni, New York. The first story of the original volume is omitted in the translation.]

—— *Oberlin's Three Stages* (Oberlin's 3 Stufen, Der Wendekreis II, 1924). 1926

A psychological study of a German aristocrat driven by his temperament to sexual excess, and only relieved by a breakdown which changes his disposition. Contains also *The Unknown Guest*, and *Sturreganz*, short stories. [Transl. by Allen W. PORTERFIELD, Harcourt, New York.]

—— *Faber; or, The Lost Years* (Faber: oder die verlorenen Jahre, 1925). 1925

A subtle and elaborate study of the mental perturbations and agonies of a man who comes back to his wife at the end of the war after six years' internment in Siberia, and finds her immersed in interests that he cannot understand. She and the women who have cast their influence over her are drawn with a strange, mystical power. [Transl. by Harry HANSEN, Harcourt, New York; Allen & Unwin, 1930.]

WASSERMAN, Jacob (*continued*). *The Triumph of Youth* (Der Aufruhr um den Junker Ernst, 1926). 1927
The revolt of an imaginative and idealistic youth against the religious bigotry and savage superstitions of the Thirty Years' war-time, the period of the "Amber Witch." He is accused of magic practises, and executed. [Transl. by Otto P. SCHINNERER, Boni, New York; Allen & Unwin.]

—— *The Maurizius Case* [Der Fall Maurizius, 1928]. 1929
After eighteen years, the father of the condemned Maurizius and the youthful son of the prosecuting counsel, both convinced of his innocence, succeed in having the case reopened. The investigation involves long and searching conversations between counsel and prisoner, the lawyer's son, who has been compared to Alyosha Karamazov, and a surviving witness; and these have an intellectual interest and a metaphysical significance typical of Herr Wassermann, whose treatment of character and motive is also far-searching. A large, massive, ponderous study of mind and motive. [Transl. by Caroline NEWTON, Liveright, New York; Allen & Unwin.]

"WAST, Hugo" [Gustava Martinez Zuviria; Spanish-Argentine; *b.* 1883]. *Stone Desert* (Desierto de Piedra). 1928
An average specimen of a number of vigorous romances which have won popularity both in Spanish and in translation. [Transl. by Louise IMBERT and Jacques LE CLERC, Longmans, New York and London.]

—— *The Strength of Lovers.* 1930
A romantic tale of the wife of a Conquistador who goes with Cabot to the Argentine in 1526, and who captures the attentions of an Indian chief. [Transl. by Louis IMBERT and Jacques LE CLERC, Longmans, New York and London.]

WATERLOO, Stanley [American; 1846–1913]. *The Story of Ab: a tale of the time of the Cave Man.* 1897
A lively reconstruction of the Stone Age and the life of the cave-men. [Doubleday, New York; Black.]

WATSON, Margaret. *Driven.* 1905
The desperate struggle for life in the west country before the repeal of the Corn Laws. Apparently a novel of purpose and in that sense not unsuccessful. [Unwin: o.p.]

WATTS, Mary [American; *née* Stanbery; *b.* 1868]. *The Tenants: an episode of the '80's.* 1908
A young girl tells of the charms of a Southern family, their balls, theatricals, picnics, and general dissipation— "on tick"—in a delightful old house in the Middle West. [McClure, New York: o.p.]

—— *Nathan Burke.* 1910
A similar picture of old-fashioned life and entertaining character; scene, Ohio during the Mexican war of 1846. [Macmillan, New York; Grosset, New York (1928).]

—— *Van Cleeve.* 1913
A novel of social life and financial affairs in New York, Florida, and Cuba, during the Spanish-American war of the eighteen-nineties. [Macmillan, New York: o.p.]

WATTS-DUNTON, Walter Theodore [1832–1914]. *Aylwin.* 1898
First edn. 1898, but written fourteen years earlier. The idea of the plot of this and *The Coming of Love* is love at war with death, and in both novel and poem the author contends that man, faced by the mysteries of fate, can but believe in the survival of the being he passionately loves. "The renascence of wonder," as he puts it, gives the novel a deeply poetical character, which is intensified by the beauty of the Snowdon chapters and the word-painting of coast scenery. Among the notable men portrayed are Rossetti, William Morris, Smetham, J. A. Symonds, James Orlando Watts, and Alfred Eugene Watts. Hurstcote is Kelmscott Manor. The gipsy heroine Sinfi is drawn from life, and the autobiographical significance of the story is patent. The action ranges from the humorous comedy of Mrs. Gudgeon to the deepest pathos and thrilling intervals of tragic suspense, ending in a scene of ideal reconciliation. [(World's Classics) Oxford Press, 1904.]

WAUGH, Alec [*b.* 1898]. *The Loom of Youth.* 1917
This life of a boy at Fernhurst (Sherborne) is a severe critical assessment of the Public School system, and an inquiry whether it is the best way of training "the future leaders of England" for "the national struggle for a right and far-sighted civilization." The boys themselves are represented as acutely conscious of the evils due to the tyranny of athleticism and the unwholesome despotism of the "bloods." Undeniable facts are massed so as to give an exaggerated impression. [Grant Richards; Cassell.]

—— *Nor Many Waters.* 1928
Mr. Waugh's competent handling of social life in fashionable circles is here directed to a serious theme—the right of a woman to divorce her husband.

—— *"Sir," She Said.* 1930
Is freedom good for the modern woman? The question is mooted but scarcely resolved in the history of one who has a liaison and is left in the lurch, and of her sister who finds a safer lot in marriage and respectability. [Chapman; Farrar, New York.]

WEBB, Mary [Mrs. Henry Bertram Law Webb, *née* Meredith; 1883–1927]. *The Golden Arrow.* 1916
True love is the golden arrow, according to the oft-quoted refrain. This is the story of two pairs of lovers and their fathers and mothers, with a strong didactic element, the contrast between the girls resembling that between Hetty and Dinah in *Adam Bede*, though the flighty maiden, "the slave of sex," gets married, and the deep and serious woman goes off with her lover. The latter's father, the sage and eloquent "Christian pantheist," is an impressive character; the comic ones are shaky constructions.

—— *Gone to Earth.* 1917
A tragic novel, of which the central event is the betrayal of an untrained, wayward, and motherless child of the mountains by a sensual Welsh squireen, and the heroine's ill-fated marriage with a chivalrous but too idealistic and inexperienced minister. There are some gleams of light, such as the poor little heroine's journey in a market-cart to her bridal, and the pen-picture of the wedding itself.

WEBB, Mary (*continued*).   *The House in Dormer Forest.*   1920
Shows up the ugliness of bigoted, pharisaic, materialist religion.   Most of the family in Dormer House are warped
   and stunted by their dull and unimaginative subservience to the convention, law of the herd, which in
   England goes for Christianity.   A repulsive set, overcharged, and drawn with more dislike than humour.
   Over against them are ranged the free-livers, the children of Nature, who are like the forest—" while
   Dormer lived by law, the forest lived by impulse."   Blake would have agreed with this and the other
   sentiments.   But these finely conceived figures are not endued with life : the moulds are beautiful, but
   the material poured in is too thin.
——— *Seven for a Secret.*   1922
Uses much the same stuff, the scenery and local characteristics of Shropshire and the Welsh border, simple,
   rustic people whose moral impulses are scrutinized, as by a Mrs. Gaskell or George Eliot rather than a
   Maria Edgeworth, and an admirable, slightly old-fashioned style that conveys poetical ideas quite as
   adequately as does her verse.   There is always a contrast between the blind and sensual and those whose
   lives are in tune with Nature.   These are exponents of her Wordsworthian philosophy of life, that
   divinity is immanent in the world about us and accessible in its beauty.
——— *Precious Bane.*   1924
Her strongest novel, strong but clumsy.   Gideon Sarn, the one-ideaed egoist, blind to everything but the
   ambition of exploiting his little property of Sarn (in the days of Waterloo and Corn Laws) and buying
   a place in county society, is of the Henchard stamp, but still more like Heathcliff, a natural force, a
   devouring passion, a troll.   The insensate egoist, out of harmony with man and nature, ends in suicide ;
   but, as usual, Mary Webb mitigates the pathos by having a subplot, in which the faithful sister, though
   no more a beauty than Jane Eyre, wins a man who shares her sympathy with the universal life around her.
   [*Collected Works*, Cape ; Dutton, New York.]
——— *Armour Wherein He Trusted.*   1929
A fragment of an historical romance of the time of the First Crusade, together with some sketches and stories—
   the latter inferior in workmanship to her novels.   [With introd. by Martin Armstrong, Cape ; Dutton,
   New York.]

WEBLING, Peggy.   *In Our Street.*   1918
Deals with the " mania of curiosity " in a man devoted to spiritualism, whose wife's happiness is sacrificed to
   his obsession.   [Hutchinson : o.p.]

WEBSTER, Henry Kitchell [American ; b. 1875].   *The Banker and the Bear : the story of a corner
in lard.*   1900
An exciting story of a commercial struggle, interwoven with a love-story.   Throws a strong light on the
   unscrupulous methods of the American business man.   See also p. 343, sub. nom. MERWIN, Samuel.
   [Macmillan, New York : o.p.]
——— *Roger Drake ; captain of industry.*   1902
An exciting business romance about the promotion of a vast combine in copper.   [Macmillan, New York : o.p.]
——— *Traitor or Loyalist ?*   1904
A tale of the blockade in N. Carolina and the excitement of the cotton trade during the Civil War time (1861).
   [Macmillan, New York : o.p.]
——— *The Painted Scene ; and other stories of the theater.*   1916
Ten stories of a second-rate variety-show in Chicago, and the stars, chorus-girls, managers, authors, musical
   directors, and " ponies," the women with their undisciplined impulses and emotions being well anatomized
   and the more sophisticated persons exposed to amusing satire.   The dialogue is in the most advanced
   American.   [Bobbs-Merrill, Indianapolis ; Constable : o.p.]
——— *The Real Adventure.*   1916
That is, marriage itself ; the problem worked out being the relations between husband and wife, and the latter's
   endeavours to justify her existence independent of home and husband.   [Bobbs-Merrill, Indianapolis ;
   Constable : o.p.].   See also MERWIN, S.

" **WEBSTER, Jean** " [Mrs. Alice Jean McKinney, *née* Chandler ; American ; 1876–1916].   *Daddy
Longlegs.*   1912
A rose-coloured romance of a charity-school girl who is adopted and educated by a wealthy patron, told in the
   form of correspondence.   [Century Co., New York ; Hodder.]

WEDGWOOD, A. Felix.   *The Shadow of a Titan.*   1910
Miscellaneous in matter, the middle part dealing with South American incidents and the rest with England.
   Remarkable for the knowledge displayed of practical affairs as well as of literature and science, and for
   the style.   The South American chapters have been compared with Hudson and Cunninghame Graham's
   studies, and favourably.   [Duckworth : o.p. ; Lane, New York : o.p.]

WEDMORE, Sir Frederick [1844–1921].   *Pastorals of France.*   1877
A Last Love at Pornic, Yvonne of Croisic, The Four Bells of Chartres.   Subtle and delicate little studies of sentiment and emotion, by a connoisseur of the mind as well as of art.   The motive in the first is an elderly
   man's love for a girl who would probably accept him, and his conscientious awakening to the probable
   wrong he would commit—a theme treated again in *The Vicar of Pimlico* (see below).   *Yvonne* is a melancholy little piece, rendering picturesquely the sense of utter solitude and remoteness of Croisic and its
   people.   [Mathews : o.p. ; Scribner, New York : o.p.]
——— *Renunciations.*   1893
Three sketches in the same genre, e.g. *A Chemist in the Suburbs*, a character-study in miniature.   All pervaded
   with a refined idealism and a connoisseur's affection for works of art.   [Mathews.]
——— *English Episodes.*   1894
The Vicar of Pimlico, a love chapter in the lives of an elderly man and a young woman ; some humorous
   anecdotes ; and *The New Marienbad Elegy*, a similar episode in soul history, with impressionist descriptions
   of skies and weather at Buxton.   [Mathews : o.p. ; Scribner, New York : o.p.]

WEDMORE, Sir Frederick (*continued*). *Orgeas and Miradou ; with other pieces.* 1896
An imaginative idyll of Provence, and other trifles, rich in landscapes sketched by an impressionist. [New ed., *sub tit. A Dream of Provence*, Pitman : o.p. ; Mosher, New York, 1907.]

—— *The Collapse of the Penitent.* 1900
A psychological narrative of the downward career and tragic end of a woman, who, a talented musician and born a bohemian, is intolerant of the bondage of commonplace wedlock. A flabby and egoistic literary man, who shrinks from the overt crime of betraying her, is morally the agent of her ruin. Full of a connoisseur's *obiter dicta* on music, architecture, and bric-à-brac. [Hutchinson : o.p.]

WELLS, Carolyn [Mrs. Hadwyn Houghton ; American]. *Patty Fairfield.* 1901
A Vassar graduate's amusing account of pranks in college. [Dodd & Mead, New York.]

—— *The Mark of Cain.* 1917
The exploits of Fleming Stone, a Yankee Sherlock Holmes, the American circumstances and American legal methods furnishing an interest of their own. [Lippincott, Philadelphia and London.]

WELLS, Herbert George [*b.* 1866]. *Select Conversations with an Uncle.* 1895
Monologues or " disarticulated essays " by an eccentric Africander, who has a low opinion of the follies and fashions of present-day society. He discusses the *Theory of the Perpetual Discomfort of Humanity, Use of Ideals, The Pains of Marriage.* Also two sketches : *A Misunderstood Artist, The Man with a Nose.* [Lane.]

—— *The Time Machine : an invention.* 1895
A scientific fantasy. The machine transports the owner at will into the past or the future. [Heinemann ; Benn ; Holt, New York.]

—— *The Wonderful Visit.* 1895
The doings of an angel who visits the earth, and is shot by a sporting vicar. [Dent ; Macmillan, New York.]

—— *The Wheels of Chance : a cycling holiday adventure.* 1896
The adventures of a poor, overworked draper on a cycling holiday in Surrey and Sussex. He plays knight-errant to a distressed damsel, his latent goodness and heroism are aroused, and he goes home with new ideas of what is good and worthy in life. [Dent ; Macmillan, New York.]

—— *The Island of Dr. Moreau : a possibility.* 1896
A ghoulish story of an island where beasts are converted by means of vivisection into a semblance of human beings. [Heinemann ; Benn ; Duffield, New York ; Doubleday, Doran, New York.]

—— *The Plattner Story ; and others.* 1897
The title-story is a fantasy in which a young schoolmaster, experimenting with an unknown chemical, is literally blown into the middle of next week. *The Sea-Raiders* imagines the shores infested with terrible octopuses. Among the tales of real life is that grim masterpiece, *The Cone.* [Benn ; Macmillan.]

—— *The Invisible Man ; a grotesque romance.* 1897
A scientist discovers a means to make himself invisible. The tremendous powers he thus acquires are, however, counterbalanced by unexpected disabilities. His first adventures are absurdly comic ; but the invisible man is driven at length to become a terror to his kind, and his last stage is a gruesome tragedy. [Macmillan ; Benn ; Harper, New York.]

—— *The War of the Worlds.* 1898
The inhabitants of Mars, a loathsome though highly organized race, invade England, and by their command of superior weapons subdue and prey on the people. Cleverly parodied in *The War of the Wenuses*, by C. L. Graves and E. V. Lucas (Arrowsmith, Bristol, 1898). [Heinemann ; Benn ; Harper, New York.]

—— *When the Sleeper Wakes.* 1899
A prophetic fantasia picturing London in A.D. 2100. A picture of topsy-turvy institutions and humanity metamorphosed, socially and morally, very much for the worse. [Macmillan ; Benn ; Harper, New York : o.p.]

—— *Tales of Space and Time.* 1899
Miscellaneous stories of the far future and the far past, for example, *A Story of the Stone Age* and *A Story of the Days to Come. The Star* describes the feelings of terrified humanity on the approach of a new star. Like the author's other fantasies, these contain a good deal of serious speculation on the future of mankind, and criticism of society. [Macmillan ; Benn ; Doubleday, New York : o.p.]

—— *Love and Mr. Lewisham.* 1900
The humours of the common lot in the person of a down-trodden usher in a private school, and especially the collapse of his ambitions through the mischance of falling in love and marrying—events which Mr. Wells always envisages as a bit of natural history, not of romance. [Macmillan ; Benn ; Scribner, New York.]

—— *The First Men in the Moon.* 1901
Making one bold postulate, the discovery of a substance that resists gravity, the author depicts, with gruesome imagination, the moon and its plants and inhabitants. [Macmillan ; Benn ; Bobbs-Merrill, Indianapolis : o.p.]

—— *The Sea Lady : a tissue of moonshine.* 1902
The visitant from the " Great Outside," who in this novel turns mundane things topsy-turvy, with absurd consequences, is a mermaid who comes ashore among a bathing-party at Sandgate. The comedy has its serious side in the criticism of our common and ignoble ideals from a far other point of view. [Methuen ; Benn ; Appleton, New York : o.p.]

—— *Twelve Stories and a Dream.* 1903
Contains *The Country of the Blind* and one or two other stories which rank among the finest short stories in English. The first-named is about a traveller's adventures in the Andes which refute the old saw, " In the country of the Blind the one-eyed man is King." [Macmillan ; Benn ; Scribner, New York.]

—— *The Food of the Gods, and How it Came to Earth.* 1904
The food is discovered by two *a priori* scientists, and every man or animal that eats of it grows to the size of a giant, with amusing consequences. [Macmillan ; Benn ; Scribner, New York.]

WELLS, Herbert George (*continued*). *Kipps: the story of a simple soul.* 1905
The comedy of class instincts. Mr. Kipps is a vulgar but estimable little draper's assistant who comes in for money and is taken up by a clique of cultured people. Their attempts to exploit and refine him are related with neat satire ; but the best of the humour is in Kipps himself, who is immensely relieved when he loses the fortune and subsides into his proper niche. This is one of Mr. Wells's most objective novels. But he has written, " I have never once ' presented ' life. My apparently most objective books are criticisms and incitements to change." [Macmillan ; Benn ; Scribner, New York.]

—— *In the Days of the Comet.* 1906
A utopia devised on old lines but inculcating very modern doctrines. The new age comes through the passage of a comet, which changes the earth's atmosphere and regenerates bodies and souls. The usual verbose discussions, and the incidents of a labour struggle and a war with Germany, mixed up with the astronomical drama. There is also a love-story, to illustrate how monogamous love and jealousy are to be superseded by a beautiful promiscuousness. [Macmillan ; Benn ; Scribner, New York.]

—— *The War in the Air ; and particularly how Mr. Bert Smallways fared while it lasted.* 1908
Here a cataclysmal war is the world-event that opens our eyes to fundamental realities. [Collins ; Macmillan, New York.]

—— *Ann Veronica : a modern love story.* 1909
A version of the " Woman who Did " ; very frank about the unruly phenomena of adolescence in the feminine case. Ann Veronica, whose impulses and perplexities are acutely analysed, escapes the penalty of her daring, the lover being set free to marry her respectably and winning an unexpected income as a playwright. Pungent satire of the Suffragettes and their male acolytes, some of whom were easily identified. [Unwin ; Benn ; Harper, New York.]

—— *Tono-Bungay.* 1909
A typical mixture of humorous realism, social criticism, and theory. The autobiographer, George Ponderevo, is the author's mouthpiece, and states his views on education and different grades of schools, and the general lack of organization in capitalistic society. George is the son of a housekeeper, and shows us the old regime from below-stairs. The pushing of a quack medicine, advertising bluffs on the largest scale, company-promoting, financial triumph and catastrophe—all are subservient to this object. [Macmillan ; Benn ; Modern Lib., New York.]

—— *The History of Mr. Polly.* 1910
The career of a young fellow of the same vulgar breed as Kipps, and the same unromantic surroundings, who has the soul of a hero of romance and the dwarfed imagination of a poet. He too falls a victim to the woman intent on marriage, and failing as a small outfitter, burns his boats—or rather his house—and escapes into the unknown, finding his destiny as potman in a village inn. The vulgar scenes are not squalid, but superbly comic, and Mr. Polly's malapropisms are admirable. [Collins ; Duffield, New York.]

—— *The New Machiavelli.* 1911
A pamphleteering study of political and sociological creeds in the guise of a biographical novel, the hero of which gets involved in irregular relations with a young lady, and wrecks his career as an epoch-making M.P. Remington is born and bred at Bromstead, Kent ; Mr. Wells's birthplace was Bromley, Kent. A number of Fabians and other well-known people are thinly caricatured. In *Ann Veronica* and *The New Machiavelli*, and to some extent also in *Tono-Bungay*, Mr. Wells may seem to hasty critics to be assailing the institution of marriage, or at any rate to be singing the praises of free love and the sanctity of passion. His later novel, *Marriage* [Macmillan, 1912], is a recantation, if such were needed, as it illustrates in a very human way the mutual compromises, the give and take, the growth of deeper sympathy, by which a happy marriage union is ultimately built up. It is risky, in short, to imagine that Mr. Wells is always preaching, or to pin our faith to this or that story as his final summing up of the sexual or the social problem. [Collins ; Benn ; Duffield, New York.]

—— *The Country of the Blind ; and other stories.* 1911
Twenty-eight of what Mr. Wells regards as his best short stories—a few appearing here for the first time. They start mostly from a contradiction of ordinary experience or established generalizations, and work out the results mathematically. The sharp, calculated sensationalism makes the process marvellously effective. The four which rise artistically and philosophically high above the rest are, the title-story, *The Door in the Wall, The Beautiful Suit,* and *The Magic Shop.* [*Vide Short Stories, infra.*]

—— *Marriage.* 1912
More debate about religion than about marriage ; but it is marriage that stultifies the man's scientific ambitions, his passion for truth. It is a very ordinary marriage—that is the point. The woman is brought up in the usual way of dull, well-to-do parents ; she is well-meaning but half-educated, and her mere inertia proves too much for the husband's finer aims. Then he throws up everything, and they go to Labrador, where both develop the qualities that have been suppressed, and they come back to England to live the real life. [Macmillan ; Duffield, New York.]

—— *The Passionate Friendship.* 1913
Attacks " the ancient limiting jealousies " that hamper man's work and development. The argument in its fictional form is not quite clear, and it is unfortunate that the supposed autobiographer abandons his intention of giving the whole story to his son. It is the history of what was at first an intellectual friendship, and then, after many years, became an illicit liaison, the ultimate issue being that the lady kills herself to avoid the scandal of a divorce. She is a symbol, she has " identified herself with something world-wide " ; but an even finer lesson might conceivably be deduced. [Macmillan ; Benn ; Cassell ; Harper, New York : o.p.]

—— *The World Set Free : a story of mankind.* 1914
The present fabric of civilization having been entirely destroyed by a great war in which atomic bombs were the chief weapon, the whole world is organized on collectivist lines and all the social and scientific reforms demanded in Mr. Wells's utopias are realized. [Macmillan ; Benn ; Dutton, New York : o.p.]

—— *The Research Magnificent.* 1915
The career of an idealist in search of the spirit of true nobility. [Macmillan.]

WELLS, Herbert George (*continued*). *Mr. Britling Sees it Through.* 1916

A running commentary on the great war and what it meant to himself and those around him, by a social thinker who talks and talks. Mr. Britling does not see the war through, at least in this book, but he does win through to a religion, after his son has been killed. It is a sincere, eloquent, and in many passages a very moving book, which may some day be a valuable document on the attitude of the intelligentsia during this period. [Cassell ; Macmillan, New York.]

—— *The Soul of a Bishop : a novel (with just a little love in it) about conscience and religion, and the real troubles of life.* 1917

Very little story, only that of the bishop's progress from orthodox churchmanship to a creedless " simple and overruling knowledge of God " and the consequent sacrifice of place and prosperity. This is a thoughtful study of the religious problem. [Cassell ; Macmillan, New York.]

—— *Joan and Peter : the story of an education.* 1918

Written in the reconstruction period. An angry arraignment of our educational methods, in the story of two young people born some years before the war, provoking the question, How different would have been the state of Europe had mankind been properly educated ? Primarily, a pamphlet, an English *Emile*, it belongs to propagandist sociology rather than fiction. [Cassell ; Macmillan, New York.]

—— *The Undying Fire : a contemporary novel.* 1919

The story of Job up to date. The Job typifies the human race. He is a Mr. Huss, a great schoolmaster (perhaps studied from Saunderson of Oundle) who is suddenly overwhelmed by a sea of troubles, and can see nothing in the universe but the triumph of evil and the vanity of man's effort to do right. But it is not a discouraging book. The Undying Fire is the spirit of life, and Mr. Huss demands such an education as will consciously and intelligently co-operate with the creative evolution which he believes in as much as does Mr. Bernard Shaw. [Cassell ; Macmillan, New York.]

—— *The Secret Places of the Heart.* 1922

Explores through the medium of conversations with a psycho-analyst the sexual reactions of a wealthy and successful man of affairs, deciding that here is not the true aristocrat of the future, for his personal relations with others rest on an entirely selfish basis, in spite of the subordination of his brilliant talents to the service of society. [Cassell ; Macmillan, New York.]

—— *Christina Alberta's Father.* 1925

Her father, Mr. Preemby, is another of Mr. Wells's stunted middle-class beings who on some accidental removal of accustomed inhibitions reveal the soul and the makings of a hero. He loses his wife, gives up his business, and goes off with his daughter to see the world. A romantic, and a believer in Atlantis, he is easily persuaded at a séance that he is a Sumerian king. Inevitably, this pleasant delusion lands him in an asylum. But the lunatic proves himself great and heroic, all which provides excellent psychological entertainment till the story lapses into general discussion. [Cape ; Macmillan, New York.]

—— *The World of William Clissold.* 1926

An immense three-decker vehicle for the elaboration of Mr. Wells's ideas on art, life, religion—in fact all departments of human life and activity. It is, as he explains, an example of what the novel of the future is to be. Perhaps only the converted will persevere to the end through the whole of Mr. Clissold's world ; Wells's ideas for general reconstruction are summed up in a chapter entitled *The Open Conspiracy*, on the same lines as his book of that title (1928). [3 vols., Benn ; 2 vols., Doubleday, Doran, New York.]

—— *Mr. Blettsworthy on Rampole Island.* 1928

A sub-title some fifteen lines in length gives a fairly accurate synopsis of the contents of this extravagant satire of modern civilization, containing indeed " much amusing and edifying matter concerning manners, customs, beliefs, warfare, crime, and a storm at sea." Blettsworthy goes out of his mind, and creates for himself a world of cannibals and megatheria, only to find, when his senses return, that the real world surpasses this in savagery and superstition. The styles of the creator of Kipps, the weaver of scientific fantasies, and the sociologist, are epitomized in the three sections of the story. [Benn ; Doubleday, Doran, New York.]

—— *The Autocracy of Mr. Parham : his remarkable adventures in this changing world.* 1930

A romance of ideas, especially the idea of big business, which is shown to be the cause of big wars. The academic autocrat Mr. Parham and the vulgar plutocrat Sir Bussy Woodcock between them manage to get a dictatorship established which involves Britain in a world war. The satire is venomous and not always impersonal, and the description of monstrous episodes, such as the mutual destruction of the British and American fleets, in the author's most telling style. [" Assisted pictorially by David Low," Heinemann ; Doubleday, Doran, New York.]

WEMYSS, Mrs. George. *The Professional Aunt.* 1910

—— *People of Popham.* 1911

Both in the *Cranford* manner. Filled with pleasant characters from village life, handsome lovers, nice girls, engaging children—the last drawn with some sentimental pathos. Stories of the rambling sort, dwelling on such things as Mary Howard's humanizing influence on the people of Popham, and bringing in some little farce. Many sayings that are worth treasuring. [(1) and (2), Constable : o.p. ; Houghton, Boston.]

—— *Impossible People.* 1918

Pathetic story of an eccentric yet lovable country clergyman, his wife, adopted daughter, and circle of friends : the merit is in the dialogue and characterization. [Constable : o.p. ; Houghton, Boston.]

WENTWORTH, Patricia [Mrs. G. F. Dillon]. *A Marriage under the Terror.* 1910

Won the 250 guinea prize in a first-novel competition. The heroine marries a revolutionary who loves her, to escape the guillotine, and the pair are brought together after thrilling adventures. Gives excellent pictures of the aristocrats mewed up in the dungeons, and of the murderous trials before Fouquier-Tinville. Danton, Robespierre, Marat, Hébert, and others make their appearance. [Melrose : o.p. ; Putnam, New York : o.p.]

WERFEL, Franz [German-Czech ; b. 1890]. *Verdi : a novel of the opera* (Verdi : Roman der Oper, 1924). 1924

An incident in the life of Verdi at Venice, in 1883. His desire to meet Wagner on friendly terms is frustrated by the latter's sudden death. Another musical composer, Boito, also figures in the story. [Transl. by Helen JESSIMAN, Jarrolds ; Simon & Schuster, New York.]

—— *The Class Reunion* (Der Abituriententag : Die Geschichte einer Jugendschuld, 1928). 1929

Psychological analysis of conduct is made to create a dramatic and tragic situation : a judge, called upon to try the murderer of a prostitute, recalls that the man before him is an old schoolfellow, whom he used to mock and dominate ; and that it is this bullying which was responsible for the man's demoralization. The conclusion is perhaps weakened by the fact that the judge is mistaken in the prisoner's identity. [Transl. by Whittaker CHAMBERS, Jarrolds ; Simon & Schuster, New York.]

WERNER, Miss Alice [South African ; b. 1859]. *The Captain of the Locusts.* 1899

Stories of European and native life in Zambesi and Natal by a lady who spent three years in the country. [Unwin : o.p.]

—— *Chapenga's White Man : a story of Central Africa.* 1901

A careful study of the growth of a little savage from Central Africa into a capable and trustworthy man. The tale is somewhat goody, but Chapenga is a real character, and whether as scapegrace or as a reformed young man engages sympathy. [Chatto : o.p.]

" WERNER, E." [Elise Bürstenbinder ; German ; 1838–1918]. *Hermann* (Hermann, 1872). 1879

Story of a young count and the girl he loves, illustrating the thesis that a curse descends on the children from the father's sins. In the end the cloud that overshadows their courtship is lifted, the sins are expiated, and a tragic conclusion is averted. [Transl., Remington : o.p.]

—— *At the Altar* (Am Altar, 1873). 1872

Protestantism versus Catholicism : the struggle in the mind of a young man trained in the priesthood from infancy, though one of his parents was a Protestant. Ultimately he throws up his vows and marries. [Lippincott, Philadelphia : o.p. ; transl. by Mrs. PARKER, 2 vols., Low (1878) : o.p.]

—— *Success : how he won it* (Glück auf, 1874). 1876

A picture of Labour struggles, and a sentimental study of the growth of respect and affection between a well-born wife and a parvenu husband, a mine-owner whose character is tried and strengthened by circumstances. [Transl. by Christina TYRRELL, Macmillan : o.p. ; by F. A. SHAW, sub tit. Good Luck, Burt, New York (1874).]

—— *Riven Bonds* (Gesprengte Fesseln, 1875). 1877

A story of matrimonial rupture, which ends satisfactorily. [Transl. by Bertha NESS, Ward & Lock : o.p.]

—— *Vineta* (Vineta, 1877). 1877

Patriotic antagonism at odds with love ; a German junker and a Polish countess are the two chief characters, and the scene is laid on the borders of Poland and Prussia. There is an ingenious plot, and a good deal of character-drawing of local and national types. [Transl. by F. A. SHAW, Dana Estes, Boston : o.p.]

—— *Banned and Blessed* (Gebannt und erlöst, 1884). 1884

A weird romance ; the principal figure a great German noble, who lives in his lonely stronghold, and is hated by all on account of a sinister mystery. All is cleared up eventually, a great flood being the instrument of poetic justice. [Transl. by Mrs. A. L. WISTER, Lippincott, Philadelphia : o.p.]

—— *St. Michael* (St. Michael, 1887). 1887

Mainly the life-story of a steadfast young man, unacknowledged grandson of a count in north Germany, of his hard struggle with adversity, his moral growth, his love, marriage, and worldly success. [Transl., Burt, New York.]

WESCOTT, Glenway [American ; b. 1901]. *The Apple of the Eye.* 1926

Three stages in the growth of a high-strung boy, on a farm in the author's native Wisconsin, related with keen imagination, a feeling for mood, and a poet's sense of natural environment. [Harper, New York ; Butterworth.]

—— *A Family Portrait.* 1927

The family chronicle of the Towers through several generations, set down from his own memory and others' reminiscences by a descendant who has an intense passion for bygone things. The Western movement and their settlement in the wilderness, the Civil War, and the gradual modernization of the primitive country and the crude towns, form the great historical panorama against which the more intimate drama is played—the tangled family relations, the loves, hates, rivalries. A refined insight and a deep sense of the tragedy of life make this a profound book. American title, The Grandmothers. [Harper, New York ; Butterworth.]

—— *Good-bye, Wisconsin.* 1928

A collection of short stories aiming to capture the spirit of Wisconsin life. The book seems to voice the author's regrets, and some measure of disillusionment. [Harper, New York ; Cape.]

" WEST, Rebecca " [Mrs. H. M. Andrews ; née Fairfield ; Irish ; b. 1892]. *The Return of the Soldier* 1918

A psycho-analytical novel. The returned soldier has had shell-shock and lost the memory of his pre-war life ; he fails to pick up the threads of his domestic relations and business affairs, and lives in a dream-land with a child-love of the past. Eventually his mind is healed by a Freudian expert. [Nisbet : o.p. ; Doubleday, Doran, New York.]

—— *The Judge.* 1922

This is very similar ; it is an illustration of the working of the Œdipus complex. Like Lawrence's young fellow in *Sons and Lovers*, the principal character is subconsciously so wrapped up in his mother, that the latter foresees trouble between him and the woman he is to marry. Tragedy is the keynote of the story from beginning to end. [Hutchinson : o.p. ; Doubleday, Doran, New York.]

WESTALL, William [1834–1903]. *The Old Factory.* 1881
A capital Lancashire story, in which the riots on the introduction of steam weaving-looms are well described. [Chatto : o.p.]

—— *With the Red Eagle.* 1897
—— *A Red Bridal.* 1898
Two war and adventure stories, centring in the career of Hofer and the Tyrolese stand against Napoleon in 1809. [(1), Chatto ; (2), *id.* : o.p.]

WESTCOTT, Edward Noyes [American ; 1847–98]. *David Harum : a story of American life.* 1898
A desultory book unified by the personality of an old banker, David Harum, a man shrewd but illiterate, more ready to cheat than to be cheated, who is averred to be a correct representation of the Yankees of rural New York. His invincible shrewdness and pawky humour, his sayings flavoured with " horse slang," made an immediate hit as a revelation of local character. [Appleton, New York and London ; Pearson ; Collins.]

WESTON, Miss Jessie Laidlay. *The Soul of the Countess.* 1900
Fairy-tales and the like by a well-known writer on comparative mythology. The title-story is a variation on the *Undine* motive ; *Our Lady of the Forest* is a supernatural tale of Crusading days ; and *The Last Valkyr* exploits the field of Scandinavian mythology. [Nutt : o.p.]

WEYMAN, Stanley John [1855–1928]. *The House of the Wolf.* 1890
A swashbuckler romance, dealing with the massacre of St. Bartholomew (1572). A grim and pitiless giant woos the beloved of a Huguenot, and seeks his life. An effort in the style of Scott, improved upon less with the art of Stevenson than with that of Dumas. [Longmans, London and New York ; Altemus Co., Philadelphia.]

—— *The Story of Francis Cludde.* 1891
A romance, in Dumas' style, of the times of Bloody Mary (1555–8). A sturdy young Protestant, slow-tongued but quick to act, tired of persecution, goes forth to win fame by a career of adventure. [Longmans, New York : o.p.]

—— *A Gentleman of France.* 1893
An excellent specimen of Mr. Weyman's historical fiction ; the hero is a Huguenot Breton (1588–9), one of Condé's veterans, flouted for his poverty and mean appearance by the courtiers. But in an important and delicate commission he acquits himself so valiantly that he wins the love of his beautiful charge, a noble kinswoman of Turenne. The writer's knowledge and accuracy, his careful reproduction of historical atmosphere, and his gifts as a story-teller, are nowhere better illustrated. [Longmans, London and New York ; Harrap.]

—— *The Man in Black.* 1894
A brief and workmanlike story of adventure and intrigue in Louis XIII's time (1636). [Longmans, New York : o.p.]

—— *Under the Red Robe.* 1894
A similar novel dealing with Béarn about 1630. An adventurer of clouded reputation is sent on a treacherous mission by Richelieu, but falls in love with the sister of the man he has to betray. He redeems his character by liberating the prisoner and giving himself up to the Cardinal. [Murray ; Longmans, New York.]

—— *My Lady Rotha.* 1894
Opens in Thuringia during the Thirty Years' War (1632), the love-story of the Countess Rotha is of secondary interest to the descriptions of strife and adventure that illustrate the devastation and demoralization of Germany overrun by mercenaries and thieves. [Ward & Lock ; Longmans, New York.]

—— *From the Memoirs of a Minister of France.* 1895
Stories in the time of Henry of Navarre (*c.* 1598–1610). [Longmans, New York : o.p.]

—— *The Red Cockade.* 1895
Adventures during the French Revolution, related by an aristocrat in sympathy with the people. Scene, Cahors and Nîmes (1789). [Longmans, London and New York.]

—— *Shrewsbury.* 1898
Deals with the inner history of Sir John Fenwick's Jacobite plot, and with other incidents of the English Revolution and the subsequent years (1688–1713). Many of the characters are cowards, bullies, and scoundrels, e.g. Robert Ferguson, " the Plotter," and the informer Matt Smith ; but the famous Duke of Shrewsbury is more attractively portrayed. [Longmans, London and New York ; (Wayfarer's Lib.) Dent.]

—— *The Castle Inn.* 1898
A tale of society and manners at Marlborough in the last days of Chatham, with descriptions of an abduction, a rescue, and other episodes of travelling during the period (1767). [Murray ; (Wayfarer's Lib.) Dent ; Longmans, New York.]

—— *Sophia.* 1900
Intrigue and social comedy in 1742. The wayward hoyden Sophia is nearly ruined at the hands of an Irish adventurer, and saved by the hero, another of the author's middle-aged gentlemen who, after many vicissitudes, win the heroine's love by sheer force of integrity and courage. The chapter " King Smallpox " shows true dramatic power. [Longmans, London and New York.]

—— *Count Hannibal : a romance of the Court of France.* 1901
Very similar to the foregoing ; ingenious and exciting as a story, not of much account as drawing of character. The massacre of St. Bartholomew (1572) is the central historical episode, and the manners and atmosphere of contemporary France are vividly reproduced. Count Hannibal is another of the somewhat unprepossessing heroes ; his bravery and magnanimity are supposed to atone for his violence and passion in the estimation of his lady-love—and of the reader. [Longmans, New York.]

WEYMAN, Stanley John (*continued*). *In Kings' Byways : short stories.* 1902
The struggles of the League and the Huguenots, Henry IV, the Duke of Guise, Cardinal Mazarin, and similar historical subjects, dealt with in the usual fashion. [Murray ; Longmans, New York.]

—— *The Long Night.* 1903
A romance of 1602–6, culminating in the famous Escalade, when D'Aubigné's Savoyards attempted to capture Geneva in time of peace. More character-drawing than usual : the Machiavellian Basterga and the treacherous syndic, bribed by the elixir vitæ, are subtle creations—the latter a departure from history, for Blondel was an honest man. [Longmans ; (Wayfarer's Lib.) Dent ; McClure, New York : o.p.]

—— *The Abbess of Vlaye.* 1904
France at the end of the sixteenth century, the plot hinging on the reduction of one of the last strongholds of revolt, Vlaye, when Henry IV has all but accomplished the settlement of the kingdom. [Longmans, London and New York ; (Wayfarer's Lib.) Dent.]

—— *Starvecrow Farm.* 1905
Touches on the industrial agitation after the great war, the Peterloo massacre and the Cato Street conspiracy (1819). But the adventures of the indiscreet and unfortunate heroine have little to do with history. [Murray ; (Wayfarer's Lib.) Dent ; Longmans, New York.]

—— *Chippinge.* 1906
Story of a reformer, a rather wrong-headed young man under a cloud, who, like so many of Mr. Weyman's heroes, wins approval by his conduct in a trying emergency. Time of the second Reform Bill (1831), Brougham, Wetherell, etc. Scenes, Malmesbury and Bristol, where the riots make a striking episode. [Murray ; (Wayfarer's Lib.) Dent ; *sub tit. Chippinge Borough,* McClure, New York : o.p.]

—— *The Wild Geese.* 1909
A novel of Kerry and an abortive rising (*c.* 1715), the chief figure a loyal Colonial, who meets with many exciting adventures. Irish critics do not accept the historical presentment of the times. [Doubleday, New York : o.p.]

—— *The Great House.* 1919
Social and more especially political life in the counties—principal scene Staffordshire—during the Corn Law agitation ; the novel ends with the repeal (1845). [Murray ; Longmans, New York.]

—— *Ovington's Bank.* 1922
Well depicts the state of the country in the great era of railways at the beginning of Victoria's reign. Scenes, on the borderland of Wales. [Murray ; Longmans, New York.]

—— *The Traveller in the Fur Cloak.* 1924
Adventures of an English emissary of the Foreign Office carrying dispatches to Austria after Napoleon's victory at Wagram (1809). [Longmans, New York.]

—— *Queen's Folly.* 1925
Not much history, but a careful study of life in Hampshire about 1805. [Murray ; Longmans, New York.]

—— *The Lively Peggy.* 1928
About a naval officer during the Napoleonic period, who is dismissed the service for drunkenness but redeems his honour as commander of a privateer. Lacks the go of earlier work. [Murray ; Longmans, New York.]
[*Works,* Thin Paper Ed., 23 vols., (excluding *The Traveller in the Fur Cloak,* and *The Lively Peggy*), Murray (new ed. 1929).]

WEYSSENHOFF, Józef [Polish ; *b.* 1860]. *The Sable and the Girl* (Soból i panna. Cykl myśliwska). 1929
The hunting scenes and the pictures of wild life in Poland are more likely to interest the English reader than the confusing story of the two hunting friends, and of the social disturbance caused by one of them who marries a peasant girl. [Transl. by Kate ZUK-SKARSZEWSKA, Allen & Unwin ; Poland, New York.]

WHARTON, Edith [Newbold, *née* Jones ; American ; *b.* 1862]. *The Greater Inclination.* 1899
Eight clever studies in the art of story-telling, dissecting various phases of social life in fashionable New York and around ; e.g. *A Coward* and *Souls Belated.* On the whole, sardonic and sad, yet not devoid of humorous relief. [Scribner, New York ; Lane.]

—— *A Gift from the Grave.* 1900
An episode in a man's moral life studied as a psychological problem. In order to win the woman he loves he sells the love-letters written to him by a distinguished lady. Later, as his better nature reasserts itself, he realizes with bitter remorse the contemptible meanness of his act. [Murray.]

—— *Crucial Instances.* 1901
Various : the American stories in the style of Messrs. James and Howells ; e.g. *Recovery, Copy,* and *The Angel at the Grave* touch on the ways of authors and the humours of the literary life. The others are of a different type. Art is of more moment than the subject in these studied essays in the short story. [Scribner, New York ; Murray.]

—— *The Valley of Decision.* 1902
A very long and slow-moving novel about a north Italian duchy (1774–95). The education and young manhood of the heir-presumptive, who assimilates Rousseau, Voltaire, and Diderot, and tries to establish a constitution, afford an elaborate study of temperament, intellect, and will during the struggle of ideas before the French Revolution. [Scribner, New York ; Murray : o.p.]

—— *Sanctuary.* 1903
A penetrating study of some difficult problems in casuistry. A woman of fine instincts marries a man whose moral nature she has found lacking, and tries to save her son from the consequences of the taint which he has inherited. The analysis of temperament is very keen. [Scribner, New York ; Macmillan ; Appleton.]

—— *The Descent of Man ; and other stories.* 1904
Mostly ironical. The man who descends is a learned professor whose clever squib at the expense of pseudo-science is taken so seriously, and brings in such big cheques, that he is tempted to join the crowd of

WHARTON, Edith (*continued*).

> sentimental religious book-makers. *The Other Two* are the previous husbands of a *divorcée*, who by the accidents of circumstance hobnob with her present adoring spouse. This unfortunate gentleman finds at last that there is nothing in her but what his predecessors have left. *Expiation* makes rather heavy game of the fact that nothing causes a book to sell better than an attack upon its morals. *The Lady Maid's Bell* is an effort in the Henry James style of ghost-story. [Scribner, New York ; Appleton.]

—— *The House of Mirth.* 1905

> Paints with harsh, metallic brilliance the garish life of the fastest and most exclusive set in New York society : the title ironical. The coarse and empty-headed husbands and their giddy and spiteful womankind, said to compose this social world, are monstrously alive. The beautiful and expensive but moneyless girl, adrift on this perilous sea, and the wishy-washy hero who fails to rescue her from her innocent entanglements, are not so easy to believe in. [*Illus.*, Scribner, New York ; Appleton.]

—— *Madame de Treymes.* 1907

> Short and compact, a characteristic novelette, detailing the sentimental and the diplomatic preliminaries to an alliance between a New Yorker and his countrywoman in Paris who had married into the French *noblesse*. [Scribner, New York ; Macmillan ; Appleton.]

—— *The Fruit of the Tree.* 1907

> A pleasure-loving woman is married to a strong, conscientious man with his heart set on social and economic reforms. Their estrangement is intensified by the advent of a woman fitted in every way to be his mate. The resulting situations are examined with microscopic analysis ; but the interest culminates in an agonizing problem of moral responsibility : whether a nurse—who happens to be the rival—is justified in cutting short the sufferings of the other woman, who has been terribly and hopelessly injured in an accident. [Scribner, New York ; Macmillan : o.p. ; Appleton.]

—— *The Hermit and the Wild Woman ; and other stories.* 1908

> The title-story is a piece of glowing imagination staged in Italy in the Middle Ages. The other six are American stories, masterly as ironical portraiture of our sophisticated civilization, and, without exception, depressing in motive. [Scribner, New York ; Macmillan : o.p. ; Appleton.]

—— *Tales of Men and Ghosts.* 1910

> Ten ingenious, bizarre, improbable stories making capital out of strange psychological situations. *The Bolted Door* is about a man whose avowal of an actual murder is received as the effect of hallucination. In *His Father's Son*, a humdrum man, with a secret thirst for romance, carries on a compromising correspondence in his wife's name with a lover. *The Debt, The Legend,* and *Full Circle* all deal with writers or thinkers and the accidents of fame, discipleship, etc. *The Eyes* is a ghost-tale, and *Afterward* a better one. [Scribner, New York ; Macmillan : o.p.]

—— *Ethan Frome.* 1911

> Recalls Hawthorne in his sternest and most tragic moods, but the method is Henry James's. A poverty-stricken, soul-stinted farmer, married to an older woman, in a bleak upland village of puritan Massachusetts, comes by imperceptible degrees to love the youthful cousin living with them as their household help. Our sympathies are sought for the lovers ; and eventually tragedy of a peculiarly horrible nature demands even more. [Scribner, New York ; Nash.]

—— *The Reef.* 1912

> A moral entanglement analysed in the detached and purely æsthetic manner of James. The favoured candidate for the hand of an American lady in France finds that her stepson has become engaged to a young woman with whom he has himself had an affair. Their secret is detected. The drama of feeling in a group of hypersensitive minds is elaborated in the minutest detail, the weak spot being the character of the man responsible for the whole predicament. He is too obviously a construction of the feminine psychologist. [Appleton, New York and London ; Macmillan.]

—— *The Custom of the Country.* 1913

> This lengthy novel is almost a comprehensive treatise on the American problem of marriage and divorce. Undine, Mrs. Wharton's hard and empty adventuress, with no fortune but her face, is married and divorced with unblushing frequency and dispatch, and her vulgar ambitions meet with rebuffs in various social spheres. The lesson implied is that the American system of keeping the women as ornaments and luxuries with no interest in the business of life is what demoralizes them. [Scribner, New York ; Appleton ; Macmillan.]

—— *Xingu ; and other stories.* 1916

> *Xingu* is a sarcastic study of literary snobbishness. The other six are stories of a pathetic or tragic turn. One of the most touching is *Bunner Sisters,* of two elderly milliners in New York. Irony of a rueful kind is the keynote of *Autres Temps*—the change of attitude in America towards divorce ;—*Coming Home*—a young Frenchman's return to his home in the Vosges after the war ;—and *The Long Run*—how two lovers sacrifice happiness to their scruples of conscience. *Kerfol* is a ghost-story, after James, picturesquely centred in a Breton château. [Scribner, New York ; Appleton ; Macmillan.]

—— *Summer.* 1917

> Another tragic story of the cabined and confined village life of puritan New England. Charity Royall is a figure of suffering entitled to stand beside Ethan Frome. [Appleton, New York and London ; Macmillan.]

—— *The Marne : a story of the War.* 1918

> A brief story in which the admiration of the French spirit acquired during her war-work in Paris is expressed through the medium of the American boy wounded at the Marne. The steady change of sentiment among average Americans is also deftly indicated. [Appleton, New York and London ; Macmillan.]

—— *The Age of Innocence.* 1920

> A drama of thwarted affection and changing manners in New York society in the eighteen-seventies, the age of propriety and inexorable convention. A woman who has incurred scandal and the man who loves her have to submit ; her reappearance only serves to hurry on the marriage which is the knell of their happiness. The man is an admirable, if perhaps too restrained, study of feeling, and competes in interest

WHARTON, Edith (*continued*).

with the case of the lady, who has become far too much Europeanized for this still old-fashioned American world. [Appleton, New York and London ; Grosset, New York.]

—— *The Glimpses of the Moon.*   1922

Two impecunious members of the pleasure-seeking, divorce-ridden crowd who flit from Venice to Rome, and from Rome to Paris and London, contract to marry for as long as their money and their friends' hospitality hold out. But the man has a sense of honour, and cannot stand some shady acts of hers. They separate, and are about to set each other free, when sentiment is too much for them. [Appleton, New York and London.]

—— *The Children.*   1928

An alarming view of the plight of the children of divorced rich people. Seven youngsters are allowed to run wild by a group of married and remarried people, living more or less promiscously in the vulgar cosmopolitan set who bathe and sport expensive frocks on the Lido. They are mothered by a child of barely sixteen, whose mingled innocence and precocious maturity is a feat of psychological portraiture. There is interest beyond the didactic purpose also in the man who befriends these waifs and the lady who cannot reconcile his position with her sense of propriety. [Appleton, New York and London ; Grosset, New York.]

—— *Certain People.*   1930

Two stand a little above the rather mediocre level of these six stories : *Atrophy* and *The Refugees.* The first is on the discomfiture of a married lady who imprudently rushes to the deathbed of her lover. The other is how an American became involved in the stream of Belgian refugees. [Appleton ; New York and London.]

—— *Hudson River Bracketed.*   1930

A sense of dissatisfaction with the shallowness and futility of American life to-day, seems to underlie this study of a novelist who learns by suffering, and who also realizes at last that he can have perfect intimacy only with the characters he has imagined, the real ones ever retaining something inscrutable. [Appleton.]

WHARTON, James B. [American]. *Squad.*   1928

A record of eight men of the American Expeditionary Force, from spring until the November of 1918, when only one remained alive. [Coward McCann, New York : Lane.]

WHATELY, Archbishop Richard [1787–1863] (ed.). *Selected Tales of the Genii.*   1840

Revised, purified, and in part remodelled, from James Ridley's *Tales of the Genii,* transl. (from the Persian) by "Sir Charles MORRELL" (1825). [(Bohn's Lib)., Bell : o.p. ; Macmillan, New York : o.p.]

WHEELWRIGHT, Edith Gray. *Anthony Graeme.*   1895

A New England story, with familiar types of character ; motive, the unforeseen growth of love in an intellectual and unimpassioned nature. [Macmillan : o.p.]

WHERRY, Edith. *The Wanderers on a Thousand Hills.*   1918

A romantic, racy, poetic story, that portrays the Chinese soul ; saturated with the learning, the mysticism, the feeling towards the material and the ideal world, characteristic of the educated Chinaman. [Lane.]

WHISHAW, Frederick J. *A Boyar of the Terrible : a romance of the Court of Ivan the Cruel, first Tsar of Russia.*   1896

A tale of adventure, giving a sketch of Ivan's lawless boyhood and tyrannical reign. Ivan loves the woman who becomes the hero's wife, and there is bitter enmity between them. Brings in Ivan's commercial relations with England, and the acquisition of Siberia (1544–84). [Longmans : o.p.]

—— *Near the Tsar, Near Death.*   1903

The unpleasant story of Peter the Great's relations with his hopeless son Alexis, who is ultimately put to death (1718). [Chatto.]

—— *A Splendid Impostor.*   1903

The story of the false Dmitri (1603–5), who impersonated the murdered son of Ivan the Terrible, and backed up by the Poles, supported also, it is said, by a Jesuit conspiracy to introduce Roman Catholicism, actually attained the crown of the Tsars, but was murdered by the Boyars. Mr. Whishaw has written a large number of readable romances of Russian history suitable for young people. [Chatto : o.p.]

WHITBY, Beatrice Jeanie [Mrs. Philip Hicks]. *Mary Fenwick's Daughter.*   1894

—— *Bequeathed.*   1900

Quiet domestic fiction and studies of womanhood, inspired by elevated ideals of conduct and of personal relations. In the second, an immaculate wife bequeaths a daughter to her husband. His marriage with a disagreeable woman, and the daughter's love-tale, are the chief matters. [(1) and (2), Hurst : o.p. ; (2), Harper, New York : o.p.]

WHITE, Edward Lucas [American ; b. 1866]. *Andivius Hedulio : adventures of a Roman Nobleman in the days of the Empire.*   1921

A nobleman, to escape the vengeance of Commodus, lives for some years as a slave. In his wanderings and the startling adventures which rain thick and fast upon his head, we are introduced to many aspects of contemporary domestic and lower-grade life, both in Rome and the provinces ; this, coupled with the racy American flavour of the hero's speech and bearing, produces an historical thriller at once instructive and ludicrous. [Dutton, New York ; Unwin.]

WHITE, Eliza Orne [American ; b. 1856]. *Miss Brooks.*   1890

Social life in Boston, and the fortunes of a small group of people. Ordinary life recorded with an eye for its humours, without idealization. [Houghton, Boston.]

—— *Winterborough.*   1892

A story of a small town in New England, with some study of character, and dialogue marked by smartness and repartee. [Houghton, Boston.]

—— *The Coming of Theodora.*   1895

Theodora has almost every excellence save tactful sympathy, and with this defect her generous efforts to

WHITE, Eliza Orne (*continued*).
assist her brother's family fail. A little comedy with Theodora's attractive person for its chief subject, that at the end turns to tragedy. [Houghton, Boston; Murray.]

—— *A Browning Courtship ; and other stories.* 1897
Browning-mania and other crazes and ineptitudes delicately satirized—e.g. *A Bismarck Dinner* and *The Queen of Clubs*. [Houghton, Boston: o.p.; Smith & Elder: o.p.]

—— *A Lover of Truth.* 1898
A study of local manners ; the virtuous and refined but colourless aristocracy of an old-fashioned country-town in New England is here drawn with a scrupulous exactness and quiet humour. [Houghton, Boston: o.p.; Murray.]

—— *The Wares of Edgefield.* 1909
The slight difficulties of married life in a young doctor and a rather conventional girl from Boston, and the difficulties of their children in their love affairs. Contrasts of life in town and country—Edgefield is apparently a little place in New Hampshire. [Houghton, Boston.]

WHITE, Percy [*b.* 1852]. *A Millionaire's Daughter.* 1899
A comedy of modern society life, with some humorous situations of love at cross purposes and smart epigrammatic dialogue. [Nash: o.p.]

—— *The West End.* 1900
A satire on smart society, its supposed vulgarity, loose morals, and frivolity, put in the mouth of a cynical parasite to a millionaire grocer, who buys his entry into the drawing-rooms of fashionable people through the services of an aristocratic but impecunious lady. [Sands: o.p.; Harper, New York: o.p.]

—— *The Grip of the Bookmaker.* 1901
Chief figure, a retired bookmaker with a shady past, engaged in a social vendetta with a proud colonel, whose daughter is loved by his son. Exploits the social stratum where mere respectability is in close contact with wealth and fashion, and portrays a number of vulgar people. [Hutchinson: o.p.; Fenno, New York: o.p.]

—— *Mr. Strudge.* 1908
An amusing satire on a coterie of " Pretorian " socialists, and a savage caricature on a young man taken by them from a greengrocer's shop to become an apostle, who tells the story himself, and, like Barry Lyndon, exposes his own heartlessness and hypocrisy. [Nash: o.p.]

WHITE, Stewart Edward [American ; *b.* 1873]. *The Westerners.* 1901
A story of the Western plains in the days of frontier wars with the Sioux. The character most fully portrayed is a detestable half-breed, whose ruthless crimes well deserve the horrible end that befalls him. [Doubleday, Doran, New York; Constable: o.p.]

—— *The Claim Jumpers.* 1901
Love-story of a young New Yorker and an unconventional girl in a Western mining district. [Doubleday, Doran, New York; Hodder: o.p.]

—— *The Blazed Trail.* 1902
Realistic account of logging or timber-getting in Michigan, with some adventure and the excitements of a struggle against a powerful firm. [Doubleday, Doran, New York; Constable.]

—— *Conjurer's House : a romance of the free forest.* 1903
The rivalry between the Hudson Bay Company and the free traders in the far North-west. Realistic pictures of the woodman, the factor, the Indian, etc., with a thrilling story of passion and adventure, a captured free trader being rescued by the factor's daughter. [McClure, New York: o.p.; Methuen.: o.p.]

—— *The Magic Forest : a modern fairy story.* 1903
About a boy who spent a summer with a tribe of Canadian Indians. [Macmillan, New York.]

—— *The Silent Places.* 1904
—— *Blazed Trail Stories ; and, Stories of the Wild Life.* 1906
—— *The Pass.* 1906
—— *Arizona Nights.* 1907
—— *The Riverman.* 1908
Present, with a most compelling magic, the real feeling of life in the vast solitudes of Michigan, north-west Canada, or the deserts and sierras of Arizona, the strain of the silence and loneliness, the desperate struggle with nature, and the characters that are tested and forged by the ordeals of such experiences. The story element in Mr. White's books sinks to insignificance beside the intense picturing of nature and the life of man. As a passionate observer he is at least the equal of Mr. C. G. D. Roberts, or Mr. Thompson Seton, and his technical knowledge of lumbering, trapping, Indian life, etc., is apparently unerring. [(1)–(5), Doubleday, Doran, New York; Hodder.]

—— *Rules of the Game.* 1910
A characteristic story of a Western forest reserve and the lumbering camp. [Doubleday, Doran, New York; Nelson.]

—— *Gold : a tale of the forty-niners.* 1913
The gold rush of 1849, scenes Panama and California. [Doubleday, Doran, New York; Hodder: o.p.]

—— *The Grey Dawn.* 1915
California in 1852 and thereafter. To cope with the turbulence and law-breaking described in the former book the San Franciscans had now set up a vigilance committee. [Doubleday, Doran, New York; Hodder: o.p.]

—— *The Rose Dawn.* 1920
An account of the Californian ranches in the last century, when the larger estates were being broken up by mortgages. Colonel Peyton, aristocratic, poor, and proud, and Kenneth Boyd, representing the new and younger spirit of enterprise, are the main characters. [Doubleday, Doran, New York; Hodder: o.p. The last three together entitled *The Story of California*, (1927), 1 vol., Doubleday, Doran, New York (also 3 vol. ed., same).]

WHITE, Stewart Edward (*continued*). *Daniel Boone, Wilderness Scout : the life story and true adventures of the great hunter, Long Knife, who first blazed the wilderness trail through the Indian country to Kentucky.*   1922
    An imaginative life of the famous pioneer who was the original of Fenimore Cooper's Hawkeye or Natty Bumppo (*c.* 1760–1800). [Doubleday, Doran, New York ; Hodder.]

—— *The Glory Hole.*   1924
    Life in a Middle West town in the eighties ; the story turns upon an inheritance, and the fulfilment of an ambitious woman's craving for social dominance. [Doubleday, Doran, New York ; Hodder : o.p.]

—— *Back of Beyond.*   1927
    An exciting account of big-game hunting in South Africa ; first appeared in the *Saturday Evening Post.* [Doubleday, Doran, New York.]

WHITE, Walter Francis [American ; *b.* 1893]. *The Fire in the Flint.*   1924
    A serious indictment of the injustice and social persecution of the negro in the South—the tragic story of a coloured doctor of high moral character in Atlanta, who is lynched by the savages of the Ku Klux Klan when leaving the house of a white woman whose child he has saved from death. [Knopf, New York ; Williams & Norgate.]

WHITE, William Hale [" Mark Rutherford," *alias* " Reuben Shapcott " ; 1831–1913]. *The Autobiography of Mark Rutherford.*   1881
    A sombre, thoughtful book—the history of a doubter, who has a strain of Bunyan's morbid self-consciousness. Beginning as an Independent minister in the eastern midlands, he passes through phases of Unitarianism to a vague theism, and finally to agnosticism and stoical resignation. In a sense, it is not only the story of his mental conflicts but also of the various currents of thought that moulded religious and philosophic attitudes in that era of scientific advance and of the birth of the higher criticism.

—— *Mark Rutherford's Deliverance* [sequel].   1885
    A narrative as rambling as the former, chief incidents a struggling journalist's attempts to preach love and undogmatic Christianity to the poor and outcast of London : contains some earnest studies of character and conduct, and is obviously grounded on autobiography. Out of his favourite teacher, the Book of Job, Mark learns his final attitude of trust in God, even though His ways are beyond our comprehension. A book that reveals the hearts of the poor struggling toilers with penetrating sympathy, ennobled by the earnestness of the autobiographer's endeavour to keep hold of the spiritual light whilst labouring in darkness and slavery. This and the following are " edited " by Mark Rutherford's imaginary friend, " Reuben Shapcott."

—— *The Revolution in Tanner's Lane.*   1887
    A sober and scrupulously honest picture of the lower middle-classes in 1814–24, especially of the times of the Bread Riots and the Blanketeers ; scenes, London, Manchester, and Cambridgeshire. Written by a man who knew what it was to be a Radical when political differences were treated as a crime. The change of ministers in an obscure Dissenting chapel, and the intrigues and abortive revolts that ensue, illustrate the gradual breaking-up of Independency ; and the trials of the socialist Coleman and others who suffered intolerable wrongs from society illustrate the history of social and political agitation in the forties. On the more personal side, the story is poignant enough, and the portrayal of domestic life and human character vivid and revealing.

—— *Miriam's Schooling ; and other papers.*   1890
    A short but penetrating character-study : how a crude and selfish girl is chastened and becomes a true woman ; a tale of lowly life sixty years ago. Also some Old Testament histories ; all ethical in purpose.

—— *Catherine Furze.*   1894
    A merciless portrayal of the cant and materialism of the lower middle-classes in the provinces ; and an earnest exposition of his views on morality and religion.

—— *Clara Hapgood.*   1896
    Mazzini is a minor character, and there is a good deal about Italian schemers in London before the Risorgimento. Mark Rutherford's ethical and religious views are further developed in the characters and their history, in Baruch Cohen, for example. The heroine bears shame rather than marry the unworthy lover who has betrayed her, and Baruch, the believer in free love, eventually gives a home to her and her child. [All, Unwin ; Doubleday, Doran, New York. (1), (2), and (3), Cape ; Oxford Press, New York.]

WHITEING, Richard [1840–1928]. *The Island : an adventure of a person of quality.*   1888
    This and the next novel together make a striking sociological study, much on the lines of Zola's experimental fiction. An English lord, revolted by the vices and sophistications of modern society in gilded London and Paris, retires from the world. Cast away on a Pacific isle, he discovers a community of English people living in peace and happy innocence, intercourse with whom renews his faith in humanity. [Longmans : o.p. ; Century Co., New York : o.p.]

—— *No. 5 John Street.*   1899
    After the peer's demise or disappearance, his friend, a rich baronet, continues his researches into social conditions by living the life of the submerged in a London slum. His journal presents a series of vividly contrasted pictures, the luxury of the rich and the misery of the poor, the former alleged to be the cause of the latter, for the two stories together are the author's plea for a radically new system of distribution. [De La More Press : o.p. ; (Wayfarer's Lib.) Dent ; Century Co., New York : o.p.]

—— *Ring in the New.*   1906
    Another story for the same purpose—the experiences of an orphaned, untrained girl who is forced to get her own living. [Hutchinson : o.p. ; Century Co., New York : o.p.]

WHITING, Mary Bradford. *The Torchbearers.*   1904
    Contains a good study of political parties and tendencies in Italy at the end of last century. Describes the Bread Riots of 1898 and the assassination of King Humbert. [Dent : o.p.]

WHITING, Mary Bradford (*continued*). *The Plough of Shame.* 1906
A crowded picture of Ferrara and Florence in the sixteenth century, Ariosto, Tasso, and Michelangelo figuring among the many characters. Poisonings, torturing, and the horrors of mediæval dungeons make it very lurid (1530). [Dent : o.p.]

WHITLOCK, Brand [American ; *b.* 1869]. *The Turn of the Balance.* 1907
A determined exposure of the legal and other delinquencies of the American social system. Mr. Whitlock was mayor of Toledo, Ohio. Unjust treatment of criminals and victims of legal injustice—both alike presented with much of the angel in their composition—the debasing effects of mammon-worship and hypocritical laws ; all illustrated with abundance of sensations. The dialogue is heavily sown with cant terms, for some of which a glossary is provided. [Bobbs-Merrill, Indianapolis (Revised ed., 1924) ; Rivers : o.p.]

WHITNEY, Adeline Dutton [*née* Train ; American ; 1824–1906]. *Boys at Chequasset.* 1862
The story of a bad boy's conversion. The hero is a slovenly boy, whose reformation is worked out in a lifelike manner, without obtrusion of the moral. [Houghton, Boston : o.p.]

—— *Faith Gartney's Girlhood.* 1863
A simple record of the life and thought of a young girl between fourteen and twenty, typical of " those young people who dream and wish and strive and err, and find, perhaps, little help to interpret their spirits to themselves." " A sort of transcendental child's book." [Houghton, Boston : o.p. ; Burt, New York ; Routledge : o.p.]

—— *The Gayworthys.* 1865
The uneventful life of an old-fashioned family living in the New England hills. There is a good deal of talk about religion ; a rough sea-captain airs his scepticism in rude metaphors, while rustics express their faith in Providence just as crudely. The book is deeply tinged with Swedenborgian mysticism. [Houghton, Boston ; Routledge : o.p.]

—— *A Summer in Leslie Goldthwaite's Life.* 1866
A girl's holiday among the mountains, and its deep, salutary effect upon her mind and heart ; simple and homely. [Houghton, Boston ; Routledge : o.p.]

—— *Hitherto : a story of yesterdays.* 1869
Home life in a New England country place some fifty years ago ; quiet Puritan folk living out their lives with eyes fixed on things above. The most prominent characters are two girls, one addicted to morbid self-questioning, the other happily trustful in Providence. A religious story interspersed with homilies. [Houghton, Boston : o.p. ; Low : o.p.]

—— *We Girls : a home story.* 1870
—— *Real Folks* [sequel]. 1871
—— *The Other Girls* [sequel]. 1873
Rambling domestic stories, of which the characters are various girls, three of whom we find living a plain life of high thinking in New York ; two others contrasted—one in the city, the other in the country ; and two, again, who go out to service, and are so deeply animated with the spirit that makes drudgery divine, that they are as happy working in the kitchen and about the house as if they were in Paradise. [(1) and (3) Houghton, Boston ; Low ; (2), *id.* ; o.p.]

—— *Ascutney Street : a neighbourhood story.* 1890
The growth of love between two people in widely different social stations, with descriptions of people and manners, and the social world dividing these two. [Houghton, Boston ; Ward & Lock : o.p.]

WIELAND, Christopher Martin [German ; 1773–1813]. *Reason Triumphant over Fancy ; Exemplified in the Singular Adventures of Don Sylvio de Rosalva : a History in which every marvellous event occurs naturally* (Don Sylvio von Rosalva, 1764). 1773
A fanciful imitation of Don Quixote, ostensibly satirizing the fairy-tales which were then in fashion. Sylvio is possessed by an absurd belief in the reality of fairy-land, and with his Sancho, Pedrillo, encounters a series of strange adventures, which eventually bring him back to sanity. Also refers, though unobtrusively, to Wieland's own emancipation from the visionary enthusiasm of his early period. [Edited by E. A. BAKER (Lib. of Early Novelists), Routledge, 1904 (Dutton, New York).]

—— *The History of Agathon* (1766–7). 1773
Wieland's own mental history in disguise. Brought up at Delphi, like the Ion of Euripides, Agathon has been initiated into the Orphic theosophy, and is imbued with the lofty idealism of Plato. But his innocence succumbs to the temptations of the world, and his philosophy to the sophisms of an Epicurean. In the conclusion that Wieland afterwards wrote, Agathon finds the ideal of his life-long quest in the sage Archytas, and learns once more to trust in wisdom and purity. [4 vols., Cadell : o.p.]

—— *The Republic of Fools : being the history of the state and people of Abdera in Thrace* (Die Abderiten, 1774). 1861
A stupid fiasco in his native Biberach, where he was town clerk, gave Wieland the idea of representing Abdera and its inhabitants at the time when the " laughing philosopher " Democritus was a citizen, and Euripides and Hippocrates were visiting the metropolis of dullness. The absurdities come to a pitch in the famous lawsuit about the ass's shadow. One of those universal satires that are a permanent rebuke to the follies of mankind. [Transl. by Henry CHRISTMAS, 2 vols., W. H. Allen : o.p.]

—— *Confessions in Elysium ; or, The Adventures of a Platonic Philosopher* (Geheime Geschichte des Philosophen Peregrinus Proteus, 1791). 1796
A Lucianic dialogue, portraying in a more merciful way a Cynic philosopher whom Lucian had branded as a hypocritical sensualist. Shows how far Wieland had travelled from the scoffing paganism of his middle period towards a nobler view of human life and conduct. [An abridged translation, 3 vols. : o.p.]

" WIGGIN, Kate Douglas " [Mrs. George Christopher Riggs ; *née* Smith ; 1856–1923]. *The Birds' Christmas Carol.* [juvenile] 1888
A little tale breathing the tenderest spirit of love and human kindness. Similar in motive to Dickens's *Christmas Carol*, but less fanciful in style. [Houghton, Boston ; Gay & Hancock.]

"WIGGIN, Kate Douglas" (continued). *A Summer in a Cañon.* [juvenile] 1889
Describes the holiday of a party of bright young people of both sexes camping out in Southern California ; their adventures and mishaps, their merry talk and very amusing letters. [Houghton, Boston ; Gay & Hancock.]

—— *Timothy's Quest.* [juvenile] 1890
A pretty little story (written for the young, but interesting to older people) of two children's venture into the great world ; the boy a figure of precocious manliness ; all the characters drawn with kindliness and humour, and the rights of the children insisted upon at every opportunity. [Houghton, Boston ; Gay & Hancock.]

—— *A Cathedral Courtship ; and, Penelope's English Experiences.* 1893
The former is an excellent example of this lady's tourist fiction ; the characters, three Americans doing the English cathedrals—a bewitching girl and an old lady, and an eligible painter who scrapes acquaintance with them. The talk and incidents that ensue abound in humour. *Penelope's English Experiences* includes the adventures and impressions of three American ladies on a visit to England ; scenes in London and the village of Belvern, fanciful sketches of a West-End ball, portraits of domestic originals, all characterized by happy strokes of humour and droll exaggeration of English traits. [In 1 vol., Houghton, Boston ; (1) and (2) separate, Gay & Hancock ; (2) alone, Black, 1930.]

—— *The Story of Patsy.* 1893
A little sketch from life, droll and tender towards the weak and unfortunate ; the hero a cripple. Far from unpleasant as a picture of slum life. [Houghton, Boston ; Gay & Hancock.]

—— *Polly Oliver's Problem.* 1893
The life of a girl on the verge of womanhood, and the problem how she shall find complete expression of her own nature within the natural limits of her sex. [Houghton, Boston ; Gay & Hancock : o.p.]

—— *Penelope's Experiences in Scotland.* 1898
The three go on to Scotland, and meet with still funnier experiences in Edinburgh and Fifeshire. Places, people, and society are depicted in a buoyant style, and old-world manners and odd characters are sketched with amiable satire. [Houghton, Boston ; Gay & Hancock : o.p.]

—— *Penelope's Irish Experiences.* 1901
The fair Americans visit Ireland, and criticize the country and people in the same genial, light-hearted style. Comic incidents, good stories, legends, and racy sayings make up the greater part of the volume. [Houghton, Boston ; Gay & Hancock : o.p.]

—— *Rebecca of Sunnybrook Farm.* 1903
—— *New Chronicles of Rebecca.* 1907
Light-hearted, tender, and humorous stories of home life in New England, racy of the soil, excellent in portraiture of girls and women-folk. Mrs. Wiggin may be described as an American Mrs. Ewing. [(1) Houghton, Boston ; Gay & Hancock ; Black ; (2) Houghton, Boston ; Hodder : o.p.]

—— *The Old Peabody Pew : a Christmas romance of a country church.* 1907
A pretty drawing of village life in New England sixty years or so since. [Grosset, New York : o.p. ; Hodder : o.p.]

—— *Susanna and Sue.* 1909
Susanna leaves a husband who has not yet awoke to the responsibilities of life, and with her sweet little daughter Sue takes refuge in a Shaker settlement. The serene life and philosophy of the Shakers is described with Mrs. Wiggin's unfailing charm. [Houghton, Boston : o.p. ; Hodder : o.p.]

—— *The Story of Waitstill Baxter.* 1913
Depicts life in a New England village about a century ago : the rebellion of the two daughters of a miserly deacon. [Houghton, Boston.]

WILDE, Oscar O'Flahertie Wills [Irish ; 1856–1900]. *The Happy Prince ; and other tales.* 1888
Fairy stories after Andersen and other fabulists, heavily charged with Wilde's æstheticism and his paradoxical and cynical wit. *The Nightingale and the Rose* exemplifies the first, and *The Remarkable Rocket* the latter quality. [Duckworth ; Putnam, New York ; Mosher, New York ; *illus.*, Brentano, New York ; Stokes, New York.]

—— *Lord Arthur Savile's Crime ; The Portrait of Mr. W. H. ; and other stories.* 1891
Lord Arthur Savile's Crime, with its cynical sub-title, "A Study of Duty," is a witty caricature of the highfalutin crime-novel. A more effective burlesque is the "high-idealistic romance," *The Canterville Ghost* (1887). *The Portrait of Mr. W. H.* (1889) unfolds a theory of the object of Shakespeare's sonnets. Two lighter *jeux d'esprit, The Sphinx without a Secret* and *The Model Millionaire,* complete the set.

—— *The Picture of Dorian Gray.* 1891
Unintentionally a severe commentary on Wilde's own pagan theory of life, the pursuit of sensuous and intellectual delight with no acceptance of moral responsibility. The plot is a variant of that of Balzac's *Peau de Chagrin,* a portrait growing old and hideous while the sensualist preserves his youthful beauty—inspired by Huysmans' portrayal of the voluptuary Des Esseintes, in *A Rebours,* and by the æsthetic ethics of Gautier, Maupassant, and Baudelaire. Hastily written—for a wager—and over-long, but enlivened by some good epigrams. [Lane ; Simpkin ; Dodd & Mead, New York ; Putnam, New York ; *illus.*, Dodd & Mead, New York.]

—— *A House of Pomegranates.* 1892
Another collection of fantastic stories which the author said was "intended neither for the British child nor the British public." [Methuen ; Dodd & Mead, New York ; Putnam, New York.]

[The last two form vols. I and VIII respectively of *Collected Works,* 16 vols., Methuen, 1907–9.]

WILDER, Thornton Niven [American ; b. 1897]. *The Cabala.* 1926
The Cabala is a set of rare personalities, living at Rome, each of whom has some unique gift of fortune or genius which makes him or her a power in the world. This is not a novel, or a series of stories. These choice souls are brought before us in a very natural and even a casual way, talking and acting ; and what they do and what happens is shown to be the inevitable outcome of individual character. The author has been described as the American Anatole France, which may be accepted with the reservation that he is

WILDER, Thornton Niven (*continued*).

essentially more of a poet than was his prototype ; nor is he ever a cynic. His pity and his irony are dispensed in terse, restrained dicta. His English prose is perhaps the finest that has come out of America. [Boni, New York ; Longmans.]

—— *The Bridge of San Luis Rey.* 1927

Another highly modern study of strange, bizarre characters, whose greatness of soul is visible only to the most searching analyst. The collapse of a bridge outside Lima in 1714 raises the question, why did Providence single out these five victims ? The wonders of human love and self-devotion, the greatness that may be discovered in the sorriest human spirit, the divinity mingled with the dross and the filth—all this is revealed with a tenderness that outbalances the irony. [*Illus.*, Boni, New York ; Grosset, New York ; *illus.* by Clare Leighton, Longmans.]

—— *The Woman of Andros.* 1930

A story adapted from the *Andria* of Terence, and expanded into a shortish novel. A young Greek, torn this way and that by love and the dictates of parental authority, and two young women of contrasted morals, are the principals. Part comedy, part sentimental drama ; in still larger part a vision of life through which Mr. Wilder's meditative soul expresses itself in reflection and comment exquisitely phrased. [Boni, New York ; Longmans.]

WILHELMSON, Carl [Finnish, writing in English]. *Midsummernight.* 1930

The saga of Otto Maki, who is carried off to sea and works as a labourer all over the United States, and then returns to Finland and courts a girl of higher degree—she is the child of a craftsman and he of a peasant. Finnish landscapes, characters, customs, and superstitions are lovingly described. [*Illus.* by Lynd Ward, Farrar & Rinehart.]

WILKINS, Mary Eleanor [Mrs. C. M. Freeman ; American ; *b.* 1862]. *A Humble Romance.* 1887

Twenty-eight terse, realistic stories and sketches of homely, penurious life in a Massachusetts village. All deal with various phases of unhappiness, a monotony which answers to a certain monotony in the characters, who are nearly all abnormal. [Harper, New York ; Ward & Lock : o.p.]

—— *A New England Nun ; and other stories.* 1891

Twenty-four humorous or pathetic stories of the same rather sombre people, showing the same compressed realism, like that of a Dutch genre-painting. [Harper, New York and London.]

—— *Jane Field.* 1894

The spiritual tragedy of a nobly natured woman, a rigid Puritan, who is tempted by maternal love and the unlawful impulse to right mundane injustice, and sins stubbornly and perseveringly. A sort of tragic humour lights up the spectacle of her austere integrity brought by her own act to a position of falsehood, which she expiates by shame and penitence. [Harper, New York : o.p.]

—— *Pembroke.* 1894

Her fullest picture of the life of a New England village, summing up her observation of these people of perverted wills—on the whole an unlovely picture, relieved against an environment of beautiful landscapes, orchards and old-world homesteads, and lightened by strokes of pathos and humour and a keen sense of the joy of life. Quarrels persisted in to the bitter end, life feuds between neighbours and kindred, stubborn and selfish pride blighting the love of youth and maid and entailing tragic consequences—such are the prevailing motives, and most of the characters are extreme developments of this attribute of the Puritan nature. [Harper, New York.]

—— *Madelon.* 1896

A tragedy in the same rural setting, romantic love playing a larger part than is usual with Miss Freeman. Here again are a series of characters all more or less under the dominion of a fixed idea—the hero, Lot Gordon, Madelon, Burr's mother, and other folk. [Harper : o.p.]

—— *Jerome : a poor man.* 1897

The poor young man makes a kind of wager that, if he become rich, he will give up all his wealth to the poor ; both which events come to pass. A study of lowly, straitened life, and a sentimental indictment of the selfish indulgence of the rich. Jerome is another example of the wrong-headed, stiff-necked New Englander, sacrificing everything to his wilful pride. [Harper : o.p.]

—— *Silence ; and other stories.* 1898

Silence is a village girl who goes mad with sorrow for her lover, carried away by the red men. *The Little Maid at the Door* is a tale of the same old days, describing Puritan superstitions and the sufferings they entailed on innocent people. *Evelina's Garden* is a fanciful story in Hawthorne's manner, more than half apologue, glorifying pure affection as the most precious thing in human life. *The Buckley Lady*, real life blent with fairyland, is a love-tale in the author's more natural style. [Harper : o.p.]

—— *The Jamesons.* 1899

A novelette, recounting the ludicrous crusade of a New York lady of advanced views against the old-fashioned habits and prejudices of a village. [Doubleday, New York : o.p. ; Dent : o.p.]

—— *The Love of Parson Lord ; and other stories.* 1900

Old Parson Lord dedicated his only daughter to missionary work, but his paternal fondness reconciles him to her frivolities, and even allows her to marry, though without his open consent. In *The Tree of Knowledge* a would-be burglar is summarily converted by a pretty, innocent maiden. *One Good Time* is the characteristic story of a penurious country woman who spends £300 in a week of enjoyment, then settles down resignedly to sober married life. A story of revolutionary times follows, and then a humorous sketch of three elderly sisters and an old beau. [Harper : o.p.]

—— *The Heart's Highway.* 1900

An historical romance, dealing with Virginia under Charles II and the tobacco riots after Nathaniel Bacon's rebellion (1682). [Doubleday, New York : o.p. ; Murray : o.p.]

—— *Understudies.* 1901

Hardly a characteristic book. Two series of fanciful stories, one of people and their pets, interpreting traits

WILKINS, Mary Eleanor (*continued*).
    of human nature by their affinities with certain animals; the other series, more poetical, about certain flowers that are shown to be symbolical of human character. [Harper: o.p.]

—— *The Portion of Labour.*   1901
    A problem-novel dealing with capital and labour in New England. A number of characters are portrayed, chiefly descendants of the old colonial stock, and counterparts in their salient traits to the types with which the authoress has familiarized us. [Harper, New York.]

—— *The Givers.*   1904
    A collection of stories: *Eglantina*, *The Reign of the Doll*, and *Lucy* are perhaps the best. [Harper: o.p.]

—— *By the Light of the Soul.*   1907
    This solemn title covers a delicate, if characteristically monotonous, story of a brave young girl and her loyalty to her mother's memory and her own conscience. [Harper: o.p.]

—— *The Shoulders of Atlas.*   1908
    Breaks away from the narrow limitations of the humble romance, and introduces plot, mystery, and other excitements. [Harper: o.p.]

—— *The Winning Lady.*   1909
    [Harper: o.p.]

—— *The Best Stories.*   1927
    Twenty-five selected tales, including *A Humble Romance* and *A New England Nun*; selected by H. W. Lanier. [Harper, New York and London.]

WILLCOCKS, Miss Mary Patricia [*b.* 1869]. *Widdicombe.*   1905
    A love-story of village and farm, relating the different histories of three girls, and bringing out the characteristics they inherit from a fine old grandmother. Scene, the west country, but the local colour is unimportant. [Lane: o.p.]

—— *The Wingless Victory.*   1907
    Scenes, Cornwall and Devon, where a village doctor, like Ibsen's "Enemy of Society," fights the local authority and makes himself unpopular by telling the truth about a sanitation scandal. His private struggle, on the other hand, is with his wife, who is out of love with him, and coquets with a foolish boy and a philandering man. [Lane: o.p.]

—— *A Man of Genius: a story of the Judgment of Paris.*   1908
    Struggle of a poor man to become an architect, and conflict of temperament with his unsuitable wife, saved from tragedy by the renunciation and good feeling of a woman to whom his heart has turned. Takes place chiefly in North Devon. [Lane: o.p.]

—— *The Way Up.*   1910
    A young ironmaster tries to remedy the ills of capitalism by founding a system of co-operative production—this is partly based on the life of Jean André Godin. Tragedy comes in through the unsympathetic conduct of his moneyed wife. Scenes, Exeter, Topsham, London, etc. [Lane: o.p.]

—— *The Sleeping Partner.*   1919
    The foremost character is a curious study of morbid introspection and inhibitions; but he is only a spectator in the story of his brother's marriage and divorce. Incidentally we are afforded an inner view of a publishing business. [Hutchinson: o.p.]

WILLIAMS, Ben Ames [American; *b.* 1889]. *The Great Accident.*   1920
    Like *Main Street*, the portrait of a small town in the Middle West, but less satirical, if not lacking in criticism. Hardiston is not new and raw, but old, well-to-do, and comfortable. But it is less than half-alive. The story is amusing enough; but it is the background that is really significant—the complacent provincialism of a self-contained little world which does not know how petty and obsolete it is. [Macmillan, New York; Mills & Boon.]

—— *Evered.*   1921
—— *The Rational Hind.*   1925
    Two quiet novels of country life in Maine. [(1) and (2), Dutton, New York; Mills & Boon.]

WILLIAMS, Charles [Irish; 1838–1904]. *John Thaddeus Mackay: a study in sects.*   1899
    A somewhat invertebrate Presbyterian minister goes round the world in search of a religion. A mixture of theological discussion and realistic delineation of the seamy side of bohemian life. The author, a well-known war-correspondent, was born at Coleraine, and made good use of his early recollections of Ulster. [Burleigh: o.p.]

WILLIAMS, Charles. *War in Heaven.*   1930
    A poet's history of a contest on this earth of to-day between the powers of goodness and evil. The Holy Grail in the shape of a cup is discovered by a scholar, and its magical powers are employed for abominable purposes by a rascally pair of confederates, who are however discomfited by the reincarnated Prester John, guardian of the Grail. [Gollancz.]

WILLIAMS, Churchill [American]. *The Captain.*   1903
    The Civil War: Grant and the Army of the Potomac (1862). [Lothrop, Boston.]

WILLIAMS, Jesse Lynch [American; *b.* 1871]. *The Stolen Story; and other newspaper stories.*   1899
    Episodes of journalist life in New York, with much information about the manners, methods, ideas, talk, and morals of newspaper people in America. Full of technicalities and of local and office slang. [Scribner, New York.]

WILLIAMSON, Mrs. Charles Norris [Alice Muriel, *née* Livingston; American by birth; *b.* 1869]. *The Newspaper Girl.*   1892
    A melodramatic novel, with delineations of the methods and manners of journalistic life—a mixture of realism and sensation that characterizes her numerous novels. [Pearson: o.p.]

WILLIAMSON, Mrs. Charles Norris (*continued*). *The Adventure of Princess Sylvia.*   1900
  A very good example of this lady's romantic novels.   A sentimental comedy, resembling *The Prisoner of Zenda* and its class in mechanism, wherein a great lady and an emperor of " Rhaetia " masquerade and make love in a highly improbable manner. [Methuen : o.p.]

WILLIAMSON, Charles Norris [1859–1920], and WILLIAMSON, Mrs. C. N.   *The Lightning Conductor.*   1902
—— *The Car of Destiny.*   1906
—— *The Botor Chaperon.*   1907
—— *The Motor Maid.*   1909
  All these are bright and amusing romances, only distinguished from many another such by the prominent place which a motor-car, or motor ride, takes in the story. [(1) and (2), Methuen ; (2), *id.* : o.p. ; (4), Hodder : o.p. ; (1), Holt, New York ; (2) McClure, New York : o.p. ; (4), Doubleday, New York : o.p.]

WILLIAMSON, Henry.   *The Beautiful Years.*   1921
  Begins a tetralogy, *The Flax of Dreams*, the life-story of Willie Maddison, who is intended to typify the generation which reached maturity about the time of the war.   His boyhood exemplifies the extreme sensitiveness to Nature and her children marking this author's work. [Revised and re-written, 1929 ; Faber ; Dutton, New York.]

—— *Dandelion Days* [sequel].   1922
  Willie Maddison's schooldays, friendship with another boy, calf-love, and the like, not very different from the ordinary run of boyish lives except in the emotionalism of his character. [Revised and re-written, 1930 ; Faber ; Dutton, New York.]

—— *The Dream of Fair Women : a tale of youth after the great war* [sequel].   1924
  Maddison is now living in an Exmoor cottage, after demobilization, engaged upon writing " The Policy of Reconstruction, or True Resurrection."   He is distracted by the appearance of a siren, follows her to Folkestone, and is disillusioned. [Collins ; revised and re-written, 1930, Faber ; Dutton, New York.]

—— *The Pathway* [sequel].   1928
  In this final volume of the tetralogy the theme is worked out to a conclusion.   It is a phase of that so often treated by Mary Webb—the conflict between the clear-sighted, sincere, and natural-minded, and the dull, conventional, self-satisfied bond-slaves of the established order.   Mary comes of a very ordinary, orthodox household, but has all the instincts for freedom.   The deliverer appears, and she inevitably falls in love.   But he only points out " the pathway."   Maddison goes through the war, which teaches him revolt ; and Blake, Richard Jefferies, Shelley, and Dostoievsky give him the new vision.   His end is a more incongruous conclusion than that of Nevil Beauchamp. [Cape ; Dutton, New York.]

—— *Tarka the Otter : his joyful water-life and death in the country of the Two Rivers.*   1927
  All that intense love of Nature, and sympathy with every form of wild life, which runs through this author's work, finds complete expression in this biography of an otter, from its babyhood to the glory of its unconquered death.   Tarka indeed is a much more satisfactory hero than Willie Maddison ; here is neither sentiment nor moralizing, but the plain joys and sorrows of life as a wild animal lives it, in which however the mingled fear and exaltation of being hunted plays a large part.   Throughout the story runs the magic of the streams of Dartmoor and Exmoor, and the river mouths of North Devon. [With introd. by Hon. Sir J. W. Fortescue, Putnam ; Dutton, New York.]

—— *The Old Stag.*   1927
  Nature-stories of English wild life.   Among the best are the two which describe a stag-hunt and the habits of a badger respectively. [Putnam ; Dutton, New York.]

WILSON, John [" Christopher North " ; Scottish ; 1785–1854].   *Lights and Shadows of Scottish Life.*   1822
  Twenty-four tales and sketches, avowedly not realistic, very sentimental in tone and abounding in pathos.   Many word-paintings of Scottish scenery in the manner of the *Recreations of Christopher North*, but more restrained.   Best known is *The Trials of Margaret Lyndsay*. [The last separately, Cassell : o.p. ; the whole collection, Blackwood : o.p. ; Claxton, Philadelphia : o.p.]

WILSON, Margaret [Mrs. G. D. Turner ; *b.* 1882].   *Trousers of Taffeta : a tale of a polygamous city.*   1929
  The life of well-born Mohammadan ladies within the zenana, in the Punjab—an indictment of the system of child-marriage.   The spiritual sufferings of the strictly-enclosed are insisted upon, and the beginnings of social progress indicated. [Cape ; Harcourt, New York.]

WILSON, Mary J.   *The Knight of the Needle Rock and his Days.*   1905
  Manners and domestic history, and glimpses of great historic events, like the voyage of the Armada and the massacre of St. Bartholomew ; gathered from family papers, the Oglander Memoirs, and other authentic sources.   In the form of a diary by a gentleman in the Isle of Wight (1571–1606). [Stock : o.p.]

" WILSON, Romer " [Mrs. E. J. Howard O'Brien ; 1891–1930].   *Martin Schüler.*   1918
  Study of a musical temperament, the owner of which remains sublimely unconscious that he owes all his gift to the self-sacrifice of others.   The selfish charm of his nature is admirably brought out, and the German background, though got up from guides and travel-books, would deceive most readers. [Methuen ; with introd. by May Sinclair, Knopf, New York, 1928.]

—— *The Death of Society.*   1921
  This *conte de fée premier*, as the authoress called it, is a fantastic story showing intuitions of genius in the extraordinary characters conjured up—the philosophic old critic and his daughters, and their mother Simple Rosa, who is allowed by her great-minded husband to love and be loved by the wandering Englishman.   It is she who tells them her oracular dream, " the Death of Society."   Scene, Trondhjem, in Norway, and the pine-forests round about. [Collins ; with introd. by Hugh Walpole, Knopf, New York, 1928.]

"WILSON, Romer" (*continued*). *The Grand Tour.* 1923

Letters and sketches by a French sculptor. Like two or three other novels of hers, not quite a success ; but it does make the reader feel that the man is a genuine artist. [Methuen ; Knopf, New York.]

—— *Greenlow.* 1927

Romer Wilson wrote a book, *All Alone ; the Life and Private History of Emily Jane Brontë* (1928), and this novel shows profound traces of the Brontë influence. It is about the very inflammable and ingenuous daughter of a Derbyshire farmer and her two sweethearts. [Collins ; Knopf, New York.]

WILSON, Theodora Wilson. *Moll o' the Toll Bar.* 1911

A good story of the hunger riots and farm-burning due to the scarcity of corn during the French war, and a good picture of uncouth characters and manners in Cumberland at the beginning of the nineteenth century. [Hutchinson : o.p.]

—— *Jack o' Peterloo.* 1924

In a similar style portrays the state of oppression, the labour troubles, and the revolutionary agitation at three successive dates, 1793, 1805, and 1819, the last being that of the Peterloo massacre. Orator Hunt is conspicuous here. [Labour Publishing Co.]

WINGATE, Mrs. Alfred [Letitia Beryl, *née* Tucker]. *Before Sunset.* 1929

A painstaking historical novel of thirteenth-century Russia, the Mongol invasion, and the heroic deeds of Alexander Nevsky. [Jenkins.]

WINGFIELD, Hon. Lewis Strange [Irish ; 1842–91]. *Lady Grizel.* 1877

Bath in the days of Earl Chatham (1747–65). [3 vols., Bentley : o.p.]

—— *My Lords of Strogue : a chronicle of Ireland from the Convention to the Union.* 1879

A fair but not accurate story, mingling history and romance (1800). The rebellion of 1798 from an Irish point of view. [3 vols., Bentley : o.p.]

"WINTER, John Strange" [Mrs. Arthur Stannard, Henrietta Eliza Vaughan, *née* Palmer ; 1856–1911]. *Bootle's Baby : a story of the Scarlet Lancers.* 1885

A pathetic story of military life in London barracks, with a foundling for heroine. [Warne : o.p. ; Warne, New York.]

—— *Cavalry Life : sketches and stories in barracks and out.* 1881
—— *Bootle's Children.* 1888
—— *A Soldier's Children.* 1892
—— *Regimental Legends.* 1897

Further stories of military life. The author's racy, if sentimental, drawing of the British soldier and regimental life in peace-time endeared her to many who were incapable of appreciating the realism of Kipling. [(1) and (4), together, Chatto ; (2), White : o.p. ; (3), Simpkin : o.p.]

—— *A Blameless Woman.* 1895

The Blameless Woman, after living with a Russian count for two years in Berlin under cover of a false marriage into which she was duped, comes home, and, in the character of a spotless maiden, marries a man she does not care for. [White : o.p.]

—— *Heart and Sword.* 1898

The conflict of ideas between husband and wife, the one a soldier, the other an actress. [o.p.]

—— *A Name to Conjure With.* 1899

A literary woman takes to alcohol as a stimulant, and, finding it efficacious, contracts the habit, with ruinous consequences. [White : o.p. ; Lippincott, Philadelphia : o.p.]

—— *A Self-made Countess : the justification of a husband.* 1900

A piquant story of smart society in London, aiming to expose snobbishness and social humbug. [White : o.p. ; Lippincott, Philadelphia : o.p.]

WINTHROP, Theodore [American ; 1828–61]. *Cecil Dreeme.* 1861

A drama of passion. The author shows how potent and profound are the struggles and emotions that may take place amid such commonplace surroundings as an average lodging-house in New York. [Holt, New York : o.p. ; W. Scott : o.p.]

—— *John Brent.* 1864

An energetic, full-blooded romance of the lawless life of the Western plains ; Helen Clitheroe, the heroine, is a novel type, and something of an enigma. [Dodd & Mead, New York : o.p. ; Paterson, Edinburgh : o.p.]

WINTLE, William James. *Paradise Row, and Some of its Inhabitants.* 1896

Short character-studies and sketches of local manners from the slums of east Leeds ; the vernacular quite unmitigated. [Milne : o.p.]

WISEMAN, Cardinal Nicholas Patrick Stephen [1802–65]. *Fabiola ; or, The Church in the Catacombs.* 1855

A story of the persecution by Diocletian (303). The Archbishop of Milan said of it that " it was the first good book that had had the success of a bad one " (*Dict. Nat. Biog.*). [Burns & Oates ; Browne & Nolan, Dublin ; Kenedy, New York ; Benziger, New York ; *illus.*, Burns & Oates.]

WISTER, Owen [American ; *b.* 1860]. *Red Man and White.* 1896

Adventures on the Indian frontier (*c.* 1866–77), a mixture of invention and actual experience, of fictitious and historical characters. General Crook is a portrait, while, presumably, Specimen Jones is a creation by the author. [Harper, New York and London.]

—— *The Virginian, a Horseman of the Plains.* 1902

A romance of Wyoming—the " Cattle Ground "—in the seventies and eighties. A young Virginian " cow puncher," a faultless hero, who quotes Shakespeare and Browning, is the sweetheart of a pretty " school-marm " from Vermont. Accepted as a classic portrayal of the real Westerner. [Macmillan, New York and London.]

WISTER, Owen (*continued*). *Lady Baltimore.* 1906
A sophisticated beauty from fashionable New York and a sensitive girl from the best society of the South contend for an honourable and chivalrous young Southerner. The *Cranford* touch is almost caught in the portrayal of the old ladies of a decayed seaport in Carolina, maintaining the palladium of their racial exclusiveness against the vulgarity of the "yellow rich." Fiercely satirical of plutocratic manners. [Macmillan, New York.]

—— *Members of the Family.* 1911
A realistic fragment rough-hewn from the strong, rich life of the West, in the days of the first settlers, and onward through the changes due to the ingress of civilization to the domestic peace and comfort of to-day. Farmers, Indians, horse-stealers, politicians, respectable people and the reverse, forcibly drawn, sometimes—e.g. *In the Back*—with something like the Kipling touch. [Macmillan, New York.]

WODEHOUSE, Pelham Grenville [*b.* 1881]. *Psmith, Journalist.* 1915
—— *The Indiscretions of Archie.* 1921
—— *The Inimitable Jeeves.* 1923
—— *Very Good, Jeeves.* 1930
Light, often extravagant comedies; Jeeves is a second Crichton, who extricates his master from all sorts of absurd situations. Society nincompoops, golf, and wealthy aunts provide material for knockabout farce, enlivened by colloquial witticisms. [(1), Black; (2)–(4), Jenkins; (2), Burt, New York; (4), Doubleday, Doran, New York.]

WOLFE, Thomas [American; *b.* 1900]. *Look Homeward, Angel.* 1929
A vehement, unchastened story of repressive family life in a little old-fashioned hill-town of North Carolina, showing imagination and an unruly sort of lyrical power. Hardness, hatred, drunkenness, sensuality, avarice, and blasphemous violence are the characteristics of the parents and brothers who thwart and blight the soul of the boy telling the story, before he wins through to freedom. The writer calls it "a story of the buried life," and is obviously under the spell of both Whitman and Joyce. [Scribner, New York; Heinemann.]

WOLFENSTEIN, Martha [American]. *Idyls of the Gass.* 1903
Stories of a town of German Jews—Maritz. Interest centres in a big-hearted old woman, who is sneered at for doing good by stealth, and a sunny, sweet-natured boy, too old to play because he knew the meaning of human pain, want, and love. Jewish observances and curious sentiments, their religion, hopes, and hideous sufferings at the hands of the anti-Semites, are set down by one who knows them intimately. [Macmillan, New York: o.p.]

WOOD, Mrs. Henry [Ellen, *née* Price; 1814–87]. *Danesbury House.* 1860
Written in the interests of the total abstinence movement. A good story, the purpose adroitly achieved by "indirection." [Ward & Lock; Collins, London and New York.]

—— *East Lynne.* 1861
The main situation is one of harrowing pathos, a divorced wife re-entering her husband's house disguised as a governess, nursing her own child and dying there, tardily forgiven. This is the climax of the plot, the basis of which is a murder, with the ultimate clearing-up of the mystery and the full proceedings of trial, cross-examination, etc. This is the best-known—perhaps the best—and the following are the next best of a large number of novels chiefly of the domestic kind, with melodramatic plots and miscellaneous excitement, but no pretensions to literary quality, except the valuable one of power to interest. [Macmillan; Collins, London and New York; Burt, New York.]

—— *The Channings.* 1862
—— *Roland Yorke* [sequel]. 1869
A pair of novels concerned with the fortunes and misfortunes of two genteel families, the dutiful and pious characters of the one being set in contrast with the Hibernian irresponsibility of the other family. The plot in the first hinges on the theft of a £20 note, suspicion falling on the good Channings and causing endless troubles. All is cleared up at last. The characters are largely young people, and the pranks of the cathedral choirboys furnish some amusement. These, and other features of life in a cathedral town, were the fruit of long residence at Worcester. In the sequel we have the ups and downs of a shiftless, good-natured fellow alongside of a murder plot of melodramatic type. [(1) and (2), Macmillan; Collins, London and New York; (1), (Everyman's Lib.) Dent (Dutton, New York).]

—— *Mrs. Halliburton's Troubles.* 1862
More domestic history: a mother's quiet endurance of adversity, a little girl's death, a family of virtuous children and a naughty boy as foil, with the little events of average life and episodes invented for the purpose of moralizing; the good young men, for instance, are rewarded with signal success in their various callings, despite initial poverty, the wicked fall into disgrace and want. [Macmillan; Collins, London and New York.]

—— *The Shadow of Ashlydyat.* 1863
Typical of a numerous class of Mrs. Wood's novels, in which the interest lies in the working out of a plot, containing romantic and supernatural elements and a good deal of family history. [Macmillan.]

—— *St. Martin's Eve.* 1866
A lady who inherits insanity marries a man with hereditary tendency to wasting disease. A day of ill-omen is among the sensational effects. The lady in one scene leaves her stepson to be burned to death. A characteristic blend of sensation and domesticity. [Macmillan.]

—— *A Life's Secret.* 1867
Concerned extensively with business matters, employers and employees, the critical incident being a strike which entails a lock-out and extreme misery for the poor workpeople and their families. [Macmillan; Collins, London and New York.]

—— *Johnny Ludlow* [6 series]. 1874–9
A number of tolerably good short stories, supposed to be told by a sagacious and observant schoolboy, each

WOOD, Mrs. Henry (*continued*).

as a rule having a distinct plot, sensational or pathetic. They abound in domestic details of lower middle-class life and in portraiture of commonplace character, and usually have a moral aim. [Macmillan.]

—— *Edina.* 1876

—— *Pomeroy Abbey.* 1878

—— *Court Netherleigh.* 1881

And a great many others showing the same characteristics, abundant details of ordinary domestic life, a sensational plot, a constant appeal to popular sentiment. [(1), (2), and (3), Macmillan.]

" **WOODROFFE, Daniel** " [Mrs. J. C. Woods, *née* Woodroffe]. *Tangled Trinities.* 1901

A Kentish vicar and his daughter, born in the West Indies, inherit a tinge of black blood. The author illustrates the effects of these inherited traits of barbarism on themselves and on their English neighbours. The girl's character is analysed, and her story is sombre in its ending. [Laurie: o.p.; Dodd & Mead, New York: o.p.]

WOODS, Edith Elmer [American; *b.* 1871]. *The Spirit of the Service.* 1903

An attempt to depict the ideals that inspire the American naval officer, by a story of service in the late Spanish War. Contrasts their true patriotism with the disreputable manœuvres and the base commercialism of the party politician. Battle of Manila described. [Macmillan: o.p.]

WOODS, Margaret Louise [*née* Bradley; *b.* 1856]. *A Village Tragedy.* 1887

An intolerably painful story admirably told—a pair of ignorant and blameless young creatures done to death by the cruelty of circumstance and the ingrained evil of humanity—the struggle for existence in its most elemental phase. [Macmillan: o.p.; Holt, New York: o.p.]

—— *Esther Vanhomrigh.* 1891

The love-story of Swift and the two Esthers, Johnson and Vanhomrigh, told anew (1712–23). A careful social, biographical, and psychological study of eighteenth-century life, introducing, besides Swift, his friends Addison and Steele, Pope and Bolingbroke. [Murray: o.p.]

—— *The Vagabonds.* 1894

A very human and appealing story of humble life; a good-natured, middle-aged clown, his pretty young wife and her lover, being the three personages of a tragedy. Describes, with friendly but conscientious realism, the daily life of a " giant circus " on tour, life in the ring and on the road. [Murray; Macmillan, New York: o.p.]

—— *Sons of the Sword: a romance of the Peninsular War.* 1901

Adventures of an Irish girl at Madrid and elsewhere in Spain (1808–9) during the Peninsular War. She comes into contact with Napoleon, who is ably portrayed; Sir John Moore also is introduced. [Heinemann: o.p.; McClure, New York: o.p.]

—— *The King's Revoke: an episode in the life of Patrick Dillon.* 1905

An Irishman attempts to rescue Ferdinand VII, rightful king, during Joseph Bonaparte's usurpation of the throne of Spain. Among the fictitious personages stands out the unscrupulous Irishman D'Haguerty, among the historical, Talleyrand (1808–13). [Murray; Dutton, New York: o.p.]

—— *A Poet's Youth.* 1923

Wordsworth's schooldays at Hawkshead, the years at Cambridge, his tours in France, and his love for Annette Vallon. [Chapman; Boni, New York.]

—— *The Spanish Lady.* 1927

Wellington and a beautiful Spaniard, during the Peninsular War; scene, Cadiz in 1813. [Cape.]

WOOLF, Leonard Sidney [*b.* 1880]. *The Village in the Jungle.* 1913

The unhappy fate of two beautiful girls, whose father is persecuted by the headman of a remote Cingalese village. The setting is interesting, and the jungle spell of greed and fear well conveyed. [Arnold; Harcourt, New York.]

—— *The Wise Virgins.* 1914

The irruption of a young artist with modern ideas into a narrow suburban family, where, of course, he meets the unsophisticated young lady. [Arnold.]

WOOLF, Virginia [Mrs. Leonard Sidney Woolf, daughter of Sir Leslie Stephen]. *The Voyage Out.* 1915

Though she eschews autobiography and describes her characters from without, Mrs. Woolf's method is analogous to Dorothy Richardson's, in so far as she shows the stream of consciousness merging into one, external things and happenings, and internal impressions. She wants to show " what really goes on, what people feel, although they generally try to hide it." Hence we see, not only a pair of lovers wondering if it is at all possible really to understand each other, but various others interested in themselves and one another, and trying to discern " the pattern of life." [Hogarth Press; Harcourt, New York.]

—— *Night and Day.* 1919

A very long novel in which readers may detect influences from Jane Austen and Meredith, as well as others discernible in the preceding novel. The scene is London, and the novelist gets as much poetic atmosphere from its vistas and its skies as others evoke from country landscapes. Several characters belong to the literary " profession," a fact that is not irrelevant to the general theme, which may perhaps be defined as the actual, workaday world set over against the other world of dreams, imagination, poetry. Their differences, their contacts, and the possibilities of reconciling them, are the inner motives of Katherine Hilbery, her love-dilemmas, and the rest of it. So too with the other three principal characters. [Duckworth; Hogarth Press.]

—— *Monday or Tuesday.* 1921

Short stories illustrating Mrs. Woolf's curious impressionism, e.g. *An Unwritten Novel*; her sceptical analysis, e.g. *A Society*; or her poetic imagination, e.g. *The Haunted House*. Notable also are *Kew Gardens* and *The Mark on the Wall*. [Hogarth Press; Harcourt, New York.]

WOOLF, Virginia (*continued*). *Jacob's Room.* 1922
" Life is not a series of gig-lamps symmetrically arranged ; life is a luminous halo, a semi-transparent envelope surrounding us from the beginning of consciousness to the end." Hence the new method of narration, in which there is no story, no effort to define the significant, the relevant to something intelligible, any connecting thread. " In short, the observer is choked with observations " (p. 113). Jacob is an infant at the start, and aged twenty-six when we leave off ; but we could only say in vague and inconsequent terms what it is that happens to him in the meantime. [Hogarth Press ; Harcourt, New York.]

—— *Mrs. Dalloway.* 1925
The incidents of a day and the accompanying visual, mental, and emotional impressions, set down from moment to moment, in the style of Dorothy Richardson, with a touch of Joyce. Mrs. Dalloway is a lady of fifty, and intent on preparations for her party this evening ; an old admirer from India calls, and there is an instant of tenderness ; she is worried about her daughter, and the broken-down spinster who is trying to convert the girl ; a shell-shocked man is going off his head, and is literally psycho-analysed before us ; and presently the day ends, much as it was expected to end. [Hogarth Press ; Harcourt, New York ; Modern Lib., New York.]

—— *To the Lighthouse.* 1927
Another experiment towards a new method. There is a houseful of people holidaying in Skye, " a houseful of unrelated passions " ; there is a project to visit the lighthouse, which never comes off till some of the most lovable are dead. There are glimpses of the steady procession of life, but no drama. Little is said : inconsequent streams of thought, longings, apprehensions, musings on life, poured out as they arise in the mind, all taking on the colours of beauty, sorrow, mystery, in the tints thrown by visible nature. Always a clear sense of ultimate significance evades us : the great revelation never comes. " Instead there were little daily miracles, illuminations, matches struck in the dark." [Hogarth Press ; Harcourt, New York.]

—— *Orlando : a biography.* 1928
The author's friend, Miss Sackville-West (Mrs. Harold Nicolson) sat at least for the photograph of Orlando, in this curious *jeu d'esprit*, which covers four centuries with the hero-heroine's experiences, born a great noble under Elizabeth, an ambassador of the Stuarts, a woman during the next two centuries, and united at last to her lover in 1928, having met him in early Victorian times. The poetical rodomontade is charming, and so is the ridicule of certain foibles of historians and of the immemorial vanity and pettiness of the literary tribe. [Hogarth Press ; Harcourt, New York.]

WOOLSON, Constance Fenimore [grand-niece of J. Fenimore Cooper ; American ; 1838–94].
Castle Nowhere : Lake Country sketches. 1876
Short stories of life near the Great Lakes, depicting a rough and ugly phase of life, but revealing the genuine humanity that lies behind it. [Harper, New York : o.p.]

—— *Rodman the Keeper.* 1880
Short stories of Georgia, Florida, and N. and S. Carolina just after the Civil War ; sympathetic in their observation of life, thoroughly feminine in their tenderness and patient delineation of ordinary existence. The physical aspects of the country, the people, black and white, and the dialects, are all carefully exhibited. [Harper, New York : o.p.]

—— *Anne.* 1882
" Scenes at Mackinac and about New York." [Harper, New York.]

—— *For the Major : a novelette.* 1883
An elderly woman, to save her husband's feelings, who has protected her and her child, tries to make herself appear young and comely, and drops the mask only at his death. Kindly sketches of village life, and of gentle, attractive people. [Harper, New York : o.p.]

—— *East Angels.* 1886
Her most elaborate novel, dealing with the love affairs and other relations of a large group of characters in Georgia before the war. The interest centres in an exalted case of self-renunciation, the magnanimous Margaret sacrificing love and erecting barriers between herself and her lover. [Harper, New York : o.p.]

—— *Jupiter Lights.* 1889
An intricate and harrowing story ; scene, a winter city on the Florida coast ; thesis, the self-abnegation of women's love. The sufferings of one woman at the hands of a fascinating man who has an inherited tendency to insanity, and, later, the mental tortures of another woman who believes she has killed him, and then falls in love with his brother, are the main episodes. [Harper, New York : o.p.]

—— *Horace Chase.* 1894
The idiosyncrasies, the tragedies, big and little, and the everyday domestic life of humble gentlefolk in an Alleghany village and at the seaside in Florida. An old but impoverished family is revolutionized by the marriage into it of the millionaire Horace Chase, whose sterling nature, lacking in culture, fails to win the sympathies of these refined people. Of deeper interest is the spiritual history of the impulsive young wife, loving her middle-aged husband, yet swayed by a passion for a younger man. [Harper : o.p.]

—— *The Front Yard ; and other Italian stories.* 1896
Six stories, elucidating character by delicate shading, deeply sympathetic in their psychological realism. [Harper, New York : o.p.]

WRIGHT, Mabel [*née* Osgood ; American ; *b.* 1859]. *Tommy-Anne and the Three Hearts.*
[juvenile] 1896

—— *Wabeno, the Magician* [sequel]. [juvenile] 1899
Diana (" Tommy-Anne ") is a little girl who wishes to know the reason for all things. A voice, which ultimately takes the form of an old man, addresses her in the woods, and informs her that he is the Heart of Nature, one of the Brotherhood of Three Hearts, which governs all things, seen and unseen ; and lends her a pair of spectacles which help her to understand some of the secrets of Nature and those of the other two brothers, Heart of God and Heart of Man. [(1) and (2), Macmillan, New York ; (1) : o.p.]

WRIGHT, Mabel (*continued*). *The Dream-Fox Story Book.* [juvenile] 1900
The dream-fox takes Billy Button through many adventures with queer animals and queer people. [Macmillan, New York.]

WRIGHT, Sydney Fowler. *The World Below.* 1929
Imagines the world half a million years hence, when the human race consists of Dwellers, chiefly male and living mostly underground, and Amphibians, chiefly female, living mostly in the sea. [Collins ; Book I was originally published separately, *sub tit. The Amphibians*, 1925.]

—— *Elfwin.* 1930
Elfwin is the daughter of Ethelfleda, the Lady of Mercia, daughter of Alfred and sister of Edward the Elder. She loves a Danish prince, and eventually finds a refuge in America. The death-struggle of Saxons and Danes is conscientiously described (915–920). [Harrap ; Longmans, New York.]

WU SHU-CHUING [Mrs. Wu Lien-teh ; Chinese]. *The Most Famous Beauty of China.* 1924
The life of Yang Kuei-Fei, wife of the Emperor of China (eighth century). [Appleton, New York.]

WYLIE, Elinor [Mrs. William Rose Benét, *née* Hoyt ; American ; 1887–1928]. *Jennifer Lorn : a sedate extravaganza.* 1923
England and India, 1773. The heroine is the wife of a Government official. [Doubleday, Doran, New York ; illus., Knopf, New York ; Richards.]

—— *The Venetian Glass Nephew.* 1925
A fantasy of eighteenth-century Venice—a cardinal gets Casanova to make him a nephew out of spun glass. [Doubleday, Doran, New York ; Heinemann.]

—— *Mortal Image.* 1926
A story of Shelley, who is supposed to have been rescued from drowning and to have begun life afresh under a new name in America. [American title, *The Orphan Angel*, Knopf, New York ; Heinemann.]

—— *Mr. Hodge and Mr. Hazard.* 1928
An amusing gloss on the foundering of romanticism at the advent of the Victorians. Mr. Hazard is a sort of composite portrait of Shelley, Byron, Keats, Landor, Coleridge, etc. High-strung, imaginative, unworldly, irascible, he comes into collision with Hodge, snobbish, mathematical, efficient, philistine ; and his victory is only of the spirit. [Knopf, New York ; Heinemann.]

" WYNNE, May " [Miss M. W. Knowles]. *A King's Tragedy.* 1905
—— *Let Erin Remember.* 1908
Two favourable examples of this prolific lady's historical romances, which usually are staged on the Continent, and serve up fictitious episodes of mediæval and later history in a spirited, and sometimes a stilted manner. The king is James I of Scotland, assassinated in 1437. The Irish tale is about Strongbow's conquest, and represents the Normans as chivalrous warriors and the Irish as defeated through their own jealousies and dissensions. Both romances are more imaginative than historical. [(1), Digby & Long : o.p. ; (2), Greening : o.p.]

—— *The Silent Captain.* 1914
The struggle between the Huguenots and Catholics (1560). Scenes, Paris, Nantes, and Amboise. The captain is Condé. [S. Paul : o.p.]

—— *Fires of Freedom.* 1916
The revolt of the Belgian provinces against Austria (1789–90). [Chapman : o.p.]

—— *A Spy for Napoleon.* 1917
The heroine is one of Napoleon's spies under Fouché, at the time of the Cadoudal-Pichegru conspiracy (1803–4). Napoleon is introduced in an unfavourable light. [Jarrold : o.p.]

—— *The Gipsy King.* 1917
North Devon in 1714. The hero is an historical figure, Bampfylde Moore Carew. [Chapman : o.p.]

—— *The King of a Day.* 1918
Stanislaus of Poland and his claim to that throne against Augustus (1733–4). [Jarrolds : o.p.]

—— *Robin the Prodigal.* 1919
An attractive sentimental picture of Defoe in his home life and his mission to Scotland, with glimpses of Harley and Godolphin. [Jarrolds : o.p.]

—— *A Prince of Intrigue : a romance of Mazeppa.* 1920
Byron's hero, Ivan Stepanovitch Mazeppa, is the hero of this story of Poland and the Ukraine, in which figure also Peter the Great and Charles XII of Sweden. [Jarrold : o.p.]

WYNNE, May, and DELL, Draycott M. *The Veiled Lady.* 1918
The Veiled Lady is the guillotine and the scenes are laid in the Reign of Terror. [Jarrolds : o.p.]

XENOPOULOS, Gregory [Greek]. *The Stepmother : a tale of modern Athens.* 1897
A short story of Greek home life, truthful in describing the features of modern Athens, and in revealing the intimate domestic life of which strangers see so little. Aims to point out the evils of the Greek practice of very early marriage. [Transl. by Mrs. EDMONDS, Lane : o.p.]

YATES, Edmund [1831–94]. *Broken to Harness : a story of English domestic life.* 1864
This and the next are the sole survivors of many novels, stories, and novelettes by the founder of *The World*. It is an ingenious plot-novel in the manner of Wilkie Collins, with character-drawing (e.g. the money-lender Scadgers) and sentimentality derived from Dickens. Kate Mellon's horse-training establishment is evidently sketched from Yates's place at Willesden. [Routledge : o.p.]

YATES, Edmund (*continued*). *Black Sheep.*   1867
> A fair example of the sensational fiction concerned not so much with objective horrors as with the motives and the mental combinations of persons intent on crime. A clever and fascinating, conscienceless woman schemes to fasten the guilt of a murder on an innocent friend. There is no secret, no mystery ; the reader's interest is absorbed in working out an intellectual problem clearly indicated from the beginning. [Edited by E. A. Baker (Half-forgotten Books), Routledge (Dutton, New York), 1903 : o.p.]

YEATS, Sidney Kilner LEVETT [Anglo-Indian]. *The Honour of Savelli.*   1896
> A romance of intrigue and action in the Italy of the Borgias, Machiavelli, etc. (*c.* 1500–4). [Low : o.p. ; Appleton, New York : o.p.]

—— *The Chevalier d'Auriac.*   1897
> Love-making, intrigue, and fighting at the Court of Henry of Navarre. [Longmans : o.p.]

—— *The Traitor's Way.*   1901
> The Huguenot conspiracy of Amboise (1560). [Longmans : o.p. ; Stokes, New York : o.p.]

—— *The Lord Protector.*   [juvenile] 1902
> Cromwell in his declining years. [Cassell : o.p. ; Longmans, New York.]

—— *Orrain.*   1904
> A second " Gentleman of France " ; the hero an invincible swordsman under a cloud, charged with the escort of a young lady through countless perils (1555). A breathless rush of adventure ; all utterly improbable and unreal. [Methuen : o.p. ; Longman, New York : o.p.]

YEATS, William Butler [Irish ; *b.* 1865]. *The Celtic Twilight : men and women, dhouls and faeries.*   1895
> A collection of Irish folk-tales of mystery and wonder by an apostle of the Celtic renaissance. Drawn chiefly from the peasants of N.E. Sligo, and retold in a style of cultivated simplicity, and with an attitude as if the writer would believe them if he could. [Bullen : o.p. ; Macmillan, New York : o.p.]

—— *The Secret Rose.*   1897
> Fairy-tales and folk-tales, original or clothed in a new imaginative form, relating to both mediæval and modern times, and together making a sort of gospel of Celtic mysticism in its latest phase. Written in exquisite prose. [*Stories of Red Hanrahan ; The Secret Rose ; Rosa Alchemica*, Macmillan, London and New York, 1914.]

YONGE, Charlotte Mary [1823–1901]. *The Heir of Redclyffe.*   1853
> An exceedingly sentimental and idealized picture of virtuous character and virtuous domestic life, manifestly inspired by Tractarian views, and intended for the moral improvement of young people. Has been neatly described as a " sweet youthful tragedy of piety and devotion."

—— *The Little Duke.*   [juvenile] 1854
> A children's story of Normandy and Richard the Fearless (943–58).

—— *The Lances of Lynwood.*   [juvenile] 1855
> A good story of the reign of Edward III and the accession of Richard II. Brings in the battle of Navarette (Nájera), where the Black Prince and Pedro the Cruel defeated Du Guesclin and Henry of Trastamare (1367).

—— *The Dove in the Eagle's Nest.*   1866
> The heroine, a maiden of Ulm, is carried off by a robber baron to his Swabian hold, and, as nurse to his sick daughter, brings an influence for peace and goodness into the house and rears her twin sons to a life of piety and noble deeds. Time of Frederick III and Maximilian I (1472–1531).

—— *The Chaplet of Pearls ; or, The White and Black Ribaumont.*   [juvenile] 1868
> A story of the times of Henry IV of France and the massacre of St. Bartholomew.

—— *The Caged Lion.*   [juvenile] 1870
> Prince James (I) of Scotland in England, under Henry V (*c.* 1407–22).

—— *Unknown to History.*   [juvenile] 1882
> A touching story that gives an account of Mary Queen of Scotland's captivity in England, the Babington plot, and her trial and execution (1568–97).

—— *Stray Pearls ; or, The Memoirs of Margaret de Ribaumont.*   [juvenile] 1883
> War of the Fronde (1648–53). Sequel to *The Chaplet of Pearls.* [o.p.]

—— *The Prince and the Page.*   [juvenile] 1884
> The reign of Henry III and the Eighth Crusade (1270–2).

—— *The Armourer's Prentices.*   [juvenile] 1884
> The adventures of two orphan brothers, who make their way from the New Forest to London in search of their fortunes. One, who has scholarly instincts, gets attached to Wolsey's household and becomes acquainted with Colet, whilst the other becomes a master-armourer.

—— *A Reputed Changeling.*   [juvenile] 1889
> Family history ; scenes, Portchester, London, St. Germain, etc. ; period Charles II to William III (1680–1700.)

—— *Beechcroft at Rockstone.*   [juvenile] 1889
> The world of district visitors, budding clergymen, school-children, and the workers of the Girls' Friendly Society, sketched in a quiet romance, ethical in tone.

—— *Two Penniless Princesses.*   [juvenile] 1891
> The sisters of James II of Scotland, in England and at the Court of René of Anjou. Time of Henry VI. [o.p.]

—— *Grisly Grisell, the Laidly Lady of Whitburn.*   [juvenile] 1894
> Wars of the Roses, Warwick the King-Maker, etc., Bruges under Philip the Good and Charles the Bold (1467). [o.p.]

—— *Modern Broods ; or, Developments Unlooked For.*   1900
> Interesting as the views and criticisms of a mid-century novelist on the young person of a later day. Crowded with characters, including several familiar types of girlhood, very similar to those that peopled her earlier

YONGE, Charlotte Mary (*continued*).

noveis. A maiden aunt in charge of four girls is a prominent figure, troubled with the anxieties and perplexities of their religious and social interests and later of their love affairs. [o.p.]

[All Macmillan, London and New York (those out of print so indicated) ; (1)-(4), also (Everyman's Lib.) Dent (Dutton, New York).]

" YORKE, Curtis " [Mrs. Susan Rowley Richmond Lee, *née* Long ; *d*. 1930]. *Jocelyn Erroll.*
1899

A novel of purpose, of the sentimental, not the intellectual, kind. Erroll is a clergyman who withdraws from the Church, but afterwards, with his freethinking wife, returns to the faith as the result of experience and family love ; he is, further, assailed by the wiles of a heartless siren, who also is brought to a sense of her errors by calamity. [Jarrold : o.p.]

—— *Carpathia Knox.* 1900

In her youth Carpathia had sacrificed her lover to her friend, and, now in old age, travelling in Spain with her niece, she meets with the son of the pair, and a warm affection grows up between the young people. A quiet narrative, the characters marked by tender humanity ; but the travel-sketches of rural Spain are the most substantial part. [Jarrold : o.p.]

—— *She Who Meant Well.* 1917

The well-meaning sister brings about a marriage between a girl and a cripple, and the results are grievous—a story told with sympathy and tenderness. [Hutchinson : o.p.]

YOUNG, Emily Hilda [*b*. 1880]. *Moor Fires.* 1916

A brooding, imaginative story of intellectual women domiciled in a notably Brontëan environment. [Murray ; Cape ; Harcourt, New York.]

—— *Miss Mole.* 1930

This plain, shrewd, self-sufficient companion-housekeeper is a delectable creation, and the play of character between her and some rather difficult people makes good comedy. [Cape ; Harcourt, New York.]

YOUNG, Florence Ethel Mills [*b*. 1875]. *Cælebs : the love-story of a bachelor.* 1917

An English village is the scene, on to which come the old-fashioned bachelor and the gardener in breeches with whom he falls in love. [Lane.]

—— *The Bigamist.* 1917

A young wife and mother discovers that her husband has a first wife still living ; she brings herself to conceal the truth ; but the relations of the pair are unsatisfactory, and she suffers acutely, especially when the husband has a fancy for another woman. [Lane.]

—— *The Laws of Chance.* 1918

After an uneventful life in London, David Curtis goes to Africa, and at Kimberley learns from a casual acquaintance a secret concerning a hoard of precious stones in England—a secret which endangers his life. [Lane.]

—— *The Barrier.* 1929

A story of Cape Town intended to illustrate " the invisible barrier which separates black from white." [Lane.]

YOUNG, Francis E. Brett [*b*. 1884]. *Deep Sea.* 1914

The sordid life of a small fishing-town in the west of England, depicted with perhaps more force and truthfulness than such sorry material is worth, artistically. [Secker : o.p. ; Collins.]

—— *The Dark Tower.* 1915

This little drama of a brother's romantic passion for his sister-in-law is avowedly inspired by Debussy's music to *Pelléas and Mélisande*. The stormy fells and ancient woods on the Welsh border in which the half-ruined Norman keep is buried are poetically described almost as a musical accompaniment. [Collins ; Knopf, New York (1926) ; Grosset, New York.]

—— *The Iron Age.* 1916

A young man of generous and sensitive temperament is driven to rebellion by the rampant industrialism which has transformed a peaceful countryside into a huge iron-foundry. After losing himself with a worthless woman, he finds a chance of redemption in the war. Both in character-drawing and in the description of scenery (Staffordshire and the Welsh border) this is at the author's highest level. [Cassell.]

—— *The Crescent Moon.* 1918

A drama of adventure and heroism, gaining in intensity from its setting in German East Africa in the early days of the war. [Collins ; Dutton, New York.]

—— *The Tragic Bride.* 1919

An inconclusive story of a young and unhappy wife who falls in love with a boy, her husband's pupil. The treatment is rather idyllic than realistic. [Cassell ; Dutton, New York.]

—— *The Young Physician.* 1919

The first part deals with the school life of a sensitive boy ; the second, with his experiences, of the usual type, as a medical student—based on the author's own recollections of his medical training. [Collins ; Dutton, New York.]

—— *The Black Diamond.* 1921

Realism combines with the picturesque in this tragedy of a young miner in South Wales. [Collins ; Dutton, New York.]

—— *The Red Knight.* 1921

Combines the adventure of a revolution in an imaginary Latin country with a character-study of a man weak and selfish but honourable. [Collins ; Dutton, New York.]

—— *Woodsmoke.* 1924

Story of a safari or expedition into the interior of Africa conjoined with a bizarre love-story, a jealous husband disappearing into the bush and haunting the lovers with his spook. The wild forest region from Mombasa to the skirts of Kilimanjaro is vividly depicted by one who knows it. [Collins ; Dutton, New York.]

YOUNG, Francis, E. Brett (*continued*). *Portrait of Claire.* 1927

A long chronicle of the life of a not extraordinary woman of good birth, her three marriages, and her devotion to the only son of the first ; gives a broad and detailed picture of English country life in the period 1899 to 1918. [Heinemann ; *sub tit. Love is Enough*, 2 vols., Knopf, New York.]

—— *The Key of Life.* 1928

A girl in doubt between two lovers, one stronger, one weaker than herself. The scene is mainly an archæological expedition's camp in Egypt. [Heinemann ; Knopf, New York.]

—— *My Brother Jonathan.* 1928

Another portrait-novel ; the hero is the son of foolish parents, and enters the medical profession ; the story of his conflicting love for two women is closely bound up with his struggles as a rising doctor. Scenes, Staffordshire, especially North Bromwich and Wednesbury. [Heinemann ; Knopf, New York.]

—— *Black Roses.* 1929

A portrait painter of mediocre attainments recalls, whilst cruising in the Mediterranean, his early life in Naples. There he had struggled against poverty, learned the meaning of friendship and romance, and lost both love and youth in the ravages of a cholera epidemic. [Heinemann ; Harper, New York.]

—— *Jim Redlake.* 1930

A very long biographical novel. The subject is the son of a doctor in the Midlands, an average young man, who goes to South Africa and serves in the East African campaign. His love affairs and marriage come in, with a lot of by-characters, superficially but recognizably drawn. [Heinemann ; Harper, New York.]

YOUNG, Francis E. Brett, and YOUNG, E. Brett. *Undergrowth.* 1913

Aims at capturing the spirit of mystery and terror of the Welsh hills ; a tale of pagan survivals, and the effect of fear on a gang of men, in especial the engineer in charge, employed in building a reservoir there. [Collins ; Dutton, New York.]

YOUNG, Margaret. *The Wreathed Dagger.* 1909

The defence of Thirlsby House, the last Royalist stronghold, and its eventual surrender to Cromwell (1648). [Cassell : o.p.]

ZAMACOIS, Eduardo [Spanish ; *b.* 1866]. *Roots.* 1929

A tragedy of hatred, the characters of which are drawn from the agricultural population of the plains of Castile. [Transl. by Eliseo VIVAS, Viking Press, New York ; Brentano.]

ZAMYATIN, Evgeny Ivanovich [Russian ; *b.* 1884]. *We.* 1924

A satire upon standardization. In the world of 3,000 A.D. the individual has completely merged into a composite human block. [Transl. by Gregory ZILBOORG, Dutton, New York.]

ZANGWILL, Israel [1864–1926]. *Children of the Ghetto ; being pictures of a Peculiar People.* 1892

The life of the Jews in London, chiefly poor and wretched immigrants but also of the aristocracy, strong in its portrayal of both ethnic and personal traits, depicted by one who knows and loves them, a Jew of the Jews. It is a succession of scenes, connected by a thread of narrative, ideas and ways of thinking, as well as ceremonial and external features. Mr. Zangwill's Jewish novels are invaluable as an historical and social document, revealing the innermost character as well as the outward life of his race. [Heinemann ; Dent ; Macmillan, New York : o.p. ; Jewish Pub. Co., New York (1916).]

—— *The King of Schnorrers : grotesques and fantasies.* 1894

A series of pictures of eighteenth-century beggars and other Hebrews, tragic and comic, the tone rather that of extravaganza, but weighted with the same intimate knowledge and copious detail. [Heinemann ; Macmillan, New York.]

—— *Dreamers of the Ghetto.* 1898

Real episodes of history thrown into the shape of fiction by an extension of Landor's method in the *Imaginary Conversations*, but with a warmer infusion of feeling. Conversations with, and imaginative memoirs of, historic representatives of the Jewish race, particularly of such as rebelled against the narrow limits of orthodox Judaism—Uriel Acosta, Maimonides, Spinoza, Heine, and Ferdinand Lassalle. [Heinemann : Jewish Pub. Co., New York.]

—— *They that Walk in Darkness : Ghetto tragedies.* 1899

Luminous pictures of the Ghetto, sombre in colour. The title-story, a pathetic fantasy, is one of the best. The simple story *Incurable* probes the deepest recesses of human agony. *Satan Mekatrig* is a weird story of temptation, with hints of the Devil's actual appearance in a Jewish community ; *The Sabbath Breaker*, a tender little anecdote of a mother's love ; *Bethulah*, a story of ancient beliefs surviving and operative amid the widely alien circumstances of modern life. [Heinemann ; Jewish Pub. Co., New York.]

—— *The Master.* 1895

The biography of a Nova Scotian lad, by nature an artist, who makes his way through almost insuperable difficulties to success, but finds the hardest struggle is to subdue himself. Deals philosophically with the deeper problems of life, presenting the ideal character of the artist, repelling the temptations of the world, and devoting body and soul to art until he attains a vision of the truth and beauty that are in the life around him. [Heinemann ; Harper, New York.]

—— *The Mantle of Elijah.* 1900

A study of the politics of the Palmerston period, with an anticipation of the Transvaal question in the Novabarba difficulty, which gives the author scope for caustic satire on jingoism and the claptrap offered as apology for war. The heroine has relations with an ambitious politician, whose personal magnetism and devotion to her father's cause lead her to become his wife. He rats, and she is disillusioned, her fastidious nature outraged by his vulgarity and selfishness. [Heinemann ; Harper, New York : o.p.]

—— *The Grey Wig : stories and novelettes.* 1903

Contains his newest and his oldest work. Mostly characterized by sparkling and epigrammatic style, both in narrative and dialogue ; the manner more studied than the matter. Title-story, a touching little comedy

ZANGWILL, Israel (*continued*).

about two aged Frenchwomen, ending in gratuitous horror. *Chassé Croisé*, still comic, but more serious of intent ; the marriage of an American " millionairess " with an English politician—love marrying ambition, and disappointed when ambition changes to love. *The Big Bow-Wow Mystery* is an attempt to " take off " the ordinary detective story. [Heinemann ; Macmillan, New York.]

—— *Ghetto Comedies.*   1907

The lighter side, but still a serious delineation of Jewish life. *The Convert* is a delicate study of a beautiful Jewess. Melchisedech Pinches reappears from *Children of the Ghetto*, in the more Rabelaisian character of a demagogue and a bragging literary quack. Satire of hypocritical pharisaism in the successful Sir Assher Abrahams, of Zionist ideals and self-immolations in Raphael. *The Model of Sorrows* is an artistic expression of the duality of the modern Jew, " king and knave in one." *The Hirelings* and *Anglicization* as well as Sir Assher in *The Jewish Trinity*, powerfully illustrate the same theme of denationalization. [Heinemann ; Macmillan, New York.]

—— *Jinny the Carrier.*   1919

A long and leisurely and uncomplicated story of Essex rustics in 1851. [Heinemann : Macmillan, New York.]

ŻEROMSKI, Stefan [Polish ; 1864–1925]. *Ashes* (Popioli, 3 vols., 1904).   1928

A tremendous panorama of Poland and Polish life at the time when, after the Hapsburg domination, nationalist sentiment was rekindled by the hopes held out by Napoleon's success in Europe. Some of the best passages in the book, indeed, are those in which the hero follows the French army in its various campaigns throughout Europe. The Polish scene (1797–1812) is reconstructed with abundant detail and exuberant vigour. [Transl. (condensed) by Helen Stankiewicz ZAND, 2 vols., Knopf.]

ZHABOTINSKY, Vladimir Evgenevich [Russian ; *b.* 1880]. *Samson the Nazarite* (Samson Nazorey).
                                                                                                                                                               1930

An imaginative reconstruction of the biblical story, in which Delilah is acquitted of her worst offences, and the Philistines are depicted with fairness and understanding. [Transl. by Cyrus BROOKS, Secker.]

ZOLA, Émile Édouard Charles Antoine [French ; 1840–1902]. *Stories for Ninon* (Contes à Ninon, 1864–74).   1897

An interesting collection of stories by Zola, the poetic romancer, written long before he conceived the experimental novel. Two series—*Contes à Ninon* (1864) and *Nouveaux contes à Ninon* (1874). *The Love Fairy*, written 1858, is a fantastic trifle in the eighteenth-century style of Crébillon ; *The Ball Programme* (1860), a Provençal story, consists chiefly of a dialogue between a young girl and her last ball programme ; *Blood* (1862) is a bit of romantic melodrama about some soldiers and a ghost ; *Simplice*, an imaginative little fairy-tale ; *The Thieves and the Ass*, the story of a picnic by the Seine, embodies reminiscences of Zola's penurious early life in Paris. *Jean Sourdon's Four Days* (*Nouveaux contes*) is longer and more important, a pastoral in four scenes, each a representative day in the life of a Provençal peasant ; youth and love, war, marriage, and paternity, sudden death, are the themes of these episodes. [Transl. by E. A. VIZETELLY, Heinemann : o.p.]

—— *A Dead Woman's Wish* (Le vœu d'une morte, 1866).   1902

Belongs to the same imaginative period of Zola's art. An idealistic story of heroism, passion, and self-effacement ; with four Parisian sketches subjoined. [Transl. by Count C. S. DE SOISSONS, S. Paul ; McKay, Philadelphia, 1928.]

—— *The Mysteries of Marseilles* (Les mystères de Marseille, 1867–8).   1895

A melodramatic novel of the old stamp, culminating in the 1848 insurrection at Marseilles. [Transl. by E. A. VIZETELLY, Hutchinson : o.p.]

—— *The Attack on the Mill* (L'attaque du moulin, 1880) ; *and other sketches of war.*   1894

L'attaque du moulin appeared in the famous collection of six naturalistic stories by as many writers, entitled *Les soirées de Médan* (1880). An intensely vivid and realistic picture of warfare by one who has constantly recognized the hideousness of war. The accompanying sketch, *Three Wars*, is a pathetic series of reminiscences of the Crimean, Franco-Italian, and Franco-German campaigns, connected by the history of two brothers : here again war is represented as perverting the moral nature of man. [Heinemann : o.p. ; Brentano, New York : o.p.]

THE ROUGON-MACQUART SERIES.

The most systematic and comprehensive attempt made since Balzac to depict on a large scale contemporary life as it is. In twenty novels, Zola traced the physiological and psychical history of a family in whose blood there was an hereditary taint. Each book illustrates a certain phase of social life ; and the work is carried out with unparalleled energy and an exhaustive research usually confined to specialists. Unprepossessing features are the commonness of the subjects, the domination of a mechanical view of life, the absence of spirituality, taste, or even selection. The avowed principle of the " experimental novel," as Zola denominates this form of fiction, is to place beings, whose physical and mental constitution is known, in a certain environment and under the influence of certain events, and then to see whether the result corresponds with the author's observation of life. Hence this family chronicle must be regarded as a serious study in human evolution, each novel showing the influence of heredity and the disturbing effect of variation, each important character exhibiting in his conduct and career the tendency of his blood.

—— *The Fortunes of the Rougons* (La fortune des Rougon, 1871).   1898

The introductory novel, which is the key to the whole series. In the preface Zola expounds the basic idea of heredity. The common ancestress of Rougons and Macquarts is the neuropathic Adelaïde Fouque, who, being widowed, takes for a lover the brutal and drunken Macquart, a gloomy and taciturn pariah. From the legitimate Pierre Rougon and the base-born Antoine and Ursula Macquart spring the divers branches of the family, and their several characteristics are constantly reproduced. Pierre domineers over his weak mother, cheats her, and turns out the other children ; then, marrying Felicité, he introduces a new strain. The effects of the *coup d'état* of 1851 in the provinces is described with local knowledge and historical

ZOLA, Émile Édouard Charles Antoine (*continued*).

accuracy, many of the incidents being founded on the statements of eye-witnesses. A touching idyll of two young lovers, Miette and Silvère, comes to a tragic conclusion through the popular upheaval. The Provençal country town of Plassans is the scene. [Transl. by E. A. VIZETELLY, Chatto.]

—— *The Rush for the Spoils* (La curée, 1871). 1885
Describes the career of Aristide Saccard, who makes an enormous fortune by building speculation, and having married a lady of social rank gains entrance to the world of vulgar profligacy and extravagance which constituted Parisian society after the establishment of the Second Empire in 1851. [Transl., Vizetelly 1885-7: o.p.; *La curée*, transl. by A. Texeira DE MATTOS, *priv. prin.*, Lutetian Soc.]

—— *The Fat and the Thin* (Le ventre de Paris, 1873). 1895
The English title refers allegorically to the incessant conflict between the fat and the lean of this world, the well-fed, prosperous bourgeois and the starving labourer. It is a study of the inhabitants of the Halles, the great central markets of Paris ; a picture of teeming, multitudinous life, full of gross contrasts. Faithful in portraiture of humble characters, shopkeepers, workpeople, fishwives, market gardeners, street-arabs, and all the motley denizens of the markets. Lisa, the selfish and worldly-wise heroine, is a Macquart ; the story hinges on her brother-in-law's return from Cayenne, his clandestine sojourn in her house, and the discontent with his idle existence which urges her at last to denounce him to the police : period, 1857 to 1860. [Transl. by E. A. VIZETELLY, Chatto.]

—— *The Conquest of Plassans* (La conquête de Plassans, 1874). 1900
Pictures the whole life of a provincial town, the petty jealousies, cliques and intrigues, and the political movements in the years following the *coup d'état.* Plassans was becoming a stronghold of the clerical party, when an arrogant and wily priest was sent to win it back for the Government. This powerful, ambitious, ascetic man makes himself head of the dominant party, and in the course of his operations wrecks the home of the Mourets. Marthe, the youngest daughter of Pierre and Felicité, weak and neurasthenic as her grandmother Adelaïde, is the pathetic heroine. She, the wife, demoralized by a fatal infatuation for the priest, which he scorns, ruins her family and dies miserably. The husband is an interesting case of a sane man believed to be a lunatic and put away, with the result that he actually goes insane. [Transl. by E. A. VIZETELLY, Chatto.]

—— *The Abbé Mouret's Transgression* (La faute de l'abbé Mouret, 1875). 1900
The Abbé is the son of this unfortunate pair, and the taint comes out, after his transgression and repentance, in the form of ecstatic and morbid spirituality verging on hysteria. He is priest of a squalid village in Provence, the degenerate inhabitants of which compose an ugly picture of country life. The central episode is a kind of mythological poem, in which the author embodies ideas from his early poem of *Genesis.* In the Paradou, the wild, neglected demesne of a ruined manor-house, amidst the unfettered exuberance of Nature, Mouret and the lovely Albine, like Adam and Eve in the garden of Eden, live their Arcadian idyll, soon to close in tragedy, and for the abbé in bitter penitence for a sin which he had committed almost involuntarily. Exposes the moral evils entailed by celibacy. [Transl. by E. A. VIZETELLY, Chatto.]

—— *His Excellency* (Son excellence Eugène Rougon, 1876). 1897
The victorious career of Eugène Rougon, the great man of the family, who becomes Prime Minister under the Empire as the result of his masterly advocacy of the regime of force, and, later, of the Liberal movement inaugurated by Napoleon III—obviously a study of Eugène Rouher (1814-84 ; Minister of State, 1861). This powerful and complex character is likewise a product of hereditary tendencies, which account for his nature and life : his father and mother were Pierre and Felicité, masculine strength and crafty intelligence. As a species of historical monograph the novel has further interest, depicting with great realism society and official life, and exposing the falsehoods and corruptions of the Imperial Court. [Transl. by E. A. VIZETELLY, Chatto : o.p.]

—— *The Dram Shop* (L'assommoir, 1877). 1897
This book first made Zola famous. The central idea is the ruinous effect, social and moral, of drinking ; and pathetic interest attaches to Gervaise, the ill-used victim of circumstances, corrupted in her very infancy yet preserving the feminine traits of tenderness and modesty. The original is appallingly outspoken, and shocked the public with its terrible revelations of the social depravity due to drink. The grossness of the argot and of the incidents is, of course, much modified here, as in all these translations. [Transl. by E. A. VIZETELLY, Chatto ; another transl., *sub tit. L'Assommoir,* Knopf. Transl. by Arthur SYMONS, Boni, 1924.]

—— *A Love Episode* (Une page d'amour, 1878). 1895
A touching story of Parisian life, full of fancy and ideality, though essentially naturalistic in its portrayal of the growth of love. A widow living with her consumptive daughter, in whom the hereditary blight reappears, enters into a passionate liaison with a doctor, and the poor little girl manages to kill herself with jealousy. The drab realism of such scenes as the child's funeral intensifies the pathos ; and, seen through a window from hour to hour, the vast ocean of Paris, moody and changeful, throws a poetic light over the story. [Transl. by E. A. VIZETELLY, Hutchinson : o.p.]

—— *Nana* (Nana, 1880). 1884
Descriptive of theatrical life and of the courtesans of Paris. Nana is a beautiful, fascinating, extravagant, and incompetent actress, who ruins a host of lovers and dies a repulsive death. [Transl. by E. A. VIZETELLY, *priv. prin.*, Victor Plarr, Lutetian Soc. ; transl. by J. STIRLING, Peterson, Philadelphia, 1880 : o.p. ; transl. by Burton RASCOE, Knopf, 1922 ; by Victor PLARR, Boni, New York.]

—— *Piping Hot* (Pot-bouille, 1882). 1885
A naturalistic painting of bourgeois domesticity, outrageous in its unveiling of private vices and of the obscene secrets of life. In pursuance of his verily Augean realism, Zola has collected into one house such a mass of ignoble characters and foul details that the whole is incredible even if the parts can be authenticated. [Transl. by Percy PINKERTON, Boni, New York, 1924.]

—— *The Ladies' Paradise* (Au bonheur des dames, 1883). 1895
A huge *magazin*, or store, with its horde of employees and throngs of customers, is the theatre of this drama

ZOLA, Émile Édouard Charles Antoine (*continued*).
of human bestiality. " The Ladies' Paradise " is, as it were, a protagonist in the play, a colossal Moloch, devouring the petty shopkeepers, who are ruined by the unequal competition.

—— *How Jolly Life Is!* (Joie de vivre, 1884). 1886
Portrays a set of selfish and unhappy people, of weak wills and diseased constitutions, who cling to life not because they find any joy in it but from morbid fear of death : scene, a seaside village in Normandy. Lazare Chanteau, a young hypochondriac, whose insane projects devour the wealth of the girl who loves him, is the most miserable decadent of them all. Pauline, on the other hand, is a fine embodiment of tireless devotion to others, in spite of ingratitude. Basely wronged by those she has saved, her hopes and affections thwarted, she yet finds consolation and joy in denying herself more and more. [Transl. by E. A. VIZETELLY, Chatto.]

—— *Germinal ; or, Master and Man* (Germinal, 1885). 1885
Describes the struggles of capital and labour in a coal-mining centre. Lantier, a scion of the Rougon-Macquarts, works as a labourer in the pits, and is one of the ringleaders when the selfish policy of the company drives the employees to strike. The life of the unhappy miners, their degradation and misery beneath the iron rule of the capitalist ; the ravages of hunger, chief weapon of their foes ; and the wild scenes of violence that signalize the strike, are painted with multitudinous details into a vast and terrible picture, calling to mind Dante's descriptions of hell. [Chatto ; transl. by Havelock ELLIS, Knopf, 1925 ; Boni, New York (*Six Masterpieces*).]

—— *His Masterpiece ; or, De Lantier's Struggle for Fame* (L'œuvre, 1886). 1886
The theme is literary and artistic work, with its vicissitudes of triumph and defeat, hope and despair. A sad tale, with more intellectual interest than usual with Zola, dealing with the unhappy life of a man of genius who is unable to bring to fruition any of his great ideas, in spite of indomitable energy. Zola makes full use of the extensive knowledge of studios and artists gained in his early work as art-critic. Claude Lantier is a composite study of the painters Cézanne and, to a less extent, the more famous Manet, whose life Zola has written, while the interesting character, Pierre Sandoz, has been identified with the novelist himself. Thus the book has exceptional interest as a *livre vécu*. Claude's insanity displays effectively the author's great pathological knowledge. [Transl. by E. A. VIZETELLY ; Chatto : o.p.]

—— *The Soil : a realistic novel* (La terre, 1887). 1888
A masterpiece of Zola's peculiar naturalism exhibiting the various excesses and fallacies of his theory of art, yet, impressing us by its sheer power of depicting, not individuals, but mankind in the mass. The agricultural population of France are depicted as a rabble of degraded beasts actuated by no motives more refined than covetousness, hatred, and lust. [Transl. by E. A. VIZETELLY, 1888 : o.p. ; Transl. by Ernest Dowson, Boni, New York, 1925.]

—— *The Dream* (Le rêve, 1888). 1893
Written as " a passport to the Academy," and well-nigh unique among Zola's fiction for its pure, idyllic grace. Angelique the foundling is taken in by an aged pair of servitors to a cathedral under whose shadow they live ; and as she grows up, sitting at her embroideries of sacred vestments, she has a vision of love and happiness which at length is realized. The mighty pile with its complex architecture, the play of light on the pinnacles and on the saints in the windows, and the solemn ritual that gives it a soul within, is the Hugoesque idea colouring the whole story. [Transl. by E. A. VIZETELLY, Chatto : o.p.]

—— *The Monomaniac* (La bête humaine, 1890). 1901
Introduces us to the railway world. Studies the business of a great line in immense detail, the picturesque side of railway life giving effect to some terrific episodes. Jacques Lantier, the monomaniac, is an engine-driver ; and Roubaud, the hero of an important episode, and other characters, work for the company in various capacities. Several threads of crime and depravity are woven into the story : Lantier has inherited from distant ancestors a hideous craving to murder women. A grim and horrible picture of life. [Transl. by E. A. VIZETELLY, Chatto : o.p.]

—— *Money* (L'argent, 1891). 1894
Explores the financial world, and brings to light the monstrous evils caused by speculation, company-promoting, the frauds and negligence of directors, and the inefficiency of existing laws. The hero, Saccard, a daring and unscrupulous financier, promotes a Universal Bank, and is opposed and ultimately ruined by the Jewish fraternity, whose power he aimed at destroying. Full of recognizable portraits, or composite portraits, of actual people—venal legislators, promoters, brokers, journalists. Reproduces actual incidents with little disguise. [Transl. by E. A. VIZETELLY, Chatto.]

—— *The Downfall* (La débâcle, 1892). 1892
A naturalistic account of the disastrous campaign that ended in Sedan as it was seen and endured by two private soldiers who were in the thick of the fight. Not only are the awful realities of modern warfare brought before the eye, but the intolerable fatigue of the marching, the agonies of the hospitals, and the degradation and misery experienced by prisoners of war are depicted with ruthless force. Still more tragic are the episodes of revolution and massacre inside beleagured Paris, where the pair of devoted friends meet again as Communist and Versaillist. [Transl. by E. A. VIZETELLY, Chatto ; by E. P. ROBINSON, Macmillan, New York : o.p.]

—— *Doctor Pascal* (1893). 1893
Here Zola concludes and sums up the results of the Rougon-Macquart cycle. Doctor Pascal, the learned student of heredity (no doubt a study of the famous savant Claude Bernard), draws up the genealogical tree, and traces the development of each branch, seeing therein an image of society and an explanation of its mysterious laws. The romantic interest centres in his passion for his niece Clotilde, which is treated as gracefully and inoffensively as a thoroughly sensuous art permits : the end is deeply tragic. Such a scene as the death of the anæmic boy in the presence of his imbecile ancestress, who has bequeathed his constitutional debility, is an epitome of the family history. [Transl. by E. A. VIZETELLY, Chatto ; by Mary J. SERRANO, Macmillan, New York : o.p.]

—— *Lourdes* (1894). 1894
First of a new series, *The Three Cities* investigating moral tendencies. A sceptical abbé, Pierre Fromont,

ZOLA, Émile Édouard Charles Antoine (*continued*).

visits Lourdes, Rome, and Paris, in search of a power sufficient for the present and future salvation of mankind. The obsolete superstition of Lourdes and the arrogant ecclesiasticism of Rome are condemned in turn, and finally, in *Paris*, the seeker examines and bans the political and social system of France. Fromont journeys first to Lourdes in the company of an invalid girl who loves him. The pilgrims' train, with its display of every disease that science can name, is described with minute and sometimes disgusting fullness ; then the processions and ceremonies before the sacred grotto are elaborately depicted, and after that the return, with the various effects on the sufferers of the religious excitement. Zola tested the cures by examining people who professed to be eye-witnesses, and was unable to authenticate a single case. [Transl. by E. A. VIZETELLY, Chatto.]

—— *Rome* (1896).   1896

His humanitarian appeal for a new religion, *La nouvelle Rome*, having been denounced by the Congregation of the Index, the abbé goes to Rome and succeeds in obtaining a personal interview with the Pope ; but his efforts to win the head of the Church to his views are fruitless. The Eternal City is described with the minuteness and exactness of a guide-book, with living pictures of the streets, the passers-by, the very dirt, and the whirl of human forces and social influences at work—a bewildering complexity. But Rome is moribund, because she fails to respond to the cry of the democracy ; she is immovable in her conservatism, and hopelessly paralysed by the material ambition of the Curia. [Transl. by E. A. VIZETELLY, Chatto (Macmillan, New York).]

—— *Paris* (1897).   1898

The abbé returns to Paris, and engages in charitable work amongst the poor. The complex life of Paris is delineated ; all parts of the community being passed in review, the governing classes with their far-reaching intrigues and personal ambitions, the world of rich financiers and licentious devotees of pleasure, the industrial classes and the very poor, the workers in the cause of scientific progress, and the underworld of agitators and conspirators. A thread of melodramatic interest is attached to an anarchist outrage, and indeed anarchism is regarded with sympathy, though the author sees health for mankind only in intelligent work. In a family of obscure fighters in the cause of humanity, Pierre Fromont, now unfrocked, finds a wife and a new career of usefulness, the lesson being that science is destined to supersede Christianity as the regenerating power. [Transl. by E. A. VIZETELLY, Chatto (2 vols., Macmillan, New York : o.p.]

—— *The Honour of the Army ; and other stories (various years).*   1887

The title-story, *Le capitaine Burle*, about an officer's loose life and dishonesty, contains an account of a duel. The next is an incredible tale of the resurrection of a buried man. Then comes an unpleasant story of loose Parisian life and immorality. *The Inundation* is one of his more imaginative essays, and *Naïs Micoulin* has much of the Southern richness of Provençal scenery. *Nantas* is one of the best short pieces, admirable in its brevity and concentration. *The Spree at Coqueville* is a Rabelaisian tale of village topers, and shows Zola in the rare character of a humorist. [Chatto.]

—— *Fruitfulness* (Fécondité, 1899).   1900

Begins another series, *Les quatres évangiles*, which he never lived to complete. The object was to give a conspectus and a criticism of modern life in France, and to shadow forth the writer's ideals of progress towards a better industrial and social organization. The offspring of Fromont appears here (in the twentieth century) as the patriarch of a hundred children, and symbolizes with his wife the principle of fruitfulness both in human procreation and in the cultivation of the earth's products. This pair is contrasted with the decadent disciple of Tolstoy, whose doctrines the teaching of the book diametrically opposes. Proclaims the hope of humanity to consist in healthy work and multiplication of the species, and in its pictures of domestic love and happiness shows the best side of Zola's nature. [Transl. by E. A. VIZETELLY, Chatto (Doubleday, New York).]

—— *Work* (Travail, 1901).   1901

Scene, a provincial town, the wretched inhabitants of which are employed in a huge factory belonging to a capitalist of the worst and most selfish type. On the one hand we are shown the tyranny of industrialism and the moral corruption of the rich man's home, on the other we watch the rise and ultimate prosperity of a co-operative factory, founded by Luc Fromont as a rival to the other. Here Zola's characteristic realism is illustrated side by side with his no less characteristic idealism, disclosing in concrete shape his hopes and aspirations towards mankind's future. [Transl. by E. A. VIZETELLY, Chatto ; Harper, New York : o.p.]

—— *Truth* (Vérité, 1903).   1903

This third novel was to have been followed by a fourth, *Justice*, but the series was cut short by Zola's death. The scene is laid in the world of French schools, and the story of a judicial crime in which a Jewish schoolmaster is the victim obviously is meant as a version of the Dreyfus case. The Church and the religious orders are attacked with implacable ferocity, and certain of the characters are open to identification. [Transl. by E. A. VIZETELLY, Chatto ; Lane, New York : o.p.]

[*Works* : edited by Ernest A. Vizetelly, 20 vols., Boni, New York ; 1924, in progress.]

ZSCHOKKE, Johann Heinrich Daniel [German ; 1771–1848]. *The Rose of Disentis.*   1873

A romance located in a Swiss village during the wars between France and Austria late in the eighteenth century. The hero of the love-story is a noble and heroic patriot, who loves a Viennese. Zschokke was a German who lived most of his life in Switzerland, and as schoolmaster, administrator, and editor was immersed in public affairs. Most of his novels and tales deal with the Swiss. [Transl. by J. J. D. TRENOR, Sheldon, New York : o.p.]

—— *The Goldmakers' Village ; or a history of the manner in which two and thirty men sold themselves to the Devil* (Das Goldmacher-Dorf, 1817).   1845

An elaborate apologue that Maria Edgeworth might have planned, telling how a country schoolmaster, by a laudable stratagem, converts the inhabitants of a village from lazy, drunken, litigious, and dissolute, into sober, industrious, prosperous, and contented people. The story is told with much poetic charm, and is the most graceful of Zschokke's didactic novels. [Burns : o.p. ; Appleton, New York : o.p.]

ZSCHOKKE, Johann Heinrich Daniel (*continued*). *Labour Stands on Golden Feet : a holiday story* (Meister Jordan, oder Handwerk hat goldenen Boden, 1845). 1852

A study of artisan life in a German town, and of the principles of healthy social progress ; the life of a pious and industrious family for three generations from Thadeus the tinker. Their prosperity is a benefit to the town by virtue of their generosity and good example. [Transl. by J. YEATS, Philip : o.p.]

—— *Tales.* 1845

A New Year's Eve, The Broken Pitcher, Jonathan Frock, Walpurgis Night : short, simple tales of village and domestic life, pleasingly sentimental or idyllic in tone, and the best of them charmingly humorous in the exaggerated portraiture of foibles and freakish personalities. [Transl. by Parke GODWIN and W. P. PRENTICE, Putnam, New York.]

ZUCCOLI, Luciano, Conte d'Ingluheim [Italian ; 1870–1929]. *Light-fingered Gentry* (La Compagnia della Leggera, 1907). 1910

Sardonic stories of Italian life showing the usual Continental mastery of the art of the short story ; the satire of national foibles is general and bitter, the cynical exposure of feminine foibles evidently the sign of an inveterate misogynist. *Through the Eyes of Love* tells how a would-be biographer gathers irreconcilable impressions from the three women his hero loved. In *Love the Sea but cling to the Shore*, a socialist preaching free love is furious when his daughter's lover proposes to enter into such a union. *The Masterpiece, Pasquina and Pif,* and *A Literary Morning* also give unattractive readings of female character among the Italian middle classes. [Transl. by Winifred HEATON, Heinemann.]

—— *Things Greater Than He* (Le Cose più grandi di lui, 1922). 1926

Analyses the contacts of a youth of introspective temperament with the outside world—hypocritical social relations, cruelty, love, and death. [Transl. by Eloïse PARKHURST, Holt, New York.]

ZWEIG, Arnold [German ; *b.* 1887]. *The Case of Sergeant Grischa* (Der Fall des Sergeanten Grischa). 1928

Grischa, a humble Russian prisoner, is caught in the vast machine of the German advance into Russia (1917). In trying to escape, he assumes the identity-disk of a dead deserter, and being captured is sentenced as a spy. The story is told on the grand scale ; it shows the multitudinous life, not only of man, but also of the animals, birds, and forests, going on continuously throughout the theatre of war, with glimpses of the world-struggle in distant regions. The rank and file of the German host come in too ; some, like the divisional general who tries to do Grischa justice, drawn with friendly insight, others, with marked resentment, as embodiments of Prussian militarism in its most inhuman phases. [Transl. by Eric SUTTON, Secker ; Viking Press, New York.]

—— *Claudia* (Die Novellen um Claudia, 1924). 1930

A rather artificial story of the happy loves of a young woman and a shy professor, in a world of painters, musicians, and literary people. [Transl. by Eric SUTTON, Secker ; Viking Press, New York.]

INDEX OF AUTHORS, TITLES, SUBJECTS, HISTORICAL NAMES AND ALLUSIONS, PLACES, CHARACTERS, ETC.

Authors' names are in small capitals (CLARK, Charles Heber), titles of books and stories in ordinary print (Aaron in the Wildwoods), subjects, etc., in italics (*Actors and Actresses*); lists of authors, grouped under their nationality in large capitals (AMERICAN NOVELISTS).

References are given from pseudonyms and hyphenated names of authors to the form adopted in the body of the book. No attempt has been made to classify stories systematically, but the cross-references from topic to topic will enable readers to find most of the fiction dealing with the larger subjects, e.g. religion and the various churches, sects, and religious movements, or illustrating literary tendencies like sentimental or chivalric romance, parody, naturalism, etc. Under such headings as " Marriage," " Plot-novels," etc., only those stories are indexed in which such topic or style of narrative is the outstanding feature.

A la recherche du temps perdu, 393
A l'ombre des jeunes filles en fleurs, 393
À un dîner d'athées, 32
Aaron in the Wildwoods, 229
Aaron's Rod, 291
Abafi, 273
Abandoned, 482
Abbaye Massacres, 280, Mademoiselle Mathilde
Abbé Aubain, The, 341
Abbé Birotteau, The, 27
Abbé Constantin, The, 221
Abbé Mouret's Transgression, The, 517
Abbés, see Priests
Abbess of Castro, The, 53
Abbess of Vlaye, The, 498
Abbot, The, 426
Abbotscourt, 22
Abditeren, Die, 503
Abel Drake's Wife, 422
Abélard, Peter, 350, Héloïse and Abélard
Abenner, King, 34, Barlaam and Josaphat
Abentheurliche Simplicissimus, Der, 216
Aberdeenshire, 313–14, G. MACDONALD'S novels
— 316, Without Conditions
Abington Abbey, 329
Abiturientag, Der, 496
Abner Daniel, 224
Abolitionists, see Slavery
About Catherine de' Medici, 30
Abraham's Sacrifice, 266
Absalom's Hair, 57
Abschied vom Paradies, 464
Absentee, The, 161
Absenteeism, see Land Questions
Absinthe-Drinking, 115, Wormwood

Absolute at Large, The, 90
Absolution, 483
Absolvo Te, 483
Abyss, The, 11
Academic Question, An, 88
Academy, French, 130, One of the Forty
Acadians, 86, Bonaventure
— 95, The Lady of Fort St. John
— 103, Bayou Folk
— 409, C. G. D. ROBERTS'S stories
— See also *Nova Scotia*
Accident, 46
Account Rendered, 48
Accused Princess, The, 479
Accuser, The, 16
Acheh, 105, A Free-Lance of To-day
Achill Island, 173, Children of Earth
Acia, 474
Acosta, Uriel, 515, Dreamers of the Ghetto
Acre, Siege of, 42, The Honour of Henri de Valois
Across the Salt Seas, 62
Act in a Backwater, An, 48
" Act of God," 164
Acte, 160, Nero
Action, 347
Action Front, 86
Actions and Reactions, 282
Active Service, 120
Actors and Actresses, 9, The House of Joy, The Improvisatore
— 12, The Flame of Life
— 38, The Chaste Diana
— 46, The Regent
— 52, The Orange Girl
— 56, The Fisher Lass
— 81, The Duke's Servants
— 89, Mummery
— 90, Joan Brotherhood
— 107, The Vagrant
— 108, Mitsou

Actors and Actresses (contd.):
109, The Inimitable Mrs. Massingham
— 128, Enter Sir John
— 129, Artists' Wives, Fromont Junior and Risler Senior
— 140, Nicholas Nickleby
— 155, Olympe de Clèves
— 184, A Mummer's Tale
— 204, Wilhelm Meister's Apprenticeship
— 221, Criquette
— 227, Allegra
— 264, The Tragic Muse
— 317, Carnival, The Vanity Girl
— 321, Out in the Open
— 341, The Man who was Good
— 342, The Position of Peggy Harper
— 348, Nell Gwyn
— 362, Pauline
— 371, In London
— 378, Less Black than We're Painted
— 392, The Good Companions
— 401, Peg Woffington
— 403, The Comedienne
— 422, The Comical Romance
— 436, The Small-Part Lady
— 446, A Gentleman Player
— 492, The Painted Scene
— 517, Nana
— Refer also to names of persons, e.g. *Bracegirdle, Mrs. ; Fenton, Lavinia ; Gwyn, Nell*
Adam and Caroline, 370
Adam and Eve, 166
Adam Bede, 164
Adam Blair, 302
Adam Hepburn's Vow, 457
Adam in Moonshine, 392

Adam of Dublin, 370
Adams, 17, The Conqueror
Adams, Parson, 172, Joseph Andrews
Addio, Amore, 429
Addison, Joseph, 308, Devereux
— 462, Henry Esmond
— 510, Esther Vanhomrigh
Adèle, 275
Adeline Mowbray, 369
Adelphi, 214
Adieu, 30
Adirondack Stories, 138
Adirondacks, 17, The Aristocrats
— 23, Eben Holden
— 138, Adirondack Stories
— 186, The Deserter
Adjutant Benôit, L', 391
Admirable Bashville, The, 431
Admirable Crichton, The, 4
Admiral of the Ocean Sea, 271
Adnam's Orchard, 211
Adolphe, 112
Adopted Husband, An, 189
Adria, 245
Adrian Glynde, 14
Adrian Savage, 322
Adrian Vidal, 362
Adrienne Mesurat, 213
Adrienne Toner, 428
Adrigoole, 363
Adultery, see Marriage and its Problems
Advanced Guard, The, 215
Adventure of the Black Lady, The, 43
Adventure of the North, An, 376
Adventures of a Bank-note, 271
Adventures of a Black Coat, 271
Adventures of a Guinea, 271

Adventures of a Man of Quality, 391

Adventures of a Rupee, 271

Adventures of a Three-guinea Watch, 402

Adventures of Akbar, 446

Adventures of an Aide-de-Camp, 211

Adventures of an Equerry, 196

Adventures of Baron Münchausen in Russia, 399

Adventures of Bindle, 267

Adventures of Captain Hatteras, 482

Adventures of Captain Horn, 451

Adventures of Captain Kettle, The, 258

Adventures of Captain Mago, The, 87

Adventures of Cyrano de Bergerac, 189

Adventures of David Simple, 173

Adventures of Dr. Whitty, The, 55

Adventures of Elizabeth in Rügen, 15

Adventures of Ferdinand, Count Fathom, 441

Adventures of François, 345

Adventures of Gerard, 150

Adventures of Gianetto, 430

Adventures of Hajji Baba of Ispahan, 351

Adventures of Harry Revel, 397

Adventures of Harry Richmond, The, 339

Adventures of Herr Baby, 346

Adventures of Huckleberry Finn, The, 476

Adventures of Joseph Andrews, 172

Adventures of Kimble Bent, The, 118

Adventures of Lady Susan, The, 71

Adventures of Launcelot Greaves, 441

Adventures of Mr. Ledbury, The, 439

Adventures of Mr. Verdant Green, The, 70

Adventures of Oliver Twist, 140

Adventures of Peregrine Pickle, 441

Adventures of Philip, The, 463

Adventures of Princess Sylvia, The, 507

Adventures of Rob Roy, 211

Adventures of Roderick Random, 441

Adventures of Sherlock Holmes, 149

Adventures of Susan, The, 71

Adventures of Telemachus, The, 171

Adventures of the Children of the King of Norway, 257

Adventures of the Comte de la Muette, 90

Adventures of the Countess of ——, 326

Adventures of the Lad of the Ferule, 257

Adventures of Tom Sawyer, 476

Adventuresses, 46, The Lion's Share

— 90, The Extraordinary Adventures of Diana Please

— 225, The Hand of Ethelberta

— 264, The Princess Casamassima

— 283, Lawrence Garthe

— 292, Hagarene

— 303, La Picara

— 317, Sylvia Scarlett

— 368, The Cuckoo in the Nest

— 458, Coquette

— 462, Vanity Fair

— 472, The Eustace Diamonds

Adventurous Simplicissimus, 216

Æmilius, 120

Æneas, 18, Dido Queen of Hearts

Æscendune, 120, Rev. A. D. CRAKE's novels

Æsop Dancing, 79

Æstheticism, 11, The Child of Pleasure

— 41, Under the Hill

— 459, Spiritual Adventures

— 504, Oscar WILDE's stories

Æthelfrith, King, 165, Fated to Win

Æthiopian History, An, 235

Affair of Dishonour, An, 139

Affair of the Clasps, The, 207

Affairs of the Heart, 255

Affair on the Bridge, The, 351

Afghanistan, 121, Doctor Claudius

— 144, The Hero of Herat, and sequel

— 157, Helen Treveryan

— 223, A Vizier's Daughter

— 368, Old For-Ever

— 450, The Minister's Son

Afield and Afloat, 451

Afloat and Ashore, 115

Africa, 134, Capt. Singleton

— 219–21, Rider HAGGARD's novels

— See also *Africa, Central, East, South, and West, Egypt, Morocco, Negroes, Savages, etc.*

Africa, Central, 26, The Golden Kingdom

— 336, Kaloolah

— 482, Five Weeks in a Balloon

Africa, East, 123, A Martyr's Servant, and sequel

Africa, East (contd.) : 187, Peter Moor's Journey

— 270, The Man who did the Right Thing

— 514, The Crescent Moon, Woodsmoke

— 515, Jim Redlake

Africa, North, 47, Atlantida

— 242, The Garden of Allah

— 304, The Romance of a Spahi

— 332, The Winding Stair

Africa, South, 57, D. BLACKBURN's novels

— 77, H. A. BRYDEN's novels

— 78, Prester John

— 175, Jock of the Bushveld

— 187, Peter Moor's Journey

— 344, The Coming of the Lord

— 411, The Colossus

— 450, Wild Honey, Blue Aloes

— 502, Back of Beyond

Africa, West, 132, African Nights' Entertainments

— 342, With Edged Tools

— 482, Dick Sands

African Nights' Entertainments, 132

Afrikaans Novelist, 300, Marie LINDE

After All, 103

After Dark, 108

After London, 267

After the Divorce, 137

After the Pardon, 429

Aftermath, 8

Aftermath, The, 43

Afterward, 499

Afterwards, 319

Against the Tide, 142

Age of Innocence, The, 499

Age of Reason, The, 198

Aged Rabbi, The, 258

Agenor de Mauléon, 155

Agent, The, 474

Agincourt, 262

Agincourt, Battle of, 222, Coronation

— 262, Agincourt

— See also *Henry V*

Agnes (by Rev. J. ABBOTT), 1

Agnès (by J. CLARETIE), 105

Agnes de Castro, 43

Agnes of Sorrento, 452

Agnes Surriage, 84

Agnosticism and Faith, 28, Ursule Mirouët

— 67, Divorce, The Weight of the Name

— 136, John Ward, Preacher

— 177, Man of the World, and Sequel

— 186, Illumination

— 241, The Children of the World

— 279, Two Years Ago

— 300, Under Which Lord

— 307, Donovan, and sequel

— 322, W. H. MALLOCK's novels

Agnosticism and Faith, 374, The Marquis of Penalta

— 375, Faith

— 382, Leon Roch, Lady Perfecta

— 423, The Story of an African Farm

— 435, Without Dogma

— 457, Maitland of Lauriston

— 487, Robert Elsmere

— 488, David Grieve, Helbeck of Bannisdale

— 502, The Autobiography of Mark Rutherford

— See also *Atheism, Freethought, Religion, Theism*

Agony Column, The, 424

Agrippina, 160, Nero

Ahab, Captain, 338, Moby, Dick

Ahnen, Die, 188

Ailell, 293, The Courtship of Ferb

Ailsa Paige, 97

Ainslie's Ju-Ju, 54

Aircraft, 282, With the Night Mail

Airy Fairy Lilian, 254

Aislinge Meic Conglinne, 343

Ak and Humanity, Tale about, 117

Akbar, Emperor, 357, The Near and the Far

— 446, A Prince of Dreamers, Adventures of Akbar

Akhila, Deacon, 307, Cathedral Folk

Akhnaton, King of Egypt, 341

AKURATERS, Janis, see MARSHALL, L. A. (tr.)

" *Alabama, The*," 71, On the Old *Kearsage*

Aladdin, 13

Aladdin O'Brien, 352

Aladore, 359

Alamo, 36, Remember the Alamo

— 152, In the Shadow of the Alamo

Alan, 49

Alard Family, 276, The End of the House of Alard

Alaric, 108, Antonina

Alas !, 75

Alas, poor Bollington !, 115

Alaska, 40, The Spoilers of the North, The Barrier, The Silver Horde

— 302–4, J. LONDON's stories

— 344, Frozen Justice

— 384, The Chicamon Stone

— 412, The Magnetic North, Come and Find Me

Albania, 306, The Captain of the Janizaries

Alberoni, Cardinal, 91, For the White Rose

— 153–4, The Chevalier d'Harmental, The Regent's Daughter

Albert Maurice of Ghent, 261, Mary of Burgundy
Albert Savarus, 27
Albertine disparue, 394
Albertine's Wooers, 244
Albrecht of Brandenburg, 360, Prince Albrecht of Brandenburg
Alcibiades, 18, Vengeful Gods
— 72, Alkibiades
— 287, Pericles and Aspasia
Alcoholism, see *Drink Questions*
Alcott (Louisa) Family, 77, The Father
— 177, O Genteel Lady
Alchemists, 23, Fryer Bacon
— 30, The Quest of the Absolute
— 94, The Star Dreamer
— 157, The Charwoman's Shadow
— 203, St. Leon
Alcyone, 387
Aldersyde, 457
Aldgate, The, 81
Aldyth, 180
Alec Forbes of Howglen, 313
Alegria del Capitán Ribot, La, 375
Alemanni, 128, A Captive of the Roman Eagles
— 188, Our Forefathers
— 231, Jetta
Aletta, 346
Alexander I (Tsar), 93, By Neva's Waters
— 216, A Brother of Girls
— 272, The Green Book
Alexander II (Tsar), 86, The White Terror and the Red
— 163, Pilgrim to the Abyss
— 342, The Vultures
Alexander VI, Pope, 341, The Forerunner
Alexandria, 2, Clitophon and Leucippe
— 117, The Tour
— 142, Tychiades
— 159, Serapis, Per Aspera, Cleopatra, Arachne
— 199, Four Sons
— 375, Paris and Vienne
— 387, Saïd the Fisherman
Alexia, 392
Alexis, Prince, 142, She That Hesitates
— 341, Peter and Alexis
Alexius I, Comnenus, 427, Count Robert of Paris
Alfgar the Dane, 120
Alfieri, Count Vittorio, 297, Gerald Fitzgerald
Alfour, 465, The Three King's Sons
Alfred the Great, 199, God Save King Alfred
Algeciras, Naval Action off, 97, Tom Bowling
Algeria, 75, Alas !
— 172, The Secret of Happiness
— 295, A Modern Legionary

Algeria (contd.): 361, Mademoiselle de Mersac
— 372, Under Two Flags
Ali Baba, 13
Ali Bey, 375, Hermann Agha
Ali Pasha, 271, The Lion of Janina
Alice, 309
Alice Adams, 460
Alice, Blind, 425, The Bride of Lammermoor
Alice-for-Short, 138
Alice Lorraine, 58
Alice of Old Vincennes, 465
Alice's Adventures in Wonderland, 93
" ALIEN," see BAKER, Mrs. L. A.
Alien, The, 348
Alien Sisters, The, 132
Aliens of the West, 159
Aliette, 172
Alise of Astra, 328
Alkibiades, 72
Alkmaar, 24, My Lady of Orange
All'erta Sentinella, 429
All Else is Folly, 2
All Fools Together, 179
All Hallows, 136
All in a Day, 14
All Men are Ghosts, 259
All on the Irish Shore, 443
All Our Yesterdays, 470
All Quiet on the Western Front, 403
All Smoke, 314
All Sorts and Conditions of Men, 52
All Souls' Day, 258
All the World Wondered, 342
Allan Quatermain, 219
Allan's Wife, 219
Alleghanies, 76, Edgar Huntly
— See also *Adirondacks, Kentucky, Smoky Mountains, White Mountains*
Allegories, 9, ANDERSEN's tales
— 22, Don Juan
— 30, the Wild Ass's Skin
— 71, The Wallet of Kai Lung
— 85, Jurgen, Figures of Earth
— 93, The Goblet
— 109, Hypnerotomachia
— 117, Psyche
— 181, Sintram
— 223, Mysteries
— 232–3, HAWTHORNE's novels and tales
— 269, Rasselas
— 281, Glimpses of Dreamlands
— 286, The Miracles of Antichrist
— 290, Such Stuff as Dreams, The God in the Thicket
— 339, The Shaving of Shagpat

Allegories (contd.): 373, Barry PAIN's stories, *passim*
— 399–400, TAGORE's stories
— 407, RICHTER's stories
— 420, Lélia
— 431, The Divine Adventure
— 446, The Crock of Gold
— 449, Dr. Jekyll and Mr. Hyde
— 455, Dame Care
— 468, Ivan Ilyitch
— 469, The Long Exile, Master and Servant, etc.
— See also *Fairy-Tales, Religious Allegory*
Allegra, 227
Allen (servant of Nelson), 97, Ben Brace
ALLEN, Charles Grant B., see " ALLEN, Grant "
Allen, Ethan, 464, The Green Mountain Boys
" ALLEN, F. M.," see DOWNEY, Edmund
Allen, Ralph, 173, Tom Jones
Allworthy, Squire, 173, Tom Jones
Almayer's Folly, 110
Almeria, 160
Alongshore, 404
Alps, 66, Footprints beneath the Snow
— 130, Tartarin on the Alps
— 347, Action
— 422, Ekkehard
— 429, Obermann
— See also *Cantabrian Alps*
Alroy, 143
Alsace, 40, The Children of Alsace
— 143, The Boundary Post
— 165–6, " ERCKMANN-CHATRIAN's " novels
— 422, R. SCHICKELÉ's novels
— 481, The Heart of Alsace
Alsatia, see *Whitefriars*
Alston, Philip, 33, Round Anvil Rock
Altar Fire, The, 47
Altar of the Dead, The, 265
Altar Steps, The, 317
Alternative, The, 33
Altiora Peto, 366
Alton Locke, 279
Altruria, 251, A Traveller from Altruria, Through the Eye of the Needle
Alva, Duke of, 24, My Lady of Orange
— 105, The Duke's Page
— 112, Ludovic and Gertrude
— 486, In Troubled Times
Am Altar, 496
Amabel and Amoris, 18
Amabel Channice, 428
Amadis of Gaul, 301
Amaryllis at the Fair, 267
Amasis, 158, An Egyptian Princess
Amateur, The, 361

Amateur Cracksman, The, 248
Amateur Emigrant, The, 449
Amateur Gentleman, 169
Amateur Peasant Girl, 395
Amazing Marriage, The, 340
Amazing Philanthropists, The, 132
Amazon, 244, The Forest Ship
— 357, The Clio
Ambales Saga, 223
Ambassadors, The, 265
Amber Witch, The (Mary Schweidler), 336
Amboise, Bussy d', 154, La Dame de Monsoreau
— 155, The Two Dianas
— 513, The Traitor's Way
Amboise, Duc d', 473, A Girl of the Multitude
Ambrosio, 298
Âme obscure, L', 128
Amelia (by Mrs. DELAND), 136
Amelia (by FIELDING), 173
America and Americans, 98, Atala, René
— 103, Penruddock
— 116, Mrs. E. COTES's novels
— 128, European Relations
— 141, Martin Chuzzlewit
— 178, An English Girl
— 221, The Abbé Constantin
— 231, Atlantis
— 283, Debits and Credits
— 366, Altiora Peto
— 376, The Right of Way
— 428, Valerie Upton, Franklin Cane
— 435, Lillian Morris, Sielanka
— 473, The Domestic Manners of the Americans, The Widow Barnaby and sequels
— 488, Daphne
— See also AMERICAN NOVELISTS, and under countries, states, cities, regions, and important persons and events, e.g. *American Revolution*, etc.
America, Discovery of, 26, The Norsemen of the West
— 114, Mercedes of Castile
— 128, Prince Madog
— 240, Gudrid the Fair
— 299, The Vinland Champions, Randvar the Songsmith
America, Central, 41, Sand and Cactus
America, Middle-West, 95, Youth and the Bright Medusa
— 189, Zona GALE's stories
— 249, The Story of a Country Town
— 251, New Leaf Mills
— 359, Otherwise Phyllis, Broken Barriers

America, Middle - West (contd.) : 506, The Great Accident

America, South, 110, Nostromo
— 131, Soldiers of Fortune
— 168, Vain Love
— 210, R. B. Cunninghame GRAHAM'S stories
— 245, A Man of Mark
— 252, El Ombú, Green Mansions
— 303, Hearts of Three
— 315, Pilgrims of Adversity
— 492, The Shadow of a Titan
— See also countries, *Argentine, Brazil, Chile*, etc.
American, The, 263
American Civil War, 5, Hospital Sketches
— 8, In Circling Camps, The Sword of Youth
— 9, Before the Dawn
— 22, Kent Fort Manor
— 23, Father Abraham
— 42, Norwood
— 47, B. K. BENSON'S novels
— 53, In the Midst of Life
— 69, Marching On
— 70, A Little Traitor to the South
— 71, The Patriots, On the Old *Kearsage*
— 81, The Shepherd of the People
— 86, John March, Southerner, The Cavalier, Kincaid's Battery
— 96, Pickets, Smith's Battery
— 97, Ailsa Paige
— 104, The Crisis
— 113, Surry of Eagle's Nest, and sequels, Pine and Palm
— 134, Miss Ravenell's conversion
— 145, T. DIXON'S novels
— 161, Debenham's Vow
— 182, The Little Shepherd of Kingdom Come
— 186, The Copperhead, Marséna, The Deserters
— 202, The Battle Ground
— 224, Henry Bourland
— 229, Tales of the Home Folks, On the Wings of Occasions, A Little Union Scout
— 238, The Limestone Tree
— 248, The Girl at the Half-way House
— 269, Arrows of the Almighty
— 270, The Long Roll, and sequel
— 275, The Challenge to Sirius
— 278, Cicily
— 318, The Washingtonians
— 345, Roland Blake, Constance Trescott, Westways
— 352, Aladdin O'Brien

American Civil War (contd.) :
353, Forever Free, and sequels
— 366, The Man from Texas
— 372, Barbe
— 373, The Burial of the Guns
— 376, My Lady of the North
— 406, The Heart of Hope
— 440, The Fortunes of Oliver Horn
— 447, They That Took the Sword
— 452, Marching On
— 466, Jack Horner
— 492, Traitor or Loyalist ?
— 506, The Captain
— See also names of generals, *Jackson, Lee*, etc., and *Abraham Lincoln*
American Claimant, The, 477
American Girl in London, An, 116
AMERICAN NOVELISTS:
Rev. J. ABBOTT, Andy ADAMS, Henry ADAMS, I. W. ADAMS, S. H. ADAMS, "Max ADELER," Louisa M. ALCOTT, T. B. ALDRICH, J. L. ALLEN, J. A. ALTSHELER, Mrs. Ada W. ANDERSON, Sherwood ANDERSON, Mrs. ATHERTON, Jane AUSTIN, Mary AUSTIN

Mrs. B. BABCOCK, W. H. BABCOCK, Irving BACHELLER, J. K. BANGS, Mrs. N. H. BANKS, J. BARNES, Amelia E. BARR, J. N. BASKETT, Frances C. BAYLOR, Rex E. BEACH, W. le C. BEARD, H. W. BEECHER, T. BEER, JESSIE BELDEN, E. BELLAMY, S. V. BENÉT, R. A. BENNET, J. BENNETT, B. K. BENSON, Ambrose BIERCE, R. M. BIRD, J. BOYD, Rev. C. T. BRADY, M. BRINIG, L. BROMFIELD, E. S. BROOKS, Mrs. Alice BROWN, C. B. BROWN, Katherine H. BROWN, W. G. BROWN, E. S. BRUDNO, Mrs. Pearl BUCK, H. C. BUNNER, Frances E. BURNETT, W. R. BURNETT, K. N. BURT, E. L. BYNNER, B. O. Donn BYRNE

J. B. CABELL, G. W. CABLE, A. CAHAN, V. F. CALVERTON, M. J. CANAVAN, Dorothy CANFIELD, Mrs. C. J. CANNON, E. C. CARPENTER, Willa S. CATHER, Mrs. Mary H. CATHERWOOD, R. W. CHAMBERS, Mrs. M. CHAPMAN, C. W. CHESNUTT,

AMERICAN NOVELISTS (*contd.*) :
Kate CHOPIN, S. CHOTZINOFF, S. H. CHURCH, W. CHURCHILL, D. H. CLARKE, C. C. COFFIN, Harriet T. COMSTOCK, J. B. CONNOLLY, Florence CONVERSE, M. D. CONWAY, Grace COOKE, J. E. COOKE, Rose COOKE, J. F. COOPER, "C. E. CRADDOCK," Pearl M. T. CRAIGIE, S. CRANE, F. M. CRAWFORD, Mary C. CROWLEY, Maria S. CUMMINS, G. W. CURTIS

R. H. DANA, C. DARROW, E. H. DAVIS, R. H. DAVIS, W. S. DAVIS, J. W. DE FOREST, Margaretta W. DELAND, F. DELL, P. DEMING, H. DICKSON, Mary G. DILLON, Beulah M. DIX, E. A. DIX, T. DIXON, N. H. DOLE, Julia C. DORR, J. R. DOS PASSOS, C. W. DOYLE, T. DREISER, Clara DRISCOLL, W. E. B. Du BOIS, P. L. DUNBAR, F. P. DUNNE

E. EGGLESTON, Sarah ELLIOTT, E. S. ELLIS, J. B. ELLIS, J. ERSKINE

J. E. FARMER, W. FAULKNER, Jessie R. FAUSET, E. FAWCETT, Rose C. FELD, Edna FERBER, C. B. FERNALD, E. FIELD, Vardis FISHER, C. M. FLANDRAU, Mary FOOTE, Esther FORBES, C. FORD, P. L. FORD, W. D. FOULKE, J. W. FOX, Harold FREDERIC, Allen FRENCH, Anna FULLER, H. B. FULLER

Zona GALE, H. GARLAND, H. GILLMAN, Ellen GLASGOW, Susan GLASPELL, Isa GLENN, Maud GOODWIN, C. GRANT, Judge R. GRANT, Anna GREEN, Sarah GREENE, J. GREGORY, Zane GREY

J. HABBERTON, E. E. HALE, H. E. HAMBLEN, A. E. HANCOCK, W. N. HARBEN, A. S. HARDY, Henry HARLAND, Mrs. C. M. W. HARRIS, J. C. HARRIS, H. S. HARRISON, F. Bret HARTE, P. L. HAWORTH, J. HAWTHORNE, N. HAWTHORNE, John HAY, Lafcadio HEARN, E. HEMINGWAY, A. HENRY, J. HERGESHEIMER, R. HERRICK, V. HERSCH, Mrs. S. J. HIGGINSON, T. W.

AMERICAN NOVELISTS (*contd.*) :
HIGGINSON, J. G. HOLLAND, O. W. HOLMES, R. HORSLEY, E. HOUGH, Blanche W. HOWARD, E. W. HOWE, W. D. HOWELLS, O. HUCKEL, C. B. HUDSON, F. P. HUMPHREY

W. IRVING, W. IRWIN

Helen M. JACKSON, H. JAMES, T. A. JANVIER, T. D. JERVEY, Sarah Orne JEWETT, Owen JOHNSON, Mary JOHNSTON, R. M. JOHNSTON, S. JUDD

R. W. KAUFFMAN, J. P. KENNEDY, Sarah B. KENNEDY, V. KESTER, Grace E. KING, W. B. B. KING, Ellen KIRK, J. KIRKLAND, L. KRONENBERGER

O. La FARGE, Elinor M. LANE, Mrs. J. LANE, Augusta LARNED, Nella LARSEN, G. P. LATHROP, P. W. LEWIS, Sinclair LEWIS, L. LEWISOHN, Ottalie A. LILJENCRANTZ, J. U. LLOYD, N. McA. LLOYD, J. LONDON, H. W. LONGFELLOW, G. H. LORIMER, R. T. S. LOWELL, J. M. LUDLOW F. LYNDE

" S. McCALL," C. McKAY, Pauline B. MACKIE, C. MAJOR, Mrs. G. MARTIN, Caroline MASON, E. L. MASTERS, J. B. MATTHEWS, H. MELVILLE, S. MERWIN, Annie MEYER, Sarah G. MILLIN, W. J. MILLS, S. W. MITCHELL, C. MORLEY, G. MORRIS, Honoré W. MORROW, W. C. MORROW, J. L. MOTT, " J. P. MowBRAY "

M. NICHOLSON, C. G. NORRIS, F. NORRIS, Kathleen NORRIS, S. L. NYBURG

H. OLDHAM, J. OPPENHEIM, W. D. ORCUTT, L. OSBOURNE, " Irene OSGOOD "

T. N. PAGE, A. B. PAINE, G. R. PARRISH, J. K. PAULDING, W. PAYNE, E. G. PEAKE, L. B. PENDLETON, Elizabeth PENNELL, B. PERRY, Mrs. PETERKIN, Elizabeth PHELPS, D. G. PHILLIPS, C. F. PIDGIN,

AMERICAN NOVELISTS (contd.):
A. S. PIER, E. A. POE, Maria L. POOL, E. POOLE, W. S. PORTER ("O. HENRY"), W. K. POST, Margaret H. POTTER, Elizabeth PRENTISS, H. PYLE

"E. QUEEN"

Emma RAYNER, O. P. READ, Myrtle REED, F. REMINGTON, Mrs. A. C. RICE, N. RICHARDSON, Martha E. RICKERT, J. A. RIIS, L. RISING, Amélie RIVES, Hallie E. RIVES, C. H. ROBERTS, Elizabeth M. ROBERTS, Elizabeth ROBINS, R. E. ROBINSON, C. ROSS, Bertha RUNKLE

E. L. SABIN, E. SALTUS, A. F. SANBORN, Mrs. SARTORIS, Evelyn SCHAEFFER, C. SCOLLARD, Evelyn SCOTT, J. R. SCOTT, Vida SCUDDER, Molly SEAWELL, Anne D. SEDGWICK, Catherine M. SEDGWICK, Adéle M. SHAW, Rev. C. M. SHELDON, W. G. SIMMS, Upton SINCLAIR, Annie SLOSSON, S. H. SMALL, Mrs. A. P. SMITH, F. H. SMITH, Minna C. SMITH, Alice SPINNER, R. N. STEPHENS, N. STEPHENSON, A. de G. STEVENS, Sheppard STEVENS, B. E. STEVENSON, F. J. STIMSON, F. R. STOCKTON, W. D. STODDARD, Grace STONE, Mrs. Beecher STOWE, Ray STRACHEY, T. S. STRIBLING, H. L. STUART, Ruth STUART, Ruth SUCKOW, J. W. SULLIVAN

B. TARKINGTON, J. TAYLER, B. TAYLOR, Mary TAYLOR, "O. THANET," D. P. THOMPSON, M. THOMPSON, N. P. THOMPSON, Mary S. TIERNAN, E. T. TOMLINSON, Jean TOOMER, A. W. TOURGÉE, J. T. TROWBRIDGE, Annie E. TRUMBULL, Mrs. TURNBULL, "Mark TWAIN"

C. VAN VECHTEN, H. K. VIELÉ

L. WALLACE, Mary E. WALLER, "A. WARD," W. WARE, C. D. WARNER, Susan WARNER, S. WATERLOO, Mary WATTS, H. K. WEBSTER, "Jean WEBSTER," Carolyn

AMERICAN NOVELISTS (contd.):
WELLS, Glenway WESCOTT, E. N. WESTCOTT, Edith WHARTON, J. B. WHARTON, E. L. WHITE, Eliza O. WHITE, S. E. WHITE, W. F. WHITE, Brand WHITLOCK, Adelaine D. WHITNEY, Kate D. W. WIGGIN, Thornton WILDER, Mary E. WILKINS, Ben A. WILLIAMS, Churchill WILLIAMS, Jesse L. WILLIAMS, Mrs. C. N. WILLIAMSON, T. WINTHROP, Owen WISTER, T. WOLFE, Martha WOLFENSTEIN, Edith WOODS, Constance F. WOOLSON, Mabel WRIGHT, Elinor WYLIE —see also 105, CLARKE and LIEBER
American Politician, An, 121
American Prisoner, The, 385
American Revolution, 8, In Hostile Red, The Sun of Saratoga
— 9, My Captive
— 35, For King or Country
— 36, The Bow of Orange Ribbon, and sequel
— 44, Spanish Bayonet
— 69, Drums
— 71, The Blue Ocean's Daughter
— 90, Love like a Gipsy
— 96, Cardigan, and sequel
— 97, The Reckoning
— 104, Richard Carvel
— 107, Daughters of the Revolution
— 114, The Spy, Lionel Lincoln, The Red Rover
— 132, Gilman of Redford
— 165, Patriot and Tory
— 169, Brinton Eliot
— 177, The Royal Americans
— 179, Janice Meredith
— 182, Erskine Dale
— 186, In the Valley
— 187, The Colonials
— 267, The King's Yard
— 277, Horseshoe Robinson
— 278, Joscelyn Cheshire
— 284, A Maid of '76
— 338, Israel Potter
— 345, Hugh Wynne, A Venture in 1777
— 390, Smith Brunt
— 418, The Carolinian
— 436, The Partizan, and sequels; Woodcraft, and sequels
— 440, The Old Manor House
— 446, Philip Winwood
— 447, The Road to Paris
— 463, The Virginians
American Tragedy, An, 151

American War of 1812, 8, A Herald of the West
— 35, Yankee Ships and Yankee Sailors, A Loyal Traitor
— 36, The Belle of Bowling Green
— 70, For the Freedom of the Sea
— 88, A Beautiful Rebel
— 126, Love Thrives in War
— 376, When Wilderness was King
— 396, Within the Capes
— 406, The Canadian Brothers
American Wives and English Husbands, 17
Amethyst Ring, The, 183
Amhurstburg, Fort, 406, The Canadian Brothers
Ami Fritz, L', 165
Amigo de la Muerte, El, 5
Amis and Amile, 352
Ammonitori, Gli, 95
Amnesia, 112, Called Back
— 138, Somehow Good
— 176, Morrison's Machine
— 294, The Whisper of a Name
— 318, The Man who Forgot
— 338, Number 56
Among Privileged People, 300
Among the Camps, 373
Among the Idol-Makers, 259
Among the Syringas, 323
Amore bendato, 169
Amorous Fiametta, 62
Amory, Blanche, 462, Pendennis
Amos Barton, 163
Amour qui pleure, L', 466
Amphibians, The, 512
Amsterdam, 145, Keetje
Amulet, The (by H. CONSCIENCE), 112
Amulet, The (by "C. E. CRADDOCK"), 119
Amy Foster, 110
Amyot Brough, Some Account of, 72
Ananias, 229
Anarchist, The, 111
Anarchists, 39, The New Antigone
— 61, The Shadow of the Cathedral
— 111, The Secret Agent
— 122, Marzio's Crucifix
— 176, Vestigia
— 228, The Bomb
— 422, SAVINKOV'S novels
Anastasius, 247
Anathema, 285
Anatole, 195
Anatomy of Society, 89
Anaxagoras, 287, Pericles and Aspasia
Ancestors, 17
Ancestral Footstep, The, 233
Anchor-Watch Yarns, 149
"Anchorites, The," 158, Homo Sum

Ancient Allan, The, 220
Ancient Heroic Romances of Ireland, 293
Ancient Mariners, 411
And Co., 61
— and Sons, 283
Andalusia, 5, The Three-Cornered Hat
— 84, The Sea-Gull
— 480, Doña Luz
Anderson, Mary, 487, Miss Bretherton
Anderson, Sir Robert, 111, The Secret Agent
Andersons, The, 320
Andes, 244, The Forest Ship
Andivius Hedulio, 500
Andorra, 421, Andorra
Andorra, 421
André, Major, 97, The Painted Minx
— 179, Janice Meredith
— 345, Hugh Wynne
André Cornélis, 67
Andreas Hofer, 355
Andrei Kolosov, 474
Andrew and his Wife, 107
Andrew Marvel and his Friends, 222
ANDREWS, Mrs. H. M., see "WEST, Rebecca"
Andrews, Joseph, 172, The Adventures of Joseph Andrews
Andromeda, 176
Ange Pitou, 155
Angel, 125
Angel at the Grave, The, 498
Angel of Pain, The, 48
Angel of the Lord, The, 251
Angel Pavement, 392
Angèle's Fortune, 464
Angelo, Michael, see Michelangelo
Angelot, 392
Anger of Olivia, The, 106
Anges gardiens, Les, 391
Anglais au Pole Nord, Les, 482
Anglesea, 15, Megan of the Dark Isles
— 75, Mrs. Bligh
— 394, John Jones, Curate
Anglican Church, 81, The Holy War
— 83, The Way of All Flesh
— 123, The Vicar of St. Luke's
— 144, Tancred
— 170, Julian Home
— 276, The End of the House of Alard, Shepherds in Sackcloth
— 317, The Altar-Steps, and sequels
— 359, Loss and Gain
— 433, John Inglesant
— 457, The Tale of a Tub
Anglicanization, 516
Anglo-Indian Life, 7, The City of Sunshine
— 101, A True Reformer
— 116, His Honour and a Lady, The Path of a Star

Anglo-Indian Life (contd.):
124, Proper Pride
— 127, The Chronicles of Dustypore
— 180, A Passage to India
— 281-2, R. KIPLING's novels and stories
— 288, The Wetherbys
— 319, A Freelance in Kashmir
— 320, Snow upon the Desert
— 381, Mrs. F. E. PENNY's novels
— 382, Alice PERRIN's novels
— 422, Banked Fires
— 445-6, Mrs. STEEL's novels
— 465, His Majesty's Greatest Subject
— See also *India*
ANGLO-INDIAN NOVELISTS: Maud DIVER, R. KIPLING, Sir G. F. MACMUNN, Mrs. F. E. PENNY, Alice PERRIN, Mrs. F. A. STEEL, S. K. Levett YEATS
Anglomaniacs in America, 170, A Gentleman of Leisure
— 263, A Passionate Pilgrim
Anglo-Norman Romancers, 188, Fulk Fitz-Warine
— 253, HUGH OF RUTLAND
Angoulême, 28, Lost Illusions
— 391, The Unhurrying Chase
Aniello, Tommaso, 234, Mas'aniello
Anima V lis, 414
Animals, 58, Crocker's Hole
— 59, Dudley and Gilderoy
— 80, The Dreams of Chang
— 100, Kashtanka
— 125, Village Tales and Jungle Tragedies
— 127, Swift Lightning
— 156, Black
— 177, Grim, Kittens
— 281, Many Inventions
— 282, The Jungle Book, and sequel, The Maltese Cat, Just-So Stories
— 283, Thy Servant a Dog
— 299, Little Grey
— 302, The Call of the Wild
— 303, White Fang, Jerry of the Islands
— 368, Owd Bob, Danny
— 409, The Heart of the Ancient Wood, Barbara Ladd
— 410, The Ledge on Bald Face
— 429, E. T. SETON's stories
— 507, Tarka the Otter, The Old Stag
— See also *Beast Fables, Nature*

Anjou, 392, The Heiress of the Forest, Angelot
Anjou, Duc d', 154, La Dame de Monsoreau
— 155, The Forty-Five Guardsmen
— 262, The Man-at-Arms
Ann Veronica, 494
Anna Karénin, 468
Anna of the Five Towns, 45
Anna St. Ives, 244
Anna, Santa, 36, Remember the Alamo
Anna Svärd, 287
Annals of a Quiet Neighbourhood, 313
Annals of an Eventful Life, 129
Annals of the Parish, 191
Anne, Queen (wife of Richard III), 369, Crouchback
Anne, Queen, 4, St. James's
— 24, The Highwayman
— 81, The Mistress of the Robes
— 145, In King's Houses
— 377, The King's Agent
— 462, Pendennis
Anne, 511
Anne Mainwaring, 408
Anne Mauleverer, 86
Anne of Austria, 154, The Three Musketeers, and sequels
— 155, The War of Women
— 195, Marie de Mancini
— 261, Richelieu, John Marston Hall
Anne of Geierstein, 427
Anne Page, 459
Anne Scarlet, 461
Anne Severn and the Fieldings, 437
Anneau d'amethyste, L', 183
Annette and Philibert, 66
Annette and Sylvie, 415
Annie Kilburn, 250
Annunciation, The, 12
Anonymous, 14, Aristocracy
— 242, High Treason
— 255, The Last Days of John Hus
— 422, Schlump
— See also under titles, e.g. Gesta Romanorum
Anonymous Story, An, 100
Another Godiva, 390
Another Good Man, 96
Another Man's Wife, 146
Another Study of Woman, 27
Antæus, 248, A Modern Antæus
Antarctic, 77, The Republic of the Southern Cross
Anthea, 435
Anthea's Guest, 434
Anthony, Captain, 111, Victory
Anthony, Saint, 175, The Temptation of St. Anthony
Anthony Garstin's Courtship, 118
Anthony Graeme, 500

Anthony the Absolute, 343
Anthony Wilding, 418
Antic Hay, 257
Antiek-Tourisme, 117
Antietam, 353, Forever Free
Antikrists mirakler, 286
Antinous, 231
Antioch, 120, Æmilius
Antiochus Epiphanes, 306, Deborah
Antiquary, The, 425
Antique Dealers, 18, The Rich Young Man
— 259, Among the Idol-Makers
Anti-Rent Party, 115, Satanstoe, and sequels
Anti-Tithe Campaign, 92, The Tithe-Proctor
Antonia (by Jessie BELDEN), 43
Antonia (by Viola MEYNELL), 344
Antonina, 108
Antonio, 366
Antony, 38, The Laughing Queen
— 131, A Friend of Cæsar
— 159, Cleopatra
Antrim, 31, The Boyne Water
— 55, The Northern Iron
— 243, Warp and Weft
— 258, A. IRVINE's novels
— 315, The Auld Meetin' Hoose Green
— 316, The Humour of Druid's Island
— 333, The Spanish Wine
— 402, Sir Ludar
Antwerp, 24, Raoul, Gentleman of Fortune
— 112, Ludovic and Gertrude
— 213, Shut In
Anvil, The, 187
Apache Indians, 372, The Heritage of Unrest
Apaches of Paris, 108, The Gentle Libertine
— See also *Paris Poor*
Apáfi, Michael, 271, 'Midst the Wild Carpathians, and sequel
Apefi, King of Egypt, 220, Queen of the Dawn
Apennines, 399, The Mysteries of Udolpho
Apes, 209, The Emotions of Polydore Marasquin
— 295, Balaoo
— 378, Melincourt
Aphrodite, 160
Apicius, 209, Neæra
Apocolocyntosis, 383
Apollo, see *Classical Mythology, Pan*
Apollo in Picardy, 377
Apollonius and Silla, The History of, 430
Apollonius of Tyre, 430
Apologues, see *Allegories, Beast Fables, Didactic Fiction*
Apostate, The, 299
Apostates, The, 386
Apothesis, 190

Appin Murder, 449, Kidnapped, Katriona
Apple of the Eye, The, 496
Apples of Gold, 133
Apprentice, The, 400
Apprenticeship, 359
April Fools, 318
April Hopes, 250
April Showers, 76
Apulia, 124, The Silver Skull
Aquinas, St. Thomas, 21, Arnoul the Englishman
Arabella Stuart, 262
Arabian Fiction, 13, The Arabian Nights
— 42, Vathek
— 197, Gesta Romanorum
— 358, New Arabian Nights
— See also *Arabs*
Arabian Nights' Entertainments, 13
Arabs, 122, Khaled
— 211, Frank Hilton
— 375, Hermann Agha
— 376, The Weavers
— 387, Knights of Araby, Oriental Encounters
— 448, The Veil, The Earthen Drum
Arachne, 159
Araminta, 442
Aran Isles, 289, Grania
— 297, Luttrell of Arran
Arbol de la Sienca Novela, El, 35
Arcadia, 434
Arcadian Adventures with the Idle Rich, 293
Arcadians, The, 176
Arcadias, 78, Scholar Gipsies
— 434, Arcadia
— See also *Heroical Romances, Pastorals, Sentimental Romances*
Arcadius, Emperor, 170, Gathering Clouds
Archæology, 188, H. B. FULLER's novels
— 454, Queen-hoo Hall
— 515, The Key of Life
Archdeacon Truggin, 390
Archibald Malmaison, 232
Architects, 46, The Roll Call
Arctic Regions, 299, The Visionary, Weird Tales
— 482, The English at the North Pole
— See also *Antarctic, Eskimoes, Yakuts*
Ardath, 115
Arden Massiter, 39
Ardennes, 181, The Four Sons of Aymon
— 225, Passe-Rose
Ardmore, 355, Nanno
Arethusa (by F. M. CRAWFORD), 123
Arethusa (by DE SELINCOURT), 140
Argalus and Parthenia, 434, The Arcadia
Argenis, 33
Argent, L', 518

Argentina, 61, The Four Horsemen of the Apocalypse, The Temptress
— 79, Tales of the Pampas
— 259, Maria
— 388, Ponce de Leon
— See also below
ARGENTINE NOVELISTS: J. ISAACS, E. LARRETA, " Hugo WAST "
Argonauci, 371
Argonauts, 279, The Heroes
Argyle, Duke of, 425, The Heart of Midlothian
Argyle, Marquess of, 355, John Splendid
— 425, A Legend of Montrose
— 448, The Red Reaper
Argyllshire, see *Highlands of Scotland*
ARI, see MORRIS, W., and MAGNÚSSON, E.
" *Ariadne, The*," 328, Frank Mildmay
Ariadne (by GRÉVILLE), 215
Ariadne (by " OUIDA "), 372
Ariel, 335
Ariosto, 503, The Plough of Shame
Aristide Froissart, 209
Aristide Pujol, Adventures of, 301
Aristocracy, 14
Aristocratic Prejudice, see *Class Feeling*
Aristocrats, The, 17
Aristodemus, 328, Japhet
Aristophanes, 287, Pericles and Aspasia
Arizona, 291, St. Mawr
— 372, The Heritage of Unrest
— 422, Isabel Stirling
— 501, Arizona Nights
Arizona Nights, 501
Ark of the Curse, The, 348
Arkansas, 377, Molly Macdonald
— 453, Backwater
— 463, Expiation (by " O. THANET "), Otto the Knight
Arm of the Lord, The, 93
Armadale, 109
Armen, Die, 323
Armenian, The (The Ghost-Seer), 422
Armiger, Rose, 265, The Other House
Armour Wherein he Trusted, 492
Armourer's 'Prentices, The, 513
Arms and the Maid, 418
Armstrong, Archibald, 104, Court Cards
Army, see *Military Novels, Regimental Life, Wars, Imaginary*, and also names of wars
Arne, 56
Arnold, Benedict, 169, Brinton Eliot
— 308, Mr. Arnold
— 423, The Son of a Tory

Arnold, Matthew, 144, Lothair
— 322, The New Republic
Arnold, Dr. Thomas, 253, Tom Brown's Schooldays
Arnold Lip, The, 290
Arnoul the Englishman, 21
Arnoux, Mme, 175, Sentimental Education
Around Old Chester, 137
Around the Moon, 482
Around the World in Eighty Days, 482
Arrah Neil, 262
Arrival of Antony, The, 113
Arrow of Gold, The, 111
Arrow of the North, The, 180
Arrows of the Almighty, 269
Arsène Lupin, 293
Arsinoë, Queen of Egypt, 159, Arachne
Art and Artists, 1, Dolorosa
— 9, The Romance of Fra Filippo Lippi
— 12, The Flame of Life
— 29, Cousin Pons.
— 33, A Triangle, Comfortless Memory
— 38, The Devil's Portrait
— 44, The Missing Masterpiece
— 47, Limitations
— 52, Gerfaut
— 57, A Princess of Thule
— 60, The Incomplete Amorist
— 61, Woman Triumphant
— 67, The Blue Duchess
— 75, Mrs. Bligh
— 88, The City of Refuge
— 89, Mendel
— 97, The Common Law
— 120, The Third Violet
— 122, Marzio's Crucifix
— 129, Artists' Wives
— 138, Alice-for-Short
— 151, The Genius
— 152, The Maker of Saints
— 156, Trilby
— 159, Arachne
— 170, Fra Lippo Lippi
— 172, An Artist's Honour
— 183, The Red Lily
— 188, H. B. FULLER's novels
— 189, Villa Rubein
— 232, Garth
— 241, In Paradise
— 249, A Fellowe and his Wife
— 252, Richard Kurt, and sequels
— 263-6, Henry JAMES's novels, *passim*
— 266, The Outcry, Colour Studies
— 281, The Light that Failed
— 294, Cynthia in the West
— 302, The Coming of Amos
— 307, The Chorus
— 312, The Dragon Painter
— 321, The Wages of Sin

Art and Artists (contd.): 323, The Golden Quill
— 327, Subsoil
— 334, The Moon and Sixpence
— 349, A Modern Lover, A Mummer's Wife, Confessions of a Young Man
— 351, Portrait in a Mirror
— 361, The Amateur, Vandover and the Brute
— 369, O. ONIONS' novels
— 372, Two Little Wooden Shoes, Ariadne
— 377, A Fair Deceiver
— 386, The Joy of Youth
— 389, Roweny in Boston, and sequel
— 393, Cities of the Plain
— 410, The Atelier du Lys, In Low Relief, The Earth-Mother
— 411, Immortal Youth
— 420, The Master Mosaic Workers
— 435, In Monte Carlo, Tales
— 442, The Life Class
— 453, The Red Room
— 479, Jenny
— 481, Peter Whiffle
— 508, The Grand Tour
— 510, The Wise Virgins
— 518, His Masterpiece
— 520, Claudia
— See also *Æstheticism, Art (Religious), Music and Musicians, Singers*, etc., and also under names of artists, *Brueghel, Crome, Gainsborough, Reynolds, Romney, Leonardo da Vinci*, etc.
Art (Religious), 257, En Route, and sequels
Art Maguire, 92
Artagnan, Chevalier d', 154, The Three Musketeers, and sequels
Artemus Ward, his book, 487
Artemus Ward, his travels, 487
Artemus Ward, in London, 487
Artevelde, Philip van, 71, The White Hoods
— 233, Suzanna
Arthur, Prince, 261, Philip Augustus
ARTHUR, Miss, see " GILBERT, G. D."
Arthur Mervyn, 76
Arthur of Little Britain, 16
Arthur O'Leary, 296
Arthurian Romances, 16, Arthur of Little Britain
— 22, Cian of the Chariots
— 132, The Road to Avalon, Uther and Igraine
— 133, Love Among the Ruins, The Seven Streams, Joan of the Tower
— 166, Galahad
— 217, The Mabinogion

Arthurian Romances (contd.): 243, The High History of the Holy Graal
— 255, Huon of Burdeux
— 269, Tom a Lincoln
— 301, Amadis of Gaul
— 322, Sir T. MALORY's Morte Darthur
— 429, The Clutch of Circumstance
— 476, A Yankee at the Court of King Arthur (burlesque)
— See also *Welsh Romances*
Arthur's Hall, 244
Artist Passes, An, 201
Artist's Honour, An, 172
Artists' Wives, 129
Artois, 313, Seraphica
Artus Hof, The, 244
Arundel, 48
Arundel, Earl of, 333, The Royal Sisters
As it Happened, 243
As the Light Led, 39
As the Twig is Bent, 105
ASBJÖRNSEN, P. Ch., see *sub nom.* DASENT, Sir G. W., 129
Ascanio, 154
Ascot, Lady, 280, Ravenshoe
Ascutney Street, 503
Ashby, Turner, 113, Surry of Eagle's Nest
Ashby-de-la-Zouche, Tournament of, 425, Ivanhoe
Ashdown Forest, 256, A Friend of Nelson
Asher, Isabel, 263, The Portrait of a Lady
Ashes (by DELEDDA), 137
Ashes (by ZEROMSKI), 516
Ashes of a God, The, 25
Ashes of Empire, 96
ASHTON, Winifred, see DANE, Clemence
Asia Minor, 103, Two Thousand Years Ago
Ask Mamma, 456
Askew, Anne, 325, Passages in the life of the faire gospeller Anne Askew
Aslauga's Knight, 181
Asmodeus, 295
Aspasia, 18, The Immortal Marriage
— 287, Pericles and Aspasia
Aspern Papers, The, 264
Aspirations of Jean Servien, The, 182
Assam, 390, His Majesty's Shirt Sleeves
Assassin, The, 364
Assassinat de M. Fualdès, L', 391
Assassination Plot (1696), 262, The King's Highway
— 497, Shrewsbury
— See also *Fenwick, Sir John*
Assassins, The, 158, Cross and Dagger
— 336, The Assassins
Assassins, The, 336
Associate Hermits, The, 451

Assommoir, L', 517
Assyria, 121, Zoroaster
— 337, Sarchedon
Astier-Réhu, 130, One of the Forty
Astonishing History of Troy Town, 396
Astrid, 286
Astronomy, 72, The Redemption of Tycho Brahe
— 94, The Star Dreamer
— 226, Two on a Tower
Asturias, 374, The Marquis of Penalta, The Fourth Estate
At a Country House, 100
At a Winter's Fire, 90
At All Costs, 6
At Christmas-time, 100
At First Sight, 136
At Home, 100
At Large, 47
At Odds, 460
At Sunwich Port, 260
At the Altar, 496
At the Back of the North Wind, 313
At the Blue Moon Again, 298
At the Casa Napoléon, 267
At the Councillor's, 326
At the Cross Roads, 348
At the Door of the Gate, 403
At the End of the Passage, 281
At the Gate of the Fold, 176
At the Grand Durbar, 445
At the River, 210
At the Sign of the Bleeding Heart, 342
At the Sign of the Blue Moon, 298
At the Sign of the Cat and Racket, 26
At the Sign of the Queen Pédauque, 183
At the Sign of the Savage, 250
At the South Gate, 406
At the Villa Rose, 331
At the Ward Toll, 210
At the Y, 208
Atala, 98
Atelier de Marie-Claire, L', 18
Atelier du Lys, The, 410
Atheism, 27, The Atheist's Mass
— 147, Crime and Punishment, *et seq.*
— 261, Niels Lyhne
— See also *Agnosticism and Faith*
Atheist's Mass, The, 27
Athelstan, King, 163, Egil's Saga
Athens, 18, The Immortal Marriage
— 287, Pericles and Aspasia
— 386, Treasures of Typhon
— 417, The Last Athenian
— 445, The Street of the Flute-Player
Athleticism, see *Muscular Novels*
Atlantida, 47
Atlantis, 231
Atlee, 297, Lord Kilgobbin

Atli the Little, 249, Howard the Halt
Atrophy, 500
Attaché, The, 222
Attack on the Mill, The, 516
Attaque du Moulin, L', 516
Atterbury Plot, 418, The Gates of Doom
Attic Philosopher, The, 443
Attila, 262, Attila
Attila, 262
ATTON, Henry, see "BARTRAM, George"
Au Bonheur des dames, 517
Auberge rouge, l', 30
Aucassin et Nicolette, 18
Auction Block, The, 40
Audrey, 270
Auf der Hohe, 19
Aufruhr um den Junker Ernst, Der, 491
Aufstand der Fischer von St. Barbara, 428
Aufzeichnungen des Malte Laurids Brigge, 408
Aughrim, Battle of, 294, Col. Torlogh O'Brien
August, 224
Augustus, Emperor, 41, Gallus
Augustus the Strong, Elector of Saxony, 285, The Countess Cosel
Auld Licht Idylls, 37
Auld Meetin' Hoose Green, The, 315
Aunt Anne, 106
Aunt Eleanor, 210
Aunt Jane and Uncle James, 113
Aunt Jo's Scrap Book, 6
Aunt Juley's Courtship, 191
Aunt Maud, 366
Aunt Trinidad, 398
Aurelian, Emperor, 489, Zenobia, and sequel
Aurelian, 489
Aurelius, Marcus, 377, Marius the Epicurean
Aurora Floyd, 69
Aurora Roja, 35
Aus einer kleinen Stadt, 188
Ausonius, 128, A Captive of the Roman Eagles
Austen, Jane, 283, The Janeites
Austerlitz, 296, Tom Burke
— 468, War and Peace
Austin Elliot, 280
Australia, 2, The Australians
— 165, Kanga Creek
— 207, The Smasher
— 208, A Chesnut Champion, The Sweep Winner
— 276, Life is Life
— 280, The Hillyars and the Burtons
— 291, Kangaroo
— 292, The Boy in the Bush
— 350, Lou of the Ranges
— 351, The Dark Fire
— See also AUSTRALIAN NOVELISTS, *passim* ; *Bush Life, Bushrangers, Convict Life, Queensland, New South Wales*, etc.

Australia Felix, 406
Australian Heroine, An, 390
AUSTRALIAN NOVELISTS : J. H. M. ABBOT, G. L. BECKE, "Rolf BOLDREWOOD," "M. A'B. BOYD," Boyd CABLE, Ada CAMBRIDGE, G. CHAMIER, M. A. H. CLARKE, "M. B. ELDERSHAW," Mary GAUNT, H. GOLDSMITH, W. G. HAY, E. W. HORNUNG, H. H. LAWSON, Emily S. LOUD, H. C. MacILWAINE, J. MOUAT, H. NISBET, Rosa C. PRAED, Mrs. K. S. PRICHARD, "H. H. RICHARDSON," "TASMA," W. S. WALKER, Price WARUNG
Australians, The, 2
Austria and Hungary, 1, The Golden Fleece
— 92, "No. 101"
— 170, Second Report of Faustus
— 186, For the Right
— 196, Orthodox
— 210, St. Vitus Day
— 231, The Good Soldier Schweik
— 267, The Stronger Wings
— 271–3, JÓKAI's novels, *passim*
— 285, Captain Zillner
— 296, The Daltons
— 339, Vittoria
— 372, John of Gerisau
— 402, The Forest of the Hanged
— 419, For Sceptre and Crown
— 519, The Rose of Disentis
— See also AUSTRIAN NOVELISTS, *Bohemia, Galicia, Hungary, Transylvania, Tyrol*, etc.
AUSTRIAN NOVELISTS : "A. HOELLRIEGEL," R. NEUMANN, P. ROSEGGER, A. SCHNITZLER
Author of "Beltraffio," The, 264
Authors, see *Literary Life*
Autobiographical Novels, 6, The Story of a Bad Boy
— 47, The House of Quiet, etc.
— 56, Blakken
— 62, Amorous Fiametta
— 73, Charlotte BRONTË's novels
— 79, The Log of a Sea Waif, Confessions of a Tradesman
— 82, The One I Knew the Best of All
— 83, The Way of All Flesh
— 93, A Childhood
— 129, Annals of an Eventful Life, Little Good-for-Nothing
— 124, Kit Kennedy
— 130, Numa Roumestan
— 141, David Copperfield

Autobiographical Novels (contd.): 146, The House of the Dead
— 191, Peace
— 200, The Unclassed, New Grub Street
— 201, The Crown of Life, Henry Ryecroft
— 223, Wanderers
— 253, Han of Iceland
— 261, Niels Lyhne
— 267, Wood Magic, Bevis
— 272, Eyes like the Sea
— 277, Slavery
— 280, The Hillyars and the Burtons
— 287, The Story of a Story
— 287, Mårbacka
— 294, Young Lives
— 295, A Hero of our Time
— 298, Our Mr. Wrenn
— 300, Christopher Kirkland
— 304, "LOTI'S" novels
— 315, P. MacGILL's novels, *passim*
— 328, Frank Mildmay, Mr. Midshipman Easy
— 338, Redburn
— 339, Evan Harrington
— 349, Confessions of a Young Man
— 351, The Wild Irish Girl
— 357, Confessions of a Child of the Century
— 359, Loss and Gain
— 402, A Terrible Temptation
— 408, Notebook of Malte Laurids Brigge
— 423, Undine
— 454, The Son of a Servant, Confessions of a Fool, Fair Haven and Foul Strand
— 467–9, TOLSTOY's novels, especially Childhood
— 472, The Belton Estate
— 473, Dr. Wortle's School
— 476, Life on the Mississippi
— 503, The History of Agathon
Autobiography of a Boy, 453
Autobiography of a Charwoman, 485
Autobiography of a Quack, 345
Autobiography of Christopher Kirkland, 300
Autobiography of Judas Iscariot, 432
Autobiography of Mark Rutherford, The, 502
Autocracy of Mr. Parham, The, 495
Autocrat of the Breakfast Table, The, 245
Automatons, 244
Automne d'une femme, L', 391
Autour de la lune, 482
Autres temps, 499
Autumn, 223
Autumn Glory, 40

Auvergne, 275, Madeleine
Avalanche, The, 389
Avalon, see *Arthurian Legend*
Avant l'amour, 466
Avanti !, 306
Avarice, see *Misers*
Avarice Chastised, 422
Avarice House, 213
Avenger, The (by Mary Beaumont), 41
Avenger, The (by De Quincey), 139
Avenger of Blood, The, 197
Avenging Children, 324
Aventure de Ladislaus Bolski, L', 101
Aventures du capitaine Mago, Les, 87
Aventures prodigieuses de Tartarin de Tarascon, 129
Average Man, An, 49
Aveu, L', 215
Avignon, 61, The Pope of the Sea
— 129, The Pope's Mule
— 212, The Reds of the Midi, and Sequels
— 407, Golden Hawk
Awakening, 65
Awkward Age, The, 265
Axe, The, 479
Axel and Anna, 71
Axholm, Isle of, 223, The MS. in the Red Box
Ayala's Angel, 473
Ayesha, 220
Aylwin, 491
Ayrshire, 123–4, S. R. Crockett's stories
— 191, Galt's novels
— 270, H. Johnstone's novels
— 424, Guy Mannering
Ayrshire Idylls, 356
Ayrshire Legatees, The, 191
Az arany ember, 271
Aziyadé, 304
Azov, 284, Kostia the Cossack
Azrael, 271, 'Midst the Wild Carpathians, and sequel
Aztecs, 267, The Aztec Treasure House
Aztec Treasure House, The, 267

B. E. N., 113
Baal Worship, 337, Sarchedon
Babbitt, 298
Babe B.A., The, 47
Baber, Emperor, 446, King Errant
Babes in the Bush, 64
Babička, 358
Babington Plot, 333, One Queen Triumphant
— 513, Unknown to History
Baboo Jabberjee, B.A., 12
Baboos, 12, Baboo Jabberjee
— 116, His Honour and a Lady

Babouc, 484
Babs the Impossible, 211
Babylon, 255, Huon of Bordeaux
— 337, Sarchedon
— 375, Paris and Vienne
Babyons, The, 128
Baby's Grandmother, The, 485
Bach, Alexander von, 272, The New Landlord
Bachelor Girl, The, 326
Bachelor of Salamanca, The, 295
Bachelor's Christmas, The, 212
Bachelor's Establishment A, 28
Back of Beyond, 502
Back to Burmah, 466
Back Trailers from the Middle Border, 192
Background for Caroline, A, 16
Backswoodsmen, The, 409
Backwater, 405
Backwater, 453
Backwoodsmen, see *Pioneers*
Bacon, Francis, Viscount Verulam, 273, In Burleigh's Days, and sequel
Bacon, Roger, 23, Fryer Bacon
— 273, The Friar's Niece
Bacon's Rebellion, 165, The Cromwell of Virginia
— 206, White Aprons
— 505, The Heart's Highway
Bad Company, see In Bad Company, 284
Bad Old Times, The, 273
Bad Times, The, 55
Bad Weather, 100
Badalia Herodsfoot, 282
Baden, 1, Trente et Quarante
— 284, Beleaguered
— 475, The Torrents of Spring
— 475, Smoke
Badman, Mr, 81, The Life and Death of Mr. Badman
Bag of Saffron, The, 256
Bagdad, 13, Arabian Nights' Entertainments
— 375, Hermann Agha
Bagenal, "King," 305, Character and Comedy
Baggaras, 150, Tragedy of the Koroško
Baiæ, 159, Quintus Claudius
Bail Up !, 360
Bailiff Yerney and his Rights, The, 89
Bairn-Keeper, The, 173
Bajani, 32
Baked Mole, The, 390
Bakunin, Michel, 22, The Devil at the Long Bridge
Balaam and his Master, 229
Balak, 58, Clara Vaughan
Balam, 58, Clara Vaughan

Balan, 98, Charles the Grete
Balance, The, 277
Balaoo, 295
Balbec, 393, Within a Budding Grove
Balcony Stories, 279
Balderstone, Caleb, 425, The Bride of Lammermoor
Balearic Isles, 342, Tomaso's Fortune
Balestier, Wolcott, see sub nom. Kipling, R., 283
Balfour, Lord, of Burley, 425, Old Mortality
Baliol Garth, 200
Balisand, 238
Balkan States, 127, The Black Pilgrim
— 215, An Uncrowned King, and sequels
— 306, The Captain of the Janizaries
— 479, The Prince of Balkistan
Ball, John, 112, Long Will
— 343, Robert Annys
— 352, The Dream of John Ball
Ball and the Cross, The, 102
Ball Programme, The, 516
Ballads of the Dauphine, The, 412
Ballarat, 406, Chronicles of Richard Mahony
Ballerina, La, 429
Ballet-Dancer, The, 429
Balloonists, 482, Five Weeks in a Balloon
Balmoral, 7
Balsamo, 155, Memoirs of a Physician, and sequel
Balthasar, 183
Baltic, 235, Her Only Brother
— 256, A Friend of Nelson
Baltimore, 363, The Chosen People
Balue, Cardinal, 426, Quentin Durward
Balzac, Honoré de, 284, Coronet
Balzac, Sieur de (Seigneur d'Entragues), 30, About Catherine de' Medici
Bamborough Castle, 52, Dorothy Forster
Banda Oriental, see *Uruguay* and *America, South*
Bandamanna Saga, 30
Bandits, The, 259
Bang, Aaron, 424, Tom Cringle's Log
Banished Man, The, 440
Banjo, 316
Banked Fires, 422
Banker and the Bear, The, 492
Banker's Love Story, A, 315
Bankruptcy, 28, The Rise and Fall of César Birotteau
Banks and Banking, 5, John Law

Banks and Banking (contd.):
52, Ready-Money Mortiboy
— 315, A Banker's Love Story
— 354, Our Mr. Dormer
— 497, David Harum
— 498, Ovington's Bank
— See also *Business, Financiers,* etc.
Banks of the Boro, The, 278
Banned and Blessed, 496
Banner of the Bull, The, 418
Bannerton's Agency, 408
Bannière bleue, La, 87
Bannlyst, 287
Bannockburn, Battle of, 335, The Chevalier of the Splendid Crest
Banquet, The, 310
Baptist Lake, 131
Baptists, 39, As the Light Led
— 260, Irresolute Catherine
— 353, Splendour of God
Bar Harbour, 122, Love in Idleness
Bar-le-Duc, 207, The Secret of Narcisse
Barabbas, 116
Barbados, 52, For Faith and Freedom
— 418, Captain Blood
Barbara Blomberg, 159
Barbara Dering, 409
Barbara Heathcote's Trials, 91
Barbara Ladd, 409
Barbara of the Thorn, 459
Barbara Rebell, 44
Barbara von Tisenhusen, 274
Barbara West, 442
Barbara Winsloe, Rebel, 165
Barbara's History, 161
Barbarian Stories, 346
Barbary Sheep, 242
Barbe of Grand Bayou, 372
Barber, Margaret F., see "Fairless, Michael," 168
Barber-Surgeon's Stories, The, 470
Barclay, Sir George, 262, The King's Highway
— See also *Assassination Plot*
Bardell, Mrs., 140, Pickwick Papers
Bardelys the Magnificent, 417
Barefooted Maiden, The (Little Barefoot), 19
Barfüssele, 19
Barge Dwellers, 237, The Water Gipsies
— 365, The Golden Barque
Bargone, Charles, see "Farrère, Claude," 170
Baring-Gould, Rev. S., see Gould, Rev. S. B., 208
Barlasch of the Guard, 342

Barletta, 22, The Challenge of Barletta
Barnaby Rudge, 140
Barnabys in America, The, 473
BARNARD, Marjorie F., see "ELDERSHAW, M. B.", 163
Barnavaux, 344
Barnavaux et quelques femmes, 344
Barnet, Battle of, 309, The Last of the Barons
Barny O'Reirdon the Navigator, 305
Baron and Squire, 360
Baron's Sons, The, 272
Barons' Wars, 120, The House of Walderne
— 122, Via Crucis
— 133, The Red Saint
— 213, A Clerk of Oxford
— 262, Forest Days
— 314, A Legend of Reading Abbey
Barque Future, The, 299
BARR, Robert, see also sub nom. CRANE, Stephen, 121
Barras, P. J. F. N., 178, Leroux
— 234, The Shadow of a Throne
Barrett, Sir Purcell, 339, Sandra Belloni
Barrier, The (by BEACH), 40
Barrier, The (by Mills YOUNG), 514
Barrington, 297
Barrow Bridge, 143, Sybil
Barrow-in-Furness, 488, Helbeck of Bannisdale
Barry Leroy, 24
Barry Lyndon, Memoirs of, 463
Barrys, The, 80
Barsetshire, 471–2, TROLLOPE'S Barsetshire Novels
Bartek the Victor, 435
Bartleby the Scrivener, 338
BARTLETT, V., see SHERRIFF, R., 433
Bashan and J, 324
Basil Netherby, 47
Basket Woman, The, 21
Basque Country, 89, Rough-Hewn
— 162, Symphonies
— 305, Ramuntcho
— 380, The Rose Garden
BASQUE NOVELIST: M. de UNAMUNO
Bass Rock, 81, My Lady of the Bass
— 124, The Cherry Riband
Basset, 222
Bastable Children, The, 60
Basterga, 498, The Long Night
Bastille, 154, The Regent's Daughter, Sylvandire
— 155, The Taking of the Bastille
— 212, The Reds of the Midi
— 261, Richelieu
— 262, The Huguenot

Bastions de l'Est, Les, 37
Batailles de la vie, La, 365
Bâtard de Mauléon, Le, 155
Batchelor's Banquet, 288
Bates, Charlie, 140, Oliver Twist
Bates, Miss, 20, Emma
Bath, Colonel, 173, Amelia
Bath, 20, Jane AUSTEN'S novels
— 93 The Bath Comedy
— 94, Love Gilds the Scene
— 165, The Moon of Bath
— 340, Chloe
— 348, A Nest of Linnets
— 411, The Taming of the Brute
— 459, Monsieur Beaucaire
— 508, Lady Grizel
— See also *Nash, Beau*
Bath Comedy, The, 93
Bâton Sinister, The, 199
Batouala, 325
Battersea, 247, My Lord Winchenden
Battle (Sussex), 133, The House of Spies
Battle Ground, The, 202
Battle of Rosnaree, 214
Battle of the Strong, The, 376
Battle of the Weak, The, 153
Battle of the White Strand, The, 214
Battledore and Shuttlecock, 118
Battlement and Tower, 404
Batu Khan, 273, 'Neath the Hoof of the Tartar
Batz Conspiracy, 194, The Red Shirts
Bavaria, 18, Gaspard Hauser
— 171, The Ugly Duchess
— 172, Success
— 460, The Initials, Quits, At Odds
BAX, A., see "O'BYRNE, D.", 363
Baxter, Richard, 98, The Draytons and the Davenants, and sequel
Bay Path, The, 244
Bayard, Chevalier de, 122, With the Immortels
— 188, Under Bayard's Banner
Bayard's Courier, 47
BAYLY, Ada Ellen, see "LYALL, Edna"
Bayonne, 89, Rough-Hewn
— 380, The Rose Garden
Bayou Folk, 103
Bazarov, 475, Fathers and Children
Beach of Dreams, The, 445
Beach of Falesá, The, 449
Beacon, The, 386
Bear Flag War, 93, Captain Courtesy
Bear-Hunting Worse than Slavery, 469
Beardsley, Aubry, 381, Our House
Bearers of the Burden, 152

Beast Fables, 129, Sir G. W. DASENT'S translations
— 167, Two Legs, etc.
— 197, Gesta Romanorum
— 211, The Wind in the Willows
— 228, Uncle Remus, Nights with Uncle Remus
— 229, Uncle Remus and his Friends
— 282, The Jungle-Book, and sequel, Just-So Stories
— 404, Reynard the Fox
— 459, Romantic Tales of the Punjab
— See also *Animals*
Beast in the Jungle, The, 266
Beasts and Super-Beasts, 355
Beat t' Harbour, A, 156
Beatrice, 241
Beatrice Cenci, 217
Beatrix, 27
Beatrix Esmond, 462, Esmond
— 463, The Virginians
Beatrix of Clare, 424
Beatrix of Venice, 381
Beatrix Randolph, 232
Beau Brocade, 370
Beauchamp's Career, 340
Beaudesert, Sedley, 309, The Caxtons
Beaufort, Henry, Cardinal, 25, The Gleaming Dawn, The Cardinal's Page
— 49, The History of Richard Raynal, Solitary
Beaufoy Romances, The, 152
Beauharnais, Josephine de, 234, The Shadow of a Throne
Beaujeu, 24
Beaumarchais, P. A. C. de, 169, Brinton Eliot
Beaumaroy Home from the Wars, 247
Beauregard Mystery, The, 215
Beau's Comedy, The, 145
Beautiful End, 245
Beautiful Rebel, A, 88
Beautiful Suit, The, 494
Beautiful Vampire, The, 195
Beautiful Years, The, 507
Beauty for Ashes, 107
Beauty of the Purple, The, 132
Because of the Angels, 247
Because of the Dollars, 111
BECH, Katharina M., see "MICHAËLIS, Karin," 344
BECK, Mrs. Lily Adams, see "BARRINGTON, E."
Becket, St. Thomas, 24, The Fool
— 343, The Saint
Beckoning Fair One, The, 369

Becquée, La, 69
"BEDE, Cuthbert," see BRADLEY, Rev. Edward
Bedford Row Conspiracy, The, 463
Bedouins, see *Arabs*,
Beechcroft at Rockstone, 513
Beechnut, 1
Beechy, 256
Bees and Bee-Keeping, 115, Oak Openings
— 161, Rev.T. EDWARDES'S novels
Beethoven, Ludwig v..n, 103, Eroica
— 361, The Moonlight Sonata
— 414, John Christopher
Beetle, 282, Stalkey & Co.
Before Adam, 303
Before Dawn, 363
Before Sunset, 508
Before the Bombardment, 438
Before the Dawn (by ALTSHELER), 9
Before the Dawn (by KAGAWA), 274
Before the Gringo Came (The Splendid Idle Forties), 17
Before Tilsit, 468
Beggar My Neighbour, 196
Beggars All, 148
Beggar's Nurse, The, 201
Beggars of the Sea, 53
Beggars on Horseback, 268
Beggar's Opera, 38, The Chaste Diana
Beginner, A, 75
Beginning and End, The, 241
Begum's Daughter, The, 84
Behaviourist Psyschology, 236, E. HEMINGWAY'S novels
Behind the Counter, 219
BEHRENS, Bertha, see "HEIMBURG, W.," 235
Beichte eines Thoren, Die, 454
BEITH, John Hay, see "HAY, Ian," 233
Belated Lover, A, 254
Beleaguered, 284
Beleaguered City, A, 367
Belfast, 295, J. H. LEPPER'S novels
— 315, A Banker's Love Story
— 403, Following Darkness, At the Door of the Gate
— See also ULSTER
Belfry, The, 437
Belgian Fiction, see RINDER, E. W., 408
Belgium, 112, H. CONSCIENCE'S stories
— 116, The Master Beggars of Belgium
— 131, The Two Crossings of Madge Swalue
— 354, The Spanish Farm Trilogy

Belgium (*contd.*): 512, The Fires of Freedom
— See also *Bruges, Flanders, Ghent, Holland, Netherlands,* etc.
Belinda (by BELLOC), 43
Belinda (by Rhoda BROUGHTON), 75
Belinda (by Maria EDGEWORTH), 160
Belisarius, 128, A Struggle for Rome, The Scarlet Banner
— 201, Veranilda
" BELL, Acton, Currer, and Ellis," see BRONTË sisters,
Bell, Colonel Ramon, 23, D'ri and I
Bell and the Arrow, The, 102
Bell Barry, 279
Bell Dundas, 452
Bella, 65
Bella Donna, 242
Bellairs, Kitty, 24, Incomparable Bellairs, Love Gilds the Scene, Pamela Pounce
Bellamy, 351
Bellarion, 418
Bellbo Heritage, The, 235
Belle Nivernaise, La, 130
Belle of Bowling Green, The, 36
Belle of Canada City, A, 230
Belle of Toorak, The, 248
Belle-rose, 1
Belles Demoiselles Plantation, The, 86
Beloved Vagabond, The, 301
Below Stairs, 434
Belshazzar, 121, Zoroaster
— 220, Belshazzar
Belshazzar, 220
Beltane the Smith, 169
Beltham, Squire, 339, Harry Richmond
Belton Estate, The, 472
Ben Brace of Nelson's " Agamemnon," 97
Ben Comee, 88
Ben Hamed el Askar, 132
Ben Hur, 486
Ben Nevis, 57, In Far Lochabar
Ben Tobit, 11
Benassis, M., 29, The Country Doctor
Benburb, Battle of, 174, The Chances of War
Bench of Desolation, The, 266
Bend of the Road, The, 319
Bending of a Twig, 107
Bendish, 240
Bendysh, Bridget, 330, By the North Sea
Benedick in Arcady, A, 456
Benedict XIII, Pope, 61 The Pope of the Sea
Benedict Kavanagh, 55
Benefactress, The, 14

BENGALI NOVELISTS: BAṄKIMACHANDRA CHAṬṬOPĀDHYĀYA, R. C. DUTT, RAVĪNDRANĀTHA THĀKURA, SARATKUMARA GHOSHA, Mrs. SATTHIANADHAN, SVARNAKUMARĪ DEVI (Mrs. GHOSAL)
Benham, 369
Benighted, 392
Benito Cereno, 338
Benjamin Parrot's Fancy, 277
Bennet, Elizabeth, 20, Pride and Prejudice
Bennet, Mr. and Mrs., 20, Pride and Prejudice
BENNETT, Arnold, see also PHILPOTTS, Eden, 387
BENOÎT DE SAINTE-MORE, see sub nom. LE FEVRE, R., 294
Benoit Castain, 391
Benoni, 224
Bent Twig, The, 88
Bente, Mrs., 290
Benthamism, 143, Popanilla
Bentinck's Tutor, 378
Beppo the Conscript, 473
Bequeathed, 500
Berengaria, 239, Richard Yea-and-Nay
— 426, The Talisman
Beresina, 27, Another Study of Woman
Bergeret, M., 183, L'histoire contemporaine
Bergson, Alexandra, 94, O Pioneers !
Bergsonian Philosophy, 393, PROUST's novels
Berkeley, Sir William, 206, White Aprons
— 270, Prisoners of Hope
Berkhamstead, 107, Minstrel Dick
Berkshire, 234, Miss HAYDEN's novels
— 346, Our Village
Berlin, 7, The Burgomaster of Berlin
— 277, The Ninth of November
— 323, Berlin
— 355, The Merchant of Berlin, and sequels
— 420, Consuelo
— 450, The Buchholtz Family
— 455, The Song of Songs
Berlin, 323
Berlin and Sans Souci, 355
Berlioz, Hector, 400, Journeyman Love
BERMANN, Richard Arnold von, see " HOELLRIEGEL, Arnold "
Bermuda, 441, Mary Paget
Bernard of Clairvaux, Saint, 122, Via Crucis
— 363, The Knight of the Cave
BERNARD, R. S., see sub nom. MAITLAND, Mrs. Ella, 321
Bernard Quesnay, 335

BERNERS, LORD (tr.), 16, Arthur of Little Britain
— 255, Huon of Bordeaux
Bernicia, 36
Berratene Jungen, 287
Berri, 420, Little Fadette
— 421, The Devil's Pool, The Country Waif
Berri, Duchesse de, 107, The Fiery Dawn
— 156, The She-Wolves of Machecoul
Berry, Mrs., 339, Richard Feverel
Berserks, 200, Gisli the Outlaw
— 214, Grettis Saga
— 249, Howard the Halt
— 483, Viga Glum
Bertha Garlan, 423
Bertram, Sir Thomas, 20, Mansfield Park
Bertram and Bimbi, 281
Bertran de Born, 239, Richard Yea-and-Nay
Bertrand of Brittany, 133
Berwick, Duke of, 262, The King's Highway
Beside Still Waters, 47
Beside the Bonnie Briar Bush, 318
Bess of the Woods, 133
Best Laid Schemes, 360
Best Man in Garotte, The, 228
Bet, The, 99
Bête humaine, La, 518
Beth Book, The, 211
BETHAM-EDWARDS, Matilda B., see EDWARDS, Matilda B. Betham, 161
Bethulah, 515
Betrayal of Shere Bahadur, The, 125
Betrayers, The, 152
Betrothed, 100
Betrothed, The (by MANZONI), 325
Betrothed, The (by SCOTT), 426
Bette, Cousine, 29, Cousin Betty
Better Dead, 37
Better Sort, The, 266
Bettesworth Book, The, 68
Bettlerin vom Pont-des-Arts, Die, 231
Betty Alden, 21
Betty Musgrave, 174
Between Heaven and Earth, 306
Between the Dark and the Daylight, 251
Between the Days, 320
Between the Heather and the Northern Sea, 300
Between the Lines, 437
Between Two Loves, 36
Between Two Thieves, 135
Bevis, 267
Bewitched, 32
Beyond, 190
Beyond Life, 85
Beyond Man's Strength, 230
Beyond the Dreams of Avarice, 52

Beyond the Frontier, 377
Beyond the Gates, 384
Beyond the Pale (by CROKER), 125
Beyond the Pale (by KIPLING), 281
Bez Dogmatu, 435
Bezushov, Pierre, 468, War and Peace
Bianchon, 28, The Muse of the Department
Bible in Spain, The, 66
Bible Society, 66, The Bible in Spain
Biblical Stories (*Old Testament*), 158, Joshua
— 166, Adam and Eve
— 212, My Head ! My Head !
— 285, Sulamith
— 516, Samson the Nazarite
Bibliothèque Nationale, 40, A Blot of Ink
BICKERSTAFFE-DREW, Mgr., see " AYSCOUGH, John "
Bicycle of Cathay, A, 451
Bidpai, Fables of, 197, Gesta Romanorum
Bienville, Governor, 142, The Black Wolf's Breed
Big Bow-Wow Mystery, The, 516
Big House of Inver, The, 443
Bigamist, The, 514
Bigamy, 69, Aurora Floyd
— 152, Folly Corner
— 169, The Nebuly Coat
— 196, A Glorious Lie
— 514, The Bigamist
Bijli the Dancer, 377
Bilbao, 61, The Intruder
Billy Bellew, 362
Billy Budd, 338
Billy Durbey, 316
Billy McCoy, 126
Binding of the Strong, The, 332
Bindle, 267
Bindles on the Rocks, 267
Bindon Parva, 56
Biography of a Grizzly, 429
Biorn and Thurid, 168, Eyrbyggja Saga
Birch, Harvey, 114, The Spy
Bird of God, 239
Bird of Passage, A, 125
Birds' Christmas Carol, The, 503
Birotteau, César, 28, The Rise and Fall of César Birotteau
Birth of Conachar, The, 254
Birth of Cuchulain, The, 214
Birth of the Gods, The, 341
Birthplace, The, 266
Birthright, 453
Biryuk, 474
Bishop, The, 100
Bishops, Trial of the Seven, 71, Trelawny of Trelawne
— 243, The Chariots of the Lord

Bishop's Gambit, The, 106
Bishra Brihkka, 32
Bismarck, Count von, 135, The Man of Iron
Bismarck Dinner, A, 501
Bismillah, 210
Bissula, 128
Bit o' Writing, The, 31
Bits from Blinkbonny, 453
Bitter Tea, 452
Bjälboarvet, 235
Black, 156
Black Arrow, The, 449
Black Bar, The, 171
Black Bartlemy's Treasure, 169
Black Belt, 77, A Gentleman of the South
Black Book of Carmarthen, 405
Black Bread, 481
Black Bryony, 390
Black Country, 61, A Son of the Forge
— 181–2, Ellen Thorneycroft FOWLER's novels
Black Cuirassier, The, 448
Black Death, 168, The Gathering of Brother Hilarius
— 220, Red Eve
— 417, Singoalla
— See also *Plague*
Black Diamond, The, 514
Black Diamonds, 272
Black Dog, The, 115
Black Douglas, The, 124
Black Dwarf, The, 425
Black Forest, 19, Village Tales, The Professor's Wife, Little Barefoot, Edelweiss
— 122, Greifenstein
— 306, Sir Raoul
Black Heart and White Heart, 219
Black Hole of Calcutta, 215, Like Another Helen, 461, Ralph Darnell
Black Jack House, 227
Black Magic, 350
Black Mary, 311
Black Mate, The, 111
Black Monk, The, 99, 100
Black Office, The, 94
Black Oxen, 18
Black Pilgrim, The, 127
Black Prince, 107, Minstrel Dick
— 155, Agenor de Mauléon
— 160, Cressy and Poictiers
— 451, With the Black Prince
— 513, The Lances of Lynwood
Black Prophet, The, 92
Black Rent, 42
Black Rock, 110
Black Roses, 515
Black Sea, 285, The Læstrygonians
Black Sheep, 513
Black Sheep Chapel, 25
Black Shilling, The, 36
Black Sparta, 346
Black Tulip, The, 155

Black, White, and Brindled, 386
Black Wolf's Breed, The, 142
Blackbird's Inspiration, 185
Blacksmith of Voe, The, 127
Blade-o'-Grass, 169
Bladys of the Stewponey, 209
Blair's Ken, 485
Blake, Admiral, 79, Sea Puritans
— 258, Prince Rupert the Buccaneer
Blake, Baby, 296, Charles O'Malley
Blake-Forster Clans, 60, The Irish Chieftains
Blakeney, Sir Percy, 370, Scarlet Pimpernel series
Blakken, 56
Blameless Woman, A, 508
Blanchardyn and Eglantine, 60
Blanche Ellerslie's Ending, 292
Blanche, Lady Falaise, 433
Blancs et les bleues, Les, 156
Blandy, Mary, 268, The Ladder
BLAUMANIS, Rudolfs, see MARSHALL, L. A. (tr.), 330
Blazed Trail Stories, 501
Blazed Trail, The, 501
Blé qui lève, Le, 40
Bleak House, 141
Bleakirk-on-Sands, 396
Blenheim, Battle of, 462, Esmond
Blennerhassett, Harman, 387, Blennerhassett
Blennerhassett, 387
Blessed are the Poor, 115
Blessed are the Rich, 3
Blick auf die Vogesen, 422
Bligh, Governor, 195, Joan of the Pilchard
— See also "*Bounty*" *Mutiny*
Blind Alley, 195
Blind Bird's Nest, A, 174
Blind Larry, 320
Blind Man, The, 291
Blind Musician, The, 284
Blind Raftery and his Wife Hilaria, 84
Blind Rosa, 112
"BLINDERS, Belinda," see "COKE, Desmond"
Blindman, 336
Blindness, 109, Poor Miss Finch
— 110, The End of the Tether
— 133, Fox Farm
— 169, Love Blinded
— 198, La symphonie pastorale
— 382, Marianela
— 493, The Country of the Blind
Blindness of Dr. Gray, The, 432

Bliss, 325
Blithedale Romance, The, 233
Blix, 361
Blocao, El, 140
Block House on the Prairie, The, 444
Blockade of Phalsbourg, 166
Blockade-Runners, 161, Debenham's Vow
— 483, The Blockade-Runners
— 492, Traitor or Loyalist
Blockhouse, The, 140
Blocus, Le, 166
Blois, 262, Henry of Guise
— 417, The Lovers of Yvonne
Blondel (of Geneva), 498, The Long Night
Blondel (Trouvère), 426, The Talisman
Blondel Parva, 378
Blood, Colonel, 412, Whitefriars
— 426, Peveril of the Peak
Blood, 516
Blood and Sand, 61
Bloom, Mr., 273, Ulysses
Bloomsbury, 276
Blot of Ink, A, 40
Blougham, Lord, 498, Chippinge
Blücher, 355, Napoleon and Blücher
Blue Aloes, 450
Blue Banner, The, 87
Blue Chamber, The, 341
Blue China, 125
Blue Duchess, The, 67
Blue-Eyed Meta Holdenis, The, 101
Blue Horizon, The, 445
Blue Jackets, 171
Blue Lagoon, The, 444
"Blue-Noses," 221, Sam Slick
Blue Ocean's Daughter, The, 71
Blue Pavilons, The, 396
Blue Peter, The, 411
Blue Roses, 139
Blue-Throated God, The, 445
Blue Trousers, 356
Bluebeard's Keys, 462
Blumen- Frucht- und Dornenstücke, 407
Blund-Ketil, 237, Hensa-Thoris Saga
BLUNDELL, Mrs. F., see "FRANCIS, M. E.," 184
BLUNDELL, Margaret, see FRANCIS, M. E., and BLUNDELL, M., 185
Blush Rose, 1
Boards of Guardians, 308, Simple Simon
Boarding House Geometry, 293
Boarding House Life, 49, Paying Guests
— 113, The Financing of Fiona
— 241, Introducing William Allison

Boarding House Life (contd.): 252, Mrs. Farrell
— 268, The Passing of the Third Floor Back
— 436, Memoirs of a Landlady
Boating Party of Two, A, 41
Bob, Snarley, 259, Mad Shepherds
Bob Burke's Duel, 320
Bob Hampton of Placer, 376
Bob, Son of Battle, 368
Bodega, La, 61
Boehme, Jacob, 30, Seraphita
Boer War, 135, The Dop Doctor
— 266, Abraham's Sacrifice
— 282, Traffics and Discoveries
— 376, The Judgement House
— 411, Taken by Assault
— 447, The Eternal Quest
Boerenkryg, De, 112
Boers, 16, The Shulamite, and sequel, Trespass
— 57, A Burgher Quixote, Richard Hartley, Prospector
— 77, H. A.BRYDEN's novels
— 197, P. GIBBON's stories
— 219, Jess, Swallow
— 220, Marie
— 300, Among Privileged People
— 327, A Daughter of the Veldt
— 346, B. MITFORD's novels
— 423, The Story of an African Farm
— See also *Africa, South, Boer War*
Bog-Myrtle and Peat, 123
Bog of Stars, The, 364
Bohemia, 25, The Cardinal's Page, The Gleaming Dawn
— 72, The Redemption of Tycho Brahe
— 93, Libussa
— 285, The Torch-Bearers of Bohemia
— See also *Czech Novelists*
Bohemian Days, 230
Bohemians of the Latin Quarter, 356
Boito, 496, Verdi
Boleyn, Anne, 4, Windsor Castle
— 333, Defender of the Faith
— 433, Cold Steel
— 461, The House of the Wizard
Bolingbroke, Viscount, 70, Mohawks
— 206, Veronica Playfair
— 308, Devereux
— 510, Esther Vanhomrigh
Bolivar, 481, Bolivar
Bolivar, 481
Bolkonsky, Prince André, 468, War and Peace
Bolli, 292, Laxdaela Saga
Bologna, 22, The Devil at the Long Bridge

Bologna (*contd.*): 470, The Lady of Laws
Bolted Door, The, 499
Bomb, The, 228
Bomb-Shell, 293
Bonaventure (by BAILEY), 25
Bonaventure (by CABLE), 86
Bond of Blood, The, 179
Bond Slaves, 32
Bondavar, 272, Black Diamonds
Bondman, The, 87
Bonds of Discipline, The, 282
Boniface IX, Pope, 61, The Pope of the Sea
Bonn, 103, Eroica
Bonnard, Sylvestre, 183, The Crime of Sylvestre Bonnard
Bonney Family, The, 455
Booby, Mrs., 172, Joseph Andrews
Book of Aneirin, 405
Book of Crafts and Characters, 401
Book of Duke Huon of Burdeux, 255
Book of Examples, The, 274
Book of Gilly, The, 289
Book of Leinster, 293
Book of Llan Dav, 405
Book of Patronio, The, 274
Book of Pity and Death, The, 304
Book of Saints and Wonders, 214
Book of Snobs, The, 462
Book of the Dun Cow, 169
Book of the Dun Cow, The, 236
Book of the Knight of La Tour-Landry, The, 288
Boone, Daniel, 104, The Crossing
— 502, Daniel Boone
— See also *Bumppo, Natty*
Booth Conspiracy, 353, The Last Full Measure
Bootleggers, 97, Marie Halkett
— See also *Gangsters*
Bootle's Baby, 508
Bootle's Children, 508
Bordeaux, 39, The Lady of Tripoli
— 155, The War of Women
— 334, Destinies
Border, Scottish, 35, Rosslyn's Raid
— 104, Court Cards
— 123, The Raiders, and sequel
— 178, The Young Lovell
— 180, The Arrow of the North, Midsummer Morn
— 182, The Hand of the North
— 223, The Outlaws of the Marches
— 277, The Keeper of the Rede

Border, Scottish (*contd.*): 380, Magnus Sinclair, With the Warden of the Marches
— 425-7, SCOTT's novels, *passim*
— See also names of counties
Border Ghost Stories, 380
Borgia, Cesare, 263, Leonora d'Orco
— 341, The Forerunner
— 412, Cæsar Borgia
— 418, The Shame of Motley
— 489, Elena
Borgia, Lucrezia, 489, Elena
Borgias, 313, The Gorgeous Borgias
— 414, Don Tarquinio
— 513, The Honour of Savelli
Börn av tiden, 224
Born in Exile, 201
Borneo, 110, An Outcast of the Islands
Borodino, 381, The Great White Army
— 468, War and Peace
Boroughmonger, The, 354
Borromeo, Cardinal Federigo, 325, The Betrothed
Borrowdale, 487, Rogue Herries
Borrowed Plumes, 427
Boscobel, 5
Boscobel Tracts, 87, Wanderer and King
BOSNIAN NOVELIST: M. MRAZOVIĆ, 354
Bosphorus, 306, Sir Raoul
— See also *Constantinople*
Boss of Taroomba, The, 247
Boss System, 104, Coniston
Bossuet, J. B., 262, The Huguenot
Boston, 23, A Candle in the Wilderness
— 36, The Black Shilling
— 43, Looking Backward
— 77, The Tether
— 107, Daughters of the Revolution
— 114, Lionel Lincoln
— 121, An American Politician
— 132, Gilman of Redford
— 177, O Genteel Lady
— 192, Jason Edwards
— 212, Judge R. GRANT's novels
— 249, A Chance Acquaintance
— 249-50, W. D. HOWELLS's novels, *passim*
— 263, The Europeans
— 264, The Bostonians
— 284, A Maid of '76
— 348, Maids of Salem
— 387, The Sentimentalists
— 389, Roweny in Boston, and sequel
— 398, Lady Good-for-Nothing
— 431, The Coast of Freedom
— 448, Old Boston
— 500, Miss Brooks

Boston, 438
Bostonians, The, 264
Boswell, James, 79, Æsop Dancing
Bosworth Field, 262, The Woodman
Botany Bay, 41, Helen Adair
Bothwell, 211
Bothwell, Earl of, 211, Bothwell
— 223, Mary Hamilton
— 239, The Queen's Quair
Botor Chaperon, The, 507
Bottle Fillers, The, 360
Bottle Imp, 449
Bouchon de Cristal, Le, 293
Bouillon, Godfrey de, 131, "God Wills It"
— 236, Helyas
— 427, Count Robert of Paris
Boule de Suif, 334
Bouncer, Mr., 70, The Adventures of Mr. Verdant Green, and sequel
Bound Together, 324
Boundary Post, The, 143
Bounderby, 141, Hard Times
Bountiful Hour, The, 182
"*Bounty*" Mutiny, 41, The Mutineer
— 195, Joan of the Pilchard
— 417, Cain's Birthday
— See also *Bligh, Governor*
Bourbon-Montpensier, Princess Charlotte of, 332, A Lily of France
Bourdaloue, Louis, 80, The Preacher and the King
Bournemouth, 322, Adrian Savage
Bouvard and Pécuchet, 175
Bouvines, Battle of, 261, Philip Augustus
Bow of Orange Ribbon, The, 36
Bowen, Elizabeth, 253, The Golden Ladder
Bowen, Richard, 97, Tom Bowling
Bowery Tales, 121
Bowling, Tom, 441, Roderick Random
Box of Sweets, A, 390
Boy in Eirinn, A, 109
Boy in the Bush, The, 292
Boy in the Woods, A, 240
Boy Life, 6, The Story of a Bad Boy
— 48, David Blaize
— 74, The Fool of Quality
— 107, D. COKE's novels
— 109, A Boy in Eirinn
— 121, His New Mittens
— 124, Kit Kennedy
— 130, Jack
— 131, Perfervid
— 167, Nash and Some Others, My Little Boy
— 169, The Chronicles of the Imp
— 181, The Wanderer
— 185, The Robber Band
— 218, Little Bob
— 233, Pip

Boy Life (*contd.*): 253, Tom Brown's Schooldays
— 267, Wood Magic, Bevis
— 282, Stalkey & Co.
— 286, Jean Gilles
— 307, The Harrovians
— 313, Alec Forbes
— 316, The White Stone
— 332, Mitch Miller, Skeeters Kirby
— 377, The Story of Dick
— 439, Running Wild
— 444, Two Little Misogynists
— 455, Tim
— 460, Penrod, and sequels
— 476, Tom Sawyer and sequels, Huckleberry Finn
— 486, Jeremy
— 503, Boys at Chequasset
— 514, The Young Physician
— See also *Child Life, School Life, Street Arabs*, etc.
Boy Life on the Prairie, 192
Boy of the First Empire, A, 74
Boy Woodburn, 368
Boyar of the Terrible, A, 500
Boyhood (by NEXØ), 359
Boyhood (by TOLSTOY), 467
Boyne, Battle of the, 31, The Boyne Water
Boys at Chequasset, 503
Boys, Stories for, 43, Tales of Greyhouse
— 47, The Story of Barnaby Lee
— 53, T. BEVAN's novels
— 59-60, M. M. BLAKE's novels
— 62, J. H. BLOUNDELLE-BURTON's novels
— 78, J. BUCHAN's novels, *passim*
— 88, Face to Face with Napoleon, and sequel
— 114-15, J. F. COOPER's novels, *passim*
— 165, E. S. ELLIS's novels
— 171, G. M. FENN's novels
— 175, Jock of the Bushveld
— 199, Rev. E. GILLIAT's stories, The Spy
— 211-12, J. GRANT's novels
— 237, G. A. HENTY's novels
— 253, Tom Brown's Schooldays, and sequel
— 258, The Captain Kettle stories
— 281, Valentin, W. H. G. KINGSTON's novels
— 289, Miss A. C. LAUT's novels
— 327-8, MARRIOTT-WATSON's novels
— 331, Martin Hyde, Jim Davis
— 345, A Venture in 1777

Boys, Stories for (contd.): 402, T. B. REED's stories
— 418, E. L. SABIN's novels
— 429, Rolf in the Woods
— 449, Treasure Island, David Balfour, The Black Arrow
— 451, W. O. STODDARD's novels
— 482-3, VERNE's novels
— See also *Children, Stories for*
Boythorn, 141, Bleak House
Bracebridge Hall, 259
Bracegirdle, Mrs., 330, In the Choir of Westminster Abbey
Bracelet, The, 242
Bracelet of Garnets, The, 285
Bracketed First, 259
Bracknels, The, 403
Braddock, General E., 448, A Soldier of Virginia
Bradford, 258, Thompson's Progress
Bradlaugh, Charles, 307, Donovan, and sequel
Bræen, 267
Brahe, Tycho, 72, The Redemption of Tycho Brahe
Brahmins, 105, The Downfall of the Gods
Brake-Fern Weir, 385
Brakespeare, 292
Bramble, Matthew, 441, Humphry Clinker
Brambletye House, 440
Bramleighs of Bishop's Folly, The, 297
Brandenburg, 7, The Burgomaster of Berlin
— 321, A Gentle Knight of Old Brandenburg
Brandon, Charles, Duke of Suffolk, 321, When Knighthood was in Flower
Brandt, Molly and Joseph, 96, Cardigan, and sequel
Brangwen, Ursula, 291 Women in Love
Brantôme, Sieur de, 203, The Lucky Prisoner
Branwen, Daughter of Llyr, 217
Brass, 361
Brass Bottle, The, 12
Brassbounder, The, 64
Brave Earth, 432
Brave Men of Eyam, The, 243
Braves gèns, Les, 326
Bravo of Venice, The, 298
Braxfield, Lord, 449, Weir of Hermiston
Bray, Madeleine, 140, Nicholas Nickleby
Bray, 319, Fancy O'Brien
Brazenhead the Great, 240
Brazil, 143, Innocentia
— 209, Canaan
BRAZILIAN NOVELIST : J. da GRAÇA ARANHA

Bread, 361
Bread Line, The, 374
Bread Riots, 502, The Revolution in Tanner's Lane, The Torchbearers
Breadwinners, The, 234
Breaker of Laws, A, 407
Breaking a Butterfly, 292
Breaking of the Storm, The, 444
Breaking Point, 16
Breath of the Gods, The, 312
Breath of the North, The, 156
Brechin, 260, Flemington
Breck, Allan, 449, David Balfour
Brecknockshire, 260, The Sheep Stealers, Aythan Waring
Breda, Peace of, 315, The Dutch in the Medway
Breeze in the Moonlight, The, 224
Breitenfeld, Battle of, 159, The Mercenary
— 470, The King's Ring
Brendon, 273, The Voyage of Maildun
Brethren, 80
Brethren, The, 220
Briary-Bush, The, 137
Bricks without Straw, 470
Bricriu's Feast, 214
Bridal March, The, 56
Bridal Wreath, The, 479
Bridau Family, 28, A Bachelor's Establishment
Bride from the Bush, A, 247
Bride of Lammermoor, The, 425
Bride of Roervig, The, 51
Bride of the Mistletoe, The, 8
Bride of the Nile, The, 159
Bride of the Sun, The, 295
Bridge Builders, The, 282
Bridge of San Luis Rey, The, 505
Bridget (by CROKER), 125
Bridget (by EDWARDS), 162
Bridget Considine, 125
Brief Candles, 257
Brigadier, The, 475
Brigand, The, 262
Brigands, 1, The King of the Mountains
— 259, The Bandits
— 272, The Poor Plutocrats
— 304, On Etna
Brigands, Les, 483
BRIGHT, Mrs. Golding, see "EGERTON, George," 162
Bright, John, 472, Phineas Finn, and sequel
Bright Metal, 453
Bright Shawl, The, 238
Brigitta, 19
Brimming Cup, The, 88
Brinton Eliot, 169
Bristol, 217, The King's Cause
— 313, Cornet Strong

Bristol (contd.) : 329, In Colston's Days, Bristol Diamonds
— 329, Under the Mendips
— 498, Chippinge
Bristol Diamonds, 329
Britain, Ancient, 22, Cian of the Chariots
— See also *Arthurian Legend, Christians, Early*, etc.
Britanny, 27, Beatrix
— 29, The Chouans
— 32, Bewitched, A Story without a Name
— 97, The Maids of Paradise
— 106, In Time of War
— 154, The Regent's Daughter
— 174, Tents of a Night
— 182, The Seven Nights
— 249, Gwenn
— 277, The Sea
— 298, The Wild Body
— 304, My Brother Yves
— 380, The White Month
— 418, Scaramouche
— 431, Green Fire
— 492 Pastorals of France
— See also *Vendée, La*
Broad Highway, The, 169
Brock, Sir Isaac, 88, A Beautiful Rebel
Broglie, Duc de, 275, The King's Indiscretion
Broke of Covenden, 442
Broken at the Fountain, 406
Broken Barriers, 359
Broken Honeymoon, The, 395
Broken Pitcher, The, 520
Broken Pitchers, 275
Broken Road, The, 331
Broken Shackles, 373
Broken Sword, The, 196
Broken to Harness, 512
Brontë Family, 437, The Three Sisters
— 508, Greenlow
— 514, Moor Fires
Brontë, Branwell, 73, The Tenant of Wildfell Hall
Bronze Eagle, The, 370
Brood of Ducklings, A, 458
Brook Kerith, The, 349
Brooksmith, 264
Broom Squire, The, 209
Brother and Sister, 186
Brother Copas, 398
Brother Gabriel, 162
Brother of Girls, A, 216
Brother Saul, 84
Brother to St. James, A, 41
Brotherhood of Consolation, 29, The Seamy Side of History
Brothers, 479
Brothers All, 311
Brothers Karamazov, The, 148
Brothers Rantzau, The, 166
Brougham, Lord, 400, A Lady of the Regency
— 490, Ten Thousand a Year
— 498, Chippinge

Broughton House, The, 382
Brown, Captain, 194, Cranford
Brown, Warder, 401, It's Never too Late to Mend
Brown, Captain John, 77, Diane
— 452, Marching On
Brown Man's Secret, The, 260
Brown Mask, The, 71
BROWNE, C. F., see "WARD, A.," 487
Browne, Sir Thomas, 259, None So Pretty
— 329, In the East Country
BROWNE, Thomas Alexander, see "BOLDREWOOD, Rolf"
Browne, William (poet), 480, The Lady Mary of Tavistock
Brownies, The, 168
Browning, Oscar, 47, The Babe B.A.
Browning, Robert, 369, Miss Barrett's Elopement
Browning Courtship, A, 501
Brownlow, Mr., 140, Oliver Twist
Bruce, Robert, 4, The Days of Bruce
— 389, The Scottish Chiefs
— 427, Castle Dangerous
Brude-Slaatten, 56
Bruden fra Rorvig, 51
Bruder und Schwester, 186
Bruder vom deutschen Hause, Die, 188
Brueghel, Pieter, 466, Droll Peter
Brueton's Bayou, 219
Bruges, 112, The Lion of Flanders
— 513, Grisly Grisell
Brugglesmith, 281
Brummell, Beau, 25, Judy Bovenden
— 38, The Gallants
— 150, Rodney Stone
— 184, Yeoman Fleetwood
Brunanburgh, Battle of, 108, Thorstein of the Mere
Brunel's Tower, 386
Brunhilde, 5
Brushwood Boy, The, 282
Brussels, 73, Villette, The Professor
— 159, Barbara Blomberg
Brust, Ben, 344, Gideon Giles
Brute, The, 111
Brutien, 405
Bryan, William Jennings, 143, The Leader
Brynhild, 484, Völsunga Saga
Bubbles of the Foam, 25
Buchan, Earl of, see *Stewart, Alexander*
Buchholz Family, The, 450
Buckingham, George Villiers, 1st Duke of, 70, In High Places
— 81, The Duke's Servants

Buckingham, George Villiers, 1st Duke of (contd.): 154, The Three Musketeers
— 426, Fortunes of Nigel
Buckingham, George Villiers, 2nd Duke of, 412, Whitefriars
— 426, Peveril of the Peak
Buckley Lady, The, 505
Budapest, 272, Black Diamonds
Buddenbrooks, 324
Buddha and Buddhism, 34, Barlaam and Josaphat
— 121, Mr. Isaacs
— 202, The Pilgrim Kamanita
Bude, 314, The Seaboard Parish
Budge and Toddie, 219
Buffer, The, 405
Bug-Jargal, 253
Builders, The, 176
Builders, The, 202
Builders of New Rome, 330
BULGARIAN
                    NOVELIST :
        I. VAZOV
Bull-Dog Drummond, 320
Bull-Fight, The, 435
Bull-Fighting, 61, Blood and Sand
— 228, Montes the Matador
— 236, Fiesta
Bull Run, 353, Forever Free
Buller-Peddington Compact, The, 451
BULLOCK, Shan F., see *sub nom.* LAWLESS, Emily, 289
Bulstrode, Mr., 164, Middlemarch
Bumble, Mr., 140, Oliver Twist
Bumppo, Natty, 114, The Leather-Stocking Tales
Bunch Grass, 480
Bundle of Life, A, 119
Bungay, 23, The famous historie of Fryer Bacon
Bunker Hill, 114, Lionel Lincoln
— 338, Israel Potter
— 447, The Road to Paris
— 448, Old Boston
Bunker 17, 72
Bunner Sisters, 499
Bunyan, John, 98, The Draytons and the Davenants, and sequel
Bunyip Land, 171
Buondelmonte's Saga, 239
Burbage, William, 442, The Great Age
— 446, A Gentleman Player
BURCHETT, G., see PUGH, E. W., 395
Burden, The (by FORBES-MOSSE), 178
Burden, The (by Mrs. Dawson SCOTT), 424
Burdett, Sir Francis, 239, The Stooping Lady
Bureau d'echange de maux, 157

Bureaucracy, 28, Buréaucracy
— 117, The Burocrats
— 311, What Not
Bureaucracy (by Balzac), 28
Bureaucrats, The, 117
Bürger, Der, 185
Burgher Quixote, A, 57
Burglars, 248, The Amateur Cracksman
— See also *Thieves*
Burglars in Paradise, 384
Burgomaster of Berlin, The, 7
Burgomaster's Wife, The, 158
Burgoyne's Invasion, 8, The Sun of Saratoga
— 97, The Little Red Foot
Burgstein, 25, The Cardinal's Page
Burgundy, 93, The Trusty Eckart
— 99, The Châtelaine of Vergi
— 261, Mary of Burgundy
— 433, The Countess Eve
Burial of the Guns, The, 373
Buried Alive, 45
Buried Alive (The House of the Dead), 146
Burke, Edmund, 63, In the Days of Goldsmith
— 348, The Jessamy Bride
Burleigh, Lord, 24, The Master of Gray
— 426, Kenilworth
— 273, In Burleigh's Days, and sequel
Burlesque Fiction, see *Parody*
Burma, 222, Thibaw's Queen, Palace Tales
— 268, The Lacquer Lady
— 353, Splendour of God
Burnbrae, 318, " Ian MACLAREN'S " novels
Burney, Fanny, 38, " The Ladies ! "
— 348, Fanny's First Novel
Burning Daylight, 303
Burning-Glass, The, 69
Burning of Rome, The, 103
Burns, Robert, 288, Nancy Stair
— 311, The Rhymer
— 356, Ayrshire Idylls
— 448, The Immortal Lover
Burr, Aaron, 17, The Conqueror
— 44, A Volunteer with Pike
— 74, A Son of the Revolution
— 84, Zachary Phips
— 248, The Magnificent Adventure
— 253, The Golden Ladder
— 270, Lewis Rand
— 387, Blennerhassett
— 452, The Minister's Wooing
Bursley, 45, A. BENNETT'S novels
BÜRSTENBINDER, Elsie, see " WERNER, E.," 496

Burtkomme faderen, Den, 191
Busca, La, 35
Buscón, La Vida del, 396
Bush Girl's Romance, A., 360
Bush Whacking, 105
Bushmen, 77, Tales of South Africa, From Veldt Camp Fires
Bushrangers, 1, Castle Vane
— 64, Robbery under Arms, The Squatter's Dream
— 169, Grif
— 280, Geoffrey Hamlyn
— 360, Hume NISBET'S stories
— 390, Outlaw and Lawmaker
—See also *Bandits*
Business, 43, H. BELLOC'S novels, *passim*
— 61, — and Co.
— 149, The Firm of Girdlestone
— 187, Debit and Credit
— 222, The General Manager's Story
— 238, Tampico
— 250, The Rise of Silas Lapham
— 293, Rain before Seven
— 298, Babbitt, The Man who knew Coolidge
— 299, The Barque Future
— 304, Letters from a Self-Made Merchant
— 308, F. LYNDE'S novels
— 324, Buddenbrooks
— 378, The Money Captain, Mr. Salt
— 379, The Darlingtons
— 392, Angel Pavement
— 402, Foul Play
— 438, Oil !, Boston, Mountain City
— 453, Fombombo, Strange Moon
— 471, When Greek meets Greek
— 492, The Banker and the Bear, Roger Drake
— 495, The Autocracy of Mr. Parham
— 518, The Monomaniac
— See also *Banks, Financial Life, Labour, Shopkeepers, Strikes,* etc.
Bustling Hours, The, 408
But Not For Love, 430
But Soft—We are Observed !, 44
But Yet a Woman, 225
Bute, Earl of, 271, Chrysal
Bute, Marquess of, 144, Lothair
Butler, Walter, 96, Cardigan, and sequel
— 423, The Son of a Tory
Buxton, 33, Forbidden to Wed
By Allan Water, 447
By Beach and Bogland, 35
By Berwen Banks, 399
By Blow and Kiss, 85
By Dulvercombe Water, 480
By Faith Alone, 40

By Lone Craig-Linnie Burn, 315
By Neva's Waters, 93
By Order of the Company, see To Have and to Hold, 270
By Order of the Czar, 231
By Order of the King, 254
By Proxy, 378
By Reef and Palm, 41
By Right of Purchase, 54
By Roaring Loom, 332
By Stroke of Sword, 26
By the Blue River, 105
By the Eternal, 401
By the Light of the Soul, 506
By the Morning Boat, 269
By the North Sea, 330
By the Open Sea, 454
By the Rise of the River, 104
By the Well, 275
By Weeping Cross, 407
By what Authority ? 49
Bye Plot, 262, Arabella Stuart
Byelinsky, 474, Rudin
Byng, Admiral, 271, Chrysal
Byron, Lord, 38, Glorious Apollo
— 143, Venetia
— 161, Lord Byron
— 230, Beyond Man's Strength
— 240, Bendish
— 379, Nightmare Abbey
— 488, The Marriage of William Ashe
Byronism, 99, René
— 122, Pietro Ghisleri
— 143, Contarini Fleming
— 177, The Woman
— 309, Ernest Maltravers
— 357, Confessions of a Child of the Century
Bystander, 207
Bythinia, 103, To the Lions
Byzantium, 170, Gathering Clouds
— 220, The Wanderer's Necklace
— 229, Theophano
— 352, King Constans
— 382, Sancta Paula
— See also *Constantinople, Eastern Empire*

C., 33
Cabala, The, 504
Cabaret de la Belle Femme, Le, 145
Cabaret up the Line, The, 145
Cabbages and Kings, 389
Cabinet des antiques, Le, 27
Cabot's Voyage, 491, The Strength of Lovers
Cade, Jack, 240, Brazenhead the Great
Cadignan, Princesse de, 28, A Princess's Secrets
Cadillac, Sieur de, 126, A Daughter of New France
— 142, The Siege of Lady Resolute

Cadiz Expedition, 74, My Lord of Essex
— 510, The Spanish Lady
Cadoudal, Georges, 155, The Companions of Jehu
— 295, The House of the Combrays
— 365, The Eagle's Talon
Cælebs, 514
Cæsar, Julius, 38, The Laughing Queen
— 122, With the Immortals
— 131, A Friend of Cæsar
— 345, The Conquered
— 346, When the Bough Breaks
Cæsar Borgia, 412
Cæsar or Nothing, 35
Caesarini, Don Gaetano, 413, Tolla
Caged Lion, The, 513
Cagliostro, Count, 155, Memoirs of a Physician, The Queen's Necklace
Cagots, 348, The Ark of the Curse
Caillou et Tili, 344
Cain's Birthday, 417
Cairo, 241, An Imaginative Man
Cakes and Ale, 334
Calabria, 122, The Children of the King
Calais, 155, The Two Dianas
— See also *Hundred Years' War*
Calcutta, 116, The Path of a Star
— 461, Ralph Darnell
— See also *Black Hole of Calcutta*
Caleb West, 440
Caleb Williams, 203
Calf Love, 39
Calhoun, J. C., 143, The Patience of John Morland
— 248, Fifty-Four Forty, or Fight
Caliban, 196
Caliban's Guide to Letters, 43
California, 17, Los Cerritos ; The Doomswoman ; Patience Sparhawk and her Times ; The Californians, The Valiant Runaways, The Splendid Idle Forties, Rezánov, Ancestors
— 21, Isidro
— 50, The Poor Man
— 58, Erema
— 93, Captain Courtesy
— 177, The Led Horse Claim
— 229, The Luck of Roaring Camp
— 260, Ramona
— 353, A Man, His Mark
— 361, McTeague, Blix, The Octopus, Shanghaied
— 449, The Silverado Squatters
— 479–80, VACHELL'S novels, *passim*

California (*contd.*): 501, Gold, and sequels
Californians, The, 17
Calisto and Melibea, 414
Call Mr. Fortune, 24
Call of the Blood, The, 242
Call of the Deep, The, 79
Call of the Wild, The, 302
Called Back, 112
Callista, 359
Calumet " K," 343
Calvert, Governor, 22, The Tower of Wye
— 47, The Story of Barnaby Lee
Calvinism, 33, Argenis
— 136, John Ward
— 231, Klytia
— 232, The Scarlet Letter
— 313–14, G. MacDONALD'S novels
— 314, Robert Falconer
— 439, The Heresy of Mehetabel Clark
— 502, Mark Rutherford's Deliverance
Camargue, 129, Letters from My Mill
Cambia Carty, 79
Cambodia, 105, The Downfall of the Gods
Cambric Mask, The, 96
Cambridge University, 47, Beside Still Waters, etc.
— 47, The Babe B.A.
— 48, David of King's
— 233, The Right Stuff
— 439, Frank Fairleigh
— See also *University Life*
Cambridge University (*Mass.*), 175, Diary of a Freshman
Cambridgeshire, 208, Cheap-Jack Zita
Cambyses, 158, An Egyptian Princess
Cameron, Archibald, 74, The Flight of the Heron, and sequels
— 457, Adam Hepburn's Vow
Camilla (by BURNEY), 83
Camilla (By ROBINS), 412
Camisards, 142, The Siege of Lady Resolute
— See also *Cavalier, Jean*
Camorra, 39, Arden Massiter
— 211, Stories of Naples
Camp and Fireside Stories, 5
Camp of Refuge, The, 314
Campaign, 336
Campaign of Ninian Jamieson, The, 131
Campion, Robert, 49, Come Rack ! Come Rope !
Can Such Things Be ?, 54
Can You Forgive Her ?, 472
Canaan, 209
Canada, 26, Snowflakes and Sunbeams
— 36, In the Midst of Alarms
— 54, H. BINDLOSS's novels
— 54, A Hazard of the Snows
— 90, Love Like a Gipsy

Canada (*contd.*): 95, Mrs. CATHERWOOD's novels, *passim*
— 97, The Drums of Aulone
— 117, The Imperialist, Cousin Cinderella
— 232, The Path of Glory
— 249, Their Wedding Journey
— 296, Arthur O'Leary
— 319, The Span o' Life
— 343, The Road to Frontenac
— 439, Montlivet
— See also *American War of 1812, Canada, North-West, Detroit, Frontenac, Hudson Bay, Labrador, Newfoundland, Nova Scotia, Riel, Rockies, Selkirks, Vancouver, Yukon*, etc.
Canada, North-West, 126, R. CULLUM's novels
— 214, Wolf Breed
— 354, The White Darkness
— 501–2, S. E. WHITE's novels
Canadian Brothers, The, 406
CANADIAN NOVELISTS : P. ACLAND ; " Grant ALLEN " ; R. BARR ; " E. BARRINGTON " ; W. CAMPBELL ; " Ralph CONNOR," Mrs. E. COTES, J. O. CURWOOD, F. P. DAY, Mazo DE LA ROCHE, Lily DOUGALL, N. DUNCAN, B. Mabel DUNHAM, V. FETHERSTONHAUGH, T. C. HALIBURTON, W. KIRBY, A. C. LAUT, S. B. LEACOCK, R. and K. M. LIZARS, J. MACKIE, Sir G. PARKER, C. PHILLIPPS - WOLLEY, Major J. RICHARDSON, C. D. G. ROBERTS, Laura SALVERSON, R. W. SERVICE, E. T. SETON, R. G. TABER
Canary Islands, 14, W. M. ARDAGH's novels
Candidate, The, 9
Candidate for Truth, A, 50
Candide, 484
Candle, A, 468
Candle in the Wilderness, A, 23
Candles in the Wind, 144
Cane, 470
Cannes, 67, A Tragic Idyll
Cannibalism, 229, Gabriel Conroy
Canning, George, 45, Vivian Grey
— 378, Melincourt
— 489, De Vere
Cannon, Parson, 245, Maxwell
Canon's Ward, The, 378
Cantabrian Alps, 35, The Lord of Labraz
Cantal, 158, Jean and Louise

Canterbury, 94, Pamela Pounce
— 377, Emerald Athwart
Canterville Ghost, The, 504
Canute, King, 120, Alfgar the Dane
— 299, The Ward of King Canute
Caoba, 165
Cape Cod Folks, 213
Cape Cod Week, A, 474
Cape Town, 77, An Exiled Scot
— 300, Among Privileged People
Capel, Mgr., 144, Lothair
Capel Sion, 167
Capello, Bianca, 348, The Cardinal's Pawn
Capitaine Burle, Le, 519
Capitaine de quinze ans, Un, 482
Capitaine Satan, Le, 189
Capital and Labour, see *Capitalism, Industrialism, Labour, Poor, Socialism, Strikes*, etc.
Capital Punishment, 11, The Seven who were Hanged
— 120, A Life for a Life
— 253, Under Sentence of Death, Claude Gueux
— 289, Would You Kill Him ?
— 474, The Jew
Capitalism, 1, Face to Face
— 43–4, BELLOC's novels
— 361, F. NORRIS's novels
— 438, Captain of Industry, A
— 519, Work
Cap'n Nat's Treasure, 295
Capri, 148, South Wind
— 168, Vain Love
Caprice, 174
Capsina, The, 48
Captain, The, 506
Captain Blood, 418
Captain Bluitt, 3
Captain Courtesy, 93
Captain Desmond, V.C., 144
Captain Dieppe, 247
Captain Digby Grand, 337
Captain Fortune, 328
Captain Fracasse, 195
Captain John Lister, 223
Captain June, 405
Captain Kettle, Adventures, and Further Adventures of, 258
Captain Kettle, K.C.B., 258
Captain Latymer, 348
Captain Macedoine's Daughter, 315
Captain Manzana, 56
Captain Margaret, 330
Captain of Industry, A, 438
Captain of the Gray-Horse Troop, The, 192
Captain of the Guard, The, 212
Captain of the Janizaries, The, 306
Captain of the Locusts, The, 496

Captain Pettifer and the U-Boats, 195
Captain Ravenshaw, 447
Captain Ribnikov, 285
Captain Satan, 189
Capt. Singleton, Life of, 134
Captain Stormfield's Visit to Heaven, 477
Captain Wyvern's Adventure, 397
Captain Zillner, 285
Captains All, 261
Captain's Book, The, 162
Captains Courageous, 282
Captain's Daughter, The, 395
Captain's Doll, The, 291
Captain's Youngest, The, 82
Captive, The (by KIPLING), 282
Captive, The (by PROUST), 394
Captive of Love, A, 281
Captive of the Roman Eagles, A, 128
Captive of the Smugglers, The, 331
Captives, The, 487
Car of Destiny, The, 507
Caracalla, Emperor, 159, Per Aspera
Caraccioli, Admiral, 156, The Neapolitan Lovers
Carancro, 86
Caravan, 190
Caravanners, The, 15
Card, The, 46
Cardigan, 96
Cardillac, 37
Cardinal and his Conscience, A, 247
Cardinal Pole, 5
Cardinal S n, A, 112
Cardinal's Page, The, 25
Cardinal's Past, The, 275
Cardinal's Pawn, The, 348
Cardinal's Snuff Box, The, 227
Career of Candida, 377
Caretaker, The, 65
Carew, 315, Grace O'Malley
Carew, Bampfylde Moore, 512, The Gipsy King
Caribbean Sea, 170, Thomas the Lambkin
Carinus, Emperor, 272, A Christian but a Roman
Carisbrooke Castle, 81, The Prisoners of Carisbrooke
— 277, The Cavaliers
— 330, The White King's Daughter
Carissima, The, 321
Carl and Anna, 185
Carleton, Captain George, 134, Memoirs of an English Officer
Carlingford, 366-7, Mrs. OLIPHANT's novels
Carlino, 416
Carlisle, 180, The Little Maister
— 331, Lawrence Clavering
Carlists, 111, The Arrow of Gold

Carlists (contd.): 342, In Kedar's Tents, The Velvet Glove
— 374, The Marquis of Penalta
Carlovingian Wars, 352, Amis and Amile
— See also *Charlemagne*
Carlowitz, 105, The Duke's Page
Carlyle, Thomas, 141, Hard Times, A Tale of Two Cities
— 279, Alton Locke
— 322, The New Republic
— 340, Beauchamp's Career
Carmarthenshire, 348, The Gate-Openers
Carmen, 341
Carmilla, 294
Carnegie, Andrew, 23, Cricket Heron
— 146, The 42nd Parallel
Carnival, 317
Carnival of Florence, The, 68
Carolina, North, 69, Drums, Marching On
— 82, Louisiana
— 511, Rodman the Keeper
Carolina, South, 134, Kate Beaumont
— 277, Horseshoe Robinson
— 278, Joscelyn Cheshire
— 418, The Carolinian
— 436, The Kassique of Kiawah
— 511, Rodman the Keeper
Caroline, 1
Caroline of Anspach (wife of George II), 425, The Heart of Midlothian
Caroline of Brunswick (wife of George IV), 109, The Queen can do no Wrong
— 191, The Ayrshire Legatees
— 400, A Lady of the Regency
Carolinian, The, 418
Carpathia Knox, 514
" *Carpet-Baggers* ", see *Reconstruction*
Carr, 50
Carriage Lamps, The, 121
Carrickfergus, 295, A Tory in Arms
" *Carrots* ", 346
Cartagena Expedition, 441, Roderick Random
Carthage, 18, Dido Queen of Hearts
— 103, Lords of the World
— 175, Salammbô
— 359, Callista
Carton, Sydney, 141, A Tale of Two Cities
Cartwright, Peter, 33, Round Anvil Rock
Carved Lions, The, 346
Casa Braccio, 122
Casa Calvo, Marquess, 93, The Code of Victor Jallot
Casa de Aizgorri, La, 35
Casaubon, Mr., 164, Middlemarch

Case-Book of Sherlock Holmes, 150
Case for the Watch, The, 43
Case of Conscience, A, 34
Case of George Dedlow, The, 345
Case of Richard Meynell, The, 488
Case of Sergeant Grischa, The, 520
Cashel Byron's Profession, 431
Cask, The, 124
" CASKODEN, Edwin " see MAJOR, C.
Casper Hauser, 490
Cast-Iron Duke, 316
Castaways, The, 261
Castelnau, 262
Castile, 303, La Picara
Casting Away of Mrs. Lecks and Mrs. Aleshine, 450
Casting of Nets, 24
CASTLE, Egerton, see also CASTLE, Agnes
Castle, The, 274
Castle Daly, 276
Castle Dangerous, 427
Castle Gay, 78
Castle in Spain, A, 90
Castle Inn, The, 497
Castle Meadow, 330
Castle Nowhere, 511
Castle of Dreams, A, 459
Castle of Ehrenstein, The, 263
Castle of Otranto, The, 486
Castle of Pictordu, The, 421
Castle of the Carpathians, The, 483
Castle Omeragh, 348
Castle Rackrent, 160
Castle to Let, A, 404
Castle Vane, 1
Castle Warlock, 314
Castlemaine, Lady, 68, Yesterdays
— 70, London Pride
— 71, Patches and Pomander
— 348, Nell Gwyn
Castlereagh, Viscount, 63, The Rebels
— 84, The Power of the Dog
— 400, A Lady of the Regency
Castles of Athlin and Dunbayne, The, 399
Castlewood, Lady, 462, Henry Esmond
— 463, The Virginians
Castries, Duchesse de, 28, The Duchess of Langeais
Castro, General, 93, Captain Courtesy
Castro, Inez de, 406, Broken at the Fountain
Casuals of the Sea, 315
Cat and the Cherub, The, 171
Catalans, 261, De l'Orme
Catfish, The, 327
Cathédrale, La, 61

Cathedral, The (by HUYSMANS), 257
Cathedral, The (by WALPOLE), 487
Cathedral Courtship, A, 504
Cathedral Folk, 307
Cathedral Life, 253, Notre-Dame de Paris
— 257, The Cathedral
— 307, Cathedral Folk
— 345, Our Father San Daniel
— 471-2, The Barsetshire novels
— 487, The Cathedral
— 509, The Channings, and sequel
— 518, The Dream
Cathedral Singer, A, 8
Catherine (by PEARD), 380
Catherine (by SANDEAU), 421
Catherine (by THACKERAY), 463
Catherine Furze, 502
Catherine of Calais, 137
Catherine of Siena, Saint, 91, The Love Story of St. Bel
— 427, The Disciple of a Saint
Catherine II of Russia, 152, Shoes of Gold
Catherine Sterling, 304
Catherine's Friends, 137
Cathie, 73, Wuthering Heights
Catholic League, 62, The King's Mignon
— 262, One in a Thousand, Henry of Guise, The Man-at-Arms, Rose d'Albret
— See also *Guises*
Cato Street Conspiracy, 498, Starvecrow Farm
Catriona, 449
Cat's Cradle, 33
Cat's Mill, The, 330
Catterick, Mrs., 108, The Woman in White
Cattle Brands, 2
Cattle-Dealers, The, 100
Cattle Farming, see *Cattle Ranch, Cowboys, Pioneers*, etc.
Cattle Raid of Cualagne, The, 169
Cattle Ranch, 64, BOLDREWOOD's novels
— 316, H. C. MACILWAINE's novels
Caucasus, 467-9, TOLSTOY's novels, *passim*
Cause of the Crime, The, 185
Cauterets, 326, The Heptameron
Cavalier, Jean, 62, The Scourge of God
— See also *Camisards*
Cavalier, The, 86
Cavalier of Tennessee, The, 360
Cavaliers, The, 277
Cavalleria Rusticana, 481
Cavalry Life, 508

Cavan, 80, Irish Pastorals
Cavanagh, Forest Ranger, 192
Cavanagh of Kultann, 457
Cave, Mary, 337, Holmby House
Caves du Vatican, Les, 198
Cavour, Count di, 24, The Pillar of Fire
— 230, Beyond Man's Strength
Caxton, Pisistratus, 309, The Caxtons, My Novel, What will he do with It
Caxton, William (tr.), 60, Blanchardyn and Eglantine
— 98, Charles the Grete
— 181, The Four Sons of Aymon
— 289, La Tour-Landry
— 294, Recuyell of the Historyes of Troy
— 404, Reynard the Fox
Caxtons, The, 309
Cease Firing, 270
Cecil, Sir Robert, 74, My Lord of Essex
— 273, The Second Cecil
Cecil, Sir William, 24, The Lonely Queen
Cecil Dreeme, 508
Cécile, 306
Cecilia (by BURNEY), 83
Cecilia (by CRAWFORD), 123
Cecilia de Noël, 232
Celebrated Jumping Frog, The, 476
Celebrity, The, 103
Celebrity at Home, The, 255
Celeste, 252
Celestial Grocery, The, 373
Celestial Omnibus, The, 180
Celestial Railroad, The, 232
Celestina (by Mrs. C. SMITH), 440
Celestina, 414
Celestines, 21, San Celestino
Celibacy, see *Sex*
Célibataires, Les, I, 27; II, 28
Cellamare Conspiracy, 153, The Chevalier d'Harmental, 154, The Regent's Daughter
Cellini, Benvenuto, 154, Ascanio
Celt and Saxon, 340
Celtic, 31, The Nowlans
— 173, Children of Earth
— 278, The Banks of the Boro
— 289, Grania
— 355, The Lost Pibroch
— 431, William SHARP's stories
— 446, Deidre, In the Land of Youth
— 513, W. B. YEATS's stories
— See also *Celtic Fiction*
Celtic doctrine of Re-birth, 343
Celtic Fiction, 214, Lady GREGORY's work (tr.)
— 236, The Feast of Bricriu

Celtic Fiction (contd.): 257, D. HYDE's work
— 273, Old Celtic Romances
— 293, A. H. LEAHY's work
— 343, Kuno MEYER's work
— 364, Silva Gadelica
— 364, The Coming of Cuchulain, and sequels
— 415, The High Deeds of Finn
— 451, The Destruction of Da Derga's Hostel
— See also *Ossianic cycle* and *Welsh Romances*
Celtic Twilight, The, 513
Cement, 202
Cénere, 137
Cent nouvelles nouvelles, 288
— See also 326, The Heptameron
Centaur, The, 59
Cercueil de cristal, Le, 416
Cerise, 337
Cerritos, Los, 17
Certain Hour, The, 85
Certain People, 500
Ces bons Normands, 218
César ó Nada, 35
Cetewayo, 219, Black Heart and White Heart
— 220, Finished
— 346, The Word of the Sorceress
Cevennes, 62, The Scourge of God
— 98, Roux the Bandit
— 142, The Siege of Lady Resolute
Ceylon, 306, Down the Sky
— 381, A Love Offensive
— 510, The Village in the Jungle
Cézanne, 518, His Masterpiece
Chabert, Colonel, 27, Colonel Chabert
Chad, 265, The Ambassadors
Chainbearers, The, 115
Chains, 360
Chair on the Boulevard, A, 342
Chaldæa, 35, The Slave of Lagash
Chaldean Magician, The, 160
Chalfont St. Giles, 324, Deborah's Diary
Challenge of Barletta, The, 22
Challenge to Sirius, The, 275
Challis, 138, It Never Can Happen Again
Challoners, The, 48
Chambéry, 65, The Will to Live
Champagne, 29, The Member for Arcis
Champion of Virtue, The, 402
Chance, 111
Chance Acquaintance, A, 249

Chancellorsville, Battle of, 120, The Red Badge of Courage
Chances of War, 174
Chand Bebee, Queen of the Deccan, 461, A Noble Queen
Chandos, Sir John, 149, The White Company
— 155, Agénor de Mauléon
Chandos, 371
Chandra Shekhar, 32
Change in the Cabinet, A, 43
Change of Air, A, 246
Change of Face, A, 106
Change of Personality, 466, John Chilcote, M.P.
— See also *Dual Personality*
Change of Treatment, A, 260
Changed Man, A, 226
Changelings, 74, The Engrafted Rose
Changing Winds, 166
Channel Islands, 254, Toilers of the Sea
Channings, The, 509
Chanson de Clarisse et Florent, La, 255
Chanson d'Esclaramonde, La, 255
Chanson d'Ide et d'Olive, La, 255
Chantemerle, 74
Chapel, The, 8
Chapelizod, 294, The House by the Churchyard
Chapenga's White Man, 496
Chaplain of the Fleet, The, 53
Chaplet of Pearls, The, 513
Chapter in the History of a Tyrone Family, 294
Chapter the Last, 224
Character and Comedy, 305
Character Writers, 3, The Spectator
Characteristics, 345
Charicles, 41
Chariot Wheels, 465
Chariots of the Lord, The, 243
Charity, 210
Charity Chance, 400
Charlemagne, 44, For the White Christ
— 98, Charles the Grete
— 181, The Four Sons of Aymon
— 184, Jacques Tournebroche
— 188, Our Forefathers
— 225, Passe Rose
— 255, Huon of Burdeux
— 375, Paris and Vienne
— 480, Valentyne and Orson
Charles V, Emperor, 22, The Maid of Florence
— 105, The Duke's Page
— 131, A Friar of Wittenberg
— 155, The Page of the Duke of Savoy
— 159, Barbara Blomberg

Charles VI, 262, Agincourt
— 483, La Reine Ysabeau
Charles I (of England), 81, The Prisoners of Carisbrooke
— 154, Twenty Years After
— 243, Follow the Gleam
— 277, The Cavaliers
— 313, Miriam Cromwell
— 330, The White King's Daughter
— 337, Holmby House
— 399, Diary of Lady W.
— 412, Whitehall
— 413, King by the Grace of God
Charles II, 4, Ovingdean Grange
— 5, Boscobel
— 10, Kelston of Kells
— 39, The Knight of the Golden Sword
— 50, Oddsfish
— 62, The King's Guerdon
— 68, Defender of the Faith
— 71, Patches and Pomander
— 81, Daniel Herrick
— 87, Wanderer and King
— 94, My Merry Rockhurst
— 133, Lantern Lane
— 211, Harry Ogilvie
— 246, Simon Dale
— 247, The Lady of Lyte
— 247, My Lord Winchenden
— 313, Yesterday's Tomorrow
— 328, The Rebel
— 412, Whitefriars
— 426, Woodstock
— 426, Peveril of the Peak
— 442, Patricia at the Inn
Charles V of France, 233, Suzanna
Charles VII, 208, Noémi
— See also *Joan of Arc*
Charles VIII, 25, Knight-at-Arms
— 341, The Forerunner
Charles IX, 154, Marguerite de Valois
— 341, Chronicle of the reign of Charles IX
— 448, Love in Armour
Charles X of Sweden, 470, Times of Battle and of Rest
Charles XI, 470, Times of Battle and of Rest
Charles XII of Sweden, 69, Kings-at-Arms
— 91, Monsieur Martin, and sequel
— 235, A King and his Campaigners, The Charles Men
— 470, The Times of Charles XII
— 512, A Prince of Intrigue
Charles Albert (of Savoy), 230, Beyond Man's Strength

Charles Edward Stuart (Young Pretender), 22, A Prince in Petto
— 69, Mr. Misfortunate
— 74, The Flight of the Heron, and sequel
— 78, The Company of the Marjolaine
— 91, Jemmy Abercraw
— 128, Oil of Spikenard
— 153, Scotland's Heir, and sequel
— 180, The Little Maister
— 243, High Treason
— 297, Gerald Fitzgerald
— 356, The Shoes of Fortune
— 366, Katie Stewart
— 424, Waverley
— 426, Redgauntlet
— 478, The Macdonald Lass
Charles the Bold, Duke of Burgundy, 275, The Duke's Vengeance
— 261, Mary of Burgundy
— 401, The Cloister and the Hearth
— 426, Quentin Durward
— 427, Anne of Geierstein
— 513, Grisly Grisell
Charles and Charlemagne, 438
Charles Auchester, 432
Charles Men, The, 235
Charles O'Malley, 296
Charles the Grete, 98
Charleston, 113, Return
— 161, Debenham's Vow
— 241, Porgy; Mamba's Daughters
— 436, The Partizan, and sequels
Charlotte, Princess, of Brunswick, 142, She That Hesitates
Charlotte, Queen, 94, Pamela Pounce
— 400, A Lady of the Regency
Charlotte Löwensköld, 287
Charlus, Baron de, 393, Remembrance of Things Past
Charm, The, 382
Charming of Estercel, The, 404
Charnock, 262, The King's Highway
Charny, Comte et Comtesse de, 155, La Comtesse de Charny
— 419, Picciola
Chartists, 143, Sybil
— 144, Endymion
— 279, Alton Locke
— 312, The Waterdale Neighbours
— 344, Gideon Giles
— See also *Reform Bill*
Chartres, 257, The Cathedral
— 377, Gaston de Latour
Chartreuse of Parma, The, 53
Charwoman's Daughter, The, 446

Charwoman's Shadow, The, 157
Chase, Jack, 338, White Jacket
Chase of Saint Castin, The, 95
Chasse aux amants, La, 52
Chassé Croisé, 516
Chasse Royale, La, 1
Chaste Diana, The, 38
Chaste Wife, The, 458
Chastelard, 239, The Queen's Quair
Chat maigre, Le, 182
Château de Pictordu, Le, 421
Château des Carpathes, Le, 483
Châtelaine of La Trinité, The, 188
Chatham, Earl of, 271, Chrysal
CHATRIAN, Alexandre, see *sub nom.* ERCKMANN, Émile, 165
Chaucer, Geoffrey, 122, Long Will
— 323, The Golden Quill
Chauvelin, Marquis de, 156, M. de Chauvelin's Will
Cheadle & Son, 197
Cheap-Jack Zita, 208
Cheats, The, 69
Chèbe, Sidonie, 129, Fromont Junior and Risler Senior
Cheeryble, the Brothers, 140, Nicholas Nickleby
Chef, Le, 210
Chef d'œuvre inconnu Le, 30
Cheggs, 140, Old Curiosity Shop
Chelkash, 206
Chelsea, 75, Mrs. Bligh
— 107, Minstrel Dick
— 182, The Bountiful Hour
— 247, My Lord Winchenden
— 325, The Old Chelsea Bun-House
Cheltenham, 94, Pamela Pounce
Chemises rouges, Les, 194
Chemist in the Suburbs, A, 492
Chénier, André, 432, The Queen's Fillet
Chéri, 108
Cherokees, 118, The Story of Old Fort Loudon
— 119, The Amulet
Cherry and Violet, 325
Cherry Blossom of a Spring Moor, 234
Cherry Gambol, 387
Cherry Riband, The, 124
Cherubina, 37, The Heroine
Cherwell, Earl of, 328, The Rebel
Chesapeake, 22, Kent Fort Manor
" *Chesapeake*," 390, Smith Brunt
Cheshire, 161, Lord Brackenbury
Chesnut Champion, A, 208

Chest of Cedar, The, 259
Chester, 32, God's Providence House
— 33, Forbidden to Wed
— 243, As it Happened
Chevalier d'Auriac, The, 513
Chevalier d'Harmental, 153
Chevalier de Maison-Rouge, The, 155
Chevalier of Pensieri-Vani, The, 188
Chevalier of the Splendid Crest, The, 335
Chevelere Assigne, 236
Chevreuse, Mme de, 277, The Silver Cross
Chicago, 10, S. ANDERSON'S novels
— 137, Moon-Calf, and sequel
— 151, Sister Carrie
— 188, The Cliff-Dwellers, With the Procession
— 192, Rose of Dutcher's Coolly
— 228, The Bomb
— 361, The Pit
— 378, The Money Captain, Mr. Salt
Chicamon Stone, The, 384
Chichester, 176, Malvery Hold
Chicot, 154, La Dame de Monsoreau
— 155, The Forty-Five Guardsmen
Chicot the Jester, see La Dame de Monsoreau, 154
Chien d'Or, Le, 53
Chiffon's Marriage, 218
Chilcoot Pass, 302, The Call of the Wild
Child, The, 117
Child Andrea, The, 344
Child at the Balustrade, The, 69
Child at the Window, 240
Child Life, 5, Years of Childhood
— 5-6, Miss ALCOTT's stories
— 8, A Cathedral Singer
— 10, Silence
— 18, Marie-Claire, Valserine
— 34, A Very Light Railway, The Keys of the Jest
— 35, Mac's Adventures
— 37, Sentimental Tommy
— 38, The Little White Bird, Peter and Wendy
— 55, The Inviolable Sanctuary, Good Conduct
— 56, Dust
— 56, The Soul of a Child, and sequel
— 59, Jimbo, The Education of Uncle Paul, and sequel, The Extra Day
— 60, Mrs. Edith BLAND's stories
— 69, Daily Bread, and sequel
— 75, Nancy, Lavinia

Child Life (contd.) : 82, Mrs. F. E. BURNETT's stories *passim*
— 100, At Home, The Cook's Wedding
— 93, A Childhood
— 114, The Cricket
— 115, Pink Furniture
— 121, Whilomville stories
— 129, Farmington
— 136, A Child in Old Chester
— 160, Early Lessons, Popular Tales
— 166, Roswitha
— 168, Mrs. EWING's stories
— 175, The Weans at Rowallan
— 180, The Goblin
— 182, My Friend's Book
— 210, The Golden Age, Dream Days
— 218, Helen's Babies
— 219, Budge and Toddie
— 226-7, Mrs. L. A. HARKER's novels
— 253, A High Wind in Jamaica
— 265, What Maisie Knew
— 277, The Thoughty Ones
— 280, The Hillyars and the Burtons, Stretton, The Harveys
— 281, Wee Willie Winkie
— 304, A Child's Romance
— 307, The Mulberry Bush
— 318, April Fools
— 323, Out in Life's Rain, Among the Syringas, Gran'ma's Jane
— 324, Memories of Ronald Love
— 324, Early Sorrow
— 325, Something Childish
— 344, Two Little Parisians
— 346, Mrs. MOLESWORTH's stories
— 347-8, Miss MONTGOMERY's novels
— 352, Thunder on the Left
— 375, Eric PARKER's stories
— 435, Yannyol
— 439, The World's Delight, The House of the Luck
— 444, Patsy
— 464, Farewell to Paradise
— 467, Childhood
— 504, Timothy's Quest
— 507, The Beautiful Years, Dandelion Days
Child Life in Town and Country, 184
Child of Chance, The, 179
Child of Pleasure, The, 11
Child of Promise, The, 459
Child of Storm, 220
Child of the Jago, A, 353
Child of the Phalanstery, The, 7
Child Saint, The, 116
Childhood, 467
Childhood, A, 93
Children, Novels by, 16, The Young Visitors

Children, Novels by (contd.):
20, Love and Freindship
Children, Stories for, 1, The Franconia Stories
— 4, Miss AGUILAR's novels
— 5–6, Miss ALCOTT's stories
— 9, J. A. ALTSHELER's novels, *passim*
— 26, R. M. BALLANTYNE's stories
— 38, The Little White Bird, Peter and Wendy
— 60, Mrs. Edith BLAND's stories
— 66, Annette and Philibert
— 70–1, Rev. C. T. BRADY's novels
— 71, Mrs. BRAY's novels
— 74, E. S. BROOKS's novels
— 79, Æsop Dancing
— 82, Mrs. F. E. BURNETT's stories, *passim*
— 87, O. V. CAINE's novels
— 88, Ben Comee
— 93, " Lewis CARROLL's " works
— 95, The Lady of Fort St. John, Old Kraskaskia
— 98, The Shadowless Man ; Mrs. CHARLES's stories
— 106, J. F. COBB's novels
— 107, Minstrel Dick
— 115, Pink Furniture
— 120, Rev. A. D. CRAKE's novels
— 127, Miss CUMMINS's novels
— 144, Beulah M. DIX's novels
— 160, The Parent's Assistant, Early Lessons, Moral Tales, Popular Tales
— 165, Miss H. ELRINGTON's novels
— 167, EWALD's stories
— 168, Mrs. EWING's stories
— 169, Gypsy and Ginger, A Window in Paris
— 172, A Little Book of Profitable Tales
— 180, The Drummer's Coat
— 211, The Wind in the Willows
— 213, Miss E. Everett GREEN's novels
— 222, Andrew Marvel and his Friends
— 229, Aaron in the Wildwood
— 233, A Wonder Book, Tanglewood Tales
— 240, Gudrid the Fair
— 249, HOWARD's novels
— 260, Saxe Holm's stories
— 279, The Heroes, The Water-Babies
— 282, The Jungle Book, and sequel, Just-So Stories, Stalky & Co., Puck of Pook's Hill, Rewards and Fairies
— 287, Wonderful Adventures of Nils, and sequel, Liliecrona's Home

Children, Stories for (contd.):
299, Miss LILJEN-CRANTZ's novels
— 306, The Slowcoach
— 313, The Light Princess, and followng
— 319, Miss L. MACMANUS's novels
— 324–5, Anne MANNING's novels
— 329, Masterman Ready, Children of the New Forest
— 329–30, Emma MARSHALL's novels
— 330, The Playfellow
— 331, The Midnight Folk
— 346, The Hostages, Mrs. MOLESWORTH's novels
— 347, Misunderstood
— 348, Thrown Together
— 358, Rev. J. M. NEALE's novels
— 363, Willoughby Manor
— 391, Mrs. PRENTISS's novels
— 396, H. PYLE's novels
— 427, Molly SEAWELL's novels
— 428, Under Cheddar Cliffs
— 439, The World's Delight
— 464, The Green Mountain Boys
— 476, Tom Sawyer, and sequels, The Prince and the Pauper
— 477, The Red Cap
— 486, Ben Hur, The Prince of India
— 487, Mrs. WALTON's stories
— 503–4, " Kate D. WIGGIN's " stories
— 511–12, Mabel WRIGHT's stories
— 513–14 Charlotte M. YONGE's novels
Children, The, 500
Children of Alsace, 40
Children of Circumstance, 86
Children of Earth, 173
Children of Gibeon, The, 52
Children of Tempest, 356
Children of the Age, 224
Children of the Bush, 292
Children of the Dawn, 91
Children of the Dead End, 315
Children of the Frost, 302
Children of the Ghetto, 515
Children of the Hills, 363
Children of the King, The, 122
Children of the King of Norway, The Adventures of the, 257
Children of the Market Place, 332
Children of the Mist, 385
Children of the New Forest, The, 329
Children of the Night, 336
Children of the Nile, 387

Children of the Sea, The, 110
Children of the Soil, 435
Children of the Tenements, 408
Children of the World, 241
Children of the Zodiac, 282
Children Reap, The, 151
Children's Children, 64
Child's Romance, A, 304
Chile, 61, Martin Rivas
CHILEAN NOVELIST : A. BLEST-GANA
Chimes, The, 140, 141
Chin Ku Ch'i Kuan, 249
China and the Chinese, 50, The Poor Man
— 71, The Wallet of Kai Lung, and sequels
— 79, East Wind, West Wind
— 126, The Travail of his Soul
— 151, Quong Lung
— 171, The Cat and the Cherub
— 194, A Wind from the Wilderness
— 195, The Surrender, The Imperial Dragon
— 199, The Indiscretions of Lin Mang
— 237, Java Head
— 343, Silk
— 378, By Proxy
— 417, Mrs. Drummond's Vocation
— 452, Bitter Tea
— 500, The Wanderers on a Thousand Hills
— See also *Chinese Novelists, Oriental*
China Clippers, The, 305
China Seas, 193
Chinatown, 81, T. BURKE's stories
— See also *East End*
Chinatown Stories, 171
Chinese Novelists and Romances, 224, HAO CH'IU CHUAN
— 395, P'U SUNG LING
— 474, TS'AO CHAN
— 512, Mrs. WU SHU-CHUING
— 249, HOWELL, E. B. (tr.)
Chingachgook, 114, The Leather-Stocking Tales
Chino-Japanese War, 467 The Heart of Nami-San
Chippendales, The, 212
Chippinge, 498
Chippings with a Chisel, 232
Chitral Expedition, 457, The Edge of Empire
Chivalry, 84
Chivalry, Romances of, 96, Don Quixote
— 178, Ladies whose Bright Eyes
— 181, The Four Sons of Aymon
— 239, The Forest Lovers, Richard Yea-and-Nay, New Canterbury Tales, Fond Adventures

Chivalry, Romances of (contd.): 240, The Song of Renny
— 288, Little Jehan de Saintré
— 289, La Tour-Landry
— 350, Palmerin of England
— 352, W. MORRIS' romances
— 359, Aladore
— 375, Paris and Vienne
— 425, Ivanhoe
— 434, The Arcadia
Chlopi, 404
Chloris of the Island, 328
Choice of Amyntas, The, 333
Choice of Three Caskets, 430
Choir Invisible, The, 8
Choiseul, Duc de, 262, Castelnau
— 275, The King's Indiscretion
CHOMLEY, C. H.—see *sub nom.* OUTHWAITE, N. L.
Chopin, F. F., 284, Coronet
— 400, Journeyman Love
— 452, The Nightingale
Chorus, The, 307
Chorus-Girl, The, 100
Chosen People, The, 363
Chosen Valley, The, 177
Chouans, The, 29
Chouette, La, 455, Mysteries of Paris
Choulette, 183, The Red Lily
Chowne, Parson, 58, The Maid of Sker
Chris, 362
Chris Gascoyne, 47
Christ, Life of, 1, Philochristus
— 11, Judas Iscariot
— 23, Vergilius
— 74, A Son of Issachar
— 116, Barabbas
— 159, The Sweet Miracle
— 187, Holyland
— 231, The Fool in Christ, Emanuel Quint
— 284, Two Thieves
— 349, The Brook Kerith
— 416, I.N.R.I.
— 419, Saint Mary Magdalene
— 431, Muime Chriosd
— 432, Autobiography of Judas Iscariot
— 486, Ben Hur
— 489, Julian
Christ and Anti-Christ, 341
Christ in Flanders, 30
Christ in the Cupboard, 390
Christ of Toro, The, 210
Christalla, 454
Christian, The, 87
Christian but a Roman, A, 272
Christian Gellert, 19
Christian Life, 74, The Fool of Quality
— 300, Joshua Davidson
— 314, Sir Gibbie

Christian Life (contd.): 502, Mark Rutherford's Deliverance
— See also *Religious Allegory*
Christian Trevalga, 459
Christian Wahnschaffe, 490
Christianity, see *Agnosticism, Anglicanism, Atheism, Cathedral Life, Church, Clergymen, Dissenters, Kirk, Presbyterians, Priests, Roman Catholics, Wesleyans*, etc.
Christians, Early, 1, Onesimus, Silanus
— 21, Faustula
— 84, Brother Saul
— 98, Conquering and to Conquer
— 99, The Two Martyrs
— 103, To the Lions, The Burning of Rome, The Crown of Pine
— 120, Æmilius
— 158, The Emperor
— 159, Serapis
— 170, Gathering Clouds
— 209, Perpetua
— 231, Antinous
— 272, A Christian but a Roman
— 295, Serenus
— 302, Valerius
— 359, Callista
— 377, Marius the Epicurean
— 417, The Last Athenian
— 435, Quo Vadis ?
— 486, Empress Octavia
— 489, Zenobia, and sequel
— 508, Fabiola
Christie Johnson, 401
Christie's Faith, 413
Christie's Old Organ, 487
Christina of Sweden, 123, Stradella
Christina Alberta's Father, 495
Christine, 213
Christmas, 503, The Birds' Christmas Carol
— See also titles below
Christmas Books, 141
Christmas Books of M. A. Titmarsh, 462
Christmas Carol, A, 140, 141
Christmas Garland, A, 42
Christmas in Possession, 70
Christmas is Christmas, 335
Christmas Stories, 141
Christopher and Columbus, 15
Christopher Columbus, 267
Christowell, 58
Christy Carew, 230
Chronic Loafer, The, 301
Chronicle of Clemendy, The, 315
Chronicle of the Reign of Charles IX, 341
Chronicles of a Russian Family, 5
Chronicles of Æscendune, The, 120
Chronicles of Aunt Minervy Ann, 229

Chronicles of Clovis, 355
Chronicles of Dustypore, The, 127
Chronicles of Glenbuckie, 270
Chronicles of Richard Mahony, 406
Chronicles of St. Tid, 386
Chronicles of the Canongate, 427
Chronicles of the Imp, 169
Chronicles of the Schönberg-Cotta Family, 98
Chrysal, 271
Chrysostom, Saint, 170, Gathering Clouds
Chucks, Mr., 328, Peter Simple
Chuckster, 140, Old Curiosity Shop
Chukchee, The, 44
Chump, Mrs., 339, Sandra Belloni
Chums, 206
Church, Sir Richard, 124, The Silver Skull
Churchill, Charles, 271, Chrysal
Churchill, John, see *Marlborough, Duke of*
Churning of the Ocean of Time, The, 25
Cian of the Chariots, 22
Cibber, Colly, 308, Devereux
Cicily, 278
Cigarette - Maker's Romance, A, 122
Cimarron, 171
Cimbrernes tog, 267
Cimbrians, The, 267
Cincinnati, 447, They that Took the Sword, Eleanor Dayton
Cinderella Jane, 113
Cinema, 381, Spider Boy
Cinq-Mars, 483
Cinq-Mars Conspiracy, 261, Richelieu
— 483, Cinq-Mars
Cinq semaines en ballon, 482
Cinque Ports, 72, God Save England !
— See also *Rye, Winchelsea*
Circassia, 295, A Hero of Our Time
Circassians, 304, Constantinople, and sequel
Circuit Rider, The, 163
Circuit-Rider's Widow, A, 228
Circuit-Rider's Wife, A, 228
Circumlocution Office, 141, Little Dorrit
Circus Life, 6, Under the Lilacs
— 392, Haxby's Circus
— 398, True Tilda
— 440, Red Wagon
— 510, The Vagabonds
Cities of the Plain, 393
Citizen Bonaparte, 166
Citizen of the World, 205
Citoyenne Jacqueline, 478
City of Dreadful Night, The, 281
City of Light, The, 195

City of Refuge, The, 88
City of Sunshine, The, 7
City of the Discreet, The, 35
Civil Service, 46, Mr. Prohack, Lord Raingo
— 141, Little Dorrit
Civilization, 267, The Journey
— 341, MEREZHKOVSKY's novels
— See also *Gulliverian Satire*
Civilization, 153
Claiborne, William, 22, The Tower of Wye
— 93, The Code of Victor Jallot
Claim Jumpers, The, 501
Clairvoyance, 28, Ursule Mirouët
— See also *Second Sight*
Clanking of Chairs, The, 320
Clansman, The, 145
Clapham, 247, My Lord Winchenore
Clara (by F. W. von HACKLÄNDER), 219
Clara (by Pett RIDGE), 308
Clara Hapgood, 502
Clara Militch, 475
Clara Vaughan, 58
Clare County, 149, The Mystery of Killard
— 355, O'Laughlin of Clare
— See also *Ennistymon*
Clare Island, 363, A Queen of Men
Clarence, 230
Clarimonde, 195
Clarissa Harlowe, 406
CLARK, Charles H., see "ADELER, Max," 3
Clark, George Rogers, 104, The Crossing
— 248, The Magnificent Adventure
— 465, The Rangers
Clark's Field, 238
Clarté, 33
Class Prejudice, 67, The Weight of the Name
— 82, A Lady of Quality, and sequel
— 133, Sorrell & Son, Old Pybus
— 167, The Way of Transgressors
— 170, A Gentleman of Leisure
— 171, Marriage
— 172, O. FEUILLET's novels
— 190, A Commentary, Fraternity
— 250, Out of the Question
— 251, A Traveller from Altruria
— 283, Margaret Kent
— 303, Martin Eden
— 308, Godolphin
— 311, Views and Vagabonds
— 312, Orphan Island
— 323, The Patten Experiment, Olivia's Summer, The Mating of a Dove

Class Prejudice (contd.): 345, Ghosts of their Ancestors
— 368, Joyce, The Cuckoo in the Nest
— 375, The Grandee
— 384, The Husband's Story
— 440, The Old Manor House
— 494, Kipps
— 508, A Self-Made Countess
— 509, Lady Baltimore
Class Reunion, The, 496
Classical Mythology, 143, Ixion in Heaven, The Infernal Marriage
— 233, A Wonder Book, Tanglewood Tales
— 240, Lore of Proserpine
— 383, see G. PETTIE
— 444, Prometheus and Epimetheus
Claude Gueux, 253
Claudia, 520
Claudier, Die, 159
Claudine at School, 108
Claudius, Emperor, 103, The Crown of Pine
Claverhouse, see *Graham of Claverhouse*
Claverings, The, 472
Claxtons, The, 257
Clay, Henry, 74, A Son of the Revolution
— 143, The Patience of John Morland
— 248, Fifty-Four Forty, or Fight
Clayhanger, 45
Clayhanger Family, The, 45
Cleg Kelly, 124
CLEGHORN, Sarah M., see 88, Hillsboro People, The Real Motive
Cleland, Colonel, 308, Devereux
Clemenceau, Georges, 133, The House of Adventure
CLEMENS, S. L., see "TWAIN, Mark," 476
Clement VI, Pope, 171, The Ugly Duchess
Clement VII, Pope, 22, The Maid of Florence
Clementina, 331
Cleopatra, 38, The Laughing Queen
— 131, A Friend of Cæsar
— 159, Cleopatra
— 219, Cleopatra
Cleopatra (by EBERS), 159
Cleopatra (by HAGGARD), 219
Clerambault, 415
Clere Family, The, 321
Clergymen, 7, The Rambling Rector
— 8, The Chapel
— 15, The Pastor's Wife
— 21, A Nameless Nobleman
— 27, Le curé de Tours
— 29, The Country Parson
— 31, Father Connell

Clergymen (contd.): 42, Norwood
— 52, The Rector of St. Luke's
— 89, Round the Corner
— 100, The Bishop
— 114, The Deacon's Week, Steadfast
— 123, The Vicar of St. Luke's
— 153, Manhood End
— 163, Scenes of Clerical Life
— 190, Saint's Progress
— 205, The Vicar of Wakefield
— 212, The Silence of Dean Maitland
— 243, Father Alphonsus
— 244, The Taming of Nan
— 246, Father Stafford
— 249, A Foregone Conclusion
— 276, Shepherds in Sackcloth
— 276, Oldbury
— 300, Grasp Your Nettle
— 305, The New Priest in Conception Bay
— 307, Cathedral Folk
— 312, Told by an Idiot
— 313, Annals of a Quiet Neighbourhood
— 314, The Seaboard Parish, Thomas Wingfold
— 329, Abington Abbey
— 363, Parson Peter
— 366-8, Mrs. OLIPHANT's novels
— 378, The Canon's Ward
— 400, A Family That Was
— 437, The Rector of Wyck
— 471-2, TROLLOPE's novels
— 473, The Vicar of Wrexhill
— 478, A Daughter of the Manse
— 487, The Captives
— 487, Robert Elsmere
— 488, The Case of Richard Meynel
— 495, The Soul of a Bishop, Impossible People
— 514, Jocelyn Erroll
— See also *Ministers, Missionaries, Preachers, Priests*
Clerk of Oxford, A, 213
Clerkenwell, 46, Riceyman Steps
— 200, The Nether World
Cleves, Duc de, 247, The Gage of Red and White
Clèves, Olympe de, 155, Olympe de Clèves
Cliff-Dwellers, The, 188
Cliff End, The, 65
Clifford, Professor, 322, MALLOCK's novels
CLIFFORD, Lady, see DE LA PASTURE, Mrs. H., 137
Clifton College, 359, The Twymans
Climats, 335

Clinton Family, 329, A. MARSHALL's novels
Clio, The, 357
Clitophon and Leucippe, 2
Cloak, The, 204
Clockmaker, The, 221
Clodd, Edward, 411, The Private Life of Henry Maitland
Clogshop Chronicles, 2
Cloister and the Hearth, The, 401
Cloisterham, 141, The Mystery of Edwin Drood
Clombrony, Lord, 161, The Absentee
Clontarf, Battle of, 360, Njals Saga
Closed All Night, 350
Closed Garden, The, 213
Closing Door, The, 423
Closing Hour, 248
Clothiers, 138, Jack of Newbery, Thomas of Reading
— 324, Colloquies of Edward Osbourne
Cloud Cuckoo Land, 346
Club of Men Misunderstood, 102, Four Faultless Felons
Clutch of Circumstance, The, 429
Cnoc-an-Air, 214
Coast of Bohemia, The, 251
Coast of Freedom, The, 431
Coat without Seam, The, 33
Cobham, Lord, 262, Arabella Stuart
Cock and Anchor, 294
Cock and Bull Story, A, 347
Cock-House at Fellsgarth, The, 402
Cockneys, 58, Clara Vaughan
— 162, Life in London, and sequel
— 167, Nash and Some Others
— 281, Soldiers Three, Life's Handicap
— 395, E. PUGH's stories
— See also *London, London Poor*
Cock's Feather, 83
Coconnat, 154, Marguerite de Valois
Code of Victor Jallot, The, 93
Cœlebs in Search of a Wife, 351
Cœur d'Alène, 177
Cœur de femme, Un, 67
Cœur virginal, Un, 209
Coffin, Long Tom, 114, The Pilot
Coffin Island, 293
Coggin, 366
Cogglesbys, 339, Evan Harrington
Coignard, Abbé Jerome, 183, At the Sign of the Queen Pédauque, The Opinions of Jérôme Coignard
— 184, Jacques Tournebroche

Coil of Carne, The, 373
Colbert, J. B., 154, The Vicomte de Bragelonne
— 159, A Demoiselle of France
Colbury, 119, The Windfall
Cold Steel, 433
Cole, Thomas, 138, Thomas of Reading
Coleraine, 297, The Bramleighs
Coleridge, S. T., 378, Melincourt
— 379, Nightmare Abbey
Colet, Dean, 513, The Armourer's 'Prentices
Colette Baudoche, 37
Coligny, Admiral, 68, "William by the Grace of God——"
— 154, Marguerite de Valois
Collaboration, 264
Collapse of the Penitent, The, 493
Collection of Antiquities, The, 27
College Life, 232, Fanshawe
— 493, Pattie Fairfield
— See also *Cambridge, Harvard, Oxford, University Life*, etc.
Collegians, The, 216
Collier de la reine, Le, 155
Colline inspirée, La, 37
Collins, Rev. Wm., 20, Pride and Prejudice
Colloquies of Edward Osborne, 324
Cologne, 340, Farina
Colomba, 341
Colonel Carter of Cartersville, 440
Colonel Carter's Christmas, 440
Colonel Chabert, 27
Colonel Enderby's Wife, 321
Colonel Fairfax, 113
Colonel Greatheart (Colonel Stow), 24
Colonel Jacque, 134
Colonel Kate, 348
Colonel Quaritch, V.C., 219
Colonel Starbottle's Client, 230
Colonel Stow, 24
COLONIAL NOVELISTS, see AUSTRALIAN, CANADIAN, SOUTH AFRICAN, and NEW ZEALAND NOVELISTS
Colonial Reformer, A, 64
Colonials, The, 187
COLONNE, Guido delle, see *sub nom.* LE FEVRE, R.
Colonna Faction, 53, The Abbess of Castro
Colorado, 44, A Volunteer with Pike
— 94, The Song of the Lark
— 259, Youth Rides West
Colossae, 346, The Triumph of Faith
Colossus, The, 411

Colour Line, 70, A Doctor of Philosophy
— 102, A Matter of Principle
— 152, W. E. B. DU BOIS' novels
— 170, There is Confusion
— 197, Margaret Harding
— 281, Without Benefit of Clergy
— 316, Banjo
— 381, The Sons of Ham
— 382, B. PERRY's novels
— 407, Out of the Cypress Swamp
— 423, Trooper Peter Halkett
— 444, A Study in Colour
— 453, T. S. STRIBLING's novels, *passim*
— 502, The Fire in the Flint
— 510, Tangled Trinities
— 514, The Barrier
— See also *Creoles, Half-Breeds, Miscegenation, Negroes, Racial Problems*
Colour Studies, 266
Colston, Edward, 329, In Colston's Days
Columbia University, 412, The Florentine Frame
Columbine, 343
Columbus, Bartholomew, 356, The Spanish Island
Columbus, Christopher, 61, Unknown Lands
— 114, Mercedes of Castile
— 267, The Long Journey
— 271, Admiral of the Ocean Sea
— 356, The Spanish Island
Column, The, 327
Comanches Indians, 248, North of 36
Combat at the Ford, 293
Combien l'amour revient aux viellards, 28
Combined Maze, The, 437
Come and Find Me, 412
Come In, 336
Come Rack! Come Rope!, 49
Comedians, The, 117
Comédie humaine, la, 26-8
Comédiens sans le savoir, les, 29
Comedies and Errors, 227
Comedies of Courtship, 246
Comedy in Spasms, A, 86
Comedy of Age, The, 107
Comendador Mendoza, 480
Comes the Blind Fury, 167
Cometh up as a Flower, 75
Comforter, 71
Comfortless Memory, 33
Comical History . . . of the Worlds of the Moon and the Sun, 127
Comical Romance, The, 422
Coming Harvest, The, 40
Coming Home, 499
Coming of Amos, The, 302
Coming of Cuculain, The, 364

Coming of the Gael, The, 214
Coming of the Lord, The, 344
Coming of the Preachers, The, 2
Coming of the Tuatha da Danaan, 214
Coming of Theodora, The, 500
Coming Race, The, 310
Comin' thro' the Rye, 332
Coming Waterloo, The, 88
Commentaries of Ser Pantaleone, 324
Commentary, A, 190
Commerce, see Business, Capital, Industrialism, etc.
Commercial Travellers, 28, Gaudissart
— 453, Fombombo
Commines, Philippe de, 152, The Justice of the King
— 426, Quentin Durward
Commission in Lunacy, The, 27
Committed to his Charge, 300
Commodore's Daughters, The, 299
Commodus, Emperor, 500, Andivius Hedulio
Common Law, The, 97
Common Lot, The, 238
Common Story, A, 205
Commonwealth, 330, Una Breakspeare
— See also Cromwell
Commune, The (1871), 39, The Dayspring
— 96, The Red Republic
— 106, In Time of War
— 166, A Man of the People
— 169, A Window in Paris
— 182, The Aspirations of Jean Servien
— 326, The Commune
— 452, The Madonna of the Barricades
— 518, The Downfall
— See also Paris, Siege of
Commune, The, 326
Communism, 22, The Devil at the Long Bridge
— 77, Diane
— 96, The Red Republic
— 206-7, GORKY's novels
— 233, The Blythedale Romance
— 364, The Informer
— 369, The Open Secret
— See also Commune, The, Russian Soviet
Compact, The, 126
Compagnia della Leggera, La, 520
Compagnon du tour de France, 420
Companions of Jehu, The, 155
Company of Death, The, 117
Company of the Marjolaine, The, 78
Compensations, 190
Compiègne, 94, Wroth

Comrades, 206
Comrades in Arms, 201
Comte Kostia, Le, 101
Comtesse de Charny, La, 155
Comtesse de Rudolstadt, La, 420
Comyns, Rev. Michael, 296, Jack Hinton
Conachar, 254, The Cuchullin Saga
Concerning Isabel Carnaby, 181
Concerning Paul and Fiammetta, 227
Conchabar, 293, The Courtship of Ferb
— 446, Deidre
Condé, Louis I de Bourbon, Prince de, 262, The Man-at-Arms
Condé, Louis II de Bourbon, Prince de, 1, Blush Rose
— 155, The War of Women
— 261, John Marston Hall
— 512, The Silent Captain
Conde, Il, 111
Conde Lucanor, El, 274
Condensed Novels, 229
Condy, Sir, 160, Castle Rackrent
Cone, The, 493
Confession, A, 207
Confessions in Elysium, 503
Confessions of a Child of the Century, 357
Confessions of a Fool, 454
Confessions of a Frivolous Girl, 212
Confessions of a Justified Sinner, The, 244
Confessions of a Little Man, 11
Confessions of a Physician, 481
Confessions of a Thug, 461
Confessions of a Tradesman, 79
Confessions of a Young Man, 349
Confessions of Con Cregan, 296
Confessions of Harry Lorrequer, 296
Confessions of Richard Plantagenet, The, 313
Confessions of Zeno, The, 457
Confidence-Man, The, 338
Confidential Communication, A, 7
Conflict of Egoisms, A, 118
Conformists, The, 31
Confounding of Camelia, The, 428
Congaree River, 436, Woodcraft, and sequels
Coningsby, 143
Coniston, 104
Coniston Water, 108, Thorstein of the Mere
Conjure Woman, The, 101
Conjurer's House, 501
Connaught, 34, Irish Idylls
— 55, The Adventures of Dr. Whitty

Connaught (contd.): 365, S. O'KELLY's stories
— 477, The Dear Irish Girl
Connecticut, 114, Steadfast
— 244, The Bay Path
— 382, B. PERRY's novels
Connecticut Yankee in King Arthur's Court, A, 476
CONNELL, F. N., see O'RIORDAN, C., 370
Connemara, 276, Castle Daly
— 296, The Martins of Cro' Martin
Connoisseur, The, 136
Conquered, The, 345
Conqueror, The, 17
Conquering and to Conquer, 98
Conquest of Canaan, The, 460
Conquest of Plassans, The, 517
Conquest of Rome, The, 429
Conquête de Plassans, La, 517
Conquista di Roma, La, 429
Conrad in Quest of his Youth, 341
Conradin V of Swabia, 479, Cristina
Conscience, 158, Good Conscience
— 322, Conscience
— 389, The Two Salomes, and sequel
— See also Crime, Didactic, etc.
Conscience, 322
Conscience of a Business Man, The, 464
Conscript, The (by BALZAC), 30
Conscript, The (by ERCKMANN-CHATRIAN), 165
Conscription, 165, The Conscript
— 304, Roman d'un spahi
Consequences, 135
Conspirators, The (The Chevalier d' Harmental), 153
Constable of the Tower, The, 5
Constance, Lake, 128, A Captive of the Roman Eagles
Constance Trescott, 345
Constant Lover, A, 231
Constant Nymph, The, 277
Constantinople, 33, The Coat without Seam
— 122, Paul Patoff
— 123, Arethusa
— 132, The Beauty of the Purple
— 229, Theophano
— 304, Constantinople, and sequel
— 305, Disenchanted
— 306, The Captain of the Janizaries, Sir Raoul
— 317, Extremes Meet
— 318, The Three Couriers
— 346, Barbarian Stories
— 350, Palmerin of England

Constantinople (contd.): 354, Flames on the Bosphorus
— 358, Theodora Phranza
— 386, Eudocia
— 394, The Pasha
— 411, The Shadow of Allah
— 427, Count Robert of Paris
— 486, The Prince of India
Constantinople, 304
Constantius Chlorus, 352, King Constans
Consuelo, 420
Contarini Fleming, 143
Conte del Graal, 242
Contes à Ninon, 516
Contes cruels, 483
Contes de Jacques Tournebroche, 184
Contes et nouvelles, 357
Contes moraux, 327
Contes tartares, 218
Contraband of War, 433
Contract, The, 311
Contrat de mariage, Le, 27
Conventionalist, The, 49
Conversion of Con Cregan, The, 113
Convert, The, 516
Converted, 37
Convicts, 41, Helen Adair
— 62, The Land of Bondage
— 105, For the Term of his Natural Life
— 109, The Inimitable Mrs. Massingham
— 131, In the Track of a Storm
— 141, Great Expectations
— 248, The Rogue's March
— 270, Prisoners of Hope
— 301, Derelicts
— 490, Price WARUNG's stories
— See also Crime, Detective Stories, Highwaymen, Prisons, Thieves, etc.
Conway Castle, 404, Battlement and Tower
Cook, Douglas, 300, Christopher Kirkland
Cook of the Gannet, The, 260
Cook's Wedding, The, 100
Coonardoo, 392
Coote, Sir Charles, 174, The Chances of War
Coote, Sir Eyre, 215, The Great Proconsul
Cope, The, 65
Copenhagen, 261, Marie Grubbe
— 359, Pelle, Ditte
Cophagus, Mr., 328, Japhet
Copperhead, The, 186
Coptic Church, 83, The Oriflamme in Egypt
Copy, 498
Coquette, 458
Coquette's Love, A, 334
Cora, 455
Coral Island, 26
Corban, 440
Corday, Charlotte, 162, The Dream Charlotte

Corday, Charlotte (contd.): 478, Citoyenne Jacqueline

Cordova, 35, The City of the Discreet

— 123, The Making and Breaking of Almansur

Cords of Vanity, The, 85

Cordwainers, 138, The Gentle Craft

Corinne, 445

Corinth, 103, Lords of the World, The Crown of Pine

" *Corinthians*," 150, Rodney Stone

Cork, 39, The Wizard's Knot

— 79, Cambia Carty

— 116, A Munster Twilight

— 296, Harry Lorrequer

— 312, Mononia

— 343, Vision of MacConglinne

— 443, Experiences of an Irish R.M.

Corleone, 121

CORMAC, see KORMAKS SAGA, 284

Corn Laws, 498, The Great House

Cornet Strong of Ireton's Horse, 313

Cornwall, 71, Romances of the West

— 106, The Watchers on the Longships

— 208-9, Rev. S. BARING-GOULD's novels, *passim*

— 228, J. H. HARRIS's stories

— 294, C. J. LEE's novels

— 305, Wreckers and Methodists, Women's Tragedies

— 317, The Heavenly Ladder

— 327, The Column, Ginevra

— 328, Chloris of the Island, Captain Fortune

— 348, The Messenger

— 379, J. H. PEARCE's novels

— 385, Lying Prophets

— 396-8, QUILLER-COUCH's stories, *passim*

— 411, Rachael Marr

— 486, Fortitude

Cornwallis, Marquess of, 416, The Scarlet Coat

Corny, King, 161, Ormond

Coronation, 222

Coronet, 284

Corporal Sam, 398

Corse de Lion, 262

Corsica, 58, Clara Vaughan

— 156, The Corsican Brothers

— 341, Colomba

— 342, The Isle of Unrest

— 397, Sir John Constantine

Corsican Brothers, The, 156

Corunna, 180, The Drummer's Coat

" CORVO, Baron," see ROLFE, F.

Coryston Family, The, 489

Coscienza di Zeno, La, 457

Cose più grandi di lui, Le, 520

Cosmopolitan, The, 436

Cossacks, 22, Red Cavalry

— 204, Taras Bulba

— 284, Kostia the Cossack

— 434, With Fire and Sword

— 468, The Cossacks

Cossacks, The, 468

Cossham, Handel, 120, John Halifax

Costaguana, 110, Nostromo

Costigan, Captain, 462, Pendennis

Côté de Guermantes, Le, 393

Cotswolds, 133, Orchards

— 317, Guy and Pauline

Cottage, The, 454

Cottage in the Chine, The, 243

Cottagers of Glenburnie, The, 222

Cotton Industry, 36, Between Two Loves

— 180, Probation

— 377, The Story of Stephen Compton

— 456, Mistress Barbara Cunliffe

— 492, Traitor or Loyalist ?

COUCH, Sir A. Q., see QUILLER-COUCH, Sir A.

Coucy, Sire de, 261, Philip Augustus

Council of Perfection, A, 321

Count Abdullah, 387

Count Bunker, 106

Count Hannibal, 497

Count Kostia, 101

Count Lucanor, 274

Count of Monte Cristo, The, 154

Count Robert of Paris, 427

Counterfeiters, The, 198

Countess Cosel, The, 285

Countess Eve, The, 433

Countess of Bellarmine, 397

Countess of Dammartin, 412

Countess of Pembroke's Arcadia, 434

Countess of Rudolstadt, 420

Countess of St. Alban, The, 219

Countess of Zelle, The, 196

Countess Tekla, The, 37

Country Air, The, 259

Country Artist, A, 435

Country By-Ways, 269

Country Doctor, A, 269

Country Doctor, The, 29

Country House, The, 190

Country House on the Rhine, The, 19

Country I Come From, The, 292

Country in Danger, The, 166

Country Neighbours, 76

Country of the Blind, The, 493

Country of the Blind, The, 494

Country of the Pointed Firs, The, 269

Country Parson, The, 29

Country People, 455

Country Waif, The, 421

Country Road, The, 76

Coupable, Le, 115

Courage (by GALSWORTHY), 190

Courage (by F. REID), 403

Court Cards, 104

Court Life, see *Royalty*, and under names of Monarchs

Court Netherleigh, 510

Court of the King of Bantam, The, 43

Court Royal, 208

Courtesans, 1, Madelon

— 28, A Harlot's Progress

— 29, Cousin Betty

— 46, The Pretty Lady

— 60, Sonnica

— 90, Our Lady of Darkness

— 108, Chéri

— 109, The New Magdalen

— 130, Sappho

— 134, Moll Flanders, Roxana

— 145, Keetje

— 151, Sister Carrie

— 156, The Lady with the Camelias

— 183, Thaïs

— 193, Nadjeja Nicolaievna

— 200, The Unclassed

— 274, Daughters of Ishmael

— 275, Broken Pitchers

— 285, Yama

— 290, Mrs. Bente

— 315, The Rat-Pit

— 317, Sylvia Scarlett

— 334, Boule de Suif

— 385, Susan Lenox

— 413, Tolla

— 414, Celestina

— 448, Magdalene

— 455, The Song of Songs

— 469, Resurrection

— 473, A Girl of the Multitude

— 483, Sardonic Tales

— 517, Nana

Courtesy Dame, The, 199

Courting of Dinah Shadd, The, 281

Courting of Mary Smith, The, 413

Courtney of Walreddon, 71

Courtrai, Battle of, 112, The Lion of Flanders

Courts of the Morning, The, 78

Courtship of Etain, The, 293

Courtship of Ferb, The, 293

Courtship of Morrice Buckler, 331

Cousin Betty, 29

Cousin Cinderella, 117

Cousin Hugh, 148

Cousin Phyllis, 194

Cousin Pons, 29

Cousin William, 245

Cousins and Others, 478

Cousins German, 253

COUVREUR, Mme, see " TASMA," 460

Covent Garden, 133, Apples of Gold

Covenanters, 10, Kelston of Kells

— 78, John Burnet of Barns, Witch Wood

— 124, Men of the Moss-Hags, The Standard-Bearer, The Cherry Riband

— 191, Ringan Gilhaize

— 211, Harry Ogilvie

— 316, R. W. MACKENNA's novels

— 380, Magnus Sinclair

— 425, Old Mortality

— See also *Graham of Claverhouse, Killie-crankie, Kirk,* etc.

Coventry, 330, The Young Queen of Hearts

Covered Wagon, The, 248

Covering End, 265

Coward, A (by CAPES), 90

Coward, A (by Edith WHARTON), 498

Coward, The, 49

Cowardice, 78, The Half-Hearted

— 90, A Coward

— 93, Schmelzle

— 331, The Four Feathers

Cowboys, 2, Andy ADAMS's stories

— 110, " R. CONNOR's " stories

— 126, C. CULLEY's novels ; The Story of the Foss River Ranch, The One-Way Trail

— 192, The Eagle's Heart, Her Mountain Lover

— 508, The Virginian

Cowper, William, 182, The Bountiful Hour

— 329, On the Banks of the Ouse

Cox's Diary, 463

Cradock Nowell, 58

Crainquebille, 184

Cranford, 194

Cranmer, Archbishop, 178, The Fifth Queen, and sequels

— 422, A Noble Wife

— 426, Quentin Durward

CRAWFORD, Mrs. Maynard, see BAKER, Amy J.

Crawley, Rawdon, 462, Vanity Fair

Cream of the Jest, The, 85

Cream Tarts, The, 448

Created Legend, The, 443

Creators, The, 437

Creatures, 136

Creatures that once were Men, 206

Crécy, Battle of, 160, Cressy and Poictiers

— 220, Red Eve

— 292, Brakespeare

Creel of Irish Stories, A, 34

Cremona, 319, Lally of the Brigade

Cremona Violin, The, 244

Creoles, 86, G. W. CABLE's novels and stories

Crescent Moon, The, 514
Cressage, 47
Cressy, 230
Cressy and Poictiers, 160
Crested Seas, The, 110
Crete, 229, Theophano
— 341, The Birth of the Gods
Crewe Train, 312
"CREYTON, P.", see TROW-BRIDGE, J. T., 473
Cricket, The, 114
Cricket Heron, 23
Cricket Match, The, 140
Cricket on the Hearth, The, 141
Crickowell, 260, Aythan Waring
Crime and Criminals, 4, Jack Sheppard
— 6, Prudence Palfrey, The Stillwater Tragedy
— 44, From the Vasty Deep
— 48, The Luck of the Vails
— 63, The Power of a Lie, The Prisoner who Sang
— 70, Eleanor's Victory, Henry Dunbar, An Open Verdict
— 76, The Prisoner
— 108-9, Wilkie COLLINS' novels, *passim*
— 140, Oliver Twist
— 146-8, DOSTOEVSKY's novels
— 173, Amelia
— 179, Payment Deferred
— 189, The Rogue in Love
— 231, Phantom
— 244, The Private Memoirs . . . of a Fanatic
— 250, The Quality of Mercy
— 254, Les misérables
— 272, Told by the Death's Head
— 276, On Trial
— 308, Falkland, Eugene Aram
— 309, Lucretia
— 322, Doctor Claude
— 336, Children of the Night
— 356, A Life's Atonement
— 364, O'FLAHERTY's novels
— 365, The Lady in Grey
— 391, The Murder of Monsieur Fualdès
— 415, Hooligan Nights
— 416, The Magistrate's Own Case
— 455, The Mysteries of Paris
— 463, Memoirs of Barry Lyndon, Catherine
— 470, Three Crosses
— See also *Burglars, Detective Fiction, Highwaymen, Thieves, Prisons,* etc.
Crime and Punishment, 147
Crime at Vanderlynden's, 354
Crime d'amour, Un, 67
Crime of Doctor Garine, The, 442

Crime of Sylvestre Bounard, The, 182
Crimean War, 61, A Son of the Forge
— 139, Véra
— 292, Sword and Gown
— 337, The Interpreter
— 373, The Coil of Carne
— 468, Sevastopol
Crimson Conquest, The, 252
Crimson Field, The, 457
Crimson Honeymoon, 243
Crimson Saga, The, 277
Crimson Tide, The, 97
Crippled Hope, A, 279
Cripps the Carrier, 58
Criquette, 221
Crisis, The, 104
Cristina, 479
Crittenden, 182
Croatan, 271
Croats, 53, A Trooper of the Finns
Crock of Gold, The, 446
Crocker's Hole, 58
Crockett, Davy, 36, Remember the Alamo
Crofters, 368, The Wizard's Son
— 446, The Gift of the Gods
Crofton Boys, 330
Crohoore of the Bill-Hook, 31
Croisée des chemins, La, 65
Croix de bois, Les, 145
Croker, John William, 143, Coningsby
— 351, Florence M'Carthy
— 462, Vanity Fair
Crome, "Old", 330, Castle Meadow
Crome Yellow, 256
Cromwell, Miriam, 313, Miriam Cromwell
Cromwell, Oliver, 24, Colonel Stow
— 36, Friend Olivia
— 68, The Governor of England
— 103, John Marmaduke, Penruddock
— 243, Follow the Gleam
— 252, A Dreamer of Dreams
— 277, The Cavaliers
— 307, To Right the Wrong, In Spite of All
— 337, Holmby House
— 380, Magnus Sinclair
— 413, King by the Grace of God
— 426, Woodstock
— 513, The Lord Protector
Cromwell, Richard, 308, Devereux
Cromwell, Thomas, 49, The King's Achievement
— 178, The Fifth Queen, and sequels
— 220, The Lady of Blossholme
— 333, Defender of the Faith
Cromwell of Virginia, The, 165
Cronica del Cid, 104
Crook, General, 372, The Heritage of Unrest
— 508, Red Man and White

Crook of the Bough, The, 148
Crooked Branch, The, 194
Crooked Mile, A, 369
Crooked Trails, 403
Croppies Lie Down, 79
Croppy, The, 31
Crosbie, Mr., 471, The Small House at Allington
Cross, The, 479
Cross and Dagger, 158
Cross at the Door, The, 432
Crossing, The, 104
Crossriggs, 174
Crotch, William, 330, Castle Meadow
Crotchet Castle, 379
Crouchback, 369
Crowborough Beacon, 256
Crowe, Capt., 441, Launcelot Greaves
Crown of Life, The, 201
Crown of Pine, The, 103
Crowned Queen, A, 215
Croy, Kate, 265, The Wings of the Dove
Crozat, Anthony, 142, The Siege of Lady Resolute
Crucial Instances, 498
Cruel City, The, 216
Cruel Enigma, A, 67
Cruelle énigme, 67
Cruise of the *Midge*, The, 424
Cruise of the *Snark*, The, 303
Cruise of the *Wild Duck*, The, 151
Crummles, Vincent, 140, Nicholas Nickleby
Crusade, First, 120, The Rival Heirs
— 131, "God Wills It"
— 427, Count Robert of Paris
— 492, Armour Wherein he Trusted
Crusade, Second, 122, Via Crucis
Crusade, Third, 270, The Fortunes of Garin
— 336, The Assassins
— 391, The Unhurrying Chase
— 426, The Talisman
Crusade, Fourth, 84, Crusade
— 87, The Blue Banner
— 306, Sir Raoul
Crusade, Sixth, 83, The Oriflamme in Egypt
Crusade, Eighth, 513, The Prince and the Page
Crusade, The "Childrens", 23, On the Forgotten Road
— 158, Cross and Dagger
— 448, The Sign of Triumph
Crusade, 84
Crusade of the *Excelsior*, The, 230
Crusoe Life, 133, Robinson Crusoe
— 329, Masterman Ready
— 375, Peter Wilkins
— 399, Swallows and Amazons

Crusoe Life (contd.): 450, The Casting Away of Mrs. Lecks and Mrs. Aleshine, and sequel (burlesque)
Cry Across the Dark Water, A, 123
Cry of Peacock, 191
Crystal Age, A, 252
Crystal Coffin, The, 416
Crystal Stopper, 293
Cuarto Poder, El, 374
Cuatro Jinetes del Apocalipsis, Los, 61
Cuba, 40, The Rainbow's End
— 112, Romance
— 120, The Open Boat
— 165, Caoba
— 182, Crittenden
— 403, F. REMINGTON's stories
Cuchulain of Muirthemne, 214
Cuchullin, 169, see Winifred FARADAY, tr.
— 214, see Lady GREGORY (tr.)
— 236, The Feast of Bricriu
— 254, The Cuchullin Saga
— 293, see LEAHY, A. H.
— 364-5, The Coming of Cuchulain, and sequel
Cuchullin Saga in Irish Literature, The, 254
Cuckoo, The, 152
Cuckoo Clock, The, 346
Cuckoo in the Nest, The, 368
Cuestion Palpitante, 375
Culloden, see *Jacobite Rebellion of 1745*
Culmstock, 58, Perlycross
Cumberland, 54, A Moorside Feud
— 87, The Shadow of a Crime, A Son of Hagar
— 108, Thorstein of the Mere
— 209, Harlaw of Sendle
— 300, Lizzie Lorton
— 368, Owd Bob
— 426, Redgauntlet
Cumberland Vendetta, A, 182
Cunning Murrell, 353
Cupid and Mr. Pepys, 459
Cupid and Psyche, 13, The Golden Ass
— 15, Melusine
Curate-in-Charge, The, 367
Curate of Churnside, The, 7
Curé de Tours, le, 27
Curé de village, le, 29
Curée, La, 517
Curran, J. P., 199, The Island of Sorrow
— 243, The King's Deputy
— 296, Jack Hinton
Curran, Sarah, 63, True Man and Traitor
— 218, Robert Emmet
Currie, Lady, 322, The New Republic
Curse Half Spoke, A, 385
Curse of the Nile, The, 439

Curse of the Village, The, 112
Cursed be the Treasure, 151
Custer, General, 9, The Last of the Chiefs
— 74, Master of the Strong Hearts
— 376, Bob Hampton
— 377, Molly Macdonald
Custody of the Child, The, 198
Custom of the Country, The, 499
Cut off from the World, 79
Cymbeline, 352, King Florus
Cynthia, 341
Cynthia in the West, 294
Cypress, Mr., 379, Nightmare Abbey
Cyprus, 475, The Royal Pawn of Venice
Cyrano de Bergerac, 189, Captain Satan
Cyrilla, 460
Cytherea, 237
CZECH NOVELISTS:
K. ČAPEK, J. HAŠEK, F. KAFKA, B. NĚMCOVÁ, A. SMILOVSKÝ, F. WERFEL (German Czech)
— See also The Last Days of John Hus (anonymous)

Dá Derga's Hostel, The Destruction of, 451
Da opposte Rive, 218
Daddy Darling's Dovecot, 168
Daddy Long-Legs, 492
Dædalus, Stephen, 273, A Portrait of the Artist as a Young Man, Ulysses
Dagonet the Jester, 319
Dagos, 210
Daily Bread, 69
Daisy and Daphne, 312
Daisy Miller, 263
Dakota, 64, The Emigrants
— 126, The Watchers of the Plains
— 192, H. GARLAND's novels, *passim*
— 415, Giants in the Earth, and sequel
— 486, Out of the Silences
Dalarna, 286, Jerusalem
Dale, Lily, 471, The Small House at Allington
Dalgetty, Captain, 425, A Legend of Montrose
Dalkeith, 346, Life of Mansie Wauch
Dally, 389
Daltons, The, 296
Daly, Mr., 276, Castle Daly
Damaged Goods, 438
Damaged Reputation, A, 54
Damascus, 387, Saïd the Fisherman
Dame aux camélias, La, 156
Dame Care, 455
Dame de Monsoreau, La, 154
Dame des Belles Cousines, La, 288, Little Jehan de Saintré

Dame en gris, La, 365
Damietta, 83, The Oriflamme in Egypt
— 158, Cross and Dagger
Damnable Life . . . of Faustus, 170
Damnation of Theron Ware, The, 186
Damsel and the Sage, The, 203
Dan Russel the Fox, 443
Dan the Dollar, 80
Danby, Earl of, 68, Defender of the Faith
Dance of Death, The, 59
Dancing Floor, The, 78
Dandelion Days, 507
Dandies, 313, The Fair Irish Maid
Danes Sketched by Themselves, The, 258
Danesbury House, 509
Danger !, 150
Dangerous Acquaintances, 286
Dangerous Age, The, 344
Dangerous Ages, 312
Dangerous Catspaw, A, 357
Dangerous Wooing, A, 56
Daniel the Prophet, 121, Zoroaster
Daniel Boone, 502
Daniel Deronda, 164
Daniel Herrick, 81
Daniel Whyte, 132
Daniele Cortis, 177
Danish Fairy Tales and Legends, 9
Danish Fiddler, A, 9
Danish Invasion of England, 120, Alfgar the Dane
— See also *Alfred the Great, Olaf, Vikings*
Danish Life, see DANISH NOVELISTS, *passim*
DANISH NOVELISTS:
H. ANDERSEN, J. H. BANG, C. V. O. BERGSOË, L. BRUUN, H. DRACHMANN, C. EWALD, S. FLEURON, K. A. GJELLERUP, B. INGEMANN, J. P. JACOBSEN, J. V. JENSEN, F. de JESSEN, "Karin MICHAËLIS," E. MIKKELSON, M. A. NEXØ, A. OEHLENSCHLÄGER, H. PONTOPPIDAN, Baron ROSENKRANTZ, H. SÖIBERG
— See also LARSEN, Hanna A. (ed.), 288
Danny, 368
Dansons la trompeuse, 167
Dante, 30, The Exiles
— 152, The Maker of Saints
— 313, The God of Love
Dantès, Edmond, 154, The Count of Monte Christo
Danton, G. J., 16, The Mysterious M. Dumont
— 162, A Storm-Rent Sky
— 222, The Giant
— 235, Rose in the Mouth
— 495, A Marriage Under the Terror

Dantzig, 342, Barlasch of the Guard
Danube, 53, A Hero in Wolf-Skin
— 259, Kyra, My Sister
— 271, Timar's Two Worlds
— 346, When the Bough Breaks
Danvers Jewels, The, 103
Danvis Folks, 413
Daphne, 488
Daphne Adeane, 33
Daphne Bruno, 400
Daphne in Fitzroy Square, 60
Daphis and Chloe, 303
DARBY, Mrs. M. H. G., see "MERRY, A."
Darcy, Mr., 20, Pride and Prejudice
Darius, 121, Zoroaster
Dark, The, 11
Dark Fire, The, 351
Dark Flower, The, 190
Dark Forest, The, 486
Dark Hester, 428
Dark Journey, The, 213
Dark Lantern, A, 412
Dark Laughter, 10
Dark Mile, The, 74
Dark Night's Work, A, 194
Dark o' the Moon, The, 123
Dark Princess, The, 152
Dark Ship, The, 77
Dark Tower, The, 514
Darkened Rooms, 198
Darling, Admiral, 58, Springhaven
Darling, The, 100
Darlingtons, The, 379
Darnley, Lord, 239, The Queen's Quair
— 337, The Queen's Maries
— See also *Mary, Queen of Scots*
Darnley, 261
Darrel of the Blessed Isles, 23
Dartada, 293
Dartmoor, 35, A Loyal Traitor
— 58, Christowell
— 91, Where England Sets her Feet
— 98, Beatrice CHASE's novels
— 120, The Last Abbot of Glastonbury
— 208–9, Rev. S. Baring GOULD's novels
— 373, My Lady of the Moor
— 385–7, Eden PHILPOTTS' novels
— 388, The French Prisoner
— 454, Dewer Rides
— 507, Tarka
Dartmoor Idylls, 209
Dashwood, Sir Francis, 178, The Portrait
— 271, Chrysal
DASHWOOD, Mrs., see "DELAFIELD, E. M.," 135
Daughter of Eve, A, 27
Daughter of Fife, A, 36
Daughter of Heth, A, 57

Daughter of Kings, A, 207
Daughter of Kings, A, 477
Daughter of New France, A, 126
Daughter of Strife, A, 173
Daughter of the Fields, A, 477
Daughter of the Manse, A, 478
Daughter of the Middle Border, A, 192
Daughter of the Veldt, A, 327
Daughter of the Vine, A, 17
Daughters of Ishmael, 274
Daughters of the Revolution, 107
Daughters of the Rich, 419
Daughters of the Vicar, 290
Dauphin Louis XVII, see *Louis XVII*
Dauphiné, 65, The Parting of the Ways
— 101, The Romance of an Honest Woman
Davenport Dunn, 297
Dave's Sweetheart, 194
David, King, 131, Giant-Killer
David, Saint, 140, Star of Mercia
David Aldin's Daughter, 21
David Arnot, 39
David Balfour, 449
David Blaize, 48
David Blaize and the Blue Door, 48
David Copperfield, 141
David Elginbrod, 313
David Golder, 358
David Harum, 497
David March, 176
David of King's, 48
David Simple, 173
Davidée Birot, 40
"*Davids*," 70, A Little Traitor to the South
Davies, Delmé, 332, The Binding of the Strong
Davis, Jefferson, 145, The Victim
Dawn, 219
Dawn of All, The, 49
Dawn on Mont Blanc, 50
Day and Night Stories, 59
Day at Laguerres, A, 440
Day in the Wilderness, A, 186
Day of Atonement (by GOLDING), 205
Day of Atonement, The (by KOROLENKO), 284
Day of Reckoning, The, 67
Day of Wrath, The, 271
Daybreak, 359
Days of Auld Langsyne, The, 318
Days of Bruce, The, 4
Days of Jeanne d'Arc, The, 95
Day's Ride, A, 297
Day's Work, The, 282
Dayspring, The, 39
Deacon Bradbury, 145
Deacon's Week, The, 114
Dead Christ, The, 407
Dead Command, The, 61

Dead Lake, The, 241
Dead Man's Plack, 253
Dead Man's Rock, 396
Dead Oppressors, 388
Dead Secret, The, 108
Dead Souls, 204
Dead Woman, A, 118
Dead Woman's Wish, A, 516
Deadlock, 405
Deadman's, 194
Deal in Cotton, A, 282
Deal in Wheat, A, 361
"DEAN, Mrs. A.," see SIDGWICK, Cecily, 433
Deans, Effie and Jeanie, 425, The Heart of Midlothian
Dean's Elbow, The, 332
Dear Irish Girl, The, 477
Dear Lady Disdain, 312
Dearborn, Fort, 376, When Wilderness was King
— 402, The Shadow of Victory
Dearmuid, 214
Dearmuid and Grania, 214
Death, 5, The Strange Friend of Tito Gill
— 235, Incurable
— 251, The Angel of the Lord
— 468, Ivan Ilyitch
— See also Capital Punishment, Future Life, Immortality
Death Comes for the Archbishop, 95
Death Dance, The, 94
Death in Venice, 324
Death of a Bachelor, The, 423
Death of a Government Clerk, The, 100
Death of a Hero, 6
Death of a Nobody, 415
Death of Ivan Ilyitch, The, 468
Death of Maurice, The, 374
Death of My Aunt, 283
Death of Pan, 157
Death of Peter Waydelin, 459
Death of Society, 507
Death of the Gods, 341
Death of the Laird's Jock, The, 427
Death of the Lion, The, 264
Death Way, The, 311
Débâcle, La, 518
Debenham's Vow, 161
Debit Account, The, 369
Debit and Credit, 187
Debits and Credits, 283
Deborah, 306
Deborah's diary, 324
Debt, The, 499
Debtor, The, 142
Debts of Honour, 272
Début dans la vie, un, 27
Decadence, 207
Decameron, The, 63
Deccan, 244, Pandurang Hari
— 461, A Noble Queen
Decatur and Somers, 427

Deceased Wife's Sister Bill, 138, It Never Can Happen Again
December the Fourteenth, 341
Decembrists, 306, The Flames of Moscow
Dechartre, 183, The Red Lily
Decius, Emperor, 120, Æmilius
— 359, Callista
Declaration of Love, 139
Decoration Day, 269
De Courcys, 471, Doctor Thorn
Deemster, The, 87
Deep Down, 26
Deep Sea, 514
Deep-Sea Plunderings, 79
Deep Sea Warriors, 305
Deep Waters, 261
Deepening Stream, The, 89
Deephaven, 268
Deeps of Deliverance, The, 162
Deerbrook, 330
Deerslayer, The, 114
Deeside, 7, Balmoral
Defeat (by HUCH), 252
Defeat (by Moss), 354
Defeat of the Amazons, The, 294
Defender of the Faith, 68
Defender of the Faith, 333
Defense Nationale, La, 326
Definite Object, The, 169
Defoe, Daniel, 512, Robin the Prodigal
Deformity, 136, Memoirs of a Midget
— 310, God's Fool
— 321, The History of Sir Richard Calmady
— 333, Of Human Bondage
— 425, The Black Dwarf
— 426, Peveril of the Peak
— 504, The Story of Patsy
— 514, She Who Meant Well
— See also Mutes
Deidre, 446
Delaney, Corney, 296, Jack Hinton
De la paix à la guerre, 481
DE LA PASTURE, E. E. M., see "DELAFIELD, E. M.," 135
De la terre à la lune, 482
Delaware, 283, A Midsummer Madness
— 401, In Castle and Colony
Delectable Duchy, The, 397
Delhi, see Indian Mutiny
Deliverance, The, 202
Delobelle, 129, Fromont Junior and Risler Senior
De l'Orme, 261
Delphine, 445
Delphine (by Mme. de Staël), 160, Leonora
Deluge, The, 434
Demerara, 413, In Guiana Wilds
Demeter's Daughter, 386

Demi-Gods, The, 446
Demi-Royal, 243
Democracy, 2
Demoiselle of France, A, 159
Demoiselles de Bienfilâtre, 483
Demon of Gold, 112
Demos, 200
Denis Duval, 463
Denmark, see DANISH NOVELISTS
Dennis O'Shaughnessy Going to Maynooth, 92
Denounced, The, 31
Denry the Audacious, 46
Densher, Lambert, 265, The Wings of the Dove
Denver, Colonel, 308, The Helpers, The Grafters, Empire Builders
Denys l'Auxerrois, 377
Denys the Dreamer, 478
Departure, 145
Deptford, 52, The World went very well then
Député d'Arcis, le, 29
Deputy was King, A, 447
Derby, Charlotte de la Trémouille, Countess of, 426, Peveril of the Peak
Derby, Earl of, 5, The Leaguer of Lathom
Derbyshire, 78, Midwinter
— 81, The Duke's Servants
— 164, Adam Bede
— 199, R. GILCHRIST's novels
— 243, The Brave Men of Eyam
— 426, Peveril of the Peak
— 488, David Grieve
Derelicts, 301
Dereonya, 80
Dermat, 274, The Fairy Palace of the Quicken Trees, etc.
Dernier amour, 365
Dernier jour d'un condamné, Le, 253
Dernière Aldini, La, 420
Dernière incarnation de Vautrin, la, 29
Derry, Siege of, 277, The Crimson Saga
Derwentwater, Earl of, 5, Preston Flight
— 52, Dorothy Forster
Désastre, Le, 326
Descent into Egypt, A, 59
Descent into the Maelstrom, A, 388
Descent of Man, The, 498
Descent of the Duchess, The, 411
Descent of the Sun, The, 25
DE SELINCOURT, Mrs. B., see SEDGWICK, Anne D., 428
Désenchantées, Les, 305
Désert de glace, Le, 482
Desert of Ice, The, 482
Deserters, The, 186
Desiderio, 192
Desierto de Piedra, 491
Desire, 436

Desire of Life, The, 429
Désirs de Jean Servien, Les, 182
Desmond, 440
Desmond's Daughter, 144
Desmond's rebellion, 165, Ralph Wynward
— 289, Maelcho
Desmoulins, Camille, 280, Mademoiselle Mathilde
Desperate Character, A, 475
Desperate Remedies, 225
Despot of Broomsedge Cove, The, 118
Dessous des cartes, Les, 32
Destinies, 334
Destiny, 171
Destiny Bay, 84
Destruction of Da Derga's Hostel, 451
Detective Stories, 23, The House of the Three Ganders
— 56, Wild Justice, The Hymn Tune Mystery
— 91, The Skeleton Key
— 102, The Father Brown Stories, etc.
— 103, Agatha CHRISTIE's novels
— 124, F. W. CROFTS' novels
— 128, Enter Sir John, Printer's Devil
— 132, Tangled Evidence
— 149, R. DOWLING's novels
— 149–50, Conon DOYLE's stories
— 169, The Mystery of M. Felix, Samuel Boyd
— 177, The Middle Temple Murder
— 187, R. A. FREEMAN's novels
— 213, Anna GREEN's novels
— 216, In Tight Places
— 254, The Mystery of a Hansom Cab
— 283, Death of My Aunt
— 293, M. LEBLANC's stories
— 293, Nonsense Novels, Winsome Winnie (burlesques)
— 331, At the Villa Rose
— 396, "E. QUEEN's" novels
— 414, The Dream-Detective
— 433, The Weird O't
— 442, The Unforeseen
— 444, A Nest of Spies
— 485, E. WALLACE's stories
— 493, The Mark of Cain
— See also Crime and Criminals
Determinism, 93, The Realization of Justus Moran
— 117, COUPERUS's novels, passim
— 225–6, HARDY's novels, passim
— See also Fatalism, Naturalism

Dethronement of the King, The, 3
De Thou, 483, Cinq-Mars
De toute son âme, 40
Detroit, 126, A Daughter of New France, The Heroine of the Strait, Love Thrives in War
— 376, A Sword of the Old Frontier
— 406, Wacousta
Deuce, The, 358
Deuceace, Mr., 463, The Yellowplush Memoirs
Deutsche Liebe, 355
Deutsche Pioniere, 444
Deux Dianes, Les, 155
Deux frères, Les, 166
De varios Colores, 480
Devaytis, 413
De Vere, Earl of Oxford, 427, Anne of Geierstein
De Vere, 489
Devereux, 308
Devil, 11, Satan's Diary
— 116, The Sorrows of Satan
— 148, They Went
— 170, Faustus
— 175, The Temptation of St. Anthony
— 433, The Countess Eve
— 515, Satan Mekatrig
— See also Diabolism, Magic, Witchcraft, etc.
Devil, The, 469
Devil, The (The Deuce), 358
Devil at the Long Bridge, The, 22
Devil in Manuscript, The, 233
Devil on Two Sticks, The, 295
Devil's Bridge, The, 6
Devil's Garden, The, 335
Devil's Half-Acre, The, 26
Devil's Keg, The, 126
Devil's Playground, The, 318
Devil's Pool, The, 421
Devil's Portrait, The, 38
Devil's Tight Rope, The, 385
Devon Boys, The, 171
Devonshire, 26, By Stroke of Sword
— 58, R. D. BLACKMORE'S novels
— 71, Romances of the West
— 71, A Royal Ward
— 179, G. FORD'S novels
— 268, Secret Bread
— 277, Tales of Dunstable Weir
— 279, Westward Ho !, Two Years Ago
— 280, R. H. KINGSLEY'S novels, passim
— 313, Henry Elizabeth
— 331, Jim Davis
— 506, Widdicombe, The Wingless Victory, A Man of Genius
— See also Dartmoor, Exmoor
Dewer Rides, 454

De Witt, Cornelius and Jan, 68, I Will Maintain
— 155, The Black Tulip
Dewpond, The, 327
Dewy Morn, The, 267
Diable boiteux, Le, 295
Diaboliques, The, 32
Diabolism, 78, The Dancing Floor
— 139, The Dice
— 244, The Private Memoirs . . . of a Fanatic
— 257, Là-Bas
— 295, Asmodeus
— 332, The Prisoner in the Opal
Dialstone Lane, 260
Diamond Necklace Case, 38, The Empress of Hearts
— 155, The Queen's Necklace
Diamond Rock, 255, His Majesty's Sloop " Diamond Rock "
Diamonds to Sit On, 258
Diana, 347
Diana Barrington, 125
Diana Mallory, 488
Diana of the Crossways, 340
Diana Please, Extraordinary Adventures of, 90
Diana Tempest, 103
Diane, 77
Diane de Poitiers, 154, Ascanio
— 155, The Two Dianas, The Page of the Duke of Savoy
— 203, The Lucky Prisoner
— 262, The Brigand
Diane de Turgis, 341
Diary, A, 71
Diary of a Freshman, 175
Diary of a Madman, The, 204
Diary of a Provincial Lady, 135
Diary of a Superfluous Man, 474
Diary of a Tutor, 435
Diary of Lady Willoughby, The, 399
Diary of Mrs. Kitty Trevelyan, 98
Diavolo al Pontelungo, Il, 22
Diaz de Bivar, Ruy, 104, The Chronicle of the Cid
Dice, The, 139
Dichter und Kauffmann, 19
Dick o' the Fens, 171
Dick Sands, 482
Dickon, 69
Dictator, The, 12
Didactic Fiction, 71-2, F. BREMER's stories
— 73, The Tenant of Wildfell Hall
— 74, The Fool of Quality
— 93, Sylvie and Bruno, and sequel
— 115, F. COPPÉE'S novels
— 119-20, Mrs. CRAIK'S novels
— 127, Miss CUMMINS's novels

Didactic Fiction (contd.) : 132, Sandford and Merton
— 160-1, Maria EDGEWORTH'S stories, passim
— 167, EWALD'S stories
— 170, Archdeacon FARRAR'S novels
— 173, Adventures of David Simple
— 197, Gesta Romanorum
— 221, If, Yes, and Perhaps
— 279, The Water-Babies
— 289, La Tour-Landry
— 300, Lynn LINTON'S novels
— 318-19, " Ian MACLAREN'S " novels, esp. Afterwards
— 348, Miss F. F. MONTRESOR'S novels
— 351, Hannah MORE'S novels
— 358, Mrs. NEEDELL'S novels
— 391, Stepping Heavenward
— 423, Dreams
— 432, John King's Question Class
— 453, Through a Needle's Eye
— 490, Susan WARNER'S novels
— 502, Miriam's Schooling
— 503, Mrs. A. D. WHITNEY'S novels
— 519, The Goldmakers Village
— See also Allegories, Girls, Stories for, Children, Stories for, Philosophical Stories, etc.
Dido, 18, Dido Queen of Hearts
Dido Queen of Hearts, 18
Dies Irae, 11
Dieux ont soif, Les, 184
Difficult People, 100
Digby Heathcote, 281
Digit of the Moon, A, 25
Dijon, 162, A Romance of Dijon
Dilemma, The, 101
Dilke, Lady, 322, The New Republic
Dingaan, 346, The Induna's Wife
Dinglefield Green, 368, Neighbours on the Green
Dinkinbar, 316
Dinmont, Dandie, 424, Guy Mannering
Dinny of the Doorstep, 395
Dinwaddie, Governor, 271, The Great Valley
Dio, 341, The Birth of the Gods
Diocletian, Emperor, 160, The Chaldean Magician
— 350, The Epicurean
— 508, Fabiola
Diplomatic Venture, A, 345
Diplomats, 297, One of Them, Tony Butler
— 323, The Royal Woman

Diplomats (contd.) : 345, A Diplomatic Venture
— See also Politics, etc.
Dipsomania, see Drink
Directory, 156, The Whites and the Blues
Dirge in Marriage, 33
Dirty Work, 261
Disaster, The, 326
Disciple, The, 67
Disciple of a Saint, The, 427
Disciple's Wife, The, 77
Discipline, 153
Discords, 162
Disenchanted, 305
Disowned, The, 308
Disraeli, Benjamin, Earl of Beaconsfield, 119, The School for Saints, and sequel
— 240, Mainwaring
D'Israeli, Isaac, 143, Vivian Grey
Dissemblers, The, 106
Dissenters, 119, The Dream and the Business
— 260, Irresolute Catherine
— 314, Paul Faber
— 366, Salem Chapel
— 367, Phœbe, Junior
— 397, Ia, Shining Ferry
— 399, Garthowen
— 440, The Minister's Guest
— 502, The Autobiography of Mark Rutherford, The Revolution in Tanner's Lane
— See also Baptists, Calvinism, Covenanters, Irvingites, Kirk, Moravians, Mormons, Quakers, Sectarianism, Shakers, Swedenborgianism, Wesleyans, etc.
Dissertations by Mr. Dooley, 157
Distaff, 414
Distinguished Provincial at Paris, A, 28
Distracted Preacher, The, 226
Ditte, 359
Diva's Ruby, The, 123
Divers Vanities, 353
Diversity of Creatures, A, 282
Diverting Adventures of Maurin, The, 4
Divided Heart, A, 241
Divine Adventure, The, 431
Divine Fire, The, 436
Divine Lady, The, 38
Divorce, 77, Mayfield
— 105, The Potter's House
— 130, Rose and Ninette
— 137, After the Divorce
— 198, The Custody of the Child
— 265, What Maisie Knew
— 279, Let Not Man Put Asunder
— 336, A Remedy against Sin
— 411, Hearts of Women
— 421, The Sin of M. Antoine

Divorce (*contd.*) : 488, Daphne
— 491, Nor Many Waters
— 499, The Custom of the Country
— 500, Glimpses of the Moon, The Children
— 509, East Lynne
— See also *Marriage*
Divorce, 67
Dix ans plus tard, 154
Djoumane, 341
Dmitri, Prince, 500, A Splendid Impostor
Dobachi, 22
Dobbin, Major, 462, Vanity Fair
Dr. Adriaan, 117
Dr. Antonio, 416
Dr. Birch and his Young Friends, 462
Doctor Breen's Practice, 250
Doctor Claude, 322
Doctor Claudius, 121
Dr. Congleton's Legacy, 270
Doctor Cupid, 75
Dr. Dumány's Wife, 272
Dr. Grenfell's Parish, 157
Doctor Grimshaw's Secret, 233
Dr. Heidegger's Experiment, 232
Dr. Jacob, 161
Dr. Jekyll and Mr. Hyde, 449
Dr. Lavendar's People, 136
Dr. Le Baron and his Daughters, 21
Doctor Luke of "The Labrador," 156
Doctor Nikola, 65
Dr. North and his Friends, 345
Doctor of Philosophy, A, 70
Doctor of the Old School, A, 318
Dr. Ox's Experiment, 482
Doctor Pascal, 518
Doctor Rameau, 365
Dr. Sevier, 86
Doctor Thorne, 471
Doctor Van Dyke, 113
Dr. Wortle's School, 473
Doctor Zay, 384
Doctor's Family, The, 366
Doctor's Lass, The, 65
Dodd Family Abroad, 296
DODGSON, Rev. C. L., see "CARROLL, Lewis"
Dodington, Bubb, 271, Chrysal
Dodo, 47
Dodo the Second, 48
Dodo Wonders, 48
Dods, Meg, 426, St. Ronan's Well
Dodsworth, 298
Dog Hervey, The, 282
Dog of Flanders, A, 372
Dog With a Bad Name, A, 402
Doge and Dogaressa, The, 244
Dogs, see *Animals*
Doings and Dealings, 35
Doll, The, 255
Dolliver Romance, The, 233

Doll's House, The, 325
Dolly, 82
Dolly Dialogues, The, 246
Dolorosa, 1
Dombey & Son, 141
Dombey Family, 141, Dombey & Son
— 270, The Gay-Dombeys
Domenico, 211
Domestic Dramas, 67
Domestic Manners of the Americans, The, 473
Domestic Servants, 46, Riceyman Steps, Elsie and the Child
— 80, A Goodly Life
— 84, Agnes Surriage
— 120, Mistress and Maid
— 126, Susan Hopley
— 323, Susannah
— 343, Lot Barrow
— 349, Esther Waters
— 374, Mrs. Murphy
— 406, Pamela
— 407, Mord Emily, Outside the Radius
— 417, Mrs. Green
— 434, Below Stairs
— 436, Mary Jane's Memoirs
— 450, Rudder Grange
— 483, Our Daily Bread
Dominion of Dreams, The, 431
Domitia, 209
Domitian, 159, Quintus Claudius
— 209, Domitia
Dommens dag, 389
Domnei, 85
Domsie, 318
Don Antonio, 211
Don des corps, Le, 415
Don Juan, 22
Don Juanes, The, 391
Don Juan's Daughters, 178
Don Orsino, 121
Don Quixote de la Mancha, 96
Don Sylvio di Rosalva, 503
Don Tarquinio, 414
Doña Luz, 480
Doña Perfecta, 382
Donal Grant, 314
Donegal, 80, The Squireen
— 91, The Passionate Hearts
— 167, A Maid of the Manse
— 218, The Old Knowledge, The Glade in the Forest
— 289, Hurrish, Grania, Book of Gilly
— 300, Where the Atlantic Meets the Land
— 315, P. MacGILL's novels
— 319, S. MacMANUS's stories
— 363, Children of the Hills, P. O'DONNELL's stories
— 402, Kilgorman
— 477, a Daughter of Kings
Doneraile Conspirators, 432, Glenaar
Donna, Una, 7
Donna Teresa, 380

Donne, Dr. John, 330, A Haunt of Ancient Peace
Donovan, 307
Doom Castle, 356
Doomed, 241
Doomed House, The, 258
Doomswoman, The, 17
Doones, 58, Lorna Doone, Slain By the Doones
Door in the Wall, The, 494
Door of the Trap, The, 10
Dop Doctor, The, 135
Dope, 414
Dopo il Divorzio, 137
Dopo il Perdone, 429
Dorastus and Fawnia, The Pleasant History of, 213
Dorchester, 71, The Brown Mask
— 226, The Mayor of Casterbridge
— See also *Dorsetshire*
Dordogne, 208, Noémi
Doris Kingsley, 401
DORLING, Commdr. H. T., see "TAFFRAIL," 459
Dormant Fires, 18
Dorothe, 7
Dorothea, 164, Middlemarch
Dorothea, 310
Dorothy Forster, 52
Dorothy Tuke, 149
Dorothy Vernon of Haddon Hall, 321
Dorrie, 466
Dorset Dear, 185
Dorsetshire, 3, "Orme AGNUS'S" stories
— 168, Moonfleet
— 225–6, HARDY's novels
— See also *Dorchester*
Dotheboys Hall, 140, Nicholas Nickleby
Double, The, 147
Double famille, Une, 27
Double Harness, 246
Double Thread, A, 181
Doubting Heart, A, 276
Doubts and Fears, 245
Doughty, Thomas, 270, Sir Mortimer
Douglas, George, 425–6, The Monastery, and sequel
"DOUGLAS, George," see BROWN, G. B.
Douglas, Sir James, 427, Castle Dangerous
Douglas, House of, 124, The Black Douglas, Maid Margaret
— 212, The Captain of the Guard
Douglass, Stephen Arnold, 332, Children of the Market Place
— 353, With Malice toward None
Dousterswivel, 425, The Antiquary
Dove in the Eagle's Nest, The, 513
Dove's Nest, The, 325
Dowdeswell, Miss, 138, Joseph Vance
Down Dartmoor Way, 385
Down in the Valley, 187

Down Our Street, 79
Down the O-hi-O, 410
Down the Sky, 306
Downfall, The, 518
Downfall of the Gods, The, 105
Downstream, 438
Doxie Dent, 2
Doyle's Rock, 454
Dracula, 451
Dragon in Shallow Waters, The, 419
Dragon Painter, The, 312
Dragonnades, 262, The Huguenot
Drake, Sir Francis, 26, By Stroke of Sword
— 35, Drake and his Yeomen
— 270, Sir Mortimer
Drake and his Yeomen, 35
Dram Shop, The, 517
Drama in Muslin, A, 349
Drama in Sunshine, A, 479
Drame au bord de la mer, Une, 30
Drames de famille, 67
Draught of the Blue, A, 25
Draytons and the Davenants, The, 98
Dreadful Dragon of Hay Hill, The, 42
Dream, The, 518
Dream and the Business, The, 119
Dream Charlotte, The, 162
Dream Children, 178
Dream Days, 210
Dream-Detective, The, 414
Dream-Fox Story Book, The, 512
Dream Life and Real Life, 423
Dream Numbers, 473
Dream of a Queer Fellow, The, 146
Dream of a Woman, The, 209
Dream of Fair Women, The, 507
Dream of John Ball, The, 352
Dream of Provence, A, 493
Dream of Rhonabwy, The, 217
Dream of the Red Chamber, The, 474
Dream Ship, The, 450
Dream Tales, 475
Dream Woman, The, 109
Dreamer of Dreams, A, 252
Dreamers, 223
Dreamers of the Ghetto, 515
Dreamer's Tales, 157
Dreams, 423
Dreams of Chang, The, 80
Dreams of Simon Usher, The, 200
Dreary Story, A, 100
Dred, 452
Drei Getreuen, Die, 187
Drender's Daughter, 459
Dresden, 24, The Gamesters
Dreyfus Case, 157, Mr. Dooley in Peace and War

Dreyfus Case (contd.): 183–4, The Elm-Tree on the Mall, etc., Penguin Island
— 393, PROUST'S later novels
— 519, Truth
D'ri and I, 23
Drift from Redwood Camp, A, 230
Drink, 17, A Daughter of the Vine, The Gorgeous Isle
— 51, The House in Demetrius Road, The Monkey Puzzle
— 61, The Fruit of the Vine
— 88, For Three Moons
— 92, Art Maguire
— 97, The Fighting Chance
— 102, The Flying Inn
— 122, Katherine Lauderdale, and sequel
— 164, Janet's Repentance
— 248, Time, Gentlemen ! Time !
— 250, Annie Kilburn
— 274, Margaret
— 303, John Barleycorn
— 336, To What Green Altar ?
— 379, The Darlingtons
— 395, The Heritage
— 409, The Long Lane's Turning
— 447, Wine on the Lees
— 508, A Name to Conjure With
— 509, Danesbury House
— 517, The Dram Shop
— See also *Absinthe Drinking, Bootleggers, Gangsters*
Dritter hof Links, 54
Driven, 491
Drogheda, Massacre of, 103, John Marmaduke
Droll Peter, 466
Dromina, 21
Drone and a Dreamer, A, 301
Dropped from the Clouds, 482
Drottningar i Kungahälla, 286
Drove Road, The, 153
Drover's Wife, The, 292
Drugs, 241, Felix
— 414, Dope
— See also *Drink*
Druidism, 91, Children of the Dawn
— 431, The Sin Eater
— See also *Celtic Romance*
Drumcondra, Dean of, 296, Roland Cashel
Drummer's Coat, The, 180
Drums, 69
Drums of Aulone, The, 97
Drumsheugh, 318, " Ian MACLAREN'S " novels
Drumtochty, 318, " Ian MACLAREN'S " novels
Dryden, John, 206, White Aprons
Du Barry, Mme, 155, Memoirs of a Physician
— 156, The Woman with the Velvet Necklace

Du Barry, Mme (contd.): 262, Castelnau
Du côté de chez Swann, 393
Du Guesclin, Bertrand, 133, Bertrand of Brittany
— 149, The White Company
— 155, Agenor de Mauléon
— 292, Brakespeare
Dual Personality, 45, Buried Alive
— 50, Lazare
— 136, The Return
— 241, Flames
— 256, Richard Greenhow
— 312, Keeping up Appearances
— 388, Late Mattia Pascal
— 449, Dr. Jekyll and Mr. Hyde
Dublin, 84, Hangman's House
— 118, A Flock of Birds
— 243, The King's Deputy
— 273, JOYCE's works
— 296–7, LEVER's novels, *passim*
— 319, Fancy O'Brien
— 355, Nanno, Tragedy of Chris
— 364, The Informer, Mr. Gilhooley
— 370–1, Adam of Dublin, and sequel
Dubliners, 273
Duchenier, 358
Duchess Laura, 44
Duchess of Langeais, The, 28
Duchess of Nona, The, 239
Duchess of Wrexe, The, 486
Duchess Veronica, The, 473
Duchesse bleue, La, 67
DUDEVANT, Baronne, see " SAND, G.," 420
Dudley, Robert, Earl of, 91, Where England sets her Feet
Dudley and Gilderoy, 59
Duel, The (by CHEKHOV), 100
Duel, The (by CONRAD), 111
Duel, The (by KUPRIN), 285
Duel, The (by SIENKIEWICZ), 435
Duelling, 77, A Gentleman of the South
— 285, The Duel
— 519, The Honour of the Army
— See also *Feuds, Holmgang, Vendettas*
Dufferin, Lord, 488, Eleanor
Duke, The, 106
Duke Carl of Rosenmold, 377
Duke of Britain, A, 335
Duke's Children, The, 473
Duke's Page, The, 105
Duke's Servants, 81
Duke's Vengeance, The, 275
Dukesborough Tales, 271
Dule Tree of Cassilis, The, 411
Dumb-Animal, 438
Dumb Foxglove, 439
Dumb Love, 93
Dumbello, Lady, 471, The Small House at Allington

Dumfries, 124, The Cherry Riband
— 316, R. W. MACKENNA's novels
Dun, The, 160, 161
Duncannon, 349, The Untilled Field
Dundee, Viscount, see *Graham of Claverhouse*
Dundonald, Earl of, 328, Frank Mildmay
Dunfermline, 288, A Monk of Fife
Dunferry Risin', The, 350
Dunham, Mabel, 114, The Pathfinder
DUNKERLEY, W. A., see " OXENHAM, J.," 372
Dunleary, 149
Dunnottar Castle, 7, Balmoral
Dunstan, Saint, 120, Edwy the Fair
Dunsterville, Maj.-Gen. L. C., 282, Stalkey & Co.
Duplessis, Cardinal, 68, Yesterdays
Durand, Alice, see " GRÉVILLE, Henri," 215
Durch Nacht zum Licht, 444
Durket Sperret, The, 165
Durtal, 257, En Route, and sequels
Dusantes, The, 451
Dust (by BJÖRNSON), 56
Dust (by HAWTHORNE), 232
Dust from the Loom, 360
Dutch in the Medway, The, 315
DUTCH NOVELISTS :
Jo van AMMERS-KÜLLER, H. CONSCIENCE, L. M. A. COUPERUS, F. W. van EEDEN, J. FABRICIUS, " M. MAARTENS," I. QUERIDO, H. J. SCHIMMEL, " S. STREUVELS," F. TIMMERMANS, S. ULFERS, " A. S. C. WALLIS "
Dutch People, 36, The Bow of Orange Ribbon, and sequel, Was it Right to Forgive ?, The Belle of Bowling Green, etc.
— 43, Antonia
— 77, Van Zanten's Happy Days
— 186, In the Valley
— 219, Lysbeth
— 223, The MS. in the Red Box
— 249, Anna HOWARTH's novels
— 258, A History of New York, Rip Van Winkle
— 288, Kitwyk
— 315, The Dutch in the Medway
— 351, The Affair on the Bridge
— 378, The Dutchman's Fireside
— 401, Free to Serve
— See also DUTCH NOVELISTS, *New York, Colonial*

Dutchman's Fireside, The, 378
Duval, Claude, 412, Whitefriars
Dwelling-Place of Light, The, 104
Dynamiter, The, 450
Dyrendal, 64

" E., A.," see RUSSELL, G. W.
Eagle's Heart, The, 192
Eagle's Nest, The, 311
Eagle's Talon, The, 365
Eames, Johnny, 471, The Small House at Allington
Earlforward, Mr., 46, Riceyman Steps
Early Autumn, 72
Early English Prose Romances, 465
Early History of Jacob Stahl, The, 50
Early Hours, The, 387
Early Lessons, 160
Early Life and Adventures of Sylvia Scarlett, 317
Early Sorrow, 324
Early Victorian, 222
Earth and the Fulness Thereof, The, 416
Earth-Mother, The, 410
Earthen Drum, The, 448
Earth's Enigmas, 409
East and West, 221
East Angels, 511
East Anglia, 323–4, Mrs. MANN's novels
— 344, Second Marriage
— 491, Aylwin
— See also *Essex, Fen Country, Norfolk, Suffolk*, and towns
East End Idylls, 3
East India Company, 215, In Furthest Ind
— See also *India*
East Lynne, 509
East of Suez, 382
East Wind, West Wind, 79
Easter Eve, 284
Eastern Empire, 170, Gathering Clouds
— See also *Byzantium, Constantinople*
Eastloom, 478
Eat, Drink, and be Merry, 307
Eatin' Crow, 228
Eaton, Mrs. J. H., see O'Neill, Margaret
Ebb Tide, The, 450
Ebbing of the Tide, The, 41
Eben Holden, 23
Eccentricities of Cardinal Pirelli, 175
Echo of Passion, An, 289
École des femmes, L', 198
Ecstasy, 117
Ecuador, 484, An Interrupted Friendship
Eddas, see *Icelandic Sagas*
Eddy and Édouard, 256
Eddy on the Floor, An, 90

Edelweiss, 19

Edgar, King, 253, Dead Man's Plack

Edgar, Prince, 120, Edwy the Fair

Edgar Huntly, 76

Edge of Circumstance, The, 360

Edge of Empire, The, 457

Edina, 510

Edinburgh, 94, The Black Office

— 124, Cleg Kelly, The Standard Bearer

— 233, The Right Stuff

— 288, Nancy Stair

— 348, Major Weir

— 424, Waverley, Guy Mannering

— 425, The Heart of Midlothian

— 425-6, The Monastery, The Abbot

— 449, Weir of Hermiston

— 470, "G. TRAVERS'" novels

Edison, Sir Thomas, 146, The 42nd Parallel

Editha's Burglar, 82

Edmund, King of East Anglia, 25, The King's Passion

Edmund Ironside, 120, Alfgar the Dane

— 299, The Ward of King Canute

Education, 19, The Country House on the Rhine

— 40, The Redeemer

— 132, Sandford and Merton

— 135, Humbug

— 166, The Brothers Rantzau

— 258, A Simple Story

— 347, Misunderstood

— 350, Zeluco

— 416, The New Heloïse

— 495, Joan and Peter, The Undying Fire

— 507, Dandelion Days, and sequels

— See also *College Life, Gentleman, Ideal, School Life, Schoolmasters, University Life*

Education of Orientals, 305, Disenchanted

— 421, The Prince of Destiny

Education of Savages, 105, Sally, Saleh

— 484, L'Ingénu

Education of Uncle Paul, The, 59

Éducation Sentimentale, L', 175

Edward I, 262, Forest Days

Edward II, 4, The Days of Bruce

— 53, In the Shadow of the Crown

— 404, The Whistling Maid

Edward III, 53, In the Shadow of the Crown

— 60, The Glory and Sorrow of Norwich

Edward III (contd.): 239, New Canterbury Tales

— 513, The Lances of Lynwood

— See also *Hundred Years' War*

Edward IV, 25, The Merchant Prince

— 60, The Glory and Sorrow of Norwich

— 309, The Last of the Barons

— See also *Roses, Wars of the*

Edward VI, 5, The Constable of the Tower

— 324, The Colloquies of Edward Osborne

— 476, The Prince and the Pauper

Edward Barry, South Sea Pearler, 41

Edwardians, The, 419

Edwin, King of Northumberland, 165, Fated to Win

Edwy, King, 120, Edwy the Fair

Edwy the Fair, 120

Een daag, 56

Egdon Heath, 225, The Return of the Native

Egil Skallagrimsson, 163, Egil's Saga

Egil's Saga, 163

Eglamore Portraits, The, 323

Eglantina, 506

Egoism, 15, Vera

— 63, Life

— 75, Mamma

— 106, Paul Ferroll, and sequel

— 127, Wheat and Tares

— 135, Zella, The Heel of Achilles

— 146, The Friend of the Family, The Insulted and Injured

— 147, Crime and Punishment, The Possessed

— 302, Jaffery, The Great Pandolfo

— 339, Richard Feverel

— 340, The Egoist

— 442, Broke of Covenden

— 492, Precious Bane

— 504, Dorian Gray

Egoist, The, 340

Egy magyar nábob, 271

Egypt, Ancient and Mediæval, 23, On the Forgotten Road

— 42, The Lost Mameluke

— 109, Hypnerotomachia

— 117, The Tour

— 158, EBERS' novels

— 195, The Romance of a Mummy

— 203, Pharaoh and the Priest

— 219, Cleopatra

— 220, Moon of Israel, The Ancient Allan, Queen of the Dawn

— 221, The World's Desire

— 235, Theagenes and Chariclea

Egypt, Ancient and Mediæval (contd.): 279, Hypathia

— 337, Sarchedon

— 341, Akhnaton

— 350, The Epicurean

— 382, Sancta Paula

— 423, A Priestess of Isis

— 486, The King's Treasure House

— See also names of Rulers

Egypt, Modern, 1, The Fellah

— 150, The Tragedy of the Korosko, The Green Flag

— 156, The Whites and the Blues

— 242, Bella Donna

— 375, Hermann Agha

— 376, The Weavers

— 439, The Curse of the Nile

— See also *Alexandria, Baggaras, Nile, Sudan,* etc.

Egyptian Princess, An, 158

Eight Cousins, 6

Eight Days, 179

Eighteen Tales, 117

Eighth Crusade, The, 156

Eighty-three Tales from Sacchetti, 418

Einer Mütter Sohn, 483

Eirikr Saga, 240, Gudrid the Fair

Eiserne Jahr, Das, 62

Ekkehard, 422

El Ombú, 252

Elaine, 166, Galahad

Elba, 60, Grantley Fenton

Elder Brother, The, 268

Elder Conklin, 228

Elder Sister, The, 458

ELDERSHAW, Flora S. P., see "ELDERSHAW, M. B."

Eldest Son, The, 329

Eldorado, 370

Eldridge, Miss, 138, It Never Can Happen Again

Eleanor, Queen, 38, The Gallants

Eleanor, Queen, wife of Henry II, 53, Westminster Cloisters

Eleanor, 488

Eleanor Dayton, 447

Eleanor of Aquitaine, 122, Via Crucis

Eleanor of Poitou, 127, The Love Story of Giraldus

Eleanor's Victory, 70

Eleazar, 11

Elections, 43, Mr. Clutterbuck's Election

— 140, Pickwick Papers

— 149, The Merchant of Killogue

— 186, Seth's Brother's Wife

— 340, Beauchamp's Career

— 378, Melincourt

Electricity, Gospel, 115-16, Marie CORELLI's novels

Elena, 489

Elephant's Child, The, 282

Élève Gilles, L', 286

Eleventh Commandment, The, 38

Elfrida of Mercia, 253, Dead Man's Plack

Elfwald II, King of Northumbria, 108, The Likeness of King Elfwald

Elfwin, 512

Elgiva, Queen, 120, Edwy the Fair

Eli of the Downs, 379

Eline Vere, 117

Elinor and Marianne, 20

Elinor Colthouse, 252

Eliot, George, 177, O Genteel Lady

Eliot, Sir John, 466, Sir Bevil

Eli's Daughter, 379

Elissa, 219

Elixir de longue vie, L', 30

Elixir of Life, see Immortality

Elixir of Life, The, 30

Eliza, 374

Eliza Getting On, 374

Eliza's Husband, 374

Elizabeth Queen, 24, The Master of Grey, The Lonely Queen, The Sea-Captain

— 25, Bonaventure

— 33, Argenis

— 49, By What Authority? The Queen's Tragedy, Come Rack, Come Rope!

— 69, The Spae-Wife

— 74, My Lord of Essex

— 91, Historical Vignettes

— 105, The Duke's Page

— 109, The Queen's Hostage

— 270, Sir Mortimer

— 313, Henry Elizabeth, The Wounds of a Friend

— 333, One Queen Triumphant, The Royal Sisters

— 426, Kenilworth

— 442, The Great Age

Elizabeth of Baden, (wife of Alexander I), 93, By Neva's Waters

Elizabeth Stuart, Queen of Bohemia, 262, Heidelberg

— 234, The Winter Queen

— 330, The Young Queen of Hearts

Elizabeth, Princess (daughter of Charles I), 330, The White King's Daughter

Elizabeth and her German Garden, 14

Elizabeth Visits America, 203

Elizabethan Romances, 23, The Famous Historie of Fryer Bacon

— 33, Argenis

— See also Greene, Nash, Lyly, Sidney, etc.

Ella non rispose, 429

Ellen Linn, 1

Ellénore, 112, Adolphe
Elliot, Ann, 20, Persuasion
Ellwood Family, 243, Demi-Royal
Elm-Tree on the Mall, The, 183
Elmer Gantry, 298
Elmslie's Drag-Net, 452
Elshander, Saunders, 131, The Pilgrimage of Strongsoul
Elsie and the Child, 46
Elsie Venner, 245
Elsket, 373
Eltham, 53, In the Shadow of the Crown
— 222, Early Victorian
Eltham House, 489
Elton, Mrs., 20, Emma
Elusive Pimpernel, The, 370
Elves, The, 93
Ely, 88, Path and Goal
— 208, Cheap-Jack Zita
— 314, The Camp of Refuge
— See also *Fen Country*
Emancipated, The, 200
Emancipation, see *Slavery*
Emancipation Act, 296, The Martins of Cro' Martin
Emancipation of Women, see *Feminism*
Emanuel, Paul, 73, Villette
Embezzlors, The, 274
Embuscades de la vie, Les, 105
Emerald Uthwart, 377
Emerson, 77, The Father
— 177, O Genteel Lady
Emigrant Ships, 164, " Act of God "
Emigrant, The, 146
Emigrants, The, 64
Emigrants of Ahadarra, The, 92
Emigrants to America, 16, The Jew
— 64, The Emigrants
— 86, The Rise of David Levinsky
— 90, Red Rust, Heirs
— 94, O Pioneers !, My Ántonia
— 415, Giants in the Earth, and sequel
— 419, The Viking Heart
— 435, In the New Promised Land
— 439, Fourscore
Émigré, L', 67
Emilie de Coulanges, 161
Emily Montague, 74
Emma, 20
Emmanuel, 389
Emmanuel Burden, 43
Emmeline, 440
Emmet, Robert, 63, True Man and Traitor
— 199, The Island of Sorrow
— 218, Robert Emmet
Emmy Lou, 330
Emotions of Polydore Marasquin, 209
Emperor, The, 158
Emperor of Portugallia, 287

Empire Builders, 308
Employés, Les, 28
Empreinte, L', 273
Empress Might-Have-Been, 18
Empress Octavia, 486
Empress of Hearts, The, 38
Empty House, The, 59
En diktares bazar, 72
En herrgårdssägen, 286
En Route, 257
Encantadas, The, 338
Enchanted Garden, The, 480
Enchantments, see CELTIC ROMANCE, *Magic, Witchcraft,* etc.
Enchantress, The, 395
Encore, An, 136
End of Evil Ways, The, 28
End of the Fianna, 214
End of the House of Alard, The, 276
End of the Road, The, 78
End of the Sermon, The, 432
End of the Tether, The, 110
Endicott and the Red Cross, 232
Endymion, 144
Endymion in Barracks, 94
Enemies, 100
Enemy to the King, An, 446
Enfant à la balustrade, L', 69
Enfant maudit, L', 30
Enfer, L', 32
Enghien, Duc d', 365, The Eagle's Talon
England, 157
England hath need of Thee, 216
England, My England, 291
English at the North Pole, The, 482
English Captain, The, 454
English Episodes, 492
English Family, An, 42
English Girl, An, 178
English Miss, The, 354
ENGLISH NOVELISTS:
Rev. E. A. ABBOTT, " John ACKWORTH," A. St. J. ADCOCK, Rev. J. G. ADDERLEY, Joseph ADDISON, J. E. AGATE, " Orme AGNUS," Grace AGUILAR, W. H. AINSWORTH, E. M. ALBANESI, Richard ALDINGTON, T. AMORY, A. J. ANDERSON, " F. ANSTEY," W. M. ARDAGH, Michael ARLEN, M. D. ARMSTRONG, Gräfin von ARNIM, Mrs. J. O. ARNOLD, Matthew ARNOLD, W. D. ARNOLD, F. ARTHUR, Daisy ASHFORD, Helen ASHTON, Mrs. Alice and C. ASKEW, G. M. ATTENBOROUGH, Stacy AUMONIER, Jane AUSTEN, Alfred AUSTIN, F. AVELING, " John AYSCOUGH."

ENGLISH NOVELISTS (*contd.*):
Francis BACON, Baron Verulam, H. BAERLEIN, R. BAGE, R. BAGOT, H. C. BAILEY, M. BAILLIE SAUNDERS, F. W. BAIN, Amy J. BAKER, G. P. BAKER, James BAKER, R. M. BALLENTYNE, G. N. BANKES, Mrs. G. L. BANKS, John BARCLAY, M. BARING, B. H. BARMBY, " John BARNETT," Michael BARRINGTON, Vernon BARTLETT, " George BARTRAM," Aubrey BEARDSLEY, Mary BEAUMONT, W. BECKFORD, D. M. BEDDOE, Max BEERBOHM, Mrs. BEHN, Lady BELL, R. S. W. BELL, Hilaire BELLOC, Mrs. BELLOC-LOWNDES, Arnold BENNETT, A. C. BENSON, E. F. BENSON, Mgr. R. H. BENSON, Stella BENSON, Wilfred BENSON, E. C. BENTLEY, P. E. BENTLEY, J. D. BERESFORD, A. BERTRAM, Sir Walter BESANT, Tom BEVAN, Mary BIDDER, Harold BINDLOSS, Otwell BINNS, D. BLACKBURN, R. D. BLACKMORE, A. BLACKWOOD, M. M. BLAKE, Mrs. E. N. BLAND, R. BLATCHFORD, J. E. BLOUNDELLE - BURTON, Florence BONE, G. H. BONE, E. C. BOOTH, G. N. BOOTHBY, George BORROW, " George BOURNE," " M. BOWEN," M. E. BRADDON, Rev. E. BRADLEY, " E. BRAMAH," Anna BRAY, A. BREBNER, P. J. BREBNER, F. BRETON, E. V. BRITON, Rev. C. H. BROMBY, Anne BRONTË, Charlotte BRONTË, Emily BRONTË, Emma F. BROOKE, Mrs. Frances BROOKE, Mrs. C. BROOKFIELD, D. K. BROSTER, Rhoda BROUGHTON, Alec BROWN, Vincent BROWN, H. A. BRYDEN, " J. E. BUCKROSE," F. T. BULLEN, G. W. BULLETT, John BUNYAN, S. H. BURCHELL, Thomas BURKE, Sir F. C. BURNAND, Fanny BURNEY, C. H. BUTCHER, Samuel BUTLER.

O. V. CAINE, Sir T. Hall CAINE, W. E. CAIRNES, Frances CAMPBELL, Gilbert CANNAN, Bernard CAPES, R. N. CAREY, Wymond CAREY, J. R. CARLING, Mrs. A. C. CARR, M. E. CARR, F.

ENGLISH NOVELISTS (*contd.*):
CARRELL, " Lewis CARROLL," Agnes and Egerton CASTLE, Capt. F. CHAMIER, Elizabeth CHARLES, R. CHARLTON, Beatrice CHASE, Sir G. T. CHESNEY, G. K. CHESTERTON, Mary CHOLMONDELEY, Agatha CHRISTIE, Rev. A. J. CHURCH, " Austin CLARE," Mrs. H. CLARKE, Isabel CLARKE, " Lucas CLEEVE," Sir Hugh CLIFFORD, Mrs. W. K. CLIFFORD, Mrs. Archer CLIVE, J. S. CLOUSTON, J. F. COBB, Thomas COBB, Richard COBBOLD, H. COCKTON, Desmond COKE, Sophie COLE, Christabel R. COLERIDGE, Hon. G. J. D. COLERIDGE, M. E. COLERIDGE, W. G. COLLINGWOOD, W. E. W. COLLINS, Wilkie COLLINS, H. E. COMPTON, A. R. CONDER, William CONGREVE, Joseph CONRAD, " Hugh CONWAY," M. B. COOKE, E. H. COOPER, A. E. COPPARD, Marie CORELLI, L. Cope CORNFORD, A. L. COTTON, John COURNOS, H. M. CRACKANTHORPE, Mrs. CRAIK, Rev. A. D. CRAKE, Sibyl CREED, C. M. CRESSWELL, A. S. CRIPPS, F. Wills CROFTS, Catherine CROWE, Dr. P. CROWTHER, Ridgewell CULLUM, G. CUMBERLAND, Sir H. S. CUNNINGHAM, Alice CUNNINGHAME, " Paul CUSHING."

T. DALIN, Moray DALTON, E. M. Smith DAMPIER, Clemence DANE, Joan DANE, " Edith DART," Sir G. W. DASENT, John DAVIS, A. J. DAWSON, C. W. DAWSON, Susanne R. DAY, Thomas DAY, Mrs. DEARMER, Mrs. P. DE CRESPIGNY, G. Warwick DEEPING, D. DEFOE, " Richard DEHAN," " E. M. DELAFIELD," Walter DE LA MARE, Mrs. DE LA PASTURE, T. DELONEY, William DE MORGAN, Charlotte DEMPSTER, Geoffrey P. DENNIS, T. DE QUINCEY, Hugh DE SELINCOURT, Blanche DEVEREUX, Charles DICKENS, Mary Angela DICKENS, A. DICKESON, G. Lowes DICKINSON, H. N. DICKINSON, Benjamin DISRAELI, Maud DIVER, Ella N. Hep-

ENGLISH NOVELISTS (contd.): worth DIXON, Catherine DODD, "Theo DOUGLAS," Mrs. M. M. DOWIE, H. B. DRAKE, J. H. DRIBERG, H. DRUMMOND, Major W. P. DRURY, Mrs. DUDENEY, George DU MAURIER, Lord DUNSANY, Sir H. M. DURAND, W. S. DURRANT.

W. J. ECCOTT, Hon. Emily EDEN, J. G. EDGAR, Amelia EDWARDES, Rev. T. EDWARDES, Matilda M. Betham EDWARDS, "George EGERTON," "George ELIOT," R. ELLIOTT, Beth ELLIS, Havelock ELLIS, Miss H. ELRINGTON, Dr. P. H. EMERSON, R. EUSTACE, C. S. EVANS, W. H. G. EWART, Mrs. EWING.

"Michael FAIRLESS," J. M. FALKNER, B. L. FARJEON, Eleanor FARJEON, Jeffery FARNOL, Archdeacon FARRAR, Margaret FARRINGTON, Allan FEA, G. M. FENN, H. FIELDING, Sarah FIELDING, Ronald FIRBANK, Sir J. P. FITZPATRICK, James Elroy FLECKER, J. S. FLETCHER, Lady H. E. FORBES, Ford Madox FORD, George FORD, C. S. FORESTER, C. E. FORREST, R. E. FORREST, E. M. FORSTER, R. H. FORSTER, Sir J. W. FORTESCUE, C. and F. FOSTER, Jessie FOTHERGILL, Ellen T. FOWLER, Marion Fox, Gilbert FRANKAU, Mrs. Hugh FRASER, Ronald FRASER, R. W. FRASER, H. W. FREEMAN, R. A. FREEMAN, Henry FRITH, J. A. FROUDE, D. K. FULTON.

Tom GALLON, John GALSWORTHY, E. G. GARDNER, David GARNETT, Olive GARNETT, Richard GARNETT, Mrs. R. S. GARNETT, Crosbie GARSTIN, Lady C. M. GASKELL, Mrs. GASKELL, P. F. GAYE, W. L. GEORGE, Dorothea GERARD, "Morice GERARD," Wiliam GERHARDI, Perceval GIBBON, A. H. GIBBS, Sir P. GIBBS, L. E. GIELGUD, Val GIELGUD, E. GIFFORD, R. Y. GILBERT, R. M. GILCHRIST, A. H. GILKES, Rev. E. GILLIAT, Capt. C. J. L. GILSON,

ENGLISH NOVELISTS (contd.): Algernon GISSING, George GISSING, Rev. G. R. GLEIG, Elinor GLYN, William GODWIN, Louis GOLDING, Samuel GORDON, Sir E. GOSSE, G. W. GOUGH, Nat GOULD, Rev. S. Baring GOULD, J. W. GRAHAM, S. GRAHAM, Kenneth GRAHAME, Richard GRAVES, Robert GRAVES, "Maxwell GRAY, E. Everett GREEN, Grahame GREENE, Robert GREENE, Sir W. T. GRENFELL, "S. C. GRIER," E. A. GRIFFIN, Major GRIFFITHS, W. E. GROGAN, Francis Hindes GROOME, C. R. GULL.

Sir H. R. HAGGARD, Miss E. B. HALL, H. F. HALL, Marie HALL, Radclyffe HALL, "John HALSHAM," B. HAMILTON, Rev. J. A. HAMILTON, Lillias HAMILTON, Margaret HAMILTON, Patrick HAMILTON, Major-General W. G. HAMLEY, Col. A. F. P. HARCOURT, Thomas HARDY, Mrs. HARKER, Beatrice HARRADEN, James HARRINGTON, Frank HARRIS, J. H. HARRIS, F. HARRISON, M. HARTLEY, J. HATTON, Marie E. HAWKER, V. HAWTREY, "Ian Hay," E. G. HAYDEN, F. W. HAYES, Richard HEAD, Adrian HEARD, E. F. HEDDLE, Rev. W. HENDERSON, G. A. HENTY, A. P. HERBERT, Maurice HEWLETT, William HEWLETT, Robert HICHENS, "Headon HILL," "Ashton HILLIERS," Rev. E. N. HOARE, Rev. Joseph HOCKING, W. B. HOCKLEY, J. L. HODSON, Thomas HOLCROFT, Ethel HOLDSWORTH, Constance HOLME, Hon. A. N. Hood, Theodore HOOK, Anthony HOPE, Miss J. G. HOPE, Thomas HOPE, Tighe HOPKINS, Norah HOULT, Clemence HOUSMAN, Laurence HOUSMAN, Edward HOWARD, "Stephen HUDSON," W. H. HUDSON, Oliver Madox HUEFFER, Richard HUGHES, Rupert HUGHES, Thomas HUGHES, Margaret HUNGERFORD, Leigh HUNT, Violet HUNT, Sir William HUNTER, Eyre HUSSEY, A. S. M. HUTCHINSON, H. G. HUTCHINSON, Ed-

ENGLISH NOVELISTS (contd.): ward HUTTON, Aldous HUXLEY, C. J. Cutcliffe HYNE.

Mrs. INCHBALD, Margaret IRWIN, L. P. JACKS, W. W. JACOBS, G. P. R. JAMES, M. R. JAMES, Alice JEANS, Richard JEFFERIES, Walter JEFFERY, H. G. JENKINS, J. E. JENKINS, Edgar JEPSON, Jerome K. JEROME, Douglas JERROLD, F. Tennyson JESSE, Richard JOHNSON, Samuel JOHNSON, Sir Harry JOHNSTON, Charles JOHNSTONE, E. Brandram JONES, E. B. C. JONES, M. W. KAYE, Sheila KAYE-SMITH, C. F. KEARY, E. KEITH, Bart KENNEDY, Margaret KENNEDY, R. M. KETTLE, Miss KIMMINS, Maude Egerton KING, Charles KINGSLEY, Henry KINGSLEY, W. H. G. KINGSTON, Rudyard KIPLING, C. H. B. KITCHIN, Emily KNIPE.

Mrs. R. S. LAFFAN, L. E. LANDON, W. S. LANDOR, John LANG, C. E. LAWRENCE, D. H. LAWRENCE, G. A. LAWRENCE, Eric LEADBITTER, "John LE BRETON," C. J. LEE, E. LEE-HAMILTON, Richard LE GALLIENNE, Rosamund LEHMANN, Charlotte LENNOX, J. P. LE POER, Amy LEVY, Arthur LEWIS, D. B. Wyndham LEWIS, M. G. LEWIS, W. S. LILLY, "Harry LINDSAY," Mary LINSKILL, Mrs. Lynn LINTON, W. J. LOCKE, Thomas LODGE, Norma LORIMER, Rupert LORRAINE, H. D. LOWRY, Basil LUBBOCK, E. V. LUCAS, F. L. LUCAS, R. J. LUCAS, Arnold LUNN, "Edna LYALL," John LYLY, Bohun LYNCH, Sylvia LYND, A. Neil LYONS, E. G. E. Bulwer LYTTON.

Rose MACAULAY, D. G. McCHESNEY, C. MACFARLANE, Arthur MACHEN, Denis MACKAIL, Stephen McKENNA, M. K. MACMILLAN, Sir G. F. MACMUNN, Shaw MacNICHOLL, Mrs. Fuller MAITLAND, Lucas MALET, W. H. MALLOCK, Sir Thomas MALORY, F. O. MANN, Mary E. MANN, Anne

ENGLISH NOVELISTS (contd.): MANNING, Frederic MANNING, "Katherine MANSFIELD," C. MARRIAGE, C. MARRIOTT, Capt. MARRYAT, Archibald MARSHALL, Emma MARSHALL, A. D. MARTIN, Mrs. H. MARTIN, Harriet MARTINEAU, John MASEFIELD, A. E. W. MASON, J. M. MATHER, Helen MATHERS, H. N. MAUGHAM, W. Somerset MAUGHAM, W. B. MAXWELL, E. C. MAYNE, W. S. MAYO, N. G. M. MEAKIN, G. J. Whyte MELVILLE, George MEREDITH, Leonard MERRICK, "H. S. MERRIMAN," Viola MEYNELL, Thomas MILLER, Hope MIRRLEES, Naomi MITCHISON, Mary R. MITFORD, Allan MONKHOUSE, C. E. MONTAGUE, Florence MONTGOMERY, F. F. MONTRESOR, F. W. MOORMAN, Elinor MORDAUNT, Hannah MORE, Sir Thomas MORE, Charles MORGAN, Lady Sydney MORGAN, J. J. MORIER, William MORRIS, Arthur MORRISON, Geoffrey MOSS, R. H. MOTTRAM, Thomas MOULT, H. H. MUNRO, D. C. MURRAY, J. M. MURRY, L. H. MYERS.

Thomas NASHE, Rev. J. M. NEALE, Mrs. J. H. NEEDELL, B. P. NEUMANN, H. NEVINSON, Sir Henry NEWBOLT, Cardinal NEWMAN, H. W. C. NEWTE, Beverley NICHOLS, Edward NOBLE, W. E. NORRIS, A. H. NORWAY, George NORWAY, Alfred NOYES, Anne C. OGLE, Ernest OLDMEADOW, Laurence OLIPHANT, A. OLLIVANT, Carola OMAN, Oliver ONIONS, Amelia OPIE, E. P. OPPENHEIM, Baroness ORCZY, "OUIDA," G. OVERTON, John OWEN, "John OXENHAM."

Violet PAGET, Barry PAIN, W. PAINTER, W. G. PALGRAVE, Robert PALTOCK, Eric PARKER, Major G. PARRY, Walter PATER, A. H. PATERSON, J. E. PATTERSON, J. B. PATTON, James PAYN, T. L. PEACOCK, C. M. A. PEAKE, J. H. PEARCE, M. F. M. PEARD, Howard PEASE, Sir Max PEMBERTON, F. E. PENNY, Dolly PENTREATH, Alice PER-

ENGLISH NOVELISTS (*contd.*):
RIN, W. C. PERRY, George PETTIE, Eden PHILLPOTTS, M. W. PICKTHALL, W. PILLING, Anna PORTER, L. PORTMAN, T. F. POWYS, E. F. POYNTER, H. F. M. PRESCOTT, E. C. PRICE, J. B. PRIESTLEY, V. S. PRITCHETT, R. O. PROWSE, E. W. PUGH, Sir A. T. QUILLER-COUCH.

Anne RADCLIFFE, A. RANSOME, Hannah RATHBONE, M. S. RAWSON, Ernest RAYMOND, Walter RAYMOND, Lorna REA, Charles READE, T. B. REED, Clara REEVE, V. H. RENDALL, Mrs. Baillie REYNOLDS, Dorothy RICHARDSON, Samuel RICHARDSON, Emily RICHINGS, Grace RICHMOND, Lady L. RIDDING, W. Pett RIDGE, Lady A. RIDLEY, W. RILEY, Mrs. D. G. RITCHIE, Margaret ROBERTS, Morley ROBERTS, Frances F. ROBERTSON, Agnes ROBINSON, Emma ROBINSON, F. W. ROBINSON, Maude ROBINSON, J. RODWAY, G. H. B. RODWELL, "Sax ROHMER," Frederick ROLFE, C. ROOK, A. R. ROPES, Sir Ronald Ross, John RUSSELL, W. C. RUSSELL, Owen RUTTER, "Mark RYCE," E. E. RYND.

Victoria SACKVILLE-WEST, M. SADLEIR, "Allan St. AUBYN," "W. St. CLAIR," J. SAUNDERS, E. W. SAVI, Mrs. C. A. Dawson SCOTT, Owen SEAMAN, Edith SEELEY, D. SENIOR, "Graham SETON," Beatrice Kean SEYMOUR, Mary Wollstonecraft SHELLEY, A. T. SHEPPARD, Elizabeth S. SHEPPARD, Mrs. Frances SHERIDAN, R. C. SHERRIFF, M. P. SHIEL, J. H. SHORTHOUSE, Cecily SIDGWICK, Ethel SIDGWICK, Sir Philip SIDNEY, Una SILBERRAD, J. G. SIME, G. R. SIMS, May SINCLAIR, Osbert SITWELL, Mrs. SKRINE, Douglas SLADEN, F. E. SMEDLEY, Albert SMITH, Bertram SMITH, Charlotte SMITH, Constance SMITH, Lady Eleanor SMITH, Horace SMITH, Isabel SMITH, Naomi Royde SMITH, W. H. SMITH, T. G. SMOLLETT,

ENGLISH NOVELISTS (*contd.*):
J. C. SNAITH, J. K. SNOWDON, Claire SPENCER, J. C. SQUIRE, G. B. STERN, Laurence STERNE, E. S. STEVENS, P. L. STEVENSON, Cynthia STOCKLEY, Christopher STONE, Marjorie STRACHEY, St. Loe STRACHEY, G. S. STREET, "Hesba STRETTON," L. A. G. STRONG, Joseph STRUTT, "Esmé STUART," H. O. STURGIS, J. F. SULLIVAN, H. SUTCLIFFE, Joan SUTHERLAND, Jonathan SWIFT, A. C. SWINBURNE, Frank SWINNERTON, Arthur SYMONS, Netta SYRETT.

"TAFFRAIL," F. C. TANSLEY, J. T. K. TARPEY, Baroness TAUTPHOEUS, Col. P. M. TAYLOR, Anne THACKERAY, W. M. THACKERAY, Edward THOMAS, E. J. THOMPSON, Sylvia THOMPSON, S. S. THORBURN, Temple THURSTON, Mrs. THURSTON, A. C. THYNNE, H. M. TOMLINSON, Paul TRENT, Anthony TROLLOPE, Frances TROLLOPE, Thomas A. TROLLOPE, W. R. H. TROWBRIDGE, Charles TURLEY, E. S. TYLEE.

E. UNDERDOWN, Allen UPWARD, H. A. VACHELL, H. VALLINGS, Mrs. E. L. VOYNICH, "Annie WAKEMAN," Edgar WALLACE, Helen WALLACE, Horace WALPOLE, Hugh WALPOLE, Mrs. O. F. WALTON, Mrs. Humphrey WARD, Lynd WARD, R. P. WARD, Mrs. Wilfrid WARD, E. B. WARDE, S. WARREN, M. WATSON, W. T. WATTS-DUNTON, Alec WAUGH, Mary WEBB, Peggy WEBLING, A. F. WEDGEWOOD, Sir F. WEDMORE, H. G. WELLS, Mrs. G. WEMYSS, P. WENTWORTH, W. WESTALL, Jessie WESTON, Stanley WEYMAN, Edith WHERRY, F. J. WHISHAW, B. J. WHITBY, Percy WHITE, William Hale WHITE, Richard WHITEING, M. B. WHITING, M. P. WILLCOCKS, Charles WILLIAMS, C. N. WILLIAMSON, Henry WILLIAMSON, Margaret WILSON, Mary J. WILSON, "Romer WILSON," Theodora W. WILSON, Mrs. Alfred WIN-

ENGLISH NOVELISTS (*contd.*):
GATE, "J. S. WINTER," W. J. WINTLE, Cardinal WISEMAN, P. G. WODEHOUSE, Mrs. Henry WOOD, "Daniel WOODROFFE," Margaret WOODS, L. S. WOOLF, Virginia WOOLF, S. F. WRIGHT, "May WYNNE," E. YATES, S. K. Levett YEATS, Charlotte M. YONGE, "Curtis YORKE," E. H. YOUNG, F. E. Mills YOUNG, F. E. Brett YOUNG, Margaret YOUNG, Israel ZANGWILL.
— See also IRISH, SCOTTISH and WELSH NOVELISTS, and for the Dominions, AUSTRALIAN, CANADIAN, NEW ZEALAND, SOUTH AFRICAN NOVELISTS.
— See also (romances and anonymous works), Fryer BACON, George À GREEN, HIGH HISTORY OF THE HOLY GRAAL, HIGH TREASON, HUGH OF RUTLAND, ROBIN HOOD. See also *Caxton, Translations by*
English Revolution, 4, James the Second
— 24, Beaujeu
— 68, I Will Maintain, and sequels
— 97, The Drums of Aulone
— 211, The Scottish Cavalier
— 314, The Sword of the King
— 422, The Lifeguardsman
— 441, Mistress Dorothy Marvin
— 497, Shrewsbury
— See also *James II*
English Rogue, The, 235
Englishwoman's Love-Letters, An, 248
Engrafted Rose, The, 74
Enlightenment of Olivia, The, 485
Ennistymon, Co. Clare, 31, The Town of the Cascades
Ennui, 160
Enough, 474
Ensorcelée, L', 32
Entail, The (by GALT), 191
Entail, The (by HOFFMANN), 244
Enter Sir John, 128
Enter, The Queen, 96
Entragues, Seigneur d', see *Balzac, Sieur de*
Entrave, L', 107
Entre Naranjos, 60
Envers de l'histoire contemporaine, l', 29
Éon, Chevalier d', 275, The King's Indiscretion
Epanchin, Mme, 147, The Idiot

Epictetus, 1, Silanus
Epicurean, The, 350
Epicurus, 386, The Treasures of Typhon
Epidemics, see *Plague*
Epiphanes, Antiochus, 306, Deborah
Episcopo and Company, 11
Episode of the Terror, An, 29
Épisodes, 326
Episodes in the Career of Shuffles, 420
Episodios Nacionales, 382
Epistolary Novels, see *Letters, Novels in*
Époque, une, 326
Epsom, 53, The Chaplain of the Fleet
Equality, see *Class Prejudice*
Erasmus, Desiderius, 72, True Heart
— 357, The Unfortunate Traveller
— 401, The Cloister and the Hearth
Erasmus, Sarel, 57, A Burgher Quixote
Erastus, 231, Klytia
Erb, 408
Erbe am Rhein, Das, 422
Erdseg, 416
Erema, 58
Erewhon, 83
Erewhon Rivisited, 83
Erfolg, 172
Eric XIV, 486, Royal Favour
Eric Brighteyes, 219
Erie, Lake, 126, Love Thrives in War
Erlach Court, 423
Erling the Bold, 26
Ernest Maltravers, 309
Eroica, 103
Eros the Slayer, 274
Erotica, 2
Errand Boy of Andrew Jackson, The, 451
Erskine Dale, Pioneer, 182
Es war, 455
Escapade, 424
Escape of Sir William Heans, The, 234
Escenas Montañesas, 382
Eschenbach, Wolfram von, 242, High History of the Holy Graal
Esclava del Senor, La, 461
Esclusa, L', 388
ESCRAGNOLLE - TAUNAY, Viscount A. d', see "DINARTE, Sylvio." 143
Esfinge Maragata, La, 167
Eskimo Life, 26, Ungava
— 344, Frozen Justice
— 412, The Magnetic North
— 459, Northern Lights and Shadows
Esmerelda, 253, Notre Dame de Paris
Espana del Cid, La, 104
Espionage, 22, Jacqueline
— 24, Barry Leroy
— 62, Napoleon Decrees

Espionage (*contd.*): 78, The Thirty-Nine Steps, and sequels
— 102, The Riddle of the Sands
— 193, The Infamous John Friend
— 277, The Pikemen
— 317, Extremes Meet
— 318, The Three Couriers
— 342, Barlasch of the Guard
— 438, The Spy
— 466, Portrait of a Spy
— See also *Pioneers*, etc.
Espuma, La, 375
Esquimaux Maiden's Romance, The, 477
Essays (*Fictional*), 3, The Spectator
— 47, A. C. BENSON's works
— 127, Prue and I
— 168, The Roadmender
— 205, The Citizen of the World
— 245, The Autocrat of the Breakfast Table, *et seq.*
— 258, Salmagundi
— 259, Bracebridge Hall
— 305, E. V. LUCAS's works, *passim*
— 321, The Saltonstall Gazette, The Etchingham Letters
— 346, Our Vllage
Essence of the Dusk, An, 25
Essenes, 349, The Brook Kerith
Essex, Countess of, 262, Arabella Stuart
Essex, Robert Devereux, Second Earl of, 74, My Lord of Essex
— 182, The Hand of the North
— 289, With Essex in Ireland
— 404, The Charming of Estercel
Essex (*County*), 179, All Fools Together
— 353, Cunning Murrell, Green Ginger
— 516, Jinny the Carrier
Este, Leonora d', 324, Ser Pantaleone
Estevanille Gonzalés, 295
Esther Happy, 28
Esther Kahn, 459
Esther Pentreath, 379
Esther Vanhomrigh, 510
Esther Waters, 349
Esthonia, 274, Mme KALLAS's novels and tales
Etain, 446, In the Land of Youth
— See also *Celtic Romance*
Étampes, Duchesse d', 154, Ascanio
Etchingham Letters, The, 321
Eternal City, The, 87
Eternal Husband, The, 147
Eternal Moment, The, 180
Eternal Quest, The, 447
Eternal Question, The, 87
Ethan Brand, 233

Ethan Frome, 499
Ethel Churchill, 287
Ethelinde, 440
Ethelred, King, the "Unready," 120, Alfgar the Dane
Ethical Problems, see *Conscience, Crime, Determinism, Marriage, Sex*, etc.
Etna, 286, The Miracles of Antichrist
Eton, 32, An Eton Boy's Letters
— 280, Austin Elliot
Eton Boy's Letters, An, 32
Etruscan Vase, The, 341
Ettore Fieramosca, 22
Etui de nacre, L', 183
Euancondit, 205
Eudocia, 386
Euergetes II, 158, The Sisters
Eugen Stielfriend, 219
Eugène, Prince, 319, Lally of the Brigade
— 355, Prince Eugene
Eugene Aram, 308
Eugenics, 459, Drender's Daughter
— See also *Marriage, Sex*
Eugénie, Empress, 323, The Royal Woman
Eugénie, 323
Eugenie Grandet, 27
Euphues Golden Legacie 302
Euphues and his England, 307
Euphues, the Anatomy of Wit, 307
Euphuism, 213, Pandosto
— 269, Tom a Lincoln
— 302, Rosalynde
— 307, Euphues
— 347, Diana
— 383, Petite Palace of Pettie his Pleasure
— 425, The Monastery
— 434, The Arcadia
Europa's Beast, 354
Europe, 265
European Relations, 128
Europeans, The, 263
Eustace Diamonds, The, 472
Eutaw, 436
Eva, 98
Evan Harrington, 339
Evander, 386
Evangelist, The, 130
Evans, Elizabeth, 164, Adam Bede
EVANS, Mary Anne, see "ELIOT, George," 164
Eve (by Baring GOULD), 208
Eve (by MAARTENS), 311
Eve and David, 28
Evelina, 83
Evelina's Garden, 505
Evelyn Innes, 349
Evenings on a Farm near Dikanka, 204
Eventyr og historier, 9
Ever-Living Ones, The, 214
Evered, 506
EVERETT, Mrs. H. J., see "DOUGLAS, Theo," 148

EVERETT-GREEN, Evelyn, see GREEN, E. E., 213
Eve's Ransom, 201
Evesham, Battle of, 262, Forest Days
Evictions, see *Fenians, Land League, Land Problems, Ribbon Men, Whiteboys*
Evil, Problem of, 10–11, ANDREEV's Stories
— 232, The Scarlet Letter
— 233, The Marble Faun
Evil May-Day, 213
Evviva la Vita, 429
EWART, Ernest Andrew, see "CABLE, Boyd"
Ex Voto, 408
Examining Magistrate, The, 100
Exchange of Souls, An, 373
Excisemen, 39, The Longshoremen
— See also *Smugglers*
Excursion, 455
Excursion, The, 74
Exemplary Novels, 96
Exeter, 68, Yesterdays
— 120, The Last Abbot of Glastonbury
— 506, The Way Up
Exile, 100
Exile of the Sons of Usnach, The, 293
Exiled Scot, An, 77
Exiles, 133
Exiles, The (by BALZAC), 30
Exiles, The (by DAVIS), 131
Exiles of Faloo, The, 374
Exmoor, 58, Lorna Doone
— 337, Katerfelto
— 507, The Dream of Fair Women, Tarka
Exodus, 337, Sarchedon
— See also *Biblical Stories*
Expédition nocturne autour de ma chambre, 320
Expedition of Humphry Clinker, The, 441
Experiment in Sincerity, An, 166
Expiation (by ARNIM), 15
Expiation (by O. THANET), 463
Expiation (by Edith WHARTON), 499
Exploits of Arsène Lupin, 293
Exploits of Brigadier Gerard, 150
Explorer, The, 333
Expressionism, 146, Dos PASSOS' novels
— 273 JOYCE's works
— 405, Pilgrimage, and sequels
— 410, Elizabeth M. ROBERTS's novels
— 510–11, Mrs. V. WOOLF's novels
Exquisite Perdita, The, 38
Extaze, 117
Exton Manor, 329
Extra Day, The, 59
Extraordinary Adventures of Diana Please, The, 90

Extraordinary Women, 318
Extravaganza, see *Facetiae, Imaginary Voyages, Oriental, Parodies*, etc.
Extremes Meet, 317
Eyck, Van, 280, Old Margaret
Eyes, The, 499
Eyes like the Sea, 272
Eyes of the Panther, The, 54
Eyrbyggja Saga, 168
Ezekiel's Sin, 379

FABER, Cecilia Boehl van, see "CABALLERO, Fernán"
Faber, 490
Fabiola, 508
Fables, see *Allegories, Beast Fables, Didactic, Fabliaux, Philosophical Stories*
Fabliaux, 13, The Arabian Nights' Entertainments
— 197, Gesta Romanorum
— 199, The Pecorone
— 326, The Heptameron
— 332, Massaccio of Salerno
— 374, Palace of Pleasure
— 418, SACCHETTI's stories
— 430, The Seven Wise Masters
— 452, STRAPAROLA's Nights
Faccio, Rina, see "ALERAMO, Sibilla"
Face of Failure, The, 464
Face of the World, The, 64
Face to Face, 1
Face to Face with Napoleon, 87
Facetiæ, 3, Out of the Hurly-Burly, Transformations
— 4, The Diverting Adventures of Maurin, and sequel
— 7, Philistia
— 12–13, "F. ANSTEY's" novels
— 31, J. K. BANGS' stories
— 37, Better Dead
— 42, Zuleika Dobson
— 43, The Green Overcoat
— 44, The Missing Masterpiece
— 55, "G. A. BIRMINGHAM's" novels
— 81, BUNNER's works
— 81–2, Sir F. C. BURNAND's stories
— 102, G. K. CHESTERTON's novels, *passim*
— 106, The Duke, The Lunatic at Large, Count Bunker
— 107, Valentine Vox, Sylvester Sound
— 129, Tartarin of Tarascon
— 130, Tartarin on the Alps, Port Tarascon
— 149, Through Green Glasses
— 157, F. P. DUNNE's stories
— 221–2, T. C. HALIBURTON's stories

Facetiæ (*contd.*): 237, The Trials of Topsy
— 241, The Green Carnation, The Londoners, The Prophet of Berkeley Square
— 245, T. HOOK's stories
— 258, Diamonds to Sit On
— 260–1, W. W. JACOBS's stories
— 267, H. G. JENKINS's stories
— 268, J. K. JEROME's stories
— 293, S. R. LEACOCK's stories
— 317, Poor Relations, The Old Men of the Sea, Vestal Fire
— 318, April Fools
— 320, MAGINN's works
— 355, H. H. MUNRO's sketches
— 374, Barry PAIN's stories
— 398, RABELAIS' works
— 439, Albert SMITH's stories
— 450–1, F. R. STOCKTON's stories
— 462, Christmas Books of M. A. Titmarsh, The Book of Snobs
— 463, Miscellanies
— 476–7, " Mark TWAIN's " stories, *passim*
— 487, "Artemus WARD's" stories
— 509, P. G. WODEHOUSE's stories
— See also *Parodies*
Facetious History of a Company of Strolling Players, 422
Facino Cane, 29
Faderen, 56
Faereyinga Saga, 466
Faggus, Tom, 58, Lorna Doone
Fagin, 140, Oliver Twist
Fair Deceiver, A, 377
Fair God, The, 486
Fair-haired Eckbert, The, 93
Fair Haven and Foul Strand, 454
Fair Irish Maid, The, 313
Fair Jilt, The, 43
Fair Maid of Perth, The, 427
Fair Margaret (by CROCKETT), 123
Fair Margaret (by HAGGARD), 220
Fair Martyr, A, 62
Fair Mississippian, The, 119
Fair Moon of Bath, The, 165
Fair Saxon, A, 312
Fairfax, Colonel, 413, King by the Grace of God
Fairservice, Andrew, 425, Rob Roy
Fairy Doll, The, 189
Fairy Gold, 317
Fairy Palace of the Quicken Trees, The, 274
Fairy-Tales, 9, ANDERSEN's Fairy Tales

Fairy-Tales (*contd.*): 12, The Brass Bottle
— 13, In Brief Authority
— 38, The Little White Bird, Peter and Wendy
— 80, Mr. Godly Beside Himself
— 93, " Lewis CARROLL's " stories
— 93, The Elves
— 98, The Shadowless Man
— 129, Sr. G. W. DASENT's translations
— 142, The Magic Flute
— 157, Lord DUNSANY's stories
— 162, Little Johannes
— 172, A Little Book of Profitable Tales
— 174, Odette
— 176, The King of Alsander
— 181, Undine, Aslauga's Knight
— 197, Germalshausen
— 279, The Heroes
— 282, Puck of Pook's Hill, Rewards and Fairies
— 287, The Wonderful Adventures of Nils, and sequel, Liliecrona's Home
— 309, The Pilgrims of the Rhine
— 313, Phantastes, The Light Princess, and following
— 330, The Cat's Mill
— 331, The Midnight Folk
— 364, Wayland Smith
— 373, The Celestial Grocery
— 402, Tales of Old Japan
— 442, The Sweet-Scented Name
— 446, The Demi-Gods
— 452, STRAPAROLA's Nights
— 504, The Happy Prince
— See also *Allegories, Fantasies*
Faith (by Cunninghame GRAHAM), 210
Faith (by J. H. HARRIS), 228
Faith (by PALACIO VALDES), 375
Faith Doctor, 163
Faith Gartney's Girlhood, 503
Faith Healing, 163, The Faith Doctor
Faith Tresilion, 386
Fakredeen, Emir, 144, Tancred
Falaise of the Blessed Voice, 131
Falcon King, The, 363
Falconer, Buckhurst, 161, Patronage
" FALCONER, Lanoe," see HAWKER, Marie E., 231
Falk, 110
Falkirk, Battle of, 159, The Hearth of Hutton
Falkland, Viscount, 307, In Spite of All

Falkland, 308
Fall des Sergenten Grischa, Der, 520
Fall Mauritizius, Der, 491
Fall of Lord Barrymore, 150
Fall of the House of Usher, 388
Fallen Fortunes, 378
Fallen Idol, A, 12
Falling Wind, The, 316
False Coin or True, 348
Falstaf, Sir John, 195, Good Sir John
— 222, Coronation
Familia de León Roch, La, 382
Familie Buchholz, 450
Familien paa Gilje, 299
Famille Profit, La, 480
Family, The, 351
Family Affair, A, 112
Family at Gilje, 299
Family Chronicles, see especially: 121, Saracinesca, and sequels
— 122, Katherine Lauderdale, and sequels
— 190, The Forsyte Saga
— 233, In a Desert Land
— 283, — and Sons
— 287, The Ring of the Löwenskölds
— 324, Buddenbrooks
— 496, A Family Portrait
Family Happiness, 469
Family Portrait, A, 496
Family That Was, A, 400
Famine, 39, The Wizard's Knot
— 92, The Black Prophet
— 229, Gabriel Conroy
— 276, Castle Daly
— 282, The Day's Work
— 325, The Betrothed
— 343, The Hunger
— 358, Tashkent
— 432, Luke Delmege
— 432, Glenaar
Famished Cat, The, 182
Famous Historie of Fryer Bacon, 23
Fancy Farm, 356
Fancy O'Brien, 319
Fane, Michael, 317, Sinister Street, and sequels
" *Fane, Violet*," see *Currie, Lady*
Fangen som sang, 63
Fanny, 172
Fanny and Jane, 108
Fanny's First Novel, 348
Fanshawe, 232
Fanshawe of the Fifth, 243
Fantasia, 429
Fantasias, 162
Fantasies, 21, Outland
— 50, Living Alone
— 90, ČAPEK's novels
— 180, The Celestial Omnibus
— 193, Lady into Fox, A Man in the Zoo
— 258, Rip Van Winkle
— 352, Thunder on the Left
— 512, The Venetian Glass Nephew

Fantasies (*contd.*): See also *Fables, Fairy-Tales, Scientific Romances, Utopias*
Fantasy, 429
Fantôme d'orient, 304
Far-away Bride, The, 50
Far Country, A, 104
Far from the Madding Crowd, 225
Far in the Forest, 345
Far och dotter, 72
Far Wandering Men, 417
Fardarougha the Miser, 92
Farewell, 30
Farewell, Love, 429
Farewell, Nikola, 65
Farewell to Arms, A, 236
Farewell to Military Profession, 430
Farewell to Paradise, 464
FARGUS, F. J., see " CONWAY, Hugh," 112
FARIGOULE, L., see " ROMAINS, J.," 415
Farina, 340
Farlige alder, Den, 344
Farm, The, 454
Farm of the Dagger, The, 385
Farmer Eli's Vacation, 76
Farmington, 129
Farnese, Pier Luigi, 418, The Strolling Saint
Fåroes, 466, Thrond of Gate
Farquhars, 7, Balmoral
Farragut, Admiral, 35, Midshipman Farragut
Farringdons, The, 181
Farthing Hall, 487
Fascism, 347, Toes Up
— 369, The Open Secret
Fashionable Adventures of Joshua Craig, 384
Fast as the Wind, 208
Fat and the Thin, The, 517
Fatal Boots, The, 463
Fatal Garland, The, 457
Fatal Gift, The, 348
Fatal Marksman, The, 139
Fatal Passion, A, 52
Fatalism, 93, Eckbert
— 117, Footsteps of Fate, Old People
— 225–6, HARDY's novels
— 253, Notre-Dame de Paris
— 254, Les misérables, Toilers of the Sea, Ninety-three
— 338, Moby-Dick
— 410, The Great Jester
— 491, Aylwin
— 496, Hermann
— 505, The Bridge of San Luis Rey
— See also *Determinism, Pessimism*
Fate, 210
Fate, The, 263
Fate of the Children of Lir, The, 214
Fate of the Children of Lir, The, 273
Fate of the Children of Muirthemne, 214
Fate of the Children of Turenn, The, 273

Fate of the Children of Usnach, 214
Fate of the Three Sons of Turenn, The, 431
Fate the Fiddler, 316
Fated to Win, 165
Father, A, 100
Father, The, 56
Father Abraham, 23
Father Alphonsus, 243
Father and Daughter, 72
Father and the Daughter, The, 369
Father Brown Stories, The, 102
Father Clancy, 187
Father Connell, 31
Father Felix's Chronicle, 102
Father Maternus, 231
Father Ralph, 364
Father Saba, 387
Father Sergius, 469
Father Stafford, 246
Fathers and Children, 475
Fathers and Sons, 475
Father's Curse, A, 30
Fathers of Men, 248
Fausse Maîtresse, La, 27
Faust (by TURGENEV), 474
Faust Legend, 416, The Revels of Orsera
Faustbuch, 170, Faustus
Faustula, 21
Faustus, John, 170, Faustus
Faute de l'abbé Mouret, La, 517
Faux monnayeurs, Les, 198
Favours from France, 478
Fawkes, Guy, see *Gunpowder Plot*
Fawn Gloves, The, 268
Fé, La, 375
Fear of Living, The, 65
Fearful Responsibility, A, 250
Feast of Bricriu, The, 236
Feather Beds, 268
Feats on the Fio d, 330
Fécondité, 519
Felicitas, 128
Felismena, 347, Diana
Felix, 241
Felix Holt, 164
Fellah, The, 1
Fellow-Townsmen, 226
Fellow Travellers, 470
Fellowe and his Wife, A, 249
Felmeres, The, 164
Felton, 81, The Duke's Servants
Female Life in Prison, 413
Female Quixote, The, 295
Feminism, 7, A Woman at Bay
— 9, The Rebel Generation, Tantalus
— 17, Julia France and her Times
— 18, The Immortal Marriage, Vengeful Gods, Dido Queen of Hearts
— 51, Goslings
— 52, The Revolt of Man
— 72, Hertha, Father and Daughter

Feminism (contd.): 74, A Superfluous Woman
— 86, Mrs. K. M. CAFFYN's novels
— 106, Love-Letters of a Worldly Woman
— 135, The War-Workers
— 145, The Story of a Modern Woman
— 160, Belinda
— 162, "George EGERTON's" stories
— 211, Mrs. Sarah GRAND's novels
— 255, The Workaday Women
— 259, Mary
— 270, Mrs. Warren's Daughter
— 270, Hagar, The Wanderers
— 299, The Pilot and his Wife, The Commodore's Daughters
— 369, Adeline Mowbray
— 377, The Career of Candida
— 384, Doctor Zay
— 414, Distaff
— 417, Women
— 461, Hannah Thurston
— 489, The Coryston Family
— 491, "Sir" She Said
— 494, Ann Veronica
Femme abandonée, La, 27
Femme au collier de velours La, 156,
Femme de trente ans, La, 26
Femmes d'artistes, Les, 129
Fen Country, 223, The MS. in the Red Box
— 280, Hereward the Wake
Fenella, 454
Fenians, 36, In the Midst of Alarms
— 231, Ismay's Children
— 278, C. J. KICKHAM's novels
— 297, Lord Kilgobbin
— 350, The Dunferry Risin'
— 363 When We were Boys
— See also *Land League, Ribbon Men, Tithe Campaign, Whiteboys*
Fennel and Rue, 251
FENOLLOSA, Mary, see "McCALL, Sidney," 312
Fenton, Lavinia, 38, The Chaste Diana
Fenwick, Sir John, 262, The King's Highway
— 497, Shrewsbury
— See also *Assassination Plot*
Fenwick's Career, 488
Feo, 381
Feodor, Tsar, 461, On the Red Staircase
Ferdinand and Isabella, 14, The Knightly Years
— 220, Fair Margaret
— 271, Admiral of the Ocean Sea
Ferdinand VII of Spain, 510, The King's Revoke

Ferdinand of Brunswick, 271, Chrysal
Ferguson, Robert, 149, Micah Clarke
— See also *Assassination Plot*
Fermanagh, 80, The Barrys, Master John
Fermata, The, 244
Ferme du Choquard, La, 101
Fermé la nuit, 350
Fern, 470
Fernando, 22
Ferozeshah, Battle of, 288, The Wetherbys
Ferragus, 28
Ferrar, Nicholas, 330, A Haunt of Ancient Peace
— 433, John Inglesant
Ferry of Fate, The, 206
Ferson, Count Axel, 39, The Reminiscences of Sir Barrington Beaumont, Bart.
— 107, The King with Two Faces
Fetches, The, 31
Feu, Le, 33
Feudalism, see *Chivalry*, and names of countries and monarchs
Feuds, see *Vendettas*
Feverel, Sir Richard, 339, Ordeal of Richard Feverel
Few Crusted Characters, A, 226
ffolliots of Redmarley, The, 227
Fiabe della virtù, Le, 375
Fiamme sul Bosforo, 354
Fiancé de Sylvie, Le, 215
Fiander's Widow, 185
Fianna, The, 214
Fiddler of Lugau, The, 410
Fidelity, 203
Fidélka, 215
Field of the Cloth of Gold, 261, Darnley
Fielding, Beau, 308, Devereux
"FIELDING, Henry," see HALL, H. F.
Fielding, Henry, 463, The Virginians
Fields of Dulditch, The, 323
Fierabras, 98
Fiery Angel, The, 77
Fiery Dawn, The, 107
Fiery Dive, The, 14
Fiery Particles, 347
Fiesta, 236
Fifeshire, 26, By Stroke of Sword
— 36, A Daughter of Fife, A Knight of the Nets
— 173, The Green Graves of Balgowrie, A Daughter of Strife
— 235, Marget at the Manse
— 339, Our Town
— 366, Katie Stewart
Fifteen Comforts (or, Joys) of Marriage, The, 288
Fifth Form at St. Dominic's, 402

Fifth Queen, The, 178
Fifth Queen Crowned, The, 178
Fifty-Four Forty, or Fight, 248
Fifty-One Tales, 157
Fight For the Crown, The, 362
Fighting Chance, The, 97
Fighting the Flames, 26
Figs and Thistles, 470
Figure in the Carpet, The, 265
Figures of Earth, 85
Fille d'Ève, Une, 27
Fille du régent, Une, 154
Filles et garçons, 184
Filleul d'un marquis, Le, 464
Fils de Titien, Le, 357
Fils Maugars, Le, 464
Final de Norma, El, 5
Finances of the Gods, The, 281
Financier, The, 151
Financiers, 44, H. BELLOC's novels
— 48, Mammon & Co.
— 53, The Golden Butterfly
— 55, Gossamer
— 80, The Gentleman from San Francisco
— 101, Jean Têterol's Idea
— 105, As the Twig is Bent
— 119, Love and the Soul Hunters
— 121, Don Orsino
— 151, The Financier, and sequel
— 186, The Market-Place
— 274, The Embezzlers
— 283, Queen Money
— 297, Davenport Dunn
— 308, Empire Builders
— 323, Berlin
— 326, Vanity
— 358, Princes of the Stock Exchange, David Golder
— 361, F. NORRIS' stories
— 371, The Modern Argonauts
— 387, The Statue
— 387, The Sentimentalists
— 433, Contraband of War
— 438, Boston
— 444, The Breaking of the Storm
— 490, A Little Journey in the World, and sequel; That Fortune
— 518, Money
— See also *Banking, Business, Millionaires*
Financing of Fiona, 113
Finer Grain, The, 266
Finest Story in the World, The, 281
Finish to the Adventures of Tom, Jerry, and Logic, 162
Finished, 220
Finland, 51, The Motherless
— 53, A Trooper of the Finns
— 286, Gosta Berling
— 470, Z. TOPELIUS' novels

Finland (contd.): See also FINNISH NOVEL-ISTS
Finn, 214, Finn, Son of Cumhal
— 274, The Fairy Palace of the Quicken Trees, etc.
Finn, Son of Cumhal, 214
FINNISH NOVELISTS: Mme Aino KALLAS, A. KIVI (STENVALL), "J. LINNAKOSKI," C. WILHELMSON
Finn's Helpers, 214
Fire and Ice, 267
Fire Brigades, 26, Fighting the Flames
Fire in the Flint, The, 502
Fire of London, 325, Cherry and Violet
— 412, Whitefriars
— See also *London*
Fire-Seeker, The, 86
Firecrackers, 481
Fires of Freedom, 512
Firm of Girdlestone, The, 149
Firm of Nucingen, The, 29
First Fleet Family, A, 41
First Hundred Thousand, The, 234
First Impressions, 20
First Love, 228
First Men in the Moon, The, 493
First the Blade, 128
First Violin, The, 180
FISHER, Mrs. Dorothea, F., see CANFIELD, Dorothy
Fisher, Bishop John, 49, The King's Achievement
Fisher-Folk, 36, A Daughter of Fife, Paul and Christina, A Knight of the Nets
— 43, The Whalers
— 60, The Mayflower
— 64, The Last of the Vikings
— 132, Rockbound
— 156-7, N. DUNCAN's stories
— 224, Benoni, and sequel
— 277, The Sea
— 282, Captains Courageous
— 285, The Læstrygonians
— 289, Grania
— 304, An Iceland Fisherman
— 314, Malcolm
— 377, J. E. PATTERSON's novels
— 379, J. H. PEARCE's novels, *passim*
— 401, Christie Johnson
— 404, S. REYNOLDS's stories
— 425, The Antiquary
— 428, The Revolt of the Fishermen
— 440, The Tides of Barnegat
— 442, The Sea-King
— 482, I Malevoglia
— 514, Deep Sea

Fisher Hill, Battle of, 376, My Lady of the North
Fisher Lass, The, 56
Fisherman, The, 216
Fisherman's Daughter, The, 112
Fisherman's Gat, 360
Fishers of the Sea, 377
Fishmonger's Fiddle, 115
Fishwife of Stand on the Green, her story, 430
Fiskerjenten, 56
Fit, The, 99
Fitz-Boodle Papers, 463
Fitz of Fitz-Ford, 71
Fitzgerald, Lord Edward, 63, Lord Edward Fitzgerald, and sequel
— 199, The Island of Sorrow
— 402, Kilgorman
FitzGerald, Maurice, 339 Richard Feverel
Fitzherbert, Mrs., 38, The Gallants
— 90, Love Like a Gipsy
— 184, Yeoman Fleetwood
— 199, To my King Ever Faithful
— 243, Demi-Royal
Five-Barred Gate, The, 466
"Five Towns," 45, A. BENNETT's novels
Five Weeks in a Balloon, 482
Fivensky, 11
Flager i byen og på havnen, Det, 56
Flamborough, 58, Mary Anerley
Flame of Fire, A, 243
Flame of Life, The, 12
Flames, 241
Flames of Moscow, The, 306
Flames on the Bosphorus, 354
Flanders, 78, John Burnet of Barns
— 92, "No. 101"
— 112, CONSCIENCE's novel
— 262, Agincourt
— 426, Quentin Durward
— 482, Dr. Ox's Experiment
— See also BELGIAN NOVELISTS, DUTCH NOVELISTS
Flat Iron for a Farthing, A, 168
Flaws, 35
Flax of Dream, The, 507
Fled' Bricrend, 236
Fleet Prison, 53, The Chaplain of the Fleet
Fleetwood, 203
Flegeljähre, 407
Flemington, 260
FLETCHER, Miss J. C., see "FLEMING, George"
Fleur-de-Blé, 408
Fleurange, 121
Fleury, Cardinal, 155, Olympe de Clèves
Flidais, 293
Flight From the Cross, The, 153
Flight of the Heron, The, 74
Flight of the King, The, 87

Flight Without End, 416
Flip, 229
"FLIT & KO," see FOSTER, C. and F., 180
Flock of Birds, A, 118
Flodden Field, 180, The Arrow of the North
— 189, The Witch's Sword
— 457, The Crimson Field
Flood, 358
Flor de Mayo, 60
Florence, 22, The Maid of Florence
— 63, The Decameron
— 68, The Carnival of Florence; Yesterdays
— 75, Alas!
— 94, Wroth
— 109, Incognita
— 128, The Sword of Love
— 164, Romola
— 168, The Gathering of Brother Hilarius
— 179, A Room with a View
— 199, The Pecorone
— 250, Indian Summer
— 285, Tales of Florence
— 291, Aaron's Rod
— 296, The Daltons
— 297, One of Them
— 302, The Old Bridge
— 386, The Joy of Youth
— 412, Cæsar Borgia
— 473, La Beata, Marietta
— 483, In Change Unchanged
— 503, The Plough of Shame
Florence M'Carthy, 351
Florentine Frame, The, 412
Florentiner Novellen, 285
Florida, 36, Remember the Alamo
— 44, Spanish Bayonet
— 294, The Romance of the Fountain
— 401, Doris Kingsley
— 448, The Sword of Justice
— 511, Constance F. WOOLSON's novels
Flosky, Mr., 379, Nightmare Abbey
Flower Beneath the Foot, The, 175
Flower, Fruit, and Thorn Pieces, 407
Flower o' the Orange, 94
Flower o' the Wheat, 105
Flower of Forgiveness, The, 445
Flower of France, The, 312
Flower of the Chapdelaines, The, 86
Flower of the Flock, The, 362
Flower of the Heather, 316
Flowers of Paradise, 76
Flucht ohne Ende, 416
Flute and Violin, 7
Fly, The, 325
Flying Cromlech, The, 132
"*Flying Dutchman*," 329, The Phantom Ship
— 333, Melmoth
Flying Inn, The, 102

Foe Farrell, 398
Foes, 271
Foes-in-Law, 75
Fogg, Phileas, 482, Around the World in Eighty Days
Folk at Furry Farm, The, 395
Folk Lore and Folk Tales, 34, Barlaam and Josaphat
— 181, Undine
— 214, Poets and Dreamers
— 235, Kwaidan
— 319, S. MACMANUS's stories
— 357, MUSAEUS
— 363, Wrack
— 364, Wayland Smith
— 373, Warriors of Old Japan, Romances of Old Japan
— 402, Tales of Old Japan
— 409, Sunrise Stories
— 411, Robin Hood
— 414, Stories Toto told Me, In His Own Image
— 431, Wm. SHARP's stories
— 445, Tales of the Punjab
— 459, Romantic Tales of the Punjab
— 465, Early English Prose Romances
— See also *Celtic Romances, Welsh Romances*
Folke Filbyter, 235
Folks from Dixie, 156
Folliott, Dr., 379, Crotchet Castle
Follow Elizabeth, 113
Follow My Leader, 402
Follow the Gleam, 243
Following Darkness, 403
Following the Equator, 476
Folly Corner, 152
Fomá Gordyéeff, 206
Fombombo, 453
Fond Adventures, 239
Fondie, 65
Fontainebleu, 262, The Brigand
Food of the Gods, The, 493
Fool, The, 24
Fool Errant, The, 239
Fool in Christ, Emanuel Quint, 231
Fool in her Folly, A, 76
Fool of Quality, The, 74
Fool of the Family, 278
Foolish Lovers, The, 167
Foolish Matrons, The, 84
Fool's Errand, A, 470
Foote, Samuel, 271, Chrysal
Footprints beneath the Snow, 66
Footsteps of a Throne, 381
Footsteps of Fate, 117
For Braganza, 275
For Ever, 190
For Faith and Freedom, 52
For Freedom, 247
For Henri and Navarre, 113
For His People, 234
For Kett and Countryside, 459
For King or Country, 35

Før kulden kommer, 408
For Maisie, 478
For Sceptre and Crown, 419
For the Freedom of the Sea, 70
For the Major, 511
For the Old Land, 278
For the Religion, 152
For the Right, 186
For the Term of his Natural Life, 105
For the White Christ, 44
For the White Rose, 91
For the White Rose of Arno, 404
For Three Moons, 88
Forayers, The, 436
Forbes of Culloden, Duncan, 318, The Lady of Hirta
Forbidden to Wed, 32, 33
Ford, Georgiana, 339, Sandra Belloni
FORD, Thomas M., see " LE BRETON, John "
FORD, W., see " ST. CLAIR, W.," 419
Foregone Conclusion, A, 249
Foreign Legion, 295, A Modern Legionary
Foreigner in the Family, The, 50
Foreigners, The, 392
Forerunner, The (by H. E. THOMAS), 464
Forerunner, The (by MEREJKOWSKI), 341
Forest Days, 262
Forest Folk, 392
Forest Lovers, The, 239
Forest of the Hanged, The, 402
Forest on the Hill, The, 386
Forest Runners, The, 9
Forest Schoolmaster, The, 416
Forest Ship, The, 244
Forester's Daughter, The, 192
Forestier, Le, 41
Forever Free, 353
Forewarners, The, 95
Forfarshire, 37-8, Sir J. M. BARRIE's stories
Forge in the Forest, The, 409
Forged Coupon, The, 469
Forgery, The, 263
Forget-me-nots, 275
Forjaettede Land, Det, 389
Formosa, 151, The Children Reap
Forrest, Gen. Nathan B., 229, A Little Union Scout
Forsaken Lady, A, 27
Forsyte Saga, The, 190
Fort Amity, 397
Fortitude, 486
Fortoellinger og Skildringer fra Norge, 299
Fortuna Chance, 392
Fortunate Lovers, The, 326
Fortunate Mistress, Lady Roxana, 134
Fortunate Union, The, 224
Fortune, 442
Fortune d'Angèle, L', 464

Fortune des Rougon, La, 516
Fortune Hunter, The, 346
Fortunes and Misfortunes of Moll Flanders, 134
Fortune's Castaway, 159
Fortune's My Foe, 62
Fortunes of Christina M'Nab, 320
Fortunes of Col. Torlogh O'Brien, 294
Fortunes of Fifi, 428
Fortunes of Garin, The, 270
Fortunes of Glencore, The, 297
Fortunes of Nigel, The, 426
Fortunes of Oliver Horn, The, 440
Fortunes of Richard Mahony, 406
Fortunes of the Rougons, The, 516
Fortunio (by GAUTIER), 195
Fortunio (by QUILLER-COUCH), 396
Forty-Five Guardsmen, The, 155
42nd Parallel, The, 146
Forward From Babelon, 205
Fosco, Count, 108, The Woman in White
Fóstbræður, 218
Fouché, Josef (Duc d' Otranto), 234, The Shadow of a Throne
— 512, A Spy for Napoleon
Foul Play, 402
Found at Blazing Star, 229
Found Wanting, 390
Founding of Fortunes, The, 34
Fountain Sealed, A (by BESANT), 52
Fountain Sealed, A (by SEDGWICK), 428
Fouque, Adelaide, 516, The Fortunes of the Rougons
Fouquet, Nicholas (Marquis de Belle-Isle), 154, The Vicomte du Bragelonne
Fouquier-Tinville, A. Q., 495, A Marriage under the Terror
Four Adventures of Richard Hannay, 78
Four Ballrooms, 336
Four Bells of Chartres, The, 492
Four Branches of the Mabinogii, The, 217
Four Chimneys, 320
Four Corners of the World, The, 332
Four Days, 193
Four Faultless Felons, 102
Four Feathers, The, 331
Four Horsemen of the Apocalypse, The, 61
Four Million, The, 389
Four Pigeons, 261
Four Roads, The, 275
Fourscore, 439
Four Sons, 199
Four Sons of Aymon, The, 181

Four Swans, The, 431
Four Winds Farm, 346
" 1492," 271
Fourth-Class Appointment, A, 136
Fourth Estate, The, 374
Fourth Magus, The, 210
Fox, Charles James, 104, Richard Carvel
— 150, Rodney Stone
— 297, Sir Jasper Carew
Fox, George, 36, Friend Olivia
— 98, The Draytons and the Davenants, and sequel
Fox Henry (Baron Holland), 271, Chrysal
— 489, Eltham House
Fox, The, 291
Fox Farm, 133
Fra den Gamle Fabrik, 51
Fra Lippo Lippi, 170
Fra Piazzo del Popolo, 51
Fragment of the Lives of Three Friends, A, 244
Fraich, 293
Framley Parsonage, 471
France, Mediæval and 17th Century, 44, For the White Christ
— 152, H. DRUMMOND's novels, *passim*
— 253, Notre Dame de Paris
— 261, Mary of Burgundy
— 261, Philip Augustus
— 263, Leonora d'Orco
— 401, The Cloister and the Hearth
— 407, By Weeping Cross
— 412, A Mediæval Garland
— 447, The Road to Paris
— See also names of Emperors, Kings, etc., and events, *Crusades, Hundred Years' War*, etc.
France, Modern, 80, The Midge
— 88, Home Fires from France
— 91, Monsieur Martin
— 107, The Fiery Dawn
— 135, Between Two Thieves
— 195, W. L. GEORGE's novels
— 225, A. S. HARDY's novels
— 256, Eddy and Edouard
— 263-6, Henry JAMES's novels
— 275, Julia KAVANAGH's novels
— 320, Between the Days
— 342, The Last Hope
— 345, Madeline
— 421, A Week in a French Country House
— 499, Madame de Treymes, The Reef, Coming Home, The Marne
— See also FRENCH NOVELISTS, *passim*, and names of characters, events, and places

Francezka, 428
Franche-Comte, 1, Blush-Rose
Francis, of Assisi, Saint, 412, The Story of Antonio
Francis I, 122, With the Immortals
— 154, Ascanio
— 155, The Two Dianas, and sequel
— 261, Darnley
Francis, Sir Philip, 150, Rodney Stone
Francis the First, 154
Franciscans, 158, Cross and Dagger
Franco-German War, 25, The Rebel
— 62, The Iron Year
— 96, Lórraine
— 135, The Man of Iron
— 139, Iseulte
— 166, The Story of the Plébiscite
— 187, Jörn Uhl
— 237, The Young Franc-Tireurs
— 281, Valentin
— 326, D. and V. MARGUÉRITTE's novels
— 372, Under the Iron Flail
— 380, The Garden of Swords
— 432, Tuck-of-Drum
— 454, The German Lieutenant
— 457, Lay Down Your Arms
— 462, Mrs. Dymond
— 518, The Downfall
— See also *Paris, Siege of*
Franco-Prussian War of 1792, 155, La Comtesse de Charny
— See also *Napoleonic Wars*
François le champi, 421
Franconia Stories, The, 1
Frank and Rosamund, 160
Frank Brown, Sea Apprentice, 79
Frank Fairleigh, 439
Frank Hilton, 211
Frank Mildmay, 328
Frankenstein, 432
Frankfurt, 24, The Gamesters
— 37, The Swordmaker
— 161, Dr. Jacob
Frankland, Sir Charles Henry, 84, Agnes Surriage
— 398, Lady Good-for-Nothing
Franklin, Benjamin, 36, The Maid of Maiden Lane
— 169, Brinton Eliot
— 206, Veronica Playfair
— 338, Israel Potter
Franklin Kane, 428
Fraser, Simon, Lord Lovat, 78, A Lost Lady of Old Years
— 153, Scotland's Heir
— 318, The Lady of Hirta
— 348, Colonel Kate
— 356, The New Road

Fraternity, 190
Frau Bürgermeisteren, Die, 158
Frau Professorin, Die, 19
Frau Sorge, 455
Fräulein Else, 423
Fräulein Schmidt and Mr. Anstruther, 15
Fraynor, Billy, 297, The Fortunes of Glencore
Freaks of Mayfair, The, 48
Fred, 191
Frédéric et Bernerette, 357
Frederic Uvedale, 256
Frederick I, Emperor (Barbarossa), 24, The Sea Captain
Frederick II (Emperor), 152, Greater than the Greatest, The Betrayers
Frederick III (Emperor), 7, The Burgomaster of Berlin
Frederick The Great, 24, The Gamesters
— 271, Chrysal
— 321, A Gentle Knight of Old Brandenburg
— 334-5, L. MÜHLBACH'S novels
— 420, Consuelo, and sequel
— 448, A Gendarme of the King
— 474, The Little Marquis of Brandenburg
Frederick I (of Sweden), 470, The Times of Frederick I
Frederick V (Elector Palatine), 262, Heidelberg
Frederick the Great and his Court, 354
Frederick the Great and his Family, 355
Frederick William, King of Prussia, 321, A Gentle Knight of Old Brandenburg
— 432, the Red Cravat
Free, Micky, 296, Charles O'Malley
Free, 151
Free Air, 298
Free Companies, 261, Philip Augustus
— 292, Brakespeare
Free Joe, 228
Free-Lance of To-day, A, 105
Free Love, 7, The Woman Who Did
— 39, The New Antigone
— 239-40, Half-Way House, and sequels
— 420, Jacques
— 431, The Irrational Knot
— 494, In the Days of the Comet
— See also *Marriage, Sex Problems*
Free Rangers, The, 9
Free to Serve, 401
Free-Will Offering, A, 125
Freelance in Kashmir, A, 319
Freelands, The, 190

Freethought, 191, Peace
— 261, Niels Lyhne
— 347, Persian Letters
— See also *Agnosticism and Faith, Atheism, Religion*
Freischütz, Der, 139
Frémont, Col., 93, Captain Courtesy
Fremsynte, Den, 299
FRENCH, Alice, see "THANET, O.," 463
French at Moscow, The, 468
French Canadians, 95, Mrs. CATHERWOOD'S novels
— 375-6, Sir Gilbert PARKER'S stories
— 439, Mrs. A. P. SMITH'S novels
— See also *Quebec*
French Nan, 94
FRENCH NOVELISTS:
E. ABOUT, L. ACHARD, O. AUBRY, M. AUDOUX, J. AICARD,

H. de BALZAC, M. BARRÈS, R. BAZAN, Quesnay de BEAUREPAIRE, M. BEDEL, J. BENDA, P. BENOIT, H. BÉRAUD, C. de BERNARD, M. H. BEYLE, A. BIRABEAU, J. R. BLOCH, H. BORDEAUX, P.C. J. BOURGET, "R. BOYLESVE," L. F. BUNGENER,

L. CAHUN, A. CHAMSON, J. CHARDONNE, F. R. vicomte de CHATEAUBRIAND, A. de CHÂTEAUBRIANT, C. V. CHERBULIEZ, J. A. A. CLARETIE, G. CLEMENCEAU, "T. COMBE," H. B. CONSTANT DE REBECQUE, F. E. J. COPPÉE, "G. COURTELINE," Mrs. A. CRAVEN, S. CYRANO DE BERGERAC,

H. DANIEL-ROPS, A. DAUDET, H. DAVIGNON, M. DEKOBRA, D. DIDEROT, R. DORGELÈS, P. DU CHAILLU, G. DUHAMEL, Alexandre DUMAS, Alexandre DUMAS *fils*, "Dominque DUNOIS," A. DUSSERRE,

"ERCKMANN - CHATRIAN," R. ESCHOLIER, "C. FARRÈRE," F. de la Mothe FÉNELON, O. FEUILLET, E.-A. FAYDEAU, G. FLAUBERT, M. FORMONT, A. FOURNIER, "A. FRANCE,"

L. GALLET, J. GALLI DE BIBIÉNA, P. GAULOT, Judith GAUTIER, T. GAUTIER, Marie GAY, A. GIDE, J. GIRAUDOUX, Count de GOBINEAU, J.

FRENCH NOVELISTS (*contd.*):
and E. de GONCOURT, Remy de GOURMONT, L. GOZLAN, J. GREEN, T. S. GUEULETTE, É. GUILLAUMIN, "GYP,"

L. HALÉVY, "M. HARRY," L. HÉMON, V. HUGO, J. K. HUYSMANS,

P. A. F. C. de LACLOS, Comtesse de LA FAYETTE, A. LAFON, A. de LA SALE, G. de LA TOUR-LANDRY, Mme LA VERGNE, M. LEBLANC, R. LE FEVRE, Marie LE FRANC, J. LE MAÎTRE, "G. LE NOTRE," G. LEROUX, A. LESAGE,

Count X. de MAISTRE, H. MALO, H. H. MALOT, René MARAN, MARGUERITE D' ANGOULÊME, P. and V. MARGUERITTE, P. MARIVAUX, J. F. MARMONTEL, G. de MAUPASSANT, F. MAURIAC, A. MAUROIS, C. MENDÈS, P. MERIMÉE, P. MILLE, de MONTESQUIEU, P. MORAND, H. MURGER, A. de MUSSET,

"H. NADEL," G. OHNET, A. PRAVIEL, M. PRÉVOST, Abbé PRÉVOST D'EXILES, M. PROUST, E. PSICHARI, F. RABELAIS, H. RABUSSON, E. ROD, E. P. RODOCANACHI, R. ROLLAND, "J. ROMAINS," M. ROSTAND, J. J. ROUSSEAU,

B. de SAINT-PIERRE, X.-B. SAINTINE, "G. SAND," L. S. J. SANDEAU, Isabelle SANDY, P. SCARRON, E. SCHURÉ, de SÉNANCOUR, E. SOUVESTRE, P. SOUVESTRE and M. ALLAIN, Mme de STAËL, E. SUE,

J. THARAUD, C. A. THEURIET, Marcelle TINAYRE, M. UCHARD, B. VALLOTTON, M. B. VAUCAIRE, J. VERNE, A. de VIGNY, Count VILLIERS DE L'ISLE ADAM, F. de VOLTAIRE, E. ZOLA
French Powder Mystery, The, 396
French Prisoner, The, 388
French Revolution, 16, The Mysterious M. Dumont
— 29, A Gondreville Mystery, An Episode of the Terror, The Seamy Side of History
— 30, The Conscript

French Revolution (contd.):
43, The Girondin
— 69, The Third Estate
— 71, A Gentleman of Virginia
— 90, The Extraordinary Adventures of Diana Please
— 90, Adventures of the Comte de la Muette
— 132, The Whirlwind
— 141, A Tale of Two Cities
— 155, Ange Pitou, and sequel
— 156, The Woman with the Velvet Necklace, The Whites and the Blues
— 162, A Romance of Dijon
— 162, A Storm-Rent Sky
— 166, The Story of a Peasant
— 178, Leroux
— 185, Noblesse Oblige
— 212, The Reds of the Midi, and sequels
— 222, The Giant
— 235, Rose in the Mouth
— 254, Ninety-Three
— 269, In the Name of Liberty
— 280, Mademoiselle Mathilde
— 309, Zanoni
— 345, Adventures of François
— 370, ORCZY'S novels
— 381, My Sword for Lafayette
— 402, Kilgorman
— 410, The Atelier du Lys
— 417, The Trampling of the Lilies
— 418, Scaramouche, The Nuptials of Corbal
— 428, The Last Duchess of Belgarde
— 432, The Queen's Fillet
— 473, A Girl of the Multitude
— 477, The Red Cap
— 478, Citoyenne Jacqueline
— 495, A Marriage under the Terror
— 497, The Red Cockade
French Romances, 15, Jean D'ARRAS
— 18, Aucassin et Nicolette
— 60, Blanchardyn and Eglantine
— 98, Charles the Grete
— 99, The Châtelaine of Vergi
— 181, The Four Sons of Aymon
— 236, Helyas
— 255, Huon of Burdeux
— 288, A. de LA SALE'S works
— 465, The Three King's Sons
— 480, Valentyn and Orson
— See also MORRIS, W. (tr.) 352

Frenchmen's Creek, 397
Frères corses, Les, 156
Frey and his Wife, 240
Freya of the Seven Isles, 111
Freydis, 240, Gudrid the Fair
Friar Observant, A, 74
Friar of Wittenberg, The, 131
Friar Rush, 465
Friar's Niece, The, 273
Friedland, Battle of, 468, War and Peace
Friend Fritz, 165
Friend of Cæsar, A, 131
Friend of Death, The, 5
Friend of Master Francis, A, 439
Friend of Nelson, A, 256
Friend of the Family, The, 146
Friend Olivia, 36
Friend with the Counter-sign, A, 47
Friends, The, 20
Friendship of Amis and Amile, 352
Friendship Village, 189
Friendship Village Love Stories, 189
Friendship's Garland, 15
Friesland, 102, The Riddle of the Sands
Frithiof the Bold, 352
Froissart, Jean, 155, Agenor de Mauléon
Frollo, Claude, 253, Notre Dame de Paris
From a Cottage in Troy, 396
From a Life of Two Months, 88
From a Swedish Home-stead, 286
From a Thatched Cottage, 234
From Day to Day, 204
From Door to Door, 90
From Moor Isles, 180
From Opposite Shores, 218
From Powder-Monkey to Admiral, 281
From Sand Hill to Pine, 230
From the Broad Acres, 176
From the Earth to the Moon, 482
From the East unto the West, 34
From the Five Rivers, 445
From the Four Winds, 189
From the Fury of the O'Flaherties, 363
From the Green Bag, 149
From the Land of the Shamrock, 34
From the Land of the Wombat, 485
From the Loom of the Dead, 379
From the Memoirs of a Minister of France, 497
From the Other Side, 188
From the Vasty Deep, 44
From Veldt Camp-Fires, 77
Fromont Family, 518-19, Lourdes, and following.

Fromont Junior and Risler Senior, 129
Fronde, The, 154, Twenty Years' After, and sequels
— 155, The War of Women
— 261, John Marston Hall
— 513, Stray Pearls
Front Lines, 86
Front Yard, The, 511
Frontenac, Count, 126, A Daughter of New France
— 343, The Road to Fron-tenac
— 376, The Power and the Glory
Frontiers of the Heart, The, 326
Frosts of June, 171
Froth, 375
Frozen Deep, The, 109
Frozen Justice, 344
Frozen Pirate, The, 417
Fruit of the Tree, The, 499
Fruit of the Vine, The, (by ATHERTON), 61
Fruit of the Vine, The (by PUGH), 395
Fruitful Vine, The, 242
Fruitfulness, 519
Fry, Elizabeth, 413, Trans-ported
Fryer Bacon, 465
Fudge Family in Paris, 350
Fulfilment of Daphne Bruno, 400
Full Circle, 499
Fuller, Margaret, 233, The Blithedale Romance
Funeral March, The, 33
Funeral March of a Marion-ette, 227
Fuoco, Il, 12
Fur Country, The, 482
Fur Traders, 289, Lords of the North, Heralds of Empire
Furnace, The, 422
Furnace of Earth, A, 409
Further Adventures of Cap-tain Kettle, 258
Further Adventures of Nils, 287
Further Adventures of Quincy Adams Sawyer, 387
Further Experiences of an Irish R.M., 443
Further Foolishness, 293
Futility, 196
Future Life, 136, The Return
— 284, Makar's Dream
— 367, A Beleaguered City, A Little Pilgrim in the Unseen
— 368, The Land of Dark-ness
— 383, The Gates Ajar
— 384, Beyond the Gates, The Gates Between
— 491, Aylwin

Gabriel, 284
Gabriel Conroy, 229
Gabriel Foot, 396

Gabriele, 211
Gadfly, The, 484
Gael, The, 308
Gaels, see *Celtic, Hebrides, Highlands, Ireland, Scotland*
Gage of Red and White, The, 247
Gainsborough, William, 330, The Parson's Daughter
Gainsborough (Lincs), 164, The Mill on the Floss
"GAK TSOK-SIN," see CROWTHER, Dr. P.
Galahad, 166, Galahad
— 243, High History of the Holy Graal
Galahad, 166
Galahad Jones, 2
Galapagos Islands, 338, The Encantadas
Galatea, 96
Galatea of the Wheatfield, 185
Galen, 377, Marius the Epicurean
Galeotti, 426, Quentin Dur-ward
Galicia, 196, Dorothea GER-ARD's novels
— 375, The Son of the Bondwoman
— 461, The Handmaid of the Lord
Gallant of Gascony, A, 448
Gallantry, 84
Gallants, The, 38
Gallegher, 131
Gallery of Women, A, 151
Gallia, 148
Gallions Reach, 469
Galloping Dick, 327
Galloway, 39, David Arnot
— 123-4, S. R. CROCKETT's novels
— 316, R. W. MACKENNA's novels
— 335, A Duke of Britain
— 424, Guy Mannering
— See also *Ayrshire, Bor-der, Covenanters*
Gallow's Orchard, 444
Gallus, 53, A Hero in Wolf-skin
Gallus, 41
Galway, 60, The Irish Chief-tains
— 276, Castle Daly
— 297, Luttrell of Arran
— 363, A Queen of Men
— See also *Aran Isles*
Gambara, 30
Gambetta, Leon, 29, Z. Marcas
— 39, The Dayspring
— 130, Numa Roumestan
Gambler, The, 147
Gambler's Luck, 244
Gambling, 1, Trente et Quarante
— 48, The Princess Sophia
— 147, The Gambler
— 381, The Footsteps of a Throne
— 390, My Little Lady
— 429, The Land of Cock-ayne

Gambling (contd.): 463, Barry Lyndon
— 467, Recollections of a Marker
Gambrinus, 285
Game, The, 302
Game and the Candle, The, 75
Game Laws, see *Poachers*
Gamelyn, 302
Gamesters, The, 24
Gammon, Father, 339, Rhoda Fleming
Gangsters in America, 82, Little Cæsar
— 105, Louis Beretti
— See also *Bootleggers, Crime*
Gaol, The, 68
Går an, Det, 8
Garçonne, La, 326
Garden by the Sea, A, 403
Garden of Allah, The, 242
Garden of Epicurus, The, 183
Garden of Survival, The, 59
Garden of Swords, The, 380
Garden Party, The, 325
Garden That I Love, The, 21
Gardener Jim, 76
Gardening, 14, Elizabeth and her German Gar-den, The Solitary Sum-mer
— 21, Alfred AUSTIN's journals
— 58, Christowell, Kit and Kitty
— 155, The Black Tulip
Gardiner, Bishop, 178, The Fifth Queen, and sequels
Gargantua, 398, RABELAIS' Works
Gargery, Joe, 141, Great Expectations
Garibaldi, Guiseppe, 24, The Pillar of Fire
— 25, The Rebel
— 133, The Lame English-man
— 144, Lothair
— 247, For Freedom
— 252, Defeat, and sequel
Garibaldi and the New Italy, 252
Garland, The, 479
Garm—a Hostage, 282
Garman and Worse, 278
Garonne, 139, The Hôtel du Petit-St.-Jean
Garrick, David, 63, In the Days of Goldsmith
— 104, Richard Carvel
— 348, The Jessamy Bride, Fanny's First Novel
Garrison, William Lloyd, 81, The Shepherd of the People
Garryowen, 444
Garth, Caleb and Mary, 164, Middlemarch
Garth, 232
Garthowen, 399

Gascons, 154, The Three Musketeers, and sequels
Gaspar Ruiz, 111
Gaspard Hauser, 18
Gaston de Latour, 377
Gate of Death, The, 47
Gate of the Hundred Sorrows, The, 281
Gate-Openers, The, 348
Gateless Barrier, The, 321
Gates Ajar, The, 383
Gates Between, The, 384
Gates of Doom, The, 418
Gates of Life, 56
Gates of Paradise, The, 242
Gates of the North, The, 365
Gathering Clouds, 170
Gathering of Brother Hilarius, The, 168
Gathering of Eagles, 199
Gaudissart, 28, Parisians in the Country, César Birotteau, 29, Cousin Pons
Gaudissart II, 29
Gauguin, Paul, 334, The Moon and Sixpence
Gaul, 345, The Conquered
— 346, When the Bough Breaks, Barbarian Stories
GAUTHIER-VILLARS, Henri, see "COLETTE and WILLY," 108
GAUTHIER-VILLARS, Sidonie Gabrielle, see "COLETTE"
Gaverocks, The, 208
Gaviota, La, 84
Gawain, Sir, 243, High History of the Holy Graal
Gay-Dombeys, The, 270
Gay House, The, 76
Gayworthys, The, 503
Gebannt und erlöst, 496
Geheime Geschichte des Philosophen Peregrinus Proteus, 503
Geisterseier, Der, 422
Gelimer, 128
Gellert, C. F., 19, Christian Gellert
Gendarme of the King, A, 448
General John Regan, 55
General Manager's Story, The, 222
General Ogle and Lady Camper, 340
General's Ring, The, 287
Generous Lover, The, 422
Generous Wine, 457
Geneva, 50, Dawn on Mont Blanc
— 101, Joseph Noirel's Revenge, Miss Rovel
— 498, The Long Night
Genevra's Money, 306
Génie du Christianisme, Le, 98
Genius, The (by DREISER), 151
Genius, The (by Mrs. POTTER), 390
Genji Monogatari, 356

Genoa, 111, Under Western Eyes
— 112, Suspense
— 397, Sir John Constantine
Gentle Craft, The, 138
Gentle Grafter, The, 389
Gentle Knight of Old Brandenburg, A, 321
Gentle Libertine, The, 108
Gentle Spirit, The, 147
Gentleman, Le, 434
Gentleman, The, 368
Gentleman, The Ideal, 74, The Fool of Quality
— 120, John Halifax
— 296, The Knight of Gwynne
— 301, Amadis of Gaul
— 307, Euphues
— 308, Pelham
— 310, Kenelm Chillingly
— 406, Sir Charles Grandison
— 462, The Newcomes
Gentleman Adventurer, A, 62
Gentleman Adventurer, The, 24
Gentleman Friend, A, 100
Gentleman from Indiana, The, 459
Gentleman from San Francisco, The, 80
Gentleman of France, A, 497
Gentleman of Leisure, A, 170
Gentleman of the South, A, 77
Gentleman of the Steppe, The, 475
Gentleman of Virginia, A, 71
Gentleman Player, A, 446
Gentleman Roger, 185
Gentleman Upcott's Daughter, 400
Gentleman Vagabond, A, 440
Gentleman's Gentleman, A, 380
Gentlewoman of France, A, 69
Geôle, La, 68
Geordie, Jingling, 426, Fortunes of Nigel
George I, 5, Preston Flight
— 91, Historical Vignettes
George II, 53, The Chaplain of the Fleet
— 62, Fortune's my Foe
— 243, High Treason
George III, 52, A Fountain Sealed
— 71, The Adventures of Lady Susan
— 132, The Orangery
— 191, Annals of the Parish
— 226, The Trumpet Major
— 284, A Maid of '76
George IV, 94, Pamela Pounce
— 150, Rodney Stone
— 169, J. FARNOL's novels, *passim*
— 184, Yeoman Fleetwood

George IV (contd.): 243, Demi-Royal
— 400, A Lady of the Regency
George Mandeville's Husband, 412
George Washington's Last Duel, 373
George's Mother, 121
Georgia, 113, Return
— 203, A Short History of Julia
— 224, W. N. HARBEN's novels
— 228-9, J. C. HARRIS's stories
— 237, Gold and Iron
— 271, R. M. JOHNSTON's novels
— 278, Cicily
— 401, Doris Kingsley
— 511, Rodman the Keeper, East Angels
Georgians, The, 224, 225
Georgie (A Lost Love), 364
Geraint, the Son of Erbin, 217
Gerald Fitzgerald the Chevalier, 297
Geraldine, 112
Geraldines, 4, Windsor Castle
— 357, The Unfortunate Traveller
Gerardo and Elena, 31
Gerard's Marriage, 464
Gerfaut, 52
Germ-Destroyer, A, 281
German in the Village, A, 335
German Lieutenant, The, 454
German Love, 355
GERMAN NOVELISTS: "Willibald ALEXIS," Bertha AUERBACH, Vicki BAUM, W. A. BECKER, Marie BERNHARD, G. BIRKENFELD, W. BLOEM, A. BRONNEN, M. BROD, K. BRÖGER, H. CAROSSA, L. C. A. von CHAMISSO DE BONCOURT, J. S. F. DAHN, LIESBIT DILL.

G. M. EBERS, E. ECKSTEIN, K. EDSCHMID, A. EGGEBRECHT, "Otto ERNST," L. FEUCHTWANGER, Irene FORBES-MOSSE, Baron de la Motte FOUQUÉ, L. FRANK, K. E. FRANZOS, G. FRENSSEN, G. FREYTAG, F. W. GERSTÄCKER, J. W. von GOETHE, J. GREGOR, F. GRIESE, H. C. GRIMMELHAUSEN, F. W. von HACKLÄNDER, W. HAUFF, G. HAUPTMANN, A. D. HAUSRATH, "W. HEIMBURG," E. T. HOFFMANN, Ricarda HUCH, W. JENSEN, B. KELLERMANN, Sophie KLOERSS, H. T. KOERNER, S. KOHN, Isolde KURZ, P. M. LAMPEL, O. LUDWIG.

GERMAN NOVELISTS (*contd.*): H. MANN, T. MANN, "E. MARLITT," J. W. MEINHOLD, C. F. MEYER, A. MOSZKOWSKI, "Louise MÜHLBACH," F. M. MÜLLER, "J. MURON," J. K. A. MUSAEUS, A. NEUMANN, H. O. NIETSCHMANN, W. NOELDECHEN, J. NORDLING, L. PERUTZ, R. E. RASPE, E. M. REMARQUE, L. RENN, F. REUTER, J. P. RICHTER, R. M. RILKE, Baron von ROBERTS, J. RODENBERG, J. ROTH.

L. von SACHER-MASOCH, "G. SAMAROW," F. SCHAÜWECKER, J. V. von SCHEFFEL, R. SCHICKELÉ, J. F. von SCHILLER, "SCHLUMP," H. SCHÜLTZ, Anna SEGHERS, F. SPIELHAGEN, E. W. J. STINDE, H. T. W. STORM, R. STRATZ, H. SUDERMANN, Bertha SUTTNER, F. THEISS, Susanne TRAUTWEIN, Clara VIEBIG, W. WALLOTH, Jacob WASSERMANN, "E. WERNER," C. M. WIELAND, J. H. D. ZSCHOKKE, A. ZWEIG
— See also 93, CARLYLE (tr.) (MUSAEUS, TIECK, and RICHTER)
— 139, DE QUINCEY (tr.)
German Romance, 170, Faustus
GERMAN-CZECH NOVELISTS: F. WERFEL,
GERMAN-SWISS NOVELISTS: Cécile LOOS, C. SPITTELER
Germany, before the 19th Century, 37, The Strong Arm
— 263, The Castle of Ehrenstein
— 74, A Friar Observant
— See also *Reformation, Seven Years' War, Thirty Years' War*, and names of monarchs and notable figures
Germany, Modern, 14-15, Gräfin von ARNIM's novels
— 161, Barbara's History, Dr. Jacob
— 213, Six Stories
— 249, Their Silver Wedding Journey
— 268, Three Men on the Bummel
— 303, Hyperion
— 325, In a German Pension
— 326, The Frontiers of the Heart
— 339, Harry Richmond

Germany, Modern (*contd.*): 354, Defeat
— 434, Anthea's Guest, Karen
— 435, Sielanka
— See also *Franco-German War*, and names of places
Germany, Post-War, 39, Calf Love
— 323, Berlin, The Patrioteer
— See also *Great War, Hitler, Kapp-Putsch, Post-War Problems*
Germelshausen, 197
Germinal, 518
Germinie Lacerteux, 206
Gervase Skinner, 245
Geschwister, Die, 188
Gesprengte Fesseln, 496
Gesta Romanorum, 197
Geste of Duke Jocelyn, The, 169
Getting of Wisdom, 406
Gettysburg, 8, In Circling Camps
— 42, Norwood
— 47, Who Goes There? and sequel
— 47, Old Squire
— 248, Stonewall's Scout
Ghent, 71, The White Hoods
— 261, Mary of Burgundy
— 280, Old Margaret
Ghetto, see *Jews*
Ghetto Comedies, 516
Ghosal, Mrs., 457, see SVARNAKUMĀRA DEVI
Ghost-Hunter and his Family, The, 31
Ghost-Seer, The, 422
Ghost-Stories, 47, Basil Netherby
— 54, Can Such Things Be?
— 59, The Empty House, *etc.*
— 90, At a Winter's Fire
— 128, Great Ghost Stories
— 136, DE LA MARE's stories
— 202, The Shadowy Third
— 214, Grettis Saga
— 265, The Turn of the Screw
— 266, M. R. JAMES's stories
— 281, The Phantom Rickshaw
— 294, In a Glass Darkly
— 379, The Shape of Fear
— 380, Border Ghost Stories
— 383, Men, Women, and Ghosts
— 397, Old Fires and Profitable Ghosts
— 403, Courage
— 449, Thrawn Janet
— 499, Tales of Men and Ghosts, Kerfol
— See also *Gothic Romance, Magic, Spiritualism, Supernaturalism, Vampires*, etc.
Ghost Stories of an Antiquary, 266

Ghosts in Daylight, 369
Ghosts of their Ancestors, The, 345
Giant, The, 222
Giant-Killer, 131
Giants in the Earth, 415
Giant's Robe, The, 12
Gibraltar, 243, As it Happened
Gideon Giles, 344
Gift from the Grave, A, 498
Gift of the Dusk, A, 394
Gift of the Gods, The, 446
Giftas, 454
Gil Blas, 167, Squire Marcos de Obregon
— 295, Gil Blas
Gil Blas, 295
Gilbert, Brian de Bois, 425, Ivanhoe
Gilbert Gurney, 245
Gilbert Neal, 224
Gilberte Swann, 393, Remembrance of Things Past
Gildas, 140, Star of Mercia
Gilded Age, The, 477
Giles Ingilby, 362
Giletta of Narbona, 430
Gilian the Dreamer, 356
Gilman of Redford, 132
Gilsland, Lord, 426, The Talisman
Ginevra, 327
Ginx's Baby, 267
Gioconda Smile, The, 256
Giovanna of Naples, 68, The Sword Decides
Giovanni Episcopo, 11
Gipsies, 66, Lavengro, The Romany Rye
— 174, The Green Grass Widow
— 217, Kriegspiel
— 341, Carmen
— 367, The Story of Valentine and his Brother
— 392, A Walking Gentleman, Fortuna Chance
— 376, The World for Sale
— 491, Aylwin
— 512, The Gipsy King
— See also *Tramps*
Gipsy King, The 512
Giraldus Cambrensis, 127, The Love Story of Giraldus
Girl Alone, A, 167
Girl at Cobhurst, The, 451
Giradin, Mme de, 400, Journeyman Love
Girl at the Gate, The, 460
Girl at the Half-way House, The, 248
Girl from the Marsh Croft, The, 287
Girl He left Behind Him, The, 185
Girl of Galway, A, 477
Girl of the Multitude, A, 473
Girls and I, The, 346
Girls' Schools, 108, Claudine at School
— 128, Regiment of Women
— 406, The Getting of Wisdom
— 492, Daddy Long-Legs

Girls, Stories for, 75–6, Miss BROUGHTON's novels, *passim*
— 91, Rosa N. CAREY's novels
— 106, Aunt Anne, Sir George's Objection
— 119–20, Mrs. CRAIK's novels
— 213, Miss E. Everett GREEN's novels
— 226–7, Mrs. L. A. HARKER's novels
— 332, Comin' thro' the Rye
— 345, Madeline
— 454, Christalla
— 457, "Annie SWAN's" novels
— 485, Lucy WALFORD's stories
— 503, Mrs. A. D. WHITNEY's novels
— See also *Children, Stories for*
Girondin, The, 43
Gisli, 200, Gisli Saga
— 240, The Outlaw
Gissing, George, 411, The Private Life of Henry Maitland
Give up your Lovers, 205
Givers, The, 506
Gjest den enøjede, 218
Glad Ghosts, 291
Glad Gut, En, 56
Glade in the Forest, The, 218
Gladiator, The, 217
Gladiators, The, 337
Gladstone, William Ewart, 240, Mainwaring
Glam, 208, Grettir the Outlaw
— 214, Grettis Saga
Glamorgan, Earl of, 314, St. George and St. Michael
Glamorganshire, 58, The Maid of Sker
Glamour, 307
Glasgow, 313, Alec Forbes
— 315, Children of the Dead End, The Rat-Pit
— 360, Justice of the Peace
— 478, St. Mungo's City
Glastonbury, 120, The Last Abbot of Glastonbury
Gleam in the North, The, 74
Gleaming Dawn, The, 25
Glen o' Weeping, The, 68
Glenaar, 432
Glencoe, 68, The Glen o' Weeping
Glencora, Lady, 472, The Prime Minister
Glendower, Owen, 180, Harry of Athol
Glengarriff, 363, When We were Boys
Glenmornan, 315
Glenshiel, Battle of, 91, For the White Rose
Glenties, 315, Children of the Dead End
Glimmer of Hunger, The, 443
Glimpse, The (novel), 46

Glimpse, The (story), 45
Glimpses of Dreamlands, 281
Glimpses of the Moon, 500
Glittering Plain, The Story of the, 352
Globe Theatre, 109, The Queen's Hostage
Gloria Mundi, 186
Glorious Apollo, 38
Glorious Lie, A, 196
Glory and Sorrow of Norwich, The, 60
Glory and the Abyss, The, 77
Glory Hole, The, 502
Glory of Clementina Wing, The, 301
Glory of Don Ramiro, The, 288
Glory of Woman, 445
Gloucester, Duke of, 330, Kensington Palace
Gloucestershire, 58, Clara Vaughan
— 212, The Spiritual Quixote
— 233, In a Desert Land
— 327, Love with Honour
" GLOUVET, Jules de," see BEAUREPAIRE, Quesnay de
Glück auf, 496
Go She Must, 193
Goat and Compasses, The, 14
Goblet, The, 93
Goblin, The, 180
Gobseck, 27
God and the King, 68
God and the Man, 79
God and Woman, 64
God in the Car, The, 246
God in the Thicket, The, 290
God of Clay, The, 24
God of his Fathers, The, 302
God of Love, The, 313
God Save England, 72
God Save King Alfred, 199
God-Seeker, The, 416
" God Wills It," 131
Gode Samvite, Det, 158
Godfather at Play, The, 439
Godfrey de Bouillon, 131, " God Wills It "
Godfrey Martin, Schoolboy, 475
Godfrey Martin, Undergraduate, 475
Godin, Jean André, 506, The Way Up
Godolphin, 308
Godolphin, Lord, 512, Robin the Prodigal
Gods and Fighting Men, 214
Gods and Mr. Perrin, The, 486
Gods are Athirst, The, 184
God's Counterpoint, 51
God's Fool, 310
God's Good Man, 116
Gods in the Schoolhouse, The, 240
God's Man, 489
Gods of Pegana, The, 157
God's Orchid, 51

God's People, 459
God's Providence House, 32
Gods, Some Mortals, and Lord Wickenham, The, 119
God's Step-Children, 344
God's Way and Man's, 469
Godson, The, 468
Godson of a Marquis, The, 464
Godunóv, Boris, 467, A Prince of Outlaws
Godwinism, 76, Wieland
Goethe, 335, Mape
GOETZ, George, see CALVERTON, V. F.
Gold, 501
Gold and Iron, 237
Gold Bug, The, 388
Gold-diggers, see *Miners*
Gold Else, 326
Gold Lace, 336
Golden Age, The, 210
Golden Arrow, The, 491
Golden Ass, The, 13
Golden Barque, The, 365
Golden Book of Torcello, The, 473
Golden Book of Venice, The, 475
Golden Bowl, The, 266
Golden Butterfly, The, 53
Golden Days, The, 307
Golden Dog, The, 283
Golden Fleece, The (by ACHARD), 1
Golden Fleece (by D. G. PHILLIPS), 384
Golden Galleon, The, 294
Golden Girl, The, 16
Golden Hawk, 407
Golden House, The, 490
Golden Key, The, 107
Golden Kingdom, The, 26
Golden Ladder, The, 253
Golden Quill, The, 323
Golden Sorrow, A, 389
Golden Straw, A, 79
Golden Thread, The, 189
Golden Triangle, 293
Golden Wedding, The, 454
Golden Wind, The, 365
Golden Windmill, The, 20
Golden Woman, The, 126
Goldmacher-Dorf, Das, 519
Goldmakers' Village, The, 519
Goldman's, 438
Goldsmith, Oliver, 63, In the Days of Goldsmith
— 79, Æsop Dancing
— 348, The Jessamy Bride
Goldsmith of Cheape, The, 81
Gollovlev Family, The, 419
Golovin, 490
Gondreville Mystery, A, 29
Gone to Earth, 491
Gone Under, 162
Good-bye, Sweetheart! 75
Good-bye, Wisconsin, 496
Good Companions, The, 392
Good Conduct, 55
Good Conscience, 158
Good Fight, A, 88
Good for the Soul, 136
Good Hour, The, 19

Good Luck, 496
Good Old Anna, 44
Good People of Pawlocz, The, 344
Good Red Earth, The, 385
Good Sir John, 195
Good Soldier Schweik, The, 231
Good Souls of Cider Land, 400
Good Stories of Man and Other Animals, 402
Good Wives, 5
Good Woman, A, 73
Goodly Life, A, 80
Goodwin Sands, 26, The Life Boat
Gopher Prairie, 298, Main Street
GORDON, Rev. Charles William, see "CONNOR, Ralph," 110
Gordon, Lord George, 140, Barnaby Rudge
"GORDON, H. R.," see ELLIS, E. S.
Gordon, General, 439, The Curse of the Nile
Gordon Keith, 373
Gorgeous Borgia, The, 313
Gorgeous Isle, The, 17
Gorilla Hunters, The, 26
Goring, Colonel, 261, Henry Masterton
Goriot, 28, Père Goriot
Gosford, Lord, 126, In Treaty with Honour
Goslings, 51
Gospel of Freedom, The, 238
Gospodin iz San Frantsisko, 80
Gossamer, 55
GOSSELIN, Louis L. T., see "LE NOTRE, G.," 295
Gossips Green, 153
Gösta Berling's Saga, 286
Gothenburg, Siege of, 107, The King with Two Faces
Gothic Romances, 20, Northanger Abbey (parody)
— 30, BALZAC's Philosophical Studies, *passim*
— 37, The Heroine (parody)
— 54, The Monk and the Hangman's Daughter
— 76, C. B. BROWN's novels
— 125, Salathiel
— 139, DE QUINCEY's stories
— 203, St. Leon, Fleetwood
— 298, The Monk
— 333, MATURIN's novels
— 388, POE's stories
— 399, Mrs. RADCLIFFE's novels
— 402, The Old English Baron
— 422, The Ghost-Seer
— 441, Ferdinand, Count Fathom
— 486, The Castle of Otranto
— See also *Ghost-Stories*
Goths, 53, A Hero in Wolf-Skin

Goths (contd.): 128, Felicitas
— 201, Veranilda
— 352, The House of the Wolfings
— See also *Totila*
Göttingen, 296, Arthur O'Leary
Gottsucher, Der, 416
Gough's Court, 107, A London Posy
Gourlay, David, 77, The House with the Green Shutters
Governesses, 297, Miss Meredith
— 391, Guardian Angels
Government, see *Communism, Law, Politics, Socialism, Utopias*, etc.
Governor, The, 344
Governor of England, The, 68
Governor of Kattowitz, The, 429
Governor's Niece, The, 33
Gower, John, 112, Long Will
Gowrie, 263
Gowrie Conspiracy, 263, Gowrie
Graal, see *Grail*
Grace Abounding, 81
Grace of Lambs, The, 284
Grace O'Malley, 315
Gradgrind, 141, Hard Times
Grǣco-Turkish War, 120, Active Service
Grafters, The, 308
Graftons, The, 329
Graham, John, of Claverhouse, 39, The Knight of the Golden Sword
— 124, Men of the Moss-Hags
— 319, Graham of Claverhouse
— 425, Old Mortality
Grail, Holy, 242, High History of the Holy Grail
— 506, War in Heaven
— See also *Arthurian Romance*
Grain Carriers, The, 360
GRAINGER, Francis Edward, see "HILL, Headon"
Grammatical Ghost, A, 379
Granada, 309, Leila
Grand Duchess, The, 56
Grand homme de province à Paris, Un, 28
Grand Hotel, 39
Grand-Louis L'innocent, 294
Grand Manner, The, 285
Grand Meaulnes, Le, 181
Grand Tour, The, 508
Grande Bretèche, la, 27
Grande Pointe, 86
Grandee, The, 375
Grandet, Eugénie, 27, Eugénie Grandet
Grandison the Second, 357
Grandissimes, The, 86
Grandmother Dear, 346
Grandmother, The, 358
Grandmothers, The, 496

Grandmother's Grandmother, 279
Grandmother's Money, 412
Grandson, The, 145
Grange, Lady, 318, The Lady of Hirta
Grania, 274, The Pursuit of Dermat and Grania, etc.
Grania (O'Malley Clan), see *O'Malley Clan*
Grania, 289
Gran'ma's Jane, 323
Grant, General Ulysses, 71, The Patriots
— 104, The Crisis, Coniston
— 376, My Lady of the North
— 506, The Captain
Grantley Fenton, 60
Grantly, Archdeacon, 471, Barchester Towers
Granvella, 105, The Duke's Page
Grape from a Thorn, A, 378
Grasp Your Nettle, 300
Grasshopper, The, 100
Grasshopper and the Ant, 136
Grattan, Henry, 243, The King's Deputy
— 400, A Lady of the Regency
GRAVES, Clotilde J. M., see "DEHAN, Richard," 135
Gray, Patrick, 24, The Master of Grey
— 239, The Queen's Quair
— 438, Queen Mary's Holdfast
Gray's Inn, 152, Men of Marlowe's
Graysons, The, 163
Great Accident, The, 506
Great Age, The, 442
Great Amulet, The, 144
Great Attempt, The, 16
Great Awakening, The, 370
Great Bluff, The, 243
Great Cañon, 135, Overland
Great Carbuncle, The, 232
Great Civil War, 5, Boscobel, The Leaguer of Lathom
— 24, Colonel Stow
— 98, The Draytons and the Davenants, and sequel
— 134, Memoirs of a Cavalier
— 144, Hugh Gwyeth
— 154, Twenty Years After
— 176, When Charles I was King, Mistress Spitfire
— 211, Harry Ogilvie
— 217, The King's Cause
— 222, Andrew Marvel and his Friends
— 223, Captain John Lister
— 261, Henry Masterton
— 262, Arrah Neil
— 313, Miriam Cromwell, Cornet Strong
— 314, St. George and St. Michael
— 319, Dagonet the Jester

Great Civil War (contd.): 328, Captain Fortune
— 329, The Children of the New Forest, Winifrede's Journal
— 330, The White King's Daughter
— 337, Holmby House
— 380, Magnus Sinclair, and sequel
— 396, The Splendid Spur
— 398, The Copernican Convoy
— 399, The Diary of Lady Willoughby
— 400, In the Smoke of War
— 404, Battlement and Tower
— 417, The Tavern Knight
— 425, A Legend of Montrose
— 440, Brambletye House
— 442, Patricia at the Inn
— 457, The White Horses
— 466, Sir Bevil
— 515, The Wreathed Dagger
Great Diamond Pipe, The, 78
Great Expectations, 141
Great Game, The, 152
Great Ghost-Stories, 128
Great God Success, The, 384
Great Good Place, The, 265
Great House, The, 498
Great Hunger, The, 63
Great Interruption, The, 335
Great Jester, The, 410
Great Lakes, 511, Castle Nowhere
Great Man, A, 45
Great Meadow, The, 410
Great Miss Driver, The, 247
Great Olaf T. Saga, The, 366
Great Pandolfo, The, 302
Great Possessions, 489
Great Proconsul, The, 215
Great Sculling Race, The, 347
Great Shadow, The, 149
Great Short Stories of the World, 105
Great Stone Face, The, 233
Great Struggle, The, 359
Great Success, A, 489
Great Unimpressionable, The, 20
Great War, 2, All Else is Folly
— 6, Death of a Hero, Roads to Glory
— 11, Confessions of a Little Man
— 33, Under Fire, Light
— 48, Up and Down, Robin Linnet
— 61, The Four Horsemen of the Apocalypse, Our Sea
— 72, Pillbox 17
— 86, Action Front, Front Lines

Great War (contd.): 88, Home Fires from France
— 89, The Deepening Stream
— 90, Pink Roses, Pugs and Peacocks
— 98, Roux the Bandit
— 145, Wooden Crosses, The Cabaret up the Line
— 146, Three Soldiers
— 153, G. DUHAMEL's novels
— 168, Way of Revelation
— 170, Soldier's Pay
— 178, Some do Not, and sequels
— 185, Carl and Anna
— 186, Peter Jackson, Cigar Merchant
— 187, Otto Babendiek
— 195, The Surrender, Blind Alley
— 204, From Day to Day
— 231, The Good Soldier Schweik
— 234, The First Hundred Thousand
— 236, A Farewell to Arms
— 237, The Secret Battle
— 244, Grey Dawn, Red Night
— 253, Cousins German
— 275, Little England
— 285, Captain Zillner
— 293, The Bomb-Shell
— 302, The Red Planet, The Rough Road
— 306, The Vermilion Box
— 311, Non-Combatants and Others
— 317, Extremes Meet
— 318, The Three Couriers
— 335, The Silence of Colonel Bramble
— 335, The Great Interruption
— 347, Toes Up
— 347, Fiery Particles
— 354, The Spanish Farm Triology
— 358, The Flood
— 402, The Forest of the Hanged
— 403, All Quiet on the Western Front, War
— 414, Pierre and Luce
— 415, Clerambault, Mother and Son
— 422, The Furnace
— 422, Schlump
— 429, The W Plan, and sequel
— 433, Journey's End
— 442, Love Lane
— 465, These Men, Thy Friends
— 466, Sacrifice
— 470, All Our Yesterdays
— 480, Susan Yellam
— 481, Potterat and the War
— 486, The Dark Forest
— 495, Mr. Britling sees it Through
— 499, The Marne
— 500, The Refugees, Squad

Great War (contd.): 520, The Case of Sergeant Grischa
— See also *Post-War Problems*
Great White Army, The, 381
Greater Glory, The, 310
Greater Inclination, The, 498
Greater Love, 268
Greater Power, The, 54
Greater than the Greatest, 152
GRECO, El, see THEOCOPULOS, Domenico
Greece, Ancient, 18, The Immortal Marriage, Vengeful Gods
— 41, Charicles
— 72, Alkibiades
— 131, A Victor of Salamis
— 158, An Egyptian Princess
— 160, Aphrodite
— 346, Mrs. MITCHISON's stories
— 347, The Temple of Gnidus
— 505, The Woman of Andros
— See also *Æneas, Alcibiades, Athens, Classical Mythology, Greek Romances, Homeric*
Greece, Modern, and Greek Characters, 1, The King of the Mountains
— 78, The Dancing Floor
— 109, Hypnerotomachia
— 246, Phroso
— 247, Anastasius
— 307, Glamour
— See also *Græco-Turkish War, Greek Novelists, Greek War of Independence*
Greek Brigand, The, 1
GREEK NOVELISTS: D. BIKÉLAS, A. EPHTALIOTIS, G. XÉNOPOULOS
— See also P. ISTRATI
Greek Romances, 2, Clitophon and Leucippe, by Achilles TATIUS
— 13, Apollonius of Tyre
— 235, HELIODORUS' Æthiopian History
— 303, Daphnis and Chloe
— 306, The True History
Greek War of Independence, 47-8, The Vintage, and sequel
— 54, Loukis Laras
— 165, Tales from the Isles of Greece
Greeley, Horace, 23, Eben Holden
Green, Professor T. H., 487, Robert Elsmere
Green, Mr. Verdant, 70, The Adventures of Mr. Verdant Green
Green Altar, The, 7
Green Apple Harvest, 276
Green Bay Tree, The, 72
Green Book, The, 272
Green Carnation, The, 241

Green Country, The, 343
Green Fire, 431
Green Flag, The, 150
Green Ginger, 353
Green-Grass Widow, A, 174
Green Groves of Balgowrie, The, 173
Green Hat, The, 14
Green Kitten, The, 206
Green Lane, 76
Green Mansions, 252
Green Mirror, The, 486
Green Mountain Boys, The, 464
Green Overcoat, The, 43
Green Patch, The, 256
Green Spectre, The, 33
Green Tea, 294
Greene Ferme Farm, 267
Greene, Richard Tobias, 337, Typee, and sequel
Greenlow, 508
Greenmantle, 78
Greenstone Door, The, 421
GREGG, Hilda, see " GRIER, S. C.," 215
Gregory VII, Pope (Hildebrand), 297, The Pilgrim
Gregory IX, Pope, 152, Greater than the Greatest
Greifenstein, 122
Grenadière, La, 26
Grenfell, Wilfred Thomason, 156-7, N. DUNCAN's stories
Grenoble, 29, The Country Doctor
— 65, A Mind Awakened
Grenville, Sir Richard, 91, Where England sets her Feet
— 279, Westward Ho !
— 294, The Golden Galleon
— 480, The Lady Mary of Tavistock
Grenzpfahl, Der, 143
Gresham, Beatrice and Mary 471, Doctor Thorne
Gretna Green, 109, The Inimitable Mrs. Massingham
Grettir the Outlaw, 208, Grettir the Outlaw
— 214, Grettis Saga
Grettir the Outlaw, 208
Grettis Saga, 214
Greville Fane, 264
Grey, Lady Jane, 4, The Tower of London
— 333, The Royal Sisters
Grey, Lord, 418, Anthony Wilding
Grey Champion, The, 232
Grey Dawn, The, 501
Grey Dawn, Red Night, 244
Grey Knight, The, 137
Grey Man, The, 124
Grey Parrot, The, 83
Grey Roses, 227
Grey Shepherd, The, 79
Grey Weather, 78
Grey Wig, The, 515
Gridiron, The, 305
Gridle, Byles, 245, The Guardian Angel

Grif, 169
Griffith Gaunt, 402
Grim, 177
Grim Smile of the Five Towns, The, 45
Grip, The, 242
Grip of the Bookmaker, The, 501
Grip of the Land, The, 218
Grippy, Leddy, 191, The Entail
Grisly Grisell, 513
Grizzle, Mrs., 441, Peregrine Pickle
Grocer Greatheart, 2
Grocers' Shops, 80, Nicky, Son of Egg
— See also Tradesmen
Growth, 460
Growth, 470
Growth of the Soil, 224
Grub-Staker, The, 192
Grub Street Nights Entertainment, The, 444
Gryll Grange, 379
Guarded Flame, The, 335
Guardian Angel, The, 245
Guardian Angels, 391
Guatemala, 312, Staying with Relations
Guavas the Tinner, 209
Gudgeon, Mrs., 491, Aylwin
Gudrid, 240, Gudrid the Fair
Gudrid the Fair, 240
Gudrun, 292, Laxdaela Saga
Guelfs and Ghibellines, 152, A Maker of Saints
— 199, The Pecorone
— 199, Provenzano the Proud
— 418, Bellarion
Guenn, 249
Guermantes Way, The, 393
Guerra, 358
Guerre des femmes, La, 155
Guert Ten Eyck, 451
Guest of Quesnay, The, 460
Guest the One-Eyed, 218
Gueux, 53, Beggars of the Sea
— 112, Ludovic and Gertrude
— 116, The Master Beggars of Belgium
— 158, The Burgomaster's Wife
Guibert, Comte de, 69, The Burning-Glass
Guiccioli, Countess, 161, Lord Byron
Guilty Man, The, 115
Guise, House of, 124, The White Plumes of Navarre
— 154-5, Marguerite de Valois, and sequels
— 155, The Two Dianas, The Page of the Duke of Savoy
— 262, One in a Thousand, Henry of Guise, The Man-at-Arms
— 446, An Enemy to the King
— 498, In Kings' Byways

Guizot, 400, Journeyman Love
Gulliverian Satire, 83, Erewhon, and sequel
— 184, Penguin Island
— 335, Voyage to the Land of the Articoles
— 336, Kaloolah
— 337, Mardi
— 354, The Isles of Wisdom
— 458, Gulliver's Travels
— 495, Mr. Blettsworthy on Rampole Island
Gulliver's Travels, 458
Gulmore the Boss, 228
Gun Runner, The, 346
Gunhild, 88
Gunnar, 360, Njals saga
Gunning, The Misses, 38, "The Ladies!"
— 348, The Fatal Gift
Gunnlaug the Wormtongue, The Story of, 352
Gunpowder Plot, 4, Guy Fawkes
Gunvor Thorsdotter til härö, 394
Gusev, 100
Gustavus I (Vasa), 268, Karine
— 486, Royal Favour
Gustavus II (Adolphus), 346, The Fortune-Hunter
— 470, The King's Ring
— See also Thirty Years' War
Gustavus III, 107, The King with Two Faces
Guten Stunde, Zur, 19
GUTHRIE, T. A., see "ANSTEY, F.," 12
Guy and Pauline, 317
Guy Fawkes, 4
Guy Livingstone, 292
Guy Mannering, 424
Guy of Tours, 225, Passe Rose
Guy of Warwick, 465
Guy Rivers, 436
Guyon, General, 230, A Sereshan
Guyon, Mme, 30, Seraphita
Guzman de Alfrache, 7, The Rogue
Gwinett, Ambrose, 234, A Kent Squire, and sequel
Gwydion, 217, Math, son of Mathonwy
Gwyn, Nell, 246, Simon Dale
— 348, Nell Gwyn
Gwynett of Thornhaugh, 234
Gyfrol, 405
Gypsy and Ginger, 169

H—— Family, The, 71
Ha Til Mi Tuliadh, 210
Haarlem, 53, Beggars of the Sea
— 155, The Black Tulip
Haas, Charles, 393, Swann's Way
Habitation Enforced, A, 282

Hackbut, Anthony, 339, Rhoda Fleming
Hackman, Francis, 349, The Rescue of Martha
Haddon Hall, 321, Dorothy Vernon
Hadji Murád, 469
Hadrian, Emperor, 158, The Emperor
— 231, Antinous
Hagar (by JOHNSTON), 270
Hagar (by LINSKILL), 300
Hagarene, 292
Hague, The, see Holland
Haïdoucs, Les, 259
Hair of the Dog, The, 336
Haiti, 253, Bug-Jargal
— 268, Moonraker
— 330, The Hour and the Man
— 350, Black Magic
— 356, The Spanish Island
Hajji Baba in England, 351
Hakon, King, 129, The Vikings of the Baltic
— 366, Olaf Saga
Haldin, Natalia, 111, Under Western Eyes
Half-a-Minute's Silence, 33
Half-Crown Bob, 490
Half-Hearted, The, 78
Half Moon, The, 178
Halfway House, 239
Halifax, 138, Thomas of Reading
Halil the Pedlar, 272
Hall, Bishop Joseph, 329, Winifrede's Journal
Hall, Nathan, 451, Guert Ten Eyck
"HALL, Owen," see DAVIS, John, 131
Hall and the Grange, The, 329
Halles de Paris, 517, The Fat and the Thin
Ham, Castle of, 57, The Mantle of the Emperor
Hamburg, 283, —— and Sons
Hamildon Hill, Battle of, 180, Harry of Athol
Hamilton, Duke of, 462, Esmond
Hamilton, Alexander, 17, The Conqueror
— 253, The Golden Ladder
— 270, Lewis Rand
— 345, The Red City
— 451, Guert Ten Eyck
Hamilton, Lady Emma, 38, The Divine Lady
— 90, Diana Please
— 120, John Halifax
— 150, Rodney Stone
— 156, The Neapolitan Lovers
HAMILTON, Eugene Lee, see LEE-HAMILTON, E., 294
Hamlet, 223, Ambales Saga
— 465, Early English Prose Romances
Hamlyn, Geoffrey, 280, The Recollections of Geoffrey Hamlyn
Hammer, The, 103
Hammer and Anvil, 444

Hammer und Amboss, 444
Hampden, John, 307, To Right the Wrong
Hampdenshire Wonder, The, 50
Hamps, Auntie, 45, Clayhanger, and sequels
Hampshire, 71, The Brown Mask
— 168, Moonfleet
— 232, Old Hampshire Vignettes
— 498, Queen's Folly
— See also New Forest, Wight, Isle of, Portsmouth, etc.
Han of Iceland, 253
Hanaud, 331-2, A. E. W. MASON's detective stories
Hand-Made Gentleman, The, 23
Hand of Ethelberta, The, 225
Hand of Destiny, The, 326
Hand of the North, The, 182
Handel, G. F., 330, The Master of the Musicians
Handel und Wandel, 219
Handley Cross, 456
Handmaid of the Lord, The, 461
Hands of Esau, 137
Handsome Brandons, The, 477
Handsome Quaker, The, 477
Handy Andy, 305
Hangman's House, 84
Hania, 436
Hankin, Shoemaker, 259, Mad Shepherds
Hannah Thurston, 461
HANNAY, Canon James O., see "BIRMINGHAM, G. A."
Hannay, Richard, 78, The Thirty-Nine Steps, and sequels
Hannibal, 60, Sonnica
— 175, Salammbô
— 199, Kallistratus
Hans Frost, 487
Hans Pfaal, 388
Hansine Solstad, 163
Hanska, Madame, 27, Modeste Mignon
Happily Ever After, 256
Happiness, 100
Happy Boy, A, 56
Happy End, The, 237
Happy Ending, 316
Happy Endings, 438
Happy-go-Lucky, 234
Happy-go-Lucky Morgans, The, 464
Happy Hunting-Ground, The, 382
Happy Mountain, The, 98
Happy Otherworld, The, 343
Happy Prince, The, 504
Happy-Thought Hall, 81
Happy Thoughts, 81
Happy Warrior, The, 256
Harbor, The, 389

Hard Cash, 401
Hard Liberty, 357
Hard Times, 141
Hard Woman, A, 255
Harding, Mr., 471-2, The Barchester novels
Harding, President, 3, Revelry
Hardinge, Mr., 322, The New Republic
Hardy, Sir Thomas Masterman, 97, Tom Bowling
Harem Life, 259, Kyra, My Sister
— 304, Constantinople, and sequel
— 305, Disenchanted
— 387, Veiled Women
— 394, Valda Hânem
— 507, Trousers of Taffeta
— See also *India, Turkey*
HÄRING, G. W. H., see "ALEXIS, Willibald"
Harington, Sir John, 38, The Gallants
Harlaw of Sendle, 209
Harlem, 316, Home to Harlem
Harley, Adrian, 339, Richard Feverel
Harley, Viscount, 4, St. James's
— 512, Robin the Prodigal
Harlot's Progress, A, 28
Harlov, 474, A Lear of the Steppes
Harmen Pols, 311
Harmer John, 487
Harm's Way, 371
Harold, 309
Harold, King of England, 120, The Rival Heirs
— 280, Hereward the Wake
— 309, Harold
Harold Fairhair, 163, Egil's Saga
— 366, Olaf Saga
Haroun-al-Raschid, 3, Arabian Nights' Entertainments
HARPER, Carrie A., see DIX, B. M. and HARPER, C. A.
Harrington, 161
Harrison, Dr., 173, Amelia
Harrison, Frederic, 411, The Private Life of Henry Maitland
— 322, The New Paul and Virginia
HARRISON, Mary St. Leger, see *sub nom.*, "MALET, Lucas," 321
"HARROD, F.," see ROBERTSON, Miss F., 411
Harrovians, The, 307
Harrow School, 307, The Harrovians
— 479, Brothers, The Hill
Harry and Lucy, 160
Harry Coverdale, 439
Harry Lorrequer, 296
Harry of Athol, 180
Harry Ogilvie, 211
Harry the Cockney, 395
Hartland Forest, 71

Harvanger, 25, The Magic Tale of Harvanger and Yolande
Harvard College, 113, Pine and Palm
— 132, Gilman of Redford
— 390, Harvard Stories
Harvard Stories, 390
Harvesters, The, 176
Harveys, The, 280
Harwich, 396, The Blue Pavilions
HASEGAWA, T., see "FUTABATEI," 189
Hassan, a fellah, 199
Hässliche Herzogin, Die, 171
Hastings, Battle of, 120, The Rival Heirs
— 309, Harold
Hastings, Warren, 215, The Great Proconsul
Hatchment, A, 210
Hatchway, Lieut., 441, Peregrine Pickle
Hatteraick, Dirk, 424, Guy Mannering
Hatteras, Captain, 482, The English at the North Pole
Haugianism, 278, Skipper Worse
Hauksbee, Mrs., 281, Plain Tales from the Hills, Under the Deodars
Haunt of Ancient Peace, A, 330
Haunted and the Haunters, The, 309
Haunted Bookshop, The, 351
Haunted Doll's House, The, 266
Haunted House, 510
Haunted Man, The, 141
Haunts of Ancient Peace, 21
Haunts of Men, The, 96
Hauser, Gaspard, 18, Gaspard Hauser
— 490, Caspar Hauser
Hausfrau Rampant, The, 450
Haut-Ton, Sir Oran, 378, Melincourt
Haute-Maurienne, 66, The House that Died
Haven, The, 386
Havisham, Miss, 141, Great Expectations
Havre, Siege of, 363, Willoughby Manor
Hawbuck Grange, 456
Hawbucks, The, 331
Hawk, Sir Mulberry, 140, Nicholas Nickleby
Hawke, Admiral, 62, Fortune's My Foe
Hawkeye, 114, The Leather-Stocking Tales
HAWKINS, Anthony Hope, see "HOPE, Anthony"
Haworths, 82
Hawthorn, Jerry, 162, Life in London, and sequel
Hawthorne, Nathaniel, 77, The Father
Haxby's Circus, 392

Haydn, Joseph, 420, Consuelo, and sequel
Haydon, Benjamin, 488, Fenwick's Career
Hazaras, 223, A Vizier's Daughter
Hazard of New Fortunes, A, 250
Hazlitt, William, 21, Hurdcott
He Knew He was Right, 472
He that Will Not when He May, 367
He Whom I Follow, 359
Head of a Hundred in the Colony of Virginia, 206
Head of the House of Coombe, The, 82
Headlong Hall, 378
Headrigg, Mause, 425, Old Mortality
Healer, The, 238
Healers, The, 311
HEARNE, Mary A., see "FARNINGHAM, Marianne," 169
Heart and Science, 109
Heart and Sword, 508
Heart of a Hero, The, 196
Heart of a Russian, The (A Hero of Our Time), 295
Heart of Alsace, The (by SCHICKELÉ), 422
Heart of Alsace, The (by VALLOTTON), 481
Heart of Darkness, 110
Heart of Hope, The, 406
Heart of Midlothian, 425
Heart of Nami-San, 467
Heart of the Ancient Firs, The, 9
Heart of the Ancient Wood, The, 409
Heart of the Hills, The, 182
Heart of the Moor, The, 98
Heart of the Northern Sea, 394
Heart of the West, The, 389
Heart of the World, 219
Heart of Toil, The, 464
Hearth of Hutton, The, 159
Hearts Courageous, 409
Heart's Highway, The, 505
Heart's Key, The, 239
Hearts of Three, 303
Hearts of Women, 411
Heartsease, 76
Heath, Charles and Peggy, 138, Alice-for-Short
Heathcliff, 73, Wuthering Heights
Heather and Snow, 314
Heather Jock, 210
Heavenly Christmas Tree, The, 146
Heavenly Ladder, The, 317
Heavenly Twins, The, 211
Heavens !, 439
Hebrides, 57, A Princess of Thule, The Maid of Killeena
— 124, Lochinvar
— 318, W. C. MACKENZIE's novels

Hebrides (contd.): 356, Children of Tempest
— 316, The Quiet Lady
— 431, Wm. SHARP's stories
— 446, The Gift of the Gods
Hector Servadac, 482
Heel of Achilles, The, 135
Heep, Uriah, 141, David Copperfield
Heidelberg, 231, Klytia, Jetta
— 234, The Winter Queen
— 262, Heidelberg
Heidelberg, 262
Heifer of the Dawn, A, 25
Heilige, Der, 343
Heine, Heinrich, 122, With the Immortals
— 400, Journeyman Lore
— 515, Dreamers of the Ghetto
Heir, The, (by "S. C. GRIER"), 215
Heir, The (by V. SACKVILLE-WEST), 419
Heir of Redclyffe, The, 513
Heir of the Ages, The, 378
Heir to Kings, 153
Heiress of the Forest, The, 392
Heirs, 90
Heiðarviga Saga, 235
Helfeck of Bannisdale, 488
Helen, 161
Helen Adair, 41
Helen of Lancaster Gate, 197
Helen of Troy, 166, The Private Life of Helen of Troy
— See also *Æneas*
Helen Ramsden, 259
Helen Treveryan, 157
Helen with the High Hand, 45
Helen's Babies, 218
Hell Fire Club, 178, The Portrait
— 271, Chrysal
— 381, Sir Richard Enscombe
Hellé, 466
Helmet of Navarre, The, 417
Héloïse and Abelard, 350
Helpers, The, 308
Helyas, The History of, 236
Hen Thorir, 30
Henchard, 226, The Mayor of Casterbridge
Henderson, Miriam, 405, Pilgrimage
Henley, Frank, 244, Anna St. Ives
Henrietta, Lady Wentworth, 170, My Lady Wentworth
Henrietta Temple, 143
Henriette, 115
Henry IV, Emperor, 297, The Pilgrim
Henry I (of England), 138, Thomas of Reading
— 209, Pabo the Priest

Henry II, 24, The Fool
— 127, The Love-Story of Giraldus
— 239, Richard Yea-and-Nay
— 343, The Saint
— 426, The Betrothed
Henry III, 21, Arnoul the Englishman
— See also *Barons' Wars*
Henry IV, 33, Argenis
— 102, Father Felix's Chronicle
Henry V, 262, Agincourt
— See also *Joan of Arc*
Henry V, 222, Coronation
Henry VI, 49, The History of Richard Raynal, Solitary
— 402, The Old English Baron
— 513, Two Penniless Princesses
Henry VII, 180, The Arrow of the North
— 220, Fair Margaret
— 262, The Woodman
Henry VIII, 4, Windsor Castle
— 49, The King's Achievement
— 178, The Fifth Queen
— 243, The Sword of the Lord
— 261, Darnley
— 333, Defender of the Faith
— 351, Utopia
— 433, Cold Steel
— 461, The House of the Wizard
Henry II (of France), 30, About Catherine de' Medici
— 155, The Two Dianas, The Page of the Duke of Savoy
— 262, The Brigand
— 286, The Princess of Cleves
— See also *Diane de Poitiers*
Henry III (of France), 4, The Admirable Crichton
— 62, The King's Mignon
— 154-5, Marguerite de Valois, and sequels
— 262, One in a Thousand, Henry of Guise
— 446, An Enemy to the King
Henry IV (of France), 113, For Henri and Navarre
— 152, A King's Pawn
— 154-5, Marguerite de Valois, and sequels
— 262, One in a Thousand
— 262, Henry of Guise, Rose d'Albret
— 417, The Helmet of Navarre
— 446, An Enemy to the King
— 448, Love in Armour
— 497, A Minister of France

Henry IV (of France) (contd.): 498, In Kings' By-ways, The Abbess of Vlaye
— 513, The Chevalier d'Auriac
Henry, Duke of York, 69, Mr. Misfortunate
Henry, Prince of Bayreuth, 321, A Gentle Knight of Old Brandenburg
Henry, Prince of Wales, 330, The Young Queen of Hearts
" HENRY, O.," see PORTER, W. S.
Henry, Patrick, 409, Hearts Courageous
Henry Bourland, 224
Henry Brocken, 136
Henry de Pomeroy, 71
Henry Dunbar, 70
Henry Elizabeth, 313
Henry Esmond, The history of, 462
Henry Masterton, 261
Henry of Guise, 262
Henry St. John, Gentleman, 113
Hensa-Thoris saga, 237
HEPBURN, T. N., see " SETOUN, G.," 430
Hephzibah Guinness, 345
Heptameron, 326
Her Best Friend, 256
Her Excellency's Daughter, 241
Her Ladyship, 478
Her Lover, 206
Her Majesty's Rebels, 308
Her Memory, 310
Her Mountain Lover, 192
Her Only Brother, 235
Her Serene Highness, 384
Her Soger Boy, 80
Herald of the West, A, 8
Heralds of Empire, 289
Herb Moon, The, 119
Herbert, George, 329, Under Salisbury Spire
— 330, A Haunt of Ancient Peace
Herdsman, The, 200
Here are Ladies, 446
Here Comes an Old Sailor, 432
Heredity, 17, A Daughter of the Vine, Ancestors
— 50-1, The Early History of Jacob Stahl, and sequels
— 52, The Children of Gibeon
— 56, The Heritage of the Kurts
— 68, The Gaol
— 78, The Path of the King
— 83, The Way of all Flesh
— 88, A Good Fight
— 127, The Poisoner
— 167, Comes the Blind Fury
— 201, Born in Exile
— 236, Lacemaker Lekholm
— 245, Elsie Venner, The Guardian Angel, A Mortal Antipathy

Heredity (contd.): 368, Two Men
— 395, The Heritage
— 418, Heritage
— 483, The Son of His Mother
— 509, St. Martin's Eve
— 510, Tangled Trinities
— 516-18, The Rougon-Macquart series
Herefordshire, 260, The Sheep Stealers
Heresy of Mehetabel Clark, The, 439
Heretic of Soana, The, 231
Hereward the Wake, 120, The Rival Heirs
— 280, Hereward the Wake
— 314, The Camp of Refuge
Hereward the Wake, 280
Heriots, The, 127
Heritage, 171
Heritage, 418
Heritage, The, 215
Heritage, The, 395
Heritage, The, 448
Heritage of the Kurts, The, 56
Heritage of Unrest, The, 372
Héritière, L', 215
Hermana San Sulpicio, La, 374
Hermann, 496
Hermann Agha, 375
Hermit, The, 207
Hermit and the Wild Woman, The, 499
Hermsprong, 23
Hero, The, 333
Hero in Wolf-Skin, A, 53
Hero of Herat, The, 144
Hero of Our Time, A, 295
Heroes, The, 279
Heroes of Smokeover, 259
Heroic Deeds of Gargantua and Pantagruel, 398
Heroine, The, 37
Heroine in Bronze, A, 8
Heroine of the Strait, The, 126
Heronshawe Main, 176
Herr Arne's Hoard, 287
Herr und Hund, 324
Herreros, 187, Peter Moor's Journey
Herridge of Reality Swamp, 234
Herself, 434
Hertford, Marquess of, 143, Vivian Grey, Coningsby
— 462, Vanity Fair
Hertha, 72
Hesper, 192
Hesperus, 407
Hester's Little Tour, 191
Het Leven, Het, 117
Hetty, 80
Hetty Wesley, 397
Hexham, 182, The Hand of the North
Hi-Spy-Hi, 398
Hic Jacet, 369
Hickson, 41
Hida no Takumi Monogatari, 414

Hidden City, The, 198
Hidden Player, The, 363
Hide and Seek, 108
Hiep-Hioup, 408
Hieroglyphics, 85
HIGGINBOTHAM, Rev. J. C., see " AGNUS, Orme," 3
High Adventure, The, 169
High Deeds of Finn, 415
High History of the Holy Graal, The, 242
High Noon, 193
High Place, The, 85
High Policy, 276
High Toby, The, 328
High Treason, 243
High Wind in Jamaica, 253
Highland Widow, The, 427
Highlands of Scotland, 7, Balmoral
— 57, William BLACK's novels, *passim*
— 77, Sir Quixote of the Moors
— 78, A Lost Lady of Old Years, Huntingtower, John MacNab, Castle Gay
— 320, The Three Miss Graemes, Us Four
— 355, John Splendid
— 355-6, N. MUNRO's novels
— 424-7, SCOTT's novels, *passim*
— 431, The Mountain Lovers
— 445, Red Rowans
— 449, David Balfour
— See also *Hebrides, Orkneys*, and counties
Hightown under Surfell, 78
Highwayman, The, 24
Highwaymen, 4, Rookwood
— 24, The Highwayman
— 71, The Brown Mask
— 91, Jemmy Abercraw
— 134, Colonel Jacque, Jonathan Wild
— 213, Tom Tufton's Travels, and sequel
— 308, Paul Clifford
— 327, Galloping Dick
— 328, The High Toby, and sequel
— 456, Willowdene Will
— See also *Bandits, Brigands*
Hilda Lessways, 45
Hilda Strafford, 228
Hill, Dr. John, 271, Chrysal
Hill, John, 267, The King's Yard
Hill, The, 479
Hill of Dreams, The, 315
Hill Rise, 335
Hilligenlei, 187
Hillingdon Hall, 456
Hillsboro, 278, Joscelyn Cheshire
Hillsboro People, 88
Hillsiders, 365
Hillyers and the Burtons, The, 280
Hilt and Hilt, 113
Himself and Mr. Raikes, 336

Hind Let Loose, A, 347
HINDENBURG, Baroness von, see HAY, Marie
Hindus, 7, The City of Sunshine
— 25, F. W. BAIN's works
— 32, The Poison Tree
— 244, HOCKLEY's works
— 281-3, KIPLING's novels
— 382, Alice PERRIN's novels
— 445-6, Mrs. STEEL's novels
— See also BENGALI NOVELISTS, India
Hirelings, The, 516
His Apparition, 251
His Cousin Betty, 380
His Daughter First, 225
His Duty, 464
His Eminence, 178
His English Wife, 453
His Excellency, 517
His Family, 389
His Father's Mate, 292
His Father's Son, 499
His First Leave, 227
His Grace of Osmonde, 82
His Great Adventure, 238
His Honour and a Lady, 116
His Honour's Pleasure, 387
His Indolence of Arras, 159
His Lost Bow, 150
His Magnificence, 10
His Magnificence, 80
His Majesty's Greatest Subject, 465
His Majesty's Shirt Sleeves, 390
His Majesty's Sloop, Diamond Rock, 255
His Masterpiece, 518
His Mistress and I, 391
His Native Wife, 41
His New Mittens, 121
His Own Father, 362
His People, 210
His Private Honour, 281
His Second Wife, 389
His Serene Highness, 24
His Vanished Star, 118
His Wedded Wife, 281
His Wife's Hand, 41
Hispaniola Plate, The, 62
Histoire comique, 184
Histoire comique des états de la lune, 127
Histoire comique des états du soleil, 127
Histoire contemporaine, L', 183
Histoire de cent trente femmes, 209
Histoire . . . de César Birotteau, 28
Histoire d'un conscrit de 1813, 165
Histoire d'un homme du peuple, 166
Histoire d'un paysan, 166
Histoire des treize, 28
Histoire du plébiscite, L', 166
Histoire of Hamblet, The, 430
Histoire sans nom, Une, 32

Historical Nights Entertainment, The, 418
Historical Novels, Early, 134, Memoirs of a Cavalier, Journal of the Plague Year
— 138, DELONEY's novels
— 188, Fulke Fitz-Warine
— 195, George à Green
— 203, St. Leon
— 286, The Princess of Clèves
— 402, The Old English Baron
Historical Vignettes, 91
History of Agathon, The, 503
History of Anthony Waring, The, 437
History of Aythan Waring, The, 260
History of David Grieve, 488
History of Egg Pandervil, The, 80
History of England, The (by Jane AUSTEN), 20
History of Fulke Fitz Warine, The, 188
History of George à Green, 195
History of Hamlet, 465
History of Helyas, Knight of the Swan, 236
History of Henry, Earl of Moreland, The, 74
History of Henry Esmond, The, 462
History of Lady Julia Mandeville, The, 74
History of Makbeth, 430
History of Margaret Catchpole, The, 107
History of Mr. Jonathan Wild, 173
History of Mr. Polly, The, 494
History of New York, A, 258
History of Over Sea, The, 352
History of Pendennis, 462
History of Pompey the Little, 271
History of Reynard the Fox, 404
History of Richard Raynal, Solitary, The, 49
History of Sir Charles Grandison, 406
History of Sir Richard Calmady, The, 321
History of Samuel Titmarsh and the Great Hoggarty Diamond, 462
History of the Caliph Vathek, The, 42
History of the Squire Marcos de Obregon, 167
History of Tom a Lincoln, 269
Hitherto, 503
Hivernage dans les glaces, 482
" HOBBES, John Oliver," see CRAIGIE, Pearl, 119

Hobhouse, 161, Lord Byron
Hocken and Huncken, 398
Hofer, Andreas, 497, With the Red Eagle
Hoffman, 156, The Woman with the Velvet Necklace
Hogan, M. P., 230
Hogni and Hedinn, 353
Hohe Lied, Das, 455
Hohensteins, The, 444
Holden, Eben, 23, Eben Holden
Holderness, 65, E. C. BOOTH's novels
— 79, A Golden Straw
— 180, C. and F. FOSTER's stories
Hole in the Wall, The, 353
Holland, 1, Blush-Rose
— 103, Penruddock
— 107, Jan van Elselo
— 112, H. CONSCIENCE's novels
— 116, The Master Beggars of Belgium
— 158, The Burgomaster's Wife
— 322, Don Luis
— 396, The Blue Pavilions
— 401, The Cloister and the Hearth
— 486, In Troubled Times
— See also Amsterdam, DUTCH NOVELISTS, Gueux, Hague, etc.
Hollow, The, 100
Holly Tree, The, 141
Holm, Peer, 63, The Great Hunger
— 64, The New Temple
Holmby House, 337
Holmes, Oliver Wendell, 177, O Genteel Lady
Holy Flower, The, 220
Holy Grail, 242
Holy Land, see Christ, Life of, Jerusalem, Jews, Palestine, etc.
Holy Orders, 116
Holy War, The, 81
Holyland, 187
Holyrood, 424, Waverley
— See also Mary Queen of Scots
Home, The (by BREMER), 71 and 72
Home (by CHEKHOV), 100
Home and the World, The, 400
Home Fires from France, 88
Home Life in Russia (Dead Souls), 205
Home-Maker, The, 89
Home to Harlem, 316
Homeric, 159, Perfection
— 166, The Private Life of Helen of Troy
— 171, The Adventures of Telemachus
— 294, Recuyell of the Historyes of Troye
— See also Classical Mythology
Homme d'affaires, Un, 29
Homme d' affaires, Un, 67

Homme de neige, L', 421
Homme qui rit, L', 254
Homme vierge, L', 391
Homo Sum, 158
Homoselle, 466
Honest Thief, An, 146
Honey-Bee, 183
Honey Bee, The, 343
Honey-Star, The, 161
Honeycomb, 405
Honeycomb, Will, 3, The Spectator
— 308, Devereux
Hong-Kong, 334, The Painted Veil
Honneur d'artiste, 172
Honorine, 27
Honorius, Emperor, 170, Gathering Clouds
Honour of Henri de Valois, 42
Honour of Savelli, The, 513
Honour of the Army, The, 519
Honourable Jim, The, 370
Hon. Peter Stirling, The, 179
Honours Easy, 347
Hook, Theodore Edward, 462, Vanity Fair
Hooligan Nights, 415
Hoosier Schoolmaster, The, 163
Hope, 210
Hope Leslie, 428
Hopeless Case, A, 170
Hopes, 71
Horace Chase, 511
Horda, La, 61
Horneck, Mary, 348, The Jessamy Bride
Horrible Suspicion, A, 163
Horse Marines, The, 283
Horse-Stealers, The, 100
Horse-Stealer's Daughter, The, 291
Horse Thieves, The, 285
Horses, see Animals
Horses and Men, 10
Horseshoe Robinson, 277
Hosen des Herrn von Bredow, Die, 7
Hospital Life, 153, G. DUHAMEL's novels
— See also Medical Life, Nurses, Sanatorium Life
Hospital Sketches, 5
Hostages, The, 346
Hosts of the Lord, The, 446
Hôtel d'Angleterre, 232
Hôtel du Petit-St.-Jean, The, 139
Hotels, 39, Grand Hotel
— 46, Imperial Palace
— See also Boarding House Life
Hototogisu, 467
Hotspur, Harry, 180, Harry of Athol
Hound from the North, The, 126
Hound of the Baskervilles, The, 150
Hounds of Fate, The, 355
Hounds of God, The, 418
Hour and the Man, The, 330
Hour of Conflict, The, 197

Hours Spent in Prison, 11
House, The, 66
House at High Bridge, The, 170
House-Boat on the Styx, A, 31
House by the Churchyard, The, 294
House by the Medlar Tree, The, 482
House by the River, The, 237
House Divided, The, 328
House in Demetrius Road, The, 51
House in Dormer Forest, The, 492
House in Marylebone, The, 106
House in the Downs, The, 328
House is Built, A, 163
House of a Thousand Candles, The, 359
House of Adventure, The, 133
House of Cobwebs, The, 201
House of De Mailly, The, 390
House of Gentlefolk, A, 474
House of Gold, The, 364
House of Hidden Treasure, The, 213
House of Islam, The, 387
House of Joy, The, 9
House of Lisronan, The, 7
House of Lynch, The, 342
House of Mirth, The (by Mrs. Wilfred WARD), 489
House of Mirth, The (by WHARTON), 499
House of Penarvan, The, 421
House of Pomegranates, A, 504
House of Quiet, The, 47
House of Seven Gables, The, 232
House of Sin, The, 466
House of Spies, The, 133
House of the Combrays, The, 295
House of the Dead, The, 146
House of the Luck, The, 439
House of the Secret, The, 170
House of the Three Ganders, The, 23
House of the Two Barbels, The, 464
House of the Whispering Pines, The, 213
House of the Wizard, The, 461.
House of the Wolf, The, 497
House of the Wolfings, A Tale of the, 352
House of Torment, The, 218
House of Walderne, The, 120
House of War, The, 387
House on Cherry Street, The, 36
House on the Beach, The, 340
House on the Hill, The, 69

House Surgeon, The, 282
House that Died, The, 66
House that Fell, The, 359
House with the Green Shutters, The, 77
Household of Sir Thomas More, 324
HOUSMAN, Laurence, see also Aucassin et Nicolette, 18
Houston, Samuel, 36, Remember the Alamo
— 248, Fifty-Four Forty, or Fight
— See also Alamo
Houyhnhnms, 458, Gulliver's Travels
How a Claim was Jumped, 460
How Conachar gained the Kingship over Ulster, 254
How I discoursed one night with an Apparition, 183
How Jolly Life Is!, 518
How the Other Half Lives, 408
How the Two Ivans Quarrelled, 204
How We Stormed the Fort, 341
Howard, Katherine, 178, The Fifth Queen Crowned
Howard the Halt, 249, Howard the Halt
Howard the Halt, 30, 249
Howard's End, 179
Howe, General, 8, In Hostile Red
— 345, Hugh Wynne
Hoxton, 52, The Children of Gibeon
Huckleberries Gathered from New England Hills, 114
Huckleberry Finn, the Adventures of, 476
Hudson, Henry, explorer, 178, The Half Moon
HUDSON, H. L., see "LINDSAY, Harry", 300
Hudson Bay Territory, 289, Lords of the North, Heralds of Empire
— 354, Jules of the Great Heart
— 375, Pierre and his People
— 376, Adventurer of the North, The Trail of the Sword
— 501, Conjurer's House
Hudson River, 43, Antonia
— 258, Rip Van Winkle
Hudson River Bracketed, 500
Hudson's Bay, 26
HUEFFER, F. M., see FORD, F. M.
Hugh, Saint, 138, The Gentle Craft
Hugh Gwyeth, 144
Hugh Rendel, 390
Hugh Trevor, 244
Hugh Wynne, 345

HUGUENIN, Mlle Adèle, see "COMBE, T.," 109
Huguenot, The, 262
Huguenots, 33, Argenis
— 62, The Scourge of God, Knighthood's Flower, The King's Mignon
— 149, The Refugees
— 154-5, Marguerite de Valois, and sequels
— 155, The Two Dianas
— 162, The Dream Charlotte
— 262, The Huguenot, Henry of Guise, The Man-at-Arms
— 332, A Lily of France
— 341, Chronicle of the Reign of Charles IX
— 363, Willoughby Manor
— 448, The Rose of Dauphiny
— 497, The House of the Wolf, A Gentleman of France, Count Hannibal
— 498, In King's Byways
— 512, The Silent Captain
— See also Guises, Henry III and IV of France, St. Bartholomew, Massacre of
Huis der Vreugden, Het, 9
Hulot family, 29, Cousin Betty
Hull, 222, Andrew Marvel
— 262, Arrah Neil
Human Boy, The, 385
Human Chord, The, 59
Human Cry, The, 409
Human Interest, The, 255
Human Odds and Ends, 201
Humanitarianism, 53, The Golden Butterfly
— 140, DICKENS's novels, esp. Oliver Twist
— 169, Blade-o'-Grass
— 278, Polly of Parker's Rents
— 420, Underneath
— 420, The Journeyman Joiner, Consuelo, and sequel
— 455, The Mysteries of Paris
— See also Social Reform, Sociological, Poor, etc.
Humbert, King, 502, The Torchbearers
— 176, Vestigia
Humbert's Invasion of Ireland, 63, The Rebels
— 289, The Race of Castlebar
Humble Lover, A, 162
Humble Romance, A, 505
Humble Romance, A, 506
Humbug, 135
Humby, Squire, 280, Ravenshoe
Humorous Stories, 374
Humour of Druid's Island, The, 316
Humphrey, Duke of Gloucester, 412, Philip the Leal
Hung Lou Meng, 474

Hunger (by HAMSUN), 223
Hunger, The (by "A. MERRY"), 343
Hungry Heart, The, 384
Hungry Stones, 399
Hundred Days, The, 26, Vengeance is Mine
— 71, The Eagle of the Empire
— 79, The Shadow of the Sword
— 87, In the Year of Waterloo
— 94, The Light of Scarthey
— 179, A Little Less Than Gods
— 370, The Bronze Eagle
— 381, The Hundred Days
— See also Napoleon, Waterloo
Hundred Days, The, 381
100%, 438
Hundred Years War, 60, The Glory and Sorrow of Norwich
— 149, The White Company
— 150, Sir Nigel
— 160, Cressy and Poictiers
— 208, Noémi
— 262, The Jacquerie, Agincourt
— See also Henry V
Hundredth Man, The, 451
Hungarian Brothers, The, 389
Hungarian Nabob, An, 271
HUNGARIAN NOVELISTS: M. JÓKAI, Baron M. JÓSIKA, K. MIKSZÁTH, Elsa S. SZÁSZ
Hungarian Revolution, 230, A Sereshan
— 267, The Stronger Wings
— 272, The Baron's Sons
Hungary, 56, The Grand Duchess
— 94, The Death Dance
— 196, The Waters of Hercules
— 271-3, JÓKAI's novels
— 297, That Boy of Norcutt's
— See also HUNGARIAN NOVELISTS, Hungarian Revolution, Hussites, Transylvania, etc.
Huns, 262, Attila
— 422, Ekkehard
Hunt, Leigh, 141, Bleak House
— 240, Bendish
Hunt the Slipper, 253
Huntings and Enchantments, 214
Hurdcott, 21
Huron Indians, 95, The Romance of Dollard
Huron, Lake, 343, The "Merry Anne"
Hurricane Harry, 281
Hurrish, 289
Hus, John, 255, The Last Days of John Hus
— 285, The Torch-Bearers of Bohemia

Husband's Story, The, 384
Husfrue, 479
Hussites, 25, The Gleaming Dawn, The Cardinal's Page
— See also *Hus, John*
Hutchinson, Lieut.-Col. G. S.—see "Seton, G.," 429
Hutton, Dr., 58, Cradock Nowell
Huxley, Thomas Henry, 322, The New Republic, The New Paul and Virginia
Hyacinth, 55
Hyaku monogatari, 235
Hymn Tune Mystery, The, 56
Hypathia, 279
Hyperion, 303
Hypnerotomachia, 109
Hypnotism, 122, The Witch of Prague
— 148, Nemo
— 156, Trilby
— 232, The House of the Seven Gables
— 250, The Undiscovered Country
— 313, David Elginbrod
— 324, Mario and the Magician
— 348, False Coin or True
— 417, Singoalla
— 429, The Land of Cockayne
Hypocrites, The, 422
Hythloday, 351, Utopia

I Crown Thee King, 381
I hafsbandet, 454
I.N.R.I., 416
I Pose, 50
I Saw Three Ships, 396
I Will Maintain, 68
I Will Repay, 370
I'd Venture all for Thee, 176
Ia, 397
Ibáñez, V. B., see V. Blasco Ibáñez
Ibsenism, 142, A Valiant Ignorance
— 162, "George Egerton's" stories
— 276, The Journalist
Iceland, 87, The Bondman
— 129, Annals of an Eventful Life
— 219, Eric Brighteyes
— 240, A Lover's Tale, The Outlaw, The Light Heart
— 253, Han of Iceland
— 304, An Iceland Fisherman
— 363, The Falcon King
— See also ICELANDIC NOVELISTS, *Icelandic Sagas, Reykjavik.*
Iceland Fisherman, An, 304
ICELANDIC NOVELISTS:
G. Gunnarsson, J. T. Thóroddsen

Icelandic Sagas, 30, Bandamanna Saga
— 163, Egil's Saga
— 168, Eyrbyggja Saga
— 200, Gisli Saga
— 214, Grettis Saga
— 223, Ambales Saga
— 235, Heiðarviga Saga
— 237, Hensa-Thoris Saga
— 249, Howard the Halt
— 284, Kormaks Saga
— 352, see Morris W. and Magnússon, E.
— 360, Njals Saga
— 466, Thrond of Gate
— 483, Viga Glum's Saga, Origines Islandicae
— 484, Völsunga Saga
— See also 208, Grettir the Outlaw; 240, Hewlett's Sagas Retold; 483, Origines Islandicae
Ida Brandt, 31
Idaho, 175, Toilers of the Hills
Ide, 255, Huon of Burdeux
Ideala, 211
Idealism, 41, The Woodman
— 173, The Ladder to the Stars
— 204, Goethe's novels
— 338, Pierre
— 359, The Twymans
— 432, Lisheen
— 433, Sir Percival
— 469, Resurrection
— 492, Sir F. Wedmore's stories
— See also *Didactic, Gentleman, Ideal, Utopias,* etc.
Idealist, The, 167
Ideals, 424
Idée de Jean Têterol, L', 101
Idiot, The, 147
Idlehurst, 222
Idolatry, 382
Idylle pendant le siège, Un, 115
Idylle tragique, Une, 67
Idylls of a Dutch Village, 478
Idylls of the Fells, 460
Idyls of the Gass, 509
Ierne, 471
If, Château d', 154, The Count of Monte Christo
If Age Could, 91
If I were King, 312
If, Yes, and Perhaps, 221
If You Neglect the Fire, 468
If Youth but Knew, 94
Ihr einziger Bruder, 235
Il fu Mattia Pascal, 388
Île des pingouins, L', 184
Île mysterieux, L', 482
Illiers, 393, Swann's Way
Illegitimate Birth, 11, The Victim
— 108, No Name
— 130, Jack
— 137, Ashes (by Deledda)
— 148, A Raw Youth
— 167, Comes the Blind Fury

Illegitimate Birth (contd.): 256, Pam, and sequel
— 260, The Interloper
— 268, Secret Bread
— 277, The Roman Road
— 293, Mis'ess Joy
— 299, One of Life's Slaves
— 301, The White Dove
— 315, Maureen
— 334, Pierre and Jean
— 348, The Alien
— 359, Ditte
— 365, Doctor Rameau
— 464, The Godson of a Marquis
— 473, Mr. Scarborough's Family
— 480, Comendador Mendoza
Illinois, 77, The Father
— 95, Spanish Peggy
— 163, The Graysons
— 283, Zury, the McVeys
— 332, E. L. Masters' novels
— 376, When Wilderness was King
— See also *Chicago*
Illumination, 186
Illusion, The, 167
Illusions perdues, 28
Illustre Gaudissart, L', 28
Illustre Maurin, L', 4
Illustrious O'Hagan, The, 312
Ilusions del Doctor Faustino, Las, 480
Im blauen Hecht, 159
Im Hause des Kommerzienrats, 326
Im Paradiese, 241
Im Schlaraffenland, 323
Im Westen Nichts Neues, 403
Image in the Sand, The, 48
Imaginary Mistress, The, 27
Imaginary Portraits, 377
Imaginary Voyages, 83, Erewhon, and sequel
— 127, L'histoire comique des états de la lune, etc.
— 235, The True History
— 375, Peter Wilkins
— 388, Poe's tales
— 458, Gulliver's Travels
— 482-3, Jules Verne's stories
— 493, The First Men in the Moon
— See also *Gulliverian Satire, Utopias*
Imaginative Man, An, 241
Imagined Life, The, 117
Immensee, 452
Immersionists, see *Pædobaptism*
Immoralist, The, 198
Immortal Lover, The, 448
Immortal Marriage, The, 18
Immortal Moment, The, 437
Immortal Youth, 411
Immortality, 30, The Elixir of Life
— 122, Khaled
— 203, St. Leon

Immortality (contd.): 333, Melmoth
— See also *Future Life, Metempsychosis, Wandering Jew*
Immortel, L', 130
Impatience de la foule, 483
Imperative Duty, An, 250
Imperfect Mother, An, 51
Imperial Dragon, The, 195
Imperial Lover, An, 461
Imperial Palace, 46
Imperialist, The, 117
Impey, Sir Elijah, 215, The Great Proconsul
Impossible People, 495
Impregnable City, The, 380
Impressionism, 42, T. Beer's novels
— 50, Stella Benson's novels
— 110-2, Conrad's novels
— 174, A. A. R. Firbank's novels
— 447, Sterne's works
— See also *Expressionism*
Impressment, 115, Afloat and Ashore
Improvisatore, The, 9
In a Canadian Canoe, 373
In a Corner of Asia, 105
In a Cornish Township, 382
In a Desert Land, 233
In a Dyke Shanty, 389
In a German Pension, 325
In a Glass Darkly, 294
In a North Country Village, 184
In a Tramp Camp, 277
In Accordance with the Evidence, 369
In Bad Company, 284
In Black and White, 281
In Blue Waters, 445
In Bohemia, 435
In Brief Authority, 13
In Burleigh's Days, 273
In Castle and Colony, 401
In Chancery, 190
In Change Unchanged, 483
In Chimney Corners, 319
In Circling Camps, 8
In Colston's Days, 329
In Connection with the De Willoughby Claim, 82
In Dagen van Strijd, 486
In Exile, 99
In Far Lochaber, 57
In Flood-Time, 281
In Furthest Ind, 215
In God's Way, 57
In Guiana Wilds, 413
In Hanging Garden Gully, 347
In Happy Hollow, 3
In her Earliest Youth, 460
In High Places, 70
In His Name, 221
In his Own Image, 414
In Homespun, 60
In Honour's Name, see The Duel, 285
In Hopefield Square, 174
In Hostile Red, 8
In Kedar's Tents, 342
In Kings' Byways, 498
In Kings' Houses, 145
In Leisler's Times, 74

In London, 371
In Love, 291
In Low Relief, 410
In Maremma, 372
In Mid Atlantic, 260
In Midsummer Days, 454
In Mio's Youth, 35
In Mr. Knox's Country, 443
In Monte Carlo, 435
In Ole Virginia, 373
In Our Street, 492
In Our Time, 236
In Paradise, 241
In Russia's Night, 193
In Sarsfield's Days, 319
In Spacious Times, 313
In Spite of All, 307
In Spite of Himself, 36
In Stanitza, 442
In Steel and Leather, 180
In Steppe, 206
In Subjection, 182
In the Arena, 460
In the Back, 509
In the Beginning, 148
In the Blue Pike, 159
In the Brooding Wild, 126
In the Cage, 265
In the Carquinez Woods, 230
In the Celtic Past, 91
In the Choir of West-
    minster Abbey, 330
In the Closed Room, 82
In the Clouds, 118
In the Day of Adversity, 62
In the Day of Battle, 447
In the Days of Drake, 176
In the Days of Goldsmith,
    63
In the Days of King James,
    81
In the Days of Serfdom, 469
In the Days of the Comet,
    494
In the Distance, 288
In the Eagle's Talons, 448
In the East Country with Sir
    Thomas Browne, 329
In the Fear of the Lord, 156
In the Gates of the North,
    365
In the Golden Shell, 483
In the Gray Goth, 383
In the Great God's Hair, 25
In the Guardianship of God,
    446
In the House of Suddhoo,
    281
In the Image of God, 3
In the Kingdom of Kerry,
    125
In the Land of Cockaigne,
    323
In the Land of Youth, 446
In the Midst of Alarms, 36
In the Midst of Life, 53
In the Morning of Time, 410
In the Name of Liberty, 269
In the New Promised Land,
    435
In the Olden Time, 410
In the Palace of the King,
    123
In the Permanent Way, 445
In the Ravine, 100
In the Roar of the Sea, 208
In the Rukh, 281

In the Same Boat, 282
In the service of Rachel,
    Lady Russell, 329
In the Shadow of the
    Alamo, 152
In the Shadow of the
    Crown, 53
In the Shadow of the
    Purple, 199
In the Smoke of War, 400
In the Stranger People's
    Country, 118
In the Tennessee Moun-
    tains, 118
In the Tideway, 445
In the Track of a Storm,
    131
In the Track of the Troops,
    26
In the Valley, 186
In the Wake of King
    James, 365
In the Wilderness (by
    HICHENS), 242
In the Wilderness (by
    UNDSET), 479
In the Wilds, 14
In the Wire Grass, 381
In the Year of Jubilee, 201
In the Year of Waterloo, 87
In the Year '13, 403
In Tight Places, 216
In Time of War, 106
In Treaty with Honour, 126
In Troubled Times, 486
In Two Moods, 284
In Vain, 434
In Veronica's Garden, 21
Incarnation of Krishna
    Mulvaney, The, 281
Incarnation of the Snow,
    An, 25
Incas, 243, The Splendid
    Knight
— 252, The Crimson Con-
    quest
— 295, The Bride of the
    Sun
Inchbracken, 105
Incident, An, 207
Inclinations, 174
Incognita, 109
Incognito, The, 139
Incomparable Bellairs, 94
Incomplete Amorist, The,
    60
Inconsequent Lives, 379
Increasing Purpose, The, 8
Incredible Adventures, 59
Incredulity of Father
    Brown, The, 102
Incurable (by HEIMBURG),
    235
Incurable (by ZANGWILL),
    515
India, 15, Oakfield
— 121, Mr. Isaacs, Doctor
    Claudius
— 179, The Bond of Blood
— 186, Silent Gods and
    Sun-Steeped Lands
— 215, Like Another Helen
— 215–16, "S. C. GRIER's"
    novels
— 255, The Old Missionary
— 281–2, R. KIPLING's
    novels and stories

India (contd.): 377, Bijli
    the Dancer
— 419, Prince Baber
— 445–6, Mrs. STEEL's
    novels
— 461, Col. P. M. TAYLOR's
    novels
— 465, E. J. THOMPSON's
    novels
— 512, Jennifer Lorn
— See also Afghanistan,
    Akbar, Anglo-Indian
    Life, ANGLO-INDIAN
    NOVELISTS, Baber,
    BENGALI NOVEL-
    ISTS, Burma, Hindus,
    Indian Fiction, India,
    North-West Frontier,
    Indian Mutiny, etc.
India, North-West Frontier,
    78, The Half-Hearted
— 215, The Warden of the
    Marches, The Ad-
    vanced Guard
— 331, The Broken Road
— 390, His Majesty's Shirt
    Sleeves
— 457, Joan SUTHERLAND's
    novels
— 465, Transgression
— See also Afghanistan
Indian Camp, 236
Indian Day, An, 465
Indian Fiction, see BEN-
    GALI NOVELISTS
— See also SWYNNERTON,
    Rev. C., 459
Indian Lily, The, 455
Indian Mutiny, 101, The
    Dilemma
— 125, Mr. Jervis
— 179, Eight Days, The
    Sword of Azrael
— 215, The Keepers of the
    Gate
— 225, Jenetha's Venture,
    The Peril of the Sword
— 445, On the Face of the
    Waters
— 446, In the Guardian-
    ship of God
— 461, Seeta
Indian Nights' Entertain-
    ment, 459
Indian Summer, 250
Indiana, 163, The Hoosier
    Schoolmaster, Roxy
— 459–60, B. TARKING-
    TON's novels, passim
— 465, Alice of Old Vin-
    cennes
Indiana, 420
Indians of America, 9, The
    Wilderness Road, The
    Last of the Chiefs
— 21, Mary AUSTIN's no-
    vels
— 23, Hermsprong
— 40, Juan and Juanita
— 44, A Volunteer with
    Pike
— 54, Nick o' the Woods
— 76, Edgar Huntly
— 86, The Grandissimes
— 95, Mrs. CATHERWOOD's
    novels, passim
— 96, Cardigan, and sequel

Indians of America (contd.):
    104, The Crossing
— 113, My Lady Poka-
    hontas
— 114–15, J. F. COOPER's
    novels, passim
— 126, A Daughter of New
    France
— 126, The Watchers of
    the Plains
— 142, The Black Wolf's
    Breed
— 165, E. S. ELLIS's no-
    vels, passim
— 171, Cimarron
— 252, El Ombú
— 260, Ramona
— 270, Audrey
— 376, Bob Hampton
— 377, Molly Macdonald
— 402, The Shadow of
    Victory
— 406, Wacousta
— 439, Montlivet
— 448, A Soldier of Vir-
    ginia
— 486, Out of the Silences
— 501–2, S. E. WHITE's
    novels
— 508, Red Man and White
— See also names of tribes,
    e.g. Apaches, Cherokees,
    Comanches, Hurons,
    Iroquois, Navajos, Ojib-
    ways
Indios, Los, 210
Indiscretion of the Duchess,
    The, 246
Indiscretions of Archie,
    The, 509
Indiscretions of Lin Mang,
    199
Individualism, 12, The Tri-
    umph of Death
— 53, Red and Black
— 198, The Immoralist
— See also Egoism
Individualist, The, 322
Induna's Wife, The, 346
Industrial Workers of the
    World, 104, The Dwell-
    ing-Place of Light
Industrialism, 45–6, A.
    BENNETT's "Five
    Towns" novels
— 104, The Dwelling-Place
    of Light
— 120, John Halifax
— 206, Comrades
— 228, The Bomb
— 236, John Goodchild
— 237, The Three Black
    Pennys
— 276, Iron and Smoke
— 299, The Barque "Fu-
    ture"
— 314, All Smoke
— 335, Bernard Quesnay
— 343, S. MERWIN's novels,
    cp. with H. K. WEB-
    STER
— 361, The Octopus
— 386, Brunel's Tower, The
    Spinners
— 403, The Promised Land
— 498, Starvecrow Farm
— 514, The Iron Age

Industrialism, 519, Work
— See also *Business, Capitalism, Financial Life, Labour, Poor, Trade Unions, Strikes,* etc.
Infamous John Friend, The, 193
Infatuation, The, 371
Infernal Marriage, The, 143
Inferno, The, 32
Infidel, The, 70
Informer, The (by CONRAD), 111
Informer, The (by O'FLAHERTY), 364
Informers, 111, The Informer (by CONRAD)
— 364, The Informer (by O'FLAHERTY)
— 432, Glenaar
— See also *Espionage, Spies*
Ingénu, L', 484
Ingénue libertine, L', 108
Ingmarsson family, 286, Jerusalem
Ingo and Ingraben, 188
Inheritor, The, 49
Inheritors, The, 171
Inimitable Jeeves, The, 509
Inimitable Mrs. Massingham, The, 109
Inisheeny, 55
Inishkey, 289, The Book of Gilly
Initials, The, 460
Initiation, 50
Inn, The, 242
Inn of the Silver Moon, The, 483
Inn of the Two Witches, The, 111
Inner Circle, 336
Inner Shrine, The, 433
Innisdoyle Neighbours, 125
Innocence of Father Brown, The, 102
Innocent II, Pope, 152, The Betrayers
Innocent Adultery, The, 422
Innocent Masqueraders, 478
Innocent Voyage, The, 253
Innocente, L', 11
Innocentia, 143
Innocents, The, 298
Innocents Abroad, The, 476
Inquisition, 4, The Vale of Cedars
— 62, The Sea Devils
— 107, Jan van Elselo
— 116, The Master Beggars of Belgium
— 176, In the Days of Drake
— 203, St. Leon
— 218, The House of Torment
— 219, Montezuma's Daughter
— 220, Fair Margaret
— 243, A Flame of Fire
— 418, The Hounds of God
Insanity, 6, The Queen of Sheba
— 23, A Roman Mystery
— 27, Eugenie Grandet
— 28, Parisians in the Country, Old Goriot

Insanity (*contd.*): 142, Against the Tide
— 147, The Idiot
— 170, The Sound and the Fury
— 202, Minna
— 203, Fleetwood
— 204, The Diary of a Madman
— 241, An Imaginative Man
— 286, Jean Gilles
— 287, The Emperor of Portugallia
— 290, The Iron Bell
— 322, A Mother
— 406, Richard Mahony
— 436, The Lady of Dreams
— 439, Seven Dreamers
— 495, Christina Alberta's Father
— 517, The Conquest of Plassans
— See also *Dual Personality, Lunatic Asylums*
Insel der grossen Mutter, Der, 231
Inside of the Cup, The, 104
Inside the Bar, 337
Inspector French and the Starvel Hollow Tragedy, 124
Inspector French's Greatest Case, 124
Insulted and Injured, The, 146
Intelligentzia, 179, E. M. FORSTER's novels
— 256, A. HUXLEY's novels
— 276, Bloomsbury
— 357, J. M. MURRY's novels
Interdiction, L', 27
Interference, 125
Interim, 405
Interloper, The (by JACOB), 260
Interloper, The (by PEARD), 380
Interlopers, The, 355
Interlopers at the Knap, 226
International Episode, An, 263
Interpreter, The, 337
Interpreters, The, 417
Interrupted Cadence, An, 244
Interrupted Friendship, An, 484
Interrupted Miracle, The, 371
Into Mexico with General Scott, 418
Into the Dark, 408
Into the Highways and Hedges, 348
" *Intrepid, The,*" 427, Decatur and Somers
Introducing William Allison, 241
Intruder, The (by D'AN-NUNZIO), 12
Intruder, The (by BLASCO IBAÑEZ), 61
Intruding Angel, The, 327

Intrusions of Peggy, The, 246
Intruso, El, 61
Inundation, The, 519
Invaders, The, 467
Invalid's Story, The, 476
Invasion, The (by GRIFFIN), 216
Invasion, The (by TOLSTOY), 468
Inveraray, 356, Gilian the Dreamer
Inverness, 57, Wild Eelin
Inviolable Sanctuary, The, 55
Invisible Empire, The, 470
Invisible Event, The, 51
Invisible Lodge, The, 407
Invisible Man, The, 493
Invisible Prince, The, 227
Invisible Tides, 430
Invoker of the Beast, The, 443
Io cerco Moglie, 375
Iona, 431
" IOTA," see CAFFYN, Kathleen M.
Iowa, 455, Miss SUCKOW's novels
— 463, Stories of a Western Town
— 464, The Missionary Sheriff
Iowa Interiors, 455
Ipané, The, 210
Ipomedon, 253, The Life of Ipomedon
Ipswich, 162, A Suffolk Courtship
Ireland, before 1640, 35, The Rebel Lady
— 91, Children of the Dawn
— 289, Maelcho
— 289, With Essex in Ireland
— 333, The Spanish Wine
— 364, The Bog of Stars
— 512, Let Erin Remember
Ireland, 1640–1798, 7, The House of Lisronan
— 60, The Irish Chieftains
— 62, The Land of Bondage
— 103, John Marmaduke
— 125, The Lost Land
— 174, The Chances of War
— 313, Kathleen Clare
— 319, In Sarsfield's Days
— 319, Nessa
— 348, Castle Omeragh, and sequel
— 353, Gerald O'Connor
— 441, The Wild Rose of Lough Gill
Ireland, Rebellion of 1798, 31, The Croppy
— 55, The Northern Iron
— 63, Lord Edward Fitzgerald, and sequel
— 188, The Two Chiefs of Dunboy
— 243, Up for the Green
— 277, The Pikemen
— 289, The Race of Castlebar
— 305, Rory O'More
— 351, The O'Briens and the O'Flahertys

Ireland, Rebellion of 1798, 477, A King's Woman
— 508, My Lords of Strogue
Ireland, 1798–1916, 84, Donn BYRNE's novels
— 312, Mononia
— 413, A Young Man from the South
Ireland, Rebellion of 1916, 118, A Flock of Birds
— 268, Greater Love
— 308, The Gael
— 371, Married Life
— See also *Irish Character,* IRISH NOVELISTS, IRISH-AMERICAN NOVELISTS, *Celtic, Celtic Sagas* ; names of counties and districts, *Aran Isles, Clare, Donegal, Ulster,* etc. ; names of organisations, *Fenians, Land League, Ribbonmen, Whiteboys,* etc.
Ireton, General, 103, John Marmaduke
— 174, The Chances of War
— 261, Henry Masterton
— 313, Cornet Strong
IRISH-AMERICAN NOVELISTS :
Rev. J. BOYCE, Donn BYRNE
Irish Brigade, 60, The Irish Chieftains
— 319, Spanish John
Irish Character, 69, The Spae-Wife
— 79, Tales of the Pampas
— 113, Dorothea CONYERS's stories
— 121, The O'Ruddy
— 132, The Amazing Philanthropists
— 157, F. P. DUNNE's stories
— 254, Molly Bawn
— 269, Strangers and Wayfarers, A Native of Winby, The Queen's Twin
— 284, Kormaks Saga
— 340, Celt and Saxon
— 351, Lady MORGAN's novels
— 419, Moody's Lodging House
— 443, SOMERVILLE and Ross's stories
— 462, Vanity Fair, Pendennis
— 471, The Macdermots of Ballycloran, The Kellys and the O'Kellys
— 504, Penelope's Irish Experiences
— See also *Celtic Fiction, Ireland,* and its subdivisions, IRISH NOVELISTS, *passim.*
Irish Chieftains, The, 60
Irish Cousin, An, 443
Irish Idylls, 34
Irish Neighbours, 35
IRISH NOVELISTS :
Eleanor J. ALEXANDER, Miriam ALEXANDER, J,

IRISH NOVELISTS
(contd.):
and M. Banim, Jane
Barlow, E. S. Barrett,
Rev. W. F. Barry, "G.
A. Birmingham," C. F.
Blake-Forster, M. M.
Donnell Bodkin, H.
Brooke, W. Buckley,
W. Bulfin, Shan F.
Bullock, Mrs. K. M.
Caffyn; "Ethna Car-
bery," Mary Carbery;
W. Carleton, Nora
Chesson, E. Childers,
P. Colum, D. Corkery,
Kathleen Coyle, Mrs. B.
M. Croker, G. Croly,
Mary Crosbie, Julia M.
Crottie, A. De Blácam,
R. Dowling, E. Dow-
ney, Conan Doyle

Charlotte O'C. Eccles,
Maria Edgworth, P.
Egan, St. John Ervine,
Erminda Esler, D.
Figgis, Rev. T. A. Fin-
lay, Kathleen Fitz-
patrick, "M. E. Fran-
cis," A. Fremdling,
"G. D. Gilbert," O.
Goldsmith, "Sarah
Grand," G. Griffin,
Miss Grimshaw, S. L.
Gwynn, Anna M. Hall,
Mrs. M. Hartley, H. A.
Hinkson, V. Hobhouse,
Eleanor Hull, A. Irvine,
J. Joyce, P. W. Joyce,
Julia Kavanagh, Annie
M. Keary, J. Keating,
Sir S. R. Keightley, P.
Kennedy, C. J. Kick-
ham, R. A. King, Emily
Lawless, J. S. Le Fanu,
J. H. Lepper, C. J.
Lever, C. Lipsett, S.
Lover, E. E. Lysaght,
S. R. Lysaght

W. McCallin, J. Mc-
Carthy, J. H. Mc-
Carthy, P. MacGill, A.
McIlroy, W. McLellan,
Ella MacMahon, Miss L.
MacManus, S. Mac-
Manus, "B. Macna-
mara," L. Macnamara,
E. McNulty, W.
Maginn, F. Mathew, C.
R. Maturin, W. H.
Maxwell, "A. Merry,"
"K. L. Montgomery,"
F. F. Moore, G. Moore,
T. Moore, J. J. Moran,
Judge Morris, Rosa
Mulholland

Hon. Caroline Norton,
W. O'Brien, "D. O'-
Byrne," W. L. O'Byrne,
P. O'Donnell, G. O'-
Donovan, E. O'Duffy,
L. O'Flaherty, S. H.
O'Grady, S. J. O'Grady,
M. O'Hanrahan, S. O'-
Kelly, C. O'Riordan,

IRISH NOVELISTS
(contd.):
P. H. Pearse, Katherine
F. Purdon, F. Reid,
Grace Rhys, L. Robin-
son, T. W. Rolleston,
G. W. Russell, Bernard
Shaw, Rev. P. A. Shee-
han, P. G. Smythe, Miss
E. Somerville and
"Martin Ross," H. de
Vere Stacpoole, James
Stephens, B. Stoker,
Mrs. Strain, W. S.
Trench, Katharine
Tynan, "Rebecca West,"
Oscar Wilde, C. Wil-
liams, Hon. L. S. Wing-
field, W. B. Yeats
— See also IRISH-
AMERICAN
NOVELISTS
Irish Pastorals, 80
Irish R. M. and his Ex-
periences, The, 443
Irish Rebellion of 1798, see
Ireland, Rebellion of,
1798
Irish Ways, 35
Irkutsk, 482, Michel Strogoff
"Iron, Ralph," see
Schreiner, Olive, 423
Iron Age, The, 514
Iron and Smoke, 276
Iron Bell, The, 290
Iron Heel, The, 303
Iron Man, 83
Iron Pirate, The, 380
Iron Year, The, 62
Ironmaster, The, 365
Iroquois Indians, 95, The
Romance of Dollard
— 97, The Little Red Foot
— 248, The Mississippi
Bubble
— 289, Lords of the North
— 439, Montlivet
Irrational Knot, The, 431
Irresolute Catherine, 260
Irvingites, 247, Because of
the Angels
Is He Popenjoy?, 473
Isaac Eller's Money, 433
Isabel Sterling, 422
Isabella, Queen, 53, In the
Shadow of the Crown
Isabella of Parma, 91, The
Pot of Basil
Isabelle, 198
Isandhlwana, 346, The
Word of the Sorceress
Isegrimm, 7
Iseute, 139
Ishmael, 70
Isidro, 21
Iskander Bey, 306, The Cap-
tain of the Janizaries
Island, The (by Royde-
Smith), 441
Island, The (by Whiteing),
502
Island Mystery, The, 55
Island Nights Entertain-
ments, 449
Island of Dr. Moreau, The,
493
Island of Sorrow, The, 199

Island of the Great Mother,
The, 231
Island Pharisees, The, 189
Islanders, 363
Islands of the Vale, 234
Isle of France, 419, Paul
and Virginia
— 420, Indiana
Isle of Thorns, 275
Isle of Unrest, The, 342
Isle of Voices, The, 449
Isles of Wisdom, The, 354
Ismay's Children, 231
Isolée, L', 40
Israel Potter, 338
Isthmian Games, 103, The
Crown of Pine
— 131, A Victor of Salamis
It is Never Too Late to
Mend, 401
It Never Can Happen
Again, 138
It Will Be All Right, 189
Italian, The, 399
Italian Influences on Early
English Fiction, see
Greene, Painter,
Pettie
ITALIAN NOVELISTS:
"Sibilla Aleramo,"
"G. d'Annunzio," M.
Taparelli d'Azeglio, R.
Bacchelli, M. Ban-
dello, A. G. Barrili,
G. Boccaccio, G. Cena,
F. Colonna, A. Fogaz-
zaro, Ser Giovanni
Fiorentino, F. D.
Guerrazzi, V. Guicci-
ardi-Fiastri, A. Man-
zoni, Massuccio of
Salerno, P. Monelli,
L. Motta, A. Panzini,
L. Pirandello, G. Ruf-
fini, F. di B. Sacchetti,
Matilde Serao, Strap-
arola, "I. Svevo," F.
Tozzi, Linda Villari,
L. Zuccoli
— See also Roscoe, T., 415
— See also Saint Mary
Magdalene, 419
— See also SARDINIAN
NOVELISTS
Italian Novelists, 415
Italian Revolution, 24, The
Pillar of Fire
— 56, Captain Mansana
— 177, The Man of the
World, and sequels
— 247, For Freedom
— 280, Silcote of Silcotes
— 297, Tony Butler
— 339, Vittoria
— 358, The Rebels, and
sequel
— 416, Lorenzo Benoni,
Dr. Antonio
— 484, The Gadfly
— 488, Eleanor
— See also Garibaldi, Maz-
zini
Italo-Turkish War, 266,
Pride of War
Italy before the 19th Century,
9, The Improvisatore
— 39, David Arnot

Italy before the 19th Century
(contd.): 53, The Char-
treuse of Parma, The
Abbess of Castro
— 192, Desiderio
— 309, Rienzi
— 319, Spanish John, Lally
of the Brigade
— 341, The Forerunner
— 357, The Unfortunate
Traveller
— 399, Mrs. Radcliffe's
novels
— 401, The Cloister and
the Hearth
— 418, Sabatini's novels,
passim
— 445, Corinne
— 447, A Sentimental
Journey
— See also Borgias, Flor-
ence, Medicis, names of
popes, etc
Italy, Modern, 1, Tolla
— 39, Arden Massiter
— 121-3, F. M. Craw-
ford's novels, passim
— 133, Exiles
— 146, The Emigrant
— 176, Vestigia, Andro-
meda
— 179, Where Angels Fear
to Tread
— 227, The Cardinal's
Snuff-Box
— 233, The Marble Faun
— 239, Fond Adventures
— 251, Ragged Lady
— 257, Young Archimedes
— 275, Silvia
— 297, The Fortunes of
Glencore, The Bram-
leighs
— 304, On Etna, Catherine
Sterling
— 321, Miserere Nobis
— 323, The Little Town
— 339, Vittoria
— 371-2, "Ouida's" novels
— 414, F. Rolfe's stories
— 473, T. A. Trollope's
novels
— 498, The Valley of Decision
— 499, The Hermit and the
Wild Woman
— 502, Clara Hapgood, The
Torchbearers
— 504, The Cabala
— 511, The Front Yard
— See also ITALIAN
NOVELISTS, passim,
SARDINIAN NOV-
ELISTS, Sicily: also
names of towns, famous
characters, events, etc.
Ivan IV (the Terrible), 467,
A Prince of Outlaws
— 500, A Boyar of the
Terrible
Ivan Greet's Masterpiece,
7
Ivan Ilyitch, 468
Ivan Ivanovich and Ivan
Nikiforovich (How the
Two Ivans Quarrelled),
204

Ivan Laude, 16
Ivan Matveyitch, 100
Ivan the Fool, 468
Ivanhoe, 425
Ivanovich, Uvar, 474, Elena
Ivar the Viking, 152
Ivolgin, General, 147, The Idiot
Ivory Child, The, 220
Ivory Tower, The, 266
Ivry, Battle of, 262, One in a Thousand, Rose d'Albret
Ixion in Heaven, 143

Jacclard, 408
Jack, 130
Jack Adams, 97
Jack and Jill (by ALCOTT), 6
Jack and Jill (by CAPES), 90
Jack and Jill of the Sierras, 230
Jack Ashore, 249
Jack Derringer, 305
Jack Hinton, 296
Jack Horner, 466
Jack of Newbery, 138
Jack o' Peterloo, 508
Jack Raymond, 484
Jack Sheppard, 4
Jack Spurlock, 304
Jack the Outlaw, 442
Jack the Painter, see *Hill, John*
Jack Wilton, Life of, 357
Jackanapes, 168
Jackson, Andrew, 74, A Son of the Revolution
— 104, The Crossing
— 143, The Patience of John Morland
— 360, The Cavalier of Tennessee
— 401, By the Eternal
— 451, The Errand Boy of Andrew Jackson
Jackson, Stonewall, 47, Bayard's Courier
— 113, Surry of Eagle's Nest
— 248, Stonewall's Scout
— 270, The Long Roll, and sequel
Jacob and John, 400
Jacob Elthorne, 173
Jacob Faithful, 328
Jacobite Admiral, A, 180
Jacobite Rebellion of 1715, 5, Preston Flight
— 7, Balmoral
— 26, To Arms !
— 52, Dorothy Forster
— 170, Over the Hills
— 171, The Silver Shoe-Buckle
— 212, Lucy Arden
— 332, Parson Kelly
— 425, Rob Roy
— 425, The Black Dwarf
Jacobite Rebellion of 1745, 16, The Great Attempt
— 36, Bernicia
— 78, A Lost Lady of Old Years, Midwinter
— 153, Winifred DUKE's novels

Jacobite Rebellion of 1745 (contd.): 159, The Hearth of Hutton
— 176, I'd venture all for thee
— 207, The Yeoman Adventurer
— 260, Flemington
— 311, Poor Sons of a Day
— 319, Spanish John, The Span o' Life
— 348, Colonel Kate
— 356, Doom Castle, The New Road
— 392, Fortuna Chance
— 404, For the White Rose of Arno
— 411, The Stone of Dunalter
— 424, Waverley
— 456, Ricroft of Withens, Under the White Cockade, The Lone Adventure
— 457, The Open Road
— 487, Rogue Herries
Jacobites, 24, The Gentleman Adventurer, The Highwayman
— 31, The Boyne Water
— 64, The Morning of To-day
— 77, An Exiled Scot, Sir Quixote of the Moors
— 81, My Lady of the Bass
— 91, For the White Rose
— 128, Oil of Spikenard
— 180, R. H. FORSTER's novels, *passim*
— 196, The Last Link
— 234, A Kent Squire, and sequel
— 262, The King's Highway
— 271, The Laird of Glenfernie, The Slave Ship
— 294, Col. Torlogh O'Brien
— 329, Snarleyyow
— 337, Cerise
— 365, In the Wake of King James
— 370, Beau Brocade, Petticoat Government
— 418, The Gates of Doom
— 426, Redgauntlet
— 447, By Allan Water
— 449, David Balfour, The Master of Ballantrae
— 478, Favours from France
— See also *Assassination Plot, Jacobite Rebellion of 1715, and of 1745*
Jacob's Room, 511
Jacqueline, 22
Jacquerie, 262, The Jacquerie
Jacquerie, The, 262
Jacques, 420
Jaffery, 302
Jalna, 137
Jamaica, 7, Ivan Greet's Masterpiece
— 376, No Defence
— 424, The Cruise of the Midge

James I, 24, The Master of Gray
— 81, In the Days of King James
— 104, Court Cards
— 262, Arabella Stuart
— 263, Gowrie
— 273, In Burleigh's Days, and sequel
— 396, The Blue Pavilions
— 426, Fortunes of Nigel
James II, 4, James the Second
— 24, Beaujeu
— 31, The Boyne Water
— 39, The Knight of the Golden Sword
— 52, For Faith and Freedom
— 62, The King's Guerdon
— 196, The Red Seal, The Broken Sword
— 330, Kensington Palace
— 365, In the Wake of King James
— See also *English Revolution, Monmouth's Rebellion, Bishops, Trial of,* etc.
James I of Scotland, 513, The Caged Lion, The Prince and the Page
James II of Scotland, 212, The Captain of the Guard
— 512, A King's Tragedy
James III, 211, The Yellow Frigate
James V, 37, A Prince of Good Fellows
— 189, The Witch's Sword
James Francis Edward (The "Old Pretender"), 331, Clementina
— 462, Henry Esmond
JAMES, Miss W. M., see "CLARE, Austin"
James River, Virginia, 62, The Land of Bondage
— 466, Homoselle
James Joyce's Ulysses, 273
James the Second, 4
JAMESON, Mrs. Annie Edith, see "BUCKROSE, J. E."
Jamesons, The, 505
Jamestown, 165, The Last Emperor of the Old Dominion
— 206, The Head of a Hundred
— 278, John o' Jamestown
Jamie Myles, 167
Jamieson, Ninian, 131, Perfervid
Jan and her Job, 227
Jan Hunkum's Money, 310
Jan of the Windmill, 168
Jan Oxber, 3
Jan van Elselo, 107
Jan Vedder's Wife, 36
Jane Cameron, 413
Jane Eyre, 73
Jane Field, 505
Jane, Our Stranger, 66
Janeites, The, 283
Janet's Home, 276
Janet's Repentance, 164

Janice Meredith, 179
Janin, Jules, 28, The Muse of the Department
Japan, 2, Shibusawa
— 45, The Shogun's Daughter
— 151, Shinju
— 186, Mrs. Hugh FRASER's stories
— 190, The Japanese Prince
— 235, Kwaidan
— 304, Catherine Sterling
— 304, Madame Chrysanthème
— 312, The Breath of the Gods, The Dragon Painter
— See also JAPANESE NOVELISTS
Japan, 304 ·
JAPANESE NOVELISTS : " FUTABATEI," Rev. T. KAGAWA, KIOKUTEI Bakin, MURASAKI, A. MUJAMORI, T. OHTA, Mme OZAKI, ROKIYIU YEN, SEI SHONAGON, K. TOKUTOMI
— See also HAYASHI, Viscount Tadasu, 234
— See also RIORDAN and TAKAYAMAGI, 409
— See also Tales of Old Japan, 402
— See also The Lady who Loved Insects, 485
Japanese Prince, The, 190
Japhet in Search of a Father, 328
Jardin d'Épicure, Le, 183
Jarl the Skyeman, 337, Mardi
Jarnac, Battle of, 262, The Man-at-Arms
Jarvie, Baillie Nicol, 425, Rob Roy
Jason Edwards, 192
Jasper Townshend's Piccaninny, 316
Jaunty Jock, 356
Java, 242, A Princess of Java
Java Head, 237
Jay of Italy, A, 91
Jealous Gods, The (Vengeful Gods), 18
Jealousies of a Country Town, The, 27
Jealousy, 335, Whatever Gods May Be
— 402, Griffith Gaunt
— 318, Julia de Roubigné
Jean and Louise, 158
Jean Christophe, 414
Jean Gilles, Schoolboy, 286
Jean Sourdon's Four Days, 516
Jean Swalue, 131
Jean Têterol's Idea, 101
Jeanne, 421
Jeanne d'Albret, 247, The Gage of Red and White
Jeanne d'Arc, see *Joan of Arc*
Jehan de Saintré, see *Little Jehan,* 288

Jefferson, Joseph, 74, A Son of the Revolution
— 248, The Magnificent Adventure
— 270, Lewis Rand
— 345, The Red City
JEFFERY, Walter—see also BECKE, G. L. and W. JEFFERY
Jeffreys, Judge, 149, Micah Clarke
— 58, Lorna Doone
— 159, Fortune's Castaway
— 165, Barbara Winslow
— 176, David March
— 196, The Red Seal
— 247, My Lord Winchenden
— 263, The Fate
— 480, By Dulvercombe Water
— See also *Monmouth's Rebellion*
Jellachich, 230, A Sereshan
Jemmy Abercraw, 91
Jena, 29, A Gondreville Mystery
— 296, Tom Burke
Jenetha's Venture, 225
Jennie Gerhart, 151
Jennifer Lorn, 512
Jennings, Sarah, see *Marlborough, Duchess of*
Jenny, 479
Jeremy, 486
Jeremy and Hamlet, 487
Jeremy at Crale, 487
Jernbauen og kirkegaarden, 56
Jerome, Saint, 98, Conquering and to Conquer
— 382, Sancta Paula
Jerome (by BEDEL), 42
Jerome (by Mary WILKINS), 505
Jerome Bonaparte, 93, Love and Honour
Jerry, 164
Jerry and Ben, 408
Jerry of the Islands, 303
Jersey, see *Channel Islands*
Jersey, Battle of, 376, The Battle of the Strong
Jerusalem, 120, The Rival Heirs
— 131, "God Wills It"
— 220, Pearl Maiden, The Brethren
— 229, The Little Daughter of Jerusalem
— 337, The Gladiators
— 448, Sarah Eden
— See also *Crusades, Zionism*
Jerusalem, 286
Jervaise Comedy, The, 51
Jess, 219
Jessamy Bride, The, 348
Jesuits, 61, The Intruder
— 123, A Martyr's Servant, and sequel
— 155, Olympe de Clève
— 273, A Portrait of the Artist as a Young Man
— 342, The Velvet Glove
— 433, John Inglesant
Jetta, 231
Jettatura, 195

Jeune fille bien élevée, La, 69
Jew, The (by KRASZEWSKI), 285
Jew, The, (by TURGENEV), 474
Jew Süss, 172
Jew who would for his debt have the flesh of a Christian, 430
Jewel of Jeopardy, The, 115
Jewel of Ynys Galon, The, 404
Jewess, The, 285
Jewish Children, 431
JEWISH NOVELISTS: E. S. BRUDNO, A. CAHAN, B. DISRAELI, L. GOLDING, S. GORDON, I. PEREZ "SHALOM 'ALEKHEM," I. ZANGWILL
Jewish Tales, 418
Jewish Trinity, The, 516
Jews, 4, The Vale of Cedars
— 16, The Mother
— 19, Olga Bardel
— 50-1, The Early History of Jacob Stahl, and sequels
— 61, and Co.
— 72, Singermann
— 72, Rubeni, The Kingdom of Love
— 86, A. CAHAN's novels
— 87, The Scapegoat
— 89, Mendel
— 143, Coningsby
— 144, Tancred
— 161, Harrington
— 164, Daniel Deronda
— 166, The Blocade
— 186, The Jews of Barnow
— 196, Orthodox, Recha
— 205, L. GOLDING's novels
— 206, S. GORDON's stories
— 227, The Yoke of the Thorah
— 231, By Order of the Czar
— 284, Gabriel
— 284, The Day of Atonement, and sequels
— 285, The Jew
— 297, Reuben Sachs
— 306, Deborah
— 344, The Coming of the Lord
— 347, Naomi's Exodus
— 358, David Golder
— 363, The Chosen People
— 371, An Obscure Apostle
— 418, Jewish Tales
— 423, The Road to the Open
— 433, Isaac Eller's Money
— 447, Tents of Israel, and sequels
— 464, The Shadow of the Cross
— 509, Idyls of the Gass
— 515-16, I. ZANGWILL's novels
— 519, Truth
— See also *Biblical Stories, Christ, Life of, Jerusalem*, JEWISH NOVELISTS, *Palestine, Zionism*, etc.

Jews of Barnow, The, 186
Jilt, The, 402
Jim Davis, 331
Jim Redlake, 515
Jimbo, 59
Jimmy and the Desperate Woman, 291
Jimmy Higgins, 438
Jingle, Mr., 140, Pickwick Papers
Jingling in the Wind, 410
Jinny the Carrier, 516
Joab, 131, Giant-Killer
Joan, 75
Joan of Arc, Saint, 95, The Days of Jeanne d'Arc
— 288, A Monk of Fife
— 312, The Flower of France
— 412, A Mediæval Garland
— 476, Personal Recollections of Joan of Arc
Joan and Peter, 495
Joan Brotherhood, 90
Joan of the Pilchard, 195
Joan of the Tower, 133
Joan Seaton, 41
Joanna Godden, 276
Job, The, 298
Job Secretary, The, 489
Jocaste, 182
Jocelyn, Rose, 339, Evan Harrington
Jocelyn Erroll, 514
Jock o'Dreams, 238
Jock of the Bushveld, 175
Jock's Ward, 330
Joe Wilson and his Mates, 292
Johanna, 125
John, King of Bohemia, 171, The Ugly Duchess
John, King of England, 133, Joan of the Tower
— 160, Runnymede
— 188, Fulk Fitz-Warine
— 261, Philip Augustus
— 344, Royston Gower
— 425, Ivanhoe
— 432, Here Comes an Old Sailor
John, Prince, 53, Westminster Cloisters
JOHN, Eugenie, see "MARLITT, Eugenie," 326
John-a-Dreams, 478
John Barleycorn, 303
John Bodewin's Testimony, 177
John Brent, 508
John Burnet of Barns, 78
John Cann's Treasure, 7
John Charity, 479
John Chilcote, M.P., 466
John Christopher, 414
John Delaroy, 265
John Doe, 31
John Goodchild, 236
John Halifax, Gentleman, 120
John Herring, 208
John Holdsworth, Chief Mate, 417
John Inglesant, 433
John Jago's Ghost, 109
John Jones, Curate, 394

John King's Question Lodge, 432
John Law, the Projector, 5
John MacNab, 78
John March, Southerner, 86
John Marchmont's Legacy, 70
John Marmaduke, 103
John Marston Hall, 261
John Marvel, Assistant, 373
John Maxwell's Marriage, 218
John Mortonson's Funeral, 54
John Newbold's Ordeal, 388
John of Austria, 68, A Knight of Spain
— 123, In the Palace of the King
— 159, Barbara Blomberg
John of Eltham, Prince, 53, In the Shadow of the Crown
John of Gerisau, 372
John o' Jamestown, 278
John of Jingalo, 248
John Paget, 165
John Riddell Murder Case, The, 178
John Saunders, Labourer, 440
John Silence, 59
John Splendid, 355
John Thaddeus Mackay, 506
John Verney, 480
John Ward, Preacher, 136
Johnny Ludlow, 509
Johnson, Esther, see "Stella"
Johnson, Doctor Samuel, 38, The Gallants
— 63, In the Days of Goldsmith
— 78, Midwinter
— 79, Æsop Dancing
— 107, A London Posy
— 122, With the Immortals
— 305, Character and Comedy
— 348, The Jessamy Bride, Fanny's First Novel
— 356, Ayrshire Idylls
— 463, The Virginians
Johnson, Sir William, 96, Cardigan, and sequel
Joie de vivre, 518
Joint Owners in Spain, 76
Jolie propriété à vendre, 215
Jonathan Wild, 173
Jones, Paul, 69, Drums
— 104, Richard Carvel
— 114, The Pilot
— 269, The Tory Lover
— 338, Israel Potter
Jonothen Frock, 520
Jonquille, 109
Jonson, Ben, 109, The Queen's Hostage
JORDAN, Mrs., see ASHTON, Helen
Jordan is a Hard Road, 376
Jörn Uhl, 187
Jorrocks, Mr., 456, Handley Cross

Jo's Boys, 6
Joscelyn Cheshire, 278
Joseph II of Austria, 91, The Pot of Basil
— 272, Rab Ráby
Joseph and his Brethren, 186
Joseph and his Friend, 461
Joseph im Schnee, 19
Joseph in the Snow, 19
Joseph Khassan, Half-Caste, 132
Joseph Noirel's Revenge, 101
Joseph Vance, 138
Josephine, Empress, 18, The Empress Might-have-Been
— 216, The Strong Hand, and sequel
Josephine, 231
Joseph's Coat, 356
Joshua, 158
Joshua Haggard's Daughter, 70
Joubert, 57, A Burgher Quixote
Journal d'un femme, Le, 172
Journal of My Other Self, The, 408
Journal of the Plague Year, 134
Journalism, 10, Winesburg, Ohio
— 17, Patience Sparhawk and her Times
— 37, When a Man's Single
— 43, Caliban's Guide to Letters
— 132, Daniel Whyte
— 137, Moon-Calf, and sequel
— 151, The Genius, Free
— 178, Mr. Fleight
— 196, Caliban
— 197, The Street of Adventure
— 200, New Grub Street
— 229, Queed
— 268, Tommy & Co.
— 276, The Journalist
— 300, Prestige
— 311, Potterism
— 312, Mystery at Geneva
— 347, True Love, A Hind Let Loose
— 361, Blix
— 374, The Bread Line, The Fourth Estate
— 442, Barbara West
— 462, Pendennis
— 463, Adventures of Philip
— 506, The Stolen Story, The Newspaper Girl
— See also *Magazine-Writing*
Journalist, The, 276
Journey by Cart, A, 100
Journey from this World to the Next, 173
Journey Round My Room, A, 320
Journey to Nature, A, 354
Journey to the Interior of the Earth, 482
Journey to Tilsit, The, 455

Journeyman Joiner, The, 420
Journeyman Love, 400
Journey's End, 433
Jowett, Benjamin, 2, The New Republic
Joy of Captain Ribot, The, 375
Joy of Youth, The, 386
Joyce, 368
Joyous Adventures of Aristide Pujol, 301
Joyous Friar, The, 10
Juan and Juanita, 40
Juan Belvidéro, Don, 30, The Elixir of Life
Juanita, 132
Juanita la Larga, 480
Jud Süss, 172
Judas Iscariot, 11, Judas Iscariot
— 74, A Son of Issachar
— 116, Barabbas
Judas Iscariot, 11
Jude the Obscure, 226
Juden von Barnow, Die, 186
Judge, The, 496
Judgement House, The, 376
Judgement of Helen, The, 106
Judgement of the Sword, The, 144
Judge's Chair, The, 386
Judson, Adoniram, 353, Splendour of God
Judy Bovenden, 25
Juicy Joe, 62
Juif errant, Le, 455
Jules of the Great Heart, 354
Julia, 416
Julia de Roubigné, 318
Julia de Trécœur, 172
Julia France and her Times, 17
Julian (The Apostate), 21, Faustula
— 173, A Journey from this World to the Next
— 341, The Death of the Gods
Julian, 489
Julian Home, 170
Julius III, Pope, 192, Desiderio
Julius Cæsar, see *Cæsar*
Julius le Vallon, 59
Jung-Stilling, H., 433, The Little Schoolmaster Mark
Jungle, The, 437
Jungle Book, The, 282
Jupiter Lights, 511
Jura Mountains, 109, Jonquille
— 433, The Countess Eve
Jurgen, 85
Jury, The, 386
Just like Aunt Bertha, 408
Just Outside, 19
Just-So Stories, 282
Justice, 519
Justice of the Duke, The, 418
Justice of the King, The, 152
Justice of the Peace, 360

Justine's Lovers, 135
Justinian, Emperor, 128, A Struggle for Rome
Jutland, 261, Niels Lyhne
— 287, The Outcast
Juvikingar, 158

Kabuis, 470
Kabul, 144, The Judgement of the Sword
— 446, Adventures of Akbar
Kadziel, 414
Kafirs, 77, From Veldt Camp-Fires
— 197, P. GIBBON's stories
— 249, Sword and Assegai
— 346, B. MITFORD's novels
— See also *Africa, South*
Kai Lung's Golden Hours, 71
Kai Lung Unrolls his Mat, 71
"Kailyard Novelists":
Sir J. M. BARRIE, S. R. CROCKETT, Susan FERRIER, Jane and Mary FINDLATER, J. GALT, Elizabeth HAMILTON, James HOGG, Henry JOHNSTON, "David LYALL," G. MacDONALD, "Ian MACLAREN," D. S. MELDRUM, J. MENZIES, D. M. MOIR, "G. SETOUN," "John STRATHESK," Annie SWAN, "Sarah TYTLER"
— See also Nonsense Novels (burlesque), 293
Kaiser, Der, 158
Kalb, Mme von, 407, Titan
Kalilah ve Dimnah, 34
Kallistratus, 199
Kaloolah, 336
Kamala, 421
Kampf um Rom, Ein, 128
Kampf ums Recht, Ein, 186
Kanga Creek, 165
Kangaroo, 291
Kansas, 94, My Ántonia
— 228, Elder Conklin
— 377, Molly Macdonald
Kapala-Kundala, 32
Kapellet, 8
Kapitanskaya Dotchka, 395
Kapp-Putsch, 287, Youth Betrayed
Kaptein van de Lijfgarde, De, 422
Kaptejn Mansana, 56
Karain, 110
Karamazovs, 148, The Brothers Karamazov
Kardinal Albrecht, 360
Karen, 434
Karine, 268
Karl und Anna, 185
Karl of Erbach, 24
Karmazinov, 147, The Possessed
Karolinerna, 235
Karoo, 249, Katrina
— 441, The Little Karoo
— See also *Africa, South*

Kashmir, 319, A Freelance in Kashmir
Kashtanka, 100
Kassa, 272, Pretty Michal
Kassique of Kiawah, The, 436
Kate Beaumont, 134
Kate Carnegie, 318
Katerfelto, 337
Katharine of Aragon, 178, The Fifth Queen, and sequels
— 461, The House of the Wizard
See also *Henry VIII*
Katherine Frensham, 228
Katherine Lauderdale, 122
Katherine Walton, 436
Kathínka Plüsch, 178
Kathleen Clare, 313
Katie Stewart, 366
Katinka, 178
Katrina, 249
Katty's Wedding, 320
Katya, 268
Katzensteg, Der, 455
Kauffmann, Angelica, 462, Miss Angel
Kazimir, King, 434, With Fire and Sword, and sequels
Kearney, Captain, 328, Peter Simple
Kearney, General Philip, 93, Captain Courtesy
"Kearsage, The," 71, On the old *Kearsage*
KECKEIS, G., see "MURON, J.," 356
KEDDIE, Henrietta, see "TYTLER, Sarah," 478
Keddy, 142
Keening Woman, The, 380
Keeper Guppy, 185
Keeper of the Castle Stores, The, 235
Keeper of the Rede, The, 277
Keeping up Appearances, 312
Keetje, 145
Keith, 69, Mr. Misfortunate
Keith of Kinnellan, 316
Kejsaren af Portugallien, 287
Kekewich, 245, Gervase Skinner
Keldar, Baron, 36, Friend Olivia
Kelly, Cleg, 123, The Stickit Minister, Cleg Kelly
Kellys and the O'Kellys, The, 471
Kelmscott Manor, 491, Aylwin
Kelston of Kells, 10
KEMBLE, Adelaide, see Mrs. SARTORIS, 421
Ken, Bishop, 247, My Lord Winchenden
— 329, Winchester Meads
Kendall, Earl of, 195, George à Green
Kenelm Chillingly, 310
Kenilworth, 120, The House of Walderne
— 426, Kenilworth

Kenilworth, 426
Kennedy Clan, 411, The Kings of Carrick, The Dule Tree of Cassilis
Kennedy, Kit, 123, Bog-Myrtle and Peat
Kennedy, Sir Thomas, 124, The Grey Man
Kennedy Square, 440
Kennedys, The, 411
Kennicott, Carol, 298, Main Street
Kensington, 38, The Little White Bird
— 68, I will Maintain, God and the King
— 330, Kensington Palace
Kensington Palace, 330
Kent, John, 123, A Martyr's Servant, and sequel
Kent, Major, 55, Spanish Gold, etc.
Kent, 15, The Caravanners
— 58, Alice Lorraine
— 60, In Homespun
— 133, The Red Saint
— 169, J. FARNOL's novels, *passim*
— 234, A Kent Squire
— 256, Crowborough Beacon
— 262, The Smuggler
— 293, Mis'ess Joy
— 330, Penshurst Castle
— 352, A Dream of John Ball
— 432, Running Horse Inn
Kent Fort Manor, 22
Kent Island, 22, The Tower of Wye
Kent Squire, A, 234
Kentons, The, 257
Kentuckians, The, 182
Kentucky, 7-8, J. L. ALLEN's novels
— 8-9, ALTSHELER's novels, *passim*
— 33, Oldfield, Round Anvil Rock
— 54, Nick o' the Woods
— 98, The Happy Mountain
— 182, J. W. Fox's novels
— 238, The Limestone Tree
— 301, Stringtown on the Pike
— 401, Visiting the Sin, A Kentucky Colonel
— 410, My Heart and My Flesh
Kentucky Cardinal, A, 8
Kentucky Colonel, A, 401
Kentucky Warbler, The, 8
Kentucky's Ghost, 383
Kepler, 72, The Redemption of Tycho Brahe
Kerfol, 499
Kerguelen's Land, 445, The Beach of Dreams
Kerrigan's Quality, 34
Kerry, 116, A Munster Twilight
— 187, Father Clancy
— 216, Tales of the Munster Festivals
— 478, The Story of Bawn, Her Ladyship
— 498, The Wild Geese

Kett, Robert, 459, For Kett and Countryside
Ketzer von Soana, Der, 231
Kew Gardens, 510
Key-Novels (Romans à clef), see *Personal Scandal*
Key of Life, The, 515
Keynote, The, 99
Keynotes, 162
Keys of Death, The, 213
Keys of the Jest, The, 34
Khaled, 122
Khazaria, 206, The Lost Kingdom
Khmer empire, 105, The Downfall of the Gods
Kickleburys on the Rhine, The, 462
Kidd, Captain, 97, The Man they Hanged
— 284, The Shadow Captain
— See also The Gold Bug, 388
Kidnapped, 449
Kiev, 72, Natasha
Kilgorman, 402
Kilhwch and Olwen, 217
Kilkenny, 31, Crohoore of the Bill-Hook, The Ghost Hunter, Father Connell
— 174, The Chances of War
— 297, Barrington
Killala, Bishop of, see *Stock, Joseph*
Killarney, 216, The Collegians
— 336, One of our Grandmothers
— 349, The Lake
— 355, The Return of Mary O'Murrough
Killiecrankie, Battle of, 211, The Scottish Cavalier
— See also *Graham of Claverhouse*
Kilmallie, 270
Kim, 282
Kincaid's Battery, 86
Kinder der Welt, Die, 241
Kindheit, Eine, 93
Kindness in a Corner, 390
Kindred, 439
King and his Campaigners, A, 235
King Appolyn of Tyre, 13
King Behind the King, The, 133
King By the Grace of God, 413
King Candaules, 195
King Coal, 438
King Coustans, The Tale of, 352
King Errant, 446
King Florus and the Fair Jehane, The Tale of, 352
King Goshawk and the Birds, 364
King Noanett, 450
King of a Day, The, 512
King of Alsander, The, 176
King of Elfland's Daughter, The, 157

King of Folly Island, The, 269
King of Hayti, The, 139
King of Schnorrers, The, 515
King of the Highland Hearts, 153
King of the Mountains, The, 1
King of Vagabonds, A, 165
King over the Water, The, 313
King Solomon, 7
King Solomon's Mines, 219
King with Two Faces, The, 107
Kingdom of Love, The, 72
King's Achievement, The, 49
King's Agent, The, 377
King's Assegai, The, 346
Kings-at-Arms, 69
King's Betrothed, The, 244
King's Cause, The, 217
King's Deputy, The, 243
King's End, 76
King's Fool, The, 39
King's Guerdon, The, 62
King's Highway, The (by G. P. R. JAMES), 262
King's Highway, The (by MARRIOT-WATSON), 328
Kings in Exile, 130
King's Indiscretion, The, 275
King's Lynn, 52, The Lady of Lynn
King's Mignon, The, 62
King's Mirror, The, 246
Kings of Carrick, The, 411
Kings of the East, The, 215
King's Own, The, 328
King's Passion, The, 25
King's Pawn, A, 152
King's Prerogative, The, 81
King's Revoke, The, 510
King's Ring, The, 470
King's Signature, The, 16
King's Spy, 165
King's Tragedy, A, 512
King's Treasure House, The, 486
King's Woman, A, 477
King's Yard, The, 267
KINGSCOTE, Mrs., see "CLEEVE, Lucas," 105
Kingston-upon-Hull, 222, Andrew Marvel and his Friends
Kinmont Willie, 104, Court Cards
Kinsmen, The, 436
Kinsmen's Clay, 125
Kiomi, 339, Harry Richmond
Kipps, 494
Kirillov, 147, The Possessed
KIRK, J. P., see "PRIOR, J.," 392
Kirk, Scottish, 37, Sir J. M. BARRIE's novels
— 105, Inchbracken
— 270, Chronicles of Glenbuckie
— 318, "Ian MACLAREN's" stories

Kirk, Scottish : See also *Covenanters, Ministers*
Kirkcaldie, 337, The Story of Margrédel
Kirkcudbright, 355, The Mystery of Muncraig
Kirriemuir, ("Thrums") 37, Sir J. M. BARRIE's novels, *passim*
KIRSCHNER, Aloisia, see "SCHUBIN, Ossip," 423
Kismet, 176
Kiss, The, 99
Kiss of Helen, The, 327
Kit, Sir, 160, Castle Rackrent
Kit and Kitty, 58
Kit Kennedy, 124
Kith and Kin (by Jessie FOSTER), 180
Kith and Kin (by BOOTH), 65
Kittens, 177
Kitty Alone, 208
Kitty Tailleur, 437
Kitwyk, 288
Kjärtan, Olaf, 292, Laxdaela Saga
Klaus Heinrich Baas, 187
Kleine Johannes, 162
Kleine Stadt, Die, 323
Kleine Tod, Der, 178
Kleine Zielen, De, 117
Kleopatra, 159
Klosterheim, 139
Klytia, 231
Kneller, Sir Godfrey, 308, Devereux
Knickerbocker, Diedrich, 258, A History of New York
Knight, A, 189
Knight-at-Arms, 25
Knight of Gwynne, The, 296
Knight of Spain, A, 68
Knight of the Cave, The, 363
Knight of the Golden Sword, The, 39
Knight of the Legion of Honour, A, 440
Knight of the Needle Rock, The, 507
Knight of the Nets, A, 36
Knight on Wheels, A, 234
Knighthood's Flower, 62
Knightly Years, The, 14
Knights of Araby, 387
Knights of the Cross, 435
Knights Templars, 84, Crusade
Knitters in the Sun (by GISSING), 200
Knitters in the Sun (by THANET), 463
Knockagow, 278
Knowle Park, 307, The Golden Days
KNOWLES, Miss W. M., see "WYNNE, May," 512
Knox, Flurry, 443, Experiences of an Irish R.M., In Mr. Knox's Country
Knox, John, 239, The Queen's Quair

Kobiety, 417
Komedianten, De, 117
Komedjanta, 403
Kommandorens dottre, 299
Konarmia, 22
Konerne ved vandposten, 224
Königliche Hoheit, 324
Kopal Kundala, 32
Kopf, Der, 323
Kormac, 240, A Lover's Tale
— 284, Kormaks Saga
Kormaks Saga, 284
Kors Davie, 408
Korset, 479
KORZENIOWSKI, F. J. C., see CONRAD, Joseph, 110
Kosciusko, 389, Thaddeus of Warsaw
Kossuth, 230, A Sereshan
Kostia the Cossack, 284
Krakatoa, Eruption of, 318, The Man who Forgot
— 360, The Pulse of Darkness
Kramer Girls, The, 455
Kransen, 479
Kreutzer Sonata, 469
Krieg, 403
Krieg und Frieden, 219
Kriegspiel, 217
Kristin Lavransdatter, 479
Kronborg, Thea, 94, The Song of the Lark
Kruger, Oom Paul, 346, Aletta
Krzyżacy, 435
Ku Klux Klan, 145, The Leopard's Spots, and sequels
— 258, Thompson's Progress
— 470, A Fool's Errand, and sequel
Kûlop Sûmbing, 105
Kumono Tayema Amayo Notsuki, 281
Kun en Spillemand, 9
KUYUMJIAN, D., see ARLEN, M., 14
Kwaidan, 235
Kyra, My Sister, 259

Là-Bas, 257
La Beata, 473
La Chanterie, Mme de, 29, The Seamy Side of History
La Cloche, James de, 69, The Cheats
— 313, Yesterdays Tomorrow
La Fontaine, 159, The Red Neighbour, A Demoiselle of France
LA FORGE, Anatole de, 29, The Seamy Side of History
La Marck, William de, 426, Quentin Durward
La Mole, 154, Marguerite de Valois
LA RAMÉE, Mdlle de, see " OUIDA "

La Rochefoucauld, 286, The Princess of Cleves
La Rochelle, 62, Knighthood's Flower
La Salle, Robert Cavalier, Sieur de, 95, The Story of Tonty
— 376, The Power and the Glory
— 377, Beyond the Frontier
LA SIPPADE, Pierre de, see Paris and Vienne, 375
La Vallière, Louise de, 1, The Golden Fleece
— 154, The Vicomte de Bragelonne
LA VILLETTE, Pierre Marie Charles de Bernard du Grail de, see BERNARD, Charles de
Labour and Labour Problems, 40, By Faith Alone
— 45, Clayhanger
— 176, Heronshawe Main
— 194, Mary Barton, Ruth, North and South, Sylvia's Lovers
— 197, The Master of Life
— 234, The Breadwinners
— 250, A Hazard of New Fortunes
— 298, Babbitt
— 359, Pelle
— 361, McTeague
— 377, Stephen Compton
— 389, The Harbor
— 464, The Heart of Toil
— 496, Success
— 497, The Old Factory
— 506, The Portion of Labour
— 508, Theodora WILSON's novels
— 518, Germinal
— 520, Labour Stands on Golden Feet
— See also Business, Industry, Strikes, Socialism, etc.
Labour Stands on Golden Feet, 520
Labrador, 26, Ungava
— 156-7, N. DUNCAN's stories
— 214, Sir W. T. GRENFELL's stories
— 354, To the Credit of the Sea
— 459, Northern Lights and Shadows
Labrador Days, 214
Lacemaker Lekholm has an Idea, 236
Lacquer Lady, The, 268
Lad and Lass, 465
Lad of the Ferule, The Adventures of the, 257
Lad of the O'Friels', A, 319
Ladder, The, 268
Ladder to the Stars, The, 173
" Ladies, The," 38
Ladies Lindores, The, 368

Ladies' Paradise, The, 517
Ladies whose Bright Eyes, 178
Lads of the Fancy, 39
Lady Audley's Secret, 69
Lady Baltimore, 509
Lady Car, 368
Lady Chatterley's Lover, 291
Lady Connie, 489
Lady Eleanore's Mantle, 232
Lady Good-for-Nothing, 398
Lady Grizel, 508
Lady in Grey, The, 365
Lady into Fox, 193
Lady Jem, 459
Lady Lucy, 185
Lady Ludlow, 194
Lady Maid's Bell, The, 499
Lady Mary of Tavistock, The, 480
Lady of Blossholme, The, 220
Lady of Dreams, The, 436
Lady of Fort St. John, The, 95
Lady of Hirta, The, 318
Lady of Laws, The, 470
Lady of Lynn, The, 52
Lady of Lyte, The, 247
Lady of Quality, A, 82
Lady of the Aroostook, The, 249
Lady of the Barge, The, 260
Lady of the Cromlech, The, 132
Lady of the Crossings, The, 360
Lady of the Deerpark, The, 365
Lady of the Fountain, The, 217
Lady of the Regency, A, 400
Lady of Tripoli, The, 39
Lady or the Tiger, The, 450
Lady Paramount, The, 227
Lady Perfecta, 382
Lady Rose's Daughter, 488
Lady Susan, 20
Lady who Loved Insects, The, 485
Lady with the Camelias, The, 156
Lady with the Dog, The, 100
Ladybird, The, 291
Lady's Glass to Dress herself by, The, 43
Laestryonians, The, 285
Lafayette, Marquis de, 17, The Conqueror
— 71, A Gentleman of Virginia
— 345, Hugh Wynne
— 381, My Sword for Lafayette
— 416, The Scarlet Coat
Lafcadio's Adventure, 198
Lagoon, The, 110
Lagos, 54, Ainslie's Ju-Ju
Laird of Glenfernie, The, 271
Laird's Luck, The, 397
Lake, General, 319, A Freelance in Kashmir

Lake, The, 349
Lake Country Sketches, 511
Lake District, 108, Thorstein of the Mere
— 331, Lawrence Clavering
— 378, Bentinck's Tutor
— 440, Ethelinde
— 487, Robert Elsmere, Helbeck of Bannisdale
— See also Borrowdale, Windermere
Lake of Wine, The, 90
Lalage's Lovers, 55
Lally of the Brigade, 319
Lamartine, Alphonse, 400, Journeyman Love
Lamb, Lady Caroline, 161, Lord Byron
— 488, The Marriage of William Ashe
Lamb, Charles, 21, Hurdcott
— 305, Character and Comedy
Lamb, William (Viscount Melbourne), 488, The Marriage of William Ashe
Lambkin's Remains, 43
Lame Dog's Diary, A, 320
Lame Englishman, The, 133
Lame Jervas, 160
Lamia, 21, Alfred AUSTIN's journals
Lamia's Winter Quarters, 21
Lamp and the Guitar, The, 397
Lamplighter, The, 127
Lancashire, 2, J. ACKWORTH's stories
— 4, The Lancashire Witches
— 5, The Leaguer of Lathom
— 82, That Lass o' Lowrie's, Haworths
— 89, Round the Corner, Three Pretty Men, The Stucco House
— 180, Probation
— 184-5, " M. E. FRANCIS's " stories
— 185, North, South, and Over Sea, Lychgate Hall
— 194, Mrs. GASKELL's stories
— 332, J. M. MATHER's stories
— 497, The Old Factory
— See also Liverpool, Manchester, etc.
Lancashire, J. R., 488, David Grieve
Lancashire Idylls, 332
Lancashire Witches, The, 4
Lancaster, Duke of, 149, The White Company
Lancelot, Sir, 243, High History of the Holy Graal
Lances of Lynwood, The, 513
Land, The, 283
Land Agents, 92, Valentine McClutchy

Land League, 55, The Bad Times
— 289, Hurrish
— 320, Misther O'Ryan
— 349, A Drama in Muslin
Land of Bondage, The, 62
Land of Cockayne, 429
Land of Darkness, The, 368
Land of the Children, The, 370
Land of the Fathers, The, 370
LANDAU, M. A., see ALDA-NOV, M. A., 6
Landes, 334, Destinies
— See also *Bordeaux*
Landhaus am Rhein, Das, 19
Landless Farmer, A, 269
Landlords, 99, The Keynote
— 160, Castle Rackrent
— 160-1, Tales from Fashionable Life
— 161, The Absentee
— 278, Sally Cavanagh
— 296, The Martins of Cro' Martin, The Daltons
— 307, In Spite of All
— 372, The Wisdom of Esau
— 471, Ierne
— 479, A Drama in Sunshine
Landmarks, 306
Landor, Walter Savage, 141, Bleak House
Landstrykere, 224
Lane that had no Turning, The, 376
LANG, Andrew, see also Aucassin et Nicolette, 18
Lange rejse, Den, 267
Langland, William, 112, Long Will
— 343, Robert Annys
Langstaff, Lancelot, 258, Salmagundi
Lansdown, Battle of, 466, Sir Bevil
Lantern Bearers, The, 434
Lantern Lane, 133
Lantier Family, 518, His Masterpiece, Germinal, The Monomaniac
Laodicean, A, 226
Lapps, 51, The Motherless
Laputa, 458, Gulliver's Travels
Large Room, A, 153
Largs, Battle of, 294, The Thirsty Sword
Larks, Captain, 58, Christowell
Larramys, The, 179
Lassalle, Ferdinand, 56, Captain Mansana
— 340, The Tragic Comedians
— 515, Dreamers of the Ghetto
Last Abbot of Glastonbury, The, 120
Last Aldini, The, 420
Last Athenian, The, 417
Last Chronicle of Barset, The, 472

Last Day, The, 430
Last Day of a Condemned Criminal, The, 253
Last Day of the Carnival, The, 284
Last Days of John Hus, The, 255
Last Days of Pompeii, 309
Last Duchess of Belgarde, The, 428
Last Empire of the Old Dominion, The, 165
Last Full Measure, The, 353
Last Galley, The, 150
Last Hope, The, 342
Last Laugh, The, 291
Last Link, The, 196
Last Load, The, 13
Last Love, A, 365
Last Love at Pornic, A, 492
Last Master of Carnandrq, 388
Last Mirage, The, 157
Last of the Barons, The, 309
Last of the Breed, The, 382
Last of the Chiefs, The, 9
Last of the Lairds, The, 191
Last of the Mohicans, The, 114
Last of the Valerii, The, 264
Last of the Vikings, The, 64
Last Post (by F. M. FORD), 178
Last Sentence, The, 213
Last Studies, 118
Last Trail, The, 215
Last Valkyr, The, 497
Late Laurels, 127
Late Mattia Pascal, 388
Late Mrs. Null, The, 451
Later Life, The, 117
Later Pratt Portraits, 188
LATEUR, F., see "STREUVELS, S.," 453
Latin Romances, 13, Lucius APULEIUS's Metamorphoses
— 383, PETRONIUS ARBITER's Satyricon
— 306, LUCIAN
Latin Quarter, 156, Trilby
— 182, The Famished Cat
— 356, Bohemians of the Latin Quarter
— 434, Le Gentleman, Herself
Latin Quarter, The, 356
Latvia, see LETTISH NOVELISTS
Laud, Archbishop, 304, The Woman and the Sword
Laudin und die Seinen, 490
Laughing Boy, 286
Laughing Man, The, 254
Laughing Queen, The, 38
Laughter of Peterkin, The, 431
Laurens, Henry, 17, The Conqueror
Lauristons, 373
Lausset, 93, The Code of Victor Jallot
Lavinia (by BROUGHTON), 75
Lavinia (by RUFFINI), 416

Lavretsky, 474, A House of Gentlefolk
Law, John, 248, The Mississippi Bubble
Law and Lawyers, 30, Bandamanna Saga
— 65, The Will to Live
— 104, A Far Country
— 141, Bleak House
— 151, An American Tragedy
— 152, Men of Marlowe's
— 163, The Graysons
— 203, Caleb Williams
— 213, The Last Sentence
— 217, The Gladiator
— 237, Hensa-Thoris Saga
— 246, Tristram of Blent
— 247, A Young Man's Year
— 283, A Lesson in Love
— 348, The One Who Looked On
— 357, A Dangerous Catspaw
— 360, Njals Saga
— 402, The Wandering Heir
— 471, Orley Farm
— 491, The Maurizius Case
— See also *Bankruptcy, Deceased Wife's Sister Bill, Detective Stories, Trials*, etc.
Law of the Gun, The, 126
Lawrence Clavering, 331
Laws of Chance, The, 514
Lawton Girl, The, 186
Laxdael Saga, 292
Lay Anthony, The, 237
Lay Confessor, The, 210
Lay Down Your Arms, 457
Lazare, 50
Lazarillo de Tormes, 338
Lazarre, 95
Lazarus, 11, Eleazar
— 419, The Life of Saint Mary Magdalene
Lazarus, 11
Lazy Laurence, 160
Leabher na L-Uidhri, 169, 293
Lead of Honour, The, 406
Leader, The, 143
Leading Note, The, 357
League of Nations, 50, Dawn on Mont Blanc
— 312, Mystery at Geneva
League of the Scarlet Pimpernel, The, 370
Leaguer of Lathom, The, 5
Lear of the Steppes, A, 474
Learoyd, Private, 281, Soldiers Three, Life's Handicap, etc.
Leather-Stocking Tales, The, 114
Leatherwood God, The, 251
Leavenworth Case, The, 213
Lebedyan, 474
Leben des Quintus Fixlein, 407
Lecco, 325, The Betrothed
Lecouvreur, Adrian, 428, Franczka
Lecture, The, 444
Led Horse Claim, The, 177

Leddy Marget, 485
Ledge on Bald Face, The, 410
Lee, General Robert E., 8, In Circling Camps
— 71, The Patriots
— 113, Surry of Eagle's Nest, Mohun
— 165, Patriot and Tory
— 376, My Lady of the North
LEE, Mrs. S. R. Richmond, see "YORKE, Curtis," 514
"LEE, Vernon," see PAGET, Violet, 373
Lee Shore, The, 311
Leeuw van Vlanderen, De, 112
Left out on Lone Star Mountain, 230
Legend, 128
Legend, The, 499
Legend of Montrose, 425
Legend of Reading Abbey, A, 314
Legend of Sleepy Hollow, A, 258
Legend of the Rhine, A, 463
Legends, 42, Romantic Legends of Spain
— 65, The Cope
— See also *Folk Lore*, etc.
Legends and Stories of Ireland, 305
Legends of Rubezahl, 357
Legends of Smokeover, 259
Legends of the Enchanted Knight, 357
Legends of the Holy Grail, The, 242
Legends of the Province House, 232
Leghorn, 176, Vestigia
Legree, Simon, 452, Uncle Tom's Cabin
Leibnitz, Baron G. von, 484, Candide
Leicester, Robert Dudley, Earl of, 426, Kenilworth
Leiden des jungen Werther, Die, 204
Leigh, Amyas, 279, Westward Ho!
Leila (by FOGAZZARO), 177
Leila (by LYTTON), 309
Leila and her Lover, 381
Leipzig, 165, The Conscript
— 188, The Lost Manuscript
— 406, Maurice Guest
Leisler, Jacob, 74, In Leisler's Times
— 84, The Begum's Daughter
Lélia, 420
Lemnian, The, 78
Lendemain des amours, Le, 365
Leningrad, see *Petersburg*
Leo the Isaurian, 132, The Beauty of the Purple
Leon Roch, 382
Leonidas, 78, The Lemnian
— 131, A Victor of Salamis
Léonie de Montbreuse, 195

Leonora (by BENNET), 45
Leonora (by EDGEWORTH), 160
Leonora d'Orco, 263
Leopard's Spots, The, 145
Leopold, Archduke of Austria, 426, The Talisman
Lepanto, Battle of, 68, A Knight of Spain
LERIGIERS, C., see "DOFF, Neel," 145
Leroux, 178
LEROY, Miss, see STUART, Esmé, 454
Leslie Castle, 20
Lespinasse, Julie de, 69, The Burning-Glass
— 488, Lady Rose's Daughter
Less Black than We're Painted, 378
Lesson, The, 268
Lesson in Love, A, 283
Lesson of the Master, The, 264
Lessways, Hilda, 45, Clayhanger, and sequels
Let Erin Remember, 512
Let Not Man Put Asunder, 279
Letter and the Lie, The, 46
Letter Bag of the Great Western, The, 221
Letter on the Floor, The, 336
Letters, Novels in, 139, Declaration of Love
— 160, Leonora
— 162, Rosa Amorosa
— 251, Letters Home
— 286, Dangerous Acquaintances
— 296, The Dodd Family Abroad
— 318, Julia de Roubigné
— 321, The Etchingham Letters, The Clere Family
— 347, Persian Letters
— 406, S. RICHARDSON's novels
— 407, Hesperus
— 416, The New Heloïse
— 429, Obermann, Souls Divided
— 441, Humphry Clinker
— 458, Love's Cross-Currents
— 487, Farthing Hall
Letters from a Self-made Merchant to his Son, 304
Letters from My Mill, 129
Letters from Troy, 397
Letters Home, 251
Letters of her Mother to Elizabeth, 474
Letters of Two Brides, 27
Letters to Sanchia upon things as they are, 240
LETTISH NOVELISTS, see L. A. MARSHALL (tr.), 330
Lettore della Principessa, Il, 38
Lettres de mon moulin, 129

Lettres d'un satyre, 209
Lettres persanes, 347
Levant, 247, Anastasius
— 315, Sailors of Fortune
LEVETT-YEATS, S. K., see YEATS, S. K. L.
Léviathan, 213
Levin, 468, Anna Karénin
Levity Hicks, 189
Lewes, Battle of, 133, The Red Saint
Lewes Priory, 49, The King's Achievement
Lewis (explorer), 248, The Magnificent Adventure
Lewis Arundel, 439
Lewis Rand, 270
Lewis Seymour and Some Women, 349
Lexington, 88, Ben Comee
— 96, Cardigan
— 107, Daughters of the Revolution
— 114, Lionel Lincoln
Leyden, 24, Raoul, Gentleman of Fortune
— 68, Prince and Heretic
— 158, The Burgomaster's Wife
Liaisons dangereuses, Les, 286
Lianhan Shee, 92
Liao-Chai-Chih-I, 395
Liber Llandaviensis, 405
Library, The, 311
Libro de Patronio, El, 274
Libro dei Morti, Il, 375
Libussa, 93
Lichtenstein, 24, Karl of Erbach
Lichtenstein, 231
Liddesdale, 380, With the Warden of the Marches
Liége, 62, The Sword of Gideon
Life, 63
Life, Adventures, and Piracies of Capt. Singleton, 134
Life and Adventures of a Cat, 271
Life and Adventures of Buscon, 396
Life and Adventures of Colonel Jacque, 134
Life and Adventures of Peter Wilkins, The, 375
Life and Death of Harriet Frean, The, 437
Life and Death of Mr. Badman, The, 81
Life and Death of Richard Yea-and-Nay, 239
Life and Gabriella, 202
Life and Opinions of John Buncle, Esq., 9
Life and Opinions of Tristram Shandy, 447
Life and Strange Adventures of Ambrose Gwinett, 234
Life Boat, The, 26
Life Class, The, 442
Life Everlasting, The, 116
Life for a Life, A (by CRAIK), 120

Life for a Life, A (by HERRICK), 238
Life in Arcadia, 176
Life in London, 162
Life in Sweden, 71, 72
Life is Life, 276
Life of a Sailor, The, 97
Life of a Simple Man, The, 218
Life of a Well-known Character, The, 244
Life of Donna Rosina, The, 303
Life of Father Vassily, The, 11
Life of Guzman de Alfarache, The, 7
Life of Ipomedon, The, 253
Life of Mansie Wauch, 346
Life of Marianne, 326
Life of Paul, the Spanish Sharper, 396
Life of Quintus Fixlein, 407
Life of St. Mary Magdalene, 419
Life of Two Cats, 304
Life on the Mississippi, 476
Lifeguardsman, The, 422
Life's Atonement, A, 356
Life's Handicap, 281
Life's Little Difficulties, 305
Life's Little Ironies, 226
Life's Morning, A, 200
Life's Secret, A, 509
Life's Trivial Round, 91
Ligeia, 388
Light, 33
Light Behind, The, 489
Light in the Clearing, The, 23
Light-Fingered Gentry (by PHILLIPS), 384
Light-Fingered Gentry (by ZUCCOLI), 520
Light Freights, 260
Light Heart, The, 240
Light of Scarthey, The, 94
Light of the Star, The, 192
Light Princess, The, 313
Light that Failed, The, 281
Lighted Candles, The, 242
Lighthouse, The, 26
Lighthouse Keeper of Aspinwall, The, 435
Lighthouses, 26, The Lighthouse
— 94, The Light of Scarthey
— 435, The Lighthouse Keeper of Aspinwall
Lightning Conductor, The, 507
Lights and Shadows of Irish Life, 222
Lights and Shadows of Scottish Life, 507
Like Another Helen, 215
Likely Story, A, 139
Likeness, 129
Likeness of King Elfwald, The, 108
Lilac Sunbonnet, The, 123
Lilian, 46
Liliecrona's Home, 287
Lilith, 166, Adam and Eve
Lilith, 115

Lilla, 44
Lilli Barr, 72
Lillian Morris, 435
Lilliesleaf, 366
Lilliput, 458, Gulliver's Travels
Lilly Dawson, 126
Lily Christine, 14
Lily of France, A, 332
Lily of the Alley, 126
Lily of the Valley, The, 27
Limbo, 256
Limehouse Nights, 87
Limerick, 31, The Boyne Water, The Denounced
— 174, The Chances of War
— 319, In Sarsfield's Days
Limerick Gloves, The, 160
Limestone Tree, The, 238
Limitations, 47
Lincoln, Abraham, 8, In Circling Camps
— 22, Mrs. BABCOCK's novels
— 23, Eben Holden, Cricket Heron, A Man for the Ages, and sequel
— 71, The Patriots
— 77, The Father
— 78, The Path of the King
— 95, Spanish Peggy
— 104, The Crisis
— 145, The Leopard's Spots, and sequels, The Southerner
— 163, The Graysons
— 283, The McVeys
— 353, Forever Free, and sequels
— 318, The Washingtonians
Lincoln (England), 160, Runnymede
— 269, Tom and Lincoln
Linda Condon, 237
Linley, Jane, 348, A Nest of Linnets
Linnæus, 470, The Times of Linnæus
Linny Lockwood, 126
Lion of Flanders, The, 112
Lion of Janina, The, 271
Lionel Lincoln, 114
Lion's Share, The, 46
Lion's Skin, The (by BERNARD), 52
Lion's Skin, The (by SABATINI), 418
Lippi, Fra Filippo, 9, The Romance of Fra Filippo Lippi
Lisa Ann, 138
Lisbeth of Jarnfjeld, 168
Lisbon, 62, The Sea Devils
— 84, Agnes Surriage
Lisconnel, 34, Strangers at Lisconnel, From the East unto the West
Lisheen, 432
Lismoyle, 125
Listener, The, 59
Listener's Lure, 305
Literary Lapses, 293
Literary Life, 8, A Heroine in Bronze

Literary Life (contd.): 17, The Aristocrats
— 19, Just Outside
— 28, Lost Illusions, and sequel
— 33, C.
— 37, Tommy and Grizel
— 42, Seven Men
— 45, A Great Man
— 48, The Oakleyites
— 49, Alan
— 51, That Kind of Man
— 52, Gerfaut
— 67, A Saint
— 75, A Beginner
— 76, A Fool in her Folly
— 77, The Tether
— 85, The Certain Hour
— 101, Prosper Randoce
— 103, The Celebrity
— 128, Legend, Printer's Devil
— 129, Artists' Wives
— 132, The Story of Ronald Kestrel
— 136, Henry Brocken
— 170, The House at High Bridge
— 172, The Love Affairs of a Bibliomaniac
— 173, Jacob Elthorne
— 177, O Genteel Lady
— 197, Pending Heaven
— 198, The Counterfeiters
— 201, Henry Ryecroft
— 223, Hunger, Shallow Soil
— 241, Telling the Truth
— 251, Fennel and Rue
— 252, Richard Kurt, and sequels
— 255, The Human Interest, The Celebrity at Home
— 256, Richard Greenhow, Crome Yellow
— 257, En Route, and sequels
— 263–6, Henry JAMES's novels, *passim*
— 284, Kormaks Saga
— 312, Staying with Relations
— 316, Morley Darville
— 327, The Dewpond, The Unpetitioned Heavens
— 330, Multitude and Solitude
— 334, Cakes and Ale
— 335, Voyage to the Land of the Articoles
— 351, C. MORLEY's novels, *passim*
— 369, The Survivor
— 378, Headlong Hall
— 379, Nightmare Abbey
— 403, The London Nights of Belsize
— 407, The Invisible Lodge, Flower, Fruit and Thorn Pieces
— 408, The Notebook of Malte Laurids Brigge
— 412, George Mandeville's Husband
— 436, The Divine Fire
— 437, Tasker Jevons

Literary Life (contd.): 442, Martin Birck's Youth
— 444, Grub Street Nights' Entertainment
— 459, Spiritual Adventures
— 465, Chariot Wheels
— 486, Fortitude
— 487, Hans Frost
— 489, A Great Success
— 498, Crucial Instances
— 518, His Masterpiece
— See also *Journalism.*
Literary Morning, A, 520
Lithuania, 413, Devaytis
— 435, The Knights of the Cross
— 455, The Journey to Tilsit
Little Angel, The, 10, 11
Little Barefoot, 19
Little Beloved, 195
Little Big Horn, Battle of, 376, Bob Hampton
Little Bob, 218
Little Book of Profitable Tales, A, 172
Little Brown Jug at Kildare, The, 359
Little Cæsar, 82
Little Countess, The, 172
Little Daughter of Jerusalem, The, 229
Little Death, The, 178
Little Demon, The, 443
Little Dinner at Timmins's, A, 463
Little Dog Laughed, The, 342
Little Dorrit, 141
Little Duke, The, 513
Little England, 275
Little Fadette, 420
Little Flutter, A, 71
Little France, 70
Little Geste of Robin Hood, A, 411
Little Gidding, see *Nicholas Ferrar*
Little Girl, The, 325
Little Good-for-Nothing, 129
Little Green World, A, 79
Little Grey, 299
Little Henry and his Bearer, 446
Little Jarvis, 427
Little Jehan de Saintré, 288
Little Johannes, 162
Little Journey in the World, A, 490
Little Karoo, The, 441
Little King, The, 321
Little Lady Mary, 256
Little Less than Gods, 179
Little Maid at the Door, The, 505
Little Maister, The, 180
Little Marquis of Brandenburg, The, 474
Little Men, 5
Little Mexican, 257
Little Minister, The, 37
Little Mr. Bouncer and his Friend, Mr. Verdant Green, 70
Little Norsk, A, 192

Little Novels (by COLLINS), 109
Little Novels (by SCHNITZLER), 423
Little Novels of Italy, 239
Little Novels of Sicily, 481
Little People, The, 227
Little Peter, 321
Little Pilgrim in the Unseen, 367
Little Princess, A, 82
Little Red Foot, The, 97
Little Regiment, The, 120
Little Saint Elizabeth, 82
Little Schoolmaster Mark, The, 433
Little Shepherd of Kingdom Come, The, 182
Little Tinker, 174
Little Town, The, 323
Little Traitor to the South, A, 70
Little Union Scout, A, 229
Little What's His Name, 129
Little White Bird, The, 38
Little Women, 5
Little Women Married, 5
Little World, A, 171
Litvinov, 475, Smoke
Liv, 63
Lively Peggy, The, 498
Liverpool, 279, Bell Barry
— 295, Cap'n Nat's Treasure
— 338, Redburn
— 363, Willoughby Manor
— 466, Dorrie
Liver's Responsibility, 41
Livery of Eve, The, 25
Living Alone, 50
Living Lie, A, 67
Living or Dead, 400
Livre de la pitié et de la mort, Le, 304
Livre de mon ami, Le, 182
Livsslaven, 299
Liza (A House of Gentlefolk), 474
Liza of Lambeth, 333
Lizerunt, 353
Lizzie Leigh, 194
Lizzie Lorton, 300
Llewellyn, Davy, 58, The Maid of Sker
Lludd and Llevelyn, 217
Llyvyr Coch o Hergest, 405
Locarno, 22, The Devil at the Long Bridge
Lochiel, 69, Mr. Misfortunate
— 74, The Flight of the Heron, and sequels
Lochinvar, 124
Lochinvárovič, 253
Lochleven Castle, 426, The Abbot
Lochnagar, 7, Balmoral
Lockhart, James, 244, The Private Memoirs . . . of a Fanatic
Lodging House Bum, A, 420
Lodsen og hans hustru, 299
Lofoten, 64, The Last of the Vikings

Loftus, Rev. Tom, 296, Jack Hinton
Log of a Cowboy, The, 2
Log of a Sea Waif, The, 79
Logic, Bob, 162, Life in London, and sequel
Logie Town, 478
Lögnerna, 266
Lohengrin, 443
Loire, 27, La Grande Bretêche
Lokis, 341
Lollards, 343, Robert Annys
— See also *Wyclif*
Lombardy, 24, Springtime
Lomond, Loch, 425, Rob Roy
London before the Stuart Period, 4, The Tower of London, Old St. Paul's
— 47, Master Skylark
— 49, By what Authority?
— 70, London Pride, In High Places
— 91, Where England sets her Feet
— 176, David March
— 213, Evil May-Day
— 323, The Golden Quill
— 447, Captain Ravenshaw
— 513, The Armourer's 'Prentices
— See also names of Kings, and historic characters, *Shakespeare,* etc.
London in Stuart and Hanoverian Times, 52, The Orange Girl, No Other Way
— 53, The Chaplain of the Fleet
— 69, Drums
— 70, Mohawks
— 81, S. H. BURCHELL's novels, *passim*
— 83, Evelina
— 87, The Christian
— 93–4, Agnes and Egerton CASTLE's novels, *passim*
— 104, Richard Carvel
— 124, The Moss-Troopers
— 134, Moll Flanders, Colonel Jacque
— 191, The Ayrshire Legatees
— 206, Veronica Playfair
— 412, Whitefriars
— 462, Henry Esmond, Pendennis
— See also events, *Fire of London, Plague,* etc., names of Monarchs and historical characters, and names of places, *Newgate, Fleet-Prison,* etc.
London Lot, A, 308
London, Modern, 50, Living Alone
— 138–9, DE MORGAN's novels
— 305, Over Bemerton's
— 306, Mr. Ingleside, London Lavender
— 316, The Square Circle

London, Modern, 352, News from Nowhere
— 510, Night and Day
— See also Cockneys, London Poor; and names of districts, Chelsea, Hoxton, New Cross, etc.
London Nights of Belsize, The, 403
London Only, 407
London Poor, 3, East End Idylls, In the Image of God
— 52, The Children of Gibeon
— 106, The House in Marylebone
— 111, The Secret Agent
— 140-1, DICKENS's novels
— 200-1, G. GISSING's novels
— 223, The Midnight Bell
— 260-1, W. W. JACOBS's stories, passim
— 278, Polly of Parker's Rents
— 290, The Iron Bell, Underneath
— 308, A Neil LYONS' stories
— 310, Kenelm Chillingly
— 333, W. S. MAUGHAM's novels, passim
— 351, The Processionals
— 353, G. MORRISON's stories
— 368, The Royal Road
— 395, E. PUGH's stories
— 407-8, Pett RIDGE's stories
— 410, Maurice Quain
— 412-3, F. W. ROBINSON's novels
— 436, The Lady of Dreams
— 447, Wine on the Lees
— 458, The Chaste Wife, Shops and Houses
— 488, Marcella
— 502, No. 5, John Street
— 515, Children of the Ghetto
— See also Cockneys
London Posy, A, 107
Londonderry, 452, A Man's Foes
Londoners, The, 241
Lone Adventure, The, 456
Loneliness, 50
Lonely Queen, The, 24
Lonewood Corner, 222
Long Exile, The, 469
Long Journey, The, 267
Long Lane's Turning, The, 409
Long Night, The, 498
Long Roll, The, 270
Long Run, The, 499
Long Trail, The, 192
Long Will, 112
Longest Journey, The, 179
Longfellow, Henry W., 177, O Genteel Lady
Longshoreman, The, 39
Longsword, 486
Look Homeward, Angel, 509
Looking Backward, 43

Loom of Youth, The, 491
Loot of Loma, 157
Lord Arthur Savile's Crime, 504
Lord Brackenbury, 161
Lord Byron, 161
Lord Dunfield, 201
Lord Edward Fitzgerald, 63
Lord Jim, 110
Lord Kilgobbin, 297
Lord of Labraz, The, 35
Lord of the Harvest, 162
Lord of the Sea, The, 433
Lord of the World, 49
Lord Ormont and his Aminta, 340
Lord Protector, The, 513
Lord Raingo, 46
Lords of High Decision, The, 359
Lords of Red Lattice, 145
Lords of the North, 289
Lords of the Sea, 360
Lords of the World, 103
Lordship of Love, The, 256
Lore of Proserpine, 240
Lorenzo Benoni, 416
Loretto School, 110, Lyndesay
Loring Mystery, The, 169
Lorle, 19, The Professor's Wife
Lorna Doone, 58
Lorraine, Cardinal de, 247, A Cardinal and his Conscience
Lorraine, 37, The Sacred Hill
— 464, Queen of the Woods
— See also Alsace, Franco-German War
Lorraine, 96
Los Angeles, 93, Captain Courtesy
Loss and Gain, 359
Lost and Saved, 363
Lost Borders, 21
Lost Endeavour, 331
Lost Faith, The, 242
Lost Father, The, 191
Lost Girl, The, 291
Lost Glove, The, 112
Lost God, The, 417
Lost Illusions, 28
Lost King, The, 18
Lost Kingdom, The, 206
Lost Kinnellan, 316
Lost Lady, A, 95
Lost Lady of Old Years, A, 78
Lost Land, The, 125
Lost Lawyer, The, 55
Lost Love, A, 364
Lost Mameluke, The, 42
Lost Manuscript, The, 188
Lost on the Steppe, 467
Lost Pibroch, The, 355
Lost Property, 407
Lost Quality, 140
Lost Sir Massingberd, 378
Lost Stradivarius, The, 168
Lost Tribes, The, 55
Lost Valley, The, 59
Lost World, The, 150
Lot Barrow, 343
Lothair, 144
Lottery, The, 160

Lotus or Laurel ?, 485
Lou, 409
Lou of the Ranges, 350
Loudon, Fort, 118, The Story of Old Fort Loudon
Loudon Hill, 425, Old Mortality
Lough Derg Pilgrim, 92
Loughsiders, The, 80
Louis IX (Saint), 21, Arnoul the Englishman
— 83, The Oriflamme in Egypt
— 131, Falaise of the Blessed Voice
Louis XI, 152, The Justice of the King
— 275, The Duke's Vengeance
— 358, The Deuce
— 426, Quentin Durward
— 427, Anne of Geierstein
— 442, Fortune
Louis XIII, 37, Cardillac
— 62, Knighthood's Flower
— 154, The Three Musketeers, and sequels
— 195, Captain Fracasse
— 261, Richelieu
— 417, Bardelys the Magnificent
— 483, Cinq-Mars
— 497, The Man in Black
Louis XIV, 1, Blush-Rose, The Golden Fleece
— 10, Kelston of Kells
— 62, Traitor and True
— 80, The Preacher and the King
— 91, Historical Vignettes
— 142, The Black Wolf's Breed
— 152, The Great Game
— 154, Sylvandire, The Vicomte de Bragelonne
— 155, Olympe de Clèves
— 159, His Indolence of Arras, A Demoiselle of France
— 196, The Countess of Zelle
— 196, A Rose of Blenheim
— 171, The Adventures of Telemachus
— 321, The Little King
— 337, Cerise
— See also Fronde, Huguenots, Mazarin, etc.
Louis XV, 92, "No. 101"
— 153, The Chevalier d' Harmental
— 154, The Regent's Daughter, Memoirs of a Physician
— 155, Olympe de Clèves
— 156, M. de Chauvelin's Will
— 234, A Kent Squire, and sequel
— 262, Castelnau
— 390, The House of De Mailly
Louis XVI, 155, The Queen's Necklace, Ange Pitou, La Comtesse de Charny

Louis XVI (contd.): 169, Briton Eliot
— 428, The Last Duchess of Belgarde
Louis XVII (Dauphin), 18, The Lost King
— 21, Dromina
— 90, A Castle in Spain
— 95, Lazarre
— 234, The Shadow of a Throne
Louis (Son of Philip Augustus), 160, Runnymede
Louis Beretti, 105
Louis Lambert, 30
Louis Philippe, 156, The She-Wolves of Machecoul
Louisa of Prussia, 355, L. Mühlbach's novels
Louisa of Prussia and her Times, 355
Louisbourg, 319, The Span o' Life
Louise and Barnavaux, 344
Louisiana, 86, Bonaventure
— 93, The Code of Victor Jallot
— 103, Bayou Folk
— 142, The Black Wolf's Breed, etc.
— 407, Out of the Cypress Swamp
Louisiana, 82
Louisiana Purchase, 44, A Volunteer with Pike
— 86, The Grandissimes
— 221, Philip Nolan's Friends
— 448, In the Eagle's Talon
Loukis Laras, 54
Lourdes, 518
Lousteau, 28, The Muse of the Department
Louves de Machecoul, Les, 156
Louvois, Marquis de, 62, In the Day of Adversity
— 152, The Great Game
— 159, The Red Neighbour
— 262, The Huguenot
— 262, Castlenau
Louvre, 262, The Brigand
Lovat, Lord, see Fraser, Simon
Love (by ARNIM), 15
Love (by CHEKHOV), 100
Love-a-Duck, The, 20
Love-Affairs of a Bibliomaniac, The, 172
Love Among the Artists, 431
Love Among the Ruins, 133
Love and a Quiet Life, 400
Love and Friendship, 20
Love and his Mask, 149
Love and Honour, 93
Love and Liberty, 156
Love and Lucy, 240
Love and Mr. Lewisham, 493
Love and the Soul Hunters, 119
Love at Arms, 418
Love Blinded, 169
Love by an Indian River, 381

Love Chase, The, 239
Love Crime, A, 67
Love Episode, A, 517
Love Fairy, The, 516
Love Gilds the Scene and Women Guide the Plot, 94
Love in a Mist, 56
Love in a Palace, 381
Love in Armour, 448
Love in Idleness, 122
Love in Old Clothes, 81
Love in Our Village, 3
Love in the Hills, 381
Love in the Woods, 279
Love is Enough, 515
Love Lane, 442
Love-Letters of a Worldly Woman, 106
Love like a Gipsy, 90
Love Like the Sea, 377
Love Me Little, Love Me Long, 401
Love o' Women, 281
Love of Comrades, 333
Love of Parson Lord, The, 505
Love of Sisters, 477
Love Offensive, A, 381
Love Passage, A, 260
Love Story of Giraldus, The, 127
Love Story of St. Bel, The, 91
Love Tangle, A, 381
Love that Prevailed, The, 348
Love the Sea but Cling to the Shore, 520
Love Thrives in War, 126
Love with Honour, 327
Lovebird, The, 438
Lovede land, Det, 394
Lovel, Mrs., 339, Rhoda Fleming
Lovel the Widower, 463
Lovelace, 406, Clarissa Harlowe
Lovells Meeting, 336
Lover Hunt, The, 52
Lover of Truth, A, 501
Lovers, The, 386
Lovers and Friends, 48
Lovers of Yvonne, The, 417
Lover's Tale, A, 240
Lover's Watch, 43
Love's Cross-Currents, 458
Love's Depths, 365
Love's Illusion, 51
Loves of Clitopho and Leucippe, 2
Loves of Pelleas and Melisande, The, 189
Loves of Poliarchus and Argenis, The, 33
Love's Pilgrim, 51
Love's Pilgrimage, 438
Lovey Mary, 405
Löwensköldska ringen, 287
Lowndes, Mrs., see Belloc-Lowndes, Marie Adelaide
Lowther, Miss (Duchess of Bolton), 196, The Heart of a Hero
— 271, Chrysal
Loyal Traitor, A, 35

Lubeck, 324, Buddenbrooks
Lucerne, 467
Lucha por la Vida, La, 35
Lucianic Satire, 122, With the Immortals
— 173, A Journey from this World to the Next
— 503, Confessions in Elysium
Lucienne, 415
Lucinda, 247
Lucino, 103
Luck of Gerald Ridgeley, The, 346
Luck of Roaring Camp, The, 229
Luck of the Barerakes, The, 327
Luck of the Bogans, The, 269
Luck of the Vails, The, 48
Luck of Wheal Veor, The, 228
Lucky Lawrences, The, 361
Lucky Mistake, The, 43
Lucky Prisoner, The, 203
Lucretia, 309
Lucy, 506
Lucy Arden, 212
Lucy Bettesworth, 68
Luddite Riots, 32, Bond Slaves
— 33, Bond Slaves
— 120, John Halifax
— 392, Forest Folk
Ludovic and Gertrude, 112
Ludvigsbakke, 31
Lugh of the Long Hand, 214
Lukardis, 490
Luke Delmege, 432
Luliban of the Pool, 41
Lumber-Men, 126, The Trail of the Axe
— 343, The Whip Hand, The "Merry-Anne"
— 501, The Blazed Trail, Conjuror's House, The Rules of the Game
Lunatic Asylums, 107, Valentine Vox
— 401, Hard Cash
— 438, Professor Hieronimus
— 517, The Conquest of Plassans
Lunatic at Large, The, 106
Lundy Island, 313, Henry Elizabeth
"Luska, Sidney," see Harland, Henry
Luther, Martin, 74, A Friar Observant
— 77, The Fiery Angel
— 98, Chronicles of the Schönberg-Cotta Family
— 105, The Duke's Page
— 131, A Friar of Wittenberg
— 159, In the Blue Pike
— 243, The Sword of the Lord
— 357, The Unfortunate Traveller
Lutherans, see Reformation
Luttrell of Arran, 297
Lwonsome Lizzie, 185

Lycanthropy, 281, The Mark of the Beast
— 369, The Master of the House
Lychgate Hall, 185
Lydgate, Mr., 164, Middlemarch
Lyf of Saynt Balaam, 34
Lying Prophets, 385
Lyme Regis, 53, 'Twas in Trafalgar's Bay
Lymington, 329, The Children of the New Forest
Lynd, Robert, see sub nom. Black, L. L. D.
Lyndesay, 110
Lynmouth, 58, Lorna Doone
Lynn, see King's Lynn
Lyons, 40, The Nun
— 221, In his Name
Lyre and Lancet, 12
"Lys, Christian," see Brebner, Percy James
Lys dans la vallée, Le, 27
Lys rouge, Le, 183
Lysbeth, 219
Lyttleton, Edith, see "Lancaster, G. B.," 287
Lytton, 1st Lord, 121, Doctor Claudius
— 462-3, The Yellowplush Memoirs

Mabel Vaughan, 127
Mabinogion, 405
Maccabæus, 103, Patriot and Hero
— 306, Deborah
McCaskey, Major, 297, Tony Butler
McClellan, General G. B., 97, Ailsa Paige
— 353, Forever Free, and sequels
MacDatho's Boar, 293
Macdermots of Ballycloran, The, 471
Macdonald, Flora, 478, The Macdonald Lass
Macdonald Lass, The, 478
McDowell, Captain John, 319, Spanish John
McFall, Mrs. Haldane, see "Grand, Sarah," 211
MacGowan, Alice, see Cooke, Grace, and A. MacGowan, 113
Macgregor Clan, 425, Rob Roy
Macgregor, Rob Roy, 211, Adventures of Rob Roy
Machiavelli, 72, Rubeni
— 341, The Forerunner
— 412, Cæsar Borgia
— 513, The Honour of Savelli
Maciej the Mazur, 44
M'Ilwraith, Jean Newton, see sub nom. McLellan, W., 319
Mackaye, Sandy, 279, Alton Locke

Mackellar, 449, The Master of Ballantrae
McKinney, Mrs. Alice, see "Webster, Jean," 492
Maclehose, Mrs. ("Clarinda"), 311, The Rhymer
"Macleod, Fiona," see Sharp, W., 431
Macleod of Dare, 57
McManus, Mrs. Seumas, see "Carbery, Ethna"
MacMurrough, Diarmid, 365, When the Norman Came
Macquart Family, 516-17, The Rougon-Macquart series
MacQuoid, Mrs., see sub nom. Keary, Annie M., 276
Mac's Adventures, 35
McTeague, 361
McVeys, The, 283
MacWhirr, Captain, 110, Typhoon
Mad Barbara, 133
Mad Professor, The, 455
Mad Shepherds, 259
Madam Prince, 408
Madame Bovary, 175
Madame Chrysanthème, 304
Madame Corentine, 40
Madame de Fleury, 160
Madame de Mauves, 263
Madame d'Orgevaut's Husband, 398
Madame de Treymes, 499
Madame Delphine, 86
Madame Firmiani, 26
Madame Prue, 439
Madame Thérèse, 165
Madagascar, 344, Barnavaux
Madcap Jane, 424
Mädchenfeinde, 444
Made in France, 81
Made out of Nothing, 259
Madeleine (by Kavanagh), 275
Madeleine (by Sandeau), 421
Madeleine at her Mirror, 466
Madeleine jeune femme, 69
Madeline, one of Love's Jansenists, 345
Madelon (by About), 1
Madelon (by Mary Wilkins), 505
Madelon Lemoine, 286
Mademoiselle de la Seiglière, 421
Mademoiselle de Maupin, 195
Mademoiselle de Mersac, 361
Mlle de Scudéri, 244
Mademoiselle Ixe, 231
Mademoiselle Mathilde, 280
Mademoiselle Miss, 227
Mademoiselle Mori, 410
Madesani-Deledda, Mme, see "Deledda, Grazia," 137

Madison, Betty, 17, Senator North
Madison, James, 17, The Conqueror
Madman's Drum, 489
Madog, 128, Prince Madog
Madonna Mary, 367
Madonna of the Barricades, The, 452
Madonna of the Future, The, 263
Madonna of the Peach-Trees, 239
Madonna of the Sleeping-Cars, The, 135
Madonna of the Trenches, A, 283
Madras, 243, As It Happened
Madre, La, 137
Madre Naturaleza, La, 375
Madrid, 35, The Struggle for Life, The Tree of Knowledge
— 61, The Mob
— 123, In the Palace of the King
— 375, Froth
— 382, The Last of the Breed
— 396, Pablo de Segovia
— 398, Lady Good-for-Nothing
Maelcho, 289
Maestrante, El, 375
Maestricht, 196, Adventures of an Equerry
Maestro Don Gesualdo, 482
Maeve, 293, The Courtship of Ferb
Mafeking, 135, The Dop Doctor
Mafia, 40, The Net
— 121, Corleone
Magada, The, 14
Magazine-Writing, 250, A Hazard of New Fortunes
— See also *Journalism*
Magdalene, 448
Magdalen's Husband, A, 77
Magdeburg, 159, The Mercenary
Maggie, 121
Maggiore, Lake, 106, Sir George's Objection
— 310, An Old Maid's Love
Magic, 42, Vathek
— 54, Ainslie's Ju-Ju
— 170, Faustus
— 203, St. Leon
— 244, Hoffman's Tales
— 249, The Restitution of the Bride
— 350, Black Magic
— 351, The Dark Fire
— 432, Frankenstein
— 515, Undergrowth
— See also *Celtic Romances, Chinese Fiction, Witchcraft*
Magic Flute, The, 142
Magic Forest, The, 501
Magic Mountain, The, 324
Magic Shadow, The, 397
Magic Shop, The, 494

Magic Tale of Harvanger and Yolande, The, 25
Magician, The, 333
Magie noire, 350
Magistrate's Own Case, The, 416
Magna Charta, 160, Runnymede
— See also *John, King*
Magnet, The, 207
Magnetic North, The, 412
Magnhild, 56
Magnificent Adventure, The, 248
Magnificent Ambersons, The, 460
Magnus Sinclair, 380
Magnússon, E., see Morris, W., 352
Magyars, see Hungarian Novelists, *Hungary*
Mahatma and the Hare, The, 220
Mahdi, The, 439, The Curse of the Nile
Mahrattas, 244, Pandurang Hari
— 319, A Freelance in Kashmir
— 461, Tara, Ralph Darnell
Maid-at-Arms, The, 96
Maid Margaret of Galloway, 124
Maid Marian, 379
Maid of Florence, The, 22
Maid of Killeena, The, 57
Maid of Maiden Lane, The, 36
Maid of '76, A, 284
Maid of Sker, The, 58
Maid of the Manse, A, 167
Maida, Battle of, 211, Adventures of an Aide-de-Camp
Maiden and Married Life of Mary Powell, 324
Maidens of the Rocks, The, 12
Maiden's Progress, The, 255
Maids' Money, 153
Maids of Paradise, The, 97
Maids of Salem, 348
Maildun, 273, The Voyage of Maildun
Maime o' the Corner, 184
Maimonides, Moses, 515, Dreamers of the Ghetto
Main Plot, 262, Arabella Stuart
Main Street (by Hawthorne), 233
Main Street (by Sinclair Lewis), 298
Main-Travelled Roads, 192
Maine, 250, A Modern Instance, Doctor Breen's Practice
— 269, The Country of the Pointed Firs, The Queen's Twin
— 452, The Pearl of Orr's Island
— 506, Evered, The Rational Hind

Maintenon, Mme de, 97, The Drums of Aulone
— 142, The Siege of Lady Resolute
— 149, The Refugees
— 154, Sylvandire
— 262, The Huguenot
Mainwaring, 240
Maironi Family, The, 177, The Patriot, and sequels
Maison, La, 66
Maison de Claudine, La, 108
Maison de Penarvan, La, 421
Maison des deux-Barbeaux, La, 464
Maison des hommes vivants, La, 170
Maison du Chat-qui-Pelote, La, 26
Maison du péché, La, 466
Maison morte, La, 66
Maison Nucingen, la, 29
Maison Vauquer, 28, Old Goriot
Maitland of Laurieston, 457
Maître Cornelius, 30
Maître de Forges, Le, 365
Maîtres mosaïstes, Les, 420
Maîtres sonneurs, Les, 421
Maiwa's Revenge, 219
Maja Desnuda, La, 60
Majesteit, 117
Majesty, 117
Major and Minor, 362
Major Lawrence, F. L. S., 289
Major Vigoureux, 398
Major Weir, 348
Majorca, 61, The Dead Command
Major's Candlesticks, The, 55
Major's Niece, The, 55
Major's Story, The, 54
Maker of Saints, A, 152
Making an Orator, 121
Making and Breaking of Almansur, The, 123
Making of a Bigot, The, 311
Making of an Englishman, 195
Making of Christopher Ferringham, The, 144
Maktub, 210
Makura Zoshi, 428
Mala Hierba, 35
Malalesta, Sigismondo Pandolfo, 256, The Mastiff of Rimini
Malay, 41, Rodman the Boatsteerer
— 105, Sir H. Clifford's novels
— 110, Almayer's Folly, and sequel, Tales of Unrest, Lord Jim
— 209, Polydore Marasquin
— 469, Gallion's Reach
Malayan Monochromes, 105
Malbone, 242
Malcolm, 314
Malcom, Mrs., 191, Annals of the Parish
Maldon, Battle of, 294, Olaf the Glorious

Malevoglia, I, 482
Malik Shah Seljuki, 145, Omar the Tentmaker
Malines, 156, The Martian
Malleville, 1
Mallow, 308, My Tower in Desmond
Malmesbury, 433, John Inglesant
— 498, Chippinge
Malombra, 177
Maltese Cat, The, 282
Malva, 206
Malvern Hills, 112, Long Will
Malvery Hold, 176
Malvina of Brittany, 268
Mam' Linda, 224
Mamma, 75
Mammon & Co., 48
Man, Isle of, 87, Sir Hall Caine's novels, *passim*
— 304, Mirry-Ann
— 426, Peveril of the Peak
Man Adrift, A, 277
Man and His Dog, A, 324
Man and his Kingdom, The, 369
Man and Maid, 60
Man and Wife, 109
Man-at-Arms, A, 423
Man-at-Arms, The, 262
Man at Odds, The, 404
Man Could Stand Up, A, 178
Man for the Ages, A, 23
Man from Australia, The, 478
Man from Egypt, The, 243
Man from Texas, The, 366
Man from the North, A, 45
Man, His Mark, A, 353
Man in Black, The, 205, The Citizen of the World
Man in Black, The, 497
Man in the Bell, The, 320
Man in the Iron Mask, The, 154, The Vicomte de Bragelonne
Man in the Moon, 127
Man in the Zoo, 193
Man of Business, A, 29
Man of Devon, A, 189
Man of Feeling, The, 318
Man of Genius, A, 506
Man of Gold, A, 271
Man of his Age, A, 152
Man of Iron, The, 135
Man of Mark, A, 245
Man of Moods, A, 305
Man of Property, The, 189
Man of Quality, Adventures of a, 391
Man of the House, The, 336
Man of the Moors, A, 456
Man of the People, A, 166
Man of the World, The, 177
Man of the World, The, 318
Man of Wrath, The, 14, Elizabeth and her German Garden
Man-Stealers, The, 433
Man that Corrupted Hadleyburg, The, 477
Man They Hanged, The, 97
Man who became a Woman, The, 10

Man who did the Right Thing, The, 270
Man who Forgot, The, 318
Man who Kept a Diary, The, 444
Man who Knew Coolidge, 298
Man who Knew Too Much, The, 102
Man who Laughs, The, 254
Man who Made Gold, The, 44
Man who Understood Women, The, 342
Man who Was, The, 281
Man who was Afraid, The (Fomá Gordyéeff), 206
Man who was Good, The, 341
Man who was Thursday, The, 102
Man with a Nose, The, 493
Man Within, The, 213
Man without a Country, The, 221
Man without a Temperament, The 325
Man You Couldn't Kill, The, 117
Manalive, 102
Manapouri, Lake, 26, The Untold Half
Manasseh, 272
Manawyddan, Son of Llyr, 217
Manchester, 3, J. AGATE's novels
— 4, Mervyn Clitheroe
— 5, The Leaguer of Lathom
— 32, Mrs. G. L. BANKS's novels
— 89, Young Earnest
— 194, Mary Barton
— 244, Grey Dawn—Red Night
— 259, Legends of Smoke-over, and sequel
— 277, Slavery
— 347, Allan MONKHOUSE's novels, A Hind Let Loose
— 502, The Revolution in Tanner's Lane
Manchuria, 33, Tinker's Leave
— 50, Tobit Transplanted
Mandalay, 268, The Lacquer Lady
Mandrake Venus, The, 162
Manet, Claude, 518, His Masterpiece
Manhattan Transfer, 146
Manhood End, 153
Manin, Daniele, 245, Adria
Mann, Horace, 77, The Father
Mannequin d'osier, Le, 183
Mannerings, The, 76
Manners, Lord George (Duke of Rutland), 143, Coningsby
Manners, Sir John, 321, Dorothy Vernon
Manœuvring, 161
Manon Lescaut, 391
Manor Farm, The, 185

Man's Foes, A, 452
Man's Man, A, 233
Man's Story, The, 10
Man's Woman, A, 361
Mansfield Park, 20
Mansie Wauch, 346
Mansourah, 83, The Oriflamme in Egypt
Mansur, 123, The Making and Breaking of Almansur
Mantalini Family, 140, Nicholas Nickleby
Mantle of Elijah, The, 515
Mantle of the Emperor, The, 57
Mantrap, 298
Manuel of Poictesme, 85, J. B. CABELL's novels, passim
MS. in the Red Box, The, 223
Manxman, The, 87
Many Captives, 372
Many Cargoes, 260
Many Inventions, 281
Many Junes, 329
Many Marriages, 10
Maoris, 64, War to the Knife
— 118, The Adventures of Kimble Bent
— 209, Tales of a Dying Race
— 322, Old New Zealand
— 337, Mardi
— 421, The Greenstone Door
Mape, 335
MAQUET, August, see sub nom. DUMAS, Alexandre
Maracot Deep, 150
Maradick at Forty, 486
Marana, les, 30
Marat, Jean Paul, 235, Rose in the Mouth
— 280, Mademoiselle Mathilde
— 495, A Marriage under the Terror
Mårbacka, 287
Marble Faun, The, 233
Marcella, 488
March, Mr. and Mrs., 249, Their Wedding Journey, and sequel
— 250, A Hazard of New Fortunes
— 251, An Open-eyed Conspiracy, A Pair of Patient Lovers
Marchesa, La, 241
Marching Men, 10
Marching On, 69
Marching On, 452
"Marchioness, The," 140, Old Curiosity Shop
Marcia, 362
Marco Fieravanti of Forli, 152, The Maker of Saints
Marco Polo, 84, Messer Marco Polo
Mardi, 337
Mare au diable, La, 421
Mare Nostrum, 61

Maréchale, La, 175, The Sentimental Education
Maremma, 91, The Love Story of St. Bel
Margaret of Anjou, 91, Historical Vignettes
— 427, Anne of Geierstein
Margaret (Daughter of James I of Scotland), 412, A Mediæval Garland
Margaret, 274
Margaret Harding, 197
Margaret Lorimer, 436
Margareta of Tyrol, 171, The Ugly Duchess
Margery of Quether, 208
Marget at the Manse, 235
Marguerite d'Angoulême, 247, The Gage of Red and White
Marguerite de Valois, 154
Mari de Mme d'Orgevaut, 398
Maria Theresa, Empress, 420, Consuelo, and sequel
Maria, 259
Maria Chapdelaine, 236
Maria Capponi, 422
Mariage dans le monde, Un, 172
Mariage d'amour, Un, 221
Mariage de Chiffon, Le, 218
Mariage de Convenance, A, 276
Mariage de Loti, Le, 304
Marianela, 382
Marie, 259
Marie Antoinette, 38, The Empress of Hearts
— 107, The King with Two Faces
— 155, The Chevalier de Maison-Rouge, The Queen's Necklace, Ange Pitou, La Comtesse de Charny
Marie-Claire, 18
Marie-Claire's Workshop, 18
Marie de Mancini, 195
Marie Grubbe, 261
Marie Halkett, 97
Marie Louise, Archduchess, 18, The Empress Might-have-Been
Marie of Lichtenstein, 231
Marie Walewska, 18
Marietta (by CRAWFORD), 123
Marietta (by TROLLOPE), 473
Mariflor, 167
Mario and the Magician, 324
Mario und der Zauberer, 324
Marion Darche, 121
Marius the Epicurean, 377
Majorie Daw, 6
Mark of Cain, The, 493
Mark o' the Deil, The, 380
Mark of the Beast, The, 281
Mark on the Wall, The, 510
Mark Rutherford's Deliverance, 502
Marka of the Pits, 103
Marked Man, A, 260

Markens gröde, 224
Market Harborough, 337
Market Place, The, 186
Markham, Gervase, 262, Arabella Stuart
Markheim, 449
Markurells i Wadköping, 51
Markus König, 188
Marlborough, Duchess of, 81, The Mistress of the Robes
— 165, The King's Spy
— 196, The Adventures of an Equerry
— 377, The King's Agent
Marlborough, 1st Duke of, 4, St. James's
— 62, Across the Salt Seas, The Sword of Gideon
— 165, The King's Spy
— 196, The Adventures of an Equerry, A Rose of Blenheim
— 234, A Kent Squire, and sequel
— 263, The Fate
— 348, Nell Gwyn
— 377, The King's Agent
— 396, The Blue Pavilions
— 441, Mistress Dorothy Marvin
— 462, Henry Esmond
Marlborough, 497, The Castle Inn
Marne, The, 499
Marneffe, Mme, 29, Cousin Betty
Marot, Clément, 154, Ascanio
Marotz, 21
Marplot, The, 308
Marquesas Islands, 337, Typee, and sequel
Marquis de St. Pelaye, 433
Marquis of Lossie, The, 314
Marquis of Penalta, The, 374
Marriage and its Problems, 7, A Woman at Bay
— 8, Sara Videbeck
— 9, Tantalus
— 10, Many Marriages
— 14, St. Christopher's Day
— 15, Love
— 19, Edelweiss, On the Heights
— 36, Was it Right to Forgive?
— 40, Those of his Own Household
— 45, Leonora, Whom God hath Joined, These Twain
— 49, Mezzanine
— 56, Magnhild
— 57, In God's Way
— 64, God and Woman
— 67, Divorce
— 69, A Gentlewoman of France
— 76, The Mannerings
— 83, Cock's Feather
— 87, The Woman Thou Gavest Me
— 88, The Brimming Cup
— 89, Rough-Hewn, The Home-Maker, The Deepening Stream

Marriage and its Problems (contd.) : 95, My Mortal Enemy
— 101, Joseph Noirel's Revenge
— 104, A Modern Chronicle
— 109, Man and Wife
— 119, The Gods, Some Mortals, and Lord Wickenham
— 122, A Rose of Yesterday
— 129, Artists' Wives
— 135, Tension, Turn back the Leaves
— 136, Philip and his Wife
— 137, Moon-Calf, and sequel
— 138, It Never Can Happen Again
— 140, Never in Vain
— 149, Love and his Mask
— 160, Leonora
— 166, Mrs. Martin's Man
— 168, Lisbeth of Jarnfjeld
— 169, Love Blinded, Signor I, Gypsy and Ginger
— 172, A Marriage in High Life, Aliette, An Artist's Honour
— 175, Madame Bovary
— 179, The Longest Journey
— 190, The Dark Flower
— 195, The City of Light, The Second Blooming
— 198, The School for Wives
— 202, Virginia
— 212, Judge R. GRANT's novels
— 226, A Group of Noble Dames
— 238, Together
— 240, Love and Lucy
— 242, The Call of the Blood, and sequel
— 246, Double Harness
— 247, Mrs. Maxon Protests, Lucinda
— 255, The Way of Marriage, The Doll
— 268, Mrs. Caudle's Curtain Lectures, Featherbeds
— 276, A Mariage de Convenance
— 281, The Gadsbys
— 288, The Fifteen Comforts of Marriage
— 289, An Echo of Passion
— 290-1, D. H. LAWRENCE's novels
— 299, The Pilot and his Wife
— 299, Stephen Escott
— 300, Sowing the Wind, Christopher Kirkland
— 311, Eve
— 316, Sonia Married, Keith of Kinellan
— 321, Colonel Enderby's Wife
— 323, The Eglamore Portraits
— 326, The Frontiers of the Heart
— 327, The Wondrous Wife

Marriage and its Problems (contd.) : 334, Une vie
— 335, W. B. MAXWELL's novels
— 339-40, MEREDITH's novels, *passim*
— 349, A Mummer's Wife
— 352, Three Northern Love-Stories
— 359, Ruth, and sequel
— 361, Brass, Bread
— 371, The Infatuation
— 374, The Fourth Estate
— 382, Leon Roch
— 384, Old Wives for New
— 398, Madame d'Orgevaut's Husband
— 408, Into the Dark
— 424, The Agony Column
— 430, Mrs. B. K. SEYMOUR's novels
— 444, The Skeleton in the House
— 458, September
— 466, The Five-Barred Gate
— 468, Anna Karénin
— 469, The Kreutzer Sonata
— 483, Absolution
— 488, David Grieve
— 489, One Poor Scruple
— 490, Wedlock, Faber
— 493, Love and Mr. Lewisham
— 494, Ann Veronica, Mr. Polly, The New Machiavelli, Marriage
— 496, Riven Bonds
— See also *Divorce, Feminism, Free Love, Jealousy, Miscegenation, Sex Problems*
Marriage (by FERRIER), 171
Marriage (by WELLS), 494
Marriage, The, 214
Marriage à la Mode, 488
Marriage in High Life, A, 172
Marriage of Cupid and Psyche, The, 13
Marriage of Gerard, The, 464
Marriage of the Dead, The, 285
Marriage of William Ashe, The, 488
Marriage Settlement, A, 27
Marriage Under the Terror, A, 495
Married, 454
Married Beneath Him, 378
Married Life, 371
Married Man, A, 212
Mars, 156, The Martian
— 493, The War of the Worlds
— 212, The Reds of the Midi, and sequels
Mar's Rebellion, see *Jacobite Rebellion of 1715*
Marseilles, 62, A Fair Martyr
— 111, The Arrow of Gold
— 316, Banjo
— 516, The Mysteries of Marseilles

Marseilles, 11
Marséna, 186
Marsh Island, A, 269
MARSHALL, Frances, see " ST. AUBYN, A.," 419
Marshalsea, 141, Little Dorrit
Marshfield the Observer, 94
Marston Moor, Battle of, 176, When Charles I was King
— 243, Follow the Gleam
— 313, Cornet Strong
Marta y Maria, 374
Marta Riquelme, 252
Martha, 253
Martha and Mary, 11
Martian, The, 156
MARTIN, Miss V., see " Ross, Martin," 443
Martin Arrowsmith, 298
Martin Birck's Youth, 442
Martin Chuzzlewit, 141
Martin Conisby's Vengeance, 169
Martin Eden, 303
Martin Hyde, 331
Martin Rivas, 61
Martin Schüler, 507
Martin Valliant, 133
Martinique, 97, Tom Bowling
— 235, Youma
— 255, His Majesty's Sloop Diamond Rock
Martins of Cro' Martin, The, 296
Martyrs, Les, 99
Martyr's Heir, A, 123
Martyr's Servant, A, 123
Maruja, 230
Marvell, Andrew, 222, Andrew Marvell and his Friends
Marvellous Tales, 249
Marx, Karl, 452, The Madonna of the Barricades
Mary I, 5, Cardinal Pole
— 24, The Sea Captain
— 49, The Queen's Tragedy
— 105, The Duke's Page
— 178, The Fifth Queen, and sequel
— 321, When Knighthood was in Flower
— 333, The Royal Sisters
— 381, I Crown Thee King
— 497, Francis Cludde, A Gentleman of France
Mary II, 68, Defender of the Faith, and sequels
— 330, Kensington Palace
Mary Queen of Scots, 24, The Master of Grey
— 49, Come Rack ! Come Rope !
— 69, The Spae Wife
— 155, The Two Dianas, The Page of the Duke of Savoy
— 211, Bothwell
— 212, Mary of Lorraine
— 223, Mary Hamilton
— 239, The Queen's Quair
— 286, The Princess of Cleves

Mary Queen of Scots (contd.): 321, Dorothy Vernon
— 333, One Queen Triumphant
— 337, The Queen's Maries
— 426, The Abbot
— 438, Queen Mary's Holdfast
— 456, Pam the Fiddler
— 513, Unknown to History
Mary (Daughter of Henry VII), 321, When Knighthood Was in Flower
Mary (by BJÖRNSON), 57
Mary (by BRADDON), 70
Mary (by L. P. JACKS), 259
Mary Amelia Spot, 277
Mary Anerley, 58
Mary Barton, 194
Mary Bray X her Mark, 460
Mary Dominie, 404
Mary Erskine, 1
Mary Fenwick's Daughter, 500
Mary Gray, 478
Mary Hamilton, 223
Mary Jane Married, 436
Mary Jane's Memoirs, 436
Mary Lee, 139
Mary Magdalene, Saint, 418, The Life of St. Mary Magdalene
Mary, Mary, 446
Mary of Burgundy, 261, Mary of Burgundy
— 321, Yolanda
Mary of Burgundy, 261
Mary of Lorraine, 212
Mary Olivier, 437
Mary Paget, 441
Mary Pechell, 44
Mary Plantagenet, 442
Mary Powell, 324
Mary Schweidler, the Amber Witch, 336
Mary Sell, 1
Mary Unwin, 419
Maryland, 22, The Tower of Wye
— 47, The Story of Barnaby Lee
— 104, Richard Carvel
— 206, Sir Christopher
— 390, The House of De Mailly
— 409, Barbara Ladd
— 440, Kennedy Square
Marzio's Crucifix, 122
Masaniello, 117, The Company of Death
— 234, Mas'aniello
Mas'aniello, 234
Masham, Mrs., 4, St. James's
— 24, The Highwayman
— 81, The Mistress of the Robes
Mashi, 400
MASOCH, see SACHER-MASOCH, L. von
Mason, Lady, 471, Orley Farm
Mason's Corner, 387, Quincy Adams Sawyer, and sequel

Masquerade, 434
Massachusetts, 84, Penelope's Suitors
— 144, The Making of Christopher Ferringham
— 232-3, HAWTHORNE'S stories
— 254, A New England Cactus
— 274, Margaret
— 452, Oldtown Folks
— 499, Ethan Frome, Summer
— 505-6, Mary E. WILKINS'S stories
— See also *New England, Boston, American Revolution,* etc.
Massacre of the Innocents, 408
Masséna, 178, Leroux
Massey, Gerald, 164, Felix Holt
Massimilla Doni, 30
Master, The, 515
Master and Maid, 227
Master and Man, 469
Master and Servant, 469
Master Beggars of Belgium, The, 116
Master Christian, The, 116
Master Christopher, 137
Master Girl, The, 243
Master Johannes Wacht, 244
Master John, 80
Master Martin the Cooper, 244
Master Mosaic-Workers, The, 420
Master of Ballantrae, The, 449
Master of Craft, A, 260
Master of Gray, The, 24
Master of Hestviken, The, 479
Master of his Fate, 36
Master of Life, A, 197
Master of Men, 370
Master of Merripit, 386
Master of Stair, The, 68
Master of the House, 369
Master of the Musicians, The, 330
Master of the Shell, The, 402
Master of the Strong Hearts, 74
Master Rogue, The, 384
Master Skylark, 47
Masterful Wilhelmine, 450
Masterman Ready, 329
Masterpiece, The, 520
Mastiff of Rimini, The, 256
Mat', 206
Matabele, 346, The King's Assegai, The Sign of the Spider
Matador of the Five Towns, The, 46
Matchmaker, The, 485
Matchmakers, The, 79
Mate of the *Daylight,* The, 269
Mated, 260
Matelot, 305

Mateo Falcone, 341
Maternity of Harriott Wicken, The, 153
Math, Son of Mathonwy, 217
Mather, Cotton, 36, The Black Shilling
— 348, Maids of Salem
— 431, The Coast of Freedom
— 461, Anne Scarlet
Mathias Sandorf, 483
Matilda Montgomerie, 406
Mating of a Dove, The, 323
Mating of Lydia, The, 489
Matka Boska, 303
Matriarch, The, 447
Matrimonial Lottery, A, 159
Matrimony, 362
Matter of Principle, A, 102
Mattie—a Stray, 413
Matty, Miss, 194, Cranford
Maugars Junior, 464
Mauprat, 420
Maureen, 315
Maureen's Fairing, 34
Maurice, Elector of Saxony, 105, The Duke's Page
Maurice, F. D., 279, Yeast
Maurice Guest, 406
Maurice Quain, 410
Maurice Tiernay, 296
Maurin des Maures, 4
Maurin the Illustrious, 4
Mauritius, 419, Paul and Virginia
Maurizius Case, The, 491
Mave, 98
Max Hensig, 59
Maximalists, 11, Sashka Jigouleff
Maximilian I of Austria, 321, Yolanda
Maximina, 374
Maxims of Morgan O'-Doherty, 320
Maxse, Admiral, 340, Beauchamp's Career
Maxwell, 319, The Span o' Life
Maxwell, 245
May, Phil, 381, Our House
May Day Eve, 59
May Fair, 14
Maya, 181
Mayenne, Duc de, 262, One in a Thousand, Rose d'Albret
Mayfield, 77
" *Mayflower,*" 144, Soldier Rigdale
Mayflower, The, 60
Maylie, Rose, 140, Oliver Twist
Mayo, County, 319, Nessa
— 451, The Snake's Pass
Mayo, Lord, 101, A True Reformer
Mayor of Casterbridge, The, 226
Mayor of Gantick, The, 396
Mayor of Troy, The, 397
Mayorazgo de Labraz, El, 35
Mazarin, Cardinal, 70, In High Places

Mazarin, Cardinal (contd.) : 154, The Vicomte de Bragelonne
— 155, The War of Women
— 195, Marie de Mancini
— 259, None So Pretty
— 261, John Marston Hall
— 277, The Silver Cross
— 417, The Lovers of Yvonne
— 498, In Kings' Byways
Mazeppa, Ivan Stepanovich, 512, A Prince of Intrigue
Mazzini, 24, The Pillar of Fire
— 133, The Lame Englishman
— 144, Lothair
— 252, Defeat, and sequel
— 416, Lorenzo Benoni
— 502, Clara Hapgood
Mea Culpa, 227
Meadow-Grass, 76
Meath, 320, The Valley of the Squinting Windows
Mecca, 447, In the Day of Battle
Mechanism, Romance of, 282, The Day's Work
Mecklenburg, 403, REUTER'S novels
Médecin de campagne, Le, 29
Mediæval Garland, A, 412
Medical Life and Problems, 29, The Country Doctor
— 31, Ida Brandt
— 39, David Arnot
— 42, Black Rent
— 55, Our Casualty
— 86, Dr. Sevier
— 133, Sincerity
— 150, Round the Red Lamp
— 238, The Web of Life, The Healer
— 250, Doctor Breen's Practice
— 298, Martin Arrowsmith
— 310, The Healers
— 311, The New Religion, Tuberculin
— 314, Paul Faber
— 345, The Autobiography of a Quack
— 366, The Doctor's Family
— 384, Though Life us do Part
— 406, Richard Mahony
— 481, Confessions of a Physician
— 490, Passages from the Diary of a Late Physician
— 499, The Fruit of the Tree
— 514, The Young Physician
— 515, My Brother Jonathan
— See also *Hospital Life, Nurses and Nursing*
Medici, Catherine de', 30, About Catherine de' Medici

Medici, Catherine de' (contd.): 124, The White Plumes of Navarre
— 154, Ascanio, Marguerite de Valois
— 155, The Two Dianas, The Page of the Duke of Savoy
— 247, A Cardinal and his Conscience
— 446, An Enemy to the King
Medici, Giovanni de', 68, The Carnival of Florence
Medici, Giuliano de', 128, The Sword of Love
Medici, Leo de', 131, A Friar of Wittenberg
Medici, Lorenzo de', 10, His Magnificence
— 128, The Sword of Love
— 164, Romola
— 285, St. Sebastian
— 333, Richard Hawkwood
Medici, Piero de', 68, The Carnival of Florence
Medicis, Marie de, 37, ·Cardillac
MEDING, O., see "SAMAROW, G.," 419
Mediterranean Sea, 24, The Sea Captain
— 61, Our Sea
— 317, Vestal Fire
Medway, 315, The Dutch in the Medway
Meer, Das, 277
Meeting, A, 210
Meeting, The, 190
Meg McIntyre's Raffle, 419
Meg of the Scarlet Foot, 467
Megan of the Dark Isles, 15
Mehalah, 208
Mehemet Ali, 42, The Honour of Henri de Valois
Meïpe, 335
Meir Ezofowicz, 371
Meister Jordan, 520
Mel, Mr. and Mrs., 339, Evan Harrington
Melanchthon, 98, Chronicles of the Schönberg-Cotta Family
— 131, A Friar of Wittenberg
— 486, Royal Favour
Melbourne, 169, Grif
— 254, The Mystery of a Hansom Cab
Melbourne, Lady, 161, Lord Byron
Meldon, Rev. J. J., 55, Spanish Gold, etc.
Melechsala, 93
Melincourt, 378
Melki Bes, 443
Mellichampe, 436
Melmoth Reconciled, 30
Melmoth the Wanderer, 333
Melrose, 425-6, The Monastery, The Abbot
Melusine, 15
Member for Arcis, The, 29
Member of the Third House, A, 192

Members of the Family, 509
Mémoires de deux jeunes mariées, 27
Mémoires d'un homme de qualité, 391
Mémoires pour servir á l'histoire de la virtu, 432
Memoirs of a Cavalier, 134
Memoirs of a Flea, 271
Memoirs of a Landlady, 436
Memoirs of a Midget, 136
Memoirs of a Person of Quality, 243
Memoirs of a Physician, 155
Memoirs of a Surrey Labourer, 68
Memoirs of an American Citizen, 238
Memoirs of an English Officer, 134
Memoirs of Barry Lyndon, 463
Memoirs of Carwin the Biloquist, 76
Memoirs of Gerald O'Connor, 353
Memoirs of Mrs. Sydney Biddulph, 432
Memoirs of Monsieur d'Artagnan, 154
Memoirs of Morgan O'Doherty, 320
Memoirs of Sherlock Holmes, 149
Memories, 355
Memories of Ronald Love, The, 324
Memories of Summer, 330
Memory Corner, 189
Memory of Parnell, A, 210
Memphis, 117, The Tour
Men and Brothers, 140
Men and Ghosts, 347
Men of Iron, 396
Men of Marlowe's, 152
Men of the Frontier Force, 144
Men of the Moss-Hags, The, 124
Men with the Bark On, 403
Men, Women, and Ghosts, 383
Ménage de garçon en province, Un, 28
Menander, 386, The Treasures of Typhon
Mendel, 89
Mendelssohn, 432, Charles Auchester
Mendelssohn, Moses, 19, Poet and Merchant
Mengraby the Magician, 358
Menhardoc, 171
Mennonites, 157, The Trail of the Conestoga
Men's Wives, 463
Menschen im Hotel, 39
Menschenwee, 396
Mensonges, 67
Mentana, 25, The Rebel
Menteith, Earl of, 425, A Legend of Montrose
Meraner Novellen, 235

Mercantile Marine, 79, F. T. BULLEN's novels
— 128, Two Years before the Mast
— 132, Daniel Whyte
— 260-1, W. W. JACOBS's stories
— 315, McFEE's novels
— 338, Redburn
— 360, The S.S. Glory, E. NOBLE's novels
Mercedes of Castile, 114
Mercenary, The, 159
Merchant of Berlin, The, 355
Merchant of Killogue, The, 149
Merchant of Venice, 34, Barlaam and Josaphat
Merchant Prince, The, 25
Mercia, 120, Edwy the Fair
Mère, La, 322
Mere Child, A, 485
Mere Cypher, A, 142
Meredith, George, 240, Mainwaring
Meridor, Diane de, 154, La Dame de Monsoreau
— 155, The Forty-Five Guardsmen
Mermaid Tavern, 113, My Lady Pokahontas
Merrie Tales of Jacques Tournebroche, 184
Merrilies, Meg, 424, Guy Mannering
Merry Adventures of Robin Hood, 396
" Merry Anne," The, 343
Merry Folk, 455
Merry Garden, 398
Merry-go-Round, The, 333
Merry Men, The, 449
Mervyn Clitheroe, 4
Mesmerism, see *Hypnotism*
Message, The, 27
Messe de l'athée, La, 27
Messenger, The, 348
Messer Marco Polo, 84
Méta Holdenis, 101
Metamorphoses, The, 13
Metastasio, 420, Consuelo, and sequel
Metempsychosis, see *Reincarnation*
Methodist Idylls, 300
Methodists, see *Wesleyans*
Metropolis, The, 438
Metternich, Prince, 267, The Stronger Wings
Mettle of the Pasture, The, 8
Metz, 37, Colette Baudoche
— 326, The Disaster
— 381, The Virgin Fortress
Meunier d'Angibault, Le, 420
MEURICE, Paul, see *sub nom.* DUMAS, The Two Dianas, 155
MEXICAN NOVELIST: AZUELA, M.
Mexican Revolution, 22, The Under Dogs

Mexico, 40, Juan and Juanita
— 44, A Volunteer with Pike
— 95, Death Comes for the Archbishop
— 126, C. CULLEY's novels
— 196, Reata
— 219, Montezuma's Daughter, Heart of the World
— 291, The Plumed Serpent
— 291, The Princess
— 296, Con Cregan
— 440, A Day at Laguerres
— 459, The Two Vanrevels
— 479, John Charity
— 486, The Fair God
— 491, Nathan Burke
Mezzanine, 49
Micah Clarke, 149
Micawber, Mr., 141, David Copperfield
Michael Firth, 271
Michael Strogoff, 482
Michelangelo, 72, Rubeni
— 341, The Forerunner
— 503, The Plough of Shame
Michigan, 501-2, S. E. WHITE's novels
Michigan, Lake, 115, Oak Openings
— 343, The Whip Hand, The " Merry Anne "
Microcosm of Empire, A, 316
Micromégas, 484
'Mid Green Pastures, 167
Midas & Son, 316
Middle Class Life, see especially : 20, Jane AUSTEN's novels
— 26-30, BALZAC's novels
— 119, The Vineyard
— 151-2, DREISER's novels
— 175, Madame Bovary, Bouvard and Pécuchet
— 349, Spring Days
— 359, The House that Fell
— 458, SWINNERTON's novels
Middle-Class Man, A, 185
Middle Classes, The, 29
Middle Temple Murder, The, 177
Middle Years, The, 264
Middlemarch, 164
Middleton, Clara, 340, The Egoist
Middy and Ensign, 171
Midge, The, 80
Midland Counties, 39, The Thirteen Evenings
— 51, Revolution
— See also *Black Country*, and names of counties
Midlander, The, 460
Midnight Bell, The, 223
Midnight Folk, The, 331
Midnight Mass, The, 92
Midshipman Farragut, 35
Midshipman Paulding, 427
'Midst the Wild Carpathians, 271
Midsummer Madness, 191
Midsummer Madness, A, 283

Midsummer Morn, 180
Midsummernight, 505
Midwinter, 78
Miggles, 229
Miggs, Miss, 140, Barnaby Rudge
Mighty Atom, The, 116
Mignon, Modeste, 27, Modeste Mignon
Miks Bumbullis, 455
" MIKULICH, V.," see VESELITSKAYA, L. I., 483
Milan, 68, The Viper of Milan
— 91, A Jay of Italy
— 169, Love Blinded
— 239, The Love Chase
— 256, Frederic Uvedale
— 325, The Betrothed
— 418, Bellarion
— 423, A Man-at-Arms
Miletus, 18, The Immortal Marriage
Military Stories, 61, Tommy Atkins of the Ramchunders
— 120-1, S. CRANE's novels, *passim*
— 144, Captain Desmond, V.C., and sequels
— 150, The Green Flag, Danger !
— 165-6, " ERCKMANN-CHATRIAN's " novels
— 211, Frank Hilton
— 281-2, R. KIPLING's stories
— 285, The Duel
— 296, C. J. LEVER's stories
— 344, P. MILLE's stories
— 347, Right Off the Map
— 516, The Attack on the Mill
— 518, The Downfall
— See also *Regimental Life*, *War*, and under names of wars and great battles
MILITSINA, E. D., see TOLLEMACHE, Mrs. B. L., 467
Milky Way, The, 268
Mill on the Floss, The, 164
Mille et un jour, Les, 382
Miller of Angibault, The, 420
Miller of Old Church, The, 202
Million, The, 196
Millionaire of Yesterday, A, 369
Millionaire, The, 16
Millionaires, 46, A. BENNETT's later novels, *passim*
— 151, The Financier, and sequel
— 258, Thompson's Progress
— 266, The Ivory Tower
— 316, Midas & Son
— 327, The Princess Xenia
— 340, One of Our Conquerors
— 368, The Railway Man
— 384, D. G. PHILLIP's novels, *passim*

Millionaires (contd.): 472, The Way We Live Now
— See also *Wealth*
Millionaire's Daughter, A, 501
Millionaire's Island, 381
MILLS, Martin, see " BOYD, Martin A'Beckett "
Milly, 265, The Wings of the Dove
Milton, John, 252, A Dreamer of Dreams
— 324, Mary Powell, Deborah's Diary
— 332, The Binding of the Strong
Mimi Pinson, 357
Mimi's Marriage, 483
Mimi's Sin, 275
Mimotchka, 483
Mind Awakened, A, 65
Minder, The, 2
Mine Host Gansendonck, 112
Mine of Faults, A, 25
Miners and Mining, 26, The Devil's Half-Acre
— 26, Deep Down
— 40, The Spoilers of the North, The Barrier
— 126, The Sheriff of Dyke Hole, The Golden Woman, The Law of the Gun
— 176, Heronshawe Main
— 229-30, Bret HARTE's stories
— 259, Youth Rides West
— 272, Black Diamonds
— 276, Son of Judith
— 290-1, D. H. LAWRENCE's novels, *passim*
— 316, The White Stone, The Undersong
— 357, Old Blazer's Hero
— 358, The Valley of Tophet
— 369, The World's Great Snare
— 379, J. H. PEARCE's novels, *passim*
— 380, H. PEASE's stories
— 428, Under Cheddar Cliffs
— 438, King Coal
— 501, Gold
— 514, The Black Diamond Mines of Falun, The, 244
Mingo, 228
Minister of Dour, The, 123
Minister of State, The, 447
Ministers, 37, The Little Minister
— 123, The Stickit Minister, The Minister of Dour
— 171, Destiny
— 173, The Story of a Mother
— 187, The Pastor of Poggsee
— 191, Annals of the Parish
— 271, The Great Valley
— 302, Adam Blair
— 318, Kate Carnegie
— 366-7, Mrs. OLIPHANT's novels
— 389, Emmanuel, and sequel

Ministers (contd.): 413, White Rocks
— 452, The Minister's Daughter
— 506, John Thaddeus Mackay
— See also *Clergymen, Kirk, Priests*
Minister's Black Veil, The, 232
Minister's Charge, The, 250
Minister's Daughter, The, 145
Minister's Guest, The, 440
Minister's Son, The, 450
Minister's Wife, The, 367
Minister's Wooing, The, 452
Minna, 202
Minnesota, 90, Red Rust
— 298, Main Street
— 415, Pure Gold
Minnie's Bishop, 55
Minor Operations, 459
Minstrel Dick, 107
MIRABEAU, Gabrielle de, see " GYP," 218
Mirabeau, 297, Gerald Fitzgerald
Miracles of Antichrist, The, 286
Miranda, 70
Miranda of the Balcony, 331
Mirandola, Pico della, 68, The Carnival of Florence
— 333, Richard Hawkwood
Miriam, 290, Sons and Lovers
Miriam, 436
Miriam Cromwell, 313
Miriam Lucas, 432
Miriam's Schooling, 502
Mirror and the Lamp, The, 335
Mirror For Witches, A, 178
Mirror of Kong-Ho, The, 71
Mirror of Shalott, A, 49
Mirry-Ann, 304
Mirthful Haven, 460
Mirthful Nine, The, 411
Miscegenation, 132, Joseph Khassan
— 311, Black Mary
— 344, God's Step-Children
— 445, Voices in the Night
— See also *Colour Line,* etc., *Half-Breeds*
Miscellaneous Studies, 377
Miser, The, 112
Misérables, Les, 254
Miserere Nobis, 321
Misers, 4, The Miser's Daughter
— 27, Eugenie Grandet
— 29, Facino Cane
— 46, Riceyman Steps
— 52, Ready-Money Mortiboy
— 91, Fardarougha the Miser
— 141, A Christmas Carol
— 164, Silas Marner
— 213, Avarice House
— 364, The House of Gold
— 415, Pure Gold
— 419, The Gollovlev Family

Misers (contd.): 438, Downstream
Miser's Daughter, The, 4
Miser's Money, 386
Misery, 100
Mis'ess Joy, 293
Misfortune, 100
Misfortunes of Elphin, The, 379
Miss Angel, 462
Miss Badsworth, M.F.H., 256
Miss Barrett's Elopement, 369
Miss Bellard's Inspiration, 251
Miss Bretherton, 487
Miss Brooks, 500
Miss Chrissie's Protégé, 167
Miss Christine Jean, 210
Miss Esperance and Mr. Wycherley, 227
Miss Gilbert's Career, 245
Miss Grace of All Souls', 467
Miss Harriet, 334
Miss Lulu Bett, 189
Miss Mannering, 408
Miss Marjoribanks, 367
Miss Meredith, 297
Miss Mole, 514
Miss Nanse, 478
Miss Parkworth, 65
Miss Ravenell's Conversion, 134
Miss Rovel, 101
Miss Shafto, 362
Miss Stuart's Legacy, 445
Miss Tarrant's Temperament, 437
Miss Tod and the Prophets, 43
Missing !, 381
Missing Masterpiece, The, 44
Missionaries, 95, Death Comes for the Archbishop
— 123, A Martyr's Servant, and sequel
— 255, The Old Missionary
— 320, Selah Harrison
— 337, Typee
— 344, God's Step-Children
— 387, The House of War
Missionary Sheriff, The, 464
Mrs. Arne, 255
Mrs. Alemere's Elopement, 327
Mrs. Ames, 48
Mrs. Bindle, 267
Mrs. Bligh, 75
Mrs. Caudle's Curtain Lectures, 268
Mrs. Cliff's Yacht, 451
Mrs. Craddock, 333
Mrs. Dalloway, 511
Mrs. Drummond's Vocation, 417
Mrs. Dymond, 462
Mrs. Erricker's Reputation, 106
Mrs. Farrell, 252
Mrs. Fitz, 442
Mrs. Galer's Business, 408
Mrs Green, 417
Mrs Grundy's Crucifix, 77
Mrs. Halliburton's Troubles, 509

Mrs. Jim Barker, 171
Mrs. Keats Bradford, 389
Mrs. Keith's Crime, 106
Mrs. Lancelot, 240
Mrs. Lathom's Extravagance, 107
Mrs. Lirriper's Lodgings, 141
Mrs. Marden, 242
Mrs. Martin's Company, 34
Mrs. Martin's Man, 166
Mrs. Maxon Protests, 247
Mrs. Murphy, 374
Mrs. Noakes, 424
Mrs. Overtheway's Remembrances, 168
Mrs. Perkins's Ball, 462
Mrs. Peter Howard, 323
Mrs. Shelmire's Djinn, 3
Mrs. Thompson, 335
Mrs. Tregaskis, 390
Mrs. Warren's Daughter, 270
Mrs. Wiggs of the Cabbage Patch, 405
Mississippi, 77, Diane
— 86, The Cavalier
— 104, The Crossing
— 118, A Spectre of Power
— 119, The Fair Mississippian
— 376, The Power and the Glory
— 406, The Lead of Honour
— 476, Tom Sawyer, and sequels, Life on the Mississippi, Hucklebury Finn
Mississippi Bubble, The, 248
Missouri, 39, As the Light Led
— 104, The Crisis
— 114, The Prairie
Mist, 479
Misted Mirror, The, 128
Mr. Antiphilos, Satyr, 209
Mr. Arnold, 308
Mr. Blettesworthy on Rampole Island, 495
Mr. Britling Sees it Through, 495
Mr. Clutterbuck's Election, 43
Mr. Crewe's Career, 104
Mr. Dooley stories, 157
Mr. Facey Romford's Hounds, 456
Mr. Fleight, 178
Mr. Fortune Speaking, 24
Mr. Gilfil's Love Story, 163
Mr. Gilhooley, 364
Mr. Godley Beside Himself, 80
Mr. Harrison's Confession, 194
Mr. Hodge and Mr. Hazard, 512
Mr. Incoul's Misadventure, 419
Mr. Ingleside, 306
Mr. Isaacs, 121
Mr. Jervis, 125
Mr. Kempe, 136
Mr. Meeson's Will, 219
Mr. Midshipman Easy, 328
Mr. Misfortunate, 69

Mr. Opp, 405
Mr. Perrin and Mr. Traill, 486
Mr. Petre, 43
Mr. Prohack, 46
" Mr. Rowl," 74
Mr. Salt, 378
Mr. Scarborough's Family, 473
Mr. Simpkinsville, 454
Mr. Smith, 485
Mr. Sponge's Sporting Tour, 456
Mr. Standfast, 78
Mr. Strudge, 501
Mr. Tangier's Vacations, 221
Mr. Tasker's Gods, 390
Mr. Teddy, 48
Mr. Tommy Dove, 136
Mr. Washington, 68
Mr. Weston's Good Wine, 390
Mr. Wildridge of the Bank, 151
Mr. Wycherley's Wards, 227
Misterton's Mistake, 400
Misther O'Ryan, 320
Mistress Barbara Cunliffe, 456
Mistress Content Cradock, 144
Mistress Dorothy Marvin, 441
Mistress of Bonaventure, The, 54
Mistress of Husaby, The, 479
Mistress of Langdale Hall, The, 278
Mistress of the Robes, The, 81
Mistress Spitfire, 176
Mistress and Maid, 120
Misunderstood, 347
Misunderstood Artist, A, 493
Mitch Miller, 332
Mithridates, 103, Two Thousand Years Ago
Mitsou, 107
Mitya's Love, 80
Mliss, 229
Mob, The, 61
Moby-Dick, 338
Moby Lane and Thereabouts, 308
Moccasin Ranch, The, 192
Mock Beggars' Hall, 162
Mockery Gap, 390
Model Millionaire, The, 504
Model of Sorrows, The, 516
Modern Antæus, A, 248
Modern Argonauts, The, 371
Modern Broods, 513
Modern Buccaneer, A, 64
Modern Chronicle, A, 104
Modern Comedy, A, 190
Modern Hero, A, see A Hero of Our Time, 295
Modern Instance, A, 250
Modern Legionary, A, 295
Modern Lover, A (by G. MOORE), 349
Modern Lovers, 343
Modern Man's Confession, A, 357

Modernism, 177, The Patriot, and sequels, Leila
— 487–8, Mrs. H. WARD'S novels
Modeste Mignon, 27
Moguls, 158, The Slave Girl of Agra
— See also *Baber*
Mohammedans, 159, The Bride of the Nile
— 387, M. PICKTHALL'S novels
— See also *Egypt, India, Turkey*, etc.
Mohawk Valley, 96, Cardigan
— 96, The Cambric Mask
— 186, In the Valley, The Copperhead
Mohawks, 70
Mohun, 113
Mohun, Lord, 462, Henry Esmond
Moldavia, 123, Recollections
Molière, 159, A Demoiselle of France
Molinoff, 42
Moll Flanders, 134
Moll o' the Toll Bar, 508
Mollmeit of the Mountains, The, 450
Molly Bawn, 254
Molly Macdonald, 377
Mom Bi, 229
Moment of Time, A, 253
Mompesson, Sir James, 4, The Star Chamber
Mon frère Yves, 304
Mon oncle Barbassou, 478
Mona Maclean, 470
Monadelschi, 123, Stradella
Monadnoc, 288, In the Distance
Monastery, The, 425
Moncontour, 262, The Man-at-Arms
Monday or Tuesday, 510
Money, 518
Money Captain, The, 378
Money-Changers, The, 438
Money Magic, 192
Mongolia, 87, The Blue Banner
Monk, General, 263, The Fate
Monk, The, 298
Monk and the Hangman's Daughter, The, 54
Monk of Fife, A, 288
Monk Wins, The, 114
Monkey Nuts, 291
Monkey Puzzle, The, 51
Monkey's Paw, The, 260
Monks, Nuns, Anchorites, and Monastic Life, 7, The White Cowl, Sister Dolorosa
— 34, Barlaam and Josaphat
— 40, The Nun
— 49, A Winnowing
— 53, The Abbess of Castro
— 74, A Friar Observant
— 84, An Untitled Story
— 98, Conquering and to Conquer
— 120, The Last Abbot of Glastonbury, The House of Walderne

Monks, Nuns, Anchorites, and Monastic Life (contd.): 133, Martin Valliant
— 142, The Nun
— 146, The Emigrant
— 162, Gabriel
— 168, The Gathering of Brother Hilarius
— 257, L'oblat
— 274, Women and Monks
— 288, A Monk of Fife
— 298, The Monk
— 314, The Camp of Refuge, A Legend of Reading Abbey
— 315, The Chronicle of Clemendy
— 326, The Heptameron
— 343, The Vision of MacConglinne
— 349, Evelyn Innes, and sequel
— 350, Héloïse and Abélard
— 359, The New June
— 366, Antonio
— 371, To a Nun Confess'd
— 374, Sister Saint Sulpice
— 422, Ekkehard
— 432, Here Comes an Old Sailor
— 465, Fryer Bacon, Friar Rush
— 469, Father Sergius
— See also *Luther, Peter the Hermit, Thebaid*
Monksbridge, 22
Monmouth, Battle of, 8, In Hostile Red
— 165, Patriot and Tory
Monmouth's Rebellion, 50, Oddsfish
— 52, For Faith and Freedom
— 68, Yesterdays
— 71, The Brown Mask
— 149, Micah Clarke
— 159, Fortune's Castaway
— 165, Barbara Winslow
— 170, My Lady Wentworth
— 196, The Red Seal
— 199, The Bâton Sinister
— 243, The Chariots of the Lord
— 263, The Fate
— 328, The Rebel
— 331, Martin Hyde, Morrice Buckler
— 418, Anthony Wilding
— 480, By Dulvercombe Water
Monomaniac, The, 518
Mononia, 312
Monsieur, Un, 210
Monsieur Beaucaire, 459
Monsieur de Camors, 172
Monsieur de Chauvelin's Will, 156
Monsieur de Lourdines, 99
Monsieur de Rochefort, 445
Monsieur Martin, 91
M. Valdemar, 388
Monsoon, Major, 296, Charles O'Malley

Monster, The, 120
Mont Blanc, 482, A Winter Amid the Ice
Mont-Cinère, 213
Montagu, Lady Mary Wortley, 38, " The Ladies ! "
— 206, Veronica Playfair
— 308, Devereux
Montagu Wycherley, 227
Montaigne, Michel de, 377, Gaston de Latour
Montalbert, 440
MONTALVO, Garcirodriguez de, see *sub nom*. LOBEIRA, V. de, 301
Montana, 126, The Sheriff of Dyke Hole, The One-Way Trail, The Golden Woman
Montcalm, Marquess of, 8, A Soldier of Manhattan
Montebello, 280, Silcote of Silcotes
Monte Carlo, 285
Montes the Matador, 228
MONTESOLE, Max, see *sub nom*. ROBERTS, M., 411
Montespan, Mme de, 154, The Vicomte de Bragelonne
Montesquiou, Count Robert de, 393, Within a Budding Grove
Montezuma's Daughter, 219
Montfort, Simon de, 133, The Red Saint
— 262, Forest Days
Montforts, The, 69
MONTGOMERY, Leslie Arthur, see " DOYLE, Lynn," 151
Montlivet, 439
Montmorency, Duc de, 417, Bardelys the Magnificent
Montreal, 248, Fifty-four Forty, or Fight
— 436, Our Little Life
Montrose, 1st Marquess of, 78, Witch Wood
— 355, John Splendid
— 425, The Legend of Montrose
— 448, The Red Reaper
Montrose (town), 260, Flemington
Moody's Lodging House, 419
Moon, 127, Comical History . . . of the Worlds of the Moon and the Sun
— 482, Around the Moon
— 493, The First Men in the Moon
Moon and Sixpence, The, 334
Moon-Calf, 137
Moon Endureth, The, 78
Moon of Bath, 165
Moon of Israel, 220
Moonfleet, 168
Moonlight Sonata, The, 361
Moonlighters, 292, Guy Livingstone
Moonraker, 268

Moonseed, 357
" Moonshiners," 118, His Vanished Star
— 119, The Windfall
Moonstone, The, 109
Moor Fires, 514
Moore, Sir John, 510, Sons of the Sword
Moore, Thomas, 240, Bendish
Moores, The, 73
Moorish Hero, A, 132
Moorland Cottage, The, 194
Moors, 104, The Cid
— 309, Leila
— 375, Paris and Vienne
— See also Morocco
Moorside Feud, A, 54
Mora, Duc de, 130, The Nabob
Mora, Marquess de, 69, The Burning-Glass
Moral Tales (by EDGEWORTH), 160
Moral Tales (by MARMONTEL), 327
Morals of Marcus Ordeyne, The, 301
Moravia, 93, The Pride of Jennico
Moravians, 459, God's People
Morayshire, 289, The Wolfe of Badenoch
Mord Em'ly, 407
Mordecai, 161, The Absentee
Mordecai, 164, Daniel Deronda
More, Hannah, 329, Bristol Diamonds
— 400, Two Men o' Mendip
— 428, Under Cheddar Cliffs
More, Sir Thomas, 49, The King's Achievement
— 324, The Household of Sir Thomas More
— 357, The Unfortunate Traveller
More Bits from Blinkbonny, 453
More Ghost Stories of an Antiquary, 266
More Happy Thoughts, 82
More Methodist Idylls, 300
More Short Sixes, 81
More Stories, 374
More Tales by Polish Authors, 44
More Tales of the Ridings, 350
More Tramps Abroad, 476
Morel Family, 290, Sons and Lovers
Morgan, Sir Henry, 404, The Jewel of Ynys Galon
Morgan, General J. H., 182, The Little Shepherd of Kingdom Come
Morgan O'Doherty, Maxims and Memoirs of, 320
Moriah's Mourning, 454
Morlac of Gascony, 400
Morley, John, 411, The Private Life of Henry Maitland
Mormon Prophet, The, 148

Mormons, 148, The Morman Prophet
— 149, A Study in Scarlet
Morning of To-day, The, 64
Morny, Duc de, 130, The Nabob
Morocco, 87, The Scapegoat
— 132, African Nights Entertainments, The Story of Ronald Kestrel, Joseph Khassan
— 242, The Garden of Allah, Barbary Sheep
Moronval Academy, 130, Jack
Morózov, General, 467, A Prince of Outlaws
Morris, Dinah, 164, Adam Bede
Morris, William, 491, Aylwin
Morrison's Machine, 176
Morrone, Pietro di, 21, San Celestino
Mors Hænder, 56
Mort de quelqu'un, 415
Mortal Antipathy, A, 245
Mortal Coils, 256
Mortal Image, 512
Mortallone, 398
Morte, La, 172
Morte amoureuse, La, 195
Morte Darthur, Le, 242, 322
Mortiboy, 52, Ready-Money Mortiboy
Mortimer, Sir Edmund, 180, Harry of Athol
Mortimer, Roger, 53, In the Shadow of the Crown
Morton, Earl of, 239, The Queen's Quair
— 425-6, The Monastery, and sequel
Mosaic, 447
Mosaics, 341
Mosca, Count, 53, The Chartreuse of Parma
Moscow, 295, The Thief
— 299, The Apostate
— 306, The Flames of Moscow
— See also Russia, French Invasion of
Moscow in Flames, 129
Moses, 212, My Head ! My Head !
Moss, Godfrey, 245, Maxwell
Moss Troopers, see Border Tales
Moss-Troopers, The, 124
MOSSE, Irene Forbes, see FORBES-MOSSE, I., 178
Mosses from an Old Manse, 232
Most, The, 33
Most Delectable and Pleasant History of Clitophon and Leucippe, 2
Mother, 206
Mother, A, 322
Mother, The (by ASCHE), 16
Mother, The (story by BARBUSSE), 33
Mother, The (by DELEDDA), 137
Mother, The (by DUNCAN), 156

Mother, The (by MAARTENS), 310
Mother, The (by PEARSE), 380
Mother, The (by PHILPOTTS), 385
Mother, The (by SVEVO), 457
Mother and Son, 415
Mother of Pearl, 183
Mother of the Man, 385
Mother-Sister, 395
Motherless, The, 51
Mother's Hands, 56
Moths, 372
Mothwise, 223
Motley, A, 190
Motor Maid, The, 507
Mount, Mrs., 339, Richard Feverel
Mount Music, 443
Mountain Blood, 237
Mountain City, 438
Mountain Europe, A, 182
Mountain Lovers, The, 431
Mountain Storm, A, 118
Mountain Tavern, The, 364
Mountains and Mountaineering, see under names of mountains and districts, e.g. Adirondacks, Alps, Caucasus, Highlands, Rockies, etc.
Mountebanks, 408
Mouret Family, 516-17, Rougon - Macquart Series
Mowbray, Lord, 489, De Vere
Mowgli, 282, The Jungle Book, and sequel
Moxon's Master, 54
Mucklewraith, 425, Old Mortality
Muertos Mandan, Los, 61
Mugby Junction, 141
Muime Chriosd, 431
Mujer de Piedra, La, 210
Mulattos, 7, Ivan Greet's Masterpiece
— 102, A Matter of Principle
Mulberry Bush, The, 307
Muld, 389
Mule, The, 342
Mulligan's Revenge, 320
MULOCK, Miss, see CRAIK, Dinah Mary, 119
Multitude and Solitude, 330
Mulvaney, Private, 281, Soldiers Three, Life's Handicap, etc.
Mummer's Tale, A, 184
Mummer's Wife, A, 349
Mummery, 89
Mummy's Foot, The, 195
Münchausen, Baron, 399, Travels of Baron Münchausen
Munich, 122, A Cigarette-Maker's Romance
— 172, Success
— 241, In Paradise
Municipal Affairs, 29, The Middle Classes
— 176, The Town of Crooked Ways

Munster, 7, The Green Altar
— 116, A Munster Twilight
— 125, Neighbours
— 149, The Merchant of Killogue, Dunleary
Munster Twilight, A, 116
Murat, J., 212, The Reds of the Midi
— 284, Coronet
Murder of Monsieur Fualdès, The, 391
Murder on the Links, The, 103
Murders in the Rue Morgue, 388
Mure of Auchendrane, John, 124, The Grey Man
— 411, The Kings of Carrick
MURFREE, Mary Noailles, see " CRADDOCK, Charles Egbert," 118
Murmuring Forest, The, 284
Murough, 257, The Lad of the Ferule
Murray of Broughton, 78, A Lost Lady of Old Years
— 425-6, The Monastery, and sequel
— 239, The Queen's Quair
MURRY, Mrs. M., see " MANSFIELD, Katherine," 325
Murtagh, Sir, 160, Castle Rackrent
MUSAEUS, J. K. A., see also CARLYLE, T. (tr.), 357
" Muscular Christianity," 253, Tom Brown's Schooldays, and sequel
— 279, C. KINGSLEY's novels
— 292, G. A. LAWRENCE's novels
Muscular Novels, 78, J. BUCHAN's novels, passim
— 273, Tom Brown's Schooldays, and sequel
— 296-7, E. J. LEVER's novels
— 302-3, Jack LONDON's novels
— 320, Bull-Dog Drummond
Muse du département, la, 28
Muse of the Department, The, 28
Music and Musicians, 29, Cousin Pons
— 30, Gambara, Massimilla Doni
— 94, The Song of the Lark
— 123, Stradella
— 127, The Poisoner
— 168, The Lost Stradivarius
— 180, The First Violin
— 242, The Way of Ambition
— 256, Beechy
— 277, The Constant Nymph
— 284, The Blind Musician
— 349, Evelyn Innes
— 406, Maurice Guest
— 414, John Christopher

Music and Musicians (contd.): 415, Lucienne
— 428, Tante
— 432, Charles Auchester
— 433, A Teacher of the Violin
— 434, Promise, and sequel
— 485, Lotus or Laurel
— 493, The Collapse of the Penitent
— 496, Verdi
— 507, Martin Schüler
— See also *Singers*, and names of musicians, *Bach, Beethoven, Crotch, Handel, Mendelssohn, Purcell, Verdi, Wagner*, etc.
Music from behind the Moon, The, 85
Muskerry, Lord, 68, Yesterdays
Muslin, 349
Musobioye Kosho Monogatari, 281
Mutes, 93, Dumb Love
— 108, Hide and Seek
— 310, God's Fool
Mutineer, The, 41
Mutiny of the *Elsinore*, The, 303
Mutual Interdependence of Things, The, 244
Muzhiks, 99, The Muzhiks
— 284, Makar's Dream
Muzhiks, The, 99
My Afterdream, 43
My Aunt Margaret's Mirror, 427
My Brother Jonathan, 515
My Brother Yves, 304
My Captive, 9
My Double, 221
My Dream, 469
My First Lie, 477
My French Master, 194
My Friend from Limousin, 199
My Friend Prospero, 227
My Friend's Book, 182
My Head ! My Head !, 212
My Heart and My Flesh, 410
My Lady Nicotine, 37
My Lady Nobody, 310
My Lady of the Bass, 81
My Lady of the Chimney Corner, 258
My Lady of the Island, 217
My Lady of the Moor, 373
My Lady of the North, 376
My Lady of the South, 376
My Lady Pokahontas, 113
My Lady Rotha, 497
My Lady Wentworth, 170
My Life, 100
My Little Boy, 167
My Little Hester, 174
My Little Lady, 390
My Little Sister, 412
My Lord of Essex, 74
My Lord the Elephant, 281
My Lord Winchenden, 247
My Lords of Strogue, 508
My Merry Rockhurst, 94
My Mortal Enemy, 95
My New Curate, 431

My Novel, 309
My Old Man, 236
My People, 167
My Poor Relations, 310
My Son, 228
My Son Richard, 439
My Sword for Lafayette, 381
My Time and What I've Done with it, 81
My Tower in Desmond, 308
My Uncle, 210
My Uncle Barbassou, 478
Myra of the Pines, 483
Myriel, Bishop, 254, Les Misérables
Myrrha, 295
Myrtle, 252
Myshkin, Prince, 147, The Idiot
Mysore War, 461, Tippoo Sultaun
Mystères de Marseille, Les, 516
Mystères de Paris, Les, 455
Mysterier, 223
Mysteries, 223
Mysteries of Marseilles, The, 516
Mysteries of Paris, The, 455
Mysteries of Udolpho, The, 399
Mysterious Affair at Styles, The, 103
Mysterious Island, The, 482
Mysterious Monsieur Dumont, The, 16
Mysterious Stranger, The, 477
Mystery at Geneva, 312
Mystery of a Hansom Cab, The, 254
Mystery of Edwin Drood, The, 141
Mystery of Killard, The, 149
Mystery of Marie Roget, The, 388
Mystery of M. Felix, 169
Mystery of Muncraig, 355
Mystery of the Tobacco Shed, 454
Mystery of 31, New Inn, The, 187
Mysticism, 256, Frederic Uvedale
— 287, The Emperor of Portugallia, The Outcast
— 290–1, D. H. LAWRENCE'S novels
— See also *Future Life, Immortality, Religion, Supernatural*, etc.
Mythological Stories, 25, F. W. BAIN's stories
— 42, The Dreadful Dragon of Hay Hill
— 79, The Grey Shepherd
— 84–5, CABELL's stories
— 148, They Went, In the Beginning
— 157, Lord DUNSANY's stories
— 193, The Twilight of the Gods

Mythological Stories (contd.): 497, The Soul of the Countess
— See also *Celtic Romances, Classical Mythology, Fairy-Tales, Folk Lore*
Mytton, John, 305, Character and Comedy

Nabob, The, 130
Nada, The Lily, 219
Nadia, 371
Nadir Shah, 158
Nadjeja Nicolaievna, 193
Nagasaki, 304, Madame Chrysanthème
Naïs Micoulin, 519
Namdalen, 158, Good Conscience
Name, The, 33
Name of Garland, 408
Name to Conjure With, A, 508
Nameless Castle, The, 272
Nameless Nobleman, A, 21
Namenlose Geschichten, 219
Nana, 517
Nance of Manchester, 3
Nancy, Battle of, 427, Anne of Geierstein
Nancy, 75
Nancy Stair, 288
Nangay Doola, 281
Nanno, 355
Nantas, 519
Nantes, 24, Storm and Treasure
— 40, Redemption
Nantes, Edict of, see *Huguenots*
Nantucket, 338, Moby-Dick
Naomi's Exodus, 347
Naples, 38, A Noble Kinsman
— 62, Amorous Fiametta
— 68, The Sword Decides
— 90, The Extraordinary Adventures of Diana Please
— 117, The Company of Death
— 156, The Neapolitan Lovers
— 211, Stories of Naples
— 216, One Crowded Hour
— 234, Mas'aniello
— 242, The Call of the Blood, and sequel
— 399, The Italian
— 416, Dr. Antonio
— 429, The Land of Cockayne
— 433, John Inglesant
Napoleon I, 6, Saint Helena
— 18, The Empress Might-have-Been
— 24, Barry Leroy
— 24, The God of Clay
— 29, A Gondreville Mystery
— 58, Springhaven
— 60, Grantley Fenton
— 70, The Two Captains

Napoleon I, (contd.): 71, The Sword Hand of Napoleon, The Eagle of the Empire
— 74, A Boy of the First Empire
— 84, The Power of the Dog
— 120, Schönbrunn
— 150, Exploits of Brigadier Gerard
— 150, Uncle Bernac
— 156, The Whites and the Blues
— 178, Leroux
— 193, Napoleon's Love Story
— 212, The White Terror
— 216, The Strong Hand, and sequel
— 284, Coronet
— 296, Tom Burke of Ours
— 311, The Eagle's Nest
— 355, L. MÜHLBACH'S novels
— 358, Taken From the Enemy
— 370, A Sheaf of Bluebells
— 428, Fortunes of Fifi
— 510, Sons of the Sword
— 512, A Spy for Napoleon
— See also *Hundred Days, Napoleonic Wars, Russia, French Invasion of*, etc.
Napoleon, Traditional Son of, 376, When Valmond Came to Pontiac
Napoleon III, 24, The Pillar of Fire
— 44, Barbara Rebell
— 57, The Mantle of the Emperor
— 70, Ishmael
— 130, The Nabob
— 135, Between Two Thieves
— 166, A Man of the People, The Story of the Plebiscite
— 323, The Royal Woman
— 345, A Diplomatic Venture
— 400, Journeyman Love
— 452, The Madonna of the Barricades
— 517, The Rush for the Spoil, His Excellency
— See also *Franco-German War*
Napoleon and Blücher, 355
Napoleon Decrees, 62
Napoleon in Germany, 355
Napoleon of Notting Hill, The, 102
Napoleonic Terror, 25, Judy Bovenden
— 149, The Great Shadow
— 150, Uncle Bernac
— 193, The Infamous John Friend
— 226, The Trumpet-Major
— 388, The French Prisoner
— 398, The Mayor of Troy, Hi-Spi-Hi
Napoleonic Wars, 58, Alice Lorraine

Napoleonic Wars (contd.):
62, Napoleon Decrees
— 79, The Shadow of the Sword
— 87, Face to Face with Napoleon, and sequel
— 94, The Black Office
— 97, Capt. F. CHAMIER's novels
— 111, The Duel
— 133, The House of Spies
— 149, The Great Shadow
— 150, Brigadier Gerard, and sequel
— 166, The Story of a Peasant
— 166, The Conscript, and sequels
— 211, Adventures of an Aide-de-Camp
— 216, The Strong Hand, and sequels
— 272, The Nameless Castle
— 296, Tom Burke of Ours, Arthur O'Leary, Maurice Tierney
— 319, Nuala
— 328, Mr. Midshipman Easy
— 328, Chloris of the Island, The House in the Downs
— 355, " L. MÜHLBACH's " novels
— 368, The Gentleman
— 380, Catherine
— 381, The Great White Army
— 410, The Fiddler of Lugau
— 468, War and Peace
— 497, With the Red Eagle, A Red Bridal
— 498, The Traveller in the Fur Cloak
— 516, Ashes
— See also *Hundred Days, Peninsular War, Russia, French Invasion of*
Napoleon's Love Story, 193
Narcissus, 344
Narr in Christo, Der, 231
Narrative of A. Gordon Pym, 388
Narrow House, The, 424
Narrow Way, A, 174
Naseby, Battle of, 313, Miriam Cromwell
— 337, Holmby House
— 404, Battlement and Tower
Nash, Beau, 93, The Bath Comedy
— 165, The Moon of Bath
— 196, The Heart of a Hero
— 459, Monsieur Beaucaire
Nash and Some Others, 167
Nastasya Filipovna, 147, The Idiot
Nat the Naturalist, 171
Natal, 496, The Captain of the Locusts
Natasha, 72
Natchez (Adam's County), 406, The Lead of Honour
Natchez, Les, 98

Nathalie, 275
Nathan Burke, 491
Native, The, 269
Native Born, 485
Natural Mother, The, 157
Naturalism: see especially: 10–11, ANDREEV's stories
— 11–12, D'ANNUNZIO's novels
— 26–8, BALZAC's novels
— 45, The Old Wives' Tale
— 53, In the Midst of Life
— 60, V. BLASCO IBAÑEZ's novels
— 118, H. M. CRACKANTHORPE's novels
— 133–4, DEFOE's stories
— 137 Grazia DELEDDA's novels
— 146–8, DOSTOEVSKY's novels
— 151–2, DREISER's novels
— 167, C. EVANS's novels
— 175, FLAUBERT's novels, especially Madame Bovary
— 205–6, J. and E. de GONCOURT's novels
— 206–7, " GORKY's " novels
— 257, HUYSMANS's novels
— 273, JOYCE's works
— 315, P. MACGILL's novels
— 317, Sinister Street and sequels
— 333–4, W. S. MAUGHAM's novels
— 334, MAUPASSANT's stories
— 349, G. MOORE's novels
— 361, F. NORRIS' stories
— 375, Froth, The Son of the Bondwoman
— 396, Toil of Men
— 455, SUDERMANN's stories
— 468, Anna Karénina, Ivan Ilyitch
— 469, Resurrection
— 516–19, ZOLA's novels
— 520, Light-Fingered Gentry
Nature, Natural Man, etc., 23, Hermsprong
— 43, Oroonoko
— 51, The Motherless
— 98, Atala
— 176, The Wonderful Wapentake, At the Gate of the Fold
— 177, S. FLEURON's novels
— 209, Mr. Antiphilos, Satyr
— 222, Idlehurst, Lonewood Corner
— 223, Pan
— 224, Growth of the Soil
— 225, The Return of the Native
— 238, The Healer
— 239–40, Half-Way House, and sequels
— 252, W. H. HUDSON's stories
— 267, J. R. JEFFERIES's novels

Nature, Natural Man, etc. (contd.): 304, Rarahu
— 354, A Journey to Nature
— 385, The Good Red Earth
— 409–10, C. D. G. ROBERTS's stories
— 419, Paul and Virginia
— 420, Indiana
— 444, The Blue Lagoon
— 464, The Marriage of Gerard, Queen of the Woods
— 491–2, Mary WEBB's novels
— 501, S. E. WHITE's novels
— 507, The Beautiful Years, and sequels
— 510, The Village in the Jungle
— See also *Animals, Beast Fables,* etc.
Nature and Art, 258
Nature and Human Nature, 222
Naulahka, The, 283
Nautical Stories, 24, The Sea Captain
— 35, Yankee Ships and Yankee Sailors, Midshipman Farragut
— 52, The World went very well then
— 62, The Hispaniola Plate, A Gentleman Adventurer, Across the Salt Seas, Fortune's My Foe
— 64, The Brassbounder
— 64, A Modern Buccaneer
— 70, Rev. C. T. BRADY's novels, *passim*
— 72, God Save England !
— 97, Capt. F. CHAMIER's novels
— 110, J. B. CONNOLLY's novels
— 110–11, J. CONRAD's novels and stories
— 114, The Pilot, The Red Rover, Mercedes of Castile, Wing-and-Wing
— 115, Afloat and Ashore
— 120, The Open Boat
— 128, Two Years before the Mast
— 149, Anchor-Watch Yarns, Dorothy Tuke
— 151, The Schooner California, Cursed be the Treasure
— 152, The Passing of the Flagship
— 171, Under the Jackstaff
— 193, China Seas
— 215, The Ship Sails On
— 258, C. HYNE's novels
— 260–1, W. W. JACOBS's stories
— 267, The King's Yard
— 279, Westward Ho !
— 281, W. H. G. KINGSTON's novels
— 294, The Golden Galleon
— 302, The Sea-Wolf,

Nautical Stories (contd.):
303, The Cruise of the *Snark*
— 305, B. LUBBOCK's stories
— 328, House in the Downs
— 328–9, MARRYAT's novels
— 331, Lost Endeavour, Sard Harker
— 337–8, MELVILLE's novels
— 342, Stranded
— 363, Walking Shadows
— 370, Admiral Quilliam
— 390, Smith Brunt
— 410, A Sea Comedy
— 411, The Blue Peter, Ancient Mariners
— 417, W. C. RUSSELL's novels
— 424, M. SCOTT's novels
— 427, Molly SEAWELL's novels, *passim*
— 441, Roderick Random
— 445, The Blue Horizon, In Blue Waters
— 459, Minor Operations
— 510, The Spirit of the Service
— See also *Mercantile Marine, Fishermen, Sea*
Navajo Indians, 286, Laughing Boy
Navvies, 3, Zike Mouldom
— 315, P. MACGILL's novels
Nazis, 172, Success
Neæra, 209
Neapolitan Lovers, The, 156
Near and the Far, The, 357
Near the Tsar, Near Death, 500
'Neath the Hoof of the Tartar, 273
Nebraska, 94, O Pioneers ! My Antonia
— 126, The Watchers of the Plains
Nebuly Coat, The, 169
Neckar, River, 262, Heidelberg
Necker, Oliver, 358, The Deuce
— 426, Quentin Durward
Necromancers, The, 49
Necromancy, 23, The Famous Historie of Fryer Bacon
— See also *Magic, Spiritualism*
Needles and Pins, 312
Ne'er do Well, The, 40
NEGRO AUTHORS:
W. E. B. DU BOIS, P. L. DUNBAR, Jessie Redmon FAUSET, Nella LARSEN, C. MCKAY, R. MARAN
Negroes, 10, Dark Laughter
— 47, Old Squire
— 101–2, C. W. CHESNUTT's novels
— 110, The Nigger of the *Narcissus*
— 120, The Monster
— 152, W. E. B. DU BOIS' novels

Negroes (contd.): 156, P. L. DUNBAR's stories
— 165, Caoba
— 175, Prancing Nigger
— 182, The Famished Cat
— 193, The Sailor's Return
— 228-9, J. C. HARRIS's stories
— 235, Youma
— 241, Du Bose HEYWARD's novels
— 253, Bug-Jargal
— 288, Passing
— 301, Stringtown on the Pike
— 316, C. McKAY's novels
— 325, Batouala
— 344, Barnavaux
— 344, God's Step-Children
— 350, Black Magic
— 373, Elsket, Red Rock
— 383, Scarlet Sister Mary
— 454, RUTH STUART's stories
— 470, Cane
— 481, Nigger Heaven
— 496, Chapenga's White Man
— See also *L'Ouverture, Toussaint,* NEGRO AUTHORS
Neige sur les pas, La, 66
Neighbourhood Stories, 189
Neighbours, 125
Neighbours, The, 71
Neighbours, The, 100
Neighbours on the Green, 368
Nekludov, Prince, 467, Youth, Lucerne
— 469, Resurrection
Nell, Little, 140, Old Curiosity Shop
Nell Gwyn, 348
Nelson, Horatio Lord, 24, Barry Leroy
— 37, The Warrior Maid
— 38, The Divine Lady
— 58, Springhaven
— 70, The Two Captains
— 90, Diana Please
— 97, Ben Brace, Tom Bowling
— 114, Wing-and-Wing
— 150, Rodney Stone
— 156, The Neapolitan Lovers
— 256, A Friend of Nelson
— 368, The Gentleman
Nemo, Captain, 482, Twenty Thousand Leagues under the Sea
Nemo, 148
Nemours, 28, Ursule Mirouët
Nero, Emperor, 103, The Burning of Rome
— 160, Nero
— 295, Myrrha
— 435, Quo Vadis?
— 486, Empress Octavia
Nero, 160
Neshdanov, 475, Virgin Soil
Nessa, 319
Nest of Linnets, A, 348
Nest of Noblemen, A, 474

Nest of Spies, A, 444
Nest of the Sparrowhawk, 370
Net, The, 40
Nether World, The, 200
Netherlands, see *Belgium, Flanders, Ghent, Holland, Leyden,* etc.
Nevada, 476, Roughing It
Never in Vain, 140
Nevermore, 64
Neveu de Rameau, Le, 142
Nevis, 17, The Gorgeous Isle
Nevsky, Aleksandr, 508, Before Sunset
New Amsterdam, 84, The Begum's Daughter
— See also *New York, Old*
New Antigone, The, 39
New Arabian Nights, The, 448
New Atlantis, The, 23
New Book of Martyrs, 153
New Broom, The, 475
New Canterbury Tales, 239
New Chronicles of Rebecca, 504
New England Cactus, A, 254
New England, 22, Dobachi
— 23, A Candle in the Wilderness
— 76, Mrs. A. BROWN's novels and stories
— 88, The Squirrel-Cage
— 114, Rose COOKE's novels
— 136, Mrs. DELAND's works
— 165, Uncrowning a King
— 242, Malbone
— 268-9, Miss JEWETT's stories
— 288, Village Photographs
— 428, Hope Leslie
— 500-1, Eliza Orne WHITE's stories
— 503-4, "Kate D. WIGGIN's" novels
— See also *Boston, Connecticut, Massachusetts, Maine, New Hampshire,* etc.
New England Nun, A, 505, 506
New Forest, 25, The Merchant Prince
— 58, Cradock Nowell
— 329, The Children of the New Forest
New France, 95, Mrs. CATHERWOOD's stories
— 126, A Daughter of New France
— 248, The Mississippi Bubble
New Friends in Old Chester, 137
New Grub Street, 200
New Guinea, 217, Miss GRIMSHAW's novels
New Hampshire, 90, Heirs
— 165, Seth Jones
— 171, Heritage
New Heloïse, The, 416

New Jersey, 35, For King or Country
— 179, Janice Meredith
— 440, The Tides of Barnegat
New June, The, 359
New Landlord, The, 272
New Leaf Mills, 251
New Machiavelli, The, 494
New Magdalen, The, 109
New Marienbad Elegy, The, 492
New Moon, The, 412
New Ohio, 221
New Orleans, 6, The Story of a Bad Boy
— 8, A Herald of the West
— 40, The Net
— 86, G. W. CABLE's novels and stories
— 93, The Code of Victor Jallot
— 401, By the Eternal
New Parishioner, The, 269
New Paul and Virginia, The, 322
New Priest in Conception Bay, The, 305
New Religion, The, 311
New Republic, The, 322
New Road, The, 356
New Saint's Tragedy, A, 388
New Salem, 22, The Soul of Ann Rutledge
New South Wales, 1, Castle Vane
— 41, A First Fleet Family
— 64, Babes in the Bush
— 85, By Blow and Kiss
— 131, In the Track of a Storm
— 132, The Story of Ronald Kestrel
— 234, Herridge of Reality Swamp
— 248, The Rogue's March
— 280, Geoffrey Hamlyn
New Temple, The, 64
New Treasure Seekers, The, 60
New Warden, The, 409
New Woman, The, 41
New Year's Eve, A, 520
New York, Colonial, 36, The Bow of Orange Ribbon, and sequel
— 36, Trinity Bells, The Belle of Bowling Green, The Strawberry Handkerchief, The House on Cherry Street
— 43, Antonia, Barnaby Lee
— 74, In Leisler's Times
— 84, The Begum's Daughter
— 115, Satanstoe, and sequels
— 179, Janice Meredith
— 258, Salmagundi, A History of New York
— 345, The Van Rensselaers
— 401, Free to Serve
— 444, The Block House on the Prairie

New York City, 8, A Heroine in Bronze
— 23, Cricket Heron
— 40, The Auction Block
— 42, Sandoval, The Road to Heaven
— 43, Antonia
— 58, Erema
— 84, The Foolish Matrons
— 97, R. W. CHAMBERS's novels, *passim*
— 80-1, H. C. BUNNER's stories
— 104, A Modern Chronicle
— 122, The Three Fates, Katherine Lauderdale, and sequel
— 123, Soprano, and sequels
— 131, Gallegher, Van Bibber
— 146, Manhattan Transfer
— 151, Sister Carrie
— 163, The Faith Doctor
— 170, E. FAWCETT's novels
— 250, A Hazard of New Fortunes
— 253, Hunt the Slipper
— 253, The Golden Ladder
— 274, Daughters of Ishmael
— 275, Broken Pitchers
— 283, Lawrence Garthe
— 304, Jack Spurlock
— 333, J. B. MATTHEWS' stories
— 481, Parties
— 490, That Fortune
— 498-9, Edith WHARTON's novels, *passim*
New York Poor, 121, Bowery Tales
— 151, Sister Carrie
— 408, J. A. RIIS' novels
— 456, Tenement Tales of New York
New York State, 23, The Light in the Clearing
— 186, H. FREDERIC's stories and novels
— 497, David Harum
New Zealand, 64, War to the Knife
— 77, Van Zanten's Happy Days
— 97, Philosopher Dick
— See also NEW ZEALAND NOVELISTS, *passim*
NEW ZEALAND NOVELISTS:
A. H. ADAMS, Mrs. L. A. BAKER, J. COWAN, A. A. GRACE, F. W. HUME, G. B. LANCASTER, Judge MANING, "Katherine MANSFIELD," H. B. MARRIOTT-WATSON, Amber REEVES, W. SATCHELL, H. S. WALPOLE
Newbury, 138, Jack of Newbury
— 337, Holmby House
Newcastle, 5th Duke of, 489, De Vere

Newcomes, The, 462
Newfoundland, 110, J. B. CONNOLLY'S novels
— 156-7, N. DUNCAN'S stories
— 305, The New Priest in Conception Bay
Newgate, 52, Dorothy Forster
— 52, The Orange Girl, No Other Way
— 140, Barnaby Rudge
— 173, Amelia
— 213, Evil May-Day
— 248, The Mississippi Bubble
— 318, The Man of the World
Newport, Andrew, 134, Memoirs of a Cavalier
Newport (Rhode Island), 452, The Minister's Wooing
News from Nowhere, 352
Newspaper Girl, The, 506
Newton, John, 182, The Bountiful Hour
— 329, On the Banks of the Ouse
Newton Forster, 328
Next Move, The, 153
Ney, Marshal, 71, The Eagle of the Empire
— 179, A Little Less Than Gods
Niagara, 249, Their Wedding Journey
Niagara Revisited, 249
Nibelungenlied, 484
Nic Revel, 171
Nicanor, 215
Niccolò dei Lapi, 22
Nice Old Man and the Pretty Girl, The, 457
Nicholas I (Tsar of Russia), 341, December the Fourteenth
Nicholas Nickleby, 140
Nicholson, General John, 179, Eight Days
Nick o' the Woods, 54
Nicky-Nan, Reservist, 398
Nicky, Son of Egg, 80
Nicole, 269
Niebla, 479
Niels Lyhne, 261
Nietzschean Philosophy, 12, The Triumph of Death
— 146-8, DOSTOEVSKY'S novels
— 206-7, "GORKY'S" stories
— 206, Fomá Gordyéeff
Nigeria, 54, Ainslie's Ju-Ju
Nigger Heaven, 481
Nigger Jeff, 151
Nigger of the *Narcissus*, The, 110
Night, 334
Night and Day, 510
Night and Morning, 309
Night Club, The, 267
Night Cometh, The, 68
Night Falls on Siva's Hill, 465
Night in Kurdestan, A, 62

Night in the Luxembourg, A, 209
Night Side of Nature, The, 126
Night Watches, 261
Nightingale, The, 452
Nightingale and the Rose, The, 504
Nightmare Abbey, 379
Nights, The, 452
Nights with Uncle Remus, 228
Nihilism, 39, The New Antigone
— 86, The White Terror and the Red
— 231, Mademoiselle Ixe
— 272, The Green Book
— 284, In Two Moods
— 342, The Vulture
— 371, Nadia
— 415, On Peter's Island
— 467, Three Deaths
— 474, Diary of a Superfluous Man
— 475, Fathers and Children, Virgin Soil
Nilbraut, Die, 159
Nile, 150, Tragedy of the Korosko
— 176, Kismet
Nile, Battle of the, 42, The Lost Mameluke
— 70, The Two Captains
Nile Novel, A, 176
Nile of St. Peter, The, 408
Nils Holgerssons underbara resa, 287
Nîmes, 209, Perpetua
— 497, The Red Cockade
Nina, 16
Nina Gordon, 452
Nine Days Wonder, A, 125
Nine Tales, 140
Nineteen, The, 168
Ninety-Three, 254
Ninth of November, The, 277
Ninth Thermidor, The, 6
Niobe, 299
Nisibis, 120, Æmilius
Nithud, 364, Wayland Smith
Nivernais, 40, By Faith Alone
Nixon, J. E., 47, The Babe B.A.
Nizamu 'l Mulk, 145, Omar the Tentmaker
No Defence, 376
No Love, 193
No More Parades, 178
No Name, 108
No New Thing, 362
No Other Tiger, 332
No Other Way, 52
No-Popery Riots (1780), 161, Harrington
No Relations, 322
No Soul above Money, 400
Noble Kinsman, A, 38
Noble Queen, A, 461
Noble Wife, A, 422
Noblesse, Ancienne, 1, Tolla, Face to Face
— 67, The Weight of the Name

Noblesse, Ancienne (contd.):
121, Fleurange
— 172, The Romance of a Poor Young Man
— 185, Noblesse Oblige
— 263, The American
— 296, The O'Donoghue
— 361, Mademoiselle de Mersac
— 375, The Grandee
— 421, Mademoiselle de la Seiglière, The House of Penarvan
— 499, Madame de Treymes
Noblesse Oblige, 185
Noblest Frailty, The, 419
Nobody's Boy, 322
Nobody's Island, 217
Nocturnal Expedition Round My Room, A, 320
Nocturne, 458
Nodier, Charles, 156, The Whites and the Blues
Noëllet, Les, 40
Noémi, 208
Non-Combatant, The, 464
Non-Combatants and Others, 311
Nonconformists, 119, The Dream and the Business
— 273, The Stars of the Revival
— 300, Scarlet Nest
— 314, Paul Faber
— 366-7, Mrs. OLIPHANT'S novels
— 399, Garthowen
— 440, The Minister's Guest
— See also *Baptists, Dissenters, Wesleyans*, etc.
None Other Gods, 49
None So Pretty, 259
Nonsense Novels, 293
Noodlot, 117
Nor Many Waters, 491
Norah Lester, 249
Nordland, 299, The Visionary, Weird Tales from Nordland, The Barque "Future"
Nördlingen, 139, Klosterheim
Nore Mutiny, 328, The King's Own
— 376, No Defence
Norfolk, 52, The Lady of Lynn
— 62, J. BLYTH'S novels
Norman Conquest, 59, The Siege of Norwich Castle
— 120, The Rival Heirs
— 280, Hereward the Wake
— 309, Harold
— 314, The Camp of Refuge
Normandy, 162, The Dream Charlotte
— 218, Those Good Normans
— 275, Nathalie, Two Lilies, Forget-me-nots
— 334, MAUPASSANT'S stories, *passim*
— 461, The Village on the Cliff

Norne, 267
Norpois, M. de, 393, Within a Budding Grove
— 394, The Sweet Cheat Gone
Norris, Mrs., 20, Mansfield Park
Norsemen in the West, The, 26
"NORTH, Christopher," see WILSON, John, 507
North and South, 194
North-East Corner, A, 295
North of Suez, 315
North of 36, 248
North Pole, 482, The English at the North Pole, and sequel
North, South, and over Sea, 185
Northanger Abbey, 20
Northborough Cross, 116
Northern Crack, A, 207
Northern Iron, The, 55
Northern Lights and Shadows, 459
Northern Pioneer, A, 488
Northumberland, Henry Percy, 6th Earl of, 333, Defender of the Faith, The Royal Sisters
Northumberland, 52, Dorothy Forster
— 74, The Engrafted Rose
— 104, By the Rise of the River
— 108, The Likeness of King Elfwald
— 180, R. H. FORSTER'S novels
— 380, J. H. PEASE'S stories
— 425, Rob Roy
Norton, Hon. Caroline, 340, Diana of the Crossways
Norton family, 456, Pam the Fiddler
Norumbega, 299, Randvar the Songsmith
Norway, 26, Erling the Bold
— 88, Gunhild
— 240, Frey and his Wife
— 267, The Long Journey
— 352, Three Northern Love-Stories
— 465, Signe's History
— 507, The Death of Society
— See also *Icelandic Sagas, passim*, NORWEGIAN NOVELISTS
NORWEGIAN NOVELISTS:
J. BOJER, B. BJÖRNSON, O. DUNN, P. EGGE, J. FALKBERGET, Arne GARBORG, N. GRIEG, K. HAMSUN, O. HANSSON, A. L. KIELLAND, R. J. KREUTZ, Jonas LIE, Ottilie A. LILJINCRANTZ, Alvide PRYDZ, Barbra RING, O. E. RÖLVAAG, Berthe SKRAM, Sigrid UNDSET
— See also Dasent, Sir G. W. (tr.)

NORWEGIAN NOVEL-ISTS (*contd.*):
See also LARSEN, Hanna A. (tr.)
Norwegian Saga, 366, The Saga of Olaf
— See also *Icelandic Sagas*
Norwich, 59, The Siege of Norwich Castle
— 60, The Glory and Sorrow of Norwich
— 219, Lysbeth
— 323, Gran'ma Jane
— 324, Memories of Ronald Love, and sequel
— 329, In the East Country
— 330, Castle Meadow
— 354, The Borough-monger
Norwood, 42
Nos enfants, 184
Nostalgia, 137
Nostromo, 110
Not All in Vain, 88
Not Convincing, 259
Not Known Here, 489
Not Like Other Girls, 91
Not on the Screen, 188
Not Wisely, but too Well, 75
Not Wooed, but Won, 378
Note in Music, A, 294
Notebooks of Malte Laurids Brigge, 408
Nothing to Pay, 167
Notre cœur, 334
Notre-Dame de Paris, 253
Notte Piacevoli, 452
Nottinghamshire, 290, The White Peacock, The Prussian Officer
— 344, T. MILLER's novels
— 392, " J. PRIOR's " novels
— 411, Robin Hood
— See also *Sherwood Forest*
Notwithstanding, 103
Noughts and Crosses, 396
Nous autres, 33
Nouveaux contes à Ninon, 516
Nouveaux contes cruels, 484
Nouveaux Pastels, 67
Nouveaux Riches, 50, The Foreigner in the Family
Nouvelle croisade des enfants, La, 66
Nouvelle Héloïse, La, 416
Nova Scotia, 110, J. B. CONNOLLY's novels
— 132, Rockbound
— 221, The Clockmaker
— 222, The Old Judge
— See also *Acadie*
Novantia, 335, A Duke of Britain
Novelas exemplares, 96
Novelle, le, 30
Novelle della Pescare, Le, 12
Novelle rusticane, 481
Novellen, 423
Novellen um Claudia, Die, 520
Novellino, 332

Novels by Eminent Hands, 463
Now !, 327
Nowlans, The, 31
Nuala, 319
Nubbles, Kit, 140, Old Curiosity Shop
Nubians, 409, Lou
Nuestro Padre San Daniel, 345
Nuit, La, 167
Nuit au Luxembourg, Une, 209
Nuit kurde, La, 62
Nùlma, 391
Numa Roumestan, 130
Number 56, 338
No. 5 John Street, 502
Number One and Number Two, 380
" No. 101," 92
Nun, The (by BAZIN), 40
Nun, The (by BEHN), 43
Nun, The (by DIDEROT), 142
Nupkins, Mr., 140, Pickwick Papers
Nuptials of Corbal, The, 418
Nuremberg, 159, In the Blue Pike
Nurses, 5, Hospital Sketches
— 19, Brigitta
— See also *Medical Life Sanatorium Life*
Nutcracker and the King of Mice, 244
Ny jord, 223
Nye novelletter, 278
Nye tempel, Det, 64

O Defunto, 159
O Genteel Lady, 177
O Pioneers !, 94
O.T., 9
Oak, Gabriel, 225, Far from the Madding Crowd
Oak Openings, 115
Oakfield, 15
Oakleyites, The, 48
Oakum, Captain, 441, Roderick Random
Oates, Titus, 16, The Accuser
— 412, Whitefriars
Obedience, 419
Oberammergau Passion Play, 460, Quits
Oberland, 405
Oberlé, Les, 40
Oberlin's Three Stages, 490
Obermann, 429
Oberon, 255, Huon of Burdeux
Oblate, The, 257
Oblomov, 205
Obrégon, 167, Squire Marcos de Obregon
" O'BRIEN, Desmond," see KING, R. A.
O'Brien, Smith, 276, Castle Daly
O'Briens and the O'Flahertys, 351
Obscure Apostle, An, 371

Observations by Mr. Dooley, 157
Occult, see *Magic, Spiritualism, Supernatural, Superstition, Witchcraft*, etc.
Oceana, 228
Ochils, 171, The Silver Shoe-Buckle
Ochiltree, Edie, 425, The Antiquary
O'Connell, Daniel, 319, A Lad of the O'Friels
— 432, Glenaar
O'Connors of Ballynahinch, The, 255
Octave of Claudius, The, 373
Octavia, 160, Nero
Octopus, The, 361
Odd Craft, 260
Odd-job Man, The, 369
Odd Number, The, 334
Odd Women, The, 201
Odds and Ends, 125
Oddsfish, 50
Odessa, 285, Sasha
Odessa, Mutiny at, 72, Natasha
Odette, 174
O'Donnel, 351
O'Donnell's Cross, 319
O'Donoghue, The, 296
Odtaa, 331
Odyssey of a Nice Girl, The, 455
Œcolampadius, 72, True Heart
Œuvre, L', 518
Of Human Bondage, 333
Of Love, 100
Of Mistress Eve, 380
O'Fay, Sir Terence, 161, The Absentee
Ogier the Dane, 181, The Four Sons of Aymon
Ogilvies, The, 119
Oglethorpe, General, 78, Midwinter
Oglethorpe, James, 401, Doris Kingsley
Ogniem i mieczem, 434
O'Halloran, Count, 161, The Absentee
O'Hara Tales, The, 31
Ohio, 104, The Crossing
— 163, The Circuit Rider
— 215, Z. GREY's novels
— 221, New Ohio
— 234, The Breadwinners
— 251, The Leatherwood God
— 410, Down the O-hi-O
— 448, The Heritage
— 470, Figs and Thistles
— 491, Nathan Burke
Oil, 438
Oil of Spikenard, 128
Oisin, 91, In the Celtic Past
— 214, Oisin and Patrick
— 274, The Fairy Palace of the Quicken Trees, etc.
Oisin and Patrick, 214
Oisin's Children, 214
Ojibway Indians, 397, Fort Amity
Oklahama, 171, Cimarron

Oktavia, 486
Olaf, Saint, 286, From a Swedish Homestead
Olaf Trygvason, 129, The Vikings of the Baltic
— 286, Sigrid Storråde
— 294, Olaf the Glorious
— 299, The Thrall of Leif the Lucky
— 366, Olaf Trygvason
Olalla, 449
Olav Audunsson, 479, The Master of Hestviken
Old Acquaintance, An, 467
Old and the Young, The, 388
Old Andy, 113
Old Bascom Place, 229
Old Blazer's Hero, 357
Old Boston, 448
Old Bridge, The, 302
Old Celtic Romances, 273
Old Chelsea Bun-House, The, 325
Old Chester, 136–7, Mrs. DELAND's stories
Old Chester Secret, An, 137
Old Chester Tales, 136
Old Commodore, The, 249
Old Corcoran's Money, 149
Old Country, The, 358
Old Creole Days, 86
Old Curiosity Shop, The, 140
Old Dark House, The, 392
Old Dominion, The (by G. P. R. JAMES), 263
Old Dominion, The (by Mary JOHNSTON), 270
Old English Baron, The, 402
Old Factory, The, 497
Old-Fashioned Farmers, 204
Old-fashioned Girl, An, 5
Old Fires and Profitable Ghosts, 397
Old For-ever, 368
Old French Romances, 352
Old French War, 114, The Last of the Mohicans
Old Fritz and the New Era, 354
Old Goriot, 28
Old Hampshire Vignettes, 232
Old House, The, 443
Old Judge, The, 222
Old Junk, 469
Old Kensington, 461
Old Knowledge, The, 218
Old Kraskaskia, 95
Old Lady's Restoration, The, 279
Old London Bridge, 413
Old Madhouse, The, 139
Old Maid, The, 27
Old Maid's Love, An, 310
Old Maid's Paradise, An, 383
Old Mam'selle's Secret, The, 326
Old Man of Visions, The, 59
Old Manor House, The, 440
Old Man's Wife, 290
Old Man's Youth, The, 139
Old Margaret, 280

Old Men of the Sea, The, 317
Old Missionary, The, 255
Old Mr. Tredgold, 368
Old Mole, 89
Old Mole's Novel, 89
Old Mortality, 425
Old New Zealand, 322
Old News, 233
Old Peabody Pew, The, 504
Old People and the Things that Pass, 117
Old Pybus, 133
Old Room, The, 167
Old St. Paul's, 4
Old Shropshire Life, 194
Old Sir Douglas, 363
Old Squire, 47
Old Stag, The, 507
Old Story of My Farming Days, An, 403
Old Thorn, An, 253
Old Ticonderoga, 233
Old Times in Middle Georgia, 271
Old Tree Blossomed, 400
Old Wives for New, 384
Old Wives' Tale, The, 45
Old-World Landowners (Old-fashioned Farmers), 204
Oldborough, Lord, 161, Patronage
Oldbuck of Monkbarns, 425 The Antiquary
Oldbury, 276
Oldest God, The, 316
Oldfield, 32
Oldham, 244, Tall Chimneys
Oldtown Folks, 452
Oléron, 304, A Child's Romance
Olga Bardel, 19
Olga Nazimov, 195
Olive, 119
Oliver, 98, Charles the Grete
Oliver Twist, 140
Oliver's Kind Women, 197
Olivia's Summer, 323
Olney, 329, On the Banks of the Ouse
— See also *Cowper*
O'Loughlin of Clare, 355
Olympe de Clèves, 155
Olympian, The, 370
O'Malley Clan, 35, The Rebel Lady
— 315, Grace O'Malley
— 363, A Queen of Men
O'Malley of Shanganagh, 84
Omar Khayyám, 145, Omar the Tentmaker
Omar the Tentmaker, 145
Ombra, 367
Ombre de l'amour, L', 466
Ombre de la croix, L' 464
Ombre s'étend sur la montagne, L', 413
Omdurman, 331, The Four Feathers
Omnibus, The, 396
Omnium, Duke of, see *Palliser, Plantagenet*
Omoo, 337
On Both Sides of the Sea, 98
On changerait plûtot l'esprit de place, 481
On Company's Service, 408

On Etna, 304
On Forsyte Change, 191
On Guard, 429
On Peter's Island, 415
On Sale, 334
On the Banks of the Ouse, 329
On the Dark Mountains, 368
On the Edge, 136
On the Eve, 474
On the Face of the Waters, 445
On the Field of Glory, 435
On the Forgotten Road, 23
On the Frontier, 230
On the Heights, 19
On the Old " Kearsage," 71
On the Red Staircase, 461
On the Road, 100
On the Staircase, 458
On the Stairs, 188
On the Track, 292
On the Will, 30
On the Wing of Occasions, 229
On Trial, 276
Once Aboard the Lugger, 397
Once More, 190
One after Another, 19
One Ash, 200
One Autumn Night, 206
One Before, The, 374
One Crowded Hour, 216
One Day, 56
One Good Time, 505
One I Knew the Best of All, The, 82
One Immortality, 222
One in a Thousand, 262
One Kind and Another, 374
One Man in his Time, 202
One of Life's Slaves, 299
One of Our Conquerors, 340
One of our Grandmothers, 336
One of Ourselves, 485
One of the Forty, 130
One of the Grenvilles, 308
One of Them, 297
One Poor Scruple, 489
One Queen Triumphant, 333
One Summer, 249
One Summer Night, 54
One-Way Trail, The, 126
One Who Looked On, The, 348
One Woman's Life, 238
One Year, 196
Oneidas, 97, The Reckoning
O'Neill, Hugh, of Tyrone, 404, The Charming of Estercel
O'Neill, Margaret, 143, The Patience of John Morland
O'Neill, Owen Roe, 174, The Chances of War
Onesimus, 1
Only a Fiddler, 9
Only Son, An, 269
Only Son of Aoife, The, 214
Only the Governess, 91
Onora, 355
Ontario, 157, The Trail of the Conestoga

Oony, 162
Open all Night, 350
Open Boat, The, 120
Open Conspiracy, The, 495
Open Country, 240
Open-Eyed Conspiracy, An, 257
Open Question, The, 412
Open Road, The, 457
Open Secret, 369
Open Verdict, An, 70
Openings in the Old Trail 230
Opimian, Dr., 379, Gryll Grange
Opinions of a Philosopher, 212
Oppenheimer, Josef Süss, 172, Jew Süss
Opstandigen, Die, 9
Optimism, 221, Ten Times One is Ten
— 484, Candide, Zadig
— See also *Utopias*
Optimist, The, 135
Options, 389
OPZOOMER, Miss A., see " WALLIS, A.S.C.," 486
Orange Girl, The, 52
Orangery, The, 132
Orchard Pavilion, The, 47
Orchards, 133
Ordeal of Richard Feverel, The, 339
Order of Release, The, 445
Ordinary People, 436
Ordination, L', 44
Oreads, 240
Oregon, 248, Fifty-Four Forty, or Fight
— 460, Mary Bray X her Mark
Orgeas and Miradou, 493
Orgreave, Janet, 45, Clayhanger, and sequels
Oriana, 301, Amadis of Gaul
Oriental Encounters, 387
Oriental Romances and Novels, 13, The Arabian Nights' Entertainments
— 34, Barlaam and Josaphat
— 42, Vathek
— 71, The Wallet of Kai Lung, and sequels
— 122, Khaled
— 125, Salathiel
— 143, Alroy
— 174, Santal
— 197, Gesta Romanorum
— 218, The Thousand and One Quarters of an Hour
— 255, Huon of Burdeux
— 285, Sulamith
— 327, Moral Tales (by MARMONTEL)
— 339, Shaving of Shagpat
— 347, Persian Letters
— 351, Hajji Baba
— 353, Roi the Fool
— 358, New Arabian Nights
— 375, Hermann Agha
— 387, M. PICKTHALL's novels

Oriental Romances and Novels (contd.): 430, The Seven Wise Masters
— 484, Visramiani
— See also *Arabian Nights, Biblical Stories, Chinese Fiction, Persian Fiction*
Orientations, 333
Oriflamme in Egypt, The, 83
Original, An, 10
Origines Islandicae, 483
Orissers, The, 357
Orkneys, 36, Paul and Christina
— 426, The Pirate
"*Orlando*," 3, The Spectator
— 308, Devereux
Orlando, 511
Orleanist Revolt, 417, Bardelys the Magnificent
Orleans, Duc de (Regent of France), 153, The Chevalier d'Harmental
— 154, Sylvandire
— 337, Cerise
Orley Farm, 471
Orloff Couple, The (Orloff and his Wife), 206
Orlov, Count, 129, The Princess Tarakanova
— 152, Shoes of Gold
Ormond (by C. B. BROWN), 76
Ormond (by EDGEWORTH), 161
Oroonoko, 43
Orphan Angel, The, 512
Orphan Dinah, 386
Orphan Island, 312
Orrain, 513
Orsini Family, 53, The Abbess of Castro
Orsino, Don, 121, Don Orsino
Ortheris, Private, 281, Soldiers Three, Life's Handicap, etc.
Orthodox, 196
O'Ruddy, The, 121
Osborne Family, 462, Vanity Fair
Osborne, Edward, 1st Duke of Leeds, 324, Colloquies of Edward Osborne
— 413, Old London Bridge
OSBOURNE, Lloyd, see also STEVENSON, R. L. B., 450
O'Shane, Sir Ulick, 161, Ormond
Ossian, see *Oisin*
Ostrogoths, 128, A Struggle for Rome
Oswald Bastable, 60
Oswego, 177, The Royal Americans
Other Girls, The, 503
Other House, The, 265
Other Main-Travelled Roads, 192
Other People's Children, 219
Other Two, The, 499

Other Woman, The, 10
Otherwise Phyllis, 359
Otsego, Lake, 114, The Pioneers
Ottilia, 339, Harry Richmond
Otto Babendick, 187
Otto of the Silver Hand, 396
Otto the Knight, 463
Où mènent les mauvais chemins, 28
Our Admirable Betty, 169
Our Brother's Burdens, 185
Our Casualty, 55
Our Cove, 228
Our Daily Bread, 483
Our Father San Daniel, 345
Our Forefathers, 188
Our Friend the Charlatan, 201
Our House and the People in It, 381
Our Kingdom, 63
Our Lady of Darkness, 90
Our Lady of Lies, 67
Our Lady of the Forest, 497
Our Lady of the Pillar, 159
Our Lady's Juggler, 183
Our Little Life, 436
Our Little Town, 294
Our Mr. Dormer, 354
Our Mr. Wrenn, 298
Our Mutual Friend, 141
— See also The Veneerings, 270
Our Sea, 61
Our Street, 462
Our Town and Some of Its People, 339
Our Village, 346
Ourselves and Our Island, 35
Out in Life's Rain, 323
Out in the Open, 321
Out of Childhood, 363
Out of Debt, out of Danger, 160
Out of Due Time, 489
Out of Gloucester, 110
Out of Nowhere into Nothing, 10
Out of Prison, 216
Out of Step, 389
Out of the Cypress Swamp, 407
Out of the Deep, 136
Out of the Hurly-Burly, 3
Out of the Question, 250
Out of the Silences, 486
Outcast, The (by LAGERLÖF), 287
Outcast, The (by PENNY), 381
Outcast, The (by PIRANDELLO), 388
Outcast of the Islands, An, 110
Outcasts, The, 207
Outcasts of Poker Flat, 229
Outcry, The, 266
Outland, 21
Outlaw, The (by GARLAND), 192
Outlaw, The (by HEWLETT), 240

Outlaw and Lawmaker, 390
Outlaw of Iceland, The, 253
Outlaws, 169, Beltane the Smith
— 214, Grettis Saga
Outlaws of the Marches, The, 223
Outlet, The, 2
Outlines in Local Colour, 333
Outpost of Progress, 110
Outside the Radius, 407
Outward Bound, 249
Ouvert la nuit, 350
Ouverture, Toussaint l', 268, Moonraker
— 330, The Hour and the Man
Over Bemerton's, 305
Over the Hills (by FARNOL), 170
Over the Hills (by FINDLATER), 174
Over the Side, 261
Over the Sliprails, 292
Overbury, Sir Thomas, 262, Arabella Stuart
— 273, In Burleigh's Days, and sequel
Overheard, 20
Overland, 135
Oviedo, 375, The Grandee
Ovingdean Grange, 4
Ovington's Bank, 498
Owd Bob, 368
"OWEN, Ashford," see OGLE, Anne C., 364
Owen—a Waif, 412
Owen Wingrave, 264
Owl's House, The, 193
Oxford, 42, Zuleika Dobson
— 70, The Adventures of Mr. Verdant Green, and sequel
— 75, Alas !
— 107, Sandford of Merton, The Comedy of Age
— 108, A Scholar of his College
— 109, The Seal of Silence
— 120, The House of Walderne
— 133, Orchards
— 142, Keddy
— 197, Cheadle & Son
— 213, A Clerk of Oxford
— 252, A Dreamer of Dreams
— 253, Tom Brown at Oxford
— 280, Stretton
— 302, Reginald Dalton
— 359, Loss and Gain
— 390, Progress of Hugh Rendel
— 412, Whitehall
— 489, Lady Connie
— See also *University Life*
Oxford, Lady, 161, Lord Byron
Oxfordshire, 58, Cripps the Carrier
— 426, Kenilworth, Woodstock
Oxney, Isle of, 275, The Challenge to Sirius

På Guds veje, 57
Pablo de Segovia, 396
Pabo the Priest, 209
Pacifism, 33, Light
— 79, The Shadow of the Sword
— 165-6, "ERCKMANN-CHATRIAN'S" novels
— 414-5, ROLLAND's novels
— 457, Lay Down Your Arms
Pactolus Prime, 470
Paddy-go-Easy and his wife Nancy, 92
Paddy Risky, 343
Paddy the Sport, 305
Padua, 424, The Vicar of the Marches
Pædobaptism, 39, As the Light Led
Paese di Cuccagna, Il, 429
Pætus Thrasea, 160, Nero
"PAGE, Stanton," see FULLER, H. B., 188
Page d'amour, Une, 517
Page of the Duke of Savoy, The, 155
Pages from Portabeg, 132
Painful Memory, A, 57
Painted Minx, The, 97
Painted Scene, The, 492
Painted Veil, The, 334
Pair of Blue Eyes, A, 225
Pair of Patient Lovers, A, 251
Paix du ménage, La, 27
Palace of Pleasure, The, 374
Palace Tales, 222
Paladin, The, 480
Palatinate, The, 71, The Turbulent Duchess
Pale Horse, The, 422
Pale Young Maiden, The, 112
Palermo, Battle of, 306, Avanti !
Palestine, 72, The Kingdom of Love
— 74, A Son of Issachar
— 144, Tancred
— 181, The Four Sons of Aymon
— 199, Hassan
— 220, The Brethren
— See also *Biblical Stories, Christ, Crusades, Jerusalem, Jews*
Palestro, 280, Silcote of Silcotes
Palliser, Plantagenet, 472, Can You Forgive Her ? Phineas Finn, and sequel, The Prime Minister
Palmerin of England, 350
Palmerston, Lord, 24, The Pillar of Fire
— 515, The Mantle of Elijah
Palmyra, 489, Zenobia
Pam, 256
Pam Decides, 256
Pam the Fiddler, 456
Pamela, 406
Pamela Pounce, 94
Pan, 290, The God in the Thicket

Pan (contd.): 291, The Last Laugh
— 316, The Oldest God
Pan, 223
Pan Michael, 434
Panama, 40, The Ne'er do Well
— 62, A Gentleman Adventurer
Panathenaic Festival, 131, A Victor of Salamis
Pandervils, The, 80
Pandosto, 213
Pandosto, 430
Pandurang Hari, 244
Panhandle and the Ghosts, 259
Panizzi, Sir Antonio, 300, Christopher Kirkland
Pan's Garden, 59
Pantagruel, 398, RABELAIS'S Works
Panurge, 398, RABELAIS'S works
Panza, Sancho, 96, Don Quixote
Paoli, 311, The Eagle's Nest
Papa del Mar, El, 61
Paphlagonian Unkind King, The, 430
Papineau, Louis Joseph, 126, In Treaty with Honour
— 376, The Pomp of the Lavilettes
Parables, see *Allegories, Beast Fables*
Paracelsus, 72, True Heart
Paradise, 76
Paradise Mystery, The, 177
Paradise Row, 508
Pardaillan, 155, The Two Dianas, The Page of the Duke of Savoy
Parent's Assistant, The, 160
Parents pauvres, Les, I and II, 29
Pariah, The, 12
Paris, Matthew, 83, The Oriflamme in Egypt
Paris before the Nineteenth Century, 26, To Arms
— 30, Seraphita
— 62, A Fair Martyr
— 68, The Quest of Glory, Yesterdays
— 68, Prince and Heretic, and sequel
— 69, The Burning-Glass, Mr. Misfortunate
— 70, In High Places
— 70, Ishmael
— 74, The Yellow Poppy
— 107, The King with Two Faces
— 142, Rameau's Nephew
— 154, Ascanio
— 195, Captain Fracasse
— 212, The Reds of the Midi, and sequels
— 233, Perronelle
— 252, A Dreamer of Dreams
— 253, Notre-Dame de Paris
— 261, Richelieu, John Marston Hall, One in a Thousand

Paris before the Nineteenth Century (*contd.*): 262, Henry of Guise
— 306, Cécile
— 345, Adventures of François
— 347, Persian Letters
— 432, The Cross at the Door
— See also *French Revolution, Henry IV, Louis XIV, Richelieu, St. Bartholomew*, etc.
Paris, Bombardment of, (in Great War), 414, Pierre and Luce
Paris, Modern, 26–30, BALZAC's novels, *passim*
— 107-8, "COLETTE'S" novels
— 148, Gallia
— 156, The Lady with the Camelias
— 156, DU MAURIER'S novels
— 175, The Sentimental Education
— 218, "GYP'S" stories
— 221, HALÉVY's novels
— 257, En Route, and sequels
— 298, Tarr
— 302, The Wonderful Year
— 310, Dorothea
— 310, The Parisians
— 322, Adrian Savage
— 342, L. MERRICK's stories
— 349, Confessions of a Young Man
— 350, The Fudge Family in Paris
— 393-4, PROUST's novels
— 400, Journeyman Love
— 463, Adventures of Philip
— 516-9, ZOLA's novels
Paris, Siege of, 39, The Dayspring
— 45, The Old Wives' Tale
— 96, Ashes of Empire
— 105, Agnès
— 106, In Time of War
— 115, Une idylle pendant la siège
— 130, Robert Helmont
— 169, A Window in Paris
— 310, The Parisians
— 326, Les tronçons du glaive
Paris, 519
Paris and Vienne, 375
Paris Churches, 257, En Route
Paris Halles, 517, The Fat and the Thin
Paris Poor, 254, Les Misérables
— 455, Mysteries of Paris
— 519, Paris
Paris, University of, 21, Arnoul the Englishman
— 127, The Love Story of Giraldus
Parish Nurse, The, 323
Parish Work, 279, Two Years Ago

Parish Work (*contd.*): 300, Grasp Your Nettle
— 313, Annals of a Quiet Neighbourhood
— 314, The Seaboard Parish
— 317, The Altar Steps, and sequels
— 323, The Parish Nurse
— 353, A Child of the Jago
— 431, My New Curate
— 432, Luke Delmege
— 513, Beechcroft at Rockstone
Parisian Points of View, 221
Parisians, The, 310
Parisians in the Country, 28
Parisiens en province, Les, 28
Parismus, Prince of Bohemia, 350
PARKS, Mrs. G. R., see ROBINS, Elizabeth, 412
Parma, 53, The Abbess of Castro
Parma, Margaret of, 486, In Troubled Times
Parma, Prince of, 24, Raoul, Gentleman of Fortune
Parnassus on Wheels, 351
Parnell, C. S., 210, His People
— 308, Her Majesty's Rebels
Parnell, Sir John, 243, The King's Deputy
Parodies, 12, Baboo Jabberjee
— 37, The Heroine
— 42, A Christmas Garland
— 107, Sandford of Merton
— 143, Ixion in Heaven
— 162, Life in London, and sequel
— 172, Adventures of Joseph Andrewes, Shamela
— 178, The John Riddell Murder Case
— 178, A Mirror for Witches
— 229, Condensed Novels
— 232, The Celestial Railroad
— 241, The Green Carnation
— 268, The White Riband
— 293, Nonsense Novels
— 293, Winsome Winnie
— 339, Shaving of Shagpat
— 357, Grandison the Second
— 373, Playthings and Parodies
— 427, Borrowed Plumes
— 441, Launcelot Greaves
— 463, Novels by Eminent Hands, Rebecca and Rowena
— 504, Lord Arthur Savile's Crime
PARR, Olive Catharine, see CHASE, Beatrice, 98
Parson Kelly, 332
Parson Peter, 363
Parson Sparrow, 390
Parson's Daughter, The, 330
Parson's Progress, 317

Parthenopean Revolt, 156, The Neapolitan Lovers
Parties, 481
Parting, A, 190
Parting of the Ways, The, 65
Partir, 145
Partizan, The, 436
Partner, The, 111
Partners, 137
Partridge, Mr., 173, Tom Jones
Party Dress, The, 238
Party Fight and Funeral, The, 92
Parzival, 242
Pascarel, 372
Pasquina and Pif, 520
Pass, The, 501
Passage of the Barque *Sappho*, The, 377
Passage to India, A, 180
Passages from the Diary of a late Physician, 490
Passages in the Life of Mistress Margaret Maitland, 366
Passages in the life of the faire Gospeller Anne Askew, 325
Passages in the Secret History of an Irish Countess, 294
Passe Rose, 225
Passing, 288
Passing of Sister Barsett, The, 269
Passing of the Flagship, The, 152
Passing of the Third Floor Back, The, 268
Passionate Elopement, The, 317
Passionate Hearts, The, 91
Passionate Pilgrim, A, 263
Passy, 156, Peter Ibbetson
Paste, 265
Pastels of Men, 67
Paston Letters, 449, The Black Arrow
Pastor of Poggsee, The, 187
Pastorals, 8, A Kentucky Cardinal, and sequel, Summer in Arcady
— 56, Synnöve Solbakken, Arne, A Happy Boy
— 79, A Little Green World
— 96, Galatea
— 129, Letters from My Mill
— 171, The Adventures of Telemachus
— 194, Cranford
— 205, The Vicar of Wakefield
— 213, Pandosto
— 226, The Woodlanders
— 236, A Princess of Arcady
— 252, Green Mansions
— 302, Rosalynde
— 303, Daphnis and Chloe
— 321, Little Peter
— 347, Diana
— 355, German Love
— 386, Evander
— 416, The Forest Schoolmaster

Pastorals (*contd.*): 416, The New Heloïse
— 419, Paul and Virginia
— 420, Little Fadette
— 421, The Devil's Pool, The Country Waif
— 434, The Arcadia
— 465, Lad and Lass
— 483, Myra of the Pines
— 516, Jean Sourdon's Four Days
Pastorals of Dorset, 185
Pastorals of France, 492
Pastor's Wife, The, 15
Patches and Pomander, 71
Pater, Walter, 322, The New Republic
Pater Maternus, 231
Path and Goal, 88
Path of a Star, The, 116
Path of Glory, The, 232
Path of Life, The, 453
Path of the King, The, 78
Path to Honour, The, 216
Pathelin, 288
Pathfinder, The, 114
Paths of the Prudent, The, 176
Pathway, The, 507
Patience of John Morland, The, 143
Patience Sparhawk and her Times, 17
Patricia, 86
Patricia at the Inn, 442
Patrician, The, 190
Patrick, Saint, 214, Gods and Fighting Men
Patrick, Master of Gray, 438, Queen Mary's Holdfast
Patrick, Sir, 160, Castle Rackrent
Patriot, The, 177
Patriot and Hero, 103
Patriot and Tory, 165
Patrioteer, The, 323
Patriotism, 71, The Patriots
— 221, The Man without a Country
— 323, The Patrioteer (Satire)
— 416, The Crystal Coffin
— 496, Vineta
Patriots, The, 71
Patriots of the South, The, 71
Patrol of the Sun-Dance Trail, 110
Patrona, Halil, 272, Halil
Patronage, 161
Patronio, 274, Count Lucanor
Patsy, 444
Patsy the Omadhaun, 63
Patten Experiment, The, 323
Pattern of Paineful Adventures, 13
Pattison, Mrs. Mark, 164, Middlemarch
Patty Fairfield, 493
Paul I (Tsar of Russia), 93, By Neva's Waters
— 306, The Flames of Moscow
Paul, Saint, 84, Brother Saul

Paul, Saint (contd.) : 103, The Crown of Pine
— 346, The Triumph of Faith
— 435, Quo Vadis ?
Paul and Christina, 36
Paul and Virginia, 419
Paul Clifford, 308
Paul Faber, 314
Paul Ferroll, 106
Paul Kelver, 268
Paul Mercer, 3
Paul Patoff, 122
Paula, Sancta, 382, Sancta Paula
Paulding, Commodore Hiram, 427, Midshipman Paulding
Paulina, 381
Pauline (by Norris), 362
Pauline (by Walford), 485
Paul's Case, 95
Pauperism, see *London Poor, Paris Poor, New York Poor, Philanthropy, Poor*, etc.
Pausanias the Spartan, 310
Pavilion on the Links, The, 448
Pawlett, Lord, 68, Yesterdays
Paying Guests, 49
Payment Deferred, 179
Payn, James, 411, The Private Life of Henry Maitland
Pays de fourrures, 482
Paysans, les, 30
Pazos de Ulloa, Los, 375
Peace, 191
Peace in Friendship Village, 189
Peace in the House, 27
Peak District, 127, The Blacksmith of Voe
— 354, Snow over Eldon
Peakland Faggot, A, 199
Pearl Maidens, 220
Pearl of Orr's Island, The, 452
Peasant and the Prince, The, 330
Peasant Marly, The, 146
Peasantry, The, 30
Peasants, for British Isles, see *Ireland, Scotland, Wales*, and names of counties
— 31, Banim's novels
— 40, This, My Son ; Autumn Glory, By Faith Alone
— 64, Children's Children, Women of the Country
— 64, God and Woman
— 89, The Bailiff Yerney
— 92, W. Carleton's stories
— 129, Rebecca Drew
— 158, The People of Juvik
— 187, Jörn Uhl, Klaus Heinrich Baas
— 200, Algernon Gissing's novels
— 216, Winter, G. Griffin's stories

Peasants (contd.) : 218, The Life of a Simple Man
— 223-4, Hamsun's novels
— 245, Miss Holme's novels
— 285, A Slav Soul
— 293, Shepherd's Warning
— 311, Harman Pols
— 323, The Fields of Dulditch
— 339, Rhoda Fleming
— 344, Mikszáth's stories
— 358, The Grandmother
— 364, O'Flahey's novels
— 367, The Minister's Wife
— 389, Emmanuel, and sequel
— 390, T. F. Powys' novels
— 395, Pushkin's stories
— 396, Toil of Men
— 404, The Peasants
— 435, Children of the Soil
— 465, Signe's History
— 467-9, Tolstoy's novels and stories
— 473, Beppo the Conscript
— 477-8, K. Tynan's novels
— 478, Idylls of a Dutch Village
— 481-2, Verga's stories
— 491, Driven
— 518, The Soil
Peasants, The, 404
Peasants' Revolt, 133, The King behind the King
— 182, The Seven Nights
— 233, In a Desert Land
— 343, Robert Annys
— 352, The Dream of John Ball
Peasants' War, 112, Veva
— 410, In the Olden Time
Peau de chagrin, Le, 30
Peau de lion, La, 52
Peché de M. Antoine, Le, 421
Pêcheur d'Islande, 304
Pecorone, Il, 199
Pedagogue, A, 439
Peder Victorious, 415
Pedro the Cruel, 155, Agenor de Mauléon
Peebles, Peter, 426, Redgauntlet
Peep Behind the Scenes, A, 487
Peep o' Day, 31
Peg Woffington, 401
Peggoty family, 141, David Copperfield
Pelham, Henry, 113, Surry of Eagle's Nest
— 243, High Treason
Pelham, 308
Pelicans, The, 135
Pelle the Conqueror, 359
Peloponnesian War, 346, Cloud Cuckoo Land
Peltonen, V., see "Linnakoski, J.," 300
Pembroke, Countess of, 270, Sir Mortimer
Pembroke, Earl of, 333, The Royal Sisters
Pembroke, 505

Penal Laws, 31, The Conformists, Crohoore of the Bill-Hook
— 60, The Irish Chieftains
— 351, O'Donnel
— 355, O'Laughlin of Clare
Penda, King of Mercia, 165, Fated to Win
Pendennis, The History of, 462
Pending Heaven, 197
Penelope Brandling, 373
Penelope's English Experiences, 504
Penelope's Experiences in Scotland, 504
Penelope's Irish Experiences, 504
Penelope's Suitors, 84
Penguin Island, 184
Peninsular War, 24, The Young Lovers
— 90, A Castle in Spain
— 124, Strong Mac
— 150, Adventures of Gerard
— 180, The Drummer's Coat
— 199, The Spy
— 203, The Subaltern
— 211, The Romance of War
— 216, A Young Man Married
— 223, Traseaden Hall
— 296, Charles O'Malley, Tom Burke of Ours
— 336, Stories of Waterloo
— 397, The Two Scouts, Harry Revel, Rain of Dollars
— 418, The Snare
— 432, The End of the Sermon
— 510, Sons of the Sword, The Spanish Lady
Pennsylvania, 237, The Three Black Pennys
— 301, The Chronic Loafer
— 345, Far in the Forest, Westways
— 447, The Road to Paris
Penny Monypenny, 174
Penrith, 72, Some Account of Amyot Brough
Penrod, 460
Penrod and Sam, 460
Penruddock of the White Lambs, 103
Penshurst Castle, 330
Pension Beaurepas, The, 264
People of Juvik, 158
People of Popham, 495
People of the Mist, The, 219
People of the Small Arrow, 152
Pepin, King, 480, Valentyne and Orson
Pepita Jiménez, 480
Peplow's Paper-Chase, 189
"Peppergrass, John," see Boyce, Rev. John
Peppiniello, 211
Pepys, Samuel, 39, The Knight of the Golden Sword

Pepys, Samuel (contd.) : 62, The King's Guerdon
— 133, Mad Barbara
— 206, White Aprons
— 315, The Dutch in the Medway
— 459, Lady Jem
Per Aspera, 159
Perceval, 217, Peredur, Son of Evrawc
— 242, High History of the Holy Graal
— 322, Morte Darthur
Perceval li Gallois, 242
"Perch, Philemon," see Johnston, R. M., 271
Percy, Henry, 6th Earl of Northumberland, 333, Defender of the Faith, The Royal Sisters
Père Antoine's Date Palm, 6
Père Goriot, 28
Peredur, Son of Evrawc, 217
Perella, 302
Perelman, O. I., see "Duimov, Osip," 153
Pérez, Fra Andrés, see sub nom. López de Ubeda, 303
Perfection, 159
Perfervid, 131
Perfume of the Rose, The, 446
Pericles, 18, The Immortal Marriage
— 287, Pericles and Aspasia
Pericles, Mr., 339, Sandra Belloni
Pericles and Aspasia, 287
Péril, 215
Peril of the Sword, The, 225
Perilous Secret, The, 402
Perlycross, 58
Permutations Among the Nightingales, 256
Perpetua, 209
Perpetual Curate, The, 367
Perpetual Fires, 293
Perrault-Harry, Mme, see "Harry, M.," 229
Perris of the Cherry-Trees, 176
Perronelle, 233
Perry, Commodore, M.C., 45, The Shogun's Daughter
Persecutions, see *Covenanters, Christians, Early, Huguenots, Inquisition, Mary I, Puritans, Roman Catholics*
Persia, 121, Zoroaster
— 145, Omar the Tentmaker
— 158, An Egyptian Princess
— 158, Nadir Shah
— 347, Persian Letters
— 351, Hajji Baba
— See also *Persian Romances*
Persian Letters, 347
Persian Romances, 382, Persian Tales
— 484, Visramiani
— 500, Tales of the Genii

Personal Recollections of Joan of Arc, 476
Personal Scandal, 14, Aristocracy
— 47, Dodo
— 130, The Nabob, Kings in Exile, One of the Forty
— 213, Cape Cod Folks
— 245, HOOK's stories
— 271, Chrysal
— 295, Asmodeus
— 322, MALLOCK's novels
— 334, Cakes and Ale
— 351, Florence M'Carthy
— 378-9, PEACOCK's novels
— 495, The Autocracy of Mr. Parham
— 518, Money
— See also The Possessed, 147
Persuasion, 20
Perth, 427, The Fair Maid of Perth
Perthshire, 311, Black Mary
— 447, The Minister of State
Peru, 252, The Crimson Conquest
— 295, The Bride of the Sun
Pessimism, 10-11, ANDREEV's stories
— 93, The Realization of Justus Moran
— 99, René
— 146-8, DOSTOEVSKY's novels
— 184, Penguin Island
— 200-1, G. GISSING's novels
— 204, The Sorrows of Werther
— 206-7, "GORKY's" stories
— 226, Tess, Jude the Obscure
— 257, En Route, and sequels
— 304-5, "LOTI'S" novels
— 357, Confessions of a Child of the Century
— 429, Obermann
— 455, SUDERMANN's stories
Peter, Saint, 435, Quo Vadis ?
Peter the Great of Russia, 69, Kings-at-Arms
— 247, The Triumph of Count Ostermann
— 341, Peter and Alexis
— 461, An Imperial Lover
— 500, Near the Tsar, Near Death
— 512, A Prince of Intrigue
Peter III (Tsar of Russia), 152, Shoes of Gold
Peter, 440
Peter and Alexis, 341
Peter Binney, 329
Peter Ibbetson, 156
Peter Jackson, Cigar Merchant, 186
Peter Moor's Journey to South-West Africa, 187

Peter Pan, 38
Peter Schlemihl's wundersame Geschichte, '98
Peter Simple, 328
Peter the Hermit, 131, "God Wills It"
Peter the Whaler, 281
Peter Whiffle, 481
Peter Wilkins, Life of, 375
Peterborough, Charles Mordaunt, Earl of, 134, Memoirs of an English Officer
— 340, Lord Ormont
Peterkin, 346
Peterloo Riots, 32, The Manchester Man
— 498, Starvecrow Farm
— 502, The Revolution in Tanner's Lane
— 508, Jack o' Peterloo
Peter's Mother, 137
Peter's Pedigree, 113
Petersburg, 33, The Coat without Seam
— 121, Fleurange
— 146, The Insulted and Injured
— 193, Petersburg Tales
— 216, The Cruel City
— 358, Princes of the Stock Exchange
— 415, On Peter's Island
— 486, The Secret City
Petersburg Tales, 193
Petit Bob, 218
Petit chose, Le, 129
Petite comtesse, La, 172
Petite Fadette, La, 420
Petite fille de Jérusalem, La, 229
Petite Palace of Pettie his Pleasure, 383
Petits bourgeois, les, 29
Petronius Arbiter, 435, Quo Vadis ?
PETROV, E., see *sub nom.* ILF, Ilya, 258
Petruchio, 447
Petticoat Government, 370
Peur de Vivre, La, 65
Peveril of the Peak, 426
Pew, 449, Treasure Island
Phalsbourg, Battle of, 165, The Conscript
— 166, The Blocade
Phantas, 369
Phantastes, 313
Phantom, 231
Phantom Army, The, 380
Phantom Chariot of Cuchullin, The, 254
Phantom from the East, A, 304
Phantom 'Rickshaw, The, 281
Phantom Ship, The, 329
Phantoms, 475
Pharais, 431
Pharaoh and the Priest, The, 203
Pharoh, 220, Moon of Israel
Pharsalia, Battle of, 131, A Friend of Caesar
Phases of an Inferior Planet, 202
Phenomena, 244

Phil Purcel the Pig Driver, 92
Philadelphia, 8, In Hostile Red
— 70, A Doctor of Philosophy
— 76, Arthur Mervyn
— 345, Hephzibah Guinness, The Red City, A Venture in 1777
Philanthropy, 74, The Fool of Quality
— 148, Beggars All
— 310, Kenelm Chillingly
— 383, The Silent Partner
— 487, Harmer John
Philibert of Savoy, 155, The Page of the Duke of Savoy
Philip I of France, 336, The Assassins
Philip II (Augustus), of France, 23, On the Forgotten Road
— 155, The Page of the Duke of Savoy
— 261, Philip Augustus
— 426, The Talisman
Philip IV (Le Bel), 112, The Lion of Flanders
Philip II (of Spain), 5, Cardinal Pole
— 24, My Lady of Orange
— 49, The Queen's Tragedy
— 107, Jan van Elselo
— 123, In the Palace of the King
— 124, The White Plumes of Navarre
— 213, The House of Torment
— 219, Lysbeth
— 288, The Glory of Don Ramiro
— 418, The Hounds of God
Philip III, 261, De L'Orme
— 365, Ulrick the Ready
Philip of Pokanoket (Mount Hope), King, 114, The Wept of the Wish-ton-Wish
— 165, Uncrowning a King
Philip and His Wife, 136
Philip Augustus, 261
Philip Nolan's Friends, 221
Philip Rollo, 211
Philip the Good (of Burgundy), 262, Agincourt
— 280, Old Margaret
Philip the Leal, 412
Philip Winwood, 446
Philippa, 428
Philistia, 7
Philochristus, 1
Philosophe sous les toits, Un, 443
Philosopher Dick, 97
Philosophers and Philosophical Stories, 9, John Buncle
— 11, The Philosopher's Stone, A Stranger in Paradise
— 18-19, AUERBACH's novels
— 23, Darrel of the Blessed Isles

Philosophers and Philosophical Stories (contd.): 23, The New Atlantis
— 23, Hermsprong
— 142, Rameau's Nephew
— 146-8, DOSTOEVSKY's novels, Crime and Punishment, *et seq.*
— 164, Adam Bede
— 191, GARBORG's novels
— 204, Wilhelm Meister's Apprenticeship
— 222, One Immortality
— 259, L. P. JACK's stories
— 269, Rasselas
— 322, MALLOCK's novels
— 377, Marius the Epicurean
— 388, PIRANDELLO's novels
— 393-4, PROUST's novels
— 441, Thorndale
— 443, The Attic Philosopher
— 479, Mist
— 490, The World's Illusion
— 503, The History of Agathon, Confessions in Elysium
— 515, The Master
— See also *Philosophers' Stone, Didactic*, etc.
Philosophers in Trouble, 259
Philosopher's Stone, 30, The Quest of the Absolute
— 203, St. Leon
Philosopher's Stone, The, 11
Philosophic Radicalism, 141, Hard Times
Phineas Finn, 472
Phineas Redux, 472
Phips, Sir William, 376, The Trail of the Sword
— 431, The Coast of Freedom
Phœbe, Junior, 367
Phœbus, Gaston, 144, Lothair
Phœbus of Halzaphron, 397
Phœnicians, 87, The Adventures of Captain Mago
— See also *Carthage, Tyre*, etc.
Phoenix, The, 33
Phœnix Park Murders, 349, A Drama in Muslin
Phroso, 246
Phyllis of the Sierras, A, 230
Piacere, Il, 11
Piazza Tales, 338
Picara, La, 303
Picaresque Romances, 7, The Rogue
— 35, The Struggle for Life
— 96, Don Quixote, Exemplary Novels
— 173, Jonothan Wild
— 201, An Artist Passes
— 216, The Adventurous Simplicissimus
— 235, The English Rogue
— 295, Gil Blas, The Bachelor of Salamanca
— 296, Con Cregan

Picaresque Romances (*contd.*): 297, Davenport Dunn
— 301, The Beloved Vagabond, Aristide Pujol
— 303, La Picara
— 317, Sylvia Scarlett and sequel
— 328, Japhet in Search of a Father
— 338, Lazarillo de Tormes
— 351, Hajji Baba
— 396, Pablo de Segovia
— 414, Celestina
— 441, Roderick Random, Ferdinand Count Fathom
Piccadilly, 366
Piccino, 82
Picciola, 419
Piccolo Mondo Antico, Il, 177
Piccolo Mondo Moderno, Il, 177
Pichegrou Conspiracy, 365, The Eagle's Talon
Pickets, 96
Pickwick Papers, 140
Picnic, The, 336
Picq Plays the Hero, 342
Picture of Dorian Gray, The, 504
Pictures, 325
Pictures from Nordland, 299
Piece of String, The, 334
Piedmont, 91, A Rogue's Tragedy
— 230, Beyond Man's Strength
Pierre, 338
Pierre and his People, 375
Pierre and Jean, 334
Pierre and Luce, 414
Pierre de la Baraque, 408
Pierre et Camille, 357
Pierre Grassou, 27
Pierre Nozière, 184
Pierrette, 27
Pieśń Przerwana, 371
Pietro Ghisleri, 122
Pig Iron, 361
Pike, Zebulon M., 44, A Volunteer with Pike
Pikemen, The, 277
Pilate, 183, The Procurator of Judæa
Pilgrim, The, 297
Pilgrim Kamanita, The, 202
Pilgrim on the Earth, The, 213
Pilgrimage (by C. E. LAWRENCE), 290
Pilgrimage (by Dorothy RICHARDSON), 405
Pilgrimage, A, 63
Pilgrimage of a Fool The, 79
Pilgrimage of Grace, 4, The Lancashire Witches
— 220, The Lady of Blossholme
Pilgrimage of Strongsoul, The, 131
Pilgrimages, 12, The Triumph of Death
— 518, Lourdes

Pilgrims of Adversity, 315
Pilgrims of the Rhine, 309
Pilgrim's Progress, The, 81
Pilgrimsgang, 63
Pillar of Fire, The, 24
Pillbox 17, 72
Pillow Sketches, 428
Pilot, The, 114
Pilot and his Wife, The, 299
Piltur og Stúlka, 465
Pine and Palm, 113
Pink Furniture, 115
Pink Roses, 90
Pioneers, 47, Who Goes There?, and sequel
— 54, H. BINDLOSS's novels
— 145, The Beau's Comedy
— 163, The Hoosier Schoolmaster
— 248, The Covered Wagon
— 289, Miss A. C. LAUT's novels
— 377, A Son of the Plains
— 410, The Great Meadow
— 444, The Blockhouse on the Prairie
— 450, King Noanett
— 509, Members of the Family
— See also *Boone, Daniel*
Pioneers, The, 114
Pip, 233
Pipes, Tom, 441, Peregrine Pickle
Piping Hot, 517
Pirate, The, 426
Pirates and Buccaneers, 36, Trinity Bells
— 62, A Gentleman Adventurer
— 64, A Modern Buccaneer
— 134, Capt. Singleton
— 169, Black Bartlemy's Treasure, and sequel
— 170, Thomas the Lambkin
— 253, A High Wind in Jamaica
— 258, Captain Kettle
— 268, Moonraker
— 338, Benito Cereno
— 380, The Iron Pirate
— 400, Jacob and John
— 404, The Jewel of Ynys Galon, The Man at Odds
— 418, The Sea-Hawk
— 426, The Pirate
— 449, Treasure Island
— 450, The Ebb Tide
— See also *Kidd, Captain*
Pisa, 108, The Yellow Mask
— 297, Miss Meredith
Pit, The, 361
Pitcairn Island, 41, The Mutineer
Pitt, William, 24, Barry Leroy
— 196, The Heart of a Hero
— 288, Nancy Stair
— 297, Sir Jasper Carew
— 489, De Vere
Pittsburg, 96, Cardigan
Pizarro, 252, The Crimson Conquest

Plague, 4, Old St. Paul's
— 60, The Glory and Sorrow of Norwich
— 62, The King's Guerdon
— 70, London Pride
— 81, Daniel Herrick
— 133, Mad Barbara
— 134, Journal of the Plague Year
— 220, Red Eve
— 243, The Brave Men of Eyam
— 255, Sir Ralph Esher
— 325, Cherry and Violet
— 325, The Betrothed
— 334, The Painted Veil
— 342, The Wandering Jew
— 445, Voices in the Night
— 459, Lady Jem
Plague of Florence, 285, The Marriage of the Dead
Plague of Marseilles, 62, A Fair Martyr
Plague of Philadelphia, 76, Arthur Mervyn
Plain or Ringlets, 456
Plain Tales from the Hills, 281
Planter of Malata, The, 111
Plasher's Mead, 317
Plaski's Tunamont, 373
Platæa, 131, A Victor of Salamis
Plated City, The, 382
Platonism, 279, Hypathia
Plato's Dream, 484
Platt-Deutsch, 403, My Farming Days, In the Year '13
Plattner Story, The, 493
Playfellow, The, 330
Playthings and Parodies, 373
Pleasant History of John Winchcomb, see Jack of Newbery
Pleasant Ways of St. Médard, The, 279
Pleasing History, The, 224
Pleggett, Mr., 328, Japhet
Pleids, The, 203
Pleydell, Councillor, 424, Guy Mannering
Pliny the Younger, 103, To the Lions
— 309, The Last Days of Pompeii
Plot, The, 25
Plot Novels, see especially:
— 7, Grant ALLEN's novels
— 101, CHERBULIEZ' novels
— 108-9, Wilkie COLLINS's novels
— 112, "Hugh CONWAY's" novels
— 122, F. M. CRAWFORD's novels, *passim*
— 149-50, Conan DOYLE's novels
— 253, Cousins German
— 327-8, H. B. MARRIOTT-WATSON's novels
— 342, "H. S. MERRIMAN's" novels
— 365, G. OHNET's novels

Plot Novels (*contd.*): 369, E. Phillips OPPENHEIM's novels
— 378, J. PAYN's novels
— 388, POE's stories
— 512, Broken to Harness
— See also *Gothic Romance, Detective Fiction*, etc.
Plough of Shame, The, 503
Ploughing of Leacana-Naomh, The, 116
Plumed Serpent, The, 291
Plunder Pit, The, 442
Plunderers, The, 411
Plutocrat, The, 460
Plymouth, New England, 21, Jane AUSTIN's novels
— 271, Croatan
Plymouth Brethren, 139, Mary Lee
Poachers, 41, The Woodman
— 78, John MacNab
— 442, Jack the Outlaw
Poe, Edgar Allan, 440, Kennedy Square
Poema del mio Cid, 104
Poet and Merchant, 19
Poet and the Composer, The, 244
Poet and the Lunatics, The, 102
Poet at the Breakfast Table, The, 245
Poets and Dreamers, 214
Poet's Bazaar, A, 72
Poet's Diary, A, 21
Poet's Love, The, 3
Poet's Youth, A, 510
Poictesme, 85, J. B. CABELL's novels, *passim*
Point Counter Point, 257
Point of View, The, 264
Point of View, The, 386
Pointed Roofs, 405
Poirot Investigates, 103
Poison, 325
Poison Belt, The, 150
Poison Island, 397
Poison of Asps, The, 394
Poison Tree, The, 32
Poisoner, The, 127
Poitiers, 150, Sir Nigel
— 195, Captain Fracasse
— 292, Brakespeare
— 358, The Old Country
— See also *Hundred Years' War*
Poitou, 99, The Keynote
— 262, The Huguenot
Pokahontas, 113, My Lady Pokahontas
Pokorsky, 474, Rudin
Poland and Polish Character, 22, Red Cavalry
— 73, S.O.S.
— 90, Heirs
— 111, Prince Roman
— 139, Blue Roses
— 204, Taras Bulba
— 285, J. I. KRASZEWSKI's novels
— 303, Mother of God
— 342, The Vultures
— 429, The Governor of Kattowitz

Poland, and Polish Character (contd.): 483, The Sleeping Army
— 496, Vineta
— See also POLISH NOVELISTS
Polchester, 487, The Cathedral, Harmer John
Pole, Cardinal, 5, Cardinal Pole
— 49, The Queen's Tragedy
Pole, Lady Helen, 17, The Aristocrats
Pole, Wilfred, 339, Sandra Belloni
Poles, Misses, 339, Sandra Belloni
Polikushka, 467
POLISH NOVELISTS:
S. ASCHE, Else C. M. BENECKE (translator), M. CZAYKOWSKI, W. GASIO-ROWSKI, A. GLOWACKY, F. GOETEL, J. J. KRAS-ZEWSKI, Mme ORZESZKO, W. St. REYMONT, Marya RODZIEWICZOWNA, Mme RYGIER-NALKOWSKA, H. SIENKIEWICZ, J. WEYS-SENHOFF, S. ZEROMSKI
Politics and Politicians, 2, Democracy
— 3, Revelry
— 9, The Candidate
— 17, Senator North
— 17, Rulers of Kings, Rezánov, Ancestors
— 18, Gaspard Hauser
— 24, His Serene Highness
— 33, The Coat without Seam
— 38, The Princess's Private Secretary
— 43, H. BELLOC's novels
— 54-5, " G. A. BIRMING-HAM'S " novels, *passim*
— 73, S.O.S.
— 82, Through One Administration
— 84, The Power of the Dog
— 104, W. CHURCHILL'S novels
— 115, Satanstoe, and sequels
— 121, An American Politician
— 127, The Heriots, Sybilla
— 143, Mary G. DILLON's novels
— 143-4, DISRAELI's novels
— 157, F. P. DUNNE'S stories
— 161, Patronage
— 166, Changing Winds
— 171-2, L. FEUCHT-WANGER'S novels
— 173, Jonathan Wild (satire)
— 177, Daniele Cortis
— 178, Mr. Fleight
— 179, The Hon. Peter Stirling
— 183, The Wickerwork Woman, and following
— 205, A Common Story
— 215, An Uncrowned King, and sequel

Politics and Politicians (contd.): 216, Writ in Water, England hath Need of Thee
— 228, Oceana
— 230, Hogan, M.P.
— 238, The Memoirs of an American Citizen
— 240, Mainwaring
— 245, A Man of Mark
— 246, The King's Mirror, Quisanté
— 271-3, JÓKAI's novels
— 276, High Policy
— 297, Reuben Sachs
— 306, When All the World is Young
— 308, F. LYNDE's novels
— 308, Her Majesty's Rebels
— 309, The Caxtons
— 312, A Fair Saxon
— 316, Sonia, and sequel
— 318, The Washingtonians
— 320, Misther O'Ryan
— 322, MALLOCK's novels
— 351, Utopia
— 354, The Boroughmonger
— 362, The Fight for the Crown
— 378, Melincourt
— 379, Maid Marian
— 384, Joshua Craig
— 429, The Conquest of Rome
— 455, The Mad Professor
— 460, The Conquest of Canaan, In the Arena
— 472, TROLLOPE's novels, *passim*, especially the Phineas Finn Series
— 474, Rudin
— 480, John Verney
— 488, Marcella, and sequel
— 489, The Coryston Family, Tremaine, De Vere
— 494, The New Machiavelli
— 495, The World of William Clissold, The Autocracy of Mr. Parham
— 498, Chippinge, The Great House
— 515, The Mantle of Elijah
— 516-8, Rougon-Macquart Series
— See also names of politicians and events, also *Diplomats, Post-War Problems, Socialism, Utopias*, etc.
POLLACK, Rt. Hon. Sir F., see *sub nom.* MAITLAND Mrs. Ella, 321
Polly, 373
Polly of Parker's Rents, 278
Polly Oliver's Problem, 504
Polperro, see *Troy Town*, 396,
Polydore Marasquin, The Emotions of, 209
Polyglots, The, 197
Polynesia, 41, G. L. BECKE's novels

Polynesia (contd.): 77, Van Zanten's Happy Days
— 305, Taurua
— 386, Black, White, and Brindled
— 417, Far Wandering Men
— 444-5, De Vere STAC-POOLE's romances
— 449, Island Nights Entertainments
Polyphili Hypneroto-machia, 109
Pomerania, 336, Mary Schweidler, Sidonia
Pomeroy Abbey, 510
Pomona's Travels, 451
Pomp of the Lavilettes, The, 376
Pompadour, Mme de, 155, Memoirs of a Physician
Pompeii, 309, The Last Days of Pompeii
— 423, A Priestess of Isis
Pompey the Little, History of, 271
Ponce de Leon, 294, The Romance of the Fountain
Ponce de Leon, 388
Pond, The, 167
Pongo and the Bull, 43
Pons, Cousin, 29, Cousin Pons
Pontefract, 176, When Charles I was King, Mistress Spitfire
Ponthieu, Countess of, 352, The History of Over Sea
Pontiac, 126, The Heroine of the Strait
— 376, When Valmond came to Pontiac, A Sword of the Old Frontier
— 406, Wacousta
Pontifex, Ernest, 83, The Way of All Flesh
Poor, 45, Clayhanger and sequels
— 46, Riceyman steps
— 61, The Mob
— 95, The Forewarners
— 132, The Amazing Philanthropists
— 146, Poor Folk, The Insulted and Injured
— 169, Blade-o'-Grass
— 189, The Rogue in Love, The Golden Thread
— 206-7, GORKY's novels and tales
— 267, Ginx's Baby
— 277, B. KENNEDY's novels
— 285, Sasha, Gambrinus
— 299, One of Life's Slaves
— 322, The Individualist
— 323, Mary E. MANN's novels, *passim*
— 355, Rosa MULHOL-LAND's novels
— 359, NEXØ's novels
— 363, Islanders, Adrigoole
— 405, Mrs. RICE's stories
— 415, Death of a Nobody
— 419, A. F. SANBORN's stories

Poor (contd.): 432, Miriam Lucas
— 440, The Under-Dog
— 466, Dorrie
— 447, Miss Grace of All Souls'
— 485, Autobiography of a Charwoman
— 508, Paradise Row
— See also *London Poor, New York Poor, Paris Poor*
Poor Elizabeth, 223
Poor Folk, 146
Poor Law Guardians, 132, The Amazing Philanthropists
Poor Liza, 274
Poor Man, The, 50
Poor Man's House, A, 404
Poor Man's Pig, The, 259
Poor Miss Finch, 109
Poor Nobleman, The, 112
Poor Plutocrats, The, 272
Poor Relations, 317
Poor Scholar, The, 92
Poor Sons of a Day, 311
Poor White, 10
Poor Women, 248
POORTEN-SCHWARTZ, J. M. W. van der, see " MAARTENS, Martin," 310
Popanilla, 143
Pope, Alexander, 206, Veronica Playfair
— 308, Devereux
— 510, Esther Vanhomrigh
Popish Plot, 16, The Accuser
— 25, The Plot
— 50, Oddsfish
— 133, Mad Barbara
— 247, The Lady of Lyte
— 412, Whitefriars
— 426, Peveril of the Peak
Pope and Chappell, 138, Alice-for-Short
Pope of the Sea, The, 61
Pope's Mule, The, 129
Popinot, Judge, 27, The Commission in Lunacy
Popioli, 516
Poppæa, 160, Nero
Popular Legends, 468
Popular Tales, 160
Popular Tales from the Norse, 129
Porgy, 241
Porgy, Captain, 436, The Partizan, and sequels; Woodcraft, and sequels
Port Philip, 354, Rise of the Australian Wool Kings
Port Said, 315, North of Suez
Port Tarascon, 130
Porte étroite, La, 198
Portent, The, 313
Porteous Riots, 425, Heart of Midlothian
Porter, Commodore W. O., 35, Midshipman Farragut
Portion of Labour, The, 506
Portrait, The, 178
Portrait in a Mirror, 351
Portrait of a Lady, The, 263

Portrait of a Spy, 466
Portrait of Claire, 515
Portrait of Mr. W. H., The, 504
Portrait of the Artist as a Young Man, A, 273
Portrait of the Misses Harlowe, 14
Portreeve, The, 385
Portsmouth, 71, The Adventures of Lady Susan
— 267, The King's Yard
Portsmouth, Duchess of, 348, Nell Gwyn
Portugal, 62, The Sea Devils
— 275, For Braganza
— 366, Antonio
— See also PORTUGUESE NOVELISTS
PORTUGUESE NOVELISTS:
"S. Dinarte," J. M. Eça de Queiroz, V. de Lobeira, J. de Montemôr, F. de Moraes
Poruks, Jans, see Marshall, L. A. (tr.)
Position of Peggy Harper, The, 342
Positivism, 50, The Hampdenshire Wonder
— 68, The Night Cometh
— 322, The New Paul and Virginia
— 466, Marcelle Tinayre's novels
— 516–19, Zola's novels
Possessed, The, 147
Possession, 72
Posson Jone, 86
Post-Girl, The, 65
Posthumous Papers of the Pickwick Club, 140
'Postle Farm, 179
Postman Chris, 185
Postmaster, The, 395
Post-War Problems, 73, S.O.S.
— 128, The Misted Mirror
— 143, The Boundary Post
— 196, Futility
— 197, The Polyglots
— 198, Venetian Lovers
— 277, The Ninth of November
— 335, Bernard Quesnay
— 350, Open all Night
— 354, Defeat
— 422, Maria Capponi, and sequel
— 429, The Governor of Kattowitz
— 452, The Valley of Indecision
— 487, The Thirteen Travellers
Pot of Basil, The, 91
Pot-bouille, 517
Potocka, Countess, 400, Journeyman Love
Potop, 434
Potterat and the War, 481
Potterism, 311
Potter's House, The, 105
Potter's Thumb, The, 445
Pottery Towns, 45, A. Bennett's novels

Pottleton Legacy, The, 439
Potts, Algernon Sydney, 297, A Day's Ride
Pougachev Rebellion, 395, The Captain's Daughter
Pounce, Peter, 172, Joseph Andrews
Poundtext, 425, Old Mortality
Poupée, La, 189
Powell, Mary, 332, The Binding of the Strong
Power, 172
Power and the Glory, The, 376
Power of a Lie, The, 63
Power of the Dog, The, 84
Powers at Play, The, 382
Powhatan, 113, My Lady Pokahontas
Powys, Merthyr, 339, Sandra Belloni
Poyser, Mrs., 164, Adam Bede
Praet, Gerhard de, 401, The Cloister and the Hearth
Prague, 25, The Cardinal's Page
— 68, The Quest of Glory
— 72, Rubeni, The Kingdom of Love
— 262, Heidelberg
— 284, Gabriel
Prairie, The, 114
Prairie Folks, 192
Prancing Nigger, 175
Prästdottern, 145
Prästdotterns son, 145
Pratt Portraits, 188
Preacher and the King, The, 80
Preachers, Itinerant, 118, The Prophet of the Great Smoky Mountains
— 164, A Simple Art
— 164, Adam Bede
— 348, Into the Highways and Hedges
Précieuses, 345, Madeline
Precious Bane, 492
Precipice, The, 205
"Preedy, George," see "Bowen, Marjorie"
Pre-Historic Times, 150, The Lost World
— 243, The Master Girl
— 267, The Long Journey
— 282, Puck of Pook's Hill
— 303, Before Adam
— 410, In the Morning of Time
— 423, When Mammoths roamed the Frozen Earth
— 491, The Story of Ab
— 493, Tales of Space and Time
Prejudged, 348
Prelude (by Mansfield), 325
Prelude (by Nichols), 359
Presbyterians, 80, The Squireen
— 167, A Maid of the Manse
— 315, The Auld Meetin' Hoose Green

Presbyterians (contd.): 316, The Humour of Druid's Island
— See also *Covenanters, Kirk, Ministers*
President's Daughter, The, 71
Press-Gangs, see *Impressment*
Pressing Forward, 391
Prester John, 78
Prestige, 300
Preston Flight, 5
"*Pretender, The Old*," see *James Francis Edward*
"*Pretender, The Young*," see *Charles Edward Stuart*
Pretty Lady, The, 46
Pretty Michael, 272
Price, Fanny, 20, Mansfield Park
Price, Judge Slocum, 278, The Prodigal Judge
Price of Harness, The, 121
Price of Love, The, 46
Pride and Prejudice, 20
Pride of Jennico, The, 93
Pride of War, 266
Prideaux, William, 36, Friend Olivia
Priestess of Isis, The, 423
Priests, Abbés, 32, Bewitched
— 137, The Woman and the Priest
— 159, A Demoiselle of France
— 187, Father Clancy
— 189, The Fairy Doll
— 196, The Supreme Crime
— 210, The Christ of Toro
— 231, The Heretic of Soana
— 349, The Untilled Field, The Lake
— 364, G. O. Donovan's novels
— 431, My New Curate
— 432, Luke Delmege, The Blindness of Dr. Gray
— 440, Corban
— 480, Pepita Jiménez, Doña Luz
— 517, The Abbé Mouret's Transgression
— See also *Clergymen, Ministers*
Prim, Marshal, 342, The Velvet Glove
Primadonna, The, 123
Primaleon, 350
Prime Minister, The, 472
Prince Albrecht of Brandenburg, 360
Prince and Heretic, 68
Prince and the Page, The, 513
Prince and the Pauper, The, 476
Prince Baber and his Wives, 419
Prince Djalinak, 132
Prince Eugene and his Times, 355
Prince Hempseed, 252
Prince in Petto, A, 22

Prince Madog, Discoverer of America, 128
Prince of Balkistan, The, 479
Prince of Bohemia, A, 29
Prince of Court Painters, A, 377
Prince of Destiny, The, 421
Prince of Dreamers, A, 446
Prince of Good Fellows, A, 37
Prince of India, The, 486
Prince of Intrigue, A, 512
Prince of Lisnover, The, 404
Prince of Outlaws, 467
Prince Otto, 449
Prince Roman, 111
Prince Rupert the Buccaneer, 258
Prince Serbryani, 467
Prince's Darling, The, 69
Princes of the Stock Exchange, 358
Princess, The, 99, 100
Princess, The, 291
Princess Aline, The, 131
Princess and the Goblin, The, 313
Princess Casamassima, The, 264
Princess of Arcady, A, 236
Princess of Cleves, The, 286
Princess of Java, A, 242
Princess of the Moor, 326
Princess of Thule, A, 57
Princess Priscilla's Fortnight, The, 15
Princess Sophia, The, 48
Princess Tarakanova, The, 129
Princess Xenia, The, 327
Princess Zoubaroff, 174
Princess's Private Secretary, The, 38
Princess's Secrets, A, 28
Prinds Otto af Danmark, 258
Pringle Family, 191, The Ayrshire Legatees
Printer's Devil, 128
Printz, Governor, 401, In Castle and Colony
Priscilla's Spies, 55
Prisoner, The, 76
Prisoner, The, 190
Prisoner in Fairyland, A, 59
Prisoner in the Opal, 332
Prisoner of Mademoiselle, The, 409
Prisoner of the Caucasus, A, 467
Prisoner of Zenda, The, 246
Prisoner Who Sang, The, 63
Prisoners—Fast Bound in Misery and Iron, 103
Prisoners of Carisbrooke, The, 81
Prisoners of Hope, 270
Prisoners of War, 74, "Mr. Rowl"
— 385, The American Prisoner
— 518, The Downfall
Prisonnier chanceux, Le, 203
Prisonnière, La, 394

Prisons, 11, Seven Who were Hanged
— 103, Prisoners
— 115, The Guilty Man
— 148, Cousin Hugh
— 189, The Rogue in Love
— 304, The Sorrow of an Old Convict
— 308, The Gael, Paul Clifford
— 320-1, Xavier de MAISTRE's works
— 385, The American Prisoner
— 401, It is Never Too Late to Mend
— 413, Female Life in Prison
— 419, Picciola
— 429, On Guard
— See also *Fleet, Marshalsea,* and *Newgate Prisons; Convicts, Crime,* etc.
Private Life of Helen of Troy, The, 166
Private Life of Henry Maitland, The, 411
Private Memoirs and Confessions of a Fanatic, The, 244
Private Papers of Henry Ryecroft, The, 201
Private Secretary, The, 101
Private Theatricals, 252
Privateers, 114, Wing-and-Wing
— 424, Tom Cringle's Log
Privilege, 419
Privilege, Lord, 328, Peter Simple
Privy Seal, 178
Probation, 180
Problem Club, The, 374
Problem of the Sea, A, 445
Problematic Characters, 444
Problematische Naturen, 444
Probus, 489
Procession of Life, The, 479
Processionals, The, 351
Procurator of Judea, The, 183
Prodigal Judge, The, 278
Prodigal Son, The, 87
Prodigal's Brother, The, 318
Prodigy, The, 12
Professional Aunt, The, 495
Professional Prince, The, 268
Professor at the Breakfast Table, The, 245
Professor Hieronimus, 438
Professor's House, The, 95
Professor's Wife, The, 19
Profit Family, The, 480
Progress (by R. B. Cunninghame GRAHAM), 210
Progress (by Cynthia STOCKLEY), 450
Progress of Hugh Rendel, 390
Promessi Sposi, I, 325
Prometheus, 193, Twilight of the Gods

Prometheus (contd.): 444, Prometheus and Epimetheus
Prometheus and Epimetheus, 444
Promise, 434
Promise of Air, The, 59
Promise of Arden, 375
Promised Land, The, 389
Promised Land, The, 403
Promises of Alice, The, 137
Promos and Cassandra, The History of, 430
Proper Pride, 124
Prophet of Berkeley Square, The, 241
Prophet of the Great Smoky Mountains, The, 118
Prophetic Marriage, The, 133
Prophet's Reward, A, 452
Prose Poems, 475
Prose Tales, 395
Proscrits, Les, 30
Prosper Randoce, 101
Protestant, The, 71
Protestantism, 71, The Protestant
— 80, The Preacher and the King
— 130, The Evangelist
— 144, Lothair
— 332, A Lily of France
— 496, At the Altar
— 497, Francis Cludde
— See also *Anglicanism, Baptists, Calvinism, Dissenters, Huguenots, Presbyterians, Kirk, Wesleyanism,* etc.
Proud Flesh, 409
Proud Woman, A, 34
Proudie, Mrs., 471-2, The Barchester Novels
Provençal Novelist, Félix GRAS, 212
Provence, 4, The Diverting Adventures of Maurin, and sequel
— 18, Aucassin et Nicolette
— 91, The Story of Fifine
— 129, A. DAUDET's tales
— 139, The Hôtel du Petit-St. Jean
— 212, The Reds of the Midi, and sequels
— 268, The Milky Way
— 301, Aristide Pujol
— 302, The Town of Tombarel
— 493, Orgeas and Miradou
— 516, The Fortunes of the Rougons
— 517, The Conquest of Plassans
Provenzano the Proud, 199
Provost, The, 191
Prudence Palfrey, 6
Prue and I, 127
" PRUS, B.," see GLOWACKY, A., 203
Prusias, 160
Prussia, see *Berlin, Brandenburg, Franco-German War, Frederick the Great, Mecklenburg,* etc.

Prussian Officer, The, 290
Prussians on the Rhine, The, 156
Psmith, Journalist, 509
Psyche, 117
Psychic Stories, 45, The Glimpse
— 59, A. BLACKWOOD's novels and stories
— 123, Cecilia
— 136, DE LA MARE's novels and stories
— 138-9, DE MORGAN's novels
— 156, DU MAURIER's novels
— 156, The Corsican Brothers
— 157, Lord DUNSANY's stories
— 168, The Lost Stradivarius
— 251, Questionable Shapes, Between the Dark and the Daylight
— 259, All Men are Ghosts
— 265, The Soft Side, The Sacred Fount
— 281-2, R. KIPLING's stories, *passim*
— 293, Nonsense Novels (burlesque)
— 299, Weird Tales
— 313, Phantastes, The Portent
— 314, Sir Gibbie
— 315, The Hill of Dreams
— 341, Mosaics
— 347, Men and Ghosts
— 367, A Beleaguered City, A Little Pilgrim in the Unseen
— 368, The Wizard's Son
— 369, Widdershins, Ghosts in Daylight, The Painted Face
— 373, The Octave of Claudius, An Exchange of Souls
— 459, Barbara of the Thorn
— 480, The Enchanted Garden
— See also *Dual Personality, Ghost-Stories, Hypnotism,* etc.
Psychical Invasion, A, 59
Psycho-Analysis, 10, Sherwood ANDERSON's novels
— 51, J. D. BERESFORD's novels
— 128, Regiment of Women
— 140, A Soldier of Life
— 185, L. FRANK's novels
— 198, The Hidden City
— 198, GIDE's novels
— 213, Julian GREEN's novels
— 257, Those Barren Leaves, Point Counter Point
— 290-1, D. H. LAWRENCE's novels and stories
— 336, Come In, Blindman
— 357, L. H. MYERS' novels
— 423, SCHNITZLER's novels

Psycho-Analysis (contd.): 436-7, May SINCLAIR's novels
— 457, " SVEVO's " stories
— 495, The Secret Places of the Heart, Christina Alberta's Father
— 496, The Class Reunion, " Rebecca WEST's " novels
— 509, Look Homeward, Angel
— 511, Mrs. Dalloway
Psychological Analysis, Novels of, 10-11, ANDREEV's stories
— 12, The Flame of Life
— 63, Treacherous Ground, The Prisoner who Sang
— 67, BOURGET's novels
— 110-12, CONRAD's novels
— 112, Adolphe
— 137, F. DELL's novels
— 139, Mary Lee
— 146-8 DOSTOEVSKY's novels
— 162, " GEORGE EGERTON's " stories
— 162, The Deeps of Deliverance
— 164, " G. ELIOT's " novels, *especially* The Mill on the Floss
— 179, E. M. FORSTER's novels
— 224, Young Ofeg's Ditties
— 237, Linda Condon
— 250, W. D. HOWELL's novels
— 252, S. HUDSON's novels, *especially* A True Story
— 257, HUYSMANS's novels
— 263-6, Henry JAMES's novels
— 283, C. H. B. KITCHIN's novels
— 324, T. MANN's novels
— 326, Life of Marianne
— 357, J. M. MURRY's novels
— 393-4, PROUST's novels
— 403, F. REID's novels
— 414, Jean Christophe
— 415, The Soul Enchanted
— 428, A. D. SEDGWICK's novels
— 455, SUDERMANN's novels and stories
— 474-5, TURGENEV's novels and stories
— 490-1, WASSERMAN's novels
— 498, A Gift from the Grave, Sanctuary
— 499, Tales of Men and Ghosts, The Reef
— See also *Behaviourism, Psycho-Analysis*
Psychology, 325
Ptolemy Philometer, 158, The Sisters
Ptolemy II, 142, Tychiades
— 159, Arachne
Public School Life, 32, An Eton Boy's Letters
— 107, D. COKE's novels
— 248, Fathers of Men

Public School Life (contd.):
259, That Sort of Thing
— 359, Prelude
— 491, The Loom of Youth
— See also *Eton, Harrow, Rugby, Shrewsbury, School Life*
Puck, 372
Puck of Pook's Hill, 282
PUDDICOMBE, Mrs. B., see "RAINE, Allen," 399
Pudd'nhead Wilson, 476
Puget Sound, 9, The Heart of the Ancient Firs
Pugilism, 39, Lads of the Fancy
— 66, Lavengro
— 83, Iron Man
— 109, Man and Wife
— 150, Rodney Stone
— 292, G. A. LAWRENCE's novels
— 302, The Game
— 431, Cashel Byron's Profession
Pugs and Peacocks, 90
Puits de Sainte Claire, Le, 183
Pulse of Darkness, The, 360
Pultava, 235, A King and his Campaigners, The Charles Men
Punishment, 157
Punjab, 459, Romantic Tales of the Punjab
Purcell, Henry, 330, In the Choir of Westminster Abbey
Purcell Papers, The, 294
Purchase Price, The, 248
Purdah, 381, Missing!
Pure Gold, 415
Puritans and Puritanism, 52, For Faith and Freedom
— 57, In Far Lochaber
— 115, Satanstoe, and sequels
— 232-3, HAWTHORNE's novels and stories
— 250, Doctor Breen's Practice
— 254, A New England Cactus
— 319, Dagonet the Jester
— 330, Una Breakspear
— 441, Mary Paget
— 457, A Tale of a Tub
— 505, Mary E. WILKINS's stories
Purloined Letter, The, 388
Purple and Fine Linen, 419
Purple Cloud, The, 433
Purple Head, The, 395
Purple Jar, The, 160
Purple Jewel, The, 102
Purple Land that England Lost, The, 252
Purse, The, 26
Purser's Own Romance, The, 132
Pursuit of Dermot and Grania, The, 274
Pursuit of the Gilla Dacher, The, 274
Pursuit of the House-Boat, The, 31

Pusey, Dr., 322, The New Republic
Put Yourself in his Place, 402
Putois, 184
Puzzle Lock, The, 187
Puzzle of Jarbek, The, 34
Pwyll, Prince of Dyfed, 217
PYESKOV, A. M., see "GORKY, M.," 206
Pyetka, 10
Pyetushkov, 475
Pyrenees, 167, The Illusion
— 261, De l'Orme

"Q," see Sir A. T. QUILLER-COUCH
Quackinboss, 297, One of Them
Quadroons, 86, Madam Delphine
— 382, The Plated City
Quaker Grandmother, A, 86
Quakeress, The, 3
Quakers, 36, Friend Olivia
— 54, Nick o' the Woods
— 87, The Shadow of a Crime
— 134, Capt. Singleton, Roxana
— 144, The Making of Christopher Ferringham
— 177, The Royal Americans
— 243, Memoirs of a Person of Quality, As it Happened, Demi-Royal
— 252, A Dreamer of Dreams
— 345, Hephzibah Guinness, Hugh Wynne, The Red City
— 410, Down the O-hi-O
— 413, The Time of her Life
— 436, Sampson Rideout
— See also *Fox, George*
Quality of Mercy, The, 250
Quand le navire . . ., 415
Quarante-cinq, Les, 155
Quasi una Fantasia, 361
Quasimodo, 253, Notre-Dame de Paris
Quatre fils Aymon, Les, 181
Quatre-vingt-treize, 254
Quatres évangiles, Les, 519
Quebec, 8, A Soldier of Manhattan
— 53, Le Chien d'Or
— 70, The Quiberon Touch
— 126, In Treaty with Honour
— 196, The Heart of a Hero
— 236, Maria Chapdelaine
— 283, The Golden Dog
— 296, Con Cregan
— 319, The Span o' Life
— 376, The Trial of the Sword, The Seats of the Mighty, The Power and the Glory
— 397, Fort Amity
— See also *Wolfe, General*

Queechy, 490
Queed, 229
Queen Bee, The, 167
Queen Can do no Wrong, The, 109
Queen Cordila, 430
Queen-hoo Hall, 454
Queen Mary's Holdfast, 438
Queen Money, 283
Queen of Clubs, The, 501
Queen of Men, A, 363
Queen of Sheba, The, 6
Queen of Spades, The, 395
Queen of the Dawn, 220
Queen of the Woods, 464
Queen versus Billy, The, 371
Queen's Fillet, The, 432
Queen's Folly, 498
Queen's Hostage, The, 109
Queen's Maries, The, 337
Queen's Necklace, The, 155
Queens of Kungahälla, The, 286
Queen's Pleasure, The, 227
Queen's Quair, The, 239
Queen's Secret, The, 69
Queen's Tragedy, The, 49
Queen's Twin, The, 269
Queensland, 316, H. C. MACILWAINE's novels
Queenstown Heights, Battle of, 88, A Beautiful Rebel
Queer-Side Stories, 456
Quentin Durward, 426
Querrils, The, 19
Quest, The (by BAROJA), 35
Quest, The (by EEDEN), 162
Quest of Glory, The, 68
Quest of the Absolute, The, 30
Quest of the Golden Fleece, 152
Quest of the Golden Girl, The, 294
Question of Habit, A, 260
Question of Taste, A, 310
Questionable Shapes, 251
Quetzalcoatl, 291
Quiberon, Battle of, 62, Fortune's My Foe
— 70, The Quiberon Touch
Quiberon Touch, The, 70
Quick and the Dead, The, 395
Quick or the Dead, The, 409
Quickening, The, 308
Quicksilver, 171
Quiet Interior, 273
Quiet Lady, The, 316
Quiet Street, A, 371
Quietists, 49, The History of Richard Raynal, Solitary
Quilp, 140, Old Curiosity Shop
Quin, 405
Quincy Adams Sawyer, 387
Quinneys', 480
Quintus Claudius, 159
Quintus Fixlein, 407
Quinze Joies de Mariage, Les, 288
Quisanté, 246
Quisisana, 444

Quits, 460
Quixotry, Romances of, 129, Tartarin of Tarascon, and sequels
— 131, Perfervid
— 212, The Spiritual Quixote
— 295, The Female Quixote
— 297, A Day's Ride
— 350, Palmerin of England
— 441, Launcelot Greaves
— 503, Reason Triumphant over Fancy
Quo Vadis?, 435

R. J.'s Mother, 136
Rab Ráby, The Strange Story of, 272
Rabelais, François de, 154, Ascanio
— 432, Brave Earth
RABINOVITZ, S., see "SHALOM ALEKHEM," 430
RABON, Charles, 29, The Middle Classes, The Member for Arcis
Rabourdin, M., 28, Bureaucracy
Race of Castlebar, The, 289
Rachael Marr, 411
Rachel Lorian, 153
Racial Problems, 7, The Rev. John Creedy
— 17, Senator North
— 80, Brethren
— 86, Madame Delphine
— 223, Poor Elizabeth
— 237, Java Head
— 250, An Imperative Duty
— 268, The Elder Brother
— 446, The Hosts of the Lord
— See also *Colour Line, Half-Breeds, Miscegenation, Negroes*
Racing, see *Sporting Novels*
Racing Rivals, 208
Radetzky, Count J. W., 230, A Sereshan
Radicals, 164, Felix Holt
— 239, The Stooping Lady
— 244, HOLCROFT's novels
— 340, Beauchamp's Career
— See also *Chartists, Socialists*, etc.
Radisson, Pierre, 289, Heralds of Empire
Radomsky, 129, The Princess Tarakanova
Radziwill, 434, With Fire and Sword, and sequels
Radziwill, Prince, 129, The Princess Tarakanova
Raeburn, Luke, 307, Donovan, We Two
Raffles, 248, The Amateur Cracksman
Raftery, Blind (Poet), 84, Blind Raftery and his Wife Hilaria
— 214, Poets and Dreamers
Ragged Lady, 251
Ragged Messenger, The, 335
Raiders, The, 123
Railroad and the Churchyard, The, 56

Railway Children, The, 60
Railway Life, 222, The General Manager's Story
— 224, The Redemption of Kenneth Galt
— 236, John Goodchild
— 379, The Darlingtons
— 408, On Company's Service
— 518, The Monomaniac
Railway Man and his Children, The, 368
" RAIMOND, C. E.," see ROBINS, Elizabeth, 412
Rain before Seven, 293
Rain of Dollars, 397
Rainbow, The, 290
Rainbow's End, The, 40
Rajah's Diamond, The, 448
Raleigh, Sir Walter, 91, Where England Sets her Feet
— 243, The Splendid Knight
— 262, Arabella Stuart
— 426, Kenilworth
Ralph Darnell, 461
Ralph the Heir, 472
Ralph Wynward, 165
Ralstons, The, 122
Rambling Rector, The, 7
Rameau's Nephew, 142
Rameses II, 158, Uarda
Rameses XIII, 203, The Pharaoh and the Priest
Ramona, 260
Ramsbottom Letters, The, 245
Ramuntcho, 305
Ranching, see *Cowboys, Pioneers, Sheep-Farming*, etc.
Rançon, La, 466
Randvar the Songsmith, 299
Rangers, The, 465
Raoul, Gentleman of Fortune, 24
Raphael Sanzio, 341, The Forerunner
Rapp, Comte, 342, Barlasch of the Guard
Rappaccini's Daughter, 232
Rapparees, 31, The Denounced
— 365, In the Wake of King James
Rarahu, 304
Rare Luck, 408
Raskolnikov, 147, Crime and Punishment
RASPAGNETTO, G., see " ANNUNZIO, Gabriele d'," 11
Rasputin, 357, Rasputin
Rasputin, 357
Rasselas, 269
Rational Hind, The, 506
Rationalism, 164, The Felmeres
— 279, Two Years Ago
Ratisbon, 159, Barbara Blombery
Rat-Pit, The, 315
Rattlin, Jack, 441, Roderick Random
Rattlin the Reefer, 249

Räuberbande, Die, 185
Raven the Skald, 352, Three Northern Love-Stories
Ravenna, 188, Under Bayard's Banner
— 346, Barbarian Stories
— 473, The Siren
Ravenshoe, 280
Ravine, The, 99
Raw Material (by CANFIELD), 89
Raw Material (by GISSING), 201
Raw Youth, A, 148
RAWLINS, E., see " EUSTACE, Robert," 167
Ray, Martha, 349, The Rescue of Martha
Reading, 138, Thomas of Reading
— 314, A Legend of Reading Abbey
Ready-Money Mortiboy, 52
Real Adventure, The, 492
Real Charlotte, The, 443
Real Folks, 503
Real Gold, 171
Real Motive, The, 88
Real People, 51
Real People, The, 369
Real Thing, The, 264
Realization of Justus Moran, The, 93
Reason Triumphant over Fancy, 503
Reata, 196
Rebecca, 463, Rebecca and Rowena
Rebecca and Rowena, 463
Rebecca Drew, 129
Rebecca of Sunnybrook Farm, 504
Rebecca Riots, 260, The Sheep Stealers
— 348, Gate-Openers
Rebel, The (by BAILEY), 25
Rebel, The, 328
Rebel Generation, The, 9
Rebel Lady, The, 35
Rebelle, La, 466
Rebellen, 358
Rebels, The (by BODKIN), 63
Rebels, The (by NEUMANN), 358
Recha, 196
Recherché de l'absolu, L', 30
Reckless Lady, The, 198
Reckoning, The, 97
Recollections from Childhood, 123
Recollections of a Marker, 467
Recollections of Geoffrey Hamlyn, The, 280
Reconstruction Period, 86, John March, Southerner
— 145, The Leopard's Spots, and sequels
— 202, The Voice of the People
— 224, Henry Bourland
— 230, Clarence
— 268, The Elder Brother
— 373, Red Rock
— 427, Throckmorton
— 470, A Fool's Errand, and sequel

Reconstruction Period (contd.): 499, Expiation (by WHARTON)
Recovery, 498
Recruit, The, 112
Rector, The, 366
Rector of Reigi, The, 274
Rector of St. Luke's, The, 52
Rector of Wyck, The, 437
Rectory Children, The, 346
Recuyell of the Historyes of Troye, 294
Red and Black, 53
Red as a Rose is She, 75
Red Axe, The, 124
Red Badge of Courage, The, 120
Red Bob of the Bismarcks, 217
Red Book of Hergest, 405
Red Bridal, A, 497
Red Cap, The, 477
Red Cavalry, 22
Red City, The, 345
Red Cockade, The, 497
Red Cravat, The, 432
Red Dawn, 35
Red Eve, 220
Red Hand of Ulster, The, 55
Red House, The (by BALZAC), 30
Red House, The, 60
Red Knight, The, 514
Red Laugh, The, 11
Red Lily, The, 183
Red Man and White, 508
Red Man's Revenge, The, 26
Red Neighbour, The, 159
Red Planet, The, 302
Red Pottage, 103
Red Reaper, The, 448
Red Republic, The, 96
Red River Expedition (Canada), 26, The Red Man's Revenge
— 318, The Prodigal's Brother
Red Rock, 373
Red Room, The, 453
Red Rose, The, 385
Red Rover, The, 114
Red Rowans, 445
Red Rust, 90
Red Saint, The, 133
Red Sand, 453
Red Seal, The, 196
Red Shirts, The, 194
Red Sky at Morning, 278
Red Soil, 198
Red Spider, 208
Red Starosta, The, 273
Red Velvet, 398
Red Wagon, 440
Redburn, 338
Redcoat Captain, 368
Redeemer, The, 40
Redemption, 40
Redemption of Kenneth Galt, The, 224
Redemption of Morley Darville, 316
Redemption of Tycho Brahe, The, 72
Redesdale, 277, The Keeper of the Rede

" REDFIELD, Martin," see BROWN, Mrs. Alice
Redgauntlet, 426
Reds of the Midi, The, 212
Redskins, The, 115
Reed Anthony, Cowman, 2
Reef, The, 499
Reef of Stars, The, 445
Reel of No. 8, A, 180
Reflections of a Married Man, 212
Reflections of Ambrosine, The, 203
Reform Bill Agitation, 58, Perlycross
— 144, Lothair
— 164, Felix Holt
— 239, The Stooping Lady
— 247, Because of the Angels
— 379, The Misfortunes of Elphin
— 442, The Plunder Pit
— 464, Trewern
— 498, Chippinge
— See also *Chartists*
Reformation, 4, Windsor Castle, The Lancashire Witches
— 74, A Friar Observant
— 120, The Last Abbot of Glastonbury
— 155, The Page of the Duke of Savoy
— 159, In the Blue Pike, Barbara Blomburg
— 231, Klytia, Father Maternus
— 243, The Sword of the Lord
— 261, Darnley
— 325, Anne Askew
— 360, Prince Albrecht of Brandenburg
— 401, The Cloister and the Hearth
— 432, Brave Earth
— See also *Huguenots, Luther, St. Bartholmew, Massacre of, Henry VIII, Mary, Charles V, Philip II*, and other contemporary monarchs and persons
Reformer's Wife, The, 446
Refugees, The, (by DOYLE), 149
Refugees, The, 500
Regamna, 293
Regamon, 293
Regency of George IV, 68, Yesterdays
— 71, A Royal Ward
— 150, Rodney Stone, The Fall of Lord Barrymore
— 328, Twisted Eglantine
— 400, A Lady of the Regency
Regent, The, 46
Regent's Daughter, The, 154
Regiment Irlandia, 319, Spanish John, Lally of the Brigade
Regiment of Women, 128
Regimental Legends, 508
Regimental Life, 223, Traseaden Hall

Regimental Life (*contd.*): 281–2, KIPLING's tales, *passim*
— 285, The Duel
— 455, The Song of Songs
— 508, "Mrs. J. S. WINTER's" novels
— 517, The Honour of the Army
— See also *Conscription, Military Stories, War,* and names of wars, battles, etc.
Regina, 455
Reginald Cruden, 402
Reginald Dalton, 302
Regulus, 283
Rehearsal, The, 207
Reign of Law, The, 8
Reign of the Doll, The, 506
Reincarnation, 59, Incredible Adventures, Julius le Vallon, The Garden of Survival
— 177, The Woman
— 281, The Finest Story in the World, The Brushwood Boy
— 511, Orlando
Reine des Bois, 464
Reine Margot, La, 154
Reine Ysabeau, La, 483
Rejuvenation, 18, Black Oxen
Rejuvenation of Miss Semaphore, The, 159
Relacciones de la Vida del Escudero Marcos de Obregón, 167
Religieuse, La, 142
Religion, 8, The Increasing Purpose
— 37, The Sacred Hill
— 47, The Orchard Pavilion
— 54, The Monk and the Hangman's Daughter
— 61, The Shadow of the Cathedral
— 63, The Great Hunger
— 64, The New Temple
— 87, The Christian, The Eternal City, The Prodigal Son, The White Prophet, The Eternal Question
— 102, The Ball and the Cross, Manalive
— 104, The Inside of the Cup
— 115–16, Marie CORELLI's novels
— 119, The School for Saints, and sequel
— 145, Saint Magloire
— 145, Deacon Bradbury
— 165, John Paget
— 177, The Patriot, and sequels, Leila
— 183, Balthasar, Mother of Pearl, The Wall of Saint-Clare
— 184, Penguin Island
— 186, Illumination
— 187, Holyland, The Pastor of Poggsee
— 191, Peace
— 197, Gesta Romanorum

Religion (*contd.*): 249, The Sheep-Fold
— 251, The Leatherwood God
— 257, En Route, and sequels
— 259, Philosophers in Trouble
— 271, Michael Firth
— 276, Green Apple Harvest
— 286, The Miracles of Antichrist, From a Swedish Homestead, Jerusalem
— 312, Told by an Idiot
— 313–14, G. MACDONALD's novels, especially Annals of a Quiet Neighborhood, and The Seaboard Parish
— 318, "Ian MACLAREN's" novels
— 322, The New Republic, The New Paul and Virginia
— 332, A Woman of Yesterday
— 341, The Death of the Gods, and sequels
— 374, The Marquis of Penalta
— 395, A Soldier's Pilgrimage
— 416, ROSEGGER's novels
— 423, Olive SCHREINER's novels
— 433, John Inglesant, A Teacher of the Violin, Blanche
— 457, Maitland of Laurieston, A Tale of a Tub
— 459, The Temple on the Hill
— 466, Marcelle TINAYRE's novels
— 484, L'Ingénu, Zadig
— 487, The Cathedral
— 487–8, Mrs. H. WARD's novels
— 492, The House in Dormer Forest
— 494, Marriage
— 495, The Soul of a Bishop, The World of William Clissold
— 518, Lourdes
— 519, Rome, Paris
— See also *Agnosticism and Faith, Atheism, Baptists, Buddhism, Calvinists, Christianity, Covenanters, Dissenters, Kirk, Monks, Mormons, Paganism, Priests, Quakers, Religious Allegory, Roman Catholics, Shakers, Swedenborgianism, Unitarians, Wesleyans,* etc.
Religious Allegory, 11, The Philosopher's Stone
— 81, J. BUNYAN's works
— 274, The Castle
— 506, War in Heaven
Religious Mania, 26, The Devil's Half-Acre

Religious Mania (*contd.*): 37, The Sacred Hill
— 130, The Evangelist
— 278, Skipper Worse
— 517, The Abbé Mouret's Transgression
Religious Orders, see *Monks,* etc.
Remarkable Rocket, The, 504
Remarkable Wreck of Thomas Hyke, The, 450
Remedy against Sin, A, 336
Remember the Alamo, 36
Remembrance of Things Past, 393
Reminiscences of Sir Barrington Beaumont, Bart., The, 39
Renard, 333, The Royal Sisters
Renaud, 181, The Four Sons of Aymon
Renaud de Montauban, 181
Renaudie, 155, The Two Dianas, and sequel
Rendelen, Thomas, 56, The Heritage of the Kurts
René, 99
René, King of Provence, 427, Anne of Geierstein
— 513, Two Penniless Princesses
Renée Mauperin, 205
Renée Néré, 107
Rennes, Battle of, 133, Bertrand of Brittany
Renunciations, 492
Repentant Sinner, The, 469
Republic of Fools, The, 503
Republic of the Southern Cross, The, 77
Reputed Changeling, A, 513
Réquisitionnaire, Le, 30
Rescue of Martha, The, 349
Responsibility, 3
Rest Cure, The, 335
Rest Harrow, 240
Restitution of the Bride, The, 249
Restoration, see *Charles II*
Resurrection, 469
"Resurrection Men," 346, Mansie Wauch
Resurrection of Mr. Wiggett, 260
Return, 113
Return, The (by CONRAD), 110
Return, The (by DE LA MARE), 136
Return, The (by MAUPASSANT), 334
Return of Imray, The, 281
Return of Joanna, 396
Return of Mary O'Murrough, 355
Return of Sherlock Holmes, 149
Return of the Native, The, 225
Return of the Soldier, 496
Return to Nature, A, 356
Returning Wave, The, 44
Reuben Sachs, 297
Reubeni, 72

Rêve, Le, 518
Revelation, 54
Revelry, 3
Revels of Orsera, The, 416
Revenge, 41, G. L. BECKE's stories, *passim*
— 73, Wuthering Heights
— 79, God and the Man
— 87, A Son of Hagar, The Bondman
— 121, To Leeward
— 154, The Count of Monte Cristo
— 249, Howard the Halt
— 276, Son of Judith
— 388, The Last Master of Carnandro
— 398, Foe-Farrell
— 483, Mathias Sandorf
— See also *Vendettas*
Revenues of the Wicked, The, 401
Reverberator, The, 264
Revere, Paul, 451, Guert Ten Eyck
Rev. John Creedy, The, 7
Revivalists, Religious, 298, Elmer Gantry
— 464, The Forerunner
— See also *Preachers, Methodists,* etc.
Revolt of Man, The, 52
Revolt of the Angels, The, 184
Revolt of the Fishermen, The, 428
Revolt of the Netherlands, 24, Raoul, Gentleman of Fortune
— 68, I will Maintain, and sequels; A Knight of Spain; Prince and Heretic, and sequel
— 112, The Year of Miracles
— 116, The Master Beggars of Belgium
— See also *Belgium, Flanders, Holland, William the Silent,* etc.
Revolution, 51
Revolution in Tanner's Lane, The, 502
Revolution of 1848, 166, A Man of the People
— 187, Debit and Credit
— 272, Eyes like the Sea
— 307, The Storm Bird
— 403, My Farming Days
— 444, Problematic Characters
— 516, Mysteries of Marseilles
— 516–8, The Fortunes of the Rougons
— See also *Hungarian Revolution, Italian Revolution*
Revolutionary Novels, see *Communism, Natural Man, Social Reform, Socialism,* etc.
Revolving Lights, 405
Reward of Virtue, The, 403
Rewards and Fairies, 282
Reynolds, Sir Joshua, 462, Miss Angel
Rezánov, 17

Rhiannon, 217, Pwyll, Prince of Dyfed
Rhine, 19, The Country House on the Rhine
— 37, The Countess Tekla, The Swordmaker
— 262, Heidelberg
Rhineland Heritage, The, 422
Rhoda Fleming, 339
Rhode Island, 254, A New England Cactus
Rhodes, Cecil, 411, The Colossus
Rhymer, The, 311
Ribbon Men, 92, Rody the Rover
RICE, James, see BESANT, Sir W., 52
Riceyman Steps, 46
Rich Man's Daughter, A, 354
Rich Young Man, The, 18
Richard I, 53, Westminster Cloisters
— 239, Richard Yea-and-Nay
— 270, The Fortunes of Garin
— 391, The Unhurrying Chase
— 336, The Assassins
— 425, Ivanhoe
— 426, The Talisman
— 513, The Little Duke
— See also *Crusade, Third*
Richard II, 112, Long Will
— 359, The New June
— See also *Peasants' Revolt*
Richard III, 25, The Merchant Prince
— 69, Dickon
— 262, The Woodman
— 313, Confessions of Richard Plantagenet
— 369, Crouchback
— 424, Beatrix of Clare
— 449, The Black Arrow
Richard Baldock, 329
Richard Cable, 208
Richard Carvel, 104
Richard Greenhow, 256
Richard Hartley, Prospector, 57
Richard Hawkwood, 333
Richard Kurt, 252
Richard, Myrtle, and I, 252
Richardson, Samuel, 463, The Virginians
Richelieu, 261
Richelieu, Cardinal, 62, Knighthood's Flower
— 154, The Three Musketeers, and sequels
— 261, Richelieu
— 275, The Cardinal's Past
— 360, Baron and Squire
— 483, Cinq-Mars
— 497, Under the Red Robe
Richmond (Virginia), 466, Suzette, Jack Horner
RICHTER, Jean Paul, see CARLYLE, 93
Ricroft of Withens, 456
Ridd, John, 58, Lorna Doone

" RIDDELL, John," see FORD, C., 178
Riddle, The, 136
Riddle of the Sands, The, 102
Rider in Khaki, The, 207
Riel, Louis, see *Red River Expedition*
Rienzi, 309
Riflemen of the Ohio, The, 9
RIGGS, Mrs. G. C., see " WIGGIN, Kate D."
Right of Way, 385
Right of Way, The, 131
Right of Way, The (novel by PARKER), 376
Right off the Map, 347
Right Stuff, The, 233
Rill from the Town Pump, A, 232
Rimini, 256, The Mastiff of Rimini
Rinconete and Cortadillo, 96
Ring in the New, 502
Ring o' Rushes, 80
Ringan Gilhaize, 191
Ringby Lass, A, 41
Ringer, The, 485
Rinuccini, 174, The Chances of War
Rio Medio, 112, Romance
Rip Van Winkle, 258
Riquelme, Marta, 252, El Ombú
Riquette, 184
Rise and Fall of César Birotteau, The, 28
Rise and Glory of the Westell-Browns, 358
Rise of David Levinsky, The, 86
Rise of Silas Lapham, 250
Rise of the Australian Wool Kings, 354
Rising Tide, The, 137
Risler aîné, 129, Fromont Junior and Risler Senior
RITCHIE, Lady, see THACKERAY, Anne, 461
Ritratto del Diavolo, Il, 38
Rival Heirs, The, 120
Rivalités, les, 27
Rivals, The, 115
Riven Bonds, 496
River, The, 385
River of Life, The, 285
Riverita, 374
Riverman, The, 501
Rivet in Grandfather's Neck, The, 85
Riviera, 241, La Marchesa
— 310, Dorothea
— 322, A Romance of the Nineteenth Century
Roach Hole, 285
Road, The, 380
Road Knight, 199
Road to Avalon, 132
Road to Calvary, The, 467
Road to Frontenac, The, 343
Road to Heaven, The, 42
Road to Paris, The, 447
Road to the Open, The, 423
Roadmender, The, 168

Roads of Destiny, 389
Roads to Glory, 6
Rob Roy, 425
Robber Band, The, 185
Robber Caliph, The, 358
Robbery under Arms, 64
Robe de laine, La, 66
Robert III (of Scotland), 427, The Fair Maid of Perth
Robert of Normandy, 138, Thomas of Reading
Robert Annys, 343
Robert Elsmere, 487
Robert Emmet, 218
Robert Falconer, 314
Robert Helmont, 130
Robert Orange, 119
Robert Peckham, 34
Robert the Deuyll, 465
Robert Urquhart, 430
ROBERTSON, John Henry, see " CONNELL, John "
Robespierre, Maximilien, 6, The Ninth Thermidor
— 16, The Mysterious M. Dumont
— 235, Rose in the Mouth
— 495, A Marriage under the Terror
— See also *French Revolution*
Robin, 82
Robin Hood, 195, George à Green
— 262, Forest Days
— 344, Royston Gower
— 396, The Merry Adventures of Robin Hood
— 411, Robin Hood
— 425, Ivanhoe
Robin Hood (by G. P. R. JAMES), 262
Robin Hood, 411
Robin Linnet, 48
Robin the Prodigal, 512
Robinson, Anastasia, 340, Lord Ormont
Robinson, Dr. John, 44, A Volunteer with Pike
Robinson, Mary, 38, The Exquisite Perdita
— 183, The Red Lily
Robinson Crusoe, 133
Robsart, Amy, 426, Kenilworth
Rochefort, Henri de, 39, The Dayspring
Roches blanches, Les, 413
Rochester, 141, The Mystery of Edwin Drood
Rochester, Earl of, 62, The King's Guerdon
— 262, Arabella Stuart
Rochester, Mr. 73, Jane Eyre
Rockbound, 132
Rockies, 110, " R. CONNOR'S " stories
— 126, In the Brooding Wild, The Law of the Gun
Rocklitz, The, 69
Röda Rummet, 453
Rodeo, El, 210
Roden's Corner, 342
Roderick Hudson, 263
Rodman the Boatsteerer, 41

Rodman the Keeper, 511
Rodney Stone, 150
Rodolphus, 1
Rody the Rover, 92
Rodzina Polanieckich, 435
Roervig Sands, 51, The Bride of Roervig
Roger Drake, 492
Roger Malvin's Burial, 232
Roger of Wendover, 25, The King's Passion
Rogers, William, 240, Bendish
— 350, The Fudge Family in Paris
Rogers's Rangers, 88, Ben Comee
Rogozhin, 147, The Idiot
Rogue, The (by ALEMAN), 7
Rogue, The (by NORRIS), 362
Rogue Bartley, 80
Rogue Herries, 487
Rogue in Love, The, 189
Rogue's March, The, 248
Rogue's Tragedy, A, 91
Rohan, Henri de, 313, Yesterday's Tomorrow
Rohan, Jacques de, see *La Cloche, James de*
Rohan, Louis de, 62, Traitor and True
Roi des montagnes, Le, 1
Roi d'Ys, 148, They Went
Roi perdu, Le, 18
Roi the Fool, 353
Rois en exil, Les, 130
Roland, 44, For the White Christ
— 98, Charles the Grete
— 181, The Four Sons of Aymon
Roland, Madame, 297, Gerald Fitzgerald
Roland Blake, 345
Roland Cashel, 296
Roland Montrevel, 155
Roland von Berlin, Der, 7
Roland Yorke, 509
Rolf in the Woods, 429
Roll Call, The, 46
Roll-Call of the Reef, The, 397
Rolling Stone, A, 206
Rolls, Old, 368, The Ladies Lindores
Roman Catholics, 21-2, AYSCOUGH's novels
— 24, Casting of Nets
— 33, Cat's Cradle, Daphne Adeane
— 34, Robert Peckham
— 49, R. H. BENSON's novels
— 67, Divorce
— 95, Death Comes for the Archbishop
— 102, G. K. CHESTERTON's novels
— 105, Isabel C. CLARKE's novels
— 116, The Master Christian
— 142, The Debtor
— 144, Lothair
— 196, The Last Link
— 218, John Maxwell's Marriage

Roman Catholics (contd.): 230, Hogan, M.P., Christy Carew
— 256, Frederic Uvedale
— 257, En Route, and sequels
— 349, Evelyn Innes, and sequel
— 351, O'Donnel
— 356, Children of Tempest
— 359, Loss and Gain
— 433, John Inglesant
— 488, Helbeck of Bannisdale
— 489, Mrs. Wilfred WARD's novels
— 496, At the Altar
— See also *Modernism, Monks, Priests*, etc.
Roman comique, Le, 422
Roman de Croissant, Le, 255
Roman de la momie, Le, 195
Roman d'un enfant, Le, 304
Roman d'un jeune homme pauvre, Le, 172
Roman d'un spahi, Le, 304
Roman Hat Mystery, The, 396
Roman Mystery, A, 23
Roman Road, The, 277
Roman Singer, A, 121
Romance, 112
Romance of a Mummy, The, 195
Romance of a Plain Man, The, 202
Romance of a Poor Young Man, The, 172
Romance of a Spahi, The, 304
Romance of an Honest Woman, The, 101
Romance of Certain Old Clothes, 264
Romance of Dijon, A, 162
Romance of Dollard, The, 95
Romance of Fra Filippo Lippi, 9
Romance of Judge Ketchum, 479
Romance of Leonardo da Vinci, 341
Romance of Palombris and Pallogris, 25
Romance of the Cape Frontier, A, 346
Romance of the Forest, The, 399
Romance of the Fountain, 294
Romance of the Nineteenth Century, A, 322
Romance of the Nursery, A, 226
Romance of the Simple, A, 439
Romance of Two Worlds, A, 115
Romance of War, The, 211
Romance of Zion Chapel, The, 294
Romances of Old Japan, 373
Romances of the Lily, 12

Romances of the Pomegranate, 12
Romances of the Rose, 12
Romances of the West, 71
Romans à clef, see *Personal Scandal*
Romans des sept sages, Li, 430
Romans of Partenay, 15
Romantic, The, 437
Romantic Adventures of a Milkmaid, 226
Romantic Comedians, The, 202
Romantic Legends of Spain, 42
Romantic Passion of Don Luis, The, 322
Romantic Tales of the Punjab, 459
Romantic Tradition, The, 430
Rome, 519
Rome, Ancient, 21, Faustula
— 23, Virgilius
— 41, Gallus
— 53, A Hero in Wolf-Skin
— 60, Sonnica
— 84, Brother Saul
— 103, The Burning of Rome, The Crown of Pine
— 117, The Comedians
— 120, Æmilius
— 159-60, ECKSTEIN's novels
— 199, Kallistratus, Four Sons
— 201, Veranilda
— 262, Attila
— 309, The Last Days of Pompeii
— 337, The Gladiators
— 345, The Conquered
— 363, The Knight of the Cave
— 341, The Death of the Gods
— 383, The Satyricon
— 435, Quo Vadis ?
— See also *Christians, Early, Cæsar, Justinian, Julius the Apostate*, and other names of emperors
Rome, Mediæval and Renaissance, 122, Pietro Ghisleri
— 123, Cecilia
— 229, Theophano
— 231, Father Maternus
— 272, Manasseh
— 309, Rienzi
— 413, Tolla
— 414, Don Tarquinio
— See also *Borgias*, and names of popes, *Clement, Innocent, Julius III*, etc.
Rome, Modern, 22, A Prince in Petto
— 23, A Roman Mystery
— 33, Cat's Cradle, Comfortless Memory, The Coat without Seam
— 87, The Eternal City
— 89, Rough-Hewn

Rome, Modern (contd.): 121, Saracinesca, and sequels
— 133, The Lame Englishman
— 242, The Fruitful Vine, The Lighted Candles
— 272, Manasseh
— 297, Gerald Fitzgerald
— 410, Mademoiselle Mori
— 429, The Conquest of Rome
— 504, The Cabala
— 519, Rome
— See also *Garibaldi*
Romeo and Juliet, 31
Romeus and Juliet, 430
Romney, George, 330, The Parson's Daughter
— 488, Fenwick's Career
Romney Marsh, 276, Joanna Godden
Romola, 164
Roncesvalles, 98, Charles the Grete
Ronds-de-cuir, Messieurs les, 117
Ronkoff, 193
Ronsard, 377, Gaston de Latour
Rooke, Admiral, 62, Across the Salt Seas
Rookwood, 4
Room in Berlin, A, 54
Room With a View, A, 179
Rooney, Mrs. P., 296, Jack Hinton
Roosevelt, President, 104, Coniston
Roots, 515
Roots of the Mountains, The, 352
" ROPSHIN, V.," see SAVINKOV, B., 422
Roquefinette, 153, The Chevalier d'Harmental
Roquevillard, Les, 65
Rory O'More, 305
Rosa, Salvator, 117, The Company of Death
Rosa, 224
Rosa Alchemica, 513
Rosa Amorosa, 162
Rosalynd, 430
Rosalynde, 302
Rosamund, Fair, 91, Historical Vignettes
Rose and Ninette, 130
Rose and the Ring, The, 462
Rose Anstey, 186
Rose Dawn, The, 501
Rose d'Albret, 262
Rose Garden, The, 380
Rose in Bloom, 6
Rose in the Mouth, 235
Rose of Blenheim, A, 196
Rose of Dauphiny, The, 448
Rose of Disentis, The, 519
Rose of Dutcher's Coolley, 192
Rose of Joy, The, 174
Rose of Lone Farm, 234
Rose of Yesterday, A, 122
Rosedew, Parson, 58, Cradock Nowell
Roses, Wars of the, 180, In Steel and Leather

Roses, Wars of the (contd.): 262, The Woodman
— 449, The Black Arrow
— 513, Grizly Grisell
— See also *Henry IV, V, VI, and VII, Edward IV, Richard III*
Rosewood Door, The, 369
Rosicrucian, The, 466
" Ross, Martin," see SOMERVILLE, Miss E., 443
Rossetti, Dante Gabriel, 491, Aylwin
Rosslyn's Raid, 35
Roswitha, 166
Rothschild's Fiddle, 99, 100
Rôtisserie de la reine Pédauque, La, 183
Rouge dóu miejour, Li, 212
Rouge et le noir, Le, 53
Rough-Hewn, 89
Rough Road, The, 302
Roughing It at Home and Abroad, 476
Rougon-Macquart Series, The, 516-8
Rouher, Eugène, 517, His Excellency
Roumania, 259, The Bandits
— See also ROUMANIAN NOVELISTS
ROUMANIAN NOVELISTS :
Ion CREANGĂ, P. ISTRATI, L. REBRENEAU
Round Anvil Rock, 32, 33
Round Cape Horn, 151
Round the Corner, 89
Round the Horn Before the Mast, 305
Round the Red Lamp, 150
Rousseauism, 23, Hermsprong
— 244, HOLCROFT's novels
— 258, Nature and Art
— 309-10, LYTTON's novels
— 378, Melincourt
— 429, Obermann
— See also *Nature and the Natural Man*
Roux the Bandit, 98
Rover, The, 111
Rowena, 425, Ivanhoe
— 463, Rebecca and Rowena
Roweny in Boston, 389
Rowlandson's Oxford, 197
Roxana, 134
Roxy, 163
Roy, Richmond, 339, Harry Richmond
Royal Americans, The, 177
Royal Favour, 486
Royal Highness, 324
Royal Pawn of Venice, The, 475
Royal Road, The, 368
Royal Runaway, The, 248
Royal Sisters, The, 333
Royal Slave, The, 43
Royal Ward, A, 71
Royal Woman, The, 323
Royalty, 19, On the Heights
— 53, The Chartreuse of Parma
— 117, Majesty
— 130, Kings in Exile

Royalty (*contd.*): 178, His Eminence
— 227, Comedies and Errors
— 246, The King's Mirror
— 248, John of Jingalo, and sequel
— 285, The Countess Cosel, The Grand Manner
— 288, Little Jehan de Saintré
— 312, The Illustrious O'Hagan
— 324, Royal Highness
— 356, The Tale of Genji
— 407, Titan
— 479, The Prince of Balkistan
— See also names of Monarchs
Royston Gower, 344
Rubempré, Lucien de, 28, Lost Illusions, and sequel, A Harlot's Progress
Rubicon, 131, A Friend of Cæsar
Rudder Grange, 450
Rudder Grangers Abroad, The, 450
Rudel, 39, The Lady of Tripoli
Rudin, 474
Rue des Filles-Dieu, 56, 338
Rue with a Difference, 91
Rugby, 253, Tom Brown's Schooldays
Ruhe ist die erste Bürgerpflicht, 7
RUIZ, José M., see "AZORIN"
Rulers of Kings, 17
Rules of the Game, 501
Runaway, The, 99
Runaway Browns, The, 81
Runenberg, The, 93
Running Horse Inn, 432
Running Wild, 439
Runnymede and Lincoln Fair, 160
Rupert, Prince, 24, Colonel Stow
— 133, Orchards
— 258, Prince Rupert the Buccaneer
— 259, None So Pretty
— 313, Rupert, Yesterday's To-morrow
Rupert, By the Grace of God, 313
Rupert of Hentzau, 246
Rush, Dr., 345, Hugh Wynne
Rush for the Spoils, The, 517
Ruskin, John, 322, The New Republic
RUSSELL, Countess, see ARNIM, Gräfin von
Russell, William, Lord, 329, In the Service of Rachel, Lady Russell
Russell, William, 353, Forever Free
Russia, see *Russia Before the 19th Century, Russia in the 19th Century, Russian Character,*

Russia (continued): see *Russian Novelists, Russian Revolution of 1905, Russian Revolution of 1917 and the Soviet*, etc.
Russia before the 19th Century, 163, Egil's Saga
— 341, Peter and Alexis
— 366, Olaf Trygvason
— 434, With Fire and Sword, and sequels
— 461, On the Red Staircase, An Imperial Lover
— 467, A Prince of Outlaws
— 500, F. WHISHAW'S novels
Russia in the 19th Century, 17, Rezánov
— 86, The White Terror and the Red
— 101, Count Kostia
— 139, Véra
— 193, Petersburg Tales
— 206, The Ferry of Fate
— 215, Nikanor
— 231, Mademoiselle Ixe
— 268, Katya
— 342, The Sowers
— 381, The Footsteps of a Throne
— 508, Before Sunset
— See also *Crimean War, Petersburg, Russia, French Invasion of, Russian Character,* RUSSIAN NOVELISTS, *Russo-Japanese War, Russo-Turkish War*
Russia, French invasion of, 30, Farewell
— 71, The Sword Hand of Napoleon
— 111, The Warrior's Soul
— 129, Moscow in Flames
— 150, Adventures of Gerard
— 165, The Conscript
— 195, Vivandière
— 199, Gathering of Eagles
— 216, A Brother of Girls
— 284, Coronet
— 306, The Flames of Moscow
— 342, Barlasch of the Guard
— 381, The Great White Army
— 468, War and Peace
— 474, The Shalonski Family
Russian Character, 33, Half-a-Minute's Silence, Tinker's Leave
— 111, Under Western Eyes
— 193, Olive GARNETT'S novels
— 196, Futility
— 197, The Polyglots
— 210, S. GRAHAM'S novels
— 520, Sergent Grischa
— See also *Crimean War,* and references under *Russia*

Russian Gentleman, A, 5
RUSSIAN NOVELISTS: S. AKSAKOV, M. A. ALDANOV (LANDAU), L. N. ANDREEV, M. P. ARTSUIBASHEV, I. BABEL, Anna BRODSKY, V. BRYUSOV, I. A. BUNIN, A. P. CHEKHOV, E. N. CHIRIKOFF, G. P. DANILEVSKY, L. T. DOSTOEVSKAYA, T. M. DOSTOEVSKY, "O. DUIMOV," A. FADYEEV, V. M. GARSHIN, F. V. GLADKOV, N. V. GOGOL, I. A. GONCHAROV, "M. GORKY," D. V. GRIGORÓVICH, N. GUBSKY, S. GUSSIEV ORENBURGSKY, Ilya ILF and E. PETROV, J. KALLINIKOV, N. M. KARAMZIN, V. KATAEV, M. KOMROFF, V. KOROLENKO, G. J. KOSTROMITIN, P. N. KRASNOV, A. I. KUPRIN, L. LEONOV, M. Y. LERMONTOV, V. LIDIN, I. LUKASH, N. LYESIKOV, D. MEREZHKOVSKY, I. F. NAZHIVIN, V. NEMIRÒVITCH-DANTCHENKO, Irene NEMIROVSKY, A. NEVYEROV, Irina ODOEVTSEVA, R. ORLOVSKY, M. OSSORGIN, I. L. PEREZ, A. S. PUSHKIN, M. E. SALTUIKOV, B. SAVINKOV, "O. SCHUBIN," "SHALOM 'ALEKHEM," B. SOKOLOV, "F. SOLOGUB," Count A. TOLSTOY, A. N. TOLSTOY, L. N. TOLSTOY, "Eugenia TUR," I. TURGENEV, "V. VERESAYEV," V. V. VERESHCHAGIN, Lidia VESELITSKAYA, E. ZAMYATIN, V. E. ZHABOTINSKY
— See also COURNOS, J., 117
— See also TOLLEMACHE, Mrs. B. L., 467
Russian Proprietor, A, 467
Russian Revolution of 1905, 16, Tales of the Revolution
— 80, The Village
— 422, What Never Happened
— 443, The Old House, The Created Legend
Russian Revolution of 1914, 341, December the Fourteenth
Russian Revolution of 1917, and Russian Soviet, 97, The Crimson Tide
— 117, Short Stories out of Soviet Russia
— 168, The Nineteen
— 198, Red Soil
— 202, Cement
— 295, The Thief
— 299, The Apostate
— 357, Rasputin
— 358, Tashkent

Russian Revolution of 1917, and Russian Soviet (*contd.*): 370, GUSSIEV ORENBURGSKY'S novels
— 371, A Quiet Street
— 383, Where will you Fall?
— 416, Flight Without End
— 442, The Crime of Dr. Garine
— 467, The Road to Calvary
— 486, The Secret City
Russian Schoolboy, A, 5
Russian Silhouettes, 100
Russian Tales by Karamsin, 274
Russo-Japanese War, 11, The Red Laugh
— 33, Tinker's Leave
— 312, "S. McCALL'S" novels
Russo-Turkish War, 26, In the Track of the Troops
— 193, Stories by GARSHIN
— 481, The War Correspondent
Ruth, 194
Ruth, the Woman who Loved, 359
Ruthenia, 196, Dorothea GERARD'S stories
— See also *Galicia*
"RUTHERFORD, Mark," see WHITE, W. H., 502
Ruthven, 239, The Queen's Quair
Rutledge, Ann, 22, The Soul of Ann Rutledge
Ruyter, Michel de, 315, The Dutch in the Medway
Rye, 48, The Oakleyites
— 178, The Half Moon
— 275, Starbrace
— 400, The Apprentice, Tales of Rye Town, Morlac of Gascony
— 463, Denis Duval
— See also *Cinque Ports*
Rye-House Plot, 50, Oddsfish
— 412, Whitefriars

S.O.S., 73
Sa maîtresse et moi, 391
Saarbrück, Battle of, 96, Lorraine
Sabbath Breaker, The, 515
Sabina, Empress, 158, The Emperor
Sable and the Girl, The, 498
Saccard, Aristide, 517, The Rush for the Spoils
Sacco-Vanzetti case, 438, Oil!, Boston
Sachem, 435
Sacheverell Case, 4, St. James's
Sack of Shakings, A, 79
Sackville, Lord George, 271, Chrysal
Sacred Cup, The, 77
Sacred Fount, The, 265
Sacred Hill, The, 37
Sacred Tree, The, 356
Sacrifice, 466
Sacrifice, The, 140

Sad Horn Blowers, The, 10
Sadie's Conquest, 54
SADYK PASHA, see CZAY-
    KOWSKI, Michael, 127
Safety Match, A, 234
Saga of Olaf Trygvason,
    The, 366
Saga om en saga, 287
Sagas (Modern), 283, Seven
    Brothers
— 286, Gösta Berling
— 417, Singoalla
— See also Icelandic Sagas,
    Norwegian Sagas
Sagas Retold, 240
Saghalien Convict, The, 284
Saguna, 422
Saguntum, 60, Sonnica
Sahara, 242, Barbary Sheep
Sahib's War, A, 282
Saïd the Fisherman, 387
Sailor Tramp, A, 277
Sailors of Fortune, 315
Sailor's Return, The, 193
Saint, A, 67
Saint, The (by FOGAZZARO),
    177
Saint, The (by MEYER), 343
St. Barbe, 144, Endymion
St. Bartholomew's Day Mas-
    sacre, 68, " William, by
    the Grace of God——"
— 113, For Henri and
    Navarre
— 124, The White Plumes
    of Navarre
— 154, Marguerite de Valois
— 203, The Lucky Prisoner
— 262, The Man-at-Arms
— 341, Chronicle of the
    reign of Charles IX
— 377, Gaston de Latour
— 497, The House of the
    Wolf, Count Hannibal
— 507, The Knight of the
    Needle Rock
— 513, The Chaplet of
    Pearls
St. Christopher's Day, 14
St. Clair, General Arthur, 9,
    The Wilderness Road
— 448, The Heritage
St. George and St. Michael,
    314
St. Germain, 44, Barbara
    Rebell
— 261, Richelieu
— 396, The Blue Pavilions
St. Gothard, 272, Dr. Du-
    mány's Wife
Saint Helena, 6
Saint Hercules, 14
St. Ives, 449
St. James's, 4
St. John's Eve, 204
St. Lawrence River, 23,
    D'ri and I
— See also Quebec
St. Leger, Col. Barry, 423,
    The Son of a Tory
St. Leon, 203
St. Louis, 104, The Crisis
Saint Magloire, 145
St. Martin's Eve, 509
St. Martin's Summer, 418
St. Mawr, 291
St. Michael, 496

St. Mungo's City, 478
St. Nicholas' Eve, 408
St. Paul's Cathedral, 330,
    Under the Dome of
    St. Paul's
St. Paul's School, 317,
    Sinister Street
St. Peter's Umbrella, 344
St. Quentin, 155, The Two
    Dianas
St. Ronan's Well, 426
Saint Sebastian, 285
St. Vitus Day, 210
Saint's Progress, 190
" Saki," see MUNRO, H. H.,
    355
Saladin, 270, The Fortunes
    of Garin
— 336, The Assassins
— 426, The Talisman
Salamis, 131, A Victor of
    Salamis
Salammbô, 175
Salathiel, the Immortal, 125
Saldar, Countess de, 339,
    Evan Harrington
Salem, 36, The Black Shil-
    ling
— 348, Maids of Salem
Salem Chapel, 366
Salem Kittredge, 382
Salisbury, 329, Under Salis-
    bury Spire
— 436, Sampson Rideout
— 471-2, Barchester novels
Sally, a Sequel, 105
Sally, a Study, 105
Sally Cavanagh, 278
Sally Dows, 230
Salm, 24, His Serene High-
    ness
Salmagundi, 258
Salt, 361
Salthaven, 261
Saltire, Lord, 280, Raven-
    shoe
Saltonstall Gazette, The, 321
SALTUIKOV, M. E., see also
    TOLLEMACHE, Mrs. B.
    L., 467
Salute to Adventurers, 78
Salvagia, 210
Salvation of a Forsyte, The,
    189, 190
Salzburg, 128, Felicitas
Sam Lawson's Oldtown
    Fireside Stories, 452
Sam Lovel's Camps, 413
Sam of Sorrow Corner, 385
Sampson, Dominie, 424,
    Guy Mannering
Sampson Rideout, Quaker,
    436
Samson and Delilah, 291
Samson the Nazarite, 516
Samuel Boyd of Catchpole
    Square, 169
Samuel Brohl and Partner,
    101
Samuel the Seeker, 438
San Celestino, 21
San Domingo, 62, The
    Hispaniola Plate
San-Felice, La, 156
San Francisco, 17, Ameri-
    can Wives and English
    Husbands

San Francisco (contd.) : 18,
    Sisters-in-Law,   Dor-
    mant Fires
— 151, Quong Lung
— 171, The Cat and the
    Cherub
— 361, Brass, F. NORRIS'
    stories, Kathleen NOR-
    RIS' novels
— 409, Proud Flesh
San Gabriel, Battle of, 93,
    Captain Courtesy
San Sebastian, 398, Cor-
    poral Sam
Sanatorium Life, 224, Chap-
    ter the Last
— 227, Ships that Pass in
    the Night
— 324, The Magic Mountain
— 394, A Gift of the Dusk
— See also Hospital Life,
    Medical Life
Sancta Paula, 382
Sanctuary, 498
Sand, George, 357, Con-
    fessions of a Child of
    the Century
— 400, Journeyman Love
— 452, The Nightingale
Sand and Cactus, 41
Sand-Man, The, 244
Sandeau, Jules, 420, Valen-
    tine
Sandford and Merton, 132
Sandford of Merton, 107
Sanditon, 21
Sandoval, 42
Sandra Belloni, 339
Sandwich, John Montague,
    4th Earl of, 271, Chrysal
— 349, The Rescue of
    Martha
Sandy, 405
Sandy Married, 113
Sanger Family, 277, The
    Constant Nymph
— 278, The Fool of the
    Family
Sangre y Arena, 61
Sanine, 16
Sanpriel, 394
Sans famille, 322
Sanseverina, Duchess, 53,
    The   Chartreuse   of
    Parma
Santee River, 436, Wood-
    craft, and sequels
Sant' Ilario, 121
Santal, 174
Santiago, 61, Martin Rivas
Santo, Il, 177
Santon Barsisa, 475
" SAPPER," see MCNEILE,
    C., 320
Sappho, 158, An Egyptian
    Princess
Sappho, 130
Sara Crewe, 82
Sara Videbeck, 8
Saracens, 98, Charles the
    Grete
— 229, Theophano
— See also Crusades
Saracinesca, 121
Saragossa, 342, The Velvet
    Glove
— 382, Saragossa

Saragossa, 382
Sarah Eden, 448
Sarah Tuldon, 3
Sarah Tuldon's Lovers, 3
Saratoga, 8, The Sun of
    Saratoga
— 251, An Open-Eyed Con-
    spiracy
Sarchedon, 337
Sard Harker, 331
Sardinia, see SARDINIAN
    NOVELISTS
SARDINIAN
            NOVELISTS :
    " Grazia DELEDDA," S.
    FARINA
Sardonic Tales, 483
Sargasso Sea, 377, The
    Passage of the Barque
    Sappho
Sarpi, Fra Paolo, 381,
    Signors of the Night
— 475, The Golden Book of
    Venice
Sarsfield, General P., 31,
    The Boyne Water
— 353, Memoirs of Gerald
    O'Connor
Sasha, 285
Sashka Jigouleff, 11
Saskatchewan, 54, Sadie's
    Conquest
Satan Mekatrig, 515
Satanella, 337
Satan's Diary, 11
Satanstoe, 115
Satire, 11, Satan's Diary
— 12, The Tinted Venus, A
    Fallen Idol, Lyre and
    Lancet
— 14, Aristocracy
— 15, Vera, Love, Expia-
    tion
— 15, Friendship's Garland
— 42, Molinoff
— 43, H. BELLOC's novels
— 51,   The   Jervaise
    Comedy, Seven Bobs-
    worth
— 55, The Red Hand of
    Ulster
— 77, V. Brown's novels
— 83, Erewhon, and se-
    quel ; The Way of All
    Flesh
— 85, J. B. CABELL'S
    works, passim
— 89, Windmills
— 96, Don Quixote
— 102, G. K. CHESTERTON'S
    novels
— 117, The Bureaucrats
— 127, Comical History
    . . . of the Worlds of
    the Moon and the Sun
— 129-30, A. DAUDET'S
    novels
— 135, " E. M. DELA-
    FIELD'S " novels
— 141, Hard Times, Little
    Dorrit
— 142, Rameau's Nephew
— 143, Ixion, The Infernal
    Marriage
— 143, Sybil
— 144, Tancred
— 145, Saint Magloire

Satire (contd.): 146, Manhattan Transfer, The 42nd Parallel
— 148, South Wind
— 157, F. P. DUNNE's stories
— 166, J. ERSKINE's novels
— 167, C. EVANS's novels
— 171, Miss FERRIER's novels
— 172, The Secret of Happiness
— 173, A Journey from this World to the Next, Jonothan Wild
— 175, Bouvard and Pécuchet
— 178, Mr. Fleight
— 182-4, "A. FRANCE's" novels and stories
— 201, In the Year of Jubilee
— 203, Transport
— 204, Dead Souls
— 205, Oblomov
— 210, R. B. Cunninghame GRAHAM's stories
— 221-2, T. C. HALIBURTON's stories
— 223, Shallow Soil
— 248, John of Jingalo, and sequel
— 251, A Traveller from Altruria, Through the Eye of a Needle
— 256-7, A. HUXLEY's novels and stories
— 258, Salmagundi, A History of New York
— 264, The Bostonians
— 267, Ginx's Baby
— 274, The Embezzlers
— 288, The Fifteen Comforts of Marriage
— 290, Pilgrimage, Youth Went Riding
— 293, S. B. LEACOCK's stories
— 295, The Female Quixote
— 295, Gil Blas, The Bachelor of Salamanca
— 295, Balaoo
— 298, At the Sign of the Blue Moon, and sequel, Sinclair LEWIS's novels
— 300, Committed to his Charge
— 306, The True History
— 308, Simple Simon
— 310, M. MAARTEN's novels, *passim*
— 311-12, Miss MACAULAY's novels
— 322, MALLOCK's novels
— 323, Berlin, The Patrioteer
— 338, The Confidence-Man
— 339, MEREDITH's novels
— 343, The Vision of Mac Conglinne
— 345, The Ghosts of their Ancestors
— 347, A Hind let Loose, Right Off the Map

Satire (contd.): 347, Persian Letters
— 351, Utopia
— 355, H. H. MUNRO's sketches
— 364, King Goshawk
— 366, Piccadilly, Altiora Peto
— 373-4, Barry PAIN's stories, *passim*
— 378-9, PEACOCK's novels
— 383, The Satyricon
— 396, QUEVEDO Y VILLEGAS' novels
— 398, RABELAIS' works
— 399, Travels of Baron Münchausen
— 404, Reynard the Fox
— 410, Jingling in the Wind
— 419, The Gollovlev Family
— 419, The Edwardians
— 422, The Comical Romance
— 435, Without Dogma
— 438, Before the Bombardment, Dumb Animal
— 441, SMOLLETT's novels
— 453, G. S. STREET's novels
— 456, Queer-Side Stories
— 457, A Tale of a Tub
— 462, The Yellowplush Papers, The Book of Snobs, The History of Samuel Titmarsh
— 473, The Widow Barnaby, and sequels
— 476-7, "Mark TWAIN's" stories
— 484, VOLTAIRE's tales
— 494, Kipps, Tono-Bungay
— 495, The Autocracy of Mr. Parham
— 498, The Descent of Man
— 501, The West End, Mr. Strudge
— 503, The Republic of Fools
— 515, We
— See also *Gulliverian Satire*, *Lucianic Satire*, *Parodies*, *Picaresque Romances*, *Personal Scandal*
Saturday's Child, 361
Satyricon, The, 383
Saucy Arethusa, The, 97
Savages, see *Africa, Education of Savages, Malay, Polynesia*, etc.
Savarus, Albert, 27, Albert Savarus
Saverne, 166, A Man of the People
Savoie, 65, A Mind Awakened
— 66, The Woollen Dress, Footprints Beneath the Snow, Annette and Philibert
— 91, A Rogue's Tragedy
— 262, The Brigand

Savoie (contd.): 399, The Romance of the Forest
Savonarola, 68, The Carnival of Florence
— 164, Romola
— 285, St. Sebastian
— 341, The Forerunner
— 452, Agnes of Sorrento
SAVOYARD NOVELIST: Xavier de MAISTRE
Sawdust, 196
Sawyer, Bob, 140, Pickwick Papers
Saxe, Marshal, 428, Franczka
Saxe Holm's Stories, 260
Saxons, 165, Fated to Win
— 512, Elfwin
— See also *Alfred the Great, Edwin, Edwy, Harold, Norman Conquest*
Saxony, 69, The Rocklitz
Sayings and Doings, 245
Sayings of Grandmamma, 203
Scanderbeg, see *Iskander Bey*
Scandinavia, see *Denmark, Norway, Sweden, Iceland*, and DANISH NOVELISTS, etc.
Scapegoat, The, 87
Scaramouche, 418
Scarborough, 65, Bella
Scarlet Banner, The, 128
Scarlet Coat, The, 416
Scarlet Letter, The, 232
Scarlet Nest, 300
Scarlet Pimpernel, The, 370
Scarlet Sister Mary, 383
Scarpe al Sole, Le, 347
Sceaux Ball, The, 26
Scènes de la vie de Bohème, 356
Scenes from Common Life, 469
Scenes of Clerical Life, 163
Schatzhaus des Königs, Das, 486
Schell, Dr., 488, Eleanor
Schlafende Heer, Das, 483
Schleswig-Holstein, 187, G. FRENSSEN's novels
Schloss, Das, 274
Schlump, 422
Schmaltz, Lowell, 298, The Man who Knew Coolidge
Schmelzle's Journey to Flaetz, 93
SCHMIDT, Otto E., see "ERNST, Otto," 166
SCHMITZ, Ettore, see "SVEVO, Italo," 457
Schmucke, 92, Cousin Pons
Scholar Gipsies, 78
Scholar of his College, A, 108
Schomburg, Marshal, 262, The Huguenot
Schönberg-Cotta Family, The, 98
Schönbrunn, Treaty of, 120, Schönbrunn
Schönbrunn, 120
Schöne Richterin, Die, 470
School across the Road, The, 107

School for Saints, The, 119
School for Wives, The, 198
School Life, 12, Vice Versâ
— 43, Tales of Greyhouse
— 170, Julian Home
— 280, Stretton, The Harveys
— 282, Stalkey & Co.
— 319, Young Barbarians
— 330, Emmy Lou
— 385, The Human Boy, and sequel
— 390, Hugh Rendel
— 402, T. B. REED's stories
— 475, Godfrey Martin, and sequel
— 487, Jeremy at Crale
— See also *College Life, Schoolmasters*, and names of schools, *Eton, Harrow, Shrewsbury*, etc.
School Life, 469
School Scenes, 469
Schoolmaster, The, 455, Mysteries of Paris
Schoolmaster, The, 100
Schoolmasters, 129, Little Good-for-Nothing
— 163, The Hoosier Schoolmaster
— 165, Kanga Creek
— 270, Dr. Congleton's Legacy
— 443, The Little Demon
— 486, Mr. Perrin and Mr. Traill
— 493, Love and Mr. Lewisham
— 495, The Undying Fire
Schoolmistress, The, 100
Schooner California, The, 151
Schuyler Family, 177, The Royal Americans
Schwarzwälder Dorfgeschichten, 19
Schwestern, Die, 158
Schwestern von Prag, Die, 214
Scientific Romances, 90, The Absolute at Large, Krakatit
— 127, The Comical History . . . of the Worlds of the Moon and the Sun
— 150, The Lost World, The Poison Belt, The Maracot Deep
— 277, The Tunnel
— 432, Frankenstein
— 433, The Lord of the Sea, The Purple Cloud
— 482-3, VERNE's novels
— 493-5, H. G. WELLS's novels, *passim*
— 512, The World Below
— See also *Imaginary Voyages, Utopias*
Scilly Isles, 305, A Man of Moods
— 331, Miranda
— 398, Major Vigoureux
Score, The, 321

Scotland before the 19th Century, 68, Yester-days
— 78, John Burnet of Barns, Witch Wood
— 104, Court Cards
— 123, CROCKETT's novels
— 191, GALT's novels
— 424-6, SCOTT's novels
— See also *Covenanters, Kirk, Jacobites, Mary Queen of Scots, Scottish War of Independence,* and names of monarchs and famous characters
Scotland's Heir, 153
SCOTT, G. F., see "HAL-SHAM, JOHN," 222
SCOTT, Hugh Stowell, see "MERRIMAN, H. S.," 342
Scott, Thomas, 456, Haw-buck Grange
Scottish Cavalier, The, 211
Scottish Character, 26, Ven-geance is Mine
— 77, The House with the Green Shutters
— 114, The Leather-Stock-ing Tales
— 160, Cressy and Poic-tiers
— 280, Austin Elliot
— 314, All Smoke
— 444, Gallow's Orchard
— 452, Elmslie's Drag-Net, A Prophet's Reward
— 504, Penelope's Experi-ences in Scotland
— See also *Highlands, Scot-land,* SCOTTISH NO-VELISTS
Scottish Chiefs, The, 389
SCOTTISH NOVELISTS: A. ALLARDYCE, Sir A. BALFOUR, Sir J. M. BAR-RIE, W. BLACK, J. J. BELL, D. W. BONE, G. B. BROWN, J. BUCHAN, R. W. BUCHANAN, R. CLELAND, Marie CORELLI, S. R. CROCKETT, J. DA-VIDSON, G. N. DOUGLAS, Winifred DUKE, R. M. FERGUSSON, Susan E. FERRIER, Jane and Mary FINDLATER, J. GALT, R. B. Cunninghame GRAHAM, J. GRANT, Elizabeth HAMILTON, Lord Ernest HAMILTON, "Ian HAY," J. HOGG, Matilda HOPE, Violet JACOB, H. JOHNSTON, A. LANG, Sir T. D. LAUDER, R. LEIGHTON, J. G. LOCKHART, "A. M'AULAY," G. MACDON-ALD, R. MACDONALD, W. MCFEE, R. MACHRAY, R. W. MACKENNA, Agnes M. MACKENZIE, C. MAC-KENZIE, H. MACKENZIE, W. C. MACKENZIE, "Ian MACLAREN," Sarah MAC-NAUGHTEN, C. MCNEILE, Sir H. E. MAXWELL,

SCOTTISH NOVELISTS (*contd.*): D. S. MELDRUM, J. MEN-ZIES, D. M. MOIR, Mrs. MOLESWORTH, J. MOORE, R. J. MUIR, N. MUNRO, Rosalind MURRAY, F. J. NIVEN, "Christopher NORTH," Margaret OLI-PHANT, Major J. RICH-ARDSON, W. ROBERTSON, Michael SCOTT, Sir W. SCOTT, "G. SETOUN," W. SHARP, Sir J. SKEL-TON, Flora Annie STEEL, Catherine STEUART, J. A. STEUART, R. L. STEVEN-SON, M. C. STIRLING, "J. STRATHESK," "An-nie SWAN," "G. TRAV-ERS," "Sarah TYTLER," Lucy WALFORD
Scottish Stories, 210
Scottish War of Independ-ence, 4, The Days of Bruce
— 335, The Chevalier of the Splendid Crest
— 389, The Scottish Chiefs
— 427, Castle Dangerous
Scoundrel, The, 366
Scourge of God, The, 62
Scout, The, 436
Scouts, 47, Who Goes There ?, A Friend with the Countersign
— 248, Stonewall's Scout
— 436, The Scout
— See also *Espionage*
Scowcroft Critics, The, 2
Scruples, 106
Scythrop, 379, Nightmare Abbey
Sea, 41, G. L. BECKE's stories
— 58, The Maid of Sker, Mary Anerley
— 79, F. T. BULLEN's novels
— 151, The Cruise of the *Wild Duck*
— 248, The Unknown Sea
— 254, Toilers of the Sea
— 268, Tom Fool, Many Latitudes
— 304, My Brother Yves, An Iceland Fisherman
— 315, MCFEE's novels
— 337, Mardi
— 360, E. NOBLE's novels
— 377, J. E. PATTERSON's novels
— 440, Caleb West
— 469, Old Junk, Gallions Reach
— See also *Fisherfolk, Mer-cantile Marine, Nautical Stories,* etc.
Sea, The, 277
"*Sea Beggars,*" see *Gueux*
Sea Captain, The, 24
Sea Comedy, A, 410
Sea Devils, The, 62
Sea-Gull, The, 84
Sea-Hawk, The, 418
Sea King, The, 442
Sea Lady, The, 493

Sea Puritans, 79
Sea-Raiders, The, 493
Sea Spray, 79
Sea Urchins, 260
Sea Whispers, 261
Sea-Wolf, The, 302
Sea Wrack, 79
Seaboard Parish, The, 314
Seacliff, 134
Seal of Silence, The, 109
Sealers, 302, The Sea-Wolf
Seamy Side of History, The, 29
Search Party, The, 55
Seaside Tragedy, A, 30
Seaton's Aunt, 136
Seats of the Mighty, The, 376
Seattle, 9, The Heart of the Ancient Firs
Seaward Lackland, 459
Sebastian Strome, 232
Sebastian von Storck, 377
Second Blooming, The, 195
Second Cecil, The, 273
Second Choice, The, 151
Second-Class Passenger, The, 197
Second Generation, The, 384
Second Home, A, 27
Second Jungle Book, The, 282
Second Marriage, 344
Second Report . . . of Faus-tus, 170
Second Sight, 69, The Spae-Wife
— 368, The Wizard's Son
Second Story, The, 445
Second Thoughts, 75
Second to None, 212
Second Wife, The, 326
SECONDAT, C. L. de, see MONTESQUIEU, Baron de, 347
Seconde, La, 108
Secret Agent, The, 111
Secret Battle, The, 237
Secret Bread, 268
Secret City, The, 486
Secret du précepteur, Le, 101
Secret in the Hill, The, 90
Secret of Father Brown, The, 102
Secret of Happiness, The, 172
Secret of Narcisse, The, 207
Secret of the Island, The, 482
Secret of the North Sea, A, 200
Secret of the Tower, The, 247
Secret Orchard, The, 94
Secret Places of the Heart, The, 495
Secret Rose, The, 513
Secret Sharer, The, 111
Secret Societies, 29, The Seamy Side of History
— 176, Vestigia
— 309, Zanoni
— See also *Anarchists, Camorra, Fenians, Ku Klux Klan, Land League, Mafia, Nihil-ists, Rapparees, Rib-bonmen.*

Secret Societies (contd.): Shanavests, Thugs, United Irishmen, Whiteboys
Secret Son, The, 153
Secret Witness, The, 258
Secret Woman, The, 385
Secrets de la Princesse de Cadignan, les, 28
Sedan, Battle of, 96, Lor-raine
— 281, Valentin
Sedgemoor, Battle of, see *Monmouth's Rebellion*
Sedley, Sir Charles, 348, Nell Gwyn
Seed-time and Harvest, 403
Seeds, 10
Seen and Heard before and after 1914, 174
Seeta, 461
Seething Pot, The, 54
Segelfoss Town, 224
SEGRAIS, Jean Regnauld, see *sub nom.* LA FAY-ETTE, Mme de, 286
Seigneur de Beaufoy, The, 152
Seine, 130, La Belle Niver-naise
Seine englishe Frau, 453
Seithenyn, 379, The Mis-fortunes of Elphin
Sejanus, 209, Neæra
Selah Harrison, 320
Selam, 354
Select Conversations with an Uncle, 493
Selected Polish Tales, 44
Selected Tales of the Genii, 500
Self-Made Countess, A, 508
Selkirk, Alexander, 133, Robinson Crusoe
Sellars, Colonel, 477, The Gilded Age, The Amer-ican Claimant
Selous, F. C., 219, Allan Quatermain
Selwyn, George, 243, High Treason
Selwyn, Bishop G. A., 64, War to the Knife
— 421, The Greenstone Door
SEMEDAWIIZ, V. V., see "VERESAYEV, V."
Semeur, Le, 179
Semi-attached Couple, The, 160
Semiramis, 337, Sarchedon
Senator North, 17
SENECA, L. Annæus, 160, Nero
Sens de la mort, Le, 68
Sensation Novels, see *Detec-tive Stories, Ghost-Stories, Magic, Super-natural,* etc.
Sensation Novels, 229
Sense and Sensibility, 20
Sense of the Past, The, 266
Sensitive Plant, A, 196
Sentimental Education, The, 175
Sentimental Journey, A, 447

Sentimental Studies, 118
Sentimental Tommy, 37
Sentimentalism, 37, Tommy and Grizel
— 74, The History of Lady Julia Mandeville
— 162, Rosa Amorosa
— 204, The Sorrows of Werther, Wilhelm Meister's Apprenticeship
— 294, The Quest of the Golden Girl
— 318, H. MACKENZIE'S novels
— 320-1, Xavier de MAISTRE'S works
— 326, Life of Marianne
— 339, Sandra Belloni, and sequel (satire)
— 371, To a Nun Confess'd
— 406, S. RICHARDSON'S novels
— 447, STERNE'S novels
— 452, Immensee
— Refer also to *Kailyard School, Pastorals*
Sentimentalists, The (by BENSON), 49
Sentimentalists, The (by PIER), 387
Sentry, The, 307
Separate Room, The, 336
Separation, 382
September, 458
Septimus, 301
Septimus Felton, 233
Seraphica, 313
Seraphita, 30
Serapion Brothers, The, 244
Serapionsbrüder, Die, 244
" Serapis," 338, Israel Potter
Serapis, 159
Serenus, 295
Sereshan, A., 230
Serf, The, 218
Serfs, see *Slavery*
Serge Panine, 365
Serious Wooing, The, 119
Sermon sous Louis XIV, Un, 80
Serre de l'aigle, La, 365
Servant of the King, A, 216
Servant of the Public, A, 247
Set of Six, A, 111
Set of Village Tales, A, 118
Seth Jones, 165
Seth's Brother's Wife, 186
Settlers at Home, 330
Sevastapol, 468
Seven, Bobsworth, 51
Seven Brothers, 283
Seven Champions of Christendom, The History of the, 269
Seven Days Darkness, 218
Seven Dials, 171, A Little World
Seven Dreamers, 439
Seven for a Secret, 492
Seven Men, 42
Seven Nights, The, 182
Seven Poor Travellers, The, 141

Seven Scots Stories, 173
Seven Streams, The, 133
Seven who were Hanged, The, 11
Seven Wise Masters, The, 430
Seven Years War, 118, The Story of Old Fort Loudon
— 439, Kindred
— 448, A Gendarme of the King
— 463, Barry Lyndon
— See also *Frederick the Great*
Seventeen, 460
Severance, 106
Severn River, 404, The Man at Odds
Severns, The, 433
Sevier, John, 104, The Crossing
Seville, 374, Sister Saint Sulpice
— 396, Pablo de Segovia
Sewanie, University of, 165, The Durket Sperret
Sex Problems, 11, The Child of Pleasure
— 16, Sanine
— 44 The Yoke of Pity
— 51, J. D. BERESFORD'S novels
— 54, Revelation
— 57, Absalom's Hair
— 61, Woman Triumphant
— 63, A Pilgrimage
— 80, The Son, Mitya's Love
— 86, A Yellow Aster
— 88, Three Strange Lovers
— 115, Henriette
— 117, Ecstasy, Eline Vere
— 128, The Misted Mirror
— 128, Regiment of Women
— 130, Rose and Ninette
— 147, The Eternal Husband
— 148, South Wind, Mrs. DOWIE'S novels
— 151-2, DREISER'S novels
— 157, The Natural Mother
— 162, Fantasias
— 179, The Child of Chance
— 185, The Story of Mary Dunne
— 186, Brother and Sister
— 194, Ruth
— 195, Mademoiselle de Maupin
— 201, The Odd Women
— 203, Fidelity
— 209, R. de GOURMONT'S novels
— 213, J. GREEN'S novels
— 222, The Well of Loneliness
— 226, Tess of the D'Urbervilles
— 236, Fiesta
— 248, Poor Women
— 273, JOYCE'S novels
— 290-1, D. H. LAWRENCE'S novels
— 294, A Note in Music
— 299, Stephen Escott
— 317, Vestal Fires

Sex Problems (contd.): 318, Extraordinary Women
— 322, A Romance of the Nineteenth Century
— 326, The Bachelor Girl
— 327, The Dewpond
— 334, A Coquette's Love
— 343, The Honey Bee
— 344, The Dangerous Age, The Governor
— 363, Lost and Saved
— 391, A Woman's Tragedy, The Don Juanes
— 393, Cities of the Plain
— 394, The Captive
— 415, The Soul Enchanted, Lucienne, and sequels
— 423, A. SCHNITZLER'S novels
— 429, Matilde SERAO'S novels
— 434, In Vain
— 436-7, May SINCLAIR'S novels
— 438, Love's Pilgrimage, Damaged Goods, Sylvia, and sequel
— 441, The Island
— 453-4, STRINDBERG'S stories
— 455, The Indian Lily
— 490, Oberlin's Three Stages
— 494, Ann Veronica, The Passionate Friendship
— 495, The Secret Places of the Heart, The World of William Clissold
— 507, Dandelion Days, and sequels
— 516-19, ZOLA'S novels, *passim*
— See also *Divorce, Feminism, Marriage, Psycho-Analysis*, etc.
Seymour, Jane, 4, Windsor Castle
Seymour, William, 262, Arabella Stuart
Seymour Charlton, 335
Seys, R. A. W., see WOODSEYS, R. A., 127
Sforza, Galeazzo Maria, 91, A Jay of Italy
Sforzas, 239, The Love Chase
— 418, Love at Arms
Shabby-Genteel Story, A, 463
Shadow Captain, The, 284
Shadow in the Rose Garden, 290
Shadow Line, The, 111
Shadow of a Crime, The, 87
Shadow of a Throne, The, 234
Shadow of a Titan, The, 492
Shadow of Allah, The, 411
Shadow of Ashlydyat, The, 509
Shadow of Love, The, 466
Shadow of Quong Lung, The, 151
Shadow of the Cathedral, The, 61

Shadow of the Cross, The, 464
Shadow of the Shark, The, 102
Shadow of the Sword, The, 79
Shadow of Victory, The, 402
Shadowed !, 44
Shadowless Man, The, 98
Shadowy Bourne, 408
Shadowy Third, The, 202
Shaftesbury, 1st Earl of, 412, Whitefriars
Shakers, 250, The Undiscovered Country
— 504, Susanna and Sue
Shakespeare, William, 47, Master Skylark
— 109, The Queen's Hostage
— 113, My Lady Pokahontas
— 273, In Burleigh's Days, and sequel
— 426, Kenilworth
— 442, The Great Age
— 446, A Gentleman Player
Shakespeare's Christmas, 397
Shakespeare's Library, 430
Shakespeare's Sources, 13, Apollonius of Tyre
— 30, Le Novelle
— 34, Barlaam and Josaphat
— 197, Gesta Romanorum
— 213, Pandosto
— 223, Hamlet in Iceland
— 302, Rosalynde
— 326, The Heptameron of Civil Discourses
— 374, The Palace of Pleasure
— 430, Shakespeare's Library
— 465, Early English Prose Romances
Shallow Soil, 223
Shalonski Family, The, 474
Shame, 121
Shame of Motley, The, 418
Shamela, 172
Shameless Wayne, 456
Shanavests, 31, John Doe
Shanghaied, 361
Shannon River, 159, Aliens of the West
" SHAPCOTT, Reuben," see WHITE, W. H., 502
Shape of Fear, The, 379
Shareholders, 261
Sharp, Becky, 462, Vanity Fair
" SHARP, Luke," see BARR, Robert, 121
SHARPE, William, see also *sub nom.* HOWARD, Blanche Willis
Shatov, 147, The Possessed,
Shaving of Shagpat, The 339
" SHCHEDRIN," see SALTUIKOV, M. E., 419
She, 219
She and Allan, 220
She Died and was Buried, 151

She that Hesitates, 142
She Walks in Beauty, 477
She Who Meant Well, 514
She-Wolves of Machecoul, 156
Sheaf of Bluebells, A, 370
Sheaf of Corn, A, 324
Sheep and the Goats, The, 324
Sheep Farming, 2, Tussock Land
— 97, Philosopher Dick
— 287, Sons o' Men
— 354, Rise of the Australian Wool Kings
Sheep Stealers, The, 260
Sheepfold, The, 249
Shelley, P. B., 143, Venetia
— 230, Beyond Man's Strength
— 335, Ariel
— 379, Nightmare Abbey
— 512, Mortal Image
Shenandoah, 113, Henry St. John, Surry of Eagle's Nest, and sequels, Colonel Fairfax
— 270, The Long Roll, and sequel
— 271, The Great Valley
— 376, My Lady of the North
— See also *American Civil War*
Shepherd of the People, The, 81
Shepherdess Felismena, The, 430
Shepherds in Sackcloth, 276
Shepherd's Warning, 293
Sherard, Mrs. R. H., see " Osgood, Irene," 371
Sheridan, R. B., 348, A Nest of Linnets
Sheriff of Dyke Hole, The, 126
Sheriffmuir, see *Jacobite Rebellion of* 1715
Sherlock Holmes stories, 149–50
Sherman, General, 104, The Crisis
Sherwood, Bishop of Durham, 178, The Young Lovell
Sherwood Forest, 262, Forest Days
— 344, Royston Gower
— See also *Robin Hood*
Shetland Isles, 36, Jan Vedder's Wife
Shibusawa, 2
Shining Ferry, The, 397
Shinju, 151
Ship of Coral, The, 445
Ship of Stars, The, 397
Ship Sails On, The, 215
Ship that Found Herself, The, 282
Ship that Sailed too Soon, The, 132
Shipowners, 278, Garman and Worse, and sequel
— 283, —— and Sons
— 360, E. Noble's stories
Ship's Company, 261

Ships that Pass in the Night, 227
Shirley, 73
Shirra, The, 318
Shirt of Nessus, The, 336
Shisen Wo Koete, 224
Shoes of Fortune, The, 356
Shoes of Gold, 152
Shogun's Daughter, The, 45
Shoot !, 388
Shopkeepers, 129, Fromont Junior and Risler Senior
— 480, Quinneys'
— 517, The Ladies' Paradise
— See also *Grocers*, *Tradesmen*, etc.
Shops and Houses, 458
Shorn Lamb, The, 302
Short History of Julia, A, 203
Short-Line War, The, 343
Short Cruises, 260
Short Stories by Mrs. Ghosal, 457
Short Stories out of Soviet Russia, 117
Shorter, C. K., 411, The Private Life of Henry Maitland
Shoulders of Atlas, The 506
Shrewsbury, 497
Shrewsbury, Duke of, 497, Shrewsbury
Shrewsbury School, 107, The Bending of a Twig
Shropshire, 194, Old Shropshire Life
— 209, Bladys of the Stewponey
— 280, Stretton
Shrouded Face, The, 404
Shueypingsin, 224
Shulamite, The, 16
Shut In, 213
Shuttlecock, The, 395
Si Gira, 388
Siberia, 146, The House of the Dead
— 284, The Vagrant, The Saghalien Convict
— 414, Anima Vilis
— 467, A Prince of Outlaws
— 469, Resurrection
— 482, Michael Strogoff
— See also *Yakuts*
Sibylla, 127
Sicca, 359, Callista
SICILIAN NOVELIST : G. Verga
Sicilian Romance, A, 399
Sicily, 21, Marotz
— 103, Two Thousand Years Ago
— 121, Corleone
— 123, Stradella
— 286, Miracles of Antichrist
— 306, Avanti !
— 481, Verga's novels and tales
Sick-Bed of Cuchulain, The, 293
Siddons, The Misses, 335, Mape

Sidney, 136
Sidney, Sir Philip, 24, The Master of Gray
— 270, Sir Mortimer
— 330, Penshurst Castle
— 357, The Unfortunate Traveller
Sidonia, 143, Coningsby
Sidonia the Sorceress, 336
Sidste kapitel, Det, 224
Siege of Howth, The, 254
Siege of Lady Resolute, The, 142
Siege of London, The, 264
Siege of Norwich Castle, The, 59
Siegfried et le Limousin, 199
Sielanka, 435
Siena, 91, The Love Story of St. Bel
— 199, Provenzano the Proud
— 427, The Disciple of a Saint
— 479, Cristina
Sign of Four, The, 149
Sign of the Spider, The, 346
Sign of the Wooden Shoes, The, 332
Sign of Triumph, The, 448
Signa, 372
Signal, The, 193
Signalled, 210
Signor Formica, 244
Signor I, 169
Signors of the Night, 381
Sigrid Storråde, 286
Sigurd, 181, Aslauga's Knight
— 484, Völsunga Saga
Sikes, Bill, 140, Oliver Twist
Sikh War, 15, Oakfield
Silanus the Christian, 1
Silas Marner, 164
Silcote of Silcotes, 280
Silence, John, 59, A. Blackwood's stories, *passim*
Silence (by Andreev), 10
Silence (by Mary E. Wilkins), 505
Silence, The, 189
Silence Farm, 431
Silence of Amor, The, 431
Silence of Colonel Bramble, The, 335
Silence of Dean Maitland, The, 212
Silent Captain, The, 512
Silent Gods and Sun-Steeped Lands, 186
Silent Partner, The, 383
Silent Places, The, 501
Silesia, 73, S.O.S.
— 187, Debit and Credit
Silk, 343
Silk of the Kine, The, 319
Silva Gadelica, 364
Silveira, Gonçalo de, 123, A Martyr's Servant, and sequel
Silver Cañon, The, 171
Silver Cross, The, 277
Silver Fox, The, 443
Silver Horde, The, 40
Silver Queen, The, 485
Silver Shoe-Buckle, The, 171

Silver Skull, The, 124
Silver Spoon, The, 190
Silver Stallion, The, 85
Silverado Squatters, The, 449
Silvia, 275
Simla, 101, A True Reformer
Simon Dale, 246
Simon the Jester, 301
Simone Turchi, 31
Simpkins Plot, The, 55
Simple Annals, 185
Simple Art, A, 164
Simple Simon, 308
Simple Story, A, 258
Simple Susan, 160
Simpleton, A, 402
Simplice, 516
Simpson, Helen de G., see *sub nom.* Dane, Clemence, 128
Sin-Eater, The, 431
Sin of Joost Avelingh, The, 310
Sin of M. Antoine, The, 421
Sinai, 158, Homo Sum
Sincerity (by Deeping), 133
Sincerity (by Erskine), 166
Sindbad, 430, The Seven Wise Masters
— 475, Turkish Tales
Singermann, 72
Singers, 94, My Ántonia
— 121, A Roman Singer
— 123, Soprano, and sequels
— 232, Beatrix Randolph
— 339, Sandra Belloni, and sequel
— 381, Feo
— 399, A Welsh Singer
— 420, The Last Aldini, Consuelo, and sequel
Singers, The, 474
Singers' Contest, The, 244
Singer's Trilogy, The, 123
Single Heart and Double Face, 402
Singoalla, 417
Sinister Street, 317
" Sinjohn, John," see Galsworthy, J., 189
Sinn Fein, 55, Up, the Rebels !
— 308, The Gael
— See also *Irish Rebellion of* 1798, and *of* 1916
Sinner and the Problem, The, 375
Sinner's Comedy, 119
Sins of Desire, 67
Sins of the Stony-hearted Man, The, 272
Sintflut, 358
Sintram and his Companions, 181
Sioux Indians, 9, The Last of the Chiefs
— 74, Master of the Strong Hearts
— 501, The Westerners
Sir Andrew Wylie, 191
Sir Bevil, 466
Sir Brooke Fossbrooke, 297
Sir Charles Danvers, 103

Sir Charles Grandison, The History of, 406
Sir Christopher, 206
Sir Edmund Orme, 264
Sir George Tressady, 488
Sir George's Objection, 106
Sir Gibbie, 314
Sir Henry Morgan the Buccaneer, 249
Sir Jasper Carew, 297
Sir John Constantine, 397
Sir Ludar, 402
Sir Luke's Return, 70
Sir Mortimer, 270
Sir Nigel, 150
Sir Patrick, the Puddock, 485
Sir Percival, 433
Sir Percy Hits Back, 370
Sir Percyvelle des Galles, 242
Sir Quixote of the Moors, 77
Sir Ralph Esher, 255
Sir Raoul, 306
Sir Richard Calmady, The history of, 321
Sir Richard Enscombe, 381
" Sir " She Said, 491
Siren, The, 473
Sisson, Aaron, 291, Aaron's Rod
Siste Athenaren, Den, 417
Siste viking, Den, 64
Sister Carrie, 151
Sister Dolorosa, 7
Sister Saint Sulpice, 374
Sister Teresa, 349
Sister to Evangeline, A, 409
Sisters, The, 158
Sisters-in-Law, 18
Sisters of Prague, The, 214
Sivtzev vrazhek, 371
Six Cents, 105
Six Mrs. Greenes, 401
Six Stories narrated by Max von Pochammer, 213
Six Worthy Yeomen of the West, 138
Sixes and Sevens, 390
Sixpence, 325
Sixty-Four, Ninety-Four !, 354
SKALBE, Karlis, see MARSHALL, L. A. (tr.), 330
Skeeters Kirby, 332
Skeleton Finger The, 243
Skeleton in the Closet, The, 221
Skeleton in the House, The, 444
Skeleton Key, The, 91
Skelett in Hause, Das, 444
Sketch of a Sinner, 458
Sketches and Travels in London, 463
Sketches by Boz, 140
Sketches in Lavender, 268
Sketches of a Siberian Tourist, 284
Sketches of Everyday Life, 71
Sketches of Irish Character, 222
Skibet gaar videre, 215
Skimpole, Harold, 141, Bleak House

Skipper of Barncraig, The, 430
Skipper Worse, 278
Skipper's Wooing, The, 260
Skirts of Happy Chance, The, 328
Sky-Blue Life, The, 207
Sky Pilot, The, 110
Slain by the Doones, 58
Slapping Sal, The, 150
Slate, The, 65
Slav Soul, A, 285
Slave, The, 241
Slave-Girl Narcissus, The, 419
Slave Girl of Agra, The, 158
Slave of Lagash, The, 35
Slave Ship, The, 271
Slavery, 7, Two Gentlemen of Kentucky
— 32, God's Providence House
— 43, Oroonoko
— 77, Diane, The Father
— 86, The Flower of the Chapdelaines
— 134, Kate Beaumont
— 160, Prusias
— 204, Dead Souls
— 228, Free Joe
— 229, Aaron in the Wildwoods
— 248, The Purchase Price
— 271, The Slave Ship
— 278, The Prodigal Judge
— 282, A Deal in Cotton
— 284, The Murmuring Forest, The Last Day of the Carnival
— 303, Mother of God
— 440, Colonel Carter of Cartersville
— 452, Uncle Tom's Cabin, Dred
— 469, Master and Servant, In the Days of Serfdom
— 470, Bricks without Straw, Pactolus Prime
— 474, A Sportsman's Sketches
— 476, Pudd'nhead Wilson
— See also Harem Life, L'Ouverture, Toussaint, Spartacus
Slavery, 277
Slaves of the Padishah, 271
Sleep and a Forgetting, A, 251
Sleeping Army, The, 483
Sleeping Fires (Dormant Fires), 18
Sleeping Fury, The, 14
Sleeping Partner, The, 506
Sleepy, 100
Slipslop, Mrs., 172, Joseph Andrews
Slop, Dr., 447, Tristram Shandy
SLOVENE NOVELIST, I. CANKAR
Slowcoach, The, 306
Slum Life, see London Poor, Poor
Smaa Fortællinger, 151
Small House at Allington, The, 471

Small-Part Lady, The, 436
Small Souls, 117
Smasher, The, 207
Smell in the Library, The, 14
Smerdyakov, 148, The Brothers Karamazov
Smetham, Henry, 491, Aylwin
Smile, 291
Smile of Fortune, A, 111
SMITH, Mrs. B., see " SWAN, Annie," 457
SMITH, Ernest Bramah, see " BRAMAH, Ernest "
SMITH, Rev. F. R., see " ACKWORTH, John," 2
SMITH, Hannah, see " STRETTON, Hesba," 453
SMITH, Herbert Huntington, see " HUNTINGTON, H. S."
Smith, Captain John, 278, John o' Jamestown
Smith, Joseph, 148, The Mormon Prophet
Smith, Sydney, 240, Bendish
Smith Brunt, 390
Smith's Battery, 96
Smoke, 475
Smokeover, Heroes of, Legends of, 259
Smoky Mountains, 118, In the Tennessee Mountains, The Prophet of the Great Smoky Mountains
Smuggler, The, 262
Smugglers, 39, The Longshoremen
— 71, A Royal Ward
— 94, The Light of Scarthey
— 123, The Raiders, and sequel
— 133, Bess of the Woods
— 168, Moonfleet
— 193, The Owl's House, and sequels
— 213, The Man Within
— 260, Aythan Waring
— 261, De l'Orme
— 262, The Smuggler
— 318, The Shirra
— 328, The House in the Downs
— 331, Jim Davis
— 363, Parson Peter
— 373, Penelope Brandling
— 386, Faith Tresilion
— See also Bootleggers
Smythe, George, 143, Coningsby
Snake-Bite, 242
Snake Pit, The, 479
Snakes and Norah, The, 34
Snake's Pass, The, 451
Snapper, 10
Snare, The, 418
Snarley Bob, 259, Mad Shepherds
Snarleyyow, 329
Snodgrass, Augustus, 140, Pickwick Papers
Snörmakar Lekholm far en idé, 236

Snorri the Priest, 168, Eyrbyggja Saga
— 235, HEIDARVIGA SAGA
— 292, Laxdaela Saga
— 360, Njals Saga
Snow Image, The, 233
Snow Man, The, 421
Snow over Eldon, 354
Snow upon the Desert, 320
Snowe, Lucy, 73, Villette
Snowflakes and Sunbeams, 26
Snowstorm, The, 395
Sobieska, Clementina, 313, The King over the Water
— 331, Clementina
Sobieski, John III, 434, With Fire and Sword, and sequels
— 435, On the Field of Glory
Sobieski, Prince Constantine, 413, Tolla
Sobieski, Count Thaddeus, 389, Thaddeus of Warsaw
Soból i panna, 498
Soboryane, 307
Social Departure, A, 116
Social Reform, 164, Felix Holt
— 238, Clark's Field
— 322, The Individualist
— 494, Tono-Bungay
— 506, The Way Up
— 519, Fruitfulness
— See also Benthamism
Social Secretary, The, 384
Socialism, 3, Stephen Remarx, Paul Mercer
— 7, Philistia
— 43, Looking Backward
— 56, Love in a Mist
— 184, The White Stone
— 200, Demos
— 250, The World of Chance
— 264, The Princess Casamassima
— 276, Bloomsbury
— 286, The Miracles of Antichrist
— 369, The Man and His Kingdom
— 417, The Interpreters
— 420-1, G. SAND's novels
— 433, Blanche, Lady Falaise
— 488, David Grieve, Marcella, and sequel
— 493-5, WELLS's novels, passim
— 502, The Revolution in Tanner's Lane
Socialism, Christian, 3, Stephen Remarx, Paul Mercer
— 279, Alton Locke, Yeast
— 332, A Woman of Yesterday
Society, A, 510
Sociological, 10, Windy McPherson's Son
— 54, A Room in Berlin
— 61, Martin Rivas
— 83, S. BUTLER's novels

Sociological (*contd.*): 89, Young Earnest, Three Pretty Men, and sequel, Anatomy of Society
— 95, The Forewarners
— 103, Marka of the Pits
— 143, Sybil
— 189, The Island Pharisees, The Man of Property
— 192, H. GARLAND's novels, *passim*
— 200–1, G. GISSING's novels
— 224, Children of the Age, and sequel
— 238, R. HERRICK's novels
— 279, Alton Locke, Yeast
— 298, Babbitt
— 309, The Caxtons, and sequels
— 310, Kenelm Chillingly
— 331, The Street of Today
— 351, Utopia
— 352, W. MORRIS' romances, especially The Dream of John Ball, News from Nowhere
— 382, Lady Perfecta
— 384–5, D. G. PHILLIPS' novels
— 404, S. REYNOLDS's stories
— 408, J. A. RIIS' novels
— 437–8, Upton SINCLAIR's novels
— 444, SPIELHAGEN's novels
— 467–9, TOLSTOY's novels
— 493–5, H. G. WELLS's novels
— 502, R. WHITEING's novels
— 503, The Turn of the Balance
— See also *Anarchists, Capitalism, Communism, Crime, Divorce, Law, Marriage, Natural Man, Nihilism, Politics, Poor, Prisons, Sex, Socialism, Strikes, Utopias*
Socrates, 287, Pericles and Aspasia
Sodome et Gomorrhe, 393
Soft Side, The, 265
Sognet, 11
Soil, The, 518
Soirées de Médan, Les, 516
— See also 334, Boule de Suif
Soissons, Comte de, 261, De l'Orme
Søkongen, 442
" SOL. SECOND THOUGHTS," see KENNEDY, J. P., 277
Soldier Born, 371
Soldier from Virginia, The, 68
Soldier of Humour, A, 298
Soldier of Life, A, 140
Soldier of Manhattan, A, 8
Soldier of Virginia, A, 448
Soldier of Waterloo, 371
Soldier Rigdale, 144

Soldier's Children, A, 508
Soldier's Home, 236
Soldiers of Fortune, 131
Soldier's Pay, 170
Soldier's Pilgrimage, A, 395
Soldiers Three, 281
Solebay, Battle of, 139, An Affair of Dishonour
Solgau, 24, Karl of Erbach
Solitary, 71
Solitary Summer, The, 14
Soll und Haben, 187
Sologne, 18, Marie-Claire
— 181, The Wanderer
Solomon, 285, Sulamith
Solomon Isles, 303, Jerry of the Islands
— 371, The Queen versus Billy
Solway Moss, 123, The Raiders, and sequel
— 124, The Moss-Troopers
Sombrero, 14
Sombrero de tres Picos, El, 5
Some Account of Amyot Brough, 72
Some Do Not, 178
Some Elderly People and their Young Friends, 320
Some Emotions and a Moral, 119
Some Experiences of an Irish R.M., 443
Some Irish Yesterdays, 443
Some Portraits of Women, 67
Some Women I have Known, 310
Somebody's Luggage, 141
Somehow Good, 138
Somers, 427, Decatur and Somers
Somerset, Duke of (*Protector*), 5, The Constable of the Tower
Somersetshire, 71, The Brown Mask
— 304, The Woman and the Sword
— 329, Under the Mendips
— 400, W. RAYMOND's novels
— 428, Under Cheddar Cliffs
— 477, The Witch Ladder
— See also *Bath, Bristol, Monmouth's Rebellion*, etc.
Something about Eve, 85
Something Childish, 325
Somnambulism, 76, Edgar Huntly
Son, The (by BUNIN), 80
Son, The (by DIXELIUS), 145
Son Avenger, The, 479
Son excellence Eugène Rougon, 517
Son of a Peasant, The, 320
Son of a Servant, The (by STRINDBERG), 454
Son of a Tory, The, 423
Son of Empire, A, 410
Son of Hagar, A, 87
Son of his Country, A, 62
Son of his Mother, The, 483

Son of Issachar, A, 74
Son of Judith, 276
Son of Royal Langbrith, The, 251
Son of the Bondwoman, The, 375
Son of the Commodore, A, 315
Son of the Forge, A, 61
Son of the Middle Border, A, 192
Son of the People, A, 370
Son of the Plains, A, 377
Son of the Revolution, A, 74
Son of the Sea, A, 79
Son of the State, A, 407
Son of the Wolf, 302
Song of Renny, The, 240
Song of Songs, The, 455
Song of the Blood-Red Flower, The, 300
Song of the Lark, The, 94
Songe d'une Femme, Le, 209
Sonia (by F. HARRIS), 228
Sonia (by McKENNA), 316
Sonia Married, 316
Sonnica, 60
Sono Omokage, 189
Sonoy, Diedrich, 24, My Lady of Orange
Sons and Lovers, 290
Sons o' Men, 287
Sons of Ham, The, 381
Sons of the Covenant, 206
Sons of the Morning, 385
Sons of the Sword, 510
Sonsonen, 145
Sophia, Tsarevna, 461, On the Red Staircase
Sophia Western, 173, Tom Jones
Sophia, 497
Sophocles, 287, Pericles and Aspasia
Sophy, 140, Old Curiosity Shop
Soprano, 123
Sorcerer's Stone, The, 217
Sorel, Julien, 53, Red and Black
Sorrell and Son, 133
Sorrow of an Old Convict, The, 304
Sorrows of Satan, The, 116
Sorrows of Werther, The, 204
Soul Enchanted, The, 415
Soul of a Bishop, The, 495
Soul of a Child, The, 56
Soul of a Serf (Fated to Win), 165
Soul of Abe Lincoln, The, 22
Soul of Ann Rutledge, The, 22
Soul of Melicent, The, 85
Soul of Susan Yellam, The, 480
Soul of the Countess, The, 497
Souls Belated, 498
Souls Divided, 429
Souls in Bondage, 197
Souls of Black Folk, 152
Souls of Poor Folk, 258
Sound and the Fury, The, 170

Soutar, Jamie, 318, " Ian MACLAREN's " novels
SOUTH AFRICAN NOVELISTS: P. GIBBON, Anna Howarth, B. MARNAN, B. MITFORD, R. L. OUTHWAITE and C. H. CHOMLEY, Olive SCHREINER, Pauline SMITH, Miss A. WERNER
South American Romances, 253
South American Sketches, 252
South Sea Bubble, 5, The South Sea Bubble
— 400, Jacob and John
— 418, The Lion's Skin
South Sea Bubble, The, 5
South Sea Islands, see *Polynesia*
South Wind, 148
South Wind, The, 59
Southampton, Earl of, 182, The Hand of the North
Southampton, 25, The Merchant Prince
Southampton Massacres, 263, The Old Dominion
Southern Charm, 203
Southern States of America, see *American Civil War*, and under names of states, cities, etc.
Southerner, The, 145
Southey, Robert, 378, Melincourt
Souvenir, 138
Sowdone of Babylone, The, 98
Sower of Wheat, A, 54
Sowers, The, 342
Sowing the Wind, 300
Spa Fields Riot, 432, Running Horse Inn
Spae-Wife, The, 69
Spain and Spaniards, 7, The Rogue
— 17, The Californians, The Valiant Runaways, The Splendid Idle Forties
— 30, El Verdugo
— 61, The Pope of the Sea
— 68, Yesterdays
— 79, Tales of the Pampas
— 111, The Inn of the Two Witches
— 155, Agenor de Mauléon
— 159, Our Lady of the Pillar
— 210, The Christ of Toro
— 239, The Spanish Jade
— 295, LESAGE's stories
— 325, The Betrothed
— 341, Carmen
— 514, Carpathia Knox
— See also SPANISH NOVELISTS, *Carlists, Inquisition*, and names of events, *Peninsular War*, etc., and of monarchs, *Philip II*, etc.
Span o' Life, The, 319
Spanish-American War, 121, Wounds in the Rain

Spanish - American War (contd.): 433, Contraband of War
— 491, Van Cleeve
— 510, The Spirit of the Service
Spanish Armada, 62, The Sea Devils
— 279, Westward Ho !
— 322, Don Luis
— 365, Ulrick the Ready
— 449, The Merry Men
— 507, The Knight of the Needle Rock
Spanish Bawd, The, 414
Spanish Bayonet, 44
Spanish Farm, The, 354
Spanish Farm Trilogy, The, 354
Spanish Gold, 55
Spanish Island, The, 356
Spanish Jade, The, 239
Spanish Jilt, The, 303
Spanish John, 319
Spanish Ladie, The, 96
Spanish Lady, The (by Margaret Woods), 510
Spanish Main, 26, By Stroke of Sword
— 150, The Last Galley
— 176, In the Days of Drake
— 243, The Splendid Knight
— 270, Sir Mortimer
— 279, Westward Ho !
— 330, Captain Margaret
— 331, Lost Endeavour
— 398, Mortallone
Spanish-Moroccan War, 140, The Blockhouse
SPANISH NOVELISTS :
F. Acebal, P. de Alarcón, M. Alemán, " Azorin," Pio Baroja, G. A. D. Bécquer, V. Blasco Ibáñez, M. de Cervantes Saavedra, C.. Espina, V. Espinel, J. Diaz Fernandez, Infante Don Juan Manuel, E. Larreta, F. López de Ubeda, Hurtado de Mendoza, G. Miro, A. Palacio Valdés, Emilia Pardo Bazán, J. M. de Pereda, B. Pérez Galdos, Quevedo de Villegas, F. de Rojàs, R. M. Tenriero, M. de Unamuno, Juan Valera, E. Zamacois
— See also Roscoe, T. (tr.), 415
Spanish Novelists, The, 415
Spanish Peggy, 95
Spanish Poniard, The, 388
Spanish Romances, 104, The Chronicles of the Cid
— 301, Lobeira
— 375, Paris and Vienne
Spanish Succession, War of, 353, Gerald O'Connor
Spanish Virgin, The, 392
Spanish War of Independence, 382, Saragossa, Trafalgar
— See also *Peninsular War*

Spanish Wine, The, 333
Sparta, 310, Pausanias
— 346, Cloud Cuckoo Land, Black Sparta
Spartacus, 103, Two Thousand Years Ago
— 160, Prusias
Spears, Mrs. E. L., see Borden, Mary
Spectator, The, 3
Spectre of Power, A, 118
Speculum Historiale, 98
Spell of the Jungle, The, 382
Sperry, Margaret, see Ohta, T., 365
Speyside, 289, The Wolfe of Badenoch
Sphinx without a Secret, The, 504
Sphinx's Children and Other People's, The, 114
Spider, The, 167
Spider and the Fly, The, 483
Spider Boy, 481
Spies, see *Espionage*
Spinners, The, 386
Spinning Wheel Stories, 6
Spinoza, 18, Spinoza
— 515, Dreamers of the Ghetto
Spinoza, 18
Spire of Caudebec, The, 289
Spirit in Prison, A, 242
Spirit of the Border, The, 215
Spirit of the Service, The, 510
Spiritual Adventures, 459
Spiritual Quixote, The, 212
Spiritualism, 44, From the Vasty Deep
— 49, The Necromancers
— 148, Nemo
— 198, Darkened Rooms
— 250, The Undiscovered Country
— 280, The Harveys
— 321, The Gateless Barrier
— 492, In Our Street
— See also *Buddhism, Future Life, Ghost Stories, Magic, Psychical Romances, Theosophy*
Splendeurs et misères des courtisanes, 28
Splendid Brother, 408
Splendid Fairing, The, 245
Splendid Idle Forties, The, 17
Splendid Imposter, A, 500
Splendid Knight, The, 243
Splendid Spur, The, 396
Splendour of God, 353
Spoil of Office, A, 192
Spoilers, The, 395
Spoilers of the North, The, 40
Spoils of Poynton, The, 265
Sporting Novels, 113, Dorothea Conyers' novels
— 114, The Monk Wins
— 140, Pickwick Papers

Sporting Novels (contd.): 207–8, Nat Gould's stories
— 256, Miss Badsworth, M.F.H.
— 337, G. J. W. Melville's novels
— 349, Esther Waters
— 368, Boy Woodburn
— 443, novels by Somerville and Ross
— 456, R. S. Surtees's novels
— See also *Pugilism*
Sportsman's Sketches, A, 474
Spree at Coqueville, The, 519
Sprightly Romance of Marsac, The, 428
Spring Days, 349
Spring Sowing, 364
Springfield (Mass.), 22, The Soul of Ann Rutledge
Springhaven, 58
Springtime, 24
Spy, The (by Fenimore Cooper), 114
Spy, The (by Gilson), 199
Spy, The (by " Gorky "), 207
Spy, The (by Upton Sinclair), 438
Spy for Napoleon, A, 512
Squad, 500
Squanders of Castle Squander, The, 92
Square Circle, The, 316
Squatter's Dream, The, 64
Squeers family, 140, Nicholas Nickleby
Squireen, The, 80
Squirrel-Cage, The, 88
Squirrel Inn, The, 451
Sredni Vashtar, 355
Staël, Mme de, 107, The King with Two Faces
— 112, Adolphe
Staffordshire, 164, Adam Bede
— 351, Bellamy
— 514, The Iron Age
— See also *Pottery Towns*
Stage, see *Actors*
Stagg, John Reginald, see " Barnett, John "
Stahl, Jacob, 50–1, The Early History of Jacob Stahl, and sequels
" Stairs, Gordon," see Austin, Mary
Stalky & Co., 282
Stamboul, 272, Halil the Pedlar
Stamford Bridge, Battle of, 309, Harold
Stamp Act, 36, The Strawberry Handkerchief
Standard Bearer, The, 124
Standish, Miles, 21, Standish of Standish, Betty Alden
— 144, Soldier Rigdale
Standish of Standish, 21
Stanislaus of Poland, 512, The King of a Day
Stannard, Mrs. A., see " Winter, J. S.", 508

Stannary Laws, 209, Guavas the Tinner
Stanwix, Fort, 96, The Maid-at-Arms
— 423, The Son of a Tory
Star, The, 493
Star Chamber, 4, The Star Chamber
— 304, The Woman and the Sword
Star Chamber, The, 4
Star Dreamer, The, 94
Star of Mercia, 140
Starbrace, 275
Stars, The, 129
Stars of the Revival, The, 273
Start in Life, A, 27
Starvecrow Farm, 498
States-General, The, 166
Statue, The, 387
Stavanger, 278, Garman and Worse, and sequel
Stavrogin, 147, The Possessed
Staying with Relations, 312
Steadfast, 114
S.S. " Atlas," 210
S.S. " Glory," The, 360
Steele, Richard, 308, Devereux
— 462, Henry Esmond
— 510, Esther Vanhomrigh
Steeplechaser, The, 208
Steerforth, 141, David Copperfield
" Stein, A.," see Nietschmann, H. O., 360
" Stella," 510, Esther Vanhomrigh
Stempenyu, 430
" Stendhal, De," see Beyle, Marie-Henri
Stenvall, see Kivi, Alexis
Stepantchikovo and its Inhabitants, 146
Stephen, King, 122, Via Crucis
— 363, The Knight of the Cave
Stephen, Leslie, 340, The Egoist
Stephen Ellicott's Daughter, 358
Stephen Escott, 299
Stephen Remarx, 3
Stepmother, The (by Auerbach), 19
Stepmother, The (by Xenopoulos), 512
Steppe, The, 100
Stepping Heavenward, 391
Stepping Westward, 185
Stepson, The, 14
Stepson of the Soil, A, 439
Steve Young, 171
Stevenson, Robert Louis, 340, The Amazing Marriage
Stewart, Alexander, 289, The Wolfe of Badenoch
Stewart, Miss C., see " M'Aulay, Allan," 311
Steyne, Lord, 462, Vanity Fair
Stickit Minister, The, 123
Stiff-Necked Generation, A, 485

Still Life, 357
Stillwater Tragedy, The, 6
Stirling, 337, The Queen's Maries
Stock, Joseph, 289, The Race of Castlebar
Stockholm, 470, The Times of Alchemy
Stockton, Admiral, 93, Captain Courtesy
Stokes, Joseph B., 245, The Guardian Angel
Stolen Emperor, The, 186
Stolen Story, The, 506
Stolen White Elephant, The, 476
Stone Age, see *Prehistoric Times*
Stone Desert, 491
Stone of Dunalter, The, 411
Stonewall's Scout, 248
Stooping Lady, The, 239
Store Frase, Den, 285
Store hunger, Den, 63
Stories and Interludes, 373
Stories for Ninon, 516
Stories from Maupassant, 334
Stories from the Irish Peasantry, 222
Stories in Grey, 374
Stories of a Western Town, 463
Stories of Irish Life, 92
Stories of Naples and the Camorra, 211
Stories of Red Hanrahan, 513
Stories of Russian Life, 99
Stories of Waterloo, 336
Stories of Wild Life, 501
Stories Revived, 264
Stories Toto Told Me, 414
Storm and Treasure, 24
Storm Bird, The, 307
Storm Centre, The, 118
Storm in a Teacup, 386
Storm-Rent Sky, A, 162
Stormfågeln, 307
Story of a Bad Boy, The, 6
Story of a Child in Old Chester, 136
Story of a Country Town, The, 249
Story of a Hida Craftsman, 414
Story of a Modern Woman, The, 145
Story of a Moorish Captain, 430
Story of a Mother, The, 173
Story of a New York House, The, 80
Story of a Novel, The, 207
Story of a Peasant, The, 166
Story of a Play, The, 251
Story of a Short Life, The, 168
Story of a Siren, The, 180
Story of a Story, The (by LAGERLOF), 287
Story of a Story, The (by J. B. MATTHEWS), 333
Story of Ab, The, 491
Story of an African Farm, The, 423

Story of Anna Beames, The, 424
Story of Antonio, The, 412
Story of Avis, The, 383
Story of Barnaby Lee, The, 47
Story of Bawn, The, 478
Story of Bessie Costrell, The, 488
Story of Burnt Njal, 360
Story of California, The, 501
Story of Dan, The, 184
Story of Dick, The, 377
Story of Elizabeth, The, 461
Story of Eva, The, 378
Story of Fifine, The, 91
Story of Francis Cludde, The, 497
Story of Gisli the Outlaw, 200
Story of Gösta Berling, The, 286
Story of Grettir the Strong, 214
Story of Hen Thorir, 237
Story of Howard the Halt, The, 249
Story of Julia Page, The, 361
Story of Krespel, The, 244
Story of Land and Sea, A, 157
Story of Lawrence Garthe, The, 283
Story of Louie, The, 369
Story of Margaret Kent, The, 283
Story of Margrédel, 337
Story of Mary Dunne, 185
Story of Monique, 275
Story of Old Fort Loudon, The, 118
Story of Patsy, The, 504
Story of Philip Methuen, The, 358
Story of Ronald Kestrel, The, 132
Story of Serapion, The, 244
Story of Stephen Compton, The, 377
Story of Susan, The, 153
Story of the Days to Come, A, 493
Story of the Foss River Ranch, 126
Story of the Gadsbys, The, 281
Story of the Glittering Plain, The, 352
Story of the Heath-Slayings, 235
Story of the Loves of Vis and Ramin, 484
Story of the Plébiscite, The, 166
Story of the Shepherdess Felismena, 347
Story of the Stone Age, A, 493
Story of the Treasure Seekers, The, 60
Story of the Volsungs and Niblungs, The, 484
Story of Thyrza, The, 76
Story of Tonty, The, 95
Story of Valentine and his Brother, The, 367

Story of Viga Glum, 483
Story of Waitstill Baxter, 504
Story without a Name, A, 32
Story without a Tail, A, 320
Strabane of the Mulberry Hills, 234
Stradella, 123
Strafford, Earl of, 216, A Servant of the King
— 243, Follow the Gleam
— 313, Kathleen Clare
— 333, Love of Comrades
Strained Allegiance, 180
Strait is the Gate, 198
Stranded, 342
Strange Adventures of a Phaeton, The, 57
Strange Case of Dr. Jekyll and Mr. Hyde, 449
Strange Case of Miss Annie Spragg, The, 73
Strange Friend of Tito Gill, The, 5
Strange Marriage, 459
Strange Moon, 453
Strange Stories from a Chinese Studio, 395
Strange Stories from the Lodge of Leisures, 395
Strange Story, A, 310
Strange Story of Rab Ráby, The, 272
Strange Vanguard, The, 46
Stranger, The, 423
Stranger Child, The, 244
Stranger in Paradise, A, 11
Strangers and Wayfarers, 269
Strangers at Lisconnel, 34
Strangford, Lord, see *Smythe, George*
Strasbourg, 326
Strasburg, 165, Madame Thérèse
— 326, Strasbourg
— 380, The Garden of Swords
Strategy, 442
Strathmore, 371
Straw, Jack, 112, Long Will
Strawberry Handkerchief, The, 36
Stray-Aways, 443
Stray Pearls, 513
Strayings of Sandy, The, 113
Street-Arabs, 124, Cleg Kelly
— 169, Grif
— 282, Kim
— 330, Jock's Ward
— 345, Adventures of François
— 407, A Son of the State
Street in Suburbia, A, 395
Street of Adventure, The, 197
Street of the Flute-Player, The, 445
Street of To-Day, The, 331
Streltzi Riot, 461, On the Red Staircase
Strength of Gideon, 156
Strength of Lovers, The, 491

Strength of Men, 156
Strether, Lambert, 265, The Ambassadors
Stretton, 280
Strictly Business, 389
Strife and Peace, 71
Strikes, 126, The Trail of the Axe
— 359, Pelle
— 428, The Revolt of the Fishermen
— 509, A Life's Secret
— 518, Germinal
— See also *Labour*
Striking Hours, The, 385
Stringtown on the Pike, 301
Striving Fire, 127
Strolling Saint, The, 418
Strong Arm, The, 37
Strong Hand, The, 216
Strong Mac, 124
Stronger Claim, The, 382
Stronger Sex, The, 44
Stronger Wings, The, 267
Struggle for Life, The (by BAROJA), 35
Struggle for Life, The (by DAUDET), 130
Struggle for Rome, A, 128
Stuart, Arabella, 262, Arabella Stuart
Stuart, J. E. B., 113, Surry of Eagle's Nest
— 47, Bayard's Courier
Stuart, Lady Margaret, 22, A Prince in Petto
Stuart of Dunleath, 362
Stucco House, The, 89
Student, The, 100
Student Life, 450, The Wrecker
— 474, Acia
— See also *College Life, Latin Quarter, University Life*
Studies in Love, 279
Studies in Love and Terror, 44
Study in Colour, A, 444
Study in Scarlet, A, 149
Study in Temptations, A, 119
Study of Woman, A, 27
Stuffed Animal House, 136
Stumbling Block, The, 395
Sturmflut, 444
Sturreganz, 490
STURT, George Bourne, see BOURNE, George
Stuyvesant, 1
Stuyvesant, Peter, 47, The Story of Barnaby Lee
— 401, In Castle and Colony
Stygt barndomsminde, Et, 57
Styria, 416, The God-Seeker
Suave Milagre, 159
Subaltern, The, 203
Subiaco, 122, Casa Braccio
Subsoil, 327
Substance of a Dream, The, 25
Substitute, The, 224
Suburb, 347
Success (by FEUCHT-WANGER), 172

Success (by Cunninghame GRAHAM), 210
Success (by "E. WERNER"), 496
Succession, 434
Such Stuff as Dreams, 290
Sudan, 439, The Curse of the Nile
— See also *Gordon, General, Nile*
Suddaby Fewster, 180
Sueños, 396
Suffolk, 62, Napoleon Decrees
— 162, The Lord of the Harvest, A Suffolk Courtship, Mock Beggars' Hall, A Humble Lover
— 186-7, H. W. FREEMAN's novels
— 218, The Serf, The House of Torment
— 372, Many Captives
Suffolk Courtship, A, 162
Suicide Club, The, 448
Suicide's Grave, The, 244
Suitors of Yvonne, The, 417
Sulamith, 285
Sult, 223
Summer (by REYMONT), 415
Summer (by WHARTON), 499
Summer Holiday or Gibraltar, 441
Summer in a Cañon, 504
Summer in Arcady, 8
Summer in Leslie Goldthwaite's Life, A, 503
Summers and Winters at Balmawhapple, 438
Summons, The, 332
Sun, 291
Sun also Rises, The, 236
Sun of Saratoga, The, 8
Sundering Flood, The, 352
Sunderland (Mass.), 145, The Beau's Comedy
Sunny Side of the Hill, The, 91
Sunrise Stories, 409
Sunshine Sketches of a Little Town, 293
Superfluous Woman, A, 74
Supernatural, 44, The Woman from Purgatory
— 73, Wuthering Heights
— 78, Grey Weather
— 99, The Two Martyrs
— 108-9, Wilkie COLLINS's novels
— 126, The Night Side of Nature
— 181, Baron de la Motte FOUQUÉ's stories
— 220, The Mahatma and the Hare
— 232, Twice-Told Tales
— 260, The Monkey's Paw
— 281-3, R. KIPLING's stories, *passim*
— 287, Herr Arne's Hoard
— 309, The Haunted and the Haunters
— 310, A Strange Story

Supernatural (contd.): 475, Dream Tales
— See also *Celtic, Celtic Romances, Diabolism, Fairy Tales, Ghost Stories, Lycanthropy, Magic, Psychical Romances, Mythology, Oriental, Vampires, Welsh Romances, Witchcraft*
Superseded, 436
Superstition, refer to references under *Supernatural*, above
Suppers, 71
Supreme Crime, The, 196
Sur Catharine de' Medici, 30
Sur la pierre blanche, 184
Sur la vaste terre, 344
Surâbhi, 446
Surgeon's Daughter, The, 427
Surprises of Life, The, 105
Surrender, The, 195
Surriage, Agnes, 398, Lady Good-for-Nothing
Surrey, Earl of, 4, Windsor Castle
— 357, The Unfortunate Traveller
Surrey, 68, G. BOURNE's works
— 70, In High Places
— 209, The Broom-Squire
Surry of Eagle's Nest, 113
Survival, A, 210
Survivor, The, 369
Susan (by Jane AUSTEN), 20
Susan (by OLDMEADOW), 366
Susan Hopley, 126
Susan Lenox, 385
Susanna and Sue, 504
Susannah, 323
Suspense, 112
Suspicious Gift, A, 59
Susquehanna, 114, The Pioneers, Wyandotté
Sussex, 24, Storm and Treasure
— 39, The Longshoremen
— 58, Alice Lorraine
— 60, In Homespun
— 77, The Glory and the Abyss
— 120, The House of Walderne
— 153, Mrs. DUDENEY's novels
— 161, Rev. T. EDWARDES's novels
— 169, The Loring Mystery
— 256, Crowborough Beacon
— 275, Sheila KAYE-SMITH's novels
— 308, Befriending Her Ladyship
— 440, Brambletye House
— See also *Smugglers*
Sussex Gorse, 275
Sutherlands, The, 245
Suzanna, 233
Suzette, 466
Sværmere, 223
Svidrigailov, 147, Crime and Punishment

Swabia, 231, Lichtenstein
— 513, The Dove in the Eagle's Nest
Swallow, 219
Swallow Barn, 277
Swallows and Amazons, 399
Swalue, Madge and Jean, 131, The Two Crossings of Madge Swalue
Swan Song, 191
Swann's Way, 393
Sweden and Swedes, 39, The Reminiscences of Sir Barrington Beaumont, Bart.
— 56, The Soul of a Child
— 91, Monsieur Martin
— 261, Marie Grubbe
— 268, Karine
— 421, The Snow Man
— 434, The Deluge
— See also *Charles XI, XII, Gustavus Adolphus, Thirty Years War*, and SWEDISH NOVELISTS
Swedenborgianism, 28, Ursule Mirouët
— 232, Garth
— 366, Piccadilly
— 503, The Gayworthys
Swedes and their Chieftains, The, 235
SWEDISH NOVELISTS: K. J. L. ALMQUIST, B. M. K. BERG, H. BERGMAN, E. A. BJÖRKMAN (Swedish-American), Fredericka BREMER, Hildur DIXELIUS, A. EJE, V. von HEIDENSTAM, E. G. HELLSTRÖM, G. JANSON, Selma LAGERLÖF, A. W. LUNDEGÅRD, H. MOLANDER, A. V. RYDBERG, S. SIWERTZ, H. E. SÖDERBERG, J. A. STRINDBURG, Z. TOPELUIS
— See also LARSEN, Hamna A. (tr.), 288
Sweep Winner, The, 208
Sweet Cheat Gone, The, 394
Sweet Miracle, The, 159
Sweet-Scented Name, The, 442
Sweetheart Gwen, 467
Sweetheart Manette, 465
Swept and Garnished, 283
Sweyn, 120, Alfgar the Dane
— 129, The Vikings of the Baltic
Swift, Jonathan, 206, Veronica Playfair
— 308, Devereux
— 510, Esther Vanhomrigh
Swift Lightning, 127
Swing of the Pendulum, The, 325
SWISS NOVELISTS: Cecile Loos, Carl SPITTELER (German-Swiss),
Switzerland, 72, True Heart
— 277, The Constant Nymph
— 303, Hyperion

Switzerland (contd.): 321, A Council of Perfection
— 427, Anne of Geierstein
— 519-20, ZSCHOKKE's stories
Swiveller, Dick, 140, Old Curiosity Shop
Swold, Battle of, 366, Olaf Saga
Sword and Assegai, 249
Sword and Gown, 292
Sword and the Distaff, The, 436
Sword Decides, The, 68
Sword Falls, The, 52
Sword Hand of Napoleon, The, 71
Sword of Azrael, The, 179
Sword of Gideon, The, 62
Sword of Justice, The, 448
Sword of Love, The, 128
Sword of the King, The, 314
Sword of the Lord, The, 243
Sword of the Old Frontier, The, 376
Sword of Welleran, The, 157
Sword of Youth, The, 8
Swordmaker, The, 37
Sworn Brothers, The, 218
Sybarite, The, 307
Sybil, 143
Sydney, Algernon, 307, The Golden Days
Sydney, 107, The History of Margaret Catchpole
— 163, A House is Built
Sydney-side Saxon, A, 6
Sydney Sovereign, A, 4604
Sylvandire, 154
Sylvester Sound, the Somnambulist, 107
Sylvia, 438
Sylvia and Michael, 317
Sylvia Scarlett, Early Life and Adventures of, 317
Sylvia's Lovers, 194
Sylvia's Marriage, 438
Sylvie and Bruno, 93
Sylvie's Betrothed, 215
SYMONDS, Miss E. M., see "PASTON, G.," 377
Symonds, J. A., 491, Aylwin
Symphonie pastorale, La, 198
Symphonies, 162
Synesius of Cyrene, 279, Hypathia
Synnöve Solbakken, 56
Syria, 87, The Blue Banner
— 306, Deborah
Syrup of the Bees, A, 25
Széchenyi, 271, An Hungarian Nabob
Szomorú Napok, 271

T. Tembaron, 82
Table Talk of Shirley, 438
Tabte land, Det, 267
Tache d'encre, Un, 40
Tagliacozzo, 199, Provenzano the Proud
— 479, Cristina
Tägliche Brot, Das, 483

TAGORE, R., see RAVĪNDRA-NĀTHA THĀKURA, 399
Tahiti, 304, Rarahu
— 334, The Moon and Sixpence
— 450, The Ebb Tide
Tahiti, 304
Tailors, 346, Life of Mansie Wauch
Tain bó Cuailgne, 169, 214
Tain bó Fraich, 293
Taken by Assault, 411
Taken from the Enemy, 358
Taking of Lungtungpen, The, 281
Taking of the Bastille, The, 155
Taking up Piccadilly, 157
Tale, The, 111
Tale of a Lonely Parish, A, 121
Tale of a Tub, A, 457
Tale of Brittany, A, 304
Tale of Chloe, The, 340
Tale of Genji, The, 356
Tale of the House of the Wolfings, 352
Tale of the Pyrenees, A, 305
Tale of Two Cities, A, 141
Tales, 435
Tales by Polish Authors, 44
Tales by STRINDBERG, 454
Tales from Fashionable Life, 160
Tales from Five Chimneys, 387
Tales from Gorky, 206
Tales from Jókai, 273
Tales from the Ægean, 54
Tales from the Fjeld, 129
Tales from the Isles of Greece, 165
Tales from the Russian of Karamsin, 274
Tales from the Telling House, 58
Tales from Welsh Hills, 467
Tales of a Dying Race, 209
Tales of Australian Early Days, 490
Tales of College Life, 70
Tales of Dunstable Weir, 277
Tales of Flemish Life, 112
Tales of Florence, 285
Tales of Greyhouse, 43
Tales of Hearsay, 111
Tales of Irish Life and Character, 222
Tales of Mean Streets, 353
Tales of Men and Ghosts, 499
Tales of My Native Town, 12
Tales of My Own Country, 260
Tales of My Own People, 132
Tales of Mystery, Imagination, and Humour, 388
Tales of Northumbria, 380
Tales of Old Japan, 402
Tales of Rye Town, 400
Tales of Soldiers and Civilians, 53
Tales of South Africa, 77

Tales of Space and Time, 493
Tales of the Crusaders, 426
Tales of the Five Towns, 45
Tales of the Genii, 500
Tales of the Home Folks in Peace and War, 229
Tales of the Isle of Death, 490
Tales of the Kirk, 124
Tales of the Labrador, 214
Tales of the Munster Festival, 216
Tales of the North Riding, 300
Tales of the Pampas (by BULFIN), 79
Tales of the Pampas (by W. H. HUDSON), 252
Tales of the Punjab, 445
Tales of the Ridings, 350
Tales of the Revolution, 16
Tales of the Riverine, 490
Tales of the Samurai, 355
Tales of the Zenana, 244
Tales of Three Hemispheres, 157
Tales of Two Countries, 207
Tales of Two Countries, 278
Tales of Two People, 247
Tales of Unrest, 110
Tales of War, 157
Tales of Wonder, 157
Tales that are Told, 174
Tales that were Told, 319
Tales Told by Simpson, 437
Taliesin, 217
Talisman, The, 426
Tall Chimneys, 244
"TALLENTYRE, S. G.," see HALL, Miss E. B., 222
Talleyrand, 24, Barry Leroy
— 432, The Queen's Fillet
— 510, The King's Revoke
Tamango, 341
Tamarisk Town, 275
Taming of Nan, The, 244
Taming of the Brute, The, 411
Tampico, 238
Tancred, 131, "God Wills It"
Tancred, 144
Tandy, Napper, 243, The King's Deputy
Tangier, 131, The Exiles
— 331, Miranda
Tangled Evidence, 132
Tangled Skein, The, 370
Tangled Trinities, 510
Tanglewood Tales, 233
Tanis, 409
Tannhaüser, 41, Under the Hill
Tansy, 161
Tantalus, 9
Tante, 428
TAPARELLI D'AZEGLIO, Marchese, see AZEGLIO, M. T.
Tapestried Chamber, The, 427
Tapestry, The, 51
Tappertit, Simon, 140, Barnaby Rudge
Taquisara, 122
Tara, 461

Taras Bulba, 204
TARDIVEAU, René, see " BOYLESVE, René "
Tarka the Otter, 507
Tarr, 298
Tarry Thou Till I Come, 125
Tartarin of Tarascon, 129
Tartarin on the Alps, 130
Tartars, 273, The Bad Old Times
— 273, 'Neath the Hoof of the Tartar
— 434, Pan Michael
Tashkent, 358
Tasker Jevons, 437
Tasmania, 105, For the Term of his Natural Life
— 234, The Escape of Sir William Heans, Strabane
Tasso, Torquato, 324, Ser Pantaleone
— 503, The Plough of Shame
Tatterdemalion, 190
Taurua, 305
Tavern Knight, The, 417
" TAYLOR, George," see HAUSRATH, A. D., 231
TAYLOR, Gertrude W., see BROSTER, D. K., and TAYLOR, G. W.
Tchaikowsky, P. F., 390, The Genius
Tchitchikoff's Journeys, 204
Tch . . ., for Russian names in this form see Ch . . ., e.g., Tchekhov, see Chekhov
Tea at Maggie Reynold's, 454
Teacher of the Violin, A, 433
TEAGUE, Rev. J. J., see " GERARD, M.," 196
Tedious Story, A, 100
Teeftallow, 453
Teeth of the Tiger, 293
Teetotal, 311
Tegelash, 197
Teheran, 411, The Plunderers
Teleki, Michael, 271, 'Midst the Wild Carpathians, and sequel
Telemachus, 171, The Adventures of Telemachus
Telepathy, 251, Though One Rose from the Dead
Telling the Truth, 241
Temple of Gnidus, The, 347
Temple of the Great Beneficence, The, 195
Temple on the Hill, The, 459
Temporal Power, 116
Temps retrouvé, Le, 394
Temptation of Burge, The, 261
Temptation of St. Anthony, 175
Temptress, The, 61
Ten-minute Stories, 59
Ten Tales, 54
Ten Thousand, The, 306, Avanti !

Ten Thousand a Year, 490
Ten Times One is Ten, 221
Ten Years Later, 154
Tenant of Wildfell Hall, The, 73
Tenants, The, 491
Ténébreuse affaire, Une, 29
Tenement Tales of New York, 456
Tennessee, 82, In Connection with the De Willoughby Claim
— 118-9, " C. E. CRADDOCK'S " novels
— 165, The Durket Sperret
— 308, The Quickening
— 453, Teeftallow, Bright Metal
— 473, The Three Scouts
Tennessee's Partner, 229
Tennyson, Alfred, Lord, 177, O Genteel Lady
— See also *Morte D'Arthur*
Tenor and the Boy, The, 211
Tension, 135
Tent, The, 364
Tentation de S. Antoine, La, 175
Tents of a Night, 174
Tents of Israel, 447
Terence, 125
Terminations, 264
Terre, La, 518
Terre qui meurt, La, 40
Terrible Czar, The, 467
Terrible Island, The, 217
Terrible Temptation, A, 402
Terror, The, 212
Terror By Night, The, 207
Tess of the D'Urbervilles, 226
Testament de M. Chauvelin, Le, 156
Testing of Diana Mallory, The, 488
TETERNIKOV, F. K., see " SOLOGUB, F.," 442
Tether, The, 77
Tetzel, Johann, 159, In the Blue Pike
— 360, Prince Albrecht of Brandenburg
Teufel, Der, 358
TEUFFEL, Mme von, see HOWARD, B. W.
Tewkesbury, 120, John Halifax
Texas, 40, Juan and Juanita
— 95, The Story of Tonty
— 164, A Simple Art
— 248, North of 36
— 296, Con Cregan
— See also *Alamo*
Texas Matchmaker, A, 2
Texts for Woodcuts, 468
Thackeray, Wm. Makepeace, 144, Endymion
Thaddeus of Warsaw, 389
Thaïs, 183
Thames, 141, Great Expectations
— 260-1, JACOBS'S stories
— 268, Three Men in a Boat
— 328, Jacob Faithful
— 439, My Son Richard
— See also *Essex, Medway*

Thanks to Sanderson, 408
That Boy o' Norcutt's, 297
That Flesh is Heir to, 438
That Fortune, 490
That Kind of Man, 51
That Lass o' Lowrie's, 82
That Sort of Thing, 259
That Sweet Enemy, 477
Thea, 455
Theagenes and Chariclea, 235
— Imitated, 96, The Travels of Pericles and Sigismunda
Thebaid, 183, Thaïs
Thebaw, King of Burma, 268, The Lacquer Lady
Thebes, 158, Uarda
Their Dear Little Ghost, 379
Their Lawful Occasions, 282
Their Lives, 255
Their Pilgrimage, 489
Their Silver Wedding Journey, 249
Their Wedding Journey, 249
Theller, Dr., 126, In Treaty with Honour
Thelma, 115
Themistocles, 131, A Victor of Salamis
Theocopulos, Domenicos, 239, Bird of God
Theodora Phranza, 358
Theodosius I, Emperor, 159, Serapis
Theology, see *Religion*
Theophano, 229
Theo's escape, 300
Theosophy, 115, Marie CORELLI's novels
— 366, Piccadilly, Altiora Peto
— See also *Spiritualism*
There is Confusion, 170
There is no Devil, 272
Therese, 423
Thermopylæ, 78, The Lemnian
— 131, A Victor of Salamis
These Little Ones, 60
These Lynnekers, 51
These Men Thy Friends, 465
These Twain, 45
They, 282
They of the High Trails, 192
They Stooped to Folly, 202
They that Took the Sword, 447
They that Walk in Darkness, 515
They Went, 148
THIBAUT, J. A., see "FRANCE, A.," 182
Thibaw's Queen, 222
Thief, The, (by BARING), 33
Thief, The (by LEONOV), 295
Thief of Virtue, The, 386
Thiers, 39, The Dayspring
Thieves, 109, The Moonstone
— 134, Moll Flanders
— 173, Jonathan Wild

Thieves (contd.): 287, Herr Arne's Hoard
— 295, The Thief
— See also *Crime, Picaresque Novels*
Thieves and the Ass, The, 516
Thin Ghost, A, 266
Things Greater than He, 520
Third Circle, The, 361
Third Estate, The, 69
Third Floor, The (by DUDENEY), 153
Third Floor, The (by SIMS), 436
Third Violet, The, 120
Third Window, The, 428
Thirsty Sword, The, 294
Thirteen, The, 28
Thirteen at Table, 157
Thirteen Evenings, The, 39
Thirteen Stories, 210
Thirteen Travellers, The, 487
Thirty-Nine Steps, The, 78
Thirty Tales and Sketches, 210
Thirty Years' War, 24, Karl of Erbach
— 53, A Trooper of the Finns
— 124, The Red Axe
— 134, Memoirs of a Cavalier
— 139, Klosterheim
— 159, The Mercenary
— 211, Philip Rollo
— 216, The Adventurous Simplicissimus
— 304, The Woman and the Sword
— 336, Mary Schweidler
— 360, Baron and Squire
— 470, The King's Ring
— 491, The Triumph of Youth
— 497, My Lady Rotha
This and That, 346
This is the End, 50
This My Son, 40
Thomas l'agnelet, 170
Thomas of Reading, 138
Thomas the Lambkin, 170
Thomas Wingfold, 314
Thompson's Progress, 258
Thoreau, 177, O Genteel Lady
Thorgar, 240, The Light Heart
Thorgils, 240, Thorgils of Treadholt
Thorgils of Treadholt, 240
Thormod, 240, The Light Heart
Thorndale, 441
"THORNE, Guy," see GULL, C. R., 218
Thorne Family, 471, Doctor Thorne
Thorny Path, A, 159
Thorpe, Dr., 138, Joseph Vance
Thorstein of the Mere, 108
Thorstein Staff-Smitten, 353

Those Barren Leaves, 257
Those Charming People, 14
Those Good Normans, 218
Those of his own Household, 40
Though Life us do Part, 384
Though One Rose from the Dead, 251
Thoughty Ones, The, 277
Thousand and One Days, The, 382
Thousand and One Quarters of an Hour, The, 218
Thrale Family, 38, The Gallants
Thrall of Leif the Lucky, The, 299
Thrawn Janet, 449
Three Admirals, The, 281
Three against the World, 275
Three Black Pennys, The, 237
Three Brothers, The (by MUNRO), 356
Three Brothers, The (by PHILPOTTS), 386
Three Cities, The, 518
Three Clerks, The, 471
Three Commanders, The, 281
Three Comrades, The, 187
Three-Cornered Hat, The, 5
Three Couriers, The, 318
Three Crosses, 470
Three Deaths, 467
Three Destinies, The, 300
Three Fair Maids, 477
Three Fates, The, 122
Three Furlongers, 275
Three-handed Reel, A, 115
Three Hostages, The, 78
Three Kings' Sons, The, 465
Three Lieutenants, The, 281
Three Maidens, The, 387
Three Marys, The, 360
Three Men, 207
Three Men in a Boat, 268
Three Men on the Bummel, 268
Three Mendicants, The, 468
Three Midshipmen, The, 281
Three Miss Graemes, The, 320
Three Miss Kings, The, 88
Three Musketeers, The, 154
Three Northern Love-Stories, 352
Three of Them (Three Men), 207
Three Pint Measures, 34
Three Pretty Men, 89
Three Scouts, The, 473
Three Sisters, The (by JACOBS), 261
Three Sisters, The (by SINCLAIR), 437
Three Soldiers, 146
Three Sons and a Mother, 89
Three Strange Lovers, 88
Three Strangers, The, 226
Three Tragic Stories of Erin, The, 273

Three Vagabonds of Trinidad, 230
Three Wars, 516
Threefold Destiny, The, 232
Threshold, The, 113
Threshold of Quiet, The, 116
Thro' a Yorkshire Window, 408
Throckmorton, Sir Nicholas, 178, The Fifth Queen, and sequels
Throckmorton, 427
Through a Needle's Eye, 453
Through Flood and Fire, 316
Through Green Glasses, 149
Through Night to Light, 444
Through One Administration, 82
Through Russia, 207
Through Sorrow's Gate, 456
Through the Chrysalis, 348
Through the Eye of the Needle, 251
Through the Eyes of Love, 520
Through the Looking-Glass, 93
Through the Turf Smoke, 319
Thrown Together, 348
Thrums, 37, Sir J. M. Barrie's novels, *passim*
Thumbs, 284
Thunder on the Left, 352
Thuringia, 306, Between Heaven and Earth
Thy Servant a Dog, 283
Thyrza, 200
Tiberius, Emperor, 117, The Tour
— 209, Neæra
Tickets, please, 291
Ticonderoga, 8, A Soldier of Manhattan
— 88, Ben Comee
— 397, Fort Amity
— 464, The Green Mountain Boys
Tides of Barnegat, The, 440
TIECK, Ludwig von, see CARLYLE, 93
Tierra de Todos, La, 61
Tierra Vasca, 35
Tigellinus, 160, Nero
Tiger of Cloud River, The, 127
Tilbury Nogo, 337
Tilly, Count of, 360, Baron and Squire
Tim, 455
Timar's Two Worlds, 271
Time and the Gods, 157
Time and Thomas Waring, 411
Time, Gentlemen! Time!, 248
Time Machine, The, 493
Time of Her Life, The, 413
Time of Man, The, 410
Time Regained, 394
Times of Alchemy, 470

Times of Battle and of Rest, The, 470
Times of Charles XII, The, 470
Times of Frederick I, The, 470
Times of Linnæus, The, 470
Timothy, 328, Japhet
Timothy's Quest, 504
Tinted Venus, The, 12
Tiphaine, 133, Bertrand of Brittany
Tipos y Paisijos, 382
Tippecanoe, Battle of, 33, Round Anvil Rock
— 163, Roxy
Tipperary, 278, Knockagow
Tipperary Joe, 296, Jack Hinton
Tippoo Sultaun, 461
Tirah Campaign, 144, Desmond's Daughter
Titan, 407
Titan, The, 151
Tithe-Proctor, The, 92
Titmouse, Tittlebat, 490, Ten Thousand a Year
Tito, 164, Romola
Tiverton Tales, 76
Tivoli, 363, The Knight of the Cave
Tjensteqvinnans son, 454
Tma, 11
To a Nun Confess'd, 371
To Arms !, 26
To Have and to Hold, 270
To Leeward, 121
To Let, 190
To London Town, 353
To-Morrow (by CONRAD), 110
To-Morrow (by EDGEWORTH), 160
To my King Ever Faithful, 199
To Right the Wrong, 307
To Tell you the Truth, 342
To the Credit of the Sea, 354
To the Lighthouse, 511
To the Lions, 103
To What Green Altar ?, 336
Tobit Transplanted, 50
Toby, Uncle, 447, Tristram Shandy
Tocsin, The, 10
TOD, John, see "STRATHESK, J.," 453
Tod in Venedig, Der, 324
TODD, Margaret G., see "TRAVERS, G.," 470
Tod's Amendment, 281
Toes Up, 347
Togail Bruidne Dá Derga, 451
Together, 238
Toil of Men, 396
Toilers of the Hills, 175
Toilers of the Sea, 254
Toison d'or, Le, 1
Tokyo, 274, Before the Dawn
Told by an Idiot, 312
Told by the Death's Head, 272
Told Under Canvas, 253
Toledo, 61, The Shadow of the Cathedral
— 338, Lazarillo de Tormes

Toll-Gatherer's Day, 232
Toll of the Bush, The, 421
Tolla, 1
Tolla the Courtesan, 413
Tolle Professor, Der, 455
Tom a Lincoln, The History of, 269
Tom Bowling, 97
Tom Brown's Schooldays, 253
Tom Burke of Ours, 296
Tom, Corinthian, 162, Life in London, and sequel
Tom Cringle's Log, 424
Tom, Dick, and Harry, 402
Tom Fool, 268
Tom Grogan, 440
Tom Jones, 173
Tom Sawyer Abroad, 476
Tom Sawyer, Detective, 476
Tom Thumb, the History of, 269
Tom Tufton's Toll, 213
Tom Tufton's Travels, 213
Tomaso's Fortune, 342
Tomb of his Ancestors, The, 282
Tommy & Co., 268
Tommy and Grizel, 37
Tommy and Thomas, 464
Tommy-Anne and the Three Hearts, 511
Tommy Atkins of the Ramchunders, 61
Tompkins, 138
Tongues of Conscience, 241
Tonio Kröger, 324
Tono-Bungay, 494
Tonquin, 295, A Modern Legionary
Tonti, Lieutenant, 95, The Story of Tonty
— 376, The Power and the Glory
— 377, Beyond the Frontier
Tontine, 450, The Wrong Box
Tony, 252
Tony Butler, 297
Tony Drum, 395
Top Speed, 408
Torch, The, 387
Torchbearers, The, 502
Torch-Bearers of Bohemia, 285
Torn Sails, 399
Torrance, Pat, 368, The Ladies Lindores, and sequel
Torrent, The, 60
Torrents of Spring, The, 475
Tory in Arms, A, 295
Tory Lover, The, 269
Tory Party, 143, Coningsby, and following
Totila, 128, A Struggle for Rome
— 201, Veranilda
Touch of Pan, The, 59
Tour, The, 117
Tour du monde en quatre-vingt jours, Le, 482
Tour in the Forest, A, 474
Tour of the World in Eighty Days, 482

Touraine, 26, La Grenadière
— 69, Daily Bread, and sequel
Tourists, see Travel Stories
TOURNEMIR, Countess de, see "TUR, E.," 474
Tours, 27, Le curé de Tours
Toute une jeunesse, 115
Tower of Dago, The, 272
Tower of London, 4, The Tower of London
— 52, Dorothy Forster
Tower of London, The, 4
Tower of Wye, The, 22
Town Mouse and a Country Mouse, A, 114
Town of Crooked Ways, The, 176
Town of the Cascades, The, 31
Town of Tombarel, The, 302
Town Poor, The, 269
Town Traveller, The, 201
Toys of Peace, The, 355
Tozer, Deacon, 366, Salem Chapel
Trabajos de Persiles y Sigismunda, Los, 96
Traddles, Thomas, 141, David Copperfield
Trade Unions, 402, Put Yourself in his Place
— 440, Tom Grogan
— See also Labour, Strikes, etc.
Trader, The, 41
Trader's Wife, The, 41
Tradesmen, 26, At the Sign of the Cat and Racket
— 40, Redemption
— 138, T. DELONEY's novels
— 201, Will Warburton
— 358, The Rise and Glory of the Westell-Browns
Trætte mænd, 191
Trafalgar, 243, Demi-Royal
— 370, The Young Days of Admiral Quilliam
— 382, Trafalgar
Trafalgar, 382
Traffics and Discoveries, 282
Tragedy of Chris, The, 355
Tragedy of Professor Denison, The, 259
Tragedy of the Korosko, 150
Tragic Bride, The, 514
Tragic Comedians, The, 340
Tragic Idyll, A, 67
Tragic Muse, The, 264
Tragical Death of Conacher, The, 254
Trail Book, The, 21
Trail-Makers of the Middle Border, 192
Trail of '98, The, 429
Trail of the Axe, The, 126
Trail of the Conestoga, The, 157
Trail of the Hawk, 298
Trail of the Lonesome Pine, 182
Trail of the Sword, The, 376
Trail Tramp, The, 192

Traitor, The, 145
Traitor and True, 62
Traitor or Loyalist ?, 492
Traitor's Way, The, 513
Traits and Confidences, 289
Traits and Stories of the Irish Peasantry, 92
Trajan, 103, To the Lions
— 302, Valerius
Trälinnan, 71
Tramp Abroad, A, 476
Tramping Methodists, The, 275
Trampling of the Lilies, The, 417
Tramps, 66, BORROW's novels
— 132, The Lady of the Cromlech
— 210, R. B. Cunninghame GRAHAM's stories
— 234, Turnpike Travellers
— 239-40, Half-Way House, and sequels
— 275, Isle of Thorns
— 277, B. KENNEDY's novels
— 322, No Relations
— 327, Love with Honour, Now !
— 392, A Walking Gentleman
Transformation, 233
Transformations, 3
Transgression, 465
Translation of a Savage, The, 376
Translations from the German, 93
Transplanted (American Wives and English Husbands), 17
Transport, 203
Transvaal, 249, Norah Lester
— See Africa, South
Transvaal, 419
Transylvania, 271, 'Midst the Wild Carpathians, and sequel
— 272, Manasseh
Trap, The, 405
Traseaden Hall, 223
Travail, 519
Travail of his Soul, The, 126
Travailleurs de la mer, 254
Travel Stories, 57, The Strange Adventures of a Phaeton, White Wings
— 88, For Three Moons
— 116, A Social Departure, A Voyage of Consolation
— 135, Overland
— 145, Departure
— 176, Kismet
— 210, R. B. Cunninghame GRAHAM's stories
— 244, The Forest Ship
— 251, The Kentons
— 291, The Plumed Serpent
— 296, The Dodd Family Abroad
— 298, Free Air, Dodsworth
— 306, The True History
— 380, Number One and Number Two

Travel Stories (*contd.*) : 447,
 A Sentimental Journey
— 451, Pomona's Travels
— 469, Old Junk, Gallions
 Reach
— 476, The Innocents
 Abroad, A Tramp
 Abroad, More Tramps
 Abroad
— 504, Penelope's English
 Experiences, and
 sequels
Traveller from Altruria, A,
 251
Traveller in the Fur Cloak,
 The, 498
Travels into several remote
 Nations of the World,
 458
Travels of Baron Mün-
 chausen, 399
Travels of Persiles and
 Sigismunda, The, 96
Travels Round Our Village,
 234
Tre Croci, 470
Treacherous Ground, 63
Treasure (Herr Arne's
 Hoard), 287
Treasure Island, 449
Treasure of Franchard, The
 449
Treasure of Heaven, The,
 116
Treasure Trove, 424
Treasures of Typhon, The,
 386
Treble Clef, The, 65
Tree of Heaven, The, 437
Tree of Knowledge (by
 BAROJA), The, 35
Tree of Knowledge (by
 WILKINS), The, 505
Tree of the Folkungs, The,
 235
Tree of the Garden, The, 65
Trelawney of Trelawne, 71
Tremaine, 489
Tremasteren Fremtiden, 299
Trembling of a Leaf, The,
 334
Tremendous Adventures of
 Major Gahagan, 463
Trente et Quarante, 1
Trent's Last Case, 50
Tres Fechas, 210
Trespass, 16
Trespasser, The, 290
Trewern, 464
Trial, The, 44
Trials, 185, The Cause of
 the Crime
— 460, Cyrilla
— 472, Phineas Redux
— See also *Crime, Law,
 Sacco-Vanzetti case*, etc.
Trials of Margaret Lyndsay,
 The, 507
Trials of the Bantocks, The,
 453
Trials of Topsy, The, 237
Triangle, A, 33
Triangle d'or, Le, 293
Tricotrin, 372
Trilby, 156
Trimalchio, 383, The Saty-
 ricon

Trimmed Lamp, The, 389
Trinity Bells, 36
Trio, 50
Trionfo della Morte, Il, 12
Tripoli, 39, The Lady of
 Tripoli
— 266, Pride of War
— 427, Decatur and Somers
Tristan (by T. MANN), 324
Tristram of Blent, 246
Triumph in Diplomacy, A,
 318
Triumph of Count Oster-
 mann, The, 247
Triumph of Death, The, 12
Triumph of Death (BEAU-
 MONT and FLETCHER),
 31
Triumph of Faith, The, 346
Triumph of Life, The, 12
Triumph of the Egg, The,
 10
Triumph of Tim, The, 480
Triumph of Youth, The, 491
Triumphs of Female Sub-
 tility, The, 303
Triumphs of Sara, The, 362
Trivial Incident, A, 100
Troglodyte, The, 363
Trois âmes d'artistes, 67
Trois mousquetaires, Les,
 154
Trojan War, see *Homeric
 Narratives*
Trold, 299
Trompe-la-Morte, 408
Tronçons du glaive, Les,
 326
Trondhjem, 64, God and
 Woman
— 163, Hansine Solstad
Trooper of the Finns, A,
 53
Trooper Peter Halkett, 423
Trotter, Job, 140, Pickwick
 Papers
Trotwood, Miss Betsy, 141,
 David Copperfield
Troubadours, 39, The King's
 Fool, The Lady of
 Tripoli
— 270, The Fortunes of
 Garin
— See also *Provence*
TROUBETZKOY, Princess, see
 RIVES, Amélie
Trough of the Wave, The,
 158
Trousers of Taffeta, 507
Troy Town, 396-8, QUIL-
 LER-COUCH's novels
True Heart, 72
True History, The, 306
True History of Joshua
 Davidson, 300
True Love, 347
True Man and Traitor, 63
True Princess, A, 90
True Reformer, A, 101
True Story, A, 252
True Story of White-Rose
 and the Fair Sibyl, 412
True Tilda, 398
Trulliber, Parson, 172,
 Joseph Andrews
Trumpet Major, The, 226

Trunnion, Commodore, 441,
 Peregrine Pickle
Trusts, 157, F. P. DUNNE's
 stories
— 303, The Iron Heel
— 342, Roden's Corner
— 343, The Whip Hand
— 361, The Octopus, The
 Pit, A Deal in Wheat
— 438, The Metropolis, and
 sequel
Trusty Eckhart, The, 93
Trusty Rebel, A, 105
Truth, 519
Trygvason, Olaf, see *Olaf*
Tryon County, 96, The
 Maid-at-Arms
Tryphena, 387
Tryphena in Love, 400
Tryst, The, 474
Tryst at an Ancient Earth-
 work, A, 226
Tubal Cain, 237
Tubber Derg, 92
Tuberculin, 311
Tuberozov, Father, 307,
 Cathedral Folk
Tuck-of-Drum, 432
Tulipe noire, La, 155
Tulliver, Maggie and Tom,
 164, The Mill on the
 Floss
Tunbridge Wells, 94, Wroth
— 256, Crowborough Bea-
 con
Tunnel, The (by KELLER-
 MANN), 277
Tunnel, The (by Dorothy
 RICHARDSON), 405
Tupman, Tracy, 140, Pick-
 wick Papers
Turandina, 443
Turbulent Duchess, The, 71
Turenne, Henri de, 71, The
 Turbulent Duchess
— 159, The Red Neighbour
— 261, John Marston Hall
— 497, A Gentleman of
 France
Turf, see *Sporting Novels*
Turgenev, Ivan, 147, The
 Possessed
Turgot, 306, Cécile
Turin, 95, The Forewarners
Turkestan, 87, The Blue
 Banner
Turkey and the Turks, 1,
 The Golden Fleece
— 78, Greenmantle
— 127, The Black Pilgrim
— 148, The Crook of the
 Bough
— 247, Anastasius
— 259, Kyra, My Sister
— 266, Pride of War
— 271, The Lion of Janina,
 'Midst the Wild Car-
 pathians, and sequel
— 305, Disenchanted
— 306, The Captain of the
 Janizaries, Sir Raoul
— 337, The Interpreter
— 354, Selam
— 387, M. PICKTHALL's
 novels
— 394, Valda Hânem, The
 Pasha

Turkey and the Turks
 (*contd.*) : 435, On the
 Field of Glory
— 475, Turkish Tales
— 481, Under the Yoke
— See also *Constantinople*
Turkish Tales, 475
Turmoil, The, 460
Turn Back the Leaves, 135
Turn of the Balance, The,
 503
Turn of the Screw, The, 265
Turnbull, Mr., 472, Phineas
 Finn, and sequel
Turnpike Travellors, 234
Turnstile, The, 331
Turpin, Archbishop, 181,
 The Four Sons of
 Aymon
Tuscany, 358, The Rebels,
 and sequel
— 473, Diamond Cut Dia-
 mond
Tussock Land, 2
Tutankhamon, 341, The
 Birth of the Gods
Tutors, 276, Janet's Home
— 280, The Tutor's Story
Tutor's Secret, The, 101
Tutor's Story, The, 280
TUTTIETT, Miss M. G., see
 "GRAY, Maxwell," 212
'Twas in Trafalgar's Bay,
 53
Tweed, River, 78, Scholar
 Gipsies
— See also *Border*
Twelve Men, 151
Twelve Stories and a Dream,
 493
Twelve Tales, 7
Twenty-Four Hours, 73
Twenty-Six Men and a Girl
 (Twenty-Six of Us),
 206
Twenty Thousand Leagues
 under the Sea, 482
Twenty-Three Tales, 469
Twenty Years After, 154
Twice-Told Tales, 232
Twilight of the Gods, The,
 193
Twilight of the Souls, The,
 117
Twinkletoes, 81
Twins, 71
Twisted Eglantine, 328
Twisting of the Rope, The,
 214
'Twixt Land and Sea, 111
Two Bites at a Cherry, 6
Two Blue Birds, 291
Two Brides, The, 381
Two Captains, The, 70
Two Chiefs of Dunboy, The,
 188
Two Crossings of Madge
 Swalue, The, 131
Two Dianas, The, 155
Two Drovers, The, 427
Two Farmers, The, 386
Two Forsyte Interludes,
 191
Two Gentlemen of Ken-
 tucky, 7
Two Helens, The, 268
Two Hussars, 467

Two Impostors and a Tinker, 113
Two Kisses, The, 369
Two Legs, 167
Two Lilies, 275
Two Little Confederates, 373
Two Little Misogynists, 444
Two Little Parisians, 344
Two Little Savages, 429
Two Little Wooden Shoes, 372
Two Lost Centuries of Britain, The, 22
Two Lovers of Pisa, The, 430
Two Magics, The, 265
Two Martyrs, The, 99
Two Men, 368
Two Men o' Mendip, 400
Two on a Tower, 226
Two or Three Graces, 257
Two Pairs of Twins, 117
Two Penniless Princesses, 513
Two Pilgrims, The, 468
Two Poets, 28
Two Prayers, 44
Two Salomes, The, 389
Two Scouts, The, 397
Two Sides to a Question, 436
Two Standards, The, 39
Two Symphonies, 198
Two Thieves, 284
Two Thousand Years Ago, 103
Two Tragedies, 99
Two Vanrevels, The, 459
Two Years Ago, 279
Two Years Before the Mast, 128
Two Young Brides, The, 27
Twrch Trwyth, The, 217
Twymans, The, 359
Tychiades, 142
Tycho Brahes Weg zu Gott, 72
Tyler, 248, Fifty-Four Forty, or Fight
Tylor, Wat, 112, Long Will
— See also *Peasants' Revolt*
Tyndall, John, 322, MALLOCK's novels
Tynedale, 104, By the Rise of the River
— See also *Northumberland*
Typee, 337
Typhoon, 110
Tyre, 2, Clitophon and Leucippe
— 18, Dido Queen of Hearts
Tyrol, 128, European Relations
— 171, The Ugly Duchess
— 176, Andromeda
— 246, Prisoner of Zenda, and sequel
— 291, The Captain's Doll
— 331, Morrice Buckler
— 410, In the Olden Time
Tyrone, 289, With Essex in Ireland
Tyranny of the Dark, The, 192

Uarda, 158
Uganda, 152, People of the Small Arrow
Ugly Duchess, The, 171
Ukraine, 204, St. John's Eve, Evenings on a Farm
— 284, The Blind Musician, The Murmuring Forest
— 512, A Prince of Intrigue
Ulrich of Würtemburg, 231, Lichtenstein
Ulrick the Ready, 365
Ulster, 7, The Rambling Rector
— 80, Hetty, The Loughsiders
— 92, Willie Reilly
— 166-7, St. John ERVINE's novels
— 312, Ulster Fireside Tales
— 315, Grace O'Malley, A. M'ILROY's stories
— 349, The Ulsterman
— 403, An Ulster Farm
— See also *Antrim, Belfast, Londonderry*, etc.
Ulster Farm, An, 403
Ulster Fireside Tales, 312
Ulsterman, The, 349
Ultima Thule, 406
Ulysses, 159, Perfection
— 221, The World's Desire
Ulysses, 273
Um Szeptor und Kronen, 419
Umbrella, The, 334
Umzilikazi, 346, The Induna's Wife
Una Breakspear, 330
Unbearable Bassington, The, 355
Uncanny Guest, The, 244
Uncertain Trumpet, The, 256
Unclassed, The, 200
Uncle Anghel, 259
Uncle Bernac, 150
Uncle 'Lisha's Friends under Bark and Canvas, 413
Uncle 'Lisha's Shop, 413
Uncle Max, 91
Uncle Piper of Piper's Hill, 460
Uncle Remus, 228
Uncle Remus and his Friends, 229
Uncle Sam in the Eyes of his Family, 166
Uncle Silas, 294
Uncle Spencer, 257
Uncle Tom's Cabin, 452
Unconscious Mummers, The, 29
Uncrowned King, An, 215
Uncrowning a King, 165
Undecimo Comandamento, L', 38
Under Bayard's Banner, 188
Under Blue Skies, 445
Under Castle Walls (Springtime), 24
Under Cheddar Cliffs, 428
Under Dog, The (by F. H. SMITH), 440

Under Dogs, The, 22
Under Fire, 33
Under Höststjernen, 223
Under Salisbury Spire, 329
Under Sentence of Death, 253
Under the Dark Star, 431
Under the Deodars, 281
Under the Dome of St. Paul's, 330
Under the Greenwood Tree, 225
Under the Hill, 41
Under the Iron Flail, 372
Under the Jackstaff, 171
Under the Lilacs, 6
Under the Mendips, 329
Under the Red Robe, 497
Under the Redwoods, 230
Under the Skylights, 188
Under the Tricolour, 344
Under the White Cockade, 456
Under the Yoke, 481
Under Two Flags, 372
Under Western Eyes, 111
Under Which Lord ?, 300
Undercurrent, The, 212
Undergrowth, 515
Underneath, 290
Undersong, The, 316
Understudies, 505
Undine (by FOUCHÉ), 181
Undine (by SCHREINER), 423
Undiscovered Country, The, 250
Undying Fire, The, 495
Undying Past, The, 455
Unfinished Song, An, 457
Unforeseen, The, 442
Unfortunate Lovers, The, 434
Unfortunate Traveller, The, 357
Ungava, 26
Unhappy Girl, An, 474
Unhurrying Chase, The, 391
Uniform and no Uniform, 117
Union of Hearts, A, 477
Unitarians, 274, Margaret
— 502, "Mark RUTHERFORD's" novels
United Irishmen, 402, Kilgorman
"*United Men*," 277, The Pikemen
United States, see *America*
Uniter of Souls, The, 443
University Life, 88, The Bent Twig, An Academic Question
— 95, The Professor's House
— 170, Julian Home
— 188, The Lost Manuscript
— 296, Arthur O'Leary
— 317, Sinister Street
— 434, In Vain
— See also *Cambridge, Oxford*, etc.
Unknown Guest, The, 490
Unknown Lands, 61

Unknown Masterpiece, The, 30
Unknown Sea, The, 248
Unknown to History, 513
Unleavened Bread, 212
Unlit Lamp, The, 200
Unordnung und frües Lied, 324
Unpetitioned Heavens, The, 327
Unpleasant Predicament, An, 146
Unsichtbare Loge, Die, 407
Unsocial Socialist, An, 431
Untertan, Der, 323
Untilled Field, The, 349
Untitled Story, An, 84
Untold Half, The, 26
Unwritten Novel, An, 510
Up and Down, 48
Up for the Green, 243
Up, the Rebels !, 55
Ups and Downs, 221
Upton Letters, The, 47
Urban II, Pope, 131, "God Wills It"
Urith, 208
Ursache, Die, 185
Ursula, Saint, 138, The Gentle Craft
Ursule Mirouët, 28
Uruguay, 252, The Purple Land
Urwaldschiff, Das, 244
Us Four, 320
Useless Precautions, The, 422
Usurper, The, 301
Ut mine Stromtid, 403
Utah, 149, A Study in Scarlet
— See also *Mormons*
Uther and Igraine, 132
Utopia, 351
Utopian Romances, 23, The New Atlantis
— 23, Hermsprong
— 43, Looking Backward
— 49, Lord of the World, The Dawn of All
— 51, Goslings
— 52, The Revolt of Man, All Sorts and Conditions of Men
— 130, Port Tarascon
— 156, The Martian
— 221, Ten Times One is Ten
— 228, Oceana
— 251, A Traveller from Altruria, Through the Eye of a Needle
— 252, A Crystal Age
— 267, After London
— 293, Nonsense Novels (burlesque)
— 310, The Coming Race
— 311, What Not
— 351, Utopia
— 352, News from Nowhere
— 419, Paul and Virginia
— 493, When the Sleeper Wakes, A Story of the Days to Come, The First Men in the Moon

Utopian Romances (contd.): 494, In the Days of the Comet, The World Set Free
— 502, The Island
Uttermost Farthing, The (by A. C. BENSON), 47
Uttermost Farthing, The (by NEUMANN), 358

"V," see CLIVE, Mrs. Archer, 106
Vacation of the Kelwyns, The, 251
Vagabond King, The, 312
Vagabonde, La, 107
Vagabondia, 82
Vagabonds, 224
Vagabonds, The, 510
Vagrant, The (by COLETTE), 107
Vagrant, The (by KOROLENKO), 284
Vain Love, 168
Vainglory, 174
Valda Hânem, 394
Valdemar Seier, 258
Vale of Cedars, The, 4
Valencia, 60, The Mayflower, The Cabin
— 104, The Cid
— 375, The Joy of Captain Ribot
Valens, 382, Sancta Paula
Valentin, 281
Valentine, 420
Valentine McClutchy, the Irish Land Agent, 92
Valentine Vox, the Ventriloquist, 107
Valentinian, 231, Jetta
— 382, Sancta Paula
Valerian, 120, Æmilius
Valerie Upton, 428
Valerius, 302
Valiant Ignorance, A, 142
Valiant Runaways, The, 17
Valjean, Jean, 254, Les misérables
Valley Forge, 345, A Venture in 1777
— See also *American Revolution*
Valley of Decision, The, 498
Valley of Fear, The, 150
Valley of Indecision, The, 452
Valley of the Beasts, The, 59
Valley of the Squinting Windows, The, 320
Valley of Tophet, The, 358
Valmouth, 174
Valmy, Battle of, 43, The Girondin
— 155, La Comtesse de Charny
— 212, The Reds of the Midi, and sequels
Valois, Chevalier de, 27, The Old Maid
Valois, François de, 122, With the Immortals
Valois, Marguerite de, 154, Marguerite de Valois

Valois, Marguerite de (contd.): 448, A Gallant of Gascony, Love in Armour
Valserine, 18
Valsolda, 177, The Patriot, and sequels
Vampires, 294, Carmilla
— 451, Dracula
Van Bibber, and Others, 131
Van Brederode, 486, In Troubled Times
Van Buren, Martin, 23, The Light in the Clearing
— 126, In Treaty with Honour
— 143, The Patience of John Moreland
Van Cleeve, 491
Van de Koele Meren des Doods, 162
Van Eycks, The, 280, Old Margaret
Van Oude Menschen, 117
Van Rensselaers of Old Manhattan, The, 345
Van Zanten's Happy Days, 77
Vandals, 128, The Scarlet Banner
— 188, Our Forefathers
Vanderbilt, Commodore, 23, Cricket Heron
Vanderdecken, Philip, 329, The Phantom Ship
Vandermast, 23, The Famous Historie of Fryer Bacon
Vandover and the Brute, 361
Vandrer spiller med sordin, 223
"*Vanessa*," 510, Esther Vanhomrigh
Vanillo Gonzales, 295
Vanished Passenger, The, 315
Vanity, 326
Vanity Fair, 462
Vanity Girl, The, 317
Vanslyperken, Lieutenant, 329, Snarleyyow
Varden, Mr. and Dolly, 140, Barnaby Rudge
Varennes, Flight to, 155, La Comtesse de Charny
Värmland, 286–7, Miss LAGERLÖF's novels
Vasco's Sweetheart, 197
Vassar College, 493, Patty Fairfield
Vathek, 42, The History of the Caliph Vathek
Vatican, see *Rome*, names of Popes, etc.
Vatican Swindle, The, 198
Vats, The, 136
Vaucelles, Katherine de, 312, Needles and Pins
Vaud, Canton, 413, White Rocks
Vaudois, see *Waldenses*
VAUGHAN, Owen, see "RHOSCOMYL, O.," 404

Vauquer, Maison, 28, Old Goriot
Vautrin, 28, A Harlot's Progress, etc.
Vautrin's Last Avatar, 28
Vauvenargues, Marquess de, 68, The Quest of Glory
VÁZQUEZ, Francisco, see Palmerin of England, 350
Vecci e i Giovanni, I, 388
Vehmgerichte of Westphalia, 37, The Strong Arm
— 427, Anne of Geierstein
Veil, The, 448
Veiled Lady, The, 512
Veiled Women, 387
Veillée des armes, La, 466
Velent Smed, 364
Velvet Glove, The (by Henry JAMES), 266
Velvet Glove, The (by "MERRIMAN"), 342
Vendée, La, 16, The Mysterious M. Dumont
— 24, Storm and Treasure
— 29, A Gondreville Mystery, etc
— 29, The Chouans
— 40, Autumn Glory
— 74, The Yellow Poppy
— 74, Chantemerle
— 155, The Companions of Jehu
— 156, The She-Wolves of Machecoul
— 254, Ninety-Three
— 295, The House of the Combrays
— 358, Duchenier
— 365, The Eagle's Talon
— 376, The Battle of the Strong
— 512, A Spy for Napoleon
Vendée, La, 156
VENDEL, H. J., see "NADEL, H.," 357
Vendetta, 115
Vendetta, La, 26
Vendettas, 26, La Vendetta
— 58, Clara Vaughán
— 115, Vendetta
— 200, Gisli Saga
— 239, The Spanish Jade
— 240, The Outlaw
— 341, Colomba
— 363, Wrack
— 411, The Kings of Carrick, The Dule Tree of Cassilis
— See also *Revenge*
Veneering Family, 141, Our Mutual Friend
— 270, The Veneerings
Veneerings, The, 270
Venetia, 143
Venetian Glass Nephew, The, 512
Venetian Lovers, 193
Venezuela, 252, Green Mansions
— 453, Fombombo, Red Sand, Strange Moon
— 481, Bolivar
Vengeance is Mine, 26
Vengeful Gods, 18

Venice, 30, Massimilla Doni
— 30, Le Novelle
— 69, Mr. Misfortunate
— 72, Rubeni
— 123, Arethusa, Stradella, Marietta
— 143, Contarini Fleming
— 188, The Chevalier of Pensieri-Vani
— 196, A Sensitive Plant
— 220, Red Eve
— 245, Adria
— 249, A Foregone Conclusion
— 250, A Fearful Responsibility
— 306, Sir Raoul
— 348, The Cardinal's Pawn
— 381, Signors of the Night, Beatrice of Venice, Paulina
— 420, The Master Mosaic Workers
— 475, Mrs. TURNBULL's novels
Ventre de Paris, Le, 517
Ventriloquism, 76, Wieland
— 107, Valentine Vox, Sylvester Sound
Venture in 1777, A, 345
Venus, 109, Hypnerotomachia
Venus of Ille, 341
Vera (by ARNIM), 15
Véra (by DEMPSTER), 139
Véra (by VILLIERS DE L'ISLE ADAM), 483
Veranilda, 201
Vercingetorix, 345, The Conquered
— 346, When the Bough Breaks
Verdens ansigt, 64
Verdi, 496, Verdi
Verdi, 496
Verdugo, El, 30
Vergilius, 23
Vergini delle Rocce, 12
Verisopft, Lord, 140, Nicholas Nickleby
Verité, La, 519
Verlaine, Paul, 183, The Red Lily
Verlorene Handschrift, Die, 188
Vermilion Box, The, 306
Vermont, 413, R. E. ROBINSON's stories
— 464, The Green Mountain Boys
Vermuyden, 223, The MS. in the Red Box
Vernon, Diana, 425, Rob Roy
Vernon, Dorothy, 321, Dorothy Vernon
Verona, 381, Beatrice of Venice
Veronica Playfair, 206
Verotchka, 100
Verrinder, 138, Alice-for-Short
Versailles, 142, The Black Wolf's Breed
— 155, Ange Pitou
— 212, The Reds of the Midi, and sequels

Versailles (contd.): 262, Castelnau
— 376, The Power and the Glory
— 390, The House of De Mailly
— 445, The Order of Release
Verteidigung Roms, Die, 252
Very Good, Jeeves, 509
Very Light Railway, A, 34
Vestal Fire, 317
Vestal Virgins, 21, Faustula
Vestigia, 176
" Vestris," 315, A Son of the Commodore
Vetrova, 193
Veva, 112
Via Crucis, 122
VIAUD, L. M. J., see " LOTI, Pierre," 304
Vicar of Bullhampton, The, 472
Vicar of Pimlico, The, 492
Vicar of St. Luke's, The, 123
Vicar of the Marches, The, 424
Vicar of Wakefield, The, 205
Vicar of Wrexhill, The, 473
Vicar's Daughter, The, 300
Vice Versâ, 12
Vich Ian Vohr, 424, Waverley
Vicissitudes of Evangeline, 203
Vicissitudes of Flynn, The, 277
Vicksburg, 345, Westways
— 406, The Heart of Hope
Vicomte de Bragelonne, 154
Victim, The (by D'ANNUNZIO), 11
Victim, The (by DIXON), 145
Victor Emanuel, King, 24, The Pillar of Fire
— See also Italian Revolution
Victor of Salamis, A, 131
Victor Olnee's Discipline, 192
Victoria, 372, The Wisdom of Esau
Victoria, 223
Victory (by CONRAD), 111
Victory (by HUCH), 252
Vida de Lazarillo de Tormes, 338
Vida y hechos del pícaro Guzmán de Alfarache, 7
Vie, Une, 334
Vie amoureuse de François Barbazanges, 466
Vie de Marianne, 326
Vie d'un simple, La, 218
Vie des martyrs, 153
Vie privée de Michel Tessier, Le, 413
Vielle Fille, la, 27
Vienna, 72, Natasha
— 103, Eroica
— 230, A Sereshan
— 307, The Storm-Bird
— 358, The Flood

Vienna (contd.): 361, The Moonlight Sonata
— 389, The Hungarian Brothers
Vieux ménage, Un, 215
Views and Vagabonds, 311
Viglund the Fair, 353
Vignettes, 118
Vignettes of Manhattan, 333
Vigo, Siege of, 62, Across the Salt Seas
Viking Heart, The, 419
Vikings, 129, The Vikings of the Baltic
— 152, Ivar the Viking
— 218, The Sworn Brothers
— 235, The Tree of the Folkungs
— 280, Hereward the Wake
— 294, The Thirsty Sword, Olaf the Glorious
— 299, Miss LILJENCRANTZ's novels
— 366, Olaf Saga
— 479, Kristin Lavransdatter
— See also Icelandic Sagas, Norwegian Sagas
Vikings of the Baltic, The, 129
Viljoen, Ben, 57, A Burglar Quixote
Villa on the Rhine, The, 19
Villa Rubein, 189
Village, The, 80
Village Commune, A, 372
Village in the Jungle, The, 510
Village Inn-Keeper, The, 112
Village on the Cliff, The, 461
Village Photographs, 288
Village Priest, The, 467
Village Tales and Jungle Tragedies, 125
Village Tales from the Black Forest, 19
Village that Voted the Earth was Flat, 283
Village Tragedy, A, 510
VILLANI, Giovanni, see The Pecorone, 199
Villette, 73
Villigen, 284, Beleaguered
Villon, François, 152, The Justice of the King
— 312, If I were King, and sequel
Vincennes, 262, Henry of Guise
Vinci, Leonardo da, 263, Leonora d'Orco
— 341, The Forerunner
Vineta, 496
Vineyard, The, 119
Vingt ans après, 154
Vingt milles lieues sous les mers, 482
Vinland, 240, Gudrid the Fair
— 299, The Vinland Champions
Vinland Champions, The, 299
Vino generoso, 457
Vintage, The, 47

Vinti, I, 482
Violante, 31
Violin Obbligato, 232
Viper of Milan, The, 68
Virgilius, 465
Virgin and the Gipsy, The, 292
Virgin Fortress, The, 381
Virgin Heart, A, 209
Virgin Man, The, 391
Virgin of the Sun, The, 220
Virgin Soil, 475
Virgin Widow, The, 98
Virginia, 22, The Tower of Wye
— 71, A Gentleman of Virginia
— 78, Salute to Adventurers
— 85, The Cords of Vanity, The Rivet in Grandfather's Neck
— 113, J. E. COOKE's novels
— 144, Soldier Rigdale, Mistress Content Cradock
— 182, Erskine Dale
— 202, Miss GLASGOW's novels, passim
— 238, Balisand
— 248, The Magnificent Adventure
— 263, The Old Dominion
— 270–1, Mary JOHNSTON's novels
— 277, Swallow Barn
— 278, The Wooing of Judith
— 308, Mr. Arnold
— 313, The Wounds of a Friend
— 373, T. N. PAGE's stories, passim
— 409, Hearts Courageous
— 410, The Great Meadow
— 427, Throckmorton
— 448, A Soldier of Virginia
— 505, The Heart's Highway
— See also Jamestown
Virginia, 202
Virginia Comedians, The, 113
Virginia of Virginia, 409
Virginian, The, 508
Virginians, The, 463
Virgins of the Rocks, The, 12
Virtue, 268
Virtuous Orphan, The, 326
Visconti, Gian Galeazzo, 68, The Viper of Milan
— 423, A Man-at-Arms
Visconti, Gian Maria, 418, Bellarion
Visconti, Lorenzo, 263, Leonora d'Orco
Vises sten, De, 11
Visigoths, 262, Attila
Vision, 400
Vision auf der Schlachtfelde von Dresden, 244
Vision of MacConglinne, The, 343
Visionary, The, 299
Visions of Dom Francisco de Quevedo y Villegas, 396
Visiting the Sin, 401

Visits of Elizabeth, The, 203
Vistas of New York, 333
Vita dei Campi, 481
Vitelli, 24, My Lady of Orange
Vitellius, 337, The Gladiators
Vittoria, 339
Vittoria Accoromboni, 473
Vittoria Savelli, 1
Vittoria Victrix, 362
Vivandière, 195
Vivandières, 165, Madame Thérèse
— 195, Vivandière
Vivian, 160, 161
Vivian Grey, 143
Vivien, 335
Vivisection, 109, Heart and Science
Viy, 204
Vizier's Daughter, A, 223
Vœu d'une morte, Le, 516
Voice, The, 137
Voice of the City, 389
Voice of the People, The, 202
Void of Understanding, 174
Volga, 103, Marka of the Pits
Volksmärchen der Deutschen, 357
Volkynia, 284, In Bad Company
Volonté, 365
Voltaire, 70, The Infidel
— 428, Francezka
Volundr, 364, Wayland Smith
Volunteer with Pike, A, 44
Von Gottes Gnaden, 413
Vor Egen Stamme, 64
Vorstengunst, 486
Vort rige, 63
Vortex, The 283
Voss, Richard, 54, The Monk and The Hangman's Daughter
Voyage, The, 357
Voyage au centre de la terre, 482
Voyage autour de ma chambre, 320
Voyage du centurion, 395
Voyage of Bran, The, 343
Voyage of Consolation, A, 116
Voyage of Maildun, The, 273
Voyage Out, The, 510
Voyage to the Land of the Articoles, 335
Voyages to the Moon and the Sun, 127
Voyageur sur la terre, Le, 213
Voyageuses, 67
Voysey, 394
Vrais riches, Les, 115
Vrouw Grobelaar's Leading Cases, 197
Vultures, The, 342
Vye, Eustacia, 225, The Return of the Native

W Plan, The, 429
"Wabash," 70, A Little Traitor to the South
Wabeno the Magician, 511
Wackles, Miss, 140, Old Curiosity Shop
Wacousta, 406
Waffen nieder, Die, 457
Wager, The (The Bet), 100
Wager, The, 319
Wages of Sin, The, 321
Wagner, Richard, 12, The Flame of Life
— 39, The Two Standards
— 349, Evelyn Innes
Wagnerbuch, 170, Faustus
Waif of the Plains, A, 230
Waif's Progress, A, 75
Wainewright, Thomas Griffiths, 309, Lucretia
Waiting, 364
Waiting for the Ferry, 207
Waiting Supper, The, 226
Wakefield, 176, David March
— 195, George à Green
Waldemar of Russia, 294, Olaf the Glorious
Waldemar III of Sweden, 235, The Tree of the Folkungs
Waldemar, 258
Waldenses, 221, In His Name
Waldheimat, 416
Waldo Trench, and Others, 188
Wales, 140, Star of Mercia
— 209, Pabo the Priest
— 276, Son of Judith
— 279, Two Years Ago
— 280, Austin Elliot
— 301, Amadis of Gaul
— 363, The Falcon King
— 426, The Talisman
— 491, Aylwin
— See also Welsh Characters, WELSH NOVELISTS, Welsh Marches
Walewska, Marie, 18, The Empress Might-have-Been
— 193, Napoleon's Love Story
Walk in Picardy, A, 157
Walkenshaw, Clementina, 69, Mr. Misfortunate
— 153, Scotland's Heir
— 356, The Shoes of Fortune
Walking Delegate, A, 282
Walking Gentleman, A, 392
Walking Shadows, 363
Wall, The, 11
Wallace, 1
Wallace, William, 4, The Days of Bruce
— 389, The Scottish Chiefs
Walladmor, 7
Wallenstein, Albrecht Eusebius von, 346, The Fortune-Hunter
— 448, The Black Cuirassier
Waller, Edmund, 39, The Knight of the Golden Sword
Wallet of Kai Lung, The, 71

Wallingford, Miles, 115, Afloat and Ashore
WALLIS, Henry M., see "HILLIERS, Ashton"
Walpole, Sir Horace, 70, Mohawks
— 207, A Daughter of Kings
Walpole, Sir Robert, 104, Richard Carvel
— 173, Jonathan Wild
— 287, Ethel Churchill
Walpurgis Night, 520
Walsingham, Sir Francis, 24, The Master of Gray
Waltheof, 59, The Siege of Norwich Castle
Wanderer, The (by BURNEY), 83
Wanderer, The (by FOURNIER), 181
Wanderer and King, 87
Wanderers, 223
Wanderers, The, 270
Wanderer's Necklace, The, 220
Wanderers on a Thousand Hills, The, 500
Wanderfoot, 450
Wandering Heath, 397
Wandering Heir, The, 402
Wandering Jew, 125, Salathiel
— 333, Melmoth
— 455, The Wandering Jew
— 486, The Prince of India
Wandering Jew, The (by MERRIMAN), 342
Wandering Jew, The (by SUE), 455
Wandering Willie's Tale, 426
Wanted—a Wife, 375
War, 78, The Courts of the Morning
— 88, The Coming Waterloo
— 120, S. Crane's stories
— 130, Robert Helmont
— 187, Peter Moor's Journey
— 266, Abraham's Sacrifice
— 347, Right Off the Map
— 433, The Yellow Danger
— 484, Babouc
— 494, The War in the Air
— 495, The Autocracy of Mr. Parham
— 516, The Attack on the Mill
— See also Military Stories, Pacifism, Regimental Life, and names of wars, Crimean, Franco-German, Great Civil War, Great War, etc.
War, 403
War and God, 214
War and Peace, 468
War Correspondent, The, 481
War for the Bull of Cuailgne, 214
War in Heaven, 506
War in the Air, The, 494
War of the Wenuses, The, 493

War of the Worlds, The, 493
War of Women, The, 155
War to the Knife, 64
War-Workers, The, 135
Warbeck, Perkin, 105, A Trusty Rebel
— 165, The King of Vagabonds
WARD, A. S., see "ROHMER, Sax," 414
Ward of King Canute, The, 299
Ward No. 6, 100
Warden, The, 471
Warden of the Marches, The, 215
Wardlaws, The, 167
Wares of Edgefield, The, 501
Warkworth Castle, 180, Harry of Athol
Warleigh, 71
Warloch o' Glenwarloch, 314
WARNER, Charles Dudley, see also "TWAIN, Mark," 477
Warning to the Curious, A, 266
Warp and Weft, 243
Warren, Joseph, 448, Old Boston
Warrington, George, 462, Pendennis
— See also The Virginians
Warrior Maid, 37
Warriors of Old Japan, 373
Warrior's Soul, The, 111
Warsaw, 342, The Vultures
Warwick "the King-Maker," 309, Last of the Barons
— 513, Grisly Grisell
Warwickshire, 330, The Young Queen of Hearts
— 388, The Spanish Poniard
— 426, Kenilworth
Wárwolf, Der, 7
Was it Right to Forgive?, 36
Washer of the Ford, The, 431
Washington, George, 17, The Conqueror
— 62, A Son of his Country
— 68, Mr. Washington
— 97, The Reckoning
— 114, The Spy
— 165, Patriot and Tory
— 179, Janice Meredith
— 271, The Great Valley
— 284, A Maid of '76
— 345, Hugh Wynne, and sequel
— 345, The Van Rensselaers
— 448, Old Boston
— 451, Guert Ten Eyck
— 463, The Virginians
Washington City, 2, Democracy
— 8, A Herald of the West
— 17, Senator North
— 22, Kent Fort Manor
— 23, The Light in the Clearing
— 58, Erema
— 81, The Shepherd of the People

Washington City (contd.): 82, Through One Administration
— 135, Justine
— 143, The Patience of John Morland
— 248, The Purchase Price
— 248, Fifty-Four Forty, or Fight
— 318, The Washingtonians
— 477, The Gilded Age
Washington Square, 263
Watcher By the Threshold, The, 78
Watchers by the Road, 450
Watchers by the Sea, 377
Watchers of the Plains, The, 126
Watchers on the Longships, The, 106
Water-Babies, The, 279
Water Gipsies, 237
Water of the Wondrous Isles, 352
Watercress Girl, The, 115
Waterdale Neighbours, The, 312
Waterford County, 355, Onora
Waterloo, 166
Waterloo, Battle of, 53, The Chartreuse of Parma
— 71, The Eagle of the Empire
— 87, In the Year of Waterloo
— 149, The Great Shadow
— 150, Adventures of Gerard
— 166, Waterloo
— 336, Stories of Waterloo
— 371, Soldier Born, and sequel
— 373, Lauristons
Watermeads, 329
Waters of Caney Fork, The, 401
Waters of Edera, The, 372
Waters of Hercules, The, 196
WATSON, Rev. J., see "MACLAREN, Ian," 318
Watsons, The, 20
Watteau, Jean Antoine, 377, A Prince of Court Painters
Watts, Alfred Eugene, 491, Aylwin
Watts, James Orlando, 491, Aylwin
Wave, The, 59
Waverley, 424
Waves of Fate, The, 360
Way Home, The, 406
Way it was with Them, The, 363
Way of all Flesh, The, 83
Way of Ambition, The, 242
Way of an Election, The, 464
Way of Escape, The, 470
Way of Marriage, The, 255
Way of Revolution, 168
Way of the Sea, The, 156
Way of Transgressors, The, 167

Way they Loved at Grimpat, The, 167
Way to Peace, The, 137
Way Up, The, 506
Way We Live Now, The, 472
Wayland Smith, 364
Waymark, 200, The Unclassed
Wayne, General Anthony, 9, The Wilderness Road
— 448, The Heritage
— See also Iroquois
Ways of Miss Barbara, The, 94
Waysiders, 365
We, 515
We and the World, 168
We Forget because We Must, 336
We Girls, 503
We Others, 33
We Two, 307
Weald of Kent, 25, Judy Bovenden
Wealth, 52, Beyond the Dreams of Avarice
— 130, The Nabob
— 154, The Count of Monte Cristo
— 203, St. Leon
— 265, The Wings of the Dove
— 271, Timar's Two Worlds
— 303, Burning Daylight
— 490, A Little Journey in the World
— 505, Jerome
— See also Banks, Financiers, Misers, Millionaires
Weans at Rowallan, The, 175
Wearing away of the Fianna, 214
Wearing of the Green, The, 279
Weavers, The, 376
Weavers and Weft, 70
Weaver's Grave, 365
Weavers and Weaving, 339, Our Town
— 351, Bellamy
Web of Life, The, 238
Webb, General, 462, Henry Esmond
Webster, Daniel, 143, The Patience of John Morland
Webster, H. K., see also Merwin, S.
Wedding Knell, The, 232
Wedding of Maine Morgor, 293
Wedlock (by "George Egerton"), 162
Wedlock (by Wasserman), 490
Wee Wifey, 91
Wee Willie Winkie, 281
Weeds, 35
Week in a French Country House, A, 421
Weg ins Freie, Der, 423
Weight of the Name, The, 67
Weir of Hermiston, 449
Weird o't, The, 433

Weird Tales, 244
Weird Tales from Northern Seas, 299
Weissenberg, Battle of, 262, Heidelberg
Weldon, A. E., see "Macnamara, B.," 320
Well at the World's End, The, 352
Well-Beloved, The, 226
Well of Loneliness, The, 222
Well of Saint-Clare, The, 183
Well-to-do Arthur, 408
Weller, Sam, 140, Pickwick Papers
Wellington, 1st Duke of, 24, The Young Lovers
— 150, Brigadier Gerard
— 319, A Freelance in Kashmir
— 433, The Man-Stealers
— 510, The Spanish Lady
— See also Peninsular War, Waterloo, etc.
Wells, Herbert George, 411, The Private Life of Henry Maitland
Welsh Characters, 167, C. Evans's novels
— 217, The Mabinogion
— 399, A Welsh Singer
— 441, Humphry Clinker
— See also Celtic Romance, Wales, WELSH NOVELISTS
Welsh Marches, 127, The Love Story of Giraldus
— 188, Fulke Fitz-Warine
— 426, The Betrothed
WELSH NOVELISTS:
C. Evans, M. Jones, Ellis Lloyd, Daisy Pryce, Gwendolen Pryce, "A. Raine," "O. Rhoscomyl," E. Rhys, H. E. Thomas, R. M. Thomas, W. E. Tirebuck
Welsh Romances, 217, The Mabinogion
— 405, Old Welsh Texts
— See also Celtic Romances
Welsh Singer, A, 399
Wendekreis, Der, 490
Wendy, 38, Peter and Wendy
Wenham, 462, Vanity Fair
Wentworth, Alice, 69, The Spae Wife
Wentworth Family, 170, My Lady Wentworth
Wentworth, Austin, 339, Richard Feverel
Wentworth, Henrietta, Lady, 159, Fortune's Castaway
— 170, My Lady Wentworth
— 199, The Bâton Sinister
Wept of the Wish-ton-Wish, The, 114
Werwolves, 124, The Black Douglas
— 274, The Wolf's Bride
— See also Lycanthropy

Wesley, John, 64, The Morning of To-day
— 74, The Fool of Quality
— 98, Diary of Mrs. Kitty Trevelyan
— 348, The Messenger
— 397, Hetty Wesley
Wesleyans and Methodists, 2, "J. Ackworth's" stories
— 36, Bernicia
— 45, Anna of the Five Towns
— 64, The Morning of To-day
— 70, The Infidel
— 93, The Arm of the Lord
— 153, The Story of Susan
— 163, The Circuit Rider
— 181, Concerning Isabel Carnaby, The Farringdons
— 182, The Bountiful Hour
— 212, The Spiritual Quixote
— 228, Mrs. C. N. W. Harris's stories
— 300, Methodist Idylls, and sequel
— 441, Humphry Clinker
Wessex, 225-6, Hardy's novels
— See also Dorsetshire, Alfred the Great
Wessex Tales, 226
West, V. S., see Sackville-West, V., 418
West End, The, 501
West Indies, 17, The Conqueror
— 24, The Gentleman Adventurer
— 39, The Thirteen Evenings
— 258, Prince Rupert the Buccaneer
— 337, Cerise
— 348, Captain Latymer
— 424, Tom Cringle's Log, The Cruise of the Midge
— See also Cuba, Haiti, Jamaica, Nevis, Panama, Spanish Main, etc.
West Wind, The, 193
Westcotes, The, 397
Westerham, 72, Some Account of Amyot Brough
Western, Squire, and Sophia, 173, Tom Jones
Western Isles, see Hebrides
Western Rebellion of 1549, 432, Brave Earth
Westerners, The, 501
Westminster, 53, Westminster Cloisters
— 168, The Gathering of Brother Hilarius
— 330, In the Choir of Westminster Abbey
Westminster Cloisters, 53
Westphalia, 93, Love and Honour
— 94, If Youth but Knew
Westward Ho ., 279
Westways, 345
Wetherbys, The, 288

Wetherell, Sir Charles, 498, Chipping
"Wetherell, Elizabeth," see Warner, Susan, 490
Wexford, 79, Croppies Lie Down
— 222, Mrs. Hall's stories
— 278, The Banks of the Boro
Weymouth, 94, Pamela Pounce
— 226, The Trumpet Major
Whaleman's Wife, A, 79
Whalers, The, 43
Whaling, 41, Rodman the Boatsteerer
— 43, The Whalers
— 127, The Tiger of Cloud River
— 338, Moby-Dick
Wharton, Duke of, 308, Devereux
What a Woman Wants, 153
What Became of Pam, 256
What I lack yet, 390
What Lay Beneath, 485
What Love Costs an Old Man, 28
What Maisie Knew, 265
What Never Happened, 422
What Not, 311
What Others Live By, 469
What She Came Through, 478
What Will He Do with It ?, 309
Whately, Archbishop, 296, Roland Cashel
Whatever Gods may Be, 335
What's Mine's Mine, 314
Wheat Industry, 90, Red Rust
— 343, Calumet "K"
— 361, The Octopus, The Pit, A Deal in Wheat
Wheat and Tares, 127
Wheel of Time, The, 264
Wheeler, Jenny P. and A. C., see "Mowbray, J. P.," 354
Wheels of Chance, The, 493
When a Man Marries, 324
When a Man's Single, 37
When All the World is Young, 306
When Charles I was King, 176
When Ghost Meets Ghost, 139
When Greek meets Greek, 471
When I was a Child, 483
When Knighthood was in Flower, 321
When Lint was in the Bell, 315
When Love flies out o' the Window, 341
When Mammoths roamed the Frozen Earth, 423
When the Bough Breaks, 346
When The King Loses His Head, 11
When the Mopoke Calls, 485

When the Norman Came, 365

When the Sleeper Wakes, 493

When the World Screamed, 150

When They Love, 33

When Valmond came to Pontiac, 376

When We were Boys, 363

When Wilderness was King, 376

When William Came, 355

Where Angels Fear to Tread, 179

Where Are You Going To ?, 412

Where England sets her Feet, 91

Where Highways Cross, 176

Where Love Is, there God is also, 468

Where the Atlantic meets the Land, 300

Where the Battle was Fought, 118

Where the Labourers are Few, 136

Where the Pavement Ends, 417

Where the Treasure Is, 398

Where will you Fall ?, 383

While Paris Laughed, 342

While the Billy Boils, 292

Whilomville Stories, 121

Whip Hand, The, 343

Whirligigs, 390

Whirlpool, The, 201

Whirlpools, 436

Whirlwind, The (by DAVIS), 132

Whirlwind, The (by NEMIROVICH - DANTCHENKO), 358

Whirlwind, The (by PHILPOTTS), 385

Whisper of a Name, The, 294

Whispers about Women, 341

Whistle and I'll come to Thee, 266

Whistler, James McNeill, 381, Our House

Whistling Maid, The, 404

Whitby, 65, The Cope

— 194, Sylvia's Lovers

White Aprons, 206

White-Caps, 126, Billy McCoy

White Company, The, 149

White Cottage, The, 277

White Cowl, The, 7

White Darkness, The, 354

White Dog, The, 443

White Dove, The, 301

White Eagles, 199

White-Faced Priest, The, 380

White Fang, 303

White Heron, A, 269

White Heron, The, 431

White Hoods, The, 71

White Horses, The, 457

White Islander, The, 95

White Jacket, 338

White King's Daughter, The, 330

White Monkey, The, 190

White Month, The, 380

White Nights, 146

White Paternoster, The, 390

White Peacock, The, 290

White Plumes of Navarre, The, 124

White Prophet, The, 87

White Queen, The, 131

White Riband, The, 268

White Robe, The, 85

White Rocks, 413

White Ship, The, 274

White Slave Traffic, 355, The Tragedy of Chris

— 412, Where Are You Going To ?

— See also Courtesans

White Stone, The (by FRANCE), 184

White Stone, The (by MACILWAINE), 316

White Terror, The, 212

White Terror and the Red, The, 86

White Wings, 57

White Wolf, 195

White Wolf, The, 397

Whiteboy, The, 222

Whiteboys, 31, Crohoore of the Bill-Hook, John Doe

— 222, The Whiteboy

Whitefield, George, 36, Bernicia

— 98, Diary of Mrs. Kitty Trevelyan

— 271, Chrysal

Whitefriars, 412, Whitefriars

— 426, The Fortunes of Nigel

Whitefriars, 412

Whitehall, 412

Whitehall Palace, 71, Patches and Pomander

— 412, Whitehall

— See also Charles I, Charles II, James I, etc.

Whiteladies, 367

Whiteoaks, 137

Whites and the Blues, The, 156

Whitewash, 480

Whitford, Vernon, 340, The Egoist

"WHITLOCK, A.," see FINLAY, Rev. T. A., 174

"WHITNEY, Harry," see KENNEDY, P., 278

Whittier, J. G., 177, O Genteel Lady

Who Goes There ?, 47

Whom God hath Joined, 45

Why Paul Ferroll Killed his Wife, 106

Why Senath Married, 268

WHYTE-MELVILLE, G. J., see MELVILLE, G. J. W., 337

Wickenham, Lord, 119, The Gods, Some Mortals, and Lord Wickenham

Wickerwork Woman, The, 183

Widdershins, 369

Widdicombe, 506

Wide Wide World, The, 490

Widecombe Fair, 386

Widow Barnaby, The, 473

Widow Married, The, 473

Widow of Ephesus, The, 14

Wieland, 76

Wife, The, 100

Wife of his Youth, The, 102

Wight, Isle of, 81, The Prisoners of Carisbrooke

— 507, The Knight of the Needle Rock

— See also Carisbrooke

Wilberforce, William, 428, Under Cheddar Cliffs

Wild Animals I have Known, 429

Wild Ass's Skin, The, 30

Wild Body, The, 298

Wild Eelin, 57

Wild Geese, The, 498

Wild Heart, The, 185

Wild Honey, 450

Wild Irish Girl, The, 351

Wild Justice, 56

Wild Oranges, 237

Wild Rose of Lough Gill, The, 441

Wild Wheat, 185

Wild Youth, 376

Wilde, Oscar O'F. W., 241, The Green Carnation

Wilder Johnsing, The, 454

Wilderness, Battle of the, 9, Before the Dawn

Wilderness Road, The, 9

Wildfire, Madge, 425, The Heart of Midlothian

Wildgoose, Geoffry, 212, The Spiritual Quixote

Wildgoose Lodge, 92

Wilhelm Meister's Apprenticeship, 204

Wilhelmina, Princess of Prussia, 321, A Gentle Knight of Old Brandenburg

Wilkes, John, 271, Chrysal

Will, 365

Will of God, The, 65

Will o' the Mill, 449

Will to Live, The, 65

Will Warburton, 201

Willet Family, 140, Barnaby Rudge

William I, see Norman Conquest

William III, 7, The House of Lisronan

— 24, The Gentleman Adventurer

— 31, The Boyne Water

— 38, The Gallants

— 68, I Will Maintain, and sequels

— 82, A Lady of Quality, His Grace of Osmonde

— 155, The Black Tulip

— 159, Fortune's Castaway

— 165, The King's Spy

William III (contd.) : 196, The Broken Sword, The Last Link

— 243, The Chariots of the Lord

— 262, The King's Highway

— 314, The Sword of the King

— 377, The King's Agent

— 396, The Blue Pavilions

— 422, The Lifeguardsman

— 486, In Troubled Times

— See also Assassination Plot, English Revolution

William IV, see Reform Bill, etc.

"William, by the Grace of God——," 68

William Jordan, Junior, 442

William of Occam, 171, The Ugly Duchess

William the Conquerer, 282

William the Quaker, 134, Capt. Singleton

William the Silent, 24, My Lady of Orange

— 68, Prince and Heretic, and sequel

— 107, Jan van Elselo

— 332, A Lily of France

— 486, In Troubled Times

Williamsburg, 113, The Virginia Comedians, and sequel

Willie Reilly and his Dear Colleen Bawn, 92

Willoughby, Lady, 399, The Diary of Lady Willoughby

Willoughby Manor, 363

Willow the King, 442

Willowdene Will, 456

Willows, 136

Willows, The, 59

"WILLY," see sub nom. "COLETTE," 108

WILSON, Wilfred, see sub nom. BLACKWOOD, Algernon

Wiltshire, 21, Hurdcott

— 94, The Star Dreamer

— 267, Wood Magic, Bevis

— 379, Eli of the Downs

— See also Salisbury, etc.

Winchelsea, 400, Morlac of Gascony

— See also Cinque Ports

Winchenden, Lord, 247, My Lord Winchenden

Winchester, 329, Winchester Meads

— 335, The Chevalier of the Splendid Crest

Winchester Meads, 329

Wind Bloweth, The, 84

Wind from the Wilderness, A, 194

Wind in the Willows, The, 211

Wind of Destiny, The, 225

Windfall, The, 119

Windfall's Eve, 306

Winding Stair, The, 332

Windischgrätz, Prince zu, 267, The Stronger Wings

Windmills, 89
Window in Paris, A, 169
Window in Thrums, A, 37
Windsor, 4, Windsor Castle
— 145, In Kings' Houses
Windsor Castle, 4
Windy McPherson's Son, 10
Windyhaugh, 470
Windyridge, 408
Windyridge Revisited, 408
Wine Beyond the World, The, 363
Wine on the Lees, 447
Winesburg, Ohio, 10
Wing-and-Wing, 114
Wingless Victory, The, 506
Wings, 443
Wings of the Dove, The, 265
Winifrede's Journal, 329
Winning Lady, The, 506
Winnipeg, 137, Jalna, and sequel
Winnowing, A, 49
Winsome Winnie, 293
Winter, 216
Winter Amid the Ice, 482
Winter Courtship, A, 269
Winter Queen, The, 234
Winterborough, 500
Wintersmoon, 487
Wire-Walker, A, 210
Wisconsin, 496, G. WESCOTT's novels
Wisdom of Esau, The, 372
Wisdom of Father Brown, The, 102
Wisdom of Fools, The, 136
Wisdom's Daughter, 220
Wise and the Wayward, The, 453
Wise Saws and Modern Instances, 222
Wise Virgins, The, 510
Wise Woods, The, 153
Wiseman, Mr., 81, Mr. Badman
Wish, The, 455
Wish House, The, 283
Witch, The, 270
Witch Hazel, 408
Witch Ladder, The, 477
Witch of Prague, The, 122
Witch Wife, The, 478
Witch Wood, 78
Witchcraft, 4, The Lancashire Witches
— 31, The Fetches
— 39, David Arnot
— 36, The Black Shilling
— 78, Witch Wood
— 105, Sir H. CLIFFORD's novels of Malay
— 178, A Mirror for Witches
— 270, The Witch
— 336, Mary Schweidler, Sidonia
— 348, Major Weir, Maids of Salem
— 478, The Witch Wife
— See also *Mather, Cotton, Magic*, etc.
Witch's Head, The, 219
Witch's Sword, The, 189
With a Diploma, 358
With Edged Tools, 342
With Essex in Ireland, 289
With Fire and Sword, 434

With George Washington into the Wilderness, 418
With Malice Toward None, 353
With Muted Strings, 223
With Sam Houston in Texas, 418
With the Black Prince, 451
With the Immortals, 122
With the Night Mail, 282
With the Procession, 188
With the Red Eagle, 497
With the Warden of the Marches, 380
Withered Arm, The, 226
Within a Budding Grove, 393
Within the Capes, 396
Within the Tides, 111
Without Benefit of Clergy, 281
Without Conditions, 316
Without Dogma, 435
Wittenberg, 170, Faustus
— 243, The Sword of the Lord
Wives and Daughters, 194
Wizard, The, 219
Wizard's Knot, The, 39
Wizard's Son, The, 368
Wogan, Chevalier, 69, Mr. Misfortunate
— 313, The King over the Water
— 331, Clementina
Wohin rollst Du, Üpfelchen ?, 383
Wolf Breed, 214
Wolfe, General, 8, A Soldier of Manhattan
— 72, Some Account of Amyot Brough
— 196, The Heart of a Hero
— 232, The Path of Glory
— 271, Chrysal
— 376, The Seats of the Mighty
Wolfe of Badenoch, The, 289
Wolff, Hermann, 375, Hermann Agha
Wolfmark, Dukes of the, 124, The Red Axe
Wolf's Bride, The, 274
Wolgast, Louis von, 336, Sidonia
Wollstonecraft, Mary, 369, Adeline Mowbray
Wolsey, Cardinal, 4, Windsor Castle
— 261, Darnley
— 513, The Armourer's 'Prentices
Wolverhampton, 181, The Farringdons
Wolves of Cernogratz, The, 355
Wolves of God, The, 59
Woman, The, 177
Woman Alone, A, 106
Woman and the Priest, The, 137
Woman and the Sword, The, 304
Woman at Bay, A, 7

Woman at the Store, The, 325
Woman Deborah, The, 16
Woman from Purgatory, The, 44
Woman Hater, A, 402
Woman in the Way, The, 369
Woman in White, The, 108
Woman of Andros, The, 505
Woman of Thirty, A, 26
Woman of Yesterday, A, 332
Woman Thou Gavest Me, The, 87
Woman Triumphant, 61
Woman Ventures, A, 384
Woman Who Did, The, 7
Woman who Rode Away, The, 291
Woman with the Fan, The, 241
Woman with the Velvet Necklace, The, 156
Woman's Heart, A, 67
Woman's Kingdom, The, 120
Woman's Life, A, 334
Woman's Reason, A, 250
Woman's Tragedy, A, 391
Woman's Vengeance, A, 32
Woman's Victory, The, 311
Women, 417
Women and Monks, 274
Women at the Pump, The, 224
Women in Love, 291
Women of the Country, 64
Women's Tragedies, 305
Won on the Post, 208
" *Wonder, Renaissance of*," 491, Aylwin
Wonder Book for Boys and Girls, 233
Wonder Tales, see *Ghost Stories, Gothic Romances, Imaginary Voyages, Magic, Oriental, Psychic, Supernatural, Utopias*, etc.
Wonderful Adventures of Nils, 287
Wonderful Mission of Earl Lavender, The, 131
Wonderful Visit, The, 493
Wonderful Wapentake, The, 176
Wonderful Year, The, 302
Wonderjaar, Het, 112
Wondrous Wife, The, 327
Wood beyond the World, The, 352
Wood-cutting Expedition, The, 467
Wood Magic, 267
Wood Pigeons and Mary, The, 346
Wood Sanctuary, 185
WOOD-SEYS, R. A., see " CUSHING, Paul," 127
Woodcraft, 436
Wooden Clara, 112
Wooden Crosses, 145
Woodlanders, The, 226
Woodman, The (by BEAUREPAIRE), 41

Woodman, The (by G. P. R. JAMES), 262
WOODS, Mrs. J. C., see " WOODROFFE, D.," 510
Woodseer, 340, The Amazing Marriage
Woodsmoke, 514
Woodstock, 426
Wooed and Married, 91
Wooing of Judith, The, 278
Wooing of Kezia, The, 3
Wooing of Sheila, The, 404
Woollen Dress, The, 66
Worcester, Marquess of, 314, St. George and St. Michael
Worcester, 509, The Channings, Roland Yorke
Worcester, Battle of, 87, Wanderer and King
— 380, Of Mistress Eve
— See also *Charles II*
Worcestershire, 148, Nemo
— 262, Forest Days
— 460, Idylls of the Fells
Word of the Sorceress, The, 346
Wordsworth, William, 378, Melincourt
— 510, A Poet's Youth
Work (by ALCOTT), 6
Work (by ZOLA), 519
Workaday Woman, The, 255
Working Bullocks, 392
Workman and Soldier, 106
World Below, The, 512
World for Sale, The, 376
World of Chance, The, 250
World of William Clissold, The, 495
World of Women, The, 51
World Set Free, The, 494
World went very well then, The, 52
Worldlings, The, 341
World's Delight, The, 439
World's Desire, The, 221
World's Ends, 490
World's Great Snare, The, 369
World's Illusion, The, 490
Wormwood, 115
Worth, Battle of, 97, The Maids of Paradise
— 380, The Garden of Swords
Would You Kill Him ?, 289
Wouldbegoods, The, 60
Wounds in the Rain, 121
Wounds of a Friend, The, 313
Wrack, 363
Wrackham Memoirs, The, 437
Wreath of Cloud, A, 356
Wreathed Dagger, The, 515
Wreck of the *Grosvenor*, The, 417
Wreckage, 118
Wrecker, The, 450
Wreckers and Methodists, 305
Wren, Sir Christopher, 176, David March
— 330, Under the Dome of St. Paul's

Wright, Silas, 23, The Light in the Clearing
Writ in Water, 216
Wrong Box, The, 450
Wroth, 94
Wrychester Paradise, 177
Wunsch, Der, 455
Wurtemberg, 172, Jew Süss
Wuthering Heights, 73
Wyandotté, 114
Wyatt, Sir Thomas, 333, The Royal Sisters
— 381, I Crown thee King
Wyclif, John, 25, The Gleaming Dawn
— 233, In a Desert Land
— 343, Robert Annys
Wye Valley, 260, Aythan Waring
Wylie, Sir Andrew, 191, Sir Andrew Wylie
Wyoming, 508, The Virginian

Xeres, 61, The Fruit of the Vine
Xerxes, 131, A Victor of Salamis
Xingu, 499

Yakov and Pasinkov, 474
Yakuts, 284, The Saghalien Convict, Makar's Dream
Yale, 169, Brinton Eliot
Yama, 285
Yankee at the Court of King Arthur, A, 476
Yankee Ships and Yankee Sailors, 35
Yankees, see Americans
Yanko the Musician, 435
Yannyol, 435
Yarmouth, Countess of, 271, Chrysal
Ye Sexes Give Ear, 397
Year of Life, A, 300
Year of Miracles, The, 112
Year One of the Republic, 166
Years of Childhood, 5
Yeast, 279
Yedo, 45, The Shogun's Daughter
Yellow Aster, A, 86
Yellow Bird, The, 102
Yellow Book of Lecan, 169
Yellow Danger, The, 433

Yellow Frigate, The, 211
Yellow God, The, 220
Yellow Mask, The, 108
Yellow Poppy, The, 74
Yellowplush Memoirs, The, 462, 463
Yeobright, Clym, 225, The Return of the Native
Yeoman Adventurer, The, 207
Yeoman Fleetwood, 184
Yerkes, Charles T., 151, The Financier
Yermolai and the Miller's Wife, 474
Yesterdays, 68
Yesterday's To-morrow, 313
Yet do not Grieve, 371
Yeux qui s'ouvrent, Les, 65
Yoke of Pity, The, 44
Yoke of the Thorah, The, 227
Yolanda, 321
Yolande, 25, The Magic Tale of Harvanger and Yolande
Yorick, Parson, 447, Tristram Shandy
York, Siege of, 457, The White Horses
York and Lancaster Rose, A, 276
Yorkshire, 33, Bond Slaves
— 36, Between Two Loves, Master of his Fate
— 41, Mary BEAUMONT's stories
— 50, Carr, Trio
— 58, Mary Anerley
— 73, Shirley, Wuthering Heights
— 176, J. S. FLETCHER's novels
— 243, Memoirs of a Person of Quality
— 256, The Bag of Saffron
— 278, The Mistress of Langdale Hall
— 300, Mary LINSKILL's novels
— 327, The Luck of Barerakes
— 350, F. W. MOORMAN's stories
— 408, W. RILEY's novels
— 442, J. K. SNOWDEN's stories
— 456-7, H. SUTCLIFFE's novels

Yorkshire (contd.): 460, Idylls of the Fells
Yorktown, 416, The Scarlet Coat
You Touched Me, 291
Youghal, 79, Cambria Carty
— 165, Ralph Wynward
— 355, Nanno
Youma, 235
Young, Robert, 377, The King's Agent
Young April, 94
Young Archimedes, 257
Young Barbarians, 319
Young Blood, 248
Young Days of Admiral Quilliam, The, 370
Young Doctor, The, 112
Young Dragon, A, 478
Young Duke, The, 143
Young Enchanted, The, 487
Young England Party, 143, Coningsby, Sybil, and following
Young Ernest, 89
Young Eve and Old Adam, 189
Young Felix, 458
Young Franc-Tireurs, The, 237
Young Fur Traders, The, 26
Young Goodman Brown, 232
Young Lives, 294
Young Lovell, The, 178
Young Lovers, The, 24
Young Man from the South, A, 413
Young Man Married, A, 216
Young Man's Year, A, 247
Young Maugars, 464
Young Mountaineers, The, 118
Young Ofeg's Ditties, 224
Young Pennymore, 356
Young Philosopher, The, 440
Young Physician, The, 514
Young Pretender, see Charles Edward Stuart
Young Queen of Hearts, The, 330
Young Sam and Sabina, 400
Young Vigilance, 69
Young Visitors, The, 16
Younger Set, The, 97
Yourself and the Neighbours, 319

Youth (by CONRAD), 110
Youth (by TOLSTOY), 467
Youth and the Bright Medusa, 95
Youth Betrayed, 287
Youth goes a-Marketing, 379
Youth Rides West, 259
Youth Went Riding, 290
Youth, Youth !, 107
Youth's Encounter, 317
Ypres, Battle of, 72, Pillbox 17
Yucatan, 181, Maya
Yukon, 302-3, Jack LONDON's stories
— 384, The Chicamon Stone
— 412, The Magnetic North, Come and Find Me
— 429, The Trail of '98
Yvette, 334
Yvonne of Croisic, 492

Zachary Phips, 84
" ZACK," see KEATS, Miss G., 276
Zadig, 484
Zadoc Pine, 81
Zalacaín el Aventurero, 35
Zanoni, 309
Zauberberg, Der, 324
Zauberreich der Liebe, 72
Zaunkönige, 188
Zayde, 286
Zealand, see Roervig
Zeilenschemering, 117
Zella Sees Herself, 135
Zeluco, 350
Zenith City, 298, Babbitt
Zenobia, 489
Zicci, 309
Ziema Obiecana, 403
Zike Mouldom, 3
Zinotchka, 100
Zionism, 72, The Kingdom of Love
Zoroaster, 121
Zossima, Father, 148, The Brothers Karamazov
Zuleika Dobson, 42
Zulus, 220, Child of Storm, Finished
— 346, B. MITFORD's novels
Zürich, 371, Nadia
Zury, 283
ZUVIRIA, G. M., see " WAST, Hugo," 491
Zwischen Himmel und Erde, 306